INTRODUCTION TO PSYCHOLOGY

INTRODUCTION

THIRD EDITION

TO PSYCHOLOGY

JAMES W. KALAT
North Carolina State University

Brooks/Cole Publishing Company
Pacific Grove, California

Brooks/Cole Publishing Company
A Division of Wadsworth, Inc.

© 1993 by Wadsworth, Inc., Belmont, California
94002. All rights reserved. No part of this book
may be reproduced, stored in a retrieval system,
or transcribed, in any form or by any means,
without the prior written permission of the
publisher, Brooks/Cole Publishing Company,
Pacific Grove, California 93950, a division of
Wadsworth, Inc.

Printed in the United States of America

10 9 8 7 6 5 4 3 2 1

**Library of Congress Cataloging-in-Publication
Data**

Kalat, James W.
    Introduction to psychology / James W. Kalat. —
3rd ed.
        p.   cm.
    Includes bibliographical references and
index.
        ISBN 0-534-17238-5
        1. Psychology.   I. Title.
BF121.K26   1992
150—dc20   92-6141

Sponsoring Editor: Kenneth King

Editorial Assistant: Gay Meixel

Development Editor: John Boykin

Production Editor: Jerilyn Emori

Designer: Carolyn Deacy

Print Buyer: Randy Hurst

Art Editor: Donna Kalal

Permissions Editors: Marion Hansen,
    Roberta Broyer

Copy Editor: Margaret Moore

Photo Researchers: Stephen Forsling,
    Andromeda Oxford Ltd.

Illustrators: Alexander Teshin Associates,
    Joel Ito, Mark Stearney, Carlyn Iverson,
    Graphic Typesetting Service, John and
    Judy Waller, Beck Visual Communications,
    Jeanne Schreiber, Darwen Hennings

Cover Photographs: Michael Scannell (door),
    Stephen Rapley

Composition and Prepress Services:
    Interactive Composition Corporation

Printing and Binding: R. R. Donnelley &
    Sons, Willard Manufacturing Division

Cover Printer: Phoenix Color Corporation

Credits continue on page R-25

To Ken King,
editor and friend

A NOTE ABOUT THE AUTHOR

Jim Kalat

Jim Kalat (rhymes with ballot) has been teaching the introductory psychology course at North Carolina State University since 1977. He received an A.B. degree summa cum laude from Duke University in 1968 and a Ph.D. in psychology from the University of Pennsylvania in 1971. Recipient of Duke's Alumni Outstanding Teacher Award and North Carolina State University's Outstanding Teacher Award, Jim is a Fellow of the American Association for the Advancement of Science, the American Psychological Association, and the American Psychological Society, of which he was the program committee chair in 1991. Besides being the author of the bestselling *Biological Psychology* (the Fourth Edition was published by Wadsworth in 1992), Jim has published articles in many psychological journals, including *Psychological Review, Teaching of Psychology,* and *Journal of Comparative and Physiological Psychology.*

CONTENTS
IN BRIEF

CONTENTS

1 WHAT IS PSYCHOLOGY?

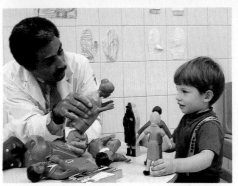

2 SCIENTIFIC METHODS IN PSYCHOLOGY

A good theory

Fits known facts

Predicts new discoveries

Is falsifiable

Is parsimonious

LET ME KNOW IF YOU HALLUCINATE.

3 BIOLOGICAL PSYCHOLOGY

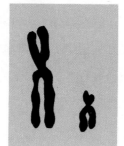

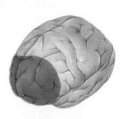

4 SENSATION AND PERCEPTION

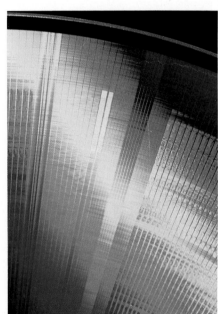

5 ALTERED STATES

6 DEVELOPMENT

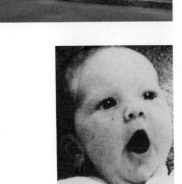

7 LEARNING

8 MEMORY

9 COGNITION AND LANGUAGE

10 INTELLIGENCE AND ITS MEASUREMENT

11 MOTIVATION

12 EMOTIONS, HEALTH PSYCHOLOGY, AND COPING WITH STRESS

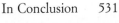

13 PERSONALITY

14 ABNORMAL BEHAVIOR

15 TREATMENT OF PSYCHOLOGICALLY TROUBLED PEOPLE

16 SOCIAL PSYCHOLOGY

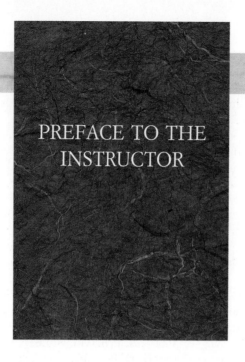

PREFACE TO THE INSTRUCTOR

Teaching psychology means far more than just changing what students know. It means changing how they think. It means ensuring that something worthwhile remains long after they have forgotten the details.

When students leave my Introduction to Psychology classroom, I certainly want them to know the field's important theories and research. But more importantly, I want them to learn the habit of questioning assertions—Freud's assertions, Skinner's, William James's, the president's, the newspaper's, their English professor's, their roommate's, mine. I want them to ask for the evidence and to know how to recognize holes in it.

I do not believe that a textbook can instill that habit of questioning assertions merely by means of boxes that are labeled "Critical Thinking." If students are going to form the habit, the author must model it in the normal course of covering the field. It should suffuse the text. I have tried to do that with this book. Consistently, I interweave material that challenges students to examine the evidence (or lack of it) behind some common assertions.

"A Guide Through the Book" following the Preface offers specifics on how this textbook can help students question for themselves, look for more than pat answers, and ultimately learn to appreciate psychology for the wondrous science that it is. And in the process, students will discover that when they begin to ask questions like psychologists that they will truly "own" the material of the course.

WHAT'S NEW IN THE THIRD EDITION

The content of this text is expanded and revised for this edition, featuring more than 500 new references, mostly from publications from 1989–1992. Every chapter has new material plus reorganization and increased clarification of old material. The illustrations are for the most part new to this edition or greatly improved. Here are a few notable changes.

- Chapter 1 (What Is Psychology?) includes a new module on the history of psychology, focusing on changes in what psychologists have considered to be interesting, answerable questions.

- Chapter 3 (Biological Psychology) has an improved explanation of how genes affect behavior, with new examples.

- The order of Chapters 4 and 5 has been reversed, putting "Sensation and Perception" before "Altered States." Note new research on olfactory receptors and on how marijuana affects the brain.

- Chapter 6 (Development) has a new module on the determinants of individual differences, including temperament, gender differences, and ethnic influences.

- Chapters 8 (Memory) and 9 (Cognition and Language) have been extensively revised and reorganized. Chapter 9 has a new module on cognitive aspects of language, including research on the psychology of reading. Chapter 6 (Development) retains material on the development of language. A new section on the psychology of gambling ties together many points from Chapters 7–9, showing how learning, memory, and cognition play a role in this often self-defeating behavior.

- Chapter 11 (Motivation) includes new research on possible biological predispositions to a homosexual orientation.

- In Chapter 13 (Personality), the second module (Personality Traits) has been significantly reorganized, putting the controversy about the trait approach at the start. A new section emphasizes the "big five" personality traits. Note also the updated material on the MMPI-2 and new research on the Rorschach.

- Chapter 15 (Treatment of Psychologically Troubled People) has an improved discussion of research on the benefits of psychotherapy.

- Much of Chapter 16 (Social Psychology) has been revised, including new or expanded treatment of racial stereotypes and prejudice, social loafing, the effects of mood on persuasion, and the equity principle in attraction. A new module highlights the power of the social situation. The module on industrial and organizational psychology has been deleted, although it appears in a separate booklet on applied psychology, which is available as a supplement.

- A brief Epilogue has been added.

TEACHING AND LEARNING AIDS FOR THIS BOOK

A number of important supplements accompany the text. Art Kohn of North Carolina Central University has prepared a very thorough and creative Instructor's Resource Guide. This volume includes suggestions for class demonstrations and lecture material; it also includes Kalat's answers to the text's "Something to Think About" questions. Ruth Maki of North Dakota State University has prepared a Study Guide that provides study aids and practice test items. Additional supplements include first- and second-year Test Item Files (also available on computer disks), videos, an interactive electronic study guide, PsychLab II (interactive software with psychology demonstrations and simulations), slides, and two sets of overhead transparencies. A separate booklet on applied psychology is provided with the text, on the instructor's request.

ACKNOWLEDGMENTS

A potential author needs self-confidence bordering on arrogance just to begin the job of writing a textbook. To complete it, the writer needs the humility to accept criticism of his or her favorite ideas and most carefully written prose. A great many people have provided helpful suggestions that have made this a far better text than it would have been otherwise.

I could not have started this book, much less completed it, without the constant support of my wife, Ann; my editor, Ken King; and my department head, Paul Thayer. To each of them: Thanks. You're the greatest.

John Boykin worked vigorously and creatively to help me organize my thoughts in revising the content of the text to develop the illustrations. He was determined to prepare illustrations that were attractive, pedagogically useful, and innovative. I am impressed, and as you page through the text, I am sure you will see why. Jerilyn Emori, who guided the production effort, has been a great pleasure to work with. Emori had the unenviable task of coordinating an author not known for great speed and a production schedule with very tight deadlines. Her sanity and sense of humor helped me keep my sanity and sense of humor. I also heartily thank Julie Davis and Carol Carreon for their work on the supplements, Joy Westberg for guiding the promotional efforts, Donna Kalal for coordinating the artists, Marion Hansen and Bobbie Broyer for taking care of permissions, Stephen Forsling for photo research, Carolyn Deacy for designing the book, and Gay Meixel for helping with all sorts of miscellaneous problems. For whatever you like about this text, these people deserve a good share of the credit.

Art Kohn has been the source of a number of creative ideas on how to approach certain topics; he has also been a stimulating person to talk to and a good friend. My colleagues at North Carolina State University provided me with encouragement, reprints and preprints, unpublished information, and free advice. I thank particularly Patricia Collins, Don Mershon, Rupert Barnes-Nacoste, Bob Pond, Paul Thayer, Bjorg Thayer, and student J. P. Thrower.

I thank the following people for their helpful reviews on earlier drafts of all or part of the book: Robert F. Bornstein, Gettysburg College; Dennis Bristow, Oklahoma State University–Stillwater; W. Jeffrey Burroughs, Clemson University; David W. Catron, Wake Forest University; Eliza T. Davies, Loyola University of Chicago; John H. Forthman, San Antonio College; Michael C. Hillard, University of New Mexico; David E. Irwin, University of Illinois at Urbana Champaign; Elizabeth M. Kurz, Indiana University at Bloomington; Dorothy L. Mercer, Eastern Kentucky University; Elaine Nocks, Furman University; Richard A. Page, Wright State University; Thomas R. Scott, University of Delaware; Donald Walter, University of Wisconsin–Parkside; Paul J. Wellman, Texas A & M University; Paul Whitney, Washington State University; Stacey B. Zaremba, Moravian College; and Otto Zinser, East Tennessee State University.

James Kalat

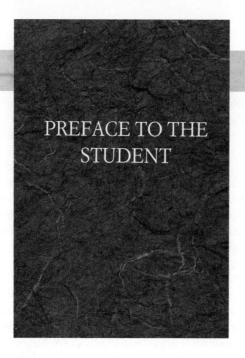

PREFACE TO THE STUDENT

Welcome to introductory psychology! I hope you will enjoy reading this text as much as I enjoyed writing it. When you finish, I hope you will write your comments on the last page of the text, tear the page out, and mail it to the publisher, who will pass it along to me. Please include a return address.

The first time I taught introductory psychology, several students complained that the book we were using was interesting to read but impossible to study. What they meant was that they had trouble finding and remembering the main points. I have tried to make this book easy to study in many ways. I have tried to make sure my discussion of each point is as clear as possible. I have tried to select material that will be as interesting as possible to you.

In addition, I have included some special features to aid your study. Each chapter begins with an outline and a brief introduction to the topic. Every chapter except Chapter 1 is divided into two or more major sections. Each of those sections begins with one or more questions—the fundamental questions that psychologists are trying to answer, the questions that motivate research. In some cases you will be able to answer the question after you read the section; in other cases you will not, because psychologists themselves are not sure about the answers. At the end of each major section you will find a summary of some important points, with page references. If you find one of the summary points unfamiliar, you should reread the appropriate section.

Throughout the text you will find certain words highlighted in **boldface.** These are important terms whose meaning you should understand. All the boldface terms in the text are listed with their definitions at the end of the chapter. They also appear in the Glossary/Subject Index at the end of the book. You might want to find the Glossary/Subject Index right now and familiarize yourself with it. Note that when you look up a term you find both its definition and page references to find it in the text. The Glossary/Subject Index also includes terms you might want to look up (such as *age differences*) that do not require definition.

You should learn the meaning of the boldface terms, but don't concentrate your study on them too heavily. I sometimes meet students who think they have mastered the course if they have memorized all the definitions. That's a mistake. You need to understand sentences that use these terms, and you should be able to recognize what is an example of the term and what is not. But memorizing definitions word for word is not a useful way to spend your time.

At various points in the text you will find a question under the heading "Concept Check." These questions enable you to test your understanding. They do not ask you simply to recall what you have read but to use or apply the information in some way. Try to answer each of these questions, rereading the previous material if necessary. Then turn to the indicated page to check your answers. If you cannot answer a Concept Check correctly, you probably have not been reading carefully enough, and you might want to reread the section in which the Concept Check occurs.

You will also find an occasional section marked "Something to Think About." These sections pose questions that require you to go beyond what is discussed in the text. In some cases there is no single right answer; there may be a number of reasonable ways to approach the question. I hope you will think about these questions, perhaps talk about them with fellow students, and maybe ask your instructor what he or she thinks.

I would like to deal with a few of the questions that students sometimes raise about their textbooks:

Do you have any useful suggestions on study habits? Whenever students ask me why they did so badly on the last test, I ask, "When did you read the assignment?" They often answer, "Well, I didn't exactly read *all* of the assignment," or "I read it the night before the test." To do your best, read each assignment *before the lecture*. Within 24 hours after the lecture, read over your lecture notes. Then, before you take the test, reread both the textbook assignment and your lecture notes. If you do not have time to reread everything, at least skim the text and reread the sections on which you need to refresh your memory.

As you read this book, try to think actively about what you are reading. One way to improve your studying is to read by the SPAR method: *Survey, Process meaningfully, Ask questions, Review*. The steps are as follows:

Survey: When you start a chapter, first look over the chapter outline to get a preview of the chapter's contents. When you start a major section of a chapter, turn to the end of the section and read the summary. When you begin to read the chapter you know what to expect and you can focus on the main points.

Process meaningfully: Read the chapter carefully. Stop to think from time to time. Tell your roommate some of the interesting things you learn. Think about how you might apply a certain concept in a real-life situation. Pause when you come to the Concept Checks and try to answer them.

Ask questions: When you finish the chapter, try to anticipate some of the questions you might be asked later. You can take questions from the Study Guide or you can compose your own questions. Write out your questions and think about them, but do not write your answers yet.

Review: Pause for a while—at least several hours, or, better yet, a day or two. If you first read a chapter before class, come back to the chapter the evening after class. Now write out the answers to the questions you wrote earlier. Check your answers against the text or against the answers given in the Study Guide. Reinforcing your memory a day or two after first reading the chapter will help you retain the material longer and with deeper understanding.

Is it worthwhile to buy and use the Study Guide? The Study Guide is designed to help students who have trouble studying, remembering the material, or answering multiple-choice questions. It is most likely to be helpful to freshmen, to students who have been away from college for a few years, and to students who have had trouble with similar courses in the past. It provides examples of multiple-choice questions, giving not only the correct answers but also explanations of why they are correct.

In the Study Guide for this text, written by Ruth Maki of North Dakota State University, you can work through each chapter in one or two hours. If you are willing to devote that much time to it, I believe the Study Guide will help you.

Does it help to underline or highlight key sentences while reading? Maybe, but don't overdo it. I have seen books in which a student underlined or highlighted more than half the sentences. What good that does, I have no idea.

What do those parentheses mean, as in "(Maki, 1990)"? Am I supposed to remember the names and dates? Psychologists generally cite references not by footnotes but in parentheses. "(Maki, 1990)" refers to a publication written by Maki and published in 1990. All the references cited are listed in alphabetical order according to the author's name in the References section at the back of the book.

You will also notice some citations that include two dates separated by a slash, such as "(Wundt, 1862/1961)." That citation refers to a publication originally published by Wundt in 1862, republished in 1961. (The original was in German; the republication was in English.)

No one expects you to memorize the names and dates in parentheses. They are there to enable you to look up the source of a statement in case you want more information. Some names *are* worth remembering, however. For instance, you will read about the research and theories of some famous psychologists, such as B. F. Skinner, Jean Piaget, and Sigmund Freud. You will certainly be expected to remember those names and a few others. But names that are important to remember are emphasized, not buried in parentheses.

Can you give me any help on how to read and understand graphs? The graphs in this book are easy to understand. Just take a minute or so to study them carefully. You will find four kinds: pie graphs, bar graphs, line graphs, and scatter plots. Let's look at each kind.

Pie graphs show how a whole is divided into parts. Figure 1 shows that more than one third

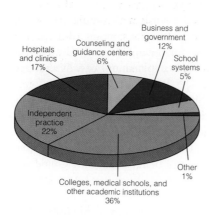

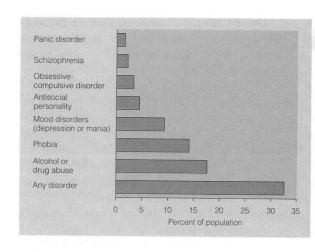

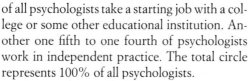

FIGURE 1
Pie graph.

FIGURE 2
Bar graph.

of all psychologists take a starting job with a college or some other educational institution. Another one fifth to one fourth of psychologists work in independent practice. The total circle represents 100% of all psychologists.

Bar graphs show the frequency of events that fall into one category or another. Figure 2 shows that about one third of all adults in the United States suffer from some type of psychological disorder. The length of the bar represents the frequency of each disorder. A fairly large number of people have a problem of alcohol or drug abuse, phobia, or affective disorders, a relatively small number have schizophrenia or panic disorder.

Line graphs show how one variable is related to another variable. In Figure 3 you see that newborn infants spend about 16 hours a day asleep. As they grow older, the amount of time they spend in two types of sleep gradually decreases.

Scatter plots are similar to line graphs, with this difference: A line graph shows averages, whereas a scatter plot shows individual data points. By looking at a scatter plot, we can see how much variation occurs among individuals.

To prepare a scatter plot, we make two observations about each individual. In Figure 4 each student is represented by one point. If you take that point and scan down to the *x*-axis, you find that student's SAT score. If you then scan across to the *y*-axis, you find that student's grade average for the freshman year. A scatter plot shows the relationship between two variables, but it also shows whether the variables are closely related or only loosely related.

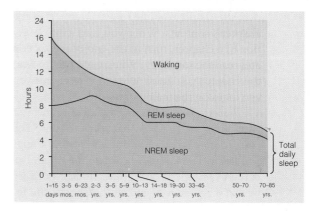

FIGURE 3
Line graph.

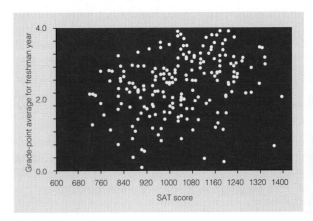

FIGURE 4
Scatter plot.

We may have to take multiple-choice tests on this material. How can I do better on those tests?

1. Read all of the choices carefully. Do not choose an answer just because it looks correct; first make sure that the other answers are wrong. Sometimes you will find a second answer that also sounds correct; decide which of the two is better.

2. If you don't know the correct answer, make an educated guess. Start by eliminating any answer that you know cannot be right. Generally, an answer that includes words such as *always* and *never* is wrong. (Psychologists are seldom sure that something is always right or always wrong.) Also eliminate any answer that includes terms that are unfamiliar to you. (Correct choices use only terms that should be familiar to a reasonably conscientious student; incorrect choices may include obscure terms or even outright nonsense.)

3. After you finish a test, go back and check your answers and rethink them. Many students insist that it is a mistake to change an answer because they think their first impulse is usually right. J. J. Johnston (1975) tested this belief by looking through the answer sheets of a number of classes that had taken a multiple-choice test. He found that of all the students who changed one or more answers, 71 students improved their scores by doing so and only 31 lowered their scores. Similar results have been reported mean that you should make changes just for the sake of making changes. But if you reconsider a question and change your mind about which answer is best, go ahead and change your answer.

Why, then, do so many students (and professors) believe that it is a mistake to change an answer? Imagine what happens when you take a test and get your paper back. When you look it over, which items do you pay attention to—the ones you got right or the ones you got wrong? The ones you got wrong, of course. You may notice three items that you originally answered correctly and then changed. You never notice the five other items you changed from incorrect to correct.

James Kalat

A GUIDE THROUGH THE BOOK

A NOTE FROM THE PUBLISHER

The scientific method is the most powerful tool in the psychologist's—and, indeed, the student's—intellectual armory. In this book, students learn that questioning assertions, challenging evidence, and evaluating results—all components of the scientific method—are second nature to the study of psychology itself. With author Jim Kalat's guidance, students are introduced to psychology in a way that will remain with them long after they may have forgotten specific theories, experiments, and results.

The material that follows demonstrates how the author uses the scientific method as a consistent theme throughout the book and how Kalat's carefully integrated learning tools clarify psychology's important theories and research.

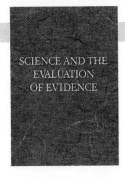

SCIENCE AND THE
EVALUATION
OF EVIDENCE

*How do scientists decide which is a better
theory and which is a worse theory?*

You will sometimes hear people say that something has been "scientifically proved." Scientists themselves seldom use the word *prove,* except when they are talking about a mathematical proof. As they collect more and better evidence, they may become confident about a given conclusion, but they still hesitate to say they are "certain" of it.

One distinguishing characteristic of science is that scientists generally agree on how to evaluate competing theories. Even when they disagree on which theory is best, they can still agree on what kinds of evidence they will accept in trying to decide. Most psychologists are quick to concede that our knowledge of psychology is less complete and less systematic than our knowledge of physics, chemistry, and biology. But like physicists, chemists, and biologists, psychologists generally agree on what constitutes good evidence and what does not. They try to rely on evidence, not on intuition.

Something to Think About

If ethicists agreed with each other on how to evaluate theories, could they make progress comparable to that of scientists? Could theologians?

STEPS IN GATHERING AND EVALUATING EVIDENCE

Above all, scientists want to know the evidence behind a given claim. If this book has one overall theme, that is it. Psychologists would like students to learn to question assertions in psychology, to ask what is the evidence behind a given claim and whether that evidence leads to an unambiguous conclusion.

In any scientific field, researchers conduct studies that go through a series of steps described in the following four paragraphs (see also Figure 2.1). Articles in scientific publications generally follow this sequence too. In each of the following chapters, you will find a section titled "What's the Evidence?" Those sections will go through one or more psychological investigations step by step, also in this order.

Hypothesis Any study begins with a **hypothesis,** which is a testable prediction of what will happen under certain conditions. In many cases the hypothesis is the product of someone's casual observations. For example, a psychologist might notice that children who like to watch violent television programs seem to be relatively violent themselves. So it seems, at any rate; we cannot always trust our impressions. The psychologist might then set out to test whether those children who watch the greatest amount of violence on television engage in the greatest amount of aggressive behavior.

Method Devising an appropriate method to test a hypothesis can be surprisingly difficult. For example, an investigator wants to measure how much violence each child watches on television. That may sound easy. But what counts as violence? Do we count minutes of violent programming, or do we count violent acts? Do some types of violence count more than others? We encounter similar problems in measuring a child's aggressive behavior. The mark of a skillful investigator is the ability to find ways to measure behaviors accurately.

FOUR STEPS

HYPOTHESIS

METHOD

33

Chapter 2 is the most important chapter in the book. It deals not only with the procedures for conducting research but also provides a conceptual guide to how psychologists evaluate evidence and theories and, in general, to how they think. For example, it highlights the importance of replicability, the criterion of falsifiability, and the principle of parsimony.

Early in Chapter 2, Kalat gives an overview of the research process. He introduces the four steps in gathering and evaluating evidence—hypothesis, method, results, and interpretation. This critical material—the heart of the scientific method—is then reinforced throughout the text.

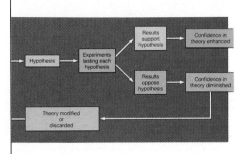

RESULTS **Results** Suppose the investigator somehow measures televised violence and aggressive behavior. Then the task is to determine the relationship between the two measures. Did the children who watched the greatest amount of violence also engage in the most aggressive behavior? If so, how strong was the relationship? Were the results convincing, or might they have arisen by accident? Here the investigator calls upon statistical techniques to evaluate the results.

INTERPRETATION **Interpretation** Finally, the task is to determine what the results mean. Sometimes the results clearly contradict the hypothesis. For example, an investigator might find that children who watch a great deal of televised violence are no more aggressive than other children, in general. In that case we might abandon the hypothesis or we might modify it: Maybe it applies only to certain kinds of children or to certain kinds of violence.

If the results match the prediction, we would look for other possible explanations before we draw a conclusion. Suppose, for example, the investigator finds that the children who watched the most violence on television were also prone to the most aggressive behavior. We would not conclude that televised violence leads to aggressive behavior, because of an alternative interpretation: Perhaps aggressive children like to watch violent television!

It is almost always possible to suggest more than one interpretation of the results of a given study. At that point the investigator sets up a second study to follow up on the results of the first and tries to decide between the two inter-

pretations. That study too may lead to further studies. Because almost any study has its limitations, the ultimate conclusion comes from a pattern of results from many studies.

REPLICABILITY

Before psychologists trust the results of a study, we like to have other investigators repeat the procedure. If they get similar results, then they have **replicable results**—that is, anyone who follows the same procedure can repeat them. If a result is replicable, we still may not be sure how to interpret it, but at least we think it is worthwhile to try. If the results cannot be replicated, then perhaps there was some hidden flaw in the first study; we base no conclusions on it.

What if a result can be replicated in some studies and not others? For example, when studying the effects of televised violence on children, certain investigators might find one set of results, while others find the opposite. Presuming that both sets of investigators conducted their studies equally well, what are we to believe?

Psychologists would look for some pattern in the results. Perhaps watching violence on television is associated with violent behavior only for children of a certain age or just for one sex. Or perhaps the results depend on the type of violent program or on the method of measuring aggressive behavior. If such a pattern seemed to emerge, psychologists would conduct additional research to confirm that pattern and try to understand it better. If no such pattern emerged, they would become skeptical of

out well; later, people forget their doubts and agree that "of course" it had been a good idea.

We can explain hindsight bias in several ways (Hawkins & Hastie, 1990). To some extent, people may misrepresent their previous beliefs to make themselves look smart. ("See how smart I am? I knew this was going to happen.") Also, people frequently cannot quite remember what they had expected before the event occurred. After the event, they remember the previous facts that fit best with the eventual outcome; they ignore other information or regard it as irrelevant. From the facts that stand out in their memory, they reconstruct an expectation of what was likely to occur—an expectation that fits the events that actually did occur, and not the expectation they really had before they knew the outcome.

Something to Think About

Can you interpret people's beliefs that they had a "psychic hunch" in terms of hindsight bias?

The Suggestibility of Eyewitness Accounts

WHAT'S THE EVIDENCE?

When people in a psychologist's laboratory distort a story or alter their recollections of previous beliefs in hindsight, no harm is done. But sometimes a great deal is riding on the accuracy of someone's memory.

You have just watched a robbery committed by a man you had never seen before. When the police ask you to describe the thief, you do your best, but you saw him for only a few seconds and cannot recall many details. The police ask, "Did he have a mustache? Did he have a tattoo on his right hand? Two other robberies were pulled off around here in the last few days by a man with a mustache and a tattoo on his right hand." Suddenly it comes back to you: "Yes, he definitely had a mustache. And I'm almost sure he had a tattoo." Did the suggestion help you to recall those details? Or did it prompt you to reconstruct details that you never actually saw?

EXPERIMENT 1

Hypothesis If people are asked questions that suggest or presuppose a certain fact, many peo-

ple will later report remembering that "fact," even if it never happened.

Method Elizabeth Loftus (1975) asked two groups of students to watch a videotape of an automobile accident. Then she asked one group, "Did you see the children getting on the school bus?" She did not ask the other group that question. In fact, there was no school bus in the videotape. A week later, she asked both groups 20 new questions about the accident, including this one: "Did you see a school bus in the film?"

Results Of the first group (those who were asked about seeing children get on a school bus), 26% reported they had seen a school bus; of the second group, only 6% said they had seen a school bus.

Interpretation The question "Did you see the children getting on the school bus?" presupposes that there was a school bus. Some of the people who heard that question added a school bus to their memory of the event. The students reconstructed what happened by combining what they actually saw with what they believed might reasonably have happened and with what someone suggested to them afterward.

What do results of this type mean? Suppose experimenters ask you whether you remember seeing children getting on the school bus. Later they ask whether you remember a school bus, and you say yes. That result might mean that the first question added a school bus to your memory. But it might also mean that you have no idea whether there was a school bus, so you are willing to go along with the experimenters' implication that there was. Or you might think, "Hmm . . . I don't remember a school bus, but the experimenters asked about one before, and I suppose they should know. So I'll say I remember a school bus." When the experimenters' suggestion leads you to give the wrong answer, does it actually change your memory or does it just change your answer?

EXPERIMENT 2

Hypothesis When people are given a misleading suggestion and then asked about what they saw, they may give answers that follow the suggestion. But if they are asked questions that eliminate the suggested information as a possible answer, they will return to the original information.

---

would talk about the student's creativity; in other cases we talk of someone's expertise. In either case, some people seem more able than other people to understand a problem or to find feasible solutions.

But what do we mean when we say "understand"? How could we determine whether someone understands, say, algebra? We would need an operational definition of *understand*. Suppose we adopt this one: Understanding is measured by how accurately someone can solve problems. That is, anyone who can solve algebra problems accurately must understand algebra.

Let's try an algebra problem: A board was sawed into two pieces. One piece was 3/4 as long as the whole board. It exceeded the length of the second piece by 2 meters. What was the length of the whole board? (Pause to calculate the answer.)

If your algebra is not too rusty, you quickly calculated that the answer is 4 meters. If you now enter the appropriate information into a computer, it too would report an answer of 4 meters. So, according to our definition of *understand*, the computer "understands."

But is the computer's understanding the same as yours? Let's try another problem similar to the first: A board was sawed into two pieces. One piece was 2/3 as long as the whole board. The second piece exceeded it in length by 2 meters. What was the length of the whole board? (Pause to calculate your answer.)

Many people answer 6 meters (Larkin, McDermott, Simon, & Simon, 1980). A computer invariably comes up with the correct answer—which is *minus* 6 meters. If you said 6 meters,

does yo[...]
derstan[...]
seems t[...]
stand t[...]
does no[...]
negativ[...]
problem[...]
the whole must be the longer of the two.

Something to Think About

The Turing Test, suggested by computer pioneer Alan Turing, proposes the following operational definition of artificial intelligence: A person poses questions to a human source and to a computer, both in another room. The human and the computer send back typewritten replies, which are identified only as coming from "source A" or "source B." If the questioner cannot determine which replies are coming from the computer, then the computer has passed a significant test of understanding.

Suppose a computer did pass the Turing Test. Would we then say that the computer "understands," just as a human does? Or would we say that it is merely mimicking human understanding?

Expert Pattern Recognition

In any field from algebra to zoology, we identify some people as "experts." One characteristic of experts is that they can look at a pattern and identify its important features almost at once. In a typical experiment (de Groot, 1966), people were shown pieces on a chessboard, as in Figure 9.10, for 5 seconds. Then they were asked to recall the position of all the pieces. When the pieces were arranged as they might occur in an actual game, expert players could recall the position of 91% of them, while novices could recall only 41%. When the pieces were arranged randomly, however, the expert players did no better than the nonexperts. Although expert chess players do not have a superior memory in general, they recognize familiar chessboard patterns far better than other people do.

Similarly, expert figure skaters can memorize a sequence of skating moves better than an average skater can. In one study, six members of the Canadian women's ice-skating team and four other, moderately skilled skaters were asked to memorize a sequence of eight skating elements and then either to describe them

FIGURE 9.10
Pieces arranged on a chessboard in a way that might actually occur in a game (a) and in a random manner (b). Master chess players can memorize the realistic pattern much better than average players can, but they are no better than average at memorizing the random pattern.

CONCEPT CHECKS

Almost 200 *Concept Checks* are strategically placed at the ends of sections throughout the book. These questions are proactive mind expanders that get students to think about, manipulate, and apply the preceding material in a conceptual fashion, rather than just repeating back what they read. Students go beyond remembering facts to *understanding* main ideas.

To further enhance continuity and clarity, these checks appear in-line with the main text, not set off in boxes. Answers are given at the end of each module.

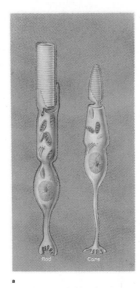

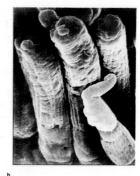

b

FIGURE 4.5
(a) A rod and a cone, the eye's two types of sensing cells. (b) Rods and cones seen through a scanning electron micrograph. The rods, which number over 120 million, help us see in dim light. The 6 million cones in the retina can distinguish gradations of color in bright light; they enable us to see that roses are red, magenta, ruby, carmine, cherry, vermilion, scarlet, and crimson—not to mention pink, yellow, orange, and white.

a

resources. More than a hundred rods send messages to the next cell in the visual system, but only a few cones converge their messages onto a given cell.

Here is another difference between rods and cones: When a light is suddenly turned off, the activity of the cones ceases almost immediately, whereas the activity of the rods declines more gradually (Jacobs, 1981). In other words, the cones give more accurate information about sudden changes in visual stimulation. Table 4.1 summarizes the key differences between rods and cones.

■ CONCEPT CHECK

1. *Why is it easier to see a faint star in the sky if you look slightly to the side of the star instead of straight at it? (Check your answer on page 133.)*

FIGURE 4.6
The consequence of having receptors mostly on the top of the retina. Birds of prey, such as these owlets, can see down much more clearly than they can see up. In flight, that arrangement is helpful. On the ground, they have to turn their heads almost upside down in order to see above them.

At first, researchers focused mostly on the role of impatience and competitiveness as the main links between Type A behavior and heart disease. When Type A people perform competitive tasks, their muscle tension increases and their sympathetic nervous system is aroused (Williams et al., 1982). Because they seek competitive tasks, their hearts are working hard much of the time.

However, later evidence has indicated that heart disease correlates more strongly with unpleasant emotions, especially depression and hostility (Booth-Kewley & Friedman, 1987). Perhaps a highly responsive sympathetic nervous system predisposes people to feel tense, while it also overstimulates the heart. Future research will tell us more about how depression and anger contribute to heart disease.

CONCEPT CHECK

5. *People with a Type A personality are likely to develop stress-related heart disease. Yet when they fill out the Social Readjustment Rating Scale, mentioned earlier, their scores are often low. Why might that scale understate the stress levels of Type A people? (Check your answer on page 524.)*

Cancer

Among the causes of cancer are genetics and exposure to toxic substances. Behavior also can influence the onset and spread of cancer, at least indirectly. For example, people who smoke cigarettes increase their risk of cancer. Women who examine their breasts regularly can detect breast cancer at an early, treatable stage. Do emotions contribute directly to cancer? Because the brain influences the immune system, which fights cancer, an emotional experience might lead to an impairment of the immune system and therefore to a greater risk of certain kinds of cancer.

The two emotional states most likely to lead to cancer are depression and stress. Many cancer patients are depressed (Weinstock, 1984), and many of them report that they were depressed, often following the death of a loved one, long before they knew they had cancer. Severe depression suppresses the activity of the immune system and leaves a person more vulnerable than usual to all sorts of infection and disease, including the spread of certain types of tumors (Anisman & Zacharko, 1983; Baker, 1987).

In research on the effects of stress in animals, increases the growth of cancer in those animals. But the animals from one duration and makeup animal studies deal with cancers caused by viruses, and viruses cause fewer than 5% of human cancers (Fox, 1983).

Depression, stress, and severe emotional problems probably do increase the risk of cancer in humans. Still, the influence is minor; emotional factors are far less important in causing cancer than are genes and toxic substances (Anisman & Zacharko, 1983; Derogatis, 1986; Fox, 1983). Keeping a positive outlook on life may help to prevent cancer; still, many people suffering from serious, long-lasting depression manage to survive to old age (Stein, Miller, & Trestman, 1991).

Psychological factors may exert a stronger influence on what happens after the onset of cancer. People who receive steady support from their family and friends have a better chance of recovery. People who decide to fight the disease have a better chance than do those who take a resigned, helpless attitude that "what will be, will be" (Geer, Morris, & Pettingale, 1979). Exactly how the patient's attitude contributes to survival we do not know, but again it probably relates to enhancing or impairing the functions of the immune system.

BIOFEEDBACK: A BEHAVIORAL METHOD OF CONTROLLING BODY FUNCTIONS

As we have seen, stress, depression, hostility, and other unpleasant emotional states can make people more vulnerable to illness. Is there anything we can do to make ourselves less vulnerable or to improve our health?

Maybe. **Biofeedback,** for example, is a method for gaining voluntary control over physiological processes that we cannot ordinarily control. Recording devices are attached to the body to monitor heart rate, blood pressure, brain waves, or other body activities (Figure 12.22). The person is given constant information ("feedback") about the activity and instructions to try to control it. For example, to reduce the effects of stress, we might monitor

QUESTIONING ASSERTIONS AS SECOND NATURE

The book's theme of questioning assertions is woven throughout the main body of the text. This material suffuses the writing, sometimes appearing as a sentence or two in the middle of a discussion, sometimes as a paragraph, a full page, or more. The result is a book that continually challenges students to think carefully about each topic as they read.

---

to begin with, and a number of those who survived continued to be reared under poor conditions (Clarke & Clarke, 1976). Still, severe deprivation of human contact early in life clearly can be extremely harmful.

● CONCEPT CHECK

8. *In what way were the unstimulating institutions similar to the Harlows' artificial monkeys? (Check your answer on page 261.)*

SOCIAL DEVELOPMENT IN CHILDHOOD

Infants less than 1 year old seldom play with one another. They show interest in one another, but they do not have enough social skills to continue any meaningful social interactions. From age 1 to 2, we can see the beginnings of social play, but still it is mostly **parallel play:** Two or more infants play at the same time, in the same place, but almost independently. After about age 2, children start playing with one another more and more. Relationships with their parents are always important, but for certain purposes they prefer to play with others their own age.

The social and emotional development of children depends in part on how successful they are in forming friendships with other children (Figure 6.29). Some children are "popular," having many friends and admirers. Others are "rejected," with most other children avoiding their company. Still others are "controversial," liked by some and rejected by others. Controversial children are generally those with some social skills but an aggressive streak.

FIGURE 6.29
Children learn their social skills by interacting with brothers, sisters, and friends close to their own age.

overworked. The healthy child in the family may react by being aggressive, impulsive, and self-destructive and engaging in other attention-getting behavior (Breslau & Prabucki, 1987).

Many studies have been made of the effects of being a firstborn child or being born later. A number of those birth-order studies report that firstborn children do better in school, are more ambitious, are more honest, and have a greater need to affiliate with others. Children born later tend to be more popular, more independent, less conforming, better adjusted emotionally, and possibly more creative. These tendencies are slight and inconsistent, however, and some of the evidence is based on poorly conducted studies (Ernst & Angst, 1983; Schooler, 1972). Be skeptical of recommendations that parents should space their children many years apart in order to give each of them the alleged benefits of the firstborn.

Something to Think About

Psychologists have offered two explanations for the effects of birth order on behavior: (1) Depending on whether there are older, younger, or no other children in the family, each child is subjected to different social influences. (2) Because the mother undergoes physical changes, such as changes in her hormones after giving birth, younger children experience different prenatal influences from those experienced by the firstborn child. What kind of evidence

---

Table 8.7	
Arnold Schwarzenegger	singer
Sandra Day O'Connor	figure skater
Michael Jordan	politician
Madonna	televangelist
Dan Rather	standup comic
Julia Roberts	inventor
Saddam Hussein	talk-show host
Boris Yeltsin	medical researcher
Martina Navratilova	movie critic
Michael Jackson	auctioneer
Barbara Bush	fashion designer
Clarence Thomas	architect
Connie Chung	golfer

committing the crime they are accused of; some say they cannot remember anything that happened that entire day. Indeed, that sort of amnesia is possible. But what about the possibility that some of these accused criminals are faking amnesia? Occasionally a claim of amnesia is made to support a plea of not guilty by reason of insanity. Suppose a psychologist or a psychiatrist is asked to determine whether such a person is truly suffering amnesia or is just faking it. How accurately can an expert distinguish the real thing from an imitation?

Daniel Schacter (1986a, 1986b) devised an experiment to answer that question. He had one group of students read a passage or watch a videotape that included many details that most people do not notice. When they were asked what certain people in the story were wearing or exactly what they said at certain times, the subjects replied (correctly) that they did not remember. A second group read the same material or watched the same videotape after being instructed to watch for those details but to *pretend* to forget them. Schacter then brought in a number of psychologists and psychiatrists who were frequently called as expert witnesses in court to determine which subjects had really forgotten and which ones were only pretending. The experts interviewed all the subjects and tried to determine which ones had really forgotten the answers and which ones were only pretending to forget. None of the experts showed much more than 50-50 accuracy, even in those cases on which they felt most certain.

The moral of the story: *If someone claims to know whether a person is suffering amnesia or faking it, be skeptical. At least ask that person to explain how he or she knows.*

SELECTIVE MEMORY

Of all the experiences you have had, you certainly remember some much more clearly than others. Generally you are most likely to remember information that is meaningful or distinctive. For example, if you try to remember the events that occurred during your junior year of high school, you are likely to recall mostly events that were highly interesting or important to you. But now suppose that the police, as part of a crime investigation, ask you to recall the details of some event that seemed uninteresting and not very important at the time. Under those circumstances your recall is likely to be accurate on some details but incomplete and inaccurate on others.

Importance of Meaningfulness

Memory is enhanced if the material is **meaningful,** fitting into a known pattern of information. If several people listen to a story about a baseball game, the ones who know the most about baseball tend to remember it best. Those who know the most about chess will remember the most from an article about chess.

J. D. Bransford and M. K. Johnson (1972) described one clever experiment illustrating the influence of meaningfulness. After looking at either picture A or picture B in Figure 8.28, two groups of people listened to the paragraph in part C (Bransford & Johnson, 1972, p. 131). Note that the paragraph makes sense if you have seen picture A but is nearly incomprehensible if you have seen only picture B. As you might expect, the people who had seen picture A remembered about twice as much of the paragraph as those who had seen only picture B.

Serial-Order Effect

When you try to remember a series of events that occurred in a temporal order, you probably find it easiest to remember the first ones and the last ones. For example, try to remember all the times you have ever applied for a job. Then try to remember all the football games you have attended. Unless you never had to apply for a job and you hate football, chances are you remember the first couple of times you applied for a

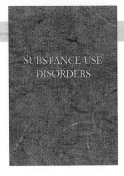

SUBSTANCE-USE DISORDERS

KEY QUESTIONS

Why do people sometimes abuse alcohol and other drugs?

What can be done to help them quit?

INTRODUCTION How would you like to volunteer for a little experiment? I want to implant a device in your head to control your brain activity—something that will automatically lift your mood and bring you happiness. There are still a few kinks in it, but most of the people who have tried it say it makes them feel good at least some of the time, and some people say it makes them feel "very happy."

I should tell you about the possible risks: My device will endanger your health and will reduce your life expectancy by, oh, 10 years or so. Some people think it may cause permanent brain damage, but they have not proved that charge, so I don't think you should worry about it. Your behavior will change a good bit, though. You may have difficulty concentrating, for example. The device affects some people more than others. If you happen to be one of those it affects strongly, you will have difficulty completing your education, getting or keeping a job, and carrying on a satisfactory personal life. But if you are lucky, you may avoid all that. Anyway, you can quit the experiment any time you want to. You should know, though, that the longer the device remains in your brain, the harder it is to get it out.

I cannot pay you for taking part in the experiment. In fact, *you* will have to pay *me*. But I'll give you a bargain rate: only $5 for the first week and then a little more each week as time passes. One other thing: Technically speaking, this experiment is illegal. We probably won't get caught, but if we do, we could both go to jail.

What do you say? Is it a deal?

I presume you will say no. I get very few volunteers. And yet if I change the term *brain device* to *drug* and change *experimenter* to *drug peddler*, it is amazing how many volunteers come forward.

For some people, using alcohol or drugs is apparently a harmless pleasure. For others, it is extremely destructive.

In Chapter 5 we examined the effects of several drugs on behavior. Instead of reviewing all of those drugs again here, we shall focus on substance abuse, principally of alcohol and opiates—addictions that have been familiar to humans for centuries and which continue to be major problems today. Substance abuse is one of the most widespread of psychological disorders.

PSYCHOACTIVE SUBSTANCE DEPENDENCE (ADDICTION)

Most people who drink alcohol or experiment with marijuana and other drugs do so in moderation. But some people are such heavy users that they jeopardize their health, their work or education, and the welfare of their family. They may use the substance daily, only on weekends, or only during sporadic binges; whatever the pattern, they know they are consuming too much. They may decide again and again to quit or cut down, but they find it impossible to change their behavior. Those who cannot quit a self-destructive habit are said to have a **dependence** on a substance or **addiction** to it.

A common estimate is that about 10% of all people in the United States and Canada have a substance dependence. Depending on where we draw the line between those with a problem

---

A MODULAR APPROACH

To give maximum flexibility to the instructor, each chapter is divided into two-to-five free-standing modules.

Helping to emphasize the book's theme of questioning assertions, these modules begin with one or more <u>key questions</u> that are important in motivating research.

Each module has its own introduction, <u>summary</u>, review of terms, and <u>answers</u>. This organization enables instructors to easily pick and choose assigned reading to meet their own course syllabi.

Each module has its own <u>recommendation of books and papers</u> for students to pursue in library research. Brief descriptions of each work are also included.

...thadone ...down a ...hey did ...orphine ...m, after discovering that they can no longer get a high from opiates, turn instead to the nonopiate drug cocaine (Kosten, Rounsaville, & Kleber, 1987). In other words, methadone maintenance programs do not eliminate the addictive behaviors. At present, there is no reliable cure for opiate dependence.

Table 14.5 Comparison of Methadone with Morphine

	Morphine	Methadone
Addictive?	Yes	Yes if taken by injection; weakly if taken orally
Administration	Usually by injection	Recommended for oral use
Onset	Rapid	Slow if taken orally
"Rush"?	Yes	Not if taken orally
Relieves craving?	Yes	Yes
Rapid withdrawal symptoms?	Yes	No

SUMMARY

■ *Substance dependence.* People who find it difficult or impossible to stop using a substance are said to be dependent on it or addicted to it. (page 598)

■ *Addictive substances.* Generally, the faster a substance enters the brain, the more likely it is to be addictive. For some people, however, almost any substance can be addictive. (page 599)

■ *Predisposition to alcoholism.* Some people may be predisposed to become alcoholics for genetic or other reasons. People at risk for alcoholism find that alcohol relieves their stress more than it does for other people. They also tend to underestimate how intoxicated they are. (page 599)

■ *Alcoholics Anonymous.* The most common treatment for alcoholism in North America is provided by the self-help group called Alcoholics Anonymous. (page 602)

■ *Antabuse.* Some alcoholics are treated with Antabuse, a prescription drug that makes them ill if they drink alcohol. (page 602)

■ *The "disease" controversy.* Whether or not alcoholism is a disease is controversial; calling it a disease may distract attention from the environmental factors that lead to drinking. (page 603)

■ *The "controlled drinking" controversy.* Whether alcoholics can be trained to drink in moderation is also a controversial, unsettled question. For severe alcoholics, no known method of treatment offers a high probability of recovery. (page 603)

■ *Treatments for opiate abuse.* Some opiate users quit using opiates, suffer through the withdrawal symptoms, and manage to abstain from further use. Others substitute methadone under medical supervision. Although methadone has less destructive effects than morphine or heroin does, it does not eliminate the underlying dependence. (page 604)

SUGGESTIONS FOR FURTHER READING

Marlatt, G. A., & Baer, J. S. (1988). Addictive behaviors: Etiology and treatment. *Annual Review of Psychology, 39,* 223–252. A review of the literature on who becomes an alcoholic or drug addict, why, and what can be done to help.

Vaillant, G. E. (1983). *The natural history of alcoholism.* Cambridge, MA: Harvard University Press. A thorough study of what happens to alcoholics over the course of their lifetime.

TERMS

dependence or **addiction** a self-destructive habit that someone cannot quit (page 598)

detoxification supervised period to remove drugs from the body (page 602)

alcoholism habitual overuse of alcohol (page 602)

Alcoholics Anonymous (AA) a self-help group of people who are trying to abstain from alcohol use and to help others do the same (page 602)

Antabuse trade name for disulfiram, a drug used in the treatment of alcoholism (page 603)

methadone a drug commonly offered as a less dangerous substitute for opiates (page 604)

ANSWERS TO CONCEPT CHECKS

8. The injection route is more likely to lead to an addiction. Other things being equal, the faster a drug reaches the brain, the more likely it is to become addictive. (page 590)

9. They are less likely than others to become alcoholics. This gene is considered the probable reason why relatively few Asians become alcoholics (Harada et al., 1982; Reed, 1985). (page 603)

Where appropriate and relevant, the text includes discussions of how culture, ethnicity, and gender influence behavior. By studying this diversity, psychologists can more thoroughly investigate the generality of psychological findings.

To determine whether a behavior is normal or abnormal, heroic or deeply disturbed, we have to know its social and cultural context. Here, Iranian worshippers flog themselves to reenact the suffering of an early Shi'ite martyr. In this context, self-flogging is a normal part of a religious ritual. In some other context, it might be a sign of psychological distress.

should accept. Some totalitarian governments have classed all political dissidents as "mentally ill."

In short, there may be no simple way to define abnormal behavior or psychological disorder. Our lack of a clear definition is a problem in some cases and not in others. For example, severely depressed people may be distressed or disordered by everyone's definition, including their own. But someone who defies the usual customs of personal hygiene and polite speech may seem "severely disordered" to some observers and merely "eccentric" to others.

Cultural Differences in Views of Abnormal Behavior

Abnormal behavior has been known in all cultures throughout history. Each time and place has interpreted such behavior according to its own worldview. People in the Middle Ages, for example, regarded bizarre behavior as a sign that the disturbed person was possessed by a demon. To exorcise the demon, priests resorted to prescribed religious rituals (Figure 14.1). During the 1800s, when the "germ" theory of illness was popular and people sought a scientific explanation for everything they observed, physicians interpreted abnormal behav-

ior as "mental illness." They tried to find its cause and a way to cure it, just as they did in treating other illnesses. In various parts of the world today, some cultures regard abnormal behaviors as biological disorders, some still talk about demon possession, and some have other interpretations.

Cultures differ not only in their views of abnormal behavior; they also differ in the behaviors themselves (Berry, Poortinga, Segal, & Dasen, 1992). For example, you probably have heard the expression "to run amok." *Running amok* is a type of abnormal behavior recognized in parts of Southeast Asia, in which someone (usually a male) runs around engaging in furious, almost indiscriminate violent behavior. *Pibloqtoq* is an uncontrollable desire to tear off one's clothing and expose oneself to severe winter weather; it is a recognized form of psychological disorder in parts of Greenland, Alaska, and the Arctic regions of Canada. *Latah* is an apparently uncontrollable tendency to imitate other people's actions, reported among women of Malaysia. *Brain fag* is a condition of headache, eye fatigue, and inability to concentrate—a common complaint among West African students just before exams. And consider our own society: We recognize *anorexia nervosa* as a psychological disorder that entails voluntary starvation. That disorder is well known in Europe, North America, and Australia, but unheard-of in many other parts of the world.

What are we to make of the fact that certain disorders occur in some cultures but not others? One interpretation is that the conditions necessary for causing them occur in some places but not others. Another interpretation is that people learn certain kinds of abnormal behavior by imitation. Perhaps if you had seen people "run amok" from time to time, you might react to some distressing situation by doing the same yourself.

Competing Views of Abnormal Behavior

Among therapists and researchers today, *one influential point of view is that many psychological disorders are the result of biological disorders*, including genetics, brain damage, chemical imbalances in the brain, hormonal abnormalities, poor nutrition, inadequate sleep, various diseases, and overuse of certain drugs, including over-the-counter medications. *A second point of view is that some psychological disorders are the result of disordered thinking caused by early ex-*

FIGURE 4.53
Retinal disparity is one cue to distance. The left and right eyes see slightly different versions of any scene; the difference between the image on the left retina and the image on the right retina indicates the distance to each object.

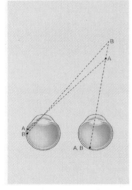

Depth Perception

Depth perception is our perception of distance; it enables us to experience the world in three dimensions. Depth perception depends on several factors.

We use **retinal disparity**—the difference in the apparent position of an object as seen by the left and right retinas—to compare the views the two eyes see (Figure 4.53). Try this: Hold one finger at arm's length. Focus on it with one eye and then with the other. Note that the apparent position of your finger shifts with respect to the background. Now hold your finger closer to your face and repeat the experiment. Notice that the apparent position of your finger shifts by a greater amount. *The discrepancy between the slightly different views the two eyes see becomes greater as the object comes closer.* We use the amount of discrepancy to gauge distance.

A second cue for depth perception is the **convergence** of our eyes—that is, the degree to which they turn in to focus on a close object (Figure 4.54). When you focus on a distant object, your eyes are looking in almost parallel directions. When you focus on something close, your eyes turn in; you can sense the pulling in of your muscles. The more the muscles pull, the closer the object must be.

Retinal disparity and convergence are called **binocular cues,** because they depend on the action of both eyes. **Monocular cues** enable a person to judge depth and distance effectively with just one eye, or if both eyes see the same image, as they do when you look at a picture. Several monocular cues help us judge the approximate distance of the objects in Figure 4.55:

- *Object size.* Other things being equal, an object close to us produces a larger image than does one farther away. This cue is useful only if we already knew the approximate actual size of the objects. For example, the roller skater in the photo produces a larger image than does the parked van, which we know is actually larger. So we see the skater as closer. The rocks in the sea, however, are not equally large in reality, so the relative sizes of their images are not a cue to their distance.

- *Linear perspective.* As parallel lines stretch out toward the horizon, they come closer and closer together. Examine the road in Figure 4.55. At the bottom of the photo (close to the viewer), the edges of the road are far apart; at greater distances, the edges of the road come closer together. The closer the lines come, the more distant we perceive them to be.

Key terms are printed in bold type, defined at their first appearance, defined again at the end of the module, and defined a third time in a combined Glossary / Subject Index at the end of the book.

This edition contains hundreds of full-color paintings, illustrations, and photographs. The captions for the illustrations are an important learning tool. Rather than simply describing the illustration, they connect the illustration with textual discussion, often helping to clarify important concepts. For increased pedagogical value, this edition has many more tables, charts, and diagrams than the second edition. All the biological art has been replaced with striking and lucid new art. Many of the figures have been streamlined for clarity. Photojournalism is used whenever possible to show that psychology often means understanding how real people function in the real world.

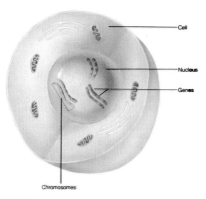

FIGURE 3.1
Genes are sections of chromosomes, which are in the nuclei of cells. Scale is exaggerated for illustration purposes.

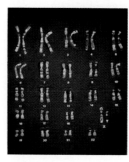

FIGURE 3.2
The nucleus of each human cell contains 46 chromosomes, 23 from the sperm and 23 from the ovum, united in pairs.

whether the individual develops as a tall red-headed woman or a short blond man.

We can locate and identify certain genes by examining chromosomes under a microscope, though most genes cannot be located so readily. If we know that a particular gene is close to some other gene that we have already located on a chromosome, then we can use that other gene as a marker. For example, if you have a particular gene that we know your father and his mother also had, then you probably also have certain other genes that are close to that gene on their chromosomes. By using such reasoning, we can identify people who have a gene that predisposes them to a particular disease even before the symptoms have become evident (Gilliam et al., 1987).

The Transmission of Genes from One Generation to Another

Because people have two of each chromosome, they have two of each type of gene, one on each of the chromosomes. They have two genes for eye color, two for hair color, two for every characteristic. The two genes for hair color, for example, may be either the same or different.

When both genes of a given pair of chromosomes are the same, the person is said to be **homozygous** (HO-mo-ZI-gus) for that gene. When the two genes are different, the person is **heterozygous** (HET-er-o-ZI-gus) for that gene (Figure 3.3). (A *zygote* is a fertilized egg. *Homozygous* means *a fertilized egg formed from the same genes; heterozygous means a fertilized egg formed from different genes.)

Certain genes are labeled **dominant genes** because they will exert their effects on development even in a person who is heterozygous for that gene. Very few human behaviors depend on a single gene, but here is one example: The gene for the ability to curl the tongue lengthwise (Figure 3.4) is a dominant gene; all people who have that gene can curl their tongue, regardless of whether they are homozygous or heterozygous for that gene. The gene for the inability to curl the tongue is said to be a **recessive gene.** Only people who are homozygous for a recessive gene show its effects. In other words, if you cannot curl your tongue, you must be homozygous for the inability-to-curl gene (not exactly a serious handicap).

A person who is heterozygous for a particu-

offer you—for a price—an opportunity to do absolutely anything you want for one day. You will not be limited by the usual constraints on what is possible. You can travel in a flash from one place on Earth to another, visiting as many places as you want, all in that single day. You can even visit outer space, exploring other worlds and seeking life (if any) on other planets. You can travel forward and backward through time, to find out what the future holds in store or to relive the great events of history—or prehistoric times. (But you will not be able to change it and it is yours.) Furthermore, I guarantee your safety: No matter what time and place you choose to visit or what you choose to do, you will not be killed or injured.

Now, how much would you be willing to pay for this once-in-a-lifetime opportunity? Oh, yes, I should mention . . . there is one catch. When the day is over, you will forget everything that happened. You will never be able to recover your memory of that day, even slightly. Any notes or photos you might have made will vanish. And anyone else who takes part in your special day will forget it, too.

Now how much would you be willing to pay? Much less, I am sure. Perhaps nothing. Living without remembering is hardly living at all. Our memories are almost the same thing as our "selves."

Kutbidin Atamkulov travels from one Central Asian village to another singing from memory the tale of the Kirghiz hero, Manas. The song, which lasts 3 hours, has been passed from master to student for centuries. Human memory can hold an amazing amount of information.

Probability of exercising vigorously (dependent variable)

Hours since end of meal (independent variable)

FIGURE 2.13
An experimenter manipulates the independent variable (in this case, the films people watch) so that two or more groups experience different treatments. Then the experimenter measures the dependent variable (in this case, pulse rate) to see how the independent variable affected it.

■ CONCEPT CHECK

5. An instructor wants to find out whether the frequency of tests in introductory psychology has any effect on students' final exam performance. The instructor gives weekly tests in one class, just three tests in a second class, and only a single mid-term exam in the third class. All three classes take the same final exam, and the instructor compares their performances. Identify the independent variable and the dependent variable. (Check your answers on page 60.)

Experimental Group and Control Group
Here is more terminology you need to understand psychological experiments: The **experimental group** receives the treatment that the experiment is designed to test. In our example, the experimental group would watch televised violence for a specific length of time. The **control group** is treated in the same way as the experimental group except for the treatment the experiment is designed to test. In other words, the control group spends the same amount of time watching television but watches only non-violent programs (Figure 2.14).

In principle, that procedure sounds easy. In practice, a difficulty arises: We are conducting a study on a group of teenagers who have a history of violent behavior. The experimental group watches a good guys versus bad guys thriller with lots of action and violence. Exactly what do we ask the control group to watch? Can we find a program without violence that is just as exciting to watch? (It's not easy.)

Random Assignment The preferred way of assigning subjects to groups is **random assignment**: The experimenter uses some chance procedure such as drawing names out of a hat to make sure that every subject has the same probability as any other subject of being assigned to a given group. Imagine what could happen if the experimenter did not assign people at random. Suppose we let the subjects choose whether they want to be in the experimental group or the control group. The people most prone to aggressive behavior might generally choose to be in the experimental group (the one that watches violent programs). Or suppose we ask people to volunteer for the study, and the first 20 people who volunteer become the experimental group and the next 20 become the con...

Table 1.2 Clinical Psychologists and Other Psychotherapists

Type of Therapist	Education	Approximate Number Practicing in U.S.A.*
Clinical psychologist	Ph.D. with clinical emphasis, or Psy.D., plus internship. Total generally 5+ years after undergraduate degree.	42,000
Psychiatrist	M.D. plus psychiatric residency. Total 8 years after undergraduate degree.	47,000
Psychoanalyst	Psychiatry or clinical psychology plus 6–8 years in a psychoanalytic institute. Some others also call themselves psychoanalysts.	3,000+
Psychiatric nurse	From 2-year (A.A.) degree to master's degree, plus supervised experience.	16,000
Clinical social worker	Master's degree plus 2 years of supervised experience. Total at least 4 years after undergraduate degree.	82,000

*Based on estimates provided by the American Psychological Association, the American Psychiatric Association, the American Psychoanalytic Association, the American Psychiatric Nurses Association, and the National Association of Social Workers.

the term only to graduates of an institute of psychoanalysis. Those institutes admit only people who are already either psychiatrists or clinical psychologists. Training in the institute lasts 6 to 8 years. Thus, if you were to become a psychoanalyst, you would be at least in your late 30s by the time you completed your training.

Table 1.2 shows the differences among various types of psychotherapists.

■ CONCEPT CHECK

1. Can psychoanalysts prescribe drugs? (Check your answer on page 18.)

Occupational Settings in Psychology

Psychologists work in many occupational settings, as shown in Figure 1.4. A little over one third work in academic institutions—colleges, universities, and medical schools. Almost 40% work in health-provider settings—independent practices, hospitals, and clinics. Others work in business, government, guidance and counseling centers, and public school systems. Those who work in business help companies make decisions about hiring, promotions, training of workers, and job design. Those who work in school systems help teachers deal with discipline problems and underachieving students.

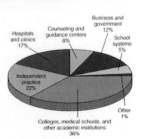

Hospitals and clinics 17%
Counseling and guidance centers 6%
Business and government 12%
School systems 5%
Independent practice 22%
Other 1%
Colleges, medical schools, and other academic institutions 36%

FIGURE 1.4
More than a third of psychologists work in academic institutions, with the remainder finding positions in a variety of settings.

Women and Minorities in Psychology

For a long time, academic psychology, like most other academic disciplines, was populated almost entirely by men. Women students were not encouraged to seek a Ph.D. degree; those who did were rarely offered employment at the

INTRODUCTION TO PSYCHOLOGY

1 WHAT IS PSYCHOLOGY?

As the space capsule opened, out sprang some little blue people. "We come from a nearby solar system," one of them said. "For years we have been listening to your radio and television programs. We have come to learn from you. Take us to your scientists!"

"Glad to," said the earthling who greeted them. "There's a fine university just down the road. I can introduce you to some physicists, chemists . . ."

"Oh, no!" interrupted one little blue person. "Not that kind of scientist! Everything you know about the physical sciences is just common sense—to us, that is. We came here to learn about your amazing advances in psychology."

Had any psychologists been on hand to meet the little blue people, they would have been as surprised as anyone else. People sometimes charge that psychologists deal only in common sense. To be complimented on the amazing advances in psychology would be a novelty.

In many cases, we must concede, the charge that psychology deals with common sense is valid. However, even when the research seems only to confirm common sense, it can be useful. After all, common sense told people that "objects fall" long before physicists started studying gravity. Similarly, psychologists' measurements of commonsense phenomena may lead to a deeper understanding of behavior.

Furthermore, common sense occasionally turns out to be wrong. Here is a test you can conduct yourself. Try to answer each of the following questions on the basis of common sense.

1. The workers at Consolidated Generic Manufacturing Company work on rotating shifts; each person works 8:00 A.M. to 4:00 P.M. for a few weeks, then midnight to 8:00 A.M., and then 4:00 P.M. to midnight. They complain of physical and mental distress, but the company insists on rotating shifts. What could be done to reduce the workers' distress?

2. Can hypnosis improve a person's memory of early childhood events or of a car accident?

3. At what age do children start using language in original ways, saying things they have never heard anyone else say?

4. How well can a newborn infant see and hear?

5. What causes infants to develop a social attachment to their mothers?

6. You talk two people into doing an unpleasant chore. You give one a small bribe and the other a large bribe. Which one will enjoy the chore more?

7. In what way are expert chess players (or experts at anything else) different from average performers?

8. After finishing a test, is it a good idea to go back and change some of your answers, or is your first impulse usually correct?

Now compare your answers with those on pages 18–19.

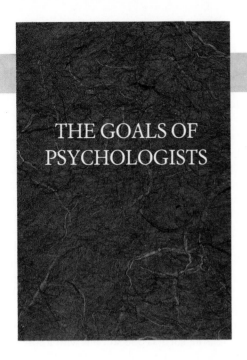

THE GOALS OF PSYCHOLOGISTS

What is psychology?

What are some of its fundamental questions?

What are the principal theoretical approaches of psychology?

What are some of psychology's main areas of study?

"Let us, then, make a fresh start and try to determine what soul is and what will be its most comprehensive definition."
ARISTOTLE (384–322 B.C.)

What do you suppose psychologists are really trying to accomplish? If you could ask any one question in psychology and be sure of getting a completely correct answer, what question would that be?

Some years ago, a student in one of my classes asked me, "When will we get to the kind of psychology we can 'use' on people?" Another student asked me whether I as a psychologist had any tips for him on how to seduce his girlfriend. (I told him I did not, and that even if I did, I would devote at least equal efforts to giving his girlfriend tips on how to resist seduction.)

Psychologists do not try to develop techniques for manipulating or tricking people. They do try to understand why people act the way they do, and try to help people to better understand themselves.

THREE MAJOR PHILOSOPHICAL ISSUES IN PSYCHOLOGY

Psychology, broadly defined, is the systematic study of behavior and experience. The term *psychology* derives from the Greek roots *psyche,* meaning "soul" or "mind," and *logos,* meaning "word" or "study." Psychology began as the analysis of the mind or soul. As with most academic disciplines, it had its roots in philosophy. Although it has moved far away from philosophy in its methods, psychology continues to be motivated by some deep philosophical issues. Three of the most profound questions are free will versus determinism, the mind-brain problem, and the nature-nurture issue.

Free Will Versus Determinism

Beginning with the Renaissance period in Europe, people began looking for scientific explanations for the phenomena they observed. One of the key points of this Scientific Revolution was a shift toward seeking the *immediate* causes of an event (what led to what) instead of the *final* causes (the ultimate purpose of the event in an overall plan). Scientists analyzed the motion of objects in terms of pushes and pulls and other laws of nature (White, 1990). That is, they made an assumption called **determinism**—the assumption that everything that happens has a cause, or *determinant,* in the observable world.

Is the same true for human behavior? We are, after all, part of the physical world. Your brain and mine are made of chemical compounds subject to the same laws of nature as anything else. According to the *determinist* assumption for human behavior, everything we do has a cause (Figure 1.1).

But what kind of cause? According to one version of this view, "hard determinism," everything we do has a cause *outside of us*; the idea that we make choices or decisions is just an illusion.

In its extreme form, hard determinism is easy to dismiss. For example, suppose you announce you are on your way from your dormitory room to the library. If I set up all sorts of

FIGURE 1.1
When this police officer risks his life to rescue someone trying to kill himself, are both choosing "freely" how to act? If so, what does "free choice" mean? According to determinism, everything we do has causes in our genetics, environment, and past experiences.

obstacles that block your usual path, you will go over them, under them, or around them until you reach the library. Clearly, your behavior depends on your internal plan or goal.

The issue is where that internal plan or goal came from. According to "soft determinism," your plan is a product of the combined influence of your genetics, your past experiences, and the current environment (Sappington, 1990). According to this view, you do make choices and set goals, but only in the way a complex machine does. For example, a robot provided with the right information could calculate whether the dormitory or the library would be a better place to process data today. If it selected the library, it could then plot out a route to get there. The robot is making choices, but those choices are determined by the way the robot was put together.

The alternative to either hard or soft determinism is **free will.** Free will is a difficult view to describe. To some extent it is merely a rejection of determinism; it claims that people sometimes make decisions not controlled by their genetics, their past experiences, or their environment. But unless people somehow create themselves,

what is left besides genetics and environment? Randomness, perhaps, although most defenders of free will are looking for something a little more noble than truly random behavior.

People's choices are seldom if ever completely random. For example, suppose you walk into a large room. You are the first one to arrive, so you could select any chair you wish. Do you choose one freely and randomly? Or is there some pattern in the way people choose? In one study, a psychologist asked students to enter a large lecture hall and take any seat. Each student left before the next entered. The psychologist simply recorded where each student sat. Most sat on the side closer to the entrance, and 60% chose an aisle seat. About 5% took the same seat where they ordinarily sat during a lecture in that room. A few selected a seat for a special reason, such as one student with a sore leg who chose a seat near the door to avoid walking farther than necessary. In short, students' seat choices were far from random (Harcum, 1991).

Granted, no one can predict exactly where a given student will sit on a given occasion; the best anyone can do is to predict where most people will sit or approximately where a given student will sit. But the same is often true in physics. When a leaf falls from a tree, a physicist can predict only approximately where it will land. That is because the leaf is subject to many competing forces, not because it is governed by a free will. Similarly, when your choice seems random or "free," perhaps it seems so because a great many determinants are at work, including perhaps some that you do not notice or fully appreciate (Nisbett & Schachter, 1966).

The philosophical question remains of how to reconcile the evidence for determinism with the strong private impression each of us has of making free choices. Still, the whole issue of free will versus determinism is one of the issues that sparks interest in psychological investigations. In a sense, every psychological investigation is a test of determinism. An investigator tries to measure how some factor influences behavior. If the study shows that it does affect behavior, then the results are a point in favor of determinism.

Something to Think About

What kind of evidence, if any, would support the concept of free will? Demonstrating that a particular theory makes incorrect predictions about behavior under given circumstances would not refute determinism. To support the concept of free will, you need to demonstrate that no conceivable theory would make correct predictions. Should a psychologist who believes in free will conduct the same kind of research that determinists conduct, or a different kind of research, or no research at all?

The Mind-Brain Problem

Every movement we make depends on muscle activity controlled by the nervous system, and every sensory experience depends on the activity of the nervous system. All activities of the nervous system follow the laws of physics and chemistry. What then is the role of the mind? We all believe that we have a conscious mind that makes decisions and controls behavior. So there must be a close relationship between the conscious mind and the physical nervous system, which includes the brain. But what is that relationship? The philosophical question of how they are related is the **mind-brain problem** (or mind-body problem). Does the brain produce the mind? If so, how and why? Or does the mind control the brain? If so, how could a

Something to Think About

One way to think about the mind-brain relationship is to ask whether something other than a brain—a computer, for example—could have a mind. How would we know?

What if we built a computer that could perform all the same intellectual functions that humans perform? Could we then decide that the computer is conscious, as human beings are conscious? If we say the computer is not conscious, must we then conclude that consciousness is unnecessary, that a brain can get along just fine without it?

The movie *Terminator 2* plays off the tension between mechanical and human natures coexisting in the same character, called a cyborg.

What accounts for the brilliance of someone like Albert Einstein? After Einstein died, scientists examined his brain for years but found nothing especially unusual about its structure. Intellectual accomplishments undoubtedly relate in some way to brain activity, but they may not relate to the easily observable aspects of brain anatomy.

nonphysical entity control a physical substance? Or are the mind and the brain just two names for the same thing? If so, what does it mean to say they are the same? (They certainly seem to be different.)

Although the mind-brain problem is a particularly difficult philosophical issue, it does lead to research. The research can determine links between brain activity on the one hand and behavior and experience on the other hand. For example, consider Figure 1.2. A technique called positron-emission tomography, discussed in Chapter 3, enables investigators to measure the amount of activity in different parts of the brain at various times. The nine photos in Figure 1.2 show brain activity while a person is engaged in nine different tasks. Red indicates the highest degree of brain activity, followed by yellow, green, and blue. As you can see, different tasks tend to activate different areas of the brain, although all areas show at least a little activity at all times (Phelps & Mazziotta, 1985).

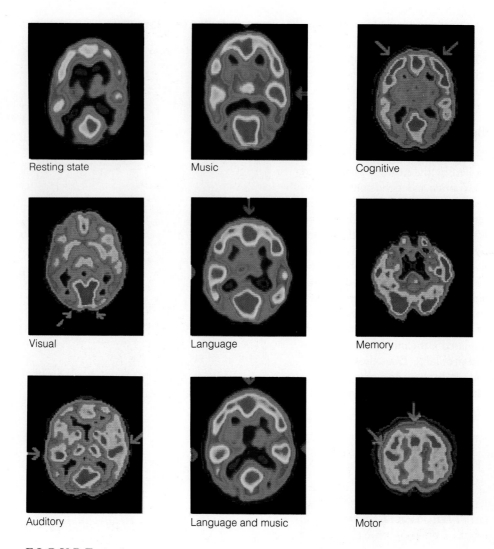

FIGURE 1.2

PET scans show brain activity of normal people engaged in different activities. Left column: Brain activity with no special stimulation and while passively watching something or listening to something. Center column: Activity while listening to music, language, or both. Right column: Activity during performance of a cognitive task, an auditory memory task, and a task of moving fingers of the right hand. Red indicates the highest activity, followed by yellow, green, and blue. Arrows indicate the most active areas.

Data such as these show a very close relationship between brain activity and psychological events. You might well ask, do these results mean that brain activity caused the associated thoughts, or did those thoughts cause that pattern of brain activity? Many brain researchers would be uncomfortable with that question. They would submit that neither brain activity nor mental activity "causes" the other; rather, brain activity and mental activity are the same thing.

Even if we accept that position, we are far from understanding the mind-brain relationship fully. Is mental activity associated with all brain activity or just with certain types? Why is there such a thing as conscious experience at all? Couldn't the brain get along without it? If one half of the brain gets cut off from the other,

FIGURE 1.3
To what extent do children resemble their parents, and why? The Burmese reform leader Aung San Suu Kyi and former Soviet President Mikhail S. Gorbachev won Nobel Peace Prizes in the 1980s. Suu Kyi was the daughter of a national hero who led Burma's struggle for independence from Britain; Gorbachev was the son of Russian peasants. The way each person develops depends on both heredity and environment, but not necessarily in ways that are easy to understand or predict.

but the person survives, does each half have its own consciousness (Natsoulas, 1991)?

Research studies are not about to resolve the mind-brain problem and put philosophers out of business. But research results do constrain the types of philosophical answers that we can seriously entertain. The hope of learning more about the mind-brain relationship is one of the ultimate goals for many psychologists, especially the psychologists whose work we shall study in Chapters 3–5.

The Nature-Nurture Issue

On the average, little boys spend more time than little girls do playing with toy guns and trucks and less time playing with dolls. Why? Are such behavioral differences mostly the result of genetic differences between boys and girls, or are they mostly the result of differences in the way society treats boys and girls?

In many countries, alcoholism is a serious problem. In other countries—Turkey, for example—alcohol abuse is less prevalent. Why the differences? Are they entirely a matter of social custom, or do certain genes influence how much alcohol people consume?

Some psychological disorders are more common in large cities than in small towns and

in the countryside. Does life in crowded cities somehow cause psychological disorders? Or do people develop such disorders because of some genetic predisposition and then move to a big city because that is the only place they can find jobs, housing, or welfare services?

Each of these questions is related to the **nature-nurture issue** (Figure 1.3). All of behavior depends on both heredity (nature) and environment (nurture), because people could not develop at all unless they had both heredity and environment. But the *differences* between one person and another may depend mostly on differences in heredity or differences in environment.

The relative contributions of hereditary differences and environmental differences vary from one instance to another. For example, how skillfully people play some video game depends mostly on how much time they have spent practicing (nurture). But how well they can distinguish red from green depends mostly on which people have a particular gene for red-green colorblindness. In other cases, the differences among people depend strongly on both environmental and hereditary differences. The nature-nurture issue shows up from time to time in practically all fields of psychology.

The Goals of Psychologists   9

WHAT PSYCHOLOGISTS DO

We have started with some major philosophical issues related to the whole enterprise of psychology. But most psychologists think explicitly about such issues only once in a while. For the most part, they deal with issues a little easier to handle, though still quite challenging.

When most people hear the term *psychologist,* they think first of **clinical psychologists,** who are **psychotherapists,** that is, specialists in helping troubled people. But many kinds of psychologists conduct research, teach, and provide nonclinical services. The interests of psychologists range from social and cultural influences on human behavior to the effects of brain damage on animal behavior, from helping corporations select among job applicants to helping mentally retarded children walk and talk. Table 1.1 lists some of the major areas of psychological research and practice and shows the percentages of Ph.D. psychologists in each of those areas.

The interests of psychologists range from highly theoretical issues to purely practical concerns. Here are a few examples of theoretical interests:

■ Will a rat that finds food in a particular place remember the place and return to it later when it is hungry?

■ What would we have to include in a computer program for it to mimic the performance of an expert chess player?

■ Can chimpanzees or other nonhumans learn to use symbols in a way that resembles the use of language by humans?

■ When people recover from brain damage, what if anything changes in the structure of the brain?

Here are a few examples of more practical interests:

■ How can someone help a compulsive gambler stop gambling?

■ What would be an effective and fair way for a company to select among many applicants for a given job?

■ Why do certain schoolchildren have academic difficulties, and what can be done to help them?

■ What design of an airplane cockpit would make it easiest for a pilot to find the controls?

As Table 1.1 shows, more than 40% of all psychologists in the United States are clinical psychologists. Notice, however, the large number and variety of *non*-clinical psychologists.

Do not confuse psychologists with psychiatrists. Psychology is an academic discipline, as are chemistry, history, and economics. If you decide to become a psychologist, you must earn a Ph.D. degree or some other advanced degree in psychology. Some psychology graduate students specialize in clinical psychology; others, in other branches of psychology. A few institutions offer the Psy.D. (Doctor of Psychology) degree, which generally requires less research experience than the Ph.D. The education for a Ph.D. or Psy.D. degree requires at least 4 or 5 years of academic work. Clinical psychologists take at least another year of supervised clinical work, called an *internship.*

Psychiatry is the branch of medicine that deals with psychological and emotional disturbances. To become a psychiatrist, you must first earn an M.D. degree and then take an additional 4 years of residency training in psychiatry. Psychiatrists and clinical psychologists provide similar services for most clients: They listen, ask questions, and provide advice. For clients with more serious problems, psychiatrists are authorized to prescribe drugs such as tranquilizers and antidepressants. Psychologists cannot prescribe drugs, because they are not medical doctors. Many clinical psychologists favor a change in the law to enable clinical psychologists with extra training to prescribe drugs. That proposal is highly controversial, and its eventual fate is hard to predict.

(Does psychiatrists' ability to prescribe drugs give them an advantage over psychologists? Not always. Ours is an overmedicated society. Some psychiatrists habitually treat anxiety and depression with drugs, whereas a psychologist would try to treat the problems by changing the person's way of living.)

Several other kinds of professionals also provide help and counsel. Psychiatric nurses and psychiatric social workers have an undergraduate or master's degree in nursing or social work plus additional training in care for emotionally troubled people.

Psychoanalysts are therapists who rely heavily on the theories and methods of the early 20th-century Viennese physician Sigmund Freud. There is some question about who may rightly call themselves psychoanalysts. Some apply the term to any psychotherapist who relies heavily on Freud's methods. Others apply

Table 1.1 Some Major Specializations in Psychology

Specialization	General Interest	Example of Specific Interest or Research Topic
Clinical psychologist	Emotional difficulties	How can people be helped to overcome severe anxiety?
Community psychologist	Organizations and social structures	Would improved job opportunities decrease certain types of psychological distress?
Counseling psychologist	Helping people to make important decisions and to achieve their potential	Should this person consider changing careers?
Developmental psychologist	Changes in behavior as people grow older	At what age can a child first distinguish between appearance and reality?
Educational psychologist	Improvement of learning in school	What is the best way to test a student's knowledge?
Environmental psychologist	The influence of noise, heat, crowding, and other environmental conditions on human behavior	How can a building be designed to maximize the comfort of the people who use it?
Ergonomist	Communication between person and machine	How can an airplane cockpit be redesigned to increase safety?
Experimental psychologist	Sensation, perception, learning, thinking, memory	Do people have several kinds of learning? Do they have several kinds of memory?
Industrial and organizational psychologist	People at work, production efficiency	Should jobs be made simple and foolproof or interesting and challenging?
Personality researcher	Personality differences among individuals	Why are certain people shy and others gregarious?
Biopsychologist	Relationship between brain and behavior	What body signals indicate hunger and satiety?
Psychometrician	Measurement of intelligence, personality, and interests	How fair or unfair are current IQ tests? Can we devise better tests?
School psychologist	Problems that affect schoolchildren	How should the school handle a child who regularly disrupts the classroom?
Social psychologist	Group behavior, social influences	What methods of persuasion are most effective in changing attitudes?

Industrial-organizational 6%
Developmental 4%
Experimental 9%
School 5%
Social and personality 4%
Educational 6%
Other 11%
Counseling 11%
Clinical 44%

Specializations of Psychologists

Table 1.2 Clinical Psychologists and Other Psychotherapists

Type of Therapist	Education	Approximate Number Practicing in U.S.A.*
Clinical psychologist	Ph.D. with clinical emphasis, or Psy.D., plus internship. Total generally 5+ years after undergraduate degree.	42,000
Psychiatrist	M.D. plus psychiatric residency. Total 8 years after undergraduate degree.	47,000
Psychoanalyst	Psychiatry or clinical psychology plus 6–8 years in a psychoanalytic institute. Some others also call themselves psychoanalysts.	3,000+
Psychiatric nurse	From 2-year (A.A.) degree to master's degree, plus supervised experience.	16,000
Clinical social worker	Master's degree plus 2 years of supervised experience. Total at least 4 years after undergraduate degree.	82,000

*Based on estimates provided by the American Psychological Association, the American Psychiatric Association, the American Psychoanalytic Association, the American Psychiatric Nurses Association, and the National Association of Social Workers.

the term only to graduates of an institute of psychoanalysis. Those institutes admit only people who are already either psychiatrists or clinical psychologists. Training in the institute lasts 6 to 8 years. Thus, if you were to become a psychoanalyst, you would be at least in your late 30s by the time you completed your training.

Table 1.2 shows the differences among various types of psychotherapists.

▪ CONCEPT CHECK

1. Can psychoanalysts prescribe drugs? (Check your answer on page 18.)

Occupational Settings in Psychology

Psychologists work in many occupational settings, as shown in Figure 1.4. A little over one third work in academic institutions—colleges, universities, and medical schools. Almost 40% work in health-provider settings—independent practices, hospitals, and clinics. Others work in business, government, guidance and counseling centers, and public school systems. Those who work in business help companies make decisions about hiring, promotions, training of workers, and job design. Those who work in school systems help teachers deal with discipline problems and underachieving students.

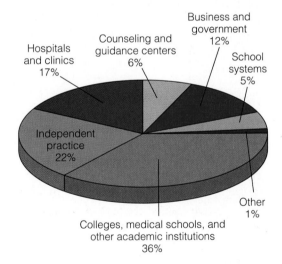

FIGURE 1.4
More than a third of psychologists work in academic institutions, with the remainder finding positions in a variety of settings.

Women and Minorities in Psychology

For a long time, academic psychology, like most other academic disciplines, was populated almost entirely by men. Women students were not encouraged to seek a Ph.D. degree; those who did were rarely offered employment at the most prestigious colleges, universities, or research institutions.

According to a survey conducted in 1983, women hold more than 30% of all Ph.D. degrees in psychology in the United States (Figure 1.5) and more than 50% of all master's degrees (Stapp, Tucker, & VandenBos, 1985). Both percentages are growing steadily. Over 50% of all current graduate students in psychology are women.

Minorities also constitute a growing percentage of psychologists, though the total number is still small (Figure 1.5). As of 1983, blacks, Hispanics, Asians, and other minorities together constituted about 5% of all American psychologists. Those numbers will grow as many graduate schools actively recruit qualified minority applicants.

SOME APPROACHES TO THE STUDY OF BEHAVIOR AND EXPERIENCE

Consider this question: Why are you reading this book right now? No doubt you could come up with a reason, but it probably would not tell the whole story. We rarely do anything for just one reason. Perhaps you are reading this book because:

- You are curious to learn something about psychology.

- You have found that reading your textbook assignments leads to better grades that will win you praise from your family and friends, increase your self-esteem, and bring you other rewards.

- You have nothing else to do right now.

- You know you will feel guilty if you spend a lot of money on a college education and then flunk out.

- Your roommate is reading a textbook, so you think you might as well do the same.

Notice that these reasons do not compete with each other. Several influences may combine and lead to a given behavior at a given time. Notice too that these reasons have to do with different things—your thoughts, your past learning, your emotions, and social influences.

Different psychologists explain the same behaviors in different ways and arrive at different answers to the same questions. In other words, they take different approaches to psy-

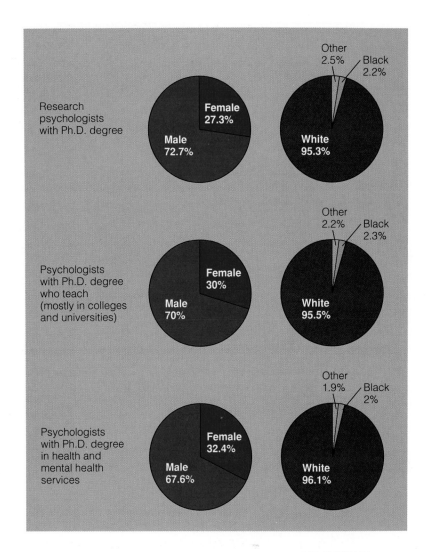

chology. Table 1.3 summarizes six examples of psychological approaches.

Let us consider a few examples of psychological approaches. To compare them, we shall examine how each approach deals with the question of individual differences: Why does one individual behave differently from another?

The Quantitative Psychology Approach

Any useful study, in psychology or in any other discipline that deals with natural phenomena, must be based on careful measurements. **Quantitative psychologists** measure individual differences and apply statistical procedures to determine what their measurements indicate. In fact, nearly all psychologists take measurements and apply statistical procedures; quantitative psychologists are those who concentrate more

FIGURE 1.5
The number of female psychologists with a Ph.D. degree is growing—about half of current graduate students are women. Although the number of minority psychologists is small, it is also growing. (Based on data of Stapp, Tucker, & VandenBos, 1985.)

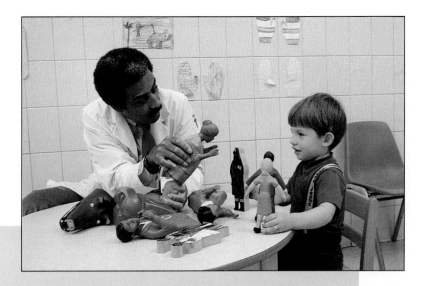

The number of minority individuals starting careers in psychology has been steadily increasing. Diversity among psychologists helps the field in many ways; people from different backgrounds tend to ask different questions and to offer different possible solutions to problems.

vised a test, they must determine whether or not it measures what it is supposed to measure.

Tests in psychology only measure; they do not explain. For example, once we determine that a particular child has a low IQ score, we can predict that the child will have trouble in school. The test score does not, however, tell us *why* the child is performing poorly—either on the test or in school. One child may perform poorly because of brain damage, another because of poor educational opportunities, yet another because he or she does not read or speak English. Measuring individual differences is a first step toward explaining them, but it is only a first step.

The Biological Approach

A **biopsychologist** (or behavioral neuroscientist) tries to explain behavior in terms of biological factors such as electrical and chemical activities in the nervous system, the effects of drugs and hormones, genetics, and evolutionary pressures. For example, Huntington's disease is a condition in which the person experiences movement disorders and eventually memory and thought disorders. Whether or not one gets this disease depends on a single gene (Chase, Wexler, & Barbeau, 1979). Although stressful experiences may hasten the onset of the disease, it appears that everyone with the disease-causing gene will eventually contract the disease.

More frequently, psychologists deal with genes that merely increase the probability of a

on mathematics and generally give less attention to the theoretical interpretations.

To measure individual differences, psychologists have devised tests of IQ, personality, interests, and attitudes, most of them requiring pencil-and-paper answers. Once they have de-

Table 1.3 Six Examples of Psychological Approaches

Approach	Description	How Psychologists Might Study, for Example, Elementary Students
Quantitative	Measures individual differences	Administer IQ tests
Biological	Studies nervous system, genetics, hormones, other biological influences	Identify indications of brain damage or disorder
Behavioral	Studies observable behavior	Observe how disruptive students are rewarded with attention
Cognitive	Studies thought and knowledge	Identify the kinds of questions a child can and cannot answer, infer thought processes
Social	Examines behavior in social context	Appraise influence of other people's expectations on child's performance
Clinical	Treats emotional troubles	Let child describe emotional conflict

given behavior or condition, depending on a number of environmental circumstances. For example, there is evidence that certain genes increase the risk that a person may abuse alcohol or become depressed (Vaillant & Milofsky, 1982; Wender et al., 1986). The person's actual alcohol use or depression, however, depends on a variety of experiences and not just on genes.

Biopsychologists also study the effects of brain damage. Brain damage may result from such things as a sharp blow to the head, a ruptured blood vessel in the brain, an interruption of oxygen supply, prolonged malnutrition, or exposure to toxic chemicals. The effects on behavior vary enormously, depending on the location and extent of the damage. For example, people with damage to one area in the right half of the brain tend to ignore what they see in the left half of the world (Pierrot-Deseilligny, Gray, & Brunet, 1986). People with damage to another area may look at a single object from two angles and fail to recognize that it is the same object (Layman & Greene, 1988).

People have long known that various drugs can alter behavior. For example, opiates generally make people quiet, passive, and insensitive to pain. Amphetamine and cocaine generally stimulate increased activity in most people. Biopsychologists try to understand what drugs do in the brain. They find that most drugs that affect behavior do so by altering the chemical communication between one neuron and another at junctions called *synapses.*

So, according to biopsychologists, why do people differ from one another? The reasons are many: People are born with different genes; they develop slightly different brains and different hormonal patterns. Some have suffered brain damage; some are under the influence of drugs or of nutritional deficiencies that affect the brain. Anything that affects the body, especially the brain, will also affect behavior.

The Behavioral Approach

Another approach to psychology is the behavioral approach. A **behaviorist** is a psychologist who studies only behaviors that can actually be observed instead of trying to analyze thought processes. Behaviorists believe that most behavior is learned, based on the consequences of past behaviors. How often we engage in a particular behavior depends on whether that behavior has usually led to positive, negative, or neutral outcomes in the past. Because many of the principles of learning are similar from one

species to another, behaviorists often use animals in their investigations.

Suppose we want to know why most first-grade children follow the teacher's instructions (most of the time) whereas a few constantly chatter, run around, and disrupt class activities. While we could imagine many possible explanations, a behaviorist would look first at the consequences of a child's disruptive behavior: Other children watch and giggle and the teacher stamps and yells. In other words, certain children learn that they can attract attention by running around noisily, but not by doing what the teacher asks them to do. How can the teacher get such children to behave better? One way is to praise them when they behave in a quiet, cooperative manner. If that approach fails, the teacher can isolate them from the other children for a few minutes after misbehaviors.

Adult behavior also is governed by its consequences. Whether adults choose to spend their time studying or socializing, running in track meets or running for political office depends in part on the rewards and frustrations their choices produced in the past. Behaviorists try to relate individual differences to the individual's record of reward and punishment.

The Cognitive Approach

Cognition refers to thinking and acquiring knowledge. A **cognitive psychologist** studies those processes. (The root *cogn* also shows up in the word *recognize*, which literally means "to know again.") Cognitive psychologists have learned much from the behaviorists. They do not simply ask people to describe their thought processes; they perform elaborate experiments to measure the consequences of those processes.

A cognitive psychologist who studies individual differences tries to identify the ways in which people think. For example, what do experts know or do that sets them apart from other people? One distinction is simply that the expert knows more facts. Consider a subject on which you are an expert: how to find your way around your college campus. A fellow student asks you, "How do I get from here to the biology building?" To answer, you can draw on the knowledge you share with the other student: "Go over toward the library. Then cut behind the library, between the library and the math building. The biology building will be right in front of you." Now a visitor who has never been on campus before asks you the same question.

You say, "Go over toward the library. . . ." "Wait, where's the library?" "Well, go out this door, make a right, go to the next street. . . ." You will find that someone with little or no previous knowledge needs detailed and extensive instructions (Isaacs & Clark, 1987).

Another distinction between the expert and the nonexpert is that the expert can identify more categories. For example, a nonexpert might look at a group of birds on a beach and say, "Hey, look at all the sea gulls." An expert bird-watcher might reply, "There are three gull species and two tern species."

Moreover, the expert can identify the *right* categories. The inexperienced bird-watcher might say, sheepishly, "Oh, I see. Some of them have darker feathers than others." The expert would reply, "No, the ones with darker feathers are just younger. To tell one species from the other you have to check the color of the beak, the color of the legs, the size of the bird, the color of the eyes . . ." The expert knows what to look for—what is relevant and what is not (Murphy & Medin, 1985).

In short, a cognitive psychologist explains individual differences partly in terms of knowledge: People differ from one another because some of them know more than others do about a particular topic. Cognitive psychologists also study the ways in which people think and remember and how they use their knowledge.

The Social Psychology Approach

Social psychologists study how an individual's actions, attitudes, emotions, and thought processes are influenced by other people. They also study how people behave in groups. When we are with other people, we tend to take our cues from them on what we should do. You arrive at a party and notice that the other guests are walking around, helping themselves to snacks, and talking. You do the same. When you go to a religious service or an art museum, you notice how other people are acting and again conform your behavior to theirs. Certainly, if you had grown up in a different country, you would have developed vastly different customs from the ones you now have.

Even within a given culture, different people acquire different behaviors because of the people around them. If for some reason you had made friends with a different set of people in high school, you might be a much different person today. According to social psychologists, people are also heavily influenced by other people's expectations. Suppose your college made

a mistake and accidentally classified you as an honors student—and let's suppose you had done nothing to earn that distinction. Because of this classification, your professors treat you differently, giving you a little extra attention, and perhaps as a result you do become an outstanding student. Results along these lines have been demonstrated for first-grade children (Rosenthal & Rubin, 1978), and we can imagine that the same might be true for more advanced students as well.

Other predictions probably have similar effects. For example, a teacher knows that a child's parents have been in trouble with the law and predicts that sooner or later the child also will get into trouble. In one way or another, that prediction may affect the child's behavior.

Or consider sex differences. Many parents expect their sons to aspire to become doctors, politicians, or professional athletes; they may or may not convey similarly high expectations to their daughters. The behavioral differences that subsequently emerge between boys and girls are partly the result of the different expectations that were conveyed to them. Social psychologists study such influences.

The Clinical Approach

Let us return to the example of first-grade children running around noisily in class. A behaviorist probably would look first for an explanation in terms of learning, such as that certain children have learned to be disruptive as a way of getting attention. Another possible explanation is that certain children are facing serious emotional troubles at home—perhaps their parents are constantly fighting; perhaps a baby brother or sister is getting all the attention; perhaps there are other problems. Clinical psychologists tend to look for explanations in terms of emotional troubles.

Sigmund Freud, the founder of psychoanalysis, became famous for his insistence that much of what we do is based on emotional problems, especially sex-related problems, of which we are not consciously aware. According to Freud, the unconscious mind retains the memory of painful thoughts and experiences, often from early childhood, that the conscious mind ignores. The unconscious may make itself felt in dreams, physical complaints, slips of the tongue, and actions that a person performs for no apparent reason. Thus, an important basis for individual differences is that different people have different unconscious thoughts and motivations.

For example, one of Freud's early patients, Dora, had frequent spells of coughing, hoarseness, and impaired breathing. She avoided any affectionate conversations with men. Freud traced these problems to Dora's being sexually abused as a child by a friend of her father (Freud, 1905/1952). Unconsciously, those early experiences intruded upon her everyday life.

We shall discuss Freud's views in more detail in Chapter 13. At this point, let us just note that his is just one of many clinical approaches. Many psychologists believe Freud overemphasized or misinterpreted human sexuality; they look for other kinds of explanations of human behavior. But many who reject the details of Freud's views agree with him that people's behavior often reflects serious emotional conflicts, including some that people seem unable or unwilling to admit to themselves. For example, the parents of a teenage girl are constantly quarreling, sometimes striking each other. The mother has a boyfriend who threatens to kill the father; the father threatens to kill the boyfriend. The girl feels threatened at home and insecure when she is away, because she never knows what she will find when she returns. Suddenly one of her legs becomes paralyzed, apparently for no medical reason. Some clinicians would regard the paralysis as an unconscious strategem to become the center of attention and to receive her parents' care. Other clinicians would offer other interpretations, but all would agree that family conflicts can lead to massive problems in school, at work, and elsewhere.

Overlap Among the Various Approaches

I have oversimplified the discussion of the approaches of psychology in several ways. First, it is only partly correct to refer to biological psychology, cognitive psychology, social psychology, and other types as approaches. True, each constitutes one way of approaching certain phenomena of interest to all psychologists. But each is also a separate field of study with its own special phenomena. Biological psychologists ask questions about how the brain works; social psychologists ask questions about group behavior. Second, the approaches just discussed are not the only approaches or the only major fields of study. In later chapters we shall consider additional approaches and topics. And third, the various approaches overlap significantly. Nearly all psychologists combine insights and information gained from a variety of approaches. To understand why one person differs from another, most psychologists are interested in their biology, their past learning experiences, the social influences that have acted on them, and much more.

As we proceed through later chapters, we shall consider one kind of behavior at a time, and generally one approach at a time. That is simply a necessity; we cannot talk intelligently about all kinds of psychological processes at once. But bear in mind that all these various processes do ultimately fit together; what you do at any moment depends on your biology, your past experiences, your social setting, your emotions, and a great deal more.

SUMMARY *

- *What psychology is.* Psychology is the systematic study of behavior and experience. Psychologists deal with theoretical questions, such as how experience relates to brain activity and how behavior relates to nature and nurture. Psychologists also deal with practical questions, such as selecting among applicants for a job or helping people to overcome bad habits. (page 5)

- *Determinism/free will.* Determinism is the view that everything that occurs, including human behavior, has a physical cause. That view is difficult to reconcile with the conviction that humans have free will—that we deliberately, consciously decide what to do. (page 5)

- *Mind-brain.* The mind-brain problem is the question of how conscious experience is related to the activity of the brain. (page 7)

- *Nature-nurture.* Behavior depends on both nature (heredity) and nurture (environment). Psychologists try to determine the influence of those two factors on differences in behavior. The relative contributions of nature and nurture vary from one behavior to another. (page 9)

- *Psychology versus psychiatry.* Psychology is an academic field whereas psychiatry is a branch of medicine. Both clinical psychologists and psychiatrists treat people with emotional problems, but only psychiatrists can prescribe medicine and other medical treatments. (page 10)

- *Quantitative approach.* Psychologists take different approaches in trying to explain the origin of individual differences. Those following the quantitative approach focus on measuring individual differences through such devices as an IQ test. (page 13)

---

*The page numbers following each item indicate where you can look to review a topic.

- *Biological approach.* Psychologists following the biological approach look for explanations of behavior in terms of genetics, brain damage, diet, and other biological factors. (page 14)

- *Behavioral approach.* Psychologists following the behavioral approach study only observable actions and generally emphasize the role of learning. (page 15)

- *Cognitive approach.* Psychologists using the cognitive approach concentrate on people's thought processes and knowledge. They demonstrate, for example, that people's performance on a given task depends largely on their factual knowledge. (page 15)

- *Social approach.* Psychologists using the social approach study how people act in groups and how an individual's behavior is affected by other people. For example, when people expect a child to do well, they treat that child in a way that may increase the probability of success. (page 16)

- *Clinical approach.* Clinical psychologists look for influences of emotional conflict on behavior, especially the role of emotional conflicts the person does not consciously recognize. (page 16)

- *Overlap.* The various approaches in psychology overlap partly in their interests, but not entirely. Each approach studies its own particular set of phenomena. (page 17)

SUGGESTIONS FOR FURTHER READING

Corsini, R. J. (1984). *Encyclopedia of psychology.* New York: Wiley. A useful reference source on all aspects of psychology.

Sechenov, I. (1965). *Reflexes of the brain.* Cambridge, MA: MIT Press. (Original work published 1863.) One of the first attempts to deal with behavior scientifically and one of the clearest statements of the argument for determinism in psychology.

TERMS

psychology the systematic study of behavior and experience (page 5)

determinism the assumption that all behavior has a cause, or *determinant,* in the observable world (page 5)

free will the alleged ability of an individual to make decisions that are not controlled by genetics, past experiences, or the environment (page 6)

mind-brain problem the philosophical question of how the conscious mind is related to the physical nervous system, including the brain (page 7)

nature-nurture issue the question of the relative roles played by heredity (nature) and environment (nurture) in determining differences in behavior (page 9)

clinical psychologist specialist in identifying and treating psychological disorders (page 10)

psychotherapist specialist who provides help for troubled people (page 10)

psychiatry the branch of medicine that deals with psychological and emotional disturbances (page 10)

psychoanalyst therapist who relies heavily on the theories of Sigmund Freud (page 10)

quantitative psychologist specialist who measures individual differences in behavior and applies statistical procedures to determine what the measurements indicate (page 13)

biopsychologist (or behavioral neuroscientist) specialist who tries to explain behavior in terms of biological factors such as electrical and chemical activities in the nervous system, the effects of drugs and hormones, genetics, and evolutionary pressures (page 14)

behaviorist psychologist who studies only observable behaviors rather than rather than trying to analyze thought processes (page 15)

cognition thinking and acquiring knowledge (page 15)

cognitive psychologist specialist who studies thought processes and the acquisition of knowledge (page 15)

social psychologist specialist who studies how an individual's actions, attitudes, emotions, and thought processes are influenced by other people and how people behave in groups (page 16)

ANSWER TO CONCEPT CHECK

1. Most psychoanalysts can prescribe drugs, because they are psychiatrists, and psychiatrists are medical doctors. However, those psychoanalysts who are psychologists instead of psychiatrists are not medical doctors and therefore cannot prescribe drugs. (page 12)

ANSWERS TO QUESTIONS IN THE TEXT *

1. Reversing the order of shifts will relieve the worker's distress. Instead of moving to an earlier shift each time, they should move to a later shift. Using very bright lights in the workplace (to simulate sunlight) would also help. (192)

---

*These questions appear on page 4. The page number following each item indicates the page in this text that provides a more detailed discussion of the topic.

2. No. Under hypnosis, people report old or forgotten memories in great detail but with low accuracy. Hypnosis stimulates acting ability more than it does memory. (page 200)

3. Children begin to make original and creative word combinations as soon as they start to link words together, around age 1 1/2 to 2. (page 237)

4. Infants can see and hear much better than was once assumed. Within the first day or two after birth, infants look longer at some patterns than others and show signs of recognizing their mothers' voice. (page 220)

5. It is not a direct result of nursing or feeding. Apparently the main reason is the warm, cuddly feeling that goes with holding and being held, plus play and other social interactions. (page 249)

6. The person who receives the small bribe will enjoy the task more. (page 693)

7. The experts can recognize a large number of complex, familiar patterns. They do not have a superior overall intelligence or a superior overall ability to recognize or remember unfamiliar materials. For tasks outside their expertise they perform about the same as anyone else. (page 374)

8. It is a good idea to check your answers and change those that now seem wrong. The idea that your first impulse is usually correct is a widespread myth. (If you missed this question, you didn't read Preface to the Student.) (page xxvi)

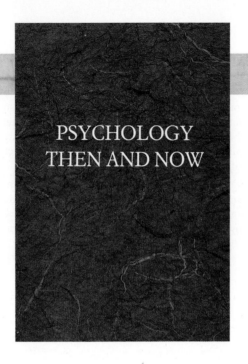

PSYCHOLOGY THEN AND NOW

What issues did the earliest psychologists address?

How has psychology changed over time?

Imagine yourself as a young scholar in, say, 1880. Enthusiastic about the new scientific approach in psychology, you have decided to become a psychologist yourself. If you are like the other early psychologists, you have a background in either biology or philosophy. You are determined to apply the scientific methods of biology to the problems of philosophy.

So far, so good. But what questions will you address? To choose a good research question in any field, a scientist considers two issues: First, what questions would be *important* to answer for either theoretical or practical reasons? Second, what questions would be *possible* to answer, given the available methods and equipment? Ideally, a research question should be both important and answerable.

Back in 1880, how do you decide which questions are important? You cannot get research ideas from the psychological journals, because the first issue won't be published until next year. (And it is going to be all in German!) You cannot follow in the tradition of previous researchers, because there haven't been any previous researchers. You are on your own.

Furthermore, back in the late 1800s and early 1900s, psychologists were not sure which questions were answerable. Sometimes they still are not sure. Many of the changes during the history of psychology have been changes in investigators' decisions about what constitutes a good research question.

In the next several pages we shall explore some of the changes in research questions over the history of psychology, featuring a few projects that dominated psychology for a while and then faded. I shall not mention Sigmund Freud or several other figures of continuing influence in psychology, simply because later chapters will discuss their work in some detail.

PSYCHOLOGY IN THE EARLY ERA (1879 to about 1920)

Philosophers at least since Aristotle (384–322 B.C.) have been debating why people act the way they do, why they have the experiences they do, and why one person is different from another. Novelists such as Chaucer, Dostoyevsky, and Goethe have also made profound observations on human behavior.

Without meaning to take anything away from the importance of these great thinkers, a number of 19th-century scholars wondered whether a scientific approach might be fruitful. They were impressed by the great strides made in physics, chemistry, and biology; they wondered whether psychology could make similar progress if it collected and evaluated evidence scientifically.

Wilhelm Wundt and the First Psychological Laboratory

The origin of psychology as we now know it is generally dated to 1879, when a medical doctor and sensory researcher named Wilhelm Wundt (pronounced "voont") set up the first psychology laboratory, in Leipzig, Germany. Wundt and others had conducted psychological experiments before then, but this was the first time anyone had established a lab exclusively for psychological research.

Wundt's fundamental question was "What are the components of experience, or mind?" He proposed that psychological experience is

FIGURE 1.6

(Left) In one of Wundt's earliest experiments, the pendulum struck the metal balls (b and d), making a sound each time. However, to an observer the ball appeared to be somewhere else at the time of the sound, generally a distance that it would travel in about 1/8 second. Wundt inferred that a person needs about 1/8 second to shift attention from one stimulus to another. (Right) The Walt Disney studios rediscovered Wundt's observation decades later: A character's mouth movements seem to be in synchrony with the sounds if the movements precede the sounds by 1/8 to 1/6 second.

composed of compounds, just as chemistry has compounds. Psychology, he maintained, has two kinds of elements—sensations and feelings (Wundt, 1896/1902). So, at a particular moment you might experience the taste of a fine meal, the sound of good music, and a certain degree of pleasure. These would merge together into a single experience, but that experience would still include the separate elements. Furthermore, Wundt maintained, your experience is partly under your control; even when the physical situation stays the same, you can shift your attention from one item to another and get a different experience.

Wundt's question about the components of experience was a philosophical one, and some of his musings about the elements of the mind were not much different from the writings of philosophers before him. But Wundt, unlike the philosophers, tried to test his statements by collecting data. He presented various kinds of lights, touches, and sounds and asked people to report the intensity and quality of their sensa-

tions. He measured the changes in people's experiences as he changed the stimulus.

Wundt also demonstrated that it was possible to conduct meaningful experiments in psychology. For example, in one of his earliest studies, Wundt set up a pendulum that struck metal balls and made a sound at two points on its swing (points b and d in Figure 1.6). Then he or another subject would watch the pendulum and determine where it appeared to be when they heard the sound. In some cases the pendulum appeared to be slightly in front of the ball and in other cases slightly behind the ball. On the average, the apparent position of the pendulum at the time of the sound differed from its actual position by about 1/8 second (Wundt, 1862/1961). Apparently we can be slightly wrong about the time when we saw or heard something. Wundt's interpretation was that it takes about 1/8 second to shift attention from one experience to another.

Wundt and his students were prolific investigators; the brief treatment here does not do him justice. He contributed a great deal (writing more than 50,000 pages), but his most lasting impact on psychology came from setting the precedent of studying psychological questions by collecting scientific data.

Edward Titchener and Structuralism

For years, most of the world's scientific psychologists received their education from Wundt himself. One of Wundt's students, Edward Titchener, came to the United States in 1892 as a psychology professor at Cornell University. Like Wundt, Titchener thought the main question of psychology was the nature of mental experiences.

Titchener (1910) typically presented a stimulus and asked his subject to analyze it into its separate features—for example, to look at an apple and describe its redness, its brightness, its shape, and so forth. Whereas Wundt believed an experience was composed of these various elements, Titchener thought people could actually *describe* the individual elements of their experience. He called his approach **structuralism,** because he was trying to describe the structures that compose the mind. He was much less interested in what those elements *do* (their functions).

If you asked some psychologists today whether they thought Titchener had the correct description of the structures of the mind, you would be likely to get a blank look or shrug of the shoulders. After Titchener died in 1927, psychologists virtually abandoned his line of research. Why? Remember that I said a good scientific question is both important and answerable. We may or may not find Titchener's question about the elements of the mind important, but after he had spent his entire adult life working on it, the question certainly seemed unanswerable. The main reason was that he and his students had to rely on observers to describe their experiences accurately. But they had no convincing way to check that accuracy. For example, suppose you are the psychologist: I look at a lemon and tell you I have an experience of brightness that is totally separate from my experience of yellowness. How do you know whether I am correct about that? I might be lying to you, telling you what I think you want me to say, or even deceiving myself. You are apparently stuck with taking my word for it, unless you have some other way of seeing into my mind. Psychologists' frustration with this approach eventually turned most of them against the whole idea of studying the mind, leaving

them eager to adopt the behaviorist alternative, which we shall discuss later.

William James and Functionalism

About simultaneously with the work of Wundt and overlapping the work of Titchener, Harvard's William James articulated some of the major issues of psychology and won eventual recognition as the founder of American psychology. James's book *The Principles of Psychology* (James, 1890) defined the questions that dominated psychology for years afterward, and still do to some extent today.

James had little patience for Wundt's or Titchener's search for the elements of the mind. He once wrote, "[A] microscopic psychology has arisen in Germany, carried on by experimental methods, asking of course every moment for introspective data, but eliminating their uncertainty by operating on a large scale and taking statistical means. This method taxes patience to the utmost, and hardly could have arisen in a country whose natives could be *bored.* Such Germans as . . . Wundt obviously cannot."

James focused concern on the actions the mind *performs,* rather than the ideas the mind *has.* That is, he did not care to isolate the elements of consciousness; he preferred to learn how the mind produces useful behaviors. For that reason we call his approach **functionalism.** He suggested the following as examples of good psychological questions (James, 1890):

- How can people strengthen good habits?
- How many objects can a person attend to at once?
- How do people recognize that they have seen something before?
- How does an intention lead to an action?

James himself did little research to answer these questions, although he proposed some reasonable possibilities. His main contribution was to inspire later researchers to address the questions he posed. In focusing on how the mind produces useful behavior, he paved the way for the behaviorists of a later generation, who focused on behavior itself and ignored "mind" altogether.

Studies of Sensation

For many early psychologists, the important question was the relationship between physical stimuli and psychological sensations. To a large extent, the study of sensation *was* psychology. The first English-language textbook of the "new," scientifically based psychology devoted almost half its pages to the senses and the related topic of attention (Scripture, 1907). By the 1930s, a standard psychology textbook devoted less than 20% of its pages to these topics (Woodworth, 1934); today, the coverage constitutes about 5–10%.

Why were the early psychologists so interested in sensation? One reason was philosophical: They wanted to understand mental experience, and experience is composed mostly if not entirely of sensations. The other reason was strategic: If they were going to demonstrate the possibility of a scientific psychology, they had to begin with questions that were *answerable,* even if some of them were not extremely interesting.

They discovered that what we see, hear, and otherwise sense is not the same as what is really "out there." For example, the *perceived* intensity of a stimulus is not directly proportional to the actual physical intensity of the stimulus. A light that is twice as intense as another light does not *look* twice as bright. Figure 1.7 shows the actual relationship between the intensity of light and its perceived brightness. The mathematical description of that relationship is called the **psychophysical function,** because it relates psychology to physics. Research such as this demonstrated that at least in the study of sensation, scientific methods can provide nonobvious answers to psychological questions.

The Influence of Darwin and the Study of Animal Intelligence

Charles Darwin's theory of evolution by natural selection (Darwin, 1859, 1871) had an enormous impact not only on biology but on psychology as well. Darwin argued that humans and other species share a remote common ancestor. That proposal implied that each species had evolved specializations adapted to different ways of life, but it also implied that all vertebrate species had certain basic features in common. It implied that nonhuman animals should exhibit varying degrees of human characteristics, including intelligence similar to human intelligence.

Presuming that we accept that implication, what should psychologists do about it? A number of early **comparative psychologists** (psychologists who compare different species) did something that seemed reasonable at the time, though we might now regard it as misguided:

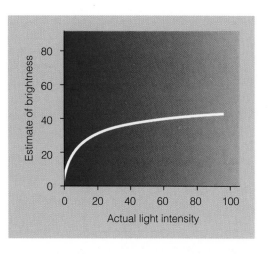

FIGURE 1.7
This graph of a psychophysical event shows the perceived intensity versus its physical intensity. When a light becomes twice as intense physically, it does not seem twice as bright. (Adapted from Stevens, 1961.)

They set out to measure animal intelligence. They apparently imagined that they would be able to rank-order all animals from the smartest to the dullest. Toward that goal, they put various species into such tasks as the delayed-response problem and the detour problem. In the *delayed-response problem,* an animal was given a signal indicating where it could find food. Then the animal was delayed in its movement toward the food (Figure 1.8a), to find out how long each species could remember the signal. In the *detour problem,* an animal was separated from food by a barrier (Figure 1.8b), to find out which species would get the idea of taking a detour away from the food at first in order to get to it later.

Comparative psychologists set their animals to other tasks as well (Maier & Schneirla, 1964). But the task of measuring animal intelligence turned out to be much more difficult than it sounded. Too often a species that seemed dull-witted on one task seemed highly capable on a very similar one. For example, zebras are generally slow to learn to approach one pattern instead of another for food, unless the patterns happen to be narrow stripes versus wide stripes, in which case zebras become geniuses (Giebel, 1958). (See Figure 1.9.) Rats perform very poorly when they have to find an object that looks different from the others, but very well when they have to find an object that smells different (Langworthy & Jennings, 1972).

Eventually psychologists realized that the relative intelligence of nonhuman animals would not be an easy question to answer; the question may even be scientifically meaningless. By the late 1920s, interest in the topic had faded (Kalat, 1983). A few investigators addressed the question from time to time, but it was never again a widespread focus of research.

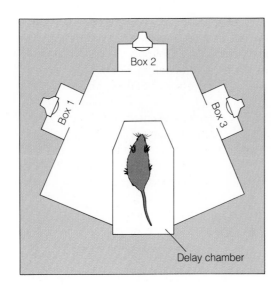

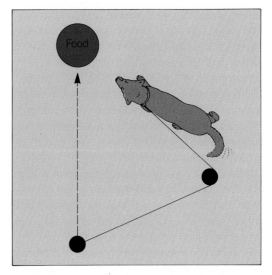

b

FIGURE 1.9
In an experiment by Giebel (1958), zebras compared stripe patterns. How "smart" a species is depends in part on what ability or skill is tested.

The Measurement of Human Intelligence

While some psychologists had studied animal intelligence, most had an even greater interest in human intelligence. Francis Galton, a first cousin of Charles Darwin, was among the first to try to measure intelligence and to ask whether intellectual variations were based on heredity. Galton was fascinated with measure-

ment of almost anything and pioneered many new methods of measurements (Hergenhahn, 1992). For example, he invented the weather map, measured degrees of boredom during lectures, suggested the use of fingerprints to identify individuals, and—presumably in the name of science—attempted to measure the degree of beauty for women of different countries.

In an effort to determine the role of heredity in human achievement, Galton (1869/1978) examined whether the sons of famous and accomplished men were likely to become equally eminent themselves. (He paid little attention to women, on the grounds that women in 19th-century England had little prospect of attaining eminence.) Galton found that the sons of judges, writers, politicians, and other noted men had a high probability of reaching high levels themselves. He attributed their edge to heredity, although today we would hardly consider his evidence persuasive. (Sons of eminent men clearly had a favorable environment, not just favorable genes.) He furthermore suggested that eminence is partly due to intelligence; thus, he believed a tendency toward high or low intelligence was inheritable.

Galton, however, had no test of intelligence. He attempted to measure intelligence by simple tests of sensory capacities and motor coordination, but none of these tests proved satisfactory. The French researcher, Alfred Binet, devised the first useful test in 1905. We shall discuss Binet's contributions and other intelligence tests in Chapter 10. At this point let us just note that the idea of intelligence testing

FIGURE 1.10
Mary Calkins, one of the first prominent women in U.S. psychology.

quickly captured a great deal of interest in the United States and other countries. Such tests were widely used during World War I as a means of eliminating "feebleminded" people from military service; soon tests were widely used by schools and sometimes by employers. Eventually psychologists developed tests of personality, interests, and other psychological characteristics.

The Role of Women in the Early Days of Psychology

In the late 1800s and early 1900s, most U.S. colleges provided only very limited opportunities for women, either as students or as faculty. Psychology was not much different from other fields in this regard, but a few women did make major contributions and achieved wide recognition.

One of the first women to make a career in psychology was Mary Calkins (Scarborough & Furomoto, 1987). When Henry Durant founded Wellesley College in 1870, he decided to hire only women to teach the all-female student body. But he could find no woman with an advanced degree in psychology. Finally, in 1890, he hired a bright young woman, Mary Calkins (Figure 1.10), who had a B.A. degree in classics, to teach psychology, promising that he would pay for her graduate education in psychology. Then the problem was to find a graduate program that would accept a female student. After much debate and stiff resistance, nearby Harvard University finally agreed to let her attend graduate classes. In 1895, when she passed the final examination for the Ph.D. degree, one of her professors remarked that she had performed better on the examination than had any other student in the history of the department.

The Harvard administration, however, was still unwilling to grant a Ph.D. degree to a woman. It suggested a compromise: It would grant her a Ph.D. degree from Radcliffe College, the recently established women's undergraduate college associated with Harvard. Calkins refused, declaring that to accept the compromise would violate the high ideals of education. She never gave in, and neither did Harvard. Although Mary Calkins never received a Ph.D. degree, she became a pioneer in psychological research, inventing a technique of studying memory, known as the paired-associates method, that is still used today. She also became president of the American Psychological Association.

The first woman to receive the Ph.D. degree in psychology was Margaret Washburn, who received it from Cornell University in 1894. She later wrote *The Animal Mind* (1908), the first text on that topic; she too served as president of the American Psychological Association. Christine Ladd-Franklin, another early psychologist, did outstanding research on vision, beginning in 1887.

THE PERIOD OF BEHAVIORIST DOMINANCE (1920? to 1970?)

Earlier in this chapter I casually tossed out a definition of psychology as "the systematic study of behavior and experience." For a substantial period in the history of psychology, most experimental psychologists would have protested violently against those words *and experience*. Some psychologists still object today, but a little less strenuously. From about 1920 to 1970, give or take a little, psychology was the study of behavior, period. Research psychologists were, with a few exceptions, firmly committed behaviorists. Psychology had nothing to say about minds, experiences, or anything of the sort.

How did psychologists ever reach that conclusion? Recall that Titchener's effort to analyze experience into its components had failed. Most psychologists concluded that questions about the mind were unanswerable. The comparative psychologists also had failed in their efforts to measure animal intelligence, but in the process they had developed techniques for studying animal learning. Behaviorists discarded the question about animal intelligence but kept the research methods.

Behaviorists' primary research question was broad and simple: What do people and other animals do under various conditions? This question is clearly answerable, although no one knew whether the answer would consist of long lists of details or a short list of general laws.

John B. Watson and the Origin of Behaviorism

We can regard John B. Watson as the founder of behaviorism. He was not the first behaviorist—actually, it is hard to say who was the first—but Watson systematized behaviorism, stated its goals and assumptions, and popularized the approach. He set forth his views in two major statements, *Psychology from the Standpoint of a Behaviorist* (Watson, 1919) and *Behaviorism* (Watson, 1925). Here are two quotes from Watson:

Psychology as the behaviorist views it is a purely objective experimental branch of natural science. Its theoretical goal is the prediction and control of behavior. (Watson, 1913, p. 158)

The goal of psychological study is the ascertaining of such data and laws that, given the stimulus, psychology can predict what the response will be; or, on the other hand, given the response, it can specify the nature of the effective stimulus. (Watson, 1919, p. 10)

Watson's books and articles set psychology's agenda for many years. The early behaviorists were extremely optimistic, expecting to discover simple, basic laws of behavior comparable to Newton's laws in physics. In the belief that behavioral laws would be more or less the same from one species to another, many experimenters studied animals, especially rats. By 1950, one psychologist found that well over half of all psychological studies on animals dealt with rats (Beach, 1950). (See Figure 1.11.)

Clark Hull and Learning Theory

Inspired by Watson, psychologists set out to study animal behavior, especially animal learning. For a time, the most influential figure in this area was Yale psychologist Clark Hull. Hull was very explicit about what he considered an important psychological question: "One of the most persistently baffling problems which confronts modern psychologists is the finding of an adequate explanation of the phenomena of maze learning" (Hull, 1932).

Hull set out to discover laws to account for the behavior of a rat in a maze. He summarized his theory in a mathematical equation showing that a rat increased its "habit strength" rapidly on the first few runs through a maze, and then more slowly on each additional trial (Figure 1.12). As Hull continued his research, he found that he had to make the equation more complicated. First he found that he had to multiply "habit strength" times "drive" to determine the probability that the rat would actually respond. Then he found that rats will run faster for a really tasty tidbit of food than for a barely edible piece. So he added to the equation another term for the amount of incentive. And then he needed another one for the effects of delaying reinforcement. And another to account for the fact that after a rat has been tested many times it starts to slow down. And other terms. Gradually his equation became longer and longer.

After the 1943 publication of Hull's major work, *Principles of Behavior,* his ideas dominated experimental psychology for years. His work was mentioned in almost a third of the articles published in the *Journal of Experimental Psychology* between 1950 and 1952. Within a few years after his death in 1952, though, his influence began to decline. Today, few psychologists take Hull's equations seriously.

What happened to Hull's theories? Not much, really. No one ever demonstrated that he was wrong. The problem was that in order to account for the behavior of a rat in a maze, Hull had to make his theory more and more complicated. The theory seemed to be getting more complicated faster than it was getting more accurate. Besides, why were psychologists studying a rat in a maze in the first place? Surely not because they cared about rats or mazes for their own sake; the hope was that psychologists would discover general principles that apply to more complex behaviors, including human behaviors. But if the behavioral laws for rats in a maze were so complicated, then perhaps psychologists should study something else. Just as psychologists of the 1920s decided that Titchener's structuralist approach was unlikely to answer his questions in a reasonable period of

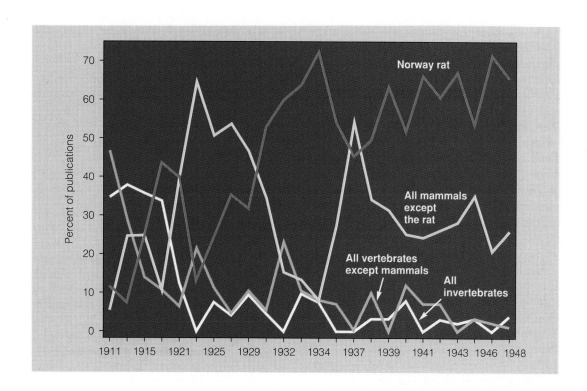

FIGURE 1.11
Frank Beach (1950) calculated the percentage of psychological studies of animals that dealt with various species in the major journal of animal behavior. Until the mid-1920s, psychologists studied a wide variety of species. Beginning in the late 1920s, most studies used rats.

time, psychologists of the late 1950s and 1960s turned away from Hull's approach.

THE CURRENT ERA IN PSYCHOLOGY

The rest of this book deals with the current era in psychology, with occasional flashbacks on the history of a particular subfield. The current era is not a "postbehaviorist" era, but we could call it a "post–behaviorist dominance" era. That is, behaviorism is still alive and well, but it does not dominate psychology in quite the same way it once did. Some psychologists continue to study animal learning, but other psychologists now study "mental images," problem solving, emotions, and other phenomena that behaviorists once rejected as "impossible to study scientifically."

But psychology has definitely *not* returned to prebehaviorist methods. Even the psychologists studying thinking and mental images are careful to do so by measuring behaviors, not by relying on people to describe their own ideas and thought processes. That is, even psychologists who ask some nonbehaviorist questions rely on solid behaviorist methods, and we are beginning to find that questions we once considered unanswerable are reasonable questions after all.

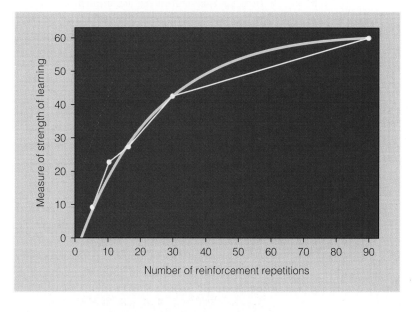

FIGURE 1.12
Clark Hull proposed the formula $_sH_R = M - Me^{-iN}$ for the strength of learning ($_sH_R$) by a rat in a maze. As the data points show, a rat improves its running speed rapidly at first and then more slowly as it approaches the maximum level, M. Hull's formula matched these results fairly well. The term i in his formula changed from one experiment to another to match the data. (Adapted from Hull, 1943.)

Throughout this discussion I have shown how psychologists over the decades have gone down some blind alleys, devoting enormous efforts on certain projects that proved to be disappointing. Not all the efforts of early psychologists were quite so fruitless; many of them have stood the test of time—for example, the Gestalt psychologists' contributions to our understanding of perception (Chapter 4), Hermann Ebbinghaus's work on memory (Chapter 8), and Sigmund Freud's concepts of unconscious motivation (Chapter 13). I have saved these for later chapters, because they are relevant to current psychology and not just of historical interest.

Still, if psychologists of the past have spent countless person-years on some currently fashionable project, only to decide later that it was mostly a waste of time, how do we know that some psychologists aren't doing the same thing right now?

Well, we don't. Thousands of psychologists are doing various kinds of research, and chances are some of them are working on projects that will never accomplish much. As you read through later chapters, you are welcome to entertain some doubts. Maybe some of psychologists' questions are not so simple as they seem; perhaps some of their answers are not so solid; perhaps you can think of a better way to approach certain topics.

In short, psychologists do not have all the answers. But that is not a cause for despair. Much like the rats in the mazes, psychologists make progress by trial and error. They pose a question, try a particular research method, and find out what happens. Sometimes the results turn out to be fascinating and rich in practical consequences. Sometimes they turn out to be puzzling or inconclusive. If one study after another proves to be disappointing, psychologists either look for a new method or change the question. By abandoning enough unsuccessful approaches, they eventually find their way to better questions and better answers.

SUMMARY

- *Choice of research questions.* During its history, psychology has several times changed its opinions of what constitutes an interesting, important, answerable question. (page 20)

- *First experiments.* In 1879 Wilhelm Wundt established the first laboratory devoted to psychological research. He demonstrated the possibility of psychological experimentation. (page 21)

- *Limits of self-observation.* One of Wundt's students, Edward Titchener, attempted to analyze the elements of mental experience, relying on people's self-observations. Other psychologists became discouraged with this approach. (page 22)

- *The founding of American psychology.* William James, generally considered the founder of American psychology, focused attention on how the mind guides useful behavior, rather than on the contents of the mind. In doing so he paved the way for the later rise of behaviorism. (page 22)

- *Early sensory research.* In the early days of psychology, many researchers concentrated on studies of the senses, partly because they were more certain to find definite answers on this topic than they were on other topics. (page 22)

- *Darwin's influence.* Charles Darwin's theory of evolution by natural selection influenced psychology in many ways; it prompted some prominent early psychologists to compare the intelligence of different species. That question turned out to be more complicated than anyone had expected. (page 23)

- *Intelligence testing.* The measurement of human intelligence was one concern of early psychologists that has persisted through the years. (page 24)

- *Women in the early days of psychology.* In spite of an environment that discouraged women from pursuing academic careers, several women including Mary Calkins and Margaret Washburn became leaders in the early days of psychology. (page 25)

- *Era of behaviorist dominance.* As psychologists became discouraged with attempts to analyze the mind, they turned to behaviorism. For many years psychological researchers concentrated on behavior, especially animal learning, to the virtual exclusion of mental experience. (page 25)

- *Mathematical models of maze learning.* Clark Hull, who attempted to describe learning with a mathematical formula, exerted great influence for a number of years. Eventually his approach became less popular because rats in mazes did not seem to generate simple or general answers to major questions. (page 26)

- *Psychological research today.* Today, psychologists study a wide variety of topics. We cannot promise that we are not going down some blind alleys, like many psychologists before us. (page 27)

SUGGESTIONS FOR FURTHER READING

Benjamin, L. T., Jr. (1988). *A history of psychology.* New York: McGraw-Hill. A collection of articles and segments of books, some old and some more recent.

Hergenhahn, B. R. (1992). *An introduction to the history of psychology.* Belmont, CA: Wadsworth. A standard textbook on the history of psychology.

Scarborough, E., & Furomoto, L. (1987). *Untold lives: The first generation of American women psychologists.* New York: Columbia University Press. A rich account of history and biography.

TERMS

structuralism an attempt to describe the structures that compose the mind (page 22)

functionalism an attempt to understand how mental processes produce useful behaviors (page 22)

psychophysical function mathematical description of the relationship between the physical properties of a stimulus and its perceived properties (page 23)

comparative psychologist specialist who compares different species (page 23)

2 SCIENTIFIC METHODS IN PSYCHOLOGY

Every year spectacular claims are published about human behavior. Some of them receive wide publicity, even if there is little or no evidence to support them. Here are some examples:

- *Biorhythms.* Some people claim that your mood and your success on a given day depend on an intellectual cycle of 33 days, an emotional cycle of 28 days, and a physical cycle of 23 days, each cycle recurring regularly from the day of birth.

- *Age regression.* Some people say that under hypnosis and similar techniques, a person can recall in great detail what it was like to be a young child, a baby, an embryo, or even a sperm cell (Sadger, 1941). (One man said that he and his fellow sperm cells had resented their father because they knew he did not want them to fertilize the egg!)

- *Psychic communication.* In 1978 a man was killed when his car plunged off a cliff. Nearly 3 weeks later his body was found, partly eaten, with his pet dog nearby. The police were about to have the dog destroyed, but then a "psychic" intervened. She claimed she could communicate with the dog, and the dog told her he had tried to defend the man's body from the coyotes and wild dogs that had eaten it. The police took her word for it and spared the dog's life (Skeptical Inquirer, 1978a).

- *The power of belief.* For a long time people were aware that the Earth had one moon and that Jupiter had at least four. They believed that Mars should have two, to fill out the mathematical progression. In 1877 two tiny moons appeared in a telescope for the first time. Why had no one seen them before? To most people the answer seemed obvious: Until 1877 there had been no telescopes powerful enough to detect such small and distant objects. But no, said one person: Those moons had not even existed before 1877! It was only because people had believed in them for so long that they had finally come into existence (Skeptical Inquirer, 1978b).

Most of us quickly dismiss the truly preposterous claims, such as the one about the moons of Mars. The one about biorhythms is not quite so easy to dismiss, although it conflicts with much of what we know about biology. Those who believe it cite isolated cases in which it seems to apply. To decide whether the idea is worthy of belief, we must evaluate the alleged evidence and collect additional evidence.

We have to be especially careful to evaluate the evidence when someone proposes a theory that sounds plausible on first hearing. It is tempting then to accept the theory without noticing possible flaws in the evidence. Not all theories that sound reasonable turn out to be correct.

In short, *we must scrutinize carefully the evidence for every claim that is made, even those that strike us as reasonable.*

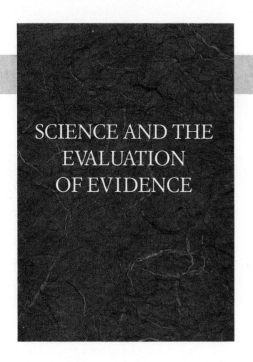

SCIENCE AND THE EVALUATION OF EVIDENCE

How do scientists decide which is a better theory and which is a worse theory?

You will sometimes hear people say that something has been "scientifically proved." Scientists themselves seldom use the word *prove,* except when they are talking about a mathematical proof. As they collect more and better evidence, they may become confident about a given conclusion, but they still hesitate to say they are "certain" of it.

One distinguishing characteristic of science is that scientists generally agree on how to evaluate competing theories. Even when they disagree on which theory is best, they can still agree on what kinds of evidence they will accept in trying to decide. Most psychologists are quick to concede that our knowledge of psychology is less complete and less systematic than our knowledge of physics, chemistry, and biology. But like physicists, chemists, and biologists, psychologists generally agree on what constitutes good evidence and what does not. They try to rely on evidence, not on intuition.

Something to Think About

If ethicists agreed with each other on how to evaluate theories, could they make progress comparable to that of scientists? Could theologians?

STEPS IN GATHERING AND EVALUATING EVIDENCE

Above all, scientists want to know the evidence behind a given claim. If this book has one overall theme, that is it. Psychologists would like students to learn to question assertions in psychology, to ask what is the evidence behind a given claim and whether that evidence leads to an unambiguous conclusion.

In any scientific field, researchers conduct studies that go through a series of steps described in the following four paragraphs (see also Figure 2.1). Articles in scientific publications generally follow this sequence too. In each of the following chapters, you will find a section titled "What's the Evidence?" Those sections will go through one or more psychological investigations step by step, also in this order.

Hypothesis Any study begins with a **hypothesis,** which is a testable prediction of what will happen under certain conditions. In many cases the hypothesis is the product of someone's casual observations. For example, a psychologist might notice that children who like to watch violent television programs seem to be relatively violent themselves. So it seems, at any rate; we cannot always trust our impressions. The psychologist might then set out to test whether those children who watch the greatest amount of violence on television engage in the greatest amount of aggressive behavior.

Method Devising an appropriate method to test a hypothesis can be surprisingly difficult. For example, an investigator wants to measure how much violence each child watches on television. That may sound easy. But what counts as violence? Do we count minutes of violent programming, or do we count violent acts? Do some types of violence count more than others? We encounter similar problems in measuring a child's aggressive behavior. The mark of a skillful investigator is the ability to find ways to measure behaviors accurately.

FIGURE 2.1
Developing a theory involves four steps to test and confirm (or disconfirm) a prediction. Confidence in the theory increases or decreases with reports of new experimental results.

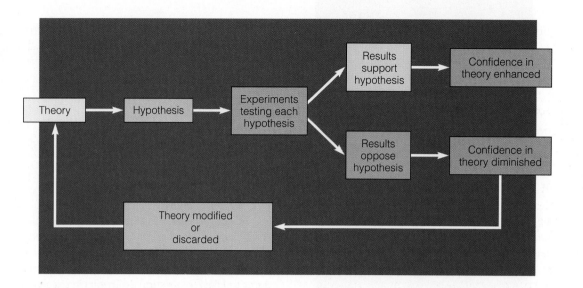

Results   Suppose the investigator somehow measures televised violence and aggressive behavior. Then the task is to determine the relationship between the two measures. Did the children who watched the greatest amount of violence also engage in the most aggressive behavior? If so, how strong was the relationship? Were the results convincing, or might they have arisen by accident? Here the investigator calls upon statistical techniques to evaluate the results.

Interpretation   Finally, the task is to determine what the results mean. Sometimes the results clearly contradict the hypothesis. For example, an investigator might find that children who watch a great deal of televised violence are no more aggressive than other children, in general. In that case we might abandon the hypothesis or we might modify it: Maybe it applies only to certain kinds of children or to certain kinds of violence.

If the results match the prediction, we would look for other possible explanations before we draw a conclusion. Suppose, for example, the investigator finds that the children who watched the most violence on television were also prone to the most aggressive behavior. We would not conclude that televised violence leads to aggressive behavior, because of an alternative interpretation: Perhaps aggressive children like to watch violent television!

It is almost always possible to suggest more than one interpretation of the results of a given study. At that point the investigator sets up a second study to follow up on the results of the first and tries to decide between the two inter-

pretations. That study too may lead to further studies. Because almost any study has its limitations, the ultimate conclusion comes from a pattern of results from many studies.

REPLICABILITY

Before psychologists trust the results of a study, we like to have other investigators repeat the procedure. If they get similar results, then they have **replicable results**—that is, anyone who follows the same procedure can repeat them. If a result is replicable, we still may not be sure how to interpret it, but at least we think it is worthwhile to try. If the results cannot be replicated, then perhaps there was some hidden flaw in the first study; we base no conclusions on it.

What if a result can be replicated in some studies and not others? For example, when studying the effects of televised violence on children, certain investigators might find one set of results, while others find the opposite. Presuming that both sets of investigators conducted their studies equally well, what are we to believe?

Psychologists would look for some pattern in the results. Perhaps watching violence on television is associated with violent behavior only for children of a certain age or just for one sex. Or perhaps the results depend on the type of violent program or on the method of measuring aggressive behavior. If such a pattern seemed to emerge, psychologists would conduct additional research to confirm that pattern and try to understand it better. If no such pattern emerged, they would become skeptical of any relationship between watching televised violence and behaving violently.

Note that a *replicable* result is not the same as a *replicated* result. Occasionally someone reports a spectacular result that a few investigators manage to replicate but most cannot. For example, one group of investigators reported that they trained some rats to respond in a certain way, then ground up the rats' brains, injected an extract into other rats, and found that the new rats remembered what the old rats had learned (Babich, Jacobson, Bubash, & Jacobson, 1965). Because this was such a surprising result, many other experimenters tried to replicate it. A few reported results somewhat similar to those of the first experimenters, but most investigators found not even a hint of such results. Even after extensive efforts, no one found a way to get transfer of training by brain extracts in a consistent way (Gaito, 1976; L. T. Smith, 1975). Therefore, we consider this result *unreplicable*. We do not know why the original investigators obtained the reported results; most psychologists now assume it was just an accident. In any case, we cannot take any results seriously unless they are consistently replicable.

CRITERIA FOR EVALUATING SCIENTIFIC THEORIES

Up to this point I have alluded to research in psychology without much detail. I shall go into the details in the sections titled "Methods of Investigation in Psychology" and "Measuring and Reporting Results." Here, let's look at the big picture: After investigators collect mounds of evidence, what do they do with it? As part of the definition of science I said that investigators agree on how to evaluate competing theories. Exactly how do they decide what is a good theory?

The goal of scientific research is to establish **theories,** comprehensive explanations of natural phenomena that lead to accurate predictions. A good theory predicts many observations in terms of a few assumptions and reduces the amount of information we must keep available for reference. For example, according to the *law of effect* (to be discussed in Chapter 7), if a person or any other animal makes some response and that response is consistently followed by a *reinforcer* (such as food to a hungry

person or water to a thirsty one), then in the future the probability of that response will increase. This law summarizes results for many species, many responses, and many reinforcers.

A good theory reveals patterns in the observations we make. It enables us to reduce many complex facts to a few facts and to identify the interactions among them. To say that "the highest mountain in the world is in the Himalayas" does not state a theory, regardless of whether the statement is true. A theory is more general than the facts it explains.

When we are confronted with several competing theories, we must evaluate them to decide which is the most acceptable. Scientists use several criteria (Figure 2.2). First, *a theory should fit the known facts.* Second, *it should predict new observations.* If I had a theory of your behavior, and it seemed to fit everything you had done in the past, the theory might seem impressive, but the real test would be to see whether it can predict what you will do in the future.

Third, *a theory should not be so vague that it fits any and all observations.* It should be **falsifiable.** In other words, we should be able to imagine some evidence that would contradict it. Here is an example of a falsifiable theory: *People identify the direction of a sound source by comparing the response in the left ear with the response in the right ear.* If we found a person who was totally deaf in one ear but who had no trouble localizing the direction of sound sources, that observation would clearly contradict, or falsify, the theory. (The fact that no one has ever found such a person supports the theory.)

Now consider a theory that is, so far as we can tell, not falsifiable: Sigmund Freud proposed that children who have certain kinds of disturbing sexual fantasies will grow up predisposed to certain kinds of adult psychological disorders. The problem is, how can we know which children have had disturbing sexual fantasies? We cannot. Fantasies being private, we cannot observe them; therefore, we cannot predict which people will or will not be predisposed to psychological disorders. Because the theory makes no testable predictions, it is not falsifiable and not a good scientific theory.

Fourth, other things being equal, *scientists prefer the theory that explains matters in the simplest possible terms and makes the simplest assumptions.* That is often a difficult criterion to apply, but it is a most important one. We shall examine it in more detail.

A good theory

Fits known facts

Predicts new discoveries

Is falsifiable

Is parsimonious

FIGURE 2.2
Scientists evaluate competing theories by these criteria and rank them as good or perhaps not so good.

THE PRINCIPLE
OF PARSIMONY

According to the principle of **parsimony** (literally, stinginess), scientists prefer the theory that accounts for the results using the simplest assumptions. In other words, they prefer a theory that is consistent with theories they have already accepted. A theory that makes radically new assumptions is acceptable only after we have made every attempt to explain the results in a simpler way.

How do we decide what is a simpler assumption? If we have previously concluded that many animals solve problems by responding to what they see, then we may simply assume that another animal, solving a new problem, might also be responding to something it sees. It would be less simple (less parsimonious) to assume that the animal solves the problem by making mathematical calculations or by reading minds. That is, making simple assumptions is partly (though not entirely) a matter of sticking to the same assumptions we have already made. Consider the following three examples.

First Example: Where Do Babies Come From?

Where babies come from is not obvious to everyone. I remember trying to explain it to my sons when they were young and getting reactions of amazement bordering on disbelief. And at least one human culture in modern times has rejected the theory that sexual intercourse causes babies.

According to Bronislaw Malinowski (1929), the Trobriand Islanders (near New Guinea) believed that the spirits of ancestors float in on the ocean tide; when they approach land, a special ghost takes one of the spirits and implants it in the head of a young woman. The young woman becomes pregnant, and the ancestral spirit becomes her baby. (Note that the theory suggests that young women can decrease their chance of pregnancy by staying far away from the ocean.)

Missionaries had repeatedly told the Trobrianders that sexual intercourse causes babies, but the Trobrianders had firmly rejected the idea. To try to convince them, Malinowski began, "Surely you must have noticed that virgins never have babies." The reply was, "Well, perhaps. But we don't have much experience with that sort of thing. There are practically no virgins around here."

While Malinowski was trying to think of other evidence that might make sense to a non-scientific people, one of the islanders said that he had evidence against the sex theory. "I was once away from the village on a journey for more than a year, and when I returned I found that my wife was pregnant. That proves that sex was not necessary."

Malinowski never did convince the Trobrianders of his theory, nor did they convince him of theirs. Why do we believe that sexual intercourse, rather than ancestral spirits floating on the water, causes babies? One reason is that to us the Trobrianders' theory is unfalsifiable. Because the supposed spirits are invisible, no one knows where they have been until after they have made a woman pregnant. Because no conceivable observation would contradict the theory, the theory is not scientific. Our other objection to the Trobriand Islanders' belief is that it is unparsimonious. It assumes that spirits float on water and enter a woman's head—an assumption that simply does not fit in with what we know or with what we think we know.

On their side, the Trobrianders rejected the sex theory because it seemed unparsimonious to them. They believed in spirits; they knew nothing of chemistry or biology. To explain to them about DNA and chromosomes and proteins would be like talking about zeta rays from outer space. For them to accept our view on where babies come from would not be a simple matter of exchanging one theory for another; they would have to change their entire view about the nature of the world.

Second Example: Clever Hans, the Amazing Horse

Early in this century, Mr. von Osten, a German mathematics teacher, set out to prove that his horse, Hans, had great intellectual abilities, particularly in arithmetic (Figure 2.3). To teach Hans arithmetic, he first showed him a single object, said "One," and lifted Hans's foot once. Then he raised Hans's foot twice for two objects, and so on. Eventually, when von Osten presented a group of objects, Hans tapped his foot by himself, and with practice he managed to tap the correct number of times. With more practice, it was no longer necessary for Hans to see the objects. Von Osten would just call out a number, and Hans would tap the appropriate number of times.

Von Osten moved on to addition and then to subtraction, multiplication, and division. Hans seemed to catch on amazingly quickly, soon responding with 90–95% accuracy. Von Osten began touring Germany to exhibit

Hans's abilities. He would give Hans a question, either orally or in writing, and Hans would tap out the answer. As time passed, Hans's abilities grew, just from being around humans, without any special training. Soon he was able to add fractions, convert fractions to decimals or vice versa, do simple algebra, tell time to the minute, and give the values of all German coins. Using a letter-to-number code, he could spell out the names of objects and even identify musical notes, such as D or B-flat. (Hans, it seems, had perfect pitch.) He responded correctly even when questions were put to him by persons other than von Osten, in unfamiliar places with von Osten nowhere in sight.

Given this evidence, many people were ready to assume that Hans had great intellectual prowess. But others were not. Why not? Certainly the evidence was replicable. The problem was parsimony. No previous research had led us to assume that a nonhuman animal could perform complex mathematical calculations. Was there a simpler explanation?

Enter Oskar Pfungst. Pfungst (1911) discovered that Hans could not answer a question correctly if the questioner had not calculated the answer first. Evidently the horse was not actually doing the calculations but was somehow getting the answers from the questioner. Next Pfungst learned that Hans had to see the experimenter. When the experimenter stood in plain sight, Hans's accuracy was 90% or better; when he could not see the experimenter, he either did not answer or made a wild guess.

Eventually Pfungst observed that any questioner who asked Hans a question would lean forward to watch Hans's foot. Hans had simply learned to start tapping whenever someone stood next to his right forefoot and leaned forward. As soon as Hans had given the correct number of taps, the experimenter would give a slight upward jerk of the head and change facial expression in anticipation that this might be the last tap. (Even skeptical scientists who tested Hans did this involuntarily.) Hans simply continued tapping until he received that cue.

In short, Hans was indeed a clever horse. But what he did could be explained in simple terms that did not involve mathematical calculations or any other advanced cognitive process. We prefer the explanation in terms of facial expressions because it is more parsimonious.

Something to Think About

If Clever Hans had died before Pfungst had discovered his secret, we would never have known

FIGURE 2.3
Clever Hans and his owner, Mr. von Osten, demonstrated that the horse could answer complex mathematical questions with great accuracy. The question was "How?" (After Pfungst, 1911, in Fernald, 1984.)

for sure how the horse was doing it. Would we be obliged to believe forever that this one horse could understand spoken language and could solve complex mathematical problems? How could we have evaluated such a hypothesis years later? (Hint: Would we have had to discover how Hans did answer the questions? Or would it be enough just to determine how he could have answered them?)

Third Example:
Extrasensory Perception

A highly controversial claim in psychology is the claim of extrasensory perception. Supporters of the idea of **extrasensory perception (ESP)** claim that certain people can acquire information without using any sense organ and without receiving any form of energy (Rhine, 1947). They claim, for instance, that a person gifted with ESP can identify another person's thoughts (telepathy) even when the two are separated by a thick lead barrier that would block the transmission of almost any form of energy. They also claim that people with telepathic powers can identify thoughts just as accurately from a distance of a thousand kilometers as from an adjacent room, in apparent violation of the inverse-square law of physics.

Some ESP supporters also claim that certain people can perceive inanimate objects that are hidden from sight (clairvoyance), predict the future (precognition), and influence such physical events as the roll of dice by sheer mental concentration (psychokinesis). In other words,

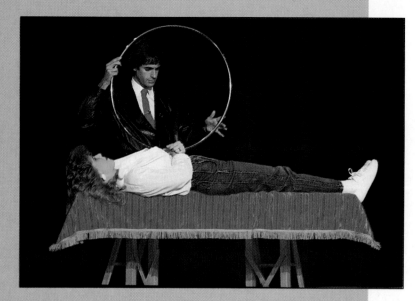

Magician David Copperfield can make people and animals seem to appear, disappear, float in the air, or do other things we know are impossible. Even if we do not know how he accomplishes these feats, we take it for granted that they are magic tricks, based on methods of misleading the audience. Other performers claim their amazing results depend on psychic powers. A more parsimonious explanation is that their feats, like Copperfield's, depend on misleading the audience.

they claim it is possible to gain information or to influence physical events without transmitting any physical energy. If any of these claims were demonstrated to be valid, then we would have to restructure our entire scientific view of nature, not just in psychology but in physics as well.

What evidence is there for ESP?

Anecdotes   One kind of evidence consists of anecdotes—people's reports of isolated events. Someone has a dream or a hunch that comes true or says something and someone else says, "I was just thinking exactly the same thing!" Such experiences may seem impressive when they occur, but they are meaningless as scientific evidence for several reasons. First, there is the possibility of coincidence. Of all the hunches and dreams that people have, eventually some are bound to come true by chance. Second, people tend to remember and talk about the hunches and dreams that do come true and to forget those that do not. They hardly ever say, "Strangest thing! I had a dream, but then nothing like it actually happened!" Third, people tend to exaggerate the coincidences that occur, both in their own memories and in the retelling. We could evaluate anecdotal evidence only if people recorded their hunches and

dreams before the predicted events and then determined how many unlikely predictions came true.

You may have heard of the "prophet Nostradamus," a 16th-century French writer who allegedly predicted many events of later centuries. Figure 2.4 presents four samples of his writings. No one knows what his predictions mean until after the "predicted" events happen. After something happens, people imaginatively reinterpret his writings to fit the event. (His "predictions" are not *falsifiable*.)

■ CONCEPT CHECK

1. *How could someone scientifically evaluate the accuracy of Nostradamus's predictions? (Check your answer on page 41.)*

Professional Psychics   A number of stage performers claim to read other people's minds and perform other psychic feats. Two of the most famous are Uri Geller and the Amazing Kreskin. Actually, Kreskin has consistently denied doing anything supernatural; he prefers to talk of his "extremely sensitive," rather than "extrasensitive" perception (Kreskin, 1991). Still, part of his success as a performer comes from letting people believe he has mental powers that defy explanation.

After carefully observing Geller, Kreskin, and others, David Marks and Richard Kammann (1980) concluded that the performers exhibited no special powers but only the kinds of deception commonly employed in magic shows. For example, Kreskin (Figure 2.5) sometimes begins his act by asking the audience to read his mind. Let's try to duplicate this trick right now: Try to read my mind. I am thinking of a number between 1 and 50. Both digits are odd numbers, but they are not the same. That is, it could be 15 but it could not be 11. (These are the instructions Kreskin gives.)

Have you chosen a number?

All right, my number was 37. Did you think of 37? If not, how about 35? You see, I started to think 35 and then changed my mind, so you might have got 35.

Probably about half the readers "read my mind." If you were one of them, are you impressed? Don't be. There are not many numbers you could have chosen. The first digit had to be 1 or 3, and the second had to be 1, 3, 5, 7, or 9. You had to eliminate 11 and 33 because both digits are the same, and you probably eliminated 15 because I cited it as a possible example. That leaves only seven possibilities. Most people like to stay far away from the example given and tend to avoid the highest and lowest possible choices. That leaves 37 as the most likely choice and 35 as the second most likely.

Second act: Kreskin asks the audience to write down something they are thinking about while he walks along the aisles talking. Then, back on stage, he "reads people's minds." He might say something like, "Someone is thinking about their mother . . ." In any large crowd, someone is bound to stand up and shout, "Yes, that's me, you read my mind!" On occasion he describes something that someone has written out in great detail. That person generally turns out to be someone sitting along the aisle where Kreskin was walking.

After a variety of other tricks (see Marks & Kammann, 1980), Kreskin goes backstage while the local mayor or some other dignitary hides Kreskin's paycheck somewhere in the audience. Then Kreskin comes back, walks up and down the aisles and across the rows, and eventually shouts, "The check is here!" The rule is that if he guesses wrong, then he does not get paid. (He hardly ever misses.)

How does he do that trick? Think for a moment before reading on.

Very simply, it is a Clever Hans trick. Kreskin studies people's faces. Most of the people are silently cheering for him to find the check. Their facial expression changes subtly as he comes close to the check and then moves away. In effect, they are saying, "Now you're getting closer" and "Now you're moving away." At last he closes in on the check. That is, Kreskin has trained himself to use his senses very well; he does not need some "extra" sense.

We can also explain the performances of many other stage performers in terms of simple tricks and illusions. Of course, someone always objects, "Well, maybe so. But there's this other guy you haven't investigated yet. Maybe he really does possess psychic powers." Until there is solid evidence to the contrary, it is simpler (more parsimonious) to assume that those other performers are also using illusion and deception.

Experiments Stage performances and anecdotal events always take place under uncontrolled conditions. So we cannot determine the probability of coincidence or the possibility of deception. The only evidence worth serious consideration comes from laboratory experiments.

For example, an experimenter shuffles a special set of ESP cards (Figure 2.6) and then

1. The great man will be struck down in the day by a thunderbolt. An evil deed, foretold by the bearer of a petition. According to the prediction another falls at night time. Conflict at Reims, London, and pestilence in Tuscany.

2. When the fish that travels over both land and sea is cast up on to the shore by a great wave, its shape foreign, smooth, and frightful. From the sea the enemies soon reach the walls.

3. The bird of prey flying to the left, before battle is joined with the French, he makes preparations. Some will regard him as good, others bad or uncertain. The weaker party will regard him as a good omen.

4. Shortly afterwards, not a very long interval, a great tumult will be raised by land and sea. The naval battles will be greater than ever. Fires, creatures which will make more tumult.

FIGURE 2.4

According to the followers of Nostradamus, each of these statements is a specific prophecy of a 20th-century event (Cheetham, 1973). Can you figure out what the prophecies mean? Compare your answers to those provided on page 41. The prophecies of Nostradamus are so vague that no one knows what they mean until after *the "predicted" event. Consequently, they are not really predictions and certainly not falsifiable.*

FIGURE 2.5
The Amazing Kreskin admits he is using magic tricks and "extremely sensitive" perception. In addition to entertaining people, he also sometimes works to combat superstition and gullibility. Some other performers claim they are using unexplainable powers. Regardless of what a performer claims to be doing, scientists look for the simplest, most parsimonious explanation available.

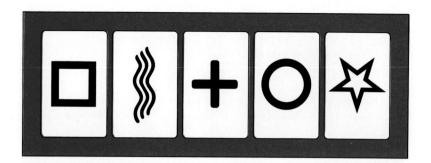

FIGURE 2.6
In one type of ESP experiment, a subject guesses the order of cards in a shuffled deck. The deck contains 25 cards, 5 each of the types shown here. Other experiments use different procedures, but the task is always to determine whether people can answer questions accurately without getting the information through their senses.

asks the subject to guess the order of the cards, from the top of the deck on down. Or the experimenter looks at a single card and asks the subject to name it. Because there are 25 cards in these decks, 5 each of 5 types, the subject should get about 5 correct just by guessing. If a subject does better than that, we can calculate the probability of accidentally doing that well. (ESP researchers, or parapsychologists, use a variety of other experimental procedures, but in each case the goal is to determine whether someone can gain information without the senses at a higher-than-chance rate.)

We can summarize the results of such experiments very simply: There is no replicable evidence that people can do better than chance (Druckman & Swets, 1988). Notice that word *replicable*. An occasional experiment does yield positive results. But of all the hundreds of experiments that have been conducted, a few are bound to show a positive result just by accident. No experiment is convincing unless other investigators, including skeptics, can repeat it and get similar results. No experiment in ESP meets the criterion of replicability.

Occasionally some researcher demonstrates an apparent psychic phenomenon in experiments that seem reasonably free from obvious flaws (e.g., Child, 1985; Nelson, Jahn, & Dunne, 1986). Before anyone has even tried to replicate the results, most psychologists are skeptical of the psychic explanation. Why? Quite simply, because they look for a more parsimonious explanation. We prefer the explanation that relies on simpler assumptions—that people use their known senses—unless the evidence absolutely forces us to reject those assumptions.

Evaluation No evidence can disprove the existence of extrasensory perception—just as no evidence can disprove the existence of unicorns. But most psychologists remain skeptical of ESP for three reasons: (1) No experiment has

yielded replicable positive results. (2) The history of ESP contains many known or strongly suspected frauds. Given that history, we insist on replicability even more strongly than usual. (3) Even if we had better evidence, we still could not explain how ESP could possibly take place. (Even its defenders offer no explanation.)

And yet many people still believe in extrasensory perception. Two California psychologists, Barry Singer and Victor Benassi, once put on a magic show for a group of college students and asked them whether they thought ESP was at work. Seventy-five percent said yes. Singer and Benassi repeated the show for another group of students, announcing in advance that everything that happened would be the result of simple tricks. Fifty percent rejected that explanation and insisted that the psychologists were using psychic powers (Marks & Kammann, 1980). Apparently some people want to believe in extrasensory perception, even when the "psychics" themselves offer more parsimonious explanations.

What have we learned about science in general?

Science does not deal with proof or certainty. All scientific conclusions are tentative and are subject to revision. Scientists always prefer the most parsimonious theory. They abandon accepted theories and assumptions only when better theories and assumptions become available. Scientists scrutinize any claim that violates the rule of parsimony. Before they will accept any such claim, they insist that it be supported by replicable experiments that rule out simpler explanations.

SUMMARY

■ *Scientific approach in psychology.* Although psychology does not have the same wealth of knowledge as other sciences have, it shares with those other fields a commitment to scientific methods, including a set of criteria for evaluating theories. (page 33)

■ *Steps in a scientific study.* A scientific study goes through the following sequence of steps: hypothesis, methods, results, interpretation. Because almost any study is subject to more than one possible interpretation, we base conclusions on a pattern of results from many studies. The results of a given study are taken seriously only if other investigators can replicate them. (page 33)

- *Criteria for evaluating theories.* Scientists seek theories that account for large amounts of information. A good theory agrees with known facts and leads to correct predictions of new information. Its predictions are sufficiently precise so that we can imagine possible results that would falsify the theory. (page 35)

- *Principle of parsimony.* Other things being equal, we prefer the theory that relies on simpler assumptions. (page 36)

- *Skepticism about extrasensory perception.* Claims of extrasensory perception are scrutinized very cautiously because evidence reported so far has been unreplicable and because careful investigation generally leads to more parsimonious explanations in terms of coincidence, magic tricks, or the use of the known senses. (page 37)

SUGGESTIONS FOR FURTHER READING

Alcock, J. E. (1987). Parapsychology: Science of the anomalous or search for the soul? *Behavioral and Brain Sciences, 10,* 553–565. An article outlining the reasons why most psychologists are skeptical of ESP. Accompanied by another article by K. R. Rao and J. Palmer favorable to ESP and 49 short commentaries by other investigators with a variety of viewpoints.

Kreskin. (1991). *Secrets of the amazing Kreskin.* Buffalo, NY: Prometheus. Kreskin explains some of his stage performances.

Kuhn, T. (1970). *The structure of scientific revolutions* (2nd ed.). Chicago: University of Chicago Press. An important book about what happens when scientists are forced to revise their basic assumptions and their way of thinking.

Marks, D., & Kammann, R. (1980). *The psychology of the psychic.* Buffalo, NY: Prometheus. A cogent scientific analysis of the exploits of alleged psychics.

Radner, D., & Radner, M. (1982). *Science and unreason.* Belmont, CA: Wadsworth. A critical survey of areas of pseudoscience and the fringes of science.

TERMS

hypothesis a testable prediction of what will happen under certain conditions (page 33)

replicable result a result that can be repeated (at least approximately) by any competent investigator who follows the same procedure as the original study (page 34)

theory a comprehensive explanation of natural phenomena that leads to accurate predictions (page 35)

falsifiable capable of being contradicted by imaginable evidence (page 35)

parsimony literally, stinginess; scientists' preference for the theory that accounts for the results using the simplest assumptions (page 36)

extrasensory perception (ESP) the alleged ability of certain people to acquire information without using any sense organ and without receiving any form of energy (page 37)

ANSWER TO CONCEPT CHECK

1. To evaluate Nostradamus's predictions, we would have to ask someone to tell us precisely what his predictions mean before the events they supposedly predict. Then we would ask someone else to estimate the likelihood of those events. Eventually we would compare the accuracy of the predictions to the advance estimates of their probability. That is, we should be impressed with "correct" predictions only if observers had rated them "unlikely" before they occurred. (page 38)

ANSWERS TO OTHER QUESTIONS IN THE TEXT

A. The prophecies of Nostradamus (see page 39), as interpreted by Cheetham (1973), refer to the following: (1) the assassinations of John F. Kennedy and Robert F. Kennedy, (2) Polaris ballistic missiles shot from submarines, (3) Hitler's invasion of France, and (4) World War II.

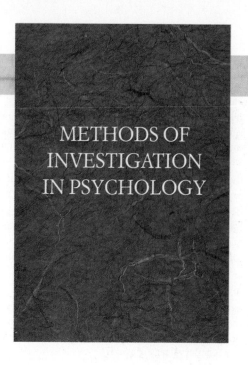

METHODS OF INVESTIGATION IN PSYCHOLOGY

How do psychologists design research studies?

What pitfalls should they try to avoid?

Psychologists try to approach questions scientifically, but they face some special problems that physicists and chemists do not face. Psychologists might ask, for example, "What is the effect of motivation on a worker's job performance?" Immediately they have to face some difficult questions: "What do we mean by motivation? How can we measure it or control it? And how should we measure job performance?" A physicist who wondered about the effect of temperature on the width of a steel bar would not pause long to ponder the true meaning of the word *temperature* or the best way to measure a steel bar.

Here is a second major difference: When physicists study subatomic particles, they find that they cannot measure events without greatly affecting those events. Physicists face that difficulty with subatomic particles, whereas psychologists face it almost all the time. If you saw me watching you and taking notes on everything you did, would you continue acting the way you ordinarily do? Probably not. Psychologists have ways of overcoming this problem (Figure 2.7), but they can seldom ignore it.

A third difference is that psychologists study some phenomena that change from time to time. Physicists' and chemists' measurements

of the properties of nitrogen or oxygen taken 50 years ago are still more or less correct today. Psychologists' measurements of sexual anxieties or attitudes toward war may hold for most people at one time and place, but suddenly become obsolete after some change in society.

GENERAL PRINCIPLES OF CONDUCTING RESEARCH

This part of the chapter will trace some of the common methods of doing research in psychology. The goal is not primarily to prepare you to conduct psychological research, although I hope that at least a few readers will eventually do just that. The primary goal is to prepare you to be an intelligent interpreter of psychological research. When you hear about some new study in psychology, you should be able to ask a few pertinent questions and to decide how good the evidence is and what conclusion (if any) it justifies.

Defining the Variables

How could you determine how strong someone's motivation is? Or whether snails have emotions? Or whether IQ tests really measure intelligence? Before you could even begin to answer such questions, you would have to decide what the terms *motivation, emotion,* and *intelligence* mean.

What do they mean? As with any other words, they mean whatever we want them to mean. At one point in Lewis Carroll's *Through the Looking Glass,* Alice objects, "But 'glory' doesn't mean 'a nice knock-down argument.'" Humpty Dumpty replies, "When *I* use a word, it means just what I choose it to mean—neither more nor less."

Similarly, psychological terms mean whatever we choose them to mean. For many purposes, the most useful definition of a term is one that makes it measurable. Psychologists often insist on an **operational definition** of a term—a definition that specifies the operations (or pro-

cedures) used to measure some variable or to produce some phenomenon (Stevens, 1935).

An operational definition is not the same as a dictionary definition. A dictionary might define *motivation* as a desire, but that definition does not tell us how to measure motivation or how to produce it. Here is one possible operational definition: "The degree of motivation is the amount of work someone will do in order to obtain a particular outcome." That definition tells us how to measure motivation; it even suggests how to determine whether a person's motivation for a particular outcome is increasing or decreasing from one time to another.

Suppose someone wishes to investigate whether children who watch violence on television are likely to behave aggressively themselves. In that case, the investigator needs operational definitions for both *televised violence* and *aggressive behavior.* No single definition is likely to be perfect. For example, the investigator might define *televised violence* as "the number of acts shown or described in which one person injures another." According to that definition, a 20-minute stalking scene counts the same as a quick attack, and a murder on screen counts the same as one that the characters just talk about. Cartoon violence does not count, because no "person" is injured. Similarly, an unsuccessful attempt to injure some-

one does not count. It is unclear from this definition whether we should count verbal insults. Another researcher might prefer a different operational definition.

Similarly, the investigator needs an operational definition of *aggressive behavior* (Figure 2.8). To define it as "the number of acts of assault or murder committed within 24 hours after watching a particular television program" probably would not be helpful. (Anyone who expected such a drastic response could not ethically perform the experiment!) A better operational definition of *aggressive behavior* specifies less extreme acts. For example, the experimenter might place a large plastic doll in front of a young child and record how often the child punches it. Again, other investigators might prefer some other operational definition. But as long as each researcher states his or her definition clearly and sticks to it, we have at least some idea what the results mean, and we know what procedure to follow if we want to try to replicate the study.

■ CONCEPT CHECK

2. Which of the following is an operational definition of intelligence: *(a) the ability to comprehend relationships, (b) a score on an IQ test, (c) the ability to survive in the real world, or (d) the product of the cerebral cortex of the brain?*

FIGURE 2.8
Aggressive behavior is difficult to define and measure. One psychologist might rate these boys' play as aggressive, whereas another might view the play as merely energetic, depending on each psychologist's definition of aggression.

What would you propose as an operational definition of hunger? *(Check your answers on page 60.)*

Random Samples and Representative Samples

In general, investigators examine the behavior of only a small number of individuals, but they want to draw conclusions about a large population, perhaps even about people in general. We say that the investigators studied a *sample* of the total population. Do the results from a limited sample really apply to the total population? The answer depends on how the sample is chosen.

Consider what can happen if the sample is greatly different from the total population: In 1936 the *Literary Digest* mailed 10 million postcards asking people their choice for president of the United States. Of the two million responses, 57% preferred the Republican candidate, Alfred Landon. As it turned out, Landon was soundly defeated by the Democratic candidate, Franklin Roosevelt. The reason for the misleading result was that the *Literary Digest* surveyed an unrepresentative sample. It selected names from the telephone and automobile registration lists. In 1936, at the end of the Great Depression, only fairly well-off people had telephones or cars, and most of them were

Republicans. The sample included very few poor people, who voted overwhelmingly Democratic.

To conduct a meaningful study, we need either a representative sample or a random sample of the population. A **representative sample** closely resembles the entire population in its percentage of males and females, blacks and whites, young and old, Republicans and Democrats, or whatever other characteristics are likely to affect the results. To get a representative sample of the people in a given city, an investigator first would determine what percentage of the city's residents belong to each category and then select people to match those percentages. The disadvantage of this method is that a group may be representative with regard to sex, race, age, and political party and yet be unrepresentative with regard to some factor the investigators ignored, such as religious preference or level of education.

In a **random sample**, every individual in the population has an equal chance of being selected. To get a random sample of city residents, an investigator might select a certain number of households at random from the most recent census listing and then select one person at random from each of those households. The resulting sample probably will not match the population's percentages by sex, race, and age, at least not as closely as a representative sample does. Still, if the random sample is large enough, the percentages are likely to be close with regard to each of those variables, as well as others that the designers of a representative sample might have overlooked.

■ CONCEPT CHECK

3. *Suppose I compare the interests and abilities of men and women students at my university. If I find a consistent difference, can I assume that it represents a difference between men in general and women in general? If not, why not? (Check your answer on page 60.)*

Single-Blind Studies and Double-Blind Studies

At some point in any psychological study, an investigator measures some aspect of behavior, perhaps by directly observing it and recording it. Imagine that you, the investigator, are recording acts of aggressive behavior by two groups of children. Imagine further that you are testing the hypothesis that Group A will be more aggressive than Group B (for whatever reason). You know that if the results support your hypothesis, then you can get your results published and you will be well on your way to becoming a famous psychologist. Now one child in Group A engages in some mildly aggressive act—a borderline case. You are not sure whether to count it or not. You want to be fair. You don't want your hypothesis to influence your decision of whether or not to count this act as aggression. Just try to ignore that hypothesis.

To overcome the potential source of error in an investigator's bias, psychologists prefer to use a **blind observer**—that is, an observer who does not know which subjects are in which group and what is expected of each. Because blind observers do not know the hypothesis, they can be objective and record observations of behavior as fairly as possible.

Ideally, the experimenter conceals the procedure from the subjects as well. For example, the experimenter could give one group a pill that might affect their behavior and give the other group an inactive pill, a **placebo,** that will have no pharmacological effect on their behavior, without telling subjects which pill they are receiving. The advantage of this kind of study is that the two groups will not behave differently just because they expected different effects. (Placebos sometimes affect behavior, but only because they alter people's expectancies.)

A study in which either the observer or the subjects are unaware of which subjects received which treatment is known as a **single-blind study** (Table 2.1).

A study in which both the observer and the subjects are unaware is known as a **double-blind study.** (Someone, of course, would have to keep a record of which subjects received which procedure. A study in which *everyone* loses track of the procedure is jokingly known as "triple blind.")

VARIETIES OF RESEARCH DESIGN

The general principles I have just discussed apply to a variety of research studies. Psychologists use various methods of investigation, each having its own advantages and disadvantages. Sometimes psychologists simply observe what one person does under certain conditions; on other occasions they perform complicated experiments on large groups. Let us examine

Table 2.1 Single-Blind and Double-Blind Studies

	Observer	Subjects
Single-blind	aware	unaware
Single-blind	unaware	aware
Double-blind	unaware	unaware

some of the major categories of research designs (see Table 2.2).

Case Histories

Psychologists are sometimes interested in conditions that rarely appear. For example, some people can remember what they have seen or heard with amazing accuracy. Others show an amazing inability to remember what they have seen or heard. People with a rare condition called Cotard's syndrome believe they are dead (Campbell, Volow, & Cavenar, 1981). A psychologist who encounters someone with a rare condition may report a **case history,** a thorough description of a single individual. It may include information about the person's medical condition, family background, unusual experiences, current behavior, and details on tasks the person can and cannot perform—in short, anything the investigator thinks might have some bearing on the person's unusual condition. In Chapter 8 you will find an example of a case history of a brain-damaged man who lost his ability to learn facts. In Chapter 14 is a case history of a woman who periodically shifted from one personality to another.

A case history is well suited to exploring special, poorly understood conditions. However, a single case history is really just an elaborate anecdote; we do not know whether or not the reported individual is typical of others with the same condition. Ideally, a series of case histories may reveal a pattern or stimulate investigators to conduct other kinds of research.

Naturalistic Observations

Whereas a case study is a careful examination of one individual, a **naturalistic observation** is a careful examination of what many people or

Table 2.2 Comparison of Five Methods of Research

Definition	Observational Study		
	Case study	*Naturalistic observation*	*Survey*
	Detailed description of a single individual	Description of what people or animals do under natural conditions	Description of selected aspects of a population of individuals
Number of individuals studied	Usually one	Usually many	Many
Manipulated by investigator	Nothing	Nothing	Questions
Advantages	Suitable for studying rare conditions	Unintrusive, natural, source of new information	Determines characteristics of a population
Example	Intensive report of the childhood of someone who became a murderer	Report on changes in society's television-watching habits	Survey of how many hours per week most people watch violent TV programs

nonhuman animals do under natural conditions. For example, Jane Goodall (1971) spent years observing chimpanzees in the wild, recording their food habits, their social interactions, their gestures, their whole way of life (Figure 2.9).

Similarly, psychologists sometimes try to observe human behavior "as an outsider." A psychologist might observe what happens when two unacquainted people get on an elevator together: Do they stand close or far apart? Do they speak? Do they look toward each other or away? Does it matter whether the people are two men, two women, or a man and a woman? **Cross-cultural psychologists** conduct naturalistic observations on people in different cul-

tures and compare their behavior. For example, they compare facial expressions in different cultures, the way different peoples settle their disputes, the way they educate their children.

Surveys

A **survey** is a study of the prevalence of certain beliefs, attitudes, or behaviors based on people's responses to specific questions. For example, in Chapter 11 we shall consider a couple of surveys of the prevalence of certain sexual behaviors. A survey is one of the most common methods of investigation in psychology, sociology, and political science. Conducting a survey is deceptively simple: Just draw up a list of ques-

CHAPTER 2: Scientific Methods in Psychology

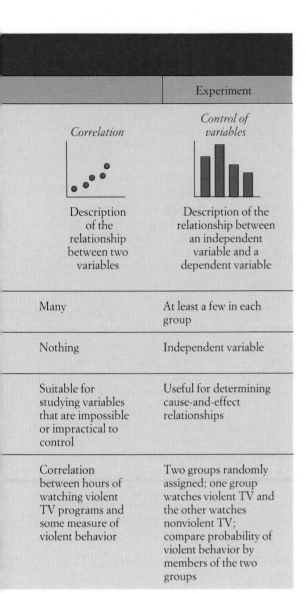

	Experiment
Correlation	*Control of variables*
Description of the relationship between two variables	Description of the relationship between an independent variable and a dependent variable
Many	At least a few in each group
Nothing	Independent variable
Suitable for studying variables that are impossible or impractical to control	Useful for determining cause-and-effect relationships
Correlation between hours of watching violent TV programs and some measure of violent behavior	Two groups randomly assigned; one group watches violent TV and the other watches nonviolent TV; compare probability of violent behavior by members of the two groups

FIGURE 2.9

In a naturalistic study, observers record the behavior of people or other species in their natural settings. Here, noted biologist Jane Goodall records her observations on chimpanzees. By patiently staying with the chimpanzees, Goodall gradually won their trust and learned to recognize individual chimps. In this manner she was able to add enormously to our understanding of chimpanzees' natural way of life.

tions, ask a number of people to answer them, and then report the results. If we are not very careful, however, the results may be misleading. We have already considered the problem of sampling; the results of a survey mean little unless we put the questions to a random or representative sample of people.

However, no matter how carefully we select the sample, the results can be only as clear as the questions are. Suppose you answer the following survey questions as shown:

Do you favor a new law to ban the sale of handguns?　　　Y　Ⓝ
Do you support the current laws on abortion?　　　Y　Ⓝ

Your answers might indicate that people should be allowed to buy handguns without restrictions and that you think the current laws put far too many restrictions on abortion. But they could also mean that you prefer a much stricter handgun law than the one proposed and that you think the current abortion laws apply too few restrictions. Or they could mean you are an anarchist opposed to all laws, regardless.

One survey asked young people of various ages how often they "felt happy the way I am." Of elementary-school girls, 67% replied "always," but only 29% of high-school girls gave that answer (Daley, 1991). Many observers interpreted these results to mean that girls lose self-esteem as they grow older. That is certainly a reasonable interpretation, but it is not the only one possible. If you say "I do not always feel happy the way I am," that could mean that you have low self-esteem, but it also could mean that you are striving to improve yourself.

Even a survey based on a representative or random sample and containing clear, unambiguous questions may still produce misleading results. Before reading further, answer each of the following survey questions:

What did you base your opinions on in question 1? You have perhaps seen some of the programs and heard about others. But at least one of them is a series you have never even heard of: There never was a program called "Space Doctor." Did you assign a rating to "Space Doctor" and to any other programs you were unfamiliar with? Most people do.

The point is clear: In examining the results of any survey, you should not assume that all the people who responded had a solid basis for their opinions. (Keep that point in mind the next time you hear the results of a political survey.)

Now on to questions 2 and 3. They are *open-ended questions;* you could answer them any way you wished. People come up with an enormous variety of answers. The results are different when we ask the same questions but suggest possible answers, as shown at the top of the next column.

When people are offered such choices as these, most will select one of the suggested answers instead of entering a "whatever else" answer of their own—even if the suggested answers are far-fetched or peculiar ones (Schuman & Scott, 1987). So how should the questions be phrased, with or without suggestions?

The purpose here is not to declare that one way of phrasing a question is right and the other is wrong. The point is simply this: The results of a survey depend on how the questions are phrased. (The next time you hear that "54% of all Americans surveyed believe such and so," inquire how the question was phrased.)

Correlational Studies

A third kind of study is the *correlational study.* A **correlation** is a measure of the relationship between two variables, both of which are outside the investigator's control. Thus, a correlational study is one in which the investigator examines the relationship between two variables, without actually manipulating either one of them.

For example, investigators have observed that children with blue eyes are likely to have an "inhibited" personality, whereas children with brown eyes are more likely to have an "uninhibited" personality (Rosenberg & Kagan, 1987). (Exceptions are numerous, of course; a correlation states only a trend, not an invariable rule.) This is a correlational study, because the investigators had no control over the children's eyes or their personality. Another example: Students who do well on the first test they take in introductory psychology generally do well on the second test as well. Again, no investigators

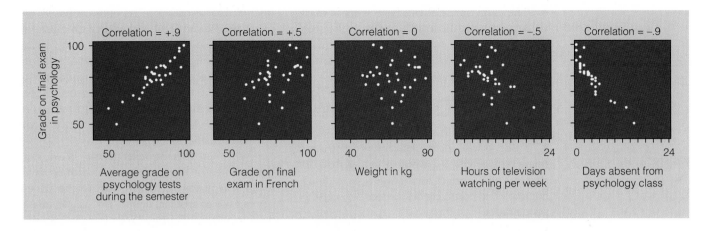

FIGURE 2.10

In a scatterplot, each dot represents data for one person; for example, in the center graph each point tells us the weight of one person and that person's grade on the psychology final exam, in this case using hypothetical data. A positive correlation indicates that as one variable increases, the other generally does also. A negative correlation indicates that as one variable increases, the other generally decreases. The closer a correlation coefficient is to +1 or −1, the stronger is the relationship.

exert any control over the two events; they merely observe the relationship (or correlation) between them.

A survey can be considered a correlational study if the interviewers compare two or more groups. For example, the interviewers might compare the beliefs of men and women or of young people and old people. The interviewer could thereby measure a relationship between one variable (sex or age) and another variable (beliefs).

The Correlation Coefficient Some correlations are strong; others are weak. For example, students who spend many hours per week reading novels tend to perform well on vocabulary tests; that is a strong correlation. Students who spend many hours per week reading novels tend to perform slightly better than average on chemistry tests; that is a weaker correlation.

Often it is helpful to have a way of measuring the direction and strength of a correlation. The standard method is known as a **correlation coefficient,** a mathematical estimate of the relationship between two variables, which can range mathematically from +1 to −1. A correlation coefficient indicates how accurately we can use measurements of one variable to predict another. A correlation coefficient of +1, for example, means that as one variable increases, the other increases also. A correlation coefficient of

−1 means that as one variable increases, the other decreases. A correlation of either +1 or −1 enables us to make perfect predictions of either variable whenever we know the other.

In real life, psychologists seldom encounter a perfect +1 or −1 correlation coefficient. The closer the correlation coefficient is to +1 or to −1, the stronger the relationship between the two variables and the more accurately we can use one variable to predict the other. Figure 2.10 shows hypothetical (not real) data demonstrating how grades on a final exam in psychology might correlate with five other variables. (This kind of graph is called a *scatterplot;* each dot represents the measurements of two variables for one person.) Grades on a psychology final exam correlate very strongly with grades on the previous tests in psychology, less strongly with grades on the French final exam, not at all with the person's weight, and negatively with the amount of time spent watching television and the number of times absent from class. Note that a correlation of +.9 is close to a straight line ascending; a correlation of −.9 is close to a straight line descending.

Here are a few examples of the findings of correlational studies:

■ The most crowded areas of a city are generally the most impoverished. (The correlation between crowdedness and poverty is positive.)

- The more time students have spent in martial-arts training, the less likely they are to seek an opportunity to fight (Nosanchuk & MacNeil, 1989). (The correlation between martial-arts training and aggressiveness is negative.)

- People's telephone numbers have no relationship to their IQ scores. (The correlation between the two is 0.)

- Students who spend many hours doing their homework generally get higher grades than do students who neglect their homework. (Doing homework is positively correlated with getting good grades.)

- People who trust other people are unlikely to cheat other people. (Trusting is negatively correlated with cheating.)

■ CONCEPT CHECK

4. Which indicates a stronger relationship between two variables, a +.50 correlation between variables A and B or a −.75 correlation between variables C and D? (Check your answer on page 60.)

Illusory Correlations It is difficult to identify a correlation between two variables solely on the basis of casual observation. You might meet four women who mention that they liked a particular movie, and then you overhear two men saying that they hated it. You start wondering why this film appeals more to women than to men. Well, maybe it does and maybe it doesn't. Those few people you overheard may not be typical of other women and men. Sometimes we think we see a correlation, even when none exists. An apparent relationship based on casual observations of unrelated or poorly related events is known as an **illusory correlation.** Much of what people believe about differences between women and men, or between blacks and whites, are examples of illusory correlations.

For another example of an illusory correlation, take the widely held belief that a full moon affects human behavior. For hundreds of years, many people have believed that crime and various kinds of mental disturbance are more common under a full moon than at other times. In fact, the term *lunacy* (from the Latin word *luna,* meaning "moon") originally meant mental illness caused by the full moon. Some police officers report that they receive more calls on nights of a full moon, and hospital workers report that more emergency cases turn up on such

nights. However, those reports are based on what people can recall rather than on carefully analyzed data. James Rotton and I. W. Kelly (1985) examined all available data relating crime, mental illness, and other phenomena to phases of the moon. They concluded that the phase of the moon has either no effect at all on human behavior or so little effect that it is almost impossible to measure.

Why then does the belief persist? We do not know when or how it first arose. (It may have been true many years ago, before the widespread use of artificial lights.) But we can guess why it persists. Suppose, for example, you are working at a hospital and you expect to handle more emergencies on full-moon nights than at other times. Sooner or later, on a full-moon night, you encounter an unusually high number of accidents, assaults, and suicide attempts. You say, "See? There was a full moon and people just went crazy!" You will remember that night for a long time. You disregard all the other full-moon nights when nothing special happened and all the non-full-moon nights when you were swamped with emergency cases.

That same selective memory might convince people that Friday the 13th brings bad luck, that dreams and hunches come true, or that people who live on the other side of the tracks are not to be trusted. The point is that an apparent correlation cannot be relied on until it has been carefully measured and confirmed by the data. The memory of a few events that seem to fit a pattern does not establish a correlation.

Correlation and Causation A correlational study tells us whether two variables are related to each other and, if so, how strongly. It does not tell us *why* they are related. *No matter how high the correlation coefficient between variables A and B, even if it is +1, it does not tell us whether A caused B, whether B caused A, or whether some third variable caused both A and B* (Figure 2.11).

For example, earlier we considered the reported correlation between blue eyes and an "inhibited" personality. Even if that correlation were extremely strong (which it is not), it would not tell us that blue eyes *cause* an inhibited personality. Perhaps people treat their blue-eyed children differently from their brown-eyed children. Perhaps blue eyes are a marker for some biochemical difference that also expresses itself in some alteration of brain activity. Perhaps blue eyes are more common in people of northern European ancestry than in people of south-

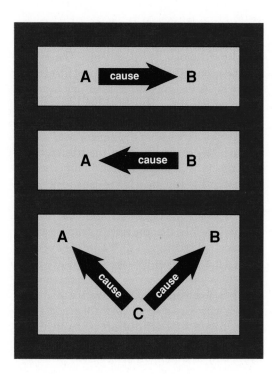

FIGURE 2.11

A strong correlation between variables A and B does not tell us whether A causes B, B causes A, or some other variable C causes both A and B.

ern European or African ancestry, and for some reason people of northern European ancestry are more inhibited. We can manufacture still other explanations; the correlation does not tell us which one to believe.

Here are some other examples of why we cannot draw cause-and-effect conclusions from correlational data:

■ *Unmarried men are more likely than married men are to wind up in a mental hospital or prison.* So we can say that, for men, marriage is negatively correlated with mental illness and criminal activity. Does the correlation mean that marriage leads to mental health and good social adjustment? Or does it mean that men who are confined to mental hospitals or prisons are unlikely to marry?

■ *Most depressed people have trouble sleeping.* Depression is negatively correlated with sleeping well. Does that mean depression causes poor sleep? Or does it mean that people who have difficulty sleeping become depressed? Or does some third variable, such as a dietary deficiency, lead to both depression and poor sleep?

Determining the size and direction of a correlation between two variables is an important first step in a study. But a correlation does not tell us about causation. To determine causation, an investigator needs to manipulate one of the variables directly, through a research design known as an *experiment*. When an investigator manipulates one variable and then observes changes in another variable, the causation is clear.

Methods of Conducting Experiments in Psychology

An **experiment** is a study in which the investigator manipulates at least one variable while measuring at least one other variable. The logic behind the simplest possible experiment is as follows: The investigator assembles a suitable sample of people (or animals), divides them randomly into two groups, and then administers some experimental procedure to one group and not to the other. Someone, preferably a blind observer, records the behavior of the two groups. If the behavior of the two groups differs in some consistent way, then the difference is presumably the result of the experimental procedure.

I shall describe psychological experiments and some of their special difficulties. For the sake of illustration, let's imagine that we are setting up an experiment to determine whether watching violent television programs leads to an increase in aggressive behavior. (We used this example in the discussion of operational definitions on page 43.)

Independent Variables and Dependent Variables An experiment is an attempt to measure the effect of an independent variable, such as watching violent television programs, on a dependent variable, such as subsequent aggressive behavior. A *variable* is anything that can have more than one value, such as age, experience, or performance on a given task. The **independent variable** is the variable the experimenter *manipulates* (Figure 2.12); for example, the experimenter varies the amount of time the subjects in an experiment spend watching violent television. The **dependent variable** is the variable that changes in response to changes in the independent variable. The dependent variable is the variable the experimenter *measures* (Figure 2.13). In our example, the experimenter measures the amount of aggressive behavior the subjects exhibit.

FIGURE 2.12
The independent variable is manipulated by the experimenter. The dependent variable is the measured outcome.

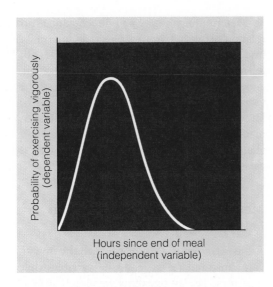

Probability of exercising vigorously (dependent variable)

Hours since end of meal (independent variable)

FIGURE 2.13
An experimenter manipulates the independent variable (in this case, the films people watch) so that two or more groups experience different treatments. Then the experimenter measures the dependent variable (in this case, pulse rate) to see how the independent variable affected it.

■ CONCEPT CHECK

5. *An instructor wants to find out whether the frequency of tests in introductory psychology has any effect on students' final exam performance. The instructor gives weekly tests in one class, just three tests in a second class, and only a single mid-term exam in the third class. All three classes take the same final exam, and the instructor compares their performances. Identify the independent variable and the dependent variable. (Check your answers on page 60.)*

Experimental Group and Control Group
Here is more terminology you need to understand psychological experiments: The **experimental group** receives the treatment that the experiment is designed to test. In our example, the experimental group would watch televised violence for a specific length of time. The **control group** is treated in the same way as the experimental group except for the treatment the experiment is designed to test. In other words, the control group spends the same amount of time watching television but watches only nonviolent programs (Figure 2.14).

In principle, that procedure sounds easy. In practice, a difficulty arises: We are conducting a study on a group of teenagers who have a history of violent behavior. The experimental group watches a good guys versus bad guys thriller with lots of action and violence. Exactly what do we ask the control group to watch? Can we find a program without violence that is just as exciting to watch? (It's not easy.)

Random Assignment The preferred way of assigning subjects to groups is **random assignment**: The experimenter uses some chance procedure such as drawing names out of a hat to make sure that every subject has the same probability as any other subject of being assigned to a given group. Imagine what could happen if the experimenter did not assign people at random. Suppose we let the subjects choose whether they want to be in the experimental group or the control group. The people most prone to aggressive behavior might generally choose to be in the experimental group (the one that watches violent programs). Or suppose we ask people to volunteer for the study, and the first 20 people who volunteer become the experimental group and the next 20 become the control group. Again, we will have trouble analyzing the results, because the people who are quickest to volunteer may be impulsive in other regards also.

Consider an animal example: We set up a rack of cages and put each rat in a cage by itself. The rack has five rows of six cages each, numbered from 1 in the upper-left corner to 30 in the lower right. Regardless of the procedures we use, we find that the rats with higher cage numbers are more aggressive than those with lower cage numbers. Why?

We might first guess that the difference has to do with location. The rats in the cages with high numbers are farthest from the lights and closest to the floor. They get fed last each day.

To test the influence of these factors, we move some of the cages to different positions in the rack, leaving each rat in its own cage. To our surprise, the rats in cages 26–30 are still more aggressive than those in cages 1–5. Why? (How could they possibly know what number is on each cage, and even if they did know, why should they care?)

The answer has to do with how rats get assigned to cages. When an investigator buys a shipment of rats, which one goes into cage 1? The one that is easiest to catch! Which ones go into the last few cages? The vicious, ornery little critters that put up the greatest resistance to being picked up! The rats in the last few cages were already the most aggressive ones before they were put into those cages.

The point is that even with rats an experimenter must assign individuals to the experimental group and the control group at random. It would not be right to assign the first 15 rats to one group and the second 15 to another group. The same is true, only more so, with humans.

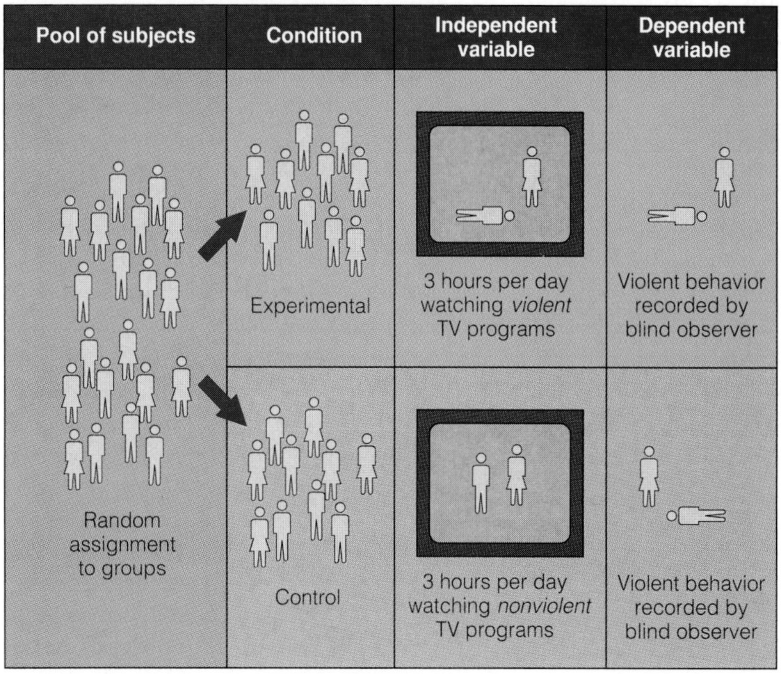

Studies of the Effects of Televised Violence on Aggressive Behavior

WHAT'S THE EVIDENCE?

We have talked in general terms about experiments on the effects of televised violence. Now let us consider some actual examples.

Part of the evidence regarding the effects of televised violence comes from correlational studies. Several such studies have found that people who watch a great deal of televised violence are more likely to engage in aggressive behavior than are people who do not (National Institute of Mental Health, 1982). Those results are suggestive but inconclusive. They do not tell us whether watching violence leads to aggressive behavior or whether people prone to aggressive behavior like to watch violence on television.

In another type of correlational study, investigators in the 1950s studied how viewers reacted when television first came to their region. Because the levels of violent behavior increased in many cities at about the time that television first appeared, some investigators suggested that violent television programs may have been responsible for the increased violent behavior (National Institute of Mental Health, 1982). Again the results are not decisive. The advent of

Pool of subjects	Condition	Independent variable	Dependent variable
	Experimental	3 hours per day watching *violent* TV programs	Violent behavior recorded by blind observer
Random assignment to groups	Control	3 hours per day watching *nonviolent* TV programs	Violent behavior recorded by blind observer

FIGURE 2.14
Once researchers decide on the hypothesis they want to test, they must design the experiment, such as these procedures for testing the effects of watching televised violence. An appropriate, accurate method of measurement is essential.

television was hardly the only change taking place in those communities at the time, and we cannot assume it was responsible for the increase in violent behavior. To examine a possible cause-and-effect relationship, we must turn to experiments.

Hypothesis Children who watch violent television programs will engage in more acts of aggression than will children who spend the same amount of time watching nonviolent programs.

Method One set of experimenters chose to study male juvenile delinquents (Parke, Berkowitz, Leyens, West, & Sebastian, 1977). The disadvantage was that the conclusions of the study might apply only to a limited group, not to young people in general. The advantage was that the experimenters could control the choice of television programs in a detention center much better than they could for youngsters living at home.

The boys were assigned randomly to two cottages. Those in one cottage watched violent films on five consecutive nights, while those in the other cottage watched nonviolent films. Throughout this period, blind observers recorded incidents of aggressive behavior by each boy. On the sixth day, each boy was put into an experimental setting in which he had an opportunity at certain times to press a button that would deliver an electric shock to another boy. (At least he thought he was delivering a shock. In fact, no shocks were given.) The experimenters recorded the frequency and intensity of shocks that each boy chose to deliver.

Results Compared to the boys who had watched nonviolent films, those who had watched the violent films engaged in more acts of aggression and pressed the button to deliver more frequent and more intense electric shocks.

Interpretation At least in this study, watching violent films led to increased violence. As with most studies, however, this one has its limitations. The boys in the experiment were not representative of boys in general, much less of people in general. Moreover, we cannot assume that we would get similar results with a different choice of violent films or a different method of measuring aggressive behavior.

The only way to get around the limitation of a given experiment is to conduct additional experiments, using different samples of people, different films, and different measures of aggressive behavior. A number of such experiments have been conducted; the results have been inconsistent. In some experiments, those who have watched violent films behave more aggressively; in others, the two groups behave about the same. In nearly all cases, the difference between the two groups is small (Cook, Kendzierski, & Thomas, 1983; Freedman, 1984, 1986; Friedrich-Cofer & Huston, 1986).

Remember what I said about a result that is *replicated* but not consistently *replicable*: It suggests that an effect occurs under certain conditions but not under others. That seems to be the case for the effect of televised violence.

WHY EXPERIMENTS SOMETIMES GO WRONG

Research on behavior poses some thorny problems because it deals with living beings. Sometimes people act strange just because they know they are in an experiment. Sometimes in the middle of a long-term experiment some of the people move out of town or simply announce that they do not want to participate any more. When psychologists cannot avoid such problems, they must at least recognize them and point out the limitations of the research results.

Demand Characteristics

The subjects who take part in a psychological experiment often try to guess what the experimenter wants them to do and say. They believe that "good" results will help the experimenter succeed and will contribute to the advancement of knowledge. As a result, some experiments reveal more about the participants' expectations than about the phenomenon the experimenter is trying to study. Martin Orne (1969) defines **demand characteristics** as cues that tell a subject what is expected of him or her and what the experimenter hopes to find. Experimenters try to minimize the influence of demand characteristics.

One example of the effects of demand characteristics surfaced in an experiment on **sensory deprivation.** In experiments of this sort, subjects are placed in an apparatus that minimizes vision, hearing, touch, and other forms of sensory stimulation. After several hours, many subjects reported hallucinations, anxiety, and difficulty in concentrating; they exhibited impaired intellectual performance. M. T. Orne and K. E. Scheibe (1964) conducted an experiment to determine whether such effects might be related to the subjects' expectations.

College students participated in the experiment, which was described to them as a study on "meaning deprivation." The experimenter interrogated the students in the experimental group about their medical history and asked them to sign a form releasing the hospital in which the experiment took place from legal responsibility for the experiment's consequences. A prominently displayed "emergency tray" contained medicines and various instruments kept on hand "as a precaution." One subject per day entered an "isolation chamber," which was actually an ordinary room that contained two chairs, a desk, a window, a mirror, a sandwich, and a glass of water. The subjects never would have guessed that the room had anything to do with sensory deprivation had they not been told so. Finally, the subjects were shown a microphone they could use to report any hallucinations or other distorted experiences and a "panic button" they could press to escape if the discomfort became unbearable. Students in the control group were led to the same room, but they were not shown the "emergency tray," they were not asked to sign a release form, and they were given no other indication that they were expected to have any unpleasant experiences.

Each subject was left alone in the room for 4 hours. Ordinarily, 4 hours by oneself is not a particularly disturbing experience. But everything the experimenter had said to the experimental group suggested that the experience would be dreadful, and the subjects acted as if it were. One pressed the panic button to demand release. Several others reported that they were hallucinating "multicolored spots on the wall," or that "the walls of the room are starting to waver," or that "the objects on the desk are becoming animated and moving about" (Figure 2.15). Some complained of anxiety, restlessness, difficulty in concentrating, and spatial disorientation. At the end of the 4 hours, most of them showed impaired performance on a series of perceptual and intellectual tasks. The subjects in the control group reported no unusual experiences.

Sensory deprivation may very well have significant effects on behavior. But as this experiment illustrates, we must carefully distinguish between the effects of the independent variable and the effects of what the subjects expect of the experiment.

In a sense, demand characteristics set up *self-fulfilling prophecies*. In designing the experiment, the experimenter has a certain expectation in mind and then conducts the experiment in a way that may inadvertently convey that expectation to the subjects, thereby influencing them to behave as expected. To eliminate demand characteristics, many experimenters take elaborate steps to conceal the purpose of the experiment from the subjects. A double-blind study serves the purpose: If two groups share the same expectations but behave differently because of the treatment they receive, then the difference in behavior is presumably not the result of their expectations.

The Hawthorne Effect

Suppose you are sorting your laundry, when suddenly I enter the room, turn on a bright blue light, and explain that I am testing whether this bright blue light will cause you to finish your laundry faster than usual. Even if the light itself has no effect on your behavior, you might indeed work harder on your laundry and finish it faster for two reasons: (1) The sheer novelty of the situation increases your arousal, and (2) be-

FIGURE 2.15
Subjects tend to report what they think the experimenter wants to hear. The cues that tell them what the experimenter hopes to find are called demand characteristics.

cause you know I am watching you, you concentrate on your work instead of taking time out for various distractions. This tendency of people to work harder and perform better just because they know they are in an experiment or because they know a change has occurred in some procedure is called the **Hawthorne effect.**

The Hawthorne effect has had a peculiar history. In the 1920s and 1930s some experimenters conducted a study of worker productivity at the Hawthorne plant of the Western Electric Company near Chicago. The experimenters variously increased and decreased the workers' rest periods and lengthened and shortened their work hours. They found that almost any change they made, in any direction, increased productivity. They concluded that productivity increased either because the workers were getting more attention than usual or simply because changes were taking place. That principle became known as the Hawthorne effect.

A reanalysis of the Hawthorne results (Parsons, 1974), however, indicated that the workers had increased their productivity not because of the attention they got or the changes that took place but simply because they had improved their job skills during the many months over which the experiments took place. Their performance probably would have improved over time even if the experimenters had done nothing.

Still, the Hawthorne effect is a real factor. Sometimes any change in procedure seems to enhance performance. Almost any change introduces variety and prompts people to pay more attention to what they are doing. People also work harder if they know someone is watching. Many joggers report that they run a little harder than usual if someone is watching, especially if it is someone the jogger would like to impress.

Something to Think About

Your college tries an experiment: It announces that courses will meet more frequently but will last only a month, instead of the usual quarter or semester. During the first year under the new system, students and faculty alike agree that more learning is taking place than before. How could the college administration determine whether 1-month classes are really superior or whether the seeming improvement is just evidence of the Hawthorne effect? (Suggest an experiment for the college to try the following year.)

Selective Attrition

At Santa Enigma State College, only 50% of all freshmen have decided on a career, whereas 90% of all seniors have decided. An observer concludes that between the freshman year and the senior year, most of the undecided students come to a decision. Sounds reasonable, right? But wait.

Suppose a creature from outer space is observing humans for the first time. He/she/it discovers that about 50% of all human children are males but that only 10–20% of 90-year-olds are males. The creature concludes that as human males grow older, most of them change into females.

You see why that conclusion is wrong. Males—with a few exceptions—do not change into females. But they do die earlier, leaving a greater proportion of older females. So can we really say that a large percentage of undecided freshmen make career decisions by the time they become seniors? Not necessarily. Perhaps undecided freshmen simply drop out of college before reaching their senior year.

This example represents the problem of **selective attrition,** also known as *differential survival,* which is the tendency for some kinds of people to be more likely than others to drop out of a study. If some subjects drop out of a

study (by dying, quitting, or moving away), then those who remain may be different from those who left. To avoid this problem, psychologists simply report the before-and-after data only for people who complete a study; they discard the data for those who leave.

■ CONCEPT CHECK

6. Decide which of the following examples represents demand characteristics, Hawthorne effect, or selective attrition:

a. The Lizard Lick State College "Fighting Nematodes" lost 22 games in a row. When a new coach was hired, the team won 3 of its next 5 games.

b. Most of the first-year teachers in the Dismalville public school system complain about the school's policies. Teachers who have been at the school for 15 years or more rarely complain and seem quite satisfied.

c. A political survey reports one set of results when people are told, "This survey is sponsored by the Democratic party," and a different set of results when they are told, "This survey is sponsored by the Republican party."

d. A study of intelligence in one group of older people reports low performance among 70-year-olds, but (surprisingly) improved mean performance when those people reach age 80.

(Check your answers on page 60.)

GENERALIZABILITY OF RESULTS

When chemists find out how two chemicals react in a test tube, they can feel confident that those chemicals will react pretty much the same way anywhere—except, perhaps, under conditions of extreme temperature or pressure or in a strong magnetic or gravitational field. Psychologists are not always so certain that they can generalize their results from one set of people to another or from one set of circumstances to another.

Generalizing the results is especially uncertain if the investigator used a very select or limited sample of people. Imagine that I advertise a study on the effects of marijuana on behavior; what kind of people are most likely to volunteer to participate? Probably people already familiar with marijuana or other drugs; probably not a random sample of the population. What if I advertised a study on hypnosis? I would expect to get mostly volunteers who are curious to experience hypnotism, perhaps people who will turn out to be easily hypnotized.

These limitations are not a cause for despair, but only for caution. If we want to generalize the results of a study to apply broadly, we need to demonstrate that we can easily obtain similar results with different populations and under a variety of circumstances.

ETHICAL CONSIDERATIONS IN EXPERIMENTATION

In any experiment, psychologists manipulate some variable to see how it affects behavior. Perhaps the idea that someone might try to alter your behavior sounds objectionable. If so, bear in mind that every time you talk to other people, you are trying to alter their behavior at least in a slight way. Most experiments in psychology produce effects that are no more lasting than the effects of a conversation.

Still, some experiments do raise ethical issues. Psychologists are seriously concerned about ethical issues, both in the experiments they conduct with humans and in those they conduct with animals.

Ethical Concerns in Experiments on Humans

Earlier in this chapter I discussed experiments on the effects of televised violence. If psychologists believed that watching violent programs on television would really transform viewers into murderers, then it would be unethical for them to conduct any experiment to find out for sure. Moreover, it would be unethical to perform any experimental procedure likely to cause people any significant pain or embarrassment or to exert any long-lasting, undesirable effects on their lives.

The main ethical principle is that experiments should include only procedures that people would agree to experience. No one should leave a study muttering, "If I had known what was going to happen, I never would have agreed to participate." To maintain high ethical standards in the conduct of experiments, psychologists ask prospective participants to give their **informed consent** before proceeding. When experimenters post a sign-up sheet asking for volunteers, or at the start of the experiment itself, they explain that the participants will receive electrical shocks, or that they will be required to drink concentrated sugar water, or whatever. Any prospective participant who objects to the procedure can simply withdraw.

In addition, experiments conducted at any college or at any other reputable institution must first be approved by a Human Subjects Committee at that institution. Such a committee judges whether or not the proposed experiments are ethical. For example, a committee would not approve an experiment that called for administering large doses of cocaine—even if some of the subjects were eager to give their informed consent. The committee also judges experiments in which the experimenters want to conceal certain procedures from the subjects. For example, suppose the experimenters plan to put subjects through a certain experience and then see whether they are more or less likely than others to obey instructions to pick up a live snake. The experimenters might not want to mention the possible snake handling in their informed-consent instructions. (The whole point of the experiment might depend on an element of surprise.) The Human Subjects Committee would then decide whether or not to permit such an experiment.

Finally, the American Psychological Association, or APA (1982), publishes a booklet detailing the ethical treatment of volunteers in experiments. Any member who disregards the principles may be censured or expelled by the APA.

Ethical Concerns in Experiments on Animals

Some types of research require human subjects—for example, research on the effects of televised violence. Animals can be used for research on biological processes, such as mechanisms of sensation, the effects of drugs on behavior, or the effects of brain damage (Figure 2.16). About 7–8% of all published studies in psychology use animals (Gallup & Suarez, 1980). Animal research would be inappropriate for addressing certain issues—such as the effects of televised violence on behavior—but it is extremely helpful for other purposes. Animal research is responsible for much of what we know about the brain, about how drugs affect behavior, and about sensory systems. Research to find treatments for schizophrenia, Huntington's disease, Parkinson's disease, brain damage, and many other conditions begins with animal studies.

FIGURE 2.16

A mirror mounted on a young owl's head enables investigators to track the owl's head movements and thereby to discover how it localizes sounds with one ear plugged. The findings may help researchers understand how blind people compensate for hearing loss. An experiment such as this subjects the animal to only a minor inconvenience. Some experiments, however, inflict pain or discomfort and are more likely to raise ethical objections.

Some people nevertheless oppose animal research. Animals, after all, are in no position to give informed consent. Animal rights supporters vary in their views. Some are willing to tolerate experiments that inflict no pain and experiments likely to help solve major human problems. Others believe animals should have all the same rights as humans (Regan, 1986). According to this view, keeping animals (even pets) in cages is slavery and killing an animal is murder. Those who accept this view oppose all animal experiments, regardless of the circumstances.

Most scientists who conduct animal research strongly support animal *welfare,* including improvements in laboratory care, but they deny that animals have the same *rights* as people (Johnson, 1990). They make the following arguments in defense of animal research:

- We certainly agree that animals should not be mistreated, but we also recognize "the right of the incurably ill to hope for cures or relief

from suffering through research using animals" (Feeney, 1987). If animal experiments were abolished, certain areas of research, such as how to promote recovery from brain damage, would be almost impossible to pursue.

- Research on animals has produced a wealth of valuable information leading to the development of antianxiety drugs, new methods of treating pain and depression, an understanding of how certain drugs impair the development of the fetus, insight into the effects of old age on memory, and methods of helping people to overcome neuromuscular disorders (N. E. Miller, 1985).

- Extremely painful experiments on animals are rare (Coile & Miller, 1984). Although they undeniably occur, their frequency has been greatly exaggerated.

- Although studies of plants, experiments with tissue cultures, and computer simulations provide useful information on a few issues, they cannot provide much information about animal or human behavior or about brain mechanisms (Gallup & Suarez, 1985).

The debate continues. Meanwhile, professional organizations such as the Neuroscience Society publish guidelines for the proper use of animals in research. Colleges and other research institutions maintain Laboratory Animal Care Committees to ensure that laboratory animals are treated humanely, that their pain and discomfort are kept to a minimum, and that experimenters consider alternatives before they impose potentially painful procedures on animals. Because such committees have to deal with competing values, their decisions are never beyond dispute. How can anyone determine whether the value of the experimental results (which are hard to predict) will outweigh the pain the animals endure (which is hard to measure)? As is often the case with ethical decisions, reasonable arguments can be raised on both sides of the question, and no compromise is fully satisfactory.

SUMMARY

- *Operational definitions.* Psychologists must begin any study by defining their terms. For many purposes they prefer operational definitions, which state how to measure a phenomenon or how to produce it. (page 43)

- *Sampling.* Because psychologists hope to draw conclusions that apply to a large population and not just to the small sample they have studied, they try to select a sample that resembles the total population. They may select either a representative sample or a random sample. (page 44)

- *Blind observers.* To ensure objectivity, investigators use blind observers—observers who do not know how each individual has been treated or what results are expected. In a double-blind study, neither the observer nor the subjects know who has received which treatment. (page 44)

- *Case histories and naturalistic observations.* A case history is a detailed research study of a single individual. Naturalistic observations observe people or other species under natural conditions. (page 45)

- *Surveys.* A survey is a report of people's answers to a questionnaire. Slight changes in the wording of a question may significantly alter the responses people give. We should not assume that everyone who answers a question has a solid basis for an opinion. (page 46)

- *Correlations.* A correlational study is a study of the relationship between variables that are outside the investigator's control. The strength of the relationship is measured by a correlation coefficient. (page 48)

- *Illusory correlations.* Beware of illusory correlations—relationships that people think they observe between variables after casual observation. (page 50)

- *Inferring causation.* A correlational study does not uncover cause-and-effect relationships, but an experiment can. (page 50)

- *Experiments.* Experiments are studies in which the investigator manipulates one variable to determine its effect on another variable. The manipulated variable is the independent variable. The one the experimenter measures to see how it was affected is the dependent variable. (page 51)

- *Random assignment.* An experimenter should use random assignment of individuals in forming experimental and control groups. That is, all individuals should have an equal probability of being chosen for the experimental group. (page 52)

- *How experiments can go wrong.* Demand characteristics, the Hawthorne effect, or selective attrition sometimes distort the results of an experiment. (page 54)

- *Generalizing conclusions.* If a study is conducted with just one population under one set of circumstances, we should be cautious about generalizing the conclusions to much different populations or different circumstances. (page 56)

- *Ethics of experimentation.* Experimentation on either humans or animals raises ethical questions. Psychologists try to minimize risk to their subjects, but they cannot avoid making difficult ethical decisions. (page 57)

SUGGESTION FOR FURTHER READING

Stanovich, K. E. (1986). *How to think straight about psychology.* Glenview, IL: Scott, Foresman. An excellent treatment of how to evaluate evidence in psychology and how to avoid pitfalls.

TERMS

operational definition a definition that specifies the operations (or procedures) used to measure some variable or to produce some phenomenon (page 43)

representative sample a selection of the population chosen to match the entire population with regard to specific variables (page 44)

random sample a group of people picked in such a way that every individual in the population has an equal chance of being selected (page 44)

blind observer an observer who does not know which subjects are in which group and what is expected of each (pag 45)

placebo an inactive pill that has no known pharmacological effect on the subjects in an experiment (page 45)

single-blind study a study in which either the observer or the subjects are unaware of which subjects received which treatment (page 45)

double-blind study a study in which neither the observer nor the subjects know which subjects received which treatment (page 45)

case history a thorough description of a single individual, including information on both past experiences and current behavior (page 45)

naturalistic observation a careful examination of what many people or nonhuman animals do under natural conditions (page 45)

cross-cultural psychologist psychologist who conducts naturalistic observations on people in different cultures and compares their behavior (page 46)

survey a study of the prevalence of certain beliefs, attitudes, or behaviors based on people's responses to specific questions (page 46)

correlation a measure of the relationship between two variables, both of which are outside the investigator's control (page 48)

correlation coefficient a mathematical estimate of the relationship between two variables, ranging from +1 (perfect positive relationship) to 0 (no linear relationship) to −1 (perfect negative relationship) (page 49)

illusory correlation an apparent relationship based on casual observation of unrelated or poorly related events (page 50)

experiment a study in which the investigator manipulates at least one variable while measuring at least one other variable (page 51)

independent variable the variable the experimenter manipulates to see how it affects the dependent variable (page 51)

dependent variable the variable the experimenter measures to see how changes in the independent variable affect it (page 51)

experimental group the group that receives the treatment that an experiment is designed to test (page 52)

control group the group that is treated in the same way as the experimental group except for the treatment the experiment is designed to test (page 52)

random assignment a chance procedure for assigning subjects to groups such that every subject has the same probability as any other of being assigned to a particular group (page 52)

demand characteristics cues that tell a subject what is expected of him or her and what the experimenter hopes to find (page 54)

sensory deprivation temporary reduction of vision, hearing, touch, and other forms of sensory stimulation (page 54)

Hawthorne effect the tendency of people to work harder and perform better just because they know they are in an experiment or because they know a change has occurred in some procedure (page 55)

selective attrition the tendency for some kinds of people to be more likely than others to drop out of a study (page 56)

informed consent a subject's agreement to take part in an experiment after being informed about what will happen (page 57)

ANSWERS TO CONCEPT CHECKS

2. The score on an IQ test is an operational definition of intelligence. (Whether it is a particularly good definition is another question.) None of the other definitions tells us how to measure or produce intelligence. One example of an operational definition of hunger is "the number of hours since one's last meal." Another is "the amount of food the individual eats when a certain type of food is available." (page 43)

3. Clearly not. It is unlikely that the men at a given college are typical of men in general or that the women are typical of women in general. Moreover, a given college may have set higher admissions standards for one sex than for the other, or it may have attracted mostly men who are interested in one major and mostly women who are interested in another. In that case, the men and women are almost certain to differ in ways that have no direct relationship to being male or female. (page 44)

4. The −0.75 correlation indicates a stronger relationship—that is, a greater accuracy of predicting one variable based on measurements of the other. A negative correlation is just as useful as a positive one. (page 50)

5. The independent variable is the frequency of tests during the semester. The dependent variable is the students' performance on the final exam. (page 52)

6. (a) Hawthorne effect. A change, perhaps any change, improves performance. (b) Selective attrition. The least satisfied teachers do not spend 15 years at the school. (c) Demand characteristics. Telling people who sponsored the survey suggests they give answers favoring that sponsor. (d) Selective attrition. Perhaps the more intelligent people were more likely to survive to age 80. (page 56)

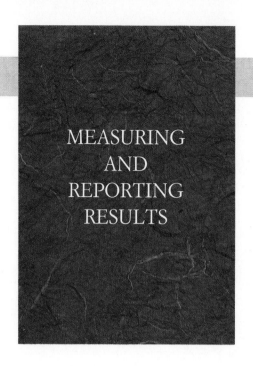

MEASURING AND REPORTING RESULTS

After psychologists have conducted a study, how can they determine whether the results are convincing or whether they demonstrate nothing but random fluctuations?

Some time ago, a television program about the alleged dangers of playing the game Dungeons and Dragons reported 28 known cases of D&D players who had committed suicide. Alarming, right?

Not necessarily. At least 3 million young people at the time were playing the game regularly. The reported suicide rate among D&D players—28 per 3 million—was considerably *less* than the suicide rate among teenagers in general.

So do the results mean that playing D&D *prevents* suicide? Hardly. The 28 reported cases probably are not a complete count of all suicides by D&D players. Besides, the correlation between playing D&D and committing suicide, regardless of its direction and magnitude, could not possibly tell us about cause and effect.

Then what conclusion should we draw from these data? *None at all.* Sometimes, as in this case, the data are meaningless because of how they were collected. Even when the data are potentially meaningful, people sometimes present them in a confusing or misleading manner (Figure 2.17). Let's consider some of the proper ways of analyzing and interpreting results.

DESCRIPTIVE STATISTICS

To explain the meaning of a study, an investigator must summarize its results in some orderly fashion. When a researcher observes the behavior of 100 people, we have no interest in hearing all the details about every person observed. We want to know what the researcher found in general, on the average. We might also want to know whether most people were similar to the average or whether they varied a great deal. An investigator presents the answers to those questions through **descriptive statistics,** which are mathematical summaries of results, such as measures of the central score and the amount of variation. The correlation coefficient, discussed earlier in this chapter, is one kind of descriptive statistic. (Descriptive statistics differ from inferential statistics, which I shall discuss later.)

Measurements of the Central Score: Mean, Median, and Mode

There are three ways of representing the central score: mean, median, and mode. The **mean** is the sum of all the scores divided by the number of scores. (Most people have the mean in mind when they say "average.") For example, the mean of 2, 10, and 3 is 5 (15/3). The mean is a useful term, especially if we are dealing with a more or less normal distribution of scores, as shown in Figure 2.18a. A **normal distribution** (or normal curve) is a symmetrical frequency of scores in which each of many independent factors produces a small, random variation in whatever we are measuring. For example, suppose we measure how long various people take to memorize a poem. Their times might form an approximately normal distribution. Most of their times will cluster around the mean, and the number of times above the mean will be about the same as the number below it.

When the actual measurements in a study do not follow the normal distribution, such as in Figure 2.18b, the mean is less useful as an indication of what happened. Suppose 19 people memorize the poem in about 15 minutes each.

FIGURE 2.17

How statistics can mislead: Both of these graphs present the same data, an increase from 20 to 22 over a year's time. But by ranging only from 20 to 22 (rather than from 0 to 22), graph B makes that increase look much more dramatic. (After Huff, 1954.)

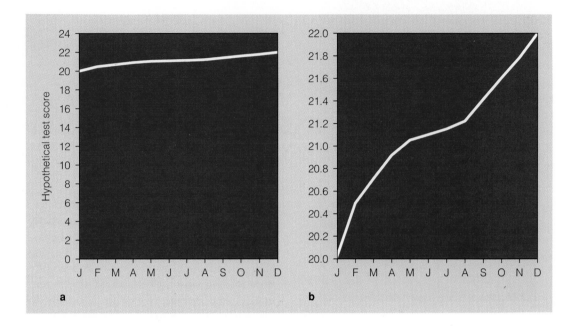

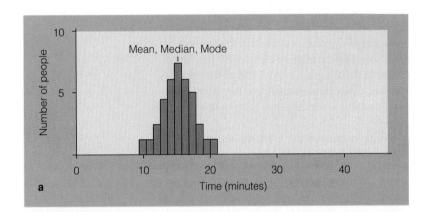

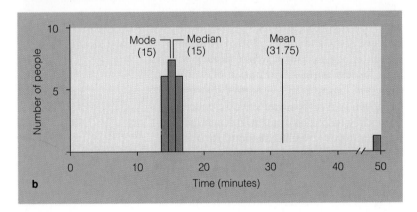

FIGURE 2.18

(a) A normal distribution. (b) The inclusion of one extreme score distorts the normal distribution and decreases the usefulness of the mean as a descriptive term.

But a 20th person falls asleep in the middle of the task and takes $5\frac{1}{2}$ hours to finish. Now the mean for the group of 20 is more than 30 minutes.

"Why not just ignore the one extreme individual?" you might ask. That could be a reasonable decision in this case, but not in others. Suppose most people solve a certain math problem in 2 to 4 minutes, a few solve it in a little more time, and about 20% fail to solve it at all, as shown in Figure 2.19. (Note that these scores definitely do not fall into the normal distribution.) While we might feel justified in ignoring the results of a single extreme individual, we can hardly ignore 20%. However, we cannot compute a mean time for solving the problem if some of the people did not solve it at all.

When the distribution of scores in a study is far from the normal distribution, the median is a more reliable indicator of what most individuals did. To determine the **median,** we arrange all the scores in order from the highest score to the lowest score. The middle score is the median. For example, if the scores are 2, 10, and 3, the median is 3. In Figure 2.19 the median score is 3 minutes.

The third way to represent the central score is the **mode,** the score that occurs most frequently. For example, in the distribution of scores 2, 2, 3, 4, and 10, the mode is 2. The mode is not particularly useful for most purposes. Here is a case, however, in which we might want to use the mode: The bar graphs in Figure 2.20 illustrate how many times people attend religious services per month in two hypothetical communities. Here the mean and the median are useless for comparison purposes, because for both populations the mean happens to be 2.4 and the median is 2. It might be more interesting to note that the mode (the most common response) is zero times per month in one population and four times per month in the other.

To recap: Roughly speaking, the mean is what most people intend when they say "average." The median is the middle score; the mode is the most common score (Figure 2.21).

■ CONCEPT CHECK

7a. *For the following distribution of scores, determine the mean, the median, and the mode: 5, 2, 2, 2, 8, 3, 1, 6, 7.*

b. *Determine the mean, median, and mode for this distribution: 5, 2, 2, 2, 35, 3, 1, 6, 7. (Check your answers on page 67.)*

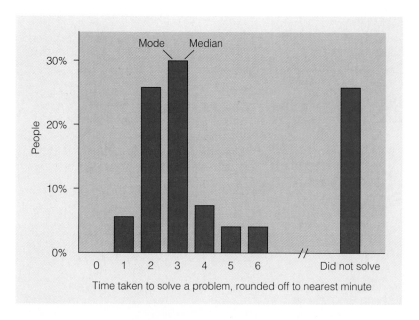

FIGURE 2.19
When a few scores are far from the rest of the distribution, the mean can be uninformative and misleading. In such cases, the median (middle value) is more meaningful.

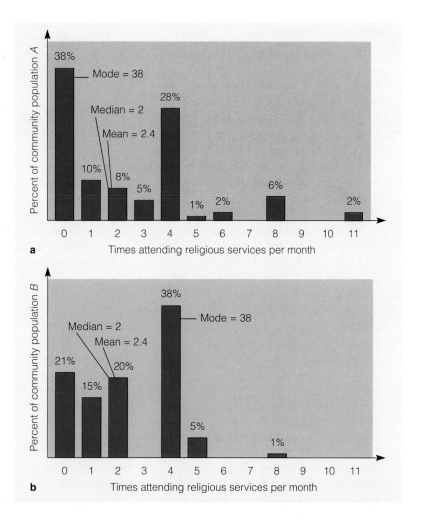

FIGURE 2.20
These two charts, which lack normal distributions, have the same median and mean. Here the difference in modes can be informative. In (a) the mode is 0; in (b) the mode is 4. (In both cases, 38% of people are on the mode, but 38 is not the mode.)

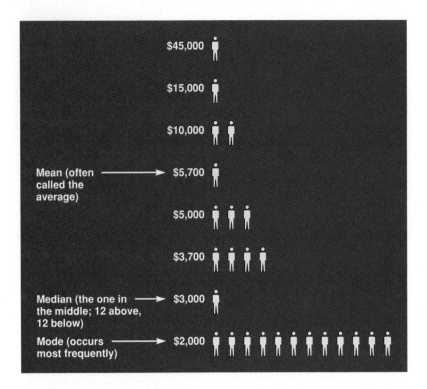

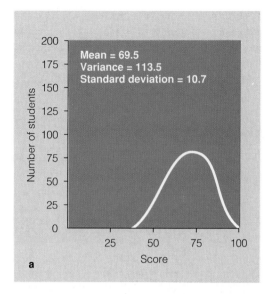

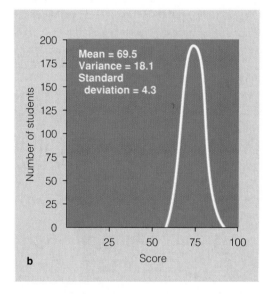

FIGURE 2.21
The monthly salaries of the 25 employees of company X, showing the mean, median, and mode. (After Huff, 1954.)

FIGURE 2.22
These two distributions of test scores have the same mean but different variances and different standard deviations.

Measures of Variation

Figure 2.22 shows two distributions of scores. Suppose they represent scores on two tests of knowledge about introductory psychology. Both tests have the same mean, median, and mode. But if you had a score of 80, then the meaning of that score would be different for the two tests. Such a score on the first test is above average, but nothing unusual. The same score on the second test would put you in the top 1% of your class.

To describe the difference between Figure 2.22a and b, we need a measurement of the variation (or spread) around the mean. The simplest such measurement is the **range** of a distribution, a statement of the highest and lowest scores. Thus, the range in Figure 2.22a is 39 to 100 and in Figure 2.22b it is 58 to 92. If we subtract the lower end of the range from the higher number, we see that the range includes more numbers in 2.22a than in 2.22b.

The range is simple but not very useful, because it takes account of only two scores. Statisticians need to know whether nearly all the scores are clustered close to the mean or whether they are more scattered. A good measure should indicate that the scores in 2.22a are much more scattered than those in 2.22b. The most useful measure is the **standard deviation,** a measurement of the amount of variation among

scores in a normal distribution. The appendix to this chapter gives a formula for calculating the standard deviation, but for our present purposes you can simply remember that when the scores are closely clustered near the mean, the standard deviation is small; when the scores are more widely scattered, the standard deviation is large.

As Figure 2.23 shows, the Scholastic Aptitude Test was originally intended to have a mean of 500 and a standard deviation of 100. (In fact, the mean is in the mid-400s, but we shall deal with the intended case.) Of all people taking the test, 68% score within one standard deviation above or below the mean (400–600); 95% score within two standard deviations (300–700). Only 2.5% score above 700; another 2.5% score below 300.

Standard deviations provide a useful way of comparing scores on two tests. For example, if you had a score one standard deviation above the mean on the SAT, you did about as well as someone who scored one standard deviation above the mean on some other test, such as the American College Test. We would say that both of you had a *deviation score* of +1.

■ C O N C E P T   C H E C K

8. *On your first psychology test, you get a score of 80. The mean for the class is 70, and the standard deviation is 5. On the second test, you get a score of 90. This time the mean for the class is again 70, but the standard deviation is 20. Compared to the other students in your class, did your performance improve, deteriorate, or stay the same? (Check your answer on page 67.)*

E V A L U A T I N G
R E S U L T S :
I N F E R E N T I A L
S T A T I S T I C S

Suppose we conduct a study comparing the performances of first-graders and second-graders at a nearby school on a set of arithmetic problems. We would probably report the means and standard deviations for each group. But we are interested in not just the performances of these two local groups but also the performances of first-graders and second-graders nationally. When we talk about the entire population, we use **inferential statistics,** which are statements about large groups based on inferences from small samples.

The most common use of inferential statistics is to decide whether the difference observed between two groups is probably real or probably accidental. Suppose, for example, we discover that the members of an experimental group who watched a series of violent television programs committed a mean of 0.38 aggressive act per person per day, while the members of a control group who did not watch violent programs committed a mean of 0.29 aggressive act. Should we conclude that watching violent programs increases aggressive behavior? Or is it

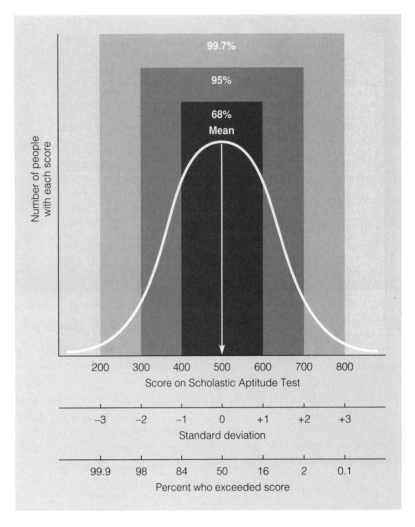

F I G U R E   2 . 2 3
In a normal distribution, the amount of variation of scores from the mean can be measured in standard deviations. In this example, scores between 400 and 600 are said to be within one standard deviation from the mean; scores between 300 and 700 are within two standard deviations.

likely that two groups chosen at random might differ by 0.09 simply by accident?

To answer that question, we use statistical techniques. Different formulas are used for different purposes. The appendix at the end of this chapter gives an example of a statistical test. A statistical test determines the probability that a study may produce, *just by accident,* results as impressive as those that were actually obtained. If that probability is low, the results can be taken seriously.

In our example, we want to know how likely it is that two groups we chose at random might differ by accident in their level of aggressiveness by at least 0.38 to 0.29. That probability depends on several factors (Figure 2.24):

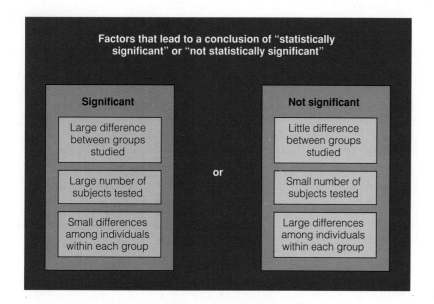

Factors that lead to a conclusion of "statistically significant" or "not statistically significant"

Significant

Large difference between groups studied

Large number of subjects tested

Small differences among individuals within each group

or

Not significant

Little difference between groups studied

Small number of subjects tested

Large differences among individuals within each group

FIGURE 2.24
We cannot draw conclusions from data until they are shown to be "statistically significant," which is why raw data must be subjected to appropriate statistical procedures. The appendix to this chapter describes some of these procedures.

1. The larger the difference between two groups, the less likely it is that the difference has arisen by accident.

2. Other things being equal, the more subjects each group has, the less likely that any difference observed between the groups is just an accident. If there are five subjects in the experimental group and five in the control group, the probability is fairly high that one group will accidentally include more aggressive people than the other. But if each group includes a thousand subjects, then the probability is slight that one group will accidentally include a much higher proportion of aggressive people than the other contains.

3. The more consistently the members of each group behave, the less likely it is that any difference between the groups has arisen through accident. For example, if almost everyone in the experimental group is found to commit about 0.38 aggressive act per day, and if almost everyone in the control group is found to commit about 0.29 aggressive act per day, then the difference between the two groups is probably not the result of accident. If both groups have a great deal of variability—that is, if the standard deviations are large—then the difference between the groups could be an accident.

To summarize the results of a statistical test, we use a value known as p, which stands for *probability* of accidentally getting results at least as impressive as the reported results. If the value of p is low, then the probability of accidentally producing such results is low. Psychologists usually regard a result as significant if the value of p is less than 5%, expressed as $p < .05$. A more cautious experimenter might insist on a stricter standard, such as $p < .01$. In either case, if the p value is lower than the standard chosen, then an experiment's results are said to be statistically significant, and the results are sufficiently convincing that we would look for an explanation. If the p value is higher than the standard chosen, the results are inconclusive.

■ CONCEPT CHECK

9. *You compare the performance of women and men on 20 tasks. On one of the tasks, you find a significant difference ($p < .01$). How could you check against the possibility that this apparent difference is the result of accident? (Check your answer on page 67.)*

Finding statistically significant results is only the first step toward drawing a conclusion. To say that an experiment has **statistically significant results** means only that the probability is low that the effect arose by chance. The question remains, if not by chance, then what caused the difference? At that point, psychologists call upon all their knowledge to try to determine the most likely interpretation of the results.

SUMMARY

■ *Descriptive statistics.* Psychologists rely on descriptive statistics to summarize their results. Descriptive statistics include measures of central score, amount of variation, and correlation. (page 61)

■ *Mean, median, and mode.* One way of presenting the central score of a distribution is the mean, determined by adding all the scores and dividing by the number of individuals. Another way is the median, which is the score in the middle after all the scores have been arranged from highest to lowest. The mode is the score that occurs most frequently. (page 61)

■ *Standard deviation.* To indicate whether most scores are clustered close to the mean or whether they are spread out, psychologists report the range of scores or the standard deviation. If we know that a given score is a certain number of standard deviations above or below the mean, then we can determine what percentage of other scores it exceeds. (page 64)

■ *Inferential statistics.* Inferential statistics are attempts to deduce the properties of a large population based on the results from a small sample. (page 65)

- *Probability of chance results.* The most common use of inferential statistics is to calculate the probability that a given research result could have arisen by chance. That probability is low if the difference between two groups is large, if the variability within each group is small, and if the number of individuals in each group is large. (page 65)

- *Statistical significance.* When psychologists say "$p < .05$," they mean that the probability that accidental fluctuations could produce the kind of results they obtained is less than 5%. They generally set a standard of 5% or less. If the results meet that standard, then they are said to be statistically significant. (page 65)

SUGGESTION FOR FURTHER READING

Agnew, N. M., & Pyke, S. W. (1987). *The science game* (4th ed.). Englewood Cliffs, NJ: Prentice-Hall. A discussion of all aspects of research, including both methods of conducting research and statistical analysis of results.

TERMS

descriptive statistics mathematical summaries of results, such as measures of the central score and the amount of variation (page 61)

mean the sum of all the scores reported in a study divided by the number of scores (page 61)

normal distribution (or normal curve) a symmetrical frequency of scores in which each of many independent factors produces a small, random variation in whatever is being measured (page 61)

median the middle score in a list of scores arranged from highest to lowest (page 62)

mode the score that occurs most frequently in a distribution of scores (page 62)

range a statement of the highest and lowest scores in a distribution of scores (page 64)

standard deviation a measurement of the amount of variation among scores in a normal distribution (page 64)

inferential statistics statements about large groups based on inferences from small samples (page 65)

$p < .05$ an expression meaning that the probability of accidentally getting results equal to the reported results is less than 5% (page 66)

statistically significant results effects that have a low probability of having arisen by chance (page 66)

ANSWERS TO CONCEPT CHECKS

7. (a) Mean = 4; median = 3; mode = 2. (b) Mean = 7; median = 3; mode = 2. Note that changing just one number in the distribution from 8 to 35 greatly altered the mean without affecting the median or the mode. (page 63)

8. Even though your score went up from 80 on the first test to 90 on the second, your performance actually deteriorated in comparison to other students' scores. An 80 on the first test was two standard deviations above the mean, a score better than 98% of all other students. A 90 on the second test was only one standard deviation above the mean, a score that beats only 84% of other students. (page 65)

9. The more comparisons one makes, the greater is the probability that at least one of them will appear to be statistically significant, just by chance. One way to avoid this difficulty would be to set a higher standard of statistical significance, such as $p < .001$, and to discount any difference that does not meet this high standard. Another way would be to repeat the study on a second population to see whether the difference is replicable. (page 66)

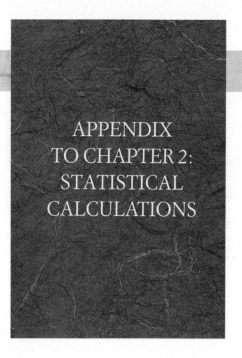

APPENDIX TO CHAPTER 2: STATISTICAL CALCULATIONS

This appendix shows how to calculate a few of the statistics mentioned in Chapter 2. It is intended primarily to satisfy your curiosity. Ask your instructor whether you should use this appendix for any other purpose.

Standard Deviation

To determine the standard deviation (SD):

1. Determine the mean of the scores.

2. Subtract the mean from each of the individual scores.

3. Square each of those results, add them together, and divide by the total number of scores.

The result is called the *variance.* The standard deviation is the square root of the variance. See Table 2.3 for examples.

Standard Error of the Mean

One way to infer whether the mean of a sample is close to the true mean of the population is to calculate the *standard error of the mean (SE).* We calculate the standard error of the mean by dividing the standard deviation of the population by $\sqrt{N - 1}$, where N is the number of individuals in the sample:

$$SE = SD/\sqrt{(N - 1)}$$

If the sample includes many individuals who vary only slightly from one another, the standard deviation will be small, N will be large, and therefore the standard error of the mean will be small. On the other hand, if the sample includes few individuals who vary greatly from one another, the standard error will be large.

A Typical Statistical Test: The *t*-test

A number of statistical tests are available to suit different kinds of data and different kinds of experiments. For the simple case of comparing two groups, both of which show results that approximate the normal distribution, one of the most popular tests is the *t-test.* Assume that for two populations the means are $\overline{x}_1$ and $\overline{x}_2$, the numbers of individuals measured are n_1 and n_2, and the standard deviations are s_1 and s_2.

Table 2.3

Individual Scores	Mean Minus the Individual Scores	Differences Squared
12.5	2.5	6.25
17.0	−2.0	4.00
11.0	4.0	16.00
14.5	0.5	0.25
16.0	−1.0	1.00
16.5	−1.5	2.25
17.5	−2.5	6.25
		36.00

Mean = 15.0

Variance = 36/7 = 5.143

Standard deviation = 2.268

We calculate t by using this formula:

$$t = \frac{(\overline{x}_2 - \overline{x}_1)\sqrt{n_1 \cdot n_2 \cdot (n_1 + n_2 - 2)}}{\sqrt{n_1 \cdot s_1^2 + n_2 \cdot s_2^2} \cdot \sqrt{n_1 + n_2}}$$

The larger the value of t, the less likely that the difference between the two groups is due to chance. The value of t will be high if the difference between the two means ($\overline{x}_2 - \overline{x}_1$) is large, if the standard deviations (s_1 and s_2) are small relative to the means, and if the number of individuals is large. For example, if a group of 50 people has a mean of 81 and a standard deviation of 7, and a group of 150 people has a mean of 73 and a standard deviation of 9, then

$$t = \frac{(81 - 73)\sqrt{150 \cdot 50 \cdot 198}}{\sqrt{(150 \cdot 81 + 50 \cdot 49)}\sqrt{(200)}} = \frac{9748.8}{120.83 \times 14.14} = 5.71$$

The larger the value of t, the less likely it is that the results have arisen by accident. Statistics books contain tables that show the likelihood of a given t value. In this case, with 200 people in the two groups combined, a t value of 5.71 is significant ($p < .001$).

Correlation Coefficients

To determine the correlation coefficient, we designate one of the variables x and the other one y. We obtain pairs of measures, x_i and y_i. Then we use the following formula:

$$r = \frac{[(\Sigma x_i y_i) - n \cdot \overline{x} \cdot \overline{y}]}{n \cdot sx \cdot sy}$$

In this formula, ($\Sigma x_i y_i$) is the sum of the products of x and y. For each pair of observations (x, y), we multiple x times y and then add together all the products. The term $n \cdot \overline{x} \cdot \overline{y}$ means n (the number of pairs) times the mean of x times the mean of y. The denominator, $n \cdot sx \cdot sy$, means n times the standard deviation of x times the standard deviation of y.

3 BIOLOGICAL PSYCHOLOGY

Biological psychology, the study of the relationship between brain activity and psychological events, is the most interesting topic in the world. I'm sure that every professor or textbook writer thinks that his or her favorite topic is "the most interesting topic in the world," and that is fine. But the others are simply wrong. This really *is* the most interesting topic in the world.

"I think, therefore I am"—René Descartes' declaration points to the mind-body problem facing psychologists: How and why does the brain's activity produce conscious experience?

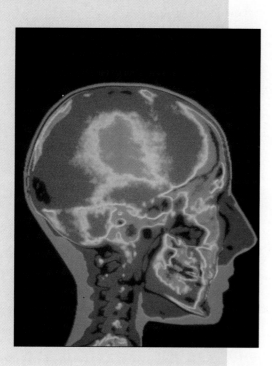

When I have made this statement—the paragraph you have just read—before a group of students or any other nonspecialist group, I have always gotten a laugh. They are amused by my self-centered assumption that my favorite topic is more interesting than anyone else's.

When I have made the same statement before a group of biological psychologists, no one laughs. They just nod their heads as if to say, "Yes, of course. This topic is not just interesting *to me*; it is inherently and *objectively* interesting. It would be everyone's favorite topic if they just *understood*!"

When I say biological psychology is extremely interesting, I am not referring to the names and locations of various parts of the brain, details about how nerve cells work, and various other facts that are no more interesting than countless other facts you have had to learn in school. I am referring to the most basic issue of biological psychology: Is the "mind" just another word for brain activity? If so, then all those molecules in the brain are somehow collectively "conscious." If *mind* is *not* just another word for brain activity, then what *is* mind and where does it come from? In either case, why is there such a thing as conscious awareness in a universe of matter and energy? To understand the mind-brain relationship would be to understand human experience at the deepest level and to understand a great deal about the nature of the universe.

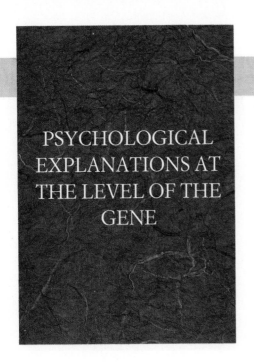

PSYCHOLOGICAL EXPLANATIONS AT THE LEVEL OF THE GENE

How does heredity affect behavior?
How does evolution influence behavior?

Everyone begins life as a fertilized egg. From then on, the way we develop is a combined product of our genes and our environment. If two people develop differently, that difference could be the result of a difference in their genes or in their environments or both.

In some cases, a gene can make an enormous difference in behavior. One condition that apparently depends largely on a single gene is **Alzheimer's disease.** People with a gene for Alzheimer's disease live a normal life until old age, when certain parts of the brain may gradually begin to deteriorate (Goldgaber, Lerman, McBride, Saffiotti, & Gajdusek, 1987; Tanzi et al., 1987). In the initial stages, people with Alzheimer's disease become forgetful. As a rule, they still remember their name and address and most of the other information they have known for years, but they have trouble remembering what they have just done and said and what has just happened. As the disease progresses, people grow confused, depressed, and unable to complete any train of thought (Schneck, Reisberg, & Ferris, 1982; Sinex & Myers, 1982). All that as the result of a single gene!

And yet the gene is not entirely responsible for the condition. Different people with the same gene have different outcomes. Whether they develop Alzheimer's disease at all, and how soon and how severely, apparently depends on many features in the environment. The same is true for many other genes of importance to psychology. Certain people have genes that make them more likely to become depressed, or to have an alcohol problem, or to develop numerous other conditions. None of those genes forces the person to develop such conditions; the outcome always depends in part on everything else that happens in the person's life.

Often psychologists have trouble determining what behavior is due to the effects of genes and what to the effects of the environment. For example, are boys generally more aggressive than girls—at least in certain circumstances—because of certain genes that directly control aggressiveness? Or do they act more aggressively because parents and other people encourage such behavior more in boys than in girls?

And why do identical twins generally resemble each other in so many ways? Is it because they have the same genes or because they have shared the same environment?

These questions illustrate the *nature-nurture* problem mentioned in Chapter 1. It shows up in practically all fields of psychology. In this section I shall discuss what genes are, how they exert their effects, and how psychologists try to determine the role of genes in human behavior. I shall also discuss a few points about the evolution of behavior.

PRINCIPLES OF GENETICS

You may have studied genetics in a biology class, but here we will explore concepts of genetics from the viewpoint of psychology, as well as biology.

Nearly every cell of every plant and animal contains a nucleus, which in turn contains strands of hereditary material called **chromosomes** (Figure 3.1). Chromosomes provide the chemical basis of heredity. Humans have 23 pairs of chromosomes; they receive one chromosome of each pair from the mother and one from the father (Figure 3.2).

Sections along each chromosome are known as **genes.** These segments control chemical reactions that ultimately direct the development of the organism. The genes determine

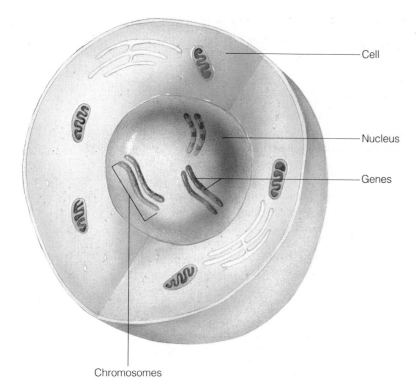

FIGURE 3.1
Genes are sections of chromosomes, which are in the nuclei of cells. Scale is exaggerated for illustration purposes.

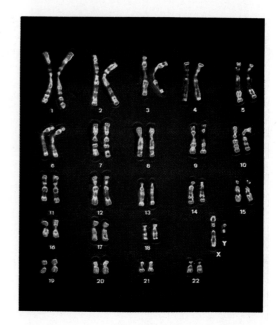

FIGURE 3.2
The nucleus of each human cell contains 46 chromosomes, 23 from the sperm and 23 from the ovum, united in pairs.

whether the individual develops as a tall red-headed woman or a short blond man.

We can locate and identify certain genes by examining chromosomes under a microscope, though most genes cannot be located so readily. If we know that a particular gene is close to some other gene that we have already located on a chromosome, then we can use that other gene as a marker. For example, if you have a particular gene that we know your father and his mother also had, then you probably also have certain other genes that are close to that gene on their chromosomes. By using such reasoning, we can identify people who have a gene that predisposes them to a particular disease even before the symptoms have become evident (Gilliam et al., 1987).

The Transmission of Genes from One Generation to Another

Because people have two of each chromosome, they have two of each type of gene, one on each of the chromosomes. They have two genes for eye color, two for hair color, two for every characteristic. The two genes for hair color, for example, may be either the same or different.

When both genes of a given pair of chromosomes are the same, the person is said to be **homozygous** (HO-mo-ZI-gus) for that gene. When the two genes are different, the person is **heterozygous** (HET-er-o-ZI-gus) for that gene (Figure 3.3). (A *zygote* is a fertilized egg. *Homozygous* means *a fertilized egg formed from the same genes; heterozygous* means *a fertilized egg formed from different genes.*)

Certain genes are labeled **dominant genes** because they will exert their effects on development even in a person who is heterozygous for that gene. Very few human behaviors depend on a single gene, but here is one example: The gene for the ability to curl the tongue lengthwise (Figure 3.4) is a dominant gene; all people who have that gene can curl their tongue, regardless of whether they are homozygous or heterozygous for that gene. The gene for the inability to curl the tongue is said to be a **recessive gene.** Only people who are homozygous for a recessive gene show its effects. In other words, if you cannot curl your tongue, you must be homozygous for the inability-to-curl gene (not exactly a serious handicap).

A person who is heterozygous for a particu-

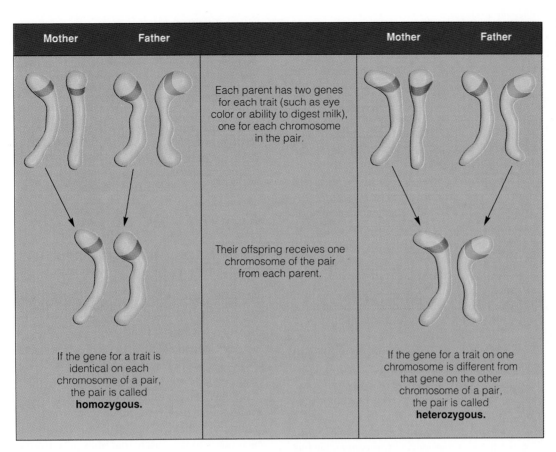

| Mother | Father | | Mother | Father |

Each parent has two genes for each trait (such as eye color or ability to digest milk), one for each chromosome in the pair.

Their offspring receives one chromosome of the pair from each parent.

If the gene for a trait is identical on each chromosome of a pair, the pair is called **homozygous.**

If the gene for a trait on one chromosome is different from that gene on the other chromosome of a pair, the pair is called **heterozygous.**

FIGURE 3.3
In a pair of homozygous chromosomes, the gene for a trait is identical on both chromosomes. In a heterozygous pair, the chromosomes contain different genes for a trait.

lar gene will show the effects of the dominant gene but may still pass the recessive gene to a son or a daughter. If parents who are heterozygous for the tongue-curling genes both pass the recessive gene to a child, the child will not develop the ability to curl his or her tongue.

Here are a few other examples of traits controlled by a single dominant gene: brown eyes, Huntington's disease, color vision, ability to taste the chemical phenylthiocarbamide (PTC), ability to metabolize alcohol into harmless acetic acid.

▪ CONCEPT CHECKS

1. The gene for tongue curling and the gene for the ability to taste PTC are both dominant genes. (PTC tastes bitter to those who can taste it at all.) Suppose you can curl your tongue but cannot taste PTC. Are you homozygous or heterozygous for the tongue-curling gene, or is it impossible to say? Are you homozygous or heterozygous for the inability to taste PTC, or is it impossible to say?

2. If two parents can curl their tongues but cannot taste PTC, what can you predict about their children? (Check your answers on page 85.)

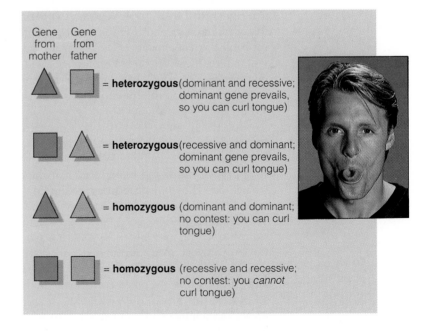

Gene from mother   Gene from father

= **heterozygous** (dominant and recessive; dominant gene prevails, so you can curl tongue)

= **heterozygous** (recessive and dominant; dominant gene prevails, so you can curl tongue)

= **homozygous** (dominant and dominant; no contest: you can curl tongue)

= **homozygous** (recessive and recessive; no contest: you *cannot* curl tongue)

FIGURE 3.4
This figure uses the ability to curl the tongue lengthwise as an example of a behavior that depends on a single gene. The gene that enables you to curl your tongue is a dominant gene, indicated by a triangle here. The square refers to a recessive gene for inability to curl tongue.

Psychological Explanations at the Level of the Gene

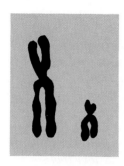

F I G U R E 3 . 5
An electron micrograph of X and Y chromosomes shows the difference in length. (From Ruch, 1984.)

Sex-Linked and Sex-Limited Genes

Some characteristics are more common in men; others are more common in women. Why? There can be many explanations, and a genetic explanation is not always a likely one. Still, genes do account for some of the differences, and it is valuable to know how genes could produce differences between the sexes.

One pair of human chromosomes are known as **sex chromosomes** because they determine whether an individual will develop as a male or as a female. The sex chromosomes are of two types, known as X and Y (Figure 3.5). A female has two **X chromosomes** in each cell; a male has one X chromosome and one **Y chromosome.** The mother contributes one X chromosome to each child, and the father contributes either an X or a Y chromosome.

Genes located on the X chromosome are known as X-linked genes, or as **sex-linked genes.** An X-linked recessive gene shows its effects more often in men than in women. For example, the most common type of colorblindness depends on an X-linked recessive gene. A man with that gene definitely will be colorblind, because he has no other X chromosome. He has a Y chromosome, but the Y chromosome contains neither the gene for colorblindness nor the gene for normal color vision. A woman who has that gene has a second X chromosome, which probably has a dominant gene for normal color vision. If so, she will not be colorblind. She will, however, be a "carrier" for colorblindness; that is, she can transmit the colorblindness gene to any of her children (Figure 3.6).

Genetically controlled differences between the sexes do not necessarily depend on sex-linked genes. For example, adult men generally have deeper voices and more facial hair than women do. Those characteristics are not controlled by genes on the X or Y chromosome. They are controlled by genes that are present in women as well as men, but these genes are activated mainly in men. **Sex-limited genes** are those that affect one sex only or affect one sex more strongly than the other, even though both sexes have the genes. The genes that control breast development in women are also sex-limited genes.

Why are men more likely to get into fistfights than women are? We do not have enough evidence to determine whether genes are responsible, but if the difference is because of their genes, the responsible genes are probably sex-*limited* genes rather than sex-linked genes.

That is, male hormones may activate certain genes that promote aggressive behavior; we have no evidence indicating an X-linked gene or a Y-linked gene for aggressive behavior.

■ C O N C E P T C H E C K

3. *Suppose a colorblind man marries a woman who is homozygous for normal color vision. What sort of color vision will their children have? (Check your answer on page 85.)*

THE EFFECTS OF GENES ON HUMAN BEHAVIOR: TYPES OF EVIDENCE

The ability to curl one's tongue lengthwise depends on the effects of a single gene and so does the ability to taste PTC. Most human behaviors, however, depend on the effects of several genes and on environmental influences as well. Researchers who study the effects of genes on human behavior concentrate on three sources of evidence: (1) the extent to which **monozygotic** (identical; literally, one-egg) **twins** resemble each other more closely than **dizygotic** (fraternal; literally, two-egg) **twins** do (Figure 3.7); (2) the extent to which monozygotic twins who are separated at birth and reared in separate environments develop greater similarities than they would simply by chance; and (3) the extent to which adopted children resemble their adoptive relatives and their biological relatives.

Comparison of Monozygotic and Dizygotic Twins

Monozygotic twins resemble each other more closely than dizygotic twins in many behaviors, including anxiety, depression, aggression, assertiveness, shyness, and tendency toward alcoholism (Loehlin, Willerman, & Horn, 1988). They generally make similar scores on IQ tests, and they both do well or poorly on the same parts of the tests (Segal, 1985).

Something to Think About

One reason that monozygotic twins resemble each other more than dizygotic twins in, say, the tendency toward depression is that they have the same genes. Can you suggest another reason?

Occasionally monozygotic twins are separated at birth and reared in separate environ-

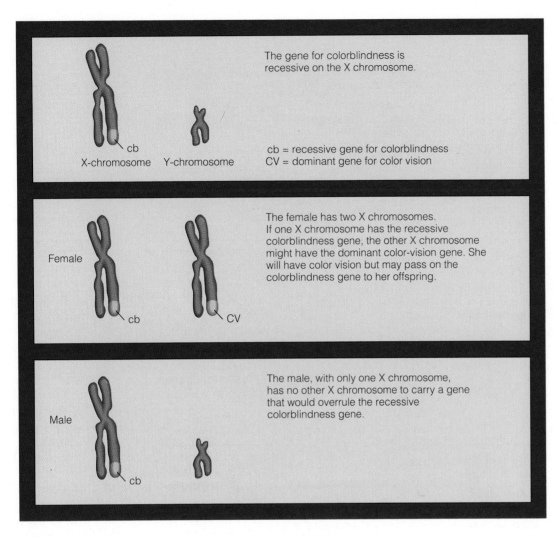

The gene for colorblindness is recessive on the X chromosome.

cb   Y-chromosome
X-chromosome

cb = recessive gene for colorblindness
CV = dominant gene for color vision

Female

The female has two X chromosomes. If one X chromosome has the recessive colorblindness gene, the other X chromosome might have the dominant color-vision gene. She will have color vision but may pass on the colorblindness gene to her offspring.

cb   CV

Male

The male, with only one X chromosome, has no other X chromosome to carry a gene that would overrule the recessive colorblindness gene.

cb

FIGURE 3.6
Why males are more likely than females to be colorblind.

ments. Any similarities between them suggest a genetic influence (Lykken, 1982), if those similarities are greater than those that might emerge by accident between two people the same age.

Adopted Children

Any strong resemblance between adopted children and their biological parents suggests a genetic influence. For example, biological children of alcohol-abusing or schizophrenic parents have an increased chance of developing alcoholism or schizophrenia themselves (Cloninger, Bohman, & Sigvardsson, 1981; Kety, 1983; Vaillant & Milofsky, 1982).

How Genes Affect Behavior

The kinds of evidence described above have demonstrated genetic contributions to some behaviors for which we might not have expected such an influence. For example, adopted children somewhat resemble their biological parents in how much time they spend watching television (Plomin, Corley, DeFries, & Fulker, 1990) and identical twins reared apart resemble each other in how deeply they care about religion (Waller, Kojetin, Bouchard, Lykken, & Tellegen, 1990). These are not enormous tendencies, but even a moderate tendency is surprising. We find it hard to imagine a "gene for watching television" or a "gene for religious devotion."

Indeed, we need not assume that the genes are exerting direct effects on television watching or religious activity. Even with such traits as eye color, the gene does not *directly* control the color; it acts by facilitating or impeding a chemical reaction somewhere in the body. Genes

Identical twins

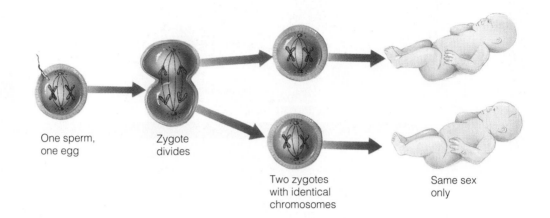

One sperm,
one egg

Zygote
divides

Two zygotes
with identical
chromosomes

Same sex
only

Fraternal twins

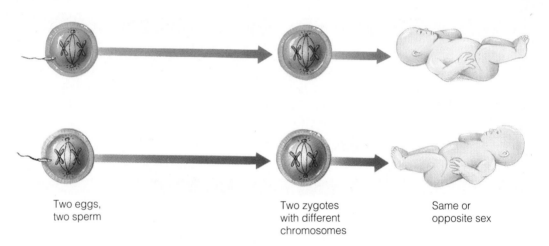

Two eggs,
two sperm

Two zygotes
with different
chromosomes

Same or
opposite sex

FIGURE 3.7
Identical (monozygotic) twins develop from the same fertilized egg. Fraternal (dizygotic) twins grow from two eggs fertilized by two different sperm.

may influence behavior by altering chemical reactions either in the brain or in other organs.

Let us consider one example: Most Asian adults, including Americans of Asian ancestry, drink little or no milk and seldom if ever eat dairy products. Within other ethnic groups, some adults enjoy consuming large amounts of dairy products, while others consume only a little. The differences in dairy consumption are known to be largely under genetic control, but we need not look for genetic differences in the taste buds or in some motivational area of the

brain. Genes alter this food preference by controlling the body's ability to digest *lactose,* the sugar in milk (Figure 3.8).

Almost all infants of all ethnic groups can digest lactose. As they grow older, most Asian children and a large number of non-Asian children lose the ability to digest lactose. (They lose that ability even if they drink milk frequently.) They can still consume a little milk, cheese, or ice cream, but if they consume very much, they become nauseated (Flatz, 1987; Rozin & Pelchat, 1988). Figure 3.9 shows how the ability to

FIGURE 3.8

Genes don't control behavior directly but through many indirect routes. They control chemical reactions in the body, which in turn influence behavior.

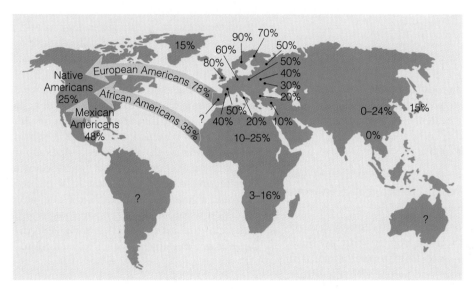

FIGURE 3.9

Adult humans vary in their ability to digest lactose, the main sugar in milk and other dairy products. In the Asian countries and other locations where most adults cannot digest lactose, cooks seldom if ever use dairy products. (Based on Flatz, 1987, and Rozin & Pelchat, 1988.)

digest dairy products varies from one part of the world to another.

The overall point is that a gene can affect a behavior—in this case, a food preference—by altering chemical reactions outside the brain itself. Similarly, genes affect the probability of alcohol abuse partly by their effects on how the liver metabolizes alcohol (Harada, Agarwal, Goedde, Tagaki, & Ishikawa, 1982; Helzer et al., 1990; Reed, 1985). At this point we have no idea how some gene alters television watching or religious activity, but we should be alert to the possibility of indirect or roundabout influences.

■ CONCEPT CHECK

4. *Why do Asian cooks almost never use cheese or milk? In what other parts of the world would you expect cooks to avoid dairy products? (Check your answers on page 85.)*

How Heredity Interacts with Environment

Genes affect chemical reactions, and chemical reactions in turn depend on a great variety of environmental influences including temperature, hormones, diet, and all the other chemical reactions going on in the body. Because the ultimate effects of a gene depend on the environment, we distinguish between the genotype and the phenotype. The **genotype** is the entire set of genes within an individual; the **phenotype** is the actual appearance of that individual, reflecting the way the genes have been expressed. For example, your genotype may contain only genes for straight hair, but, depending on your health, your diet, and your grooming habits, you may have straight hair, curly hair, or no hair at all.

In some cases, altering the environment counteracts the usual effects of a gene. For example, **phenylketonuria (PKU)** is an inherited disorder in which a person lacks the chemical reactions that break down a substance called *phenylalanine,* a common constituent of the diet, into other chemicals. On an ordinary diet, the affected person accumulates phenylalanine in the brain and becomes mentally retarded. However, an affected person who stays on a diet low in phenylalanine for at least the first 12 to 15 years of life does not become mentally retarded.

The effect of diet on PKU is worth remembering. Occasionally you may hear someone say that "because such-and-so condition is under genetic control, we cannot do anything to change it." The example of PKU shows that this conclusion is incorrect.

EVOLUTION

Our genes are a product of evolution. Evolution is more than a well-established theory supported by fossil evidence; it is a logical necessity based on what we know about genetics. The argument goes as follows:

1. The genes an organism inherits from its parents largely control its characteristics. In short, like begets like.

2. On occasion, genetic variations will cause an organism to differ from its parents. Such variations may arise from recombinations of genes (some from one parent and some from the other) or from **mutations** (random changes in the structure of genes). Recombinations and mutations alter the appearance or activity of the organism. Most mutations are disadvantageous, although an occasional mutation will give an individual an advantage in coping with some situation.

3. If individuals with a certain gene or gene combination reproduce more successfully than others do, the genes that confer an advantage will spread. Over many generations, the frequency of those genes will increase while the frequency of others will decrease. Such changes in the gene frequencies of a species constitute **evolution.** Because we know that mutations sometimes occur in genes and that an occasional mutation may lead to greater success in reproduction, we can logically deduce that evolution *must* occur.

Animal and plant breeders discovered a long time ago that they could develop new strains through **artificial selection,** or selective breeding. By purposefully breeding only those animals with certain traits, breeders developed cocker spaniels, thoroughbred race horses, and chickens that lay enormous numbers of eggs. Charles Darwin's theory of evolution stated that **natural selection** can accomplish the same thing as selective breeding. If, in nature, individuals with certain genetically controlled characteristics reproduce more successfully than others do, then the species will come to resemble those individuals more and more as time passes.

Some people assume, mistakenly, that evolution means "the survival of the fittest." But what really matters in evolution is not survival but *reproduction* (Figure 3.10). Someone who lives to the age of 100 without having a child has failed to spread his or her genes. By contrast, a person who has five healthy children before dying at age 30 is a big success, evolutionarily speaking.

A gene that increases a person's chance of surviving long enough to reproduce will be favored over a gene that causes death in infancy. But genes that have no influence on the individual's survival may also be favored. For example, a gene that makes an individual more successful at attracting mates would certainly be favored, as would a gene that makes an individual more successful at protecting his or her offspring or other close relatives. Selection for a gene that benefits one's relatives is called **kin selection.**

■ CONCEPT CHECK

5. Infertile worker bees are sisters of the queen bee, which lays all the eggs. In comparison with species in which all individuals are fertile, would you expect worker bees to be more likely or less likely to risk their lives to defend their sister? Would you expect a queen bee to be more or less likely than a worker bee to risk her life? (Check your answers on page 85.)

Occasionally people say something like "every generation our little toes get smaller and smaller because we don't use them," or "through evolution we will gradually get rid of the human appendix because we don't need it." Such statements reflect a misunderstanding about evolution. We do not add, change, or lose genes because of the way we use some part of the body. A lack of need for an appendix has no effect on the genes controlling the appendix. The only way people could evolve, say, a reduction of the size of the little toe would be if people with genes for "smaller than average little toe" had some reproductive advantage over other people.

ETHOLOGY AND COMPARATIVE PSYCHOLOGY

Psychologists learn about the genetics of behavior and the evolution of behavior largely through studies of animals. The study of animal behavior grew out of two separate pursuits: ethology and comparative psychology. **Ethology** is the branch of biology that studies animal behavior under natural or nearly natural conditions. Ethologists emphasize unlearned or **species-specific behaviors**—behaviors that are widespread in one animal species but not others. Species-specific behaviors are sometimes described as *instinctive,* although many investigators shun that term. (Many people use the term *instinct* as if it constituted an explanation. For example, they would say a mother squirrel takes care of her young because of her "maternal instinct." But simply naming what is happening is hardly an explanation.)

Comparative psychology is the branch of psychology that compares the behaviors of various animal species. A comparative psychologist might study which species are best at localizing sounds, how species differ in their means of finding food, or why some species solve a particular problem faster than other species do. Both ethologists and comparative psychologists study how behavioral capacities evolve. They distinguish between the proximate causes and the ultimate causes of a behavior. The **proximate causes** are the stimuli that prompt the behavior. (The root *prox-* means "near," as in the word *approximate.*) The **ultimate causes** are the reasons for which the behavioral tendency evolved, the functions it serves. For example, during the mating season, a male stickleback fish will attack anything with a red underside—even a piece of wood painted red underneath (Figure 3.11). The *proximate* cause of the attack behavior is the red underside. The *ultimate* cause is the fact that a male stickleback can increase his chance of reproducing if he drives other males out of his territory. (Adult male sticklebacks have a red belly during the mating season.)

Evolution adapts the behavior of an animal, as well as its anatomy, to its way of life. Consider the mating behavior of the kittiwake, a member of the gull family (Tinbergen, 1958). Kittiwakes, unlike other gulls, nest on narrow ledges of steep cliffs (Figure 3.12). Because there are just so many suitable ledges, kittiwakes fight ferociously to claim a territory. By contrast, her-

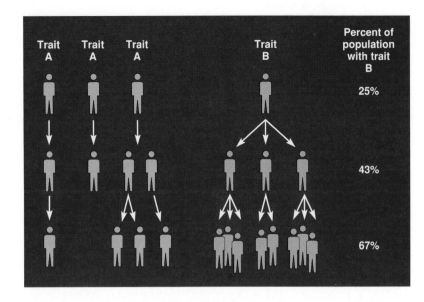

FIGURE 3.10
What's important in evolution is reproduction, not survival. Here, the population starts with three people carrying trait A and one with trait B. The person with B and his or her descendants produce more children, on the average, than people with A do. Consequently, the genes controlling trait B increase in prevalence from one generation to the next.

FIGURE 3.11
To ensure successful reproduction, male sticklebacks defend their territory against intruders and will even attack a model if the bottom of the model is painted red (the color of the male fish's belly during the mating season).

FIGURE 3.12
The nesting behavior of kittiwakes is superbly adapted for their survival. For example, the parents build a mud barrier on the edge of the nest, and the young remain motionless until they are able to fly.

ring gulls, which nest on the ground, rarely fight over territory, because for them one nesting site is about as good as any other. Kittiwakes use mud to build a hard nest with a barrier to prevent their eggs from rolling off the ledge. Herring gulls make no such effort. When kittiwake chicks hatch, they remain virtually motionless until they are old enough to fly. The ultimate cause of this behavior is clear: A chick that takes even a step or two may fall off the ledge. Herring gull chicks, in contrast, begin to wander out of their nest long before they can fly.

Each of these kittiwake behaviors—fighting over territory, building secure nests, and remaining motionless—is well adapted to life on a narrow ledge. But have these behaviors been built into the animal by evolution, or are they learned anew by each individual? In the rare cases when kittiwakes nest on the ground, the chicks remain motionless anyway, even though they are in no danger of falling. When the egg of a gull species that does not nest on cliff ledges is placed in a kittiwake's nest, the kittiwakes accept the foreign egg and care for the chick after it hatches. But the chick invariably takes a few steps and falls to its death. Evidently some behavioral differences are a product of the evolution of each species rather than anything the individual learns.

SOCIOBIOLOGY

Sociobiology is a field that tries to relate the social behaviors of a species to its biology, particularly to its evolutionary history. According to sociobiologists, an animal interacts with others

of its species in a particular way because doing so provides a survival or reproductive advantage. That is, certain genes increase the probability that the animal will successfully mate and pass on those same genes to the next generation.

Animal Examples of Sociobiological Explanations

Sociobiologists try to understand how various social behaviors may have helped animals to survive and reproduce. Here are three examples (Wilson, 1975):

■ The largest males of the South American leaf fish build a nest and then try to attract females to deposit their eggs in it. Many of the smaller males, especially after being defeated in fights with larger males, change their appearance and behavior to resemble females. They enter the nests of the larger males and deposit their sperm, much as a female would deposit eggs. What is the reason for this unusual behavior? The smaller males are unable to defend a territory and attract females on their own. If they can fool a larger male into letting them deposit their sperm, however, some of those sperm might fertilize eggs when a female comes by.

■ Lions generally live in groups made up of one adult male, several adult females, and their young. If a new male succeeds in driving off the old male, he is likely to kill all the young. Why? Female lions are not sexually receptive so long as they are nursing their young. By killing the young, the new male brings the females into sexual receptivity and increases the likelihood of spreading his genes.

■ Starlings in flight flock tightly together when a hawk appears. Why? A hawk can descend on a lone starling at enormous speed and seize it with its talons. If a hawk descends on a dense flock, however, it may miss its prey and be jostled by the other birds, possibly sustaining a serious injury. The more tightly packed the flock, the less likely the hawk will attack.

Speculations on Human Sociobiology

Human social behavior also is partly the product of our evolutionary history. In principle that result is a logical necessity, yet citing precise examples is difficult because we are less certain about which human behaviors are strongly influenced by our genes and which ones are learned from our culture. Consider a couple of speculative, controversial examples:

- People will work very hard to help one another, sometimes even risking their own lives to help other people. Doing something to help others with no direct benefit to oneself is called **altruistic behavior** (Figure 3.13). Similarly, other species engage in some behaviors that appear to be altruistic; for example, a goose that sees a hawk overhead utters an alarm call that warns other geese. One explanation for altruistic behavior is that kin selection has favored certain genes that somehow promote altruistic behaviors (Trivers, 1972). That is, individuals that help their offspring and other relatives tend to spread their genes, simply because those relatives have many of the same genes as the altruistic individual. In principle, this explanation makes sense. In practice, we have trouble knowing whether human altruistic behavior depends on genes or on the way we rear children.

- Men are more likely than women are to seek multiple sexual partners. A sociobiological interpretation is that a man who impregnates several women is spreading his genes far and wide. A woman gains no such advantage in taking multiple sexual partners. Moreover, if she were to do so, she might have trouble getting any one of them to help her rear her children. Therefore, the sociobiologists say, we may have evolved some sex-limited genes that increase males' interest in multiple partners or decrease females' interest. Perhaps. The problem is that this explanation is difficult to test. Human cultures have traditionally encouraged, or at least tolerated, multiple sexual partners for men, while they have held a very different attitude for women. What sociobiologists consider evidence for a biological influence may appear to someone else to support a cultural explanation. (As we shall see in Chapter 11, sexual customs vary significantly from one culture to another.)

What then is the relationship between human behavior and human biology? Like other animals, we are the product of our evolutionary history. We must spend effort eating, drinking, regulating our body temperature, and dealing with other biological functions. We show interest in others of our species. We react with fear to loud noises and other intense stimuli, even before we have learned what those stimuli mean. Our capacities for behavior are a product of our evolutionary history. But the actual behaviors are also a product of our experiences, including what we learn from our culture.

FIGURE 3.13

A Tibetan boy gives money to an impoverished monk. Why do people and some other species sometimes engage in behaviors to help others? One possibility (kin selection) is that natural selection has favored behaviors that help our relatives, and we sometimes extend those behaviors to nonrelatives. Especially with humans, however, we can also imagine nongenetic explanations.

SUMMARY

- *Genes.* Genes, which are segments of chromosomes, control heredity. Because chromosomes come in pairs, every person has two of each gene, one received from the father and one from the mother. (page 73)

- *Dominant and recessive genes.* A dominant gene exerts its effects even in people who have only one dominant gene. People must have two of a recessive gene, one on each chromosome, in order to show its effects. (page 74)

- *Sex-linked and sex-limited genes.* Genes on the X chromosome are sex linked. A sex-linked recessive gene will show its effects more frequently in males than in females. A sex-limited gene may be present in both sexes, but it exerts its effects more strongly in one than in the other. (page 76)

- *Evidence for genetic influences.* Most important human behaviors depend on many genes. We determine the contribution of genes by seeing whether monozygotic twins resemble each other more than dizygotic twins do, by comparing monozygotic twins reared in separate environments, and by examining how adopted children resemble their biological parents and their adoptive parents. (page 76)

■ *How genes affect behavior.* Genes can affect behavior indirectly, such as by altering digestion, and not just by altering the brain itself. (page 77)

■ *Influence of the environment on gene expression.* The effect of a gene depends on the total environment, including the chemistry of the body. Sometimes a change in diet can alter the effect of a gene. (page 79)

■ *Evolution.* Evolution by natural selection is a logical necessity, given the principles of heredity and the fact that individuals with certain genes leave more offspring than do individuals with other genes. (page 80)

■ *Study of animal behavior.* Ethologists and comparative psychologists study animal behavior and try to understand how it evolved. (page 81)

■ *Sociobiology.* Sociobiologists try to explain social behaviors in terms of the survival and reproductive advantages of those behaviors. Human social behaviors are difficult to interpret in those terms, however, because of the strong influence of tradition and culture. (page 82)

SUGGESTIONS FOR FURTHER READING

Crawford, C. B. (1989). The theory of evolution: Of what value to psychology? *Journal of Comparative Psychology, 103,* 4–22. Includes some thought-provoking suggestions about the evolution of human behavior.

Lorenz, K. (1949). *King Solomon's ring.* New York: Crowell. Delightful observations on animal behavior.

Tinbergen, N. (1958). *Curious naturalists.* New York: Basic Books. One of the best books for stimulating interest in animal behavior.

TERMS

Alzheimer's disease a disease of old age marked by gradual damage to the brain leading to the gradual loss of memory and other abilities (page 73)

chromosome a strand of hereditary material found in the nucleus of a cell (page 73)

gene a segment of a chromosome that controls chemical reactions that ultimately direct the development of the organism (page 73)

homozygous having the same gene on both members of a pair of chromosomes (page 74)

heterozygous having different genes on a pair of chromosomes (page 74)

dominant gene a gene that will exert its effects on development even in a person who is heterozygous for that gene (page 74)

recessive gene a gene that will affect development only in a person who is homozygous for that gene (page 74)

sex chromosomes the chromosomes that determine whether an individual will develop as a female or as a male (page 76)

X chromosome a sex chromosome of which females have two per cell and males have one (page 76)

Y chromosome a sex chromosome of which males have one per cell and females have none (page 76)

sex-linked gene a gene situated on the X chromosome (page 76)

sex-limited gene a gene that affects one sex only or affects one sex more strongly than the other, even though both sexes have the gene (page 76)

monozygotic twins (literally, one-egg twins) identical twins who develop from the same fertilized egg (page 76)

dizygotic twins (literally, two-egg twins) fraternal twins who develop from two eggs fertilized by two different sperm. Dizygotic twins are no more closely related than are any other children born to the same parents. (page 76)

genotype the entire set of genes within an individual (page 79)

phenotype the actual appearance of the individual, reflecting the way the genes have been expressed (page 79)

phenylketonuria (PKU) an inherited disorder in which a person lacks the chemical reactions that break down a substance called phenylalanine, a common constituent of the diet, into other chemicals; unless the diet is carefully controlled, the affected person becomes mentally retarded (page 79)

mutation a random change in the structure of a gene (page 80)

evolution changes in the gene frequencies of a species (page 80)

artificial selection the purposeful breeding, by humans, of animals with certain traits; also known as selective breeding (page 80)

natural selection the tendency, in nature, of individuals with certain genetically controlled characteristics to reproduce more successfully than others do; eventually the species will come to resemble those individuals more and more (page 80)

kin selection selection for a gene that benefits one's relatives (page 80)

ethology the branch of biology that studies animal behavior under natural or nearly natural conditions (page 81)

species-specific behavior a particular behavior that is widespread in one animal species but not in others (page 81)

comparative psychology the branch of psychology that compares the behaviors of various animal species (page 81)

proximate cause stimulus that prompts a behavior (page 81)

ultimate cause reason for which a behavioral tendency evolved, the function it serves (page 81)

sociobiology a field that tries to relate the social behaviors of a species to its biology, particularly to its evolutionary history (page 82)

altruistic behavior behavior that benefits others without directly benefiting the individual showing the behavior (page 83)

ANSWERS TO CONCEPT CHECKS

1. It is impossible to say whether you are homozygous or heterozygous for the tongue-curling gene. Because that gene is a dominant gene, it produces the same effects in both the homozygous and the heterozygous conditions. If you cannot taste PTC, however, you must be homozygous for the nontasting gene. (page 75)

2. Because both of the parents must be homozygous for the inability to taste PTC, all their children will be unable to taste it also. Because both parents may be heterozygous for the tongue-curling gene, we cannot predict whether or not some of their children will be noncurlers. (page 75)

3. The woman will pass a dominant gene for normal color vision to all the children, so they will all have normal color vision. The man will pass a gene for deficient color vision on his X chromosome; the daughters will be carriers for color blindness. (page 76)

4. Oriental cooks almost never use cheese or milk because most Oriental adults cannot digest lactose, the primary sugar in dairy products. We also should expect to find little use of dairy products in those parts of Africa and southeastern Europe where few people can digest much lactose. (page 79)

5. Because the infertile worker bees cannot reproduce, the only way they can pass on their genes is by helping the queen bee. Consequently, they will sacrifice their own lives to defend the queen. They will also risk their lives to defend other workers in the hive, because these workers also try to defend the queen. The queen, however, will do little to defend a worker, because doing so would not increase her probability of reproducing. (page 80)

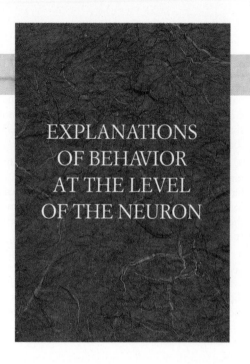

EXPLANATIONS OF BEHAVIOR AT THE LEVEL OF THE NEURON

Is the brain the mind?

Can we explain our experiences and our behavior in terms of the actions of single cells in the nervous system?

Your brain, which controls everything you do, is composed of cells. Does this mean that every one of your experiences—every sight, every sound, every thought—represents the activity of cells in your brain?

A highly productive strategy in science is **reductionism**—the attempt to explain complex phenomena by reducing them to combinations of simpler components. Biologists explain breathing, blood circulation, and metabolism in terms of chemical reactions and physical forces. Chemists explain chemical reactions in terms of the properties of the 92 naturally occurring elements. Physicists explain the structure of the atom and the interactions among atoms in terms of a few fundamental forces.

Does reductionism apply to psychology? Can we explain human behavior and experience in terms of chemical and electrical events in the brain? Here we deal with attempts to answer those questions.

THE CELLS OF THE NERVOUS SYSTEM

You experience your "self" as a single entity that senses, thinks, and remembers. And yet neuroscientists find that the nervous system responsible for your experience consists of an enormous number of separate cells. The brain processes information in **neurons** (NOO-rons), or nerve cells. Many of the neurons in the human nervous system are extremely small; the best current estimate is that the nervous system contains about 100 billion neurons (Williams & Herrup, 1988), as shown in Figure 3.14. The nervous system also contains another kind of cells called **glia** (GLEE-uh), which support the neurons in many ways without actually transmitting information themselves. The glia are about one tenth the size of neurons but about 10 times more numerous. Until shortly after the year 1900, many researchers thought it likely that all the neurons physically merged, that the tip of each neuron actually joined the next neuron. We now know that it does not; each neuron remains separate. How do so many separate neurons and glia combine forces to produce the single stream of experiences that is "you"?

The secret is communication. Each neuron receives information and transmits it to other cells by conducting electrochemical impulses. Sensory neurons carry information from the sense organs to the central nervous system; neurons of the central nervous system process that sensory information and compare it to past information; motor neurons convey commands to the muscles and glands. Within the central nervous system, each neuron sends information to many others, which send information to still others; eventually some of those neurons may send information back to the first one. Out of all this rapid exchange of information, about 100 billion neurons produce a single functioning system.

To understand the nervous system, we must understand the properties of both the individual neurons and the connections among them. Neurons have a variety of shapes, depending on whether they receive information from a few sources or from many and whether they send impulses over a short distance or over a long distance (Figure 3.15).

A neuron consists of three parts—a cell body, dendrites, and an axon (Figure 3.16). The **cell body** contains the nucleus of the cell. The **dendrites** (from a Greek word meaning "tree") are widely branching structures, usually short; they receive transmissions from other neurons. The **axon** is a single, long, thin, straight fiber with branches near its tip. Some vertebrate axons are covered with *myelin,* an insulating sheath that speeds up the transmission of impulses along an axon. As a rule, an axon transmits information to other cells, and the dendrites or cell body of each other cell receives that information. That information can be either excitatory or inhibitory; that is, it can increase or decrease the probability that the next cell will send a message of its own.

The structure of the brain, unlike the structure of a computer, is not fixed throughout its life. Although the human brain gains no additional neurons after early infancy, the existing neurons frequently grow new branches of their axons and dendrites and retract other branches (Purves & Hadley, 1985), as shown in Figure 3.17. For example, an enriched social environment leads to increased branching of the dendrites. Rats kept in large cages with other rats and with a variety of objects to explore develop a wider pattern of dendritic branching than do rats kept in individual cages (Camel, Withers, & Greenough, 1986; Greenough, 1975). The increased branching enables each dendrite to integrate information from a greater number of sources. Animals with increased dendritic branching tend to perform better on a variety of learning and memory tasks.

In humans, the dendritic branching changes with advancing age. Although the amount and type of change differ from person to person, nearly all people gradually lose some neurons as they grow older. In people who remain healthy and alert, the surviving neurons *increase* their branching pattern and tend to compensate for the neurons that have been lost. Each neuron that survives makes contact with so many other neurons that the total number of connections in the brain remains almost as high as it was earlier in life. In people who become senile, however, the surviving neurons fail to increase their branching; the branching may even decrease. As a result, the number of connections in the brain decreases and the capacity to process information declines (Buell & Coleman, 1981). (We do not know *why* neurons increase their branching pattern in some aging people and not in others.)

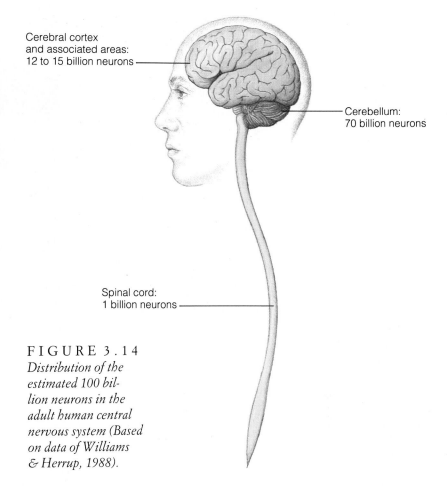

Cerebral cortex and associated areas: 12 to 15 billion neurons

Cerebellum: 70 billion neurons

Spinal cord: 1 billion neurons

FIGURE 3.14
Distribution of the estimated 100 billion neurons in the adult human central nervous system (Based on data of Williams & Herrup, 1988).

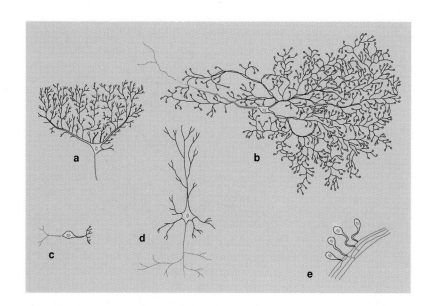

FIGURE 3.15
Neurons vary enormously in their shapes. In each case the neuron consists of its cell body and all the branched attachments, called axons and dendrites. The neurons in (a) and (b) receive input from many sources, the neuron in (c) from only a few sources, and the neuron in (d) from an intermediate number of sources. The neurons in (e) are sensory neurons, which carry messages from sensory receptors to the brain or spinal cord. The axons are coded blue for easy identification. (Part b courtesy of Richard Coss.)

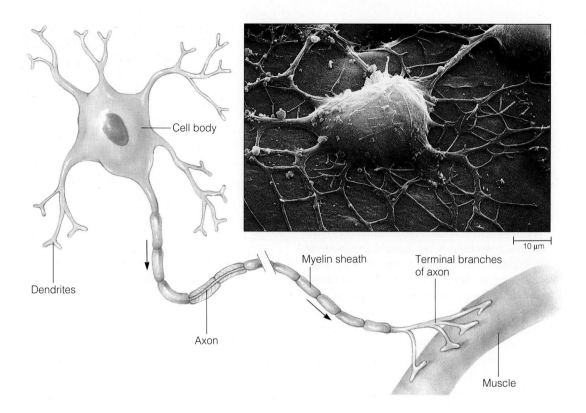

FIGURE 3.16
The generalized structure of a motor neuron shows the dendrites, the branching structures that receive transmissions from other neurons; and the axon, a single, long, thin, straight fiber with branches near its tip. Axons, which range in length from 1 millimeter to more than a meter, carry information toward other cells. (inset) A photomicrograph of a neuron.

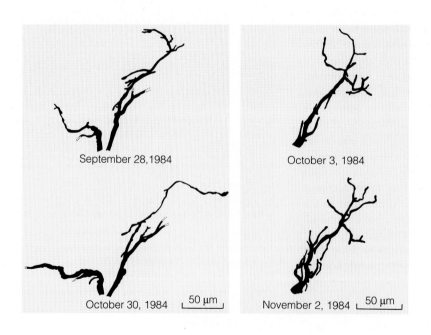

September 28, 1984

October 3, 1984

October 30, 1984   50 µm

November 2, 1984   50 µm

FIGURE 3.17
Dendrites, such as these from rat brains, gradually change their structures. Between one viewing and a second viewing a month later, some branches elongate and others contract. (From Purves & Hadley, 1985.)

THE ACTION POTENTIAL

An axon can transmit information over a great distance. For example, sensory neurons carry information all the way from your toes or fingers to your spinal cord. If the information grew weaker and weaker as it traveled along an axon, a touch on your fingers might feel very faint; a touch on your shoulder would feel much more intense, because it did not have to travel so far to reach your spinal cord.

Axons convey information by a special process called an *action potential,* which maintains the impulse at a constant strength, no matter how far it has to travel. Ordinarily, there is an electrical charge across the membrane (or covering) of an axon. The **action potential** is a sudden decrease or reversal in that charge, produced by the movement of sodium ions across the membrane (Figure 3.18). After sodium ions cross at one point, the electrical excitation opens channels at the next point along the axon, enabling sodium ions to cross there, as shown in Figure 3.19b. This process repeats at one point after another along the axon; in this manner, the action potential remains equally strong all the way to the end of the axon.

The chemical mechanism of the action potential is well understood. For illustration, consider the axon of a sensory neuron in your finger. When the axon is at rest, positively charged sodium ions are more concentrated outside the axon than inside it. As a result, the axon's interior has a negative electrical potential with respect to its exterior. If someone pinches your finger, that stimulus opens small channels in the axon's membrane, enabling sodium ions to enter (Figure 3.19a), bringing with them their positive electrical charge. This flow of positive charge into the relatively negative interior of the axon constitutes the action potential. Just after the sodium ions enter the membrane, potassium ions leave, thereby restoring the original charge across the membrane (Figure 3.19b).

Because the transmission of information along an axon depends on the flow of sodium ions across its membrane, anything that prevents the opening and closing of sodium gates will silence the neuron. For example, scorpion venom paralyzes neurons by keeping their sodium gates permanently open (Pappone & Cahalan, 1987; Strichartz, Rando, & Wang, 1987). Anesthetic drugs (such as Novocaine) si-

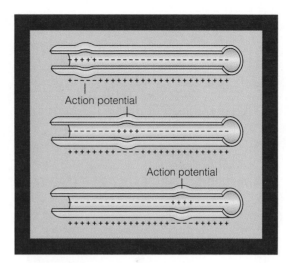

FIGURE 3.18
Ion movements conduct an action potential along an axon. At each point along the membrane, sodium ions enter the axon and alter the distribution of positive and negative charges. As one point along the membrane returns to its original state, the action potential flows to the next point.

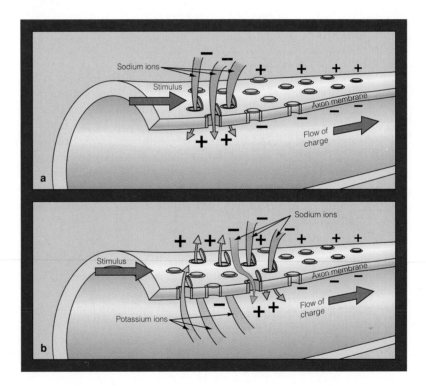

FIGURE 3.19
(a) During an action potential, sodium gates in the neuron membrane open, and sodium ions enter the axon, bringing a positive charge with them. (b) After an action potential occurs at one point along the axon, the sodium gates close at that point and open at the next point along the axon. When the sodium gates close, potassium gates open, and potassium ions flow out of the axon, carrying a positive charge with them. (Modified from Starr & Taggart, 1989.)

FIGURE 3.20
A synapse, magnified thousands of times in an electron micrograph, includes small round structures in the middle cell called synaptic vesicles, which store neurotransmitter molecules. The thick, dark area at the bottom of the cell is the synapse.

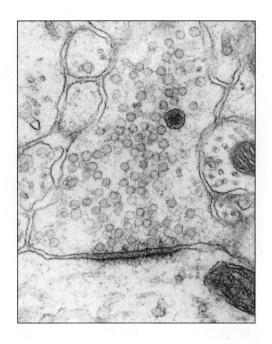

lence neurons by clogging the sodium gates (van Dyke & Byck, 1982). When your dentist drills a tooth, the neurons in your tooth send out the message "Pain! Pain! Pain!" But that message does not get through to the brain, because a shot of Novocaine has prevented the sensory axons from sending their message.

■ CONCEPT CHECKS

6. *What do you suppose happens to the sodium ions after they enter the axon or to the potassium ions after they leave? What can you infer must be true in order for the system to continue to work?*

7. *If you stub your toe, do you feel it immediately or is there a delay before you feel it? Why? (Check your answers on page 96.)*

SYNAPSES: THE JUNCTIONS BETWEEN NEURONS

Ultimately, each neuron must communicate with other neurons. Communication between one neuron and the next follows a different process from the transmission along an axon. At a **synapse** (SIN-aps), the specialized junction between one neuron and another (Figure 3.20), one neuron releases a chemical that either excites or inhibits the next neuron. The following paragraph relates the process.

A typical axon has several branches; each branch ends with a little bulge called a *presynaptic ending,* or a **terminal button** (Figure 3.21).

When an action potential reaches the terminal button, it causes the release of molecules of a **neurotransmitter,** a chemical that has been stored in packets called *synaptic vesicles* and elsewhere in the interior of the terminal button (Figure 3.21). Different neurons use different chemicals as their neurotransmitters, but each neuron uses the same chemical (or the same combination of two or three chemicals) at all times and at all branches of its axon (Eccles, 1986). The neurotransmitter molecules then diffuse across a narrow gap called a *synaptic cleft* to the neuron on the receiving end of the synapse, the **postsynaptic neuron.** There the neurotransmitter molecules attach to receptors, which may be located on the neuron's dendrites or cell body or (for special purposes) on the tip of its axon. The neural communication process is summarized in Figure 3.22.

Depending on the chemical used as a neurotransmitter and on the type of receptor, the result may be either excitation or inhibition of the neuron. The postsynaptic neuron may be receiving nearly simultaneous excitation and inhibition from a great many other neurons. It produces an action potential of its own if the total amount of excitation outweighs the total amount of inhibition. If the inhibitory signals outweigh the excitatory signals, then the neuron is temporarily silent. This process resembles a decision: When you are trying to decide whether to do something, you weigh all the pros and cons and act if the pros outweigh the cons.

What would happen if the excitation and inhibition were equal, or if for a time the postsynaptic neuron received no excitation or inhibition at all? The outcome would vary. A few neurons would be silent; most would produce action potentials at a moderate rate. *Spontaneous firing* refers to the action potentials that occur under such conditions.

Note that inhibition is not just the absence of excitation; it is an active braking process. For example, when a pinch on your foot causes you to raise it, contracting one set of muscles, inhibitory synapses in your spinal cord block activity in the opposing set of muscles, those that extend your leg. Those inhibitory synapses prevent your spinal cord from sending messages to raise your leg and extend it at the same time.

■ CONCEPT CHECKS

8. *As mentioned earlier, under some conditions the axons and dendrites of a neuron increase their branching. How will that affect the number of synapses?*

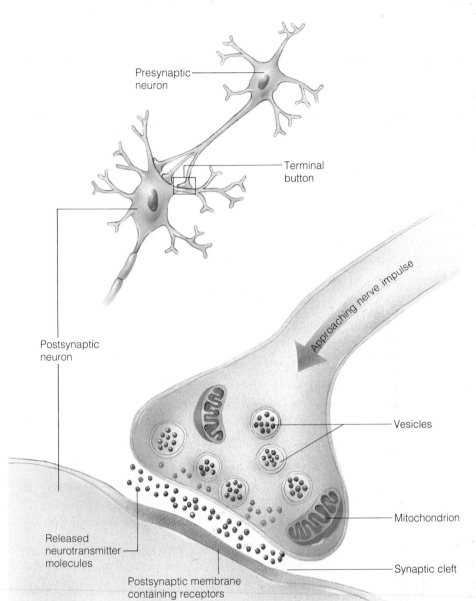

FIGURE 3.21
The synapse is the junction of the presynaptic (message-sending) cell and the postsynaptic (message-receiving) cell. At the end of the presynaptic axon is the terminal button, which contains many molecules of the neurotransmitter, ready for release.

Presynaptic neuron

Terminal button

Approaching nerve impulse

Vesicles

Mitochondrion

Postsynaptic neuron

Released neurotransmitter molecules

Synaptic cleft

Postsynaptic membrane containing receptors

9. *Norepinephrine is a neurotransmitter that inhibits postsynaptic neurons. If a drug were injected that prevents norepinephrine from attaching to its receptors, what would happen to the postsynaptic neuron?*
(Check your answers on page 96.)

Neurons Communicate by Releasing Chemicals

WHAT'S THE EVIDENCE?

I have just finished telling you that neurons communicate by releasing chemicals at synapses. Perhaps you are perfectly content to take my word for it and go on with something else. Still, it is good to pause and contemplate the kinds of evidence responsible for an important conclusion like this one. After all, one could certainly imagine other means by which neurons might communicate, such as by electrical charges or mechanical stimulation.

Today, neuroscientists have a wealth of evidence that neurons release chemicals at synapses. They can work with radioactively labeled chemicals that enable investigators to trace where chemicals go and what happens when they get there; they also can inject purified chemicals at a synapse and use extremely fine electrodes to measure the response of the postsynaptic neuron. But scientists have known since the 1920s that neurons communicate by releasing chemicals; at that time they had none of the fancy equipment they have today. Otto Loewi found evidence of chemical transmission by a very simple, clever experiment, as he later described in his autobiography (Loewi, 1960).

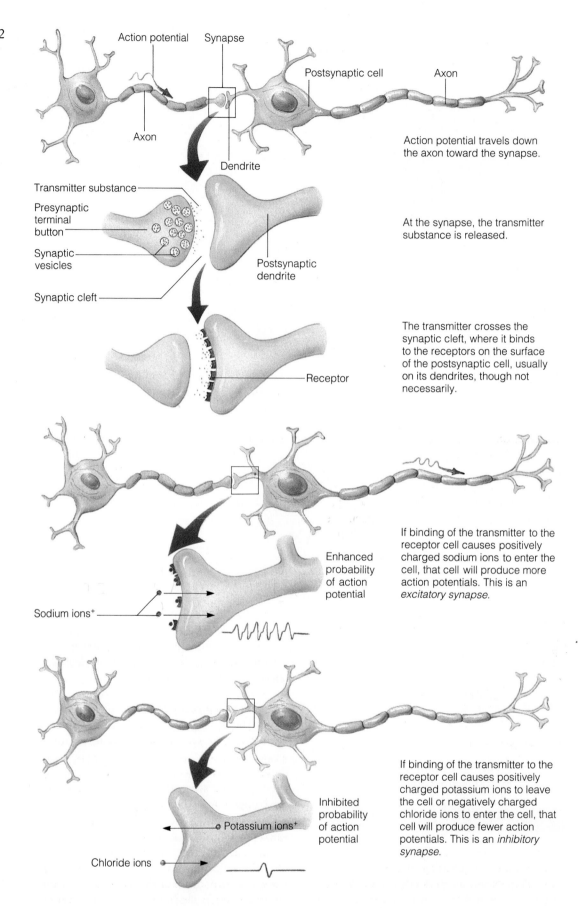

FIGURE 3.22
The complex process of neural communication actually takes only 1 to 2 milliseconds.

Action potential   Synapse
Axon   Postsynaptic cell   Axon
Dendrite

Action potential travels down the axon toward the synapse.

Transmitter substance
Presynaptic terminal button
Synaptic vesicles
Synaptic cleft
Postsynaptic dendrite

At the synapse, the transmitter substance is released.

Receptor

The transmitter crosses the synaptic cleft, where it binds to the receptors on the surface of the postsynaptic cell, usually on its dendrites, though not necessarily.

Enhanced probability of action potential
Sodium ions+

If binding of the transmitter to the receptor cell causes positively charged sodium ions to enter the cell, that cell will produce more action potentials. This is an *excitatory synapse*.

Inhibited probability of action potential
Potassium ions+
Chloride ions

If binding of the transmitter to the receptor cell causes positively charged potassium ions to leave the cell or negatively charged chloride ions to enter the cell, that cell will produce fewer action potentials. This is an *inhibitory synapse*.

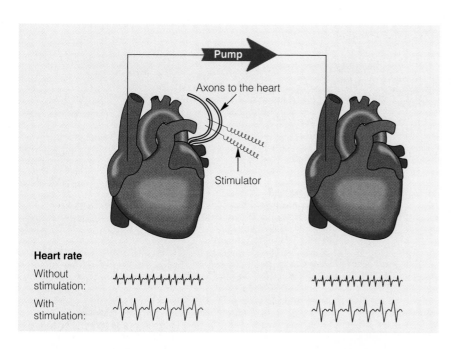

FIGURE 3.23
Otto Loewi demonstrated that axons release chemicals that can affect other cells. Using a frog, he electrically stimulated a set of axons known to decrease the heart rate. Then he collected some fluid from around that heart and transferred it to the surface of another frog's heart. When that heart slowed its beat, Loewi concluded that the axons of the first heart must have released a chemical that slows the heart rate.

Hypothesis If a neuron releases chemicals, an investigator should be able to collect some of those chemicals and transfer them from one animal to another and thereby get the second animal to do what the first animal had been doing. Loewi had no way to collect chemicals released within the brain itself, so he worked with axons communicating with the heart muscle. (Much later research confirmed, as Loewi suspected, that the communication between a neuron and a muscle is similar to that between two neurons.)

Method Loewi began by electrically stimulating some axons connected to a frog's heart. These particular axons slowed down the heart rate. As he continued stimulating those axons, he collected some of the fluid on and around that heart and transferred it to the heart of a second frog.

Results When Loewi transferred the fluid from the first frog's heart, the second frog's heart rate slowed down also (Figure 3.23).

Interpretation Evidently the stimulated axons had released some chemical that slows heart rate. At least in this case, neurons send messages by releasing chemicals.

This was a remarkably clever experiment; indeed, Loewi eventually won a Nobel Prize in physiology for this experiment and others related to it. Even outstanding experiments have limitations, however. In this case, the main limi-

tation was the uncertainty about whether the conclusion applied only to frog hearts or whether it applied to all communication by neurons. Answering *that* question required enormous efforts and much more elaborate equipment. (The answer is that *almost* all communication by neurons depends on the release of chemicals. A few exceptional neurons communicate electrically.)

THE ROLE OF DIFFERENT NEUROTRANSMITTERS IN BEHAVIOR

Each neuron releases the same chemical or the same combination of chemicals at all branches of its axon. But different neurons release different chemicals. Investigators believe that dozens of chemicals serve as neurotransmitters (Snyder, 1984) and that different transmitters control different aspects of behavior (see Table 3.1). That likelihood has profound implications: If different transmitters control different aspects of behavior, then an excess or a deficit of a particular transmitter will cause some sort of abnormal behavior. Such imbalances may be caused by genetic factors, by brain damage, by drugs, and even by changes in the amount of some ingredient in a person's diet.

One example of a behavioral disorder related to a particular neurotransmitter is **Parkinson's disease,** a condition that affects many elderly people. Its main symptoms are difficulty

Table 3.1 Important Neurotransmitters and Some of Their Functions

Neurotransmitter	Behavioral Consequences of Neurotransmitter Excess	Behavioral Consequences of Neurotransmitter Deficit	Comments
Acetylcholine	Muscle paralysis or convulsions, sometimes death	Memory impairment	Acetylcholine is also released at the junction between motor neuron and muscle.
Dopamine	Involuntary movements; schizophrenia?	Impaired movement (Parkinson's disease); memory impairment; depression?	The brain has several dopamine paths. Some are important for movement; others for thought and emotion.
Norepinephrine	Autonomic arousal; anxiety; symptoms resembling schizophrenia	Memory impairment; depression?	Several transmitters contribute to depression in complex ways not yet understood.
Serotonin	?	Increased aggressive behavior; sleeplessness; depression?	Serotonin synapses are disrupted or damaged by LSD, ecstasy, and several other abused drugs.
GABA (gamma-amino-butyric acid)	?	Anxiety	Tranquilizers facilitate GABA synapses and thereby reduce anxiety.
Glutamate; glycine; other amino acids	Various, including cell death	Various	The most abundant transmitters in the central nervous system; their functions are diverse.
Endorphins	Inhibition of pain	Increased pain	The effects of endorphins are partly mimicked by morphine, heroin, and other opiates.
Neuropeptides	Various	Various	These are small chains of amino acids. The brain uses many neuropeptides; their functions vary and remain mostly unknown.

Sources: Kalat, 1992; Spring, Chiodo, & Bowen, 1987.

in initiating voluntary movement, slowness of movement, and tremors. It is accompanied by serious depression, which may be a symptom of the disease rather than just a reaction to it. Without medical treatment, Parkinson's disease generally grows worse and worse as time passes, until the person dies.

In Parkinson's disease one set of neurons gradually die (Figure 3.24). Those neurons give rise to a path of axons that all use the same neurotransmitter, a chemical known as **dopamine** (DOPE-uh-meen), which promotes activity levels and facilitates movement. One way to treat Parkinson's disease is the drug *deprenyl,* which slows the loss of neurons (Tetrud & Langston, 1989). However, deprenyl does not restore the lost neurons or compensate for the damage already done. Another treatment is to furnish the brain with extra dopamine to compensate for the lost neurons. Dopamine, like many other chemicals, cannot cross directly from the blood into the brain. But another chemical, L-DOPA,

taken in the form of pills, can enter the blood and cross into the brain, where it is converted into dopamine. This treatment does not reverse the disease; the neurons continue to die. The extra dopamine does, however, reduce the symptoms of the disease and gives the victim additional years of normal, active life. (The movie *Awakenings* showed L-DOPA's spectacular, though temporary, benefits for *encephalitis lethargica,* a rare and extremely severe condition similar to Parkinson's disease.

Although the cause of Parkinson's disease probably differs from one case to another, one possible cause is exposure to toxic substances. In 1982 several young adults (ages 22 to 42) developed Parkinson's disease after using illegal drugs that they had all bought from the same dealer. Investigators eventually identified the drug as a mixture of two chemicals known as MPPP and MPTP. L-DOPA reduced the symptoms for these people, as it does for more typical Parkinson's patients. Experiments with animals disclosed that MPTP causes damage to the substantia nigra, the same part of the brain known to be damaged in Parkinson's disease (Chiueh, 1988).

MPTP is occasionally released as an atmospheric pollutant by certain industrial and chemical processes. It is chemically similar to a number of herbicides and pesticides, including *paraquat.* Extensive exposure to such toxic substances may increase the risk of developing Parkinson's disease.

■ CONCEPT CHECK

10. *People suffering from certain disorders are given haloperidol, a drug that blocks activity at dopamine synapses. How would haloperidol affect a person suffering from Parkinson's disease? (Check your answer on page 96.)*

CHEMICAL INTERFERENCE WITH THE FUNCTIONING OF NEURONS

Many factors can interfere with the healthy functioning of neurons. One is a lack of adequate vitamin B_1 (thiamine), a substance abundant in yeast, grain, beans, peas, liver, and pork. Although most other organs of the body can use a variety of fuels, most cells in the brain use only **glucose** (GLOO-kose), a sugar. However, for the brain to use glucose, it must have an adequate supply of vitamin B_1. If a person's diet is deficient in that vitamin over a period of weeks, parts of the brain deteriorate or die, and other parts function below their normal capacity. Vitamin B_1 deficiency is common among severe alcoholics and causes some of them gradually to develop a kind of brain damage known as Korsakoff's syndrome, characterized by severe memory loss.

A number of drugs can interfere with the activity of a particular type of synapse. Common-cold remedies, for example, decrease the flow of sinus fluids by blocking acetylcholine synapses and stimulating norepinephrine synapses. Because the same neurotransmitters are used at other synapses as well, cold remedies have the side effects of increasing heart rate, decreasing salivation, and impeding sexual arousal.

Lysergic acid diethylamide (LSD) and most other hallucinogenic drugs (drugs that cause hallucinations) also are believed to act on the synapses. LSD is chemically similar to the neu-

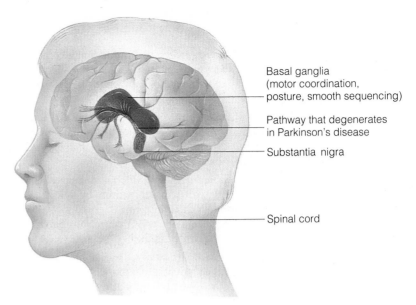

Basal ganglia (motor coordination, posture, smooth sequencing)

Pathway that degenerates in Parkinson's disease

Substantia nigra

Spinal cord

FIGURE 3.24
In Parkinson's disease, one path of axons from the substantia nigra gradually dies. Patients can gain years of active life by taking a chemical called L-DOPA, which is converted to the neurotransmitter dopamine in the brain.

rotransmitter **serotonin,** which plays an important role in sleep and mood changes. LSD stimulates one of several kind of serotonin synapses (Jacobs, 1987). Mescaline (the active substance in peyote), "angel dust," "ecstasy," and other hallucinogenic drugs also stimulate or block serotonin synapses and other kinds of synapses. Heroin and morphine stimulate the synapses that normally respond to **endorphins** (en-DOR-fins), neurotransmitters that inhibit the sensation of pain, even though those drugs are not very similar to endorphins chemically.

■ CONCEPT CHECK

11. *One way in which society could prevent Korsakoff's syndrome would be to prevent alcoholism. What would be another way? (Check your answer on page 96.)*

SUMMARY

■ *Neuron structure.* A neuron, or nerve cell, consists of a cell body, dendrites, and an axon. The axon conveys information to other neurons, where it is received by the dendrites or cell body or occasionally by another axon. (page 86)

■ *Changes in neuron structure.* The branching of a neuron's axon and dendrites changes over time as a result of experience; it also changes during aging. (page 87)

- *The action potential.* Information is conveyed along an axon by an action potential, which is regenerated without loss of strength at each point along the axon. (page 89)

- *Mechanism of the action potential.* An action potential depends on the flow of sodium and potassium ions. Anything blocking that flow will block the action potential. (page 89)

- *How neurons communicate.* A neuron communicates with another neuron by releasing a chemical called a neurotransmitter at a specialized junction called a synapse. A neurotransmitter can either excite or inhibit the next neuron. (page 90)

- *Neurotransmitters and behavioral disorders.* An excess or a deficit of a particular neurotransmitter may lead to abnormal behavior, such as Parkinson's disease. (page 93)

- *Chemical impairment of neuronal activity.* The functioning of neurons may be impaired by a deficit of vitamin B_1 or by certain chemicals that resemble neurotransmitters. (page 95)

SUGGESTIONS FOR FURTHER READING

Kalat, J. W. (1992). *Biological psychology* (4th ed.). Belmont, CA: Wadsworth. Chapters 1 through 5 deal with the material discussed in this chapter, but in more detail.

Levitan, I. B., & Kaczmarek, L. K. (1991). *The neuron.* New York: Oxford University Press. For those who want a *lot* more information about neurons and synapses.

TERMS

reductionism the attempt to explain complex phenomena by reducing them to combinations of simpler components (page 86)

neuron a cell of the nervous system that receives information and transmits it to other cells by conducting electrochemical impulses (page 86)

glia a cell of the nervous system that insulates neurons, removes waste materials (such as dead cells), and performs other supportive functions (page 86)

cell body the part of the neuron that contains the nucleus of the cell (page 86)

dendrite one of the widely branching structures of a neuron that receive transmission from other neurons (page 86)

axon a single long, thin, straight fiber that transmits information from a neuron to other neurons or to muscle cells (page 87)

action potential a sudden decrease or reversal in electrical charge across the membrane (or covering) of an axon (page 89)

synapse the specialized junction between one neuron and another at which one neuron releases a neurotransmitter, which either excites or inhibits the next neuron (page 90)

terminal button a bulge at the end of an axon from which the axon releases a chemical called a neurotransmitter (page 90)

neurotransmitter a chemical that is stored in the terminal of an axon and periodically released at a synapse (page 90)

postsynaptic neuron a neuron on the receiving end of a synapse (page 90)

Parkinson's disease a behavioral disorder caused by the deterioration of a path of axons, characterized by difficulty in initiating voluntary movement (page 93)

dopamine a neurotransmitter that promotes activity levels and facilitates movement (page 94)

glucose a sugar, the main source of nutrition for the brain (page 95)

lysergic acid diethylamide (LSD) a chemical that can affect the brain, sometimes producing hallucinations (page 95)

serotonin a neurotransmitter that plays an important role in sleep and mood changes (page 95)

endorphin a neurotransmitter that inhibits the sensation of pain (page 95)

ANSWERS TO CONCEPT CHECKS

6. The membrane gradually pumps the sodium ions out while simultaneously pumping potassium ions in. (page 90)

7. You will not feel the pain immediately because the action potential must travel from your foot to your brain. (If the action potentials travel at, say, 10 meters per second and your toe is about 1.5 meters from your brain, you will feel the pain about 0.15 second after you stub your toe.) (page 90)

8. Increased branching of the axons and dendrites will increase the number of synapses. (page 90)

9. Under the influence of a drug that prevents norepinephrine from attaching to its receptors, the postsynaptic neuron will receive less inhibition than usual. If we presume that the neuron continues to receive a certain amount of excitation, it will produce action potentials more frequently than usual. (page 91)

10. Haloperidol would increase the severity of Parkinson's disease. In fact, large doses of haloperidol can induce symptoms of Parkinson's disease in anyone. (page 95)

11. Another way to prevent Korsakoff's syndrome would be to require all alcoholic beverages to be fortified with vitamin B_1. (page 95)

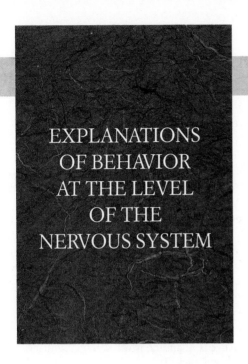

EXPLANATIONS OF BEHAVIOR AT THE LEVEL OF THE NERVOUS SYSTEM

What do different parts of the brain do?
Does a person who loses part of the brain also
lose part of the mind?

Every community has some division of labor among its members. Some people farm, some sell shoes, some build houses, some write psychology textbooks. Yet the division is not absolute. Many people who are not farmers grow a few vegetables in their backyard. And hardly anyone does only one job or does a job without the help of others.

The same is true of areas of the nervous system. Different areas contribute in different ways, but no one area is in complete control of any behavior. So even though we say that a particular structure is important for vision or for the control of movement, we know that it does not carry out that function without the participation of other areas.

SPECIALIZATION BY AREAS OF THE BRAIN

Why should psychologists care what different parts of the brain do? There are at least two reasons, one practical and the other theoretical.

The practical reason is that we want to distinguish between people who act strangely because they have had bad experiences and people who act strangely because they have suffered brain damage. To do so, we have to know how brain damage affects behavior.

The theoretical reason is simply that the study of brain damage can help us understand the organization of behavior. In some manner or another, behavior must be made up of component parts. But what are those parts? Is behavior composed of ideas? Sensations? Movements? Personality characteristics?

Brain damage from one cause or another is rather common. For young people, the most common cause is a blow to the head from a fall, an automobile accident, a fight, or other sudden trauma. An estimated 400,000 people per year suffer brain damage from such causes in the United States (Peterson, 1980). In old age, the most common cause of brain damage is **stroke,** an interruption of blood flow, and thus of oxygen supply, to part of the brain. A 60-year-old has a little less than a 1% chance per year of having a stroke; by age 85 that chance increases to more than 5% per year (Kurtzke, 1976). People also can suffer brain damage from diseases, drugs and poisons, bullets, radiation, and nutritional deficits.

Depending on the location of the brain damage, the result may be impaired vision, faulty hearing, inability to perform certain movements, increased or decreased eating, fluctuations in body temperature, and a great variety of other outcomes. Each of those outcomes provides us with some clues as to how behavior is organized. Each outcome also helps to document the conclusion that *if part of the brain is lost, part of behavior and experience is lost as well.* So far as we can tell, *brain activity and "mind" are inseparable; we cannot have one without the other.*

AN OVERVIEW OF THE NERVOUS SYSTEM

Psychologists and biologists distinguish between the central nervous system and the peripheral nervous system. The **central nervous system** consists of the brain and the spinal cord. The **peripheral nervous system** consists of the **nerves** (bundles of axons) that carry messages from the sense organs to the central nervous system and from the central nervous system to

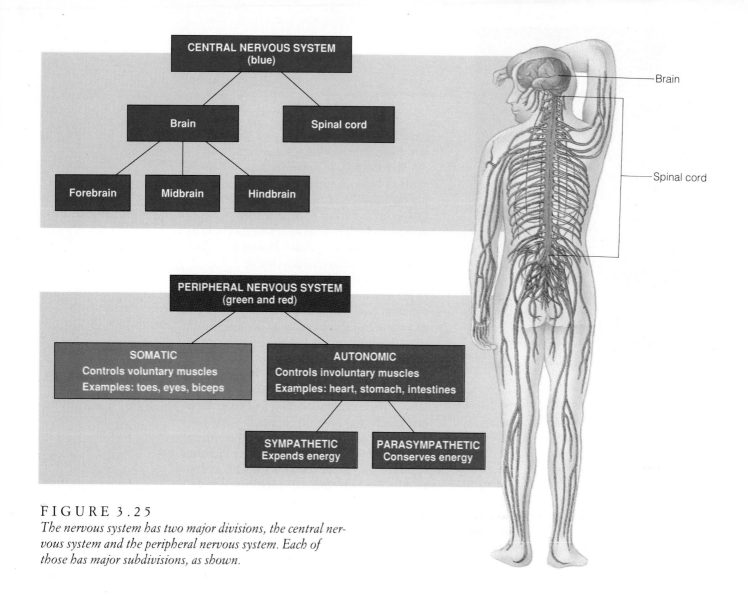

Brain

Spinal cord

FIGURE 3.25
The nervous system has two major divisions, the central nervous system and the peripheral nervous system. Each of those has major subdivisions, as shown.

the muscles and glands. The peripheral nervous system has two divisions, the **somatic nervous system,** which controls the muscles, and the **autonomic nervous system,** which controls the organs, such as the heart. Figure 3.25 summarizes the major divisions of the nervous system.

Early in its embryological development, the central nervous system of vertebrates, including humans, is a tube with three lumps, as shown in Figure 3.26. Those lumps develop into the **forebrain,** the **midbrain,** and the **hindbrain;** the rest of the tube develops into the spinal cord. The hindbrain and the midbrain are more prominent in fish, reptiles, and birds than in mammals (Figure 3.27). The forebrain, the most anterior (forward) part of the brain, contains the cerebral cortex and other structures. It is by far the dominant portion of the brain in mammals, especially humans.

The Spinal Cord

The **spinal cord** communicates with the body below the level of the head by means of sensory neurons and motor neurons (Figure 3.28). The **sensory neurons** carry information about touch, pain, and other senses from the periphery of the body to the spinal cord. The **motor neurons** transmit impulses from the central nervous system to the muscles and glands. In Figure 3.28, note that all the sensory nerves enter on one side (the person's back); all the motor nerves leave on the other side (the stomach side).

The spinal cord serves both reflexive and voluntary behavior. A **reflex** is a rapid, automatic response to a stimulus. For example, suppose you put your hand on a hot stove. Stimulation of pain receptors in your finger sends

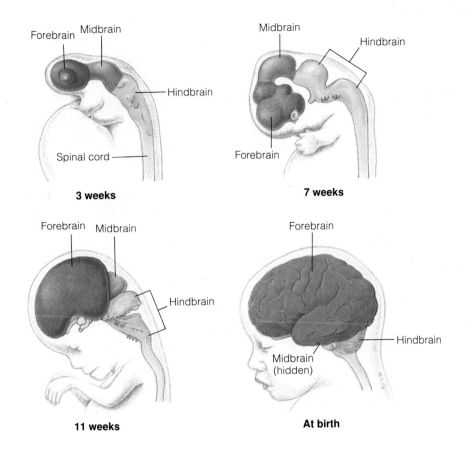

3 weeks

7 weeks

11 weeks

At birth

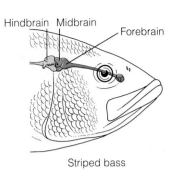

Striped bass

Grass snake

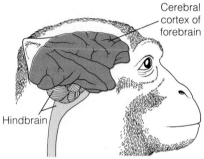

Macaque monkey

FIGURE 3.26
The human brain begins development as three lumps. By birth, the fore-brain grows much larger than the midbrain and hindbrain, although all three structures perform essential functions.

FIGURE 3.27
In mammals, such as macaque monkeys, the forebrain is larger in proportion to the rest of the brain than it is in other vertebrates. The midbrain is surrounded by the forebrain and therefore is not visible from the outside surface of the brain.

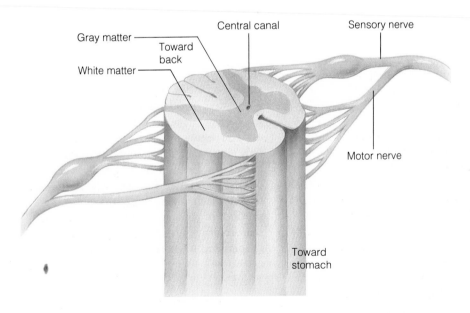

FIGURE 3.28
The spinal cord receives sensory information from all parts of the body except the head. Through its motor nerves it sends messages to control the muscles and glands.

FIGURE 3.29

The sympathetic nervous system prepares the body for brief bouts of vigorous activity; the parasympathetic nervous system promotes digestion and other nonemergency functions. Although both systems are active at all times, the balance may shift from predominance of one to predominance of the other.

Sympathetic system
generates energy

Parasympathetic system
conserves energy

Sympathetic	Parasympathetic
Pupils open	Pupils constrict
Saliva decreases	Saliva flows
Pulse quickens	Pulse slows
Sweat increases	
Stomach less active	Stomach churns
Epinephrine (adrenaline) secretes	

messages along sensory neurons; within the spinal cord these neurons send messages via interneurons to motor neurons, which send impulses to the muscles that jerk your hand away from the hot stove.

The spinal cord is also necessary for voluntary behaviors. All the information your brain receives about touch stimulation comes to it by way of the spinal cord; every command to move a muscle goes by way of axons from the brain to the spinal cord.

Spinal injury is a common outcome of automobile accidents, other accidents, and certain diseases. If the spinal cord is completely cut near its lower end, then the person may lose control of only the legs, bowel, and bladder—the body parts controlled by the lowest part of the spinal cord. If the cut is higher, then the person loses control of a greater area of the body, because a larger part of the spinal cord is disconnected from the brain. If the cord is cut near the top, then the person may lose control of the arms as well as the legs. And if a cut goes only part way through the cord, then a person may lose control of just the left side or just the right side.

The Autonomic Nervous System

The autonomic nervous system, closely associated with the spinal cord, controls the internal organs such as the heart. The term *autonomic* means involuntary or automatic. The auto-

nomic nervous system is partly, though not entirely, automatic. We are generally not aware of its activity, although it does receive information from, and send information to, the brain and spinal cord.

The autonomic nervous system consists of two parts: (1) The *sympathetic nervous system,* controlled by a chain of neurons lying just outside the spinal cord, increases heart rate and breathing rate and readies the body for vigorous "fight or flight" activities. (2) The *parasympathetic nervous system,* controlled by neurons in the very top and very bottom levels of the spinal cord, decreases heart rate, increases digestive activities, and in general promotes the body's activities that take place during rest (Figure 3.29).

The autonomic nervous system is particularly important for emotions. When you are nervous, your heart beats rapidly, you cannot catch your breath, and you feel "butterflies in the stomach." All those responses are the product of your autonomic nervous system. I shall return to this topic in more detail in the chapter about emotions (Chapter 12).

The Endocrine System

Although the endocrine system is not part of the nervous system, it is closely related to it, especially to the autonomic nervous system. The **endocrine system** is a set of glands that produce hormones and release them into the blood. Figure 3.30 shows some of the major endocrine glands.

Hormones are chemicals released by certain glands and conveyed by the blood to other parts of the body, where they alter activity. They are similar to neurotransmitters in that both affect the nervous system. The same chemical may be used both as a hormone and as a neurotransmitter. The difference is that when a chemical is used as a neurotransmitter, it is released immediately adjacent to the cell that it is to excite or inhibit. When it is used as a hormone, it is released into the blood, which diffuses it throughout the body.

Hormones are important for controlling relatively long-term effects on behavior, such as readying an animal's body for the mating season, migration, or hibernation. Some hormonal effects are nearly permanent. For example, the amount of the male sex hormone testosterone present during prenatal development determines whether one develops a penis and scrotum or a clitoris and labia. Hormones also control the onset of puberty. Other effects of hormones are more temporary. For example, hormones control blood pressure, the rate of energy use, and the rate of urine production.

■ CONCEPT CHECK

12. *Just after a meal, the pancreas produces increased amounts of the hormone insulin, which increases the conversion of the digested food into fats in many cells throughout the body. In what way is a hormone more effective for this purpose than a neurotransmitter would be? (Check your answer on page 115.)*

The Hindbrain

The **medulla** and **pons,** structures located in the hindbrain (Figure 3.31), are an elaboration of the spinal cord. Both structures receive sensory input from the head (taste, hearing, touch sensations on the scalp) and send impulses for motor control of the head (for example, chewing, swallowing, and breathing). They also send axons to the body's organs as part of the parasympathetic nervous system. Because the medulla and pons control breathing, heart rate, and other life-preserving functions, almost any damage to them is fatal. An overdose of heroin or other opiate drugs can be fatal, largely because it suppresses activity in the hindbrain.

The **reticular formation** is a diffuse set of neurons that extend from the medulla into the forebrain. (The term reticular means "netlike.")

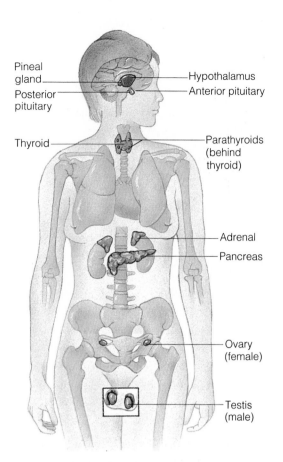

FIGURE 3.30
Glands in the endocrine system produce hormones and release them into the blood.

As the name implies, neurons of the reticular formation are extensively interconnected with one another as well as with neurons that relay sensory information. They are largely responsible for variations in the level of arousal of the brain; they react to all types of sensory stimulation by sending impulses throughout much of the forebrain. Damage to the reticular formation makes a person inactive and unresponsive.

The **cerebellum** (Latin for "little brain"), another part of the hindbrain, is active in the control of movement, especially for complex, rapid motor skills, such as playing the piano or dribbling a basketball (Kornhuber, 1974). A person who suffers damage to the cerebellum can still make muscular movements, but has to plan each series of movements slowly, one at a time, instead of executing them in a smooth sequence. Such a person has difficulty walking a straight line and speaks haltingly, slurring the words. (Words have to be planned as units; you cannot speak a word clearly by pronouncing one sound at a time.)

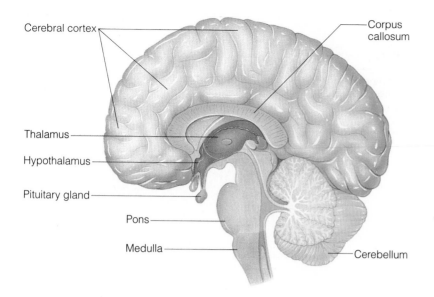

FIGURE 3.31
This view shows the midline structures of the human brain. The pons, medulla, and cerebellum constitute the hindbrain.

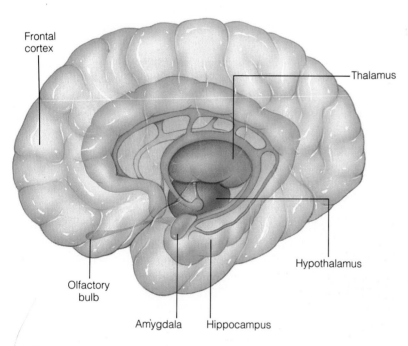

FIGURE 3.32
The limbic system, a set of subcortical structures, forms a border (or limbus) around the brain stem.

One way of testing for damage to the cerebellum is the **finger-to-nose test.** A person is told to hold one arm out straight and then, with eyes closed, to touch the nose as quickly as possible. Although most people have little difficulty with this task, someone with a damaged cerebellum may move the finger slowly and haltingly or may miss the nose altogether.

The effects of damage to the cerebellum are similar to the effects of alcohol abuse. A person who has drunk too much alcohol generally has slow, slurred speech and cannot walk a straight line. The cerebellum is one of the first brain areas to be impaired by alcohol.

The Midbrain and the Subcortical Structures of the Forebrain

When you look at a picture of the human brain, ordinarily all you see is the cerebellum, the medulla and pons, and the cerebral cortex. The word *cortex* means "bark," or outer covering. Unlike the bark of a tree, the cerebral cortex constitutes about 90% of the total human brain. It surrounds and dwarfs some core structures of the midbrain and subcortical forebrain; these structures are not visible from the outside.

Figures 3.31 and 3.32 show a few of the numerous structures of the midbrain and subcortical forebrain. Neuroscientists have devoted great efforts to determining the functions of each structure as precisely as possible. They now understand some of those structures fairly well. For example, the *thalamus* serves as an area of intermediate processing of sensory information on its way to the cerebral cortex. The *hypothalamus* has tiny subareas that make critical contributions to eating, drinking, sexual behavior, and other motivated or emotional behaviors. The *hippocampus* is essential for storing certain kinds of memories; we shall consider research on the hippocampus in Chapter 8. Some other areas are a little more difficult to characterize. For example, researchers regard the *basal ganglia* as important for control of movement and certain aspects of cognition, but the exact nature of that contribution is not yet as clear as we would like it to be (Phillips & Carr, 1987; Stelmach & Phillips, 1991).

THE CEREBRAL CORTEX

The **cerebral cortex** is the outer surface of the forebrain, consisting of two **hemispheres,** the left and the right. Each hemisphere is responsible for sensation and motor control on the op-

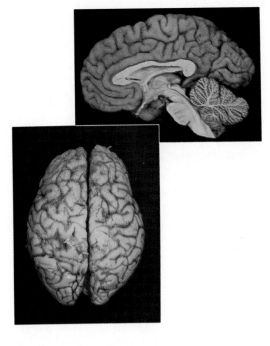

FIGURE 3.33
The human cerebral cortex: (bottom) left and right hemispheres; (top) inside view of a complete hemisphere. The folds greatly extend its surface area.

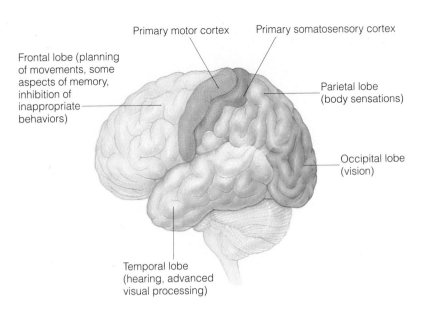

Frontal lobe (planning of movements, some aspects of memory, inhibition of inappropriate behaviors)

Primary motor cortex

Primary somatosensory cortex

Parietal lobe (body sensations)

Occipital lobe (vision)

Temporal lobe (hearing, advanced visual processing)

FIGURE 3.34
The four lobes of the human cerebral cortex, with indications of some of their major functions.

posite side of the body. The cell bodies of neurons are arrayed on or near the outer surface of the cerebral cortex; an inner core consists of axons. You have probably heard people talk about "having a lot of gray matter." The *gray matter* of the forebrain is the cerebral cortex. It is called gray matter because it contains a great many cell bodies, which are grayer than the axons. The interior of the forebrain beneath the cerebral cortex contains large areas of *white matter,* composed entirely of axons. (Many axons are covered with *myelin,* a white insulation.) You can see the colors in Figure 3.38.

The number of cell bodies in the cerebral cortex is proportional to the surface area. In humans, the cerebral cortex has a large number of folds and grooves (Figure 3.33), which make its total surface area quite large. Although it is customary to divide each hemisphere of the cerebral cortex into four "lobes," as shown in Figure 3.34, the borders between the lobes are arbitrary.

The Occipital Lobe

The **occipital lobe,** the rear portion of each hemisphere of the cerebral cortex, plays a critical role in vision. Damage to the occipital lobe results in loss of vision in part of the visual field, as if part of both eyes had been destroyed. (The

visual field is the world as someone sees it. For example, your left visual field is what appears on your left.) Someone who suffers damage to the occipital lobe in the left hemisphere loses vision in the right half of the visual field. If the damage occurs in the right hemisphere, the loss is in the left half of the visual field. People with occipital lobe damage have no conscious experience of seeing anything in the "blind" field; however, such people can point toward an object that they do not consciously see—to their own surprise! They also can move their eyes toward an object in the blind field (Rafal, Smith, Krantz, Cohen, & Brennan, 1990). Evidently some subcortical areas respond to the visual stimulus and direct a few simple movements, even though the information never reaches the cortex.

The Parietal Lobe

The **parietal** (puh-RIGH-eht-l) **lobe** is the main receiving area for the sense of touch. It is essential for body perception in general, including the perception of the location and movement of body parts and the orientation of the body in space. Many neurons in the parietal lobe also contribute to motor control.

A strip in the anterior (forward) part of the parietal lobe receives most touch sensation and other information about the body. This is the

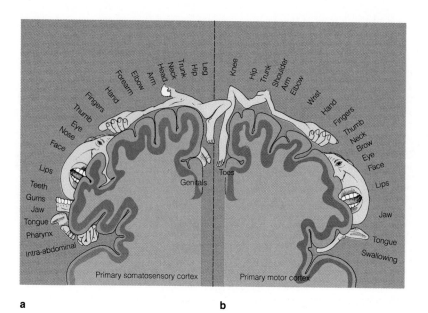

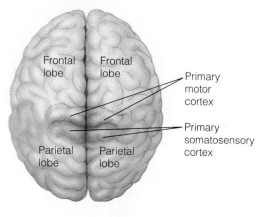

c

FIGURE 3.35
(a) The primary somatosensory cortex and (b) the primary motor cortex, illustrating which part of the body each brain area controls. Larger areas of the cortex are devoted to body parts that need to be controlled with great precision, such as the face and hands. The figure shows the left primary somatosensory cortex, which receives information from the right side of the body, and the right primary motor cortex, which controls the muscles on the left side of the body. (c) Locations of the primary somatosensory cortex and the primary motor cortex. (From Geschwind, 1979.)

FIGURE 3.36
A person with damage to the right parietal lobe will draw only the right side of an object, as this attempt to copy a picture of a flower shows. (From Heilman, 1979.)

primary somatosensory (body-sensory) **cortex.** Damage to this strip in one hemisphere impairs perception on the opposite side of the body. Each location along the primary somatosensory cortex receives sensation from a different part of the body, as shown in Figure 3.35a.

Damage to an area in the parietal lobe just behind the primary somatosensory cortex disorganizes sensations of touch. A person with such damage can still feel objects but may ignore what he or she is feeling. A person with damage in the right parietal cortex may show **neglect** of the left side of the body and the left side of the world (Levine, Warach, Benowitz, & Calvanio, 1986). Such people may fail to dress or groom the left side of the body, insisting that it is "someone else." They read only the right side of a page and draw only the right side of an object, using only the right side of the paper (Figure 3.36). If asked to describe from memory what they would see if they walked down a particular street, they describe only what they would see on the right side. If then asked what they would see if they came *back* along that street, they describe the opposite side!

The Temporal Lobe

The **temporal lobe** of each hemisphere, located toward the temples, is the main processing area for hearing. It also plays an important role in some of the more complex aspects of vision. Damage to the temporal lobe does not leave a person blind, as damage to the occipital lobe does, but it does impair the ability to recognize complex patterns such as faces (Benton, 1980) or to identify which direction an object is moving (Newsome & Paré, 1988). Similarly, an irritation of the occipital lobe (from a brain tumor, for example) merely produces the experience of seeing flashing lights. An irritation in the temporal lobe may evoke elaborate, dreamlike hallucinations.

One area in the temporal lobe in the left hemisphere is important for language comprehension. Damage centered here impairs people's ability to understand what other people are saying; they also have trouble remembering the names of objects when they are speaking themselves.

The temporal lobe also apparently plays an important role in emotional behavior. Tumors, epilepsy, or other abnormalities affecting the temporal lobe sometimes cause severe emotional outbursts. Some people, for example, exhibit unprovoked violent behavior (Mark & Ervin, 1970). Others suffer periods of uncontrollable laughter (Swash, 1972). Still others, including the Russian novelist Fyodor Dostoyevsky (who had temporal lobe epilepsy), experience periods of ecstatic pleasure and a feeling of "oneness with the universe" (Cirignotta, Todesco, & Lugaresi, 1980). Dostoyevsky declared that such experiences brought him the purest, most intense pleasure he ever had—though only for a moment.

The Frontal Lobe

The **frontal lobe** is the large anterior portion of each cerebral hemisphere; it is apparently not necessary for any type of sensation, although it receives some information from each of the sensory systems (Stuss & Benson, 1984). A strip along the rear portion of the frontal lobe, the **primary motor cortex** (Figure 3.35b), is important for the control of fine movements, such as moving one finger at a time. As with the primary somatosensory cortex, each part of the primary motor cortex controls a different part of the body. A person who suffers damage to the primary motor cortex of one hemisphere experiences weakness and an impairment of fine movements on the opposite side of the body.

An area in the left frontal lobe is important for human language production. People with extensive damage centered in this area have trouble speaking, writing, or gesturing in sign language (Bellugi, Poizner, & Klima, 1983; Geschwind, 1970). What they say makes sense, although they generally omit prepositions, conjunctions, and word endings.

Functions of the Prefrontal Cortex
The **prefrontal cortex** (Figure 3.37) is the portion of the frontal lobe in front of the motor cortex. The prefrontal cortex is critical for planning movements, for integrating movements with information that has just been received, for the inhibition of inappropriate behaviors, and for certain aspects of memory. For example, after damage to the prefrontal cortex, both humans and monkeys learn to respond to stimuli that are present at the time of the response, but they perform poorly if they have to respond after the stimulus is removed (Goldman-Rakic, 1988). They also fail on a task that requires them to keep track of objects they have just seen and to pick up any object they have not recently seen

(Bachevalier & Mishkin, 1986). Evidently the prefrontal cortex contributes in some way to keeping track of recent memories and planning actions based on them.

Prefrontal Lobotomies
In the 1940s and early 1950s, an operation known as **prefrontal lobotomy** became a common treatment for depression, schizophrenia, and other disorders for which no other treatment was available at the time. This surgery damaged part of the prefrontal cortex or severed its connections with other areas of the brain (Figure 3.38). The operation was popularized by Dr. Walter Freeman, who performed more than a thousand lobotomies (Valenstein, 1986). The theoretical rationale behind the surgery was vague and ill founded, and the procedure itself was crude, even by the standards of that time.

Did lobotomies help any mental patients? It is hard to say for sure. Prefrontal lobotomies did sometimes provide relief from anxiety and made some of the most agitated patients easier to handle. The surgeons themselves did some follow-up studies on limited aspects of the patients' behavior and pronounced most of the patients "improved."

Something to Think About

What reasons can you think of for regarding such reports of "improved" lobotomy patients as scientifically unsatisfactory? (You may want to use some of the pointers in Chapter 2 as a checklist.)

However, the side effects of the surgery often included a loss of initiative, planning, and emotional expression; decreased ability to concentrate; confusion; loss of social skills; and

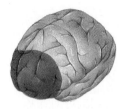

FIGURE 3.37
The prefrontal cortex of the human brain (shaded area) contributes to planning movements, inhibiting inappropriate movements, and certain aspects of memory.

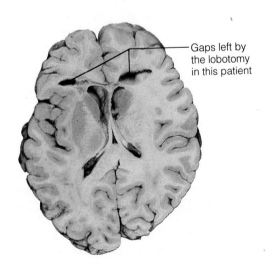

Gaps left by the lobotomy in this patient

FIGURE 3.38

Prefrontal lobotomy was applied to thousands of people in the 1940s and 1950s, sometimes relieving agitation but generally causing serious deficits such as a loss of initiative and emotional expressions. Here, two holes in the frontal cortex are visible signs of a lobotomy conducted many years previously.

FIGURE 3.39
This apparatus records regional cerebral blood flow (rCBF) in the brain, allowing investigators to measure activity in different parts of the brain.

certain defects of memory and cognition. Because of these behavioral effects, lobotomies fell out of favor in the mid-1950s. After the introduction of drugs to control depression and schizophrenia, the use of lobotomies was almost immediately abandoned.

▪ CONCEPT CHECK

13. *The following five people are known to have suffered damage to the cerebral cortex. From their behavioral symptoms, determine the probable location of the damage for each person: (a) impaired perception of the left half of the body and a tendency to ignore the left half of the body and the left half of the world, (b) impaired hearing and some changes in emotional experience, (c) inability to make fine movements with the right hand, (d) loss of vision in the left visual field, and (e) failure to inhibit inappropriate behaviors and difficulty remembering what has just happened. (Check your answers on page 115.)*

Different Brain Areas Control Different Behavioral Functions

WHAT'S THE EVIDENCE?

In the sections just completed, I have described the different behavioral functions of different parts of the brain. As evidence, I have described the effects of damage in different areas. For example, damage to the occipital lobe impairs vision and damage to part of the frontal lobe impairs speech.

Should we be satisfied with that evidence? Perhaps not, at least not entirely. Scientists learn to be skeptical of almost any conclusion that rests on a single line of evidence. Sometimes a particular line of evidence has some hidden flaw. For example, perhaps the frontal lobe is not directly responsible for speech; maybe it performs some function that is necessary for some other area to mediate speech. (For analogy, we could prevent a car from moving if we removed a piece of a tire or a piece of the gas tank. Those pieces do not exactly make the car move, but they have to be present in order for the engine to do its job.)

For any kind of conclusion, scientists try to find separate kinds of evidence. (The same is true in courts of law; an eyewitness plus a fingerprint is much more convincing than either one would be by itself.) We have, in fact, many kinds of evidence identifying the behavioral functions of different brain areas. Here is an example using up-to-date technology.

Hypothesis If a particular brain area is responsible for a particular behavioral function, then neuron activity in that area should increase during that kind of behavior.

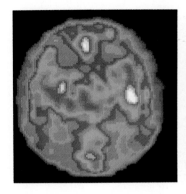 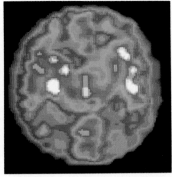 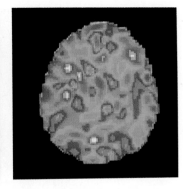

a   b   c

FIGURE 3.40

These rCBF records indicate the relative amounts of blood flow to various brain areas of a normal human brain under differing conditions. Red indicates the greatest amount of blood flow, and therefore brain activity; yellow indicates the next-greatest amount, followed by green, blue, and purple. (a) Blood flow to the brain at rest. (b) Blood flow while the person describes a magazine story. (c) Difference between (b) and (a). The record in (c) indicates the areas that increased their activity during speech. Note the widespread areas of activity, especially in the left hemisphere. (From Wallesch, Henriksen, Kornhuber, & Paulson, 1985.)

Method Investigators can measure the activity in various parts of the brain by recording the amount of blood flow to each area, referred to as the **regional cerebral blood flow technique (rCBF).** Because blood flow increases to the most active areas, a measurement of blood flow is a fairly accurate measurement of brain activity.

To measure rCBF, investigators inject into the person's blood a small amount of radioactively labeled xenon, an inert gas. The more active a certain area of the brain is, the greater the amount of xenon-carrying blood that will enter that area. Figure 3.39 shows the apparatus used in measuring rCBF. Investigators measure rCBF while a person is engaged in several tasks, and then they compare the results across tasks to find out how brain activity changes. In one study, they compared rCBF during rest and during speech (Wallesch, Henriksen, Kornhuber, & Paulson, 1985).

Results Figure 3.40 shows the results. Reds indicate areas of highest activity; yellows, greens, blues, and purples indicate progressively lower activity. This figure demonstrates that while a person is speaking, blood flow increases to much of the left hemisphere, including the left frontal cortex but other areas as well.

Interpretation and Comment Evidently the left frontal cortex is important for speech, as previous methods had already indicated. How-

ever, other cortical areas are important as well.

Research using the rCBF method and related methods can identify the brain areas associated with any given task. Nearly any behavior, it turns out, activates much of the cerebral cortex, though it activates some areas more than others.

THE CORPUS CALLOSUM AND THE SPLIT-BRAIN PHENOMENON

Earlier in this chapter I noted that billions of individual neurons produce one overall conscious "you" via communication. What would happen if one large set of neurons were unable to communicate with another large set? Would that unity of experience split up into two or more separate spheres of consciousness? Research on some unusual surgical patients suggests that the answer is yes.

As we have seen, sensory information from each side of the body travels primarily to the opposite hemisphere of the cerebral cortex. The two hemispheres normally communicate with each other by means of a large set of axons called the **corpus callosum** (Figure 3.41). So ordinarily each hemisphere has access to information from both sides of the body. If the corpus

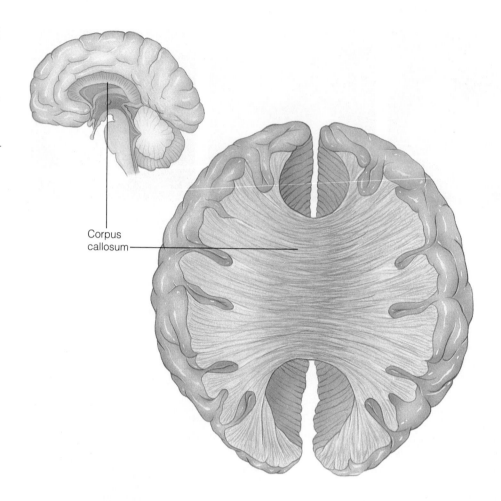

FIGURE 3.41
The corpus callosum is a large set of axons that convey information between the two hemispheres of the cerebral cortex. (left) A midline view showing the location of the corpus callosum. (right) A horizontal section, showing how each axon of the corpus callosum links a spot in the left hemisphere to a corresponding spot in the right hemisphere.

Corpus callosum

callosum is cut, however, the hemispheres are almost completely isolated from each other.

Several teams of brain surgeons have disconnected the left hemisphere of the cerebral cortex from the right hemisphere. The purpose of such an operation is to relieve a condition called **epilepsy,** in which neurons somewhere in the brain begin to emit abnormal rhythmic, spontaneous impulses. Those impulses originate in different locations for different people. They quickly spread to other areas of the brain, including neurons in the opposite hemisphere. The effects on behavior can vary widely, depending on where the epilepsy originates in the brain and where it spreads. Most people with epilepsy respond well to antiepileptic drugs and live normal lives. A few people, however, do not respond to any of the known drugs and continue to have major seizures so frequently that they cannot work, go to school, or travel far from medical help. Such people are willing to try almost anything to get relief.

And so surgeons decided to sever the corpus callosum of people with severe, otherwise untreatable epilepsy. The reasoning was that although the epileptic seizures would still occur,

they would be prevented from spreading across the corpus callosum to the other hemisphere and so would be less severe.

The operation was more successful than expected. Not only were the seizures limited to one side of the body, but they also became far less frequent. A possible explanation is that the operation interrupted the feedback loop between the two hemispheres that allows an epileptic seizure to echo back and forth. These split-brain patients were able to return to work and to resume other normal activities. There were, however, some interesting behavioral side effects. But before I can discuss them, we need to consider the links between the eyes and the brain.

Connections Between the Eyes and the Brain

Note: This section presents a simple concept that is contrary to most people's expectations. Even when students are warned that this material will appear on a test and are practically told what the question will be, many of them still miss it. So pay attention!

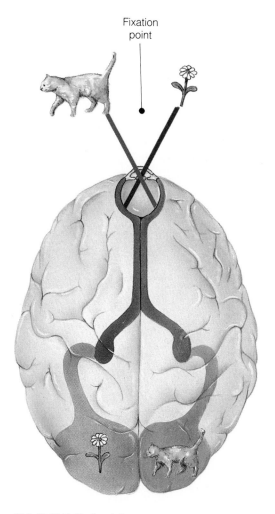

FIGURE 3.42

A mythical beast, the cyclops, sees each side of the world in the opposite side of its one retina. Humans have two eyes like that of the cyclops: For each eye, the left half of the retina sees the right half of the world and the right half of the retina sees the left half of the world.

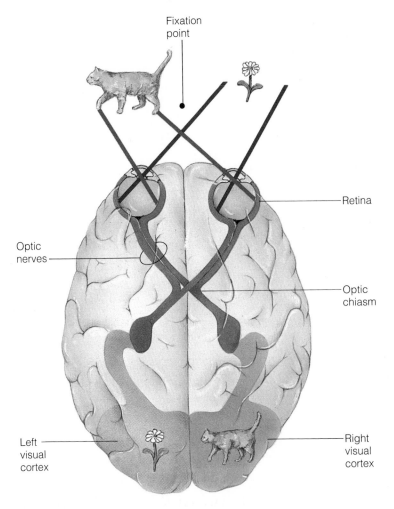

FIGURE 3.43

In the human visual system (viewed here from above), light from either half of the world crosses through the pupils to strike the opposite side of each retina. Axons from the left half of each retina travel to the left hemisphere of the brain; axons from the right half of each retina travel to the right hemisphere of the brain.

Because each hemisphere of the brain controls the muscles on the opposite side of the body, it needs to see the opposite side of the world. This does *not* mean that your left hemisphere sees with the right eye or that your right hemisphere sees with the left eye. Convince yourself: Close one eye, then open it and close the other. Note that you see almost the same view with both eyes. You see the left half of the world with part of your left eye and part of your right eye.

To illustrate, consider Figure 3.42, which shows the visual system of the mythical one-eyed beast, the cyclops. In this view, you are looking at the head of the cyclops from above. Light from either half of the world crosses

through the pupil to strike the opposite side of the **retina** (the visual receptors lining the back of the eyeball). That is, light from the left strikes the right half of the retina and light from the right strikes the left half of the retina. Then axons from each half of the retina go to their own side of the brain.

The human visual system is organized just like that of the cyclops, except that humans have two "cyclopean" eyes. Figure 3.43, which shows the human system, warrants careful study. In us as in the cyclops, light from each half of the world strikes receptors on the opposite side of the retina, but we (unlike the cyclops) have two such retinas. Information from the left half of *each* retina travels via the **optic**

(a) A woman with a severed corpus callosum can name something she touches with her hidden right hand, but she cannot name an object that she feels with her left hand. Information from the left hemisphere goes to the right hemisphere, which cannot talk.
(b) When the word hatband *is flashed on a screen, a woman with a split brain can report only what her left hemisphere saw,* band. *However, with her left hand she can point to a hat, which is what the right hemisphere saw.*

Left field:
can't name or describe;
can identify by touch
with left hand

Right field:
named with ease;
can identify by touch
with right hand

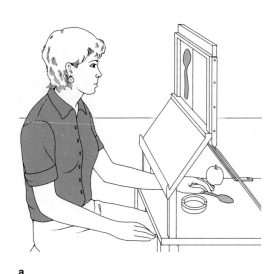

a

Fixation
Point

H A T ● B A N D

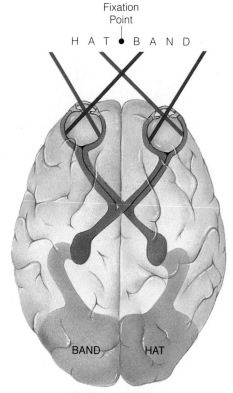

BAND   HAT

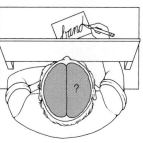

b

nerves to the left hemisphere of the cerebral cortex; information from the right half of each retina travels via the optic nerves to the right hemisphere.

Here is one way to remember this material: *Light from each side of the world strikes the opposite side of the retina. The brain is connected to the eyes in such a way that each hemisphere sees the opposite side of the world.* If you remember those two statements, you should be able to sketch the connections shown in Figure 3.43.

What about the very center of the retina? Cells in a thin strip down the center of each retina send axons to both sides of the brain.

Behavioral Effects of Severing the Corpus Callosum

For almost all right-handed people and for about 60% of left-handed people, the brain area that controls speech is located in the left hemisphere of the brain. When visual or other information comes into your right hemisphere, you have no difficulty talking about it, because the corpus callosum readily transfers information between the hemispheres.

But what happens when the corpus callosum is severed? When a woman with a severed corpus callosum touches something with her right hand without looking at it, she can say what it is, because the touch information reaches her left hemisphere (Nebes, 1974; Sperry, 1967). However, if she touches something with her left hand, then she cannot say what it is, because the information reaches only her right hemisphere. If she is given several choices and is asked to point to what her left hand has felt, she can point to it correctly—but only with her left hand. In fact, she will sometimes point to the correct object with her left hand while saying, "I have no idea what it was. I didn't feel anything." Evidently the right hemisphere can understand the instructions and answer with the hand it controls, but it cannot talk. Roger Sperry won a Nobel Prize in physiology and medicine in 1981 for these pioneering discoveries (Figure 3.44a).

Now consider what happens when this split-brain woman looks at something (Figure 3.44b). Under ordinary conditions, when her eyes are free to move about, she sees almost the same thing in both hemispheres. In the laboratory, however, it is possible to restrict information to one side or the other by presenting it faster than the eyes can move. The woman in Figure 3.45b focuses her eyes on a point in the middle of the screen. The investigator flashes a word such as *hatband* on the screen for a split second so that the woman does not have enough time to move her eyes. If she is asked what she saw, she replies, "band," which is what the left hemisphere saw. Information from the right side of the screen, you will recall, goes to the left side of each retina and from there to the left hemisphere. If she is asked what *kind* of band it might be, she is puzzled: "I don't know. Jazz band? Rubber band?" What the right hemisphere saw cannot get to the left hemisphere, which does the talking. However, if the investigator displays a set of objects and asks the woman to *point* to what she just saw, using her *left* hand, she points to a hat, which is what the right hemisphere saw! The left hemisphere and right hemisphere answer questions independently, as if they were separate people.

Split-brain people get along reasonably well in everyday life. Walking, for example, is no problem; it is controlled largely by subcortical areas of the brain that exchange information through connections below the corpus callosum.

In special circumstances, the two hemispheres find clever ways to cooperate. In one experiment, a split-brain person was looking at pictures flashed on a screen, as in Figure 3.44b. He could not name most of the objects flashed in the left visual field, but after some delay, he could name such simple shapes as round, square, or triangular. Here is how he did it: After seeing the object (with the right hemisphere), he let his eyes move around the room. (Both hemispheres have control of the eye muscles.) When the right hemisphere saw something with the same shape as the object it had seen on the screen, it would stop moving the eyes. The left hemisphere just waited for the eyes to stop moving and then called out the shape of the object it saw.

■ CONCEPT CHECK

14. *After damage to the corpus callosum, a person can describe some of what he or she sees, but not all. Where does the person have to see something in order to describe it in words? One eye or the other? One half of the retina? One visual field or the other? (Check your answer on page 115.)*

Split-brain surgery is extremely rare. We study such patients not because you are likely to encounter one but because they teach us something about the organization of the brain: The

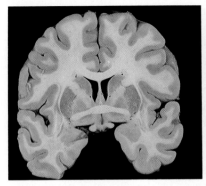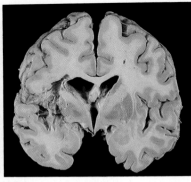

a   b

FIGURE 3.45
Comparison of a cross section through the brain of (a) a normal person and (b) a person who had had a stroke demonstrates the loss of cells in the brain of the stroke victim.

unity of our experience depends on communication among different parts of the brain. If that communication is disrupted, different parts of the brain may start dealing with their own tasks separately, as if they were different people.

BRAIN DAMAGE AND BEHAVIORAL RECOVERY

You may have heard the expression "They say we use only 10% of our brain." Stop and think about that for a moment. Who are "they"? No brain researcher ever says anything of the sort. What does the statement really mean? Does it mean that someone could lose 90% of the brain and still function normally? If so, the statement is false. Does it mean that only 10% of the neurons in the brain are active at any given time? If so, false again. Perhaps it means simply that we could all know more and do more than we know and do now. That is undeniably true, though it has nothing to do with the estimated 10% (or any other numerical estimate). I am not much of an athlete, but that does not mean that I am using only 10% of my muscles.

We all use all of our brain (even those who do not seem to be using their brains very well). Any loss of brain cells leads to behavioral limitations. Figure 3.45 compares a normal brain with the brain of a stroke victim. Note the areas of lost cells in the stroke victim's brain. A person who survives a stroke will suffer certain behavioral deficits, depending on the location of the damage. As time passes, however, the deficits usually decrease. For example, recall what happens after damage to the right parietal lobe: The person at first neglects the left side of the body and the left side of the world. If the damage is not too severe, however, the stroke victim gradually begins attending to stimuli on the left side, at least when there are no stimuli on the right side competing for attention. As recovery progresses over a period of weeks, the person comes to attend to both sides about equally, although he or she may still attend to stimuli on the right side first.

The reason for the recovery is not obvious. Dead neurons cannot be replaced by new ones, as dead skin cells can. A simple theory might be that one of the surviving brain areas takes over the functions of the damaged area. The evidence, however, contradicts that suggestion, except in children below the age of about 3–5, whose brains are not yet fully developed. After certain kinds of brain injury, children recover from the direct effects (such as loss of muscle control) better than adults do, although they suffer some generalized deficits (such as loss of intelligence) never seen in adults (Taylor, 1984). It is as if the undamaged areas assumed some of the functions of the damaged areas, but in so doing they lost certain functions of their own.

After damage to an adult brain, however, the brain has only a very limited capacity to reorganize. How then does recovery take place?

Therapies for Brain Damage

After brain damage, certain structural changes occur within the brain. Some axons and dendrites sprout new branches; some of the surviving synapses in the damaged area become more sensitive to neurotransmitters (Marshall, 1985). In some cases, these and other structural changes contribute to recovery. Various therapies can aid these physiological recovery processes. We shall look at two therapies, one structural and one behavioral.

Partial Brain Transplants Suppose you suffered damage to part of your brain. What would happen if a surgeon took the corresponding part of someone else's brain and transplanted it into yours? Never mind, for the moment, where the surgeon might find a donor or what kind of identity crisis you might experience. Let's just consider whether the operation might work.

If the surgeon took brain tissue from an adult donor, then the answer is simple: The operation would not work. Chances would be better if the donor was a **fetus** (an individual at an

early stage of prenatal development). The neurons of a fetus are still growing and are primed to make connections with other neurons. In laboratory experiments, investigators have damaged part of a rat's brain, waited until the animal had recovered as much as it could by itself, and measured its behavioral deficits. Then they took the corresponding area from the brain of a fetal rat and transplanted it into the damaged brain of the adult. In a number of experiments, the rats that received the brain transplants showed substantial behavioral recovery (Gash, Collier, & Sladek, 1985; Kimble, 1990).

Does this therapy have any potential for humans? The obvious problem is finding donors. One possibility is to transplant tissue from aborted fetuses. Although that procedure is theoretically the most likely to succeed, it faces legal problems in the United States and presents practical difficulties. For the transplant to succeed, the tissue would have to be taken at just the right stage of development and would have to be implanted almost immediately into the recipient's brain. Several attempts have been made to relieve Parkinson's disease by transplanting tissue from aborted fetuses; so far the results have been mixed but mostly discouraging (Lindvall et al., 1989).

Another possibility is to take brain tissue from the fetus of a related species. Theoretically, such a procedure might work; brain tissue has been transplanted successfully from mice to rats (Björklund, Stenevi, Dunnett, & Gage, 1982).

Still another possibility has been tried as a treatment for Parkinson's patients—substituting adrenal gland tissue for brain tissue. Because adrenal gland cells produce dopamine, they can stand in for the lost neurons that released dopamine as their neurotransmitter. A few Parkinson's patients in Sweden, Mexico, and the United States have received adrenal gland transplants, but most of them experienced only slight benefits or none at all (Backlund et al., 1985; Lewin, 1988). Evidently brain-tissue grafts are not useful with our present methods. With additional research, some variant of this technique may become practical.

Behavioral Therapies for Brain Damage Many brain-damaged people are capable of doing more than they initially realize. For example, someone who has lost all sensation in one arm may stop using it, relying instead on the arm with normal sensation. If forced to try using the impaired arm, that person may be surprised at his or her success. People who have suffered damage to certain parts of the occipital lobe of the cerebral cortex lose their peripheral vision. However, if they simply learn to turn their heads back and forth, they can gain the missing information (Marshall, 1985). Furthermore, after certain kinds of brain damage, people tend to neglect certain kinds of stimuli; for example, they may pay attention to what they feel and ignore what they see. Their vision is impaired but not altogether lost; with sufficient practice they can learn to attend to what they see. Physical therapists and other medical personnel work with brain-damaged people, encouraging them to practice their impaired skills.

Psychologists also work with patients who have lost certain social skills. Some people with frontal-lobe damage seem to lose their inhibitions. They insult others, make obscene sexual comments in public, and fail to bathe themselves. Therapists cannot undo the brain damage, but they can train the person to behave acceptably, using the same training techniques one might use with an ill-behaved child (McGlynn, 1990).

The Precarious Nature of Recovery

As we have seen, people can gradually recover some of the behaviors that are lost through brain damage. For example, a rat with damage to part of its hypothalamus at first neither eats nor drinks and seldom moves. If it is kept alive by tube feeding, it gradually begins to eat and drink a little of highly tasty substances, then a little more, and then begins to accept less tasty substances until eventually it eats enough of a normal diet to keep itself alive. Meanwhile, the rat begins to make a few simple movements and then more until eventually it has a full range of movements.

However, the recovered rat is still different from normal rats; its behavior deteriorates rapidly in the presence of stressors that would hardly bother a normal rat. For example, if the room gets too cold, or if the rat loses a little blood, then the rat stops eating, drinking, and moving (Snyder & Stricker, 1985; Stricker, Cooper, Marshall, & Zigmond, 1979).

Similarly, many people who have recovered from a stroke deteriorate badly under conditions that a normal person tolerates with relative ease. A man who has recovered the ability to speak, for instance, may be able to utter only garbled nonsense after he has had a couple of alcoholic drinks.

Furthermore, long after people have recov-

After a stroke at age 39, actress Patricia Neal had to learn how to walk and talk again. Dominoes and jigsaw puzzles were part of her therapy. Within 3 years she resumed her career.

ered more or less normal behavior following brain damage, they may suffer a relapse in old age. An older person's behavior may deteriorate, eventually ending up about the same as it was just after the damage (Schallert, 1983).

This deterioration has interesting implications. If you suffer mild or gradual brain damage as a young adult—perhaps from a concussion, a brain infection, or the use of drugs—you may not notice any change in your behavior at the time. Your young brain compensates for the loss of neurons, and the surviving neurons may work a little harder to keep your behavior about the same. In old age, however, as natural processes lead to an additional loss of neurons and to less vigorous brain activity, the compensation begins to fail and the symptoms finally appear.

Something to Think About

Many young people who are exposed to toxins or brain infections show no symptoms at the time, but develop Parkinson's disease in old age. How might you explain this phenomenon, given what you have just learned about recovery from brain damage and deterioration in old age?

SUMMARY

■ *Division of labor in the brain.* Although nearly every structure of the brain contributes in some way to almost every behavior, each structure performs specialized functions. (page 97)

■ *Central and peripheral nervous systems.* The central nervous system consists of the brain (forebrain, midbrain, and hindbrain) and the spinal cord. The peripheral nervous system consists of nerves that communicate between the central nervous system and the rest of the body. (page 97)

■ *Peripheral nervous system.* One division of the peripheral nervous system is the somatic nerves, which convey sensory information from the periphery to the central nervous system and which convey impulses from the central nervous system to the muscles. The other division of the peripheral nervous system is the autonomic nervous system, which regulates the activity of the internal organs. (page 98)

■ *Autonomic nervous system.* The autonomic nervous system is closely related to the endocrine system, organs that release hormones into the blood. (page 100)

■ *Lobes of the cerebral cortex.* The occipital lobe of the cerebral cortex is critical for vision. The parietal lobe is vital for touch and body sensations. The temporal lobe is essential for hearing, complex aspects of vision, and emotional behaviors. The frontal lobe contains the motor cortex, which controls fine movements. The anterior portion of the frontal lobe, the prefrontal cortex, is critical for planning movements and relating them to recent experiences. (page 103)

■ *Corpus callosum.* The corpus callosum is a set of axons through which the left and right hemispheres of the cortex communicate. After it is damaged, information that reaches one hemisphere cannot be shared with the other. (page 107)

■ *Connections from eyes to brain.* In humans, information from the left visual field strikes the right half of both retinas, from which it is sent to the right hemisphere of the brain. Information from the right visual field strikes the left half of both retinas, from which it is sent to the left hemisphere. (page 108)

■ *Split-brain patients.* The left hemisphere is specialized for language in most people. Split-brain patients can describe information only if it enters the left hemisphere. Because of the lack of direct communication between left and right hemispheres in split-brain patients, such people show signs of having separate spheres of awareness. (page 110)

■ *Recovery from brain damage.* Most brain-damaged people recover partly, although their behavioral capacities remain more precarious than those of people who have not suffered brain damage. Currently, the most successful therapy for brain damage is simply for the person to practice the impaired behaviors. (page 111)

SUGGESTIONS FOR FURTHER READING

Blakemore, C. (1977). *Mechanics of the mind.* New York: Cambridge University Press. A captivating, well-illustrated discussion of brain functioning.

Valenstein, E. S. (1986). *Great and desperate cures.* New York: Basic Books. A fascinating history of the rise and fall of prefrontal lobotomies.

TERMS

stroke an interruption of blood flow, and thus of oxygen supply, to part of the brain (page 97)

central nervous system the brain and the spinal cord (page 97)

peripheral nervous system the nerves that convey messages from the sense organs to the central nervous system and from the central nervous system to the muscles and glands (page 97)

nerve a bundle of axons carrying messages from the sense organs to the central nervous system or from the central nervous system to the muscles and glands (page 97)

somatic nervous system the nerves that control the muscles (page 98)

autonomic nervous system a set of neurons lying in and alongside the spinal cord that receive information from and send information to the organs, such as the heart (page 98)

forebrain the most anterior (forward) part of the brain, including the cerebral cortex and other structures (page 98)

midbrain the middle part of the brain, more prominent in fish, reptiles, and birds than in mammals (page 98)

hindbrain the most posterior (hind) part of the brain, including the medulla, pons, and cerebellum (page 98)

spinal cord the part of the central nervous system that communicates with sensory neurons and motor neurons below the level of the head (page 98)

sensory neuron a neuron that carries information about touch, pain, and other senses from the periphery of the body to the spinal cord (page 98)

motor neuron a neuron that transmits impulses from the central nervous system to the muscles or glands (page 98)

reflex a rapid, automatic response to a stimulus (page 98)

endocrine system a set of glands that produce hormones and release them into the blood (page 101)

hormone a chemical released by a gland and conveyed by the blood to other parts of the body, where it alters activity (page 101)

medulla a structure located in the hindbrain that is an elaboration of the spinal cord; controls many muscles in the head and several life-preserving functions, such as breathing (page 101)

pons a structure adjacent to the medulla that receives sensory input from the head and controls many muscles in the head (page 101)

reticular formation a diffuse set of neurons, extending from the medulla into the forebrain, that is largely responsible for variations in the level of arousal of the brain (page 101)

cerebellum (Latin for "little brain") a hindbrain structure that is active in the control of movement, especially for complex, rapid motor skills (page 101)

finger-to-nose test a test to assess possible damage to the cerebellum in which a person is asked to hold one arm out straight and then, with eyes closed, to touch the nose as quickly as possible (page 102)

cerebral cortex the outer surface of the forebrain (page 102)

hemisphere the left or the right half of the brain; each hemisphere is responsible for sensation and motor control on the opposite side of the body (page 102)

occipital lobe the rear portion of each hemisphere of the cerebral cortex, critical for vision (page 103)

visual field what you see (page 103)

parietal lobe a portion of each hemisphere of the cerebral cortex that is the main receiving area for the sense of touch, for perception of one's own body, and to some extent for voluntary movement (page 103)

primary somatosensory cortex a strip in the anterior (forward) part of the parietal lobe that receives most touch sensation and other information about the body (page 104)

neglect tendency to ignore stimuli on one side of the body or one side of the world (page 104)

temporal lobe a portion of each hemisphere of the cerebral cortex that is the main processing area for hearing, complex aspects of vision, and emotional behavior (page 104)

frontal lobe the anterior portion of each hemisphere of the cerebral cortex, containing the primary motor cortex and the prefrontal cortex (page 105)

primary motor cortex a strip along the rear portion of the frontal lobe, critical for the control of fine movements (page 105)

prefrontal cortex the portion of the frontal lobe in front of the motor cortex, critical for planning movements and for certain cognitive functions (page 105)

prefrontal lobotomy an operation in which part of the prefrontal cortex is damaged or in which the connections are cut between the prefrontal cortex and other brain areas (page 105)

regional cerebral blood flow technique (rCBF) a technique for estimating the level of activity in an area of the brain by dissolving radioactive xenon in the blood and measuring the radioactivity emitted in that area (page 107)

corpus callosum a large set of axons connecting the left and right hemispheres of the cerebral cortex and enabling the two hemispheres to communicate with each other (page 107)

epilepsy a condition characterized by abnormal rhythmic activity of brain neurons (page 108)

retina the visual receptors lining the back of the eyeball (page 109)

optic nerve bundle of axons from the retina to the brain (page 109)

fetus an individual at an early stage of prenatal development (page 112)

ANSWERS TO CONCEPT CHECKS

12. The storage of fats takes place at many sites throughout the body. A hormone diffuses throughout the body; a neurotransmitter exerts its effects only on the neurons immediately adjacent to where it was released. (page 100)

13. The damage probably is in: (a) the right parietal lobe, (b) one of the temporal lobes, (c) the primary motor cortex in the left frontal lobe, (d) the right occipital lobe, and (e) at least part of the prefrontal cortex. (page 106)

14. To describe something, the person must see it with the left half of the retina of either eye. The left half of the retina sees the right visual field. (page 111)

4 SENSATION AND PERCEPTION

When my son Sam was 8 years old, he asked me, "If we went to some other planet, would we see different colors?" He did not mean just a new shade or a new mixture of familiar colors. He meant colors that were truly new, as different from familiar colors as yellow is from red or blue. I told him no, that would be impossible, and I tried to explain why. I am not sure he understood.

No matter where we might go in outer space, no matter what unfamiliar objects or atmospheres we might encounter, we could never experience a color, or a sound, or any other sensation that would be fundamentally different from what we experience on Earth. Different combinations, perhaps. But fundamentally different sensory experiences, no.

Three years later, Sam told me he was wondering whether people who look at the same thing are all having the same experience. When different people look at something and call it "green," how can we know whether they are all seeing the same "green"? I agreed that there was no sure way of knowing.

Why am I certain that colors on a different planet would look the same as they do on Earth and yet uncertain that colors look the same to different people here? You may find the answer obvious. If not, I hope it will be after you have read this chapter.

Sensation is the conversion of energy from the environment into a pattern of response by the nervous system. It is the registration of information. **Perception** is making sense of that information. Light rays striking your eyes or sound waves striking your ears give rise to sensation. When you say, "I see my roommate" or "I hear the call of a mourning dove," you are expressing your perception of what those sensations mean.

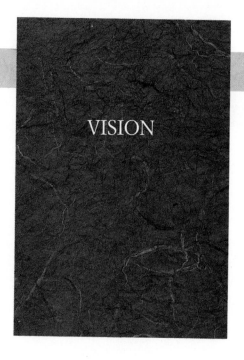

VISION

How do our eyes convert light energy into something we can experience?

How do we perceive colors?

We live in a world full of **stimuli**—energies that affect what we do. Our eyes, ears, and other sensory organs are packed with **receptors**—specialized cells that convert environmental energies into signals for the nervous system. Somehow the nervous system builds a representation of the useful information in the outside world. But how?

When we think about vision, we easily fall into the trap of imagining that the brain simply builds a little copy of what the eyes see. For example, if you see a ball on top of a table, perhaps that is because a set of neurons somewhere in your brain represents the ball and some other set *under* the first set represents the table. Maybe the neurons representing the ball are themselves arranged in a spherical pattern so that a ball-shaped set of neurons gets active every time you see a ball.

Today, neuroscientists consider such a proposal ridiculous, but people of long ago assumed it must be true. Both philosophers and anatomists tried to figure out how the connections from the eyes to the brain might curve around to form an image that was "right-side-up" in the brain. That question would not even make sense unless we assume that the brain has to form copies of what the eyes see.

Even today, many people find it hard to shake the idea that the brain forms copies of the visual image. To get away from that problem, let us consider for a moment the way your brain represents odors. Although no one yet knows the details of this process, we are not even tempted to assume that the brain builds little copies of what we smell. Are the neurons that smell a rose arranged in the shape of a rose? Are they arranged in the shape of some molecule in the rose? Of course not. The way the brain represents the smell of a rose need not physically resemble anything about the rose.

The same goes for vision. The representation of a visual stimulus in the brain need not physically resemble what we see, any more than the representation of a smell resembles the flower. Furthermore, what we experience is not the same as what is "out there." As a light grows more intense, we see it as "brighter," but brightness is not the same thing as intensity. If the wavelength of a light changes, we see it as a different color, but color is not the same thing as wavelength. Our experiences do not *copy* the outside world; they *translate* it into a very different language.

THE DETECTION OF LIGHT

What we refer to as *light* is just one part of the electromagnetic spectrum. As Figure 4.1 shows, the **electromagnetic spectrum** is the continuum of all the frequencies of radiated energy, from gamma rays and X rays, which have very short wavelengths, through ultraviolet, visible light, and infrared to radio and TV transmissions, which have very long wavelengths.

What makes "visible light" visible? The answer is "our receptors," which are equipped to respond to wavelengths from 400 nm to 700 nm. With different receptors, we might see a different range of wavelengths. Some species—bees, for example—see some wavelengths shorter than 350 nm, which are invisible to humans. However, bees fail to see some of the longer wavelengths, those that appear red to most humans.

FIGURE 4.1
Visible light, what human eyes can see, is a small part of the electromagnetic spectrum. Experimenting with prisms, Isaac Newton discovered that white light is a mixture of all colors, and color is a property of light. A carrot looks orange because it reflects orange and absorbs all the other colors.

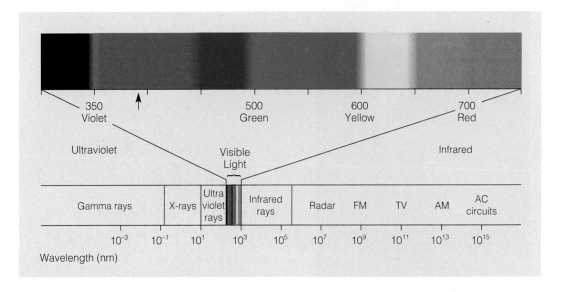

The red you see in some snapshots is the color of the retina, reflecting light from a flash that is mounted on the camera so that light bounces straight back.

Structure of the Eye

When we see an object, light reflected from that object passes through the **pupil,** an adjustable opening in the eye through which light enters. The **iris** is the colored structure on the surface of the eye, surrounding the pupil. It is the structure we describe when we say someone has brown eyes, blue eyes, or whatever. When the light is dim, muscles open the pupil to let in more light. When the light is bright, muscles narrow the pupil.

After light passes through the pupil, it travels through the *vitreous humor* (a clear, jellylike substance) and strikes the retina at the back of the eyeball. The **retina** is a layer of visual receptors covering the back surface of the eyeball. As light passes through the eye, the cornea and the lens focus the light on the retina as shown in Figure 4.2.

The **cornea,** a rigid transparent structure on the outer surface of the eyeball, focuses light in the same way at all times. The **lens,** however, is a flexible structure that can vary in thickness, enabling the eye to focus on objects at different distances. When we look at a distant object, for example, our eye muscles relax and let the lens become thinner and flatter, as shown in Figure 4.3a. When we look at a close object, our eye muscles tighten and make the lens thicker and rounder (Figure 4.3b). In old age, the lens becomes less flexible. That is why many older people need eyeglasses, or corrective lenses, in order to focus on nearby objects.

The lens filters out some light, especially blue and ultraviolet light. A *cataract* is a disorder in which the lens becomes cloudy. People with severe cataracts may have a lens surgically removed and replaced with a contact lens. Sometimes they report seeing colors, especially blue, more clearly and distinctly than they did before the operation (Davenport & Foley, 1979). They do, however, suffer increased risk of damage to the retina from ultraviolet light.

Our vision is best when our eyeballs are nearly spherical. A person whose eyeballs are elongated, as shown in Figure 4.4a, can focus well on nearby objects but has difficulty focus-

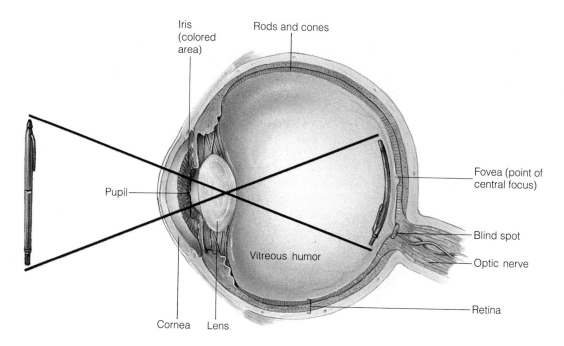

Iris (colored area)

Rods and cones

Pupil

Fovea (point of central focus)

Blind spot

Optic nerve

Vitreous humor

Retina

Cornea   Lens

FIGURE 4.2

The lens gets its name from Latin for lentil, *referring to its shape—an appropriate choice, as this cross section of the eye shows. The names of other parts of the eye also refer to their appearance.*

ing on distant objects. Such a person is said to be *nearsighted,* or to have **myopia** (mi-O-pea-ah). About half of all 20-year-olds are nearsighted and must wear glasses or contact lenses in order to see well at a distance. A person whose eyeballs are flattened, as shown in Figure 4.4b, is *farsighted.* Such a person can focus well on distant objects but has difficulty focusing on close objects. Farsightedness is less common than nearsightedness.

Some nearsighted people have undergone a form of surgery known as *radial keratotomy* (CARE-ah-TOT-oh-mee). In this operation, the surgeon makes small incisions, generally 16 or fewer, in the eyeball (Bores, 1983). As the eyeball heals, it flexes and changes shape. If the surgery is performed properly, the eye will more or less regain its normal shape. Most people experience an overall improvement of vision after the operation, although a few experience *overcorrection*—that is, they end up being farsighted instead of nearsighted (Waring et al., 1987).

The Visual Receptors

The visual receptors of the eye are specialized neurons in the retina, at the back of the eyeball. They are so sensitive to light that they are capa-

ble of responding to a single photon, the smallest possible quantity of light.

These visual receptors are of two types: cones and rods. The two differ in appearance, as Figure 4.5 shows, and in function. The **cones** are adapted for color vision, daytime vision, and detailed vision. The **rods** are adapted for vision in dim light.

About 5–10% of all the visual receptors in the human retina are cones. Most birds have about the same proportion or a higher proportion of cones than humans have; they also have good color vision. Species with very few cones in their retina—rats, for example—make little use of color vision. Every species of mammal that has been tested has at least a small number of cones and at least a slight ability to respond to differences in color (Jacobs, 1981).

The proportion of cones is highest toward the center of the retina. The **fovea** (FOE-vee-uh), the central area of the human retina, is adapted for highly detailed vision (Figure 4.2). The fovea has a greater density of receptors than any other part of the retina; also, receptors in the fovea send their information to a great number of cells at later stages in the nervous system. If you want to see something in detail, you focus it on the fovea; for example, you can read letters of the alphabet only if you see them in or near the fovea.

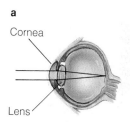

a

Cornea

Lens

Focus on distant object (lens thin)

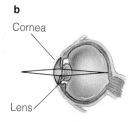

b

Cornea

Lens

Focus on close object (lens thick)

FIGURE 4.3

Changing shape so that objects (a) far and (b) near can come into focus, the flexible, transparent lens bends entering light rays so that they fall on the retina. In old age, the lens becomes rigid and people find it harder to focus on nearby objects.

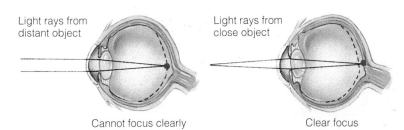

Light rays from distant object

Light rays from close object

Cannot focus clearly

Clear focus

a Nearsighted eyes

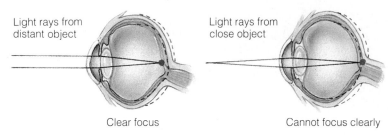

Light rays from distant object

Light rays from close object

Clear focus

Cannot focus clearly

b Farsighted eyes

F I G U R E 4 . 4

The structure of (a) nearsighted and (b) farsighted eyes distort vision. Because the nearsighted eye is elongated, light from a distant object focuses in front of the retina. Because the farsighted eye is flattened, light from a nearby object focuses behind the retina. (The dashed line shows the position of the normal retina in each case.)

Other animal species have eyes that are organized somewhat differently from human eyes. For example, hawks, owls, and other predatory birds have a greater density of receptors on the top of the retina (looking down) than on the bottom of the retina (looking up). When these birds are flying, this arrangement enables them to see the ground beneath them in detail. When they are on the ground, however, they have trouble seeing above themselves (Figure 4.6).

The fovea consists solely of cones (Figure 4.2). Away from the fovea, the proportion of cones drops sharply. That is why you have poor color vision, or none at all, in the far periphery of your eye. Try this experiment: Hold several pens or pencils of different colors behind your back. (Any objects will work so long as they have about the same size and shape and approximately the same brightness.) Pick one at random without looking at it. Hold it behind your head and bring it very slowly into your field of vision. When you just barely begin to see it, you will probably not be able to tell what color it is. (If glaucoma or some other medical problem has impaired your peripheral vision, you will have to bring the object closer to your fovea before you can see it at all.)

The rods are more effective than the cones in detecting dim light for two reasons: First, a rod is slightly more responsive to faint stimulation than a cone is. Second, the rods pool their

These photographs simulate (a) near-sightedness and (b) farsightedness.

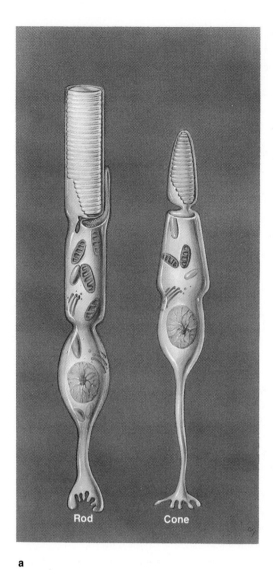

a

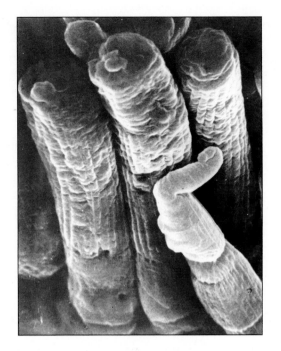

b

FIGURE 4.5
(a) A rod and a cone, the eye's two types of sensing cells. (b) Rods and cones seen through a scanning electron micrograph. The rods, which number over 120 million, help us see in dim light. The 6 million cones in the retina can distinguish gradations of color in bright light; they enable us to see that roses are red, magenta, ruby, carmine, cherry, vermilion, scarlet, and crimson—not to mention pink, yellow, orange, and white.

resources. More than a hundred rods send messages to the next cell in the visual system, but only a few cones converge their messages onto a given cell.

Here is another difference between rods and cones: When a light is suddenly turned off, the activity of the cones ceases almost immediately, whereas the activity of the rods declines more gradually (Jacobs, 1981). In other words, the cones give more accurate information about sudden changes in visual stimulation. Table 4.1 summarizes the key differences between rods and cones.

■ CONCEPT CHECK

1. Why is it easier to see a faint star in the sky if you look slightly to the side of the star instead of straight at it? (Check your answer on page 133.)

FIGURE 4.6
The consequence of having receptors mostly on the top of the retina. Birds of prey, such as these owlets, can see down much more clearly than they can see up. In flight, that arrangement is helpful. On the ground, they have to turn their heads almost upside down in order to see above them.

Table 4.1 Differences Between Rods and Cones

	Rods	Cones
Shape	Nearly cylindrical	Tapered at one end
Prevalence in human retina	90–95%	5–10%
Greatest incidence by species	In species that are active at night	In birds, primates, and other species that are active during the day
Area of the retina	Toward the periphery	Toward the fovea
Contribution to color vision	No direct contribution	Critical for color vision
Response to dim light	Strong	Weak
Contribution to perception of detail	Little	Much
Response to sudden change in visual stimulation	Slow	Rapid

In a coal mine or a dark movie theater, we see little at first. As our eyes adapt to the dim light, we see more and more.

Dark Adaptation

You go into a basement at night trying to find your flashlight. The only light bulb in the basement is burned out. A little moonlight comes through the basement windows, but not much. At first you can hardly see anything. A couple of minutes later, you are beginning to see well enough to find your way around. After 10 minutes, you can see well enough to find the flashlight. This gradual improvement in the ability to see under dim light is called **dark adaptation.**

Dark adaptation occurs because the visual receptors gradually become more sensitive as they "rest" in dim light. The cones and rods adapt to the dark at different rates. Ordinarily during the day our vision relies overwhelmingly on cones, and even as we begin adapting to the dark we are seeing mostly with cones. However, if we stay long enough in a very dim location, the rods continue adapting longer than the cones do, until eventually the rods become significantly more sensitive than the cones. At that point we are seeing mostly with rods.

Here is how a psychologist can demonstrate this process of dark adaptation (Goldstein, 1989): You are taken from a well-lit room into a room that is completely dark except for one tiny flashing light. You have a knob that controls the intensity of the light; you are told to make the light so dim that you can barely see it. Over the course of 3 or 4 minutes you will gradually decrease the intensity of the light, as shown in Figure 4.7a. Note that a decrease in the intensity of the light indicates an increase in the sensitivity of your eyes.

If you stared straight at the point of light, your results demonstrate the adaptation of your cones to the dim light. (You have been focusing the light on your fovea, which has no rods.) Now the psychologist repeats the study, with one change in procedure: You are told to stare at a very faint light while another light flashes in the periphery of your vision, where it stimulates rods as well as cones. You turn a control knob until the flashing light in the periphery is just barely visible. Figure 4.7b shows the results.

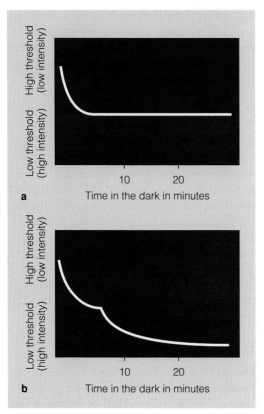

FIGURE 4.7

These graphs show dark adaptation to (a) a light you stare at directly, using only cones, and (b) a light in your peripheral vision, which you see with both cones and rods. (Based on Goldstein, 1989.)

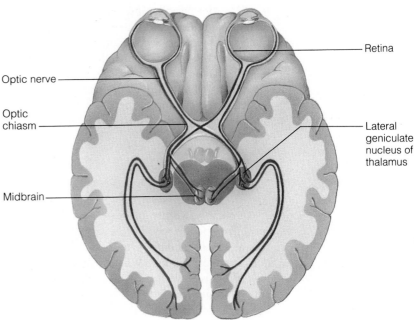

FIGURE 4.8

Axons from cells in the retina depart the eye at the blind spot and form the optic nerve. In humans about half the axons in the optic nerve cross to the opposite side of the brain at the optic chiasm. Some optic nerve axons carry information to the midbrain; others carry it to the thalamus, which relays information to the cerebral cortex.

During the first 7 to 10 minutes, the results are the same as before. But then your rods become more sensitive than your cones, and you begin to see even fainter lights. Your rods continue to adapt to the dark over the next 20 minutes or so.

■ CONCEPT CHECKS

2. You may have heard people say that cats can see in the dark. Is that possible?

3. After you have thoroughly adapted to extremely dim light, will you see more objects in your fovea or in the periphery of your eye? (Check your answers on page 133.)

The Visual Pathway

If you were designing an eye, you would probably run the axons of the cones and rods straight to the brain. Nature chose a different method. The visual receptors send their impulses *away from* the brain, toward the center of the eye, where they make synaptic contacts with other neurons called bipolar cells. The *bipolar cells* in turn make contact with still other neurons, the **ganglion cells.** The axons from the ganglion cells join to form the **optic nerve,** which exits the eye, as Figures 4.2 and Figure 4.8 show. Half of each optic nerve crosses to the opposite side of the brain at the optic chiasm. Axons from the optic nerve separate and go to several locations in the brain. In humans the largest number go to the thalamus, which then sends information to the occipital lobe, the primary area of the cortex for visual processing. (In some species, especially nonmammals, the route to the midbrain is larger.)

The area at which the optic nerve exits the retina is called the **blind spot.** There is no room for receptors here because the exiting axons take up all the space. You can find your own blind spot by covering your left eye and staring at the X or by covering your right eye and staring at the O below. Then slowly move the page forward and backward. At a certain distance the letter you are not staring at will disappear, because you focus that letter onto the blind spot of your eye.

X   O

Ordinarily we are unaware of our blind spot. Even people who have a very large blind spot as a result of damage to the retina are seldom aware of their loss. What accounts for this lack of awareness? Figure 4.9 may suggest an answer. Cover your left eye and stare at the X in the center of Figure 4.9, then slowly move the

FIGURE 4.9
Close your left eye and focus your right eye on the x. *Move the page toward your eyes and away from them until you find a point at which the* o *on the right disappears. At that point the* o *is focused on the blind spot of your retina, where you have no receptors. Note what you see in its place—not a blank spot, but a continuation of the square.*

page forward and backward, as you did with the first demonstration. Notice what happens when this O disappears: You see a complete square! Your brain fills in the gap at the blind spot to complete the pattern.

COLOR VISION

As Figure 4.1 shows, different colors of light correspond to different wavelengths of electromagnetic energy. (White light consists of an equal mixture of all the visible wavelengths.) How does the visual system convert those wavelengths into our perception of color? Although no one theory answers all questions about color vision, we can account for the main phenomena of color vision with a combination of three theories—the trichromatic (or Young-Helmholtz) theory, the opponent-process theory, and the retinex theory.

The Trichromatic Theory

The **trichromatic theory,** also known as the **Young-Helmholtz theory,** was proposed by Thomas Young and modified by Hermann von Helmholtz in the 19th century. According to this theory, color vision depends on the relative rate of response of three types of cones. Each type of cone is most sensitive to a particular range of light wavelengths (Figure 4.10). One type is most sensitive to short wavelengths, another to medium wavelengths, and another to long wavelengths. Each wavelength prompts varying levels of activity in the three types of cones. We perceive *blue* when the short-wavelength cones are more active than the other two. We see *green* when the medium-wavelength cones are the most active. We perceive *red* when the long-wavelength cones are the most active. When the long-wavelength and the medium-wavelength cones are equally active and the short-wavelength cones are less active, we see *yellow.* When all three types of cones are equally active, we see *white* or *gray.* Each color is the result of a unique ratio of responses. We perceive *black* when a group of cones is inactive and is bordered by an area where all three types of cones are active. The contrast is necessary for the perception of black.

Young and Helmholtz proposed their theory long before experiments had confirmed that people do indeed have three types of cones (Wald, 1968). They relied entirely on a behavioral observation: They found that observers could choose three different colors of light and then, by mixing them in various proportions, match all other colors of light. (Note that mixing light of different colors is not the same as mixing paints of different colors. Mixing yellow and blue *paints* produces green; mixing yellow and blue *light* produces white.)

The short-wavelength cones, which respond most strongly to blue, are less numerous than the other two types, especially in the fovea. Consequently a tiny blue point may look black. In order for the retina to detect blueness, the blue must extend over a moderately large area. Figure 4.11 illustrates this effect. Count the red spots and then the blue spots. Then stand farther away and count the spots again. You will probably see as many red spots as before but fewer blue spots.

- ■ CONCEPT CHECK

4. According to the trichromatic theory, how do we tell the difference between bright yellow-green and dim yellow-green light? (Check your answer on page 133.)

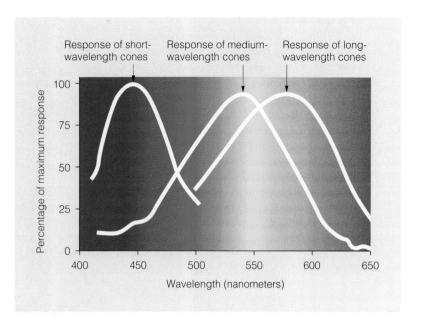

FIGURE 4.10
Sensitivity of three types of cones to different wavelengths of light.

The Opponent-Process Theory

The trichromatic theory was only partly right. Young and Helmholtz were right about how many cones we have, but they were not simply trying to predict the number of cone types. They were trying to explain color vision. On many points, too detailed to consider here, their trichromatic theory could not easily account for the results.

Another 19th-century scientist, Ewald Hering, having noticed that color perceptions seem to occur in pairs, proposed the **opponent-process theory** of color vision, which accounts for much of what happens after the cones send their information to the bipolar cells and ganglion cells. According to this theory, we perceive color not in terms of independent colors but in terms of a system of paired opposites: red versus green, yellow versus blue, and white versus black. Any light stimulus leads to a perception somewhere along each of the three dimensions. Although Hering did not know it, the dimensions correspond to specific responses by

bipolar cells in the eye, and all the later neurons to which they send their information (DeValois, 1965; Michael, 1978). Some bipolar cells are excited when green light strikes the cones that connect to them and inhibited when red light strikes. Other bipolar cells are excited by red and inhibited by green. Still other cells are excited by yellow and inhibited by blue or excited by blue and inhibited by yellow. The white-black system is more complicated: If a cell is excited by white light, we cannot say exactly that it is inhibited by black. Rather, the cell is inhibited when the light on neighboring areas of the retina is brighter than the light in its own area.

For example, in Figure 4.12, bipolar cell 1 receives an excitatory synaptic message from the long-wavelength cone and an inhibitory synaptic message from the medium-wavelength cone. The cell increases its response in the presence of red light and decreases its response in the presence of green light. Bipolar cell 2 receives excitatory synaptic messages from the short-wavelength cone; it is therefore excited by blue light. Cell 2 receives inhibitory messages from both the long-wavelength cone and the medium-wavelength cone; it will be inhibited by red, yellow, or green light.

Figure 4.13 lends support to the opponent-process theory. Pick a point near the center of the figure and stare at it for a minute or so, preferably under a bright light, without moving

FIGURE 4.11
Black or blue? Blue spots look black unless they cover a sizable area. Count the red dots, then count the blue dots. Try again while standing farther away from the page.

FIGURE 4.12

According to the opponent-process theory of color vision, the responses of three kinds of cones excite and inhibit bipolar cells, which relay their responses to later cells in the visual system. For example, red light excites the long-wavelength cone and thereby excites bipolar cell 1; green light excites the medium-wavelength cone and thereby inhibits bipolar cell 1. Therefore, bipolar cell 1 increases its response in the presence of red light and decreases its response in the presence of green light. After prolonged exposure to red light, the cell will "rebound" to an inhibition of response, and therefore report a message of "green."

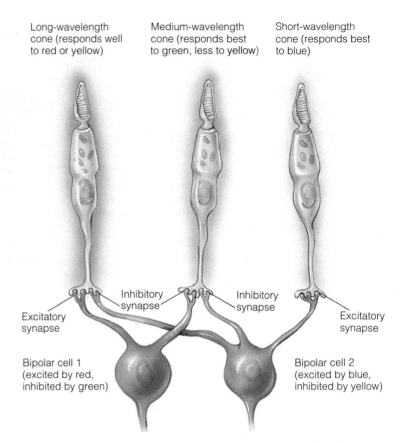

Long-wavelength cone (responds well to red or yellow)

Medium-wavelength cone (responds best to green, less to yellow)

Short-wavelength cone (responds best to blue)

Inhibitory synapse

Inhibitory synapse

Excitatory synapse

Excitatory synapse

Bipolar cell 1 (excited by red, inhibited by green)

Bipolar cell 2 (excited by blue, inhibited by yellow)

To ganglion cells   To ganglion cells

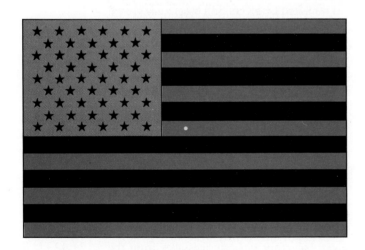

FIGURE 4.13
Use this flag to see the negative afterimages of opposite colors, which rebound after sufficient stimulation.

your eyes or your head. Then look at a plain white or gray background. *Do this now.*

If you have normal or near-normal vision, you saw the red, white, and blue United States flag when you looked away. After the cells in your visual system have been activated in one direction long enough, removal of the stimulus makes them rebound in the opposite direction. Thus, if you stare at something bright green and then look away, you will see red; if you stare at something yellow and then look away, you will see blue. The rebound colors are called **negative afterimages.**

■ CONCEPT CHECKS

5. *How would bipolar cell 1 in Figure 4.12 respond to yellow light? Why?*

6. *The negative afterimage that you created by staring at Figure 4.13 may seem to move against the background. Why doesn't it stay in one place?*

(Check your answers on page 133.)

The Retinex Theory

The opponent-process theory accounts for many phenomena of color vision, but not all. Suppose you look at a full-color illustration in daylight; you see objects of all colors. Then you look at the same illustration under a mostly green light or while you are wearing green-tinted glasses. (See Figure 4.14.) Does everything look green to you? The illustration probably looks greener than it used to, especially at first. And yet you still see objects as yellow, red, blue, or whatever color they were before. This tendency of an object to appear nearly the same color under a variety of lighting conditions is called **color constancy.**

In response to such observations, Edwin Land (the inventor of the Polaroid Land camera) proposed the **retinex theory.** According to this theory, we perceive color through the cerebral cortex's comparison of various retinal patterns (Figure 4.15). (*Retinex* is a combination of *retina* and *cortex.*) The cerebral cortex compares the patterns of light coming from different areas of the retina and synthesizes a color perception for each area (Land, Hubel, Livingstone, Perry, & Burns, 1983; Land & McCann, 1971). Even when the light is mostly green, different objects reflect different amounts of green and other light; these differences enable the cortex to compare one object with another.

Two kinds of evidence support the retinex theory. First, if you look at a lemon under green light in a room full of other objects, you see the lemon as yellow. But if you look at the same lemon under green light against a black background, the lemon looks undeniably green. To maintain color constancy, we have to compare the light coming from a variety of objects. Only the visual cortex is in a position to compare information from areas across the entire visual field.

Second, after monkeys suffer damage to an anterior portion of the occipital cortex, they no longer show color constancy (Wild, Butler, Carden, & Kulikowski, 1985). They still see colors, and they still can learn to pick up only orange objects, for example. But if the light is shifted from white to some other color, they no longer pick up the correct object. As the retinex theory predicts, the phenomenon of color constancy depends on the activity of the cerebral cortex.

Note that each of the three theories of color vision explains different phenomena and that

FIGURE 4.14
You can identify the various colors in these photographs, despite the green and red filters. You experience this constancy when you wear tinted sunglasses. Looking through green lenses, you see corn as yellow, not as green or even as yellow-green.

they are not directly in competition with one another. That is, the retinex theory does not deny that we see colors in terms of three pairs of opposites, and all theories agree that color vision begins with the stimulation of three kinds of cones.

Something to Think About

If you stare for a minute at a small green object on a white background and then look away, you

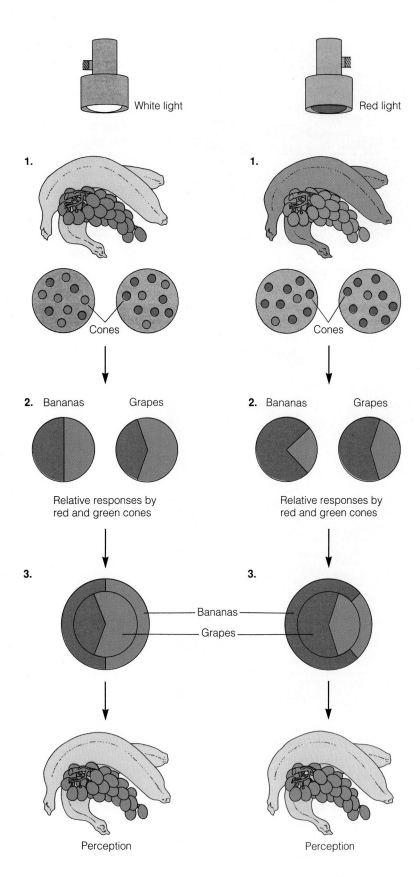

White light

1.

Cones

2. Bananas   Grapes

Relative responses by
red and green cones

3.

Bananas
Grapes

Perception

Red light

1.

Cones

2. Bananas   Grapes

Relative responses by
red and green cones

3.

Perception

FIGURE 4.15
When bananas and grapes reflect red light, they excite a higher percentage of long-wavelength (red) cones than usual. According to the retinex theory, brain cells determine the red-green percentage for each fruit. Then cells in the visual cortex divide the "red-greenness" of the bananas by the "red-greenness" of the grapes to produce color sensations. In red and white light, the ratios between the fruits are nearly constant.

see a red afterimage. But if you stare at a green wall near you so that you see nothing but green in all directions, then when you look away you do not see a red afterimage. Why not?

Colorblindness

For a long time, people apparently assumed that anyone with normal vision could see and recognize colors (Fletcher & Voke, 1985). Then, during the 1600s, the phenomenon of colorblindness was unambiguously recognized. Here was the first clue that color vision is a function of our eyes and brains, and not just of the light itself.

The total inability to distinguish one color from another is extremely rare, except as the result of certain kinds of brain damage. However, about 4% of all people are *partially* colorblind. Investigators believe that most cases of colorblindness result from either the absence of one of the three types of cones or an abnormality in the responsiveness of one of those types (Fletcher & Voke, 1985). For example, one type of cone may have less than the normal amount of **photopigment,** a chemical in the cones and rods that releases energy when it is struck by light. People with a deficiency of the medium-wavelength cones are relatively insensitive to green light. I do not mean that such people are blind to green light; I mean rather that they have trouble discriminating green from other colors. Such people perceive a green patch as almost gray, although they might see very large green patches as green (Boynton, 1988).

The most common type of colorblindness is sometimes known as **red-green colorblindness.** People with red-green colorblindness have difficulty distinguishing red from green and either red or green from yellow. Actually, red-green colorblindness has two forms, *protanopia* and *deuteranopia*. People with protanopia lack long-wavelength cones; people with deuteranopia lack medium-wavelength cones. People with the rare *yellow-blue colorblindness* (also known as *tritanopia*) have trouble distinguishing yellows and blues. They are believed to lack short-wavelength cones.

Figure 4.16 gives a crude but usually satisfactory test for red-green colorblindness. What do you see in each part of the figure? (To interpret your answers, refer to answer A on page 133.)

How does the world look to colorblind people? Their descriptions use all the usual color words: Roses are red, violets are blue, bananas are yellow, grass is green. But that does not mean that they perceive red, green, or any other color the same way a person with normal color vision does. Can they tell us what the rose they say is red actually looks like to them? In most cases, they cannot. Certain rare individuals, however, are red-green colorblind in one eye but have normal vision in the other eye. Because they know what the color words really mean (from experience with their normal eye), they can tell us what their colorblind eye sees. They say that objects that look red or green to the normal eye look yellow or yellow-gray to the colorblind eye (Marriott, 1976).

If you have normal color vision, Figure 4.17 will show you what it is like to be red-green colorblind. First cover part b, a typical item from a colorblindness test, and stare at part a, a red field, under a bright light for about a minute. Then look at part b. Staring at the red field has

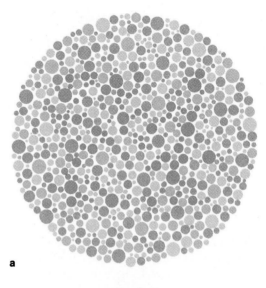

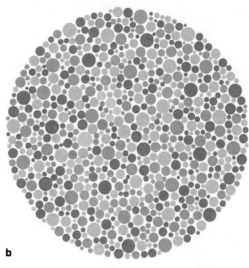

a

b

F I G U R E   4 . 1 6
These items provide an informal test for red-green colorblindness, an inherited condition that affects mostly men. What do you see? Compare your answers to answer A, page 133.

a

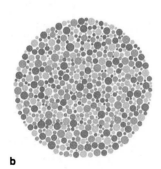

b

c

F I G U R E   4 . 1 7
These stimuli induce temporary red-green colorblindness and temporarily enhance color vision. First stare at pattern a under a bright light for about a minute, then look at b. What do you see? Next stare at c for a minute and look at b again. Now what do you see? Compare your answer to answer B, page 133.

fatigued your red cones, and you now have only a weak sensation of red. As the red cones recover, you will see part b normally. If you are red-green colorblind, the effect will be weak.

Now stare at part c, a green field, for about a minute and look at part b again. Because you have fatigued your green cones, the figure in b will stand out even more strongly than usual. In fact, certain red-green colorblind people may be able to see the number in b only after staring at c. (Refer to answer B on page 133.)

Something to Think About

The introduction to this chapter suggested that we would see no new colors on another planet and that we cannot be certain that different people on Earth really have the same color experiences. Try now to explain the reasons behind those statements.

SUMMARY

■ *The coding of sensory information.* The brain does not build little copies of the stimuli it senses. It converts or translates sensory stimuli into an arbitrary code that represents the information. (page 119)

■ *Focus.* The cornea and lens focus the light that enters through the pupil of the eye. If the eye is not spherical or if the lens is not flexible, corrective lenses may be needed. (page 120)

■ *Cones and rods.* The retina contains two kinds of receptors: cones and rods. Cones are specialized for detailed vision and color perception. Rods detect dim light. (page 121)

■ *Blind spot.* The blind spot is the area of the retina through which the optic nerve exits; this area has no receptors and is therefore blind. (page 125)

■ *Three types of cones.* Color vision depends on three types of cones, each most sensitive to a particular range of light wavelengths. The cones transmit messages so that the bipolar and ganglion cells in the visual system are excited by light of one color and inhibited by light of the opposite color. Then the cerebral cortex compares the responses from different parts of the retina to determine the color of light coming from each area of the visual field. (page 126)

■ *Colorblindness.* Complete colorblindness is rare. Certain people have difficulty distinguishing reds from greens; in rare cases, some have difficulty distinguishing yellows from blues. (page 130)

SUGGESTIONS FOR FURTHER READING

Goldstein, E. B. (1989). *Sensation and perception* (3rd ed.). Belmont, CA: Wadsworth. An excellent textbook covering sensory processes.

Hubel, D. H. (1988). *Eye, brain, and vision.* New York: Scientific American Library. A treatment by an investigator who shared the Nobel Prize in physiology and medicine for his research on the physiology of vision.

TERMS

sensation the conversion of energy from the environment into a pattern of response by the nervous system (page 118)

perception the interpretation of sensory information (page 118)

stimulus an energy in the environment that affects what we do (page 119)

receptor a specialized cell that converts environmental energies into signals for the nervous system (page 119)

electromagnetic spectrum the continuum of all the frequencies of radiated energy (page 119)

pupil the adjustable opening in the eye through which light enters (page 120)

iris the colored structure on the surface of the eye, surrounding the pupil (page 120)

retina a layer of visual receptors covering the back surface of the eyeball (page 120)

cornea a rigid, transparent structure on the surface of the eyeball (page 120)

lens a flexible structure that can vary its thickness to enable the eye to focus on objects at different distances (page 120)

myopia nearsightedness, the inability to focus on distant objects (page 121)

cone the type of visual receptor that is adapted for color vision, daytime vision, and detailed vision (page 121)

rod the type of visual receptor that is adapted for vision in dim light (page 121)

fovea the central part of the retina that has a greater density of receptors, especially cones, than any other part of the retina (page 121)

dark adaptation a gradual improvement in the ability to see under dim light (page 124)

ganglion cells neurons in the eye that receive input from the visual receptors and send impulses via the optic nerve to the brain (page 125)

optic nerve a set of axons that extend from the ganglion cells of the eye to the thalamus and several other areas of the brain (page 125)

blind spot the area of the retina through which the optic nerve exits (page 125)

trichromatic theory or **Young-Helmholtz theory** the theory that color vision depends on the relative rate of response of three types of cones (page 126)

opponent-process theory (of color vision) the theory that we perceive color in terms of a system of paired opposites: red versus green, yellow versus blue, and white versus black (page 127)

negative afterimage a color that a person sees after staring at its opposite color for a while (page 128)

color constancy the tendency of an object to appear nearly the same color under a variety of lighting conditions (page 129)

retinex theory the theory that color perception results from the cerebral cortex's comparison of various retinal patterns (page 129)

photopigment a chemical in the cones and rods that releases energy when it is struck by light (page 130)

red-green colorblindness the inability to distinguish red from green and either red or green from yellow (page 130)

ANSWERS TO CONCEPT CHECKS

1. The center of the retina consists entirely of cones. If you look slightly to the side, the light falls on an area of the retina that consists partly of rods, which are more sensitive to faint light. (page 123)

2. As with people, cats can adapt well to dim light. No animal, however, can see in complete darkness. Vision is the detection of light that strikes the eye. (Similarly, the X-ray vision attributed to the comic book character Superman is impossible. Even if he could send out X rays, he would not see anything unless those X rays bounced off some object and back into his eyes. (page 125)

3. You will see more objects in the periphery of your eye. The fovea contains only cones, which cannot become as sensitive as the rods do in the periphery. (page 125)

4. Although bright yellow-green and dim yellow-green light would evoke the same ratio of firing by the three cone types, the total amount of firing would be greater for the bright yellow-green light. (page 127)

5. Ganglion cell 1 would be almost unaffected by yellow light. Yellow light would stimulate the long-wavelength cone, which excites ganglion cell 1, but it would stimulate the medium-wavelength cone, which inhibits ganglion cell 1, about equally. (page 128)

6. The afterimage is on your eye, not on the background. When you try to focus on a different part of the afterimage, you move your eyes and the afterimage moves with them. (page 128)

ANSWERS TO OTHER QUESTIONS IN THE TEXT

A. In Figure 4.16a, a person with normal-color vision sees the numeral 74; in Figure 4.16b, the numeral 8.

B. In Figure 4.17b, you should see the numeral 29.

THE NONVISUAL SENSES

How do hearing, the vestibular sense, skin senses, pain, taste, and olfaction work?

Consider these common expressions:

I *see* what you mean.

I *feel* sympathetic toward your plight.

I am deeply *touched* by everyone's support and concern.

The Senate will *hold* hearings on the budget proposal.

She is a person of great *taste*.

He was *dizzy* with success.

The policies of this company *stink*.

That *sounds* like a good job offer.

Each sentence expresses an idea in terms of sensation, though we know that the terms are not meant to be taken literally. When we say, "He has great taste," we are not talking about his tongue. Rather, we use such terms to describe a wide variety of concepts.

That usage is not accidental. Most of our thinking and brain activity is devoted to processing sensory stimuli. Sensations bring us in contact with the energies of the outside world. We have already considered the detection of light. Here we deal with the detection of mechanical energies such as touch and vibration and with the detection of chemicals (taste and smell).

HEARING

Fish detect vibrations in the water by means of a long row of touch receptors along their sides, called the *lateral line system.* The mammalian ear, which probably evolved as a modification of the lateral line system, converts sound waves into mechanical displacements of a membrane that a row of receptor cells can detect.

Sound waves are vibrations of the air or of some other medium. They vary in both frequency and amplitude (Figure 4.18). The *frequency* of a sound wave is the number of cycles (vibrations) it goes through per second. **Pitch** is a perception closely related to frequency. We perceive a high-frequency sound wave as high pitched and a low-frequency sound as low pitched. **Loudness** is our perception that depends on the amplitude of a sound wave—the vertical range of its cycles. Other things being equal, the greater the *amplitude* of a sound, the louder it sounds to us. Because pitch and loudness are psychological concepts, however, they can sometimes be influenced by factors other than the physical frequency and amplitude of sound waves.

The ear, a complicated organ, converts relatively weak sound waves into more intense waves of pressure in the fluid-filled canals of the snail-shaped **cochlea** (KOCK-lee-uh), which contains the receptors for hearing (Figure 4.19). When sound waves strike the eardrum, they cause it to vibrate. The eardrum is connected to three tiny bones: the hammer, the anvil, and the stirrup (also known by their Latin names: malleus, incus, and stapes). As the weak vibrations of the large eardrum travel through these bones, they are transformed into stronger vibrations of the much smaller stirrup. The stirrup in turn transmits the vibrations to the fluid-filled cochlea, where the vibrations displace hair cells along the **basilar membrane,** a thin structure within the cochlea. These hair cells, which act much like touch receptors on the skin, are connected to neurons whose axons form the auditory nerve. Impulses are transmitted along this pathway to the areas of the brain responsible for hearing.

A person can lose hearing in two ways. One is **conductive deafness,** which results if the bones connected to the eardrum fail to transmit

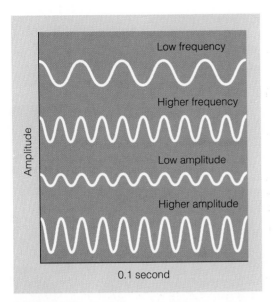

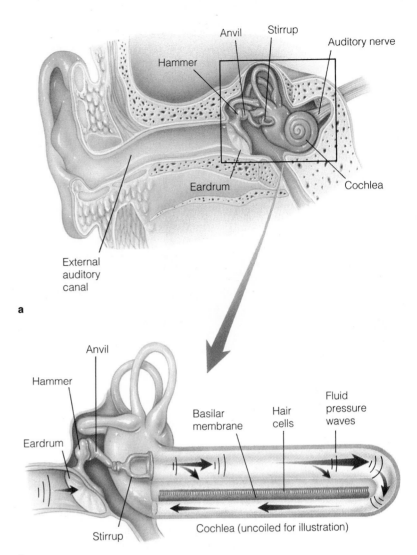

FIGURE 4.18

The period (time) between the peaks of a sound wave determines the frequency of the sound; we experience frequencies as different pitches. The vertical range, or amplitude, of a wave determines the sound's intensity and loudness.

FIGURE 4.19

When sound waves strike the eardrum (a), they cause it to vibrate. The eardrum is connected to three tiny bones—the hammer, anvil, and stirrup—that convert the sound wave into a series of strong vibrations in the fluid-filled cochlea (b). Those vibrations displace the hair cells along the basilar membrane in the cochlea, which is aptly named from the Greek word for snail. Here the dimensions of the cochlea have been changed to make the general principles clear.

sound waves properly to the cochlea. Sometimes surgery can correct conductive deafness by removing whatever is obstructing the movement of those bones. A person with conductive deafness can still hear his or her own voice, because it can be conducted through the skull bones to the cochlea, bypassing the eardrum altogether. The other type of hearing loss is **nerve deafness,** which results from damage to the cochlea, the hair cells, or the auditory nerve. Nerve deafness can result from heredity, from multiple sclerosis and other diseases, and from prolonged exposure to loud noises. Nerve deafness is permanent and cannot be corrected by surgery.

Hearing aids can compensate for the hearing loss in most people with either conductive deafness or nerve deafness (Moore, 1989). Hearing aids merely increase the intensity of the sound, so they are of little help to people with severe damage to the cochlea or the auditory nerve. Many people have hearing impairments only for certain frequencies. For example, people with damage to certain parts of the cochlea have trouble hearing high frequencies or medium-range frequencies. Modern hearing aids can be adjusted to intensify only a certain range of sounds so that they do not intensify the sounds that were already loud enough.

Pitch Perception

The adult human ear responds to sound waves from about 15–20 hertz to about 15,000-20,000 hertz (Hz). (A **hertz,** named for German physicist Heinrich Hertz, is a unit of frequency equaling one cycle per second.) The low frequencies are perceived as deep tones of low pitch; the high frequencies are perceived as tones of high pitch. The upper limit of hearing

135

declines suddenly after exposure to loud noises and declines steadily as a person grows older.

Other species can hear somewhat different ranges of sounds. You probably know about high-frequency whistles made for summoning dogs; the dogs can hear the whistle but people cannot. Some species of bats produce calls around 100,000 Hz and then listen for echoes to locate insects (Roeder, 1967).

The ability to perceive pitch depends on three mechanisms: *frequency, volley,* and *place.* At low frequencies (up to about 100 Hz), the basilar membrane in the cochlea vibrates in synchrony with the sound waves; that is, it produces action potentials at the same frequency as the sound. This is the **frequency principle.** A sound with a frequency of 50 Hz excites each hair cell along the membrane 50 times per second, sending 50 impulses per second to the brain.

At intermediate frequencies (about 100–5000 Hz), the basilar membrane continues to vibrate in synchrony with the sound waves. However, the individual hair cells are unable to send an impulse to the brain every time the membrane vibrates. (A neuron cannot fire more than about 1,000 action potentials per second, and it cannot maintain that pace for long.) Even so, each vibration of the membrane excites at least a few hair cells, and groups of them, volleys, respond to each vibration by producing an action potential (Rose, Brugge, Anderson, & Hind, 1967). This is the **volley principle.** Thus, a tone at 2000 Hz might send impulses to the brain 2,000 times per second, even though no neuron by itself could produce all those impulses.

At high frequencies, sound waves of different frequencies cause vibrations at different locations along the basilar membrane. The membrane is thin and stiff near the stirrup and wide and floppy at the other end. Consequently, high-frequency sounds cause maximum vibration near the stirrup end, and lower-frequency sounds cause maximum vibration at points farther along the membrane. During a high-frequency sound, hair cells near the stirrup become active; during a low-frequency sound, hair cells at the opposite end become active. This is the **place principle.** The brain can identify the frequency by noting which cells are most active.

The reason we can discriminate among pitches is that different pitches excite different hair cells along the basilar membrane (Zwislocki, 1981). Figure 4.20 shows how we perceive pitches of low, medium, and high frequency.

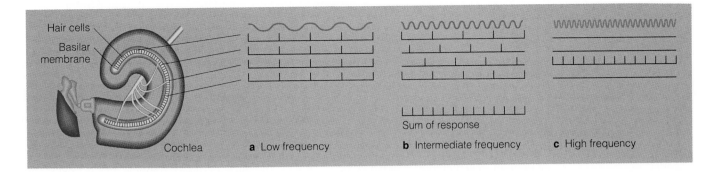

FIGURE 4.20

The auditory system responds differently to low-, medium-, and high-frequency tones. (a) At low frequencies, hair cells at many points along the basilar membrane produce impulses in synchrony with the sound waves. (b) At medium frequencies, different cells produce impulses in synchrony with different waves, but the group as a whole still produces one or more impulses for each wave. (c) At high frequencies, only one point along the basilar membrane vibrates; hair cells at other locations are silent.

■ CONCEPT CHECK

7. *When hair cells at one point along the basilar membrane produce 50 impulses per second, we hear a tone at 5000 Hz. What do we hear when those same hair cells produce 100 impulses per second? (Check your answer on page 148.)*

Localization of Sounds

When you hear something, the stimulus is actually on the basilar membrane of your ear, but you do not experience it as such. You experience it as "out there," and you can generally estimate approximately where it came from. How do you do that?

The auditory system determines the direction of a source of sound by comparing the messages coming from the two ears. If a sound is coming from a source directly in front, the messages will arrive at the two ears at the same time and will be equal in loudness. If the sound is coming from a source on the left, however, it will arrive at the left ear slightly before it arrives at the right ear, and it will be louder in the left ear (Figure 4.21). Yet you do not hear two sounds; you have an experience of a single sound coming from the left. A difference between the messages in the two ears indicates how far the sound source is to the left or right of center.

The auditory system also can detect the approximate distance of a sound source. If a

FIGURE 4.21

The stereophonic hearing of our ears enables us to determine where a sound is coming from. The ear located closest to the sound will receive the sound waves first. A change of less than one ten-thousandth of a second can alter our perception of the location of a sound source.

sound grows louder, you interpret it as coming closer. If one sound includes more high-frequency tones than another does, you assume the one with the high-frequency tones is closer. (Low-frequency tones carry better over a long distance than high-frequency tones do.) However, loudness and frequency tell you only the *relative* distances of sound sources; neither one provides information about the *absolute* distance. The only cue for absolute distance is the amount of reverberation (Mershon & King, 1975). In a closed room, you first hear the sound waves that come directly from the source and then, after a delay, the waves that are reflected off the walls, floor, ceiling, and objects in the room. The more distant the source, the greater the percentage of reflected and delayed sound you hear. When you hear many reflected sounds (echoes), you judge the source of the sound to be far away. In a noisy room, the noise interferes mostly with the weakest sounds, the echoes. In such a room, people have trouble estimating the distances of sounds; because they hear few echoes, they interpret all sounds as coming from short distances (McMurtry & Mershon, 1985).

■ CONCEPT CHECKS

8. Why is it difficult to tell whether a sound is coming from directly in front of or from directly behind you?

9. Suppose you are listening to a radio with just one speaker (not stereo). Can the station play sounds that you will localize as coming from different directions, such as left, center, and right? Can it play sounds that you will localize as coming from different distances? Why or why not? (Check your answers on page 148.)

RECEPTORS OF MECHANICAL STIMULATION

Certain receptors are called **mechanoreceptors** because they respond to mechanical stimulation like pressing and pulling. Hearing and vestibular sensation also detect mechanical stimulation.

The Vestibular Sense

In the inner ear on each side of the head, adjacent to the structures responsible for hearing, is a structure called the *vestibule*. The **vestibular sense** that it controls tells us the direction of tilt

and amount of acceleration of our head and the position of our head with respect to gravity. It plays a key role in posture and balance and is responsible for the sensations we experience when we are riding on a roller coaster or sitting in an airplane during takeoff.

The vestibular sense also enables us to keep our eyes focused even when our head is moving. When you walk down the street, you can keep your eyes focused on a distant street sign even though your head is bobbing up and down. The vestibular sense detects each head movement and controls the movement of your eyes to compensate for it.

Do this experiment: Try to read this page while you are jiggling the book up and down and from side to side, keeping your head steady. Now hold the book steady and move your head up and down and from side to side, keeping the book steady. If you are like most people, you will find it much easier to read when you are moving your head than when you are jiggling the book. That is because your vestibular sense keeps your eyes focused on the print during head movements. People who have suffered injury to their vestibular sense report that they have to hold their head perfectly steady in order to read street signs or clocks. If they move their head even a bit, their vision becomes blurred.

The vestibular system is composed of three semicircular canals, oriented in three separate directions, and two otolith organs (Figure 4.22b). The *semicircular canals* are lined with hair cells and filled with a jellylike substance. When the body accelerates in any direction, the jellylike substance in the corresponding semicircular canal pushes against the hair cells, which send messages to the brain. The two *otolith organs* shown in Figure 4.22b also contain hair cells (Figure 4.22c), which lie next to the *otoliths* (calcium carbonate particles). Depending on which way the head tilts, the particles move about in the direction of gravitational pull and excite different sets of hair cells. The otolith organs report the direction from which gravity is pulling and tell us which way is "up."

At least that is true when the body is at rest. If you walk forward, inertia drags the calcium carbonate particles in your otolith organs backward. Yet you do not grow confused and think that "down" is behind you. How do you know which direction is up and which is down while you are moving?

Apparently the brain integrates information from the vestibular system with information from the eyes and from the feet or from whatever other part of the body is in contact with the

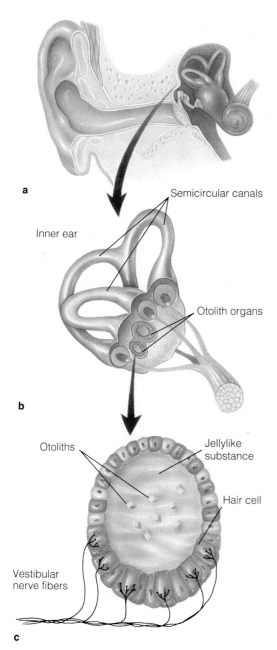

a

Semicircular canals

Inner ear

Otolith organs

b

Otoliths

Jellylike substance

Hair cell

Vestibular nerve fibers

c

In orbit, the otolith organs provide no useful information about "up" and "down." Astronauts rely entirely on visual cues for a sense of direction. But Alan Shepard, the first U.S. astronaut in space, was grounded for years by attacks of vertigo caused by excess fluid in his cochlea and semicircular canals, a condition known as Ménière's disease.

FIGURE 4.22
(a) Location of and (b) structures of the vestibule. (c) Moving your head or body displaces hair cells that report the tilt of your head and the direction and acceleration of movement.

ground (Stoffregen & Riccio, 1988). When the rest of your body tells you that you are keeping your balance, you are likely to feel that your head is up and your feet are down, even if your otolith organs are telling you something else and even if you are not standing perpendicular to the Earth's gravity. For this reason, a pilot feels "right-side-up" with respect to the airplane even when the airplane is executing a steep turn.

The Cutaneous Senses

What we commonly think of as the sense of touch actually consists of several partly independent senses: pressure on the skin, warmth, cold, pain, vibration, movement across the skin, and stretch of the skin. These sensations depend on several kinds of receptors in the skin, as Figure 4.23 shows (Iggo & Andres, 1982). A pinch on the skin feels different from a tickle, and both feel different from a cut or a burn, because each of these stimuli excites different receptors. Collectively, these sensations are known as the **cutaneous senses,** meaning the *skin senses.* Although they are most prominent in the skin, we have some of the same receptors in our internal organs as well, enabling us to feel internal pain, pressure, or temperature changes. Therefore, the cutaneous senses are sometimes known by the broader term *somatosensory system,* meaning *body-sensory system.*

On the fingertips, the lips, and other highly sensitive areas of skin, the receptors are densely packed, and each receptor detects stimulation in only a small area of the skin. On the back and other less sensitive areas, the receptors are scattered more widely, and each one is responsible

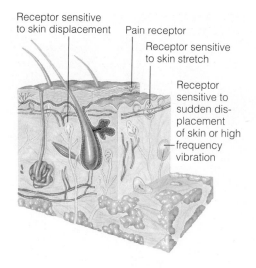

Receptor sensitive
to skin displacement

Pain receptor

Receptor sensitive
to skin stretch

Receptor
sensitive to
sudden dis-
placement
of skin or high
frequency
vibration

FIGURE 4.23
Cutaneous sensation is the product of many kinds of receptors, each sensitive to a particular kind of information.

FIGURE 4.24
Sighted and blind subjects felt these raised-line drawings and tried to identify what they represented. Most sighted subjects and subjects blind since birth found the task very difficult and seldom answered correctly. Subjects who had become blind later in life performed much better (From Heller, 1989).

for detecting stimulation over a large surface. Similarly, much more of the parietal lobe is devoted to sensation from the lips and fingers than from the less sensitive areas.

Humans are far better than most other species at identifying objects by touch, although raccoons provide some tough competition (Rensch & Dücker, 1963). Most people are quite adept at feeling common objects such as spoons or pencils and identifying them, based on hardness and texture (Klatzky, Lederman, & Reed, 1987).

With practice, most people probably could use touch for even more complex identifications. Subjects in one study felt raised-line drawings, like those in Figure 4.24, without seeing them. Some of the subjects were sighted; some were blind since birth; and some had become blind later in life. Most sighted people found it very difficult to identify what the drawings represented, presumably because they had little practice at paying close attention to touch. People blind since birth also had little success on this task, but for a different reason: A raised-line drawing of an umbrella or similar objects makes little sense to someone who has never seen a visual drawing of the same object. In contrast, people who had lost their vision later in life were able to identify many of the objects (Heller, 1989). They had the advantage of previous experience with visual drawings, plus years of practice in paying close attention to touch.

Pain

We experience pain in many ways: when we cut a finger, spill an irritating chemical on our skin, or suffer exposure to extreme heat or cold. Pain receptors are simple, bare nerve endings that send messages to the spinal cord. The sensation of pain, however, is far more complex than the simple relaying of stimulation from the skin to the central nervous system (Liebeskind & Paul, 1977; Melzack & Wall, 1983). Many cutaneous stimuli—including warmth, cold, and pressure—become painful when they are intense. Moreover, many kinds of mild cutaneous stimuli can *reduce* pain. For example, you can make a cut on your leg hurt less if you rub the skin around it or apply cold packs or hot packs (Rollman, 1991). People may also feel more pain or less as a result of the other events going on in their lives. An injured athlete, for example, may show no signs of pain until the game is over. Other people report severe pain after what seems to be just a minor injury. And some people continue to feel pain long after an injury has healed, almost as if pain had become a learned habit. Because of observations such as these, Ronald Melzack and P. D. Wall (1965) proposed the **gate theory** of pain, the idea that pain messages have to pass through a gate in the spinal cord on their way to the brain. The brain and receptors in the skin can send messages to the spinal cord to open or close that gate. Although some details of Melzack and Wall's theory are apparently wrong, their basic idea is valid: The activity of the rest of the brain can facilitate or inhibit the transmission of pain messages (Figure 4.25).

One way to reduce the sensation of pain is to provide some distraction. In terms of the gate theory, the distraction closes the pain gate. For example, surgery patients in a room with a pleasant view complain less about pain, take less painkilling medicine, and recover faster than do patients in a windowless room or a room with a poor view (Ulrich, 1984). Many people relieve their pain by listening to music, by playing games, or by recollecting some pleasant experience (Lavine, Buchsbaum, & Poncy, 1976; McCaul & Malott, 1984).

Many, if not all, of the axons transmitting pain messages in the spinal cord release a neurotransmitter called *substance P*. An injection of the chemical *capsaicin* into the spinal cord of a laboratory animal causes the pain axons suddenly to release large quantities of substance P, and causes the animal to show signs of pain (Yarsh, Farb, Leeman, & Jessell, 1979). Capsaicin is the chemical that makes jalapeños and similar peppers taste hot. When you bite down on a hot pepper, the capsaicin releases minute amounts of substance P from the tongue, causing a stinging, hot sensation.

One way to control pain is to take morphine or similar drugs that stimulate the **endorphin** synapses. The term *endorphin* is a combination of the terms *endogenous* (self-produced) and *morphine*. Endorphins act as neurotransmitters that inhibit the release of substance P, thus decreasing the sensation of pain and inducing pleasant feelings (Reichling, Kwiat, & Basbaum, 1988; Terman, Shavitt, Lewis, Cannon, & Liebeskind, 1984). (See Figure 4.26.)

Pain alerts us to an injury. (People who are totally insensitive to pain have a short life expectancy!) However, once the brain has received a pain message, the prolonged sensation of pain can disrupt behavior. Presumably, endorphin synapses evolved as a means of

FIGURE 4.25
The Lamaze method of giving birth emphasizes control of pain sensations by changing attitudes, controlling fears and anxieties, and concentrating on breathing. It is one example of how the brain can close "pain gates" and thereby alter pain sensation. Here a midwife trains an expectant mother.

reducing the pain signal after it has served its function.

A variety of stimuli can release endorphins. Under some circumstances, a painful stimulus itself releases endorphins so that exposure to one painful stimulus decreases sensitivity to the next painful stimulus (Terman & Liebeskind, 1986). Pleasant stimuli may also release endorphins. (That may help explain why a pleasant view helps to ease postsurgical pain.) In short, endorphins are a powerful method, perhaps the main method, of closing pain "gates."

■ CONCEPT CHECK

10. *Naloxone, a drug used as an antidote for an overdose of morphine, is known to block the endorphin synapses. How could we use naloxone to determine whether a pleasant stimulus releases endorphins? (Check your answer on page 148.)*

FIGURE 4.26
Substance P is the neurotransmitter most responsible for pain sensations. Endorphins are neurotransmitters that block the release of substance P, thereby decreasing pain sensations. Opiates decrease pain by mimicking the effects of endorphins.

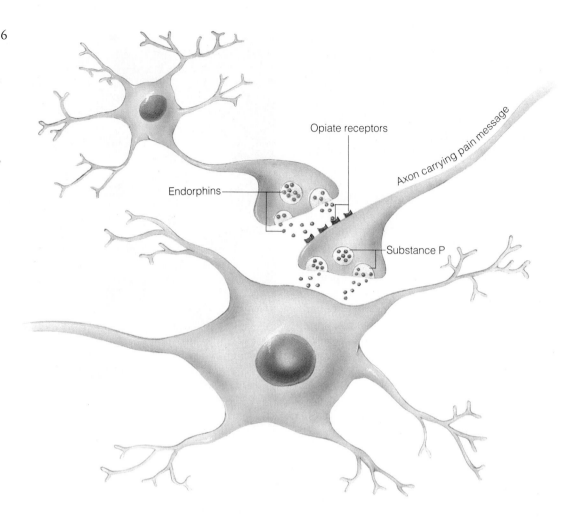

THE CHEMICAL SENSES: TASTE AND SMELL

Most textbooks on sensation spend most of their pages on vision and hearing; some ignore taste and smell or include them in a chapter titled "The Other Senses" or even "The Minor Senses." For most of the animal kingdom, however, these senses are not so minor. If rats or raccoons wrote sensation textbooks, they would probably devote as much coverage to taste and smell as they would to hearing; vision would be one of "The Minor Senses."

The **chemical receptors** responsible for taste and smell are evolutionarily ancient and found throughout the animal kingdom (unlike vision and hearing, which are found in some species and not others). In the mammalian brain, taste and smell have extensive connections to the subcortical areas associated with motivations and emotions; consequently, they tend to evoke strong emotional responses.

Taste

Vision and hearing enable us to do many different things: to find food and water, to avoid danger, to keep our balance, and to find suitable mates. But the sense of **taste,** which detects chemicals on the tongue, serves just one function: It tells us what to eat and drink. The cells in the brain that receive information from the taste receptors are closely related to the cells that control food intake (Yamamoto, 1987).

The taste receptors are located in **taste buds** found in tiny folds on the surface of the tongue (Figure 4.27). They respond to chemicals dissolved in the saliva. We can describe most tastes in terms of four qualities—sweet, sour, salty, and bitter—and we can match most tastes by combining those qualities in varying proportions (Schiffman & Erickson, 1971).

Different Types of Taste Receptors In the 1980s, neuroscientists made major progress in

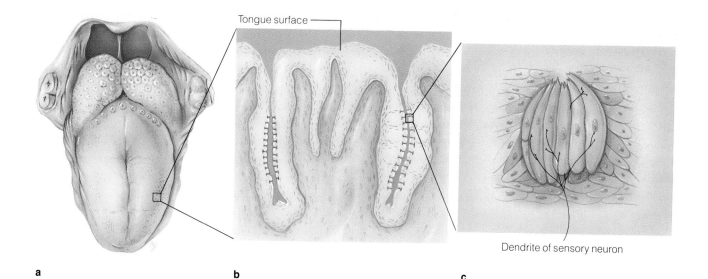

Tongue surface

Dendrite of sensory neuron

a   b   c

FIGURE 4.27

(a) The tongue, a powerful muscle used in speaking and eating. Taste buds, which react to chemicals dissolved in saliva, are located primarily on the tongue papillae (protuberances). (b) A cross section of one of the larger papillae, showing taste buds. (c) A cross section of one taste bud. Each taste bud has about 50 transducer cells within it that continuously replace others as they wear out; these cells last about 10 days. Taste buds are most concentrated at the tip and back of the tongue.

identifying and characterizing the taste receptors. We now have a reasonably clear understanding of how salty receptors and sour receptors work (Avenet & Kinnamon, 1991). Sweet receptors and bitter receptors are less well understood; many researchers believe we have several kinds of sweet and bitter receptors.

Actually, long before the neuroscientists began characterizing taste receptors, behavioral researchers had solid evidence that different tastes depend on different kinds of receptors, probably four or more kinds. That conclusion rested partly on the demonstrations that people can match almost any taste by mixing sweet, sour, salty, and bitter substances (Schiffman & Erickson, 1971). The conclusion was also supported by evidence that certain procedures can affect one taste without affecting others, presumably by acting on only one type of receptor. Here are four examples:

■ Cooling the tongue decreases one's sensitivity to the taste of sucrose and other sweet substances without affecting the taste of salty or sour substances and with only a slight effect on the taste of bitter substances (Frankmann & Green, 1988). This finding suggests that the receptors for sweet tastes have different properties from the receptors for other tastes. (It also

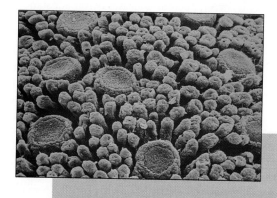

The tongue is one of the most sensitive parts of the body—something you may have discovered if you've accidentally bitten or burnt your tongue or eaten a potent chili pepper. This scanning electron micrograph of the tongue's surface shows the filiform (filamentlike) papillae, which help move food without tasting it.

implies that soft drinks would taste sweeter hot than cold.)

■ Have you ever drunk a glass of orange juice just after brushing your teeth? How can something that ordinarily tastes so good suddenly taste so bad? The reason is that most toothpastes contain sodium lauryl sulfate, a chemical that weakens our response to sweet tastes and intensifies our response to sour and bitter tastes (Schiffman, 1983). Again, the implication is that different taste receptors have different properties.

■ The chemical amiloride prevents sodium ions from crossing the membrane of a cell. This chemical weakens the taste of sodium chloride (common table salt) and other salts as well as sugars but has no effect on the taste of bitter or sour substances (Schiffman, Simon, Gill, & Beeker, 1988). Evidently the salty receptor differs in some respects from the bitter and sour receptors.

■ The artificial sweetener saccharin tastes both sweet and bitter, though some people experience one taste more strongly than the other. If you taste caffeine before tasting saccharin, both the sweet and the bitter tastes of saccharin will be intensified. Preexposure to caffeine has no effect, however, on substances that taste only sweet, such as sucrose, or on substances that taste only bitter, such as quinine (Schiffman, Diaz, & Beeker, 1986). Because we can affect the taste of saccharin without affecting the taste of sucrose or quinine, it seems likely that saccharin stimulates a separate receptor. In other words, we may have separate receptors for sweet, bitter, and sweet-bitter, as well as for salty and sour.

Olfaction

Olfaction is the sense of smell. The olfactory receptors, located on the mucous membrane in the rear air passages of the nose (Figure 4.28b), detect the presence of certain airborne molecules. Chemically, these receptors are much like synaptic receptors, except that they are stimulated by chemicals from the environment instead of chemicals released by other neurons. The axons of the olfactory receptors form the olfactory tract, which extends to the olfactory bulbs at the base of the brain.

How many kinds of olfactory receptors do we have? Neuroscientists have believed since the 1800s and known since the 1960s that color vision depends on three kinds of receptors.

Similarly, they have known about the receptors for hearing, touch, and pain for decades. In taste, debate continues about whether we have just four kinds of receptors or whether we might have a few more than that. Still, the approximate number has been known for a long time. In olfaction, however, until 1991 researchers had virtually no idea how many types of receptors might exist.

In principle, researchers can determine the number of receptor types through behavioral data, without chemically isolating the receptors. In color vision, for example, researchers have long known that people can mix three colors of light in various amounts to match any other color. Therefore, even before they had the technology to examine the cones in the retina, they had reason to believe that the retina has three kinds of cones. In taste, the fact that we can mix sweet, sour, salty, and bitter substances to match almost any other taste implies that the tongue has perhaps only four kinds of taste receptors. When we come to olfaction, no one knew how many kinds of receptors to expect. Can people match all possible odors by mixing appropriate amounts of three, four, seven, or ten "primary" odors? Or do they need fifty, a hundred, or what? No researcher had ever demonstrated that it was possible to match all the possible odors by mixing some number of primaries.

Perhaps it is just as well that no one spent a lifetime trying. In 1991, Linda Buck and Richard Axel used the latest biochemical technology to demonstrate that the nose has at least a hundred types of olfactory receptors (Buck & Axel, 1991). In addition to the hundred or so they found, the nose could easily have more, perhaps several hundred. Each receptor responds to a fair number of odorant molecules, not just one, and each odorant molecule stimulates several or many kinds of receptors. Exactly how the brain makes sense of all this information, we do not know (Figure 4.29). What we can say is that our olfactory system is set up to detect and discriminate among an enormous number of possible molecules. When perfume chemists synthesize some brand-new molecule, people do not need to evolve a new receptor to detect it; we can detect the chemical with some combination of the receptors we already have.

The sense of smell is more acute in most other mammals than it is in humans. A single olfactory receptor is probably about as sensitive in humans as it is in any other species, but other species have a greater number of receptors.

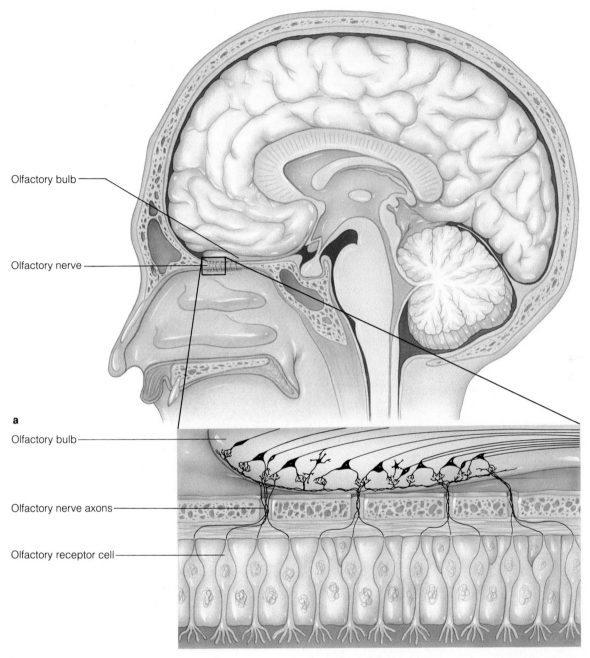

Olfactory bulb

Olfactory nerve

a

Olfactory bulb

Olfactory nerve axons

Olfactory receptor cell

b

FIGURE 4.28

The olfactory receptor cells lining the nasal cavity send information to the olfactory bulb in the brain. There are at least a hundred types of receptors with specialized responses to airborne chemicals.

Specially trained dogs can track a person's olfactory trail across fields and through woods. Dogs also recognize one another by odor. A male dog claims a territory by scent-marking it—depositing a few drops of urine at key locations.

Many mammals identify one another by means of **pheromones,** odorous chemicals they release into the environment. In nearly all nonhuman mammals, the males rely on pheromones to distinguish sexually receptive females from unreceptive females.

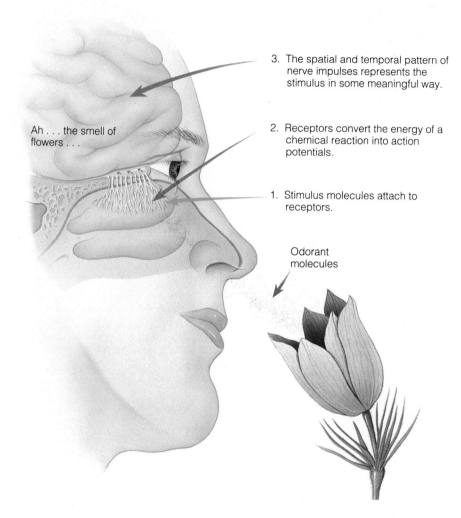

3. The spatial and temporal pattern of nerve impulses represents the stimulus in some meaningful way.

Ah . . . the smell of flowers . . .

2. Receptors convert the energy of a chemical reaction into action potentials.

1. Stimulus molecules attach to receptors.

Odorant molecules

FIGURE 4.29
Olfaction, like any other sensory system, converts a physical energy into a complex pattern of brain activity.

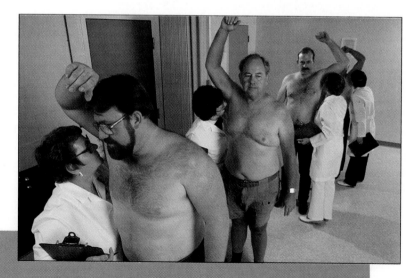

Secret, Ban, Arrid—as their names suggest, U.S. industries spend millions developing and promoting deodorants and antiperspirants so we can secretly banish sweat and have arid armpits. In the past, people used strong perfume to mask odors.

Humans prefer *not* to recognize one another by smell. The deodorant and perfume industries exist for the sole purpose of removing and covering up human odors. But perhaps we respond to pheromones anyway, at least under certain conditions. For example, young women who are in frequent contact with one another, such as roommates in a college dormitory, tend to synchronize their menstrual cycles, probably as a result of pheromones they secrete. (If the women are taking birth-control pills, the synchronization does not occur.) In one experiment, women who were exposed daily to another woman's underarm secretions became synchronized to her menstrual cycle (Russell, Switz, & Thompson, 1980). (*Why* this occurs is not clear. Female dogs, cats, and rats do not synchronize their periods of fertility. Why should humans?)

Human males also secrete an odorous chemical in their sweat, in an amount proportional to the amount of testosterone in their blood. In one experiment, when samples of this chemical were placed in certain bathroom stalls, other men tended to avoid using those stalls (Gustavson, Dawson, & Bonett, 1987).

In addition to its role in responding to pheromones, olfaction plays a key role in food selection. What we call the flavor of a food is produced by both its taste and its smell. When a meat or other food is spoiled, olfaction alerts us to that fact before we even try to taste it.

Something to Think About

Why might it be that humans as well as monkeys and chimpanzees are less sensitive to odors and more responsive to vision than are most other mammals? For an animal living in trees, which is more useful—vision or olfaction?

SUMMARY

- *Pitch.* At low frequencies of sound, we identify pitch by the frequency of vibrations on the basilar membrane. At intermediate frequencies, we identify pitch by volleys of responses from a number of neurons. At high frequencies, we identify pitch by the area of the basilar membrane that vibrates most strongly. (page 135)

- *Localizing sounds.* We localize the source of a sound by detecting differences in the time and loudness of sounds our two ears receive. We localize the distance of a sound source mostly by the amount of reverberation, or echoes, following the main sound. (page 137)

- *Vestibular system.* The vestibular system tells us about the movement of the head and its position with respect to gravity. The vestibular system enables us to keep our eyes focused on an object while the rest of our body is in motion. (page 138)

- *Cutaneous receptors.* We experience many types of sensation on the skin, each dependent on different receptors. The fingertips, lips, and face have especially rich supplies of such receptors. (page 139)

- *Pain.* The sense of pain can be alleviated by a variety of events that release endorphins in the central nervous system. (page 140)

- *Taste receptors.* Researchers have characterized taste receptors for salty and sour tastes; the nature of sweet and bitter receptors is less certain. Even before the receptors were characterized, investigators knew there had to be several kinds, because certain procedures affect one taste quality (such as sweetness) without affecting the others. (page 142)

- *Olfactory receptors.* The olfactory system— the sense of smell—depends on at least a hundred types of receptors, each with its own special sensitivity. (page 144)

- *Pheromones.* Other mammals and perhaps humans use odorous chemicals called pheromones for certain types of communication. (page 145)

SUGGESTIONS FOR FURTHER READING

Heller, M. A., & Schiff, W. (1991). *The psychology of touch.* Hillsdale, NJ: Erlbaum. Describes research on touch and how people learn to use it for Braille reading and other functions.

Melzack, R., & Wall, P. D. (1983). *The challenge of pain.* New York: Basic Books. Discussion of factors that evoke and inhibit pain.

Snyder, S. (1989). *Brainstorming: The science and politics of opiate research.* Cambridge, MA: Harvard University Press. Fascinating account of the research that led to the discovery of endorphins, written by one of the key researchers.

Zwislocki, J. J. (1981). Sound analysis in the ear: A history of discoveries. *American Scientist, 69,* 184–192. Review of research on the mechanisms of hearing.

TERMS

sound waves vibrations of the air or of some other medium (page 134)

pitch a perception closely related to the frequency of sound waves (page 134)

loudness a perception that depends on the amplitude of sound waves (page 134)

cochlea the snail-shaped, fluid-filled structure that contains the receptors for hearing (page 134)

basilar membrane a thin structure in the cochlea that vibrates after sound waves strike the eardrum (page 134)

conductive deafness hearing loss that results if the bones connected to the eardrum fail to transmit sound waves properly to the cochlea (page 134)

nerve deafness hearing loss that results from damage to the cochlea, the hair cells, or the auditory nerve (page 135)

hertz a unit of frequency representing one cycle per second (page 135)

frequency principle identification of pitch by the frequency of action potentials in neurons along the basilar membrane of the cochlea, synchronized with the frequency of sound waves (page 136)

volley principle identification of pitch by the fact that groups of hair cells respond to each vibration by producing an action potential (page 136)

place principle identification of pitch by which auditory neurons, coming from which part of the basilar membrane, are most active (page 136)

mechanoreceptors receptors that respond to mechanical stimulation (page 138)

vestibular sense a specialized sense that detects the direction of tilt and amount of acceleration of the head and the position of the head with respect to gravity (page 138)

cutaneous senses the skin senses, including pressure on the skin, warmth, cold, pain, vibration, movement across the skin, and stretch of the skin (page 139)

gate theory a theory that pain messages have to pass through a gate in the spinal cord on their way to the brain and that the brain and receptors in the skin can send messages to the spinal cord to open or close that gate (page 141)

endorphin any of the neurotransmitters that decrease the perception of pain and induce pleasant feelings (page 141)

chemical receptors the receptors that respond to the chemicals that come into contact with the nose and mouth (page 142)

taste the sensory system that responds to chemicals on the tongue (page 142)

taste bud the site of the taste receptors, located in one of the folds on the surface of the tongue (page 142)

olfaction the sense of smell, the detection of chemicals in contact with the membranes inside the nose (page 144)

pheromone an odorous chemical released by an animal that changes the way other members of its species respond to it socially (page 145)

ANSWERS TO CONCEPT CHECKS

7. We still hear a tone at 5000 Hz, but it is louder than before. For high-frequency tones, the pitch we hear depends on which hair cells are most active, not on how many impulses per second they fire. (page 137)

8. We localize sounds by comparing the input into the left ear with the input into the right ear. If a sound comes from straight ahead or from straight behind (or from straight above or below), the input into the left ear is identical with the input into the right ear. (page 138)

9. Various sounds from the radio cannot seem to come from different directions, because your localization of the direction of a sound depends on a comparison between the responses of the two ears. However, the radio can play sounds that seem to come from different distances, because distance localization does not depend on a difference between the ears. It depends on the amount of reverberation, loudness, and high-frequency tones, all of which can be varied with a single speaker. Consequently, the radio can easily give an impression of people walking toward you or away from you, but not of people walking left to right or right to left. (page 138)

10. First determine how much the pleasant stimulus decreases the experience of pain for several people. Then give half of them naloxone and half of them a placebo. Again measure how much the pleasant stimulus decreases the pain. If the pleasant stimulus decreases pain by releasing endorphins, then naloxone should impair its painkilling effects. (page 141)

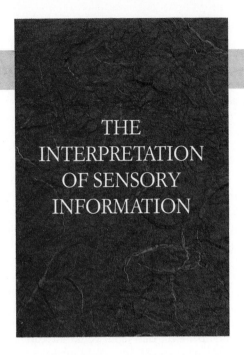

THE INTERPRETATION OF SENSORY INFORMATION

What is the relationship between the real world and the way we perceive it?

How do we make sense of what we see?

Why are we sometimes wrong about what we think we see?

No doubt you have heard people say that "a picture is worth a thousand words." If so, what is one one-thousandth of a picture worth? One word? Ordinarily, one one-thousandth of a picture is worth nothing. (Of course, I grant, "nothing" is *one word*!)

Figure 4.30 shows part of a photograph composed entirely of dots. If you look at it closely, you can see the dots. In fact, if you get close enough or if you use a magnifying glass, you may see nothing but the dots. If you stand back a little farther, you may still be aware of the dots, but now you see combinations of dots as "a hand." From a still greater distance, you can no longer see individual dots; you see only the hand.

Actually, our vision is like this all the time. Your retina is composed of about 126 million rods and cones, each of which sees one dot of the visual field. Granted, that is an enormous number of dots; still, they are dots. What you perceive is not dots, however, but lines, curves, and complex objects. In a variety of ways your nervous system starts with an enormous array of details and extracts the meaningful information.

PERCEPTION OF MINIMAL STIMULI

Right now your receptors are no doubt bombarded by a large number of sensory stimuli. You are (evidently) focusing much of your attention on what you see in this book. But you are also at least vaguely aware of a few other things you see in the periphery of your vision and a few background sounds. You ignore a great many other stimuli, although you could easily shift your attention to them if you had a reason to do so. For example, you probably have not been aware of the feeling of your clothes against your skin, but now that I have called your attention to it, you do notice it.

In addition to the stimuli you sometimes notice, are there other stimuli so weak that you cannot detect them? More controversially, are there some stimuli you do not consciously detect, but which nevertheless influence your behavior?

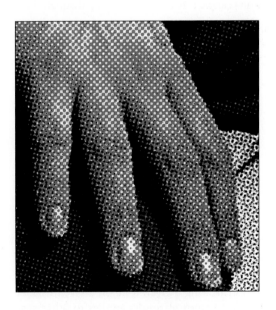

FIGURE 4.30
Although this photograph is composed entirely of dots, we see an overall pattern, a hand. The principles at work in our perception of this photograph are at work in all our perceptions.

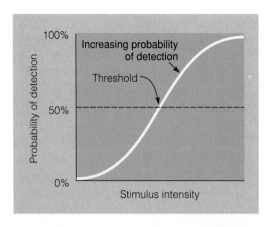

FIGURE 4.31
Typical results of an experiment to measure a sensory threshold. There is no sharp boundary between stimuli that you can perceive and stimuli that you cannot perceive.

Sensory Thresholds

Under ideal circumstances, your sensory receptors can respond to extremely weak stimuli. Once your eyes have become adapted to darkness, the rods will respond to as little as a single photon of light (Baylor, Lamb, & Yau, 1979). An olfactory receptor can respond to a single molecule of an odorant. Human hearing is so acute that some people under certain conditions can hear the blood coursing through their ears.

How intense does a stimulus have to be for us to detect it under ordinary conditions? Many experiments have been conducted to determine the threshold of hearing—that is, the minimum intensity at which we can detect sound. Typically, subjects are presented with tones of varying intensity in random order; sometimes no tone at all is presented. On each trial the subjects are asked to say whether or not they heard a tone. Figure 4.31 presents some typical results. Notice that there is no precise dividing line between the tones that are always heard and those that are never heard. Generally, as loudness increases, the probability of detection also increases. Still, over a certain range of loudness, we cannot be sure whether or not a person will report hearing a given tone on a given trial. A similar pattern of results applies to other sensory systems.

For this reason, perception researchers define a **sensory threshold** as the minimum intensity at which a given individual can detect a

stimulus 50% of the time. Note, however, that an individual will frequently detect stimuli that are weaker than the threshold and sometimes fail to detect stimuli above the threshold.

An individual's sensory threshold may change from time to time—perhaps as a result of **sensory adaptation,** the tendency of a sensory threshold to rise or fall after a period of strong or weak stimulation. The sensory threshold falls after a period when the sensory receptors have not been stimulated. A low threshold means you can detect faint stimuli. For example, if you have been outdoors on a bright, sunny day and you now walk into a movie theater, you have trouble seeing the seats at first. After a few minutes your threshold drops and you see the seats well. If you stayed in the dark theater after the movie ended, your ability to detect dim light would increase still further. The sensory threshold at the time of maximum sensory adaptation is called the **absolute threshold.**

When people try to detect weak stimuli, they can make two kinds of error: They can fail to detect a stimulus (a "miss"), or they can say they detected a stimulus when none was present (a "false alarm"). **Signal-detection theory** is the study of people's tendencies to make correct judgments, misses, and false alarms (Green & Swets, 1966). (Psychologists borrowed signal-detection theory from engineering, where this system is applied to such matters as detecting radio signals in the presence of interfering noise.) According to signal-detection theory, people's responses depend both on the ability of their senses to detect a stimulus and on their willingness to risk a miss or a false alarm. (When in doubt, they have to risk one or the other.)

Suppose we tell a subject that a 10-cent reward will be paid every time he or she correctly reports that a light is present, while a 1-cent penalty will be imposed for reporting that a light was present when it was not. Whenever the subject is not sure that a light is present, he or she will say yes, taking a risk of making a false alarm. The results will resemble those in Figure 4.32a. Now suppose we inform other subjects that they will receive a 1-cent reward for correctly reporting that they saw a light and will suffer a 10-cent penalty *and* an electric shock for reporting that they saw a light when none was present. These subjects will say yes only when they are certain that a light was present. That is, they are more willing to risk a miss than a false alarm. The results will look like those in

Figure 4.32b. *Clearly, if we want to determine which subjects are more sensitive to light, we have to take into account their misses and false alarms as well as their correct judgments.* Subjects whose measured thresholds are high may simply be exercising great caution in making their responses.

This same tendency toward caution shows up when subjects are tested to determine their threshold for recognizing words. For example, in one experiment the subjects were asked to try to read words that were flashed on a screen for just a split second. They performed well when ordinary words like *river* or *peach* were shown. For emotionally loaded words like *penis* or *bitch*, however, they performed poorly. In fact, the words had to be held on the screen for a substantially longer time before the subjects could identify them. Psychologists have suggested a number of possible explanations for such results (e.g., Blum & Barbour, 1979); one possibility is that subjects hesitate to blurt out an emotionally charged word unless they are certain they are right.

Subliminal Perception

You probably have heard of **subliminal perception,** the idea that a stimulus can influence our behavior even when it is presented so faintly or briefly or along with such strong distractors that we do not perceive it consciously. (*Limen* is Latin for "threshold"; thus, subliminal means subthreshold.) Some people claim that subliminal perception can have a powerful, even manipulative, effect on human behavior.

Are such claims plausible or outright nonsense? Problem number one is to define *subliminal*. I just finished telling you that *subliminal* means *subthreshold*. Fine, except that I already told you there is no sharp threshold dividing perceptible stimuli from imperceptible stimuli. If we define *subliminal* or *subthreshold* stimuli as stimuli that people detect on less than 50% of occasions, then subthreshold perception is neither unusual nor surprising. In practical terms, when psychologists refer to a "subliminal stimulus," they generally mean "a stimulus that a person *did not* consciously detect on a given occasion," regardless of whether the person *could have* detected it under other circumstances.

That definition does not end the problem, however. How do we know whether or not someone *did* detect a given stimulus? We ask, of course. But how do we know what the person's

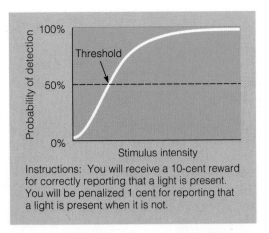

Instructions: You will receive a 10-cent reward for correctly reporting that a light is present. You will be penalized 1 cent for reporting that a light is present when it is not.

a

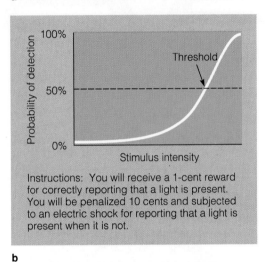

Instructions: You will receive a 1-cent reward for correctly reporting that a light is present. You will be penalized 10 cents and subjected to an electric shock for reporting that a light is present when it is not.

b

FIGURE 4.32
Results of experiments to measure a sensory threshold using two different sets of instructions.

answers really mean? Suppose someone insists that he or she "did not see" some word an experimenter flashed instantaneously on a screen. That reply could mean "I never saw anything," "I'm unsure what I saw," or "I forget what I saw." You can see why this kind of research is often difficult to interpret.

Brief Attention to Stimuli We Seem to Ignore
Sometimes you cannot report a stimulus even a few seconds after you saw it or heard it, and yet you probably did process it, for at least a moment. Here is the evidence:

Neville Moray (1959) fitted some college students with earphones attached to a tape recorder that transmitted a different message to each ear, at a rate of 150 words per minute (see Figure 4.33). He asked each student to repeat, word for word, everything that came into one ear or the other. (To see how much attention this requires, turn on two radios tuned to different stations with someone talking. Choose one

This ad pokes fun at the idea of subliminal perception, since it's so obvious.
Yet the technique effectively conveys two messages simultaneously.

With a little imagination, people can "find" subliminal messages almost anywhere. However, research indicates that subliminal messages have only limited effects (if any) on behavior.

of the stations and try to repeat everything the announcer says.)

With a little practice, the students became reasonably adept at this task. Then the experimenter asked them some questions to see how much they remembered of what they had heard in the other ear. Most of them remembered almost nothing. They could remember whether they had heard a man's voice or a woman's voice or just a series of sounds, but they could not remember any of the content. Even when the announcer read a short list of simple words and repeated it 35 times, the students did not remember the words. They apparently had tuned out that ear so completely that nothing got through to their consciousness.

Was that information heard at all? To find out, Moray repeated the experiment, but this time, halfway through the tape, the voice in the tuned-out ear spoke the student's name: "You can quit this task now, Judy Callahan." About half the students remembered hearing the instruction, although most of them assumed that it was meant to be a distraction and ignored it.

The conclusion here is that many stimuli which we cannot report—stimuli that never make it to consciousness—do get processed, at least briefly. These stimuli are capable of capturing our attention.

FIGURE 4.33
In this binaural test, the subject hears different tapes—one for the left ear, another for the right—playing at the same time. She is told to listen only to what one ear receives.

The rock group Judas Priest was sued by the families of two teenage boys who shot themselves. The families claimed that subliminal messages on the rock group's album Stained Class *prompted the boys to suicide. A witness for the families demonstrated that if one song was filtered, slowed down, and played backward, people could hear the phrase "Do it." The defense replied that the band had not intentionally inserted this backward message, and that even if they had, the message would not drive a person to suicide. The court found the band not guilty.*

What Subliminal Perception Cannot Do

Although subliminal perception may have some effects on behavior, they tend to be very modest effects. Unfortunately, many of the claims regarding subliminal effects have been so wild, and so lacking in evidence, that many scientists became very skeptical that subliminal perception could have any effect at all.

Many years ago, claims were made that subliminal messages could control people's buying habits. For example, an unscrupulous theater owner might insert a single frame reading "EAT POPCORN" in the middle of a film. Customers not consciously aware of the message could not resist it, so they would flock to the concession stand to buy popcorn. That claim has been tested many times; no one has found any strong or replicable effect (Bornstein, 1989).

Another claim is that certain rock records contain satanic messages that have been recorded backward and superimposed on the songs. Some people allege that listeners unconsciously perceive and follow these messages to turn to drugs or devil worship. So far as psychology is concerned, the issue is whether people who heard a backward message could understand it and whether it would influence their behavior. Psychologists have recorded various messages (fairly tame, nothing "satanic") and asked people to listen to them played backward. So far, no one listening to the backward messages has been able to discern what they would sound like forward. And listening to those messages has not influenced anyone's behavior in any detectable way (Vokey & Read, 1985). In other words, even if certain records do contain backward messages, we have no reason to believe that listeners will be influenced by them.

A third unsupported claim: Many book stores and music stores sell "subliminal audiotapes" that claim they can help you improve your memory, quit smoking, lose weight, raise your self-esteem, and so forth. In one study, psychologists asked more than 200 volunteers to listen to a popular brand of audiotape. But they intentionally mislabeled some of the tapes. That is, some tapes with "self-esteem" messages were labeled "memory tapes" and some tapes with "memory" messages were labeled "self-esteem tapes." After a month of listening, most who *thought* they were listening to self-esteem tapes said they had greatly improved their self-esteem; those who *thought* they were listening to memory tapes said their memory had greatly improved. What they were *actually* hearing had no bearing on the results. In other words, if people improved their memory—and some of them did improve, although not nearly as much as they thought they did—the improvement depended on their expectations, and not on the tapes themselves (Greenwald, Spangenberg, Pratkanis, & Eskanazi, 1991).

What Subliminal Perception Can Do

That was a sampling of what subliminal messages *cannot* do. Now let's consider examples of what they apparently *can* do:

If people are subliminally exposed to a simple picture and then asked to choose between that picture and another one (both now plainly visible), about 60–65% choose the picture they had seen subliminally. Although this is not a very strong effect, it does last a week or more (Bornstein, 1989).

If people see a word subliminally, it influences their later perception of an easily visible stimulus (Dixon, 1981). For example, people watch a screen where the word PENCIL is flashed briefly in the midst of a cluttered background. Then they see a set of letters such as TERIW or WRITE and they are supposed to say, as quickly as possible, whether it is a word. People who have just seen the subliminal stimulus PENCIL respond a little quicker than usual that WRITE is a word. This is a fairly dependable effect, although it apparently wears off within seconds after the subliminal stimulus.

A number of researchers have made claims that brief, subliminal exposure to an emotional message produces an emotional response. In one study, undergraduate students showed mild signs of nervousness or discomfort after viewing a very brief presentation of the message NO ONE LOVES ME, but not after viewing the unemotional message NO ONE LIFTS IT (Masling, Bornstein, Poynton, Reid, & Katkin,

1991). This study was not set up to measure how long the effect might last. Other studies have reported fairly long-lasting emotional effects of subliminal stimuli (Hardaway, 1990), but these results remain highly controversial.

With various refinements in technique, could subliminal perception become an effective means of influencing people, for either worthwhile or dangerous purposes? Maybe, say some psychologists (e.g., Bornstein, 1989); very unlikely, say others (e.g., McConnell, 1989). So far, however, the best-documented effects are either weak or short-lived (Balay & Shevrin, 1988; Creed, 1987; Wolitzky & Wachtel, 1973).

PERCEPTION AND THE RECOGNITION OF PATTERNS

Most of our perception deals with clear, strong, well-above-threshold stimuli. The issue to explain is not how we perceive that something is there, but how we perceive what it *is*.

Human perception of complex scenes, especially faces, can be quite amazing. Suppose you look at several photographs of faces you have never seen before (perhaps in the yearbook of a college you have never visited). Five days later, half of the photographs are shifted around and mixed with an equal number of new ones. Can you identify the faces you saw before? If you are like most people, you will get more than 90% correct (Galper & Hochberg, 1971; Hochberg & Galper, 1967). How do we do that?

When you go back to your 25th-year high-school reunion, will you recognize the people you haven't seen since graduation? You probably will recognize many of them, even though they will have changed much in the meantime. Can you match the high-school photos in Figure 4.34 with the photos of the same people as they looked 25 years later? Probably not, but other people who had gone to that same high school succeeded with a respectable 49% accuracy (Bruck, Cavanagh, & Ceci, 1991).

People are remarkably skilled at recognizing faces as well as other familiar items (Diamond & Carey, 1986). Apparently this ability requires some specialized brain circuitry; people with certain rare kinds of brain damage lose the ability to recognize faces or describe them from memory, although they still can see everything else (Etcoff, Freeman, & Cave, 1991). To

FIGURE 4.34
High school photos and the same people 25 years later. Can you match the photos in the two sets? (Check answer C on page 177.) (From Bruck, Cavanagh, & Ceci, 1991.)

explain how we identify faces is quite challenging. In fact, explaining how we recognize even a letter of the alphabet is difficult enough.

The Feature-Detector Approach

According to one explanation, we begin recognition by breaking a complex stimulus into its component parts. For example, when we look at the letter *K,* some part of the brain might identify a vertical line and two slanted lines on the right connected to the center of the vertical line. Another part of the brain might compare that analysis with information held in memory and say, "Oh. That combination of lines makes up the letter *K.*" As we shall see, investigators

have identified neurons in the visual system of the brain that respond to particular lines or other features of a visual stimulus; these cells are **feature detectors.**

Investigators of artificial intelligence have tried to build machines that could recognize patterns by means of feature detectors. The task turns out to be more difficult than it sounds. Suppose we want to instruct such a machine to recognize the letter *A.* We have the machine scan a page of handwriting and break each character into points of light and dark, as in Figure 4.35. We then have it look for slanted lines meeting at a point at the top, with a horizontal line in the middle. If it finds all these characteristics, then it identifies the letter as an *A.*

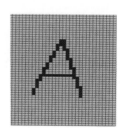

FIGURE 4.35
The letter A *broken down into points of light and dark in the first stages of feature detection.*

FIGURE 4.36
Legibility is in the eye of the beholder. Everyone's handwriting is distinctive. Could a machine be programmed to identify each of these (and more) as the letter a?

So far, so good. But people's handwriting varies. The machine would have to identify each of the scrawls in Figure 4.36 as an *A*. Furthermore, humans learn to perceive things in context. We perceive the words in Figure 4.37a as CAT and HAT, even though the A in CAT is identical to the H in HAT. Likewise, the character in the center of 4.37b can be read as either the letter *B* or the number 13. Apparently, visual perception depends on something more than just feature detectors. Even so, feature detectors are probably an important part of visual perception, at least in the early stages of the process.

Feature Detectors in the Human Visual System

WHAT'S THE EVIDENCE?

We know that certain parts of the human brain, including the occipital cortex, contribute to vision. But what is the role of the individual neurons? And how could investigators determine that role? After all, they can hardly insert electrodes into the human brain. Let's look at two studies.

EXPERIMENT 1

Hypothesis Neurons in the visual cortex of cats and monkeys will respond specifically when light strikes the retina in a particular pattern, such as a line.

Method Two pioneers in the study of the visual cortex, David Hubel and Torsten Wiesel (1981 Nobel Prize winners in physiology and medicine), inserted thin electrodes into cells of the occipital cortex of cats and monkeys and then recorded the activity of those cells when various light patterns struck the animals' retinas (Figure 4.38).

Results They found that each cell has a preferred stimulus (Hubel & Wiesel, 1968). Some cells become active only when a vertical bar of light strikes a given portion of the retina. Others become active only when a horizontal bar or a bar tilted at a particular angle strikes the retina. In other words, the cells act as feature detectors.

In later experiments, Hubel and Wiesel and other investigators found a variety of other feature detectors, including some that respond to lines moving in a particular direction.

Interpretation Hubel and Wiesel found feature-detector cells in both cats and monkeys. If the organization of the occipital cortex is similar in species as distantly related as cats and monkeys, it is likely (though not certain) to be similar in humans as well.

A second line of evidence is based on the following reasoning: If the human cortex does contain feature-detector cells, one type of cell should become fatigued after we stare for a time at the features that excite it. When we look away, we should see an aftereffect created by the inactivity of that type of cell. (Recall the negative afterimage in color vision, as shown by Figure 4.13.)

One example of this phenomenon is the waterfall illusion: If you stare at a waterfall for a minute or more and then turn your eyes to nearby cliffs, the cliffs will appear to flow *upward*. In staring at the waterfall, you fatigue cells that respond to downward motion. When you look away those cells become inactive, but other cells that respond to upward motion continue their normal activity. Even though the motionless cliffs stimulate those cells only weakly, the stimulation is enough to produce an illusion of upward motion.

Here's a second example: If you stare at a pinwheel while it is rotating in a counterclockwise direction, you will fatigue the cells that respond to motion toward the center. After the pinwheel stops, it appears to be rotating in the opposite direction, with the lines apparently moving away from the center.

For another example, here is a demonstration you can perform yourself.

a

b

FIGURE 4.37
We perceive elements differently depending on their context. In (a), the A in CAT is the same as the H in HAT, but we perceive them differently. In (b), the central character can appear to be a B or the number 13, depending on whether we read horizontally or vertically. (b from Kim, 1989.)

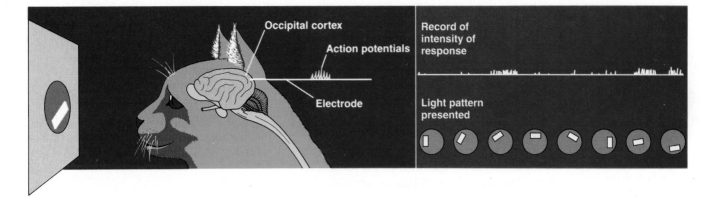

FIGURE 4.38
Hubel and Wiesel implanted electrodes to record the activity of neurons in the occipital cortex of a cat. Then they compared the responses evoked by various patterns of light and darkness on the retina. In most cases, a neuron responded vigorously when a portion of the retina saw a bar of light oriented at a particular angle. When the angle of the bar changed, that cell became silent but some other cell (not shown) responded.

EXPERIMENT 2

Hypothesis After you stare at one set of vertical lines, you will fatigue the feature detectors that respond to lines of a particular width. If you then look at lines slightly wider or narrower than the original ones, they will appear to be even wider or narrower than they really are.

Method Cover the right half of Figure 4.39 and stare at the little rectangle in the middle of the left half for at least 1 minute. (The effect will grow stronger the longer you stare.) Do not stare at just one point; move your focus around within the rectangle. Then look at the square in the center of the right part of the figure, and compare the spacing between the lines of the top and bottom gratings (Blakemore & Sutton, 1969).

Results What did you perceive in the right half of the figure? People generally report that the top set of lines looks narrower than it really is and that the bottom set of lines looks wider.

Interpretation Staring at the left part of the figure fatigues one set of cells sensitive to wide lines in the top part of the figure and another set sensitive to narrow lines in the bottom part. Then when you look at intermediate lines, the fatigued cells become inactive. Therefore, your perception is dominated by cells sensitive to narrower lines in the top part and to wider lines in the bottom part.

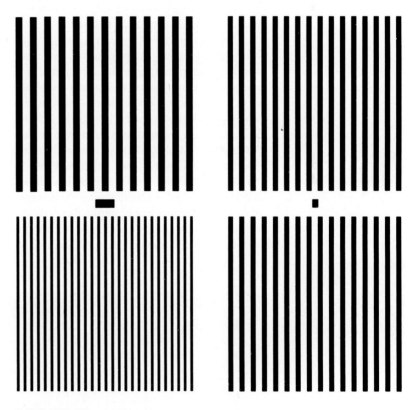

FIGURE 4.39
Use this display to fatigue your feature detectors and create an afterimage. Follow the directions in Experiment 2. (From Blakemore & Sutton, 1969.)

To summarize, two types of evidence suggest that the human brain contains visual feature detectors: (1) The brains of other species contain cells with the properties of feature detectors, and (2) after staring at certain patterns, we see aftereffects that can be explained as fatigue of feature-detector cells in the brain.

Note one important point here about scientific evidence: A single line of evidence—even excellent, Nobel Prize–winning evidence—is seldom enough to establish a conclusion to our complete satisfaction. Whenever possible, we look for independent lines of evidence that confirm the same conclusion.

Do Feature Detectors Explain Perception?

The feature detectors I have been describing are active during the early stages of visual processing. They detect lines of a certain width and angle and objects moving in a certain direction, for example. How do you perceive something more complicated, such as your grandmother's face, the Eiffel Tower, or even the letter *A*?

One possibility is that the brain contains increasingly complex feature detectors. One set of cells responds to single lines. Another set receives input from the first set and responds only to certain combinations of lines—such as the lines that make up the letter *A* (Selfridge, 1959). Still other cells respond to even more complex patterns, such as the pattern of a hand or a face (Desimone, Albright, Gross, & Bruce, 1984).

We run into problems, however, if we try to account for visual perception entirely in terms of feature detectors. For example, if everything we see depends on its own specific feature detector, then there should be people with some

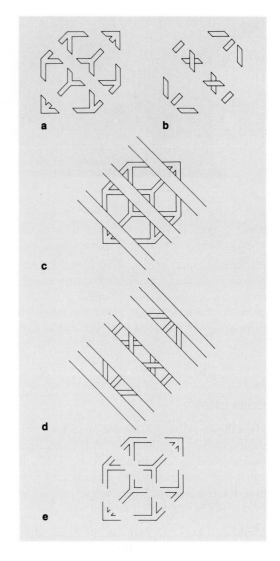

FIGURE 4.40
This picture is a puzzle until a context is introduced. Then a cube "emerges" from meaningless lines. (From Kanizsa, 1979.)

FIGURE 4.41
Someone familiar with only the Hebrew or Arabic alphabet would not "see" meaningful patterns emerge in part b.

CHAPTER 4: Sensation and Perception

FIGURE 4.42
According to Gestalt psychology, the whole is more than the sum of its parts. Here we perceive an assembly of several hundred people as an airplane.

very limited kind of brain damage who can perceive, say, every letter *except F* or all faces *except* that of the prime minister of Great Britain. But such effects never occur. Apparently no neuron is involved in one and only one perception. Although feature detectors are active in the early stages of perception, something else must supplement their activity.

Furthermore, we do not perceive a scene simply by adding up points, lines, or other simple features. The way we perceive part of a scene depends on the context provided by the rest of the scene. In Figure 4.40 (based on Kanizsa, 1979) parts a and b are composed of small geometric forms. Although we might guess that part a is made up of segments of a three-dimensional cube, we cannot "see" the cube. Part b does not even suggest a cube. In parts c and d, the added lines provide a context that enables us to see the cube. In part e, the deletion of short lines from a enables us to "see" imaginary lines that provide the same context. In c, d, and e, we have perceptually organized the meaningless forms of a and b into a meaningful pattern; we are perceiving something that is not really there.

Similarly, in Figure 4.41a we see a series of meaningless patches. No matter how hard we try, we can perceive no real pattern. Yet in Figure 4.41b, the addition of some black glop immediately enables us to perceive those same patches as the word *psychology* (Bregman, 1981). Note that the letters are not "there" in part b any more than they are in part a; we perceive them as being there only because we are imposing an active interpretation on the pattern.

Another example of our imposing an inter-

pretation is an illusion known as the **autokinetic effect:** If you sit in a darkened room and stare at one small stationary point of light, the point eventually will seem to move. Moreover, how much it appears to move and in which direction are subject to the power of suggestion. If someone says, "I see it moving in a zigzag manner" or "I see it moving slowly in a counterclockwise direction," you are likely to perceive it the same way. Because you expect to see it move, and because you have no frame of reference to show that it is not moving, you do see it move.

The Gestalt Psychology Approach

Figure 4.42 is a photo of several hundred people. Yet you probably see the overall shape of an airplane. Is any one of those people by himself or herself a tiny piece of an airplane? Of course not. Out of context, one person is no more a piece of an airplane than a piece of anything else. The plane is not the sum of the people; it is the overall pattern.

Such observations derive from **Gestalt psychology.** *Gestalt* (geh-SHTALT) is a German word for which there is no exact English equivalent; *configuration* and *overall pattern* come close. The founders of Gestalt psychology rejected the idea that a perception can be broken down into its component parts. If a melody is broken up into individual notes, the melody is lost. Their slogan was "The whole is more than the sum of its parts."

According to Gestalt psychologists, visual perception is an active production, not just the passive adding up of lines and dots. We considered examples of this principle in Figures 4.40 and 4.41. Here are some further examples:

This assemblage, Celia, Los Angeles, *is by the English artist David Hockney. According to Gestalt psychologists, the whole picture is more than its 32 parts together. Imagine these 32 photos jumbled together in a shoe box, like your vacation snapshots. Looked at individually and in random order, they would simply be 32 photos. Yet with the correct arrangement, they form a meaningful pattern. How do repetitions in* Celia *add to your information?*

Figure 4.43 shows a photo and a drawing of two animals. When you first look at these pictures, you will probably see nothing but meaningless black and white patches. As you continue to look at them, you may suddenly see the animals. (If you give up, check answer D, page 177.) And once you have seen them, you will see them again whenever you look at the pictures. To perceive the animals, you must separate **figure and ground**—that is, you must distinguish the object from the background. Ordinarily that process takes place almost instantaneously; only in special cases like this one do you become aware of the process.

Figure 4.44 contains five **reversible figures,** stimuli that may be perceived in more than one way. In effect, we test hypotheses: "Is this the front of the object or is that the front? Is this object facing left or facing right? Is this section the foreground or the background?" Depending on what we are looking for, we may organize the scene in different ways. In Figure 4.44, part a is

called the *Necker cube,* after the psychologist who first called attention to it. Which is the front face of the cube? If you look long enough, you will see it two ways. In fact, you can choose to see it one way or the other. You can see part b either as a vase or as two profiles. Part c is a very minimal stimulus; you have to use some imagination to see anything meaningful. You might see nothing at all, or a man blowing a horn, or a woman's face. (If you need help, check answer E on page 177.) Parts d and e are more difficult for most people to see two ways. Part d (from Boring, 1930) shows both an old woman and a young woman. Almost everyone sees one or the other immediately, but many people lock into one perception so tightly that they cannot see the other one. Part e was drawn by an 8-year-old girl who intended it as the picture of a face. Some people claim it looks like an apple. There is a third possibility. Can you find it? (If you have trouble with parts d or e, check answer F, page 177.) Note that when you change from one

a

b

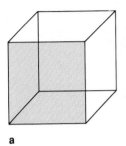

a

b

c

d

e

FIGURE 4.44
Reversible figures. (a) The Necker cube. Which is the front face? (b) Faces or a vase. (c) Sax player and woman's face ("Sara Nader"). (d) An old woman and a young woman. (e) A face or what? (Part c from Shepard 1990; part d from Boring, 1930.)

perception to another on any of these reversible figures, you suddenly reinterpret each piece of the figure. For example, in part c, when you see the man's face and nose, that context almost forces you to see another part of the figure as a horn.

It is difficult to explain in any scientific way *how* we perceive organized wholes, though the Gestalt psychologists offered a few principles of how we organize perceptions. Figure 4.45 gives examples of each principle. **Proximity** is the tendency to perceive objects that are close together as belonging to a group. The objects in part a form two groups because of proximity. The tendency to perceive objects that resemble each other as forming a group is called **similarity.** The objects in b group into Xs and Os because of similarity. When lines are interrupted, as in c, we may perceive a **continuation** of the lines. We can perceive this illustration as a green rectangle covering the front of one horse and the rear of another, but we can also per-

ceive it as a rectangle covering the center of one very elongated horse.

When a familiar figure is interrupted, as in d, we perceive a **closure** of the figure—that is, we imagine the rest of the figure. (Because of closure you perceive the head, two arms, and two legs as belonging to the same woman. How might magicians use this principle?)

Finally, we tend to perceive a **good figure**— a simple, symmetrical figure—even when the pattern can be perceived in some other way. In e, even after we see that the right-hand drawing is a green backward L overlapping part of an irregular object, we continue to perceive it as a red square overlapping a green square. In general, a good figure is a symmetrical figure or a figure composed of continuous lines.

■ CONCEPT CHECK

11. Which of the Gestalt principles were operating in your perception of Figures 4.40 and 4.41? (Check your answer on page 177.)

People who are looking for an image or a message in some random pattern sometimes convince themselves that they have found what they were seeking. Crowds in one town believed they saw the image of a recently murdered girl (inset) on a blank billboard. Perception results from a combination of sensory stimulation and our expectations.

This jumbled pattern of pieces of letters suggests the word read. We see that word from the overall array, not from the sum of its elements. (Designed by Timothy Bassford for Literary Volunteers of America, Inc.)

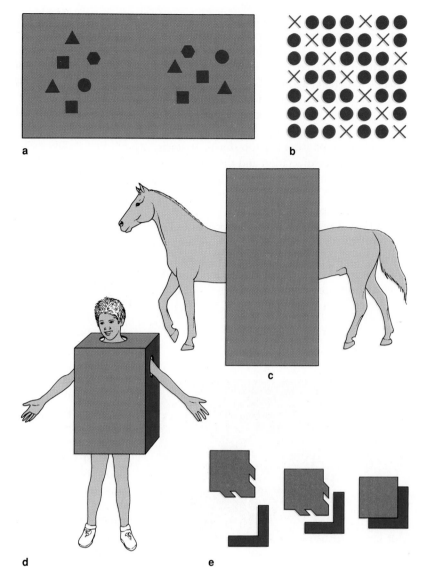

a

b

c

d   e

Gestalt Principles in Hearing

The perceptual organization principles of Gestalt psychology apply to hearing as well as to vision. There are reversible figures in sound, just as there are in vision. For instance, you can hear the sound of a clock as "tick, tock, tick, tock" or as "tock, tick, tock, tick." You can hear your windshield wipers going "dunga, dunga" or "gadung, gadung."

As with visual reversible figures, people occasionally get so locked into one interpretation of something they hear that they have trouble hearing it any other way. For example, read this sentence to a friend: "The matadors fish on Friday." Pause long enough to make sure your friend has understood the sentence. Then say: "The cat on the mat adores fish on Friday." If

you read the second sentence normally, without pausing between mat and adores, your friend is likely to be puzzled. "Huh? The cat on the matadors . . . ?" Had you not read the first sentence, your friend would not have had trouble understanding the second sentence.

Feature Detectors and Gestalt Psychology: Bottom-Up Versus Top-Down Processing

The Gestalt approach to perception does not conflict with the feature-detector approach as much as it might seem. The two approaches merely describe perception in different ways. The feature-detector approach describes how perception, especially vision, develops from the bottom up. It takes the individual points of light identified by the receptors and connects them into lines and then connects lines into more complex features. According to the feature-detector approach, the brain says, "I see these points here, here, and here, so there must be a line. I see a line here and another line connecting with it here, so there must be a letter *L*."

The Gestalt approach describes how perception develops from the top down. It starts with an overall expectation and then fits in the pieces. According to the Gestalt interpretation, the brain says, "I see what looks like a circle, so the missing piece must be part of a circle too."

Which view is correct? Both, of course. Our perception has to assemble the individual points of light or bits of sound, but once it forms a tentative interpretation of the pattern, it uses that interpretation to organize the rest of the information.

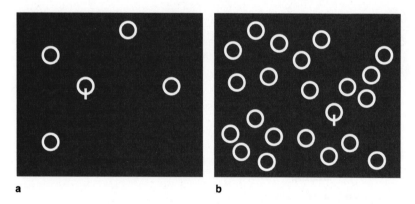

a **b**

FIGURE 4.46
Demonstration of the preattentive processes. Find the vertical line in parts a and b. Most people find it about equally fast in both.

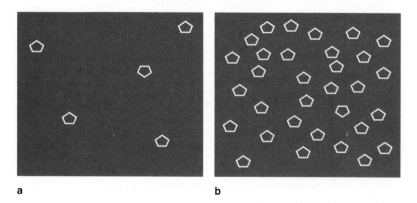

a **b**

FIGURE 4.47
Demonstration of attentive processes. Find the pentagon pointing down in parts a and b. Most people take longer to find it in b.

Preattentive and Attentive Processes in Vision

When you look at a scene made up of many shapes and relationships among objects, you automatically notice certain details even if you are not intentionally looking for them. Consider Figures 4.46a and b. In each figure, find the circle that is intersected by a vertical line. Most people spot the vertical line in b about as quickly as the vertical line in a, even though b has far more distractors (circles without lines) (Treisman & Souther, 1985). The vertical line simply stands out in both figures. Apparently people examine all the circles *in parallel*, rather than attending to them one at a time. That is, they can look at all the circles at once. Their zeroing in on the vertical line does not require attention; it is the result of a **preattentive process**—a process that takes place automatically and simultaneously across a large portion of the visual field. Our preattentive processes probably use feature detectors to identify simple elements (Enns & Rensink, 1990).

Now look at Figures 4.47a and b. Each part contains several pentagons, most of them pointing upward. Find the one pentagon in each part that points downward.

Most people take longer to find the pentagon pointing down in part b than in part a, because part b contains more distractors. The greater the number of distractors, the longer it takes to find the pentagon that is different. People must turn their attention to one pentagon at a time until they come to the correct one. In contrast to the preceding example, this task requires an **attentive process**—that is, a procedure that considers only one part of the visual field at a time. An attentive process is a *serial* process because a person must pay attention to each part in the series. Under natural conditions our perception results from a mixture of preattentive processes and attentive processes.

PERCEPTION OF MOVEMENT AND DEPTH

As an automobile drives away from us, its image on the retina grows smaller, yet we perceive it as moving, not as shrinking. That perception illustrates **visual constancy**—our tendency to perceive objects as being unchanging in shape, size, and color, even though what actually strikes our retina may be something quite different. When we sit off to the side in a movie theater, for example, the images that strike our retina may be

FIGURE 4.48
A photograph of a photo taken from the side appears distorted. Yet when you view a movie screen from an angle, you are seldom aware of the distortion.

FIGURE 4.49
(a) Shape constancy. We perceive all three doors as rectangles. (b) Size constancy. We perceive all three hands as equal in size.

badly distorted (see Figure 4.48). And yet they seem almost normal (Cutting, 1987). Figure 4.49 shows examples of two visual constancies: shape constancy and size constancy. Constancies depend on our familiarity with objects and on our ability to estimate distances and angles of view. For example, we know that a door is still rectangular even when we view it from an odd angle. But to recognize that an object has kept its shape and size, we have to perceive movement or changes in distance or angle. How do we do so?

Perception of Movement

It is common sense to assume that anyone who can see at all, can see everything there is to see. That is, someone who sees a rabbit should be able to see its size, shape, color, and direction and speed of movement. That is common sense, but it is wrong. You already know that some people are colorblind. You may not have known that some people are motion blind. Motion blindness results from damage to a small area in the temporal lobe of the cortex (Newsome & Paré, 1988). It is an extremely rare condition, but the fact that it occurs at all illustrates a major point: The visual system of the brain has separate pathways that analyze different aspects of what we see. One pathway analyzes shape; another analyzes color; another analyzes movement (Livingstone, 1988; Livingstone & Hubel, 1988; Zeki & Shipp, 1988). How we manage to see each object as a unified whole is a major research problem—one that would never occur to us based on common sense.

The detection of motion in the visual world raises some interesting issues, including how we distinguish between our own movement and the movement of objects. Try this simple demonstration: Hold an object in front of your eyes and then move it to the right. Now hold the object in front of your eyes and move your eyes to the left. The image of the object moves across your retina in the same way, regardless of whether you move the object or move your eyes. Yet you perceive the object as moving in one case and not in the other. Why is that?

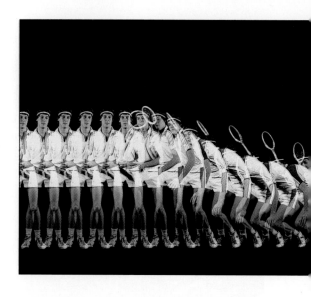

FIGURE 4.50

Motion pictures: When you watch a movie, you are unaware of its thousands of still photographs flickering by at a rate of 86,400 an hour. The sequence of photographs printed here conveys a sense of motion in another way.

FIGURE 4.51

Gestalt psychology began in 1910 when Max Werthimer first used a strobo-scope to study the phi phenomenon—the illusion of motion when similar objects appear in rapid succession, as in these blinking lights.

There are two reasons why the object does not appear to move when you move your eyes. One reason is that the vestibular system constantly keeps the visual areas of the brain informed of movements of your head. Other systems keep the visual areas informed of eye movements. When your brain knows that your eyes have moved to the left, it interprets the change in what you see as being a result of that movement. In fact, when people are moving, they notice other moving objects *less* than when

they are motionless. For example, you are more likely to notice a tree blowing in the wind when you are standing still than while you are driving a car (Probst, Krafczyk, Brandt, & Wist, 1984). (Under certain conditions, this tendency may be hazardous to drivers.)

The second reason is that we perceive motion when an object moves *relative to the background* (Gibson, 1968). When you walk forward, everything you see seems to be passing by. If certain objects pass by faster or slower than the objects around them, you perceive them as moving.

What do we perceive when an object is stationary and the background is moving? That hardly ever happens, but when it does, we incorrectly perceive the object as moving and the background as stationary. For example, when you watch clouds moving slowly across the moon from left to right, you generally perceive the clouds as a stationary background and the moon as an object moving from right to left. This perception, known as **induced movement,** is a form of *apparent movement,* as opposed to *real movement.*

I have already mentioned two other examples of apparent movement: the waterfall illusion (page 156) and the autokinetic effect (page 159). Yet another example is **stroboscopic movement,** an illusion of movement created by a rapid succession of stationary images. When a scene is flashed on a screen and is followed a split second later by a second scene slightly different from the first, you perceive the objects as having moved smoothly from their location in the first scene to their location in the second

scene (Figure 4.50). Motion pictures are actually a series of still photos flashed on the screen at a rate of 24 per second. Thus, the perceived movement is an illusion produced by the rapid succession of photos.

We also experience an illusion of movement when two or more stationary lights separated by a short distance blink on and off at regular intervals (Figure 4.51). Your brain creates the sense of motion in what is called the **phi effect,** or phi movement. You may have noticed signs in front of restaurants or motels that make use of this effect. As the lights blink on and off, an arrow seems to be moving and inviting you to come in.

Our perception of movement relies on a combination of preattentive and attentive processes (Dick, Ullman, & Sagi, 1987). When an object moves fairly steadily, we detect it at once by a preattentive process. If you are sitting outdoors you can immediately detect a squirrel running along the ground or a bird hopping through the treetops, even if you are not particularly attending to it. However, if a squirrel goes behind a bush and later emerges on the other side, you can perceive it as a single squirrel that moved from one side of the bush to the other, but only if you are paying attention.

The preattentive detection of movement played an interesting role in the history of astronomy. In 1930, Clyde Tombaugh was searching the skies for any unknown planet beyond Neptune. He photographed each region of the sky twice, several days apart. A planet, unlike a star, would move from one photo to the next. However, how would he find one tiny dot

FIGURE 4.52
Clyde Tombaugh used preattentive detection of movement to discover the planet Pluto. He photographed each area of the sky twice, several days apart. Then he had a machine flip back and forth between the two photos of each pair. When he came to one part of the sky, he immediately (preattentively) noticed one dot that moved between the two photos. That dot was the planet Pluto.

that moved, among all the countless unmoving dots in the sky? If he had to check each spot one at a time (attentively), the task would be almost impossible. Instead, he put each pair of photos on a machine that would flip back and forth between showing one photo and showing the other. When he came to the correct pair of photos, the machine flipped back and forth between them and he immediately—preattentively—noticed the one moving dot (Tombaugh, 1980). We now know that little dot as the planet Pluto (Figure 4.52).

F I G U R E 4 . 5 3
Retinal disparity is
one cue to distance.
The left and right
eyes see slightly dif-
ferent versions of
any scene; the differ-
ence between the im-
age on the left retina
and the image on the
right retina indicates
the distance to each
object.

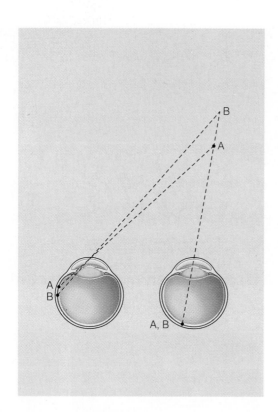

Depth Perception

Depth perception is our perception of distance; it enables us to experience the world in three dimensions. Depth perception depends on several factors.

We use **retinal disparity**—the difference in the apparent position of an object as seen by the left and right retinas—to compare the views the two eyes see (Figure 4.53). Try this: Hold one finger at arm's length. Focus on it with one eye and then with the other. Note that the apparent position of your finger shifts with respect to the background. Now hold your finger closer to your face and repeat the experiment. Notice that the apparent position of your finger shifts by a greater amount. *The discrepancy between the slightly different views the two eyes see becomes greater as the object comes closer.* We use the amount of discrepancy to gauge distance.

A second cue for depth perception is the **convergence** of our eyes—that is, the degree to which they turn in to focus on a close object (Figure 4.54). When you focus on a distant object, your eyes are looking in almost parallel directions. When you focus on something close, your eyes turn in; you can sense the pulling in of your muscles. The more the muscles pull, the closer the object must be.

Retinal disparity and convergence are called **binocular cues,** because they depend on the action of both eyes. **Monocular cues** enable a person to judge depth and distance effectively with just one eye, or if both eyes see the same image, as they do when you look at a picture. Several monocular cues help us judge the approximate distance of the objects in Figure 4.55:

- *Object size.* Other things being equal, an object close to us produces a larger image than does one farther away. This cue is useful only if we already knew the approximate actual size of the objects. For example, the roller skater in the photo produces a larger image than does the parked van, which we know is actually larger. So we see the skater as closer. The rocks in the sea, however, are not equally large in reality, so the relative sizes of their images are not a cue to their distance.

- *Linear perspective.* As parallel lines stretch out toward the horizon, they come closer and closer together. Examine the road in Figure 4.55. At the bottom of the photo (close to the viewer), the edges of the road are far apart; at greater distances, the edges of the road come closer together. The closer the lines come, the more distant we perceive them to be.

FIGURE 4.55
Thanks to several cues, we can judge depth and distance with one eye as well as we do with both eyes. (1) Closer objects occupy more space on the retina (or on the photograph) than do distant objects of the same type. (2) Nearer objects show more detail. (3) Closer objects overlap certain distant objects. (4) Objects in the foreground look sharper than do objects on the horizon. These are known as monocular cues.

■ *Detail.* We see nearby objects, such as the roller skater, in much detail. More distant objects are increasingly hazy and less detailed.

■ *Interposition.* A nearby object interrupts our view of a more distant object. Interposition is our surest way of seeing which rocks are closer than others.

■ *Texture gradient.* Notice the posts on the safety rail on the right side of the road. At greater distances, the posts come closer and closer together. The "packed together" appearance of objects gives us another cue to their approximate distance.

■ *Shadows.* Shadows are hardly prominent in Figure 4.55, but when present they can provide another cue to help us interpret a picture (Figure 4.56).

Motion parallax, another monocular cue, helps us to perceive depth when we are actually looking at a scene, though it is of no help when we are looking at a photograph. When we are moving—riding along in a car, for example—close objects seem to pass by swiftly while distant objects seem to pass by very slowly. The faster an object passes by, the closer it must be. That principle is motion parallax.

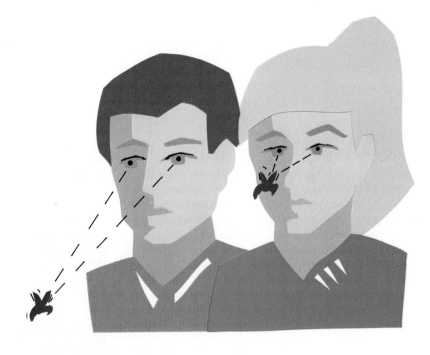

FIGURE 4.54
Convergence of the eyes as a cue to distance. The more this viewer has to converge her eyes toward each other in order to focus on an object, the closer the object must be.

This photo of people from Monterrey, Mexico, includes several monocular cues to distance, especially size. We interpret the people shown larger to be closer. Linear perspective and detail also contribute to our perception of distance.

FIGURE 4.56

The direction of light and placement of shadow can create the illusion that objects are either (a) round objects sitting on a surface or (b) concave depressions in the surface. We are accustomed to seeing objects lit from above. Shadows therefore give us cues to "below." See what happens when you turn the book and look at this figure upside down.

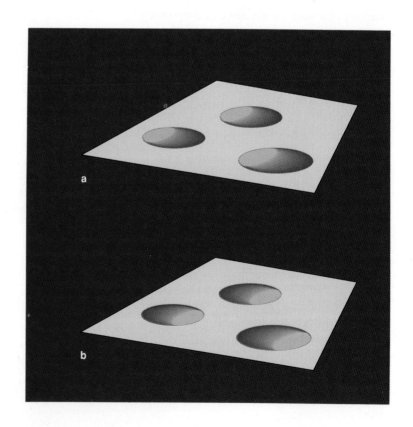

If you were a passenger on this train, the ground beside the tracks would appear to pass by more quickly than the more distant elements in the landscape. The photo's version of motion parallax is that the ground is blurred, the more distant objects crisp.

■ CONCEPT CHECK

12. In three-dimensional photography, cameras take two views of the same scene from different locations through lenses with different color filters or with different polarized-light filters. The two views are then superimposed. The viewer looks at the composite view through special glasses so that one eye sees the view taken with one camera and the other eye sees the view taken with the other camera. Which depth cue is at work here? (Check your answer on page 177.)

OPTICAL ILLUSIONS

Many people claim to have seen strange things: ghosts, flying saucers, the Loch Ness monster, Bigfoot, Santa's elves, or people floating in the air. Maybe they are lying; maybe they did see something extraordinary. Another possibility is that they saw something ordinary but misinterpreted it. An **optical illusion** is a misinterpretation of a visual stimulus as being larger or smaller or straighter or more curved than it really is. Figure 4.57 shows some examples of optical illusions. Psychologists would like to come up with a single explanation for all optical illusions. (Remember the principle of parsimony from Chapter 2.) Although they have not fully succeeded, they can explain a fair number of optical illusions based on the relationship between size perception and depth perception.

FIGURE 4.57
Many paintings rely on some optical illusion, but we are more aware of it in geometric figures. (Check your answers with a ruler and a compass.)

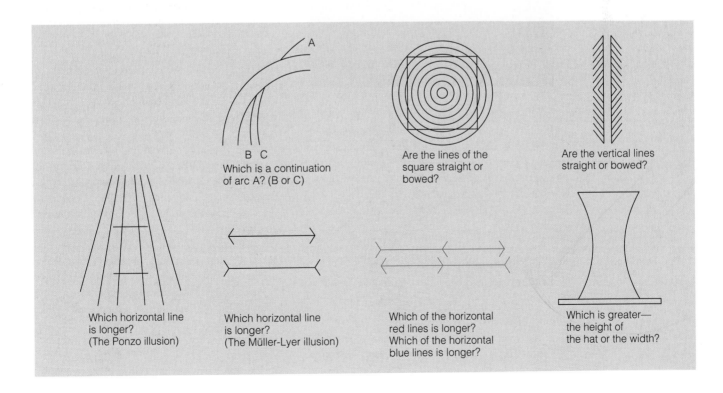

Which is a continuation of arc A? (B or C)

Are the lines of the square straight or bowed?

Are the vertical lines straight or bowed?

Which horizontal line is longer? (The Ponzo illusion)

Which horizontal line is longer? (The Müller-Lyer illusion)

Which of the horizontal red lines is longer? Which of the horizontal blue lines is longer?

Which is greater—the height of the hat or the width?

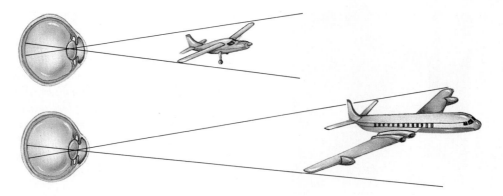

FIGURE 4.58

The trade-off between size and distance. A given image on the retina may indicate either a small, close object or a large, distant object.

FIGURE 4.59

Because fish come in all sizes, we can estimate the size of a fish only if we know how far away it is or if we can compare its size to other nearby objects. See what happens when you cover the man and then cover the hand.

The Relationship Between Depth Perception and Size Perception

If you can estimate the size of an object, you can deduce its distance. If you can estimate its distance, you can deduce its size. Figure 4.58 shows that an image of a given size on the retina may represent either a small, close object or a large, distant object. Watch what happens when you take a single image and change its apparent distance: Stare at Figure 4.13 again to form a negative afterimage. First examine the afterimage while you are looking at the wall across the room. Your afterimage looks like a fairly large flag. Then look at the afterimage against the palm of your hand. Suddenly it has become a very small flag. Move your hand backward and forward; you can make the apparent size of the flag grow and then shrink.

In the real world, we seldom have trouble estimating the size and distance of objects. When you walk along the street, for instance, you never wonder whether the people you see are very far away or are only a few inches tall. Even so, judging size and distance is sometimes confusing (Figure 4.59). I once saw an airplane overhead and for a minute or two was unsure whether it was a small, remote-controlled toy airplane or a distant, full-size airplane. Familiarity with the size of airplanes was of no help to me, and in the sky there are few cues to distance.

The same difficulty arises in reported sightings of UFOs. When people see an unidentified object in the sky, there is usually nothing to help them estimate its distance. And if they overestimate its distance, they also will overestimate its size and speed.

What does all this have to do with optical illusions? Whenever we misjudge distance, we are likely to misjudge size as well. For example, Figure 4.60a shows people in the Ames room (named for its designer, Adelbert Ames). The room is designed to look like a normal rectangular room, though its true dimensions are as shown in Figure 4.60b. The right corner is much closer than the left corner. The two young

a

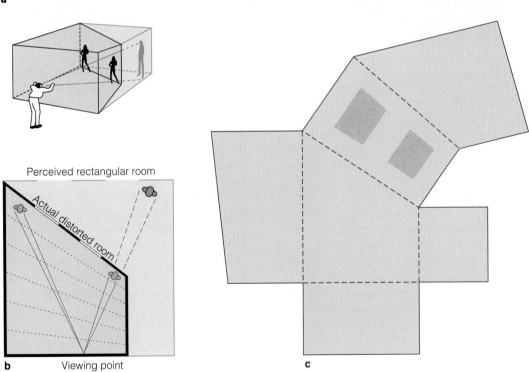

Perceived rectangular room

Actual distorted room

b   Viewing point

c

FIGURE 4.60

A study in deceptive perception, the Ames room is designed to be viewed through a peephole with one eye. (a) Both of these people are actually the same height. We are so accustomed to rooms with right angles that we can't imagine how this apparently ordinary room creates this optical illusion. (b) This diagram shows the positions of the people in the Ames room and demonstrates how the illusion of distance is created. (c) You can use this illustration to create a miniature Ames room. (Part b from Wilson et al., 1964.)

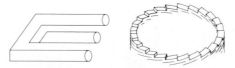

FIGURE 4.61

Expectations shape perceptions. These two-dimensional drawings puzzle us because we try to interpret them as three-dimensional objects.

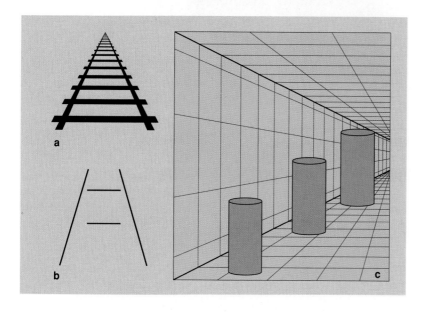

FIGURE 4.62

Some optical illusions depend on misjudgment of distances. In b, the top line looks longer because the perspective (resembling the railroad tracks in a) suggests a difference in distance. In c, the jar on the right seems larger because the context makes it appear farther away.

women are actually the same height. If we eliminated all the background cues, then we would correctly perceive the women as being the same size but at different distances. However, the apparently rectangular room provides such powerful (though misleading) cues to distance that the women appear to differ greatly in height. You can make your own model of the Ames room by copying Figure 4.60c, cutting it out and folding it.

Even a two-dimensional drawing on a flat surface may offer cues that lead to erroneous depth perception. Apparently we have a strong tendency to interpret two-dimensional drawings as if they were three-dimensional. Figure 4.61 shows a bewildering two-prong/three-prong device and a round staircase that seems to run uphill all the way clockwise or downhill

all the way counterclockwise. Both drawings puzzle us because we try to interpret them as three-dimensional objects.

In Figure 4.62a, we interpret the railroad track as heading into the distance. Similarly, because the background cues in part b suggest that the upper line is farther away than the lower line, we perceive the upper line as being larger. The same is true of the right-hand cylinder in part c. Recall from Figure 4.58 that when two objects produce the same-size image on the retina, we perceive the more distant one as being larger. In short, by perceiving two-dimensional representations as if they were three-dimensional, we misjudge distance and consequently misjudge size. When we are somehow misled by the cues that ordinarily ensure constancy in size and shape, we end up experiencing an optical illusion (Day, 1972).

We can also experience an *auditory illusion* by a similar principle: If we misestimate the distance to a sound source, we will misestimate other characteristics of the sound. In one study, experimenters misled students about the distance of a sound by using the **visual capture effect,** the tendency of people to hear a sound as coming from a visually prominent source. (You experience this effect when you "hear" a voice coming from a ventriloquist's dummy or from a movie or television screen.) The experimenters had an unchanging sound source that the students never saw, plus a silent "dummy loudspeaker" that moved. The students always thought they heard the sound coming from the dummy loudspeaker, regardless of where the experimenters put it. When the loudspeaker was far away, most students said the sound was *louder* than when the speaker was close (Mershon, Desaulniers, Kiefer, Amerson, & Mills, 1981). Remember, the actual sound was the same in all cases. When people thought they heard such a sound from a great distance, they interpreted it as a strong, intense sound.

The Moon Illusion

The moon close to the horizon appears about 30% larger than it appears when higher in the sky. This is one of the largest, most impressive, most dependable of all optical illusions and the one we experience most frequently in everyday life. Some people try to explain this **moon illusion** by referring to the bending of light rays by the atmosphere or to some other physical phenomenon. The seeming difference, however, is caused by a psychological rather than a physical phenomenon. If you actually measure the moon image with navigational or photographic equipment, you will find that its size is the same at the horizon as it is higher in the sky. For example, Figure 4.63 shows the moon at two positions in the sky; you can measure the two images to demonstrate that they really are the same size. (The atmosphere's bending of light rays makes the moon look orange near the horizon, but it does not increase the size of the image.) However, photographs never seem to capture the full strength of the moon illusion as we see it in real life. In Figure 4.63 (or any similar pair of photos), the moon looks almost the same at each position; in the actual night sky the moon at the horizon looks enormous.

Two possible explanations of the moon illusion agree that it depends on the vast terrain between the viewer and the horizon. The question, then, is how that terrain exerts its effects. One possibility is that it provides a basis for size comparison. When you see the moon at the horizon, you can compare it to the other objects you see at the horizon, all of which look tiny. By contrast, the moon looks large. When you see the moon high in the sky, however, it is surrounded only by the vast, featureless sky, and in contrast the moon appears relatively small (Baird, 1982; Restle, 1970).

A second possibility is that the terrain between the viewer and the horizon gives an impression of great distance. When the moon is high in the sky, we have no basis to judge distance, and perhaps we unconsciously see the overhead moon as closer than the moon is at the horizon. If we see the horizon moon as more distant, we will perceive it as larger (Kaufman & Rock, 1989; Rock & Kaufman, 1962). This explanation is appealing, because it relates the moon illusion to our misperceptions of distance, a factor already accepted as important for many other illusions.

Many psychologists are not satisfied, however, mostly because they are not convinced that the horizon moon looks farther away than the overhead moon. If we ask people which looks farther away, many hesitate or say they are not sure. If we prevail upon them to answer, most say the horizon moon looks *closer,* in direct contradiction to the theory. Some psychologists reply that the situation is complicated: Unconsciously we perceive the horizon as farther away; consequently we perceive the horizon moon as very large; because of the perceived large size of the horizon moon, we secondarily and consciously perceive it as closer (which is what people report), while we con-

FIGURE 4.63
Ordinarily, the moon at the horizon looks much larger than the moon overhead. In photographs this illusion disappears completely or almost completely, but the photographs do serve to demonstrate that the physical image of the moon is the same in both cases. The moon illusion requires a psychological explanation, not a physical explanation.

tinue to unconsciously perceive it as farther away (Rock & Kaufman, 1962).

That theory is worth taking seriously, even if it sounds a bit far-fetched. But many psychologists continue to search for other explanations that do not require such awkward assumptions. Possibilities include differences in eye movements, differences in the angle of view, changes in the way the eye muscles focus vision, and a wealth of others (Hershenson, 1989). In spite of extensive research, for unknown reasons the moon illusion remains difficult to explain.

One major message arises from work on optical illusions, and indeed from all the research on visual perception: What we perceive is not the same as what is "out there." The visual system does an amazing job of providing us with useful information about the world around us, but under unusual circumstances we can be very wrong about what we think we saw.

SUMMARY

■ *Perception of minimal stimuli.* There is no sharp dividing line between sensory stimuli that can be perceived and sensory stimuli that cannot be perceived. A threshold stimulus is one that is intense enough to be perceived 50% of the time. (page 149)

■ *Subliminal perception.* Under some circumstances, a weak stimulus that we do not consciously identify may influence our behavior, at least weakly or briefly. However, the claims of powerful or irresistible effects of subliminal perception are unfounded. (page 150)

- *Detection of simple visual features.* In the first stages of the process of perception, feature-detector cells identify lines, points, and simple movement. Feature detectors cannot account for many of the active, interpretive aspects of perception, however. (page 155)

- *Perception of organized wholes.* According to Gestalt psychologists, we perceive an organized whole by identifying similarities and continuous patterns across a large area of the visual field. (page 159)

- *Attentive and preattentive perception.* We can identify some features of the visual field immediately even without paying attention to them. We identify others only by attending to one part of the visual field at a time. (page 164)

- *Visual constancies.* We ordinarily perceive the shape, size, and color of objects as constant even though the pattern of light striking the retina varies from time to time. (page 164)

- *Motion perception.* We perceive an object as moving if it moves relative to its background. We can generally distinguish between an object that is actually moving and a similar pattern of retinal stimulation that results from our own movement. (page 165)

- *Depth perception.* To perceive depth, we use retinal discrepancy between the views our two eyes see. We also use other cues that are just as effective with one eye as with two. (page 168)

- *The size-distance relationship.* Our estimate of an object's size depends on our estimate of its distance from us. If we overestimate its distance, we will also overestimate its size. (page 172)

- *Optical illusions.* Many, but not all, optical illusions result from interpreting a two-dimensional display as three-dimensional or from other faulty estimates of depth. One of the strongest illusions, the moon illusion, has still not been convincingly explained. (page 172)

SUGGESTIONS FOR FURTHER READING

Kanizsa, G. (1979). *Organization in vision.* New York: Praeger. Emphasizes the Gestalt approach to vision.

Livingstone, M. S. (1988, January). Art, illusion, and the visual system. *Scientific American, 258* (1), 78–85. Discusses implications of the finding that different parts of the brain deal with different aspects of visual information, such as shape, color, and movement.

Rock, I. (1984). *Perception.* New York: Scientific American Books. Includes discussions of visual constancies, illusions, motion perception, and the relationship between perception and art.

TERMS

sensory threshold the minimum intensity at which a given individual can detect a sensory stimulus 50% of the time; a low threshold indicates ability to detect faint stimuli (page 150)

sensory adaptation the tendency of a sensory threshold to fall after a period when the sensory receptors have not been stimulated and to rise after exposure to intense stimuli (page 150)

absolute threshold the sensory threshold at a time of maximum sensory adaptation (page 150)

signal-detection theory the study of people's tendencies to make correct judgments, misses, and false alarms (page 150)

subliminal perception the ability of a stimulus to influence our behavior even when it is presented so faintly or briefly or along with such strong distractors that we do not perceive it consciously (page 151)

feature detector a neuron in the visual system of the brain that responds to particular lines or other features of a visual stimulus (page 155)

autokinetic effect the illusory perception that a point of light in a darkened room is in motion (page 159)

Gestalt psychology an approach to psychology that seeks explanations of how we perceive overall patterns (page 159)

figure and ground an object and its background (page 160)

reversible figure a stimulus that you can perceive in more than one way (page 160)

proximity in Gestalt psychology, the tendency to perceive objects that are close together as belonging to a group (page 161)

similarity in Gestalt psychology, the tendency to perceive objects that resemble each other as belonging to a group (page 161)

continuation in Gestalt psychology, the tendency to fill in the gaps in an interrupted line (page 161)

closure in Gestalt psychology, the tendency to imagine the rest of an incomplete familiar figure (page 161)

good figure in Gestalt psychology, the tendency to perceive simple, symmetrical figures (page 161)

preattentive process a perceptual activity that occurs automatically and simultaneously across a large portion of the visual field (page 164)

attentive process a perceptual activity that considers only one part of a visual field at a time (page 164)

visual constancy the tendency to perceive objects as being unchanging in shape, size, and color, despite variations in what actually reaches the retina (page 164)

induced movement a perception that an object is moving and the background is stationary when in fact the object is stationary and the background is moving (page 166)

stroboscopic movement an illusion of movement created by a rapid succession of stationary images (page 166)

phi effect the illusion of movement created when two or more stationary lights separated by a short distance flash on and off at regular intervals (page 167)

depth perception the perception of distance, which enables us to experience the world in three dimensions (page 168)

retinal disparity the difference in the apparent position of an object as seen by the left and right retinas (page 168)

convergence the degree to which the eyes turn in to focus on a close object (page 168)

binocular cues visual cues that depend on the action of both eyes (page 168)

monocular cues visual cues that are just as effective with one eye as with both (page 168)

motion parallax the apparently swift motion of objects close to a moving observer and the apparently slow motion of objects farther away (page 169)

optical illusion a misinterpretation of a visual stimulus as being larger or smaller or straighter or more curved than it really is (page 171)

visual capture effect tendency to localize a sound as coming from a prominent visual feature (such as a loudspeaker or a ventriloquist's dummy) (page 174)

moon illusion the apparent difference between the size of the moon at the horizon and its size higher in the sky (page 174)

11. In Figure 4.40, continuation, closure, and perhaps good figure; in Figure 4.41, closure. (page 161)

12. Retinal disparity. (page 171)

ANSWERS TO OTHER QUESTIONS IN THE TEXT

C. a (7). b (1). c (5). d (9). e (4).

D.

E.

F.

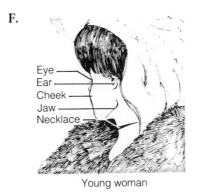
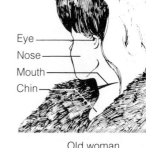

Young woman

Old woman

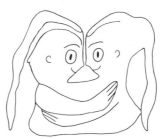

5 ALTERED STATES

My colleague Art Kohn tells a story of an old man who displayed what he said had been Abraham Lincoln's hand-ax. Of course, the man explained, the blade had worn out some years after Lincoln died, so it had to be replaced. And some years later the handle broke and had to be replaced. But this was still Lincoln's ax.

Was it? In a sense, no: Not one scrap of material remained from the ax Lincoln had used. In another sense, yes: We see an unbroken continuity between the ax Lincoln used and this ax.

Now, what about *you*: Are you still the same person as that little 5-year-old who toddled off to kindergarten so many years ago? Since childhood, your body has repeatedly replaced its skin cells, blood cells, and many other cells. As you have grown, you have added new cells throughout your body. Daily, each cell replaces many of its molecules with new ones. Only a minuscule fraction of the material currently in your body is the same as the material that composed your 5-year-old body. The material in your body has been replaced far more times than Lincoln's ax could ever be. It is the same *you* only in the same sense that "Lincoln's ax" is still the same ax as the one Lincoln used long ago.

And yet, you may reply, the exchange of chemicals in your body is irrelevant to your sense of identity. What really constitutes *you* is not the particular molecules in your body at any given instant; the real *you* is your continuing experience, your unbroken "stream of consciousness," in the phrase of William James (1899/1962).

In this chapter we consider some factors that can alter that "stream" of consciousness. When we sleep, we are less conscious than usual of the world around us, as if the stream had been dammed up. When we dream, we experience a world where illogical or impossible events take place readily, as if the stream had been diverted into a new, unfamiliar channel. Under the influence of hypnosis or certain drugs, we may experience distortions of experience. I'm not sure how to force hypnosis into this stream analogy, but taking drugs is a little like polluting the stream. In any case, sleep, hypnosis, and drugs alter our usual way of experiencing the world.

Since the time of your birth, you have repeatedly replaced the material in your body and added new material. Only a minuscule fraction of the molecules in your body today are the same as the molecules that were present in infancy. What makes you the same person from one year to the next is your continuous stream of conscious experience.

SLEEP AND DREAMS

Why do we sleep?
What accounts for the content of our dreams?

Ground squirrels hibernate during the winter, a time when they would have trouble finding enough food. Something in their bodies has to tell them exactly when in the spring is a good time to wake up. The females awaken at almost exactly the time when food becomes available. The males also need to awaken in time to eat, but they have another concern as well: The females are ready to mate as soon as they come out of their winter burrows, and each female mates only once a year. So the males need to be ready and waiting for the females. If some of the males woke up before the females and some woke up afterward, the late risers would pay for their extra sleep by missing out on their mating opportunity for a *whole year.* So the males don't take any chances; they all awaken from hibernation a full week before the females are due. And then they sit around waiting for a week . . . with no females, no food to eat, and nothing to do except to fight with one another (French, 1988).

The point is that all species have evolved timing mechanisms to prepare their behavior for the situations they are likely to encounter. Male ground squirrels have some mechanism that awakens them from hibernation while the air is still cold and well before food is available.

They awaken not in response to their current situation but in preparation for their future situation. Similarly, most migrating birds start south in the fall well before their northern homes become inhospitable.

Humans have built-in timing mechanisms also. We do not have any annual mechanism to prepare us to migrate or hibernate, but we do have mechanisms to prepare us for activity during the day and sleep during the night.

OUR CIRCADIAN RHYTHMS

Humans and other animals that rely on vision for survival are active during the day and inactive at night (Figure 5.1). Rats, mice, and other less visual animals are active at night and inactive during the day. Each species generates a rhythm of activity and inactivity lasting about one day. We call these rhythms **circadian rhythms.** (The term *circadian* comes from the Latin roots *circa* and *dies,* meaning "about a day.") The rising and setting of the sun provides a cue to reset our rhythm each day and keep it at exactly 24 hours; in an environment with no cues to time, most people generate a waking-sleeping rhythm lasting 24 1/2 to 25 hours (Moore-Ede, Czeisler, & Richardson, 1983).

One of the earliest demonstrations of humans' circadian rhythms was a study of two people who spent a few weeks in a remote part of Mammoth Caves in Kentucky, isolated from the outside world (Kleitman, 1963). For 24 hours a day, the temperature was a constant 12° Celsius, and the relative humidity was a steady 100%. They saw no light except the light from lamps that they could control, and they heard no noises except the ones they made themselves. Nothing prevented them from staying awake all the time, from sleeping all the time, or from waking and sleeping by fits and starts. Yet, they went to sleep and awoke at about the same time every day. In later studies, people adjusted easily to an artificial 23-hour day or a 25-hour day, but most had trouble adjusting to more extreme schedules (Czeisler, Weitzman, Moore-Ede, Zimmerman, & Knauer, 1980; Folkard, Hume, Minors, Waterhouse, & Watson, 1985). Evidently, our circadian rhythms depend on a

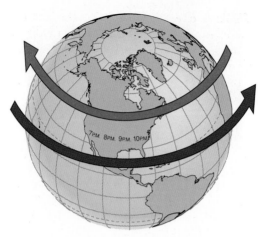

FIGURE 5.2
Jet lag: time zones and sleeping times.

rhythm generated within our own bodies, not one supplied by the environment.

Shifting Sleep Schedules

When you travel across time zones, your internally generated cycles of waking and sleeping are thrown out of phase with the outside world. For example, if you travel from the west coast of North America to western Europe, it will be 7:00 A.M. (time to get up and go) when your body says it is 11:00 P.M. (time to go to bed). The resulting jet lag will make it difficult for you to fall asleep at night, to awaken in the morning, and to function during the day. Over a few days you will gradually adjust to your new schedule, but you will experience jet lag again when you return home. Back on the west coast, your body will scream, "Bedtime! Bedtime!" before anyone else thinks it is time for dinner.

Most people find it easier to adjust to flying west, where they go to bed later, than to flying east, where they go to bed earlier (Désir et al., 1981). East-coast people adjust to west-coast time more easily than west-coast people adjust to east-coast time (Figure 5.2). Adjusting to a new time zone is more difficult for some people than for others, and a few people find it almost impossible to adjust, especially after flying east. If they have to move from the west coast to the east coast, they suffer **insomnia,** difficulty in getting to sleep or staying asleep. The same thing happens when they stay awake very late for a few nights in a row in their own home-town. Their bodies cannot shift back to the earlier schedule once they have adjusted to the later schedule, and the result is insomnia.

Companies that want to keep their factories going nonstop run three work shifts, generally midnight–8:00 A.M., 8:00 A.M.–4:00 P.M., and 4:00 P.M.–midnight. Because it is difficult to find people to work regularly on the "graveyard shift" (midnight–8:00 A.M.), many companies ask their workers to rotate among the three shifts. According to one survey, 26% of U.S. men and 18% of U.S. women work on variable time schedules. Workers on variable shifts report more use of alcohol, tranquilizers, and sleeping pills than do other workers; they also report more job stress and emotional problems (Gordon, Cleary, Parker, & Czeisler, 1986). People working the night shift, especially those who have just switched to the night shift, are responsible for a disproportionate number of industrial accidents. Even people who work the night shift month after month may not fully adjust; they continue feeling groggy on the job and sleeping fitfully during the day.

Employers can ease the burden on their workers in two ways: First, when they transfer workers from one shift to another, they should transfer workers to a *later* shift, not an earlier shift (Czeisler, Moore-Ede, & Coleman, 1982) (Figure 5.3). That is, someone working the 8:00 A.M.–4:00 P.M. shift should switch to the 4:00 P.M.–midnight shift (equivalent to traveling west), instead of the midnight–8:00 A.M. shift (equivalent to traveling east).

Second, employers can help workers adjust to the night shift by providing bright lights to mimic sunlight. In one study, young men exposed to very bright lights at night adjusted well to working at night and sleeping during the day.

Within 6 days, their circadian rhythms had shifted to the new schedule. Another group of men who worked on the same schedule but under less bright lights showed no indications of altering their circadian rhythms (Czeisler et al., 1990).

■ CONCEPT CHECK

1. Suppose you are the president of Consolidated Generic Products in the U.S.A., and you are negotiating a difficult business deal with someone from the opposite side of the world. Should you prefer a meeting place in Europe or on an island in the Pacific Ocean? (Check your answer on page 196.)

Something to Think About

What advice would you give someone who suffered severe, lasting insomnia because that person's body was not ready for sleep until 3:00 A.M.? Remember, the internal clock can shift more easily to a later time than to an earlier time. How could such a person reset his or her internal clock to the correct time?

WHY WE SLEEP

We would not have been born with a mechanism that forces us to sleep for 8 hours or so out of every 24 unless sleep did us some good. But what good does it do? Scientists have proposed two theories.

The Repair and Restoration Theory of Why We Sleep

According to the **repair and restoration theory,** the purpose of sleep is to enable the body to recover from the exertions of the day. During sleep the body increases its rate of cell division and the rate at which it produces new proteins (Adam, 1980). It also digests food. There is no doubt that these and perhaps other restorative processes do occur during sleep. However, nearly all of the same processes also take place when we are awake but sitting quietly. Evidently we do not need sleep in order to rest the muscles or any other tissues, other than perhaps the brain (Horne, 1988). We have several other reasons to doubt that sleeping is like resting to catch your breath after extensive exercise.

First, if sleep were simply a means of recovering from the exertions of the day, it would resemble the rest periods we have after bouts of activity. But people need only a little more sleep

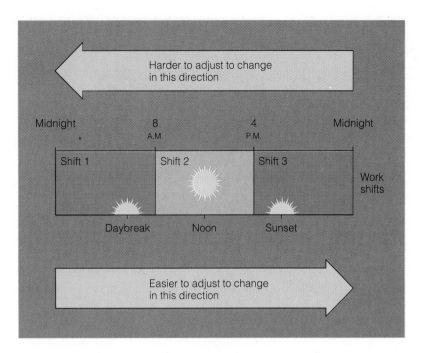

FIGURE 5.3

The graveyard shift is aptly named—serious industrial accidents, including those at nuclear power plants, usually occur at night, when workers are least alert. Night-shift jobs providing emergency services are essential. But few people want to work at night permanently, so workers rotate among three shifts. As in jet lag, the direction of change is critical. Moving forward—clockwise—is easier than going backward.

after a day of extreme physical or mental activity than after a day of inactivity (Horne & Minard, 1985).

Second, some people get by with much less than the "normal" 7 1/2 to 8 hours of sleep a day. An extreme case was a 70-year-old woman who claimed that she slept only about 1 hour a night. Researchers who observed her over a number of days confirmed her claim; some nights she did not sleep at all (Meddis, Pearson, & Langford, 1973). Nevertheless, she remained healthy.

Third, some people have intentionally gone without sleep for a week or more, suffering less severely than we might have expected (Figure 5.4). In 1965 a San Diego high-school student, Randy Gardner, stayed awake for 264 hours and 12 minutes—11 days—in a project for a high-school science fair. Gardner suffered no serious psychological consequences (Dement, 1972). On the last night of his ordeal he played about a hundred arcade games against sleep researcher William Dement and won every game. Just before the end of the 264 hours he held

a television press conference and handled himself well. After sleeping 14 hours and 40 minutes, he awoke refreshed and apparently fully recovered.

You may have heard that unscrupulous people have used sleep deprivation as a means of brainwashing or torturing prisoners. Why would sleep deprivation produce so many more drastic effects on prisoners than it did on, say, Randy Gardner? Two reasons: First, Gardner may have been better able to tolerate sleep deprivation than most other people. After all, we never would have heard about him if he had given up on his project and gone to sleep after 3 days, as most people would have. Second, Gardner knew he was in control of the situation. If he became unbearably miserable, he could simply quit and go to sleep. Tortured prisoners do not have that option; if they stay awake night after night, they do so because of constant prodding, not because of their own decision. For the same reason, rats that have been forced to go without sleep for several days suffer severe health problems that human volunteers seldom experience after similar periods of sleep deprivation (Rechtschaffen, Gilliland, Bergmann, & Winter, 1983).

If you go without any sleep some night—as most college students do at one time or another—you probably will grow very sleepy by about 4:00 or 5:00 A.M. But if you are still awake at 7:00 or 8:00 A.M., you will feel much less sleepy than you did before. For the rest of the day you may feel a little strange, but you probably will have little difficulty staying awake and keeping reasonably alert. That night, however, you will feel very sleepy indeed. Apparently, the need to sleep is tied to particular time periods.

In one study, volunteers went without sleep for three nights; an experimenter periodically took their temperature and measured their performance on logical reasoning tasks. Both temperature and logical reasoning declined during the first night and then increased almost to their normal level the next morning. During the second and third nights, temperature and logical reasoning decreased more than they had the first night, but again they improved the following morning (Figure 5.5). Thus, sleep deprivation produces a pattern of progressive deterioration that is superimposed on the normal circadian cycle of rising and falling body temperature and reasoning ability (Babkoff, Caspy, Mikulincer, & Sing, 1991).

In short, sleepiness apparently depends partly on how long one has gone without sleep and partly on the time of day (that is, where one is within the circadian rhythm). Evidently, sleep contributes to repair and restoration of the body, but that must not be its only reason for existence.

The Evolutionary Theory of Why We Sleep

Sleep may be a way of conserving energy. If we built a solar-powered robot to explore the planet Mars, we probably would program it to shut down almost all its activities at night in order to conserve fuel and in order to avoid walking into rocks that it could not see.

According to the **evolutionary theory of sleep,** evolution equipped us with a regular pattern of sleeping and waking for the same reason (Kleitman, 1963; Webb, 1979). The theory does not deny that sleep provides some important restorative functions. It merely says that evolution has programmed us to perform those functions at a time when activity would be inefficient and possibly dangerous.

Note, however, that sleep protects us only from the sort of trouble we might walk into; it does not protect us from trouble that comes looking for us! So we sleep well when we are in a familiar, safe place; but we sleep lightly, if at all, when we fear that burglars will break into the room or that bears will nose into the tent.

The evolutionary theory accounts well for differences in sleep among species (Campbell & Tobler, 1984). Why do cats, for instance, sleep

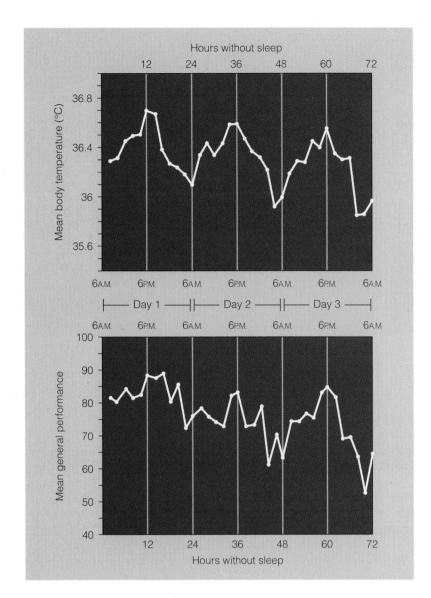

FIGURE 5.5
Cumulative effects of 3 days without sleep. Both body temperature and logical reasoning decrease each night and increase the next morning. They also deteriorate from one day to the next. (From Babkoff, Caspy, Mikulincer, & Sing, 1991).

so much, whereas horses and sheep sleep so little? Surely cats do not need five times as much repair and restoration as horses do. But cats can afford to have long periods of inactivity because they spend little time eating and are unlikely to be attacked while they sleep. Horses and sheep must spend almost all their waking hours eating, because their diet is very low in calories (Figure 5.6). Moreover, they cannot afford to sleep too long or too soundly, because their survival depends on their ability to run away from attackers. (Woody Allen once said, "The lion and the calf shall lie down together, but the calf won't get much sleep.")

Which of the two theories of sleep is correct? Both are, to a large degree. Supporters of the repair and restoration theory concede that the timing and even amount of sleep depend on when the animal is least efficient at finding food and defending itself. Supporters of the evolutionary theory concede that during a time that evolution has set aside for an animal to conserve energy, the animal takes that opportunity to perform repair and restoration functions.

STAGES OF SLEEP

In the mid-1950s, Michel Jouvet, a French scientist, discovered that brain activity and body activity vary from time to time during sleep. While trying to record the very small head movements that a severely brain-damaged cat made while asleep, he found periods in which its brain was relatively active even though its muscles were completely relaxed. Further research indicated that such periods occur not

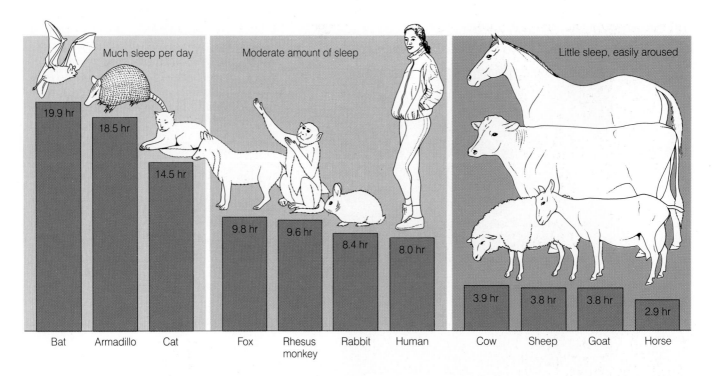

Much sleep per day			Moderate amount of sleep				Little sleep, easily aroused			
19.9 hr	18.5 hr	14.5 hr	9.8 hr	9.6 hr	8.4 hr	8.0 hr	3.9 hr	3.8 hr	3.8 hr	2.9 hr
Bat	Armadillo	Cat	Fox	Rhesus monkey	Rabbit	Human	Cow	Sheep	Goat	Horse

FIGURE 5.6
Sleep time for mammals varies widely. Animals that are rarely attacked sleep a lot; those in danger of attack sleep only a few hours. Diet also relates to sleep. (Based on data from Zepelin & Rechtschaffen, 1974.)

only in brain-damaged cats but also in normal cats (Jouvet, Michel, & Courjon, 1959). Jouvet referred to these periods as *paradoxical sleep.* (A paradox is an apparent self-contradiction.) The paradox is that such sleep is very light in some respects but very deep in other ways. The brain is active, and the body's heart rate, breathing rate, and temperature fluctuate substantially (Parmeggiani, 1982). In these respects paradoxical sleep is very light. And yet most of the muscles, especially the large muscles involved in posture and locomotion, are very relaxed, and it is difficult to awaken someone during paradoxical sleep. In these respects paradoxical sleep is deep sleep.

At about the same time, American researchers William Dement and Nathaniel Kleitman (1957a, 1957b) observed that in one recurrent stage of human sleep, the sleeper's eyes move rapidly back and forth under the closed lids (Figure 5.7). They referred to this stage as **rapid eye movement (REM) sleep.** (All other stages of sleep are known as **non-REM,** or **NREM, sleep.**) Almost at once investigators realized that REM sleep is the same as paradoxical sleep. When Dement and Kleitman awakened people during REM sleep, the sleepers usually reported that they had been dreaming. Apparently, the rapid eye movements were external indications of an internal event; for the first time, it became possible to undertake scientific studies of dreaming.

Sleep Cycles During the Night

Sleep researchers have identified four stages of sleep: After we fall asleep, we progress from stage 1 sleep, in which the brain remains fairly active, through stages 2, 3, and 4. They can detect the stages by recording brain waves with electrodes attached to the scalp (Figure 5.8). A device called an **electroencephalograph,** abbreviated **EEG,** measures and amplifies slight electrical changes on the scalp that reflect patterns of activity in the brain. An awake, alert brain produces an EEG record with many short, choppy waves like the one shown in Figure 5.9a. In sleep stages 1 through 4, the brain produces an increasing number of long, slow waves, as shown in Figure 5.9b through e. These waves indicate *decreased* brain activity. They grow larger from one stage to the next because a larger proportion of the neurons are active at the same time. During wakefulness, by contrast, the neurons are out of synchrony and their activities nearly cancel each other out, rather like the voices of a crowd of people talking at the same time.

After we have reached stage 4 of sleep, we gradually move back through stages 3 and 2 to stage 1 again. A normal young adult cycles from stage 1 to stage 4 and back to stage 1 again in about 90 to 100 minutes. Then he or she repeats the sequence, again and again, all through the night (Figure 5.10). The first time through the

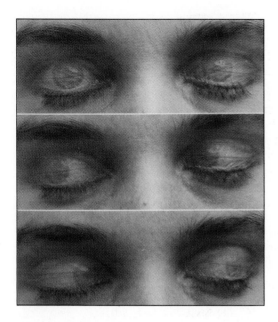

FIGURE 5.7
Rapid eye movements like those in these double-exposure photographs indicate when a sleeping person is dreaming.

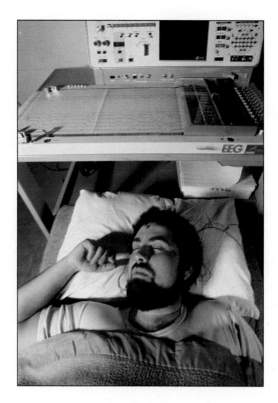

FIGURE 5.8
These electrodes monitor the activity in a sleeper's brain, and an EEG then records and displays brain-wave patterns.

cycle, stages 3 and 4 last the longest; later in the night the duration of stages 3 and 4 declines (and may disappear entirely), and the duration of stages 1 and 2 increases. Except for the first occurrence of stage 1 (when the person is just entering sleep), REM periods replace many or most of the stage 1 periods. Figure 5.9f shows a period of REM sleep. Note both the active EEG recordings and the eye movements.

■ CONCEPT CHECK

2. Would REM sleep and dreaming be more common toward the end of the night's sleep or toward the beginning? (Check your answer on page 196.)

Sleep Stages and Dreaming

Dement's early research indicated that people who were awakened during REM sleep almost always reported they had been dreaming but that people who were awakened during any other period almost never reported dreaming. So, for a time, REM sleep was thought to be almost synonymous with dreaming. However, later studies found a fair amount of dreaming during non-REM sleep as well, although non-REM dreams are less vivid, less visual, less

bizarre, and less likely to be experienced as something really happening. People's reports as to whether or not they were dreaming depended on how they defined *dream.*

The link between REM sleep and highly vivid dreams enabled sleep investigators to determine with fair accuracy whether or not someone was sleeping. Scientific progress frequently depends on an improved way of measuring something; in this case, a method of measuring dreaming enabled researchers to answer some basic questions.

For example, does everyone dream? People who claim they do not dream have been taken into the laboratory so that researchers could examine brain waves and eye movements. The people who claimed not to dream all had normal periods of REM sleep. If awakened during one of these periods, they reported dreams (to their own surprise). Apparently, these people dream as much as anyone else; they simply forget their dreams faster.

Another question: How long do dreams last? Before the discovery of REM sleep, this was an unanswerable question; now, suddenly, we had a method to answer it. William Dement and Edward Wolpert (1958) awakened people after REM periods of various durations and asked them to describe their dreams, if any. A

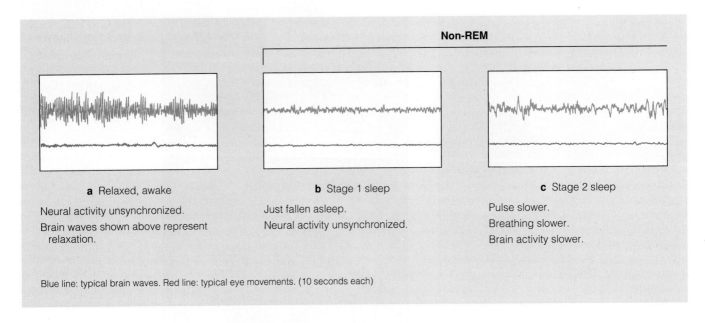

a Relaxed, awake

Neural activity unsynchronized.
Brain waves shown above represent relaxation.

b Stage 1 sleep

Just fallen asleep.
Neural activity unsynchronized.

c Stage 2 sleep

Pulse slower.
Breathing slower.
Brain activity slower.

Blue line: typical brain waves. Red line: typical eye movements. (10 seconds each)

FIGURE 5.9
During sleep, people progress through stages that vary in brain activity. The blue line indicates brain waves, as shown by an EEG. The red line shows eye movements. Note that REM sleep resembles stage 1 sleep except for the addition of rapid eye movements.

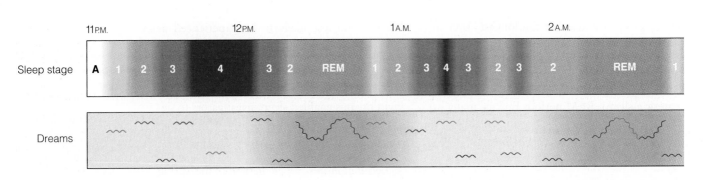

FIGURE 5.10
Condensing hundreds of pages of EEG recordings over a night, this graph shows that a person had five cycles of REM and non-REM sleep and woke up briefly three times (A = Awake). The large amount of stage 3 and 4 sleep early in the night is typical of most people. During such non-REM sleep, the body uses little energy. Brain activity, respiration, and temperature decrease. (From Dement, 1972.)

person awakened after 1 minute of REM sleep usually would tell a brief story; a person awakened after 5 minutes of REM sleep usually would tell a story about 5 times as long, and so on. Evidently, dreams take place in "real time." That is, a dream is not over in a split second; if it seemed to last several minutes, it probably did.

The discovery of REM also enabled sleep researchers to pose some questions that turned out to be surprisingly difficult to answer. One such question is, Why do we have REM sleep (or dreams) at all?

The Function of REM Sleep:

WHAT'S THE EVIDENCE?

Given that people spend about 20–25% of an average night in the specialized state of REM sleep, presumably REM sleep serves some important function. But what is that function? The most direct way to approach this question is to deprive people of REM sleep and see how the deprivation affects their health or behavior.

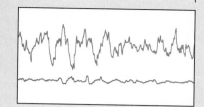

Non-REM

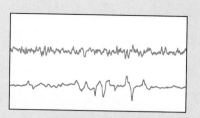

d Stage 3 sleep

Pulse, breathing, and brain activity
  slower yet.

Neural activity more synchronized.

Stages 3 and 4 dominate first half of
  night.

e Stage 4 sleep

Pulse, breathing, and brain activity
  slowest.

Neural activity highly synchronized.

f REM (paradoxical) sleep

Eyes move back and forth.

Dreams more frequent, vivid,
  complex.

Hardest to waken.

Postural muscles most relaxed.

Duration gets longer toward morning.

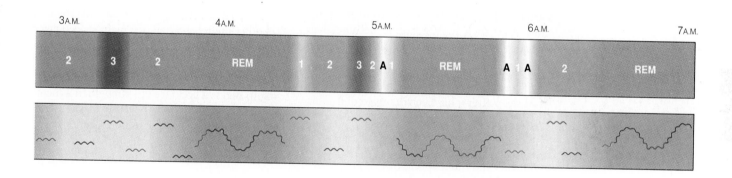

EXPERIMENT 1

Hypothesis People who are deprived of REM sleep will show some sign of needing more REM sleep. In particular, they should show an increased amount of REM sleep after the deprivation period. During the days following a night of REM deprivation, people might show other (unpredictable) signs of disturbance. (This is a somewhat unusual kind of research, in which the investigators perform a new procedure and then try to notice whatever happens. Succeeding at this kind of research requires an alert, observant investigator.)

Method Dement (1960) monitored the sleep of eight young men for seven consecutive nights and awakened them for a few minutes when-

ever their EEG and eye movements indicated the onset of REM sleep. He awakened the members of a control group the same number of times but at random, so that he did not necessarily interrupt their REM sleep.

Results Over the course of a week, Dement found it harder and harder to prevent REM sleep. On the first night, the average subject in the experimental group had to be awakened 12 times. By the seventh night, the average subject had to be awakened 26 times, often with great difficulty. On the eighth night, all the subjects were permitted to sleep without interruption. Most of them showed a "REM rebound," spending 29% of the night in REM sleep as compared with 19% before the experiment

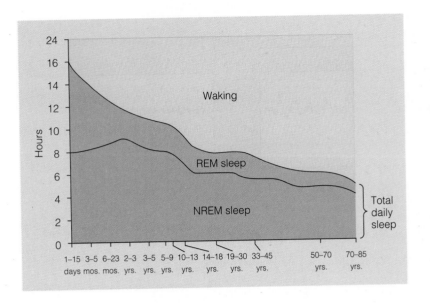

FIGURE 5.11
The percentage of time in REM and non-REM sleep varies with age. As the total amount of sleep declines over age, the percentage of REM sleep also declines. Thus it is uncertain whether REM is particularly important for infants, or just particularly prevalent in those who spend many hours asleep. (From Roffwarg, Muzio, & Dement, 1966).

started. The subjects in the control group showed no such REM rebound because they had not been deprived of REM sleep.

Interpretation REM sleep appears to satisfy some need, because the body tries to get more REM sleep after it has been deprived of it. This initial study led to a series of follow-up studies in which investigators measured the effects of REM deprivation on many aspects of behavior in humans and other species. Most people deprived of REM sleep report an increase in anxiety and irritability and some difficulty in concentrating (Ellman, Spielman, Steiner, & Halperin, 1978; Hoyt & Singer, 1978). Many report a ravenous appetite. Cats that have been deprived of REM sleep often engage in increased and indiscriminate sexual behavior. This behavior has not been reported in humans.

In general, the effects of REM deprivation are not catastrophic and in some cases not even unpleasant. Selective deprivation of REM sleep may even bring about a striking improvement in the mood of some severely depressed people (Vogel, Thompson, Thurmond, & Rivers, 1973). Although REM-deprivation studies indicate that we do have a need for REM sleep, they tell us little about *why* we need it.

A second way to approach the question is to determine which people get more REM sleep

than others. One clear pattern is that infants get more REM sleep than children do and that children get more than adults do (Figure 5.11).

From that observation, a number of people have inferred that REM sleep serves some function that is more acute in younger people. Maybe so, but we should be cautious about interpreting this evidence. Infants not only get more REM sleep but also get more total sleep. If we compare species, we find that the species that get the most total sleep (such as cats) also generally have the greatest percentage of REM sleep. Among adult humans, those who sleep 9 or more hours per night spend much of that time in REM sleep; those who sleep 6 hours or less spend a smaller percentage of time in REM sleep. In short, the individuals with the greatest amount of total sleep time spend the greatest percentage of that time in REM. It is as if a certain amount of non-REM sleep is necessary each night, and additional amounts of REM sleep can be added if sleep continues long enough (Horne, 1988).

There is another way to study the function of REM sleep: Most people get less than 10% REM sleep during the first half of a night's sleep and more than 30% during the second half. Based on this fact, researchers have investigated whether the second half of a night's sleep gives us any special benefits that the first half does not. For example, psychologists have long known that learning something just before going to bed is a good way to strengthen a memory. Perhaps that is because REM sleep strengthens memories. If so, the second half of the night's sleep (richer in REM) should be more helpful than the first half is.

EXPERIMENT 2

Hypothesis Mary Fowler, Michael Sullivan, and Bruce Ekstrand (1973) reasoned that if REM sleep promotes memory, then memory should improve more during the second half of a night's sleep, which includes a higher proportion of REM sleep.

Method Three groups of 16 college students each tried to memorize a list of 15 words. The first experimental group was awakened soon after they went to sleep. They then studied the list and returned to sleep; 3 1/2 hours later they were reawakened and tested. The second experimental group was awakened 4 hours after they went to sleep. They then studied the list and returned to sleep, to be reawakened and tested 3 1/2 hours later. The control group

FIGURE 5.12
The content of most dreams comes from what we think about or do in the day or two prior to the dream. If you came across these sculptures outside a ghost town in Nevada, perhaps you would dream about zombies the next night.

studied the list during the day and was tested 3 1/2 hours later. The difference among the three groups was whether their retention interval occurred during normal waking activities, the first half of a night's sleep, or the second half.

Results   The first experimental group, whose retention interval was the first half of their night's sleep, had the best memory of the word list. The second experimental group, whose retention interval was the second half of their night's sleep, had the second-best memory. The control group, whose retention interval was filled with normal waking activities, had the worst memory.

Interpretation   Evidently, REM sleep is not particularly beneficial to memory. Memory was better after 3 1/2 hours of sleep than after 3 1/2 hours of wakefulness, but it was better if that sleep included little REM sleep (the first half of the night) than if it included more than 30% REM sleep.

These results suggest that non-REM sleep is better for memory than REM sleep is. But other interpretations are also possible: For example, maybe it is more difficult to store memories when one is awakened in the middle of the night than if one is awakened early in the night. Although the two groups were equally fast in memorizing the list, it is difficult to eliminate the possibility that they had not learned equally well.

At any rate, these results indicate that REM sleep is not particularly helpful for strengthening memories. Why then do we need REM sleep? At this point, we still do not know. Psychologists have no shortage of guesses, ranging from REM sleep as a means of discarding useless memories (Crick & Mitchison, 1986) to REM as a means of controlling brain temperature (Wehr, 1990). Research does not always lead to an immediate answer to a question, not even with a question as apparently simple as the function of REM sleep.

THE CONTENT OF OUR DREAMS

What do we dream about and why? At one time, people believed that dreams foretold the future. Sometimes, of course, they do, either by coincidence or because the dreamer had some reason to expect a certain event to happen. Sigmund Freud maintained that dreams reveal a person's unconscious thoughts and motivations (Chapter 15). To some extent they do; the content of most dreams comes from events the person experienced or thought about in the previous day or two (Arkin & Antrobus, 1978). (See Figure 5.12.) For example, people deprived of fluids frequently dream about drinking; people who have been kept in isolation

"Even a saint is not responsible for what happens in his dreams."
ST. THOMAS AQUINAS

For 50,000 years, Australia's aborigines have been interpreting their dreams through music, dance, and art about their Dreamtime, a mythical period when spirit ancestors created everything on the earth. The paintings, which were once done on the sandy soil of the desert, are now created on canvas, with dots of acrylic paint to reproduce the stones or clumps of plant matter that made up the traditional designs. Here a father is explaining his dreaming to his children.

dream about talking in groups. People who have watched violent movies tend to have unusually clear, vivid, and emotional dreams, though not necessarily violent ones. After watching movies with a great deal of explicit sexual content, people who are asked about their dreams frequently say, "I, uhh . . . forget what I was dreaming about."

Furthermore, a frequently repeated dream may suggest that something is worrying the person. People who have the same dream over and over tend to report more anxiety, depression, and stress in their waking lives than do other people (Brown & Donderi, 1986).

However, the fact that dreams generally relate to recent experiences and concerns does not necessarily mean that interpreting dreams is a dependable way to understand someone's innermost thoughts. Many psychotherapists imaginatively overinterpret dreams, thereby probably revealing more about the therapists themselves than about their clients.

Dreams are a product of brain activity, and even a sleeping brain experiences a fair amount of sensory information. While you sleep, you hear, feel, and smell the world around you, and

your vestibular system detects the position of your head. Meanwhile, especially during REM sleep periods, many parts of your brain, especially the visual areas, have substantial amounts of spontaneous activity. According to the **activation-synthesis theory of dreams,** the brain experiences this spontaneous activity as sensations, links the sensations together, and tries to synthesize them into a coherent pattern (Hobson, 1988). A dream is your brain's best effort to make sense of the limited information it is receiving.

This theory suffers the flaws of being vague and not easily testable. Still, as the theory assumes, people who are experiencing various stimuli often incorporate them into their dreams (Arkin & Antrobus, 1978; Dement, 1972). For example, if you happened to feel a spray of water on your face, you might dream about standing in the rain or going swimming. A sudden loud noise might become a dream about an earthquake or a plane crash. A bright light might become a dream about flashes of lightning or a fire.

We can relate certain common dreams to sensory stimuli, although the explanations are admittedly based more on speculation than on evidence. For example, most people have occasional dreams of flying or falling. Perhaps those dreams relate to the fact that you are lying down when you sleep; your vestibular system detects your prone position and your brain interprets the sensation as if you were flying (Hobson & McCarley, 1977). Most people also have occasional dreams in which they are trying to run away from something but find that they cannot move. A possible reason is that the major postural muscles really are paralyzed during REM sleep. Thus, your brain could send messages telling your muscles to move but then receive sensory feedback indicating that they have not moved at all.

As I said, these explanations are speculative. One objection is that most people almost always sleep in a prone position but only occasionally dream of flying, and that our muscles are always paralyzed during REM sleep but we only occasionally dream of being unable to move.

Most people experience visual imagery during their dreams. Blind people may or may not, depending on when and how they became blind. A person who has had vision and then lost it because of damage to the eyes continues to see during dreams. (The visual cortex is still intact and becomes spontaneously active during REM sleep.) But a person who has never had vision or who has lost it because of damage to the visual cortex does not see during dreams. People with any degree of visual impairment are more likely than sighted people to dream about things they have touched (Sabo & Kirtley, 1982).

Many questions about dreams are more easily asked than answered. For example, many people ask, "Do we dream in color?" That sounds like a simple question, perhaps one that should be simple to answer. However, the very fact that people ask this question reveals why it is difficult to answer. People ask because they do not remember whether or not their dreams were in color. But how can an investigator determine whether people dream in color except by asking them? The best answer we have is that when people are awakened during REM sleep, when their recall should be as sharp as possible, they report color half the time or more (Herman, Roffwarg, & Tauber, 1968; Padgham, 1975). This does not mean that their other dreams are necessarily in black and white; it may mean only that the colors in those dreams are not memorable.

ABNORMALITIES OF SLEEP

Comedian Steven Wright says that someone asked him, "Did you sleep well last night?" He replied, "No, I made a few mistakes."

We laugh because sleep isn't the kind of activity on which a person makes mistakes; sleep just happens. Sometimes, however, sleep doesn't happen, or it happens at the wrong time, or it does not seem restful, or we have bad dreams. We probably do not wish to call these unpleasant experiences "mistakes," but in one way or another, our sleep is not what we wanted it to be.

Insomnia

The term *insomnia* literally means "lack of sleep." However, we cannot usefully define insomnia in terms of the number of hours someone sleeps. Some people feel well rested after less than 6 hours of sleep per night; others feel poorly rested after 8 or 9. Furthermore, many people who seek help for their insomnia greatly underestimate how much they sleep. Some of the insomniacs who have been studied in sleep laboratories get to sleep almost as fast as other people and accumulate almost a normal amount of sleep per night. However, when they are awakened, even from stage 4 sleep, they claim they were not asleep! Evidently they are getting many hours of sleep, but their sleep is for some reason not restful. Many of these same people report feeling "much better rested" after a night when they took sleeping pills, even though the sleeping pills increased their total sleep time by only about half an hour (Mendelson, 1990). In short, insomnia is a subjective condition. *A complaint of insomnia indicates that the person feels poorly rested at the end of the night.* By this definition, about one third of all adults have occasional insomnia and about one tenth have serious or chronic insomnia (Lilie & Rosenberg, 1990).

It is convenient to distinguish three main types of insomnia: People with **onset insomnia** have trouble falling asleep. Those with **termination insomnia** awaken early and cannot get back to sleep. Those with **maintenance insomnia** awaken frequently during the night, though they get back to sleep each time. In many cases, onset insomnia and termination insomnia are related to a circadian rhythm that is out of synchrony with the outside world. At 11:00 P.M. a person with onset insomnia may feel as if it were still only 6:00 P.M. At 2:00 A.M. a person with termination insomnia may already feel as if it were 7:00 A.M. In such cases, therapy is a matter of trying to readjust the circadian rhythms so that the person can feel sleepy and wakeful at the normal times.

In addition to an out-of-synch circadian rhythm, we can identify many other causes of insomnia (Kales & Kales, 1984). People sometimes have trouble sleeping because of noise, worries, uncomfortable temperatures, use of various drugs, indigestion, and miscellaneous other problems. Many people drink alcohol as a way of relaxing and getting to sleep, but excessive use of alcohol can lead to prolonged sleep impairments (Johnson, Burdick, & Smith, 1970).

Overuse of tranquilizers can also become a cause of insomnia. That statement may be surprising, because people often take tranquilizers as a way of *preventing* insomnia. Tranquilizers do induce sleep and help people get a restful sleep. The problem is, no pill exerts its effects for exactly the period of time that someone wanted to sleep. Some tranquilizers produce brief effects that wear off before morning, so the person may awaken early (Kales, Soldatos, Bixler, & Kales, 1983). Others have effects that last too long, so the person remains sleepy for part of the next day.

An additional problem with tranquilizers is that a consistent user may come to depend on them to get to sleep (Kales, Scharf, & Kales, 1978). When such a person tries to sleep without taking a pill, he or she may experience more severe insomnia than the original insomnia the pill was supposed to relieve.

Sleep Apnea

One cause of extremely poor sleep is known as **sleep apnea** (AP-nee-uh). *Apnea* means "no breathing." Many people have irregular breathing or occasional periods of 10 seconds or so without breathing during their sleep. People with sleep apnea, however, may fail to breathe for a minute or more and then wake up gasping for breath (Weitzman, 1981). When they do manage to breathe during their sleep, they generally snore. They may lie in bed for 8 to 10 hours a night but actually sleep less than half that time. During the following day they are likely to feel sleepy.

Many people with sleep apnea are obese and unable to find a sleeping position that lets them breathe easily. Others have brain abnormalities, especially in the medulla, that interfere with breathing during sleep. Sleep apnea can be

a serious problem, especially in older people. In many cases in which old people die in their sleep, physicians suspect that the actual cause of death was sleep apnea (Bliwise, Bliwise, Partinen, Pursley, & Dement, 1988).

Narcolepsy

Narcolepsy is a condition in which people fall asleep or at least feel very sleepy, often suddenly, in the middle of the day (Kellerman, 1981; Mahowald & Schenck, 1989). They may also experience sudden attacks of muscle weakness, especially after a period of anger, excitement, or other strong emotions. Sometimes they have dreamlike experiences that they have trouble distinguishing from reality. Each of these symptoms could be interpreted as a sudden intrusion of sleep, especially REM sleep, into the waking period of the day. People with narcolepsy show less arousal than most other people do during the day, but more arousal at night (Meyer, Ishikawa, Hata, & Karacan, 1987). Evidently they have some problem in their separation of waking and sleeping.

The causes of narcolepsy are unknown. Physicians prescribe stimulant drugs and antidepressant drugs, both of which are somewhat helpful. They also advise affected people to avoid situations that arouse strong emotions.

Sleep Talking, Sleepwalking, Nightmares, and Night Terrors

Many people who may or may not suffer insomnia have certain unusual experiences during their sleep. Sleep talking is probably the most common and least troublesome. Most people talk in their sleep, at least once in a while (Arkin, 1978). The frequency with which sleep talking occurs is generally underestimated, because sleep talkers do not remember it themselves and usually no one else is awake to hear it. Sleep talking occurs with about equal probability in REM sleep and non-REM sleep. It may range from a single, indistinct word or grunt to a clearly articulated paragraph. Sleep talkers sometimes pause between utterances, as if they were carrying on a conversation. In fact, you can sometimes engage them in a dialogue. Sleep talking is nothing to worry about. It is not related to any mental or emotional disorder, and sleep talkers rarely say anything they would be embarrassed to say when awake.

Sleepwalking tends to run (walk?) in families. A person who appears to be sleepwalking may really be awake but confused. True sleep-walking occurs mostly in children during stage 4 sleep and lasts less than 15 minutes. Few children hurt themselves when sleepwalking, and most children outgrow it (Dement, 1972). You have no doubt heard people say, "You should never awaken a sleepwalker." This is another of those statements like "We only use 10 percent of our brain" in which people are quoting each other, each person confident that the others know what they are talking about. In fact, sleep researchers report that waking a sleepwalker is neither dangerous nor harmful, although the person may be disoriented and confused (Moorcroft, 1989).

Finally, what about nightmares? Psychologists distinguish between nightmares and night terrors. A nightmare is an unpleasant dream, but a dream nevertheless. A night terror, however, creates a sudden arousal from sleep accompanied by extreme panic, including a heart rate three times the normal rate. Night terrors occur during stage 3 or stage 4, never during REM sleep. They are fairly common in young children, but their frequency declines with age (Salzarulo & Chevalier, 1983).

■ CONCEPT CHECK

3. *Why would it be unlikely, if not impossible, for sleepwalking to occur during REM sleep? (Check your answer on page 196.)*

If You Have Trouble Sleeping . . .

Insomnia can be a brief, minor annoyance or a sign of some potentially serious disorder. If you suffer prolonged insomnia, you should consult a physician, but for occasional or minor insomnia there are some steps you can try yourself (Hauri, 1982; Lilie & Rosenberg, 1990):

■ Try to wake up at the same time each day. (It is hard to get to sleep at a regular time if you don't also wake up at a regular time.)

■ Avoid caffeine and nicotine, especially in the evenings.

■ Avoid habitual use of alcohol or sleeping pills. (Either may help you get to sleep occasionally, but they become counterproductive after repeated use.)

■ Avoid trying to sleep in a room that is too warm or too noisy.

■ Get a steady amount of exercise daily. (Irregular exercise does little good.)

■ If you find that you just can't get to sleep, don't lie in bed worrying about it. Get up, do something else, and try again later.

SUMMARY

■ *Circadian rhythms.* Sleepiness depends on the time of day. Even in an unchanging environment, people become sleepy in cycles of approximately 24 hours. (page 181)

■ *Theories of the need for sleep.* A number of repair and restoration functions take place during sleep. Sleep also serves to conserve energy at times of relative inefficiency. (page 183)

■ *Sleep stages.* During sleep, people cycle through sleep stages 1 through 4 and back through stages 3 and 2 to 1 again. The cycle beginning and ending with stage 1 lasts about 90 to 100 minutes. (page 185)

■ *REM sleep and dreams.* A special stage known as REM sleep replaces many of the stage-1 periods. REM sleep is characterized by rapid eye movements, a high level of brain activity, and relaxed muscles. People usually dream during this stage. (page 186)

■ *Insomnia.* Insomnia—subjectively unsatisfactory sleep—may result from many influences, including a biological rhythm that is out of phase with the outside world, sleep apnea, narcolepsy, and overuse of sleeping pills. (page 193)

SUGGESTIONS FOR FURTHER READING

Dement, W. C. (1992). *The sleepwatchers.* Stanford, CA: Stanford Alumni Association. Account by one of the founders of sleep research.

Moorcroft, W. (1989). *Sleep, dreaming, and sleep disorders: An introduction.* Lanham, MD: University Press of America. An excellent review of research on many aspects of sleep and dreams.

TERMS

circadian rhythm rhythm of increase and decrease in some process lasting approximately one day (page 181)

insomnia difficulty in getting to sleep or staying asleep (page 182)

repair and restoration theory the theory that the purpose of sleep is to enable the body to recover from the exertions of the day (page 183)

evolutionary theory of sleep the theory that sleep evolved primarily as a means of forcing animals to conserve their energy when they are relatively inefficient (page 184)

rapid eye movement (REM) sleep a stage of sleep characterized by rapid eye movements, a high level of brain activity, and deep relaxation of the postural muscles; also known as paradoxical sleep (page 186)

non-REM (NREM) sleep all stages of sleep other than REM sleep (page 186)

electroencephalograph (EEG) a device that measures and amplifies slight electrical changes on the scalp that reflect brain activity (page 186)

activation-synthesis theory of dreams the theory that parts of the brain are spontaneously activated during REM sleep and that a dream is the brain's attempt to synthesize that activation into a coherent pattern (page 192)

onset insomnia trouble falling asleep (page 193)

termination insomnia a tendency to awaken early and to be unable to get back to sleep (page 193)

maintenance insomnia trouble staying asleep, with a tendency to awaken briefly but frequently (page 193)

sleep apnea a condition in which a person has trouble breathing while asleep (page 194)

narcolepsy a condition characterized by suddenly falling asleep, or at least feeling very sleepy, during the day (page 194)

ANSWERS TO CONCEPT CHECKS

1. You should prefer to schedule the meeting on a Pacific island so that you will travel west and the other person will travel east. (page 183)

2. REM sleep and dreaming are more common toward the end of the night's sleep. (page 187)

3. During REM sleep the major postural muscles of the body are completely relaxed. (page 195)

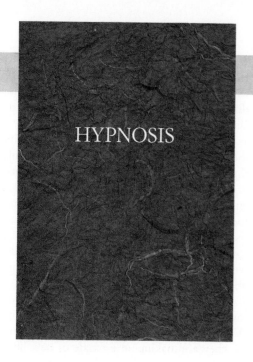

HYPNOSIS

What can hypnosis do?
What are its limitations?

If a hypnotist told you that you were 4 years old, and you suddenly starting acting like a 4-year-old, we would say that you were a good hypnotic subject. If the hypnotist said that you see your cousin sitting in the empty chair in front of you, and you said yes, you see her, then again we would remark on the fact that you are deeply hypnotized.

But what if you had *not* been hypnotized and you started acting like a 4-year-old? Or insisted that you see someone in that empty chair? In that case, psychologists would suspect that you were suffering from some psychological disorder—probably something fairly serious. Hypnosis induces a temporary state that is sometimes bizarre. No wonder we find it so fascinating.

Psychologists define **hypnosis** as a condition of increased suggestibility that occurs in the context of a special hypnotist-subject relationship. The term *hypnosis* comes from Hypnos, the Greek god of sleep. Although it has long been assumed that hypnosis is somehow related to sleep, the connection is rather superficial. It is true that in both states the eyes are usually closed and the person is without initiative. Moreover, in both hypnosis and dreams, a person accepts contradictory information without protest. A hypnotized person resembles a waking person, however, in his or her ability to move about and to respond to stimuli.

Hypnosis was first practiced by an Austrian philosopher and physician, Franz Anton Mesmer (1734–1815). In treating certain medical problems, Mesmer would pass a magnet back and forth across the patient's body to redirect the flow of blood, nerve activity, and certain undefined "fluids." His novel form of therapy seemed to help some patients dramatically.

Later, Mesmer discovered that he could dispense with the magnet; a piece of wood, or even his own hand, would work just as well. We would now conclude that his therapy, when it worked, did so through the power of suggestion on people whose problems were psychological in origin. But Mesmer clung to the conviction that it depended on an "animal magnetism" that came from his own body.

In his later years Mesmer grew stranger and stranger. After his death, his followers carried out serious studies of "animal magnetism" or "Mesmerism," eventually giving it the name "hypnotism." But by that time, many physicians and scientists associated hypnosis with eccentrics, charlatans, and other practitioners of hocus-pocus. Legitimate users of hypnosis have had to fight against that reputation ever since.

WAYS OF INDUCING HYPNOSIS

Mesmer thought that hypnosis was a power emanating from his own body, like the power a magnet exerts on metals. If so, only certain people would have the power to hypnotize others. Today we believe that becoming a successful hypnotist requires a certain amount of skill and training but no unusual powers or personality traits.

Some people still use hypnosis as part of a stage act. We should carefully distinguish stage hypnotists from psychologists and psychiatrists who are licensed to practice hypnosis. Hypnosis can be useful for many therapeutic purposes, including pain reduction and breaking bad habits.

There are several ways of inducing hypnosis. The first step toward being hypnotized is simply agreeing to give it a try. Contrary to what you may have seen in movies or on television, no one can hypnotize someone who does not agree to cooperate.

A hypnotist might then ask the subject to concentrate while the hypnotist monotonously repeats such suggestions as, "You are starting to fall asleep. Your eyelids are getting heavy. Your eyelids are getting very heavy. They are starting to close. You are falling into a deep, deep sleep" (Figure 5.13).

In another popular technique, described by R. Udolf (1981), the hypnotist suggests, "After you go under hypnosis, your arm will begin to rise automatically." (Some people, eager for the hypnosis to succeed, shoot their arm up immediately and have to be told, "No, not yet. Just relax; that will happen later.") Then the hypnotist encourages the subject to relax and suggests that the arm is starting to feel lighter, as if it were tied to a helium balloon. Later the hypnotist suggests that the arm is beginning to feel a little strange and is beginning to twitch. The timing of this suggestion is important, because after people stand or sit in one position long enough, their limbs really do begin to feel strange and twitch a bit. If the hypnotist's suggestion comes at just the right moment, the subject thinks, "Wow, that's right, my arm does feel a little strange. This is really starting to work!" Wanting to be hypnotized or believing that you are being hypnotized is a big step toward actually being hypnotized.

A little later the hypnotist may suggest that the subject's arm is starting to rise. If that fails, the suggestion may be revised a bit: "Your arm is so light that when I push it upward a little, it will keep rising by itself." If the arm rises and then begins to waver and drop, a skilled hypnotist may say, "Now you can lower your arm." At some point along the way the subject's eyelids will close, even if the hypnotist has said nothing about closing them.

Gradually, the hypnotist brings the subject into a condition of heightened suggestibility. When people talk about the "depth" of hypnosis, they are making an estimate of how likely the subject is to do what the hypnotist suggests. A "deeply" hypnotized person will do what the hypnotist says to do and will experience (or at least will *report* experiencing) what the hypnotist says to experience.

What happens in hypnosis is not altogether different from what happens in ordinary experience. When you watch a good movie or play or read a good novel, you may become captivated by its "suggestions" (Figure 5.14). You may focus your attention on the story and experience the emotions just as strongly as if you were one of the characters. Hypnosis has much the same effect (Barber, 1979).

Hypnosis, nevertheless, produces some paradoxical effects. A hypnotist says, "Your hand is rising; you can do nothing to stop it," and the person's hand does indeed rise. When asked about it later, people who have been through this experience often insist that they had "lost control" over their own behavior. Still, the behavior is neither reflexive nor involuntary in any usual sense of the word *involuntary;* the hypnotized people are certainly producing the behavior themselves. Psychologists have wrestled with this problem of how a behavior can be both voluntary and involuntary. One resolution is that the hypnotized people have voluntarily *decided* to be open to this new experience of hypnosis. Having done so, these people regard the hypnotist's words as the cause of their behavior. They experience the behavior as "just happening," and they do not have the usual feeling of deciding whether or not to do something (Lynn, Rhue, & Weekes, 1990).

FIGURE 5.13
A hypnotist induces hypnosis by repeating suggestions, relying on the hypnotized person's cooperation and willingness to accept suggestions. No one can enforce hypnosis on an unwilling person.

FIGURE 5.14
Hypnosis, which gets its name from a word for sleep, *resembles the suspended consciousness of sleep. When a novel draws you deeply into its world, you are entranced or "hypnotized" by it.*

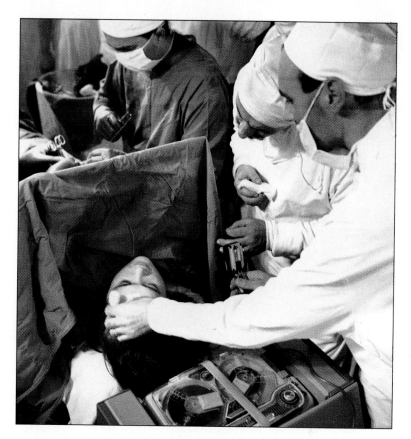

FIGURE 5.15
This woman is undergoing an appendectomy with only hypnotic suggestions as pain reducers. In patients sufficiently responsive to hypnotic suggestions, this procedure reduces the risks associated with anesthesia.

THE USES (AND NON-USES) OF HYPNOSIS

Hypnosis can produce relaxation, concentration, temporary changes in behavior, and sometimes changes that persist beyond the end of the hypnotic state. There is no evidence, however, that it enables you to do anything you could not do ordinarily, with sufficient motivation.

What Hypnosis Can Do

One well-established effect of hypnosis on perception is the inhibition of pain. A hypnotic suggestion to feel no pain is sometimes so effective (with some people) that medical or dental surgery can be performed without anesthesia. Apparently, hypnosis has only a slight effect on the intensity of pain but a significant effect on the *distress* that accompanies pain (Hilgard, 1979). A painful stimulus produces as much change in heart rate and blood pressure in hypnotized people as in nonhypnotized people

(Hilgard, 1973). However, in many cases the hypnotized people are simply not bothered by the pain. Hypnotic reduction of pain is particularly useful in certain kinds of surgery that are safer when performed without anesthetic drugs (Figure 5.15). Hypnosis also provides some relief for people who have developed a great tolerance to painkilling opiates or who for some reason cannot take opiates.

Another constructive use of hypnosis is a **posthypnotic suggestion,** a suggestion that the person will do or experience something particular after coming out of hypnosis. The posthypnotic suggestion could be to do something trivial, such as to smile at the end of the hypnotic session, to dream about a certain topic that night, or to scratch one's left ear at exactly nine o'clock. Posthypnotic suggestions also have more practical applications, such as helping people give up tobacco or alcohol, lose weight, stop nail biting, become more sexually responsive, stop having night terrors, or change some

FIGURE 5.16
The U.S. Supreme Court ruled in 1987 that criminal defendants may testify about details they recalled under hypnosis. Its decision sparked this protest by the magician known as "the Amazing Kreskin." Kreskin borrowed a stunt usually used to demonstrate the power of hypnosis—standing on a person suspended between two chairs. Many psychologists and physicians doubt the accuracy of testimony obtained under hypnosis. Details reported with confidence under hypnosis often turn out to be factually inaccurate.

other behavior (Kihlstrom, 1979; Udolf, 1981). Posthypnotic suggestions seem to be quite effective in helping people change their habits, although the effects tend to wear off in a few days or weeks. The suggestions do not force any change in behavior; the people who agree to be hypnotized have already decided to try to quit smoking or to break some other habit. The hypnosis underscores that resolve.

What Hypnosis Cannot Do

Some spectacular claims have been made for the power of hypnotic suggestion, but on closer scrutiny most of them turn out to be less impressive. For instance, people under hypnosis can become as stiff as a board, so stiff that they can balance their head and neck on one chair and their feet on another chair and allow someone to stand on their body (Figure 5.16)! Amazing? Not really. You probably can make yourself stiff enough to balance in this way without

being hypnotized. It is easier than it looks. (But I do not recommend that you invite anyone to stand on you. Someone who does not balance just right could injure you.)

Many hypnotists have attempted to use hypnosis to enhance people's memory, but the evidence indicates that this use is unreliable. In one case, a woman disappeared without a trace. When weeks passed with no word from her, the police became suspicious and hypnotized her son. The son reported having seen his father murder his mother and then chop up her body and dispose of the pieces. On the basis of that testimony, the father was convicted and sentenced to life in prison. A few months later, the conviction was reversed when the woman turned up alive and well in another state. She had merely deserted her family.

Hypnotized people are highly suggestible. When told to recall something, they will almost surely report that they remember it. But what they report may be incorrect or may be a mixture of real memories and fantasies (Gibson, 1982). Even after they come out of hypnosis, they may continue to report the same memories, real or imagined, that they recalled under hypnosis.

In some laboratory experiments, hypnosis has improved memory (Stager & Lundy, 1985), but in most cases it has led to false reports. In one study (Dwyman & Bowers, 1983), researchers showed subjects photos and then asked them to recall as many as they could. After the subjects had done their best, they were hypnotized and asked to try again. Under hypnosis, the subjects recalled more items than before, but most of the additional items were wrong. Even so, they were just as sure about the additional wrong items as they were about the additional correct ones.

In response to such findings, a panel appointed by the American Medical Association (1986) concluded that testimony elicited under hypnosis should not be used in courts of law. This does not mean, however, that the police should never use hypnosis. If an investigation has reached a dead end, hypnotizing a witness may yield information that leads the police to solid evidence (Figure 5.17). If it does not lead to solid evidence, they can simply ignore the witness's hypnotized report.

An even more doubtful claim is that hypnosis can help people recall their early childhood. A hypnotist might say, "You are getting younger. It is now the year ___; now it is ___;

now you are only 6 years old." Under hypnosis a person may give a convincing performance of being a 10-year-old, a 6-year-old, or a 3-year-old, even playing with teddy bears and blankets as a 3-year-old would (Nash, Johnson, & Tipton, 1979).

But is the subject really reliving early childhood experiences? Evidently not. First, the childhood "memories" that the hypnotized subject so confidently recalls, such as the names of friends and teachers and the details of birthday parties, are generally inaccurate (Nash, 1987). Second, a person who has presumably regressed under hypnosis to early childhood retains spelling and other skills learned later in life. When asked to draw a picture, the subject does not draw as children draw but as adults imagine that children draw (Orne, 1951). (See Figure 5.18.) Third, hypnotized subjects will respond to suggestions that they are growing older as well as to suggestions that they are growing younger. They give just as convincing a performance of being an older person (and "remembering" events in the future) as of being a younger person (Rubenstein & Newman, 1954). Because they must be acting out an imagined future, we should assume they are doing the same for the past.

Finally, the most preposterous claim of all is that hypnosis can help someone to recall memories from a previous life. Hypnotized people who claim to be recollecting a previous life generally describe the life of a person similar to themselves and married to someone who bears an uncanny resemblance to their current boyfriend or girlfriend. If subjects are asked whether their country (in their past life) is at war or what kind of money is in use, their guesses are seldom correct (Spanos, 1987–88).

The Still-Uncertain Limits of Hypnosis

If a hypnotist asked you to do something immoral or dangerous, what would you do? "You don't have to worry," a hypnotist will reassure you. "People never do anything under hypnosis that they would ordinarily refuse to do." Although nearly all hypnotists seem to believe that statement is true, they offer little solid evidence pro or con.

In one experiment (Orne & Evans, 1965), hypnotized college students were asked to perform three acts. First, they were told to go to a box in a corner of the room and pick up a poisonous snake. There actually was a poisonous, potentially deadly snake in the box. If a subject

FIGURE 5.17
Los Angeles has used special "hypnocops" who hypnotize witnesses to a crime to get additional (or more confident) testimony. It also sends some witnesses to psychotherapists who practice hypnosis. Critics of this procedure point to research showing that hypnosis often leads to confident but inaccurate recall.

got too close to the snake, he or she was restrained at the last moment. Second, the hypnotist poured some highly concentrated, fuming nitric acid into a large container and said distinctly that it was nitric acid. To dispel any doubts, he threw a coin into the acid and let the subjects watch it as it started to dissolve. The hypnotist then told a subject to reach into the acid with bare hands and remove the coin. Here there was no last-second restraint. Anyone who followed the instructions was told to wash his or her hands in warm soapy water immediately afterward. (This was before procedures were adopted to protect subjects in psychological experiments.) Third, the hypnotist told a subject to throw the nitric acid into the face of the hypnotist's assistant. Unnoticed, the hypnotist had swapped the container of nitric acid for a container of water, but the hypnotized subject had no way of knowing that. The results: Five of the six hypnotized people followed all three directions.

Does this mean that you would do something under hypnosis that you would not ordinarily do? Before we can answer that, we need to know what people will do when they are not under hypnosis. M. T. Orne and F. J. Evans (1965) asked some subjects to *pretend* they were hypnotized and then asked them to pick up the snake, stick their hands into the fuming nitric acid, and throw the acid at an assistant. All six

FIGURE 5.18

Regression or role playing? One person made drawing (a) at age 6 and the other three drawings (b, c, d) as a college student under hypnosis. While under hypnosis, the person was asked to regress to age 6. The drawings under hypnosis are not like drawings done in childhood. Orne (1951) concluded that the hypnotized students played the role of a 6-year-old and drew as they thought a child would.

pretenders followed all three commands! So did two of six people who were just told to take these actions as part of an experiment, with no mention of hypnosis. (They did, however, hesitate much longer than the hypnotized subjects.) Why would people do such extraordinary things? They explained that they simply trusted the experimenter: "If he tells me to do something, it can't really be dangerous."

In short, people under hypnosis will do some strange things, but so will some people who are not under hypnosis. We simply do not have adequate evidence to decide whether people under hypnosis will do anything that they would utterly refuse to do otherwise.

DISTORTIONS OF PERCEPTION UNDER HYPNOSIS

A few people report visual or auditory **hallucinations** (sensory experiences not corresponding to reality) under hypnosis; a larger number report touch hallucinations (Udolf, 1981). A hypnotist can bring about a touch hallucination by such suggestions as "Your nose itches" or "Your left hand feels numb."

When hypnotized people say that they see or hear something, or that they fail to see or hear something, are they telling the truth or are they just saying what the hypnotist wants them to say? Or do they perhaps believe what they say, even though the visual or auditory information does get through to the nervous system?

In one experiment to test this question, people who were highly susceptible to hypnosis looked at the Ponzo illusion, shown in Figure 5.19a. Like other people, they reported that the top horizontal line looked longer than the bottom horizontal line. Then they were hypnotized and told not to see the radiating lines, just the two horizontal ones. Those who said that they no longer saw the radiating lines still perceived the top line as longer than the bottom one (Miller, Hennessy, & Leibowitz, 1973). If the radiating lines had truly disappeared, then the subjects would have seen something like Figure 5.19b, in which the horizontal lines look equal.

In another experiment, hypnotized subjects were told that they would hear nothing. From that point on, they appeared to be deaf, ignoring even shouts. The experimenter spoke a word such as *dream,* showed the subjects four written words, and signaled for them to choose one—any way they wished. In each case, one of the words rhymed with the original word (such as *cream*) and one had a related meaning (such as *sleep*). The other two words were unrelated to the original word. A person who really did not hear the word *dream* would have a 50% chance of choosing one of the related words. The hypnotized subjects chose a related word 40% of the time—significantly less than they would have by random choice (Nash, Lynn, Stanley, & Carlson, 1987). Evidently the hypnotized subjects did hear the word, but in some manner rejected it to make themselves appear to be deaf. (We cannot say whether they did so deliberately.)

So, does hypnosis alter perception? Yes and no. Hypnosis does not screen out sensory information altogether, as if the sensory receptors had been destroyed. Evidently the information gets into the nervous system and persists long enough to exert some influence on behavior, even when hypnotized people deny that they saw or heard anything.

■ CONCEPT CHECK

4. In the experiment in which hypnotized people were told that they were deaf, what conclusion would we draw if they chose one of the related words more than 50% of the time? (Check your answer on page 205.)

IS HYPNOSIS AN ALTERED STATE OF CONSCIOUSNESS?

Because I have included hypnosis in a chapter titled "Altered States," you may take it for granted that hypnosis is an altered state, whatever that means. But not all psychologists concede that point. Some claim that hypnosis does not really alter a person's state of awareness in anything like the manner of sleep or drugs. Rather, they suggest, a hypnotized person is in a normal, waking state but playing a role, much like a performer in a play. Just as actors and actresses do what the author and play director tell them to do, hypnotized people do what the hypnotist tells them to do. But in both cases, people are fully awake and acting voluntarily.

One way to determine whether hypnosis is a special state of consciousness is to see whether nonhypnotized people can do everything that hypnotized people do. That is, if you agreed to pretend you were hypnotized, could you fake it well enough to convince an experienced hypnotist?

Can an Unhypnotized Person Pretend to Be Hypnotized?

In several experiments, one group of college students was hypnotized while another group was told to pretend they were hypnotized. An experienced hypnotist then examined all the people and tried to determine which ones were really hypnotized.

Fooling the hypnotist turned out to be easier than expected. The pretenders were able to tolerate sharp pain without flinching and could recall or pretend to recall old memories. They could make their bodies as stiff as a board and lie rigid between two chairs. When told to sit down, they did so immediately (like hypnotized people) without first checking to make sure there was a chair behind them (Orne, 1959, 1979). When told to experience anger or some other emotion, they exhibited physiological changes such as increased heart rate and sweating, just like hypnotized people (Damaser, Shor, & Orne, 1963). Not even highly experienced hypnotists could identify the pretenders with confidence.

However, a few differences did emerge (Orne, 1979). The pretenders did certain things differently from the way the hypnotized subjects did them—not because they were unable to do them but because they did not know how a hypnotized subject would act. For instance, when the hypnotist suggested, "You see Professor Schmaltz sitting in that chair," people in both groups reported seeing the professor. Some of the hypnotized subjects, however, said they were puzzled. "How is it that I see the professor there, but I can also see the entire chair?" Pretenders never reported seeing this "double reality."

At that point in the experiment, Professor Schmaltz actually walked into the room. "Who is that entering the room?" asked the hypnotist. The pretenders either would say they saw no one or would identify Schmaltz as someone else. The hypnotized subjects would say, "That's Professor Schmaltz." Some of them said that they were confused by seeing the same person in two places at the same time. For some of them the hallucinated professor faded at that moment, whereas others continued to accept the double image.

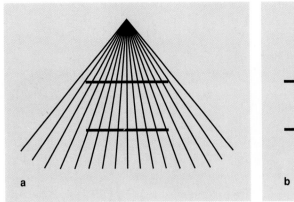 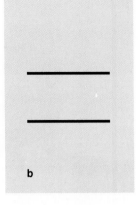

FIGURE 5.19
Horizontal lines of equal length in (a) the Ponzo illusion and (b) without the optical illusion. Researchers employ such visual stimuli to determine how hypnosis may alter sensory perception.

FIGURE 5.20
Kenneth Bianchi, accused of being the Hillside strangler, pleaded not guilty on the grounds that he had a "multiple personality" and that his evil second personality was responsible for the crimes. Psychiatrist Martin Orne, however, persuaded the court that Bianchi was faking his second personality and, indeed, that he was only pretending to be hypnotized.

So . . . what is the conclusion? Is hypnosis an altered state, or are hypnotized people just playing a role? This is not an easy question. Apparently, nonhypnotized people playing the role of "hypnotized subjects" can mimic most of the effects of hypnosis, and they probably could have mimicked some of the other effects if they had just known what those effects were. However, the fact that nonhypnotized role players resemble hypnotized people does not necessarily mean that hypnosis is "nothing but" role playing (Hilgard, 1971). The induction of hypnosis produces a variety of effects that other people have to learn to imitate; those effects happen spontaneously for the hypnotized subjects.

Faked Hypnosis by a Criminal Defendant

In 1979 Kenneth Bianchi was arrested for raping and strangling two women. He was suspected of raping and strangling many others in similar fashion—of being the "Hillside Strangler" who had been terrifying the Los Angeles area. While he was awaiting trial, a psychiatrist hypnotized him and claimed to uncover a second personality, "Steve Walker," who had first appeared when Bianchi was 9 and who had, Bianchi said, actually committed the crimes. Bianchi pleaded not guilty by reason of insanity.

But was Bianchi really insane, or was he faking the second personality and, indeed, only pretending to be hypnotized (Figure 5.20)? Six psychiatrists were asked to examine Bianchi and try to answer these questions. One of them was Martin Orne, the psychiatrist who had conducted the research on whether college students could effectively pretend to be hypnotized. He knew how hard it was to detect the pretenders, but he had also picked up a few tricks in the course of the research. And, more important, he had cultivated a healthy skepticism. At first, the six psychiatrists were divided on whether Bianchi was insane or faking. Eventually, Orne convinced them that Bianchi was faking, for a variety of reasons including the following (Orne, Dinges, & Orne, 1984):

- Bianchi behaved under hypnosis in ways that Orne had never seen in other hypnotized people. When Orne suggested that someone was sitting in the empty chair opposite Bianchi, Bianchi not only claimed to see that person but also reached out to shake hands with the imaginary person! He also tried to get Orne to talk to the imaginary person. Orne concluded that Bianchi was trying too hard to prove that he was hypnotized.

- In one hypnosis session, Bianchi's "Steve" personality tore the filter tip off a cigarette. After the hypnosis was over, the "Ken" personality expressed amazement at the filter tip and said he couldn't imagine who might have torn it off. This episode might suggest that Bianchi had completely forgotten the experience under hypnosis. However, Orne observed that Bianchi did exactly the same thing with three other hypnotists. Again, the natural conclusion was that Bianchi was trying to convince everyone that he had been deeply hypnotized.

- At one point Orne told Bianchi that he doubted Bianchi was a true case of multiple personality because "real" multiple personalities have three personalities, not just two. (This is not true; Orne just wanted to see what would happen.) Later that day, Bianchi developed a third personality.

By uncovering these facts, Orne exposed Bianchi's pretense. Bianchi agreed to plead guilty in return for the state's dropping its request for the death penalty. He also stopped claiming to have multiple personalities.

In short, it is sometimes possible to distinguish between hypnotized people and those who are only pretending. But it is not easy.

SUMMARY

■ *Nature of hypnosis.* Hypnosis is a condition of increased suggestibility that occurs in the context of a special hypnotist-subject relationship. Psychologists try to distinguish the genuine phenomenon, which deserves serious study, from exaggerated claims. (page 197)

■ *Hypnosis induction.* To induce hypnosis, a hypnotist asks a person to concentrate and then makes repetitive suggestions. The first steps toward being hypnotized are to be willing to be hypnotized and to believe that one is becoming hypnotized. (page 197)

■ *Uses.* Hypnosis can alleviate pain, and through posthypnotic suggestions it can help someone overcome bad habits, at least temporarily. (page 199)

■ *Nonuses.* Hypnosis does not give people special strength or unusual powers. Most of the new "memories" evoked under hypnosis are incorrect. (page 200)

■ *Uncertain limits.* Although many hypnotists insist that a subject never will do anything under hypnosis that he or she would refuse to do otherwise, little solid evidence backs this claim. In experiments, it is difficult to find anything that either a hypnotized person or an unhypnotized person will refuse to do. (page 201)

■ *Sensory distortions.* People under hypnosis can be induced to ignore certain stimuli as if they were blind or deaf. However, the visual or auditory information still reaches the nervous system and influences behavior in subtle or indirect ways. (page 202)

■ *Hypnosis as an altered state.* Controversy continues about whether hypnosis is a special state of consciousness or whether it is the product of role playing. (page 203)

SUGGESTIONS FOR FURTHER READING

Hilgard, E. R. (1971). Hypnotic phenomena: The struggle for scientific acceptance. *American Scientist, 59,* 567–577. A brief history of hypnosis and an introduction to the research controversies.

Udolf, R. (1981). *Handbook of hypnosis for professionals.* New York: Van Nostrand Reinhold. A thorough review of research on all aspects of hypnosis.

TERMS

hypnosis a condition of increased suggestibility that occurs in the context of a special hypnotist-subject relationship (page 197)

posthypnotic suggestion a suggestion made to hypnotized subjects that they will do or experience something particular after coming out of hypnosis (page 199)

hallucination a sensory experience not corresponding to reality, such as seeing or hearing something that is not present or failing to see or hear something that is present (page 202)

ANSWER TO CONCEPT CHECK

4. We would conclude that they really had heard the words. Note that this is the same conclusion we drew when people chose the related words less than 50% of the time. If they really did not hear anything, then they would choose a related word 50% of the time; any other result indicates that they heard. (page 203)

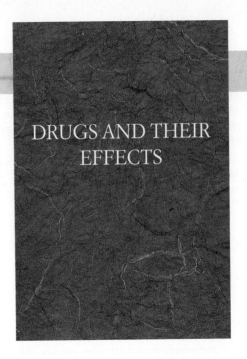

DRUGS AND THEIR EFFECTS

What experiences do drugs of abuse produce?
Why do people experiment with such drugs?

Many people assume (incorrectly) that any drug they get from a physician or a pharmacy must be safe. In fact, almost any drug has unwanted side effects and many legal drugs can become habit-forming after repeated use. Furthermore, many abused drugs (including amphetamine, morphine, and even cocaine) have legitimate medical uses. The dividing line between "good drugs" and "bad drugs" is a blurry one; it depends more on the quantities used and reasons for use than it does on the chemistry of the drugs themselves.

Alcohol and other drugs have been part of human experience throughout history. People sometimes experiment with unfamiliar drugs just to have new experiences. They may use drugs familiar to them because they like the experiences the drugs induce. In either case, they are trying to produce an altered state of consciousness. The abuse of alcohol and other drugs is one of the most widespread problems of our society. In Chapter 14 I shall take up the question of addictions and what can be done about them. Here I briefly survey some common drugs of abuse, what experiences they produce, and how the effects change after repeated use.

A SURVEY OF ABUSED DRUGS AND THEIR EFFECTS

Some abused drugs—such as alcohol, tranquilizers, and opiates—have predominantly calming effects. Others—such as amphetamines and cocaine—have predominantly stimulating effects. Some drug users are content to use either the "downers" or the "uppers." Apparently they want a *change* in their experience—any change. Table 5.1 lists some of the commonly abused drugs and their most prominent effects.

Alcohol

Alcohol is a class of molecules that includes methanol, ethanol, propyl alcohol (rubbing alcohol), and others. Ethanol is the one that people drink; the others are highly dangerous if consumed. Alcohol acts primarily as a relaxant (Sudzak et al., 1986), although it may have certain stimulating effects as well. It leads to heightened aggressive, sexual, or playful behavior, mainly by depressing the brain areas that ordinarily inhibit such behaviors. Moderate use of alcohol serves as a tension reducer and a social lubricant. It helps people forget their problems, at least for the moment (Cowan, 1983).

Excessive use impairs judgment, memory, and motor control (Hashtroudi & Parker, 1986; Hull & Bond, 1986). (See Figure 5.21.) After years of use, alcohol may lead to a long-lasting impairment of memory that persists even during periods of abstinence (Forsberg & Goldman, 1987). Alcohol abuse is particularly harmful to memory in older people (Nelson, McSpadden, Fromme, & Marlatt, 1986). It can also lead to damage of the liver and other organs; it can aggravate and prolong many medical conditions.

Alcohol exerts many of its behavioral effects by facilitating transmission at synapses using the neurotransmitter GABA (Sudzak et al., 1986). Tranquilizers also act by facilitating those synapses, though they do so in a slightly different way. Because of this similarity of mechanism, the effects of alcohol resemble those of tranquilizers. Taking alcohol and tranquilizers together can be dangerous. Together they can suppress GABA transmission more effectively than either alcohol or tranquilizers

Table 5.1 Commonly Abused Drugs and Their Effects

Drug Category	Effects on Behavior	Effects on Central Nervous System and Organs
Depressants		
Alcohol	Relaxant; relieves inhibitions; impairs memory and judgment	Widespread effects on membranes of neurons; facilitates activity at GABA synapses
Tranquilizers: barbiturates; benzodiazepines (Valium, Xanax)	Relieve anxiety; relax muscles; induce sleep	Facilitate activity at GABA synapses
Opiates: morphine, heroin	Decrease pain; decrease attention to real world; unpleasant withdrawal effects as drug leaves synapses	Stimulate endorphin synapses
Stimulants		
Caffeine	Increases energy, alertness	Increases heart rate; indirectly increases activity at glutamate synapses
Amphetamines; cocaine	Increase energy, alertness	Increase or prolong activity at dopamine synapses
Mixed Stimulant-Depressant		
Nicotine	Stimulates brain activity, but most smokers say cigarettes relax them	Stimulates activity at some (not all) acetylcholine synapses; increases heart rate
Distortion of Experience		
Marijuana (THC)	Intensifies sensory experiences; distorts perception of time; can relieve glaucoma, nausea; sometimes impairs learning, memory	Attaches to receptors found in hippocampus and other areas; normal role of these receptors is unknown
Hallucinogens		
LSD; mescaline	Cause hallucinations, sensory distortions, and occasionally panic	Alter pattern of release and binding of serotonin

could alone; sometimes they suppress it to a dangerously low level.

Tranquilizers

Tranquilizers help people to relax and fall asleep; they have miscellaneous other effects including suppression of epileptic seizures. Tranquilizers are widely prescribed for medical reasons; sometimes people continue using them long after it is medically advisable.

Barbiturates were once the most commonly used tranquilizing drug. When it turned out that they were highly habit-forming, however, and that an overdose could easily be fatal, investigators looked for a substitute. Today the most commonly used tranquilizers are a class of chemicals called *benzodiazepines,* which include the drugs Valium and Xanax (Simonsen, 1990). Thousands of tons of benzodiazepines are taken in pill form every year in the United States. Benzodiazepines relieve anxiety and induce sleep; like alcohol, they act by facilitating transmission at GABA synapses (Macdonald, Weddle, & Gross, 1986). Benzodiazepines can be habit-forming, although they are less so than barbiturates.

Opiates

Opiates are either natural drugs derived from the opium poppy or synthetic drugs with a chemical structure similar to that of the natural opiates. Shortly after taking an opiate drug, in most cases the user feels happy, is nearly insensitive to pain, and tends to ignore real-world stimuli; he or she feels warmth, contentment, a loss of anxiety, and (on the unpleasant side)

FIGURE 5.21

It's not what you drink—beer, wine, or whiskey—but how much and how quickly you consume alcohol that determines your state of intoxication. What you eat before or while drinking and your physical size also influence alcohol's impact on you. This chart shows rising levels of alcohol in the bloodstream of a 150-lb person with an empty stomach. (Based on Time, *1974.)*

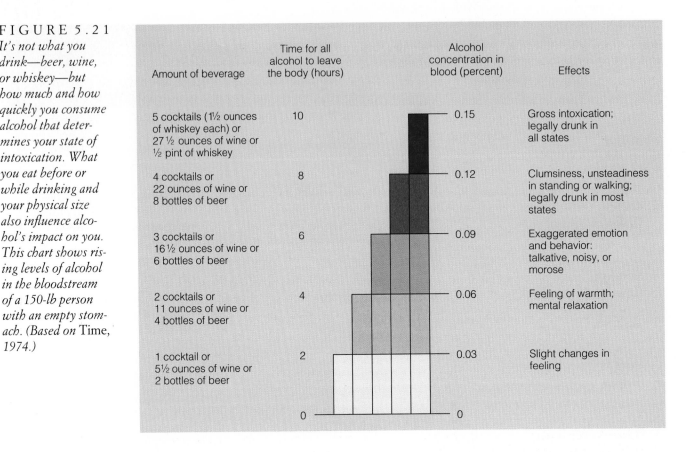

Amount of beverage	Time for all alcohol to leave the body (hours)	Alcohol concentration in blood (percent)	Effects
5 cocktails (1½ ounces of whiskey each) or 27½ ounces of wine or ½ pint of whiskey	10	0.15	Gross intoxication; legally drunk in all states
4 cocktails or 22 ounces of wine or 8 bottles of beer	8	0.12	Clumsiness, unsteadiness in standing or walking; legally drunk in most states
3 cocktails or 16½ ounces of wine or 6 bottles of beer	6	0.09	Exaggerated emotion and behavior: talkative, noisy, or morose
2 cocktails or 11 ounces of wine or 4 bottles of beer	4	0.06	Feeling of warmth; mental relaxation
1 cocktail or 5½ ounces of wine or 2 bottles of beer	2	0.03	Slight changes in feeling
	0	0	

nausea. Once these drugs have left the brain, the affected synapses become understimulated and the user enters withdrawal. Elation gives way to anxiety, heightened sensitivity to pain, and acute sensitivity to external stimuli. Morphine (named after Morpheus, the Greek god of dreams) has medical use as a painkiller.

The most common opiate drugs—morphine and heroin—bind to a specific set of synaptic receptors in the brain (Pert & Snyder, 1973). This discovery prompted neuroscientists to look for naturally occurring brain chemicals that bind to those receptors, as it hardly seemed likely that evolution would equip us with receptors just to respond to extracts of the opium poppy. Researchers found that the brain produces several chemicals, called **endorphins,** that bind to the opiate receptors (Hughes et al., 1975), as noted in Chapter 3. Endorphins are important in the brain's self-suppression of prolonged or repetitive pain (Barbaro, 1988).

Marijuana

Marijuana produces a variety of distortions of experience; in the doses that people ordinarily use, the effects are not extreme. People smoke marijuana because it produces a "high" and intensifies their sensory experiences (Weil, Zinberg, & Nelson, 1968). It also makes them a bit drowsy and gives them the illusion that time is passing very slowly. Although people are aware of its effects for no more than 2 or 3 hours after using it, more subtle effects may persist much longer. Marijuana dissolves in the fats of the body, and traces of it persist for weeks after it has been used (Dackis, Pottash, Annitto, & Gold, 1982).

A number of early reports claimed that marijuana use leads to crime, mental illness, sexual debauchery, and a loss of motivation and ambition. It now appears, however, that those reports confused correlation with causation (see page 50.) Although marijuana use tends to be prevalent among people with a history of such behaviors, it does not cause them. Marijuana may, however, aggravate those behaviors in people who are already predisposed toward them (Hollister, 1986). By interfering with the ability to concentrate, it may also impair learning and memory (Miller & Branconnier, 1983), especially among people using marijuana for the first time. Some marijuana users experience a general loss of motivation.

Marijuana does have certain medical uses.

By reducing pressure in the eyes, it helps relieve glaucoma, a common cause of blindness. It reduces nausea and acts as a weak painkiller. Marijuana suppresses tremors and other involuntary movements that are a problem for people with certain kinds of brain damage.

The active ingredient in marijuana (*Cannabis*) is THC, or tetrahydrocannabinol. For many years, researchers were unable to find any brain receptor to which THC attached and believed it operated by altering neuronal membranes in general. Apparently they failed to find THC receptors because they used chemical procedures that were appropriate for finding other kinds of brain receptors, but not THC receptors. THC does indeed attach to some specialized receptors, which are found mostly in the hippocampus (an important brain area for memory) and several areas that are important for the control of movement (Herkenham et al., 1990). Additional THC receptors are found scattered in much of the forebrain. In fact, THC receptors appear to be among the most numerous receptor types in the brain (Herkenham, Lynn, deCosta, & Richfield, 1991).

Presumably, evolution did not give us an abundance of THC receptors in order to experience marijuana, any more than it gave us opiate receptors to experience opiates. The brain must have some naturally occurring chemicals that stimulate the THC receptors. At this point we do not know what those chemicals are or what they contribute to normal behavior.

Although marijuana use is certainly not good for one's health, it does not produce sudden or immediate harmful consequences. Many people die of an overdose of opiates; hardly anyone dies of an overdose of marijuana. We now understand why: Opiate receptors are densely located in the medulla and other brain areas that control heart rate and breathing, whereas those same areas have very few THC receptors (Herkenham et al., 1990). So even rather large dosages of marijuana are unlikely to stop the heart or to interfere with breathing. According to studies with rats and monkeys, exposure to marijuana smoke can shrink the dendrites of neurons in the hippocampus. (The animals were exposed to piped-in marijuana smoke; don't picture them sitting around with tiny cigarettes in their mouths.) However, these effects are apparently temporary; the brains eventually returned to normal, even if the animals had been exposed to constant marijuana smoke over a period of months (Westlake et al., 1991).

■ CONCEPT CHECK

5. *Some employers conduct urine tests at random times to determine whether their employees have been taking drugs on the job. What special problem is likely to arise when they test for marijuana? (Check your answer on page 213.)*

Stimulants

Stimulants are drugs that boost energy, heighten alertness, increase activity, and produce a pleasant feeling. Coffee, tea, and caffeinated soft drinks are mild stimulants. People drink these beverages partly for their taste and partly for their stimulant effects (Cines & Rozin, 1982). People who drink much coffee become dependent on caffeine; if someone replaces their regular coffee with decaffeinated coffee, they experience headaches and drowsiness (Hughes et al., 1991). Caffeine exerts its effects by an indirect route that ultimately increases the release of the neurotransmitter glutamate (Silinsky, 1989).

Amphetamine and cocaine are powerful stimulants with wide-ranging effects. Amphetamine increases the release of the neurotransmitter dopamine (page 94), which increases activity levels and pleasure. Amphetamine and cocaine both prevent neurons from reabsorbing the dopamine they have released; they thereby prolong the effects of the dopamine (Ritz, Lamb, Goldberg, & Kuhar, 1987). Cocaine also prolongs the activity of the neurotransmitter norepinephrine and has additional anesthetic (sensation-blocking) effects, similar to the effects of Novocaine and Lidocaine.

We regard cocaine as a stimulant, because it increases heart rate, makes people feel excited, and interferes with their sleep. However, cocaine actually *decreases* the overall activity within the brain (London et al., 1990). That may seem to contradict the statement that cocaine prolongs activity of a couple of neurotransmitters; however, those transmitters are inhibitory transmitters at many synapses. Thus, by increasing dopamine and norepinephrine activity, cocaine decreases the activity of many brain neurons (Figure 5.22).

Cocaine has long been available in the powdery form of cocaine hydrochloride, a chemical that can be sniffed or injected. When sniffed, it produces mostly enjoyable effects that increase gradually over a few minutes and then decline gradually over about half an hour. It also anes-

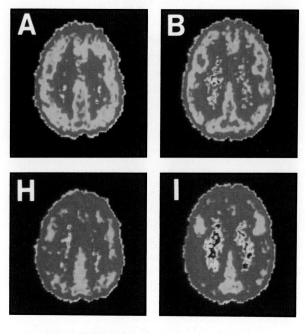

FIGURE 5.22
"Your brain on drugs." Parts A and B show the activity of a normal brain in horizontal section, as measured by PET scans. Parts H and I show activity of the same brain under the influence of cocaine. Red indicates the highest amount of activity, followed by yellow, green, and blue. Note that cocaine has decreased the total amount of activity in the brain.

FIGURE 5.23
Because crack is smoked, this form of cocaine reaches the brain in 8 seconds, much faster—and in a more potent form—than most drugs, which is why it is so popular and addictive.

thetizes the nostrils and in some cases damages the lungs.

Before 1985, the only way to get a more intense effect from cocaine hydrochloride was to treat it with ether to convert it into *free-base cocaine*—cocaine with the hydrochloride removed. Smoking free-base cocaine enables a high percentage of it to enter the body rapidly and thereby to enter the brain rapidly. The faster a drug enters the brain, the more intense the resulting experience.

The drug known as *crack* first became available in 1985. Crack is cocaine that has already been converted to the free-base form, ready to be smoked (Brower & Anglin, 1987; Kozel & Adams, 1986). (See Figure 5.23.) Crack produces a rush of potent effects within a few seconds, much faster than sniffed cocaine hydrochloride. Crack's effects also decline much faster, provoking a withdrawal state marked by headache, irritability, and depression. People sometimes experience a strong craving for additional crack as a way of escaping the unpleasant withdrawal state. Repeated use of any drug, especially one with rapid and powerful effects, is

dangerous to the brain. Compared to other cocaine users, crack users experience more hallucinations, disordered thinking, and suicidal thoughts and are more likely to attack other people violently (Honer, Gewirtz, & Turey, 1987). Crack can also easily provoke heart attacks, other medical complications, and psychological disorders; a large dose can easily be fatal.

Crack is both highly addictive and reasonably inexpensive; it has become one of the most widely used illegal drugs. Because selling crack is so lucrative, rival gangs in large cities compete with one another to control the sales. The resulting violence has created a problem for society that goes beyond the direct harm done by the drug itself.

Cigarettes

Tobacco cigarettes deliver nicotine; curiously, although nicotine stimulates the central nervous system, most smokers say that they find cigarettes relaxing (Gilbert, 1979). People also smoke cigarettes and cigars because smoking gives them something to do with their hands, a kind of fidgeting.

Smoking cigarettes is highly addictive, much more so than cigars. The main reason is that smokers inhale cigarette smoke more deeply, enabling the nicotine in the smoke to reach the brain more quickly (Bennett, 1980). Nontobacco cigarettes, which contain no nicotine, have never proved popular. Smokers who switch to low-nicotine cigarettes tend to increase the number of cigarettes they smoke, as if they were trying to maintain a constant level of nicotine in their body (Kumar, Cooke, Lader, & Russell, 1977; McMorrow & Foxx, 1983). Moreover, many smokers who try to quit smoking find it easier to do so if they chew gum that contains nicotine (Fagerström, 1981; Jarvis, 1983; Lichtenstein, 1982).

Hallucinogens

Drugs that induce sensory distortions are **hallucinogens** (Jacobs, 1987). Most of them are derived from certain mushrooms or other plants (Figure 5.24); some are manufactured in chemistry laboratories. The hallucinogenic drugs LSD, PCP, and mescaline intensify sensations and sometimes produce a dreamlike state or an intense mystical experience. They occasionally prompt a panic response or violent behavior, and a few users report flashback experiences long after they have used the drugs.

The physiological action of the hallucinogens varies from drug to drug. LSD attaches mainly to one kind of brain receptor sensitive to the neurotransmitter serotonin (Jacobs, 1987). It stimulates those receptors at irregular times and prevents the brain's neurotransmitter from stimulating the receptors at the normal times. Consequently it produces varied distortions of experience. To understand why it produces the particular distortions it does, we shall need to know more about those serotonin receptors than we do now.

Other Drugs

Every year new drugs make their appearance; some have a major potential to become addictive or to impair people's health. In the middle 1980s a new synthetic drug made its appearance on college campuses and elsewhere: MDMA, popularly known as "ecstasy," which produces a mixture of stimulant and hallucinogenic effects. Unlike users of other drugs, ecstasy users gradually lose interest in the drug. One possible explanation for the loss of interest is that the drug at first stimulates serotonin synapses (hence its consciousness-altering effects), but in the process destroys them so that on later occasions the drug produces little effect (Price, Ricaurte, Krystal, & Heninger, 1989).

"Ice" is a pure form of methamphetamine, closely related to amphetamine. It produces effects similar to those of cocaine and amphetamine, except that methamphetamine's effects start quicker and last longer (Cho, 1990); consequently, its potential for addiction is great.

FIGURE 5.24
Tablas, or yarn paintings, created by members of the Huichol tribe (Mexico), evoke the beautiful lights, vivid colors, and "peculiar creatures" experienced after the people eat the hallucinogenic peyote cactus in highly ritualized ceremonies.

WITHDRAWAL AND TOLERANCE

The intended effects of any drug are temporary. Initially they produce some effect, such as excitement, relaxation, or a distortion of experience. As the drug leaves the brain and the effects wear off, the person experiences **withdrawal effects,** which may be more or less the opposite of the initial effects. After someone has taken a given drug repeatedly, its effects grow weaker and weaker, unless the person increases the dosage. This decrease in effect is called **tolerance**. Drug users often seek the drug as a way of fighting the withdrawal effects; they increase their dosage to compensate for the tolerance. That is, these two effects tend to promote increased use of a drug.

Drug Withdrawal

When habitual users suddenly stop using alcohol or opiate drugs (such as morphine or heroin), they gradually enter a state of withdrawal (Gawin & Kleber, 1986). With alcohol, the typical withdrawal symptoms are sweating, nausea, sleeplessness, and, in severe cases, hallucinations and seizures (Mello & Mendelson, 1978). With opiate drugs, the typical withdrawal symptoms are anxiety, restlessness, loss of appetite, vomiting, diarrhea, sweating, and gagging (Mansky, 1978). Users who quit tranquilizers may experience sleeplessness and nervousness. Generally, people who quit marijuana report only mild withdrawal symptoms or none at all.

Some researchers explain drug withdrawal as a special case of the opponent-process theory of emotions, in which removing the stimulus for one emotion causes a rebound to the opposite emotion (Solomon, 1980; Solomon & Corbit, 1974). A drug provides the stimulus for a mostly pleasant emotional state. As the drug wears off, however, the user rebounds to the opposite emotional state. Opiates, for example, overstimulate certain brain receptors and cause them to become fatigued (Herz & Schulz, 1978). The overstimulation produces one effect; the fatigue afterward produces the opposite effect.

After many repetitions, the initial high grows weaker and the withdrawal grows more intense and more unpleasant. To escape the withdrawal symptoms, users are compelled to take the drug again.

Drug Tolerance

People who take a drug repeatedly develop a tolerance to its effects. To achieve the desired high, drug users have to increase the dose. Some longtime users inject three or four times more heroin or morphine into their veins than it would take to kill a nonuser.

What brings about drug tolerance? It may result in part from automatic chemical changes that occur in cells throughout the body to counteract the drug's effects (Baker & Tiffany, 1985). It may also result in part from psychological causes. For example, alcohol impairs the coordination of rats as well as that of humans. If rats are simply injected with alcohol every day for 24 days and then tested, the results show that their coordination has been seriously impaired. Apparently such rats develop no tolerance to the alcohol. However, if their coordination is tested after each of the 24 injections, each test session offers the rats an opportunity to practice their coordination, and their performance steadily improves (Wenger, Tiffany, Bombardier, Nicholls, & Woods, 1981). In

other words, by practicing coordination while under the influence of the alcohol, the rats develop a tolerance to alcohol. Similarly, though amphetamine suppresses appetite, rats or people that eat a little food after each amphetamine dose gradually develop tolerance to the drug's effects (Streather & Hinson, 1985; Wolgin & Salisbury, 1985). For this reason, "diet pills" based on amphetamine or related compounds become less and less effective over time.

▪ CONCEPT CHECK

6. *People who use amphetamines or related drugs as appetite suppressants generally find that the effect wears off after a week or two. How could they prolong the effect? (Check your answer on page 213.)*

SUMMARY

▪ *Alcohol.* Alcohol, the most widely abused drug in our society, relaxes people and relieves their inhibitions. It can also impair judgment and reasoning. (page 206)

▪ *Tranquilizers.* Benzodiazepine tranquilizers are widely used to relieve anxiety; they are also sometimes used to relax muscles or to promote sleep. (page 207)

▪ *Opiates.* Opiate drugs bind to endorphin receptors in the nervous system. The immediate effect of opiates is pleasure and relief from pain. (page 207)

▪ *Marijuana.* Marijuana's active compound, THC, acts on abundant receptors, found mostly in the hippocampus and certain brain areas important for control of movement. Because it dissolves in the body's fats, it can exert subtle effects over a period of days or weeks after use. Because the medulla has few THC receptors, a large dose of marijuana is seldom fatal. (page 208)

▪ *Stimulants.* Stimulant drugs such as amphetamine and cocaine increase activity levels and pleasure. Compared to other forms of cocaine, crack produces more rapid effects on behavior, greater risk of addiction, and greater risk of damage to the heart and other organs. (page 209)

▪ *Nicotine.* Nicotine, found in cigarettes, is a stimulant to the brain, although smokers say they smoke to relax. (page 210)

▪ *Hallucinogens.* Hallucinogens induce sensory distortions. Some hallucinogens are believed to lead to brain damage. (page 211)

- *Withdrawal.* After using a drug, the user enters a rebound state known as withdrawal. Drug users often crave drugs as a way of decreasing the withdrawal symptoms. (page 211)

- *Tolerance.* People who use certain drugs repeatedly become less and less sensitive to them. (page 212)

SUGGESTIONS FOR FURTHER READING

Hamilton, L. W., & Timmons, C. R. (1990). *Principles of behavioral pharmacology.* Englewood Cliffs, NJ: Prentice-Hall. Clear, interesting descriptions of the effects of both medical drugs and abused drugs.

Hoffman, F. G. (1983). *A handbook on drug and alcohol abuse* (2nd ed.). New York: Oxford University Press. A description of the effects of commonly abused drugs.

TERMS

alcohol a class of molecules that includes ethanol, methanol, propyl alcohol (rubbing alcohol), and others (page 206)

tranquilizers drugs that help people to relax (page 207)

opiates drugs derived from the opium poppy or drugs that produce effects similar to those of opium derivatives (page 207)

endorphins chemicals produced by the brain that have effects resembling those of opiates (page 208)

hallucinogens drugs that induce sensory distortions (page 211)

withdrawal effects experiences that occur as a result of the removal of a drug from the brain (page 211)

tolerance the weakened effect of a drug after repeated use (page 211)

ANSWERS TO CONCEPT CHECKS

5. Because marijuana dissolves in the fats and leaves the body very slowly, people may still test positive for the drug weeks after the last time they used it. (page 209)

6. Instead of taking a pill just before a meal, they should take it between meals, when they are not planning to eat right away or when they plan to skip a meal altogether. If they eat right after taking a pill, they soon develop a tolerance to its appetite-suppressing effects. However, even if they follow the advice to take the pills when planning to eat nothing, people are not likely to lose weight in the long run. After their appetite is suppressed for a while, they are likely to experience increased appetite later. (page 212)

6 DEVELOPMENT

Suppose you buy a robot. When you get it home, you discover that it does nothing useful. It cannot even maintain its balance. It makes irritating, high-pitched noises, moves its limbs about haphazardly, and leaks. The store you bought it from refuses to take it back. And you discover that, for some reason, it is illegal to turn it off. So you are stuck with this useless machine.

A few years later, your robot can walk and talk, read and write, draw pictures, and do arithmetic. It will follow your directions (most of the time), and sometimes it will even find useful things to do without being told. It beats you consistently at Chinese checkers and destroys you at memory games.

How did all this happen? After all, you knew nothing about how to program a robot. Did your robot have some sort of built-in programming that simply took a long time to phase in? Or was it programmed to learn all these skills by imitating what it saw?

Children are a great deal like that robot. Nearly every parent wonders, "How did my children get to be the way they are?" The goal of developmental psychology is to understand everything that influences human behavior "from womb to tomb."

As we grow older, we change in many ways—we gain in some ways and lose in others. Developmental psychologists seek to understand the changes in our behavior and the reasons behind them.

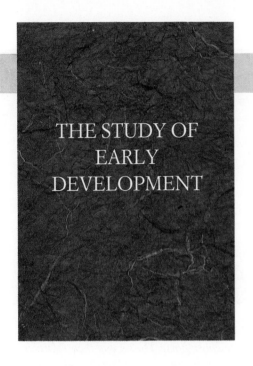

THE STUDY OF
EARLY
DEVELOPMENT

*What are the capacities of the newborn and
the young infant?*

*How can psychologists determine those
capacities?*

The art works of young children can be amazingly inventive and can reveal a great deal of what the children are thinking. One toddler, 1 1/2 years old, showed off a drawing that consisted only of dots on a sheet of paper. Puzzled adults did not understand the drawing. It was a rabbit, the child explained, while making more dots: "Look: Hop, hop, hop . . ." (Winner, 1986).

When my daughter, Robin, was 6 years old, she drew a picture of a boy and a girl drawing pictures (Figure 6.1). The overall picture has a number of miscellaneous features that may not be clear, such as the fact that both children are wearing Halloween costumes. For the little girl's drawing, Robin pasted on some wildlife photos. This array, she maintained, was what the little girl had drawn. Now look at the little boy's drawing: It's just a scribble. I asked why the little girl's drawing was so much better than

FIGURE 6.1
*A drawing of two children drawing pictures,
courtesy of 6-year-old Robin Kalat.*

217

the little boy's. Robin replied, "Don't make fun of him, Daddy. He's doing the best he can."

Sometimes, as in this case, a child's drawing is not just art; it's almost a philosophy of life. As children grow older, their art changes. Today, 10-year-old Robin Kalat produces drawings that are much neater, technically much more skilled than anything she could have done a few years ago. But most of them don't have the same charm and expressiveness as her earlier drawings.

The point is this: As we grow older, we develop; we gain many new abilities and skills. But we lose something too.

Studying the abilities of children, especially very young children and infants, is extremely challenging. The very young are often capable of far more than we realize, simply because they misunderstand our questions or because we misunderstand their answers. Sometimes the same is true for the very old. Developmental psychologists have made much of their progress by devising increasingly careful and sensitive ways to measure what people can and cannot do.

THE FETUS AND THE NEWBORN

Early one morning while a human mother is giving birth, a horse is also giving birth. By mid-afternoon, the newborn horse is following its mother around the field; within a few days it is starting to run (Figure 6.2). By age 2 or 3 years it approaches its potential as a race horse or a work horse.

In contrast, that human baby needs several months of development before it can crawl, much less run. When we look at a helpless human baby, we are tempted to assume that it cannot do anything, other than the obvious—sleeping and crying. Actually, the newborn can do quite a lot; it can see, hear, learn . . . but I am getting ahead of the story. The point is that a substantial degree of development takes place before birth.

Prenatal Development

During **prenatal** (before-birth) development, everyone starts life as a fertilized egg cell. That fertilized egg quickly becomes an **embryo,** dividing into many cells and starting to grow. A human embryo does not look much different from a chicken embryo or any other vertebrate embryo (Figure 6.3).

FIGURE 6.2
A newborn horse. Horses and their relatives are born much more mature than human infants. Many other species, however, are born far less mature than humans.

From about 2 months after conception until birth, we call the developing human a **fetus.** The fetus looks more human than the embryo did, but it still has a long way to go. All of its organs, including the brain, must mature a great deal before birth. Different structures and substructures mature at different times; consequently, traumas and poisons produce different kinds of impairments at different ages.

The growing body receives its nutrition from the mother. If she eats little, the baby receives little nourishment. If she takes drugs, the baby gets them too. Undernourished mothers generally give birth to small babies (Figure 6.4), and investigators have long known that newborns weighing less than about 1,750–2,000 grams (4 pounds) have a high risk of dying in infancy (Kopp, 1990). Such babies who survive have a considerable risk of eventual mental retardation, low academic achievement, and various behavior problems (Morgan & Winick, 1989). Those facts are beyond dispute, but consider how difficult it is to interpret what they mean.

The apparently obvious interpretation is that a low birth weight leads to impaired brain development, and thus to later academic and behavior problems. But the apparently obvious interpretation may not be correct. Most low-birth-weight babies are born to unmarried

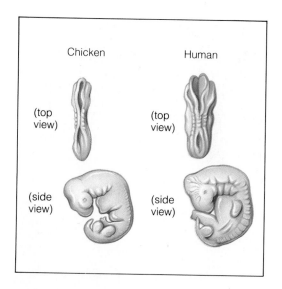

FIGURE 6.3

During the earliest stages, a human embryo looks much the same as the embryo of any other vertebrate species. The differences emerge later.

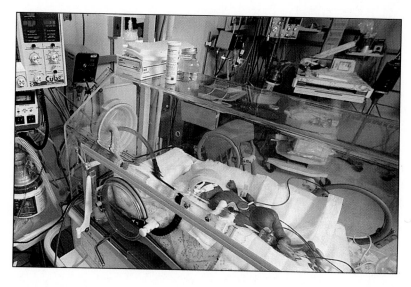

FIGURE 6.4

Low-birth-weight babies are prone to a number of physical and behavioral difficulties later in life; however, we cannot be sure that low birth weight causes these problems. Many of these babies are born to mothers who fail to provide good prenatal and postnatal nutrition and care.

teenage mothers or to other mothers who are poor, uneducated, living under difficult circumstances, and unlikely to get good medical care (McCormick, 1985). These mothers did not get adequate nutrition or medical care before giving birth, and they may not provide their babies a very good environment afterward. In short, these mothers' babies probably would have troubles growing up, regardless of birth weight (Brooks-Gunn & Furstenberg, 1986).

How, then, could we determine the effect of low birth weight on later development? Answering this question might seem impossible, because birth weight is so hopelessly entangled with the mother's age, health, financial situation, education, and so forth. But one clever research strategy minimizes these problems: Psychologists have examined pairs of twins in which one twin was born much heavier than the other. In such cases we have a low-birth-weight child *and* a "control group" child with a higher birth weight but the same parents, the same diet, the same medical care (or lack of it), and the same environment. Investigators find that if the low-birth-weight infant gets adequate care, it generally develops about as well as the heavier twin (Wilson, 1987). In short, low birth weight *by itself* is not an insurmountable problem for a child's long-term development; it correlates with developmental difficulties largely because

many low-birth-weight babies encounter other disadvantages later in life.

A more severe risk arises if the fetus is exposed to alcohol or other substances. If the mother drinks alcohol during pregnancy, the infant may show signs of the **fetal alcohol syndrome,** a condition marked by decreased alertness and other signs of impaired development after birth (Streissguth, Barr, & Martin, 1983). The more alcohol the mother drinks and the longer she drinks during pregnancy, the greater the risk to the fetus (see Figure 6.5). Cocaine, opiates, and tobacco are also dangerous to the fetus; so are certain prescription drugs the mother may take to help combat depression, schizophrenia, anxiety, and other psychological disorders (Kerns, 1986). Many drugs simply have not been in use long enough for investigators to determine the long-term effects of exposing fetuses to them. To be safe, pregnant women should get a physician's advice before taking even routine, over-the-counter drugs.

Still, it is remarkable that an occasional "high risk" child—small at birth, perhaps exposed to alcohol or other drugs before birth, perhaps from an impoverished or very turbulent family—overcomes all odds and becomes a healthy, productive, even outstanding person (Werner, 1989). What makes some children so "resilient" to such severe stress is unknown.

The Study of Early Development

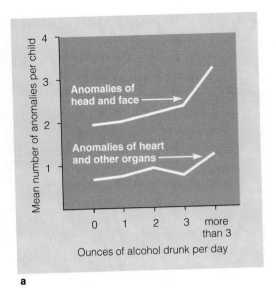

FIGURE 6.5

(a) The more alcohol a woman drinks during pregnancy, the more likely her baby is to have anomalies of the head, face, and organs. (Based on data of Ernhart et al., 1987.) (b) A child with fetal alcohol syndrome. Notice especially the wide separation between the eyes, a common feature of this syndrome.

BEHAVIORAL CAPACITIES OF THE NEWBORN

A human newborn is a little like a computer that is not attached to a monitor: It may be processing a great deal of information, but it cannot tell us about it. The challenge of studying the newborn is to figure out how to attach some sort of "monitor" to find out what is going on in the newborn's head.

Newborns have very little control of their muscles. At first they cannot keep their head from flopping over, and their arms and legs flail about aimlessly. About the only useful movements they can make are mouth movements and eye movements. As the months pass, and as their control spreads from the head muscles downward, they are able to make progressively finer movements, eventually culminating in the ability to move a single finger at a time.

If we want to test the infant's sensory and learning abilities, we have to test them by means of responses the infant can control. For example, if we want to test what an infant can see, we should examine eye movements or head movements; we should not try to train the infant to

reach out and grab something. Researchers insensitive to this problem have frequently underestimated the sensory and learning capacities of infants.

The Vision of Newborns

William James, a pioneer in American psychology, once said that so far as an infant can tell, the world is a "buzzing confusion," full of meaningless sights and sounds. How can we tell what an infant really sees, given that the infant cannot describe anything?

One way is to record the infant's eye movements. Infants direct their eyes toward some objects longer than others, sometimes because they see them more clearly. For example, infants less than 3 months old spend very little time looking at narrow diagonal stripes, and many investigators believe infants simply cannot see any difference between such stripes and a plain gray field (Leehy, Moskowitz-Cook, Brill, & Held, 1975). In many cases, infants direct their eyes toward (or pay attention to) the same kinds of objects that attract the attention of adults. For example, even at the age of 2 days infants spend more time looking at drawings of human faces than at other patterns with similar areas of light and dark (Fantz, 1963). (See Figure 6.6.) They can also imitate facial expressions (Meltzoff & Moore, 1977), another indication of perception (Figure 6.7). (How and why they imitate, we do not know.)

In the retina of the newborn, the periphery is closer to reaching maturity than the fovea is; consequently, infants cannot see so much detail as older children and adults do (Johnson, 1990). Still, infants look directly at brightly colored or otherwise interesting objects; they don't try to look "out the corner of the eye."

Although infants tend to look mostly at the same kinds of objects that adults look at—colorful objects, faces, rotating objects, and so forth—they do not control their visual attention in the same way that adults do. Infants less than 3 or 4 months old have trouble shifting their attention *away* from an attractive display (Johnson, Posner, & Rothbart, 1991). For example, once they begin looking at a set of moving dots on a computer screen, they seem unable to turn their eyes away from it, even to look at an equally interesting display nearby. Sometimes, 1-month-old infants continue staring at something until they begin literally crying in distress!

As infants become slightly older (about 3 to 6 months old), they can shift their eyes from one object to another, but then they are likely to shift their gaze *back* to the first object. Adults who look at a complicated scene generally look at one object, then another, then another, and may check most of the objects in the display be-

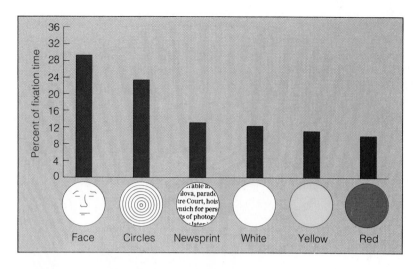

FIGURE 6.6
Infants pay more attention to faces than to other patterns. (Based on Fantz, 1963.) These results suggest that infants are born with certain visual preferences that do not depend on learned associations. The preference for faces facilitates the development of social attachments.

fore returning to the first object; infants seem unable to inhibit their eyes from turning back to an object they have already examined (Clohessy, Posner, Rothbart, & Veccra, 1991). This peculiarity is apparently due to the immaturity of a path in the brain from the cerebral cortex to an area in the midbrain that controls eye movements. In effect, the cortex cannot tell the midbrain that it has seen enough of one object and that it is ready to move on to something else.

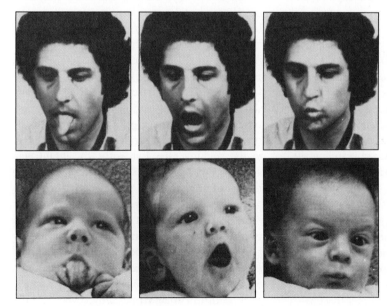

FIGURE 6.7
Infants 2 to 3 weeks old sometimes imitate adults' facial expressions without knowing what they express. (Photos at left from Meltzoff & Moore, 1977.)

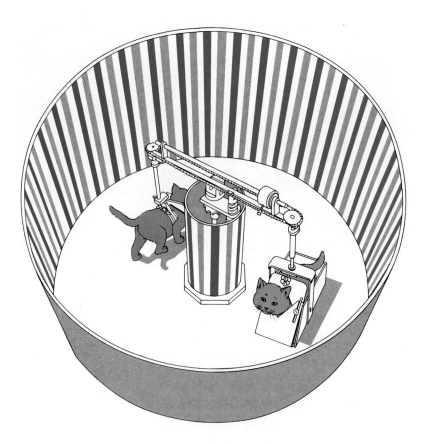

FIGURE 6.8

As the kitten carousel experiment demonstrates, experience influences development. These two kittens see the same thing, but only one can correlate what it sees with its own movements. Only the active kitten develops normal paw-eye coordination. (Modified from Held & Hein, 1963.)

Although visual-motor coordination develops quickly, infants need practice to maintain and improve that coordination. Several studies have been made of kittens, which are ideal for such studies because kittens can move about quite well by the time they first open their eyes. In one experiment, kittens were permitted to walk around in a dark room for 21 hours a day (Held & Hein, 1963). For the other 3 hours, half the kittens (the "active" group) were permitted to walk around in a well-lit cylindrical room, as Figure 6.8 shows. The other kittens (the "passive" group) were confined to boxes that were propelled around the room by the active kittens.

The active kittens gradually developed good paw-eye coordination, but the passive kittens lagged far behind. In fact, the passive kittens' coordination actually grew worse instead of better as the experiment continued. Evidently, kittens need to see and move at the same time in order to maintain and improve their visually guided behavior. The same is almost certainly true for humans as well.

The Hearing of Newborns

At first it might seem difficult to measure newborns' responses to sounds; after all, we cannot observe anything similar to eye movements. However, we can record the effects of sounds on the infant's sucking. Infants suck more vigorously when they are aroused, and certain sounds arouse them more than others do.

In one study, the experimenters played a brief sound and noted how it affected the infant's sucking rate (Figure 6.9). On the first few occasions, the sound increased the sucking rate. After the sound had been played repeatedly, it produced less and less effect. We say that the infant **habituated** to the sound (that is, the infant showed less response after the sound had been repeated). But when the experimenters substituted a new sound, it produced a sharp increase in the sucking rate. Evidently, the infant was aroused because he or she heard a new, unfamiliar sound.

Psychologists use this technique to determine whether an infant hears a difference between two sounds (Jusczyk, 1985). For example, an infant who has habituated to the sound *ba* will increase the sucking rate in response to the sound *pa* (Eimas, Siqueland, Jusczyk, & Vigorito, 1971). Apparently, even month-old infants can tell the difference between *ba* and *pa*.

The Development of Visual-Motor Coordination

By age 5 months or so, infants have had extensive visual experience but almost no experience at crawling or reaching for objects. Suddenly, as they start to gain control of their arm and leg movements, they have to reach out to pick up toys, crawl around objects, avoid crawling off ledges, and in other ways coordinate what they see with what they do.

All that happens rather quickly; evidently, infants can judge visual distances reasonably well without extensive practice. In one study, researchers found that 5-month-old infants consistently reach for the closer of two objects (Yonas & Granrud, 1985). As they grow older, they start using more and more depth cues—such as binocular disparity, convergence, and motion parallax—to guide their movements.

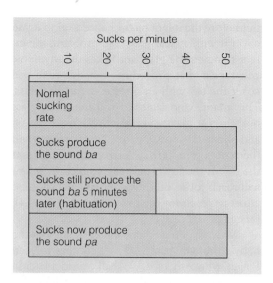

Sucks per minute

| | | | | |
|10|20|30|40|50|

Normal sucking rate

Sucks produce the sound ba

Sucks still produce the sound ba 5 minutes later (habituation)

Sucks now produce the sound pa

FIGURE 6.9

After 5 minutes of hearing the same sound, the infant's sucking habituates. When a new sound, pa, follows, the sucking rate increases, indication that infants hear a difference between the sounds ba and pa. (Based on results of Eimas, Siqueland, Juscyk, & Vigorito, 1971.)

FIGURE 6.10

Inspired by research showing that a fetus learns to recognize its mother's voice, some women have made special efforts to talk to their fetuses—and some enterprising capitalists have sold them "pregaphones," manuals, tapes, and lessons. (Don't count on the fetus to be the one getting the greatest benefit from all of this.)

The Learning and Memory of Newborns

Infants certainly cannot describe their memories to us. But if they respond differently to some stimulus because of previous experience with it, we can infer that they remember it.

Several studies have begun with the fact that infants learn to suck harder on a nipple if their sucking turns on some sound. Investigators then tried to determine whether the infants will work harder to turn on certain sounds than they will for others. In one study, 26 babies less than 3 days old could turn on a tape recording of their mother's voice by sucking on a nipple at certain times and at certain rates. By sucking at different times or at different rates, they could turn on a tape recording of some other woman's voice. When their manner of sucking produced their own mother's voice, their rate of sucking increased significantly (DeCasper & Fifer, 1980); it increased less when it produced a different voice. Apparently, even very young infants recognized their own mother's voice and preferred it to an unfamiliar voice. Because they showed this preference so early—in some cases, on the day of birth—developmental psychologists believe the infants are displaying a memory for what they heard *before birth* (Figure 6.10).

▪ CONCEPT CHECK

1. Suppose a newborn sucks to turn on a tape recording of its father's voice. Eventually the baby habituates and the sucking rate decreases. Now the experimenters substitute the recording of a different man's voice for the father's. What would you conclude if the sucking rate increased? What would you conclude if it remained the same? What would you conclude if it decreased? (Check your answers on page 226.)

Investigators have also demonstrated infant learning and memory by studying head movements—another of the few types of movements an infant can control. For example, in certain studies an experimenter tickled an infant's cheek while sounding either a tone or a buzzer. A movement of the infant's head after one sound (tone for half the infants, buzzer for the other half) brought a reward of sugar water; a movement after the other sound brought no reward. Newborns learned to turn their head more often in response to whichever sound was paired with reward (Clifton, Siqueland, & Lipsitt, 1972; Siqueland & Lipsitt, 1966).

Using somewhat older infants, Carolyn Rovee-Collier (1984) demonstrated an ability to

FIGURE 6.11
By the age of 8 weeks, infants can rapidly learn to kick one of their legs to activate a mobile attached to their ankle with a ribbon. After just a little practice, they can keep the mobile going for a full 45-minute session. In addition, these infants remember how to activate the mobile from one session to the next. (From Rovee-Collier, 1984.)

learn a response and remember it for days afterward. She attached a ribbon to one ankle so that an infant could activate a mobile by kicking with one leg (Figure 6.11). Two-month-old infants quickly learned this response and generally kept the mobile going nonstop for a full 45-minute session. (I know I said infants cannot control their leg muscles, but they don't need much control to keep the mobile going.) Once they have learned, they quickly remember what to do when the ribbon is reattached several days later—to the infants' evident delight.

THE DIFFICULTIES OF INFERRING THE INFANT'S THOUGHTS AND KNOWLEDGE

When we watch the behavior of an infant, we are tempted to speculate on what the infant is thinking. Sometimes we can make a reasonable inference, but we should always use great caution.

Consider an example: You place a toy in front of a 6-month-old, who reaches out and grabs it. Later you place a toy in the same place,

but before the infant has a chance to grab it you cover it with a clear glass. No problem; the infant removes the glass and takes the toy. Now you repeat that procedure, but this time you cover the toy with an opaque (nonclear) glass. The infant, who watched you place the glass over the toy, makes no effort to remove the glass and obtain the toy. Or you put the toy down and then put a thin barrier between the infant and the toy. If the toy is partially visible, the infant will reach for it; otherwise, he or she makes no effort to reach for the toy (Piaget, 1937/1954). (See Figure 6.12.)

Why not? And what can we infer about the baby's thought processes? According to Jean Piaget, whose theories we shall consider later in this chapter, the baby's failure to reach out for the toy means that the baby *does not know* the toy is there. "How could that be?" you might ask. "If the baby watched me hide the toy, of course the baby knows where the toy is." Not necessarily; perhaps babies have not yet gained the concept of **object permanence,** the idea that objects continue to exist even when we do not see or hear them.

Still, instead of unquestioningly accepting Piaget's interpretation, we should test babies under other conditions, to find out whether they will ever reach for something they do not see. Here are two other observations to consider before drawing a conclusion:

First observation: If we show an infant a toy and then turn off the lights before the infant can grab it, the infant will still reach out to grab it in the dark (Bower & Wishart, 1972).

Possible interpretation: Evidently, infants can reach out for something they do not see, provided that they see nothing else. In other words, it's wrong to assume that the infant believes the unseen toy has ceased to exist. Maybe the infant concentrates so completely on the seen objects that he or she simply ignores the unseen objects.

Second observation: From about 9 to 11 months, an infant who watches you hide a toy will reach out to retrieve it. But if you hide the toy several times on the right side and then hide it on the left side, the infant will continue to reach out to the right side.

Interpretation: One possibility is that the infant even at this age does not understand that a hidden object remains in place. Another possibility is that infants quickly for-

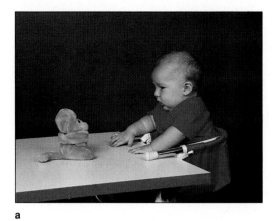 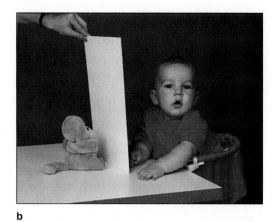

a   b

FIGURE 6.12

During the sensorimotor period, a child will reach for a visible toy (a) but not one that is hidden behind a barrier (b)—even if he or she sees someone hide the toy. According to Piaget, this observation indicates the child lacks the concept of object permanence.

get where the object was hidden. Still another possibility is that the infant simply gets into a motor habit of reaching in one direction, regardless of what he or she sees (or thinks).

Which interpretation is correct? What is the *real* reason why 6-month-old infants will not reach out to grab a toy they just saw you hide? We don't really know, and I apologize if our uncertainty frustrates you. (If it does, you might want to choose a career outside psychology. Psychologists have to get used to uncertainty.)

The main point is that we should not jump to conclusions, particularly when we are dealing with infants or anyone else whose thought processes are likely to be very different from our own. When we study an infant, we get very different results depending on exactly how we conduct the study. We may believe we understand the infant's vision, hearing, memory, or thinking, but we should always be prepared to modify our conclusions if someone finds a better way to measure the infant's capacities.

the damaging effects of alcohol and other drugs. Babies who are very small at birth have a high risk of later problems, but mostly because many such babies do not get good care or stimulation later in life. (page 218)

- *Inferring infant capacities.* It is easy to underestimate the capacities of newborn human infants because they have so little control over their muscles. With careful testing procedures, we can demonstrate that newborns can see, hear, and remember more than we might have supposed. Unlike adults, however, they have great trouble shifting their visual attention from one stimulus to another. (page 220)

- *Inferring infant thought processes.* Infants behave differently from older children in many ways. For example, infants fail to reach for a toy after watching someone hide it within their reach. We can try to draw inferences about infants' thinking, but we have to be cautious about those inferences. An infant might fail to reach for a toy because she does not know the toy still exists, because she is distracted by other things she sees, because she has forgotten the hiding place, or because she is following a motor habit inconsistent with reaching in the correct direction. (page 224)

SUMMARY

- *Prenatal development.* Behavioral development begins before birth. During prenatal development, an individual is especially vulnerable to

SUGGESTION FOR FURTHER READING

Horowitz, F. D. (Ed.). (1989). Special issue: Children and their development. *American Psychologist, 44* (2). A special issue devoted to all aspects of the development of behavior.

TERMS

prenatal before birth (page 218)

embryo an organism at a very early stage of development (from conception to about 2 months in humans) (page 218)

fetus an organism more developed than an embryo but not yet born (from about 2 months until birth in humans) (page 218)

fetal alcohol syndrome a condition marked by decreased alertness and other signs of impaired development, caused by exposure to alcohol prior to birth (page 219)

habituate to decrease a person's response to a stimulus when it is presented repeatedly (page 222)

object permanence the concept that an object continues to exist even when one does not see, hear, or otherwise sense it (page 224)

ANSWER TO CONCEPT CHECK

1. If the rate increased, we would conclude that the infant recognizes the difference between the father's voice and the other voice. If it remained the same, we would conclude that the infant did not notice a difference. If it decreased, we would assume that the infant for some reason preferred the sound of the father's voice to that of the other man. (That would be a puzzler, because it is difficult to imagine how a newborn would recognize his or her father's voice.) (page 223)

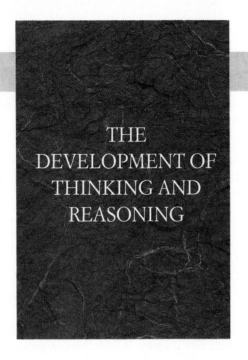

THE DEVELOPMENT OF THINKING AND REASONING

What goes on in the mind of a small child?

How does the thinking of children differ from that of adults?

How do language abilities and moral reasoning develop?

Preschool children ask some profound questions: "Why is the sky blue? What makes ice cubes cold? If it's dangerous to look at the sun, why is it safe to look at a picture of the sun? Where does the sun go at night?" They are relentlessly curious about how things work and why. (Moreover, when you answer their questions, they never interrupt to ask, "Is this going to be on the test?")

These same budding little scientists also believe in Santa Claus, the Easter Bunny, and the Tooth Fairy. The child who asks "Why is there snow?" seems equally content with either an explanation of how moisture condenses in the upper atmosphere or the simple reply, "So children can play in it."

Adults find it difficult to recapture what it was like to be a child. It is clear that children think differently from adults in a number of ways, but it is not easy to specify those ways. Nevertheless, we try.

THE DEVELOPMENT OF THOUGHT AND KNOWLEDGE: PIAGET'S CONTRIBUTIONS

Attending a rousing political rally may have a profound effect on a young adult, much less effect on a preteen, and no effect at all on an infant. However, playing with a pile of blocks will be a more stimulating experience for a young child than for someone older. *The effect of a certain experience on a person's thinking processes and knowledge depends on that person's maturity and previous experiences.* The theorist who made this point most strongly and most influentially was Jean Piaget (peah-ZHAY) (1896–1980). (See Figure 6.13.)

Early in his career, Piaget administered IQ tests to French-speaking children in Switzer-

FIGURE 6.13
Jean Piaget (1896–1980), the most influential theorist on intellectual development in children, demonstrated that an experience's influence on a person's way of thinking depends on that person's age and previous experience.

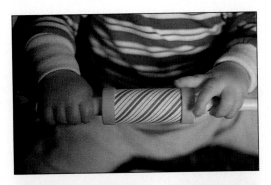

FIGURE 6.14

According to Piaget, assimilation and accommodation occur whenever we deal with an object. Here, the infant assimilates new objects to the grasp schema, applying an established behavior to them. However, the infant also accommodates the grasp schema, adjusting it to fit objects of different shapes and sizes.

land. He grew bored with the IQ tests because he felt he was not learning anything about intelligence, but he was fascinated by the incorrect answers that children consistently gave to certain questions. For example, when asked, "If you mix some water at a temperature of 50 degrees with an equal amount of water at 70 degrees, what temperature will the mixture be?" most 9-year-olds answer, "120 degrees" (Jensen, 1980).

Unless someone was going around mischievously misinforming all the children in Switzerland, the children must be coming to some incorrect conclusions on their own. In other words—and this is one of Piaget's central insights—*children's thought processes are different from those of adults.* Children are not merely inexperienced adults, and they are not just less skillfully going through the same thought processes adults use. The difference between children's thought processes and those of adults is

qualitative as well as *quantitative*—that is, it is a difference in kind and a difference in degree. Piaget supported this conclusion with extensive longitudinal studies of children, especially his own.

How Thought Processes and Knowledge Grow: Some Piagetian Terminology

According to Piaget, a child's intellectual development is not merely an accumulation of experience or a maturational unfolding. Rather, the child constructs new mental processes as he or she interacts with the environment.

In Piaget's terminology, behavior is based on schemata (plural of *schema*). A **schema** is an organized way of interacting with objects in the world. For instance, infants have a grasping schema and a sucking schema. Older infants gradually add new schemata to their repertoire and adapt their old ones. This adaptation takes place through the processes of assimilation and accommodation.

In **assimilation** a person applies an old schema to new objects—for example, an infant may suck an unfamiliar object or use the grasp response in trying to manipulate it. In **accommodation** a person modifies an old schema to fit a new object—for example, an infant may suck a breast, a bottle, and a pacifier in different ways or may modify the grasp response to accommodate the size or shape of a new toy (Figure 6.14).

Infants shift back and forth from assimilation to accommodation. For example, an infant who tries to suck on a rubber ball (assimilating it to her sucking schema) may find that she cannot fit it into her mouth. First she may try to accommodate her sucking schema to fit the ball; if that fails, she may try to shake the ball. She is assimilating her grasping schema to the new object—expanding her motor repertoire to include it. But at the same time, she is accommodating that schema—changing it—to fit the ball.

Adults do much the same thing. You are given a new mathematical problem to solve. You try several of the methods you have already learned until you hit on the one schema that works. In other words, you assimilate your old schema to the new problem. If, however, the new problem is quite different from any problem you have ever solved before, you modify (accommodate) your schema until you work out a solution. Through processes like these, said Piaget, intellectual growth occurs.

Piaget's Stages of Intellectual Development

Piaget contended that children progress through four major stages of intellectual development:

1. *The sensorimotor stage* (from birth to about 1 1/2 years)
2. *The preoperational stage* (from about 1 1/2 to 7 years)
3. *The concrete-operations stage* (from about 7 to 11 years)
4. *The formal-operations stage* (from about 11 years onward)

The ages given here are approximate. Many people do not reach the stage of formal operations until well beyond age 11, if they reach it at all. Piaget recognized that some children develop at a faster rate than others, but he insisted that all children go through these four stages in the same order. Let us consider the capacities of children at each of these stages.

The Sensorimotor Stage: Infancy

Piaget called the first stage of intellectual development the **sensorimotor stage** because at this early age (birth to 1 1/2 years) behavior consists mostly of simple motor responses to sensory stimuli—for example, the grasp reflex and the sucking reflex. Infants respond to what is present, rather than to what is remembered or imagined. Piaget concluded that infants in the sensorimotor stage are incapable of representational thought—that is, they do not think about objects they cannot see, hear, feel, or otherwise sense. We have already discussed some of the pros and cons of this proposal. We cannot be sure what the infant thinks, but we do observe that infants less than 1 to 1 1/2 years old respond mostly to what they see and hear. By the end of this period they begin to talk. The fact that they can now talk about unseen objects is evidence that they have acquired the concept of object permanence.

During the course of this first stage of development, children also appear to gain some concept of self. The data are as follows: A mother puts a spot of unscented rouge on an infant's nose and then places the infant in front of a mirror. Infants less than 1 1/2 years old either ignore the red spot they see on the baby in the mirror or reach out to touch the red spot on the mirror. At some point after age 1 1/2 years, infants in the same situation touch themselves on

FIGURE 6.15
If someone places a bit of unscented rouge on a child's nose, a child older than about 2 years shows self-recognition by touching his or her own nose. A younger child ignores the red spot or points at the mirror.

the nose, indicating that they recognize themselves in the mirror (Figure 6.15). Different infants show this sign of self-recognition at somewhat different ages; the age at which they start to show self-recognition is also the age at which they begin sometimes to act embarrassed (Lewis, Sullivan, Stanger, & Weiss, 1991). That is, they show a sense of self either in both situations or in neither.

The Preoperational Stage: Early Childhood

By about age 1 1/2, most children are learning to speak; within a few years they have nearly mastered their language. Nevertheless, they do not understand everything the same way adults do. For example, they have difficulty understanding that a mother can be someone else's daughter. A boy with one brother will assert that his brother has no brother. Piaget refers to this period as the **preoperational stage.** The child is said to lack **operations,** which are reversible mental processes. For example, for a boy to understand that his brother has a brother, he must be able to reverse the concept "having a brother."

Distinguishing Appearance from Reality in the Preoperational Stage Children in the early preoperational stage do not distinguish clearly between appearance and reality. A child who sees you put a white ball behind a blue filter will say that the ball is blue. When you ask, "Yes, I know the ball *looks* blue, but what color is it *really*?" the child grows confused. So far as the child is concerned, any ball that *looks* blue *is* blue (Flavell, 1986).

Children in the early part of the preoperational stage also have trouble using one object as a symbol or representation for another. For example, a psychologist shows a child a playhouse room that is a scale model of a full-size room. Then the psychologist hides a tiny toy in the small room and explains that a bigger toy just like it is "in the same place" in the bigger room. (For example, if the little toy was behind the sofa in the little room, the big toy would be behind the sofa in the big room.) Most 2 1/2-year-old children look haphazardly for the big toy in the big room without using the little room as a "map." By age 3, most children who see the little toy hidden in the little room go immediately to the correct location in the big room (DeLoache, 1989).

Egocentric Thinking in the Preoperational Period Piaget concluded that children's thought processes are **egocentric.** In using this term, Piaget did *not* mean that children are selfish; instead, he meant that the child sees the world as centered around himself or herself and cannot take the perspective of another person. If you and a preschool child sit on opposite sides of a pile of blocks and you ask the child to draw what the blocks would look like from your side, the child will draw them as they look from his or her own side. When speaking, children often omit to describe the necessary background information, as if assuming that the listener understands everything the speaker understands. At age 6, my daughter, Robin, told me that the children in her class liked their teacher so much that "she can't put her feet down." I eventually elicited the explanation that the teacher sometimes invited the children to sit around her while she read a story, and they sat so close that she had nowhere to put her feet.

Later researchers have pointed out, however, that children's tendency to be egocentric is not absolute (Gelman & Baillargeon, 1983). If the pile-of-blocks task is greatly simplified, a child may accurately describe the other person's point of view (Figure 6.16). For instance, you show a child a card with one picture on the front and a different picture on the back, and then you sit across from the child and show the card again. Three-year-olds and even some 2-year-olds will describe what *they* see *and* what

FIGURE 6.16
In a test for egocentric thinking, a child is asked how a pile of blocks would look from someone else's viewpoint. Preschool children generally fail to describe someone else's viewpoint for a large pile of blocks, but they succeed with a small, simple pile of only two or three blocks.

you see. When a child is looking at a card with a picture on only one side and you ask, "May I see it?" the child will turn it toward you. Apparently, young children do recognize that perspectives differ.

Moreover, a 4-year-old will describe a scene differently depending on whether he or she is talking to a blindfolded adult, an adult who is not blindfolded, or a 2-year-old. When talking to a younger child, the 4-year-old will speak slowly and use simple language. In other words, a child is more egocentric than an adult, but not completely egocentric, as Piaget claimed.

■ CONCEPT CHECK

2. Which of the following is the clearest example of egocentric thinking?
  a. A writer who uses someone else's words without giving credit
  b. A politician who blames others for everything that goes wrong
  c. A professor who gives the same complicated lecture to a freshman class that she gives to a convention of professionals
  (Check your answer on page 244.)

Lack of the Concept of Conservation in the Preoperational Period According to Piaget, preoperational children lack the concept of **conservation.** Just as they fail to understand

Table 6.1 Typical Tasks Used to Measure Conservation

Conservation of number

Preoperational children say that the two rows have the same number of pennies.

Preoperational children say that the second row has more pennies.

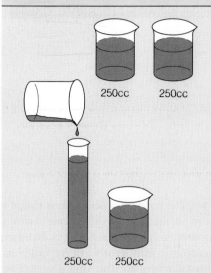

Conservation of volume

Preoperational children say that the two same-size containers have the same amount of water.

Preoperational children say that the taller, thinner container has more water.

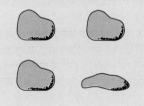

Conservation of mass

Preoperational children say that the two same-size balls of clay have the same amount of clay.

Preoperational children say that a squashed ball of clay contains a different amount of clay from the same-size round ball of clay.

---

that something can still be white even though it looks blue, they fail to understand that objects conserve such properties as number, length, volume, area, and mass after the shape or arrangement of the objects has changed. They cannot perform the mental operations necessary to understand such transformations. (Table 6.1 shows some typical conservation tasks.)

For example, if we set up two glasses of the same size containing the same amount of water and then pour the contents of one glass into a taller, thinner glass, preoperational children will say that the second glass contains more water (Figure 6.17).

I once doubted whether children really believed what they were saying in such a situation.

Perhaps, I thought, the way the questions are phrased somehow tricks them into saying something they do not believe. Then something happened to convince me that preoperational children really believe their answers. One year, when I was discussing Piaget in my introductory psychology class, I invited my son Sam, then 5 1/2 years old, to take part in a class demonstration. I started with two glasses of water, which he agreed contained equal amounts of water. Then I poured the water from one glass into a wider glass, lowering the water level. When I asked Sam which glass contained more water, he confidently pointed to the tall, thin one. After class he complained, "Daddy, why did you ask me such an easy question? Everyone could see that there was more water in that

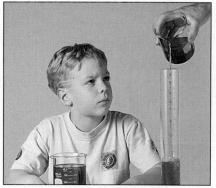

FIGURE 6.17

Looks can be deceptive: The conservation concept shows one way children think less logically than adults do. Preoperational children, up to about age 7 years, don't understand that some property of a substance—such as the volume of water—remains constant despite changes in its appearance. At around age 7, during the transition from preoperational thinking to concrete operations, the conservation tasks seem difficult and confusing.

glass! You should have asked me something harder to show how smart I am!"

The following year I brought Sam to class again for the same demonstration. He was now 6 1/2 years old, about the age at which children make the transition from preoperational thinking to the next stage. I again poured the water from one of the tall glasses into a wider one and asked him which glass contained more water. He looked and paused. His face got red. Finally he whispered, "Daddy, I don't know!" After class he complained, "Why did you ask me such a hard question? I'm never coming back to any of your classes again!" The question that was embarrassingly easy a year ago had become embarrassingly difficult.

The next year, when he was 7 1/2, I tried again (at home). This time he answered confidently, "Both glasses have the same amount of water, of course. Why? Is this some sort of trick question?"

The Concrete-Operations Stage: Later Childhood

At about age 7, children enter the stage of concrete operations and begin to understand the conservation of physical properties. The transition is not sharp, however. The ability to understand the conservation of various properties emerges sequentially, at different ages. For instance, a 6-year-old child may understand that squashing a ball of clay will not change its weight, but may not realize until years later that squashing the ball will not change the volume of

water it displaces when it is dropped into a glass.

The **stage of concrete operations** is Piaget's term for the stage when children can perform mental operations on concrete objects. But they still have trouble with abstract or hypothetical ideas. For example, ask this question: "How could you move a 4-mile-high mountain of whipped cream from one side of the city to the other?" Older children find the question amusing and try to think of an imaginative answer. But children in the concrete-operations stage (or younger) are likely to complain that the question is silly.

Or ask, "If you could have a third eye anywhere on your body, where would you put it?" Children in this stage generally respond immediately that they would put it right between the other two, on their forehead. They seem to regard the question as not very interesting. Older children come up with more imaginative possibilities, such as on the back of their head or at the tip of a finger (so they could peek around corners).

The Formal-Operations Stage: Adolescence and Adulthood

The **stage of formal operations** is Piaget's term referring to the mental processes used in dealing with abstract, hypothetical situations. Those processes demand logical, deductive reasoning and systematic planning.

Piaget set the beginning of the formal-operations stage at about age 11. He attributed some

Table 6.2 Summary of Piaget's Stages of Cognitive Development

Stage and Approximate Age	Achievements and Activities	Limitations
Sensorimotor (birth to $1\frac{1}{2}$ years)	Reacts to sensory stimuli through reflexes and other responses	Little use of language; seems not to understand object permanence; does not distinguish appearance from reality
Preoperational ($1\frac{1}{2}$ to 7 years)	Develops language; can represent objects mentally by words and other symbols; can respond to objects that are remembered but not present at the moment	Lacks operations (reversible mental processes); lacks concept of conservation; focuses on one property at a time (such as length or width), not on both at once; still has some trouble distinguishing appearance from reality
Concrete operations (7 to 11 years)	Understands conservation of mass, number, and volume; can reason logically with regard to concrete objects that can be seen or touched	Has trouble reasoning about abstract concepts and hypothetical situations
Formal operations (11 years onward)	Can reason logically about abstract and hypothetical concepts; develops strategies; plans actions in advance	None beyond the occasional irrationalities of all human thought

fairly sophisticated abilities to children in this stage, although later research indicates that many children take much longer to reach it and some people never do get there.

Suppose we ask three children, ages 6, 10, and 14, to arrange a set of 12 sticks in order from longest to shortest. The 6-year-old (preoperational) child fails to order the sticks correctly. The 10-year-old (concrete operations) eventually gets them in the right order, but only after a great deal of trial and error. The 14-year-old (formal operations) holds the sticks upright with their bottom ends on the table and then removes the longest one, the second-longest one, and so on.

A second example: We set up five bottles of clear liquid and explain that it is possible, by mixing the liquids together in a certain combination, to produce a yellow liquid. The task is to find the right combination. Children in the concrete-operations stage plunge right in with an unsystematic trial-and-error search. They try combining bottles A and B, then C and D, then perhaps A, C, and E, and so on. By the time they work through five or six combinations they forget which ones they have already tried. They may try one combination several times and others not at all; if and when they do stumble onto the correct combination, it is mostly luck.

Children in the formal-operations stage approach the problem more systematically. They may first try all the two-bottle combinations: AB, AC, AD, AE, BC, and so forth. If all those fail, they turn to three-bottle combinations: ABC, ABD, ABE, ACD, and so on. By adopting a strategy for trying every possible combination one time and one time only, they are bound to succeed.

Children do not reach the stage of formal operations any more suddenly than they reach the concrete-operations stage. Before they can reason logically about a particular problem, they must first have had a fair amount of experience in dealing with that problem. A 9-year-old who has spent a great deal of time playing chess reasons logically about chess problems and plans several moves ahead. The same child reverts to concrete reasoning when faced with an unfamiliar problem.

Table 6.2 summarizes Piaget's four stages.

■ CONCEPT CHECK

3. *You are given the following information about four children. Assign each of them to one of Piaget's stages of intellectual development. (Check your answers on page 244.)*

    a. *Has mastered the concept of conservation; still has trouble with abstract and hypothetical questions*

    b. *Performs well on tests of object permanence; still has trouble with conservation*

    c. *Has schemata; does not speak in complete sentences; fails tests of object permanence*

    d. *Performs well on tests of object permanence, conservation, and hypothetical questions*

Are Piaget's Stages Distinct?

WHAT'S THE EVIDENCE?

According to Piaget, the four stages of intellectual development are distinct, and each transition from one stage to the next requires a major reorganization of the child's way of thinking. He contended that children in the sensorimotor stage fail certain tasks because they lack the concept of object permanence and that children in the preoperational stage fail conservation tasks because they lack the necessary mental processes.

Was Piaget right? One way to find out is to test whether the transition from one stage to the next is sharp or blurry. If the stages are distinct, then a child in, say, the preoperational stage should be unable to perform the tasks characteristic of concrete operations, no matter how we set up the situation or phrase the question. But if one stage merges gradually into the next, we should be able to find children who show concrete operational reasoning at some times and not others. Furthermore, it should be possible to advance a child from one stage to the next by careful training.

Hypothesis A child who fails a conservation task (which requires concrete-operational reasoning) may be able to answer correctly a much simplified version of the same problem. After practicing on very simple problems, the child may be able to solve the more difficult version.

Method Ordinarily, preoperational children (before about age 7) fail the conservation-of-number task: An investigator presents two rows of coins or candies with seven or more objects in each row, then spreads out one row and asks which row "has more." Preoperational children reply that the spread-out row has more.

Rochel Gelman (1982) gave preschool children a much simplified version of this task: She presented two rows of just three objects each (Figure 6.18). After she spread out one of the rows, she asked which row had more. She repeatedly presented two rows of three items each, and then rows of four items each. After a child had much practice with rows of three and four items, Gelman presented rows with eight to ten items in each.

Results With rows of only three or four items each, even 3- and 4-year-old children answered that the rows had the same number of items. (Most of the 3-year-olds counted first, to make sure.) After much practice with these short rows, most of the 3- and 4-year-olds also answered correctly that the spread-out row of eight items had the same number as the tightly packed row of eight.

Interpretation The difference in reasoning between preoperational children and concrete-operational children is largely quantitative, and the transition is gradual. If we take a task on which the preoperational children ordinarily

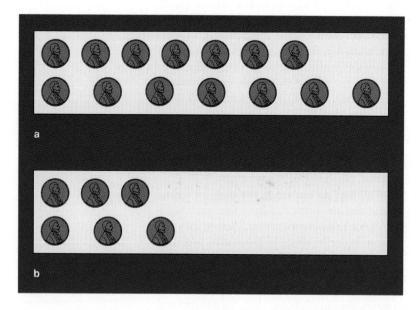

FIGURE 6.18
(a) With the standard conservation-of-number task, preoperational children answer that the lower row has more. (b) With a simplified task, the same children say that both rows have the same number.

fail and we greatly simplify it, those children are likely to solve it. (Perhaps if we took tasks on which the older children succeed and we made the task much more complicated, those children might fail.) That is, the difference between older children and younger children is not so much a matter of "having" an ability or of "lacking" it; the difference is one of readily using the ability and using it only in simple tasks.

Evaluation of Piaget's Theories

Piaget's major contribution was to demonstrate that children's thinking differs from that of adults. Young children really do approach certain questions differently from adults and sometimes arrive at very different answers.

What is less certain is whether children go through distinct stages and whether children at higher stages have capacities that children at lower stages lack altogether. As we have seen, depending on how someone poses the questions, infants may or may not show signs of understanding object permanence. Children less than about 7 years old are highly egocentric in some situations but less so in others. A child who fails the conservation-of-number task does nevertheless understand the concept of number; the same child can answer the questions correctly if we direct his or her attention to the key aspects. In short, Piaget seems to have underestimated the capacities of young children. They apparently have some fairly advanced capacities, even if they do not always use them. (And Piaget may have overestimated adolescents and adults. Even rather bright adults sometimes revert to egocentric and other illogical thinking.)

Moreover, children do not seem to pass suddenly from one stage of development to another. An 8-year-old child may give correct answers in some conservation tasks and not others. The same child may appear to be at the preoperational stage at some times, but at other times appear to be at the stage of concrete operations or even at the stage of formal operations. Although Piaget directed psychologists to some important aspects of how thinking develops, he may have overstated some of his conclusions.

Implications of Piaget's Findings for Education

One implication of Piaget's findings is that children have to discover certain concepts, such as the concept of conservation, mainly on their own. Teaching such concepts is mostly a matter of directing children's attention to the key aspects and then letting them discover the concepts for themselves.

A second implication is that teachers should be aware of each child's capacities and should work within them. Children in the lower grades can learn about concrete objects more easily than they can deal with symbolic and abstract concepts or with deductive logic. Recognizing a child's current stage of maturation and encouraging the child to go slightly beyond it is better than insisting that the child behave in a manner appropriate to a higher stage of development.

LANGUAGE DEVELOPMENT

Susan Carey (1978) has estimated that children between the ages of 1 1/2 and 6 learn an average of nine new words per day—almost one new word per hour—thereby increasing their ability to tell us what they know and think (see Table 6.3). Imagine what it is like for a young child to learn a language. Deciphering the meanings of words would be extraordinarily difficult unless the infant in effect made some assumptions to simplify the task (Markman, 1990). When an adult points at an object and says "bed," the infant refers the sound to the type of object the adult is pointing at. That assumption seems so natural that we may not even recognize it as an assumption. But so far as the infant knows, the sound *could* have referred to "thing that is important at bedtime," in which case it would refer also to pajamas, darkened rooms, and goodnight kisses.

Table 6.3 Conversations with Some Children at the Preoperational Stage

Q: Are you an American?
A: No, my father is an American. I'm a girl.

Q: Do you have to go to the bathroom?
A: No. Don't have to go. Mine peanut not working. Don't have any juice in it.

Q: Do you understand what's happening in this movie (a nature film)?
A: Yes. When the baby skunks grow up, they turn into raccoons.

Table 6.4 Stages of Language Development in Children

Average Age	Language Abilities
3 months	Random vocalizations and cooing
6 months	Babbling
1 year	More babbling; some language comprehension; probably a few words, including "Mama"
1½ years	Some individual words, mostly nouns, but no phrases
2 years	Large vocabulary (more than 50 words); many 2-word phrases; no sentences
2½ years	Good language comprehension; longer phrases and short sentences; still many errors
3 years	Vocabulary around a thousand words; fewer errors; longer sentences
4 years	Close to basic adult speech competence

But infants *do* make the key assumption that most words refer to a type of object or a type of action, as Ellen Markman and Jean Hutchinson (1984) demonstrated. They showed 2-year-old and 3-year-old children pictures of common objects, gave the objects nonsense names, and then found out what other objects the children would apply those names to. For example, the experimenters called a birthday cake a *zig*. Then they showed pictures of a chocolate cake and a birthday present and asked which of them was another *zig*. Eighty-three percent of the children chose the chocolate cake. Evidently, even 2- and 3-year-old children know that a particular word applies to various objects in the same category, not to objects that are part of the same "theme."

Stages of Language Development

Language development in children follows a distinct sequence. Table 6.4 lists the average ages at which children reach various stages of language ability (Lenneberg, 1969; Moskowitz, 1978). Although there is great variation from one child to another, the rate of language development is not closely related to intelligence. A child who advances through these stages faster or slower than the average is not necessarily more intelligent or less intelligent than the average child.

Infants begin by babbling. For the first 6 months or so, their babbling has no apparent

relationship to what they hear; deaf infants babble as much as hearing infants do. Beyond about age 6 months, hearing infants babble more and deaf infants babble less. By the time they are a year old, infants begin to understand language and most of them can say at least a word or two. For most infants throughout the world, one of the first sounds is *muh*. Parents in most parts of the world have defined *muh-muh* (or something similar to it) as meaning "mother." Infants also typically make the sounds *duh, puh,* and *buh;* they almost never make the sound *s*. In many languages, the word for father is similar to *daddy* or *papa. Baba* is the word for grandmother in several languages. In effect, infants tell their parents what words to use for certain concepts.

By age 1 1/2, most toddlers can say a few words. Their vocabulary may be small or large—the average is about 50 words—but they almost never link words together. Thus, a toddler who can say "Daddy" and "bye-bye" may be unable to say "Bye-bye, Daddy." These one-word utterances generally convey a great deal of information, however, and parents can usually make out their meaning from the context. *Mama* might mean "That's a picture of Mama," "Take me to Mama," "Mama went away and left me here," or "Mama, get me something to eat." Most of the words children use at this stage are nouns, along with a few verbs and adjectives. Their speech consists mostly of words for objects and actions, corresponding to what Piaget said was central to children's thinking at this age (Rice, 1989).

Some toddlers follow a pattern of language development different from the usual one (Nelson, 1981). Instead of speaking one word at a time and learning the names of objects, they speak poorly articulated, compressed phrases, such as "Do-it-again" or "I-like-read-Goodnight-Moon." At first these expressions are so poorly pronounced that adults, unless they listen carefully, may not realize that the child is doing anything but babbling. Children who start off by generating complex requests and phrases tend to do so consistently over much of the period of language development (Nelson, Baker, Denninger, Bonvillian, & Kaplan, 1985).

At about age 2, children start to produce many two-word phrases and occasional longer phrases (see examples in Table 6.5). Children pick up useful phrases very rapidly. In one study, a 20-month-old child asked the experimenter for an extra cookie and was teasingly told, "Okay, one for the road." On her next visit, the child ate one cookie and then asked, "One for the road?" (Nelson, 1985).

Still, even at this early stage, much of what children say is creative rather than just imitative. It is unlikely that they have ever heard their parents say, "More page," "Allgone sticky," or "Allgone outside." Such statements are contrary to adult speech habits and adult thought. A child who says "Allgone outside" seems to be saying that the outside is not there any more. (As Piaget said, young children do seem to think differently from adults.)

By age 2 1/2 to 3 years, most children are generating full sentences, though each child maintains a few peculiarities. For example, many children have their own rules for making negative sentences. One of the most common is to add *no* or *not* to the beginning or end of a sentence, such as, "No I want to go to bed!" One little girl made her negatives just by saying something louder and at a higher pitch; for instance, if she shrieked, "I want to share my toys," she meant, "I do not want to share my toys." Presumably she had learned this "rule" by remembering that people screamed at her when they told her not to do something. My son Sam made negatives at this stage by adding the word *either* to the end of a sentence: "I want to eat lima beans either." Apparently he had heard people say, "I don't want to do that either," and had decided that an *either* at the end of the sentence made it an emphatic negative.

At this same age, children act as if they were applying grammatical rules. (I say "as if" because they cannot state the rules. By the same token, baseball players who anticipate exactly where a fly ball will come down act "as if" they understood complex physics and calculus.) For example, a child may learn the word *feet* at an early age and then, after learning other plurals, abandon it in favor of *foots*. Later, he or she begins to compromise by saying "feets," "footses," or "feetses" before eventually returning to "feet." Children at this stage say many things they have never heard anyone else say, such as "The mans comed" or "The womans goed and doed something." Clearly, they are applying rules of how to form plurals and past tenses, although they overgeneralize those rules. My son David invented the word *shis* to mean "belonging to a female." He had apparently generalized the rule "He—his, she—shis." Note that all these inventions imply that children are doing something more than just

Table 6.5 Sample Two-Word Phrases Spoken by a 2-Year-Old Child

Phrase	Meaning
Mommy bath.	Mommy is taking a bath.
Throw Daddy.	Throw it to Daddy.
More page.	Don't stop reading.
More high.	More food is up there on top.
Allgone sticky.	My hands have been washed.
Allgone outside.	Someone closed the door.
No hug!	I'm angry at you!

Toddlers can communicate a great deal with a single word combined with gestures and intonation.

imitating, and more than just producing responses that win them reinforcements. They are trying their best to learn rules.

Eventually, children learn both the rules ("add an *s* to make a plural") and the common exceptions (*feet, mice,* and so forth), even though most parents make little effort to correct their children's mistakes. In fact, many parents find the errors rather charming. One child once said, "Mommy, Tommy fall my truck down." The mother turned with a smile and said, "Tommy, did you fall Stevie's truck down?" By age 4, most children have nearly mastered the use of language. Their vocabulary is still limited, and they still make an occasional irregular statement, such as "Are we all out of cookies or are we still in them?" And adults can still confuse them by speaking in complex, compound, or passive sentences. For most purposes, however, these children are using language well.

■ CONCEPT CHECK

4. At what age do children begin to string words into novel combinations that they have never heard anyone say before? Why do psychologists believe that even very young children learn some of the rules of grammar? (Check your answers on page 244.)

Language Development as Maturation

Language development depends largely on maturation rather than on the mere accumulation of experience (Lenneberg, 1967, 1969). Part of the evidence for this conclusion is that the sequence of stages outlined in Table 6.4 is about the same in all known cultures. The average ages differ a bit from one culture to another, but the various stages are easily recognizable worldwide, in all languages, at approximately the same ages.

Furthermore, parents who expose their children to as much language as possible find that they hardly speed up the children's language development at all (Figure 6.19). The children may acquire a slightly larger vocabulary than usual, but they still go through each stage at about the normal age. At the opposite end in terms of exposure to language, hearing children of deaf parents are exposed to very little spoken language, but if they have periodic contact with speaking people, they progress through the various stages almost on schedule.

If children weren't exposed to any language at all, would they make up one of their own? Some parents of deaf children have unintentionally conducted such an experiment on their own children. A child who cannot hear well enough to learn speech and who never sees anyone using sign language is effectively isolated from all language. The results are consistent: The children make up their own sign language (Goldin-Meadow, 1985). As they grow older, they make the system more complex, linking signs together into sentences with some consistency of word order. Most of the children manage to teach their system, or at least part of it, to one or both parents. Children who spend much time together adopt each other's signs and eventually develop a unified system.

We consider language further in Chapter 9.

FIGURE 6.19
Some overeager parents try to coach their children on language usage at a very early age. The attention may be enjoyable, but it is not likely to accelerate progress through the stages of language development.

DEVELOPMENT OF MORAL REASONING

As children develop their reasoning powers, they apply their new reasoning abilities to moral issues. Just as 11-year-olds reason differently from 5-year-olds about what happens when water is poured from one beaker to another, they also reason differently about issues of right and wrong.

Kohlberg's Method of Evaluating Levels of Moral Reasoning

Morality used to be regarded as a set of arbitrary rules with no logical basis that people learn from their culture. Lawrence Kohlberg (1969; Kohlberg & Hersh, 1977) rejected that view, arguing instead that moral reasoning is the result of a reasoning process that resembles Piaget's stages of intellectual development. Young children mostly equate "wrong" with "punished." Adults understand that certain acts are wrong even though they may never lead to punishment and that other acts are right even if they do lead to punishment. Children younger than about 6 years old think that accidentally breaking something valuable is worse than intentionally breaking something of less value; older children and adults give more regard to people's intentions.

Kohlberg proposed that people pass through distinct stages as they develop moral reasoning. Although those stages are analogous to Piaget's stages, they do not follow the same time sequence. For example, an individual may progress rapidly through Piaget's stages while moving more slowly through Kohlberg's stages.

Kohlberg suggested that moral reasoning should not be evaluated according to the decisions a person makes but according to the reasoning behind them. For example, in George Bernard Shaw's play *The Doctor's Dilemma,* two men are dying of tuberculosis. The doctor can save either one of them but not both. One man has little talent but is honest and decent. The other man, a young artistic genius, is dishonest, rude, and thoroughly disagreeable. Which one should the doctor save? According to Kohlberg, we cannot evaluate the doctor's moral reasoning by asking which man he decided to save. Instead, we should ask *on what basis* the doctor made his decision. In Shaw's play, the doctor saves the untalented man and lets the genius die in hopes that he can marry the widow. (You can evaluate the doctor's moral reasoning for yourself.)

Kohlberg believed that we all start with a low level of moral reasoning and mature through higher stages. (Shaw's doctor apparently did not get very far.) To measure the maturity of a person's moral judgments, Kohlberg devised a series of **moral dilemmas**—problems that pit one moral value against another. Each dilemma is accompanied by a question, such as "What should this person do?" or "Did this person do the right thing?" Actually, there is no one "right" answer to the questions. More revealing than the answer is the explanation and justification the respondent gives. The respondent's explanations are then matched to one of Kohlberg's six stages, which are grouped into three levels (see Table 6.6). Note that, in Kohlberg's scheme, what counts is not the decision you make but the reasons behind it. There are no moral or immoral decisions, just moral and immoral reasons for a decision (Darley & Shultz, 1990). (See Figure 6.20.)

Something to Think About

Suppose a military junta overthrows a democratic government and sets up a dictatorship. In which of Kohlberg's stages of moral reasoning would you classify the members of the junta? Would your answer depend on the reasons they gave for setting up the dictatorship?

The responses people make to Kohlberg's moral dilemmas suggest the level of moral reasoning at which they *usually* operate. Few people are absolutely consistent in their moral views, and their responses may differ from one time to another or even from one question to another. For example, someone with a mature grasp of medical ethics may lie to a police officer about how fast he or she was driving.

What does seem to be consistent in societies throughout the world is that people begin at the first stage and progress through the others in the order Kohlberg suggests, although they may not all reach the highest stages. (The order of progression is an important point. If people were as likely to progress in the order 3-5-4 as in the order 3-4-5, then we would have no justification for regarding stage 5 as higher than stage 4.) Apparently, people do not skip a stage, and few revert to an earlier stage after reaching a higher one.

Figure 6.21 shows that most 10-year-olds' judgments are at Kohlberg's first or second stage, but that the mode of 16-year-olds' judgments is at stage 5. What accounts for this rather swift development of moral reasoning? Kohlberg suggests that it results from cognitive growth: Sixteen-year-olds are capable of more mature reasoning than are 10-year-olds. Rachael Henry (1983) proposes a different possibility: Adolescents reject parental authority. In stages 1 and 2, parents are the source of moral judgments, and what they say determines what is right and what is wrong. In stage 3, other people become the source of moral judgments. In stage 4, the source is the law; in stages 5 and 6, society as a whole or some abstract truth is the source of moral judgments. As adolescents continue to mature, they move farther and farther away from regarding their parents as the ultimate authority on questions of morality.

■ CONCEPT CHECK

5. *For the moral dilemma described at the top of Table 6.6, suppose someone says that Heinz was wrong to steal the drug to save his wife. Which level of moral reasoning is characteristic of this judgment? (Check your answer on page 244.)*

Table 6.6 Responses to One of Kohlberg's Moral Dilemmas by People at Six Levels of Moral Reasoning

The dilemma: Heinz's wife was near death from a type of cancer. A druggist had recently discovered a drug that might be able to save her. The druggist was charging $2,000 for the drug, which cost him $200 to make. Heinz could not afford to pay for it, and he could borrow only $1,000 from friends. He offered to pay the rest later. The druggist refused to sell the drug for less than the full price paid in advance. "I discovered the drug and I'm going to make money from it." Late that night Heinz broke into the store to steal the drug for his wife. Did Heinz do the right thing?

Level/Stage	Typical Answer	Basis for Judging Right from Wrong	Description of Stage
The Level of Preconventional Morality			
1. Punishment and obedience orientation	"No. If he steals the drug he might go to jail." "Yes. If he can't afford the drug, he can't afford a funeral, either."	Wrong is equated with punishment. What is good is whatever is in the man's immediate self-interest.	Decisions are based on their immediate consequences. Whatever is rewarded is "good" and whatever is punished is "bad." If you break something and are punished, then what you did was bad.
2. Instrumental relativist orientation	"He can steal the drug and save his wife, and he'll be with her when he gets out of jail."	Again, what is good is whatever is in the man's own best interests, but his interests include delayed benefits.	It is good to help other people, but only because they may one day return the favor: "You scratch my back and I'll scratch yours."
The Level of Conventional Morality			
3. Interpersonal concordance, or "good boy/nice girl" orientation	"People will understand if you steal the drug to save your wife, but they'll think you're cruel and a coward if you don't."	Public opinion is the main basis for judging what is good.	The "right" thing to do is whatever pleases others, especially those in authority. Be a good person so others will think you are good. Conformity to the dictates of public opinion is important.
4. "Law and order" orientation	"No, because stealing is illegal." "It is the husband's duty to save his wife even if he feels guilty afterward for stealing the drug."	Right and wrong can be determined by duty, or by one's role in society.	You should respect the law—simply because it *is* the law—and should work to strengthen the social order that enforces it.
The Level of Postconventional or Principled Morality			
5. Social-contract legalistic orientation	"The husband has a right to the drug even if he can't pay now. If the druggist won't charge it, the government should look after it."	Laws are made for people's benefit. They should be flexible. If necessary, we may have to change certain laws or allow for exceptions to them.	The "right" thing to do is whatever people have agreed is best for society. As in stage 4, you respect the law, but in addition recognize that a majority of the people can agree to change the rules. Anyone who makes a promise is obligated to keep the promise.
6. Universal ethical principle orientation	"Although it is legally wrong to steal, the husband would be morally wrong not to steal to save his wife. A life is more precious than financial gain."	Right and wrong are based on absolute values such as human life. Sometimes these values take precedence over human laws.	In special cases it may be right to violate a law that conflicts with higher ethical principles, such as justice and respect for human life. Among those who have obeyed a "higher law" are Jesus, Mahatma Gandhi, and Martin Luther King, Jr.

Source: Kohlberg, 1981.

FIGURE 6.20
Here is a real-life moral dilemma: Michigan physician Jack Kevorkian developed a device to help terminally ill patients kill themselves painlessly. Is it morally right or wrong to aid in someone's suicide? According to Kohlberg's viewpoint, the morality of an act does not depend on the act itself, but on the reasoning behind the act.

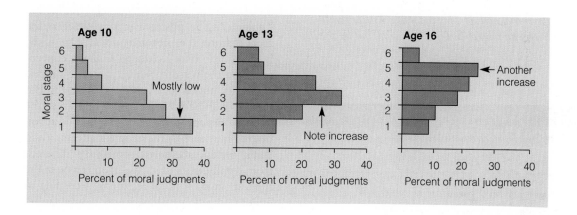

FIGURE 6.21
Distinguishing right from wrong: The development of moral reasoning. Most younger adolescents give answers corresponding to Kohlberg's earlier moral stages. By age 16, most are at Kohlberg's fourth and fifth stages. (Based on Kohlberg, 1969.)

Criticisms of Kohlberg's Views of Moral Development

Although Kohlberg's theories have had an enormous impact on psychology, they do have certain limitations. Some critics point out that moral reasoning is just one part of moral behavior. James Rest (1983) divides moral behavior into four components:

1. Interpreting the situation

2. Deciding the morally correct thing to do

3. Deciding what you actually will do, which may not be the same as the morally correct thing to do

4. Actually doing what you've decided to do

Kohlberg's stages relate only to the first and second of these components. Many juvenile delinquents and adult criminals make mature re-sponses to Kohlberg's moral dilemmas but then engage in behavior that is anything but moral (Jurkovic, 1980; Link, Sherer, & Byrne, 1977). Apparently a person can distinguish between right and wrong in the abstract and then ignore that distinction in the way he or she behaves (Figure 6.22).

Another criticism is that Kohlberg's theories imply that moral reasoning is entirely a logical process. For example, we decide that it is wrong to hurt another person because human life and welfare are fundamentally valuable. But moral reasoning is partly an emotional process. We do not want to hurt other people because we feel bad when we see other people suffering (Kagan, 1984).

Still another criticism is that Kohlberg concentrated entirely on one type of moral reasoning, which we might call the "justice" orienta-

FIGURE 6.22
Critics of Kohlberg's approach to moral reasoning point out that moral reasoning is not the same thing as moral action. This cadet at a Russian military academy probably could explain why cheating is immoral, but he cheats nevertheless.

Table 6.7 Carol Gilligan's Stages of Moral Development

Stage	Basis for Deciding Right from Wrong
Preconventional	What is helpful or harmful to myself?
Conventional	What is helpful or harmful to other people?
Postconventional	What is helpful or harmful to myself as well as to others?

tion (what is right and what is wrong). Carol Gilligan (1977, 1979) pointed out a different way of approaching moral decisions, the "caring" orientation (what would help or hurt other people). For example, consider a situation during the Vietnam War, in which a group of soldiers were ordered to kill a group of unarmed civilians. One soldier, who regarded the order as immoral, refused to shoot. However, his actions did not make any difference, as the other soldiers killed all the civilians. In terms of "justice," this soldier acted at a high moral level, following a "higher law" that required him not to kill. But in terms of "caring," his actions were not especially moral. A better action would have been to find a way to hide a few of the Vietnamese civilians (Linn & Gilligan, 1990).

Initially, Gilligan (1977, 1979) proposed that the "justice" and "caring" orientations represented a sex difference. Men, she said, focus mostly on rights and duties; women focus more on caring and relationships. For example, when asked about the ethics of abortion, men might say that abortion is wrong because it takes a life, or they might say it is acceptable because a woman has the right to make decisions about her own body. Either answer could get a high evaluation in Kohlberg's system, if explained clearly. But a woman might answer the same question by saying the ethics of abortion depends on many of the details of the situation. An "it depends" answer does not get high marks in Kohlberg's system, because it does not rely on abstract principles of right and wrong. Nevertheless, it may reflect a sympathetic, caring approach to solving people's problems.

Gilligan therefore proposed an alternative set of stages of moral development, outlined in Table 6.7. The postconventional stage is the most mature; the preconventional stage is the least mature. Like Kohlberg, Gilligan concentrates on the reasons behind someone's moral decisions, not on the decisions themselves. But unlike Kohlberg, Gilligan emphasizes the "caring" aspect of the reasons: Will this action help or hurt each of the people it affects? Gilligan's system measures something different from Kohlberg's system; a person can be in the highest stage of moral reasoning according to either Gilligan or Kohlberg and a low stage according to the other (Walker, 1989).

Later research found that men and women do not differ greatly or consistently in how they approach moral dilemmas (Brabeck, 1983). Men may be a little more likely than women to talk about justice and women a little more likely than men to show concern about caring (Gilligan & Attanucci, 1988). But both sexes show concern with both kinds of moral reasoning.

Gilligan has therefore modified her position: Each of us has within ourselves two "voices" of morality—a voice of justice and rights, and a voice of caring and relationships. One voice may speak a little louder in some people and the other voice in other people, but both voices are valid (Gilligan & Attanucci, 1988). Sometimes the two voices are in conflict; that is, one may feel an obligation to help some person and yet find that the only way to help requires breaking some general principle of justice (Linn & Gilligan, 1990). In short, sometimes situations are complicated and moral reasoning difficult. (See Figure 6.23.)

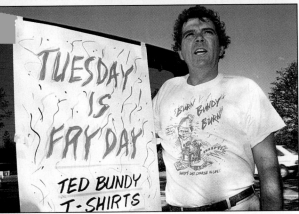

FIGURE 6.23

In controversial areas such as abortion and the death penalty, competing sides may disagree vigorously, even while each side believes it bases its decision on morality. Sometimes the disagreement represents different interpretations of justice. Sometimes it represents conflict between a justice perspective and a caring perspective.

SUMMARY

■ *Piaget's view of children's thinking.* According to Jean Piaget, children's thought processes are more intuitive, less logical, and more egocentric than adults' thought processes are. (page 227)

■ *Piaget's stages of development.* Piaget described four stages of development of thought processes and knowledge. Children progress through those stages in order. (page 229)

■ *Possibility of advancing progress.* We can teach children to give correct answers to questions that they ordinarily cannot answer until a later stage of development. (page 234)

■ *Restricted uses of abilities.* Young children do not always use all the abilities they have. Although children in the preoperational stage ordinarily fail to demonstrate conservation of number, it is clear from other tasks that they do understand the concept of number. (page 234)

■ *Language development.* Children begin rapidly learning language at about age 1 1/2. From the start, their speech is creative and not just imitative. (page 235)

■ *Kohlberg's view of moral reasoning.* Lawrence Kohlberg contended that moral reasoning also can be described in terms of stages. According to Kohlberg, a person's moral reasoning should be evaluated on the basis of the reasons the person gives for a decision, rather than on the basis of the decision itself. (page 238)

■ *Gilligan's view of moral reasoning.* Carol Gilligan demonstrated that not all people decide moral dilemmas primarily on the basis of principles of justice. Some (more women than men) decide primarily on the basis of a caring orientation. (page 242)

SUGGESTION FOR FURTHER READING

Wadsworth, B. J. (1989). *Piaget's theory of cognitive and affective development* (4th ed.). White Plains, NY: Longman. A clear description of Piaget's main contributions.

TERMS

schema (plural: schemata) an organized way of interacting with objects in the world (page 228)

assimilation Piaget's term for the application of an established schema to new objects (page 228)

accommodation Piaget's term for the modification of an established schema to fit new objects (page 228)

sensorimotor stage according to Piaget, the first stage of intellectual development, in which an infant's behavior is limited to making simple motor responses to sensory stimuli (page 229)

preoperational stage according to Piaget, the second stage of intellectual development, in which children lack operations (page 229)

operation according to Piaget, a mental process that can be reversed (page 229)

egocentric an inability to take the perspective of another person, a tendency to view the world as centered around oneself (page 230)

conservation the concept that objects retain their weight, volume, and certain other properties in spite of changes in their shape or arrangement (page 230)

stage of concrete operations according to Piaget, the third stage of intellectual development, in which children can deal with the properties of concrete objects but cannot readily deal with hypothetical or abstract questions (page 232)

stage of formal operations according to Piaget, the fourth and final stage of intellectual development, in which people deal with abstract, hypothetical situations, which demand logical, deductive reasoning and systematic planning (page 232)

moral dilemma a problem that pits one moral value against another (page 239)

ANSWERS TO CONCEPT CHECKS

2. (c) is the clearest case of egocentric thought, a failure to recognize another person's point of view. It is not the same thing as selfishness. (page 230)

3. (a) Stage of concrete operations; (b) preoperational stage; (c) sensorimotor stage; (d) stage of formal operations. (page 234)

4. Children begin to string words into novel combinations as soon as they begin to speak two words at a time. We believe that they learn rules of grammar because they overgeneralize those rules, saying such "words" as *womans* and *goed*. (page 238)

5. Not enough information is provided to answer this question. In Kohlberg's system, any judgment can represent either a high or a low level of moral reasoning. We evaluate a person's moral reasoning entirely by the explanation for the judgment, not by the judgment itself. (page 239)

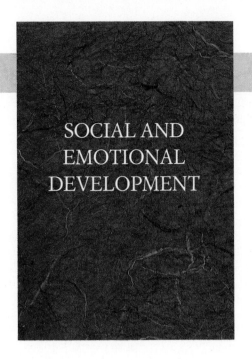

SOCIAL AND EMOTIONAL DEVELOPMENT

What are the special social and emotional problems that people face at different ages of life?

What determines how we develop socially and emotionally?

You are a contestant on a new TV game show called "What's My Worry?" Behind the curtain is someone with an overriding concern. You are to identify that concern by questioning a psychologist who knows what it is. (You can neither see nor hear the person.) You must ask questions that can be answered with a single word or a short phrase. If you identify the concern correctly, you can win up to $50,000.

But there is one catch: The more questions you ask, the smaller your prize. If you guess correctly after one question, you win $50,000. After two questions, you win $25,000. And so on. It would be poor strategy to go on asking questions until you were sure of the answer; instead, you should ask one or two questions and then guess.

What would your first question be? Mine would be: "How old is this person?" The principal worries of teenagers are different from those of most 20-year-olds, which in turn differ from those of most 40-year-olds and 70-year-olds. Each age has its own characteristic concerns and decisions, opportunities and pleasures.

RESEARCH DESIGNS FOR STUDYING DEVELOPMENT

Comparing the psychology of people of different ages sounds easy: We study a group of, say, 10-year-olds and a group of 20-year-olds and see how they differ. But how do we know whether those differences are due to age or to some other difference between the groups? We may get different results depending on exactly how we conduct the study. Depending on circumstances, psychologists can use either cross-sectional studies or longitudinal studies. A **cross-sectional study** compares groups of individuals of different ages all at the same time. For example, we could compare the drawing abilities of 6-year-olds, 8-year-olds, and 10-year-olds.

A **longitudinal study** follows a single group of individuals as they develop. For example, we could study a group of 6-year-olds, and then restudy the same children when they reach ages 9 and 12. Table 6.8 contrasts the two kinds of studies.

Longitudinal studies face certain obvious practical difficulties. A longitudinal study of children from age 6 to 12 necessarily requires 6 years to complete; some longitudinal studies last decades. To make matters worse, many of the children who begin in a study at, say, age 6 may move out of town by age 9 or 12. A longitudinal study of the elderly faces the problem that many people will die or become seriously ill before the end of the study. (This is the problem of "selective attrition" mentioned in Chapter 2.) By choosing a cross-sectional study, we avoid such problems.

A longitudinal study also faces the difficulty of separating the effects of age from the effects of changes in society. For example, suppose we found that a group of people who were 20 years old in 1970 became politically more conservative by age 40. We would not know whether these people became more conservative because of age or because of changes in the political situation between 1970 and 1990.

Why, then, would investigators ever conduct a longitudinal study? One reason is that

Table 6.8 Cross-sectional and Longitudinal Studies

	Description	Advantages	Disadvantages	Example
Cross-sectional	Several groups of subjects of various ages studied at one time	1. Quick 2. No risk of confusing age affects with effects of changes in society	1. Risk of sampling error by getting different kinds of people at different ages 2. Risk of cohort effects	Compare memory abilities of 3-, 5-, and 7-year-olds.
Longitudinal	One group of subjects studied repeatedly as they grow older	1. No risk of sampling differences 2. Can study effects of one experience on later development 3. Can study consistency within individuals over time	1. Takes long time 2. Some subjects quit 3. Sometimes hard to separate effects of age from changes in society	Study social and emotional behavior of children at time of parents' divorce and at various times afterward.

FIGURE 6.24

One reason why the young people of today differ from their elders is that they grew up in a different historical era, with different education, nutrition, and health care. Differences among age groups based on such influences are called cohort effects.

certain questions logically require a longitudinal study. For example, to study the effects of divorce on children, we learn much by comparing how each child reacts at first with how that same child reacts several years later. To study whether happy children are likely to become happy adults, we would have to follow a single group of people for a substantial period of time.

What happens if a cross-sectional study gives one result and a longitudinal study gives another? Psychologists do not just throw up their hands in despair; they look for reasons behind the different results. For example, suppose someone conducting a study in 1955 finds that the mean IQ score of the 20-year-olds is much higher than that of the 60-year-olds. However, on a retest in 1995, the former-20-year-olds (now 60 years old) score as high as they did in 1955. Thus, the longitudinal part of the study indicates that IQ scores are fairly stable from age 20 to age 60. Why, then, did the 20-year-olds score so much higher than the 60-year-olds in 1955? Two possible reasons: First, perhaps the investigators in 1955 selected a particularly bright group of 20-year-olds or a dull group of 60-year-olds. Second, maybe the generation of people who were 20 years old in 1955 were healthier and better educated than the older generation had ever been. That is, the 20-year-olds of 1955 may have performed better than the 20-year-olds of 1915 would have. Psychologists call this a *cohort effect* (Figure 6.24). A **cohort** is a group of people born at a particular time or a group of people who entered some organization at a particular time. Psychologists try to distinguish whether a difference among people of different ages is really due to age or whether it is a difference among cohorts.

6. Suppose you want to study the effect of age on artistic abilities, and you want to be sure that any apparent differences are due to age and not to a cohort effect. Which should you use, a longitudinal study or a cross-sectional study?

7. Suppose you want to study the effect of age on choice of clothing, but you are worried because clothing fashions change from one year to the next. (It would not be fair to compare the people of today with people of previous years.) Which should you use, a longitudinal study or a cross-sectional study?
(Check your answers on page 261.)

Using a combination of cross-sectional and longitudinal studies, psychologists study changes in people's abilities, but also changes in their life situations. The decisions and social environment young adults face are very different from the experiences of children on one hand or old people on the other.

ERIKSON'S AGES OF HUMAN DEVELOPMENT

How people spend their time and what they think about are largely determined by their current role in life—preschool child, student, worker, or retired person. And a person's role in life is determined largely, though not entirely, by his or her age. To understand why people behave as they do, we need to know the decisions they are facing at their current stage of life.

Erik Erikson (Figure 6.25), a pioneer in child psychoanalysis, divided the human lifespan into eight ages, each with its own social and emotional conflicts. First is the age of the newborn infant, whose main conflict is **basic trust versus mistrust.** The infant asks, in effect, "Is my social world predictable and supportive?" The most significant step in the social development of a newborn infant is arriving at a basic trust that the parents will meet his or her needs. An infant whose early environment is supportive, nurturing, and loving will form an attachment to the parents that will also influence future relationships with other people (Erikson, 1963).

Erikson's second age is the age of the toddler, 1 to 3 years old, whose main conflict is **autonomy versus shame and doubt.** The toddler faces the issue "Can I do things by myself or

FIGURE 6.25
Erik Erikson, a highly influential theorist, argued that each age has its own special social and emotional conflicts.

must I always rely on others?" Experiencing independence for the first time, the toddler begins to walk and talk, to be toilet trained, to obey some instructions and defy others, and to make choices. Depending on how the parents react, children may develop a healthy feeling of autonomy (independence) or a self-critical sense of shame and doubt that they can accomplish things on their own.

Erikson's third age is the age of the preschool child, whose main conflict is **initiative versus guilt.** At ages 3 to 6, as children begin to broaden their horizons, their boundless energy comes into conflict with parental restrictions. Sooner or later the child breaks something or makes a big mess. The child faces the question "Am I good or bad?" In contrast to the previous stage, where the child was concerned about what he or she is *capable of doing,* at this state the child is concerned about the morality or acceptability of his or her actions.

In the fourth age, preadolescence (about ages 6 to 12), **industry versus inferiority** is the main conflict. The question is "Am I successful or worthless?" Children widen their focus from the immediate family to society at large and begin to prepare for adult roles. They fantasize about the great successes ahead, and they begin to compete with their peers in an effort to excel in the activities of their age. Children who feel that they are failing may be plagued with long-lasting feelings of inferiority. Children who take pride in their accomplishments gain a long-lasting feeling of competence.

Erikson's fifth age is adolescence (the early teens), in which the main conflict is **identity versus role confusion.** Adolescents begin to seek independence from their parents and try to answer the question "Who am I?" or "Who will I be?" They may eventually settle on a satisfactory answer—an identity—or they may continue to experiment with goals and life-styles—a state of role confusion.

Erikson's sixth age is young adulthood (the late teens and the 20s), in which **intimacy versus isolation** is the main conflict. Shall I share my life with another person or shall I live alone? Young adults who marry or who live with a friend find that they have to adjust their habits in order to make the relationship succeed. Those who choose to live alone may experience loneliness and pressure from their parents and friends to find a suitable partner.

Erikson's seventh age is middle adulthood (from the late 20s through retirement), in which the major conflict is **generativity versus stagnation.** Will I produce something of real value? Will I succeed in my life, both as a parent and as a worker? Or will the quality of my life simply dwindle with the years?

Erikson's eighth age is old age (the years after retirement), in which the main conflict is **ego integrity versus despair.** Have I lived a full life or have I failed? Integrity is a state of contentment about one's life, past, present, and future. Despair is a state of disappointment about the past and the present, coupled with fear of the future. Table 6.9 summarizes Erikson's ages.

Is Erikson's view of development correct? That is almost an unanswerable question. Some psychologists find Erikson's description of development a useful way to organize our thinking about human life; others find it less useful; almost no one finds it easy to test scientifically. Erikson described development; he did not explain it. For example, he hardly addressed the question of how or why a person progresses from one stage to the next Still, Erikson called attention to the fact that the social and emotional concerns of one age differ from those of another, and his writings inspired interest in development across the entire lifespan.

Now let's take a closer look at some of the major issues that confront people in their social and emotional development at different ages. Beyond the primary conflicts that Erikson highlighted, development is marked by a succession of other significant problems.

Table 6.9 Erikson's Ages of Human Development

Age	Main Conflict	Typical Question
Infant	Basic trust versus mistrust	Is my social world predictable and supportive?
Toddler (ages 1–3)	Autonomy versus shame and doubt	Can I do things by myself or must I always rely on others?
Preschool child (ages 3–6)	Initiative versus guilt	Am I good or bad?
Preadolescent (ages 6–12)	Industry versus inferiority	Am I successful or worthless?
Adolescent (early teens)	Identity versus role confusion	Who am I?
Young adult (late teens and early 20s)	Intimacy versus isolation	Shall I share my life with another person or shall I live alone?
Middle adult (late 20s to retirement)	Generativity versus stagnation	Will I succeed in my life, both as a parent and as a worker?
Older adult (after retirement)	Ego integrity versus despair	Have I lived a full life or have I failed?

INFANCY: FORMING THE FIRST ATTACHMENTS

Before the late 1950s, if someone had asked, "What causes an infant to develop an attachment to its mother?" almost all psychologists would have replied, "Mother's milk." They were wrong.

Studies of Attachment Among Monkeys

Attachment—a long-term feeling of closeness between a child and a care giver—depends on more than just being fed. Attachment is part of trust, in Erikson's sense of "trust versus mistrust." That attachment or trust comes only partly from the satisfaction of biological needs. It also depends on the emotional responses provoked by such acts as hugging.

Some highly influential evidence comes from an experiment that Harry Harlow conducted with monkeys. Harlow (1958) separated eight newborn rhesus monkeys from their mothers and isolated each of them in a room containing two artificial mothers. Four of the infant monkeys had a mother made out of wire and equipped with a milk bottle in the breast position and a mother made out of cloth with no bottle; the other four had a cloth mother with a bottle and a wire mother with no bottle. Harlow wanted to find out how much time the baby monkeys would spend with the artificial mother that fed them.

Figure 6.26 shows the mean number of hours per day that the monkeys spent with the two kinds of mothers. Regardless of whether they got their milk from the cloth mother or from the wire mother (Figure 6.27), they all spent more than half their time clinging to the cloth mother and very little time with the wire mother. Evidently their attachment depended more on *contact comfort*—comfortable skin sensations—than on the satisfaction of their hunger or sucking needs.

At first Harlow thought that the cloth mothers were serving the infants' emotional needs adequately. He discovered, however, that the monkeys failed to develop normal social and sexual behavior (Harlow, Harlow, & Suomi, 1971). (See Figure 6.28.) When some of the females finally became pregnant, they proved to be woefully inadequate mothers, rejecting every attempt their babies made to cling to them or to be nursed. Clearly, the monkeys that had been reared by artificial mothers did not know how to react to other monkeys.

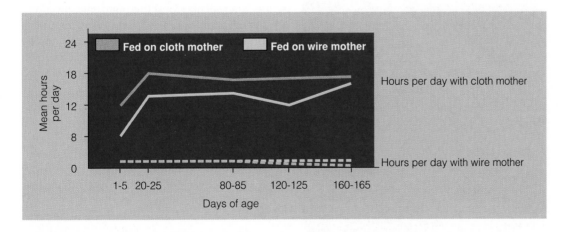

FIGURE 6.26

Regardless of which artificial mother fed them, all the baby monkeys preferred the cloth mothers; the bottom two lines show hours per day with the wire mothers.

In Harlow's studies, monkeys who got milk from the wire mother still clung to the cloth mother as much as they could.

F I G U R E 6 . 2 8
Much of what we learn and need depends on interaction with others. This mother monkey reared in isolation ignores her baby.

Physical contact and cuddling are essential for the attachment that develops between parent and child. The early parent-child relationship serves as a prototype for later social attachments.

What are the messages of this study for humans? The data do *not* mean that an infant needs a mother's constant attention. They do mean that an infant needs social attention from *someone*. In later studies, Harry Harlow and Margaret Harlow (1965) found that infant monkeys reared by artificial mothers could develop fairly normally if they had frequent opportunities to play with other infant monkeys.

Early Attachment in Humans

Early social experience is, we would assume, at least equally important for human social development. Although we cannot conduct deliberate experiments to test this point, all indications support it. In the early 1900s, many foundling homes and orphanages raised infants under conditions that were little better than those of the Harlows' monkeys. The supervisors, trained to believe that unnecessary stimulation should be avoided, ruled that each infant be kept in a crib in a narrow cubicle. The nurses seldom cuddled the infants or played with them, and the infants rarely had an opportunity even to see other babies.

In various institutions, 30–100% of the babies died within 1 year (Spitz, 1945, 1946). Those who survived were retarded in physical growth and in language and intellectual development; they were socially inept and unresponsive to their environment (Bowlby, 1952). We cannot ascribe these results solely to early social isolation because many of the children were ill to begin with, and a number of those who survived continued to be reared under poor conditions (Clarke & Clarke, 1976). Still, severe deprivation of human contact early in life clearly can be extremely harmful.

■ CONCEPT CHECK

8. *In what way were the unstimulating institutions similar to the Harlows' artificial monkeys? (Check your answer on page 261.)*

SOCIAL DEVELOPMENT IN CHILDHOOD

Infants less than 1 year old seldom play with one another. They show interest in one another, but they do not have enough social skills to continue any meaningful social interactions. From age 1 to 2, we can see the beginnings of social play, but still it is mostly **parallel play:** Two or more infants play at the same time, in the same place, but almost independently. After about age 2, children start playing with one another more and more. Relationships with their parents are always important, but for certain purposes they prefer to play with others their own age.

The social and emotional development of children depends in part on how successful they are in forming friendships with other children (Figure 6.29). Some children are "popular," having many friends and admirers. Others are "rejected," with most other children avoiding their company. Still others are "controversial," liked by some and rejected by others. Controversial children are generally those with some social skills but an aggressive streak. A child's status as popular, rejected, or controversial tends to be fairly consistent from year to year (Coie & Dodge, 1983). Children with few friends tend to suffer low self-esteem and to do poorly in both schoolwork and athletics. (But does the lack of friends lead to poor performance or does poor performance lead to the lack of friends?)

The behavior of brothers and sisters also influences a child's development. Siblings can exert a positive influence by acting as teachers and playmates or a negative influence by acting in a hostile or abusive manner. They may also exert an indirect effect by influencing the behavior of the parents. For example, when a brother or sister has a major physical disability, the parents are likely to become distressed and

FIGURE 6.29
Children learn their social skills by interacting with brothers, sisters, and friends close to their own age.

overworked. The healthy child in the family may react by being aggressive, impulsive, and self-destructive and engaging in other attention-getting behavior (Breslau & Prabucki, 1987).

Many studies have been made of the effects of being a firstborn child or being born later. A number of those birth-order studies report that firstborn children do better in school, are more ambitious, are more honest, and have a greater need to affiliate with others. Children born later tend to be more popular, more independent, less conforming, better adjusted emotionally, and possibly more creative. These tendencies are slight and inconsistent, however, and some of the evidence is based on poorly conducted studies (Ernst & Angst, 1983; Schooler, 1972). Be skeptical of recommendations that parents should space their children many years apart in order to give each of them the alleged benefits of the firstborn.

Something to Think About

Psychologists have offered two explanations for the effects of birth order on behavior: (1) Depending on whether there are older, younger, or no other children in the family, each child is subjected to different social influences. (2) Because the mother undergoes physical changes, such as changes in her hormones after giving birth, younger children experience different prenatal influences from those experienced by the firstborn child. What kind of evidence would you need to decide whether one explanation was more satisfactory than the other?

ADOLESCENCE

Adolescence begins when the body shows signs of sexual maturation. In North America, the mean ages are around 12 to 13 in girls and about a year or two later in boys. It is more difficult to say when adolescence ends. Adolescence merges into adulthood, and adulthood is more a state of mind than a condition of the body. Some 12-year-olds act like adults, and some 30-year-olds act like adolescents.

Adolescence is a time of transition from childhood to adulthood. Children think of themselves as part of their parents' family; young adults are ready to start their own family. Adolescents are somewhere in between, still closely tied to their parents but spending more and more time with their peer group. Their relationship with their parents changes, often in turbulent ways. From the parents' standpoint, adolescents are no longer acting like dutiful, obedient children, but they are also not acting like responsible adults. The adolescents are asserting their independence, but they are sometimes making big mistakes, at least in the parents' judgment. The relationship between the parents and teenagers may include episodes of serious conflict (Paikoff & Brooks-Gunn, 1991).

Adolescence is a time of "finding yourself," of determining "Who am I?" or "Who will I be?" As Erikson said, identity is a major issue at this age.

Identity Crisis

In some societies, children are expected eventually to enter the same occupation as their parents and to live in the same town. The parents may even choose marriage partners for their children. In such societies, adolescents have few major choices to make.

Our society offers young people a great many choices. They can decide how much education to get, what job to seek, and where to live. They can decide whether to marry and whom and when. They can choose their own political and religious affiliation. They can choose their own standards of behavior for sex, alcohol, and drugs. In making each of these choices, they may face conflicting pressures from peers, parents, and teachers.

Adolescents, realizing that they must make such decisions within a few years, face an **identity crisis.** The search for identity or self-understanding may lead an adolescent in several directions (Marcia, 1980). **Identity foreclosure,** for example, is the passive acceptance of a role defined by one's parents. An adolescent's father may declare, for example, "When you graduate from high school, you will go on to college and study electrical engineering, just as I did when I was your age. Then you will go into the family business with me." Adolescents who accept such parental prescriptions enjoy at least one advantage: They avoid the uncertainty and anxiety that other adolescents endure while trying to "find themselves."

Until fairly recently, identity foreclosure was the norm for most young women. Parents and society both decreed, "You will be a full-time wife and mother." Today, young women have greater freedom to choose what to do with their life. That greater freedom has made it more likely that they will experience an identity crisis during adolescence.

The search for identity may also lead to **role diffusion.** The uncertain sense of identity and the low self-esteem that many adolescents experience may prompt them to experiment with a variety of roles, alternately playing the "party goer," the "rebel," the "serious student," the "loner," and the "class clown." Role diffusion is not necessarily a bad thing, at least as a temporary measure. It is natural to experiment with several roles before a person finds the one that seems most suitable.

Another possible outcome is a **moratorium**—a delay in resolving an identity crisis. The adolescent simply postpones making any lasting decision.

Finally, the search for identity may lead to **identity achievement.** Some adolescents deliberately decide what their values, goals, and place in society will be. That identity may or may not be permanent; we all continue to change in various ways throughout life, and from time to time we need to rethink our values and goals.

The "Personal Fable" of Teenagers

Respond to the following statements. Are they true or false?

- Other people will fail to realize their life ambitions, but I will realize mine.

- I understand love and sex in a way my parents never did.

FIGURE 6.30
Some teenagers seriously risk their health and safety. According to David Elkind, one reason for such risky behavior is the "personal fable," the secret belief that "nothing bad will happen to me."

- Tragedy may strike other people, but it will probably never strike me.
- Almost everyone notices how I look and how I dress.

You know perfectly well that all these statements are false, and yet you may nurture a secret belief in them too. According to David Elkind (1984), teenagers are particularly likely to harbor such beliefs. Taken together, he calls them the "personal fable," the conviction that "I am special; what is true for everyone else is not true for me." Up to a point, that fable may actually foster psychological well-being. It helps us to maintain a cheerful, optimistic outlook on life. It becomes dangerous when it leads people to take foolish chances: "I can drive when I'm drunk and never have an accident." "I won't get pregnant." "I'm going to be a success whether or not I study." (See Figure 6.30.)

Teenage Sexuality

The decision about "Who am I?" or "What am I going to do with my life?" includes the question "How shall I behave sexually?" Generally, sexual behavior is not an issue before **puberty,** the time of onset of sexual maturation. Beginning at puberty, it suddenly becomes a very important issue indeed. A fairly high percentage of teenagers become sexually active, as shown in Figure 6.31, although the figures vary from year to year (Brooks-Gunn & Furstenberg, 1989). Their motives for sex vary. It can be a search for pleasure, a way of strengthening a relationship with a boyfriend or girlfriend, a way of coping with frustrations, a way of becoming accepted by a peer subculture, or a way of proving "I am an adult."

When a young couple goes out on a first date, each party may be uncertain what the other party has in mind. Some people look forward to sex on the first date; others are adamant about having no sex before marriage. F. Scott Christopher and Rodney Cate (1985) found that college-age couples progressed toward intimacy at vastly different rates. Perhaps no one pattern of dating and intimacy is best for all people. In Christopher and Cate's study, couples who were quick to reach sexual intimacy reported loving each other about the same amount as couples who were slower to become intimate. However, the rapid-involvement couples did report more conflict early in their relationship.

Perhaps the most important concern is that both members of a couple should be in agreement about what sexual intimacy implies or does not imply about their relationship. In general, more men than women are willing to have

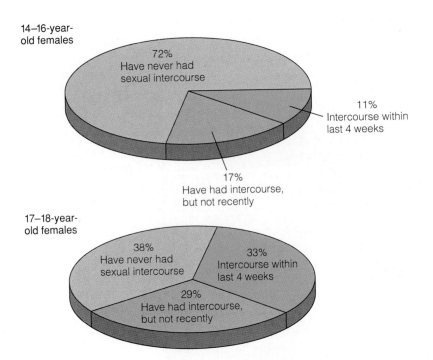

14–16-year-old females

72%
Have never had sexual intercourse

11%
Intercourse within last 4 weeks

17%
Have had intercourse, but not recently

17–18-year-old females

38%
Have never had sexual intercourse

33%
Intercourse within last 4 weeks

29%
Have had intercourse, but not recently

FIGURE 6.31
According to one survey of 1,032 teenage females in Philadelphia, most have had intercourse before age 19, although they vary greatly in their frequency of intercourse. (Based on data of Loewenstein & Furstenberg, 1991.)

sex casually with many partners (Hendrick, Hendrick, Slapion-Foote, & Foote, 1985). If a man regards intercourse as a casual act while his partner considers intercourse as an implied engagement to be married, then someone is headed for trouble.

Over the past several decades sexual activity among teenagers has grown increasingly common, in part because of the ready availability of birth-control pills and other contraceptive devices. And yet a large percentage of teenage couples fail to use contraceptives or to use them consistently (Finkel & Finkel, 1983); about 10–15% of teenage girls have unwanted pregnancies (Zelnik & Kantner, 1977, 1978).

Despite the increase in teenage sexual activity, misinformation about sex still abounds (Morrison, 1985). Many sexually active teenagers mistakenly believe that:

■ Young teenagers cannot get pregnant.

■ It is impossible to get pregnant the first time you have sex.

■ A woman must have sex frequently in order to become pregnant.

■ Someone who has had sex several times without getting pregnant must be safe.

■ A woman has to have an orgasm in order to get pregnant.

■ A woman will not get pregnant unless she wants to.

Even teenagers who are better informed may fail to use contraceptives because they would be embarrassed to purchase them. Some believe that it is all right to have sex but wrong to plan for it. Still others fall victim to their "personal fables," as discussed earlier. They believe that "other people get pregnant, but it won't happen to me."

YOUNG ADULTHOOD

In young adulthood, marriage and career no longer lie in the future. Ready or not, the future has arrived. According to Erikson, the main concern at this age is "Shall I live by myself or share my life with another person?"

Attraction and Partner Selection

The custom of dating serves both short-term and long-term purposes. The short-term purpose is to have a pleasant time. The long-term purpose is to choose a marriage partner. The two are not always in harmony.

When people decide whom to date, one major determinant is familiarity. You are more likely to date someone you see frequently than someone you see rarely. The same is true when you choose friends. But extensive familiarity does not always lead to romantic attraction. In Israel, many children are reared in kibbutzim, collective farms, from infancy to adolescence. And yet young Israelis generally avoid dating people who grew up in the same kibbutz (Shepher, 1971). They regard one another almost like brother and sister.

Another major determinant of who dates whom is physical appearance. The best-looking girls tend to date the best-looking boys. Dating couples tend to resemble each other physically almost as much as married couples do (Plomin, DeFries, & Roberts, 1977). However, the superficial considerations that lead to casual dating are rarely substantial enough to sustain a lasting relationship. Couples who differ sharply in education and interests may date for a while, but they are not likely to marry (Plomin, DeFries, & Roberts, 1977).

Dating and Learning About Each Other

Dating couples gradually share a great deal of information about themselves, including their political and religious beliefs, their feelings toward their parents, and their deepest hopes and fears (Rubin, Hill, Peplau, & Dunkel-Schetter,

1980). Generally, women reveal more about themselves than men do—to friends as well as to dating partners (Caltabiano & Smithson, 1983). Still, both men and women are generally reluctant at first to reveal themselves fully to a dating partner and to enter into intimate communication. What causes that reluctance?

As a rule, people exchange information about their private lives only after a long, gradual, give-and-take process (Figure 6.32). If an old friend opens up to you about his failure at work or tells you about his brother in jail, you may feel privileged. If the man who just moved in next door shares the same sort of information, you probably wonder what strange sort of person he is.

When people feel they have nothing to lose, they are more likely to reveal themselves. For instance, couples who are facing serious difficulties in their marriage speak more candidly to each other than happily married couples do (Tolstedt & Stokes, 1984). Zick Rubin (1974) found that strangers who meet by accident on a train or a plane on their way to different destinations often reveal intimate information they would never reveal even to their closest friends.

Dating couples who have many acquaintances in common feel that they have a great deal to lose if they open up too freely or too quickly. Until they have actually decided to get married, many couples do not explore the matters that most often cause friction after marriage.

Answer the questions in Table 6.10 *as you think your boyfriend or girlfriend* would answer them. Were you uncertain about how your boyfriend or girlfriend would answer any of the questions? If so, you are in the majority. And yet disagreements on such questions are among the most common reasons for divorce.

Balancing Family and Career

In early adulthood, most people start both a family and a career. Sometimes the two come into conflict, most frequently for women. Traditionally in Europe and the United States, mothers have devoted much more time to care for small children than fathers have. The amount of time mothers devoted has been variable; wealthy European mothers might leave their children with "nannies" during most of the day or send them to a boarding school at an early age. Still, most mothers stayed at home while their children were young.

FIGURE 6.32
Dating is marked by cautious self-disclosure. Both partners want to get to know each other, but each also wants to avoid saying anything that could make the wrong impression.

Table 6.10 Premarital Questionnaire

1. After marriage, how often would you want to visit your parents? Your in-laws?

2. How many children do you want to have? How soon?

3. How do you want to raise your children? Should the mother stay home with the children full-time while they are young? Or should the father and mother share the responsibility for child care? Or should the children be put in a day-care center?

4. Suppose the husband is offered a good job in one city and the wife is offered a good job in a city a hundred miles away. Neither spouse can find a satisfactory job in the other's city. How would you decide where to live?

5. Suppose a sudden financial crisis strikes. Where would you cut expenses to balance the budget? Clothes? Food? Housing? Entertainment?

6. How often do you plan to attend religious services?

7. Where and how do you like to spend your vacations?

8. How often would you expect to spend an evening with friends, apart from your spouse?

Did that interrupt their careers? Well, staying at home does not interrupt your career if you do not have a career. Before the late 1960s and early 1970s, career opportunities for women were distinctly limited. Job discrimination against women still exists today, but it is much less severe than in times past. Many young women are in the midst of promising careers when they contemplate having a baby.

Today it is common for a woman to have a career and to be the primary caretaker for one or more children. Balancing the demands of career and family can be taxing.

Suddenly they have a difficult decision to face: After delivering the baby, do they return to work at least part-time? And if so, how soon? Most families need the income from the mother's job; even if they don't, the mother may enjoy working outside the home. But getting affordable, high-quality day care is difficult in most areas (Scarr, Phillips, & McCartney, 1989).

Different families make different decisions. The mother may interrupt her career to stay with the baby; less frequently the father may stay with the baby full-time; in some cases, the mother and father arrange their work schedules so that they can take turns being with the baby. In still other families, both parents work full-time and try to find decent day-care facilities.

In any of these cases, but especially if both parents work full-time, the parents discover that they do not have enough hours in the day. One survey found many families in which each parent worked a full-time job and spent an average of 3 to 5 hours per day on house work and child care (Burley, 1991). Under those circumstances, the parents have little time left for recreation or romance.

In many such families, the father and mother find very little time to spend with each other, and their relationship may encounter some tensions. One study reported an interesting, hard-to-interpret correlation: In two-income families, the *more* time the father spent with the child, the *less* the father reported lov-

ing the mother (Crouter, Perry-Jenkins, Huston, & McHale, 1987). What does that correlation mean: The less time he spends with the child, the more time he has for the mother? Or the less he loves the mother, the more he prefers to spend his time with the child instead? Or what? In any event, balancing career needs and family needs is a serious, widespread problem.

Later in this chapter we will discuss two-paycheck families from the child's point of view.

MIDDLE ADULTHOOD

From the 20s until retirement, the main concern of most adults is "What and how much will I produce? Will I make a valuable contribution and achieve significant success?"

These are generally highly productive years in which people take pride and satisfaction in their accomplishments. Middle adulthood lacks some of the excitement of young adulthood but brings a greater sense of security and accomplishment. Middle-aged adults generally have a good sense of how successful they are going to be in their marriage and career.

Job Satisfaction

Adults who are satisfied with their job are generally satisfied with their life, and people who like their life generally like their job (Keon & McDonald, 1982). Some adults manage to be happy even though they work at an unrewarding job, but the daily work routine is bound to have an enormous influence on their satisfaction with life.

How satisfied *are* most workers with their job? The answer depends on how we word the question. When pollsters ask simply, "Are you satisfied with your job?" about 85–90% say yes (Weaver, 1980). But when pollsters ask, "If you could start over, would you seek the same job you have now?" less than half of white-collar workers and only one fourth of blue-collar workers say yes. Although most workers say they are "satisfied" with their job, they could easily imagine being *more* satisfied.

The level of satisfaction is lower, on the average, among young workers than among long-term workers (Bass & Ryterband, 1979). (See Figure 6.33.) One explanation is that older workers have better, higher-paying jobs that offer greater responsibility and challenge. Another is that today's young people are harder to satisfy. But neither of those explanations ac-

Possible reasons why older workers report greater job satisfaction than younger workers

Better pay

Greater responsibility

Greater challenges

Comfort of status quo

Lower expectations

Previous experience in less suitable jobs

FIGURE 6.33
Most older workers report higher job satisfaction than younger workers do. Psychologists identify several reasons.

counts for all the results (Janson & Martin, 1982). Another possibility is that many young workers start in the wrong job and find a more suitable one later on. Yet another is that many young people are still considering the possibility of changing jobs; by age 40 it becomes more difficult to change, and people reconcile themselves to the job they have.

Your choice of career has a profound effect on the quality of your life. A student once told me that he found the courses in his major boring, but at least they were preparing him for a job. I cautioned him that he probably would find that job just as boring. Between the ages of 20 and 70 you will probably spend about half your waking hours on the job—a long time to live with work you find unsatisfying.

The Midlife Transition

People enter adulthood with a great many hopes and goals. Then as they settle into the daily round of activities, they tend to postpone their ambitions. Around age 40, some adults experience a **midlife transition,** a reassessment of their personal goals. Up to this point, they clung to the personal fable that their life would be a success in every way. There was always plenty of time to get that better job, start that family, write that great novel, take that trip up the Amazon, or get that graduate degree. But at

some point they begin to realize that the opportunity to do all these things is rapidly fading, and that if they do not enjoy life now, it probably will not get better later.

The Russian novelist Leo Tolstoy wrote at age 47:

I have lived through the period of childhood, adolescence and youth when I climbed higher and higher up the mysterious hill of life, hoping to find at its summit a result worthy of the effort put in; I have also lived through the period of maturity during which, having reached the summit, I went on calmly and contentedly . . . searching all round me for the fruits of life which I had attained . . . and I have lived through the conviction that nothing of what I expected on this summit was there and that now, only one thing remained to me—to descend to the other side to the place where I came from. And I have begun that descent. . . . I call such a condition old age, and at the present moment I have reached that condition. (Tolstoy, 1875/1978, pp. 288–289).

Daniel Levinson (1977, 1978) reports that about 80% of all adults experience such a midlife transition. Other psychologists deny that the experience is anywhere near that common. The disagreement may be a matter of definition. Most middle-aged adults do not experience a painful midlife transition like the one

"Adults hope that life begins at 40—but the great anxiety is that it ends there."
DANIEL LEVINSON
(1978)

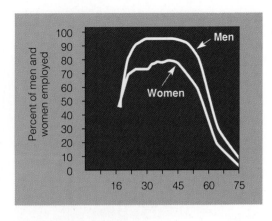

FIGURE 6.35
The percent of people employed rises and falls as a function of age. These figures include students, patients in hospitals, and others who are not looking for a job. (Based on data from U.S. Department of Labor, 1989.)

Tolstoy described, but many go through a minor, nontraumatic readjustment. They review their successes and failures, examine the direction their life is taking, and set new, more realistic goals.

Some adults who go through a midlife transition accept their life as it is. Others refuse to abandon their early goals. Declaring "It's now or never," they train for a new job or take some other positive step—sometimes over the protests of family members who would prefer to play it safe. Still others become depressed and may turn to alcohol or some other means of escape.

■ CONCEPT CHECK

9. *In what way does a midlife transition resemble an adolescent identity crisis? (Check your answer on page 261.)*

OLD AGE

The percentage of people who live into their 70s and 80s has grown steadily throughout the 20th century. An unprecedented number of them retire and remain healthy, active, and independent. Evidently that is particularly true for old African Americans and Native Americans. Members of these two groups have a high probability of dying young, but those who survive to about 75 are generally stronger and healthier

than most European Americans of the same age (Markides & Machalak, 1984). Presumably, minority individuals *have* to be strong and healthy to survive that long in a disadvantaged environment, and once they have made it to 75 they have a good chance to last quite a while longer.

Different people age in different ways. Some people, especially those with Alzheimer's disease or other serious ailments, deteriorate both intellectually and physically, in some cases rapidly. Other older people remain almost as active and alert as ever, well into their 80s or even 90s. One study of intellectually gifted men found that most of them had very little loss of vocabulary after age 70. The main exception to this rule was that they gradually decreased their use of words pertaining to jobs, health, and death (Shneidman, 1989). Presumably, they simply did not wish to discuss these topics.

One common concern of old age is to maintain a sense of dignity and self-esteem. How well older people maintain their dignity depends in large part on how they are treated by their family, their community, and their society (Figure 6.34). Some cultures, including the people of Korea, observe a special ceremony to celebrate a person's retirement or 70th birthday (Damron-Rodriguez, 1991). African-American and Native American families traditionally honor their elders, giving them a position of status and calling upon them for advice. Japanese families follow a similar tradition at least publicly, although many admit in private that they have a less positive attitude toward the elderly (Koyano, 1991).

Many of the changes that people experience as they grow older are determined by society rather than by biology (Schlossberg, 1984). One of those changes is enforced (or encouraged) retirement. Figure 6.35 shows the percentage of people in the United States employed at various ages (U.S. Department of Labor, 1989). For about 40 to 50 years of their life, people spend much of their time at work, taking pride in their accomplishments and enjoying their status. Then sometime between 60 and 70 they face voluntary or mandatory retirement. Many continue to be active, doing volunteer work, taking a part-time job, or serving as a U.S. senator.

People adjust to retirement in different ways (Atchley, 1980). Those who had a variety of interests and engaged in different activities before retirement usually find the adjustment easiest. Most retirees go through a "honeymoon" period at first, doing all the things they never had time to do before. However, their reborn hopes for great achievement soon fade. Just as many 20-year-olds start out with goals they can never achieve, many 65-year-olds enter retirement with hopes that are sure to be disappointed. Within a few months or a few years, they experience something similar to the midlife transition, review their prospects, and settle for more realistic goals.

It is helpful for old people to maintain some sense of control over their lives even if and when their health begins to fail. Consider a person who has spent half a century managing a household or running a business. Now he or she may be living in a nursing home where staff members make all the decisions, from scheduling meals to choosing television programs. The loss of control can be frustrating and degrading. If the staff lets its residents make certain choices on their own and perform some tasks by themselves, their health, alertness, and memory tend to improve (Rodin, 1986; Rowe & Kahn, 1987).

THE PSYCHOLOGY OF FACING DEATH

We commonly associate death with old people, although a person can die at any age. But even a young person who expects to live many years must cope with anxiety about eventually dying.

Not only do we have trouble dealing with the prospect of our own death, but we also find it difficult to deal with the death of others. A dying person finds few listeners who are comfortable talking about death.

Most people deal with anxiety about death by telling themselves that their death is far in the future. When they learn they have a fatal disease, they react in special ways. In her book *On Death and Dying,* Elisabeth Kübler-Ross (1969) suggests that dying people go through five stages of adjustment (see Table 6.11).

Kübler-Ross suggests that all dying people progress through these five stages in the same order. Other observers, however, report that dying people may move from stage to stage in any order and may skip some stages altogether. In any case, these stages represent five common ways of coping with the imminent prospect of death.

Something to Think About

Do Kübler-Ross's stages apply only to people who are dying? Or do people react in similar fashion to lesser losses, such as a poor grade or the loss of a job? Have you ever had a personal experience in which you went through some of these same stages?

SUMMARY

- *Cross-sectional and longitudinal studies.* Psychologists study development by means of cross-sectional studies, which examine people of different ages at the same time, and by means of longitudinal studies, which look at a single group of people at different times as they grow older. Each method has its advantages and disadvantages. (page 245.)

- *Cohort effects.* In some cases a difference between young people and old people is not due to age itself but to a cohort effect: The people born in one era differ from those born in a different era. (page 246)

- *Erikson's ages of development.* Erik Erikson described the human lifespan as a series of eight ages, each with its own social and emotional conflicts. (page 247.)

- *Infant attachment.* The attachment of an infant to his or her mother depends on the comfort of physical contact rather than on being fed. Both infant monkeys and infant humans need social

"A man who has not found something he is willing to die for is not fit to live."
MARTIN LUTHER KING, JR.

"This is perhaps the greatest lesson we learned from our patients: LIVE, so you do not have to look back and say, 'God, how I have wasted my life!'"
ELISABETH KÜBLER-ROSS (1975)

"The worst thing about death is the fact that when a man is dead it's impossible any longer to undo the harm you have done him, or to do the good you haven't done him. They say: live in such a way as to be always ready to die. I would say: live in such a way that anyone can die without you having anything to regret."
LEO TOLSTOY (1865/1978, p. 192)

Table 6.11 Kübler-Ross's Five Stages of Adjustment to Death

Stage	Behavior or Experience of People Who Are Dying	Characteristic Expression
Denial	Refuse to acknowledge their condition; may visit several physicians or faith healers in search of someone to restore their health	"No, not me; it cannot be true"
Anger	Criticize and rage at doctors, nurses, and relatives	"Why me?"
Bargaining	Promise good behavior in exchange for the granting of a wish, usually the extension of life; those who do not believe in God may try to strike a bargain with the doctor	"Get me through this, God, and I'll give half my money to the church" or "Doc, give me some medicine that will make me well again, and here's what I'll do for you"
Depression	Sadness at losing what is past and sadness because of impending losses	"All I can do is wait for the bitter end"
Acceptance	Show little emotion of any sort; do not wish to be stirred up by news of the outside world, even by a potential new treatment to prolong life; psychologically ready to die	"The final rest before the long journey"

Source: Kübler-Ross, 1969.

contact and attention if they are to develop normal social behaviors. (page 249)

■ *Social development of children.* The social development of a child depends on the influences of other children, including brothers and sisters. (page 251)

■ *Adolescent identity crisis.* Adolescents have to deal with an identity crisis, the question "Who am I?" Many experiment with several identities before deciding which one seems right. (page 252)

■ *Adolescent sexual concerns.* Adolescents also have to make decisions about sexual behavior. Dating couples vary to a great degree in how intimate they become sexually and how soon. (page 253)

■ *Young adults' concerns.* One of the main concerns of young adults is the decision to marry or to establish some other lasting relationship. Many also have to deal with the competing demands of family and career. (page 254)

■ *Middle adulthood.* For most adults, satisfaction with life is closely linked with satisfaction on the job. Some adults experience a midlife transition in which they reevaluate their goals. (page 256)

■ *Old age.* In old age, people make new adjustments, including the adjustment to retirement. Maintaining dignity and independence is a key concern. (page 258)

■ *Facing death.* People at all ages have to face the anxieties associated with the fact that we eventually die. People go through some characteristic reactions when they know that they are likely to die soon. (page 259)

SUGGESTIONS FOR FURTHER READING

Elkind, D. (1984). *All grown up and no place to go.* Reading, MA: Addison-Wesley. An account of the problems teenagers and young adults face.

Sheehy, G. (1977). *Passages.* New York: Bantam. Describes the problems and crises that people face from young adulthood through old age.

Tavris, C., & Offir, C. (1977). *The longest war.* New York: Harcourt Brace Jovanovich. A highly engaging account of sex roles, the differences between women and men, and the relationships that form between women and men.

TERMS

cross-sectional study a study of groups of individuals of different ages all at the same time (page 245)

longitudinal study a study of a single group of individuals over time (page 245)

cohort a group of people born at a particular time (as compared to people born at different times) (page 246)

basic trust versus mistrust the conflict between trusting and mistrusting that one's parents and other key figures will meet one's basic needs; first conflict in Erikson's eight ages of human development (page 247)

autonomy versus shame and doubt the conflict between independence and doubt about one's abilities (page 247)

initiative versus guilt the conflict between independent behavior and behavior inhibited by guilt (page 247)

industry versus inferiority the conflict between feelings of accomplishment and feelings of worthlessness (page 247)

identity versus role confusion the conflict between the sense of self and the confusion over one's identity (page 248)

intimacy versus isolation the conflict between establishing a long-term relationship with another person and remaining alone (page 248)

generativity versus stagnation the conflict between a productive life and an unproductive life (page 248)

ego integrity versus despair the conflict between satisfaction and dissatisfaction with one's life; final conflict in Erikson's eight ages of human development (page 248)

attachment a long-term feeling of closeness between people, such as a child and a care giver (page 249)

parallel play simultaneous but independent play, common in young children (page 251)

identity crisis the search for self-understanding (page 252)

identity foreclosure the acceptance of a role that a person's parents prescribe (page 252)

role diffusion experimentation with various roles or identities (page 252)

moratorium a delay in resolving an identity crisis (page 252)

identity achievement the deliberate choice of a role or identity (page 252)

puberty the time of onset of sexual maturation (page 253)

midlife transition a time of reassessment of one's goals (page 257)

ANSWERS TO CONCEPT CHECKS

6. Use a longitudinal study. A longitudinal study studies the same people repeatedly instead of comparing one cohort with another. (page 247)

7. Use a cross-sectional study, comparing people of different ages all in the same year. (page 247)

8. Both the institutions and the Harlows' monkeys failed to provide the social contact necessary for infants to learn how to relate to others. (page 251)

9. In both a midlife transition and an adolescent identity crisis, people reexamine their goals, plan for the future, and decide who they are or who they want to be. (page 258)

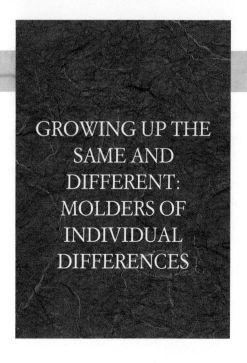

GROWING UP THE SAME AND DIFFERENT: MOLDERS OF INDIVIDUAL DIFFERENCES

Are people's temperamental differences consistent as they grow older?

How does family life guide children's social and emotional development?

In what ways do boys and girls differ, and why?

How does ethnic identity influence development?

If you have ever read *Uncle Tom's Cabin,* you were no doubt dumbstruck by the unrelenting cruelty of the slave-owner Simon Legree. You may have remarked to yourself, "If I had been Simon Legree, I wouldn't have acted that way." An interesting comment, that. If you had been Simon Legree, you wouldn't have been *you!* You would have been born in a different time and a different place, perhaps of a different race and a different sex, and surrounded by a different family. If a child born in that setting had most of the same genes you have, perhaps that child would develop to be somewhat similar to the person you are today. But "somewhat similar" is as much as we can expect.

Each of us is a unique individual, influencing our environment as well as being influenced by it. But each of us is also male or female and a member of a particular family, a particular society, and a particular ethnic group. You and I are complex products of what we bring to the situation (our personality and temperament) and what the situation does to us. Let us begin with temperament.

TEMPERAMENT AND LIFELONG DEVELOPMENT

People differ markedly in their **temperament**—their tendency to be active or inactive, outgoing or reserved. Would you rather go to a party where you will meet new people, or would you prefer to spend a quiet evening with a few old friends? Do you like to try a new, somewhat risky adventure, or would you prefer to watch while someone else tries it first? In general, are you more impulsive or more reserved than most of the people you know?

Now, the way you just described yourself: Is that the way you have always been, more or less? Or have you changed considerably? Were you at one time a great deal more outgoing and adventurous, or more shy and reserved, than you are now?

According to the research, most people are fairly consistent in their temperament over long periods of time, at least in certain regards. We can begin to measure temperament even in young children. Jerome Kagan and Nancy Snidman (1991) measured how often 4-month-old infants kicked, how often they cried, and how tense their hands were. A few months later they examined the same infants' responses to mildly frightening situations. (For example, the experimenter might uncover a rotating toy, frown, and scream a nonsense phrase.) Infants who showed the most kicking, crying, and tension at age 4 months tended to show the most fears at ages 9 and 14 months. That is, their temperament was consistent from one test to the next.

▪ CONCEPT CHECK

10. *Was Kagan and Snidman's study longitudinal or cross-sectional? (Check your answer on page 273.)*

Infants who seldom kick, cry, or show fears are called "easy" or "uninhibited" (Thomas & Chess, 1980; Thomas, Chess, & Birch, 1968). Easy infants develop regular sleeping and eating habits, show interest in new people and new objects, and are easily comforted. The kicking, crying, highly fearful infants are, as you might guess, termed "difficult" or "inhibited." Their eating and sleeping habits are irregular, they show frequent signs of tension, and they are hard to comfort (Kagan, 1989). They are also more likely to contract various contagious diseases (Lewis, Thomas, & Worobey, 1990). Evidently, temperament is connected to all aspects of how the body functions. Not all infants fit into either the "inhibited" or "uninhibited" categories; many are intermediate. Some fit the special category "slow to warm up": They withdraw at first from unfamiliar people and new experiences, but after repeated exposures they begin to react positively.

How long do temperaments last? In many cases for years. Infants identified as highly inhibited at the age of 21 months end up, with few exceptions, as shy, quiet, nervous, and fearful 7 1/2-year-olds (Kagan, Reznick, & Snidman, 1988). Infants identified as uninhibited develop into socially interactive, highly talkative 7 1/2-year-olds. Eventually, longitudinal studies will follow such children into adulthood to tell us whether temperament is constant over a lifetime.

What causes differences in temperament? Genetic differences make some contribution. Monozygotic (identical) twins resemble each other in temperament more than dizygotic (fraternal) twins do (Matheny, 1989). Even monozygotic twins reared in separate and apparently rather different environments generally end up with similar temperaments (Bouchard, Lykken, McGue, Segal, & Tellegen, 1990). Environmental factors obviously play a major role also; otherwise, monozygotic twins would always match each other exactly in temperament.

Heredity and environment can interact in some complex ways to influence temperament. Furthermore, a child's developing temperament can alter the environment, which in turn influences the further development of temperament (Bouchard et al., 1990; Collins & Gunnar, 1990). For example, a child with an uninhibited temperament will meet more people and try more new experiences than an inhibited child will; in doing so, the child learns new skills and develops new behaviors that alter later reactions to new situations.

THE FAMILY

One of the most powerful influences in the human environment is the family. How children feel about themselves—good or bad, successful or worthless—depends to a large degree on their relationship with family members. Children in a loving family learn, "I am a lovable person." They also gain a sense of security. By playing with brothers, sisters, or other children, they begin to learn social skills. They also learn social skills by observation, especially by watching how their parents relate to each other. How do variations in early family environments affect a child's social and emotional development?

Parental Employment and Child Care

For many years, psychologists assumed that most children grew up in a so-called traditional family, which consisted of a working father, a housekeeping mother, and one or more children. At one time psychoanalysts believed young children needed to develop an almost exclusive relationship with their mother or a single mother-substitute in order to develop a good adjustment. Today, a clear majority of mothers have at least a part-time job (a situation discussed from the adult's perspective in the previous module), and most young children develop attachments to several adult care givers. How does that experience affect their development?

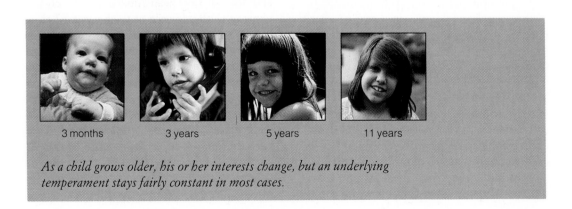

3 months   3 years   5 years   11 years

As a child grows older, his or her interests change, but an underlying temperament stays fairly constant in most cases.

FIGURE 6.36

As you might guess, the effects of day care on children's development depend on the quality of that care, and the quality varies enormously in the United States.

Two-Paycheck Families In 1960, only one fifth of American mothers of preschool children had jobs outside the home. In the 1980s, half or more had jobs (Rubenstein, 1985). When both the father and the mother spend most of the day at work and have only a limited amount of time to spend with their children, how does that affect the child?

The results vary. Some mothers of young children work at unsatisfying jobs because they need the money. If they are unhappy about working, they return from work in an unpleasant mood that interferes with their effectiveness as mothers (Lamb, 1982). Other mothers work because they enjoy their careers. They return from work with high self-esteem; they make good use of the time they have available with their children. They become role models for their daughters, who are likely to develop career aspirations of their own (Hoffman, 1989).

Preschool children in two-paycheck families are left in various day-care arrangements while the parents are at work (Figure 6.36). The effects on the children depend on the quality of the day care and the age of the child. When children less than a year old are entrusted to day-care centers where the staff is indifferent and unstable, the children are likely to feel insecure. If the day care is reasonably good, however, and if the parents provide good attention at night and on weekends, the children seem to develop about as well as children who spend all

day with a parent (Scarr, Phillips, & McCartney, 1990). Children who spend much of their first year of life in day care tend to be a bit "bossy" and disobedient, but they also develop self-confidence and social skills in dealing with other children (Clarke-Stewart, 1989).

Fathers as Care Givers of Young Children
Traditionally, mothers have spent more time than have fathers taking care of children, especially young children. But fathers have always played an important role (Lamb, 1974). They engage more often in vigorous, stimulating play with their children and serve as role models for both sons and daughters. In homes where the father is absent or where the parents are hostile toward each other, the children often have difficulty relating to the opposite sex in later years.

In some families, the mother works full-time and the father stays home as the primary care giver of young children. Fathers in such families resemble other fathers more than they resemble mothers. They are about as strict and disciplinary as more traditional fathers are (Radin, 1982). Although they play with their children more than the mothers do, they hug them less and talk to them less (Lamb, Frodi, Hwang, & Frodi, 1982). Generally, these untraditional fathers seem to make adequate parents, and their children seem to develop normally.

Parental Conflict and Divorce

At an earlier time in the United States, divorce was unusual and frowned upon. When Adlai Stevenson was defeated in the presidential campaign of 1952, one explanation was that "American voters will never elect a divorced candidate as President." By 1980 when Ronald Reagan was elected President, his having divorced and remarried was not an issue at all. Divorce was simply a fact of life.

An estimated 75% of African-American and 38% of European-American children will experience the divorce of their parents before the children reach age 16. Most of those children show a variety of academic, social, and emotional problems, compared to children in two-parent households. One reason is that children in divorced families receive less attention and suffer greater economic hardships. The main reason, however, is that children in divorced families have to endure prolonged conflict and hostility between their parents (Amato & Keith, 1991). If the divorce is completed while the children are still too young to realize what is happening, the effects on the children are milder (Tschann, Johnston, Kline, & Wallerstein, 1990).

Mavis Hetherington and her associates have conducted longitudinal studies of middle-class elementary-school children and their families following a divorce (Hetherington, 1989; Hetherington, Cox, & Cox, 1982). In each case, the mother had custody of the children. Hetherington found that most of the children and many of the parents suffered considerable upheaval after the divorce, especially during the first year.

During this first year the children resorted to pouting and seeking attention. They were generally angry about their parents' divorce, and they let the parents know about it. Many of the mothers had very difficult relationships with their sons; one exasperated divorced mother described the relationship as "like getting bitten to death by ducks." Boys in particular became very aggressive toward other children, and much of their aggressive behavior was unprovoked and ineffective (Figure 6.37). After 2 years they became better adjusted, but by then they had been rejected by their peers. Boys who changed schools after the first year managed to escape their reputation and make a fresh start.

The degree of distress varied from one child to another. Generally, a child's distress was greater if the mother had not worked before the divorce and had taken a job immediately afterward—often an economic necessity. The children in such families felt they had lost both their father and their mother. In the studies by Hetherington and her associates, boys showed more distress and more negative behavior than girls did, partly because the mothers retained custody of the children. When the father had custody, the boys reacted better than the girls did (Santrock, Warshak, & Elliott, 1982). (However, because many other factors are at work, we cannot conclude that a father should always be granted custody of sons or that a mother should always be granted custody of daughters.)

In families in which the mother remarried, girls generally had more trouble accepting the stepfather than boys did. Hetherington (1989) found that many of the girls rejected every attempt their stepfathers made to establish a positive relationship; eventually the stepfather simply gave up. When stepfathers were asked to name all the "members of your family," most did not even mention their stepdaughters.

Hetherington's studies concentrated on white middle-class children, and the results are

FIGURE 6.37
Sons of divorced parents often go through a period in which they act out their frustrations by starting fights.

somewhat different for other cultures. Divorce is more common in African-American families, and in most cases less stressful (Fine & Schwebel, 1987). Apparently, most African-American families accept the idea of single parenthood better than most white families do. In addition, many African-American families ease the burden of single parenthood by having a grandmother or other relative share in the child care. As in white families, the more upset the mother is by the divorce, the more upset the children are likely to be (Phillips & Alcebo, 1986).

To almost any generalization about the effects of divorce on children, exceptions can be found (Hetherington, Stanley-Hagan, & Anderson, 1989). Some children show emotional distress for a year or two and then gradually feel better. Others continue to act depressed 5 or 10 years after the divorce. A few seem to do well for a while and then show signs of distress years later, especially during adolescence. Some children are amazingly resilient through their parents' divorce and afterward. They keep their friends; they do all right in school; they maintain good relationships with both parents. Generally these are children who were well adjusted before the divorce and whose parents displayed a minimum of conflict toward each other (Hetherington, 1989; Kline, Tschann, Johnston, & Wallerstein, 1989).

Given the emotional trauma commonly associated with divorce, should parents stick together? Staying together is not always a workable solution. Children who grow up in households in which the parents are constantly in conflict develop emotional problems similar to those of children in divorced families (Emery, 1982). Indeed, most children (especially boys) in divorced families begin to show signs of distress years *before* the divorce itself, perhaps in response to the parental conflict they already see (Cherlin et al., 1991).

THE INFLUENCE OF GENDER

In what ways would you be different if you had been born female instead of male, or male instead of female? We all have certain impressions of how boys act differently from girls, and men from women. But how many of those impressions are correct, how many are exaggerations, and how many are simply false? Remember the phenomenon of *illusory correlations* from Chapter 2: We tend to remember most clearly the examples that fit some pattern we expect to find; we therefore convince ourselves that our expectations were correct. Sex differences do occur, but we have to base our conclusions on systematic data and not on casual impressions.

Sex Differences in Behavior

In 1974, Eleanor Maccoby and Carol Jacklin published an extensive review of the literature on sex differences in behavior. They concluded that the evidence supported a few generalizations. For example, females tend to perform better on certain aspects of language use, whereas males tend to perform better on certain mathematical and visual-spatial tasks. Those differences are marked in adolescents and adults, but doubtful in children. In addition, males tend to fight more. Sex differences in other aspects of behavior were possible, but not clear from the evidence (Maccoby & Jacklin, 1974).

Maccoby and Jacklin's review drew two kinds of criticisms. First, some argued that they had ignored or understated many behavioral differences between the sexes: On the average, men swear more than women. Women tend to know more than men do about flowers. Men and women generally carry books and packages in different ways (Figure 6.38). A list of miscellaneous differences could go on.

Second, others argued that Maccoby and Jacklin had overstated the differences, and that

FIGURE 6.38
One of many poorly understood differences between the sexes: Beyond the age of puberty, most males carry packages at their side, whereas females carry them in an elevated position.

in fact males and females hardly differ at all. According to this point of view, boys and girls—and men and women—act differently only because our society tells them to. (Actually, even if true, this is not a fair criticism of Maccoby and Jacklin, who were trying to describe the differences, not to explain them.)

Much time has passed since Maccoby and Jacklin's 1974 review. Most of the same conclusions still hold, although we must modify them somewhat (Maccoby, 1990). For example, the advantage of females on verbal tasks seems to have faded (for reasons unknown). New evidence has indicated that women are, on the average, more easily influenced by other people's opinions. (Depending on your point of view, you could say that women are more "conformist" or that men are more "stubborn.") New evidence also indicates sex differences in helping behavior. It is not a simple case of one sex being more helpful than the other; men and women tend to help in different ways. For example, men are generally more likely to help a stranger change a flat tire; women are more

FIGURE 6.39
One girl tested alone behaves about the same as one boy tested alone. But when boys play together, they "show off" to one another and to other observers.

likely to help people who need long-term nurturing support (Eagly & Crowley, 1986).

Sex Differences in Social Situations   It is now clear that certain important differences between males and females emerge only in a social context (Maccoby, 1990). Psychologists ordinarily test people in isolation. When tested one at a time, boys and girls tend to behave about the same in most regards. However, in a group setting, boys usually get together with other boys while girls get together with other girls; suddenly the two groups act very differently (Figure 6.39).

Girls sometimes play competitive games, but they are more likely than boys to spend long times at quiet, cooperative play. They take turns; they present their desires as "suggestions" instead of demands; they exchange compliments; and they generally try to avoid hurting each other's feelings.

Meanwhile, boys are almost always competing with each other. They compete even when they are just talking: They shout orders, they interrupt, they make threats and boasts, and they exchange insults. Their play is often rough and aggressive and almost always competitive. That is, someone wins and someone loses. When a group of elementary-school boys play baseball, sooner or later they have some dispute about the rules; invariably they work out some compromise and continue playing, but they may continue screaming "you cheater" or "you liar" while they continue playing. Still, when the game is over, they almost always part as friends.

When they grow up, do boys change their way of interacting with one another? Not entirely. Deborah Tannen (1990) reports one episode at a college basketball game: At the University of Michigan, student tickets have seat numbers on them, but students generally ignore those assignments and take seats on a first-come, first-served basis. One night several men from the visiting team, Michigan State, tried to go to the seats listed on their tickets, only to find some University of Michigan students already seated there, including both men and women. The Michigan State students asked the others to get out of their seats; the men in those seats then replied rudely, and the dispute quickly grew loud, heated, and insulting. The women with these men were mortified with embarrassment. Within a few minutes, however, the Michigan State men settled into seats next to the University of Michigan students, and before long the two sets of men were happily discussing basketball strategies. The women didn't understand; they would not have screamed insults at anyone in the first place, but if they had done so, they would have become enemies for life. They certainly would not have enjoyed a friendly conversation with them a few minutes later.

Male-Female Relationships in Childhood and Adulthood What do you suppose happens when boys and girls play together? If they are working on a task that requires cooperation, few sex differences are evident (Powlishta & Maccoby, 1990). However, in an unsupervised situation with no need to cooperate, the boys often dominate and intimidate the girls. In some cases, the boys play and the girls simply watch (Maccoby, 1990).

When boys and girls become young men and women, romantic interests may draw them together. Both are ill prepared to deal with the other sex. Men are used to demanding their way; women are used to a cooperative give-and-take. Men worry about their status in relation to other men; women often do not understand these status contests. When women discuss their problems, they expect their listeners to express sympathy; men often do not understand this need. Here are some examples of the resultant misunderstanding (Tannen, 1990):

■ A man invites an out-of-town friend to spend the night in a guest bedroom. The man's wife is upset that her husband did not check with her before inviting his friend. He replies that he would feel embarrassed to say "I have to ask my wife first."

■ A woman asks her husband to get their VCR to record movies off television. The husband says this particular kind of VCR plays tapes but cannot record. The woman then asks their next-door neighbor to check the VCR. He too tells her the VCR cannot record tapes. The husband remains angry about this episode for years, because his wife implied he was incompetent to understand their VCR.

■ A woman who has breast surgery tells her husband she is unhappy about the scar left by the surgery. Instead of expressing sympathy, he replies, "You can have plastic surgery. . . ." She is upset with the implication that he doesn't like the way she looks. He replies that he doesn't care about the scar; he was trying to help because *she* said she was unhappy.

Are male-female relationships always like this? Of course not. Men are not all the same; neither are women. Men can sometimes be very sympathetic, just as women can sometimes be very competitive. The point is that the sexes dif-fer on the average, and that men and women need to work at understanding one another's point of view.

Gender Roles

Given that men and women differ on the average in many social behaviors, the question is: Why? Chances are, there are several reasons. Biology is probably one factor. Competition among males for status is extremely widespread in the animal kingdom; it is probably part of our basic nature. But people are also molded by culture. Even if males are biologically predisposed to be more aggressive or females to be more cooperative, their culture channels the ways they express those tendencies.

In one way or another, each society teaches its children how they are expected to behave. In particular, it prepares boys for the tasks expected of men and it prepares women for the tasks expected of women. That is, it teaches them their *gender role*. A gender role is the psychological aspect of being male or female, as opposed to sex, which is the biological aspect. **Gender role** is the role each person is expected to play because of being male or female.

When we say that "society" teaches children their gender role, that does not necessarily mean that *adults* teach children their gender role, or that *anyone* teaches gender roles deliberately or intentionally. Adults, especially parents, do teach children gender roles to some extent. Parents dress boys differently from girls, give them different toys, and offer them different kinds of experiences (Figure 6.40). The choice of toys in turn determines how much the parents talk with the children while they are playing. When parents and their children play with dolls, they talk a great deal; when they play with cars and trucks, they talk less (O'Brien & Nagle, 1987). Adults also teach gender roles by example. Boys tend to imitate their father, and girls tend to imitate their mother. Television presents certain images of what men and women do. Children also pay attention to role models outside the home. For instance, a girl who goes to a female pediatrician may think of becoming a doctor herself.

However, in our society, most adults do *not* teach boys that they are supposed to fight with one another. In fact, they usually try to curb the fighting. Little boys tend to be bossy and aggressive toward little girls if they think no adults are watching; with an adult present, they become more cooperative (Powlishta & Maccoby, 1990).

FIGURE 6.40
Children learn their gender roles partly from their parents. But parents who try to treat their sons and daughters alike discover that children also learn roles from other children.

And yet, clearly, little boys do learn to compete and fight with one another, even if adults are trying to teach them to stop. Where does this part of their gender role come from? From whom are they learning it? Quite simply, they learn it from other children. Children have a "playground culture" of their own; each cohort of children teaches the slightly younger set what is expected of them. Even parents who try to raise their sons and daughters exactly the same find that their children come back from the playground with strong prejudices about what boys do and what girls do.

Gender roles are not altogether independent of biology; they interact with biology. For example, consider boys' tendency to fight more than girls do. Assuming that boys have, on the average, at least a slight biological predisposition to be aggressive and competitive, boys learn by observation on the playground that other boys tend to be aggressive. To get along in that child society, they have to learn to compete, and what they learn augments their biological predisposition.

In many cases, of course, gender roles have no close or direct relationship with biology. In Western society, tradition tells us that women should wear their hair longer than men, that women will do more of the cooking, and that men will try to repair cars and other machinery.

Such differences seem arbitrary. Certainly, the roles of men and women vary drastically from one society to another (Figure 6.41) and from one time to another in a given society. In the United States early in the 20th century, women could not vote, few attended college, and employment opportunities for women were very limited. In a period of decades all those customs and more have changed. Our biology does not dictate our customs.

Gender roles are not necessarily harmful in all cases, but they sometimes limit the choices children feel will be open to them in later life. Imagine an artistically inclined boy who is told that "real men like sports, not art." Or imagine a girl who wants to become an electrical engineer until someone tells her that "engineering is not a good career for a woman." Ideally, children (and adults) should feel free to develop their own interests and their own talents, whatever they may be.

■ CONCEPT CHECK

11. *Which of the following (if any) are examples of people following gender roles? (Check your answer on page 273.)*

    a. A woman's ability to nurse a baby
    b. A boy's interest in playing football
    c. A girl's interest in ballet
    d. A man's beard growth

FIGURE 6.41
Gender roles vary greatly from one culture to another. In the United States, gender roles are more flexible now than they once were. Many women hold jobs previously reserved for men.

ETHNIC AND CULTURAL INFLUENCES

Minority-group children are subject to several influences that mold their behavior differently from that of others. First, the customs and attitudes of their own ethnic group may be different from those of other people. Second, the mere fact of belonging to a minority group implies "I am different." Third, the discrimination against certain minority groups sometimes leads to economic and emotional hardship (McLoyd, 1990), but also encourages extra efforts in the areas of achievement where the barriers are weakest. For example, one explanation for the high academic success of so many Asian-Americans (Figure 6.42) is that they have limited opportunities for employment, so they take pride in their education (Sue & Okazaki, 1990).

Minority Children's Self-Esteem

One of the unfortunate facts of life for minority-group members is that many people treat them as group members and not as individuals. Consequently, their self-esteem is closely tied to their image of the whole group. That is, it is hard to think highly of yourself unless you also think highly of your ethnic group.

For many years, especially prior to the 1950s, studies in the United States reported that most African-American children had a relatively low self-esteem. For example, Kenneth Clark and Mamie Clark (1947) offered 252 African-American children ages 3 to 7 a choice among two white dolls and two black dolls, and then asked some questions about the dolls. Most of these children (67%) chose one of the white dolls to play with. In response to questions, most picked a white doll as the one that looked "nice" and a black doll as the one that looked "bad." Finally the experimenters asked which doll "looks like you." Most hesitated and then selected a black doll, often with signs of great distress. Several cried at this point, and two ran out of the testing room.

The Clarks argued that school segregation was one of the main reasons for the low self-esteem of African-American children. At this time, African-American children in the southeastern states were not permitted to attend the same schools as white children. The state governments defended this system by saying that the two school systems were "separate but

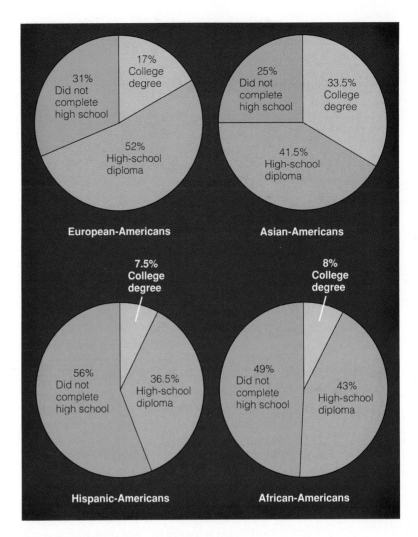

FIGURE 6.42
More Asian-Americans complete high school and college than do members of other ethnic groups in the United States. The percentages change for each group from year to year.

equal." The Clarks and other psychologists replied that even if the two systems really did offer equal educations (which they did not), the fact of segregation itself made them inherently unequal. Segregation necessarily told the African-American children, "You are not as good as others."

In 1954, Kenneth Clark and other psychologists presented their evidence and arguments to the U.S. Supreme Court, in one of the first cases in which psychological evidence influenced the Court. In the now-famous decision of *Brown vs. Board of Education,* the Supreme Court ruled that segregated schools violated the rights of all children to equal protection under the law; it ordered school districts to open all public schools equally to members of all races.

In 1954 the U.S. Supreme Court required the racial integration of all public schools, partly because it believed integration would aid minority children's self-esteem. Their self-esteem did increase, but not until much later.

At that point, many psychologists expected that the schools would quickly desegregate, that minority children's self-esteem would climb, and that minority children's academic accomplishments would soon catch up with those of white children. Those expectations turned out to be naive (Stephan, 1978). School districts found creative ways to delay desegregation, and when it finally did occur it often took place amid hostile attitudes, hardly supportive of minority children's self-esteem or accomplishments. Furthermore, little attention was given to helping minority children overcome years of poor preparation (Cook, 1979; Gerard, 1983). Imagine a sixth-grade African-American child from a poorly equipped school that did not even have textbooks, who is suddenly thrust into a competitive classroom with white children who had been receiving a much better education.

The self-esteem of African-American children remained low for years but began to improve after the 1960s; today it is about equal to that of European-American children (Spurlock, 1986). The reasons for this improvement are not obvious. Perhaps desegregated schools eventually had the desired effects. Self-esteem may also have increased because of the civil rights movement of the 1960s, Black History month, and many other influences.

Minority Children's Academic Performance

Academic achievement has been gradually increasing among minority children, although much room for improvement still remains. In an effort to understand the reasons behind disappointing academic achievement, many educators have looked for ethnic or cultural differences in how children learn. That is, some children might learn better with one style of teaching while other children learn better with a different style (Dunn & Griggs, 1990). For example, several studies have found that Native American children have special strengths in visual memory and observational learning. However, so far no one has demonstrated that styles of teaching based on these strengths make any significant difference in children's academic achievement (Kleinfeld & Nelson, 1991).

According to Diane Scott-Jones, who conducted extensive observations of impoverished African-American children in their own homes, it may be difficult to help low-achieving children unless we can help their parents as well. She found that many mothers of low-achieving children spent much time trying to help their children with schoolwork; however, in many cases the mothers (who were poorly educated themselves) were teaching the children incorrect information (Scott-Jones, 1984).

CLOSING COMMENTS

Each of us can easily fall into the trap of thinking that our own way of growing up and of relating to other people is the "right" way, the "normal" way. In fact, people differ substantially in their social development; we have examined some of the major reasons—temperament, family influences, gender, and ethnic and cultural identity. As a society, we are coming both to recognize and to appreciate the resulting diversity of behavior.

SUMMARY

- *Temperament.* Even infants only a few months old show clear differences in temperament, their characteristic way of reacting to new experiences and new people. Temperament is fairly consistent as a person grows older. (p. 262)

- *Changes in the U.S. family.* As U.S. society has changed over the decades, the role of women has changed and therefore family life has changed. The research suggests that children who spend much of their early life in a day-care arrangement can develop without difficulties, provided that the day care is of good quality. (page 263)

- *Effects of divorce.* Children of divorcing families often show signs of distress, sometimes even before the divorce. The distress is generally more marked in European-American families than in African-American families. (page 264)

- *Male-female differences.* Behavioral differences between males and females are small, on the average, when people are tested one at a time. However, in social settings males tend to associate with other males while females associate with females. Males tend to be more competitive, sometimes aggressively. (page 266)

- *Gender roles.* Men and women differ in their behavior partly as a result of gender roles, the behaviors each society specifies for men and for women. (page 268)

- *Ethnic and cultural differences.* People also differ because of ethnic and cultural influences. Decades ago, African-American children had very low self-esteem; their self-esteem has, however, increased. African-American and Native American children have shown some improvement in their academic performance over the years; psychologists are not certain what methods would encourage further improvement. (page 271)

SUGGESTIONS FOR FURTHER READING

Hetherington, E. M. (1989). Coping with family transitions: Winners, losers, and survivors. *Child Development, 60,* 1–14. Review of the effects of divorce on children.

Kagan, J., & Snidman, N. (1991). Infant predictors of inhibited and uninhibited profiles. *Psychological Science, 2,* 40–44. Discussion of research on temperament in young children.

Maccoby, E. E. (1990). Gender and relationships. *American Psychologist, 45,* 513–520. Review of findings concerning sex differences in social behavior.

Tannen, D. (1990). *You just don't understand.* New York: William Morrow. A popular book discussing the ways in which men and women fail to understand one another.

TERMS

temperament people's tendency to be active or inactive, outgoing or reserved (page 262)

gender role the role each person is expected to play because of being male or female (page 268)

ANSWERS TO CONCEPT CHECKS

10. Kagan and Snidman's study was longitudinal; they studied the same children at more than one age. (page 262)

11. A boy who becomes interested in football and a girl who becomes interested in ballet are examples of people following gender roles. The other two are not. (Gender roles are psychological, not physical.) (page 269)

7 LEARNING

Suppose we set up a simple experiment on animal learning. We put a monkey midway between a green wall and a red wall. If it approaches the green wall, we give it a few raisins; if it approaches the red wall, it gets nothing. After a few trials, the monkey always approaches the green wall. After it has made the correct choice, say, 15 times in a row, we are satisfied that the monkey has learned.

Now let's suppose we conduct the same experiment on an alligator. We use the same procedure as with the monkey, but we get different results. The alligator strains our patience, sitting for hours at a time without approaching either wall. When it finally moves, it is as likely to approach one wall as the other. After hundreds of trials, *we* have learned something: not to go into the trained-alligator business. But we see little evidence that the alligator has learned anything.

Does this mean that alligators are slow learners? Not necessarily. Maybe they are just not motivated to seek food. Maybe they cannot see the difference between red and green. Maybe they learn but also forget fast, so that they can never put together a long streak of consecutive correct turns. To decide whether or not alligators can learn, we would have to test them under a wide variety of circumstances. (I don't know whether you care, but yes, alligators can learn. They're not much good at learning to find food, but they can learn how to get away from unpleasant stimuli, according to Davidson, 1966.)

Some similar problems arise in evaluating human learning. Suppose little Joey is having great academic troubles. Should we consider him a "slow learner"? Not necessarily. Like the alligator, Joey may not be properly motivated, or he may have trouble seeing or hearing, or he may have a tendency to forget. Maybe he has trouble in school because he is distracted by his emotional troubles at home. (That's a possibility we probably wouldn't consider for the alligator.) We can imagine all sorts of other reasons why he might be having trouble.

Psychologists have spent an enormous amount of time studying animal learning. One of the main things they have learned is how important it is to consider all sorts of confounding influences that might interfere with learned performance. That is one of many important messages we gain from the experimental study of learning.

This chapter is about learning *behaviors*: why you lick your lips at the sight of tasty food, why you turn away from a food that once made you sick, why you get nervous if a police car starts to follow you, and why you shudder at the sight of a ferocious person with a chain saw. It is also about why you work harder at some tasks than at others and why you sometimes take so long before you give up. Chapter 8 deals with the learning of facts and ideas—the kind of learning that schools try to promote.

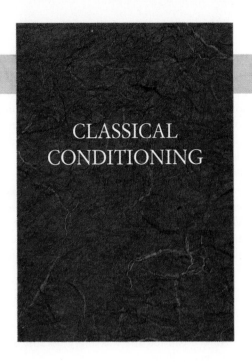

CLASSICAL CONDITIONING

When we learn a relationship between two stimuli, what happens?

Do we start responding to one stimulus as if it were the other?

Or do we learn how to use information from one stimulus to predict something about the other?

Y ou are sitting alone in your room when you hear the doorknob turn. You look up because you know your roommate is about to enter the room. A few moments later you can see from a facial expression that your roommate is in a foul mood, so you say nothing. Your roommate flicks a switch on the stereo and you flinch because you know the stereo is set to a deafening noise level.

You are responding to sensory stimuli, but you are not just responding to the stimuli themselves; you are responding to what they predict. The turn of the doorknob by itself would be of little interest except that it means someone is about to enter the room. The flick of a switch on the stereo by itself is a soft sound; you flinch because this sound predicts a much louder one. At some point you learned what each of these stimuli predicts.

Much of our behavior consists of learned responses to simple signals. Can all behavior be analyzed into such simple units? Some psychol-

ogists have said yes: Behavior is the sum of many simple stimulus-response connections.

However, even those apparently simple responses to simple stimuli no longer seem as simple as they once did. To explain even the simplest learned responses, we have to give the individual credit for having processed a great deal of information.

In their efforts to discover what takes place during learning, psychologists have conducted thousands of experiments, many of them on nonhuman animals. The underlying idea is that the behavior of a rat or a fish is likely to be easier to understand than that of a human. Furthermore, if we discover that the learned behavior of, say, a rat is highly complex, then it is safe to assume that the learned behavior of a human is at least that complex.

THE RISE OF BEHAVIORISM

Most of the pioneering work in the scientific study of learning can be credited to *behaviorists,* psychologists who emphasized behavior rather than thought. The psychology of learning can be clearly understood only within the historical context in which it arose.

Charles Darwin's theory of evolution by natural selection inspired psychologists of the early 1900s to study animal learning and intelligence (Kalat, 1983). At first they were interested in comparing the intelligence of different species; as most psychologists began losing interest in that question, they began using animal studies as a way of understanding the general principles of learning. If nonhumans learn more or less the same way as humans, they reasoned, then it should be possible to discover the basic laws of learning by studying the behavior of any species in any convenient laboratory task.

Eventually the study of animal learning became dominated by psychologists who called themselves **behaviorists** (Watson, 1913). Behaviorists try to explain the causes of behavior by studying only those behaviors that scientists can observe and measure, without reference to unobservable mental processes.

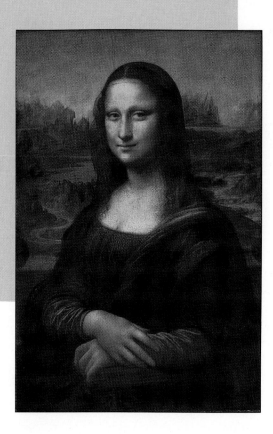

The original behaviorists were, in part, protesting against the views of the *structuralists* (see Chapter 1) and others who had asked people to describe their thoughts and ideas. The behaviorists pointed out that it was useless to ask people for reports on their own experience, because there is no way to check on the accuracy of such reports. If someone says, "I hear singing," or "I see the moon," we can check the reports against our own observations. But if someone says, "My idea of roundness is stronger than my idea of color," we have no way to check the accuracy of the statement. We are not even certain what it means. *If psychology is to be a scientific enterprise, behaviorists insist, it must deal only with observable, measurable events—that is, behaviors.*

Behaviorists make several assumptions:

1. *All behavior is caused or determined in some way.* (Recall the discussion of free will and determinism in Chapter 1.) In other words, all behavior obeys certain laws. The reason psychologists cannot always predict what you will do is that they do not know enough about you and about the stimuli that are acting upon you. Moreover, their theories of behavior are not yet sufficiently well developed for them to make full, comprehensive predictions.

2. *The environment molds behavior.* Each sensory stimulus gives rise to a response. Learning consists of a change in the connections between stimuli and responses. For this reason, behaviorism is sometimes referred to as *stimulus-response psychology,* or *S-R psychology.*

3. *Explanations of behavior based on internal causes and mental states are generally useless.* We commonly "explain" people's behavior in terms of their motivations, or emotions, or mental state. However, behaviorists insist that such explanations explain nothing:

> **Q.** Why did she yell at that man?
> **A.** She yelled because she was angry.
> **Q.** How do you know she was angry?
> **A.** We can tell she was angry because she was yelling.

B. F. Skinner, probably the most influential of all behaviorists, objected to mental terms as simply sloppy use of the language. For example, he argued, when you say, "I *intend* to . . . ," what you really mean is "I am about to . . . ," or "In situations like this I usually . . . ," or "This is in the preliminary stages of happening. . . ." That is, any statement about intentions or motivations can be converted into a descriptive statement or a self-observation (Skinner, 1990).

Most behaviorists today are a little more willing than those of the past to talk about anger, hope, motivation levels, and other internal states. Indeed, some criticize Skinner's extreme focus on description and apparent lack of interest in the underlying processes that produce behavior (Staddon & Bueno, 1991).

Still, most psychologists want to modify behaviorism rather than abandon it. They may wish to discuss *anger* or *hope* or some other mental-sounding concept, but they do not introduce these terms casually. They insist on precise operational definitions to specify how to measure such concepts. Even cognitive psychologists who want to broaden the scope of psychology to include thinking use behavioristic methods to measure the responses that presumably reflect thinking. The conclusions we draw about psychological processes must be grounded on observations of behavior.

The behaviorist approach has been by far the dominant approach to the psychology of learning. Because psychologists of the early 20th century were inclined to accept the behavioristic assumptions, they were quick to adopt

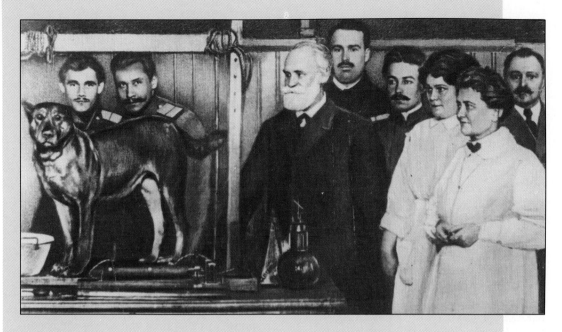

Ivan P. Pavlov (with the white beard) with students and an experimental dog. Pavlov focused on limited aspects of the dog's behavior—mostly salivation—and found some apparently simple principles to describe that behavior.

certain relatively simple interpretations of what happens during learning. As we shall see, those interpretations were good descriptions in many regards but require modification in light of later research.

PAVLOV AND CLASSICAL CONDITIONING

Suppose you always feed your cat at 4:00 P.M. with food you keep in the refrigerator. As 4:00 P.M. approaches, your cat goes to the kitchen, claws at the refrigerator, meows, and salivates. You might explain the cat's behavior by saying that it "expects" food, that it "knows" there is food in the refrigerator, or that it is "trying to get someone to feed it." Behaviorists reject such explanations in favor of a more mechanical interpretation based on stimuli and responses. When Ivan P. Pavlov proposed a simple, highly mechanical theory of learning, it was widely accepted almost overnight. The mood of the times was ready for what he had to say.

Pavlov, a Russian physiologist, won a Nobel Prize in physiology in 1904 for his research on digestion (Gantt, 1973). He continued his research by measuring the secretion of digestive

juices in a dog's stomach when food was placed in its mouth or in its stomach. One day he noticed that a dog would salivate or secrete digestive juices as soon as it saw or smelled food. Because this secretion presumably depended on the dog's previous experiences with food, Pavlov called it a "psychological" secretion.

Pavlov's Procedures

Pavlov guessed that animals are born with certain automatic connections—he called them **unconditioned reflexes**—between a stimulus such as food and a response such as secreting digestive juices in the digestive system. He conjectured that animals also acquire certain reflexes as a result of experience. If so, he reasoned, it might be possible to transfer a reflex from one stimulus to another. For example, if a neutral stimulus—say, a flashing light or a buzzer—always preceded food, an animal might begin to make the same digestive response to the light that it would make if food were already in its mouth. Thus, the flashing light or buzzer would also prompt digestive secretions. The process by which an organism learns a new association between two paired stimuli—a neutral one and one that already

FIGURE 7.1

Ivan P. Pavlov used dogs for his experiments on classical conditioning of salivation. The experimenter can ring a bell (CS), present food (UCS), and measure the response (CR and UCR). Pavlov himself collected saliva with a simple measuring pouch attached to the dog's cheek; later, his colleagues used a more complex device.

evokes a reflexive response—has come to be known as **classical conditioning** or **Pavlovian conditioning.** (It is called classical simply because it has been known and studied for a long time.)

Pavlov used an experimental setup like the one Figure 7.1 shows (Goodwin, 1991). First he carefully selected dogs with a moderate degree of arousal. (Highly excitable dogs would not hold still long enough; docile dogs would fall asleep during the study.) Then he attached a tube to one of the salivary ducts in the dog's mouth to measure salivation. He could have measured stomach secretions, but it was easier to measure salivation.

Pavlov found that whenever he gave the dog food, saliva flowed into the dog's mouth. This happened automatically; no training was required. He referred to the food as the **unconditioned stimulus (UCS)** and to the salivation as the **unconditioned response (UCR).** In other words, before Pavlov started to train the dog, the unconditioned stimulus (UCS) elicited the unconditioned response (UCR) consistently, automatically, reflexively. The unconditioned stimulus continues to elicit the unconditioned response throughout any experiment in classical conditioning.

Next, Pavlov introduced a new stimulus, a buzzer. On hearing the buzzer, the dog made certain orienting responses: It got up, lifted its ears, and looked around. It did not salivate, however, so the stimulus was essentially neutral initially. Pavlov sounded the buzzer a few seconds before giving food to the dog and did this over and over again; after enough repetitions, the dog would salivate as soon as it heard the buzzer (Pavlov, 1927/1960).

Pavlov called the buzzer the **conditioned stimulus (CS),** because the dog's response to it depended on the preceding conditions. He called the salivation that followed the sounding of the buzzer the **conditioned response (CR).** The conditioned response is simply whatever response the conditioned stimulus begins to elicit *as a result* of the conditioning (training) procedure. The conditioned stimulus does *not* elicit this response at the start of the conditioning procedure.

In Pavlov's experiments, the unconditioned response was salivation and so was the conditioned response; the only difference was whether the dog salivated because of the conditioned stimulus or because of the unconditioned stimulus. In other experiments, however, the conditioned response may be different from the unconditioned response. *Whatever the conditioned stimulus elicits as a result of training is the conditioned response.*

To summarize: The *unconditioned stimulus* (UCS), such as food or shock, automatically elicits the *unconditioned response* (UCR) at all times. A neutral stimulus, such as a tone or buzzer, that is paired with the UCS becomes a *conditioned stimulus* (CS). At first it elicits either no response at all or some irrelevant response, such as just looking around. After some number of pairings of the CS with the UCS, the conditioned stimulus elicits the *conditioned response* (CR). Figure 7.2 diagrams these relationships.

Here is another example of classical conditioning: Suppose your alarm clock makes a faint clicking sound a couple of seconds before the actual alarm goes off. At first, the click by itself does not awaken you, but the alarm does. After a week or so, however, you awaken as soon as you hear the click, not waiting for the alarm. Here, the alarm is the unconditioned stimulus that automatically elicits awakening, the unconditioned response. The click is the conditioned stimulus, and awakening in response to the click is a conditioned response.

The unconditioned stimulus may be almost any stimulus that evokes an automatic response. The conditioned stimulus may be almost any

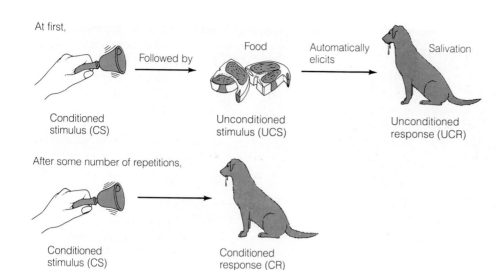

FIGURE 7.2

In classical conditioning, a conditioned stimulus is followed by an unconditioned stimulus. At first the conditioned stimulus elicits no response, while the unconditioned stimulus elicits the unconditioned response. After sufficient pairings, the conditioned stimulus begins to elicit the conditioned response, which may resemble the unconditioned response.

detectable stimulus—a light, a sound, the interruption of a constant light or sound, a touch, a smell, or some combination of stimuli. Other things being equal, conditioning occurs more rapidly when the conditioned stimulus is unfamiliar than when it is familiar. For example, if someone hears a tone a thousand times and then the tone is paired with a puff of air in the person's eyes, the person will take a long time to show any signs of conditioning. The person has difficulty learning that the tone predicts the air puff because it has never predicted anything in the past (Kalat, 1977; Mackintosh, 1973). Similarly, imagine two people who are bitten by a snake. The one who has never been close to a snake before may develop an intense fear of snakes; the one who has spent the past 5 years tending snakes at the zoo will develop little if any fear. In both cases, the snake is a conditioned stimulus and the bite is an unconditioned stimulus, but the familiarity of the snake (CS) determines whether the person will develop a strong association or a weak one.

We shall start with mostly laboratory studies, but eventually come to an application of classical conditioning to the human phenomenon of drug tolerance. Later in this book we shall consider the role of classical conditioning in the development of phobias (Chapter 14).

■ CONCEPT CHECK

1. A nursing mother consistently responds to her baby's crying by putting the baby to her breast. The baby's sucking causes the release of milk. Within a few days, as soon as the mother hears the baby crying, the milk starts to flow, even before she puts the baby to her breast. What is the conditioned stimulus? The conditioned response? The unconditioned stimulus? The unconditioned response? (Check your answers on page 292.)

The Phenomena of Classical Conditioning

The process that establishes or strengthens a conditioned response is known as **acquisition.** Figure 7.3 shows how the strength of a conditioned response increases as the conditioned and unconditioned stimuli are repeatedly presented together. However, acquisition is not the end of the story, because any response that can be learned can also be unlearned or changed.

Once Pavlov had demonstrated the manner in which classical conditioning occurs, inquisitive psychologists wondered what would happen after various changes in the procedures. Their investigations, prompted by practical concerns, theoretical concerns, or mere curiosity, have revealed many phenomena that are related to classical conditioning. Here are a few of the main ones:

Extinction Suppose I sound a buzzer and then blow a puff of air into your eyes. After a few repetitions, you start closing your eyes as soon as you hear the buzzer (Figure 7.4). Now I sound the buzzer repeatedly without puffing any air. What do you do?

If you are like most people, you will blink your eyes the first time and perhaps the second and third times, but before long you will stop

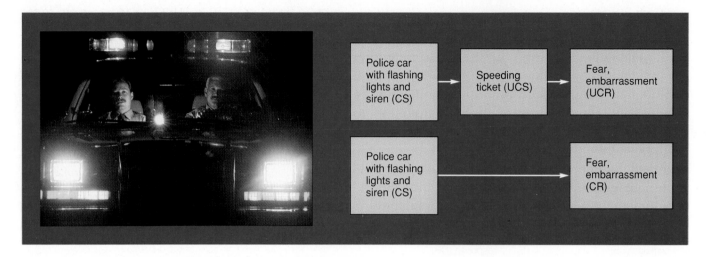

Classical conditioning is not just for dogs. A stimulus that signals some other event can develop the ability to evoke strong conditioned responses.

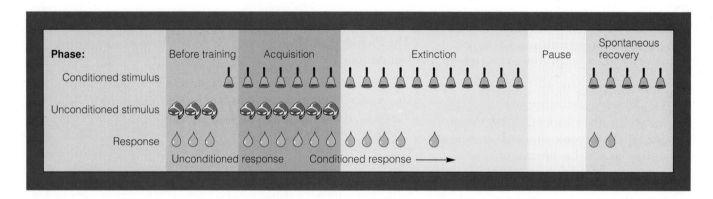

FIGURE 7.3

Phases of classical conditioning. Classical conditioning proceeds through several phases, depending on the time of presentation of the two stimuli. If the conditioned stimulus regularly precedes the unconditioned stimulus, acquisition occurs. If the conditioned stimulus is presented by itself, extinction occurs. A pause after extinction yields a brief spontaneous recovery.

blinking. This dying out of the conditioned response is called **extinction** (Figure 7.3). *To extinguish a classically conditioned response, repeatedly present the conditioned stimulus (CS) without the unconditioned stimulus (UCS).*

As with acquisition, extinction involves learning; just as acquisition establishes a connection between the conditioned stimulus and the unconditioned stimulus, extinction establishes a connection between the conditioned stimulus and the *absence* of the unconditioned

stimulus. The factors that facilitate or impair acquisition have similar effects on extinction. For example, the sudden presentation of a loud noise or other distraction temporarily interferes with either acquisition or extinction (Pavlov, 1927/1960).

Be careful to distinguish between extinction and forgetting. Both serve to weaken a learned response, but they arise from different sources. Forgetting occurs when we have no opportunity to practice a certain behavior over a long time. Extinction occurs as the result of a specific experience—namely, the presentation of the conditioned stimulus without the unconditioned stimulus.

Spontaneous Recovery Suppose we classically condition a response and then extinguish

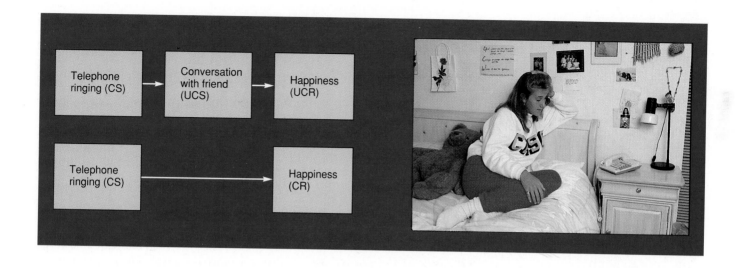

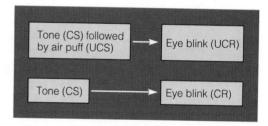

it. Several hours or days later, we present the conditioned stimulus again. In many cases, the conditioned response will reappear. But this return is temporary, lasting only one or a few trials, unless CS-UCS pairings are resumed. **Spontaneous recovery** refers to this temporary return of an extinguished response after a delay (Figure 7.3). For example, the sound of a buzzer (CS) is followed by a puff of air blown into the eyes (UCS) many times until the person learns to blink at the sound of the buzzer. Then the buzzer is presented repeatedly by itself until the person learns to stop blinking. Neither the buzzer nor the puff of air is presented for the next few hours. Then the buzzer is sounded again and the person blinks—not strongly, perhaps, but more than at the end of the extinction training.

Why does spontaneous recovery take place? Think of it this way: At first, the buzzer predicted a puff of air blown into the eyes. Then it predicted nothing. The two sets of experiences conflict with each other, but the more recent one predominates and the person stops blinking. Hours later, neither experience is much more recent than the other and the effects of the original acquisition are almost as strong as the effects of the extinction.

■ CONCEPT CHECK

2. In Pavlov's experiment on conditioned salivation in response to a buzzer, what procedure

FIGURE 7.4
The procedure for classical conditioning of the eyeblink response.

could you use to produce extinction? What procedure could you use to produce spontaneous recovery? (Check your answers on page 292.)

Stimulus Generalization Suppose I play a tone—say, middle C—and then blow a puff of air into your eyes. After a few repetitions you start to blink your eyes as soon as you hear middle C. What happens if I play some other note?

You probably will blink your eyes in response to the new tone as well. The closer the new tone is to the training note (middle C), the more likely you will be to blink (Figure 7.5). **Stimulus generalization** is the extension of a conditioned response from the training stimulus to similar stimuli.

Although I have described the conditioned stimulus as a particular tone, it actually includes the entire set of sensory stimuli impinging on

Classical Conditioning   283

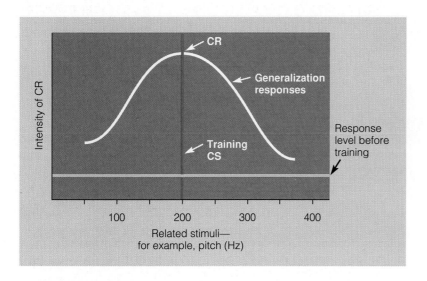

FIGURE 7.5
Stimulus generalization is the process of extending a learned response to new stimuli that resemble the one used in training. As a rule, a stimulus similar to the training stimulus elicits a strong response; a less similar stimulus elicits a weaker response.

you at the time—the tone itself, the lab room, the presence of the experimenter, and any other background stimuli. Thus, a perceptible change in the tone or in any of the background stimuli will decrease the conditioned response. If the changes are drastic enough, the conditioned response will disappear altogether (Pearce, 1987). For example, if a middle C is always paired with a puff of air in a psychology lab room, you will blink your eyes when you hear a tone in that setting but not when you hear it at a piano recital.

Discrimination   Now suppose I always follow middle C with a puff of air but never follow F-sharp with a puff of air. Eventually you will **discriminate** between the two tones: You will respond differently to the two stimuli because different outcomes followed them. You will blink your eyes when you hear middle C but not when you hear F-sharp. We rely constantly on discrimination in everyday life: We learn that one bell signals that it is time for class to start and a different bell signals a fire.

Something to Think About

We can easily determine how well human subjects discriminate between two stimuli. We can simply ask, "Which note has the higher pitch?" or "Which light is brighter?" How could we determine how well an animal can discriminate between these stimuli?

DRUG TOLERANCE AS AN EXAMPLE OF CLASSICAL CONDITIONING

Classical conditioning occurs in many laboratory settings; it also occurs in the outside world, sometimes in settings where we might not have expected it. One such setting is **drug tolerance**, the fact that users of certain drugs experience progressively weaker effects after taking those drugs repeatedly.

Drug tolerance occurs for a variety of reasons, which vary from one case to another (Poulos & Cappell, 1991). In many cases, however, drug tolerance is learned. When drug users inject themselves with morphine or heroin, the injection procedure is a stimulus that reliably predicts a second stimulus, the drug's entry into the brain. The drug alters experience but it also triggers a variety of body defenses and countermeasures against the drug's effects—for example, changes in hormone secretions, heart rate, and breathing rate.

Whenever one stimulus predicts another stimulus that produces a response, we have the conditions necessary for classical conditioning. Shepard Siegel (1977, 1983) has demonstrated that classical conditioning does indeed take place during drug-injecting episodes. Initially, the injection ritual is a neutral stimulus that gives rise to no relevant response. After many pairings of that stimulus with the entry of the drug into the brain, however, the injection procedure by itself is able to evoke the body's antidrug defenses (Figure 7.6).

How might classical conditioning contribute to drug tolerance? The first time someone takes a drug, there is a certain delay between the time the drug enters the brain and the time the brain mobilizes its defenses. After classical conditioning has taken place, the injection procedure, acting as a conditioned stimulus, may itself trigger the defense reactions, even before the drug has entered the brain. As the defense reactions are aroused earlier and earlier, the effects of the drug grow weaker and the user can tolerate heavier and heavier dosages.

Here is an example of the evidence that supports the classical-conditioning interpretation of drug tolerance. If we assume that the injection procedure serves as a conditioned stimulus, then the body's defense reactions should be stronger when the drug is given with the usual injection procedure (the conditioned stimulus) than when it is given by some other means, in some unfamiliar setting. The evidence strongly supports this prediction (Eikelboom & Stewart, 1982; Lê, Poulos, & Cappell, 1979; Poulos, Wilkinson, & Cappell, 1981; Siegel, 1983; Tiffany & Baker, 1981). *To show strong tolerance in a particular environment, the individual must have previously received the drug in that environment.*

Why do some people die of a drug overdose that is no greater than the dose they normally tolerated? According to the classical-conditioning interpretation, they probably took the fatal overdose in an unfamiliar setting. Because that setting did not serve as a CS, it failed to trigger the usual tolerance.

- ■ CONCEPT CHECKS

3. *When an individual develops tolerance to the effects of a drug injection, what are the conditioned stimulus, the unconditioned stimulus, the conditioned response, and the unconditioned response?*

4. *Within the classical-conditioning interpretation of drug tolerance, what procedure should extinguish tolerance?*
(Check your answers on page 292.)

EXPLANATIONS OF CLASSICAL CONDITIONING

What is classical conditioning, really? At first, psychologists thought it was a fairly simple process of transferring a response from one stimulus to another. As is often the case, further investigation indicated that the apparent simplicity was an illusion.

Pavlov's Theory of the Causes of Classical Conditioning

Pavlov believed that in order for classical conditioning to occur, the conditioned stimulus and the unconditioned stimulus must be close together in time. Nearness in time is called **temporal contiguity.** With rare exceptions, the conditioned stimulus must be presented first, followed quickly by the unconditioned stimulus. In some cases, the conditioned stimulus (such as a tone) continues until the presentation of the unconditioned stimulus; in other cases, the conditioned stimulus stops before the unconditioned stimulus. In either case, however, the delay is short between the start of one stimulus and the start of the other. All other things

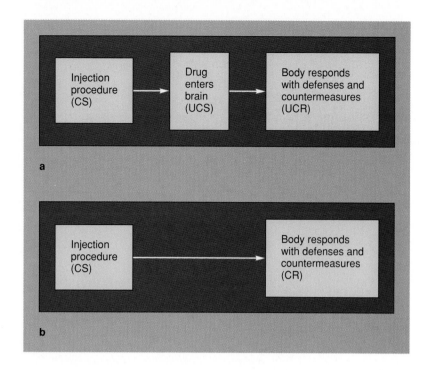

FIGURE 7.6
If a particular injection procedure consistently predicts the entry of a drug, an individual can develop a conditioned response to defend himself or herself against the drug. This conditioned response is an important part of drug tolerance.

being equal, the longer the delay between CS and UCS, the weaker the conditioning will be.

Pavlov believed not only that temporal contiguity facilitated conditioning but also that temporal contiguity actually *caused* it. According to his theory, every stimulus excites a specific area of the brain. A buzzer excites a "buzzer center," and meat excites a "meat center." Exciting both centers at the same time establishes and strengthens a connection between them. From then on, any excitation of the buzzer center (CS) also excites the meat center (UCS) and evokes salivation (Figure 7.7).

Pavlov's theory appealed to behaviorists at the time because it offered a simple, mechanical explanation of learning. It still provides a useful description of the biochemical mechanisms of learning in invertebrate animals (see, for example, Kandel & Schwartz, 1982). However, most psychologists now believe classical conditioning requires a more complex explanation.

Conditioning: More Than a Transfer of Responses

According to Pavlov's view of classical conditioning, an animal comes to respond to the conditioned stimulus as if it were the unconditioned stimulus. For his results, that interpreta-

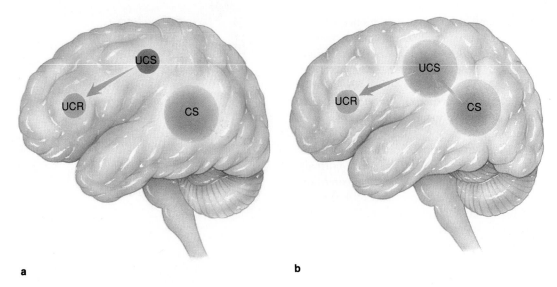

a   b

FIGURE 7.7
Pavlov believed that conditioning depended on temporal contiguity. (a) At the start of conditioning, activity in the UCS center automatically causes activation of the UCR center. At this time activity of the CS center does not affect the UCS center. (b) After sufficient pairings of the CS and UCS, their simultaneous activity causes the growth of a connection between the CS and UCS centers. Afterward, activity in the CS center will flow to the UCS center and therefore excite the UCR center.

tion was reasonable; the conditioned response was virtually the same as the unconditioned response.

However, in some situations the conditioned response can be quite different from the unconditioned response. For example, if a buzzer (CS) signals a forthcoming shock (UCS), animals respond to the buzzer by freezing in position. They do not react to it as if it were a shock; they react to it as they would to signals of possible danger in the real world. *In short, the conditioned response serves to prepare the individual for the unconditioned stimulus.*

Temporal Contiguity Is Not Enough

WHAT'S THE EVIDENCE?

Contrary to what Pavlov believed, repeatedly pairing a conditioned stimulus with an unconditioned stimulus may, under certain conditions, establish very little connection between the two stimuli. We shall consider two experiments, both of which have been very influential in the study of animal learning:

EXPERIMENT 1

Hypothesis If classical conditioning depends on temporal contiguity, then an animal should associate any novel stimulus with an immediately following unconditioned stimulus. But perhaps the animal will not form an association if some other stimulus tells it to expect the unconditioned stimulus. That is, conditioning may depend on the "surprising" or "unexpected" appearance of the unconditioned stimulus.

Method For some rats, a light was repeatedly followed by a shock (UCS) until the rats showed a clear, consistent response to the light. For other rats, a tone was followed by the shock until the rats consistently responded to the tone. Then the experimenter presented a light and a tone simultaneously, followed by the same shock. Later the experimenter tested the rats' reactions to the light and the tone, each presented separately (Kamin, 1969). (See Figure 7.8.)

Results After pairing of the combined light-plus-tone with shock, rats continued to respond as before to whichever stimulus they had originally associated with shock (light for some rats, tone for others). However, they responded very

Group 1

Frozen in
fear position

Calm

Group 2

Calm

Frozen in
fear position

FIGURE 7.8

In Kamin's experiment, each rat learned first to associate either light or sound with shock. Then it received a compound of both light and sound followed by shock. Even after many pairings, each rat continued showing fear of its old stimulus (the one that already predicted shock). The rat showed little response to the new stimulus.

weakly to the new, added stimulus. That is, even though the new stimulus was always followed by the shock, animals developed little response to it. These results demonstrate the **blocking effect:** The previously established association to one stimulus blocks the formation of an association to the added stimulus.

Interpretation If temporal contiguity were the main factor responsible for learning, the rats should have learned a strong response to both the light and the tone, because both were presented just before the shock. However, the new stimulus was uninformative. Rats had previously learned that one stimulus predicted the shock; the new stimulus added nothing whatever to that prediction.

EXPERIMENT 2

Hypothesis A conditioned stimulus that immediately precedes an unconditioned stimulus may or may not be a useful predictor, depending on how often the UCS occurs without the

CS. If the unconditioned stimulus is just as likely to occur with or without the conditioned stimulus, then the animal will not strongly associate one with the other.

Method For some rats, conditioned stimulus and unconditioned stimulus were presented in the sequence shown in Figure 7.9 (top). The horizontal line represents time; the vertical arrows represent times of stimuli presentation. For other rats, the two stimuli were presented in the sequence shown for Group 2. In both cases, every presentation of the conditioned stimulus immediately preceded a presentation of the unconditioned stimulus. But in the second case the unconditioned stimulus also occurred frequently in the *absence* of the conditioned stimulus; therefore, the CS was a poor predictor of the UCS (Rescorla, 1968, 1988).

Results Rats given the first sequence of stimuli formed a strong association between conditioned stimulus and unconditioned stimulus. Those given the second sequence of stimuli

Classical Conditioning   287

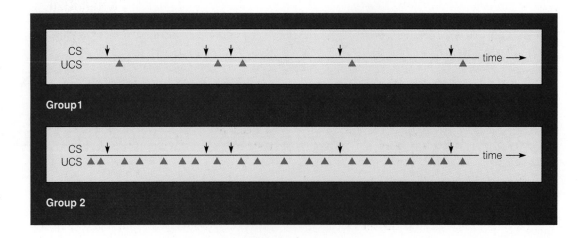

formed little or no association between the two stimuli and thus failed to respond to the conditioned stimulus (Rescorla, 1968, 1988).

Interpretation The results support the same conclusion as the first experiment: *Animals (including humans) associate a conditioned stimulus with an unconditioned stimulus only when the CS predicts the occurrence of the UCS.* If the conditioned stimulus comes immediately before the unconditioned stimulus but provides no new information, the animal will not associate the CS with the UCS.

- **CONCEPT CHECK**

5. If temporal contiguity were the only factor responsible for classical conditioning, what result should the experimenters have obtained in Experiment 2? (Check your answer on page 292.)

Conditioning, Contiguity, and Contingency

The results just discussed indicate that classical conditioning depends on more than just contiguity. For an animal to form a strong association between two stimuli, the first stimulus must be a good predictor of the second. Therefore, one possible explanation of conditioning is that it depends not on contiguity (being close together in time) but on **contingency** (predictability).

However, contingency probably is not the whole explanation either (Papini & Bitterman, 1990). It is hard to imagine, for example, that a rat calculates the probability of a shock after a tone versus the probability of a shock during a period without a tone.

Psychologists have been searching for an explanation of classical conditioning that ac-

counts for the importance of both contiguity and contingency. One possibility goes as follows: We all enter life with a predisposition to respond to the unusual and the unexpected. If you hear an unusual sound and then quickly receive an unexpected shock, you are likely to associate the sound with the shock. But if you had heard that sound many times before, you have already associated it with "nothing particular happening afterward." You would then be very slow to associate the sound with the shock. That is, we can associate a stimulus with either an event (shock) or a *non-event* (no shock), and association with one impairs association with the other.

Furthermore, you will also be slow to associate the sound with the shock if you had already expected the shock. For example, you might have already seen a flash of light that predicted the shock. Or you might have received many unpredicted shocks in this location. Even if no particular stimulus predicted a shock at this particular moment, the shock was still expected; in a sense, all the background cues, including the room itself, provide a prediction of the shock. *In short, we tend to associate unusual or unexpected stimuli with one another, especially if those stimuli come close together in time* (Holyoak, Koh, & Nisbett, 1989).

Specialized Learning: Conditioned Taste Aversions

At one time, psychologists believed that all learning follows the same laws; if they could describe what happens in any one convenient situation, they would understand learning in all situations. That was a reasonable starting assumption, but only an assumption. For many years, psychologists studied only a few examples of learning and never seriously tested the assumption that all learning follows the same laws. Eventually they discovered that associating a food with illness is a special situation that calls forth a specialized type of learning.

We see that specialization most clearly when we examine associations over long delays. For many kinds of conditioned responses, such as salivating and blinking, learning is greatest with a short delay between the conditioned stimulus and the unconditioned stimulus—on the order of 1 or 2 seconds. Under ordinary conditions, we see little evidence of learning if the delay is greater than 20 seconds (Kimble, 1961).

However, animals (including people) have no trouble learning which foods are safe to eat and which are harmful, even though they may not feel the consequences of a spoiled food until long after eating it. John Garcia and his colleagues (Garcia, Ervin, & Koelling, 1966) demonstrated that rats can associate food with illness over delays lasting minutes, even hours. They gave rats a saccharin solution that the rats had never tasted before. Ordinarily, rats will readily drink saccharin and show a strong preference for it. But 15 minutes or more after the rats had stopped drinking, the experimenters injected mild doses of poisons to make them slightly ill. When the rats had recovered, the experimenters again offered them a saccharin solution. All of them avoided it, even though they readily drank plain water. Evidently the rats had learned a connection between taste and illness, in spite of the long delay and having experienced the pairing only once. **Conditioned taste aversion** is the phenomenon of avoiding eating something that has been followed by illness when eaten in the past.

An animal that learns a conditioned taste aversion to a food treats that food as if it were foul-tasting (Garcia, 1990). Some ranchers in the western United States occasionally use this type of learning to deter coyotes from eating sheep. They offer the coyotes sheep meat containing low levels of lithium salts or similar poisons. Afterward, as shown in Figure 7.10, the coyotes no longer attack sheep, and they treat sheep meat as if it tasted bad. This technique has the advantage of protecting the ranchers' sheep without killing the coyotes, which are a threatened species.

Research has shown that taste aversion is not the result of a lingering aftertaste of the food but is truly the result of an association between events separated by a long delay. For example,

FIGURE 7.10
This coyote previously got ill by eating sheep meat containing a mild dose of lithium salts. Now it reacts toward both live and dead sheep as it would toward bad-tasting food. (From Garcia, 1990.)

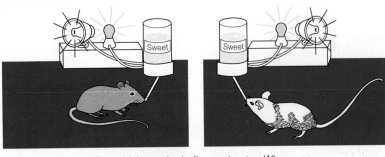

Rats drink saccharin-flavored water. Whenever they make contact with the tube, they turn on a bright light and a noisy buzzer.

Then

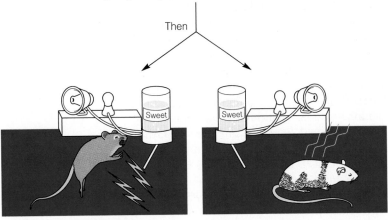

Some rats get electric shock.

Some rats are made nauseated by X rays.

Next day: Rats are given a choice between a tube of saccharin-flavored water and a tube of unflavored water hooked up to the light and the buzzer.

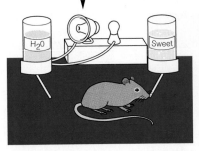

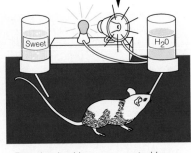

Rats that had been shocked avoided the tube with the lights and noises but drank the saccharin-flavored water.

Rats that had been nauseated by X rays avoided the saccharin-flavored water but drank the water with the lights and the buzzer.

FIGURE 7.11
The experiment by Garcia and Koelling (1966). Rats "blame" tastes for their illness, lights and sounds for their pain.

rats can learn that drinking one concentration of a solution will make them sick and that another will not, even though both concentrations leave the same aftertaste (Rozin, 1969).

John Garcia and R. A. Koelling (1966) demonstrated another specialization of learning: Animals are predisposed to associate poison with foods but not with lights and sounds. They are also predisposed to associate shocks with lights and sounds but not with foods. In Garcia and Koelling's experiment, rats were al-

lowed to drink saccharin-flavored water from tubes that were set up so that whenever the rats licked the water a bright light flashed and a loud noise sounded. Some of the rats were exposed to X rays (which can induce nausea) while they drank. Others were given electric shocks to their feet 2 seconds after they had begun to drink. After the training was complete, each rat was tested separately with a tube of saccharin-flavored water and with a tube of unflavored water that produced lights and noises. Figure 7.11 illustrates the experiment.

The rats that had been exposed to X rays avoided only the flavored water. The rats that had received shocks while drinking avoided only the tube that produced lights and noises. Evidently, rats (and other species) have a built-in predisposition to associate illness mostly with what they have eaten or drunk and to associate skin pain mostly with what they have seen or heard. Such predispositions are presumably beneficial because foods are more likely to cause internal events, and lights and sounds are more likely to signal external events.

The tendency to associate certain foods with sickness helps us to learn which substances are safe and which are harmful. For cancer patients, however, the tendency creates a special problem: Patients undergoing certain kinds of chemotherapy feel nauseated after every treatment. Over time, they may learn an aversion to every food they ate before every treatment (Bernstein, 1985; Bernstein & Borson, 1986). They may end up eating almost nothing.

One way to avoid that problem is for a cancer patient to eat the same food before every chemotherapy session. The patient makes that one food the "scapegoat" and associates the ensuing nausea with that food and not with others (Mattes, 1988). This procedure is successful with many patients but not with all; for some patients the cancer itself causes nausea and therefore foods eaten at any time become aversive (Bernstein & Borson, 1986).

CLASSICAL
CONDITIONING
AS INFORMATION
PROCESSING

Classical conditioning is important for some aspects of our behavior, less important for others. It alters our motivational or emotional reactions to stimuli, our "gut feelings"—including responses related to fear, preparations for eating, preparations for a drug injection, and so forth. But it does not control our body movements toward or away from various stimuli. That is, classical conditioning might tell us to be afraid, but it does not tell us how to get away from whatever is frightening us. It might tell us to salivate in preparation for eating, but it does not tell us where to look for food. We have other types of learning to answer these other questions, as we shall see later in this chapter.

According to the current view of classical conditioning, the learner is an active processor of information. Psychologists no longer view conditioning as the passive connection of two stimuli that happened to come close together in time. Each individual enters the world with certain predispositions—such as the predisposition to associate illness with what it eats instead of what it sees or hears. When it experiences a series of stimuli, it determines what each predicts. If a given stimulus provides reliable information about what is about to happen, the animal learns to respond to that stimulus. Otherwise, it does not. In a sense, an individual undergoing classical conditioning resembles a scientist who is trying to figure out what causes what (Rescorla, 1985).

SUMMARY

- *Historical background.* The scientific study of learning grew out of attempts to compare the intelligence of various animal species. (page 277)

- *Behaviorism.* Behaviorism is an attempt to explain behavior without reference to unobservable mental processes. Behaviorists assume that all behavior is caused in some way, that mental states do not explain behavior, and that behavior is molded by sensory stimuli. (page 277)

- *Classical conditioning.* Ivan Pavlov discovered classical conditioning, the process by which an organism learns a new association between two stimuli that have been paired with each other—a neutral stimulus (the conditioned stimulus) and one that already evokes a reflexive response (the unconditioned stimulus). The organism displays this association by responding in a new way (the conditioned response) to the conditioned stimulus. (page 279)

- *Extinction.* After classical conditioning has established a conditioned response to a stimulus, the response can be extinguished by presenting that stimulus repeatedly by itself. (page 281)

- *Spontaneous recovery.* If the conditioned stimulus is not presented at all for some time after extinction and then is presented again, the conditioned response may return to some degree. That return is called spontaneous recovery. (page 282)

- *Discrimination.* An animal or person who has been trained to respond to one stimulus will respond similarly to similar stimuli. However, if one stimulus is followed by an unconditioned stimulus and another is not, the individual will come to discriminate between them. (page 284)

- *Drug tolerance.* Drug tolerance is partly a form of classical conditioning in which the drug administration procedure becomes associated with the effects of the drug. (page 284)

- *Temporal contiguity versus contingency.* Pavlov believed that temporal contiguity between two stimuli caused classical conditioning. We now believe that conditioning depends also on contingency, or the extent to which the occurrence of the first stimulus predicts the occurrence of the second. (page 285)

- *Predispositions.* Conditioning is based on certain predispositions, such as the predisposition to associate illness with foods rather than with other events. (page 288)

SUGGESTION FOR FURTHER READING

Rescorla, R. A. (1988). Pavlovian conditioning: It's not what you think it is. *American Psychologist, 43,* 151–160. A theoretical review by an investigator who has contributed significantly to changing views of classical conditioning.

TERMS

behaviorist a psychologist who tries to explain the causes of behavior by studying only those behaviors that he or she can observe and measure, without reference to unobservable mental processes (page 277)

unconditioned reflex an automatic connection between a stimulus and a response (page 279)

classical conditioning or **Pavlovian conditioning** the process by which an organism learns a new association between two paired stimuli—a neutral stimulus and one that already evokes a reflexive response (page 280)

unconditioned stimulus (UCS) a stimulus that automatically elicits an unconditioned response (page 280)

unconditioned response (UCR) an automatic response to an unconditioned stimulus (page 280)

conditioned stimulus (CS) a stimulus that comes to evoke a particular response after being paired with the unconditioned stimulus (page 280)

conditioned response (CR) a response that the conditioned stimulus elicits only because it has previously been paired with the unconditioned stimulus (page 280)

acquisition the process by which a conditioned response is established or strengthened (page 281)

extinction in classical conditioning, the dying out of the conditioned response after repeated presentations of the conditioned stimulus unaccompanied by the unconditioned stimulus (page 282)

spontaneous recovery the temporary return of an extinguished response after a delay (page 283)

stimulus generalization the extension of a conditioned response from the training stimulus to similar stimuli (page 283)

discrimination making different responses to different stimuli that have been followed by different outcomes (page 284)

drug tolerance the weakened effect of a drug after repeated use (page 284)

temporal contiguity nearness in time (page 284)

blocking effect tendency for a previously established association to one stimulus to block the formation of an association to an added stimulus (page 287)

contingency the degree to which the occurrence of one stimulus predicts the occurrence of a second stimulus (page 288)

conditioned taste aversion the tendency to avoid eating a substance that has been followed by illness when eaten in the past (page 289)

ANSWERS TO CONCEPT CHECKS

1. The conditioned stimulus is the baby's crying. The unconditioned stimulus is the baby's sucking at the breast. Both the conditioned response and the unconditioned response are the release of milk. Many nursing mothers experience this classically conditioned reflex. (page 281)

2. To bring about extinction, present the buzzer repeatedly without presenting any food. To bring about spontaneous recovery, first bring about extinction and then wait hours or days and present the buzzer again. (page 283)

3. The conditioned stimulus is the injection procedure. The unconditioned stimulus is the entry of the drug into the brain. Both the conditioned response and the unconditioned response are the body's defenses against the drug. (page 285)

4. To extinguish tolerance, present the injection procedure (conditioned stimulus) without injecting the drug (unconditioned stimulus). Instead, inject just water or salt water. Shepard Siegel (1977) demonstrated that repeated injections of salt water do reduce tolerance to morphine in rats. (page 285)

5. If temporal contiguity were the main factor responsible for classical conditioning, rats exposed to the first sequence of stimuli should have responded the same as those exposed to the second sequence of stimuli. (page 288)

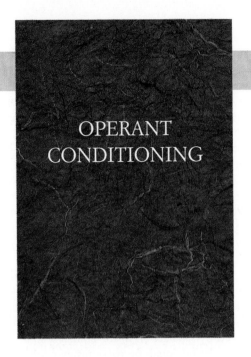

OPERANT CONDITIONING

How do rewards and punishments guide our behavior?

How can we most effectively use rewards and punishments to guide the behavior of others?

John B. Watson, one of the founders of behaviorism, once said, "Give me a dozen healthy infants, well-formed, and my own specified world to bring them up in and I'll guarantee to take any one at random and train him to become any type of specialist I might select—doctor, lawyer, artist, merchant-chief, and yes, even beggar-man thief, regardless of his talents, penchants, tendencies, abilities, vocations, and race of his ancestors" (1925, p. 82).

We shall never know whether Watson was right. No one ever said, "Okay, John, here are your twelve healthy infants; tell us how you want to arrange the world." Today, few psychologists share Watson's conviction that differences in experience are responsible for virtually all differences in behavior. Still, experience clearly has a strong influence on behavior. Whether we choose to do something is largely determined by whether we have been rewarded or punished for doing it in the past.

THORNDIKE AND OPERANT CONDITIONING

Shortly before Pavlov performed his innovative experiments, Edward L. Thorndike (1911/1970), a Harvard graduate student, had begun to train and test some cats in his basement. Saying that earlier experiments had dealt only with animal intelligence, never with animal stupidity, he devised a simple, behavioristic explanation of learning.

Thorndike put cats into puzzle boxes (Figure 7.12) from which they could escape by pressing a lever, pulling a string, or tilting a pole. Sometimes he placed a food reward outside the box. (Usually, though, just escaping from a small box seemed reward enough.) The cats learned to make whatever response led to the reward. Thorndike discovered that they learned faster if they got the reward immediately after making the response. The longer the delay between response and reward, the less improvement there was in the rate of response.

When the cat had to tilt a pole in order to escape, it would first paw or gnaw at the door, scratch the walls, or pace back and forth. Eventually, by accident, it would bump against the pole and open the door. The next time, the cat

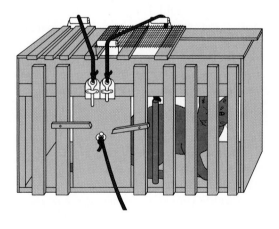

FIGURE 7.12
Each of Thorndike's puzzle boxes had a device that could open it. Here, tilting the pole will open the door. (Based on Thorndike, 1911/1970.)

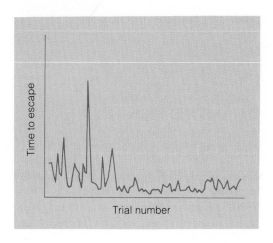

FIGURE 7.13

Trial and error or insight? As data from one of Thorndike's experiments show, the time a cat needs to escape from a puzzle box gradually grows shorter, but in an irregular manner. Thorndike concluded that the cat did not at any point "suddenly get the idea." Instead, reinforcement gradually increased the probability of one behavior.

would go through the same repertoire of behaviors but might bump against the pole a little sooner. Over many trials, the time it took the cat to escape grew shorter, in a gradual and irregular fashion. Figure 7.13 shows a learning curve to represent this behavior. A *learning curve* is a graph of the changes in behavior that occur over successive trials in a learning experiment.

Had the cat "figured out" how to escape? Had it come to "understand" the connection between bumping against the pole and opening the door? No, said Thorndike, a true behaviorist. If the cat had gained some new insight at some point along the way, he explained, its speed of escaping would have increased suddenly and would have remained constant for all later trials. Actually, the cat's performance improved only slowly and gradually. Clearly, something other than understanding must have been at work.

Thorndike concluded that learning occurs only as certain behaviors are strengthened at the expense of others. An animal enters a given situation with a certain repertoire of responses—pawing the door, scratching the walls, pacing, and so forth (labeled R_1, R_2, R_3, . . . in Figure 7.14a). First, the animal engages in its most probable response for this situation (response R_1 in the figure). If nothing special happens, it proceeds to other responses. Eventually, it gets to a lower-probability response—for example,

bumping against the pole that opens the door (response R_7 in the figure). The opening of the door serves as a reinforcement.

A **reinforcement** is an event that increases the probability that the preceding response will be repeated in the future. In other words, it "stamps in," or strengthens, the response. The next time Thorndike's cat is in the puzzle box, it may have a .04 probability of bumping the lever instead of .03; after another reinforcement, the probability may go up to .05. Eventually, the pole-bumping response has a greater probability than any other response, and the cat escapes quickly (Figure 7.14c).

Thorndike summarized his views in the **law of effect** (Thorndike, 1911/1970, p. 244): "Of several responses made to the same situation, those which are accompanied or closely followed by satisfaction to the animal will, other things being equal, be more firmly connected with the situation, so that, when it recurs, they will be more likely to recur." In other words, the animal becomes more likely to repeat the responses that led to favorable consequences. This process does not require that the animal "think" or "understand." Someone could easily program a machine to increase responses that led to reinforcement.

The process of changing behavior by following a response with reinforcement is known as **operant conditioning** (because the subject operates on the environment to produce an outcome) or **instrumental conditioning** (because the subject's behavior is *instrumental* in producing the outcome). The difference between operant conditioning and classical conditioning is one of procedure: *In operant conditioning, the subject's behavior determines what the outcome will be and when it will occur. In classical conditioning, the subject's behavior has no effect on the outcome (the presentation of either the CS or the UCS).*

Some psychologists have suggested that classical conditioning and operant conditioning may differ in other ways as well. For example, they have suggested that classical conditioning applies only to **visceral** responses (responses of the internal organs), such as salivation and digestion. In this view, operant conditioning applies only to **skeletal** responses—that is, movements of muscles such as those of the legs. But this distinction is cloudy. If a tone is followed by an electric shock in a classical-conditioning procedure, the tone will make the animal freeze in position as well as increase its heart rate. And a few investigators have reported that reinforce-

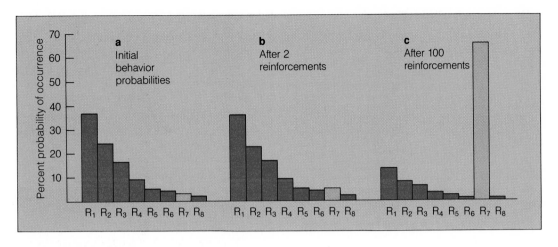

FIGURE 7.14

According to Thorndike, an animal enters any situation with a repertoire of responses (R₁ through R₈ here, with R₁ representing its most likely response). If reinforcement always follows R₇, the probability steadily increases that the animal will make that response in that situation. Note that learning occurs by increasing the probability of one response, not by insight or understanding.

ment in operant conditioning can increase the frequency of heart rate, intestinal contractions, and other visceral responses (Miller, 1969); later studies have failed to replicate those results (Dworkin & Miller, 1986). In short, psychologists distinguish between classical and operant conditioning, but we are not certain whether or not the brain distinguishes between them.

■ CONCEPT CHECK

6. *When I ring a bell, an animal sits up on its hind legs and drools; then I give it some food. Is that an example of classical conditioning or of operant conditioning?*

Well, actually this is a trick question; you do not have enough information to answer it. What else would you have to know before you could answer? (Check your answer on page 310.)

Why Are Certain Responses Learned More Easily Than Others?

Thorndike's cats quickly learned to push and pull various devices in their efforts to escape from his puzzle boxes. But when Thorndike tried to teach them to scratch themselves or lick themselves to receive the same reinforcement, they learned slowly and never performed at a high level. Why not?

One possible reason is **belongingness,** the concept that certain stimuli "belong" together,

or that a given response might be more readily associated with certain outcomes than with others. Belongingness is an idea Thorndike himself suggested, although psychologists neglected it for decades, preferring to believe that animals could associate almost any stimulus with any response equally easily. Eventually, psychologists had to revive the concept of belongingness (Seligman, 1970). I mentioned one example of this principle in the discussion of classical conditioning: Rats are predisposed to associate illness with something they ate rather than with something they saw or heard. Another example: Dogs can readily learn that a sound coming from one location means "raise your left leg," while a sound coming from another location means "raise your right leg." But it takes them virtually forever to learn that a ticking metronome means raise the left leg while a buzzer means raise the right leg (Dobrzecka, Szwejkowska, & Konorski, 1966). (See Figure 7.15.) Somehow the location of a sound and a location on the body "belong" together; a type of sound does not belong with a location on the body.

Presumably, Thorndike's cats were slow to associate scratching themselves with escaping from a box because the two activities do not "belong" together. (Cats evolved the ability to learn "what leads to what" in the real world, and scratching oneself is very unlikely to open doors in the real world.) But there is another possible explanation for why cats have trouble

FIGURE 7.15
According to Thorn-dike's principle of belongingness, some items are easy to associate with each other because they "belong" together, while others do not. For example, dogs easily learn to use the direction of a sound as a signal for which leg to raise, but they have trouble using the type *of sound as a signal for which leg to raise.*

Dog easily learns to raise the leg closer to the sound source.

Dog does not easily learn to raise one leg when it hears a metronome and a different leg when it hears a buzzer.

learning to scratch themselves for reinforcement: Perhaps a cat can scratch itself only when it itches (Charlton, 1983). Consider what would happen if you knew that you would be handsomely reinforced for swallowing rapidly and repeatedly. You would no doubt increase your rate of swallowing a little, for a short time. But after those first few swallows, you find additional swallows more and more difficult. (If you doubt me, go ahead and try.) Some behaviors are just not easy to produce in large quantity.

Extinction, Generalization, and Discrimination

No doubt you are familiar with the saying "If at first you don't succeed, try, try again." That is good advice in some situations but not in others. For example, the first time you tried to ride a bicycle you probably fell, but you kept trying until eventually you could ride with ease. However, what if you tried riding your bicycle on icy or snowy roads and found that you kept slipping and sliding? Should you try, try again? Or what if you inserted some coins in a vending machine and got nothing in return? Should you keep on trying? No. Sometimes you need to learn to quit something altogether, or to try it under some conditions and not others. (You ride your bicycle on safe, dry roads; you insert your coins in vending machines that have a history of paying off.)

In other words, you extinguish your unsuccessful responses, you generalize your successful ones to new situations, and you learn to discriminate between appropriate and inappropriate occasions for a given behavior. In operant conditioning, we achieve **extinction** by omitting the reinforcement after a subject has made a response. For example, you have been in the habit of asking your roommate to join you for supper. The last five times you asked, your roommate said no. You stop asking. (In classical conditioning, you will recall, extinction is achieved by presenting the CS without the UCS.)

If a subject receives reinforcement for making a particular response in the presence of a certain stimulus, the subject will make the same response in the presence of a similar stimulus. The greater the difference between the original stimulus and the new stimulus, however, the less vigorously the subject is likely to respond. This phenomenon is known as **stimulus generalization.** For example, you might smile at a stranger who reminds you of an old friend. Or you might reach for the turn signal in a rented car in the place you would find it in your own car. In both cases you are responding to a new stimulus in the same way you have learned to respond to an old stimulus.

If a subject is reinforced for responding to one stimulus and is reinforced less strongly (or not at all) for responding to another stimulus, then the subject will learn to use **discrimination** between them and will respond more vigorously to one than to the other. For example, you walk toward a parked car you think is yours and then you realize it is not. After several such experiences you learn to identify your own car from a distance.

Table 7.1 compares operant conditioning and classical conditioning.

B. F. SKINNER AND THE SHAPING OF RESPONSES

The most influential behaviorist was B. F. Skinner (1904-1990), who demonstrated many uses of operant conditioning. In a sense, Skinner was an ardent practitioner of parsimony, always seeking simple explanations in terms of reinforcement histories rather than complex or mysterious explanations in terms of mental states.

Although we ordinarily expect scientific progress to emerge from a logical sequence of experiments designed to test certain hypotheses, it sometimes results from simple accident. For example, in one of Skinner's early experiments, he arranged for rats to run down an 8-foot-long alley to get food. But after a while he grew tired of picking the rats up every time and returning them to the starting position. So he built a circular runway. Now the rats, after getting the food, could run around the circle and back to the start box on their own. But Skinner still had to replenish the food in the goal box each time. He rigged it so the rats could do that too. Eventually he decided there was no need for the alley to be 8 feet long. In fact, he dispensed with the alley altogether. What was left

If a response (such as inserting a coin into a vending machine) is not reinforced, we either extinguish the response (stop inserting coins) or learn to discriminate (using a different vending machine that delivers the promised goods).

was a simple box, now called the *Skinner box* (Figure 7.16), in which a rat presses a lever or a pigeon pecks an illuminated disk (or "key") to receive food (Skinner, 1956).

Shaping Behavior

Suppose we want to train a rat to press a lever. We could simply put the rat in the box and wait, just as Thorndike waited for cats to find their way out of his puzzle boxes. However, the rat might never press that lever. To avoid interminable waits, Skinner devised a powerful technique, called **shaping,** for establishing a new

---

Table 7.1 Comparison of Classical Conditioning and Operant Conditioning

	Classical Conditioning	Operant Conditioning
Terminology	CS, UCS, CR, UCR	Response, reinforcement
Subject's behavior . . .	Does not control UCS	Controls reinforcement
Paired during acquisition	Two stimuli (CS and UCS)	Response and reinforcement (in the presence of certain stimuli)
Responses studied	Mostly visceral (internal organs)	Mostly skeletal (movements)
Extinction procedure	CS without UCS	Response without reinforcement

FIGURE 7.16
B. F. Skinner examines one of his laboratory animals in an operant-conditioning chamber, or "Skinner box." When the light above the bar is on, pressing the bar is reinforced. A food pellet rolls out of the storage device (left) and down the tube into the cage.

response by reinforcing successive approximations to it.

We might begin by reinforcing the rat for standing up. Because that is a common behavior for rats, the rat soon gets its first reinforcement. Before long the rat has received several reinforcements and is beginning to stand up more frequently. Now we change the rules. We give the rat food only when it stands up while facing in the general direction of the lever. Soon the rat spends much of its time standing up and facing the lever. (It extinguishes its behavior of standing and facing any other direction, because those responses are not reinforced.) Now we provide reinforcement only when the rat stands in the part of the cage nearest the lever. Gradually the rat moves closer and closer to the wall on which the lever is mounted, until it is

touching the wall. Then the rat must touch the lever and finally apply weight to it. This whole shaping of behavior can sometimes be completed in minutes. The rat learns to make the response through a series of short, easy steps.

From a theoretical standpoint, Skinner's view of shaping leaves one important question unanswered: In order for a psychologist to reinforce successive approximations to some behavior, those first approximations had to come from somewhere. But where did those first behaviors come from? Neither Skinner nor his followers believe those behaviors are truly spontaneous; they must have been the product of the animal's previous experiences and its competing responses to all the stimuli in its environment (Epstein, 1991). Still, admittedly, the animal's natural variations in behavior from moment to moment are complex and hard to explain.

Chaining Behavior

To produce more complex sequences of behavior, psychologists use a procedure called **chaining.** Assume that you want to train an animal to go through a sequence of actions in a particular order. For example, you might be training a seeing eye dog for a blind person or a dolphin for Sea World. You want the animal to go through the whole sequence and not to stop and wait for a reinforcement after each behavior. You could *chain* the behaviors, reinforcing each one by the opportunity to make the next behavior. That is, first the animal learns the final behavior for some reinforcement; then it learns the next-to-last behavior, which is reinforced by the opportunity to perform the final behavior. And so on.

For example, a rat might first be placed on the top platform in Figure 7.17, where it eats food. Then it is placed on the intermediate platform with a ladder in place to the top platform. It learns to climb the ladder. After it has done so repeatedly, it is placed on the intermediate platform but the ladder is not present. The rat has to learn to pull a string to raise the ladder so that it can climb to the top platform. Finally the rat is put on the bottom platform. It has to learn to climb the ladder to the intermediate platform, pull a string to raise the ladder, and then climb the ladder again. For each response in the chain, the reinforcement is the opportunity to engage in the next behavior, until the final response in the chain leads to a primary reinforcement.

Humans learn to make chains of responses, too. As an infant you learned to eat with a fork and a spoon. Later you learned to put your own food on the plate before eating. Eventually you learned to plan a menu, go to the grocery store, buy the ingredients, cook the meal, put it on the plate, and then eat it. Each behavior is reinforced by the opportunity to engage in the next behavior.

To show how effective shaping and chaining can be, Skinner sometimes performed this demonstration: First, he trained a rat to go to the center of a cage. Then he trained it to do so only when he was playing a certain record. Then he trained it to wait for the record to start, go to the center of the cage, and sit up on its hind legs. Step by step Skinner eventually trained the rat to wait for the record to start (which happened to be the "Star-Spangled Banner"), move to the center of the cage, sit up on its hind legs, put its claws on a string next to a pole, pull the string to hoist a flag, and then salute the flag until the record had finished. Only then did it get its food reinforcement. Needless to say, a show of patriotism is not part of a rat's natural repertoire of behavior; it learns to go through the motions only by successive approximations.

INCREASING AND DECREASING THE FREQUENCY OF RESPONSES

To a large extent our behavior is governed by its consequences. We engage in acts that increase the number of good things that happen to us and decrease the number of bad things. Investigators of operant conditioning try to determine in detail how those good things and bad things change our behavior.

Reinforcement and Punishment

A few pages back, I defined *reinforcement* as an event that increases the probability that the preceding response will be repeated in the future. Psychologists distinguish two kinds of reinforcement: positive reinforcement and negative reinforcement. You might at first suppose that if positive reinforcement is the presentation of something pleasant, negative reinforcement must be the presentation of something unpleasant. But it is not. Negative reinforcement is the *omission* of something that would have been *unpleasant*. Many people find this definition confusing, and some prominent psychologists have advocated either changing the definition or dropping the term altogether (Kimble, 1981).

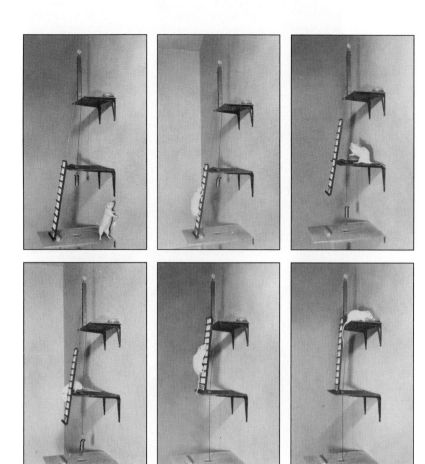

FIGURE 7.17

Chaining is a procedure in which the reinforcement for one behavior is the opportunity to engage in the next behavior. To reach food on the top platform, this rat must climb a ladder and pull a string to raise the ladder so that it can climb up again. Behavior chains longer than this can be sustained by one reward at the end.

But once a field has accepted a definition of some term, changing it is quite difficult. (Think of the United States' eternal resistance to adopting the metric system.)

So let's just accept the usual definitions of positive and negative reinforcement and try to make them understandable: *Both* positive and negative reinforcement *increase* the responses they are paired with. **Positive reinforcement** is the presentation of a favorable event, such as food, water, or access to a sexual partner. **Negative reinforcement** (also called escape or avoidance learning) is the omission or removal of an unfavorable event. Just remember that reinforcement always strengthens a response; the terms *positive* and *negative* refer to whether something is presented or removed. Food is a positive reinforcer; turning off an electric shock

Squirrels on vacation? These water-skiers learned to ski through shaping and chaining, methods of reinforcing desired behavior and building on it. Standing still would be just the first of many steps in gradually training these animals to ski.

is a negative reinforcer. Practice this distinction with the items in Concept Check 7.

▪ C O N C E P T C H E C K

7. *Identify each of the following as positive reinforcement or negative reinforcement:*

a. The judge cancels your speeding ticket because you promise not to speed again.

b. A friend compliments you for your (now) excellent driving habits.

c. Your employer gives you bonus pay for working overtime.

d. You turn off a dripping faucet, ending the "drip drip drip" sound.
(Check your answers on page 310.)

Punishment, the opposite of reinforcement, is an event that decreases the probability that the preceding response will be repeated.

Inhibiting a response in order to avoid punishment is known as passive avoidance. For example, we avoid jumping off cliffs in order to avoid injury; we do not steal because we would expect to be punished if we did.

Just as we distinguish between positive and negative reinforcement, we can distinguish between positive and negative punishment (McConnell, 1990). **Negative punishment** (also called omission training) is the weakening of a response by the omission of a favorable stimulus. For example, a teenager who drives recklessly loses the privilege of driving the family car. The loss of a favorable opportunity suppresses the tendency toward reckless driving.

Table 7.2 summarizes the four varieties of operant conditioning. Remember these key points: *All reinforcement increases a behavior; all punishment decreases it. "Positive" means that a response leads to some event; "negative" means that a response prevents the event.*

▪ C O N C E P T C H E C K

8. *Identify each of the following as positive punishment or negative punishment:*

a. Your professor gives you a poor grade because you wrote a paper with many misspellings.

b. Your parents "ground" you (forbid you to go out at night) because of a poor test grade.

c. Your swimming coach requires you to clean the pool after a poor swimming effort.

d. Your swimming coach says you cannot go to the next swim meet (which you were looking forward to), because you broke a training rule.
(Check your answers on page 310.)

How effective is punishment? Should children sometimes be spanked? Should retarded people be punished for engaging in dangerous behaviors? Psychologists are not in full agreement on these matters.

If an individual has a strong motivation to engage in a certain behavior and has no other way to satisfy that motivation, punishment is generally ineffective. In one experiment, B. F. Skinner (1938) first trained some rats to press a bar to get food and then switched procedures so that pressing the bar no longer produced food. For some of the rats, Skinner arranged the apparatus so that the bar slapped their paws every time they pressed it during the first 10 minutes of the extinction period. The other rats received no punishment. For the first 10 minutes, the

Table 7.2 The Four Categories of Operant Conditioning

	Pleasant Stimulus	Unpleasant Stimulus
Presented	Positive reinforcement (increases frequency of response) Example: You write an outstanding short story and *receive a prize* for it	Punishment (decreases frequency of response) Example: You write an insulting letter to someone who later *slaps* your face as punishment
Removed	Negative punishment (also called omission training—decreases frequency of response) Example: You write an ungrammatical letter of application to graduate school and as a result you *do not receive admission* to the program	Negative reinforcement (also called escape or avoidance learning—increases frequency of response) Example: You write an outstanding term paper in a course and as a result you *do not have to take* the final exam

punished rats lowered their response rate. In the long run, however, they made as many total responses as the unpunished rats did.

Skinner concluded that punishment temporarily suppresses a behavior but does not permanently weaken it. Later research, however, indicates that under certain circumstances punishment exerts lasting effects on behavior. The problem with Skinner's study is that the hungry rats had no alternative response available for obtaining food. If you got a shock every time you touched the refrigerator door but knew there was no food available elsewhere, you would go on trying to open the door.

Psychologists now believe that punishment can be effective so long as it is delivered promptly and consistently after a response is made and so long as some alternative response is available (Walters & Grusec, 1977). Even so, the effectiveness of punishment depends on many factors. For example, children respond more readily to mild punishment accompanied by a parent's explanation of why they were punished than they do to more intense punishment without an explanation. Punishment is ineffective if children learn that they can get more attention for "bad" behavior than for "good" behavior. It may even stimulate the very behaviors it is meant to discourage. For example, a parent who spanks a child for nervous fidgeting may find that the spanking makes the child even more nervous and fidgety.

In practical situations, the question is not whether punishment will work but whether it is the best way to achieve the desired results. If you want to teach your young son or daughter not to touch a hot stove, you may get good results from a swift but gentle slap on the wrist or even a sharp NO! A few years later, if you want to teach the same child to speak politely to others, an occasional reinforcement for politeness is likely to work better than punishment for rudeness. The government has found that it can elicit more cooperation from business firms by granting them tax credits for desirable actions than by fining them for undesirable actions.

Something to Think About

Your local school board proposes to improve class attendance by lowering the grades of any student who misses a certain number of classes. How might it achieve the same goal through positive reinforcement?

What Constitutes Reinforcement?

In operant conditioning, the probability of some response increases because a reinforcement follows it. But what is a reinforcement? It is "something that increases the probability of the preceding response." So far we are just going around in circles, unless we can find some way to specify what will be a reinforcement and what will not. We want to specify that for a practical reason as well: When we want to reinforce a child for doing well in school or a worker for doing well on the job (or anyone for doing

Different items can serve as reinforcements for different people. This man has devoted enormous time, effort, and money to collecting license plates, parts of old cars, and other items that other people would throw away as worthless. Some people pay thousands of dollars for old comic books, stamps, coins, or baseball cards.

well at anything), we have to know what will be an effective reinforcement.

Thorndike suggested a trial-and-error approach to finding reinforcers: We could simply try a number of likely reinforcers and see what works. If some event serves as a reinforcer for one behavior in one situation, it will also serve as a reinforcer for other behaviors in other situations. The problem with that approach is that a given reinforcer may be more effective at one time than at others. You might walk a mile for a cold drink today but not tomorrow. The opportunity to talk to a long-lost friend might be a great reinforcer at one time, a weak reinforcer or even an annoyance at some other time. Tickets to an opera might be a strong reinforcer for one person but not for another. We need to understand not only *what* can be a reinforcer, but also *when* and *for whom* it will be an effective reinforcer.

The Premack Principle David Premack (1965) proposed that a reinforcer is not really a stimulus; it is the opportunity to do something. For example, we often speak of food as a reinforcer, but the real reinforcer is the opportunity to eat. Furthermore, Premack suggested, the opportunity for a higher-probability behavior will reinforce any lower-probability behavior. This relationship is known as the **Premack principle.** Thus, to determine what will be an effec-

tive reinforcer, we could simply observe what some person or animal ordinarily does. For example, suppose a fourth-grade teacher finds that Jenny spends as much time on the playground as possible and spends little of her time studying. The teacher could get Jenny to study more by allowing her some extra play time if she completes a certain amount of studying. The reverse is also true: Suppose Juanita is shy and studious; she stays inside reading while the other children are at play. The teacher might offer Juanita a special book to keep if she spends a certain amount of time playing outside with the other children.

The key point of the Premack principle is that a given opportunity could be a reinforcer at one time and not another, or for one person and not another. For one person the opportunity for response A reinforces response B; for someone else the opportunity for response B reinforces response A.

■ CONCEPT CHECK

9. Anorexia nervosa is a condition in which an otherwise healthy person refuses to eat enough to survive and is obsessed with weight loss. Suppose you are a psychologist trying to encourage such a person to eat and you wish to use positive reinforcement. According to the Premack principle, how should you begin? (Check your answer on page 310.)

The Disequilibrium Principle The Premack principle is a major step toward understanding reinforcement, but it needs some fine-tuning. Its weakness is its assumption that low-frequency behaviors are unimportant to us and probably not reinforcing. But consider, for example, the low-frequency, very nonglamorous behavior of trimming your toenails: Over the course of an average week, you probably spend almost no time at all on this activity; consequently, the Premack principle implies that the opportunity to clip your toenails should be an extremely weak reinforcer. But if you are overdue for trimming those nails, the opportunity to trim them may take priority over some much more common activities. The same is true of sexual activity, watching movies, making long-distance phone calls, and a variety of other infrequent but important activities.

Evidently the key to reinforcement is not just how much time we spend on a given activity, but whether we are spending as much time on it as we would like. According to the **disequi-**

librium principle of reinforcement, each of us has a normal, or "equilibrium," state in which we divide our time among various activities in some preferred way. If for any reason we have spent less time than usual on one of these activities, then we are in a state of disequilibrium. An opportunity to engage in the deprived activity will be a reinforcer because it restores equilibrium (Timberlake & Farmer-Dougan, 1991). That is, even the opportunity for a rare behavior can be a reinforcer after a period of deprivation.

Primary and Secondary Reinforcement We can easily see why food and water are reinforcers; we all need to eat and drink in order to survive. But we will also work for a dollar bill or a college diploma. We distinguish between **primary reinforcers** such as food and water, which satisfy biological needs, and **secondary reinforcers** such as dollar bills, which become reinforcing because of their association with a primary reinforcer in the past. Dollar bills have no value to us at first, but become reinforcing once we learn that we can exchange them for food or other primary reinforcers. A student learns that good grades will win the approval of parents and teachers; an employee learns that increased sales will win the approval of the employer. We spend most of our time working for secondary reinforcers.

Reinforcement as Learning What Leads to What Thorndike, you will recall, held that reinforcement strengthens the response that preceded it. According to that view, reinforcement is a mechanical process; the person who experiences reinforcement simply engages in the response more frequently, without understanding *why.*

According to another view that E. C. Tolman (1932) first proposed, individuals learn what leads to what. A rat may learn that running down an alley leads to food. Having learned that, the rat does not automatically go running down the alley all the time. It runs down the alley only when it needs food.

For example, suppose an animal has managed to find its way through a maze. We reward it by giving it something it may not need at the moment, such as food just after it has eaten a meal. Despite this reinforcement, the animal does not repeat the behavior, at least not right away. But if we retest the animal several hours later, we find that it suddenly increases the frequency of the behavior (Tolman & Honzik, 1930).

David Nathanson, a psychologist in Florida, uses the Premack principle in teaching children with Down syndrome or other mental disabilities. The goal is to improve their ability to learn by increasing their short attention spans; the positive reinforcement is the opportunity to "play" with a dolphin. The children, ranging in age from 2 to 10, first receive individual instruction in a classroomlike setting. Then the teacher takes a child to the pool to meet the dolphin. A card with a picture and word on it is shown to the child and then thrown into the water; the dolphin pushes it back to the child with its nose. If the child identifies the picture with the correct word, he or she gets a "kiss" from the dolphin or gets to throw the card back in the water. The children tend to give correct answers more often with the dolphins than in the classroom.

Another example: A rat is reinforced with sugar water for making response A and is reinforced with food pellets for making response B. After both responses have become well established, the rat is made ill after consuming, say, the sugar water and quickly learns to avoid it. Now the rat is put in a cage where it can make both response A and response B, although neither response produces any reinforcement. The rat spends most of its time making response B and seldom, if ever, makes response A (Colwill & Rescorla, 1985). Clearly something more is at work here than reinforcement increasing the frequency of responses. Evidently the rat has learned which response produced which outcome.

In other words, we must distinguish between learning and performance. A subject's behavior depends on what outcome is associated with that behavior and on how strongly motivated the subject is to achieve that outcome.

Some secondary reinforcers are surprisingly powerful. Consider, for example, how hard some first-graders work for a little gold star that the teacher pastes on an assignment.

Schedules of Reinforcement

The simplest procedure in operant conditioning is to provide reinforcement every time the correct response occurs. **Continuous reinforcement** refers to reinforcement for every correct response. As you know, not every response in the real world leads to reinforcement. Generally, we need fairly steady reinforcement when we are first learning some skill, but after a while we can continue with only occasional reinforcement. For example, when you first learned to write, your teachers and others told you, "That's very good. . . . You make your letters very neatly. . . . You spelled all these words correctly!" Sometimes they gave you a gold star or some other little prize for writing clearly or spelling well. Today, you receive only an occasional compliment on your neat writing or good spelling, but that is enough.

Reinforcement for some responses and not others is known as **partial reinforcement.** We behave differently when we know that only some of our responses will be reinforced. Psychologists have investigated the effects of many **schedules of reinforcement,** which are rules for

the delivery of reinforcement. Continuous reinforcement is the simplest schedule of reinforcement. Four schedules for partial reinforcement are fixed ratio, fixed interval, variable ratio, and variable interval. (See Table 7.3.) A ratio schedule provides reinforcements depending on the number of responses. An interval schedule provides reinforcements depending on the timing of responses.

Fixed-Ratio Schedule A **fixed-ratio schedule** provides reinforcement only after a certain (fixed) number of correct responses have been made—after every fifth response, for example. Even with a fixed-ratio schedule that reinforces every one-hundredth or every two-hundredth response, some animals will continue to respond until they get reinforcement. We see similar behavior among pieceworkers in a factory, whose pay depends on how many pieces they turn out or among fruit pickers who get paid by the bushel.

The response rate on a fixed-ratio schedule tends to be rapid and steady. However, if the schedule requires a large number of responses for a reinforcement, there may be a temporary interruption. For example, an animal that has just finished pressing a lever 50 times to get a piece of food will pause for a while before starting to press again. The more responses that are required, the longer the pause will be. The same is true of humans. A student who has just completed 10 calculus problems may pause briefly before starting her French assignment; after completing 100 problems, she will pause even longer.

Variable-Ratio Schedule A **variable-ratio schedule** is the same as a fixed-ratio schedule except that the number of responses necessary for reinforcement varies from time to time. Reinforcement may come after 10 responses, then after 17 more responses, then after another 9. Variable-ratio schedules generate steady response rates. Gambling is reinforced on a variable-ratio schedule, because the gambler receives payment for some responses and not others on an irregular basis.

In everyday life we sometimes perform some behavior for which the chance of reinforcement is fairly low and independent of how many times we have performed this behavior. When that is true, we are reinforced on a variable-ratio schedule. For example, a radio station announces it will give free concert tickets to the next 40 people who call. When you call, you find that the line is busy. Each time you call you may have, say, one chance in twenty of getting a free line. So if you call repeatedly, you are reinforced for an average of one twentieth of your calls. (In this case, of course, you would be reinforced only once.)

Buying raffle tickets also leads to variable-ratio reinforcement. Each ticket has some small chance of being a winner. You might have to buy just a few tickets before you buy a winner, or you might have to buy hundreds, thousands, even millions.

Fixed-Interval Schedule   A **fixed-interval schedule** provides reinforcement for the first response made after a specific time interval. For instance, an animal might get food only for the first response it makes after each 2-minute interval. Then it would have to wait another 2 minutes before another response would count. Animals (including humans) on such a schedule usually learn to pause after each reinforcement and begin to respond again only as the end of the time interval approaches.

Checking your mailbox is an example of behavior on a fixed-interval schedule. If your mail is delivered at about 3 P.M., you will get no reinforcement for checking your mailbox at 2:00 P.M. If you are eagerly awaiting an important letter, you will begin to check around 2:30 and continue checking every few minutes until it arrives.

Variable-Interval Schedule   In a **variable-interval schedule,** the time interval varies between one reinforcement opportunity and the next. For example, reinforcement may come for the first response after 2 minutes, then for the first response after 7 seconds, then for the first response after 3 minutes 20 seconds, and so forth. There is no way of knowing how long it will be before the next response is reinforced. Consequently, animals usually respond to a variable-interval schedule at a slow but steady rate. In an office where employees are rewarded if they are at work when the boss appears, they will work steadily but not necessarily vigorously so long as the boss's appearances are irregular and unpredictable.

Stargazing is another example of a response reinforced on a variable-interval schedule. The reinforcement for stargazing—seeing a comet, a nova, or some other unusual phenomenon—appears at irregular, unpredictable intervals. Consequently, both professional and amateur astronomers scan the skies regularly.

Table 7.3 Some Schedules of Reinforcement

Type	Description
Continuous	Reinforcement for every response of the correct type
Fixed ratio	Reinforcement for a certain number of responses, regardless of their timing
Variable ratio	Reinforcement for an unpredictable number of responses that varies around some mean value
Fixed interval	Reinforcement for the first response that follows a given delay since the previous reinforcement
Variable interval	Reinforcement for the first response that follows an unpredictable delay since the previous reinforcement

Extinction of Responses Maintained by Ratio or Interval Reinforcement   After a schedule of partial reinforcement (either a ratio schedule or an interval schedule), the extinction of responses tends to be slower than it is after a schedule of continuous reinforcement (reinforcement for every response). That tendency is known as the **partial-reinforcement extinction effect.** If a subject has become accustomed to reinforcement for every response it makes, a sudden cessation of reinforcement is very noticeable and extinction sets in rapidly. On a ratio or an interval schedule, however, the subject learns that it may have to respond many times before getting reinforcement. Consequently, a long time may pass before it discovers that its responses will never be reinforced again. So extinction occurs slowly.

■ CONCEPT CHECKS

10. The reinforcement for studying hard is getting a good score on a test. Which schedule of reinforcement is in force in each of the following situations? When will students study in each case?

a. The professor gives unannounced tests ("pop quizzes") at unpredictable times.

b. The professor gives a test on the last day of every month.

c. Students work at their own pace and take a test as soon as they finish a chapter.

Reinforcements—continuous or partial—encourage us to continue trying. Whatever the job, all employees are on a schedule of reinforcement. This factory worker is paid on a fixed-ratio schedule—her wages depend on the number of items she produces. Businesses that adopt incentive-pay systems usually increase productivity. Gambling offers reinforcement on a variable-ratio schedule. Some people play blackjack or roulette for hours at a time with few rewards for their efforts. The unpredictability is part of the appeal to gamblers. But never knowing whether or not the next bet will be the big payoff makes it hard to quit. "Just one more" may become one more hour.

11. *A novice gambler and a longtime gambler both lose 20 bets in a row. Which is more likely to continue betting? Why?*
(Check your answers on page 310.)

SOME PRACTICAL APPLICATIONS OF OPERANT CONDITIONING

Although operant conditioning arose from purely theoretical concerns, it has had a long history of practical applications. Here are four examples.

Animal Training

Most animal acts today are based on training methods similar to Skinner's. To get an animal to perform a trick, the trainer first trains it to perform some simple act that is similar to its natural behavior. Then the trainer shapes the animal, step by step, to perform progressively more complex behaviors. Most animal trainers rely on positive reinforcement rather than on punishment.

During the Second World War, Skinner proposed a military application of his training methods (Skinner, 1960). The military was having trouble designing a guidance system for its air-to-ground missiles. It needed apparatus that could recognize a target and guide a missile toward it but that would be compact enough to leave room for explosives. Skinner said that he could teach pigeons to recognize a target and peck in its direction. If pigeons were placed in the nose cone of a missile, the direction of their pecking would guide the missile to the target. Skinner demonstrated that pigeons would do the job more cheaply and more accurately than the apparatus then in use and would take up less space. But the military laughed off the whole idea.

Persuasion

How could you get someone to do something he or she did not want to do? To take an extreme example, how could you convince a prisoner of war to cooperate with the enemy?

The best way is to start by reinforcing a very small degree of cooperation and then working up from there. This principle has been applied by people who probably never had heard of B. F. Skinner, positive reinforcement, or shaping. During the Korean War, for example, the

Chinese Communists forwarded some of the letters written home by prisoners of war but intercepted others. (The prisoners could tell from the replies which letters had been forwarded.) The prisoners began to suspect they would have better luck getting their letters through if they said something mildly favorable about their captors. So from time to time they would include a brief remark that the Communists were not really so bad, or that certain aspects of the Chinese system seemed to work pretty well, or that they hoped the war would end soon. After a while the Chinese captors ran essay contests in which the soldier who wrote the best essay (in the captors' opinion) would win a little extra food or some other privilege. Most of the winning essays contained a statement or two that complimented the Communists on some minor matter or that admitted "the United States is not perfect." Gradually, more and more soldiers started to include such statements in their essays. Occasionally, the Chinese might ask one of them, "You said the United States is not perfect. We wonder whether you could tell us some of the ways in which it is not perfect, so that we can better understand your system." Then they would ask the soldiers who cooperated to read aloud their lists of what was wrong with the United States. And so on. Gradually, without torture or coercion, and with only modest reinforcements, the Chinese induced many prisoners to make public statements denouncing the United States, to make false confessions, to inform on fellow prisoners, and even to reveal military secrets (Cialdini, 1985).

The point is clear: Whether we want to get rats to salute the flag or soldiers to denounce it, the most effective training technique is to start with natural behaviors, to reinforce those behaviors, and then gradually to shape more complex behaviors.

Behavior Modification

Say what you will about ethics, we often try to change people's behavior—in prisons, for example, and mental hospitals and schools. The principles of operant conditioning have proved very useful in efforts to modify behavior.

In **behavior modification,** someone sets a specific behavior goal and then systematically reinforces the subject's successive approximations to it. For example, Donald Whaley and Richard Malott (1971) describe a 9-year-old boy who would talk loudly and rapidly for more than 10 minutes at a time without ever pausing

The high-tech hope of robots handling housekeeping chores has yet to materialize, but in the meantime, simian aides— trained monkeys—are helping the disabled. Monkeys are proving useful for doing indoor tasks for people with limited mobility—such as the simian aide above with a quadriplegic man. The monkey at left is being trained to retrieve objects identified with a laser beam. Such training relies on shaping behavior Skinner-style—building a new response by reinforcing sequential approximations to it.

long enough for others to get a word in. As you might imagine, the boy's parents, teachers, and indeed everyone who knew him were eager to modify his behavior.

A psychologist began by searching out a behavior that the boy preferred even to talking (recall the Premack principle). That turned out to be firing a cap pistol. (Perhaps because it made even more noise than talking?) Whenever the boy paused for at least 3 seconds, he earned some caps. In the first session, he earned only 20 reinforcements in 90 minutes (see Figure 7.18). (He was silent for only 60 seconds during those 90 minutes!) Over successive sessions, he earned more reinforcements. Then the psychologist shifted to a fixed-ratio schedule, reinforcing only every fifth pause. By the sixth session,

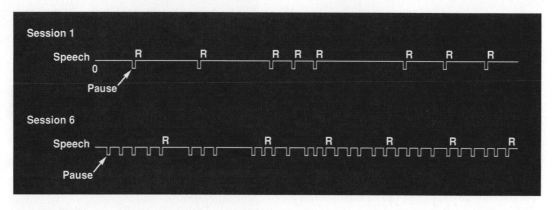

FIGURE 7.18
In one example of behavior modification, a psychologist gave a gabby boy a reinforcement (caps for a cap gun) whenever he paused from talking for 3 seconds. In the first session he earned only 20 caps in 90 minutes. By the sixth session his pauses had become more frequent.

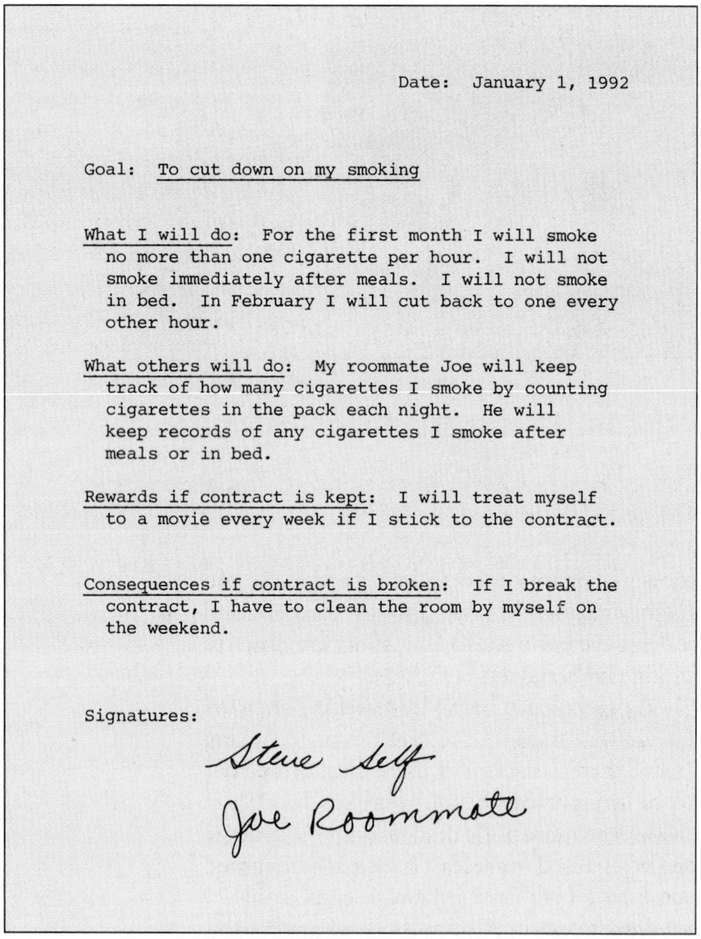

Date: January 1, 1992

Goal: <u>To cut down on my smoking</u>

<u>What I will do</u>: For the first month I will smoke no more than one cigarette per hour. I will not smoke immediately after meals. I will not smoke in bed. In February I will cut back to one every other hour.

<u>What others will do</u>: My roommate Joe will keep track of how many cigarettes I smoke by counting cigarettes in the pack each night. He will keep records of any cigarettes I smoke after meals or in bed.

<u>Rewards if contract is kept</u>: I will treat myself to a movie every week if I stick to the contract.

<u>Consequences if contract is broken</u>: If I break the contract, I have to clean the room by myself on the weekend.

Signatures:

Steve Self
Joe Roommate

FIGURE 7.19
Sometimes people try to change their own behavior by setting up a system of reinforcements and punishments.

the boy was pausing about once per minute. He was still gabby, but at least other people were getting some chance to talk.

■ CONCEPT CHECK

12. Which type of operant conditioning was used in the preceding example of the gabby boy: positive reinforcement, negative reinforcement (active avoidance), punishment (passive avoidance), or negative punishment (omission training)? (Check your answer on page 310.)

Breaking Bad Habits

Some people learn to conquer their own bad habits by means of reinforcements, with a little outside help. Nathan Azrin and Robert Nunn (1973) recommend this three-step method:

1. Become more aware of your bad habit. Interrupt the behavior and isolate it from the chain of normal activities. As an extension of this step, Brian Yates (1985) suggests you imagine an association between the behavior and something repulsive. For example, to break a fingernail-biting habit, imagine your fingernails covered with sewage.

2. If no one else will reinforce you for making progress, provide your own reinforcements. For example, buy yourself a special treat for abandoning your bad habit for a certain period of time.

3. Do something incompatible with the offending habit. For example, if you have a nervous habit of hunching up your shoulders, practice depressing your shoulders.

Figure 7.19 shows an example in which a college student set up a list of reinforcements and punishments to support his goal of decreased smoking. If he successfully limited his smoking, he would treat himself to a movie. If he exceeded the limit he had set for himself, he would have to clean the room by himself on the weekend, and he would not go to a movie. Many people set up similar patterns of reinforcement and punishment for themselves, generally without a written contract.

You might try drawing up for yourself a plan to change some of your own habits. For example, you might set a goal to study your assignments on a more regular basis (if you do not do so already). Choose some realistic reinforcers, and see whether this program actually improves your study habits. If not, you might try modifying the plan.

SUMMARY

■ *Reinforcement.* Edward Thorndike introduced the concept of reinforcement. A reinforcement increases the probability that the preceding response will be repeated. (page 293)

■ *Operant conditioning.* Operant conditioning is the process of controlling the rate of a behavior through reinforcement. (page 294)

■ *Extinction.* In operant conditioning, a response becomes extinguished if it is no longer followed by reinforcement. (page 296)

■ *Shaping.* Shaping is a technique for training subjects to perform acts that are remote from their natural behavior by reinforcing them for successive approximations to the desired behavior. (page 297)

■ *Punishment.* Punishment, the omission of a reinforcement, or the omission of a punishment also will change the rate of a behavior. (page 300)

■ *The nature of reinforcement.* The opportunity to engage in a frequent behavior will reinforce a less frequent behavior. Something that an individual can exchange for a reinforcer becomes a reinforcer itself. (page 301)

■ *Learning what leads to what.* Animals (and people) learn which reinforcement is associated with which behavior. The frequency with which they repeat a given behavior depends on the strength of their motivation to receive the associated reinforcement at the moment. (page 303)

■ *Schedules of reinforcement.* The timing of a response depends on the schedule of reinforcement. In a ratio schedule of reinforcement, an individual is given reinforcement after a fixed or variable number of responses. In an interval schedule of reinforcement, an individual is given reinforcement after a fixed or variable period of time. (page 304)

■ *Applications.* People have applied operant conditioning to animal training, persuasion, behavior modification, and habit breaking. (page 306)

SUGGESTIONS FOR FURTHER READING

Glaser, R. (1990). The reemergence of learning theory within instructional research. *American Psychologist, 45,* 29–39. Discussion of applications of operant conditioning to education.

Schwartz, B. (1988). *Psychology of learning and behavior* (3rd ed.). New York: Norton. An excellent comprehensive text on learning.

Skinner, B. F. (1948). *Walden two.* New York: Macmillan. A novel about an attempt to devise an ideal society according to the principles of operant conditioning.

TERMS

reinforcement an event that increases the probability that the preceding response will be repeated in the future (page 294)

law of effect Thorndike's theory that a response which is followed by favorable consequences becomes more probable and a response which is followed by unfavorable consequences becomes less probable (page 294)

operant conditioning or **instrumental conditioning** the process of changing behavior by following a response with reinforcement (page 294)

visceral pertaining to the internal organs (page 294)

skeletal pertaining to the muscles that move the limbs, trunk, and head (page 294)

belongingness the concept that certain stimuli are readily associated with each other and that certain responses are readily associated with certain outcomes (page 295)

extinction in operant conditioning, the weakening of a response after a period of no reinforcement (page 296)

stimulus generalization in operant conditioning, the tendency to make a similar response to a stimulus that resembles one that has been associated with reinforcement (page 296)

discrimination in operant conditioning, the learning of different behaviors in response to stimuli associated with different levels of reinforcement (page 297)

shaping a technique for establishing a new response by reinforcing successive approximations to it (page 297)

chaining a procedure for developing a sequence of behaviors in which the reinforcement for one response is the opportunity to engage in the next response (page 298)

positive reinforcement the presentation of a favorable event (page 299)

negative reinforcement the omission or removal of an unfavorable event (page 299)

punishment an event that decreases the probability that the preceding response will be repeated (page 300)

negative punishment the weakening of a response by the omission of a favorable stimulus (page 300)

Premack principle the principle that the opportunity to engage in a frequent behavior will reinforce a less frequent behavior (page 302)

disequilibrium principle principle that an opportunity to engage in any deprived activity will be a reinforcer because it restores equilibrium (page 302)

primary reinforcer an event that satisfies a biological need (page 303)

secondary reinforcer an event that becomes reinforcing when it is associated with a primary reinforcer (page 303)

continuous reinforcement reinforcement for every correct response (page 304)

partial reinforcement reinforcement for some responses and not others (page 304)

schedule of reinforcement a rule for the delivery of reinforcement following various patterns of responding (page 304)

fixed-ratio schedule a rule for delivering reinforcement only after the subject has made a certain number of responses (page 304)

variable-ratio schedule a rule for delivering reinforcement after varying numbers of responses (page 304)

fixed-interval schedule a rule for delivering reinforcement for the first response the subject makes after a specified period of time has passed (page 305)

variable-interval schedule a rule for delivering reinforcement after varying amounts of time (page 305)

partial-reinforcement extinction effect the tendency for extinction to occur more slowly on ei-

ther a ratio or an interval schedule than on a schedule of continuous reinforcement (page 305)

behavior modification a procedure for modifying behavior by setting specific behavior goals and reinforcing the subject for successive approximations to those goals (page 307)

ANSWERS TO CONCEPT CHECKS

6. You would have to know whether the bell was always followed by food (classical conditioning) or whether food was presented only if the animal sat up on its hind legs (operant conditioning). (page 295)

7. (a) Negative reinforcement—the omission of something (a fine) that would have been unpleasant. (b) Positive reinforcement. (c) Positive reinforcement. (d) Negative reinforcement. (page 300)

8. (a) Positive punishment. (b) Negative punishment—the omission of an opportunity to do something enjoyable. (c) Positive punishment. (d) Negative punishment. (page 300)

9. Begin by determining how this person spends his or her time—for example, exercising, reading, watching television, visiting with friends. Offer those opportunities as reinforcers for gaining weight. (We shall discuss this approach more fully in Chapter 15.) (page 302)

10. (a) Variable interval; students will study at a steady rate each day. (b) Fixed interval; students will study vigorously as they get close to the end of the month and will pause for some time after each test. (c) Fixed ratio; students will study at a steady pace (except for interruptions from other courses and other commitments). (page 305)

11. The habitual gambler will continue longer, because he or she has a history of being reinforced for gambling on a variable-ratio schedule, which retards extinction. (For the same reason, an alcoholic who has had both good experiences and bad experiences while drunk is likely to keep on drinking even after several consecutive bad experiences.) (page 305)

12. If you consider "silence" an active response, you could regard this as an example of positive reinforcement for silence. Otherwise, it is an example of negative punishment for the response of talking. The response (talking) is decreased because its occurrence leads to the omission of the reinforcer (the caps). (page 308)

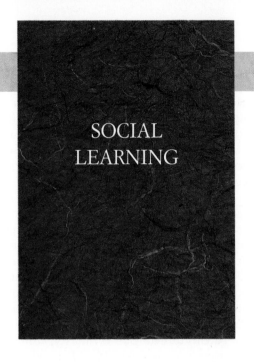

SOCIAL
LEARNING

How do we learn from the successes and failures of others without trying every response ourselves?

How do you learn how fast you should drive your car? Classical conditioning plays a role: You notice that your speedometer has hit 70 and a few seconds later you hear a police siren. The next time you notice your speedometer hitting 70, you experience a conditioned response: nervousness.

Reinforcement too plays a role in your behavior: When you drive at a steady 55 mph, the fact that you reach your destination sooner than if you had driven at 45 provides positive reinforcement. When you drive at 70, reaching your destination even sooner will provide further reinforcement. But it may also bring punishment, causing you to reach your destination both later and poorer.

You also learn from observing the behavior of others. You read that the police plan to enforce the speed laws more rigorously than usual during a holiday weekend, so you stay within the limit. But you notice that everyone is passing you, so you speed up. Then you pass a three-car wreck and recognize some of the cars that had passed you a minute before, so you slow down again. Note that you speed up and slow down even though you are experiencing no direct reinforcement or punishment. You learn about the reinforcements and punishments that your own behavior is likely to provoke by observing what happens to others.

THE SOCIAL-LEARNING APPROACH

According to the **social-learning approach** (Bandura, 1977, 1986), just about everything we do has been learned, even what we call "personality." But not all of it is learned by trial and error with reinforcement; we learn about many behaviors before we try them the first time. Much learning, especially in humans, results from observing the behavior of others and from imagining the consequences of our own behavior. That is, we can learn what leads to what, long before we actually perform any of the actions.

Although psychologists frequently speak of "social-learning theory," it is not a theory in the sense described in Chapter 2. The social-learning approach is more a point of view or a field of emphasis. It focuses on the effects of observation, imitation, setting goals, and self-reinforcement. In this sense, much of human behavior depends on social learning; after all, most school learning is an attempt to learn from the experiences and discoveries of other people.

Modeling and Imitation

When you join a religious organization, a fraternity, or a sorority or when you start a new job, you discover that the people already there observe certain customs. They will explain some of those customs to you, but the only way you will learn about other customs is by watching. Those who already know them serve as models (or examples) for you; when you copy their example, we say that you are **modeling** your behavior after theirs, or that you are **imitating.**

We are selective in choosing whom to imitate. We imitate people we regard as successful, people with whom we identify, people we want to be like. Advertisers are keenly aware of this tendency. They try to identify the consumers who are most likely to buy their products and the people those consumers are most likely to

According to the social-learning approach, we learn many behaviors by observing what others do, imitating behaviors that are reinforced, and avoiding behaviors that are punished.

Learning a new skill, such as how to hunt with bow and arrow, may require a combination of verbal instruction, imitating a model, and trial-and-error learning. That is, social learning combines with classical or operant conditioning.

admire and imitate. Cereal and candy advertisements feature happy, healthy children; soft-drink ads feature attractive young adults; ads for luxury cars feature wealthy executives and their impeccably groomed spouses.

The advertisers of Miller Lite beer have used this approach in a particularly effective manner. Earlier attempts to market a low-calo-rie beer had all failed. Beer drinkers perceived low-calorie beer as "diet beer" or "sissy beer." So Miller's ads featured well-known, middle-aged former athletes drinking Lite beer and getting into he-man disputes about why people should drink Lite beer—because it tastes great or because it is less filling. The campaign was so successful that the demand for *all* low-calorie beers, not just Miller's, skyrocketed.

This tendency to identify with role models is especially powerful among children. Parents sometimes tell their children, "Do as I say and not as I do." But children are more likely to copy what the parents do (Young-Ok & Stevens, 1987). They also learn how to be a parent by watching their own parents. If and when you become a parent, you probably will treat your own children in much the same way your own parents treated you—even if you *disliked* the way your parents treated you. For example, many people who were yelled at, spanked, slapped, and paddled as children tend to yell at, spank, slap, and paddle their own children (Simons, Whitbeck, Conger, & Wu, 1991). It is, of course, *possible* for you to treat your children differently from the way your parents treated you, but the natural tendency is to imitate what you have observed.

Children also take behavioral cues from other adults and from television characters. They tend to imitate adults of their own sex more than adults of the opposite sex, even when the behaviors are fairly trivial. In one experiment, children watched adults choose between an apple and a banana. If all the men chose, say, the apple and all the women chose the banana, the boys who were watching wanted an apple and the girls wanted a banana (Perry & Bussey, 1979). In other words, children learn about gender roles and sex stereotypes by observation.

Albert Bandura, Dorothea Ross, and Sheila Ross (1963) studied the role of imitation in learning aggressive behavior. They had two groups of children watch films in which an adult or a cartoon character violently attacked an inflated "Bobo" doll. They had another group watch a film in which the characters did not attack the doll. Then they left the children in a room with a Bobo doll. The children who had watched films showing attacks on the doll (and only those children) attacked the doll vigorously, using many of the same movements they had just seen (Figure 7.20). The clear implication is that children copy the aggressive behavior they have seen in others.

Is the same true for adolescents and adults? This issue is worth much concern, because so many popular movies include so much violence. As we saw in Chapter 2, the available evidence does not demonstrate that watching violence on television or in movies necessarily causes violent behavior. However, some individuals are more highly influenced than others; some viewers (especially adolescents with a history of violent behavior) may identify strongly with a highly violent character in a film. Others may be highly influenced by a film because it resembles some event they have witnessed in their own lives. Many cases have been reported in which people have re-enacted scenes they had just seen in a film (Snyder, 1991).

■ CONCEPT CHECK

13. *Many people complain that they cannot tell much difference between the two major political parties in the United States, because so many American politicians campaign in similar styles and take similar stands on the issues. Explain this observation in terms of social learning. (Check your answer on page 315.)*

Vicarious Reinforcement and Punishment

Six months ago your best friend quit a job with Consolidated Generic Products in order to open a restaurant. Now you are considering whether you should quit your own job with Consolidated Generic and open your own restaurant in a different part of town. How do you decide whether or not to take this step?

Perhaps the first thing you do is to find out how successful your friend has been. You do not automatically imitate the behavior of someone else, even someone you admire. Rather, you imitate behavior that has proved reinforcing for that person. In other words, you learn by **vicarious reinforcement** or **punishment**—that is, by substituting someone else's experience for your own.

When a new business venture succeeds, other companies try to figure out the reasons for that success and try to follow the same course. When a venture fails, other companies try to learn the reasons for that failure and try to avoid making the same mistakes. When a football team wins consistently, other teams copy its style of play. And when a television program wins high ratings, other producers are sure to present look-alikes the following year.

FIGURE 7.20
A child will mimic an adult's behavior even when neither one is reinforced for the behavior. This girl attacks a doll after seeing a film of a woman hitting it. People who witness violent behavior, including violence at home, may be more prone than others to turn to violent behavior themselves.

Something to Think About

Might vicarious learning lead to a certain monotony of behavior? Might it contribute to the lack of variety in the television programs and movies that are offered to the public? How can we learn vicariously without becoming like everyone else?

In many cases, vicarious punishment seems to affect behavior less than vicarious reinforcement does. We are bombarded by reminders that failure to wear seat belts will lead to injury or death, and yet many of us fail to buckle up, even though failure to use seat belts is illegal in some states. Despite widespread publicity about the consequences of driving drunk, using addictive drugs, or engaging in "unsafe sex," many people ignore the danger. Even the death

In most cases, vicarious punishment is not very effective; people discount what happened to someone else and assure themselves "I'm different. It can't happen to me." When basketball star Magic Johnson revealed he had HIV, his statement had an enormous impact. People who had admired Johnson and wanted to be like him could not tell themselves "I'm different."

penalty, an extreme example of vicarious punishment, has little demonstrable effect on the murder rate.

Why does vicarious punishment so frequently produce such weak effects? One explanation is that to be influenced, we must identify with the person who is receiving a vicarious reinforcement or punishment. Most of us think of ourselves as successful people; we see someone who is getting punished as a "loser" and "not like us." We can therefore continue to ignore the dangers.

The Role of Self-Efficacy in Social Learning

You watch an Olympic diver win a gold medal for a superb display of physical control. Presumably you would like to earn an Olympic medal too; so because of this vicarious reinforcement you should go out and try to make some spectacular dives into a pool. Do you? Probably not. Why not? Why does that vicarious reinforcement fail to motivate you to engage in imitative behavior?

If you are like most people, the reason is that you doubt you are capable of duplicating the diver's performance. People imitate someone else's behavior only if they have a sense of **self-**

efficacy—the perception that they themselves could perform the task successfully.

We achieve or fail to achieve a sense of self-efficacy in two ways. One way is by observing ourselves. If I have tried and failed to develop even simple athletic skills, I will have no sense of self-efficacy when I think of trying to duplicate the behavior of an Olympic medalist. A student who has studied hard and has done well on several exams will have a strong sense of self-efficacy when faced with the next exam.

We also learn about self-efficacy from role models. If your older cousin has studied hard and has gained admission to medical school, you may believe that you can do the same. Psychologists sometimes help students overcome test anxiety by having them watch students similar to themselves displaying good test-taking skills (Dykeman, 1989).

People's persistence or lack of persistence in coping with a difficult task is strongly influenced by their sense of self-efficacy. For example, kidney patients undergoing dialysis treatment are advised to curtail their fluid intake sharply. Patients who are confident they can follow the instructions generally restrict their intake and respond well to the treatment. Those who confess that they "can't tolerate frustration" generally yield to temptation, go on drinking fluids, and soon die (Rosenbaum & Smira, 1986).

Similarly, people who believe they can quit smoking have a reasonable chance of succeeding. People who doubt their ability to quit may try hard at first, but sooner or later they have one cigarette, decide they are a hopeless case, and give up (Curry, Marlatt, & Gordon, 1987).

Self-Reinforcement and Self-Punishment in Social Learning

We learn by observing others who are doing what we would like to do. If our sense of self-efficacy is strong enough, we try to imitate their behavior. But actually succeeding is another matter, which often requires prolonged efforts. People typically set a goal for themselves and monitor their progress toward it. They even provide reinforcement or punishment for themselves just as if they were training someone else. They say to themselves, "If I finish this math assignment on time, I'll treat myself to a movie and a new magazine. If I don't finish on time, I'll make myself clean the stove and the sink." (Self-punishments are usually pretty mild.)

People who have never learned to use self-reinforcement can be taught to do so. Donald Meichenbaum and Joseph Goodman (1971) worked with a group of elementary-school children who acted impulsively, blurting out answers and failing to consider the consequences of their actions. To encourage them to set appropriate goals for themselves and to practice self-reinforcement in achieving them, Meichenbaum and Goodman taught the children to talk to themselves while working on a task. For example, a child might say, "Okay, what do I have to do? You want me to copy the picture. . . . Okay, draw the line down, down, good; then to the right, that's it; now down some more and to the left. Good, I'm doing fine so far. Remember, go slowly. Now back up again. No, I was supposed to go down. That's okay. Just erase the line carefully. . . ." After only four training sessions, the children had learned to pause before answering questions and were answering more questions correctly.

Unfortunately, self-reinforcement and self-punishment do not always work. One psychologist, Ron Ash (1986), tried to teach himself to stop smoking by means of punishment. He decided to smoke only while he was reading *Psychological Bulletin* and other highly respected but tedious publications. By associating smoking with boredom, he hoped to eliminate his desire to smoke. Two months later he was smoking as much as ever, but he was starting to *enjoy* reading *Psychological Bulletin!*

IN CLOSING: WHY WE DO WHAT WE DO

Almost everything you have done today was a learned behavior—from getting dressed and combing your hair this morning through reading this book right now. In fact, you probably would have trouble listing many things you have done today that were not learned. Even your bad habits are examples of learning, or mislearning.

One point that I hope has emerged in this chapter is that learning takes many forms. Classically conditioned salivation, conditioned taste aversions, operantly conditioned movements, and socially learned behaviors occur under diverse circumstances. The underlying mechanisms in the brain may overlap, but at a descriptive level these types of learning differ in some important ways. In short, your behavior is subject to a wide variety of learned influences.

SUMMARY

- *Learning by observation.* We learn much by observing what other people do and what consequences they experience. (page 311)

- *Whom we imitate.* We are more likely to imitate the actions of people we admire and people with whom we identify. (page 311)

- *What we imitate.* We tend to imitate behaviors that have led to reinforcement for other people. We are less consistent in avoiding behaviors that have led to punishment. (page 313)

- *Self-efficacy.* Whether or not we decide to imitate a behavior that has led to reinforcement for others depends on whether we believe we are capable of duplicating that behavior. (page 314)

- *Self-reinforcement and self-punishment.* Once people have decided to try to imitate a certain behavior, they set goals for themselves and may even provide their own reinforcements and punishments. (page 314)

SUGGESTION FOR FURTHER READING

Bandura, A. (1986). *Social foundations of thought and action.* Englewood Cliffs, NJ: Prentice-Hall. A review of social learning by its most influential investigator.

TERMS

social-learning approach the view that people learn by observing and imitating the behavior of others and by imagining the consequences of their own behavior (page 311)

modeling or **imitating** copying a behavior or custom (page 311)

vicarious reinforcement or **vicarious punishment** reinforcement or punishment observed to have been experienced by someone else (page 313)

self-efficacy the perception of one's own ability to perform a task successfully (page 314)

ANSWER TO CONCEPT CHECK

13. One reason why most American politicians run similar campaigns and take similar stands is that they all tend to copy the same models—candidates who have won elections in the past. One other reason is that they all pay attention to the same public-opinion polls. (page 313)

8 MEMORY

Suppose I offer you—for a price—an opportunity to do absolutely anything you want to do for one day. You will not be limited by any of the usual constraints on what is possible. You can travel in a flash from one place on Earth to another, visiting as many places as you care to crowd into that single day. You can even travel into outer space, exploring other worlds and observing life (if any) on other planets. You can travel forward and backward through time, finding out what the future holds in store and witnessing the great events of history—or even of prehistoric times. (But you will not be able to alter history.) Anything you want to do—just name it and it is yours. Furthermore, I guarantee your safety: No matter what time and place you choose to visit or what you choose to do, you will not be killed or injured.

Now, how much would you be willing to pay for this once-in-a-lifetime opportunity? Oh, yes, I should mention . . . there is one catch. When the day is over, you will forget everything that happened. You will never be able to recover your memory of that day, even slightly. Any notes or photos you might have made will vanish. And anyone else who takes part in your special day will forget it, too.

Now how much would you be willing to pay? Much less, I am sure. Perhaps nothing. Living without remembering is hardly living at all. Our memories are almost the same thing as our "selves."

Kutbidin Atamkulov travels from one Central Asian village to another singing from memory the tale of the Kirghiz hero, Manas. The song, which lasts 3 hours, has been passed from master to student for centuries. Human memory can hold an amazing amount of information.

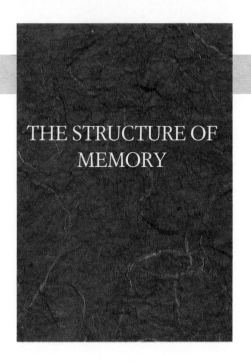

THE STRUCTURE OF MEMORY

Are there different types of memory?
Do we remember some types of material
better than others?

"Memory is a record of past events." That definition sounds reasonable enough, though it includes far more than what we usually mean when we speak of memory. The rings of a tree provide a record of the rainfall and other weather conditions in past years. The dirt on the soles of your shoes provides a record of where you were this morning. If you fold a sheet of paper, the crease provides a permanent record of the event. All of these are records of past events, but none of them is a memory.

Can you explain why they are not memories? "Well, for one thing," you may reply, "the paper cannot describe the occasion on which the crease was made." True, but the same holds true for much of human memory as well. Even though you remember how to tie your shoes, you probably cannot describe the occasion when you first formed that memory.

So what is memory? How can we define it to include all of human memory without including tree rings, the dirt on your shoes, or the crease in a sheet of paper? Defining *memory* is not easy. Nevertheless, psychologists have learned much about the circumstances that strengthen or weaken memory and about the ways in which memory differs from one situation to another.

EBBINGHAUS AND THE ASSOCIATIONIST APPROACH TO MEMORY

Since the time of John Locke, David Hume, David Hartley, and other British philosophers of the 1600s and 1700s, *association* (the linking of sensations or ideas) has been regarded as central to all thought processes. By the 1800s, associationism had become the dominant view of memory and related processes. Its influence is evident in the 20th-century writings of Pavlov, Thorndike, and the other researchers mentioned in Chapter 7. According to associationism in its original form, all experience consists of simple sensations or other psychological "elements." Similarity or contiguity in time and space links those simple elements together— "associates" them—into more complex assemblages, much as chemical bonds associate atoms into compounds.

Such was the theoretical environment in which the German psychologist Hermann Ebbinghaus (1850–1909) undertook his study of memory. Like many other psychologists of his time, Ebbinghaus began by interpreting memory in terms of association. Unlike the others, however, he devised a way of studying memory experimentally. Previously, when investigators asked people to describe their memories, they had no way of determining whether the descriptions were accurate.

Ebbinghaus simply tested memory for newly learned material. This procedure enabled him to control the amount of learning and the delay between learning and testing. It also enabled him to measure the accuracy of each memory. His method gradually became the dominant approach to the study of memory (Newman, 1987).

To make sure that the material to be memorized would be unfamiliar, Ebbinghaus invented the **nonsense syllable,** a meaningless three-letter combination such as REK or JID. He wrote out 2,300 such syllables and arranged them in random lists (Figure 8.1). His goal was to determine how rapidly people could memorize such lists and how long they could remember them. He had no cooperative introductory psychology students to draw on for his study, so

FIGURE 8.1
Hermann Ebbinghaus pioneered the scientific study of memory by observing his own capacity for memorizing lists of nonsense syllables.

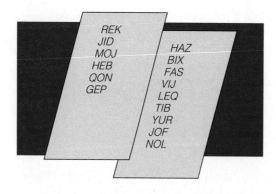

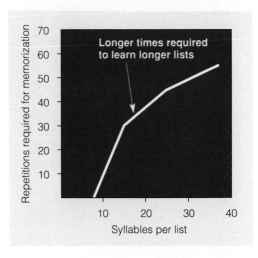

Longer times required to learn longer lists

FIGURE 8.2

Before Ebbinghaus it was obvious to common sense that people need more time to memorize a long list than a short list. Ebbinghaus's contribution was to measure how much more time people need for a long list.

he ran all the tests on himself. Over the course of about 6 years he memorized thousands of lists of nonsense syllables. (He must have been unusually dedicated to his science or uncommonly tolerant of boredom.) Let us consider two examples of Ebbinghaus's findings.

First, Ebbinghaus demonstrated that it takes longer to memorize a long list than it takes to memorize a short one. That may strike you as obvious, but it is also obvious that when you drop an object, it falls. Physicists made great advances by measuring *how fast* an object falls, and Ebbinghaus's great contribution was in measuring *how much* more time people need to memorize long lists than to memorize short lists. Figure 8.2 gives the results. Note that he was able to memorize a list of up to seven syllables in a single reading, but each additional syllable increased the number of repetitions required to recall the list. These results are similar to those that other, later investigators have obtained.

Second example: To measure how long a memory lasts, Ebbinghaus memorized several lists of 13 nonsense syllables each and then tested his memory after various delays. The results appear in Figure 8.3. He forgot a mean of more than half of each list after an hour and still more after 24 hours.

These results were based on memorization of meaningless lists, and they would no doubt differ if Ebbinghaus had been memorizing something important. Even so, if these results represent a general tendency, they suggest something very disturbing. Think of it from the standpoint of an educator: If students forget much of what they learn within one day, how much will they remember a year from now? However, later researchers, generally using college students, found results very different from those of Ebbinghaus: Most students remember most of the words on a memorized list when they are tested 24 hours later (Koppenaal, 1963).

Why do you suppose most college students remember a list so much better than Ebbinghaus did? You may be tempted to say college students did so well because they are so intelligent. True, no doubt, but Ebbinghaus was no dummy either. Or you might suggest that college students have had "so much practice at memorizing nonsense." (Sorry if you think that's true.) But Ebbinghaus had memorized a lot of nonsense himself. In fact, that was the problem: Poor Hermann Ebbinghaus had memorized *too much* nonsense—literally thousands of lists of syllables (Figure 8.4). As we shall see later in this chapter, memory of previously learned material can greatly interfere with memory of new material. Because Ebbinghaus had memorized so many lists of syllables, he tended to confuse one list with another and therefore to forget new lists very rapidly.

Ebbinghaus's methods of research remained popular for decades. They made possible such basic discoveries as the fact that people who memorize a great many similar lists (as Ebbinghaus did) are likely to forget them faster than other people do.

Today, few psychologists study memorization of nonsense syllables, and most regard memory as a more complex process than Ebbinghaus imagined it to be. Nevertheless, Ebbinghaus's influence can still be seen in the usual methods of studying memory: Investiga-

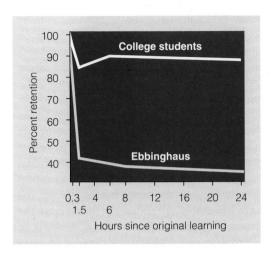

FIGURE 8.3
Yellow line: Recall of lists of syllables by Ebbinghaus (1913) after delays of various lengths. White line: Recall of lists of words by college students after delays of various lengths. (Based on Koppenaal, 1963.) Ebbinghaus learned as fast as other people but forgot faster.

FIGURE 8.4
Ebbinghaus could learn new lists of nonsense syllables, but he forgot them quickly because of interference from all the previous lists he had learned. People who memorize many similar lists start to confuse them with one another.

tors expose people to a list of words, a story, or some other experience and later test the subjects' recall. The basic assumption is that we can study the principles of memory in a laboratory just as we can study any other natural phenomenon.

THE INFORMATION-PROCESSING MODEL OF MEMORY

Ebbinghaus apparently thought of memory as a haphazard collection of associations, with no one memory being much different from another. One overall theme of memory research since his time has been the search for distinctions among types of memory.

You remember some experiences for less than a minute, other experiences for hours or days, and still others for a lifetime. Is that because you simply lose certain memories faster than others, or does it indicate that you have different kinds of memory—some temporary and some permanent?

According to one view, the **information-processing model** of memory, human memory is analogous to the memory system of a computer: Information enters the system, is processed and coded in various ways, and is then stored (Figure 8.5). According to one popular

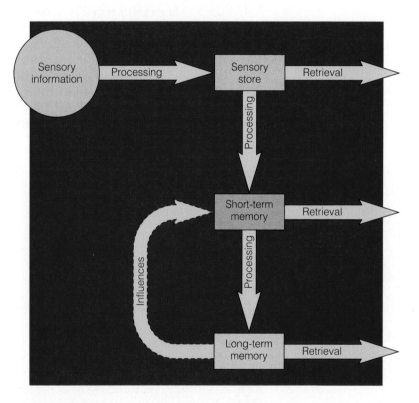

FIGURE 8.5
The information-processing model of memory resembles a computer's memory system, including temporary and permanent memory.

FIGURE 8.6
George Sperling flashed arrays like this on a screen for 50 milliseconds. After the display went off, a signal told the viewer which row to recite.

version of the information-processing model, memory first enters temporary storage (as when information is typed into a computer) and then enters permanent storage (as when information is entered onto a disk). Later, in response to a retrieval cue, a person can recover the information (Atkinson & Shiffrin, 1968). Investigators working in this tradition generally distinguish among several types of memory: a very brief sensory store, short-term memory, and long-term memory.

The Sensory Store

Every memory begins as an exposure to a sensory stimulus. After you see or hear something for even a split second, you can report minor details about it before the memory vanishes. This recall is possible because it has been temporarily entered into the **sensory store,** a very brief storage of sensory information. However, unless you immediately and actively attend to this sensory information, it will fade in less than a second as new information replaces it in the sensory store.

George Sperling (1960) tested how much information people can retain in the sensory store. He flashed an array like the one shown in Figure 8.6 onto a screen for 50 milliseconds (50 × .001 second). When he asked viewers to report as much of the whole array as they could, he found that they could recall a mean of only about four items. If he had stopped at that

point, he might have concluded that viewers could store only a small fraction of an array.

But Sperling knew that it takes several seconds for a person to report even a few items, and he knew it was likely that memories in the sensory store would fade over those seconds. In other words, much of the array, perhaps even all of it, may have entered the sensory store but may have faded in the time it took to report more than a few items. To test that possibility, he told viewers he would ask them to report only one row of the array, but he did not tell them which row. After flashing the array on the screen, he immediately used a high, medium, or low tone to signal which row the viewers were to recall. Most people could name all of the items in that row, regardless of which row he indicated. Evidently, nearly all of the information in the array was available to them for a split second. When he waited for even a second before signaling which row to recall, viewers could recall few, if any, of the items in that row.

Something to Think About

Sperling demonstrated the capacity of the sensory store for visual information. How could you demonstrate the capacity of the sensory store for *auditory* information?

Unless the information that enters the sensory store is immediately used in some way, it fades rapidly. In fact, the same information may enter the sensory store repeatedly without ever forming a permanent memory. My neighbor once told me he worked at the Wardlaw Building. "Where's that?" I asked. When he explained, I realized I had driven past that clearly marked building on my way to work every day for the previous 11 years. Although I had seen the sign thousands of times, it had never remained in my memory.

Here is an exercise you can try on yourself: Figure 8.7 shows a real U.S. penny and 14 fakes. Can you identify the real one? Are you sure? In one study (Nickerson & Adams, 1979), only 15 of 36 U.S. citizens chose the correct coin. (If you do not have a penny in your pocket, check your answer A on page 335.) Now try drawing (from memory) a nickel or the back of a penny. (If you are not from the United States, draw a coin common in your own country.) If you are like most people, the detailed appearance of the coin has passed through your sensory store repeatedly but has never entered your lasting memory.

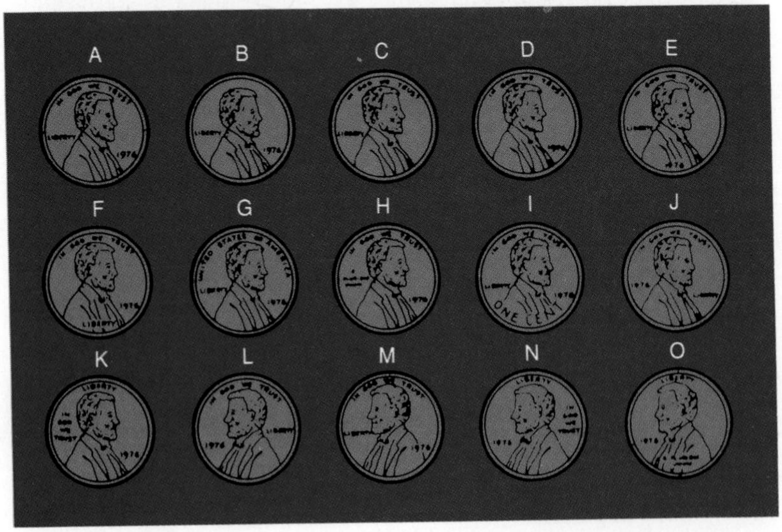

FIGURE 8.7
Can you spot the geniune penny among 14 fakes? (Based on Nickerson & Adams, 1979.) If you're not sure (and you don't have a penny with you), check answer A on page 335.

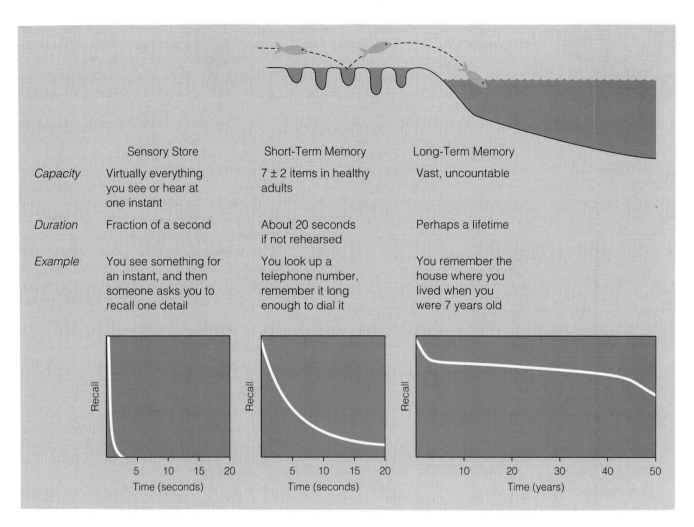

	Sensory Store	Short-Term Memory	Long-Term Memory
Capacity	Virtually everything you see or hear at one instant	7 ± 2 items in healthy adults	Vast, uncountable
Duration	Fraction of a second	About 20 seconds if not rehearsed	Perhaps a lifetime
Example	You see something for an instant, and then someone asks you to recall one detail	You look up a telephone number, remember it long enough to dial it	You remember the house where you lived when you were 7 years old

Short-Term Memory Versus Long-Term Memory

Beyond the extremely brief sensory store, psychologists distinguish two types of memory, according to duration. **Long-term memory** is a relatively permanent store of (mostly) meaningful information. **Short-term memory** is the particular subset of information a person is dealing with at the moment. (Figure 8.8 compares the rates of decay of the sensory store and short- and long-term memory.) Many investigators today have various doubts and reservations about the short-term versus long-term distinction, but most agree that we need some distinction at least similar to this.

Information in short-term memory is available only temporarily. After attention is distracted, the information rapidly becomes less and less available, though perhaps not lost altogether. Someone comes up to you at a party and says, "Hello, I'm Sally Davis." "I'm pleased to meet you, Sally," you reply. Two minutes later

you want to introduce her to someone else, but you have already forgotten her name. (Curiously, you seem to remember what her name was *not*. For example, if someone asks whether her name might have been "Beulah Budweiser," you say you are sure it was not, even though you have no idea what her name really was.)

In contrast, the information stored in long-term memory can be available at any time. To get information from long-term memory, a person needs a *retrieval cue,* an association that facilitates retrieval. A retrieval cue serves as a reminder. Some retrieval cues work better than others. For example, the retrieval cue "the city you were born in" should enable you to retrieve the name of one city from your long-term memory. The retrieval cue "U.S. city whose name is also the name of a type of animal" probably does not enable you to retrieve anything quickly. You laboriously go through all the cities (or animals) you can think of until eventually

FIGURE 8.8
After about 1 second, you cannot recall information from the sensory store. Short-term memories can be recalled up to about 20 seconds without rehearsal—much longer if you keep rehearsing them. Long-term memories decline somewhat, especially at first, but you may be able to retrieve them for a lifetime. Your address from years ago is probably in your long-term memory and will continue to be for the rest of your life.

FIGURE 8.9
Short-term memory is like a hand full of eggs; it can store only a limited number of items at a time.

you come upon an answer, most likely Buffalo, New York. (Conceivably, you might think of Caribou, Maine; Cuckoo, Virginia; Anaconda, Montana; or Deadhorse, Alaska.) Retrieving long-term memories is sometimes a difficult, effortful task.

For many years, psychologists thought of short-term memory and long-term memory as separate stages: Information first enters short-term memory and stays there a while; some but not all of the information in short-term memory gradually enters a separate long-term memory. Like many theories in psychology, that theory is not exactly wrong, but it oversimplifies some important points.

Characteristics of Short-Term Memory

If short-term memory is qualitatively different from long-term memory, it should have some special properties. Let us consider the reported characteristics of short-term memory, and the strengths and weaknesses of certain items of evidence.

The Limited Capacity of Short-Term Memory People can store a vast amount of information in their long-term memory. The musical conductor Arturo Toscanini knew every note for every instrument for 250 symphonies, 100 operas, and many other compositions (Marek, 1975). Storing something in long-term memory is like putting books on the shelves of a library; you need not discard an old book to make room for a new one.

In contrast, short-term memory can apparently store only a sharply limited amount of information. When you read or listen to a long list of items and then try to recite them (short-term memory), you discover that you can recall only a few. Read each of the following sequences of letters and then look away and try to repeat them from memory. Or read each aloud and ask a friend to repeat it.

EHGPH

JROZNQ

SRBWRCN

MPDIWFBS

ZYBPIAFMO

BOJFKFLTRC

XUGJDPFSVCL

Most normal adults can repeat a list of approximately seven items (letters in this case), about the same number of items that Ebbing-

haus managed to memorize after reading a list once (Figure 8.2). Some people can remember eight or nine; others, only five or six. George Miller (1956) referred to the short-term memory capacity as "the magical number seven, plus or minus two." When people try to repeat a longer list, however, they may fail to remember even the first seven items. It is somewhat like trying to hold several eggs in one hand: You can hold a certain number, depending on their size, but if you try to hold too many you drop them all (Figure 8.9).

Ways of Storing More Information in Short-Term Memory Although we speak of approximately seven "items" in short-term memory, the size of each item can vary. For illustration, read this sequence of numbers once, then try to repeat it:

3141627182814141732

Could you do it? Most people cannot even come close to repeating all 19 digits. If you have a strong background in mathematics, however, you may have recognized this sequence as the approximate values of four mathematical constants (pi, 3.1416 . . . ; *e*, 2.71828 . . . ; the square root of two, 1.414 . . . ; and the square root of three, 1.732). If you recognized those constants, you had only 4 items to store instead of 19, and the capacity of your short-term memory was more than adequate.

Here is an easier example that illustrates the same point. Try to repeat the following sequence of 12 digits:

106614921776

If you recognized that this sequence consists of three historical dates (the Norman invasion of England in 1066, Columbus's arrival in America in 1492, and the Declaration of Independence in 1776), then you could repeat all 12 digits. You stored the sequence as 3 items (years) instead of 12 items (digits). The process of grouping digits or letters into meaningful sequences is known as **chunking.** Note that chunking uses knowledge previously stored in long-term memory.

Note also that when you store memory in chunks, you still store close to seven items, but now each item is larger than before (Figure 8.10). Still, your short-term memory can more easily handle seven little items than seven big items. In particular, it is easier to remember seven short words than seven long words. You need more time to repeat "cauliflower, broccoli, rutabaga, asparagus, . . ." than to repeat "nine, two, four, six, . . ." You may also need more mental effort to store the word *cauliflower* than to store the word *nine*.

One study demonstrated that tendency, using people who were fluent in both Welsh and English. The Welsh words for the numbers 0 through 9 take longer to say than the corresponding English words. (In Welsh, they are *dim, un, dau, tri, pedwar, pump, chwech, saith, wyth,* and *naw.*) Even people who are more fluent in Welsh than in English speak a randomized list of digits about 10% faster in English than in Welsh. Those same people have a mean short-term memory capacity of about 6.5 English digits or 5.8 Welsh digits (Ellis & Hennelley, 1980). Evidently it is easier to remember a list that we can say fast than a list that we say more slowly. However, the speed of saying a list is only one (relatively minor) factor controlling the limits of short-term memory. Even if you need more than twice as long to speak a list like "cauliflower, broccoli, rutabaga, . . ." than to say "nine, two, four, . . ." you do not remember twice as many words from the second list as from the first. More words, yes, but not twice as many (Schweickert, Guentert, & Hersberger, 1990).

Can people increase the capacity of their short-term memory through practice? No. However, they can learn to use larger and larger chunks. One student from Carnegie-Mellon University, described only as a "typical male undergraduate" (Ericsson, Chase, & Falcon, 1980), volunteered for an experiment on the memorization of digits. At the beginning, he could repeat only about 7 digits at a time. Over the course of a year and a half, working 3 to 5 hours a week, he gradually improved his ability, as shown in Figure 8.11, until he could repeat a sequence of up to 80 digits.

However, he had not expanded his short-term memory capacity. When tested with letters instead of numbers, his capacity was still 7. Instead, he had developed some extraordinary strategies for chunking, many of which were more meaningful to him than they would be to most people. He was a competitive runner, so he might store the sequence "3492 . . ." as "3 minutes, 49.2 seconds, a near world-record time for running a mile." He might store the next set of numbers as a good time for running a kilometer, a mediocre marathon time, or a date in history. He had organized his memory in such a way that he could fit an impressive amount of information into each chunk.

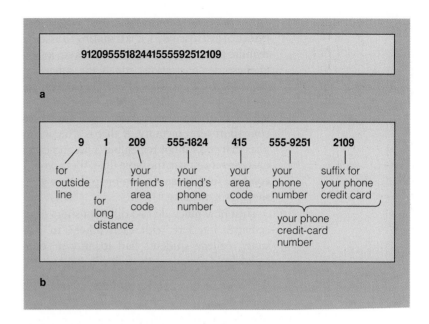

FIGURE 8.10
We overcome the limits of short-term memory through chunking. You probably could not remember the 26-digit number in (a), but by breaking it up into a series of chunks, you remember it and dial the number correctly.

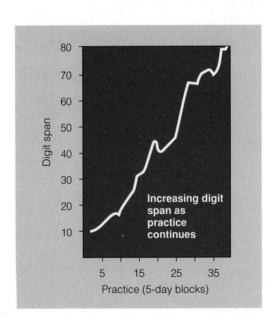

FIGURE 8.11
Most people can repeat a list of about 7 numbers. One college student gradually increased his ability to repeat a list of numbers, over 18 months of practice. With practice, he greatly expanded his short-term memory for digits but not for letters or words. (From Ericsson, Chase, & Falcon, 1980.)

The Structure of Memory   325

Is Short-Term Memory Unitary? Given the evidence just discussed, it is tempting to assume that the short-term memory we measure in any of these demonstrations equals the sphere of immediate consciousness. That is, whatever you are attending to—a list of words, a page of reading, or a conversation with a friend—occupies your short-term memory. If that is true, it implies that you cannot remember a list and carry on a conversation at the same time. (Both would compete for the same seven or so slots in your short-term memory.)

Just how much do two different short-term activities interfere with each other? In one study, college students had to answer some true-false questions of the following type:

A follows B: B A
B is not preceded by A: A B

(The first of these is true. The second is false.) On some trials the students simply answered the questions without any interference; on other trials they were given a set of six digits, such as "384176," to say repeatedly while they figured out the answer to one of the questions. Then they got a new set of six digits to repeat during the next question. The students remembered the digits and answered the questions accurately under either condition. Reciting the digits did slow them down, especially on more difficult items such as "B is not preceded by A." On the hardest questions, they took about $3\frac{1}{2}$ seconds without interference, about 6 seconds with interference (Baddeley & Hitch, 1974).

These results indicate that two short-term tasks compete with each other somewhat, but not so much as we might have expected. After all, remembering six letters should almost completely occupy one's short-term memory, leaving almost nothing available to process a complicated sentence. Evidently, your immediate attention span can handle different kinds of information at the same time, storing them in ways that do not completely interfere with each other.

Forgetting Short-Term and Long-Term Memories

Defenders of a strong distinction between short-term and long-term memory contend that the mechanisms of forgetting are different for the two types of memory. One possibility is that unrehearsed short-term memories simply decay over time, while long-term memories become unavailable for a greater variety of reasons, such as interference.

Certainly the *rate* of forgetting is vastly different for the two kinds of memory. We enter many facts into our short-term memory—an address, a telephone number, the price of something at a store—that we use briefly and then forget. By contrast, some well-established long-term memories last a lifetime. Granted, your memories for the events of last week are clearer than for those of a year ago. Still, with proper reminders, even people 70 and 80 years old can remember many childhood experiences.

Role of Interference in Forgetting of Long-Term Memories **Interference** is a competition among related memories. If you have trouble remembering the name of your acquaintance John Stevenson, it may well be because of interference from the memory of a similar-looking acquaintance named Steve Johnson. Finding a pearl in a bucket of white marbles is harder than finding a pearl in a bucket of black marbles.

For convenience, psychologists distinguish between two types of interference: proactive interference and retroactive interference. **Proactive interference** is the hindrance an older memory produces on a newer one. **Retroactive interference** is the impairment a newer memory produces on an older one. Figure 8.12 shows the difference. Take an example: Suppose you memorize a list of the major rivers in Africa; two days later you memorize a list of the major rivers in Asia. You will tend to forget the African rivers because of retroactive interference (the new material interfering with the old). You will also tend to forget the Asian rivers because of proactive interference (the old interfering with the

Proactive interference: Old memory impairs recall of newer memory.

Retroactive interference: New memory impairs recall of older memory.

FIGURE 8.12
Suppose you have two memories. Call the first one O and the second one X. If they are similar but not identical, each will interfere with the other. The interference of the first (O) on the second (X) is proactive interference. Interference of the second (X) on the first (O) is retroactive interference.

new). Thus, your brother who memorized only the African rivers will remember them better than you; your sister who memorized only the Asian rivers will remember them better than you.

One moral of the story is this: When you want to memorize something, avoid studying anything else too similar immediately beforehand or afterward.

▪ CONCEPT CHECKS

1. Professor Tryhard learns the names of his students every semester. After a number of years, he finds that he learns them as quickly as ever but forgets them faster. Is that an example of retroactive interference or proactive interference?

2. Remember spontaneous recovery from Chapter 7, page 282? Can you explain it in terms of proactive interference? (What is learned first? What is learned second? What would happen if the first interfered with the second?)
(Check your answers on page 335.)

Decay of Short-Term Memories over Time

In contrast to long-term memory, which is forgotten mostly because of interference, short-term memory is more vulnerable to loss through simple decay. That is, unless people continually rehearse the material in short-term memory, it gradually fades away.

Lloyd Peterson and Margaret Peterson (1959) demonstrated the decay of short-term memory with a simple experiment that you can easily repeat if you can trick some friend into volunteering. First read aloud a meaningless sequence of letters, such as HOZDF. Then wait for a bit and ask your friend to repeat it. He or she will have no difficulty doing so. The reason is that your friend suspected you would ask for a recall of the letters and spent the delay rehearsing, "H-O-Z-D-F, H-O-Z-D-F, . . ." A 5-year-old child might forget the letters within 10 to 20 seconds because young children do not routinely rehearse material.

If you prevent rehearsal during the delay period, however, your adult friend will forget just as quickly as a child will. Say "I am going to read you a list of letters, such as HOZDF. Then I'm going to tell you a number, such as 231. When you hear the number, begin counting backward by threes: 231, 228, 225, 222, 219, and so on. When I tell you to stop, I'll ask you to repeat the sequence of letters." You can record your data as in Table 8.1.

Table 8.1			
Letter Sequence	Starting Number	Delay in Seconds	Correct Recall?
BKLRE	712	5	
ZIWOJ	380	10	
CNVIU	416	15	
DSJGT	289	20	
NFMXS	601	25	

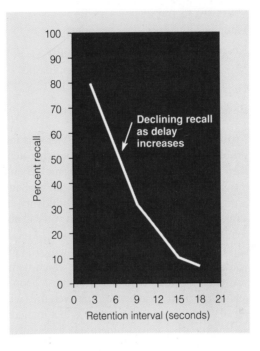

FIGURE 8.13
In the study by Peterson and Peterson (1959), people remembered a set of letters well after a short delay, but their memory faded greatly over 20 seconds.

Try this experiment with several friends, and compute the percentage of those who recalled the letters correctly after various delays. Figure 8.13 gives the results Peterson and Peterson obtained. Note that only about 10% of their subjects could recall the letters correctly after a delay of 18 seconds. In other words, if we fail to rehearse something that has entered short-term memory, it will generally fade away within 20 seconds or less.

This demonstration works well, however, only when the person is trying to memorize something fairly meaningless, like HOZDF. If you ask your friend to memorize "There is a poisonous snake under your chair," he or she is likely to remember it well even after counting backward by threes from 231. Highly meaningful material enters long-term memory quickly and does not rapidly decay.

Here is an interesting consequence of the fact that short-term memories fade rapidly: Suppose I ask you to try to memorize some unfamiliar material, such as the nicknames of some college teams:

University of Alaska, Southeast	Humpback Whales
Heidelberg College	Student Princes
Humboldt State	Lumberjacks
Arkansas Tech	Wonder Boys
University of California, Santa Cruz	Banana Slugs
University of Akron	Zips
Hamline University	Pipers
Kearney State College	Antelopes
Mankato State University	Golden Flashes
University of Idaho	Vandals
Boston University	Terriers

I pause after some pairs and ask, "What is the probability that you will remember this item (say, the University of Akron nickname) when I test you at some later time?" You can give any estimate from 100% (complete confidence in your memory) to 0% (certainty that you will not remember). Estimating the probability of recall can be quite useful: If you know which items you have learned best, you know which items you need to keep studying. But most people make very poor estimates of how well they will recall various items. The reason is that immediately after they learn something, it is still in short-term memory. The memory still seems strong at that point, and they have no way of knowing how strong their long-term memory will be after the short-term memory fades. If they wait a minute, look at a few other items, and then come back, they can give a highly accurate estimate of how well they will remember, say, the University of Akron nickname (Nelson & Dunlosky, 1991). The short-term memory has faded by that time, and they can gauge the strength of the long-term memory.

Role of Interference in Forgetting of Short-Term Memories If the forgetting of short-term memories depends only on decay and not on interference, this finding would constitute persuasive evidence that short-term and long-term memory depend on separate and distinct processes. However, interference turns out to play a significant role in both cases.

For example, let's reconsider the demonstration I asked you to try a little while ago: You read off "BKLRE," asked someone to count backward by threes for 5 seconds, and then probably found that the person could recall the letters. After two more trials you came to "DSJGT" and a 20-second delay. At that point the person probably did not give the correct answer. But DSJGT was the fourth trial, potentially subject to a fair amount of proactive interference. Suppose you try this with another volunteer, but now you *start* with DSJGT and a 20-second delay. Under these conditions, most subjects remember DSJGT without difficulty (Keppel & Underwood, 1962; Wickens, 1970). Evidently the forgetting that occurs in this situation depends partly on interference.

This does not mean that the results previously discussed were wrong. If you give people a substantial number of trials, varying the delay before recall, you will obtain results similar to those in Figure 8.13. That is, short-term memory really is stronger after a 5-second delay than it is after a 20-second delay.

Still, even in that case the forgetting may depend partly on interference. Counting backward is, after all, a verbal task and saying "289, 286, 283 . . ." is likely to interfere with the memory "DSJGT." In a follow-up study, Judith Reitman (1974) found that people forgot a sequence of words faster if they spent the delay on a verbal task than if they spent the delay listening for tones. That is, verbal activity weakens the memory by interference. However, the memory did fade somewhat even when the subjects spent the time listening for tones. The point is that forgetting of short-term memories depends on both decay and interference, and therefore that forgetting of short-term and long-term memories depends on partly overlapping mechanisms.

■ CONCEPT CHECK

3. Name one way in which short-term memory and long-term memory are evidently different, and one way in which they are similar. (Check your answer on page 335.)

The Transfer from Short-Term Memory to Long-Term Memory

Consolidation is the formation and strengthening of long-term memories. But just how do we form long-term memories? Originally, psychologists thought of short-term memory and long-

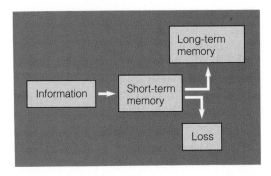

FIGURE 8.14
According to the original conception of the relationship between short-term and long-term memory, if a short-term memory is rehearsed long enough, it becomes a long-term memory. Without consolidation, it is lost. This view is now considered oversimplified.

FIGURE 8.15
People experience "flashbulb memories" for the details surrounding intense emotional events, such as an earthquake or other natural disaster, a personal tragedy, or hearing of the assassination of a political leader. The emotional surge may fix the memory of even such trivia as the time of day, the weather, who else was present, and what they said.

term memory as containers. New information went first into the short-term container; if rehearsal kept it there long enough, it would enter the long-term container (Figure 8.14).

According to this hypothesis, all we must do to form a long-term memory is to keep something in short-term memory long enough. But the data contradict this simple view. Simply holding an item in short-term memory does not make it highly available for recall later, and how long it stays in short-term memory does not, by itself, make much difference.

In one experiment (Craik & Watkins, 1973), college students were asked to listen to a long list of words and then to report the last word on the list that began with the letter *g*. For example, in the list *table, giraffe, frog, key, banana, pencil, spoon, grass, garden, house,* the correct answer would be *garden*. Note what the students had to do: When they heard the first *g* word, *giraffe,* they had to hold it in short-term memory until they heard *grass,* six words later. At that point they replaced the word *giraffe* in short-term memory with the word *grass,* which they immediately replaced with the next word, *garden*. After students had given the correct answer (*garden*), the experimenter asked (to the students' surprise) for all the words on the list that began with *g*. The students remembered *grass* and *giraffe* about equally well (or equally poorly) even though they had stored *giraffe* in short-term memory six times as long as they had stored *grass*. Evidently, how long a word stays in short-term memory has little to do with whether it moves into long-term memory.

Information moves most rapidly into your long-term memory if you register it as highly important. For instance, a large percentage of the people who are old enough to remember the assassination of John F. Kennedy, the assassination of Martin Luther King, Jr., or the explosion of the *Challenger* spacecraft can recall a wealth of unimportant details associated with the event, such as exactly where they were when they first heard the news, who they were with, what they said, and what the weather was like. Such memories are known as "flashbulb memories" (Brown & Kulik, 1977). Similarly, you may remember a number of details from your first day at college, or you may remember where you were and what you were doing when you heard the war in Iraq had started (Figure 8.15).

Most of our memories do not have that "flashbulb" quality, but we do tend to remember mainly the events that strike us as important. Something happens and you think, "Ah. That was important." Such events move quickly into long-term memory.

One way in which this process operates is that some important or exciting experience arouses your sympathetic nervous system, releasing epinephrine (adrenaline) into your bloodstream. Substantial evidence now indicates that increased epinephrine secretion enhances consolidation of a memory, up to an optimum level (McGaugh, 1990). Excessive epinephrine has a less beneficial effect, and sometimes even a harmful effect. (This is one reason why people in a panic often have trouble remembering details of the situation later.)

Epinephrine enhances the formation of long-term memory indirectly, by converting stored glycogen to glucose and therefore raising the level of glucose available to the brain. In fact, injecting glucose shortly after an experience enhances future memory of it, even if the epinephrine level stays constant (Gold, 1987; Hall & Gold, 1990; Lee, Graham, & Gold, 1988). Recall from Chapter 3 that glucose is the brain's primary fuel; elevating the glucose level facilitates brain functioning.

■ CONCEPT CHECK

4. *Immediately after memorizing something, a person sits down to a meal. Would you expect eating to improve or impair the memory? (Check your answer on page 335.)*

POSSIBLE MODIFICATIONS OF THE INFORMATION-PROCESSING MODEL

The information-processing model of memory focuses on the distinction between short-term memory and long-term memory. While that distinction is useful in many ways, we have also reached some conclusions that are not exactly what the original proponents of this distinction would have expected:

1. While retaining a list of only seven or so items in short-term memory, we can still understand complex sentences or perform other tasks that presumably require short-term memory. So the "limit" of short-term memory is not as simple as we once thought it to be.

2. Interference contributes to forgetting in both short-term and long-term memory. So the two types of memory rely on processes that are at least similar, perhaps overlapping.

3. Consolidation depends more on how important a memory is than it depends on the passage of time. Forming a long-term memory requires some sort of active processing.

In response to such challenges as these, many psychologists have looked for some other way of characterizing memory. They want to keep the idea that a person retains and strengthens some memories while losing others. But instead of assuming that all short-term memories are either lost or consolidated into long-term memories, these psychologists try to account for the varying strengths of long-term memories, which can range from a clear, easily recalled memory to a weak memory that shows up only after extensive prodding.

Depth of Processing

According to the **depth-of-processing principle** (Craik & Lockhart, 1972), information may be stored at various levels, either superficially or deeply, depending on the number and type of associations formed with it. For example, a typical short-term memory is stored at a superficial level; I tell you "HOZDF" and you retain those letters, probably by rehearsing their sounds. At a slightly deeper level of processing, you might study some assigned but uninteresting material just well enough to recall it on a test. At a still deeper level, you have certain topics of great personal interest in which you ponder new information, think about it from every angle, and remember it well from then on. Table 8.2 summarizes this model.

Note that the depth-of-processing view distinguishes among various levels or strengths of memories. Even if we maintain the term *long-term memory,* this view enables us to describe differences between old memories easy to recall and old memories difficult to recall.

For analogy, consider what happens when a librarian files a new book in the library. Simply to place the book somewhere on the shelves without recording its location would be a very low level of processing, and the librarian's chances of ever finding it again would be slight—analogous to a short-term memory. So the librarian fills out file cards for the book and puts them into the card catalog. To fill out just a title card for the book would be an intermediate level of processing. To fill out several cards—one for title, one for author, and one or more for subject matter—is a deeper level of processing. Someone who came to the library later looking for that book would have an excellent chance of finding it. Similarly, when you are trying to memorize something, the more "cards" you fill out (that is, the more ways you link it to other information), the greater your chances of finding the memory when you want it.

For example, imagine several groups of students who study a list of 20 words in several ways. One group simply reads the list over and over. This is a superficial level of processing and an inefficient way to memorize material (Greene, 1987). Actors and public speakers who have to memorize lengthy passages spend little time simply repeating the words and more time thinking about them. A second group counts the letters in each word. This is also a superficial level of processing, because it does not focus on the meaning of the words. A third group tries to think of a synonym for each word or tries to use each word in a sentence. As they think about the words, they store them at a relatively deep level of processing. Even though all the students spent the same amount of time studying the list, the third group remembers the words far better than the other two. That is, the deeper the level of processing, the easier it is to recall the material.

Something to Think About

How can you use the depth-of-processing principle to develop good study habits?

We can distinguish two types of processing: processing of individual items and processing of list organization (Einstein & Hunt, 1980; McDaniel, Einstein, & Lollis, 1988). If you go through a list of words thinking about the meaning of each, you are processing *individual items.* If you go through the list looking for relationships among the items, you are processing the *organization* of the list. You might notice, for example, that the list consists of five animals, six foods, four methods of transportation, and five objects made of wood. Even sorting items into such simple categories as "words that apply to me" and "words that do not apply to me" will enhance your sense of how the list is organized and therefore your ability to recall it (Klein & Kihlstrom, 1986).

▪ CONCEPT CHECK

5. Here are two arrangements of the same words:

a. Be a room age to the attend hall will over party across be there 18 you after wild in the class must.

b. There will be a wild party in the room across the hall after class; you must be over age 18 to attend.

Why is it easier to remember b than a—because of processing of individual items or because of processing of organization? (Check your answer on page 335.)

The main contribution of the depth-of-processing principle is its account for the relative ease of recalling some long-term memories and the comparative difficulty of recalling others. That is, it distinguishes levels of long-term

Table 8.2 Depth-of-Processing Model of Memory

Superficial processing	Simply repeat the material to be remembered: "Hawk, Oriole, Tiger, Timberwolf, Blue Jay, Bull."
Deeper processing	Think about each item. Note that two start with *T* and two with *B*.
Still deeper processing	Note that three are birds and three are mammals. Also, three are major league baseball teams, and three are NBA basketball teams.

memories, instead of lumping them all together. However, the limitation of this view is that it does not tell us how to *measure* the depth of processing, independently of the memory it is supposed to explain (Baddeley, 1978). For example, if you or I came up with a new way of studying the words on a list (like drawing an abstract picture corresponding to each word, for example), it would be hard to guess how deep the resultant processing would be.

Encoding Specificity

The depth-of-processing principle implies that the way you think about a memory when you store it determines what cues will help to remind you of the memory later. Let us return to our library analogy for a moment:

A new book titled *Brain Mechanisms in Mental Retardation* arrives in the library. The librarian places it on the appropriate shelf and fills out three cards for the card catalog: one for the author, one for the title, and one for the subject, *mental retardation.* I happen to read a section in this book on the physiological basis of learning. Three years later I want to find the book again, but I cannot remember the author or title. I go to the card catalog and look under the subject headings *physiology* and *learning.* But the book I want is not listed. Why not? Simply because the librarian filed the book under a different heading. Unless I use the same subject heading the librarian used, I cannot find the book. (Had the librarian filled out several subject cards instead of just one, I would have had a better chance of finding it.)

A similar principle applies to memory. (Note that I say *similar.* Your brain does not actually store each memory in a separate place, as a librarian stores books.) When you store a memory, you attach to it certain retrieval cues,

FIGURE 8.16

According to the principle of encoding specificity, the way we code a word during original learning determines which cues will remind us of that word later. For example, when you hear the word queen *you may think of that word in any of several ways. If you think of* queen bee, *then the cue* playing card *will not remind you of it later. If you think of the* Queen of England, *then* chess piece *will not be a good reminder.*

Table 8.3a		
Clergyman	—	Cardinal
Trinket	—	Charm
Social event	—	Ball
Shrubbery	—	Bush
Inches	—	Feet
Take a test	—	Pass
Baseball	—	Pitcher
Geometry	—	Plane
Tennis	—	Racket
Stone	—	Rock
Magic	—	Spell
Envelope	—	Seal
Cashiers	—	Checkers

like file cards. These retrieval cues are the associations you use both when you store a memory and when you try to recall it. Depending on your depth of processing, you may set up many retrieval cues or only one or two. No matter how many cues you set up, however, it helps if you use those same cues when you try to find the memory again. This statement is known as the **encoding specificity principle** (Tulving & Thomson, 1973). Although cues that were not present when you stored the memory may help somewhat to evoke the memory (Newman et al., 1982), they are less effective than cues that were present at the time of storage (Figure 8.16).

Here is an example of encoding specificity (modified from Thieman, 1984). First, read the list of paired associates in Table 8.3a. Then turn to Table 8.3b on page 334. For each of the words on the list there, try to recall a related word on the list you just read. *Do this now.*

The answers are on page 335, answer B. Most people find this task difficult and make only a few of the correct pairings. Because they initially coded the word *cardinal* as a type of clergyman, for example, the retrieval cue *bird* does not remind them of the word *cardinal.* The cue *bird* is most effective for people who think of *cardinal* as a bird at the time of storage. In

short, you can improve your memory by storing information in terms of retrieval cues and by using the same retrieval cues when you try to recall the information.

Additional and Alternative Distinctions

The distinction between short-term and long-term memory, even as modified by the depth-of-processing principle, may not be the only or best distinction to draw among types of memories. For example, some psychologists distinguish **working memory,** information you are working with, from **reference memory,** permanent memory you can refer to (Baddeley, 1986). Working memory can hold a great deal of temporary information until it is replaced by something new. For example, working memory includes the current time of day, how long before you have to go to your next class, the weather outside, where you parked your car, what you ate for lunch today, and how long until your library books are due. A number of animal studies suggest that the brain handles temporary, changeable information (working memories) differently from the way it handles more permanent information (reference memories) (Malamut, Saunders, & Mishkin, 1984; Sakurai, 1990; Zola-Morgan & Squire, 1986; Zola-Morgan, Squire, & Mishkin, 1982). (See Figure 8.17.)

Many psychologists also distinguish **semantic memory,** memory for factual information, from **episodic memory,** memory for specific

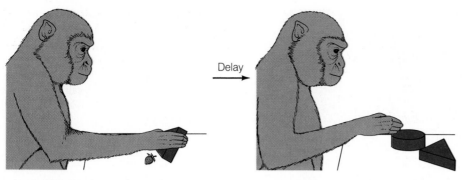

Monkey lifts sample object to get food.

Food is under the new object.

Table 8.4 Distinctions Among Types of Memory

	Description	Examples
Working memory	Memory of temporary information you are working with; will be replaced with new information later	Where you parked your car today, today's schedule, where you left off sweeping the floor, your current bank balance
Reference memory	Permanent memory you can refer back to	Your social security number, what jobs you've had, what a red light means
Semantic memory	Memory of factual information	Who is the president, how many cups in a gallon, where you bought your car
Episodic memory	Memory of specific events in your life	Your first kiss, the time your dog died, your first day of college
Procedural memory	How to do something	How to change a tire, how to ice skate
Declarative memory	Facts	Where you parked your car, your social security number, who is president, your first kiss

events in a person's life (Tulving, 1989). Under some circumstances, episodic memories can be more fragile. For example, people sometimes remember some fact they have heard (a semantic memory) but forget when, where, and from whom they heard it (an episodic memory). As with the case of working and reference memory, the brain apparently handles episodic memory differently from semantic memory (Tulving, 1989). Table 8.4 summarizes these different types of memory, plus two that will be discussed later.

■ CONCEPT CHECKS

6. *Is your memory for the rules of tennis a working memory or a reference memory? What about your memory for the current score in a tennis match?*

7. *Is your memory of your current mailing address a semantic memory or an episodic memory? What about your memory of the events of moving to your current address?*
(Check your answers on page 335.)

In Retrospect: Different Ways of Categorizing Memories

We began with the distinction between short-term memory and long-term memory. That distinction still has much to recommend it, although our conceptions of it have changed significantly since it was first proposed. If we do not accept that distinction, then we would presumably choose something similar—perhaps something like the depth-of-processing principle, which recognizes a continuum of long-term memories. The most solid conclusion is that memory is not a single process; we have different mechanisms to serve different purposes.

Table 8.3b

Instructions: For each of these words, write a related word that you remember from the second column of the list in Table 8.3a.

Pottery	_____
Animal	_____
Part of body	_____
Transportation	_____
Football	_____
Crime	_____
U.S. politician	_____
Music	_____
Personality	_____
Write	_____
Bird	_____
Board game	_____
Sports	_____

SUMMARY

■ *Ebbinghaus's approach.* Hermann Ebbinghaus and other early investigators tested memorization of lists of nonsense syllables or other items. They interpreted memory as an association, or link, among items. (page 319)

■ *The information-processing model.* Psychologists now distinguish among various types of memory. According to the information-processing model of memory, information is stored first as short-term memories and later processed to become long-term memories. (page 321)

■ *Memory capacity.* Short-term memory has a capacity of only about seven items in normal adults, although chunking can enable us to store much information in each item. Long-term memory has a very large, not easily measured capacity. (page 324)

■ *Forgetting.* Long-term memory fades mostly because of interference from similar items. Short-term memory fades partly because of interference and partly because of decay over time. (page 326)

■ *Forming long-term memories.* Merely holding material in short-term memory for a while does not enter it into long-term memory. We form long-term memories mostly when we regard something as important or interesting. (page 328)

■ *Depth of processing principle.* Some long-term memories are stronger than others. According to the depth-of-processing principle, a memory becomes stronger (and easier to recall) if we think about the meaning of the material and relate it to other material. (page 330)

■ *Encoding specificity.* When we form a memory, we store it with links to the way we thought about it at that time. When we try to recall the memory, a cue is most effective if it is similar to the links we formed at the time of storage. (page 331)

■ *Other memory distinctions.* Some psychologists also distinguish between working memory and reference memory, or between semantic memory and episodic memory. We apparently have different kinds of memory to serve different purposes. (page 332)

SUGGESTION FOR FURTHER READING

Schacter, D. L. (1989). Memory. In M. I. Posner (Ed.), *Foundations of cognitive science* (pp. 683–725). Cambridge, MA: MIT Press. Review of current issues by one of the leading investigators.

TERMS

nonsense syllable a meaningless three-letter combination (page 319)

information-processing model view that information is processed, coded, and stored in various ways in human memory as it is in a computer (page 321)

sensory store a very brief storage of sensory information (page 322)

long-term memory a relatively permanent store of information (page 323)

short-term memory the particular subset of information someone is dealing with at the moment (page 323)

chunking process of grouping digits or letters into meaningful sequences (page 324)

interference competition among related memories (page 326)

proactive interference the hindrance an older memory produces on a newer one (page 326)

retroactive interference the impairment a newer memory produces on an older one (page 326)

consolidation the formation and strengthening of long-term memories (page 328)

depth-of-processing principle principle that information may be stored at various levels, either superficially or deeply, depending on the number and type of associations formed with it (page 330)

encoding specificity principle principle that memory is strengthened by using the same retrieval cues when retrieving a memory as when storing it (page 332)

working memory memory for what one is working with at the moment (page 332)

reference memory memory for general principles and events of long ago (page 332)

semantic memory memory for factual information (page 332)

episodic memory memory for specific events in a person's life (page 332)

ANSWERS TO CONCEPT CHECKS

1. It is due to proactive interference—interference from memories learned earlier. Much of the difficulty in retrieving long-term memories is due to proactive interference. (page 327)

2. First, the subject learns the response; second, the subject learns the extinction of the response. If the first learning proactively interferes with the later learning, spontaneous recovery will result. (page 327)

3. Short-term memory has a capacity limited to about seven items in normal adults, whereas long-term memory has an extremely large capacity (difficult to estimate). Both short-term memory and long-term memory are more rapidly forgotten in the presence of interference. (page 328)

4. Eating increases the amount of circulating glucose; therefore, we should expect it to improve memory. One study with rats confirmed this prediction (Flood, Smith, & Morley, 1987). (page 330)

5. It is easier to remember b because of processing of organization. (page 331)

6. Your memory for the rules of tennis is a reference memory. Your memory for the current score in a tennis match is a working memory. (page 333)

7. Your memory of your current address is a semantic memory. Your memory of the events of moving is an episodic memory. (page 333)

ANSWERS TO OTHER QUESTIONS IN THE TEXT

A. The correct coin is A. (page 322)

B. (page 332)

Pottery	Pitcher
Animal	Seal
Part of body	Feet
Transportation	Plane
Football	Pass
Crime	Racket
U.S. politician	Bush
Music	Rock
Personality	Charm
Write	Spell
Bird	Cardinal
Board game	Checkers
Sports	Ball

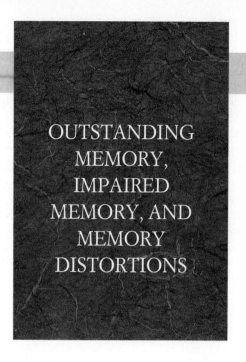

OUTSTANDING MEMORY, IMPAIRED MEMORY, AND MEMORY DISTORTIONS

Why do we sometimes forget?
Why do we sometimes think we remember
something, when in fact we are wrong?

At one point while I was doing the research for this book, I went to find an article that I remembered reading, which I thought would nicely illustrate a particular point I wanted to make. I was pretty sure I remembered the author, the name of the journal, and the date of the article within a year. I was certain it would not take me long to find the article.

About 4 hours later I finally located it. I was right about the author, but I was wrong about the journal and the year. Worst of all, I discovered that the results the article reported were quite different from what I remembered. (The way I remembered the results made a lot more sense than the actual results!)

Why do we sometimes forget things? And why do we sometimes remember something all wrong and think we are right?

MEMORY FOR SELDOM-USED INFORMATION

Quickly now, what is the capital of Missouri? What was the name of your seventh-grade English teacher? What is the formula for finding the volume of a sphere? To whom did you last write a check, and what was the amount? What is the correct definition of the term *demand characteristics?*

All of us enter an enormous amount of information into our memories, but we vary in how well we can recall the memories we need, when we need them. Some people consistently recall seemingly everything they have ever known, in amazing detail; others forget what you just told them 15 seconds ago and need extensive reminders to recall even the most basic and familiar material. Most of us find that we sometimes have embarrassing difficulty recalling some personal experience or some fact we once knew perfectly well (Crovitz & Schiffman, 1974; Rubin, Wetzler, & Nebes, 1986). And yet at other times we may be surprised that we remember something far better than we would have expected. Given a good enough reminder, we may remember even more.

Long-Term Retention of Personal Experiences

No doubt you remember a great percentage of the important events in your life, but how could you measure that percentage? Marigold Linton (1982) wrote notes about at least two important personal events each day for 6 years and recorded the date on the back of each note. At various times she drew notes at random from the pile and tested her ability to recall the approximate date of each event. She found that she remembered the dates of about 95% of events a year old and a slightly lower percentage of older events. Similarly, Willem Wagenaar (1986) made cards recording 2,400 personal events over 6 years. At the end of the 6 years, he tested himself by reading part of each card (for example, "what happened") and trying to recall the rest (for example, who, where, and when). Although he remembered the recent events more clearly than the older events, he was able to recall at least a little information about almost every event.

Harry Bahrick (1984) tested people who had studied Spanish in school 1 to 50 years previously on their current memory of Spanish. Nearly all agreed that they had rarely used Spanish and had not refreshed their memories at all since their school days. (That is a dis-

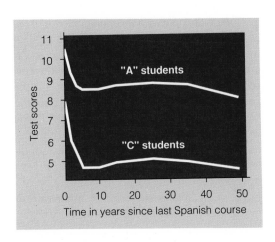

FIGURE 8.18

(Left) Spanish vocabulary as measured by a recognition test shows a rapid decline in the first few years but then long-term stability. (From Bahrick, 1984.) (Right) Within a few years after taking your last foreign-language course, you may think you have forgotten it all. You have not, and even the part you have forgotten will come back (through relearning) if you visit a country where you can practice the language.

turbing comment, but beside the point.) Their retention of Spanish dropped noticeably in the first 3 to 6 years, but remained fairly stable from then on (Figure 8.18). In other words, we do not completely forget even very old memories that we seldom use.

Dependence of Memory on the Method of Testing

So we remember a great deal from long ago. Even when we seem to have forgotten something, is it completely lost? Or might we retrieve it under the right circumstances?

Sometimes people remember better than they realize; how well they remember something depends on how we test them. The simplest way is to ask for **recall.** To recall something is to produce it. For instance, I might ask you, "Please name all the children in your third-grade class." Suppose you correctly name very few of them, even none. That does not necessarily indicate that you have totally forgotten those children. You tend to confuse the names of the children in your third-grade class with those you knew in first, second, and later grades. (Remember the influence of proactive and retroactive interference.)

You probably will demonstrate much better recall by means of **cued recall,** in which you get significant hints to aid your recall. For example, I might show you a photograph of all the children in your third-grade class or I might give

FIGURE 8.19

Could you recall the names of the students in your third-grade class? Trying to remember without any hints is recall. Using a photo or a list of initials is cued recall. If you tried to choose the correct names from a list, you would be engaged in recognition. If you compared how fast you relearned the correct names and how fast you learned another list, you would be using the savings (or relearning) method.

you a list of their initials (Figure 8.19). Try this: Cover the right side of Table 8.5 with a piece of paper and try to identify each of the people described. (This is the recall method.) Then uncover the right side, revealing each person's initials, and try again. (This is cued recall.)

Table 8.5 Illustration of the Difference Between Recall and Cued Recall

Instructions: First try to identify each person in the left column while covering the right column (recall method). Then expose the right column, which gives each person's initials, and try again (cued recall).

Author of *Moby Dick*	H. M.
Only woman with face on a U.S. coin ($1)	S. B. A.
Author of Hercule Poirot stories	A. C.
President of the Soviet Union when it collapsed	M. G.
Discoverer of classical conditioning	I. P.
Baseball's all-time career home-run leader	H. A.
Author of Sherlock Holmes stories	A. C. D.
First U.S. woman astronaut	S. R.
Author of this book	J. K.
Author of *Gone with the Wind*	M. M.
First names of the Wright brothers (airplane inventors)	W. & O.
Democratic nominee for vice president in 1984	G. F.

For answers, see page 357.

In **recognition,** a third method of testing the persistence of memory, a person is asked to choose the correct item from among several items. People can usually recognize a number of names or facts that they could not recall. For example, I might give you a list of 60 names and ask you to check off the correct names of children in your third-grade class. Multiple-choice tests use the recognition method to test memory.

A fourth method, the **savings,** or **relearning, method,** will sometimes detect weaker memories than any of the other methods will. Suppose you cannot name some of the children in your third-grade class (recall method) and cannot pick out their names from a list of choices (recognition method). If I presented you with the correct list of names, you might learn it faster than you would learn an unfamiliar list of names. The fact that you *relearn* something more quickly than you learn something new is evidence that some memory has persisted (MacLeod, 1988). In other words, you *save time* when you relearn material that you learned in the past. The amount of time saved (time needed for original learning minus the time for relearning) is a measure of memory.

Finally, people who show no evidence of explicit memory may show substantial implicit memory. The tests we have considered so far are **explicit** tests; a person has to state the correct answer, generally recognizing that it *is* the correct answer. For example, to the question "Who is your psychology instructor?" you would have to state the name or choose it from a list of choices. In contrast to such explicit or direct tests of memory, an **implicit** or *indirect* test does not require any conscious recognition of a memory. In fact, the subjects may not even realize that they are taking part in a memory test.

For example, you might read a list of words, including CHAIRMAN, LECTURES, PENDULUM, and DONATION. You read them just once, perhaps not even realizing that you will be tested on them, and when you are asked to repeat the list a few minutes later, you cannot. Then you are asked to fill in the missing letters to make words from the following:

```
__ H A __ R __ __ N
M __ __ N __ T __ C
__ E __ D __ L __ M
__ E C __ __ R __ S
A __ __ A __ __ I N
```

You probably will find it easy to fill in the letters for the words you had read (CHAIRMAN, PENDULUM, and LECTURES) but more difficult for the other words (MAGNETIC and ASSASSIN). Reading a word temporarily primes the word and increases the chance that you will recognize it in a word fragment (Graf & Mandler, 1984; Schacter, 1987a).

Here is another example of implicit memory: People are shown a series of drawings like those in Figure 8.20 and asked to identify whether each drawing is possible or impossible as a three-dimensional object. People who have once discovered that a drawing is "possible" identify it as "possible" more quickly when they see the same drawing again later. Both college students and patients with amnesia show this improvement, even though the patients say they do not recognize having seen the drawing previously (Schacter, Cooper, Delaney, Peterson, & Tharan, 1991; Schacter, Tharan, Cooper, & Rubens, 1991). In short, an explicit memory of seeing the drawing does not facilitate an implicit memory of how to see it as a three-dimensional object. Table 8.6 summarizes these various ways of testing memory.

The conclusion from all of these studies:

People who cannot answer a question correctly may not have forgotten the information completely. If tested in a different way, they may show at least subtle signs of retaining the information.

■ CONCEPT CHECKS

8. *Each of the following is an example of one method of testing memory. Identify each method.*

  a. *Although you thought you had completely forgotten your high-school French, you do much better in your college French course than does your roommate, who never had French in high school.*

  b. *You don't have a telephone directory and are trying to remember the phone number of the local pizza parlor.*

  c. *After witnessing a robbery, you have trouble describing the thief. The police show you*

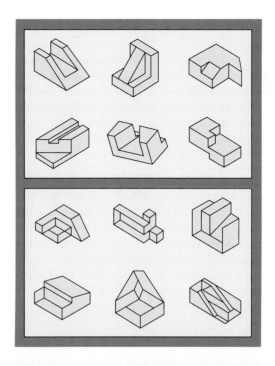

FIGURE 8.20
Which of these are possible as three-dimensional figures and which are not? Eventually, people discover that the top six are possible and the bottom six are not. If they are shown the same figures later, they identify the possible figures more rapidly, showing implicit memory, even if they do not remember seeing them before. (From Schacter, Cooper, Delaney, Peterson, & Tharan, 1991.)

Table 8.6 Five Ways to Test Memory

	Description	Example
Explicit (direct) tests		
Recall	You are asked to say what you remember.	Name the Seven Dwarfs.
Cued recall	You are given significant hints to help you remember.	Name the Seven Dwarfs. Hint: One was always smiling, one was smart, one never talked, one seemed always to have a cold. . . .
Recognition	You are asked to choose the correct item from among several items.	Which of the following were among the Seven Dwarfs: Sneezy, Sleazy, Dopey, Dippy, Hippy, Happy?
Savings (relearning)	You are asked to relearn something: If it takes you less time than when you first learned that material, some memory has persisted.	Try memorizing this list: Sleepy, Sneezy, Doc, Dopey, Grumpy, Happy, Bashful. Can you memorize it faster than this list: Sleazy, Snoopy, Duck, Dippy, Gripey, Hippy, Blushy?
Implicit (indirect) tests	You are asked to generate words, without necessarily recognizing them as memories.	You hear the story "Snow White and the Seven Dwarfs." Some time later you are asked to fill in these blanks to make words: __ L __ __ P __ / __ N __ __ Z __ / __ __ C / __ O __ E __ / __ R __ __ P __ / __ __ __ P P __ / __ A __ H __ U __

several photographs and ask whether any of them was the robber

d. *You go to a restaurant that you say you do not remember, although you went there in early childhood. To your surprise, you find your way to the restroom without directions.*

e. *Your friend asks, "What's the name of our chemistry lab instructor? I think it's Julie or Judy something."*

f. *Two people near you are talking about Central America, and you are paying no attention. After they leave, someone asks you what they had been talking about and you reply that you have no idea. A few minutes later you spontaneously comment, "I wonder what's going on in Central America these days."*

9. *The results shown in Figure 8.18 demonstrate how well people recall the Spanish they studied years ago. Might they actually remember more than this figure indicates? If so, how might you determine how much more they remember?* (Check your answers on page 357.)

EXCEPTIONAL MEMORY

If you listen as 30 strangers say their names, you probably will find that you can recall only a few of those names, if any. If someone tested you by the cued recall, recognition, or savings method, you probably would demonstrate more memory than appeared at first. Still, your immediate recall would be very limited.

Some people can listen once and then recall all 30 names. Other people have other spectacular memory abilities; for example, one person became famous for his ability to recite the digits of pi (3.14159265 . . .) to an enormous number of decimal places. Such abilities are not often useful in everyday life. Perhaps someone who excels at memorizing names could get paid for doing a stage act, much the way other people juggle or perform magic tricks. But not many people will pay for tickets to listen to someone recite the digits of pi.

Still, some people have demonstrated an ability to remember wider varieties of more useful information. And others have developed techniques that all of us can learn to use, that enable people to memorize a long list of items quickly.

Example of a Person with an Exceptional Memory

The mathematician Alexander Aitken excelled in logical reasoning, mathematics, and many other skills (Hunter, 1977). A few examples of his memory: As a schoolboy, he was once told to work out the decimal for 1/97; he noticed that it had an interesting repeating pattern and from then on could recite it from memory. He memorized whole books of Virgil (in Latin!) and *Paradise Lost.* His memory for detail was so good that committees often used him as a walking record book of all their past deliberations and decisions. As part of an experiment, a psychologist once asked him to memorize a list of 25 words. After reading them once, he was able to recite the first 12. After reading them four times, he recited them all. He was tested four more times over the next 15 months; three of those four times he got all 25 correct. Twenty-seven years later, he wondered whether he could still remember the list, not having thought about it during all that time. It took him a few minutes, but he got all 25.

Whenever he wanted to memorize something, he did not concentrate; he relaxed. "One must be relaxed, yet possessed, in order to do this well. . . . Interest is the thing. Interest focuses the attention. . . . The thing to do is to learn by heart, not because one has to, but because one loves the thing and is interested in it. Then one has moved away from concentration to relaxation."

Mnemonic Devices

Few of us have the memory gifts of Alexander Aitken. But almost anyone can learn a few tricks to enhance certain kinds of memorization.

If you had to memorize something lengthy—a speech, for example, or a list of all the bones in the body—what would you do? Some people would simply repeat the list over and over again. That is the way Ebbinghaus memorized his lists of nonsense syllables, but it is a very inefficient way of learning.

One way to facilitate memorization is to use a **mnemonic device,** which is any memory aid that is based on encoding each item in some special way. The word *mnemonic* ("nee-MAHN-ik") comes from a Greek root meaning "memory." (The same root appears in the word *amnesia,* "lack of memory.")

Mnemonic devices come in many varieties.

When Mozart was a boy he visited the Vatican, where he heard a performance of a piece of music. The next day he had a handwritten score of the piece. The pope was furious, because he had decreed that no one could copy the score of that music. Mozart had written down the entire piece from memory—eight voice parts—after one hearing. The pope was so impressed, he awarded him a medal.

Nobel Peace Prize Winners

1901 H. Dunant and F. Passy
1902 E. Ducommun and A. Gobat
1903 Sir W. R. Cremer
1904 Institute of International Law
1905 Baroness von Suttner
1906 T. Roosevelt
1907 E. T. Moneta and L. Renault
1908 K. P. Arnoldson and F. Bajer
1909 A. M. F. Beernaert and
        Baron d'Estournelles de Constant
1910 International Peace Bureau
1911 T. M. C. Asser and A. H. Fried

1957 L. B. Pearson
1958 G. Pire
1959 P. J. Noel-Baker
1960 A. Luthuli
1961 D. Hammarskjöld (posthumously)
1962 L. Pauling (awarded 1963)

1990 M. Gorbachev
1991 A. S. Suu Kyi

FIGURE 8.21
A list of Nobel Peace Prize winners. Mnemonic devices can be useful when people try to memorize long lists like this one.

Some are simple, as in thinking up a little story that reminds you of each item to be remembered (such as "Every Good Boy Does Fine" to remember the notes EGBDF on the musical staff). Suppose you had to memorize the list of Nobel Peace Prize winners (Figure 8.21). You might try making up a little story: "Dun (Dunant) passed (Passy) the Duke (Ducommun) of Gob (Gobat) some cream (Cremer). That made him internally ILL (Institute of International Law). He suited (von Suttner) up with some roses (Roosevelt) and spent some money (Moneta) on a Renault (Renault). . . ." You still have to study the names, but your story might help you to remember them all in order.

One of the oldest and most effective mnemonic devices is the **method of loci** (method of places). First you memorize a series of places and then you use some vivid image to associate each of these locations with something you want to remember. For example, you might start by memorizing every location along the route from your dormitory room to, say, your psychology classroom. Then you link the locations, in order, to the names.

For example, suppose the first three locations you pass are the desk in your room, the door to your room, and the corridor. You should first form a mental image linking the first pair of Nobel Peace Prize winners, Dunant and Passy, to the first location, your desk. You might imagine a Monopoly game board on your desk, with a big sign "DO NOT (Dunant) PASS (Passy) GO." Then you link the second pair of names to the second location, your door: A DUKE (as in Ducommun) is standing at the door, giving confusing signals. He says "DO COME IN (Ducommun)" and "GO BACK (Gobat)." Then you link the corridor to Cremer, perhaps by imagining someone has spilled CREAM (Cremer) all over the floor (Figure 8.22). You continue in this manner until you have linked every name to a location. Now, if you can remember all those locations in order and if you have imagined good images for each

FIGURE 8.22
The method of loci is one of the oldest mnemonic devices. First learn a list of places, such as "my desk, the door of my room, the corridor, . . ." Then link each of these places to the items on a list of words or names, such as a list of the names of Nobel Peace Prize winners.

FIGURE 8.23
In the movie The Dirty Dozen, *a group of soldiers planning an attack used a mnemonic device to remember their plan: One—Guards at the roadblock; we've just begun. Two—The guards are through. Three—The major's men are on a spree. Four—The major and Wladislaw go through the door. They memorized sixteen steps this way.*

one, you can recite the list of Nobel Peace Prize winners.

A similar mnemonic device is called the *peg* method (Figure 8.23). You start by memorizing a list of objects, such as "One is a bun, two is a shoe, three is a tree, . . ." Then you form mental images to link the names with these peg words, just as you would with the method of loci. For example, for number one, "I ate a BUN at the DUNE (Dunant) PASS (Passy)," imagining *dune pass* as a passageway between sand dunes. Later you use all your peg words to help remember the list of names. One trouble with the method of loci and the peg method is the difficulty of thinking of good images for all the items. (When you eventually get to Nobel Peace Prize winner Gorbachev, your image may have to be rather far-fetched.)

How useful are elaborate mnemonic devices, such as the method of loci or the peg method? That depends. For remembering your school assignments or how to drive a car or most other common tasks, few people rely on mnemonic devices. But if you have to memorize long lists of unrelated words in order, mnemonic devices can be very helpful.

AMNESIA AND ITS IMPLICATIONS FOR MEMORY

Some people suffer **amnesia,** a loss of memory, either as a result of brain damage or for other reasons. Even in the most severe cases, people do not forget everything they have ever learned. They may lose one kind of memory while performing normally on another kind. The specific deficits of amnesic patients tell us much about the types of memory that people have. We shall consider amnesia based on several types of brain damage, amnesia of infancy and old age, and amnesia based on emotional traumas.

The Case of H. M., a Man with Hippocampal Damage

In 1953 a man with the initials H. M. was subjected to unusual brain surgery in an attempt to control his extreme epilepsy. H. M. had suffered such frequent and severe seizures that he was unable to keep a job or live a normal life; he had failed to respond to antiepileptic drugs. In desperation, surgeons removed from his brain the **hippocampus** and several neighboring structures (Figure 8.24), where they believed his epileptic seizures were originating. Although the surgeons did not know what to expect from the operation, they acted on the belief that desperate cases call for desperate measures.

The results of the surgery were favorable in some regards. H. M.'s epileptic seizures decreased in frequency and severity. His personality and intellect remained the same; in fact, his IQ score increased slightly after the operation, presumably because of the decreased epileptic interference.

However, he suffered severe memory problems (Corkin, 1984; Milner, 1959), particularly a massive **anterograde** (ANT-eh-ro-grade) **amnesia** (inability to store new long-term memories). For years after the operation, he gave the year as 1953 and his own age as 27. Later, he took wild guesses (Corkin, 1984). He would read the same issue of a magazine repeatedly without realizing that he had read it before. He could not even remember where he had lived for the last few years. He also suffered a moderate **retrograde amnesia** for long-term factual memories (loss of memory for events that occurred shortly prior to brain damage from trauma or disease; see Figure 8.25). That is, he had some trouble recalling events that happened within the last 1 to 3 years before the operation, although he could recall still older events. He could still form normal short-term memories, such as repeating a brief list of items. With constant rehearsal and no distraction, he could even retain those memories for several minutes. He could also learn new skills, as we shall see in a moment.

H. M. is a modern Rip van Winkle who becomes more and more out of date with each passing year (Gabrieli, Cohen, & Corkin, 1988; Smith, 1988). He does not recognize the names or faces of people who became famous after the mid-1950s. He could not name the president of the United States even when Ronald Reagan was president, though he remembered Reagan as an actor from before 1953. He does not understand the meaning of words that entered the English language after the time of his surgery. For example, he guessed that *biodegradable* means "two grades," that *soul food* means "forgiveness," and that a *closet queen* is a "moth." For H. M., watching the evening news is like visiting another planet.

In spite of H. M.'s massive memory difficulties, he can acquire new skills and retain them later. We refer to skill retention as **procedural memory,** in contrast with **declarative memory,** the ability to recall factual informa-

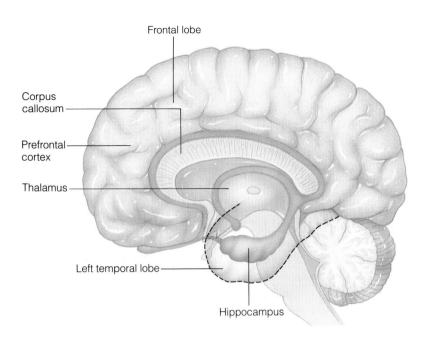

FIGURE 8.24
The hippocampus is a large subcortical structure of the brain. After damage to the hippocampus and related structures, patient H. M. had great trouble storing new long-term memories.

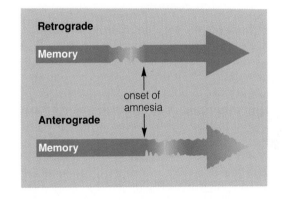

FIGURE 8.25
Retrograde amnesia is loss of memory for events in a certain period before brain damage or some other trauma. Anterograde amnesia is a difficulty forming new memories after some trauma.

tion. For example, H. M. has learned to read material written in mirror fashion (Cohen & Squire, 1980):

with the words reversed like this

Although he has learned to read mirror writing, he does not remember having learned it. He has also learned a simple finger maze, and he has learned the correct solution to the Tower of Hanoi puzzle shown in Figure 8.26 (Cohen, Eichenbaum, Deacedo, & Corkin, 1985). He

FIGURE 8.26
In the Tower of Hanoi puzzle, the task is to transfer all the disks to another peg, while moving only one at a time and never placing a larger disk onto a smaller disk. Patient H. M. learned the correct strategy and retained it from one test period to another, although he did not remember ever seeing the task before. That is, he showed procedural memory but not declarative memory.

does not *remember* learning these skills, however. He claims he has never seen any of these tasks before, and he is always a bit surprised by his success.

Frontal-Lobe Amnesia

Amnesia can also arise after damage to the frontal lobes, especially the prefrontal cortex (Figure 8.24). Because the frontal lobes receive a great deal of input from the hippocampus, the symptoms of frontal-lobe damage overlap those of hippocampal damage. However, frontal-lobe damage produces some special memory impairments of its own.

Frontal-lobe damage can be the result of a stroke or of trauma to the head. Frontal-lobe deterioration is also commonly associated with **Korsakoff's syndrome,** also known as the *alcohol amnestic disorder,* a condition caused by a prolonged deficiency of vitamin B_1, usually as a result of chronic alcoholism. The vitamin deficiency leads to a loss or shrinkage of neurons in many parts of the brain, especially the prefrontal cortex and parts of the thalamus. Patients suffer multiple impairments of memory, apathy, and confusion (Oscar-Berman, 1980; Squire, Amaral, & Press, 1990). Patients with Korsakoff's syndrome suffer severe retrograde amnesia, generally covering most events beginning about 15 years before the onset of their illness (Squire, Haist, & Shimamura, 1989). They also suffer from anterograde amnesia. Although they can memorize a list of words, they forget the list rapidly, especially if they are tested in a room different from the room in which they learned it (Winocur, Moscovitch, & Witherspoon, 1987). They have particular trouble remembering when and where various events took place (Schacter, 1987b). For example, if asked what they ate this morning or what they did last night, they describe something they did some time in the past. In spite of their severe loss of declarative memories, they acquire new procedural memories reasonably well.

Patients with frontal-lobe damage, whatever the cause, have a characteristic pattern of answering questions with a bewildering mixture of correct information, out-of-date information (because they cannot remember what is correct right now), and wild guesses. Their guesses, or **confabulations,** are apparent attempts to fill in the gaps in their memory. The result is sometimes self-contradictory or preposterous, as the following example illustrates (Moscovitch, 1989, pp. 135–136):

> **Psychologist:** How old are you?
> **Patient:** I'm 40, 42, pardon me, 62.
> **Psychologist:** Are you married or single?
> **Patient:** Married.
> **Psychologist:** How long have you been married?
> **Patient:** About 4 months.
> **Psychologist:** What's your wife's name?
> **Patient:** Martha.
> **Psychologist:** How many children do you have?
> **Patient:** Four. (He laughs.) Not bad for 4 months.
> **Psychologist:** How old are your children?
> **Patient:** The eldest is 32; his name is Bob. And the youngest is 22; his name is Joe.
> **Psychologist:** How did you get these children in 4 months?
> **Patient:** They're adopted.
> **Psychologist:** Who adopted them?
> **Patient:** Martha and I.
> **Psychologist:** Immediately after you got married you wanted to adopt these older children?
> **Patient:** Before we were married we adopted one of them, two of them. The eldest girl Brenda and Bob, and Joe and Dina since we were married.
> **Psychologist:** Does it all sound a little strange to you, what you are saying?
> **Patient:** I think it is a little strange.
> **Psychologist:** I think when I looked at your record it said that you've been married for over 30 years. Does that sound more reasonable to you if I told you that?

Patient: No.
Psychologist: Do you really believe that you have been married for 4 months?
Patient: Yes.

Like most patients with frontal-lobe damage, this man denies that he has a bad memory. So far as he is concerned, he answers every question and he thinks his answers are correct, so his memory must be okay.

Alzheimer's Disease

A third example of amnesia caused by brain damage is **Alzheimer's disease,** a degenerative condition that generally occurs in old age (Coyle, Price, & DeLong, 1983). The cerebral cortex, hippocampus, and other areas lose cells, as Figure 8.27 shows (Hyman, van Hoesen, Damasio, & Barnes, 1984). According to one estimate, about 20% of all people develop Alzheimer's disease by age 80 (Mortimer, Schuman, & French, 1981). The symptoms start with minor forgetfulness and progress (sometimes rapidly) to more serious memory loss, confusion, depression, restlessness, hallucinations, delusions, and disturbances of eating, sleeping, and other daily activities (Cummings & Victoroff, 1990). Many Alzheimer's patients are not fully aware of their own memory loss (McGlynn & Kaszniak, 1991).

Alzheimer's disease has both genetic and nongenetic causes. The son or daughter of a person with Alzheimer's disease has almost a 50 percent probability of eventually developing the disease (Mohs, Breitner, Silverman, & Davis, 1987). Some people with no family history of Alzheimer's disease also develop the condition (Hardy, 1990); however, they generally do so later in life, after about age 80.

People in an early stage of Alzheimer's disease can recall events from long ago, but they have trouble remembering new information. When one investigator played a round of golf with an Alzheimer's patient (Schacter, 1983), the patient could remember the rules and terminology of golf perfectly well but could never remember how many strokes he had taken on a hole. He often forgot whether he had already teed off or was still waiting his turn. Unless he went directly to his ball after hitting it, he could not remember where it was. He could not say what label was on his ball, although when he picked up a ball he could recognize whether it was his.

As with H. M. and Korsakoff's patients, Alzheimer's patients retain procedural memo-

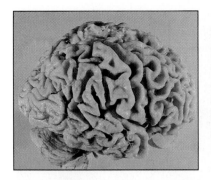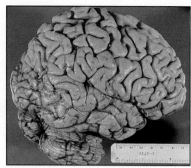

FIGURE 8.27
In the brain of an Alzheimer's patient (left), the cerebral cortex and other areas show significant shrinkage compared with a normal brain (right). As the brain shrinks, patients also show deficits of memory and reasoning.

ries more easily than declarative memories. In one study, Alzheimer's patients who could not memorize a list of words had little trouble learning the skill of maintaining contact between a hand-held pointer and a moving object (Eslinger & Damasio, 1986).

Sparing of Implicit Memory in Amnesic Patients

Although H. M., frontal-lobe patients, and Alzheimer's patients all have severe memory deficits, certain aspects of their memory remain almost intact. For example, they acquire new procedural memories. Moreover, although amnesic patients perform poorly on explicit tests of memory (such as recall, cued recall, or recognition), H. M. and frontal-lobe patients perform about normally on *implicit* tests of memory (Shimamura, Salmon, Squire, & Butters, 1987). Generally, Alzheimer's patients do not.

For example, brain-damaged amnesic patients are asked to read a list of words, such as DEFEND, TINSEL, and BATHED. When they are tested later, they are unable to remember any of the words on the list. Then they are given three-letter combinations and asked to complete each stem to make a complete word, any word:

DEF_____   TIN_____   BAT_____

Each of these fragments can be completed in several ways; for example, DEF_____ can become DEFEAT, DEFECT, DEFACE, DEFINE, DEFROST, and so on. Instead of coming up with other words that could be built on the stems, frontal-lobe patients and other amnesic patients generally fill in the letters that will

People with Alzheimer's disease lose their use of factual memory. Procedural memory is less impaired; those with the disease forget to do things more than they forget how *to do them. Posting reminders to turn off appliances is often useful.*

form the words on the original list (Schacter, 1985).

Moreover, when the experimenter flashes a series of blurred words on a screen, the brain-damaged people can read and identify the words DEFEND, TINSEL, and BATHED more easily than they can recognize other six-letter words. Somehow these words are "activated" in the patients' brains. The people are likely to see them and say them even though they insist they do not remember seeing them on the original list (Richardson-Klavehn & Bjork, 1988). (Some people do not even remember that there *was* a list.) Severely depressed people also show normal implicit memory, even though they perform poorly on most explicit tests of memory (Danion et al., 1991).

■ CONCEPT CHECKS

10. *(a) Is remembering how to tie your shoes a procedural memory or a declarative memory? (b) You remember an event that happened to you the first day of high school. Is that a procedural or a declarative memory? Short-term memory or long-term memory?*

11. *Which kinds of memory are most impaired in H. M., frontal-lobe patients, and Alzheimer's patients? Which kinds are least impaired? (Check your answers on page 357.)*

Implications of Amnesia for Memory

Studies of amnesic patients reveal, first, that the ability to recall old events is different from the ability to store new memories and that procedural memories are different from declarative memories. Second, they reveal that certain memories that seem to be forgotten, at least as far as the person's conscious memory is concerned, are still alive somewhere in the brain and still capable of influencing behavior on implicit tests of memory. In short, we have several kinds of memory that are vulnerable in different ways.

Infant Amnesia

Most adults can recall very few experiences from before the age of 5. That relative lack of memories is known as **infant amnesia** or *childhood amnesia.* Memories from that period are forgotten, but not just because they are old (Wetzer & Sweeney, 1986). After all, a 60-year-old can remember more from age 20 than a 20-year-old can remember from age 3.

Psychologists have proposed a number of theories to explain why our early memories are so vulnerable. The explanation probably does not have much to do with the maturation of language ability or any other uniquely human process, because nonhumans also forget most of what they learned as infants (Bachevalier & Mishkin, 1984).

One possible explanation is that young children fail to organize their memories as adults do. Most adults, when given a list of items to remember, sort them into groups or look for patterns that will aid recall. Preschool children almost never use such aids (Kail & Strauss, 1984; Moely, Olson, Halwes, & Flavell, 1969).

Another possibility is that infant amnesia may be related to the slow maturation of the hippocampus (Moscovitch, 1985). Although we recall few factual memories from before age 5, we retain an enormous number of procedural memories from that time—how to walk, talk, put on clothing, keep ourselves clean, and conduct other daily activities. That pattern of retaining procedural memories while losing factual memories is characteristic of H. M. and of other humans and animals with damage to the hippocampus.

Something to Think About

Does the encoding specificity principle (page 331) suggest another possible explanation for infant amnesia? (Hint: Your physiological condition always differs somewhat at the time of attempted recall from what it was at the time of original learning.)

Amnesia of Old Age

Most elderly people also experience a certain amount of memory loss—in most cases, far less severe than that of Alzheimer's disease. Memory skills vary from one person to another and from one time to another. On the average, older adults show only mild deficits on the simplest memory tasks, such as short-term retention of a list of words; they show greater deficits on more complex memory tasks (Babcock & Salthouse, 1990; Salthouse, Mitchell, Skovronek, & Babcock, 1989). If given a short narrative to remember, older adults remember the central points of the narrative almost as well as younger adults but they show a substantial deficit in memory of the odd and irrelevant details (Hess, Donley, & Vandermaas, 1989).

One aspect likely to suffer especially is memory for context and time. Older people may wonder, "Did I already tell this story to my daughter, or was it someone else?" "Where did I park my car today?" "Is my appointment for today or for tomorrow?" In one study, young people (20–30 years) and old people (65–87 years) tried to memorize a long list of words. When recalling the words, the older people were more likely to say the same word two or three times, forgetting that they had already said it (Koriat, Ben-Zur, & Sheffer, 1988).

The memory deficits of older people resemble the memory deficits typical of people with damage to the hippocampus and the prefrontal cortex. Old people typically lose some cells in the hippocampus and certain kinds of synapses in the prefrontal cortex; those losses are probably responsible for much of the memory impairment in old age (Arnsten & Goldman-Rakic, 1985a, 1985b; Gallagher & Pelleymounter, 1988).

B. F. Skinner (1983) devised various techniques to compensate for the memory decline he experienced as he grew older. Skinner trusted as little as possible to memory. He wrote notes to himself whenever he wanted to remember something. If he decided he should take an umbrella when he left the house, he immediately placed an umbrella near the front door. He avoided long, complex sentences, lest he forget where he was going before he reached the end.

People retain many procedural memories from early childhood, such as how to eat with chopsticks or a fork and spoon, but they forget nearly all the events from that time of their life.

Emotionally Induced Amnesia

Some people experience severe retrograde amnesia following a traumatic emotional experience. Many psychologists, following the theories of Sigmund Freud, believe that the amnesia may be a means of escape from memories too unpleasant to deal with. However, this belief is easy to assert and much more difficult to demonstrate with evidence. Emotionally induced amnesia probably occurs more often in soap operas and movies than it does in real life, although it is nevertheless possible.

One patient who was suffering severe retrograde amnesia for no apparent biological reason was still able to learn and remember new material. He was asked to memorize a list of paired associates in which famous people were paired with professions other than their own, such as the one in Table 8.7. He actually learned a list similar to this faster than normal people did. Most people are hindered by proactive interference, but this patient, who had completely forgotten what various people were really famous for, had no trouble remembering the new pairings (Kapur, Heath, Meudell, & Kennedy, 1986).

Accused criminals frequently claim that they are suffering emotionally induced amnesia. From one fourth to more than half of all convicted murderers claim they cannot remember

Table 8.7

Arnold Schwarzenegger	singer
Sandra Day O'Connor	figure skater
Michael Jordan	politician
Madonna	televangelist
Dan Rather	standup comic
Julia Roberts	inventor
Saddam Hussein	talk-show host
Boris Yeltsin	medical researcher
Martina Navratilova	movie critic
Michael Jackson	auctioneer
Barbara Bush	fashion designer
Clarence Thomas	architect
Connie Chung	golfer

committing the crime they are accused of; some say they cannot remember anything that happened that entire day. Indeed, that sort of amnesia is possible. But what about the possibility that some of these accused criminals are faking amnesia? Occasionally a claim of amnesia is made to support a plea of not guilty by reason of insanity. Suppose a psychologist or a psychiatrist is asked to determine whether such a person is truly suffering amnesia or is just faking it. How accurately can an expert distinguish the real thing from an imitation?

Daniel Schacter (1986a, 1986b) devised an experiment to answer that question. He had one group of students read a passage or watch a videotape that included many details that most people do not notice. When they were asked what certain people in the story were wearing or exactly what they said at certain times, the subjects replied (correctly) that they did not remember. A second group read the same material or watched the same videotape after being instructed to watch for those details but to *pretend* to forget them. Schacter then brought in a number of psychologists and psychiatrists who were frequently called as expert witnesses in court to determine which subjects had really forgotten and which ones were only pretending. The experts interviewed all the subjects and tried to determine which ones had really forgotten the answers and which ones were only pretending to forget. None of the experts showed much more than 50-50 accuracy, even in those cases on which they felt most certain.

The moral of the story: *If someone claims to know whether a person is suffering amnesia or faking it, be skeptical. At least ask that person to explain how he or she knows.*

SELECTIVE MEMORY

Of all the experiences you have had, you certainly remember some much more clearly than others. Generally you are most likely to remember information that is meaningful or distinctive. For example, if you try to remember the events that occurred during your junior year of high school, you are likely to recall mostly events that were highly interesting or important to you. But now suppose that the police, as part of a crime investigation, ask you to recall the details of some event that seemed uninteresting and not very important at the time. Under those circumstances your recall is likely to be accurate on some details but incomplete and inaccurate on others.

Importance of Meaningfulness

Memory is enhanced if the material is **meaningful,** fitting into a known pattern of information. If several people listen to a story about a baseball game, the ones who know the most about baseball tend to remember it best. Those who know the most about chess will remember the most from an article about chess.

J. D. Bransford and M. K. Johnson (1972) described one clever experiment illustrating the influence of meaningfulness. After looking at either picture A or picture B in Figure 8.28, two groups of people listened to the paragraph in part C (Bransford & Johnson, 1972, p. 131). Note that the paragraph makes sense if you have seen picture A but is nearly incomprehensible if you have seen only picture B. As you might expect, the people who had seen picture A remembered about twice as much of the paragraph as those who had seen only picture B.

Serial-Order Effect

When you try to remember a series of events that occurred in a temporal order, you probably find it easiest to remember the first ones and the last ones. For example, try to remember all the times you have ever applied for a job. Then try to remember all the football games you have attended. Unless you never had to apply for a job and you hate football, chances are you remember the first couple of times you applied for a

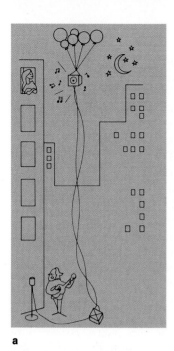

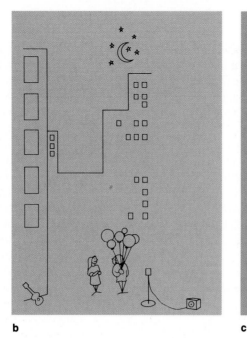

If the balloons popped, the sound would not be able to carry since everything would be too far away from the correct floor. A closed window would also prevent the sound from carrying since most buildings tend to be well insulated. Since the whole operation depends on a steady flow of electricity, a break in the middle of the wire would also cause problems. Of course, the fellow could shout, but the human voice is not loud enough to carry that far. An additional problem is that a string could break on the instrument. Then there could be no accompaniment to the message. It is clear that the best situation would involve less distance. Then there would be fewer potential problems. With face to face contact, the least number of things could go wrong.

a   b   c

FIGURE 8.28
In an experiment by Bransford and Johnson (1972), one group of people looked at picture a and another group looked at picture b. Then both groups heard the paragraph in part c. The paragraph is meaningful only if you have seen picture a.

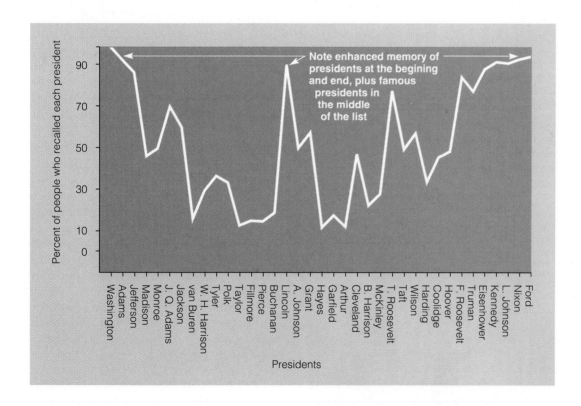

FIGURE 8.29
In the mid-1970s, a group of students tried to recall as many U.S. presidents as they could. Note the increased recall near the beginning and end of the list. (Based on Roediger & Crowder, 1976.)

job and the first one or two football games, the most recent one or two of each, and perhaps a few of the ones in between.

Now try to write the names of all the presidents of the United States (or any similar list). If you are like most people, you will have no difficulty naming the first few or the last few, but you will falter on many of the names near the middle of the list. Figure 8.29 shows the percentage of students in the mid-1970s who recalled each of the presidents up to Gerald Ford (Roediger & Crowder, 1976).

The **serial-order effect** is the tendency to remember the first and last items on a list better than those in the middle. The *primacy effect* is the tendency to remember the first items; the *recency effect* refers to the tendency to remember the last items.

The first few items in a list are easy to remember because we can rehearse them by themselves for a time without any interference from other items. The last item on a list stands out simply because it is the last. Depending on circumstances, it may still be in your short-term memory or working memory at the time you try to recall it.

Importance of Distinctiveness

When confronted with a series of mostly similar items, we tend to remember the unusual or distinctive ones (Figure 8.30). Read the following list and then recall immediately, in any order, as many items as you can:

potato, asparagus, cauliflower, turnip, broccoli, Alabama, beans, corn, peas, rutabaga, squash, cabbage

One of the items you are most likely to recall is *Alabama,* because it is different from the others: It is the only word beginning with a capital letter and the only word that refers to anything other than a vegetable.

Similarly, we tend to remember unusual people or people with unusual names. If you meet several men with rather ordinary appearances and similar names, like John Stevens, Steve Johnson, and Joe Stevenson, it may take you a long time to get their names straight. You would have much less trouble remembering a 7-foot-tall red-headed man named Stinky Rockefeller. The tendency to remember unusual items better than the more common items is known as the **von Restorff effect,** after the psychologist who first demonstrated it (von Restorff, 1933).

Although, other things being equal, we remember distinctive events better than more common events, other things are usually not equal. For example, people sometimes try to help themselves remember where they put something by placing it in a distinctive, unusual place: "I won't need this plane ticket for two months. So I'll put it in this really unusual place so I'll be sure to remember it—right under my stereo set." Two months later it is easy to remember that the ticket is tucked away in some unusual place. But *which* unusual place? That may be forgotten (Winograd & Soloway, 1986). It would be better to put the ticket in a meaningful place somehow related to travel—in a suitcase, inside a travel book, or with the swimsuit you plan to take on the trip (Figure 8.31).

RECONSTRUCTION OF PAST EXPERIENCES

Ebbinghaus and others following in his tradition studied people's ability to memorize sequences word for word, in precise order. In everyday life, some of our memory tasks require us to remember some sequence exactly. If you want to call someone on the phone, you won't gain much from remembering the "approximate" telephone number. If you try to recite a famous poem, or the Pledge of Allegiance, or the Twenty-third Psalm, no one will be impressed if you can "explain the main idea," even though you can't remember any of the exact words.

In many other circumstances, however, your goal is just to remember the main events. If your roommate asks you how the basketball game turned out last night, he or she probably wants only the most meaningful information (such as the final score) and the distinctive information (a few unusual or exciting plays). Here the memory task is not quite the same as the ones Ebbinghaus studied.

When you try to describe an experience, you start with the meaningful or distinctive details that you remember clearly and you **reconstruct** the rest to fill in the gaps. (During an original experience we *construct* a memory. When

FIGURE 8.30
Which of these four men are you most likely to remember? Other things being equal, we remember the most unusual individuals.

we try to retrieve that memory, we *reconstruct* it from what survives.) For example, suppose you try to recall your experience of studying in the library last night. You may remember where you sat, what you were reading, who sat down next to you, and where you went for a snack afterward. As time passes, many of those details, perhaps all of them, will fade like an old photo. However, if you happen to fall in love with the person who sat down next to you and went with you for a snack, you may remember the experience forever. In that case, however, you probably will remember meeting that person and probably where you went for a snack, but you are likely to forget which book you were reading. If you wanted to recall which book it was, you might reconstruct the memory this way: "Let's see, that semester I was taking a chemistry course that took a lot of study, so maybe I was reading a chemistry book. No, wait, I remember that when we went out for a snack we talked about politics. So maybe I was reading a political science text."

We also reconstruct the time and circumstances of a particular experience: "That happened while I was still in high school. I remember talking about it with the other guys working at the Pizza Palace, so it must have been before I quit my job there. And it was before I started taking guitar lessons. So it must have been about October of my senior year." We use political landmarks for the same purpose, such as, "I think that happened during the first part of the Bush administration, so it must have been about 1989 or 1990" (Brown, Shevell, & Rips, 1986).

Sometimes what we call a memory is just a reasonable guess. In answering the question "How many hours did you spend studying last month?" very few students will try to remember all the hours and count them up. They recall a day they consider "typical," estimate how long they studied that day, and then multiply by 30 to get the number of hours they studied in a month (Bradburn, Rips, & Shevell, 1987).

DISTORTIONS OF MEMORY

Have you ever described something that you remembered "clearly," only to discover later that you were wrong about many of the details? If so, you are not alone. We sometimes confuse memories of what really happened with our guesses about what "must have" happened.

Schematic Memory

When we reconstruct a memory of an experience, we generally fit it into a series of expectations, which F. C. Bartlett called a **schema.** For example, if you try to recall your last trip to the dentist, you probably will fill in the gaps with a schema of what usually happens at the dentist's office.

Bartlett demonstrated this tendency by asking some British people to read stories and then try to retell them after various delays (Bartlett, 1932). One of the stories, "The War of the Ghosts," was a Native American tale about two young men who met five other men who later turned out to be ghosts; one of the young men went home, while the other went with the ghosts to a battle in which he sustained an injury that later killed him. Most of Bartlett's subjects found the story confusing, even incoherent. It contained the unfamiliar place names "Egulac" and "Kalama," an unfamiliar sequence of events, and an assortment of seemingly unimportant details. In short, it did not fit neatly into any of the subjects' schemas.

When Bartlett's subjects retold the story, most of them omitted the place names, said nothing about ghosts, and altered other details. Subjects who retold the story on several occasions, weeks or months apart, told it with progressively greater distortions. Most of the later versions, though inaccurate, made more sense than the original—at least to the British, though perhaps not to Native Americans. In other words, we distort memories to make them more logical, to make them fit our inferences of what "must have happened."

Sometimes our inferences are correct, sometimes not. In one study (Brewer & Treyens, 1981), students waited in a room described as "the experimenter's office," without any instruction to pay attention to anything in the room or to try to remember it. After leaving, they were asked to describe the room. Most of them described the desk, chair, walls, and other items that are ordinarily found in an office; but about a third of them also described a bookcase, which was not there. That is, some of what people describe as a "memory" is actually just a reasonable guess.

Our memories are not entirely dependent on inferences, however. As you learned earlier, in the discussion of distinctiveness, people tend to remember highly unusual items better than they remember the ordinary items. In one study, one group of subjects spent a short time

F I G U R E 8 . 3 1 *These four factors affect memorization of items on a list. For long-term recall, meaningfulness is usually the most helpful factor.*

in a graduate student's office and later tried to recall what was in it. Most of them remembered the surprising items, such as fingerpaints and a stuffed bear, better than the more customary items, such as textbooks and a calculator. A second group of subjects tried to recall what they had seen in an elementary-school classroom, which had in fact been stocked with the same items as the graduate student's office. This second group remembered the (for them) surprising textbooks and calculator better than they remembered the fingerpaints and stuffed bear (Pezdek, Whetstone, Reynolds, Askari, & Dougherty, 1989).

To what extent will people reconstruct a memory based on inferences of what must have been true, and to what extent will they remember mainly the surprising, unexpected items? The difficulty in answering this question is that the results vary, depending on the exact procedure used (Maki, 1990). When people listen to a reasonably coherent story, they may remember a surprising detail (such as "he got his bicycle out of the kitchen") better than a more expected detail (such as "he got his bicycle out of the garage"). But if the story is full of confusing and irrelevant details, as in Bartlett's "War of the Ghosts," people impose some order on it and reconstruct a story focusing on the details that fit into an organizing schema.

Something to Think About

Is real life full of "confusing and irrelevant details"? If so, does that account for the frequency of people's memory distortions?

Hindsight Bias

To illustrate another way in which we reconstruct memories, let's try a little demonstration. First read the following paragraph, then answer the question after it:

For some years after the arrival of Hastings as governor-general of India, the consolidation of British power involved serious war. The first of these wars took place on the northern frontier of Bengal where the British were faced by the plundering raids of the Gurkas of Nepal. Attempts had been made to stop the raids by an exchange of lands, but the Gurkas would not give up their claims to country under British control, and Hastings decided to deal with them once and for all. The campaign began in November, 1814. It

was not glorious. The Gurkas were only some 12,000 strong; but they were brave fighters, fighting in territory well-suited to their raiding tactics. The older British commanders were used to war in the plains where the enemy ran away from a resolute attack. In the mountains of Nepal it was not easy even to find the enemy. The troops and transport animals suffered from the extremes of heat and cold, and the officers learned caution only after sharp reverses. Major-General Sir D. Octerlony was the one commander to escape from these minor defeats. (Woodward, 1938, pp. 383–384)

Question In the light of the information appearing in the passage, what was the probability of occurrence of each of the four possible outcomes listed below? (The probabilities should sum to 100%.)

a. a British victory   _____ %

b. a Gurka victory   _____ %

c. military stalemate with no peace settlement   _____ %

d. military stalemate with a peace settlement   _____ %

Note that some of the facts pointed in one direction and some pointed in another direction; each of the possible outcomes had some probability of occurring. Now that you have made your estimates of the probabilities, I can tell you what really happened: The two sides had a military stalemate without any settlement. The British had the advantages of superior numbers and superior equipment, but the Gurkas knew the territory and refused to give up. Battles continued sporadically and indecisively for years.

Now that you know the outcome, would you like to revise your estimates of the probabilities? Perhaps if you reread the paragraph you will decide that you had overestimated the probabilities of some outcomes and underestimated others.

Subjects in one experiment read the preceding passage about the British and the Gurkas. Some were told the correct outcome, and others were told one of the other outcomes; all were then told to estimate the probabilities of the four possible outcomes. Each group gave a high estimate to the probability of the outcome they had been told (Fischhoff, 1975). That is, once they knew what "really" happened (or incorrectly *thought* they knew), they reinterpreted the previous interpretation to make that outcome seem likely, or perhaps even necessary (Figure 8.32). The subjects' behavior illustrates **hindsight bias,** the tendency to mold our recollection of the past to fit the way later events turned out. Something happens and we say, "I *knew* that was going to happen!"

(Oh, incidentally, I lied about the outcome of the British-Gurkas war. Really the British won. Because of their poor leadership and strategy, the war dragged out for 2 years, but eventually their superior power and resources prevailed. Now would you like to re-evaluate your estimates *again*?)

Hindsight bias can be a powerful, almost irresistible influence. After the British-versus-Gurkas experiment described earlier, the experimenters repeated the procedure with new groups who were specifically told to "ignore" the outcome and try to base their probability estimates on the other information. Subjects proved unable to ignore the outcome. Even when told to ignore it, they gave a high estimate to the probability of the outcome they thought had occurred (Fischhoff, 1975).

In another study, college students in 1972 were asked to predict what would happen during an upcoming visit of then-President Nixon to China and the Soviet Union. For example, they were asked to estimate the probability that Nixon would meet with Chinese premier Mao Tse-Tung and the probability that the United States and the Soviet Union would agree to establish a joint space program. After the end of the visit, the same students were asked to recall the probabilities they had assigned to each event. In their recollections they overestimated how likely they had considered the events that actually happened; they underestimated the probabilities they had assigned to events that ultimately failed to occur (Fischhoff & Beyth, 1975).

Examples of hindsight bias are abundant in many phases of life. A couple announces they are getting a divorce and their friends say, "I *knew* that marriage was doomed." Later the couple cancel their plans for a divorce and the same friends say, "I knew they would get back together." A basketball announcer tells us, "After that key play at the start of the second half, I knew the home team was going to lose." Historians look at the events over a period of time and perceive a "trend" in those events that "had to" turn out the way they did. The government makes a controversial decision that turns

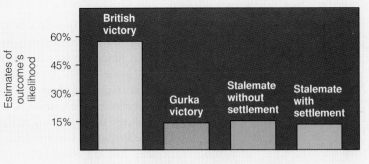

a Subjects told outcome was a British victory

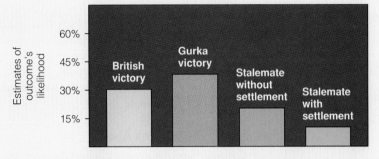

b Subjects told outcome was a Gurka victory

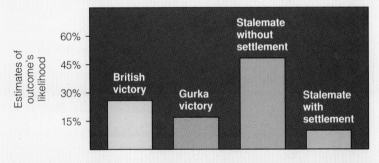

c Subjects told outcome was a stalemate without settlement

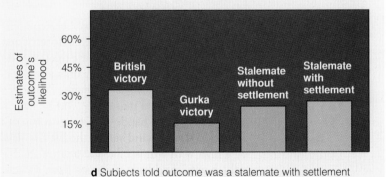

d Subjects told outcome was a stalemate with settlement

FIGURE 8.32
Mean estimates of the likelihood of four outcomes varied, depending on what each group was told about the "actual" outcome. Those who thought the British had won said that under the circumstances, the British had a very high probability of victory. Those who thought the Gurkas had won said that was the most likely outcome under the circumstances. And so forth. (Based on data of Fischhoff, 1975.)

out well; later, people forget their doubts and agree that "of course" it had been a good idea.

We can explain hindsight bias in several ways (Hawkins & Hastie, 1990). To some extent, people may misrepresent their previous beliefs to make themselves look smart. ("See how smart I am? I knew this was going to happen.") Also, people frequently cannot quite remember what they had expected before the event occurred. After the event, they remember the previous facts that fit best with the eventual outcome; they ignore other information or regard it as irrelevant. From the facts that stand out in their memory, they reconstruct an expectation of what was likely to occur—an expectation that fits the events that actually did occur, and not the expectation they really had before they knew the outcome.

Something to Think About

Can you interpret people's beliefs that they had a "psychic hunch" in terms of hindsight bias?

The Suggestibility of Eyewitness Accounts

WHAT'S THE EVIDENCE?

When people in a psychologist's laboratory distort a story or alter their recollections of previous beliefs in hindsight, no harm is done. But sometimes a great deal is riding on the accuracy of someone's memory.

You have just watched a robbery committed by a man you had never seen before. When the police ask you to describe the thief, you do your best, but you saw him for only a few seconds and cannot recall many details. The police ask, "Did he have a mustache? Did he have a tattoo on his right hand? Two other robberies were pulled off around here in the last few days by a man with a mustache and a tattoo on his right hand." Suddenly it comes back to you: "Yes, he definitely had a mustache. And I'm almost sure he had a tattoo." Did the suggestion help you to recall those details? Or did it prompt you to reconstruct details that you never actually saw?

EXPERIMENT 1

Hypothesis If people are asked questions that suggest or presuppose a certain fact, many peo-

ple will later report remembering that "fact," even if it never happened.

Method Elizabeth Loftus (1975) asked two groups of students to watch a videotape of an automobile accident. Then she asked one group, "Did you see the children getting on the school bus?" She did not ask the other group that question. In fact, there was no school bus in the videotape. A week later, she asked both groups 20 new questions about the accident, including this one: "Did you see a school bus in the film?"

Results Of the first group (those who were asked about seeing children get on a school bus), 26% reported they had seen a school bus; of the second group, only 6% said they had seen a school bus.

Interpretation The question "Did you see the children getting on the school bus?" presupposes that there was a school bus. Some of the people who heard that question added a school bus to their memory of the event. The students reconstructed what happened by combining what they actually saw with what they believed might reasonably have happened and with what someone suggested to them afterward.

What do results of this type mean? Suppose experimenters ask you whether you remember seeing children getting on the school bus. Later they ask whether you remember a school bus, and you say yes. That result might mean that the first question added a school bus to your memory. But it might also mean that you have no idea whether there was a school bus, so you are willing to go along with the experimenters' implication that there was. Or you might think, "Hmm . . . I don't remember a school bus, but the experimenters asked about one before, and I suppose they should know. So I'll say I remember a school bus." When the experimenters' suggestion leads you to give the wrong answer, does it actually change your memory or does it just change your answer?

EXPERIMENT 2

Hypothesis When people are given a misleading suggestion and then asked about what they saw, they may give answers that follow the suggestion. But if they are asked questions that eliminate the suggested information as a possible answer, they will return to the original information.

Method   College students saw a series of slides about a man who entered a room, stole some money and a calculator, and left (Figure 8.33). One of the slides showed a coffee jar on a file cabinet. At the end of the slides, the students were asked a series of questions. Some were asked a question designed to mislead them: They were asked whether they saw a jar of sugar on the file cabinet. Others were just asked about a jar. Later, some of the misled students and some of the other students were asked what kind of jar they saw on the file cabinet, a jar of coffee or a jar of sugar. The remaining students were asked whether they saw a jar of coffee or a jar of cookies (Zaragoza, McCloskey, & Jamis, 1987).

Results   Of those who were asked whether they saw a jar of sugar or a jar of coffee, 39% of those who had heard the misleading question about a jar of sugar said they remembered a jar of sugar. Of those who had not heard the misleading question, only 18% said they remembered a jar of sugar.

However, of students who were asked whether they saw a jar of coffee or a jar of cookies, about the same percentage remembered the jar of coffee, regardless of whether they had heard the misleading question about a jar of sugar.

Interpretation   A misleading suggestion does sometimes lead people to answer a question incorrectly by substituting the suggested information for the original information. But evidently the suggestion does not impair the original memory. If someone asks a question that excludes the suggested information, people remember the original information as well as if the suggestion had never been made.

There is a message in all this about how psychologists do research: What seems like the obvious interpretation for a given set of results may not be the only one and perhaps not even the best one. The psychologists who conducted Experiment 1 proposed what seemed a reasonable interpretation—that the misleading suggestions had actually changed people's memories. But other psychologists doubted that interpretation and conducted their own study, which led to a different interpretation.

This whole issue of how much to trust eyewitness testimony becomes especially troublesome when a child is the witness to a crime. A

FIGURE 8.33
Subjects in one experiment saw this slide (among others) and later answered a series of questions. Some subjects answered a question about whether they remembered seeing the jar of sugar on the file cabinet. Many said they did. However, when they were also asked what brand of coffee was on the file cabinet, they remembered just as well as people who had not been asked the misleading question about a jar of sugar.

child claims to have been sexually molested, for example, or a child is the only witness to a murder. How trustworthy is the child's testimony, especially when the case comes to trial many months later, after parents and police have asked who-knows-what kinds of questions?

In one experiment, children listened as an adult read a short story about a girl who got a stomachache from eating eggs too fast. When the children were later asked simple questions about the story, children at all ages from 3 through 12 replied correctly about 90% of the time. But some of the children were first asked, "Do you remember the story about Loren, who had a headache because she ate her cereal too fast?" After hearing this question, younger children were more heavily influenced than were older children, as shown in Figure 8.34. They reported remembering headaches instead of stomachaches and cereal instead of eggs (Ceci, Ross, & Toglia, 1987). Such results do not mean that we should discount the testimony of young children. (To do so would virtually legalize crimes against children!) But they do mean that anyone who questions young children must be especially careful not to word the questions in a way that will suggest one answer or another.

Children who were asked misleading questions were less likely than other children were to give correct answers later. The effect of misleading questions was greater on younger children than on older children. (From Ceci, Ross, & Toglia, 1987.)

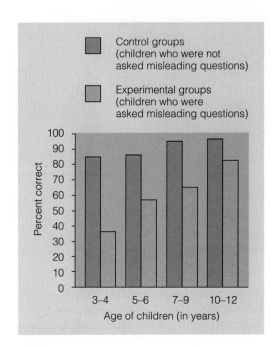

SUMMARY

■ *Long-term retention.* Most people remember a high percentage of the significant events of their lives and a fair amount of the material they learned in school, even if they seldom use the information. (page 336)

■ *Results of different ways of testing memory.* When people seem to have forgotten something, they may remember it better with a different method of testing, such as cued recall, recognition, or savings. (page 337)

■ *Implicit memory.* Even when people have no conscious recollection of an event, that event may influence their behavior on implicit tests of memory. (page 338)

■ *Exceptional memory.* Some people have exceptionally good memories. Others can improve their ability to memorize by using mnemonic devices. (page 340)

■ *Brain damage and amnesia.* People with damage to the hippocampus, the frontal cortex, and related structures suffer severe amnesia, especially in their ability to recall factual information they encountered after the onset of their disorder. Many of them still have nearly normal short-term memory and implicit memory. (page 342)

■ *Infant amnesia.* Most adults have trouble recalling events from before about age 5, possibly because the hippocampus was not mature in infancy. (page 346)

■ *Old-age amnesia.* Many elderly people have memory troubles, possibly because of deterioration of the hippocampus in old age. (page 347)

■ *Other amnesia.* Emotionally induced amnesia is possible, but rare. Even experts have difficulty distinguishing between people with real amnesia and people pretending to have amnesia. (page 347)

■ *Selective memory.* People are most likely to remember meaningful information, distinctive or unusual information, and the first and last items on a list. (page 348)

■ *Reconstruction.* In remembering stories or events from their own lives, people recall some of the facts and fill in the gaps based on logical inferences of what must have happened. (page 350)

■ *Memory distortions.* People tend to misremember the past in certain ways, emphasizing those facts that seem to fit with the way events finally turned out and deemphasizing facts that seemed to point in a different direction. (page 351)

■ *Distorted eyewitness memory.* Misleading questions can bias an eyewitness to report events inaccurately, although psychologists do not all agree that the misleading questions actually alter people's memories. (page 354)

SUGGESTIONS FOR FURTHER READING

Cermak, L. S. (1975). *Improving your memory.* New York: McGraw-Hill. A lively book about mnemonic devices and other ways to improve memory.

Squire, L. R. (1987). *Memory and brain.* New York: Oxford University. An excellent review focusing on amnesia and the biological foundations of memory.

TERMS

recall method of testing memory by asking someone to produce a certain item (such as a word) (page 337)

cued recall method of testing memory by asking someone to remember a certain item after being given a hint (page 337)

recognition method of testing memory by asking someone to choose the correct item from a set of alternatives (page 338)

savings method or **relearning method** method of testing memory by measuring how much faster someone can relearn something learned in the past than something being learned for the first time (page 338)

explicit memory test test in which a person has to state the correct answer, generally recognizing that it is the correct answer (page 338)

implicit memory test test that does not require any conscious recognition of a memory (page 338)

mnemonic device any memory aid that is based on encoding each item in some special way (page 340)

method of loci mnemonic device that calls for linking the items on a list with a memorized list of places (page 341)

amnesia loss of memory (page 342)

hippocampus forebrain structure believed to be important for certain aspects of memory (page 342)

anterograde amnesia inability to store new long-term memories (page 343)

retrograde amnesia loss of memory for events that occurred shortly prior to brain damage (page 343)

procedural memory retention of learned skills (page 343)

declarative memory recall of factual information (page 343)

Korsakoff's syndrome condition caused by prolonged deficiency of vitamin B$_1$, which results in both retrograde amnesia and anterograde amnesia (page 344)

confabulation guesses made by an amnesic patient to fill in the gaps in his or her memory (page 344)

Alzheimer's disease degenerative condition that generally occurs in old age, characterized by progressive loss of memory (page 345)

infant amnesia relative lack of declarative memories from before about age 5 in humans (page 346)

meaningfulness ability of a given item to fit into a known pattern of information (page 348)

serial-order effect tendency to remember the first and last items on a list better than those in the middle (page 350)

von Restorff effect tendency to remember the most distinctive items on a list better than other items (page 350)

reconstruction putting together an account of past events, based partly on memories and partly on expectations of what must have happened (page 350)

schema in memory, a series of expectations used to guide one's reconstruction of events (page 351)

hindsight bias tendency to mold our recollection of the past to fit the way later events turned out (page 353)

ANSWERS TO CONCEPT CHECKS

8. (a) savings; (b) recall; (c) recognition; (d) implicit; (e) cued recall; (f) implicit. (page 339)

9. People would remember even more if they were tested by the recognition method, as Bahrick (1984) demonstrated. They probably would show even greater retention if they were tested by the savings method. (page 339)

10. (a) procedural; (b) declarative, long-term. (page 346)

11. H. M., Korsakoff's patients, and Alzheimer's patients have anterograde amnesia, a difficulty in storing new memories, especially declarative memories. They are relatively normal in their ability to store new procedural memories. H. M. and Korsakoff's patients perform about normally on implicit tests of memory. (page 346)

ANSWERS TO OTHER QUESTIONS IN THE TEXT

Hermann Melville, Susan B. Anthony, Agatha Christie, Mikhail Gorbachev, Ivan Pavlov, Henry Aaron, Arthur Conan Doyle, Sally Ride, James Kalat, Margaret Mitchell, Wilbur and Orville, Geraldine Ferraro (page 338)

9 COGNITION AND LANGUAGE

How does a television set work? We can answer that question in two ways: One way is to describe the internal wiring and what each electronic device does. The other way is to describe how the set as a whole operates. (For example, if I flip a certain switch, the set comes on. If I turn a dial, the channel changes.)

How does a human work—that is, behave? We can also answer that question in two ways: One way is to describe what each neuron does and how the various neurons communicate with one another. The other way is to describe the behavior of the person as a whole. (For ex-

ample, when the weather turns cold or rainy, I go indoors. At certain times of day I walk toward a restaurant.)

Do we need a third way of describing behavior? Might we describe behavior as something caused by thoughts, knowledge, expectations, and desires?

As we saw in Chapter 7, traditional behaviorists say no. We do not need such terms to describe how a television works or to describe human behavior. Moreover, neurons and behavior are easily observed and measured. Thoughts and knowledge are not. A scientific study, say the behaviorists, should deal only with what can be observed and measured.

And yet each of us is directly aware of our own thoughts. Even if we cannot observe or measure other people's thoughts directly, we are sure of the reality of our own. In fact, my own conscious mind is the thing I am most sure of. (After all, the external world might be just an illusion.)

Granted that thoughts exist, we ask, What are they? Even if we cannot observe them directly, can we measure them indirectly through their effects on behavior? This chapter deals with the attempts of psychologists to grapple with such questions.

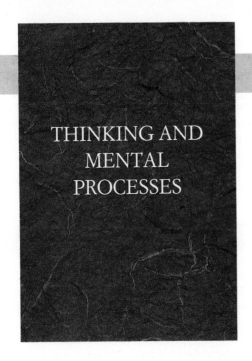

THINKING AND MENTAL PROCESSES

How is it possible to measure thought processes?

Are mental images similar to visual images?

How do people categorize items?

In 1986 investigators located the remains of the luxury liner *Titanic,* which had sunk in 1912. With great expense and effort they maneuvered a remote-control device to photograph various parts of the ship. Why did they bother? Did they plan to recover valuable cargo from the ship? No. Did they expect to learn anything about why the ship sank? Maybe, although the causes of the disaster were already well established. Actually, the investigators did not expect to learn anything especially useful. They wanted to know more about the ship just because they wanted to know. And so did all the rest of us who eagerly pored over the pictures.

Once we saw the pictures, we knew something that we had not known before. But was that the end of it? Hardly. The pictures started us thinking. We imagined what the ship must have looked like in 1912 and how we would have felt if we had been on board when it sank. To a limited extent, we shared the experiences of the people who went down with the *Titanic.* Perhaps this is why we seek new information about the *Titanic* or about anything else: The new information gives us something new to think about.

People spend a great deal of time just thinking. We imagine what life was like in the past and what it will be like in the future, how life would be different today if we had done something different in the past.

The relationship of all this thinking to actual behavior is not altogether obvious. At the end of one speech in the 1930s, in which the learning theorist Edward Tolman described how a rat learns the layout of its environment, a member of the audience, Edwin Guthrie, objected that Tolman had left the rat "buried in thought." That is, Guthrie did not see how the rat's thought processes could ever lead to actions. Psychologists today still wrestle with that problem, but the fact remains that both humans and rats generally think (or "process information," if you prefer) long before they act.

Cognition is psychologists' word for thinking, gaining knowledge, and dealing with knowledge. Cognitive psychology is the study of how people think, how they acquire knowledge, how they imagine, how they plan, and how they solve problems. It also deals with how people organize their thoughts into language and communicate their thoughts to others. In short, cognitive psychology deals with some of the most complex and most interesting processes in human experience.

MEASURING MENTAL ACTIVITY

For decades many psychologists, especially behaviorists, neglected and even ridiculed the study of mental activity. Mental experiences are private, they claimed; a scientific field cannot deal with phenomena that it cannot observe and measure.

And yet each of us knows that mental activity is real. The French philosopher René Descartes said the one statement he could not doubt was "I think, therefore I am." I could conceivably doubt the existence of *your* mental activity, but I can hardly doubt my own.

Psychologists were therefore in an awkward position. As individuals, they knew the reality of their own mental activity; but as scientists, they had nothing to say about it. The only way

Psychologists cannot observe thinking itself, but they can measure its effects. By timing people's responses under various conditions and comparing speeds, psychologists can infer what thought processes people went through and how long each one took.

out of this dilemma was to find a way to measure mental activity.

Granted, we cannot observe mental activity directly—just as physicists cannot observe magnetic fields directly. We can, however, measure the effects of mental activity. Saul Sternberg and other psychologists demonstrated that they could time people's delays in making certain responses and thereby infer something about people's thought processes. By measuring the speed and accuracy of people's responses, cognitive psychologists can deal with questions such as the following: Are mental images similar to visual images? Do people look for information by scanning their memories one item at a time or all at once? How do we think about categories of objects, such as the categories *bird* and *vehicle*? And what is the relationship between belief and disbelief? *The underlying theme of this chapter is that psychologists really can answer questions about how people think, using scientific studies rather than self-reports.*

MENTAL IMAGERY

Let's start with one common self-report about thinking: When people think about three-dimensional objects or about places where they have been, they generally report that they "see" images in their head. How closely do those mental images resemble actual vision? Indeed, do we really "see" visual images at all? "Well, of course we do," you might reply. "We do it all the time."

But self-reports are not solid evidence. After all, people sometimes insist that they have a clear mental image of some object and then find that they cannot correctly answer simple questions about it.

To illustrate: Imagine a simple cube balanced with one point (corner) on the table and the opposite point straight up. Imagine that you hold the highest point with one finger. Now, with a finger of the opposite hand, point to all the remaining corners of the cube. How many corners do you touch?

You probably will say that you answered this question by "picturing" a cube in your mind as if you were actually seeing it. However, most people answer the question incorrectly, and few people get the right answer quickly (Hinton, 1979). (Check answer A, page 372.)

So our mental images are sometimes wrong. Further, it is not obvious that we need mental images to answer visual or spatial questions. Computers can answer such questions quite ac-

curately without drawing little pictures inside themselves. Can we demonstrate that mental images are at least sometimes useful and that they have some of the properties we ordinarily associate with vision? Answering this question was a triumph of the experimental method in cognitive psychology.

Mental Imagery

Roger Shepard and Jacqueline Metzler (1971) conducted a classic study of how humans solve visual problems. They reasoned that if people actually visualize mental images, then the time it takes them to rotate a mental image should be similar to the time it takes to rotate a real object.

Hypothesis When people have to rotate a mental image to answer a question, the farther they have to rotate it, the longer it will take them to answer the question.

Method The experimenters showed subjects pairs of two-dimensional drawings of three-dimensional objects, as in Figure 9.1, and asked whether the drawings in each pair represented the same object rotated in different directions or whether they represented different objects. (Try to answer this question yourself before reading further. Then check answer B, page 372.)

The subjects could answer by pulling one lever to indicate *same* and another lever to indicate *different*. When the correct answer was *same,* a subject might determine that answer by rotating a mental image of the first picture until it matched the second. If so, the delay should depend on how far the image had to be rotated.

The delays before answering *different* were generally longer and less consistent than those for answering *same*—as is generally the case. Subjects could answer *same* as soon as they found a way to rotate the first object to match the second. However, to be sure that the objects were different, subjects might have to double-check several times and imagine more than one way of rotating the object.

Results Subjects were almost 97% accurate in determining both *same* and *different*. As predicted, their reaction time for responding *same* depended on the angular difference in orientation between the two views. For example, if the first image of a pair had to be rotated 30 degrees to match the second image, the subject took a certain amount of time to pull the *same* lever. If the two images looked the same after the first one had been rotated 60 degrees, the subject took twice as long to pull the lever. In other words, the subjects reacted as if they were actually watching a little model of the object rotate in their head; the more the object needed to be rotated, the longer they took to determine the answer.

Interpretation Viewing a mental image is at least partly like real vision.

In a related experiment, subjects were shown pairs of cubes. Each face of a particular cube was labeled with a different letter or number. For each pair, subjects were asked whether it was possible that the two cubes were identical. To answer, they had to imagine the rotation of one of the cubes. The rotation could be completed either by one turn through an oblique angle, as process A in Figure 9.2 shows, or by two 90-degree turns, as process B in Figure 9.2 shows. Those who reported that they could imagine turns through oblique angles answered the questions more accurately even though they answered faster than other subjects did (Just & Carpenter, 1985). An experiment such as this helps us to understand why certain people answer a problem faster or more accurately than others do: They go through different identifiable mental processes.

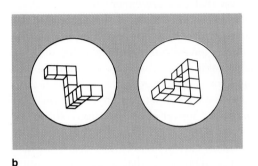

FIGURE 9.1
Examples of pairs of drawings used in an experiment by Shepard and Metzler (1971). Do the drawings for each pair represent the same object being rotated, or are they different objects? (See answer B on page 372.)

a

b

c

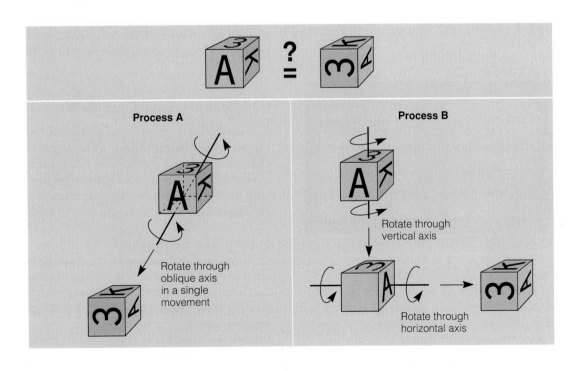

Process A

Rotate through oblique axis in a single movement

Process B

Rotate through vertical axis

Rotate through horizontal axis

FIGURE 9.2
People solved the problem of the identity of the two cubes in either of two ways. Process A requires one step, and process B requires two steps. Those who used process A solved the problem more quickly—and more accurately.

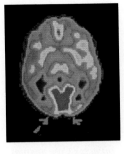

FIGURE 9.3
PET scans like this and similar technologies tell us how much activity is occurring in each part of the brain. Red indicates the greatest activity level, followed by yellow, green, and blue. Studies have found increasing activity in the visual cortex of the brain while people form mental images.

Something to Think About

Some people report that they have auditory images as well as visual images. They "hear" words or songs "in their head." What kind of evidence would we need to test that claim?

Has the evidence so far convinced you that people really do experience mental images? Here is a different kind of evidence: When people say that they are experiencing mental images, the parts of their brain that are responsible for vision become more active (Farah, 1988). Subjects have been asked such questions as: What color is a football? Are the hind legs of a kangaroo shorter than its front legs? In those subjects who say that they are relying on visual images to answer these questions, the blood flow increases to the occipital cortex (the visual area of the cortex; Figure 9.3). People who have suffered damage to that area cannot answer such questions.

Note an important point about scientific procedure: We almost never base a conclusion on just one experiment or even on one kind of evidence. Although the experiment on rotating mental images is a classic, we look for additional evidence that points to the same conclusion.

The Piecemeal Formation of Mental Images

We have just considered evidence to demonstrate the existence of mental images—a point that may have struck you as obvious from the start. The experimental evidence is nevertheless valuable for two reasons.

First, it reassures us that our intuitions were correct. (They are not always, after all.) Second, in the process of conducting the experiments we have just described, psychologists developed methods that they can employ to address other questions—questions whose answers are far from obvious. For example, when you form a mental image of, say, your house, does it appear all at once or bit by bit?

Subjects in one experiment first memorized a series of block letters, like the letter shown in Figure 9.4a. Then they were shown a grid with an x on one spot and were asked whether or not a given letter—in this case, F—would cover the x. When the x was in the upper left-hand corner of the grid, as in Figure 9.4b, the subjects answered quickly. If they were drawing the letter F, that is the position they would fill in first. When the x was in some other position farther from the upper left, as in Figure 9.4c, they took longer to answer. Evidently they formed a mental image of the letter gradually, starting in the upper left where they would start to draw it and then proceeding to the rest of the letter (Kosslyn, 1988). That is, the image forms piece by piece, not all at once.

Try this demonstration of the same point: Form a mental image of a dog. Once you have formed it, does it seem complete? If so, answer two questions: First, what breed of dog is it? Second, does it have a collar? Most people have little hesitation in identifying the breed; the breed was part of their initial image. But most people pause before saying whether they saw a collar. The dog in the initial image neither had a collar nor lacked a collar; that part of the image was simply unformed. When asked about a collar, people have to add another feature to the image.

Using Mental Images: Cognitive Maps

You are staying at a hotel in an unfamiliar city. You walk a few blocks to get to a museum; then you turn and walk in another direction to get to a restaurant; after dinner you turn again and walk to a theater. After the performance, how do you get back to the hotel? Do you retrace all of your steps? Can you find a shorter route? Or do you give up and hail a cab?

If you can find your way back, you do so by using a **cognitive map,** a mental image of a spatial arrangement. One way to measure the accuracy of people's cognitive maps is to test how well they can find the route from one place to another. Another way is to ask them to draw a

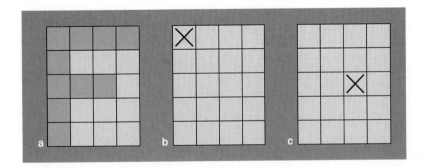

FIGURE 9.4
After subjects memorize block letters like the one in a, they are shown a pattern such as b or c and then asked whether the letter F would cover the x. People respond faster when the x is in the upper left and slower when it is toward the lower right. Such results suggest that a mental image forms gradually, starting in the upper left corner, rather than all at once.

map. As you might expect, people draw a more complete map of the areas they are most familiar with. When students try to draw a map of their college campus, they generally include the central buildings on campus and the buildings they enter most frequently (Saarinen, 1973). The longer students have been on campus, the more detail they include (Cohen & Cohen, 1985).

The errors people make in their cognitive maps follow some interesting patterns. First, they tend to remember street angles as being close to 90 degrees, even when they are not (Moar & Bower, 1983). We can easily understand that error. For practical purposes, all we need to remember is "go three blocks and turn left" or "go two blocks and turn right"; we do not burden our memory by recalling "turn 72 degrees to the right."

Second, people generally image geographic areas as being aligned neatly along a north-to-south axis and an east-to-west axis (Stevens & Coupe, 1978; B. Tversky, 1981). Try these questions, for example: Which city is farther west—Reno, Nevada; or Los Angeles, California? And which is farther north—Philadelphia, Pennsylvania; or Rome, Italy? Most people reason that, because California is west of Nevada, Los Angeles is "obviously" west of Reno. (Figure 9.5 shows the true position of the cities.) Rome is in southern Europe, and Philadelphia is in the northern part of the United States; therefore, Philadelphia should be north of Rome. In fact, Rome is north of Philadelphia.

You see now the differences between a cognitive map and a real map: Cognitive maps, like other mental images, highlight some details, distort some, and omit some. Nevertheless, they are accurate enough for most practical purposes.

SEARCHING THROUGH MENTAL LISTS

Some mental representations are nonvisual. For example, I give you a name and you try to decide whether it is the name of a famous person. To answer correctly, you have to look for a match between that name and the name of any famous person you have ever heard of. How do you do something like that? Do you go through all the famous names one by one, or do you somehow compare them all at once? And what if I made it a little more difficult: I am interested

FIGURE 9.5
Logical versus actual: Location of Reno and Los Angeles. Most people imagine that Los Angeles is the farther west because California is west of Nevada.

only in people who became famous by being a classical music composer, or a poet, or a National League baseball player. (If the person became famous in some other way, you say no.) Would you have to go through any different mental processes with this task than with the simpler, "famous or not famous," task?

As before, we cannot rely on you to describe your mental processes. But we can learn something about those processes by measuring how long it takes you to answer various questions.

Subjects in one classic experiment watched a number flashed on a screen (Sternberg, 1967). They were told to pull one lever if the number was, say, either 3 or 7, and a different lever if it was any other number. To make the correct response, the subjects had to go through three steps: First, they had to perceive what number was being flashed on the screen. Second, they had to compare that number to the numbers they had memorized (3 and 7) to determine whether it was one of them. Third, they had to pull a lever.

To perform that second step, determining whether the number was either a 3 or a 7, did subjects ask first "Was it a 3?" and then "Was it a 7?" Or did they somehow compare it to both the 3 and the 7 simultaneously?

Saul Sternberg (1967) measured their reaction times under various conditions. Sometimes the subjects had to decide whether the number on the screen was a single number, such as 3. Sometimes they had to decide whether it was either of two numbers, such as 3 or 7. Sometimes they had to decide whether it was one of four numbers, such as 3, 4, 6, or 7. Figure 9.6 gives the results.

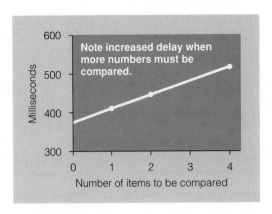

FIGURE 9.6
When people were asked to compare a number on the screen to one, two, or four memorized numbers, they took longer when they had to compare it to more numbers. The line is extrapolated to zero to show how much time is taken for other elements of the response besides the comparison process. These results suggest that people compare the number on the screen to those in memory one at a time (in series), not all at once (in parallel). (Based on Sternberg, 1967.)

When the subjects had memorized two numbers to compare to the displayed number, they took 35 msec (milliseconds) longer per response than when they had one number. When they had four numbers, they took 71 msec longer than when they had two. Apparently, they took about 35 msec to compare the displayed number to each of the memorized numbers. Because the relationship was so regular, Sternberg concluded that the subjects were comparing the number on the screen to each of the numbers they had memorized, one at a time. That is, they conducted their comparisons *in serial,* not *in parallel.*

That one study did not settle the matter, though. Other research has shown that people sometimes *do* conduct a parallel search. If the task is to decide whether the number on the screen was 2, 4, 6, 8, or 0—that is, an even number—they answer very rapidly, implying a parallel search. The same is true if the task is to decide whether the number was 1, 2, 3, 4, or 5. That is, depending on the difficulty of the task, people may search through a mental list of items either in series or in parallel. And sometimes the results are difficult to interpret (Townsend, 1990). But in any case, psychologists try to understand people's cognitive processes not by asking them to describe their own thought processes but by timing their responses.

1. In studies similar to Sternberg's, experimenters made it harder to perceive the numbers on the screen by making them blurry. The results were slightly different from those shown in Figure 9.6: The slope of the graph line was the same, but the line started higher. Which step in a subject's response was affected by the blurred numbers: perceiving the number, comparing it to the numbers in memory, or pulling the lever?

2. Figure 9.6 shows the results for subjects who are making a serial comparison of an item they just saw to one or more items held in memory. What would the results look like if they conducted their comparisons in parallel?
(Check your answers on page 372.)

CATEGORIZATION

We started with a couple of questions about mental images and memory searches, on which you may have had confident (if not necessarily accurate) self-reports. Now let's turn to a cognitive psychology question on which common sense offers no answer: How do people divide the world's objects into categories? That is, when we add a new word or phrase to our language, such as *endangered species, toxic waste,* or *yuppie,* that term refers to a category we have devised which includes some items and excludes others. What kinds of categories do we ordinarily form?

If we form useful categories, they enable us to make educated guesses about features we have never seen for ourselves (Anderson, 1991). For example, if you see a leopard and someone asks you whether it has taste buds, you can confidently answer yes, without even thinking of checking the animal's mouth to find out. You know a leopard must have taste buds, because you categorize it as a mammal and all mammals have taste buds.

We often take our categories for granted, as if our own way of categorizing objects were the only possible way (Figure 9.7). But people in other cultures sometimes use categories that seem strange to us (Lakoff, 1987). The Japanese word *hon* refers to long, thin things, including sticks, pencils, trees, and hair. It also includes items that do not strike English-speaking people as obvious examples of long, thin things: hits in baseball, shots in basketball, telephone calls, television programs, a mental contest between a Zen master and a student, and medical injections. Clearly, people from different cultures categorize objects in different ways.

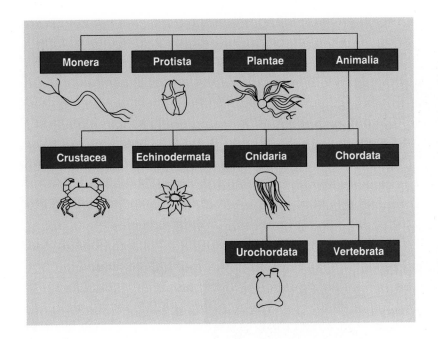

Those that belong to the emperor

Embalmed ones

Trained animals

Suckling pigs

Mermaids

Fabulous ones

Stray dogs

Those that are included in this classification

Those that tremble as if they were mad

Innumerable ones

Those drawn with a very fine camel's hair brush

Others

Those that have just broken a flower vase

Those that resemble flies from a distance

FIGURE 9.7

Left: A much-abridged chart of the current scientific classification of the animal kingdom. Right: an alleged listing from an ancient Chinese encyclopedia—actually the creation of someone's imagination (Rosch, 1978). The point is, there are many ways to categorize animals or anything else, and some methods of categorizing are better than others.

How do people decide how to categorize objects? That question is part of the more basic question, How do we think?

Categorization by Levels

According to one view, the **categorization by levels** approach (Collins & Quillian, 1969, 1970), we categorize each item at a level with similar items; several categories at one level combine into a single category at the next higher level, as in Figure 9.8. For example, *salmon* and *shark* are both fish; *fish* and *bird* are both *animals.* Each lower-level category has all the defining features of the higher-level category plus certain distinctive features of its own. For example, *canary* has the distinctive features *can sing* and *is yellow;* it also necessarily has all the features of the higher-level category, *bird,* such as *has feathers* and *can fly.*

Categorizing objects in this way simplifies our memory task. Once we learn, for example, that a yellow warbler is a kind of bird, we do not have to memorize that it has wings and feathers, lays eggs, and can fly. When necessary, we memorize the exceptions, such as the fact that ostriches and penguins, unlike most birds, cannot fly.

The evidence for this view comes from measurements of reaction times. Suppose you are asked true-false question about canaries. To the statement "A canary is yellow," you respond rapidly, because *yellow* is a distinctive feature of *canary.* To the statement "A canary lays eggs," you respond more slowly, because *laying eggs* is not a particularly distinctive feature of *canaries.* You have to reason, "Canaries are birds, and birds lay eggs. So canaries lay eggs." Finally, to the statement "Canaries have skin," your reaction time is slower yet. *Skin* is not a distinctive feature of either *canaries* or *birds.* So you have to go from the *canary* level to the *bird* level to the *animal* level before you find the distinctive feature *skin.*

The categorization by levels approach accounts for some of the data but not all. Robins, canaries, and penguins are all birds; therefore, according to this approach, they should all be at the same level. And yet people are quicker to agree that robins and canaries have feathers than they are to agree that penguins or ostriches have feathers.

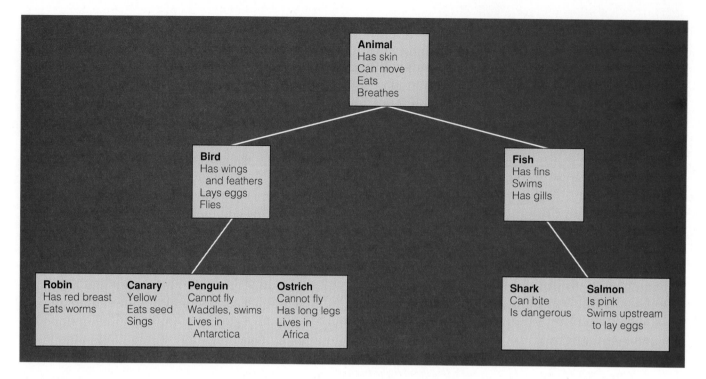

FIGURE 9.8
According to the categorization by levels approach, we form categories that include each of the categories in the level below it. We learn the special properties of a category such as canary, *but we also know that* canary *has all the properties of the higher categories.*

■ CONCEPT CHECK

3. *Which would take longer to decide: whether Eskimos wear parkas or whether Eskimos wear clothes? Why? (Check your answer on page 372.)*

Categorization by Features

Why do people take longer to agree that penguins have feathers than they take to agree that robins have feathers? Perhaps because it also takes longer to decide whether penguins are birds than to decide whether robins are birds (Rips, Shoben, & Smith, 1973; Smith, Shoben, & Rips, 1974). When we **categorize by features,** we define the category *bird* in terms of wings, feathers, flight, egg laying, a typical size and shape, and so forth. We decide whether something fits that category by determining how many of those features it has. Robins are "typical" birds; penguins are not.

In some cases, the "features" get a little more complicated. A picture of a mother robin with her baby is, most would agree, similar to a picture of a robin by itself. But it is also similar (in a different way) to a picture of a mother tiger with her cub. That is, the "features" relevant to categorizing some item can vary depending on what else we are comparing it to (Medin, Goldstone, & Gentner, 1990).

Categorization by Prototypes

Categorization by features accounts for a great deal of reaction-time data, so we probably do think of certain categories, such as *bird,* in terms of a list of features. But frequently we also deal with such loosely defined categories as "interesting novels" or "embarrassing experiences," in which we could not list the defining features.

According to Eleanor Rosch (1978; Rosch & Mervis, 1975; see also Nosofsky, 1986), loose categories are defined by their most familiar or most typical examples, called **prototypes.** According to the **categorization by prototypes** approach, we decide whether an object belongs to a category by determining how well it resembles the protypical members of the category.

For example, we define the category *vehicle* by giving examples: car, bus, train, airplane, boat. To decide whether some other object is a vehicle, we compare it to these examples. People have short reaction times to *truck;* they have longer reaction times to the atypical example *blimp* and still longer reaction times to *elevator* or *water skis.*

The main point of Rosch's prototype approach is that category membership is sometimes a matter of degree. When we are asked whether a penguin is a bird, there is a correct answer ("yes"), but when we are asked whether an elevator is a vehicle or whether our next-door neighbor is intelligent, we have to answer "sort of" or "not exactly."

Do we always define categories by proto-types? No. We can deal with odd categories such as *repentant turtles* or *sarcastic toddlers,* even though we probably cannot think of a clear example of either category (Smith, Osherson, Rips, & Keane, 1988).

The overall message is that we categorize different items in different ways. We can think of a category in terms of features (like the features of *bird*), in terms of prototypes (such as a typical *vehicle*), or in terms of combinations of properties (such as *sarcastic toddler*).

BELIEF AND DISBELIEF

Now that we are armed with solid scientific methods of investigating cognition, we can begin to deal with some challenging questions that used to be fit only for speculation. For example: Is it in general easier to believe something or to disbelieve?

Many parents tell their children all sorts of preposterous things: "The tooth fairy will take your tooth and give you money in return." "The Easter Bunny brings baskets of colored eggs on Easter morning." "You're really going to enjoy first grade!"

And young children tend to believe almost everything they are told, at least until something happens to change their mind. When we become adults, do we outgrow that childlike tendency? Or do we too have a tendency to believe everything we hear?

Two philosophical traditions have offered different answers to this question (Gilbert, 1991). The French philosopher René Descartes offered a suggestion that seems almost self-evident: When we hear a new idea, we first comprehend its meaning. Then we weigh the pros and cons to decide whether to believe it or to reject it. The Dutch philosopher Spinoza, how-ever, suggested that when we comprehend something, we simultaneously believe it; we cannot understand an idea without imagining what it means for the idea to be true. Later we may weigh the evidence and decide to confirm our initial belief, reject it, or regard it as uncertain. Under some conditions we may reject it within a second or two, but according to Spinoza the rejection always comes after at least a brief period of acceptance. In short, believing is easy; disbelief takes some extra effort.

Which philosopher was right? Both had to rely on speculation and argument; psychologists would like to have evidence. Self-observations will not do. It may seem to you that you heard some ridiculous statement and rejected it "immediately," but you cannot eliminate the possibility that you may have accepted it for just an instant before marshalling your forces against it. One way to evaluate this possibility is to examine reaction times when people say they agree or disagree with some statement. Research has shown that people generally take longer to answer a question "no" than to answer "yes," longer to disagree than to agree.

Here is another way to test Spinoza's proposal: If disbelief requires more effort than belief, then people who are exhausted, distracted, or otherwise impaired may not be able to muster the extra effort. Under such circumstances they may be inclined to believe something they would ordinarily reject.

In one experiment, college students read a series of sentences allegedly based on the way people learn a foreign language. For example, one of the sentences was "A twyrin is a doctor." After each such sentence appeared on a computer screen, the word *true* or *false* appeared on the screen to indicate whether the previous statement had been correct. Thus the student should try to remember the "true" statements and reject the "false" ones. Intermixed with these sentences, the students had to perform a second task: From time to time they would hear a tone; they were supposed to respond by press-ing a button as quickly as possible. Conse-quently, the students were exposed to four kinds of sentences: "true" statements with dis-tractions (button pressing), "true" statements without distractions, and "false" statements with and without distractions.

At the end, the experimenters asked ques-tions of the form "Is a twyrin a doctor?" If the statement was supposedly "true," the distrac-tion made no difference; students were likely to remember it as true, with or without distrac-tion. But if they were distracted during a "false" statement, they generally misremembered it as "true" (Gilbert, Krull, & Malone, 1990).

These results support Spinoza's suggestion that disbelief takes more effort than belief. The pattern of results is the same in a variety of other experiments: If people are frequently distracted while listening to a speech, they are more likely

Saboteur or scapegoat? *Hartwig's sister Kathy Kubicina called the conclusion that he caused the blast 'obscene'*

The Navy Blames a Dead Man

The Iowa report cites sabotage but fails to prove it

It was a full-dress attempt to close the books on one of the Navy's most harrowing peacetime tragedies. A team of admirals was deployed to unveil the 1,100-page report on the explosion that killed 47 seamen aboard the battleship USS Iowa last April. But they left most listeners at sea with a troubling list of unanswered questions. The brass depicted 24-year-old Petty Officer Clayton Hartwig as a moody loner who fulfilled his fantasies of dying valiantly in the line of duty by slipping a homemade detonator between bags of gunpowder, immolating himself and fellow crew members of gun turret number two in a 3,000-degree fireball. But the Navy backed away from suggestions, which had been leaked earlier to credulous news organizations—including NEWSWEEK—that Hartwig was distraught over the end of a homosexual affair with a crew member he had named as beneficiary of his $100,000 life-insurance policy. In fact, the Navy says its psychologists did *not* conclude that Hartwig was emotionally unstable and offered no evidence that he was homosexual. Even so, the report, which took four months, $4 million and hundreds of interviews, concluded that Hartwig "most likely" caused the disaster in an act of suicidal sabotage.

Critics—including Hartwig's family—quickly accused the Navy of being more intent on fingering a scapegoat than probing the catastrophe. Investigators say they recovered traces of a detonator, possibly fashioned by Hartwig and hidden between bags of powder inserted into the 16-inch gun. But authorities are unable to duplicate the kind of detonating device he supposedly used. Nor can they come up with convincing evidence that he even had the knowledge or wherewithal to build one. They found no traces in his personal effects to match the detonator residue recovered from the gun; only an Army munitions manual and a book called "Getting Even: The Complete Book of Dirty Tricks" remotely suggested that he had any pertinent knowledge. If he did have the know-how, it was unlikely he had the time. Hartwig was unaware he would be serving as gun captain that day until hours before the blast.

Poor supervision: According to the Navy's scenario, part of Hartwig's duty was to supervise another sailor, known as a rammer, who shoved the powder bags up the gun barrel. As gun captain, he would give a thumbs-up sign when he saw the bags reach the proper position—21 inches from the breech. But Hartwig allowed the bags to be rammed too far up, hitting a loaded projectile and triggering the fiery explosion—right in his face. Again, the Navy's reconstruction of events is leaky. Although the rammer was new to the job, and perhaps susceptible to Hartwig's misdirection, the regular gun captain was standing right next to Hartwig. Hartwig would have had to pull off his sabotage without the experienced officer seeing him—a difficult feat.

The Navy also chose to discount serious safety problems it uncovered in turret 2 as a possible cause of the explosion. Investigators found poor supervision and seamen improperly trained for gun operations. Officials said the Iowa's top officers, including Capt. Fred Moosally, have been recommended for disciplinary action. Hartwig himself emerges as only a shadowy figure in the Navy's findings. Psychologists sketch him as an introvert with delusions of grandeur (a photo found in his possession shows him posing in a Navy commander's uniform with a sword). While he had a history of forging close personal relationships with other men, there was no finding that his relationships were anything more than platonic. And while he had spoken in the past of suicide, his last letters from the Iowa were upbeat.

Hartwig's family members charge that the Navy is covering up its own transgressions by slandering a dead sailor. His sister, Kathy Kubicina of Cleveland, called the report's conclusions "obscene." If Hartwig had survived the blast, there would not be sufficient evidence for a conviction, says family lawyer Kreig Brusnahan. "Is it fair that he should be convicted in death when he could not be convicted in life?" he asks. Hartwig's family is not the only party angered by the report. Although the Navy has absolved Gunner's Mate Kendall Truitt of any responsibility for the blast, his naval career has been seriously damaged by the leaks alleging a homosexual relationship with Hartwig and the suggestion that he benefited from the Iowa tragedy thanks to the life-insurance policy. Truitt's lawyer, Ellis Rubin, says he is considering lawsuits against the news organizations that carried the original reports. For Truitt, at least, there is the possibility of recompense. For the dead of gun turret number two, there will be no such solace.

BILL TURQUE *with* RICHARD SANDZA
in Washington

Disbelief takes more effort than belief; consequently, an accusation is generally more influential than a denial is. When a gun exploded on the navy battleship Iowa, the navy at first blamed a sailor, suggesting the explosion was part of a murder-suicide plot. Later it withdrew these charges, admitting it had little evidence for them. In a case such as this, the original accusation hurts the reputation of the accused and the later retraction receives much less publicity, possibly none at all. Even if people do read a retraction ("This man probably did not sabotage the ship"), the retraction may hurt again instead of helping.

than usual to accept what the speaker had to say (Baron, Baron, & Miller, 1973).

A further consequence: Suppose people hear some claim, which turns out to be based on no evidence at all. Logically, we should expect them to reject the idea completely. But if rejection takes some extra effort, not everyone will give it that extra effort. In an experiment to test this prediction, college students read a series of headlines, supposedly about candidates for public office. Different students read different headlines so that each student would read one of the following headlines about "Bob Talbert":

Bob Talbert linked with Mafia.

Bob Talbert not linked with Mafia.

Is Bob Talbert linked with Mafia?

Bob Talbert celebrates birthday.

Similarly, for a number of other candidates, one headline charged wrongdoing, one denied wrongdoing, one raised a question of wrongdoing, and one made an irrelevant comment. Each group saw just one of those headlines per candidate. Afterward the students were asked for their opinions of the candidates. Curiously, being told "Bob Talbert not linked with Mafia" or being asked "Is Bob Talbert linked with Mafia?" left most people with a low opinion of Talbert. Evidently, once the charge was made, many people tended to believe it (Wegner, Wenzlaff, Kerker, & Beattie, 1981).

(You can see the diabolical implications: If you want to smear your political opponent, leak some rumors that he or she has been involved in a sex scandal, or has embezzled funds, or has committed some other shameful act. The initial headline alleging these charges hurts your opponent, and the later headline denying them actually hurts your opponent again.)

At one point in the late 1800s, a man in Russia was charged with murdering his father. Although the jury found him not guilty, the tsar sentenced him to 20 years in prison anyway. The tsar's explanation was that the crime was so severe that the state should not take any chances of letting someone get away with it (Belknap, 1990). That is, once the charges had been made, the tsar assumed they must be partly true.

One final demonstration of this tendency to believe: Students in one study watched as an experimenter poured sugar into two jars. Then they were told to place two labels on the jars, putting whichever label they wanted on each jar. One label said "sucrose, table sugar." The

FIGURE 9.9

Most students preferred Kool-Aid made with sugar labeled "sugar" instead of sugar labeled "not cyanide," even though they had placed the labels themselves. Evidently, we tend to believe an accusation ("cyanide") to some extent even if it is denied immediately ("not"). Disbelief takes more effort than belief does. (Based on results of Rozin, Markwith, & Ross, 1990.)

other said "not sodium cyanide, not poison." Then the experimenter made two cups of Kool-Aid, one with sugar from one jar and one from sugar in the other jar (Figure 9.9). Finally the experimenter asked the students to choose one cup of Kool-Aid. Almost half the students said they had no preference, but of those who did have a preference, 35 of 44 wanted the Kool-Aid made from the jar marked "sucrose," not from the one that denied having cyanide and poison (Rozin, Markwith, & Ross, 1990). The students acted as if the label "not cyanide" meant something was wrong with the sugar in that jar. Evidently, we have some problem in fully understanding and believing the word *not*.

(It is particularly difficult to understand double negatives, such as "She is not unfriendly." Each negative requires rejecting the positive statement; a double negative requires rejecting a rejection. I once came across a quadruple negative in a news article: "The legislature failed to repeal the law preventing school districts from abolishing corporal punishment." (How long does it take you to understand *that* sentence?)

SUMMARY

■ *Timing.* Although psychologists cannot directly observe thought, they can infer its properties by timing people's response delays. (page 361)

- *Mental images.* One line of evidence for the reality of mental images comes from studies of the rotation of mental images. When people answer whether or not one picture could be rotated to match another, their delay is proportional to the distance an actual object would have to rotate. (page 362)

- *Cognitive maps.* People learn to find their way by using cognitive maps, but they make certain consistent errors in their cognitive maps, such as remembering all turns as being close to 90-degree angles. (page 364)

- *Mental searches.* When people search through a mental list, they can search the items either in series or in parallel, depending on the difficulty of the task. (page 365)

- *Categorizing.* People can form categories of objects either by lists of common features or by examples or prototypes that represent a category. (page 366)

- *Belief vs. disbelief.* Evidence suggests that when we understand some statement we tend to believe it initially; disbelief requires a second, effortful step. (page 369)

SUGGESTIONS FOR FURTHER READING

Hearst, E. (1991). Psychology and nothing. *American Scientist, 79,* 432–443. Interesting article about how we react to nonevents, related to the psychology of disbelief.

Lakoff, G. (1987). *Women, fire, and dangerous things.* Chicago: University of Chicago Press. A discussion of how we conceptualize categories.

Posner, M. I. (Ed.) (1989). *Foundations of cognitive science.* Cambridge, MA: MIT Press. A collection of chapters by outstanding investigators of memory and cognition.

TERMS

cognition the processes that enable us to imagine, to gain knowledge, to reason about knowledge, and to judge its meaning (page 361)

cognitive map a mental representation of a spatial arrangement (page 364)

categorization by levels theory that we categorize each item at a level with similar items; each item has distinctive features of its own plus all the features of higher-level categories that include it (page 367)

categorization by features theory that we categorize objects by determining how many features they have that are characteristic of the members of a category (page 368)

prototype a highly typical member of a category (page 368)

categorization by prototypes theory that we decide whether an object belongs to a category by determining how well it resembles the prototypes of the category (page 368)

ANSWERS TO CONCEPT CHECKS

1. Making the letters blurry slowed the perception of the number. If it had slowed the process of comparing a number to the numbers in memory, the slope of the line would have become steeper. (page 366)

2. The line in Figure 9.6 would be horizontal instead of increasing. (page 366)

3. It should take longer to respond that Eskimos wear clothes. Wearing parkas is a distinctive feature of Eskimos, along with living in igloos. To answer whether Eskimos wear clothes we have to go a level up, either to "Eskimos are human; humans wear clothes" or to "parkas are clothes." (page 368)

ANSWERS TO OTHER QUESTIONS IN THE TEXT

A. The cube has six (not four) remaining corners. (page 362)

B. The objects in pair a are the same; in b they are the same; and in c they are different. (page 362)

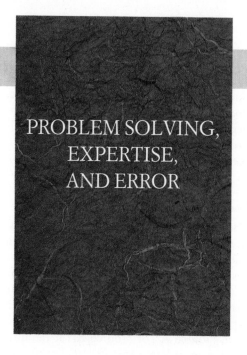

PROBLEM SOLVING, EXPERTISE, AND ERROR

What do experts know or do that sets them apart from other people?

How can we improve our ability to solve problems?

Why do people sometimes reason illogically?

On a college physics exam, a student was once asked how to use a barometer to determine the height of a building. He answered that he would tie a long string to the barometer, go to the top of the building, and carefully lower the barometer until it reached the ground. Then he would cut the string and measure its length.

When the professor marked this answer incorrect, the student asked why. "Well," said the professor, "your method would work, but it's not the method I wanted you to use." The student objected. The professor then offered, as a compromise, to let the student try again.

"All right," the student said. "Take the barometer to the top of the building, drop it, and measure the time it takes to hit the ground. Then from the formula for the speed of a falling object, using the gravitational constant, calculate the height of the building."

"Hmmm," replied the professor. "That too would work. And it does make use of physical principles. But it still isn't the answer I had in mind. Can you think of another way to use the barometer to determine the height of the building?"

"Another way? Sure," replied the student. "Place the barometer next to the building on a sunny day. Measure the height of the barometer and the length of its shadow. Also measure the length of the building's shadow. Then use the formula

$$\frac{\text{height of barometer}}{\text{length of barometer's shadow}} = \frac{\text{height of building}}{\text{length of building's shadow}}$$

The professor was becoming more and more impressed with the student, but he was still reluctant to give credit for the answer. He asked for yet another way.

The student suggested, "Measure the barometer's height. Then walk up the stairs of the building, marking it off in units of the barometer's height. At the top, take the number of barometer units and multiply by the height of the barometer to get the height of the building."

The professor sighed. "Just give me one more way—any other way—and I'll give you credit, even if it's not the answer I wanted."

"Really?" asked the student with a smile. "Any other way?"

"Yes, any other way."

"All right," said the student. "Go to the man who owns the building and say, 'Hey buddy, if you tell me how tall this building is, I'll give you this neat barometer!'"

We sometimes face a logical or practical problem that we have never tried to solve before. We have to devise a new solution; we cannot rely on a memorized or practiced solution. Sometimes people develop creative, imaginative solutions, like the ones the physics student proposed. Sometimes they offer less imaginative, but still reasonable, solutions. Sometimes they suggest something quite illogical, and sometimes they cannot think of any solution at all. Psychologists study problem-solving behavior partly to understand the thought processes behind it and partly to look for ways to help people reason more effectively.

EXPERTISE

People vary in their performance on problem-solving and decision-making tasks. In the barometer story just described we probably would talk about the student's creativity; in other cases we talk of someone's expertise. In either case, some people seem more able than other people to understand a problem or to find feasible solutions.

But what do we mean when we say "understand"? How could we determine whether someone understands, say, algebra? We would need an operational definition of *understand*. Suppose we adopt this one: Understanding is measured by how accurately someone can solve problems. That is, anyone who can solve algebra problems accurately must understand algebra.

Let's try an algebra problem: A board was sawed into two pieces. One piece was 3/4 as long as the whole board. It exceeded the length of the second piece by 2 meters. What was the length of the whole board? (Pause to calculate the answer.)

If your algebra is not too rusty, you quickly calculated that the answer is 4 meters. If you now enter the appropriate information into a computer, it too will report an answer of 4 meters. So, according to our definition of *understand,* the computer "understands."

But is the computer's understanding the same as yours? Let's try another problem similar to the first: A board was sawed into two pieces. One piece was 2/3 as long as the whole board. The second piece exceeded it in length by 2 meters. What was the length of the whole board? (Pause to calculate your answer.)

Many people answer 6 meters (Larkin, McDermott, Simon, & Simon, 1980). A computer invariably comes up with the correct answer—which is *minus* 6 meters. If you said 6 meters,

does your answer mean that the computer understands better than you do? The computer seems to understand algebra, but you understand the real world. (The computer evidently does not.) You know that boards cannot have negative lengths and that (contrary to what the problem said) the piece that constitutes 2/3 of the whole must be the longer of the two.

Something to Think About

The Turing Test, suggested by computer pioneer Alan Turing, proposes the following operational definition of artificial intelligence: A person poses questions to a human source and to a computer, both in another room. The human and the computer send back typewritten replies, which are identified only as coming from "source A" or "source B." If the questioner cannot determine which replies are coming from the computer, then the computer has passed a significant test of understanding.

Suppose a computer did pass the Turing Test. Would we then say that the computer "understands," just as a human does? Or would we say that it is merely mimicking human understanding?

Expert Pattern Recognition

In any field from algebra to zoology, we identify some people as "experts." One characteristic of experts is that they can look at a pattern and identify its important features almost at once. In a typical experiment (de Groot, 1966), people were shown pieces on a chessboard, as in Figure 9.10, for 5 seconds. Then they were asked to recall the position of all the pieces. When the pieces were arranged as they might occur in an actual game, expert players could recall the position of 91% of them, while novices could recall only 41%. When the pieces were arranged randomly, however, the expert players did no better than the nonexperts. Although expert chess players do not have a superior memory in general, they recognize familiar chessboard patterns far better than other people do.

Similarly, expert figure skaters can memorize a sequence of skating moves better than an average skater can. In one study, six members of the Canadian women's ice-skating team and four other, moderately skilled skaters were asked to memorize a sequence of eight skating elements and then either to describe them

a   b

FIGURE 9.10
Pieces arranged on a chessboard in a way that might actually occur in a game (a) and in a random manner (b). Master chess players can memorize the realistic pattern much better than average players can, but they are no better than average at memorizing the random pattern.

or to perform them. If the elements were arranged in a haphazard order, the two groups of skaters remembered about equally well. But when the elements were choreographed in a logical order, the expert skaters remembered much better (Deakin & Allard, 1991). In this and other situations, an expert excels at recognizing and memorizing meaningful patterns of information.

Expert Problem Solving

Some people manage to solve unfamiliar problems, while other people fail to do so. For example, try this difficult problem: Given a triangle, as shown in Figure 9.11, find the line parallel to the base that will divide the area of the triangle in half.

Alan Schoenfeld (1985) observed the steps people went through as they tried to solve this problem. One pair of college students who had just completed a calculus course began by guessing that the line should be drawn halfway between the base and the vertex of the triangle. After carefully drawing that line, they realized it was wrong. Then they drew a line from the vertex to the midpoint of the base, forgetting that the line had to be parallel to the base. One of them suggested that they go back to the problem and "underline the important parts." When the allotted 30 minutes expired, they were no closer to a solution than when they began.

By contrast, one professional mathematician noticed that any line drawn parallel to the base will create a small triangle *Xyz* similar to the large triangle *XYZ*, as shown in Figure 9.12. Because the angles of the two triangles are the same, the height-to-base ratio of the small triangle (*h/b*) must be the same as the height-to-base ratio of the large triangle (*H/B*). Because the problem specified that the area of the small triangle is half the area of the large triangle, he calculated that the ratio of *h* to *H* must be the ratio of 1 to the square root of 2 (Figure 9.12).

The two students knew how to do everything the professional mathematician did. Why, then, could they not solve the problem? The expert almost immediately picked out the relevant information, rejected some fruitless approaches, and plotted a direct route to the solution. The nonexperts wasted much time on wild-goose chases without realizing that they were doing something irrelevant. Evidently, expertise is a matter not just of having the right tools but also of knowing which tools to use and when.

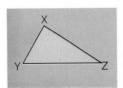

FIGURE 9.11
A question to test mathematical problem-solving skills: What line drawn parallel to the base of the triangle will divide the area in half?

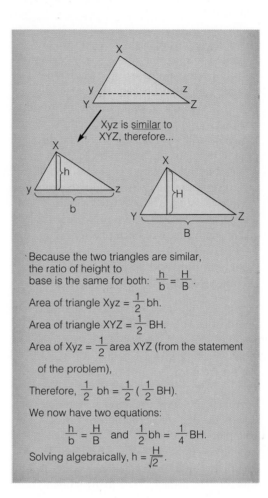

Because the two triangles are similar, the ratio of height to base is the same for both: $\frac{h}{b} = \frac{H}{B}$.

Area of triangle Xyz = $\frac{1}{2}$ bh.

Area of triangle XYZ = $\frac{1}{2}$ BH.

Area of Xyz = $\frac{1}{2}$ area XYZ (from the statement of the problem),

Therefore, $\frac{1}{2}$ bh = $\frac{1}{2}$ ($\frac{1}{2}$ BH).

We now have two equations:

$\frac{h}{b} = \frac{H}{B}$ and $\frac{1}{2}$ bh = $\frac{1}{4}$ BH.

Solving algebraically, h = $\frac{H}{\sqrt{2}}$.

FIGURE 9.12
An expert solution for how to divide the area of a triangle in half by a line drawn parallel to the base. The impossible may seem easy once you see the answer.

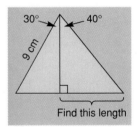

FIGURE 9.13
Experts and novices approach this geometric problem in different ways. People with less expertise in geometry generally start with the question to be answered and work backward. Those with greater expertise start with what was given and work forward until they answer the question. For the answer, see answer C, page 391. (Based on Sweller, 1989.)

Experts also tend to approach problems in a different way from novices. As a rule, novices start with the question to be answered and work backward, whereas experts usually start with the material given and work forward (Sweller, 1989; Sweller, Mawer, & Ward, 1983). For example, consider the problem in Figure 9.13. People with less knowledge of math generally start with the line they want to measure, find a formula for determining its length, and then work backward from there. People with a stronger grasp of math generally start with the information given and then start calculating the other angles and lengths until they arrive at the line they are supposed to determine.

FIGURE 9.14
The four steps in solving problems.

PROBLEM SOLVING

No one is born an expert; people learn their expertise. Can people also learn general skills of problem solving, which they could apply even in fields where they have only a moderate amount of knowledge and experience? To some extent, yes.

Generally we go through four phases when we set about solving a problem (Polya, 1957): (1) understanding the problem, (2) generating one or more hypotheses, (3) testing the hypotheses, and (4) checking the result (Figure 9.14). A scientist goes through those four phases in approaching a new, complex phenomenon, and you probably would go through them in trying to assemble a bicycle that came with garbled instructions. To at least a small extent, people can be trained to solve problems more successfully (Bransford & Stein, 1984). We shall go through the four phases of problem solving, with advice on each phase.

Understanding and Simplifying a Difficult Problem

You are facing a question or a problem, and you have no idea how to begin. You may even think the problem is unsolvable. Then someone shows you how to solve it and you realize, "I could have done that, if I had only thought of trying it that way."

When you do not see how to solve a problem, try starting with a simpler version of it. For example, here is what may appear to be a difficult, even an impossible, problem: A professor hands back students' test papers at random. On the average, how many students will accidentally receive their own paper? (Note that the problem fails to specify how many students are in the class.)

At first you may not see any way to approach the problem, but see what happens if we start with simpler cases: How many students will get their own paper back if there is only one student in the class? One, of course. What if there are two students? There is a 50% chance that both will get their own paper back and a 50% chance that neither will. On the average, one student will get the correct paper. What if there are three students? Each student has one chance in three of getting his or her own paper. One-third chance times three students means that, on the average, one student will get the correct paper. Having worked through a few simple examples, we suddenly see the pattern: The number of students in the class does not matter; on the av-

erage, one student will get his or her own paper back.

Often you can also find ways to simplify a factual question and to generate a decent estimate of the correct answer (von Baeyer, 1988). For example, what is the circumference of the Earth? Even if you do not know the answer, you might know the distance from New York to Los Angeles—about 3,000 miles (4,800 km). The distance from New York to Los Angeles is also a change of three time zones. How many times zones would a traveler cross in going completely around the Earth? Twenty-four (one for each hour in the day). So the distance from New York is 3/24 (or one eighth) of the distance around the Earth. Eight times the distance from New York to Los Angeles is 8 × 3,000 miles (4,800 km) = 24,000 miles (38,400 km). That is a decent approximation of the circumference of the Earth, 24,902.4 miles (40,068 km).

Generating Hypotheses

Suppose that after simplifying a problem as well as possible, you realize that many answers are possible. At that point you need to generate hypotheses—preliminary interpretations that you can evaluate or test.

In some cases, you can generate more hypotheses than you can test. Consider the traveling-salesperson problem in Figure 9.15. Starting and finishing at Ames, how could you travel through each of the marked cities while keeping your total travel distance to a minimum? You could set up an algorithm to solve the problem. An **algorithm** is a mechanical, repetitive mathematical procedure for solving a problem such as "Calculate the distance from Ames to a first city, then to a second city, and so on through all cities and back to Ames again. Repeat the same procedure for all possible orders of the cities. Compare the distances of all the possible routes."

That algorithm tests all the possible hypotheses (routes) and is sure to lead to the best answer . . . eventually. But even with just 10 cities to visit, there are nearly 2 million possible routes (10 factorial divided by 2). As the number of cities increases, the task becomes unmanageable even for computers. To make the problem manageable, we must narrow the number of hypotheses. We do so by resorting to **heuristics,** strategies for simplifying a problem or for guiding an investigation. A heuristic is a rule for checking the most likely possibilities. For instance, we might decide to test only those routes in which each move takes us to one of the four closest cities, rejecting all routes in which the salesperson has to go from one end of the state to the other. Or we might limit the search to routes in which the salesperson finishes one part of the state before starting a new one.

Heuristics are important for many kinds of problem solving. Suppose you and a friend you haven't seen for years find you are both visiting the same state at the same time and decide to meet halfway between where you are and where your friend is. But that is a city where neither of you has ever been before, so neither of you can suggest a landmark where you can meet. You might think of some heuristic to simplify the problem. For example, "Go to the city limits on the western side and look for the nearest fast-food place." Once you arrived, you might have to look for your friend in several nearby fast-food places, but at least you would have narrowed the search. (Perhaps you could think of a better heuristic for solving this problem.)

■ CONCEPT CHECK

4. The government wants to know how much the average citizen pays for groceries each week. So it finds a city with only one grocery store, asks the store manager how much money he or she receives for sales in a given week, and divides that amount by the number of people who live in the city. Is that approach to the problem an example of an algorithm or an example of heuristics? (Check your answer on page 391.)

Testing Hypotheses and Checking the Results

If you think you have solved a problem, test your idea to see whether it will work. Many people who think they have a great idea never bother to try it out, even on a small scale. One inventor applied for a patent on the "perpetual motion machine" shown in Figure 9.16. Rubber balls, being lighter than water, rise in a column of water and overflow the top. Being heavier than air, they fall, moving a belt and thereby generating energy. At the bottom, they reenter the water column. Do you see why this system could never work? You would if you tried to build it. (Check your answer on page 391, answer D.)

The final step in solving a problem is to check the results. You think you have the solution; you think your hypothesis works. Fine, but to make sure, check it again. In scientific research, checking may mean repeating an experiment to see whether the results are replicable.

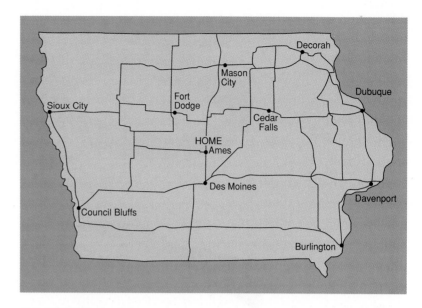

FIGURE 9.15
In the "traveling salesman problem," the task is to find the shortest route from home through all the other destinations. If the number of destinations is large, the number of possible routes can be extremely large. Therefore, we look for some heuristic to simplify the problem.

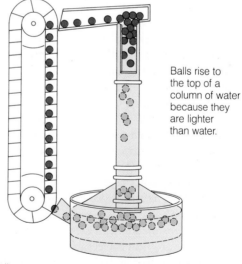

Balls overflow onto conveyor belt and pull it down because they are heavier than air.

Balls rise to the top of a column of water because they are lighter than water.

Balls reenter column of water.

FIGURE 9.16
What is wrong with this perpetual motion machine?

In mathematics, checking may be a matter of repeating the calculations or at least of thinking about whether the answer you calculated is plausible. For example, if you have calculated that the answer to some question is "40 square IQ points per cubic second," you might realize that the answer is inherently meaningless and that something must have gone wrong.

Problem Solving, Expertise, and Error   377

FIGURE 9.17
(a) Draw the trajectory of water as it flows out of a coiled garden hose. (b) Draw the trajectory of a bullet as it leaves a coiled gun barrel.

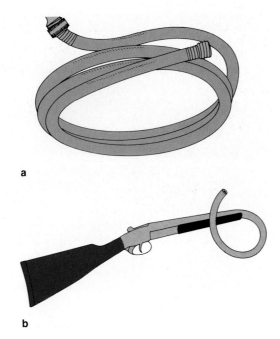

a

b

Generalizing Solutions to Similar Problems

After laboriously solving one problem, can people then solve a related problem more easily? Can they at least recognize that the new problem is related to the old problem, so they know where to start?

Sometimes yes, but all too frequently no. Many people who understand the laws of probability fail to see how those laws might apply to real-life situations (Nisbett, Fong, Lehman, & Cheng, 1987). For example, most people who flipped a coin 10 times and got 10 consecutive heads would not expect more than 5 heads out of the next 10 flips. But the same people might expect a basketball team that won 10 consecutive games to win the next 10 games as well. The basketball situation is not exactly the same as coin flipping, but it does have some similarity: A long winning streak depends partly on skill but partly on chance also.

In other situations as well, people who have solved one problem correctly fail to solve a second problem that is basically similar, unless someone gives them a hint explaining that the problems are similar (Gick & Holyoak, 1980). For example, Figure 9.17a shows a coiled garden hose. When the water spurts out, what path will it take? (Draw it.) Figure 9.17b shows a curved gun barrel. When the bullet comes out, what path will it take? (Draw it.)

Almost everyone draws the water coming out of the garden hose in a straight path. Even after doing so, however, many people draw a bullet coming out of a gun in a curved path, as if the bullet remembered the curved path it had just taken (Kaiser, Jonides, & Alexander, 1986). The physics is the same in both situations: Both the water and the bullet will follow a straight path (except for the effects of gravity).

Sometimes we recognize similar problems and use our solution to an old problem as a guide to solving a new one (Figure 9.18); sometimes we do not. What accounts for the difference? One reason is that it is easier to generalize a solution after we have seen several examples of it; if we have seen only a single example, we may think of the solution in only that one context (Gick & Holyoak, 1983). For example, one group of high-school students had learned to solve arithmetic-progression problems in algebra, practicing on a variety of problems. When they were given a fundamentally similar problem in physics, they recognized the similarity and solved it (Figure 9.19). A different group of students had been taught to solve the physics problem; when they were given the related problem in algebra, most of them failed to recognize the similarity (Bassok & Holyoak, 1989). Apparently the physics students associated the solution entirely with physics, and they failed to see it as a general principle that could be applied more widely.

Although people often fail to transfer a solution from one problem to an analogous problem, most people transfer general approaches to problems. For example, people might learn to represent certain kinds of problems graphically or to break up a problem into subproblems. Once they have learned these skills, they readily apply them to other problems (Novick, 1990).

SPECIAL FEATURES OF INSIGHT PROBLEMS

Some of the problems we have been discussing are "insight" problems or "Aha!" problems—the kind in which you think of the correct answer suddenly, if you think of it at all. Here is a clear example of an insight problem (Gardner, 1978): Figure 9.20 shows an object that was made by just cutting and bending an ordinary piece of cardboard. How was it made? If you think you know, take a piece of paper and try to make it yourself.

People react to this problem in different ways. Some see the solution almost at once; oth-

FIGURE 9.18
The computer mouse was invented by a computer scientist who was familiar with an engineering device called a planimeter and decided that it could be modified for use with computers. Such insights are unusual; most people do not generalize a solution from one task to another.

ers take a long time before insight suddenly strikes them; still others never figure it out. Some people have looked at this illustration and told me that it was impossible, that I must have pasted two pieces together or bought a custom-made piece of "trick" cardboard. (The correct answer is on page 391, answer E.)

Insightful Problem Solving: Sudden or Gradual?

Solving insight problems differs from solving, say, algebra problems. Most people can look at an algebra problem and rather accurately predict whether or not they will be able to solve it, and if so how quickly. As they work on it, they can estimate how close they are to reaching a solution. On insight problems, however, they give poor estimates of whether they are about to solve the problem or not (Metcalfe & Wiebe, 1987). Frequently someone will say, "I have no idea whether I will ever solve this problem," and then suddenly announce the correct answer a minute or so later.

So it appears that the answer comes suddenly, all or none. But does it really? If you were groping your way around in a dark room, you would have no idea how soon you were going to find the door, but that does not mean that you had made no progress. You would have learned much about the room, including many places where the door was *not*.

So maybe people are making progress without realizing it when they struggle with insight problems. To test this possibility, psychologists gave students problems of the following form:

The three words below are all associated with one other word. What is that word?

color   numbers   oil

In this case, the correct answer is *paint*. Like other insight questions, subjects reported that they got the answer suddenly or not at all and that they could not tell whether they were about to think of the answer or not. Then the experimenters gave the subjects paired sets of three words each, like those shown here in Sets 1 and 2, to examine for 12 seconds. In each pair, one set had a correct answer (like *paint* in the example just given). For the other set, no one word was associated with all three items. Subjects were to try to generate a correct answer if they could; if not, they were to guess *which* set had a correct answer and say how confident they were of their guess. Examples:

a An arithmetic-progression problem in algebra:

Q: A boy was given an allowance of 50 cents a week beginning on his sixth birthday. On each birthday following this, the weekly allowance was increased 25 cents. What is the weekly allowance beginning on his 15th birthday?

Solution: Let a_n = allowance beginning on nth birthday.
d = difference added on each birthday

a_{15} = a_6 + (9)d

↖ Number of birthdays from age 6 to 15

= \$.50 + (9) × .25 = \$2.75

---

b A constant-acceleration problem in physics:

Q: An express train, traveling at 30 meters per second at the start of the third second of its travel, uniformly accelerates increasing in speed 5 meters per second each succeeding second. What is its final speed at the end of the 9th second?

Solution: Let s_n = speed at beginning of nth second
d = difference added each second

s_{10} = s_3 + (7)d

↗ Speed at beginning of 10th second (end of 9th)   ↖ Number of seconds from the start of 3rd second to end of the 9th

= 30 + (7) × 5 = 65 mph

FIGURE 9.19

An arithmetic-progression problem in algebra (a) is similar to a constant-acceleration problem in physics (b). Students who had learned to solve the algebra problem recognized the physics problem as similar and solved it successfully. Most students who had learned to solve the physics problem, however, failed to recognize the algebra problem as similar and failed to solve it. (From Bassok and Holyoak, 1989.)

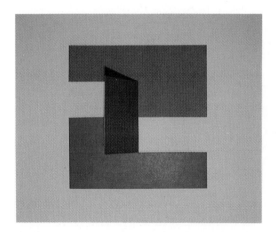

FIGURE 9.20

An object made by cutting and folding an ordinary piece of cardboard with nothing left over. How was it done?

Set 1		Set 2	
playing	still	town	ticket
credit	pages	root	shop
report	music	car	broker

(You can check your answers on page 391, answer F.)

The main result was that when subjects could not find the correct answer, they still guessed with greater than 50% accuracy which was the set that had a correct answer (Bowers, Regehr, Balthazard, & Parker, 1990). Even on pairs for which subjects said they had "no confidence" at all in their guesses, they were still right more often than not. In short, insight solutions are not altogether sudden; people may be "getting warm" even without realizing it.

Creative Problem Solving

Solving a problem or developing a new product is always to some extent a creative activity, but we identify certain solutions and products as especially creative. Psychologists frequently define **creativity** as the development of novel, socially valued products (Mumford & Gustafson, 1988). In principle that is a reasonable definition, but in practice it can be hard to apply. Many unusual works of art and literature were very lightly regarded in their own time and later hailed as classics. By the usual definition of *creative,* these works became creative many decades after they were produced!

What does it take to be creative? As a rule, each person is much more creative in some situations than in others (Barron & Harrington, 1981). That is, someone who thinks of creative solutions to mathematical or engineering problems may show little creativity as a poet or a painter.

An example of creative problem solving: United Nations field worker Peter Dalglish, wanting to help homeless orphans in Khartoum, Sudan, decided to put their knowledge of the streets to good use as bicycle couriers in a city where telephones are unreliable. On another occasion, Dalglish caught a boy breaking into his car. Instead of calling the police, he thought, "This kid would make a great mechanic" and set up a technical school for homeless children.

Still, many investigators treat creativity as a kind of talent that varies among people. If so, it should be measurable. The Torrance Tests of Creative Thinking use items similar to the one shown in Figure 9.21 to measure creativity. Children who score high are more likely than others to make creative achievements as adults, including inventions, publications, artistic and musical compositions, and clothing designs (Torrance, 1980, 1981, 1982).

Based on the assumption that creativity is a talent that each of us might or might not have, many psychologists (and others) have assumed that only people with extraordinary creative talent are responsible for great advances in science or in the arts. According to this view, only one person in a million, perhaps one in a billion, could figure out a great theory, write a great play, or pioneer a new field of painting or music. But is that true? Or could someone of fairly normal abilities make the same contributions, if given the right opportunity?

That question is difficult to answer in the arts, but not too difficult in math and science. Suppose we offer some bright but reasonably normal person—a college student, for example—all the information that was available to some scientist who devised some great and famous theory. Could a "normal" person develop the same theory?

To find out, experimenters asked 14 university students to try to find a mathematical formula to describe a certain set of information. Four managed to produce the great theory and one more came close. Before I explain in more detail, you might want to try your hand at these data yourself. Below is a table of five pairs of

FIGURE 9.21
A "what-is-it?" picture similar to those in one part of the Torrance Tests of Creative Thinking.

numbers, arbitrarily labeled s and q. The numbers s and q are measurements of two physical variables, but I won't tell you what the variables are, because you might be familiar with the theory in question. Examine each of the pairs of variables and see whether you can find a single mathematical equation relating s to q.

The students in the experiment were allowed up to 1 hour; you can take as long as you wish. You may use a calculator. Recommendation: Either copy these data onto another sheet of paper or cover the text below the data so that you do not accidentally read the correct formula.

s	q
36	88
67.25	224.7
93	365.3
141	687
483.8	4332.1

The data represent measurements on the first five planets of our solar system. Column s gives the distance from the sun in millions of miles; column q gives the time (in Earth days) required for rotation around the sun. The German astronomer Johannes Kepler (1571–1630) is regarded as a great genius and the founder of modern astronomy for discerning the relationship between these two sets of data. He worked on this problem for weeks before figuring it out; four university students figured it out within an hour (Qin & Simon, 1990). To be fair to Kepler, I should point out that the university students used calculators and that they knew the problem was solvable, whereas Kepler had only a pencil and paper and had to guess that the problem was solvable.

The correct formula can be expressed in any of the following ways:

$$s^3/q^2 = 6.025$$
$$s^3/6.025 = q^2$$
$$q^{2/3} = 0.55s$$
$$s^{1.5} = 2.45q$$

That is, the cube of the distance from the sun is related to the square of the period of rotation. What can we conclude from the fact that bright (but not one in a billion) college students with calculators can quickly reconstruct the theory that made Kepler famous? We don't want to take credit away from Kepler. After all, he posed the question and assembled the data, as well as figuring out the answer to the question.

However, it does appear that many people, not just the talented few, are capable of creative insights in math and science.

Something to Think About

Are people of normal talents also capable of great creative achievements in art and literature? How could we test that ability?

DECISION MAKING

Although we humans pride ourselves on our intelligence and on our ability to solve problems, we sometimes err on fairly simple problems. After someone points out the correct answer, we are surprised at our own mistake. Sometimes we err because we relied on inappropriate heuristics. Recall that heuristics are methods for simplifying a problem and facilitating an investigation. Ordinarily, relying on heuristics enables us to find a reasonable, if not perfect, answer. Occasionally, however, certain heuristics can lead us astray. Let's now consider several reasons why people sometimes arrive at illogical conclusions.

Premature Commitment to a Hypothesis

Sometimes we make mistakes because we commit ourselves prematurely to a particular hypothesis and fail to consider other possibilities. Suppose a psychologist asks subjects to look at a photo way out of focus, as in Figure 9.22a, and asks them what they think the photo shows. Then the psychologist shows them a series of

a

FIGURE 9.22
People who form a hypothesis based on the first photo look at succeeding photos trying to find evidence that they are right. Because their first guess is generally wrong, they do less well than do people who look at the later photos before making any preliminary guesses. Try to guess what this shows. Then examine parts b and c on the following pages.

photos, each one in slightly sharper focus, until they correctly identify what is shown in the photos. Some people try to simplify the task by forming a hypothesis such as, "Maybe it's a picture of a roulette wheel." That is a heuristic of sorts; it guides further exploration of the photos. However, if the initial hypothesis is wrong, it can mislead. Subjects who first see an extremely blurry photo are generally *less* accurate at identifying a slightly blurry photo than are subjects who looked first at the slightly blurry photo (Bruner & Potter, 1964). Those who see the extremely blurry photo are impaired even if they check their initial hypothesis and find out that it is wrong (Snodgrass & Hirshman, 1991). Somehow, their initial interpretation continues to interfere with any new interpretation.

Peter Wason (1960) asked students to discover a certain rule he had in mind for generating sequences of numbers. One example of the numbers the rule might generate, he explained, was "2, 4, 6." He told the students that they could ask about other sequences, and he would tell them whether or not those sequences fit the rule. As soon as they thought they had enough evidence, they could guess what the rule was.

Most students started by asking, "8, 10, 12?" When told "yes," they proceeded with, "14, 16, 18?" Each time, they were told, "yes, that sequence fits the rule." Soon most of them guessed, "The rule is three consecutive even numbers."

"No," came the reply. "That is not the rule."

Many students persisted, trying "20, 22, 24?" "26, 28, 30?" "250, 252, 254?" And so forth. Eventually they would say, "Three even numbers in which the second is two more than the first and the third is two more than the second." Again, they were told that the guess was wrong. "But how can it be wrong?" they complained. "It always works!"

The rule Wason had in mind was, "Any three positive numbers of increasing magnitude." For instance, 1, 2, 3, would be acceptable; so would 4, 19, 22, or 3, 76, 9 million. Where many students went wrong was in testing only the cases that their hypothesis said would fit the rule. One must also examine the cases that the hypothesis says will not fit the rule (Klayman & Ha, 1987).

A follow-up study used the same procedure but added one complication: Investigators told the students that when they asked about a sequence, the answers they received might be wrong on 0 to 20% of all occasions. Under these conditions, students were even less likely than usual to discover the rule. Whenever they got a result that did not match their hypothesis, they "explained it away" by assuming this was one of those occasions on which they received an incorrect answer (Gorman, 1989).

Scientists sometimes do the same thing, pursuing a single hypothesis, disregarding alternative hypotheses, and assuming that contradictory data are probably wrong (Frishhoff & Beyth-Marom, 1983). To a certain extent, this is a reasonable and defensible strategy. After all, the results of a few studies here and there may be inaccurate, and we should not be quick to discard a hypothesis that fits a large percentage of the data. The hard decision is to determine when to continue defending a hypothesis that usually works and when to look for a substitute.

The Representativeness Heuristic and Base-Rate Information

Some years ago I heard a clever saying: "If something looks like a duck, waddles like a duck, and quacks like a duck, chances are it's a duck." This saying is an example of the **representativeness heuristic,** the tendency to assume that if an item is similar to members of a particular category, it is probably a member of that category itself. It is generally a reasonable assumption that serves us well.

It can lead us astray, however, if we are dealing with something unusual. For example, suppose you see a bird that looks like an Eskimo curlew, walks like an Eskimo curlew, and whistles like an Eskimo curlew. Does that mean you have found an Eskimo curlew? Not likely. Eskimo curlews are extremely rare, almost extinct; chances are, you have sighted some more common shore bird that resembles an Eskimo curlew.

Similarly, suppose your answers on a personality test resemble the answers typically given by people with schizophrenia. Does that mean you have schizophrenia yourself? Maybe, but probably not. Normal people who give a few schizophrenic answers are more common than schizophrenic people themselves are.

When we have to decide whether something belongs in category A or category B, for example Eskimo curlew versus other shore bird, or schizophrenic person versus non-schizophrenic person, we should consider three questions: (1) How closely does it resemble the items in category A? (2) How closely does it resemble the items in category B? (3) Which is more common, category A or category B? The answer to the third question is known as **base-rate information**—that is, data about the frequency or probability of a given item, how rare or how common it is.

People frequently overlook the base-rate information and follow only the representativeness heuristic. As a result, they identify something as a member of some uncommon category, disregarding the more likely category. For example, consider the following question (modified from Kahneman & Tversky, 1973):

Psychologists have interviewed 30 engineers and 70 lawyers. One of them is Jack, a 45-year-old married man with four children. He is generally conservative, careful, and ambitious. He shows no interest in political and social issues and spends most of his free time on home carpentry, sailing, and mathematical puzzles. What is the probability that Jack is one of the 30 engineers in the sample of 100?

Most people think that the description is more representative of engineers than it is of lawyers. Based on representativeness, they estimate that Jack is probably an engineer. But what about the fact that the sample includes more than twice as many lawyers as engineers? That base-rate information should influence their estimates. In fact, however, most people pay little attention to the base-rate information. They make about the same estimates of how likely Jack is to be an engineer, regardless of whether the sample includes 30% engineers or 70% engineers (Kahneman & Tversky, 1973). However, people do use the base-rate information if they have paid attention to it. If people actually count out cards saying "engineer" or "lawyer," they use that information in estimating how likely it is that Jack is an engineer (Gigerenzer, Hell, & Blank, 1988).

Here is another example of overreliance on the representativeness heuristic. Read the following description, and then answer the questions following it:

Linda was a philosophy major. She is 31, bright, outspoken, and concerned with issues of discrimination and social justice.

Now, what would you estimate is the probability that Linda is a bank teller? What is the probability that she is a *feminist* bank teller? (Answer before you read on.)

It is hard to know what the true probabilities are, but that is not the point. The interesting result is that most people estimate a higher

In 1988, a U.S. Navy ship in the Persian Gulf shot down an Iranian civilian airplane after mistaking it for an attacking fighter plane. To discriminate between a civilian plane and a fighter plane, or between any two items, we should consider not only the appearance of the object but also the base-rate information—how common the two kinds of objects are.

probability that Linda is a feminist bank teller than the probability that she is a bank teller (Tversky & Kahneman, 1983). That is self-contradictory, as she clearly could not be a feminist bank teller without being a bank teller. The reason is that people regard the description as fairly typical for a feminist, and therefore also for a feminist bank teller (or feminist anything else). But it is not especially typical for bank

FIGURE 9.22
(continued)

b

Table 9.1 The Representativeness Heuristic and the Availability Heuristic

	Is a tendency to assume that . . .	Leads us astray when . . .	Example
Representativeness heuristic	any item that resembles members of some category is probably itself a member of that category.	an item resembles members of a rare category.	You see something that looks the way you think a UFO would look, so you decide it is a UFO.
Availability heuristic	how easily we can think of examples of some category indicates how many examples really occur.	one kind of example is easier to think of than another is.	You remember more newspaper reports of airline crashes than of car crashes, so you assume that air crashes are more common than car crashes.

tellers in general (Shafir, Smith, & Osherson, 1990). Because of the representativeness heuristic, most people overestimate the probability that Linda is a feminist bank teller.

■ CONCEPT CHECK

5. *Suppose an improved lie-detector test can determine with 90% accuracy whether people are telling the truth. An employer proposes to administer the test to all employees, asking them whether they have ever stolen from the company and firing everyone who fails the test. Is that policy reasonable? Assume that the company has 1,000 employees, of whom only 20 have ever stolen anything. Hint: Think about the base-rate*

probability of finding a dishonest employee. (Check your answer on page 391.)

The Availability Heuristic

When asked how common something is, or how often something happens, we generally start by trying to think of examples. Try this question: In the English language, are there more words that start with k or more words that have k as the third letter? If you are like most people, you guessed that there are more words that start with k. How did you decide that? You tried to think of words that start with k: "king, kitchen, kangaroo, key, knowledge, . . ." Then you tried to think of words that have k as the third letter: "ask, ink, bake, . . . uh . . ." You were relying on the **availability heuristic,** the strategy of assuming that how many memories of an event are available indicates how common the event actually is (Table 9.1). Because it was easier to think of words that start with k than words with k as the third letter, you assumed that there really are more words that start with k. In fact, however, words with k as the third letter are considerably more common.

The availability heuristic leads to illusory correlations, as we saw in Chapter 2. Someone asks, "Do people act strange on nights of a full moon?" If you have always expected people to act strange on such nights, you may be able to remember more examples when they did act strange than examples when they did not.

Here is another example of the availability heuristic: Professor Gomez says, "Today's students seem less impressive than the ones I remember from 20 years ago. The educational system must be going downhill." The professor probably remembers mainly her best students

Table 9.2 Your Odds of Dying

How much do you think each of the following activities increases your chance of dying? Rank them from most dangerous (7) to least dangerous (1). Compare your ranking with answer G on page 391.

_____ Traveling 50 miles in a motor vehicle (cause of death: accident)

_____ Traveling 400 miles in a school bus (cause: accident)

_____ Flying 4 minutes, general aviation (cause: accident)

_____ Flying 4 hours, scheduled airline (cause: accident)

_____ Getting a chest X ray in a good hospital (cause: cancer from radiation)

_____ Working for 3 hours as a miner (cause: accident)

_____ Drinking 2 glasses of wine (cause: alcohol-related cirrhosis and automobile accident)

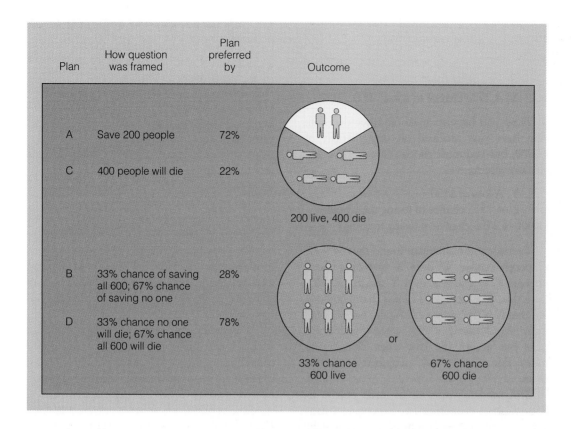

Plan	How question was framed	Plan preferred by	Outcome
A	Save 200 people	72%	
C	400 people will die	22%	

200 live, 400 die

Plan	How question was framed	Plan preferred by	Outcome
B	33% chance of saving all 600; 67% chance of saving no one	28%	
D	33% chance no one will die; 67% chance all 600 will die	78%	

33% chance 600 live   or   67% chance 600 die

FIGURE 9.23
When Amos Tversky and Daniel Kahneman (1981) offered these choices to more than 150 people, 72% chose A over B and 78% chose D over C. However, plan A is exactly the same as plan C (200 live, 400 die), and plan B is exactly the same as plan D. Why then did so many people choose both A and D? The reason, according to Tversky and Kahneman, is that most people avoid taking a risk when a question is phrased in terms of gain, but they are willing to take a risk when a question is phrased in terms of loss.

from 20 years ago; she incorrectly assumes that most students 20 years ago were like the outstanding ones she remembers.

You can guard against overuse of the availability heuristic. When you try to estimate whether one type of event is more common than another, look for systematic data. Don't just trust your memory of how often various events occur. See Table 9.2.

The Framing of Questions

If we were truly logical beings, we would give the same answer to a question no matter how it was reworded. In fact, we do not. Most people give one answer to a question that is phrased in terms of gain and give a different answer to the same question when it is phrased in terms of loss.

For example: You have recently been appointed head of the Public Health Service. A new contagious disease has been detected, and you have to choose between two plans for combating it. If you do nothing, 600 people will die. If you adopt plan A, you will save the lives of 200 people. If you adopt plan B, there is a 33% chance that you will save all 600 and 67% chance that you will save no one. (Choose one of the plans before reading further.)

Now another contagious disease breaks out; you must again choose between two plans. If you adopt plan C, 400 people will die. If you adopt plan D, there is a 33% chance that no one will die and a 67% chance that 600 will die. (Choose one now, then compare your choices with the results in Figure 9.23.)

FIGURE 9.22
(continued)

c

Consider another example, this one dealing with money instead of lives. Which would you rather have?

> W. A gain of $240
>
> or   X. A 25% chance to win $1,000

Now you have to make another decision. You have just received an outright gift of $1,000, but you must choose between two unpleasant alternatives:

> Y. A loss of $750
>
> or   Z. A 75% chance of losing the whole $1,000 (a 25% chance of losing nothing)

Tversky and Kahneman found that 84% of all people chose W over X (avoiding risk), whereas 87% chose Z over Y (taking a risk). Note that W is actually $10 less than choice Y and that X is the same as Z. Again, people generally avoid taking a risk when considering gains but accept the risk when considering losses. Put another way, people try to avoid losses.

This tendency sometimes leads people to decisions that economists would consider irrational. For example, 2 months ago you bought an expensive ticket to a football game. Today, the day of the game, the weather is cold and rainy. The team you were cheering for is having a dismal season, and several key players are out with injuries. You do not look forward to attending. In fact, if you did not have tickets and someone offered you a free one, you would refuse. And yet, you may decide to go to the game anyway, because you already paid for the tickets and you "don't want to take a loss." (In fact, you lose twice—first by buying the tickets and second by attending an uninteresting game in the rain.) People can, however, learn to make rational decisions in situations like this (Larrick, Morgan, & Nisbett, 1990).

■ CONCEPT CHECK

6a. Someone says, "More than 90% of all college students like to watch late-late night television, whereas only 20% of older adults do. Therefore, more watchers of late-late night television are college students." What error in thinking has this person made?

b. Someone tells me that if I say "abracadabra" every morning I will stay healthy. I say it daily, and, sure enough, I stay healthy. I conclude that saying this magic word really does ensure health. What error of thinking have I made?
(Check your answers on page 391.)

LEARNING, MEMORY, COGNITION, AND THE PSYCHOLOGY OF GAMBLING

Gambling sometimes becomes a serious problem, analogous to drug addiction. Here is one case: Joan (not her real name) began buying tickets in the state lottery, at first buying only a few tickets at a time and occasionally winning up to $500 or $2,000. Gradually she started buying more and more tickets, eventually spending an average of more than $2,000 on lottery tickets per day. She worked as an accountant for a large company, where she found a way to make false claims. Over 2 years she embezzled half a million dollars, but all she had to show for it were several bags of losing lottery tickets (Lorenz, 1990).

Why would an intelligent person engage in such self-defeating behavior? Let us try to address this question using some of the principles of learning, memory, and thinking that we have encountered in the last three chapters.

Risk taking is an unavoidable part of life. Even if you would never think of entering a gambling casino, you often have to decide about other risks you might take. Investing in the stock market is a gamble; so is putting your money in a bank instead of the stock market. An intelligent person cannot avoid taking risks but tries to take "good" risks instead of "bad" risks. Suppose you are considering two job offers. You could have a desk job with a moderate starting salary and high job security, but little chance of advancement. Or you could take a job in the entertainment industry with a much lower starting salary and almost no job security, but a 5% chance of becoming rich and famous. Whichever you choose, you are gambling that your choice will be the better one.

How would an intelligent person choose? According to one point of view, people evaluate the merit of a choice in terms of its **expected value,** which is the mean of all the possible values of that choice, weighted according to their probabilities. For example, you might estimate the value of the desk job at $33,000 (its annual salary). The value of the entertainment job is a weighted mean of several possible outcomes. We do not know the actual probabilities, but we might make a guess such as the following:

$20\% \times \$\ 20,000 = \$\ 4,000$ (moderate chance of low salary)

$$+ \;75\% \;\times\; \$ \quad\quad 0 \;= \quad\quad 0 \quad\text{(high chance of earning nothing)}$$

$$+ \;\;5\% \;\times\; \$500{,}000 \;=\; \underline{\$25{,}000} \quad\text{(small chance of huge income)}$$

TOTAL $29,000

According to the figures above, the expected value of the desk job is a little higher than that of the entertainment job. Of course, you may add other considerations, such as the interest level of the two jobs and the fact that if you fail at the entertainment job you could undoubtedly get some other job, so you would not really end up with a salary of zero.

For this choice of jobs, the riskier decision (to try the entertainment job) is defensible. In other cases, the expected value of the riskier decision is so low that we wonder why anyone would choose it. For example, consider the expected value of spending $1 on a state lottery ticket. The exact figures vary from one lottery to another, but Table 9.3 gives figures for one typical lottery. Some lotteries offer larger prizes, but they also have smaller chances of winning.

Unlike the job example, in which you had to guess your chances of succeeding or failing and the monetary consequences in each case, the odds of winning a state lottery are public knowledge. In the example above, it is clear that the expected value of a lottery ticket is far less than its $1 cost. And yet people who know the odds persist in buying lottery tickets. Why? Psychologists have suggested several possibilities, some of them based on principles of learning, memory, and cognition.

Gambling is an inevitable part of life; even people who would never enter a casino or bet on a horse race take many gambles with their time and energies. For example, hundreds of people may try out for a part in a play or a movie, even though they realize that they have only a slim chance of winning the part. To have any chance of success in life, one must take intelligent gambles and not foolish ones.

Overestimation of Control

Rationally, you should not spend $1 on a 1-in-21-thousand chance at winning $5,000 in a lottery. But what if you thought that *your* chances (unlike everyone else's) were significantly better than that? Perhaps you believe that you have some special skill or luck that will enable you to pick winning numbers. If so, then gambling might make sense for you. Most gamblers do believe that some people can win consistently at

---

Table 9.3 Expected Winnings on a $1 Decco Ticket (a California Lottery Game)

	Probability	×	Payoff	=	Expected Value
	.9573084	×	$0	=	$0.000
	.040404	×	$5	=	$0.202
	.0022409	×	$50	=	$0.112
	.0000467	×	$5,000	=	$0.233
Total	1.0				$0.547

Note: Someone who purchases a $1 ticket has more than a 95% chance of winning nothing, slightly more than a 4% chance of winning $5, and so forth. Overall, the person should expect to receive about 55 cents back for the $1. No one actually receives this 55 cents for a single ticket, but that should be the average payoff after someone has bought many Decco tickets.

FIGURE 9.24
Most chronic gamblers believe that some people can win consistently at games of chance. Even with slot machines, many people believe their skill in pulling the handle can influence their results.

games of chance. Even most people who play the slot machines (Figure 9.24) believe that their skill in pulling the arm can influence their winnings (Griffiths, 1990).

In fact, this is part of a more general principle: Most people are overconfident about the accuracy of their own judgments. For example, we ask people questions of the form "What is *absinthe*—a precious stone, a liqueur, or a Caribbean island?" After each question we ask people to estimate their probability of being correct. Most people overestimate (Lichtenstein, Fischhoff, & Phillips, 1982). That is, on questions where they estimate 60% accuracy, they are correct less than 60% of the time; when they estimate 70% accuracy, they are correct less than 70% of the time. So, when confronted with a roulette wheel or some other game of chance, it is not surprising that people overestimate their chances of winning.

People are particularly prone to overestimate their chance of success if they perceive the game as one of skill and not pure luck. And when they *do* something—even pulling a lever or choosing a number—they tend to believe that what they are doing has some control over the outcome. If they regard themselves as skillful people, as most of us do, they expect to win more than they lose (Burger, 1986).

Here is a quote from one habitual lottery gambler who makes clear his beliefs about the possibility of skillfully picking winning numbers: "Working the lottery is a lot of work and you need the time between games to work on your systems and number combinations. You need to get books with systems, and work out possible repeat combinations and go over your charts to check the highs and lows [numbers with many hits and numbers with few hits], and

the number of times since a number hit last, if a number is hot, and combinations of pairs that are hot, etc., etc." (in Lorenz, 1990, p. 385). (This man's gambling eventually led him to criminal offenses that landed him in prison.)

In one study, people were given a chance to buy $1 lottery tickets for a $50 prize (Langer, 1975). Some of them were simply handed a ticket, while others were permitted to choose their own ticket. Those who chose their own ticket thought they had a better chance of winning. Days later, all the ticket-holders were asked whether they were willing to sell their ticket to someone else. Those who had been handed a ticket were generally willing to sell, asking for a price only slightly higher than what they had paid for their ticket. Those who had chosen their own ticket asked a mean of more than $8 per ticket, and some refused to sell for less than the full $50 they expected to win!

The Enhanced Value of a Big Win

Most people would prefer a certain gain of $1 to a 50% chance of gaining $2, even though the expected value is the same in both cases. They would also prefer a certain $1 to a 1% chance of $100. But something strange happens at very large values: Many people would exchange their certain $1 for 1 chance in a million of winning a million dollars . . . or even 1 chance in 2 million of winning a million dollars. Evidently they reason, "Here's a chance to become rich, perhaps my only chance. Even an extremely slim chance is worth a dollar." For this reason, most people are more likely to enter a lottery with one enormous prize than one with lots of small prizes, even though their chance of winning the enormous prize is extremely small (Brenner, 1990; Wagenaar, 1988).

Schedules of Reinforcement

Most gamblers make a long series of bets, not just one bet. They win some; they lose some. They get reinforced on a variable-ratio schedule; that is, the more bets they place, the more times they win, but the order of wins and losses is random. As we discussed in Chapter 7, such a schedule induces a steady rate of responding, even during a long period without reinforcement.

Still, some people who have never won a lottery persist in buying tickets, whereas other people quit buying tickets immediately after winning a million-dollar jackpot (Kaplan, 1988). That is, a win does not always reinforce gambling and a loss may not particularly weaken it. Howard Rachlin (1990) suggests that a gambler evaluates his or her success at the end of a string of bets that ends in a win. For example, suppose you lose bets on six horse races and then bet on a winner. If your bet on the winner pays more than the amount you lost on the first six bets, then you don't count your progress as "six losses, one win," but as "a net gain on the day, one overall win." (Horse-race gamblers who have lost money on the first few races of the day generally make large bets on the final race. Do you see why?)

Similarly, if you bet on a single number at roulette (at a payoff of 35 to 1), you would count yourself as a winner if you picked a winning number before losing $35. The situation is a little like a pigeon pecking at a disk, receiving rare but very large reinforcements.

Now, imagine Wally Witless who buys tickets in a state lottery. Every year he spends hundreds of dollars, maybe thousands, without winning anything. Does he give up? If so, he admits that all that he invested was a loss. If he continues buying tickets, he maintains the hope of eventually hitting the jackpot, winning more than enough to make up for all the money he lost. A single payoff could make the whole string of bets a net win.

Vicarious Reinforcement and Punishment

Recall from the discussion of social-learning theory that people learn what to do and what to avoid by observing what happens to others. Recall also that vicarious reinforcement tends to be more effective than vicarious punishment.

State governments want to encourage people to buy lottery tickets (because they provide revenue for the government), so what do you suppose they do? They encourage massive publicity for everyone who wins a big jackpot (Figure 9.25). You will often see news reports showing some instant millionaire, delirious with excitement. (The state hopes this vicarious reinforcement will induce you to buy lottery tickets.) You seldom see reports about the millions of people who bought tickets and won nothing.

The Influence of Heuristics

Using the availability heuristic, people assume that if they can recall many examples of an event, the event must be common. You can see

FIGURE 9.25
States that sponsor lotteries provide publicity and an exciting atmosphere for each big payoff. They hope this publicity will provide vicarious reinforcement to encourage other people to buy lottery tickets. They do not publicize all the people who lost money on the lottery.

how this combines forces with vicarious reinforcement. Someone who sees a big lottery winner on television almost every week remembers many such examples and therefore overestimates the likelihood of winning a lottery.

The representativeness heuristic also plays a role in gambling. Suppose you are flipping a coin, recording the order of heads (H) and tails (T). Which of these sequences do you think is more likely:

1. H H H H H H H H
2. H H H H T T T T

Most of the people not trained in probability theory choose sequence 2, although in fact the two sequences are equally likely (Kahneman & Tversky, 1973). People know that in a sequence of coin flips, the numbers of heads and tails usually come close to balancing out, so sequence 2 seems more *representative* of a typical sequence. However, that does not alter the odds: After a run of four heads, a sequence of four more heads is just as likely as four tails.

The gambler's fallacy is an example of the representativeness heuristic. The **gambler's fallacy** is the belief that if a particular outcome has not occurred for a while, its "turn" has come. For example, if the last seven spins on the roulette wheel landed on black numbers, the next spin probably will land on a red number. If your last 20 bets have lost, your next one will probably win. But because each random event is really independent of all the preceding events, the gambler's fallacy leads to misplaced confidence.

In summary, we have the following explanations for why some people continue to gamble despite consistent losses:

- They believe that by skillfully choosing the right numbers they can increase their probability of winning a game of chance.

- They are willing to accept an almost certain loss in order to have a slim chance of winning a fortune, especially if they see no other way of getting rich.

- They can continue through a long losing streak if the (imagined) eventual payoff is big enough to repay all the losses.

- They remember seeing or hearing about many people who have won big jackpots. Thus they receive vicarious reinforcement for gambling and they overestimate the probability of winning.

- They may believe that after a long series of losses, the probability of winning increases.

Similar explanations apply to the gambles people take in everyday life. If you drink and drive, or go out on a date with someone who mistreated you in the past, you are taking a gamble—perhaps a foolish gamble. People take such risks for some of the same reasons just described.

One general point from all this is that people usually have multiple reasons for their behavior. People do not gamble for just one reason any more than you went to college for just one reason. A second general point is that the principles of learning, memory, and cognition do not apply to separate domains; we can apply all of those principles to a single behavior, such as gambling.

Something to Think About

Recall the discussion on page 385 of how the phrasing of a question may influence someone's decision. For example, most people will take more risks to avoid a loss than they will to increase a gain. Can you use this principle to explain why many gamblers on a losing streak will continue betting, sometimes increasing their bets? Is there a different way for a gambler to think about the situation so as to decrease the temptation to continue gambling?

SUMMARY

- *Expert pattern recognition.* Experts recognize and memorize familiar and meaningful patterns more rapidly than less experienced people do. (page 374)

- *Expert problem solving.* Experts solve problems in their field rapidly because they recognize the appropriate method and avoid wasting time on ineffective methods. (page 375)

- *Steps in solving a problem.* People go through four steps in solving a problem: understanding the problem, generating hypotheses, testing the hypotheses, and checking the result. (page 376)

- *Algorithms and heuristics.* People can solve problems through algorithms (repetitive means of checking every possibility) or heuristics (ways of simplifying the problem to get a reasonable solution). (page 376)

- *Generalizing.* Many people who have learned how to solve a problem fail to apply that solution to a similar problem. (page 378)

- *Insight.* With insight problems, people have trouble estimating how close they are to a solution. However, they may be making progress even if they do not realize they are. (page 378)

- *Creativity.* Under favorable conditions, even people of fairly normal abilities can achieve outstanding creative insights. (page 380)

- *Reasons for errors.* People use various heuristics that sometimes lead to certain patterns of errors. Common mistakes include premature commitment to a hypothesis and overreliance on the representativeness heuristic and the availability heuristic. (page 381)

- *Reasons for gambling.* Gambling illustrates the combined influences of learning, memory, and cognition. Many people gamble despite consistent losses because they overestimate their control, because they imagine a large payoff, because they experience vicarious reinforcement, and because they believe a series of losses makes an eventual win more likely. (page 386)

SUGGESTIONS FOR FURTHER READING

Bransford, J. B., & Stein, B. S. (1984). *The ideal problem solver.* New York: Freeman. Advice on how to approach and solve both "mind-bender" problems and practical problems.

Dostoevsky, F. (1972). *The gambler.* Chicago: University of Chicago Press. (Original work written 1866.) A classic novel that captures the enticement of gambling.

Kahneman, D., Slovic, P., & Tversky, A. (Eds.) (1982). *Judgment under uncertainty.* Cambridge, England: Cambridge University Press. Describes research on the representativeness heuristic, the availability heuristic, and other heuristics that can lead to systematic errors in decision making.

TERMS

algorithm a mechanical, repetitive mathematical procedure for solving a problem (page 376)

heuristics strategies for simplifying a problem or for guiding an investigation (page 376)

creativity the development of novel, socially valued products (page 380)

representativeness heuristic the tendency to assume that if an item is similar to members of a particular category, it is probably a member of that category itself (page 382)

base-rate information data about the frequency or probability of a given item (page 383)

availability heuristic the strategy of assuming that the number of available memories of an event indicates how common the event actually is (page 384)

expected value mean of all the possible values of a choice, weighted according to their probabilities (page 386)

gambler's fallacy belief that if a particular outcome has not occurred for a while, its "turn" has come (page 389)

ANSWERS TO CONCEPT CHECKS

4. It is an example of heuristics; someone has devised a simple way to obtain an approximate answer. A possible example of an algorithm would be to collect grocery receipts from a random sample of all the people in the country and then divide the total of the receipts by the number of people sampled. (page 377)

5. The employer would fire 18 dishonest employees (90% of the 20 who had stolen). The employer would also fire 98 honest employees (10% of the 980 who had not stolen). Because the base rate of dishonesty is low, a clear majority of those identified as dishonest are actually honest. (page 384)

6. (a) Failure to consider the base rate: 20% of all older adults is a larger number than 90% of all college students; (b) Premature commitment to one hypothesis without considering other hypotheses (such as that one could stay healthy without any magic words). (page 386)

ANSWERS TO OTHER QUESTIONS IN THE TEXT

C. 6.54 cm (page 375)

D. The water in the tube would leak out of the hole in the bottom. Any membrane heavy enough to keep the water in would also keep the rubber balls out. (page 377)

E. The illustration here shows how to cut and fold an ordinary piece of paper or cardboard to match the figure with nothing left over. (page 379)

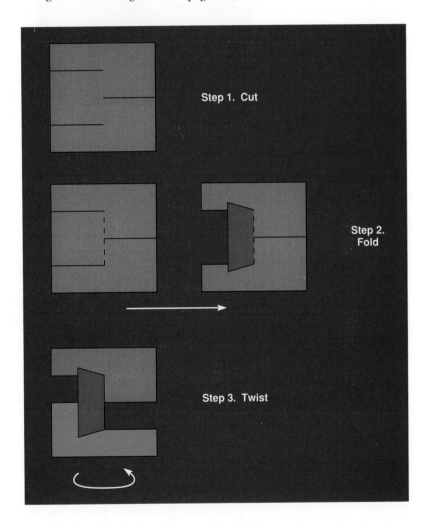

F. Set 1: The words *playing, credit,* and *report* are all associated with *card.* Set 2: The words *ticket, shop,* and *broker* are all associated with *pawn.* (page 379)

G. All of the activities listed increase your odds of dying equally, by one in a million (source: Failure Analysis Associates). Some of these activities may seem more dangerous than others seem, because some kinds of accidents and risks receive more publicity than others do. That is, our overestimation of certain risks is another example of the availability heuristic. (page 384)

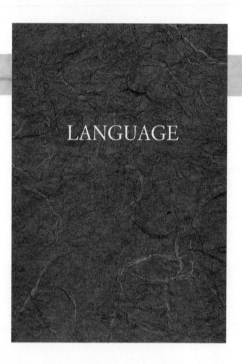

LANGUAGE

How do we learn to understand language, to speak, and to read?

Does language have special properties that set it apart from other intelligent behaviors?

Rats can learn mazes about as fast as humans can. Given enough practice, a chimpanzee or an elephant can learn to perform some rather complicated tasks. Apparently, other species have many intellectual abilities similar to those of humans.

And yet the achievements of humans far surpass those of other species. We build bridges, discover cures for diseases, cultivate crops, write and read psychology textbooks, and put other species into zoos. What enables us to do so much more than other animals?

One answer to that question is language, a complex system that enables us to convert our thoughts into words and to convert other people's words into thoughts. By age 3, almost all children have learned language well enough to put it to some very important uses: They use it to acquire knowledge. ("Don't touch the stove!" "Stay away from the poison ivy.") They use it to inform others. ("Swing me around some more, Daddy!" "Not so fast, Daddy!") A few years later they are using language to learn history, science, and the accumulated knowledge and wisdom of humanity.

NONHUMAN PRECURSORS TO LANGUAGE

Language is an immensely useful ability. Without it, each of us would have only the benefit of our own experiences. With it, we can profit from the experiences of people on the other side of the world and people who lived thousands of years ago.

So, if language is such a useful ability, why have no other species evolved it? Or do some nonhumans have certain abilities related to language? Some psychologists once believed that language was simply the product of having *enough* brain and/or *enough* training. In its simple form, we can discard that view. No amount of training enables dolphins, whales, chimpanzees, or other large-brained animals to match the language abilities of normal children or even of certain brain-damaged children whose total brain mass is relatively small. Language is definitely a human specialization (See Figure 9.26.)

But saying that does not tell us whether or not other species might have some primitive abilities similar to language. According to one school of thought, language is a separate, uniquely human skill. Adding language to a species is like adding speech synthesis to a computer: One needs to attach a separate piece of hardware. According to this point of view, humans gained speech simply because we added this extra brain hardware.

According to a different school of thought, human language is an elaboration or modification of intellectual abilities present in other species. Evolution seldom builds anything from scratch. For example, the wings of birds and bats are modifications of the forelimbs present in other land vertebrates. The quills of porcupines are modified hairs. An elephant's trunk is a modified nose. Similarly, human language presumably evolved from some other capacity present in other species. If so, it should be possible to train other species to do something that at least resembles language.

FIGURE 9.26

Nonhuman species certainly communicate with each other, and with training many species can learn to communicate with people. However, so far as we can determine, no nonhumans develop a language comparable to human languages.

Attempts to Teach Language to Chimpanzees

During the 1920s and 1930s, a number of psychologists were optimistic about the possibility of teaching chimpanzees to talk. Winthrop Kellogg and Luella Kellogg (1933), psychologists at Florida State University, tried to rear a baby chimpanzee, Gua, in the same way as they were rearing their son Donald, who was about the same age. Gua did learn certain human habits, including drinking from a cup and eating with a spoon. She never learned to speak, however, although she seemed to understand a few spoken words.

Later, another couple (Hayes, 1951) reared a chimpanzee named Viki, giving her their undivided attention and free run of the house. (Imagine what their house looked like. Visitors sometimes asked whether the Hayeses lived there too or just the chimpanzee.) Viki, like Gua, learned a number of human habits and understood some spoken language, but her own speaking vocabulary was limited to some poorly articulated approximations to *cup, up,* and *mama* (Figure 9.27). With the failure of

these and other attempts to teach chimpanzees to talk, most psychologists doubted that chimpanzees could ever learn anything resembling human language.

Then in the 1960s and 1970s, Allen Gardner and Beatrice Gardner (1969), psychologists at the University of Nevada, taught a chimpanzee, Washoe, to use the sign language that American deaf people use (Ameslan). Sign language is closer to the hand gestures that chimpanzees use naturally, and it does not require them to imitate human voice sounds, for which their vocal tracts are poorly adapted. Washoe started slowly, but eventually she learned the symbols for about a hundred words. She occasionally linked symbols together into meaningful combinations, such as "cry hurt food" for a radish and "baby in my drink" when someone put a doll into her cup.

At about the same time, Ann Premack and David Premack (1972) taught chimpanzees to communicate by means of colored magnets that represented words, including such complex relational words as *same, if . . . then,* and *is the color of.* For a while it appeared, at least to some observers, that chimpanzees could use visual symbols and hand gestures in a way very similar to human language (Figure 9.28).

But how similar was it, really? Careful analysis of the chimpanzees' use of signs revealed that many of their symbols were an imitation of symbols their human trainers had used recently (Terrace, Petitto, Sanders, & Bever, 1979). Moreover, they used their symbols almost exclusively to make requests, rarely if ever to describe things (as humans do). The chimps had learned the meanings of many symbols, but they seldom linked them together in anything like a sentence (Pate & Rumbaugh, 1983; Terrace et al., 1979; Thompson & Church, 1980). By contrast, a child with a vocabulary of a hundred words or so starts linking them together to make many original combinations and short sentences. Also, the chimps understood the symbols only if they were arranged in the familiar order; if an experimenter tried to communicate something with a sightly different word order, the chimps became confused (Rumbaugh, 1990). In short, the chimps' use of symbols showed little of the flexibility of human language.

That, at any rate, was the conclusion from studies of the common chimpanzee, *Pan troglodytes.* Closely related to the common chimp is a rare and endangered species, *Pan*

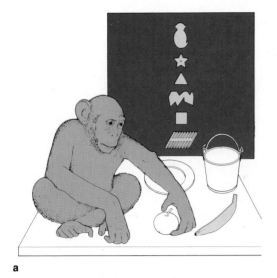

a

b

c

d

FIGURE 9.27

Speaking is physically impossible for chimpanzees, but some psychologists have tried to teach them to communicate by gesture or symbols. (a) The Premacks' chimp uses a board to communicate. (b) Viki in her human home, helping with the housework. After years with the Hayeses, she could make only a few sounds similar to English words. (c) Kanzi, a bonobo, presses symbols to indicate words. Bonobos have shown the most promising ability to acquire language among the higher primates. (d) A chimp signing toothbrush. *(e) Roger Fouts with Alley the chimp, who is signing* lizard.

e

paniscus, sometimes known as the pygmy chimpanzee (a misleading term because these animals are almost as large as common chimpanzees) and sometimes known as the bonobo. The social behavior of *Pan paniscus* resembles that of humans in several regards: Males and females form strong, long-lasting attachments; females are sexually responsive throughout the

month, not just during their fertile period; males contribute much more to infant care than other nonhuman primate males do; and adults often share food with one another.

In the mid-1980s Sue Savage-Rumbaugh, Duane Rumbaugh, and their associates began trying to teach a female bonobo, Matata, to press symbols that light up when touched; each symbol represents a word. She made very disappointing progress. However, her infant son Kanzi, who stood by during her training, seemed to learn a great deal just by watching. When given his first chance to use the symbol board, he almost immediately surpassed the performance of his mother and of every common chimp that had been tested.

Kanzi and his younger sister Mulika have used symbols in ways that go beyond the productions of common chimpanzees. First, they use the symbols to name and describe objects even when they are not requesting them. Second, they occasionally use the symbols to relate events of the past. For example, Kanzi once punched the symbols "Matata bite" to explain the cut he had received on his hand an hour previously. Third, Kanzi and Mulika frequently make original, creative requests. For example, after Kanzi had learned to press the symbols to ask someone to play "chase" with him, he asked one person to chase another person while Kanzi watched!

Furthermore, Kanzi has shown considerable understanding of spoken English, even though no one tried to teach him to understand it. By age 5 1/2 he understood about 150 spoken words and responded correctly to complex, unfamiliar spoken commands such as "throw your ball to the river" and "go to the refrigerator and get out a tomato" (Savage-Rumbaugh, 1990; Savage-Rumbaugh, Sevcik, Brakke, & Rumbaugh, 1992). Kanzi even passed the test of

FIGURE 9.28
One of David and Ann Premack's chimpanzees arranges plastic chips to make a "sentence" request for food.

responding to commands over earphones, when no one in the room with him could inadvertently signal what he was supposed to do (Figure 9.29). That was an important test, because it demonstrated Kanzi was not just responding to subtle gestures or facial expressions, as Clever Hans did (Chapter 1).

FIGURE 9.29
Kanzi points to answers on a board in response to questions he hears through earphones. Experimenter Rose Sevcik sits with him but does not hear the questions and cannot intentionally or accidentally signal the correct answer.

Why have Kanzi and Mulika been so much more successful than other chimpanzees? Part of the explanation probably pertains to species differences: Perhaps bonobos have greater language capacities than common chimpanzees, or perhaps they simply have a better ability to code and remember the kinds of sounds humans use in speech. Another part of the explanation may pertain to the method of training: Learning by observation and imitation probably promotes better understanding than do the formal training methods used in previous studies. (Savage-Rumbaugh, Sevcik, Brakke, & Rumbaugh, 1992). Finally, Kanzi and Mulika began their language experience early in life.

Nonprimate Language?

Can any nonprimates learn any aspect of language? Maybe. Alex, an African gray parrot (Figure 9.30), has learned to make human sounds in ways that seem to indicate understanding. Parrots are, of course, famous for imitating human sounds, and Irene Pepperberg has argued that parrots can learn the meanings of sounds. She kept Alex in a stimulating environment and taught him to say the names of certain objects. First she and the other trainers would say a word repeatedly, then they would offer rewards if Alex approximated the same

sound. Here is a short excerpt from a "conversation" with Alex early in training (Pepperberg, 1981):

Pepperberg: Pasta! [takes pasta] Pasta! [Alex stretches from his perch, appears to reach for pasta.]
Alex: Pa!
Pepperberg: Better . . . what is it?
Alex: Pah-ah.
Pepperberg: Better!
Alex: Pah-ta.
Pepperberg: Okay, here's the pasta. Good try.

Although this example concerns pasta, Pepperberg generally used toys for rewards. For example, if Alex said *paper, wood,* or *key,* she would give him what he asked for. In no case did she reward him for saying *paper* or *wood* by giving him a piece of food.

Alex made gradual progress, apparently learning to give spoken answers to spoken questions (Pepperberg, 1990). He can answer such questions as "What color is the key?" (answer: "green") and "What object is gray?" (answer: "circle"). Is Alex really speaking English? Most scientists are reluctant to accept such a surprising conclusion; recall from Chapter 2 the importance of replicating any surprising result and of exploring alternative explanations before settling on the best one. However, if Alex really does understand and speak English, we will have to rethink some assumptions about what sort of brain development is necessary for language.

What do we learn about language from studies of nonhuman language abilities? At a practical level, we may gain some insights into how best to teach language to those who do not learn it easily (e.g., Glass, Gazzaniga, & Premack, 1973). At a more theoretical level, we find out something about how special humans are—and are not. We learn that the brain structures necessary for language are not entirely limited to the human brain. Although humans undeniably develop language far more readily than any other species does, our language abilities are an elaboration of abilities found to some degree in other species.

■ CONCEPT CHECK

7. Based on the studies of Kanzi and Mulika, what would be good advice on how to teach language to children born with some disability that impairs language learning? (Check your answer on page 409).

FIGURE 9.30
Alex, an African gray parrot, answers questions such as "What color is the circle?" He receives no food reinforcements.

LANGUAGE AND THOUGHT

How is language related to thought? Many years ago certain psychologists maintained that they are identical; thought was just "subvocal" speech, and we could in principle figure out what someone is thinking by recording muscle movements in the throat. Among other problems with that theory, it seems to imply that preverbal children, brain-damaged adults, and nonhuman animals cannot think at all. Today we look for more subtle and complex ways in which language and thought influence each other.

The Productivity of Language

Language is productive—that is, we can use language to express a never-ending variety of new ideas. Every day we say and hear a few stock sentences, such as "Nice weather we're having," but we also say and hear sentences that probably no one has ever said before.

You might doubt that statement. You might ask, "How can you *know* that no one has ever said some particular sentence before?!" Well, of course, we *cannot* know that a *particular* sentence is new, but we can be confident that *some* sentences are new (not specifying which ones). The number of possible sentences in English alone is staggering—about 10^{30} sentences of 20 words or fewer. Expressed another way, if every human on the planet produced a new sentence every second of every day for an entire century, they would come nowhere near reaching that total. Try this exercise (Slobin, 1979): Pick any sentence of 10 to 20 words from any book you choose. How long would you have to keep reading, in that book or any other, until you found exactly the same sentence again?

In short, we do not memorize all the sentences we will ever use; instead, we learn rules for making sentences and for interpreting other people's sentences. Noam Chomsky (1980) has described those rules as a transformational grammar, which is a system for converting a deep structure into a surface structure. The deep structure is the underlying logic of the language. The surface structure is the sequence of words as they are actually spoken or written (Figure 9.31). According to this theory, whenever we speak we transform the deep structure of the language into a surface structure. Two surface structures may resemble each other without representing the same deep

FIGURE 9.31

According to transformational grammar, we can transform a sentence with a given surface structure into any of several other sentences with different surface structures. All of them represent the same deep structure, which is the underlying logic of the sentence.

structure, or they may represent the same deep structure without resembling each other.

For example, "John is easy to please" has the same deep structure as "Pleasing John is easy" and "It is easy to please John." They all represent the same underlying idea: When people try to please John, they find it easy to do.

In contrast, consider the sentence "Never threaten someone with a chain saw." The surface structure of that one sentence maps into two quite different deep structures:

1. It is not nice to swing a chain saw around and threaten someone with it.

2. If you meet someone carrying a chain saw, don't make any threatening gestures.

Transformational grammar consists of a set of rules for converting one surface structure into another. For example, it specifies that we can transform "John is easy to please" into "Pleasing John is easy." But we cannot transform "John is eager to please" into "Pleasing John is eager."

Ordinarily, when we listen to language, we attend only briefly to the surface structure, quickly extracting and remembering the deep structure—that is, the meaning (Sachs, 1967). To illustrate: Several paragraphs ago you read one of the following sentences. Without peeking, can you remember which one it was?

1. Two surface structures may represent the same deep structure without resembling each other, or they may resemble each other without representing the same deep structure.

2. Two surface structures may resemble each other without representing the same deep structure, or they may represent the same deep structure without resembling each other.

3. Two deep structures may resemble each other, but two surface structures cannot.

If you are like most people, you had trouble remembering whether it was 1 or 2. (If you thought it was 3, you haven't been reading very carefully.) Generally, once people understand a sentence, they remember its meaning, not its word-for-word sequence.

Understanding a sentence is a complex matter that requires knowledge about the world. For example, consider the following sentences (from Just & Carpenter, 1987):

That store sells horse shoes.

That store sells alligator shoes.

We would not interpret the second sentence as referring to "shoes for alligators to wear," because alligators do not wear shoes. But that is a fact you had to know; the sentences themselves do not tell you that horses wear horse shoes but people wear alligator shoes. Here is another example:

I'm going to buy a pet hamster at the store, if it's open.

I'm going to buy a pet hamster at the store, if it's healthy.

You understand at once that *it* in the first sentence refers to the store and in the second sentence to the hamster. Nothing about the sentence structure tells you that, however. (If you were communicating with a computer or a being from another planet, you would have to specify what each *it* meant.) You understood because you know that stores (but not hamsters) can be open, whereas hamsters (but not stores) can be healthy. In short, language comprehension depends on assumptions that the speaker and the listener—or writer and reader—share.

The Whorf Hypothesis

Language is our means of expressing thought, and we learn rules for converting thoughts into sentences. But once we learn a particular language, does that language guide our thought? According to one view, the **Whorf hypothesis** (or *Sapir-Whorf hypothesis*), our language determines the way we think (Whorf, 1941): People who speak different languages think differently.

This hypothesis is vaguer than most scientific hypotheses; it does not specify *how* language affects thought, just *that* it affects thought in some way. Therefore, testing the hypothesis is a matter of trying to find a good example, any example, of some such effect.

For the most part, the search for such effects has led to little that is convincing. For many years the most widely cited example was the supposed fact that Eskimos had dozens of words for snow, enabling them to describe some of the fine points of snow that speakers of other languages would necessarily overlook. Even if true, this would hardly be powerful evidence. Ornithologists know hundreds of words for birds; astronomers have a great vocabulary for stars and galaxies; every expert knows many specialized words. But having a large vocabulary on a topic is not the same as thinking *differently* about it.

Furthermore, most of the claims about Eskimo snow words came from people who never met an Eskimo in their lives, much less talked with one. A 1911 publication identified four Eskimo snow words, roughly corresponding to snowflake, snow on the ground, drifting snow, and snowdrift. Later authors who had read this publication (or heard about it by word of mouth) exaggerated its findings; still later authors exaggerated still further. Eventually, people were quoting each other without any idea of where the original information had come from—a bit like the widespread, nonsensical statement that "we use only 10% of our brains." By the 1970s, magazines and encyclopedias variously announced that Eskimos had 50, 100, or 200 words for snow (Martin, 1986; Pullum, 1991).

(You may wonder how many snow words the Eskimos actually have. We cannot give a precise number. Actually, "Eskimo" is a family of languages, and the vocabulary varies from one language to another. According to Laura Martin [1986], West Greenlandic has two roots, meaning snowflake and snow-on-the-ground. It can add suffixes to these roots to make many additional words, just as English can: *snowed, snowing, snowy, snowfall,* and so forth. And, like English, it has words that can apply to snow as well as to other objects, depending on context: *drift, powder, avalanche,*

. . . If we count all of these as "snow" words, then West Greenlandic has a large number of snow words. But then so does English.)

Can we find a better example to support the Whorf hypothesis? Anthropologists tell us that the Quechua people of the Andes have no word for *flat*. If that is correct, presumably they have trouble expressing the idea of *flatness* and perhaps difficulty even thinking about it. Similarly, languages in some nontechnological societies have no words for numbers other than "one," "two," and "many." A speaker of such a language probably would find it difficult to deal with even the simplest mathematical questions (Hunt & Agnoli, 1991). According to Benjamin Whorf (1941), the Hopi language has no way of saying "ten days," although one can say "after the tenth day." According to Whorf, the consequence is that Hopi speakers cannot easily think about lengths of time or about time as an abstract concept.

How convincing is this evidence? Well, we might be skeptical. One reason why so much false information spread about Eskimo words for snow is that hardly anyone knew enough about the Eskimo languages to check the claims. So how do we know whether someone has misled us about the Quechuan language or about the ability of Hopi speakers to think about time? (Do you know anyone who knows anyone who speaks Quechuan?) If the Whorf hypothesis is valid, and if it has far-reaching significance, we should be able to support it with examples from many languages, and not just from remote and exotic languages.

Perhaps speakers of different European languages think differently in some ways. For example, many languages have gender endings on nouns. The German word for pigeon (*Taube*) is female; the Italian word (*piccione*) is masculine. So Germans call a pigeon "she" and Italians call it "he." Conversely, Germans call a buzzard "he," while Italians call it "she." Do Germans and Italians think about pigeons and buzzards differently from each other, and from English speakers, who call both kinds of bird "it"? Unfortunately, research on this question is surprisingly sparse (Hunt & Agnoli, 1991).

Similarly, English has many words with multiple meanings. For example, *well* can mean "in a good way" or "a hole from which water comes." *Park* can mean "stop a car" or "a public place with trees and walkways." Italian, by contrast, has relatively few words with more than one meaning. Do Italians therefore think

Years ago, the favorite example to illustrate the Whorf hypothesis was the supposed fact that Eskimos have countless words for snow. Laura Martin (1986) demonstrated that this claim was enormously exaggerated. Even if true, it would be a poor example of the Whorf hypothesis.

differently, and perhaps understand sentences faster or more clearly, than English-speakers? Presumably they tell fewer puns.

Russian speakers can identify exactly how close they feel to another person by using various shades of nicknames. Because English has far fewer shades of nicknames (at most something like "James, Jim, and Jimmy"), certain fine points of Russian novels get lost in English translations.

We do have evidence to support the Whorf hypothesis in one case: The effects of gender-related words in various situations. In English it used to be customary to use the pronoun *he* to refer to a person of unknown gender—such as "a doctor should do what he thinks is best," or "a professor should know his topic well." Many people objected that this custom implied that doctors, professors, and so forth were necessarily *men*. And indeed the language does have this effect. In one study, students read sentences such as

The average American believes he watches too much TV.

or

The average American believes he or she watches too much TV.

or

Average Americans believe they watch too much TV.

After each sentence, students described the image it suggested. Students who read the *he* sentence almost always described a man. When they read a sentence with *he or she,* men described an image with a man; women described an image with a woman. When they heard a *they* sentence, most described a group composed of both men and women (Gastil, 1990). In short, the way we speak does influence the way we think, at least in this situation. For that reason, speakers and writers today are encouraged to use gender-neutral expressions, such as "a doctor should do what *he or she* thinks is best," or "professors should know *their* topics well."

UNDERSTANDING LANGUAGE

Making sense of what we see and hear is a complex process. A single letter, such as *a,* sounds different in different words, sounds different for different speakers, and looks different in different handwritings. Yet we learn to treat all of these expressions as the same. A single word can have different meanings in different contexts; for example, *net* can refer to something on a basketball or tennis court, something to catch fish or butterflies, or the profit of a corporation. Even a sentence has different meanings in different contexts (Just & Carpenter, 1987). (See Figure 9.32.) For example, we generally interpret the proverb "Time flies like an arrow" to mean that time passes quickly. But consider the same sentence in two other contexts:

> **Q:** You taught me how to use this device to time the motion of cars, and a different way to time the flight of arrows. But how should I time the flight of houseflies?
> **A:** *Time flies like an arrow.*

> There were all sorts of weird insects in this place—space flies, gravity flies, and time flies. They all eat wood, but each fly likes a different kind. Space flies like to eat a desk. Most gravity flies like chairs. *Time flies like an arrow.*

Language comprehension is immensely complicated, as people discover when they try to program a computer to understand language (Just & Carpenter, 1987). And yet most of the time we understand what we hear and read without any noticeable effort. Although many questions remain to be answered, researchers have also made some discoveries about how all this takes place.

Hearing a Word as a Whole

We customarily describe the word *cat* as being composed of three sounds, *Kuh, Ah,* and *Tuh.* In a sense that is misleading: The first sound in *cat* is not quite the same as the consonant sound in *Kuh;* the *A* and *T* sounds are changed also. Each letter changes its sound depending on the other sounds that precede it and follow it. We cannot hear the separate letters of a word; we must hear the word as a whole.

One of the clearest demonstrations was an experiment in which students listened to a tape recording of a sentence with one sound missing (Warren, 1970). The sentence was "The state governors met with their respective legislatures convening in the capital city." However, the sound of the first *s* in the word *legislatures,* along with part of the adjacent *i* and *l,* had been replaced by a cough or a tone. The students were asked to listen to the recording and try to identify the location of the cough or tone. None of the 20 students identified the location correctly, and half thought the cough or tone interrupted one of the other words on the tape. They all claimed to have heard the *s* plainly. In fact, even those who had been told that the *s* sound was missing insisted that they had heard the sound. Apparently the brain had used the context to fill in the missing sound.

Understanding Words in Context

Many words have different meanings in different contexts. Some words have meanings that seem almost completely unrelated to one another. *Rose* can refer to a flower, or it can be the past tense of the verb *to rise.* Consider the word *mean* in this sentence: "What did that mean old statistician mean by asking us to find the mean and mode of this distribution?"

Just as we hear the word *legislatures* as a whole, not as a string of separate letters, we interpret a sequence of words as a whole, not one at a time. For example, suppose you hear a tape-recorded sound that is carefully engineered to sound halfway between *dent* and *tent*. If you simply hear it and have to say what you heard, you might reply "dent," "tent," or "something sort of intermediate between dent and tent." But now suppose you hear that same sound in context:

1. When the *ent in the fender was well camouflaged, we sold the car.

2. When the *ent in the forest was well camouflaged, we began our hike.

People who hear sentence 1 tend to report the word *dent*. People who hear sentence 2 tend to report *tent*. Now consider two more sentences:

3. When the *ent was noticed in the fender, we sold the car.

4. When the *ent was noticed in the forest, we stopped to rest.

For sentences 3 and 4, the context does not matter. People are as likely to report hearing *dent* in one sentence as they are in the other (Connine, Blasko, & Hall, 1991). Think for a moment what this means: In the first two sentences, the fender or forest showed up three syllables after *ent*. In the second pair, the fender or forest showed up six syllables later. Evidently, when you hear an ambiguous sound you can hold it in some temporary "undecided" state for about three syllables to find out whether the context helps you to understand it. Beyond that point it is too late for the context to help; you hear it one way or the other and stick with it even if the later context contradicts your decision.

Although a delayed context cannot help you hear an ambiguous word correctly, it can help you understand what it means. Consider the following sentence from Karl Lashley (1951):

> Rapid righting with his uninjured hand saved from loss the contents of the capsized canoe.

If you hear this sentence spoken aloud, so that spelling is not a clue, you are likely to interpret the second word as "writing." That is a perfectly reasonable interpretation until we come to the final two words of the sentence. Suddenly the phrase *capsized canoe* changes the whole scenario; now we understand that "righting" meant pushing with a paddle. In summary, the immediate context can influence what you think you heard, but even a much delayed context can influence what you think the sentence means.

READING

Before the abolition of slavery in the United States, it was illegal in many states to teach a slave how to read. Slaves who could read might be dangerous, the reasoning went. They might get new ideas; they might learn things their masters did not want them to know.

Since then, many totalitarian governments probably wished they could prevent people

Great wall of china.

Our new china patterns underscore Gorham's commitment to dinnerware that can proudly stand next to our highly popular crystal stemware and our inveterately successful sterling flatware. To see it all, talk to your Gorham representative or write Gorham, P.O. Box 6150, Providence, RI 02940.

GORHAM THE PERFECT SETTING

FIGURE 9.32
Many clever ads take advantage of the fact that a given word can have several meanings and that people will figure out the intended meaning based on context.

from reading, but because that was impossible, they tried to control *what* people read. Anything opposing the government in power was banned; so were some nonpolitical works that might stimulate new thoughts.

Reading can be a powerful force against a repressive government; it can also be a powerful force to strengthen a modern, progressive society. In a highly technological society, an illiterate person is unqualified for most jobs and seriously disadvantaged in so many aspects of everyday life.

To figure out how best to teach reading, we need to understand what people do when they read. As they pass their eyes over a page, do they read one letter at a time, a word at a time, or more? Do they have to finish reading one item before they start on the next, or can they start on a new one before they finish the last one? Do they have to think of the sound of a word before they understand it, or can they go directly from a printed word to its meaning? If we knew more

Reading is a complex skill that includes stages from eye movements through understanding and using the material. Investigators find that they cannot separate these stages; how well a reader understands the material influences the speed of the eye movements. By studying reading, psychologists hope to improve methods of teaching reading.

about reading, we might be able to help people to read faster and with better comprehension.

Reading and Eye Movements

One of the basic skills of reading is to pass your eyes over the words, left to right and top to bottom in English. Do you read one word at a time, one letter at a time, or perhaps a whole phrase at a time? And do you move your eyes steadily or in a jerky fashion?

The movements are so fast that you cannot answer these questions by self-inspection. Psychologists have arranged devices to monitor people's eye movements during reading. Their first discovery was that a reader's eyes move in a jerky fashion, not steadily. You can move your eyes steadily when they are following a moving object, but when you are scanning a stationary object such as a page of print, your eyes move from one focal point to another in quick jumps called **saccades.** An average person reading an average page of text focuses on each point for about 200 milliseconds (msec) on the average. The fixation varies from a duration of less than 100 msec on short, familiar words like *girl* to a second or more on difficult words like *ghoul.* Good readers generally have shorter fixations than poor readers do (Just & Carpenter, 1987). After each fixation, the saccade lasts about 25–50 msec. Thus, a typical person has about four fixations per second while reading.

How much can a person read during one fixation? Many people have the impression that they see quite a bit of the page at each instant. Like many informal impressions, that one is wrong. The research says that we generally read only one word at a time, sometimes two or three if they are short. Recall from Chapter 4 that human vision has its greatest acuity in the fovea, an area in the center of the retina. You can read letters when you fixate them in the fovea, but your

ability to read drops sharply in the surrounding area. To demonstrate this phenomenon, focus on the point marked by an arrow (↓) in the sentences below.

1. This is a sentence with no misspelled words.

2. Xboc lx z rxuhce with no mjvvgab zucn.

3. Xboc lx z rxuhmj with zw cjvvgab zucn.

If you permit your eyes to wander back and forth, you quickly notice that sentences 2 and 3 are gibberish. But as long as you dutifully keep your eyes on the fixation point in sentence 2, it may look all right. You can read the letter on which you fixated your eyes plus about three or four characters (including spaces) to the left and about seven to the right. This is enough for you to see *—ce with no m—*. You cannot see the more distant letters well enough to be sure whether or not they spell out real words.

In sentence 3, however, you do notice something wrong. Even while keeping your eyes carefully fixated on the *i* in *with,* you can see that the next word is the nonsense combination *zw* and that the previous word ends with *j,* unlike any English word you can think of. Evidently you can read about 11 characters in one fixation.

In a study documenting this phenomenon, college students read text on a computer screen while a machine monitored their eye positions and fed that information to the computer. The computer correctly displayed whatever word a student was fixating on, plus a certain number of letters on each side of it. Beyond those letters, the computer displayed only gibberish. Students almost never noticed that anything was unusual, unless the computer started displaying gibberish letters closer than three characters to the left or seven characters to the right of the fixation point (Underwood & McConkie, 1985). Evidently we read in a "window" of about 11 letters—the fixated letter, about three characters to its left, and about seven to its right.

■ CONCEPT CHECKS

8. *Why can we sometimes read two or three short words at a time, whereas we need a saccade or two to read the same number of longer words?*
9. *If a word is longer than 11 letters, will a reader need more than one fixation to read it? (Check your answers on page 409.)*

In many cases, that window includes one word plus a fragment of the next word. For example, suppose you have fixated on the point shown by an arrow in the sentence below:

↓
The government made serious mistakes.

Because of the research just described, we know that readers can see the word *serious* plus about the first three letters of *mistakes*. That does not provide enough information to read the word *mistakes;* from what the reader knows, that next word could be *misspellings, misbehavior, missiles, mishmash,* or any of a number of other *mis*-things that a government might make. Does that little "preview" of the next word facilitate reading? Yes. In one study, college students again read passages on a computer screen while a machine monitored their eye movements. The computer correctly displayed the word the student fixated on plus the next zero, three, or four letters. So the display would look like this:

↓
The government made xxxxxxx xxxxxxxx.

↓
The government made serious xxxxxxxx.

↓
The government made serious mistakes.

or like this:

↓
The government made serxxxx xxxxxxxx.

↓
The government made serious misxxxxx.

↓
The government made serious mistakes.

Students who could preview the first three or four letters of the next word read significantly faster than those who could not (Inhoff, 1989). Evidently we do not read just one word at a time. While we are reading one word, we are getting started on the next.

Some people read much faster than others, and you might wonder, for example, what "speed readers" do differently from normal readers. Some people who have learned to speed-read can cover a page in less than one fifth the time a normal reader takes. However, they see only the same number of letters in one eye fixation as anyone else does. Speed readers save time partly by keeping each fixation short and partly by skipping over many words altogether. Compared to most other readers, speed

a

c Did you see C or J?

b

d Was the first letter C or J?

readers generally understand the basic points of their reading quite well; however, they do miss a fair amount of detail (Just & Carpenter, 1987).

The Word-Superiority Effect

When we read a word, do we identify the letters one at a time, or do we process several letters simultaneously, in parallel? Beginning readers have to sound out a word one letter at a time—for example, "Kuh . . . Ah . . . Tuh . . . CAT." When experienced readers come to an unfamiliar word, like *eleemosynary* or *metrorrhagia,* they sound out it out one syllable at a time. But with short, familiar words we apparently attend to all letters simultaneously.

In one experiment, the investigator flashed a single letter on a screen for less than a quarter of a second and then flashed an interfering pattern on the screen and asked, "What was the letter, *C* or *J?*" Then the experimenter flashed a whole word on the screen for the same length of time and asked, "What was the first letter of the word, *C* or *J?*" (Figure 9.33). Which question do you think the subjects answered correctly more often? Most of them identified the letter more accurately when it was part of a whole

FIGURE 9.33
Do you C a J? (a, b) A student watches either a word or a single letter flashed on a screen. (c, d) An interfering pattern is then flashed on the screen and the student is asked, "Which was presented, C or J?" More students were able to identify the letter correctly when it was part of a word.

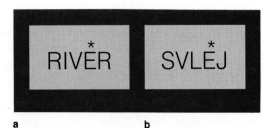

FIGURE 9.34
Students were better at identifying an indicated letter when they focused on an entire word (a) than when they were asked to remember a single letter in a designated spot among random letters (b).

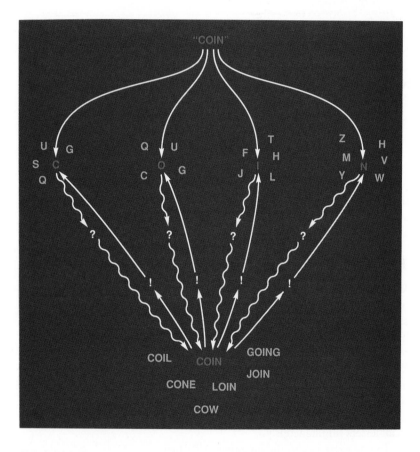

FIGURE 9.35
According to one version of the connectionist model, a visual stimulus activates certain letter units, some more strongly than others. Those letter units then activate a word unit, which in turn strengthens the letter units that compose it. For this reason, we recognize a whole word more easily than we recognize a single letter.

word than when it was presented by itself (Reicher, 1969; Wheeler, 1970). This is known as the **word-superiority effect.**

In a follow-up experiment, James Johnston and James McClelland (1974) briefly flashed words on the screen and asked students to identify one letter (whose position was marked) in each word (Figure 9.34). On some trials they told the students to focus on the center of the area where the word would appear and to try to see the whole word. On other trials they showed the students exactly where the critical letter would appear on the screen and told them to focus on that spot and ignore the rest of the screen. Most students did better at identifying the critical letter when they were told to look at the whole word than when they focused on just the letter itself!

The context of other letters aids recognition only if the combination is a word or something close to a word. For example, it is easier to recognize the difference between *COIN* and *JOIN* than the difference between *C* and *J*. But it is easier to recognize the difference between *C* and *J* than the difference between *XQCF* and *XQJF* (Rumelhart & McClelland, 1982).

You may have experienced the word-superiority effect yourself. A common game on long car trips is to try to find every letter of the alphabet on the billboards along the way. Many people find it easier to spot a particular letter by reading whole words than by checking each word letter by letter.

The Connectionist Model

What accounts for the word-superiority effect? One possibility is the **connectionist model.** Actually, psychologists have proposed several connectionist models. According to one version (McClelland, 1988; Rumelhart, McClelland, & the PDP Research Group, 1986), our perceptions and memories are represented by vast numbers of connections among "units," presumably corresponding to neurons or sets of neurons. Each unit is connected to other units (Figure 9.35).

Each unit, when activated, excites some of its neighbors and inhibits others to varying degrees. Suppose that at a given moment units corresponding to the letters *C, O, I,* and *N* are moderately active—not quite active enough for a firm identification of each letter. These units excite a higher-order unit corresponding to the word *COIN*. Although none of the four letter units sends a strong message by itself, the collective impact is strong (McClelland & Rumelhart, 1981). This higher-level perception *COIN* then feeds excitation back to the letter-identifying units and confirms their tentative decisions because they make sense in the context.

Figure 9.36 is an example of the kind of phenomenon this model attempts to explain. Why do you see the top word in that figure as *RED* instead of *PFB*? After all, in the other three words of that figure, you do see those letters as *P, F,* and *B.* But in the top word, one ambiguous figure activates some *P* units and some *R* units; the next figure activates *E* and *F* units, and the third figure activates *D* and *B* units. All of those units in turn activate other, more complex units corresponding to *RFB, PFB, PFD,* and *RED.* Because *RED* is the only English word in the group, the units that correspond to *RED* are easier to activate than those for *PFB* and the others. Consequently, you perceive the word as *RED.* As the *RED* unit becomes active, it in turn provides feedback to strengthen the activity of the *R, E,* and *D* units.

The Role of Sound in Reading

The word-superiority effect indicates that we deal with all the letters of a short word at the same time, but it does not tell us how we identify the word. Specifically, do we convert the word into a sound before we understand its meaning? In an alphabetic language such as English, each letter (such as *f*) or short combination of letters (such as *sh*) represents a **phoneme,** a unit of sound. A word consists of one or more **morphemes,** units of meaning. For example, *cats* has two morphemes (*cat* and *s*). (The final *s* is a unit of meaning because it indicates that the word is plural.) (See Figure 9.37.)

When we read, do we sound the word out phonemically, or can we go directly from the printed word to the meaning? That is, when you see the word *shoe,* do you first convert it into its sound, or can you simply look at the letters and at once think of a protective garment for your feet?

It is undeniable that we do convert the letters into sound at least in certain cases. If you see an unfamiliar word, you may sound it out and then think, "Oh, that must be the word *khaki!* I didn't know it was spelled that way!" Consider also the following passage. At a glance it looks meaningless, but if you read it aloud, you will discover a surprising pattern:

Abe E seedy E effigy ate shy Jake hay yell lemon nope peak you arrest tea you've E dub bull you wax wise E.

(If you read this aloud and you're still puzzled, check answer H, page 409.)

But the question is, Do we *always* read a word by converting it to sound? As usual with questions like this one, we cannot rely on our self-observations. When you look at a word, you determine its meaning and you generally, maybe always, determine its sound. But all of that happens so fast that you cannot reliably report the order in which the events occurred.

▪ CONCEPT CHECK

10. How many phonemes are in the word thoughtfully? *How many morphemes? (Check your answers on page 409.)*

Experiments on Word Identification

One way to address the relationship of sound to reading is to see whether people have more trouble reading words that violate the usual pronunciation rules. In some languages, such as Italian, all spellings are phonetic, without exception. English has many exceptions. *Have* does not rhyme with *cave, one* does not rhyme with *lone, laugh* does not sound the way it looks.

FIGURE 9.37
The word thankfulness *has ten phonemes (units of sound) and three morphemes (units of meaning).*

All of these irregularities make life difficult for anyone trying to learn English, but they make possible some interesting experiments in the psychology of language.

For example, students in one experiment viewed letter combinations on a computer screen and pressed one of two levers to indicate whether the letters formed an English word. Sometimes the letters did not; sometimes they formed a word that follows the usual pronunciation rules (like *grill* or *treat*), and sometimes they formed a word with an irregular pronunciation (like *yacht* or *gauge*). On the average, students responded just as fast to words with irregular pronunciations as to words with regular pronunciations (Coltheart, Besner, Jonasson, & Davelaar, 1979).

Those results seemed to imply that people could understand written words directly without worrying about their sounds. But many psychologists were not ready to concede the point. They looked carefully at the word list and discovered that some of the "regular pronunciation" words followed somewhat inconsistent pronunciation rules. For example, consider the word *treat:* Not all words that end with *-eat* rhyme with *treat; great* rhymes with *ate,* and *threat* rhymes with *jet.* Similarly, *base* appears to have a "regular" pronunciation, but *phase* ends with the same letter combination and does not rhyme with *base.* So a reader who sees the word *treat* or *base* may have some difficulty determining the correct pronunciation, perhaps comparable to the difficulties with the word *yacht* or *gauge.*

In a follow-up study, experimenters eliminated words like *treat* and *base;* they presented students with a mixture of nonwords, words with an irregular pronunciation (like *laugh*), and words with a regular, no-exceptions pronunciation (like *nerve*). With these improved lists, students responded faster to the words with regular pronunciations than to those with irregular pronunciations (Bauer & Stanovich, 1980).

In a further study, subjects were given a category, such as "articles of clothing." Then they viewed a computer screen that displayed a set of letters, which might or might not be a word. The subjects' task was to decide whether or not the string of letters spelled a word that fit the category. They would respond "yes" to *skirt,* "no" to *truck* or *zurg.* The key result was that subjects frequently made the mistake of responding "yes" to *sute,* while seldom respond-

ing "yes" to *surt.* That is, they responded to letter strings that *sounded* like an article of clothing (in this case a suit), but not to strings that were spelled like an article of clothing (Van Orden, Johnson, & Hale, 1988). Overall, these and similar studies provide evidence that people consistently attend to pronunciation when reading (Van Orden, Pennington, & Stone, 1990).

These results do not imply that we always sound out each word as if we were seeing it for the first time. Experienced readers quickly notice something wrong with "blue up the balloon" (which a 6-year-old just learning to read would accept without question). The point is not that sound is the *only* factor in reading, but just that it is consistently one important factor.

Reading as an Automatic Habit: The Stroop Effect

Experienced readers identify familiar words almost without effort. It is difficult for us to avoid reading them as words, even if we try. For example, read the following instructions and then examine Figure 9.38 on the next page and follow them:

> Notice the blocks of color at the top of the figure. Scanning from left to right, give the name of each color as fast as you can. Then notice the nonsense syllables printed in different colors in the center of the figure. Don't try to pronounce them; just say the color of each one as fast as possible. Then turn to the real words at the bottom. Don't read them; quickly say the color in which each one is printed.

If you are like most people, you found it very difficult not to read the words at the bottom of the figure. After all the practice you have had reading English, you can hardly bring yourself to look at the word *RED,* written in green letters, and say "green." This is known as the **Stroop effect,** after the psychologist who discovered it. Because you can read familiar words faster than you can name colors, the tendency to say "red" seriously interferes with your saying "green" (Cohen, Dunbar, & McClelland, 1990). (One way to read the colors instead of the words, reported by bilingual students, is to name the colors in a language other than English. Another way is to blur your vision intentionally so that you cannot make out the letters.)

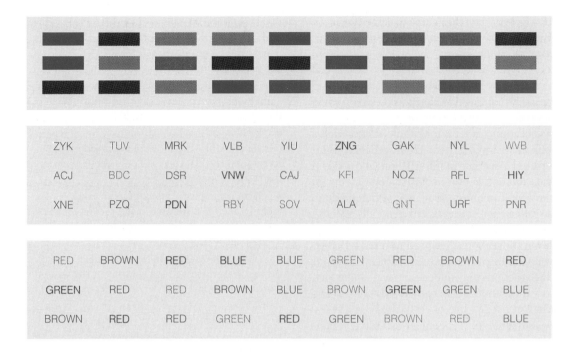

FIGURE 9.38
Read (left to right) the color of the ink in each part. Try to ignore the words themselves. Your difficulties on the lowest part illustrate the Stroop effect.

Good Readers and Poor Readers

Every competent reader converts the letters into sounds to identify the words. But good readers do more; they interpret the meaning of each sentence and each paragraph.

One major key to good reading is to determine the meaning of an ambiguous word. For example, the word *dove* could refer to a bird in the pigeon family, or it could be the past tense of the verb *to dive*. When people come across that word in their reading, it initially activates both meanings, but a good reader suppresses the meaning that does not fit the context. In one experiment, college students read sentences; about 1 second after each sentence they saw another word and they were asked whether that word was related to the meaning of the sentence. Sometimes the task was easy:

Sentence	Test Word	Related?
She dropped the plate.	Break.	yes
He dug with the shovel.	Ace.	no

In cases such as these, good readers and poor readers performed about equally well. But sometimes the test word was related to an irrelevant meaning of one word in the sentence:

Sentence	Test Word	Related?
He dug with the spade.	Ace.	no

In a case such as this, good readers responded "no" very promptly after seeing the word *ace*, but poor readers responded slowly and sometimes inaccurately (Gernsbacher & Faust, 1991). Evidently, good readers suppressed the irrelevant meaning of *spade* as a playing card, while the poor readers suppressed it more slowly or less completely.

Another characterisic of good readers is that they monitor their own reading comprehension; that is, they keep track of whether or not they understand what they are reading. Occasionally in reading, you come across a sentence that is complicated, confusing, or just badly written. Here is an example from the student newspaper at North Carolina State University:

> He said Harris told him she and Brothers told French that grades had been changed.

What do you do when you come across a sentence like that? If you are monitoring your own understanding, you notice that you are confused. Good readers generally read fairly quickly, but when they come to something confusing they stop and reread the confusing sentence or, if necessary, the whole paragraph. Poor readers tend to read at their same speed for both easy and difficult materials; they are less likely than good readers to slow down when they come to difficult sentences.

The same is true for whole sections of a book. You should read quickly when you understand a section well but should slow down when the text is more complicated. To do so, you have to monitor your own understanding. Above-average students can generally identify which sections they understand best; they single out the sections they need to reread. Below-average students have more trouble picking out which sections they understand well and which ones they understand poorly (Maki & Berry, 1984).

Actually, most people—including bright college students who get good grades—could improve their comprehension through better self-monitoring (Glenberg, Sanocki, Epstein, & Morris, 1987; Zabrucky, Moore, & Schultz, 1987). Many educators recommend that you pause at regular intervals to check your understanding. The Concept Checks in this text are intended to encourage you to do so.

A self-monitoring system you can use with any text is the SPAR method: Survey, Process meaningfully, Ask questions, and Review and test yourself. Start with an overview of what a passage is about, read it carefully, and then see whether you can answer questions about the passage or explain it to others. If not, go back and reread.

SUMMARY

■ *Language in animals.* The ability to acquire language evolved from precursors present in our ancestors and still detectable in other species. Certain species, such as the bonobo, have made striking progress in language use, although their exact potential is still uncertain. (page 392)

■ *Thought and language.* People are capable of expressing an enormous number of ideas in words, linking them in creative ways. Understanding what others say requires a great deal of factual knowledge as well as an understanding of the language. (page 397)

■ *Whorf hypothesis.* According to the Whorf hypothesis, our language influences how we think.

Good evidence to support this theory is hard to find, although the effects of gender-related words may be one example. (page 398)

■ *Ambiguity.* We hear a word as a whole, not as a sequence of parts. We can change how we hear an ambiguous word, depending on approximately the next three syllables. (page 400)

■ *Reading.* When we read, we have fixation periods separated by eye movements called saccades. Even good readers can read only about 11 letters per fixation. (page 401)

■ *Word-superiority effect.* Good readers can identify a letter faster and more accurately when they see it as part of a word than when they see it by itself. (page 403)

■ *Converting words into sound.* The evidence indicates that when we read we convert the written words into sound in order to understand them. (page 405)

■ *Good readers.* Good readers suppress the irrelevant meanings of ambiguous words; they also monitor their own understanding, pausing to reread the parts they did not understand well. (page 407)

SUGGESTIONS FOR FURTHER READING

Adams, M. J. (1990). *Beginning to read.* Cambridge, MA: MIT Press. Excellent review of research on how people read.

Just, M. A., and Carpenter, P. A. (1987). *The psychology of reading and language comprehension.* Boston: Allyn and Bacon. Discussion of many aspects of language use and comprehension, with an emphasis on computer modeling of language.

TERMS

Whorf hypothesis hypothesis that our language determines the way we think (page 398)

saccade a quick jump in the focus of the eyes from one point to another (page 402)

word-superiority effect greater ease of identifying a letter when it is part of a whole word than when it is presented by itself (page 404)

connectionist model theory that our perceptions and memories are represented by vast numbers of connections among "units," each of them connected to other units (page 404)

phoneme a unit of sound (page 405)

morpheme a unit of meaning (page 405)

Stroop effect the difficulty of naming the colors in which words are written instead of reading the words themselves (page 406)

ANSWERS TO CONCEPT CHECKS

7. Start language learning when a child is young. Rely on imitation as much as possible instead of providing direct reinforcements for correct responses. (page 396)

8. Two or three short words can fall within the "window" of about 11 letters that we can fixate on the fovea at one time. If the words are longer, it may be impossible to get them all onto the fovea at once. (page 408)

9. Probably, but not always. Suppose your eyes fixate on the fourth letter of *memorization*. You should be able to see the three letters to its left and the seven to its right—in other words, all except the final letter. Because there is only one English word of the form *memorizatio-*, you have enough information to recognize the word. (page 402)

10. *Thoughtfully* has seven phonemes: th-ough-t-f-u-ll-y. (A phoneme is a unit of sound, not necessarily a letter of the alphabet.) It has three morphemes: thought-ful-ly. (Each morpheme has a distinct meaning.) (page 405)

ANSWER TO OTHER QUESTION IN THE TEXT

H. It's the alphabet: a, b, c, d, . . . (page 405)

10 INTELLIGENCE AND ITS MEASUREMENT

The famous mathematician Alan Turing bicycled to and from work each day. Occasionally the chain fell off his bicycle and he had to replace it. Eventually, Turing began keeping records and noticed that the chain fell off at mathematically regular intervals. In fact, it fell off after exactly a certain number of turns of the front wheel. Turing then calculated that this number was an even multiple of the number of spokes in the front wheel, the number of links in the chain, and the number of cogs in the pedal. From these data he deduced that the chain came loose whenever a particular link in the chain came in contact with a particular bent spoke on the wheel. He identified that spoke, repaired it, and never again had trouble with the chain (Stewart, 1987).

Turing's solution to his problem qualifies as highly intelligent, according to what we usually mean by *intelligent*. But hold your applause. Your local bicycle mechanic could have solved the problem in just a few minutes, without using any mathematics at all.

So, you might ask, what's my point? Is it that Turing was unintelligent? Not at all. He was highly intelligent, and if you have some new, complicated, unfamiliar problem to solve, you probably should take it to someone like Turing, not to your favorite bicycle mechanic.

My point is that intelligence is a combination of general abilities and practiced skills. The term *intelligence* can refer to the highly practiced skills shown by a good bicycle mechanic, a Micronesian sailor, a hunter-gatherer of the Serengeti plains, or any other person with extensive experience and special expertise in a particular area. *Intelligence* can also refer to the generalized problem-solving ability that Turing displayed—the kind of ability that can compensate for a lack of experience. But even that ability develops gradually, reflecting contributions of many kinds of experience.

Micronesian sailors navigate accurately among distant locations, relying on landmarks and the position of the sun and the stars. This highly developed skill is one kind of intelligent behavior.

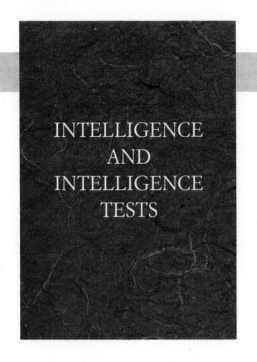

INTELLIGENCE AND INTELLIGENCE TESTS

What is intelligence?
What is the purpose of IQ tests?
What do the scores on IQ tests mean?

Intelligence testing has a long history of controversy, partly because of misconceptions about its purpose. Consider this analogy:

You and I have just been put in charge of choosing members of the next U.S. Olympic team. To choose the best-qualified people, we decide to hold tryouts in basketball, gymnastics, high jumping, and all the other events. Suddenly the Olympic rules are changed: Each country can send only 30 men and 30 women, and each athlete must compete in every event. Furthermore, the competitive events will be new ones, not exactly like any of the familiar events, and the Olympic Committee will not publish the rules for any of the new events until all of our athletes have arrived at the Olympic site. Clearly, we cannot hold regular tryouts. How shall we choose the team?

Our best bet would be to devise a test of "general athletic ability." We would measure the abilities of all the applicants to run, jump, change direction, maintain balance, throw and catch, kick, lift weights, respond rapidly to signals, and perform other athletic feats. Then we would choose the applicants who had the best scores.

That might not be the best possible test, and we would no doubt make some mistakes in our selection of athletes. But if we must choose 60 athletes, and if we want to maximize their chances of winning, we certainly have to use some sort of test. So we go ahead with our Test of General Athletic Ability.

As time passes, other people begin to use our test. It becomes well accepted and widely used. Does its acceptance imply that athletic ability is a single quantity, like speed or weight? No. When we devised the test, it merely suited our purposes to combine various scores of skills as if athletic ability were a single quantity, even though we knew it was not. (Some athletes are good at one sport but not at others.)

WHAT IS INTELLIGENCE?

Intelligence tests resemble our imaginary test of athletic ability. If we have to choose from among applicants to a school or college, we want to select those who will profit most from the experience. Because students may be studying subjects that they have never studied before, we want to measure their general ability to profit from education rather than any specific knowledge or specialized ability. By the same token, if we want to identify children who belong in a special education program for retarded children, we need to measure their general ability to handle schoolwork.

Intelligence tests were developed for the practical function of selecting students for special classes. They were not based on any theory of intelligence, and those who administer them are usually content to define *intelligence* as the ability to do well in school. Given that definition, IQ tests do measure intelligence.

For theoretical purposes, however, that definition is far from satisfactory. But what would be a better definition? Here are some of the ways that psychologists have defined *intelligence* (Wolman, 1989):

- The ability to cope with the environment through learning

- The ability to judge, comprehend, and reason

- The ability to understand and deal with people, objects, and symbols

413

a   **b**

FIGURE 10.1
In the two photos above, which person is the supervisor and which is the worker? Robert Sternberg has used these photos to evaluate people's "practical intelligence"—their ability to understand nonverbal cues.

- The ability to act purposefully, think rationally, and deal effectively with the environment.

Note that these definitions use such terms as *judge, comprehend, understand,* and *think rationally*—terms that are themselves only vaguely defined. One survey of over a thousand specialists in intelligence testing found that 53% believed that a consensus exists on what *intelligent* means (Snyderman & Rothman, 1987). (Think about that: A consensus is a general agreement. Here, a bare majority, just over 50%, says that a "general agreement" exists. How general can it be?)

Some psychologists contend that traditional definitions of intelligence have been too narrow, ignoring many important abilities. For example, Robert Sternberg (1985) and Richard Weinberg (1989), for example, include social and practical intelligence, that is, the ability to:

- Respond to facial cues and gestures that mean "I'd like to talk to you" or "Please don't bother me"

- Watch two people at work and figure out which one is the supervisor (Figure 10.1)

- Look at a couple and tell whether they have an ongoing relationship or whether they have just met

- Figure out what is most important for success on a job

Psychologists would like to organize this list of intelligent abilities more intelligently. Intelli-gence should not consist of a haphazard set of unrelated abilities; the list should have some structure or organization. Just as all the objects in the world are composed of compounds of 92 elements, most psychologists expect to find that all the kinds of intelligence are compounds of a few basic abilities. They have proposed several models of how intelligence is organized.

Spearman's Psychometric Approach and the *g* Factor

Charles Spearman (1904) took a **psychometric** approach to intelligence. Psychometric means the measurement (*metric*) of individual differences in behaviors and abilities. Spearman began by measuring how well a variety of people performed a variety of tasks, such as following complex directions, judging musical pitch, matching colors, and performing arithmetic calculations. He then found that their performance on each task correlated positively with their performance on all the other tasks. He deduced that all the tasks must have something in common. To perform well on any test of mental ability, Spearman argued, people need a certain "general" ability, which he called **g.** The *g* factor has to do with perceiving and manipulating relationships; it relates to abstract reasoning rather than to the recall of factual information.

To account for the fact that performance on various tasks does not correlate perfectly, Spearman suggested that each task requires the

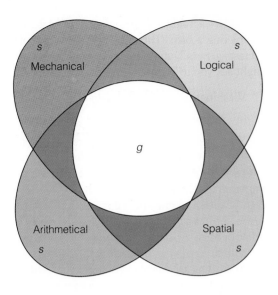

FIGURE 10.2
According to Spearman, all intelligent abilities have an area of overlap, which he called g (for "general"). Each ability also depends partly on an s (for "specific") factor.

use of a "specific" ability, **s,** in addition to the general ability, *g*, that all tasks require (Figure 10.2). Thus, intelligence consists of a general ability plus an unknown number of specific abilities, such as mechanical, musical, arithmetical, logical, and spatial. Spearman called his theory a "monarchic" theory of intelligence because it included a dominant ability, or monarch, which ruled over the lesser abilities.

Later, Spearman discovered that some of the specific abilities he had identified correlated fairly highly with one another. So he proposed that in addition to the general factor and the specific factors, intelligence included "group" factors that were broader than the specific factors, but not so broad as the *g* factor.

Most, but not all, investigators of intelligence have accepted the concept of a *g* factor. J. P. Guilford (1973), for example, has argued that people have many independent mental abilities that do not necessarily correlate significantly with one another.

Fluid Intelligence and Crystallized Intelligence

Raymond Cattell followed Spearman's psychometric approach but proposed an important modification of Spearman's concept of *g*. According to Cattell (1987), the *g* factor has two components: fluid intelligence and crystallized

intelligence. The analogy is to water: Fluid water can take any shape, whereas ice crystals are rigid. **Fluid intelligence** is the power of reasoning and using information. It includes the ability to perceive relationships, deal with unfamiliar problems, and gain new types of knowledge. **Crystallized intelligence** consists of acquired skills and knowledge and the application of that knowledge to specific content in a person's experience. Crystallized intelligence includes the skills of a good auto mechanic, salesperson, or accountant.

Fluid intelligence, according to Cattell and his colleagues, reaches its peak well before age 20; beyond that age it may either remain constant or begin to decline. Crystallized intelligence, on the other hand, continues to increase as long as a person remains active (Cattell, 1987; Horn & Donaldson, 1976). A 20-year-old may be more successful than a 65-year-old at solving some problem that is unfamiliar to both of them, but the 65-year-old will excel in solving problems in his or her area of specialization.

In some cases, people can solve a problem only by thinking about it in familiar terms— that is, by using crystallized intelligence. In one study, for example, workers at a dairy plant were relatively poor at solving such simple multiplication problems as 17 × 68. Those same workers, however, could quickly calculate the price of 17 quarts of milk at 68 cents a quart, without even using pencil and paper (Scribner, 1986).

While the distinction between crystallized intelligence and fluid intelligence is appealing, it is not always easy to apply in practice. We ordinarily rely on a combination of the two, though we may rely more on one than on the other.

■ CONCEPT CHECK

1. Was Alan Turing's solution to the slipping bicycle chain (at the start of this chapter) an example of fluid or crystallized intelligence? Is the solution provided by a bicycle mechanic an example of fluid or crystallized intelligence? (Check your answers on page 426.)

Sternberg's Triarchic Theory of Intelligence

Spearman and Cattell concluded that most of intelligence consists of one or two major abilities. That conclusion reflects to some extent their choice of what skills to test. To illustrate, let us return to the analogy of a test of general athletic ability: Suppose we developed an athletic test that included a 100-meter run, a 1,000-meter run, broad jump, high jump, and pole vault. We would quickly discover that performance on each item correlates positively with performance on each of the others, and we might conclude that all athletic skills reflect a "general athletic ability." But that conclusion would depend on the fact that all of our items had something to do with running. If we substituted weight lifting and archery for two of those items, we would find that the correlations among items were relatively low, and we would be less convinced of a general athletic ability.

Similarly, as Robert Sternberg (1991) and others have pointed out, psychologists find strong evidence for a *g* factor in intelligence because their intelligence tests focus on overlapping skills. If psychologists broadened the scope of intelligence tests to include some practical skills and creativity, they probably would find lower correlations between one part of the IQ test and another. In short, people may well have some "non-*g*" types of intelligence that the IQ tests ignore.

Sternberg has raised another criticism: Too many psychologists have been content to measure IQ and not sufficiently interested in the nature of the mental abilities that constitute intelligence. That is, when people do something intelligent, exactly what are they doing?

In contrast to Spearman's monarchic theory, Sternberg (1985) has proposed a "triarchic" theory of intelligence. As its name suggests, the **triarchic theory** posits that intelligence is governed by three types of process, which he refers to as metacomponents, knowledge-acquisition components, and performance components.

Metacomponents are the mental abilities we use in planning an approach to a problem. When you encounter an unfamiliar question, you map out a strategy for analyzing the question, assembling relevant information, and testing possible solutions to the problem.

Knowledge-acquisition components are the mental abilities we use in gaining new knowledge. Learning is a more active process than simply memorizing what someone else tells you; you gain knowledge (or *should* gain knowledge) by various activities you initiate. For example, you learn how to operate a new computer by reading sections of the manual, trying out your understanding on the computer, then returning to the manual.

Performance components are the mental

abilities we actually use in solving a problem or completing a task. These are the abilities that IQ tests generally measure. For example, a test might ask you to complete an analogy, such as

Washington is to 1 as Lincoln is to:

(a) 5,   (b) 10,   (c) 20,   (d) 50.

Your performance components take you through several steps, as you try to find a way to interpret the question that will lead to one of the four available answers. Ultimately you decide that the question must be talking about George Washington and the $1 bill and that the answer is (a), because Abraham Lincoln's picture is on the $5 bill.

According to Sternberg, intelligent behavior depends on all three kinds of components—metacomponents, knowledge-acquisition components, and performance components. Furthermore, psychologists should work to identify the ways in which we use the three kinds of components. Sternberg (1985) himself has conducted experiments to determine what components are required for solving various problems and to describe some of the differences among the three types of components.

Gardner's Theory of Multiple Intelligences

Whereas Sternberg has criticized most intelligence tests for being too narrow, Howard Gardner (1985) has pushed that criticism further, claiming that people have **multiple intelligences**—numerous unrelated forms of intelligence. Gardner defines intelligence as the ability to do something that other people value within one's culture. Given that definition, intelligence is not a single process, and various types of intelligence may not even be related to one another. Gardner distinguishes language abilities, musical abilities, logical and mathematical reasoning, spatial reasoning, body movement skills, and social sensitivity. He points out that people may be outstanding in one type of intelligence but not in others. For example, a *savant* (literally, "learned one") is a person who has an outstanding ability in one area such as music or calendar calculations but poor abilities in other areas. (The movie *Rain Man* depicted one such person.)

Gardner certainly makes an important point: People do have a variety of socially valued abilities, and most of us are very strong on one or more of these abilities and weak on others. Whether or not we want to call all of these

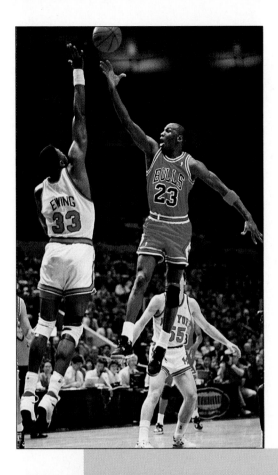

According to Howard Gardner, we have not one intelligence but many intelligences, including mathematics, artistic skill, muscle skills, and musical abilities.

abilities "intelligences" is a matter of personal preference. However, many of the skills Gardner discusses are difficult to measure, and so far his approach has not led to any new method of testing intelligence. Table 10.1 summarizes these four theories of intelligence.

Theories of Intelligence and Tests of Intelligence

The standard IQ tests, which we shall consider momentarily, were devised decades ago, before most of the discoveries about memory and cog-

Table 10.1 Four Theories of Intelligence

Theory	Principal Theorist	Key Ideas and Terms	Examples
Psychometric approach	Charles Spearman (1904)	g factor: general abstract reasoning ability common to various tasks	Perceiving and manipulating relationships
		s factor: specific ability required for a given task	Mechanical, verbal, spatial abilities
Fluid and crystallized intelligence	Raymond Cattell (1987)	Divides Spearman's g factor into two components:	
		1. Fluid intelligence (reasoning and using information; peaks before age 20)	Fluid: finding a solution to an unfamiliar problem
		2. Crystallized intelligence (acquired skills and knowledge; keeps growing as long as you live)	Crystallized: knowing how to play the piano, build a cabinet, write a novel, calculate the price of 17 quarts of milk
Triarchic theory	Robert Sternberg (1985, 1991)	Criticizes Spearman's and Cattell's theories for ignoring important non-g types of intelligence	
		Says intelligent behavior depends on three types of processes:	
		1. Metacomponents (abilities used to approach a problem)	Deciding what steps to take and in which order to design a new factory
		2. Knowledge-acquisition components (abilities used to gain new knowledge)	Collecting information on factory design from books and experts in the field
		3. Performance components (abilities used to actually solve a problem or complete a task)	Actually designing the factory, after planning the procedure and collecting the information
Multiple intelligences	Howard Gardner (1985)	People have numerous unrelated forms of intelligence	Music, social sensitivity, math
		Intelligence is defined as the ability to do something that other people value within your culture	Fill a tooth, sell Chryslers, dance

nition that we discussed in the last two chapters. Today we have several theories about intelligence, such as Sternberg's triarchic theory, and a variety of intelligence tests, but little relationship between the theories and the tests.

Can we measure something—in this case intelligence—without our fundamentally understanding what it is? Possibly so, even though the idea may seem preposterous. Physicists measured gravity and magnetism long before they had any sophisticated understanding of these forces. Maybe psychologists can do the same with intelligence.

But then again, maybe not. The fact that physicists successfully measured gravity and magnetism without understanding them is no guarantee that all measurements of poorly understood phenomena will turn out to be valid.

Many psychologists are dissatisfied with the currently available intelligence tests, and some are working in hopes of eventually producing a fundamentally better test. In the meantime, the currently available tests have serious strengths as well as weaknesses. Let us examine some of those tests.

IQ TESTS

Regardless of whether we are trying to identify the best students or the worst, we should base our judgments on accurate, objective, fair information. We look at the students' grades and the recommendations of their teachers, even though we know that such evidence can be inaccurate and unfair. (Some schools are better than others; some teachers grade harder than others.) We also look at students' scores on standardized tests.

Intelligence quotient (IQ) tests attempt to measure an individual's probable performance in school and similar settings. (The term *quotient* dates from the time when IQ was determined by dividing *mental age* by *chronological age*. That method is now obsolete, but the term remains.) The first IQ tests were devised for a practical purpose by two French psychologists, Alfred Binet and Theophile Simon (1905). The French Ministry of Public Instruction wanted a fair way to identify children who had such serious intellectual deficiencies that they could not succeed in the public school system of Paris. Those children were to be put into special classes for the retarded. Formerly, the task of identifying retarded children had been left entirely to medical doctors. But different doctors had different standards for judging retardation, and there was no way to resolve their disagreements. An equitable, impartial test of some sort was needed. Binet and Simon produced a test to measure the skills that children need for success in school, such as understanding and using language, computational skills, memory, and the ability to follow instructions.

Such a test can make useful predictions. It can tell us that Susie is likely to do well in school but that Nancy is not. But suppose Susie does well and Nancy does poorly. Can we say that Susie does better in school *because* she has a higher IQ score?

No. Consider this analogy: Suppose we ask why a certain baseball player strikes out so often. Someone answers, "Because he has a low batting average." Clearly, that explains nothing. (The reason for the low batting average is that he strikes out so often.) Similarly, saying that a student does poorly in school because he or she does poorly on an IQ test isn't much of an explanation; after all, the IQ test was designed to measure the very skills schoolwork requires. *An IQ score is like any other score: It measures current performance. A test measures differences among people; it does not explain the differences.*

IQ tests have gained a special mystique in our society. Many schools routinely administer IQ tests to all of their students, but few ever tell the students the results. Why not? School administrators say that they fear the students will compare scores with one another and that those who made lower scores will feel discouraged. Maybe so, but the main point of IQ tests is to predict how well students will perform in school, and schools always tell students their

grades. Students can compare grades and make one another feel just as bad as if they were comparing IQ scores. Perhaps the secrecy surrounding IQ scores makes them seem more important than they really are.

The Stanford-Binet Test

The test Binet and Simon designed was later modified for English speakers by Lewis Terman and other Stanford psychologists and published as the **Stanford-Binet IQ test**. This test is administered to individual students by someone who has been carefully trained in how to present each item and how to score each answer. It contains items that range in difficulty, as designated by age (see Table 10.2). An item designated as "age 8," for example, will be answered correctly by 60–90% of all 8-year-olds. (A higher percentage of older children will answer it correctly, as will a lower percentage of

Table 10.2 Examples of the Types of Items on the Stanford-Binet Test

Age	Sample Test Item
2	Test administrator points at pictures of everyday objects and asks, "What is this?" "Here are some pegs of different sizes and shapes. See whether you can put each one into the correct hole."
4	"Why do people live in houses?" "Birds fly in the air; fish swim in the _____."
6	"Here is a picture of a horse. Do you see what part of the horse is missing?" "Here are some candies. Can you count how many there are?"
8	"What should you do if you find a lost puppy?" "Stephanie can't write today because she twisted her ankle. What is wrong with that?"
10	"Why should people be quiet in a library?" "Repeat after me: 4 8 3 7 1 4."
12	"What does *regret* mean?" "Here is a picture. Can you tell me what is wrong with it?"
14	"What is the similarity between *high* and *low*?" "Watch me fold this paper and cut it. Now, when I unfold it, how many holes will there be?"
Adult	"Make up a sentence using the words *celebrate, reverse,* and *appointment.*" "What do people mean when they say, 'People who live in glass houses should not throw stones'?"

Source: Modified from Nietzel and Bernstein, 1987.

Table 10.3 Items from the Wechsler Intelligence Scale for Children (WISC)

Test	Example
Verbal Scale	
Information	From what animal do we get milk? (Either "cow" or "goat" is an acceptable answer.)
Similarities	How are a plum and a peach similar? (Correct answer: "They are both fruits." Half credit is given for "Both are food." or "Both are round.")
Arithmetic	Count these blocks: ■ ■ ■ ■ ■ ■ ■ ■
Vocabulary	Define the word *letter*.
Comprehension	What should you do if you see a train approaching a broken track? (A correct answer is "Stand safely out of the way and wave something to warn the train." Half credit is given for "Tell someone at the railroad station." *No* credit is given for "I would try to fix the track.")
Digit Span	Repeat these numbers after I say them: 3 6 2.
Performance Scale	
Picture completion	What parts are missing from this picture?
Picture arrangement	Here are some cards with a gardener on them. Can you put them in order?
Block design	See how I have arranged these four blocks? Here are four more blocks. Can you arrange your blocks like mine?
Object assembly	Can you put these five puzzle pieces together to make a dog?
Coding	Here is a page full of shapes. Put a slash (/) through all the circles and an × through all the squares.
Mazes	Here is a maze. Start with your pencil here and trace a path to the other end of the maze without crossing any lines.

Source: Based on Wechsler, 1949.

younger children.) Those who take the test are asked to answer only those items that are pegged at or near their level of functioning. For example, the psychologist testing an 8-year-old might start with the items designated for 6- or 7-year-olds. If the child missed many of them, the psychologist would go back to the items for 5-year-olds. But if the child answered all or nearly all of the 6- and 7-year-old items correctly, the psychologist would proceed to the items for 8-year-olds, 9-year-olds, and so forth. When the child begins to miss item after item, the test is over.

Ordinarily, the entire test lasts no more than an hour to an hour and a half. However, unlike most other IQ tests, the current edition of the Stanford-Binet imposes no time limit; people are allowed to think about each item as long as they wish (McCall, Yates, Hendricks, Turner, & McNabb, 1989).

Stanford-Binet IQ scores are computed from tables set up to ensure that a given IQ score will mean the same thing at different ages. A 6-year-old with an IQ score of, say, 116 has performed better on the test than 84% of other 6-year-olds. Similarly, an adult with an IQ score of 116 has performed better than 84% of other adults. The mean IQ at each age is 100. In addition to the overall IQ, the Stanford-Binet provides subscores reflecting verbal reasoning, quantitative reasoning, and abstract visual reasoning (McCall et al., 1989).

In Table 10.2 notice that the Stanford-Binet test includes questions designated for ages as low as 2 years. It is possible to make rough estimates of intelligence in infants as young as 6 months, mostly by determining whether they pay more attention to a changing visual stimulus than to a stimulus that remains constant (Bornstein & Sigman, 1986; Rose & Wallace, 1985). Nevertheless, estimates of intelligence are relatively unstable for children under the age of 4 or 5. Before 4 or 5, scores are likely to fluctuate more widely than scores obtained at later ages (Honzik, 1974; Morrow & Morrow, 1974).

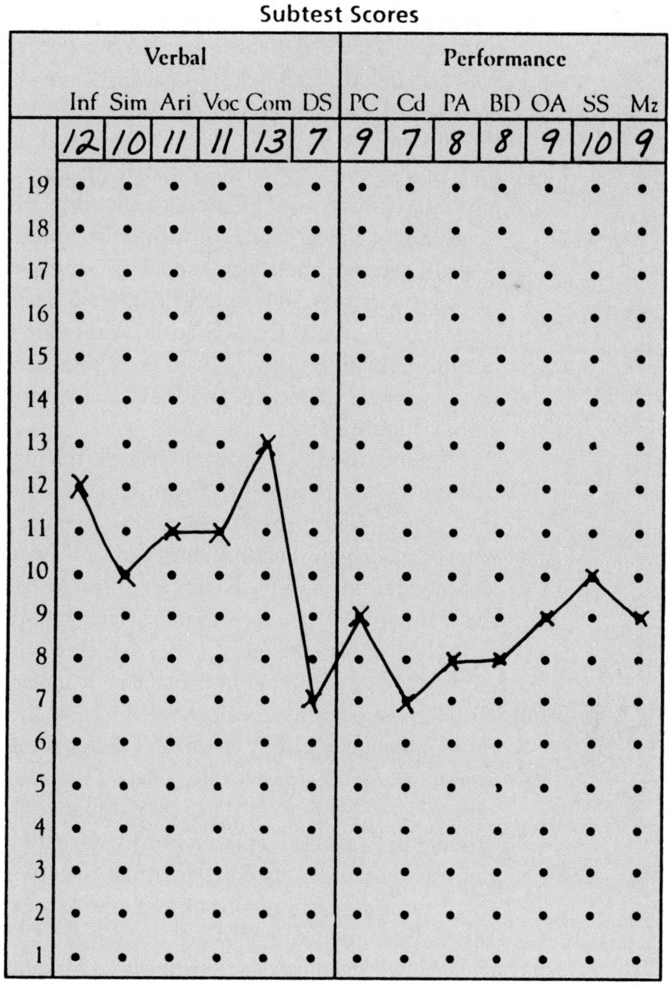

The Wechsler Tests

Two IQ tests devised by David Wechsler are now more commonly used than the Stanford-Binet. Known as the **Wechsler Adult Intelligence Scale–Revised (WAIS-R)** and the **Wechsler Intelligence Scale for Children–Third Edition (WISC-III)**, these tests produce the same average, 100, and almost the same distribution of scores as the Stanford-Binet pro-

FIGURE 10.3
A score profile for one child on the WISC-III IQ test. Each subtest score represents this child's performance on one type of task compared with other children of the same age. In addition to providing an overall IQ score, a profile such as this highlights an individual's strengths and weaknesses. Note this child's better performance on verbal tasks than on performance tasks. (Data courtesy of Patricia Collins)

duces. As with the Stanford-Binet, the Wechsler tests are administered to one individual at a time. The main advantage of the Wechsler tests is that in addition to an overall score, they provide scores in two major categories (verbal and performance), each of which is divided into component abilities. (Table 10.3 shows examples of test items, and Figure 10.3 shows one individual's test profile.) Thus, the Wechsler tests may indicate the individual's pattern of strengths and weaknesses. For example, Navajo children whose families speak Navajo as well as

English generally get higher scores on the performance scales than they do on the verbal scales (Naglieri, 1984).

Each of the 12 parts of the WISC-III and the WAIS-R begins with very simple questions that almost everyone answers correctly; each part then progresses to increasingly difficult items. Six of the 12 parts constitute the Verbal Scale of the test; these parts require the use of spoken or written language. The other 6 parts constitute the Performance Scale. Although a person must know English well enough to understand the instructions, the answers are nonverbal (Figure 10.4).

The inclusion of questions that ask for factual information (such as "From what animal do we get milk?") has caused much controversy. Critics complain that such items measure knowledge, not ability. Defenders reply, first, that "intelligent" people tend to learn more facts than others do, even if they have had no more exposure to the information. Furthermore, as we saw in Chapter 9, expertise and problem-solving ability require a substantial amount of factual knowledge. Finally, the purpose of the test is to predict performance in school, and in that respect it works. Granted, the test measures current performance rather than raw ability. But no one knows how to measure ability independent of performance.

We will examine such criticisms of intelligence tests in greater depth in the second module of this chapter.

FIGURE 10.4
Much of the WAIS-R involves nonverbal tests in which a person is asked to perform certain tasks. Here, to evaluate visual-spatial organization, a woman arranges colored blocks according to a specified pattern while a psychologist times her.

Raven's Progressive Matrices

The Stanford-Binet and Wechsler tests, though useful for many purposes, have certain limitations. First, they call for specific information that may be much more familiar to some people than to others. Second, because they require comprehension and use of the English language, they are unfair to people who do not speak English well, including immigrants and hearing-impaired people. "Why not simply translate them into other languages?" you might ask. The situation is not that simple. For example, one part of the Stanford-Binet gives people certain words and asks for words that rhyme with them. Generating rhymes is fairly easy in English, extremely easy in Italian, and virtually impossible in Zulu (Smith, 1974).

To overcome such problems, psychologists have tried to devise a culture-fair or a culture-reduced test that would make minimal use of language and would not ask for any specific facts. One example of a culture-reduced test is

the **Progressive Matrices** test devised by John C. Raven. Figure 10.5 presents matrices of the type this test uses. These matrices, which "progress" gradually from easy items to difficult items, attempt to measure "abstract reasoning"; to answer them, a person must generate hypotheses, test them, and infer rules (Carpenter, Just, & Shell, 1990).

The Progressive Matrices test calls for no verbal responses and no specific information. The instructions are simple enough to be explained to a person who does not speak English or to a preschool child. Spanish-speaking immigrants to the United States score about the same, on the average, as the rest of the U.S. population (Powers, Barkan, & Jones, 1986) on this test; deaf people perform about as well as hearing people (Vernon, 1967). The Progressive Matrices test cannot be used with blind people.

How "culture fair" is the Progressive Matrices test? Certainly, it is fairer than the Wech-

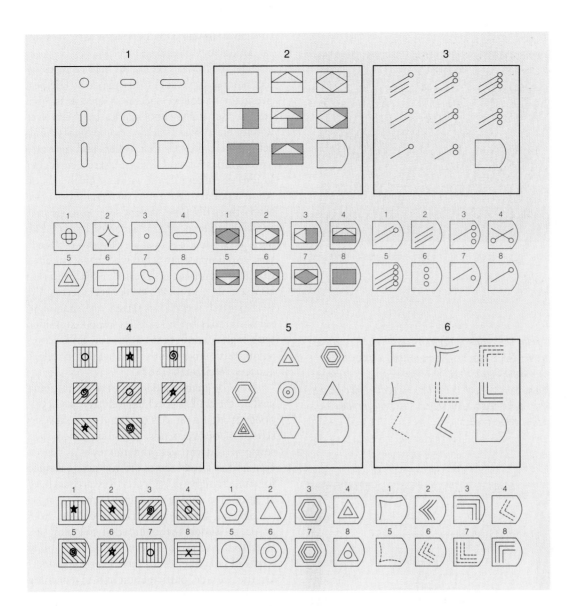

FIGURE 10.5
Items similar to those in Raven's Progressive Matrices test. The instructions are: "Each pattern has a piece missing. From the eight choices provided, select the one that completes the pattern, both going across and going down." (You can check your answers against answer A, page 426.)

sler or Stanford-Binet test is for most non-English-speaking people. But the Progressive Matrices test does assume that the test-taker is at least familiar with pencil-and-paper tests and with the idea of looking for visual patterns. A person from a nontechnological society may be quite baffled by the Progressive Matrices.

For disadvantaged subcultures within the United States, the Progressive Matrices test offers no clear advantage. On the average, African Americans and European Americans differ just as much on the Progressive Matrices as they do on the Wechsler and Stanford-Binet tests. In fact, the Progressive Matrices test has one possible disadvantage (Sternberg, 1991): By reporting only a single overall score, the test fails to show an individual's areas of strength and weakness, as the other IQ tests do.

The Scholastic Aptitude Test

Although most people do not regard the **Scholastic Aptitude Test (SAT)** as an intelligence test, it serves the same function: It predicts performance in college. (Figure 10.6 shows the relationship between SAT scores and grade-point average during the freshman year in college at one university.) Administered to large groups of students at one time, the SAT consists of multiple-choice items divided into two sets, verbal and quantitative. Each set is scored on a scale from 200 to 800. The designers of the test intended that the mean score would be 500 on each scale. Now that a higher percentage of high-school students take the test, the mean score is actually about 450. Figure 10.7 presents examples of the types of items found on the SAT. As a college student, you are

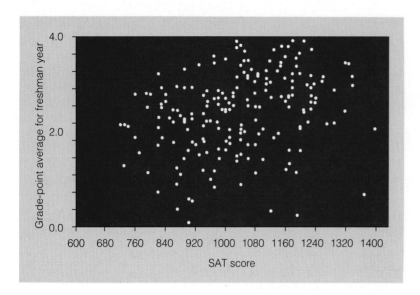

FIGURE 10.6

In this scatterplot, each point represents one freshman student at a particular state university. That student's SAT score is given on the x-axis; his or her grade-point average on the y-axis. Note that SAT scores predict college grades moderately well, with a correlation of .3 for this sample. Note also a number of exceptions—students with high SAT scores but poor grades and students with low SAT scores but good grades.

FIGURE 10.7

These two sample items from the Scholastic Aptitude Test reflect its two parts, which measure mathematical and verbal skills. (From the College Entrance Examination Board and the Educational Testing Service.)

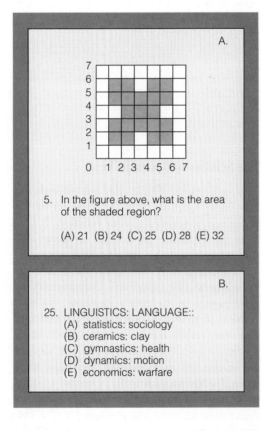

probably familiar with the SAT or with the similar American College Test (ACT).

The SAT was designed to help colleges select among applicants for admission. The best predictor of college success is success in high school. But high-school grades by themselves are not entirely satisfactory. Some high schools set higher standards than others and may give lower grades for work that would receive higher grades elsewhere. Even within a given school, some students take more challenging courses than others do. One student's B− average may indicate higher academic accomplishment than another student's A average. The SAT offers a way to compare students who have attended different high schools and taken different courses. As a predictor of college success, the SAT by itself is even less satisfactory than high-school grades by themselves. When combined with high-school grades, however, SAT scores significantly improve the prediction of college success (Weitzman, 1982).

Because many students worry about doing well on the SAT, a coaching industry has developed. Students can pay to attend sessions after school or on weekends. If you attended such sessions, did you get your money's worth? If you did not attend them, did you miss a chance for a much higher SAT score? Researchers have attempted to answer these questions.

Several studies have compared the SAT scores of students who attended coaching sessions to the scores of students of similar ability who did not. The results have been consistent: On the average, participation in SAT-coaching sessions raises a student's score by about 10 to 20 points (on a scale from 200 to 800). Students who attend longer, more intensive coaching sessions score only slightly higher than those who attend briefer sessions. To improve scores by more than about 30 points, a student has to spend almost as much time in the coaching sessions as in school (Kulik, Bangert-Drowns, & Kulik, 1984; Messick & Jungeblut, 1981).

Testing Aptitude Versus Testing Achievement

The SAT and IQ tests are considered aptitude or ability tests. (Note the term *aptitude* in Scholastic Aptitude Test.) Psychologists and educators distinguish aptitude tests from *achievement* tests, which are intended to measure the skills or knowledge someone has gained in a particular area of study. For example, the tests you take in your college courses are considered achievement tests.

In fact, however, the two kinds of tests overlap and no one can test aptitude or achievement separately from the other. People with good reasoning ability have an advantage on any achievement test, and those people who have achieved a great deal of knowledge can use it on supposed tests of reasoning ability.

Here is a demonstration of the difficulty of measuring aptitude separately from knowledge: The SAT includes many reading passages, each followed by a set of questions concerning the reading. Supposedly, these items measure the students' ability to draw conclusions from what they just read. However, one study found that college students could answer almost half the questions correctly even *without* reading the passages (Katz, Lautenschlager, Blackburn, & Harris, 1990). That is, they could call upon their knowledge of related material to choose the most likely answers. These items were supposed to measure how well students could learn from their readings, but they in fact measured (in part) how much the students already knew.

The point to remember is this: *No test measures pure ability, and perhaps no test ever will. Every test necessarily measures some complex mixture of abilities and knowledge.*

Tests of the Future

The standard IQ tests and the SAT have lasted for decades, despite persistent criticisms, with relatively minor revisions. The format of these tests may change in the future; for example, before long people may be reading the questions on a computer screen and typing their answers on a keyboard. But that change does not alter the fundamental nature of the test.

Some psychologists hope to develop new IQ tests that differ from the current tests in more fundamental ways—perhaps tests that focus less on knowledge and more on ability to learn or tests that cover a wider range of abilities (Sternberg, 1991). But producing a significantly improved IQ test is not as easy as it may sound. A test that measures ability to learn or one that covers a wide range of abilities is likely to require a great deal of the test-taker's time. And some skills are more difficult than others to measure.

In the next module of this chapter we shall consider the ways in which psychologists evaluate tests, including the currently available IQ tests and any new tests that might be proposed to take their place. Psychologists have worked out some clear criteria for evaluating tests and deciding which tests are better than others.

At this point let us simply stress that the value of an IQ test, like that of any tool, depends on how it is used. A hammer can be used to build a door or to break one down; similarly, a test score can be used to open the doors of opportunity or to close them. A test score, if cautiously interpreted, can aid schools in making placement decisions. If it is treated as an infallible guide, it can be seriously misleading.

SUMMARY

- *Defining intelligence.* The designers of the standard IQ tests defined intelligence simply as the ability to do well in school. Psychologists with a more theoretical interest have defined intelligence by listing the abilities it includes. (page 413)

- *g factor.* A number of "intelligent" abilities apparently share a common element, known as the *g* factor, which is closely related to abstract reasoning and the perception of relationships. However, people may have other intelligent abilities that relate less closely to *g*. (page 414)

- *Fluid and crystallized intelligence.* Psychologists distinguish between fluid intelligence (a basic reasoning ability that a person can apply to any problem, including unfamiliar types) and crystallized intelligence (acquired abilities to solve familiar types of problems). (page 415)

- *Abilities that make up intelligence.* Different psychologists have drawn up different lists of the abilities that make up intelligence. Some define intelligence fairly narrowly; others include such abilities as social attentiveness, musical abilities, and motor skills. (page 415)

- *Triarchic theory.* According to the triarchic theory of intelligence, intelligence has three types of components: metacomponents (which guide the planning of an approach to a problem), knowledge-acquisition components (which guide the acquisition of new knowledge), and performance components (which guide the actual solving of a problem). (page 415)

- *Multiple-intelligences theory.* According to the multiple intelligences view, people possess many types of intelligence that are independent of one another. (page 416)

- *IQ tests.* The Stanford-Binet and other IQ tests were devised to predict the level of performance in school. (page 418)

- *Wechsler IQ tests.* The Wechsler IQ tests measure 12 separate abilities, grouped into a Verbal Scale of six parts and a Performance Scale of six parts. (page 421)

- *Culture-reduced tests.* Culture-reduced tests such as Raven's Progressive Matrices can be used with people who are unfamiliar with English. (page 422)

- *SAT.* The Scholastic Aptitude Test is similar to IQ tests because it predicts performance in school, specifically in college. (page 423)

SUGGESTIONS FOR FURTHER READING

Ceci, S. J. (1990). *On intelligence . . . more or less.* Englewood Cliffs, NJ: Prentice-Hall. Perceptive critique of traditional assumptions about intelligence.

Sternberg, R. J. (Ed.). (1982). *Beyond IQ.* Cambridge, England: Cambridge University. An influential effort to describe the mental abilities that constitute intelligence, urging a broader, more inclusive concept of intelligence.

TERMS

psychometric the measurement of individual differences in abilities and behaviors (page 414)

g Spearman's "general" factor that all IQ tests and all parts of an IQ test are believed to have in common (page 414)

s a "specific" factor that is more important for performance on some scales of an intelligence test than it is on others (page 415)

fluid intelligence the basic power of reasoning and using information, including the ability to perceive relationships, deal with unfamiliar problems, and gain new types of knowledge (page 415)

crystallized intelligence acquired skills and knowledge and the application of that knowledge to specific content in a person's experience (page 415)

triarchic theory Sternberg's theory that intelligence is governed by three types of processes, which he refers to as metacomponents, performance components, and knowledge-acquisition components (page 416)

multiple intelligences Gardner's theory that intelligence is composed of numerous unrelated forms of intelligent behavior (page 416)

intelligence quotient (IQ) a measure of an individual's probable performance in school and in similar settings (page 419)

Stanford-Binet IQ test a test of intelligence, the first important IQ test in the English language (page 419)

Wechsler Adult Intelligence Scale–Revised (WAIS-R) an IQ test originally devised by David Wechsler, commonly used with adults (page 421)

Wechsler Intelligence Scale for Children–Third Edition (WISC-III) an IQ test originally devised by David Wechsler, commonly used with children (page 421)

Progressive Matrices an IQ test that attempts to measure abstract reasoning without use of language or recall of facts (page 422)

Scholastic Aptitude Test (SAT) a test of students' likelihood of performing well in college (page 423)

ANSWER TO CONCEPT CHECK

1. Turing's solution reflected fluid intelligence, a generalized ability that he could apply to any topic. The solution provided by a bicycle mechanic reflects crystallized intelligence, ability developed in a particular area of experience. (page 415)

ANSWERS TO OTHER QUESTIONS IN THE TEXT

A. (page 423)

1. (8)

2. (6)

3. (3)

4. (4)

5. (6)

6. (2)

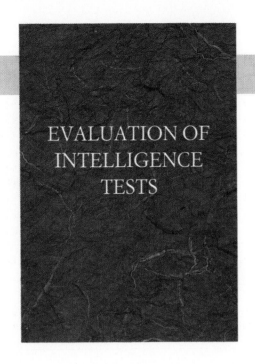

EVALUATION OF INTELLIGENCE TESTS

What do the scores on IQ tests mean?
Are variations in intelligence between groups of people the result of differences in genes?

Edward Thorndike, a pioneer in the study of both animal and human learning, is often quoted as saying, "If something exists, it exists in some amount. If it exists in some amount, it can be measured." Douglas Detterman (1979) countered, "Anything which exists can be measured incorrectly."

We can apply both of these quotes to intelligence: If intelligence exists at all, it can be measured. But it can also be measured incorrectly. One of the major tasks for researchers in this field is to test the tests—to determine whether the tests measure what their designers claim they measure, whether they measure it accurately, and whether they apply fairly to all groups. This is an area of heated arguments, an area in which it is often difficult to separate science from politics and social beliefs.

THE STANDARDIZATION OF IQ TESTS

In order to specify what various scores mean, those who devise a test must *standardize* it. **Standardization** is the process of establishing rules for administering a test and for interpreting its scores. One of the main steps in stan-

dardization is to find the **norms**, which are descriptions of the frequencies at which particular scores occur.

Psychologists try to standardize a test on a large, representative population. For example, if a test is to be used with children throughout the United States and Canada, psychologists need to measure the norms for a large random or representative sample of U.S. and Canadian children, not just for children of one ethnic group or one geographic region.

The Distribution of IQ Scores

Binet, Wechsler, and the other pioneers who devised the first IQ tests chose items and arranged the scoring method to establish the mean score at 100 with a standard deviation of 15 for the Wechsler test as Figure 10.8 shows, and 16 for the Stanford-Binet. (The standard deviation, you may recall from Chapter 2, is a measure of the degree of variability of performance. If most scores are close to the mean, the standard deviation is small; if scores vary widely, the standard deviation is larger.)

In any normal distribution, 68% of all people are within one standard deviation above or below the mean; 96% are within two standard deviations. Someone with a score of 115 on the Wechsler test exceeds the scores of those people within one standard deviation from the mean, plus all of those more than one standard deviation below the mean—a total of 84% of all people, as shown in Figure 10.8. We say that such a person is "in the 84th percentile." Someone with an IQ score of 130 is in the 98th percentile, which means that his or her score is higher than the scores of 98% of others of the same age.

Psychologists sometimes refer to people more than two standard deviations above the mean as "gifted." That designation is arbitrary. There is not much difference between an allegedly "gifted" child with an IQ of 130 and an allegedly "nongifted" child with an IQ of 129.

Psychologists also classify people more than two standard deviations below the mean as "retarded." Many retarded children, especially those who are severely retarded, suffer from biological disorders, including chromosomal abnormalities and fetal alcohol syndrome (Zigler

FIGURE 10.8
The scores on an IQ test form an approximately bell-shaped curve. The curve shown here represents scores on the Wechsler IQ test, with a standard deviation of 15 (15 points above and below the mean, 100). The results on the Stanford-Binet test are very similar, except that the standard deviation is 16, so the spread is slightly wider.

IQ score	55	70	85	100	115	130	145
Standard deviations from the mean	−3	−2	−1	0	+1	+2	+3
Percent who exceed this score	99.9	98	84	50	16	2	0.1
Percent below this score (percentile)	1	2	16	50	84	98	99+

People with IQ scores at least two standard deviations below the mean are classed as "retarded." Many can be "mainstreamed" in regular classes; severely retarded children are taught in special classes.

& Hodapp, 1991). Since 1975, U.S. law has required schools to provide "free, appropriate" education to all retarded children. Those with severe retardation are placed in separate classes; those with milder problems are "mainstreamed" (placed in regular classes with some extra attention).

Restandardization of IQ Tests

Over the years, the standardization of any IQ test becomes obsolete. In 1920 a question that asked people to identify "Mars" was fairly difficult, because most people knew little about the planets. Today, in an era of space exploration, the same question is easy for most people. Periodically, the publishers of each IQ test update it, reword the questions, and change the scoring standards.

The result has been to make IQ tests harder. To keep the mean score at 100, items that were once considered difficult but that have since become easy have been replaced with more difficult items (Flynn, 1984, 1987). In other words, people are doing better and better at answering the questions that used to appear in IQ tests. Why? Psychologists are not certain. Evolution is not a plausible explanation for such a rapid change. The explanation may lie in improved education, in better health and nutrition, in exposure to a wider range of information via television, or in other changes in the environment.

EVALUATION OF TESTS

At some point in your academic career, you probably complained that a test was unfair.

You were sure you knew the important material, but the test concentrated on minor details or penalized you for not saying something in quite the right way. Your instructor may have replied that what you considered "minor" details were actually important or that the way you worded your answers suggested that you did not really understand the material. You and your instructor may not have come to any agreement on what was important and on how to determine whether the test measured it.

Similarly, many people complain that intelligence tests unfairly focus on various facts that are familiar to some test-takers and not to others. Much is at stake in this dispute; intelligence tests substantially influence the future of millions of people. Along with school grades, test scores help to determine which children will attend regular classes, which will be placed in special classes for slow learners, and which will attend courses designed for gifted students.

Psychologists try to avoid simply arguing about whether or not a test seems fair; they look at specific kinds of evidence to determine whether the test achieves what it is intended to achieve. The two basic ways of evaluating any test are to check its reliability and its validity.

Reliability

The **reliability** of a test is defined as the repeatability of its scores (Anastasi, 1988). A reliable test measures something consistently. To measure the reliability of a test, psychologists use a correlation coefficient. They may test the same people twice, either with the same test or with equivalent versions of it, and compare the two sets of scores. Or they may compare the scores on the first and second halves of the test or the scores on the test's odd-numbered and even-numbered items. If all the items measure approximately the same abilities, the scores on one set of items should be highly correlated with the scores on the other set of items. As with any other correlation coefficient, the reliability of a test can (theoretically) range from +1 to −1. In the real world, however, reliabilities are always positive. (A negative reliability would mean that people who do better than average the first time they take a test will do worse than average the next time. That simply never happens.) Figure 10.9 illustrates **test-retest reliability**.

If a test's reliability is perfect (+1), the person who scores the highest on the first test will also score highest on the retest, and the person

In some countries test scores can determine a student's future almost irrevocably. Students who perform well are almost assured of future success; those who perform poorly may have very limited opportunities.

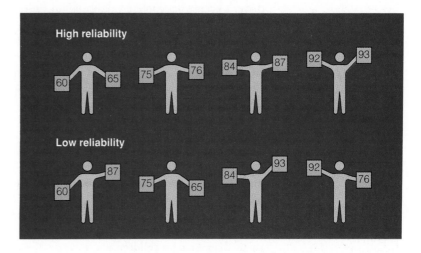

FIGURE 10.9

On a test with high reliability, people who score high one time will score high again when they take the test a second time. On a test with low reliability, scores fluctuate randomly.

who receives the 127th-best score will again make the 127th-best score. If the reliability is 0, a person's scores will vary randomly from one test to another. The reliability of the WISC-III has been measured at about .95; the reliabilities of the Stanford-Binet, Progressive Matrices, and SAT are also in the range of about .90 to .95 (Anastasi, 1988; Burke, 1985; Siegler & Richards, 1982). These figures indicate that the

IQ tests are measuring *something* in a consistent, repeatable manner. (They do not tell us what that something is.)

■ C O N C E P T C H E C K S

2. I have just devised a new "intelligence test." I measure your intelligence by dividing the length of your head by its width and then multiplying by 100. Would that be a reliable test?

3. Most students find that if they retake the SAT, their scores increase the second time. Does that improvement indicate that the test is unreliable? (Check your answers on page 440.)

Validity

A test's **validity** is a determination of how well it measures what it claims to measure. One type of validity is **content validity**. We say that a test has high content validity if its items accurately represent the information the test is meant to measure. For example, a licensing examination for psychologists would have high content validity if it tested all the major points a practicing psychologist is expected to know. A test for a driver's license has content validity if it includes all the important laws and regulations that pertain to driving.

A second type of validity is **construct validity**. A test has construct validity if what it measures corresponds to a theoretical construct. For example, intelligence is a theoretical construct. Psychologists expect it to have certain properties, such as increasing as a child grows older. They also expect it to include several component abilities, such as mathematics, memorization, and verbal reasoning. For an IQ test to have construct validity, it must reflect those properties. For example, older children should, as a rule, answer more questions correctly than younger children do.

Predictive validity, a third type of validity, is the ability of a test's scores to predict some real-world performance. For example, an interest test that accurately predicts what courses a student will like has predictive validity. Similarly, an IQ test that accurately predicts how well a student will perform in school has predictive validity.

As with reliability, psychologists measure predictive validity by means of a correlation coefficient. For example, to determine the predictive validity of an IQ test or of the SAT, psychologists determine how well those scores predict students' grades. A validity of +1 would

mean that the scores perfectly predicted performance; a validity of 0 would mean that the scores were worthless as predictors. The predictive validity of such tests as the WISC-III, Stanford-Binet, Progressive Matrices, and SAT generally ranges from about .3 to .6, varying from one school to another (Anastasi, 1988; Siegler & Richards, 1982). As these figures suggest, success in school depends on many factors, not just on the skills the tests measure.

IQ tests also have some validity for predicting success on a variety of jobs, especially for performance on entry-level jobs (Barrett & Depinet, 1991). That is true partly because people with higher IQ scores generally have more or better education than do people with lower IQ scores. How well IQ predicts job success *independently of education* is less clear. Also, IQ scores are doubtful predictors of the skills people will develop after extensive experience. Many experienced workers with mediocre test scores display impressively intelligent behaviors on their jobs (Ceci, 1990).

Sometimes the reported predictive validity of a test such as the SAT can be misleading. Consider some data for the Graduate Record Examination (GRE), a test similar to the SAT: For graduate students in physics, the verbal part of the GRE has higher predictive validity than does the quantitative (mathematical) part. For graduate students in English, the quantitative part has higher predictive validity than does the verbal part (Educational Testing Service, 1990). How can we explain these surprising results? Simply, graduate departments in physics select students largely on the basis of their quantitative scores, whereas English departments look mainly at the verbal scores. Consequently, almost all graduate students in physics have about the same (very high) score on the quantitative test, and almost all English graduate students have the same (very high) score on the verbal test. When almost all the students in a department have practically the same score, that score cannot predict which students will be more successful than others. *A test can have a high predictive validity only for a population whose scores vary over a substantial range.*

■ C O N C E P T C H E C K S

4. Can a test have high reliability and low validity? Can a test have low reliability and high validity?

5. If physics graduate departments tried admitting some students with low GRE quantitative scores and English departments tried admitting some students with low GRE verbal scores, what would happen to the predictive validity of those tests?

(Check your answers on page 441.)

Utility

In addition to reliability and validity, a good test should have utility. **Utility** is defined as usefulness for a practical purpose. Not every test that is reliable and valid is also useful. For example, a test of infant intelligence would be of interest to researchers, but it would have little practical usefulness. (Most IQ tests are used for placing students in special classes; infants are not ready for *any* classes.)

Some psychologists have questioned the utility of the SAT (for example, Gottfredson & Crouse, 1986). We can predict students' college grades moderately well by means of high-school grades alone. Adding SAT scores improves the prediction, but does it improve the prediction enough to be worth the cost, the time, and the anxiety? That is, even if the test has respectable reliability and validity, does it have enough utility to justify requiring it? Psychologists have different points of view on this question. Table 10.4 summarizes criteria for evaluating intelligence tests.

Interpreting Fluctuations in Scores

Suppose you make a score of 94% correct on the first test in your psychology course. On the second test (which was equally difficult), you make a score of 88%. Does that score indicate that you studied harder for the first test than for the second test? Not necessarily. Whenever you take tests that are not perfectly reliable, your scores are likely to fluctuate. The lower the reliability, the greater the fluctuation.

When people lose sight of that fact, they sometimes try to explain apparent fluctuations in performance that are really due to the unreliability of the test. In one well-known study, Harold M. Skeels (1966) identified a group of low-IQ infants in an orphanage and then placed them in an institution where they received more personal attention. Several years later, most of those infants showed great increases in their IQ scores. Should we conclude, as many psychologists did, that the extra attention improved the children's IQ performances? Not necessarily (Longstreth, 1981). IQ tests for infants have low reliabilities—in other words, the scores fluctuate widely from one time to another. If someone selects a group of infants with low IQ scores and retests them a few years later, the mean IQ score is almost certain to improve, simply because the early scores were poor estimates of the children's abilities. Or, to put it another way, the scores had nowhere to go but up.

Something to Think About

What would be the proper control group for the study by Skeels?

Table 10.4 Evaluating Intelligence Tests

Reliability	Validity	Utility	Bias
How consistent are the same person's scores?	How well does the test measure what it claims to measure?	How useful is the test for some practical purpose?	Do test scores make equally accurate predictions for all groups?
	Content—Do the test items represent the pertinent information?		
	Construct—Do the results match theoretical expectations?		
	Prediction—Do the test scores predict real-world performance?		

GROUP DIFFERENCES IN IQ SCORES

Binet and the other pioneers in IQ testing discovered that girls tend to do better than boys on language tasks, whereas boys tend to do better than girls on some visual-spatial and mathematical tasks. By loading the test with one type of item, they could have "demonstrated" that girls are smarter than boys or that boys are smarter than girls. Instead, they carefully balanced the two types of items to ensure that the mean score of both girls and boys would be 100.

Girls' mean performance continues to be better than boys' on certain verbal tasks, especially those that depend on speech fluency. In mathematics, girls perform better than boys on the average in elementary school, but boys perform somewhat better in high school and college. Over the second half of the 20th century, however, the differences between the sexes in both verbal and mathematical tasks have been gradually decreasing (Feingold, 1988; Hyde, Fennema, & Lamon, 1990). (Why they are decreasing is unknown, as is the reason for their existence in the first place.)

Even the reported sex differences may be exaggerations, because of the problem of **selective reporting**—the fact that investigators are more likely to publish findings when they match predictions than when they do not. For example, what would you do if you conducted a study of spatial ability and found no difference between males and females? If you had expected to find males performing better than females, you might doubt your own results and decline to publish them. Someone else who found the expected difference between males and females might be more likely to submit the results for publication (Fausto-Sterling, 1985). Consequently, we should be cautious when interpreting reports concerning sex differences.

Whites and blacks in the United States also differ in their mean performance on IQ tests. The mean score of whites is 100. The mean score of blacks is generally said to be 85, although that figure is based largely on old studies. The gap between blacks and whites on the SAT has been slightly but steadily decreasing over the years; the gap on IQ tests may also be decreasing. As with sex differences, we should interpret the reported differences with caution; not all data are published, and the published data may be a less-than-perfect representation of the population. The reasons for the apparent race differences have proved hard to identify and consequently have become the subject of much controversy.

ARE IQ TESTS BIASED?

One possible explanation for group differences in IQ scores is that the tests are biased against certain groups. If a test is meant to measure intelligence (or anything else), then it should measure it accurately no matter who is taking the test. Do IQ tests meet that standard?

Some people apparently believe that any test showing a difference between two groups *must* be biased against the lower-scoring group. But that charge is not necessarily true. The test could be accurately reporting a real difference between the groups. If the term *test bias* is to be useful, it must indicate that the test scores either exaggerate a difference between groups or report a difference that does not really exist at all. A test that correctly reports a real difference is not biased.

We say a test is **biased** against a group if it *systematically underestimates* that group's performance. (A test can be biased in favor of a group if it systematically overestimates the group's performance.) To determine whether a test is biased, we have to find out whether certain groups perform better than the test predicts they will. Psychologists try to identify bias both in individual test items and in the test as a whole.

Evaluating Possible Bias in Single Test Items

To determine whether a particular test item is biased, psychologists have to go beyond an "armchair analysis" that says "this item looks unfair." For example, in a 1980 court case, a group of parents challenged the use of IQ tests by school systems in the Chicago area because they believed the tests were biased against black children. Although the judge ruled that the tests were not biased, he suggested that certain individual items might be biased. For example, one item on the WISC-III asks what you should do if a smaller child starts a fight with you. The correct answer, according to the test manual, is that you should show restraint. The judge suggested that some black children might be taught always to strike back, even against a smaller child, so that item might be biased against blacks.

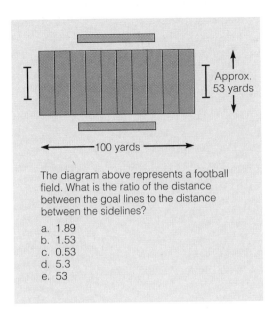

The diagram above represents a football field. What is the ratio of the distance between the goal lines to the distance between the sidelines?

a. 1.89
b. 1.53
c. 0.53
d. 5.3
e. 53

Approx. 53 yards

←— 100 yards —→

FIGURE 10.10
This item was once included on the SAT until psychologists determined that it was biased against women. Many women did not know which were the goal lines and which were the sidelines.

A test is biased if its scores underpredict the performance of some group. But if its scores make equally accurate predictions for all groups, then it is not biased; group differences in scores evidently report an actual difference among groups. Note that calling a test "unbiased" does not mean its scores measure fixed or innate potential. It just means that whatever is responsible for group differences in school performance or some other performance shows up in test scores as well.

Although the judge's suggestion sounds reasonable, it is based on an armchair analysis rather than data. The data, it turns out, reveal that the "fight with a smaller child" item is slightly easier for black children than it is for white children (Koh, Abbatiello, & McLoughlin, 1984).

To determine whether a particular item is biased, psychologists ask whether or not the item is significantly more difficult for one group than for another (Schmitt & Dorans, 1990). If they find, for example, that a particular item or a particular type of item is one of the easiest on the test for whites but one of the more difficult ones for blacks or Hispanics, they replace the item or revise its wording to try to make it equally fair for all groups.

Figure 10.10 presents an item that psychologists determined was biased against women. This item, which once appeared on the SAT, shows a diagram of a football field and asks for the ratio of the distance between the goal lines to the distance between the sidelines. For men, this was one of the easiest items on the test, and their performance on it correlated highly with their performance on the rest of the test. That is,

nearly all the men who missed it did poorly on the rest of the test as well. However, this item was more difficult for women than for men. A higher percentage of women missed it, including some women who did very well on the rest of the test. The reason was that a number of women did not know which were the goal lines and which were the sidelines. When the publishers of the SAT realized that this item was biased against women, they replaced it with one that had nothing to do with football.

Evaluating Possible Bias in a Test as a Whole

By definition, a biased test is one that systematically underestimates the performance of a group. If an IQ test is indeed biased against blacks, for example, then blacks who score, say, 100 are really more intelligent than whites who have the same score.

Bias Against Immigrants Given this definition, the Stanford-Binet and Wechsler tests are undeniably biased against people who do not understand English well, including the foreign born and many deaf people. When I say that the tests are "biased" against these groups, I do not mean that the authors intentionally built in any bias. I mean only that the tests make inaccurate predictions for those people. People who do not speak English well do poorly on the Stanford-Binet and Wechsler tests, but in the long run they perform better in school and on the job than their scores predict. Most immigrant children with an IQ score of, say, 70 do poorly in school at first, but as they master the English language, their performance steadily improves.

Psychologists, unfortunately, have not always been sensitive to the problem of test bias. In the late 1910s and early 1920s, hostility toward immigrants was widespread among U.S. citizens, including many psychologists. One prominent psychologist claimed that the results of IQ tests showed that over 80% of recent Russian, Jewish, Polish, and Hungarian immigrants were "feebleminded" (Gelb, 1986). Today it seems obvious that those immigrants were greatly impaired by their lack of familiarity with the English language and U.S. culture and that the tests were heavily biased against them. At the time, though, many Americans were prepared to believe the worst about immigrants, and the test results were widely accepted. Laws enacted in 1924 greatly restricted immigration. It is difficult to reconstruct exactly how much influence psychologists had on the passage of that law (Snyderman & Herrnstein, 1983), but they certainly contributed to the regrettable climate of the time.

The Charge of Racial Bias   Many people have raised charges of racial bias in IQ tests and in the SAT. A large part of their argument is that some of the items ask for factual information or for definitions of words that are more familiar to whites than they are to blacks. To illustrate this point, some critics have developed tests with a "reverse bias," favoring blacks over whites. Figure 10.11 shows examples from one such test, the Black Intelligence Test of Cultural Homogeneity (BITCH). Back in the 1970s, tests such as this one received a fair amount of attention. They certainly underscored the point that some information is more familiar to members of one race than it is to members of another race. However, we cannot reasonably regard the BITCH as an intelligence test; even for blacks, high scores on this test do not predict good performance in school or on the job (Matarazzo & Wiens, 1977).

Circle the letter that indicates the correct meaning of the word or phrase.

1. *running a game*
   a. writing a bad check
   b. looking at something
   c. directing a contest
   d. getting what one wants from another person or thing
2. *to get down*
   a. to dominate
   b. to travel
   c. to lower a position
   d. to have sexual intercourse
3. *cop an attitude*
   a. leave
   b. become angry
   c. sit down
   d. protect a neighborhood
4. *alley apple*
   a. brick
   b. piece of fruit
   c. dog
   d. horse
5. *boogie jugie*
   a. tired
   b. worthless
   c. old
   d. well put together

FIGURE 10.11
Some items from the Black Intelligence Test of Cultural Homogeneity (BITCH). Check your answers against answer B, page 441.

The best way to measure possible bias of standard IQ tests or the SAT is to determine whether those tests underestimate minority students' likely performance. The evidence indicates that they do not. Minority-group students with a given IQ score generally do about as well in school and at school-related tasks as do middle-class whites with the same IQ score (Barrett & Depinet, 1991; Cole, 1981; Lambert, 1981; Svanum & Bringle, 1982). Likewise, minority-group students with a given SAT score generally do about as well in college as do white students with the same scores (McCornack, 1983). The unpleasant fact is that on the average, white students get better grades in school than do black students in the United States. The IQ tests accurately report that fact. Perhaps instead of "blaming the messenger" (the IQ tests) for the bad news, we should try to address the reasons behind the difference.

"Students will rise to your level of expectation," says Jaime Escalante, the high-school teacher portrayed by Edward James Olmos in Stand and Deliver. The movie chronicles his talent for inspiring average students to excel in calculus. School counselors warned that he was asking too much of his students; parents said their kids didn't need calculus. And when his students first passed the advance placement test in calculus, they were accused of cheating, a charge that seemed to reflect bias against the students, who were not white, middle-class, college-prep types. What does this success suggest about intelligence?

Note that when I say the IQ tests show no demonstrable bias against minority groups, I am *not* saying that the differences in scores are due to differences in innate ability. Remember, the tests are not pure measures of ability, much less "innate ability." We can imagine many possible explanations for the difference between the races—the most obvious reason being the effects of poverty and decreased opportunity. We shall return to this question later in this section.

■ CONCEPT CHECKS

6. *A test of driving skills includes items requiring people to describe what they see. People with visual impairments score lower than do people with good vision. Is the test therefore biased against people with visual impairments?*

7. *Suppose someone devises a new IQ test and we discover that tall people generally get higher scores on this test than short people do. How could we determine whether or not this test is biased against short people?*
(Check your answers on page 441.)

How Do Heredity and Environment Affect IQ Scores?

The British scholar Francis Galton (1869/1978) was the first to offer evidence that a tendency toward high intelligence is hereditary. As evidence, he simply pointed out that eminent and distinguished men—politicians, judges, and the like—generally had a number of distinguished relatives. We no longer consider that evidence convincing, because distinguished people share environment as well as genes with their relatives. Besides, becoming distinguished is only partly a matter of intelligence. (You probably can name a few distinguished people whom you would not regard as especially intelligent.)

The question of how heredity affects intelligence has persisted to this day and has turned out to be difficult to answer to everyone's satisfaction. If we could control people as we control experimental animals, we could answer the question conclusively. We could take hundreds of babies from high-IQ parents and hundreds from low-IQ parents and then randomly assign half of each group to either high-IQ or low-IQ adoptive parents, as Figure 10.12 shows. We could see to it that none of the parents would "adopt" their own child and that none would know whether their adoptive child was from high-IQ or low-IQ parents. A few years later we could test the children to see whether their IQs matched those of their biological parents or those of their adoptive parents. Of course, we cannot conduct any such experiment.

For many years an extensive study of British twins reported by Cyril Burt seemed to provide decisive evidence. Burt's data conformed almost perfectly to the hypothesis that genetic differences are responsible for differences in IQ. Suspicious because the data conformed too perfectly, Leon Kamin (1974) carefully reexamined Burt's publications and uncovered numerous instances of vague procedures and some extremely unlikely patterns in the results. For instance, over a period of decades, as Burt added more and more children to his studies, he continued to get exactly the same correlation coefficients between the IQ scores of twins, even to the third decimal place! Moreover, he published some papers with two "coworkers" who were unknown to his university and to his colleagues. Burt died before the controversy arose, so we shall never know exactly what happened. The suspicion is strong, however, that he either distorted or fabricated much or all of his data. At any rate, we no longer take his reported findings seriously.

A number of other investigators (whose honesty is not in doubt) have also looked at the relationship of heredity and environment to intelligence. We shall consider the various types of evidence they have produced and note the strengths and weaknesses of each. The issues here are not limited to studies of IQ tests; they extend to any discussion of the influence of human heredity and environment.

Identical and Fraternal Twins

Figure 10.13, which is based on a review of the literature by Thomas Bouchard and Matthew McGue (1981), shows the correlations of IQ scores for monozygotic (identical) twins, dizygotic (fraternal) twins, and individuals with several other degrees of relationship. Note the stronger correlation between monozygotic twins than between dizygotic twins. The correlation in IQ scores is high for monozygotic twins even if they are reared in separate environments.

A single individual will usually get somewhat different scores on two successive tries at any IQ test, because no IQ test is perfectly reliable. On the average, that difference is about six points. Identical twins who take the same test at the same time differ from each other by about that same amount, and therefore their IQ scores

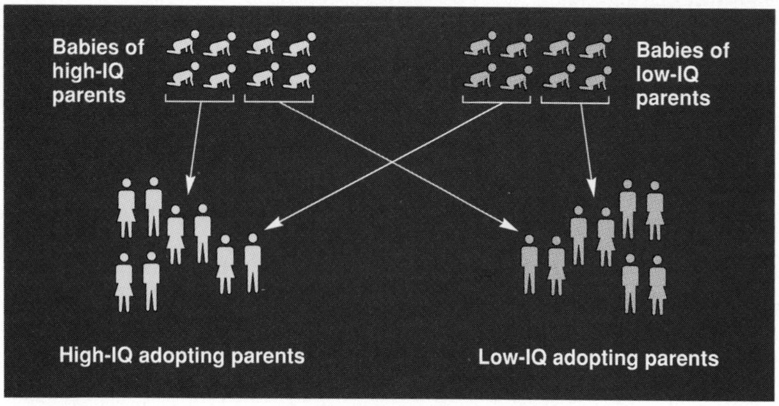

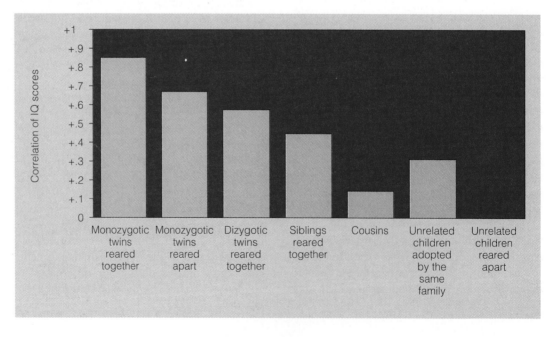

FIGURE 10.12

In a scientifically ideal study of the role of heredity in IQ scores, an investigator would randomly assign some babies of high-IQ biological parents to low-IQ adopting parents and some babies of low-IQ biological parents to high-IQ adopting parents. Because such a study is not feasible, psychologists do their best to interpret the results of various less-than-ideal studies.

FIGURE 10.13
Mean correlations for the IQs of children with various degrees of genetic and environmental similarity. (Adapted from Bouchard & McGue, 1981.)

correlate highly (Plomin & DeFries, 1980). Fraternal twins differ by a larger amount and nontwins by a still larger amount. Remoter relatives, such as cousins, have IQ scores that correlate positively, but not strongly.

These results are usually interpreted to mean that identical twins resemble each other more in IQ scores than fraternal twins do because their heredity is the same. Some psychologists have challenged this interpretation, saying that identical twins resemble each other more than fraternal twins do only because their parents and others probably treat identical twins more similarly than they treat fraternal twins. However, researchers have found that identical twins who always *thought* they were fraternal twins resemble each other as much as other identical twins; fraternal twins who always *thought* they were identical twins resemble each other only as much as other fraternal twins, not as much as identical twins (Scarr, 1968; Scarr & Carter-Saltzman, 1979). That is, the main determinant of similarity in IQ is whether twins are actually identical, not whether they think they are identical. The reason for the similarity is more likely genetic than environmental.

Identical Twins Reared Apart

Several studies have reported that identical twins who have been adopted by different parents and reared in separate environments strongly resemble each other in IQ scores (Bouchard & McGue, 1981; Farber, 1981). That resemblance seems to suggest a strong genetic contribution to IQ. What happens, however, is that the "separate" environments have often been very similar (Farber, 1981; Kamin, 1974). In some cases, the biological parents raised one twin and close relatives or next-door neighbors raised the other twin. Consequently, these results are difficult to interpret.

A further complication: The IQ scores of children are significantly affected by small differences in age, and "8-year-old children" vary in age from exactly 8 years to 8 years and 11+ months. So twins, who are exactly the same age, will almost certainly resemble each other more than will two children "of the same age" chosen at random.

Adopted Children

Many psychologists believe that the most convincing evidence for a genetic influence comes from studies of adopted children. The IQ scores of children who are reared by their bio-

In most cases, a pair of identical twins have nearly the same IQ score. Generally, identical twins resemble each other in IQ score more closely than do fraternal twins, even in cases in which the identical twins did not know they were identical.

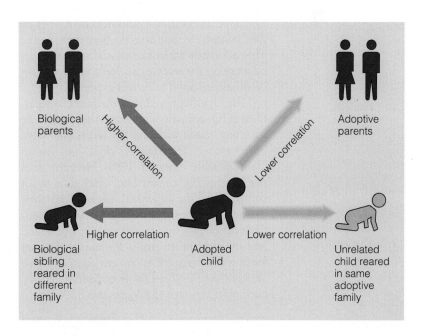

FIGURE 10.14

The IQ scores of adopted children correlate more highly with the IQ scores of their biological relatives than they do with the IQ scores of their adoptive relatives. Such data point to a hereditary influence on IQ scores.

logical parents generally resemble their parents' IQ scores (Figure 10.14). The IQ scores of children who are reared by adoptive parents have less resemblance to their adoptive parents' IQ scores. In fact, the IQs of adopted children resemble the IQs of their biological parents more than they resemble the IQs of their adoptive parents (Scarr & Carter-Saltzman, 1979). Furthermore, the IQ scores of unrelated children adopted by the same family resemble each other less closely than do the IQs of related children who are adopted by separate families (Teasdale & Owen, 1984).

The interpretation of these results is confounded to some extent by the policies of adoption agencies. Many adoption agencies place children of high-IQ parents with the brightest available adoptive parents. Thus, adopted children with high-IQ parents may develop high IQs themselves not just because of their heredity but also because of their environment. Still, the fact that adopted children resemble their biological parents *more* than they resemble their adoptive parents implies a significant role of heredity in IQ scores.

Extensive and careful reviews of the literature have concluded that both hereditary and environmental differences do contribute to variations in human intelligence (Thompson, Detterman, & Plomin, 1991; Turkheimer, 1991). The important question is no longer *do* they contribute, but *how* do they contribute? That is, how do various genes and various experiences alter the way we develop and the way we eventually respond to certain experiences?

The fact that heredity contributes to variations in IQ scores does not mean that people are somehow stuck with the IQ score they were born with. "Hereditary" does not mean "unmodifiable" (Angoff, 1988). Heredity does not control IQ (or anything else) directly; it controls how the individual reacts to the environment. It is possible that the "best" environment for one group of children may not be the best for some other group. Perhaps those who are at a disadvantage in one environment have an advantage in some other environment. We need more research to address this question.

Race and IQ Scores

WHAT'S THE EVIDENCE?

On the average, blacks in the United States score about 85 on IQ tests, 15 points lower than the average for whites. The difference is fairly constant on a variety of IQ tests. But measuring the difference does not explain its origin. Arthur Jensen (1969) argued that the difference is due largely to hereditary differences between the races. That was a highly controversial suggestion, to say the least, and a difficult one to test. Most of Jensen's data had to do with the contribution of heredity to IQ differences among whites; he argued that if hereditary differences are responsible for much of the variation in IQ within a race, they are likely to be responsible for part of the difference between races as well. However, the validity of that point is far from certain. Many black families suffer from levels of poverty and other hardships that few white families experience.

How could we test the contributions of heredity and environment to the race differences? One way would be to trade environments—have some black families raise white children and some white families raise black children. Psychologists cannot conduct such an experiment, but they have examined what happens when white families do adopt black children. (Black families seldom adopt white children.) They have also looked for a relationship between the IQs of black children and the relative degrees of their European and African ancestry. Let's examine two of the most carefully conducted studies.

STUDY 1

Hypothesis If the IQ difference between the races is due partly to early experiences, then black children reared by white families will perform better on IQ tests than most other black children will.

Method Sandra Scarr and Richard Weinberg (1976) located black children who had been adopted by white families in Minnesota. Many of these families also had adopted white children, and many had biological children of their own. IQ tests were administered to all the adopting parents and all the children.

Results The mean IQ scores are shown in Figure 10.15.

Interpretation The mean IQ score of the adopted black children was not only higher than the mean of other black children (85) but also higher than the mean for the white population (100). This result provides impressive support for the idea that the difference in IQ between the races is due largely to environmental differences. The results, however, also suggest a possible role for heredity because both sets of adopted children scored lower than the adopting parents and their biological children scored. (Adoption agencies are very selective about

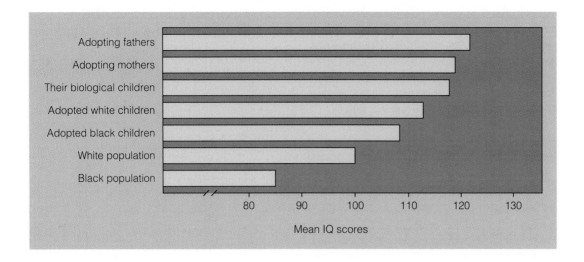

FIGURE 10.15
Results of the Scarr-Weinberg (1976) study. Black children and white children reared under similar conditions had similar, though not identical, IQ scores.

adopting parents, and most adopting parents have high IQ scores.) Because the results of this study were ambiguous, Scarr and her colleagues conducted a second study.

STUDY 2

Hypothesis If heredity is responsible for even part of the difference between the races in IQ performance, then blacks with a high percentage of European ancestry should obtain higher IQ scores than blacks with a lower percentage. (Few U.S. blacks have 100% African ancestry. The mean for the U.S. black population is about 75–80% African ancestry and 20–25% European ancestry.)

Method The investigators (Scarr, Pakstis, Katz, & Barker, 1977) estimated the percentage of African ancestry for 362 black children in Philadelphia by means of blood typing. They examined 14 different blood factors—the familiar ABO blood types, the Rh factor, the Duffy factor, and 11 others. Some blood factors are more common in Europe than in Africa and vice versa. For example, type B blood is present in only 9% of Europeans but in 21% of Africans. No Europeans have Duffy type A−B− blood, whereas 94% of Africans do. By comparing each child's blood factors to the frequency of those blood factors in both Europe and Africa, the investigators estimated the degree of European ancestry for each child. They were under no illusion that their estimates were highly precise, but that was of no great concern. All that mattered was that, in general, children with higher estimated European ancestry had more actual European ancestry. Then they correlated their estimates of European ancestry

with performance on Raven's Progressive Matrices and four other tests of intellectual performance.

Results The investigators tried several methods of weighting the importance of various blood factors to estimate European and African ancestry. Regardless of which method they used, they found virtually no correlation between the estimates of European ancestry and measures of performance.

Interpretation No one or two studies can ever resolve a question like this completely, and additional research would be helpful. (For example, as with any study, the investigators may have used a sample of children that was not representative of the entire population.) Still, we can safely say that the best available evidence indicates that hereditary factors account for little if any of the race differences in IQ.

Closing Comments

In the early years after the invention of IQ tests, psychologists and educators spread the belief that IQ tests offer a measurement of innate ability, some sort of fixed potential for each person. They had no real evidence for that belief, and today we have reasons to reject it. IQ tests measure an inseparable mixture of ability and achievement, not a person's innate potential. They reflect both hereditary and environmental influences, and the environmental influences are apparently responsible for the race differences in the United States.

IQ tests serve the practical function of identifying approximately how well an individual is likely to perform in school or in school-related tasks, and of identifying people with special strengths and weaknesses. If used for those purposes, even the imperfect tests of today can be valuable. When people start to revert to thinking of IQ tests as measures of innate ability, problems and confusion are sure to arise.

SUMMARY

- *Standardization.* To determine the meaning of a test's scores, the authors of a test determine the mean and the distribution of scores for a random or representative sample of the population. IQ tests are revised periodically. To keep the same mean, test authors have made the tests more difficult from time to time. (page 427)

- *Distribution of IQ scores.* IQ tests have a mean of 100 and a standard deviation of about 15 or 16, depending on the test. Items are carefully selected so that performance on each item correlates positively with performance on the test as a whole. (page 427).

- *Reliability and validity.* Tests are evaluated in terms of reliability and validity. Reliability is a measure of a test's consistency, or the repeatability of its scores. Validity is a determination of how well a test measures what it claims to measure. (page 429)

- *Test bias.* Psychologists try to remove from a test any item that is easy for one group of people but difficult for another. They also try to evaluate the possible bias of a test as a whole. Bias is defined as a systematic underestimation or overestimation of the performance of a group. By that definition, IQ tests are biased against immigrants but apparently not against racial minorities; they predict the school performance of blacks about as accurately as that of whites. (page 432)

- *Hereditary and environmental influences.* To determine the contribution of heredity to the variation in scores on IQ tests, investigators consider three types of evidence: comparison of identical twins and fraternal twins, studies of identical twins reared apart, and studies of adopted children. Both heredity and environment have important influences, although we know too little about how they exert their influences. (page 435)

- *Nonhereditary basis of racial differences in IQ.* Black children with a higher percentage of European ancestry have about the same mean IQ score as do black children with a lower percentage of European ancestry. These results suggest that heredity is not responsible for the difference in IQ scores between blacks and whites. (page 438)

SUGGESTION FOR FURTHER READING

Anastasi, A. (1988). *Psychological testing* (6th ed.). New York: Macmillan. A thorough treatment of the design and interpretation of IQ tests and other psychological tests.

TERMS

standardization the process of establishing rules for administering a test and for interpreting its scores (page 427)

norms descriptions of the frequencies at which particular scores occur (page 427)

reliability repeatability of a test's scores (page 429)

test-retest reliability repeatability of a test's scores between a test and a retest (page 429)

validity determination of how well a test measures what it claims to measure (page 430)

content validity similarity between the items in a test and the information the test is meant to measure (page 430)

construct validity correspondence of a test's measurements to a theoretical construct (page 430)

predictive validity ability of a test's scores to predict some real-world performance (page 430)

utility usefulness of a test for a practical purpose (page 431)

selective reporting tendency for investigators to be more likely to publish findings when they match predictions than when they do not (page 432)

bias tendency for test scores to exaggerate a difference between groups or to report a difference that does not exist at all (page 432)

ANSWERS TO CONCEPT CHECKS

2. Yes! To say that a test is "reliable" is simply to say that its scores are repeatable—that and only that. My test would give perfectly reliable (repeatable) measurements. True, they would be utterly useless, but that is beside the point. Reliability is not a measure of usefulness. (page 430)

3. No. An individual's score may be higher on the retest, either because of the practice at taking the test or because of the additional months of education. But the rank order of scores does not change much. That is, if a number of people retake the test, all of them are likely to improve their scores, but those who had the highest scores the first time probably will have the highest scores the second time. (page 430)

4. Yes, a test can have high reliability and low validity. A measure of intelligence determined by dividing head length by head width has high reliability (repeatability) but presumably no validity. A test with low reliability cannot have high validity, however. Low reliability means that the scores fluctuate randomly. If the test scores cannot even predict a later score on the same test, then they can hardly predict anything else. (page 430)

5. The predictive validity of the tests would increase. Predictive validity tends to be low when almost all students have practically the same score; it is higher when students' scores are highly variable. (page 430)

6. No, this test is not biased against people with visual impairments. It correctly determines that they are likely to be poor drivers. (page 435)

7. We would have to determine whether the test accurately predicts the school performances of both short and tall people. If short people with, say, an IQ score of 100 perform better in school than tall people with an IQ score of 100, then the test is underpredicting the performances of short people and we can conclude the test is biased against them. (The mere fact that the test reports a difference between short people and tall people is not in itself evidence of test bias.) (page 435)

ANSWERS TO OTHER QUESTIONS IN THE TEXT

B. 1. d **2.** d **3.** b **4.** a **5.** b

11 MOTIVATION

NASA is searching for a volunteer to make a solo trip to Mars. If you volunteer, you will journey for 2 or 3 years in a small, uncomfortable spacecraft, eating monotonous food and having no human companionship. You will have about a 20% chance of coming back to Earth alive. What you are offered in return is a chance to be the first human being to set foot on Mars. How would you respond to this opportunity? When I pose this question to large groups of students, most decline, but at least a few say they are ready to volunteer.

What moves people to risk their lives scaling cliffs or sky diving? Some say they feel most alive when courting danger.

If we assume that humans are rational beings who try to maximize their probability of surviving and passing on their genes, then volunteering for that trip to Mars does not make a whole lot of sense. Neither does it make sense to risk one's life for a political or religious cause. And yet many people do. For many people, various abstract goals take priority over all of their practical goals, such as surviving and reproducing. Why? How do these abstract goals become so strong, and why are they so much stronger for some people than for others?

A great deal about human motivation is puzzling. Unfortunately, it will remain puzzling at the end of this chapter. This chapter deals with some of the better understood aspects of motivation. We begin with an overview of some general principles of motivation. Then we shall explore three examples of motivated behaviors: hunger, sexual activity, and striving for achievement.

I have selected these examples for emphasis largely because they are an important part of human life but also because they illustrate how our biology interacts with the social setting. Hunger is based on a biological need, but what, when, and how much we eat also depends on what we learn from other people. Sexual motivation also serves a biological need, but the search for a suitable partner is fundamentally a social behavior. Striving for achievement is learned as a method of pleasing and impressing others. Although it is primarily a social motivation, it is an outgrowth of the competition for dominance that we can observe throughout the animal kingdom.

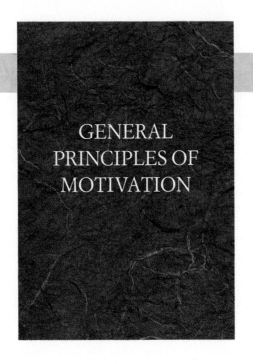

GENERAL PRINCIPLES OF MOTIVATION

What is motivation?
How could a psychologist determine whether
or not an act is motivated?

You are sitting quietly, reading a book, when suddenly you hear a loud noise. You jump a little and gasp. Was that action motivated? "No," you say. "I jumped involuntarily." Now I tell you that I want to do a little experiment. I shall tap my pencil; as soon as you hear it, you should try to jump and gasp just as you did the first time. I tap my pencil and, sure enough, you jump and gasp—not exactly as you did the first time, but approximately so. Was that action motivated? "Yes," you reply.

In both cases, I accept your answer. If I had not asked you whether or not your behavior was motivated, or if I did not trust your answer, could I have figured it out in any other way? Remember, your motivated behavior and your unmotivated behavior looked about the same. Sometimes we cannot trust people's self-reports. Someone accused of murder says, "I didn't mean to kill. It was an accident." Your friend, who promised to drive you somewhere and then left without you, says, "I didn't do it on purpose. I just forgot." Maybe so and maybe not. How do we decide whether or not a behavior is motivated? We need a clear understanding of how motivated behaviors differ from unmotivated behaviors.

VIEWS OF MOTIVATION

What is motivation? Let's try some definitions: "Motivation is what activates and directs behavior." Will that do? That description fits motivation fairly well, but it also fits some other, nonmotivational phenomena. For example, light activates and directs the growth of plants, but we would hardly say that light "motivates" plants.

"Motivation is what makes our behavior more vigorous and energetic." That definition ignores some important motivational phenomena. For example, some people are strongly motivated to lie motionless for hours on end.

How about this: "Motivation is what changes one's preferences or choices"? That might do, except that we would first have to define preference and choice.

To be honest, it is hard to state precisely what we mean by motivation. Psychologists have repeatedly altered their views of motivation. By considering one theory after another, they have seen the shortcomings of each and have developed some idea of what is and is not motivation.

Motivation as an Instinctive Energy

Motivation, which comes from the same root as *motion,* is literally something that "moves" a person. So we might think of it as a type of energy. Sigmund Freud, the founder of psychoanalysis, proposed that the human nervous system is a reservoir of **libido,** a kind of sexual energy. As libido builds up, it demands an outlet, like air in an overinflated balloon or hot water trapped under a geyser. If its normal outlet is blocked, it will discharge itself through some other channel. Freud used this concept to explain why people who are unable to release their libido in a normal way sometimes engage in irrational, self-defeating behaviors. If, for example, you had an impulse or an energy for engaging in some forbidden sex act, it might manifest itself in the form of nervous twitches (Freud, 1908/1963).

Konrad Lorenz, a pioneer in the field of ethology (the study of animal behavior under

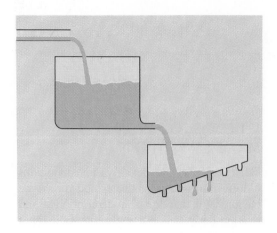

FIGURE 11.1
According to Konrad Lorenz, energy (represented as a fluid) builds up in a "reservoir" in the brain; it needs to be discharged. Ordinarily, an instinct is released through natural or preferred outlets. If those are blocked, however, energy spills into another outlet, and the animal engages in an irrelevant behavior. (After Lorenz, 1950.)

natural conditions), proposed a similar theory. According to Lorenz (1950), animals engage in instinctive acts when specific energies reach a critical level. For example, a male stickleback fish outside the breeding season has no specific energy for mating, and it will not respond sexually. At the start of the breeding season, it has a small amount of mating energy and it will court female stickleback fish, as well as attack male stickleback fish. At the height of the breeding season, it has a great amount of mating energy and it will court females vigorously; it may even respond sexually to a piece of wood painted to resemble a female of its species.

Figure 11.1 illustrates Lorenz's model. A specific kind of energy builds up in the reservoir and flows into the tray below. The outlets in that tray represent ways of releasing the energy. If conditions are right, the energy is released through the lowest outlet—for example, mating with a normal partner. If that outlet is blocked and energy continues to build up, the energy will spill through one of the higher, less preferred outlets.

Both Freud and Lorenz based their theories on a conception of the nervous system that is now obsolete. They believed that every impulse to action had to be carried out in one way or another. We now know that under certain circumstances an impulse for a given behavior can simply be canceled or inhibited.

Drive Theories

Closely related to the instinctive energy theories, such as those of Freud and Lorenz, are theories that describe motivation as a **drive,** an internal state of unrest or irritation that energizes one behavior after another until one of them removes the irritation (Hull, 1943). For example, when you get a splinter in your finger, the discomfort motivates you to engage in various actions until you get rid of the splinter.

According to *drive-reduction theory,* popular among psychologists of an earlier era, animals including humans strive to reduce their needs and drives as much as possible. That is, they eat to reduce their hunger, drink to reduce their thirst, have sexual relations to reduce their sex drive, and so forth. This view implies that one's ideal condition is to have no unmet needs or drives; an individual in this state would become completely inactive.

This view also implies that we are equally satisfied to reduce our drives one way as another. Note the contrast with instinct theories: According to instinct theories, each motivation prompts a particular action; for example, a hungry person seeks to eat. According to drive theories, a motivation will prompt any action that reduces the drive; for example, a hungry person will be equally content to eat, to pump food into the stomach, or to reduce hunger in any other conceivable way.

The principal shortcoming of drive theory is that it implies that people (and other animals) always try to reduce their drives and thereby their level of stimulation. In fact, we all seek variety and activity in our lives; the ideal state is one with a moderate amount of stimulation, not one with as little as possible.

Another flaw in drive theory is that it ignores the role of external stimulation. For example, a person's interest in food depends not only on hunger (an internal drive) but also on what foods are available. Similarly, interest in sex depends partly on an internal drive and partly on the presence or absence of a suitable partner.

Homeostasis

An important advance from the idea of drive reduction is the concept of **homeostasis,** the maintenance of biological conditions within an organism at an optimum level (Cannon, 1929). The idea of homeostasis recognizes that we are motivated to seek an intermediate state of stimulation, not to reduce all drives and stimuli to zero. For example, people maintain body temperature at about 37°C (98.6°F) through a combination of physiological and behavioral means. Each of us also maintains a fairly steady body weight, a nearly constant amount of water in the body, a reasonably stable level of sensory stimulation while we are awake, and so on.

Unlike a rock, which remains static only because nothing is acting on it, the homeostasis of the body is more like a spinning top; someone has to apply additional energy from time to time to keep it spinning. For example, we maintain constant body temperature partly by shivering, sweating, and other involuntary physiological responses and partly by putting on extra clothing, taking off excess clothing, or finding a more comfortable location.

Human motivated behaviors are not exactly homeostatic, however; or at least they do not resemble the actions that a home thermostat controls. When your home is neither hot nor cold, the thermostat triggers neither the air conditioning system nor the heater. But human behavior often acts in anticipation of future needs. For example, you might eat a large breakfast some morning, even though you are not hungry, just because you know that you are going to be too busy to stop for lunch. Thus, one fruitful way of describing motivation is that it maintains current homeostasis and anticipates future needs to maintain future homeostasis (Appley, 1991).

Still, even that conception of motivation overlooks the power of new stimuli to arouse motivated behaviors. For example, nonhungry people may eat or drink just to be sociable or just because someone has offered them something especially tasty.

Incentive Theories

Why do people ride roller coasters? It is doubtful that they have any special need to go thundering down a steep decline. Or suppose you have just finished a big meal and someone offers you a slice of a very special cake. If you are like most people, you eat it but hardly because you need it. Evidently, motivation includes more than the internal forces that push us toward certain behaviors; it also includes **incentives**—external stimuli that *pull* us toward certain actions.

The distinction between a drive and an incentive is not clear-cut. Jumping into a swimming pool on a hot summer day may satisfy your biological drive to maintain normal body temperature, but the prospect of splashing around

in the water may serve as a strong incentive as well.

Most motivated behaviors are controlled by a combination of drives and incentives. You eat because you are hungry (a drive) and because you see appealing food in front of you (an incentive). How much you eat depends on both the strength of the drive and the appeal of the incentive.

Intrinsic and Extrinsic Motivations

Similar to the distinction between drives and incentives, let us distinguish between intrinsic motivations and extrinsic motivations. An **intrinsic motivation** is a motivation to engage in an act for its own sake; an **extrinsic motivation** is based on the rewards and punishments the act may bring. For example, if you eat because you are hungry, you are following an intrinsic motivation; if you eat something you don't like in order to please the cook, you are following an extrinsic motivation. Most of our behavior is motivated by a combination of intrinsic and extrinsic motivations. An artist paints partly for the joy of creation (intrinsic) and partly for the eventual profit (extrinsic). You read this book partly because you enjoy reading it (I hope) and partly because you want to get a good grade on a test.

When people describe themselves as "highly motivated," they are generally referring to an extrinsic motivation. For example, people who say they are motivated to succeed at their jobs are in most cases motivated by the rewards they have been receiving or the ones they expect to receive. They may or may not actually enjoy the work itself or gain any sense of accomplishment from it (McClelland, Koestner, & Weinberger, 1989).

We eat because of both intrinsic and extrinsic motivations. Even when the hunger (an intrinsic motivation) is satisfied, we eat because of the taste and the desire to socialize (extrinsic motivations).

Why would someone devote enormous time and energy to building up muscles, as Arnold Schwarzenegger has? We assume such people have both intrinsic and extrinsic motivations. An intrinsic motivation is the enjoyment of exercising and body-building for their own sake. An extrinsic motivation is to obtain the attention and admiration of other people.

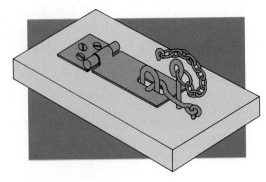

FIGURE 11.2
Monkeys learned to open this device by removing the pin, the hook, and the hasp, in order. At first they received no reward, opening the device just for the fun of it. Then when they could open it to obtain a raisin, their performance deteriorated. Evidently in some cases an individual performs better with just intrinsic motivation (here, the joy of the task itself) than with a combination of intrinsic and extrinsic motivations.

Does a combination of intrinsic and extrinsic motivations lead to more persistent and effective performance than, say, an intrinsic motivation alone? Not always. In a classic study, researchers gave four monkeys a device like the one in Figure 11.2 to play with. To open it, a monkey had to remove the pin, lift the hook, and lift the hasp, in that order. The monkeys played with the device from time to time over a period of 10 days. They received no reinforcements; they played with it apparently just for the fun of it (an intrinsic motivation). By the end of the 10 days, each monkey was able to open the device quickly, almost never getting the steps out of order. Then the device was placed over a food well in a place where the monkeys were accustomed to finding a raisin (an extrinsic motivation). If they opened the device they could get it. Suddenly their ability to open the device deteriorated. Instead of patiently removing the pin, the hook, and the hasp as they had done before, they attacked the hasp forcefully. They took longer to open the device for food than they had for play. Later, when they were given the device by itself with no food available, they opened it less frequently than before and made more errors in their attempts (Harlow, Harlow, & Meyer, 1950). Evidently, opening the device for food had become work, and the monkeys no longer saw it as play.

The same principle applies to human behavior: If people are given extrinsic reinforce-ments just for participating in an interesting activity, they become less interested in that activity, at least temporarily (Bates, 1979). For example, college students in one experiment were asked to try to arrange seven plastic pieces with complex shapes to match figures in a drawing. At one point halfway through the experiment, students in the experimental group were paid $1 for each correct match. (Students in the control group did not know that the experimental group was being paid.) Then the experiment continued without pay for anyone. So long as the students in the experimental group were being paid, they worked harder than the students in the control group. After pay was suspended, the experimental group worked less than the control group did (Deci, 1971). Results such as these illustrate the **overjustification effect**: When people are given more extrinsic motivation than necessary to perform a task, their intrinsic motivation declines. According to one interpretation, people ask themselves, "Why am I doing this task?" They answer, "It's not because I enjoy the task. It's because I'm being paid." Once the extrinsic motivation is removed, the task seems uninteresting. The overjustification effect has been reported in a variety of settings, among both children and adults (Kassin & Lepper, 1984).

The demonstration of this effect implies that children should not be rewarded for reading, drawing, or other activities they enjoy. The

Table 11.1 Four Views of Motivation

View	Basic Position	Major Weaknesses
Instinct theories	Motivations are energies that accumulate; each energy specifies a preferred action, although it might spill over into a less preferred outlet.	Based on obsolete view of the nervous system.
Drive theories	Motivations are based on needs or irritations that we try to reduce; they do not specify particular actions.	Implies that we always try to reduce stimulation, never to increase it. Also overlooks importance of external stimuli.
Homeostasis (plus anticipation)	Motivations tend to maintain body states near some optimum, intermediate level. They may anticipate future needs as well as reacting to current needs.	Overlooks importance of external stimuli.
Incentive theories	Motivations are responses to attractive stimuli.	Incomplete unless combined with drive or homeostasis.

reward may change their perception of the task to "work" instead of "fun." Does the overjustification effect imply that children should not be rewarded for doing their homework? Maybe, maybe not. Faced with a page of addition or subtraction problems, most children have so little intrinsic motivation that an extrinsic motivation could do no harm. They may have to be bribed to complete such tedious arithmetic until they can get to the kinds of mathematics that are intrinsically more interesting.

Does the overjustification effect imply that workers would enjoy their job more and work harder if they were not paid? Of course not. On the job, extrinsic motivators such as salary and bonuses are essential for good performance (Scott, 1976). But people do sometimes stay at a job for intrinsic reasons; many people who could afford to retire continue working at their jobs.

Table 11.1 summarizes four views of motivation.

■ CONCEPT CHECK

1. Many college students play tennis in their spare time. Are they following an intrinsic motivation or an extrinsic motivation? One student

practices especially hard in hopes of becoming a professional player. Is that student following an intrinsic motivation or an extrinsic motivation? Given the overjustification effect, would you expect retired professional players to enjoy playing tennis more or less than other people do? (Check your answers on page 453.)

TYPES OF MOTIVATIONS

How many motivations do people have? They are motivated to obtain food, water, shelter, clothing, companionship, sexual activity. . . . The list could go on. Can we group these into a few coherent categories?

Primary and Secondary Motivations

One way to categorize motivations is to distinguish primary motivations from secondary motivations. **Primary motivations**—such as the desire for food and water—serve obvious biological needs. **Secondary motivations** develop as a result of specific learning experiences; they do not serve any biological need directly, although they may lead indirectly to the satisfaction of primary motivations. Primary motivations and secondary motivations are analogous

Table 11.2 Four Lists of Primary Motivations

W. McDougall (1932)	P. T. Young (1936)	H. A. Murray (1938)	K. B Madsen (1959)
Food seeking	Hunger	Inspiration	Hunger
Disgust	Nausea	Water	Thirst
Sex	Thirst	Food	Sex
Fear	Sex	Sentience	Nursing
Curiosity	Nursing	Sex	Temperature
Protective/parental	Urinating	Lactation	Pain avoidance
Gregarious	Defecating	Expiration	Excretion
Self-assertive	Avoiding heat	Urination	Oxygen
Submissive	Avoiding cold	Defecation	Rest/sleep
Anger	Avoiding pain	Pain avoidance	Activity
Appeal	Air	Heat avoidance	Security
Constructive	Fear/anger	Cold avoidance	Aggression
Acquisitive	Fatigue	Harm avoidance	
Laughter	Sleep		
Comfort	Curiosity		
Rest/sleep	Social instinct		
Migratory	Tickle		
Coughing/breathing			

Note: I have rephrased some of the words in more familiar language—for example, *pain avoidance* instead of *noxavoidance*.

to *primary reinforcers* and *secondary reinforcers*, discussed in Chapter 7. In both cases, *primary* implies the satisfaction of a biological need. *Secondary* implies learned.

Presumably, we learn secondary motivations because they help us to satisfy primary motivations. For example, we learn a desire for money (a secondary motivation) because it helps us to obtain food, water, and shelter (primary motivations). In some cases, however, a secondary motivation seems to develop a momentum of its own, becoming apparently independent of the original primary motivations associated with it. For example, someone may start collecting coins or stamps (a secondary motivation) in hopes of making a profit or because the collection leads to praise from other coin or stamp enthusiasts. Eventually some collectors devote enormous money and effort to their collections, demonstrating that they have become interested in the stamps for their own sake and not just as a means to make money or impress friends.

People can have an unlimited number of secondary motivations. Because the biological needs of the body are limited, psychologists expect to find only a limited number of primary motivations. Table 11.2 presents four examples of psychologists' attempts to list all the primary motivations.

If you study the lists closely, you may see the complexity of the task. Each list includes one or more debatable entries, and none of them seems complete. Moreover, none of these lists has any structure or organization. Each implies that all motivations are equally important and that every motivation is independent of the others. Wouldn't it make sense to group certain motivations together, such as the several kinds of avoidance? And shouldn't some motivations be distinguished as more important, or at least more urgent, than others?

■ CONCEPT CHECK

2. *Is your interest in graduating from college a primary motivation or a secondary motivation? (Check your answer on page 453.)*

Maslow's Hierarchy of Needs

Abraham Maslow (1970) listed human motivations in a more organized, structured way. His influential proposal includes both primary motivations and secondary motivations. According to Maslow, our behavior is governed by a **hierarchy of needs**. The most basic are the physiological needs for food, drink, oxygen, and warmth, as shown at the bottom level of Figure 11.3. Maslow holds that these basic needs ordinarily take priority over all others (Figure 11.4). For example, people who are gasping for breath will not take time out to do something else before they have satisfied their need for oxygen. Once people have satisfied all of their physiological needs, they seek to satisfy their safety needs, such as security from attack and avoidance of pain. When those needs are satisfied, they proceed to the needs for love and belonging—making friends and socializing with them. Next come the needs for esteem, such as gaining prestige and a feeling of accomplishment. At the apex of Maslow's hierarchy is the need for **self-actualization**, the need to achieve one's full potential.

Maslow's theory is appealing because it recognizes a wide range of human motivations—from satisfying our biological needs to savoring the joy of accomplishment. Moreover, it suggests that the various motivations are not equal. When they conflict, the basic physiological needs take priority over safety needs, which take priority over the need for love, and so on.

Maslow's hierarchy has been widely accepted, although it has inspired little research, and what research has been done has often failed to support the theory (Wahba & Bridwell, 1976). No evidence supports the idea that motivations fall into five distinct categories. That is, the differences between the need for oxygen and the need for food (both basic physiological needs) are as great as the differences between the need for love and the need for self-esteem. More important, people sometimes work to satisfy higher-level needs before they satisfy lower-level needs. Even when you are ravenously hungry, you might skip a meal to be with someone you love, or to study for a test, or to accept an award. Martyrs have willingly sacrificed their lives to advance some political or religious cause. Depending on the circumstances, almost any motivation may take priority over the others, at least temporarily.

GENERAL PROPERTIES OF MOTIVATED BEHAVIOR

What, if anything, do various types of motivated behavior have in common? The foremost characteristic of motivated behaviors is that they are goal directed (Pervin, 1983). They have a quality of "persistence until." A person or an

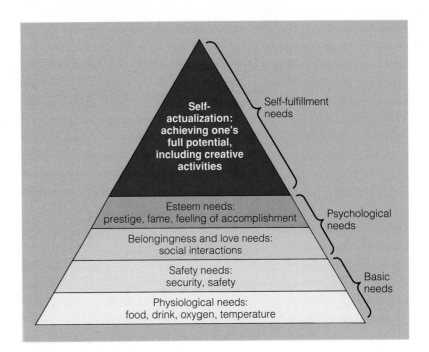

FIGURE 11.3

Maslow's hierarchy of needs suggests a hierarchical order to human motivations. If you are thirsty, you will want to drink something to meet that basic need. If your primary physical needs are met, you can focus on meeting psychological needs for companionship and achievement. Your final efforts will be devoted to reaching your full potential. But do all people follow this principle? Some people, including Olympic performers, sacrifice eating, drinking, and companionship to strive toward athletic accomplishment and prestige. Artists might also give up some physical comforts and social pleasures to focus on an inner vision and to realize their creative potential.

FIGURE 11.4

According to Maslow's hierarchy of needs, we concentrate first on the lowest level of needs—such as the need for food, oxygen, and temperature—until we meet them. Then we move on to higher and higher needs. Thus, an impoverished and homeless person would be unlikely to devote much effort to creative endeavors. (Some exceptions to that rule do occur, however.)

animal engages in one behavior after another until reaching the goal. When you feel cold, you do not always do one particular thing. You may go inside, put on a sweater, huddle with others, run around, or just stand and shiver, depending on the circumstances. Similarly, when you are hungry, you may act in a number of ways to obtain food. To determine whether a particular behavior is motivated, as opposed to automatic or reflexive, an observer needs to watch the individual over a period of time in a variety of circumstances. If the individual varies the behavior at different times and persists until reaching a goal, then the behavior is motivated, or intentional.

Something to Think About

A frog flicks its tongue at a passing insect, captures it, and swallows it. The behavior serves to satisfy the frog's need for food, so we might guess that it is motivated. However, the behavior appears to be as constant as a reflex. How might you determine whether or not the behavior is motivated?

A second characteristic of motivated behaviors is that they vary from time to time, under the influence of both internal (biological) and external (social) controls (Pervin, 1983). For example, you wear clothes to keep warm, to look attractive, to display your exquisite taste, and to avoid arrest for indecent exposure. Exactly what clothing and how much clothing you wear depends on what you feel like doing, today's weather, and the people you expect to see. We have more than one motivation for almost everything we do.

Motivated behaviors vary from person to person as well as from situation to situation. People do not differ much in their drive for oxygen, but they differ significantly in their search for food, still more in their motivation for sexual activity, self-esteem, and self-fulfillment—the needs near the top of Maslow's hierarchy. In the rest of this chapter, we shall return periodically to the ways in which people differ in their motivations.

SUMMARY

■ *Motivation as an energy.* Sigmund Freud and Konrad Lorenz viewed motivated behaviors as outlets for instinctive energies. They believed that specific energies accumulated in the nervous sys-

tem and had to be released in one way or another. Their theories were based on a now-obsolete concept of the nervous system. (page 445)

■ *Motivation as drive reduction.* Some psychologists have described motivation as a drive that energizes behaviors which persist until they reduce the drive. This view implies that we strive to achieve a state of minimal drive and minimal stimulation. (page 446)

■ *Motivation as a way of maintaining homeostasis.* To a large degree, motivated behaviors tend to maintain body conditions and stimulation at a near-constant, or homeostatic, level. This view of motivation can account for much behavior if we also assume that behaviors anticipate future needs instead of just responding to current needs. However, the homeostatic view of motivation overlooks the role of external stimuli in arousing behavior. (page 446)

■ *Motivation as incentive.* Motivations are partly under the control of incentives—external stimuli that pull us toward certain actions. Both drives and incentives control most motivated behaviors. (page 447)

■ *Intrinsic and extrinsic motivations.* People and animals engage in some actions because the actions themselves are interesting or pleasing (intrinsic motivation). Providing an external reinforcement (extrinsic motivation) for the actions may actually reduce the interest or pleasure they provide. (page 447)

■ *Types of motivations.* Psychologists have made several attempts to list or categorize various motivations. One prominent attempt, offered by Abraham Maslow, arranged needs in a hierarchy ranging from basic physiological needs at the bottom to the need for self-actualization at the top. His claim that people satisfy their lower needs before their higher needs does not apply in all cases. (page 449)

■ *Characteristics of motivated behaviors.* Motivated behaviors persist until the individual reaches a goal. They are controlled by internal and external forces and by biological and social forces. Motivated behaviors vary from time to time, from situation to situation, and from person to person. (page 451)

SUGGESTION FOR FURTHER READING

Mook, D. G. (1987). *Motivation: The organization of action.* New York: Norton. A theoretical treatment of the basic principles of motivation.

TERMS

libido according to Sigmund Freud, a kind of sexual energy (page 445)

drive an internal state of unrest or irritation that energizes one behavior after another until one of them removes the irritation (page 446)

homeostasis the maintenance of biological conditions within an organism at an optimum level (page 446)

incentive an external stimulus that prompts an action to obtain the stimulus (page 447)

intrinsic motivation motivation to engage in an act for its own sake (page 447)

extrinsic motivation motivation based on the rewards and punishments an act may bring (page 447)

overjustification effect tendency for people who are given more extrinsic motivation than necessary to perform a task to experience a decline in their intrinsic motivation (page 448)

primary motivation motivation that serves biological needs (page 449)

secondary motivation motivation that serves no biological need directly but develops as a result of specific learning experiences (page 449)

hierarchy of needs Maslow's categorization of human motivations, ranging from basic physiological needs at the bottom to the need for self-actualization at the top (page 450)

self-actualization the need to achieve one's full potential (page 451)

ANSWERS TO CONCEPT CHECKS

1. College students who play tennis for recreation are following an intrinsic motivation. A student who practices tennis in hopes of a professional career is following an extrinsic motivation. According to the overjustification effect, you should expect a retired professional tennis player to enjoy playing tennis less than other people do—at least less than other players of high ability. (page 449)

2. Your interest in graduating from college is a secondary motivation, because it is something you had to learn to value. Such secondary motivations can become very strong. (page 450)

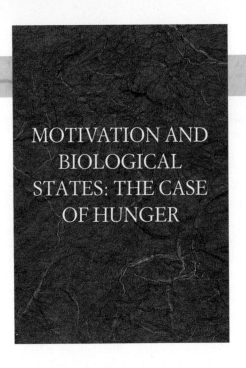

MOTIVATION AND BIOLOGICAL STATES: THE CASE OF HUNGER

What causes us to feel hungry?

How do we choose which foods to eat?

Why do some people gain excessive weight and others deliberately lose weight to a dangerous level?

In the 1970s, the United States suffered a gasoline shortage. Sometimes, drivers found that every service station in their area was out of gas. After a few such experiences, they stopped taking chances. Whenever they saw a station with gas, they would stop and fill their tank, even if it was already more than half full.

If you expect to have trouble finding food from time to time, a good strategy is to fill up your "tank" whenever you can. Throughout most of human existence, people have had to contend with periodic food shortages and famines. To many of our ancestors, the idea of going on a diet to lose weight would have made no sense at all. The same is true for many impoverished people today.

However, most people in the United States, Canada, and western Europe have more than enough to eat at all times. The strategy of filling the tank as often as possible is no longer helpful, and many people habitually overeat.

Social pressures make matters even worse. When you visit friends or relatives, they may offer you food as a gesture of affection, and they may act hurt if you refuse their hospitality. Say you visit the family of your boyfriend or girl-friend, and you want to make a good impression. "Dinner's ready!" someone calls. You go into the dining room and find a huge meal, which your hosts clearly expect you to enjoy. Do you explain that you are not hungry because you already made a pig of yourself at lunch? Probably not.

Eating is controlled by many motives, both physiological and social. We eat to get needed nutrition but also to experience tastes and to socialize (Figure 11.5).

PHYSIOLOGICAL MECHANISMS OF HUNGER

Hunger is a (partly) homeostatic drive that serves to keep fuel available for the body to use. Specialized mechanisms in the brain monitor how much fuel is available; when supplies begin to drop, the brain triggers behaviors that lead to eating. But how does the brain know how much fuel is available and therefore how much a person should eat and how often?

The problem is far more complex than keeping enough fuel in a car's gas tank. When the fuel gauge shows that the tank is running low, you fill it with gas. By contrast, keeping track of how much fuel is in your stomach does not tell you how much more you need. Right now, in addition to the fuel in your stomach and intestines, a fair amount of fuel is present in every cell of your body, ready to be used. Additional fuel is circulating in your blood, ready to enter cells that need it. Still more fuel is stored in fat cells, available to be converted into a form that can enter the blood. If necessary, your body can break down muscle tissues to provide additional fuel. Whereas your car will stop within seconds after it uses all the fuel in the gas tank, your body can keep going for days, even weeks, after your stomach is empty.

Unlike your car, which uses only gas, your body needs a complex mixture of proteins, fats, and carbohydrates, plus assorted vitamins and minerals. How much you should eat at a given meal depends both on how much nutrition you need and on exactly what combination of nutrients is present in the foods you are eating. How can your brain possibly get it right?

Fortunately, it doesn't need to. The brain monitors how much fuel you need, based on the fuel available in your cells and circulating in your blood. When the need for more fuel is great enough, you feel hungry. How much you eat in your next meal corresponds only loosely to how much you need. If you eat too little, you will feel hungry again soon. If you eat too much, part of the excess will be temporarily stored as fat and later converted from fat to sugars that can enter your bloodstream. As a result, you won't feel hungry again as soon as usual. You do not have to eat exactly the correct amount in a given meal; you can correct your errors over the next few meals.

The Short-Term Regulation of Hunger

To determine how much fuel your body needs at a given moment, your brain keeps track of several factors (Friedman & Stricker, 1976). One of the most important factors is **glucose,** the most abundant sugar in your blood. Many of the foods you eat can be converted into glucose; so can your body's fats. An important source of energy for all parts of the body, glucose is the main source of energy for the brain. The brain monitors the amount of glucose and other fuels entering the cells. If the amount is insufficient, certain parts of the brain produce the sensation of hunger. The **lateral hypothalamus** (Figure 11.6) of the brain is known to contribute to this process, although it is hardly the only important area. After damage to the lateral hypothalamus, individuals eat less and lose weight; some starve to death in the presence of good food.

One cause of hunger is a decreased supply of glucose and other nutrients to the cells (Figure 11.7). Ordinarily, the amount of nutrients present in the blood does not vary widely from time to time; what varies is the amount leaving the blood and entering the cells. The flow of nutrients into the cells depends largely on **insulin,** a hormone which the pancreas releases. Insulin is the body's way of preventing enormous fluctuations in blood glucose and other nutrients (Woods, 1991).

At the beginning of a meal, long before the nutrients have started entering the blood, the brain sends messages to the pancreas to increase its secretion of insulin. Insulin promotes movement of nutrients out of the blood and into the cells—both the cells that need fuel and the cells that can convert nutrients to fat or other stores for later use. As the meal contin-

FIGURE 11.5
Mealtime is more than just an opportunity to satisfy hunger: It is an occasion to bring the family and sometimes friends together, to share a pleasant experience, to discuss the events of the day, and even to pass on a culture from one generation to the next. We expect people to participate in the family's meals, even if they are not hungry.

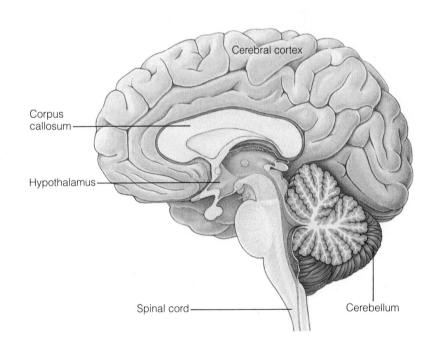

FIGURE 11.6
The hypothalamus, a small area on the underside of the brain, contains a number of subareas that contribute in various ways to eating, drinking, sexual behavior, and other motivated activities. Damage to the lateral hypothalamus inhibits eating; damage to other hypothalamic areas can provoke overeating.

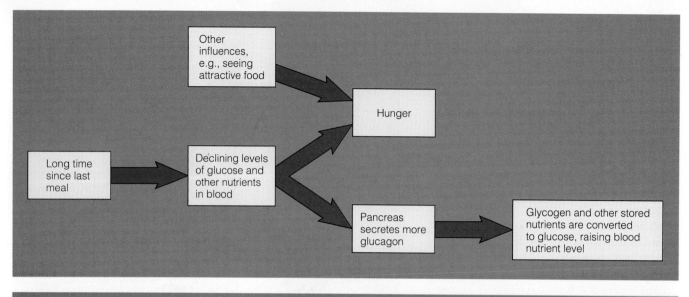

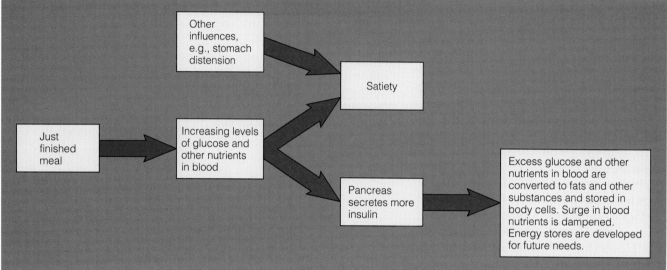

FIGURE 11.7

The short-term regulation of eating depends on the levels of glucose and other nutrients in the blood; it also depends on the appearance and flavor of the food, social influences, and so forth. Varying secretions of the hormones insulin and glucagon help to keep the blood nutrient levels reasonably constant. During and shortly after a meal, insulin moves blood nutrients into storage in the liver and fat cells; during a period without food, glucagon converts stored nutrients into blood glucose.

ues, the digested food enters the blood, but almost as fast as it enters, insulin helps to move excess nutrients out of the blood and into the liver or fat cells. In that manner the insulin holds down the surge of glucose and other nutrients in the blood. Later, long after the meal, when the nutrient supply in the blood starts to drop, the pancreas secretes the hormone **glucagon** instead of insulin. Glucagon helps to convert stored energy supplies back into blood glucose; it continues to do so until the next meal.

At least that is what happens in healthy peo-

ple. Consider what happens if insulin levels stay too high or too low for long times: When insulin levels are consistently low, as in the medical condition diabetes, nutrients enter the cells very slowly and the person feels hungry (Figure 11.8). People with diabetes may eat a great deal without gaining weight because the food they eat cannot enter the cells—not even the fat cells (Lindberg, Coburn, & Stricker, 1984). They simply excrete much of what they eat.

At the opposite extreme, if insulin levels are consistently high, nutrients enter the cells easily, but a high percentage of every meal is converted to fats and stored in fat cells. Because the insulin level remains high, the food stored in fat cells simply stays there; glucagon cannot mobilize it back into blood glucose a couple of hours later. Consequently, as soon as a person with high insulin levels finishes digesting one meal, he or she is hungry for the next one (Johnson & Wildman, 1983). (Figure 11.9 shows the relationship between glucose level and food intake.) Note that if the insulin level is either consistently low or consistently high, the result will be an increased appetite; however, very low insulin leads to weight loss and very high insulin leads to weight gain.

One cause of a high insulin level is damage to axons near the **ventromedial hypothalamus** in the brain, which can occur because of tumors in the area. People or animals with such damage store much of each meal as fats; they gain weight but they are constantly hungry (Friedman & Stricker, 1976; King, Smith, & Frohman, 1984). (See Figure 11.10.)

■ CONCEPT CHECK

3. Insulin levels fluctuate cyclically over the course of a day. Would you guess that they are higher in the middle of the day, when hunger is high, or late at night, when hunger is generally low? (Check your answer on page 468.)

Satiety

The brain monitors the levels of glucose and other nutrients in the cells to determine when the body needs more fuel. But when you start to eat, how does your brain know when you should stop?

Satiety (sah-TI-uht-ee) is the experience of being full, of feeling no more hunger. Ordinarily, satiety depends mostly on stomach distention. When the stomach is full, you feel satiated (Deutsch, Young, & Kalogeris, 1978). Food entering the small intestine may also contribute to the feeling of satiety, possibly by causing the intestine to release a certain hormone (Smith & Gibbs, 1987). Moreover, if you are eating a familiar, calorie-rich diet, you may stop eating long before your stomach is full because you have learned how much energy to expect from the food (Deutsch, 1983). With familiar foods, satiety occurs at about the point when the digestive system has taken in as much food as it can handle. Thus, satiety is a way of preventing an excessive surge of nutrients in the blood (Woods, 1991).

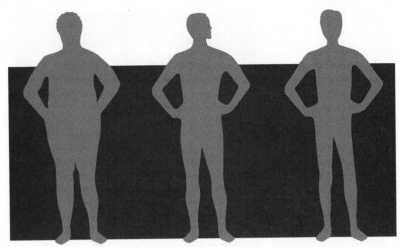

High insulin
Food is stored as fat.
Little glucose in blood.
Appetite increases.
Weight increases.

Lower insulin
Fat supplies are converted to glucose.
Appetite is lower.

Very low insulin
Glucose cannot enter cells. Appetite is high but much of nutrition is excreted.
Weight decreases.

FIGURE 11.8
How insulin affects glucose, appetite, and weight.

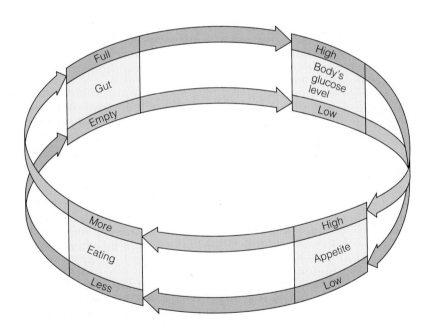

FIGURE 11.9
To maintain equilibrium, homeostatic regulating systems, such as the one for food intake shown here, provide a feedback mechanism. Low levels of glucose—the brain's primary energy source—stimulate the hypothalamus, which prompts the pancreas to release insulin and raise the levels of glucose. Once the glucose reaches a certain level, control mechanisms act to lower it.

FIGURE 11.10
An obese rat with a damaged ventromedial hypothalamus (left) can eat less than an ordinary rat (right) does and still gain weight. This rat's excess fat prevents it from grooming its fur.

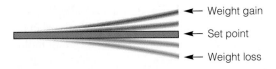

FIGURE 11.11
For most people most of the time, weight fluctuates around a set point, somewhat like a diving board that bounces up and down from a central position.

We also have ways of becoming satiated on a specific food, to prevent an excessive buildup of a particular kind of nutrient (Mook, 1990). For example, after eating a high-protein meal, you might be interested in eating some sweets, but not more proteins. If you had just finished eating sweets, you might be willing to eat a high-protein food, but not more sweets.

The Long-Term Regulation of Hunger

You eat some meals that are rich in calories and some that are low in calories. You probably never eat a meal that contains exactly the number of calories you have burned since your last meal. What would happen if you made a slight but consistent error in the size of each meal? If you consistently ate just 5% more than you needed, you would gain 15 pounds (7 kilograms) per year (Jéquier, 1987). If you consistently ate 5% less than you needed, you would eventually starve to death.

The brain prevents this kind of error by monitoring body weight over time. That long-term mechanism compensates for errors made by the short-term mechanisms of hunger and satiety. When you lose weight, for whatever reason, you feel hungrier and eat more until you gain the weight back. Conversely, when you gain weight, you feel less hungry and cut back on your eating until you lose the weight again. All of this happens automatically; you do not need to check the scales each day. Over the course of months, most people maintain a nearly constant body weight. That weight is referred to as a **set point**—a level that the body attempts to maintain (Figure 11.11).

When someone eats less food than usual for a few days, appetite increases during the next few days; conversely, after a huge meal (Thanksgiving dinner, for example), appetite decreases. Note that the physiological regula-

tors maintain a constant weight, but not necessarily a normal or healthy weight. Some people fluctuate around a low weight; others fluctuate around a much higher weight. Most adults maintain almost the same weight year after year, unless they become ill, change their way of life, or make a deliberate effort to lose weight.

■ CONCEPT CHECK

4. After damage to the ventromedial hypothalamus, an animal's weight eventually reaches a higher than usual level and then fluctuates around that amount. What has happened to the set point? (Check your answer on page 468.)

MOTIVES IN FOOD SELECTIONS

So far I have discussed how you determine when and how much to eat. A separate issue, just as important, is how you determine which foods to eat. Within a fairly wide range, you can vary your choices from day to day without noticing much effect. Consider the following analogy.

One day the chef made soup out of nothing but vegetables: broccoli, potatoes, carrots, peas, beans, onions, corn, a pinch of salt, and lots of water. The next day the chef used chicken, beef, tomatoes, cheese, spices, and some fruit. Surprisingly, the soup turned out almost the same as it did the day before. It filled up the pot a bit more, but it was basically the same soup. In fact, no matter how exotic the ingredients the chef added, the soup always ended up about the same.

That "soup" is your body. The chef (your hand) throws in different ingredients every day, and sometimes you fill up the pot a little more than usual. But your body stays about the same. The human digestive system has an amazing

FIGURE 11.12

Infants and young children will try eating almost anything and refuse a food only if it tastes bad. As they grow older they learn to avoid foods for other reasons. People avoid eating some substances to avoid getting sick; they avoid other substances because the very idea of eating them is disgusting.

ability to turn almost any food into tissues and energy.

Not all ingredients are acceptable, of course. Sand and furniture polish are definitely out. And the system needs some variety. If you eat just one food day after day, you are likely to end up ill. Yet, within a fairly wide range, you can exert much freedom in your choice of foods.

Nevertheless, most people acquire strong food preferences. How do we decide what to eat? Mainly we learn what *not* to eat. Toddlers around the age of 1 ½ will put almost anything into their mouth and try to eat it (Figure 11.12). Gradually they learn to avoid insects, hair, soap, paper, leaves, and other items that adults consider inedible (Rozin, Hammer, Oster, Horowitz, & Marmora, 1986). Up to age 7 or 8, almost the only reason children give for refusing to eat something is that they think it would taste

bad (Rozin, Fallon, & Augustoni-Ziskind, 1986). As they grow older, they give a wider variety of reasons for accepting certain foods and rejecting others. Food selection is a complex matter; as with other motivations, it depends on a combination of physiological, social, and cognitive factors. Let's consider some of the most important factors.

Acceptance or Rejection of Foods Based on Taste

Some taste preferences are present at birth. Infants readily consume sweet liquids; when they taste something bitter or sour, they turn their head and spit it out.

At least one taste preference can be triggered by an abnormal condition within the body. One boy showed a strong craving for salt. As an infant, he licked the salt off crackers and bacon but refused to eat the food itself. One of the first words he learned was *salt*. He put a thick layer of salt on everything he ate, and sometimes he ate salt by itself. When deprived of salt, he ate almost nothing and began to waste away. At the age of 3 ½, he was taken to the hospital and fed the usual hospital fare. He soon died of salt deficiency (Wilkins & Richter, 1940).

It turned out that the boy's adrenal glands were defective. These glands secrete hormones that enable the body to retain salt. The boy craved such great amounts of salt because salt was being excreted so rapidly from his body. (We are often told to limit our salt intake for health reasons, but too little salt can also be dangerous.)

Research on animals confirms that a deficiency of salt in the body triggers an immediate craving for salty foods. As soon as animals, including humans, become salt deficient, they show a heightened preference for salty tastes (Rozin & Kalat, 1971). People who have lost large quantities of salt as a result of bleeding or heavy sweating often express a craving for salt. Apparently, salt actually tastes better to salt-deficient individuals than it does to others (Jacobs, Mark, & Scott, 1988). In short, changes in body chemistry can alter a person's motivation to choose a particular food.

Preference for Familiar Foods

Although people eat a wide variety of foods, they are cautious about eating foods they have never eaten before. Think about the first time

FIGURE 11.13
People associate the foods they eat, especially unfamiliar foods, with the way they feel afterward. If you ate corn dogs and cotton candy just before getting on a wild roller coaster ride and then got sick from the ride, you would find that something in your brain had "blamed" the food for your feeling ill, even though you consciously believe that the food had nothing to do with your illness. Ordinarily, however, this kind of learning enables us to learn to avoid harmful substances.

Crispy Cajun Crickets

(Adapted from a recipe in the *Food Insects Newsletter*, March 1990)

Tired of the same old snack food? Perk up your next party with Crispy Cajun Crickets ("pampered" house crickets, *Acheta domesticus*, available from Flucker's Cricket Farm, P.O. Box 378, Baton Rouge, LA 70821, 800-735-8537).

   1 cup crickets
   1 pinch oatmeal
   4 ounces butter, melted
      Salt
      Garlic
      Cayenne

1. Put crickets in a clean, airy container with oatmeal for food. After one day, discard sick crickets and freeze the rest.
2. Wash frozen crickets in warm water and spread on a cookie sheet. Roast in a 250-degree oven until crunchy.
3. Meanwhile, heat butter with remaining ingredients and sprinkle this sauce on crickets before serving.

Yield: 1 serving

FIGURE 11.14
People avoid eating some potential foods because they are disgusted by the very idea of eating them. For example, most people would refuse to eat insects, regardless of any assurances that the insects were nutritious and harmless.

much as any other children do, but by the time they reach adulthood, many insist on having them with almost every meal. Cuisine is one of the most stable features of human cultures. In the United States, for example, the children and grandchildren of immigrants tend to follow the food choices of their forebears long after they have discarded other old-country customs.

Learned Associations with Foods

As mentioned in Chapter 7, animals associate foods with the gastrointestinal consequences of eating them. The same is true of humans. When you eat something and later get sick, you may form a strong aversion to that food, especially if it was unfamiliar. Ordinarily, that aversion occurs because something in the food made you ill, but the same learning takes place even if something else caused the illness. A person who eats a greasy corn dog at an amusement park and then goes on a wild ride and gets sick may find corn dogs repulsive from then on (Figure 11.13). The person may "know" the ride was at fault, but somehow an area deep in the brain associates the food with the sickness.

Moreover, people sometimes reject safe, nutritious foods because they have learned to associate them with something that evokes repulsive associations (Rozin & Fallon, 1987; Rozin, Millman, & Nemeroff, 1986). In our society, most people refuse to eat brains or any part of a dog, cat, or horse. How would you like to try the tasty morsels described in Figure 11.14? Most people find the idea of eating insects repulsive, even if the insects were sterilized to kill all germs (Rozin & Fallon, 1987). They also say they would refuse to drink a glass of apple juice after a dead, sterilized cockroach had been dipped into it. After seeing a cockroach dipped into a glass of apple juice, some people even refuse to drink other apple juice poured into a different glass (Rozin, Millman, & Nemeroff, 1986).

you tried artichokes, jalapeño peppers, or coffee, for example. Although you probably enjoy new combinations of familiar ingredients, you tend to be wary of a new food or drink. If you ever become ill after eating something, you are likely to be even more cautious about eating something new (Rozin, 1968).

Members of every culture and every ethnic group become familiar with its preferred ways of preparing and seasoning foods. Children who grow up in Italian families come to prefer foods flavored with tomato, garlic, and olive oil. Mexican children at first dislike jalapeños as

EATING DISORDERS

The mechanisms I have discussed so far enable most people to select a reasonable, well-balanced diet and to maintain their weight within normal limits. In some individuals, the motivational mechanisms go awry. They feel hungry all the time and eat too much, or they alternate between stuffing themselves and starving themselves, or they feel hungry but refuse to eat.

Some of these disorders result from physiological abnormalities; others result from social and cognitive influences that compete with the normal physiological mechanisms.

Obesity

Obesity is the excessive accumulation of body fat. A body weight 20–40% above the standard for a person's height is considered mild obesity. Weight 41–100% above the standard is considered moderate obesity. Weight more than 100% above the standard is considered severe obesity (Berkow, 1987). Why do some people become seriously overweight? Obviously because they take in more calories than they use up. But *why* do they do that? One reason, as we have seen, is that some people have high levels of insulin, which causes much of the food they eat to be stored as fats. Let's consider some other possible explanations.

Emotional Disturbances

One prevalent idea is that people overeat in response to anxiety, depression, or some other emotional problem. Some people do try to cheer themselves up by overeating. In one survey of 100 adults (Edelman, 1981), 40 said that they overeat three or more times a month when they fall into an unpleasant mood. When they feel nervous, tired, lonely, or sorry for themselves, they set out on a binge of eating. The binge enables them to focus their attention on eating and away from their other concerns (Heatherton & Baumeister, 1991). Afterward, they feel bloated and regret having eaten so much, but they also feel calm and relaxed.

Although people temporarily gain weight after one of these binges, that weight gain does not become a permanent overweight condition. Edelman's study revealed that as many normal-weight people as overweight people engage in eating binges. Moreover, other evidence indicates that overweight people, on the average, experience about the same emotional problems as other people do. The prevalence of anxiety, depression, and other psychological concerns is no greater among obese people than among other people of the same age and the same overall health (Wadden & Stunkard, 1987). Apparently, the only difference is that severely overweight people often feel lonely and depressed *as a result* of being overweight. In short, emotional disturbance is not a plausible explanation for why certain people are overweight.

Each culture has its own traditional way of preparing and flavoring its foods. Immigrants to the United States may encounter difficulties in obtaining all the ingredients familiar to them; some will go to great lengths to obtain various spices. If they cannot obtain the spices they want, they may find some way to combine other spices and ingredients to approximate the desired flavor.

Overresponsiveness to the Taste of Foods

Like humans, rats will become obese under certain conditions. We can make a rat obese either by damaging parts of its brain or by feeding it a diet rich in sweet and fatty foods (Blundell, 1987). As rats grow more and more obese, they become increasingly finicky about their food. They overeat when they are offered highly palatable foods, but they undereat when they are offered less tasty foods (Sclafani & Springer, 1976; Teitelbaum, 1955). Apparently their eating is guided more by incentives (the taste of food) than by drives (the body's need for food).

Might the same be true of overweight people? According to the **externality hypothesis** (Schachter, 1971; Schachter & Rodin, 1974), overweight people are motivated more strongly by external cues (such as the taste and appearance of food) than by internal cues (the physiological mechanisms that control hunger). Perhaps the tendency to overeat tasty foods leads people to gain weight.

Stanley Schachter (1968, 1971) supported this hypothesis with some very simple experiments. In one case, college students were told they were taking part in a taste experiment. They were all given a milkshake and were told to drink as much of it as they wanted. Then they

FIGURE 11.15
According to the externality hypothesis, overweight people base their eating habits mostly on taste, not on hunger. In one experiment, overweight people drank more than average when their milkshakes tasted good, but less than average when their milkshakes tasted bad. Only some overweight people show this tendency, not all.

were asked to rate its flavor. Overweight students drank more than the normal-weight students when the milkshake tasted good, but less when it tasted bad (Figure 11.15). Not all overweight people show this tendency, but some do.

Does this result indicate that people become overweight *because* they are motivated more strongly by taste than by the need for food? Maybe, maybe not. It is equally plausible that they respond more strongly to external cues *after* becoming overweight.

Decreased Energy Output

Many overweight people consistently eat normal or even small meals and still fail to lose weight (DeLuise, Blackburn, & Flier, 1980). They become and remain overweight because they expend too little energy. I refer here not just to their lack of exercise but also to their failure to burn off enough calories in their overall metabolism, either because of low levels of thyroid hormones or for other reasons.

Obesity tends to run in families (Stunkard et al., 1986). By studying infants born to obese parents, we may be able to learn something about what predisposes individuals to obesity. One group of investigators compared the infants of 12 overweight mothers and 6 normal-weight mothers over their first year of life. All the babies weighed about the same at birth, but

6 of the babies of the overweight mothers had become overweight by the end of the year. Those babies also had been relatively inactive since birth. During the first 3 months they had expended about 20% less energy per day than had the babies who maintained normal weight (Roberts, Savage, Coward, Chew, & Lucas, 1988).

Low energy expenditure is a good predictor of weight gain in adults as well. Eric Ravussin and his associates (1988) found that the adults with the lowest energy expenditure over a 24-hour period were the most likely to gain weight over the next 2 to 4 years. Figure 11.16 summarizes factors involved in being overweight.

Losing Weight

The best way to lose weight is to eat less—no surprise in that conclusion. Most dieters do in fact succeed in losing weight, and some keep it off permanently (Schachter, 1982). Others, however, despite good intentions, consistently fail to lose weight or alternate between losing it and gaining it back. Some become so desperate they will try almost anything—including surgery to remove fat, implanting a balloon in the stomach (to reduce its capacity), taking drugs that suppress appetite, and having the jaws wired shut (Munro, Stewart, Seidelin, Mackenzie, & Dewhurst, 1987). Even these

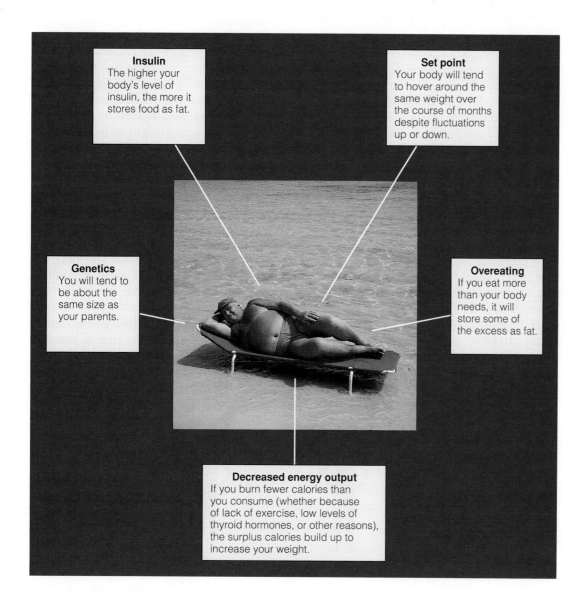

FIGURE 11.16
Why are some people fat and other people thin? Many factors contribute; some are within the individual's control and some are not.

Insulin
The higher your body's level of insulin, the more it stores food as fat.

Set point
Your body will tend to hover around the same weight over the course of months despite fluctuations up or down.

Genetics
You will tend to be about the same size as your parents.

Overeating
If you eat more than your body needs, it will store some of the excess as fat.

Decreased energy output
If you burn fewer calories than you consume (whether because of lack of exercise, low levels of thyroid hormones, or other reasons), the surplus calories build up to increase your weight.

desperate solutions are often ineffective, and they frequently produce health problems of their own.

Besides decreasing their eating, dieters are also advised to get regular exercise, as a way of both burning off extra calories and improving overall health. The difficulty is that most overweight people have trouble sticking to a regular exercise program, and even if they do stick to it, they do not lose much weight unless they also eat less (Segal & Pi-Sunyer, 1989). In one study, 13 obese women exercised fairly vigorously for 90 minutes a day, 4 or 5 times a week, for 14 months. By the end of that time, their mean weight had dropped from 90 kilograms (198 pounds) to 86.3 kilograms (190 pounds). Even that mild weight loss is beneficial, but the point is that exercise by itself is unlikely to turn

a fat person into a thin person (Després et al., 1991).

For people who cannot stick to a diet by themselves, therapists have devised programs based on the belief that people have multiple motivations for most behaviors. People who enter a weight-loss program want to feel healthier and look more attractive. The therapist provides additional motivations, including praise and support from other members of the weight-loss group. The therapist also tries to make clients more aware that their eating is controlled by external cues, such as the aroma and appearance of foods. Sometimes simply getting snack foods out of sight helps people stick to a diet. Because weight is based on long-established eating habits, dieters are advised to learn new habits of eating in moderation, not to starve themselves temporarily and become "gluttons in reverse" (Cummings, 1979). Unfortunately, most supervised weight-loss programs produce disappointing results (Brownell, 1982). One reason for the poor results is that most of the clients are people who have already demonstrated that they cannot stick to a diet—people who have repeatedly failed to lose weight on their own.

The Effect of Intentional Weight Loss on Appetite

Many people in our society, especially women, believe they should lose weight even though their weight is already well within normal limits. The motivation to lose weight is a product of cultural standards that depict thin women as especially attractive. April Fallon and Paul Rozin (1985) asked women to indicate on a diagram which body figure they thought men considered most attractive. The investigators also asked

men which female figure *they* considered most attractive. As Figure 11.17 shows, women thought that men preferred thinner women than most men actually do. (Curiously, the same study found that men thought women preferred heavier men than most women actually do.)

Given the social pressure to be thin, many people deprive themselves of food they would like to eat (Polivy & Herman, 1987). By consistently depriving themselves of food, normal-weight dieters hold their weight below the set point that is natural for their body. Despite their determination, however, nature drives normal-weight dieters to increase their intake. When they fall off their diet at one meal, for whatever reason, they are likely to indulge themselves on the next as well.

In one experiment, normal-weight subjects were told that they were taking part in market research on the flavors of ice creams. Some of them were first asked to drink a milkshake, while others were not. Then they were all asked to taste three flavors of ice cream. (The depen-

FIGURE 11.17
In a study by Fallon and Rozin (1985), women and men were asked which figure they considered most attractive in the opposite sex and which figure they thought the opposite sex considered most attractive. Each sex had systematic misestimates of the other's preferences.

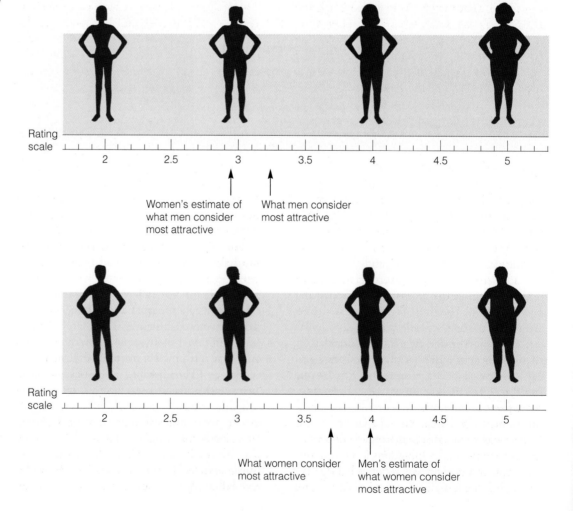

CHAPTER 11: Motivation

dent variable was how much ice cream they ate.) When this experiment was conducted with people who were not dieting, the ones who had first drunk a milkshake ate *less* ice cream than those who had not (Figure 11.18). No surprise here; those who had drunk a milkshake were simply feeling less hungry. But when the experiment was conducted with normal-weight people who were dieting, those who had first drunk a milkshake ate just as much ice cream and sometimes even *more* than those who had not drunk a milkshake (Ruderman, 1986; Ruderman & Christensen, 1983). The tendency was particularly pronounced among dieters with low self-esteem (Polivy, Heatherton, & Herman, 1988). Apparently the dieters said to themselves, "What the heck. As long as I've already eaten more than I should have, I may as well eat all I want."

Anorexia Nervosa

Some people go beyond reasonable limits in their passion to lose weight. The Duchess of Windsor once said, "You can't be too rich or too thin." That may be true about being too rich, but it is definitely wrong about being too thin. Some people are so strongly motivated to be thin (for social and cognitive reasons) that they manage to overrule their physiological drives almost completely.

Here is a case history: A somewhat chubby 11-year-old girl, who weighed 118 pounds (53 kilograms), was told to watch her weight (Bachrach, Erwin, & Mohr, 1965). She did so all through her teens. Along the way she suffered certain hormonal difficulties, including menstrual irregularity, heavy menstrual bleeding, and deficient activity of her thyroid gland. At age 18 she still weighed 118 pounds (53 kilograms), but with her taller frame that weight was normal for her.

After she was married, she moved from her home in Virginia to her husband's place of employment in California. She immediately became homesick. Because the couple could afford only a small apartment with no cooking facilities, they ate most of their meals at a very cheap restaurant. Soon she began to lose weight and stopped menstruating. Sexual relations were painful and unpleasant for her. Her physician warned her that she was losing far too much weight and said that if she did not start regaining some of it he would be forced to send her home to her parents. He intended this as a threat, but she took it as a promise. By the time

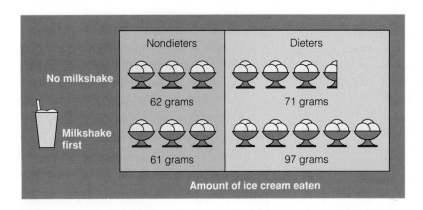

she visited the physician again, she had lost even more weight. She went back to Virginia.

Even after returning to familiar surroundings and home cooking, however, she continued to lose weight. The weight loss seemed to have developed a momentum of its own, and she continued to get thinner, eventually reaching a weight of only 47 pounds (21 kilograms).

This is a case of **anorexia nervosa**, a condition in which a person refuses to eat adequate food and steadily loses weight. (*Anorexia* means "loss of appetite." *Nervosa* means "for nervous reasons," as opposed to organic reasons.) At the outset, the person may have decided to lose weight for health reasons, or to become a dancer, or for some other reason. But the weight loss continues long after the original motivation has vanished.

Anorexia nervosa occurs in about 0.5% of white teenage girls. Anorexia is almost unheard of before the teens; it is rare in boys and uncommon in black girls. Although the problem seldom arises later than the early 20s, it may persist through the 20s and beyond. Because relatively little is known about males with anorexia, our discussion here focuses entirely on females.

As with other psychological conditions, anorexia nervosa comes in all degrees. Of those who are so seriously afflicted that they consult a physician, about 5–10% die of starvation. The prevalence of anorexia has been gradually increasing over the past several decades (Mitchell & Eckert, 1987), perhaps because of society's increasing pressure on women to be thin.

Anorexia nervosa has been described as a "pathological fear of fatness." Even when anorexic women become painfully thin, they often describe themselves as "looking fat" and "needing to lose weight" (Figure 11.19). They suppress their eating, although they generally continue to feel hungry. Anorexia might be described as a special case of Maslow's hierarchy

Dieters who drank a milkshake before tasting ice cream ate more ice cream than did dieters who had not drunk a milkshake. Apparently those who drank a milkshake thought, "I've broken my diet anyway, so I may as well eat all I want." (Data from Ruderman & Christensen, 1983.)

FIGURE 11.19
A fun house mirror causes a temporary distortion of anyone's body appearance. People with anorexia nervosa experience a similar distortion of body image at all times, seeing themselves as much fatter than they really are.

of needs: An anorexic woman manages to suppress her lower-level hunger needs in order to pursue higher-level goals of self-esteem. But her biology does not give up; even while she refuses to eat, her thoughts may be preoccupied with food.

Bulimia

Other people, again mostly young women, starve themselves at times but occasionally throw themselves into an eating binge. They may consume up to 20,000 calories at a time (Schlesier-Stropp, 1984)—the equivalent of about 30 Big Macs, 10 helpings of french fries, and 10 chocolate milkshakes. Some, but not all, force themselves to vomit or use laxatives after gorging on these enormous meals. People who alternate between self-starvation and excessive eating are said to suffer from **bulimia** (literally, "ox hunger"). Like anorexic women, they are preoccupied with food and show an exaggerated fear of growing fat (Striegel-Moore, Silberstein, & Rodin, 1986). Unlike anorexic women, they do not necessarily remain thin.

We might imagine that people who go on eating binges might starve themselves for a while to make up for it. According to Janet Po-

livy and Peter Herman (1985), however, the causation goes in the other direction: It is the dieting that causes the binges. Bulimic people starve themselves far below their normal weight; they then fight their persistent feelings of hunger for a while and then go on an eating binge.

Implications

The research on anorexia and bulimia underscores an important point about motivation in general: Our motivations are controlled by a complex mixture of physiological, social, and cognitive forces. People become overweight (or perceive themselves as overweight) for a variety of reasons, and then try to lose weight mostly for social reasons, such as trying to look attractive. Sometimes the physiological factors and the social factors collide, as when normal-weight people try to make themselves thinner and thinner.

The prevalence of anorexia and bulimia also illustrates the risks that accompany societal pressures for people, especially women, to conform to current standards of beauty (Figure 11.20). Sometimes, healthy people make themselves unhealthy while trying to make their normal bodies "perfect."

Surprisingly, even when they are on the verge of starvation, anorexic women have unusually high energy levels (Falk, Halmi, & Tryon, 1985). They run long distances, engage in sports, work diligently on their school assignments, and sleep very little.

What motivates someone to become anorexic? First, many women who become anorexic have always prized self-control. Their extreme weight loss demonstrates extreme self-control and thereby raises their self-esteem.

Second, by becoming so thin that they lose their secondary sexual characteristics, including breast development, they stop being attractive to men. At least some young women with anorexia have a fear of sex and a fear of accepting an adult role. By becoming extremely thin, they can retreat into looking like, acting like, and being treated like little girls again.

Third, maintaining a dangerously low weight is a way of rebelling quietly and of attracting attention. Before the onset of the disorder, most anorexic girls are described as having been obedient, conforming, and highly intelligent perfectionists—girls who never gave their parents or teachers any trouble (Bruch, 1980; Goldstein, 1981; Rowland, 1970). Perhaps as a

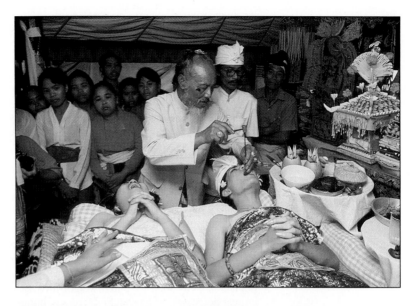

FIGURE 11.20

At various times and places, societies have pressured women to alter their appearance to be considered "attractive"—to emphasize or hide some part of the body, to gain weight or lose weight, even to mutilate body parts. (The photo in the upper right shows an Indonesian tooth-filing ceremony.) In some cases excessive dieting leads to anorexia or bulimia.

result, their parents and others took them for granted and gave them little attention. Their severe weight loss makes the parents and friends suddenly attentive and concerned. The anorexic girl comes to enjoy the attention; she

becomes reluctant to lose it by gaining weight.

There are probably other reasons behind anorexia. As with most complex human behaviors, anorexia is based on a combination of motivations, not just one.

SUMMARY

- *Hunger.* Mechanisms that monitor the amount of glucose and other fuels in the cells regulate hunger. The availability of glucose depends on the hormone insulin, which facilitates the entry of glucose into the cells. (page 454)

- *Satiety.* We stop eating when food distends the stomach, if not before. With familiar foods, we can learn how much to eat, based on the number of calories in the food. (page 457)

- *Long-term regulation of intake.* An individual meal may be larger or smaller than necessary to provide the energy the body needs. In the long run, a person compensates for such fluctuations by regulating body weight. When weight increases, hunger decreases; when weight decreases, hunger increases. (page 458)

- *Food selection.* Food preferences can be altered by changes in body chemistry, such as a deficiency of salt. Other things being equal, we tend to prefer familiar foods. We avoid foods that have been followed by illness and foods that we associate with something repulsive, even if the food itself is harmless. (page 458)

- *Causes of being overweight.* Several factors contribute to a person becoming overweight. High levels of insulin increase weight by causing blood glucose to be stored as fats. People who are motivated more by the tastes of foods than by the need for nutrition may be likely to gain weight. Inactive people are more likely to gain weight than active people. (page 461)

- *Weight-loss techniques.* People in our society resort to a variety of strategies to lose weight, with varying degrees of success. Regular exercise can help severely overweight people to lose weight. (page 462)

- *Effects of unnecessary weight loss.* Normal-weight people who follow a strict diet have a strong desire to eat more than they do. On occasion, they abandon their diet and indulge in eating binges. (page 464)

- *Anorexia nervosa.* People suffering from anorexia nervosa deprive themselves of food, sometimes to the point of starvation. They suppress their physiological drives to satisfy other motivations, including self-esteem. People suffering from bulimia alternate between periods of strict dieting and brief but spectacular eating binges. (page 465)

SUGGESTIONS FOR FURTHER READING

Logue, A. W. (1986). *The psychology of eating and drinking.* New York: Freeman. Discusses normal and abnormal eating, including anorexia and bulimia.

Rozin, P., & Vollmecke, T. A. (1986). Food likes and dislikes. *Annual Review of Nutrition, 6.* 433–456. A review of the factors that influence our choice of foods.

Wurtman, R. J. (1987). Human obesity [Special issue]. *Annals of the New York Academy of Sciences, 499.* A collection of articles by specialists in research and therapy with severely overweight people.

TERMS

glucose the most abundant sugar in the blood (page 455)

lateral hypothalamus an area of the brain that contributes to the control of hunger (page 455)

insulin a hormone which the pancreas releases to increase the entry of glucose and other nutrients into the cells (page 455)

glucagon a hormone which the pancreas releases to convert stored energy supplies into blood glucose (page 456)

ventromedial hypothalamus an area of the brain in which damage leads to weight gain via an increase in the secretion of insulin (page 457)

satiety the experience of being full, of feeling no more hunger (page 457)

set point a level of some variable (such as weight) that the body attempts to maintain (page 458)

obesity the excessive accumulation of body fat (page 461)

externality hypothesis hypothesis that overweight people are motivated more strongly by external cues (such as the taste and appearance of food) than by internal cues (the physiological mechanisms that control hunger) (page 461)

anorexia nervosa a condition in which a person refuses to eat adequate food and steadily loses weight (page 465)

bulimia a condition in which a person alternates between self-starvation and excessive eating (page 466)

ANSWERS TO CONCEPT CHECKS

3. Insulin levels are higher in the middle of the day (LeMagnen, 1981). As a result, much of the food you eat is stored as fats and you become hungry again soon. Late at night, when insulin levels are lower, some of your fat supplies are converted to glucose, which enters the blood. (page 457)

4. The set point has increased. (page 458)

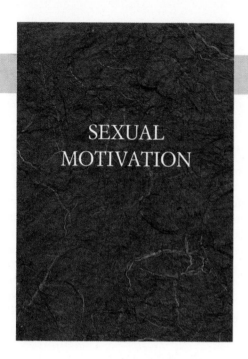

SEXUAL MOTIVATION

What causes sexual arousal?

What sexual customs are prevalent in our society?

What accounts for some of the variations in sexual practices?

In most mammalian species, male and female come together just long enough to mate; then they go their separate ways. In other species, male and female stay together after mating to care for the young. With few exceptions, however, the sex act occurs only when the female is fertile. When she is incapable of becoming pregnant, she does not give off the odors that attract males, and even if a male approaches her sexually, she rejects his advances. Although neither male nor female knows the relationship between mating and pregnancy, their sexual motivations serve the purpose of reproduction.

Humans are exceptions in this regard. We are interested in sex even at times of the month when a woman is unlikely to get pregnant; in fact, we often take measures to prevent pregnancy. Most couples stay together not only long enough to rear children but also long after the children are grown up. Sexual motivation is a force that binds people together in powerful and intimate relationships. Jealousy based on sex drives people apart; it is one of the leading causes of murder (Daly, Wilson, & Weghorst, 1982). In one way or another, our sexual motivation influences many of the social customs that define our civilization.

Sexual motivation, like hunger, depends on both a physiological drive and available incentives. Again as with hunger, the sex drive increases during a time of deprivation, at least up to a point, and it can be inhibited for social and symbolic reasons, including religious vows.

However, the sex drive differs from hunger in important ways. Many people experience little sex drive in the absence of such incentives as a loving partner or erotic stimuli. Moreover, people differ greatly in the incentives that arouse them sexually. Some people are aroused by the sight of shoes or undergarments, the feel of rubber or leather, the experience of inflicting or receiving pain, and other preferences that most people do not share and find hard to understand.

Sexual customs vary sharply from one society to another. These people play "kiss-a-girl" in traditional Ukrainian costumes while riding galloping horses. The point of the game is ostensibly to develop horse-riding skills, but clearly that is not the only motivation.

THE VARIABILITY OF HUMAN SEXUALITY

Sexual motivation varies enormously from one person to another. This point was first demonstrated by Alfred C. Kinsey (Figure 11.21), who was in many ways an unlikely person to become a sex expert. Kinsey, shy and studious, went through high school, college, and graduate school without ever having had a date (Pomeroy, 1972). After earning a doctorate in zoology in 1920, he met a young woman who shared his interest in the study of insects. They were married the following year.

Some years later, in 1938, Indiana University persuaded Kinsey to coordinate a new course on marriage. Faculty members from other departments were to participate in the course, but Kinsey, being a biologist, was to teach the section on sexual relations. Finding little useful information in the library, he set out to interview people about their sexual behavior. Within a few years, what began as a modest effort had become a substantial research program involving lengthy interviews with 18,000 people from all walks of life throughout the United States.

Kinsey conducted all of his interviews face to face. To put people at ease, he assured them that everything they said would be kept confidential and that nothing they said would shock him. To describe the sex organs and sex acts, he used whatever words, technical or slang, that the other person used. Most people said that he enabled them to relax and to talk more freely about sex than they ever had to anyone else.

(Legitimate sex survey researchers take every precaution to assure the anonymity and confidentiality of all replies; for example, they might ask you to fill out and return an anonymous written questionnaire or to answer questions face to face in private. Researchers are unlikely to conduct sex surveys by telephone, because you could not be sure that your answers would be confidential or anonymous, or even that you were talking with a legitimate researcher. If anyone asks you to answer some sex questions over the telephone, *do not* participate. Treat the request as an obscene phone call.)

Kinsey published tables reporting the frequencies of various sex acts among people in the United States in the 1940s. Unfortunately, he could not obtain a random or representative sample of the population. He obtained most of his interviews by going to organizations, ranging from fraternities to nunneries, and trying to get everyone in the organization to talk to him. His sampling of organizations was neither representative nor random, and the statistical data he reported may have been far from accurate. For example, 37% of the men he interviewed reported having at least one homosexual experience. More recent studies with more representative samples have reported percentages around 20% (for example, Fay, Turner, Klassen, & Gagnon, 1989). Even if some of Kinsey's data were inaccurate, his studies paved the way for other surveys and scientific studies of sex.

One of Kinsey's undisputed findings was that human sexual behavior is highly variable (Kinsey, Pomeroy, & Martin, 1948; Kinsey, Pomeroy, Martin, & Gebhard, 1953). Figure 11.22 shows the reported frequencies of orgasm per week by males from adolescence to age 30. Although Kinsey's percentages may not be exactly accurate, the enormous range is clear. While most men were having orgasms zero to four times a week, others were averaging two or three times a day. At the extremes, one 30-year-old man reported that he had experienced orgasm only once in his life, whereas another man reported an average of four to five orgasms a day over the preceding 30 years.

The range of variation was equally great among females. For example, Figure 11.22 also shows the reported frequencies of orgasm in single women age 16 to 20. About 10% of all women reported having never had an orgasm, whereas a few said they had had 50 or more orgasms within 20 minutes.

The mean frequency of orgasm gradually declines as one grows older, as Figure 11.23 shows. But these figures can be very misleading for several reasons. Primarily, these are the results of a cross-sectional study; the results of a longitudinal study might well be different. Furthermore, the data in Figure 11.23 represent means of large groups; the behavior of a given individual may be very different from that of the group mean. Some older people remain almost as active sexually as they ever were, whereas others become almost completely inactive (Martin, 1981).

Something to Think About

Why is it likely that the results of a longitudinal study of aging and sexual activity might be different from those of a cross-sectional study? Think about the possibilities of sampling error and of cohort effects. (Review page 246.)

Kinsey found that most people were unaware of the great variation in sexual behavior in the population at large. For example, when he asked people whether they believed that "excessive masturbation" causes physical and mental illness, most said they did. (We now know it does not.) He then asked what would constitute "excessive." For each person, "excessive" meant a little more than what he or she did. One young man who masturbated about once a month said he thought three times a month would be excessive and would cause mental illness. Another man, who masturbated three times a day, said he thought five times a day would be excessive. (In reaction to these findings, Kinsey once defined *nymphomaniac* as "someone who wants sex more than you do.")

Cultural Variations

Sexual behaviors that are considered acceptable or even normal in one society may be regarded as strange, deviant, or even criminal in another. However, we must approach comparative studies of sexual practices with caution. Imagine what would happen if an anthropologist from New Guinea spent a few months talking to people in one U.S. city and then wrote a book about the sexual customs of American society. The possibilities for distortion and error

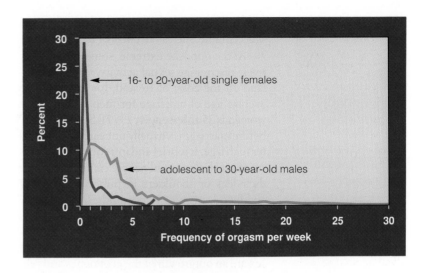

FIGURE 11.22
Frequency of orgasm per week varies widely among adolescent to 30-year-old males and single females age 16 to 20 (Kinsey, Pomeroy, & Martin, 1948; Kinsey, Pomeroy, Martin, & Gebhard, 1953). The actual percentages may be inaccurate, but the frequency of sexual outlets clearly is highly variable.

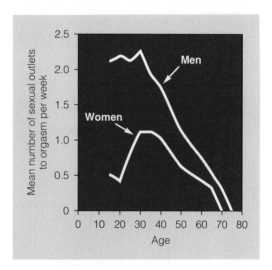

FIGURE 11.23
In Kinsey's samples, the median frequency of orgasm, or climax, began to decline after age 30 to 35, although large differences occur at each age. (From Kinsey, Pomeroy, & Martin, 1948; and Kinsey, Pomeroy, Martin, & Gebhard, 1953.)

are obvious. Although reports about sex in other societies may not be altogether reliable, we know that sexual customs differ strikingly from one society to another.

At one extreme are certain societies in Polynesia that encourage premarital sex, sometimes at an early age, on the theory that intercourse is necessary for sexual maturation (Davenport, 1977). The rules about who are acceptable partners for premarital sex differ from one island to another. On some islands, only potential marriage partners are acceptable. On other islands, only someone who *cannot* be a marriage partner is acceptable, such as an uncle or an aunt.

At the opposite extreme, some societies actively discourage sexual activity. On a small island off the coast of Ireland, for example, the average age of marriage for men is 36 and for women is 25 (Messenger, 1971). Sexual activity before marriage is virtually unheard-of; even after marriage, it is brief and infrequent. Nudity is strictly forbidden, and people cannot even bare their legs or shoulders in public. After early childhood, people do not undress completely even to take a bath. No one on the island knows how to swim. (Swimming would require removing too much clothing.) Their attitudes toward sex are an outgrowth of the economics and religion of the island. Because farm land is limited, they cannot afford to allow population growth. Because their Roman Catholic religion forbids the use of contraceptives, they must hold sexual activity to a minimum.

Anthropological studies of this sort imply that sexual customs are not the direct result of any biological necessity. Human societies can survive with a vast variety of sexual customs; as economic conditions and other circumstances change, attitudes toward sex are likely to change as well.

The custom of "no sex before marriage" probably was easier to follow when people expected to marry young. Through most of the history of Judeo-Christian societies, teenage marriages were typical. The same is true in many nontechnological societies today.

Sexual Behavior and Customs in the United States

In most Judeo-Christian societies, the standard teaching (if not always the standard practice) has long been "no premarital or extramarital sex, especially for women." Centuries ago, when people married younger than they do today, that teaching may have been easier to follow. Today, the mean age at first marriage is almost 23 for women and 25 for men (National Center for Health Statistics, 1988). The mean age of reaching puberty is about 13 or 14 (Kumar, 1975). A delay of 10 years (often more) between puberty and marriage makes the prohibition against premarital sex a more serious strain than it used to be.

In an earlier era, young people were urged to abstain from masturbation as well as from intercourse. In the late 1800s, Graham's crackers and Kellogg's cornflakes were created to provide intentionally bland foods that would help young people suppress their sexual desires (Money, 1983). The theory was that if people don't enjoy their food very much, then they won't crave other pleasures, either. (Can you imagine an advertisement today, "Buy our cereal; it will lower your sex drive"?)

One reason for the rule of no sex before marriage was society's desire to avoid the birth of fatherless children. Today the availability of contraceptive devices has made it possible to reduce the number of unwanted pregnancies. Moreover, the manner in which sex is treated in the movies and other media has encouraged people to engage in premarital intercourse with greater freedom than before.

Not everyone in the United States is sexually permissive, of course (Brooks-Gunn & Furstenberg, 1989; Christopher & Cate, 1985). Some often have casual sexual relations; others have sex only after establishing a serious relationship; others only after marriage. The expectations governing sexual activity in our society are not so well defined as they are in many other cultures.

Something to Think About

Sexual customs vary significantly from one society to another, but most societies have a fairly clear, unambiguous standard that most people follow. Would our society be better off or worse off if nearly all people followed the same set of sexual customs?

Sexual Behavior in the AIDS Era

During the 1980s, a new factor entered into people's sexual motivations: the fear of **acquired immune deficiency syndrome (AIDS),** a new and deadly sexually transmitted, or venereal, disease that gradually destroys the body's immune system.

For the AIDS virus to spread from one person to another, it must enter the second person's blood. (Outside the blood or the body's cells, the virus cannot survive.) There are three common routes of transmission: transfusions of contaminated blood, sharing needles used for intravenous injections, and sexual contact.

In vaginal intercourse, there is an estimated 3% chance that an infected male will transmit the virus to a female, and no more than a 2% chance that an infected female will transmit it to a male (Kaplan, 1988). The likelihood of transmission increases if either partner has an open wound on the genitals or if the woman is menstruating. The probability of transmission during anal intercourse is much higher, about 7–10%, because the lining of the rectum is likely to be torn (Kaplan, 1988). None of these estimates can be completely accurate, of course.

For generations, people have known how to avoid contracting syphilis, gonorrhea, and other **venereal diseases:** Don't have sex with someone who might be infected, or when in doubt, use a condom. (To be completely safe, don't have sex at all.) Because AIDS is life-threatening and (so far) incurable, it has had a greater impact on sexual customs than other venereal diseases have had. Since the advent of AIDS, many people, especially homosexual men, have grown more cautious. More homosexual males are choosing long-term sexual partners, and more are using condoms to reduce the likelihood of transmitting the virus (William, 1984). One study of men leaving a homosexual bathhouse found that only 10% were engaging in anal sex without a condom—a far lower percentage than was common prior to the AIDS crisis (Richwald et al., 1988).

Some heterosexual couples also have become more cautious. As in other areas of life, some people habitually take greater risks than others, either because they do not think about the risks or because they think "it can't happen to me." According to one survey of sexually active teenage girls in Philadelphia, about one fourth to one third of the girls had used no contraceptives at all during their most recent sexual intercourse (Loewenstein & Furstenberg,

1991). However, the use of condoms as a method of contraception has increased since the start of the AIDS scare; at one college, the use of condoms increased from 6% of sexually active couples in 1975 to 25% in 1989 (De-Buono, Zinner, Daamen, & McCormack, 1990).

Right to life

AIDS is a preventable disease. By using condoms during sex and by not sharing injection needles with other people, one can greatly decrease the probability of transmitting or receiving the AIDS virus. Advertisements such as this one have prompted many people to change their behaviors.

SEXUAL AROUSAL

Sexual motivation depends on both physiological and cognitive influences. William Masters and Virginia Johnson (1966), who pioneered the study of human sexual response, discovered that physiological arousal during the sex act is about the same in men and women. They observed hundreds of people engaging in masturbation and sexual intercourse in a laboratory and monitored their physiological responses, including heart rate, breathing, muscle tension, blood engorgement of the genitals and breasts, and nipple erection. Masters and Johnson identified four physiological stages in sexual arousal (Figure 11.24). During the first stage,

FIGURE 11.24
Sexual arousal usually proceeds through four stages—excitement, plateau, orgasm, and resolution. Each line represents the response of a different individual. (After Masters & Johnson, 1966.)

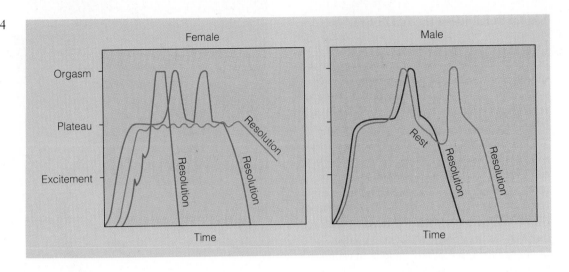

excitement, a man's penis becomes erect and a woman's vagina becomes lubricated. Breathing grows rapid and deep. Heart rate and blood pressure increase. Many people experience a flush of the skin, which sometimes resembles a measles rash. Women's nipples become erect, and, if they have never nursed a baby, their breasts swell slightly. Although this stage is referred to as excitement, it actually requires some level of relaxation. Nervousness interferes with sexual excitement; so do stimulant drugs (even coffee).

During the second stage, called the *plateau,* excitement remains fairly constant. This stage lasts for varying lengths of time, depending on the person's age and the intensity of the stimulation. During the third stage, excitement becomes intense and is followed by a sudden relief of tension known as *climax* or *orgasm,* which is felt throughout the entire body. During the fourth and final stage, *resolution,* the person returns to an unaroused state.

As Figure 11.24 shows, the pattern of excitation varies from one person to another. Some women experience no orgasm at all; others experience a single orgasm or multiple orgasms consecutively. Men do not experience multiple orgasms, although they may achieve orgasm again following a rest (or refractory) period. In both sexes, the intensity of orgasm ranges from something like a sigh to an extremely intense experience over the whole body.

At any rate, that is the usual pattern. Some people are unable to complete the four stages of arousal. Some men cannot get or maintain an erection. Others have premature ejaculations; they advance from excitement to orgasm sooner than they or their partners wish. A substantial number of women, perhaps as many as 10%, and relatively few men advance to the plateau stage but seldom or never experience orgasm. The reasons for such sexual dysfunctions include both physiological disorders and competing motivations. For example, some people are inhibited in their sexual arousal because they have been taught that sex is shameful. When the problems are motivational rather than physiological, a therapist can work with people to reduce their anxieties or to help them learn new patterns of sexual activity more satisfactory to both themselves and their partners (Andersen, 1983).

SEXUAL IDENTITY AND ORIENTATION

Just as hunger includes two major aspects—how much food to eat and which foods to choose—sexual motivation includes two aspects: how frequently to have sex and with whom. We begin by developing a clear preference for male or female partners. What is responsible for that preference?

Psychologists distinguish two aspects of being male or female: sexual identity and sexual orientation. **Sexual identity** is the sex the person regards himself or herself as being. That is, people think of themselves as being men or women, and they identify with others of that sex. **Sexual orientation** is the person's preference for male or female sex partners (or both). Someone who thinks of himself as a man and who prefers other men as sex partners has a male sexual identity and a homosexual (or "gay") sex orientation. Sexual identity is based partly on anatomical and physiological factors, partly on social influences. Psychologists do not yet fully understand the causes of sexual orientation.

Influences on Sexual Anatomy

In the earliest stages of development, the human fetus has a "unisex" appearance (Figure 11.25a). One structure subsequently develops into either a penis or a clitoris; another structure develops into either a scrotum or labia. The direction that development takes depends on hormonal influences during prenatal development. Genetic male fetuses generally secrete relatively high levels of the hormone **testosterone,** and their structures develop into a penis and a scrotum. Genetic female fetuses generally secrete lower levels of testosterone, and their structures develop into a clitoris and labia. High levels of the hormone **estrogen** are present in the mother at this time, and some of that hormone enters the circulation of the fetus. However, because sexual development depends mostly on the testosterone levels, the mother's hormones do not alter the appearance of either male or female fetuses.

In rare cases, the fetus may secrete an intermediate level of testosterone early in development, or the mother may take medications similar to testosterone. The structures may then develop into something about halfway between male and female (Money & Ehrhardt, 1972).

Some psychologists believe that the psychological makeup of adults reflects this early bisexuality. According to this view, we go through life with the potential to adopt either the male or the female role in our relationships with others and to respond sexually to either male or female partners. For most people, only half of that potential expresses itself. What activates one half or the other—or both? It may be that hormonal levels in the fetus influence subsequent sexual behavior, as they influence sexual anatomy. However, the evidence is not conclusive (Hines, 1982). I shall discuss some of it later in this section.

■ CONCEPT CHECK

5. *If a human fetus were exposed to very low levels of both testosterone and estrogen throughout prenatal development, how would the sexual anatomy appear? (Check your answer on page 482.)*

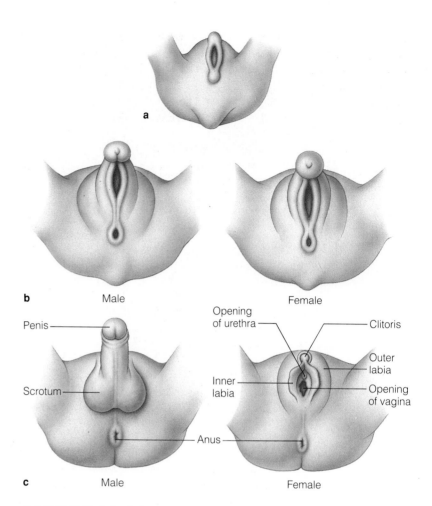

FIGURE 11.25
The human genitals look the same for male and female for about the first 6 weeks after conception (a). Differences begin to emerge in the second trimester (b) and are well developed at birth (c).

Influences on Sexual Orientation

No doubt you developed your sexual identity at an early age, soon after your parents told you whether you were a boy or a girl. With rare exceptions, people's sense of sexual identity matches their sexual anatomy. Sexual anatomy is a less certain determinant of sexual orientation. While most people feel sexual attraction to members of the opposite sex (heterosexuality), a significant number are sexually attracted to members of their own sex (homosexuality).

Prevalence of Homosexual Orientations
How large is that "significant number" of people who have a homosexual orientation? We

How common is homosexuality in the United States? Many people state the number "ten percent" with great confidence, but the evidence on this point is shaky. Sexual orientation probably depends on the combined influences of many factors, some biological and some experiential, but the full explanation is far from certain at this point.

might imagine that the percentage should be easy to determine, and indeed many people announce the figure "ten percent" as if it were an established fact. The exact percentage is difficult to specify, however, for two reasons. First, homosexuality versus heterosexuality is not an all-or-none matter; many people have at least briefly experimented with both types of activity, even if their orientation is predominantly one or the other. Second, it is difficult to get a large, representative sample of the population to answer sex surveys, and to answer them honestly.

In the 1940s and 1950s, Alfred Kinsey and his associates interviewed about 18,000 people. Kinsey reported that about 37% of the men he interviewed reported having at least one homosexual experience and about 13% had a predominantly homosexual orientation. About 7% of women had a predominantly homosexual orientation, although only 4% had extensive homosexual experience. The often-quoted figure that "10% of people are predominantly homosexual" is simply the mean of Kinsey's 13% of men and 7% of women. As Bruce Voeller (1990, p. 36) pointed out, "the 10% figure is regularly used by scholars, by the press, and in government statistics. As with so many pieces of knowledge (and myth), repeated telling made it so." However, Kinsey's data

were based on interviews with people willing (and sometimes eager) to be interviewed, not with a representative or random sample of the population. Moreover, his interviews were mostly limited to white people in the midwestern and northeastern states; we should beware of extending his conclusions to people of all races in all places half a century later.

A more recent survey with a more representative but smaller sample (1,450 U.S. men) indicated that at least 20% had had at least one sexual contact to orgasm with another male (Fay, Turner, Klassen, & Gagnon, 1989). For most of those men, however, their only such experience was some adolescent sex play, such as teenage boys masturbating together. A little more than 3% said they had "occasionally" or "often" had sexual contact with other males after the age of 19.

Possible Explanations of Sexual Orientation Differences Adult homosexuals often report that their sexual preference was apparent to them from as early an age as they can remember. They did not choose it voluntarily, and they could not change it easily. What causes some people to develop a heterosexual preference and others to develop a homosexual preference? There probably are several contributing factors. I shall deal here only with males, mainly because most of the research has been done with males.

Society's attitudes toward homosexuality have changed repeatedly over time. So far as we can tell, the ancient Greeks and Romans considered it fairly typical for men to engage in occasional sexual activities with each other as well as with women (Boswell, 1990). (The Greek and Roman writers had little to say about women's sexual interests.) In a later era, Europeans regarded male homosexuality as sinful or criminal. By the early 20th century, the "enlightened" view was that homosexuality was not sinful, but merely a sign of disease or mental illness. For many years, psychologists and psychiatrists attributed male homosexuality to the effects of a domineering or rejecting mother who lived in conflict with a detached, indifferent father (Wakeling, 1979). Their evidence, however, was based on a badly distorted sample: They were acquainted with various homosexual men who had sought help for psychological troubles. But homosexual men without psychological problems never consulted therapists, and therefore the therapists did not know that such men existed (Hoffman, 1977). Studies of homosexual men who have never gone to a therapist conflict with the view that homosexuality is a psychological disorder; many homosexual men are content and well adjusted (Siegelman, 1974). Furthermore, many homosexual men who do suffer anxiety and other problems may simply be responding to the manner in which society treats them. Consequently, psychologists and psychiatrists today consider a homosexual orientation to be a natural variation in sexual motivation.

What, then, accounts for this variation in sexual orientation? There are probably a variety of reasons, differing from one person to another. Genetics is one possible contributing factor. Figure 11.26 shows the results of one study concerning homosexuality in the twin brothers and adopted brothers of adult homosexual men (Bailey & Pillard, 1991). Note that homosexuality is more prevalent in the monozygotic (identical) twins than in the dizygotic (fraternal) twins. That trend suggests that some gene may predispose men toward homosexuality, although a gene could hardly be the only factor. (If it were, then 100% of the monozygotic twins would have homosexual orientations.) Note also that homosexuality is more common among the dizygotic twins than among adopted brothers. That trend also suggests a genetic factor, although it could also indicate the influence of some factor in the prenatal environment, shared by twins but not by boys who simply grow up in the same family.

Genes are clearly not the only influence on sexual orientation, and perhaps not even the only biological influence. Prenatal hormones constitute another possible influence; here the evidence is suggestive but hardly conclusive. Let us examine it carefully.

Hormonal Influences on Sexual Orientation

WHAT'S THE EVIDENCE?

Hormonal influences at certain stages of pregnancy can alter the anatomy of the genitals and of certain parts of the brain; perhaps prenatal hormonal influences can alter the brain in ways that eventually influence sexual orientation. (Adult hormone levels do not control sexual orientation.)

In an area such as this, laboratory experiments on humans are out of the question. Inves-

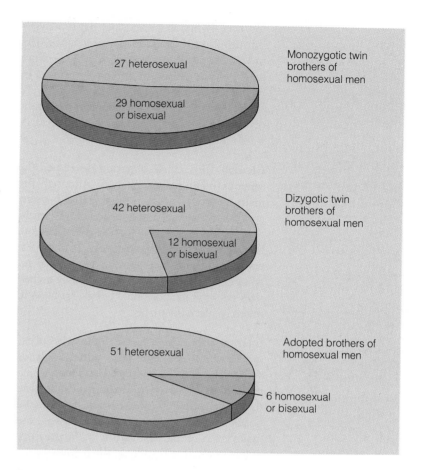

FIGURE 11.26
The probability of a homosexual orientation is higher among monozygotic twin brothers of homosexual men than among dizygotic twin brothers of homosexual men. The probability is still lower among adopted brothers of homosexual men. These data suggest a possible role of genes in the development of sexual orientation. (Based on results of Bailey & Pillard, 1991.)

tigators combine experiments on animals and correlational studies with humans. Let's begin with an animal study.

AN EXPERIMENT WITH RATS
Hypothesis Because the hormones of a pregnant rat pass through her blood into the blood of her fetuses, hormonal changes in the mother might alter the brain development of the fetuses. Based on previous studies measuring the times that certain parts of the brain develop, Ingeborg Ward (1972, 1977) proposed that an alteration of the rat mother's hormones during the last week of her pregnancy might lead to long-term changes in the sexual orientation of her offspring.

Method Ward confined pregnant rats in a small, tight, brightly lighted Plexiglas enclosure for three 45-minute periods per day on days 14 through 21 of the rats' 23-day pregnancy. This procedure produced a stress response, which increased the release of adrenal hormones by the mother. After the babies were born, Ward let them develop without any further stress. She observed their sexual behavior in adulthood toward both males and females.

Results The female offspring developed the same as other female rats do. Although the males developed nearly normal sexual anatomy and nearly normal adult testosterone levels, they responded sexually to male partners more than they did to female partners. In the presence of females, they showed few sexual responses. In the presence of males, they arched their backs in the position a female rat takes to invite a male to mount her.

Interpretation In response to the stressful experience, the mother rats' adrenal glands secreted high levels of adrenal hormones, which apparently competed with the male hormone testosterone for entry to the brain. The adrenal hormones also temporarily suppressed the males' testosterone production. In the presence of low levels of testosterone, the hypothalamus (a part of the brain) developed in a manner that increased the probability of a sexual interest in males.

Even in rats, sexual orientation depends on experiences and not just on brain anatomy. In a later study, Ingeborg Ward and Jonathan Reed (1985) found that a prenatally stressed male rat that shared a cage with a female for the first 2 months of life was likely to develop a stronger sexual interest in female partners than in male partners. A prenatally stressed male caged with a male was likely to respond sexually either to other males or equally to both males and females. (Males that had not been exposed to prenatal stress were more interested in females than in other males, regardless of their early experiences.) Prenatal stress does not necessarily cause a male rat to develop a sexual interest in males; it alters the way he reacts to various experiences after birth.

A CORRELATIONAL STUDY WITH HUMANS
Although prenatal hormones influence sexual orientation in rats, we cannot assume that human development depends on the same factors as rat development does. Still, the rat experiment shows us something to look for in humans.

Hypothesis Perhaps women whose adrenal glands are highly activated by stress during some stage of pregnancy give birth to sons with a preference for male sexual partners.

Method Investigators asked 283 mothers of adult sons and daughters to recall any stressful experiences they had before or during pregnancy (Ellis, Ames, Peckham, & Burke, 1988). The investigators sent a separate questionnaire to the sons and daughters to determine their sexual orientation.

Results On a scale of stress severity ranging from a low of 1 to a high of 4, the mothers of male homosexuals rated the middle third of their pregnancy at 2.3. The mean for the other mothers was 1.5. There were no significant differences among the mothers of heterosexual men, bisexual men, heterosexual women, and homosexual women.

Interpretation These results support the hypothesis that prenatal stress increases the probability that a male will develop a homosexual orientation. They do not suggest any relationship between prenatal stress and bisexuality or lesbianism. At most, prenatal hormones increase the probability of a given sexual orientation; sexual orientation develops through a person's experiences as well, in ways that psychologists do not yet clearly understand (Ellis & Ames, 1987).

Although these results are suggestive, we cannot draw a firm conclusion. First, the mothers of homosexual men reported only slightly more prenatal stress than did the other mothers. Second, it is difficult to reconstruct accurate memories of pregnancy 20 years or more after the fact. An ideal study would measure stress during pregnancy and then determine the sexual orientation of the sons and daughters many years later.

Nevertheless, these results suggest a possible influence of prenatal hormones. We have another way to test this hypothesis: Prenatal testosterone levels control the development of certain brain areas, especially in the hypothalamus. If prenatal hormones have some effect on the eventual development of sexual orientation, then examination of the brain should reveal measurable differences between homosexual and heterosexual men.

A CORRELATIONAL STUDY ON THE HUMAN BRAIN
Animal studies have demonstrated that one section of the anterior hypothalamus is generally

larger in males than it is in females and that it is necessary for the display of male-typical sexual activity. Its growth is known to depend on prenatal hormones. This, then, is an interesting area to compare in the brains of homosexual and heterosexual men.

Hypothesis A particular cluster of neurons in the anterior hypothalamus will be larger, on average, in the brains of heterosexual men than in the brains of homosexual men or heterosexual women.

Method Simon LeVay (1991) examined the brains of 41 young or middle-aged adults (ages 26–59), who had died of AIDS or other causes. AIDS was the cause of death for all 19 of the homosexual men in the study, 6 of the 16 heterosexual men, and 1 of the 6 heterosexual women. No brains of homosexual women were available for study. LeVay measured the sizes of four clusters of neurons in the anterior hypothalamus, including two clusters for which sex differences are common and two which do not differ between the sexes.

Results LeVay found no systematic variation in the size of three of the neuron clusters. However, he did find substantial differences in one cluster, known as the third interstitial nucleus. This area was, on the average, about twice as large in heterosexual men as it was in homosexual men, and about the same size in homosexual men as it was in heterosexual women. Figure 11.27 shows results for two representative individuals. The results probably do not simply reflect the cause of death; among heterosexual men, the size of this brain area did not depend on whether the men died of AIDS or of other causes.

Interpretation These results suggest that the size of part of the anterior hypothalamus may be related to heterosexual versus homosexual orientation, at least for some individuals. These results are consistent with the idea that genes or prenatal hormones guide brain development, thus altering the probabilities of developing various sexual orientations. But they are not entirely conclusive. Conceivably, a homosexual or heterosexual life-style might alter brain anatomy instead of the other way around. Also, we do not know whether the people LeVay studied were representative of other people; certainly we must await replications on other samples. Finally, the variations in brain structure from one person to another indicate that brain anatomy does not completely control sex-

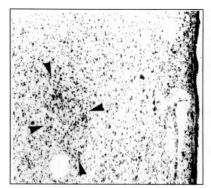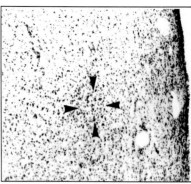

FIGURE 11.27
One section of the anterior hypothalamus (marked with arrow) is larger, on the average, in the brains of heterosexual men than in the brains of homosexual men or heterosexual women (LeVay, 1991). Review Figure 11.6 for the location of the hypothalamus.

ual orientation. (The third interstitial nucleus was fairly large in some homosexual men and fairly small in some heterosexual men.)

So, where do all these studies leave us? At this point, we can say more about the possible biological influences on sexual orientation than we can about the role of various experiences. Experiences undoubtedly do exert a major influence, but we do not know which experiences are most crucial. Even with regard to the biological influences, the results indicate only that genes and prenatal hormones *may* influence the development of sexual orientation. We shall need to await additional studies before we can draw any confident conclusion.

Uncertainty and tentative conclusions are not unusual in psychology. If you decide to become a psychologist, you will have to get used to the words *maybe* and *probably*. Here, the combined effect of three kinds of evidence (the rat study and two very different human studies) leads to a louder "maybe" than any one study would by itself, but the conclusion is still "maybe." As I pointed out in Chapter 2, psychologists rarely talk about "proving" a conclusion; they merely increase or decrease their confidence in a conclusion.

■ CONCEPT CHECK

6. *Most studies find that adult homosexual men have approximately the same levels of testosterone in their blood as heterosexual men of the same age have. Do such results conflict with the*

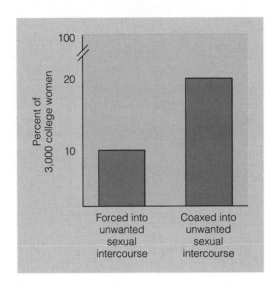

suggestion that prenatal hormonal conditions predispose certain men to homosexuality? (Check your answer on page 482.)

MOTIVATION AND RAPE

Up to this point we have been considering sexual behavior among consenting adults. Not all behavior meets that description. **Rape** is sexual contact obtained through violence, threats, or intimidation. The perpetrator may be guided by various combinations of sexual and violent motivations.

Only a small proportion of raped women report the rape to the police; consequently, police statistics vastly understate the prevalence of rape. Women who are forced into sex by a date may not even perceive the event as rape (Allgeier, 1987). In a survey of more than 3,000 women at 32 colleges, 9% reported that they had been forced into unwanted sexual intercourse, and 25% said they had participated in unwanted intercourse in response to verbal coaxing or while under the influence of alcohol (Koss, Gidycz, & Wisniewski, 1987; see Figure 11.28). Most cases were date rapes, rather than assaults by strangers.

In a survey of men at the same colleges, 4.4% admitted that they had forced themselves sexually on a woman at least once, and an additional 3.3% said they had attempted to do so (Koss & Dinero, 1988). Perhaps these 4.4% of the men were responsible for the rapes reported by 25% of the women. But it is more likely that many men understated the sexual coercion they had used, and some may have misperceived what happened. Some men convince themselves that the woman they raped did not really mean it when she said no.

What motivates men to rape? That is a hard question to answer, because most of our data are based on men who have been actually *convicted* of rape. Most of the rapes that come to the attention of the police and the public are violent attacks by strangers. The men most likely to be convicted are repeat offenders. Those who commit repeated, violent attacks are probably not representative of other rapists; indeed, it is hard to imagine how researchers could obtain a representative sample. Based on an admittedly unrepresentative sample, psychologists' tentative assessment is that rapists feel anger toward women and a need to dominate or control them. Some rapists feel that they have been hurt or belittled by women in the past. (Maybe that is true and maybe that is just an excuse they use.) Although much less is known about date rapists, one survey of admitted date rapists found that they also reported anger toward women and a drive to dominate them (Lisak & Roth, 1988).

Some psychologists distinguish between rapists who intended to humiliate and injure their victims and those who used only enough force to subdue their victims. However, there is no way to determine for sure whether a rapist is using force just to obtain compliance or is indulging in violence for its own sake (Prentky, Knight, & Rosenberg, 1988).

We do know that most convicted rapists have a long history of hostility and violence toward both men and women (Gebhard, Gagnon, Pomeroy, & Christenson, 1965; Groth, 1979). Many of them were sexually abused in childhood; in committing their assaults, they may be reenacting their own experiences, sometimes more closely than they realize (Burgess, Hazelwood, Rokous, Hartman, & Burgess, 1988).

Some rapists have a weak sex drive or are almost impotent; they hope to find sexual satisfaction by being "completely in charge," something they cannot manage with a willing partner. They are sexually aroused by photos and audiotapes of rape, whereas most other men are either unaroused or repulsed (Earls, 1988). To judge whether a convicted rapist is still dangerous, measurements of his sexual arousal are sometimes made while he listens to tapes. Men who develop erections while listening to descriptions of rape are considered to be still dangerous.

Something to Think About

Rapists and child molesters sometimes pore over sexually explicit magazines and videotapes just before committing an offense (Malamuth & Donnerstein, 1982; Marshall, 1988). Can we conclude that such materials lead to the offenses? (Remember, correlation does not mean causation.) What kind of evidence would we need to determine whether sexually explicit materials lead to sex offenses?

Rape is a complex matter, and, like other motivated behaviors, it has a variety of causes. While a rapist may have been an abused child or may feel anger toward women, these circumstances do not explain why he commits an attack at a particular moment. In many cases, he is so intoxicated from alcohol or other drugs that he sheds the inhibitions that would ordinarily prevent such an attack (Lisak & Roth, 1988). Psychologists have much to learn before they can understand rape and contribute to its prevention.

Unless people call attention to the phenomenon of date rape, it is easily ignored. Women raped on a date seldom report it to the police; the men who force a woman to have sex on a date seldom perceive their act as rape.

SUMMARY

■ *Variability in human sexual behavior.* Alfred Kinsey, who conducted the first extensive survey of human sexual behavior, found that sexual activity varies more widely than most people realize. (page 470)

■ *Cultural variations in sexual customs.* Some societies are highly permissive in their attitudes toward sexual practices; others are extremely restrictive. In the United States, sexual freedom has been on the rise throughout much of the 20th century, although the AIDS epidemic has made some people more cautious in their sexual activities. (page 471)

■ *Sexual arousal.* Sexual arousal proceeds through four stages: excitement, plateau, orgasm, and resolution. For a combination of physiological and motivational reasons, some people fail to pass through all four stages or pass through them more quickly than they wish. (page 473)

■ *Development of genitals.* In the early stages of development, the human fetus possesses anatomical structures that may develop into either male genitalia (if testosterone levels are high enough) or female genitalia (if testosterone levels are lower). How much prenatal hormones affect human sexual behavior is uncertain. (page 475)

■ *Homosexuality.* The reasons are not clear as to why some people develop a heterosexual orientation and others develop a homosexual orientation. Among biological determinants, possibilities include genetics and the effects of prenatal stress, which can alter prenatal hormones. (page 476)

■ *Rape and related offenses.* Rape, especially date rape, and other sex offenses occur far more often than police records indicate. Convicted rapists generally have a long history of violence; for many of them, the motivation seems to be more aggressive than sexual. Many rapists were sexually abused as children. (page 480)

SUGGESTION FOR FURTHER READING

Hyde, J. S. (1989). *Understanding human sexuality* (2nd ed.). New York: McGraw-Hill. A comprehensive textbook on human sexual behavior.

TERMS

acquired immune deficiency syndrome (AIDS) a disease often transmitted sexually that gradually destroys the body's immune system (page 473)

venereal disease a disease that is spread through sexual contact (page 473)

sexual identity the sex a person regards himself or herself as being (page 474)

sexual orientation a person's preference for male or female sex partners (page 474)

testosterone a hormone present in higher quantities in males than in females (page 475)

estrogen a hormone present in higher quantities in females than in males (page 475)

rape sexual contact obtained through violence, threats, or intimidation (page 480)

ANSWERS TO CONCEPT CHECKS

5. A fetus exposed to very low levels of both testosterone and estrogen throughout prenatal development would develop a normal female appearance. High levels of testosterone lead to male anatomy; low levels lead to female anatomy. The level of estrogen does not play a decisive role. (page 475)

6. Not necessarily. The suggestion is that prenatal stress (or any other condition with equivalent effects) may interfere with the effect of testosterone on the brain during a critical stage of its development, even though the testosterone levels may be within the normal range. After the stress is removed, the testosterone levels remain normal, but certain aspects of brain development have already been determined. (page 480)

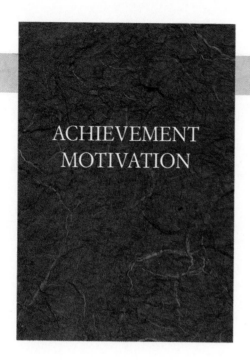

ACHIEVEMENT MOTIVATION

What motivates some people to work harder than others?

How do we learn an achievement motivation?

How do people with a strong achievement motivation differ from others?

Your 2-year-old nephew is building a stack of blocks. You say, "Here, let me help you," and you finish stacking the blocks. Will he smile and thank you? Hardly. He is more likely to cry, "I wanted to do it myself!" His goal was not to *have* a tall stack, but to *build* a tall stack.

Now you are doing something creative yourself—painting a picture, writing a story, playing chess perhaps—something you do moderately well. Someone more expert than you says, "Here, let me help you. I see you're having a little trouble, and I think I can fix it." How do you react? You might not burst into tears, but you probably resent the help. You are more interested in completing the task yourself than in having a perfect final product.

Most of us strive for the joy of accomplishment, some more than others. What occupation do you hope to enter after graduation? Have you chosen it because it is your surest way to earn a lot of money? Or have you chosen it because it will enable you to take pride in your achievements? Many people forgo a better-paying job to take one that gives them a greater opportunity to achieve. (I bet your psychology professor is one such person.)

THE MEASUREMENT OF NEED FOR ACHIEVEMENT

The **need for achievement** is a striving for accomplishment and excellence. That sounds like a rather straightforward definition, but it confuses two quite distinct types of motivation (McClelland, Koestner, & Weinberger, 1989). As a rule, when people describe themselves as having a strong achievement motivation, they refer to an extrinsic motivation. That is, they are impelled by the rewards they have been receiving or expect to receive for various accomplishments. But, as we saw in the first module of this chapter, there is a second kind of need for achievement, a more intrinsic motivation. People with this intrinsic kind of need for achievement may or may not describe themselves as striving for achievement, but they take pleasure in accomplishing goals for their own sake. They are likely to persist at a task for a long time and probably develop great skills in the long run. For example, people who spend every spare moment playing or studying chess may be driven by an intrinsic motivation to excel at chess, even if they do not think of themselves as "highly motivated" for achievement. (They may even think of themselves as wasting their time.) We shall concentrate here on the intrinsic need for achievement.

The intrinsic need for achievement was first inferred from the performance of schoolchildren. Some children are much more successful in school than others who, so far as we can tell, are equal in ability and equally interested in the rewards that good grades might eventually bring. The same is true in athletics, business, and other aspects of life. Apparently, some people simply try harder than others. If that is true, then we should be able to measure and study this tendency as a personality variable.

But how? If you wanted to determine which workers or schoolchildren were most highly motivated to achieve, what would you measure and how? You could not simply measure how much people achieve because you are trying to explain *why* some people achieve more than others. You would need some measure of the need for achievement that is separate from the achievements themselves.

The artist who created this wooden cow desk probably hoped for recognition and money (an extrinsic motivation), but also must have enjoyed the creative process itself (an intrinsic motivation).

FIGURE 11.29
In the Thematic Apperception Test, each person looks at a series of pictures similar to this one and tells a story about each one. Psychologists count the number of achievement themes to measure the person's need for achievement. They can also measure other motivations by counting other kinds of themes.

Another way *not* to measure the need for achievement is to ask people whether they are strongly motivated for success. Many people say yes because they believe it is socially desirable to do so. Psychologists measure achievement motivation indirectly, without even telling people what they are measuring.

One of the most popular methods of measuring need for achievement makes use of the *Thematic Apperception Test,* which we shall look at again in Chapter 13. Investigators show people pictures like the one in Figure 11.29 and ask them to tell a story about each picture, including what is going on, what led up to this scene, and what will happen next (McClelland, Atkinson, Clark, & Lowell, 1953). The investigators then count the number of times each person mentions striving for goals and achievements.

For example, this story would score high:

This girl is taking an important test. First she went through the test and answered all the items she knew well. Now she is trying to remember the answer to one of the more difficult questions. She gazes off into the distance, trying to remember everything she has read about this topic. She finally remembers, writes down the correct answer, and gets a perfect score. Later she goes on to college, becomes a Rhodes scholar, and eventually becomes a famous inventor.

Contrast that story with this one:

This girl is sitting through a very boring class. She is gazing off into the distance, thinking about the party she went to last weekend. As soon as class is over, she goes out and has a good time with her friends.

Such a story would rate a zero on need for achievement.

Need for Achievement and Setting Goals

Suppose you have a choice of three video games to play. One game is easy; you know you can get a high score on it, but so could anyone else. The second game is more difficult; you are not sure how well you would do. The third is the most difficult; you would expect to lose quickly, as most people do. Which do you choose? Most people prefer the game of intermediate difficulty, especially people with a strong need for achievement (Atkinson & Birch, 1978).

For example, in one study, children were asked to throw 10 rings to try to hit a peg from any distance they chose, from 1 to 15 feet (0.3 to 4.6 meters). Because the others stood around watching as each child threw the rings, there was an element of competition even though no one was keeping score. Children who had scored high on need for achievement generally chose intermediate distances and managed to hit the peg a little less than half the time (McClelland, 1958).

According to one interpretation of these results, the value of a goal is a product of its expectancy and its value (Atkinson, 1957). The **expectancy** is the perceived probability of achieving a goal, such as 50% or 99%. The value is, simply, what the goal would be worth. Easy goals (such as "running 1,500 meters without falling down") have a high expectancy but a low value. The most difficult goals (such as "setting the Olympic record in the 1,500-meter race") have a high value but almost zero expectancy. Intermediate goals (such as "winning a local 1,500-meter race") have a fairly high expectancy and a fairly high value; the product of multiplying the two is also high.

Many psychologists doubt that this *expectancy-value interpretation* applies in all cases. It assumes that people mentally calculate the probability of success and multiply by the pride they would feel in success—hardly a simple undertaking. Even preschool children usually prefer tasks of intermediate difficulty, even though they have trouble estimating how well they will do on the task and even though they do not seem to value accomplishing difficult tasks much more than accomplishing simple tasks (Schneider, 1984).

According to an alternative explanation, the *competency interpretation,* people prefer intermediate tasks because the results are more informative (Heckhausen, 1984; Schneider, 1984). According to that explanation, even preschool children want to know their own competence. People who attempt a task that is too easy or too difficult learn little about their competence. They learn about their competence by attempting an intermediate task (Fig-

Most people, especially those with a high need for achievement, prefer goals that are challenging but not impossible. According to the competency interpretation, we prefer such goals because they are likely to teach us something about our own abilities. We would learn little about ourselves by attempting something too easy or too difficult.

ure 11.30), one on which they might or might not succeed. The competence interpretation is not necessarily inconsistent with the expectancy-value interpretation; as is often the case in psychology, both theories may be valid, perhaps for different people or under different circumstances.

Most people, not just people with a strong need for achievement, prefer tasks with intermediate difficulty. However, people with a strong need for achievement show an even stronger preference than other people do (Schneider, 1984). A few people prefer especially easy or especially difficult tasks. Such people are dominated by a **fear of failure**. By adopting a strategy of taking no risks and setting low goals, they avoid failure, although they never achieve any remarkable success. When they set extremely high goals for themselves, at least they have an excuse for failure. Apparently, they would rather fail at an impossible task than run the risk of failing at a realistic task.

People with a strong fear of failure make a normal effort, or even an extraordinary effort, on an easy task or in a relaxed, low-pressure situation. But if they are told, "This is an important test; you are going to be evaluated, so do your best," they lower their effort. (Fear of failure is closely related to test anxiety.) By contrast, people with a strong need for achievement

FIGURE 11.31
Conditions for high activity toward achieving goals.

Setting goals leads to vigorous activity if:

The goal is realistic.

A serious commitment is made, especially if it is made publicly.

Feedback is received.

make little effort on an easy task or when the situation puts little pressure on them. When they are told that they are going to be evaluated, they try harder (Nygard, 1982).

When people receive feedback on their performance, such as "You got 82% correct on the first test," those with a strong need for achievement usually increase their efforts, whereas those with a lower need do not increase their efforts and sometimes decrease them. Apparently those with a strong need for achievement set such high goals that they interpret almost any feedback as meaning that they are behind schedule and need to try harder. People with a low need for achievement set lower goals, and almost any feedback they receive reassures them that they are doing all right (Matsui, Okada, & Kakuyama, 1982).

Something to Think About

Some people have suggested that our society has become less ambitious and less motivated by achievement than it once was. How could we test that hypothesis?

■ CONCEPT CHECK

7. *The new football coach at Generic Tech has set up a schedule for next year. The team will play only opponents that had a won-lost record of 5-6 or 6-5 last year. Does this coach have a high need for achievement or a high fear of failure? (Check your answer on page 489.)*

Effective and Ineffective Goals

High but realistic goals are especially effective in motivating people with a strong need for achievement. To a lesser degree, they can motivate almost anyone. At the start of the college semester, four young women are asked to state their goals. One is aiming for a straight-A average. Another hopes to get at least a C average. A third plans to "do as well as I can." A fourth has no set goals. Which student will work hardest and get the best grades?

The student aiming for a straight-A average will do the best, under certain circumstances:

■ She must have enough ability for the goal to be realistic. If she has always had to struggle just to get a passing grade, she will quickly become discouraged.

■ She must take her goal seriously. If she only says she is aiming for straight A's and then never thinks about it again, it will make no difference

to her. She can increase her commitment to the goal by stating it publicly. The more people who know about her goal, the harder it will be for her to ignore it.

■ She must get some feedback from periodic test scores and grades on assignments to tell her what she needs to study harder (Figure 11.31).

The same conditions hold for workers (Locke, Shaw, Saari, & Latham, 1981). A high yet realistic goal leads to better performance than does an easy goal. A vague "do your best" goal is no better than no goal at all. For a goal to be effective, workers must be committed to achieving it and must receive periodic feedback on their progress. Once they reach their goal, they must be rewarded; otherwise, they will be indifferent toward setting goals later on.

■ CONCEPT CHECK

8. *Under what conditions would people be most likely to keep their New Year's resolutions? (Check your answer on page 489.)*

AGE AND SEX DIFFERENCES IN NEED FOR ACHIEVEMENT

Some people have such a strong need for achievement that they will devote every available moment to an ambitious task they have set for themselves. They are so highly motivated by achievement for its own sake that they need no other reward. An extrinsic incentive, such as extra pay for high accomplishment, does not enhance their performance (D. C. McClelland, 1985). The challenge itself is all the motivation they need. Others place a lower value on achievement. How does the need for achievement develop, and why does it become stronger in some people than in others?

The Development of Need for Achievement in Childhood

Given that the need for achievement is a secondary motivation (one that is learned) rather than a primary motivation (one that serves a direct biological need), we might imagine that people would take a long time to develop it. In fact, children 18 months old clearly show pride in their accomplishments, such as building a tall stack of blocks. By age 2 1/2, they understand the idea of competition; they show pleasure at beating someone else, disappointment at losing (Heckhausen, 1984).

Although preschool children show great pleasure at completing a task, they seldom appear distressed by their inability to complete it. Heinz Heckhausen (1984) tried to find out how children less than 4 years old would react to failure. He rigged up various contraptions so that a child's stack of blocks would topple or fall through a trap door. He often managed to arouse the children's curiosity, never their discouragement. Eventually he began to suspect that children learn the experience of success long before they understand failure.

Preschool children are highly optimistic about their own abilities. Even if they have failed a task repeatedly, they announce confidently that they will succeed the next time. An adult asks, "Who is going to win this game the next time we play?" Most preschool children shout "Me!" even if they have lost time after time in the past (Stipek, 1984).

Perhaps optimism comes naturally to humans. We quickly learn how it feels to succeed; we learn more slowly what it means to fail. When children enter school, their teachers force them to compare themselves to one another. Within a few years, some children approach tasks with a fear of failure instead of a joyful striving for success (Stipek, 1984).

Psychologists have not yet determined when and why children change their attitudes toward success and failure, but they suspect teachers unintentionally convey the message, "You probably aren't going to like this or do it very well, but you have to do it anyway." Jere Brophy (1987, p. 190) reports the following quotes from junior-high teachers:

- "If you get done by ten o'clock, you can go outside."

- "This penmanship assignment means that sometimes in life you just can't do what you want to do. The next time you have to do something you don't want to do, just think: 'Well, that's part of life.'"

- "You'll have to work real quietly, otherwise you'll have to do more assignments."

- "This test is to see who the really smart ones are."

Sex Differences in Need for Achievement

According to some reports, women score lower than men do on need for achievement as measured by the Thematic Apperception Test. The difference is subject to both biological and environmental interpretations. Male hormones may encourage aggressiveness and competition in humans, as they clearly do in other species. Aggressiveness and competition are not the same as striving for achievement, but they may facilitate it. In addition, our society encourages boys to set high goals and to begin competing at an early age, while it encourages girls to concentrate more on being sensitive to the needs of others (Honig, 1983).

Perhaps one reason for the sex difference in need for achievement has to do with neither hormones nor early experiences but with social influences in adolescence and later life. The goals that high-school girls set for themselves are about as high as those of high-school boys (Farmer, 1983). Within several years after high school, many women lower their goals. Why?

One explanation is that women are more influenced by criticism than men are (Roberts, 1991). A woman who is told that she is doing poorly or that she is unlikely to succeed often takes the advice seriously. Many men tend to ignore such criticisms and proceed as before. Ignoring criticism is not necessarily a good idea, but the net result is that women may become discouraged faster than men.

Furthermore, women have historically faced serious discrimination against them in most jobs; consequently, many have chosen to enter certain fields where women predominate.

Preschool children show delight in their successes, but show no clear sign of discouragement after their failures. Perhaps they are ever-confident of their eventual success, or perhaps they simply do not understand the concept of failure.

For many years, women had almost no chance of achieving great success in business or politics; after changes in society's attitudes and policies, an increasing number of women have reached high levels of achievement and recognition. With that change has come a change in young women's ambitions. Traditionally, women have scaled back their ambitions either because they thought they had no chance for achievement or because they feared social rejection. Today, those barriers are breaking down.

In one study, a group of adult women filled out a job-interest questionnaire. The interests they checked most frequently included secretary, elementary teacher, home economics teacher, and dietician. Two weeks later they filled out the questionnaire again, but this time they were given these instructions:

I want you to pretend with me that men have come of age and that: (1) Men like intelligent women; (2) Men and women are promoted equally in business and the professions; and (3) Raising a family well is very possible for a career woman. (Farmer & Bohn, 1970, p. 229).

After hearing these instructions, the women showed a significantly increased interest in becoming an author, psychologist, lawyer, insurance salesperson, or physician. They largely lost interest in becoming a secretary, teacher, or dietician (Farmer & Bohn, 1970). Evidently, women lower their career aspirations because they fear that high ambitions will scare men away, or because they believe businesses will not promote them fairly, or because they fear

that a full-time career will interfere with raising a family (Farmer, 1987).

Women have often been led to believe, perhaps correctly, that men resent and dislike highly successful women. Matina Horner (1972) proposed that women have low motivation for achievement because they have a *fear of success*. She did not mean that women try to fail, but merely that they might try to avoid high, conspicuous levels of success. Horner asked 90 college women to complete a story beginning, "After the first-term finals, Anne finds herself at the top of her medical school class." She asked 88 men to do the same, except that she substituted "John" for "Anne." Almost two thirds of the women told stories in which Anne quit medical school or suffered social rejection or other misfortunes. Less than one tenth of the men said that anything unpleasant happened to John. Horner concluded that women have been taught that high levels of achievement are unfeminine; once they approach those levels, they begin to fear the consequences.

However, these results have been difficult to replicate. They have a "now you see it, now you don't" quality. In most later studies, about an equal percentage of men and women raised concerns about fear of success (Zuckerman & Wheeler, 1975). Was Horner therefore wrong? Not necessarily. The results could have differed because of changes in procedure, including slight changes in instructions. They could also have differed because of a change in society. Since the late 1960s, when Horner collected her first results, our society has developed a more supportive attitude toward women with career aspirations. Perhaps women today have less reason to fear success than women of the past had.

Are women right in believing that businesses will not promote them fairly? It is difficult to say. On the one hand, many businesses make a deliberate effort to recruit and promote women. On the other hand, as one observer has pointed out, "Two facts matter to business: Only women have babies and only men make rules" (Schwartz, 1989, p. 65). Although many women want to take an extended leave from a job after they give birth, many employers prefer that they quit altogether. The result is that everyone loses: The woman leaves a promising career and later returns to the work force with much lower aspirations. The company loses a talented worker permanently. And observers conclude that it is a mistake to hire women for top jobs, because they are likely to quit (Schwartz, 1989). Perhaps our society will find better ways to enable women (and men) to combine career ambitions with family commitments.

SUMMARY

- *Measurement of need for achievement.* Some people work harder than others because of their strong need for achievement. Need for achievement can be measured by the stories a person tells when looking at a picture in the Thematic Apperception Test. (page 483)

- *Goal setting.* People with a strong need for achievement prefer to set goals that are high but realistic. Given such a goal, they will work as hard as possible. In contrast, people with a low need for achievement or a strong fear of failure prefer goals that are either easy to achieve or so difficult that they provide a ready excuse for failure. (page 484)

- *Effectiveness of goal setting.* Almost everyone is motivated to achieve a goal if the goal is realistic, if the person makes a serious commitment to achieving it, and if the person gets feedback on his or her efforts to reach the goal. (page 486)

- *Achievement motivation in children.* Children begin showing delight in their accomplishments by age 1 1/2. Preschool children are highly optimistic about their own abilities. After they enter school, they learn the meaning of failure and start to show discouragement. (page 486)

- *Sex differences in need for achievement.* According to some reports, men have, on the average, a stronger need for achievement than women have, although some of the results are difficult to replicate. To some extent, women lower their aspirations because they fear that their high success may displease men or because they believe that employers will not promote them fairly. Studies in the 1960s indicated that women were inhibited by a fear of success, but that fear is no longer evident. (page 487)

SUGGESTION FOR FURTHER READING

McClelland, D. C. (1985). *Human motivation.* Glenview, IL: Scott, Foresman. A text by one of the pioneers in the study of achievement motivation.

TERMS

need for achievement a striving for accomplishment and excellence (page 483)

expectancy the perceived probability of achieving a goal (page 485)

fear of failure a preoccupation with avoiding failure, rather than taking risks in order to succeed (page 485)

ANSWERS TO CONCEPT CHECKS

7. You were right if you said the coach has a high need for achievement, because he chose a schedule that will pose an intermediate challenge—not too easy, not too difficult. You were also right if you objected that I did not give you enough information to answer the question. I did not tell you how Generic Tech's team fared last season. If they went undefeated last year, then the new schedule may be too easy. If Tech has not won a game in years, then the schedule is too difficult. If the schedule is either too easy or too difficult, then the coach probably has a fear of failure. (page 486)

8. A New Year's resolution is like any other goal: People are more likely to keep it if it is realistic, if they state the resolution publicly, and if they receive feedback on how well they are achieving it. (page 486)

12

EMOTIONS, HEALTH PSYCHOLOGY, AND COPING WITH STRESS

The *Star Trek* character Mr. Spock is reputed to feel very little emotion because he is half Vulcan—and people from the planet Vulcan feel little or no emotion. Suppose you are the first astronaut to land on Vulcan. The Vulcans gather around and ask you, their first visitor from Earth, what *emotion* is. What do you tell them?

"Well," you might say, "emotion is how you feel when something surprisingly good or surprisingly bad happens to you."

"Wait a minute," they reply. "We don't understand these words *feel* and *surprisingly*."

"All right, how about this: Emotions are experiences like anger, fear, happiness, sadness. . . ."

"Anger, fear—what do those terms mean?" the Vulcans ask.

Defining such terms would be like trying to explain *color* to a blind person—maybe

harder. Even though blind people cannot experience color, they can determine whether someone else has color vision by showing cards like the ones in Chapter 4. Anyone who reports seeing one pattern in the cards has color vision; anyone who reports seeing another pattern does not. Could you set up a similar test that would let the Vulcans determine whether someone was experiencing an emotion? If so, what sort of test could you use? The problem is clear: *Color vision* has a well-established meaning; *emotion* has an imprecise meaning that is defined mostly by example.

In this chapter we shall consider what psychologists have learned so far about emotions, which still leaves some major questions unanswered. We begin with general theories and principles. Then we turn to the role of emotions in health and the ways in which people cope with the emotions associated with stress.

When we experience emotions, we are in some way moved. (Movement *is the root of* emotion.) *Our feeling of disturbance is a positive or negative excitement; sometimes we cry for joy, sometimes for grief.*

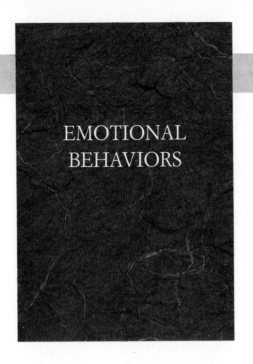

EMOTIONAL BEHAVIORS

What causes us to feel one emotion or another?

What determines the intensity of the emotion?

What causes anger?

What causes happiness?

Y_ou may have heard the expression "as happy as a clam." This expression probably originated because a clam's shells meet in a shape that resembles a smile. However, a smile or other facial expression is not always a faithful indicator of someone's emotions (even in people, never mind clams). I once met a woman who had had plastic surgery to mold her mouth into a permanent smile, but she had about the sourest, angriest disposition you can imagine. She certainly confused people when she smiled while insulting them.

People's self-reports of emotions are not always accurate, either. Angry people sometimes insist they are not angry; depressed people say, "Leave me alone; I'm not depressed." Because of the difficulties of measuring people's internal emotional experiences, any scientific study of emotion must begin with systematic studies of the observable aspects of emotion—its physiology, expressions, and effect on behavior.

EMOTION AND PHYSIOLOGICAL AROUSAL

Originally, the word *emotion* was a general term for any sort of turbulent movement. People used to talk about thunder as an "emotion of the atmosphere." Eventually, the word came to refer only to feelings that give rise to vigorous motion of the body, such as fear, anger, and joy.

In contemporary terms, an emotion is "an inferred complex sequence of reactions to a stimulus [including] cognitive evaluations, subjective changes, autonomic and neural arousal, impulses to action, and behavior designed to have an effect upon the stimulus that initiated the complex sequence" (Plutchik, 1982, p. 551). According to that definition, emotion has many aspects, presumably linked to one another. One aspect—autonomic and neural arousal—is relatively easy to investigate scientifically. Most emotional states include increased arousal of the autonomic nervous system, which prepares the body for vigorous action.

We experience emotional arousal when we have a strong tendency either to approach or to avoid something, generally in an energetic way (Arnold, 1970). For example, love includes a strong drive to come close to another person. Anger includes a tendency to charge toward someone and to attack through either speech or action. Fear and disgust are associated with a tendency to escape. All emotions share certain features related to physiological arousal. So although anger, fear, and happiness are very different emotional states, we may express any one of them by screaming or by engaging in frenzied activity.

"But wait," you say. "Sometimes when I feel highly emotional I can hardly do anything at all. Like the time I borrowed a friend's car and then wrecked it. When I had to explain what had happened to the car, I could hardly speak." True, but even then your emotion was associated with a tendency to take vigorous action. While you were reporting the wreck to your friend, you undoubtedly felt a strong urge to run away. Although you suppressed that urge, it made itself apparent in your trembling voice and shaking hands.

Ordinarily an emotional state elicits a tendency toward vigorous action, even if we suppress that tendency. Here, a soldier disarms a mine during the war in the former Yugoslavia. No doubt he feels an emotional desire to run away, and no doubt his heart is racing, but he manages to restrain his actions.

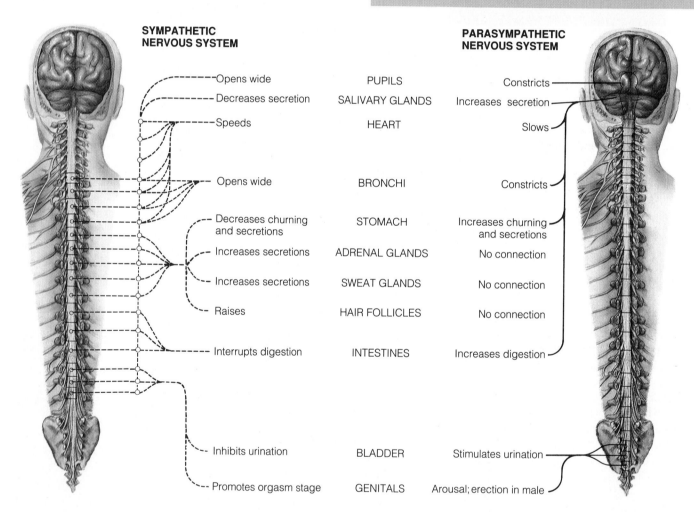

SYMPATHETIC NERVOUS SYSTEM		PARASYMPATHETIC NERVOUS SYSTEM
Opens wide	PUPILS	Constricts
Decreases secretion	SALIVARY GLANDS	Increases secretion
Speeds	HEART	Slows
Opens wide	BRONCHI	Constricts
Decreases churning and secretions	STOMACH	Increases churning and secretions
Increases secretions	ADRENAL GLANDS	No connection
Increases secretions	SWEAT GLANDS	No connection
Raises	HAIR FOLLICLES	No connection
Interrupts digestion	INTESTINES	Increases digestion
Inhibits urination	BLADDER	Stimulates urination
Promotes orgasm stage	GENITALS	Arousal; erection in male

FIGURE 12.1

The automatic nervous system consists of the sympathetic and parasympathetic nervous systems, which act sometimes in opposing ways and sometimes in cooperative ways. The sympathetic nervous system readies the body for emergency actions; the parasympathetic nervous system supports digestive and other nonemergency actions.

The intensity of emotional behaviors is strongly influenced by the autonomic nervous system, a good place to begin our study of emotion.

The Autonomic Nervous System

Any stimulus that arouses an emotion—such as a hug, a fire alarm, or a slap on the face—alters the activity of the **autonomic nervous system,** the section of the nervous system that controls the functioning of the internal organs. The word *autonomic* means independent; biologists once believed that the autonomic nervous system operated independently of the brain and the spinal cord. We now know that the brain and the spinal cord send messages to alter the activity of the autonomic nervous system, but we continue to use the term *autonomic*.

The autonomic nervous system consists of the sympathetic nervous system and the parasympathetic nervous system (Figure 12.1). Two chains of neuron clusters just to the left and right of the spinal cord make up the **sympathetic nervous system**. These clusters are richly interconnected and tend to respond as a unit. Thus a stimulus that arouses any part of the sympathetic nervous system arouses the rest of it as well. Its axons extend to the heart, intestines, and other internal organs. The **parasympathetic nervous system** consists of neurons whose axons extend from the medulla (Figure 3.32) and the lower part of the spinal cord to neuron clusters near the internal organs. These clusters are not directly interconnected; they operate independently.

The sympathetic nervous system arouses the body for "fight or flight" (Figure 12.2). For example, if someone charges at you, you may have to choose between fighting and running away; in either case, your sympathetic nervous system prepares you for a burst of vigorous activity. It does so by increasing your heart rate, breathing rate, production of sweat, and flow of epinephrine (EP-i-NEF-rin; also known as adrenaline). The parasympathetic nervous system decreases the heart rate, promotes digestion, and in general supports nonemergency functions.

Both systems are constantly active, though one may be more active than the other at any given time. An emergency that demands a vigorous response will predominantly activate the sympathetic system; a restful situation predominantly activates the parasympathetic system. Some situations activate or inhibit parts of both systems at once (Berntson, Cacioppo, & Quigley, 1991). For example, a frightening situation may increase your heart rate and sweating (sympathetic responses) and promote bowel and bladder emptying (parasympathetic responses). Remember the last time you were seriously frightened—perhaps your professor asked you to explain why your term paper was so similar to one that another student turned in last semester, or perhaps your boss asked

FIGURE 12.2
Escaping from an attacker mobilizes the sympathetic nervous system, which prepares the body for a brief but vigorous burst of activity.

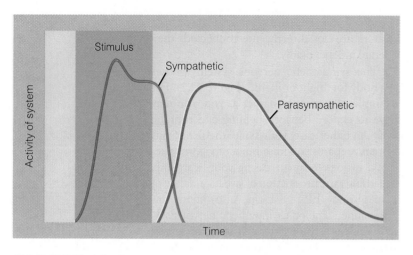

FIGURE 12.3
After removal of the stimulus eliciting the sympathetic response, the sympathetic response is reduced, while the opposing parasympathetic response is enhanced. This is why people feel almost faint at the end of an exciting experience.

The Opponent-Process Principle of Emotions

After a stimulus that has excited sympathetic activity ceases, there is sometimes a "rebound" of increased parasympathetic activity (Gellhorn, 1970). (See Figure 12.3.) For example, while you are running away from an attacker, your sympathetic nervous system increases your heart rate and your breathing rate. If the police suddenly intercept your attacker, your sympathetic arousal ceases, and your parasympathetic system becomes highly activated as a rebound. If the rebound is great enough, a person who has just escaped from danger may faint because of the sudden decrease in heart rate.

This tendency is related to a larger, general principle, the **opponent-process principle of emotions** (Solomon, 1980; Solomon & Corbit, 1974). According to this principle, the removal of a stimulus that excites one emotion causes a swing to an opposite emotion (Figure 12.4). This principle is similar to the opponent-process principle of color vision (discussed in Chapter 4). Recall that when you stare for a long time at one color and then look away, you see its opposite. (After staring at yellow, you see blue.) Solomon and Corbit suggest that the same principle holds for emotional states.

For example, suppose you make a parachute jump for the first time. As you start to fall,

whether you knew why $500 was missing from the cash register. Chances are, your heart was beating wildly, you found yourself gasping for breath, and you were afraid you were going to lose your bladder control. Both your sympathetic and parasympathetic systems were responsible for those responses.

FIGURE 12.4
According to the opponent-process principle of the emotions, removing the stimulus for one emotion elicits a rebound to the opposite emotion. A hiker who sees a snake may feel terrified; when the threat passes, the terror gives way to relief and elation.

you probably experience a state akin to terror. As you continue to fall and your parachute opens, your terror begins to subside. When you land safely, your emotional state does not simply return to normal; it rebounds to relief. As time passes, your relief gradually fades until at last you return to a normal state. Figure 12.5 shows these changes in emotional response over time. Solomon and Corbit refer to the initial emotion as the A state and the opposite, rebound emotion as the B state.

Here is another example: You hear on the radio that you have just won a million dollars in a lottery. You immediately experience elation and joy. Later you discover that you are not the winner after all. Someone with a similar name has won. Now you feel sad, even though you "lost" something you never had.

Solomon and Corbit further propose that repetition of an experience strengthens the B state but not the A state. For example, after you have made several parachute jumps, your rebound pleasure becomes greater and starts to occur earlier and earlier. Over time, you may not be aware of any initial terror at all; the entire experience becomes pleasant.

Figure 12.5 illustrates the changes in emotional response that occur when the experience-and-rebound cycle is repeated many times. Note that the A state has become weaker and the B state has become stronger and more prolonged.

■ CONCEPT CHECKS

1. When you ride a roller coaster, does your heart rate increase or decrease? What happens after you get off?

2. If we apply the opponent-process principle to the experiences drugs produce, we can describe the initial "high" as the A state and the subsequent unpleasant withdrawal experience as the B state. If someone takes a drug repeatedly, how will the A state and the B state change? (Check your answers on page 512.)

Measuring the Activity of the Sympathetic Nervous System

Any new stimulus, such as a sudden flash of light or an unexpected loud noise, briefly activates the sympathetic nervous system. One way to measure this activation is to check the **galvanic skin response (GSR)**—that is, a brief increase in the electrical conductivity of the skin. An investigator may place two electrodes on the skin, pass a weak, even imperceptible current

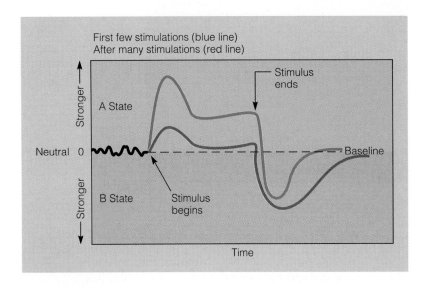

FIGURE 12.5
According to the opponent-process theory of emotions, removal of the stimulus for one emotion (A state) induces the opposite emotion (B state). The blue line shows emotional responses to a stimulus that is introduced and then withdrawn. The red line shows emotional responses to a stimulus that has been introduced and withdrawn repeatedly. Note how the intensity of the responses alters over time. (Based on Solomon & Corbit, 1974.)

between them, and measure changes in the flow of the current. Any activation of the sympathetic nervous system causes a slight sweat that moistens the skin and increases its ability to conduct electricity (Richter, 1929).

A more elaborate way of measuring activation of the sympathetic nervous system is by means of a **polygraph,** a special instrument that simultaneously records physiological changes including blood pressure, heart rate, breathing rate, and GSR (Figure 12.6).

The polygraph is occasionally used in psychological research, but its most common use is as a so-called lie detector. The assumption is that people feel anxious when they lie—especially when they are hooked up to a lie detector—and consequently their sympathetic nervous system will show more arousal than when they are telling the truth.

But does lying really produce more arousal than telling the truth does? Not necessarily. Some honest people become anxious and tense when they are asked about possible wrongdoing, even though they answer all questions truthfully. Other people, especially those who do not believe the polygraph test can catch them in a lie, manage to remain calm when they are lying (Waid & Orne, 1982).

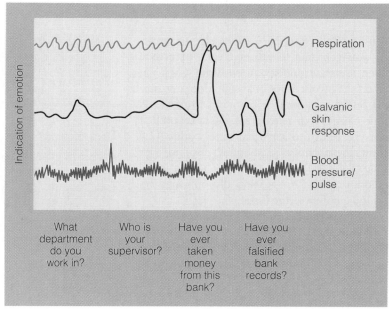

Respiration

Galvanic skin response

Blood pressure/pulse

Indication of emotion

What department do you work in?

Who is your supervisor?

Have you ever taken money from this bank?

Have you ever falsified bank records?

b

FIGURE 12.6

The polygraph, a method for detecting nervous arousal, is the basis for the so-called lie detector test. The polygraph operator asks a series of nonthreatening questions to establish baseline readings of the subject's autonomic responses, then asks questions relevant to some investigation. The underlying assumption is that an increase in arousal indicates nervousness, which in turn indicates lying. Unfortunately, a large percentage of innocent people also become nervous. Several studies have found that polygraph operators typically identify more than 50% of all innocent people as "liars."

People who try to detect lying without using a polygraph are correct only slightly more than half the time. In one study, a variety of specialists watched videotapes of five honest women and five women who were lying; each specialist tried to determine whether or not each woman was telling the truth. Of those tested, only Secret Service agents were correct more often than not. (The Secret Service is the agency that protects the U.S. president and other top government officials.) CIA and FBI agents, police, judges, psychiatrists, and assorted others performed around chance levels (Ekman & O'Sullivan, 1991). Why the Secret Service agents did so well is uncertain, but it is clear that most people have trouble identifying liars.

The polygraph detects lying more accurately than most people do, but not enough more accurately. Typically, polygraph examiners correctly identify about 77–87% of the liars they test. That is, about 13–23% of liars "beat" the polygraph test. Unfortunately, examiners also identify about 51–56% of *honest* people as lying (Forman & McCauley, 1986; Horvath,

1977; Patrick & Iacono, 1989). In other words, if you honestly told a polygraph examiner that you had nothing to do with some crime, more likely than not the polygraph would say you were lying.

In the past, many employers relied on polygraph tests to screen job applicants or current employees, asking such questions as "Have you ever stolen from your employer?" Many honest people get nervous when asked such a question; consequently, employers who used polygraph tests rejected many worthy applicants and cast suspicion on many honest employees. In 1988 the U.S. Congress passed a law prohibiting private employers from using polygraph tests except under special circumstances (Camara, 1988).

The **guilty-knowledge test,** a modified version of the polygraph test, produces more accurate results by asking a different type of question (Lykken, 1979). Instead of asking, "Did you rob the gas station?" the interrogator asks, "Was the gas station robbed at 8 o'clock? At 10:30? At midnight? At 1:30 in the morning? Did the robber carry a gun? A knife? A club?" So long as the questions deal with facts that have not yet been publicized, innocent people should be no more nervous about one question than about another. A person who shows greater arousal when asked about the correct details of the crime than when asked other questions must have "guilty knowledge"—knowledge that only someone who had committed the crime or had talked to the person who committed it could possess. The guilty-knowledge test, when properly administered, identifies guilty people at least as accurately as the standard lie-detector test does, but almost never identifies an innocent person as guilty (Lykken, 1988).

Something to Think About

How might the results of the guilty-knowledge test be biased by a questioner who knows the correct details of the crime? How should the test be administered to minimize that bias?

THREE GENERAL THEORIES OF EMOTION

Psychologists generally agree that emotions are related to the activity of the autonomic nervous system and the activity of the body in general. What is less clear is the nature of that relationship. Let us consider three theories that have offered different descriptions of that relationship.

The James-Lange Theory of Emotions

We have seen that any emotion triggers arousal of the autonomic nervous system. In 1884, William James and Carl Lange independently proposed that autonomic arousal is more than just an *indication* of emotion—in their view, it *is* the emotion (Figure 12.7).

Common sense suggests that an outside stimulus causes an emotion and that the emotion in turn causes autonomic changes and body movements: We cry because we are sad, we tremble because we are afraid, we attack because we are angry. James and Lange turned this concept around. According to the **James-Lange theory,** a stimulus evokes autonomic changes and body movements *directly,* and what we call an emotion is merely our perception of those changes and movements. We decide we are sad *because* we cry, we feel afraid *because* we tremble, we feel angry *because* we attack. Similarly, the act of smiling makes us happy and frowning makes us unhappy.

But what about anger, fear, or happiness you feel when you are just sitting still? How do you know which emotion you are experiencing? According to the James-Lange theory, you can tell by your autonomic state. You feel one way when you are angry, another way when you are happy, another way when you are frightened or sad. (Remember, according to this theory, an emotion is the *perception* of what is happening in your body, not the *cause* of that change.) But

FIGURE 12.7
Three traditional theories of emotion differ concerning the relationship between physiological arousal and the cognitive experience of emotion. According to the James-Lange theory, the physiological arousal determines the nature of the emotion. According to the Cannon-Bard theory, the physiological arousal is independent of the cognitive experience. According to Schachter and Singer's theory, the physiological arousal determines the intensity of the emotion, but it does not determine which emotion one experiences.

is the autonomic state associated with anger noticeably different from the state associated with anxiety or any other emotion?

Heart rate and respiration increase during almost any emotion. Beyond that basic similarity, each emotional state has certain distinguishing physiological features (Levenson, 1992). With its "butterflies in the stomach" sensation, anxiety is probably the most distinctive emotional experience (Neiss, 1988). Your heart rate increases a little more when you are angry or frightened than when you are happy; the temperature of your hands increases more when you are angry than when you feel any other emotion. Your facial muscles respond in different ways when you experience different emotions, even though you are not actually smiling or frowning (Tassinary & Cacioppo, 1992).

Granted that emotional states produce different physiological states, do those differences account for the differences in emotions, as James and Lange proposed? If you begin to breathe rapidly and your heart begins to race, do you decide whether you are angry or frightened by checking the temperature of your hands—or any other physiological indicator? Or do you decide you are afraid because you see a tiger charging at you? If the tiger influences your decision, then James and Lange underestimated the importance of cognition in determining emotions. Several other psychologists have tried to clarify the role of cognition with other theories of emotions.

The Cannon-Bard Theory of Emotions

Walter Cannon (1927), a prominent American physiologist, proposed that an emotional state consists of autonomic changes and cognitions, which arise independently of the autonomic changes. This view, as modified by Philip Bard (1934), is known as the **Cannon-Bard theory of emotions** (Figure 12.7). According to this theory, certain areas of the brain evaluate sensory information and, when appropriate, send one set of impulses to the autonomic nervous system and another set to the forebrain, which is responsible for the subjective and cognitive aspects of emotion.

The key assumption here is that the cognitive aspect of emotions is independent of the autonomic aspect. That assumption is only partly true. After spinal cord damage, people experience little sensation from their heart beat, stomach fluttering, and other autonomic responses. Most such people continue to experience fear, anger, and other emotions; that is, they experience the cognitive aspect of the emotion without the autonomic aspect. However, they may report that their emotions feel less intense than they did before. For example, one man with spinal cord damage reported that he occasionally *acted* angry without actually feeling angry, just because he knew that if he did not respond to some situation with anger, other people would take advantage of him (Hohmann, 1966).

Similarly, after people with an intact nervous system take tranquilizing drugs, they generally report that their emotions, especially anxiety, seem less intense than before. That is, the cognitive aspect of emotions may be partly independent of the autonomic changes, but it is more connected than Cannon and Bard suggested.

Schachter and Singer's Theory of Emotions

Suppose we wire you to another person in such a way that you share the other person's heart rate, breathing rate, skin temperature, and muscle tension. When the other person feels a particular emotion, will you feel it too? (If so, the results would support the James-Lange theory.)

We cannot perform that experiment, but we can do the next best thing: We can use a drug to induce nearly the same physiological state in two people and then see whether they both report the same emotion. To make things a little more interesting, we can put them in different situations. If emotion depends only on a person's physiological state, as the James-Lange theory says, then both people will report the same emotion, even if they happen to be in different situations. Stanley Schachter and Jerome Singer (1962) put these ideas to a test in a now-famous experiment.

Schachter and Singer gave injections of the hormone epinephrine (adrenaline) to a group of college students who agreed to participate in their experiment. (Epinephrine mimics the effects of arousal of the sympathetic nervous system for about 20 to 30 minutes.) The experimenters told some of the subjects that the injections were vitamins; they did not warn them about the likely autonomic effects. Others were told to expect increased heart rate, butterflies in the stomach, and so forth. (Therefore, when they did have such experiences, they would attribute the effects to the pill, not to the situation.)

Subjects were then placed in different situations. Some were placed, one at a time, in a situation designed to arouse euphoria, or excited happiness. The others were placed in a situation designed to arouse anger.

Each student in the euphoria situation was asked to wait in a room with a very playful confederate, or accomplice, of the experimenter. The confederate flipped wads of paper into a trash can, sailed paper airplanes, built a tower with manila folders, shot paper wads at the tower with a rubber band, and played with a Hula-Hoop. He encouraged the subject to join him in play.

Each subject in the anger situation was put in a waiting room with an angry confederate and asked to fill out an insulting questionnaire that included such items as these:

Which member of your immediate family does not bathe or wash regularly?

With how many men (other than your father) has your mother had extramarital relationships?

4 or fewer   5–9   10 or more

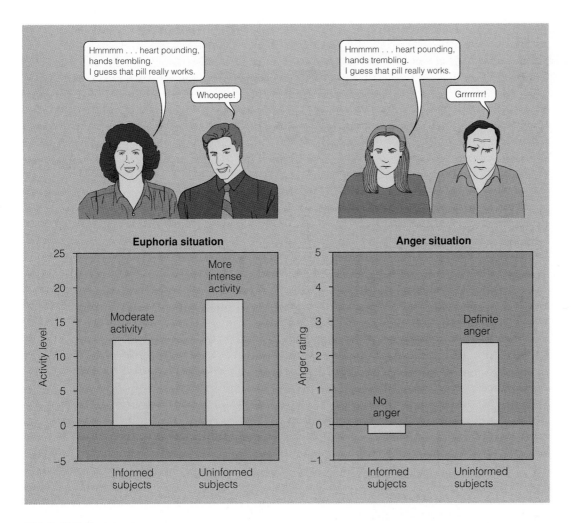

FIGURE 12.8

In Schachter and Singer's experiment, people who were uninformed about the effects of epinephrine reported strong emotions appropriate to their situation. According to Schachter and Singer, the autonomic arousal controls the strength of the emotion, but cognitive factors tell us which emotion we are experiencing.

Most students in the euphoria situation showed strong emotional responses. Some joined the confederate in his play (Figure 12.8), and some of them initiated play of their own. (One jumped up and down on the desk, and another opened a window and threw paper wads at passersby.) The students in the anger situation responded with different emotions; some muttered angry comments, and some refused to complete the questionnaire.

But another factor was important in this experiment. Some of the subjects had been informed beforehand that the injections would produce certain autonomic effects, including hand tremor and increased heart rate. No matter which situation they were in, those subjects showed only slight emotional responses. When they felt themselves sweating and their hands trembling, they said to themselves, "Aha! I'm getting the side effects, just as they said I would."

What can we conclude from this experiment? According to **Schachter and Singer's theory of emotions,** a given physiological state is not the same thing as an emotion (see Figure 12.7). The intensity of the physiological state—that is, the degree of sympathetic nervous system arousal—determines the intensity of the emotion. But that physiological state could be perceived as any of several emotions. Depending on all the information people have about themselves and the situation, they could interpret a particular type of arousal as anger, as euphoria, or just as an interesting side effect of

Table 12.1 Three Theories of Emotion

Theory		Comment

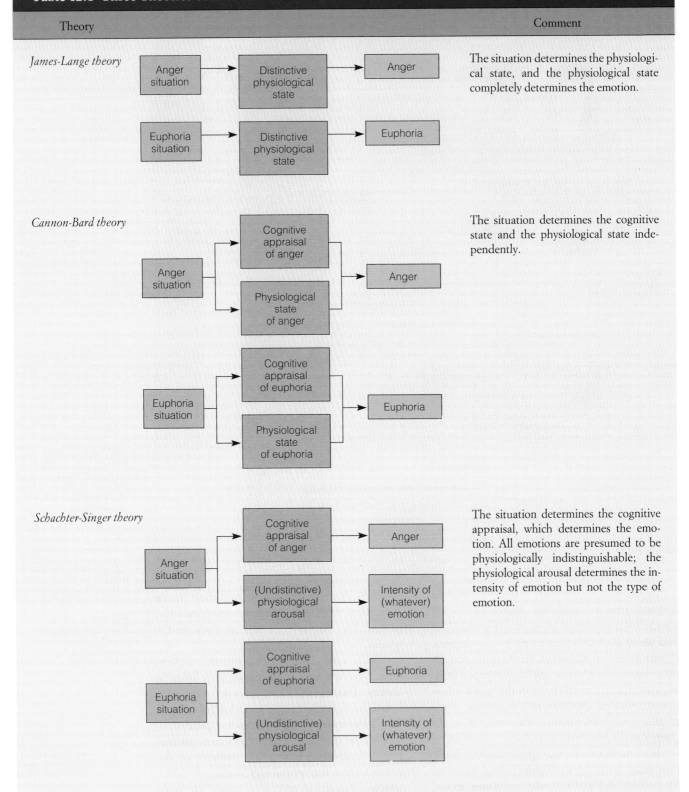

James-Lange theory

Anger situation → Distinctive physiological state → Anger

Euphoria situation → Distinctive physiological state → Euphoria

The situation determines the physiological state, and the physiological state completely determines the emotion.

Cannon-Bard theory

Anger situation → Cognitive appraisal of anger / Physiological state of anger → Anger

Euphoria situation → Cognitive appraisal of euphoria / Physiological state of euphoria → Euphoria

The situation determines the cognitive state and the physiological state independently.

Schachter-Singer theory

Anger situation → Cognitive appraisal of anger → Anger / (Undistinctive) physiological arousal → Intensity of (whatever) emotion

Euphoria situation → Cognitive appraisal of euphoria → Euphoria / (Undistinctive) physiological arousal → Intensity of (whatever) emotion

The situation determines the cognitive appraisal, which determines the emotion. All emotions are presumed to be physiologically indistinguishable; the physiological arousal determines the intensity of emotion but not the type of emotion.

taking a pill. That is, arousal intensifies an emotion, but cognitive appraisal of the situation tells us *which* emotion we are feeling. Table 12.1 contrasts Schachter and Singer's theory with the James-Lange and Cannon-Bard theories.

Unfortunately, these conclusions neglect another group of subjects—subjects whose results raise problems for Schachter and Singer's theory. These subjects were given placebo injections and then placed in the euphoria situation or the anger situation. According to the theory, these subjects should have experienced little emotion, because they had not been given any treatment to increase their autonomic arousal. However, they showed about as much euphoria in the euphoria situation and as much anger in the anger situation as did the subjects injected with epinephrine. Therefore, critics argue, the epinephrine injections may have had nothing to do with the results. If we accept that possibility, we are left with this summary of Schachter and Singer's experiment: People in a euphoria situation act happy; people in an anger situation act angry. That result is neither surprising nor theoretically important (Plutchik & Ax, 1967).

A further problem: Two separate studies failed to replicate Schachter and Singer's results. When students in those experiments were given a treatment to increase their arousal (either an epinephrine injection or a posthypnotic suggestion) and were then placed in a euphoria situation, they did not label their arousal as euphoria. Most of them identified it as anger (Marshall & Zimbardo, 1979; Maslach, 1979). Contrary to Schachter and Singer, we have no solid evidence that a given physiological state can be identified as different emotions at different times.

Schachter and Singer were right in calling attention to the importance of cognition, but they may have gone too far. In emphasizing how cognition determines our emotions, they downplayed the contributions of physiological states. To some extent, fear, anger, and happiness really do feel different physiologically, and those physiological differences contribute to emotions. Cognitions also contribute to emotions but not just as a way of labeling the physiological arousal.

So where are we in our quest for an understanding of emotions? As is often the case in psychology, we have several theories that seem to be partly right, but no one theory that fits all the data. We look to further research to develop and improve our theories.

At present, few investigators seem concerned with the general question of what emotions really are. Most believe that a more fruitful strategy is to explore the nature of specific emotions and their causes and expressions. Perhaps some day after we know enough about specific emotions we can come back to the issue of emotions in general.

■ CONCEPT CHECK

3. You are in a small boat far from shore, and you see a storm approaching. You feel frightened and start to tremble. According to the James-Lange theory, which came first, the fright or the trembling? According to Schachter and Singer's theory, which came first? (Check your answers on page 512.)

THE EXPRESSION
OF EMOTIONS

We experience certain emotions—anger, for example—primarily in the presence of other people. Embarrassment occurs almost exclusively in the presence of an audience, at least an imagined audience (Miller, 1986). We can feel happy or sad when we are alone, but our facial expressions of emotions are most pronounced when others are watching. One study found that people bowling with friends often smiled after making a strike or a spare; people bowling alone seldom smiled (Kraut & Johnston, 1979). Even 10-month-old infants at play smile more when their mothers are watching than when their mothers are sitting nearby but reading a magazine (Jones, Collins, & Hong, 1991). Evidently our expressions of emotions are not simply reflexes but serve as a means of communication.

Facial expressions are ordinarily a fairly accurate indicator of what emotions people are feeling and whether those emotions are growing more intense or are decreasing (Ekman, Friesen, & Ancoli, 1980). Some people are better at judging emotions than others are. For reasons unknown, women tend to be somewhat more accurate than men are at detecting people's emotions in a variety of situations (Hall, 1978).

Can you make yourself happy by smiling or sad by frowning? James Laird (1974) molded people's faces into a smile or a frown by telling

a   b

FIGURE 12.9

Facial expression can influence mood. When people hold a pen with their teeth (a), they rate cartoons as funnier than when they hold a pen with their protruded lips (b).

them to contract first this muscle, then that one, without ever using the words *smile* or *frown*. He found that an induced smile made people more likely to feel happy and that an induced frown made them more likely to feel sad or angry.

But remember the problem of *demand characteristics:* Subjects in an experiment often report what they think the experimenter expects them to report. Even though Laird never used the words *smile* or *frown,* the subjects may have identified their expressions and guessed that they were supposed to be related to their mood.

In another study, the experimenters found a clever way to conceal their purpose. They told subjects that the experiment had to do with how people with disabilities learn to write after losing control of their arms. The subjects were told to hold a pen either with their teeth or with their protruded lips, as Figure 12.9 shows. Then they were to use the pen in various ways, such as drawing lines between dots, underlining words on a page, and making checkmarks to rate the funniness of cartoons. When they held the pen with their teeth, their face was forced into a near-smile and they rated the cartoons as very funny. When they held the pen with protruded lips, they rated the cartoons as significantly less funny (Strack, Martin, & Stepper, 1988). (You might try holding a pen in one way and then the other while reading newspaper cartoons. Do you notice any difference?)

Cross-Cultural Similarities in Facial Expressions of Emotions

If we assume that the ancient ancestors of humans had anything in common with today's monkeys, then we can assume that they communicated their emotional states through gestures,

FIGURE 12.10

The facial expressions of chimpanzees are similar to those of humans.

FIGURE 12.11
People throughout the world, such as this man from New Guinea, raise their eyebrows as a greeting. (From Eibl-Eibesfeldt, 1973.) Traveling around the world, you could communicate anywhere by using such universal facial expressions of emotion as smiling and frowning. But you might give the wrong message if you didn't know that nodding your head in some cultures means "no" or which hand and foot gestures are insulting.

facial expressions, and tone of voice (Redican, 1982). (See Figure 12.10.) When we evolved spoken language, we superimposed that upon the previous system without replacing it. We still use facial expressions to communicate our emotions more often than we use words. You wink, nod, or smile to show a romantic interest; you withhold such expressions to indicate a lack of interest. You signal your eagerness to end a conversation by checking your watch, by edging toward the door, or by some other non-verbal means. To say you are bored would be considered rude.

Many common facial expressions of emotions are similar throughout the world. Charles Darwin (1872/1965) asked missionaries and other people stationed in remote parts of the world to describe the facial expressions of the people who lived there. He found that people everywhere laugh, cry, smile, and frown and use similar facial expressions to pout, sneer, and blush and to express grief, determination, anger, surprise, terror, and disgust. Although the frequency and the circumstances in which people used those expressions varied, the expressions themselves were about the same.

A century later, Irenus Eibl-Eibesfeldt (1973, 1974) photographed people in different cultures to document the similarities in their facial expressions. He confirmed that people throughout the world laugh, cry, smile, and frown; he also found that people in nearly all cultures wink, kiss, and stick out their tongue, although again the frequencies and the circumstances vary. He found that to express a friendly greeting, people raise their eyebrows briefly (Figure 12.11). The mean duration of that expression is the same in all cultures: one third of a second from start to finish, including one sixth of a second in the fully elevated position.

People in various cultures also interpret the meaning of facial expressions in much the same way. Paul Ekman and his associates (Ekman, 1972; Ekman, Sorenson, & Friesen, 1969) took photographs of Americans whose faces were showing happiness, anger, fear, disgust, sur-

prise, and sadness and then asked people in the United States, Japan, Brazil, Chile, and Argentina to name the emotion that each face displayed (Figure 12.12). People in all of these countries identified the expressions with greater than 80% accuracy.

In a later study, people from 10 cultures were shown photographs of faces and were asked to identify both the primary emotion in each case (the emotion expressed most strongly) and the secondary emotion that might also be present—for example, mostly anger plus a little disgust. People in all 10 cultures generally agreed on both the primary and the

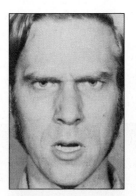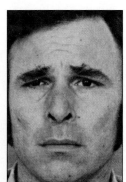
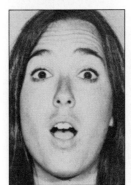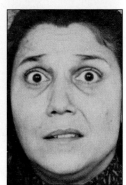

FIGURE 12.12
Ekman has used these faces in experiments on people's ability to recognize expressions of emotions. Can you identify which face conveys anger, disgust, fear, happiness, sadness, and surprise? Check your answers on page 512. (From Ekman & Friesen, 1984.)

Emotional Behaviors 505

secondary emotion and on the intensity of the emotion in each case (Ekman et al., 1987). People are even better at identifying emotions when they can observe body position, voice quality, and speech content in addition to facial expressions (O'Sullivan, Ekman, Friesen, & Scherer, 1985).

Each culture has its own special expressions and gestures, as well as special rules that govern the use of facial expressions (Klineberg, 1938). For example, although people in all cultures laugh, they laugh at different things. The Chinese have elaborate rules on how to display grief. The Japanese are taught when to smile and when not to smile. The Maori of New Zealand cry when they meet a friend after a long absence.

The Origin of Expressions and Gestures

The universality of any behavior may be the result of genetic similarities, learned responses to similar experiences, or both. For example, the reason people throughout the world are afraid of the dark may be that we all have genes favoring fear of the dark or that we all have learned that dark places really are dangerous.

Either explanation—similar genes or similar learning—seems to account for the origin of certain expressions and gestures. The best evidence for a genetic influence is that children who are born deaf and blind quickly develop normal expressions of smiling, frowning, laughing, and crying, even though they have had little or no opportunity to learn such expressions (Figure 12.13). The blind boy in Figure 12.14 covers his face in embarrassment just as a sighted person would. This response is particularly striking because the boy does not know what it means to see or to be seen.

Many common gestures are probably learned modifications or extensions of built-in behaviors. For example, people in many, but not all, parts of the world shake their head to indicate "no." The origin of this gesture may be the infant's unlearned response of turning away from unwanted food. Later, a child learns to shake his or her head as a general indication of rejection.

Once the meaning of a gesture or an expression has become well established, people may use an opposite expression to convey the opposite meaning. Darwin called this the "principle

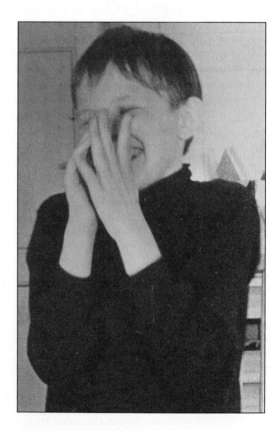

FIGURE 12.14
*A boy, blind since birth, covering his face in embarrassment. (From Eibl-Eibesfeldt, 1973.)
He prevents others from seeing his face, even though he has never experienced sight himself.*

FIGURE 12.13
This laughing girl was born deaf and blind. (From Eibl-Eibesfeldt, 1973.)

of antithesis." For example, Eibl-Eibesfeldt (1973, 1974) has observed that some cultures use an "antigreeting" expression that is the opposite of the eyebrow-raising greeting. Instead of raising their eyebrows and slightly opening their mouth, these people close their eyes, lower their eyebrows, and tighten their lips. The message: "I close you out."

EXPERIENCING EMOTIONS

How many different emotions do humans experience? That sounds like a simple, straightforward question that should have a simple, straightforward answer: Perhaps we have a few "basic" emotions that are biologically given; those few might combine to form our other emotional experiences, just as three basic colors combine to produce all the other colors we see.

However, if this simple question does have a simple answer, no one has found it so far. Several psychologists have proposed lists of "basic" emotions, but they do not agree on what to include on the list. Some lists are very short, such as "pain and pleasure" or "happiness, sadness, and anger." Others are longer, such as "interest, joy, surprise, distress, anger, disgust, contempt, fear, shame, and guilt" (Izard, 1977). Some cultures identify emotions for which the English language has no word; for example, the Japanese identify a special emotion *amae,* "the need to be loved" (Lazarus, Averill, & Opton, 1970). Unfortunately, we have no clear criteria for deciding which emotions are basic and which are not. For example, are *shame* and *guilt* separate emotions, or are they related? What about *disgust* and *contempt?* Are *surprise, courage, wonder, expectancy,* and *hope* basic emotions, compound emotions, or not emotions at all? Is *fear* a single emotion, or is the fear of a killer with a chain saw different from, say, the fear of cancer?

So far, psychologists have no consensus about which emotions are basic or even how to decide which ones are basic. In fact, some are beginning to doubt that the whole idea of "basic" emotions is a useful one. Perhaps all the familiar emotions are compounds of various "basic" subcomponents (Ortony & Turner, 1990). For example, anger may be a compound of four or so separate behavioral components that often occur simultaneously, as shown in Figure 12.15.

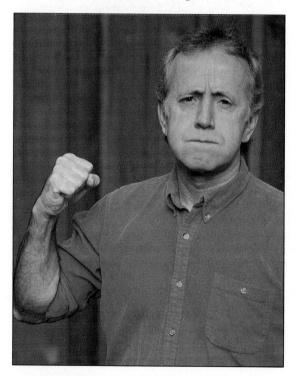

FIGURE 12.15
For years psychologists sought a list of "basic" emotions but found no consensus. An alternative approach is to discard the concept of basic emotions. Perhaps even anger is a compound of "basic" components that have separate causes and meanings even though they often occur together.

I shall not try to discuss each type of emotion, partly because no one is sure how many types there are. Instead, I shall focus on two important types of emotional experience, anger and happiness. What makes us angry and what do we do about it? And what makes us happy?

Anger and Aggressive Behavior

Anger is experienced as a desire to hurt another person or to drive another person away. It is a familiar and normal human emotion that can be destructive, either by leading to violent behavior or, if suppressed, by undermining relationships between people.

Most people become angry far more often than they become physically aggressive. In one study, some people were asked to describe their most recent experience of anger; others kept an "anger diary" for a week (Averill, 1983). They reported that in more than half their experiences of anger, their anger was directed against family or friends. They usually dealt with their anger by saying something to the person who had aroused it or by talking about the experience to someone else. Very rarely did they physically attack the person who had provoked their anger.

Factors That Elicit Anger and Aggression A great many factors can increase the probability of anger and aggression. Aggressive behavior correlates positively, though not very highly, with high levels of the hormone testosterone (Dabbs & Morris, 1990; Moyer, 1974); it tends to be more frequent when the temperature is high (Anderson, 1989). Sometimes people become angry just because someone else comes too close. For example, imagine how you would feel if a stranger sat right next to you on a park bench even though many other nearby benches were empty. We all like to have some space to ourselves, some opportunities for privacy. This is one reason why college roommates sometimes get on each other's nerves.

We also feel angry with our competitors, especially if we think someone has competed unfairly. A special kind of competition is rivalry between two men interested in the same woman or two women interested in the same man. Of human murders other than those committed in the act of robbery or other crimes, an estimated 20% are motivated by sexual rivalry (Daly, Wilson, & Weghorst, 1982).

A great many instances of anger fall under the heading "times when I felt mistreated." For example, you may get angry when a storekeeper sells you shoddy merchandise or when your boss denies you a promotion you think you deserve. According to the **frustration-aggression hypothesis,** much or all of anger and aggressive behavior is caused by "frustration" (Dollard, Miller, Doob, Mowrer, & Sears, 1939). You experience frustration when some obstacle prevents you from reaching some expected goal, such as when a barking dog prevents you from sleeping or a traffic jam prevents you from reaching an important appointment on time. Frustration leads to anger and hostile aggression; it is not a factor in the calm aggressive behaviors that people learn as strategies for getting what they want (Berkowitz, 1989).

However, the frustration-aggression hypothesis appears to be an oversimplification. Unpleasant events that do not cause frustration sometimes lead to aggressive behavior. Leonard Berkowitz (1983) has proposed a more comprehensive theory: All unpleasant events—including frustration, pain, foul odors, a hot environment, and frightening information—give rise to both the impulse to fight and the impulse to flee. Which impulse dominates depends on the circumstances, such as the availability of avoidance responses, the targets available for attack, and the individual's previous experiences with fighting and fleeing. For example, if someone bumps into you and spills hot coffee all over you, do you scream angrily? Perhaps. But if that person is your boss, or the loan and scholarship officer at your college, or the biggest and meanest-looking person you have ever seen, you may smile and apologize for being in the way.

Prediction and Control of Violent Behavior People who cannot control their anger sometimes commit acts of violence, even criminal acts. Anger is hardly the only cause of violence, but because it is one primary cause, let's now consider how psychologists try to predict violent behavior.

A parole board is trying to decide whether or not to release a prisoner who is eligible for parole. The staff of a mental hospital is debating whether or not to discharge a patient with a history of violent behavior. A judge is trying to decide whether or not to send a first-time offender to jail. In each case, the authorities ask a psychologist or a psychiatrist for a professional opinion on whether the person is dangerous.

How accurate are such opinions? If they are based mainly on interviews, they are accurate

The facial expression of anger represents a threat of possible attack, but for most of us that threat seldom develops into a reality. We deal with our anger by discussing the problem or by walking away from the situation; rarely if ever do we strike someone.

only a little more often than they would be by chance (Monahan, 1984). Some dangerous people manage to convince others that they are harmless.

The most accurate predictions are those based on biographical information. People who were physically abused as children and who witnessed violence between their parents are more likely than others are to commit repeated acts of violence, including murder (Eron, 1987; Lewis et al., 1983, 1985, 1987). The physical pain of being beaten may provoke future violence, and a violent parent provides a model for the child eventually to imitate. (Recall the principles of social learning from Chapter 7.) Even this predictor is far from foolproof, however; only about one third of abused children become abusive parents (Widom, 1989).

Many other biographical factors are associated with a tendency toward violent behavior (Eron, 1987; Lewis et al., 1983, 1985):

- A history of acting violently during childhood

- Not feeling guilty after hurting someone

- Symptoms of brain damage or of major psychological disorders

- Being closely related to someone who has been committed to a psychiatric hospital

- A history of suicide attempts

- Watching a great deal of violence on television

How can anyone help people to control their violent behavior? Punishment is sometimes effective and may be necessary in extreme cases, but it is often counterproductive. Excessively painful punishment actually triggers aggressive behavior.

Sometimes cognitive approaches are effective. People can be taught to stop making unrealistic, perfectionistic demands on themselves and others. They can be taught to tolerate frustration.

Encouraging people to learn new behaviors is another way to control violent behavior (Fehrenbach & Thelen, 1982). Eliminating reinforcement may extinguish or reduce the offensive behavior. If a child has learned to win attention by throwing temper tantrums, for example, then parents and teachers should ignore the tantrums. Or they can impose "time-out" periods after an episode of violent behavior, perhaps by temporarily isolating a child who regularly attacks other children. Finally, they can reinforce acceptable behavior, perhaps by giving points toward a reward for every hour spent in calm interaction with others.

Happiness

What makes you happy? What makes you unhappy? The answers are more elusive than you might expect. The following quote is from Leo Tolstoy, the author of *War and Peace, Anna*

Some violent behavior is learned and can be extinguished. One technique is a form of deprivation, isolating a child after he or she hits others. Another method reinforces good behavior—an approach used for the chatterbox in Chapter 7.

Karenina, and other famous novels. At the time of this writing, Tolstoy was rich and famous, but desperately unhappy:

I wandered about in the forest of human knowledge. . . . From one branch of human knowledge I received an endless number of precise answers to questions I had not asked, answers concerning the chemical composition of the stars, the movement of the sun toward the constellation Hercules, the origin of the species and of man, the forms of infinitely small atoms. . . . But the answer given by this branch of knowledge to my question about the meaning of my life was only this: You . . . are a temporary, random conglomeration of particles. The thing that you have been led to refer to as your life is simply the mutual interaction and alteration of these particles. This conglomeration will continue for a certain period of time; then the interaction of these particles will come to a halt, and the thing you call your life will come to an end and with it all your questions. You are a little lump of something randomly stuck together. The lump decomposes. . . . There is no more to be said.

My life came to a stop. . . . There was no life in me because I had no desires whose satisfaction I would have found reasonable. . . . If a fairy had come and offered to fulfill my every wish, I would not have known what to wish for. . . . I did not even want to discover truth anymore because I had guessed what it was. The truth was that life is meaningless. (Tolstoy, 1882/1983, pp. 40–41, 27–28)

What would it take to make Tolstoy happy? Fame, wealth, family, and friends had failed to bring him happiness. If he were alive today, no doubt someone would recommend giving him antidepressant drugs. But I wouldn't count on drugs to do him much good either. What Tolstoy needed was a belief—a belief that the universe made sense and that life had meaning.

Eventually he found contentment, if not exactly happiness, by changing his life, seeking spiritual (though not church-oriented) values, and giving away much of his wealth—over the protests of his wife and children.

Many things can make people happy, but mere *things* don't keep people happy for long. Within a given country, at a given time, wealthy people tend to be happier than poor people are, but we can find many exceptions to this rule. Furthermore, as a given country—say, the United States—becomes wealthier and wealthier, the average person in that country does not become happier and happier (Diener, 1984).

Then what does make people happy? We can list many possibilities—having a belief in the value of life, having goals to work toward, having the freedom to choose our own way of life, and so on. But it is difficult to conduct research on the contribution of each factor. Good scientific research requires good measurement, and measuring happiness is difficult.

Most frequently psychologists measure happiness simply by asking people how happy they are. Based on people's self-reports, psychologists find that religious people and people with many friends tend to be happier than nonreligious people and people with few social contacts. Also, people who are healthy and who are achieving their goals tend to be happy (Diener, 1984). However, these trends represent correlational data and therefore tell us nothing about cause and effect. (For example, we do not know whether having friends makes a person happy or whether being happy helps someone attract friends.)

Moreover, people's self-reports of happiness may not be entirely accurate. For example, consider Figure 12.16, which shows that *reported* happiness is nearly constant from young adulthood through old age (Russell & Megaard, 1988). If we take these results at face value, we would conclude that age is virtually unrelated to happiness. Are people in their 70s really just as happy as young adults are? Maybe. But it is also possible that "I feel very happy" means something different to an older person than it does to a younger person.

As a rule, people with many social contacts are happier than people with few contacts. However, the underlying causes of happiness are elusive. Some people with little wealth, such as these friends in Estonia, are happy, and some rich and famous people are desperately unhappy.

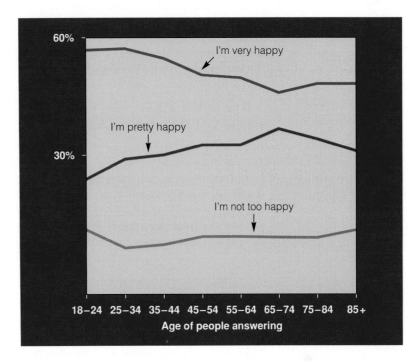

FIGURE 12.16
Between 1972 and 1986, more than 20,000 U.S. people were asked how happy they were— very happy, pretty happy, or not too happy. Results varied only slightly from one age to another or from one year to another. (Based on data of Russell & Megaard, 1988).

SUMMARY

■ *Emotions and autonomic arousal.* Emotions are generally associated with arousal of the sympathetic or parasympathetic branch of the autonomic nervous system. The sympathetic nervous system readies the body for emergency action. The parasympathetic nervous system promotes digestion and other less vigorous activities. (page 493)

■ *Opponent-process principle.* As the opponent-process principle of emotions points out, the removal of the impetus for a given emotion brings about a sudden swing to the opposite emotion. (page 496)

■ *Polygraph.* The polygraph measures the activity of the sympathetic nervous system through such variables as heart rate, breathing rate, blood pressure, and electrical conductance of the skin. The polygraph is sometimes used as a "lie detector," although its accuracy for that purpose is low. (page 497)

■ *James-Lange theory.* According to the James-Lange theory of emotions, an emotion is the perception of a change in the body's physiological state. (page 499)

■ *Cannon-Bard theory.* According to the Cannon-Bard theory, the cognitive experience of an emotion is independent of physiological arousal. (page 500)

■ *Schachter and Singer's theory.* According to Schachter and Singer's theory, autonomic arousal determines the intensity of an emotion but does not determine what that emotion will be. We identify an emotion on the basis of how we perceive the situation. (page 500)

■ *Limitations of these theories.* None of these three theories of emotion is fully satisfactory. Physiological and cognitive influences interact in complex ways to produce emotional experiences. (page 503)

■ *Facial expressions.* Facial expressions are closely tied to emotions. When people move their facial muscles into something that resembles a smile, they are more likely to be happy than if they maintain other expressions. (page 503)

■ *Cultural similarities.* Many human facial expressions are largely the same for cultures throughout the world. (page 504)

■ *Anger.* People experience anger frequently, although it seldom leads to violent acts. Aggressive behavior often occurs in defense of territory or in competition for a mate. Frustration or other unpleasant experiences often prompt aggressive behavior. (page 508)

■ *Predicting violence.* Psychologists and psychiatrists find it difficult to predict whether a particular prisoner would be dangerous if released. Currently, the best way to make such predictions is to review the prisoner's biographical information, especially the history of violent behavior. (page 508)

- *Measuring happiness.* Happiness is difficult to measure, and most of what we know about it is based on correlational data. Possessions alone cannot guarantee happiness. (page 509)

SUGGESTIONS FOR FURTHER READING

Jones, W., Cheek, J., & Briggs, S. (Eds.) (1986). *Shyness: Perspectives on research and treatment.* New York: Plenum. See especially R. S. Miller's chapter on embarrassment.

Mandler, G. (1984). *Mind and body: Psychology of emotion and stress.* New York: Norton. Perhaps the best scholarly work on the emotions.

TERMS

autonomic nervous system a section of the nervous system that controls the functioning of the internal organs (page 495)

sympathetic nervous system a system composed of two chains of neuron clusters lying just to the left and right of the spinal cord; the neurons send messages to the internal organs to prepare them for a burst of vigorous activity (page 495)

parasympathetic nervous system a system of neurons located at the top and bottom of the spinal cord; the neurons send messages to the internal organs that prepare the body for digestion and related processes (page 495)

opponent-process principle of emotions principle that the removal of a stimulus that excites one emotion causes a swing to an opposite emotion (page 496)

galvanic skin response (GSR) a brief increase in the electrical conductivity of the skin, indicating increased arousal of the sympathetic nervous system (page 497)

polygraph a machine that simultaneously measures heart rate, breathing rate, blood pressure, and galvanic skin response (page 497)

guilty-knowledge test a test that uses the polygraph to measure whether a person has information that only someone guilty of a certain crime could know (page 498)

James-Lange theory the theory that emotion is merely our perception of autonomic changes and movements evoked directly by various stimuli (page 499)

Cannon-Bard theory of emotions theory that certain areas of the brain evaluate sensory information and, when appropriate, send one set of impulses to the autonomic nervous system and another set to the forebrain, which is responsible for the subjective and cognitive aspects of emotion (page 500)

Schachter and Singer's theory of emotions theory that emotions are our interpretation of autonomic arousal in light of all the information we have about ourselves and the situation (page 501)

frustration-aggression hypothesis the theory that frustration leads to aggressive behavior (page 508)

ANSWERS TO CONCEPT CHECKS

1. When you ride a roller coaster, your heart rate increases (sympathetic activity). After you get off, your heart rate falls to lower than usual (rebound increase in parasympathetic activity). (page 497)

2. After someone takes a drug repeatedly, the A state becomes weaker. (That is known as tolerance, as discussed in Chapter 7.) The B state (withdrawal) becomes stronger. (page 497)

3. According to the James-Lange theory, the trembling and shaking came first. Schachter and Singer's theory agrees. However, according to the James-Lange theory, your perception of the trembling and shaking leads immediately and automatically to the experience of fear. According to Schachter and Singer's theory, you first interpret your trembling on the basis of circumstances before you experience fear: "Am I shaking because of that pill I took? Because someone made me angry? Because I'm excited? Because I'm frightened?" (page 503)

ANSWERS TO OTHER QUESTIONS IN THE TEXT

Figure 12.12, page 505: From left to right, top to bottom, the faces express happiness, anger, sadness, surprise, disgust, and fear.

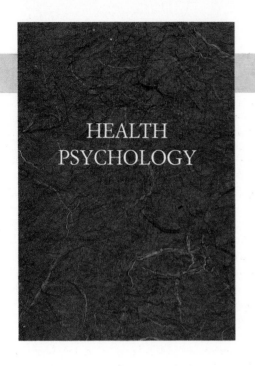

HEALTH PSYCHOLOGY

How do our emotions affect our health?

Imagine you meet a man who is suffering from, say, multiple sclerosis. Would you say, "It's his own fault he's sick; he's being punished for his sins"? I presume you would neither say nor believe anything so cruel. However, in the Middle Ages and in ancient times, many people believed just that. We congratulate ourselves today on having advanced beyond that way of thinking; we know it is wrong to "blame the victim."

Or do we? We may think cigarette smokers are at least partly at fault if they develop lung cancer. We note that AIDS usually occurs in people with a history of intravenous drug use or unsafe sex. If women drink alcohol during pregnancy, we hold them partly responsible for the deformities or mental retardation of their infants. As we learn more and more about the causes of various illnesses, we expect people to accept more responsibility for their own health, even if we do not exactly use the word *blame* when people become ill.

People's behavior does, in fact, influence their health. Unfortunately, we can easily overstate the amount of that influence. Some people are always as careful as possible about their diet, exercise regularly, and have healthy habits but develop serious illnesses anyway. Psychological factors influence our health, but they are not the only influence.

Health psychology deals with the ways in which people's behavior can enhance health and prevent illness and how behavior contributes to recovery from illness (Brannon & Feist, 1992). It deals with such issues as why people smoke, why they may ignore their physician's advice, and how to reduce pain. In this section, we shall focus mainly on how stress and other emotional conditions affect health.

STRESS

Have you ever gone without sleep several nights in a row trying to finish an assignment before a deadline? Or waited what seemed like forever for someone who was supposed to pick you up? Or had a close friend suddenly not want to see you anymore? Or tried to explain why you no longer want to date someone? Each of these experiences provokes an emotional response and causes stress.

Selye's Concept of Stress

According to Hans Selye (1979), an Austrian-born physician who worked at McGill University in Montreal, **stress** is *the nonspecific response of the body to any demand made upon it.* Every demand on the body evokes certain specific responses as well. The body responds in one way to the loss of blood, in another way to the lack of sleep. But all demands on the body evoke generalized, nonspecific responses. For example, they all activate the sympathetic nervous system, increase the release of the hormone epinephrine, and interfere with your ability to concentrate.

When people say, "I've been under a lot of stress lately," they are generally referring to a string of unpleasant experiences. Selye's concept of stress is broader than that: He includes any experience that brings about some change in a person's life. For example, getting married or being promoted is presumably a pleasant experience, but it also demands that you make a number of changes in the way you live, and so in Selye's sense it produces stress. It is unclear, however, whether a favorable stressor makes the same demands on the body as does an unfavorable stressor.

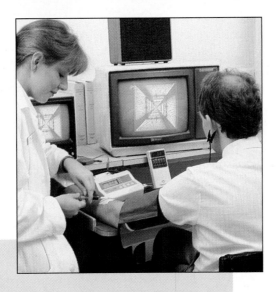

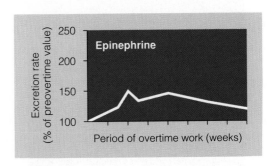

FIGURE 12.17

Epinephrine levels rose for a group of women before, during, and after a long period of working overtime. To establish a baseline, each woman's epinephrine level prior to the overtime period was taken as 100%; thus any number above 100% represents an increase. (From Frankenhaeuser, 1980.)

In recent years, stress management has become a growth industry. Some stress is inevitable and appropriate, but too much for too long can be dangerous. In this measurement of stress, blood samples are taken from this subject before he begins a video game designed to reduce emotional stress. Once he finishes the game, a second blood sample will be taken to compare levels of epinephrine in his blood before and after the game.

According to Selye, the body goes through three stages in its response to a stressor: The first is **alarm,** a brief period of high arousal of the sympathetic nervous system, readying the body for vigorous activity. However, some stressors last longer than the body can maintain this high state of arousal. Perhaps you live down the street from a nuclear power plant, or you have a high-stress job. If so, you cannot overcome your problem with a brief burst of intense activity. You enter **resistance,** a stage of prolonged but moderate arousal. Your epinephrine levels remain at a high level day after day, week after week (Figure 12.17). Your adrenal cortex secretes **cortisol** and several other hormones that elevate blood sugar and enhance metabolism. The increased fuel supply to the cells enables them to sustain a high, steady level of activity to endure prolonged stress. However, you no longer feel ready for vigorous activity; you feel withdrawn and inactive much of the time, your performance deteriorates, and you complain of emotional distress (Baum, Gatchel, & Schaeffer, 1983; Frankenhaeuser, 1980).

If the stress is even more intense and long-lasting, the body enters the third stage, **exhaustion.** As cortisol and other hormones shift energy toward increasing blood sugar and metabolism, they shift it away from synthesis of proteins, including the proteins necessary for

the immune system. In the short term that shift may not be a problem; however, severe stress over many months may weaken the immune system and leave the individual vulnerable to a variety of illnesses (O'Leary, 1990). The end result is what Selye calls the **general adaptation syndrome,** which is characterized by weakness, fatigue, loss of appetite, and a general lack of interest.

Posttraumatic Stress Disorder

Perhaps the most powerful demonstration of the effects of severe stress is **posttraumatic stress disorder (PTSD),** a condition in which people who have endured extreme stress feel prolonged anxiety and depression (Pitman, Orr, Forgue, deJong, & Claiborn, 1987). This condition has been recognized after wars throughout history, under such names as "battle fatigue" or "shell shock." One nationwide survey reported posttraumatic stress disorder in 20% of the American veterans who were wounded in Vietnam (Helzer, Robins, & McEnvoy, 1987). It also occurs in rape or assault victims, torture victims, survivors of an airplane crash or a severe automobile crash, and witnesses to a murder. In rare cases, a person may experience only mild distress immediately after the event but develop PTSD a few months later (Burstein, 1985).

People with posttraumatic stress disorder may suffer from frequent nightmares, outbursts of anger, constant unhappiness, and guilt. The guilt is a special kind of experience, often called *survivor's guilt,* common in people who survive a catastrophe in which many other people died. People with PTSD may have difficulty concentrating or relating emotionally to other people (Keane, Wolfe, & Taylor, 1987). A brief reminder of the tragic experience can trigger a flashback that borders on panic. Many day-to-day events become stressful, even years after the original event (Solomon, Mikulincer, & Flum, 1988). In one study, eight Vietnam veterans with PTSD watched a 15-minute videotape of dramatized combat. Watching the film elevated their endorphin levels in the same way in which people generally react to an actual injury (Pitman, van der Kolk, Orr, & Greenberg, 1990).

One obstacle for psychologists who deal with PTSD victims is that some of them actively resist recovery (Krystal, 1991). For example, some Jewish survivors of the Nazi concentration camps say that if they accepted the past and became happy again, that would be like approving the Holocaust and "giving Hitler a posthumous victory."

This group of Vietnam vets met regularly for a year to work on problems related to posttraumatic stress. Since the group disbanded, one member has had a show of his hand-colored photographs. (This group portrait is a sample of his work.) Another member has started his own company. Some members have created new careers; some have been in and out of substance-abuse programs. Most continue to experience vivid dreams full of war images.

Measuring Stress and Its Effect on Health

Most investigators agree that severe stress can endanger a person's health. For example, prolonged job stress is significantly correlated with anxiety and depression (deWolff, 1985). People who experience severe stress on the job report frequent illnesses as well. (At least they often call in sick and stay home from work!)

How much stress is injurious to one's health? Is it true that the more stress a person experiences, the more that person's health suffers?

To answer such questions, we need to measure both stress and health. Measuring health is tough enough; measuring stress is even more difficult. One approach is to give people a checklist of stressful experiences. For example, Thomas Holmes and Richard Rahe (1967) devised a Social Readjustment Rating Scale (Table 12.2) that assigns points for both desirable and undesirable events, in accordance with Selye's idea that any change in a person's life is stressful. Note, for example, that you could get 35 points for "change in number of arguments with spouse"—the same number of stress points for an increase or a decrease in argu-

ments! To measure your amount of stress, you are supposed to check off all the experiences you have had within a given period of time, such as the last 6 months, and total up the points assigned to each.

Although this scale has been widely used, it is subject to many criticisms: First, the assumption that we can add stress points from various events is probably wrong (Birnbaum & Sotoodeh, 1991). For example, suppose you graduate from college (26 points), treat yourself to a vacation (13), and then start a new job (36). That adds up to 75 points—more than you would get for a divorce (73) or the death of a close family member (63).

Second problem: The scale includes 53 points for suffering the stress associated with "personal injury or illness." It also ascribes points for sex difficulties, change in sleeping habits, and change in eating habits—all symptoms of illness. So it is not very impressive to find that people with high stress scores have an increased probability of being ill.

Third, the scale fails to measure some important stressors. Selye defined stress as a response to changes in one's life, and accordingly this scale ignores the stress of coping with unchanging problems, such as racism or poverty.

Table 12.2 Social Readjustment Rating Scale

Rank	Life Event	Point Value	Rank	Life Event	Point Value
1	Death of spouse	100	22	Change in responsibilities at work	29
2	Divorce	73	23	Son or daughter leaving home	29
3	Marital separation	65	24	Trouble with in-laws	29
4	Jail term	63	25	Outstanding personal achievement	28
5	Death of close family member	63	26	Wife begin or stop work	26
6	Personal injury or illness	53	27	Begin or end school	26
7	Marriage	50	28	Change in living conditions	25
8	Fired at work	47	29	Revision of personal habits	24
9	Marital reconciliation	45	30	Trouble with boss	23
10	Retirement	45	31	Change in work hours or conditions	20
11	Change in health of family member	44	32	Change in residence	20
12	Pregnancy	40	33	Change in schools	20
13	Sex difficulties	39	34	Change in recreation	19
14	Gain of new family member	39	35	Change in church activities	19
15	Business readjustment	39	36	Change in social activities	18
16	Change in financial state	38	37	Mortgage or loan less than $10,000	17
17	Death of close friend	37	38	Change in sleeping habits	16
18	Change to different line of work	36	39	Change in number of family get-togethers	15
19	Change in number of arguments with spouse	35	40	Change in eating habits	15
20	Mortgage over $10,000	31	41	Vacation	13
21	Foreclosure of mortgage or loan	30	42	Christmas	12
			43	Minor violations of the law	11

Source: Homes & Rahe, 1967.

It also ignores the stress we experience from events that *almost* happened. For example, all year long you expect to be laid off from your job. You keep waiting, but the rumored plant closing never happens. Or you have been counting on a promotion at work, and you have told all your friends that you are expecting it, but then you do not get promoted. You get no points on the rating scale for "not getting fired" or "not being promoted." And yet anyone who has lived through such an experience can tell you that it was very stressful.

Something to Think About

Can you think of a better way to measure stress? Some psychologists have given people a list of events and have asked them both to check off events they have experienced and to assign a value to each event on the basis of how stressful they found it. Is that an improvement, or does it introduce problems of its own?

Lazarus's Approach to Stress

Aside from the problems with the Social Readjustment Rating Scale, however, many psychologists challenge the basic assumption that a particular life change produces a specific amount of stress and that a given event will be equally stressful for all people. As Richard Lazarus (1977) pointed out, the stress evoked by an event depends on how people interpret the event and what they can do about it. Pregnancy may be much more stressful for a 16-year-old unmarried woman than it is for a 27-year-old married woman. Being fired may be a disaster for a 50-year-old who expects to have trouble finding another job; it may be only a minor annoyance to a 19-year-old.

According to Lazarus, *stress is a situation that someone regards as threatening and as possibly exceeding his or her resources* (Lazarus, 1977). (See Figure 12.18.) Note that this view includes a major role for people's knowledge,

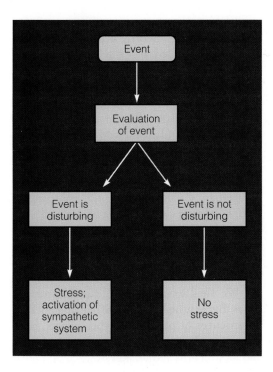

FIGURE 12.18
Lazarus believes that evaluation of some kind, conscious or unconscious, always precedes emotion. Thus a given event may be highly stressful for one person, only slightly stressful or not at all for a second person.

experience, and cognitions: Two women are bitten by a snake. The first woman panics; the second woman remains calm, because she recognizes the snake as a harmless variety. Two men are criticized by their boss. One is deeply hurt; the other (who has seen the boss act this way before) shrugs and says, "I guess the boss is in a bad mood again today."

To the extent that stress depends on our interpretation of an event, not simply on the event itself, people can learn to cope with potentially stressful events, as we shall see later in this chapter. They can learn to deal with events actively instead of feeling threatened by them. Given this view, the proper measure of stress would have to include not only the unpleasant events ("hassles") that we have to deal with but also the pleasant events ("uplifts") that brighten our day and help to cancel out the unpleasant events (Kanner, Coyne, Schaefer, & Lazarus, 1981). Table 12.3 presents one example of this approach.

Table 12.3 Ten Most Frequent Hassles and Uplifts

Hassles	Uplifts
1. Concerns about weight	1. Relating well with your spouse or lover
2. Health of a family member	2. Relating well with friends
3. Rising prices of common goods	3. Completing a task
4. Home maintenance	4. Feeling healthy
5. Too many things to do	5. Getting enough sleep
6. Misplacing or losing things	6. Eating out
7. Yard work or outside home maintenance	7. Meeting your responsibilities
8. Property, investment, or taxes	8. Visiting, phoning, or writing someone
9. Crime	9. Spending time with family
10. Physical appearance	10. Home (inside) pleasing to you

Source: Kanner, Coyne, Schaefer, & Lazarus, 1981.

We can conclude this section by emphasizing that stress is difficult to measure accurately. Nevertheless, we can identify particular kinds of stressful experiences that endanger many people's health. Studying the effects of experience on health and illness can offer us insights into the relationship among stressful experiences, interpretation of those experiences, and body functioning.

STRESS AND PSYCHOSOMATIC ILLNESS

A **psychosomatic illness** is an illness that is influenced by a person's experiences—particularly stressful experiences—or by his or her reactions to those experiences. It is *not* an imagined or a pretended illness. And it is not entirely the result of psychological factors. High blood pressure, for example, is caused by a combination of a genetic predisposition, stress, and salt in the diet (Friedman & Iwai, 1976).

For many years, physicians looking for the sources of illness concentrated on physical agents such as germs or injuries, giving no thought to the possibility of a psychosomatic influence. Then, in the early 1800s, they found soldiers who were suffering from what we would now call posttraumatic stress disorder. Some of the soldiers showed serious (though temporary) physical ailments, including blindness or paralysis, even though they had never been hit by a bullet or shrapnel. A few even died on the battlefield when a cannon ball landed nearby without striking them. Physicians of the time suggested that the soldiers were injured by the wind of the cannon ball passing by, or by atmospheric electricity stirred up by the wind, or by the heat or the temporary vacuum it left in its wake. Today those hypotheses sound extremely far-fetched; at the time they seemed more reasonable than the "ridiculous" idea that mere fear or other psychological states could influence someone's health (McMahon, 1975).

Physicians and psychologists still have trouble explaining how emotional states affect the body. They do not assume that emotions lead directly to illness. They know, however, that people who have certain emotional experiences are more likely than others to overeat, to smoke, or to engage in other habits that increase the risk of illness. Certain behaviors and experiences can damage the immune system and increase a person's vulnerability to a variety of disorders ranging from minor infections to cancer (Shavit et al., 1985).

One young woman died of fear in a most peculiar way: When she was born, on Friday the 13th, the midwife who delivered her and two other babies that day announced that all three were hexed and would die before their 23rd birthday. The other two did die young. As the third woman approached her 23rd birthday, she checked into a hospital and informed the staff of her fears. The staff noted that she dealt with her anxiety by extreme hyperventilation (deep breathing). Shortly before her birthday, she hyperventilated to death.

How did that happen? Ordinarily, when people do not breathe voluntarily they breathe reflexively; the reflex is triggered by carbon dioxide in the blood. By extreme hyperventilation, this woman had exhaled so much carbon dioxide that she did not have enough left to trigger reflexive breathing. When she stopped breathing voluntarily, she stopped breathing altogether ("Clinicopathologic conference," 1967). This is a clear example of a self-fulfilling prophecy: The fact that the woman believed in the hex caused its fulfillment. It is also a clear example of an indirect influence of emotions on health.

We shall examine three examples of diseases that may be linked to particular emotional experiences or personality types: ulcers, heart disease, and cancer. In each case, the evidence has its strengths and weaknesses.

Ulcers and Stress:

WHAT'S THE EVIDENCE?

An **ulcer** is an open sore on the lining of the stomach or duodenum (the upper part of the small intestine) that is caused in part by excess digestive acids. People who experience severe work-related stress are especially vulnerable to ulcers; for example, ulcers are common among immigrant workers who are forced to work long hours to make a living (Sonnenberg, 1988). Ulcers are also likely to form in hospital patients with serious illnesses (Peura, 1987).

How could we test the relationship between stress and ulcers? Because of the manifest difficulties of conducting such studies with humans, Joseph Brady, Robert Porter, Donald Conrad, and John Mason (1958) used monkeys. A monkey's digestive system works the same way as a human's and responds similarly to stress.

Hypothesis Monkeys that are responsible for turning off shocks for both themselves and their partners will get ulcers. Monkeys that get the same number of shocks without having any control over them will be less likely to get ulcers.

Method The experimenters fastened two monkeys into chairs. One of the monkeys, the so-called executive monkey, could prevent electric shock by pressing a lever at least once every 20 seconds. If it failed to do so, *both* monkeys would receive a shock to their feet once every 20 seconds until the executive monkey pressed the lever again. Both monkeys got the same shock, but only the executive monkey had to cope with the work and worry. The shock-avoidance sessions lasted for 6 hours, twice a day, seven days a week, until one monkey or the other showed signs of illness.

Results Four pairs of monkeys were used over the course of the experiment. Within the first hour or two of the first session, every executive monkey became highly adept at pressing the lever; neither monkey received many shocks after that. All four executive monkeys developed severe ulcers, and three of them died. None of the passive partners developed ulcers.

Interpretation Actually, it is not easy to draw any firm conclusion. First, the design of the experiment was flawed: Instead of assigning monkeys randomly to the executive and passive roles, the experimenters put all the monkeys through a brief training period and then chose the fastest learners to be the executives. Conceivably, fast learners may be more likely than slow learners to get ulcers. It is even remotely conceivable that the fast-learning monkeys would have developed ulcers without being put into the shock apparatus. That suggestion may or may not strike you as plausible, but it illustrates the importance of proper control groups: When experimenters use inadequate control groups, they cannot eliminate alternative explanations of the results.

Actually, even if we ignore the methodological flaw in this study, it could not provide decisive evidence about the causes of ulcers. That is, even if we accept that the executive monkeys are more likely than the passive monkeys are to get ulcers, we do not know whether the executive monkeys are at risk because they have to "worry" or just because they have to work. To answer that question, we need additional studies. This is an important point about scientific progress: *Because the results of almost any single experiment can be interpreted in several ways, most conclusions rest on a whole series of experiments.*

In the wake of this monkey experiment, investigators conducted a number of similar experiments with rats. They also conducted experiments on humans, relying on various short-term measures of distress, rather than actually trying to induce ulcers. To summarize a mass of results: In general, the "worry" caused by "being in charge" of shocks or loud noises is not a serious health problem. In fact, having control over unpleasant events generally *decreases* the stress they evoke (Glass, Singer, & Pennebaker, 1977; Guile, 1987; Sherrod, Hage, Halpern, & Moore, 1977; Weiss, 1968). The original executive-monkey experiment was an exception to this rule because the executive monkeys became so good at avoiding shocks. The passive monkeys suffered little stress because they rarely received a shock.

All the studies agree on one point, however: Stress increases the risk of ulcers. When animals are exposed to either shocks or the threat of shocks, at least some of them get ulcers; animals that are simply left in their cages for the same time have little risk of ulcers. Similarly, people who undergo prolonged stressful experiences have a serious risk of ulcers.

How does stress cause ulcers? A stressful experience activates mostly the sympathetic nervous system, increasing heart rate, breathing rate, and epinephrine secretions. However, ulcers do not form during the stress session itself; they form afterward during the rest period (Desiderato, MacKinnon, & Hissom, 1974). Once the stress session is over, the autonomic nervous system rebounds from a state of high sympathetic arousal to a state of parasympathetic dominance, increasing the digestive secretions even if there is no food in the digestive system. Those excess secretions eat away at the lining of the stomach and intestines and produce an ulcer (Figure 12.19).

In addition to digestive secretions, the rest period after a stressful experience is marked by decreased blood flow to the stomach and many slow but intense stomach contractions. These contractions tend to break up the protective mucus lining of the stomach and expose parts of the stomach wall to the digestive secretions (Garrick, 1990; Garrick, Minor, Bauck, Weiner, & Guth, 1989).

Ulcers are becoming less common than they once were. People who are highly vulnerable to ulcers, including long-term hospital patients, are given various medications to prevent excess stomach acid secretions or antacid pills to soak up the excess acids (Miller, 1987).

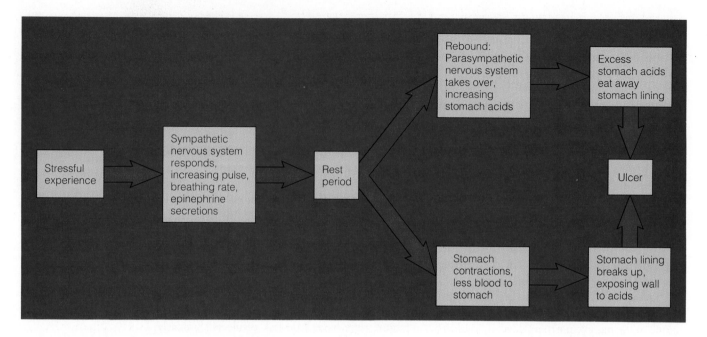

FIGURE 12.19
A prolonged stressful experience can lead to ulcers, partly by rebound overactivity of the parasympathetic nervous system, which increases the secretion of digestive acids, and partly by increased stomach contractions.

■ CONCEPT CHECK

4. *Last week your physician told you that you are prone to ulcers and gave you some antacids and other pills to take. You have just completed five midterm exams in two days, an experience you found very stressful, and you discover that you have misplaced all the pills. What could you do to guard against developing an ulcer? (Check your answer on page 524.)*

Heart Disease

The upholsterer repairing the chairs in a physician's waiting room once noticed that the fronts of the chairs wore out before the backs. To figure out why, the physician began watching patients in the waiting room. He noticed that his heart patients habitually sat on the front edges of their seats, waiting impatiently to be called in for their appointments. This observation led the physician to hypothesize a link between heart disease and an impatient, success-driven personality, now known as the Type A personality (Friedman & Rosenman, 1974).

People with a **Type A personality** are highly competitive; they must always win. They are impatient, always in a hurry, and often angry and hostile. By contrast, people with a **Type B personality** are relatively easygoing, less hurried, and less hostile. For example, Gary Schwartz (1987) describes observations of two men fishing: One (a Type B) slowly baited his hook, dropped his line into the water, and sat back watching the gulls and waiting for a bite. An-

other man (a Type A), fishing with two poles, spent much of his time rushing back and forth between the two poles, cursing when the two lines got tangled with each other. When another fisher caught a large fish, this man pulled up his anchor in frustration and raced his boat off to another part of the bay. (Are you a Type A or a Type B? Check yourself by answering the questions in Figure 12.20.)

Statistically, a link does exist between Type A personality and susceptibility to heart disease, although that link is not overwhelmingly strong (Harbin, 1989). Part of the evidence for a linkage comes from studies comparing heart disease in various cultures (Levine, 1990). Some cultures have a hurried pace of life; people walk fast; they talk fast; almost everyone wears a watch; storekeepers pay prompt attention to their customers. Other cultures have a more relaxed pace of life; people are seldom in a rush; few people wear watches; the buses and trains seldom arrive on schedule but no one seems to care (Figure 12.21). As you might guess, the rate of heart disease is higher in countries with a hurried pace of life than it is in countries with a more relaxed pace. In the United States, the pace of life is generally fastest in large northeastern cities; it is slowest in small towns of the west and the south. Note, of course, that these are correlational data; they do not demonstrate conclusively that a frantic pace of life causes heart problems. (For example, something about cultural differences in diet or climate might simultaneously influence people's activity levels and their heart muscles.)

Measuring the Type A Personality

_____ 1. Do you find it difficult to restrain yourself from hurrying others' speech (finishing their sentences for them)?

_____ 2. Do you often try to do more than one thing at a time (such as eat and read simultaneously)?

_____ 3. Do you often feel guilty if you use extra time to relax?

_____ 4. Do you tend to get involved in a great number of projects at once?

_____ 5. Do you find yourself racing through yellow lights when you drive?

_____ 6. Do you need to win in order to derive enjoyment from games and sports?

_____ 7. Do you generally move, walk, and eat rapidly?

_____ 8. Do you agree to take on too many responsibilities?

_____ 9. Do you detest waiting in lines?

_____ 10. Do you have an intense desire to better your position in life and impress others?

FIGURE 12.20

If you answer yes to a majority of these items, Friedman and Rosenman (1974) would say you probably have a Type A personality. But they would also consider your explanation of your answers, so this questionnaire gives only a rough estimate of your personality. Friedman and Rosenman classified everyone as either Type A or Type B, but most psychologists believe people can have any degree of Type A traits from low to high.

FIGURE 12.21

People in some cultures have a frantic pace of life: Everyone seems to be in a rush; people walk fast, talk fast, and push one another around; their main concern may be about whether Federal Express is better than UPS for overnight delivery. In other cultures, no one is sure what time it is and no one cares. The risk of heart disease is greatest in cultures or subcultures with a frantic pace of life.

At first, researchers focused mostly on the role of impatience and competitiveness as the main links between Type A behavior and heart disease. When Type A people perform competitive tasks, their muscle tension increases and their sympathetic nervous system is aroused (Williams et al., 1982). Because they seek competitive tasks, their hearts are working hard much of the time.

However, later evidence has indicated that heart disease correlates more strongly with unpleasant emotions, especially depression and hostility (Booth-Kewley & Friedman, 1987). Perhaps a highly responsive sympathetic nervous system predisposes people to feel tense, while it also overstimulates the heart. Future research will tell us more about how depression and anger contribute to heart disease.

■ CONCEPT CHECK

5. *People with a Type A personality are likely to develop stress-related heart disease. Yet when they fill out the Social Readjustment Rating Scale, mentioned earlier, their scores are often low. Why might that scale understate the stress levels of Type A people? (Check your answer on page 524.)*

Cancer

Among the causes of cancer are genetics and exposure to toxic substances. Behavior also can influence the onset and spread of cancer, at least indirectly. For example, people who smoke cigarettes increase their risk of cancer. Women who examine their breasts regularly can detect breast cancer at an early, treatable stage. Do emotions contribute directly to cancer? Because the brain influences the immune system, which fights cancer, an emotional experience might lead to an impairment of the immune system and therefore to a greater risk of certain kinds of cancer.

The two emotional states most likely to lead to cancer are depression and stress. Many cancer patients are depressed (Weinstock, 1984), and many of them report that they were depressed, often following the death of a loved one, long before they knew they had cancer. Severe depression suppresses the activity of the immune system and leaves a person more vulnerable than usual to all sorts of infection and disease, including the spread of certain types of tumors (Anisman & Zacharko, 1983; Baker, 1987).

In research on the effects of stress in ani-

mals, investigators have found that stress increases the spread of cancer and shortens the animal's survival. But it is difficult to generalize those results to humans. First, the results vary from one study to another, depending on the duration and type of stress and the genetic makeup of the animals. Second, nearly all the animal studies deal with cancers caused by viruses, and viruses cause fewer than 5% of human cancers (Fox, 1983).

Depression, stress, and severe emotional problems probably do increase the risk of cancer in humans. Still, the influence is minor; emotional factors are far less important in causing cancer than are genes and toxic substances (Anisman & Zacharko, 1983; Derogatis, 1986; Fox, 1983). Keeping a positive outlook on life may help to prevent cancer; still, many people suffering from serious, long-lasting depression manage to survive to old age (Stein, Miller, & Trestman, 1991).

Psychological factors may exert a stronger influence on what happens after the onset of cancer. People who receive steady support from their family and friends have a better chance of recovery. People who decide to fight the disease have a better chance than do those who take a resigned, helpless attitude that "what will be, will be" (Geer, Morris, & Pettingale, 1979). Exactly how the patient's attitude contributes to survival we do not know, but again it probably relates to enhancing or impairing the functions of the immune system.

BIOFEEDBACK: A BEHAVIORAL METHOD OF CONTROLLING BODY FUNCTIONS

As we have seen, stress, depression, hostility, and other unpleasant emotional states can make people more vulnerable to illness. Is there anything we can do to make ourselves less vulnerable or to improve our health?

Maybe. **Biofeedback,** for example, is a method for gaining voluntary control over physiological processes that we cannot ordinarily control. Recording devices are attached to the body to monitor heart rate, blood pressure, brain waves, or other body activities (Figure 12.22). The person is given constant information ("feedback") about the activity and instructions to try to control it. For example, to reduce the effects of stress, we might monitor

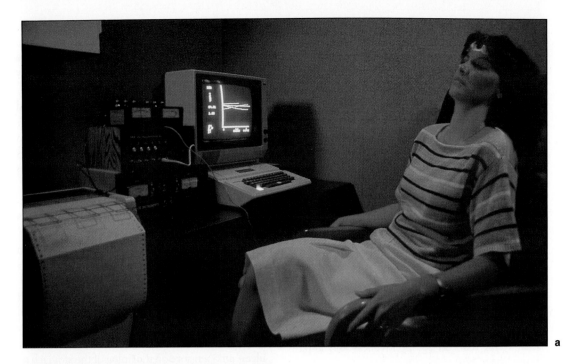

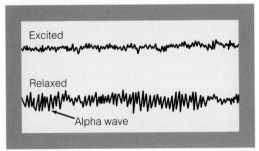

b

FIGURE 12.22

(a) To aid mental fitness, people may calm themselves using biofeedback machines. Brain researcher James Hardt helped develop a computerized biofeedback program, Mind Fitness, which translates brain waves into musical tones; people "hear" their alpha waves (Hollandsworth, 1989, p. 24). Although biofeedback helps people control their arousal, its long-term medical value is still doubtful for most purposes. (b) EEG patterns showing relaxed (alpha) states.

the person's blood pressure and the electrical activity of the brain. We could sound a tone whenever the person's blood pressure dropped below a certain level or whenever the brain began to emit alpha waves. (These brain waves occur at a rate of 8 to 12 per second; they generally indicate a state of relaxation.) So long as the person remains calm and relaxed, the tone sounds continuously (Schwartz, 1975). As soon as the person tenses up, the tone ceases.

Biofeedback has proved effective in certain specific applications, such as control of pain, gaining certain motor skills, and increasing relaxation (Schneider, 1987). But its effectiveness is more difficult to evaluate in other instances. Most practitioners use biofeedback in combination with other techniques, so it is difficult to determine the contribution of biofeedback itself. Many common applications of biofeedback provide only doubtful medical benefits (Roberts, 1985). For example, the lowered blood pressure and other effects produced by biofeedback generally do not persist after the monitoring devices have been detached (Blanchard & Young, 1973, 1974).

SUMMARY

- *Selye's concept of stress.* According to Hans Selye, stress is "the nonspecific response of the body to any demand made upon it." Any event, pleasant or unpleasant, that brings about some change in a person's life produces some measure of stress. (page 513)

- *Stages of response to stress.* The body goes through three stages in response to a stressful experience: alarm, resistance, and exhaustion. In resistance and exhaustion, prolonged channeling of energy toward resisting stress may weaken the immune system. (page 514)

- *Influence of past experiences.* The degree of stress an event evokes depends not only on the event itself but also on the person's interpretation of the event. People with posttraumatic stress disorder react strongly to daily events because of their previous experiences with war, rape, or other deeply upsetting events. (page 514)

- *Difficulties of measuring stress.* The stress an individual experiences is difficult to measure. Two people who have gone through similar experiences may show different levels of stress. (page 515)

■ *Psychosomatic illness.* Stress, hostility, and other emotional experiences may increase the probability of certain illnesses. A psychosomatic illness is somehow related to a person's experiences or to his or her reactions to those experiences. (page 518)

■ *Ulcers.* Ulcers form because of excess digestive secretions that can be produced by the parasympathetic rebound following a period of excess sympathetic nervous system activity. (page 518)

■ *Heart disease.* People with a Type A personality are competitive, impatient, and hostile. They are more likely than others to suffer heart disease, although the strength of that relationship and the reasons behind it are still in dispute. The emotional states of depression and hostility pose a greater risk than do competitiveness and impatience. (page 520)

■ *Cancer.* Depression and stress may increase the risk of cancer, at least slightly. People who take a fighting attitude toward their cancer generally survive longer than do those with a helpless attitude. (page 522)

■ *Biofeedback.* Biofeedback is a method of trying to gain control over such physiological processes as heart rate and blood pressure. Some of its common uses have not been demonstrated to be medically useful. (page 522)

SUGGESTION FOR FURTHER READING

Brannon, L., & Feist, J. (1992). *Health psychology* (2nd ed.). Belmont, CA: Wadsworth. A textbook that surveys the relationship between behavior and health.

TERMS

health psychology field of psychology that deals with the ways in which people's behavior can enhance health and prevent illness and how behavior contributes to recovery from illness (page 513)

stress according to Hans Selye, the nonspecific response of the body to any demand made upon it; according to Lazarus, a situation that someone regards as threatening and as possibly exceeding his or her resources (page 513)

alarm first stage of response to stress, a brief period of high arousal of the sympathetic nervous system, readying the body for vigorous activity (page 514)

resistance second stage of response to stress, a stage of prolonged but moderate arousal (page 514)

cortisol hormone that elevates blood sugar and enhances metabolism (page 514)

exhaustion third stage of response to stress, when the body's prolonged response to stress decreases the synthesis of proteins, including the proteins necessary for the immune system (page 514)

general adaptation syndrome condition characterized by weakness, fatigue, loss of appetite, and a general lack of interest (page 514)

posttraumatic stress disorder (PTSD) condition in which people who have endured extreme stress feel prolonged anxiety and depression (page 514)

psychosomatic illness an illness that is influenced by a person's experiences—particularly stressful experiences—or by his or her reactions to those experiences (page 518)

ulcer an open sore on the lining of the stomach or duodenum (page 518)

Type A personality personality characterized by constant competitiveness, impatience, anger, and hostility (page 520)

Type B personality personality characterized by easy-goingness, lack of hurry, and lack of hostility (page 520)

biofeedback method for gaining voluntary control over physiological processes that we cannot ordinarily control through sensory feedback (page 522)

ANSWERS TO CONCEPT CHECKS

4. To avoid an ulcer, eat something to absorb the excess stomach acids. (Don't consume alcohol, fruit juices, or anything else that is acidic itself.) Theoretically, we should expect that calming down gradually would be better than relaxing suddenly and completely. However, researchers find that adding some mild stressors during the rest period does not help someone to calm down gradually; the mild stressors may even increase the risk of ulcers (Murison & Overmier, 1990; Overmier, Murison, Ursin, & Skoglund, 1987). (page 520)

5. The Social Readjustment Rating Scale measures events that change a person's life; it does not measure constant sources of stress such as the pressures of work. It also fails to measure how people react to events, such as impatience, competitiveness, and hostility. (page 522)

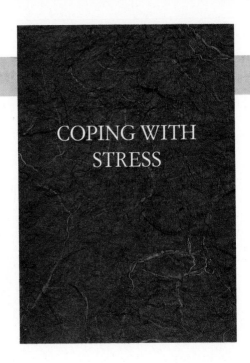

COPING WITH STRESS

How can we reduce the harmful effects of stress on the body?

How can we learn to cope with stress?

An eccentric millionaire whom you have never met before hands you a $10 bill for no apparent reason, no strings attached. How do you feel? Happy, I presume.

Now let's change the circumstances a bit: That generous person had been handing out $100 bills until it was your turn. Then the millionaire said, "Sorry, I just ran out of $100 bills. So I'll have to give you a $10 bill instead." Now how do you feel? Disappointed, sad, angry? You may even feel *cheated*, although you have just received something for nothing.

Just as your reaction to a free $10 bill depends on the circumstances, so does your reaction to bad news. How would you feel if you had studied hard for a test and then got a C–? Unhappy, I presume. But if you then discovered that everyone around you had failed the test, your C– would seem good by comparison. You would begin to feel much better.

How you feel about an event depends not just on the event itself but also on how you interpret it (Frijda, 1988; Lazarus, Averill, & Opton, 1970). Was it better or worse than you had expected? Better or worse than what happened to someone else? Was it a one-time event, or did it carry some hint of what might happen in the future? How you feel about an event also depends on your personality. Some people man-

age to keep their spirits high even in the face of tragedy while others are devastated by lesser setbacks.

Coping with stress is the process of developing ways to decrease its effects, to get through difficult tasks despite the stress. How do people cope with disappointments, anxieties, and stress? And can we learn to cope more successfully?

RELAXATION

As we have seen, the sympathetic nervous system prepares us to respond vigorously to emergencies. But sometimes it gets aroused when there is no call for action. We become angry at someone we have no intention of fighting. We worry about something that will happen tomorrow or next week, or about something that *may* happen. Some people have a highly responsive sympathetic nervous system, frequently producing intense changes in heart rate and epinephrine secretions (Manuck, Cohen, Rabin, Muldoon, & Bachen, 1991). Other people show weaker sympathetic arousal under almost all circumstances.

Nearly all of us can learn to relax or to curb our arousal to prevent excessive strain. If you want to relax, here are some suggestions that may help (Benson, 1985):

- Find a quiet place. Do not insist on absolute silence; just find a spot where the noise is least disturbing.

- Adopt a comfortable position, relaxing your muscles (Figure 12.23). If you are not sure how to do so, start with the opposite: *Tense* all your muscles so you become fully aware of how they feel. Then relax them one by one, starting from your toes and working systematically toward your head.

- Reduce all sources of stimulation, including your own thoughts. Focus your eyes on some simple, unexciting object. Or repeat something over and over—a sentence, a phrase, a prayer, or even a meaningless sound like "om"—whatever feels comfortable to you.

- Don't worry about anything, not even about relaxing. If worrisome thoughts keep popping

FIGURE 12.23
Some people adopt special yoga or meditation techniques to reduce stress. Others find they can reduce stress without any formal procedure, just by finding a relaxing position, reducing their muscle tension, and taking a break from their most stressful concerns.

Exercise can be a way of working off excess energy, especially when you are waiting for something to happen. Exercise also helps by improving overall condition; people in poor physical condition sometimes show excessive arousal to mild stressful events.

into your head, dismiss them with an "Oh, well."

Some people call this practice meditation. People who spend a little time each day practicing this technique report that they feel less stress. Many of them also lower their blood pressure and improve their overall health (Benson, 1977, 1985).

Another step toward relaxation is to learn to interpret situations realistically. Some people fret forever about disasters that *might* happen or about something someone said that *might* be taken as an insult. Psychologists encourage people to reinterpret situations and events in less threatening ways.

EXERCISE

Exercise also can help to reduce stress. It may seem contradictory to say that both relaxation and exercise reduce stress, but exercise helps people relax. Exercise is a particularly helpful way to deal with nervousness about an anticipated stressful event (Mobily, 1982). Suppose you are tense about something you have to do tomorrow. Your sympathetic nervous system becomes highly aroused in preparation for that event, yet there is nothing you can do about it. Under those conditions, the best approach may be to work off some of your excess energy through exercise and relax afterward.

Regular exercise also prepares people for the unexpected. People in good physical condition react less strongly than other people to stressful events (Crews & Landers, 1987). An event that would elevate the heart rate enor-

mously in other people elevates it only moderately in a person who has been exercising regularly.

PREDICTING AND CONTROLLING EVENTS

Another way of coping with stress is to try to gain some sense of control over events or at least a feeling that you know what is likely to happen next. In the winter of 1988, an unusually severe snowstorm hit my hometown of Raleigh, North Carolina. Because the city had little snow-clearing equipment, and because most residents had scant experience driving through snow, the schools and many businesses closed down for five days. By the end of the fifth day, many people were complaining of "cabin fever": "I can't stand being cooped up in this house another

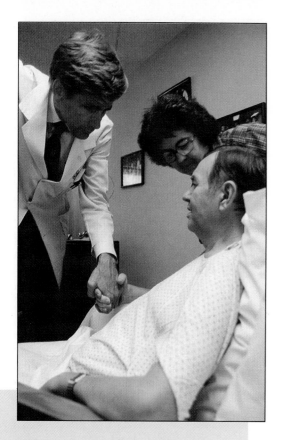

Surgical patients recover more quickly when they are told what is going to happen. They are better able to cope with pain if they are told what to do when it arises (Ludwick-Rosenthal & Neufeld, 1988). Such information gives them a slight feeling of control.

day! I've got to get out!" Staying at home, in itself, was not the problem. The problem was that people had no way of knowing whether they would be staying home the next day or going to school or work. And the answer was beyond their control.

In general, an event is less stressful if we can predict or control it than if we cannot (Thompson, 1981). In several experiments, people were asked to perform difficult tasks while listening to loud bursts of noise that might impair their performance. Some subjects were shown a switch and were told that they could cut off the noise if they chose to, although the experimenters preferred that they leave it on. Even though none of the subjects flipped the switch, simply knowing that they *could* turn off the noise made it less disturbing to them. They performed better on a proofreading task than did subjects who had no control over the noise (Glass, Singer, & Pennebaker, 1977; Sherrod, Hage, Halpern, & Moore, 1977).

As a rule, people who consistently blame someone else for their misfortunes tend to have a poor psychological adjustment (Tennen & Affleck, 1990). Apparently the reason is their lost sense of control. If you think your misfortunes are your own fault, you may feel somewhat depressed about your failure, but at least you have some control. You can say, "I won't make that mistake again" or "Next time I'll try harder." But if you think other people are maliciously thwarting your plans, you no longer feel control. You are also likely to feel mistrustful and suspicious of other people.

■ CONCEPT CHECK

6. *Which would disrupt your studying more, your own radio or your roommate's radio? Why? (Check your answers on page 531.)*

How Do Predictability and Controllability Help?

Why does a predictable or controllable event produce less stress than an unpredictable or uncontrollable event does? One possibility is that we fear an unpredictable, uncontrollable event may grow so intense that it will eventually become unbearable (Thompson, 1981). So long as we know what probably will happen next, we assume that things won't get any worse. And so long as we have some measure of control over an event, we tell ourselves that we can take some action if the situation becomes unbearable.

A second possibility is that when an event is predictable we have a chance to prepare ourselves for it. In animal experiments, a signal that warns of an imminent shock enables a rat to adopt a protective posture that will reduce the pain.

There is a third possibility: When we have no way of predicting or controlling a stressful event, we have to keep ourselves in a constant state of arousal. Suppose you dread being called on in class to answer questions. If your professor calls on students at random, you have no way of predicting when your name will be called. You must stay ready and alert every minute. If your professor calls out names in alphabetic order, however, you can relax until just before your turn comes.

Is Predictability Always Helpful?

As a general rule, knowing what to expect reduces the stressfulness of an experience. But if you are not likely to face the experience for some time, and if there is nothing you can do about it anyway, then just knowing about it may not be helpful. If someone could tell you when and how you were going to die—and you knew you could do nothing to avoid it—would you want to know? Maybe you would, on the grounds that you could make better decisions about how to live whatever life was left to you. But you might prefer not to know.

People with a family history of Huntington's disease are faced with precisely that decision. Huntington's disease is an uncommon, inherited disorder that typically strikes at about age 40. People with the disease undergo a gradual deterioration in their muscle control and mental functioning until they die about 15 years later. If your father or mother had the disease, you would have a 50% chance of getting it too.

Before the 1980s, people with a family history of Huntington's disease had to live with uncertainty until they either got the disease themselves or grew old without getting it. Today, medical technicians can examine an individual's chromosomes, compare them to the chromosomes of relatives with and without Huntington's disease, and determine with up to 95% accuracy whether the individual will fall victim to the disease (Gusella et al., 1983). However that information turns out, it helps people to make important decisions about their future, particularly about whether or not to have children. But they have no way of preventing or delaying the onset of the disease. Some people who know they are at risk decide to have their chromosomes examined. Others choose to remain uncertain. In short, people are not always sure they want to know what to expect if they can do nothing about it.

INOCULATION

Any stressful experience is less disturbing if you know what to expect, but it is hard to know what to expect if you have not been through the experience before. Sometimes a good solution is to provide people with a small-scale preview of a stressful experience they may have to face later.

In other words, we can inoculate or immunize someone against certain kinds of stressful experience (Burchfield, 1979). For example, a medical school may show students films of surgical operations before they watch live operations. Even painful electric shocks cause less distress if they are preceded by milder shocks (Sines, 1979).

One way to inoculate people against stressful events is to have them practice ways of dealing with such events beforehand (Janis, 1983; Meichenbaum, 1985; Meichenbaum & Cameron, 1983). For example, the army has soldiers practice combat skills under realistic conditions, sometimes under actual gunfire. Another way is through role playing. A police trainee might pretend to intervene while two people act like a husband and wife engaged in a violent quarrel. If you are nervous about going to your landlord with a complaint, you might get a friend to play the part of the landlord and then practice what you plan to say.

Inoculation has proved successful with young people suffering from "dating anxiety." Some young people are so nervous about saying or doing the wrong thing that they avoid all opportunities to go out on a date. By means of role playing, in which they practice dating behaviors with assigned partners, they can be helped to feel less apprehensive (Jaremko, 1983).

■ CONCEPT CHECK

7. *Suppose you are nervous about giving a speech before a group of 200 strangers. How could you inoculate yourself to reduce the stress? (Check your answer on page 531.)*

SOCIAL SUPPORT

A great many people have had a severely painful experience at one time or another. Perhaps you were beaten or sexually molested; perhaps you were responsible for someone else's injury; perhaps you attempted suicide; perhaps someone humiliated you in public. Whatever your experience, you may decide it was too painful even to think about, much less talk about. And therefore the pain builds up within.

People who have had painful experiences report that they feel much better after they get a chance to talk about them to someone—almost anyone (Pennebaker, 1990). A sympathetic friend or relative may provide not only a shoulder to cry on but also help in getting through the day. Some people who worry about their friends' or relatives' reactions will open up about their most private experiences to a near-stranger, especially someone they meet on a plane or out of town. (They do not worry about making a bad impression on someone they do not expect to meet again.)

In many cases, people gain the greatest support by talking with people who have lived

People who work together often like to talk together after work or on weekends. One reason is that they can provide social support for one another concerning the stresses and difficulties they have faced on the job.

through similar crises. Alcoholics Anonymous, for example, is composed of recovering alcoholics who try to help one another. For another example, the nurses who work in the intensive care units of hospitals undergo constant, often severe stress (Hay & Oken, 1977). The unspoken (but rigidly obeyed) rule is never to refuse help to either a patient or a fellow nurse. They are surrounded by the sight, sound, and smell of patients who are suffering and dying. When a patient dies, it is often the nurse, not the doctor, who has to inform the relatives. At the end of the day, the nurses cannot simply go home and resume life as usual. They have to unwind, and they often do so by sharing their experiences with other nurses.

Social support also helps people to cope with the common, everyday situations that all of us experience. According to one study, medical students who married while they were in school reported a sharp drop in stress levels (Coombs & Fawzy, 1982). They said that their spouse provided care, concern, and reaffirmation of their self-esteem when it was threatened.

DISTRACTION

People who are trying to cope with stress caused by mild but persistent pain often resort to some sort of distraction. Pain includes the emotional response to an injury as well as the sensation of the injury, and one way to reduce that response is to concentrate on something unrelated to the pain. Many people find they can reduce dental or postsurgical pain by playing video games, watching comedies on television, imagining that they are arguing with someone, or thinking about some meaningful event in their lives (McCaul & Malott, 1984). The Lamaze method teaches women to cope with the pain of childbirth by concentrating on breathing exercises. One reason hypnosis tends to reduce pain may be that it distracts the sufferer's attention.

How effective a distraction is depends partly on whether or not a person believes that it will help. In one experiment, college students were asked to hold their fingers in ice water until the sensation became too painful to endure (Melzack, Weisz, & Sprague, 1963). Some of them listened to music of their own choice and were told that listening to music would lessen the pain. Others also listened to music but were given no suggestion that it would ease the pain. Still others heard nothing but were told that a special "ultrasonic sound" was being transmitted that would lessen the pain. The group that heard music and expected it to lessen the pain tolerated the pain better than the other two groups did. Evidently, neither the music nor the suggestion of reduced pain is as effective as both are together.

Does distraction really reduce pain, or do people just report that it does because they think they are expected to? We know that music sometimes acts like a painkilling drug: It causes certain pathways in the nervous system to release neurotransmitters known as endorphins, which excite the same receptors that heroin and morphine excite (Goldstein, 1980).

"Have you ever had a secret too shameful to tell? Have you stopped yourself from disclosing a personal experience because you thought others would think less of you? . . . Have you ever lied to yourself by claiming that a major upheaval in your life didn't affect you or, perhaps, didn't occur?

If so you may be hurting yourself. Not because you have had a troubling experience but because you can't express it."
JAMES W. PENNEBAKER
(1990)

Trying to ignore pain won't eliminate it, but distractions can make it more tolerable—as with this boy recovering from heart surgery. Most adults develop distractions: playing cards, reading mysteries, knitting.

Recordings of brain activity show less response to electric shock while music is playing than during silence (Lavine, Buchsbaum, & Poncy, 1976).

Distraction also helps us to cope with stress that is not painful. People who are concentrating on a difficult task find it helpful to take a break once in a while. They may go to a movie, read something entertaining, play a round of golf, or just daydream. Finally, trying to find the humor in a stressful situation often provides an effective distraction.

Something to Think About

Many experiments report that a placebo by itself serves as an effective painkiller for certain patients. Why might that be?

BELIEFS AS COPING STRATEGIES

- In the long run, I shall be more successful than most other people are.

- Sure I have my strengths and weaknesses, but my strengths are in areas that are important; my weaknesses are in areas that don't really matter.

- When I fail, it is because I didn't try hard enough or because I got some bad breaks. It is not because of any lack of ability.

- No matter how bad (or good) things are, they are going to get better.

- Right now I'm sad that my wife (husband) left me, but in the long run I'll be better off without her (him).

- I lost my job, but in many ways it was a crummy job. The more I think about it, the happier I am that I lost it. I can get a better one.

For a given person at a given time, any of these statements may be correct or incorrect; but even if incorrect, believing in it can be very comforting and stress-reducing. Remember the "personal fable" of adolescence in Chapter 6? Most normal, happy people nurture various versions of that fable throughout their life. They emphasize their strengths, downplay their weaknesses, and distort bad news to make it seem less bad, maybe even good (Taylor & Brown, 1988).

When a situation is undeniably bad, people may still find ways to deny it. Medics serving in the Vietnam War knew they were risking their lives every time they boarded a helicopter to go to the aid of wounded soldiers. Because they had no way to predict or control the enemy's actions, we might expect that they would have experienced extreme stress. In general, however, measurements of the activity of their autonomic nervous system showed low levels of arousal on both flight days and nonflight days (Bourne, 1971). Why? They had managed to convince themselves of their own invulnerability. They even told exaggerated stories about their close brushes with death as evidence to prove that they led a charmed life.

One study of 78 women who had surgery for the removal of breast cancer found that they coped with their stress and anxiety in three ways (Taylor, 1983):

First, they searched for some meaning in the experience. Many of them said they had become better people and had developed a new attitude toward life.

Second, they tried to regain a feeling of mastery over their lives. They wanted to believe that they knew why they had developed cancer and that they knew how to avoid a recurrence.

Third, they all sought to boost their self-esteem by comparing themselves with someone else who was worse off: "I'm glad I had only one breast removed instead of both, like some other women." "Sure, I had both breasts removed, but at least I was 70 years old at the time. It would have been worse if it happened when I was young." "It was terrible to have both breasts removed at age 25, but I was already married, and my husband has been sympathetic and supportive."

Psychologists sometimes try to help people develop a more optimistic self-image, even if that image is partly illusion (Försterling, 1985). They encourage people to think of their successes as an indication of ability and to think of their failures as an indication of lack of effort. An improved self-image helps some people to feel less depressed and more in control of their lives.

IN CONCLUSION

We discuss various aspects of psychology in different chapters—cognition, motivation, emotion, and so forth. That seems a reasonable way to organize a psychology textbook, but our experiences do not divide up so neatly into separate parts. As you have seen in this chapter, our emotions are closely linked to our biology, our motivations, and our memory and cognitions. Any factor that changes one aspect of our experience—say, cognition—has rippling effects on emotions and motivations as well.

Before, during, and after the 1991 war in Iraq, Iraqi leader Saddam Hussein put on a brave, confident front. Perhaps he truly expected to succeed; perhaps he was just bluffing. In any case, a hopeful belief can reduce the stressfulness of threatening events.

SUMMARY

■ *Interpreting stressful events.* How successfully we cope with a stressful event depends largely on how we interpret the event. (page 525)

■ *Relaxation.* One way of coping with stress is to find a quiet place, relax the muscles, and eliminate distracting stimuli. Exercise can be a helpful way of handling nervous energy and enabling later relaxation. (page 525)

■ *Prediction and control.* Events are generally less stressful when people think they can predict or control them. However, being able to predict a stressful event without being able to control it is much less helpful. (page 526)

■ *Inoculation.* Someone who has experienced a mild sample of a stressful experience is less stressed than are other people by a later, more intense version of the same experience. (page 528)

■ *Social support.* Support and encouragement from friends and family help to alleviate stress. Many people cope with problems by talking with other people who have dealt with similar problems, such as members of self-help groups. (page 528)

■ *Distraction.* Distracting a person's attention from the source of stress helps to reduce the stress. (page 529)

■ *Beliefs.* A belief in one's capacity to succeed may help to reduce stress even if the belief is not entirely accurate. (page 530)

SUGGESTION FOR FURTHER READING

Pennebaker, J. W. (1990). *Opening up.* New York: William Morrow and Company. A description of the stress-relieving values of discussing your most painful experiences, either with other people or to yourself in writing.

TERMS

inoculation protection against the harmful effects of stress by earlier exposure to a small amount of it (page 528)

ANSWERS TO CONCEPT CHECKS

6. Your roommate's radio would be more disruptive. You can turn your own radio on or off, switch stations, or reduce the volume. You have no such control over your roommate's radio (unless your roommate happens to be very cooperative). (page 527)

7. Practice giving your speech to a small group of friends. If possible, practice giving it in the room where you are to deliver it. (page 528)

13 PERSONALITY

Several thousand people have the task of assembling the world's largest jigsaw puzzle, which contains over a trillion pieces. Connie Conclusionjumper examines 20 pieces very closely, stares off into the distance, and announces, "When the puzzle is fully assembled, it will be a picture of the Houston Astrodome!" Prudence Plodder says, "Well, I don't know what the whole puzzle will look like, but I think I've found two little pieces that fit together."

Which of the two is making the greater contribution to completing the puzzle? We could argue either way. Clearly the task will require an enormous number of little, unglamorous accomplishments like Prudence's. But if Connie is right, her flash of insight will be extremely valuable in assembling all the little pieces. Of course, if the puzzle turns out to be a picture of two sailboats on Lake Erie, then Connie will have made us waste time looking for connections that are not there.

Some psychologists have offered grand theories about the nature of personality. Others have investigated why people with a certain type of personality act the way they do in a specific situation. We need both contributions. We begin with the grand, overall theories of personality. Then we turn to investigations of more limited aspects of personality. Finally, we consider methods of measuring personality characteristics.

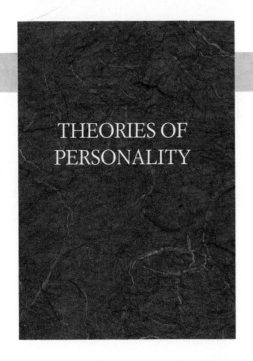

THEORIES OF
PERSONALITY

Is personality rooted in one or two dominant motivations, such as sexuality or the desire for superiority?

Is personality influenced by unconscious motivations and thoughts?

What is a "healthy" personality?

What makes us tick? What makes us the way we are? Way down deep, are humans good, bad, or somewhere in between?

The 17th-century philosopher Thomas Hobbes argued that humans are by nature selfish. Life in a state of nature, he said, is "nasty, brutish, and short." If we are to protect ourselves from one another, we must be restrained by a watchful government.

The 18th-century political philosopher Jean-Jacques Rousseau disagreed. He maintained that humans are good by nature and that "civilized" governments are the problem, not the solution. Although he conceded that society could never return to "noble savagery," he believed that education and government should promote the freedom of the individual. Rational people acting freely, he maintained, would advance the welfare of all.

The debate between those two viewpoints survives in modern theories of personality (Figure 13.1). Some theorists, including Sigmund Freud, have held that people are born with sexual and destructive impulses that must be held in check if civilization is to survive. Others, including Carl Rogers, have held that people will

achieve good and noble goals once they have been freed from unnecessary restraints.

Which point of view is correct? Do not decide too quickly. Many people reject Freud's theory without having read any of his works. Others embrace it without fully understanding it and then proceed to "analyze" the behavior of their friends. The personality theories we shall consider are complex, and we cannot do them full justice in just a few pages. For a deeper understanding, read the books listed under "Suggestions for Further Reading" at the end of this section on personality theories.

PERSONALITY AND CONCEPTIONS OF ITS ORIGIN

The term *personality* comes from the Latin word *persona*, meaning "mask." In the plays of ancient Greece and Rome, actors wore masks to indicate whether they were happy, sad, or angry. Unlike a mask that one can put on or take

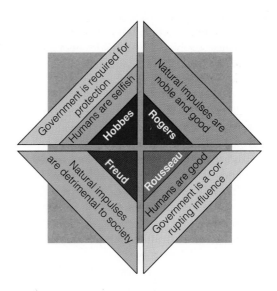

FIGURE 13.1

Philosophers Thomas Hobbes and Jean-Jacques Rousseau expressed opposite views on human nature. Psychologists Sigmund Freud and Carl Rogers also expressed opposite views. Freud, like Hobbes, stressed the more negative aspects of human nature; Rogers, the more positive or optimistic aspects.

FIGURE 13.2
According to the second-century Greek physician Galen, people's personalities depended on four humors. From left to right: Someone with an abundance of blood, or sanguine, has a changeable temperament. Someone with an excess of black bile is melancholy. A person with too much yellow bile, or choleric, is easily angered. And someone with too much phlegm is generally inactive. Accepted in Europe and the Arab world, Galen's theory remained popular throughout the Renaissance. Scholars were thought those most prone to melancholy, and an Oxford scholar, Robert Burton, wrote a large volume on it, The Anatomy of Melancholy, *first published in 1621.*

"Every individual is virtually an enemy of civilization. . . . Thus civilization has to be defended against the individual. . . . For the masses are lazy and unintelligent . . . and the individuals composing them support one another in giving free rein to their indiscipline."
SIGMUND FREUD
(1927/1953)

"It has been my experience that persons have a basically positive direction. In my deepest contacts with individuals in therapy, even those whose troubles are most disturbing, whose behavior has been most anti-social, whose feelings seem most abnormal, I find this to be true."
CARL ROGERS
(1961)

off, however, the term *personality* implies something stable. **Personality** consists of all the consistent ways in which the behavior of one person differs from that of others.

The ancient Greeks believed that personality depended on which of four different "humors" (chemicals) predominated in a person's body (Figure 13.2). A predominance of yellow bile made people hot tempered. A predominance of black bile made people depressed. An excess of phlegm made people sluggish and apathetic. An excess of blood made people courageous, hopeful, and amorous. The ancient Greek theory persists in the English language in such terms as *phlegmatic* and *melancholic* (literally, "black-bile-ic").

Today, although we no longer believe in the four humors, we do believe that personality is influenced by other chemicals, such as hormones and neurotransmitters. It is further influenced by our experiences, including our observation and imitation of other people's behavior.

According to some historically influential theories of personality, differences in personality arise from the different ways in which people try to satisfy one central motive, such as the sex drive, the desire for superiority, or the drive to achieve one's full potential. We begin with Sigmund Freud, who concentrated on the sex drive and its ability to influence behavior indirectly, perhaps even unconsciously.

SIGMUND FREUD AND PSYCHOANALYSIS

Sigmund Freud's theory was the first of several psychodynamic theories. A **psychodynamic theory** relates personality to the interplay of conflicting forces within the individual, including some that the individual may not recognize consciously. Freud (1856–1939; Figure 13.3), an Austrian physician, developed theories on personality development that have had an enormous influence on psychologists and other students of human behavior. In fact, his influence went well beyond his data. Sometimes this happens; a theory somehow fits the mood of the times and many people accept it, some of them uncritically. Why Freud's theory became as popular as it did is an important issue for historians, but for our purposes it would take us too far afield. Let's just say that psychologists today differ substantially in their opinions of Freud's theories.

Freud's main interests were cultural history and anthropology, and he wrote several books and articles about those topics in his later years. As a Jew in late 19th-century Austria, however, he knew he had little chance of becoming a university professor. The only professional careers open to Jews in his time and place were in law, business, and medicine.

Freud chose to study medicine, though he was never deeply committed to it. He took over

FIGURE 13.3
Sigmund Freud offered interpretations of dreams, slips of the tongue, psychological disorders, and other behaviors that people had previously considered "random" or "unexplainable." According to Freud, even apparently purposeless behaviors reveal the influence of unconscious thoughts and motivations. Freud's theories have had an immense influence on many people, not just on psychologists. For example, many literary commentators have offered psychoanalytic interpretations of novels and plays. Most psychological researchers, however, are skeptical of Freud's approach. Many of his theories are difficult to test scientifically, and some are so vague that they are not falsifiable.

7 years to complete medical school because he spent much of his time taking elective courses in biology and philosophy. After receiving his medical degree, he worked in brain research and began to practice medicine only when it became financially necessary. His interest in theory persisted throughout his life. Even the methods he devised for treating psychological disorders had more to do with *understanding* the disorders than with *relieving* them.

Freud's Concept of the Unconscious

Early in his career, Freud worked with the psychiatrist Josef Breuer, who had been treating a young woman with physical complaints that seemed to have no medical basis. As she talked with Breuer about her past and recalled various traumatic, or emotionally damaging, experiences, her symptoms gradually subsided. Breuer proposed that the memory of those experiences was somehow associated with tension and that recalling the experiences released the tension. He called this release of pent-up tension **catharsis,** a term Freud adopted in his own theory.

Freud began to apply Breuer's "talking cure" to some of his own emotionally disturbed patients. He referred to his method of explaining and dealing with personality as **psychoanalysis,** and to this day psychoanalysts remain loyal to that method and to the theories behind it (Figure 13.4).

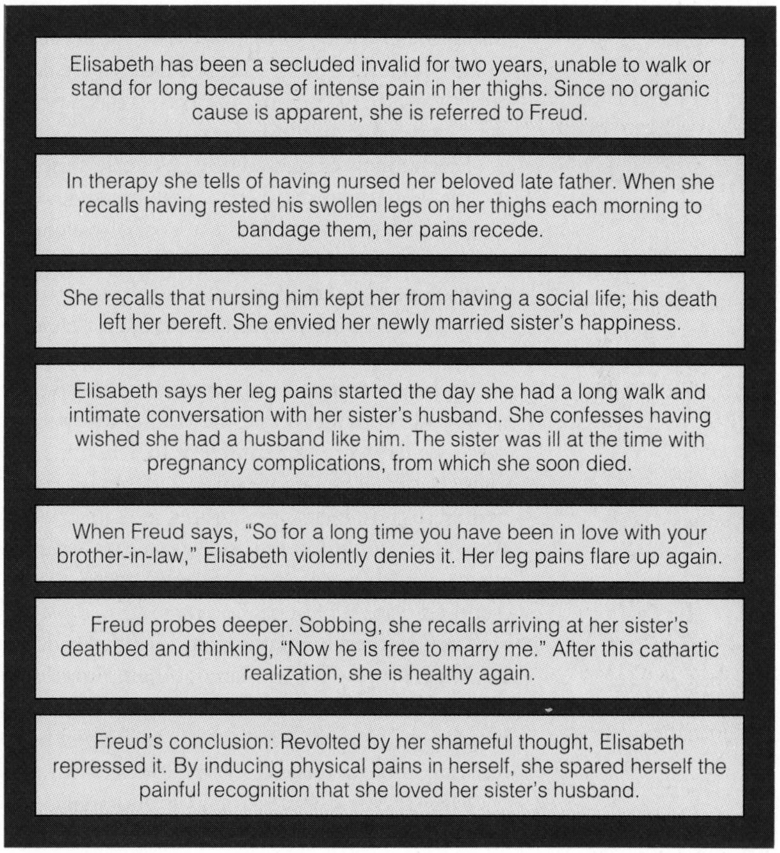

Elisabeth has been a secluded invalid for two years, unable to walk or stand for long because of intense pain in her thighs. Since no organic cause is apparent, she is referred to Freud.

In therapy she tells of having nursed her beloved late father. When she recalls having rested his swollen legs on her thighs each morning to bandage them, her pains recede.

She recalls that nursing him kept her from having a social life; his death left her bereft. She envied her newly married sister's happiness.

Elisabeth says her leg pains started the day she had a long walk and intimate conversation with her sister's husband. She confesses having wished she had a husband like him. The sister was ill at the time with pregnancy complications, from which she soon died.

When Freud says, "So for a long time you have been in love with your brother-in-law," Elisabeth violently denies it. Her leg pains flare up again.

Freud probes deeper. Sobbing, she recalls arriving at her sister's deathbed and thinking, "Now he is free to marry me." After this cathartic realization, she is healthy again.

Freud's conclusion: Revolted by her shameful thought, Elisabeth repressed it. By inducing physical pains in herself, she spared herself the painful recognition that she loved her sister's husband.

FIGURE 13.4
An example of Freud's psychoanalysis. (Based on Breuer & Freud, 1895/1957.)

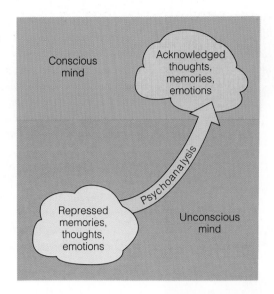

Conscious mind

Acknowledged thoughts, memories, emotions

Psychoanalysis

Repressed memories, thoughts, emotions

Unconscious mind

Psychoanalysis is based on the assumption that each of us has an unconscious mind as well as a conscious mind (Figure 13.5). The **unconscious** has thoughts, memories, and emotions just as the conscious mind does, though it acts in a less logical fashion. Even though we are not directly aware of the unconscious, it has a profound influence on our behavior.

Psychoanalysis started out as a fairly simple theory: The unconscious contains memories of traumatic experiences, and the goal of psychoanalysts is to bring those memories to consciousness. That effort produces catharsis and relieves the patient of irrational and self-defeating impulses.

As Freud listened to his patients, however, he became convinced that the traumatic events they recalled were not sufficient to account for their abnormal behavior. Some patients reacted strongly to past events that others took in stride. Why? He concluded that still earlier traumatic events, which were even harder to recall, predisposed certain patients to overreact.

Freud urged his patients to recall ever-earlier experiences. When many of them reported experiences of sexual abuse in early childhood, he proposed that all emotionally disturbed behavior could be traced to such experiences.

Over the next few years, as Freud analyzed himself and others, he changed his mind: Sexual abuse of children, he decided, was not common enough to account for all the disturbed behavior he observed. When his patients reported that they had been sexually abused as children, he concluded that they were reporting fantasies.

Regardless of whether the recollections of sexual abuse were real or fantasy, they were clearly disturbing to Freud's patients. So he modified his theory: The ultimate cause of a disturbed personality is the *sexual fantasies* of young children, including imagined sexual abuse.

That revision of Freud's original theory made it very difficult to test the theory scientifically. It is possible to test the effects of early experiences on subsequent behavior but hard to test the effects of fantasies.

Was Freud correct in changing his mind? Maybe not. Today we recognize that sexual abuse of children occurs far more often than it is reported and that it can leave long-lasting psychological scars. In some ways Freud's earlier writings now sound more up-to-date than his later ones. Historians are not sure why Freud changed his mind. Jeffrey Masson (1984) suggests that Freud simply lost the courage to defend his earlier views and that for a long time he nurtured doubts about whether he had been right to abandon them.

Stages of Psychosexual Development in Freud's Theory of Personality

Freud believed that psychosexual interest and pleasure begin long before the individual achieves sexual maturity. He used the term **psychosexual pleasure** in a broad sense to include the good feelings arising from the stimulation of parts of the body. He maintained that the way we deal with psychosexual development influences nearly all aspects of our personality.

Freud proposed that young children have sexual tendencies that resemble those of more primitive mammals. Just as nonhuman mammals respond sexually to stimuli that do not excite most adult humans, children respond "sexually" to stimulation of the mouth, the anus, and other body zones. Freud collected no direct evidence for this view and in fact made no extensive observations of children. Rather, he reconstructed childhood experiences from the memories of his patients and other adults.

According to Freud (1905/1925), people have a psychosexual energy, which he called **libido** (lih-BEE-doh), from a Latin word meaning "desire." The libido provides the energy for much behavior throughout life, as I mentioned in Chapter 11. At different ages it focuses on different parts of the body. Normally, it starts in the mouth and "flows" to other parts as the child grows older. Children go through five stages of **psychosexual development,** each with a characteristic sexual focus that leaves its mark on adult personality. If normal sexual development is blocked or frustrated at any stage, Freud said, a **fixation** occurs. Part of the libido becomes fixated at that stage; that is, it continues to be preoccupied with the pleasure area associated with that stage. Table 13.1 summarizes the stages.

The Oral Stage   In the **oral stage,** from birth through the first year or so (Freud was vague about the age limits of all his stages), the infant derives intense psychosexual pleasure from stimulation of the mouth, particularly while sucking at the mother's breast. In the later part of the oral stage, the infant begins to bite as well as suck.

According to Freud, an infant who receives either too little or too much opportunity to suck can become fixated at the oral stage. The consequence is that much libido remains attached to the mouth; throughout life the person may continue to receive great pleasure from eating, drinking, smoking, and kissing. He or she may also take pleasure from being "fed" information. Someone who is fixated at the later part of the oral stage may be inclined to "biting" sarcasm and ridicule. People with an oral fixation have lasting concerns with dependence and independence, according to Freud.

The Anal Stage   Around 1 to 3 years of age, children enter the **anal stage**. At this time they get psychosexual pleasure from their bowel movements. They may enjoy either the sensation of excreting feces or the sensation of holding them back.

A child can develop a fixation at the anal stage if toilet training is too strict or if it starts too early or too late. People with an anal fixation either go through life "holding things back"—being orderly, stingy, and stubborn—or, less commonly, may go to the opposite extreme and become wasteful, messy, and destructive.

The Phallic Stage   Beginning at about age 3, in the **phallic stage,** children begin to play with their genitals. They become more aware of what it means to be male or female. If parents teach children that touching their genitals is shameful, the children may become fixated at the phallic stage. According to Freud, boys with a

| Table 13.1 Freud's Stages of Psychosexual Development |||
Stage (approximate ages)	Sexual Interests	Effect of Fixation at This Stage
Oral stage (birth to 1 year)	Sucking, swallowing, biting	Lasting concerns with dependence and independence; pleasure from eating, drinking, other oral activities
Anal stage (1 to 3 years)	Expelling feces, retaining feces	Orderliness, stinginess, stubbornness
Phallic stage (3 to 5 or 6 years)	Touching penis or clitoris; Oedipus complex or Electra complex	Difficulty feeling closeness; males: fear of castration; females: penis envy
Latency period (5 or 6 to puberty)	Sexual interests suppressed	—
Genital period (puberty onward)	Sexual contact with other people	—

The beginning of psychosexual development is the oral stage, in which infants enjoy stimulation of their mouth—which for them means sucking, swallowing, and biting. They like putting things in their mouth and gnawing on them. According to Freud, if normal sexual development is blocked at this stage, the child will grow up continuing to get much pleasure from drinking and eating, as well as kissing and smoking. Perhaps this pipe smoker's mother weaned him too quickly—or let him nurse too long. And perhaps such an explanation is wrong. Like many of Freud's ideas, this one is difficult to test.

Freud proposed that a "fixation" at an early stage of psychosexual development can alter the development of personality. For example, if toilet training is either too harsh or too lenient, someone may develop an "anal" personality, characterized by either extreme orderliness or extreme messiness. This hypothesis is difficult to evaluate scientifically, because it is not easily falsifiable. When we observe neat and orderly behavior, we can reinterpret that person's early toilet training as either too lenient or too harsh.

phallic fixation are afraid of being castrated; girls with such a fixation develop "penis envy." Both males and females with a phallic fixation may find it difficult to experience closeness and love.

According to Freud, boys in the phallic stage experience an **Oedipus complex**. (Oedipus—EHD-ah-puhs—was a figure in an ancient Greek play by Sophocles. Oedipus unknowingly murdered his father and married his mother.) Freud claimed that a boy develops a sexual interest in his mother and competitive aggression toward his father. But the boy realizes that his father is larger and stronger; he learns to identify with his father and to shift his own sexual interests to someone other than his mother. A boy who fails to resolve the Oedipus complex may forever feel anxiety and hostility toward other men.

Similarly, Freud asserted, young girls experience an **Electra complex,** named after a character in an ancient Greek play who persuades her brother to kill their mother, who had murdered their father. A girl with an Electra complex feels a romantic attraction toward her father and hostility toward her mother. Freud was vague about how girls resolve the Electra complex; he implied that they never resolve it com-

pletely and therefore remain partly fixated at the phallic stage.

Freud's writings about boys' fear of castration, girls' penis envy, the Oedipus complex, and the Electra complex have long been controversial. Freud inferred these ideas from the recollections of his adult patients, not from his observations of children. Most developmental psychologists deny that children ordinarily show such tendencies.

The Latent Period From about age 5 or 6 until adolescence, Freud said that most children suppress their psychosexual interest. They enter a **latent period,** a time when they play mostly with peers of their own sex. Most psychologists call this a "period" instead of a "stage of development" because psychosexual interest is not developing (changing); it is just waiting. According to Freud, no one becomes fixated at the latent period.

Apparently a product of the way we rear children in Europe and North America, the latent period may not occur in certain unindustrialized societies.

The Genital Stage Beginning at puberty, young people take a strong sexual interest in other people. This is known as the **genital stage**. According to Freud, anyone who has fixated a great deal of libido at earlier stages has little libido left for the genital stage. But people who have successfully negotiated the earlier stages can now derive primary satisfaction from sexual intercourse; other types of stimulation reinforce this primary source of pleasure.

Evaluation of Freud's Stages Was Freud right about these stages and about the consequences of fixation? Many psychologists are uncertain about whether his views can even be tested. Recall from Chapter 2 that a good scientific theory is falsifiable—that is, its predictions should be clear enough for us to imagine data that would contradict them. Freud's theory makes such vague predictions that psychologists are not sure what results would contradict them (Grünbaum, 1986; Popper, 1986). For example, consider Freud's views concerning anal fixation: If the parents are too strict in their toilet training, or if they begin it too early or too late, the child will become either orderly, stingy, and stubborn *or* messy and wasteful. That is hardly a precise prediction.

Suppose we make the prediction more precise, concentrating on what Freud considered the most common result of anal fixation: Does strict toilet training lead to a combination of orderly, stingy, and stubborn behavior? Phrasing the question in that way at least makes it scientifically testable. Most of the studies that have tested that hypothesis fail to support it; strict toilet training is not consistently related to orderly, stingy, or stubborn behavior (Fisher & Greenberg, 1977). The evidence relating early oral experience (such as duration of breast-feeding) to a later "oral personality" (characterized by dependence and a craving for eating, drinking, and smoking) is slightly stronger (Fisher & Greenberg, 1977). Even so, many psychologists are skeptical of the relationship because many of the studies that report it were poorly designed. To the extent that Freud's theory of psychosexual development is testable, the evidence is as yet unconvincing.

Defense Mechanisms Against Anxiety

According to Freud, an individual's personality is determined to a large degree by the way the unconscious mind deals with anxiety. To reduce the anxiety that certain thoughts and motivations cause, Freud said, we reject highly un-

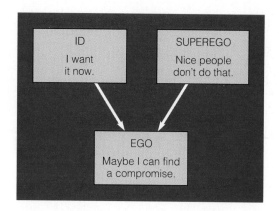

FIGURE 13.6
Freud described personality as a collection of three parts that are often in conflict with one another. The id *asks for immediate gratification of biological urges, such as the sex drive. The* superego *counters these impulses with lists of rules that we learned from our parents. The* ego, *torn between these two forces, makes the decision of what to do. According to Freud, we can understand certain people's behavior by assuming that their id is stronger than their superego or that their superego is stronger than their id.*

pleasant thoughts from the conscious mind and force them into the unconscious.

Personality, Freud claimed, consists of three aspects: the id, the ego, and the superego (Figure 13.6). (Actually, he used German words that mean *it, I,* and *over-I.* A translator used Latin equivalents instead of English words.) The **id** consists of all our biological drives, such as sex and hunger. The id demands immediate gratification. The **ego** is the rational, decision-making aspect of the personality. The **superego** contains the memory of our parents' rules and prohibitions, such as, "Nice little boys and girls don't do that." Sometimes the id produces sexual or other motivations that the superego considers repugnant, evoking feelings of guilt. The ego may side with either the id or the superego; if it sides with the superego, it tries to avoid even thinking about the id's unacceptable impulses.

Most psychologists today find it difficult to imagine the mind in terms of three warring factions. They regard Freud's description as an occasionally useful metaphor at best.

According to Freud, the ego defends itself against conflicts and anxieties by relegating unpleasant thoughts and impulses to the unconscious. Among the **defense mechanisms** that

FIGURE 13.7
The ego—the rational I—has numerous ways of defending itself against anxiety, that apprehensive state named for the Latin word meaning "to strangle." These defense mechanisms try to ignore or avoid facing unpleasant reality, and they are part of an internal battle in which you fight against yourself.

the ego employs are repression, denial, rationalization, displacement, regression, projection, reaction formation, and sublimation (Figure 13.7). These processes are ordinarily unconscious; we are not aware of our own repressions, rationalizations, and so forth. Defense mechanisms are normal ways of suppressing anxiety and are often adaptive. They become a problem only if they are carried to extremes, or if they prevent a person from dealing with reality.

■ CONCEPT CHECK

1. What kind of behavior would you expect of someone with a strong id and a weak superego? What behavior would you expect of someone with an unusually strong superego? (Check your answers on page 553.)

Repression The defense mechanism of **repression** is motivated forgetting—the active re-

jection of unacceptable thoughts, desires, and memories and their relegation to the unconscious. Repression is perhaps the most central concept in Freud's theory.

For example, a woman sees someone beating another person to death. Later she cannot remember what she saw. She has repressed the painful memory. Another example: A man gives a speech and several members of the audience raise serious objections to what he says. Later he forgets their objections. People sometimes repress their own unacceptable thoughts as well.

Although repression continues to be a highly influential concept, researchers have struggled to find any unambiguous evidence to support it. Investigators have exposed subjects to various unpleasant or threatening experiences, in the expectation that repression would interfere with their memories of such events. However, in cases when subjects did have trouble remembering the events, a variety of alternative explanations appear to be possible (Holmes, 1990). As with many of Freud's other concepts, repression is an appealing idea but one that is difficult to support scientifically.

Denial   The refusal to believe information that provokes anxiety is called **denial**. Whereas repression is the motivated forgetting of certain information, denial is an assertion that the information is incorrect.

For example, a doctor tells a woman that her child is mentally retarded. She refuses to accept this opinion and shops around for another doctor who will tell her the child is not retarded.

Rationalization   When people attempt to prove that their actions are rational and justifiable and thus worthy of approval, they are using **rationalization**. For example, a student who wants to go to the movies instead of studying says, "More studying won't do me any good anyway." Someone who misses a deadline to apply for a job says, "I didn't really want that job anyway."

Displacement   By diverting a behavior or a thought away from its natural target toward a less threatening target, **displacement** lets people engage in the behavior they prefer without experiencing severe anxiety.

For example, a man who is angry at his boss comes home and kicks his dog. He really wants to kick his boss, but that would cause him too much anxiety. Or a student who fails an examination blames her professor for giving an unfair test and her roommate for distracting her when she was trying to study. To admit that the fault was her own would cause anxiety.

Regression   A return to a more juvenile level of functioning, **regression** is an effort to avoid the anxiety of facing one's current role in life. By adopting a childish role, a person can escape responsibility and return to an earlier, perhaps more secure way of life. A person may also regress to an earlier stage of psychosexual development in response to emotionally trying circumstances.

For example, after a new sibling is born, a 5-year-old child may start wetting the bed again. Following a divorce or a business setback, a man may resort to daydreaming, getting drunk, or other immature behaviors.

Projection   The attribution of one's own undesirable characteristics to other people is

John McEnroe comments on a referee's call in a juvenile manner. Which defense mechanisms are athletes using in the following comments: "They had the home-field advantage," "The referees sided against us," "You gotta play rough to win"?

known as **projection**. When people project their own faults onto others, they generally do not deny that they themselves possess those faults (Holmes, 1978; Sherwood, 1981). However, by suggesting that the faults are widespread, they make them more acceptable and less anxiety provoking.

For example, someone says, "Everyone cheats on their income taxes," or "Every student cheats on a test now and then." People who make such statements probably cheat a little themselves.

Reaction Formation   In an effort to reduce anxiety and to keep undesirable characteristics repressed, people may use **reaction formation** to present themselves as the opposite of what they really are. In Shakespeare's play *Hamlet,*

Gertrude says, "The lady protests too much, methinks." People who insist too vehemently that something is "absolutely" true often harbor secret doubts about whether it really is true.

For example, someone with strong deviant sexual impulses may become a crusader against pornography, demonstrating, "See? I was afraid I might have this terrible fault, but that can't be true because I'm working for the exact opposite." (Not everyone who opposes pornography is a secret deviate, of course. Different people can be attracted to a cause for very different reasons.)

Sublimation The transformation of an unacceptable impulse into an acceptable, even an admirable, behavior is **sublimation**. According to Freud, sublimation enables a person to express the impulse without admitting its existence. For example, painting and sculpture may represent a sublimation of sexual impulses. Someone with unacceptable aggressive impulses may sublimate them by becoming a surgeon. Whether Freud is correct about sublimation is difficult to say; if the true motives of a painter are sexual, they are hidden well indeed. However, if Freud is correct, sublimation is the one defense mechanism that leads to socially constructive behavior.

■ CONCEPT CHECK

2. Match the Freudian defense mechanisms in the top list with the situations in the list that follows.

1. Repression	*5. Regression*
2. Denial	*6. Projection*
3. Rationalization	*7. Reaction formation*
4. Displacement	*8. Sublimation*

a. ____ *A man who is angry with his neighbor goes hunting and kills a deer.*

b. ____ *Someone with a smoking habit insists that there is no convincing evidence that smoking impairs health.*

c. ____ *A woman with doubts about her religious faith tries to convert others to her religion.*

d. ____ *A man who beats his wife writes a book arguing that people have an instinctive need for aggressive behavior.*

e. ____ *A woman forgets a doctor's appointment for a test for cancer.*

f. ____ *Someone who has difficulty dealing with certain people resorts to pouting, crying, and throwing tantrums.*

g. ____ *A boss takes credit for a good idea suggested by an employee because, "It's better for me to take the credit so that our department will look good and all the employees will benefit."*

h. ____ *Someone with an unacceptable impulse to shout obscenities becomes a writer of novels.*

(Check your answers on page 553.)

Manifestations of the Unconscious in Everyday Life

Freud believed that the unconscious made itself felt in nearly all aspects of ordinary life. Even an act that may be explained as "just a meaningless accident" reflects an unconscious motivation. For example, when one of Freud's patients "forgot" an appointment, Freud assumed the patient did not want to keep it. When a patient left something behind in Freud's office and had to come back to get it, Freud assumed that the patient enjoyed being with him and was unconsciously planting an excuse to return. Much of people's behavior and personality, Freud said, was based on unconscious motivations.

Freud also interpreted *slips of the tongue,* or what have come to be called "Freudian slips," as revelations of unconscious thoughts and motives. If you said "I leave you" when you intended to say "I love you," Freud would assume that your error revealed an unconscious rejection of your professed love.

Today, psychologists believe that most slips of the tongue and other such errors have multiple causes (Norman, 1981). For example, President Jimmy Carter once introduced former Vice-President Hubert Horatio Humphrey as "Hubert Horatio Hornblower." It may be that Carter thought of Humphrey as someone who "blows his own horn" too much. But even if we accept this as a Freudian slip, that is not the whole explanation. Horatio Hornblower was a character in a series of novels. Carter may have referred to Horatio Hornblower many times before, and after saying "Hubert Horatio" it would have been easy for him to substitute Hornblower for Humphrey.

Freudian Slips

WHAT'S THE EVIDENCE?

Freud claimed that what we say "by accident" reveals hidden motives. Many of Freud's claims are virtually impossible to test scientifically. This one can be tested, though not easily.

We could follow people around and record all their slips of the tongue, or we could ask them to record all their own slips. But we would still have to guess or infer the hidden motives of the people we were following. And the people who were recording their own slips would have to decide which slips to record. If they were familiar with Freud's theory, they might record only the errors that seemed to fit the theory and ignore those that did not.

A second method would be to induce a motive—hunger, for example—for the purposes of an experiment. Then we could ask the hungry subjects to read a certain passage, and we could count how many of their slips of the tongue had something to do with eating. We could repeat the experiment with people in whom we had induced a different motive, to see whether they made different slips.

But most people make so few slips of the tongue that the experiment might go on for months without yielding significant results. To test Freud's theory, we need a procedure that increases the frequency of slips of the tongue. Michael Motley and Bernard Baars (1979) devised such a procedure.

Hypothesis When people are performing a difficult task on which they are likely to make slips of the tongue, the kinds of slips they make will depend on the kinds of motivations they are feeling at the moment.

Method The experimenters divided 90 male college students into three groups: a "sex" group, a "shock" group, and a control group. Those in the sex group were greeted by a very attractive female experimenter dressed in a sexy outfit and behaving in a seductive manner. Those in the shock group were met by a male experimenter who attached electrodes to their arms and told them the electrodes were connected to a "random shock generator" that might or might not give them one or more painful shocks at unpredictable times during the experiment. (No shocks were actually given.) Those in the control group were met by a male experimenter who attached no electrodes to them and made no mention of shocks. Thus one group should have a heightened sexual motivation, one group should have a strong fear of shock, and one group should be concerned with neither sex nor shock during the experiment.

The students watched a screen on which the experimenters flashed pairs of words or nonsense syllables, such as "HAT-RAM" and

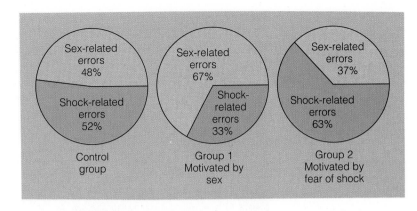

"RUF-GAM." Each pair was flashed for 1 second. A buzzer sounded 0.4 second after each pair appeared, telling the students to speak aloud the *previous* pair. So, for example, after seeing "RUF-GAM," they would have to say "HAT-RAM" (the previous pair), and remember "RUF-GAM" to say after the next pair. About 30% of the time, students made slips of the tongue. For example, they would say "HAT-RAM" as "RAT-HAM" and "RUF-GAM" as "GUF-RAM."

Some of the syllable pairs were designed to promote sex-related slips. For example, "GOXI-FURL" and "LOOD-GEGS" might be pronounced as "FOXY-GIRL" and "GOOD-LEGS." Other pairs were designed to promote shock-related slips. For example, "SHAD-BOCK" and "WOT-HIRE" might be pronounced as "BAD-SHOCK" and "HOT-WIRE." Still other pairs did not suggest any slips related to either sex or shock.

Results The men in the sex group made more than twice as many sex-related slips as shock-related slips. The opposite was true for the men in the shock group. Those in the control group made both types of errors about equally. Figure 13.8 illustrates the results.

Interpretation The results support Freud's claim that a strong motivation can increase the frequency of slips of the tongue related to that motivation. Slips of the tongue may indeed tell us something about a person's thoughts and desires.

But the results do not support Freud's contention that hidden motivations are the main cause of slips of the tongue. Slips were common in this experiment because the task was so difficult. Having to say one pair while preparing to say another produced conflict between the two pairs that a subject was trying to remember.

FIGURE 13.8
In the presence of an attractive woman, men made many sex-related slips of the tongue. When they were worried about shocks, they made shock-related slips of the tongue.

FIGURE 13.9

Karen Horney, a major neo-Freudian, revised some of Freud's theories and gave greater attention to cultural influences. She was a pioneer in the development of feminine psychology.

The Legacy of Freud

Among Freud's contributions to the study of personality were his recognition of the importance of childhood experiences and the sex drive. His methods of treating psychological disorders led to the whole range of psychotherapeutic techniques, which we shall consider in Chapter 15. Still, it is difficult to evaluate how much of his theory is correct. Psychologists today express a wide range of opinions about Freud. Some follow his ideas closely, and others reject his whole approach as pseudoscience.

Some psychologists, known as **neo-Freudians,** have remained faithful to parts of Freud's theory while modifying other parts. One of the most influential neo-Freudians was the German physician Karen Horney (HOR-nigh; 1885–1952; Figure 13.9), who believed that Freud had exaggerated the role of the sex drive in human behavior and had misunderstood the sexual motivations of women. She believed, for example, that the conflict between a child and his or her parents was a reaction to parental hostility and intimidation, not a manifestation of a sexual Oedipus complex or Electra complex. Horney contended that Freud had slighted the importance of cultural influences on personality and was more interested in tracing the childhood sources of anxiety than he was in helping people deal with current problems. Still, Hor-

ney's views were more a revision than a rejection of Freud's theories. Other theorists, including Carl Jung and Alfred Adler, broke more sharply with Freud.

CARL G. JUNG AND THE COLLECTIVE UNCONSCIOUS

Carl G. Jung (YOONG; 1875–1961; Figure 13.10), a Swiss physician, was an early member of Freud's inner circle. Freud regarded Jung as a son, the "heir apparent" or "crown prince" of the psychoanalytic movement. But their father-son relationship gradually deteriorated (Alexander, 1982). At one point, Freud and Jung agreed to analyze each other's dreams. Freud described one of his dreams, but then refused to provide the personal associations that would enable Jung to interpret it, insisting that "I cannot risk my authority."

Jung was more forthcoming. He described a dream in which he explored the upper stories of a house, then explored its basement, and finally, discovering that the house had a subbasement, began to explore that. Jung thought the dream referred to his explorations of the mind. The top floor was the conscious; the basement was the unconscious; and the subbasement was a still deeper level of the unconscious, yet to be explored. Freud, however, insisted that the dream referred to Jung's personal experiences and frustrations (Hannah, 1976).

Jung's own theory of personality incorporated many of Freud's insights but put greater emphasis on people's search for a spiritual meaning in life and on the continuity of human experience, past and present. Jung believed that every person has a conscious mind, a "personal unconscious" (equivalent to Freud's "unconscious"), and a collective unconscious. The personal unconscious represents a person's own experience. The **collective unconscious,** which is present at birth, represents the cumulative experience of preceding generations. Because all humans share a common ancestry, all have nearly the same collective unconscious. (Jung never explained how the collective unconscious might develop biologically.)

Jung drew his evidence for the collective unconscious from observations of various cultures. He pointed out that similar images emerge in the art of cultures throughout the world (Figure 13.11) and that similar themes emerge in religions, myths, and folklore. Those images and themes also appear in dreams and in

a

FIGURE 13.10
Carl G. Jung rejected Freud's concept of dreams hiding their meaning from the conscious mind: "To me dreams are a part of nature which harbors no intention to deceive but express something as best it can" (June, 1965).

b

c

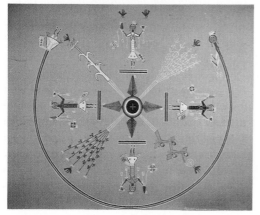

d

FIGURE 13.11
Carl Jung was fascinated with the similar images that show up in the artworks of different cultures. One recurring image is the mandala, which Jung believed to be a symbol of the self's striving for unity and wholeness. These mandalas are (a) a Hindu painting; (b) a mosaic from Beth Alpha Synagogue, Israel, from about 500 A.D.; (c) a Greek ceramic from about 550 B.C.; and (d) a Navajo sand painting, Southwestern United States.

the hallucinations of people with severe psychological disorders.

Jung's impact on contemporary psychology is hard to judge. Some psychotherapists make extensive use of his ideas, and most are at least aware of them. Many of his ideas are vague and mystical, however, and difficult to deal with scientifically.

ALFRED ADLER AND INDIVIDUAL PSYCHOLOGY

Alfred Adler (1870–1937; Figure 13.12), an Austrian physician who, like Jung, had been one of Freud's early followers, broke with Freud because he believed Freud was overemphasizing the sex drive and neglecting other, more important influences on personality. Their disagreement reached a peak in 1911, with Freud insisting that women experience "penis envy" and with Adler contending that women were more likely to envy men's status and power. The two were never reconciled.

Adler founded a rival school of thought, which he called **individual psychology**. To Adler this term did not mean "psychology of the individual." Rather, it meant "indivisible psychology," a psychology of the person as a whole rather than a psychology of parts, such as id, ego, and superego. Adler agreed with Freud that childhood experiences have a crucial effect on personality, that many motives are outside conscious awareness, and that people can be helped to overcome their problems through a "talking cure." He put far more emphasis, however, on conscious, goal-directed behavior.

Adler's Description of Personality

Several of Adler's early patients were acrobats who had had an arm or a leg damaged by a childhood illness or injury. Determined to overcome their disabilities, they had worked hard to develop the strength and coordination they needed to perform as acrobats. Perhaps, Adler surmised, people in general try to overcome their weaknesses and transform them into strengths (Adler, 1932/1964).

As infants, Adler pointed out, we are small, dependent creatures; we strive to overcome our inferiority. Some people never succeed, however, and go through life with an **inferiority complex,** an exaggerated feeling of weakness, inadequacy, and helplessness. Even those who do manage to overcome their feelings of inferiority persist in their efforts to achieve.

According to Adler, everyone has a natural **striving for superiority,** a desire to seek personal excellence and fulfillment. Each person creates a **style of life,** or "master plan," for achieving a sense of superiority. That style of life may be directed toward success in business, sports, politics, or some other competitive activity. Or it may be directed toward "success" of a different sort: For example, someone who withdraws from life may gain a sense of accomplishment or superiority from being uncommonly self-sacrificing. Someone who constantly complains about real or imagined illnesses or disabilities may, by demanding help from friends and family, win a measure of control or superiority over them. Or someone may commit crimes in order to savor the attention they bring.

Adler recognized that people may not be aware of their own style of life and the assumptions behind it and may fail to realize that the real motive behind some word or action is to manipulate others. They may engage in self-defeating behavior because they have not admitted to themselves what their goals really are. Adler tried to determine people's real motives. For example, he would ask someone who complained of a backache, "How would your life be different if you could get rid of your backache?" Those who said they would become more active were presumably suffering from real ailments that they were trying to overcome. Those who said they could think of no way in which their life would change, or said only that they would get less sympathy from others, were presumably suffering from psychologically caused ailments or at least were exaggerating their discomfort.

▪ CONCEPT CHECK

3. In Adler's theory, what is the relationship between striving for superiority and style of life? (Check your answer on page 553.)

Adler's View of Psychological Disorders

Any personality based on a selfish style of life is unhealthy, Adler (1928/1964) said. People's need for one another requires that they develop a **social interest,** a sense of solidarity and identification with other people. People with a strong social interest strive for superiority in a way that contributes to the welfare of the whole human race, not just to their own welfare. They want to cooperate with other people, not to compete. In equating mental health with a strong social interest, Adler saw mental health as a positive state, not just the absence of impairments.

In Adler's view, people with psychological disorders are not suffering from an "illness." Rather, they have set immature goals, are following a faulty style of life, and show little social interest. Their response to new opportunity is "Yes, but . . ." (Adler, 1932/1964). They are striving for superiority in ways that are useless to themselves and to others.

For example, one of Adler's patients was a man who lived in conflict with his wife because he was constantly trying to impress her and dominate her (Adler, 1927). In discussing his problems, the man revealed that he had been very slow to mature physically and had not reached puberty until he was 17 years old. Other teenagers had ignored him and had treated him like a child. He was now a physically normal adult, but he was overcompensating for those years of feeling inferior by trying to seem bigger and more important than he really was.

Adler tried to get patients to understand their own style of life and to correct the faulty assumptions on which it rested. He urged them to strengthen their social interest and to strive for superiority in ways that would benefit both themselves and others.

Adler's Legacy

Adler's influence on psychology exceeds his fame. His concept of the "inferiority complex" has become part of the common culture. He was the first to talk about mental health as a positive state rather than as merely the absence of impairments. Many later forms of therapy drew on Adler's innovations, especially his emphasis on the assumptions underlying a patient's behavior. Humanistic psychologists followed Adler in urging people to take responsibility for their own behavior and for modifying their style of life.

HUMANISTIC PSYCHOLOGY

Another general perspective on personality, **humanistic psychology,** deals with consciousness, values, and abstract beliefs, including the spiri-

FIGURE 13.12
Like Horney, Alfred Adler thought Freud overemphasized the sex drive. Adler was very interested in feelings of self-esteem. He was the first to talk about the possibility of a "healthy" personality, and not just a personality free from disorders. According to Adler, the key to a healthy personality was "social interest," a desire for the welfare of other people.

tual experiences and the beliefs that people live by and die for. According to humanistic psychologists, personality depends on what people believe and how they perceive the world. If you *believe* that a particular experience was highly meaningful, then it *was* highly meaningful. A psychologist can understand your behavior only by asking you for your own evaluations and interpretations of the events in your life.

(In theology, a *humanist* glorifies humans, generally denying or at least giving little attention to a supreme being. The term *humanistic psychologist* implies nothing about a person's religious beliefs.)

Humanistic psychology emerged in the 1950s and 1960s as a protest against both behaviorism and psychoanalysis, the dominant

FIGURE 13.13

Carl Rogers maintained that people naturally strive toward positive goals; they do not need special urging. He recommended that people relate to one another with "unconditional positive regard."

viewpoints in psychology at that time (Berlyne, 1981). Those two approaches, despite their many differences, are both rooted in *determinism* (the belief that every behavior has a cause) and in *reductionism* (the attempt to explain behavior in terms of its component elements). Humanistic psychologists turn away from these attempts to explain behavior in terms of its component parts or unconscious causes. They claim that people make deliberate, conscious decisions about what to do with their lives. People may decide to devote themselves to a great cause, to sacrifice their own well-being, and to risk their lives. To the humanistic psychologist, it is pointless to try to ascribe such behavior to past rewards and punishments or to unconscious thought processes.

Humanistic psychologists seldom conduct research—at least not the kind of research that leads to reports of means and medians and other statistical data. In spite of the risks of relying on anecdotal evidence, they prefer to study unique individuals and unique experiences— the exceptions to the rule, not just the rule itself.

For example, humanistic psychologists study growth experiences—the moments that people identify as points of transition, when they may say, "Aha! Now I have become an adult," or "Now I have truly committed my life to this goal" (Frick, 1983). They also study **peak experiences,** moments in which a person feels truly fulfilled, content, and at peace. Some people report that they "feel at one with the universe" when they hear "thrilling" music, or take part in an emotional religious ceremony, or

achieve some great accomplishment. Some mountain-climbers who have scaled Mount Everest report what is literally a "peak" experience (Lester, 1983).

Carl Rogers and the Goal of Self-Actualization

Carl Rogers, an American psychologist, studied theology before turning to psychology, and the influence of those early studies is apparent in his view of human nature. Rogers (Figure 13.13) became probably the most influential humanistic psychologist.

Rogers (1980) holds that human nature is basically good. People have a natural drive toward **self-actualization,** which means the achievement of their full potential. According to Rogers, it is as natural for people to strive for excellence as it is for a plant to grow. The drive for self-actualization is the basic drive behind the development of personality. (To some extent, Rogers's concept of self-actualization is similar to Adler's concept of striving for superiority.)

Beginning at an early age, children evaluate themselves and their actions. They learn that what they do is sometimes good and sometimes bad. They develop a **self-concept,** an image of what they really are, and an **ideal self,** an image of what they would like to be. Rogers measured a person's self-concept and ideal self by handing the person a stack of cards containing statements such as "I am honest" and "I am suspicious of others." The person would then sort the statements into two piles: *true of me* and *not true of me*. Then Rogers would provide an identical stack of cards and ask the person to sort them into two piles: *true of my ideal self* and *not true of my ideal self*. In this manner he could determine whether someone's self-concept was similar to his or her ideal self. People who perceive a great discrepancy between the two generally experience distress. Humanistic psychologists try to help people overcome that distress, either by improving their self-concept or by changing their ideal self.

To promote human welfare, Rogers maintains, people should relate to one another with **unconditional positive regard,** a relationship that Thomas Harris (1967) has described with the phrase "I'm OK, you're OK." Unconditional positive regard is the complete, unqualified acceptance of another person as he or she is, much like the love of a parent for a child. If someone expresses anger, or even a desire to kill, the listener should accept that as an understandable feeling, even while discouraging the other person from acting on the impulse. This view resembles the Christian admonition to "hate the sin but love the sinner."

Abraham Maslow and the Self-Actualized Personality

Abraham Maslow (Figure 13.14), another of the founders of humanistic psychology, proposed that people have a hierarchy of needs, an idea we considered in Chapter 11. The highest of those needs is *self-actualization,* the fulfillment of a person's potential. What kind of person achieves self-actualization, and what is the result of achieving it? Maslow (1962, 1971) sought to describe the self-actualized personality. He complained that psychologists concentrate on disordered personalities, reflecting the medical view that health is merely the absence of disease. They seem to assume that all personality is either "normal" (that is, bland) or undesirable. Maslow insisted, as Adler had, that personality may differ from the "normal" in positive, desirable ways.

To determine the characteristics of the self-actualized personality, Maslow made a list of people who in his opinion had achieved their full potential. His list included people he knew personally as well as figures from history (Figure 13.15). He then sought to discover what they had in common.

According to Maslow (1962, 1971), people with a self-actualized personality show the following characteristics:

- An accurate perception of reality. They perceive the world as it is, not as they would like it to be. They are willing to accept uncertainty and ambiguity when necessary.

- Independence, creativity, and spontaneity. They follow their own impulses.

- Acceptance of themselves and others. They treat people with unconditional positive regard.

- A problem-centered outlook, rather than a self-centered outlook. They think about how best to solve a problem, not how to make themselves look good.

- Enjoyment of life. They are open to positive experiences, including "peak experiences."

- A good sense of humor.

Critics have attacked Maslow's description on the grounds that, because it is based on his own choice of subjects, it may simply reflect the

FIGURE 13.14
Abraham Maslow, one of the founders of humanistic psychology, introduced the concept of a "self-actualized personality," a better-than-merely-normal personality, associated with high productivity and enjoyment of life.

FIGURE 13.15
Harriet Tubman, one of the people Maslow identified as having a self-actualized personality, was one of the leaders of the Underground Railroad, a system for helping black slaves to escape from the Southern states during the period before the Civil War. Maslow described the self-actualized personality by identifying similarities between Tubman and other highly productive and accomplished people.

characteristics he himself admired. In any case, Maslow set a precedent for other attempts to define a healthy personality as something more than personality without disorder. Like Adler, he pointed to the possibility of a "healthier than normal" personality.

SUMMARY

- *Personality theories as views of human nature.* Personality consists of all the stable, consistent ways in which the behavior of one person differs from that of others. Theories of personality are closely related to conceptions of human nature. Some observers believe that human beings are basically hostile and need to be restrained (Hobbes, Freud). Others believe that human beings are basically good and are hampered by restraints (Rousseau, Rogers). (page 535)

- *Freud.* Sigmund Freud, the founder of psychoanalysis, proposed that human behavior is greatly influenced by unconscious thoughts and motives. (page 536)

- *Freud's view of the unconscious.* According to Freud, unacceptable thoughts and impulses are relegated to the unconscious because they are threatening or anxiety provoking. People engage in repression and other defense mechanisms to exclude such thoughts and impulses from the conscious mind. (page 537)

- *Freud's psychosexual stages.* Freud believed that many unconscious thoughts and motives are sexual in nature. He proposed that people progress through stages or periods of psychosexual development—oral, anal, phallic, latent, and genital—and that frustration at any one stage can lead to a lasting fixation of libido at that stage. (page 538)

- *Slips of the tongue.* Unconscious thoughts influence many aspects of everyday life, including slips of the tongue, although other influences may be more important. (page 544)

- *Jung.* Carl Jung believed that all people share a "collective unconscious" that represents the entire experience of humanity. (page 546)

- *Adler.* Alfred Adler proposed that people's primary motivation is a striving for superiority. Each person adopts his or her own "style of life," or method of striving for superiority. (page 548)

- *Adler's view of a healthy personality.* According to Adler, the healthiest style of life is one that emphasizes "social interest"—that is, concern for the welfare of others. (page 548)

- *Humanistic psychology.* Humanistic psychologists emphasize conscious, deliberate decision making; they oppose attempts to reduce behavior to its elements or to seek explanations in terms of unconscious influences. (page 549)

- *Rogers.* Carl Rogers focused attention on the discrepancies between a person's self-concept and his or her ideal self. He recommended that people relate to one another with unconditional positive regard. (page 550)

- *Maslow.* Abraham Maslow described a self-actualized personality, which he said was characteristic of people who achieve their full potential. (page 551)

SUGGESTIONS FOR FURTHER READING

Adler, A. (1954). *Understanding human nature.* Greenwich, CT: Fawcett. (Original work published 1927.) Adler's most general and most popular book.

Freud, S. (1924). *Introductory lectures on psychoanalysis.* New York: Boni & Liveright. Available in various paperback editions, this is Freud's attempt to describe the fundamentals of his theory to a general audience.

Maslow, A. H. (1962). *Toward a psychology of being.* Princeton, NJ: Van Nostrand. A good introduction to humanistic psychology.

TERMS

personality all the stable, consistent ways in which the behavior of one person differs from that of others (page 536)

psychodynamic theory a theory that relates personality to the interplay of conflicting forces within the individual, including some that are unconscious (page 536)

catharsis the release of pent-up tension (page 537)

psychoanalysis Freud's approach to personality, based on the interplay of conscious and unconscious forces (page 537)

unconscious according to Freud, an aspect of the mind that influences behavior, although we are not directly aware of it (page 538)

psychosexual pleasure according to Freud, any enjoyment arising from stimulation of parts of the body (page 538)

libido in Freud's theory, a psychosexual energy (page 538)

psychosexual development in Freud's theory, progression through a series of five developmental stages, each with a characteristic psychosexual focus that leaves its mark on adult personality (page 539)

fixation in Freud's theory, a persisting preoccupation with an immature psychosexual interest as a result of frustration at that stage of psychosexual development (page 539)

oral stage Freud's first stage of psychosexual development, in which psychosexual pleasure is focused on the mouth (page 539)

anal stage Freud's second stage of psychosexual development, in which psychosexual pleasure is focused on the anus (page 539)

phallic stage Freud's third stage of psychosexual development, in which psychosexual interest is focused on the penis or clitoris (page 539)

Oedipus complex according to Freud, a young boy's sexual interest in his mother accompanied by competitive aggression toward his father (page 540)

Electra complex according to Freud, a young girl's romantic attraction toward her father and hostility toward her mother (page 540)

latent period according to Freud, a period in which psychosexual interest is suppressed or dormant (page 540)

genital stage Freud's final stage of psychosexual development, in which sexual pleasure is focused on sexual intimacy with others (page 541)

id according to Freud, the aspect of personality that consists of all our biological drives and demands for immediate gratification (page 541)

ego according to Freud, the rational, decision-making aspect of personality (page 541)

superego according to Freud, the aspect of personality that consists of memories of rules put forth by one's parents (page 541)

defense mechanism a method employed by the ego to protect itself against anxiety caused by conflict between the id's demands and the superego's constraints (page 541)

repression motivated forgetting; the relegation of unacceptable impulses or memories to the unconscious (page 542)

denial the refusal to believe information that provokes anxiety (page 543)

rationalization attempting to prove that one's actions are rational and justifiable and thus worthy of approval (page 543)

displacement the diversion of a thought or an action away from its natural target toward a less threatening target (page 543)

regression the return to a more juvenile level of functioning as a means of reducing anxiety or in response to emotionally trying circumstances (page 543)

projection the attribution of one's own undesirable characteristics to other people (page 543)

reaction formation presenting oneself as the opposite of what one really is in an effort to reduce anxiety (page 543)

sublimation the transformation of an unacceptable impulse into an acceptable, even an admirable, behavior (page 544)

neo-Freudians personality theorists who have remained faithful to parts of Freud's theory while modifying other parts (page 546)

collective unconscious according to Jung, an inborn level of the unconscious that symbolizes the collective experience of the human species (page 546)

individual psychology the psychology of the person as an indivisible whole, as formulated by Adler (page 548)

inferiority complex an exaggerated feeling of weakness, inadequacy, and helplessness (page 548)

striving for superiority according to Adler, a universal desire to seek personal excellence and fulfillment (page 548)

style of life according to Adler, a person's master plan for achieving a sense of superiority (page 548)

social interest a sense of solidarity and identification with other people (page 548)

humanistic psychology a branch of psychology that emphasizes the capacity of people to make conscious decisions about their own lives (page 549)

peak experience an experience that brings fulfillment, contentment, and peace (page 550)

self-actualization the achievement of one's full potential (page 550)

self-concept a person's image of what he or she really is (page 550)

ideal self a person's image of what he or she would like to be (page 550)

unconditional positive regard complete, unqualified acceptance of another person as he or she is (page 550)

ANSWERS TO CONCEPT CHECKS

1. Someone with a strong id and a weak superego would be expected to give in to a variety of sexual and other impulses that other people would inhibit. Someone with an unusually strong superego would be unusually inhibited and dominated by feelings of guilt. (page 542)

2. a. 4, displacement; b. 2, denial; c. 7, reaction formation; d. 6, projection; e. 1, repression; f. 5, regression; g. 3, rationalization; h. 8, sublimation. (page 544)

3. In Adler's theory, a person's style of life is his or her method of striving for superiority. (page 548)

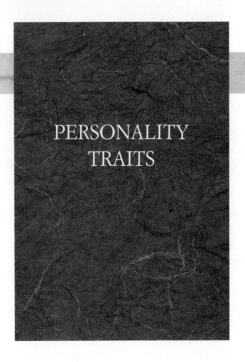

PERSONALITY TRAITS

Is personality consistent over time and from one situation to another?

What are personality traits?

In many ways all rocks are the same. If you plan to drop a rock and you want to predict when it will hit the ground, you do not need to know what kind of rock it is. If you skip a rock across a lake, throw it against a window, or use it to crack open a coconut, you can pretty well predict what will happen.

For certain other purposes, however, you need to know something about the rock. If you want to predict what will happen if you run an electric current through it, you have to know what kind of rock it is. If you want to determine a fair sale price for the rock, you need to know whether it is a diamond or a piece of granite.

Similarly, people resemble one another in some ways and differ in others. Psychologists investigate individual differences in two ways, called the nomothetic and the idiographic approaches. The word *nomothetic* (NAHM-uh-THEHT-ick) comes from the Greek *nomothetes*, meaning "legislator"; the **nomothetic approach** seeks general laws about how some aspect of personality affects behavior, often based on statistical comparisons of large groups of people. For example, we might make the nomothetic statement that people with a more *Machiavellian* personality tend to be highly manipulative and that people with a less Machiavellian personality tend to cooperate with oth-

ers. We could apply that statement fairly directly to anyone, simply by measuring that person's amount of "Machiavellianism."

In contrast, the word *idiographic* is based on the root *idio-*, meaning "individual." The **idiographic approach** concentrates on intensive studies of individuals (Pervin, 1990). For example, certain psychologists have studied how people's goals in life affect their moods and their reactions to various events. Because different people have different goals, the investigators draw carefully qualified conclusions about how people with one kind of goal behave and how people with some other kind of goal behave (Emmons, 1991). The idiographic approach may lead to a conclusion that applies to more than just one person, but it is not meant to generalize to everyone.

PERSONALITY TRAITS AND STATES

Suppose I meet you and decide that you seem quiet and shy. Until I have known you for a while, I will not know whether you usually act this way or only at times. Each of us has both temporary and long-lasting personality tendencies.

A consistent, long-lasting tendency in behavior, such as shyness, hostility, or talkativeness, is known as a **trait**. In contrast, a **state** is a temporary activation of a particular behavior. People's behavior varies from time to time because they are in different states. For example, Don, who has a trait of being highly talkative at most times, seldom talks in a library, because the library induces a state of silence. Donna, who has a trait of being reticent, talks a great deal while she is working at an information booth. Although Don and Donna's behavior changes drastically from one situation to another, they still have consistent traits that would become apparent, for example, if they both attended the same dinner party.

Note that both traits and states are descriptions of behavior, not explanations. To say that someone is talkative or quiet does not explain the person's behavior; it merely tells us what we are trying to explain.

4. Two psychologists agree that a particular person is showing anxiety, but they argue about whether the anxiety is "trait anxiety" or "state anxiety." What do they mean by that distinction? How could they settle their argument? (Check your answers on page 561.)

PROS AND CONS OF THE TRAIT APPROACH

A funny thing happened on the way to an understanding of personality traits: Researchers in this field spent many years debating whether traits even exist!

The idea of describing people's behavior in terms of personality traits is more than just an act of convenience. It implies the theoretical idea that personality is composed of traits—that you are the way you are because of the sum of various measurable personality tendencies. That in turn implies that personality traits are fairly consistent from time to time and from one situation to another. Are they?

Criticisms of the Trait Approach

Psychologists critical of the trait approach have focused mainly on the question of whether traits are consistent across situations. Their consistency over time is easy enough to document. For example, if I measure your honesty or almost any other trait today, and then measure it again *in the same way* a few months or even a few years later, I can expect to find your scores about the same (Stein, Newcomb, & Bentler, 1986). That is, someone who returns a lost wallet to its owner today probably will do the same thing 6 months from now.

However, consistency across situations is harder to demonstrate. Walter Mischel (1973, 1981) argued that personality varies so much from one situation to another that we should abandon the idea of broadly defined traits. For example, someone who returns a lost wallet to its owner may cheat on income taxes or may tell a current boyfriend or girlfriend "You are the only one I have ever loved." Consequently, Mischel argued, a broad trait such as "honesty" is useless for describing a person's behavior. Instead, we should talk about narrow traits such as "honesty in returning lost objects" and "honesty to romantic partners."

According to Mischel, behavior varies so strongly from one situation to another because

In Geronimo with His Spirit *(1984), the artist, Frederick Brown, implies that each of us has a "true self" that differs from the self we show the world. Personality includes underlying traits that remain stable over long periods of time as well as temporary states that can change from time to time, as easily as a person takes off one mask and puts on another.*

most of our social behaviors are learned. (Recall the discussion of social learning in Chapter 7.) In familiar situations, people learn to follow **scripts**—the rules governing who will do what and when (Abelson, 1981). For example, the script for a lecture class or a religious service dictates who will do the talking and when; to some extent it even specifies what they will say. When we follow well-defined scripts, as we do most of the day, our personality traits have little to do with our behavior. Even when people do display different personality traits, Mischel insists, they are narrow traits specific to limited situations.

Why then do most of the people we know *seem* to have a consistent personality? One possibility is that this apparent consistency is mostly an illusion (Schweder, 1982). When we see someone behaving in a friendly way in a certain situation, we may assume that he or she is friendly in other situations as well. When someone is shy in our presence, we may assume that

the person is shy with other people as well. Once we have decided that we know someone's personality, we tend to remember those occasions when people behave in a way that fits our expectation, dismissing other observations as "exceptions to the rule."

■ CONCEPT CHECK

5. *Given the ways in which people distort their memories of others, why does a person have a hard time trying to escape his or her reputation? (Check your answer on page 561.)*

Defense of the Trait Approach

Personality researchers took these criticisms of the trait approach seriously, but most eventually concluded that traits are not just an illusion. Furthermore, some sort of understanding of traits is not only sensible but quite necessary for many purposes. For example, if someone offers you a present, you would like to know whether this person is *generous* or *manipulative*. If you do not stop to ask such questions, you will often get yourself into trouble (Funder, 1991).

Defenders of the concept of traits point out, first, that no one should reasonably expect any trait to be consistent across all situations. For example, a person who is friendly and talkative at a party sits quietly during a lecture. That is hardly a sign of an inconsistent personality. It merely reminds us that personality traits show up most clearly in situations without a well-defined script (Buss, 1989).

Second, people may appear to be inconsistent on a given trait for a very good reason: *They are being consistent on some other trait* (Bem & Allen, 1974). For example, a woman who seems honest in many situations confronts an embarrassing question from her neighbor: "Why didn't you invite me to your party next Saturday?" The woman replies, "Oh, it's just a party for people from my office." That is a lie; the real reason is that the neighbor always starts arguments. This woman may have a strong trait of being honest, but she has an even stronger trait of being tactful. When the two traits come into conflict, one of them wins out. A psychologist who was measuring *only* honesty might conclude that the woman's personality is inconsistent, but that would ignore the fact that she is being highly consistent on her most central or dominant trait (Kenrick & Stringfield, 1980).

Third, many of the studies reporting low consistency of traits were based on inadequate measurements (Epstein & O'Brien, 1985). If I measured your degree of honesty in three or four situations and found it to be inconsistent, one possibility is that your behavior really does vary as much as it seems. Another possibility is that I did not measure your behavior carefully enough. When psychologists improve their measurements by taking repeated observations, they find that the apparent consistency of personality traits improves (Epstein, 1979; Moskowitz, 1982).

THE SEARCH FOR BROAD PERSONALITY TRAITS

Suppose we agree that reasonably broad personality traits do exist. If so, how many personality traits are there? Gordon Allport and H. S. Odbert (1936) plodded through an English dictionary and found almost 18,000 words that might be used to describe personality. Not all of those were trait words; some were terms for temporary states (such as *confused*), and some were evaluative words (such as *nasty*). Furthermore, many terms were synonyms of other terms, such as *affectionate, warm,* and *loving.* Others were opposites, such as *honest* and *dishonest.* By analyzing clusters of synonyms and antonyms, R. B. Cattell narrowed the list down to 35 traits.

So 35 was, according to Cattell, the number of personality traits that the English language recognizes. But psychologists are not obligated to accept precisely that number. For the purpose of a simple description of personality, they would like to reduce the number of traits as far as possible, while still being able to characterize most of what people do. The idea is similar to the principle of parsimony, from Chapter 2: If we can explain most of personality with, say, 5 or 10 traits, we should not talk about 35 or more traits.

Psychologists use a method called *factor analysis* to find which traits correlate with one another and which ones do not. For example, if measurements of *warmth, gregariousness,* and *assertiveness* correlate positively with one another, we can group them together into a single trait. But if *warmth* does not correlate highly with self-discipline, then they should be separate traits and not grouped together.

Using this approach, many researchers have found that they can describe most of the usual variation in human personality with what they call the **big five personality dimensions**: neuroticism, extraversion, agreeableness, conscientiousness, and openness to new experience (McCrae & Costa, 1987). These five factors offer a powerful description of personality because each pertains to behavior in a wide variety of situations and because each of these dimensions is nearly independent of the others. The big five dimensions are described as follows (Costa, McCrae, & Dye, 1991):

Neuroticism is a tendency to experience unpleasant emotions relatively easily. People high in neuroticism are relatively likely to experience anxiety, hostility, depression, self-consciousness, and impulsiveness.

Extraversion is a tendency to seek new experiences and to enjoy the company of other people. Extraversion is associated with warmth, gregariousness, assertiveness, and excitement seeking. People high in extraversion tend not to become excited easily (Stelmack, 1990). This is perhaps one reason why they tend to seek new and exciting experiences, and perhaps also a reason why they are not shy about meeting new people. Moreover, extraverts tend to maintain a fairly stable, positive mood under most circumstances (Williams, 1990). The opposite of extraversion is *introversion*.

Agreeableness is a tendency to be compassionate toward others and not antagonistic. It implies a concern for the welfare of other people, closely related to Adler's concept of social interest. People high in agreeableness

generally trust other people and expect other people to trust them.

Conscientiousness is a tendency to show self-discipline, to be dutiful, and to strive for achievement and competence. Research has shown that people high in conscientiousness tend to be better than average workers on almost any job (Barrick & Mount, 1991). They are likely to complete whatever task they say they will perform.

Openness to experience is the hardest of the big five to describe, and sometimes not an easy trait to demonstrate in certain populations. Roughly speaking, it is a tendency to enjoy new experiences, especially intellectual experiences, the arts, fantasies, and anything that exposes the person to new ideas.

These five traits have proved to be a useful way of describing personality not just in the United States and other English-speaking countries but in other European countries as well. Preliminary research indicates that these traits are a less satisfactory way of describing personality in certain non-European cultures (John, 1990). Certainly we shall need additional research to determine whether these traits apply to human nature in general or just to a particular range of cultures.

We also need more research to determine how people develop their personality traits. The results of twin studies suggest that extraversion and neuroticism have strong hereditary components (Bouchard & McGue, 1990; Eysenck, 1990). However, we do not know *how* heredity influences personality development or how it combines its influence with various kinds of experience.

■ CONCEPT CHECK

6. Some psychologists suggest that we should divide extraversion into two traits—which they call ambition *and* sociability—*changing the big five into the big six. How should psychologists determine whether or not to do so? (Check your answer on page 561.)*

SELECTED RESEARCH TOPICS

For special purposes, psychologists investigate a variety of personality topics, not just the big five. Let us consider two examples of personality topics that have received a great deal of research attention. The first, androgyny, relates to the issue of personality differences between men and women. It is an important and interesting topic, as well as one that illustrates some special research issues. The second topic, locus of control, plays a key role in several theories about depression and other clinical disorders.

Masculinity, Femininity, and Androgyny

Two of the most obvious personality traits are masculinity and femininity, which are not the same as being biologically male or female. Not all males are equally masculine; not all females are equally feminine.

When we use the terms *masculine* and *feminine* to describe someone's behavior, exactly what do we mean? If you consider yourself masculine, try to describe what it means to be masculine; if you consider yourself feminine, try to describe what it means to be feminine. Most people find it difficult to list many characteristics; you may not regard any of them as absolutely essential.

Androgyny is a personality trait marked by the flexibility to use both masculine (andro-) and feminine (gyne-) characteristics at different times and in different situations. Judit Polgar, a Hungarian teenager, is modest and soft-spoken in most of her dealings with other people, but becomes aggressive and ambitious when playing chess. At the age 15 years and 5 months, she became the youngest person ever to achieve the rank of grandmaster at chess, and only the fourth woman of any age.

According to the usual or stereotypical meanings of these terms, it is masculine to be ambitious, to be self-assertive, and to be interested in sports. It is feminine to enjoy caring for children, to be sympathetic and understanding, and to enjoy beautifying the house and garden.

Is it healthy to accept these roles wholeheartedly? Not entirely, perhaps—at least not if they limit one's choices. A man who loves taking care of children and who hates sports may worry that he is not very masculine. A highly assertive woman may be told that she is unfeminine. Perhaps people would be healthier and happier if they felt free to combine masculinity and femininity in whatever way they like—to be, for example, ambitious, assertive, interested in children, *and* sympathetic to the needs of others.

Reasoning along these lines, Sandra Bem (1974) identified a psychological trait called **androgyny** (from the Greek roots *andr-* meaning "man" and *gyne-* meaning "woman"). According to Bem, androgynous people, as she originally conceptualized the trait, are equally masculine and feminine. They are not limited by one stereotype or the other; they can display masculine or feminine traits with equal ease, depending on what the situation requires.

Table 13.2 presents part of a checklist of masculine and feminine traits. According to Bem, you can measure your degree of androgyny by checking all the items that apply to yourself. If you check about the same number of masculine and feminine items, you are said to be androgynous. Such people, Bem predicted, are more likely to be mentally healthy and flexible in their behavior than are other people.

Table 13.2 Sample Items from the Bem Sex-Role Inventory	
Masculine Items	Feminine Items
Ambitious	Affectionate
Assertive	Cheerful
Competitive	Compassionate
Makes decisions easily	Loves children
Self-reliant	Loyal
Willing to take risks	Sympathetic

Source: Bem, 1974, p. 156.

Note that Bem made an important theoretical point: *Masculine* and *feminine* are not opposite poles of a single dimension. It is possible for a person to be both (or neither).

Bem's original method of measuring androgyny probably is not the best (Spence, 1984). The checklist does not measure all aspects of masculinity or femininity. It tends, in fact, to focus heavily on self-assertiveness and sympathy with other people.

More important, a person can make a score that is *equal* in masculinity and femininity either by scoring high in both or by scoring low in both. Someone who is assertive, self-reliant, cheerful, and compassionate has the advantages of both masculinity and femininity; such a person is likely to have high self-esteem and a good ability to get along with others. Someone who is unassertive, highly dependent, gloomy, and indifferent to others is also considered androgynous because the masculinity and femininity scores are equal—at zero! But such a person is at a disadvantage in many regards. For this reason, most investigators now define androgyny as a personality high in both masculinity and femininity.

Does androgyny confer any benefits that are greater than the sum of the benefits provided by masculinity and the benefits provided by femininity? Said another way, does being high in both masculinity and femininity give people some special kind of flexibility in their behavior, because of their ability to switch from one to the other? Most of the research has failed to find any such special benefit, although many researchers continue to look for better evidence. To date, the evidence suggests that masculinity and femininity provide separate, independent benefits (Marsh & Byrne, 1991; Spence, 1984).

Locus of Control

Do you think your success in life will depend mostly on your own efforts or mostly on circumstances beyond your control? People who believe they are largely in control of their lives are said to have an **internal locus of control**. Those who believe they are controlled mostly by external forces are said to have an **external locus of control** (Rotter, 1966). Table 13.3 lists some items from a questionnaire designed to measure locus of control. Many personality researchers and clinical psychologists use this questionnaire.

People's perception of their locus of control tends to be fairly consistent from one situation to another (Lefcourt, 1976). Those with an internal locus of control tend to take responsibility for their own behavior—for both their successes and their failures (see Figure 13.16). When someone of the opposite sex finds them attractive, they assume it is because of their charm. By contrast, people with an external locus of control assume that the other person was just easy to please.

People with an internal locus of control know that they are not *always* in control. If they buy a lottery ticket or play a game of chance, they realize that they have no control over the outcome. In fact, they tend to be less interested in games of chance than people with an external locus of control are (Lefcourt, 1976). They not only *believe* they are generally in control but also *like* to be in control.

Locus of control correlates with a number of other personality traits (Lefcourt, 1976). For

---

Table 13.3 Sample Items from the Internal-External Scale

For each item, choose the statement you agree with most closely.

1. a. Without the right breaks one cannot be an effective leader.

   b. Capable people who fail to become leaders have not taken advantage of their opportunities.

2. a. Becoming a success is a matter of hard work; luck has little or nothing to do with it.

   b. Getting a good job depends mainly on being in the right place at the right time.

3. a. As far as world affairs are concerned, most of us are the victims of forces we can neither understand nor control.

   b. By taking an active part in political and social affairs, the people can control world events.

4. a. Many times I feel that I have little influence over the things that happen to me.

   b. It is impossible for me to believe that chance or luck plays an important role in my life.

Source: Rotter, 1966, pp. 11–12.

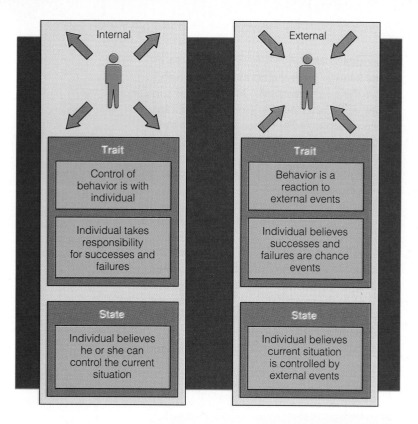

FIGURE 13.16
Locus of control can exist either as a lasting personality trait or as a tempo-rary state of behavior.

Regardless of whether people have an internal or an external locus of control, some people's ability to control events is limited. These Catholic refugees have fled the North Vietnamese army. They cannot defeat the army, but rather than live in the communist state it supports, they have chosen to leave. Would you guess that people who take such risky actions have an internal locus of control or an external one?

example, people with an internal locus of control tend to work longer on a problem before giving up. They are more likely to choose a larger reward next week over a smaller reward today. People with an external locus of control are more likely to feel depressed and helpless.

Locus of control may show itself as a tempo-rary state as well as a lasting trait. In other words, we may display an internal locus of control under certain circumstances and an exter-nal locus of control under others. For example, people generally display an internal locus of control when they are engaged in tasks that re-quire skill, when they make choices, and when they are competing against others.

THE FUTURE OF TRAIT RESEARCH

At the start of the discussion of traits, I re-marked that just as rocks are the same in some ways and different in others, personalities are the same in some ways and different in others. Let me push that analogy one step further: If we want to know *why* one rock differs from an-other, we have to start by describing the differ-ences among rocks as carefully as possible. Sim-ilarly, if we are ever going to understand what makes one personality different from another, we have to start with a description of personali-ties.

Psychologists do conduct research on the causes of personality differences. The discus-sion here has scarcely hinted at that research. Instead, I have emphasized the attempts to de-scribe personality, a challenging enough goal in itself. In the future, psychologists hope to have more to say about the underlying causes.

SUMMARY

- *Nomothetic and idiographic laws.* Psycholo-gists seek both nomothetic laws, which apply to all people, and idiographic laws, which apply to indi-vidual differences. (page 554)

- *Traits and states.* Traits are personality charac-teristics that persist over time; states are tempo-rary changes in behavior in response to particular situations. (page 554)

- *Criticisms of the trait approach.* Some personal-ity theorists have criticized the trait concept on the grounds that behavior seems to be inconsistent from one situation to another. (page 555)

■ *Defense of the trait approach.* Defenders of the trait concept point out that (1) we should not expect traits to be apparent at all times or in all situations, (2) people sometimes appear to be inconsistent in one trait only because they are more consistent in some other trait, and (3) traits sometimes appear to be inconsistent only because they have been measured inadequately. (page 556)

■ *Five major traits.* Psychologists seek a short list of traits that describes as much of behavior as possible. Much can be explained by these five traits: neuroticism, extraversion, openness to new experience, agreeableness, and conscientiousness. (page 557)

■ *Androgyny.* Androgyny is a trait that combines the features of masculinity and femininity. Psychologists are not sure whether it confers any special benefits beyond the separate benefits of its two components. (page 558)

■ *Locus of control.* People with an internal locus of control believe that for the most part they are in control of their lives. People with an external locus of control believe that their lives are controlled mostly by outside forces. (page 559)

SUGGESTION FOR FURTHER READING

Pervin, L. A. (1990). *Handbook of personality.* New York: Guilford Press. Contains summaries of contemporary theory and research on a wide variety of topics related to personality.

TERMS

nomothetic approach approach to the study of individual differences that seeks general laws about how some aspect of personality affects behavior, often based on statistical comparisons of large groups of people (page 554)

idiographic approach approach to the study of individual differences that concentrates on intensive studies of individuals (page 554)

trait a consistent, long-lasting tendency in behavior (page 554)

state a temporary activation of a particular behavior (page 554)

scripts rules of social behavior governing who will do what and when (page 555)

big five personality dimensions five traits that account for a great deal of human personality differences: neuroticism, extraversion, agreeableness, conscientiousness, and openness to new experience (page 557)

neuroticism tendency to experience unpleasant emotions relatively easily (page 557)

extraversion tendency to seek new experiences and to enjoy the company of other people (page 557)

agreeableness tendency to be compassionate toward others and not antagonistic (page 557)

conscientiousness tendency to show self-discipline, to be dutiful, and to strive for achievement and competence (page 557)

openness to experience tendency to enjoy new experiences, especially intellectual experiences, the arts, fantasies, and anything that exposes the person to new ideas (page 557)

androgyny tendency to be both masculine and feminine (page 558)

internal locus of control belief that one is largely in control of the major events of one's life (page 559)

external locus of control belief that external forces control the major events of one's life (page 559)

ANSWERS TO CONCEPT CHECKS

4. "Trait anxiety" is a tendency to experience anxiety in a wide variety of settings. "State anxiety" is anxiety evoked by a particular situation. Psychologists could observe whether this person's anxiety declines sharply when the situation changes. If it does, it is state anxiety. If not, it is trait anxiety. (page 555)

5. People tend to remember the occasions when someone's behavior matches his or her reputation. They regard occasions when behavior does not match the reputation as exceptions. (page 556)

6. They should determine whether measures of ambition correlate strongly with measures of sociability. If they do, then ambition and sociability are two aspects of a single trait, extraversion. If they do not correlate strongly, then they are indeed separate personality traits. (page 557)

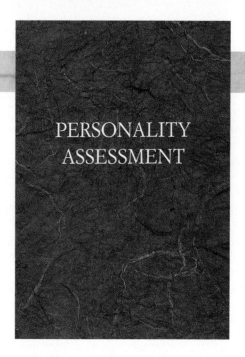

PERSONALITY
ASSESSMENT

How can we measure personality?

How can we use measurements of personality?

A new P. T. Barnum Psychology Clinic has just opened at your local shopping mall and is offering a Grand Opening Special on personality tests. You have always wanted to know more about yourself, so you sign up. Here is Barnum's true-false test.

Questionnaire for Universal Assessment of Zealous Youth (QUAZY)

1. I have never met a cannibal I didn't like.   T F

2. Robbery is the only major felony I have ever committed.   T F

3. I eat "funny mushrooms" less frequently than I used to.   T F

4. I don't care what people say about my nose-picking habit.   T F

5. Sex with vegetables no longer disgusts me.   T F

6. This time I am quitting glue-sniffing for good.   T F

7. I generally lie on questions like this one.   T F

8. I spent much of my childhood sucking on telephone cords.   T F

9. I find it impossible to sleep if I think my bed might be clean.   T F

10. Naked bus drivers make me nervous.   T F

11. Some of my friends don't know what a rotten person I am.   T F

12. I usually find laxatives unsatisfying.   T F

13. I spend my spare time playing strip solitaire.   T F

You turn in your answers. A few minutes later a computer prints out your individual personality profile:

You have a need for other people to like and admire you, and yet you tend to be critical of yourself. While you have some personality weaknesses, you are generally able to compensate for them. You have considerable unused capacity that you have not turned to your advantage. Disciplined and self-controlled on the outside, you tend to be worrisome and insecure on the inside. At times, you have serious doubts as to whether you have made the right decision or done the right thing. You prefer a certain amount of change and variety and become dissatisfied when hemmed in by restrictions and limitations. You also pride yourself as an independent thinker and do not accept others' statements without satisfactory proof. But you have found it unwise to be too frank in revealing yourself to others. At times you are extraverted, affable, and sociable, while at other times you are introverted, wary, and reserved. Some of your aspirations tend to be rather unrealistic. (Forer, 1949, p. 120)

Do you agree with this assessment?

An experiment along these lines has been conducted a number of times with psychology classes (Forer, 1949; Marks & Kammann, 1980; Ulrich, Stachnik, & Stainton, 1963). Students started by filling out a questionnaire—one that looked fairly reasonable, not something as preposterous as the QUAZY. Several days later, each student received a sealed envelope with his or her name on it. Inside was a "personality profile," supposedly based on the student's answers to the questionnaire. The students were asked, "How accurately does this profile describe you?" About 90% rated it good or excellent. Some expressed amazement at its accuracy: "I didn't realize until now that psychology was an exact science." Of course, none of them realized that everyone had received exactly the same personality profile—the same one you just read.

The students accepted this personality profile partly because it vaguely and generally describes almost everyone and partly because people tend to accept almost *any* statement that an "expert" makes about them. Richard Kammann repeated the experiment but substituted a strange, unflattering personality profile that included statements like "Your boundless energy is a little wearisome to your friends" and "You seem to find it impossible to work out a satisfactory adjustment to your problems." More than 20% of the students rated this unlikely assortment of statements a "good to excellent" description of their own personality (Marks & Kammann, 1980).

The moral of the story is this: Psychological testing is tricky. If we want to know whether a particular test measures a particular person's personality, we cannot simply ask whether or not that person thinks it does. Even if a test is totally worthless—horoscopes, palm reading, or the QUAZY—many people will describe its results as a "highly accurate" description of themselves. To devise a psychological test that not only *appears* to work but also actually *does* work, we need to go through some elaborate procedures to design the test carefully and to determine its reliability and validity.

STANDARDIZED PERSONALITY TESTS

Psychologists have devised a great variety of personality tests; they add new ones every year. A **standardized test** is one that is administered according to specified rules and whose scores are interpreted in a prescribed fashion. An important step in standardizing a test is to determine the distribution of scores for a large number of people. We need to know the mean score and the range of scores for people in general and the mean and the range for various special populations, such as severely depressed people. Given such information, we can determine whether a given individual's score on the test is within the normal range or whether it is more typical of people with some disorder.

Most of the tests published in popular magazines have never been standardized. A

Most people tend to accept almost any personality assessment someone offers them, especially if it is stated in vague, general terms that each person can interpret to fit himself or herself. To determine the accuracy of a personality test, we need objective information, not just self-reports by satisfied customers.

magazine may herald its article "Test Yourself: How Good Is Your Marriage?" or "Test Yourself: How Well Do You Control the Stress in Your Life?" After you have taken the test and compared your answers to the scoring key, the article may tell you that "if your score is greater than 80, you are doing very well . . . if it is below 20, you need to work on improving yourself!"—or some such nonsense. Unless the magazine states otherwise, you can take it for granted that the author pulled the scoring norms out of thin air and never even bothered to make sure that the items were clear and unambiguous.

Many of the best-known and most widely used standardized personality tests were devised with almost no theoretical basis. Their authors simply wanted to measure some of the ways in which one person differs from another, and they were almost indifferent to whether their tests had any connection with Freudian theory, Adlerian theory, or even the latest research on personality traits. We shall discuss some examples of well-established personality tests, but these may not be the final word. New tests with a clearer theoretical basis are on the way, including some that concentrate on measuring the "big five" personality dimensions (Costa, McCrae, & Dye, 1991).

OBJECTIVE TESTS OF PERSONALITY

Some of the most widely used personality tests are based on simple pencil-and-paper responses. We shall consider one of them—the MMPI—in some detail because it illustrates so many general points about personality testing. We shall then consider the 16-PF more briefly.

The Minnesota Multiphasic Personality Inventory (MMPI)

The **Minnesota Multiphasic Personality Inventory** (mercifully abbreviated **MMPI**) consists of a series of true-false questions. The original MMPI, developed in the 1940s and still in use, has 550 items; the second edition, **MMPI-2**, published in 1990, has 567. Typical items are "My mother never loved me" and "I think I would like the work of a pharmacist." (The items I give in this text are rewordings of the actual items.)

The original MMPI was devised *empirically*—that is, by trial and error (Hathaway & McKinley, 1940). The authors asked hundreds of people to answer hundreds of true-false questions about themselves. Then they posed the same questions to groups of depressed people, paranoid people, and people with other clinical disorders. They selected those items that most of the people in a given clinical group answered differently from the way most other people answered them. Their assumption was that if you answer many questions the way depressed people usually answer, you may be depressed too. The MMPI had 10 scales, for reporting a depression score, a paranoia score, a schizophrenia score, and others.

The result was a test that worked in practice. For example, the higher a person's score on the depression scale, the more likely that person would be diagnosed as depressed. Some of the items on the MMPI made sense theoretically; some did not. For example, some items on the depression scale asked about feelings of helplessness or worthlessness, which are an important part of depression. But two other items were "I attend church regularly" and "Occasionally I tease animals." If you answered *false* to either of those items, you would get a point on the depression scale! These items were included simply because in the original sample of people, depressed people were more likely than were nondepressed people to answer *false* on these items. Perhaps there was some good (if

nonobvious) reason for that tendency, or perhaps the tendency was just a coincidence. In either event, the items were included on the depression scale.

The MMPI-2

The MMPI was standardized in the 1940s. As time passed, the meaning of certain items, or at least of certain answers to them, changed. For example, how would you respond to the following item?

I believe I am important. T F

In the 1940s, fewer than 10% of all people marked this item true. At the time, "important" meant about the same as "famous," and people who called themselves important were thought to have an inflated view of themselves. Today most people mark this item true. After all, we now believe that every person is important.

What about this item?

I like to play drop the handkerchief. T F

Drop the handkerchief is a game similar to tag. It dropped out of popularity in the 1950s, and most people born since then have never even heard of the game, much less played it.

To bring the MMPI up to date, a group of psychologists rephrased some of the items, eliminated some, and added new ones to deal with drug abuse, suicidal ideas, Type A personality, and other issues that did not concern the psychologists of the 1940s (Butcher, Graham, Williams, & Ben-Porath, 1990). They removed items that had no theoretical connection to the personality dimensions they were supposed to measure. (For example, they deleted "Occasionally I tease animals" from the depression scale.) Then they tried out the new MMPI-2 on 2,600 people selected to resemble the current mix of age, sex, race, and education in the United States. In other words, the psychologists restandardized the test. (Any test has to be restandardized from time to time. You may recall from the discussion of IQ tests that certain items once considered difficult are now considered relatively easy.)

The MMPI-2 has 10 clinical scales, as shown in Table 13.4. The various scales have 32 to 78 items each, scattered throughout the test, rather than clustered. Most people get at least a few points on each scale; psychologists look for any score that is much higher than average as a sign of possible difficulties. Figure 13.17 shows how MMPI-2 scores are plotted.

Table 13.4 The Ten MMPI Clinical Scales

Scale	Typical Item
Hypochondriasis (Hs)	I have chest pains several times a week. (T)
Depression (D)	I am glad that I am alive. (F)
Hysteria (Hy)	My heart frequently pounds so hard I can hear it. (T)
Psychopathic deviate (Pd)	I get a fair deal from most people. (F)
Masculinity-femininity (Mf)	I like to arrange flowers. (T = female)
Paranoia (Pa)	There are evil people trying to influence my mind. (T)
Psychasthenia (obsessive-compulsive) (Pt)	I save nearly everything I buy, even after I have no use for it. (T)
Schizophrenia (Sc)	I see, hear, and smell things that no one else knows about. (T)
Hypomania (Ma)	When things are dull I try to get some excitement started. (T)
Social introversion (Si)	I have the time of my life at parties. (F)

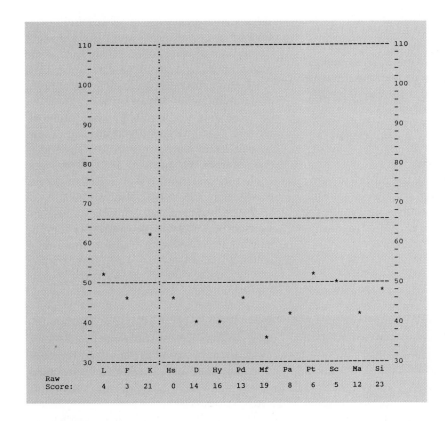

FIGURE 13.17

For the MMPI-2's 10 clinical scales, a score is plotted to profile an individual, as shown here. This is the profile of a middle-aged man with no psychological problems. A person with a disorder such as hypochondria or paranoia would have certain scores in the range of 65 or higher. (Source: Minnesota Multiphasic Personality Inventory-2, © by the Regents of the University of Minnesota. Data courtesy of R. J. Huber.)

The Generalizability of the MMPI

Your personality is such an integral part of what you are; is it really possible for one test to measure personality for all kinds of people? In particular, is the MMPI (or MMPI-2) a fair measure of personality for people of different racial and cultural backgrounds?

This is a difficult question to answer for many reasons, perhaps the main one being that race is a loose concept. The personality differences that occur within a given race are enormous compared to the very small differences that occur on the average between one race and another (Zuckerman, 1990). The MMPI reveals only small or inconsistent differences among African-Americans, European-Americans, Asian-Americans, Native Americans, and Hispanics (Greene, 1987b). With regard to the small differences that do emerge, we do not know whether they reflect real differences in personality or differences in understanding what certain questions mean. Consequently, psychologists use the same norms for all races, but they are slightly more cautious about interpreting the scores of racial minorities, especially for those people who are most impoverished and least educated (Gynther, 1989).

Detection of Deception on the MMPI and Elsewhere

Suppose you were taking the MMPI or some other personality test and you wanted to make yourself look mentally healthier than you really are. Could you lie on the test? Yes. Could anyone catch you in your lies? Again, yes.

The designers of both the MMPI and the MMPI-2 included in their test certain items designed to identify people who are consistently lying (Woychyshyn, McElheran, & Romney, 1992). For example, consider the items "I like every person I have ever met" and "Occasionally I get angry at someone." If you answer true to the first question and false to the second, you are either a saint or a liar. The test authors, convinced that there are more liars than saints, would give you two points on a special "lie scale." If you get too many points on the lie scale, a psychologist will refuse to trust your answers on the other items. Some people lie on the test to try to make themselves look *bad,* strangely enough. The test has some special items to detect that kind of faking also.

A similar method is used to detect deception on other types of tests. For example, many employers ask job applicants to fill out a questionnaire that asks them how much experience they have had with certain job-related skills. What is to prevent eager applicants from exaggerating or even lying about their experience? To find out whether applicants are lying, some employers include among the authentic items a few bogus items referring to nonexistent tasks, as shown in Table 13.5.

According to the results of one study, almost half of all job applicants claimed experience at one or more nonexistent tasks (Anderson, Warner, & Spencer, 1984). Moreover, applicants who claimed a great deal of experience at nonexistent tasks also overstated their ability on real tasks. An employer can use answers on bogus items as a correction factor. The more skill an applicant claims to have on a

Table 13.5 Part of an Employment Application, Designed to Determine Whether Applicants Are Lying About Their Skills

How much experience have you had at:	None	A Little	Much
Matrixing solvency files?	___	___	___
Typing from audio-fortran reports?	___	___	___
Determining myopic weights for periodic tables?	___	___	___
Resolving disputes by isometric analysis?	___	___	___
Stocking solubility product constants?	___	___	___
Planning basic entropy programs?	___	___	___
Operating a matriculation machine?	___	___	___

nonexistent task, the more the employer discounts that applicant's claims of skill on real tasks.

Something to Think About

Could you use this strategy in other situations? Suppose a political candidate promises to increase aid to college students. You are skeptical. How could you use the candidate's statements on other issues to help you decide whether or not to believe this promise?

Uses of the MMPI

The MMPI is useful to researchers who want to measure personality traits to see how they correlate with other traits or to test a theory of personality development. It is also useful to clinical psychologists who want to learn something about a client before beginning therapy or who want an independent measure of how much a client's personality has changed during the course of therapy (McReynolds, 1985).

How informative are the results to the client who actually takes the test? In some cases, they point out some problem to which the person had paid little attention. In other cases, however, the results do little more than restate the obvious. For example, suppose you gave the following answers on the MMPI or MMPI-2:

I doubt that I will ever be successful.	True
I am glad that I am alive.	False
I have thoughts about suicide.	True
I am helpless to control the important events in my life.	True

A psychologist analyzes your answer sheet and tells you, "Your results show indications of depression." In a sense, this may seem so self-evident that you begin to question the whole point of taking the test. But even in a case like this, the results can be useful—not just for telling you that you are depressed (which you already knew), but for measuring *how* depressed you are at this moment (a basis for comparison of future results).

The 16-PF Test

The **16-PF Test** is another widely used standardized personality test. The term "PF" stands for personality factors. The test measures 16 factors, or traits, of personality. Unlike the

MMPI, which was intended primarily to identify abnormal personalities, the 16-PF Test was devised to assess various aspects of normal personality. Raymond Cattell (1965) used factor analysis to identify the traits that contribute most significantly to personality. As we saw earlier in this chapter, other psychologists using factor analysis identified 5 major traits; Cattell found 16. He then devised a test to measure each of those traits. Because of the large number of factors, the results of his test apply to a rather wide range of behaviors (Krug, 1978).

When someone takes the 16-PF Test, the results are printed out as a **personality profile**, as Figure 13.18 shows. By examining such a profile, an experienced psychologist can determine the person's dominant personality traits.

Although the 16-PF Test was originally designed to assess normal personality, it does enable clinicians to identify various abnormalities, such as schizophrenia, depression, and alcoholism (Kerzendorfer, 1977). Each disorder is associated with a characteristic personality profile (Figure 13.19). As with any test, it should be used cautiously, especially with people from different cultural backgrounds. Psychologists have translated this test into other languages, but often something gets lost in translation. One study found that Mexican-Americans taking the 16-PF in Spanish had substantially different personality profiles than did Mexican-Americans taking supposedly the "same" test in English (Whitworth & Perry, 1990).

PROJECTIVE TESTS

The MMPI, the 16-PF, and similar personality tests are easy to score and easy to handle statistically, but they restrict how a person can respond to a question. To find out more, psychologists ask open-ended questions that permit an unlimited range of responses.

Simply to say "Tell me about yourself" rarely evokes much information. In fact, most people find such invitations threatening. They may not be fully honest even with themselves, much less with a psychologist they have just met.

Many people find it easier to discuss their problems in the abstract than in the first person. For instance, they might say, "I have a friend with this problem. Let me tell you my friend's problem and ask what my friend should do." They then describe their own problem. They are "projecting" their problem onto someone

FIGURE 13.18
Personality profiles on the 16-PF test for airline pilots, creative artists, and writers. A personality profile shows whether people are high or low on a given trait. In this sample, writers were the most imaginative group. (Adapted from Handbook for the Sixteen Personality Factors, *copyright 1970 by the Institute for Personality and Ability Testing, Inc. Reproduced by permission of the copyright owners.)*

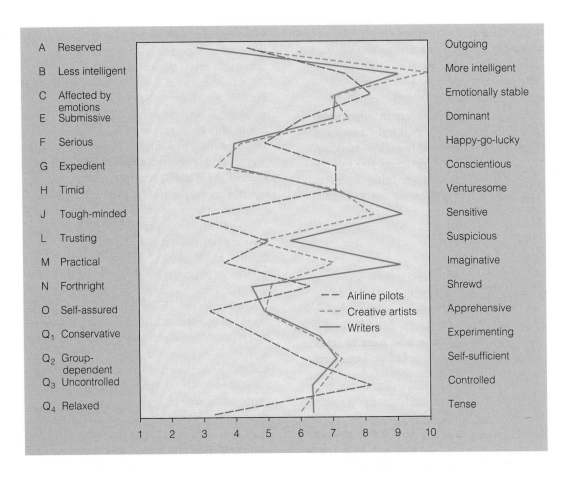

FIGURE 13.19
This personality profile, based on the 16-PF Test, shows that this person is high in guilt, low in "ego strength." Cattell made up his own words for familiar concepts so that he could provide a precise definition that would not be confused with the everyday and vague meaning of a term such as depression. For example, surgency means something similar to cheerfulness and sociability. Parmia resembles adventurousness or boldness. (From Cattell, 1965).

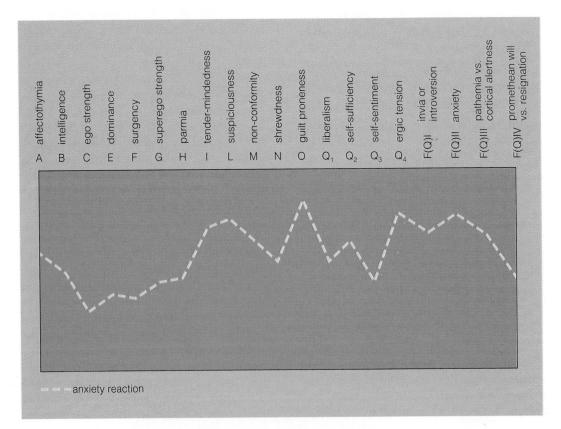

else, in Freud's sense of the word—attributing their own characteristics to someone else.

Rather than discouraging projection, psychologists often make use of it. They use projective tests, which are designed to encourage people to project their personality characteristics onto ambiguous stimuli. This strategy helps people reveal themselves more fully than they normally would to a stranger, or even to themselves. Let's consider two of the best-known projective tests.

■ CONCEPT CHECK

7. Which of the following is a projective test? (a) A psychologist gives a child a set of puppets with instructions to act out a story about a family. (b) A psychologist hands you a stack of cards, each containing one word such as tolerant, *with instructions to sort them into two piles—a stack of cards that apply to you and a stack of cards that do not apply to you. (Check your answer on page 573.)*

Rorschach Inkblot Test

The **Rorschach Inkblot Test** is probably the most famous projective test of personality. It was created by Hermann Rorschach, a Swiss psychiatrist, who was interested in art and the occult. He read a book of poems by Justinus Kerner, a mystic writer, who had made a series of random inkblots and had then written a poem about each one. Kerner believed that anything that happens at random reveals the influence of occult, supernatural forces.

Rorschach made his own inkblots but put them to a different use. He was familiar with a word-association test then in use in which a person was given a word and was asked to say the first word that came to mind. Rorschach combined this approach with his inkblots: He showed people an inkblot and then asked them to say what came to mind (Pichot, 1984).

After testing a series of inkblots on his patients, Rorschach noticed that they reported seeing different things in the inkblots. In a book published in 1921 (English translation, 1942) he presented the 10 inkblots that still constitute the Rorschach Inkblot Test. (Originally he had worked with a larger number, but the publisher insisted on cutting the number to 10 to save printing costs.) As other psychiatrists and psychologists began using these blots, the Rorschach gradually evolved into the projective test we know today.

The Rorschach Inkblot Test consists of 10 cards similar to the one in Figure 13.20. Five are black and white; five are in color. If you take this test, a psychologist will hand you a card and ask, "What might this be?" (Figure 13.21). The instructions are intentionally vague. The assumption is that everything you do in an ill-defined situation will reveal something significant about your personality to the psychologist—and the more poorly defined the situation, the better. The psychologist may keep a record of almost everything you do, including what you say you see, where and how you hold the cards, the length of any pauses between your responses, and so forth.

Because everything you do, down to blinking your eyes, is considered significant, the psychologist avoids suggesting what you should do. (If you want to get a psychologist really flustered, say that you do not understand what is expected and you would like an example of what to say. The one thing a psychologist can never do with the Rorschach is to give an example.)

Sometimes people's answers are highly revealing. For example, one woman, who was having serious marital difficulties, gave the following responses:

(Card 1) Outer looks like wings of a butterfly . . . and inner details, a stolid woman. Butterfly may in a sense be pulling at the woman in two different directions. One is responsibility and obligation, and the other direction is pursuit of a [long pause] well, love, selfish but satisfying.

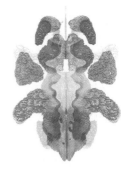

FIGURE 13.20
In the Rorschach Inkblot Test, people look at a pattern similar to this one and tell what it looks like to them. The underlying theory is that when the situation is ambiguous, whatever someone does will reveal the individual's personality.

FIGURE 13.21
In the Rorschach Inkblot Test, there are no wrong or right answers. The psychologist records the client's visual associations and behavior and later interprets them.

(Card 3) Seems to suggest two human forms . . . facing each other. . . . Myself, both myself . . . one part tells me one way; another portion, a completely contradictory way. . . . Red in center seems to suggest . . . almost in a romantic sense . . . the heart. . . . This is feminine form, and they are connected to this, the right and the left of it. Therefore, two sides. The right meaning which is right or constructive, the left which would be the destructive or the shortsighted way. The immediate impact was two figures facing each other. Both emanate from one female form and it seemed to be concerned with the romantic affair of the heart. I'm all three. (Beck, 1960, pp. 58–59)

Granted that people's answers on the Rorschach often contain a wealth of personal information, the key issue is whether or not psychologists can find a dependable way to interpret that information. In the 1950s and 1960s, certain psychologists made wild and unsupportable claims, even calling the Rorschach "an X ray of the mind." Those claims provoked equally enthusiastic criticisms. Part of the trouble with the Rorschach is that each person sees different things in different cards and that someone who takes the Rorschach at several different times may give different responses each time. Hence the reliability of the test (the repeatability of its scores) is not outstanding—about .83 according to one review (Parker, 1983).

A more serious difficulty is that for many years different psychologists were interpreting the Rorschach results in different ways. In the 1960s five different systems of interpreting the Rorschach were in use by various psychologists, and more than one fifth of all psychologists were using their own personally invented method or were just drawing subjective impressions from people's answers (Exner, 1986). In other words, if you had taken the Rorschach test in the 1960s with 5 to 10 different psychologists, each might have drawn a different conclusion about your personality, even though you gave each one the same answers. (The situation was similar to taking a final exam in some course and having different students' papers graded by different answer keys.)

Since the 1980s, a scoring system devised by James Exner (1986) has become the dominant approach, and different psychologists are more likely today than in the past to agree on their interpretations of someone's Rorschach re-

sponses. Its validity is still controversial. For a personality test we measure the validity by asking whether the test results can identify which people have serious psychological problems and which people do not. The answer is, yes, at least statistically speaking, the test can make such discriminations. For example, on the average, people who are just starting psychotherapy make many responses suggesting psychological distress; after months or years of psychotherapy they give fewer such responses (Weiner & Exner, 1991). People who (according to their therapists) rely heavily on repression give characteristic answers that other people seldom give (Viglione, Brager, & Haller, 1991). So far, so good. The controversy concerns whether or not these statistical differences are powerful enough to make decisions about a given individual. That is, can the test identify someone's psychological disorder with, say, 90–95% accuracy? According to one study, the Rorschach can identify schizophrenia with about that accuracy. For other disorders, it can tell us that a given person has *some* sort of problem, but it cannot identify the particular problem with much certainty (Vincent & Harman, 1991).

■ CONCEPT CHECK

8. *Why would it be impossible to receive a copy of the Rorschach Inkblot Test by mail, fill it out, and mail it back to a psychologist to evaluate your answers? (Check your answer on page 573.)*

The Thematic Apperception Test

The **Thematic Apperception Test (TAT)** consists of 20 pictures like the one shown in Figure 13.22. It was devised by Christiana Morgan and Henry Murray as a means of measuring people's needs; it was revised and published by Murray (1943). Different sets of pictures are used for women, men, boys, and girls. The subject is asked to make up a story for each picture, describing what is happening, what events led up to the scene, and what will happen in the future. The pictures are all somewhat ambiguous but, except for the 20th card (which is blank!), they provide a better-defined stimulus than does the Rorschach.

People who take the TAT are expected to identify with the people shown in the pictures. That is why men are given pictures showing mostly men, and women are given pictures showing mostly women. People usually tell stories that relate to recent events and concerns in their own lives, possibly including concerns they would be reluctant to talk about openly.

For example, one young man told the following story about a picture of a man clinging to a rope:

This man is escaping. Several months ago he was beat up and shanghaied and taken aboard ship. Since then, he has been mistreated and unhappy and has been looking for a way to escape. Now the ship is anchored near a tropical island and he is climbing down a rope to the water. He will get away successfully and swim to shore. When he gets there, he will be met by a group of beautiful native women with whom he will live the rest of his life in luxury and never tell anyone what happened. Sometimes he will feel that he should go back to his old life; but he will never do it. (Kimble & Garmezy, 1968, pp. 582–583)

This young man had entered divinity school, mainly to please his parents, but was quite unhappy there. He was wrestling with a secret desire to "escape" to a new life with greater worldly pleasures. In his story, he described someone doing what he really wanted to do but could not openly admit.

The TAT is often used in a clinical setting to get clients to speak freely about their problems. It is also used for research purposes. For instance, an investigator might measure someone's "need for achievement" by counting all the stories he or she tells about achievement. The same might be done for aggression, passivity, control of outside events, or dominance. The investigator could use the findings to study the forces that strengthen or weaken various needs and why certain groups of people express different needs.

For most purposes, the reliability of the TAT is rather low, in some studies as low as .3 or .4. (That is, someone who takes the test on two occasions is likely to give different answers each time.) Psychologists have identified two reasons for this low reliability. First, the instructions imply that the person should tell a "creative" (that is, a new) story, not the same story he or she told the last time. A change in the instructions can increase the reliability (Lundy, 1985). Second, a person's responses on the TAT may vary considerably from time to time because the test measures current concerns, which change over time (Lundy, 1985). Generally, TAT results correspond better to what a person *has done recently* than to what he or she

will do in the future (Anastasi, 1988). For that reason, it might be better to say that the TAT measures "current concerns" rather than "needs."

USES AND MISUSES OF PERSONALITY TESTS

Before any drug company can market a new drug in the United States, the Food and Drug Administration (FDA) requires that it be carefully tested. If the FDA finds it safe and effective, it approves the drug for certain purposes, with a warning label that lists precautions, such as an advisory that certain kinds of people should avoid taking it. After it is approved, however, the FDA cannot prevent a physician from prescribing it for some unapproved purpose and it cannot keep it out of the hands of people who should not be taking it.

Personality tests are a little like drugs: They ought to be used with great caution, and only for the purposes for which they have demonstrable usefulness. They are, at a minimum, helpful to psychologists as an interviewing technique, to help "break the ice" and get a good conversation started with a client. Tests can also be useful as an aid in personality assessment by a clinical psychologist. Note that I said "as an aid." The test results should not be used by themselves to determine someone's problem. For example, suppose someone has an MMPI personality profile that resembles the profile typical for schizophrenia. Identifying schizophrenia or any other unusual condition is a signal-detection problem, as we discussed in Chapter 4—a problem of detecting a stimulus when it is present without reporting it when it is absent. Suppose (realistically) that people without schizophrenia outnumber people with schizophrenia by 100 to 1. Suppose further that a particular personality profile on the MMPI-2 is characteristic of 95% of people with schizophrenia and only 5% of other people. As Figure 13.23 shows, 5% of the normal population is a *larger* group than 95% of the schizophrenic population. Thus, if we called everyone "schizophrenic" who had a high score, we would be wrong more often than right. (Recall the representativeness heuristic and the issue of base-rate information, discussed in Chapter 9: Someone who seems "representative" of people in some rare category may not necessarily belong to that category.) Therefore, a conscientious

FIGURE 13.22
In the Thematic Apperception Test, people look at a picture such as this one and tell a story about what is going on. Most people include material that relates to current concerns in their lives.

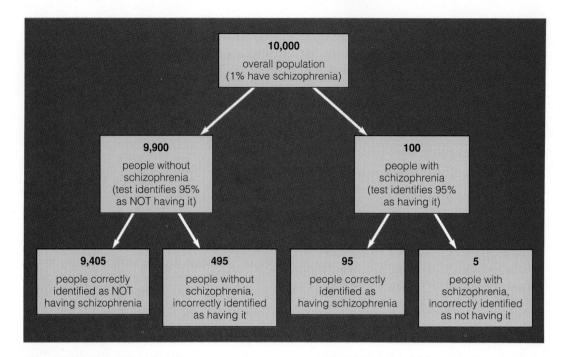

FIGURE 13.23

Even the best personality tests make mistakes. A test to detect an unusual condition will often identify normal people as having the condition. Here, we assume that a certain profile occurs in 95% of people with schizophrenia and 5% of other people. If we relied entirely on this test, we would correctly identify 95 schizophrenic people, but we would also identify 495 normal people as schizophrenic.

psychologist uses a test score as only one line of evidence; he or she will look for other confirmatory evidence before deciding what someone's problem is.

Some employers use personality tests to screen job applicants, selecting only those who have the "right" personality. For example, some companies want to hire only people with an "aggressive" personality for sales jobs. Others want to eliminate anyone who shows signs of any psychological abnormality. As a rule, personality tests have a rather low predictive validity for this purpose; in many cases they have no demonstrated validity at all. For example, a personality test that claims to measure an "aggressive" personality may not measure the kind of aggressiveness that presumably helps in a sales job. For ethical, legal, and practical reasons, employers should use personality tests *only* when they have clear evidence that the results help them to select the best job applicants more accurately than they could select without the tests.

SUMMARY

- *People's tendency to accept personality test results.* Because most people are inclined to accept almost any interpretation of their personality based on a personality test, tests must be carefully scrutinized to ensure that they are measuring what they claim to measure. (page 562)

- *Standardized personality tests.* A standardized test is one that is administered according to explicit rules and whose results are interpreted in a prescribed fashion. Standards are based on the scores of people who have already taken the test. (page 563)

- *The MMPI.* The MMPI, a widely used personality test, consists of a series of true-false questions selected in an effort to distinguish among various personality types. The MMPI-2 is a modernization of the version developed in the 1940s. (page 564)

- *Detection of lying.* The MMPI and certain other tests guard against lying by including items on which nearly all honest people will give the same answer. Any other answer is probably a lie. An unusual number of "lying" answers will invalidate the results. (page 566)

■ *The 16-PF Test.* The 16-PF Test, another standardized personality test, measures 16 personality traits. Although it was designed primarily to measure normal personality, its results do distinguish between normal and abnormal personalities. (page 567)

■ *Projective tests.* A projective test—such as the Rorschach Inkblot Test or the Thematic Apperception Test—lets people describe their concerns indirectly while talking about "the person in the picture" or about some other ambiguous stimulus. Projective tests can provide a wealth of information about a person, but that information is difficult to interpret. (page 567)

■ *Uses and misuses of personality tests.* Personality tests can be an aid to assessing personality, but their results should be interpreted cautiously in conjunction with other evidence. They should be used for selection only when evidence clearly indicates that the results are valid for this purpose. (page 571)

SUGGESTION FOR FURTHER READING

Anastasi, A. (1988). *Psychological testing* (6th ed.). New York: Macmillan. A good textbook on both personality testing and IQ testing.

TERMS

standardized test a test that is administered according to specified rules and whose scores are interpreted in a prescribed fashion (page 563)

Minnesota Multiphasic Personality Inventory (MMPI) a standardized personality test consisting of true-false items, intended to measure various clinical conditions (page 564)

MMPI-2 the modernized edition of the MMPI (page 564)

16-PF Test a standardized personality test that measures 16 personality traits (page 567)

personality profile a graph that shows an individual's scores on scales measuring a number of personality traits (page 567)

Rorschach Inkblot Test a projective personality test in which people are shown 10 inkblots and asked what each might be (page 569)

Thematic Apperception Test (TAT) a projective personality test in which a person is asked to tell a story about each of 20 pictures (page 570)

ANSWERS TO CONCEPT CHECKS

7. (a) The puppet activity could be a projective test, because the child is likely to project his or her own family concerns onto the puppets, using them to enact various problems. (page 569)

8. The Rorschach Inkblot Test must be administered in person by a psychologist who observes how you hold the cards, whether you rotate them, and anything else you do. The psychologist may also ask you to explain where you see something or why it looks the way you say it does. (page 570)

14 ABNORMAL BEHAVIOR

Over the past 4 months, George has struck and injured several dozen people, most of whom he hardly knew. Two of them had to be sent to the hospital. George expresses no guilt, no regrets. He says he would attack every one of them again if he got the chance. What should society do with George?

1. Send him to jail?

2. Commit him to a mental hospital?

3. Give him an award for being the best defensive lineman in the league?

Before you can answer, you must know the context of George's behavior. Behavior that seems normal at a party might seem bizarre at a business meeting. Behavior that earns millions for a rock singer might earn a trip to the mental hospital for a college professor. Behavior that is perfectly routine in one culture might be considered criminal in another.

Even when we know the context of someone's behavior, we may wonder whether it is "normal." Suppose your rich Aunt Tillie starts to pass out $5 bills to strangers on the street corner and vows that she will keep on doing so until she has exhausted her entire fortune. Is she mentally ill? Should the court commit her to a mental hospital and turn her fortune over to you as her trustee?

A man claims to be Jesus Christ and asks permission to appear before the United Nations to announce God's message to the world. A psychiatrist is sure that he can relieve this man of his disordered thinking by giving him antipsychotic drugs, but the man refuses to take them and insists that his thinking is perfectly normal. Should we force him to take the drugs, just ignore him, or put his address on the agenda of the United Nations?

What is normal? Rock musicians can earn fortunes from behavior that would get most people fired. Groups like the Plasmatics vie for attention by deliberately looking provocatively strange.

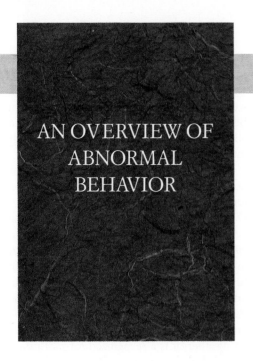

AN OVERVIEW OF ABNORMAL BEHAVIOR

Why do some people behave abnormally?

What are the most common kinds of abnormal behavior?

Students in medical school often contract what is known as "medical students' disease." Imagine that you are just beginning your training in medicine. One of your textbooks describes "Cryptic Ruminating Umbilicus Disorder":

"The symptoms are very minor until the condition becomes hopeless. The first symptom is a pale tongue." (You go to the mirror. You can't remember what your tongue is supposed to look like, but it *does* look a little pale.) "Later a hard spot forms in the neck." (You feel your neck. "Wait! I never felt *this* before! I think it's something hard!") "Just before the arms and legs fall off, there is shortness of breath, increased heart rate, and sweating." (Already distressed, you *do* have shortness of breath, your heart *is* racing, and you *are* sweating profusely.)

Sooner or later, most medical students decide they have some dreaded illness. The problem is imaginary; they merely confuse the description of some disease with their own normal condition. When my brother was in medical school, he diagnosed himself as having a rare, fatal illness, checked himself into a hospital, and wrote a will. (Today he is a successful physician.)

"Medical students' disease" is even more common among students of psychological dis-

orders. As you read this chapter and the next, you may decide that you are suffering from some such disorder: "That sounds exactly like me! I must have Deteriorating Raving Odd Omnivorous Lycanthropy!"

Well, maybe you do and maybe you don't. Psychological disorders are just exaggerations of tendencies that nearly all of us have. The difference between "normal" and "psychologically disordered" is a matter of degree.

CONCEPTS OF ABNORMAL BEHAVIOR

What constitutes abnormal behavior or psychological disorder? In a descriptive sense, "normal" is average, and anything that differs very much from the average is said to be abnormal. But by that definition, unusually happy or unusually successful people would be considered abnormal.

We might define abnormal behavior as any behavior that distresses a person, any behavior that a person wants to escape from. But some people say they are doing just fine, even though their behavior strikes everyone else as bizarre.

The American Psychiatric Association (1987) has defined psychological disorders as patterns of behavior associated with distress (pain) or disability (impaired functioning) or with an increased risk of death, pain, or loss of freedom. We can question that definition as well. For example, when Martin Luther King, Jr., fought for the rights of African-Americans, he engaged in behaviors that brought the risk of death, pain, and loss of freedom. But we regard his acts as heroic, not abnormal.

Another definition is that abnormal behavior is behavior that a particular culture regards as troublesome or unacceptable. For example, someone who is frequently intoxicated with alcohol may be considered normal in one society, abnormal in another. People whose only problem is that they see things and hear things that no one else does may be put into a mental hospital, or they may be revered as visionaries, depending on the beliefs of their society (Leff, 1981). The difficulty with defining abnormal behavior as a behavior a society does not accept is that it does not tell us what behavior a society

To determine whether a behavior is normal or abnormal, heroic or deeply disturbed, we have to know its social and cultural context. Here, Iranian worshippers flog themselves to reenact the suffering of an early Shi'ite martyr. In this context, self-flogging is a normal part of a religious ritual. In some other context, it might be a sign of psychological distress.

ior as "mental illness." They tried to find its cause and a way to cure it, just as they did in treating other illnesses. In various parts of the world today, some cultures regard abnormal behaviors as biological disorders, some still talk about demon possession, and some have other interpretations.

Cultures differ not only in their views of abnormal behavior; they also differ in the behaviors themselves (Berry, Poortinga, Segal, & Dasen, 1992). For example, you probably have heard the expression "to run amok." *Running amok* is a type of abnormal behavior recognized in parts of Southeast Asia, in which someone (usually a male) runs around engaging in furious, almost indiscriminate violent behavior. *Pibloqtoq* is an uncontrollable desire to tear off one's clothing and expose oneself to severe winter weather; it is a recognized form of psychological disorder in parts of Greenland, Alaska, and the Arctic regions of Canada. *Latah* is an apparently uncontrollable tendency to imitate other people's actions, reported among women of Malaysia. *Brain fag* is a condition of headache, eye fatigue, and inability to concentrate—a common complaint among West African students just before exams. And consider our own society: We recognize *anorexia nervosa* as a psychological disorder that entails voluntary starvation. That disorder is well known in Europe, North America, and Australia, but unheard-of in many other parts of the world.

What are we to make of the fact that certain disorders occur in some cultures but not others? One interpretation is that the conditions necessary for causing them occur in some places but not others. Another interpretation is that people learn certain kinds of abnormal behavior by imitation. Perhaps if you had seen people "run amok" from time to time, you might react to some distressing situation by doing the same yourself.

should accept. Some totalitarian governments have classed all political dissidents as "mentally ill."

In short, there may be no simple way to define abnormal behavior or psychological disorder. Our lack of a clear definition is a problem in some cases and not in others. For example, severely depressed people may be distressed or disordered by everyone's definition, including their own. But someone who defies the usual customs of personal hygiene and polite speech may seem "severely disordered" to some observers and merely "eccentric" to others.

Cultural Differences in Views of Abnormal Behavior

Abnormal behavior has been known in all cultures throughout history. Each time and place has interpreted such behavior according to its own worldview. People in the Middle Ages, for example, regarded bizarre behavior as a sign that the disturbed person was possessed by a demon. To exorcise the demon, priests resorted to prescribed religious rituals (Figure 14.1). During the 1800s, when the "germ" theory of illness was popular and people sought a scientific explanation for everything they observed, physicians interpreted abnormal behav-

Competing Views of Abnormal Behavior

Among therapists and researchers today, *one influential point of view is that many psychological disorders are the result of biological disorders,* including genetics, brain damage, chemical imbalances in the brain, hormonal abnormalities, poor nutrition, inadequate sleep, various diseases, and overuse of certain drugs, including over-the-counter medications. *A second point of view is that some psychological disorders are the result of disordered thinking caused by early ex-*

periences. That is essentially the Freudian point of view. Even many theorists who disagree with Freud believe that traumatic experiences early in life may later distort people's thinking. *A third point of view is that some psychological disorders are learned reactions to a stressful or unsupportive environment* that the person is trying to cope with as well as possible.

For illustration, consider alcohol abuse. Someone may become an alcohol abuser because of a genetic tendency or other biological factors, the effects of early family life, or the stresses of current life. Naturally, these explanations are compatible with one another; a given individual may develop an alcohol problem for a combination of several reasons. Tracking down the causes of psychological disorders turns out to be quite a challenge.

THE PREVALENCE OF PSYCHOLOGICAL DISORDERS

It is difficult to estimate how widespread psychological disorders are because only about one third of all people suffering from them seek professional help, and even those who do seek help are as likely to go to their family doctor as to a psychiatrist or a psychologist (Shapiro et al., 1984). The only way to assemble accurate data on the prevalence of various disorders is to survey a large random sample of people over a wide geographic area.

Such a survey, of about 20,000 people, was conducted in Baltimore, St. Louis, and New Haven (Eaton et al., 1984; Regier et al., 1984). Trained interviewers tried to reach all the "usual residents" of each selected neighborhood, including those who lived at home and those who lived in institutions such as prisons, mental hospitals, and nursing homes. They found that about one fifth of all adults were suffering from a psychological disorder of some sort (as defined by the American Psychiatric Association) and that close to one third had suffered from such a disorder at some time during their life (Myers et al., 1984; Robins et al., 1984).

The most common psychological disorders are phobia and other anxiety disorders, alcohol or drug abuse, and mood disorders (including depression). As Figure 14.2 shows, each of these three problems affects about 10–20% of all people at some time during their life. That figure is only approximate because each disorder occurs in varying degrees and because dif-

FIGURE 14.1
Peculiar behavior was once explained as demon possession. Here St. Zenobius exorcises devils, fleeing from the mouths of the possessed. At the time of this late 15th-century work, attributed to Botticelli, the priest Savonarola was exorcising the city with public burnings of luxury goods.

ferent psychologists set different cutoffs for what constitutes a "disorder."

THE CLASSIFICATION OF PSYCHOLOGICAL DISORDERS

Any scientific study must be based on some accepted method for classifying information. Imagine what biology would be like if biologists had no systematic way of classifying animals: Someone publishes an article about the mating behavior of a "black bird." You try to replicate the study, but you get different results. Then you discover that the black bird the first researcher studied was a crow, whereas you have

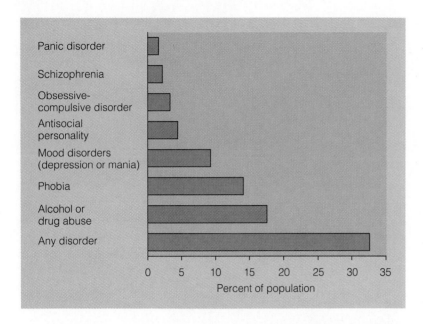

FIGURE 14.2

Almost 20% of the people surveyed in three U.S. cities had some psychological disorder at some time during their lifetime (Myers et al., 1984; Robins et al., 1984). These figures—a combination of self-reports and the assessment of trained interviewers—are estimates that do not indicate the severity of the disorder in individuals. The total percentage for disorders (32%) is less than the total of the seven categories (49%) because some people have two or more disorders. The homeless were not surveyed.

been studying a raven. To avoid such confusion, biologists use a system of classification in which each term refers to one and only one species.

Similarly, we need a clear, unambiguous system of classifying psychological disorders. Psychiatrists and clinical psychologists have been trying for years to devise such a system of classification, though they have not yet fully succeeded. One difficulty is that many psychological disorders are poorly understood, and it is difficult to classify items that we do not understand. A second difficulty is that many people have more than one disorder or what seems to be a mixture of disorders.

Currently, the most widely used classification scheme is the one adopted by the American Psychiatric Association (1987) in its ***Diagnostic and Statistical Manual of Mental Disorders, Third Edition—Revised,*** commonly known as **DSM III-R.** It lists the acceptable labels for all psychological disorders (alcohol intoxication, exhibitionism, pathological gambling, anorexia nervosa, sleepwalking disorder, stuttering, and hundreds of others), with a description of each and guidelines on how to dis-

tinguish it from similar disorders. DSM III-R describes disorders as they appear in North America and Europe; other societies have variations on these disorders and additional disorders that we do not see (Leff, 1981). I shall use the terminology of DSM III-R in this chapter. The American Psychiatric Association plans to publish a new edition, DSM IV, in the 1990s.

The clinicians and researchers who use DSM III-R classify each client along five separate *axes* (lists). A person may have more than one disorder on a given axis—for example, alcohol abuse and depression—or may have none at all. Axes 1 to 3 categorize specific disorders. Axis 1 lists disorders that have their onset at some time after infancy. These are the disorders that psychologists and psychiatrists deal with most frequently; in most cases the person has a realistic chance of recovery. Table 14.1 lists some of the categories of disorder on Axis 1.

Axis 2 lists disorders that generally persist throughout life, such as mental retardation and personality disorders (see Table 14.2). These conditions are almost part of the person himself or herself, rather than something the person has acquired. A **personality disorder** is a maladaptive, inflexible way of dealing with the environment and other people, such as antisocial behavior or an avoidance of other people. While many other psychological disorders resemble medical disease to some extent, personality disorders clearly do not. They seem to be an integral part of the person, like being tall, or left handed, or red headed. People with personality disorders seldom complain about their condition. When they seek treatment, it is generally at the insistence of their family, acquaintances, or employer.

Axis 3 lists physical disorders, such as diabetes or alcoholic cirrhosis of the liver, that may affect a person's behavior. Ordinarily a psychotherapist does not treat a person for an Axis 3 disorder, but awareness of the Axis 3 disorder might affect interpretation or treatment of some disorder listed on Axis 1 or 2.

Stress may intensify a psychological disorder and may affect the course of treatment. Axis 4 indicates how much stress the person has had to endure, on a scale from 0 (almost no stress) to 6 (stress equivalent to being held hostage or to the death of one's child).

Some people with a psychological disorder are able to go on with their normal work and social activities; others are not. Axis 5 evaluates a person's overall level of functioning, on a scale from 1 (serious attempt at suicide or complete

Table 14.1 Some Major Categories of Psychological Disorders, According to Axis 1 of DSM III-R

Disorders usually first evident in childhood or adolescence	*Examples:* *attention-deficit hyperactivity disorder* Impulsivity; hyperactivity; inability to pay attention to school or work *anorexia nervosa* Abnormal fear of fatness; voluntary starvation *pica* The eating of inedible objects such as hair or dirt *gender identity disorders* Rejection of one's own sex; insistence that one is, or wants to be, a member of the opposite sex (*not* homosexuality) *Tourette's disorder* Repetitive movements, such as blinking an eyelid or twitching a hand; chanted sounds—in many cases, obscene words *elimination disorders* Bed-wetting; urinating or defecating in one's clothes *stuttering* Frequent repetition or prolongation of sounds, interfering with speech
Organic mental disorders	The result of deterioration of the brain or of temporary interference with brain functioning, as in opiate intoxication or opiate withdrawal
Psychoactive substance abuse disorders	Alcohol abuse, cocaine abuse, opiate abuse, and abuse of other mind-altering substances
Schizophrenia	Deterioration of everyday functioning, along with either a lack of emotional response, or thought disorders, or hallucinations or delusions
Delusional (paranoid) disorder	Irrational beliefs, such as the belief that "everyone is talking about me behind my back" or that "I have discovered the secret that will solve all the world's problems if I can just get people to listen to me"
Mood disorders	Periods of depression serious enough to interfere with daily life, sometimes alternating with periods of mania, which is the opposite of depression
Anxiety disorders	Lingering anxiety at almost all times, unpredictable attacks of severe anxiety, or periods of anxiety that regularly occur when the person is confronted with a particular object or thought
Somatoform disorders	*Examples:* *conversion disorder* One or more physical ailments, such as blindness or paralysis, that are caused at least in part by psychological factors but are not intentionally produced *hypochondriasis* Repetitive, exaggerated complaints of illness *somatization disorder* Recurrent, multiple complaints of pain and other ailments that are apparently not due to any physical disorder
Dissociative disorders	Loss of the memory of a person's own identity or the memory of past events, not caused by brain damage
Sexual disorders	*Examples:* *pedophilia* Sexual attraction to children *exhibitionism* Sexual pleasure from exposing oneself in public *voyeurism* Sexual arousal primarily from watching other people undressing or engaging in sexual intercourse *fetishism* Sexual arousal primarily from leather or other inanimate objects
Sleep disorders	*Examples:* *insomnia* Frequent feeling of not being rested after a night's sleep *sleep terror disorder* Repeated periods of awakening suddenly in an experience of panic *sleepwalking disorder* Repeated episodes of leaving the bed, walking about, and not remembering the episode later
Impulse control disorders	A tendency to act on impulses that other people usually inhibit, such as the urge to gamble large amounts of money foolishly, the urge to steal something, or the urge to strike someone

> **Table 14.2 Some Major Categories of Psychological Disorders, According to Axis 2 of DSM III-R**

Developmental disorders	*Examples:* *mental retardation* Intellectual functioning significantly below average; significant deficits in adaptive behavior *autistic disorder* Lack of social behavior; impaired communication; restricted repertoire of activities and interests
Personality disorders	Maladaptive personalities *Examples:* *paranoid personality disorder* Suspiciousness; habitual interpretation of other people's acts as threatening *schizotypal personality disorder* Poor relationships with other people; odd thinking; neglect of normal grooming. This disorder is similar to schizophrenia but less extreme *antisocial personality disorder* Lack of affection for other people; tendency to manipulate other people without feeling guilty; high probability of getting into trouble with the law; low probability of keeping a job *borderline personality disorder* Lack of a stable self-image; trouble establishing lasting relationships with other people or making lasting decisions about values, career choice, even sexual orientation; repeated self-endangering behavior, such as drug abuse, reckless driving, casual sex, binge eating, shoplifting, and running up large debts *histrionic personality disorder* Excessive emotionality and attention-seeking; constant demand for praise *narcissistic personality disorder* Exaggerated opinion of one's own importance and a lack of regard for others. (Narcissus was a figure in Greek mythology who fell in love with himself.) *avoidant personality disorder* Avoidance of social contact; lack of friends *dependent personality disorder* Preference for letting other people make decisions; lack of initiative and self-confidence

inability to take care of oneself) to 90 (happy, productive, with many interests).

- ### CONCEPT CHECK

1. Earlier I suggested three definitions of abnormal behavior: (1) behavior that gives a person discomfort, (2) behavior that leads to distress, disability, or an increased risk of pain or loss of freedom, and (3) behavior that society finds troublesome or unacceptable. By which of those definitions does a personality disorder qualify as an abnormal behavior? (Check your answer on page 585.)

EXAMPLES OF AXIS 1 DISORDERS

Later in this chapter we shall consider in detail the three most common Axis 1 disorders—anxiety disorders and phobias, alcohol and drug abuse, and mood disorders—as well as schizophrenia, which can be especially disabling. At this point, we shall briefly consider somatoform disorders and dissociative disorders. These are interesting, important Axis 1 disorders that we do not consider elsewhere.

Somatoform Disorders

The term *somatoform* is derived from the Greek root *soma,* meaning body. **Somatoform disorders** are conditions in which a person has physical symptoms that seem to have no medical cause. The person is not pretending or imagining the symptoms; they are real, but they result from psychological rather than medical problems. Diagnosis of somatoform disorders is difficult; sometimes someone really does have an undetected medical problem. You can imagine the consequences of treating someone for psychological troubles and ignoring a tumor or other ailment.

Somatoform disorders affect only about one person in a thousand (Myers et al., 1984; Robins et al., 1984). For unknown reasons, they tend to be more common in females than in males, possibly because they are a reaction to the dominating behavior of men toward women (Chodoff, 1982).

Hypochondriasis (HI-po-KON-DRI-ah-sis) is a type of somatoform disorder in which a person exaggerates physical complaints or complains of ailments that a physician cannot detect. In **conversion disorder,** a person, for no apparent medical reason, exhibits such symptoms as paralysis, blindness, deafness, dizziness, or an inability to speak. Some women (and, rarely, men too!) show symptoms of pregnancy, complete with morning sickness and a swollen abdomen, although they are not pregnant. Such symptoms are clearly not imaginary. The term *conversion* implies that the person has "converted" an anxiety-producing conflict into a physical symptom. For example, according to psychoanalysts, a person who is anxious about the possibility of hitting someone might develop a paralysis of the arm.

A person who experiences a long series of diverse ailments that seem to have no medical basis is said to be suffering from **somatization disorder.** The common symptoms are nausea and vomiting, pain, shortness of breath, difficulty swallowing, and a burning sensation in the genitals or rectum. This diversity of complaints contrasts with conversion disorder, in which a person typically has a single, well-defined physical complaint.

Many theorists believe that somatoform disorders develop and persist because they bring the sufferer two advantages. First, they enable the person to avoid facing a serious emotional conflict by converting it into a physical symptom. Second, they bring **secondary gain**—indirect benefits such as the attention and sympathy of others and an excuse for avoiding unpleasant activities.

Dissociative Disorders

Dissociation is the separation of one set of memories from another for no discernible medical reason. For instance, a person suffering from amnesia may forget only a particularly traumatic set of memories, such as being sexually molested, observing wartime atrocities, or committing a violent act in a moment of rage. Or the amnesia may be more general, extending to the person's identity and past experiences or to the person's entire store of factual information. Such global amnesia usually lasts only a few days.

In a state known as **psychogenic fugue** (FYOOG), people wander about, sometimes over great distances, lose track of their identity, and perhaps assume a new name. They are generally disoriented and fail to respond appropriately to their surroundings. The fugue state usually ends abruptly; the person "wakes up" mystified at being in a strange place and generally unaware of what happened during the fugue.

In a rare, extreme type of dissociation, the personality separates into several identities, a condition known as **multiple personality disorder** (Solomon & Solomon, 1982). The person may shift abruptly from one personality to another, each with its own behavioral patterns, memories, and even name, almost as if each personality were really a different person.

Many people, including some who should know better, describe multiple personality as "schizophrenia." They are wrong. People with multiple personality disorder have several personalities, any one of which by itself might be considered normal, whereas people suffering from schizophrenia have just one seriously disordered personality.

One famous case of multiple personality was Chris Costner White Sizemore, who was described in the book and the movie *The Three Faces of Eve* (Thigpen & Cleckley, 1957) and who eventually told her own story in the book *I'm Eve* (Sizemore & Pittillo, 1977). (See Figure 14.3.) Chris Sizemore is not sure how her problem began but, so far as she can recall, it started during early childhood. As a 2-year-old, she had seen the dead body of a man and had been told that a "monster" had killed him. She felt that it was some other girl in her body who was seeing the dead man, and not she herself. Soon after, she saw a man at a sawmill who had accidentally been sawed into three pieces. Then, when Chris was 6, her grandmother died. At the funeral, when her aunt tried to get her to kiss her dead grandmother, she reacted with horror. Faced with this series of traumatic experiences, she dissociated herself from them. From her perspective, another girl simply took over her body at various times.

The psychiatrist who treated Chris in adulthood described her 10th, 11th, and 12th personalities in *The Three Faces of Eve.* One, whom he called "Eve White," was a shy, inhibited woman. Another, "Eve Black," was a fun-lov-

FIGURE 14.3
Chris Sizemore, the real "Eve" in The Three Faces of Eve, *displays one of her paintings. She exhibited a total of 22 personalities, including her final, permanent identity. A person who periodically changes personality and identity is said to have* multiple personality. *Each of those personalities by itself seems reasonably normal. Films, television, and other media often mistakenly refer to this condition as "schizophrenia." People with schizophrenia have only one personality; that personality, however, is abnormal in serious ways.*

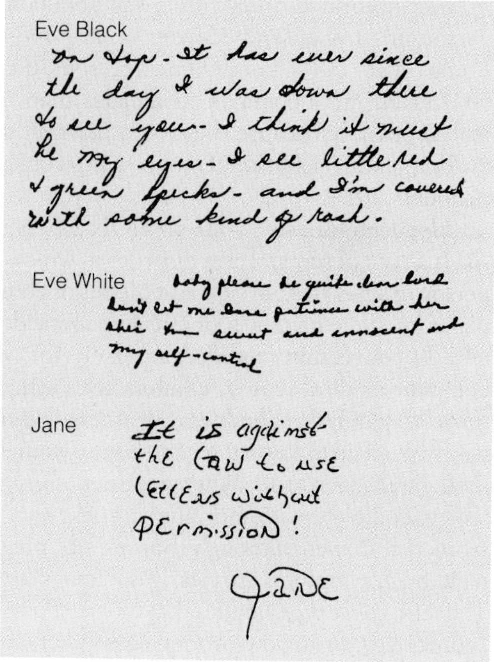

Eve Black

Eve White

Jane

FIGURE 14.4
Chris Sizemore's personalities differed in their memories, their skills, and even their handwriting.

ing party-goer, who once "came out" just long enough to leave poor Eve White in a sexy dress, drunk, in a bar surrounded by soldiers who wondered why she suddenly seemed not to know them. Yet another was "Jane," a calm, intelligent woman who claimed to have a college education. At the end of treatment, the psychiatrist believed that Jane would emerge as the single, permanent personality. She divorced and remarried, and at first her difficulties seemed to be over.

In fact, 10 more personalities were yet to emerge—in groups of 3, except for the final personality. Each had some memory of past personalities but little or no knowledge of her other current "selves." Sometimes one self would write notes to the other selves. Each had a different handwriting (Figure 14.4). One of her total of 22 personalities was mute and left handed. Two had allergies that the others did not have. Chris's daughter became fairly adept at identifying and dealing with the separate personalities, but occasionally she would have to ask, "Who are you today, Mommy?"

Many psychiatrists' bills later, a single personality emerged that has remained Chris's only personality since the mid-1970s. Today Chris is a healthy, pleasant woman and a talented painter. She remembers each of her past selves. Curiously, she does not remember how to sew—a skill some of her previous personalities had learned.

Multiple personality appears to be a means of coping with an intolerable reality. We do not know why a few people resort to this means of coping while others do not. As we saw in Chapter 5, psychologists and psychiatrists sometimes find it difficult to distinguish between true cases of multiple personality and people who pretend to have multiple personalities, including criminals seeking to use an insanity defense.

■ CONCEPT CHECK

2. People with Alzheimer's disease forget most of their factual memories. Why then is Alzheimer's disease not considered a dissociative disorder? (Check your answer on page 585.)

SUMMARY

■ *Multiple causes of abnormal behavior.* Abnormal behavior is the result of various combinations of biological factors, early experiences, and learned responses to a stressful or unsupportive environment. (page 577)

■ *The Diagnostic and Statistical Manual.* Psychological disorders are classified in the *Diagnostic and Statistical Manual of Mental Disorders, Third Edition—Revised* (DSM III-R). This manual classifies disorders along five axes. Axis 1 and Axis 2 deal with psychological disorders; Axis 3 deals with physical ailments that may affect behavior; Axes 4 and 5 provide means for evaluating a person's stress level and overall functioning. (page 579)

■ *Axis 1—disorders that last part of a person's life.* Axis 1 of DSM III-R lists disorders that usually begin after infancy and that have at least some likelihood of recovery. The three most common disorders of this sort are anxiety disorders, substance abuse, and depression. (page 580)

■ *Axis 2—lifelong disorders.* Axis 2 of DSM III-R lists conditions that arise early and persist throughout a lifetime such as mental retardation and personality disorders. (page 580)

■ *Personality disorders.* Personality disorders are stable characteristics that impair a person's effectiveness or ability to get along with others. Examples of personality disorders are excessive dependence on others and excessive self-centeredness. (page 580)

■ *Somatoform disorders.* Somatoform disorders are conditions in which a person has physical ailments that have no apparent organic basis but are in some way based on psychological problems. (page 582)

■ *Dissociative disorders.* People with dissociative disorders lose access to a particular set of memories. One type of dissociative disorder is multiple personality, in which a person alternates among two or more personalities, each with its own set of memories. (page 583)

SUGGESTION FOR FURTHER READING

American Psychiatric Association. (1987). *Diagnostic and statistical manual of mental disorders* (3rd ed.-rev.). Washington, DC. The standard guide to the classification and description of psychological disorders.

TERMS

***Diagnostic and Statistical Manual of Mental Disorders, Third Edition—Revised* (DSM III-R)** book that lists the acceptable labels for all psychological disorders with a description of each and guidelines on how to distinguish it from similar disorders (page 580)

personality disorder a maladaptive, inflexible way of dealing with the environment and other people (page 580)

somatoform disorder condition in which a person has physical symptoms that seem to have no medical cause (page 582)

hypochondriasis type of somatoform disorder in which a person exaggerates physical complaints or complains of ailments that a physician cannot detect (page 583)

conversion disorder condition in which a person, for no apparent medical reason, exhibits such symptoms as paralysis, blindness, deafness, dizziness, or an inability to speak (page 583)

somatization disorder condition in which a person experiences a long series of diverse ailments that have no apparent medical basis (page 583)

secondary gain indirect benefits from a disorder, such as the attention and sympathy of others and an excuse for avoiding unpleasant activities (page 583)

dissociation separation of one set of memories from another for no discernible medical reason (page 583)

psychogenic fugue condition in which people wander about, sometimes over great distances, lose track of their identity, and perhaps assume a new name (page 583)

multiple personality disorder rare type of dissociation in which the personality separates into several identities (page 583)

ANSWERS TO CONCEPT CHECKS

1. A personality disorder qualifies as abnormal by the third definition because society considers the behavior troublesome. Some personality disorders qualify as abnormal by the second definition because they lead to an increased risk of loss of freedom (through unemployment or imprisonment). As a rule, personality disorders do not qualify as abnormal by the first definition because people generally do not complain about their personality disorders. (page 582)

2. Alzheimer's disease is associated with brain deterioration. A disorder is considered "dissociative" only if it occurs for psychological rather than organic reasons. (page 584)

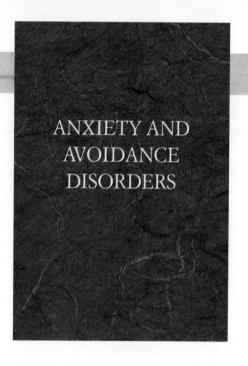

ANXIETY AND AVOIDANCE DISORDERS

Why do some people take extreme measures to avoid something that is harmless or only slightly dangerous?

Why do some people develop strange habits and rituals?

You go to the beach, looking forward to an afternoon of swimming and surfing. Someone tells you that a shark attacked two swimmers yesterday and has just been sighted close to shore. Do you venture into the water? What if the shark attack occurred a month ago and no shark has been seen in the area since then? Now would you go in? What if no shark has attacked anyone in this area, but someone saw a small shark there a few days ago?

What if no shark has ever been seen within 50 miles of this particular beach, but recently you read a magazine story about shark attacks?

How much fear and caution is normal? Staying out of the water because you see a large shark is perfectly reasonable. Staying out of the water because of sharks you have read about is, by most people's standards, excessively cautious. If you refuse even to look at photographs of the ocean because they might *remind* you of sharks, you have a serious problem indeed.

It is normal to have a certain amount of fear and to avoid situations that might provoke fear. But excessive fear and caution are linked to some of the most common psychological disorders.

DISORDERS WITH APPARENTLY UNPROVOKED ANXIETY

Many psychological disorders are marked by a combination of fear, anxiety, and attempts to avoid anxiety. Anxiety, unlike fear, is generally not associated with a specific situation. We feel fear in the presence of a hungry tiger, but our fear passes as soon as we get away. But we cannot escape the anxiety we experience about dying or about our personal inadequacies. Some degree of anxiety is normal; it becomes a problem only when it interferes with our ability to cope with everyday life.

Generalized Anxiety Disorder

People with **generalized anxiety disorder** are constantly plagued by exaggerated worries. They worry that "I might get sick," "My daughter might get sick," "I might lose my job," or "I might not be able to pay my bills." Although these people have no realistic reason for such worries—at least no more reason than anyone else—their worries persist and interfere with daily life. They grow tense, restless, irritable, and fatigued.

Panic Disorder

Panic disorder is an emotional disturbance found in about 1–2% of all American adults, women more than men; it is rare among children (McNally, 1990; Myers et al., 1984; Robins et al., 1984). People with this disorder have a fairly constant state of moderate anxiety and an overresponsive sympathetic nervous system; they respond to even mild stressors or mild exercise with a sudden increase in heart rate and blood adrenaline (Liebowitz et al., 1985; Nutt, 1989). That arousal sometimes provokes a full-fledged panic attack, accompanied by chest pains, difficulty in breathing, sweating, faintness, and shaking (see Figure 14.5). A panic attack generally lasts only a few minutes, although it may last an hour or more. During an attack, most people worry about fainting, dying, or going crazy (Argyle, 1988). People often interpret a panic attack as a heart attack or as a sign of an impending heart attack. After a few such attacks, those worries may grow more intense and may even trigger further panics.

Panic disorder can become self-perpetuating (Figure 14.6). Many people deal with anxiety by taking a deep breath or two, to help calm themselves down. On the theory that "if a little is good, a whole lot will be better," they may continue breathing deeply, or hyperventilating. **Hyperventilation** expels carbon dioxide and therefore lowers the carbon dioxide level in the blood. Then if something happens that increases the carbon dioxide level, such as sudden physical activity or an experience that excites the sympathetic nervous system, the carbon dioxide level in the blood increases by a large percentage and stimulates an increased heart rate, trembling, and other symptoms of a panic attack—the very thing the person was trying to avoid (Gorman et al., 1988; Woods et al., 1986). After a few such episodes, the likelihood of further attacks increases. One treatment for panic disorders is to teach the person to avoid hyperventilating (Wolpe & Rowan, 1988). Another is to teach the person to recognize sudden increases in heart rate and trembling as a sign of carbon dioxide fluctuations, and not as a sign of an impending heart attack.

When people discover that physical exertion sometimes triggers a panic attack, they may decide to avoid any sort of physical activity. As a result, they grow even more sensitive to the effects of physical activity; even slight exertion will raise the level of carbon dioxide in their blood. Consequently, some authorities recommend regular exercise as a treatment for panic disorder (Ledwidge, 1980).

Panic disorder is frequently linked with **agoraphobia**—an excessive fear of open places or public places, from *agora*, the ancient Greek word for "marketplace" (Reich, 1986). Most psychologists believe that the people with panic disorder are not primarily afraid of the open places themselves; they are afraid of being incapacitated or embarrassed by having a panic attack in a public place. In a sense, they are afraid of their own fear (McNally, 1990). To avoid the prospect of a public panic attack, they stay home as much as possible and almost never go out alone.

■ CONCEPT CHECK

3. *Some psychologists advise people with panic attacks to stop worrying about their attacks, to*

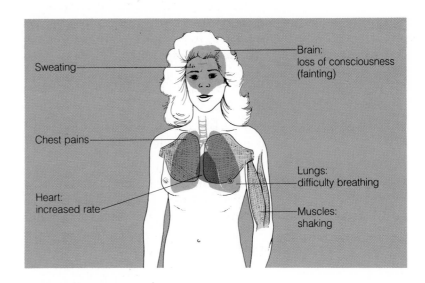

FIGURE 14.5
People subject to panic attacks experience moderate anxiety almost constantly, as well as occasional periods of intense anxiety. During a panic attack, the sympathetic nervous system intensely activates the heart and other organs. People are generally frightened by this experience; some believe they are having a heart attack.

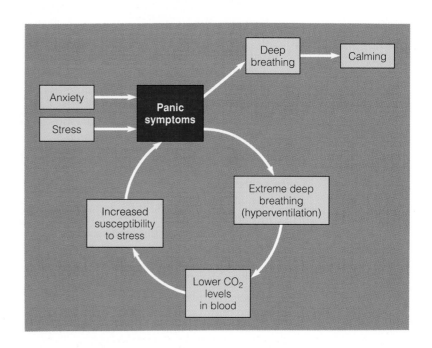

FIGURE 14.6
Deep breathing helps to calm a person, but extreme deep breathing increases the probability of another panic attack.

take an attitude, "If it happens, it happens." Why would they make this recommendation? (Check your answer on page 597.)

DISORDERS WITH EXAGGERATED AVOIDANCE BEHAVIORS

People learn to avoid punishment, as we saw in Chapter 7. In some cases, their efforts to avoid punishment become so extreme and persistent that they begin to interfere with daily activities. We begin with some general observations on avoidance learning, which will be relevant to the later discussion of phobias (extreme fears) and compulsions (rituals designed to avoid unpleasant thoughts or events).

Avoidance Learning and Its Persistence

If you learn to do something for a positive reinforcement, you will extinguish your response soon after you stop receiving reinforcements. Avoidance behaviors are different, however. Suppose you learn to press a lever to avoid electric shocks. Soon you are responding steadily and receiving no shocks. Now the experimenter disconnects the shock generator, without telling you. The extinction procedure has begun; you no longer need to press the lever. What will you do? You will continue pressing, of course. So far as you can tell, nothing has changed; the response still "works." *Avoidance behaviors are highly resistant to extinction;* once someone learns a response to avoid mishap, the response continues long after it ceases to be necessary.

You can see how this tendency would support superstitions: Suppose you believe that Friday the 13th is a dangerous day. You are very cautious every Friday the 13th, but occasionally some misfortune happens anyway. The misfortune confirms your belief that Friday the 13th is dangerous. The next Friday the 13th, nothing goes wrong. You conclude, "It helps to be careful on Friday the 13th. I was cautious all day long, and I avoided bad luck." *In other words, so long as you engage in avoidance behavior, you will never find out that your behavior is useless.*

■ CONCEPT CHECK

4. Suppose you are an experimenter, and you have trained someone to press a lever to avoid

shocks. Now you disconnect the shock generator. Other than telling the person what you have done, what procedure could you use to facilitate extinction of the lever-pressing? (Check your answer on page 597.)

Phobias

Terror is the only thing that comes close to how I feel when I think of moths. Their willowy, see-through wings always seem filthy. I remember being stuck in a car with a huge moth and my date, not knowing how terrified I was of moths, thought I was kidding when I told him I was afraid. It was terrible! I can feel it right now . . . the . . . feeling trapped and the moth with its ugly body flitting around so quickly, I couldn't anticipate where it would go next. Finally that creature hit me in the arm and I screamed—it felt dirty and sleazy and then it hit me in the face and I began to scream uncontrollably. I had the terrible feeling it was going to fly into my mouth while I was screaming, but I couldn't stop. (Duke & Nowicki, 1979, p. 244)

Phobias are extreme and persistent fears leading to avoidance behaviors, similar to a superstitious fear of Friday the 13th. Phobias are sometimes defined as "irrational fears," but that definition is inadequate. A fear of snakes or spiders is not irrational—some of them are dangerous. Yet such a fear is often regarded as a phobia. Some people have such a strong fear of these creatures that they keep away from fields in which they might be lurking, stay away from unfamiliar buildings, avoid books that might have pictures of snakes or spiders, and don't talk to strangers who, after all, might like to *talk* about snakes or spiders.

A **phobia** is best defined as *a fear so extreme that it interferes with normal living.* Confronting the object of the phobia may lead to sweating, trembling, and rapid breathing and heart rate. Often fear of the object is compounded by a fear that the fear itself will provoke a heart attack. In many ways, phobias are like panic disorder, except that phobias are aroused by a specific object or event, whereas panic attacks occur at less predictable times.

Because most people with phobias are well aware that their fears are exaggerated, it does no good to tell them not to be afraid. In fact, attempts to reduce phobias by providing information sometimes backfire. One city tried to combat the phobia of elevators by posting signs on elevators throughout the city: "There is no reason to be afraid of elevators. There is almost no chance at all that the cable will break or that you will suffocate." The signs actually *increased* the phobia of elevators.

The Prevalence of Phobias How many people suffer from phobias? As with most other psychological disorders, phobias are exaggerations of normal behaviors. Depending on where we draw the line between phobias and normal fears, estimates of the prevalence of phobias range from 5% to 13% of the population (Myers et al., 1984). About twice as many women as men experience phobias. Figure 14.7 shows the most frequently reported phobias. Figure 14.8 shows the prevalence of phobias by age. Note the early onset; phobias often begin in the teenage years (Burke, Burke, Regier, & Rae, 1990).

The Learning of Phobias Although people seem to be born with a few fears, such as a fear of sudden loud noises, most fears are learned. Apparently even the fear of heights is learned. Infants begin to show a fear of heights shortly after they begin to crawl—presumably also the age when they have their first experiences of slipping and falling. Infants who crawl early develop fear of heights early; infants who are late to crawl are also late to develop fear of heights (Campos, Bertenthal, & Kermoian, 1992).

John B. Watson, one of the founders of behaviorism, was the first to demonstrate the possibility of learning a fear (Watson & Rayner, 1920). Today, we would consider it unethical to try to create a fear, especially in humans, but in 1920 such restraint was less common. Watson and Rosalie Rayner studied an 11-month-old child, "Albert B.," who had previously shown no fear of white rats or other animals (Figure 14.9). They set a white rat down in front of Albert, and then, just behind him, they struck a large steel bar with a hammer. The sudden sound made Albert whimper and cover his face. After seven repetitions, the mere sight of the rat would make Albert cry and crawl away. Watson and Rayner declared that they had created a strong fear and that phobias in general might develop along similar lines.

Although Watson and Rayner's study is open to several methodological criticisms (Harris, 1979; Samelson, 1980), it led the way for later interpretations of phobias as learned responses. Their explanation of phobias failed to answer some important questions: Why do people develop phobias toward objects that have never injured them? Why are some phobias

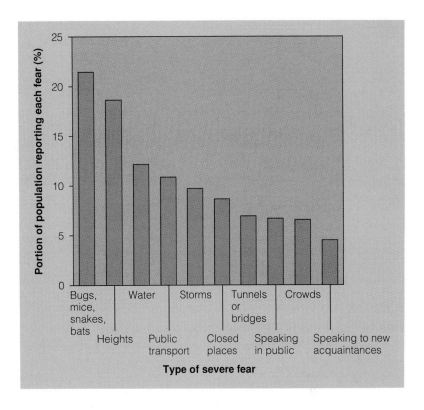

FIGURE 14.7

The most common phobias include snakes and other animals, heights, open places and crowds, and storms. Here, people reported their severe fears. Not all severe fears qualify as phobias, however.

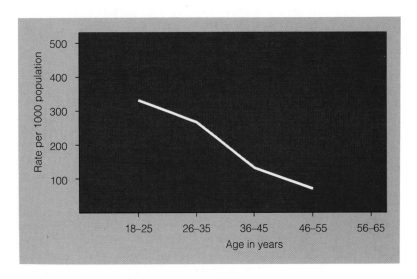

FIGURE 14.8

Most phobias are not lifelong conditions. Most young people with phobias lose their phobias by middle age, either spontaneously or because of therapy.

Anxiety and Avoidance Disorders   589

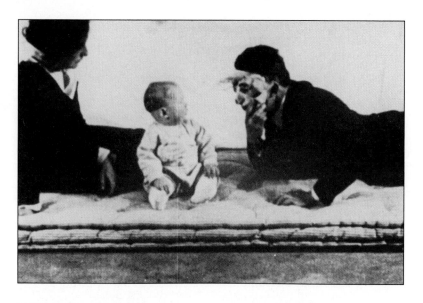

FIGURE 14.9

John B. Watson argued that most fears, including phobias, are learned. Watson first demonstrated that this child, Little Albert, showed little fear of small animals. Then Watson paired the presentation of a white rat with a loud, frightening noise. Little Albert became afraid of the white rat; he also began showing fears of other small animals, odd-looking masks, and other objects he had not previously feared. (Courtesy of Professor Benjamin Harris.)

much more common than others? And why are phobias so persistent?

■ CONCEPT CHECK

5. *In classical-conditioning terms, what was the CS in Watson and Rayner's experiment? The UCS? The CR? The UCR? (Check your answers on page 597.)*

Learning Fear by Observation

WHAT'S THE EVIDENCE?

Contrary to Watson and Rayner's explanation, almost half of all people with phobias have never had a painful experience with the object they fear (Öst & Hugdahl, 1981). Are you afraid of snakes? Most people have at least a moderate fear of snakes, and a fair number have phobias about them. Have you ever been injured by a snake? Chances are, no. Why do so many people fear snakes when so few have ever been injured by one?

As noted in our consideration of social learning in Chapter 7, we learn many things by watching or listening to others. Perhaps we hear that someone has been injured by a snake, and we become afraid too.

That hypothesis is probably correct, but how can we demonstrate it? Susan Mineka and her colleagues demonstrated how monkeys learn fears by observing other monkeys (Mineka, 1987; Mineka, Davidson, Cook, & Keir, 1984). Her experiments show how animal studies can shed important light on important human issues.

EXPERIMENT 1

Hypothesis Monkeys that have seen other monkeys show fear of a snake will develop such a fear themselves.

Method Monkeys that live in the wild generally show a strong fear of snakes. They are not born with that fear, however; monkeys reared in a laboratory show no fear of snakes. Mineka put a laboratory-reared monkey together with a wild-born monkey and let them both see a snake (Figure 14.10a). The lab monkey watched the wild monkey show signs of fear. Later she tested the lab monkey by itself to see whether it had acquired a fear of snakes.

Results When the lab monkey saw how frightened its partner was of the snake, it became frightened too (Figure 14.10b). It continued to be afraid of the snake when tested by itself even months later.

Interpretation The lab monkey may have learned a fear of snakes because it saw that its partner was afraid of snakes. But Mineka considered another possible, though less likely, interpretation: The lab-reared monkey may have become fearful simply because it observed the other monkey's fear. That is, maybe it did not matter *what* the wild-reared monkey was afraid of. To test this possibility, Mineka conducted a second experiment.

EXPERIMENT 2

Hypothesis A monkey that sees another monkey show fear but does not know what the second monkey is afraid of will not develop the same fear itself.

Method A monkey reared in a lab watched a monkey reared in the wild through a plate of glass. The wild monkey could see a snake through a window that the lab monkey could not see. Thus the lab monkey saw the wild monkey show fear, but did not know what it was afraid of. Later the lab monkey was put close to a snake to see whether it would show fear.

Results The lab monkey showed no fear of the snake.

Interpretation To develop a fear of snakes, the observer monkey had to see that the other monkey was frightened of snakes, not just that it was frightened (Figure 14.10c).

Note that although the observer monkey had to see *what* the other monkey was afraid of, it did not have to see *why* it was afraid. Just seeing the other monkey's fear of the snake in Experiment 1 was enough. Humans not only observe other people's fears but also can tell one another what we are afraid of and why.

Why Some Phobias Are More Common Than Others Imagine that you survey your friends. (You can survey them in fact, if you like, but in this case it's pretty easy to imagine what the results will be.) You ask them the following questions *in this order*:

- Are you afraid of snakes?
- Are you afraid of cars?
- Have you ever been bitten by a snake or seen someone else get bitten by a snake?
- Have you ever been injured in a car accident or seen someone else get injured in a car accident?

I think you know what results to expect: A fair number of people will admit being afraid of snakes, some of them extremely afraid, even though very few have any firsthand experience with snake bites. Almost no one is afraid of cars, even though almost everyone has experienced or witnessed a car accident in which someone got injured. Why do people develop some fears more readily than others?

The most common phobias are of open spaces, closed spaces, heights, lightning and thunder, animals, and illness. In contrast, few people have phobias of cars, guns, or tools—even though injuries from cars, guns, and tools are quite common. One explanation for this tendency is that, as Martin Seligman (1971) put it, people may be inherently "prepared" to learn certain phobias. For millions of years people who quickly learned to avoid snakes, heights, and lightning probably have had a good chance to survive and to transmit their genes. We have not had enough time to evolve a tendency to fear cars and guns.

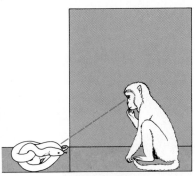
Wild-reared monkey   Lab-reared monkey

Wild-reared monkey shows fear of snake.

Lab-reared monkey shows no fear of snake.

a

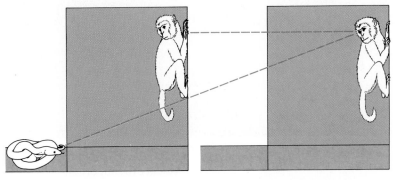

Lab-reared monkey learns fear of snake by observing wild-reared monkey and snake.

b

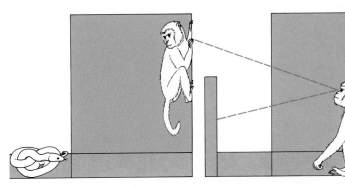

Barrier masks snake from view of lab-reared monkey.

Lab-reared monkey does not learn fear when snake is not visible.

c

FIGURE 14.10
A laboratory-reared monkey learns to fear snakes from the reaction of a monkey reared in the wild. But if the snake is not visible, the lab-reared monkey fails to learn fear.

Phobias are most likely to develop for dangerous events that we can neither predict nor control. They also develop for events that give us occasional unpleasant experiences without any safe or pleasant experiences. Can you therefore explain why so many people have phobias of lightning and so few people have phobias of cars?

We have evidence to support this view from both monkey and human studies. Monkeys who watch a videotape of another monkey running away from a snake learn to fear snakes; monkeys who watch a monkey running away from a flower show no fear of flowers (Mineka, 1987). People who receive electric shocks paired with pictures of snakes quickly develop a strong and persistent response to snake pictures; people who receive shocks paired with pictures of houses show a much weaker response (Öhman, Eriksson, & Olofsson, 1975).

There may be other reasons why some phobias are more common than others. One is that we have many safe experiences with cars and tools to outweigh any bad experiences. We have few safe experiences with snakes or with falling from high places. Another possibility is that people generally develop phobias for objects they cannot predict or control. Danger is more stressful when it takes us by surprise (Mineka, 1985; Mineka, Cook, & Miller, 1984). If you are afraid of spiders, for example, you have to be constantly on the alert for those tiny, unpredictable critters. You never know where they might be or when they might strike, so you can never completely relax. Lightning is also unpredictable and uncontrollable. In contrast, you don't have to worry that electric outlets will take you by surprise. You have to be on the alert

for cars when you are near a road, but not at other times.

The Persistence of Phobias Well-established phobias can last a lifetime. If you remember the discussion about avoidance learning, you can see why phobias are so difficult to extinguish: If you have learned to press a lever to avoid shock, you may not stop pressing long enough to find out that your response is no longer necessary. Similarly, if you stay away from snakes or heights or closed places because you are afraid of them (a phobia), you will never learn that your fear is exaggerated. In other words, extinction never takes place.

Therapies for Phobias We shall consider general principles of psychotherapy in Chapter 15. Here, however, let us examine two therapies that are intended specifically for phobias—systematic desensitization and flooding.

As we have seen, phobias are persistent because people consistently avoid the object of the phobia. As long as people continue making their avoidance response, they cannot learn that the response is unnecessary; extinction does not take place. Therefore, the best way to extinguish a phobia is to expose a person to the object that arouses the fear. When nothing bad happens, the phobia fades.

The most common and most successful treatment for phobia is **systematic desensitization,** a method of reducing fear by gradually exposing people to the object of their fear (Wolpe, 1961). Someone with a phobia of snakes, for example, is first given training in methods of relaxation. Then the patient is asked to lie on a comfortable couch with relaxing music playing in the background and with the therapist nearby. The therapist asks the patient to imagine a small black-and-white photo of a snake. Next the patient is asked to imagine a full-color photo and then to imagine a real snake. After the patient has handled all of those images without distress, the same sequence is repeated with real photos and eventually with a real snake (Figure 14.11).

The process resembles Skinner's shaping procedure (page 297): The patient is given time to master one step before going on to the next. The patient can say stop if the distress becomes too severe; the therapist then goes back several steps and repeats the sequence. Some people get through the whole procedure in a single, 1-hour session; others need weekly sessions for

2 or 3 months. Systematic desensitization can easily be combined with social learning: The person with a phobia watches other people who display a fearless response to the object.

Flooding or **implosion** is a treatment in which the person is exposed to the object of the phobia suddenly rather than gradually (Hogan & Kirchner, 1967; Rachman, 1969) (Figure 14.12). (It is called "flooding" because the patient is "flooded" with fear.) If you had a phobia of rats, for example, you might be told to imagine that you were locked in a room full of rats crawling all over you and viciously attacking you. The image arouses your sympathetic nervous system enormously, and your heart rate and breathing rate soar to high levels (Lande, 1982).

The human sympathetic nervous system is not capable of maintaining extreme arousal for very long, however, and within a few minutes your heart rate and breathing rate begin to decline. A little later, you report that you feel more relaxed, even though the therapist continues to suggest gory images of what rats are doing to you. Once you have reached this point, the battle is half won.

■ CONCEPT CHECKS

6. In what way does systematic desensitization resemble extinction of a learned shock-avoidance response?

7. How is the flooding procedure related to the James-Lange theory of emotions, discussed in Chapter 12?

(Check your answers on page 597.)

Obsessive-Compulsive Disorder

People with **obsessive-compulsive disorder** have two kinds of problems: An **obsession** is a repetitive, unwelcome stream of thought. For example, such people might find themselves constantly imagining gruesome scenes, worrying that they are about to kill someone, dwelling on doubts about their religion, or thinking "I hate my sister, I hate my sister." The harder they try to escape such thoughts, the more repetitive they become. A **compulsion** is a repetitive, almost irresistible action. Obsessions generally lead to compulsions, as an itching sensation leads to scratching.

The Persistence of Obsessions People with obsessive-compulsive disorder feel a combination of guilt and anxiety over certain thoughts

FIGURE 14.11
One of the most effective therapies for phobia is systematic desensitization, in which a therapist gradually exposes a client to the object of the phobia, first in imagination and later in reality. A similar procedure is exposure therapy; the therapist demonstrates a lack of fear of the object and encourages the client to do the same.

FIGURE 14.12
Flooding is a procedure similar to systematic desensitization, except that in flooding the person is exposed suddenly, not gradually, to the object of fear. At first the person is terrified, but as the autonomic arousal decreases (as it inevitably does), the person realizes "I can handle this situation."

or impulses. They feel persistent, frightening impulses—perhaps an impulse to engage in some sexual act they consider shameful, an impulse to hurt someone they love, or an impulse to commit suicide. They decide, "Oh, what a terrible thing to think. I don't want to think such a thing ever again." And so they resolve to shut the thought or impulse out of their consciousness.

However, it is very difficult to exclude a particular thought. The harder one tries to prevent the thought, the more intrusive it becomes. As a child, the Russian novelist Leo Tolstoy once organized a club with a most unusual qualification for membership: A prospective member had to stand alone in a corner *without thinking about a white bear* (Simmons, 1949). If you think that sounds easy, try it. You probably go months at a time without thinking about white bears, but when you try *not* to think about them, you can think of nothing else.

In one experiment, college students were asked to tape-record everything that came to mind during 5 minutes but to try *not* to think about white bears. If they did, they were to mention it and ring a bell. Subjects reported thinking about a bear a mean of more than six times during the 5 minutes (Wegner, Schneider, Carter, & White, 1987). Afterward, they reported that almost everything in the room reminded them of white bears. Evidently, attempts to suppress a thought are likely to backfire, even with an emotionally trivial thought such as "white bears." You can imagine what it must be like with severely upsetting thoughts.

One Type of Compulsion: Cleaning People with obsessive-compulsive disorder can have several kinds of compulsions. Some collect things. (One man collected newspapers under his bed until they raised the bed so high it almost touched the ceiling.) Others have odd habits, such as touching everything they see, trying to arrange objects in a completely symmetrical manner, walking back and forth through a door nine times before leaving a building, or spending their spare moments counting various objects. (The Obsessive-Compulsive Foundation produces a button that says "Every Member Counts"!)

The most common compulsions are cleaning and checking. Obsessive-compulsive cleaning is similar to a phobia of dirt. Here is a description of a severe cleaning compulsion (Nagera, 1976):

"R.," a 12-year-old boy, had a long standing habit of prolonged bathing and hand washing, dating from a film about germs he had seen in the second grade. At about age 12, he started to complain about "being dirty" and having "bad thoughts," but he would not elaborate. His hand washing and bathing became longer and more frequent. When he bathed, he carefully washed himself with soap and washcloth all over, including the inside of his mouth and the inside of each nostril. He even opened his eyes in the soapy water and carefully washed his eyeballs. The only part he did not wash was his penis, which he covered with a washcloth as soon as he entered the tub.

Coupled with his strange bathing habits, he developed some original superstitions. Whenever he did anything with one hand, he immediately did the same thing with the other hand. Whenever anyone mentioned a member of R.'s family, he would mention the corresponding member of the other person's family. He always walked to school by the same route, being careful never to step on any spot he had ever stepped on before. (After a while this became a serious strain on his memory.) At school, he would wipe the palm of his hand on his pants after any "good" thought; at home, he would wipe his hand on his pants after any "bad" thought.

R.'s problems were traced to a single event. Just before the onset of his exaggerated behaviors, R. and another boy had pulled down their pants and looked at each other. Afterward he felt guilty and full of anxiety that he might do the same thing again. The constant bathing was apparently an attempt to wash away his feelings of "dirtiness." The superstitious rituals were an attempt to impose rigid self-control. His underlying reasoning could be described as, "If I can keep myself under perfect control at all times, even following these rigid and pointless rules, I will never again lose control and do something shameful."

Another Type of Compulsion: Checking An obsessive-compulsive checker "double-checks" everything. Before going to bed at night, he or she checks to make sure that all the doors and windows are locked and that all the water taps and gas outlets are turned off. But then the question arises, "Did I *really* check them all, or did I only imagine it?" So everything has to be checked again. And again. "After all, I may accidentally have unlocked one of the doors when I was checking it." Obsessive-compulsive checkers can never decide when to stop checking; they may go on for hours, and even then not be satisfied.

Obsessive-compulsive checkers have been known to check every door they pass to see whether anyone has been locked in, to check trash containers and bushes to see whether anyone has abandoned a baby, to call the police every day to ask whether they have committed a crime that they have forgotten, and to drive back and forth along a street to see whether they ran over anyone the last time through (Pollak, 1979; Rachman & Hodgson, 1980).

Why do checkers go on checking? According to some reports, they do not trust their memory of what they have done (Sher, Frost, Kushner, Crews, & Alexander, 1989). In one study, the experimenters asked several people—among them some obsessive-compulsive checkers—to read a list of words and to think their opposites. (For instance, when they saw "NORTH-S . . . ," they would think *south*.) Then the experimenters combined the two sets of words—the words on the list and their opposites—and asked the subjects to identify which words they had read and which ones they had only thought. The obsessive-compulsive checkers remembered about as well as the control group did, but their confidence in their answers was significantly lower. Compared to the control group, the checkers were less confident of their ability to distinguish between what had actually happened and what they had just imagined (Sher, Frost, & Otto, 1983).

Table 14.3 summarizes key differences between obsessive-compulsive cleaners and checkers. Table 14.4 lists some items from a questionnaire on obsessive-compulsive tendencies (Rachman & Hodgson, 1980). Try answering these questions yourself, or try guessing how an obsessive-compulsive person would answer them. The most common obsessive-compulsive answers are given on page 597. (The few items listed here are not sufficient to diagnose someone as obsessive-compulsive. So don't worry if you give all the obsessive-compulsive answers.)

Possible Predispositions or Causes About 2–3% of all people in the United States suffer from obsessive-compulsive disorder at some time during their life (Karno, Golding, Sorenson, & Burnam, 1988). The disorder occurs most frequently among hard-working, perfectionistic people of average or above-average intelligence. It may develop either suddenly or

Table 14.3. Obsessive-Compulsive Cleaners and Checkers

	Cleaners	*Checkers*
Sex distribution	Mostly female	About equally male and female
Dominant emotion	Anxiety, similar to phobia	Guilt, shame
Speed of onset	Usually rapid	More often gradual
Life disruption	Dominates life	Usually does not disrupt job and family life
Ritual length	Less than 1 hour at a time	Some go on indefinitely
Feel better after rituals?	Yes	Usually not

Source: Rachman & Hodgson, 1980.

Table 14.4 Questionnaire for Obsessive-Compulsive Tendencies

1. I avoid using public telephones because of possible contamination.   T F

2. I frequently get nasty thoughts and have difficulty in getting rid of them.   T F

3. I usually have serious doubts about the simple everyday things I do.   T F

4. Neither of my parents was very strict during my childhood.   T F

5. I do not take a long time to dress in the morning.   T F

6. One of my major problems is that I pay too much attention to detail.   T F

7. I do not stick to a very strict routine when doing ordinary things.   T F

8. I do not usually count when doing a routine task.   T F

9. Even when I do something very carefully, I often feel that it is not quite right.   T F

Source: Rachman & Hodgson, 1980.

gradually, usually beginning between the ages 10 and 25. Nearly all people with obsessive-compulsive disorder have some insight into their own behavior and realize that their rituals are inappropriate. However, that realization does not stop the rituals.

Obsessive-compulsive disorder tends to run in families, suggesting a possible genetic basis. Certain drugs have demonstrated substantial ability to suppress obsessions and compulsions, including Anafranil (generic name clomipramine). All such drugs inhibit the reuptake of the neurotransmitter serotonin after its release by presynaptic neurons; that is, the drugs prolong the effects of serotonin. The effectiveness of such drugs suggests that some disorder of the brain's serotonin synapses may be a cause or at least a predisposition to obsessive-compulsive disorder (Goodman et al., 1990; Leonard et al., 1989; Yaryura-Tobias, 1977). The details of this relationship are far from clear, as a whole new area of research is opening up.

IN CLOSING

Phobia and obsessive-compulsive disorder illustrate some of the possible links between emotions and cognitions. At the risk of seriously oversimplifying, we could say that people with phobias experience emotional attacks because of their cognitions about some object, whereas people with obsessive-compulsive disorder experience repetitive cognitions for emotional reasons. In both conditions, most people are cognitively aware that their reactions are exaggerated, but mere awareness of the problem does not correct it. Dealing with such conditions requires attention to emotions, cognitions, and the links between them.

SUMMARY

- *Anxiety disorder and panic disorder.* People with generalized anxiety disorder or panic disorder experience extreme anxiety. Panic disorder is characterized by episodes of disabling anxiety, some of which may be triggered by hyperventilation. (page 586)

- *Persistence of avoidance behaviors.* Once an individual has learned a shock-avoidance response, the response may persist long after the possibility of shock has been removed. As with shock-avoidance responses, phobias and obsessive-compulsive disorder persist because people do not discover that their avoidance behaviors are unnecessary. (page 588)

- *Phobia.* A phobia is a fear so extreme that it interferes with normal living. Phobias are learned through observation as well as through experience. (page 588)

- *Common phobias.* People are more likely to develop phobias of certain objects than of others; for example, snake phobias are more common than car phobias. The objects of the most common phobias have menaced humans throughout evolutionary history. They pose dangers that are difficult to predict or control, and they are generally objects with which we have had few safe experiences. (page 591)

- *Systematic desensitization of phobias.* A common therapy for phobia is systematic desensitization, in which the patient is taught to relax and is then gradually exposed to the object of the phobia. Flooding is similar except that the person is exposed to the object suddenly. (page 592)

- *Obsessive-compulsive disorder.* People with obsessive-compulsive disorder try to avoid certain thoughts or impulses that cause anxiety or guilt. They also have repetitive behaviors. (page 593)

- *Types of obsessive-compulsive disorder.* Two common types of compulsion are cleaning and checking. Cleaners try to avoid any type of contamination. Checkers constantly double-check themselves and invent elaborate rituals. (page 594)

SUGGESTION FOR FURTHER READING

Wegner, D. (1989). *White bears and other unwanted thoughts.* New York: Viking Penguin. An account of experiments on obsessive thinking.

TERMS

generalized anxiety disorder disorder in which people are constantly plagued by exaggerated worries (page 586)

panic disorder disorder characterized by a fairly constant state of moderate anxiety and occasional attacks of sudden increased heart rate, chest pains, difficulty in breathing, sweating, faintness, and shaking (page 586)

hyperventilation deep breathing (page 587)

agoraphobia excessive fear of open places or public places (page 587)

phobia a fear so extreme that it interferes with normal living (page 588)

systematic desensitization method of reducing fear by gradually exposing people to the object of their fear (page 592)

flooding or **implosion** a therapy for phobia in which the person is suddenly exposed to the object of the phobia (page 593)

obsessive-compulsive disorder condition with repetitive thoughts and actions (page 593)

obsession a repetitive, unwelcome stream of thought (page 593)

compulsion a repetitive, almost irresistible action (page 593)

ANSWERS TO CONCEPT CHECKS

3. Worrying about anything—even panic attacks themselves—often prompts these people to hyperventilate, and hyperventilation can lead to another panic attack. (page 588)

4. Temporarily prevent the person from pressing the lever. Only when the person stops pressing does he or she discover that pressing is not necessary. (page 588)

5. The CS was the white rat. The UCS was the loud noise. The CR and the UCR were a combination of crying and other reactions of fear. (page 590)

6. The method of extinguishing a learned shock-avoidance response is to prevent the response so that the individual learns that the failure to respond is not followed by shock. Similarly, in systematic desensitization the patient is prevented from fleeing the feared stimulus; he or she therefore learns that the danger is not as great as imagined. (page 593)

7. The flooding procedure is compatible with the James-Lange theory of emotions, which holds that emotions follow from perceptions of body arousal. In flooding, as arousal of the autonomic nervous system decreases, the person perceives, "I am calming down. I must not be as frightened of this situation as I thought I was." (page 593)

ANSWERS TO OTHER QUESTIONS IN THE TEXT

Typical answers for obsessive-compulsive people (page 595):

1. T, **2.** T, **3.** T, **4.** F, **5.** F, **6.** T, **7.** F, **8.** F, **9.** T

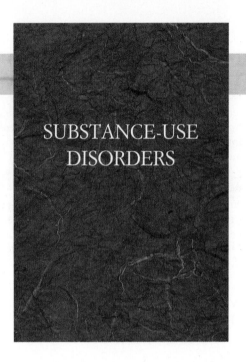

SUBSTANCE-USE DISORDERS

Why do people sometimes abuse alcohol and other drugs?

What can be done to help them quit?

How would you like to volunteer for a little experiment? I want to implant a device in your head to control your brain activity—something that will automatically lift your mood and bring you happiness. There are still a few kinks in it, but most of the people who have tried it say it makes them feel good at least some of the time, and some people say it makes them feel "very happy."

I should tell you about the possible risks: My device will endanger your health and will reduce your life expectancy by, oh, 10 years or so. Some people think it may cause permanent brain damage, but they have not proved that charge, so I don't think you should worry about it. Your behavior will change a good bit, though. You may have difficulty concentrating, for example. The device affects some people more than others. If you happen to be one of those it affects strongly, you will have difficulty completing your education, getting or keeping a job, and carrying on a satisfactory personal life. But if you are lucky, you may avoid all that. Anyway, you can quit the experiment any time you want to. You should know, though, that the longer the device remains in your brain, the harder it is to get it out.

I cannot pay you for taking part in the experiment. In fact, *you* will have to pay *me*. But I'll give you a bargain rate: only $5 for the first week and then a little more each week as time passes. One other thing: Technically speaking, this experiment is illegal. We probably won't get caught, but if we do, we could both go to jail.

What do you say? Is it a deal?

I presume you will say no. I get very few volunteers. And yet if I change the term *brain device* to *drug* and change *experimenter* to *drug peddler,* it is amazing how many volunteers come forward.

For some people, using alcohol or drugs is apparently a harmless pleasure. For others, it is extremely destructive.

In Chapter 5 we examined the effects of several drugs on behavior. Instead of reviewing all of those drugs again here, we shall focus on substance abuse, principally of alcohol and opiates—addictions that have been familiar to humans for centuries and which continue to be major problems today. Substance abuse is one of the most widespread of psychological disorders.

PSYCHOACTIVE SUBSTANCE DEPENDENCE (ADDICTION)

Most people who drink alcohol or experiment with marijuana and other drugs do so in moderation. But some people are such heavy users that they jeopardize their health, their work or education, and the welfare of their family. They may use the substance daily, only on weekends, or only during sporadic binges; whatever the pattern, they know they are consuming too much. They may decide again and again to quit or cut down, but they find it impossible to change their behavior. Those who cannot quit a self-destructive habit are said to have a **dependence** on a substance or **addiction** to it.

A common estimate is that about 10% of all people in the United States and Canada have a substance dependence. Depending on where we draw the line between those with a problem and those without a problem, the estimate might be either higher or lower. But without question, the problem is widespread.

Some substances are much more likely than others are to be addictive. Other things being equal, the more rapidly a substance enters the brain, the more likely it is to be addictive. Cigarettes are more addictive than cigars, for example, because smokers inhale cigarette smoke more deeply, allowing the nicotine to enter the bloodstream and reach the brain more quickly (Bennett, 1980). Similarly, gulped alcohol is more addictive than sipped alcohol, injected cocaine is more addictive than sniffed cocaine, and crack cocaine is more addictive than injected cocaine.

Roy Wise and Michael Bozarth (1987) have proposed that all addictive substances have one property in common: They activate the dopamine synapses responsible for locomotion. Even opiates, barbiturates, and alcohol—which act mainly as depressants—stimulate movement, especially in small doses.

Almost any substance, however, can be addictive under certain circumstances. In one hospital ward where alcoholics were being treated, one of the patients moved his bed into the men's room (Cummings, 1979). At first the hospital staff ignored this curious behavior. Then, one by one, other patients moved their beds into the men's room. Eventually the staff realized what was going on. These men, deprived of alcohol, had discovered that they could get a "high" by drinking enormous amounts of water! By drinking about 7.5 gallons (30 liters) of water a day and urinating the same amount (which was why they moved into the men's room), they managed to alter the acid-to-base balance of their blood enough to produce something like drunkenness. They had become "water addicts." Is water addictive? *The addiction is not in the drug but in the user.*

___

Something to Think About

Are any addictive behaviors beneficial? (If a behavior is beneficial, can we call it *addictive*?)

___

■ CONCEPT CHECK

8. *Methadone, an opiate drug, can be taken either as an injection (entering the blood rapidly) or as a pill (entering the blood slowly). Which route is more likely to lead to an addiction? (Check your answer on page 605).*

Addiction is in the user, not in the drug. Some people will continue using drugs even though they know the drugs endanger their health, limit their opportunities, and provide them with little pleasure.

PREDISPOSITION TO ADDICTION

Although only a minority of alcohol drinkers become alcoholics, many alcoholics become addicted before they reach age 25 (Cloninger, 1987). Some people try heroin once or twice and then quit; others inject themselves so frequently they eventually destroy every vein they can find (Dole, 1978). Why do some people become addicted while others do not?

Most of the research has dealt with alcoholism, the most common addiction, so we shall focus on predisposition to alcoholism. Might it be possible to determine in advance which people are most likely to develop into alcoholics? If we could identify those people early enough, we might be able to train them to drink in moderation or to abstain altogether.

Genetics and Family Background

There is convincing evidence that genetics plays a role in predisposition to alcoholism. The close biological relatives of alcoholics are more likely to become alcoholics themselves than are the relatives of nonalcoholics (Gabrielli & Plomin, 1985). That holds true even when the children of alcoholics are adopted by people who are not alcoholics (Cloninger, Bohman, & Sigvardsson, 1981; Vaillant & Milofsky, 1982).

The incidence of alcoholism is greater than average among adults who have grown up in families marked by conflict between the parents, poor relationships between parents and children, and inadequate parental supervision of the children (Maddahian, Newcomb, &

Not everyone who uses alcohol or other drugs—not even everyone who uses them regularly—suffers the same fate. Some people continue to live a normal life; others experience serious problems with their health and well-being; a few continue to deteriorate until they can no longer take care of themselves. Psychologists would like to be able to identify the people at greatest risk early—before they reach a point of no return.

Bentler, 1988; Schulsinger, Knop, Goodwin, Teasdale, & Mikkelsen, 1986; Zucker & Gomberg, 1986). Once they reach adolescence, many children who grow up in such an environment respond by missing school, engaging in impulsive behaviors, and experimenting with alcohol and other drugs. As adults, they are vulnerable to both alcoholism and drug addiction.

The culture in which children are raised also plays a role. For example, most Jewish families emphasize drinking in moderation, and relatively few Jews become alcoholics (Cahalan, 1978). That is more or less true of Italians as well. By contrast, the Irish tend to be more tolerant of heavy drinking, and alcoholism is more prevalent among people of Irish background (Vaillant & Milofsky, 1982).

Still, individuals differ. Not all children of alcoholic parents become alcoholics themselves, and not all children who grow up in a culture that tolerates heavy drinking become alcoholics. Again, how can we predict which people are most vulnerable to alcoholism?

Ways of Predicting Alcoholism

WHAT'S THE EVIDENCE?

Perhaps a person's early behavior might offer some indicator of who is more likely or less likely to become an alcoholic. One way to find such a clue would be to record the presence or absence of various behaviors in hundreds of young people. Twenty years later we find out which of them have become alcoholics and determine which early behaviors would have predicted those outcomes. Such a study would take 20 years. Moreover, it might be difficult to find some of the subjects after that time, especially the alcoholics.

A more feasible approach would be to compare children of an alcoholic parent with children of parents who are not alcoholics. From previous studies, we know that more children of alcoholics will become alcoholics. Therefore, behaviors that are significantly more prevalent among the children of alcoholics may predict vulnerability to alcoholism.

In the first of the following studies, experimenters tested whether alcohol might be more rewarding to the sons of alcoholics than to the sons of nonalcoholics (Levenson, Oyama, & Meek, 1987).

Experiment 1

Hypothesis When people are put into a stressful situation, an opportunity to drink alcohol will reduce that stress for almost everyone, but it will have a greater effect on the adult sons of an alcoholic parent than on other men the same age.

Method The experiment was conducted on young men, half of them sons of an alcoholic father and half of them sons of nonalcoholic parents. (The study focused on men because alcoholism is about twice as common in men as in women.) The men were told that at a certain time they would receive an electric shock and at another time they would have to give a 3-minute speech on "What I like and dislike about my body." They watched a clock tick off the waiting time. Half of each group were given alcohol to drink at the start of the waiting period, and everyone who was offered alcohol drank it.

Results All of the men showed considerable stress, as measured by heart rate, restlessness, and self-reports of emotions. All of those who drank alcohol showed a lower heart rate and reported less anxiety. The easing of stress was more pronounced in those who had an alcoholic father (Figure 14.13.)

Interpretation Men who are genetically vulnerable to alcoholism experience greater stress-reducing effects from alcohol than other men the same age. Perhaps the degree to which alcohol relieves stress may provide a measure of vulnerability to alcoholism.

Two other experiments examined the possibility that young men who are vulnerable to alcoholism might have trouble estimating their own degree of intoxication (O'Malley & Maisto, 1985; Schuckit, 1985). Because these two experiments used practically the same method and reported the same pattern of results, I shall report them as one.

Experiment 2

Hypothesis Sons of an alcoholic father will underestimate how much they have been affected by the alcohol they have drunk.

Method Young men, some sons of alcoholic fathers and some sons of nonalcoholic parents, consumed drinks containing various amounts of vodka. None of them knew how much vodka was in the drinks. (Vodka has virtually no taste or smell.) After consuming the drinks, they performed various motor and cognitive tasks. They also estimated how much vodka they had drunk and how intoxicated they were.

Results The sons of alcoholic fathers were just as much affected as the sons of nonalcoholics were in their motor and cognitive perfor-

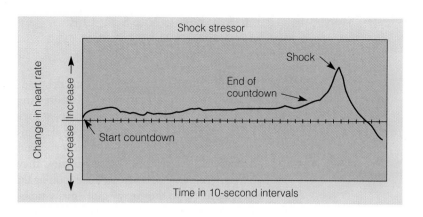

FIGURE 14.13
Changes in stress over time for a typical subject. The line goes up to indicate an increase in heart rate. Note that heart rate increased as soon as the countdown began and then remained stable. It rose toward the end of the countdown and again at the time of the shock or speech. Alcohol suppressed these signs of stress, especially for the sons of alcoholics. (From Levenson, Oyama, & Meek, 1987).

mance. However, they consistently underestimated how much vodka they had drunk and how intoxicated they were.

Interpretation Men who are not especially vulnerable to alcoholism are quick to recognize when they have started to become tipsy and generally stop drinking at that time. Men who are genetically more vulnerable to alcoholism are slower to recognize the signs of intoxication and continue drinking. Again, it may be possible to identify individuals who are particularly prone to alcoholism by testing their ability to monitor their own level of intoxication.

Every study has its strengths and its limitations, and you probably have noticed one of the major limitations of these studies on predisposition to alcohol abuse: They deal entirely with men. Starting with men is reasonable; after all, alcohol abuse is more common in men than in women. Still, someone needs to repeat these studies with women. The studies just discussed have other limitations, too; for example, they tested people's responses just once instead of repeatedly, and in laboratory settings instead of normal drinking environments (Newlin & Thomson, 1990). As with most areas of research, investigators start with a fairly simple but limited design and then proceed with additional research to find out how broadly the conclusions apply.

TREATMENTS FOR ALCOHOLISM AND DRUG ADDICTION

At some point, most alcoholics and drug addicts decide that the occasional pleasures the drugs give them are not worth all the pain they bring. So they decide to quit. Some people manage to quit on their own, although few succeed on their first attempt. More frequently, they quit and then relapse into drug use, quit again and relapse again; they may "quit" many times before they finally succeed on a long-term basis. A relapse after a period of abstention is not necessarily a failure; it may provide the addict with "practice" toward long-term abstention. In the long run, about 10–20% of alcohol and drug users manage to quit without help (Cohen et al., 1989).

People who seek professional help have a little higher probability of long-term abstention, although hardly a guarantee. Clinical psychologists spend an estimated one fifth to one fourth of their time with patients suffering from substance-abuse problems (Cummings, 1979). Addicts who check into a hospital for treatment can be supervised 24 hours a day to ensure full abstinence. **Detoxification** refers to a supervised period to remove drugs from the body. In the long run, however, most addicts respond just as well to outpatient treatment as they do to hospital treatment (Miller & Hester, 1986).

Therapists use many methods for helping people overcome substance-abuse disorders. In Chapter 15 we shall consider methods of therapy in general, as they apply to all types of disorders. Here we focus on methods that apply exclusively to substance abuse.

Treating Alcoholism

Alcoholism, the habitual overuse of alcohol, is the most common and most costly form of drug abuse in the United States and Europe. An estimated 25–40% of all hospital patients suffer from complications caused by alcohol abuse (Holden, 1987).

Alcoholics Anonymous The most widespread treatment for alcoholism in North America is **Alcoholics Anonymous (AA),** a self-help group of people who are trying to abstain from alcohol use and to help others do the same. In all large cities, and in many smaller cities and towns, AA meetings are held regularly in community halls, church basements, and other available spaces (Figure 14.14). New members are strongly encouraged to attend 90 meetings during the first 90 days. (Those who miss one day can compensate by attending two or more meetings another day.) From then on, members attend as often as they like.

Millions of people worldwide have participated in the AA program. One reason for its appeal is that all the members have gone through similar experiences. If someone tries to make an excuse for drinking, saying "You just don't understand how I feel," others can retort, "Oh, yes we do!" Fellow sufferers make very understanding listeners. A member who feels the urge to take a drink, or who has already had one, can call a fellow member day or night for support. There is no charge for attendance at meetings; members simply contribute what they can toward the cost of the meeting place. AA has inspired other "anonymous" self-help groups whose purpose is to help drug addicts, compulsive gamblers, compulsive eaters, and so forth.

Although AA members themselves have no doubt about the value of the program, research on its effectiveness has been scarce. One reason is that the organization is serious about its members' anonymity; it does not provide a list of members, and many of its meetings are closed to nonmembers.

About 50% of AA members abstain from alcohol altogether for at least a year and a half after joining; others try to abstain but suffer occasional relapses (Emrick, 1987; Thurstin, Alfano, & Nerviano, 1987). Those results compare favorably to the results for alcoholics in other programs and for alcoholics who try to quit on their own. Still, because assignment to groups is not random, we cannot draw a firm conclusion. (Perhaps people who join AA are more highly motivated to quit than other alcoholics are.)

Antabuse In addition to or instead of attendance at AA meetings, many alcoholics seek medical treatment. Many years ago, investigators noticed that the workers in a certain rubber-manufacturing plant drank very little alcohol. The investigators eventually linked this behavior to disulfiram, a chemical that was used in the manufacturing process. Ordinarily, the liver converts alcohol into a toxic substance, acetaldehyde (ASS-eh-TAL-de-HIDE), and then converts acetaldehyde into a harmless substance, acetic acid. Disulfiram, however, blocks the conversion of acetaldehyde to acetic acid. Whenever the workers drank alcohol, acetaldehyde accumulated in their body and they became ill. Over time, they learned to avoid all use of alcohol.

Disulfiram, under the trade name **Antabuse,** is now commonly used in the treatment of alcoholism (Peachey & Naranjo, 1983). Alcoholics who take a daily Antabuse pill become very sick whenever they have a drink. They develop a sensation of heat in the face, a headache, nausea, blurred vision, and anxiety. The threat of sickness is probably more effective than the sickness itself (Fuller & Roth, 1979). By taking a daily pill, a recovering alcoholic renews a decision not to drink. Those who actually do take a drink in spite of the threat get quite ill, at which point they may decide not to drink again, or they may decide not to take the pill again!

- # CONCEPT CHECK

9. *About 50% of Asians have a gene that makes them unable to convert acetaldehyde to acetic acid. Would such people be more likely or less likely than others to become alcoholics? (Check your answer on page 605.)*

Controversy: Is Alcoholism a "Disease"? Alcoholics Anonymous has traditionally regarded alcoholism as a disease. What that means is not exactly clear, because the medical profession makes no precise definition of *disease,* and neither does AA. Apparently, AA means that alcoholism is the problem itself, not just a sign of some other psychological or moral weakness, and that alcoholics should feel no guiltier about their alcoholism than they would about having pneumonia.

Labeling something as a disease has consequences, however. For example, the United States' 1992 Americans with Disabilities Act prohibits employers from discriminating against otherwise qualified job applicants with disabilities, including alcoholism and drug abuse. In other words, an employer cannot refuse to hire alcoholics or drug addicts.

Also, the "disease" concept of alcoholism implies that alcoholics gradually progress to drinking more and more. Supporters of this view hold that the only hope for an alcoholic lies in complete abstention from alcohol; one drink, or one sip, will cause a reformed alcoholic to revert to uncontrolled drinking (Peele, 1984). Many researchers regard that view as an overgeneralization, because different alcoholics deteriorate to different degrees (Vaillant, 1983). Most alcoholics who go on drinking eventually

FIGURE 14.14

Alcoholics Anonymous (AA) is the prototypical example of self-help groups. AA meetings are held throughout the United States and in many other countries throughout the world. Members share their experiences with one another and provide encouragement and help to members in need. A member who is fighting a craving for alcohol can call a fellow member for help at any time; each understands the problems that others are having. AA makes many recommendations, but its only requirement is that members try to overcome their alcohol problems.

reach a stable level, though not necessarily a desirable level. Some actually cut back on their drinking even though they continue to drink to excess (Hodgson, Rankin, & Stockwell, 1979; Moos & Finney, 1983; Wanberg & Horn, 1983).

Finally, to regard alcoholism strictly as a disease ignores the possibility that environmental factors may have some influence on drinking behavior (Marlatt, 1978). Excessive drinking can sometimes be brought under control by altering the environment. One approach is to provide reinforcers that compete with the reinforcers provided by drinking. For example, a therapist might help an alcoholic to find a full-time job, provide marital counseling, and get the person interested in a social club or a hobby (Azrin, 1976).

Another Controversy: Controlled Drinking Most physicians agree with Alcoholics Anonymous that the only hope for an alcoholic is total abstinence. Drinking in moderation, they insist, is out of the question.

A few psychologists disagree, claiming that at least some alcoholics can be trained to cut back on their drinking. They do not claim that alcoholics can start drinking in moderation simply by deciding to do so, nor do they claim that moderate drinking is an appropriate goal for most alcoholics. But they suggest it might be appropriate for a small number.

Mark Sobell and Linda Sobell (1976) reported that they had trained some severe alcoholics to drink in a controlled manner. As part of the treatment, they had alcoholics watch videotapes of themselves drinking out of control. The investigators counseled each alcoholic on when, where, and how to drink in moderation. They reported that an experimental group of 20 alcoholics treated in this manner fared as well as or better than a control group of 20 alcoholics who received treatments emphasizing total abstinence.

Those claims were greeted with great skepticism. A follow-up study found that only 1 of the 20 alcoholics in the experimental group could be considered a "controlled" drinker 10 years later (Pendery, Maltzman, & West, 1982). Of the others, 8 were excessive drinkers, and 4 had died from alcohol-related causes. Six had been in and out of jails and hospitals because of alcohol problems until at last they gave up on controlled drinking and entered an abstinence program. The last person from the original study could not be found 10 years later but was known to have been drinking excessively at last report.

The 20 alcoholics in the control group, whose treatment had centered on total abstinence, did just as poorly. After 10 years, 6 of them had died from alcohol-related causes and the rest were still drinking in excess (Sobell & Sobell, 1984). In other words, for this sample of quite severe alcoholics, neither treatment had succeeded. With other individuals under other circumstances, controlled drinking might be a suitable goal.

Treating Opiate Addiction

Before the year 1900, opiate drugs such as morphine and heroin were considered far less dangerous than alcohol (Siegel, 1987). In fact, many medical doctors used to urge their alcoholic patients to switch from alcohol to morphine. Then, around 1900, the use of opiates was made illegal in the United States, except by prescription for relief from pain. Since then, research on opiate use has been limited by the fact that only law-breakers now use opiates.

Some users of heroin and other opiates try to break their habit by going "cold turkey"—abstaining altogether until the withdrawal symptoms subside, sometimes under medical supervision. Many people, however, experience a recurring urge to take the drug, even long after the withdrawal symptoms have subsided. For those who cannot quit, researchers have sought to find a nonaddictive substitute that would satisfy the craving for opiates without creating their harmful effects. Heroin was originally introduced as a substitute for morphine. Soon, however, physicians discovered that heroin is even more addictive and troublesome than morphine.

Today, the most common substitute for opiates is **methadone** (METH-uh-don). Methadone is chemically similar to both morphine and heroin and can itself be addictive. (Table 14.5 compares methadone and morphine.) When taken in pill form, however, it takes hours to enter and leave the bloodstream (Dole, 1980). (If morphine or heroin is taken as a pill, most of the drug is broken down in the digestive system and never reaches the brain.) Thus methadone does not produce the "rush" associated with intravenous injections of opiates; nor does it produce rapid withdrawal symptoms. Although methadone satisfies the craving for opiates without seriously disrupting the user's behavior, it does not eliminate the addiction itself. If the dosage is reduced, the craving returns.

Going cold turkey: Heroin withdrawal resembles a severe bout of the flu, with aching limbs, intense chills, vomiting, and diarrhea; it lasts a week on average. Unfortunately, even after people have suffered through withdrawal, they are likely to experience periods of craving for the drug.

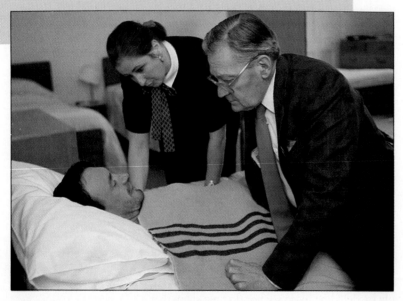

Many addicts who stick to a methadone maintenance program are able to hold down a job and commit fewer crimes than they did when they were using heroin or morphine (Woody & O'Brien, 1986). Some of them, after discovering that they can no longer get a high from opiates, turn instead to the nonopiate drug cocaine (Kosten, Rounsaville, & Kleber, 1987). In other words, methadone maintenance programs do not eliminate the addictive behaviors. At present, there is no reliable cure for opiate dependence.

Table 14.5 Comparison of Methadone with Morphine

	Morphine	Methadone
Addictive?	Yes	Yes if taken by injection; weakly if taken orally
Administration	Usually by injection	Recommended for oral use
Onset	Rapid	Slow if taken orally
"Rush"?	Yes	Not if taken orally
Relieves craving?	Yes	Yes
Rapid withdrawal symptoms?	Yes	No

SUMMARY

■ *Substance dependence.* People who find it difficult or impossible to stop using a substance are said to be dependent on it or addicted to it. (page 598)

■ *Addictive substances.* Generally, the faster a substance enters the brain, the more likely it is to be addictive. For some people, however, almost any substance can be addictive. (page 599)

■ *Predisposition to alcoholism.* Some people may be predisposed to become alcoholics for genetic or other reasons. People at risk for alcoholism find that alcohol relieves their stress more than it does for other people. They also tend to underestimate how intoxicated they are. (page 599)

■ *Alcoholics Anonymous.* The most common treatment for alcoholism in North America is provided by the self-help group called Alcoholics Anonymous. (page 602)

■ *Antabuse.* Some alcoholics are treated with Antabuse, a prescription drug that makes them ill if they drink alcohol. (page 602)

■ *The "disease" controversy.* Whether or not alcoholism is a disease is controversial; calling it a disease may distract attention from the environmental factors that lead to drinking. (page 603)

■ *The "controlled drinking" controversy.* Whether alcoholics can be trained to drink in moderation is also a controversial, unsettled question. For severe alcoholics, no known method of treatment offers a high probability of recovery. (page 603)

■ *Treatments for opiate abuse.* Some opiate users quit using opiates, suffer through the withdrawal symptoms, and manage to abstain from further use. Others substitute methadone under medical supervision. Although methadone has less destructive effects than morphine or heroin does, it does not eliminate the underlying dependence. (page 604)

SUGGESTIONS FOR FURTHER READING

Marlatt, G. A., & Baer, J. S. (1988). Addictive behaviors: Etiology and treatment. *Annual Review of Psychology, 39,* 223–252. A review of the literature on who becomes an alcoholic or drug addict, why, and what can be done to help.

Vaillant, G. E. (1983). *The natural history of alcoholism.* Cambridge, MA: Harvard University Press. A thorough study of what happens to alcoholics over the course of their lifetime.

TERMS

dependence or **addiction** a self-destructive habit that someone cannot quit (page 598)

detoxification supervised period to remove drugs from the body (page 602)

alcoholism habitual overuse of alcohol (page 602)

Alcoholics Anonymous (AA) a self-help group of people who are trying to abstain from alcohol use and to help others do the same (page 602)

Antabuse trade name for disulfiram, a drug used in the treatment of alcoholism (page 603)

methadone a drug commonly offered as a less dangerous substitute for opiates (page 604)

ANSWERS TO CONCEPT CHECKS

8. The injection route is more likely to lead to an addiction. Other things being equal, the faster a drug reaches the brain, the more likely it is to become addictive. (page 590)

9. They are less likely than others to become alcoholics. This gene is considered the probable reason why relatively few Asians become alcoholics (Harada et al., 1982; Reed, 1985). (page 603)

MOOD
DISORDERS

Why do people become depressed?
What can be done to relieve depression?
How are depression and suicide related?

Even when things are going badly, most people remain optimistic that all will be well in the end. After the hurt and disappointment we feel when a relationship breaks up, we say, "Oh, well, at least I learned something from the experience." When we lose money, we say, "It could have been worse. I still have my health."

But sometimes we feel depressed. Nothing seems as much fun as it used to be, and the future seems ominous. For some people, the depression is severe and long-lasting. Why?

DEPRESSION

Sometimes someone says "I'm depressed" to mean "I am sad; life isn't going very well for me right now." In psychology, **depression** refers to a prolonged condition, lasting most of the day, day after day, with a loss of interest or pleasure and a lack of productive activity. Even if life starts going well for the person, the depression persists.

Depressed people have trouble concentrating. Their appetite and sex drive decline. Their facial expression is typically sad. They feel worthless, fearful, guilty, and powerless to control what happens to them. Most of them consider suicide and many attempt it.

Nearly all depressed people experience sleep abnormalities (Carroll, 1980; Healy & Williams, 1988). (See Figure 14.15.) They enter REM sleep in less than 45 minutes after falling asleep (an unusually short time for most people). Most depressed people wake up too early and cannot get back to sleep. When morning comes they feel poorly rested. In fact, early morning is usually the time when they feel most depressed. During most of the day they feel a little sleepy.

Depression, like any other psychological disorder, can vary in degree. For some people an episode of depression persists for months at a time and may recur periodically year after year. **Bipolar disorder,** also known as *manic-depressive disorder,* is a related condition in which a person alternates between periods of depression and periods of mania, which is the opposite extreme. We shall return to bipolar disorder later.

Many psychologists also distinguish between reactive and endogenous depressions (Zimmerman, Coryell, Pfohl, & Stangl, 1986). A **reactive depression** develops suddenly in reaction to a severe loss, such as the death of a spouse. An **endogenous depression** develops more gradually and cannot be traced to any single traumatic experience. Rather, it seems to result from internal, biological influences.

In practice, this distinction is difficult to draw. In many cases, depression apparently results from a combination of a biological predisposition and a history of unpleasant experiences. Moreover, classifying someone's depression as reactive or endogenous is of little help in deciding how to treat it (Arana, Baldessarini, & Ornsteen, 1985; Keller et al., 1986).

About 5% of all people in the United States suffer from a major depression at some time during their life (Robins et al., 1984). For unknown reasons, depression is more common among women than among men (Nolen-Hoeksema, 1987). The most common age of onset for major depression is about 40; for bipolar disorder, about 30. Over the decades there has been a trend toward diagnosis at younger ages (Burke, Burke, Rae, & Regier, 1991). We do not know whether that means that depression has

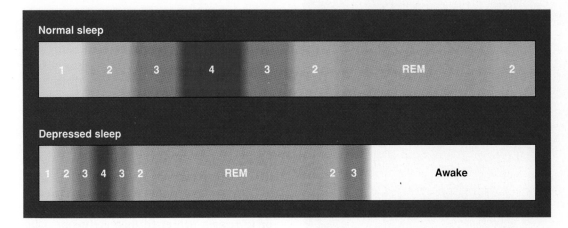

Normal sleep

1 2 3 4 3 2 REM 2

Depressed sleep

1 2 3 4 3 2 REM 2 3 Awake

FIGURE 14.15
When most people go to sleep at their normal time of day, they progress slowly to stage 4 and then back through stages 3 and 2, reaching REM toward the end of their first 90-minute cycle. Depressed people, however, reach REM more rapidly, generally in less than 45 minutes. They also tend to awaken frequently during the night.

started having its onset at younger and younger ages, or just that therapists have become more expert at detecting early-onset depression.

Biological Predisposition to Depression

The fact that depression tends to run in families suggests that some people have a genetic predisposition to depression (see Figure 14.16). It is two to five times more common among the close relatives of a depressed person than it is in the population at large (Beardslee, Bemporad, Keller, & Klerman, 1983; Weissman, Kidd, & Prusoff, 1982). It is particularly common among the relatives of people who themselves became severely depressed before age 30 (Price, Kidd, & Weissman, 1987). Adopted children who become depressed usually have more biological relatives than adopting relatives who are depressed (Wender et al., 1986). So far we do not have consistent evidence to indicate whether depression depends on one gene or several (Faraone, Kremen, & Tsuang, 1990). Chances are, a disposition to depression depends on different genes or gene combinations in different families; a number of different biological abnormalities may lead to the same behavioral result.

Many relatives of depressed people suffer from severe anxiety (Kendler, Heath, Martin, & Eaves, 1987) or alcohol abuse (Cook &

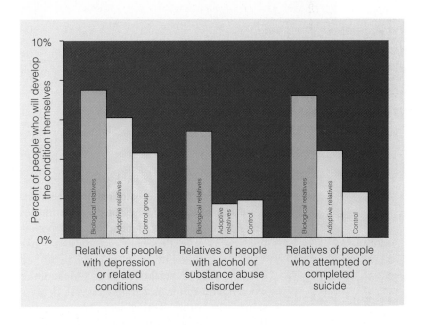

FIGURE 14.16
When compared with incidences of depression in the general public, which is 5–10%, blood relatives of a depressed person are more likely to suffer depression themselves. The closer the genetic relationship is, the greater is the probability of depression.

Winokur, 1985). It is possible that certain families have genes that express themselves in different ways, leading to depression in some people and to other disorders in other people.

Fluctuations in the level of sex hormones and other hormones may trigger episodes of depression, especially in women. Shortly after giv-

Mood Disorders 607

The appearance of depressed people mirrors their feelings of sadness and hopelessness, as this painting by Rafael Coronel shows. Downcast eyes and sagging head and shoulders accompany slow movement. Suggestions to "smile" or "cheer up" fall on deaf ears.

ing birth, a time of massive hormonal changes, some women enter a **postpartum depression.** Estimates of the frequency of postpartum depression vary widely, depending on whether one counts only the severe cases (about 1 per 1,000), the moderate cases (about 1 in 10), or even the mild cases (about 3 in 10). Most of the women who suffer moderate to severe depression have a history of other depressive episodes; the hormonal swing after giving birth is not so much a *cause* of depression as it is a trigger for an additional depressive episode (O'Hara, Schlechte, Lewis, & Wright, 1991).

Other Risk Factors in Depression

What kind of person becomes depressed? Biological predisposition is only part of the answer. Another part is that people become depressed when bad things happen to them. But why do some people become deeply depressed after a loss that upsets other people only a little?

A severe loss early in life seems to make some people overresponsive to losses later on. For example, adolescents who lose a parent through death or divorce are particularly vulnerable to depression later in life (Roy, 1985). Breaking up with a boyfriend or girlfriend, or the death of another close relative, may bring back the feelings of desertion they felt over the loss of the parent.

People with poor social support also tend to be vulnerable to depression. As we saw in Chapter 12, social support helps people to cope with stress. People with a happy marriage and close friends are less likely to become depressed or to remain depressed than are people who have no one to talk to about their troubles (Barnett & Gotlib, 1988; Flaherty, Gaviria, Black, Altman, & Mitchell, 1983).

Finally, people who are undergoing severe pain are likely to become depressed (Katon, Egan, & Miller, 1985; Romano & Turner, 1985). However, the correlation between the two does not establish that pain leads to depression. Many people show signs of depression before complaining of pain.

COGNITIVE ASPECTS OF DEPRESSION

Most people believe that every cloud has a silver lining. Show depressed people a silver lining and they wrap it in a cloud. Somehow they think differently from people who are not depressed. Do their thoughts lead to their depression?

In one experiment, depressed and undepressed people were asked to imagine certain events that might happen to them and then to explain why those events might have happened (Peterson, 1983). The undepressed people often suggested explanations that turned bad events into good ones. For example, to the statement "You have a date that goes badly," they might explain that "the weather was bad, and I slipped in the mud and got my good clothes all messy. But then the two of us had a good laugh, I went back and changed clothes, and we ended up having a better time than ever." The depressed people suggested explanations that made the bad event even worse. For example, "The date went badly because I said something stupid and my date was embarrassed and refused to see me ever again." Even to good news like "you got rich," a depressed person might say, "I got rich because one of my favorite relatives died and left me some money. And then all my friends got jealous of my wealth and wouldn't talk to me anymore."

Why do some people see only the unpleasant side of life? According to the **learned-helplessness theory,** their experiences have taught them that they have no control over the major events in their lives.

Learned Helplessness: Animal Experiments

The learned-helplessness theory of depression grew out of some experiments with animals. While testing theories about avoidance learning in animals, Steven Maier, Martin Seligman, and Richard Solomon (1969) trained some dogs in shuttle boxes. First, the dog hears a tone and then, 5 seconds later, it receives a 5-second shock to its feet. Most dogs quickly learn to jump across the barrier as soon as they hear the tone and manage to avoid the shocks altogether.

In one variation of this procedure, the experimenters first strapped dogs with no previous experience into restraining harnesses and then repeatedly sounded a tone that was followed by a shock to the dogs' feet. The dogs soon learned that the tone predicted shock. They struggled to escape but could not. When the experimenters put the same dogs into the shuttle box the next day (without the harness), they discovered to their surprise that the dogs were extremely slow to learn the avoidance response. Most of them failed to learn it at all. Why? Besides learning on the first day that the tone predicted shock, the dogs had also learned that they could not escape the shock. On the second day, even though they were no longer restrained, the dogs did not jump when they received the shocks. They had learned that they were helpless.

These "helpless" dogs resembled depressed people in several respects. The dogs were inactive and slow to learn. Even their posture and "facial expressions" suggested sadness. The experimenters proposed that the same process might operate in humans: People who, despite their best efforts, meet only with defeat and loss may come to feel "helpless" and fall into depression.

Learned Helplessness: Studies with Humans

In later experiments (for example, Price, Tryon, & Raps, 1978), human subjects were asked to perform certain tasks. Some of them were given tasks that were much more difficult than they seemed to be—so difficult, in fact, that the subjects were bound to fail. Then they

were given a second task, this one only moderately difficult. Those who had been forced to fail on the first task performed the second task worse than others who had never attempted the first task (Figure 14.17). Apparently they had lost their self-esteem, felt "low," and were somewhat depressed. The depression was mild, however, and vanished as soon as the experimenter explained that they had not really "failed" on the first task. Experiments of this type indicate that humans can learn helplessness, at least as a temporary tendency.

Do Depressed People Underestimate Their Control of Events?

According to the learned-helplessness theory, some people become depressed because they believe they have little control over events. But do they really underestimate their control, or do they just seem to underestimate it, because everyone else overestimates it? Lauren Alloy and Lyn Abramson (1979) set up an experiment to answer those questions.

First, students were asked to fill out a questionnaire designed to measure depression. Those with higher-than-average scores were considered depressed; the others were considered undepressed. (We do not know whether depressed college students are representative of other depressed people.)

Then the students were told to try to get a green light to come on, either by pressing a button or by not pressing it. Pressing the button might either increase or decrease the probability that the light would come on. Consequently, the students should try both pressing and not pressing to see what would happen. The apparatus was set up so that some students had a great deal of control: One response (either pressing or not pressing) would turn the light on 75% of the time, whereas the other response would never turn it on. Other students had less control, and some had no control at all.

Afterward, the experimenters asked subjects to estimate how much control they had had over the outcome. Both sets of subjects estimated their control fairly accurately when they had at least 25% control, but the undepressed people seriously overestimated when they had no control (see Figure 14.18). In other words, the depressed people did not underestimate their control over the light. On the contrary, the normal, undepressed people had an illusion of control when, in fact, they had no control.

We could interpret that result in two ways

FIGURE 14.17
According to the learned-helplessness theory, people who try as hard as they can and still fail (perhaps because the task was more difficult than it appeared) learn that they are helpless. They lose self-confidence and stop trying. If this feeling of helplessness continues, they may be on their way to depression.

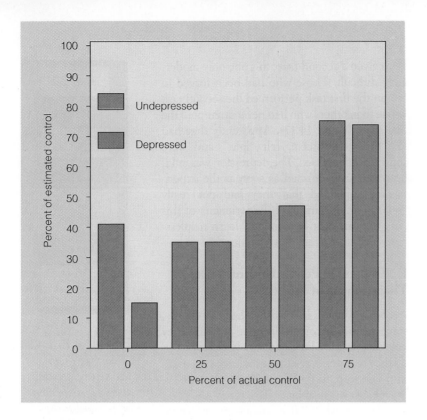

FIGURE 14.18

Depressed and undepressed people estimated their amount of control of a light in a situation in which actual control varied from 0% to 75%. Note the results when subjects had no control. Depressed subjects believed they had a slight amount of control; undepressed subjects believed they had more than 40% control! (Based on data of Alloy & Abramson, 1979.)

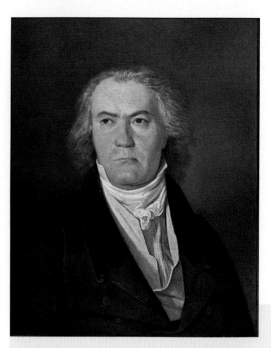

Depressed people are sometimes quite accurate in their appraisal of a gloomy situation. As Beethoven began to lose his hearing, he tried every doctor he could find. None could help him. He became severely depressed, accurately recognizing that his deafness was permanent.

(Schwartz, 1981). First, some people become depressed because they perceive—rightly or wrongly—that they have no control. And perhaps other people do not become depressed because they maintain an illusion of controlling their fate even when it is out of their hands. Depressed people say, "I'm not pessimistic, just realistic." Maybe they are right. Second, perhaps people become depressed for other reasons, but after becoming depressed they begin to recognize their lack of control. We do not know which interpretation is correct.

For whatever reason, people who are not depressed tend to take an optimistic view of their ability to control events, and of their abilities in general. They regard themselves as well liked; if anything, they overestimate other people's opinions of them (Lewinsohn, Mischel, Chaplin, & Barton, 1980).

■ CONCEPT CHECK

***10.** Why do most students predict that they will raise their grades in the future? And why does al-* most every sports coach predict that his or her team will do better this year than last? Would depressed people be more or less likely than undepressed people to buy a lottery ticket? (Check your answers on page 615.)*

Learned Helplessness and Attributions for Failure

Having an unpleasant experience is usually not enough in itself to make a person depressed. People feel helpless and become depressed only if they believe they are somehow to blame for the unpleasant experience. Suppose you fail a French test. How bad do you feel? The answer depends on why you think you failed. You might attribute your failure to any of a number of causes:

■ I failed because the test was so hard. This prof always makes the first test of the semester extra difficult just to scare us into studying harder.

■ I failed because I'm the only one in the class who didn't take French in high school.

- I failed because I was sick and didn't get a chance to study.
- I failed because I'm stupid.

With any of the first three attributions for failure, you probably wouldn't feel very depressed. You would be attributing your failure to a temporary, specific, or correctable situation—a problem that has nothing to do with your abilities. But the fourth attribution applies to you at all times in all situations. If you make that attribution—and if your grades are important to you—you are likely to feel depressed. And if you are already depressed, you are likely to make that attribution (Abramson, Seligman, & Teasdale, 1978; Peterson, Bettes, & Seligman, 1985).

Depressed people tend to attribute their failures to factors that are stable (long-lasting), global (applicable to many situations), and internal (within themselves). For example, "I'm stupid. I'm lazy. I'm unattractive. I'm uncoordinated." However, they attribute their successes to external forces or to luck. In terms of the "locus of control" personality trait discussed in Chapter 13, depressed people tend to show an external locus of control; they believe they have little control over the important events in their life (Benassi, Sweeney, & Dufour, 1988; Costello, 1982).

Something to Think About

Are nations as well as individuals subject to learned helplessness? If so, might this principle explain why some nations decide that it is pointless to negotiate with other nations? Can you think of other examples in an international setting?

Helplessness and Depression

Results such as those we have examined indicate that depressed people tend to feel helpless, that they tend to have a low opinion of their ability to control events. But which came first: the depression or the feeling of helplessness? It is difficult to determine what caused what, because many people become depressed and develop attitudes of helplessness at about the same time (Barnett & Gotlib, 1988; Silverman, Silverman, & Eardley, 1984).

Some prominent theorists believe, however, that feelings of helplessness and hopelessness are a cause for at least some cases of depression (Abramson, Metalsky, & Alloy, 1989). When

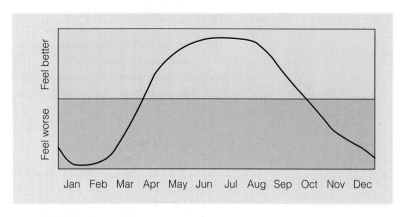

FIGURE 14.19

Most people have a slightly more pleasant mood during the summer (when the sun is out most of the day) than during the winter (when the day has fewer hours of sunlight). A small number of people—those with seasonal affective disorder—show an exaggerated tendency, feeling extremely good in the summer and seriously depressed in the winter. Seasonal affective disorder is more common in far-northern locations such as Alaska, where the summer days have many hours of sunlight and the winter days have few. It is unheard-of in tropical locations such as Hawaii, where the amount of sunlight per day differs only slightly between summer and winter.

people come to expect bad outcomes and believe that they have little control over those outcomes, they are likely to become depressed. That theory, however, still leaves open the question of how people come to hold these depression-producing beliefs in the first place.

SEASONAL AFFECTIVE DISORDER

One variety of depression is known as **seasonal affective disorder,** or *depression with a seasonal pattern* (Figure 14.19). People with this disorder become seriously depressed every winter. In summer they are either normal or slightly manic (the opposite of depressed). Unlike most other depressed patients, they tend to sleep and eat excessively during their depressed periods (Jacobsen, Sack, Wehr, Rogers, & Rosenthal, 1987).

People with seasonal affective disorder respond to the amount of sunlight they see each day. Most of us are more cheerful when the sun is shining than we are on cloudy days, but these people are particularly sensitive to the effects of sunlight. Seasonal affective disorder can be relieved by sitting for a few hours each day in front of a bright light after the sun sets or before it rises—artificially lengthening the day and resetting the body's biological clock (Wehr et al., 1986).

11. *In the Southern Hemisphere, would seasonal affective disorder occur in January and February, as it does in the Northern Hemisphere, or would it occur at some other time? (Check your answer on page 615.)*

BIPOLAR DISORDER

People with bipolar disorder (also known as manic-depressive disorder) alternate between the extremes of mania and depression. In most respects, **mania** is the opposite of depression. When people with bipolar disorder are in the depressed phase, they are slow, inactive, and inhibited. When they are in the manic phase, they are constantly active and uninhibited. When depressed, they feel helpless, guilt ridden, and sad. When manic, they are either happy or angry. About 1% of all adults in the United States suffer from bipolar disorder at some time during their life (Robins et al., 1984).

People in a manic phase have trouble inhibiting their impulses. Mental hospitals cannot install fire alarms in certain wards because manic patients pull the alarm repeatedly. They make costly mistakes of judgment, such as investing large sums of money in highly risky or poorly considered ventures. Even after their friends warn them of the risks, they plunge ahead.

The rambling speech of a manic person has been described as a "flight of ideas." The person starts talking about one topic, which suggests another, which suggests another. Here is a quote from a manic patient:

I like playing pool a lot, that's one of my releases, that I play pool a lot. Oh what else? Bartend, bartend on the side, it's kind of fun to, if you're a bartender you can, you can see how people reacted, amounts of alcohol and different guys around, different chicks around, and different situations, if it's snowing outside, if it's cold outside, the weather conditions, all types of different types of environments and types of different types of people you'll usually find in a bar. (Hoffman, Stopek, & Andreasen, 1986, p. 835)

Some people experience a mild degree of mania ("hypomania") almost always. They are productive, popular, extraverted, "life-of-the-party" types. Mania may become so serious, however, that it makes normal life impossible. The theatrical director Joshua Logan has described his own experiences with depression and mania. A few excerpts follow.

A Self-Report: Depressive Phase

I had no faith in the work I was doing or the people I was working with. . . . It was a great burden to get up in the morning and I couldn't wait to go to bed at night, even though I started not sleeping well. . . . I thought I was well but feeling low because of a hidden personal discouragement of some sort—something I couldn't quite put my finger on. . . . I just forced myself to live through a dreary, hopeless existence that lasted for months on end. . . .

My depressions actually began around the age of thirty-two. I remember I was working on a play, and I was forcing myself to work. . . . I can remember that I sat in some sort of aggravated agony as it was read aloud for the first time by the cast. It sounded so awful that I didn't want to direct it. I didn't even want to see it. I remember feeling so depressed that I wished that I were dead without having to go through the shame and defeat of suicide. I couldn't sleep well at all, and sleep meant, for me, oblivion, and that's what I longed for and couldn't get. I didn't know what to do and I felt very, very lost. (Fieve, 1975, pp. 42–43)

A Self-Report: Manic Phase

Here, Logan describes his manic experiences:

Finally, as time passed, the depression gradually wore off and turned into something else, which I didn't understand either. But it was a much pleasanter thing to go through, at least at first. Instead of hating everything, I started liking things—liking them too much, perhaps. . . . I

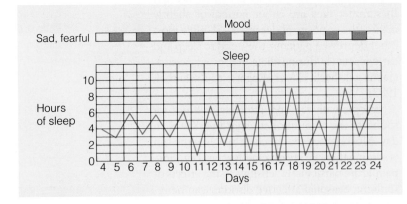

FIGURE 14.20
These records show one woman's 1-day manic periods alternating with 1-day depressed periods. Her days of cheerfulness alternated with days of fearfulness and sadness. (Based on Richter, 1938).

put out a thousand ideas a minute: things to do, plays to write, plots to write stories about. . . .

I decided to get married on the spur of the moment. . . . I practically forced her to say yes. Suddenly we had a loveless marriage and that had to be broken up overnight. . . .

I can only remember that I worked constantly, day and night, never even seeming to need more than a few hours of sleep. I always had a new idea or another conference. . . . It was an exhilarating time for me.

It finally went too far. In the end I went over the bounds of reality, or law and order, so to say. I don't mean that I committed any crimes, but I could easily have done so if anyone had crossed me. I flew into rages if contradicted. I began to be irritable with everyone. Should a man, friend or foe, object to anything I did or said, it was quite possible that I could poke him in the jaw. I was eventually persuaded by the doctors that I was desperately ill and should go into the hospital. But it was not, even then, convincing to me that I was ill.

There I was, on the sixth floor of a New York building that had special iron bars around it and an iron gate that had slid into place and locked me away from the rest of the world. . . . I looked about and saw that there was an open window. I leaped up on the sill and climbed out of the window on the ledge on the sixth floor and said, "Unless you open the door, I'm going to climb down the outside of this building." At the time, I remember feeling so powerful that I might actually be able to scale the building. . . . They immediately opened the steel door, and I climbed back in. That's where manic elation can take you. (Fieve, 1975, pp. 43–45)

Bipolar Cycles

A manic period or a depressed period may last for months or for just a day. Figure 14.20 shows the mood ratings for a manic-depressive woman over 3 weeks (Richter, 1938). Note that she alternated day by day. She slept more on her cheerful days than on her sad days. Figure 14.21 shows the mood and body weight fluctuations for a manic-depressive man who had 3-day manic periods and 3-day depressed periods (Crammer, 1959). In many patients the depressed periods last longer than the manic periods.

SUICIDE

Many psychologically disturbed people attempt suicide, especially those who are depressed.

Suicide is one of the most common causes of death among young people. Figure 14.22 shows the estimated rates of suicide as a function of age (Boyd, 1983). Accurate records are hard to come by, because an unknown number of people disguise their suicides to look like accidents, either to reduce their family's anguish or to enable their survivors to collect life insurance.

Women make more suicide attempts than men, yet more men than women die by suicide (Cross & Hirschfeld, 1986). Most men who attempt suicide use guns or other violent means.

Résumé
Razors pain you;
Rivers are damp;
Acids stain you;
And drugs cause cramp.
Guns aren't lawful;
Nooses give;
Gas smells awful;
You might as well live.
DOROTHY PARKER
(1944)

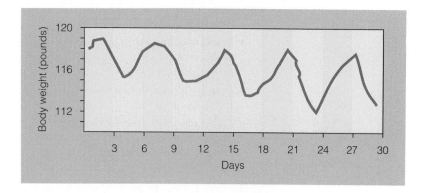

FIGURE 14.21
Records for a man who had 3-day manic periods (pink) alternating with 3-day depressed periods (blue). Note that he lost weight during manic times because of his high activity level. (Based on Crammer, 1959.)

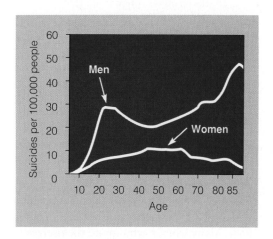

FIGURE 14.22
At every age, men are more likely than women are to commit suicide, although a very large number of women (especially young women) make suicide attempts from which they survive. For women, the probability of suicide is greatest in middle age. For men, it is high at about age 20, decreases during middle age, and rises again in old age.

Mood Disorders   613

Table 14.6 People Most Likely to Attempt Suicide

- Depressed people, especially those with disordered thinking (Roose, Glassman, Walsh, Woodring, & Vital-Herne, 1983)
- People who have untreated psychological disorders (Brent et al., 1988)
- People who have recently suffered the death of a spouse and men who have recently been divorced or separated, especially those who have little social support from friends and family (Blumenthal & Kupfer, 1986)
- People who during their childhood or adolescence lost a parent through death or divorce (Adam, 1986)
- Drug and alcohol abusers (Beck & Steer, 1989)
- People who made a previous suicide attempt and took precautions against being discovered in that attempt (Beck & Steer, 1989)
- Children and adolescents who are not living with both parents, who have a family history of psychiatric disorders, or who have a history of drug abuse (Garfield, Froese, & Hood, 1982)
- People with guns in their home, particularly those with a history of violent attacks on others (Brent et al., 1988)
- People whose relatives have suffered depression or who have committed suicide (Blumenthal & Kupfer, 1986)
- People with low activity of the neurotransmitter serotonin in the brain (Mann, McBride, & Stanley, 1986)

Women are more likely to try poison, drugs, or other relatively slow, nonviolent, uncertain methods (Rich, Ricketts, Fowler, & Young, 1988). Many women who injure themselves in suicide attempts are believed to be crying out for help and not really trying to kill themselves (Barnes, 1985). That is particularly true of young women. Unfortunately, some of them actually die, and others are disabled for life.

Warning Signs of Possible Suicide

Suicide follows no dependable pattern. The fact that someone has talked about suicide—or has not talked about suicide—gives little clue about whether or not the person will attempt it. You may have heard people say that "someone who attempts suicide but survives will never actually commit suicide." That is simply untrue. In fact, about one third of those who survive one attempt eventually kill themselves (Blumenthal & Kupfer, 1986). Many people who attempt suicide give warning signals well in advance, but some do not. One study found that more than half of the people who made a serious suicide attempt decided on suicide less than 24 hours before making the attempt (Peterson, Peterson, O'Shanick, & Swann, 1985).

However, certain factors are associated with an increased probability of attempting suicide. Anyone working with troubled people should be aware of these warning signals. Suicide attempts are most common among the types of people in Table 14.6.

If you suspect that someone you know is thinking about suicide, what should you do? Treat the person like a normal human being. Don't assume that the person is so fragile that one wrong word will be disastrous. Don't be afraid to ask, "You have been looking depressed. Have you been thinking about suicide?" You may do the person a favor by showing that you are not frightened by the thought and that you are willing to talk about it.

Most people who threaten suicide are crying out for help; they are feeling pain, either mental or physical. You may not be able to guess what kind of pain someone is feeling. Be prepared to listen.

Urge the person to get professional help. Most large cities have a suicide prevention hotline listed in the white pages of the telephone directory.

SUMMARY

- *Symptoms of depression.* A depressed person takes little interest or pleasure in life, feels worthless, powerless, and guilty, and may consider suicide. Such a person has trouble sleeping, loses interest in sex and eating, and cannot concentrate. (page 606)
- *Predispositions.* Some people are predisposed to depression by genetic or other biological factors, by early experiences such as the loss of a parent, or by poor social support in adulthood. (page 607)

- *Helplessness.* Depressed people interpret disappointing experiences as personal failures. They act as if they believe they are helpless in the face of adversity. (page 609)

- *Perception of control or noncontrol.* Depressed people accurately assess their lack of control in situations in which they do have low control, whereas people who are not depressed generally believe they have more control than they do. (page 609)

- *Seasonal affective disorder.* Seasonal affective disorder is an uncommon condition in which people become depressed during the winter and somewhat manic during the summer. (page 611)

- *Bipolar disorder.* People with bipolar disorder alternate between periods of depression and periods of mania, in which they engage in constant, driven, uninhibited activity. (page 612)

- *Suicide.* Although it is difficult to know who will or will not attempt suicide, it is common among depressed people and people who show certain other warning signs. (page 613)

SUGGESTIONS FOR FURTHER READING

Beers, C. W. (1948). *A mind that found itself.* Garden City, NY: Doubleday. (Original work published 1908.) An autobiography of a man who recovered from a severe case of bipolar disorder.

Seligman, M. E. P. (1975). *Helplessness.* San Francisco, CA: W. H. Freeman. Well-written discussion of the role of helplessness in depression and other aspects of life.

TERMS

depression condition lasting most of the day, day after day, with a loss of interest or pleasure and a lack of productive activity (page 606)

bipolar disorder condition in which a person alternates between periods of depression and periods of mania (page 606)

reactive depression depression that develops suddenly in reaction to a severe loss (page 606)

endogenous depression depression that develops gradually, not traceable to any single traumatic experience (page 606)

postpartum depression period of depression some women experience shortly after giving birth (page 608)

learned-helplessness theory theory that some people become depressed because they have learned that they have no control over the major events in their lives (page 609)

seasonal affective disorder condition in which people become seriously depressed every winter, when the amount of sunlight per day is short (page 611)

mania condition in which people are constantly active, uninhibited, and either happy or angry (page 612)

ANSWERS TO CONCEPT CHECKS

10. Most people who are not depressed overestimate their own positive qualities and their own control of the situation. That is why most students predict greater success in the future, even though the number of students who will get lower grades in the future is the same as the number who will get higher grades. The same is true of sports coaches. Depressed people are less likely than others to buy a lottery ticket because they would accurately perceive that their chance of success is low. (page 610)

11. In the Southern Hemisphere, seasonal affective disorder should occur in July and August, when the amount of sunlight per day is low. (page 612)

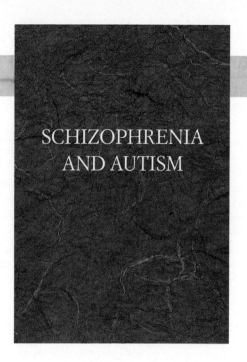

SCHIZOPHRENIA AND AUTISM

What is schizophrenia?
What causes it?
What can be done about it?
What is autism?

How would you like to live in a world all your own? You can be the supreme ruler. No one will ever criticize you or tell you what to do. You can tell other people—and even inanimate things—what to do, and they will immediately obey. Every one of your fantasies becomes a reality.

Perhaps that world sounds like a heaven to you; I suspect it soon would be more like a hell. Most of us enjoy the give and take with other people; we enjoy struggling to achieve our fantasies more than we would enjoy the actual fulfillment of our fantasies.

Some people live almost "in a world of their own," not always distinguishing betweeen fantasy and reality. They have trouble understanding what others say and trouble making themselves understood. Eventually they may retreat into a private existence, paying little attention to others. We shall consider two conditions that impair social interactions—schizophrenia, a moderately common condition in adulthood, and autism, a rare condition with onset in infancy.

THE SYMPTOMS OF SCHIZOPHRENIA

Schizophrenia is a generally severe, widely misunderstood psychological disorder. The term *schizophrenia* is based on Greek roots meaning "split mind." It does *not* refer to a split into two minds or personalities, but a split between the intellectual and emotional aspects of the personality, as if the intellect and the emotions were no longer in contact with each other. It also implies a split from reality. (Television programs and movies sometimes confuse schizophrenia with *multiple personality*. A person with schizophrenia has an abnormal personality but has only one personality.)

A person suffering from schizophrenia may seem happy or sad without cause or may fail to show emotions in a situation that normally evokes them. Such a person may even report bad news cheerfully or good news sadly. To be diagnosed with **schizophrenia,** according to DSM III-R, a person must exhibit a deterioration of daily activities over a period of at least 6 months, including work, social relations, and self-care. He or she must *also* exhibit either hallucinations, delusions, flat or inappropriate emotions, certain movement disorders, or thought disorders. If the hallucinations are not prominent or the delusions are not bizarre, then the person must exhibit one of the other symptoms as well.

Approximately 1–2% of Americans are afflicted with schizophrenia at some point in their life (Robins et al., 1984). Some sources cite slightly higher or lower figures depending on how many borderline cases they include. Schizophrenia occurs in all countries and in all ethnic groups, although it is apparently rare in the tropics and especially prevalent in densely populated areas of cities. It is about as common among men as among women.

Schizophrenia is most frequently diagnosed in young adults in their teens or 20s. A first diagnosis is rare after age 30 and unheard of after age 45. The onset is sometimes sudden but is usually gradual. Most people with schizophrenia are described as having been "strange" children who had a short attention span, made few friends, often disrupted their classroom with "unusual" behaviors, and had mild thought disorders (Arboleda & Holzman, 1985; Parnas, Schulsinger, Schulsinger, Mednick, & Teasdale, 1982).

Something to Think About

When we ask people to recall the childhood behavior of someone who later developed schizophrenia, what kinds of memory errors are likely, and why? (Recall the issues raised in Chapters 8 and 9.)

Hallucinations

A person subject to **hallucinations** has sensory experiences that do not correspond to anything in the outside world. Most commonly, people with schizophrenia hear voices and other sounds that no one else hears. Not all schizophrenic people hear voices, but most people who do are suffering from schizophrenia. The "voices" may speak only nonsense, or they may tell the person to carry out certain acts. Sometimes hallucinating people think the voices are real, sometimes they know the voices are coming from within their own head, and sometimes they are not sure (Junginger & Frame, 1985). Few people with schizophrenia have visual hallucinations, which are more characteristic of drug abusers. Occasionally, some have distorted or exaggerated visual experiences. (See Figure 14.23.)

Delusions

Delusions are unfounded beliefs. Three of the more common types of delusions are persecution, grandeur, and reference: A **delusion of persecution** is a belief that one is being persecuted, that "people are out to get me." A **delusion of grandeur** is a belief that one is unusually important, perhaps a special messenger from God or a person of central importance to the future of the world. A **delusion of reference** is a tendency to interpret all sorts of messages as if they were meant for oneself. Someone with a delusion of reference may interpret a headline in the morning newspaper as a coded message or may take a television announcer's comments as personal insults. People with delusions do not always hold them with great conviction (Rudden, Gilmore, & Allen, 1982), but they sometimes act on them nevertheless.

FIGURE 14.23

These portraits graphically illustrate their artist's progressive psychological deterioration. When well-known animal artist Louis Wain (1860–1939) began suffering delusions of persecution, his drawings showed a schizophrenic's disturbing distortions in perception.

Disorders of Emotion and Movement

Many people with schizophrenia show little sign of emotion. Their faces seldom express emotion, and they speak without the inflections most people use for emphasis. When they do show emotions, the expressions are inappropriate, such as laughing for no reason (Figure 14.24).

Some people with schizophrenia have a movement disorder called catatonia. **Catatonia** may take the form of either rigid inactivity or excessive activity; in either case, the person's movements or lack of movements seems to be unrelated to stimuli in the outside world.

FIGURE 14.24
A patient with disorganized schizophrenia may giggle for no apparent reason or engage in other bizarre behaviors.

The Thought Disorder of Schizophrenia

One characteristic of schizophrenic thought is the use of *loose and idiosyncratic associations,* somewhat like the illogical leaps that occur in dreams. For example, one man used the words *Jesus, cigar,* and *sex* as synonyms. When he was asked to explain, he said they were all the same because Jesus has a halo around his head, a cigar has a band around it, and during sex people put their arms around each other.

Another characteristic of schizophrenic thought is *difficulty in using abstract concepts* (Wright, 1975). For instance, many people with schizophrenia have trouble sorting objects into categories. Many also give strictly literal responses when asked to interpret the meaning of proverbs. Here are some examples (Krueger, 1978, pp. 196–197):

> *Proverb:* People who live in glass houses shouldn't throw stones.
> *Interpretation:* "It would break the glass."
> *Proverb:* All that glitters is not gold.
> *Interpretation:* "It might be brass."
> *Proverb:* A stitch in time saves nine.
> *Interpretation:* "If you take one stitch for a small tear now, it will save nine later."

Because of this tendency to interpret everything literally, people with schizophrenic thought disorder often misunderstand simple statements. On being taken to the admitting office of a hospital, one person said, "Oh, is this where people go to admit their faults?"

Many schizophrenic people use vague, round about ways of saying something simple. For instance, one such person said, "I was born with a male sense" instead of "I'm a man." They often take many words to say almost nothing. They ramble aimlessly when they speak and write, as in this excerpt from a letter one man wrote to his mother:

> *I am writing on paper. The pen which I am using is from a factory called "Perry & Co." This factory is in England. I assume this. Behind the name of Perry Co. the city of London is inscribed; but not the city. The city of London is in England. I know this from my school-days. Then, I always liked geography. My last teacher in that subject was Professor August A. He was a man with black eyes. I also like black eyes. There are also blue and gray eyes and other sorts, too. I have heard it said that snakes have green eyes. All people have eyes. There are some, too, who are blind. These blind people are led about by a boy. It must be very terrible not to be able to see. There are people who can't see and, in addition, can't hear. I know some who hear too much. (Bleuler, 1911, p. 17)*

The Distinction Between Positive and Negative Symptoms

Many investigators distinguish between positive symptoms and negative symptoms of schizophrenia (Andreasen & Olsen, 1982; Crow, 1985). (In this case, *positive* means *present* and *negative* means *absent;* they do not mean *good* and *bad.*) **Positive symptoms** are characteristics present in people with schizophrenia and absent in others—such as hallucinations, delusions, abnormal movements, and thought disorder. **Negative symptoms** are behaviors that are present in other people—such as the ability to take care of themselves—but absent in schizophrenic people. Other common negative symptoms include the lack of emotional expression, a lack of social interaction, a deficit of speech, and a lack of pleasure.

Some patients have mostly positive symptoms; others have mostly negative symptoms. As a rule, those with many negative symptoms have earlier onset, worse educational and occupational performance, and a weaker prospect for recovery (Andreasen, Flaum, Swayze, Tyrrell, & Arndt, 1990).

TYPES OF SCHIZOPHRENIA

In some schizophrenic patients, a particular set of symptoms may be especially prominent. Depending on which symptoms they exhibit, they are said to be suffering from one of four types of schizophrenia: undifferentiated, catatonic, paranoid, or disorganized schizophrenia.

Undifferentiated schizophrenia is characterized by the basic symptoms—a deterioration of daily activities, plus some combination of hallucinations, delusions, inappropriate emotions, movement disorders, and thought disorders. However, none of these symptoms is unusually pronounced or bizarre.

Catatonic schizophrenia is characterized by the basic symptoms plus prominent movement disorders. The affected person may go through periods of extremely rapid, mostly repetitive activity alternating with periods of total inactivity.

During the inactive periods he or she may hold a given posture without moving and may resist attempts to alter that posture (Figure 14.25). Catatonic schizophrenia has become less common over the years and is now fairly rare.

Disorganized schizophrenia is characterized by incoherent speech, extreme lack of social relationships, and "silly" or "odd" behavior. For example, one man gift-wrapped one of his feces and proudly presented it to his therapist. Here is a conversation with someone suffering from disorganized schizophrenia (Duke & Nowicki, 1979):

Interviewer: How does it feel to have your problems?

Patient: Who can tell me the name of my song? I don't know, but it won't be long. It won't be short, tall, none at all. My head hurts, my knees hurt—my nephew, his uncle, my aunt. My God, I'm happy . . . not a care in the world. My hair's been curled, the flag's unfurled. This is my country, land that I love, this is the country, land that I love.

Interviewer: How do you feel?

Patient: Happy! Don't you hear me? Why do you talk to me? (barks like a dog). (Duke & Nowicki, 1979, p. 162)

Paranoid schizophrenia is characterized by the basic symptoms plus strong or elaborate hallucinations and delusions, especially delusions of persecution and delusions of grandeur. Compared to other types of schizophrenia, paranoid schizophrenia generally has a later age of onset and a better prospect for recovery (Fenton & McGlashan, 1991). Most people with paranoid schizophrenia can manage their own lives reasonably well, except for their constant suspicion—for example, a suspicion that "I am surrounded by spies" or that "evil forces from Mars are trying to control my mind."

Paranoid schizophrenia tends not to run in the same families as other types of schizophrenia do (Farmer, McGuffin, & Gottesman, 1987). In some ways, it resembles depression more than it resembles other types of schizophrenia (Zigler & Glick, 1988).

Although the distinctions among these types of schizophrenia are convenient, they are not absolute. Some people fall on the borderline of two or more types of schizophrenia, perhaps switching back and forth between them. Switching is especially common between undifferentiated schizophrenia and one of the other types (Kendler, Gruenberg, & Tsuang, 1985).

FIGURE 14.25
A person suffering from catatonic schizophrenia may hold a bizarre posture for hours and alternate this rigid stupor with equally purposeless, excited activity. Such people may stubbornly resist attempts to change their behavior, but they need supervision to avoid hurting themselves or others. Catatonic schizophrenia is uncommon.

■ CONCEPT CHECK

12. Why are people more likely to switch between undifferentiated schizophrenia and one of the other types than, say, between disorganized schizophrenia and one of the other types? (Check your answer on page 625.)

CAUSES OF SCHIZOPHRENIA

From all indications, schizophrenia has multiple causes. Certain people may have a biological predisposition to schizophrenia, but not everyone with a biological predisposition develops schizophrenia. Even people who do develop schizophrenia vary in the type and severity of their symptoms. Psychologists are still far from a thorough understanding of the factors that cause schizophrenia and how those various factors combine their influences. We shall examine what psychologists currently understand, but bear in mind that this understanding is tentative.

Brain Damage

Unlike people suffering from other psychological disorders, people suffering from schizophrenia show minor but widespread brain damage (see Figure 14.26). The cerebral cortex is somewhat shrunken in one fourth to one third of all schizophrenic patients, and the cerebral ventricles (fluid-filled spaces in the brain) are enlarged on the average (Raz & Raz, 1990). Enlargement of the cerebral ventricles implies decreased space for neurons; thus it suggests mild brain damage. Most people with schizophrenia have cognitive and memory deficit similar to those of people with damage to the prefrontal cortex or the temporal cortex (Rubin et al., 1991; Saykin et al., 1991).

The causes of this brain damage are not certain. One possibility is that people with schizophrenia produce some chemical within themselves that causes brain damage. Another possibility is that through some combination of genetic and other influences, their brains developed abnormally during prenatal life and infancy (Weinberger, 1987). To decide between these possibilities, we need to know whether the brain damage found in schizophrenic people has been present since early childhood or whether it develops gradually throughout their lives. So far, the answer is uncertain.

■ CONCEPT CHECK

13. *Following a stroke a patient shows symptoms similar to schizophrenia. Where is the brain* *damage probably located? (Check your answer on page 625.)*

Dopamine Imbalance

Schizophrenia is commonly treated with drugs. All the effective drugs share one characteristic: They block dopamine synapses in the brain. In fact, the therapeutic effectiveness of these drugs is nearly proportional to their tendency to block those synapses (Seeman & Lee, 1975). Furthermore, large doses of amphetamine, cocaine, or other drugs that increase dopamine activity can induce a temporary state that closely resembles schizophrenia. These phenomena have led to the **dopamine theory of schizophrenia,** which holds that the underlying cause of schizophrenia is excessive stimulation of certain types of dopamine synapses. That stimulation may occur in part because other, competing synapses are being destroyed.

Genetics

What causes the brain damage often associated with schizophrenia and the apparent overactivity of dopamine synapses? Perhaps a particular gene produces chemicals that damage certain neurons or that make certain neurons more active than others. Substantial evidence supports this genetic predisposition for schizophrenia.

First, for adopted children who eventually

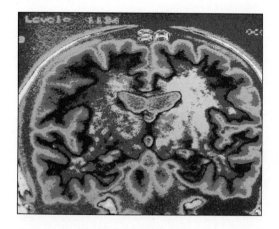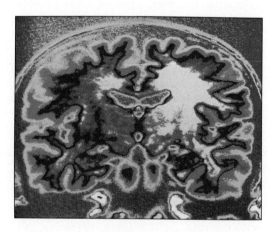

FIGURE 14.26
Many (though not all) people with schizophrenia show signs of mild loss of neurons in the brain. Here we see views of the brains of twins. The twin on the left has schizophrenia; the twin on the right does not. Note that the ventricles (near the center of each brain) are larger in the twin with schizophrenia. The ventricles are fluid-filled cavities; an enlargement of the ventricles implies a loss of the brain tissue. (Photos courtesy of E. F. Torrey & M. F. Casanova/NIMH.)

develop schizophrenia, schizophrenia is more common among their biological relatives than it is among their adoptive relatives (Kety, 1977, 1983; Lowing, Mirsky, & Pereira, 1983). Second, if one member of a pair of identical twins develops schizophrenia, there is almost a 50% chance that the other will develop it too (Gottesman, 1991). (See Figure 14.27.) That figure understates the role of genetics in schizophrenia, however, because a high percentage of the twins who do not develop schizophrenia will suffer from other serious psychological disturbances, including "borderline" schizophrenia (Farmer, McGuffin, & Gottesman, 1987; Kendler & Robinette, 1983). Furthermore, the schizophrenic twin and the nonschizophrenic twin run an equal risk of passing schizophrenia on to their children (Gottesman & Bertelson, 1989; Kringlen & Cramer, 1989). Apparently some gene or genes tend to increase the likelihood of schizophrenia. Even if a person with those genes does not actually develop schizophrenia, he or she still passes the genes to the next generation.

One focus of current research is to identify those people who have the genes for schizophrenia but who do not show the symptoms. Identifying them could be useful for better understanding the genetics and for understanding how genetic influences combine with environmental influences. One possible "marker" for such people is an impairment of **pursuit eye movements,** the movements necessary for keeping one's eyes focused on a moving object. About 80% of people with schizophrenia move their eyes in a series of rapid jerks instead of moving them smoothly (Holzman, 1985); they show this same impairment before they develop schizophrenia, during a schizophrenic episode, and after successful therapy (Holzman, 1988). The same impairment occurs in many of their close relatives, but in very few people who are unrelated to someone with schizophrenia (Blackwood, St. Clair, Muir, & Duffy, 1991; Clementz & Sweeney, 1990). Thus it may prove to be a way of identifying people who have the genes for schizophrenia.

Something to Think About

People suffering from schizophrenia are less likely than others to have children. This is particularly true of schizophrenic men, partly because they have a weaker-than-average sex drive and partly because they are socially inept. So it is difficult to imagine how a gene that leads to schizophrenia could spread enough to affect 1% of the population. Can you imagine a possible explanation?

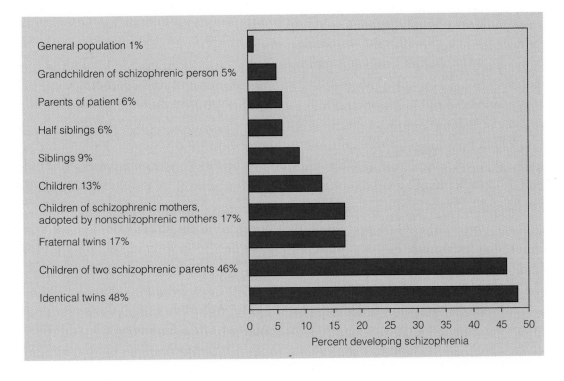

FIGURE 14.27
The relatives of a schizophrenic person have an increased probability of developing schizophrenia themselves. Note that children of a schizophrenic mother have a 17% risk of schizophrenia even if adopted by a family with no schizophrenic members. (Based on data from Gottesman, 1991.)

Experience

Assuming that genes predispose certain people to schizophrenia, what environmental factors determine whether or not those genes will be expressed as schizophrenia? Some years ago, psychologists suggested that mothers who gave a confusing mixture of "come here" and "go away" signals were likely to induce schizophrenia in their children. That theory has been discarded, for several reasons.

One reason is that it does not fit the data on adoptions. The child of a schizophrenic parent who is adopted by normal parents has a high risk of developing schizophrenia, whereas other adopted children reared in the same family generally do not become schizophrenic. So it seems unlikely that confusing verbal signals from the mother are responsible for schizophrenia.

Another reason is that the suggested cause does not seem sufficient to produce the effect. Even abused and battered children seldom develop schizophrenia. It is hard to believe that confusing verbal signals would cause even greater damage.

Finally, the "bad mother" theory does not fit the course of the disorder over time. If the mother's behavior were the main cause of the problem, we would expect the child to improve when separated from her. In fact, schizophrenia usually develops in early adulthood—when most people become independent of their parents—and gradually grows more severe from then on unless drugs are administered.

A more reasonable hypothesis is that the onset of schizophrenia may be *triggered* by stress. Note the word *triggered*. Although stress probably does not *cause* schizophrenia, it may aggravate the symptoms. The effect of stress is difficult to measure, however, because the term *stress* is imprecise and subjective; events that are stressful for one person may not be stressful for another.

Judith Rabkin (1980) reviewed studies in which schizophrenic people were asked to report any stressful events that had occurred during the months just before they developed schizophrenia. The frequency of stressful events turned out to be only slightly higher than normal. This finding could mean any of several things: The schizophrenic people may have forgotten the stressful events they experienced; stress may not be particularly significant in the onset of schizophrenia; the critically stressful events may have occurred more than a few months before the onset of the disorder; or people who are susceptible to schizophrenia may overrespond to very mild stress. We shall need further studies, preferably longitudinal studies, to decide among these possibilities.

Infections During Early Development

A person born in the winter months is slightly more likely to develop schizophrenia than a person born at any other time (Bradbury & Miller, 1985). No other psychological disorder has this characteristic. Moreover, investigators have clearly demonstrated this **season-of-birth effect** only in the northern climates, not near the equator. Evidently, something about the weather near the time of birth contributes to some people's vulnerability to schizophrenia.

One possible explanation relates to the fact that influenza and other epidemics are most common in the fall, especially in northern climates. Suppose a woman catches influenza or some similar disease in the fall. If she happens to be in the second trimester of pregnancy at the time, her illness may affect her fetus during a critical stage for brain development; she delivers that baby in the winter. According to several studies, in years of a major influenza epidemic in the fall, the babies born 3 months later (in the winter) are at increased risk for schizophrenia, as diagnosed 20 or more years later (Kendell & Kemp, 1989; Mednick, Machon, & Huttunen, 1990; Torrey, Rawlings, & Waldman, 1988).

You might ask, if the brain damage occurs before or near the time of birth, why do the symptoms emerge so much later? One answer is that certain parts of the brain, especially the prefrontal cortex, go through a critical stage of development during the second trimester of pregnancy but do not become fully functional until adolescence. As the brain begins to rely more and more on those areas, the effects of the damage become more evident (Weinberger, 1987).

The causes of schizophrenia are still not understood; what is clear is that schizophrenia depends on a number of influences, not just a single cause. Genetics, stress, and prenatal exposure to illness are likely influences on schizophrenia, but exactly how these and other influences interact will be a topic of research for years to come.

A U T I S M

Autism is a disorder that resembles schizophrenia in certain ways, although the underlying causes are apparently quite different. The term *autism* literally means "self-ism." (It comes from the same Greek root as does *automobile*, which literally means "self-mover.") Autistic children live in a world of their own, socially unresponsive to other people.

Both childhood autism and schizophrenia are characterized by extreme social isolation, repetitive movements, and a failure to communicate with others. Autism and schizophrenia do not as a rule run in the same families, however, and the drugs that are effective in treating schizophrenia are not helpful for autistic children. Table 14.7 summarizes the distinctions between schizophrenia and autism.

A rare condition that affects only about 1 child in 2,500, autism has an early onset. Parents often recognize that "something is wrong" by the time the child is 6 months old and invariably by age 3 years. Autism usually persists for a lifetime, although some improvement may occur. More than 75% of all autistic children are boys. Because it is generally a lifelong disorder, DSM III-R lists it on Axis 2.

Symptoms

The following list contains the main symptoms of autism (Creak, 1961; Kanner, 1943; Ornitz & Ritvo, 1976):

■ *Social isolation.* Autistic children almost never seek social contact with others. They pay little attention to what others are doing and learn almost nothing by imitation (Varni, Lovaas, Koegel, & Everett, 1979).

■ *Stereotyped behaviors.* Autistic children repeat movements such as biting the hands, rotating an object, or flapping the arms.

■ *Resistance to change in routine.* Autistic children protest any change in daily activities.

■ *Abnormal responses to sensory stimuli.* Autistic children ignore much of what they see and hear and are extremely unresponsive to painful stimuli. They focus their attention narrowly on one stimulus or one activity and ignore everything else (Lovaas, Koegel, & Schreibman, 1979).

■ *Inappropriate emotional expressions.* Autistic children engage in occasional outbursts of laughter or crying for no apparent reason. Emotions seem to arise from internal rather than external sources.

■ *Great fluctuations in activity level.* Autistic children have periods of either inactivity or uncontrollably high activity.

Table 14.7 Distinctions Between Schizophrenia and Autism		
Characteristics	Schizophrenia	Autism
Usual age at first diagnosis	15 to 30 years old	A few months to 3 years old
Sex ratio	Equal numbers of males and females	Mostly males
Genetics	Clear genetic tendency	Uncertain; usually does not appear in same family with other autistics or schizophrenics
Response to neuroleptic drugs	Symptoms generally reduced	Little effect other than sedation

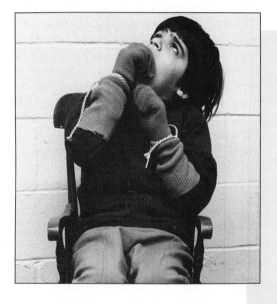

Children with autism relate poorly to other people, show little response to painful stimuli at most times, and engage in repetitive acts such as biting themselves. The condition develops early in life; no specific treatment is known. Sometimes therapists put gloves on the children's hands to protect them from the biting.

■ *Poor development of language.* Autistic children are very slow in learning to speak and to understand language. Some learn to speak as a parrot does, showing little evidence of comprehension. Many confuse the pronouns *me* and *you*.

■ *Wide variation in performance between one intellectual task and another.* Many autistic children perform extraordinarily well on one task, such as memorization or music or mathematical calculations, but perform at the level of retarded people on other tasks.

What is it like to be autistic? Most autistic people can never answer that question for us.

However, one man made a substantial recovery and described the experience (White & White, 1987). He said that he often experienced stimuli as being extremely intense. Noises were so loud and lights were so bright that he retreated into a world of his own as a means of escape.

Possible Causes

Autism was first described by the psychiatrist Leo Kanner in 1943. Early studies reported that the condition occurs most often in families with highly intellectual, emotionally cold mothers, giving rise to the theory that children become autistic in reaction to such mothers. That theory has been abandoned, for two main reasons. One is that autistic children have been identified in all kinds of families—rich and poor, educated and uneducated (DeMyer, 1979). The other is that 98% of the brothers and sisters of autistic children are psychologically normal. If the behavior of the mother were really the cause of autism, we would expect all her children to be at least somewhat abnormal.

Genetic factors apparently contribute to autism; when one identical twin has autism, the other twin almost always does also (Ritvo, Freeman, Mason-Brothers, Mo, & Ritvo, 1985). However, the fact that only about 2% of the brothers and sisters of autistic children are affected indicates that no single gene contributes strongly to autism. If genetic factors have any influence at all, we must assume that the impact comes either from a combination of several genes or from the interaction of genes with abnormal factors in the environment. Another possibility is that autism may be caused by complications during the mother's pregnancy or around the time of birth (Links, Stockwell, Abichandani, & Simeon, 1980).

One biological abnormality may be particularly important: Many autistic children have unusually high levels of endorphins, the brain chemicals that resemble morphine and inhibit pain (Gillberg, Terenius, & Lönnerholm, 1985; Sandman et al., 1990). Several of the symptoms of autism resemble those of morphine users, including social withdrawal, insensitivity to pain, and a tendency to overrespond to stimuli at some times and to ignore them at others (Kalat, 1978; Panksepp, Herman, & Vilberg, 1978).

Treatment and Outcome

Although the ultimate causes of autism may be biological, the most effective treatment available today is special education. Autistic children learn best in a highly structured environment with a highly predictable routine (Schopler, 1987). An autistic child will pay attention to another person only if that person constantly demands the child's attention on a one-to-one basis. Autistic children gradually learn language under careful tutoring that combines spoken language and sign language—much as one teaches deaf children (Barrera, Lobato-Barrera, & Sulzer-Azaroff, 1980). Stereotyped behaviors can be eliminated by reducing the sensory stimulation they produce (Rincover, 1978). For instance, a hand-biting habit can be suppressed by forcing the child to wear gloves.

What happens to autistic children when they reach adulthood? According to one follow-up study of 80 autistic children, more than half spent their adult lives in mental institutions. Some lived with their parents or other relatives; a few progressed far enough to live independently and hold jobs. All but a few had continuing problems, including poor development of speech (Wolf & Goldberg, 1986).

SUMMARY

- *Symptoms of schizophrenia.* A person with schizophrenia is someone whose everyday functioning has deteriorated over a period of at least 6 months and who shows at least one of the following symptoms: hallucinations (mostly auditory), delusions, weak or inappropriate emotional expression, catatonic movements, and thought disorder. (page 616)

- *Onset.* Schizophrenia is usually first diagnosed in young adults. However, certain signs are evident in children, including mild thought disorder, lack of emotional contact with others, and impaired pursuit eye movements. (page 616)

- *Thought disorder of schizophrenia.* The thought disorder of schizophrenia is characterized by loose associations, impaired use of abstract concepts, and vague, wandering speech that conveys little information. (page 618)

- *Types of schizophrenia.* Psychologists distinguish four types of schizophrenia: undifferentiated, catatonic, disorganized, and paranoid. Some authorities believe paranoid schizophrenia resembles depression more than it does other types of schizophrenia. (page 618)

- *Brain damage.* Many people with schizophrenia show indications of mild brain damage. (page 619)

- *Role of dopamine.* Schizophrenia is relieved by various drugs that block dopamine synapses in the brain. For that reason, many people believe schizophrenia is due to overactivity at certain types of dopamine synapses. (page 620)

- *Combined forces of genetics and experience.* A predisposition to schizophrenia may be inherited. However, experience influences the timing and intensity of schizophrenic behavioral episodes. (page 620)

- *Season-of-birth effect.* Schizophrenia is more common in people born in the winter months, especially in cold climates. For that reason, some investigators believe that some cases of schizophrenia may be caused by a virus or bacterium contracted before or shortly after birth. (page 622)

- *Autism.* Autism is a childhood condition that resembles schizophrenia in certain ways. Autistic children fail to seek social contact with other people. The causes of autism are uncertain, and no treatment produces reliably good results. (page 622)

SUGGESTION FOR FURTHER READING

Gottesman, I. I. (1991). *Schizophrenia genesis.* New York: W. H. Freeman. Review of research on the causes of schizophrenia.

TERMS

schizophrenia condition marked by deterioration of daily activities over a period of at least 6 months, plus either hallucinations, delusions, flat or inappropriate emotions, certain movement disorders, or thought disorders (page 616)

hallucination sensory experience that does not correspond to anything in the outside world (page 617)

delusion unfounded belief (page 617)

delusion of persecution belief that one is being persecuted (page 617)

delusion of grandeur belief that one is unusually important (page 617)

delusion of reference tendency to interpret all sorts of messages as if they were meant for oneself (page 617)

catatonia movement disorder, consisting of either rigid inactivity or excessive activity (page 617)

positive symptoms characteristics present in people with schizophrenia and absent in others—such as hallucinations, delusions, abnormal movements, and thought disorder (page 618)

negative symptoms behaviors that are present in other people—such as the ability to take care of themselves—but absent in schizophrenic people (page 618)

undifferentiated schizophrenia type of schizophrenia characterized by the basic symptoms but no unusual or especially prominent symptoms (page 618)

catatonic schizophrenia type of schizophrenia characterized by the basic symptoms plus prominent movement disorders (page 618)

disorganized schizophrenia type of schizophrenia characterized by incoherent speech, extreme lack of social relationships, and "silly" or "odd" behavior (page 619)

paranoid schizophrenia type of schizophrenia characterized by the basic symptoms plus strong or elaborate hallucinations and delusions (page 619)

dopamine theory of schizophrenia theory that the underlying cause of schizophrenia is excessive stimulation of certain types of dopamine synapses (page 620)

pursuit eye movements the movements necessary for keeping one's eyes focusing on a moving object (page 621)

season-of-birth effect tendency for people born in the winter months to be slightly more likely than other people are to develop schizophrenia (page 622)

autism condition with onset in early childhood, characterized by extreme social isolation, repetitive movements, and a failure to communicate with others (page 622)

ANSWERS TO CONCEPT CHECKS

12. With any disorder, symptoms are more severe at some times than at others. Whenever any of the special symptoms of catatonic, disorganized, or paranoid schizophrenia become less severe, the person is left with undifferentiated schizophrenia. To shift between any two of the other types, a person would have to lose the symptoms of one type and gain the symptoms of the other type. (page 619)

13. The damage probably is located in the frontal or temporal lobes of the cerebral cortex, the areas that are generally damaged in people with schizophrenia. (page 620)

15

TREATMENT OF PSYCHOLOGICALLY TROUBLED PEOPLE

Vaclav Havel spent years as a political prisoner because of his criticisms of the Communist government of Czechoslovakia. Later, after he became president in the new, non-Communist government, he reflected on the tribulations his country was suffering:

People . . . are in a state of shock caused by freedom. It is similar to coming out of prison: When you are inside, you yearn for the moment when they will release you, but when it happens, you are suddenly helpless. You do not know what to do and even have a yen to go back, because at least you know what awaits you. You do not know what freedom will bring. ("A conversation with President Havel," 1992)

Some people are, in a sense, prisoners within themselves. Their freedom is limited by their own fears, thoughts, and habits. In a way they want to be released from all that, but in a way they also may resist freedom. They are not sure how to live without the limitations they have had for so long or how to accept full responsibility for their own decisions. Freedom, even psychological freedom, can be a bit intimidating.

Psychotherapists try to help people free themselves from their psychological shackles. We could compare the role of a psychotherapist to that of a physician, an educator, a member of the clergy, or a friend. Better yet, let's think of a psychotherapist as a kindly parole officer—someone who tries to help another person make the adjustment from a self-imposed prison into a world of new opportunities.

A psychotherapist serves many roles, like those of a friend, teacher, physician, even parole officer. A psychotherapist tries to help clients through their difficult times to reach a better, freer future.

PSYCHOTHERAPY

What methods are used to help people overcome psychological disorders?

How effective are these methods?

Psychotherapy is a treatment of psychological disorders, by methods that generally include a personal relationship between a trained therapist and a client. But psychotherapy does little good unless a client gives the proverbial damn.

Before the Second World War, almost all psychotherapists were psychiatrists, and most of them used Freudian methods. Since then, clinical psychologists, social workers, counseling psychologists, and others have begun to practice psychotherapy. Table 15.1 contrasts the practices of psychiatrists and clinical psychologists (Knesper, Belcher, & Cross, 1989).

Both the number of therapists and the variety of methods they use have increased enormously (Garfield, 1981). Well over 100 forms of psychotherapy are available today. Psychotherapy is used for certain well-defined disorders, such as phobia, depression, and addiction, and for a wide variety of adjustment and coping problems that do not fall into any set category. In fact, about a third of the people who consult psychotherapists have no psychological disorder (Shapiro et al., 1984). They are the "worried well" or the "nervous normals"—fairly healthy, normal people hoping to improve some aspect of their life. They consult a therapist not like a sick person seeing a physician but like an athlete seeking advice from a coach.

In some types of psychotherapy, the therapist does most of the talking; in others, the therapist says little. Some emphasize past emotions; others emphasize current emotions; still others emphasize current behaviors. Some concentrate on helping clients understand the reasons behind their behaviors; others concentrate on changing the behaviors, and never mind where the behaviors came from in the first place. Some focus on the problems of the individual; some focus on problems of families or whole communities.

In the following survey of the most common forms of therapy and some less common ones, we shall see how therapists use different methods depending on what they consider the central problem of troubled people.

PSYCHOANALYSIS

A number of types of psychotherapy, known as **psychodynamic therapies,** attempt to unravel people's underlying drives and motivations. For example, both Sigmund Freud's procedure, looking for underlying sexual motives, and Alfred Adler's procedure, looking for underlying power and superiority motives, are considered psychodynamic. Here we shall focus on Freud's procedure.

Psychoanalysis, Freud's method of psychotherapy, was the first of the "talk" therapies. It is a method based on identifying unconscious thoughts and emotions and bringing them to consciousness. Psychoanalysts try to help clients achieve insight into why they do what they do and think what they think (Figure 15.1). Psychoanalysis is therefore described as an "insight-oriented therapy" in contrast to therapies that focus on changing thoughts and behaviors.

Freud believed that psychological problems were the result of unconscious thought processes and that the only way to control self-defeating behaviors was to make those processes conscious. Bringing them to consciousness, he thought, would produce **catharsis,** a release of pent-up emotions associated with unconscious thoughts and memories.

At first, Freud sought to gain access to his clients' unconscious through hypnosis. He

Observation
If I don't drive around
the park,
I'm pretty sure to
make my mark.
If I'm in bed each
night by ten,
I may get back my
looks again.
If I abstain from fun
and such,
I'll probably amount
to much.
But I shall stay the way
I am,
Because I do not give a
damn.
DOROTHY PARKER
(1944)

Table 15.1 Comparison of Psychiatrists and Clinical Psychologists

	Education	Mean Time Spent with Each Client per Month	Types of Patients Seen
Psychiatrist	M.D. degree plus residency in psychiatry. Can prescribe drugs.	About 4 hours (some psychiatrists reported means less than 2 hours; some reported means above 6 hours)	Much diversity; includes some with severe disorders and some with minor disorders
Clinical psychologist	Ph.D. degree with specialization in clinical psychology. Cannot prescribe drugs.	About 4 hours (some reported means as low as 2 hours; some as high as 4.7 hours)	Less diversity; includes few patients with schizophrenia and other severe disorders

Source: Adapted from data of Knesper, Belcher, & Cross, 1989.

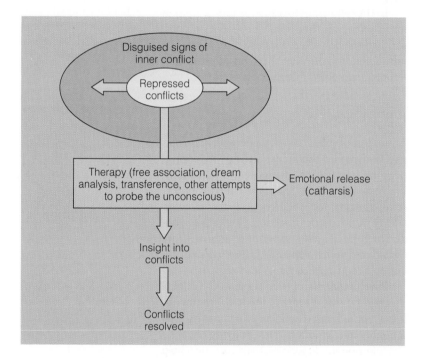

FIGURE 15.1
The goal of psychoanalysis is to resolve psychological problems by bringing to consciousness the unconscious thought processes that are responsible for the difficulty. Analysis literally means "to loosen or break up, to look at the parts."

abandoned that approach, however, after he discovered that many clients immediately forgot the insights they had gained while under hypnosis. He developed other methods of bringing unconscious material to consciousness: free association, dream analysis, and transference.

Free Association

Free association is a method that Freud and his patients developed together. (Actually, a more accurate translation of the German expression would be "free intrusion.") In **free association,** the client lies on a couch, starts thinking about a particular symptom or problem, and then reports everything that comes to mind—a word, a phrase, a visual image. The client is instructed not to omit anything, not to censor anything that might be embarrassing, and not to worry about trying to express everything in complete sentences.

The therapist listens for links and themes that might tie the patient's fragmentary remarks together. Freud believed that all behavior is determined, that nothing happens without a cause. (You will recall that behaviorists make the same assumption; see page 278.) Even when the client jumps from one thought to another, the thoughts must be related in some way.

Here is a paraphrased excerpt from a free-association session:

A man begins by describing a conference he had with his boss the previous day. He did not like the boss's policy, but he was in no position to contradict the boss. He had had a dream. It was something about an ironing board, but that was all he remembered of the dream. He comments that his wife has been complaining about the way their maid irons. He thinks his wife is being unfair; he hopes she does not fire the maid. He complains that his boss did not give him credit for some work he did recently. He recalls a childhood episode: He jumped off a cupboard and bounced off his mother's behind while she was leaning over to do some ironing. She told his father, who gave him a spanking. His father never let him explain; he was always too strict. (Munroe, 1955, p. 39)

To a psychoanalyst, the links in this story suggest that the man is associating his wife with his mother. His wife was unfair to the maid about the ironing, just as his mother had been unfair to him. Moreover, his boss is like his father, never giving him a chance to explain his errors and never giving him credit for what he did well.

Dream Analysis

For thousands of years, people have been trying to divine the meaning of dreams. Some have said that dreams predict the future, others that they reveal the dreamer's personality.

Freud (1900/1955) agreed that dreams reveal something about personality, but he rejected the view that each detail has the same meaning for everyone. To understand a dream, he said, one must determine what associations each detail has for the dreamer. Each dream has a **manifest content**—the content that appears on the surface—and a **latent content**—the hidden content that is represented only symbolically in the actual experience. The only way a psychoanalyst can discover the latent content of a dream is to ask what each detail of the manifest content means to the dreamer.

To illustrate, Freud (1900/1905) interpreted one of his own dreams, in which he dreamed that one of his friends was his uncle. He worked out the following associations: Both this friend and another friend had been recommended for an appointment as professor at the university. Both had been turned down, probably because they were Jews. Freud himself had recently been recommended for the same appointment, but he feared he too would be turned down because he was Jewish. Freud's only uncle had once been convicted of illegal business dealings. Freud's father had said, however, that the uncle was not a bad man but just a simpleton.

What was the relationship between the two friends and the uncle? One of the friends was, in Freud's reluctant judgment, a bit simple-minded. The other had once been taken to court by a woman who accused him of sexual misconduct. Although these charges were dropped, some people might still feel that being accused was as bad as being convicted. By linking these two friends to his uncle, Freud interpreted the dream as meaning, "Maybe they didn't get rejected for the university appointment because they were Jews, but because one was a simpleton (like my uncle) and the other was regarded as a criminal (like my uncle). If so, I still have a chance to get the appointment."

To Freud, every dream represents a wish

fulfillment. The wish may be disguised, but it is always there. For example, in his dream Freud was not wishing that his friend were his uncle. Rather, he was wishing that he would get the university appointment, and he was wishing that his friends had been rejected for some reason other than for being Jews.

Freud's theory seems to apply to many dreams. For example, people who have been deprived of food and water—and who, presumably, are wishing for food and water—have more frequent and more elaborate dreams about eating and drinking than other people do (O'Nell, 1965). Note, however, Freud's leap of logic: Some dreams seem rather clearly to represent wish fulfillment, and certain others can be interpreted as wish fulfillments with a little effort; therefore, *all* dreams are wish fulfillments. Most psychologists today do not accept that conclusion.

▪ CONCEPT CHECK

1. A popular paperback purports to tell you what your dreams mean. It says that every element of a dream has a symbolic meaning, in many cases a sexual meaning. A ballpoint pen represents a penis, for example, and walking up a flight of stairs represents sexual arousal. Do you think Freud would agree or disagree with this book? (Check your answer on page 644.)

Transference

Some clients show exaggerated love or hatred for their therapist that seems inappropriate under the circumstances. Psychoanalysts call this reaction **transference,** by which they mean that clients are transferring onto the therapist what they actually feel toward their father or mother or some other important figure. Transference often provides a clue to the client's feelings about those people.

Psychoanalysts are fairly active in **interpretation** of what the client says—that is, they explain the underlying meaning—and may even argue with the client about interpretations. They may regard the client's disagreement as **resistance,** continued repression that interferes with the therapy. Resistance can take many forms; for example, a client who has begun to touch on some extremely anxiety-provoking topic may turn the conversation to something trivial or may simply "forget" to come to the next session.

Although psychoanalysis has evolved considerably since Freud's time, its goal is still to bring about a major reorganization of the personality, changing a person from the inside out. The assumption is that people who understand the reasons behind their actions will be better able to make rational and productive decisions.

THERAPIES THAT FOCUS ON THOUGHTS AND BELIEFS

Someone says to you, "Look how messy your room is! Don't you ever clean it?" How do you react? You might say, "Big deal. Maybe I'll clean it tomorrow." Or you might feel worried, angry, even depressed. If you get upset, it may not merely be because you were criticized, but because you want everyone to believe that you are scrupulously clean and tidy at all times. Some therapists focus on the thoughts and beliefs that underlie people's emotional reactions. Unlike psychoanalysts, these therapists are more concerned about what people are thinking right now than about early experiences that may have led to their thoughts.

Rational-Emotive Therapy

Rational-emotive therapy is based on the assumption that people's emotions depend on their "internal sentences" such as "I can't be happy unless everyone thinks my room is clean" (Ellis & Harper, 1961). This therapy is called "rational-emotive" because it assumes that thoughts (rationality) lead to emotions.

Rational-emotive therapists (Ellis, 1987) hold that abnormal behavior often results from such irrational beliefs as these:

- I must perform certain tasks successfully.
- I must perform well at all times.
- I must have the approval of certain people at all times.
- Others must treat me fairly and with consideration.
- I must live under easy, gratifying conditions.

It is the word *must* that makes these beliefs irrational. Rational-emotive therapists try to identify people's irrational beliefs (which they may never have verbalized) and then contradict them. They urge clients to substitute other, more realistic "internal sentences." These therapists try to stop their clients from constantly evaluating their own performance and comparing themselves to others (Orth & Thebarge,

1984). Rational-emotive therapists intervene directly, instructing, persuading, and doing much of the talking. Here is an excerpt from a rational-emotive therapy session with a 25-year-old physicist:

Client: The whole trouble is that I am really a phony. I am living under false pretenses. And the longer it goes on, the more people praise me and make a fuss over my accomplishments, the worse I feel.

Therapist: What do you mean you are a phony? I thought that you told me, during our last session, that your work has been examined at another laboratory and that some of the people there think your ideas are of revolutionary importance.

Client: But I have wasted so much time. I could be doing very much better. . . . Remember that book I told you I was writing . . . it's been three weeks now since I've spent any time on it. And this is simple stuff that I should be able to do with my left hand while I am writing a technical paper with my right. I have heard Bob Oppenheimer reel off stuff extemporaneously to a bunch of newspaper reporters that is twice as good as what I am mightily laboring on in this damned book!

Therapist: Perhaps so. And perhaps you're not quite as good—yet—as Oppenheimer or a few other outstanding people in your field. But the real point, it seems to me, is that . . . here you are, at just twenty-five, with a Ph.D. in a most difficult field, with an excellent job, much good work in process, and what well may be a fine professional paper and a good popular book also in progress. And just because you're not another Oppenheimer or Einstein quite yet, you're savagely berating yourself.

Client: Well, shouldn't I be doing much better than I am?

Therapist: No, why the devil should you? As far as I can see, you are not doing badly at all. But your major difficulty—the main cause of your present unhappiness—is your utterly perfectionistic criteria for judging your performance. (Ellis & Harper, 1961, pp. 99–100)

■ CONCEPT CHECK

2. How does the idea behind rational-emotive therapy compare to the James-Lange theory of emotions, page 499? (Check your answer on page 644.)

Cognitive Therapy

Cognitive therapy seeks to improve people's psychological well-being by changing their cognitions—their thoughts and beliefs. Cognitive therapy is best known through the work of Aaron Beck with depressed patients (Beck, 1976; Hollon & Beck, 1979). According to Beck, depressed people are guided by some thoughts or assumptions of which they are only dimly aware. He refers to the "negative cognitive triad of depression":

- I am deprived or defeated.
- The world is full of obstacles.
- The future is devoid of hope.

Based on these assumptions, which Beck calls "automatic thoughts," depressed people interpret ambiguous situations to their own disadvantage. When something goes wrong, they blame themselves: "I'm worthless and I can't do anything right." When an acquaintance walks past without smiling, they think, "He/she doesn't like me." They do not even look for alternative interpretations of the situation (Beck, 1991). Research has confirmed that depressed people are more likely than other people are to agree with such statements as "I'm a loser," or "Nothing ever works out right for me and it's all my fault," or "I never have a good time" (Hollon, Kendall, & Lumry, 1986).

The task of a cognitive therapist is to help people substitute more favorable beliefs. Unlike rational-emotive therapists, who in many cases simply tell their clients what to think, cognitive therapists try to get their clients to make discoveries for themselves. The therapist focuses on one of the client's beliefs such as "No one likes me." The therapist points out that this is a hypothesis, not an established fact, and invites the client to test the hypothesis as a scientist would: "What evidence do you have for this hypothesis?"

"Well," a client may reply, "when I arrive at work in the morning, hardly anyone says hello."

"Is there any other way of looking at that evidence?"

"Hmm. . . . I suppose it's possible that the others are busy."

"Does anyone ever seem happy to see you?"

"Well, maybe. I'm not sure."

"Then let's find out. For the next week, keep a notebook with you and record every time that anyone smiles or seems happy to see you. The next time I see you we'll discuss what you find."

Striving for excellence is admirable, in ballet or any other endeavor. It becomes a problem only if people decide "I must be the best at everything I do." Rational-emotive therapists try to help people replace such irrational demands with more realistic ones.

The therapist's goal is to get depressed clients to discover that their automatic thoughts are incorrect, that things are not so bad as they seem, and that the future is not hopeless. If one of the client's thoughts does turn out to be correct—for example, "My boyfriend is interested in someone else"—then the therapist asks, "Even if it's true, is that the end of the world?"

HUMANISTIC THERAPY

As we saw in Chapter 13, humanistic psychologists believe that people can decide consciously and deliberately what kind of person to be and that people naturally strive to achieve their full

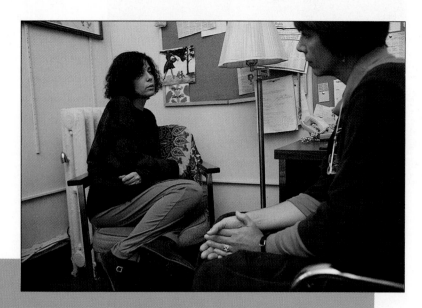

Therapy for anorexia nervosa can take many directions. Therapists often rely on behavior modification to make sure the person eats enough to survive and to gain a little weight. In addition, they talk to the woman and, if possible, to her family to try to uncover conflicts and communication problems.

potential. However, people sometimes learn to dislike themselves because others criticize and reject them. They become distressed by the **incongruence** (mismatch) between their self-concept and their ideal self. Humanistic therapists hold that once people are freed from the inhibiting influences of a rejecting society they can solve their own problems.

The best-known version of humanistic therapy is **person-centered therapy,** pioneered by Carl Rogers. It is also known as nondirective or client-centered therapy. The therapist listens to the client sympathetically, with total acceptance and *unconditional positive regard,* like the love of a parent for a child. Most of the time the therapist restates what the client has said in order to clarify it, conveying the message, "I'm trying to understand your experience from your point of view." The therapist strives to be genuine, empathic, and caring; rarely does he or she offer any interpretation or advice. Here is an example (shortened from Rogers, 1951, pp. 46–47):

> **Client:** I've never said this before to anyone. This is a terrible thing to say, but if I could just find some glorious cause that I could give my life for I would be happy. I guess

maybe I haven't the guts—or the strength—to kill myself—and I just don't want to live.
> **Counselor:** At the present time things look so black to you that you can't see much point in living.
> **Client:** Yes. I wish people hated me, because then I could turn away from them and could blame them. But no, it is all in my hands. I either fight whatever it is that holds me in this terrible conflict, or retreat clear back to the security of my dream world where I could do things, have clever friends, be a pretty wonderful sort of person.
> **Counselor:** It's really a tough struggle, digging into this like you are, and at times the shelter of your dream world looks more attractive and comfortable.
> **Client:** My dream world or suicide.
> **Counselor:** Your dream world or something more permanent than dreams.
> **Client:** Yes. (A long pause. Complete change of voice.) So I don't see why I should waste your time. I'm not worth it. What do you think?
> **Counselor:** It's up to you, Gil. It isn't wasting my time. I'd be glad to see you, whenever you come, but it's how you feel about it. If you want to come twice a week, once a week, it's up to you.
> **Client:** You're not going to suggest that I come in oftener? You're not alarmed and think I ought to come in every day until I get out of this?
> **Counselor:** I believe you are able to make your own decision. I'll see you whenever you want to come.
> **Client:** I don't believe you are alarmed about . . . I see. I may be afraid of myself, but you aren't afraid for me.

The therapist provides an atmosphere in which the client can freely explore feelings of guilt, anxiety, and hostility. By accepting the client's feelings, the therapist conveys the message, "You can make your own decisions. Now that you are more aware of certain problems, you can deal with them constructively yourself."

BEHAVIOR THERAPY

Behavior therapists assume that human behavior is learned and that it can be unlearned. They identify the behavior that needs to be changed, such as a phobia or an addiction or a nervous twitch, and then set about changing it through reinforcement, punishment, and other principles of learning. They may try to understand the causes of the behavior as a first step toward changing it, but unlike psychoanalysts, they are more interested in directly changing behaviors than in understanding their origins.

Behavior therapy begins with clear, well-defined behavioral goals, such as eliminating test anxiety or getting the client to quit smoking, and then attempts to achieve those goals through learning. Setting clear goals enables the therapist to judge whether or not the therapy is succeeding. If the client shows no improvement after a few sessions, the therapist tries a different procedure.

Systematic desensitization to treat phobias, which we examined in Chapter 14, is one example of behavior therapy. For other problems, behavior therapists use a variety of methods.

Behavior Modification for Anorexia Nervosa

One of the quickest and most successful ways of treating anorexia nervosa (Chapter 11) is behavior modification, a system in which the therapist provides reinforcement whenever the person exhibits a clearly defined target behavior. One woman with severe anorexia nervosa was isolated from her family and placed in a small, barren hospital room (Bachrach, Erwin, &

Mohr, 1965). She was told that she could not leave the room and could see no one except the nurse who came at mealtimes. She could obtain privileges—such as having a radio, television, or reading material; the right to leave the room; or the right to have visitors—only as a reward for gaining weight. This method may seem heartless, but life-threatening cases like this one demand drastic measures. The woman gradually gained weight and was released from the hospital when she reached 77 pounds (35 kilograms). After leaving, she lost some of the weight she had gained but not enough to endanger her life.

Behavior modification can be combined with other therapeutic methods. In cases of anorexia nervosa, it is most effective when combined with family counseling designed to alter the family interactions that may have led to the problem (Russell, Szmukler, Dare, & Eisler, 1987).

Table 15.2 contrasts four major types of psychotherapy.

Behavior Therapy for Bed-Wetting

Some children continue to wet the bed long after the usual age of toilet training. Most of them outgrow the problem, but occasionally it lingers on to age 5, 10, or even into the teens.

We now know that most bed-wetters have small bladders and thus have difficulty getting

Table 15.2 Comparison of Four Major Types of Psychotherapy

Type of Psychotherapy	Theory of What Causes Psychological Disorders	Goal of Treatment	Therapeutic Methods	Role of the Therapist
Psychoanalysis	Unconscious thoughts and motivations	To bring unconscious thoughts to consciousness; to achieve insight	Free association, dream analysis, and other methods of probing the unconscious mind	To interpret associations
Rational-emotive and cognitive therapy	Irrational beliefs and unrealistic goals	To establish realistic goals and expectations	Dialogue with the therapist	To help client reexamine assumptions
Humanistic (person-centered) therapy	Reactions to a rejecting society; incongruence between self-concept and ideal self	To enable the client to make personal decisions; to promote self-acceptance	Client-centered interviews	To focus the client's attention; to provide unconditional positive regard
Behavior therapy	Learned inappropriate, maladaptive behaviors	To change behaviors	Positive reinforcement and other learning techniques	To develop and direct the behavior modification program

FIGURE 15.2
A child can be trained not to wet the bed through use of classical-conditioning techniques. At first the sensation of a full bladder (the CS) produces no response, and the child wets the bed. This causes the buzzer to sound (the UCS), and the child wakes up (the UCR). By associating the sensation of a full bladder with a buzzer, the child soon begins waking up to the sensation of a full bladder alone, and he or she will not wet the bed.

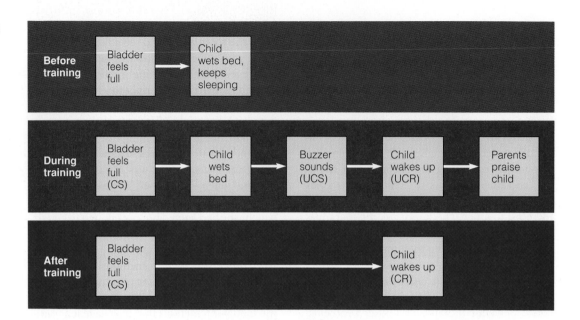

through the night without urinating. We also know that they are unusually deep sleepers who do not wake up when they wet the bed (Stegat, 1975).

The most effective procedure uses a simple device, sold by Sears, that makes use of classical conditioning. It trains the child to wake up at night and go to the bathroom without wetting the bed (Hansen, 1979). Here is how it works: Two thin pieces of metal foil separated by a piece of cloth are placed under the bottom sheet. The top piece of foil has holes in it, and wires connect the two pieces of foil to an alarm. If the child wets the bed, the moisture completes a circuit and triggers the alarm. In the early stages of conditioning, the alarm awakens both the child and the parents, and the child is taken to the bathroom to finish urinating.

The buzzer acts as an unconditioned stimulus (UCS) that evokes the unconditioned response (UCR) of waking up. In this instance, the body itself generates the conditioned stimulus (CS): the sensation produced by a full bladder (Figure 15.2). Whenever that sensation is present, it serves as a signal that a buzzer will soon sound. After a few pairings (or more), the sensation of a full bladder is enough to wake the child.

Actually the situation is a little more complicated, because the child is positively reinforced with praise for waking up to go to the toilet. Training with this device enables most, but not all, bed-wetting children to cease bed-wetting after 1 to 3 months of treatment (Bollard, 1982; Dische, Yule, Corbett, & Hand, 1983).

Aversion Therapy

Although behavior therapists rely mostly on positive reinforcement, they occasionally use punishments to try to teach clients an aversion (dislike) of some stimulus. For example, they might ask someone who is trying to quit smoking to smoke twice as many cigarettes as usual for a few days, to inhale rapidly (one puff every 6 seconds), or to smoke nonstop in a small, airtight room with overflowing ashtrays until there is little oxygen left to breathe. The goal is to teach the client an aversion to smoking. At the end of this treatment, most people stop smoking at least temporarily, although they are likely to start again within a year (Poole, Sanson-Fisher, & German, 1981). Apparently, it is difficult to undo years of enjoyable smoking with a few unpleasant sessions.

■ CONCEPT CHECK

3. Answer the following questions with reference to psychoanalysis, cognitive therapy, humanistic therapy, and behavior therapy.

   a. In which type of therapy is the therapist least likely to offer interpretations of behavior and advice?

   b. Which type focuses more on changing what people do than on exploring what they think?

   c. Which two types try to change what people think?
   (Check your answers on page 644.)

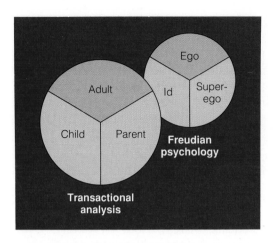

FIGURE 15.3
The three aspects of the personality in transactional analysis are analogous to the three aspects of the personality in Freudian psychology.

Aversion therapy attempts to break a bad habit by associating it with something unpleasant. For example, someone trying to quit cigarettes might smoke in a small, poorly ventilated room until breathing becomes difficult. In other cases, a person might learn to associate cigarettes or some other undesirable habit with electric shocks or another kind of punisher.

SOME LESS COMMON THERAPIES

Besides the common forms of therapy there are countless methods that come and go like fads (Appelbaum, 1979). To cure what ails you, you can climb naked into a hot tub to reenact the moment of birth, or you can sprawl on the floor and scream, or you can take LSD, or you can get "Rolfed," a treatment consisting of vigorous, even painful, massage. Here is a look at three examples of uncommon but "mainstream" forms of therapy.

Transactional Analysis

In **transactional analysis**, often abbreviated **TA**, psychologists attempt to analyze people's "transactions," or communication patterns (Berne, 1964). Transactional analysts assume that each of us has three aspects of personality: a childlike aspect, a rational adult aspect, and a parenting aspect. These are analogous to the Freudian concepts of id, ego, and superego (see Chapter 13). (See Figure 15.3.)

When we speak, we speak as a child, or as an adult, or as a parent. Moreover, we speak to someone as if that person were a child, an adult, or a parent. A "transaction" (or communication) is "balanced" if each person is speaking to the same aspect of the other person who is replying. For example, if I ask you how to get downtown and you give me directions, our transaction is balanced. I speak to you as adult to adult, and you reply as adult to adult. If I say,

"Kids nowadays are lazy," and you reply, "Yes, they're awful," both of us are speaking as parent to parent.

Problems arise when a transaction is "crossed." For example, you tell your parents, "Some of my friends and I are planning to go to Florida for spring break." But your father replies, "No way! I've heard about spring break in Florida. No child of mine is going to go down there and. . . ." You were trying for an adult-adult transaction, but your father came back with a parent-child transaction (Figure 15.4).

How do you respond? You might pick up the cue and respond as child to parent: "You never let me do anything! All my friends get to go except me!" Or you might continue to speak as adult to adult and try to get your father to do the same: "I understand how you feel. Let me reassure you that we're not going to drink and party with all those rowdies you've heard about. We're going to spend our time visiting the museums and sightseeing. It will be very educational."

According to transactional analysts, many interpersonal conflicts develop as a result of crossed transactions. People make trouble for themselves because they are not really communicating. The analysts try to teach people to be aware of how they are addressing each other and how they are being addressed so that they can keep their transactions parallel.

FIGURE 15.4

According to transactional analysis, "balanced" transactions occur when each person is talking to the aspect of the other person that is responding (a). "Crossed" transactions occur when a person is talking to one aspect and a different aspect is responding (b). Crossed transactions often lead to confusion and misunderstanding.

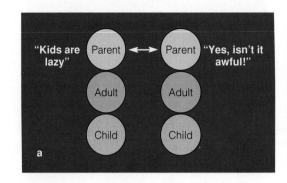

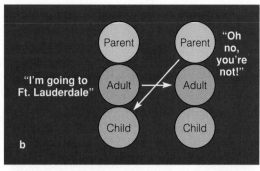

■ CONCEPT CHECK

4. *Linda and Maria are shopping for a VCR. Linda says, "This is the nicest one, but you can't afford it." Maria replies, "Oh, yeah? Well, that's the one I'm going to buy." Is this a parallel transaction or a crossed transaction? (Check your answer on page 644.)*

Gestalt Therapy

In Chapter 4 we considered Gestalt psychology, the study of how people integrate perceptions into a whole. **Gestalt therapy** (Perls, 1973) is loosely based on the same idea. It deals with the person "as a whole," including body as well as mind. For example, a Gestalt therapist, noticing a client's body language, might say, "You say you are no longer upset with your mother, but whenever you mention her you clench your fists." Or the therapist might say, "Notice how your eyes are wandering about instead of looking at the person you are talking to. Does that mean you are trying to avoid something?"

Unlike psychoanalysts and many other therapists, Gestalt therapists discourage clients from dwelling on the past. They concentrate on the person's immediate experience and current behavior. They believe it does little good for you to discover that you are acting strangely because your mother was too harsh with you during toilet training. Instead, they urge you to accept responsibility for your own actions and find solutions to your problems here and now.

Paradoxical Intervention

Sometimes psychotherapists have to cope with patients who have no interest in helping themselves and who *like* being considered "mentally ill." Their behavior wins them attention and sympathy and gives them an excuse for not carrying out their obligations at home or at work

(Fontana, Marcus, Noel, & Rakusin, 1972). Others enjoy being told that they are a "juvenile delinquent" or "the thinnest anorexic I've ever seen."

You are a psychotherapist trying to deal with someone who does not want to change. What do you do? You might decide that the patient should be left free to make that choice. Or you might decide that people should *not* be permitted to engage in self-defeating behavior. If you choose the latter approach, how might you intervene?

One method is known as **paradoxical intervention**. A paradox is an apparently self-contradictory statement. Paradoxical intervention consists of telling a person to do something but giving such an undesirable reason for doing it that the person will want to stop.

For example, a school psychologist was trying to deal with a teenage student who seldom attended school and misbehaved when he did attend. After a long series of other approaches had failed, the psychologist told him:

Psychologists sometimes find that children, somewhat younger than you, go through a phase in which they like to misbehave before they are able to become mature young men. This pattern is sort of like a last fling. . . . It seems that you have not passed through this childish phase yet. It is expected that you will be misbehaving and getting into trouble for a while longer than your mature friends until you grow up like them. . . . It seems it would be best for you if you didn't go to school until you grow through this childish stage; we don't want you to fight the urge to misbehave because you apparently aren't mature enough to control it.

After this conversation, the student's attendance and grades improved and his misbehavior declined (Kolko & Milan, 1983, p. 657).

Paradoxical intervention is used only as a last resort after more conventional forms of therapy have failed. Even then, it must be used with caution. Some people practice what they call "reverse psychology," which consists simply of telling someone to do the opposite of what they want the person to do; that practice can easily backfire (Haley, 1984). Paradoxical intervention is more than reverse psychology; it requires convincing the person that if he or she does the "recommended" action, it will be interpreted as a sign of childishness or some other undesirable characteristic. As with any other treatment, the therapist must constantly monitor the effects of the treatment.

GENERAL TRENDS IN PSYCHOTHERAPY

The early practitioners of each type of psychotherapy were, in some cases, fairly rigid in their beliefs about exactly what the therapist and client should do, when they should do it, and how long the whole procedure should last. Today, many psychotherapists have modified some of these procedures or combined parts of one therapy with parts of another. We shall consider two major trends, eclectic therapy and brief therapy.

Eclectic Therapy

In 1950, almost half of all the psychotherapists in the United States relied mostly on psychoanalysis or closely related methods. Since then, psychoanalysis has declined in popularity (Mahoney, 1990). Today, almost half of all psychologists practice **eclectic therapy,** meaning that they use a combination of methods and approaches. For example, an eclectic therapist might use behavior modification, psychoanalysis, and rational-emotive techniques in different combinations, depending on each client's needs (Garfield, 1980).

Brief Therapy

For many years, psychoanalysts expected to see each client for at least an hour a week for years. Even therapists who rejected the psychoanalytic approach regarded psychotherapy as a long-term commitment. They regarded any client who quit after a few sessions as a dropout, a failure. Eventually they realized that some of the apparent "failures" were really "premature successes" who did not need further treatment (Rockwell & Pinkerton, 1982). In fact, about half of all the people who enter psychotherapy show significant improvement within 8 ses-

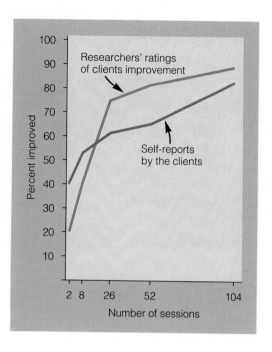

FIGURE 15.5
The relationship of the number of psychotherapy sessions and the percentage of clients improved. (From Howard et al., 1986.)

sions, and three-fourths show improvement within 26 sessions (Howard, Kopta, Krause, & Orlinsky, 1986). (See Figure 15.5.)

Now, many therapists realize that it is sometimes desirable to limit the duration of therapy. At the start of **brief therapy,** or *time-limited therapy* (Clarkin & Frances, 1982), the therapist and client make an agreement about what they can expect from each other and how long the treatment will last—generally between 2 and 6 months (Koss & Butcher, 1986).

As the deadline approaches, both the therapist and the client are strongly motivated to bring the therapy to a successful conclusion. How hard would you work on a term paper if you had no deadline to meet? Advocates of brief therapy believe that when people know that their therapy may go on forever, they feel no need to come to grips with their problems quickly. They may even resist doing so for fear of breaking off a satisfying relationship with their therapist. When they know they have a deadline, they deal with their main problems promptly.

Moreover, with a deadline agreed on in advance, clients do not feel "deserted" when the therapy ends. They may return for an occasional session months later (Bennett, 1983), but for a time they must get along without help. Any client who fails to make progress by the time the deadline nears should think about going to a different therapist.

Research has found that brief therapy is about as successful as long-term therapy for

Group therapy offers an opportunity for people to discuss their problems with others who have similar problems, under a therapist's supervision. Participants learn from one another's successes and failures; they also practice social skills.

most clients. Brief therapy is least successful with clients who have complex, severe problems and clients who fail to form a working relationship with the therapist during the early sessions (DeLeon, Vanden Bos, & Cummings, 1983; Dush, Hirt, & Schroeder, 1983; Koss & Butcher, 1986). However, those clients are likely to have trouble in long-term therapy also.

THERAPY IN A GROUP

Freud and the other early pioneers of psychotherapy dealt with their clients on a one-to-one basis. Individual psychotherapy has its advantages, most of all privacy. But for many purposes it is helpful to treat clients in groups.

Group Therapy

Group therapy is therapy that is administered to a group of people all at one time. It first came into vogue for economic reasons. Most psychotherapists charge substantial fees for the usual 50-minute session. (They have to charge more per patient than most medical practitioners simply because they see only one patient per hour.) Because many middle-class and poor people in need of psychotherapy cannot afford those fees, some therapists began to treat small groups of people, spreading the cost among them.

Group therapy has other advantages as well. Therapists typically try to set up a group of about seven or eight people who are about the same age and have similar problems—people who have as much in common with one another as possible. For example, a group might be composed of people who are all struggling with poor interpersonal skills, eating disorders, or compulsive gambling. Members learn from each other and are encouraged by each other's successes.

Group therapy sessions give people an opportunity to explore how they relate to others. Clients become aware of how they irritate others and how they can be useful to others. They use group therapy to develop and practice social skills (Bloch, 1986).

Family Therapy

In **family therapy,** the group consists of members of one family. It is based on the assumption that many psychological disorders are related to problems of communication and interaction within a family. Family therapy is not exactly an alternative to other forms of therapy; a family therapist may use psychoanalysis, cognitive therapy, behavior therapy, or any other technique. What distinguishes family therapists is that they prefer to talk with two or more members of a family together; even when they talk with just one member they focus on how that individual fits into the family (Hazelrigg, Cooper, & Borduin, 1987).

For example, one young man who had been caught stealing a car was taken to a psychologist. The psychologist, a family therapist, asked to talk with the parents as well. As it turned out, the father had been a heavy drinker until his boss pressured him to quit drinking and join Alcoholics Anonymous. Until that time, the mother had made most of the family decisions in close consultation with her son, who had become almost a substitute husband. When the father quit drinking, he began to assume more authority over the family, and his son came to resent him. The mother felt less needed and grew depressed.

Each member of the family had problems that could not be resolved by an individual. The therapist worked to help the father improve his relationship with both his son and his wife and to help all three find satisfying roles within the family (Foley, 1984). Because so many psychological problems arise from family relationships, family therapy has been growing more and more popular (Gurman, Kniskern, & Pinsof, 1986).

Self-Help Groups

Self-help groups, such as Alcoholics Anonymous (page 602), operate much like group therapy sessions, except that they do not include a therapist. Everyone in the group both gives and receives help. People who have experienced a problem themselves can offer special insights to others with the same problem. Self-help groups have another advantage: The members are available to help one another whenever someone needs help—often or seldom, without appointment, without charge.

Some self-help groups are composed of current or former mental patients. The members feel a need to talk to others who have gone through a similar experience, either in addition to or instead of treatment by a therapist. The Mental Patients' Association in Canada was organized by former patients who were frustrated and angry at the treatment they had received (or failed to receive), especially in mental hospitals (Chamberlin, 1978). Similar organizations in the United States and Europe enable former patients to share experiences with one another, provide support, and work together to defend the rights and welfare of mental patients.

EVALUATING THE EFFECTIVENESS OF PSYCHOTHERAPY

How well does psychotherapy work? Hans Eysenck (1952b) called attention to this question by pointing out that about 65% of the people who never receive therapy for their psychological problems nevertheless improve in a year or two. Improvement without therapy is called **spontaneous remission;** it is a fairly common finding with phobia, depression, and certain other disorders. According to the statistics available at that time, people who did receive therapy improved at about the same rate as those without therapy. Eysenck therefore suggested that psychotherapy is generally ineffective and almost worthless.

Eysenck's conclusions, which were highly influential at the time, were based on weak data. No one had actually conducted an experiment in which troubled people were randomly assigned to a therapy group and a control group. Instead, the therapy groups were composed of people who *chose* to enter therapy; the control

The novelist Leo Tolstoy observed, "All happy families resemble one another, but each unhappy family is unhappy in its own way." While one family may be aware of shared problems, another may make one member the scapegoat. As impartial referees, family therapists can help people deal with what's wrong in their family even when some members resist participating.

Self-help groups operate on the assumption that people relate best to others who share the same problem. The excuses and rationalizations an alcoholic might use with a therapist are unlikely to get far with fellow alcoholics.

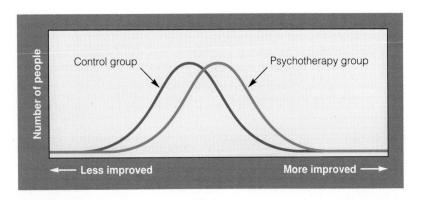

FIGURE 15.6
According to one review of 475 studies, the average person receiving psychotherapy shows more improvement than do 80% of similar, randomly assigned people not in therapy. Note that both groups show substantial variation; some untreated people progress better than some treated people. This comparison lumps together all kinds of therapy and all kinds of troubled people. (From Smith, Glass, & Miller, 1980.)

groups were composed of people who chose *not* to enter therapy. Let's suppose—quite realistically—that the people with the most severe troubles might opt for therapy, whereas those with milder problems might decide they could get by on their own. In that case it is unfair to compare the degree of improvement by the two groups. Furthermore, investigators' definition of "improvement" was often much more stringent for the therapy group than it was for the control group.

Since then, researchers have conducted better studies, comparing people who were randomly assigned to therapy and control groups. In many cases, the people in the control group were put on a "waiting list" to begin therapy later. A month or more after the start of the study, researchers measured the amount of improvement by the people in therapy and the improvement by people still on the waiting list. According to one review of 475 such studies, the average person in therapy shows greater improvement than 80% of people not in therapy (Smith, Glass, & Miller, 1980). Figure 15.6 illustrates this effect. This overall summary combines the effects of many kinds of therapy on many kinds of troubles; it is a little like saying that "medicine is better than no medicine." A more detailed analysis of the data indicated that, as a rule, therapists using cognitive or cognitive-behavioral methods produced more dependable benefits than did those using other methods. Also, benefits were generally largest for people suffering from depression or a single

phobia and smallest for people with vague, general complaints or all-pervasive problems (Singer, 1981; Smith, Glass, & Miller, 1980). Surveys of additional, more recent research have indicated that depressed people receiving cognitive or behavioral therapy improve more than about 98% of people not in therapy (Dobson, 1989; Robinson, Berman, & Neimeyer, 1990). In short, psychotherapy produces dependable benefits.

Why Nearly All Therapies Are Helpful

Although the research indicates that certain kinds of therapies produce somewhat better results than others do, the surprising fact remains that every therapy which has been tested produces clear benefits (Stiles, Shapiro, & Elliott, 1986). I call this a "surprising" fact because various therapies are based on highly discrepant theories of the nature of psychological disorders. Advocates of a particular therapy sometimes claim that a particular, unique procedure in their method is critical to success. But if behavior therapy, psychoanalysis, and person-centered therapy all produce benefits, then their methods must have some valuable features in common, more so than appears at first (Horvath, 1988; Strupp, 1986).

The various forms of psychotherapy do share some important features. For example, they all rely on the "therapeutic alliance"—a relationship between therapist and client that is characterized by acceptance, caring, respect, and attention. This relationship provides social support that helps clients deal with their problems and acquire social skills that they can apply to other relationships.

Moreover, in nearly all forms of therapy, clients talk about their beliefs and emotions, how they act, and why they act that way. They examine aspects of themselves that they ordinarily take for granted; in so doing, they gain self-understanding.

The mere fact of entering therapy, whatever the method, improves clients' morale. The therapist conveys the message "You are going to get better." Clients begin to think of themselves as people who can cope with their problems and overcome them. Just expecting improvement can lead to improvement.

Finally, every form of therapy requires clients to commit themselves to making some sort of change in their lifestyle (Klein, Zitrin, Woerner, & Ross, 1983). Simply by coming to the therapy session, they are reaffirming their commitment—to drink less, to feel less depressed, or to overcome a fear. They are also obliged to work on that change between sessions so that they can come to the next session and report, "I've been doing a little better lately." Improvement may depend as much on what clients do between sessions as on what happens in the sessions themselves.

Let us close this section with an example of how some therapists attempt to strengthen their clients' commitment to change (Haley, 1984). Suppose the problem is cigarette smoking. After discussing the habit with the client, the therapist casually mentions a "guaranteed cure" and then changes the subject. The client asks skeptically about the guaranteed cure, and the therapist says that it is not for everyone. "You probably wouldn't be interested."

"What do you mean I wouldn't be interested? What is it?"

"Well," replies the therapist, "part of the deal is that I can't tell you what the method is unless you agree to follow it."

"But how can I do that if I don't know what it is?"

"You're absolutely right. As I said, I don't think you would be interested."

Over the next few weeks the client keeps returning to the topic of the guaranteed cure, becoming more and more curious. Each time, the therapist refuses to describe it and tries to change the subject. Eventually the client says, "All right. Whatever this guaranteed cure thing is, I'll do it." The therapist encourages the client to discuss this decision with friends and return the next week. At that point the therapist finally reveals the plan:

"I want you to carry a little notebook with you and record every time you smoke a cigarette. When you come back next week I'll ask you to show it to me. For the first cigarette, you'll owe me a penny, in addition to my usual fee. For the second cigarette, you'll owe me two pennies. The next one will cost you four pennies, and so on. The price doubles for each cigarette."

The client leaves, disappointed by this unimpressive scheme but committed to follow it. The next week the client returns with $40.95, the charge for 12 cigarettes. "You dirty so-and-so! The first few cigarettes were cheap. But now they're getting expensive! I've smoked my last cigarette!"

The therapist pretends to be disappointed. "Nuts, there goes my trip to the Bahamas."

This treatment succeeds only because the client makes an irrevocable commitment to follow the therapist's plan. Once that commitment has been made, the battle is half-won. Without such a commitment, success would be doubtful. Even with other therapies that do not make such an ordeal of it, the client's commitment to change is essential.

SUMMARY

- *Psychoanalysis.* Psychoanalysts try to uncover the unconscious reasons behind self-defeating behaviors. To bring the unconscious to consciousness, they rely on free association, dream analysis, and transference. (page 629)

- *Rational-emotive and cognitive therapies.* Rational-emotive therapists and cognitive therapists try to get clients to give up their irrational beliefs and unrealistic goals and to replace defeatist thinking with more favorable views of themselves and the world. (page 632)

- *Humanistic therapy.* Humanistic therapists, including person-centered therapists, assume that if people accept themselves as they are, they can solve their own problems. Person-centered therapists listen with unconditional positive regard but seldom offer interpretations or advice. (page 633)

- *Behavior therapy.* Behavior therapists set specific goals for changing a client's behavior and use a variety of learning techniques to help a client achieve those goals. (page 634)

- *Some other therapies.* Among the many other forms of psychotherapy available are transactional analysis, Gestalt therapy, and paradoxical intervention. (page 637)

- *Eclectic therapy.* About half of all psychotherapists today call themselves "eclectic"—that is, they use a combination of methods, depending on the circumstances. (page 639)

- *Brief therapy.* Many therapists set a time limit on the treatment, usually ranging from 2 to 6 months. Brief therapy is about as successful as long-term therapy if the goals are limited. (page 639)

- *Group therapies and self-help groups.* Psychotherapy is sometimes provided to people in groups, often composed of people with similar problems or members of a family. Self-help groups provide sessions similar to group therapy but without a therapist. (page 640)

- *Effectiveness of psychotherapy.* The average troubled person in therapy improves more than at least 80% of people not in therapy; the improvement is greater with certain kinds of therapy, including cognitive therapy. It is also greater with certain disorders, such as depression and phobia. (page 641)

- *Similarities among therapies.* A wide variety of therapies share certain features: All rely on a caring relationship between therapist and client. All promote self-understanding. All improve clients' morale. And all require a commitment by clients to try to make changes in their lives. (page 642)

SUGGESTIONS FOR FURTHER READING

Goleman, D., & Speeth, K. R. (1982). *The essential psychotherapies.* New York: New American Library. Includes excerpts from the writings of pioneers in psychotherapy.

Haley, J. (1984). *Ordeal therapy.* San Francisco: Jossey-Bass. Describes a clever, inventive approach to therapy.

TERMS

psychotherapy treatment of psychological disorders by methods that generally include a personal relationship between a trained therapist and a client (page 629)

psychodynamic therapies treatments that attempt to unravel people's underlying drives and motivations (page 629)

psychoanalysis a method of psychotherapy founded by Sigmund Freud based on identifying unconscious thoughts and emotions and bringing them to consciousness (page 629)

catharsis release of pent-up emotions associated with unconscious thoughts and memories (page 629)

free association procedure in which a client lies on a couch, starts thinking about a particular symptom or problem, and then reports everything that comes to mind (page 630)

manifest content the content that appears on the surface of a dream (page 631)

latent content the hidden content of a dream that is represented only symbolically (page 631)

transference extension of a client's feelings toward a parent or other important figure onto the therapist (page 631)

interpretation a therapist's explanation of the underlying meaning of what a client says (page 631)

resistance according to psychoanalysts, continued repression that interferes with therapy (page 631)

rational-emotive therapy treatment based on the assumption that people's emotions depend on their "internal sentences" such as "I can't be happy unless everyone thinks my room is clean" (page 632)

cognitive therapy treatment that seeks to improve people's psychological well-being by changing their cognitions (page 633)

incongruence a mismatch between someone's self-concept and ideal self (page 634)

person-centered therapy (also known as nondirective or client-centered therapy) procedure in which a therapist listens to the client sympathetically, provides unconditional positive regard, and offers little interpretation or advice (page 634)

behavior therapy treatment that begins with clear, well-defined behavioral goals, such as eliminating test anxiety, and then attempts to achieve those goals through learning (page 635)

transactional analysis (TA) treatment in which a psychologist attempts to analyze "transactions," or communication patterns (page 637)

Gestalt therapy treatment that deals with the person "as a whole," with emphasis on body language and the here-and-now (page 638)

paradoxical intervention procedure in which a psychologist tells a person to do something but gives an undesirable reason for doing it in hopes that the person will want to stop (page 638)

eclectic therapy treatment that uses a combination of methods and approaches (page 639)

brief therapy (or time-limited therapy) treatment that begins with an agreement on what therapist and client can expect from each other and how long the treatment will last (page 639)

group therapy treatment administered to a group of people all at one time (page 640)

family therapy treatment provided for members of one family, generally meeting as a group (page 640)

spontaneous remission improvement of a psychological condition without therapy (page 641)

ANSWERS TO CONCEPT CHECKS

1. Freud would disagree with the premise of this paperback. Freud believed that the symbolism of dream elements differed from one person to another. (page 631)

2. Rational-emotive therapy assumes that many thoughts lead to emotions. This assumption is the reverse of the James-Lange theory, which argues that emotion-related changes in the body give rise to thoughts. (page 632)

3. (a) Humanistic therapy; (b) behavior therapy; (c) psychoanalysis and cognitive therapy. (page 636)

4. This is a parallel transaction. Linda is speaking as parent to child, and Maria is responding as child to parent. (page 638)

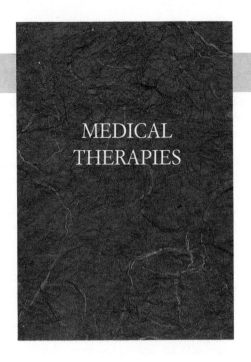

MEDICAL THERAPIES

How do drugs and other medical interventions alleviate psychological disorders?

How effective are medical therapies?

Under what circumstances should they be used?

In his novel *The Idiot,* the Russian novelist Fyodor Dostoyevsky (1868/1969, pp. 245–246) described in the third person what he experienced just before each epileptic seizure: For a brief moment "it seemed his brain was on fire, and in an extraordinary surge all his vital forces would be intensified. The sense of life, the consciousness of self were multiplied tenfold in these moments. . . . His mind and heart were flooded with extraordinary light; all torment, all doubt, all anxieties were relieved at once, resolved in a kind of lofty calm, full of serene, harmonious joy and hope, full of understanding and knowledge of the ultimate cause of things."

Afterward Dostoyevsky debated with himself what to make of these moments of supreme bliss. Were they glimpses of the supreme beauty and harmony of the universe, moments when he could be at peace with his Creator? Or were all of these experiences just by-products of a diseased state of the brain?

This issue is not just a curiosity for scholars of Russian literature; it is central to medical therapies for psychological disorders. Said in other terms: Does happiness really "count" if it

is induced by a physical change in the brain? In general, our society's answer to this question has been mixed. On the one hand, we do not want "normal" people to make themselves happier by taking drugs (or by trying to acquire the kind of epilepsy that Dostoyevsky had). We consider drug-induced happiness to be artificial, a poor substitute for the happiness people can find in real life. On the other hand, we *do* offer drugs to elevate the mood of depressed people, artificially bringing their mood up to "normal." If one of those depressed people, having recovered to normal mood, now wanted to increase the dosage to try for an even better mood, we probably would object (Nesse, 1991).

Medical therapies face philosophical issues of this type as well as practical and scientific issues. What are the effects of drugs and other medical treatments on people with psychological disorders? How do they work? And do they do more good than harm?

THE RATIONALE BEHIND MEDICAL THERAPIES

The various talk therapies we examined in the first module of this chapter all try to change people's thoughts and actions by providing new experiences. They rely on conversations between the client and the therapist or among members of a therapy group. The clients must be committed, or at least willing, to change certain aspects of their life.

Medical therapies differ from talk therapies in some important regards. They attempt to change brain functioning directly, rather than through experience. Once the physician and client have agreed to try a drug or some other medical treatment, there is no need for further talk. To be sure, they will meet periodically to evaluate the client's progress, but those discussions are not a critical part of the therapy itself. Moreover, clients do not need to make a commitment to changing their lives. They must agree to receive the treatment—or, if they are considered legally incompetent to decide, a legal guardian must agree—but no additional cooperation is necessary. The goal of medical

Psychiatric drugs have become a major industry. Drugs are available for the relief of anxiety, depression, schizophrenia, and other conditions. Two difficult issues arise: How effective are these drugs, in comparison to other methods of treatment? And under what circumstances do the benefits outweigh the disadvantages?

therapies is to restore the brain to a normal physiological state, on the theory that normal physiology leads to normal behavior and experience. (Medical therapies are often, though not always, combined with some form of talk therapy.)

Medical therapy for psychological disorders has a long and not very glorious history. We have already discussed prefrontal lobotomies in Chapter 3. Another early medical therapy was insulin shock, a procedure in which people with schizophrenia were given an overdose of insulin to precipitate an epileptic-type convulsion, on the theory that people could not have epilepsy and schizophrenia at the same time. Insulin shock provided little if any benefit for people with schizophrenia and constituted an extremely unpleasant experience. Patients were exposed to heat, cold, water, and miscellaneous

other treatments, generally on no theory other than the idea that "nothing else is working so we may as well give it a try." The medical therapies of today have to struggle to overcome the (deservedly) bad reputation established by the medical therapies of times past.

We shall discuss some of the current medical therapies for anxiety and avoidance disorders, depression, and schizophrenia. In Chapter 14, we already considered the use of Antabuse for alcohol abuse and methadone for opiate abuse.

DRUG THERAPIES FOR ANXIETY AND AVOIDANCE DISORDERS

Tranquilizers are among the most widely prescribed drugs in the United States (Robinson, 1987). The most common tranquilizers are the *benzodiazepines,* including drugs with the trade names Valium, Librium, and Xanax. Benzodiazepines relieve anxiety, relax the muscles, induce sleep, and inhibit epileptic seizures. Sometimes they are prescribed for people with panic disorder, phobia, or other anxiety disorders; frequently, however, they are prescribed for people with no diagnosable disorder. For such people the drugs serve as a means of relieving an occasional episode of anxiety or as a sleeping pill. Benzodiazepines can be habit-forming, especially if used as sleeping pills.

Brain researchers now understand in reasonable detail how benzodiazepines work. The neurotransmitter GABA stimulates receptors on a neuron's membrane, as shown in Figure 15.7. On its own, GABA attaches moderately easily to this receptor, opening a channel for chloride ions (Cl^-) to enter the neuron. Benzodiazepines alter the shape of the receptor complex to enable GABA molecules to attach more readily. Thus they indirectly facilitate transmission at these synapses (Macdonald, Weddle, & Gross, 1986). Facilitation of those synapses decreases anxiety and promotes sleep. Tranquilizers also reduce anxiety indirectly: People who have tranquilizers available "as a crutch" are less worried about having an anxiety attack and are consequently less likely to have such an attack. Unfortunately, some people come to rely on tranquilizers for problems they could handle without drugs.

For people with obsessive-compulsive disorder, the drug clomipramine (Anafranil) and

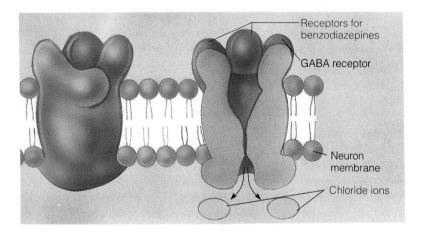

FIGURE 15.7
Benzodiazepine tranquilizers such as Valium and Librium attach to a site on the receptor complex for the neurotransmitter GABA. When they attach, they modify the shape of the receptor complex, making it easier for GABA to stimulate its receptor. Thus the benzodiazepines indirectly facilitate transmission at this synapse, enabling chloride molecules to enter the neuron. The effect on behavior is to relieve anxiety.

Receptors for benzodiazepines
GABA receptor
Neuron membrane
Chloride ions

related drugs have demonstrated considerable usefulness. Within 2 weeks on clomipramine, 50–60% of obsessive-compulsive patients experience noticeable relief from their symptoms (Clomipramine collaborative study group, 1991). Clomipramine prolongs the effects of the neurotransmitter serotonin by preventing the presynaptic neuron from reabsorbing it. That is, after an axon releases serotonin from its terminal button, clomipramine causes the serotonin to remain longer than usual in the synapse, reexciting the postsynaptic neuron. The effectiveness of this drug suggests (but does not conclusively demonstrate) a biological basis for obsessive-compulsive disorder.

▪ CONCEPT CHECK

5. *Alcohol facilitates transmission at GABA synapses. What effect should we expect if someone took both alcohol and a benzodiazepine tranquilizer? (Check your answer on page 652.)*

BIOLOGICAL THERAPIES FOR DEPRESSION

Three types of drugs are used as antidepressants: tricyclics, serotonin reuptake blockers, and monoamine oxidase inhibitors. **Tricyclic drugs** (such as Tofranil) block the reabsorption of several neurotransmitters—dopamine, norepinephrine, and serotonin—after they are released by the terminal button (Figure 15.8). Thus tricyclics prolong the effect of these neurotransmitters on the receptors of the postsynaptic cell. **Serotonin reuptake blockers** (such as Prozac) also block reuptake of released neurotransmitters, but their effect is more narrowly limited to the neurotransmitter serotonin. **Monoamine** (MAHN-oh-ah-MEEN) **oxidase inhibitors (MAOIs)** (such as Nardil) block the metabolic breakdown of released dopamine, norepinephrine, and serotonin (Figure 15.8c). Thus MAOIs also prolong the ability of released neurotransmitters to stimulate the postsynaptic cell. MAOIs are not widely used, except for patients who suffer from a combination of severe anxiety and depression (Joyce & Paykel, 1989).

The effects of antidepressant drugs build up slowly. Some depressed people begin to experience relief within 1 week; most people have to take the drugs for 2 to 3 weeks before they notice any effects. The relief from depression continues to increase over 6 to 8 weeks (Blaine, Prien, & Levine, 1983). What is happening so gradually over that time?

Two changes are taking place: First, while the drugs increase the stimulation of certain

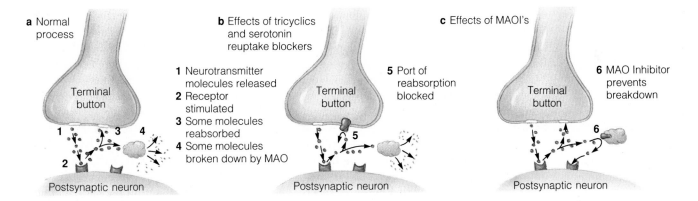

a Normal process

1 Neurotransmitter molecules released
2 Receptor stimulated
3 Some molecules reabsorbed
4 Some molecules broken down by MAO

Terminal button

Postsynaptic neuron

b Effects of tricyclics and serotonin reuptake blockers

5 Port of reabsorption blocked

Terminal button

Postsynaptic neuron

c Effects of MAOI's

6 MAO Inhibitor prevents breakdown

Terminal button

Postsynaptic neuron

FIGURE 15.8

Antidepressant drugs prolong the activity of the neurotransmitters dopamine, norepinephrine, and serotonin by two major routes. (a) Ordinarily, after the release of one of the neurotransmitters, some of the molecules are reabsorbed by the terminal button and other molecules are broken down by the enzyme MAO (monoamine oxidase). (b) Serotonin reuptake blockers prevent reabsorption of serotonin. The tricyclic drugs are less specific, preventing the reabsorption of dopamine, norepinephrine, or serotonin. (c) MAO inhibitors block the enzyme MAO. The result of any of these antidepressant drugs is to increase the stimulation of receptors on the postsynaptic neuron.

synaptic receptors, they slowly decrease the sensitivity of those receptors (McNeal & Cimbolic, 1986; Sulser, Gillespie, Mishra, & Manier, 1984). Apparently, relief from depression requires both increased stimulation and decreased sensitivity.

Second, the prolonged use of antidepressant drugs gradually improves the timing of the person's sleep patterns. Most depressed people have disorders of their 24-hour cycles. They are not as alert as other people during the day and not as sleepy at night. They wake up too early and cannot get back to sleep. Antidepressant drugs slowly restore their 24-hour cycles to normal at about the same rate at which they relieve their depression (Healy & Williams, 1988).

■ CONCEPT CHECK

6. *The drug mianserin prolongs the release of dopamine, norepinephrine, and serotonin from the terminal button (Leonard, 1982). Would mianserin increase or decrease the intensity of depression? (Check your answer on page 652.)*

Advantages and Disadvantages of Antidepressant Drugs

Antidepressant drugs alleviate depression for most people. The drugs are convenient to use and relatively inexpensive. Double-blind studies have consistently found that 50–70% of the people who take tricyclic drugs experience an improvement in their mood, as compared to 20–30% of people who take placebos (Blaine, Prien, & Levine, 1983; Gerson, Plotkin, & Jarvik, 1988; Morris & Beck, 1974).

Overall, cognitive therapy is beneficial to a somewhat higher percentage of depressed patients than drug therapy is (Robinson, Berman, & Neimeyer, 1990). Cognitive therapy also has the advantage of producing no side effects. You might then wonder why anyone would choose drug therapy. There are two reasons: First, drug therapy tends to work more quickly. (Remember, 2 months of psychotherapy is considered "brief psychotherapy." The drugs show benefits within 1 to 3 weeks.) Second, drug therapy is decidedly less expensive.

To a large extent, drug therapies are limited by the drugs' side effects. About one third of the people who take tricyclic drugs experience dry mouth, dizziness, sweating, and constipation. A smaller number experience tremor, blurred vision, rapid heartbeat, impaired concentration, and other side effects (Blaine, Prien, & Levine, 1983). In many cases, the side effects

are severe enough to force people to stop taking the drugs or to reduce their dosage. The fact that many people cannot tolerate a large dosage is one major reason why only 50–70% of people gain significant benefits from the drugs.

The serotonin reuptake blockers, such as Prozac, became available in the 1980s. The advantage of these drugs is that they produce fewer side effects for most people; consequently most people can take them in larger dosages and experience greater relief from depression (Burrows, McIntyre, Judd, & Norman, 1988; Stark & Hardison, 1985). The use of Prozac became controversial when certain people reported that the drug provoked them to suicidal thoughts. Unfortunately it is difficult to predict which Prozac users will experience such thoughts, although the research suggests that only a small percentage will (Mann & Kapur, 1991).

Electroconvulsive Shock Therapy

Another well-known but controversial treatment for depression is **electroconvulsive therapy,** abbreviated **ECT** (Figure 15.9). In ECT, a brief electrical shock is administered across the patient's head to induce a convulsion similar to epilepsy. First used in the 1930s, ECT became popular in the 1940s and 1950s as a treatment for schizophrenia, depression, and many other disorders. It then fell out of favor, partly because antidepressant drugs and other therapeutic methods had become available and partly because ECT had been widely abused. Some patients were subjected to ECT 100 times or more without their consent. In many cases, it was used as a threat to enforce patients' cooperation.

Beginning in the 1970s, ECT has made a comeback in modified form. Today it is used more selectively than it was in the past, mostly for severely depressed people who fail to respond to antidepressant drugs, whose thinking is seriously disordered, or who have strong suicidal tendencies (Scovern & Kilmann, 1980). For suicidal patients, this treatment has the advantage of taking effect more quickly than antidepressant drugs do—in about 1 week instead of 2 or 3. When a life is at stake, rapid relief is important.

ECT is now used only with patients who have given their informed consent, and its use is generally limited to six to eight applications on alternate days. The shock is less intense than it used to be, and the patient is given muscle relaxants and anesthetics to prevent injury and to reduce discomfort.

Exactly how ECT works is uncertain. Some have suggested that it relieves depression by causing people to forget certain depressing thoughts and memories. However, the data do not support that suggestion. Although ECT usually does impair memory, at least temporarily, there are ways to reduce the memory loss without lessening the antidepressant effect (Miller, Small, Milstein, Malloy, & Stout, 1981). Among the many effects of ECT on the brain, one may be of critical importance: By decreasing the sensitivity of synapses that inhibit certain neurons from releasing dopamine and norepinephrine, ECT increases the stimulation of those synapses (Chiodo & Antelman, 1980).

The use of ECT continues to be controversial. According to extensive reviews of the literature, ECT relieves depression for about 80% of the patients and generally produces fewer side effects than antidepressant drugs do (Fink, 1985; Janicak et al., 1985; Weiner, 1984). The brain shows no signs of damage, either immediately after the treatment or months later (Coffey et al., 1991). However, other researchers question those benefits and believe that the long-term side effects have been underestimated. Patients' rights groups, aware of how ECT has been abused at times, generally oppose its use. Because of the controversy and opposition, most psychiatrists hesitate to recommend it.

LITHIUM THERAPY FOR BIPOLAR DISORDER

Many years ago, researcher J. F. Cade had the idea that uric acid might be effective in treating mania. To get the uric acid to dissolve in water, he mixed it with lithium salts. The resulting mixture proved effective, but eventually researchers discovered that the lithium salts, not the uric acid, were therapeutic.

Lithium salts were soon adopted in the Scandinavian countries, but they were slow to be accepted in the United States. One reason was that drug manufacturers had no interest in marketing lithium pills. (Lithium is a natural substance and cannot be patented.) A second reason was that lithium salts produce toxic side effects unless the dosage is carefully monitored. If the dosage is too low, it does no good. If it is slightly higher than the recommended level, it produces nausea and blurred vision.

Properly regulated dosages of lithium are

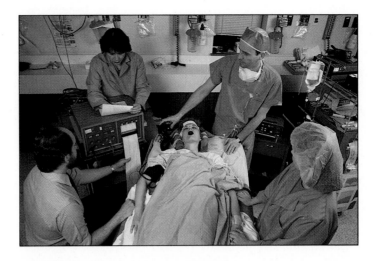

FIGURE 15.9
Electroconvulsive therapy today is administered only with the person's informed consent. It is given in conjunction with muscle relaxants and anesthetics to minimize discomfort.

the most effective known treatment for bipolar disorder (manic-depressive illness). Lithium reduces mania and protects the patient from relapsing into either mania or depression. It does not provide a permanent "cure," however; the person must continue to take lithium pills every day. When someone whose mood has become normal decides to quit taking the pills, mania or depression is likely to return within about 5 months (Suppes, Baldessarini, Faedda, & Tohen, 1991).

At this point, no one is certain how lithium relieves bipolar disorder. Many researchers believe its primary effects are on chemical pathways within neurons, not on transmission at a particular kind of synapse (Manji et al., 1991; Risby et al., 1991).

DRUG THERAPIES FOR SCHIZOPHRENIA

Before the discovery of effective drugs, the outlook for people with schizophrenia was bleak. Usually they underwent a gradual deterioration interrupted by periods of partial recovery. Many spent virtually their entire adult life in a mental hospital.

During the 1950s, researchers discovered the first effective antischizophrenic drug: chlorpromazine (klor-PRAHM-uh-ZEEN; trade name: Thorazine). Drugs that relieve schizophrenia are known as **neuroleptic drugs**. Chlorpromazine and other neuroleptic drugs, including haloperidol (HAHL-o-PAIR-ih-dol; trade

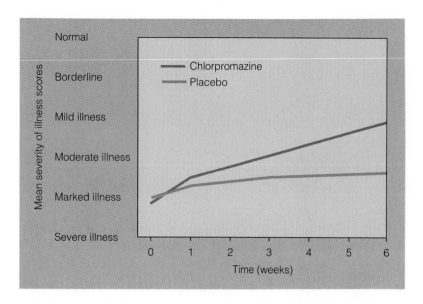

FIGURE 15.10

Antipsychotic drugs reduce psychotic symptoms gradually over several weeks. Placebo pills are noticeably less effective. (Data from Cole, Goldberg, & Davis, 1966; Davis, 1985.)

name: Haldol), have enabled many schizophrenic people to escape lifelong confinement in a mental hospital. Although these drugs do not "cure" the disorder, a daily dosage does help to control it, much as daily insulin shots control diabetes. Since the 1950s, a majority of people with schizophrenia have improved enough to leave mental hospitals or to avoid ever entering one (Harding, Brooks, Ashikaga, Straus, and Breier,1987).

All neuroleptic drugs block dopamine receptors in the brain, and their effectiveness in blocking those receptors is proportional to their effectiveness in relieving schizophrenia (Seeman, Lee, Chau-Wong, & Wong, 1976). Presumably, neuroleptic drugs relieve a condition in which dopamine overstimulates certain synapses.

Neuroleptic drugs take effect gradually and produce a variable degree of recovery. Figure 15.10 shows one set of data concerning the rate of improvement with neuroleptics; however, few studies have been conducted on this issue (Keck, Cohen, Baldessarini, & McElroy, 1989).

As a rule, neuroleptic drugs produce their clearest effects if treatment begins shortly after a sudden onset of schizophrenia. The greater someone's deterioration before drug treatment begins, the slighter the recovery. Most of the recovery that will ever take place emerges gradu-

ally during the first month (Szymanski, Simon, & Gutterman, 1983). Beyond that point, the drugs merely maintain behavior but do not improve it. If an affected person stops taking the drugs, the symptoms are likely to return and to grow worse, though not in all cases (Figure 15.11). For a given patient, it is difficult to predict what will happen (Lieberman et al., 1987).

Side Effects of Drug Therapies for Schizophrenia

Neuroleptic drugs produce some very unwelcome side effects in certain people. Prolonged use of these drugs leads to impotence in men (Mitchell & Popkin, 1982). They also produce a movement disorder, **tardive dyskinesia** (TAHRD-eev DIS-ki-NEE-zhuh), characterized by tremors and involuntary movements (Chouinard & Jones, 1980). Tardive dyskinesia is presumably related to activity at dopamine synapses, some of which control movement; however, the chemical basis of tardive dyskinesia is uncertain (Andersson et al., 1990). Tardive dyskinesia is often a permanent condition, although a patient who quits taking neuroleptic drugs at an early age has a good chance of recovery (Smith & Baldessarini, 1980). So far, physicians are unable to predict which patients will develop tardive dyskinesia and which ones will not.

Researchers have sought new drugs that could combat schizophrenia without causing tardive dyskinesia. Certain *atypical antipsychotic drugs,* including clozapine, have shown much promise in this regard; they block dopamine synapses in parts of the cerebral cortex but not the dopamine synapses in the subcortical areas essential for control of movement (White & Wang, 1983).

▪ CONCEPT CHECK

7. *In Chapter 14, we considered the efforts that are made to diagnose schizophrenia as early as possible. Given what we know about neuroleptic drugs, why is early diagnosis so important? (Check your answer on page 652.)*

Drug Therapy and Psychotherapy for Schizophrenia

The degree of recovery produced by antischizophrenic drugs varies, and drug therapy by itself is not a perfect solution. Some people with schizophrenia never have to enter a mental hospital, but others spend years in hospitals and still others are in and out of hospitals throughout their life (Pokorny, 1978).

Although most psychologists and psychiatrists believe that psychotherapy by itself is not a very powerful treatment for schizophrenia, it can be a valuable adjunct to drug therapies. Highly stressful experiences sometimes aggravate schizophrenia and may cause a flare-up of problems that had been brought under control. If a patient faces constant criticism and hostility from relatives, the schizophrenic symptoms are likely to grow worse (Vaughn, Snyder, Jones, Freeman, & Falloon, 1984). Helping people with schizophrenia cope with their environment can reduce the need for drugs. In some cases, psychotherapy for the family improves the situation. In extreme cases, it may be necessary to separate the patient from his or her family.

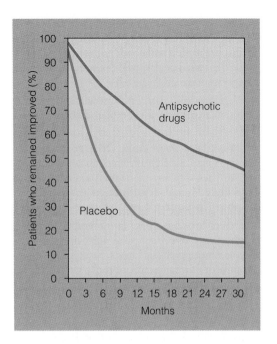

FIGURE 15.11
This graph indicates that during 2½ years, the percentage of schizophrenic patients who remained "improved" is higher in the group that received drug treatment than in the placebo group. But it also shows that antipsychotic drugs do not always prevent relapse. (Based on Baldessarini, 1984.) Both the benefits and the side effects vary from one patient to another.

A MAJOR UNANSWERED QUESTION

Suppose we have a group of people seeking help for some disorder—for sake of illustration, let's say depression. The research tells us that various kinds of talk therapy would be effective for most depressed people. It also tells us that antidepressant drugs are helpful for most people. What it does not tell us is whether talk therapy and drug therapy are helpful to the *same* people. That is, are there some people who would respond better to talk therapy and others who would respond better to drug therapy? And within each category: Are there some people who would respond better to cognitive therapy and others who would respond better to, say, behavior therapy or psychoanalysis? Are there some who would respond better to one drug and others to a different drug? If so, how can we identify which treatment is best for a given individual?

So far, psychologists have been unable to answer such questions, although a number have tried (Dance & Neufeld, 1988). One study did find that people with phobias who had the opportunity to choose their method of therapy made better progress than people who were given a method of therapy at random (Devine & Fernald, 1973). Still, we do not know whether those people somehow knew which method would be right for them or whether they simply started with a more favorable attitude because they had been offered a choice. The issue of predicting which treatment is best for which person is inherently difficult, but also important enough to justify major research efforts in the future.

SUMMARY

- *Goal of medical therapies.* Medical therapies are designed to alter brain activity directly. (page 645)

- *Drugs for anxiety and avoidance disorders.* Tranquilizers are often used to control excessive anxiety. Clomipramine and related drugs have shown an ability to relieve the symptoms of obsessive-compulsive disorder. (page 646)

- *Effects of antidepressant drugs on the brain.* Tricyclic drugs and MAOIs are used to treat depression. Both types of drugs prolong the stimulation of synaptic receptors by dopamine, norepinephrine, and serotonin. Serotonin reuptake inhibitors also relieve depression, producing fewer side effects than the other drugs do, for most people. (page 647)

- *Effects of antidepressant drugs on behavior.* The effects of antidepressant drugs build up slowly over weeks. About 50–70% of depressed people benefit from taking these drugs, as compared to 20–30% of those who take placebos. (page 648)

- *Electroconvulsive therapy.* Electroconvulsive therapy has a long history of abuse; in modified form it has made a comeback and is now helpful to some depressed people who fail to respond to antidepressant drugs. (page 648)

- *Lithium treatment.* Lithium salts are the most effective treatment for bipolar disorder. (page 649)

- *Antischizophrenic drugs.* Drugs that block dopamine synapses often alleviate schizophrenia. Results are best if treatment begins before the person has suffered serious deterioration. (page 649)

- *Side effects of antischizophrenic drugs.* Drug treatment for schizophrenia sometimes produces a movement disorder called tardive dyskinesia. Atypical antipsychotic drugs have shown some promise of relieving schizophrenia without inducing tardive dyskinesia. (page 650)

SUGGESTION FOR FURTHER READING

Solomon, S. H. (1980). *Biological aspects of mental disorder.* New York: Oxford University Press. Discussion of research on biological causes and treatments of psychological disorders.

TERMS

tricyclic drugs drugs that block the reabsorption of the neurotransmitters dopamine, norepinephrine, and serotonin, after they are released by the terminal button, thus prolonging the effect of these neurotransmitters on the receptors of the postsynaptic cell (page 647)

serotonin reuptake blockers drugs that block the reuptake of the neurotransmitter serotonin by the terminal button (page 647)

monoamine oxidase inhibitors (MAOIs) drugs that block the metabolic breakdown of released dopamine, norepinephrine, and serotonin after their release from the terminal button, thus prolonging the effect of these neurotransmitters on the receptors of the postsynaptic cell (page 647)

electroconvulsive therapy (ECT) treatment in which a brief electrical shock is administered across the patient's head to induce a convulsion similar to epilepsy, sometimes used as a treatment for certain types of depression (page 648)

neuroleptic drugs drugs that relieve schizophrenia (page 649)

tardive dyskinesia a movement disorder characterized by tremors and involuntary movements (page 650)

ANSWERS TO CONCEPT CHECKS

5. The combined effect of alcohol and a benzodiazepine tranquilizer would decrease anxiety, relax the muscles, and induce sleep more effectively than either alcohol or a benzodiazepine could by itself. In fact, the combined effect can be so strong as to be dangerous, even fatal. People given prescriptions for benzodiazepine tranquilizers are warned not to take them in conjunction with alcohol. (page 647)

6. Mianserin should relieve depression and has in fact been used as an antidepressant. Although it acts by a different route from that of the tricyclics and MAOIs, it prolongs the stimulation of dopamine, norepinephrine, and serotonin receptors. (page 648)

7. Neuroleptics are more helpful to people in the early stages of schizophrenia than to those who have deteriorated severely. However, psychiatrists do not want to administer neuroleptics to people who do not need them because of the risk of tardive dyskinesia. Consequently, early and accurate diagnosis of schizophrenia is important. (page 650)

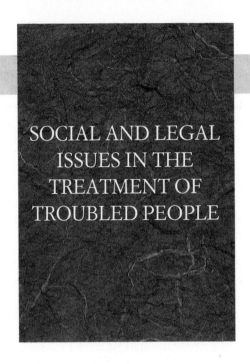

SOCIAL AND LEGAL ISSUES IN THE TREATMENT OF TROUBLED PEOPLE

What should society do about psychological disorders?

Can anything be done to prevent them?

A group of nearsighted people, lost in the woods, were trying to find their way home. One of the few who wore glasses said, "I think I know the way. Follow me." The others burst into laughter. "That's ridiculous," said one. "How could anybody who needs glasses be our leader?"

In 1972 the Democratic party nominated Senator Thomas Eagleton for vice-president of the United States. Shortly after his nomination he revealed that he had once received psychiatric treatment for depression. He was subjected to merciless ridicule: "How could anybody who needs a psychiatrist be our leader?" In 1988 rumors circulated that the Democratic nominee for president, Michael Dukakis, had once received psychotherapy for depression. Although the rumors were apparently unfounded, they hurt Dukakis's standing in the polls.

About one fourth to one third of all Americans suffer from a psychological disorder at some time during their life. Unfortunately, many people in our society consider it shameful to seek help for a psychological disorder. They struggle along on their own, like a nearsighted person who refuses to wear glasses, rather than admit they need help.

As a citizen and voter, you will have to deal with numerous issues relating to psychological disorders and therapies: Who, if anyone, should be confined to a mental hospital? Should mental patients have the right to refuse treatment? Under what circumstances, if any, should a criminal defendant be acquitted because of "insanity"? Can society as a whole take steps to prevent certain types of psychological disorders? We shall examine each of these questions, beginning with the issue of confining people to mental hospitals.

MENTAL HOSPITALS

About once every 8 seconds someone in the United States is admitted to a hospital or a nursing home because of a psychological problem (Kiesler, 1982b). Most of those people stay less than a month, but some stay years, even a lifetime. Hospitalization for psychological problems accounts for 25% of hospitalizations for all types of illness in the United States. Traditionally, we have told one another that we put people in these institutions "for their own sake." Sometimes that has been true, but often we have put people into mental hospitals for our own sake, because we found their behavior disturbing.

Until the 1950s, people with severe psychological disturbances were generally confined in large mental hospitals supported by their state or county. At the time most of those hospitals were built, severely disturbed mental patients had little hope of ever returning to society. The hospitals, which were designed to provide long-term custodial care, were usually located in some remote country area far from the patients' homes. Frequently they resembled prisons (Okin, 1983). Patients were dependent on hospital attendants who cooked the food, did the laundry, and made all the decisions. Little thought was given to helping patients learn the skills they would need if they were ever to leave. State hospitals claimed to provide psychiatric care, but most patients seldom saw a psychiatrist or a psychologist. Moreover, state legislatures rarely furnished enough financial support to attract well-qualified, professional personnel. Some hospitals were better than others, but most of them were pretty grim places.

Most large state mental hospitals were built long ago, when the goal of such institutions was to provide custodial care for patients who were likely to remain in the hospital for years, perhaps for life. Today, the goal of mental hospitals is to return people to society within a short time. Still, although the quality of such hospitals varies widely, many remain rather grim and uninviting.

With the advent of antidepressant and anti-schizophrenic drugs in the 1950s, advances in psychotherapy, and changes in the commitment laws, the number of long-term residents in mental hospitals began to decline, eventually reaching a level about one third what it was in 1950 (Pepper & Ryglewicz, 1982). The goal of mental hospitals is no longer to provide long-term custody. Instead, it is to supply short-term care until a patient is ready to return home.

Unfortunately, however, many mental hospitals are still prisonlike institutions, ill suited to their new goals. Moreover, with the decline in mental-hospital populations, state legislatures have shown little interest in spending money on new, modern facilities.

Life in Mental Hospitals

To find out what life is like in mental hospitals, eight healthy adults—three psychologists, a psychiatrist, a psychology graduate student, and three others—each approached a different mental hospital and asked to be voluntarily committed (Rosenhan, 1973). Some repeated the experience until as a group they had entered 12 mental hospitals. When asked why they thought they belonged in a mental hospital, they said they sometimes heard voices saying "empty," "hollow," and "thud." Without further ado, each pseudopatient was admitted at once, generally with a diagnosis of schizophrenia. (One was given a diagnosis of bipolar disorder.)

D. L. Rosenhan reports that he and the other pseudopatients were immediately degraded to a status less than human. First they were given a physical examination in a semipublic room where a number of other people came and went. Then they were assigned to a ward where the staff paid little attention to them.

At first, the pseudopatients tried to conceal the fact that they were "spying" on the hospital and jotted down their notes in secret. Later, when they realized that none of the staff members were paying much attention, they grew bolder and bolder. Eventually they followed the staff around, taking notes on everything the staff did. Far from being intimidated by this behavior, the staff regarded this note taking as a "symptom" of the patients' "illness"!

One day a nurse unbuttoned her uniform to adjust her bra while standing in the middle of a men's ward. Rosenhan noted that she showed no embarrassment and paid no attention to the men. Her action told them that she did not regard them as *men*. They were just *mental patients*.

Eventually all the pseudopatients were discharged with a diagnosis of "schizophrenia in remission"—meaning that they still had schizophrenia but were no longer showing symptoms. None of the psychiatrists or other staff showed any suspicion that the pseudopatients were really healthy; none expressed any doubt about the diagnosis of schizophrenia. Actually, it is not surprising that the staff members were so easily taken in by the fake mental patients—healthy people rarely try to get admitted to mental hospitals. The significance of the report is that the hospitals showed scant respect for the privacy and self-respect of their patients.

When the staff at another mental hospital heard about these results and expressed doubt that they would ever admit a fake patient,

Rosenhan offered an experiment. He told them that one or more healthy people would attempt to be admitted to the hospital within the next 3 months, and he challenged the staff to identify the impostors. No pseudopatients actually showed up, but one or more staff members pointed out 41 new patients (from a total of 193) as "probable impostors." Evidently, even experienced professionals have trouble identifying who has a psychological disorder and who does not.

Deinstitutionalization: The Concept and the Reality

Given the degrading atmosphere at many mental hospitals, many critics claim that people with mild to moderate problems are better off in community mental-health centers close to their own home. There they receive supervision and treatment, but they also enjoy some degree of independence, some freedom to come and go, and some contact with the "real world." Certain patients may even live at home, getting their professional care either by visiting a treatment center or by having a mental-health worker visit them at home. Still others may rely on a self-help group.

Several studies have compared these "alternative" forms of care with full-time confinement in mental hospitals. Every study has found that well-planned alternate care is as good as or better than care in mental hospitals in promoting psychological adjustment, in helping patients return to their school or job, and in restoring them to independent living (Braun et al., 1981; Kiesler, 1982a). Alternative care is also less expensive.

Such research prompted a movement toward **deinstitutionalization,** the removal of patients from mental hospitals. The idea is to give people the least restrictive care possible. Only those few patients who cannot care for themselves or who are considered dangerous to society would be confined to mental hospitals. The rest would live in their own home or in group homes and would receive care at community mental-health centers.

Unfortunately, many states got only half the message. They discharged great numbers of patients from their mental hospitals *without* planning adequate alternatives for care and housing (Pepper & Ryglewicz, 1982). They unwittingly created a population of mentally disturbed people with no home, no job, and little opportunity for professional care (Teplin, 1983).

Community mental-health centers provide an alternative to state mental hospitals. A community mental-health center serves as a "halfway house"; people receive the amount of attention and supervision they need, but they are free to come and go and to live as normal a life as they can. Studies show that such alternatives to mental hospitals provide consistent advantages.

Deinstitutionalization is the process of releasing most mental patients from mental hospitals. Ideally, the released patients receive high-quality care in community mental-health centers or alternatives to the mental hospital. Unfortunately, in some cases mental hospitals have merely released patients without providing any alternative care. As a result, some former mental patients have no home, no job, and little prospect for a better life.

LEGAL ISSUES IN THE TREATMENT OF DISORDERED PEOPLE

In a democratic society, we treasure both freedom and security. Sometimes these values are in conflict. For example, the right of a psychologically disordered person to freedom may conflict (or appear to conflict) with the right of other people to feel safe and secure. We shall consider several ways in which this conflict arises and the difficulties we have in resolving the conflict.

Involuntary Commitment and Treatment

A psychiatrist believes that Charles is severely schizophrenic. He cannot hold a job, he does not pay his bills or take care of his personal hygiene, and his neighbors consider him a nuisance. His family wants to commit him to a mental hospital, and the psychiatrist wants to give him drugs. But Charles refuses both courses, claiming that his family is "out to get him." Should he be permitted to refuse treatment?

We can argue this question either way. On the one hand, some seriously disordered people fail to recognize that there is anything wrong with them. On the other hand, some families have been known to commit aging or otherwise unwelcome relatives to mental hospitals just to get them out of the way. And some psychiatrists have given drugs and ECT treatments to people with only minor problems, doing them more harm than good. People need protection from inappropriate treatment.

Which people (if any) should be confined to a mental hospital against their will? In the United States, laws vary from state to state. In some states, a court can commit patients to a mental hospital only if they are suffering from a mental disorder and are dangerous to themselves or others. The American Psychiatric Association has recommended that the laws be changed to allow commitment of any patient who "lacks capacity to make an informed decision concerning treatment" and who has a severe but treatable disorder (Bloom & Faulkner, 1987; Hoge, Sachs, Appelbaum, Greer, & Gordon, 1988). That is, they would rely on a judgment of the patient's competence rather than on whether the patient was dangerous. Regardless of how the law is stated, a judge has to make the final decision after a court hearing; the outcome of such hearings varies haphazardly (Bloom & Faulkner, 1987).

Under a practice known as **preventive detention,** psychologically disturbed people who are considered dangerous to society can be involuntarily committed to a mental hospital to prevent them from committing crimes. This option raises some tricky problems. Suppose a client tells a therapist, "Sometimes I feel like killing my boss." A few days later the client actually does kill the boss. Is the therapist legally to blame for failure to prevent this murder? Some courts have said yes, the therapist has a duty to warn anyone whom a client has threatened to murder or to impose preventive detention.

That ruling may sound reasonable, but now imagine what happens in practice. You are the therapist; I am your client. I tell you that I felt like killing my neighbor yesterday because his barking dog kept me awake all night. You believe this was just an exaggerated way of saying that I was angry, not a serious threat of murder. But you're not completely certain of that, and you don't want to get in trouble with the law if I go on a rampage tonight. So you order me committed to a mental hospital, even though you doubt that commitment is in my best interests. Moral of the story: Legal decisions sometimes have unintended consequences (Appelbaum, 1988).

Patients in a mental hospital have the right to refuse certain forms of treatment even if they have been involuntarily committed by a judge who decided that they needed those treatments (Appelbaum, 1988a). What patients are likely to refuse treatment? According to their psychiatrists, many of them exhibit hostility, emotional withdrawal, and disorganized thinking (Marder et al., 1983). According to the patients themselves, they have good reason to be hostile and withdrawn; the hospital staff is trying to force them to submit to a treatment they consider unnecessary. Figure 15.12 compares patients with schizophrenia who refused drug treatment and patients who agreed to drug treatment. Understandably, decisions about enforced treatment can be very difficult.

Something to Think About

Thomas Szasz (1982) proposed that psychologically "normal" people write a "psychiatric will" specifying what treatments to give them, and what treatments to avoid, if they ever de-

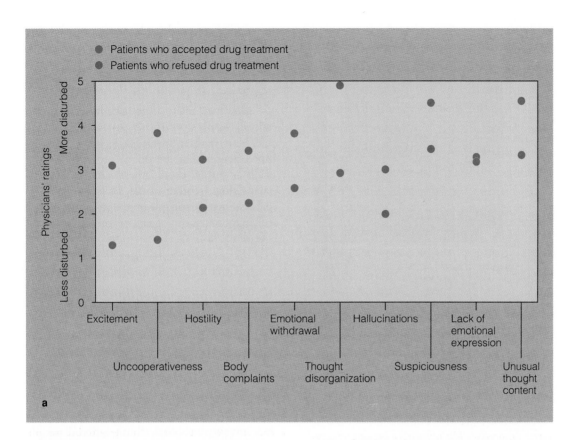

a

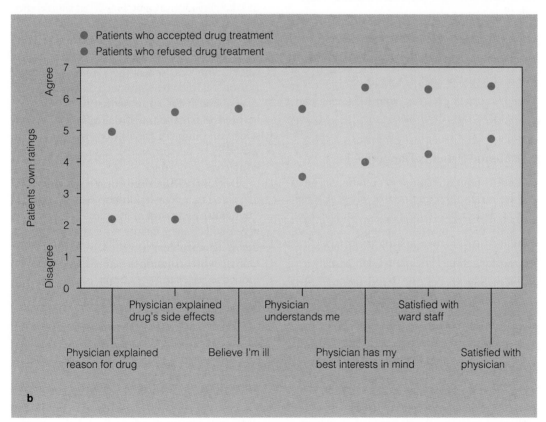

b

FIGURE 15.12

*People with schizo-
phrenia who refuse
drug therapy impress
their physicians as
being seriously dis-
turbed. The patients
rate themselves as
dissatisfied with
their physicians and
their treatments.
(a) Physicians' rat-
ings of their patients.
High scores indicate
greater disturbance.
Those refusing treat-
ment showed greater
indications of distur-
bance on most scales.
(b) Patients' self-
ratings. The higher
scores of patients
who agreed to drug
treatment indicate
their higher satisfac-
tion with how they
have been treated.
(Based on data from
Marder et al., 1983.)*

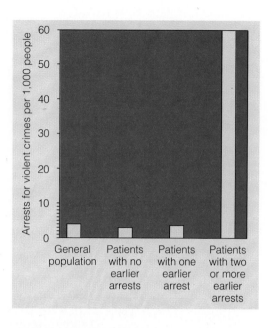

FIGURE 15.13

These arrest rates compare levels of violent crimes among the general population and mental patients. (After data reported by Cocozza, Melick, & Steadman, 1978.) A few mental patients with a previous criminal history continue to be dangerous. The others are no more dangerous than anyone else.

velop a severe psychological disorder. If you wrote such a will, what would you put in it? Or would you prefer to trust your judgment later, at the time of the disorder?

Are Mental Patients Dangerous?

Disputes about involuntary commitment often revolve around the question of whether someone is dangerous. Newspaper and television publicity about "mentally deranged" killers implies that many psychologically disordered people are dangerous. The impression of danger is compounded by selective reporting—we hear about the few mental patients who commit crimes and seldom about the many who do not. As a result, we perceive an *illusory correlation,* an apparent relationship between two unrelated variables.

That fear of mental patients is mostly unjustified. A small number of people who are arrested for a crime get sent to a mental hospital instead of a prison. When released, they have a high probability of committing further crimes. Other patients who are sent to a mental hospital—those who have not been arrested—are

nearly always harmless. After their release, they are no more likely than any other citizen to become a suspect in a crime (Cocozza, Melick, & Steadman, 1978; Rabkin, 1979; Teplin, 1985). (See Figure 15.13.)

However, many cities have homeless mentally ill people whom no one knows how to handle. Many of them are arrested and jailed for minor offenses that the police ordinarily ignore such as public drunkenness, panhandling, or jaywalking. In other words, society uses the legal system to get people off the streets instead of relying on psychological or medical reasons (Teplin, 1984).

■ **CONCEPT CHECK**

8. *Why is it probably true that the mental hospitals in some states contain more dangerous people than in other states? (Check your answer on page 663.)*

THE INSANITY DEFENSE

Not many psychologically disordered people are dangerous, but some are. What should society do if such a person commits a felony?

Suppose in the midst of an epileptic seizure you flail your arms about and accidentally knock someone down the stairs, killing that person. Should you be convicted of murder? Of course not. Now, suppose that in the midst of severe hallucinations and delusions, you attack what you think is a giant insect, but in fact you are killing a person. In that case should you be convicted of murder?

British and American courts have traditionally ruled that you should not, because you are "not guilty by reason of insanity." Most people agree with that principle, at least for extreme cases. The problem is where to draw the line. Under what conditions should someone be judged legally insane? *Insanity* is a legal term, not a psychological or medical one, and its definition has gone through many changes over the years (Shapiro, 1985).

One point on which most authorities agree is that the crime itself, no matter how atrocious, does not demonstrate insanity. In Chapter 5 we considered the case of the "Hillside Strangler" who committed a long series of rapes and murders, but who was eventually ruled sane and sentenced to prison. The same decision was made for David Berkowitz, the "Son of Sam" murderer who killed a large number of women in the mid-1970s and claimed he was carrying out orders from "Sam," his neighbor's dog (Abrahamsen, 1985). In 1991, Jeffrey Dahmer was arrested after not only murdering a series of men but even cannibalizing them. The court found Dahmer sane also. In each of these cases, the crimes were ghastly and bizarre, but their bizarre nature did not demonstrate that the murderer was insane. In fact, each of the murderers knew what he was doing, knew it was wrong, and took steps to avoid getting caught. The juries therefore considered them sane.

In many other cases, a decision about sanity or insanity is very difficult; lawyers, physicians, and psychologists have long struggled to establish a clear and acceptable definition of *insanity*. One of the oldest, and perhaps the most famous definition, the **M'Naghten rule,** written in Britain in 1843, states:

To establish a defense on the ground of insanity, it must be clearly proved that, at the time of the committing of the act, the party accused was laboring under such a defect of reason, from disease of the mind, as not to know the nature and quality of the act he was doing; or if he did know it, that he did not know he was doing what was wrong. (Shapiro, 1985)

In other words, to be regarded as insane under the M'Naghten rule, people must be so disordered that they do not realize they are committing a criminal act. Many observers have considered that rule somewhat too narrow. They would like to broaden the definition of insanity to include "irresistible impulses"—acts similar to sneezing or hiccuping, which someone could not completely inhibit even if they were illegal. Under the **Durham rule,** established in 1954 in the case of a man named Durham, a U.S. court held that a defendant is not criminally responsible if the activity was "a product of mental disease or defect." That rule confused more than it clarified. Almost anything can be considered a mental disease or defect. And what does it mean to say that an act is a "product" of such a defect?

The **Model Penal Code,** written in the 1950s, attempted to clarify the definition of insanity:

A person is not responsible for criminal conduct if at the time of such conduct as a result of mental disease or defect he lacks substantial capacity either to appreciate the criminality (wrongfulness) of his conduct or to conform his conduct to the requirements of law. (Shapiro, 1985)

Courts have consistently ruled that the bizarreness of a crime does not by itself demonstrate insanity. In 1992, Jeffrey Dahmer was convicted of murdering and dismembering 15 men, cannibalizing some of them. The court ruled that he was sane; it granted that he was "abnormal" but maintained that he knew what he was doing.

When John Hinckley, Jr., who had tried to assassinate President Reagan, was found not guilty by reason of insanity in 1982, laws were proposed across the country to limit the insanity defense—despite the fact that it is seldom used and even less often successful.

The rules on the determination of insanity differ from country to country and from state to state within the United States. In any event, fewer than 1% of people accused of felonies in the United States are acquitted by reason of insanity (Insanity Defense Work Group, 1983).

One question under debate is whether the prosecution or the defense should bear the "burden of proof" in establishing insanity. In some cases, the judge instructs the jury that, in order to convict the defendant, the prosecution has to prove that the defendant was sane. In other cases, the defense has to prove that the defendant was insane in order to win an acquittal.

A second question is whether those who are called to give "expert testimony" should state their opinion of the defendant's sanity or just describe the defendant's mental condition. A growing number of lawyers, psychiatrists, and psychologists would prefer to limit expert testimony to descriptive statements, leaving the legal question of insanity to the judge and jury (Insanity Defense Work Group, 1983).

PREDICTING AND PREVENTING MENTAL ILLNESS

If our society decided to do whatever it could to prevent mental illness, how effective could it be? Throughout the early history of psychology and psychiatry, the emphasis was on treatment of people who were already ill, not on prevention. One wonders how history might have been different if Sigmund Freud had stuck with his early view that psychological disorders result from childhood sexual abuse (Freud & Breuer, 1893). Whether right or wrong, that theory implied that psychological disorders were preventable, if we could only find ways to combat childhood sexual abuse. But Freud changed his theory, arguing that the cause of psychological disorders was childhood sexual *fantasies*. With that change, he implied that psychological disorders are unpredictable and unpreventable.

Decades later, certain psychologists, especially community psychologists, began to pay more attention to prevention. **Community psychologists** focus on the needs of large groups rather than those of individuals. They distinguish between **primary prevention,** preventing a disorder from starting, and **secondary prevention,** identifying a disorder in its early stages and preventing it from becoming more serious.

Methods of Prevention

Just as our society puts fluoride into drinking water to prevent tooth decay and immunizes people against contagious diseases, it can take action to prevent certain types of psychological disorders (Albee, 1986; Goldston, 1986; Long, 1986). For example, it can take the following actions:

- *Banning toxins.* The sale of lead-based paint has been banned because children who eat flakes of lead-based paint sustain brain damage. Other toxins in the air and water have yet to be controlled.

- *Educating pregnant women about prenatal care.* For example, women need to be informed that the use of alcohol or other drugs during pregnancy may cause brain damage to the fetus and that certain bacterial and viral infections during pregnancy may impair fetal brain development and increase the risk of psychological disorders.

- *Jobs.* Helping people who lose their jobs to find new work enables them to regain their self-esteem.

- *Child care.* Providing better day-care facilities would contribute to the psychological health of both parents and children.

These techniques are aimed at primary prevention for the entire community. Secondary prevention techniques can be targeted at specific individuals who are just beginning to show symptoms of a particular disorder. For example, if we could identify people who are just in the preliminary stages of developing alcoholism or schizophrenia, psychologists might be able to intervene more effectively than they can if they wait until a later stage.

Although psychologists already know a certain amount about prevention, a great deal more remains to be discovered. Prevention turns out to be a difficult matter, requiring research and not just common sense. For example, it is still unclear how effectively strict antidrug laws prevent drug abuse or how effective it is to tell children to "just say no." Or consider suicide: What happens if a television station shows a program about suicide, stressing its tragic effects on grieving friends and relatives? Do such programs help to prevent suicide (as the stations hoped and expected)? Do they backfire? Or do the results depend on other factors?

Can the Media Cause or Prevent Suicide?

WHAT'S THE EVIDENCE?

During late 1984 and early 1985, U.S. television networks broadcast four programs about suicide in well-meaning attempts to dramatize the pain that suicide causes to families. They hoped these programs would, if anything, decrease the suicide rate. Although the networks did not intend this as a scientific study, Madelyn Gould and David Shaffer (1986) analyzed the results as if it were one.

Hypothesis The suicide rate will either increase or decrease—we do not know which—during the 2 weeks after a fictional suicide is portrayed on television.

Method Gould and Shaffer (1986) collected data about suicides and suicide attempts by teenagers who had been admitted to six hospitals in the New York City area. (They concentrated on teenagers because the TV programs portrayed teenagers.) They determined the teenage suicide rates for the 2 weeks immediately after each of the four TV shows on suicide, when viewers were most likely to be influenced by them. They then compared those rates to the rates during other weeks in the fall and winter of 1984–85.

Results During the 2 weeks just after each show, teenagers in the area committed a mean of 1.6 suicides per week plus 11 uncompleted attempts. During other weeks in the fall and winter of 1984–85, the means were 1.1 suicides plus 7.8 uncompleted attempts (Figure 15.14) The increase in suicide attempts was statistically significant ($p < .05$), but the increase in completed suicides was not.

Interpretation The publicity had backfired. There were more suicide attempts just after the shows than at other times. Evidently some people who attempt suicide are responding to suggestion. Knowing that someone else has taken that action may make it seem more acceptable to them.

David Phillips and Lundie Carstensen (1986) reported similar results in a study on the effects of reports of actual suicides. From 1973 to 1979, the teenage suicide rate generally went

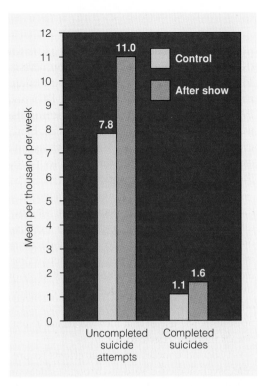

FIGURE 15.14
During the 2 weeks after four televised programs about teenage suicide, the suicide rate among teenagers increased. That is, a well-meaning attempt to prevent suicide (by publicizing its tragic nature) had evidently backfired.

up during the week after a news story about a teenage suicide. (This was true for both newspaper and TV accounts.) The greater the publicity, the greater the increase in the suicide rate. Phillips (1974) reported similar results for adults.

These results suggest an odd strategy for suicide prevention: Instead of publicizing the horrors of suicide, we should encourage the media to *ignore* suicides. Still, it is difficult to interpret before-and-after studies like these. Perhaps the suicide rates went up or down at particular times for reasons unrelated to the TV programs.

Two other studies attempted to replicate Gould and Shaffer's results. David Phillips and Daniel Paight (1987) examined records in Pennsylvania and California, and A. L. Berman (1988) looked at suicide rates throughout the United States. Neither study found a significant change in suicide rates after the broadcast of television programs about suicide.

Another study examined suicide rates throughout the country following TV news stories about actual (not fictional) suicides (Kessler, Downey, Milafsky, & Stipp, 1988). This study confirmed the finding by Phillips and Carstensen (1986) that between 1973 and 1980 the teenage suicide rate rose during the weeks following the airing of such stories. However, between 1981 and 1984 the teenage suicide rate *decreased* during the weeks following the broadcast of similar stories.

What conclusions can we draw? First, it is hard to draw any conclusion about whether televised stories about suicide, either fictional or factual, will lead to an increase or a decrease in the suicide rate. However, the evidence does indicate that some people copy the *method* of suicide described in such stories. For example, after a story about suicide by carbon monoxide poisoning, the use of that method shows a temporary increase (Berman, 1988).

A second conclusion is that efforts to prevent psychological disorders through education do not always succeed. Before we invest major efforts on an educational program about some preventable condition—suicide, drug abuse, AIDS, or whatever—we need research to measure the effects of the program.

Third, the results underline an important point about the scientific method: the need for replication. Even when a study has been carefully conducted, other investigators must repeat the procedures to see whether they get the same results in other times and places.

SUMMARY

■ *Mental hospitals.* Most mental hospitals were designed and built at a time when society expected mental patients to remain in them for a long time, even for a lifetime. Today, most patients stay a month or less. Large mental hospitals are not well designed to help restore people to society. In many of them, patients receive little attention and little respect. (page 653)

■ *Deinstitutionalization.* Community mental-health centers provide psychological care while permitting people some measure of freedom. The care they provide is equal or superior to the care provided by large mental hospitals. However, many states have released patients from mental hospitals without supplying adequate community mental-health facilities. (page 655)

■ *Involuntary commitment.* Laws on involuntary commitment to mental hospitals vary. In some states, people can be committed only if they are

dangerous; in others, people can be committed if they are judged incompetent to decide about their own treatment. It is difficult to frame laws that ensure treatment for those who need it, while also protecting the rights of those who have good reasons for refusing it. (page 656)

■ *Controversy concerning danger of mental patients.* Mental patients are rarely dangerous, except for those few who had committed crimes before being admitted to a mental hospital. Yet some mental patients are arrested to keep them off the streets, and others are involuntarily committed to mental hospitals to prevent them from committing crimes, even when it is highly unlikely that they will do so. (page 658)

■ *The insanity defense.* Some defendants accused of a crime are acquitted for reasons of insanity, which is a legal rather than a medical or psychological concept. The criteria for establishing insanity are vague and controversial. (page 658)

■ *Prevention of psychological disorders.* Psychologists and psychiatrists are increasingly concerned about preventing psychological disorders. Many preventive measures require the cooperation of society as a whole. (page 660)

■ *Suicide prevention.* It may be possible to lower suicide rates by curtailing media publicity about suicide, although the evidence is not conclusive. (page 661)

SUGGESTIONS FOR FURTHER READING

Ewing, C. P. (Ed.). (1985). *Psychology, psychiatry, and the law: A clinical and forensic handbook.* Sarasota, FL: Professional Resource Exchange. A review of procedures governing commitment to mental hospitals, the insanity defense, the right to refuse treatment, and other legal issues.

Sheehan, S. (1982). *Is there no place on earth for me?* Boston: Houghton Mifflin. The story of a young woman with schizophrenia and her life in and out of mental hospitals.

TERMS

deinstitutionalization removal of patients from mental hospitals (page 655)

preventive detention practice of involuntarily committing psychologically disturbed people to a mental hospital to prevent them from committing crimes (page 656)

M'Naghten rule rule that a defendant is not criminally responsible if, at the time of committing the act, the person was laboring under such a defect of reason, from disease of the mind, as not to know the nature and quality of the act he was doing; or if he did know it, that he did not know he was doing what was wrong (page 659)

Durham rule rule that a defendant is not criminally responsible if the activity was "a product of mental disease or defect" (page 659)

Model Penal Code rule that a person is not responsible for criminal conduct if at the time of such conduct as a result of mental disease or defect he lacks substantial capacity either to appreciate the criminality (wrongfulness) of his conduct or to conform his conduct to the requirements of law (page 659)

community psychologist psychologist who focuses on the needs of large groups rather than those of individuals (page 660)

primary prevention preventing a disorder from starting (page 660)

secondary prevention identifying a disorder in its early stages and preventing it from becoming more serious (page 660)

ANSWER TO CONCEPT CHECK

8. In some states, people can be involuntarily committed to mental hospitals only if they are dangerous. In other states, they can be committed if they are judged incompetent to make their own decisions. (page 658)

16

SOCIAL PSYCHOLOGY

In the *Communist Manifesto*, Karl Marx and Friedrich Engels wrote, "Mankind are more disposed to suffer, while evils are sufferable, than to right themselves by abolishing the forms to which they are accustomed. But when a long train of abuses and usurpations, pursuing invariably the same object, evinces a design to reduce them under absolute despotism, it is their right, it is their duty, to throw off such government." Vladimir Lenin later wrote, "A little rebellion, now and then, is a good thing."

Do you agree with those statements? Why or why not? Can you think of anything that would change your mind?

Oh, pardon. . . . That first statement was not from the *Communist Manifesto*—it was from the United States' Declaration of Independence. Sorry. And that second statement was a quote from Thomas Jefferson, not Lenin.

Do you agree more with these statements now that you know they were written by the founding fathers of the United States rather than by the founding fathers of communism?

What determines whether or not you will agree with someone who is trying to influence you? This question is one example of the issues of interest to **social psychologists**—the psychologists who study social behavior and how an individual influences other people and is influenced by other people.

Social psychology is a broad, diverse field that is difficult to define. I know I have just defined it as the study of social behavior and influence, but that term *social behavior* in turn gets defined very broadly, to include such matters as attitudes, persuasion, and certain aspects of self-understanding. A more useful characterization, if not exactly a definition, is that social psychology is a field that studies the everyday behaviors of more-or-less normal people, generally in their relationships with other people. In this chapter we shall consider several of the major fields of research and application in social psychology.

Social psychologists find that our reactions to other people's behavior depends not only on what they do and say but also on who does it and says it. Would you react the same way to a speech by this Viennese street preacher as you would to a similar speech by someone with more impressive credentials and more conventional attire?

666

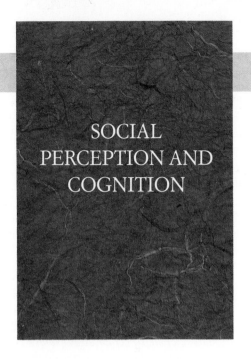

SOCIAL PERCEPTION AND COGNITION

How do we form impressions of other people?

How do we decide why someone behaves in a certain way?

I n 1991, Clarence Thomas, a nominee for the U.S. Supreme Court, was accused of sexually harrassing a woman who once worked in his office. Later the same year, Bill Clinton, a candidate for the Democratic nomination for presi-dent, was accused of having an extramarital sexual affair. Both Thomas and Clinton claimed the charges were a lie. In each case, the public listened and tried to decide what to believe and whether the charges should disqualify the accused person from public office. Also in each case, some observers ultimately believed the accuser and others believed the accused.

Every day people try to make a good impression on you: a candidate for public office, a classmate who wants to borrow some money, a used-car salesperson. How do you decide what you think of these people, whether you like or dislike them, trust or distrust them? That is, how do you form *social perceptions*—interpretations of the feelings, intentions, and personalities of other people?

In 1991 the U.S. Senate held confirmation hearings concerning the appointment of Clarence Thomas to the Supreme Court. As part of that hearing, it considered charges by Anita Hill that Thomas had sexually harassed her. To weigh her charges against his denials, the senators considered not only what the two said but also the way they said it, their appearance, and their past behavior. That is, the senators formed social perceptions of each of them. (In this case, the impressions were about equally positive and many senators had trouble deciding whom to believe.)

FIRST IMPRESSIONS

When you talk to someone you have never met before—say, the student sitting next to you in class—you begin to form an impression of how intelligent he or she is, how friendly, how energetic. Right or wrong, many people trust their first impressions. What information do we use in forming first impressions?

The Primacy Effect

Our first impressions of others, correct or incorrect, are influential simply because they are first. Other things being equal, the first information we learn about someone influences us more than later information does (Belmore, 1987; Jones & Goethals, 1972). This tendency is known as the **primacy effect.**

Subjects in one study watched a man answer 30 questions on an intelligence test. All the subjects saw him answer 15 questions correctly and 15 incorrectly. However, some saw him answer most of the early questions correctly, whereas the others saw him miss most of the early ones and then answer most of the last questions correctly. Those who saw him start off strong judged him to be significantly more intelligent than did those who saw him start off weak (Jones, Rock, Shaver, Goethals, & Ward, 1968). When the subjects were asked to guess how many questions the man got right, those who saw him correctly answer the first ones guessed his total was about 21. Those who saw him miss the first ones but finish strong guessed his total was about 13. (Remember, both groups saw him answer 15 questions correctly.)

Why are first impressions so influential? Perhaps we simply pay more attention at first. Also, if our first impression of someone is unfavorable, we may not spend enough time with that person to form an alternative view. Moreover, the first information we receive influences our interpretation of later information (Anderson & Hubert, 1963; Zanna & Hamilton, 1977). Compare these two pairs of sentences:

a. Today I saw Julie kick a dog. Julie is usually kind to animals.

b. Julie is usually kind to animals. Today I saw Julie kick a dog.

In a, the first thing we learn about Julie is that she kicked a dog. The second statement doesn't improve her image very much because it sounds as though someone were trying to make excuses for her. In b, the first thing we learn about Julie is that she is usually kind to animals. When we hear that she kicked a dog, we try to reconcile that information with what we already know. We think, "Maybe it was just a little playful kick. Or maybe the dog had attacked Julie's pet hamster. There must be some reason."

Something to Think About

In a criminal trial, the prosecution presents its evidence first. Might that give the jury an unfavorable first impression of the defendant and increase the probability of a conviction?

■ CONCEPT CHECK

1. Why do some professors avoid looking at students' names when they grade essay exams? Why is it more important for them to do so on the tests later in the semester than on the first test? (Check your answer on page 679.)

Physical Characteristics

Many people hold strong (and often incorrect) beliefs that physical characteristics are related to psychological traits. As a rule, people regard their physically attractive acquaintances as highly sociable, dominant, sexually responsive, mentally healthy, intelligent, and socially skilled (Feingold, 1992). One group of experimenters asked subjects to rate the personality and intelligence of students in a series of yearbook photographs (Dion, Berscheid, & Walster, 1972). The photographs had been selected to include equal numbers of attractive, average-looking, and less attractive students. The subjects rated the attractive students as more sensitive, kind, poised, and sociable than the others. They also predicted that the more attractive students would enjoy highly successful careers and happy marriages. Unattractive people, however, may be perceived as unpleasant, perhaps even threatening.

Physical characteristics have a great deal to do with how people are treated in various settings. Other things being equal, teachers expect better performance from attractive children than from unattractive children (Clifford & Walster, 1973). Attractive people are on average paid higher salaries than unattractive people are (Quinn, 1978). Juries often treat attractive defendants less harshly than unattractive defendants, unless the jury believes a defendant used his or her good looks to gain people's trust and then swindle them (Sigall & Ostrove, 1975; Stewart, 1980).

Nonverbal Behavior

We also form impressions of others simply by watching them. For example, we judge people's emotions and personality traits by observing their facial expressions and their body movements (Lippa, 1983). You may infer that one woman is introverted because she makes small, tight gestures and that another is extraverted because she makes large, expansive gestures. You decide that one man is anxious and "uptight" because he twitches, fidgets, and trembles and that another is calm and composed because he makes smooth, controlled gestures.

Research suggests that when nonverbal information conflicts with verbal information, we are more likely to trust the nonverbal information, perhaps because nonverbal behavior is hard to modify voluntarily (Figure 16.1). That is, people lie with their words more often than they lie with their gestures (DePaulo, 1992). When a friend says, "I love you," but frowns, stands far away, and refuses to look at you, which do you believe—the verbal statement or the nonverbal statement?

SOCIAL COGNITION

Eventually we progress beyond first impressions. **Social cognition** is the process by which we combine and remember information about others and make inferences based on that information (Sherman, Judd, & Park, 1989).

Impression Formation

Suppose I say to you, "My friend Dave is intelligent, skillful, and industrious. He's also warm, determined, practical, and cautious." How do you combine those pieces of information to form an overall impression of Dave?

In early research on impression formation, Solomon Asch (1946) proposed that when people try to organize a list of traits into an integrated pattern, certain traits are more influential than others; these *central traits* serve to organize the total list. They may even influence the meaning or connotation of the other traits. For example, compare the expression "warm and determined" to the expression "cold and determined." Does the implication of

FIGURE 16.1
People convey their feelings and attitudes both by what they say and by their body language— their posture, arm and leg positions, smile or frown, eye movements, and so forth. When someone's words conflict with the body language, we tend to trust the body language more. We know that people lie with their words more easily than they do with their posture.

determined change from one expression to the other?

Asch found that changing "warm" to "cold" in a list of traits drastically changed people's impression of a person. Changing other traits in the list had less effect. So Asch identified "warm" and "cold" as central traits.

Other researchers suggest that we form our impressions of others simply by averaging the information we have about them (Anderson, 1974). Suppose I ask you how likable you think Dave is based on the traits listed above. You might assign a likability score to each trait, ranging from highly positive to highly negative, and then intuitively average all the scores. You might, of course, weight some of the scores more highly than others; for example, Dave's "warmth" might influence your overall opinion much more heavily than his "cautiousness" does.

We also pay more attention to unusual information than we do to ordinary information (Skowronski & Carlston, 1987). Suppose I write a letter of recommendation for a student who is applying to medical school. If I say the student is "bright, motivated, and neat," I doubt the admissions committee will be very impressed. If I say the student wrote the longest, most thorough term paper I have ever seen and turned it in a week before it was due, the admissions committee is likely to pay attention to that unusual information.

Because most people try to describe others in favorable terms, any unfavorable comments tend to catch our attention (Kanouse & Hanson, 1972). If I included in my letter of recommendation such phrases as "socially inept" or "not always reliable," the admissions committee probably would pay more attention to those comments than to any of my favorable comments.

Schematic Processing of Social Information

We form impressions not only of individuals but also of what we perceive as "types" of individuals. For example, you might react favorably to a tall red-headed woman you just met because she reminds you of some other woman you once knew and liked. Or you might react to a mortician based on your perception of the "typical" mortician. In many cases, our impression of some group or type is based on just a single person we once met, or even someone that we just heard about (Smith & Zárate, 1992). We refer to such impressions or expectations about a particular type of people as **schemas.**

Schemas can strongly influence what we notice and remember about others. For example, Claudia Cohen (1981) showed subjects a videotape of a woman having dinner with her husband. Some of the subjects were told that she was a waitress; others were told that she was a librarian. The videotape showed the woman doing certain things that fit popular expectations of a waitress (drinking beer, listening to popular music) and doing other things that fit common expectations of a librarian (wearing glasses, reading historical novels). When the subjects were later tested on their memory of what they had seen, they chiefly remembered the facts that matched their expectations. For example, those who had been told the woman was a waitress were more likely to remember that she drank beer; those who were told she was a librarian were more likely to remember that she read historical novels. In short, schemas have a strong effect on what we perceive and remember about other people.

Stereotypes and Racial Prejudice

Our schemas are not always accurate, because we recall some events more readily than others. You are more likely to recall the three times your next-door neighbors were rude to you than the thousands of times they were not. You therefore form an inaccurate schema about your neighbors.

Schemas about large categories of people, such as a whole ethnic group, are called **stereotypes** (overgeneralizations of either positive or negative attitudes) or **prejudices** (negative prejudgments of people). For example, some people believe that Germans are hard-working, the Irish are temperamental, and the Japanese are polite. Some stereotypes may be partly true (even if exaggerated); others can be altogether false. People can develop false stereotypes as illusory correlations, which arise because we remember unusual events more clearly than ordinary events (see Chapter 2). For example, if you are white and 90% of the people you ordinarily see in the course of a day are white, you probably will remember what black people do more readily than what white people do. If, in addition to *looking different* from the majority, a few members of a minority group *do* something unusual—such as being extra-polite, driving a car recklessly, or talking loudly in public—the combination is likely to make an especially strong impression (Hamilton & Gifford, 1976). Moreover, as we have seen, we usually look for an explanation of unusual behavior and tend to attribute it to whatever we notice most clearly about the person who engages in it. So when we see a member of some minority group do something unusual, we tend to think, "Ah, that's the way *those* people act." Once such a stereotype forms, it can be quite persistent; when we meet someone who does not fit the stereotype we explain away the discrepancy as an "exception to the rule" (Rothbart & John, 1985).

A stereotype or prejudice can distort people's perceptions of other people's behavior. For example, in one study, white college students watched a videotape of an argument between a white student and a black student (Duncan, 1976). The argument grew heated and at last one student shoved the other. In one version of the videotape, the white student shoved the black student; in another version, the black student shoved the white student. Subjects who saw the white student shove the black student described the action as "playing around" or "dramatizing"; those who saw the black student shove the white student described the action as "violent."

White people's stereotypes and prejudices about black people have been of special concern to both social psychologists and the public at large. Before the 1960s, many white Americans stated their prejudices quite openly and unapologetically. Then, after the Civil Rights

Act of 1964, the civil rights movement, and the assassination of Martin Luther King, Jr., the mood changed. At least in public, most white Americans seemed to embrace the principles of equal opportunity and equal rights. Psychologists therefore expected—naively, it now appears—that white people's stereotypes and prejudices about black people would steadily decrease.

What has actually happened is that many white people who report themselves as having "little or no racial prejudice" sometimes display racial discrimination, acting in ways that imply definite racial prejudice. What are we to make of this? One possibility, of course, is that the denials of racial prejudice are either lies or self-deceptions. But that is not necessarily so. Some white people frankly admit that they were taught some unfavorable stereotypes and prejudices, which emerge from time to time as automatic habits. For example, in one study white college students were asked for their reactions under various circumstances, such as "suppose a black person sits next to you on a bus," or "suppose a black family moves into the house next-door to yours." In each case, the students were to describe how they believe they *would* respond and also how they *should* respond. Some students acknowledged large discrepancies, saying they would react one way but should react a very different way. They said they felt uncomfortable about this discrepancy and were trying to change it (Devine, Monteith, Zuwerink, & Elliot, 1991).

In other cases, a white person's attitude toward black people may be marked with **ambivalence** (literally, *both values*)—a mixture of favorable and unfavorable beliefs. For example, a white person may believe that black people are in general ill-educated or incompetent in certain ways, yet also hold great admiration for the ways in which black people have struggled to overcome barriers and disadvantages. As a result of this ambivalence, white people tend to overstate their praise for black people who do well and to overstate their criticism of black people who make mistakes (Figure 16.2).

In one study college students, mostly white, were assembled into teams to compete for prizes by answering "trivia" questions. Each team had a captain, who was selected by a rigged drawing. For half the teams that captain was black; for the other half, white. All the captains were in fact confederates of the experimenter and were told exactly what to do. In

Serbs and Croats have lived side by side for hundreds of years, intermittently fighting. Each generation learns its prejudices from the older generation.

Stereotypes and prejudices often form when two groups of people remember each other's unusual behaviors. White police officers in certain cities tend to remember their experiences with black criminals; similarly, black citizens remember their experiences with cruel or brutal police officers. Each group tends to think of the other group, "They're all like that."

FIGURE 16.2
Many white people in the United States hold ambivalent attitudes toward blacks; that is, they hold a mixture of strongly positive and strongly negative beliefs. They tend to admire and praise successful blacks even more strongly than they admire and praise equally successful whites. However, they tend to be harsher toward unsuccessful or criminal blacks than they are toward similar whites.

some cases, the captains performed their tasks well and their teams won prizes; in other cases, the captains made one blunder after another and cost their team any chance of winning. Afterward, the members of each team were asked to evaluate their captain's performance. As Figure 16.3 shows, successful black captains got higher evaluations than successful white captains, but unsuccessful black captains got lower evaluations than unsuccessful white captains (Hass, Katz, Rizzo, Bailey, & Eisenstadt, 1991).

The apparent interpretation is that white students were showing their ambivalence toward blacks: They like blacks in some ways and dislike blacks in others; they admire blacks who succeed and scorn blacks who fail. We shall await further research to clarify the nature of white students' ambivalent attitudes. It would also be interesting to find out how black students would react to successful and unsuccessful white and black captains. As is often the case in research, one interesting study raises new questions that may inspire further studies.

Overcoming Prejudice

After prejudices and hostility have arisen between two groups, what can anyone do to break

down those barriers? Simply getting to know each other better may help, but prejudices are sometimes rather stubborn. A more effective technique is to get the two groups to work toward a common goal.

Many years ago, psychologists demonstrated the power of this technique using two arbitrarily chosen groups, not different races (Sherif, 1966). At a summer camp at Robbers' Cave, Oklahoma, 11-to-12-year-old boys were divided into two groups in separate cabins. The groups competed for prizes in sports, treasure hunts, and other activities. With each competition the antagonism between the two groups grew more intense. The boys made threatening posters, shouted insults, and threw apples at one another's cabins. Clearly each group had developed prejudice and hostility toward the other.

Up to a point the "counselors" (the experimenters) allowed the hostility to take its course, neither encouraging it nor prohibiting it. Then they tried to reverse it by stopping the competitions and setting common goals. First they had the two groups work together to find and repair a leak in the water pipe that supplied the camp. Later they had the groups pool their treasuries

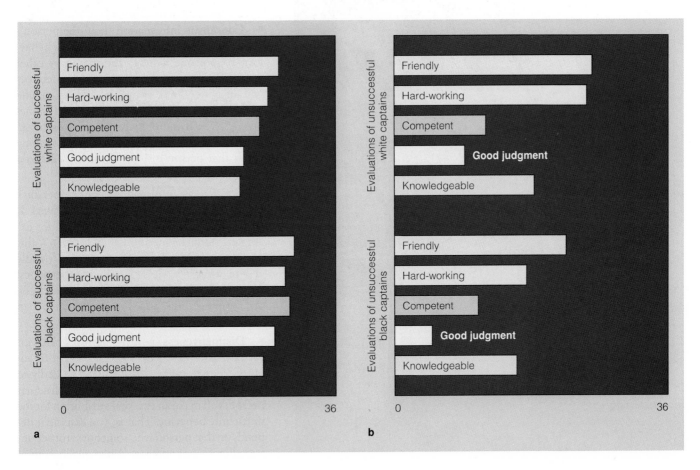

FIGURE 16.3
In the study by Hass, Katz, Rizzo, Bailey, & Eisenstadt (1991), white students evaluated the performances of their team captains (who were actually confederates of the experimenter). Successful black captains received higher ratings than successful white captains, but unsuccessful black captains received lower ratings than unsuccessful white captains. These results suggest that many white people have "ambivalent" feelings about black people—a mixture of favorable and unfavorable beliefs.

to rent a movie that both groups wanted to see. Still later they had the boys pull together to get a truck out of a rut. Gradually hostility turned to friendship—except for a few holdouts who nursed their hatred to the bitter end! The point of the study is that competition leads to hostility; cooperation leads to friendship.

ATTRIBUTION

We often try to figure out why the people we observe behave as they do. Yesterday you won a million dollars in the state lottery. Today a classmate who had never seemed to notice you before asks you for a date. You wonder whether this sudden interest is the result of your charming personality or your new wealth. When we

are not sure what is causing the behavior of someone we are observing, we *attribute* causes that seem appropriate. **Attribution** is the set of thought processes we use to assign causes to our own behavior and the behavior of others.

Internal Causes Versus External Causes

Fritz Heider, the founder of attribution theory, maintained that people often try to decide whether someone's behavior is the result of internal causes or external causes (Heider, 1958). Internal causes come from the person's stable characteristics, such as attitudes, personality traits, or abilities. External causes come from the situation, such as stimuli in the environment, the events of the day, and the rewards and

Social Perception and Cognition 673

Working together toward a shared goal is an excellent way to overcome prejudice. When people owe their success to someone else's efforts, they naturally come to like that person and they may generalize that attitude to similar others.

- **Consensus information** (how the person's behavior compares with other people's behavior). If someone behaves the same way other people do in some situation, or the same way you imagine other people would, then you probably make an external attribution. If someone behaves in an unusual way, you look for an internal attribution, pertaining to something about that person instead of something about the situation.

- **Consistency information** (how the person's behavior varies from one time to the next). If someone seems almost always friendly, for example, you make an internal attribution ("this person is friendly"). If someone seems friendly at some times and less friendly at other times, you look for external attributions ("something just happened to put this person in a bad mood").

- **Distinctiveness** (how the person's behavior varies from one object or social partner to another). For example, if someone is friendly to most people, but unfriendly to one particular person, you make an external attribution for the unfriendly behavior. That is, you assume it depends on that person who somehow arouses unfriendliness, not on a stable personality trait of the person who suddenly acted unfriendly.

■ CONCEPT CHECK

2. *Your friend Juanita returns from watching a movie and says it was excellent. The other people you heard commenting on this film disliked it. Will you probably make an internal or an external attribution for Juanita's enjoyment of this movie? Why? (Distinctiveness, consensus, or consistency?) (Check your answer on page 679.)*

The Discounting Principle

Kelley's theory of attribution suggests that we usually engage in fairly complex thought processes when we search for the cause of another person's behavior. Kelley also recognized, however, that in certain cases we pay strong attention to one feature of the situation, which guides our interpretation of the others. According to the **discounting principle,** when we attribute a person's behavior to one obvious cause, we tend to discount the likelihood of other possible causes (Kelley, 1972). For example, you learn that Senator Philip Buster, who voted against gun-control legislation last month, received a $100,000 donation from the

penalties associated with certain acts. For example, your brother decides to walk to work every morning instead of driving. You could attribute his action to an internal cause ("He likes fresh air and exercise") or to an external cause ("He saves money" or "It allows him to walk past the house of that woman he's trying to meet").

We look for internal causes when someone does something unexpected, something that makes us say, "I wouldn't have done that." For example, if someone laughs and talks boisterously at a funeral, we look for an internal cause, such as "immaturity and lack of respect" (Jones & Davis, 1965). But if someone laughs and talks boisterously at a party, we attribute the behavior to the situation.

Harold Kelley (1967) proposed that we rely on three types of information in deciding whether to make an internal or an external attribution for someone's behavior:

National Rifle Association a while back. So you attribute his vote to an external cause (the large donation) rather than to an internal cause (his opposition to gun control). In other words, the clear external cause leads you to discount the less certain internal cause (Kruglanski, 1970; Strickland, 1958).

We also apply the discounting principle to our own behavior. In one clever experiment, investigators asked a group of undergraduate women to read two joke books, listening to a tape-recorded laugh track while reading one of them. They told some of the women (and not others) that listening to the laugh track would increase their smiling and laughter. In fact it had very little effect. Here is where the discounting principle comes in: Imagine yourself in the position of one of the women who expect to laugh more while reading the book accompanied by the laugh track. When you do laugh while reading that book, you attribute your laughter to the laugh track, *discounting* the effect of the joke itself. When you laugh while reading the other book, you attribute your laughter only to the book. Later in this experiment the women were given an opportunity to read whichever book they wanted during "free time." Most of the women who had expected to laugh more during the laugh track chose to read the book *not* associated with the laugh track. Apparently they reasoned "That book made me laugh just as hard even without the laugh track, so it must really be funnier." Women in the control group, who did not expect the laugh track to affect their responses, showed no preference between the two books (Olson, 1992).

Still, people do not discount internal causes completely, even in the presence of strong external causes. In one experiment, subjects were asked to read an essay another student had written, which either praised Fidel Castro, the Communist leader of Cuba, or criticized him. The subjects were then asked to judge the writer's real attitude toward Castro. It might seem natural for them to assume that the writer meant what he or she said—that is, to attribute the content of the essays to internal causes (Jones & Harris, 1967).

But the investigators told some of the subjects that the writer of the pro- or anti-Castro essay had been assigned, almost forced, to write it. Did the revelation of that strong external cause lead those subjects to discount the internal cause? Not completely. Most of the subjects still thought the writer was pro-Castro. Figure 16.4 shows the results.

When someone behaves in an unusual way—such as wearing a wedding dress while riding a motorcycle—we generally make an internal attribution. That is, we assume there is something unusual about this person; we do not assume that other people in the same situation would have behaved the same way. (If we knew more about the situation, we might be less confident of this attribution.)

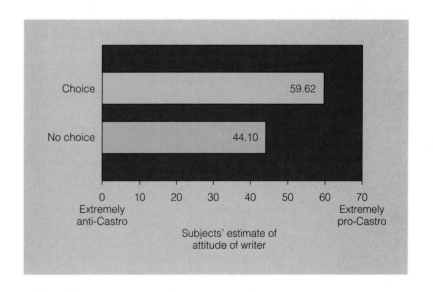

FIGURE 16.4
When subjects were told that a person chose to write a pro-Castro essay, they attributed pro-Castro attitudes to the writer. Even when they were told that the writer had been required to write the essay, they still attributed mildly pro-Castro attitudes to the writer. (Based on data from Jones & Harris, 1967.)

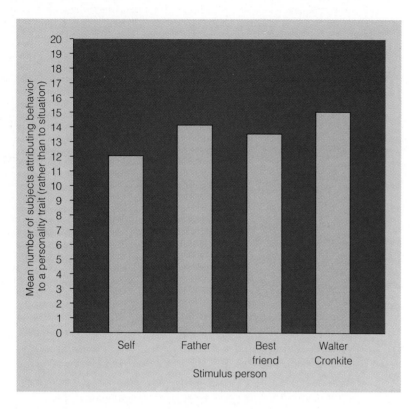

FIGURE 16.5
Subjects were asked whether certain people had certain traits, such as "leniency," or the opposite traits, such as "firmness," or whether "it depended on the situation." They attributed the most personality traits to news announcer Walter Cronkite (the person they knew least) and the fewest to themselves. That is, they were most likely to say their own behavior depended on the situation. (Based on data of Nisbett, Caputo, Legant, & Marecek, 1973.)

Errors and Biases

As the preceding experiment suggests, we often assume that people's behavior results from internal causes even when we know that some strong external cause may have been operating. Lee Ross (1977) calls this tendency to overemphasize internal explanations of other people's behavior the **fundamental attribution error.**

Moreover, people are more likely to attribute internal causes to other people's behavior than they are to their own behavior (Jones & Nisbett, 1972). This tendency is called the **actor-observer effect.** You are an "actor" when you try to explain the causes of your own behavior and an "observer" when you try to explain someone else's behavior.

The actor-observer effect has been demonstrated in a number of studies (Watson, 1982). In one of them, Richard Nisbett and his colleagues (1973) asked college students to rate themselves, their fathers, their best friends, and Walter Cronkite (a television news announcer at the time) on a number of personality traits. For each trait (such as "leniency"), the subjects had three choices: (1) the person possesses the trait, (2) the person possesses the opposite trait, and (3) the person's behavior "depends on the situation." Subjects checked "depends on the situation" most frequently when they were rating themselves, less frequently when they were rating their fathers and friends, and least often when they were rating Walter Cronkite. These results are consistent with the actor-observer effect; subjects made external attributions for their own behavior ("depends on the situation") and internal attributions for others' behavior ("they possess certain traits"). Figure 16.5 shows the results.

Why do we tend to explain our own behavior differently from that of others? There are several possibilities (Jones & Nisbett, 1972; Watson, 1982). First, because we observe our own behavior in many different situations, we realize how much it varies from one situation to another. (Recall Kelley's theory: You make external attributions when someone's behavior varies across time and across situations.)

Second, we tend to attribute unexpected, surprising behavior to internal causes. Our own behavior seldom surprises us, so we do not attribute it to internal causes.

A third reason is perceptual. We do not see ourselves as objects, because our eyes look outward and focus on our environment. We see other people, however, as objects in our visual field.

The perceptual explanation for the actor-observer effect has an interesting implication: If you could somehow become an object in your own visual field, then you might explain your own behavior in terms of internal traits, just as you tend to explain the behavior of others. In one innovative study, Michael Storms (1973) videotaped several subjects as they carried on a conversation. Before showing them the videotape, he asked them why they had said certain things and why they thought the others had said what they had. At first, most of the subjects attributed their own remarks to external causes ("I was responding to what the other person said") and attributed what the other people had said to internal causes "He was showing off" or "She always says things like that"). Then Storms showed them the videotape and asked them the same questions. This time, many of them attributed their own behavior more to internal causes ("I was being smart-alecky. . . . I was trying to act friendly").

■ CONCEPT CHECK

3. *You go along with a crowd to see* Return of the Son of Sequel Strikes Back Again, Part 2. *Are you more likely to think that you really want to see the movie or that the others do? (Check your answer on page 679).*

Something to Think About

Try to explain these examples of behavior:

- Why did you choose to go to the college you are attending?

- Why did your roommate choose this college?

- Why are you reading this book right now?

- Why does your roommate study so much (or so little)?

Did you attribute internal causes or external causes to these behaviors? Did you rely more on external causes to explain other people's behavior or to explain your own?

Using Attributions to Protect Our Self-Esteem

Although we generally attribute our own behavior largely to external causes, we vary our attributions to protect our self-esteem. For example, you may credit your intelligence for the good grades you get (an internal attribution) and blame unfair tests for your bad grades (an external attribution). Members of groups that are frequent victims of discrimination often blame prejudice and discrimination for a large portion of their failures and defeats (Crocker & Major, 1989). Such attributions are undoubtedly correct in many cases, but not necessarily in all cases. Attributions that we adopt in an effort to maximize our credit for success and minimize our blame for failure are called **self-serving biases** (Miller & Ross, 1975; Van Der Pligt & Eiser, 1983).

We can also protect our self-esteem by adopting **self-handicapping strategies,** in which we create external causes as "decoy" excuses for our failures. Suppose you expect to do poorly on a final exam. You go to a party the night before and stay out until three in the morning. Now you can blame your low score on your lack of sleep and avoid having to admit that you would have done poorly anyway.

In an experiment on self-handicapping strategies, Steven Berglas and Edward Jones

We tend to attribute our own behavior to external causes and other people's behavior to their personality traits. For example, if you bounce a check, you probably attribute your error to inaccurate information about your bank balance, some temporary fluctuation in your financial situation, or some other external cause. But when your congressional representative (or a former representative) discusses why he or she bounced some bad checks (as a number of them tried to explain in 1992), you are likely to make a less generous attribution about your representative's error than you did about your own.

(1978) had college students work on problems; some students were given solvable problems and some were given unsolvable problems. Then the experimenters told all the subjects that they had done well. They wanted the subjects who had been given solvable problems to believe that they had performed skillfully and the subjects who had been given unsolvable problems to believe that they had been lucky. (It had to be luck because the subjects knew they had not understood the problems!)

Next they told the subjects that the experiment's purpose was to investigate the effects of drugs on problem solving and that they were now going to pass out another set of problems. The subjects could choose between taking a drug that supposedly impaired problem solving and another drug that supposedly improved it. The subjects who had worked on unsolvable problems the first time were more likely than the others were to choose the drug that supposedly impaired performance. Because they did not expect to do well on the second set of problems anyway, they provided themselves with a convenient excuse.

Social Perception and Cognition   677

The performer who does poorly at an audition may attribute this result to external circumstances to maintain self-esteem: "She must have slept with the director," "They only wanted a certain type," or "The whole show was cast beforehand." This is a self-serving bias in attribution.

In closing, we can see that attributions play an important role in social interactions. We are seldom fully aware of the reasons for our own behavior, much less someone else's. Consequently our attributions are based partly on our observations and partly on what we wish or imagine to be true. If someone you know passes by without saying hello, you might attribute that person's behavior to absent-mindedness, indifference to you, or outright hostility. If someone acts unusually friendly, you might attribute that response to your own personal charm, the other person's extraverted personality, or the other person's devious and manipulative personality. Whatever attributions you make are sure to influence your own social behaviors.

SUMMARY

- *First impressions.* We form first impressions of others on the basis of their appearance and their nonverbal behavior. (page 668)

- *Primacy effect.* Other things being equal, we pay more attention to the first information we learn about someone than to later information. (page 668)

- *Impression formation.* People organize the information they have about other people into an overall impression. They ascribe greater weight to certain central traits, such as "warmness" or "coldness," than they do to other traits, and they weigh some kinds of information more heavily than others. (page 669)

- *Schemas.* People tend to perceive and remember other people's behavior in ways that match their expectations. (page 670)

- *Stereotypes.* Stereotypes are generalized beliefs about groups of people. They are sometimes illusory correlations that arise from people's tendency to remember unusual actions clearly, especially unusual actions by members of minority groups. (page 670)

- *Racial prejudice.* White people in the United States sometimes show prejudice against blacks even though they deny having racial prejudice. One reason is that some whites have habits of prejudice that sometimes emerge, despite conscious efforts to overcome them. Another reason is that many whites have ambivalent attitudes toward blacks, exaggerating both their praise for success and their criticism for mistakes. (page 670)

- *Attribution.* Attribution is the set of thought processes by which we assign causes to behavior. We attribute behavior either to internal causes or to external causes. According to Harold Kelley, we are likely to attribute behavior to an internal cause if it is consistent over time, different from most other people's behavior, and directed toward a variety of other people or objects. (page 673)

- *Discounting principle.* We tend to discount one possible cause for behavior when we become aware of a more obvious cause for it. (page 674)

- *Fundamental attribution error.* We are more likely to attribute the behavior of other people to internal causes than we are to attribute our own behavior to internal causes. (page 676)

■ *Self-handicapping.* We sometimes try to protect our self-esteem by attributing our successes to skill and our failures to outside influences. (page 677)

SUGGESTION FOR FURTHER READING

Fiske, S. T., & Taylor, S. E. (1984). *Social cognition.* New York: Random House. A discussion of research on how people perceive, process, and remember information about others.

TERMS

social psychologists psychologists who study social behavior and how an individual influences others and is influenced by them (page 666)

primacy effect tendency to be influenced more by the first information learned about someone than by later information about the same person (page 668)

social cognition the process of combining and remembering information about others and making inferences based on that information (page 669)

schemas impressions or expectations about a particular type of people (page 670)

stereotypes overgeneralizations of either positive or negative attitudes toward people (page 670)

prejudices negative prejudgments of people (page 670)

ambivalence a mixture of favorable and unfavorable beliefs about some person or group (page 671)

attribution the set of thought processes we use to assign causes to our own behavior and the behavior of others (page 673)

consensus information observations of how some person's behavior compares with that of others (page 674)

consistency information observations of how some person's behavior varies from one time to another (page 674)

distinctiveness observations of how some person's behavior varies from one object or social partner to another (page 674)

discounting principle tendency of people who have already made one attribution for some behavior to discount the likelihood of other possible causes of the behavior (page 674)

fundamental attribution error tendency to overemphasize internal explanations of other people's behavior (page 676)

actor-observer effect tendency to attribute internal causes more to other people's behavior than to one's own behavior (page 676)

self-serving biases attributions people adopt in an effort to maximize their credit for success and minimize their blame for failure (page 677)

self-handicapping strategies techniques for protecting self-esteem by creating external causes as decoy excuses for failures (page 677)

ANSWERS TO CONCEPT CHECKS

1. They want to avoid being biased by their first impressions of the students. That procedure is less important on the first test because they do not yet have a strong impression of the students. (page 668)

2. You probably will make an internal attribution for Juanita's enjoyment, attributing it to the fact that she is easy to please instead of attributing it to the quality of the movie. The reason is *consensus*: When one person's behavior differs from that of others, we make an internal attribution. (page 674)

3. You are likely to think that the others really want to go to the movie (an internal attribution) and that you are going because of the external situation (peer pressure). (page 677)

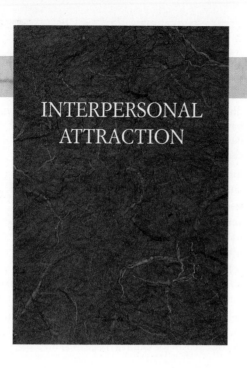

INTERPERSONAL ATTRACTION

Why do we like some people better than others?

Why are we more eager to be with other people at some times than at other times?

What is the difference between loving and liking?

Willliam Proxmire, a former U.S. senator, used to give "Golden Fleece Awards" to those who, in his opinion, were most flagrant in wasting the taxpayers' money. He once bestowed an award on some psychologists who had received a federal grant to study how people fall in love. He declared that their experimental design was flawed. (It is not clear what his qualifications were for judging that.) Anyway, he went on, it is pointless to study love because people do not want to understand love. They prefer, he said, to let such matters remain a mystery, and therefore psychologists should stop doing research on love.

This section is about the information Senator Proxmire did not want you to know.

SHORT-TERM, CASUAL AFFILIATIONS

Let us begin with brief relationships. Sometimes we want to be with other people, but we have no intention of developing a long-term relationship with any of them. For example, you might want to get together with some other students in a particular class to study for a test, or you might get together with a group for recreational sports.

Brief, casual affiliations can also be important to us for our own self-understanding. If you have just had some intense and trying emotional experience, you might want to be with other people who have had a similar experience, to compare your reactions to theirs and (you hope) demonstrate that you coped with the experience at least as well as they did (Kruglanski & Mayseless, 1990). People also like to associate with people who can set a good example. For example, cancer patients generally like to associate with other cancer patients, especially patients who are showing signs of recovery, who can provide an encouraging role model (Taylor & Lobel, 1989).

When people expect to face some difficult experience in the near future, they generally like to be with other people facing a similar predicament. The old saying goes, "Misery loves company." To test this saying, Stanley Schachter (1959) told subjects he was trying to measure the effects of electric shock on their heart rate and blood pressure. He told one group to expect substantial shocks; he told the other group to expect mild tickling or tingling sensations. Then he told subjects that they would have to wait about 10 minutes while the experimenter made some last-minute adjustments of the equipment. Some subjects were given a choice between waiting alone or waiting with other subjects in the same experiment. Other subjects were given a choice between waiting alone and waiting with students who just happened to be in the building (not subjects in the experiment). Subjects who expected only mild shocks had little preference; they were willing to wait anywhere or with anybody. But the subjects who expected strong shocks strongly preferred to wait with other subjects in the same experiment, as Figure 16.6 shows. In short, people in distress crave the company of people in similar distress. That is, misery loves *miserable* company. Short-term relationships like these can serve a variety of purposes, even if they do not develop into anything deeper or more lasting.

ESTABLISHING MORE LASTING RELATIONSHIPS

The world's population includes billions of people. During your lifetime you may personally see millions of them; you probably will get to know thousands of them by name at one time or another. But you will develop meaningful or lasting relationships with relatively few. How do you choose those people, or how do they choose you? We shall examine several of the most dependable factors—proximity, mere exposure, physical attractiveness, and similarity.

Proximity

Proximity means closeness. (It comes from the same root as *approximate*.) We tend to choose as friends people who are in close proximity to us, who cross our path frequently. In one study, residents of a graduate housing project at the Massachusetts Institute of Technology were asked to list their three closest friends (Festinger, Schachter, & Back, 1950). The residents lived in two-story buildings with five apartments on each floor (Figure 16.7). On the average, they reported that about two thirds of their closest friends lived in the same building, and of those about two thirds lived on the same floor. People were most likely to make friends with their next-door neighbors.

In another study, college dormitory residents reported that they were more likely to be friends with students who lived one door away than with students who lived two doors away (Priest & Sawyer, 1967). At the start of a school year, Robert Hays (1985) asked college students to name two other students with whom they thought they might become friends. After 3 months, he found that more of the potential friends who lived close together had become friends than had those who lived farther apart.

Proximity influences romantic relationships as well. In an early study, James Bossard (1931) analyzed 5,000 marriage-license applications in Philadelphia and observed a clear relationship between proximity and marriage rates. More couples who lived one block apart got married than those who lived two blocks apart, and so forth. People tend to be more mobile today than they were when this study was conducted in 1931, but still you are more likely to marry someone who lives in your own town or attends your own college than you are to marry someone you once met while out of town.

People who are facing an emotionally trying experience, such as soldiers on the eve of battle, prefer to be with others who have undergone or expect to undergo the same experience.

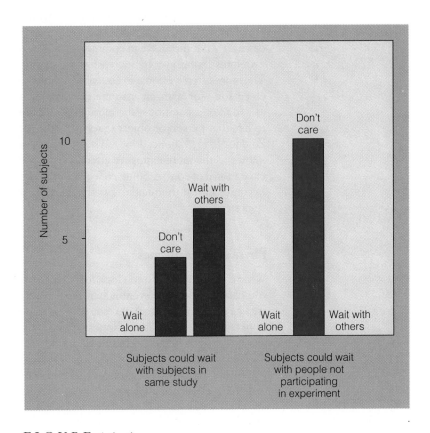

FIGURE 16.6

In Schachter's experiment, people who thought they were waiting for a procedure in which they would receive strong shocks preferred to wait with others who were about to undergo the same procedure. They had no particular desire to wait with people who were not participating in the same study. That is, miserable people like to be with other miserable people. In more general terms, we like to compare our reactions to those of other people who have had, or expect to have, similar experiences.

Interpersonal Attraction 681

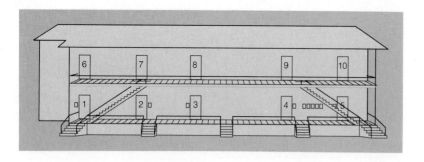

FIGURE 16.7
Students who lived in this graduate housing project generally chose friends who lived nearby. (From Festinger, Schachter, & Back, 1950.)

For the initial stage of attraction between a man and a woman, or even between two friends, physical appearance is highly important. In the long run, however, a couple must have some similar interests and values if their relationship is to thrive.

Mere Exposure

Proximity promotes liking by increasing the number of opportunities two people have to discover what they have in common. But it also promotes liking just by increasing familiarity. The more often we come in contact with another person—or with an inanimate object such as a food or a painting—the more likely we are to like that person or object (Saegert, Swap, & Zajonc, 1973; Zajonc, 1968). This tendency is known as the **mere-exposure effect.** (There are exceptions, of course. Some college roommates become almost homicidal by the end of a semester.)

Physical Attractiveness

What characteristics do you look for in a person you date and perhaps eventually marry? If you are like most college students, you say you want "a person who is intelligent, honest, easy to talk to, . . . and who has a good sense of humor."

Now imagine a friend of yours says, "Hey, you're not doing anything this weekend, are you? How about going out on a blind date with my cousin who is visiting here for the weekend?"

"Well, I don't know," you reply. "Tell me about your cousin."

"My cousin is intelligent, honest, easy to talk to, . . . has a good sense of humor."

Do you go on the date? No. Why not? After all, your friend's description matches your description of a "dream date"! The trouble is, your friend did not mention the cousin's appearance, so you infer that the cousin must be

ugly. (Were you being hypocritical when you said you wanted someone intelligent, honest, and easy to talk to? I think not. You expected people to assume that you preferred someone with an acceptable appearance.)

Some time ago Elaine Walster and her colleagues (1966) set up "computer dates" for over 700 freshmen at the University of Minnesota. All the participants were asked to complete attitude scales, personality tests, and academic aptitude tests. Unknown to the subjects, Walster's research assistants rated the physical attractiveness of each subject while he or she was filling in the forms.

Actually, the dates were assigned at random, with no regard for the information the students had provided about themselves. The researchers then organized a big dance at the university gymnasium. During an intermission, they asked the students to fill out a questionnaire that asked how much they liked their dates.

The students with physically attractive dates liked their dates much more than did those with less attractive dates. How much they liked their dates had almost nothing to do with their dates' attitudes or personality. In other words, physical attraction seemed to be all-important.

In a way, that almost had to be the result, given the procedures of this study. Each couple had spent only an hour or two together, and they spent most of that time dancing to the music of a loud rock band. They hardly had an opportunity to explore each other's deepest thinking about politics and religion. Still, we can concede that physical attraction is the first step in bringing a couple together; if two people do not find each other attractive, they will not spend enough time together to compare notes on their interests and values.

■ CONCEPT CHECK

4. *An attractive person your own age from another country moves in next-door to you. Neither of you speaks the other's language. Are you likely to become friends? What factors will tend to strengthen the likelihood of your becoming friends? What factors will tend to weaken it? (Check your answers on page 687.)*

The Similarity Principle

If you could travel back in time and become close friends with any famous historical figure you chose, whom would you choose? Benjamin Franklin, Martin Luther King, Jr., Marie Curie, Agatha Christie, Confucius, Chief Sitting Bull, Susan B. Anthony, Joan of Arc, Sigmund Freud? Those are just suggestions; choose anyone you wish. How would you decide? Many historical figures probably would be interesting to meet, but in choosing a *friend,* you probably would look for someone similar to you or someone you would like to resemble.

How about your close friends? Most people choose friends who resemble themselves in age, ethnic background, physical attractiveness, political and religious beliefs, intelligence, academic interests, and attitudes toward sex and drugs (Laumann, 1969). Most people also date and eventually marry people who resemble themselves in many ways (Burgess & Wallin, 1953; Buss, 1985; Osborne, Noble, & Wey, 1978). The tendency to associate with people similar to oneself is known, not surprisingly, as the **similarity principle.**

Is it ever true that "opposites attract"? Sometimes, but not often (Winch, 1958). For example, a dominant person may choose a submissive friend, or a nurturing person may pair with someone who likes to be "babied." But such cases are exceptions; the rule is that people seek partners who resemble them.

The Equity Principle

A business deal works best if both of the parties entering into it believe they are getting as much as they are giving. The same is true of friendships and romantic relationships. According to one category of social psychological theories, called **exchange** or **equity theories,** social relationships are transactions in which partners exchange goods and services. In some cases, the businesslike nature of this exchange is fairly blatant. In the "Singles' Ads" sections of some newspapers, those seeking a relationship describe what they have to offer ("35-year-old divorced male, 6′1″, business executive, athletic. . .") and what they want in return ("seeks warm, caring, attractive woman, age 27–33 . . ."). The ads resemble the "asked" and "bid"

Similarity of interests brings together these New Zealand lawn bowlers. We like other people like ourselves because we think their attitudes and interests are right—in harmony with ours.

columns for the stock exchange (Kenrick & Trost, 1989).

As with a business deal, each participant hopes to get as good a deal as possible. If partner A is much more desirable than partner B, then B will be very pleased to have a relationship with A, but A will be much less pleased. Such a relationship will be unstable, compared to one in which the two partners are about equally desirable. To illustrate, let's imagine that you compare the pluses and minuses of a relationship you have with someone you are dating, as shown in Table 16.1. You probably would make these comparisons informally or intuitively instead of writing them out in such a formal manner, but the idea is the same. Note that the table shows that you consider yourself more desirable than your partner is in some regards, less desirable in other regards. You probably would note some additional pluses and minuses not listed in the table. Depending on which factors you think are most important, you might think you are getting a good deal or a poor one from this relationship. Simultaneously, your partner thinks about the pluses and minuses and also decides whether the exchange seems fair.

As you can begin to suspect by examining Table 16.1, it is difficult to develop an equal exchange in a relationship between people who are very different from each other. Here, one person is richer, more intelligent, and more loyal; the other is more attractive and more popular. Do the advantages equal or exceed the disadvantages for both parties? Perhaps neither one is quite sure. Now imagine a relationship between two people who resemble each other. Both are equally attractive, equally popular, equally intelligent, and so forth. Therefore the exchange is fair; neither party is getting a better deal than the other is. In short, *the equity principle implies the similarity principle;* someone who seeks a fair, equitable relationship can achieve it most easily with a highly similar partner.

ROMANTIC AND PASSIONATE LOVE

A good romantic relationship requires a fair exchange between two people, but we also know it is more than just a business deal. At its best, a romantic relationship includes liking and loving, and perhaps several kinds of loving.

Defining and Measuring Love

The poet Elizabeth Barrett Browning once asked, "How do I love thee? Let me count the ways." How do social psychologists count the ways of love?

In one of the first attempts to measure love, Zick Rubin (1970, 1973) developed scales of liking and loving. According to Rubin, liking includes a feeling of respect and admiration for someone. Two items from his liking scale are "In my opinion, _____ is an exceptionally mature person" and "_____ is one of the most likable people I know." (Fill in the name of a friend or romantic partner in the blank spaces.)

Table 16.1 The Pluses and Minuses of a Hypothetical Dating Relationship from the Standpoint of One Partner

	You	Your Partner	Net Advantage/Disadvantage to You
Physical appearance	Average	Outstanding	Advantage
Prestige	Not well known	Popular	Advantage
Finances	Pay for most date expenses and occasional presents, provide nice car	Contributes very little	Disadvantage
Intelligence	Very high	Above average	Disadvantage
Annoying habits	Occasional swearing	Bad table manners	Uncertain
Loyalty	Dating no one else	Dates others often	Disadvantage
Attitudes	Conservative on most issues	Liberal on most issues	Disadvantage (to both people)

Loving has to do with feelings of intimacy, absorption, and possessiveness. Sample items are "I feel that I can confide in _____ about virtually everything" and "It would be hard for me to get along without _____."

In one study, Rubin (1973) asked 182 college couples to rate their dating partners and their best friends on his liking and loving scales. Not surprisingly, the subjects rated both friends and romantic partners high on the liking scale, but they rated their romantic partners significantly higher on the loving scale. The scores on the two scales were positively correlated, though not perfectly. Apparently, you like almost all the people you love, but you may not love all the people you like. When Rubin asked the subjects how likely they were to marry their dating partner, they reported high probabilities only if they both liked and loved their partner.

Is love a single experience, or does it have multiple dimensions? Robert Sternberg (1986; Sternberg & Grajek, 1984) asked subjects questions about their experience of love and then analyzed the results to see whether the answers to each question correlated with the answers to others. He concluded that love has three main dimensions: *intimacy* (how well you can talk with and confide in your partner), *passion* (erotic attraction and the feeling of being in love), and *commitment* (an intention to continue in the relationship).

According to Sternberg, these three dimensions are somewhat independent. For example, a passionate relationship might be low in intimacy and commitment. And a marriage high in intimacy and commitment might be low in passion, more like a solid friendship. Most of us aspire to romantic relationships that are high on all counts: intimacy, passion, and commitment. Sternberg terms such ideal relationships "consummate loves."

Clyde and Susan Hendrick (1986) have identified three primary styles of love: *eros* (passionate, erotic love), *ludus* (uncommitted, game-playing love), and *storge* (friendship love). (The strange-sounding labels are borrowed from Greek.) Hendrick and Hendrick also describe three secondary styles of love: *mania* (possessive and obsessive love), *pragma* (practical, list-of-benefits love), and *agape* (ah-GAH-pay; selfless, spiritual love). Table 16.2 shows some of the items used on a questionnaire to measure these six styles of love.

Hendrick and Hendrick (1986) also found that men tend to be more ludic (game playing and uncommitted), whereas women tend to be more storgic and pragmatic (inclined to see love as friendship or as a relationship based on practical considerations). Couples tend to share the same love style—that is, erotic partners choose erotic partners, and storgic partners choose storgic partners (Hendrick, Hendrick, & Adler, 1988). Relationships in which both partners

According to Robert Sternberg, romantic love has three partly independent dimensions: intimacy (the ability to confide in each other), passion (erotic attraction), and commitment (an intention to make the relationship last).

Table 16.2 Example Items from a Questionnaire to Identify Types of Love

Eros	My lover and I have the right physical "chemistry" between us.
Ludus	I enjoy playing the "game of love" with a number of different partners.
Storge	My most satisfying love relationships have developed from good friendships.
Pragma	I consider what a person is going to become in life before I commit myself to him/her.
Mania	When my lover doesn't pay attention to me, I feel sick all over.
Agape	I cannot be happy unless I place my lover's happiness before my own.

Source: Hendrick & Hendrick, 1986.

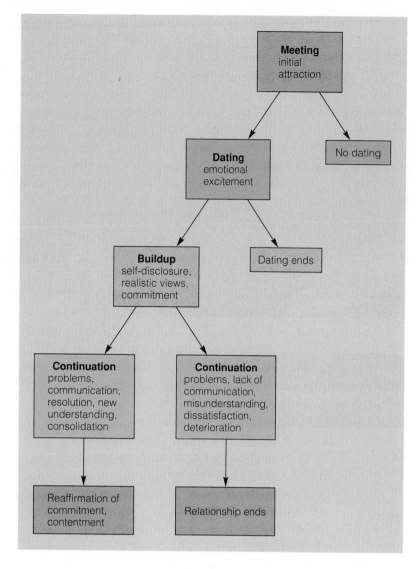

```
                    ┌─────────────┐
                    │   Meeting   │
                    │   initial   │
                    │  attraction │
                    └─────────────┘
                       │       │
                       ▼       ▼
              ┌─────────────┐  ┌───────────┐
              │   Dating    │  │ No dating │
              │  emotional  │  └───────────┘
              │  excitement │
              └─────────────┘
                 │       │
                 ▼       ▼
          ┌────────────┐  ┌─────────────┐
          │  Buildup   │  │ Dating ends │
          │self-disclosure,│└─────────────┘
          │realistic views,│
          │ commitment │
          └────────────┘
            │       │
            ▼       ▼
┌──────────────┐  ┌──────────────┐
│ Continuation │  │ Continuation │
│ problems,    │  │ problems, lack│
│ communication,│ │ of           │
│ resolution, new│ │ communication,│
│ understanding,│ │ misunderstanding,│
│ consolidation│  │ dissatisfaction,│
└──────────────┘  │ deterioration │
      │           └──────────────┘
      ▼                  │
┌──────────────┐         ▼
│ Reaffirmation of│  ┌──────────────┐
│ commitment,   │  │Relationship ends│
│ contentment   │  └──────────────┘
└──────────────┘
```

FIGURE 16.8

A romantic relationship begins with initial attraction. Of all the couples that experience initial attraction, a small percentage proceed to the dating stage; some of those advance to the buildup stage, and so forth. At each stage, the relationship can develop further or it can end.

share the same view of love tend to be more successful than relationships in which the partners have different views.

The Life Cycle of Romantic Relationships

Romantic relationships have a beginning, a middle, and sometimes an intentional end. George Levinger (1980, 1983) suggests that relationships go through five stages: initial attraction, buildup, continuation and consolidation, deterioration, and ending (Figure 16.8). Not all relationships, of course, go through all five stages. Here are some of the factors that affect each stage.

We have already considered the variables that influence *initial attraction.* Generally, we form relationships with people we meet at school, at work, or near where we live and who are similar to us in age, socioeconomic status, ethnic background, and physical appearance.

The emotional excitement that often develops during initial attraction tends to fade over time (Berscheid, 1983; Solomon & Corbit, 1974). As couples enter the *buildup* stage, partners learn new things about each other, gradually revealing intimate, sometimes even embarrassing information about themselves. Even at this point, however, the relationship may not be stable. In one study at the beginning of an academic year, 250 undergraduates each identified their "closest, deepest" relationship. Of these, almost half (47%) identified a romantic partner. Presumably those relationships were well into the buildup stage, if not beyond. But almost half of those "closest, deepest" relationships broke up by the end of the academic year (Berscheid, Snyder, & Omoto, 1989).

In the *continuation stage,* the relationship reaches a stable "middle age." By this time the partners have worked out a complex system of shared work and understandings. The excitement of constantly discovering new things about each other is over, and the partners may not arouse each other's emotions as intensely or as frequently as before (Berscheid, 1983). This does not mean that they no longer love each other. The emotion that persists in a mature relationship may become apparent only when the relationship is terminated by the death or departure of one of the partners.

Although the partners in a successful mature relationship may not live in a constant state of rapturous passion, they enjoy their intimacy and their ease in communicating with each other. John Gottman (1979) notes that the partners in a successful marriage listen to each other and validate each other's opinions, whereas the partners in an unsuccessful marriage engage in "cross complaining," nagging and criticizing each other without really listening.

As time passes, some relationships enter a stage of *deterioration.* Why? Exchange theories offer one explanation (Levinger, 1976): One of the partners has changed, for better or worse, and the exchange is no longer equally fair to both. According to one survey of 2,000 married people, the subjects who felt they were not getting their fair share out of the relationship were more likely to engage in extramarital affairs, apparently to even the score (Walster, Traupman, & Walster, 1978). (Or was it the other way around? Did they first commit adultery and then justify their behavior by saying that their marriage was unrewarding?)

When problems arise in a relationship, how do the partners deal with them? In one study,

50 college students described how they reacted when they confronted problems in their romantic relationships (Rusbult & Zembrodt, 1983). Most of their responses fell into one of four categories: *voice* (talking about the problems and trying to work them out), *loyalty* (passively waiting and hoping things will improve), *neglect* (allowing the relationship to deteriorate), and *exit* (withdrawing from the relationship).

Some relationships finally arrive at an *ending*. One partner may decide to end the relationship before the other partner is even aware that a problem exists (Vaughan, 1986). It is rare that both partners decide to end a relationship at the same time. As a rule, college men are less sensitive to problems in their relationships than college women are, and men are less likely to foresee a breakup (Rubin, Peplau, & Hill, 1981). When the breakup comes, the men usually seem more upset than the women do (Bloom, White, & Asher, 1979). Perhaps women monitor relationships more carefully and prepare themselves for what lies ahead.

In a mature, lasting relationship, a couple can count on each other for care and affection through both the good times and the bad times. Here, two weary travelers wait for a train in Salzburg, Austria.

SUMMARY

■ *Short-term affiliation.* People in distress or need gain strength from associating even briefly with other people, especially others who have undergone or who expect to undergo similar distressing experiences. (page 680)

■ *Attraction.* People generally choose friends and romantic partners who live near them, frequently come in contact with them, resemble them in various ways, and seem physically attractive. (page 681)

■ *Equity or exchange.* Relationships are most likely to survive and grow if both parties believe that they receive about as much from the relationship as they contribute to it. Relationships between similar people are most likely to achieve this kind of balance. (page 683)

■ *Liking and loving.* Although people generally like the people they love, loving and liking can be measured separately. (page 684)

■ *Dimensions and types of love.* Love has several dimensions, including intimacy, passion, and commitment. Psychologists distinguish several types of love. (page 684)

■ *Development of relationships.* Romantic relationships go through some or all of five stages: initial attraction, buildup, continuation and consolidation, deterioration, and ending. (page 686)

SUGGESTIONS FOR FURTHER READING

Brehm, S. S. (1985). *Intimate relationships.* New York: Random House. A readable discussion of research on close relationships.

Hendrick, C. (Ed.). (1989). *Close relationships.* Newbury Park, CA: Sage. A collection of articles by noted researchers, covering friendships as well as romantic relationships.

TERMS

proximity (literally, closeness) tendency to choose as friends people with whom we come in frequent contact (page 681)

mere-exposure effect tendency to increase liking for everything and everyone that has become familiar (page 682)

similarity principle tendency to associate with people similar to oneself (page 683)

exchange or **equity theories** theories holding that social relationships are transactions in which partners exchange goods and services (page 683)

ANSWER TO CONCEPT CHECK

4. Three factors will strengthen the likelihood of your becoming friends: proximity, exposure, and attractiveness. The similarity principle will weaken it. Because of the difference in languages, you will have little chance, at least at first, to discover any similarities in interests or attitudes. In fact, proximity probably will not be a potent force because it serves largely as a means of enabling people to discover what they have in common. (page 683)

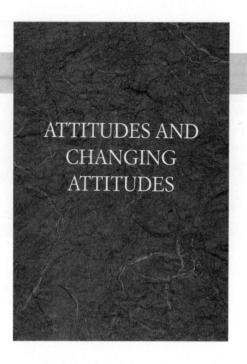

ATTITUDES AND CHANGING ATTITUDES

What are attitudes?
How do attitudes affect behavior?
What are the most effective means of
persuading people to change their attitudes?

"If you want to change people's behavior, first you have to change their attitudes." Do you agree?

Suppose you say yes. Now answer two more questions: (1) What is your attitude toward paying higher taxes? (2) If the government raises taxes, will you pay the higher taxes?

If you're like most people, you will say that (1) your attitude toward paying higher taxes is unfavorable, but that (2) if the taxes are raised, you will pay them. In other words, by changing the law, the government can change your behavior without changing your attitude.

So what effects do attitudes have on behavior? And what leads people to change their attitudes?

ATTITUDES AND THEIR INFLUENCE

An **attitude** is a learned like or dislike of something or somebody that influences our behavior toward that thing or person (Allport, 1935; Bem, 1970; Petty & Cacioppo, 1981). You probably hold attitudes toward all sorts of things and people: final exams, nuclear power plants, used-car dealers, vegetarians, mimes.

Your attitudes include an emotional component (the way you feel about something), a cognitive component (what you know or believe), and a behavioral component (what you are likely to do).

A common way of measuring attitudes is through the use of attitude scales, such as Likert scales, also known as summated rating scales (Dawes & Smith, 1985). On a Likert scale (named after the psychologist Rensis Likert), a person checks some point along a line ranging from 1, meaning "strongly disagree," to 5 or 7, meaning "strongly agree," on each of several statements about some topic (Figure 16.9). Then someone adds all the numerical values. The higher the total, the more favorable the person's attitude toward the topic.

Attitudes as Predictors of Behavior

It may seem obvious that attitudes influence behavior. If you have a positive attitude toward a certain brand of toothpaste, you probably will buy it. If you have a negative attitude toward your senator, you probably will vote for someone else.

Surprisingly, however, behavior often correlates rather weakly with attitudes (McGuire, 1985; Wicker, 1969). Why might that be? One reason is that many variables other than attitudes also influence our behavior (Fishbein & Ajzen, 1975). For example, your favorable attitude toward new Porsches may not influence your buying behavior if you cannot afford an expensive car. Your favorable attitude toward getting good grades is no guarantee that you will be a straight-A student.

The behavior of some people is more consistent with their attitudes than is the behavior of others. Some people are consistently inconsistent: Whenever they face an unfamiliar situation, the first thing they do is determine what is expected of them and what everyone else is doing. Such people, referred to as **high self-monitors** because they are constantly monitoring their own behavior to try to make the right impression (Snyder, 1979), often behave in ways that do not match their attitudes.

Finally, attitudes are better predictors of people's overall behavior than they are of any

FIGURE 16.9

Indicate your level of agreement with the items below using the following scale:

	Strongly disagree		Neutral		Strongly agree
1. Labor unions are necessary to protect the rights of workers.	1	2	3	4	5
2. Labor union leaders have too much power.	1	2	3	4	5
3. If I worked for a company with a union, I would join the union.	1	2	3	4	5
4. I would never cross a picket line of striking workers.	1	2	3	4	5
5. Striking workers hurt their company and unfairly raise prices for the consumer.	1	2	3	4	5
6. Labor unions should not be permitted to engage in political activity.	1	2	3	4	5
7. America is a better place for today's workers because of the efforts by labor unions in the past.	1	2	3	4	5

Note: Items 2, 5, and 6 are scored the opposite of 1, 3, 4, and 7.

specific behavior (Ajzen & Fishbein, 1980; Fishbein & Ajzen, 1975). For example, people's attitudes toward religion correlate well with a composite score measuring a long list of religious behaviors—praying before meals, attending services, contributing money, reading religious books, and so forth. But it correlates less highly with any single one of those behaviors (Fishbein & Ajzen, 1974).

ATTITUDE CHANGE AND PERSUASION

A great many people in this world will try to persuade you to change your attitudes and to do something that may or may not be in your best interests. They will ask you to give them your time, your money, your vote, your allegiance. Sometimes they will persuade you and sometimes they will not. The effectiveness of persuasion depends on *who says what, how,* and to *whom* (Hovland, Janis, & Kelley, 1953; Hovland, Lumsdaine, & Sheffield, 1949).

Two Routes of Persuasion

Suppose you see a television advertisement in which your favorite actor or actress endorses some brand of cat food. The next time you go to the grocery store, will you buy that brand—presuming that you have a cat? You might; certainly many people would. Both advertisers and social psychologists have concluded that attractive or famous people tend to be highly persuasive, at least under certain conditions.

Now suppose that a little later you see your favorite actor or actress again, but this time endorsing a candidate for governor of your state. Now how do you react? Suddenly the celebrity has become much less persuasive. You probably think something like, "What makes him/her an expert on politics?"

Why didn't you ask the same question before? After all, great acting ability doesn't qualify someone as an expert on cat food any more than it does for politics. The difference is that your decision about cat food did not seem very important; you take the governor's race more seriously.

Richard Petty and John Cacioppo (1981, 1986) have proposed that certain kinds of persuasive influences weigh more heavily for some decisions than they do for others. When people take a decision seriously, they invest the necessary time and effort to evaluate carefully the evidence and logic behind each message. Petty and Cacioppo call this logical approach the **central route to persuasion.** In contrast, when people listen to a message on a topic of little importance to them, they may pay more attention to such superficial factors as the speaker's appearance and reputation or the sheer number of arguments presented, regardless of their quality. This superficial approach is the **peripheral route to persuasion.**

■ CONCEPT CHECK

5. You listen to someone who is trying to persuade you to change your major from astrology to psychology. Your future success may depend on making the right decision. You also listen to someone explain why a trip to the Bahamas is better than a trip to the Fiji Islands. You had no intention of going to either place. In which case will you pay more attention to the evidence and logic, following the central route to persuasion? (Check your answer on page 697.)

Mood and Persuasion

Have you ever had the experience in which someone flatters you, acts unusually friendly, tells a few jokes, and then asks for a favor? Many people seem to believe that if they can get you into a good mood, they will be able to persuade you more easily than if you are in a normal or bad mood. Is that belief correct?

It depends. According to the evidence, people who are in a good mood tend to follow the peripheral route to persuasion (Schwarz, Bless, & Bohner, 1991). That is, they are influenced by superficial factors such as the speaker's appearance and apparent sincerity; they can be persuaded about equally easily by a solid argument or a flimsy one. (More or less, when people are in a really good mood, their brain turns to mush. They will agree to almost anything.)

However, when people are in a bad mood—a temporary state of disappointment, not a long-term depressed state—they turn to the central route to persuasion. Suddenly they start evaluating evidence carefully, perhaps to avoid making any mistakes that would make their bad situation even worse. If you offer a weak argument, the person in a bad mood will devote the effort to find and expose the errors. However, if your evidence and logic are solid, you can persuade a person in a bad mood even more strongly than you can a person in a good mood (Figure 16.10).

You can see how to apply this finding: If you want to persuade someone of something, and you are confident of your evidence and logic, you might actually *prefer* to talk to the person when he or she is in a bad mood, when the person will be most likely to devote some effort to your message. But if you know your case is weak, wait for a good mood.

(On the other hand, when people wait for you to be in a good mood to try to persuade you of something, be suspicious. They may be trying to convince you of something illogical.)

Delayed Influence of Messages

In certain cases, a message may have no apparent influence on you at the time you hear it, but an important effect later. There are several reasons why a message can have a delayed effect; we shall consider two examples.

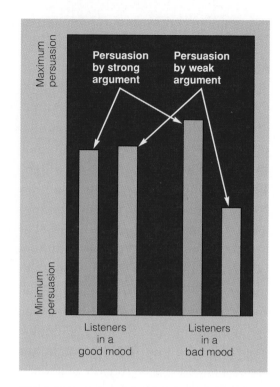

FIGURE 16.10

In one study, subjects were put into a good mood or a bad mood by asking them to spend 15 minutes describing either one of the most pleasant or one of the least pleasant events that ever happened to them. Then they listened to either strong, logical arguments or weak, flimsy arguments in favor of raising student fees at the university. Students in a bad mood were heavily persuaded by the strong arguments but not by the weak arguments. Students in a good mood were equally persuaded by either argument. (Based on study by Bless, Bohner, Schwarz, & Strack, 1990.)

The Sleeper Effect   Suppose you reject some message because of peripheral route influences. For example, you reject some new idea without giving it much thought, because you have a low opinion of the person who suggested it. If the idea is a good one, it may have a delayed effect. Weeks or months later, you may forget where you heard the idea and remember only the idea itself; at that time you evaluate it on its merits (Hovland & Weiss, 1951; Pratkanis, Greenwald, Leippe, & Baumgardner, 1988). Psychologists use the term **sleeper effect** to describe delayed persuasion by an initially rejected message (Figure 16.11).

Minority Influence   Delayed influence also occurs if a political minority, especially one that

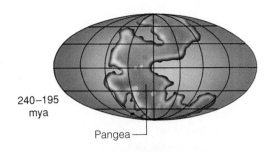

240–195
mya

Pangea

40–25
mya

present

FIGURE 16.11

The theory of plate tectonics and continental drift is one example of the sleeper effect. In 1912, Alfred Wegener proposed that until 225 million years ago, all of the Earth's land was joined as a single supercontinent, Pangaea, from which our current continents divided and separated. At first, geologists dismissed and even ridiculed this theory, partly because Wegener was a meteorologist, not a geologist. Four decades later, new evidence forced geologists to accept the idea of continental drift.

is not widely respected, proposes a worthwhile idea: The majority may reject the idea at first but adopt it in some form later.

For example, the Socialist Party of the United States ran candidates for president and other elective offices from 1900 through the 1950s. The party made its best showing in 1912 when it received 6% of the vote in the presidential election. None of the Socialists' candidates was ever elected senator or governor; only a few were elected to the House of Representatives (Shannon, 1955). Beginning in the 1930s the party's membership and support began to dwindle, until eventually the party stopped nominating candidates. Was that because the Socialists had given up? No. *It was because they had already accomplished most of their original*

Table 16.3 The Political Platform of the U.S. Socialist Party, 1900

Proposal	Eventual Fate of Proposal
Women's right to vote	Established by 19th amendment to U.S. Constitution, ratified 1920
Old-age pensions	Included in the Social Security Act of 1935
Unemployment insurance	Included in the Social Security Act of 1935; also guaranteed by other state and federal legislation
Health and accident insurance	Included in part in Social Security Act of 1935 and in Medicare Act of 1965
Increased wages, including minimum wage	First minimum-wage law passed in 1938; periodically updated since then
Reduction of working hours	Maximum 40-hour work week (with exceptions) established by Fair Labor Standards Act of 1938
Public ownership of electric, gas, and other utilities and of the means of transportation and communication	Utilities not owned by government, but heavily regulated by federal and state governments since the 1930s
Initiative, referendum, and recall (mechanisms for private citizens to push for changes in legislation and for removal of elected officials)	Adopted by most state governments at various times

Source: Foster, 1968, and Leuchtenburg, 1963.

goals. Most of the major points in the party's 1900 platform had been enacted into law (see Table 16.3). Of course, the Democrats and Republicans who voted for these changes always claimed the ideas were their own. Still, the Socialist party, though always a minority, had exerted an enormous influence on the majority.

If a minority group keeps repeating a single, simple message and if its members seem to be united, eventually it has a good chance of influencing the majority's decision (Moscovici & Mugny, 1983; Nemeth, 1986). By expressing its views, a minority can also prompt the majority to generate new ideas of its own (Nemeth, 1986). That is, by demonstrating the possibility of disagreement, the minority opens the way for other individuals to offer new suggestions different from the original views of both the majority and the minority.

Mahatma Gandhi (1869–1948). With the ambitious goal of unifying a vast nation divided by social and religious differences and using unconventional methods of nonviolent resistance, Gandhi managed gradually to free India from its position as the jewel in the crown of the British Empire. Beginning as a minority of one, he developed a huge following, the respect of his opponents, and worldwide admiration for his steadfastness. Other minority leaders, most notably Martin Luther King, Jr., have effectively drawn from Gandhi's examples of active but peaceful protest.

■ CONCEPT CHECK

6. *At a meeting of your student government, you suggest a new method of testing and grading students. The other members immediately reject your plan. Should you become discouraged and give up? If not, what should you do? (Check your answer on page 697.)*

Ways of Presenting Persuasive Messages

In the presidential campaign of 1964, Lyndon Johnson claimed that the election of his opponent, Barry Goldwater, would mean extremist policies and an increased probability of war. Johnson's tactics succeeded and he won a landslide victory. In the campaign of 1980, Jimmy Carter claimed that the election of his opponent, Ronald Reagan, would mean extremist policies and an increased probability of war. This time the scare tactics failed, and Reagan defeated Carter handily. Why does fear help to persuade people sometimes and not at other times?

Fear messages are effective only if they convince people that the danger is real (Leventhal, 1970). Most voters in 1964 knew little about Goldwater and were prepared to believe he was an extremist. Reagan had been a familiar face for years, and most voters did not believe he would do anything rash. Johnson's charges seemed realistic; Carter's did not.

Moreover, a fear message is effective only if people believe they can do something to prevent the threatened disaster. Frightening messages about AIDS have changed many people's sex practices. Frightening messages about the "greenhouse effect" have proved less persuasive because most people do not see what, if anything, they can do about it.

Finally, if a message is too frightening, people may reject it or ignore it altogether (Chaiken, 1987). If the consequences of AIDS or the greenhouse effect strike people as too severe, they may simply refuse to listen.

Audience Variables

Some people are more easily persuaded than others are, and a given individual may be more easily influenced at some times than at others. The ease of persuading someone depends on both person variables and situation variables.

Person Variables Would you guess that highly intelligent people are persuaded more easily, or less easily, than less intelligent people are? Actually, it depends on the message (McGuire, 1968; Petty & Cacioppo, 1981). Highly intelligent people are quicker to accept a new, complex scientific theory because they can understand the evidence better than less intelligent people can. However, less intelligent people are more likely to accept an illogical or poorly supported idea (Eagly & Warren, 1976).

People's self-esteem also relates to their ease of persuasion. Generally, persuasive messages seem to have their greatest influence on people with an *intermediate* amount of self-esteem (Rhodes & Wood, 1992). Apparently the people with the highest degree of self-esteem resist most attempts to influence them. People with the lowest degree of self-esteem often have some trouble even understanding the persuasive messages.

Situation Variables A persuasive message can become ineffective if people can generate arguments against it. For example, simply informing subjects a few minutes ahead of time that they are about to hear a persuasive speech on a certain topic weakens the effect of the talk on their attitudes (Petty & Cacioppo, 1977); this is called the **forewarning effect.**

In the **inoculation effect,** people first hear a weak argument, then a stronger argument for the same conclusion. After they have rejected the first argument, they are likely to reject the second one also. In one experiment, subjects listened to speeches *against* brushing their teeth after every meal. Some of them heard just a strong argument (for example, "Brushing your teeth too frequently wears away tooth enamel, leading to serious disease"). Others heard first a weak argument, then 2 days later the strong argument. Still others first heard an argument *for* toothbrushing, then the strong argument against it. Only the subjects who heard the weak antibrushing argument before the strong one resisted its influence; the other two groups found it highly persuasive (McGuire & Papageorgis, 1961).

- CONCEPT CHECK

7. *If you want your children to preserve the beliefs and attitudes you try to teach them, should you give them only arguments that support those beliefs or should you also expose them to attacks on those beliefs? Why? (Check your answer on page 697.)*

COGNITIVE DISSONANCE

A few pages back, we considered whether people's behavior will change when their attitudes change. The theory of cognitive dissonance reverses the direction: It holds that when people's behavior changes, their attitudes will change (Festinger, 1957).

Cognitive dissonance is a state of unpleasant tension that people experience when they hold contradictory attitudes or when they behave in a way that is inconsistent with their attitudes. People try to reduce that tension in several ways: They can change their behavior to match their attitudes, change their attitudes to match their behavior, or adopt a new attitude that justifies their behavior under the circumstances (Wicklund & Brehm, 1976). (See Figure 16.12.) For example, Jane, a heavy smoker, believes that cigarette smoking is bad because it causes lung cancer and heart disease. Yet she smokes two packs a day. The inconsistency between her attitudes and her behavior creates dissonance, an unpleasant state of arousal. To

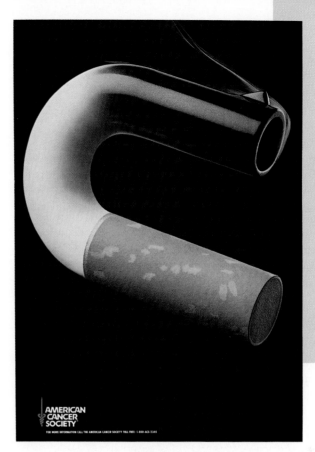

AMERICAN CANCER SOCIETY
FOR MORE INFORMATION CALL THE AMERICAN CANCER SOCIETY TOLL FREE: 1-800-ACS-2345

A fear message may be persuasive if the danger seems realistic and if people see a way to decrease the danger. However, people often ignore excessively frightening messages. An anti-smoking message such as this one may be effective for some viewers, less so for others.

reduce the dissonance, Jane can stop smoking, she can change her attitude—by deciding that cigarette smoking is not really dangerous after all—or she can adopt a new attitude, such as "smoking reduces my tension and keeps me from gaining weight." Although a person might adopt any of these three options, most of the research has focused on ways in which cognitive dissonance changes people's attitudes.

Evidence Favoring Cognitive Dissonance Theory

Leon Festinger and J. Merrill Carlsmith (1959) carried out a classic experiment demonstrating that cognitive dissonance can lead to attitude change. They created dissonance in college students by inducing them to lie to another student. Here's how the experiment worked: Seventy-one male undergraduates were invited to take part in an experiment on "motor behavior." Each subject was individually asked to perform a boring task—for example, rotating pegs on a board over and over again—for an hour. (The task was made as boring as possible, for reasons you will learn in a moment.) Afterward, the experimenter thanked each subject and explained that the study's actual purpose was to see whether the subjects' performance was affected by their attitudes toward the task.

FIGURE 16.12
Cognitive dissonance is a state of tension that arises when people perceive that their attitudes do not match their behaviors. Theoretically, they could resolve this discrepancy by changing either their attitudes or their behavior, or by developing a new attitude or excuse to explain the discrepancy. Most of the research, however, has focused on ways in which cognitive dissonance leads to a change of attitudes.

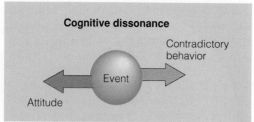

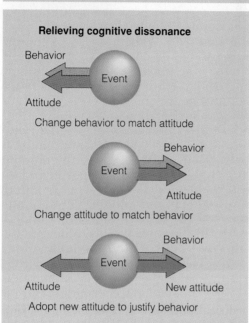

Cognitive dissonance

Contradictory behavior

Event

Attitude

Relieving cognitive dissonance

Behavior

Event

Attitude

Change behavior to match attitude

Behavior

Event

Attitude

Change attitude to match behavior

Behavior

Event

Attitude   New attitude

Adopt new attitude to justify behavior

(This was not in fact the purpose.) The experimenter further explained that some subjects and not others were told that the experiment would be fun and interesting before starting.

As a matter of fact, the experimenter continued, right now the research assistant is supposed to inform the next subject, a young woman waiting in the next room, that the experiment will be fun and interesting. The experimenter excused himself to find the research assistant and then returned distraught a few minutes later. The assistant was nowhere to be found, he said. He turned to the subject and asked, "Would you be willing to tell the next subject that you thought this was an interesting, enjoyable experiment? If so, I will pay you."

Some students were offered $1; others were offered $20. Most of them, regardless of how much they were offered, agreed to tell the woman in the next room that the experiment was interesting. Presumably they experienced cognitive dissonance as they told this whopper of a lie. As they left, thinking the experiment was over, they were met by a representative of the psychology department who explained that the department wanted to find out what kinds of experiments were being conducted and whether they were educationally worthwhile. (The answers to these questions were the real point of the experiment.) Each subject was asked how enjoyable he considered the experiment and whether he would be willing to participate in a similar experiment later.

Which subjects do you think said they liked the experiment more, those who were paid $20 or those who were paid only $1? The students who received $20 said they thought the experiment was boring and that they wanted nothing to do with another such experiment. Those who received just $1 said they enjoyed the experiment and would be glad to participate again (Figure 16.13).

Why? According to the theory of cognitive dissonance, those who accepted $20 to tell a lie experienced little conflict. They knew they were lying, but they also knew why: for the $20. (In the 1950s, when this experiment took place, $20 was worth much more than it is now.) They had no reason to change their original opinion of the experiment—that they were bored to tears.

However, the students who had told a lie for only $1 felt a conflict between their true attitude toward the boring experiment and what they had said about it. The small payment did not provide them with a good reason for lying, so they experienced cognitive dissonance. Because it was too late to take back their lie, the only way they could reduce their dissonance was to change their attitude, to decide that the experiment really was interesting after all. ("I learned a lot of interesting things about myself, like . . . uh . . . how good I am at rotating pegs.")

In a second experiment (Aronson & Carlsmith, 1963), 4-year-old children (one at a time) were shown five toys: a tank, a steam shovel, plastic gears, a fire engine, and a set of dishes and pans. Each child was asked which toy looked like the best one, the second best, and so on. Then the experimenter said he would have to leave the room. He invited the child to play with the toys while he was gone, except, he insisted, "I don't want you to play with the _____," filling in whichever toy the child had ranked second. To some of the children he made a mild threat: "If you played with it, I would be annoyed." To others he made a more severe threat: "If you played with it, I would be very angry. I would have to take all my toys and go home and never come back again. . . . I would think you were just a baby."

The experimenter left for 10 minutes and watched each child through a one-way mirror. All the children dutifully avoided the forbidden toy. Then he returned and asked each child to tell him again which was the best toy, the second best, and so on.

All the children who had received the severe threat ranked the forbidden toy either first or second. They knew why they had avoided the toy, and they had no reason to change their mind about how much they wished they could play with it. However, almost half the children who had heard the mild threat lowered their evaluation of the forbidden toy. They had dissonant beliefs: "I really like that toy" and "I didn't play with it." Why hadn't they played with it? They didn't know. Was it because a man they had never met before said he would be "annoyed"—whatever *that* means? That didn't sound like much of a reason. The only way they could relieve their dissonance was to convince themselves that they did not really like the toy very much.

Whether or not cognitive dissonance arises during the course of an experiment depends on some subtle points of procedure. For example, subjects who behave in ways inconsistent with their attitudes are most likely to experience dissonance if they believe they have chosen their actions freely. They also experience more dissonance if they believe they cannot undo their actions. Subjects in one experiment were asked to say unkind things to another student (Davis & Jones, 1960). Some of them were told they could withdraw from the experiment if they chose; others were told they must perform the task. Independently, some of the subjects were told that they could meet the other student later on and take back the unkind things they had said; other subjects were told that they would have no opportunity to apologize.

Which subjects experienced the greatest amount of dissonance? Those who believed that they had freely chosen to say unkind things and that they could not retract their statements (Figure 16.14). They were also the subjects who changed their attitudes the most during the experiment. In order to justify their actions and relieve their dissonance, they decided that the other student was in fact unlikable and deserved their unkind comments.

■ CONCEPT CHECK

8. *Suppose your parents pay you to make a good grade in some course you consider boring. According to cognitive dissonance theory, are you*

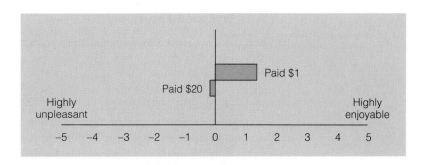

FIGURE 16.13
In a classic experiment demonstrating cognitive dissonance, subjects were paid $1 or $20 for telling another subject that they enjoyed an experiment (which actually was boring). Later they were asked for their real opinions. Those subjects who were paid the smaller amount said they enjoyed the study more. (Based on data from Festinger & Carlsmith, 1959.)

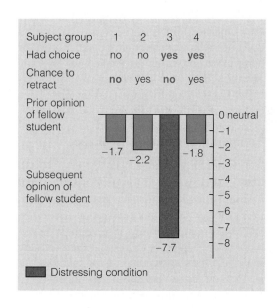

FIGURE 16.14
Students were told to tell another student, "My first impression of you . . . was not too favorable. . . . Your general interests and so on just strike me as those of a pretty shallow person. . . . Frankly, I just wouldn't know how much I could trust you." Students who were told participation was optional but an apology was not possible felt the worst and changed their attitudes the most. (Based on data from Davis & Jones, 1960.)

more likely to develop a positive attitude toward your studies if your parents pay you $10 or $100? Would the theory of intrinsic and extrinsic motivation, discussed in Chapter 11, lead to the same prediction or a different one? (Check your answers on page 697.)

Self-Perception Theory

According to cognitive dissonance theory, people change their attitudes to reduce the tension they experience when their attitudes do not match their behavior. Self-perception theory explains the change in attitude in a different manner. According to **self-perception theory,** subjects in dissonance experiments are simply trying to attribute their behavior to reasonable causes (Bem, 1967, 1972).

For example, in the experiment in which students lied about the boring experiment, they heard themselves saying, "This was a fun experiment," and then asked themselves why they had said that. Those who were paid $20 attributed their behavior to an external cause—they had told a lie for the money. (In other words, they discounted any internal cause for their behavior.) But those who were paid only a dollar for telling the lie could not attribute their behavior to any strong external cause. The only way they could explain their behavior was to attribute it to an internal cause—they must have really enjoyed the experiment.

Comparing Cognitive Dissonance and Self-Perception Theories

Cognitive dissonance theory assumes that arousal is necessary for changes in attitude to take place, whereas self-perception theory assumes that people simply observe their behavior and try to infer logically what their attitude must be. One way to compare the two theories is to ask subjects to behave in ways inconsistent with their attitudes and then measure their heart rate and other physiological indicators of arousal. Such studies find, as cognitive dissonance theory predicts, that situations designed to provoke dissonance do produce heightened arousal (Croyle & Cooper, 1983; Elkin & Leippe, 1986).

A further test: According to dissonance theory, if we could somehow *reduce* the subjects' arousal in dissonance experiments, the subjects should not alter their attitudes much, whereas if we could *increase* their arousal, they should alter their attitudes to a greater degree than usual. In one experiment, subjects in one group were given tranquilizers (to reduce their arousal), and subjects in a second group were given amphetamines (to heighten it). Subjects in a third group were given a placebo. All the subjects were then asked to write an essay in favor of a position the experimenters knew they disagreed with. Writing such an essay produces

cognitive dissonance; the subjects think, "Why am I writing this? I thought I disagreed with this." Frequently subjects relieve their dissonance by changing their attitudes to match what they are writing. In this experiment, as predicted, the subjects who had received amphetamines changed their attitudes the most, and the subjects who had received tranquilizers changed them the least. In short, the greater the tension, the greater the attitude change.

Does this result mean that self-perception theory is wrong? No. Self-perception theory can explain some phenomena that dissonance theory cannot. For example, when you are rewarded for doing something you enjoy, your behavior is fully consistent with your attitudes and dissonance theory does not apply. However, self-perception theory correctly predicts that when you are rewarded for doing something enjoyable, you discount the internal cause of your behavior and enjoy the activity less than usual.

One suggestion is that dissonance theory and self-perception theory apply to different situations (Fazio, Zanna, & Cooper, 1977). We feel strong dissonance when our behavior is highly inconsistent with our firmly established attitudes. We are influenced by self-perception when our behavior is only mildly inconsistent with our attitudes or when our attitudes were not clearly formed to begin with (Fazio, 1987). As is often the case in psychology, separate processes—here, cognitive dissonance and self-perception—lead to the same result.

SUMMARY

■ *Attitudes.* An attitude is a learned like or dislike of something or somebody that influences our behavior toward that thing or person. (page 688)

■ *Relationship between attitudes and behavior.* Attitudes are rather poor predictors of behavior, especially a single behavior in a single situation, because many other factors influence behavior. (page 688)

■ *Two routes to persuasion.* When people are in a good mood, or when they are considering an appeal on a topic of little importance, they are easily persuaded by the speaker's appearance and other superficial factors, regardless of the strength or weakness of the evidence. When people are in a bad mood, or when they consider an appeal on a matter of importance to them, they pay more attention to the quality of the evidence and logic. (page 689)

- *Sleeper effect*. When people reject a message because of their low regard for the person who proposed it, they sometimes forget where they heard the idea and come to accept it later. (page 690)

- *Minority influence*. Although a minority may have little influence at first, it may, through persistent repetition of its message, eventually persuade the majority to adopt its position or to consider other alternatives. (page 690)

- *Influence of fear-inducing messages*. Whether or not messages that appeal to fear prove effective depends on whether people perceive the danger as real and on whether they think they can do anything about it. (page 692)

- *Forewarning and inoculation effects*. People evaluate the reasoning behind the persuasive messages they hear. If they have been warned that someone will try to persuade them of something, or if they have previously heard a weak version of the persuasive argument, they tend to resist the persuasive argument more strongly than they otherwise would have. (page 692)

- *Cognitive dissonance*. Cognitive dissonance is a state of unpleasant tension that arises from contradictory attitudes or from behavior that conflicts with a person's attitudes. When people behave in a way that does not match their attitudes, they reduce the inconsistency by changing either their behavior or their attitudes. (page 693)

- *Self-perception theory*. Self-perception theory holds that people try to find reasonable causes to which they can attribute their behavior. (page 696)

SUGGESTION FOR FURTHER READING

Petty, R. E., & Cacioppo, J. T. (1981). *Attitudes and persuasion: Classic and contemporary approaches.* Dubuque, IA: Wm. C. Brown. A complete yet readable review of research on attitudes and attitude change.

TERMS

attitude a learned like or dislike of something or somebody that influences our behavior toward that thing or person (page 688)

high self-monitor person who constantly monitors his or her own behavior to try to make the right impression (page 688)

central route to persuasion method of persuasion based on careful evaluation of evidence and logic (page 689)

peripheral route to persuasion method of persuasion based on such superficial factors as the speaker's appearance and reputation or the sheer number of arguments presented, regardless of their quality (page 689)

sleeper effect delayed persuasion by an initially rejected message (page 690)

forewarning effect tendency of a brief preview of a message to decrease its persuasiveness (page 693)

inoculation effect tendency of a persuasive message to be weakened if people first hear a weak argument for the same conclusion (page 693)

cognitive dissonance a state of unpleasant tension that people experience when they hold contradictory attitudes or when they behave in a way that is inconsistent with their attitudes (page 693)

self-perception theory theory that subjects in dissonance experiments are simply trying to attribute their behavior to reasonable causes (page 696)

ANSWERS TO CONCEPT CHECKS

5. You will pay more attention to the evidence and logic, following the central route to persuasion, for the decision about your major. (page 690)

6. The fact that your idea was overwhelmingly rejected does not mean that you should give up. If you and a few allies continue presenting this plan in a simple way, showing apparent agreement among yourselves, the majority may eventually endorse some plan similar to it—even if they fail to give you credit for suggesting the idea. (page 692)

7. You should expose them to weak attacks on their beliefs so that they will learn how to resist such attacks. Otherwise, they will be like children who grow up in a germ-free environment: They will develop no "immunity" and will be vulnerable when their beliefs are attacked. (page 693)

8. You will come to like your studies more if you are paid $10 than if you are paid $100. If you are paid only $10, you won't be able to tell yourself you are doing it only for the money. Instead, you will tell yourself that you must be really interested. The theory of intrinsic and extrinsic motivation leads to the same prediction: If you study hard in the absence of any strong external reason, you will perceive that you have internal reasons for studying. (page 695)

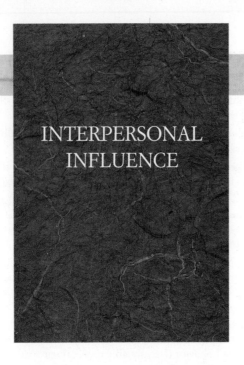

INTERPERSONAL INFLUENCE

Under what circumstances do we conform to the behavior of others?

Under what circumstances do we behave as others tell us to?

Why do people act differently in groups from when they are alone?

In the spring of 1983, a strange epidemic swept through a Palestinian village in one of the territories occupied by Israel. The hospitals were flooded with people, mostly adolescents, complaining of headaches, dizzy spells, stomach pains, blurred vision, and difficulty breathing. The Palestinians accused the Israelis of poisoning the air or the water, perhaps in an effort to sterilize the young Palestinian women. The Israelis replied with heated denials.

Meanwhile, although physicians conducted extensive tests on all the patients, they could find nothing medically wrong. They studied the food, the air, the water, every possible source of poison or of contagious disease. They found no signs of anything that could cause illness. Finally they concluded that all the symptoms were the result of anxiety, coupled with the power of suggestion (Paicheler, 1988). The Palestinians, understandably nervous about the political tensions in the region, *believed* they had been poisoned; this belief and the accompanying symptoms of illness spread from person to person just like a contagious disease.

We live in an ambiguous world. Often we do not understand what is happening or what we should do about it; when in doubt, we take our cues from what other people are doing or what they tell us to do. And that is fine—provided that the other people are better informed or wiser than we are.

CONFORMITY

We often conform our actions to those of the group around us. **Conformity** means maintaining or changing one's behavior to match the behavior of others. Sometimes we conform because we want to be like others; for example, we might intentionally copy the way other people dress, especially people we like or admire. At other times we might simply use other people's behavior as a guide to what is normal or acceptable behavior. For example, if we see someone drop a piece of trash in an already littered environment, we conclude that doing so is acceptable and we become more likely to drop our own trash (Cialdini, Kallgren, & Reno, 1991).

Do people conform more in some situations than in others? Early research suggested that people conform strongly when they are not confident of their own opinions and look to others for guidance (Sherif, 1935). Do people conform even when they are confident of their own opinions? To answer that question, Solomon Asch (1951, 1956) carried out a now-famous series of experiments.

Asch assembled groups of students and asked them to look at a vertical bar, as shown at left in Figure 16.15, which was defined as the model. He also showed them three other vertical bars (right half of Figure 16.15), and asked them which bar was the same length as the model. As you can see, the task is simple. Asch asked the students to give their answers aloud. He repeated the procedure with 18 sets of bars.

Only one student in each group was a real subject. All the others were confederates who had been instructed to give incorrect answers on 12 of the 18 trials. Asch arranged for the real subject to be the next-to-the-last person in the group to announce his answer so that he would hear most of the confederates' incorrect re-

FIGURE 16.15
Choosing conformity: In Asch's conformity studies, subjects asked to match a line with one of three other lines on another card were surrounded by experimental accomplices who gave obviously wrong answers.

sponses before giving his own (Figure 16.16). Would he go along with the crowd?

To Asch's surprise, 37 of the 50 subjects conformed to the majority at least once, and 14 of them conformed on more than 6 of the 12 trials on which the majority was wrong. When faced with a unanimous wrong answer by the other group members, the mean subject conformed on 4 of the 12 trials. Asch was disturbed by these results: "That we have found the tendency to conformity in our society so strong . . . is a matter of concern. It raises questions about our ways of education and about the values that guide our conduct" (Asch, 1955, p. 34).

Why did the subjects conform so readily? When they were interviewed after the experiment, some said they thought the rest of the group was correct or that they guessed some optical illusion was influencing the appearance. Others said they knew their conforming answers were wrong, but went along with the group for fear of being ridiculed or thought "peculiar." Reactions of the nonconforming subjects were interesting too: Some were very nervous but felt duty-bound to tell how the bars looked to them. A few seemed socially withdrawn, as if they paid no attention to anyone

A religious assembly poses powerful forces toward conformity. People take their cues for behavior from what other people are doing; anyone who fails to conform may be discouraged from continued membership in the group.

FIGURE 16.16
Three of the eight subjects in one of Asch's experiments on conformity. The one in the middle is the real subject; the others are the experimenter's confederates. (From Asch, 1951.) In this test of group pressure's power to induce conformity, people had only to disagree with strangers for a short time. The correct answers were clear—yet most subjects felt a strong pressure to conform to what the majority said.

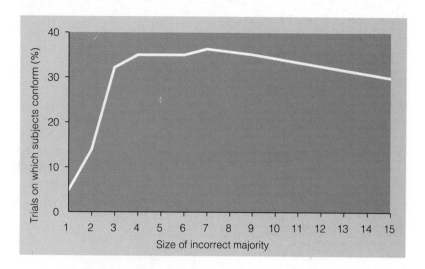

FIGURE 16.17
Asch (1955) found that conformity became more frequent as group size increased up to about three and then leveled off. But when subjects had an "ally," conformity decreased considerably.

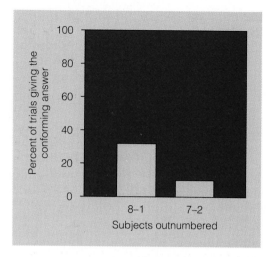

FIGURE 16.18
In Asch's experiments, subjects who were faced with a unanimous majority giving wrong answers conformed to the majority view on 32% of trials. Subjects who had one "ally" giving the correct answer were less likely to conform. Evidently it is difficult to be in a minority of one, but less difficult to be in a minority of two.

else. Still others were supremely self-confident, as if to say, "I'm right and everyone else is wrong. It happens all the time."

Asch (1951, 1955) found that one of the situational factors that influence conformity is the size of the opposing majority. In a series of studies, he varied the number of confederates who gave incorrect answers from 1 to 15. He found that the subjects conformed to a group of 3 or 4 as readily as they did to a larger group (Figure 16.17). However, the subjects conformed much less if they had an "ally." In some of his experiments, Asch instructed one of the confederates to give correct answers. In the presence of this nonconformist, the real subjects conformed only occasionally (Figure 16.18). Apparently, it is difficult to be a minority of one but not so difficult to be part of a minority of two.

ACCEPTING OR DENYING RESPONSIBILITY TOWARD OTHERS

Sometimes other people encourage us to do something we would not have done on our own, as in the case of Asch's studies. Sometimes other people inhibit us from doing something we would have done on our own. We look

around and see what others are doing—or *not* doing—and we say, "Okay, I'll do that too. I'll do my fair share—no more, no less." Why do people sometimes work together to help one another, and sometimes ignore the needs of others?

Bystander Helpfulness or Apathy

Suppose while you are waiting at a bus stop you see me trip and fall down, just 30 meters away from you. I am not screaming in agony but I am not getting up right away either, so you are not sure whether or not I need help. Do you think you probably would come over and offer your help? Or would you just stand there apathetically (without showing signs of caring)? Before you answer, try imagining the situation two ways: First, you and I are the only people in sight. Second, there are a lot of other people nearby, none of whom is rushing to my aid. Does the presence of those other people make any difference to your response? (Note that it doesn't change *my* predicament. I am in the same amount of pain, regardless of whether it is one person or many people who are ignoring me.)

Late one night in March, 1964, Kitty Genovese was stabbed to death near her apartment in Queens, New York. For 30 minutes, 38 of her neighbors listened to her screams. A few stood at their windows watching. None of them came to her aid or called the police. Why?

Bibb Latané and John Darley (1969) proposed that one reason the neighbors failed to help was **diffusion of responsibility**—the fact that we feel less responsibility for helping when other people are around than when we know that no one else can help. Latane and Darley suggest that no one helped Kitty Genovese because everyone knew that there were many other people on the scene who *could* help her.

In an experiment designed to test this hypothesis, a young woman ushered either one student or two students into a room and asked them to wait a few minutes for the start of a market research study (Latané & Darley, 1968, 1969). She then went into the next room, closing the door behind her. There she played a tape recording that made it sound as if she had climbed onto a chair and had fallen off. For about 2 minutes she could be heard crying and moaning, "Oh . . . my foot . . . I can't move it. Oh . . . my ankle. . . ." Of the subjects who were waiting alone, 70% went next-door and offered to help. Of the subjects who were waiting with someone else, only 13% offered to help.

Diffusion of responsibility is one possible explanation. Each person thinks, "It's not my responsibility to help any more than it is the other person's. And if we get blamed for not helping, it's as much that person's fault as it is mine." A second possible explanation is that the presence of another person changes the way we react to an ambiguous situation: "Does that woman need help or not? I'm not really sure. This other person isn't doing anything, so maybe she doesn't."

Social Loafing

Sometimes your success and rewards depend entirely on your own efforts. For example, when you take a test in one of your college courses, you must work alone. (You can get into real trouble if you and a fellow student decide to "cooperate"!) In other cases, however, you work with other people as part of a team. For example, if you work for a company that gives workers a share of the profits, your rewards depend on both your own productivity and that of other workers. Do you work as hard when rewards depend on the group's productivity as when they depend on your own efforts alone?

In a tug-of-war or other task in which individuals pool their efforts, most people do not work as hard as they would when working alone. This is called "social loafing." However, if participants know that each individual's contribution will be measured separately, social loafing ceases and everyone puts out a full effort.

The answer is, probably not—at least under certain circumstances. In one experiment, students were told to scream and clap and try to make as loud a noise as possible, like cheerleaders at a sports event. Sometimes each student screamed and clapped alone; sometimes students acted in groups of 2 to 6; and sometimes they acted alone but *thought* that other people were screaming and clapping too. (They wore headphones so that they could not hear anyone else.) As a rule, a student who screamed and clapped alone made more noise than a student who was (or thought he or she was) screaming and clapping as part of a group (Latané, Williams, & Harkins, 1979). Social psychologists call this observation **social loafing**—the tendency to "loaf" (or work less hard) when sharing the work with other people. Social loafing has been demonstrated for several other behaviors, not just for screaming. For example, suppose you were asked to "name all the uses you can think of for a brick" (such as *crack nuts, anchor a boat,* or *use as door stop*) and write each one on a card. You probably would need a tall stack of cards if you were working by yourself, but you would fill out fewer cards if you were tossing them into a pile along with other peo-

FIGURE 16.19
During an emergency, people abandon their usual tendencies toward bystander apathy and social loafing. During the 1989 earthquake in the San Francisco area, authorities ordered the residents in one area to evacuate their residences within 15 minutes. People who usually ignored one another immediately pitched in to help one another move their valuables.

ple's suggestions, to be evaluated as a group (Harkins & Jackson, 1985).

At this point you may be thinking, "Wait a minute. When I'm playing on a basketball team, I try as hard as I can. I don't think I do any social loafing." And you are right; social loafing seldom occurs in team sports. The reason is that observers, including teammates, can easily see who is contributing and who is not. Even though the team wins or loses as a group, individual players also compete for recognition as individuals. Even for behaviors such as yelling and screaming or thinking of odd uses for a brick, people put out their full effort on a group task if they know that their own contribution can be evaluated afterward (Harkins & Jackson, 1985; Williams, Harkins, & Latané, 1981).

Participants also put out a full effort if they believe their contribution will make a difference in achieving success. For example, if you and your partner are both trying to think of odd uses for a brick, and the two of you are throwing your cards into the same stack, then you know that most of the uses you generate will duplicate your partner's, so an extra effort may not make much difference. But if you have reason to believe your partner is not very good at this task, you will work as hard as if you were on your own (Williams & Karau, 1991). Also, if you are part

of a group in which each person is trying to think of odd uses for a different object (instead of all trying to think of uses for a brick or any other single object), then your ideas will not duplicate anyone else's contributions. Under such circumstances, social loafing disappears (Harkins & Petty, 1982).

■ CONCEPT CHECKS

9. *Given what we have learned about social loafing, why are most people unlikely to work hard to clean up the environment?*

10. *Suppose the head of a large library wants the library staff to pay more attention to getting all the books into their correct locations. Currently many of the books are misplaced and the staff seem to be "loafing" at rearranging them. What could be done to encourage greater efforts? (Check your answers on page 707.)*

Volunteerism

The preceding sections may have given an exaggerated impression. Perhaps you inferred that "no one ever takes responsibility for helping anyone else" and that "everyone is content to let someone else do the work." That conclusion is not correct, at least not for all the people all the time.

When serious needs and problems arise in society, great numbers of volunteers respond with their time and money (Figure 16.19). For example, consider the problem of AIDS victims, some of whom find themselves shunned by strangers and virtually deserted by their family and friends. To meet this need, volunteer organizations have developed in many cities to provide "AIDS buddies," healthy people who offer comfort, assistance, and companionship to AIDS victims. Most of the people who volunteer to become AIDS buddies do not consider themselves to be at high risk for developing AIDS themselves; they do not have careers in psychology or medicine; they expect no reward or recognition for themselves. Apparently they volunteer simply as a way of expressing their values and their desire to help others (Omoto & Snyder, 1990). Volunteers also staff many other organizations devoted to health, education, environmental protection, and similar important causes. In short, some people—somehow—resist the pressures of bystander apathy and social loafing.

GROUP DECISION MAKING

An organization that needs to make some decision will frequently set up a committee to look into the issues and make recommendations. We prefer a committee to an individual because the committee has more time, more total information, and fewer peculiarities and biases than any individual has. Nevertheless, as we have just seen, a group is subject to the influences of conformity and social loafing, which sometimes interfere with its reaching the best possible decisions.

Group Polarization

If a group is composed of people who nearly all lean the same direction on a particular issue, then as they discuss that issue, the group as a whole will tend to move even further in that direction. Consequently, the group probably will vote for a more extreme decision than most of its members favored at the start (Lamm & Myers, 1978). This phenomenon is known as **group polarization.** Note that in this case *polarization* does not mean that the group breaks up into fragments who favor different positions. Rather, it means that the members of a group, after discussing the issues, move together toward one *pole* (extreme position) or the other.

For example, in one study in the 1960s, French students were asked first to report their attitudes toward Americans and toward Charles de Gaulle, then president of France. Most of them expressed negative attitudes toward Americans and positive attitudes toward de Gaulle. After discussing the questions as a group, most of them became more extreme in their anti-American and pro-de Gaulle attitudes (Moscovici & Zavalloni, 1969).

Group polarization occurs for at least two reasons: increased information and the pressure to conform (Isenberg, 1986). During the group discussion, the members become aware of new arguments and new information. If most of the members were leaning in one direction at the start, the group hears arguments mostly favoring that side of the issue (Burnstein & Vinokur, 1973, 1977). And as the members of the group become aware of the consensus during the discussion, they feel pressure to conform. But notice that the pressure to conform is strongest for people who only slightly supported the group's position at the start. The people who at first supported that view most

vigorously feel little if any pressure to soften or moderate their stance.

Limits on Conformity and Group Polarization

Group polarization will occur much more strongly in some groups than in others. Let's consider two examples.

First, suppose you join a society opposed to the death penalty. At first you are, say, moderately opposed to the death penalty, although you have some mixed feelings. After attending a few meetings, you hear many arguments against the death penalty and you discover that you win people's friendship by expressing your own opposition to the death penalty. We can safely predict that your opinions will become stronger and more extreme.

Second example: Suppose you go to law school and you find that the first-year law students spend a great deal of time discussing the pros and cons of the death penalty. Here, 85% of your fellow students support the death penalty; you are part of the minority who oppose it. However, although you hear mostly arguments supporting the death penalty, you will not necessarily switch your views to conform to that of the majority. A group that starts with a nearly unanimous opinion generally becomes more extreme (group polarization), but a group that starts with a significant difference of opinion can remain permanently divided.

For a long time, social psychologists were puzzled by that observation. Why shouldn't the pressure from the majority eventually persuade everyone to conform? Apparently the main reason is that people holding the minority view associate with others who hold that view. They influence one another and thereby immunize themselves from the majority view. A speaker who seems very persuasive to other people may seem biased, unfair, and totally unpersuasive to holders of the minority view. In that manner the holders of the minority view resist pressures toward conformity (Nowak, Szamrej, & Latané, 1990).

Groupthink

An extreme form of group polarization is known as **groupthink,** in which the members of a group actively silence all dissenters and move quickly toward a poorly thought-out decision (Janis, 1972, 1985). Groupthink is most likely to occur in a highly cohesive group, such as a

Many organizations try to resist the tendency toward group-think—the tendency to stifle dissenting views and proceed to a possibly disastrous decision. During the Renaissance, European kings sometimes called on a "fool" (or court jester) to describe some proposal in a fresh and possibly amusing light. In a court composed largely of yes-men, the fool sometimes was the only one who could publicly point out the folly of some proposed action. (From Roger von Oech's Creative Whack Pack; *art by George Willett; © Roger von Oech 1992.)*

fraternal or religious organization, in which the members think it would be rude to criticize one another's views. Rather than spoil the harmony, they keep silent and pretend to agree. Group-think also occurs when the group leaders make it clear that they do not wish to hear objections to their plans.

One dramatic example of groupthink led to the Bay of Pigs fiasco of 1962 (Janis, 1972). U.S. President John F. Kennedy and his advisers were considering a plan to support a small-scale invasion of Cuba at the Bay of Pigs. The assumption was that a small group of Cuban exiles could overwhelm the Cuban army and trigger a spontaneous rebellion of the Cuban people against Fidel Castro and the Communist government. Kennedy's advisers raised few questions to challenge that assumption. When one adviser expressed doubts, he was told that he was being disloyal and that he should support the president, who had already made up his mind. Within a few hours after the invasion began, all the invaders were killed or captured. The decision makers (and everyone else) wondered how they could have made such a stupid decision.

Another example of groupthink was NASA's decision to launch the space shuttle *Challenger* on a cold morning in 1986 despite protests from the project engineers that the rocket booster was unsafe at low temperatures. The top decision makers let it be known that there were strong economic and public-relations reasons for launching the shuttle on schedule and that they wanted to hear no objections. Seventy-three seconds after the launch, the *Challenger* exploded because of an O-ring that was unable to function at low temperatures.

In both the Bay of Pigs incident and the *Challenger* disaster, a cohesive group under strong leadership made a disastrous decision. The leaders and some of the group members discouraged dissent and created an illusion of unanimous support.

Irving Janis (1985) suggests several techniques for reducing the likelihood of groupthink: Leaders should encourage dissent. The group can be divided into subgroups to see whether, in independent discussions, they arrive at the same conclusions. Leaders should consult their advisers one by one in private. The group should seek the advice of outside experts, including those with dissenting opinions. Regardless of whether a leader takes such steps or not, members with their doubts about a decision should remember the lessons of the Bay of Pigs and the *Challenger*: When much is at stake, it is better to risk angering one's leader than to go along with a possibly disastrous decision.

The Psychology of Juries

Jury trials offer an important and rather unusual example of group decision making. Ordinarily the people who make an important decision for a company have been selected for their special competence, and they know that they will reap the rewards or suffer the consequences for their decisions. By contrast, a jury is composed of people with no special competence, who probably do not know one another, and who need not even explain their decision, much less accept any consequences from it. The results of a jury trial depend, of course, largely on the evidence, but they also depend on the selection of jurors and the judge's instructions to the jury.

Jury Selection Before a trial begins, the judge, the prosecuting attorney, and the defense attorney interview prospective jurors in a process called *voir dire,* an Old French term meaning "to tell the truth." Prospective jurors are asked whether they have already formed an opinion based on accounts in the media, and whether for any other reason they would be unable to render a fair and impartial verdict. The judge excuses "for cause" anyone who could not render an impartial judgment. The two attorneys can ask the prospective jurors additional questions and make a certain number of **peremptory challenges,** rejecting prospective jurors without explanation. The permitted number of peremptory challenges may be only 2 or 3 in a routine case, but 20 or more in a heavily publicized case. The attorneys use their peremptory challenges to eliminate jurors who seem to have a bias in favor of the other side. Presumably those who survive all the challenges by both sides constitute a fair, impartial jury.

Special problems arise in jury selection for death-penalty cases. Prior to 1968, any prospective juror who opposed the death penalty was excluded "for cause" from the jury of a murder trial. In the *Witherspoon* decision of that year, the Supreme Court ruled that opponents of the death penalty can be excluded for cause only if they are so opposed that they would vote against the death penalty in all cases, regardless of the evidence. People who are unconditionally opposed to the death penalty are referred to as **death-scrupled.** Those who are willing to consider the death penalty under certain circumstances are referred to as **death-qualified**— that is, they are qualified to serve on death-penalty cases. (*Death-qualified* does not mean "qualified to die.")

Many social psychologists have challenged the wisdom of excluding death-scrupled people from juries. One reason is that more blacks than whites are death-scrupled, as well as more women than men and more young people than older people (Fitzgerald & Ellsworth, 1984). Consequently, a young black defendant in a murder case often faces a jury composed mostly of older white men. A second reason for objecting is that death-qualified people tend to be more sympathetic to the prosecution, while death-scrupled people tend to be more sympathetic to the defense. A fair jury should include both kinds of people. Psychologists have found, for example, that death-qualified people are more likely than death-scrupled people are to agree with this statement: "All laws should be strictly enforced, no matter what the results." They are less likely to agree with this statement:

A jury trial begins with the voir dire, *a process of interviewing and eliminating potential jurors. Some jurors are eliminated for cause because they have already formed an opinion. Others are eliminated by* peremptory *challenges by either the prosecutor or the defense attorney. One controversial issue is whether it is fair to eliminate potential jurors in a death-penalty case for cause just because they oppose the death penalty. Critics argue that eliminating such people stacks the jury with jurors more likely than most people are to find the defendant guilty.*

"It is better for society to let some guilty people go free than to risk convicting an innocent person" (Fitzgerald & Ellsworth, 1984).

Several studies have compared the reactions to mock trials of death-qualified people and death-scrupled people. In a particularly thorough study (Cowan, Thompson, & Ellsworth, 1984), adult (nonstudent) subjects watched a realistic 2 1/2 hour videotape of a dramatized murder trial. They were then assigned to 12-person juries and asked to deliberate for an hour. Ten of the juries consisted entirely of death-qualified people; ten included 2 to 4 death-scrupled people. The videotape had been designed to present a borderline case. Evidently it succeeded, because no jury reached a verdict within the allotted hour. The juries that included death-scrupled people were more critical of the evidence presented by both the prosecution and the defense, and the death-scrupled people were more likely to vote for acquittal than the death-qualified people (Figure 16.20).

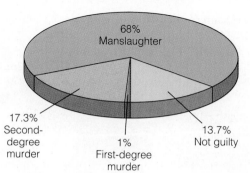

Death-qualified people

68% Manslaughter

17.3% Second-degree murder

1% First-degree murder

13.7% Not guilty

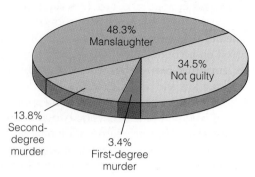

Death-scrupled people

48.3% Manslaughter

34.5% Not guilty

13.8% Second-degree murder

3.4% First-degree murder

FIGURE 16.20

Death-qualified people are those qualified to serve on a jury for a death-penalty case. Death-scrupled people are those who say they could never vote in favor of the death penalty; under current U.S. law, such people cannot serve on juries when the prosecution is seeking the death penalty. In one experiment, mock juries considered the guilt or innocence of a defendant. They were given evidence designed to make the case difficult to decide. Death-scrupled people were far more likely than death-qualified people were to vote "not guilty." This evidence suggests that excluding death-scrupled people tilts the jury toward conviction. (Based on data of Cowan, Thompson, & Ellsworth, 1984.)

Apparently, then, the exclusion of death-scrupled people makes juries less representative and decreases the defendant's chances of getting a fair trial in a murder trial.

Many attorneys as well as psychologists have argued for keeping death-scrupled people on juries, at least for the phase of the trial that considers guilt or innocence. So far, the courts and legislatures have asked for more research before they make any such decision.

The Judge's Instructions At various points during a trial, the judge may instruct the jury to ignore certain statements made by one of the attorneys or witnesses. According to the research, most jurors find that instruction difficult to follow (Sue, Smith, & Caldwell, 1973). Imagine yourself as a juror: You just heard someone say that the defendant failed a lie-detector test, but the judge says to ignore that statement, because the evidence is not admissible. How thoroughly could you ignore it?

At the end of a trial, the judge explains to the jury the relevant portions of the law as they apply to the case at hand. For example, the judge might explain that the prosecution has the "burden of proof"; if in doubt about the de-

fendant's guilt, the jury should vote to acquit. For many years, judges and lawyers paid relatively little attention to this phase of the trial, apparently believing it was important to *state* the law but not important to be sure the jury *understands* the law. However, research has shown that alterations in the judge's instructions can greatly alter the jury's understanding and its probability of convicting or acquitting the defendant (Luginbuhl, 1992).

Again, some special problems arise in death-penalty cases. During the voir dire for a death-penalty case, the judge informs prospective jurors that if they find the defendant guilty in this case, they may be asked to decide about the death penalty. The judge then asks whether or not each person could consider the death penalty under various possible circumstances. Unfortunately, simply asking all of these questions about "whether you might vote for the death penalty if you find the defendant guilty" implies that the jury probably *will* find the defendant guilty (Haney, 1984). In short, decision making by a jury is like other examples of group decision making: They can be strongly influenced by seemingly minor changes in procedures, instructions, or the makeup of the group.

SUMMARY

■ *Conformity.* Many people conform to the majority view even when they are confident that the majority is wrong. An individual is as likely to conform to a group of three as to a larger group, but an individual who has an ally is less likely to conform to the majority. (page 698)

■ *Diffusion of responsibility.* People in groups are less likely than an isolated individual to come to the aid of another because they experience a diffusion of responsibility. (page 700)

■ *Social loafing.* People working together on a task tend to exert less effort than people who are working independently. However, they will work just as hard on the group task if they are evaluated on their individual performances or if they believe their contributions will make a big difference to the group's success. (page 701)

■ *Group polarization.* Groups of people who lean mostly in the same direction on a given issue often make decisions that are more extreme than the decisions most individuals would have made on their own. However, if a group is divided in their opinions at the start, some support for the minority opinion may remain in the group permanently. (page 703)

■ *Groupthink.* Groupthink occurs when members of a cohesive group fail to express their opposition to a decision or when the leaders of the group try to silence dissent. (page 703)

■ *Psychology of juries.* Juries are groups of non-experts who make important, even life-or-death, decisions. Social psychologists have investigated the influence of the judge's instructions and the selection of people to compose the jury. (page 704)

SUGGESTIONS FOR FURTHER READING

Cialdini, R. B. (1988). *Influence: Science and practice* (2nd ed.). Glenview, IL: Scott, Foresman. A book full of instructive and entertaining examples on how people try to influence one another. Highly recommended.

Janis, I. (1982). *Groupthink: Psychological studies of policy decisions and fiascoes.* (2nd ed.) Boston: Houghton Mifflin. Gives fascinating examples of how groups sometimes make disastrous decisions by stifling dissent.

TERMS

conformity maintaining or changing one's behavior to match the behavior of others (page 698)

diffusion of responsibility tendency to feel less responsibility for helping when other people are around than when we know that no one else can help (page 701)

social loafing tendency to "loaf" (or work less hard) when sharing the work with other people (page 701)

group polarization tendency for a group whose members lean in the same direction on a particular issue to become more extreme in its opinion after discussing the issue (page 703)

groupthink process in which the members of a group actively silence all dissenters and move quickly toward a poorly thought-out decision (page 703)

peremptory challenge rejection of a prospective juror by an attorney without explanation (page 705)

death-scrupled a person who opposes the death penalty under all circumstances (page 705)

death-qualified a person who is qualified to serve on death-penalty cases because of willingness to consider voting for the death penalty (page 705)

ANSWERS TO CONCEPT CHECKS

9. For the task of protecting the environment, each person is part of a "group" with billions of other people. Social loafing is likely because many one-person contributions, such as picking up litter, would not earn individual credit or recognition. Also, each person thinks, "What good could one person do on such a gigantic problem?" When people believe their own contribution would not make a noticeable difference, they tend to engage in social loafing. (page 702)

10. One approach would be to make the contributions of each staff member more apparent (because social loafing is common when people do not see that their own efforts make much difference). For example, assign each person a different set of shelves and report data on which shelves have shown the greatest improvement in their orderliness. A similar approach can be used for other examples of loafing on the job. (page 702)

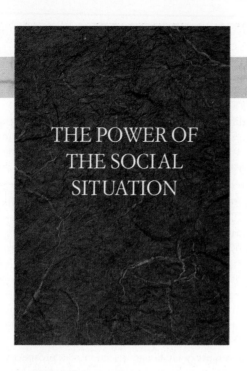

THE POWER OF THE SOCIAL SITUATION

Why do people sometimes engage in self-defeating behaviors?

How can we change the situation to minimize such behaviors?

Back in the 1960s, a number of world problems seemed to threaten the very future of civilization. The Vietnam War seemed to go on forever; the nations of the world seemed to be preparing for global nuclear war; racial injustice and discrimination were widespread in the United States; we were beginning to recognize how badly people were damaging the environment. As a high school and then college student at the time, I had grandiose dreams that I was going to save the world. I wasn't sure how—maybe through my great moral leadership (I told you I had "grandiose dreams"!), maybe through politics, maybe through psychological research. I hoped somehow to change human nature so that people would stop being so cruel and selfish.

Now here we are 30 years later, and I reflect on the people who really did improve the world in major and spectacular ways. Some of the first such people who come to mind made their impact through moral leadership or politics—Martin Luther King, Jr., Mother Teresa, Mikhail Gorbachev, Boris Yeltsin, and others. But there have also been some people who improved the world through technology—a route that I never even contemplated during my

youthful "save the world" fantasies. For example, the engineers who devised spy satellites made possible the international treaties banning tests of nuclear weapons. (Without the capacity to watch one another, competing countries would never have agreed to such treaties.) The engineers who developed computers, printers, and modems spread freedom of the press to every technologically advanced country. (Any country that lets people have computers lets them have printing presses.) These technological advances changed human *behavior* without changing human *nature*.

The general point here is that much of our behavior is controlled by the situation—sometimes the technological situation, sometimes the social situation. On occasion some person or a social situation pressures us, or virtually compels us, to behave in cruel, uncooperative, even self-defeating ways. We need to recognize the power of these situations so that we can deal with them, change them, or avoid them altogether.

BEHAVIOR TRAPS

What would you think of someone who knowingly paid a great deal more for something than it was worth? Or someone who confessed to a crime even though the police admitted they did not have enough evidence for a conviction? Or someone who used up all of his or her resources at once instead of saving some for later? You probably would question that person's intelligence or sanity. And yet under certain circumstances you might find yourself engaging in similar behaviors yourself. Sometimes we get into a **behavior trap**—a situation that almost forces us into self-defeating behaviors. We call such situations "traps" because people wander into them without realizing the danger; once they see the danger, they cannot find their way out of the situation. We shall consider three examples—the dollar auction, the prisoner's dilemma, and the commons dilemma.

The Dollar Auction

Imagine you and I and a few other people are at an auction. The auctioneer explains that the next item up for bids is a dollar bill, which she will sell to the highest bidder, even if the highest bid is only a few cents. There is one catch, however; at the end, when someone finally buys the dollar bill, the second-highest bidder must pay his or her bid to the auctioneer also, receiving nothing in return. So, for example, if I bid 5 cents, you bid 10 cents, and the bidding stops there, you would buy the dollar bill for 10 cents and I would simply lose my 5 cents.

Suppose we think this sounds like fun and we plunge right in. I bid 5 cents, you bid 10, I bid 15, and the bidding continues. Eventually you bid 90 cents and I bid 95. Now what do you do? If you let me have the dollar bill for 95 cents, you will lose 90 cents. So you bid a dollar, hoping at least to break even. What do I do? If I stop bidding, I lose 95 cents. But if I can buy the dollar for $1.05, I sustain a net loss of only 5 cents. So I bid $1.05. Then you bid $1.10, because you would rather lose 10 cents than lose a whole dollar. And so on. After a while we start to lose track of the economics and we start to get angry with each other. After all, as soon as one of us quits bidding, the other one "wins."

Psychologists have repeatedly set up such a situation to see what would happen. They have usually managed to sell their dollar bills for prices over $1, usually in the range of $3 to $5, and once for $25 (Brockner & Rubin, 1985). As soon as the bidding went over $1, bidders became increasingly distressed—sweating, trembling, sometimes even crying. Many of them offered excuses for themselves, such as "I'm sorry I behaved so irrationally, but I had a couple of beers before I came over here." (At the end of the experiment the psychologists always returned the money that the bidders paid them, but they had not let anyone know they were going to do so.)

The point of this study is not "here's a good scam you can use to work your way through college." The point is that once a person gets into a situation like this, it is hard to get out. And similar situations do arise in real life. The arms race between the United States and the Soviet Union was a classic example: From the end of World War II until 1991 (when the Soviet Union collapsed), the two countries devoted enormous sums of money to building weapons. Periodically critics asked, "Does it really make sense to spend this much money on weapons?" And the reply was, "We have already spent an enormous amount. Having spent so much already, we may as well spend a little more to be sure that we have more weapons than the other side."

Another example: Suppose you are presi-

People are often fond of citing ways in which technology has damaged human life: air and water pollution, the possibility of nuclear war, and so forth. But technology also enhances communication, education, and problem solving for people throughout the world. When people behave in self-defeating ways, we should look for ways to change the situation—through technology or other means—as an alternative to trying to change human nature.

dent of Colossal Airlines and you are barely breaking even on your flights from New York to Los Angeles. Now your main competitor, Planetary Airlines, decreases their ticket prices on their New York to Los Angeles flights. If you match or beat their prices, you know you will lose money on the flights. But if you charge more than Planetary does, most of your customers will switch to the other airline, your flights will be empty, and you will lose even more than if you had lowered prices. So you are trapped into lowering Colossal's prices, possibly spurring Planetary into lowering their prices still further, and so on.

Perhaps you can think of additional examples analogous to the dollar auction. Note that in each case, people behave in irrational ways, but not because of something wrong with their reasoning abilities. They simply get trapped by the situation.

Cooperation and Competition in the Prisoner's Dilemma

In some situations you have a choice between two actions. If you think in terms of what would be best for yourself, you will choose one action; if you think in terms of what is best for the

The Power of the Social Situation

A prolonged labor strike offers a behavior trap similar to the dollar auction: After a while it becomes clear that both sides will lose more money through the strike than they could possibly gain in the final settlement. However, each side reasons, "We have already lost a great deal, but if we give in now, we have lost it all in vain. Better to hold out a little longer in hopes of gaining at least something."

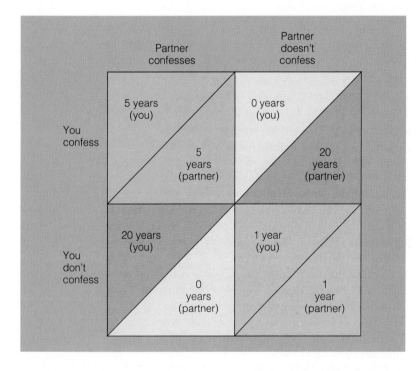

FIGURE 16.21
In the prisoner's dilemma, each person considering the choice alone finds it beneficial to confess. But when both people confess, they suffer worse consequences than if both had refused to confess.

group, you will choose the other action. If you choose what seems best for you, and everyone else chooses what seems best for himself or herself, everyone may suffer. The problem is not simply human selfishness; the problem is inherent in the situation itself.

For example, consider the **prisoner's dilemma:** You and a friend are arrested and charged with armed robbery. The police take each of you into separate rooms and ask you to confess. If neither of you confesses, the police will not have enough evidence to convict you of armed robbery, but they can convict you of a lesser offense that carries a sentence of 1 year in prison. If either of you confesses and testifies against the other, the one who confesses will go free and the other will get 20 years in prison. If you both confess, you will each get 5 years in prison. And each of you knows that the other person has the same options. Figure 16.21 illustrates your choices.

If your friend does not confess, it is to your own advantage to confess—you go free instead of spending a year in prison. (Your friend will get 20 years in prison, but let's assume you are mostly interested in your own welfare.) If your friend does confess, it is still to your advantage to confess—you get only 5 years in prison instead of 20. So you confess. Your friend, reasoning the same way, also confesses, and you both get 5 years in prison. You both would have been better off if you had both kept quiet. The situation has fostered and almost compelled uncooperative behavior.

If you and your friend could have talked things over in advance, you would have agreed not to confess. Then when the police took you to separate rooms, you would each hope that the other would keep the bargain. And if your friend did keep the bargain, what should you do? Confess, of course! We're back where we started.

The two of you will behave cooperatively only if you can stay in constant communication with each other (Nemeth, 1972). If you and your friend agree not to confess and then listen to everything the other one says, you both keep the bargain. You know that if one confesses, the other will retaliate immediately.

For experiments on the prisoner's dilemma, social psychologists have invented games in which each player chooses between two moves, one cooperative and the other competitive. The moves the players make determine their costs and rewards (Figure 16.22). To complicate matters (and make them more interesting), the game continues for many trials. If one player chooses the competitive response on one trial, the other player can retaliate on the next trial. Players earn the most rewards if both choose the cooperative move. Frequently, however, one player chooses the competitive response, the other retaliates, both begin making only the competitive response, and both players lose rewards (Brickman, Becker, & Castle, 1979; Rosenbaum, 1980).

The prisoner's dilemma is analogous to many actual decisions that many of us face. For example, suppose you agree to buy my stamp collection for $300. I agree I will mail you the collection and you agree you will mail me the check. But then I wonder whether you are really sending me a check, so I decide to wait until I receive it before sending the stamps. You don't trust me to mail the stamps, so you decide to wait for the stamps before you send the check. As a result, we do not carry out the deal we both had agreed on.

The Commons Dilemma

The commons dilemma is another case in which people hurt themselves as well as others by considering only their own short-term interests (Hardin, 1968). The **commons dilemma** takes its name from this parable: You are a shepherd in a small village with a piece of land—the commons—that everyone is free to share. Most of the time, your sheep graze on your own land, but when a few of them need a little extra grass, you are free to take them to the commons. There are 50 shepherds in the village, and the commons can support about 50 sheep a day. So if each shepherd takes an average of one sheep a day to the commons, everything works out fine. But suppose a few shepherds decide to take several sheep a day to the commons and save the grass on their own land. Not to be outdone, other shepherds do the same. Soon the commons is barren, useless to all.

The same holds true for any situation in which people overuse a resource that has a fixed rate of replacement. If we cut down forests faster than trees can grow back and catch fish faster than they can reproduce, then sooner or later we exhaust our supplies of trees and fish (Figure 16.23).

Social psychologists have simulated the commons dilemma, like the prisoner's dilemma, in laboratory games. In one study, col-

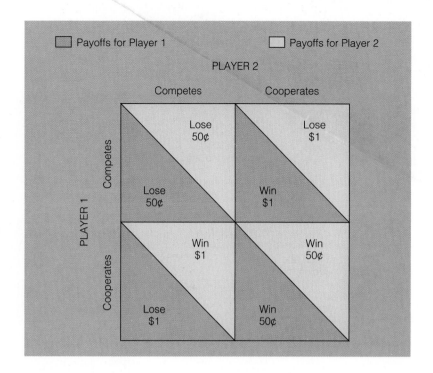

FIGURE 16.22
In this game based on the prisoner's dilemma, each player can choose the cooperative move or the competitive move. If both cooperate, each wins 50 cents; in other choices, one or both players lose money.

lege students were asked to sit around a bowl that contained 10 nuts (Edney, 1979). They were told that they could take as many nuts as they wanted any time they chose. Every 10 seconds, the number of nuts remaining in the bowl would be doubled. The object of the game was to collect as many nuts as possible. Clearly, the rational strategy is to let the nuts double every 10 seconds for a while and then to "harvest" some to divide among the participants. But most of the groups never made it past the first 10 seconds. The subjects simply plunged in and grabbed as many nuts as they could, immediately exhausting the resources.

Fortunately, there are ways to avoid the tragedy of the commons. In some experiments (as in some real situations), people have resisted the temptation to gobble up resources for short-term profits by talking over the situation and agreeing on a sensible method for distributing the available resources (Messick et al., 1983; Samuelson, Messick, Rutte, & Wilke, 1984). By studying group behavior, social psychologists hope to find ways to help preserve our air, water, forests, petroleum, and the other resources of our worldwide commons.

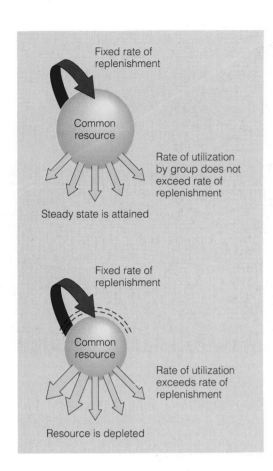

FIGURE 16.23

The commons dilemma: Unless the users agree to moderate their utilization of a resource, it will soon be used up. This dilemma is occurring on a global scale now, as 50 million acres of tropical rain forest disappear each year—100 acres a minute.

STRATEGIES TO ELICIT COMPLIANCE

Compliance is the tendency to do what someone asks us to do. Sometimes people find ways to trap us into complying more than we would choose to do voluntarily. These are worth knowing about so that you can resist being tricked into doing something contrary to your best interests.

One technique is to make a modest request at first and then to follow it up with a much larger second request. This is called the **foot-in-the-door technique.** When Jonathan Freedman and Scott Fraser (1966) asked suburban residents in Palo Alto, California, to put a small "Drive Safely" sign in their window, most of them agreed to do so. A couple of weeks later, other researchers asked the same residents to let them set up a large, unsightly "Drive Safely" billboard in their front yard for 10 days. They

made the same request to a group of residents whom the first group of researchers had not approached. Of those who had already agreed to display the small sign, 76% agreed to let them set up the billboard. Only 17% of the others agreed. Even agreeing to make such a small commitment as signing a petition to support a cause significantly increases the probability that people will later donate money to that cause (Schwarzwald, Bizman, & Raz, 1983).

In another approach, called the **door-in-the-face technique** (Cialdini et al., 1975), someone follows an outrageous initial request with a much more reasonable second one, implying an obligation that if you refused the first request you should at least compromise by agreeing to the second one. For example, I once received a telephone call from a college alumni association, asking me to show my loyalty by contributing a thousand dollars. When I apologetically declined, the caller asked whether I could contribute 500. And if not 500, how about 200? And so forth. I believe the original request for a thousand dollars was not an honest statement of the expected contribution, but merely a manipulation to guarantee my compliance with one of the lower requests.

Robert Cialdini and his colleagues (1975) demonstrated the power of the door-in-the-face technique with a clever experiment. They asked college students to agree to spend 2 hours a week for 2 years working as counselors to juvenile delinquents. Not surprisingly, every student refused. Then the researchers asked, "If you won't do that, would you chaperone a group from the juvenile detention center for one trip to the zoo?" Half the subjects complied with this more modest request, as compared to only 17% of the subjects who had not first been asked to make the larger commitment.

Why did presenting the larger request first make the students more willing to comply with the smaller request? Apparently they felt that the researchers were conceding a great deal and that it was only fair to meet them halfway.

In the **that's-not-all technique,** someone makes an offer and then, before anyone has a chance to reply, improves the offer. The television announcer says, "Here's your chance to buy this amazing combination paper shredder and coffee maker for only $39.95. But wait, there's more! We'll throw in a can of dog deodorant! And this handy windshield-wiper cleaner and a subscription to *Modern Lobotomist!* And if you act now, you can get this amazing offer, which usually costs $39.95, for only $19.95! Call this number!" People who hear the first offer and then the "improved" offer are more likely to comply than are people who begin with the "improved" offer (Burger, 1986).

■ CONCEPT CHECK

11. *Identify each of the following as an example of the foot-in-the-door technique, the door-in-the-face technique, or the that's-not-all technique.*

a. *Your boss says, "We need to cut costs drastically around here. I'm afraid I'm going to have to cut your salary by 50%." You protest vigorously. Your boss replies, "Well, I suppose we could cut expenses some other way. Maybe I can give you just a 5% cut." "Thanks," you reply. "I can live with that."*

b. *A store marks its prices "25% off," then scratches that out and marks them "50% off!" Though the prices are now about the*

Many stores use the "that's not all" technique, showing a high price that has been crossed off and replaced with a lower price. Have you ever wondered why the price is often at the bottom of the sales tag? Here's why: If the store owners want to raise the price, they can cut off the price at the bottom, write in a new (much higher) price, and then mark that one "down" to the new price. The price now in effect appears to be a bargain; the customer does not know that it is higher than last week's price.

same as at competing stores, customers flock in to buy.

c. *A friend asks you to help carry some supplies over to the elementary school for an afternoon tutoring program. When you get there, the principal says that one of the tutors is late and asks whether you could take her place until she arrives. You agree and spend the rest of the afternoon tutoring. The principal then talks you into coming back every week as a tutor.*

(Check your answers on page 717.)

Obedience to Authority

WHAT'S THE EVIDENCE?

Ordinarily, if someone you hardly know orders you to do something unpleasant, saying "You *have* to do this," you probably would refuse quite vehemently. Sometimes, however, you may get into a situation in which you feel obligated to obey unreasonable orders from someone who has no right to insist on your obedience. We might have thought that only people with some rigid, authority-worshiping personality would follow objectionable orders, but evidence has shown that some situations build up such powerful pressures that almost anyone obeys.

Research on this topic was inspired by reports of atrocities in the Nazi concentration camps during the Second World War. Those who had committed the atrocities defended themselves by saying they were only obeying orders. International courts rejected that defense, and outraged people throughout the world told themselves, "If I had been there, I would have refused to follow such orders" and "It couldn't happen here."

What do you think? Could it happen here? Stanley Milgram (1974) set up an experiment to discover whether a carefully designed situation could trap people into obeying apparently dangerous orders. Milgram's experiment quickly became one of the most famous studies in psychology, with major ethical as well as scientific implications.

Hypothesis When an authority figure gives normal people instructions to do something that might hurt another person, at least some of them will obey, under carefully designed circumstances.

Method Two adult male subjects arrived at the experimental room—the real subject and a confederate of the experimenter pretending to be a subject. (They were not college students. The experimenters wanted results that would generalize to a broad population. They also wanted to minimize the risk that the subjects would guess the true purpose of the experiment.) The experimenter told the subjects that this was an experiment on learning and that one subject would be the "teacher" and the other the "learner." The teacher would read lists of words through a microphone to the learner, who would sit in a nearby room. The teacher would then test the learner's memory for the words. Every time the learner made a mistake, the teacher was to deliver an electric shock as punishment.

The experiment was rigged so that the real subject was always the teacher and the confederate was always the learner. The teacher watched as the learner was strapped into the shock device, so he knew that the learner could not escape (Figure 16.24). In one version of the experiment, the learner was a middle-age man who said he had a heart condition. The learner never actually received any shocks, but the teacher was led to believe that he did.

The experiment began uneventfully. The teacher read the words and tested the learner's memory for them. The learner made many mistakes. The teacher sat at a shock generator that had levers to deliver shocks ranging from 15 volts up to 450 volts, in 15-volt increments (Figure 16.25). The experimenter instructed the teacher to deliver a shock every time the learner made a mistake, beginning with the 15-volt switch and raising the voltage by 15 volts for

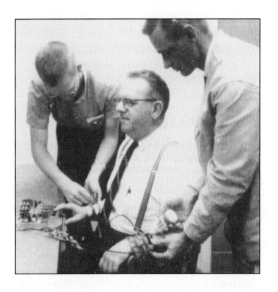

FIGURE 16.24
In Milgram's experiment, a rigged drawing selected a confederate of the experimenter to be the "learner." Here, the learner is strapped to a device that is said to deliver shocks.

FIGURE 16.25
The "teacher" in Milgram's experiment flipped switches on this box, apparently delivering stronger and stronger shocks for each successive error the "learner" made. The situation was designed to appear realistic, although the device did not actually shock the learner.

each successive mistake. As the voltage went up, the learner in the next room cried out in pain and even kicked the wall.

If a teacher asked who would take responsibility for any harm to the learner, the experimenter replied that he (the experimenter) would take responsibility, but he insisted that "while the shocks may be painful, they are not dangerous." When the shock reached 150 volts, the learner called out in pain and begged to be let out of the experiment, complaining that his heart was bothering him. Beginning at 270, he responded to shocks with agonized screams. At 300 volts he shouted that he would no longer answer any questions. After 330 volts he made no response at all. Still, the experimenter ordered the teacher to continue asking questions and delivering shocks. (Remember, the learner was not really being shocked. The screams of pain were played on a tape recorder.)

Results Of 40 subjects, 25 continued to deliver shocks all the way up to 450 volts. The people who did so were not sadists. They were normal adults, recruited from the community through newspaper ads. They were paid a few dollars for their services, and those who asked were told that they could keep the money even if they quit. (Not many asked.) People from all walks of life obeyed the experimenter's orders, including blue-collar workers, white-collar workers, and professionals. Most of them grew quite upset and agitated while they were supposedly delivering shocks to the screaming learner, but they kept right on.

Interpretation The obedience Milgram observed depended on certain factors he put into the situation. One was that the experimenter agreed to take responsibility. (Remember the diffusion of responsibility principle.) Another factor was that the experimenter started with a small request, asking the subject to press the lever for a 15-volt shock, and then gradually progressed to stronger shocks. (Remember the foot-in-the-door principle; remember also Skinner's shaping principle.) We can identify many other contributing factors, and we can imagine many ways to change the procedure that probably would change the results. Figure 16.26 and Figure 16.27 illustrate the results of a few variations in procedure. Still, the remarkable conclusion remains that many normal people followed orders from an experimenter they just met, even though they thought they might hurt or even kill another person. Imagine how

FIGURE 16.26
In one variation of his standard procedure, Milgram asked the teacher to hold the learner's hand on the shock electrode. This close contact with the learner decreased obedience to less than half of its usual level; still, some teachers continued following orders to deliver shocks. (From Milgram's 1965 film, Obedience.)

much stronger would be the pressure to obey orders from a government or military leader.

Ethical Issues Milgram's experiment told us something about ourselves that we did not want to hear. No longer could we say, "Something like the Nazi concentration camps could never happen here." We found that most of us tend to follow orders, even quite offensive orders. We are indebted to Milgram's study for this important, if unwelcome, information.

However, although I am glad to know about Milgram's results, I am not sure I would have wanted to be a subject in his experiment. Most of his subjects were emotionally drained by the experience and some were visibly upset to discover how readily they had obeyed orders to deliver dangerous shocks to another person.

Milgram's study prompted psychology researchers to establish much clearer and stricter rules about what an experimenter can ask a subject to do. Today, before the start of any psychological experiment—even the simplest and most innocuous—the experimenter must submit a plan to a Human Subjects Committee that must approve the ethics of the experiment before it can begin.

Because of the current rules of Human Subjects Committees, no research similar to Mil-

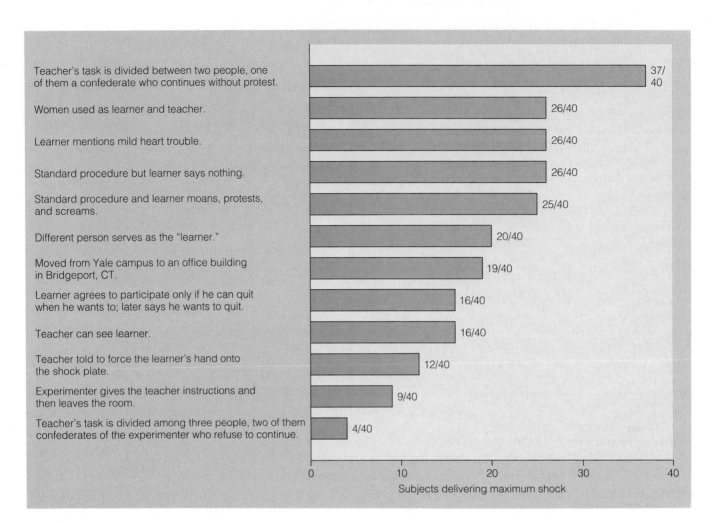

Teacher's task is divided between two people, one of them a confederate who continues without protest.	37/40
Women used as learner and teacher.	26/40
Learner mentions mild heart trouble.	26/40
Standard procedure but learner says nothing.	26/40
Standard procedure and learner moans, protests, and screams.	25/40
Different person serves as the "learner."	20/40
Moved from Yale campus to an office building in Bridgeport, CT.	19/40
Learner agrees to participate only if he can quit when he wants to; later says he wants to quit.	16/40
Teacher can see learner.	16/40
Teacher told to force the learner's hand onto the shock plate.	12/40
Experimenter gives the teacher instructions and then leaves the room.	9/40
Teacher's task is divided among three people, two of them confederates of the experimenter who refuse to continue.	4/40

Subjects delivering maximum shock

FIGURE 16.27
Milgram varied his procedure in many ways to find out what elements promoted or inhibited obedience. Division of responsibility increased obedience; an implication of personal responsibility decreased obedience. Under all conditions, some people obeyed and others did not.

gram's study could be done today. However, if the same procedures had been in place *at the time of Milgram's study*, would a committee have prohibited his study? The curious fact is, we aren't sure. Before Milgram's research, very few people expected his results to turn out the way they did. Milgram had asked a number of psychologists and psychiatrists to predict the results; nearly all replied that only a rare psychopathic weirdo would press levers to deliver severe shocks. A Human Subjects Committee that shared this expectation might have foreseen little ethical difficulty with Milgram's study. The unforeseen ethical problem underscores just how surprising Milgram's results were.

Something to Think About

Here is a version of the experiment that Milgram never tried: At the start of the experiment, we announce that the teacher and the learner will trade places halfway through the experiment so that the previous "learner" will start delivering shocks to the teacher. How do you think the teachers would behave then? What other changes in procedure can you imagine that might influence the degree of obedience?

SUMMARY

■ *Behavior traps.* Certain situations—such as the dollar auction, the prisoner's dilemma, and the commons dilemma—pressure even intelligent and rational people into self-defeating behavior. To avoid self-defeating behavior, people need to avoid or change such situations. (page 708)

- *Compliance.* The likelihood that people will comply with the requests of others is increased when someone starts with a small request that is accepted and then makes a large request or if someone starts with a large request that is refused and then makes a small request. (page 712)

- *Obedience.* Many people obey the orders of a person in authority even if they believe their action will injure someone else. They are less likely to obey if they can see the person who would be injured. They are more likely to obey if other people are following orders without protest. (page 713)

TERMS

behavior trap situation that almost forces people into self-defeating behaviors (page 708)

prisoner's dilemma situation in which people have to choose between an act beneficial to themselves but harmful to others, and an act that is moderately beneficial to all (page 710)

commons dilemma situation in which people who share a common resource tend to overuse it and therefore make it unavailable in the long run (page 711)

foot-in-the-door technique method of eliciting compliance by first making a modest request and then following it with a much larger request (page 712)

door-in-the-face technique method of eliciting compliance by first making an outrageous request and then replying to the refusal with a more reasonable request (page 712)

that's-not-all technique method of eliciting compliance in which someone makes an offer and then, before anyone has a chance to reply, improves the offer (page 713)

SUGGESTIONS FOR FURTHER READING

Brockner, J., & Rubin, J. Z. (1985). *Entrapment in escalating conflicts.* New York: Springer-Verlag. Describes research on the dollar auction and similar behavior traps.

Milgram, S. (1975). *Obedience to authority.* New York: Harper & Row. Describes Milgram's classic experiments on obedience.

ANSWERS TO CONCEPT CHECK

11. (a) Door-in-the-face technique; (b) that's-not-all technique; (c) foot-in-the-door technique. (page 713)

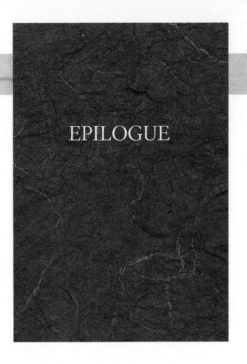

EPILOGUE

Here we are at the end of the book. As I have been writing and revising this book, I have imagined you sitting there reading it. I have generally imagined a student somewhat like I was when I was a college student, reading about psychology for the first time and often growing excited about something I had just read. I remember periodically telling my roommate (or my family, when I was home for a vacation), "Guess what I just learned in psychology! Isn't this interesting?" And I remember occasionally thinking, "Hmm. The book says such-and-so, but I'm not convinced. I wonder whether psychologists ever considered a different explanation. . . ." And I started thinking about possible research I might do if I ever became a psychologist.

I hope that you have had some of those same experiences yourself. I hope you have occasionally become excited about something you read, so that you thought about it and talked to other people about it. In fact, I hope you told your roommate so much about psychology that you started to become annoying. And I hope you have sometimes reacted with doubts or misgivings about some conclusion, imagining some research project you might like to conduct to test and challenge that conclusion.

Now, as I picture you reaching the end of the course, I'm not sure how you will react. You might be thinking, "Wow, I sure have learned a lot!" Or you might be thinking, "Is that all?" Maybe you are even reacting both ways: "I really have learned a lot. But it seems like there ought to be more. I still don't understand what conscious experience is all about, and I don't understand why I react the way I do sometimes. And this book—*wonderful as it is*—hardly mentioned certain important topics. Like why do we laugh? Or how do we sense the passage of time? Or why do I feel like yawning whenever I see someone else yawn?"

If I didn't answer all your questions, there are two good reasons. One is that this is an introductory text; if you want to learn more, you should take additional courses or do some additional reading. The other reason is that psychologists do not know all the answers.

Perhaps some day you will become a psychological researcher yourself and add to the sum of our knowledge. If not, you can try to keep up to date on current developments in psychology by reading newspaper and magazine articles and an occasional book. One of the main goals of this book has been to prepare you to continue learning about psychology in that fashion. Try to read critically. If you pick up a book in the psychology section of your local bookstore, try to determine whether it is based on scientific evidence or just the author's own pronouncements. If you read an article in the newspaper, try to judge whether its conclusions follow from decent evidence. If it reports a survey, were the survey's questions unambiguous? If the article implies a cause-and-effect relationship, was the evidence based on experiments or only correlations? No matter what the evidence, can you think of a more reasonable, more parsimonious explanation than the one the author suggests?

Above all, remember that nearly all our conclusions are tentative. Psychological researchers seldom use the word *prove*; they have many ways of indicating moderate confidence. I once suggested to my editor, half-seriously, that we should include in the index to this book the entry "*maybe*—see pages 1–718." We did not include such an entry because our understanding of psychology is not really that bad—at least, not always. But be leery of anyone who seems a little too certain about some great new insight in psychology; the route from *maybe* to *definitely* is long and arduous.

Abelson, R. P. (1981). Psychological status of the script concept. *American Psychologist, 36,* 715–729. (13)

Abrahamsen, D. (1985). *Confessions of Son of Sam.* New York: Columbia University Press. (15)

Abramson, L. Y., Metalsky, G. I., & Alloy, L. B. (1989). Hopelessness depression: A theory-based subtype of depression. *Psychological Review, 96,* 358–372. (14)

Abramson, L. Y., Seligman, M. E. P., & Teasdale, J. D. (1978). Learned helplessness in humans: Critique and reformulation. *Journal of Abnormal Psychology, 87,* 49–74. (14)

"A conversation with President Havel." (1992, March). *World Press Review, 39*(3), 14–16. (15)

Adam, K. (1980). Sleep as a restorative process and a theory to explain why. In P. S. McConnell, G. J. Boer, H. J. Romijn, N. E. van de Poll, & M. A. Corner (Eds.), *Progress in brain research: Vol. 53, Adaptive capabilities of the nervous system* (pp. 289–305). Amsterdam: Elsevier/North Holland Biomedical. (5)

Adam, K. S. (1986). Early family influences on suicidal behavior. *Annals of the New York Academy of Sciences, 487,* 63–76. (14)

Adler, A. (1927). *Understanding human nature.* New York: Greenberg. (13)

Adler, A. (1928/1964). Brief comments on reason, intelligence, and feeble-mindedness. In H. L. Ansbacher & R. R. Ansbacher (Eds.), *Superiority and social interest* (pp. 41–49). New York: Viking. (Original work published 1928) (13)

Adler, A. (1932/1964). The structure of neurosis. In H. L. Ansbacher & R. R. Ansbacher (Eds.), *Superiority and social interest* (pp. 83–95). New York: Viking. (Original work published 1932) (13)

Ajzen, I., & Fishbein, M. (1980). *Understanding attitudes and predicting social behavior.* Englewood Cliffs, NJ: Prentice-Hall. (16)

Albee, G. W. (1986). Toward a just society: Lessons from observations on the primary prevention of psychopathology. *American Psychologist, 41,* 891–898. (15)

Alexander, I. E. (1982). The Freud-Jung relationship—the other side of Oedipus and countertransference. *American Psychologist, 37,* 1009–1018. (13)

Allgeier, E. R. (1987). Coercive versus consensual sexual interactions. *The G. Stanley Hall Lecture Series, 7,* 11–63. (11)

Alloy, L. B., & Abramson, L. Y. (1979). Judgment of contingency in depressed and nondepressed students: Sadder but wiser? *Journal of Experimental Psychology: General, 108,* 441–485. (14)

Allport, G. W. (1935). Attitudes. In C. Murchison (Ed.), *A handbook of social psychology* (pp. 798–844). Worcester, MA: Clark University. (16)

Allport, G. W., & Odbert, H. S. (1936). Trait-names: A psycholexical study. *Psychological Monographs, 47* (Whole No. 211). (13)

Amato, P. R., & Keith, B. (1991). Parental divorce and the well-being of children: A meta-analysis. *Psychological Bulletin, 110,* 26–46. (6)

American Medical Association. (1986). Council Report: Scientific status of refreshing recollection by the use of hypnosis. *International Journal of Clinical and Experimental Hypnosis, 34,* 1–12. (5)

American Psychiatric Association. (1987). *Diagnostic and statistical manual of mental disorders* (Third edition-Revised.) Washington, DC: Author. (14)

American Psychological Association. (1982). *Ethical principles in the conduct of research with human participants.* Washington, DC: Author. (2)

Anastasi, A. (1988). *Psychological testing* (6th ed.). New York: Macmillan. (10, 13)

Andersen, B. L. (1983). Primary orgasmic dysfunction: Diagnostic considerations and review of treatment. *Psychological Bulletin, 93,* 105–136. (11)

Anderson, C. A. (1989). Temperature and aggression: Ubiquitous effects of heat on occurrence of human violence. *Psychological Bulletin, 106,* 74–96. (12)

Anderson, C. D., Warner, J. L., & Spencer, C. C. (1984). Inflation bias in self-assessment examinations: Implications for valid employee selection. *Journal of Applied Psychology, 69,* 574–580. (13)

Anderson, J. R. (1991). The adaptive nature of human categorization. *Psychological Review, 98,* 409–429. (9)

Anderson, N. H. (1974). Cognitive algebra: Integration theory applied to social attribution. In L. Berkowitz (Ed.), *Advances in experimental social psychology* (Vol. 7, pp. 1–101). New York: Academic Press. (16)

Anderson, N. H., & Hubert, S. (1963). Effects of concomitant verbal recall on order effects in personality impression formation. *Journal of Verbal Learning and Verbal Behavior, 2,* 379–391. (16)

Andersson, U., Eckernäs, S.-Å., Hartvig, P., Ulin, J., Långström, B., & Hägström, J.-E. (1990). Striatal binding of ^{11}C-NMSP studied with positron emission tomography in patients with persistent tardive dyskinesia: No evidence for altered dopamine D_2 receptor binding. *Journal of Neural Transmission, 79,* 215–226. (15)

Andreasen, N. C., Flaum, M., Swayze, V. W., II, Tyrrell, G., & Arndt, S. (1990). Positive and negative symptoms in schizophrenia. *Archives of General Psychiatry, 47,* 615–621. (14)

Andreasen, N. C., & Olsen, S. (1982). Negative v. positive schizophrenia. Definition and validation. *Archives of General Psychiatry, 39,* 789–794. (14)

Angoff, W. H. (1988). The nature-nurture debate, aptitudes, and group differences. *American Psychologist, 43,* 713–720. (10)

Anisman, H., & Zacharko, R. M. (1983). Stress and neoplasia: Speculations and caveats. *Behavioral Medicine Update, 5,* 27–35. (12)

Anonymous. (1955). *Alcoholics anonymous* (2nd ed.). New York: Alcoholics Anonymous World Services. (14)

Appelbaum, P. S. (1988). The new preventive detention: Psychiatry's problematic responsibility for the control of violence. *American Journal of Psychiatry, 145,* 779–785. (15)

Appelbaum, S. A. (1979). *Out in inner space.* Garden City, NY: Anchor Press/Doubleday. (15)

Appley, M. H. (1991). Motivation, equilibration, and stress. In R. Dienstbier (Ed.), *Nebraska Symposium on Motivation 1990* (pp. 1–67). Lincoln, NE: University of Nebraska Press. (11)

Arana, G. W., Baldessarini, R. J., & Ornsteen, M. (1985). The dexamethasone suppression test for diagnosis and prognosis in psychiatry. *Archives of General Psychiatry, 42,* 1193–1204. (14)

Arboleda, C., & Holzman, P. S. (1985). Thought disorder in children at risk for psychosis. *Archives of General Psychiatry, 42,* 1004–1013. (14)

Argyle, N. (1988). The nature of cognitions in panic disorder. *Behaviour Research and Therapy, 26,* 261–264. (14)

Arkin, A. M. (1978). Sleeptalking. In A. M. Arkin, J. S. Antrobus, & S. J. Ellman (Eds.), *The mind in sleep* (pp. 513–532). Hillsdale, NJ: Lawrence Erlbaum. (5)

Arkin, A. M., & Antrobus, J. S. (1978). The effects of external stimuli applied prior to and during sleep on sleep experience. In A. M. Arkin, J. S. Antrobus, & S. J. Ellman (Eds.), *The mind in sleep* (pp. 351–391). Hillsdale, NJ: Lawrence Erlbaum. (5)

Arnold, M. B. (1970). Perennial problems in the field of emotion. In M. B. Arnold (Ed.), *Feelings and emotions* (pp. 169–185). New York: Academic Press. (12)

Arnsten, A. F. T., & Goldman-Rakic, P. S. (1985a). Alpha₂-adrenergic mechanisms in prefrontal cortex associated with cognitive decline in aged nonhuman primates. *Science, 230,* 1273–1276. (8)

Arnsten, A. F. T., & Goldman-Rakic, P. S. (1985b). Catecholamines and cognitive decline in aged nonhuman primates. *Annals of the New York Academy of Sciences, 444,* 218–234. (8)

Aronson, E., & Carlsmith, J. M. (1963). Effect of the severity of threat on the devaluation of forbidden behavior. *Journal of Abnormal and Social Psychology, 66,* 584–588. (16)

Asch, S. E. (1946). Forming impressions of personality. *Journal of Abnormal and Social Psychology, 41,* 258–290. (16)

Asch, S. E. (1951). Effects of group pressure upon the modification and distortion of judgments. In H. Guetzkow (Ed.), *Groups, leadership, and men* (pp. 177–190). Pittsburgh, PA: Carnegie Press. (16)

Asch, S. E. (1955, November). Opinions and social pressure. *Scientific American, 193*(5), 31–35. (16)

Asch, S. E. (1956). Studies of independence and conformity: I. A minority of one against a unanimous majority. *Psychological Monographs, 70*(9, Whole No. 416). (16)

Ash, R. (1986, August). An anecdote submitted by Ron Ash. *The Industrial-Organizational Psychologist, 23*(4), 8. (7)

Atchley, R. C. (1980). *The social forces in later life* (3rd ed.). Belmont, CA: Wadsworth. (6)

Atkinson, J. W. (1957). Motivational determinants of risk taking behavior. *Psychological Review, 64,* 359–372. (11)

Atkinson, J. W., & Birch, D. (1978). *Introduction to motivation* (2nd ed.). New York: D. Van Nostrand. (11)

Atkinson, R. C., & Shiffrin, R. M. (1968). Human memory: A proposed system and its control. In K. W. Spence & J. T. Spence (Eds.), *The psychology of learning and motivation* (Vol. 2, pp. 89–105). New York: Academic Press. (8)

Avenet, P., & Kinnamon, S. C. (1991). Cellular basis of taste reception. *Current Opinion in Neurobiology, 1,* 198–203. (4)

---

*The number in parentheses after each entry is the chapter in which the reference appears.

Averill, J. R. (1983). Studies on anger and aggression: Implications for theories of emotion. *American Psychologist, 38,* 1145–1160. (12)

Azrin, N. H. (1976). Improvements in the community-reinforcement approach to alcoholism. *Behaviour Research and Therapy, 14,* 339–348. (14)

Azrin, N. H., & Nunn, R. G. (1973). Habit-reversal: A method of eliminating nervous habits and tics. *Behaviour Research and Therapy, 11,* 619–628. (7)

Babcock, R. L. & Salthouse, T. A. (1990). Effects of increased processing demands on age differences in working memory. *Psychology & Aging, 5,* 421–428. (8)

Babich, F. R., Jacobson, A. L., Bubash, S., & Jacobson, A. (1965). Transfer of a response to naive rats by injection of ribonucleic acid extracted from trained rats. *Science, 149,* 656–657. (2)

Babkoff, H., Caspy, T., Mikulincer, M., & Sing, H. C. (1991). Monotonic and rhythmic influences: A challenge for sleep deprivation research. *Psychological Bulletin, 109,* 411–428. (5)

Bachevalier, J., & Mishkin, M. (1984). An early and a late developing system for learning and retention in infant monkeys. *Behavioral Neuroscience, 98,* 770–778. (8)

Bachevalier, J., & Mishkin, M. (1986). Visual recognition impairment follows ventromedial but not dorsolateral prefrontal lesions in monkeys. *Behavioral Brain Research, 20,* 249–261. (3)

Bachrach, A. J., Erwin, W. J., & Mohr, J. P. (1965). The control of eating behavior in an anoretic by operant conditioning techniques. In L. P. Ullmann & L. Krasner (Eds.), *Case studies in behavior modification* (pp. 153–163). New York: Holt, Rinehart, & Winston. (11, 15)

Backlund, E.-O., Granberg, P. O., Hamberger, B., Sedvall, G., Seiger, A., & Olson, L. (1985). Transplantation of adrenal medullary tissue to striatum in Parkinsonism. In A. Björklund & U. Stenevi (Eds.), *Neural grafting in the mammalian CNS* (pp. 551–556). Amsterdam: Elsevier. (3)

Baddeley, A. D. (1978). The trouble with levels: A reexamination of Craik and Lockhart's framework for memory research. *Psychological Review, 85,* 139–152. (8)

Baddeley, A. D. (1986). *Working memory.* Oxford, England: Clarendon Press. (8)

Baddeley, A. D., & Hitch, G. (1974). Working memory. In G.H. Bower (Ed.), *Psychology of Learning and Motivation* (Vol. 8, pp. 47–89). New York: Academic Press. (8)

Bahrick, H. (1984). Semantic memory content in permastore: 50 years of memory for Spanish learned in school. *Journal of Experimental Psychology: General, 113,* 1–29. (8)

Bailey, J. M., & Pillard, R. C. (1991). A genetic study of male sexual orientation. *Archives of General Psychiatry, 48,* 1089–1096. (11)

Baird, J. C. (1982). The moon illusion: A reference theory. *Journal of Experimental Psychology: General, 111,* 304–315. (4)

Baker, G. H. B. (1987). Invited review: Psychological factors and immunity. *Journal of Psychosomatic Research, 31,* 1–10. (12)

Baker, T. B., & Tiffany, S. T. (1985). Morphine tolerance as habituation. *Psychological Bulletin, 92,* 78–108. (5)

Balay, J., & Shevrin, H. (1988). The subliminal psychodynamic activation method: *A critical review. American Psychologist, 43,* 161–174. (4)

Baldessarini, R. J. (1984). Antipsychotic drugs. In T. B. Karasu (Ed.), *The psychiatric therapies. I. The somatic therapies* (pp. 119–170). Washington, DC: American Psychiatric Press. (15)

Bandura, A. (1977). *Social learning theory.* Englewood Cliffs, NJ: Prentice-Hall. (7)

Bandura, A. (1986). Social foundations of thought and action. Englewood Cliffs, NJ: Prentice-Hall. (7)

Bandura, A., Ross, D., & Ross, S. A. (1963). Imitation of film-mediated aggressive models. *Journal of Abnormal and Social Psychology, 66,* 3–11. (7)

Barbaro, N. M. (1988). Studies of PAG/PVG stimulation for pain relief in humans. In H. L. Fields & J. M. Besson (Eds.), *Progress in brain research* (Vol. 77, pp. 165–173). Amsterdam: Elsevier. (5)

Barber, T. X. (1979). Suggested ("hypnotic") behavior: The trance paradigm versus an alternative paradigm. In E. Fromm & R. E. Shor (Eds.), *Hypnosis: Developments in research and new perspectives* (2nd ed.) (pp. 217–271). New York: Aldine. (5)

Bard, P. (1934). On emotional expression after decortication with some remarks on certain theoretical views. *Psychological Review, 41,* 309–329. (12)

Barnes, R. (1985). Women and self-injury. *International Journal of Women's Studies, 8,* 465–474. (14)

Barnett, P. A., & Gotlib, I. H. (1988). Psychosocial functioning and depression: Distinguishing among antecedents, concomitants, and consequences. *Psychological Bulletin, 104,* 97–126. (14)

Baron, R. S., Baron, P. H., & Miller, N. (1973). The relation between distraction and persuasion. *Psychological Bulletin, 80,* 310–323. (9)

Barrera, R. D., Lobato-Barrera, D., & Sulzer-Azaroff, B. (1980). A simultaneous treatment comparison of three expressive language training programs with a mute autistic child. *Journal of Autism and Developmental Disorders, 10,* 21–37. (14)

Barrett, G. V., & Depinet, R. L. (1991). A reconsideration of testing for competence rather than intelligence. *American Psychologist, 46,* 1012–1024. (10)

Barrick, M. R., & Mount, M. K. (1991). The big five personality dimensions and job performance: A meta-analysis. *Personnel Psychology, 44,* 1–26. (13)

Barron, F., & Harrington, D. M. (1981). Creativity, intelligence, and personality. *Annual Review of Psychology, 32,* 439–476. (9)

Bartlett, F. C. (1932). *Remembering.* Cambridge, England: Cambridge University Press. (8)

Bass, B. M., & Ryterband, E. C. (1979). *Organizational psychology* (2nd ed.). Boston: Allyn & Bacon. (6)

Bassok, M., & Holyoak, K. J. (1989). Interdomain transfer between isomorphic topics in algebra and physics. *Journal of Experimental Psychology: Learning, Memory, and Cognition, 15,* 153–166. (9)

Bates, J. A. (1979). Extrinsic reward and intrinsic motivation: A review with implications for the classroom. *Review of Educational Research, 49,* 557–576. (11)

Bauer, D. W., & Stanovich, K. E. (1980). Lexical access and the spelling-to-sound regularity effect. *Memory & Cognition, 8,* 424–432. (9)

Baum, A., Gatchel, R. J., & Schaeffer, M. A. (1983). Emotional, behavioral, and physiological effects of chronic stress at Three Mile Island. *Journal of Consulting and Clinical Psychology, 51,* 565–572. (12)

Baylor, D. A., Lamb, T. D., & Yau, K.-W. (1979). Responses of retinal rods to single photons. *Journal of Physiology* (London), *288,* 613–634. (4)

Beach, F. A. (1950). The snark was a boojum. *American Psychologist, 5,* 115–124. (1)

Beardslee, W. R., Bemporad, J., Keller, M. B., & Klerman, G. L. (1983). Children of parents with major affective disorder: A review. *American Journal of Psychiatry, 140,* 825–832. (14)

Beck, A. T. (1976). *Cognitive therapy and the emotional disorders.* New York: New American Library. (15)

Beck, A. T. (1991). Cognitive therapy: A 30-year retrospective. *American Psychologist, 46,* 368–375. (15)

Beck, A. T., & Steer, R. A. (1989). Clinical predictors of eventual suicide: A 5- to 10-year prospective study of suicide attempters. *Journal of Affective Disorders, 17,* 203–209. (14)

Belknap, R. L. (1990). *The genesis of the Brothers Karamazov.* Evanston, IL: Northwestern University Press. (9)

Bellugi, U., Poizner, H., & Klima, E. S. (1983). Brain organization for language: Clues from sign aphasia. *Human Neurobiology, 2,* 155–170. (3)

Belmore, S. M. (1987). Determinants of attention during impression formation. *Journal of Experimental Psychology: Learning, Memory, and Cognition, 13,* 480–489. (16)

Bem, D. J. (1967). Self-perception: An alternative interpretation of cognitive dissonance phenomena. *Psychological Review, 74,* 183–200. (16)

Bem, D. J. (1970). *Beliefs, attitudes, and human affairs.* Pacific Grove, CA: Brooks/Cole. (16)

Bem, D. J. (1972). Self-perception theory. *Advances in Experimental Social Psychology, 6,* 1–62. (16)

Bem, D. J., & Allen, A. (1974). On predicting some of the people some of the time. *Psychological Review, 81,* 506–520. (13)

Bem, S. L. (1974). The measurement of psychological androgyny. *Journal of Consulting and Clinical Psychology, 42,* 155–162. (13)

Benassi, V. A., Sweeney, P. D., & Dufour, C. L. (1988). Is there a relation between locus of control orientation and depression? *Journal of Abnormal Psychology, 97,* 357–367. (14)

Bennett, M. J. (1983). Focal psychotherapy—terminable and interminable. *American Journal of Psychotherapy, 37,* 365–375. (15)

Bennett, W. (1980). The cigarette century. *Science 80, 1*(6), 36–43. (5, 14)

Benson, H. (1977). Systemic hypertension and the relaxation response. *New England Journal of Medicine, 296,* 1152–1156. (12)

Benson, H. (1985). Stress, health, and the relaxation response. In W. D. Gentry, H. Benson, & C. J. de Wolff (Eds.), *Behavioral medicine: Work, stress and health* (pp. 15–32). Dordrecht, Netherlands: Martinus Nijhoff. (12)

Benton, A. L. (1980). The neuropsychology of facial recognition. *American Psychologist, 35,* 176–186. (3)

Berglas, S., & Jones, E. E. (1978). Drug choice as a self-handicapping strategy in response to noncontingent success. *Journal of Personality and Social Psychology, 36,* 405–417. (5, 16)

Berkow, R. (Ed.) (1987). *The Merck Manual* (15th ed.). Rahway, NJ: Merck Sharp & Dohme Research Laboratories. (11)

Berkowitz, L. (1983). Aversively stimulated aggression: Some parallels and differences in research with animals and humans. *American Psychologist, 38,* 1135–1144. (12)

Berkowitz, L. (1989). Frustration-aggression hypothesis: Examination and reformulation. *Psychological Bulletin, 106,* 59–73. (12)

Berlyne, D. E. (1981). Humanistic psychology as a protest movement. In J. R. Royce & L. P. Mos (Eds.), *Humanistic psychology: Concepts and criticisms* (pp. 261–293). New York: Plenum. (13)

Berman, A. L. (1988). Fictional depiction of suicide in television films and imitation effects. *American Journal of Psychiatry, 145,* 982–986. (15)

Berne, E. (1964). *Games people play.* New York: Grove. (15)

Bernstein, I. L. (1985). Learned food aversions in the progression of cancer and its treatment. *Annals of the New York Academy of Sciences, 443,* 365–380. (7)

Bernstein, I. L., & Borson, S. (1986). Learned food aversion: A component of anorexia syndromes. *Psychological Review, 93,* 462–472. (7)

Berntson, G. G., Cacioppo, J. T., & Quigley, K. S. (1991). Autonomic determinism: The modes of autonomic control, the doctrine of autonomic space, and the laws of autonomic constraint. *Psychological Review, 98,* 459–487. (12)

Berry, J. W., Poortinga, Y. H., Segal, H., & Dasen, P. R. (1992). *Cross-cultural psychology.* Cambridge, England: Cambridge University Press. (16)

Berscheid, E. (1983). Emotion. In H. H. Kelley, E. Berscheid, A. Christensen, J. H. Harvey, T. L. Huston, G. Levinger, E. McClintock, L. A. Peplau, & D. R. Peterson, *Close relationships* (pp. 110–168). New York: W. H. Freeman. (16)

Berscheid, E., Snyder, M., & Omoto, A. M. (1989). Issues in studying close relationships. In C. Hendrick (Ed.), *Close relationships* (pp. 63–91). Newbury Park, CA: Sage. (16)

Binet, A., & Simon, T. (1905). Méthodes nouvelles pour le diagnostic du niveau intellectuel des anormaux [New methods for the measurement of the intellectual level of the abnormal]. *L'Année Psychologique, 11,* 191–244. (10)

Birnbaum, M. H., & Sotoodeh, Y. (1991). Measurement of stress: Scaling the magnitudes of life changes. *Psychological Science, 2,* 236–243. (12)

Björklund, A., Stenevi, U., Dunnett, S. B., & Gage, F. H. (1982). Cross-species neural grafting in a rat model of Parkinson's disease. *Nature, 298,* 652–654. (3)

Blackwood, D. H. R., St. Clair, D. M., Muir, W. J., & Duffy, J. C. (1991). Auditory P300 and eye tracking dysfunction in schizophrenic pedigrees. *Archives of General Psychiatry, 48,* 899–909. (14)

Blaine, J. D., Prien, R. F., & Levine, J. (1983). The role of antidepressants in the treatment of affective disorders. *American Journal of Psychotherapy, 37,* 502–520. (15)

Blakemore, C., & Sutton, P. (1969). Size adaptation: A new aftereffect. *Science, 166,* 245–247. (4)

Blanchard, E. B., & Young, L. D. (1973). Self-control of cardiac functioning: A promise as yet unfulfilled. *Psychological Bulletin, 79,* 145–163. (12)

Blanchard, E. B., & Young, L. D. (1974). Clinical applications of biofeedback training: A review of evidence. *Archives of General Psychiatry, 30,* 573–589. (12)

Bless, H., Bohner, G., Schwarz, N., & Strack, F. (1990). Mood and persuasion: A cognitive response analysis. *Personality and Social Psychology Bulletin, 16,* 331–345. (16)

Bleuler, E. (1911/1950). Dementia praecox, or the group of schizophrenias (J. Zinkin, Trans.). New York: International Universities Press. (Original work published 1911) (14)

Bliwise, D. L., Bliwise, N. G., Partinen, M., Pursley, A. M., & Dement, W. C. (1988). Sleep apnea and mortality in an aged cohort. *American Journal of Public Health, 78,* 544–547. (5)

Bloom, B. L., White, S. W., & Asher, S. J. (1979). Marital disruption as a stressful life event. In G. Levinger & O. C. Moles (Eds.), *Divorce and separation* (pp. 184–200). New York: Basic Books. (16)

Bloom, J. D., & Faulkner, L. R. (1987). Competency determinations in civil commitment. *American Journal of Psychiatry, 144,* 193–196. (15)

Blum, G. S., & Barbour, J. S. (1979). Selective inattention to anxiety-linked stimuli. *Journal of Experimental Psychology: General, 108,* 182–224. (4)

Blumenthal, S. J., & Kupfer, D. J. (1986). Generalizable treatment strategies for suicidal behavior. *Annals of the New York Academy of Sciences, 487,* 327–340. (14)

Blundell, J. E. (1987). Nutritional manipulations for altering food intake. *Annals of the New York Academy of Sciences, 499,* 144–155. (11)

Bollard, J. (1982). A 2-year follow-up of bedwetters treated by dry-bed training and standard conditioning. *Behaviour Research and Therapy, 20,* 571–580. (15)

Booth-Kewley, S., & Friedman, H. S. (1987). Psychological predictors of heart disease: A quantitative review. *Psychological Bulletin, 101,* 343–362. (12)

Bores, L. D. (1983). Historical review and clinical results of radial keratotomy. *International Ophthalmology Clinics, 23,* 93–118. (4)

Boring, E. G. (1930). A new ambiguous figure. *American Journal of Psychology, 42,* 444–445. (4)

Bornstein, M. H., & Sigman, M. D. (1986). Continuity in mental development from infancy. *Child Development, 57,* 251–274. (10)

Bornstein, R. F. (1989). Subliminal techniques as propaganda tools: Review and critique. *Journal of Mind and Behavior, 10,* 231–262. (4)

Bossard, J. H. S. (1931). Residential propinquity as a factor in marriage selection. *American Journal of Sociology, 38,* 219–224. (16)

Boswell, J. (1990). Sexual and ethical categories in premodern Europe. In D. P. McWhirter, S. A. Sanders, & J. M. Reinisch (Eds.), *Homosexuality/heterosexuality* (pp. 15–31). New York: Oxford University Press. (11)

Bouchard, T. J., Lykken, D. T., McGue, M., Segal, N. L., & Tellegen, A. (1990). Sources of psychological differences: The Minnesota study of twins reared apart. *Science, 250,* 223–228. (6)

Bouchard, T. J., Jr., & McGue, M. (1981). Familial studies of intelligence: A review. *Science, 212,* 1055–1059. (10)

Bouchard, T. J., Jr., & McGue, M. (1990). Genetic and rearing environmental influences on adult personality: An analysis of adopted children reared apart. *Journal of Personality, 58,* 263–292. (13)

Bourne, P. G. (1971). Altered adrenal function in two combat situations in Viet Nam. In B. E. Eleftheriou & J. P. Scott (Eds.), *The physiology of aggression and defeat* (pp. 265–290). New York: Plenum. (12)

Bower, T. G. R., & Wishart, J. G. (1972). Effects of motor skill on object permanence. *Cognition, 1,* 165–172. (6)

Bowers, K. S., Regehr, G., Balthazard, C., & Parker, K. (1990). Intuition in the context of discovery. *Cognitive Psychology, 22,* 72–110. (9)

Bowlby, J. (1952). *Maternal care and mental health.* Geneva: World Health Organization. (6)

Boyd, J. H. (1983). The increasing rate of suicide by firearms. *New England Journal of Medicine, 308,* 872–874. (14)

Boynton, R. M. (1988). Color vision. *Annual Review of Psychology, 39,* 69–100. (4)

Brabeck, M. (1983). Moral judgment: Theory and research on differences between males and females. *Developmental Psychology, 3,* 274–291. (6)

Bradburn, N. M., Rips, L. J., & Shevell, S. K. (1987). Answering autobiographical questions: The impact of memory and inference on surveys. *Science, 236,* 157–161. (8)

Bradbury, T. N., & Miller, G. A. (1985). Season of birth in schizophrenia: A review of evidence, methodology, and etiology. *Psychological Bulletin, 98,* 569–594. (14)

Brady, J. V., Porter, R. W., Conrad, D. G., & Mason, J. W. (1958). Avoidance behavior and the development of gastroduodenal ulcers. *Journal of the Experimental Analysis of Behavior, 1,* 69–72. (12)

Brannon, L., & Feist, J. (1992). *Health psychology* (2nd ed.). Belmont, CA: Wadsworth. (12)

Bransford, J. D., & Johnson, M. K. (1972). Contextual prerequisites for understanding: Some investigations of comprehension and recall. *Journal of Verbal Learning and Verbal Behavior, 11,* 717–726. (8)

Bransford, J. D., & Stein, B. S. (1984). *The ideal problem solver.* New York: W. H. Freeman. (9)

Braun, P., Kochansky, G., Shapiro, R., Greenberg, S., Gudeman, J. E., Johnson, S., & Shore, M. F. (1981). Overview: Deinstitutionalization of psychiatric patients: A critical review of outcome studies. *American Journal of Psychiatry, 138,* 736–749. (15)

Bregman, A. S. (1981). Asking the "what for" question in auditory perception. In M. Kubovy & J. R. Pomerantz (Eds.), *Perceptual organization* (pp. 99–118). Hillsdale, NJ: Lawrence Erlbaum. (4)

Brenner, R. (1990). *Gambling and speculation.* Cambridge, England: Cambridge University Press. (9)

Brent, D. A., Perper, J. A., Goldstein, C. E., Kolko, D. J., Allan, M. J., Allman, C. J., & Zelenak, J. P. (1988). Risk factors for adolescent suicide. *Archives of General Psychiatry, 45,* 581–588. (14)

Breslau, N., & Prabucki, K. (1987). Siblings of disabled children. *Archives of General Psychiatry, 44,* 1040–1046. (6)

Breuer, J., & Freud, S. (1957). *Studies on Hysteria* (J. Strachey, Trans. and ed.). New York: Basic Books. (Original work published 1895) (13, 15)

Brewer, W. F., & Treyens, J. C. (1981). Role of schemata in memory for places. *Cognitive Psychology, 13,* 207–230. (8)

Brickman, P., Becker, L. J., & Castle, S. (1979). Making trust easier and harder through forms of sequential interaction. *Journal of Personality and Social Psychology, 37,* 515–521. (16)

Brockner, J., & Rubin, J. Z. (1985). *Entrapment in escalating conflicts.* New York: Springer-Verlag. (16)

Brooks-Gunn, J., & Furstenberg, F. F., Jr. (1986). The children of adolescent mothers: Physical, academic, and psychological outcomes. *Developmental Review, 6,* 224–251. (6)

Brooks-Gunn, J., & Furstenberg, F. F., Jr. (1989). Adolescent sexual behavior. *American Psychologist, 44,* 249–257. (6, 11)

Brophy, J. (1987). Socializing students' motivation to learn. *Advances in Motivation and Achievement, 5,* 181–210. (11)

Brower, K. J., & Anglin, M. D. (1987). Adolescent cocaine use: Epidemiology, risk factors, and prevention. *Journal of Drug Education, 17,* 163–180. (5)

Brown, N. R., Shevell, S. K., & Rips, L. J. (1986). Public memories and their personal context. In D. C. Rubin (Ed.), *Autobiographical memory* (pp. 137–158). Cambridge, England: Cambridge University Press. (8)

Brown, R., & Kulik, J. (1977). Flashbulb memories. *Cognition, 5,* 73–99. (8)

Brown, R. J., & Donderi, D. C. (1986). Dream content and reported well-being among recurrent dreamers, past-recurrent dreamers, and nonrecurrent dreamers. *Journal of Personality and Social Psychology, 50,* 612–623. (5)

Brownell, K. D. (1982). Obesity: Understanding and treating a serious, prevalent, and refractory disorder. *Journal of Consulting and Clinical Psychology, 50,* 820–840. (11)

Bruch, H. (1980). Preconditions for the development of anorexia nervosa. *American Journal of Psychoanalysis, 40,* 169–172. (11)

Bruck, M., Cavanagh, P., & Ceci, S. J. (1991). Fortysomething: Recognizing faces at one's 25th reunion. *Memory & Cognition, 19,* 221–228. (4)

Bruner, J. S., & Potter, M. C. (1964). Interference in visual recognition. *Science, 144,* 424–425. (9)

Buck, L., & Axel, R. (1991). A novel multigene family may encode odorant receptors: A molecular basis for odor recognition. *Cell, 65,* 175–187. (4)

Buell, S. J., & Coleman, P. D. (1981). Quantitative evidence for selective growth in normal human aging but not in senile dementia. *Brain Research, 214,* 23–41. (3)

Burchfield, S. R. (1979). The stress response: A new perspective. *Psychosomatic Medicine, 41,* 661–672. (12)

Burger, J. M. (1986). Increasing compliance by improving the deal: The that's-not-all technique. *Journal of Personality and Social Psychology, 51,* 277–283. (9)

Burgess, A. W., Hazelwood, R. R., Rokous, F. E., Hartman, C. R., & Burgess, A. G. (1988). Serial rapists and their victims: Reenactment and repetition. *Annals of the New York Academy of Sciences, 528,* 277–295. (11)

Burgess, E. W., & Wallin, P. (1953). *Engagement and marriage.* Philadelphia: Lippincott. (16)

Burke, H. R. (1985). Raven's Progressive Matrices (1938): More on norms, reliability, and validity. *Journal of Clinical Psychology, 41,* 231–235. (10)

Burke, K. C., Burke, J. D., Jr., Rae, D. S., & Regier, D. A. (1991). Comparing age at onset of major depression and other psychiatric disorders by birth cohorts in five U.S. community populations. *Archives of General Psychiatry, 48,* 787–795. (14)

Burke, K. C., Burke, J. D., Jr., Regier, D. A., & Rae, D. S. (1990). Age at onset of selected mental disorders in five community populations. *Archives of General Psychiatry, 47,* 511–518. (14)

Burley, K. A. (1991). Family-work spillover in dual-career couples: A comparison of two time perspectives. *Psychological Reports, 68,* 471–480. (6)

Burnstein, E., & Vinokur, A. (1973). Testing two classes of theories about group-induced shifts in individual choice. *Journal of Experimental Social Psychology, 9,* 123–137. (16)

Burnstein, E., & Vinokur, A. (1977). Persuasive arguments and social comparison as determinants of attitude polarization. *Journal of Experimental Social Psychology, 13,* 315–332. (16)

Burrows, G. D., McIntyre, I. M., Judd, F. K., & Norman, T. R. (1988, August). Clinical effects of serotonin reuptake inhibitors in the treatment of depressive illness. *Journal of Clinical Psychiatry, 49* (Suppl. 8), 18–22. (15)

Burstein, A. (1985). How common is delayed posttraumatic stress disorder? *American Journal of Psychiatry, 142,* 887. (12)

Buss, D. M. (1985). Human mate selection. *American Scientist, 73,* 47–51. (16)

Buss, A. H. (1989). Personality as traits. *American Psychologist, 44*, 1378–1388. (13)

Butcher, J. N., Graham, J. R., Williams, C. L., & Ben-Porath, Y. S. (1990). *Development and use of the MMPI-2 content scales.* Minneapolis: University of Minnesota Press. (13)

Cahalan, D. (1978). Subcultural differences in drinking behavior in U.S. national surveys and selected European studies. In P. E. Nathan, G. A. Marlatt, & T. Løberg (Eds.), *Alcoholism: New directions in behavioral research and treatment* (pp. 235–253). New York: Plenum. (14)

Caltabiano, M. L., & Smithson, M. (1983). Variables affecting the perception of self-disclosure appropriateness. *Journal of Social Psychology, 120*, 119–128. (6)

Camara, W. J. (1988). Reagan signs ban of polygraph testing for job applicants. *The Industrial-Organizational Psychologist, 26*, 39–41. (12)

Camel, J. E., Withers, G. S., & Greenough, W. T. (1986). Persistence of visual cortex dendritic alterations induced by postweaning exposure to a "superenriched" environment in rats. *Behavioral Neuroscience, 100*, 810–813. (3)

Campbell, S. S., & Tobler, I. (1984). Animal sleep: A review of sleep duration across phylogeny. *Neuroscience & Biobehavioral Reviews, 8*, 269–300. (5)

Campbell, S., Volow, M. R., & Cavenar, J. O. (1981). Cotard's syndrome and the psychiatric manifestations of typhoid fever. *American Journal of Psychiatry, 138*, 1377–1378. (2)

Campos, J. J., Bertenthal, B. I., & Kermoian, R. (1992). Early experience and emotional development. *Psychological Science, 3*, 61–64. (14)

Cannon, W. B. (1927). The James-Lange theory of emotion. *American Journal of Psychology, 39*, 106–124. (12)

Cannon, W. B. (1929). Organization for physiological homeostasis. *Physiological Reviews, 9*, 399–431. (11)

Caplan, L. (1984). *The insanity defense and the trial of John W. Hinckley, Jr.* Boston: Godine. (15)

Carey, S. (1978). The child as word learner. In M. Halle, J. Bresnan, & G. A. Miller (Eds.), *Linguistic theory and psychological reality* (pp. 264–293). Cambridge, MA: MIT Press. (6)

Carpenter, P. A., Just, M. A., & Shell, P. (1990). What one intelligence test measures: A theoretical account of the processing in the Raven Progressive Matrices test. *Psychological Review, 97*, 404–431. (10)

Carroll, B. J. (1980). Implications of biological research for the diagnosis of depression. In J. Mendlewicz (Ed.), *New advances in the diagnosis and treatment of depressive illness* (pp. 85–107). Amsterdam: Excerpta medica. (14)

Cattell, R. B. (1965). *The scientific analysis of personality.* Chicago: Aldine. (13)

Cattell, R. B. (1987). *Intelligence: Its structure, growth and action.* Amsterdam: North-Holland. (10)

Ceci, S. J. (1990). *On intelligence . . . more or less.* Englewood Cliffs, NJ: Prentice-Hall. (10)

Ceci, S. J., Ross, D. F., & Toglia, M. P. (1987). Suggestibility of children's memory: Psycholegal implications. *Journal of Experimental Psychology: General, 116*, 38–49. (8)

Chaiken, S. (1987). The heuristic model of persuasion. In M. P. Zanna, J. M. Olson, & C. P. Herman (Eds.), *Social influence: The Ontario symposium* (Vol. 5, pp. 3–39). Hillsdale, NJ: Lawrence Erlbaum. (16)

Chamberlin, J. (1978). *On our own.* New York: Hawthorn. (15)

Charlton, S. G. (1983). Differential conditionability: Reinforcing grooming in golden hamsters. *Animal Learning & Behavior, 11*, 27–34. (7)

Chase, T. N., Wexler, N. S., & Barbeau, A. (Eds.) (1979). *Advances in Neurology: Vol. 23, Huntington's disease.* New York: Raven Press. (1)

Cheetham, E. (1973). *The prophecies of Nostradamus.* New York: Putnam's. (2)

Cherlin, A. J., Furstenberg, F. F., Jr., Chase-Lansdale, P. L., Kiernan, K. E., Robins, P. K., Morrison, D. R., & Teitler, J. O. (1991). Longitudinal studies of effects of divorce on children in Great Britain and the United States. *Science, 252*, 1386–1389. (6)

Child, I. L. (1985). Psychology and anomalous observations: The question of ESP in dreams. *American Psychologist, 40*, 1219–1239. (2)

Chiodo, L. A., & Antelman, S. M. (1980). Electroconvulsive shock: Progressive dopamine autoreceptor subsensitivity independent of repeated treatment. *Science, 210*, 799–801. (15)

Chiueh, C. C. (1988). Dopamine in the extrapyramidal motor function. *Annals of the New York Academy of Sciences, 515*, 226–238. (3)

Cho, A. K. (1990). Ice: A new dosage form of an old drug. *Science, 249*, 631–634. (5)

Chodoff, P. (1982). Hysteria and women. *American Journal of Psychiatry, 139*, 545–551. (14)

Chomsky, N. (1980). *Rules and representations.* New York: Columbia University Press. (9)

Chouinard, G., & Jones, B. D. (1980). Neuroleptic-induced supersensitivity psychosis: Clinical and pharmacological characteristics. *American Journal of Psychiatry, 137*, 16–21. (15)

Christopher, F. S., & Cate, R. M. (1985). Premarital sexual pathways and relationship development. *Journal of Social and Personal Relationships, 2*, 271–288. (6, 11)

Cialdini, R. B. (1985). *Influence: Science and practice.* Glenview, IL: Scott, Foresman. (7)

Cialdini, R. B., Kallgren, C. A., & Reno, R. R. (1991). A focus theory of normative conduct: A theoretical refinement and reevaluation of the role of norms in human behavior. *Advances in Experimental Social Psychology, 24*, 201–234. (16)

Cialdini, R. B., Vincent, J. E., Lewis, S. K., Catalan, J., Wheeler, D.,'& Darby, B. L. (1975). Reciprocal concessions procedure for inducing compliance: The door-in-the-face technique. *Journal of Personality and Social Psychology, 31*, 206–215. (16)

Cines, B. M., & Rozin, P. (1982). Some aspects of the liking for hot coffee and coffee flavor. *Appetite: Journal for Intake Research, 3*, 23–34. (5)

Cirignotta, F., Todesco, C. V., & Lugaresi, E. (1980). Temporal lobe epilepsy with ecstatic seizures (so-called Dostoevsky epilepsy). *Epilepsia, 21*, 705–710. (3)

Clark, K. B., & Clark, M. P. (1947). Racial identification and preference in Negro children. In T. M. Newcomb & E. L. Hartley (Eds.), *Readings in social psychology* (pp. 169–178). New York: Henry Holt. (6)

Clarke, A. M., & Clarke, A. D. B. (1976). *Early experience: Myth and evidence.* New York: Free Press. (6)

Clarke-Stewart, K. A. (1989). Infant day care: Maligned or malignant? *American Psychologist, 44*, 266–273. (6)

Clarkin, J. F., & Frances, A. (1982). Selection criteria for the brief psychotherapies. *American Journal of Psychotherapy, 36*, 166–180. (15)

Clementz, B. A., & Sweeney, J. A. (1990). Is eye movement dysfunction a biological marker for schizophrenia? A methodological review. *Psychological Review, 108*, 77–92. (14)

Clifford, M. M., & Walster, E. (1973). The effect of physical attractiveness on teacher expectation. *Sociology of Education, 46*, 248–258. (16)

Clifton, R., Siqueland, E. R., & Lipsitt, L. P. (1972). Conditioned head-turning in human newborns as a function of conditioned response requirements and states of wakefulness. *Journal of Experimental Child Psychology, 13*, 43–57. (6)

"Clinicopathologic conference." (1967). *Johns Hopkins Medical Journal, 120*, 186–199. (12)

Clohessy, A. B., Posner, M. I., Rothbart, M. K., & Veccra, S. P. (1991). The development of inhibition of return in early infancy. *Journal of Cognitive Neuroscience, 3*, 345–350. (6)

Clomipramine collaborative study group. (1991). Clomipramine in the treatment of patients with obsessive-compulsive disorder. *Archives of General Psychiatry, 48*, 730–738. (15)

Cloninger, C. R. (1987). Neurogenetic adaptive mechanisms in alcoholism. *Science, 236*, 410–416. (14)

Cloninger, C. R., Bohman, M., & Sigvardsson, S. (1981). Inheritance of alcohol abuse: Cross-fostering analysis of adopted men. *Archives of General Psychiatry, 38*, 861–868. (3, 14)

Cocozza, J., Melick, M., & Steadman, H. (1978). Trends in violent crime among ex-mental patients. *Criminology, 16*, 317–334. (15)

Coffey, C. E., Weiner, R. D., Djang, W. T., Figiel, G. S., Soady, S. A. R., Patterson, L. J., Holt, P. D., Spritzer, C. E., & Wilkinson, W. E. (1991). Brain anatomic effects of electroconvulsive therapy. *Archives of General Psychiatry, 48*, 1013–1021. (15)

Cohen, C. E. (1981). Person categories and social perception: Testing some boundaries of the processing effects of prior knowledge. *Journal of Personality and Social Psychology, 40*, 441–452. (16)

Cohen, J. D., Dunbar, K., & McClelland, J. L. (1990). On the control of automatic processes: A parallel distributed processing account of the Stroop effect. *Psychological Review, 97*, 332–361. (9)

Cohen, N. J., Eichenbaum, H., Deacedo, B. S., & Corkin, S. (1985). Different memory systems underlying acquisition of procedural and declarative knowledge. *Annals of the New York Academy of Sciences, 444*, 54–71. (8)

Cohen, N. J., & Squire, L. R. (1980). Preserved learning and retention of pattern-analyzing skill in amnesia: Dissociation of knowing how and knowing that. *Science, 210*, 207–211. (8)

Cohen, S., Lichtenstein, E., Prochaska, J. O., Rossi, J. S., Gritz, E. R., Carr, C. R., Orleans, C. T., Schoenbach, V. J., Biener, L., Abrams, D., DiClemente, C., Curry, S., Marlatt, G. A., Cummings, K. M., Emont, S. L., Giovino, G., & Ossip-Klein, D. (1989). Debunking myths about self-quitting: Evidence from 10 prospective studies of persons who attempt to quit smoking by themselves. *American Psychologist, 44*, 1355–1365. (14)

Cohen, S. L., & Cohen, R. (1985). The role of activity in spatial cognition. In R. Cohen (Ed.), *The development of spatial cognition* (pp. 199–223). Hillsdale, NJ: Lawrence Erlbaum. (9)

Coie, J. D., & Dodge, K. (1983). Continuities and change in children's social status: A five-year longitudinal study. *Merrill-Palmer Quarterly, 29*, 261–282. (6)

Coile, D. C., & Miller, N. (1984). How radical animal activists try to mislead humane people. *American Psychologist, 39*, 700–701. (1)

Cole, J. O., Goldberg, S. C., & Davis, J. M. (1966). Drugs in the treatment of psychosis. In P. Solomon (Ed.), *Psychiatric drugs* (pp. 153–180). New York: Grune & Stratton. (15)

Cole, N. S. (1981). Bias in testing. *American Psychologist, 36*, 1067–1077. (10)

Collins, A. M., & Quillian, M. R. (1969). Retrieval time from semantic memory. *Journal of Verbal Learning and Verbal Behavior, 8*, 240–247. (9)

Collins, A. M., & Quillian, M. R. (1970). Does category size affect categorization time? *Journal of Verbal Learning and Verbal Behavior, 9*, 432–438. (9)

Collins, W. A., & Gunnar, M. R. (1990). Social and personality development. *Annual Review of Psychology, 41*, 387–416. (6)

Coltheart, M., Besner, D., Jonasson, J. T., & Davelaar, E. (1979). Phonological recoding in the lexical decision task. *Quarterly Journal of Experimental Psychology, 31*, 489–508. (9)

Colwill, R. M., & Rescorla, R. A. (1985). Post-conditioning devaluation of a reinforcer affects instrumental responding. *Journal of Experimental Psychology: Animal Behavior Processes, 11*, 120–132. (7)

Connine, C. M., Blasko, D. G., & Hall, M. (1991). Effects of subsequent sentence context in auditory word recognition: Temporal and linguistic constraints. *Journal of Memory and Language, 30*, 234–250. (9)

Cook, B. L., & Winokur, G. (1985). Separate heritability of alcoholism and psychotic symptoms. *American Journal of Psychiatry, 142*, 360–361. (14)

Cook, S. W. (1979). Social science and school desegregation: "Did we mislead the Supreme Court?" *Personality and Social Psychology Bulletin, 5*, 420–437. (6)

Cook, T. D., Kendzierski, D. A., & Thomas, S. V. (1983). The implicit assumptions of television research: An analysis of the 1982 NIMH report on television and behavior. *Public Opinion Quarterly, 47,* 161–201. (2)

Coombs, R. H., & Fawzy, F. I. (1982). The effect of marital status on stress in medical school. *American Journal of Psychiatry, 139,* 1490–1493. (12)

Corkin, S. (1984). Lasting consequences of bilateral medial temporal lobectomy: Clinical course and experimental findings in H.M. *Seminars in Neurology, 4,* 249–259. (8)

Costa, P. T., Jr., McCrae, R. R., & Dye, D. A. (1991). Facet scales for agreeableness and conscientiousness: A revision of the NEO personality inventory. *Personality and Individual Differences, 12,* 887–898. (13)

Costello, E. J. (1982). Locus of control and depression in students and psychiatric outpatients. *Journal of Clinical Psychology, 38,* 340–343. (14)

Cowan, C. L., Thompson, W. C., & Ellsworth, P. C. (1984). The effects of death qualification on jurors' predisposition to convict and on the quality of deliberation. *Law and Human Behavior, 8,* 53–79. (16)

Cowan, J. D. (1983). Testing the escape hypotheses: Alcohol helps users to forget their feelings. *Journal of Nervous and Mental Disease, 171,* 40–48. (5)

Coyle, J. T., Price, D. L., & DeLong, M. R. (1983). Alzheimer's disease: A disorder of cortical cholinergic innervation. *Science, 219,* 1184–1190. (8)

Craik, F. I. M., & Lockhart, R. S. (1972). Levels of processing: A framework for memory research. *Journal of Verbal Learning and Verbal Behavior, 11,* 671–684. (8)

Craik, F. I. M., & Watkins, M. J. (1973). The role of rehearsal in short-term memory. *Journal of Verbal Learning and Verbal Behavior, 12,* 599–607. (8)

Crammer, J. L. (1959). Water and sodium in two psychotics. *Lancet, 1*(7083), 1122–1126. (14)

Creak, M. (1961). Schizophrenic syndrome in childhood. *British Medical Journal, 2,* 889–890. (14)

Creed, T. L. (1987). Subliminal deception: Pseudoscience on the college lecture circuit. *Skeptical Inquirer, 11,* 358–366. (4)

Crews, D. J., & Landers, D. M. (1987). A meta-analytic review of aerobic fitness and reactivity to psychosocial stressors. *Medicine & Science in Sports & Exercise, 19,* S114–S120. (12)

Crick, F., & Mitchison, G. (1986). REM sleep and neural nets. *Journal of Mind and Behavior, 7,* 229–249. (5)

Crocker, J., & Major, B. (1989). Social stigma and self-esteem: The self-protective properties of stigma. *Psychological Review, 96,* 608–630. (16)

Cross, C. K., & Hirschfeld, R. M. A. (1986). Psychosocial factors and suicidal behavior. *Annals of the New York Academy of Sciences, 487,* 77–89. (14)

Crouter, A. C., Perry-Jenkins, M., Huston, T. L., & McHale, S. M. (1987). Processes underlying father involvement in dual-earner and single-earner families. *Developmental Psychology, 23,* 431–440. (6)

Crovitz, H. F., & Schiffman, H. (1974). Frequency of episodic memories as a function of their age. *Bulletin of the Psychonomic Society, 4,* 517–518. (8)

Crow, T. J. (1985). The two-syndrome concept: Origins and current status. *Schizophrenia Bulletin, 11,* 471–486. (14)

Croyle, R. T., & Cooper, J. (1983). Dissonance arousal: Physiological evidence. *Journal of Personality and Social Psychology, 45,* 782–791. (16)

Cummings, J. L., & Victoroff, J. I. (1990). Noncognitive neuropsychiatric syndromes in Alzheimer's disease. *Neuropsychiatry, Neuropsychology, & Behavioral Neurology, 3,* 140–158. (8)

Cummings, N. A. (1979). Turning bread into stones: Our modern antimiracle. *American Psychologist, 34,* 1119–1129. (11, 14)

Curry, S., Marlatt, A., & Gordon, J. R. (1987). Abstinence violation effect: Validation of an attributional construct with smoking cessation. *Journal of Consulting and Clinical Psychology, 55,* 145–149. (7)

Cutting, J. E. (1987). Rigidity in cinema seen from the front row, side aisle. *Journal of Experimental Psychology: Human Perception and Performance, 13,* 323–334. (4)

Czeisler, C. A., Johnson, M. P., Duffy, J. F., Brown, E. N., Ronda, J. M., & Kronauer, R. E. (1990). Exposure to bright light and darkness to treat physiologic maladaptation to night work. *New England Journal of Medicine, 322,* 1353–1359. (5)

Czeisler, C. A., Moore-Ede, M. C., & Coleman, R. M. (1982). Rotating shift work schedules that disrupt sleep are improved by applying circadian principles. *Science, 217,* 460–463. (5)

Czeisler, C. A., Weitzman, E. D., Moore-Ede, M. C., Zimmerman, J. C., & Knauer, R. S. (1980). Human sleep: Its duration and organization depend on its circadian phase. *Science, 210,* 1264–1267. (5)

Dabbs, J. M., & Morris, R. (1990). Testosterone, social class, and antisocial behavior in a sample of 4,462 men. *Psychological Science, 1,* 209–211. (12)

Dackis, C. A., Pottash, A. L. C., Annitto, W., & Gold, M. S. (1982). Persistence of urinary marijuana levels after supervised abstinence. *American Journal of Psychiatry, 139,* 1196–1198. (5)

Daley, S. (1991, January 9). Girls' self esteem is lost on way to adolescence, new study finds. *New York Times,* Jan. 9, p. B1. (2)

Dallenbach, K. M. (1951). A puzzle picture with a new principle of concealment. *American Journal of Psychology, 64,* 431–433. (4)

Daly, M., Wilson, M., & Weghorst, S. J. (1982). Male sexual jealousy. *Ethology & Sociobiology, 3,* 11–27. (11, 12)

Damaser, E. C., Shor, R. E., & Orne, M. E. (1963). Physiological effects during hypnotically requested emotions. *Psychosomatic Medicine, 25,* 334–343. (5)

Damron-Rodriguez, J. (1991). Commentary: Multicultural aspects of aging in the U.S.: Implications for health and human services. *Journal of Cross-cultural Gerontology, 6,* 135–143. (6)

Dance, K. A., & Neufeld, R. W. J. (1988). Aptitude-treatment interaction research in the clinical setting: A review of attempts to dispel the "patient uniformity" myth. *Psychological Bulletin, 104,* 192–213. (15)

Danion, J.-M., Willard-Schroeder, D., Zimmermann, M.-A., Grangé, E., Schlienger, J.-L., & Singer, L. (1991). Explicit memory and repetition priming in depression. *Archives of General Psychiatry, 48,* 707–711. (8)

Darley, J. M., & Shultz, T. R. (1990). Moral rules: Their content and acquisition. *Annual Review of Psychology, 41,* 525–556. (6)

Darwin, C. (1859). *On the origin of species by means of natural selection.* London: Murray. (1)

Darwin, C. (1871). *The descent of man.* New York: D. Appleton. (7)

Darwin, C. (1872/1965). *The expression of emotions in man and animals.* Chicago: University of Chicago Press. (Original work published 1872) (12)

Davenport, D., & Foley, J. M. (1979). Fringe benefits of cataract surgery. *Science, 204,* 454–457. (4)

Davenport, W. H. (1977). Sex in cross-cultural perspective. In F. A. Beach (Ed.), *Human sexuality in four perspectives* (pp. 62–86). Baltimore: Johns Hopkins University Press. (11)

Davidson, R. S. (1966). Laboratory maintenance and learning of *Alligator mississippiensis. Psychological Reports, 19,* 595–601. (7)

Davis, J. M. (1985). Maintenance therapy and the natural course of schizophrenia. *Journal of Clinical Psychiatry, 46,* 18–21. (15)

Davis, K. E., & Jones, E. E. (1960). Changes in interpersonal perception as a means of reducing cognitive dissonance. *Journal of Abnormal and Social Psychology, 61,* 402–410. (16)

Dawes, R. M., & Smith, T. L. (1985). Attitude and opinion measurement. In G. Lindzey & E. Aronson (Eds.), *Handbook of social psychology* (Vol. 1, pp. 509–566). New York: Random House. (16)

Day, R. H. (1972). Visual spatial illusions: A general explanation. *Science, 175,* 1335–1340. (4)

Deakin, J. M., & Allard, F. (1991). Skilled memory in expert figure skaters. *Memory & Cognition, 19,* 79–86. (9)

DeBuono, B. A., Zinner, S. H., Daamen, M., & McCormack, W. M. (1990). Sexual behavior of college women in 1975, 1986, and 1989. *New England Journal of Medicine, 322,* 821–825. (11)

DeCasper, A. J., & Fifer, W. P. (1980). Of human bonding: Newborns prefer their mothers' voices. *Science, 208,* 1174–1177. (6)

Deci, E. L. (1971). Effects of externally mediated rewards on intrinsic motivation. *Journal of Personality and Social Psychology, 18,* 105–115. (11)

de Groot, A. D. (1966). Perception and memory versus thought: Some old ideas and recent findings. In B. Kleinmuntz (Ed.), *Problem solving* (pp. 19–50). New York: Wiley. (9)

DeLeon, P. H., Vanden Bos, G. R., & Cummings, N. A. (1983). Psychotherapy—Is it safe, effective, and appropriate? *American Psychologist, 38,* 907–911. (15)

DeLoache, J. S. (1989). The development of representation in young children. *Advances in Child Development and Behavior, 22,* 1–39. (6)

DeLuise, M., Blackburn, G. L., & Flier, J. S. (1980). Reduced activity of the red-cell sodium-potassium pump in human obesity. *New England Journal of Medicine, 303,* 1017–1022. (11)

Dement, W. (1960). The effect of dream deprivation. *Science, 131,* 1705–1707. (5)

Dement, W. C. (1972). *Some must watch while some must sleep.* Stanford, CA: Stanford Alumni Association. (5)

Dement, W. (1992). *The Sleepwatchers.* Stanford, CA: Portable Stanford Book Series. (5)

Dement, W., & Kleitman, N. (1957a). Cyclic variations in EEG during sleep and their relation to eye movements, body motility, and dreaming. *Electroencephalography and Clinical Neurophysiology, 9,* 673–690. (5)

Dement, W., & Kleitman, N. (1957b). The relation of eye movements during sleep to dream activity: An objective method for the study of dreaming. *Journal of Experimental Psychology, 53,* 339–346. (5)

Dement, W., & Wolpert, E. A. (1958). The relation of eye movements, body motility, and external stimuli to dream content. *Journal of Experimental Psychology, 55,* 543–553. (5)

DeMyer, M. K. (1979). *Parents and children in autism.* Washington, DC: V. H. Winston. (14)

DePaulo, B. M. (1992). Nonverbal behavior and self-presentation. *Psychological Bulletin, 111,* 203–243. (16)

Després, J.-P., Pouliot, M.-C., Moorjani, S., Nadeau, A., Tremblay, A., Lupien, P. J., Thériault, G., & Bouchard, C. (1991). Loss of abdominal fat and metabolic response to exercise training in obese women. *American Journal of Physiology, 261,* E159–E167. (11)

Derogatis, L. (1986). Psychology in cancer medicine: A perspective and overview. *Journal of Consulting and Clinical Psychology, 54,* 632–638. (12)

Desiderato, O., MacKinnon, J. R., & Hissom, H. (1974). Development of gastric ulcers in rats following stress termination. *Journal of Comparative and Physiological Psychology, 87,* 208–214. (12)

Desimone, R., Albright, T. D., Gross, C. G., & Bruce, C. (1984). Stimulus-selective properties of inferior temporal neurons in the macaque. *Journal of Neuroscience, 4,* 2051–2062. (4)

Désir, D., VanCauter, E., Fang, V. S., Martino, E., Jadot, C., Spire, J.-P., Noël, P., Refetoff, S., Copinschi, G., & Golstein, J. (1981). Effects of jet lag on hormonal patterns. I. Procedure variations in total plasma proteins, and disruption of adrenocorticotropin-cortisol periodicity. *Journal of Clinical Endocrinology and Metabolism, 52,* 628–641. (5)

Detterman, D. K. (1979). Detterman's laws of individual differences research. In R. J. Sternberg & D. K. Detterman (Eds.), *Human intelligence* (pp. 165–175). Norwood, NJ: Ablex. (10)

Deutsch, J. A. (1983). Dietary control and the stomach. *Progress in Neurobiology, 20,* 313–332. (11)

Deutsch, J. A., Young, N. G., & Kalogeris, T. J. (1978). The stomach signals satiety. *Science, 201,* 165–167. (11)

DeValois, R. L. (1965). Behavioral and electrophysiological studies of primate vision. In W. D. Neff (Ed.), *Contributions to sensory physiology* (Vol. 1, pp. 137–178). New York: Academic. (4)

Devine, D. A., & Fernald, P. S. (1973). Outcome effects of receiving a preferred, randomly assigned, or nonpreferred therapy. *Journal of Consulting and Clinical Psychology, 41,* 104–107. (15)

Devine, P. G., Monteith, M. J., Zuwerink, J. R., & Elliot, A. J. (1991). Prejudice with and without compunction. *Journal of Personality and Social Psychology, 60,* 817–830. (16)

deWolff, C. J. (1985). Stress and strain in the work environment: Does it lead to illness? In W. D. Gentry, H. Benson, & C. J. deWolff (Eds.), *Behavioral medicine: Work, stress, and health* (pp. 33–43). Dordrecht, Netherlands: Martinus Nijhoff. (12)

Diamond, R., & Carey, S. (1986). Why faces are and are not special: An effect of expertise. *Journal of Experimental Psychology: General, 115,* 107–117. (4)

Dick, M., Ullman, S., & Sagi, D. (1987). Parallel and serial processes in motion detection. *Science, 237,* 400–402. (4)

Diener, E. (1984). Subjective well-being. *Psychological Bulletin, 95,* 542–575. (12)

Dion, K. E., Berscheid, E., & Walster, E. (1972). What is beautiful is good. *Journal of Personality and Social Psychology, 24,* 285–290. (16)

Dische, S., Yule, W., Corbett, J., & Hand, D. (1983). Childhood nocturnal enuresis: Factors associated with outcome of treatment with an enuresis alarm. *Developmental Medicine and Child Neurology, 25,* 67–80. (15)

Dixon, N. F. (1981). *Preconscious processing.* New York: Wiley. (4)

Dobrzecka, C., Szwejkowska, G., & Konorski, J. (1966). Qualitative versus directional cues in two forms of differentiation. *Science, 153,* 87–89. (7)

Dobson, K. S. (1989). A meta-analysis of the efficacy of cognitive therapy for depression. *Journal of Consulting and Clinical Psychology, 57,* 414–419. (15)

Dole, V. P. (1978). A clinician's view of addiction. In J. Fishman (Ed.), *The bases of addiction* (pp. 37–46). Berlin: Dahlem Konferenzen. (14)

Dollard, J., Miller, N. E., Doob, L. W., Mowrer, O. H., & Sears, R. R. (1939). *Frustration and aggression.* New Haven, CT: Yale University Press. (12)

Dostoyevsky, F. (1868/1969). *The idiot.* New York: New American Library. (Original work published 1868) (15)

Druckman, D., & Swets, J. A. (1988). *Enhancing human performance.* Washington, DC: National Academy Press. (2)

Duke, M., & Nowicki, S., Jr. (1979). *Abnormal psychology: Perspectives on being different.* Monterey, CA: Brooks/Cole. (14)

Duncan, B. L. (1976). Differential social perception and attribution of intergroup violence: Testing the lower limits of stereotyping of blacks. *Journal of Personality and Social Psychology, 34,* 590–598. (16)

Dunn, R., & Griggs, S. A. (1990). Research on the learning style characteristics of selected racial and ethnic groups. *Journal of Reading, Writing, & Learning Disabilities International, 6,* 262–280. (6)

Dush, D. M., Hirt, M. L., & Schroeder, H. (1983). Self-statement modification with adults: A meta-analysis. *Psychological Bulletin, 94,* 408–422. (4, 15)

Dworkin, B. R., & Miller, N. E. (1986). Failure to replicate visceral learning in the acute curarized rat preparation. *Behavioral Neuroscience, 100,* 299–314. (7)

Dwyman, J., & Bowers, K. (1983). The use of hypnosis to enhance recall. *Science, 222,* 184–185. (5)

Dykeman, B. (1989). A social-learning perspective of treating test-anxious students. *College Student Journal, 23,* 123–125. (7)

Eagly, A. H., & Crowley, M. (1986). Gender and helping behavior: A meta-analytic review of the social psychological literature. *Psychological Bulletin, 100,* 283–308. (6)

Eagly, A. H., & Warren, R. (1976). Intelligence, comprehension, and opinion change. *Journal of Personality, 44,* 226–242. (16)

Earls, C. M. (1988). Aberrant sexual arousal in sexual offenders. *Annals of the New York Academy of Sciences, 528,* 41–48. (11)

Eaton, W. W., Holzer, C. E., von Korff, M., Anthony, J. C., Helzer, J. E., George, L., Burnam, A., Boyd, J. H., Kessler, L. G., & Locke, B. Z. (1984). The design of the epidemiologic catchment area surveys. *Archives of General Psychiatry, 41,* 942–948. (14)

Ebbinghaus, H. (1913). *Memory.* New York: Teachers College. (Original work published 1885) (8)

Eccles, J. C. (1986). Chemical transmission and Dale's principle. In T. Hökfelt, K. Fuxe, & B. Pernow (Eds.), *Progress in brain research* (Vol. 68, pp. 3–13). Amsterdam: Elsevier. (3)

Edelman, B. (1981). Binge eating in normal weight and overweight individuals. *Psychological Reports, 49,* 739–746. (11)

Edney, J. H. (1979). The nuts game: A concise commons dilemma analog. *Environmental Psychology and Nonverbal Behavior, 3,* 252–254. (16)

Educational Testing Service. (1990). *Guide to the use of the Graduate Record Examinations program.* Princeton, NJ: Author. (10)

Eibl-Eibesfeldt, I. (1973). *Der vorprogrammierte Mensch* [The preprogrammed human]. Vienna: Verlag Fritz Molden. (12)

Eibl-Eibesfeldt, I. (1974). *Love and hate.* New York: Schocken. (12)

Eikelboom, R., & Stewart, J. (1982). Conditioning of drug-induced physiological responses. *Psychological Review, 89,* 507–528. (7)

Eimas, P. D., Siqueland, E. R., Jusczyk, P., & Vigorito, J. (1971). Speech perception in infants. *Science, 171,* 303–306. (6)

Einstein, G. O., & Hunt, R. R. (1980). Levels of processing and organization: Additive effects of individual item and relational processing. *Journal of Experimental Psychology: Human Learning and Memory, 6,* 588–598. (8)

Ekman, P. (1972). Universals and cultural differences in facial expressions of emotion. In J. K. Cole (Ed.), *Nebraska symposium on motivation 1971* (pp. 207–283). Lincoln, NE: University of Nebraska Press. (12)

Ekman, P., & Friesen, W. V. (1984). *Unmasking the face* (2nd ed.). Palo Alto, CA: Consulting Psychologists Press. (12)

Ekman, P., Friesen, W. V., & Ancoli, S. (1980). Facial signs of emotional experience. *Journal of Personality and Social Psychology, 39,* 1125–1134. (12)

Ekman, P., Friesen, W. V., O'Sullivan, M., Chan, A., Diacoyanni-Tarlatzis, I., Heider, K., Krause, R., LeCompte, W. A., Pitcairn, T., Ricci-Bitti, P. E., Scherer, K., Tomita, M., & Tzavaras, A. (1987). Universals and cultural differences in the judgments of facial expressions of emotion. *Journal of Personality and Social Psychology, 53,* 712–717. (12)

Ekman, P., & O'Sullivan, M. (1991). Who can catch a liar? *American Psychologist, 46,* 913–920. (12)

Ekman, P., Sorenson, E. R., & Friesen, W. V. (1969). Pan-cultural elements in facial displays of emotion. *Science, 164,* 86–88. (12)

Elkin, R. A., & Leippe, M. R. (1986). Physiological arousal, dissonance, and attitude change: Evidence for a dissonance-arousal link and a "don't remind me" effect. *Journal of Personality and Social Psychology, 51,* 55–65. (16)

Elkind, D. (1984). *All grown up and no place to go.* Reading, MA: Addison-Wesley. (6)

Ellis, A. (1987). The impossibility of achieving consistently good mental health. *American Psychologist, 42,* 364–375. (15)

Ellis, A., & Harper, R. A. (1961). *A guide to rational living.* Englewood Cliffs, NJ: Prentice-Hall. (15)

Ellis, L., & Ames, M. A. (1987). Neurohormonal functioning and sexual orientation: A theory of homosexuality-heterosexuality. *Psychological Bulletin, 101,* 233–258. (11)

Ellis, L., Ames, M. A., Peckham, W., & Burke, D. (1988). Sexual orientation of human offspring may be altered by severe maternal stress during pregnancy. *Journal of Sex Research, 25,* 152–157. (11)

Ellis, N. C., & Hennelley, R. A. (1980). A bilingual word-length effect: Implications for intelligence testing and the relative ease of mental calculation in Welsh and English. *British Journal of Psychology, 71,* 43–52. (8)

Ellman, S. J., Spielman, A. J., Luck, D., Steiner, S. S., & Halperin, R. (1978). REM deprivation: A review. In A. M. Arkin, J. S. Antrobus, & S. J. Ellman (Eds.), *The mind in sleep* (pp. 419–457). Hillsdale, NJ: Lawrence Erlbaum. (5)

Emery, R. W. (1982). Interparental conflict and the children of discord and divorce. *Psychological Bulletin, 92,* 310–330. (6)

Emmons, R. A. (1991). Personal strivings, daily life events, and psychological and physical well-being. *Journal of Personality, 59,* 453–472. (13)

Emrick, C. D. (1987). Alcoholics Anonymous: Affiliation processes and effectiveness as treatment. *Alcoholism: Clinical & Experimental Research, 11,* 416–423. (14)

Enns, J. T., & Rensink, R. A. (1990). Sensitivity to three-dimensional orientation in visual search. *Psychological Science, 1,* 323–326. (4)

Epstein, R. (1991). Skinner, creativity, and the problem of spontaneous behavior. *Psychological Science, 2,* 362–370. (7)

Epstein, S. (1979). The stability of behavior: I. On predicting most of the people much of the time. *Journal of Personality and Social Psychology, 37,* 1097–1126. (13)

Epstein, S., & O'Brien, E. J. (1985). The person-situation debate in historical and current perspective. *Psychological Bulletin, 98,* 513–537. (13)

Ericsson, K. A., Chase, W. G., & Falcon, S. (1980). Acquisition of a memory skill. *Science, 208,* 1181–1182. (8)

Erikson, E. H. (1963). *Childhood and society* (2nd ed.). New York: Norton. (6)

Ernhart, C. B., Sokol, R. J., Martier, S., Moron, P., Nadler, D., Ager, J. W., & Wolf, A. (1987). Alcohol teratogenicity in the human: A detailed assessment of specificity, critical period, and threshold. *American Journal of Obstetrics and Gynecology, 156,* 33–39. (6)

Ernst, C., & Angst, J. (1983). *Birth order: Its influence on personality.* New York: Springer-Verlag. (6)

Eron, L. D. (1987). The development of aggressive behavior from the perspective of a developing behaviorism. *American Psychologist, 42,* 435–442. (12)

Eslinger, P. J., & Damasio, A. R. (1986). Preserved motor learning in Alzheimer's disease: Implications for anatomy and behavior. *Journal of Neuroscience, 6,* 3006–3009. (8)

Etcoff, N. L., Freeman, R., & Cave, K. R. (1991). Can we lose memories of faces? Content specificity and awareness in a prosopagnosic. *Journal of Cognitive Neuroscience, 3,* 25–41. (4)

Exner, J. E., Jr. (1986). *The Rorschach: A comprehensive system* (2nd ed.). New York: Wiley. (13)

Eysenck, H. J. (1952). The effects of psychotherapy: An evaluation. *Journal of Consulting Psychology, 16,* 319–324. (15)

Eysenck, H. J. (1990). Genetic and environmental contributions to individual differences: The three major dimensions of personality. *Journal of Personality, 58,* 245–261. (13)

Fagerström, K.-O. (1981). A comparison of psychological and pharmacological treatment in smoking cessation. *Uppsala Psychological Reports,* No. 302. (5)

Falk, J. R., Halmi, K. A., & Tryon, W. W. (1985). Activity measures in anorexia nervosa. *Archives of General Psychiatry, 42,* 811–814. (11)

Fallon, A. E., & Rozin, P. (1985). Sex differences in perceptions of desirable body shape. *Journal of Abnormal Psychology, 94,* 102–105. (11)

Fantz, R. L. (1963). Pattern vision in newborn infants. *Science, 140,* 296–297. (6)

Farah, M. J. (1988). Is visual imagery really visual? Overlooked evidence from neuropsychology. *Psychological Review, 95,* 307–317. (9)

Faraone, S. V., Kremen, W. S., & Tsuang, M. T. (1990). Genetic transmission of major affective disorders: Quantitative models and linkage analyses. *Psychological Bulletin, 108,* 109–127. (14)

Farber, S. L. (1981). *Identical twins reared apart: A reanalysis.* New York: Basic Books. (10)

Farmer, A. E., McGuffin, P., & Gottesman, I. I. (1987). Twin concordance for DSM-III schizophrenia. *Archives of General Psychiatry, 44,* 634–641. (14)

Farmer, H. (1983). Career and homemaking plans for high school youth. *Journal of Counseling Psychology, 30,* 40–45. (11)

Farmer, H. S. (1987). Female motivation and achievement: Implications for interventions. *Advances in Motivation and Achievement, 5,* 51–97. (11)

Farmer, H., & Bohn, M. (1970). Home-career conflict reduction and the level of career interest in women. *Journal of Counseling Psychology, 17,* 228–232. (11)

Fausto-Sterling, A. (1985). *Myths of gender.* New York: Basic Books. (2, 9)

Fay, R. E., Turner, C. F., Klassen, A. D., & Gagnon, J. H. (1989). Prevalence and patterns of same-gender sexual contact among men. *Science, 243,* 338–348. (11)

Fazio, R. H. (1987). Self-perception theory: A current perspective. In M. Zanna, J. M. Olson, & C. P. Herman (Eds.), *Social influence: The Ontario symposium* (Vol. 5, pp. 129–150). Hillsdale, NJ: Lawrence Erlbaum. (16)

Fazio, R. H., Zanna, M. P., & Cooper, J. (1977). Dissonance and self-perception: An integrative view of each theory's proper domain of application. *Journal of Experimental Social Psychology, 13,* 464–479. (16)

Feeney, D. M. (1987). Human rights and animal welfare. *American Psychologist, 42,* 593–599. (2)

Fehrenbach, P. A., & Thelen, M. H. (1982). Behavioral approaches to the treatment of aggressive disorders. *Behavior Modification, 6,* 465–497. (12)

Feingold, A. (1988). Cognitive gender differences are disappearing. *American Psychologist, 43,* 95–103. (10)

Feingold, A. (1992). Good-looking people are not what we think. *Psychological Bulletin, 111,* 304–341. (16)

Fenton, W. S., & McGlashan, T. H. (1991). Natural history of schizophrenia subtypes. I. Longitudinal study of paranoid, hebephrenic, and undifferentiated schizophrenia. *Archives of General Psychiatry, 48,* 969–977. (14)

Fernald, D. (1984). *The Hans legacy: A story of science.* Hillsdale, NJ: Lawrence Erlbaum. (2)

Festinger, L. (1957). *A theory of cognitive dissonance.* Stanford, CA: Stanford University Press. (16)

Festinger, L., & Carlsmith, J. M. (1959). Cognitive consequences of forced compliance. *Journal of Abnormal and Social Psychology, 58,* 203–210. (16)

Festinger, L., Schachter, S., & Back, K. (1950). *Social pressures in informal groups: A study of human factors in housing.* New York: Harper. (16)

Fieve, R. R. (1975). *Moodswing.* New York: William Morrow. (14)

Fine, M. A., & Schwebel, A. I. (1987). An emergent explanation of differing racial reactions to single parenthood. *Journal of Divorce, 11,* 1–15. (6)

Fink, M. (1985). Convulsive therapy: Fifty years of progress. *Convulsive Therapy, 1,* 204–216. (15)

Finkel, M. L., & Finkel, D. J. (1983). Male adolescent sexual behavior, the forgotten partner: A review. *Journal of School Health, 53,* 544–547. (6)

Fischhoff, B. (1975). Hindsight ≠ foresight: The effect of outcome knowledge on judgment under uncertainty. *Journal of Experimental Psychology: Human Perception and Performance, 1,* 288–299. (8)

Fischhoff, B., & Beyth, R. (1975). "I knew it would happen"—Remembered probabilities of once-future things. *Organizational Behavior & Human Performance, 13,* 1–16. (8)

Fishbein, M., & Ajzen, I. (1974). Attitudes towards objects as predictors of single and multiple behavioral criteria. *Psychological Review, 81,* 59–74. (16)

Fishbein, M., & Ajzen, I. (1975). *Belief, attitude, intention and behavior: An introduction to theory and research.* Reading, MA: Addison-Wesley. (16)

Fisher, S., & Greenberg, R. P. (1977). *The scientific credibility of Freud's theories and therapy.* New York: Basic Books. (13)

Fitzgerald, R., & Ellsworth, P. C. (1984). Due process vs. crime control: Death qualification and jury attitudes. *Law and Human Behavior, 8,* 31–51. (16)

Flaherty, J. A., Gaviria, F. M., Black, E. M., Altman, E., & Mitchell, T. (1983). The role of social support in the functioning of patients with unipolar depression. *American Journal of Psychiatry, 140,* 473–476. (14)

Flatz, G. (1987). Genetics of lactose digestion in humans. *Advances in Human Genetics, 16,* 1–77. (3)

Flavell, J. (1986). The development of children's knowledge about the appearance-reality distinction. *American Psychologist, 41,* 418–425. (6)

Fletcher, R., & Voke, J. (1985). *Defective colour vision.* Bristol, England: Adam Hilger. (4)

Flood, J. F., Smith, G. E., & Morley, J. E. (1987). Modulation of memory processing by cholecystokinin: Dependence on the vagus nerve. *Science, 236,* 832–834. (8)

Flynn, J. R. (1984). The mean IQ of Americans: Massive gains 1932 to 1978. *Psychological Bulletin, 95,* 29–51. (10)

Flynn, J. R. (1987). Massive IQ gains in 14 nations: What IQ tests really measure. *Psychological Bulletin, 101,* 171–191. (10)

Foley, V. D. (1984). Family therapy. In R. J. Corini (Ed.), *Current psychotherapies* (3rd ed.) (pp. 447–490). Itasca, IL: F. E. Peacock Publishers. (15)

Folkard, S., Hume, K. I., Minors, D. S., Waterhouse, J. M., & Watson, F. L. (1985). Independence of the circadian rhythm in alertness from the sleep/wake cycle. *Nature, 313,* 678–679. (5)

Fontana, A. F., Marcus, J. L., Noel, B., & Rakusin, J. M. (1972). Prehospitalization coping styles of psychiatric patients: The goal-directedness of life events. *Journal of Nervous and Mental Disease, 155,* 311–321. (15)

Forer, B. R. (1949). The fallacy of personal validation: A classroom demonstration of gullibility. *Journal of Abnormal and Social Psychology, 44,* 118–123. (13)

Forman, R. F., & McCauley, C. (1986). Validity of the positive control polygraph test using the field practice model. *Journal of Applied Psychology, 71,* 691–698. (12)

Forsberg, L. K., & Goldman, M. S. (1987). Experience-dependent recovery of cognitive deficits in alcoholics: Extended transfer of training. *Journal of Abnormal Psychology, 96,* 345–353. (5)

Försterling, F. (1985). Attributional retraining: A review. *Psychological Bulletin, 98,* 495–512. (12)

Foster, W. Z. (1968). *History of the Communist Party of the United States.* New York: Greenwood Press. (16)

Fowler, M. J., Sullivan, M. J., & Ekstrand, B. R. (1973). Sleep and memory. *Science, 179,* 302–304. (5)

Fox, B. H. (1983). Current theory of psychogenic effects on cancer incidence and prognosis. *Journal of Psychosocial Oncology, 1,* 17–31. (12)

Frankenhaeuser, M. (1980). Psychoneuroendocrine approaches to the study of stressful person-environment transactions. In H. Selye (Ed.), *Selye's guide to stress research* (pp. 46–70). New York: Van Nostrand Reinhold. (12)

Frankmann, S. P., & Green, B. G. (1988). Differential effects of cooling on the intensity of taste. *Annals of the New York Academy of Sciences, 510,* 300–303. (4)

Freedman, J. L. (1984). Effect of television violence on aggressiveness. *Psychological Bulletin, 96,* 227–246. (2)

Freedman, J. L. (1986). Television violence and aggression: A rejoinder. *Psychological Bulletin, 100,* 372–378. (2)

Freedman, J. L., & Fraser, S. C. (1966). Compliance without pressure: The foot in the door technique. *Journal of Personality and Social Psychology, 4,* 195–202. (16)

French, A. R. (1988). The patterns of mammalian hibernation. *American Scientist, 76,* 568–575. (5)

Freud, S. (1900/1955). *The interpretation of dreams* (J. Strachey, Trans.). New York: Basic Books. (Original work published 1900) (15)

Freud, S. (1905/1925). *Three contributions to the theory of sex* (A. A. Brill, Trans.). New York: Nervous and Mental Disease Pub. Co. (Original work published 1905) (13)

Freud, S. (1905/1952). *The case of Dora and other papers.* New York: Norton. (Original work published 1905) (1)

Freud, S. (1908/1963). "Civilized" sexual morality and modern nervousness. In P. Rieff (Ed.), *Freud: Sexuality and the psychology of love* (pp. 20–40). New York: Collier Books. (Original work published 1908) (11)

Freud, S. (1927/1953). *The future of an illusion* (J. Strachey, Trans.). New York: Liveright. (Original work published 1927) (13)

Frick, W. B. (1983). The symbolic growth experience. *Journal of Humanistic Psychology, 23,* 108–125. (13)

Friedman, M., & Rosenman, R. H. (1974). *Type-A behavior and your heart.* New York: Knopf. (12)

Friedman, M. I., & Stricker, E. M. (1976). The physiological psychology of hunger: A physiological perspective. *Psychological Review, 83,* 409–431. (11)

Friedman, R., & Iwai, J. (1976). Genetic predisposition and stress-induced hypertension. *Science, 193,* 161–162. (12)

Friedrich-Cofer, L., & Huston, A. C. (1986). Television violence and aggression: The debate continues. *Psychological Bulletin, 100,* 364–371. (2)

Frijda, N. H. (1988). The laws of emotion. *American Psychologist, 45,* 349–358. (12)

Frishhoff, B., & Beyth-Marom, R. (1983). Hypothesis evaluation from a Bayesian perspective. *Psychological Review, 90,* 239–260. (9)

Fuller, R. K., & Roth, H. P. (1979). Disulfiram for the treatment of alcoholism: An evaluation in 128 men. *Annals of Internal Medicine, 90,* 901–904. (14)

Funder, D. C. (1991). Global traits: A neo-Allportian approach to personality. *Psychological Science, 2,* 31–39. (13)

Gabrieli, J. D. E., Cohen, N. J., & Corkin, S. (1988). The impaired learning of semantic knowledge following bilateral medial temporal-lobe resection. *Brain and Cognition, 7,* 157–177. (8)

Gabrielli, W. F., Jr., & Plomin, R. (1985). Drinking behavior in the Colorado adoptee and twin sample. *Journal of Studies on Alcohol, 46,* 24–31. (14)

Gaito, J. (1976). Molecular psychobiology of memory: Its appearance, contributions, and decline. *Physiological Psychology, 4,* 476–484. (2)

Gallagher, M., & Pelleymounter, M. A. (1988). Spatial learning deficits in old rats: A model for memory decline in the aged. *Neurobiology of Aging, 9,* 549–556. (8)

Gallup, G. G., Jr., & Suarez, S. D. (1980). On the use of animals in psychological research. *Psychological Record, 30,* 211–218. (2)

Gallup, G. G., Jr., & Suarez, S. D. (1985). Alternatives to the use of animals in psychological research. *American Psychologist, 40,* 1104–1111. (2)

Galper, R. E., & Hochberg, J. (1971). Recognition memory for photographs of faces. *American Journal of Psychology, 84,* 351–354. (4)

Galton, F. (1978). *Hereditary genius.* New York: St. Martin's. (Original work published 1869) (1, 10)

Gantt, W. H. (1973). Reminiscences of Pavlov. *Journal of the Experimental Analysis of Behavior, 20,* 131–136. (7)

Garcia, J. (1990). Learning without memory. *Journal of Cognitive Neuroscience, 2,* 287–305. (7)

Garcia, J., Ervin, F. R., & Koelling, R. A. (1966). Learning with prolonged delay of reinforcement. *Psychonomic Science, 5,* 121–122. (7)

Garcia, J., & Koelling, R. A. (1966). *Psychonomic Science, 4,* 123–124. (7)

Gardner, H. (1985). *Frames of mind.* New York: Basic Books. (10)

Gardner, M. (1978). Mathematical games. *Scientific American, 239*(5), 22–32. (9)

Gardner, R. A., & Gardner, B. T. (1969). Teaching sign language to a chimpanzee. *Science, 165,* 664–672. (9)

Garfield, S. L. (1980). *Psychotherapy: An eclectic approach.* New York: Wiley. (15)

Garfield, S. L. (1981). Psychotherapy: A 40-year appraisal. *American Psychologist, 36,* 174–183. (15)

Garrick, T. (1990). The role of gastric contractility and brain thyrotropin-releasing hormone in cold restraint-induced gastric mucosal injury. *Annals of the New York Academy of Sciences, 597,* 51–70. (12)

Garrick, T., Minor, T. R., Bauck, S., Weiner, H., & Guth, P. (1989). Predictable and unpredictable shock stimulates gastric contractility and causes mucosal injury in rats. *Behavioral Neuroscience, 103,* 124–130. (12)

Gash, D. M., Collier, T. J., & Sladek, J. R., Jr. (1985). Neural transplantation: A review of recent developments and potential applications to the aged brain. *Neurobiology of Aging, 6,* 131–150. (3)

Gastil, J. (1990). Generic pronouns and sexist language: The oxymoronic character of masculine generics. *Sex Roles, 23,* 629–642. (9)

Gawin, F. H., & Kleber, H. D. (1986). Abstinence symptomatology and psychiatric diagnosis in cocaine abusers. *Archives of General Psychiatry, 43,* 107–113. (5)

Gebhard, P. H., Gagnon, J. H., Pomeroy, W. B., & Christenson, C. V. (1965). *Sex offenders: An analysis of types.* New York: Harper & Row. (11)

Geer, S., Morris, T., & Pettingale, K. W. (1979). Psychological response to breast cancer: Effect on outcome. *Lancet, ii*(8146), 785–787. (12)

Gelb, S. A. (1986). Henry H. Goddard and the immigrants, 1910–1917: The studies and their social context. *Journal of the History of the Behavioral Sciences, 22,* 324–332. (10)

Gellhorn, E. (1970). The emotions and the ergotropic and trophotropic systems. *Psychologische Forschung, 34,* 48–94. (12)

Gelman, R. (1982). Accessing one-to-one correspondence: Still another paper about conservation. *British Journal of Psychology, 73,* 209–220. (6)

Gelman, R., & Baillargeon, R. (1983). A review of some Piagetian concepts. In P. H. Mussen (Ed.), *Handbook of child psychology* (4th ed.) (Vol. 3, pp. 167–230). New York: Wiley. (6)

Gerard, H. B. (1983). School desegregation: The social science role. *American Psychologist, 38,* 869–877. (6)

Gernsbacher, M. A., & Faust, M. E. (1991). The mechanism of suppression: A component of general comprehension skill. *Journal of Experimental Psychology: Learning, Memory, and Cognition, 17,* 245–262. (9)

Gerson, S. C., Plotkin, D. A., & Jarvik, L. F. (1988). Antidepressant drug studies, 1964 to 1986: Empirical evidence for aging patients. *Journal of Clinical Pharmacology, 8,* 311–322. (15)

Geschwind, N. (1970). The organization of language and the brain. *Science, 170,* 940–944. (3)

Gibson, H. B. (1982). The use of hypnosis in police investigations. *Bulletin of the British Psychological Society, 35,* 138–142. (5)

Gibson, J. J. (1968). What gives rise to the perception of movement? *Psychological Review, 75,* 335–346. (4)

Gick, M. L., & Holyoak, K. J. (1980). Analogical problem solving. *Cognitive Psychology, 12,* 306–355. (9)

Gick, M. L., & Holyoak, K. J. (1983). Schema induction and analogical transfer. *Cognitive Psychology, 15,* 1–38. (9)

Giebel, H. D. (1958). Visuelles Lernvermögen bei Einhufern [Visual learning capacity in hoofed animals]. *Zoologisches Jahrbücher Abteilung für Allgemeine Zoologie, 67,* 487–520. (7)

Gigerenzer, G., Hell, W., & Blank, H. (1988). Presentation and context: The use of base rates as a continuous variable. *Journal of Experimental Psychology: Human Perception and Performance, 14,* 513–525. (9)

Gilbert, D. G. (1979). Paradoxical tranquilizing and emotion-reducing effects of nicotine. *Psychological Bulletin, 86,* 643–661. (5)

Gilbert, D. T. (1991). How mental systems believe. *American Psychologist, 46,* 107–119. (9)

Gilbert, D. T., Krull, D. S., & Malone, P. S. (1990). Unbelieving the unbelievable: Some problems in the rejection of false information. *Journal of Personality and Social Psychology, 59,* 601–613. (9)

Gillberg, C., Terenius, L., & Lönnerholm, G. (1985). Endorphin activity in childhood psychosis. *Archives of General Psychiatry, 42,* 780–783. (14)

Gilliam, T. C., Bucan, M., MacDonald, M. E., Zimmer, M., Haines, J., Cheng, S. V., Pohl, T. M., Meyers, R. H., Whaley, W. L., Allitto, B. A., Faryniarz, A., Wasmuth, J. J., Frischauf, A.-M., Conneally, P. M., Lehrach, H., & Gusella, J. F. (1987). A DNA segment encoding two genes very tightly linked to Huntington's disease. *Science, 238,* 950–952. (3)

Gilligan, C. (1977). In a different voice: Women's conceptions of self and morality. *Harvard Educational Review, 47,* 481–517. (6)

Gilligan, C. (1979). Woman's place in man's life cycle. *Harvard Educational Review, 49,* 431–446. (6)

Gilligan, C., & Attanucci, J. (1988). Two moral orientations: Gender differences and similarities. *Merrill-Palmer Quarterly, 34,* 223–237. (6)

Glass, A. V., Gazzaniga, M. S., & Premack, D. (1973). Artificial language training in global aphasics. *Neuropsychologia, 11,* 95–103. (9)

Glass, D. C., Singer, J. E., & Pennebaker, J. W. (1977). Behavioral and physiological effects of uncontrollable environmental events. In D. Stokols (Ed.), *Perspectives on environment and behavior* (pp. 131–151). New York: Plenum. (12)

Glenberg, A. M., Sanocki, T., Epstein, W., & Morris, C. (1987). Enhancing calibration of comprehension. *Journal of Experimental Psychology: General, 116,* 119–136. (9)

Gold, P. E. (1987). Sweet memories. *American Scientist, 75,* 151–155. (8)

Goldgaber, D., Lerman, M. I., McBride, O. W., Saffiotti, U., & Gajdusek, D. C. (1987). Characterization and chromosomal localization of a cDNA encoding brain amyloid of Alzheimer's disease. *Science, 235,* 877–880. (3)

Goldin-Meadow, S. (1985). Language development under atypical learning conditions: Replication and implications of a study of deaf children of hearing parents. In K. E. Nelson (Ed.), *Children's language* (Vol. 5, pp. 197–245). Hillsdale, NJ: Lawrence Erlbaum. (6)

Goldman-Rakic, P.S. (1988). Topography of cognition: Parallel distributed networks in primate association cortex. *Annual Review of Neuroscience, 11,* 137–156. (3)

Goldstein, A. (1980). Thrills in response to music and other stimuli. *Physiological Psychology, 8,* 126–129. (12)

Goldstein, E. B. (1989). *Sensation and perception* (3rd ed.). Belmont, CA: Wadsworth. (4)

Goldstein, M. J. (1981). Family factors associated with schizophrenia and anorexia nervosa. *Journal of Youth and Adolescence, 10,* 385–405. (11)

Goldston, S. E. (1986). Primary prevention. *American Psychologist, 41,* 453–460. (15)

Goodall, J. (1971). *In the shadow of man.* Boston: Houghton Mifflin. (2)

Goodman, W. K., Price, L. H., Delgado, P. L., Palumbo, J., Krystal, J. H., Nagy, L. M., Rasmussen, S. A., Heninger, G. R., & Charney, D. S. (1990). Specificity of serotonin reuptake inhibitors in the treatment of obsessive-compulsive disorder. *Archives of General Psychiatry, 47,* 577–585. (14)

Goodwin, C. J. (1991). Misportraying Pavlov's apparatus. *American Journal of Psychology, 104,* 135–141. (7)

Gordon, N. P., Cleary, P. D., Parker, C. E., & Czeisler, C. A. (1986). The prevalence and health impact of shiftwork. *American Journal of Public Health, 76,* 1225–1228. (5)

Gorman, J. M., Fyer, M. R., Goetz, R., Askanazi, J., Liebowitz, M. R., Fyer, A. J., Kinney, J., & Klein, D. F. (1988). Ventilatory physiology of patients with panic disorder. *Archives of General Psychiatry, 45,* 31–39. (14)

Gorman, M. E. (1989). Error, falsification and scientific inference: An experimental investigation.

Quarterly Journal of Experimental Psychology, 41A, 385–412. (9)

Gottesman, I. I. (1991). *Schizophrenia genesis.* New York: W.H. Freeman. (14)

Gottesman, I. I., & Bertelson, A. (1989). Confirming unexpressed genotypes for schizophrenia. *Archives of General Psychiatry, 46,* 867–872. (14)

Gottfredson, L. S., & Crouse, J. (1986). Validity versus utility of mental tests: Example of the SAT. *Journal of Vocational Behavior, 29,* 363–378. (10)

Gottman, J. M. (1979). Marital interaction: Experimental investigations. New York: Academic Press. (16)

Gould, M. S., & Shaffer, D. (1986). The impact of suicide in television movies. *New England Journal of Medicine, 315,* 690–694. (15)

Graf, P., & Mandler, G. (1984). Activation makes words more accessible, but not necessarily more retrievable. *Journal of Verbal Learning and Verbal Behavior, 23,* 553–568. (8)

Green, D. M., & Swets, J. A. (1966). *Signal detection theory and psychophysics.* New York: Wiley. (4)

Greene, R. L. (1987a). Effects of maintenance rehearsal on human memory. *Psychological Bulletin, 102,* 403–413. (8)

Greene, R. L. (1987b). Ethnicity and MMPI performance: A review. *Journal of Consulting and Clinical Psychology, 55,* 497–512. (13)

Greenough, W. T. (1975). Experiential modification of the developing brain. *American Scientist, 63,* 37–46. (3)

Greenwald, A. G., Spangenberg, E. R., Pratkanis, A. R., & Eskanazi, J. (1991). Double-blind tests of subliminal self-help audiotapes. *Psychological Science, 2,* 119–122. (4)

Griffiths, M. D. (1990). The cognitive psychology of gambling. *Journal of Gambling Studies, 6,* 31–42. (9)

Groth, A. N. (1979). Men who rape: The psychology of the offender. New York: Plenum. (11)

Grünbaum, A. (1986). Précis of The Foundations of Psychoanalysis: A philosophical critique. *Behavioral and Brain Sciences, 9,* 217–284. (13)

Guile, M. N. (1987). Differential gastric ulceration in rats receiving shocks on either fixed-time or variable-time schedules. *Behavioral Neuroscience, 101,* 139–140. (12)

Guilford, J. P. (1973). Theories of intelligence. In B. B. Wolman (Ed.), *Handbook of general psychology* (pp. 630–643). Englewood Cliffs, NJ: Prentice-Hall. (10)

Gurman, A. S., Kniskern, D. P., & Pinsof, W. M. (1986). Research on the process and outcome of marital and family therapy. In S. L. Garfield & A. E. Bergin (Eds.), *Handbook of psychotherapy and behavior change* (pp. 565–624). New York: Wiley. (15)

Gusella, J. F., Wexler, N. S., Conneally, P. M., Naylor, S. L., Anderson, M. A., Tanzi, R. E., Watkins, P. C., Ottina, K., Wallace, M. R., Sakachi, A. Y., Young, A. B., Shoulson, I., Bonilla, E., & Martin, J. B. (1983). A polymorphic DNA marker genetically linked to Huntington's disease. *Nature, 306,* 234–238. (12)

Gustavson, A. R., Dawson, M. E., & Bonett, D. G. (1987). Androstenol, a putative human pheromone, affects human (Homo sapiens) male choice performance. *Journal of Comparative Psychology, 101,* 210–212. (4)

Gynther, M. D. (1989). MMPI comparisons of blacks and whites: A review and commentary. *Journal of Clinical Psychology, 45,* 878–883. (13)

Haley, J. (1984). *Ordeal therapy.* San Francisco: Jossey-Bass. (15)

Hall, J. A. (1978). Gender effects in decoding nonverbal cues. *Psychological Bulletin, 85,* 845–857. (12)

Hall, J. L., & Gold, P. E. (1990). Adrenalectomy-induced memory deficits: Role of plasma glucose levels. *Physiology & Behavior, 47,* 27–33. (8)

Hamilton, D. L., & Gifford, R. K. (1976). Illusory correlation in interpersonal perception: A cognitive basis of stereotypic judgments. *Journal of Experimental Social Psychology, 12,* 392–407. (16)

Hannah, B. (1976). *Jung: His life and work.* New York: Putnam's. (13)

Hansen, G. D. (1979). Enuresis control through fading, escape, and avoidance training. *Journal of Applied Behavior Analysis, 12,* 303–307. (15)

Harada, S., Agarwal, D. P. Goedde, H. W., Tagaki, S., & Ishikawa, B. (1982). Possible protective role against alcoholism for aldehyde dehydrogenase isozyme deficiency in Japan. *Lancet, ii,* 827. (3)

Harbin, T. J. (1989). The relationship between the Type A behavior pattern and physiological responsivity: A quantitative review. *Psychophysiology, 26,* 110–119. (12)

Harcum, E. R. (1991). Behavioral paradigm for a psychological resolution of the free will issue. *Journal of Mind and Behavior, 12,* 93–114. (1)

Hardaway, R. A. (1990). Subliminally activated symbiotic fantasies: Facts and artifacts. *Psychological Bulletin, 107,* 177–195. (4)

Hardin, G. (1968). The tragedy of the commons. *Science, 162,* 1243–1248. (16)

Harding, C. M., Brooks, G. W., Ashikaga, T., Straus, J. S., & Breier, A. (1987). The Vermont longitudinal study of persons with severe mental illness, II: Long-term outcome of subjects who retrospectively met DSM-III criteria for schizophrenia. *American Journal of Psychiatry, 144,* 727–735. (15)

Hardy, J. (1990). Molecular genetics of the dementias. *Seminars in the Neurosciences, 2,* 109–115. (8)

Harkins, S. G., & Jackson, J. M. (1985). The role of evaluation in eliminating social loafing. *Journal of Personality and Social Psychology, 11,* 457–465. (16)

Harkins, S., & Petty, R. (1982). Effects of task difficulty and task uniqueness on social loafing. *Journal of Personality and Social Psychology, 43,* 1214–1229. (16)

Harlow, H. F. (1958). The nature of love. *American Psychologist, 13,* 673–685. (6)

Harlow, H. F., & Harlow, M. K. (1965). The affectional systems. In A. M. Schrier, H. F. Harlow, & F. Stollnitz (Eds.), *Behavior of nonhuman primates* (Vol. 2, pp. 287–334). New York: Academic Press. (6)

Harlow, H. F., Harlow, M. K., & Meyer, D. R. (1950). Learning motivated by a manipulative drive. *Journal of Experimental Psychology, 40,* 228–234. (11)

Harlow, H. F., Harlow, M. K., & Suomi, S. J. (1971). From thought to therapy: Lessons from a primate laboratory. *American Scientist, 59,* 538–549. (6)

Harris, B. (1979). What ever happened to Little Albert? *American Psychologist, 34,* 151–160. (14)

Harris, T. (1967). *I'm OK—You're OK.* New York: Avon. (13)

Hashtroudi, S., & Parker, E. S. (1986). Acute alcohol amnesia: What is remembered and what is forgotten. *Research Advances in Alcohol and Drug Problems, 9,* 179–209. (5)

Hass, R. G., Katz, I., Rizzo, N., Bailey, J., & Eisenstadt, D. (1991). Cross-racial appraisal as related to attitude ambivalence and cognitive complexity. *Journal of Personality and Social Psychology, 17,* 83–92. (16)

Hathaway, S. R., & McKinley, J. C. (1940). A multiphasic personality schedule (Minnesota): I. Construction of the schedule. *Journal of Psychology, 10,* 249–254. (13)

Hauri, P. (1982). *The sleep disorders.* Kalamazoo, MI: Upjohn. (5)

Hawkins, S.A., & Hastie, R. (1990). Biased judgments of past events after the outcomes are known. *Psychological Bulletin, 107,* 311–327. (16)

Hay, D., & Oken, D. (1977). The psychological stresses of intensive care unit nursing. In A. Monat & R. S. Lazarus (Eds.), *Stress and coping* (pp. 118–140). New York: Columbia University Press. (12)

Hayes, C. (1951). *The ape in our house.* New York: Harper. (9)

Hays, R. B. (1985). A longitudinal study of friendship development. *Journal of Personality and Social Psychology, 48,* 909–924. (16)

Hazelrigg, M. D., Cooper, H. M., & Borduin, C. M. (1987). Evaluating the effectiveness of family therapies: An integrative review and analysis. *Psychological Bulletin, 101,* 428–442. (15)

Healy, D., & Williams, J. M. G. (1988). Dysrhythmia, dysphoria, and depression: The interaction of learned helplessness and circadian dysrhythmia in the pathogenesis of depression. *Psychological Bulletin, 103,* 163–178. (14)

Heatherton, T. G., & Baumeister, R. F. (1991). Binge eating as escape from self-awareness. *Psychological Bulletin, 110,* 86–108. (11)

Heckhausen, H. (1984). Emergent achievement behavior: Some early developments. *Advances in Motivation and Achievement, 3,* 1–32. (11)

Heider, F. (1958). *The psychology of interpersonal relations.* New York: Wiley. (16)

Heilman, K. M. (1979). Neglect and related disorders. In K. M. Heilman & E. Valenstein (Eds.), *Clinical neuropsychology* (pp. 268–307). New York: Oxford University Press. (3)

Held, R., & Hein, A. (1963). Movement-produced stimulation in the development of visually guided behavior. *Journal of Comparative and Physiological Psychology, 56,* 872–876. (6)

Heller, M. A. (1989). Picture and pattern perception in the sighted and the blind: The advantage of the late blind. *Perception, 18,* 379–389. (4)

Helzer, J. E., Canino, G. J., Yeh, E.-K., Bland, R. C., Lee, C. K., Hwu, H.-G., & Newman, S. (1990). Alcoholism—North America and Asia. *Archives of General Psychiatry, 47,* 313–319. (3)

Helzer, J. E., Robins, L. N., & McEnvoy, L. (1987). Post-traumatic stress disorder in the general population. *New England Journal of Medicine, 317,* 1630–1634. (12)

Hendrick, C., & Hendrick, S. (1986). A theory and method of love. *Journal of Personality and Social Psychology, 50,* 392–402. (16)

Hendrick, C., Hendrick, S., & Adler, N. L. (1988). Romantic relationships: Love, satisfaction, and staying together. *Journal of Personality and Social Psychology, 54,* 980–988. (16)

Hendrick, S., Hendrick, C., Slapion-Foote, M. J., & Foote, F. H. (1985). Gender differences in sexual attitudes. *Journal of Personality and Social Psychology, 48,* 1630–1642. (6)

Henry, R. M. (1983). The cognitive versus psychodynamic debate about morality. *Human Development, 26,* 173–179. (6)

Hergenhahn, B. R. (1992). *An introduction to the history of psychology* (2nd ed.). Belmont, CA: Wadsworth. (1)

Herkenham, M., Lynn, A. B., deCosta, B. R., & Richfield, E. K. (1991). Neuronal localization of cannabinoid receptors in the basal ganglia of the rat. *Brain Research, 547,* 267–274. (5)

Herkenham, M., Lynn, A. B., Little, M. D., Johnson, M. R., Melvin, L. S., deCosta, B. R., & Rice, K. C. (1990). Cannabinoid receptor localization in brain. *Proceedings of the National Academy of Sciences, 87,* 1932–1936. (5)

Herman, J., Roffwarg, H., & Tauber, E. S. (1968). Color and other perceptual aspects of REM and NREM sleep. *Psychophysiology, 5,* 223. (5)

Hershenson, M. (Ed.) (1989). *The moon illusion.* Hillsdale, NJ: Lawrence Erlbaum. (4)

Herz, A., & Schulz, R. (1978). Changes in neuronal sensitivity during addictive processes. In J. Fishman (Ed.), *The bases of addiction* (pp. 375–394). Berlin: Dahlem Konferenzen. (5)

Hess, T. M., Donley, J., & Vandermaas, M. O. (1989). Aging-related changes in the processing and retention of script information. *Experimental Aging Research, 15,* 89–96. (8)

Hetherington, E. M. (1989). Coping with family transitions. Winners, losers, and survivors. *Child Development, 60,* 1–14. (6)

Hetherington, E. M., Cox, M., & Cox, R. (1982). Effects of divorce on parents and children. In M. E. Lamb (Ed.), *Nontraditional families* (pp. 233–288). Hillsdale, NJ: Lawrence Erlbaum. (6)

Hetherington, E. M., Stanley-Hagan, M., & Anderson, E. R. (1989). Marital transitions: A child's perspective. *American Psychologist, 44,* 303–312. (6)

Hilgard, E. R. (1971). Hypnotic phenomena: The struggle for scientific acceptance. *American Scientist, 59,* 567–577. (5)

Hilgard, E. R. (1973). A neodissociation interpretation of pain reduction in hypnosis. *Psychological Review, 80,* 396–411. (5)

Hilgard, E. R. (1979). Divided consciousness in hypnosis: The implications of the hidden observer. In E. Fromm & R. E. Shor (Eds.), *Hypnosis: Developments in research and new perspectives* (2nd ed.) (pp. 45–79). New York: Aldine. (5)

Hines, M. (1982). Prenatal gonadal hormones and sex differences in human behavior. *Psychological Bulletin, 92,* 56–80. (11)

Hinton, G. (1979). Some demonstrations of the effects of structural descriptions in mental imagery. *Cognitive Science, 3,* 231–250. (9)

Hobson, J. A. (1988). *The dreaming brain.* New York: Basic Books. (4)

Hobson, J. A., & McCarley, R. W. (1977). The brain as a dream state generator: An activation-synthesis hypothesis of the dream process. *American Journal of Psychiatry, 134,* 1335–1348. (4)

Hochberg, J., & Galper, R. E. (1967). Recognition of faces: I. An exploratory study. *Psychonomic Science, 9,* 619–620. (4)

Hodgson, R., Rankin, H., & Stockwell, T. (1979). Alcohol dependence and the priming effect. *Behaviour Research and Therapy, 17,* 379–387. (14)

Hoffman, L. W. (1989). Effects of maternal employment in the two-parent family. *American Psychologist, 44,* 283–292. (6)

Hoffman, M. (1977). Homosexuality. In F. A. Beach (Ed.), *Human sexuality in four perspectives* (pp. 164–189). Baltimore, MD: Johns Hopkins University Press. (11)

Hoffman, R. E., Stopek, S., & Andreasen, N. C. (1986). A comparative study of manic vs. schizophrenic speech disorganization. *Archives of General Psychiatry, 43,* 831–838. (14)

Hogan, R. A., & Kirchner, J. H. (1967). Preliminary report of the extinction of learned fears via short-term implosive therapy. *Journal of Abnormal Psychology, 72,* 106–109. (14)

Hoge, S. K., Sachs, G., Appelbaum, P. S., Greer, A., & Gordon, C. (1988). Limitations on psychiatrists' discretionary civil commitment authority by the Stone and dangerousness criteria. *Archives of General Psychiatry, 45,* 764–769. (15)

Hohmann, G. W. (1966). Some effects of spinal cord lesions on experienced emotional feelings. *Psychophysiology, 3,* 143–156. (12)

Holden, C. (1987). Is alcoholism treatment effective? *Science, 236,* 20–22. (14)

Hollandsworth, S. (1989, August-October). Have you exercised your mind today? *Special reports: Health,* pp. 18–26. (12)

Hollister, L. E. (1986). Health aspects of cannabis. *Pharmacological Reviews, 38,* 1–20. (5)

Hollon, S. D., & Beck, A. T. (1979). Cognitive therapy of depression. In P. C. Kendall & S. D. Hollon (Eds.), *Cognitive-behavioral interventions* (pp. 153–203). New York: Academic Press. (15)

Hollon, S. D., Kendall, P. C., & Lumry, A. (1986). Specificity of depressogenic cognitions in clinical depression. *Journal of Abnormal Psychology, 95,* 52–59. (15)

Holmes, D. S. (1978). Projection as a defense mechanism. *Psychological Bulletin, 85,* 677–688. (13)

Holmes, D. S. (1990). The evidence for repression: An examination of sixty years of research. In J. L. Singer (Ed.), *Repression and dissociation* (pp. 85–102). New York: Wiley. (13)

Holmes, T., & Rahe, R. (1967). The social readjustment rating scale. *Journal of Psychosomatic Research, 11,* 213–218. (12)

Holyoak, K. J., Koh, K., & Nisbett, R. E. (1989). A theory of conditioning: Inductive learning within rule-based default hierarchies. *Psychological Review, 96,* 315–340. (7)

Holzman, P. S. (1985). Eye movement dysfunctions and psychosis. *International Review of Neurobiology, 27,* 179–205. (14)

Holzman, P. S. (1988). A single dominant gene can account for eye tracking dysfunctions and schizophrenia in offspring of discordant twins. *Archives of General Psychiatry, 45,* 641–647. (14)

Honer, W. G., Gewirtz, G., & Turey, M. (1987). Psychosis and violence in cocaine smokers. *Lancet, ii*(8556), 451. (5)

Honig, A. S. (1983). Sex role socialization in early childhood. *Young Children, 38*, 57–70. (11)

Honzik, M. P. (1974). The development of intelligence. In B. B. Wolman (Ed.), *Handbook of general psychology* (pp. 644–655). Englewood Cliffs, NJ: Prentice-Hall. (10)

Horn, J. L., & Donaldson, G. (1976). On the myth of intellectual decline in adulthood. *American Psychologist, 31*, 701–719. (10)

Horne, J. A. (1988). *Why we sleep.* Oxford, England: Oxford University Press. (5)

Horne, J. A., & Minard, A. (1985). Sleep and sleepiness following a behaviorally "active" day. *Ergonomics, 28*, 567–575. (5)

Horner, M. S. (1972). Toward an understanding of achievement-related conflicts in women. *Journal of Social Issues, 28*, 157–175. (11)

Horvath, F. (1977). The effect of selected variables on interpretation of polygraph records. *Journal of Applied Psychology, 62*, 127–136. (12)

Horvath, P. (1988). Placebos and common factors in two decades of psychotherapy research. *Psychological Bulletin, 104*, 214–225. (15)

Hovland, C. I., Janis, I. L., & Kelley, H. H. (1953). *Communication and persuasion.* New Haven: Yale University Press. (16)

Hovland, C. I., Lumsdaine, A. A., & Sheffield, F. D. (1949). *Studies in social psychology in World War II: Vol. 3, Experiments on mass communications.* Princeton, NJ: Princeton University Press. (16)

Hovland, C. I., & Weiss, W. (1951). The influences of source credibility on communication effectiveness. *Public Opinion Quarterly, 15*, 635–650. (16)

Howard, K. I., Kopta, S. M., Krause, M. S., & Orlinsky, D. E. (1986). The dose-effect relationship in psychotherapy. *American Psychologist, 41*, 159–164. (15)

Hoyt, M. F., & Singer, J. L. (1978). Psychological effects of REM ("dream") deprivation upon waking mentation. In A. M. Arkin, J. S. Antrobus, & S. J. Ellman (Eds.), *The mind in sleep* (pp. 487–510). Hillsdale, NJ: Lawrence Erlbaum. (5)

Hubel, D. H., & Wiesel, T. N. (1968). Receptive fields and functional architecture of monkey striate cortex. *Journal of Physiology* (London), *195*, 215–243. (4)

Huff, D. (1954). *How to lie with statistics.* New York: Norton. (2)

Hughes, J. R., Higgins, S. T., Bickel, W. K., Hunt, W. K., Fenwick, J. W., Gulliver, S. B., & Mireault, G. C. (1991). Caffeine self-administration, withdrawal, and adverse effects among coffee drinkers. *Archives of General Psychiatry, 48*, 611–617. (5)

Hughes, J., Smith, T. W., Kosterlitz, H. W., Fothergill, L. A., Morgan, B. A., & Morris, H. R. (1975). Identification of two related pentapeptides from the brain with potent opiate antagonist activity. *Nature, 258*, 577–579. (5)

Hull, C. L. (1932). The goal gradient hypothesis and maze learning. *Psychological Review, 39*, 25–43. (1)

Hull, C. L. (1943). *Principles of behavior: An introduction to behavior theory.* New York: D. Appleton. (1, 11)

Hull, J. G., & Bond, C. F., Jr. (1986). Social and behavioral consequences of alcohol consumption and expectancy: A meta-analysis. *Psychological Bulletin, 99*, 347–360. (5)

Hunt, E., & Agnoli, F. (1991). The Whorfian hypothesis: A cognitive psychology perspective. *Psychological Review, 98*, 377–389. (9)

Hunter, I. M. (1977). An exceptional memory. *British Journal of Psychology, 68*, 155–164. (8)

Hyde, J. S., Fennema, E., & Lamon, S. J. (1990). Gender differences in mathematics performance: A meta-analysis. *Psychological Bulletin, 107*, 139–155. (10)

Hyman, B. T., van Hoesen, G. W., Damasio, A. R., & Barnes, C. L. (1984). Alzheimer's disease: Cell-specific pathology isolates the hippocampal formation. *Science, 225*, 1168–1170. (8)

Iggo, A., & Andres, K. H. (1982). Morphology of cutaneous receptors. *Annual Review of Neuroscience, 5*, 1–31. (4)

Inhoff, A. W. (1989). Lexical access during eye fixations in sentence reading: Are word access codes used to integrate lexical information across interword fixations? *Journal of Memory and Language, 28*, 444–461. (9)

Insanity defense work group. (1983). American Psychiatric Association statement on the insanity defense. *American Journal of Psychiatry, 140*, 681–688. (15)

Isaacs, E. A., & Clark, H. H. (1987). References in conversation between experts and novices. *Journal of Experimental Psychology: General, 116*, 26–37. (1)

Isenberg, D. J. (1986). Group polarization: A critical review and meta-analysis. *Journal of Personality and Social Psychology, 50*, 1141–1151. (16)

Izard, C. E. (1977). *Human emotions.* New York: Plenum. (12)

Jacobs, B. L. (1987). How hallucinogenic drugs work. *American Scientist, 75*, 386–392. (5)

Jacobs, G. H. (1981). *Comparative color vision.* New York: Academic Press. (4)

Jacobs, K. M., Mark, G. P., & Scott, T. R. (1988). Taste responses in the nucleus tractus solitarius of sodium-deprived rats. *Journal of Physiology, 406*, 393–410. (11)

Jacobsen, F. M., Sack, D. A., Wehr, T. A., Rogers, S., & Rosenthal, N. E. (1987). Neuroendocrine 5–hydroxytryptophan in seasonal affective disorder. *Archives of General Psychiatry, 44*, 1086–1091. (14)

James, W. (1884). What is an emotion? *Mind, 9*, 188–205. (12)

James, W. (1890). *The principles of psychology.* New York: Henry Holt. (1)

James, W. (1899/1962). *Talks to teachers on psychology.* New York: Dover. (Original work published 1899) (9)

Janicak, P. G., Davis, J. M., Gibbons, R. D., Ericksen, S., Chang, S., & Gallagher, P. (1985). Efficacy of ECT: A meta-analysis. *American Journal of Psychiatry, 142*, 297–302. (15)

Janis, I. L. (1972). *Victims of groupthink.* Boston: Houghton Mifflin. (16)

Janis, I. L. (1983). Stress inoculation in health care. In D. Meichenbaum & M. E. Jaremko (Eds.), *Stress reduction and prevention* (pp. 67–99). New York: Plenum. (12)

Janis, I. L. (1985). Sources of error in strategic decision making. In J. M. Pennings and associates (Eds.), *Organizational strategy and change* (pp. 157–197). San Francisco: Jossey-Bass. (16)

Janson, P., & Martin, J. K. (1982). Job satisfaction and age: A test of two views. *Social Forces, 60*, 1089–1102. (6)

Jaremko, M. E. (1983). Stress inoculation training for social anxiety, with emphasis on dating anxiety. In D. Meichenbaum & M. E. Jaremko (Eds.), *Stress reduction and prevention* (pp. 419–450). New York: Plenum. (12)

Jarvis, M. (1983). The treatment of cigarette dependence. *British Journal of Addiction, 78*, 125–130. (5)

Jensen, A. R. (1969). How much can we boost I.Q. and scholastic achievement? *Harvard Educational Review, 39*, 1–123. (10)

Jensen, A. R. (1980). *Bias in mental testing.* New York: Free Press. (6)

Jéquier, E. (1987). Energy utilization in human obesity. *Annals of the New York Academy of Sciences, 499*, 73–83. (11)

John, O. P. (1990). The "big five" factor taxonomy: Dimensions of personality in the natural language and in questionnaires. In L.A. Pervin (Ed.), *Handbook of personality* (pp. 66–100). New York: Guilford Press. (13)

Johnson, D. (1990). Animal rights and human lives. Time for scientists to right the balance. *Psychological Science, 1*, 213–214. (2)

Johnson, L. C., Burdick, J. A., & Smith, J. (1970). Sleep during alcohol intake and withdrawal in the chronic alcoholic. *Archives of General Psychiatry, 22*, 406–418. (5)

Johnson, M. H. (1990). Cortical maturation and the development of visual attention in early infancy. *Journal of Cognitive Neuroscience, 2*, 81–95. (6)

Johnson, M. H., Posner, M. I., & Rothbart, M. K. (1991). Components of visual orienting in early infancy: Contingency learning, anticipatory looking, and disengaging. *Journal of Cognitive Neuroscience, 3*, 335–344. (6)

Johnson, W. G., & Wildman, H. E. (1983). Influence of external and covert food stimuli on insulin secretion in obese and normal subjects. *Behavioral Neuroscience, 97*, 1025–1028. (11)

Johnston, J. C., & McClelland, J. L. (1974). Perception of letters in words: Seek not and ye shall find. *Science, 184*, 1192–1194. (9)

Johnston, J.J. (1975). Sticking with first responses on multiple-choice exams: For better or for worse? *Teaching of Psychology, 2*, 178–179. (Preface)

Jones, E. E., & Davis, K. E. (1965). From acts to dispositions: The attribution process in person perception. In L. Berkowitz (Ed.), *Advances in Experimental Social Psychology* (Vol. 2, pp. 219–266). New York: Academic Press. (16)

Jones, E. E., & Goethals, G. R. (1972). Order effects in impression formation: Attribution context and the nature of the entity. In E. Jones, D. Kanouse, H. Kelley, R. Nisbett, S. Valins, & B. Wiener (Eds.), *Attribution: Perceiving the causes of behavior* (pp. 27–46). Morristown, NJ: General Learning Press. (16)

Jones, E. E., & Harris, V. A. (1967). The attribution of attitudes. *Journal of Experimental Social Psychology, 13*, 1–24. (16)

Jones, E. E., & Nisbett, R. E. (1972). The actor and the observer: Divergent perception of the causes of behavior. In E. Jones, D. Kanouse, H. Kelley, R. Nisbett, S. Valins, & B. Wiener (Eds.), *Attribution: Perceiving the causes of behavior* (pp. 79–94). Morristown, NJ: General Learning Press. (16)

Jones, E. E., Rock, L., Shaver, K. G., Goethals, G. R., & Ward, L. M. (1968). Pattern of performance and ability attribution: An unexpected primacy effect. *Journal of Personality and Social Psychology, 10*, 317–340. (16)

Jones, S. S., Collins, K., & Hong, H.-W. (1991). An audience effect on smile production in 10-month-old infants. *Psychological Science, 2*, 45–49. (12)

Jouvet, M., Michel, F., & Courjon, J. (1959). Sur un stade d'activité électrique cérébrale rapide au cours du sommeil physiologique [On a state of rapid electrical cerebral activity during physiological sleep]. *Comptes Rendus des Séances de la Société de Biologie, 153*, 1024–1028. (5)

Joyce, P. R., & Paykel, E. S. (1989). Predictors of drug response in depression. *Archives of General Psychiatry, 46*, 89–99. (15)

Jung, C. G. (1965). *Memories, dreams, reflections* (A. Jaffe, Ed.). New York: Random House. (13)

Junginger, J., & Frame, C. L. (1985). Self-report of the frequency and phenomenology of verbal hallucinations. *Journal of Nervous and Mental Disease, 173*, 149–155. (14)

Jurkovic, G. J. (1980). The juvenile delinquent as a moral philosopher: A structural-developmental perspective. *Psychological Bulletin, 88*, 709–727. (6)

Jusczyk, P. W. (1985). The high-amplitude sucking technique as a methodological tool in speech perception research. In G. Gottlieb & N. A. Krasnegor (Eds.), *Measurement of audition and vision in the first year of postnatal life* (pp. 195–222). Norwood, NJ: Ablex. (6)

Just, M. A., & Carpenter, P. A. (1985). Cognitive coordinate systems: Accounts of mental rotation and individual differences in spatial ability. *Psychological Review, 92*, 137–172. (9)

Just, M. A., & Carpenter, P. A. (1987). *The psychology of reading and language comprehension.* Boston: Allyn & Bacon. (9)

Kagan, J. (1984). *The nature of the child.* New York: Basic Books. (6)

Kagan, J. (1989). Temperamental contributions to social behavior. *American Psychologist, 44*, 668–674. (6)

Kagan, J., Reznick, J. S., & Snidman, N. (1988). Biological bases of childhood shyness. *Science, 240,* 167–171. (6)

Kagan, J., & Snidman, N. (1991). Infant predictors of inhibited and uninhibited profiles. *Psychological Science, 2,* 40–44. (6)

Kahneman, D., & Tversky, A. (1973). On the psychology of prediction. *Psychological Review, 80,* 237–251. (9)

Kail, R., & Strauss, M. S. (1984). The development of human memory: An historical overview. In R. Kail & N. E. Spear (Eds.), *Comparative perspectives on the development of memory* (pp. 3–22). Hillsdale, NJ: Lawrence Erlbaum. (8)

Kaiser, M. K., Jonides, J., & Alexander, J. (1986). Intuitive reasoning about abstract and familiar physics problems. *Memory & Cognition, 14,* 308–312. (9)

Kalat, J. W. (1977). Status of "learned safety" or "learned noncorrelation" as a mechanism in taste-aversion learning. In L. M. Barker, M. R. Best, & M. Domjan (Eds.), *Learning mechanisms in food selection* (pp. 273–293). Waco, TX: Baylor University Press. (7)

Kalat, J. W. (1978). Letter to the editor: Speculations on similarities between autism and opiate addiction. *Journal of Autism and Childhood Schizophrenia, 8,* 477–479. (14)

Kalat, J. W. (1983). Evolutionary thinking in the history of the comparative psychology of learning. *Neuroscience & Biobehavioral Reviews, 7,* 309–314. (1, 7)

Kalat, J. W. (1992). *Biological Psychology* (4th ed.). Belmont, CA: Wadsworth. (3)

Kales, A., & Kales, J. D. (1984). *Evaluation and treatment of insomnia.* New York: Oxford. (5)

Kales, A., Scharf, M. B., & Kales, J. D. (1978). Rebound insomnia: A new clinical syndrome. *Science, 201,* 1039–1041. (5)

Kales, A., Soldatos, C. R., Bixler, E. O., & Kales, J. D. (1983). Early morning insomnia with rapidly eliminated benzodiazepines. *Science, 220,* 95–97. (5)

Kamin, L. J. (1969). Predictability, surprise, attention, and conditioning. In B. A. Campbell & R. M. Church (Eds.), *Punishment and aversive behavior* (pp. 279–296). New York: Appleton-Century-Crofts. (7)

Kamin, L. J. (1974). *The science and politics of IQ.* New York: Wiley. (10)

Kandel, E. R., & Schwartz, J. H. (1982). Molecular biology of learning: Modulation of transmitter release. *Science, 218,* 433–443. (7)

Kanizsa, G. (1979). *Organization in vision.* New York: Praeger. (4)

Kanner, A. D., Coyne, J. C., Schaefer, C., & Lazarus, R. S. (1981). Comparison of two modes of stress measurement: Daily hassles and uplifts versus major life events. *Journal of Behavioral Medicine, 4,* 1–39. (12)

Kanner, L. (1943). Autistic disturbances of affective contact. *Nervous Child, 2,* 217–250. (14)

Kanouse, D. E., & Hanson, L. R., Jr. (1972). Negativity in evaluations. In E. Jones, D. Kanouse, H. Kelley, R. Nisbett, S. Valins, & B. Wiener (Eds.), *Attribution: Perceiving the causes of behavior* (pp. 47–62). Morristown, NJ: General Learning Press. (16)

Kaplan, E. H. (1988). Crisis? A brief critique of Masters, Johnson and Kolodny. *Journal of Sex Research, 25,* 317–322. (11)

Kaplan, H. R. (1988). Gambling among lottery winners: Before and after the big score. *Journal of Gambling Behavior, 4,* 171–182. (9)

Kapur, N., Heath, P., Meudell, P., & Kennedy, P. (1986). Amnesia can facilitate memory performance: Evidence from a patient with dissociated retrograde amnesia. *Neuropsychologia, 24,* 215–221. (8)

Karno, M., Golding, J. M., Sorenson, S. B., & Burnam, A. (1988). The epidemiology of obsessive-compulsive disorder in five US communities. *Archives of General Psychiatry, 45,* 1094–1099. (14)

Kassin, S. M., & Lepper, M. R. (1984). Oversufficient and insufficient justification effects: Cognitive and behavioral development. *Advances in Motivation and Achievement, 3,* 73–106. (11)

Katon, W., Egan, K., & Miller, D. (1985). Chronic pain: Lifetime psychiatric diagnoses and family history. *American Journal of Psychiatry, 142,* 1156–1160. (14)

Katz, S., Lautenschlager, G. J., Blackburn, A. B., & Harris, F. H. (1990). Answering reading comprehension items without passages on the SAT. *Psychological Science, 1,* 122–127. (10)

Kaufman, L., & Rock, I. (1989). The moon illusion thirty years later. In M. Hershenson (Ed.), *The moon illusion* (pp. 193–234). Hillsdale, NJ: Lawrence Erlbaum. (4)

Keane, T. M., Wolfe, J., & Taylor, K. L. (1987). Posttraumatic stress disorder: Evidence for diagnostic validity and methods of psychological assessment. *Journal of Clinical Psychology, 43,* 32–43. (12)

Keck, P. E. Jr., Cohen, B. M., Baldessarini, R. J., & McElroy, S. L. (1989). Time course of antipsychotic effects of neuroleptic drugs. *American Journal of Psychiatry, 146,* 1289–1292. (15)

Keller, M. B., Lavori, P. W., Klerman, G. L., Andreasen, N. C., Endicott, J., Coryell, W., Fawcett, J., Rice, J. P., & Hirschfeld, R. M. A. (1986). Low levels and lack of predictors of somatotherapy and psychotherapy received by depressed patients. *Archives of General Psychiatry, 43,* 458–466. (14)

Kellerman, H. (1981). *Sleep disorders: Insomnia and narcolepsy.* New York: Brunner/Mazel. (5)

Kelley, H. H. (1967). Attribution theory in social psychology. In D. Levine (Ed.), *Nebraska symposium on motivation* (Vol. 15, pp. 192–238). Lincoln, NE: University of Nebraska Press. (16)

Kelley, H. H. (1972). Causal schemata and the attribution process. In E. Jones, D. Kanouse, H. Kelley, R. Nisbett, S. Valins, & B. Wiener (Eds.), *Attribution: Perceiving the causes of behavior* (pp. 151–174). Morristown, NJ: General Learning Press. (16)

Kellogg, W. N., & Kellogg, L. A. (1933). *The ape and the child.* New York: McGraw-Hill. (6)

Kendall, R. W., & Kemp, I. W. (1989). Maternal influenza in the etiology of schizophrenia. *Archives of General Psychiatry, 46,* 878–882. (14)

Kendler, K. S., Gruenberg, A. M., & Tsuang, M. T. (1985). Subtype stability in schizophrenia. *American Journal of Psychiatry, 142,* 827–832. (14)

Kendler, K. S., Heath, A. C., Martin, N. G., & Eaves, L. J. (1987). Symptoms of anxiety and symptoms of depression: Same genes, different environments? *Archives of General Psychiatry, 122,* 451–457. (14)

Kendler, K. S., & Robinette, C. D. (1983). Schizophrenia in the National Academy of Sciences-National Research Council twin registry—A 16-year update. *American Journal of Psychiatry, 140,* 1551–1563. (14)

Kenrick, D. T., & Stringfield, D. O. (1980). Personality traits and the eye of the beholder: Crossing some traditional philosophical boundaries in the search for consistency in all of the people. *Psychological Review, 87,* 88–104. (13)

Kenrick, D. T., & Trost, M. R. (1989). A reproductive exchange model of heterosexual relationships. In C. Hendick (Ed.), *Close relationships* (pp. 92–118). Newbury Park, CA: Sage. (16)

Keon, T. L., & McDonald, B. (1982). Job satisfaction and life satisfaction: An empirical evaluation of their interrelationship. *Human Relations, 35,* 167–180. (6)

Keppel, G., & Underwood, B. J. (1962). Proactive inhibition in short-term retention of single items. *Journal of Verbal Learning and Verbal Behavior, 1,* 153–161. (8)

Kerns, L. L. (1986). Treatment of mental disorders in pregnancy: A review of psychotropic drug risks and benefits. *Journal of Nervous and Mental Disease, 174,* 652–659. (6)

Kerzendorfer, M. (1977). Diagnostic usefulness of Cattell's 16PF. *Zeitschrift für Klinische Psychologie, 6,* 259–280. (13)

Kessler, R. C., Downey, G., Milafsky, J. R., & Stipp, H. (1988). Clustering of teenage suicides after television news stories about suicides: A reconsideration. *American Journal of Psychiatry, 145,* 1379–1383. (15)

Kety, S. S. (1977). Genetic aspects of schizophrenia: Observations on the biological and adoptive relatives of adoptees who became schizophrenic. In E. S. Gershon, R. H. Belmaker, S. S. Kety, & M. Rosenbaum (Eds.), *The impact of biology on modern psychiatry* (pp. 195–206). New York: Spectrum. (14)

Kety, S. S. (1983). Mental illness in the biological and adoptive relatives of schizophrenic adoptees: Findings relevant to genetic and environmental factors in etiology. *American Journal of Psychiatry, 140,* 720–727. (14)

Kiesler, C. A. (1982a). Mental health and alternative care. *American Psychologist, 37,* 349–360. (15)

Kiesler, C. A. (1982b). Public and professional myths about mental hospitalization. *American Psychologist, 37,* 1323–1339. (15)

Kihlstrom, J. F. (1979). Hypnosis and psychopathology: Retrospect and prospect. *Journal of Abnormal Psychology, 88,* 459–473. (5)

Kimble, D. P. (1990). Functional effects of neural grafting in the mammalian central nervous system. *Psychological Bulletin, 108,* 462–479. (3)

Kimble, G. A. (1961). *Hilgard and Marquis' Conditioning and Learning* (2nd ed.). New York: Appleton-Century-Crofts. (7)

Kimble, G. A. (1981). Biological and cognitive constraints on learning. *The G. Stanley Hall Lecture Series, 1,* 11–60. (7)

Kimble, G. A., & Garmezy, N. (1968). *Principles of general psychology* (3rd ed.). New York: Ronald. (13)

King, B. M., Smith, R. L., & Frohman, L. A. (1984). Hyperinsulinemia in rats with ventromedial hypothalamic lesions: Role of hyperphagia. *Behavioral Neuroscience, 98,* 152–155. (11)

Kinsey, A. C., Pomeroy, W. B., & Martin, C. E. (1948). *Sexual behavior in the human male.* Philadelphia: W. B. Saunders. (11)

Kinsey, A. C., Pomeroy, W. B., Martin, C. E., & Gebhard, P. H. (1953). *Sexual behavior in the human female.* Philadelphia: W. B. Saunders. (11)

Kite, M. E., & Deaux, K. (1986). Attitudes toward homosexuality: Assessment and behavioral consequences. *Basic and Applied Social Psychology, 7,* 137–162. (16)

Klatzky, R. L., Lederman, S., & Reed, C. (1987). There's more to touch than meets the eye: The salience of object attributes for haptics with and without vision. *Journal of Experimental Psychology: General, 116,* 356–369. (4)

Klayman, J., & Ha, Y.-W. (1987). Confirmation, disconfirmation, and information in hypothesis testing. *Psychological Review, 94,* 211–228. (9)

Klein, D. F., Zitrin, C. M., Woerner, M. G., & Ross, D. C. (1983). Treatment of phobias. II. Behavior therapy and supportive psychotherapy: Are there any specific ingredients? *Archives of General Psychiatry, 40,* 139–145. (15)

Klein, S. B., & Kihlstrom, J. F. (1986). Elaboration, organization, and the self-reference effect in memory. *Journal of Experimental Psychology: General, 115,* 26–38. (8)

Kleinfeld, J., & Nelson, P. (1991). Adapting instruction to Native Americans' learning styles: An iconoclastic view. *Journal of Cross-cultural Psychology, 22,* 273–282. (6)

Kleitman, N. (1963). *Sleep and wakefulness* (revised and enlarged edition). Chicago: University of Chicago Press. (5)

Kline, M., Tschann, J. M., Johnston, J. R., & Wallerstein, J. S. (1989). Children's adjustment in joint and sole physical custody families. *Developmental Psychology, 25,* 430–438. (6)

Klineberg, O. (1938). Emotional expression in Chinese literature. *Journal of Abnormal and Social Psychology, 33,* 517–520. (12)

Knesper, D. J., Belcher, B. E., & Cross, J. G. (1989). A market analysis comparing the practices of psychiatrists and psychologists. *Archives of General Psychiatry, 46,* 305–314. (15)

Koh, T.-H., Abbatiello, A., & McLoughlin, C. S. (1984). Cultural bias in WISC subtest items: A response to Judge Grady's suggestion in relation to the PASE case. *School Psychology Review, 13,* 89–94. (10)

Kohlberg, L. (1969). Stage and sequence: The cognitive-developmental approach to socialization. In D. A. Goslin (Ed.), *Handbook of socialization theory and research.* Chicago: Rand McNally (6)

Kohlberg, L. (1981). *The meaning and measurement of moral development.* Worcester, MA: Clark University Press. (6)

Kohlberg, L., & Hersh, R. H. (1977). Moral development: A review of the theory. *Theory into Practice, 16,* 53–59. (6)

Kolko, D. J., & Milan, M. A. (1983). Reframing and paradoxical instruction to overcome "resistance" in the treatment of delinquent youths: A multiple baseline analysis. *Journal of Consulting and Clinical Psychology, 51,* 655–660. (15)

Kopp, C. B. (1990). Risks in infancy: Appraising the research. *Merrill-Palmer Quarterly, 36,* 117–139. (6)

Koppenaal, R. J. (1963). Time changes in the strengths of A-B, A-C lists: Spontaneous recovery? *Journal of Verbal Learning and Verbal Behavior, 2,* 310–319. (8)

Koriat, A., Ben-Zur, H., & Sheffer, D. (1988). Telling the same story twice: Output monitoring and age. *Journal of Memory and Language, 27,* 23–39. (8)

Kornhuber, H. H. (1974). Cerebral cortex, cerebellum, and basal ganglia: An introduction to their motor functions. In F. O. Schmitt & F. G. Worden (Eds.), *The neurosciences: Third study program* (pp. 267–280). Cambridge, MA: MIT Press. (3)

Koss, M. P., & Butcher, J. N. (1986). Research on brief psychotherapy. In S. L. Garfield & A. E. Bergin (Eds.), *Handbook of psychotherapy and behavior change* (pp. 627–670). New York: Wiley. (15)

Koss, M. P., & Dinero, T. E. (1988). Predictors of sexual aggression among a national sample of male college students. *Annals of the New York Academy of Sciences, 528,* 133–147. (11)

Koss, M. P., Gidycz, C. A., & Wisniewski, N. (1987). The scope of rape: Incidence and prevalence of sexual aggression and victimization in a national sample of higher education students. *Journal of Consulting and Clinical Psychology, 55,* 162–170. (11)

Kosslyn, S. M. (1988). Aspects of a cognitive neuroscience of mental imagery. *Science, 240,* 1621–1626. (9)

Kosten, T. R., Rounsaville, B. J., & Kleber, H. D. (1987). A 2.5-year follow-up of cocaine use among treated opioid addicts. *Archives of General Psychiatry, 44,* 281–284. (14)

Koyano, W. (1991). Japanese attitudes toward the elderly: A review of research findings. *Journal of Cross-cultural Gerontology, 4,* 335–345. (6)

Kozel, N. J., & Adams, E. H. (1986). Epidemiology of drug abuse: An overview. *Science, 234,* 970–974. (5)

Kraut, R. E., & Johnston, R. E. (1979). Social and emotional messages of smiling: An ethological approach. *Journal of Personality and Social Psychology, 37,* 1539–1553. (12)

Kreskin. (1991). *Secrets of the amazing Kreskin.* Buffalo, NY: Prometheus. (2)

Kringlen, E., & Cramer, G. (1989). Offspring of monozygotic twins discordant for schizophrenia. *Archives of General Psychiatry, 46,* 873–877. (14)

Krug, S. E. (1978). Reliability and scope in personality assessment: A comparison of the Cattell and Eysenck inventories. *Multivariate Experimental Clinical Research, 3,* 195–204. (13)

Kruglanski, A. W. (1970). Attributing trustworthiness in supervisor-worker relations. *Journal of Experimental Social Psychology, 6,* 214–232. (16)

Kruglanski, A. W., & Mayseless, O. (1990). Classic and current social comparison research: Expanding the perspective. *Psychological Bulletin, 108,* 195–208. (16)

Krystal, H. (1991). Integration and self-healing in post-traumatic states: A ten-year retrospective. *American Imago, 48,* 93–118. (12)

Kübler-Ross, E. (1969). *On death and dying.* New York: Macmillan. (6)

Kübler-Ross, E. (1975). *Death: The final stage of growth.* Englewood Cliffs, NJ: Prentice-Hall. (6)

Kulik, J. A., Bangert-Drowns, R. L., & Kulik, C. C. (1984). Effectiveness of coaching for aptitude tests. *Psychological Bulletin, 95,* 179–188. (10)

Kumar, J. (1975). The recent level of age at menarche and the effect of nutrition level and socio-economic status on menarche: A comparative study. *Eastern Anthropologist, 28,* 99–131. (11)

Kumar, R., Cooke, E. C., Lader, M. H., & Russell, M. A. H. (1977). Is nicotine important in tobacco smoking? *Clinical Pharmacology & Therapeutics, 21,* 520–529. (5)

Kurtzke, J. R. (1976). An introduction to the epidemiology of cerebrovascular disease. In F. Scheinberg (Ed.), *Cerebrovascular diseases* (pp. 239–253). New York: Raven. (3)

Laird, J. D. (1974). Self-attribution of emotion: The effects of expressive behavior on the quality of emotional experience. *Journal of Personality and Social Psychology, 29,* 475–486. (12)

Lakoff, G. (1987). *Women, fire, and dangerous things.* Chicago: University of Chicago Press. (9)

Lamb, M. (1974). Paternal influences and the father's role. *American Psychologist, 34,* 938–943. (6)

Lamb, M. E. (1982). Maternal employment and child development: A review. In M. E. Lamb (Ed.), *Nontraditional families* (pp. 45–69). Hillsdale, NJ: Lawrence Erlbaum. (6)

Lamb, M. E., Frodi, A. M., Hwang, C.-P., & Frodi, M. (1982). Varying degrees of paternal involvement in infant care: Attitudinal and behavioral correlates. In M. E. Lamb (Ed.), *Nontraditional families* (pp. 117–137). Hillsdale, NJ: Lawrence Erlbaum. (6)

Lambert, N. M. (1981). Psychological evidence in *Larry P. v. Wilson Riles:* An evaluation by a witness for the defense. *American Psychologist, 36,* 937–952. (10)

Lamm, H., & Myers, D. G. (1978). Group-induced polarization of attitudes and behavior. *Advances in Experimental Social Psychology, 11,* 145–195. (16)

Land, E. H., Hubel, D. H., Livingstone, M. S., Perry, S. H., & Burns, M. M. (1983). Colour-generating interactions across the corpus callosum. *Nature, 303,* 616–618. (4)

Land, E. H., & McCann, J. J. (1971). Lightness and retinex theory. *Journal of the Optical Society of America, 61,* 1–11. (4)

Lande, S. D. (1982). Physiological and subjective measures of anxiety during flooding. *Behaviour Research and Therapy, 20,* 81–88. (14)

Langer, E. J. (1975). The illusion of control. *Journal of Personality and Social Psychology, 32,* 311–328. (9)

Langworthy, R. A., & Jennings, J. W. (1972). Oddball, abstract olfactory learning in laboratory rats. *Psychological Record, 22,* 487–490. (1)

Larkin, J., McDermott, J., Simon, D. P., & Simon, H. A. (1980). Expert and novice performance in solving physics problems. *Science, 208,* 1335–1342. (9)

Larrick, R. P., Morgan, J. N., & Nisbett, R. E. (1990). Teaching the use of cost-benefit reasoning in everyday life. *Psychological Science, 1,* 362–370. (9)

Lashley, K. S. (1951). The problem of serial order in behavior. In L. A. Jeffress (Ed.), *Cerebral mechanisms in behavior* (pp. 112–146). New York: Wiley. (9)

Latané, B., & Darley, J. M. (1968). Group inhibition of bystander intervention in emergencies. *Journal of Personality and Social Psychology, 10,* 215–221. (16)

Latané, B., & Darley, J. M. (1969). Bystander "apathy." *American Scientist, 57,* 244–268. (16)

Latané, B., Williams, K., & Harkins, S. (1979). Many hands make light the work: The causes and consequences of social loafing. *Journal of Personality and Social Psychology, 37,* 823–832. (16)

Lavine, R., Buchsbaum, M. S., & Poncy, M. (1976). Auditory analgesia: Somatosensory evoked response and subjective pain rating. *Psychophysiology, 13,* 140–148. (4, 12)

Layman, S., & Greene, E. (1988). The effects of stroke on object recognition. *Brain and Cognition, 7,* 87–114. (1, 3)

Lazarus, R. S. (1977). Cognitive and coping processes in emotion. In A. Monat & R. S. Lazarus (Eds.), *Stress and coping* (pp. 145–158). New York: Columbia University Press. (12)

Lazarus, R. S., Averill, J. R., & Opton, E. M., Jr. (1970). Towards a cognitive theory of emotion. In M. B. Arnold (Ed.), *Feelings and emotions* (pp. 207–232). New York: Academic Press. (12)

Lê, A. D., Poulos, C. X., & Cappell, H. (1979). Conditioned tolerance to the hypothermic effect of ethyl alcohol. *Science, 206,* 1109–1110. (7)

Ledwidge, B. (1980). Run for your mind: Aerobic exercise as a means of alleviating anxiety and depression. *Canadian Journal of Behavioral Science, 12,* 126–140. (14)

Lee, M. K., Graham, S. N., & Gold, P. E. (1988). Memory enhancement with post-training intraventricular glucose injections in rats. *Behavioral Neuroscience, 102,* 591–595. (8)

Leehy, S. C., Moscowitz-Cook, A., Brill, S., & Held, R. (1975). Orientational anisotropy in infant vision. *Science, 190,* 900–902. (6)

Lefcourt, H. M. (1976). *Locus of control: Current trends in theory and research.* New York: Wiley. (13)

Leff, J. (1981). *Psychiatry around the globe.* New York: Marcel Dekker. (14)

LeMagnen, J. (1981). The metabolic basis of dual periodicity of feeding in rats. *Behavioral and Brain Sciences, 4,* 561–607. (11)

Lenneberg, E. H. (1967). *Biological foundations of language.* New York: Wiley. (6)

Lenneberg, E. H. (1969). On explaining language. *Science, 164,* 635–643. (6)

Leonard, H. L., Swedo, S. E., Rapoport, J. L., Koby, E. V., Lenane, M. C., Cheslow, D. L., & Hamburger, S. D. (1989). Treatment of obsessive-compulsive disorder with clomipramine and desipramine in children and adolescents. *Archives of General Psychiatry, 46,* 1088–1092. (14)

Lester, J. T. (1983). Wrestling with the self on Mount Everest. *Journal of Humanistic Psychology, 23,* 31–41. (13)

Leuchtenburg, W. E. (1963). *Franklin D. Roosevelt and the New Deal 1932–1940.* New York: Harper & Row. (16)

LeVay, S. (1991). A difference in hypothalamic structure between heterosexual and homosexual men. *Science, 253,* 1034–1037. (11)

Levenson, R. W. (1992). Autonomic nervous system differences among emotions. *Psychological Science, 3,* 23–27. (12)

Levenson, R. W., Oyama, O. N., & Meek, P. S. (1987). Greater reinforcement from alcohol for those at risk: Parental risk, personality risk, and sex. *Journal of Abnormal Psychology, 96,* 242–253. (14)

Leventhal, H. (1970). Findings and theory in the study of fear communication. In L. Berkowitz (Ed.), *Advances in Experimental Social Psychology* (Vol. 5, pp. 119–186). New York: Academic Press. (16)

Levine, D. N., Warach, J. D., Benowitz, L., & Calvanio, R. (1986). Left spatial neglect: Effects of lesion size and premorbid brain atrophy on severity and recovery following right cerebral infarction. *Neurology, 36,* 362–366. (3)

Levine, R. V. (1990). The pace of life. *American Scientist, 78,* 450–459. (12)

Levinger, G. (1976). A social psychological perspective on marital dissolution. *Journal of Social Issues, 32,* 21–47. (16)

Levinger, G. (1980). Toward the analysis of close relationships. *Journal of Experimental Social Psychology, 16,* 510–544. (16)

Levinger, G. (1983). Development and change. In H. H. Kelley, E. Berscheid, A. Christensen, J. H. Harvey, T. L. Huston, G. Levinger, E. McClintock, L. A. Peplau, & D. R. Peterson (Eds.), *Close relationships* (pp. 315–359). New York: W. H. Freeman. (16)

Levinson, D. J. (1977). The mid-life transition: A period in adult psychosocial development. *Psychiatry, 40*, 99–112. (6)

Levinson, D. J. (1978). *The seasons of a man's life.* New York: Ballantine. (6)

Lewin, R. (1988). Cloud over Parkinson's therapy. *Science, 240*, 390–392. (3)

Lewinsohn, P. M., Mischel, W., Chaplin, W., & Barton, R. (1980). Social competence and depression: The role of illusory self-perceptions. *Journal of Abnormal Psychology, 89*, 203–212. (14)

Lewis, D. O., Moy, E., Jackson, L. D., Aaronson, R., Restifo, N., Serra, S., & Simos, A. (1985). Biopsychosocial characteristics of children who later murder: A prospective study. *American Journal of Psychiatry, 142*, 1161–1167. (12)

Lewis, D. O., Pincus, J. H., Lovly, R., Spitzer, E., & Moy, E. (1987). Biopsychosocial characteristics of matched samples of delinquents and nondelinquents. *Journal of the American Academy of Child and Adolescent Psychiatry, 26*, 744–752. (12)

Lewis, D. O., Shanok, S. S., Grant, M., & Ritvo, E. (1983). Homicidally aggressive young children: Neuropsychiatric and experiential correlates. *American Journal of Psychiatry, 140*, 148–153. (12)

Lewis, M., Sullivan, M. W., Stanger, C., & Weiss, M. (1991). Self development and self-conscious emotions. In S. Chess & M. E. Hertzig (Eds.), *Annual Progress in Child Psychiatry and Child Development 1990* (pp. 34–51). New York: Brunner/Mazel. (6)

Lewis, M., Thomas, D. A., & Worobey, J. (1990). Developmental organization, stress, and illness. *Psychological Science, 1*, 316–318. (6)

Lichtenstein, E. (1982). The smoking problem: A behavioral perspective. *Journal of Consulting and Clinical Psychology, 50*, 804–819. (5)

Lichtenstein, S., Fischhoff, B., & Phillips, L. D. (1982). Calibration of probabilities: The state of the art to 1980. In D. Kahneman, P. Slovic, & A. Tversky (Eds.), *Judgment under uncertainty: Heuristics and biases* (pp. 306–334). Cambridge, England: Cambridge University Press. (9)

Lieberman, J. A., Kane, J. M., Sarantakos, S., Gadaleta, D., Woerner, M., Alvir, J., & Ramos-Lorenzi, J. (1987). Prediction of relapse in schizophrenia. *Archives of General Psychiatry, 44*, 597–603. (15)

Liebeskind, J. C., & Paul, L. A. (1977). Psychological and physiological mechanisms of pain. *Annual Review of Psychology, 28*, 41–60. (4)

Liebowitz, M. R., Gorman, J. M., Fyer, A. J., Levitt, M., Dillon, D., Levy, G., Appleby, I. L., Anderson, S., Palij, M., Davies, S. O., & Klein, D. F. (1985). Lactate provocation of panic attacks: II. Biochemical and physiological findings. *Archives of General Psychiatry, 42*, 709–719. (14)

Lilie, J. K., & Rosenberg, R. P. (1990). Behavioral treatment of insomnia. *Progress in Behavior Modification, 25*, 152–177. (5)

Lindberg, N. O., Coburn, C., & Stricker, E. M. (1984). Increased feeding by rats after subdiabetogenic streptozotocin treatment: A role for insulin in satiety. *Behavioral Neuroscience, 98*, 138–145. (11)

Lindvall, O., Rehncrona, S., Brundin, P., Gustavii, B., Åstedt, B., Widner, H., Lindholm, T., Björklund, A., Leenders, K. L., Rothwell, J. C., Frackowiak, R., Marsden, D., Johnels, B., Steg, G., Freedman, R., Hoffer, B. J., Seiger, A., Bygdeman, M., Strömberg, I., & Olsen, J. (1989). Human fetal dopamine neurons grafted into the striatum in two patients wih severe Parkinson's disease. *Archives of Neurology, 46*, 615–631. (3)

Link, N. F., Sherer, S. E., & Byrne, P. N. (1977). Moral judgment and moral conduct in the psychopath. *Canadian Psychiatric Association Journal, 22*, 341–346. (6)

Links, P. S., Stockwell, M., Abichandani, F., & Simeon, J. (1980). Minor physical anomalies in childhood autism. Part I. Their relationship to pre- and perinatal complications. *Journal of Autism and Developmental Disorders, 10*, 273–285. (14)

Linn, R., & Gilligan, C. (1990). One action, two moral orientations—The tension between justice and care voices in Israeli selective conscientious objectors. *New Ideas in Psychology, 8*, 189–203. (6)

Linton, M. (1982). Transformations of memory in everyday life. In U. Neisser (Ed.), *Memory observed* (pp. 77–91). San Francisco: W. H. Freeman. (8)

Lippa, R. (1983). Expressive behavior. In L. Wheeler & P. Shaver (Eds.), *Review of personality and social psychology* (Vol. 4, pp. 181–205). Beverly Hills, CA: Sage. (16)

Lipsitt, L. P. (1963). Learning in the first year of life. *Advances in Child Development and Behavior, 1*, 147–195. (6)

Lisak, D., & Roth, S. (1988). Motivational factors in nonincarcerated sexually aggressive men. *Journal of Personality and Social Psychology, 55*, 795–802. (11)

Livingstone, M. S. (1988, January). Art, illusion, and the visual system. *Scientific American, 258*(1), 78–85. (4)

Livingstone, M. S., & Hubel, D. (1988). Segregation of form, color, movement, and depth: Anatomy, physiology, and perception. *Science, 240*, 740–749. (4)

Locke, E. A., Shaw, K. N., Saari, L. M., & Latham, G. P. (1981). Goal setting and task performance: 1969–1980. *Psychological Bulletin, 90*, 125–152. (11)

Loewenstein, G., & Furstenberg, F. (1991). Is teenage sexual behavior rational? *Journal of Applied Social Psychology, 21*, 957–986. (6, 11)

Loewi, O. (1960). An autobiographic sketch. *Perspectives in Biology, 4*, 3–25. (3)

Loftus, E. F. (1975). Leading questions and the eyewitness report. *Cognitive Psychology, 7*, 560–572. (8)

London, E. D., Cascella, N. G., Wong, D. F., Phillips, R. L., Dannals, R. F., Links, J. M., Herning, R., Grayson, R., Jaffe, J. H., & Wagner, H. N. (1990). Cocaine-induced reduction of utilization in human brain. *Archives of General Psychiatry, 47*, 567–574. (5)

Long, B. B. (1986). The prevention of mental-emotional disabilities. *American Psychologist, 41*, 825–829. (15)

Longstreth, L. E. (1981). Revisiting Skeels' final study: A critique. *Developmental Psychology, 17*, 620–625. (10)

Lorenz, K. (1950). The comparative method in studying innate behaviour patterns. *Symposia of the Society for Experimental Biology, 4*, 221–268. (11)

Lorenz, V. C. (1990). State lotteries and compulsive gambling. *Journal of Gambling Studies, 6*, 383–396. (9)

Lovaas, O. I., Koegel, R. L., & Schreibman, L. (1979). Stimulus overselectivity in autism: A review of research. *Psychological Bulletin, 86*, 1236–1254. (14)

Lowing, P. A., Mirsky, A. F., & Pereira, R. (1983). The inheritance of schizophrenia spectrum disorders: A reanalysis of the Danish adoptee study plan. *American Journal of Psychiatry, 140*, 1167–1171. (14)

Ludwick-Rosenthal, R., & Neufeld, R. W. J. (1988). Stress management during noxious medical procedures: An evaluative review of outcome studies. *Psychological Bulletin, 104*, 326–342. (12)

Luginbuhl, J. (1992). Comprehension of judges' instructions in the penalty phase of a capital trial: Focus on mitigating circumstances. *Law and Human Behavior, 16*, 203–218. (16)

Lundy, A. (1985). The reliability of the thematic apperception test. *Journal of Personality Assessment, 49*, 141–145. (13)

Lykken, D. T. (1979). The detection of deception. *Psychological Bulletin, 86*, 47–53. (12)

Lykken, D. T. (1982). Research with twins: The concept of emergenesis. *Psychophysiology, 19*, 361–373. (3)

Lykken, D. T. (1988). Detection of guilty knowledge: A comment on Forman and McCauley. *Journal of Applied Psychology, 73*, 303–304. (12)

Lynn, S. J., Rhue, J. W., & Weekes, J. R. (1990). Hypnotic involuntariness: A social cognitive analysis. *Psychological Review, 97*, 169–184. (5)

Maccoby, E. E. (1990). Gender and relationships. *American Psychologist, 45*, 513–520. (6)

Maccoby, E. E., & Jacklin, C. N. (1974). *The psychology of sex differences.* Stanford, CA: Stanford University Press. (6)

Macdonald, R. L., Weddle, M. G., & Gross, R. A. (1986). Benzodiazepine, beta-carboline, and barbiturate actions on GABA responses. *Advances in Biochemical Psychopharmacology, 41*, 67–78. (5, 15)

Mackintosh, N. J. (1973). Stimulus selection: Learning to ignore stimuli that predict no change in reinforcement. In R. A. Hinde & J. Stevenson-Hinde (Eds.), *Constraints on learning* (pp. 75–100). London: Academic Press. (7)

MacLeod, C. M. (1988). Forgotten but not gone: Savings for pictures and words in long-term memory. *Journal of Experimental Psychology: Learning, Memory, and Cognition, 14*, 195–212. (8)

Maddahian, E., Newcomb, M. D., & Bentler, P. M. (1988). Risk factors for substance use: Ethnic differences among adolescents. *Journal of Substance Abuse, 1*, 11–23. (14)

Madsen, K. B. (1959). *Theories of motivation.* Copenhagen: Munksgaard. (11)

Mahoney, M. J. (1990). *Human change processes.* New York: Basic Books. (15)

Mahowald, M. W., & Schenck, C. H. (1989). Narcolepsy. In G. Adelman (Ed.), *Neuroscience year* (pp. 114–116). Boston: Birkhäuser. (5)

Maier, N. R. F., & Schneirla, T. C. (1964). *Principles of animal psychology* (enlarged edition). New York: Dover. (7)

Maier, S. F., Seligman, M. E. P., & Solomon, R. L. (1969). Pavlovian fear conditioning and learned helplessness: Effects on escape and avoidance behavior of (a) the CS-US contingency and (b) the independence of the US and voluntary responding. In B. A. Campbell and R. M. Church (Eds.), *Punishment and aversive behavior* (pp. 299–342). New York: Appleton-Century-Crofts. (7)

Maki, R. H. (1990). Memory for script actions: Effects of relevance and detail expectancy. *Memory & Cognition, 18*, 5–14. (8)

Maki, R., & Berry, S. (1984). Metacomprehension of text material. *Journal of Experimental Psychology: Learning, Memory, and Cognition, 10*, 663–679. (9)

Malamut, B. L., Saunders, R. C., & Mishkin, M. (1984). Monkeys with combined amygdalo-hippocampal lesions succeed in object discrimination learning despite 24-hour intertrial intervals. *Behavioral Neuroscience, 98*, 759–769. (8)

Malamuth, N. M., & Donnerstein, E. (1982). The effects of aggressive-pornographic mass media stimuli. In L. Berkowitz (Ed.), *Advances in experimental social psychology* (Vol. 15, pp. 103–136). New York: Academic Press. (11)

Malinowski, B. (1929). *The sexual life of savages in Northwestern Melanesia.* New York: Harcourt, Brace, & World. (2)

Manji, H. K., Hsiao, J. K., Risby, E. D., Oliver, J., Rudorfer, M. V., & Potter, W. Z. (1991). The mechanisms of action of lithium. I. Effects on serotoninergic and noradrenergic systems in normal subjects. *Archives of General Psychiatry, 48*, 505–512. (15)

Mann, J. J., & Kapur, S. (1991). The emergence of suicidal ideation and behavior during antidepressant pharmacotherapy. *Archives of General Psychiatry, 48*, 1027–1033. (15)

Mann, J. J., McBride, P. A., & Stanley, M. (1986). Postmortem monoamine receptor and enzyme studies in suicide. *Annals of the New York Academy of Sciences, 487*, 114–121. (14)

Mansky, P. A. (1978). Opiates: Human psychopharmacology. In L. L. Iversen, S. D. Iversen, & S. H. Snyder (Eds.), *Handbook of psychopharmacology: Vol. 12, Drugs of abuse* (pp. 95–185). New York: Plenum. (5)

Manuck, S. B., Cohen, S., Rabin, B. S., Muldoon, M. F., & Bachen, E. A. (1991). Individual differences in cellular immune response to stress. *Psychological Science, 2*, 111–115. (12)

Marcia, J. E. (1980). Identity in adolescence. In J. Adelson (Ed.), *Handbook of adolescent psychology* (pp. 159–187). New York: Wiley. (6)

Marder, S. R., Mebane, A., Chien, C., Winslade, W. J., Swann, E., & Van Putten, T. (1983). A comparison of patients who refuse and consent to neuroleptic treatment. *American Journal of Psychiatry, 140,* 470–472. (15)

Marek, G. R. (1975). *Toscanini.* London: Vision. (8)

Mark, V. H., & Ervin, F. R. (1970). *Violence and the brain.* New York: Harper & Row. (3)

Markides, K. S., & Machalak, R. (1984). Selective survival, aging and society. *Archives of Gerontology & Geriatrics, 3,* 207–222. (6)

Markman, E. M. (1990). Constraints children place on word meanings. *Cognitive Science, 14,* 57–77. (6)

Markman, E. M., & Hutchinson, J. E. (1984). Children's sensitivity to constraints on word meaning: Taxonomic versus thematic relations. *Cognitive Psychology, 16,* 1–27. (6)

Marks, D., & Kammann, R. (1980). *The psychology of the psychic.* Buffalo, NY: Prometheus. (2, 13)

Marlatt, G. A. (1978). Craving for alcohol, loss of control, and relapse: A cognitive-behavioral analysis. In P. E. Nathan, G. A. Marlatt, & T. Løberg (Eds.), *Alcoholism: New directions in behavioral research and treatment* (pp. 271–314). New York: Plenum. (14)

Marriott, F. H. C. (1976). Abnormal colour vision. In H. Davson (Ed.), *The eye* (2nd ed.) (pp. 533–547). New York: Academic Press. (4)

Marsh, H. W., & Byrne, B. M. (1991). Differentiated additive androgyny model: Relations between masculinity, femininity, and multiple dimensions of self-concept. *Journal of Personality and Social Psychology, 61,* 811–828. (13)

Marshall, G. D., & Zimbardo, P. G. (1979). Affective consequences of inadequately explained physiological arousal. *Journal of Personality and Social Psychology, 37,* 970–988. (12)

Marshall, J. R. (1985). Neural plasticity and recovery of function after brain injury. *International Review of Neurobiology, 26,* 201–247. (3)

Marshall, W. L. (1988). The use of sexually explicit stimuli by rapists, child molesters, and nonoffenders. *Journal of Sex Research, 25,* 267–288. (11)

Martin, C. E. (1981). Factors affecting sexual functioning in 60–79-year-old married males. *Archives of Sexual Behavior, 10,* 399–420. (11)

Martin, L. (1986). "Eskimo words for snow": A case study in the genesis and decay of an anthropological example. *American Anthropologist, 88,* 418–423. (9)

Maslach, C. (1979). Negative emotional biasing of unexplained arousal. *Journal of Personality and Social Psychology, 37,* 953–969. (12)

Masling, J. M., Bornstein, R. F., Poynton, F. G., Reid, S., & Katkin, E. S. (1991). Perception without awareness and electrodermal responding: A strong test of subliminal psychodynamic activation effects. *Journal of Mind and Behavior, 12,* 33–48. (4)

Maslow, A. H. (1962). *Toward a psychology of being.* Princeton, NJ: Van Nostrand. (13)

Maslow, A. H. (1970). *Motivation and personality* (2nd ed.). New York: Harper & Row. (11)

Maslow, A. H. (1971). *The farther reaches of human nature.* New York: Viking. (13)

Masson, J. M. (1984). *The assault on truth.* New York: Farrar, Straus, and Giroux. (13)

Masters, W. H., & Johnson, V. E. (1966). *Human sexual response.* Boston: Little, Brown. (11)

Matarazzo, J. D., & Wiens, A. N. (1977). Black Intelligence Test of Cultural Homogeneity and Wechsler Adult Intelligence Scale scores of black and white police applicants. *Journal of Applied Psychology, 62,* 57–63. (10)

Matheny, A. P., Jr. (1989). Children's behavioral inhibition over age and across situations: Genetic similarity for a trait to change. *Journal of Personality, 57,* 215–235. (6)

Matsui, T., Okada, A., & Kakuyama, T. (1982). Influence of goal setting, performance, and feedback effectiveness. *Journal of Applied Psychology, 67,* 645–648. (11)

Mattes, R. D. (1988). Blocking learned food aversions in cancer patients receiving chemotherapy. *Annals of the New York Academy of Sciences, 510,* 478–479. (7)

McCall, V. W., Yates, B., Hendricks, S., Turner, K., & McNabb, B. (1989). Comparison between the Stanford-Binet: L-M and the Stanford-Binet: Fourth edition with a group of gifted children. *Contemporary Educational Psychology, 14,* 93–96. (10)

McCaul, K. D., & Malott, J. M. (1984). Distraction and coping with pain. *Psychological Bulletin, 95,* 516–533. (4, 12)

McClelland, D. C. (1958). Risk taking in children with high and low need for achievement. In J. W. Atkinson (Ed.), *Motives in fantasy, action, and society* (pp. 306–321). Princeton, NJ: Van Nostrand. (11)

McClelland, D. C. (1985). How motives, skills, and values determine what people do. *American Psychologist, 40,* 812–825. (11)

McClelland, D. C., Atkinson, J. W., Clark, R. A., & Lowell, E. L. (1953). *The achievement motive.* New York: Appleton-Century-Crofts. (11)

McClelland, D. C., Koestner, R., & Weinberger, J. (1989). How do self-attributed and implicit motives differ? *Psychological Review, 96,* 690–702. (11)

McClelland, J. L. (1988). Connectionist models and psychological evidence. *Journal of Memory and Language, 27,* 107–123. (9)

McClelland, J. L., & Rumelhart, D. E. (1981). An interactive activation model of context effects in letter perception: Part 1. An account of basic findings. *Psychological Review, 88,* 375–407. (9)

McConnell, J. V. (1990). Negative reinforcement and positive punishment. *Teaching of Psychology, 17,* 247–249. (7)

McConnell, J. W. (1989, Summer). Reinvention of subliminal perception. *Skeptical Inquirer, 13,* 427–429. (4)

McCormick, M. C. (1985). The contribution of low birth weight to infant mortality and childhood morbidity. *New England Journal of Medicine, 312,* 82–90. (6)

McCornack, R. L. (1983). Bias in the validity of predicted college grades in four ethnic minority groups. *Educational & Psychological Measurement, 43,* 517–522. (10)

McCrae, R. R., & Costa, P. T., Jr. (1987). Validation of the five-factor model of personality across instruments and observers. *Journal of Personality and Social Psychology, 52,* 81–90. (13)

McDaniel, M. A., Einstein, G. O., & Lollis, T. (1988). Qualitative and quantitative considerations in encoding difficulty effects. *Memory & Cognition, 16,* 8–14. (8)

McDougall, W. (1932). *The energies of men.* New York: Charles Scribner's Sons. (11)

McGaugh, J. L. (1990). Significance and remembrance: The role of neuromodulatory systems. *Psychological Science, 1,* 15–25. (8)

McGlynn, S. M. (1990). Behavioral approaches to neuropsychological rehabilitation. *Psychological Bulletin, 108,* 420–441. (3)

McGlynn, S. M., & Kaszniak, A. W. (1991). When metacognition fails: Impaired awareness of deficit in Alzheimer's disease. *Journal of Cognitive Neuroscience, 3,* 182–189. (8)

McGuire, W. J. (1968). Personality and attitude change: An information-processing theory. In A. G. Greenwald et al. (Eds.), *Psychological foundations of attitudes* (pp. 171–196). New York: Academic Press. (16)

McGuire, W. J. (1985). Attitudes and attitude change. In G. Lindzey & E. Aronson (Eds.), *Handbook of social psychology* (Vol. 2, pp. 233–346). New York: Random House. (16)

McGuire, W. J., & Papageorgis, D. (1961). The relative efficacy of various types of prior belief-defense in producing immunity against persuasion. *Journal of Abnormal and Social Psychology, 62,* 327–337. (16)

McLoyd, V. C. (1990). The impact of economic hardship on black families and children: Psychological distress, parenting, and socioeconomic development. *Child Development, 61,* 311–346. (6)

McMahon, C. E. (1975). The wind of the cannon ball: An informative anecdote from medical history. *Psychotherapy & Psychosomatics, 26,* 125–131. (12)

McMorrow, M. J., & Foxx, R. M. (1983). Nicotine's role in smoking: An analysis of nicotine regulation. *Psychological Bulletin, 93,* 302–327. (5)

McMurtry, P. L., & Mershon, D. H. (1985). Auditory distance judgments in noise, with and without hearing protection. *Proceedings of the Human Factors Society* (Baltimore, MD), pp. 811–813. (4)

McNally, R. J. (1990). Psychological approaches to panic disorder: A review. *Psychological Bulletin, 108,* 403–419. (14)

McNeal, E. T., & Cimbolic, P. (1986). Antidepressants and biochemical theories of depression. *Psychological Bulletin, 99,* 361–374. (15)

McReynolds, P. (1985). Psychological assessment and clinical practice: Problems and prospects. *Advances in Personality Assessment, 4,* 1–30. (13)

Meddis, R., Pearson, A. J. D., & Langford, G. (1973). An extreme case of healthy insomnia. *EEG and Clinical Neurophysiology, 35,* 213–214. (5)

Medin, D. L., Goldstone, R. L., & Gentner, D. (1990). Similarity involving attributes and relations: Judgments of similarity and difference are not inverses. *Psychological Science, 1,* 64–69. (9)

Mednick, S. A., Machon, R. A., & Huttunen, M. O. (1990). An update on the Helsinki influenza project. *Archives of General Psychiatry, 47,* 292. (14)

Meichenbaum, D. (1985). *Stress inoculation training.* New York: Pergamon. (12)

Meichenbaum, D., & Cameron, R. (1983). Stress inoculation training. In D. Meichenbaum & M. E. Jaremko (Eds.), *Stress reduction and prevention* (pp. 115–154). New York: Plenum. (12)

Meichenbaum, D. H., & Goodman, J. (1971). Training impulsive children to talk to themselves: A means of developing self-control. *Journal of Abnormal Psychology, 77,* 115–126. (7)

Mello, N. K., & Mendelson, J. H. (1978). Behavioral pharmacology of human alcohol, heroin and marihuana use. In J. Fishman (Ed.), *The bases of addiction* (pp. 133–158). Berlin: Dahlem Konferenzen. (5)

Meltzoff, A. N., & Moore, M. K. (1977). Imitation of facial and manual gestures by human neonates. *Science, 198,* 75–78. (6)

Melzack, R., & Wall, P. D. (1965). Pain mechanisms: A new theory. *Science, 150,* 971–979. (5)

Melzack, R., & Wall, P. D. (1983). *The challenge of pain.* New York: Basic Books. (5)

Melzack, R., Weisz, A. Z., & Sprague, L. T. (1963). Stratagems for controlling pain: Contributions of auditory stimulation and suggestion. *Experimental Neurology, 8,* 239–247. (12)

Mendelson, W. G. (1990). Do studies of sedative/hypnotics suggest the nature of chronic insomnia? In J. Montplaisir & R. Godbout (Eds.), *Sleep and biological rhythms* (pp. 209–218). New York: Oxford University Press. (5)

Mershon, D. H., Desaulniers, D. H., Kiefer, S. A., Amerson, T. L., Jr., & Mills, J. T. (1981). Perceived loudness and visually determined auditory distance. *Perception, 10,* 531–543. (4)

Mershon, D. H., & King, L. E. (1975). Intensity and reverberation as factors in the auditory perception of egocentric distance. *Perception and Psychophysics, 18,* 409–415. (4)

Mesmer, F. A. (1980). *Mesmerism: A translation of the original medical and scientific writings of F. A. Mesmer.* Los Altos, CA: William Kaufmann. (12)

Messenger, J. C. (1971). Sex and repression in an Irish folk community. In D. S. Marshall & R. C. Suggs (Eds.), *Human sexual behavior: Variations in the ethnographic spectrum* (pp. 3–37). New York: Basic Books. (11)

Messick, S., & Jungeblut, A. (1981). Time and method in coaching for the SAT. *Psychological Bulletin, 89,* 191–216. (10)

Metcalfe, J., & Wiebe, D. (1987). Intuition in insight and noninsight problem solving. *Memory & Cognition, 15,* 238–246. (9)

Meyer, J. S., Ishikawa, Y., Hata, T., & Karacan, I. (1987). Cerebral blood flow in normal and abnormal sleep and dreaming. *Brain and Cognition, 6,* 266–294. (5)

Michael, C. R. (1978). Color vision mechanisms in monkey striate cortex: Dual-opponent cells with concentric receptive fields. *Journal of Neurophysiology, 41,* 572–588. (4)

Milgram, S. (1974). *Obedience to authority.* New York: Harper & Row. (16)

Miller, D. T., & Ross, M. (1975). Self-serving biases in the attribution of causality: Fact or fiction? *Psychological Bulletin, 82,* 213–225. (16)

Miller, G. A. (1956). The magical number seven, plus or minus two: Some limits on our capacity for processing information. *Psychological Review, 63,* 81–97. (8)

Miller, L. L., & Branconnier, R. J. (1983). Cannabis: Effects on memory and the cholinergic limbic system. *Psychological Bulletin, 93,* 441–456. (5)

Miller, M. J., Small, I. F., Milstein, V., Malloy, F., & Stout, J. R. (1981). Electrode placement and cognitive change with ECT: Male and female response. *American Journal of Psychiatry, 138,* 384–386. (15)

Miller, N. E. (1969). Learning of visceral and glandular responses. *Science, 163,* 434–445. (7)

Miller, N. E. (1985). The value of behavioral research on animals. *American Psychologist, 40,* 423–440. (2)

Miller, R. J., Hennessy, R. T., & Leibowitz, H. W. (1973). The effect of hypnotic ablation of the background on the magnitude of the Ponzo perspective illusion. *International Journal of Clinical and Experimental Hypnosis, 21,* 180–191. (5)

Miller, R. S. (1986). Embarrassment: Causes and consequences. In W. Jones, J. Cheek, & S. Briggs (Eds.), *Shyness: Perspectives on research and treatment* (pp. 295–311). New York: Plenum. (12)

Miller, T. A. (1987). Mechanisms of stress-related mucosal damage. *American Journal of Medicine, 83* (Suppl. 6A), 8–14. (12)

Miller, W. R., & Hester, R. K. (1986). Inpatient alcohol treatment: Who benefits? *American Psychologist, 41,* 794–805. (14)

Milner, B. (1959). The memory defect in bilateral hippocampal lesions. *Psychiatric Research Reports, 11,* 43–52. (8)

Mineka, S. (1985). The frightful complexity of the origin of fears. In F. R. Brush & J. B. Overmier (Eds.), *Affect, conditioning, and cognition* (pp. 55–73). Hillsdale, NJ: Lawrence Erlbaum. (14)

Mineka, S. (1987). A primate model of phobic fears. In H. Eysenck & I. Martin (Eds.), *Theoretical foundations of behavior therapy* (pp. 81–111). New York: Plenum. (14)

Mineka, S., Cook, M., & Miller, S. (1984). Fear conditioned with escapable and inescapable shock: The effects of a feedback stimulus. *Journal of Experimental Psychology: Animal Behavior Processes, 10,* 307–323. (14)

Mineka, S., Davidson, M., Cook, M., & Keir, R. (1984). Observational conditioning of snake fear in rhesus monkeys. *Journal of Abnormal Psychology, 93,* 355–372. (14)

Mischel, W. (1973). Toward a cognitive social learning reconceptualization of personality. *Psychological Review, 80,* 252–283. (13)

Mischel, W. (1981). Current issues and challenges in personality. In L. T. Benjamin, Jr. (Ed.), *The G. Stanley Hall Lecture Series* (Vol. 1, pp. 81–99). Washington, DC: American Psychological Association. (13)

Mitchell, J. E., & Eckert, E. D. (1987). Scope and significance of eating disorders. *Journal of Consulting and Clinical Psychology, 55,* 628–634. (11)

Mitchell, J. E., & Popkin, M. K. (1982). Antipsychotic drug therapy and sexual dysfunction in men. *American Journal of Psychiatry, 139,* 633–637. (15)

Moar, I., & Bower, G. H. (1983). Inconsistency in spatial knowledge. *Memory & Cognition, 11,* 107–113. (9)

Mobily, K. (1982). Using physical therapy activity and recreation to cope with stress and anxiety: A review. *American Corrective Therapy Journal, 36,* 77–81. (12)

Moely, B. E., Olson, F. A., Halwes, T. G., & Flavell, J. H. (1969). Production deficiency in young children's clustered recall. *Developmental Psychology, 1,* 26–34. (6)

Mohs, R. C., Breitner, J. C. S., Silverman, J. M., & Davis, K. L. (1987). Alzheimer's disease: Morbid risk among first-degree relatives approximates 50% by 90 years of age. *Archives of General Psychiatry, 44,* 405–408. (8)

Monahan, J. (1984). The prediction of violent behavior: Toward a second generation of theory and policy. *American Journal of Psychiatry, 141,* 10–15. (12)

Money, J. (1983). The genealogical descent of sexual psychoneuroendocrinology from sex and health theory: The eighteenth to the twentieth centuries. *Psychoneuroendocrinology, 8,* 391–400. (11)

Money, J., & Ehrhardt, A. A. (1972). *Man and woman, boy and girl.* Baltimore, MD: Johns Hopkins University Press. (11)

Mook, D. G. (1990). Satiety, specifications, and stop rules: Feeding as voluntary action. *Progress in Psychobiology and Physiological Psychology, 14,* 1–65. (11)

Moorcroft, W. J. (1989). *Sleep, dreaming, & sleep disorders.* Lanham, MD: University Press of America. (5)

Moore, B. C. J. (1989). *An introduction to the psychology of hearing* (3rd ed.). London: Academic Press. (4)

Moore-Ede, M. C., Czeisler, C. A., & Richardson, G. S. (1983). Circadian timekeeping in health and disease. *New England Journal of Medicine, 309,* 469–476. (5)

Moos, R. H., & Finney, J. W. (1983). The expanding scope of alcoholism treatment evaluation. *American Psychologist, 38,* 1036–1044. (14)

Moray, N. (1959). Attention in dichotic listening: Affective cues and the influence of instructions. *Quarterly Journal of Experimental Psychology, 11,* 56–60. (4)

Morgan, B. L. G., & Winick, M. (1989). Malnutrition, central nervous system effects. In G. Adelman (Ed.), *Neuroscience year* (pp. 97–99). Boston: Birkhäuser. (6)

Morris, J. B., & Beck, A. T. (1974). The efficacy of antidepressant drugs. *Archives of General Psychiatry, 30,* 667–674. (15)

Morrison, D. B. (1985). Adolescent contraceptive behavior: A review. *Psychological Bulletin, 98,* 538–568. (6)

Morrow, R. S., & Morrow, S. (1974). The measurement of intelligence. In B. B. Wolman (Ed.), *Handbook of general psychology* (pp. 656–670). Englewood Cliffs, NJ: Prentice-Hall. (10)

Mortimer, J. A., Schuman, L. M., & French, L. R. (1981). Epidemiology of dementing illness. In J. A. Mortimer & L. M. Schuman (Eds.), *Epidemiology of dementia* (pp. 3–23). New York: Oxford University Press. (8)

Moscovici, S., & Mugny, G. (1983). Minority influence. In P. B. Paulus (Ed.), *Basic group processes* (pp. 41–64). New York: Springer-Verlag. (16)

Moscovici, S., & Zavalloni, M. (1969). The group as a polarizer of attitudes. *Journal of Personality and Social Psychology, 12,* 125–135. (16)

Moscovitch, M. (1985). Memory from infancy to old age: Implications for theories of normal and pathological memory. *Annals of the New York Academy of Sciences, 444,* 78–96. (8)

Moscovitch, M. (1989). Confabulation and the frontal systems: Strategic versus associative retrieval in neuropsychological theories of memory. In H. L. Roediger, III, & F. I. M. Craik (Eds.), *Varieties of memory and consciousness: Essays in honour of Endel Tulving* (pp. 133–160). Hillsdale, NJ: Lawrence Erlbaum. (8)

Moskowitz, B. A. (1978). The acquisition of language. *Scientific American, 239*(5), 92–108. (6)

Moskowitz, D. S. (1982). Coherence and cross-situational generality in personality: A new analysis of old problems. *Journal of Personality and Social Psychology, 43,* 754–768. (13)

Motley, M. T., & Baars, B. J. (1979). Effects of cognitive set upon laboratory induced verbal (Freudian) slips. *Journal of Speech and Hearing Research, 22,* 421–432. (13)

Moyer, K. E. (1974). Sex differences in aggression. In R. C. Friedman, R. M. Richart, & R. L. VandeWiele (Eds.), *Sex differences in behavior* (pp. 335–372). New York: Wiley. (12)

Mumford, M. D., & Gustafson, S. B. (1988). Creativity syndrome: Integration, application, and innovation. *Psychological Bulletin, 103,* 27–43. (9)

Munro, J. F., Stewart, I. C., Seidelin, P. H., Mackenzie, H. S., & Dewhurst, N. G. (1987). Mechanical treatment for obesity. *Annals of the New York Academy of Sciences, 499,* 305–312. (11)

Munroe, R. (1955). *Schools of psychoanalytic thought.* New York: Dryden. (15)

Murison, R., & Overmier, J. B. (1990). Proactive actions of psychological stress on gastric ulceration in rats—Real psychobiology. *Annals of the New York Academy of Sciences, 597,* 191–200. (12)

Murphy, G. L., & Medin, D. L. (1985). The role of theories in conceptual coherence. *Psychological Review, 92,* 289–316. (1)

Murray, H. A. (1938). *Explorations in personality.* New York: Oxford University Press. (11)

Murray, H. A. (1943). *Thematic Apperception Test manual.* Cambridge, MA: Harvard University Press. (13)

Myers, J. K., Weissman, M. M., Tischler, G. L., Holzer, C. E., III, Leaf, P. J., Orvaschel, H., Anthony, J. C., Boyd, J. H., Burke, J. D., Jr., Kramer, M., & Stoltzman, R. (1984). Six-month prevalence of psychiatric disorders in three communities. *Archives of General Psychiatry, 41,* 959–967. (14)

Naglieri, J. A. (1984). Concurrent and predictive validity of the Kaufman Assessment Battery for children with a Navajo sample. *Journal of School Psychology, 22,* 373–380. (10)

Nash, M. (1987). What, if anything, is regressed about hypnotic age regression? A review of the empirical literature. *Psychological Bulletin, 102,* 42–52. (5)

Nash, M. R., Johnson, L. S., & Tipton, R. D. (1979). Hypnotic age regression and the occurrence of transitional object relationships. *Journal of Abnormal Psychology, 88,* 547–555. (5)

Nash, M. R., Lynn, S. J., Stanley, S., & Carlson, V. (1987). Subjectively complete hypnotic deafness and auditory priming. *International Journal of Clinical and Experimental Hypnosis, 35,* 32–40. (5)

National Center for Health Statistics. (1988). *Vital Statistics of the United States, 1984* (Vol. 3). Washington, DC: U.S. Government Printing Office. (11)

National Institute of Mental Health. (1982). Television and behavior: Ten years of scientific progress and implications for the eighties. Rockville, MD: Author. (2)

Natsoulas, T. (1991). Consciousness and commissurotomy: III. Toward the improvement of alternative conceptions. *Journal of Mind and Behavior, 12,* 1–32. (1)

Nebes, R. D. (1974). Hemispheric specialization in commissurotomized man. *Psychological Bulletin, 81,* 1–14. (3)

Neiss, R. (1988). Reconceptualizing arousal: Psychobiological stakes in motor performance. *Psychological Bulletin, 103,* 345–366. (12)

Nelson, K. (1981). Individual differences in language development: Implications for development and language. *Developmental Psychology, 17,* 170–187. (6)

Nelson, K. (1985). Making sense: The acquisition of shared meaning. Orlando, FL: Academic Press. (6)

Nelson, K. E., Baker, N. D., Denninger, M., Bonvillian, J. D., & Kaplan, B. J. (1985). Cookie versus Do-it-again: Imitative-referential and personal-social-syntactic-initiating language styles in young children. *Linguistics, 23,* 433–454. (6)

Nelson, R. D., Jahn, R. G., & Dunne, B. J. (1986). Operator-related anomalies in physical systems and information processes. *Journal of the Society for Psychical Research, 53,* 261–285. (2)

Nelson, T. O., & Dunlosky, J. (1991). When people's judgments of learning (JOLs) are extremely accurate at predicting subsequent recall: The "delayed-JOL effect." *Psychological Science, 2,* 267–270. (8)

Nelson, T. O., McSpadden, M., Fromme, K., & Marlatt, G. A. (1986). Effects of alcohol intoxication on metamemory and on retrieval from long-term memory. *Journal of Experimental Psychology: General, 115,* 247–254. (5)

Nemeth, C. (1972). A critical analysis of research utilizing the prisoner's dilemma paradigm for the study of bargaining. In L. Berkowitz (Ed.), *Advances in Experimental Social Psychology* (Vol. 6, pp. 203–234). New York: Academic Press. (16)

Nemeth, C. J. (1986). Differential contributions of majority and minority influence. *Psychological Review, 93,* 23–32. (16)

Nesse, R. M. (1991, November/December). What good is feeling bad? *The Sciences, 31*(6), 30–37. (15)

Newlin, D. B., & Thomson, J. B. (1990). Alcohol challenge with sons of alcoholics: A critical review and analysis. *Psychological Bulletin, 108,* 383–402. (14)

Newman, S. E. (1987). Ebbinghaus' *On memory:* Some effects on early American research. In D. S. Gorfein & R. R. Hoffman (Eds.), *Memory and learning: The Ebbinghaus centennial conference* (pp. 77–87). Hillsdale, NJ: Lawrence Erlbaum. (8)

Newman, S. E., Cooper, M. H., Parker, K. O., Sidden, J. A., Gonder-Frederick, L. A., Moorefield, K. M., & Nelson, P. A. (1982). Some tests of the encoding specificity and semantic integration hypotheses. *American Journal of Psychology, 95,* 103–123. (8)

Newsome, W. T., & Paré, E. B. (1988). A selective impairment of motion perception following lesions of the middle temporal visual area (MT). *Journal of Neuroscience, 8,* 2201–2211. (3, 4)

Nickerson, R. S., & Adams, M. J. (1979). Long-term memory for a common object. *Cognitive Psychology, 11,* 287–307. (8)

Nietzel, M. T., & Bernstein, D. A. (1987). *Introduction to clinical psychology.* Englewood Cliffs, NJ: Prentice-Hall. (10)

Nisbett, R. E., Caputo, C., Legant, P., & Marecek, J. (1973). Behavior as seen by the actor and as seen by the observer. *Journal of Personality and Social Psychology, 27,* 154–164. (16)

Nisbett, R. E., Fong, G. T., Lehman, D. R., & Cheng, P. W. (1987). Teaching reasoning. *Science, 238,* 625–631. (9)

Nisbett, R. E., & Schachter, S. (1966). Cognitive manipulation of pain. *Journal of Experimental Social Psychology, 2,* 227–236. (9)

Nolen-Hoeksema, S. (1987). Sex differences in unipolar depression: Evidence and theory. *Psychological Bulletin, 101,* 259–282. (14)

Norman, D. A. (1981). Categorization of action slips. *Psychological Review, 88,* 1–15. (13)

Nosanchuk, T. A., & MacNeil, C. (1989). Examination of the effects of traditional and modern martial arts training on aggressiveness. *Aggressive Behavior, 15,* 153–159. (2)

Nosofsky, R. M. (1986). Attention, similarity, and the identification-categorization relationship. *Journal of Experimental Psychology: General, 115,* 39–57. (9)

Novick, L. R. (1990). Representational transfer in problem solving. *Psychological Science, 1,* 128–132. (9)

Nowak, A., Szamrej, J., & Latané, B. (1990). From private attitude to public opinion: A dynamic theory of social impact. *Psychological Review, 97,* 362–376. (16)

Nutt, D. J. (1989). Altered central alpha$_2$-adrenoceptor sensitivity in panic disorder. *Archives of General Psychiatry, 46,* 165–169. (14)

Nygard, R. (1982). Achievement motives and individual differences in situational specificity of behavior. *Journal of Personality and Social Psychology, 43,* 319–327. (11)

O'Brien, M., & Nagle, K. J. (1987). Parents' speech to toddlers: The effect of play context. *Journal of Child Language, 14,* 269–279. (6)

O'Hara, M. W., Schlechte, J. A., Lewis, D. A., & Wright, E. J. (1991). Prospective study of postpartum blues. *Archives of General Psychiatry, 48,* 801–806. (14)

Öhman, A., Eriksson, A., & Olofsson, C. (1975). One-trial learning and superior resistance to extinction of autonomic responses conditioned to potentially phobic objects. *Journal of Comparative and Physiological Psychology, 88,* 619–627. (14)

Okin, R. L. (1983). The future of state hospitals: Should there be one? *American Journal of Psychiatry, 140,* 577–581. (15)

O'Leary, A. (1990). Stress, emotion, and human immune function. *Psychological Bulletin, 108,* 363–382. (12)

Olson, J. M. (1992). Self-perception of humor: Evidence for discounting and augmentation effects. *Journal of Personality and Social Psychology, 62,* 369–377. (16)

O'Malley, S. S., & Maisto, S. A. (1985). Effects of family drinking history and expectancies on responses to alcohol in men. *Journal of Studies on Alcohol, 46,* 289–297. (14)

Omoto, A. M., & Snyder, M. (1990). Basic research in action: Volunteerism and society's response to AIDS. *Personality and Social Psychology Bulletin, 16,* 152–165. (16)

O'Nell, C. W. (1965). A cross-cultural study of hunger and thirst motivation manifested in dreams. *Human Development, 8,* 181–193. (15)

Orne, M. T. (1951). The mechanisms of hypnotic age regression: An experimental study. *Journal of Abnormal and Social Psychology, 46,* 213–225. (5)

Orne, M. T. (1959). The nature of hypnosis: Artifact and essence. *Journal of Abnormal and Social Psychology, 58,* 277–299. (5)

Orne, M. T. (1969). Demand characteristics and the concept of quasi-controls. In R. Rosenthal & R. L. Rosnow (Eds.), *Artifact in behavioral research* (pp. 143–179). (2)

Orne, M. T. (1979). On the simulating subject as a quasi-control group in hypnosis research: What, why, and how. In E. Fromm & R. E. Shor (Eds.), *Hypnosis: Developments in research and new perspectives* (2nd ed.) (pp. 519–565). New York: Aldine. (5)

Orne, M. T., Dinges, D. F., & Orne, E. C. (1984). On the differential diagnosis of multiple personality in the forensic context. *International Journal of Clinical and Experimental Hypnosis, 32,* 118–169. (5)

Orne, M. T., & Evans, F. J. (1965). Social control in the psychological experiment: Antisocial behavior and hypnosis. *Journal of Personality and Social Psychology, 1,* 189–200. (5)

Orne, M. T., & Scheibe, K. E. (1964). The contribution of nondeprivation factors in the production of sensory deprivation effects: The psychology of the "panic button." *Journal of Abnormal and Social Psychology, 68,* 3–12. (2)

Ornitz, E. M., & Ritvo, E. R. (1976). Medical assessment. In E. R. Ritvo (Ed.), *Autism* (pp. 7–23). New York: Spectrum. (14)

Orth, J. E., & Thebarge, R. W. (1984). Helping clients reduce self-evaluative behavior: Consider the consequences. *Cognitive Therapy and Research, 8,* 13–18. (15)

Ortony, A., & Turner, T. J. (1990). What's basic about basic emotions? *Psychological Review, 97,* 315–331. (12)

Osborne, R. T., Noble, C. E., & Wey, N. J. (Eds.) (1978). *Human variation: Biopsychology of age, race, and sex.* New York: Academic Press. (16)

Oscar-Berman, M. (1980). Neuropsychological consequences of long-term chronic alcoholism. *American Scientist, 68,* 410–419. (8)

Öst, L.-G., & Hugdahl, K. (1981). Acquisition of phobias and anxiety response patterns in clinical patients. *Behaviour Research and Therapy, 19,* 439–447. (14)

O'Sullivan, M., Ekman, P., Friesen, W., & Scherer, K. (1985). What you say and how you say it: The contribution of speech content and voice quality to judgments of others. *Journal of Personality and Social Psychology, 48,* 54–62. (12)

Overmier, J. B., Murison, R., Ursin, H., & Skoglund, E. J. (1987). Quality of post-stressor rest influences the ulcerative process. *Behavioral Neuroscience, 101,* 246–253. (12)

Padgham, C. A. (1975). Colours experienced in dreams. *British Journal of Psychology, 66,* 25–28. (5)

Paicheler, G. (1988). *The psychology of social influence.* Cambridge, England: Cambridge University Press. (16)

Paikoff, R. L., & Brooks-Gunn, J. (1991). Do parent-child relationships change during puberty? *Psychological Bulletin, 110,* 47–66. (6)

Panksepp, J., Herman, B., & Vilberg, T. (1978). An opiate excess model of childhood autism. *Neuroscience Abstracts, 4*(Abstract 1601), 500. (14)

Papini, M. R., & Bitterman, M. E. (1990). The role of contingency in classical conditioning. *Psychological Review, 97,* 396–403. (7)

Pappone, P. A., & Cahalan, M. D. (1987). *Pandinus imperator* scorpion venom blocks voltage-gated potassium channels in nerve fibers. *Journal of Neuroscience, 7,* 3300–3305. (3)

Parke, R. D., Berkowitz, L., Leyens, J. P., West, S. G., & Sebastian, R. J. (1977). Some effects of violent and nonviolent movies on the behavior of juvenile delinquents. In L. Berkowitz (Ed.), *Advances in experimental social psychology* (Vol. 10, pp. 135–172). New York: Academic Press. (2)

Parker, D. (1944). *The portable Dorothy Parker.* New York: Viking. (14, 15)

Parker, K. (1983). A meta-analysis of the reliability and validity of the Rorschach. *Journal of Personality Assessment, 47,* 227–231. (13)

Parmeggiani, P. L. (1982). Regulation of physiological functions during sleep in mammals. *Experientia, 38,* 1405–1408. (5)

Parnas, J., Schulsinger, F., Schulsinger, H., Mednick, S. A., & Teasdale, T. W. (1982). Behavioral precursors of schizophrenia spectrum. *Archives of General Psychiatry, 39,* 658–664. (14)

Parsons, H. M. (1974). What happened at Hawthorne? *Science, 183,* 922–932. (2)

Pate, J. L., & Rumbaugh, D. M. (1983). The language-like behavior of Lana chimpanzee: Is it merely discrimination and paired-associate learning? *Animal Learning & Behavior, 11,* 134–138. (9)

Patrick, C. J., & Iacono, W. G. (1989). Psychopathy, threat, and polygraph test accuracy. *Journal of Applied Psychology, 74,* 347–355. (12)

Pavlov, I. P. (1927/1960). *Conditioned reflexes.* New York: Dover. (Original work published 1927) (7)

Peachey, J. E., & Naranjo, C. A. (1983). The use of disulfiram and other alcohol-sensitizing drugs in the treatment of alcoholism. *Research Advances in Alcohol and Drug Problems, 7,* 397–431. (14)

Pearce, J. M. (1987). A model for stimulus generalization in Pavlovian conditioning. *Psychological Review, 94,* 61–73. (7)

Peele, S. (1984). The cultural context of psychological approaches to alcoholism. *American Psychologist, 39,* 1337–1351. (14)

Pendery, M. L., Maltzman, I. M., & West, L. J. (1982). Controlled drinking by alcoholics? New findings and a reevaluation of a major affirmative study. *Science, 217,* 169–175. (14)

Pennebaker, J. W. (1990). *Opening up.* New York: William Morrow. (12)

Pepper, B., & Ryglewicz, H. (1982). Testimony for the neglected: The mentally ill in the post-deinstitutionalized age. *American Journal of Orthopsychiatry, 52,* 388–392. (15)

Pepperberg, I. M. (1981). Functional vocalizations by an African gray parrot. *Zeitschrift für Tierpsychologie, 55,* 139–160. (9)

Pepperberg, I. M. (1990). Cognition in an African gray parrot (*Psittacus erithacus*): Further evidence for comprehension of categories and labels. *Journal of Comparative Psychology, 104,* 41–52. (9)

Perls, F. (1973). *The Gestalt approach and eye witness to therapy.* Ben Lomond, CA: Science and Behavior Books. (15)

Perry, D. G., & Bussey, K. (1979). The social learning theory of sex differences: Imitation is alive and well. *Journal of Personality and Social Psychology, 37*, 1699–1712. (7)

Pert, C. B., & Snyder, S. H. (1973). The opiate receptor: Demonstration in nervous tissue. *Science, 179*, 1011–1014. (5)

Pervin, L. A. (1983). The stasis and flow of behavior: Toward a theory of goals. In M. M. Page (Ed.), *Nebraska symposium on motivation 1982* (pp. 1–53). Lincoln, NE: University of Nebraska Press. (11)

Pervin, L. A. (1990). A brief history of modern personality theory. In L. A. Pervin (Ed.), *Handbook of personality* (pp. 3–18). New York: Guilford Press. (13)

Peterson, C. (1983). Clouds and silver linings: Depressive symptoms and causal attributions about ostensibly "good" and "bad" events. *Cognitive Therapy and Research, 7*, 575–578. (14)

Peterson, C., Bettes, B. A., & Seligman, M. E. P. (1985). Depressive symptoms and unprompted causal attributions: Content analysis. *Behaviour Research and Therapy, 23*, 379–382. (14)

Peterson, G. C. (1980). Organic mental disorders associated with brain trauma. In H. I. Kaplan, A. M. Freedman, & B. J. Sadlock (Eds.), *Comprehensive textbook of psychiatry* (3rd ed.) (Vol. 2, pp. 1422–1437). Baltimore, MD: Williams & Wilkins. (3)

Peterson, L. G., Peterson, M., O'Shanick, G. J., & Swann, A. (1985). Self-inflicted gunshot wounds: Lethality of method versus intent. *American Journal of Psychiatry, 142*, 228–231. (14)

Peterson, L. R., & Peterson, M. J. (1959). Short-term retention of individual verbal items. *Journal of Experimental Psychology, 58*, 193–198. (8)

Petty, R. E., & Cacioppo, J. T. (1977). Effects of forewarning of persuasive intent and involvement on cognitive responses and persuasion. *Personality and Social Psychology Bulletin, 5*, 173–176. (16)

Petty, R. E., & Cacioppo, J. T. (1981). *Attitudes and persuasion: Classic and contemporary approaches.* Dubuque, IA: Wm. C. Brown. (16)

Petty, R. E., & Cacioppo, J. T. (1986). *Communication and persuasion: Central and peripheral routes to attitude change.* New York: Springer-Verlag. (16)

Peura, D. A. (1987). Stress-related mucosal damage: An overview. *American Journal of Medicine, 83* (Suppl. 6A), 3–7. (12)

Pezdek, K., Whetstone, T., Reynolds, K., Askari, N., & Dougherty, T. (1989). Memory for real-world scenes: The role of consistency with schema expectation. *Journal of Experimental Psychology: Learning, Memory, and Cognition, 15*, 587–595. (8)

Pfungst, O. (1911). *Clever Hans.* New York: Holt. (2)

Phelps, M. E., & Mazziotta, J. C. (1985). Positron emission tomography: Human brain function and biochemistry. *Science, 228*, 799–809. (1)

Phillips, A. G., & Carr, G. D. (1987). Cognition and the basal ganglia: A possible substrate for procedural knowledge. *Canadian Journal of Neurological Science, 14* (3 Suppl.), 381–385. (3)

Phillips, D. P. (1974). The influence of suggestion on suicide: Substantive and theoretical implications of the Werther effect. *American Sociological Review, 39*, 340–354. (15)

Phillips, D. P., & Carstensen, L. L. (1986). Clustering of teenage suicides after television news stores about suicide. *New England Journal of Medicine, 315*, 685–689. (15)

Phillips, D. P., & Paight, D. J. (1987). The impact of televised movies about suicide. *New England Journal of Medicine, 317*, 809–811. (15)

Phillips, R. T., & Alcebo, A. M. (1986). The effects of divorce on black children and adolescents. *American Journal of Social Psychology, 6*, 69–73. (6)

Piaget, J. (1937/1954). *The construction of reality in the child* (M. Cook, Trans.). New York: Basic Books. (Original work published 1937) (6)

Pichot, P. (1984). Centenary of the birth of Hermann Rorschach. *Journal of Personality Assessment, 48*, 591–596. (13)

Pierrot-Deseilligny, C., Gray, F., & Brunet, P. (1986). Infarcts of both inferior parietal lobules with impairment of visually guided eye movements, peripheral visual inattention and optic ataxia. *Brain, 109*, 81–97. (1)

Pitman, R. K., Orr, S. P., Forgue, D. F., deJong, J. B., & Claiborn, N. M. (1987). Psychophysiologic assessment of posttraumatic stress disorder imagery in Vietnam combat veterans. *Archives of General Psychiatry, 44*, 970–975. (12)

Pitman, R. K., van der Kolk, B. A., Orr, S. P., & Greenberg, M. S. (1990). Naloxone-reversible analgesic response to combat-related stimuli in posttraumatic stress disorder. *Archives of General Psychiatry, 47*, 541–544. (12)

Plomin, R., Corley, R., DeFries, J. C., & Fulker, D. W. (1990). Individual differences in television viewing in early childhood: Nature as well as nurture. *Psychological Science, 1*, 371–377. (14)

Plomin, R., & DeFries, J. C. (1980). Genetics and intelligence: Recent data. *Intelligence, 4*, 15–24. (10)

Plomin, R., DeFries, J. C., & Roberts, M. K. (1977). Assortative mating by unwed biological parents of adopted children. *Science, 196*, 449–450. (6)

Plutchik, R. (1982). A psychoevolutionary theory of emotions. *Social Science Information, 21*, 529–553. (12)

Plutchik, R., & Ax, A. F. (1967). A critique of "determinants of emotional state" by Schachter and Singer (1962). *Psychophysiology, 4*, 79–82. (12)

Pokorny, A. D. (1978). The course and prognosis of schizophrenia. In W. E. Fann, I. Karacan, A. D. Pokorny, & R. L. Williams (Eds.), *Phenomenology and treatment of schizophrenia* (pp. 21–37). New York: Spectrum. (15)

Polivy, J., Heatherton, T. F., & Herman, C. P. (1988). Self-esteem, restraint, and eating behavior. *Journal of Abnormal Psychology, 97*, 354–356. (11)

Polivy, J., & Herman, C. P. (1985). Dieting and binging: A causal analysis. *American Psychologist, 40*, 193–201. (11)

Polivy, J., & Herman, C. P. (1987). Diagnosis and treatment of normal eating. *Journal of Consulting and Clinical Psychology, 55*, 635–644. (11)

Pollak, J. M. (1979). Obsessive-compulsive personality: A review. *Psychological Bulletin, 86*, 225–241. (14)

Polya, G. (1957). *How to solve it.* Garden City, NY: Doubleday Anchor. (9)

Pomeroy, W. B. (1972). *Dr. Kinsey and the Institute for Sex Research.* New York: Harper & Row. (11)

Poole, A. D., Sanson-Fisher, R. W., & German, G. A. (1981). The rapid-smoking technique: Therapeutic effectiveness. *Behaviour Research and Therapy, 19*, 389–397. (15)

Popper, K. (1986). Predicting overt behavior versus predicting hidden states. *Behavioral and Brain Sciences, 9*, 254–255. (13)

Poulos, C. X., & Cappell, H. (1991). Homeostatic theory of drug tolerance: A general model of physiological adaptation. *Psychological Review, 98*, 390–408. (7)

Poulos, C. X., Wilkinson, D. A., & Cappell, H. (1981). Homeostatic regulation and Pavlovian conditioning in tolerance to amphetamine-induced anorexia. *Journal of Comparative and Physiological Psychology, 95*, 735–746. (7)

Powers, S., Barkan, J. H., & Jones, P. B. (1986). Reliability of the Standard Progressive Matrices Test for Hispanic and Anglo-American children. *Perceptual & Motor Skills, 62*, 348–350. (10)

Powlishta, K. K., & Maccoby, E. E. (1990). Resource utilization in mixed-sex dyads: The influence of adult presence and task type. *Sex Roles, 23*, 223–240. (6)

Pratkanis, A. R., Greenwald, A. G., Leippe, M. R., & Baumgardner, M. H. (1988). In search of reliable persuasion effects: III. The sleeper effect is dead. Long live the sleeper effect. *Journal of Personality and Social Psychology, 54*, 203–218. (16)

Premack, A. J., & Premack, D. (1972). Teaching language to an ape. *Scientific American, 227* (4), 92–99. (9)

Premack, D. (1965). Reinforcement theory. In D. Levine (Ed.), *Nebraska symposium on motivation* (pp. 123–188). Lincoln, NE: University of Nebraska Press. (7)

Prentky, R. A., Knight, R. A., & Rosenberg, R. (1988). Validation analyses on a taxonomic system for rapists: Disconfirmation and reconceptualization. *Annals of the New York Academy of Sciences, 528*, 21–40. (11)

Price, K. P., Tryon, W. W., & Raps, C. S. (1978). Learned helplessness and depression in a clinical population: A test of two behavioral hypotheses. *Journal of Abnormal Psychology, 87*, 113–121. (14)

Price, L. H., Ricaurte, G. A., Krystal, J. H., & Heninger, G. R. (1989). Neuroendocrine and mood responses to intravenous L-tryptophan in 3,4–methylene dioxymethamphetamine (MDMA) users. *Archives of General Psychiatry, 46*, 20–22. (5)

Price, K., Kidd, K. K., & Weissman, M. M. (1987). Early onset (under age 30 years) and panic disorder as markers for etiologic homogeneity in major depression. *Archives of General Psychiatry, 44*, 434–440. (14)

Priest, R. F., & Sawyer, J. (1967). Proximity and peership: Bases of balance in interpersonal attraction. *American Journal of Sociology, 72*, 633–649. (16)

Probst, T., Krafczyk, S., Brandt, T., & Wist, E. R. (1984). Interaction between perceived self-motion and object-motion impairs vehicle guidance. *Science, 225*, 536–538. (4)

Pullum, G. K. (1991). *The Great Eskimo vocabulary hoax.* Chicago: University of Chicago Press. (9)

Purves, D., & Hadley, R. D. (1985). Changes in the dendritic branching of adult mammalian neurons revealed by repeated imaging *in situ. Nature, 315*, 404–406. (3)

Qin, Y., & Simon, H. A. (1990). Laboratory replication of scientific discovery processes. *Cognitive Science, 14*, 281–312. (9)

Quinn, R. P. (1978). Physical deviance and occupational mistreatment: The short, the fat, and the ugly. Master's thesis, University of Michigan Survey Research Center, University of Michigan, Ann Arbor. (16)

Rabkin, J. G. (1979). Criminal behavior of discharged mental patients: A critical appraisal of the research. *Psychological Bulletin, 86*, 1–27. (15)

Rabkin, J. G. (1980). Stressful life events and schizophrenia: A review of the research literature. *Psychological Bulletin, 87*, 408–425. (14)

Rachlin, H. (1990). Why do people gamble and keep gambling despite heavy losses? *Psychological Science, 1*, 294–297. (9)

Rachman, S. (1969). Treatment by prolonged exposure to high intensity stimulation. *Behaviour Research and Therapy, 7*, 295–302. (14)

Rachman, S. J., & Hodgson, R. J. (1980). *Obsessions and compulsions.* Englewood Cliffs, NJ: Prentice-Hall. (14)

Radin, N. (1982). Primary caregiving and role-sharing fathers. In M. E. Lamb (Ed.), *Nontraditional families* (pp. 173–204). Hillsdale, NJ: Lawrence Erlbaum. (6)

Rafal, R., Smith, J., Krantz, J., Cohen, A., & Brennan, C. (1990). Extrageniculate vision in hemianopic humans: Saccade inhibition by signals in the blind field. *Science, 250*, 118–121. (3)

Ravussin, E., Lillioja, S., Knowler, W. C., Christin, L., Freymona, D., Abbott, W. G. H., Boyce, V., Howard, B. V., & Bogardus, C. (1988). Reduced rate of energy expenditure as a risk factor for bodyweight gain. *New England Journal of Medicine, 318*, 467–472. (11)

Raz, S., & Raz, N. (1990). Structural brain abnormalities in the major psychoses: A quantitative review of the evidence from computerized imaging. *Psychological Bulletin, 108*, 93–108. (14)

Rechtschaffen, A., Gilliland, M. A., Bergmann, B. M., & Winter, J. B. (1983). Physiological correlates of prolonged sleep deprivation in rats. *Science, 221*, 182–184. (5)

Redican, W. K. (1982). An evolutionary perspective on human facial displays. In P. Ekman (Ed.), *Emotion in the human face* (pp. 212–280). Cambridge, England: Cambridge University Press. (12)

Reed, T. E. (1985). Ethnic differences in alcohol use, abuse, and sensitivity: A review with genetic interpretation. *Social Biology, 32,* 195–209. (3)

Regan, T. (1986). The rights of humans and other animals. *Acta Physiologica Scandinavica, 128* (Suppl. 554), 33–40. (2)

Regier, D. A., Myers, J. K., Kramer, M., Robins, L. N., Blazer, D. G., Hough, R. L., Eaton, W. W., & Locke, B. Z. (1984). The NIMH epidemiologic catchment area program. *Archives of General Psychiatry, 41,* 934–941. (14)

Reich, T. (1986). The epidemiology of anxiety. *Journal of Nervous and Mental Disease, 174,* 129–136. (14)

Reicher, G. M. (1969). Perceptual recognition as a function of meaningfulness of stimulus material. *Journal of Experimental Psychology, 81,* 275–280. (9)

Reichling, D. B., Kwiat, G. C., & Basbaum, A. I. (1988). Anatomy, physiology, and pharmacology of the periaqueductal gray contribution to antinociceptive controls. In H. L. Fields & J.-M. Besson (Eds.), *Progress in brain research* (Vol. 77, pp. 31–46). Amsterdam: Elsevier. (4)

Reitman, J. S. (1974). Without surreptitious rehearsal, information in short-term memory decays. *Journal of Verbal Learning and Verbal Behavior, 13,* 365–377. (8)

Rensch, B., & Dücker, G. (1963). Haptisches Lernund Unterscheidungs-Vermögen bei einem Waschbären [Tactile learning and discrimination abilities in a racoon]. *Zeitschrift für Tierpsychologie, 20,* 608–615. (4)

Rescorla, R. A. (1968). Probability of shock in the presence and absence of CS in fear conditioning. *Journal of Comparative and Physiological Psychology, 66,* 1–5. (7)

Rescorla, R. (1985). Associationism in animal learning. In L.-G. Nilsson & T. Archer (Eds.), *Perspectives on learning and memory* (pp. 39–61). Hillsdale, NJ: Lawrence Erlbaum. (7)

Rescorla, R. A. (1988). Pavlovian conditioning: It's not what you think it is. *American Psychologist, 43,* 151–160. (7)

Rest, J. R. (1983). Morality. In P. H. Mussen (Ed.), *Handbook of child psychology* (4th ed.) (Vol. 3, pp. 556–629). New York: Wiley. (6)

Restle, F. (1970). Moon illusion explained on the basis of relative size. *Science, 167,* 1092–1096. (4)

Rhine, J. B. (1947). *The reach of the mind.* New York: William Sloane. (2)

Rhodes, N., & Wood, W. (1992). Self-esteem and intelligence affect influenceability: The mediating role of message reception. *Psychological Bulletin, 111,* 156–171. (16)

Rice, M. L. (1989). Children's language acquisition. *American Psychologist, 44,* 149–156. (6)

Rich, C. L., Ricketts, J. E., Fowler, R. C., & Young, D. (1988). Some differences between men and women who commit suicide. *American Journal of Psychiatry, 145,* 718–722. (14)

Richardson-Klavehn, A., & Bjork, R. A. (1988). Measures of memory. *Annual Review of Psychology, 39,* 475–543. (8)

Richter, C. P. (1929). Physiological factors involved in the electrical resistance of the skin. *American Journal of Physiology, 88,* 596–615. (12)

Richter, C. P. (1938). Two-day cycles of alternating good and bad behavior in psychotic patients. *Archives of Neurology and Psychiatry, 39,* 587–598. (14)

Richwald, G. A., Morisky, D. E., Kyle, G. R., Kristal, A. R., Gerber, M. M., & Friedland, J. M. (1988). Sexual activities in bathhouses in Los Angeles county: Implications for AIDS prevention education. *Journal of Sex Research, 25,* 169–180. (11)

Rincover, A. (1978). Sensory extinction: A procedure for eliminating self-stimulatory behavior in developmentally disabled children. *Journal of Abnormal Child Psychology, 6,* 299–310. (14)

Rips, L. J., Shoben, E. J., & Smith, E. E. (1973). Semantic distance and the verification of semantic relations. *Journal of Verbal Learning and Verbal Behavior, 12,* 1–20. (9)

Risby, E. D., Hsiao, J. K., Manji, H. K., Bitran, J., Moses, F., Zhou, D. F., & Potter, W. Z. (1991). The mechanisms of action of lithium: II. Effects on adenylate cyclase activity and beta-adrenergic receptor binding in normal subjects. *Archives of General Psychiatry, 48,* 513–524. (15)

Ritvo, E. R., Freeman, B. J., Mason-Brothers, A., Mo, A., & Ritvo, A. M. (1985). Concordance for the syndrome of autism in 40 pairs of afflicted twins. *American Journal of Psychiatry, 142,* 74–77. (14)

Ritz, M. C., Lamb, R. J., Goldberg, S. R., & Kuhar, M. J. (1987). Cocaine receptors on dopamine transporters are related to self-administration of cocaine. *Science, 237,* 1219–1223. (5)

Roberts, A. H. (1985). Biofeedback: Research, training, and clinical roles. *American Psychologist, 40,* 938–941. (14)

Roberts, S. B., Savage, J., Coward, W. A., Chew, B., & Lucas, A. (1988). Energy expenditure and intake in infants born to lean and overweight mothers. *New England Journal of Medicine, 318,* 461–466. (11)

Roberts, T.-A. (1991). Gender and the influence of evaluations on self-assessments in achievement settings. *Psychological Bulletin, 109,* 297–308. (11)

Robins, L. N., Helzer, J. E., Weissman, M. M., Orvaschel, H., Gruenberg, E., Burke, J. D., Jr., & Regier, D. A. (1984). Lifetime prevalence of specific psychiatric disorders in three sites. *Archives of General Psychiatry, 41,* 949–958. (14)

Robinson, B. (1987, Feb. 16). Major classes of drugs continue on comeback trail. *Drug Topics, 131* (4), 67. (15)

Robinson, L. A., Berman, J. S., & Neimeyer, R. A. (1990). Psychotherapy for the treatment of depression: A comprehensive review of controlled outcome research. *Psychological Bulletin, 108,* 30–49. (15)

Rock, I., & Kaufman, L. (1962). The moon illusion, II. *Science, 136,* 1023–1031. (4)

Rockwell, W. J. K., & Pinkerton, R. S. (1982). Single-session psychotherapy. *American Journal of Psychotherapy, 36,* 32–40. (15)

Rodin, J. (1986). Aging and health: Effects of the sense of control. *Science, 233,* 1271–1276. (6)

Roeder, K. D. (1967). *Nerve cells and insect behavior.* Cambridge, MA: Harvard University Press. (4)

Roediger, H. L., III, & Crowder, R. G. (1976). A serial position effect in recall of United States presidents. *Bulletin of the Psychonomic Society, 8,* 275–278. (8)

Roffwarg, H. P., Muzio, J. N., & Dement, W. C. (1966). Ontogenetic development of human sleep-dream cycle. *Science, 152,* 604–609. (5)

Rogers, C. (1951). *Client-centered therapy.* Boston: Houghton Mifflin. (15)

Rogers, C. R. (1961). *On becoming a person.* Boston: Houghton Mifflin. (13)

Rogers, C. (1980). *A way of being.* Boston: Houghton Mifflin. (13)

Rollman, G. B. (1991). Pain responsiveness. In M. Heller & W. Schiff (Eds.), *The psychology of touch* (pp. 91–118). Hillsdale, NJ: Lawrence Erlbaum. (4)

Romano, J. M., & Turner, J. A. (1985). Chronic pain and depression: Does the evidence support a relationship? *Psychological Bulletin, 97,* 18–34. (14)

Roose, S. P., Glassman, A. H., Walsh, B. T., Woodring, S., & Vital-Herne, J. (1983). Depression, delusions, and suicide. *American Journal of Psychiatry, 140,* 1159–1162. (14)

Rosch, E. (1978). Principles of categorization. In E. Rosch & B. B. Lloyd (Eds.), *Cognition and categorization* (pp. 27–48). Hillsdale, NJ: Lawrence Erlbaum. (9)

Rosch, E., & Mervis, C. B. (1975). Family resemblances: Studies in the internal structure of categories. *Cognitive Psychology, 7,* 573–605. (9)

Rose, J. E., Brugge, J. F., Anderson, D. J., & Hind, J. E. (1967). Phase-locked response to low-frequency tones in single auditory nerve fibers of the squirrel monkey. *Journal of Neurophysiology, 30,* 769–793. (4)

Rose, S. A., & Wallace, I. F. (1985). Cross-modal and intramodal transfer as predictors of mental development in full-term and preterm infants. *Developmental Psychology, 21,* 949–962. (10)

Rosenbaum, M., & Smira, K. B. (1986). Cognitive and personality factors in the delay of gratification of hemodialysis patients. *Journal of Personality and Social Psychology, 51,* 357–364. (11)

Rosenbaum, M. E. (1980). Cooperation and competition. In P. B. Paulus (Ed.), *The psychology of group influence.* Hillsdale, NJ: Lawrence Erlbaum. (16)

Rosenberg, A., & Kagan, J. (1987). Iris pigmentation and behavioral inhibition. *Developmental Psychobiology, 20,* 377–392. (2)

Rosenhan, D. L. (1973). On being sane in insane places. *Science, 179,* 250–258. (15)

Rosenthal, R., & Rubin, D. B. (1978). Interpersonal expectancy effects: The first 345 studies. *Behavioral and Brain Sciences, 3,* 377–415. (1)

Ross, L. (1977). The intuitive psychologist and his shortcomings: Distortions in the attribution process. In L. Berkowitz (Ed.), *Advances in experimental social psychology* (Vol. 10, pp. 173–220). New York: Academic Press. (16)

Rothbart, M., & John, O. P. (1985). Social categorization and behavioral episodes: A cognitive analysis of the effects of intergroup contact. *Journal of Social Issues, 41,* 81–104. (16)

Rotter, J. B. (1966). Generalized expectancies for internal versus external control of reinforcement. *Psychological Monographs, 80* (Whole No. 603). (13)

Rotton, J., & Kelly, I. W. (1985). Much ado about the full moon: A meta-analysis of lunar-lunacy research. *Psychological Bulletin, 97,* 286–306. (2)

Rovee-Collier, C. (1984). The ontogeny of learning and memory in human infancy. In R. Kail & N. E. Spear (Eds.), *Comparative perspectives on the development of memory* (pp. 103–134). Hillsdale, NJ: Lawrence Erlbaum. (6)

Rowe, J. W., & Kahn, R. L. (1987). Human aging: Usual and successful. *Science, 237,* 143–149. (6)

Rowland, C. V., Jr. (Ed.) (1970). *Anorexia and obesity.* Boston: Little, Brown. (11)

Roy, A. (1985). Early parental separation and adult depression. *Archives of General Psychiatry, 42,* 987–991. (14)

Rozin, P. (1968). Specific aversions and neophobia as a consequence of vitamin deficiency and/or poisoning in half-wild and domestic rats. *Journal of Comparative and Physiological Psychology, 66,* 82–88. (11)

Rozin, P. (1969). Central or peripheral mediation of learning with long CS-US intervals in the feeding system. *Journal of Comparative and Physiological Psychology, 67,* 421–429. (7)

Rozin, P., & Fallon, A. E. (1987). A perspective on disgust. *Psychological Review, 94,* 23–41. (11)

Rozin, P., Fallon, A., & Augustoni-Ziskind, M. L. (1986). The child's conception of food: The development of categories of acceptable and rejected substances. *Journal of Nutrition Education, 18,* 75–81. (11)

Rozin, P., Hammer, L., Oster, H., Horowitz, T., & Marmora, V. (1986). The child's conception of food: Differentiation of categories of rejected substances in the 16 months to 5 year age range. *Appetite, 7,* 141–151. (11)

Rozin, P., & Kalat, J. W. (1971). Specific hungers and poison avoidance as adaptive specializations of learning. *Psychological Review, 78,* 459–486. (11)

Rozin, P., Markwith, M., & Ross, B. (1990). The sympathetic magical law of similarity, nominal realism and neglect of negatives in response to negative labels. *Psychological Science, 1,* 383–384. (9)

Rozin, P., Millman, L., & Nemeroff, C. (1986). Operation of the laws of sympathetic magic in disgust and other domains. *Journal of Personality and Social Psychology, 50,* 703–712. (11)

Rozin, P., & Pelchat, M. L. (1988). Memories of mammaries: Adaptations to weaning from milk. *Progress in Psychobiology and Physiological Psychology, 13,* 1–29. (3)

Rubenstein, J. L. (1985). The effects of maternal employment on young children. *Applied Developmental Psychology, 2*, 99–128. (6)

Rubenstein, R., & Newman, R. (1954). The living out of "future" experiences under hypnosis. *Science, 119*, 472–473. (5)

Rubin, D. C., Wetzler, S. E., & Nebes, R. D. (1986). Autobiographical memory across the lifespan. In D. C. Rubin (Ed.), *Autobiographical memory* (pp. 202–221). Cambridge, England: Cambridge University Press. (8)

Rubin, P., Holm, S., Friberg, L., Videbech, P., Andersen, H. S., Bendsen, B. B., Stømsø, N., Larsen, J. K., Lassen, N. A., & Hemmingsen, R. (1991). Altered modulation of prefrontal and subcortical brain activity in newly diagnosed schizophrenia and schizophreniform disorder. *Archives of General Psychiatry, 48*, 987–995. (14)

Rubin, Z. (1970). Measurement of romantic love. *Journal of Personality and Social Psychology, 16*, 265–273. (16)

Rubin, Z. (1973). *Liking and loving: An invitation to social psychology.* New York: Holt, Rinehart, & Winston. (16)

Rubin, Z. (1974). Lovers and other strangers: The development of intimacy in encounters and relationships. *American Scientist, 62*, 182–190. (6)

Rubin, Z., Hill, C. T., Peplau, L. A., & Dunkel-Schetter, C. (1980). Self-disclosure in dating couples: Sex roles and the ethic of openness. *Journal of Marriage and the Family, 42*, 305–317. (6)

Rubin, Z., Peplau, L. A., & Hill, C. T. (1981). Loving and leaving: Sex differences in romantic attachments. *Sex Roles, 7*, 821–835. (16)

Ruch, J. (1984). *Psychology: The personal science.* Belmont, CA: Wadsworth. (3)

Rudden, M., Gilmore, M., & Allen, F. (1982). Delusions: When to confront the facts of life? *American Journal of Psychiatry, 139*, 929–932. (14)

Ruderman, A. J. (1986). Dietary restraint: A theoretical and empirical review. *Psychological Review, 99*, 247–262. (11)

Ruderman, A. J., & Christensen, H. C. (1983). Restraint theory and its applicability to overweight individuals. *Journal of Abnormal Psychology, 92*, 210–215. (11)

Rumbaugh, D. M. (1990). Comparative psychology and the great apes: Their competency in learning, language, and numbers. *Psychological Record, 40*, 15–39. (9)

Rumelhart, D. E., & McClelland, J. L. (1982). An interactive activation model of context effects in letter perception: Part 2, The contextual enhancement effect and some tests and extensions of the model. *Psychological Review, 89*, 60–94. (9)

Rumelhart, D. E., McClelland, J. L., & the PDP Research Group. (1986). *Parallel distributed processing.* Cambridge, MA: MIT Press. (9)

Rusbult, C. E., & Zembrodt, I. M. (1983). Response to dissatisfaction in romantic involvements: A multidimensional scaling analysis. *Journal of Experimental Social Psychology, 19*, 274–293. (16)

Russell, C., & Megaard, I. (Eds.). (1988). *The general social survey, 1972–1986.* New York: Springer-Verlag. (12)

Russell, G. F. M., Szmukler, G. I., Dare, C., & Eisler, I. (1987). An evaluation of family therapy in anorexia nervosa and bulimia nervosa. *Archives of General Psychiatry, 44*, 1047–1056. (15)

Russell, M. J., Switz, G. M., & Thompson, K. (1980). Olfactory influences on the human menstrual cycle. *Pharmacology, Biochemistry, and Behavior, 13*, 737–738. (4)

Saarinen, T. F. (1973). The use of projective techniques in geographic research. In W. H. Ittelson (Ed.), *Environment and cognition* (pp. 29–52). New York: Seminar Press. (9)

Sabo, K. T., & Kirtley, D. D. (1982). Objects and activities in the dreams of the blind. *International Journal of Rehabilitation Research, 5*, 241–242. (5)

Sachs, J. S. (1967). Recognition memory for syntactic and semantic aspects of connected discourse. *Perception and Psychophysics, 2*, 437–442. (9)

Sadger, J. (1941). Preliminary study of the psychic life of the fetus and the primary germ. *Psychoanalytic Review, 28*, 327–358. (2)

Saegert, S., Swap, W., & Zajonc, R. B. (1973). Exposure, context, and interpersonal attraction. *Journal of Personality and Social Psychology, 25*, 234–242. (16)

Sakurai, Y. (1990). Cells in the rat auditory system have sensory-delay correlates during the performance of an auditory working memory task. *Behavioral Neuroscience, 104*, 856–868. (8)

Salthouse, T. A., Mitchell, D. R., Skovronek, E., & Babcock, R. L. (1989). Effects of adult age and working memory on reasoning and spatial abilities. *Journal of Experimental Psychology: Learning, Memory, and Cognition, 15*, 507–516. (8)

Salzarulo, P., & Chevalier, A. (1983). Sleep problems in children and their relationship with early disturbances of the waking-sleeping rhythms. *Sleep, 6*, 47–51. (5)

Samelson, F. (1980). J. B. Watson's Little Albert, Cyril Burt's twins, and the need for a critical science. *American Scientist, 35*, 619–625. (14)

Samuelson, C. D., Messick, D. M., Rutte, C. G., & Wilke, H. (1984). Individual and structural solutions to resource dilemmas in two cultures. *Journal of Personality and Social Psychology, 47*, 94–104. (16)

Sandman, C. A., Barron, J. L., Demet, E. M., Chicz-Demet, A., Rothenberg, S. J., & Zea, F. J. (1990). Opioid peptides and perinatal development: Is beta-endorphin a natural teratogen? *Annals of the New York Academy of Sciences, 579*, 91–108. (14)

Santrock, J. W., Warshak, R. A., & Elliott, G. L. (1982). Social development and parent-child interaction in father-custody and stepmother families. In M. E. Lamb (Ed.), *Nontraditional families* (pp. 289–314). Hillsdale, NJ: Lawrence Erlbaum. (6)

Sappington, A. A. (1990). Recent psychological approaches to the free will versus determinism issue. *Psychological Bulletin, 108*, 19–29. (1)

Savage-Rumbaugh, E. S. (1990). Language acquisition in a nonhuman species: Implications for the innateness debate. *Developmental Psychology, 23*, 599–620. (9)

Savage-Rumbaugh, E. S., Sevcik, R. A., Brakke, K. E., & Rumbaugh, D. M. (1992). Symbols: Their communicative use, communication, and combination by bonobos (*Pan paniscus*). In L. P. Lipsitt & C. Rovee-Collier (Eds.), *Advances in infancy research* (Vol. 7, pp. 221–278). Norwood, NJ: Ablex. (9)

Saykin, A. J., Gur, R. C., Gur, R. E., Mozley, D., Mozley, L. H., Resnick, S. M., Kester, B., & Stafiniak, P. (1991). Neuropsychological function in schizophrenia. *Archives of General Psychiatry, 48*, 618–624. (14)

Scarborough, E., & Furomoto, L. (1987). *Untold lives: The first generation of American women psychologists.* New York: Columbia University Press. (1)

Scarr, S. (1968). Environmental bias in twin studies. *Eugenics Quarterly, 15*, 34–40. (10)

Scarr, S., & Carter-Saltzman, L. (1979). Twin method: Defense of a critical assumption. *Behavior Genetics, 9*, 527–542. (10)

Scarr, S., Pakstis, A. J., Katz, S. H., & Barker, W. B. (1977). The absence of a relationship between degree of white ancestry and intellectual skills within a black population. *Human Genetics, 39*, 69–86. (10)

Scarr, S., Phillips, D., & McCartney, K. (1989). Working mothers and their families. *American Psychologist, 44*, 1402–1409. (6)

Scarr, S., Phillips, D., & McCartney, K. (1990). Facts, fantasies and the future of child care in the United States. *Psychological Science, 1*, 26–35. (6)

Scarr, S., & Weinberg, R. A. (1976). IQ test performance of black children adopted by white families. *American Psychologist, 31*, 726–739. (10)

Schachter, D. L. (1983). Amnesia observed: Remembering and forgetting in a natural environment. *Journal of Abnormal Psychology, 92*, 236–242. (8)

Schacter, D. L. (1985). Priming of old and new knowledge in amnesic patients and normal subjects. *Annals of the New York Academy of Sciences, 444*, 41–53. (8)

Schachter, D. L. (1986a). Amnesia and crime: How much do we really know? *American Psychologist, 41*, 286–295. (8)

Schachter, D. L. (1986b). Feeling-of-knowing ratings distinguish between genuine and simulated forgetting. *Journal of Experimental Psychology: Learning, Memory, and Cognition, 12*, 30–41. (8)

Schacter, D. L. (1987a). Implicit memory: History and current status. *Journal of Experimental Psychology: Learning, Memory, and Cognition, 13*, 501–518. (8)

Schachter, D. L. (1987b). Memory, amnesia, and frontal lobe dysfunction. *Psychobiology, 15*, 21–36. (8)

Schacter, D. L., Cooper, L. A., Delaney, S. M., Peterson, M. A., & Tharan, M. (1991). Implicit memory for possible and impossible objects: Constraints on the construction of structural descriptions. *Journal of Experimental Psychology: Learning, Memory, and Cognition, 17*, 3–19. (8)

Schacter, D. L., Tharan, M., Cooper, L. A., & Rubens, A. B. (1991). Preserved priming of novel objects in patients with memory disorders. *Journal of Cognitive Neuroscience, 3*, 117–130. (8)

Schachter, S. (1959). *The psychology of affiliation.* Stanford, CA: Stanford University Press. (16)

Schachter, S. (1968). Obesity and eating. *Science, 161*, 751–756. (11)

Schachter, S. (1971). Some extraordinary facts about obese humans and rats. *American Psychologist, 26*, 129–144. (11)

Schachter, S. (1982). Recidivism and self-cure of smoking and obesity. *American Psychologist, 37*, 436–444. (11)

Schachter, S., & Rodin, J. (1974). *Obese humans and rats.* New York: Wiley. (11)

Schachter, S., & Singer, J. (1962). Cognitive, social, and physiological determinants of emotional state. *Psychological Review, 69*, 379–399. (12)

Schallert, T. (1983). Sensorimotor impairment and recovery of function in brain-damaged rats: Reappearance of symptoms during old age. *Behavioral Neuroscience, 97*, 159–164. (3)

Schiffman, S. S. (1983). Taste and smell in disease. *New England Journal of Medicine, 308*, 1275–1279, 1337–1343. (4)

Schiffman, S. S., Diaz, C., & Beeker, T. G. (1986). Caffeine intensifies taste of certain sweeteners: Role of adenosine receptor. *Pharmacology, Biochemistry, & Behavior, 24*, 429–432. (4)

Schiffman, S. S., & Erickson, R. P. (1971). A psychophysical model for gustatory quality. *Physiology & Behavior, 7*, 617–633. (4)

Schiffman, S. S., Simon, S. A., Gill, J. M., & Beeker, T. G. (1988). Bretylium tosylate enhances salt taste via amiloride-sensitive pathway. *Annals of the New York Academy of Sciences, 510*, 584–586. (4)

Schlesier-Stropp, B. (1984). Bulimia: A review of the literature. *Psychological Review, 95*, 247–257. (11)

Schlossberg, N. K. (1984). Exploring the adult years. *The G. Stanley Hall Lecture Series, 4*, 101–154. (6)

Schmitt, A. P., & Dorans, N. J. (1990). Differential item functioning for minority examinees on the SAT. *Journal of Educational Measurement, 27*, 67–81. (10)

Schneck, M. K., Reisberg, B., & Ferris, S. H. (1982). An overview of current concepts of Alzheimer's disease. *American Journal of Psychiatry, 139*, 165–173. (3)

Schneider, C. J. (1987). Cost effectiveness of biofeedback and behavioral medicine treatments: A review of the literature. *Biofeedback and Self-Regulation, 12*, 71–92. (12)

Schneider, K. (1984). The cognitive basis of task choice in preschool children. *Advances in Motivation and Achievement, 3*, 57–72. (11)

Schoenfeld, A. H. (1985). *Mathematical problem solving.* Orlando, FL: Academic Press. (9)

Schooler, C. (1972). Birth order effects: Not here, not now! *Psychological Bulletin, 78*, 161–175. (6)

Schopler, E. (1987). Specific and nonspecific factors in the effectiveness of a treatment system. *American Psychologist, 42*, 376–383. (14)

Schuckit, M. A. (1985). Ethanol-induced changes in body sway in men at high alcoholism risk. *Archives of General Psychiatry, 42,* 375–379. (14)

Schulsinger, F., Knop, J., Goodwin, D. W., Teasdale, T. W., & Mikkelsen, U. (1986). A prospective study of young men at high risk for alcoholism. *Archives of General Psychiatry, 43,* 755–760. (14)

Schuman, H., & Scott, J. (1987). Problems in the use of survey questions to measure public opinion. *Science, 236,* 957–959. (2)

Schwartz, B. (1981). Does helplessness cause depression, or do only depressed people become helpless? Comment on Alloy and Abramson. *Journal of Experimental Psychology: General, 110,* 429–435. (14)

Schwartz, F. N. (1989, January-February). Management women and the new facts of life. *Harvard Business Review,* 65–76. (11)

Schwartz, G. E. (1975). Biofeedback, self-regulation, and the patterning of physiological processes. *American Scientist, 63,* 314–324. (12)

Schwartz, G. E. (1987). Personality and health: An integrative health science approach. *The G. Stanley Hall Lecture Series, 7,* 125–157. (12)

Schwarz, N., Bless, H., & Bohner, G. (1991). Mood and persuasion: Affective states influence the processing of persuasive messages. *Advances in Experimental Social Psychology, 24,* 161–199. (16)

Schwarzwald, J., Bizman, A., & Raz, M. (1983). The foot-in-the-door paradigm: Effects of second request size on donation probability and donor generosity. *Personality and Social Psychology Bulletin, 9,* 443–450. (16)

Schweder, R. (1982). Fact and artifact in trait perception: The systematic distortion hypothesis. *Progress in Experimental Personality Research, 11,* 65–100. (13)

Schweickert, R., Guentert, L., & Hersberger, L. (1990). Phonological similarity, pronunciation rate, and memory span. *Psychological Science, 1,* 74–77. (8)

Sclafani, A., & Springer, D. (1976). Dietary obesity in adult rats: Similarities to hypothalamic and human obesity syndromes. *Physiology & Behavior, 17,* 461–471. (11)

Scott, W. E. (1976). The effects of extrinsic rewards on "intrinsic motivation." *Organizational Behavior & Human Performance, 15,* 117–129. (11)

Scott-Jones, D. (1984). Family influences on cognitive development and school achievement. *Review of Research in Education, 11,* 259–304. (6)

Scovern, A. W., & Kilmann, P. R. (1980). Status of electroconvulsive therapy: Review of the outcome literature. *Psychological Bulletin, 87,* 260–303. (15)

Scribner, S. (1986). Thinking in action: Some characteristics of practical thought. In R. J. Sternberg & R. K. Wagner (Eds.), *Practical intelligence* (pp. 13–30). Cambridge, England: Cambridge University Press. (10)

Scripture, E. W. (1907). *Thinking, feeling, doing* (2nd ed.). New York: G. P. Putnam's Sons. (1)

Seeman, P., & Lee, T. (1975). Antipsychotic drugs: Direct correlation between clinical potency and presynaptic action on dopamine neurons. *Science, 188,* 1217–1219. (14)

Seeman, P., Lee, T., Chau-Wong, M., & Wong, K. (1976). Antipsychotic drug doses and neuroleptic/dopamine receptors. *Nature, 261,* 717–719. (15)

Segal, K. R., & Pi-Sunyer, F. X. (1989). Exercise and obesity. *Medical Clinics of North America, 73,* 217–236. (11)

Segal, N. (1985). Monozygotic and dizygotic twins: A comparative analysis of mental ability profiles. *Child Development, 56,* 1051–1058. (3)

Selfridge, O. (1959). Pandemonium: A paradigm for learning. In *Symposium on the mechanisation of thought processes* (Vol. 1, pp. 513–526). London: H. M. Stationery Office. (4)

Seligman, M. E. P. (1970). On the generality of the laws of learning. *Psychological Review, 77,* 406–418. (7)

Seligman, M. E. P. (1971). Phobias and preparedness. *Behavior Therapy, 2,* 307–320. (14)

Selye, H. (1979). Stress, cancer, and the mind. In J. Taché, H. Selye, & S. B. Day (Eds.), *Cancer, stress, and death* (pp. 11–27). New York: Plenum. (12)

Shafir, E. B., Smith, E. E., & Osheron, D. N. (1990). Typicality and reasoning fallacies. *Memory & Cognition, 18,* 229–239. (9)

Shannon, D. A. (1955). *The Socialist Party of America.* New York: Macmillan. (16)

Shapiro, D. L. (1985). Insanity and the assessment of criminal responsibility. In C. P. Ewing (Ed.), *Psychology, psychiatry, and the law: A clinical and forensic handbook* (pp. 67–94). Sarasota, FL: Professional Resource Exchange. (15)

Shapiro, S., Skinner, E. A., Kessler, L. G., Von Korff, M., German, P. S., Tischler, G. L., Leaf, P. J., Benham, L., Cottler, L., & Regier, D. A. (1984). Utilization of health and mental health services. *Archives of General Psychiatry, 41,* 971–978. (14, 15)

Shavit, Y., Terman, G. W., Martin, F. C., Lewis, J. W., Liebeskind, J. C., & Gale, R. P. (1985). Stress, opioid peptides, the immune system, and cancer. *Journal of Immunology, 135,* 834S-837S. (12)

Shepard, R. N., & Metzler, J. N. (1971). Mental rotation of three-dimensional objects. *Science, 171,* 701–703. (9)

Shepher, J. (1971). Mate selection among second-generation kibbutz adolescents and adults: Incest avoidance and negative imprinting. *Archives of Sexual Behavior, 1,* 293–307. (6)

Sher, K. J., Frost, R. O., Kushner, M., Crews, T. M., & Alexander, J. E. (1989). Memory deficits in compulsive checkers: Replication and extension in a clinical sample. *Behaviour Research and Therapy, 27,* 65–69. (14)

Sher, K. J., Frost, R. O., & Otto, R. (1983). Cognitive deficits in compulsive checkers: An exploratory study. *Behaviour Research and Therapy, 21,* 357–363. (14)

Sherif, M. (1966). *In common predicament.* Boston: Houghton Mifflin. (16)

Sherman, S. J., Judd, C. M., & Park, B. (1989). Social cognition. In M. R. Rosenzweig & L. W. Porter (Eds.), *Annual Review of Psychology* (Vol. 40, pp. 281–326). Palo Alto, CA: Annual Reviews. (16)

Sherrod, D. R., Hage, J. N., Halpern, P. L., & Moore, B. S. (1977). Effects of personal causation and perceived control on responses to an aversive environment: The more control, the better. *Journal of Experimental Social Psychology, 13,* 14–27. (12)

Sherwood, G. G. (1981). Self-serving biases in person perception: A reexamination of projection as a mechanism of defense. *Psychological Bulletin, 90,* 445–459. (13)

Shimamura, A. P., Salmon, D. P., Squire, L. R., & Butters, N. (1987). Memory dysfunction and word priming in dementia and amnesia. *Behavioral Neuroscience, 101,* 347–351. (8)

Shneidman, E. (1989). The Indian summer of life: A preliminary study of septuagenarians. *American Psychologist, 44,* 684–694. (6)

Siegel, S. (1977). Morphine tolerance as an associative process. *Journal of Experimental Psychology: Animal Behavior Processes, 3,* 1–13. (7)

Siegel, S. (1983). Classical conditioning, drug tolerance, and drug dependence. *Research Advances in Alcohol and Drug Problems, 7,* 207–246. (7)

Siegel, S. (1987). Alcohol and opiate dependence: Reevaluation of the Victorian perspective. *Research Advances in Alcohol and Drug Problems, 9,* 279–314. (14)

Siegelman, M. (1974). Parental background of male homosexuals and heterosexuals. *Archives of Sexual Behavior, 3,* 3–18. (11)

Siegler, R. S., & Richards, D. D. (1982). The development of intelligence. In R. J. Sternberg (Ed.), *Handbook of human intelligence* (pp. 897–971). Cambridge, England: Cambridge University Press. (10)

Sigall, H., & Ostrove, N. (1975). Beautiful but dangerous: Effects of offender attractiveness and nature of the crime on juridic judgment. *Journal of Personality and Social Psychology, 31,* 410–414. (16)

Silinsky, E. M. (1989). Adenosine derivatives and neuronal function. *Seminars in the Neurosciences, 1,* 155–165. (5)

Silverman, J. S., Silverman, J. A., & Eardley, D. A. (1984). Do maladaptive attitudes cause depression? *Archives of General Psychiatry, 41,* 28–30. (14)

Simmons, E. J. (1949). *Leo Tolstoy.* London: John Lehmann. (14)

Simons, R. L., Whitbeck, L. B., Conger, R. D., & Wu, C.-I. (1991). Intergenerational transmission of harsh parenting. *Developmental Psychology, 27,* 159–171. (7)

Simonsen, L. (1990, April). What are pharmacists dispensing most often? *Pharmacy Times,* pp. 56–64. (5)

Sines, J. O. (1979). Non-pharmacological and non-surgical resistance to stress ulcers in temperamentally and physiologically susceptible rats. *Journal of Psychosomatic Research, 23,* 77–82. (12)

Sinex, F. M., & Myers, R. H. (1982). Alzheimer's disease, Down's syndrome, and aging: The genetic approach. *Annals of the New York Academy of Sciences, 396,* 3–13. (3)

Singer, J. L. (1981). Clinical intervention: New developments in methods and evaluation. *The G. Stanley Hall Lecture Series, 1,* 101–128. (15)

Siqueland, E. R., & Lipsitt, L. P. (1966). Conditioned head-turning in human newborns. *Journal of Experimental Child Psychology, 3,* 356–376. (6)

Sizemore, C. C., & Pittillo, E. S. (1977). *I'm Eve.* Garden City, NY: Doubleday. (14)

Skeels, H. M. (1966). Adult status of children with contrasting early life experiences. *Monographs of the Society for Research in Child Development, 31,* 1–65. (10)

Skeptical Inquirer (1978a). Psychic vibrations. *Skeptical Inquirer, 3*(2), 13. (2)

Skeptical Inquirer (1978b). Psychic vibrations. *Skeptical Inquirer, 2*(2), 23. (2)

Skinner, B. F. (1938). *The behavior of organisms.* New York: D. Appleton-Century. (7)

Skinner, B. F. (1956). A case history in scientific method. *American Psychologist, 11,* 221–233. (7)

Skinner, B. F. (1960). Pigeons in a pelican. *American Psychologist, 15,* 28–37. (7)

Skinner, B. F. (1983). Intellectual self-management in old age. *American Psychologist, 38,* 239–244. (8)

Skinner, B. F. (1990). Can psychology be a science of mind? *American Psychologist, 45,* 1206–1210. (7)

Skowronski, J. J., & Carlston, D. E. (1987). Social judgment and social memory: The role of cue diagnosticity in negativity, positivity, and extremity biases. *Journal of Personality and Social Psychology, 52,* 689–699. (16)

Slobin, D. I. (1979). *Psycholinguistics* (2nd ed.). Glenview, IL: Scott, Foresman. (9)

Smith, E. E., Osherson, D. N., Rips, L. J., & Keane, M. (1988). Combining prototypes: A selective modification model. *Cognitive Science, 12,* 485–527. (9)

Smith, E. E., Shoben, E. J., & Rips, L. J. (1974). Structure and process in semantic memory: A featural model for semantic decisions. *Psychological Review, 81,* 214–241. (9)

Smith, E. R., & Zárate, M. A. (1992). Exemplar-based model of social judgment. *Psychological Review, 99,* 3–21. (16)

Smith, G. P., & Gibbs, J. (1987). The effect of gut peptides on hunger, satiety, and food intake in humans. *Annals of the New York Academy of Sciences, 499,* 132–136. (11)

Smith, J. M., & Baldessarini, R. J. (1980). Changes in prevalence, severity, and recovery in tardive dyskinesia with age. *Archives of General Psychiatry, 37,* 1368–1373. (15)

Smith, L. T. (1975). The interanimal transfer phenomenon: A review. *Psychological Bulletin, 81,* 1078–1095. (2)

Smith, M. L. (1988). Recall of spatial location by the amnesic patient H. M. *Brain and Cognition, 7,* 178–183. (8)

Smith, M. L., Glass, G. V., & Miller, T. I. (1980). *The benefits of psychotherapy.* Baltimore, MD: Johns Hopkins University Press. (15)

Smith, M. W. (1974). Alfred Binet's remarkable questions: A cross-national and cross-temporal analysis of the cultural biases built into the Stanford-Binet intelligence scale and other Binet tests. *Genetic Psychology Monographs, 89,* 307–334. (10)

Snodgrass, J. G., & Hirshman, E. (1991). Theoretical explorations of the Bruner-Potter (1964) interference effect. *Journal of Memory and Language, 30,* 273–293. (9)

Snyder, G. L., & Stricker, E. M. (1985). Effects of lateral hypothalamic lesions on food intake of rats during exposure to cold. *Behavioral Neuroscience, 99,* 310–322. (3)

Snyder, M. (1979). Self-monitoring process. *Advances in Experimental Social Psychology, 12,* 85–128. (16)

Snyder, S. (1991). Movies and juvenile delinquency: An overview. *Adolescence, 26,* 121–132. (7)

Snyder, S. H. (1984). Drug and neurotransmitter receptors in the brain. *Science, 224,* 22–31. (3)

Snyderman, M., & Herrnstein, R. J. (1983). Intelligence tests and the Immigration Act of 1924. *American Psychologist, 38,* 986–995. (10)

Snyderman, M., & Rothman, S. (1987). Survey of expert opinion on intelligence and aptitude testing. *American Psychologist, 42,* 137–144. (10)

Sobell, M. B., & Sobell, L. C. (1976). Second-year treatment outcome of alcoholics treated by individualized behavior therapy: Results. *Behaviour Research and Therapy, 14,* 195–215. (14)

Sobell, M. B., & Sobell, L. C. (1984). The aftermath of heresy: A response to Pendery et al.'s (1982) critique of "individualized behavior therapy for alcoholics." *Behaviour Research and Therapy, 22,* 413–440. (14)

Solomon, R. L. (1980). The opponent-process theory of acquired motivation. *American Psychologist, 35,* 691–712. (5, 12)

Solomon, R. L., & Corbit, J. D. (1974). An opponent-process theory of motivation: I. Temporal dynamics of affect. *Psychological Review, 81,* 119–145. (5, 12, 16)

Solomon, R. S., & Solomon, V. (1982). Differential diagnosis of the multiple personality. *Psychological Reports, 51,* 1187–1194. (14)

Solomon, Z., Mikulincer, M., & Flum, H. (1988). Negative life events, coping responses, and combat-related psychopathology: A prospective study. *Journal of Abnormal Psychology, 97,* 302–307. (12)

Sonnenberg, A. (1988). Factors which influence the incidence and course of peptic ulcer. *Scandinavian Journal of Gastroenterology, 155* (Suppl.), 119–140. (12)

Spanos, N. P. (1987–88). Past-life hypnotic regression: A critical view. *Skeptical Inquirer, 12,* 174–180. (5)

Spearman, C. (1904). "General intelligence," objectively determined and measured. *American Journal of Psychology, 15,* 201–293. (10)

Spence, J. T. (1984). Masculinity, femininity, and gender-related traits: A conceptual analysis and critique of current research. *Progress in Experimental Personality Research, 13,* 1–97. (13)

Sperling, G. (1960). The information available in brief visual presentations. *Psychological Monographs, 74*(11, Whole No. 498). (8)

Sperry, R. W. (1967). Split-brain approach to learning problems. In G. C. Quarton, T. Melnechuk, & F. O. Schmitt (Eds.), *The neurosciences: A study program* (pp. 714–722). New York: Rockefeller University Press. (3)

Spitz, R. A. (1945). Hospitalism: An inquiry into the genesis of psychiatric conditions in early childhood. *Psychoanalytic Study of the Child, 1,* 53–74. (6)

Spitz, R. A. (1946). Hospitalism: A follow-up report. *Psychoanalytic Study of the Child, 2,* 113–117. (6)

Spring, B., Chiodo, J., & Bowen, D. J. (1987). Carbohydrates, tryptophan, and behavior: A methodological review. *Psychological Bulletin, 102,* 234–256. (3)

Spurlock, J. (1986). Development of self-concept in Afro-American children. *Hospital & Community Psychiatry, 37,* 66–70. (6)

Squire, L. R., Amaral, D. G., & Press, G. A. (1990). Magnetic resonance imaging of the hippocampal formation and mammillary nuclei distinguish medial temporal lobe and diencephalic amnesia. *Journal of Neuroscience, 10,* 3106–3117. (8)

Squire, L. R., Haist, F., & Shimamura, A. P. (1989). The neurology of memory: Quantitative assessment of retrograde amnesia in two groups of amnesic patients. *Journal of Neuroscience, 9,* 828–839. (8)

Staddon, J. E. R., & Bueno, J. L. O. (1991). On models, behaviorism and the neural basis of learning. *Psychological Science, 2,* 3–11. (7)

Stager, G. L., & Lundy, R. M. (1985). Hypnosis and the learning and recall of visually presented material. *International Journal of Clinical and Experimental Hypnosis, 33,* 27–39. (5)

Stapp, J., Tucker, A. M., & VandenBos, G. R. (1985). Census of psychological personnel: 1983. *American Psychologist, 40,* 1317–1351. (1)

Stark, P., & Hardison, C. D. (1985, March). A review of multicenter controlled studies of fluoxetine vs. imipramine and placebo in outpatients with major depressive disorders. *Journal of Clinical Psychiatry, 46* (3, Sec. 2), 53–58. (15)

Starr, C., & Taggart, R. (1992). *Biology: The unity and diversity of life* (6th ed.). Belmont, CA: Wadsworth.

Stegat, H. (1975). Die Verhaltenstherapie der Enuresis und Enkopresis [Behavior therapy for enuresis and encopresis]. *Zeitschrift für Kinder- und Jugendpsychiatrie, 3,* 149–173. (15)

Stein, J. A., Newcomb, M. D., & Bentler, P. M. (1986). Stability and change in personality: A longitudinal study from early adolescence to young adulthood. *Journal of Research in Personality, 20,* 276–291. (13)

Stein, M., Miller, A. H., & Trestman, R. L. (1991). Depression, the immune system, and health and illness. *Archives of General Psychiatry, 48,* 171–177. (12)

Stelmach, G. E., & Phillips, J. G. (1991). Movement disorders—limb movement and the basal ganglia. *Physical Therapy, 71,* 60–69. (3)

Stelmack, R. M. (1990). Biological bases of extraversion: Psychophysiological evidence. *Journal of Personality, 58,* 293–311. (13)

Stephan, W. G. (1978). School desegregation: An evaluation of predictions made in Brown vs. Board of Education. *Psychological Bulletin, 85,* 217–238. (6)

Sternberg, R. J. (1985). *Beyond IQ.* Cambridge, England: Cambridge University Press. (10)

Sternberg, R. (1986). A triangular theory of love. *Psychological Review, 93,* 119–135. (16)

Sternberg, R. J. (1991). Death, taxes, and bad intelligence tests. *Intelligence, 15,* 257–269. (10)

Sternberg, R. J., & Grajek, S. (1984). The nature of love. *Journal of Personality and Social Psychology, 47,* 312–329. (16)

Sternberg, S. (1967). Two operations in character recognition: Some evidence from reaction-time measurements. *Perception and Psychophysics, 2,* 45–53. (9)

Stevens, A., & Coupe, P. (1978). Distortions in judged spatial relations. *Cognitive Psychology, 10,* 422–437. (9)

Stevens, S. S. (1935). The operational definition of psychological concepts. *Psychological Review, 42,* 517–527. (2)

Stevens, S. S. (1961). To honor Fechner and repeal his law. *Science, 133,* 80–86. (4)

Stewart, I. (1987). Are mathematicians logical? *Nature, 325,* 386–387. (10)

Stewart, J. E. (1980). Defendant's attractiveness as a factor in the outcome of criminal trials: An observational study. *Journal of Applied Social Psychology, 10,* 348–361. (16)

Stiles, W. B., Shapiro, D. A., & Elliott, R. (1986). "Are all psychotherapies equivalent?" *American Psychologist, 41,* 165–180. (15)

Stipek, D. J. (1984). Young children's performance expectations: Logical analysis or wishful thinking? *Advances in Motivation and Achievement, 3,* 33–56. (11)

Stoffregen, T. A., & Riccio, G. E. (1988). An ecological theory of orientation and the vestibular system. *Psychological Review, 95,* 3–14. (4)

Storms, M. D. (1973). Videotape and the attribution process: Reversing actors' and observers' points of view. *Journal of Personality and Social Psychology, 27,* 165–175. (16)

Strack, F., Martin, L. L., & Stepper, S. (1988). Inhibiting and facilitating conditions of the human smile: A nonobtrusive test of the facial feedback hypothesis. *Journal of Personality and Social Psychology, 54,* 768–777. (12)

Streather, A., & Hinson, R. E. (1985). Neurochemical and behavioral factors in the development of tolerance to anorectics. *Behavioral Neuroscience, 99,* 842–852. (5)

Streissguth, A. P., Barr, H. M., & Martin, D. C. (1983). Maternal alcohol use and neonatal habituation assessed with the Brazelton scale. *Child Development, 54,* 1109–1118. (6)

Strichartz, G., Rando, T., & Wang, G. K. (1987). An integrated view of the molecular toxinology of sodium channel gating in excitable cells. *Annual Review of Neuroscience, 10,* 237–267. (3)

Stricker, E. M., Cooper, P. H., Marshall, J. F., & Zigmond, M. J. (1979). Acute homeostatic imbalances reinstate sensorimotor dysfunctions in rats with lateral hypothalamic lesions. *Journal of Comparative and Physiological Psychology, 93,* 512–521. (3)

Strickland, L. H. (1958). Surveillance and trust. *Journal of Personality, 26,* 200–215. (16)

Striegel-Moore, R. H., Silberstein, L. R., & Rodin, J. (1986). Toward an understanding of risk factors for bulimia. *American Psychologist, 41,* 246–263. (11)

Strupp, H. H. (1986). Psychotherapy: Research, practice, and public policy (How to avoid dead ends). *American Psychologist, 41,* 120–130. (15)

Stunkard, A. J., Sørensen, T. I. A., Hanis, C., Teasdale, T. W., Chakraborty, R., Shull, W. J., & Schulinger, F. (1986). An adoption study of human obesity. *New England Journal of Medicine, 314,* 193–198. (11)

Stuss, D. T., & Benson, D. F. (1984). Neuropsychological studies of the frontal lobes. *Psychological Bulletin, 95,* 3–28. (3)

Sudzak, P. D., Glowa, J. R., Crawley, J. N., Schwartz, R. D., Skolnick, P., & Paul, S. M. (1986). A selective imidazobenzodiazepine antagonist of ethanol in the rat. *Science, 234,* 1243–1247. (5)

Sue, S., & Okazaki, S. (1990). Asian-American educational achievements. *American Psychologist, 45,* 913–920. (6)

Sue, S., Smith, R. E., & Caldwell, C. (1973). Effects of inadmissible evidence on the decisions of simulated jurors: A moral dilemma. *Journal of Applied Social Psychology, 3,* 345–353. (16)

Sulser, F., Gillespie, D. D., Mishra, R., & Manier, D. H. (1984). Desensitization by antidepressants of central norepinephrine receptor systems coupled to adenylate cyclase. *Annals of the New York Academy of Sciences, 430,* 91–101. (14)

Suppes, T., Baldessarini, R. J., Faedda, G. L., & Tohen, M. (1991). Risk of recurrence following discontinuation of lithium treatment in bipolar disorder. *Archives of General Psychiatry, 48,* 1082–1088. (15)

Svanum, S., & Bringle, R. G. (1982). Race, social class, and predictive bias: An evaluation using the WISC, WRAT, and teacher ratings. *Intelligence, 6,* 275–286. (10)

Swash, M. (1972). Released involuntary laughter after temporal lobe infarction. *Journal of Neurology, Neurosurgery, and Psychiatry, 35,* 108–113. (3)

Sweller, J. (1989). Cognitive technology: Some procedures for facilitating learning and problem solving in mathematics and science. *Journal of Educational Psychology, 81,* 457–466. (9)

Sweller, J., Mawer, R. F., & Ward, M. R. (1983). Development of expertise in mathematical problem solving. *Journal of Experimental Psychology: General, 112,* 639–661. (9)

Szymanski, H. V., Simon, J. C., & Gutterman, N. (1983). Recovery from schizophrenic psychosis. *American Journal of Psychiatry, 140,* 335–338. (15)

Tannen, D. (1990). *You just don't understand.* New York: William Morrow. (6)

Tanzi, R. E., Gusella, J. F., Watkins, P. C., Bruns, G. A. P., St. George-Hyslop, P., VanKeuren, M. L., Patterson, D., Pagan, S., Kurnit, D. M., & Neve, R. L. (1987). Amyloid beta protein gene: cDNA, mRNA distribution, and genetic linkage near the Alzheimer's locus. *Science, 235,* 880–884. (3)

Tassinary, L. G., & Cacioppo, J. T. (1992). Unobservable facial actions and emotion. *Psychological Science, 3,* 28–33. (12)

Taylor, H. G. (1984). Early brain injury and cognitive development. In C. R. Almli & S. Finger (Eds.), *Early brain damage* (pp. 325–345). Orlando, FL: Academic Press. (3)

Taylor, S. E. (1983). Adjustment to threatening events: A theory of cognitive adaptation. *American Psychologist, 38,* 1161–1173. (12)

Taylor, S. E., & Brown, J. D. (1988). Illusion and well-being: A social psychological perspective on mental health. *Psychological Bulletin, 103,* 193–210. (12)

Taylor, S. E., & Lobel, M. (1989). Social comparison activity under threat: Downward evaluation and upward contacts. *Psychological Review, 96,* 569–575. (16)

Teasdale, T. W., & Owen, D. R. (1984). Heredity and familial environment in intelligence and educational level: A sibling study. *Nature, 309,* 620–622. (10)

Teitelbaum, P. (1955). Sensory control of hypothalamic hyperphagia. *Journal of Comparative and Physiological Psychology, 48,* 156–163. (11)

Tennen, H., & Affleck, G. (1990). Blaming others for threatening events. *Psychological Bulletin, 108,* 209–232. (12)

Teplin, L. A. (1983). The criminalization of the mentally ill: Speculation in search of data. *Psychological Bulletin, 94,* 54–67. (15)

Teplin, L. A. (1984). Criminalizing mental disorder: The comparative arrest rate of the mentally ill. *American Psychologist, 39,* 794–803. (15)

Teplin, L. A. (1985). The criminality of the mentally ill: A dangerous misconception. *American Journal of Psychiatry, 142,* 593–599. (15)

Terman, G. W., & Liebeskind, J. C. (1986). Relation of stress-induced analgesia to stimulation-produced analgesia. *Annals of the New York Academy of Sciences, 467,* 300–308. (4)

Terman, G. W., Shavitt, Y., Lewis, J. W., Cannon, J. T., & Liebeskind, J. C. (1984). Intrinsic mechanisms of pain inhibition: Activation by stress. *Science, 226,* 1270–1277. (4)

Terrace, H. S., Petitto, L. A., Sanders, R. J., & Bever, T. G. (1979). Can an ape create a sentence? *Science, 206,* 891–902. (9)

Tetrud, J. W., & Langston, J. W. (1989). The effect of deprenyl (Selegiline) on the natural history of Parkinson's disease. *Science, 245,* 519–522. (3)

Thieman, T. J. (1984). A classroom demonstration of encoding specificity. *Teaching of Psychology, 11,* 101–102. (8)

Thigpen, C., & Cleckley, H. (1957). *The three faces of Eve.* New York: McGraw-Hill. (14)

Thomas, A., & Chess, S. (1980). *The dynamics of psychological development.* New York: Brunner/Mazel. (6)

Thomas, A., Chess, S., & Birch, H. G. (1968). *Temperament and behavior disorders in children.* New York: New York University Press. (6)

Thompson, C. R., & Church, R. M. (1980). An explanation of the language of a chimpanzee. *Science, 208,* 313–314. (9)

Thompson, L. A., Detterman, D. K., & Plomin, R. (1991). Associations between cognitive abilities and scholastic achievement: Genetic overlap but environmental differences. *Psychological Science, 2,* 158–165. (10)

Thompson, S. C. (1981). Will it hurt less if I can control it? A complex answer to a simple question. *Psychological Bulletin, 90,* 89–101. (12)

Thorndike, E. L. (1898). Animal intelligence: An experimental study of the associative processes in animals. *Psychological Monographs, 2*(No. 8). (7)

Thorndike, E. L. (1911/1970). *Animal intelligence.* Darien, CT: Hafner. (Original work published 1911) (7)

Thurstin, A. H., Alfano, A. M., & Nerviano, V. J. (1987). The efficacy of AA attendance for aftercare of inpatient alcoholics: Some follow-up data. *International Journal of the Addictions, 22,* 1083–1090. (14)

Tiffany, S. T., & Baker, T. B. (1981). Morphine tolerance in rats: Congruence with a Pavlovian paradigm. *Journal of Comparative and Physiological Psychology, 95,* 747–762. (7)

Timberlake, W., & Farmer-Dougan, V. A. (1991). Reinforcement in applied settings: Figuring out ahead of time what will work. *Psychological Bulletin, 110,* 379–391. (7)

Time. (April 22, 1974). Alcoholism. (5)

Tinbergen, N. (1958). *Curious naturalists.* New York: Basic Books. (3)

Titchener, E. B. (1910). *A textbook of psychology.* New York: Macmillan. (1)

Tolman, E. C. (1932). *Purposive behavior in animals and men.* New York: Century. (7)

Tolman, E. C., & Honzik, C. H. (1930). Introduction and removal of reward, and maze performance in rats. *University of California Publications in Psychology, 4,* 257–275. (7)

Tolstedt, B. E., & Stokes, J. P. (1984). Self-disclosure, intimacy, and the depenetration process. *Journal of Personality and Social Psychology, 46,* 84–90. (6)

Tolstoy, L. (1865, 1875/1978). *Tolstoy's letters, Vol. I: 1828–1879.* New York: Charles Scribner's Sons. (Original works written 1828–1879) (6)

Tolstoy, L. (1983). *Confession.* New York: Norton. (Original work written 1882 but blocked from publication by the Russian censor) (12)

Tombaugh, C. W. (1980). *Out of the darkness, the planet Pluto.* Harrisburg, PA: Stackpole. (4)

Torrance, E. P. (1980). Growing up creatively gifted: A 22-year longitudinal study. *Creative Child and Adult Quarterly, 5,* 148–159. (9)

Torrance, E. P. (1981). Empirical validation of criterion-referenced indicators of creative ability through a longitudinal study. *Creative Child and Adult Quarterly, 6,* 136–140. (9)

Torrance, E. P. (1982). "Sounds and images" productions of elementary school pupils as predictors of the creative achievements of young adults. *Creative Child and Adult Quarterly, 7,* 8–14. (9)

Torrey, E. F., Rawlings, R., & Waldman, I. N. (1988). Schizophrenic births and viral diseases in two states. *Schizophrenia Research, 1,* 73–77. (14)

Townsend, J. T. (1990). Serial vs. parallel processing: Sometimes they look like Tweedledum and Tweedledee but they can (and should) be distinguished. *Psychological Science, 1,* 46–54. (9)

Treisman, A., & Souther, J. (1985). Search asymmetry: A diagnostic for preattentive processing of separable features. *Journal of Experimental Psychology: General, 114,* 285–310. (4)

Trivers, R. L. (1972). Parental investment and sexual selection. In B. Campbell (Ed.), *Sexual selection and the descent of man, 1871–1971* (pp. 136–179). Chicago: Aldine. (3)

Tschann, J. M., Johnston, J. R., Kline, M., & Wallerstein, J. S. (1990). Conflict, loss, change and parent-child relationships: Predicting children's adjustment during divorce. *Journal of Divorce, 13,* 1–22. (6)

Tulving, E. (1989). Remembering and knowing the past. *American Scientist, 77,* 361–367. (8)

Tulving, E., & Thomson, D. M. (1973). Encoding specificity and retrieval processes in episodic memory. *Psychological Review, 80,* 352–373. (8)

Turkheimer, E. (1991). Individual and group differences in adoption studies of IQ. *Psychological Bulletin, 110,* 392–405. (10)

Tversky, A., & Kahneman, D. (1981). The framing of decisions and the psychology of choice. *Science, 211,* 453–458. (9)

Tversky, A., & Kahneman, D. (1983). Extensional versus intuitive reasoning: The conjunctional fallacy in probability judgment. *Psychological Review, 90,* 293–315. (9)

Tversky, B. (1981). Distortions in memory for maps. *Cognitive Psychology, 13,* 407–433. (9)

U.S. Department of Labor. (1989, April). *Employment and Earnings* (Vol. 36, No. 4). Washington, DC: U.S. Government Printing Office. (6)

Udolf, R. (1981). *Handbook of hypnosis for professionals.* New York: Van Nostrand Reinhold. (5)

Ulrich, R. E., Stachnik, T. J., & Stainton, N. R. (1963). Student acceptance of generalized personality interpretations. *Psychological Reports, 13,* 831–834. (13)

Ulrich, R. S. (1984). View through a window may influence recovery from surgery. *Science, 224,* 420–421. (4)

Underwood, N. R., & McConkie, G. W. (1985). Perceptual span for letter distinctions during reading. *Reading Research Quarterly, 20,* 153–162. (9)

Vaillant, G. E. (1983). *The natural history of alcoholism.* Cambridge, MA: Harvard University Press. (14)

Vaillant, G. E., & Milofsky, E. S. (1982). The etiology of alcoholism: A prospective viewpoint. *American Psychologist, 37,* 494–503. (1, 3, 14)

Valenstein, E. S. (1986). *Great and desperate cures.* New York: Basic Books. (3)

Van Der Pligt, J., & Eiser, J. R. (1983). Actors' and observers' attributions, self-serving bias, and positivity. *European Journal of Social Psychology, 13,* 95–104. (16)

van Dyke, C., & Byck, R. (1982). Cocaine. *Scientific American, 246*(3), 128–141. (3)

Van Orden, G. C., Johnston, J. C., & Hale, B. L. (1988). Word identification in reading proceeds from spelling to sound to meaning. *Journal of Experimental Psychology: Learning, Memory, and Cognition, 14,* 371–386. (9)

Van Orden, G. C., Pennington, B. F., & Stone, G. O. (1990). Word identification in reading and the promise of subsymbolic psycholinguistics. *Psychological Review, 97,* 488–522. (9)

Varni, J. W., Lovaas, O. I., Koegel, R. L., & Everett, N. L. (1979). An analysis of observational learning in autistic and normal children. *Journal of Abnormal Child Psychology, 7,* 31–43. (14)

Vaughan, D. (1986). *Uncoupling.* New York: Vintage Books. (16)

Vaughn, C. E., Snyder, K. S., Jones, S., Freeman, W. B., & Falloon, I. R. H. (1984). Family factors in schizophrenia relapse. *Archives of General Psychiatry, 41,* 1169–1177. (15)

Vernon, M. (1967). Relationship of language to the thinking process. *Archives of General Psychiatry, 16,* 325–333. (10)

Viglione, D. J., Brager, R., & Haller, N. (1991). Psychoanalytic interpretation of the Rorschach: Do we have better hieroglyphics? *Journal of Personality Assessment, 57,* 1–9. (13)

Vincent, K. R., & Harman, M. J. (1991). The Exner Rorschach: An analysis of its clinical validity. *Journal of Clinical Psychology, 47,* 596–599. (13)

Voeller, B. (1990). Some uses and abuses of the Kinsey scale. In D. P. McWhirter, S. A. Sanders, & J. M. Reinisch (Eds.), *Homosexuality/heterosexuality* (pp. 32–38). New York: Oxford University Press. (11)

Vogel, G. W., Thompson, F. C., Jr., Thurmond, A., & Rivers, B. (1973). The effect of REM deprivation on depression. In W. P. Koella & P. Levin (Eds.), *Sleep: Physiology, biochemistry, psychology, pharmacology, clinical implications* (pp. 191–195). Basel, Switzerland: Karger. (5)

Vokey, J. R., & Read, J. D. (1985). Subliminal messages: Between the devil and the media. *American Psychologist, 40,* 1231–1239. (4)

von Baeyer, C. (1988, September/October). How Fermi would have fixed it. *The Sciences, 28*(5), 2–4. (9)

von Restorff, H. (1933). Analyse von Vorgängen im Spurenfeld. I. Uber die Wirkung von Bereichsbildungen im Spurenfeld [Analysis of the events in memory. I. Concerning the effect of domain learning in the memory field]. *Psychologische Forschung, 18,* 299–342. (8)

Wadden, T. A., & Stunkard, A. J. (1987). Psychopathology and obesity. *Annals of the New York Academy of Sciences, 499,* 55–65. (11)

Wagenaar, W. A. (1986). My memory: A study of autobiographical memory over six years. *Cognitive Psychology, 18,* 225–252. (8)

Wagenaar, W. A. (1988). *Paradoxes of gambling behaviour.* Hillsdale, NJ: Lawrence Erlbaum. (9)

Wahba, M. A., & Bridwell, L. G. (1976). Maslow reconsidered: A review of research on the need hierarchy theory. *Organizational Behavior & Human Performance, 15,* 212–240. (11)

Waid, W. M., & Orne, M. T. (1982). The physiological detection of deception. *American Scientist, 70,* 402–409. (12)

Wakeling, A. (1979). A general psychiatric approach to sexual deviation. In I. Rosen (Ed.), *Sexual deviation* (2nd ed.) (pp. 1–28). Oxford: Oxford University Press. (11)

Wald, G. (1968). Molecular basis of visual excitation. *Science, 162,* 230–239. (4)

Walker, L. J. (1989). A longitudinal study of moral reasoning. *Child Development, 60,* 157–166. (6)

Waller, N. G., Kojetin, B. A., Bouchard, T. J., Jr., Lykken, D. T., & Tellegen, A. (1990). Genetic and environmental influences on religious interests, attitudes, and values: A study of twins reared apart and together. *Psychological Science, 1,* 138–142. (3)

Wallesch, C.-W., Henriksen, L., Kornhuber, H. H., & Paulson, O. B. (1985). Observations on regional cerebral blood flow in cortical and subcortical structures during language production in normal man. *Brain and Language, 25,* 224–233. (3)

Walster, E., Aronson, E., Abrahams, D., & Rottman, L. (1966). Importance of physical attractiveness in dating behavior. *Journal of Personality and Social Psychology, 4,* 508–516. (16)

Walster, E., Traupman, J., & Walster, G. W. (1978). Equity and extramarital sexuality. *Archives of Sexual Behavior, 7,* 127–142. (16)

Walters, G. C., & Grusec, J. E. (1977). *Punishment.* San Francisco: W. H. Freeman. (7)

Wanberg, K. W., & Horn, J. L. (1983). Assessment of alcohol use with multidimensional concepts and measures. *American Psychologist, 38,* 1055–1069. (14)

Ward, I. L. (1972). Prenatal stress feminizes and demasculinizes the behavior of males. *Science, 175,* 82–84. (11)

Ward, I. L. (1977). Exogenous androgen activates female behavior in noncopulating, prenatally stressed male rats. *Journal of Comparative and Physiological Psychology, 91,* 465–471. (11)

Ward, I. L., & Reed, J. (1985). Prenatal stress and prepubertal social rearing conditions interact to determine sexual behavior in male rats. *Behavioral Neuroscience, 99,* 301–309. (11)

Waring, G. O., III, Lynn, M. J., Culbertson, W., Laibson, P. R., Lindstrom, R. D., McDonald, M. B., Myers, W. D., Obstbaum, S. A., Rowsey, J. J., & Schanzlin, D. J. (1987). Three-year results of the prospective evaluation of radial keratotomy (PERK) study. *Ophthalmology, 94,* 1339–1354. (4)

Warren, R. M. (1970). Perceptual restoration of missing speech sounds. *Science, 167,* 392–393. (9)

Washburn, M. F. (1908). *The animal mind.* New York: Macmillan. (1)

Wason, P. C. (1960). On the failure to eliminate hypotheses in a conceptual task. *Quarterly Journal of Experimental Psychology, 12,* 129–140. (9)

Watson, D. (1982). The actor and the observer: How are their perceptions of causality divergent? *Psychological Bulletin, 92,* 682–700. (16)

Watson, J. B. (1913). Psychology as the behaviorist views it. *Psychological Review, 20,* 158–177. (1, 7)

Watson, J. B. (1919). *Psychology from the standpoint of a behaviorist.* Philadelphia: Lippincott. (1)

Watson, J. B. (1925). *Behaviorism.* New York: Norton. (1, 7)

Watson, J. B., & Rayner, R. (1920). Conditioned emotional reactions. *Journal of Experimental Psychology, 3,* 1–14. (14)

Weaver, C. N. (1980). Job satisfaction in the United States in the 1970s. *Journal of Applied Psychology, 65,* 364–367. (6)

Webb, W. B. (1979). Theories of sleep functions and some clinical implications. In R. Drucker-Colín, M. Shkurovich, & M. B. Sterman (Eds.), *The functions of sleep* (pp. 19–35). New York: Academic Press. (5)

Wechsler, D. (1949). *WISC manual.* New York: Psychological Corporation. (10)

Wegner, D. M., Schneider, D. J., Carter, S. R., III, & White, T. L. (1987). Paradoxical effects of thought suppression. *Journal of Personality and Social Psychology, 53,* 5–13. (14)

Wegner, D. M., Wenzlaff, R., Kerker, R. M., & Beattie, A. E. (1981). Incrimination through innuendo: Can media questions become public answers? *Journal of Personality and Social Psychology, 40,* 822–832. (9)

Wehr, T. A. (1990). Effects of wakefulness and sleep on depression and mania. In J. Montplaisir & R. Godbout (Eds.), *Sleep and biological rhythms* (pp. 42–86). New York: Oxford University Press. (5)

Wehr, T. A., Jacobsen, F. M., Sack, D. A., Arendt, J., Tamarkin, L., & Rosenthal, N. E. (1986). Phototherapy of seasonal affective disorder. *Archives of General Psychiatry, 43,* 870–875. (14)

Weil, A. T., Zinberg, N. E., & Nelson, J. M. (1968). Clinical and psychological effects of marihuana in man. *Science, 162,* 1234–1242. (5)

Weinberg, R. A. (1989). Intelligence and IQ: Landmark issues and great debates. *American Psychologist, 44,* 98–104. (10)

Weinberger, D. R. (1987). Implications of normal brain development for the pathogenesis of schizophrenia. *Archives of General Psychiatry, 44,* 660–669. (14)

Weiner, I. B., & Exner, J. E., Jr. (1991). Rorschach changes in long-term and short-term psychotherapy. *Journal of Personality Assessment, 56,* 453–465. (13)

Weiner, R. D. (1984). Does electroconvulsive therapy cause brain damage? *Behavioral and Brain Sciences, 7,* 1–53. (15)

Weinstock, C. (1984). Further evidence on psychobiological aspects of cancer. *International Journal of Psychosomatics, 31,* 20–22. (12)

Weiss, J. M. (1968). Effects of coping responses on stress. *Journal of Comparative and Physiological Psychology, 65,* 251–260. (12)

Weissman, M. M., Kidd, K. K., & Prusoff, B. A. (1982). Variability in rates of affective disorders in relatives of depressed and normal probands. *Archives of General Psychiatry, 39,* 1397–1403. (14)

Weitzman, E. D. (1981). Sleep and its disorders. *Annual Review of Neuroscience, 4,* 381–417. (5)

Weitzman, R. A. (1982). The prediction of college achievement by the Scholastic Aptitude Test and the high school record. *Journal of Educational Measurement, 19,* 179–191. (10)

Wender, P. H., Kety, S. S., Rosenthal, D., Schulsinger, F., Ortmann, J., & Lunde, I. (1986). Psychiatric disorders in the biological and adoptive families of adopted individuals with affective disorders. *Archives of General Psychiatry, 43,* 923–929. (1, 14)

Wenger, J. R., Tiffany, T. M., Bombardier, C., Nicholls, K., & Woods, S. C. (1981). Ethanol tolerance in the rat is learned. *Science, 213,* 575–576. (5)

Werner, E. E. (1989). High-risk children in young adulthood: A longitudinal study from birth to 32 years. *American Journal of Orthopsychiatry, 59,* 72–81. (6)

Westlake, T. M., Howlett, A. C., Ali, S. F., Paule, M. G., Scallet, A. C., & Slikker, W., Jr. (1991). Chronic exposure to Δ^9-tetrahydrocannabinol fails to irreversibly alter brain cannabinoid receptors. *Brain Research, 544,* 145–149. (5)

Wetzer, S. E., & Sweeney, J. A. (1986). Childhood amnesia: An empirical demonstration. In D. C. Rubin (Ed.), *Autobiographical memory* (pp. 191–201). Cambridge, England: Cambridge University Press. (8)

Whaley, D. L., & Malott, R. W. (1971). *Elementary principles of behavior.* Englewood Cliffs, NJ: Prentice-Hall. (7)

Wheeler, D. D. (1970). Processes in word recognition. *Cognitive Psychology, 1,* 59–85. (9)

White, B. B., & White, M. S. (1987). Autism from the inside. *Medical Hypotheses, 24,* 223–229. (14)

White, F. J., & Wang, R. Y. (1983). Differential effects of classical and atypical antipsychotic drugs on A9 and A10 dopamine neurons. *Science, 221,* 1054–1057. (15)

White, P. A. (1990). Ideas about causation in philosophy and psychology. *Psychological Bulletin, 108,* 3–18. (1)

Whitworth, R. H., & Perry, S. M. (1990). Comparison of Anglo- and Mexican-Americans on the 16-PF administered in Spanish or English. *Journal of Clinical Psychology, 46,* 857–863. (13)

Whorf, B. L. (1941). The relation of habitual thought and behavior to language. In L. Spier, A. I. Hallowell, & S. S. Newman (Eds.), *Language, culture, and personality* (pp. 75–93). Menasha, WI: Sapir Memorial Publication Fund. (9)

Wickens, D. D. (1970). Encoding categories of words: An empirical approach to meaning. *Psychological Review, 77,* 1–15. (8)

Wicker, A. W. (1969). Attitudes vs. action: The relation of verbal and overt behavioral responses to attitude objects. *Journal of Social Issues, 25*(4), 47–78. (16)

Wicklund, R. A., & Brehm, J. W. (1976). *Perspectives on cognitive dissonance.* Hillsdale, NJ: Lawrence Erlbaum. (16)

Widom, C. S. (1989). Does violence beget violence? A critical examination of the literature. *Psychological Bulletin, 106,* 3–28. (12)

Wild, H. M., Butler, S. R., Carden, D., & Kulikowski, J. J. (1985). Primate cortical area V4 important for colour constancy but not wavelength discrimination. *Nature, 313,* 133–135. (4)

Wilkins, L., & Richter, C. P. (1940). A great craving for salt by a child with corticoadrenal insufficiency. *Journal of the American Medical Association, 114,* 866–868. (11)

William, D. C. (1984). The prevention of AIDS by modifying sexual behavior. *Annals of the New York Academy of Sciences, 437,* 283–285. (11)

Williams, D. G. (1990). Effects of psychoticism, extraversion, and neuroticism in current mood: A statistical review of six studies. *Personality and Individual Differences, 11,* 615–630. (13)

Williams, K., Harkins, S. G., & Latané, B. (1981). Identifiability as a deterrent to social loafing: Two cheering experiments. *Journal of Personality and Social Psychology, 40,* 303–311. (16)

Williams, K. D., & Karau, S. J. (1991). Social loafing and social compensation: The effects of expectations of co-worker performance. *Journal of Personality and Social Psychology, 61,* 570–581. (16)

Williams, R. B., Jr., Lane, J. D., Kuhn, C. M., Melosh, W., White, A. D., & Schanberg, S. M. (1982). Type A behavior and elevated physiological and neuroendocrine responses to cognitive tasks. *Science, 218,* 483–485. (12)

Williams, R. W., & Herrup, K. (1988). The control of neuron number. *Annual Review of Neuroscience, 11,* 423–453. (3)

Wilson, E. O. (1975). *Sociobiology: The new synthesis.* Cambridge, England: Belknap. (3)

Wilson, J. R., and the editors of *Life.* (1964). *The mind.* New York: Time. (4, 10)

Wilson, R. S. (1987). Risk and resilience in early mental development. In S. Chess & A. Thomas (Eds.), *Annual Progress in Child Psychiatry & Child Development 1986* (pp. 69–85). New York: Brunner/Mazel. (6)

Winch, R. (1958). *Mate-selection: A study of complementary needs.* New York: Harper. (16)

Winner, E. (1986, August). Where pelicans kiss seals. *Psychology Today,* 24–35. (6)

Winocur, G., Moscovitch, M., & Witherspoon, D. (1987). Contextual cuing and memory performance in brain-damaged amnesics and old people. *Brain and Cognition, 6,* 129–141. (8)

Winograd, E., & Soloway, R. M. (1986). On forgetting the locations of things stored in special places. *Journal of Experimental Psychology: General, 115,* 366–372. (8)

Wise, R. A., & Bozarth, M. A. (1987). A psychomotor stimulant theory of addiction. *Psychological Review, 94,* 469–492. (14)

Wolgin, D. L., & Salisbury, J. J. (1985). Amphetamine tolerance and body weight set point: A dose-response analysis. *Behavioral Neuroscience, 99,* 175–185. (5)

Wolitzky, D. L., & Wachtel, P. L. (1973). Personality and perception. In B. B. Wolman (Ed.), *Handbook of general psychology* (pp. 826–857). Englewood Cliffs, NJ: Prentice-Hall. (4)

Wolman, B. B. (1989). *Dictionary of behavioral science* (2nd ed.). San Diego, CA: Academic Press. (10)

Wolpe, J. (1961). The systematic desensitization treatment of neuroses. *Journal of Nervous and Mental Disease, 132,* 189–203. (14)

Wolpe, J., & Rowan, V. C. (1988). Panic disorder: A product of classical conditioning. *Behaviour Research and Therapy, 26,* 441–450. (14)

Woods, C. W., Charney, D. S., Loke, J., Goodman, W. K., Redmond, E. E., Jr., & Heninger, G. R. (1986). Carbon dioxide sensitivity in panic anxiety. *Archives of General Psychiatry, 43,* 900–909. (14)

Woods, S. C. (1991). The eating paradox: How we tolerate food. *Psychological Review, 98,* 488–505. (11)

Woodward, E. L. (1938). *The age of reform.* London: Oxford University Press. (8)

Woodworth, R. S. (1934). *Psychology* (3rd ed.). New York: Henry Holt. (1)

Woody, G. E., & O'Brien, C. P. (1986). Update on methadone maintenance. *Research Advances in Alcohol and Drug Problems, 9,* 261–277. (14)

Woychyshyn, C. A., McElheran, W. G., & Romney, D. M. (1992). MMPI validity measures: A comparative study of original with alternative indices. *Journal of Personality Assessment, 58,* 138–148. (13)

Wright, D. M. (1975). Impairment in abstract conceptualization in schizophrenia. *Psychological Bulletin, 82,* 120–127. (14)

Wundt, W. (1902). *Outlines of psychology* (C. H. Judd, Trans.). New York: Gustav Sechert. (Original work published 1896) (1)

Wundt, W. (1961). Contributions to the theory of sensory perception. In T. Shipley (Ed.), *Classics in psychology* (pp. 51–78). New York: Philosophical Library. (Original work published 1862) (1)

Yamamoto, T. (1987). Cortical organization in gustatory perception. *Annals of the New York Academy of Sciences, 510,* 49–54. (4)

Yarsh, T. L., Farb, D. H., Leeman, S. E., & Jessell, T. M. (1979). Intrathecal capsaicin depletes substance P in the rat spinal cord and produces prolonged thermal analgesia. *Science, 206,* 481–483. (4)

Yaryura-Tobias, J. A. (1977). Obsessive-compulsive disorders: A serotonergic hypothesis. *Journal of Orthomolecular Psychiatry, 6,* 317–326. (14)

Yates, B. (1985). Self-management. Belmont, CA: Wadsworth. (7)

Yonas, A., & Granrud, C. E. (1985). Reaching as a measure of infants' spatial perception. In G. Gottlieb & N. A. Krasnegor (Eds.), *Measurement of audition and vision in the first year of postnatal life* (pp. 301–322). Norwood, NJ: Ablex. (6)

Young, P. T. (1936). *Motivation of behavior.* New York: Wiley. (11)

Young-Ok, K., & Stevens, J. H., Jr. (1987). The socialization of prosocial behavior in children. *Childhood Education, 63,* 200–206. (7)

Zabrucky, K., Moore, D., & Schultz, N. R., Jr. (1987). Evaluation of comprehension in young and old adults. *Developmental Psychology, 23,* 39–43. (9)

Zajonc, R. B. (1968). Attitudinal effects of mere exposure. *Journal of Personality and Social Psychology, 9,* Monograph Supplement 2, part 2. (16)

Zanna, M., & Hamilton, D. L. (1977). Further evidence for meaning change in impression formation. *Journal of Experimental Social Psychology, 13,* 224–238. (16)

Zaragoza, M. S., McCloskey, M., & Jamis, M. (1987). Misleading postevent information and recall of the original event: Further evidence against the memory impairment hypothesis. *Journal of Experimental Psychology: Learning, Memory, and Cognition, 13,* 36–44. (8)

Zeki, S., & Shipp, S. (1988). The functional logic of cortical connections. *Nature, 335,* 311–317. (4)

Zelnik, M., & Kantner, J. F. (1977). Sexual and contraceptive experience of young unmarried women in the United States, 1976 and 1971. *Family Planning Perspectives, 9,* 55–71. (6)

Zelnik, M., & Kantner, J. F. (1978). Contraceptive patterns and premarital pregnancy among women aged 15–19 in 1976. *Family Planning Perspectives, 10,* 135–142. (6)

Zepelin, H., & Rechtschaffen, A. (1974). Mammalian sleep, longevity, and energy metabolism. *Brain, Behavior, and Evolution, 10,* 425–470. (5)

Zigler, E., & Glick, M. (1988). Is paranoid schizophrenia really camouflaged depression? *American Psychologist, 43,* 284–290. (14)

Zigler, E., & Hodapp, R. M. (1991). Behavioral functioning in individuals with mental retardation. *Annual Review of Psychology, 42,* 29–50. (10)

Zimmerman, M., Coryell, W., Pfohl, B., & Stangl, D. (1986). The validity of four definitions of endogenous depression. II. Clinical, demographic, familial, and psychosocial correlates. *Archives of General Psychiatry, 43,* 234–244. (14)

Zola-Morgan, S., & Squire, L. R. (1986). Memory impairment in monkeys following lesions limited to the hippocampus. *Behavioral Neuroscience, 100,* 155–160. (8)

Zola-Morgan, S., Squire, L. R., & Mishkin, M. (1982). The neuroanatomy of amnesia: Amygdala-hippocampus versus temporal stem. *Science, 218,* 1337–1339. (8)

Zucker, R. A., & Gomberg, E. S. L. (1986). Etiology of alcoholism reconsidered. *American Psychologist, 41,* 783–793. (14)

Zuckerman, M. (1990). Some dubious premises in research and theory on racial differences. *American Psychologist, 45,* 1297–1303. (13)

Zuckerman, M., & Wheeler, L. (1975). To dispel fantasies about the fantasy-based measure of fear of success. *Psychological Bulletin, 82,* 932–946. (11)

Zwislocki, J. J. (1981). Sound analysis in the ear: A history of discoveries. *American Scientist, 69,* 184–192. (4)

Page 3: CHAPTER 1: Photo by Pierre-Yves Goavec, San Francisco

Page 6: Figure 1.1: Photo by N. Tomalin/Bruce Coleman, Ltd.

Page 7: Top photo by Zade Rosenthal. © 1992 Carolco. Courtesy Arnold Schwarzenegger/Oak Productions/Lightstorm Entertainment, Inc. Bottom photo from AP/Wide World Photos

Page 8: Photos courtesy of Michael E. Phelps and John C. Mazziotta, UCLA, School of Medicine

Page 9: Figure 1.3: Left photo © Apesteguy/Simon/Gamma Liaison. Right photo © Sandro Tucci/*Time* Magazine

Page 14: Photo by Michael Heron/Woodfin Camp

Page 21: Figure 1.6: Right photo © The Walt Disney Company

Page 25: Figure 1.10: Photo courtesy of Wellesley College

Page 31: CHAPTER 2: Photo by Greg Pease

Page 37: Figure 2.3: After Pfungst, 1911, in Fernald, 1984

Page 38: Photo by Chip Mitchell/Picture Group

Page 39: Figure 2.5: Photo courtesy CFB Productions, Inc.

Page 43: Figure 2.7: Photo by Bohdan Hrynewych/Stock Boston

Page 44: Figure 2.8: Photo by Sally and Richard Greenhill

Page 47: Figure 2.9: Photo by Penelope Breese/Gamma Liaison

Page 58: Figure 2.16: Photo © David Madison

Page 71: CHAPTER 3: Photo by Barbara Kasten/Ehlers Caudill Gallery, Ltd., Chicago

Page 72: Photo from ZEFA/Stockmarket

Page 74: Figure 3.2: Photo from Science Photo Library

Page 75: Figure 3.4: Photo from ZEFA

Page 76: Figure 3.5: Image © 1984 by Wadsworth, Inc. Used by permission of the publisher

Page 81: Figure 3.11: Photos by David Thompson/Oxford Scientific Films

Page 82: Figure 3.12: Photo by Gordon Langsbury/Bruce Coleman, Ltd.

Page 83: Figure 3.13: Photo by Galen Rowell/*Mountain Light*

Page 87: Figure 3.15b from J. G. Brandon and R. G. Coss, *Brain Research,* 252:51–61, 1982. Used by permission of R. G. Coss

Page 88: Figure 3.17 reprinted by permission from *Nature,* 315:404–406 and Dale Purves. Copyright © 1985 Macmillan Magazines Ltd.

Page 88: Figure 3.16: Photo © Manfred Kage/Peter Arnold, Inc.

Page 90: Figure 3.20: Photo by Dennis D. Kunkel/Biological Photo Service

Page 100: Figure 3.29: Photo by Paul J. Sutton/Duomo

Page 103: Figure 3.33: Photos by Dr. Colin Chumbley/Science Photo Library

Page 104: Figure 3.35 from Norman Geschwind, "Specializations of the Human Brain," September 1979. Copyright © 1979 by Scientific American, Inc. All rights reserved. Figure 3.36 from *Clinical Neuropsychology* by Kenneth M. Heilman and Edward

Valenstein. Copyright © 1979 by Oxford University Press, Inc. Reprinted by permission

Page 105: Figure 3.38: Photo courtesy of Dana Copeland

Page 106: Figure 3.39: Photo by Burt Glinn/Magnum

Page 107: Figure 3.40 from Wallesch, Henriksen, Kornhuber, and Paulson, 1985

Page 111: Figure 3.45: Photos courtesy of Dana Copeland

Page 113: Photo from Rex Features

Page 117: CHAPTER 4: Photo from Eric Jacobson Studio, New York

Page 118: Photo by R. P. Carr/Bruce Coleman, Ltd.

Page 120: Photo courtesy of Mike and Donna Durrenberger

Page 122: Photos from ZEFA

Page 123: Figure 4.5: Photo courtesy of E. R. Lewis, F. S. Werblin, and Y. Y. Zeevi. Figure 4.6: Photo © Chase Swift

Page 124: Photo from The Image Bank

Page 129: Figure 4.14: Photo by Klaus Benser/ZEFA

Page 131: Figures 4.16 and 4.17 reproduced from *Ishihara's Test for Colour Blindness,* Kanehara & Co., Ltd., Tokyo, Japan. A test for color blindness cannot be conducted with this material. Used by permission

Page 136: Left photo from Trippett/Sipa Press. Right photo from Rex Features

Page 139: Figure 4.22: Left photo from The Image Bank. Right photo from NASA

Page 140: Figure 4.24 from "Picture and Pattern Perception in the Sighted and the Blind: The Advantage of the Late Blind" by M. A. Heller, *Perception,* 18:379–389, 1989. Reprinted by permission from Pion, London

Page 141: Figure 4.25: Photo by Stuart Franklin/Magnum

Page 143: Photo from Omikron/Science Photo Library

Page 146: Photo by Louise Psimoyos/Contact Press Images/Colorific!

Page 152: Top photo courtesy and © Toyota Motor Sales, U.S.A., Inc. Bottom photo courtesy of American Association of Advertising Agencies

Page 153: Figure 4.33: Left photo by Van Bucher, University of Florida, Department of Clinical Psychology/Photo Researchers. Right photo © Marilyn Newton

Page 155: Figure 4.34 from "Fortysomething: Recognizing Faces at One's 25th Reunion" by M. Bruck, P. Cavanagh, and S. J. Ceci, *Memory and Cognition,* 19:221–228, 1991. Reprinted by permission of M. Bruck

Page 156: Figure 4.37b from *Inversions* by Scott Kim. Copyright 1989 by Scott Kim. Reprinted by permission of W. H. Freeman and Company

Page 158: Figure 4.40 from *Organization in Vision: Essays on Gestalt Perception* by Gaetano Kanizsa. Copyright © 1979 by Gaetano Kanizsa. Reprinted with permission of Praeger Publishers, an imprint of Greenwood Publishing Group, Westport, CT

Page 159: Figure 4.42: Photo courtesy McDonnell Douglas

Page 160: Collage by David Hockney, *Celia. Los Angeles,* April 10, 1982. Composite polaroid, 18x40 in. © David Hockney, 1982

Page 161: Figure 4.43b from "A Puzzle Picture with a New Principle of Concealment" by K. M. Dallenbach,

American Journal of Psychology, 54:431–433, 1951. Copyright © by The Board of Trustees of the University of Illinois. Figure 4.44c from *Mind Sights* by Roger N. Shepard. Copyright © 1990 by Roger N. Shepard. Reprinted by permission of W. H. Freeman and Company

Page 162: Left photo from San Diego Union/Russ Gilbert. Right photo from AP/Wide World Photos

Page 165: Figure 4.48: Photo from Wide World Photos

Pages 166–167: Figure 4.50: Photo from Globus Brothers/ZEFA/Stock Market

Page 166: Figure 4.51: Photo by Larry Dale Gordon/Image Bank

Page 167: Figure 4.52: Photo from Lowell Observatory

Page 168: Figure 4.53: Photos © Lara Hartley

Page 169: Top photo by John Boykin

Page 170: Figure 4.55: Photo from Budge/Liaison/Frank Spooner Pictures

Page 171: Photo by Steve McGurry/Magnum

Page 172: Figure 4.59: Photo by Andrew Brillant

Page 173: Figure 4.60a: Photo by S. Schwartzenberg. © The Exploratorium. All rights reserved

Page 175: Figure 4.63: Photos © Mark Antman/The Image Works

Page 179: CHAPTER 5: Photo by Cheryl Fenton, San Francisco

Page 180: Photo © Joel Simon

Page 182: Figure 5.1: Photo © Joel Simon

Page 184: Figure 5.4: Photo from San Diego Historical Society

Page 185: Figure 5.5 from "Monotonic and Rhythmic Influences: A Challenge for Sleep Deprivation Research" by H. Babkoff, T. Caspy, M. Mikulincer, and H. C. Sing, *Psychological Bulletin,* 109:411–428, 1991. Copyright 1991 by the American Psychological Association. Adapted by permission of the APA and H. Babkoff

Page 187: Figure 5.7: Photos by Dr. J. Allan Hobson, Harvard Medical School. Figure 5.8: Photo by Richard Nowitz/Black Star/Colorific!

Page 188: Figure 5.9: EEG recordings provided by T. E. LeVere. Figure 5.10 based on data from *Some Must Watch While Some Must Sleep* by William C. Dement. Copyright © 1972, 1974, 1976 by William C. Dement. Used by permission of William C. Dement and the Stanford Alumni Association

Page 190: Figure 5.11 from "Ontogenetic Development of Human Sleep-Dream Cycle" by H. P. Roffwarg, J. N. Muzio, and W. C. Dement, *Science,* 152:604–609, 1966. Copyright 1966 by the AAAS. Used by permission of the AAAS and W. C. Dement

Page 191: Figure 5.12: Photo by Garry Gay/The Image Bank

Page 192: Photo by Penny Tweedie/Impact

Page 193: Photo by David Gifford/Science Photo Library

Page 198: Figure 5.13: Photo from *Newsweek*/James Wilson

Page 199: Figure 5.14: Photo by Sally and Richard Greenhill. Figure 5.15: Photo from UPI/Bettmann

Page 200: Figure 5.16: Photo from Wide World Photos

Page 201: Figure 5.17: Photo courtesy Martin Reiser, Los Angeles Police Department

Page 204: Figure 5.20: Photo © 1979 Los Angeles Times. Photo by R. L. Oliver

Page 434: Figure 10.11 from Black Intelligence Test of Cultural Homogeneity. Copyright © 1972 by Robert L. Williams, Ph.D. Reprinted by permission
Page 435: Photo from Frank Spooner Pictures
Page 436: Figure 10.13 adapted from "Familial Studies of Intelligence: A Review" by T. Bouchard et al., *Science*, 212:1055–1059, 1981. Copyright 1981 by the AAAS. Reprinted by permission of the AAAS and T. Bouchard
Page 437: Photo by David Moscroft/Rex Features

Page 443: CHAPTER 11: Photo © David Madison/DUOMO, 1991
Page 444: Photo by Galen Rowell/Peter Arnold, Inc.
Page 447: Photo by G. Rogers/Image Bank
Page 448: Photo by George Butler/Visions Photo Inc.
Page 451: Figure 11.4: Photo by Les Stone/Sygma
Page 455: Figure 11.5: Photo by Stephanie Maze/Woodfin Camp
Page 458: Figure 11.10: Photo by Yoav Levy/Colorific!
Page 459: Figure 11.12: Photo by Sally and Richard Greenhill
Page 460: Figure 11.13: Photo by Bower/The Image Bank. Figure 11.14 reprinted by permission of Gene DeFoliart from *The Food Insects Newsletter*, March 1990
Page 461: Photo by Ethan Hoffman/Colorific!
Page 462: Photo from Rex Features
Page 463: Figure 11.16: Photo from ZEFA
Page 466: Figure 11.19: Photo by Tony Freeman/PhotoEdit
Page 467: Figure 11.20: Top left photo from Mary Evans Picture Library. Top right photo © R. Ian Lloyd. Bottom left and right photos from Kobal Collection/Super Stock
Page 469: Photo by Jay Dickman
Page 470: Figure 11.21: Reproduced by permission of The Kinsey Institute for Research in Sex, Gender, and Reproduction, Inc. Photography by Dellenback
Page 471: Figures 11.22 and 11.23 adapted from *Sexual Behavior in the Human Male* by A. C. Kinsey, W. B. Pomeroy, and C. E. Martin, 1948, W. B. Saunders Company and *Sexual Behavior in the Human Female* by A. C. Kinsey, W. B. Pomeroy, C. E. Martin, and P. H. Gebhard, 1953, W. B. Saunders Company. Reprinted by permission of The Kinsey Institute for Research in Sex, Gender, and Reproduction, Inc.
Page 472: Photo by Alain Evrard/Photo Researchers
Page 473: Photo courtesy San Francisco AIDS Foundation
Page 476: Photo from Foulon/Sipa/Rex Features
Page 479: Figure 11.27 from "A Difference in Hypothalmic Structure Between Heterosexual and Homosexual Men" by S. LeVay, *Science*, 253:1034–1037, 1991. Copyright 1991 by the AAAS. Reprinted by permission of the AAAS and S. LeVay
Page 481: Photo by Donna Binder/Impact Visuals
Page 484: Photos © Michael Speaker. Figure 11.29: Photo © Elizabeth Crews
Page 485: Figure 11.20: Photo by Bob Daemmrich/Stock Boston
Page 487: Photo by Schaeier/ZEFA
Page 488: Photo by Shelly Katz/Black Star

Page 491: CHAPTER 12: Photo by Susan Lapides/Woodfin Camp
Page 492: Photo by Jim Anderson/Colorific!
Page 494: Photo from Reuters/Bettmann
Page 495: Figure 12.2: Left photo by Les Stone/Sygma. Right photo from Animals Animals/Stouffer Productions, Ltd.
Page 497: Figure 12.5 based on "An Opponent-Process Theory of Motivation: I. Temporal Dynamics of Affect" by R. L. Solomon and J. D. Corbit, *Psychological Review*, 81:119–145, 1974. Copyright 1974 by the American Psychological Association. Reprinted by permission of the APA and R. L. Solomon
Page 498: Figure 12.6: Photo by Alon Reininger/Contact Press Images/Colorific!
Page 504: Figure 12.9: Photos by Ann Dowie. Figure 12.10: Photo from Chanloup/TV Magazine/Frank Spooner Pictures

Page 505: Figure 12.11: Photos from *Der Vorprogrammierte Mensch* by I. Eibl-Eibesfeldt, 1973. Used by permission of I. Eibl-Eibesfeldt. Figure 12.12: Photos from *Unmasking the Face* (2d ed.) by P. Ekman and W. Friesen, 1984. Used by permission of P. Ekman
Page 506: Figures 12.13 and 12.14: Photos from *Der Vorprogrammierte Mensch* by I. Eibl-Eibesfeldt, 1973. Used by permission of I. Eibl-Eibesfeldt
Page 507: Figure 12.15: Photos by Ann Dowie
Page 509: Left photo by Ann Dowie. Right photo by Grey Villet/Black Star
Page 510: Photo by John Sturrock/Network
Page 511: Photo © Cary Wolinsky/Stock Boston
Page 514: Photo from St. Bartholomew's Hospital, London/Science Photo Library
Page 515: Photo by Frankee (Jim Lenoir)
Page 516: Table 12.2 from "The Social Readjustment Rating Scale" by T. H. Holmes and R. H. Rahe in *Journal of Psychosomatic Research*, 11:213-218, 1967. Copyright 1967 by Pergamon Press, Ltd. Reprinted by permission of Pergamon Press and T. H. Holmes
Page 517: Left photo by Barbara Campbell/Gamma Liaison. Right photo by Gale Zucker/Stock Boston. Table 12.3 adapted from "Comparison of Two Modes of Stress Measurement: Daily Hassles and Uplifts Versus Major Life Events" by A. D. Kanner, J. C. Coyne, C. Schaefer, and R. S. Lazarus, *Journal of Behavioral Medicine*, 4:14, 1981. Copyright 1981 by Plenum Publishing Corporation. Adapted by permission of the publisher and A. D. Kanner
Page 521: Figure 12.20: Photo by Bob Krist/Black Star/Colorific! Right from *Type-A Behavior and Your Heart* by Meyer Friedman and Ray H. Rosenman. Copyright © 1974 by Meyer Friedman. Reprinted by permission of Alfred A. Knopf, Inc. Figure 12.21: Left photo by Alain Buu/Gamma Liaison. Right photo by Bill Horsman/Stock Boston
Page 523: Figure 12.22: Photo by Marc St. Gil/Image Bank
Page 526: Figure 12.23: Left photo by Zao-Grimberg/The Image Bank. Right photo from ZEFA
Page 527: Photo by William Strode/Black Star/Colorific!
Page 529: Photo from ZEFA
Page 530: Photo by Burt Glinn/Magnum
Page 531: Photo from F. Demulder Collection/Sipa Press

Page 533: CHAPTER 13: Photo by Michael S. Yamishita/Woodfin Camp
Page 534: Photo by Bonnie Schiffman
Page 536: Figure 13.2: Illustrations from the Granger Collection.
Page 537: Figure 13.3: Photo from The Mary Evans Picture Library/Sigmund Freud Collection
Page 539: Left photo by Kindra Clineff/Picture Cube. Right photo by Carol Palmer/Picture Cube
Page 540: Left photo © Seny Norasingh. Right photo by Kindra Clineff/Picture Cube
Page 543: Photo by Robin Anderson/Rex Features
Page 546: Figure 13.9: Photo from the Bettmann Archive, New York
Page 547: Figure 13.10: Photo from Culver Pictures, Inc. Figure 13.11a–d: Hindu mandala from The Granger Collection. All other photos from the Archive for Research in Archetypal Symbolism, San Francisco
Page 549: Figure 13.12: Photo from Wide World Photos
Page 550: Figure 13.13: Photo from The Bettmann Archive
Page 551: Figure 13.14: Photo from The Bettmann Archive. Figure 13.15: Photo from The Granger Collection
Page 555: Painting by Frederick Brown, "Geronimo with His Spirit," 1984. Oil on linen, 80x80 inches. Collection Fondacion Culturaltelevisa. Marlborough Gallery, New York
Page 556: Photo by Steve Liss/Gamma Liaison
Page 558: Photo from Sipa Press
Page 560: Photo by Yves-Guy Berges/Sipa Press/Rex Features
Page 563: Photo by Margot Granitsas/The Image Works

Page 565: Figure 13.17: Minnesota Multiphasic Personality Inventory-2. Copyright © by the Regents of the University of Minnesota 1942, 1943 (renewed 1970), 1989. This profile form 1989. All rights reserved
Page 568: Figure 13.18 adapted from *Handbook for the Sixteen Personality Factors* by Raymond B. Cattell. Copyright 1970, 1988 by the Institute for Personality and Ability Testing, Inc. All rights reserved. Reproduced by permission. Figure 13.19 from *The Scientific Analysis of Personality* by Raymond B. Cattell, 1965, Penguin Library. Reprinted by permisssion of Raymond B. Cattell
Page 569: Figure 13.21: Photo from Science Photo Library
Page 571: Figure 13.22 from *Thematic Apperception Test* by Henry A. Murray, Harvard University Press, Cambridge, MA. Copyright © 1943 by the President and Fellows of Harvard College, © 1971 by Henry A. Murray. Reprinted by permission of the publisher

Page 575: CHAPTER 14: Photo from Eric Jacobson Studio, New York
Page 576: Photo from Stills/Lynn Goldsmith Inc./Rex Features
Page 578: Photo by Anis Hamdani/Gamma Liaison
Page 579: Figure 14.1: "Three Miracles of St. Zenobius" (detail) by Botticelli/The National Gallery, London
Page 580: Figure 14.2 adapted from Meyers et al., *Archives of General Psychiatry*, 41:949–958, 1984 and Robins et al., Archives of General Psychiatry, 41:959–967, 1984. Copyright 1984 by the American Medical Association
Page 584: Figure 14.3: Photo from Wide World Photos. Handwriting from *I'm Eve* by Chris Costner Sizemore and Élen Sain Pitillo. Copyright © 1977 by Chris Costner Sizemore and Élen Sain Pitillo
Page 590: Figure 14.9: Photo courtesy Professor Benjamin Harris, Department of Psychology, University of Wisconsin
Page 592: Photo by Kent Wood/Photo Researchers
Page 593: Figure 14.11: Photo © Andrew Sacks. Figure 14.12: Photo by Jacques Chenet/Woodfin Camp
Page 595: Figure 14.13: Tables 14.3 and 14.4 from *Obsessions and Compulsions* by Stanley J. Rachman and Ray J. Hodgson. Copyright © 1980. Reprinted by permission of Prentice-Hall, Inc., Englewood Cliffs, NJ
Page 599: Photo form Hrechorowica/Delta/Sipa Press
Page 600: Left photo by Julian Calder/Impact Photos. Right photo from Rex Features
Page 601: Figure 14.13 adapted from Levenson et al., "Greater Reinforcement from Alcohol for Those at Risk: Parental Risk, Personality Risk, and Sex," *Journal of Abnormal Psychology*, 96:242–253, 1987. Used by permission of the author
Page 603: Figure 14.14: Photo by Jim McHugh/Visages/Colorific!
Page 604: Photo by Mike Goldwater/Network
Page 607: Figure 14.15 adapted from *Sleep* by J. Allan Hobson. Copyright © 1989 by J. Allan Hobson. Reprinted by permission of W. H. Freeman and Company
Page 608: Painting by Rafael Coronel, "Mujer." Courtesy B. Lewin Galleries
Page 610: Painting by Ferdinand Georg Waldmuller. "Ludwig van Beethoven." Archiv fur Kunst und Geschichte, Berlin
Page 612: Figure 14.20 adapted from "Two–day Cycles of Alternating Good and Bad Behavior in Psychotic Patients" by C. P. Richter in *Archives of Neurology and Psychology*, 39:587–598, 1938. Copyright 1938 by the American Medical Association
Pages 612–613: Excerpts from Joshua Logan in *Moodswing* by Ronald R. Fieve. Copyright © 1975 by Ronald R. Fieve. Used by permission of William R. Morrow & Co.
Page 613: Poem from *The Portable Dorothy Parker*, edited by Brendan Gill. Copyright 1926, renewed 1954 by Dorothy Parker. Reprinted by permission of Viking Penguin Inc. Figure 14.21 based on "Water and Sodium in Two Psychotics" by J. L. Crammer in

Lancet, 1(7083):1122–1126, 1959. Used by permission of Lancet Ltd. Figure 14.22 from "The Increasing Rate of Suicide by Firearms" by J. H. Boyd in *New England Journal of Medicine,* 308:872–874, 1983. Used by permission

Page 617: Figure 14.23: Photos of Wain's paintings by Derek Bayes, *Life* Magazine, © Time, Inc.

Page 618: Figure 14.24: Photo by Benyas Kaugman/Black Star

Page 619: Figure 14.25: Photo by Grunnitos/Monkmeyer Press

Page 620: Figure 14.26: Photos courtesy of E.F. Torrey and M.F. Casanova/NIMH

Page 623: Photo © Joel Gordon

Page 627: CHAPTER 15: Photo by Craig Aurness/Woodfin Camp

Page 628: Photo by Steve Goldberg/Monkmeyer Press Photos

Page 629: From *The Portable Dorothy Parker,* edited by Brendan Gill. Copyright 1926, renewed 1954 by Dorothy Parker. Reprinted by permission of Viking Penguin Inc.

Page 632: Excerpt from *A Guide to Rational Living* by Albert Ellis, Ph.D., and Robert A. Harper, Ph.D. Copyright © 1989, 1961 by Institute for Rational Living Inc. Reprinted by permission of the publisher, Prentice–Hall/A Division of Simon & Schuster, Englewood Cliffs, NJ

Page 633: Photo from Davies/Network

Page 634: Photo © Joel Gordon

Page 637: Photo by Mimi Forsyth/Monkmeyer Press Photos

Page 639: Figure 15.5 based on "The Dose–Effect Relationship in Psychotherapy" by Kenneth I. Howard et al., in *American Psychologist,* 41:159–164, 1986. Used by permission of Kenneth I. Howard

Page 640: Photo by Mike Goldwater/Network

Page 641: Top photo by Scott Witte/Third Coast Stock Source. Bottom photo by E. Sander/Liaison/Gamma/Frank Spooner Pictures

Page 642: Figure 15.6 adapted from *The Benefits of Psychotherapy* by M. L. Smith, G. V. Glass, and T. I. Miller, The Johns Hopkins University Press, 1980. Used by permission

Page 646: Photo by Steve Goldberg/Monkmeyer Press Photos. Figure 15.7 based on "Studies on Endogenous Ligands (Endacoids) for the Benzodiazepine/Beta–Carboline Binding Sites" by A. Guidotti, P. Ferrero, M. Fujimoto, R. M. Santi, and E. Costa, *Advances in Biochemical Psychopharmacology,* 41:137–148, 1986

Page 649: Figure 15.9: Photo by James D. Wilson/Woodfin Camp

Page 650: Figure 15.10 based on "Drugs in the Treatment of Psychosis" by J. O. Cole et al., in *Psychiatric Drugs,* P. Solomon (ed.), 1966, Grune & Stratton. Used by permission

Page 654: Photo by Jack Sprat/Black Star

Page 655: Top photo by Stack Pick/Stock Boston. Bottom photo by Bill Anderson/Monkmeyer Press Photos

Page 659: Top photo from Sygma. Bottom photo by D. Halstear/Frank Spooner Pictures

Page 665: CHAPTER 16: Photo by Greg Pease

Page 666: Photo by John Boykin

Page 667: Left photo by Dennis Brack/Black Star. Right photo by Rob Crandall/Picture Group

Page 669: Figure 16.1: Photo by Lara Hartley

Page 671: Top photo by Jacques Langevin/Sygma. Bottom photo by Rob Crandall/Picture Group

Page 672: Figure 16.2: Left photo © David Madison. Right photo by Ken Kobre/Picture Group

Page 674: Photo by Barbara Filet/Tony Stone Worldwide

Page 675: Photo © Maggie Hallahan

Page 677: Photo by Rob Crandall/Picture Group

Page 678: Photo from Photofest

Page 681: Photo by J. Langevin/Sygma

Page 682: Figure 16.7 reprinted from *Social Pressures in Informal Groups: A Study of Human Factors in Housing* by Leon Festinger, Stanley Schachter, and Kurt Back, with the permission of the publishers, Stanford University Press. © 1950 by Leon Festinger, Stanley Schachter, and Kurt Back. Photo by Henley & Savage/Tony Stone Worldwide

Page 683: Photo by Heinz Stucke/Frank Spooner Pictures

Page 685: Photo by Baldwin/ZEFA

Page 687: Photo by John Boykin

Page 692: Photo by Paul Popper, Ltd.

Page 693: Photo courtesy American Cancer Society

Page 699: Photo by David Reed/Impact Photos. Figure 16.16: Photo by William Vandivert

Page 700: Figure 16.17 adapted from "Opinion and Social Pressure" by Solomon Asch, *Scientific American,* November 1955. Copyright © 1955 by Scientific American, Inc. All rights reserved

Page 701: Photo by John Boykin

Page 702: Figure 16.19: Photo by Chuck Nacke/Black Star

Page 704: Image © and courtesy Roger von Oech, from the Creative Whack Pack. Art by George Willet

Page 705: Photo by Jim Howard/Colorific!

Page 709: Photo © R. Ian Lloyd

Page 710: Photo by David Sutton/Picture Group

Page 712: Figure 16.23: Photo by Stephen Ferry/J.B. Pictures

Page 713: Photo by Ann Dowie

Page 714: Figures 16.24 and 16.25: Photos © 1965 by Stanley Milgram. From the film *Obedience,* distributed by Pennsylvania State University Audio Visual Services

Page 715: Figure 16.26: Photos © 1965 by Stanley Milgram. From the film *Obedience,* distributed by Pennsylvania State University Audio Visual Services

appetite, weight loss and, 464–65
aptitude testing, 424–25
arousal, 696
artificial intelligence, 7, 155
artificial mother experiment, 249–50
artificial selection the purposeful selection, by humans, of certain animals for breeding purposes. 80
Asian Americans, academic achievement of, 271
Asians
  dairy products and, 78–79
  in psychology, 13
  See also race differences
assimilation Piaget's term for the application of an established schema to new objects. 228
association, 319
attachment a long-term feeling of closeness between people, such as a child and a care giver. 249–51
attention-deficit disorder, 581
attentive process paying attention to only one part of a visual field at a time. 164
  cognitive dissonance and, 693–96
  influence of, 688–89
  persuasion and change of, 689–93
attitude a learned like or dislike of something or somebody that influences our behavior toward that thing or person. 688
attraction, 254–55, 680–87
attractive people, 254, 668, 682–83
attribution the set of thought processes we use to assign causes to our own behavior and the behavior of others. 673
  discounting principle and, 674–75
  errors and bias in, 676–77
  internal versus external causes of, 673–74
  self-esteem and, 677–78
atypical antipsychotic drugs, 650
audition. *See* hearing
auditory illusion, 174
autism condition with onset in early childhood, characterized by extreme social isolation, repetitive movements, and a failure to communicate with others. 622–23
  causes of, 624
  symptoms of, 623–24
  treatments for, 624
autokinetic effect the illusory perception that a point of light in a darkened room is in motion. 159
autonomic nervous system a set of neurons lying in and alongside the spinal cord, which receives information from and sends information to the internal organs such as the heart. 98, 100–101, 494–96, 519, 527
autonomy versus shame and doubt the conflict between independence and doubt about one's abilities. 247, 248
availability heuristic the strategy of assuming that the number of available memories of an event indicates how common the event actually is. 384–85, 389
average. *See* **mean**
aversion therapy, 638
avoidance disorders, 588
  drug therapies for, 646–47
  obsessive-compulsive, 593–96
  persistence of, 588
  phobias, 588–93
axes of DSM III-R, 580–82
axon a single long, thin fiber that transmits impulses from a neuron to other neurons or to muscle cells. 87, 89–90, 125, 141, 144

babbling, 236
babies. *See* infancy
bad habits, 308–9
bait shyness. *See* **conditioned taste aversion**
balance, 138–39
balanced transactions, 637, 638
barbiturates, 207
basal ganglia, 102
base-rate information information about the frequency or probability of a given item. 383
basic trust versus mistrust the conflict between trusting and mistrusting that one's parents and other key figures will meet one's basic needs; first conflict in Erikson's eight ages of human development. 248
basilar membrane a thin membrane in the cochlea that vibrates after sound waves strike the eardrum. 134, 135, 136, 137
bats, hearing in, 136
Bay of Pigs, 704
bed-wetting, 635–36
bees, vision of, 119
behaviorism
  basic assumptions of, 278–79
  origin of, 25–26
  rise of, 277–78
behaviorist a psychologist who tries to explain the causes of behavior by studying only those behaviors that he or she can observe and measure, without reference to unobservable mental processes. 15, 277–78
behavior modification a procedure for modifying behavior by setting specific behavior goals and reinforcing the subject for successive approximations to those goals. 307–8
behavior therapy treatment that begins with clear, well-defined behavioral goals, such as eliminating test anxiety, and then attempts to achieve those goals through learning. 634–35
behavior trap situation that almost forces people into self-defeating behaviors. 708
beliefs, as coping strategies, 530–31
belongingness the concept that certain stimuli are readily associated with each other and that certain responses are readily associated with certain outcomes. 295–96
benzodiazepines, 207, 646
Bianchi case, 204, 658
bias tendency for test scores to exaggerate a difference between groups or to report a difference that does not exist at all. 432–38
big five personality dimensions five traits that account for a great deal of human personality differences: neuroticism, extraversion, agreeableness, conscientiousness, and openness to new experiences. 557, 563
binge eating, 461, 466
binocular cues visual cues that depend on the action of both eyes. 168
biofeedback method for gaining voluntary control over physiological processes that we cannot ordinarily control through sensory feedback. 522–23
biographical information, 508
biological cycles, 181, 183
biological psychology
  ethology, comparative psychology, and, 81–82
  genes and, 73–80
  nerve system and, 97–113

  neurons and, 86–95
  sociobiology and, 82–85
biopsychologist (or *behavioral neuroscientist*) a psychologist who tries to relate behavior to activities of the brain and other organs. 14–15
biorhythms, 32
bipolar cells, 125, 127–28
bipolar disorder condition in which a person alternates between periods of depression and periods of mania. 606, 612–13, 649
birds, vision of, 121, 122
birth order, 251
birth weight, development and, 218–19
Black Intelligence Test of Cultural Homogeneity, 434
blacks. *See* African Americans
blindness
  cutaneous senses and, 140
  dreaming and, 192–93
  emotional expression and, 506
blind observer an observer who does not know which subjects are in which group and what results are expected. 45
blind spot the area of the retina through which the optic nerve exits. 125–26
blind study, 44–45
blocking effect tendency for a previously established association to one stimulus to block the formation of an association to an added stimulus.
blood pressure, 497
blood types, 439
bonding. *See* **attachment**
bonobos, language acquisition of, 394–96
borderline personality disorder, 582
bottom-up processing, 164
brain
  activity while sleeping, 186–87, 188, 192
  aging and, 87, 97
  cerebral cortex, 102–6
  chemical mechanisms of, 88–95
  corpus callosum, 107–11
  damage, 15, 97, 101–5, 108, 110–13, 619–20
  electrical stimulation of, 7, 8
  feature detectors, in 155–58
  hind-, mid-, and fore-, 101–2
  homosexuality and, 478–79
  hunger and, 454–57
  maturation, 98, 99
  measuring activity in, 7–8
  pain and, 141
  species differences in, 87, 98, 99
  structure of, 86–88
  surgery, 108, 110, 112
  therapy, 112–13
  vision and, 108–10
brain fag, 578
brief therapy (or time-limited therapy) treatment that begins with an agreement on what therapist and client can expect from each other and how long the treatment will last. 639–40
Brown vs. Board of Education, 271
bulimia condition in which a person alternates between self-starvation and excessive eating. 466–67
bystander apathy, 700–701

cabin fever, 526–27
caffeine, 207, 209
cancer, 522, 530–31
Cannon-Bard theory of emotions theory that certain areas of the brain evaluate sensory

information and, when appropriate, send one set of impulses to the autonomic nervous system and another set to the forebrain, which is responsible for the subjective and cognitive aspects of emotion. 499, 500, 502

capsaicin, 141

careers
family and, 255–56
satisfaction with, 256–57

case history a thorough description of a single individual, including information on both past experiences and current behavior. 45

cataracts, 120

catatonia movement disorder, consisting of either rigid inactivity or excessive activity. 617

catatonic schizophrenia type of schizophrenia characterized by the basic symptoms plus prominent movement disorders. 618–19

categorization by features theory that we categorize objects by determining how many features they have that are characteristic of the members of a category. 368

categorization by levels theory that we categorize each item at a level with similar items; each item has features of its own plus all the features of higher-level categories that include it. 367–68

categorization by prototypes theory that we decide whether an object belongs to a category by determining how well it resembles the prototypes of the category. 368–69

catharsis release of pent-up emotions associated with unconscious thoughts and memories. 537, 629

cats
feature detectors in, 156
operant conditioning of, 293–94, 295–96
sleep habits of, 184–85
visual-motor coordination of, 222

causation, 50–51

cell body the part of the neuron that includes the nucleus. 86

central nervous system the brain and the spinal cord. 86, 97

central route to persuasion method of persuasion based on careful evaluation of evidence and logic. 689

central tendency, 61–63

central traits, 669

cerebellum (Latin for "little brain") a hindbrain structure. 101

cerebral cortex the outer surface of the forebrain, consisting of six distinct layers of cells and fibers. 102–3

cerebral ventricles, 620

chaining a procedure for developing a sequence of behaviors in which the reinforcement for one response is the opportunity to engage in the next response. 298–99

Challenger disaster, 704

checking, 594–95. *See also* **obsessive-compulsive disorder**

chemical receptors the receptors that respond to the chemicals that come into contact with the nose and mouth. 142

chess, 374

child abuse, 509

child care, 263–64

childhood
gender roles in, 268–69
imitative behavior in, 312
intellectual development in, 229–32, 233

language development in, 235–38
male-female relationships in, 268
moral reasoning in, 238–42
punishment in, 301
sexuality in, 538–40
social-emotional development in, 247–48, 251–52

child psychology. *See* developmental psychology

child-rearing practices, 263–65

chimpanzees, language acquisition by, 393–96

chlorpromazine, 649–50

chromosome a strand of hereditary material found in the nucleus of a cell. 73–76

chunking process of grouping digits or letters into meaningful sequences. 324–25

cigarettes, 210–11, 314, 599

circadian rhythm rhythm of increase and decrease in some process lasting approximately one day. 181–83

clairvoyance, 37

classical conditioning or **Pavlovian conditioning** the process by which an organism learns a new association between two stimuli paired with each other—a neutral stimulus and one that already evokes a reflexive response. 280–81
drug tolerance as example of, 284–85
explanations of, 285–90
as information processing, 290–91
operant conditioning versus, 294–95, 297
Pavlovian procedures, 279–82
phenomena of, 281–84

cleaning, 594. *See also* **obsessive-compulsive disorder**

Clever Hans, 36–37

clinical psychologist one who specializes in identifying and treating psychological disorders. 10, 12, 630

clinical social worker, 12

clomipramine, 646–47

closure in Gestalt psychology, the tendency to imagine the rest of an incomplete familiar figure. 161, 163

clozapine, 650

cocaine, 15, 207, 209–10, 599

cochlea the snail-shaped, fluid-filled structure that contains the receptors for hearing. 134, 135

coffee, 209

cognition the processes that enable us to imagine, to gain knowledge, to reason about knowledge, and to judge its meaning. 15, 361
belief, disbelief, and, 369–71
categorization and, 366–69
language and, 397–400
mental imagery and, 362–65
mental lists and, 366
social perception and, 667–78

cognitive dissonance a state of unpleasant tension that people experience when they hold contradictory attitudes or when they behave in a way that is inconsistent with their attitudes. 693–96

cognitive map a mental representation of a spatial arrangement. 364–65

cognitive psychologist a psychologist who studies thought processes and the acquisition of knowledge. 15–16

cognitive therapy treatment that seeks to improve people's psychological well-being by changing their cognitions. 633

cohort a group of people born at a particular time (as compared to people born at a different time). 246

cohort effect, 246

collective unconscious according to Jung, an inborn level of the unconscious that symbolizes the collective experience of the human species. 546

color blindness, 76, 130–32

color constancy the tendency of an object to appear nearly the same color under a variety of lighting conditions. 129

color vision, 126
color blindness, 76, 130–32
opponent-process theory of, 127–28
retinex theory of, 129
trichromatic theory of, 126–27

commitment, 685

commons dilemma situation in which people who share a common resource tend to overuse it and therefore make it unavailable in the long run. 711–12

communication. *See* language

community psychologist psychologist who focuses on the needs of large groups rather than on individuals. 660

comparative psychologist psychologist who compares different species. 23

comparative psychology the branch of psychology that compares the behaviors of various animal species. 81

competency interpretation, 485

compliance, 712–16

compulsion a repetitive, almost irresistible action. 593, 594–95

conditioned response (CR) a response that the conditioned stimulus elicits only because it has previously been paired with the unconditioned stimulus. 280, 281

conditioned stimulus (CS) a stimulus that comes to evoke a particular response after being paired with the unconditioned stimulus. 280, 281

conditioned taste aversion or **bait shyness** the tendency to avoid eating a substance that has been followed by illness when eaten in the past. 289–90

condoms, 473

conduction velocity of axon, 89

conductive deafness hearing loss that results if the bones connected to the eardrum fail to transmit sound waves properly to the cochlea. 134–35

cone the type of visual receptor that is adapted for color vision, daytime vision, and detailed vision. 121, 122–23

confabulation guesses made by an amnesic patient to fill in the gaps in his or her memory. 344

conformity maintaining or changing one's behavior to match the behavior of others. 698–700, 703

connectionist model theory that our perceptions and our memories are represented by vast numbers of connections among "units," each of them connected to other units. 404–5

conscientiousness tendency to show self-discipline, to be dutiful, and to strive for achievement and competence. 557

consensus information observations of how some person's behavior compares with that of others. 674

conservation the concept that objects retain their weight, volume, and certain other properties in spite of changes in their shape or arrangement. 230–32, 234, 235

consistency information observations of how some person's behavior varies from one time to another. 674

consolidation the formation and strengthening of long-term memories. 328–29, 330

construct validity correspondence of a test's measurements to a theoretical construct. 430, 431

contact comfort, 249, 250

content validity similarity between the items in a test and the information the test is meant to measure. 430, 431

contingency the degree to which the occurrence of one stimulus predicts the occurrence of a second stimulus. 288

continuation in Gestalt psychology, the tendency to fill in the gaps in an interrupted line. 161, 163

continuous reinforcement reinforcement for every response. 304, 305

contraceptives, 254, 472, 473

control group the group that is subjected to the same procedures as the experimental group except for the treatment that is being tested. 52

controlled drinking, 603–4

convergence the turning in of the eyes as they focus on close objects. 168, 169

conversion disorder condition in which a person, for no apparent medical reason, exhibits such symptoms as paralysis, blindness, deafness, dizziness, or an inability to speak. 583

cooperation, 709–12

cornea a rigid, transparent structure in the eye. 120, 121

corpus callosum a large set of axons connecting the left and right hemispheres of the cerebral cortex and enabling the two hemispheres to communicate with each other. 107–8

correlation a measure of the relationship between two variables, neither of which is controlled by the investigator. 48–51

correlation coefficient a mathematical estimate of the relationship between two variables, ranging from +1 (perfect positive relationship) to 0 (no linear relationship) to –1 (perfect negative relationship). 49, 69

cortex. *See* cerebral cortex

cortisol hormone that elevates blood sugar and enhances metabolism

counseling psychologist, 11

coyotes, taste aversion in, 289

CR. *See* conditioned response

crack, 210

creativity the development of novel, socially valued products. 380

criminals
  amnesia in, 347–48
  moral reasoning in, 241
  multiple personalities of, 204, 583
  psychiatric assessments of, 508–9

cross-cultural comparisons. *See* cultural differences

cross-cultural psychologist psychologist who compares the behavior of people in different cultures. 46

crossed transactions, 637, 638

cross-sectional study a study of individuals of different ages all at the same time. 245, 246

crystallized intelligence acquired skills and knowledge and the application of that knowledge to specific content in a person's experience. 415, 418

CS. *See* **conditioned stimulus**

cuddling, 249–50

cued recall method of testing memory by asking someone to remember a certain item after being given a hint. 337, 338, 339

cultural differences
  in abnormal behavior, 577–78
  in academic performance, 271–72
  in alcohol consumption, 600
  in art and folklore, 546–47
  in dating, 254
  in emotional expression, 507
  in facial expressions, 504–7
  in food choice, 460, 461
  in language and thought, 398–400
  in life choices, 252
  in life pace and heart disease, 520, 521
  in personality traits, 557, 566
  in self-esteem, 271
  in sexual behavior, 469, 471–72
  in treatment of elderly, 258–59
  in understanding of reproduction, 36
  See also race differences

culture-fair tests, 422–23

cutaneous senses the skin senses, including pressure, warmth, cold, pain, vibration, movement across the skin, and stretch of the skin. 139–40

cyclops, 109

Dahmer case, 659

daily rhythms, 181, 183

dark adaptation a gradual improvement in the ability to see under dim light. 124–25

dating, 253, 254–55, 682–83

dating anxiety, 528

day care, 264

deafness, 134–35, 238, 506

death anxiety, 259–60

death-qualified a person who is qualified to serve on death-penalty cases because of willingness to consider voting for the death penalty. 705–6

death-scrupled a person who opposes the death penalty under all circumstances. 705–6

decision making. *See* problem solving

declarative memory recall of factual information. 333, 343

defense mechanism a method of protecting oneself against anxiety caused by conflict between the id's demands and the superego's constraints. 541–42

deinstitutionalization removal of patients from mental hospitals. 655

delayed-response problem, 23, 24

delusion unfounded belief. 617

delusion of grandeur belief that one is unusually important. 617

delusion of persecution belief that one is being persecuted. 617

delusion of reference tendency to interpret all sorts of messages as if they were meant for oneself. 617

demand characteristics cues that reveal to the participants what results the experimenter expects. 54–55, 504

dendrite one of the widely branching structures of a neuron that generally receive transmission from other neurons. 86–87, 88

denial the refusal to believe information that provokes anxiety. 543

dependence. *See* addiction

dependent personality disorder, 582

dependent variable the variable the experimenter measures to see how changes in the independent variable affect it. 51

deprenyl, 94

depression condition lasting most of the day, day after day, with a loss of interest or pleasure and a lack of productive activity. 606–7
  biological predisposition to, 607–8
  bipolar disorder, 612–13
  cancer and, 522
  cognitive aspects of, 608–11
  drug therapy for, 647–48
  eating disorders and, 461
  ECT and, 648–49
  learned helplessness and, 609–11
  MMPI and, 564
  risk factors in, 608
  seasonal affective disorder, 611, 612
  suicide and, 613–14

depth-of-processing principle principle that information may be stored at various levels, either superficially or deeply, depending on the number and type of associations formed with it. 330–31

depth perception the perception of distance. 168–70

descriptive statistics mathematical summaries of results, such as measures of the central score and the amount of variation. 61–65
  correlation coefficient, 49–50, 69
  measures of central score, 61–64
  measures of variation, 64–65, 68–69

determinism the view that all behavior has a physical cause. 5, 550

detour problem, 23, 24

detoxification supervised period to remove drugs from the body. 602

deuteranopia, 130–31

development
  of brain, 98, 99
  of intellect, 229–35
  of knowledge, 228
  of language, 235–38
  of learning, 223–23
  of memory, 222–23
  of moral reasoning, 238–42
  of muscle control, 220, 222
  of sensory organs, 220–22
  of social-emotional behavior, 245–57
  of thinking, 228
  of visual-motor coordination, 222

developmental psychology, 11

diabetes, 456

Diagnostic and Statistical Manual of Mental Disorders, Third Edition—Revised (DSM III-R) book that lists the acceptable labels for all psychological disorders with a description of each and guidelines on how to distinguish it from similar disorders. 580

dieting, 462–64

diffusion of responsibility tendency to feel less responsibility for helping when other people are around than when we know that no one else can help. 701

digestion, 455–56, 458–59

discounting principle tendency of people who have already made one attribution for some behavior to discount the likelihood of other possible causes of the behavior. 674–75

discrimination making different responses to different stimuli that have been followed by different outcomes; in operant conditioning, the learning of different behaviors

explicit memory test test in which a person has to state the correct answer, generally recognizing it as the correct answer. 338, 339

expression of emotions, 503–7

externality hypothesis hypothesis that overweight people are motivated more strongly by external cues (such as the taste and appearance of food) than by internal cues (the physiological mechanisms that control hunger). 461–62

external locus of control belief that external forces control the major events of one's life. 559–60

extinction in classical conditioning, the dying out of the conditioned response after repeated presentations of the conditioned stimulus unaccompanied by the unconditioned stimulus; in operant conditioning, the weakening of a response after a period of no reinforcement. 282, 296

extrasensory perception (ESP) the alleged ability of certain people to obtain information without using any sense organ and without receiving any form of energy. 37–40

extraversion tendency to seek new experiences and to enjoy the company of other people. 557

extrinsic motivation motivation based on the rewards and punishments an act may bring. 447–48, 449

eye movement, 186, 220–21, 402–3
eye structure, 120–21
eyewitness reports, 354–55

face recognition, 154–55
facial expressions, 503–7
factor analysis, 557
falsifiable capable of being contradicted by imaginable evidence. 35
familiar foods, 459–60
family
conflict in, 264–66
employment and, 255–56, 263–64
family therapy treatment provided for members of one family, generally meeting as a group. 640–41
farsightedness, 121, 122
father, as care giver, 264
fear, 493, 495–97, 499, 589
fear of failure a preoccupation with avoiding failure, rather than taking risks in order to succeed. 485
fear of success, 488
feature detector a neuron in the visual system of the brain that responds to particular lines or other features of a visual stimulus. 155–59, 163–64
femininity, 558–59
fetal alcohol syndrome a condition marked by decreased alertness and other signs of impaired development, caused by exposure to alcohol prior to birth. 219, 220
fetus an organism more developed than an embryo but not yet born (from about two months until birth in humans). 112, 475
fight-or-flight response, 100, 495, 508
figure and ground an object and its background. 160, 163
finger-to-nose test a test to assess possible damage to the cerebellum in which a person is asked to hold one arm straight out and then touch the nose as quickly as possible. 102

firstborn child, 251
first impressions, 668–69
fixation in Freud's theory, a persisting preoccupation with an immature psychosexual interest as a result of frustration at that stage of psychosexual development. 539, 540
fixed-interval schedule a rule for delivering reinforcement for the first response the subject makes after a specified period of time has passed. 305
fixed-ratio schedule a rule for delivering reinforcement only after the subject has made a certain number of responses. 304, 305
flight of ideas, 612
flooding or **implosion** a therapy for phobia in which the person is suddenly exposed to the object of the phobia. 593
fluctuation in scores, 431
fluid intelligence the basic power of reasoning and using information, including the ability to perceive relationships, deal with unfamiliar problems, and gain new types of knowledge. 415, 418
food selection, 458–60
foot-in-the-door technique method of eliciting compliance by first making a modest request and then following it with a much larger request. 712
forebrain the most anterior (forward) part of the brain, including the cerebral cortex and the limbic system. 98, 99
forewarning effect tendency of a brief preview of a message to decrease its persuasiveness. 692–93
forgetting, 282, 326–28. *See also* **amnesia; memory**
formal operations stage, 232–33
fovea the central part of the retina that consists solely of cones. 121, 122, 402
fraternal twins. *See* **dizygotic twins**
free association procedure in which a client lies on a couch, starts thinking about a particular symptom or problem, and then reports everything that comes to mind. 630–31
free-base cocaine, 210
free will the alleged ability of an individual to make decisions that are not determined by heredity, past experience, or the environment. 6
frequency of sound waves, 134
frequency principle identification of pitch by the frequency of action potentials in an auditory neuron axon, synchronized with the frequency of sound waves. 136
Freudian slip, 544–45
frontal lobe the anterior portion of each hemisphere of the cerebral cortex, containing the motor cortex and the prefrontal cortex. 105, 344
frowning, 503–4
frustration-aggression hypothesis the theory that frustration leads to aggressive behavior. 508
full moon, 50
functionalism an attempt to understand how mental processes produce useful behaviors. 22
fundamental attribution error tendency to overemphasize internal explanations of other people's behavior. 676

g Spearman's "general" factor that all IQ tests and all parts of an IQ test are believed to have in common. 414–15

GABA (gamma-aminobutyric acid) 94, 206, 646
galvanic skin response (GSR) a brief increase in the electrical conductivity of the skin, indicating increased arousal of the sympathetic nervous system. 497
gambler's fallacy belief that if a particular outcome has not occurred for a while, its "turn" has come. 389–90
gambling, 304, 386–90
ganglion cells neurons in the eye that receive input from the visual receptors and send impulses via the optic nerve to the brain. 125
gang violence, 210
gate theory a theory that pain messages have to pass through a gate in the spinal cord on their way to the brain and that messages from the brain can open or close that gate. 141
gender role the role each person is expected to play because of being male or female. 268–69, 270
androgyny and, 538–39
language and, 399–400
social learning and, 312
See also sex differences
gene a segment of a chromosome that indirectly controls development. 73–74
effects of, on human behavior, 76–80
evolution of, 80, 81
sex-linked and sex-limited, 76, 77
transmission of, 74–75
general adaptation syndrome condition characterized by weakness, fatigue, loss of appetite, and a general lack of interest. 514
generalizability of test results, 56–57
generalized anxiety disorder disorder in which people are constantly plagued by exaggerated worries. 586
generativity versus stagnation the conflict between a productive life and an unproductive life. 248
genetics
of alcoholism, 59, 77, 79
of Alzheimer's disease, 73
of autism, 624
of depression, 607
of emotional expression, 506
homosexuality and, 477
Huntington's disease and, 14
of intelligence, 435–38
principles of, 73–76
of schizophrenia, 620–21
genitals, 475, 539
genital stage Freud's final stage of psychosexual development, in which sexual pleasure is focused on sexual intimacy with others. 539, 540–41
genotype the entire set of genes within an individual. 79
Gestalt psychology an approach to psychology that seeks explanations of how we perceive overall patterns. 159
hearing principles, 163, 164
perceptual organization principles, 159–61, 164
Gestalt therapy treatment that deals with the person "as a whole," with emphasis on body language and the here-and-now. 638
giftedness, 527
glaucoma, 209
glia a cell of the nervous system that insulates neurons, removes waste materials (such as dead cells), and performs other supportive functions. 86

glucagon a hormone which the pancreas releases to convert stored energy supplies into glucose. 456

glucose the most abundant sugar in the blood, the main source of nutrition for the brain. 95, 330, 455–57

glutamate, 209

goal setting, 486

good figure in Gestalt psychology, the tendency to perceive simple, symmetrical figures. 161, 163

Graduate Record Exam (GRE), 430

grammatical rules, 237

graveyard shift, 182–83

gray matter, 102

GRE. *See* Graduate Record Exam

group decision making, 703–7

group polarization tendency for a group whose members lean in the same direction on a particular issue to become more extreme in its opinion after discussing the issue. 703

group therapy treatment administered to a group of people all at one time. 640

groupthink process in which the members of a group actively silence all dissenters and move quickly toward a poorly thought-out decision. 703–4

guilty-knowledge test a test that uses the polygraph to measure whether a person has information that only someone guilty of a certain crime could know. 498–99

gum chewing, 211

habituate to decrease a person's response to a stimulus when it is presented repeatedly. 222, 223

hair cells, 134, 135, 136

hallucination a sensory experience not corresponding to reality, such as seeing or hearing something that is not present or failing to see or hear something that is present. 202, 617, 618, 619

hallucinogens drugs that induce sensory distortions. 95, 211

haloperidol, 649

hammer, 134, 135

happiness, 493, 499, 509–10

"hard" determinism, 5–6

hassles, 517

Hawthorne effect the tendency for people's performance to improve not because of the independent variable but simply because they know a change has occurred in some procedure or because they know they are being observed. 55–56

health psychology field of psychology that deals with the ways in which people's behavior can enhance health and prevent illness and how behavior contributes to recovery from illness. 513

hearing
   of infants, 222
   localization of sound, 137–38
   pitch perception, 135–37
   structure of ear, 134–35
   threshold of, 150

hearing aids, 135

heart disease, 520

heart rate, 499

helplessness. *See* **learned-helplessness theory**

hemisphere the left or the right half of the brain. 102–5, 107–10, 111

heredity. *See* genetics; **nature-nurture issue**

heroin, 95, 101, 208, 599, 604

hertz (Hz) a unit of frequency representing one cycle per second. 135

heterozygous having different genes on a pair of chromosomes. 74, 75

heuristics strategies for simplifying a problem or for guiding an investigation. 376–77

hierarchy of needs Maslow's categorization of human motivations, ranging from basic physiological needs at the bottom to the need for self-actualization at the top. 450–51

high self-monitor person who constantly monitors his or her own behavior to try to make the right impression. 688–89

Hillside Strangler case, 204, 658

hindbrain the most posterior (hind) part of the brain, including the medulla, pons, and cerebellum. 98, 99, 101–2

hindsight bias tendency to mold our recollection of the past to fit the way later events turned out. 353–54

hippocampus forebrain structure believed to be important for certain aspects of memory. 342–43

Hispanics, in psychology, 13

history of psychology, 20–27

histrionic personality disorder, 582

homelessness, 658

homeostasis the maintenance of biological conditions within an organism at an optimum level. 446–47, 449

homosexuality, 470, 473, 474–77

homozygous having the same gene on both members of a pair of chromosomes. 74, 75

hormone a chemical released by a gland and conveyed by the blood to other parts of the body, where it alters activity. 101, 477–79

humanistic psychology a branch of psychology that emphasizes the capacity of people to make conscious decisions about their own lives. 549–52, 633–34

humanistic therapy, 633–34

Human Subjects Committee, 57

hunger
   motives in food selection, 458–60
   physiological mechanisms of, 454–58

Huntington's disease, 14, 528

hyperactivity, 581

hyperventilation deep breathing. 518, 587

hypnosis a condition of increased suggestibility that occurs in the context of a special hypnotist-subject relationship. 197
   age regression and, 32, 201, 202
   as altered state, 203–4
   crime and, 200, 201, 204
   faking, 203–4
   inducing, 197–98
   limits of, 201–2
   memory, and, 200–201
   pain and, 197, 199
   perception and, 202–3
   posthypnotic suggestions and, 199–200

hypochondriasis type of somatoform disorder in which a person exaggerates physical complaints or complains of ailments that a physician cannot detect. 583

hypothalamus, 101–102

hypothesis a testable prediction of what will happen under certain conditions. 33
   generating, 376–77
   premature commitment to, 381–82
   testing, 377

Hz. *See* **hertz**

"ice," 211

id according to Freud, the aspect of personality that consists of biological drives and demands for immediate gratification. 541

ideal self a person's image of what he or she would like to be. 550

identical twins. *See* **monozygotic twins**

identity achievement the deliberate choice of a role or identity. 252

identity crisis the search for self-understanding. 252

identity foreclosure the acceptance of a role that a person's parents prescribe. 252

identity versus role confusion the conflict between the sense of self and confusion over one's identity. 248

idiographic approach approach to the study of individual differences that concentrates on intensive studies of individuals. 554

idiosyncratic associations, 618

illness, stress and, 514, 515–16

illogical reasoning, 383–86

illusory correlation an apparent relationship between two variables based on casual observation, even though the variables are actually unrelated. 50, 266

imitation. *See* **modeling**

immigrants, test bias and, 433–34

immunization. *See* **inoculation**

implicit memory test test that does not require any conscious recognition of a memory. 338, 339

impression formation, 668–70

impulse control disorders, 581

incentive an external stimulus that prompts an action to obtain it. 447, 449

incongruence a mismatch between someone's self-concept and ideal self. 634

independent variable the variable the experimenter manipulates to see how it affects the dependent variable. 51

individual psychology the psychology of the person as an indivisible whole, as formulated by Adler. 548–49

induced movement a perception that an object is moving and the background is stationary when in fact the object is stationary and the background is moving. 166

industrial and organizational psychologist, 11

industry versus inferiority the conflict between feelings of accomplishment and feelings of worthlessness. 247–48

infancy
   attachment in, 249–50
   hearing in, 222
   inferring abilities of, 224–25
   intellectual development in, 224–25
   language development in, 235–37
   learning and memory in, 222–23
   sexuality in, 539
   social-emotional development in, 247
   temperament in, 262–63
   vision in, 220–21
   visual-motor control in, 222

infant amnesia relative lack of declarative memories from before about age 5 in humans. 346

inferential statistics statements about large groups based on inferences from small samples. 65–66

inferiority complex an exaggerated feeling of weakness, inadequacy, and helplessness. 548, 549

influenza, 622

information-processing model view that information is processed and coded in various ways in human memory as it is in a computer. 321–22

informed consent a subject's agreement to take part in an experiment after being informed about what will happen. 57

inhibition, 262–63

initiative versus guilt the conflict between independent behavior and behavior inhibited by guilt. 247, 248

injection procedure, 284

inkblots, 569, 570

inoculation (in the context of coping with stress) protection against the harmful effects of stress by earlier exposure to a small amount of it. 528

inoculation effect (in the context of persuasion) tendency of a persuasive message to be weakened if people first hear a weak argument for the same conclusion. 693

insanity defense, 658–60

insight, 378–79

insomnia difficulty in getting to sleep or in staying asleep. 182–83

instinctive behavior, 81, 445–46

institutionalized infants, 250–51

instrumental conditioning the process of changing behavior by following a response with reinforcement. 294

insulin a hormone which the pancreas releases to increase the entry of glucose and other nutrients into the cells. 455–57, 463

insulin shock, 646

intellect
  age and, 258
  developmental stages of, 229–35

intelligence, 412, 413–14
  in animals, 23–24
  early measures of, 24–25
  fluid and crystallized, 415, 418
  heredity, environment, and, 435–38
  multiple, 416–17, 418
  psychometric approach to, 414–15, 418
  triarchic theory of, 415–16, 418

intelligence quotient (IQ) a measure of an individual's probable performance in school and in similar settings. 419

intelligence testing, 413. *See also* IQ tests

interference competition among related memories. 326, 328, 330

internal locus of control belief that one is largely in control of the major events of one's life. 559–60

internships, 10

interpersonal attraction
  lasting relationships, 684–87
  romantic and passionate love, 681–84
  short-term, casual affiliations, 680

interpersonal influence
  conformity, 698–700
  group decision making, 703–6
  responsibility for others, 700–702

interpretation a therapist's explanation of the underlying meaning of what a client says. 631

intimacy, 685

intimacy versus isolation the conflict between establishing a long-term relationship with another person and remaining alone. 248

intrinsic motivation motivation to engage in an act for its own sake. 447–48, 449

introversion, 557

IQ tests, 246, 418–19
  aptitude versus achievement, 424–25
  bias in, 432–40
  evaluation of, 428–30
  future tests, 425
  group differences in scores on, 432
  Progressive Matrices, 422
  race and, 432, 434–35, 438–39
  Scholastic Aptitude Test, 423–24
  standardization of, 427–28
  Stanford-Binet test, 419–21
  Wechsler tests, 421–22

iris the colored structure on the surface of the eye, surrounding the pupil. 120, 121

James-Lange theory the theory that emotion is merely our perception of autonomic changes and movements evoked directly by various stimuli. 499–500, 502

Japanese, elderly and, 528–59

jet lag, 182

job applicants, 566–67, 572

job satisfaction, 256–57

juries, 704–7

kin selection selection for a gene that benefits one's relatives. 80, 83

kittiwake, evolution and, 81–82

knowledge-acquisition components, 416

Korsakoff's syndrome condition caused by prolonged deficiency of vitamin B_1, which results in both retrograde amnesia and anterograde amnesia. 95, 344

Laboratory Animal Care Committee, 59

lactose, 78–79

language, 392
  in chimpanzees, 393–96
  development of, 229, 235–38
  nonhuman precursors to, 392–96
  reading and, 401–8
  thought and, 397–400
  understanding, 400–401

latah, 578

latent content the hidden content of a dream that is represented only symbolically in the actual experience. 631

latent period according to Freud, a period in which psychosexual interest is suppressed or dormant. 539, 540

lateral hypothalamus an area of the brain that contributes to the control of hunger. 455–57

lateral line system, 134

law of effect Thorndike's theory that a response that is followed by favorable consequences becomes more probable and a response that is followed by unfavorable consequences becomes less probable. 294

L-DOPA, 94, 95

leaf fish, sociobiology and, 82

learned aggression, 509–10

learned-helplessness theory theory that some people become depressed because they have learned that they have no control over the major events in their lives. 609–11

learning
  classical conditioning and, 277–91
  in infancy, 222–23
  operant conditioning and, 293–309
  social, 311–14
  while asleep, 190–91

learning curve, 294

left hemisphere of brain, 102–3, 104, 110–11

lens a structure that varies its thickness to enable the eye to focus on objects at different distances. 120, 121

lesbians, 476

libido according to Sigmund Freud, a kind of sexual energy. 445, 538–39

Librium, 646

Lidocaine, 209

lie-detector test, 497–99

light detection, 119
  dark adaptation, 124–25
  eye structure and, 120–21
  visual pathways, 125–26
  visual receptors for, 121–23

light waves, 119, 126–27

Likert scale, 688, 689

lion, sociobiology and, 82

list organization, 330, 331

lithium, 649

lobes, of cerebral cortex, 102–5

lobotomy. *See* **prefrontal lobotomy**

localization of sound, 137–38

locus of control, 559–60

logical reasoning, 232–33, 376–78

longitudinal study a study of a single group of individuals over time. 245–46

long-term memory a relatively permanent store of information. 323–24
  interference with, 326–27
  transfer from short-term memory to, 328–30

loose associations, 618

lotteries, 387, 388, 389

loudness a perception closely related to the amplitude of sound waves. 134, 143

love, 493, 684–87

LSD. *See* **lysergic acid diethylamide**

ludus love, 685

lysergic acid diethylamide (LSD) a chemical that can affect the brain, sometimes producing hallucinations. 95, 207, 211

magic tricks, 38, 40

mainstreaming, 428

maintenance insomnia trouble staying asleep, with a tendency to awaken briefly but frequently. 193

mania condition in which people are constantly active, uninhibited, and either happy or angry. 612–13

mania love, 685

manic-depressive disorder, 606, 612–13, 649

manifest content the content that appears on the surface of a dream. 631

MAOIs. *See* **monoamine oxidase inhibitors**

marijuana, 208–9

marriage, 255–56, 269

masculinity, 558–59

mastectomy, 530–31

masturbation, 471, 472

maturation. *See* development

mean the sum of all the scores reported in a study divided by the number of scores. 61–62

meaningfulness ability of a given item to fit into a known pattern of information. 348

mechanoreceptors receptors that respond to mechanical stimulation.

media, 661

median the middle score in a list of scores aranged from highest to lowest. 62

medical therapies, 645
  electroconvulsive shock, 648–49
  rationale for, 645–46
  See also drug therapy

laws about how some aspect of personality affects behavior, often based on statistical comparisons of large groups of people. 554

nonexpert performance, 16

non-REM (NREM) sleep all stages of sleep other than REM sleep. 186, 188

nonsense syllable a meaningless three-letter combination. 319–21

nontraditional family, 263–65

nonverbal communication, 669

norepinephrine, 91, 94, 209

normal distribution a symmetrical frequency of scores produced by many factors, each of which produces small, random variations. 61

norms descriptions of the frequencies at which particular scores occur. 427

Novocain, 209

nursing, 12, 509

nutrition, fetal, 218

obesity the excessive accumulation of body fat. 461, 462

object permanence the concept that an object continues to exist even when one does not see, hear, or otherwise sense it. 224

observational studies
case history, 45, 46
correlational study, 46, 48–52
naturalistic observation, 45–46
survey, 46–48

obsession a repetitive, unwelcome stream of thought. 593–94

obsessive-compulsive disorder condition marked by repetitive thoughts and actions. 593–96

occipital lobe the rear portion of each hemisphere of the cerebral cortex, critical for vision. 103

odor. *See* **olfaction**

Oedipus complex according to Freud, a young boy's sexual interest in his mother accompanied by competitive aggression toward his father. 540

old age, 94, 248, 258, 347

olfaction the sense of smell, the detection of chemicals in contact with the membranes inside the nose. 144–47

olfactory bulb, 102

onset insomnia trouble falling asleep. 193

openness to experience tendency to enjoy new experiences, especially intellectual experiences, the arts, fantasies, and anything that exposes the person to new ideas. 557

operant conditioning the process of changing behavior by following a response with reinforcement. 293–94
applications of, 306–9
basic concepts in, 294–97
classical conditioning versus, 294–95, 297
frequency of responses in, 299–306
shaping of responses in, 297–99

operation according to Piaget, a mental process that can be reversed. 229

operational definition a definition that specifies the procedures used to measure some variable or to produce some phenomenon. 43

opiates drugs derived from the opium poppy or drugs that produce effects similar to those of opium derivatives. 207–8
addiction to, 604–5
effects of, 15, 207–8
overdose of, 101
withdrawal from, 211, 212

opponent-process principle of emotions principle that the removal of a stimulus that excites one emotion causes a swing to an opposite emotion. 496–97

opponent-process theory (of color vision) the theory that we perceive color in terms of a system of paired opposites: red versus green, yellow versus blue, and white versus black. 127–28

optical illusion a misinterpretation of a visual stimulus as being larger or smaller or straighter or more curved than it really is. 171

optic nerve a set of axons that extend from the ganglion cells of the eye to the thalamus and several other areas of the brain. 109–10, 125

oral stage Freud's first stage of psychosexual development, in which psychosexual pleasure is focused on the mouth. 539

orgasm, 470–71, 474

otolith organs, 138–39

overcorrection, 121

overjustification effect tendency for people who are given a great deal of extrinsic motivation to experience a decline in their intrinsic motivation. 448–49

overweight, 461

***p* < .05** an expression meaning that the probability of accidentally getting results equal to the reported results is less than 5%. 66

pain, 99–100, 140–41
depression and, 608
drugs and, 207, 208, 209
hypnosis and, 197, 199

pancreas, 455

panic disorder disorder characterized by a fairly constant state of moderate anxiety and occasional attacks of sudden increased heart rate, chest pains, difficulty in breathing, sweating, faintness, and shaking. 586–87

paradoxical intervention procedure in which a psychologist tells a person to do something but gives an undesirable reason for doing it in hopes that the person will want to stop. 638–39

paradoxical sleep, 186

parallel play simultaneous but independent play, common in young children. 251

paranoia, 582

paranoid schizophrenia type of schizophrenia characterized by the basic symptoms plus strong or elaborate hallucinations and delusions. 619

paraquat, 95

parasympathetic nervous system a system of neurons located at the top and bottom of the spinal cord; the neurons send messages to the internal organs that prepare the body for digestion and related processes. 100, 495–96

parental behavior, 264–65

parietal lobe a portion of each hemisphere of the cerebral cortex that is essential for touch, for perception of one's own body, and to some extent for voluntary movement. 103–4

Parkinson's disease a disease caused by the deterioration of a path of axons using dopamine as their neurotransmitter, characterized by difficulty in initiating voluntary movement. 93–95, 112

parrots, language development in, 396

parsimony literally, stinginess; the avoidance of new theoretical assumptions. 36

partial brain transplant, 112

partial reinforcement reinforcement for some responses and not others. 304, 305

partial-reinforcement extinction effect the tendency for extinction to occur more slowly on either a ratio or an interval schedule than on a schedule of continuous reinforcement. 305

partner selection, 254–55

passionate love, 684–87

pattern recognition, 154–55
expert, 374–75
feature-detector approach, 155–59, 163–64
Gestalt psychology approach, 159–64
preattentive and attentive vision processes, 164

Pavlovian conditioning. *See* **classical conditioning**

PCP, 121

peak experience an experience that brings fulfillment, contentment, and peace. 550

peg method, 342

penis envy, 540

perception the interpretation of the meaning of sensory information. 118
of depth, 168–70
of distance, 137–38
hypnosis and, 202–3
of location, 137–38
of minimal stimuli, 149–54
of movement, 165–67
of pattern, 155–64, 374–75
subliminal, 151–54

peremptory challenge rejection of a prospective juror by an attorney without explanation. 705

performance components, 416

peripheral nervous system the nerves that convey messages from the sense organs to the central nervous system and from the central nervous system to the muscles and glands. 97–98

peripheral route to persuasion method of persuasion based on such superficial factors as the speaker's appearance and reputation or the sheer number of arguments presented, regardless of their quality. 689

peripheral vision, 122

perpetual motion machine, 377

personal fable, 252–53, 257, 530

personality all the stable, consistent ways in which the behavior of one person differs from that of others. 536
collective unconscious and, 546–48
humanistic psychology and, 549–51
individual psychology and, 548–49
objective tests of, 564–67
origins of, 535–36
projective tests of, 567–71
psychoanalysis and, 536–46
standardized tests of, 563
test uses and misuses, 571–72
traits and states, 554–57

personality disorder a maladaptive, inflexible way of dealing with the environment and other people. 580–82

personality profile a graph that shows an individual's scores on scales measuring a number of personality traits. 567

personality researcher, 11

personal unconsciousness, 546

person-centered therapy (also known as *nondirective* or *client-centered therapy*) procedure in which a therapist listens to the client sympathetically, provides unconditional positive regard, and offers little interpretation or advice. 634

persuasion, 306–7, 689–93

phallic stage Freud's third stage of psychosexual development, in which psychosexual interest in focused on the penis or clitoris. 539–40

phenotype the actual appearance of the individual, reflecting the way the genes have been expressed. 79

phenylalanine, 80

phenylketonuria (PKU) an inherited disorder in which a person cannot break down phenylalanine, a common constituent of the diet; unless the diet is carefully controlled, the affected person becomes mentally retarded. 79–80

pheromone an odorous chemical released by an animal that changes the way other members of its species respond to it socially. 145–47

phi effect the illusion of movement created when two or more stationary lights flash on and off at regular intervals. 167

phobia a fear so extreme that it interferes with normal living. 588–93

phoneme a unit of sound. 405

photon, 121

photopigment a chemical that releases energy when struck by light and thereby enables rods and cones to respond to light. 130

physical attractiveness, 254, 668, 682–83

physiological arousal, 493–99

physiological basis of hunger, 454–58

physiological psychologist, 11

pibloqtoq, 578

pigeons, 306

pinwheel illusion, 156

pitch a perception closely related to the frequency of sound waves. 134

PKU. *See* **phenylketonuria**

placebo an inactive pill that has no known biological effect on the subjects in an experiment. 45

place principle identification of pitch by which auditory neurons, coming from which part of the basilar membrane, are most active. 136

plateau, 414

polygraph a machine that simultaneously measures heart rate, breathing rate, blood pressure, and galvanic skin response. 497–99

pons a structure adjacent to the medulla that receives sensory input from the head and controls many muscles in the head. 101

positive reinforcement the presentation of a favorable event. 299, 301

positive symptoms characteristics present in people with schizophrenia and absent in others—such as hallucinations, delusions, abnormal movements, and thought disorder. 618

positron-emission tomography, 7–8

posthypnotic suggestion a suggestion made to hypnotized subjects that they will do something or experience something particular after coming out of hypnosis. 199–200

postpartum depression period of depression some women experience shortly after giving birth. 608

postsynaptic neuron a neuron on the receiving end of a synapse. 90, 91

posttraumatic stress disorder (PTSD) condition in which people who have endured extreme stress feel prolonged anxiety and depression. 514–15, 518

pragma love, 685

preattentive process a procedure that occurs automatically and simultaneously across a large portion of the visual field. 164

precognition, 37

predictability. *See* **contingency**

prediction
  and control of stressful events, 526–28
  of violent behavior, 509

predictive validity ability of a test's scores to predict some real-world performance. 430, 431

predisposition
  to alcoholism, 77, 79, 577
  to depression, 607–8
  to schizophrenia, 620–21
  to suicide, 614
  to violent behavior, 508–9

prefrontal cortex the most anterior portion of the frontal lobe, critical for planning movements and for certain cognitive functions. 105, 344

prefrontal lobotomy an operation in which part of the prefrontal cortex is damaged or in which the connections are cut between the prefrontal cortex and other brain areas. 105–6

pregnancy, 218–19

prejudice schema or prejudgment about a large category of people, such as an ethnic group. 670–73

Premack principle the principle that the opportunity to engage in a frequent behavior will reinforce a less frequent behavior. 302

premarital questionnaire, 255

premature ejaculation, 474

prenatal before birth. 218–20

preoperational stage according to Piaget, the second stage of intellectual development, in which children lack the concept of conservation. 229–32, 233

preschool child, 247, 248

presynaptic ending, 90, 91

preventive detention practice of involuntarily committing psychologically disturbed people to a mental hospital to prevent them from committing crimes. 656

primacy effect tendency to be influenced more by the first information learned about someone than by later information about the same person. 668

primary motivation motivation that serves a biological need. 449–50

primary motor cortex a strip of cerebral cortex in the rear of the frontal lobe, critical for fine control of the muscles. 105

primary prevention preventing a disorder from starting. 660

primary reinforcer an event that satisfies a biological need. 303

primary somatosensory cortex a strip of cerebral cortex in the parietal lobe that is specialized for touch and related information. 104

principle of antithesis, 507–8

prisoners, 184

prisoner's dilemma situation in which people have to choose between an act beneficial to themselves but harmful to others, and an act that is moderately beneficial to all. 710–11

proactive interference the hindrance an older memory produces on a newer one. 326

problem solving, 376
  creative, 380–81
  errors in, 381–86
  expert, 375
  generalizing solutions, 378
  generating hypotheses, 376–77
  insightful, 379–80
  testing hypotheses, 377
  understanding and simplifying, 376

procedural memory retention of learned skills. 333, 343

Progressive Matrices an IQ test that attempts to measure abstract reasoning without use of language or recall of facts. 422–23

projection the attribution of one's own undesirable characteristics to other people. 543

projective tests, 567–69
  Rorschach Inkblot Test, 569–70
  Thematic Apperception Test, 570–71

protanopia, 130–31

prototype a highly typical member of a category. 368

proximate cause stimulus that prompts a behavior. 81

proximity in Gestalt psychology, the tendency to perceive objects that are close together as belonging to a group. 161, 163

proximity in social behavior, the tendency to choose as friends people with whom we come in frequent contact. 681–82

Prozac, 648

psychiatric will, 656–57

psychiatry the branch of medicine that specializes in identifying and treating psychological disorders. 10

psychics, 32, 38–39

psychoanalysis Freud's approach to personality, based on the interplay of conscious and unconscious forces. 537–38, 629–32.

psychoanalyst therapist who relies heavily on the theories of Sigmund Freud. 10

psychodynamic theory a theory that relates personality to the interplay of conflicting forces within the individual, including some that are unconscious. 536

psychodynamic therapies treatments that attempt to unravel people's underlying drives and motivations. 629

psychogenic fugue condition in which peple wander about, sometimes over great distances, lose track of their identity, and perhaps assume a new name. 583

psychokinesis, 37

psychological disorders
  anxiety, 586–88
  autism, 622–24
  avoidance, 588–96
  bipolar, 606, 612–13, 649
  classifications of, 579–82
  depression, 461, 522, 564, 608–14
  examples of Axis 1 disorders, 582–84
  legal issues in treatment of, 656–58
  prevalence of, 579
  schizophrenia, 570–72, 616–22, 649–51
  seasonal affective disorder, 611
  substance abuse, 598–99
  suicide, 241, 613–14, 661

psychology the systematic study of behavior and experience. 5
  approaches to, 13–17
  branches of, 10–12
  free will versus determinism, 5–7
  history of, 20–27

mind-brain problem, 7–9
nature-nurture issue, 9
occupational settings in, 12
research designs in, 45–54
research principles in, 42–45
scientific method and, 33–40
women and minorities in, 12–13, 25

psychometric the measurement of individual differences in abilities and behaviors. 414, 418

psychophysical function mathematical description of the relationship between the physical properties of a stimulus and its perceived properties. 23

psychosexual development in Freud's theory, progression through a series of developmental periods, each with a characteristic psychosexual focus that leaves its mark on adult personality. 539–41

psychosexual pleasure according to Freud, any enjoyment arising from stimulation of part of the body. 538

psychosomatic illness an illness that is influenced by a person's experiences or by his or her reactions to those experiences. 518

psychotherapist professional who provides help for troubled people. 10

psychotherapy treatment of psychological disorders by methods that generally include a personal relationship between a trained therapist and a client. 629
behavior therapy, 634–36
effectiveness of, 641–43
group therapy, 640–41
humanistic therapy, 633–34
less common forms of, 637–39
psychoanalysis, 537–38, 629–32
thought and belief therapies, 632–33
trends in, 639–40

puberty the time of onset of sexual maturation. 253, 540–41

punishment an event that decreases the probability that the preceding response will be repeated in the future. 300–301

pupil the opening in the eye through which light enters. 120, 121

pursuit eye movements the movements necessary for keeping one's eyes focusing on a moving object. 621

quantitative psychologist a psychologist who measures individual differences in behavior and applies statistical procedures to analyze those measurements. 13–14

race differences
in academic achievement, 271
in death scruples, 705
in food selection, 78–79, 459–60
in IQ tests, 432, 434–35, 438–39
in personality tests, 566
in self-esteem, 271
See also minority groups
racial prejudice, 670–73
radial keratotomy, 121

random assignment a chance procedure for assigning subjects to groups such that every subject has the same probability as any other of being assigned to a particular group. 52

random sample a group of people picked in such a way that every individual in the population has an equal chance of being selected. 44

range a statement of the highest and lowest scores in a distribution of scores. 64

rape sexual contact obtained through violence, threats, or intimidation. 480–81

rapid eye movement (REM) sleep a stage of sleep characterized by rapid eye movements, a high level of brain activity, and deep relaxation of the postural muscles; also known as paradoxical sleep. 186, 187, 188–91

rational-emotive therapy treatment based on the assumption that people's emotions depend on their "internal sentences" such as "I can't be happy unless everyone thinks my room is clean." 632

rationalization attempting to prove that one's actions are rational and justifiable and thus worthy of approval. 543

rats
alcohol tolerance of, 212
brain damage in, 113
chaining, 299
classical conditioning of, 286–88, 289, 290
in mazes, 26–27
obesity in, 461
operant conditioning of, 297–98, 299
punishment of, 300–301
sexual orientation of, 477–78

Raven's Progressive Matrices, 422–23

rCBF. *See* **regional cerebral blood flow technique**

reaction formation presenting oneself as the opposite of what one really is in an effort to reduce anxiety. 543–44

reactive depression depression that develops suddenly in reaction to a severe loss. 606

reading, 401–2
connectionist model of, 404–5
eye movement and, 402–3
good and poor readers, 407–8
role of sound in, 405–6
Stroop effect of, 406
word-superiority effect of, 403–4

reasoning, 232–33, 376–79

rebound effect. *See* **opponent-process theory**

recall method of testing memory by asking someone to produce a certain item (such as a word). 337, 338, 339

receptor a specialized cell that responds to a particular form of energy and conveys its response to other cells in the nervous system. 119

recessive gene a gene that will affect development only in a person who is homozygous for that gene. 74

recognition method of testing memory by asking someone to choose the correct item from a set of alternatives. 338, 339

reconstruction putting together an account of past events, based partly on memories and partly on expectations of what must have happened. 350–51

red-green color blindness the inability to distinguish between red and green. 130–32

reductionism the attempt to explain complex phenomena in terms of simpler components or events. 86, 550

reference memory memory for general principles and events of long ago. 332, 333

reflex an automatic response to a stimulus. 98–100

regional cerebral blood flow technique (rCBF) a technique for estimating the level of activity in an area of the brain by dissolving radioactive xenon in the blood and measuring the radioactivity emitted in that area. 107

regression the return to a more juvenile level of functioning as a means of reducing anxiety or in response to emotionally trying circumstances. 543

reinforcement an event that increases the probability that the response that preceded it will be repeated in the future. 294, 295, 296–97, 298, 299–300, 301–5

relationships
brief, 680
long-lasting, 681–84
romantic, 684–87

relaxation, 525–26

relearning method. *See* **savings method**

reliability repeatability of a test's scores. 429–30, 431, 570, 571

REM sleep. *See* **rapid eye movement sleep**

repair and restoration theory the theory that the purpose of sleep is to enable the body to recover from the wear and tear of the day. 183, 185

replicable result a result that can be repeated (at least approximately) by any competent investigator who follows the original procedure. 34–35

representativeness heuristic the tendency to assume that if an item is similar to members of a particular category, it is probably a member of that category itself. 382–84

representative sample a selection of the population chosen to match the overall population with regard to specific variables. 44

repression motivated forgetting; the relegation of unacceptable impulses or memories to the unconscious. 542–43

research
design varieties, 42–54
ethics in, 57–59
generalizability of, 56–57
problems in, 54–56
principles of conducting, 42–45

resistance second stage of response to stress, a stage of prolonged but moderate arousal. 514

resistance in psychoanalysis, continued repression that interferes with therapy. 631

resolution, 474

retardation, 427–28, 582

reticular formation a diffuse set of neurons, extending from the medulla into the forebrain, that is largely responsible for variations in the level of arousal of the brain. 101

retina the rear surface of the eye, lined with visual receptors. 109, 120, 121

retinal disparity the difference in the apparent position of an object as seen by the left retina and by the right retina. 168

retinex theory the theory that color perception results from the cerebral cortex's comparison of various retinal patterns. 129–30

retirement, 259

retrieval cue, 323

retroactive interference the impairment a newer memory produces on an older one. 326

retrograde amnesia loss of memory for events that occurred shortly prior to brain damage. 343

reversible figure a stimulus that you can perceive in more than one way. 160–61, 163

right hemisphere of brain, 102–3, 110

right to refuse treatment, 656

rod the type of visual receptor that is adapted for dim light. 121, 122–23

role diffusion experimentation with various roles or identities. 252

romantic love, 684–87

Rorschach Inkblot Test a projective personality test in which people are shown 10 inkblots and asked what each might be. 569–70

running amok, 578

s a "specific" factor that is more important for performance on some scales of an intelligence test than it is on others. 415

saccade a quick jump in the focus of the eyes from one point to another. 402

salivation, 279, 280

salt deficiency, 459

salt taste preference, 459

SAT. *See* **Scholastic Aptitude Test**

satanic messages, 153

satiety the experience of being full, of feeling no more hunger. 457–58

savant, 416

savings method or **relearning method** method of testing memory by measuring how much faster someone can relearn something learned in the past than something being learned for the first time. 338, 339

scatterplot, 49

Schachter and Singer's theory of emotions theory that emotions are our interpretation of autonomic arousal in light of all the information we have about ourselves and the situation. 500–503

schedule of reinforcement a rule for the delivery of reinforcement following various patterns of responding. 304, 388–89

schema (plural: schemata) in Piaget's theory, an organized way of interacting with objects in the world. 228

schema in memory, a series of expectations used to guide one's reconstruction of events. 351

schemas in social cognition, impressions or expectations about a particular type of people. 670

schizophrenia condition marked by deterioration of daily activities over a period of at least six months, plus either hallucinations, delusions, flat or inappropriate emotions, certain movement disorders, or thought disorders. 616

causes of, 619–22, 651

drug therapy for, 649–51

identifying, 570, 571–72

symptoms of, 616–18

types of, 618–19

Scholastic Aptitude Test (SAT) a test of students' likelihood of performing well in college. 423–25

school psychologist, 11

scientific method

basic steps in, 33–34

ethical considerations, 57–59

generalizability, 56–57

measuring and representing results, 61–66, 68, 69

principle of parsimony, 36–40

psychology research designs, 45–54

replicability, 34–35

research principles, 42–45

theory evaluation, 35

varieties of research design, 45–54

why experiments go wrong, 54–56

scripts rules of social behavior governing who will do what and when. 555

seasonal affective disorder condition in which people become seriously depressed every winter, when the amount of sunlight per day is short. 611

season of birth effect tendency for people born in the winter months to be slightly more likely than other people are to develop schizophrenia. 622

secondary gain indirect benefits from a disorder, such as the attention and sympathy of others and an excuse for avoiding unpleasant activities. 583

secondary motivation motivation that serves no direct biological need but develops as a result of specific experiences. 449–50

secondary prevention identifying a disorder in its early stages and preventing it from becoming more serious. 660

secondary reinforcer an event that becomes reinforcing when it is associated with a primary reinforcer. 303, 304

sedatives. *See* **tranquilizers**

selective attrition the tendency for some kinds of people to be more likely than others to drop out of a study. 56

selective memory, 348–50

selective reporting tendency for investigators to be more likely to publish findings when they match predictions than when they do not. 432

self-actualization the achievement of one's full potential, or the need to achieve one's full potential. 451, 550, 551

self-actualized personality, 551–52

self-concept a person's image of what he or she really is. 550

self-efficacy the perception of one's own ability to perform a task successfully. 314

self-esteem

attribution and, 677–78

in cancer victims, 530–31

of elderly, 258–59

of minority-group children, 271–72

self-fulfilling prophecy, 55

self-handicapping strategies techniques for protecting self-esteem by creating external causes as decoy excuses for failures. 677

self-help groups, 641

self-perception theory theory that subjects in dissonance experiments are simply trying to attribute their behavior to reasonable causes. 696

self-serving biases attributions people adopt in an effort to maximize their credit for success and minimize their blame for failure. 677

semantic memory memory for factual information. 332, 333

semicircular canal, 138, 139

senility, 87

sensation the conversion of energy from the environment into a pattern of response by the nervous system. 118

action potential and, 89–90

chemical senses, 142–47

color vision, 126–32

early studies of, 22–23

hearing, 134–38

light detection, 119–26

mechanical stimulation, 138–41

sensorimotor stage according to Piaget, the first stage of intellectual development, in

which an infant's behavior is limited to making simple motor responses to sensory stimuli. 229, 233

sensory adaptation the tendency of a sensory threshold to fall after a period when the sensory receptors have not been stimulated and to rise after exposure to intense stimuli. 150

sensory deprivation temporary reduction of visual, auditory, and other stimulation of senses. 54–55

sensory neuron a neuron that conveys sensory information to the central nervous system. 98, 99

sensory store a very brief storage of sensory information. 322, 323

sensory threshold the minimum intensity at which an individual can detect a sensory stimulus 50% of the time; a low threshold indicates ability to detect faint stimuli. 150–51

serial-order effect tendency to remember the first and last items on a list better than those in the middle. 350

serotonin a neurotransmitter that plays an important role in sleep and mood changes. 94, 95

serotonin reuptake blockers drugs that block the reuptake of the neurotransmitter serotonin by the terminal button. 647

set point a level of some variable (such as weight) that the body attempts to maintain. 458, 463

sex chromosomes the chromosomes that determine whether an individual will develop as a female or as a male. 76

sex differences

in aggressive behavior, 269

in anorexia nervosa, 465

in behavior, 266–67

in dating behavior, 254–55

in depression, 606

in desire to be thin, 464–68

in detecting emotions, 503

in employment opportunities, 255–56

in gender roles, 268–69

genetics of, 76

in identity foreclosure, 252

in intellectual abilities, 432, 433

in moral reasoning, 242

in need for achievement, 487–88

olfaction and, 146–47

in panic disorder, 586

in personality, 558–59

in phobias, 589

in psychology careers, 12–13

in reaction to divorce, 264–65

in sexual behavior, 83, 253–54, 470–71, 474

in social behavior, 267–68

social expectations and, 16

social learning and, 312

in suicide attempts, 613–14

See also women in psychology

sex-limited gene a gene that exerts its effects on one sex only or on one sex more than on the other, even though both sexes have the gene. 76

sex-linked gene a gene situated on the X chromosome. 76

sexual abuse, 480, 538

sexual arousal, 473–74

sexual behavior

adolescent, 253–54

identity and orientation, 474–79

rape, 480–81
variability of, in humans, 470–73
sexual fantasies, 35, 473–74
sexual identity the sex a person regards himself or herself as being. 474–75
sexual orientation a person's preference for male or female sex partners. 474–75
shaping a technique for establishing a new response by reinforcing successive approximations to it. 297–98
shift work, 182–83
short-term memory the particular subset of information someone is dealing with at the moment. 323–24
characteristics of, 324–26
decay in, 327–28
forgetting in, 326, 328
interference with, 328
transfer to long-term memory, 329–31
shyness, 555–56
siblings, 251
sight. *See* vision
signal-detection theory the study of people's tendencies to make correct judgments, misses, and false alarms. 150
sign language, 238, 393
similarity in Gestalt psychology, the tendency to perceive related objects as belonging to a group. 161, 163
similarity principle tendency to associate with people similar to oneself. 683
single-blind study a study in which either the observer or the subjects are unaware of which subjects received one treatment and which received another treatment. 45
16-PF TEST a standardized personality test that measures 16 personality traits. 567, 568
skeletal pertaining to the muscles that move the limbs, trunk, and head. 294–95
Skinner box, 297
sleep
abnormalities, 193–95, 606
cycles, 182, 186–87
depression and, 606
deprivation, 183–84
dreams and, 186, 187–88, 191–93
memory and, 190–91
reasons for, 183, 184–85
schedules for, 182–83
stages, 185–87
sleep apnea a condition in which a person has trouble breathing while asleep. 194
sleeper effect delayed persuasion by an initially rejected message. 690
sleep talking, 194
sleepwalking, 194–95
slips of the tongue, 544–45
smell. *See* **olfaction**
smoking. *See* cigarettes; nicotine
social cognition the process of combining and remembering information about others and making inferences based on that information. 669
impression formation, 669–70
prejudice and, 670–73
schematic information processing, 669
social-emotional development
in adolescence, 252–54
in adulthood, 254–59
in childhood, 251–52
Erikson's ages of, 247–49
in infancy, 247, 249–50
in middle adulthood, 256–58

in old age, 258–59
research designs for, 245–47
in young adulthood, 254–56
social interest a sense of solidarity and identification with other people. 548–49
social isolation, 250–51
social-learning approach the view that people learn by observing and imitating the behavior of others and by imagining the consequences of their own behavior. 311–15
social loafing tendency to "loaf" (or work less hard) when sharing the work with other people. 701
social perception, 667
attribution and, 673–78
cognition and, 669–73
first impressions, 668–69
social psychologist a psychologist who studies social behavior and how an individual's behavior is influenced by other people. 16
Social Readjustment Rating Scale, 515, 516
social support, 522, 528–29, 608
sociobiology a field that tries to explain the social behaviors of animals in terms of their survival and reproductive advantages. 82–84
sociopathic personality, 582
sodium ion, 89–90
"soft" determinism, 6
somatic nervous system the nerves that control the muscles. 98
somatization disorder condition in which a person experiences a long series of diverse ailments that have no apparent medical basis. 583
somatoform disorder condition in which a person has physical symptoms that seem to have no medical cause. 581, 582–83
somatosensory system. *See* **cutaneous senses**
Son of Sam case, 658–59
sound, reading and, 405
sound localization, 137–38, 295
sound waves vibrations of the air or of some other medium. 134, 135
SPAR method, 408
species differences
in brain, 87, 88, 99
in cutaneous senses, 140
in embryos, 218, 219
in hearing, 136
in intelligence, 23
in language, 392–96
in learning, 277–78
in maturity at birth, 218
in olfaction, 144–45
in recovery from brain damage, 113
in sexual motivation, 469
in sleep, 181, 184–85, 186
in vision, 119, 121, 122, 123
species-specific behavior a particular behavior that is widespread in one animal species but not in others. 81
speech. *See* language
speed reading, 403
spinal cord the part of the central nervous system that communicates with sense organs and muscles below the level of the head. 98, 99, 500
split brain, 107–11
spontaneous firing, 90
spontaneous recovery the return of an extinguished response after a delay. 283
spontaneous remission improvement of a psychological condition without therapy. 641

squirrels, hibernation of, 181
stage of concrete operations according to Piaget, the third stage of intellectual development, in which children can deal with the properties of concrete objects but cannot readily deal with hypothetical or abstract questions. 232, 233
stage of formal operations according to Piaget, the fourth and final stage of intellectual development, in which people use logical, deductive reasoning and systematic planning. 232–33
stages
of adjustment to dying, 259, 260
of intellectual development, 228–33
of language development, 235–38
of moral reasoning development, 239–42
of psychosexuality, 538–41
of romantic relationships, 684–87
of sleep, 185–88
of social-emotional development, 247–48
standard deviation a measurement of the amount of variation among scores in a normal distribution. 64–65, 68
standard error of the mean, 68
standardization the process of establishing rules for administering a test and for interpreting its scores. 427
standardized test a test that is administered according to specified rules and whose scores are interpreted in a prescribed fashion. 563
Stanford-Binet IQ test a test of intelligence, the first important IQ test in the English language. 419–21, 427, 429, 430
starling, sociobiology and, 82
state a temporary activation of a particular behavior. 554
statistically significant results results that have a low probability of having arisen by chance. 66
statistics
calculations, 68–69
descriptive, 61–65
inferential, 65–66
stereotype schema or prejudgment about a large category of people, such as an ethnic group. 670–71
stickleback fish, breeding habits of, 81, 446
stimulant drugs, 194, 206, 209–10
stimulus an energy in the environment that can influence action. 119
stimulus generalization the extension of a learned response from the training stimulus to similar stimuli; in operant conditioning, the tendency to make a similar response to a stimulus that resembles one that has been associated with reinforcement. 283–84, 296
stimulus-response (S-R) psychology, 278
stirrup, 134, 135
storge love, 685
stress according to Selye, the nonspecific response of the body to any demand made upon it; according to Lazarus, a situation that someone regards as threatening and as possibly exceeding his or her resources. 513–14
alcohol and, 601
biofeedback and, 522–23
conceptions of, 513–14, 516–17
coping with, 525–31
measuring effects of, 515–16
posttraumatic stress disorder, 514–15

psychological disorders and, 580
psychosomatic illness and, 578
schizophrenia and, 622, 651
ulcers, heart disease, cancer, and, 518–22
striving for superiority according to Adler, a
universal desire to seek a personal feeling
of excellence and fulfillment. 548
stroboscopic movement an illusion of movement created by a rapid succession of stationary images. 166–67
stroke an interruption of blood flow, and thus
of oxygen supply, to part of the brain. 97,
111–12
Stroop effect the difficulty of naming the colors
in which words are written instead of reading the words themselves. 406, 407
structuralism an attempt to describe the structures that compose the mind. 22, 278
style of life according to Adler, a person's master plan for achieving a sense of superiority. 548
sublimation the transformation of an unacceptable impulse into an acceptable, even an
admirable, behavior. 544
subliminal perception the alleged influence on
behavior of a stimulus that is below the
threshold for conscious recognition.
151–54
substance abuse, 598–99. *See also* **addiction**
substance P, 141, 142
substantia nigra, 94
sucking, 222–23, 228
suicide, 241, 613–14, 661
superego according to Freud, the aspect of personality that consists of memories of rules
put forth by one's parents. 541
survey a study of the prevalence of certain beliefs, attitudes, or behaviors based on people's responses to specific questions.
46–48
survivor's guilt, 515
sympathetic nervous system a system composed of two chains of neuron clusters lying just to the left and right of the spinal
cord; the neurons send messages to the internal organs to prepare them for a burst
of vigorous activity. 495–96, 519, 525
synapse the specialized junction at which one
neuron releases a neurotransmitter, which
excites or inhibits another neuron. 90, 91
synaptic cleft, 90, 91
synaptic vesicles, 90, 91
systematic desensitization method of reducing
fear by gradually exposing people to the
object of their fear. 592–93

TA. *See* **transactional analysis**
tardive dyskinesia a movement disorder characterized by tremors and involuntary
movements. 650
taste the sensory system that responds to chemicals on the tongue. 142–44
taste bud the site of the taste receptors, located
in one of the folds on the surface of the
tongue. 142, 143
tea, 209
teenagers. *See* adolescence
telepathy, 37
television
aggression and, 33–34, 43, 53–54, 313
gender roles and, 268
violence on, 33–34, 43, 53–54, 313
temperament people's tendency to be active or
inactive, outgoing or reserved. 262–63

temporal contiguity being close together in
time. 285
temporal lobe a portion of each hemisphere of
the cerebral cortex that is critical for hearing, complex aspects of vision, and emotional behavior. 104–5
terminal button a bulge at the end of an axon
from which the axon releases a neurotransmitter. 90, 91
termination insomnia a tendency to awaken
early and to be unable to get back to sleep.
193
testosterone a hormone present in higher quantities in males than in females. 100, 475
test-retest reliability repeatability of a test's
scores between a test and a retest. 429
tetrahydrocannabinol (THC), 209
thalamus, 102
that's-not-all technique method of eliciting
compliance in which someone makes an
offer and then, before anyone has a chance
to reply, improves the offer. 713
THC. *See* tetrahydrocannabinol
Thematic Apperception Test (TAT) a projective personality test in which a person is
asked to tell a story about each of 20 pictures. 484, 570–71
theory a comprehensive explanation of natural
phenomena that leads to accurate predictions. 35
thiamine, 95
thinking. *See* **cognition**
thought disorders, 618
Three Faces of Eve, 583, 584
time-limited therapy, 639
toddlers
language development of, 236–38
preoperational stage and, 229–32
social-emotional development of, 247–48
tolerance the weakened effect of a drug after
repeated use. 211, 212, 284–85
tongue, 142, 143
tongue curling, 74, 75
top-down processing, 164
Torrance Test of Creative Thinking, 380
touch sensation, 140–41
Tourette's disorder, 581
Tower of Hanoi puzzle, 343, 344
trait a consistent, long-lasting tendency in behavior. 554, 555–57, 560
tranquilizers drugs that help people to relax.
207
anxiety and avoidance disorders and, 646
effects of, 206, 207
insomnia and, 194
transactional analysis (TA) treatment in which
a psychologist attempts to analyze
"transactions," or communication patterns. 637–38
transference extention of a client's feelings toward a parent or other important figure
onto the therapist. 631
transformational grammar, 397
triarchic theory Sternberg's theory that intelligence is governed by three types of process, which he refers to as metacomponents, performance components, and
knowledge-acquisition components. 416,
418
trichromatic theory or **Young-Helmholtz theory** the theory that color vision depends on
the relative rate of response of three types
of cones. 126–27

tricyclic drugs drugs that block the reabsorption of the neurotransmitters dopamine,
norepinephrine, and serotonin, after they
are released by the terminal button, thus
prolonging the effect of these neurotransmitters on the receptors of the postsynaptic cell. 647
tritanopia, 131
Tobriand Islanders, 36
t-test, 68–69
tumor, 104–5
Turing test, 374
twins, 76, 219, 263, 435–37, 621, 624
two-paycheck families, 264
Type A personality personality characterized
by constant competitiveness, impatience,
anger, and hostility. 520, 521, 522
Type B personality personality characterized
by easy-goingness, lack of hurry, and lack
of hostility. 520, 521

UFOs, 172
ulcer an open sore on the lining of the stomach
or duodenum. 518
ultimate cause reason for which a behavioral
tendency evolved, the function it serves.
81
unconditional positive regard complete, unqualified acceptance of another person as
he or she is. 550–51
unconditioned reflex an automatic connection
between a stimulus and a response. 279
unconditioned response (UCR) an automatic
response to an unconditioned stimulus.
280, 281
unconditioned stimulus (UCS) a stimulus that
automatically elicits an unconditioned response. 280, 281
unconscious according to Freud, an aspect of
the mind that influences behavior, although we are not directly aware of it. 16,
537–38, 544
undifferentiated schizophrenia type of
schizophrenia characterized by the basic
symptoms but no unusual or especially
prominent symptoms. 618
uplifts, 517
utility usefulness of a test for a practical purpose. 431

validity determination of how well a test measures what it claims to measure. 430, 431,
570, 571
Valium, 646
variable-interval schedule a rule for delivering
reinforcement after varying amounts of
time. 305
variable-ratio schedule a rule for delivering reinforcement after varying numbers of responses. 304–5
variation, 64–65
venereal disease a disease that is spread
through sexual contact. 473
ventromedial hypothalamus an area of the
brain in which damage leads to weight
gain via an increase in the secretion of insulin. 457, 458
vestibular sense a specialized sense that detects
the direction of tilt and amount of acceleration of the head. 138–39
vicarious reinforcement or **vicarious punishment** reinforcement or punishment observed to have been experienced by someone else. 313–14

Vietnam veterans, 514–15, 530
violence. *See* aggressive behavior
visceral pertaining to the internal organs. 294–95
vision, 149
  brain damage and, 103
  color, 126–32
  eye-brain connections, 109–10
  in infancy, 220–21
  light detection, 119–26
  threshold of, 150–51
visual capture effect tendency to localize a sound as coming from a prominent visual feature (such as a loudspeaker or a ventriloquist's dummy). 174
visual constancy the tendency to perceive objects as unchanging in shape, size, and color, despite variations in what actually reaches the retina. 164–65
visual cortex, 129
visual field what you see. 103
visual-motor coordination, 222
vitamin B_1, 95, 344
vitreous humor, 120
volley principle identification of pitch by volleys of action potentials in a series of auditory neurons, each volley synchronized with a sound wave. 136

volunteerism, 702
von Restorff effect tendency to remember the most distinctive items on a list better than other items. 350

WAIS-R. *See* **Wechsler Adult Intelligence Scale—Revised**
walking, 111
waterfall illusion, 156
wavelengths, 119, 126, 127
Wechsler Adult Intelligence Scale—Revised (WAIS-R) an IQ test originally devised by David Wechsler, commonly used with adults. 421–22
Wechsler Intelligence Scale for Children—Revised (WISC-R) an IQ test originally devised by David Wechsler, commonly used with children. 420–22, 427, 429, 430
weight loss, 458, 462–64
weight regulation, 458
white matter, 103
Whorf hypothesis hypothesis that our language influences the way we think. 398–99
WISC-R. *See* **Wechsler Intelligence Scale for Children—Revised**
withdrawal effects experiences that occur as a result of the removal of a drug from the brain. 211

women. *See* sex differences
women in psychology, 12–13, 25
word-superiority effect greater ease of identifying a letter when it is part of a whole word than when it is presented by itself. 403–4
worker productivity, 55–56
working memory memory for what one is working with at the moment. 332, 333
working mothers, 256, 263–64
work shifts, 182–83

Xanax, 646
X chromosome a sex chromosome of which females have two per cell and males have one. 76

Y chromosome a sex chromosome found in males but not in females. 76
yellow-blue color blindness, 131
yoga, 526
young adulthood, 248, 254–56

zebra, intelligence of, 23
zygote, 74

To the Owner of This Book

I hope that you have enjoyed *Introduction to Psychology,* Third Edition as much
as I enjoyed writing it. I would like to know as much about your experience
as you would care to offer. Only through your comments and those of others
can I learn how to make this a better text for future readers.

School _____ Your instructor's name _____

1. What did you like the most about *Introduction to Psychology,* Third Edition? _____

_____

_____

_____

2. Do you have any recommendations for ways to improve the next edition of this text? _____

_____

_____

_____

3. In the space below or in a separate letter, please write any other comments you have about the book. (For example, were
any chapters or concepts particularly difficult?) I'd be delighted to hear from you!

_____

_____

_____

_____

_____

_____

_____

_____

_____

_____

_____

Optional:

Your name _____ Date _____

May Brooks/Cole quote you, either in promotion for *Introduction to Psychology* or in future publishing ventures?

Yes ☐   No ☐

Thanks!

FOLD HERE

FOLD HERE

BUSINESS REPLY MAIL

FIRST CLASS   PERMIT NO. 358   PACIFIC GROVE, CA

Postage will be paid by addressee

James W. Kalat
Brooks/Cole Publishing Company
511 Forest Lodge Road
Pacific Grove, CA 93950

Deep excavations

A practical manual

Second edition

Deep excavations

A practical manual

Malcolm Puller, CEng, DIC, FICE, FIStrucE

Second edition

Thomas Telford

Published by Thomas Telford Publishing, Thomas Telford Ltd, 1 Heron Quay, London E14 4JD.
www.thomastelford.com

Distributors for Thomas Telford books are
USA: ASCE Press, 1801 Alexander Bell Drive, Reston, VA 20191-4400, USA
Japan: Maruzen Co. Ltd, Book Department, 3–10 Nihonbashi 2-chome, Chuo-ku, Tokyo 103
Australia: DA Books and Journals, 648 Whitehorse Road, Mitcham 3132, Victoria

First published 1996
Second edition 2003

A catalogue record for this book is available from the British Library

ISBN: 0 7277 3150 5

Typeset by Academic + Technical, Bristol
Printed and bound in Great Britain by MPG Books, Bodmin

Preface

The opportunity to revise, correct and augment the previous publication in a second edition is gratefully accepted. Two rather obvious opportunities present themselves. Firstly, the first edition contained some errors for which the Author must accept responsibility; hopefully some applied diligence and care have corrected these. Secondly, and perhaps more importantly, the past seven years have given both consultants and contractors the opportunity to show analytical and design skills and practical boldness in underground construction works which may have been difficult to match in recent previous times. The marriage of numerical analysis and practical construction becomes a reality as further validation of analytical methods is made. It is unfair, perhaps, to draw attention to such progress by citing one individual contract, but with the risk of irritating engineers elsewhere the Author believes the deep excavation for the new Westminster underground station made for the Jubilee Line in the late 1990s deserves such attention. More details are to be found on pages 124–126 and 533 of this second edition of *Deep Excavations* and in recent technical publications by others.

Once more, the Author gratefully acknowledges the patient assistance given by the staff of the library of the Institution of Civil Engineers and the kindness of copyright holders in giving permission to quote from published papers and reports.

Grateful thanks are also given to Brian Bell, David Puller, Chris Harnan and John Dixon for all their helpful comments and assistance, and to Carolyn and Jeremy King for the preparation of the typed text.

Above all, the Author believes past experience and engineering skills should remain critically allied in the design and construction of deep excavation works and trusts that the reader may agree and follow this principle, rather than rely unduly on formal standards and regulations.

A cynic once said that 'engineering is the art of modelling materials we do not wholly understand, into shapes we cannot precisely analyse so as to withstand forces we cannot entirely assess in such a way that the public has no reason to suspect the extent of our ignorance'. The Author trusts that study of the following pages may dispel this view.

M J Puller
Sevenoaks, Kent

September 2003

Conversion factors

Some of the cases and examples cited in this book use Imperial units. For convenience of readers, the following list of conversion factors is provided. (The conversion factors have been rounded-up where appropriate).

Linear measure

1 in.	$= 25 \cdot 4\,mm$	1 mm	$= 0 \cdot 03937\,in.$
1 ft	$= 0 \cdot 3048\,m$	1 cm	$= 0 \cdot 3937\,in.$
1 yd	$= 0 \cdot 9144\,m$	1 m	$= 3 \cdot 2808\,ft$
			or $1 \cdot 0936\,yd$
1 mile	$= 1 \cdot 6093\,km$	1 km	$= 0 \cdot 6214\,mile$

Square measure

1 sq. in.	$= 645 \cdot 16\,mm^2$	1 cm^2	$= 0 \cdot 155\,sq.\,in.$
1 sq. ft	$= 0 \cdot 0929\,m^2$	1 m^2	$= 10 \cdot 7639\,sq.\,ft$
1 sq. yd	$= 0 \cdot 8361\,m^2$		or $1 \cdot 196\,sq.\,yds$
1 acre	$= 0 \cdot 4047\,hectare$	1 hectare	$= 2 \cdot 471\,acres$
1 sq. mile	$= 259\,hectares$		
1 hectare	$= 10\,000\,m^2$	1 km^2	$= 247 \cdot 1\,acres$

Cubic measure

1 cubic in.	$= 16 \cdot 387\,cm^3$	1 mm^3	$= 0 \cdot 000\,061\,cubic\,in.$
1 cubic ft	$= 0 \cdot 0283\,m^3$	1 m^3	$= 35 \cdot 3147\,cubic\,ft$
1 cubic yd	$= 0 \cdot 7645\,m^3$		or $1 \cdot 308\,cubic\,yds$

Measure of capacity

1 pint	$= 0 \cdot 568\,litre$	1 litre	$= 1 \cdot 7598\,pints$
1 gallon	$= 4 \cdot 546\,litres$		or $0 \cdot 22\,gallon$

Weight

1 oz	$= 28 \cdot 35\,g$	1 g	$= 0 \cdot 0353\,oz$
1 lb	$= 0 \cdot 4536\,kg$	1 kg	$= 2 \cdot 2046\,lb$
1 ton	$= 1 \cdot 016\,tonnes$		
	or $1016\,kg$		

Load, pressure, density

1 lbf	$= 4 \cdot 448\,N$
1 pound per linear foot	$= 1 \cdot 4882\,kg\,per\,linear\,m$
1 pound per square foot	$= 4 \cdot 882\,kg\,per\,m^2$
1 tonf per linear foot	$= 32 \cdot 69\,kN\,per\,linear\,m$
1 tonf per square inch	$= 15 \cdot 444\,N\,per\,mm^2$
1 tonf per square foot	$= 107 \cdot 25\,kN\,per\,m^2$
100 lb per cubic foot	$= 1602\,kg\,per\,m^3$

Other parameters

1 ft^3/s	$= 0 \cdot 0283\,m^3/s$
1 Imperial gall/min	$= 4 \cdot 546\,l/m$
1 inch unit of moment of inertia	$= 41 \cdot 6198\,cm\,units$
1 inch unit of modulus of section	$= 16 \cdot 3860\,cm\,units$

Contents

1 Introduction

The purpose of the book is to present, in a selective way, design and construction for deep excavations made for civil engineering purposes. Emphasis is placed on descriptions of work constructed, in some instances within the Author's personal responsibility, but for the most part as observed by the Author and as described and reported by others.

Both temporary construction and permanent works are described. The design of temporary construction to support soil and rock at the excavation periphery, and to exclude groundwater, frequently becomes the responsibility of the contractor, and there may be incentives to devise methods that economize in construction time and cost. The term 'temporary' may mislead; on major works, measures of peripheral soil support and groundwater exclusion may require sufficient strength and durability to last several years. The difficult task of the temporary works designer, to provide an adequate but time-related solution without waste, should not be underestimated. The final cost of temporary works may also depend upon the ease of their eventual removal. In some cases, their incorporation into the permanent works, as with diaphragm walls, can mitigate against the cost of soil support during the construction period.

Permanent construction is divided in the text, for the sake of convenience, into work in shafts and caissons, basements and cut-and-cover construction, with some obvious overlap with temporary works. Traditionally, the design of permanent work and responsibility for its adequacy lies with the consulting engineer. The exceptions are those projects designed by the owner's organization or which are the subject of a turnkey or design-and-construct arrangement where a contracting firm may assume professional responsibility for permanent construction. The designers of temporary and permanent works are therefore often not the same persons on a particular job, and in many instances they are not employed by the same organization.

The choice of which deep excavation works to include in the book has been guided by a definition used in the CIRIA Report on trenching practice[1]. This report covered trench excavations to a depth of 6 m. As an approximate division between shallow and deep excavations, this 6 m depth has been adopted by the Author: for the most part, this book features work greater than this depth. Mention should nevertheless be made of the high risk of excavations less than 6 m deep. Of those accidents involving fatalities or major injuries in relatively shallow excavations from 1996 to 2001 where details are available, analysis shows the following causes:

- unsupported excavation: 54% of cases
- working ahead of support: 12% of cases
- inadequate support: 16% of cases
- unstable slopes of open cut: 6% of cases
- other causes (principally unsafe machine operation): 12% of cases.

Within these statistics an underlying cause in accidents involving inadequate support and working ahead of support involves misuse of drag boxes and trench boxes. There is insufficient evidence within this period to make a correlation with particular soil conditions but there is some evidence that the proximity of existing services and backfilled trenchworks and the effects of wet weather are not adequately considered as stability risks. Throughout, a prime reason for these accidents is the absence of capable supervision on site.

Safety and avoidance of damage

The design of soil support to deep excavations on land must ensure an adequate factor of safety against collapse in the short term, that is, during the construction period, and an adequate factor of safety against collapse for the design life of the permanent substructure. In addition, in both the short and long term the design of the works must be such as to contain deformation of the soil or rock adjacent to the excavation to limits which do not cause distress to existing structures or services. Standards of construction at each stage must be such that the work complies with the strength assumptions used in the design and is sufficiently durable to avoid deterioration and movement or collapse. Additionally, construction standards must be such as to avoid loss of ground into the excavation which might cause an unacceptable risk of subsidence or collapse. In the United Kingdom, legislation extends to the rights of neighbours sharing a common party wall between their properties and any damage that occurs due to construction work, including excavations, on one side of the wall (see the section on Party walls at the end of this chapter).

Deep excavations below river or sea beds require specific design consideration. For the most part, deformation or subsidence will be less important than excavations on land unless existing works are nearby. The risk of scour effects to the sea or river bed, which are possible as a result of the new works themselves, may prove to be an additional hazard which could cause structural collapse, and must be guarded against. Variations in sea and river states in terms of tide, storm swells, current and wave conditions all require assessment in terms of risk to safety and to structure; given the likely consequences of collapse during construction or thereafter to foundation works at sea or on major rivers, strenuous care is required in the assessment of such factors.

The risk to construction personnel and users of the permanent structure must be defined separately to the risk of subsidence damage to property and services. In the former case, the awesome consequences of inadequate standards of design and construction in deep excavation works should be self-evident, and particularly so on the site of the works. Frequent reference is made to modes of failure throughout the text; the experience of previous failures is seldom reported, and the advantage that should be gained for future works is lost.

Design and construction works for the support of deep excavations require investigations of the site topography, the subsoil and groundwater conditions, the states of sea and river water and the stability of sea and river beds (where applicable), the risk of seismic loading, the extent of superimposed loads, the state of existing structures and services, and the availability and quality of available structural materials. None of these matters is treated specifically, although without such information of adequate quality prior to design of both the temporary and permanent works, all reference to avoidance of risk to life and reduction of damage to property becomes meaningless.

Construction regulations: safety

In many developed countries, the design and site works of deep excavations are subject to statutory regulations that are devised to maintain minimum standards of site construction safety.

In the UK the principal legislation is the Health and Safety at Work etc. Act 1974[2], which specifies the responsibility of employers, suppliers and employees for all work together with the Management of Health and Safety at Work Regulations 1999[3]. This legislation is complementary to the Construction (Health, Safety and Welfare) Regulations 1996[4], which apply to any type of building works and most types of civil engineering construction. These UK regulations list specific work operations, section by section, for example: section 9 covers stability of structures; section 10, demolition or dismantling; section 11, explosives; section 12, excavations; section 13, cofferdams and caissons. Other legislation refers to operations and specialist activities, for example, the Lifting Operations and Lifting Equipment Regulations 1998[5], the Provision and Use of Work Equipment Regulations 1998[6], the Work in Compressed Air Regulations 1996[7], the Confined Space Regulations 1997[8], and the Control of Explosives Regulations 1991[9]. An explanatory manual to the Construction Regulations, published by CIP Ltd[10], is continuously updated.

In the UK, the Health and Safety Executive is responsible for the implementation of the Health and Safety at Work Act and the Construction Regulations. These pieces of legislation place duties on both employer and employee: while the employer must provide safe access, a safe place of work and a safe system of work for employees, every employee must take reasonable care for the safety of others and must cooperate with the employer in such matters. The employer must not intentionally or recklessly interfere with or misuse anything provided in pursuance of the requirements for health, safety and welfare. All cofferdams and caissons must be properly constructed, altered or dismantled under competent supervision and, wherever possible, by experienced operatives. Every cofferdam or caisson must be provided, so far as is reasonably practical, with ladders or other means of escape in case of flooding. Inspections of cofferdams, caissons and trenches must be made when work is in progress and, in addition, they must be thoroughly examined and records made whenever explosive charges have been fired, whenever any damage has occurred, or, in any case, every seven days. Other regulations require the inspection of lifting plant and excavators, and the management is held responsible for the competence of designers, supervisors and operatives.

In 1992 an extension to the Management of Health and Safety at Work Act required all employers in the UK, not only those in construction, to carry out assessments of risks to safety. A further widening of responsibility was made in 1995 when the Construction (Design and Management) Regulations 1994[11] placed a duty on designers to avoid, so far as is practicable, risks to safety and health during the demolition, construction and maintenance of construction works. A recent amendment to these regulations in October 2000 placed responsibility not only on designers but also on staff under their control.

The above in no way gives a complete explanation of safety legislation applying to deep excavation sites in the UK but shows the change, particularly at site, made first in 1961 and thereafter with the introduction of statutory regulations for site safety.

Permanent works for building construction such as basements, are also the subject of building standard control legislation either nationally or by city in all developed countries.

Contractual responsibility: client, engineer and contractor

In addition to the responsibility spelt out in statutory regulations for works on site and the design of temporary and permanent works, the contracts between employer and contractor and between client and consultant will define responsibility for the adequacy of both the temporary and permanent soil support. Contract conditions will vary between countries and from job

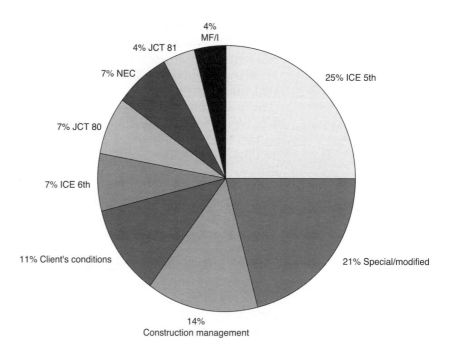

Fig. 1.1. Conditions of contract currently used in construction in the UK[12]

to job. Standard forms of contract between employer and contractor for deep excavation work include recent editions of the ICE contract, FIDIC international conditions, the New Engineering Contract and other design-and-build contracts and management contracts. The range of conditions of contract in use in the UK was reviewed by Clayton[12] in 2001 for general construction works and is summarized in Fig. 1.1. The ICE contract still remains in use, however, in particular the sixth edition first published in 1991.

In the UK, an earlier standard form of contract between contractor and client for civil engineering works, the ICE form (fifth edition), was commented on by Abrahamson[13] who concluded that the responsibility for temporary works was complex. He examined four issues.

(a) *Responsibility of the contractor to the employer.* The contractor's responsibility to the employer is clear by virtue of the clause wording: 'The contractor shall take full responsibility for the adequacy, stability and safety of all site operations and methods of construction'. So, if any temporary works design by the contractor, or subcontractors (whether nominated or not), is inadequate, the deficiency must be remedied by the contractor, and if any damage to either permanent or temporary works is caused by the deficiency the contractor becomes liable to rectify this also. Temporary works designed by the engineer do not become the design responsibility of the contractor under this clause.

(b) *Responsibility of the engineer to the client.* The engineer has a plain duty to the client to ensure that the permanent works are not distressed by loads induced from the temporary works and that the temporary works are built in accordance with the design whether by the contractor or the engineer. In addition, the engineer carries a duty to the client to design the temporary works where it would not be satisfactory to allow the contractor to make the design.

(c) *Responsibility (or perhaps lack of responsibility) of the employer, via the engineer, to the contractor.* The engineer has no obligation to the contractor to detect or prevent faults in the temporary works. While the engineer has rights of control under the contract, the contractor cannot excuse bad workmanship in temporary works on the basis that the engineer made no objection.

(d) *Responsibility of the employer, engineer and contractor to employees and members of the public.* The contractor is liable to employees and other third parties if a duty of care is not discharged in designing or constructing temporary works, and the contractor is probably also liable for a defective design by the engineer when an experienced contractor would have known it to be defective. Abrahamson concluded that the engineer's liability to third parties as a result of temporary works failure was most difficult to define. Without doubt the contractor, under this particular form of contract, does hold much of the responsibility for the safe design and performance of temporary works, such as temporary soil support. In particular, he holds responsibility towards the client for the adequacy in design and construction of such temporary support works by subcontractors and even nominated subcontractors.

It is evident that works such as piling or diaphragm walls, which at different stages serve functions both of temporary and permanent soil support, require specific reference in the conditions of contract for such work. The case law on such matters remains sparse and the division of responsibility between contractor and engineer may be without legal precedent. In the UK it is not unusual for a subcontractor to provide the design of a specialist soil support system, say a diaphragm wall, to act both during construction and as part of the permanent structure. Presumably, under ICE conditions, the engineer's approval of the subcontractor's design for the permanent performance of the wall element would to some extent relieve the contractor's responsibility in that direction, whereas the performance of the same element during construction would remain solely the contractor's responsibility. It is interesting to note that severe distress of such a wall panel, should it occur during construction, say below formation level, would not necessarily become apparent at that time and may only be revealed by the non-performance of the permanent works. The assessment of fact and the legal position of works designed to act in temporary and permanent stages may prove to be complicated.

Causes of failure in deep excavations

The failure of a soil support system does not necessarily occur by structural collapse; other types of failure include excessive deformation of the soil and soil support structure, inadequate groundwater exclusion, and insufficient durability of the soil support structure resulting in failure over time.

In the Author's experience the causes of failure may be summarized as follows.

(a) Open excavations
   (i) inadequate site investigation resulting in optimistic design assumptions of soil, rock strength and groundwater conditions
   (ii) inadequate appreciation by the designer of susceptibility to settlement of adjacent structures and services
   (iii) lack of appreciation by the designer and constructor of the effects of weathering and time on soil strength.

(b) Braced excavations
   (i) inadequate site investigations resulting in optimistic design assumptions of soil and rock homogeneity, strength of soil and rock fabric, and groundwater conditions
   (ii) inadequate quality of structural detailing
   (iii) inadequate coordination between designer and constructor

(iv)   lack of appreciation by the designer of the limitations of specialist techniques such as diaphragm walling and anchoring

(v)   lack of appreciation by the designer of the influence of deflections in the soil support structure and retained soil deformations

(vi)   changes in loading from natural conditions – groundwater, tidal states, waves, temperature – and lack of appreciation by the constructor of the possible consequences of these changes

(vii)   changes in soil and rock conditions and the lack of appreciation by the constructor of the possible consequences

(viii)   overloading of soil support structure by temporary plant loads

(ix)   bad workmanship in site temporary works.

Sowers and Sowers[14] stated that, within their experience, failures of anchored sheet pile walls and braced excavations seldom occur as the result of inadequacies of modern earth pressure theories. Instead, they are caused by the more obvious neglect of backfill loads, construction operations that produce excessive earth pressures, poorly designed support systems and inadequate allowances for deflections, deterioration and corrosion, and poor design in construction details.

In the Author's experience, structural failure of braced and anchored walls has usually occurred within the strutting or anchorage, or by passive soil failure below formation level caused by inadequate sheeting penetration. In other instances, fewer in number, very bad standards have caused gaps within walls allowing cofferdams to blow with extensive loss of ground from behind the walls.

Deflections caused by loads applied to soil support systems observed by the Author have generally been less than the tolerances allowed for in construction of the systems and frequent actual settlements and deformation to adjacent existing structures have been less than those predicted by calculation unless workmanship standards have been poor.

The extent of soil deformations around large excavations is referred to in published work more readily than records of structural failure; Peck[15] and Clough and Davidson[16] reviewed the likely range of horizontal and vertical movements. Clough and Schmidt[17], in considering the design and performance of excavations in soft clay, used data from Peck[15], D'Appolania[18] and Goldberg et al.[19] to show that settlements associated with excavations where basal stability is a problem exceed those where no such stability problem exists.

Records of soil deformations caused by particular excavations in London were referred to by Cole and Burland[20] and by Wood and Perrin[21]. Burland et al.[22] examined movements near excavations into London clay and stated that while the magnitude of ground movement will depend on methods of construction and day-to-day sequences of work made on site, it should be possible to make reasonable estimates of upper and lower limits of movement, especially when field measurements add to knowledge of the conditions. Calculated predictions of deformation using numerical methods rely on accurate assessment of soil deformation parameters; back analysis of field measurements from nearby excavations may provide these values.

Clough and Davidson[16] concluded that for a given depth of excavation the amount of ground movement depends on the properties of the retained soil and not on the stiffness of the temporary supporting wall, but Goldberg et al.[19] stated that wall stiffness is an important factor in such soil deformation. Defining wall stiffness by a parameter given by EI/h^4, where EI is the flexural stiffness of the wall and h is the vertical distance between supports, and plotting this against the stability number for excavation in clays H/c_u (where H is the total depth of excavation and c_u is the undrained shear strength of the clay), boundary lines were given to show orders of expected lateral wall movement.

The use of temporary berms and other construction procedures to reduce movements were referred to by Clough and Schmidt[17] and will be treated in detail in the following chapters.

Subsidence may occur near excavations as a result of the installation process of walling, sheeting and anchorages in addition to deformations caused by loading. Deformations which occur during installation of unlined borings for piles and diaphragm walls and movements caused by pre-loading of ground anchors are rarely appreciated at the design stage. White[23] referred to several cases where the declination of rock anchors used to support temporary sheeting caused settlement to occur as a result of the vertical load component overstressing rock below the tip of soldier piles.

More recently, the response of buildings to induced settlements caused by nearby deep excavations and tunnelling works has been the subject of both analytical and observational research (see Boscardin and Cording[24] and the Proceedings of the Conference on Building Response to Tunnelling 2001[25]). This aspect is further discussed in Chapter 11.

Risk evaluation

Casagrande[26] emphasized that risks were inherent in any project, their existence should be recognized and, using steps representing a balance between economy and safety, these risks should be treated systematically. Casagrande defined 'calculated risk' in two parts:

(a) the use of imperfect knowledge, guided judgement and experience, to estimate the possible ranges for all pertinent quantities that enter into the solution of the problem
(b) decisions on an appropriate margin of safety, or degree of risk, taking into consideration economic factors and the magnitude of losses that would result from failure.

Casagrande did not quantify risk. Later, Whitman[27] reported considerable advances in reliability and probabilistic theory, but stressed that the use of such methods was no substitute for physical measurements and sound engineering interpretation. Concluding, Whitman said that the satisfactory evaluation of risk could be answered in two ways.

(a) If a relatively large probability of failure (0·05 or more) under design loading were tolerable, then this risk could be evaluated (by reliability theory) with sufficiency accuracy for decision-making purposes. This situation applies only when economic loss and not safety are of concern.
(b) If a very small probability of failure (say less than 0·001) under design loading conditions is required, the actual risk cannot be evaluated by analysis. However, conducting a formal evaluation of the probability of failure can help greatly in understanding the risk and what might best be done to reduce it.

The design of many deep excavation schemes must certainly lie within the second category where the acceptance of failure probability must be very low indeed because of the risk to life.

Whitman illustrated his paper with applications of reliability theory to examine systematic and random errors when evaluating risk in slope stability, factors of safety in risk analysis of liquefaction, and the use of system analysis techniques for quantifying risk on a project basis. Examples of risk evaluation were given for an industrial plant built on potentially liquefiable sands and for earth dam construction.

Hoeg and Muraka[28] considered the conventional design of a simple gravity retaining wall and carried out a statistical analysis. For given soil properties and backfill height, this design used factors of safety of 1·9, 3·7 and 1·6 against overturning, bearing failure and sliding respectively, yet despite these apparently conservative values the statistical analysis showed that the corresponding failure probabilities were 1/10 000, 13/1000 and 3/1000. The probability of bearing failure is particularly high, and large differences were also indicated in failure probabilities between each failure. This example shows the ease with which conventional factors of safety are able to mislead.

Hoeg and Muraka then redesigned the gravity wall using probabilistic methods, evaluating initial costs, construction costs, costs of failure and the probabilities of failure by overturning, bearing and sliding, to determine the expected total cost. The optimum design was the system with minimum expected total cost.

The principle of risk assessment is within the scope of this book, but probability is not (for this see Whitman[27] and Hoeg and Muraka[28] and the references therein).

The primary intent of Hoeg and Muraka was to provide a model for the probabilistic design, by similar methods, of more complicated structures such as braced and anchored walls, but despite their intrinsic logic there is little indication that such methods have gained acceptance by designers.

Risk management

The management of geotechnical risk, including that associated with deep excavations, was reviewed by Clayton[12] in 2001. Clayton also comments that procurement methods have an important influence on geotechnical risk management and refers to the extent to which geotechnical risk is shared between client and contractor as the type of contract is varied. Figure 1.2 (Flanagan and Norman[29]) suggests a broad risk division for forms of contract which have gained increasing acceptance and do not conform to the traditional fully designed, remeasured type of contract such as the ICE Conditions of Contract.

Examples of risk registers compiled by both designers and contractors are given by Clayton together with a summary of software for risk management from a 1998 survey. A recent edition of the *Project Risk Management Software Directory*[30] lists over 40 different software titles although their use in risk management in geotechnical work is limited in the Author's experience. Generally, the Prima Vera programme appears to be the most popular software for this purpose at present.

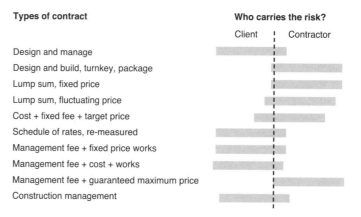

Fig. 1.2. Risk management: division by forms of contract[12]

Party walls

Although outside the scope of this book, mention should be made of the statutory rights of building owners and their tenants regarding construction works, such as excavation and underpinning affecting party walls. In the UK the Party Wall Act applies to this matter; Ensom et al.[31] and Anstey[32] should be consulted.

References

1. Irvine D.J. and Smith R.J. *Trenching practice*. CIRIA, London, 1992, Report 97.
2. *Health and Safety at Work Act 1974*. HMSO, London.
3. *Management of Health and Safety at Work Regulations 1999*. HMSO, London.
4. *The Construction (Health, Safety and Welfare) Regulations 1996*. HMSO, London.
5. *The Lifting Operations and Lifting Equipment Regulations 1998*. HMSO, London.
6. *The Provision and Use of Work Equipment Regulations 1998*. HMSO, London.
7. *Work in Compressed Air Special Regulations 1996*. HMSO, London.
8. *The Confined Space Regulations 1997*. HMSO, London.
9. *Control of Explosives Regulations 1991*. HMSO, London.
10. *Construction: Health and Safety Manual*. CIP Ltd, Birmingham, 2000.
11. *Construction (Design and Management) Regulations 1994*. HMSO, London.
12. Clayton C.R. *Managing geotechnical risk*. Thomas Telford Ltd., London, 2001.
13. Abrahamson M.W. *Engineering law and the ICE contracts*. Applied Science, London, 1983.
14. Sowers G.B. and Sowers G.F. Failures of bulkhead and excavation bracing. *Civ. Engng*, 1967, **107**, No. 1, 72–77.
15. Peck R.B. Deep excavations and tunnelling in soft ground. *Proc. 7th Int. Conf. S.M.F.E.*, Mexico City, 1969, State of the art volume, Vol. 2, 225–290. Sociedad de Mexicana de Mecanica de Suelos, Mexico City, 1969.
16. Clough G.W. and Davidson R.R. Effects of construction on geotechnical performance. *Proc. 9th Int. Conf. S.M.F.E.*, Tokyo, 1977, 15–53. Japanese Society of Soil Mechanics and Foundation Engineering, Tokyo.
17. Clough G.W. and Schmidt B. Design and performance of excavations and tunnels in soft clay. *Soft clay engineering*. Ed. E.W. Brand and R.P. Brenner, Elsevier, London, 1981, 567–634.
18. D'Appolonia D.J. Effects of foundation construction on nearby structures. *Proc. 4th Pan American Conf. S.M.F.E.*, San Juan, 1971, Vol. 1, 189–236 (discussion Vol. 3, 171–178).
19. Goldberg D.T. *et al*. *Federal Highway Administration Reports*. National Technical Information Service, Washington, DC, 1976.
20. Cole K.W. and Burland J.B. Observations on retaining wall movements associated with a large excavation. *Proc. 5th Euro. Conf. S.M.F.E.*, Madrid, 1972, Vol. 1, 445–453.
21. Wood L.A. and Perrin A.J. The performance of a deep foundation in London clay. *Proc. 11th Int. Conf. S.M.F.E.*, San Francisco, 1985, 2277–2280. Balkema, Rotterdam, 1985.
22. Burland J.B. *et al*. Movements around excavations in London clay. *Proc. 7th Euro. Conf. S.M.F.E.*, Brighton, 1979, Vol. 1, 13–29. British Geotechnical Society, London, 1979.
23. White R.E. Anchored walls adjacent to vertical rock cuts. *Proc. Conf. Diaphragm Walls*. Institution of Civil Engineers, London, 1974, 181–188.
24. Boscardin M. and Cording E. Building settlement to excavation induced settlement. *ASCE J. Geotech. Engng*, **115**, No. 1, 1–21. Jan. 1989.
25. *Proc. of Conference on Building Response to Tunnelling*, London, 2001. Thomas Telford Ltd., London, 2001.
26. Casagrande A. Role of the calculated risk in earthwork and foundation engineering. *ASCE J.S.M.*, 1965, **91**, No. 4, July 1.
27. Whitman R.V. Evaluating calculated risk in geotechnical engineering (17th Terzaghi Lecture). *ASCE J. Geotech. Engng*, 1984, **110**, No. 2, 145–188.
28. Hoeg K. and Muraka P.P. Probabilistic analysis and design of a retaining wall. *ASCE J. Geotech. Engng*, 1974, **100**, No. 3, 349–366.

29. Flanagan R. and Norman G. *Risk management and construction*. Blackwell Science, London, 1993.
30. *Project risk management software directory*. Association of Project Management. Euro Log Ltd., 2000.
31. Ensom D., Roe E. and Anstey J. *The party wall act explained*. Pyramus and Thisbe, Parrot House Press, Weedon 1996.
32. Anstey J. *Party walls*. Royal Institution of Chartered Surveyors, 5th edition, 1998.

Bibliography

Benjamin J.R. and Cornell G.R. *Probability statistics and decisions for civil engineers*. McGraw-Hill, New York, 1970.

Health and Safety Commission. *Management of health and safety at work*. HMSO, London, 1992.

Health and Safety Executive. *Successful health and safety management*. HMSO, London, 1991.

Lamb P. *Applications of statistics in soil mechanics*. Newnes-Butterworth, London, 1974.

Newmark N.M. Rankine lecture: Effects of earthquakes on dams and foundations. *Géotechnique*, 1965, **15**, 139–160.

Peck R.B. 9th Rankine lecture: Advantages and limitations of the observational method in applied soil mechanics. *Géotechnique*, 1969, **19**, No. 2, 171–187.

2 The control of groundwater

The occurrence of groundwater on site directly influences construction methods, permanent works design and, thereby, construction time and cost; possibly, in the longer term, the durability of the structure and its maintenance costs will also be affected. This chapter considers only the first of these, construction methods of dewatering deep excavations. It addresses groundwater control in three ways: the problem presented to constructors; the techniques available to them; and the calculation methods to assist in the design of groundwater control. The chapter draws on data from four references, CIRIA Report C515[1], BS 8004[2] and textbooks by Cashman and Preene[3] and Powers[4].

Groundwater problems

The sources of groundwater on a particular site may be threefold: rainfall, run-off or groundwater flow through pervious soils or rock from streams, rivers or the sea. Variations in soil and rock conditions, in particular permeability, horizontally and vertically, cause variations in groundwater flow both on the ground surface and below it. The degree to which groundwater is contained by relatively impermeable soil above or below a permeable stratum will in turn influence any excess or artesian pressure within stored groundwater.

Reducing the quantity of groundwater within subsoil adjacent to an excavation by a dewatering process such as pumping will increase the strength of the soil as the groundwater pressure, or pore pressure, is reduced. Reduction in groundwater head therefore reduces the load, say on the bracing to a deep excavation, and provides a method of improving soil strength.

The effective stress is the difference between the applied, total stress and the pressure induced by loading to groundwater within the pores of saturated soil. As the soil is loaded, say from a building foundation, the increase in load is shared between the soil structure and the pore-water within the soil. The stress carried by the soil structure, known as the effective stress σ', is therefore equal to total stress σ less the pore-water pressure u. Since water possesses no strength, the soil reduces in volume as the water is displaced. The time-dependent rate of this change in volume and change in pore pressure depends on the permeability of the soil fabric and physical drainage conditions. The dissipation of pore pressure and the volume change stops when equilibrium is reached with external forces applied to the soil mass.

So, the shear strength of the soil τ' depends on the effective stress and at failure is

$$\tau' = c' + \sigma' \tan \phi' \tag{1}$$

where c' is the cohesion of the soil in effective stress terms, and ϕ' is the angle of shearing resistance in effective stress terms. The total stress, therefore, is a stress state which applies only at one instant, whereas the fully drained equilibrium condition when effective stress is maximized occurs after some

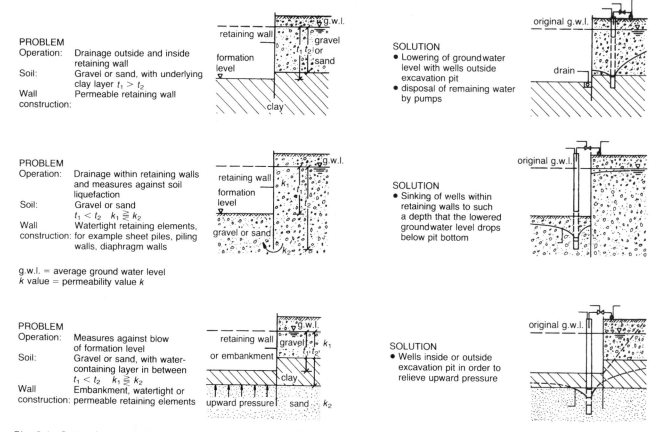

PROBLEM
Operation: Drainage outside and inside retaining wall
Soil: Gravel or sand, with underlying clay layer $t_1 > t_2$
Wall construction: Permeable retaining wall

SOLUTION
• Lowering of groundwater level with wells outside excavation pit
• disposal of remaining water by pumps

PROBLEM
Operation: Drainage within retaining walls and measures against soil liquefaction
Soil: Gravel or sand $t_1 < t_2$ $k_1 \gtreqqless k_2$
Wall construction: Watertight retaining elements, for example sheet piles, piling walls, diaphragm walls

g.w.l. = average ground water level
k value = permeability value k

SOLUTION
• Sinking of wells within retaining walls to such a depth that the lowered groundwater level drops below pit bottom

PROBLEM
Operation: Measures against blow of formation level
Soil: Gravel or sand, with water-containing layer in between $t_1 < t_2$ $k_1 \gtreqqless k_2$
Wall construction: Embankment, watertight or permeable retaining elements

SOLUTION
• Wells inside or outside excavation pit in order to relieve upward pressure

Fig. 2.1. Groundwater control applied to a deep sheeted excavation in various ground conditions

time. This time is relatively short with a granular, permeable soil but longer with a cohesive, impermeable soil.

Reduction of groundwater within an excavation may be necessary for access by workers and machines. However, removal of groundwater from below the excavated level and externally to the excavation may be required to improve soil stability below and around the excavation itself. Examples of groundwater control applied to a deep sheeted excavation in various ground conditions are shown in Fig. 2.1. Reduction in groundwater levels and piezometric head allows progressive excavation in the dry, reduces pressure on the sheeting, reduces the risk of base uplift at formation level of the completed excavation, and allows the strength of the soil to increase progressively as effective stress conditions apply to a fully drained, dewatered soil condition. Figure 2.2 shows a similar improvement to working conditions and soil strength in a battered, open excavation.

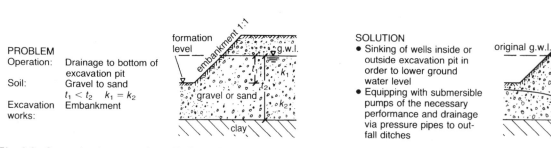

PROBLEM
Operation: Drainage to bottom of excavation pit
Soil: Gravel to sand $t_1 < t_2$ $k_1 = k_2$
Excavation works: Embankment

SOLUTION
• Sinking of wells inside or outside excavation pit in order to lower ground water level
• Equipping with submersible pumps of the necessary performance and drainage via pressure pipes to out-fall ditches

Fig. 2.2. Groundwater control applied to a battered excavation

The quantity of groundwater that may be abstracted from individual sites may be restricted by local legislation. In Berlin, for example, a maximum discharge from any one site into watercourses has for some years been limited to 1.5 litres/s for every 1000 m^2 of wetted wall and base slab areas. Any discharge into watercourses or public sewers may be controlled by legislation regarding the quality of the discharge water. In the United Kingdom such discharge may be considered to be trade waste.

Available methods of groundwater control

The four main methods used to exclude groundwater from deep excavations are[1]:

(a) stopping surface water from entering the excavation by using, for example, cut-off ditches, low walls and embankments
(b) allowing water to flow into the excavation and subsequently pumping it from drainage sumps, grips, ditches or French drains
(c) pre-draining the soil by lowering the groundwater level ahead of the excavation, for example, by use of wellpoints or deep wells
(d) stopping the groundwater from entering the excavation by a cut-off wall within the soil, such as a cement–bentonite slurry wall.

Table 2.1 shows the wide range of available techniques, which fall broadly into these four categories. Selection of the most effective method at minimum cost will depend on a number of factors, such as the dimensions of the excavation (in particular its depth), the thickness and type of soil strata, the depth of the excavation relative to soil types, the magnitude of groundwater pressure in each stratum, the prevention of damage to nearby structures and services, and the length of time the excavation is to remain open.

Preliminary guidance on choosing the best method may be gained from Table 2.2, which shows the influence of the width and depth of the excavation. The range of application of dewatering techniques (related to permeability and drawdown) is shown in Fig. 2.3, and similarly the range of groundwater exclusion methods varying by soil particle size is shown in Fig. 2.4.

In very broad terms, open excavations are frequently dewatered using single- or multi-stage wellpointing systems and sheeted excavations for basements and cut-and-cover construction often use sump pumping where the sheeting can be economically driven or excavated into an impermeable stratum to get a natural seal. Where a natural cut-off cannot be obtained, a horizontal grout plug can be injected to obtain a cut-off. Where artesian pressure heads need to be relieved in deep strata below excavations, this may be done by relief wells or deep pumped wells. For both open and sheeted excavations, deep wells with submersible pumps at the well screens are often used to obtain a drawdown which would not have been possible by wellpointing or sump pumping. The use of vertical cut-off walls to isolate construction areas from inundated surrounding areas of subsoil can be applied to achieve economies in pumping resources and construction time.

A site investigation is necessary before choosing a dewatering method. This will accurately define the depths and types of strata, from which permeabilities may be estimated and groundwater levels assessed. The site investigation must disclose any tidal influences. Where groundwater is to be removed from the site, its method of disposal must be investigated and any risk of contaminants within the groundwater carefully evaluated.

The contractor is therefore faced with a choice of dewatering or groundwater exclusion methods which will each have advantages and disadvantages in terms of cost, overall efficiency, time and convenience. Some indication of

Table 2.1 Methods of groundwater control[38]

Method	Soils suitable for treatment	Uses	Advantages	Disadvantages
Group 1: surface water control				
1. Ditches 2. Training walls 3. Embankments	All soils if used in conjunction with polythene sheeting	Open excavations	Simple methods of diverting surface water	May be an obstruction to construction traffic
Group 2: temporary groundwater control				
Internal pumping				
4. Sump pumping	Clean gravels and coarse sands	Open, shallow excavations	Simple pumping from ground	Fines easily removed. Encourages instability of formation
5. Gravity drainage	Impermeable soils	Open excavation especially on sloping sites	Simple pumping equipment	
Groundwater lowering				
6. Wellpoint systems with suction pumps (including the machine-laid horizontal system)	Sandy gravels down to fine sands (with proper control can also be used in silty sands)	Open excavation including progressive trench excavations. Horizontal drain system particularly pertinent for pipe trench excavations outside urban areas	Quick and easy to install in suitable soils. Economical for short pumping periods of a few weeks	Difficult to install in open gravels or ground containing cobbles and boulders. Pumping must be continuous and noise of pump may be a problem in a built-up area. Suction lift is limited to about 4·0–5·5 m, depending on soils. If greater lowering is needed, multi-stage installation is necessary
7. Eductor system using high-pressure water to create vacuum as well as to lift the water	Silty sands and sandy silts	Deep excavations in space so confined that multi-stage wellpointing cannot be used. More appropriate to low-permeability soils	No limitation on amount of drawdown. Raking holes are possible	Initial installation is fairly costly. Risk of flooding excavation if high-pressure water main is ruptured
8. Shallow bored wells with suction pumps	Sandy gravels to silty fine sands and water bearing rocks but particularly suitable for high-permeability soils	More appropriate for installations to be pumped for several months or for use in silty soils where correct filtering is important	Generally costs less to run than a comparable wellpoint installation, so if pumping is required for several months costs should be compared. Correct filtering can be controlled better than with wellpoints to prevent removal of fines from silty soils	Initial installation is fairly costly. Pumping must be continuous and noise of pump may be a problem in a built-up area. Suction is limited to about 4·0–5·5 m, depending on soils, If greater lowering is needed, multi-stage installation is necessary
9. Deep-bored filter wells, i.e. those with submersible pumps (line-shaft pumps with motor mounted at well head used in some countries)	Gravels to silty fine sand and water-bearing rocks	Deep excavations in, through or above water-bearing formations	No limitation on amount of drawdown as there is for suction pumping. A well can be constructed to draw water from several layers throughout its depth. Vacuum can be applied to assist drainage of fine soils. Wells can be sited clear of working area. No noise problem if mains electricity supply is available	High installation cost

Table 2.1 continued

Method	Soils suitable for treatment	Uses	Advantages	Disadvantages
10. Electro-osmosis	Silts, silty clays and some peats	Open excavations in appropriate soils or to speed dissipation of water during construction	In appropriate soils can be used when no other water-lowering method is applicable	Installation and running costs are usually high
11. Drainage galleries	Any water-bearing strata underlain by low permeability strata suitable for tunnelling	Removal of large quantities of water for dam abutment, cut-offs, etc.	Very large quantities of water can be drained into gallery and disposed of by conventional large-scale pumps	Very expensive, galleries may need to be concreted and grouted later
12. Collector well	Clean sands and gravel	Dewatering deep confined aquifers	Minimizes number of pumping points	Only suitable for large excavations

Group 3: exclusion methods
Temporary methods

Method	Soils suitable for treatment	Uses	Advantages	Disadvantages
13. Ammonium/brine refrigeration	All types of saturated soils and rock	Formation of ice in the voids stops water flow	Imparts temporary mechanical strength to soils. Treatment effective from working surface outwards. Better for large applications of long duration	Treatment takes time to develop. Installation costs are high and refrigeration plant is expensive. Requires strict site control. Some ground heave
14. Liquid nitrogen refrigeration	As for 13	As for 13	As for 13, but better for small applications of short duration or where quick freezing is required	Liquid nitrogen is expensive. Requires strict site control. Some ground heave
15. Compressed air	All types of saturated soils and rock	Confined chambers such as tunnels, shafts and caissons	Gives stability to sides of chamber by limiting ingress of water. Reduces pumping to a minimum	High set-up costs; possible health hazards
16. Slurry trench cut-off with bentonite or native clay	Silts, sands, gravels and cobbles	Practically unrestricted. Extensive curtain walls round open excavation	A rapidly installed, cheaper form of diaphragm wall. Can be keyed into impermeable strata such as clays or soft shales	Must be adequately supported. Cost increases greatly with depth. Costly to attempt to key into hard or irregular bedrock surfaces. Not effective in soils of greater permeability than 5×10^{-3} m/s
17. Impervious soil barrier	Silts, sands, gravels and cobbles	As for 16	Relatively cheap. Local materials may be used	Must be placed some distance from excavation. Restricted depth of installation
18. Sheet piling (can be permanent)	All types of soil (except boulder beds and where natural or unnatural obstructions exist — particularly timber baulks)	Practically unrestricted	Well understood method using readily available plant. Rapid installation. Steel can be incorporated in permanent works or recovered	Difficult to drive and maintain seal in boulders. Vibration and noise of driving may not be acceptable. Capital investment in piles can be high if re-usage is restricted. Seal may not be perfect; proprietary seals may be expensive

Table 2.1 continued

Method	Soils suitable for treatment	Uses	Advantages	Disadvantages
Permanent methods — diaphragms				
19. Diaphragm walls (structural concrete)	All soil types including those containing boulders (rotary percussion drilling suitable for penetrating rocks and boulders by reverse circulation using bentonite slurry)	Deep basements. Underground car parks. Underground pumping stations. Shafts. Dry docks. Cut-and-cover construction, etc.	Can be designed to form part of a permanent foundation. Particularly efficient for circular excavations. Can be keyed into rock. Minimum vibration and noise. Treatment is permanent. Can be used in restricted space. Can be put down very close to existing foundations	High cost may prove uneconomical unless it can be incorporated into permanent structure. There is an upper limit to the density of steel reinforcement that can be accepted
20. Secant (interlocking) and contiguous bored piles	All soil types, but penetration through boulders may be difficult and costly	As for 19. Underpasses in stiff clay soils	Can be used on small and confined sites. Can be put down very close to existing foundations. Minimum noise and vibration. Treatment is permanent	Ensuring complete contact of all piles over their full length may be difficult in practice. Joints may be sealed by grouting externally. Efficiency of reinforcing steel not as high as for 19
Permanent methods — grouted cut-offs				
21. Thin, grouted membrane	Silts and sands	As for 16	As for 16	The driving and extracting of the H pile or sheet pile element used to form the membrane limits the depth achievable and the type of soil. Also as for 16
22. Jet grouting	All types of soil and weak rocks	Practically unrestricted	As for 16	Expensive
23. Cementitious	Fissured and jointed rocks	Filling fissures to stop water flow (filler added for major voids)	Equipment is simple and can be used in confined spaces. Treatment is permanent	Treatment needs to be extensive to be effective
24. Clay/cementitious grouts	Sands and gravels	Filling voids to exclude water. To form relatively impermeable barriers (vertical or horizontal). Suitable for conditions where long-term flexibility is desirable, e.g. cores of dams	Equipment is simple and can be used in confined spaces. Treatment is permanent. Grout is introduced by means of a sleeved grout pipe which limits its spread. Can be sealed to an irregular or hard stratum	A comparatively thick barrier is needed to ensure continuity. At least 4 m of natural cover needed (or equivalent)
25. Silicates, Joosten, Guttman and other processes	Medium and coarse sands and gravels	As for 24, but non-flexible	Comparatively high mechanical strength. High degree of control of grout spread. Simple means of injection by lances. Indefinite life. Favoured for underpinning works below water level	Comparatively high cost of chemicals. Requires at least 2 m of natural cover or equivalent. Treatment can be incomplete in silty material or in presence of silt or clay lenses

Table 2.1 continued

Method	Soils suitable for treatment	Uses	Advantages	Disadvantages
26. Resin grouts	Silty fine sands	As for 24, but only some flexibility	Can be used in conjunction with clay/cementitious grouts for treating finer strata	High cost, so usually economical only on larger civil engineering works. Requires strict site control
Permanent methods — soil strengthening				
27. Electrochemical consolidation	Soft clays	Improving shear strength of soft clay without causing settlement	See 'Uses'	Installation and running costs are usually high

Table 2.2 Depth and width restrictions for excavations that use groundwater control methods[38]

	Depth limits	Width limits	Other limits
Groundwater control by pumping			
1. Sump pumping	Limits of excavation: Up to 8 m below pump installation level	Increasing width increases required sump and ditch capacity	Flatter slopes may be required for unsupported excavations in silts and fine sands
2. Single system wellpoints	Maximum limit of drawdown: 3–4 m in silty fine sands, 5–6 m generally	Limited by soil cone of depression (R_0)	Space required for unsupported side slopes
3. Multi-stage wellpoints	Unlimited	Limited by soil cone of depression (R_0)	Requires increasingly larger land-take for side slopes
4. Horizontal wellpointing	Limits in installation below ground level: 4 m normally, 6 m maximum	As for 2	Segmental installation lengths usually 100 m long. Space required for a machine 13 m by 3 m
5. Eductor	Unlimited but for wellpoint type drawdown usually restricted to 25 m	As for 7	As for 7
6. Shallow wells	Limit of drawdown: 6–8 m below pump installation level	Not usually critical, but the wider the excavation the more wells are required. Limited then by cone of depression (R_0)	
7. Deep bored wells	Unrestricted using submersible pumps	Not usually critical, but the wider the excavation the more wells are required	Extremely large excavation may require ancillary wells within the excavation
8. Electro-osmosis	Limits of excavation: 8 m below pump installation level	Not critical	Available power supply
9. Drainage galleries	Can be installed at any depth where access is available	Unlimited	May require large working space at installation level
10. Collector well	As for 7	As for 7	As for 7

Table 2.2 continued

	Depth limits	Width limits	Other limits
Groundwater control by exclusion			
11. Freezing	Unlimited (cases recorded to >900 m below ground level). Depends on depth to which receiving holes can be drilled. Liquid nitrogen required for deeper projects	Not critical, excavation base can be frozen. However, because of economics usually confined to narrow excavation	Circular construction highly desirable for stability. Long time required for installation and freezing
12. Compressed air	See statutory regulations	Depends on depth below ground level	Must be used in an enclosed environment, as in tunnels and shafts
13. Slurry trenching	25 m below ground level or as restricted by reach of digging plant employed	None	
14. Impervious soil barrier	Usually 5 m or less	None, since cut-off achieved	Must be placed some distance from excavation. Space is required for construction
15. Sheet piling	Recommended maximum below ground level 20 m. Have been used to >30 m, but piles may not then be recoverable	None, providing adequate penetration achieved. Wide excavation may require ancillary central dewatering	Overhead space for driving required. When used as double wall cofferdam, ratio of width to retained height >0·8. Noise problem
16. Diaphragm wall	Installation below ground level to 40 m normal. Up to 100 m can be achieved	None, but minimum diameter of a circular cut-off about 4·5 m	Space required for a stabilizing bund if wall is not tied or propped
17. Secant (interlocking) and contiguous bored piles	Maximum depth of installation 30 m below ground level or to hard strata		Overhead space for boring rig required
18. Thin grouted membrane	Limits of installation below ground level: 15 m if driven (usual) 25 m if vibrated	None	
19. Jet grouting	Cannot be used through hard rock		
20. Grouting processes	Determined by depth to which receiving hole can be drilled and presence of strata which cannot be penetrated by chosen grout. 12 m below ground level for driven lance methods (e.g. Joosten). >250 m for tube-à-manchette methods in soft deposits	Unlimited, but more efficient in confined areas rather than as curtains	
21. Electrochemical consolidation	Not critical, but preferably <8 m	Not critical	Available power supply

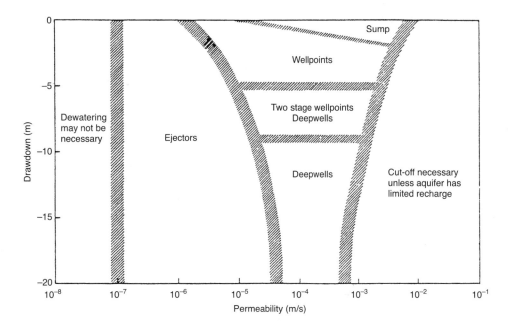

Fig. 2.3. Tentative range of application of dewatering techniques related to soil permeability and drawdown[37]

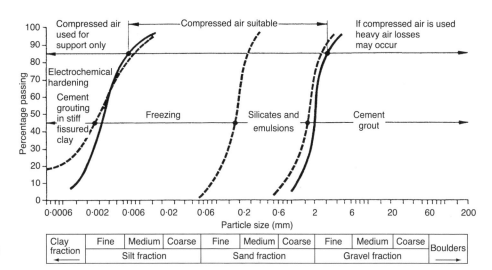

Fig. 2.4. Tentative ranges of soils for groundwater exclusion methods[38]

the cost of each method can be seen from Tables 2.3–2.5, originally included in CIRIA Report C515[1] but here augmented and corrected to 2003 prices.

In terms of overall efficiency, BS 8004[2] recommends that the following conditions should be fulfilled when dewatering excavations.

(a) The lowered groundwater level should be kept under full control at all times, to avoid fluctuations that could affect the stability of the excavations (and presumably the continuity of construction work within it).

(b) The method adopted should be chosen so that the excavation remains stable at all times, that is, slips do not occur in the sides of the excavation and excessive heaving of the base does not arise.

(c) When the aquifer to be drained consists of a fairly uniformly graded granular material, it can establish itself as a material filter to prevent loss of ground as a result of the pumping. (If this is not the case, filter material needs to be placed around the well screen to avoid the transport of fines, particularly in sandy silts and fine sands. The

Table 2.3. Approximate costs of groundwater control[38]

Method	Cost approximation
Sump pumping	Cheapest. Cost of excavating sumps, pump hire, attendance and operation. Note high relative cost of fuel: for 150 mm pump, fuel costs approx. £30 per 24 h pump hire £190 per week
Wellpointing	Very competitive for reasonable length excavations to moderate depth over short period. Approximate cost for 100 m nominal length of wellpoint equipment with wellpoints at 1·5 m centres: mobilization, installation and demobilization allow £3000 (sum). Hire of equipment including two 150 mm pumps £600–£700 per week. Cost of operating system and fuel costs: £650–750 per week. Disposable wellpoints are cheaper for long-term projects
Shallow wells	More expensive than wellpoints of same depth, but competitive on confined sites with medium- to high-permeability soils
Eductors	Expensive but may be the best engineering solution
Deep bored wells	Relatively costly depending on number installed, depth and strata. Usually only economic for large projects. Installation only costs approx. £250 per linear metre of well, with operating costs extra
Horizontal wellpoints	Dependent on plant availability. Expensive mobilization but can be competitive for the right job, e.g. pipelines or drainage. Installation only £15 to £20 per linear metre installed plus pump hire/operation
Electro-osmosis	Very high energy costs
Electrochemical consolidation	Very high energy costs

Note. 2003 UK prices; costs are only approximate and vary from job to job, influenced by job size and location, access conditions, ground conditions and period of dewatering. Mobilization and demobilization costs are not included.

Table 2.4. Relative costs of permanent methods of excluding groundwater[38]

Method	Relative cost
Impervious soil barrier	Inexpensive form of cut-off for shallow depths but dependent on availability of local clay soil. May require dewatering during construction
Shallow concrete cut-off	If local soils are permeable, mass concrete walls of limited depth may be feasible
Slurry trench with soil backfill	Relatively inexpensive cut-off. Performance not necessarily adequate. Often undertaken with extended backhoe without concrete guide walls
Thin grouted membrane	An inexpensive cut-off particularly in granular subsoils where H pile former can be inserted by vibration economically
Jet grouting and intrusion grouting	Secant walls in jet grouted soils and intrusion grouting may be cost feasible depending on soil conditions
Soil mix walls	Use of overlapping columns in soil mix may be feasible depending on type of soil and availability of local expertise
Slurry trenching	Competitive at moderate depths where extended backhoe excavation is feasible. Plastic sheets may be inserted to improve performance
Diaphragm walling	Expensive but feasible to depths in excess of 50 m by use of cutter rigs where high quality is required. May be integrated into permanent structural walls to improve overall expense
Piled wall cut-offs	Contiguous piled walls with possible later jet grouting or hard/soft secant pile construction are feasible in most subsoils to moderate depths. Expensive

Table 2.5. *Approximate costs of geotechnical processes for excluding groundwater*[38]

Method	Relative cost per m^3 of grouted soil
Grouting	
Clay	Cheapest
Cement/fly ash	£30–£40
Cement	£50–£100
Cement/bentonite	£50–£120
Bentonite gel	£50–£120
Jet grouting	£150–£200
Silicates	Joosten £50
	Aluminates £100
	Esters £120
Resins	£250–£350
Chemicals	Up to £300–£400
Compressed air	Very expensive
Freezing	Extremely expensive. Usually regarded as a last resort. More expensive than electro-osmosis. Only economic at great depth

Note. Installation methods, periods, soil and rock types, job size and location all influence site-specific prices. The above prices (2003 UK prices) are given only for broad comparison purposes.

quantity of fines pumped should be checked by using a silt trap within the discharge pipework.)

(*d*) There should be an adequate margin of pumping capacity and standby power plant.

(*e*) Water removed by pumps should be discharged clear of the excavation areas, avoiding erosion, silting or contamination of existing drains or watercourses.

(*f*) The pumping methods adopted for groundwater lowering should not lead to damage of existing structures (in particular, the risk of removal of fines by pumping and the long-term consolidation of soils, especially fine-grained soils, should be carefully evaluated; care in filter and well screen design will determine the extent of the transport of fines by pumping). The risk of settlement caused by removal of groundwater will be determined by the extent of drawdown and the consolidation characteristics of the soil, and both should be examined carefully, especially when nearby buildings are sensitive to settlement.

(*g*) At least for economy in pumping, the water level should not be lowered further than necessary to keep the excavation clear of water at all times.

(*h*) The method applied should avoid excessive loss of ground by seepage from the sides of the excavation.

The methods available to implement these conditions are described in more detail below.

Surface drainage

It is prudent to avoid surface run-off entering the excavation by the use of a cut-off ditch or French drain (using a porous pipe with a granular surround). This applies particularly on sloping ground where the cut-off drain is placed on the side of the excavation with greater elevation.

Gravity drainage

In relatively impermeable soils water can be conducted to sumps by open-jointed pipework surrounded by gravel with very little fall. Some advantageous drawdown will occur if the trench excavations are lowered when groundwater levels are close to the main formation level.

In deep cofferdams with a clay formation, gravity drainage is frequently used to conduct groundwater to a sump sited outside the plan area of the permanent works. These temporary drains should be grouted on completion of the permanent works construction to avoid introducing a weak bearing area below the permanent works and a source of free water which could cause leakage through the permanent structure. Where possible, cofferdam widths should be increased to accommodate these drains outside the permanent works and to accommodate any tolerance required in the installation of the sheeting to the cofferdam.

Sump pumping

Sump pumping is the traditional method of removing groundwater from within a sheeted deep excavation. The sump, ideally formed within the sheeted enclosure outside the plan area of the permanent construction, is equipped with a suction head to a lift pump, or with a filter head to a submersible pump where the lift would be more than 6 m or so below a suction pump. The suction or filter head can often be made with a perforated 45 gallon oil drum surrounded by a gravel filter medium. Frequently, a greater pump capacity is needed to pull the groundwater down in the sump, either prior to bulk excavation or during the course of excavation, than is required thereafter to maintain the depressed level of groundwater. It may be convenient to install the pumps in multiple units so that the pumping capacity can be reduced in the steady-state pumping condition.

Pumping from wellpoints or wells

Wellpoints and deep well systems installed prior to excavation and outside the excavation area can be used to cause groundwater to flow away from the excavation to improve stability to its side batters and base, and to allow construction works to proceed in the dry.

Traditionally, wellpoints have been an easily installed system in loose to medium-dense and well-graded sandy gravels. With a drawdown limit for each wellpoint of 5 or 6 m from the level of the pump suction, either single- or multi-tier systems can be used in battered excavations. Multi-tier systems are installed progressively as drawdown is achieved at each level of wellpointing. The wellpoints consist of small-diameter (50 mm) wellscreens and are generally spaced at regular intervals around the perimeter of the excavation. When wellpoints are spaced relatively close to one another, the completed overlapping cones of depression of the installation are such that the depressed water level is brought below the final formation level (Fig. 2.5). The wellpoints are normally jetted in, although soils such as open gravels may lead to high jetting-water loss, and other soils such as compact sands, stiff clays and boulder clays may be difficult to penetrate by jetting, in which case pre-boring may be needed. The wellpoints, once installed, are connected to a header pipe, typically 150 mm in diameter, by swing-joint connections equipped with a gate valve to each wellpoint. The header pipe is joined to the suction side of a vacuum-assisted centrifugal pump with delivery to a convenient point of discharge. Figure 2.6 gives an indication of the soil grading in which wellpoints are economical. Wellpoints are extracted after use by jetting out, although this may prove difficult if the dewatering system has been in place for a long time. Where soil contamination constitutes a serious risk of corrosion to the wellpoint screen, a disposal wellpoint with a plastic slotted tube and nylon filter fabric may prevent the screen from blocking during long-term pumping.

Pumping groundwater out of a
well results in a lowering of the
groundwater level in the vicinity
of the well, thereby forming a drainage
funnel, known as a cone of depression.

By sinking several wells at appropriate
distances from each other, an even
lowering of the groundwater level
is achieved, as the cones of
depression overlap.

Well 1 in operation

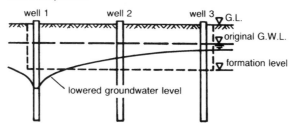

Well 1 + 2 in operation

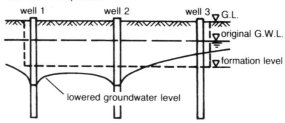

Well 1 + 2 + 3 in operation

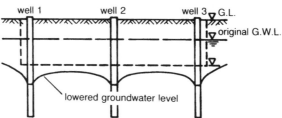

Fig. 2.5. Overlapping cones of
depression in a wellpoint
installation to produce a
depressed water level below
the formation level

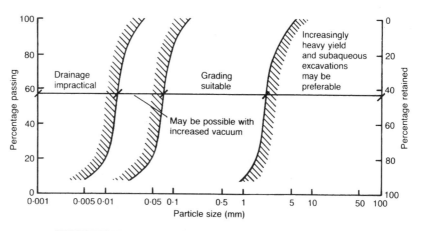

Fig. 2.6. Approximate soil
grading limits for effective
wellpoint dewatering[38]

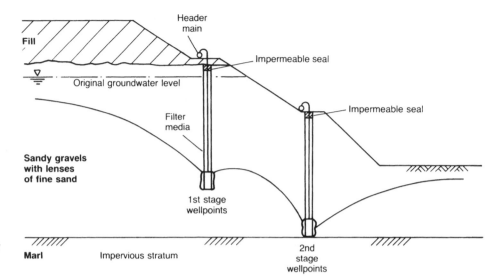

Fig. 2.7. Cross-section of a large open excavation showing typical wellpoint installation applied in two stages

Typical wellpoint installations for large open excavations of increasing depth are shown in Fig. 2.7. After drawdown has been obtained, it may be possible to remove the highest tier of wellpoints for reuse at a lower level. It should be noted that multi-stage systems often impose large construction widths to accommodate the batters and the berm widths at each wellpoint tier. Heavy construction plant may damage header pipework and it is usual to install valves within the header pipework to allow speedy isolation and replacement of any damaged sections.

Wellpoints are spaced 1 to 4 m apart, depending on soil conditions and drawdown requirements. Nomograms for spacing wellpoint installations in clean, uniform sands and gravels and stratified clean sand and gravel are shown in Fig. 2.8. The spacing should be based on the most permeable of the strata, and it should be noted that the lower the permeability of the ground, the steeper the drawdown curve. Variations between horizontal and vertical soil permeability should be noted; in stratified sands the horizontal

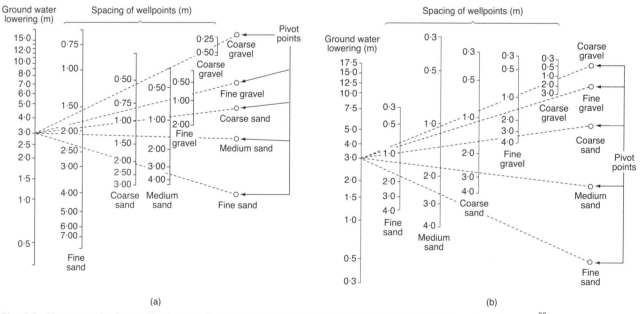

Fig. 2.8. Nomographs for wellpoint spacing: (a) uniform sands and gravels; (b) stratified sand and gravel[38]

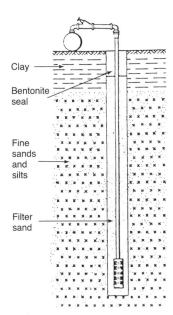

Fig. 2.9. Vertical cross-section of a sealed vacuum wellpoint

permeability (expressed in cm/s) may be up to one order less than the vertical soil permeability.

The design of wellpoint systems is considered in more detail by Cashman and Preene[3] and by Powers[4], who gives methods for estimating yield and drawdown for confined and unconfined aquifers for various well layouts.

Drawdown by wellpoints becomes progressively slower as soil grain size reduces, and becomes very slow in silts, silty sands and soils with a D_{10} grain size less than about 0·05 mm. Friction losses within pipework become critical in such soils and efficient drawdown is less likely. In these circumstances, vacuum wellpointing can be used to advantage. A bentonite clay seal is used to maintain a high vacuum at the well screen and although a conventional drawdown of groundwater is not achieved, continuous pumping and close spacing of the vacuum wellpoints prevent groundwater flow from the soil towards the excavation. A typical sealed vacuum wellpoint is shown in Fig. 2.9.

Wellpointing is often advantageous for dewatering trenchworks and can be applied to either one or both trench sides. The system can be installed progressively for long trenchworks by leapfrogging in increments of 100 to 120 m. Within this length successive operations of wellpoint installation, operation, trench excavation, trench backfilling and wellpoint extraction are carried out prior to moving forward to the next length. Although systems installed to one trench side only allow favourable access for construction activities, the extent of drawdown over the trench width may not be sufficient other than in homogeneous permeable soils. The effective depth of trench dewatering is limited of course by the 5 to 6 m maximum depth of the wellpoint itself. Figure 2.10 shows a typical installation for a single-sided wellpoint system.

Some improvement to drawdown in a layered depth can be achieved by vertical sand drains to improve vertical permeability. The use of a granular soil surround to the wellpoint, known as 'sanding-in', achieves the same purpose. The use of a double-sided wellpoint system for trenchworks is shown in Fig. 2.11. This system provides a more effective drawdown and allows a greater trench width than the single-sided system for similar soil conditions. The improvement in drawdown reduces the risk of instability at the bottom of the trench. This also results from groundwater flow towards the wellpoints and away from the bottom of the trench.

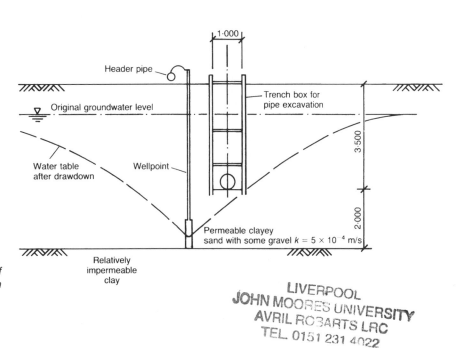

Fig. 2.10. Typical installation of a single-sided wellpoint system

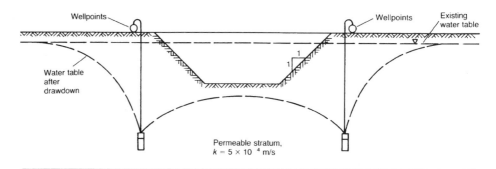

Fig. 2.11. Typical installation of a double-sided wellpoint system

Where fine-grained soils predominate, a vacuum can be applied to the well-points to improve system effectiveness, although the time taken to achieve full drawdown may prove to be longer than desired. Some reduction in efficiency may also occur with time as air is drawn into the system through ineffective seals and joints. The effective depth of drawdown may be increased in all soils by a multi-stage system, as shown in Fig. 2.7.

The use of a dewatering system outside a sheeted excavation such as trench-works reduces the groundwater pressure from the sheeting and trench bracing, but means an increased drawdown of the water table from the area outside the excavation which is limited in extent only by the permeability of the soil itself and the volume of the aquifer. Similarly, the yield of groundwater to achieve this drawdown and the pump capacity needed is controlled by the permeability of the subsoil and the aquifer volume. Where the drawdown curve is flat, in relatively permeable strata, the removal of groundwater, sometimes un-intended, from beneath existing structures and services a considerable distance from the excavation may cause settlement and subsidence damage.

In addition to vertical drainage, horizontal drains and wellpoints are also used, particularly for trenchworks. In layered soils the difference between horizontal and vertical permeability of the soil fabric may be as large as one order of magnitude when permeability is measured in cm/s. It is therefore illogical to install dewatering that relies on the vertical flow of groundwater to the wellpoint or well screen if the means are available to lay a horizontal drain at the required depth to achieve drawdown. Trenches for drains are dug by backhoe or, alternatively, specially built machines for laying a perforated pipe within a gravel surround may be used. The maximum depth for the operation of these excavator/pipelayer machines is only of the order of 6 m, but they find application for shallow trenchworks in homogeneous sandy soils and have attractive installation outputs of up to 1000 linear metres of drain per day. Although currently available in Holland and North America these machines are now less commonly available in the United Kingdom than previously.

Ejector systems, also known as eductor systems, may provide an alternative to both conventional and vacuum wellpointing, although their adoption probably requires a more reliable and detailed knowledge of subsoil and groundwater conditions. Overall, the plant and installation costs are likely to be less than those for deep wells, and although individual ejector efficiency is low, the operational depths are not limited in the same way as wellpointing and therefore multi-tier systems become unnecessary.

Both twin- and single-pipe ejectors are used; typical pipe layouts are shown in Fig. 2.12. In the twin-pipe ejector, high-pressure water through the supply pipe and the body of the ejector is fed through the tapered nozzle. A partial

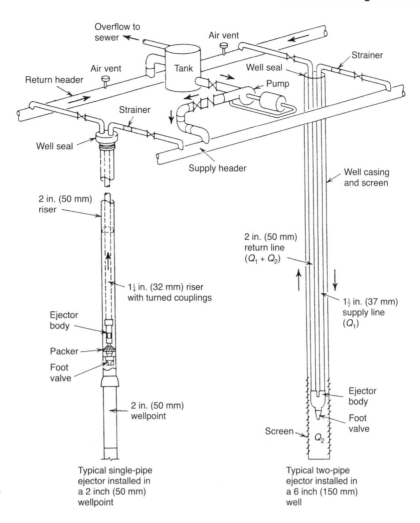

Fig. 2.12. Single- and twin-pipe
wellpoint ejector systems[4]

vacuum is caused in the suction chamber, causing groundwater to be sucked through the foot valve. Incoming supplies from the downward supply pipe and through the foot valve mix in the suction chamber and pass into the Venturi where the velocity decreases and the pressure increase is sufficient to send the combined supplies through the second pipe to ground level. This twin-pipe system is usually installed in a casing and well screen, unlike the single-pipe system, which is shown in section detail in Fig. 2.13. The single-pipe ejector can be installed within a 50 mm diameter wellpoint and, like the twin-pipe model, is self-priming and will evacuate air from its own well screen. The single-pipe system relies on downward flow of water (this time in the annular space between the casing and the inner return pipe) to a suction chamber and then, with groundwater sucked in, the water passes into a Venturi chamber where increased pressure causes the supply and the groundwater to flow upward to ground level for disposal.

Ejectors are best suited for removal of groundwater from finer-grained, low-permeability soils and are used in deep excavations and shafts beyond the depths economically operated by multi-tier wellpointing. Their operation depends on submergence below groundwater level, otherwise cavitation occurs. Deep well systems are likely to be used in preference to ejectors unless this submergence condition is reasonably certain to be maintained. Case studies of the use of ejectors and vacuum wellpoints in fine-grained Eocene soils in the UK were described by Preene[5], and methods of estimating steady-state flow rate discussed.

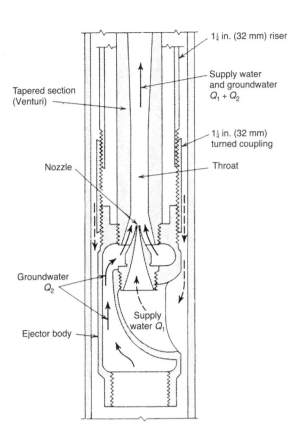

1¼ in. (32 mm) riser

Supply water
and groundwater
$Q_1 + Q_2$

Tapered section
(Venturi)

1¼ in. (32 mm)
turned coupling

Nozzle

Throat

Groundwater
Q_2

Supply
water Q_1

Ejector body

*Fig. 2.13. Cross-section of
single-pipe ejector[4]*

The most convenient subsoil conditions for excavation through inundated soils are where an impermeable stratum can be economically reached by sheeting driven, or a cut-off installed to penetrate below excavation level. Some penetration of the impermeable stratum will be needed to form a seal, and this may be achieved with difficulty in hard soils or rock strata. Grout injection may improve this seal. In these circumstances, groundwater flow below the sheeting or cut-off will be small, and providing there are no serious openings or 'windows' within the sheeting or cut-off below excavation level, there will be no risk of base failure and heave of the completed excavation at formation level. It is only necessary to pump out the volume of groundwater within the sheeting near formation level and to maintain the dewatered level. Where such a cut-off does not occur at convenient depth, a seal can be obtained with a horizontal cut-off by jet grouting or by intrusion grouting where soil permeability makes this feasible. In these circumstances, again, only limited dewatering is needed within the sheeting to keep the formation dry, providing the sheeting or cut-off is effective below formation level and leakage through the grout plug is small.

Where an impermeable stratum does not occur at a convenient depth or the use of a horizontal grout curtain is not feasible, the flow of water through permeable strata occurs downwards, under the sheeting, and then upwards to formation level. As the penetration depth of the sheeting is increased, the flow path is increased and the quantity of exit water and its exit velocity are reduced proportionally. This ingress of groundwater upwards to formation level may have serious effects because of the induced seepage forces on the passive wedge of soil below excavation level supporting the external sheeting. Marsland[6] showed the relevance of this seepage force in model tests and, later, Soubra and Kestner[7] considered the effects of this seepage force on alternative passive failure mechanisms. The risk of instability below formation level within a sheeted excavation is described later in this chapter. In finer-grained

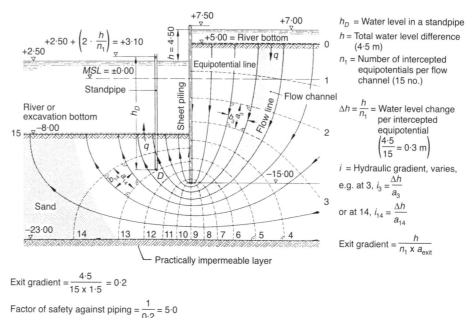

h_D = Water level in a standpipe

h = Total water level difference (4·5 m)

n_1 = Number of intercepted equipotentials per flow channel (15 no.)

$\Delta h = \dfrac{h}{n_1}$ = Water level change per intercepted equipotential

$\left(\dfrac{4·5}{15} = 0·3\ \text{m}\right)$

i = Hydraulic gradient, varies, e.g. at 3, $i_3 = \dfrac{\Delta h}{a_3}$

or at 14, $i_{14} = \dfrac{\Delta h}{a_{14}}$

Exit gradient = $\dfrac{h}{n_1 \times a_{\text{exit}}}$

Fig. 2.14. Effect of seepage pressure on base stability within an excavation in sand: calculation of exit gradient and factor of safety against piping

Exit gradient = $\dfrac{4·5}{15 \times 1·5} = 0·2$

Factor of safety against piping = $\dfrac{1}{0·2} = 5·0$

If groundwater is reduced to −8.00 at excavation bottom, exit gradient = $\dfrac{15}{15 \times 1·5} = 0·67$

and factor of safety against piping = $\dfrac{1}{0·67} = 1.5$

soils where the differential head of groundwater between the outside and inside of the sheeting to the excavation is high, soil liquefaction can occur when the vertical effective stress within the soil reaches zero, a condition caused by the seepage pressure. This condition can be examined by considering the critical exit velocity with the use of a flow net, as shown in Fig. 2.14, and will give an early indication of risk. Figure 2.15 shows the reduction in factor of safety against piping as the width of a trench in fine sand is progressively reduced. The possibility of base instability within excavations in soft clays should be examined, as described in Chapter 7 on cofferdam design.

Where the ingress of groundwater below sheeting is such that seepage pressures are excessive or the quantity of water is too great to remove by horizontal drains and sump pumping, the use of deep wells near the toe of the sheeting becomes necessary. Screens for these deep wells may be sited below the toe of the sheeting to reduce flow and upward seepage pressures, but at the expense of greater yield of groundwater and increased radius of drawdown.

A cross-section through a deep well is shown in Fig. 2.16[8]. Methods of boring for the installation of deep wells are summarized in Table 2.6 from the CIRIA report[1]. The diameter of the bore is dependent largely on the diameter of the submersible pump required. The initial equipment and installation costs for a deep well scheme are higher than those for wellpoint systems, although pumping efficiency is generally better and similar to that in water well schemes. The wells typically consist of a plastic well casing surrounded by granular filter media over the screen length with a bentonite seal above the filter. A geotextile or nylon sock is usually placed over the well screen to avoid any movement of the filter media towards the pump. More durable and stronger screens from galvanized or stainless steel are employed where long-term performance in fine-grained soils is required. An electric submersible pump of the required power and capacity is suspended within the well screen depth and connected to riser and header pipes.

BS 8004[2] provides a useful guide to the design of filters to surround deep well installations, pumping sumps or blankets to control seepage:

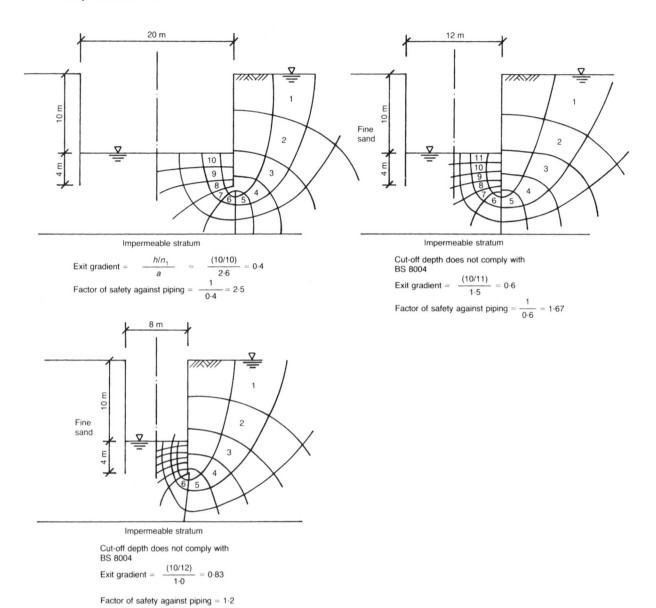

Exit gradient $= \dfrac{h/n_1}{a} = \dfrac{(10/10)}{2 \cdot 6} = 0 \cdot 4$

Factor of safety against piping $= \dfrac{1}{0 \cdot 4} = 2 \cdot 5$

Cut-off depth does not comply with BS 8004

Exit gradient $= \dfrac{(10/11)}{1 \cdot 5} = 0 \cdot 6$

Factor of safety against piping $= \dfrac{1}{0 \cdot 6} = 1 \cdot 67$

Cut-off depth does not comply with BS 8004

Exit gradient $= \dfrac{(10/12)}{1 \cdot 0} = 0 \cdot 83$

Factor of safety against piping $= 1 \cdot 2$

Fig. 2.15. *Reduction in the factor of safety against piping as cofferdam width is reduced, shown by flow net calculations*

(a) The 15% size of the filter should not be greater than four times the 85% size of the natural soil of the protected material surrounding the filter (point A, Fig. 2.17).

(b) The 15% size of the filter should not be less than four times the 15% size of the protected material (point B, Fig. 2.17).

(c) Filters should not contain more than 5% material passing through a 75 mm sieve (point C, Fig. 2.17), and such material should be cohesionless. Where the size given by (b) is less than that given by (c), the latter should apply.

(d) The grading curve of the filter material should roughly follow the same shape as the grading curve of the protected material.

(e) The 50% size of the filter should not exceed 25 times the 50% size of the protected material (point E, Fig. 2.17).

(f) Where the protected material contains a large proportion of gravel or coarser material, the filter should be designed on the basis of the

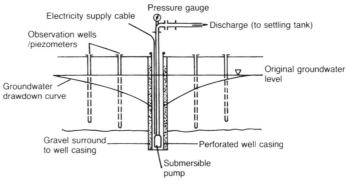

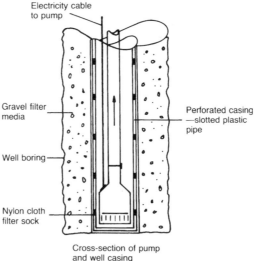

Fig. 2.16. Cross-section of a typical deep well with observation wells[8]

grading of that proportion of the protected material finer than the 19 mm sieve.

(g) Where the soil is gap graded (e.g. a silty fine sand with some gravel) the coarser particles cannot prevent the finer particles from migrating through the large pore spaces in the filter, if the latter is designed on the complete grading curve of the soil. Therefore, the coarse particles should be ignored and the grading limits for the filter should be selected on the grading curve of the finer soil.

(h) Where a filter is placed against a variable soil, the filter has to be designed to protect the finest soil. Generally, rule (a) should be applied to the finest soil and rule (b) to the coarsest.

(i) Filter material should be well graded within the limits permitted by the range of particle sizes to avoid segregation when placing.

(j) The maximum size of the filter material should not be more than about 80 mm.

BS 8004 adds that in practice slightly coarser grading may be needed to ensure reasonable flow of water to the well without initial loss of an unreasonable quantity of fines.

Deep well systems are often applied in deep excavations within temporary cofferdams or basement excavations to remove groundwater from sands and gravels or to intercept flow from water-bearing rocks. In particular, they can be used to relieve artesian groundwater pressure at depth from contained aquifers. In order that pumping prior to excavation may be effective, the period required to achieve reduction of head should not be estimated too

Table 2.6 Summary of principal drilling techniques used for dewatering well installations[38]

Method	Resources	Typical diameter and depth of bore	Notes
Jetting with hammer-action placing tube	Supervisor Labourers Crane operator Hammer-action tube Large jetting pump Large compressor Crane, twin roped, free fall	300 mm cased to 20 m depth	Not widely used. Not usually cost-effective for installation of just a few wells. Can be difficult to monitor and control. Special safety measures may be necessary
Cable percussion	Drill rig operator Assistant drillers Cable percussion drill and casing	150–600 mm cased to about 50 m depth in unstable ground with casing telescoped 100 m depth or more in stable formations uncased	Widely available. Effective at penetrating granular and cohesive soils. Slow penetration if rock or cobbles and boulders present
Rotary open-hole with mud, direct circulation	Drill rig operator Assistant driller Rotary drill and rods Mud Mud handling system	150–600 mm uncased to 100 m depth or more with appropriate rig	Rapid installation rates achievable in granular and cohesive soils. Cobbles and boulders can cause difficulty
Rotary open-hole with mud, reverse circulation	Drill rig operator Assistant driller Rotary drill and rods Mud Mud handling system	400 mm plus uncased to 100 m depth or more with appropriate rig	Similar to direct circulation system, but usually used for larger holes
Rotary cased hole with water flush	Drill rig operator Assistant driller Jetting pump Rotary drill and casing	100–250 mm cased to 30 m depth or more with appropriate rig	An appropriate rig can penetrate virtually any ground from hard rock to soft clay
Rotary down the hole hammer	Drill rig operator Assistant driller Large compressor Rotary drill and rods Down the hole hammer (Foam)	76–600 mm to 100 m depth or more with appropriate rig	Requires the use of duplex systems in unstable formations

optimistically. Failure to achieve sufficient drawdown may limit excavation progress or, worse, induce base failure of the formation where reduction of the artesian head is not measured or taken into account.

Design of a deep well system for a sheeted or enclosed excavation should be made with reliable data regarding groundwater level, soil stratification and soil fabric permeability. Due to the importance of the installation and the capital costs related to the number of wells required, soil permeability values should be assessed from full-scale pumping tests wherever possible. Where buildings or services are nearby, it is essential that settlement risk due to dewatering is assessed and, where necessary, the cost and construction time of local recharge schemes allowed for.

An example of the successful application of a deep well dewatering scheme is shown in Fig. 2.18. The site for an underpass some 600 m long and maximum depth 12 m had been reclaimed using hydraulic fill from the coastline at Jeddah. The subsoil conditions are also shown in Fig. 2.18: 1 m thick loose sand and gravel fill overlaid the reclamation material consisting of

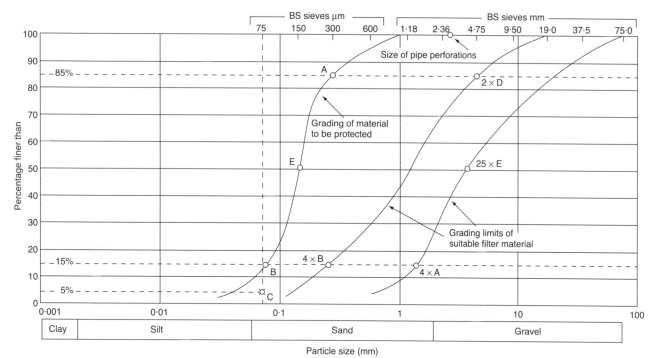

Fig. 2.17. Design rules for filters[2]

very loose sand and a medium dense to dense clayey sand to a depth of 7 m. Below this reclamation a layer of soft coral limestone interbedded with dense coralline sand 7 m thick overlaid dense clayey sand. The existing groundwater level was generally 1 m deep over the whole of a fairly flat site. The underpass walls were designed to be built in structural diaphragm walls and the whole structure was anchored by tension piles. The structural walls, spanned by a reinforced concrete floor slab, resembled a floating structure anchored by the piles. The structural walls did not achieve either a temporary or permanent seal into impermeable soil or rock at depth. Cross-diaphragms in self-hardening slurry works subdivided the excavation into three compartments, but none of these walls achieved a cut-off with depth. The three compartments were successively excavated and dewatered by a total of 29 deep wells. The specification for the wells and the pumps is shown in Fig. 2.19. The cost of the four cross-diaphragm slurry walls was significantly less than savings made from reducing the programme time; early commencement of excavation within the first compartment was possible prior to completion of the structural diaphragm walls further along the underpass. Compartment working also reduced drawdown of groundwater at the shallower excavation levels at each end of the underpass. The dewatering scheme was particularly successful, bearing in mind the limited opportunity for pumping prior to bulk excavation within a very short construction programme worked on a 24-hour, seven-day basis. At the deepest section of the underpass, the deep wells reduced groundwater to a metre or so below formation level with two to three weeks of pumping prior to excavation.

In such conditions, the penetration depth of the external diaphragm walls is selected to meet the most severe of four design criteria: first, the minimum depth to avoid piping of loose sand below formation level; second, the minimum depth to give sufficient passive resistance to support the external walls prior to casting the floor slab to the underpass; third, the optimum depth to extend the drainage path to formation level for external groundwater;

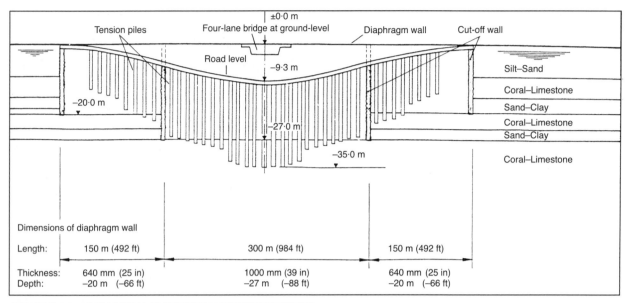

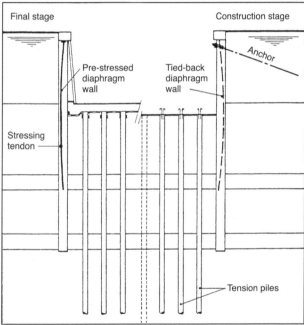

Fig. 2.18. Diwan Underpass, Jeddah, Saudi Arabia, longitudinal and transverse section

last, to site the well heads within the walls at the most economical depth. The optimum depth for the well heads minimizes the number of wells required to achieve drawdown, at the same time reducing the quantities to be pumped in terms of available pump capacity and energy used. Wall penetration and the design of the dewatering scheme in sheeted deep excavations is referred to later in this chapter.

Use of relief wells

The use of vertical relief wells each consisting of a granular filter backfill placed within and surrounding a slotted well screen can be effective, without pumping, for transferring perched water tables to lower, partly-filled aquifers below deep excavations. Ward[9] also referred to the use of this simple

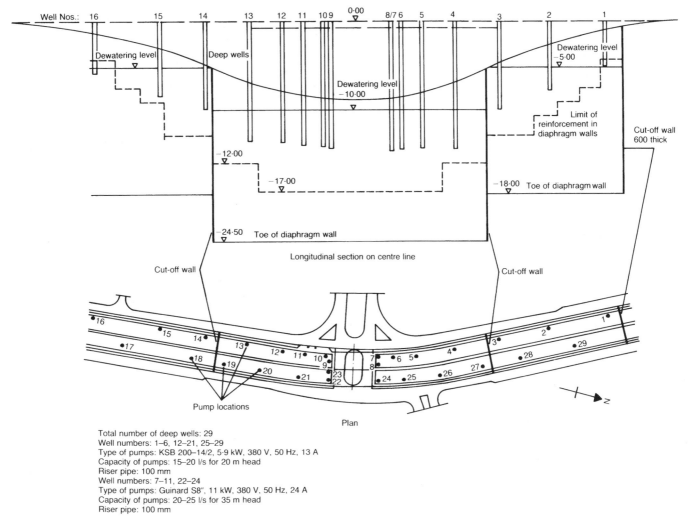

Fig. 2.19. Location of cut-offs and deep wells for the Diwan Underpass, Jeddah, Saudi Arabia (courtesy of Bauer)

procedure to relieve the artesian pressure which had caused uplift of the formation and damage to pipework in a trench excavation penetrating laminated sand and silty clay with entrapped artesian groundwater.

Groundwater control by cut-offs

Relatively impermeable walls or cut-offs can be effective in temporarily excluding groundwater from deep excavations, reducing the need for removal of groundwater by pumping. The use of cut-offs can therefore materially improve construction progress by dividing a basement or cut-and-cover excavation into compartments, allowing excavation to proceed below the water table in construction areas where perimeter soil-retaining walls have been completed, the cut-off achieving a seal into an impermeable stratum below the aquifer prior to the completion of the whole perimeter wall. Cut-offs can also be effective in restricting the flow of groundwater from aquifers exposed by battered, open excavations.

The cut-off may possess both flexural strength and relative impermeability, such as walls built from sheet piling, reinforced concrete piling and diaphragm walling, or the cut-off may have low permeability, relatively high flexibility and low flexural strength. Cut-offs in the latter category include unreinforced diaphragm walls in plastic concrete, thin diaphragm cut-offs made by grout

Table 2.7 Summary of cut-off methods[8]

Method	Soils suitable for treatment	Uses
1. Sheet piling	All types of soil (except boulder beds and rock)	Practically unrestricted
2. Diaphragm walls (structural concrete)	All soil types including those containing boulders (rotary percussion drilling suitable for penetrating rocks and boulders by reverse circulation using bentonite slurry)	Deep basements Underground car parks Underground pumping stations Shafts Dry docks
3. Slurry trench cut-off	Silts, sands, gravels and cobbles	Practically unrestricted Extensive curtain walls round open excavations
4. Thin grouted membrane	Silts and sands	As for 3
5. Contiguous and secant bored pile walls (and mix-in-place pile walls)	All soil types but penetration through boulders may be difficult and costly	As for 2
6. Cement grouts	Fissured and jointed rocks	Filling fissures to stop water flow (filler added for major voids)
Grouted cut-offs		
7. Clay/cement grouts	Sands and gravels	Filling voids to exclude water. To form relatively impermeable barriers — vertical or horizontal. Suitable for conditions where long-term flexibility is desirable, e.g. cores of dams
8. Silicates: Joosten, Guttman and other processes	Medium and coarse sand and gravels	As for 7, but non-flexible
9. Resin grouts	Silty fine sands	As for 7, but only some flexibility
Freezing		
10. Ammonium/brine refrigeration	All types of saturated soils and rocks	Formation of ice in the voids stops water flow
11. Liquid nitrogen refrigerant	As for 10	As for 10

injection, mix-in-place pile walls, unreinforced bentonite slurry walls, cement–bentonite slurry walls and membranes. These low strength cut-offs rely for their support above formation level on soil berms between the cut-off and the excavation, and find economic application in temporary works where only the property of relative impermeability is needed. Specialist methods such as installation of freeze soil barriers using ammonia/brine or liquid nitrogen find application in particular locations in fine-grained saturated soils which justify relatively high installation and running costs. Table 2.7 summarizes cut-off methods[8].

The effectiveness of cut-offs constructed from grout curtains and slurry trenches was discussed by Ambrasseys[10] and later by Brauns[11] and others. The effectiveness of cut-off walls using jointed methods such as sheet piling, concrete piling and concrete diaphragm walls was reviewed by Telling *et al.*[12], referring to the use of the cut-offs below dam structures. Analytical appraisal of cut-off efficiency, while important for permanent cut-offs below dams, is not of prime importance for temporary works in deep excavations, although the practical aspects of avoiding local windows caused by bad workmanship and leading to leakages in temporary cut-offs may prove to be vital.

Fig. 2.20. Triple auger rig used in mix-in-place piling (courtesy of Raito Inc.)

Mix-in-place pile walls

The use of mix-in-place methods, combining cement additives, water and soil, was first applied by the Japanese Ministry of Transportation in 1975 using multi-shaft augers. The method, now popular in Japan and the United States is finding progressive application in Europe, as plant manufacturers develop equipment to efficiently mix in place either powdered additives to the soil or wet grout pre-mixed and achieved to the requisite depth through the hollow stem of a deep auger. Figure 2.20 shows a typical triple auger rig.

Cut-off construction using slurry wall techniques

The development of slurry cut-off walls began in the mid 1940s when the US Corps of Engineers used permanent cut-off construction below levees on the Mississippi river. Wide cut-offs excavated by dragline were put down under bentonite slurry, and the excavated soils were later backfilled by dozer. The slurry stabilizes the trench during excavation and is left in place, with the backfilled soil used to form the cut-off. A filter cake slurry deposit forms on the trench sides during excavation and acts compositely with the backfilled soil and slurry to resist the flow of water across the trench. Many cut-offs of this type were subsequently made in the United States to depths of 30 m or more and widths varying up to 3 m for temporary and permanent control of seepage into excavations, as foundation and embankment cut-offs for water-retaining structures, and to prevent seepage of various pollutants from contaminated groundwater. D'Appolonia[13] described construction methods by dragline and backhoe and provided values of wall permeability as a function of the bentonite content of completed backfill and the permeability of soil–bentonite backfill related to fines content. Overall, however, the application of such wide, deep soil–bentonite slurry cut-offs has been replaced in deep excavation works by bentonite–cement slurry membranes which are installed by backhoe with long booms to relatively shallow depths up to 10 m, to greater depths using conventional diaphragm wall equipment, or a combination of both. These cut-offs are narrower than the earlier soil–bentonite walls and vary between 600 mm and 1 m, and may also be backfilled with excavated soil, as described by Hetherington et al.[14] where impermeability requirements are less rigorous and a cheaper membrane material is needed. This innovation was first used in 1975 at Alton Water Dam, Ipswich, UK, for the construction of a permanent seepage cut-off to an impounded area. Initially, the 600 mm wide trench was excavated by backhoe and then by conventional diaphragm wall equipment, a hydraulic grab mounted on kelly bar equipment. Conventional, temporary tubular stop ends were used at the end of each working day, but guide trench construction was limited to the use of timber baulks. An initial site trial used six panels with varying cement contents for the slurry. With a constant bentonite content of 4% by weight, the cement was varied in increments from a minimum of $70 \, kg/m^3$ to a maximum of $150 \, kg/m^3$: permeability test results varied from 1×10^{-8} to $1 \times 10^{-9} \, m/s$ at the lower and higher cement contents, respectively. The water bleed did not appear to vary with cement content; a final cement content of $125 \, kg/m^3$ was used.

The properties of bentonite–cement slurry cut-off walls, known as self-hardening slurry walls, were described by Caron[15]. He examined the characteristics of the slurry in its two separate phases, initially as a means of trench support and subsequently as the hardened trench fill mixture. During the excavation phase the initial properties of the self-hardening slurry are similar to those of a bentonite slurry, but over time the cement content causes stiffening and, as excavation proceeds, the bentonite–cement slurry progressively combines with soil particles. Later, water bleed from the slurry and filtration through the sides of the trench causes further stiffening. The change in slurry stiffness and the increase in viscosity with time in the initial excavation phase were described by Caron for a range of cement types, retarder additives and soil addition to the slurry. Hardened slurry properties were also examined, but as a first approximation Caron concluded that slurry strength was governed by the cement/water ratio, viscosity by the bentonite/water ratio, and the setting time by the retarder/water ratio. More detailed analysis showed the relationships were a little more complicated, as shown in Table 2.8.

The principal characteristics to be addressed by the designer are cut-off strength, minimum strain at failure and permeability. For a typical self-hardening slurry for groundwater cut-off, these properties would be specified as follows:

Table 2.8 Hardened slurry properties[15]

Characteristic	Principal factor	Secondary factors
Strength	Cement/water ratio	Bentonite/water, retarder/water ratios
Viscosity	Bentonite/water ratio	Cement/water, retarder/water ratios
Settling time	Retarder/water ratio	Cement/water, bentonite/water ratios

- unconfined compressive strength: at 28 days, samples from panels, 90% of all results in the range 100–500 kN/m^2
- permeability: target value less than 1×10^{-9} m/s; test results from control samples from panel: all samples less than 1×10^{-8} m/s and at least 50% of all samples less than 1×10^{-9} m/s
- consolidated drained triaxial testing: all results of samples tested from panels to demonstrate strain at failure in excess of 5%.

On a cut-off contract (Kielder Water Dam, Icos, 1976) the mix proportions to achieve a similar specification were, in kilograms per cubic metre of slurry: bentonite, 54 kg/m^3; water, 942 kg/m^3; Portland cement, 28·8 kg/m^3; ground blast furnace slag, 67·2 kg/m^3; retarder additive, nil. The parameters specified were:

- permeability: 500 h after placing under a hydraulic gradient of 1:450, the sample first saturated under a back pressure of 150 kN/m^2:10^{-8} m/s
- deformation: minimum deformation under a deviator stress of 125 kN/m^2 at 2% strain per hour with cell pressure of 500 kN/m^2, 90 days after mixing: 5%.

The cut-off at Kielder was 19 m deep and 600 mm wide.

Overall, it is rare that the minimum compressive strength of the slurry proves difficult to achieve with economical cement contents. Caron proposed an empirical relationship using test results with bentonite from various sources, and concluded that a 28-day compressive strength $R = 10^4 \times$ (cement/water ratio)^2 kPa was dependable for cement/water ratios between 0·1 and 0·7. Caron commented that deviations from this relationship could be attributed to the nature of the bentonite, but considered that this contradicted the more reasoned assumption that the cement should have a more important influence on slurry strength than the colloidal agent that keeps it in suspension. Tornaghi[16] in a review of self-hardening slurries using Italian cements, commented that the value of the multiplier to the square of the cement/water ratio could vary considerably, depending on the nature of the cement, from a value of 10^3 to more than 10^4 kPa for cement/water ratios between 0·15 and 1.

The specified values of minimum deformation at failure, commonly of the order of 5% axial strain, imply a plastic failure and preclude brittleness from the failure mechanism, presumably to accommodate lateral ground movement during the performance of the cut-off. In practice, this value is not difficult to achieve with normal bentonite and cement contents in drained tests, although as Tornaghi reminded us, the rate of strain in drained tests on cement–bentonite mixes is critical in its effect on test values of axial strain at failure.

The permeability of the cut-off material is generally of the order of 10^{-8} m/s after one month, according to Tornaghi, a somewhat higher figure than that shown by Caron (Fig. 2.21).

The effects of mixing methods on the properties of slurries were reported by Jefferis[17]. He concluded that poorly mixed slurries never develop cut-off properties that are as good as those of efficiently mixed slurries and, for cement–bentonite slurries in particular, good mixing reduces bleeding of the fluid material and the permeability of the set material, although some increase in strength and brittleness also occurs.

The design of cement–bentonite slurry mixes can be varied (as at Kielder) by the inclusion of cement-replacement materials such as Pulverized Fuel Ash and ground blast furnace slag for economy. The use of ground clays other than bentonite can also reduce material cost. Apart from material costs, the largest cost variables are the provision and type of guide walls and the means of slurry trench excavation. The risk of 'windows' occurring

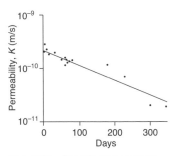

Fig. 2.21. Development over time of the permeability of a bentonite–cement slurry[15]

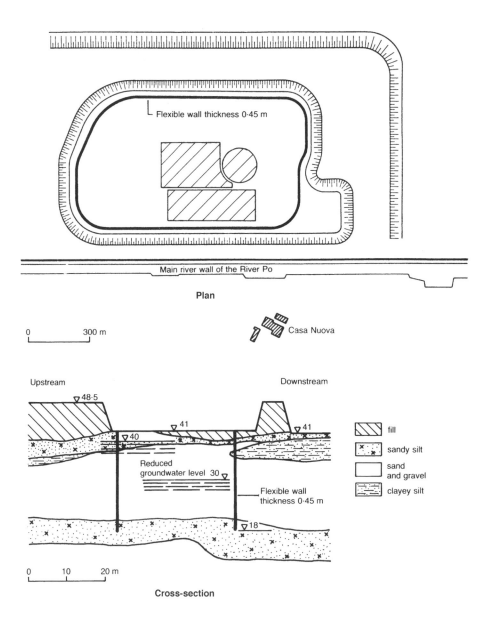

Fig. 2.22. Plan and cross-section of cut-off construction for deep excavation at Caorso, Italy[16]

within cut-offs excavated by backhoe should be noted as it can affect overall cut-off performance detrimentally and lead to wash-out through scour.

Tornaghi described two examples of the use of cement–bentonite cut-offs to exclude groundwater in deep excavations. The first, installed by Rodio in 1970, was used to cut off groundwater flow through fill, silty sands and sands and gravels in a deep excavation at a nuclear power complex at Caorso, near Milan. A plan and cross-section through the excavation is shown in Fig. 2.22. The cut-off is 450 mm thick and has a mean depth of 23·5 m. The second example, installed in 1982 for a deep excavation at the nuclear power complex at Montalto di Castro, near Rome, is shown in plan and cross-section in Fig. 2.23. The cut-off, 800 mm wide, was taken through silty sands containing silty clay layers and through a conglomerate rock to obtain a cut-off into clay. The total depth of the wall was 36 m and the depth of cut-off into the clay was 2 m. The required drawdown of the groundwater was approximately 20 m, which was maintained by ten deep wells shown in plan position in Fig. 2.23.

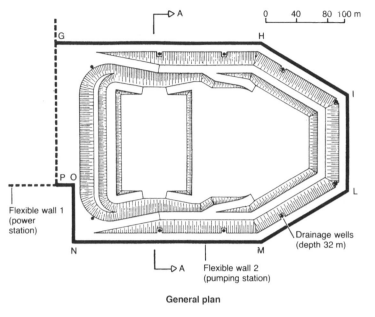

General plan

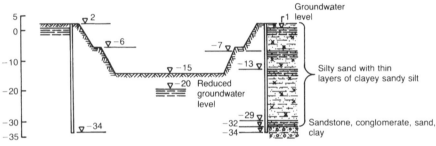

Section A–A

Fig. 2.23. Plan and cross-section of deep excavation with cut-off and ten deep wells at Montalto di Castro, Italy[16]

Cut-off construction using grout curtains installed by intrusion grouting or jet grouting

Where peripheral walls to a deep excavation are required to resist soil pressures and provide a barrier to the ingress of groundwater, structural walls are necessary. Where such walls need to be extended in depth to prevent ingress of groundwater or where the waterproofing of structural wall elements requires improvement, it may be economical to use grout injections or jet grouting techniques.

The process of grout injection into soils is used both to strengthen the soil mass and to reduce its overall permeability. The acceptance of grout by the soil structure and the travel of the grout within it is governed by the permeability of the soil fabric. Where soil permeability is insufficient for grout take and grout pressure is adequate, the grout enters the soil mass as a grout body and does not permeate between soil grains. Such an effect, known as claquage or hydrofracture, is the basis of compaction and squeeze grouting. In contrast, jet grouting is used to destroy the soil structure deliberately and replace it with a soil/grout mixture. Jet grouting can be used in most soil types but is particularly effective in sands and cohesionless silts. Although very high jet pressures are used, hydrofracture pressures are not likely to be reached in jet grouting, the grouted void being formed by the erosive action of the jets and the high pore-water pressures set up at shallow depth in the soil near the jet.

The jet grouting process deserves more explanation. The process was originally introduced in Pakistan by the UK contractor Cementation, but was later

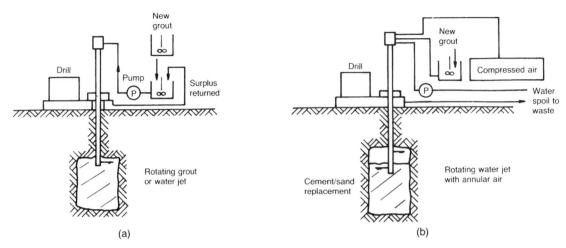

Fig. 2.24. Jet grouting systems: (a) mix-in-place; (b) replacement method

developed by Japanese firms. In the early 1980s the process was imported to Europe from Japan.

The two systems most frequently used are mix-in-place and replacement grouting, as shown in Fig. 2.24. Both systems use water or air/water jets with diameters in the range 2 to 3 mm. The first is the simpler method in which a single grout jet at a pressure of 300 to 500 bar is rotated during extraction from a pre-drilled hole. Rotation speed is 10 to 20 rpm and the rate of extraction is low (about 100 to 150 mm/min). Since grout loss has to be low, mix-in-place is carried out in a tight hole. Eroded soil brought to the surface is recirculated with additional grout. To improve the cutting action a shroud of air (at low pressure, 5 to 7 bar) can be used to wrap the cutting jet. Columns between 400 and 800 mm in diameter are formed in sands – more in coarse sands and less in cohesive soils.

The second method, replacement grouting (known originally as the Kajima–Keller process), uses a triple-tube drill stem to grout from an open hole. The tube delivers a jet of water at very high pressure (400 to 500 bar) which breaks up the soil at the periphery of the bore. The cuttings are returned to the ground surface by this water by direct circulation. Air encapsulation can also be used in the second method. This air jet improves soil cutting performance and the efficiency of soil cuttings returning to the ground surface. Grout is then pumped down the third tube at a pressure of 5 to 7 bar to enter below the eroding jet. The system, cutting and grouting simultaneously, is rotated and lifted simultaneously at about 5 rpm and 50 mm/min, respectively. Column and panel construction by the triple-jet process is shown in Fig. 2.25.

The grout holes can be located within 300 mm of existing foundations so that the jet can undercut them by as much again and bores can be inclined below existing foundations. Drilling can often be made through existing footings with inclined bores to treat below them. The process has been used to depths in excess of 40 m. A wide range of soils above and below groundwater level can be treated, from gravels to clays, although stones tend to fall to the base of the column in open gravels.

Typical dimensions and properties of the soil/cement grout mass are shown in Table 2.9.

Quality control may be applied on site by pre-contract trials of column construction. Site measurements are made of lift speed and rotation, depth, pressures and flow rates of grout, water and air. Grout mix quality tests and core sampling are used where appropriate, and the specific gravity of

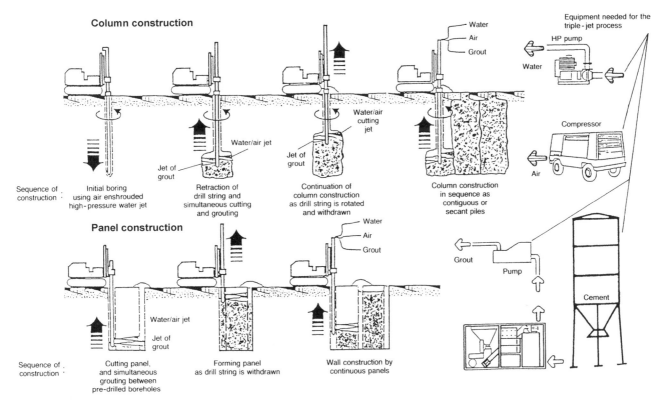

Fig. 2.25. Jet grouting: column and panel construction by the triple-jet process (courtesy of Soletanche–Bachy)

Table 2.9 Typical dimensions and properties of the soil/cement grout mass

	Granular soils	Cohesive soils
Diameter (m)	0·8 to 1·8	0·5 to 1·5
Unconfined compressive strength (N/mm^2)	1 to 10	0·5 to 5
Shear strength (kN/m^2)	500	250
Permeability (cm/s)	10^{-4} to 10^{-7}	10^{-4} to 10^{-7}

the grout waste slurry is measured. Both cement and cement/Pulverized Fuel Ash grouts may be used, the latter weaker but costing less than the cement grout alternative.

Two examples are presented to show the use of jet grouting to improve grout water exclusion from deep excavations. Figure 2.26 shows the use of a jet-grouted cut-off to allow a new underground railway tunnel construction in Rotterdam to pass under the existing Blaak station built on a wall in H-section steel profiles (the 'D' wall) which terminated in the middle of the Pleistocene bed of fine sands at level −24. To allow excavation under the station without considerably reducing the water level, the H pile wall was extended downwards by a cut-off in secant jet grout columns to a cut-off in clay at level −30 using the triple-jet method. The grouting was made from a working platform at level −8 under Blaak station with a headroom of only 4·3 m. The groundwater was reduced temporarily to level −0·5 during the jet grouting works. To avoid risk of instability of the existing station during installation of the cut-off, the row of jet-grouted columns was offset a small distance from the line of the H pile wall and the gap between the H piles and the jet grout secant wall was plugged with a double row of short jet grout columns.

The second example shown in Fig. 2.27 is the use of jet-grouted columns at the rear of a hand-dug caisson for a peripheral basement wall to a commercial

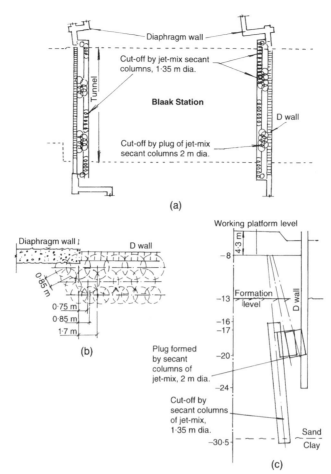

Fig. 2.26. Example of jet grouting for cut-off construction at the Blaak metro station, Rotterdam: (a) plan of cut-off walls; (b) jet mix column installation; (c) cross-section of deep and shallow jet mix walls (courtesy of Soletanche–Bachy)

development in Hong Kong. The soil on the west side of the basement was retained by conventional diaphragm wall construction to depths greater than 20 m, while hand-dug caissons were used at shallower depths on the side where bedrock was at depths between 5 and 20 m. Prior to the installation of the caisson wall a cut-off was necessary to avoid groundwater drawdown outside the site and the consequent settlement to neighbouring structures. The cut-off was made by a grout curtain where soils were groutable using bentonite–cement grout in the first phase followed by silicate gel injection using tubes à manchette. Where the fine silty sands overlying bedrock were not easily grouted, the cut-off was made from secant jet mix columns. The columns, shown in Fig. 2.27, were generally 0·8 m in diameter and a pressure of 200 bar was used to install them with a cement grout proportion of 350 kg/m³ of soil cement grout.

Horizontal grout curtains
Within a sheeted or walled deep excavation a horizontal grout curtain may be needed to reduce the vertical inflow of groundwater from permeable strata below formation level where the peripheral sheeting or walls do not achieve a cut-off into bedrock or a relatively impermeable stratum. Such a situation arises where a deep permeable stratum or layered permeable strata exist. The depth of a peripheral vertical cut-off wall may prove uneconomic in these soil conditions and the alternative of a box-like cut-off using a horizontal grout curtain to seal the base of the excavation enclosure may be attractive.

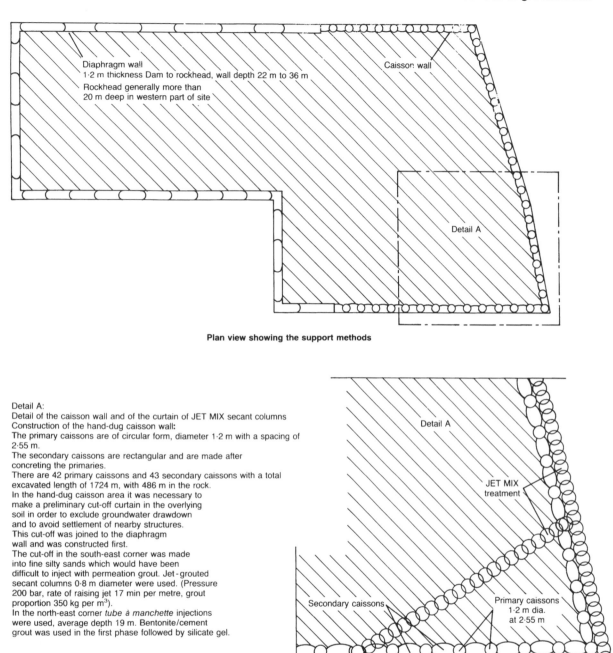

Plan view showing the support methods

Detail A:
Detail of the caisson wall and of the curtain of JET MIX secant columns
Construction of the hand-dug caisson wall:
The primary caissons are of circular form, diameter 1·2 m with a spacing of 2·55 m.
The secondary caissons are rectangular and are made after concreting the primaries.
There are 42 primary caissons and 43 secondary caissons with a total excavated length of 1724 m, with 486 m in the rock.
In the hand-dug caisson area it was necessary to make a preliminary cut-off curtain in the overlying soil in order to exclude groundwater drawdown and to avoid settlement of nearby structures. This cut-off was joined to the diaphragm wall and was constructed first.
The cut-off in the south-east corner was made into fine silty sands which would have been difficult to inject with permeation grout. Jet-grouted secant columns 0·8 m diameter were used. (Pressure 200 bar, rate of raising jet 17 min per metre, grout proportion 350 kg per m^3).
In the north-east corner *tube à manchette* injections were used, average depth 19 m. Bentonite/cement grout was used in the first phase followed by silicate gel.

Fig. 2.27. *Example of jet grouting for cut-off treatment at the rear of hand-dug caissons at Kowloon, Hong Kong (courtesy of Soletanche–Bachy)*

Two options are available. A shallow horizontal curtain may be formed by jet grouting or, where soil conditions allow, a deeper horizontal curtain may be formed by intrusion grouting, using either clay–cement (ultrafine grain size cement can be used) or silicate grouts, depending on soil permeability. It is often economical to anchor shallow grout curtains with mini piles or deeper jet-grouted tensile anchors, which reduces the effective span of the grout curtains and resists the upward groundwater pressure upon the removal of the significant dead weight of the overburden pressure of the soil above it. The installation of jet-grouted columns improves the subsoil strength below formation level and increases the subsoil passive resistance, giving support to the peripheral walls. The shallow jet-grouted, anchored cut-off therefore has the prime objective of excluding groundwater, but it can also materially assist in supporting the peripheral walls. Deeper silicate grout curtains, which in turn require deeper peripheral walls, may be formed more economically by intrusion grouting rather than jet grouting where soil permeability allows. These deeper cut-offs benefit from the dead weight of the retained soil above the grout curtain to resist the upward groundwater pressure and probably avoid the need for intermediate anchoring from jet-grouted columns. Specified maximum leakage rates in the range 2 to 5 litres/s per 1000 m^2 of plan area would be typical of this type of construction in cohesionless soils. More traditional methods of underwater concreting may prove economical as horizontal cut-offs, particularly in long, narrow excavations. Additives are vital with underwater concrete to prevent the cement from being washed out and to improve flowability, waterproofness and control setting time. Most recent innovations include the incorporation of steel fibre reinforcement in tremie concrete plugs.

Mention should also be made of the installation of horizontal curtains by horizontal drilling and grouting from shafts for special projects.

Design of dewatering systems

Design objectives

The objectives of the methods described to control groundwater in the previous sections, by exclusion (with surface drains or by cut-off walls) or by removal of groundwater (by drainage or by pumping), are to:

(a) lower the water table and intercept seepage which would otherwise enter the excavation and interfere with the work
(b) improve the stability of slopes and prevent slippages
(c) prevent heave in the bottom of excavations
(d) reduce lateral pressures on temporary sheeting and bracing.

Design methods to remove groundwater by pumping, either by various well-pointing methods or deep wells, will be considered in the remainder of this chapter. It is assumed that the means of dewatering has been selected, the soil properties, including permeability, are known or can be estimated, and the depths of each stratum and the head of groundwater have been determined. The design will determine the number and spacing of wellpoints or wells to achieve the required drawdown and the required capacity of pumping to remove the groundwater yield at the well heads. The design yield, or quantity of water to be pumped, depends on various factors including the permeability of the soil fabric, the groundwater source (whether flow is radial or from a line source such as a river or shoreline), whether the wells penetrate fully or partly to the base of the aquifer, the plan shape of the excavation and the plan layout of wells.

The design methods make fundamental assumptions regarding soil and groundwater flow which are only partly fulfilled on site; therefore, a balance has to be struck between the results of such calculations and experience, preferably local experience, of the selected dewatering method. The assumptions made include the following.

(a) The aquifer extends horizontally with uniform thickness in all directions without encountering recharge or barrier boundaries.
(b) The aquifer is isotropic, that is, the permeability is the same in all directions.
(c) The aquifer releases water from storage instantly when the head is reduced.

(d) The pumping well is frictionless and has a very small diameter.

(e) Under steady-state seepage conditions, Darcy's law applies and flow is laminar (Darcy's law states that for a given soil the velocity of flow is directly proportional to the hydraulic gradient and the soil permeability, $v = ki$, where v is velocity of flow, i is the hydraulic gradient and k is the soil permeability).

Numerical modelling of groundwater flow may be used either with spreadsheet programs to allow speedy calculation of established design equations or by groundwater modelling packages which provide design solutions too complex for traditional computation. These latter methods are described by Anderson and Woessner[18]. The use of these packages is likely to increase as reliance on computer design increases; their principal application at present is in the initial design of large complex schemes and the sensitivity analyses applied to layouts, pump depths and capacities in such schemes.

Standard well formulae still remain a practical, albeit approximate, basis of design for typical dewatering systems as described here. Relationships for discharge into a slot from a line source or sources are used with empirical expressions for radius of influence to model flow quantities to wellpoints or wells for trenchworks. Formulae for radial flow to a single well are used to model flow to a whole excavation, often square or rectangular in plan. The application of two-dimensional flow nets is convenient, although not necessarily accurate, to obtain estimates of quantities of groundwater flow into sheeted excavations and to verify the stability of the formation soils due to seepage pressures as a result of the dewatering. The design is therefore a process of approximation and does not replace either previous experience or common sense.

Powrie and Preene[19] compared flow rate/drawdown relationships computed by equivalent well and infinite slot techniques with finite element methods, and advised the range of validity of the equivalent well method for various excavation plan geometries. The same authors compared case records of 30 dewatering schemes in fine-grained soils[20] to assess the validity of analysis methods in steady-state conditions. They concluded that equivalent well/slot methods could be effectively used to estimate flow ratio for dewatering systems in these soils providing the method of analysis is appropriate to the boundary conditions in the field. Close sources of recharge were found to increase flow ratio considerably, and it was recommended their effects be modelled by flow net techniques.

Both two-dimensional steady-state flow programs and equivalent well formulae therefore provide means of estimating flow rates, each with advantages and disadvantages. The importance of accurate selection of a value for soil fabric permeability nevertheless remains common to both. The CIRIA report on groundwater control[1] provides a tentative guide to the reliability of permeability estimates from various methods (see Table 2.10), but concludes that some uncertainty of permeability values is inevitable. Powrie and Preene[19] confirmed the widely held practical opinion that the most reliable permeability estimates are obtained from field pumping tests with drawdown measured by piezometers. The method of analysis should be varied according to the aquifer boundary conditions, using the well formula where the recharge aquifer is not close to the well, and finite element analysis otherwise.

Where no pumping test is available and the soil has isotropic permeability and contains less than approximately 20% of silt and clay size particles, Hazen's rule may be used to estimate permeability from grading curves, providing representative particle size test results are available. (Hazen's rule

Table 2.10 Tentative guide to reliability of permeability estimates by various methods[38]

Method	Notes	Reliability
Groundwater control trials	Appropriate for large-scale works or where observational method is being used. Costs high but can be offset against main works	Good if appropriately analysed
Pumping tests	Test a large volume of soil. Provide information on well yields, water chemistry and distance of influence. Costs high to moderate depending on complexity (simple tests can sometimes be very useful)	Good if appropriately analysed. May be difficult to carry out and analyse in fine-grained soils (e.g. silt) or if there are different strata with significant variations in permeability (e.g. gravel over fine sand). Good instrumentation is essential, adequate number of piezometers, etc.
Inverse numerical modelling	Uses groundwater monitoring data (e.g. piezometer readings) to back analyse permeability. Costs low to moderate	Good if adequate groundwater data are available and are appropriately analysed
Tests in boreholes	Only a small volume of soil tested; affected by soil disturbance from drilling	
Falling head	Very prone to clogging of borehole. Costs very low	Very poor
Rising head	Prone to clogging or loosening of borehole base. Costs very low	Poor to moderate. Better results in coarser, less silty soils
Constant head	Inflow tests prone to clogging. Costs low	Poor to moderate. Better results in coarser, less silty soils
Packer test	Normally carried out in rock. Results are hugely influenced by fissure network. Costs low to moderate	Poor to good. Can confirm presence of fissures depending on fissure spacing
Tests in piezometers and standpipes	Only a small volume of soil tested; dependent on the design and quality of piezometer installation and on any soil disturbance	
Falling head	Prone to clogging. Costs very low	Very poor
Rising head	Costs very low	Poor to moderate. Better results in coarser, less silty soils
Constant head	Inflow tests prone to clogging. Costs low	Poor to moderate. Better results in coarser, less silty soils
Specialist in situ tests, e.g. piezocone, in situ parameter	Can identify small stratigraphic changes and provide permeability profile with depth. Costs moderate	Can be good in fine-grained soils (silts and clays). Can be difficult to use in coarser soils or weak rocks
Laboratory tests	Only a small volume of soil tested; sample disturbance can affect results	
Particle size distribution (PSD) analysis of bulk samples	Loss of fines during sampling may lead to overestimates of permeability. Costs very low	Very poor, especially in laminated or structured soils
Particle size analysis of tube samples	Not representative in structured soils or if silt and clay content is more than about 10 to 20 per cent. Costs very low to low	Moderate to good in uniform sands with low silt and clay content; poor in laminated or structured soils
Permeameter testing, e.g. triaxial cell, Rowe consolidation cell, oedometer consolidation cell	Soil fabric and structure means sample size affects results: smaller samples tend to underestimate in situ permeability. Costs low to moderate	Good in clays and some silts where minimally disturbed samples, large enough to be representative, can be obtained

is $k = CD_{10}^2$, where k is permeability (in m/s), D_{10} is the 10% particle size (in mm) and the constant C is usually taken in the range 0·01 to 0·0125.) From tube samples the mean value of permeability from all curves should be used, but from bulk samples the minimum value is likely to be more reliable.

If the soil contains more than 20% of silt and clay particles or, less significantly, anisotropic permeability, in situ rising or falling head tests should be used in boreholes. Providing that an adequate number of tests are made, the maximum result should be used. The use of permeability results from laboratory testing is not recommended.

In the next section, well formulae are described as a series of cases depending upon the source of water, confinement of the aquifer and penetration of the well. Design methods are then proposed which use either well formulae or flow net methods to determine the quantity of water flowing towards the pumps, and hence the number, and size, of pumps required.

Well formulae

Mansur and Kaufman[21] estimated discharge and drawdown from various well configurations for the cases presented below.

Dewatering for trenchworks

Case 1. Partial penetration by a single row of wellpoints of an unconfined aquifer with gravity flow fed from a single line source (Fig. 2.28(a)). Application: narrow trench work, wellpoints to single side, unconfined aquifer, river or similar line source.

The total discharge Q (in m³/s) from wellpoints is

$$Q = \left[\left(0·73 + 0·27 \frac{(H - h_0)}{H} \right) \frac{kx}{2R_0} (H^2 - h_0^2) \right] \qquad (2)$$

and the maximum residual head h_D downstream from the slot is

$$h_D = h_0 \left(\frac{1·48}{R_0} (H - h_0) + 1 \right) \qquad (3)$$

where x is the length of the trench (m), H is the height of the static water table (m), h_0 is the height of the water table in wells (m), h_s is the difference in head between the outside and inside of the well (it is small, approximately $0·001H$), k is the soil permeability (m/s), and R_0 is the distance of the line source, taken as equal to the radius of influence R_0 (m). Mansur and Kaufman stated that these expressions for Q and h_D are valid for the ratio of radius of influence to the height of the static water table (R_0/h_0) equal to or greater than 3·0. This ratio covers most site conditions.

Case 2. For artesian conditions, partial penetration of a single row of wellpoints fed from a single line source. Application: narrow trench work, wellpoints to single side, artesian conditions, river or similar line source (Fig. 2.28(b)).

The total discharge (in m³/s) is

$$Q = \left(\frac{kDx(H - h_e)}{R_0 + E_A} \right) \qquad (4)$$

where E_A is an extra length factor which depends upon the ratio of slot penetration to the thickness of pervious stratum, and is obtained from Fig. 2.28(b); h_e is the head of water at the well above the base of the aquifer, and D is the thickness of the aquifer. The maximum residual head (in m)

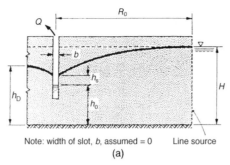

Note: width of slot, *b*, assumed = 0   Line source

(a)

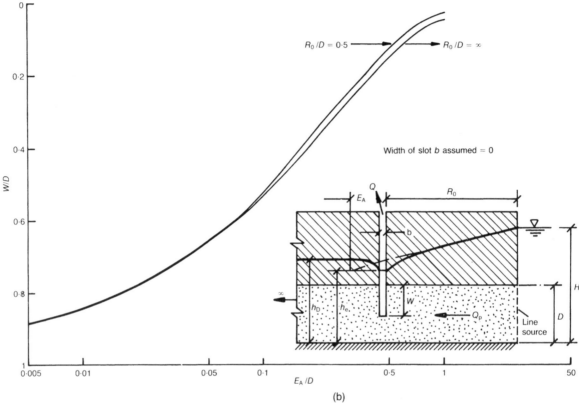

Width of slot *b* assumed = 0

(b)

Fig. 2.28. Partial penetration by a single row of wellpoints from a single line source: (a) gravity conditions; (b) artesian conditions, plot of W/D against E_A/D [38]

downstream from the slot is

$$h_D = \frac{E_A(H - h_e)}{R_0 + E_A} + h_e. \tag{5}$$

Case 3. Partial penetration by a single row of wellpoints of an unconfined aquifer with gravity flow midway between parallel line sources (Fig. 2.29(a)). Application: narrow trench work, wellpoints to single side, unconfined aquifer, two line sources, say two rivers, a trench midway between them.

The discharge is

$$Q = \left[\left(0{\cdot}73 + 0{\cdot}27 \frac{(H - h_0)}{H} \right) \frac{kx}{R_0} (H^2 - h_0^2) \right]. \tag{6}$$

Mansur and Kaufman reported that this expression, as in cases 1 and 2, is based on model studies by Chapman[22] for gravity flow from a line source to a single partially penetrating slot. The model test showed slight irregularities

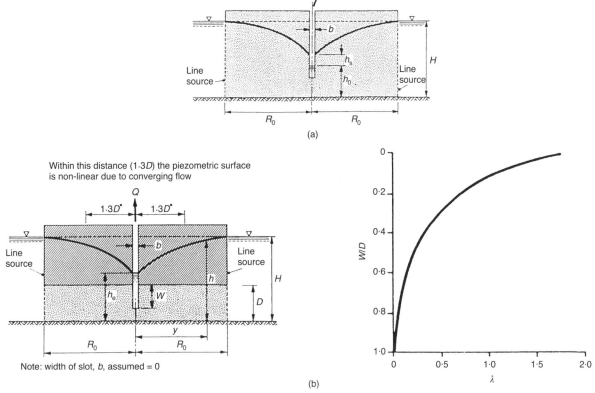

Fig. 2.29. Partial penetration by a single row of wellpoints midway between parallel line sources: (a) gravity conditions; (b) artesian conditions, plot of W/D against λ [38]

and the equation should therefore be regarded only as an estimate of the flow required to provide the given head reduction.

Case 4. For artesian conditions, partial penetration by a line of wellpoints midway between two parallel line sources (Fig. 2.29(b)). Application: narrow trench work, wellpoints to single side, artesian conditions, two line sources, say two rivers, a trench midway between them.

The total discharge is

$$Q = \frac{2kDx(H - h_{e})}{R_0 + \lambda D}. \tag{7}$$

At distance y from the slot, when y exceeds $1\cdot3D$, the head h increases linearly as y increases and can be expressed as

$$h = h_{e} + (H - h_{e})\left(\frac{y + \lambda D}{R_0 + \lambda D}\right) \tag{8}$$

where λ is a factor dependent upon the ratio of slot penetration to aquifer thickness (see Fig. 2.29(b) in which W is the depth of the base of the well below the upper horizon of the aquifer).

Dewatering for a wide trench or narrow rectangular excavation
Case 5. Partial penetration by a double row of wellpoints of an unconfined aquifer with gravity flow midway between two parallel line sources (Fig. 2.30(a)). Application: trench works with double row of wellpoints, unconfined aquifer, two line sources, a trench midway between them.

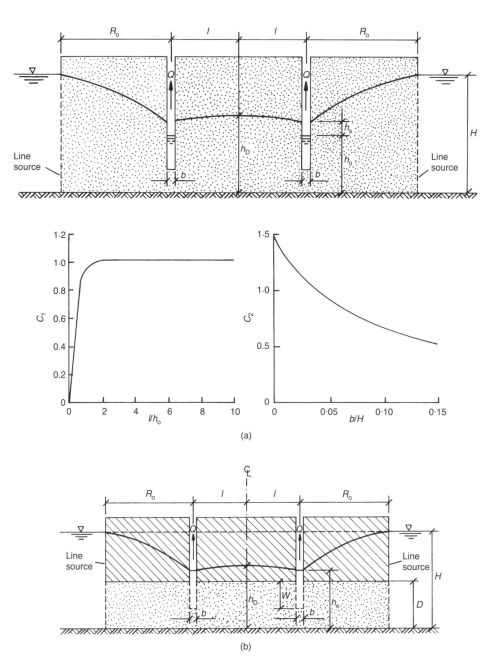

Fig. 2.30. Partial penetration
by a double row of wellpoints
midway between parallel line
sources: (a) gravity
conditions, plots of C_1 against
l/h_0 and C_2 against b/H;
(b) artesian conditions[38]

Q is the total combined flow from both slots and is twice that for a single line source (see Eq. (2) in Case 1). The head is

$$h_{\mathrm{D}} = h_0 \left[\frac{C_1 C_2}{R_0} (H - h_0) + 1 \right]$$

(9)

and C_1 and C_2 are obtained from Fig. 2.30(a).

Note that for large or square excavations, wellpoints will be required on all four sides of the excavation. A conservative approximation of the pumping capacity needed can be made by calculating the values of Q separately for opposite sides of the excavation.

Case 6. For artesian conditions, partial penetration by a double row of wellpoints midway between two parallel line sources (Fig. 2.30(b)). Application:

trench works with double row of wellpoints, artesian conditions, two line sources, a trench midway between them.

Again, Q is the total combined flow from both slots and is twice that for single line sources (Eq. (4)). Values of E_A from Fig. 2.28(b) are as for case 2. The head h_D midway between the slots can be calculated as before from Eq. (5) (except where the slots are very close; in this case, a conservative estimate results from the calculation).

Dewatering for square or rectangular plan shape unsheeted excavations

Forchheimer[23] derived a formula from a system of perfect gravity flow wells of equal length and capacity. This work forms the basis of the design of dewatering systems based on radial flow to a number of wells.

Case 7. Full penetration by a single well of unconfined aquifer with gravity flow fed by circular source. Application: square and rectangular plan shape excavations, unconfined aquifer (Fig. 2.31(a)).

From Darcy's law it can be shown that

$$Q = \frac{\pi k (H^2 - h_w^2)}{\log_e(R_0/r_w)} \tag{10}$$

and drawdown $(H - h)$ at a distance r from the well can be obtained from

$$(H^2 - h^2) = \frac{Q}{\pi k} \log_e \left(\frac{R_0}{r} \right). \tag{11}$$

Case 8. For artesian conditions, full penetration by single well fed by circular source (Fig. 2.31(b)). Application: square or rectangular plan shape excavations, artesian conditions.

$$Q = \frac{2\pi k D (H - h_w)}{\log_e(R_0/r_w)} \tag{12}$$

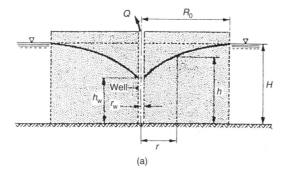

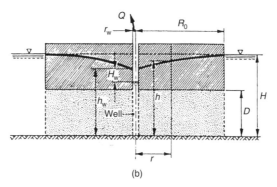

(a)

(b)

Fig. 2.31. Full penetration by a single well fed by a circular source: (a) gravity conditions; (b) artesian conditions[38]

and drawdown $(H - h)$ at distance r from the well can be obtained from

$$H - h = \frac{Q}{2\pi kD} \log_e \frac{R_0}{r}.$$ (13)

Case 9. Full penetration of circular arrangement of wells in an unconfined aquifer. Application: square or rectangular plan shape excavations, unconfined aquifer. From Forchheimer's work it can be shown that for a circular arrangement of wells

$$Q = \frac{\pi k (H^2 - h_e^2)}{\log_e R_0 - \log_e a}$$ (14)

where Q is the total flow to the circular well array (m^3/s), a is the radius of the wells from the centre of the circular well array (m), and h_e is the height of water above the impermeable stratum at the centre of the circular well array (m).

Design methods
Formulae which estimate flow and drawdown from line sources to slots, radial flow to a single or circular array of wells, and flow nets used to model two-dimensional flow conditions, are explained and illustrated in the remainder of this chapter to solve design problems for dewatering excavations of different sizes and construction. The design work of estimating pump resources, pump depths and locations should all be considered as much art as science, with adequate allowance for in situ conditions which may differ from those presumed in the calculations.

Dewatering of trench using progressive wellpoint system: design procedure
   (a) Determine the geometry of the trench cross-section, the extent of drawdown required and the permeability of strata.
   (b) Determine the extent of the dewatered length of the trench works. Assume the dewatered length will need to be twice the excavated length at any one stage.
   (c) Determine the side slopes to the excavation and whether single- or double-sided wellpoint installation is required.
   (d) Check that the wellpoint will partially penetrate the aquifer.

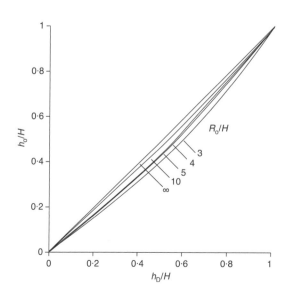

Fig. 2.32. Plot of h_0/H against h_D/H for various R_0/H[38]

(e) Consider the radius of influence R_0 for the required drawdown

$$R_0 = 1500(H - h_D)k^{1/2} \qquad (15)$$

Check that $R_0/H \geq 3$.

(f) If a double line of wellpoints is required, check the operating level at the line of wellpoints from the relationships h_0/H and h_D/H for different R_0/H (Fig. 2.32). Check the required drawdown at the line of wellpoints from the header pipe level to the top of the wellpoint does not exceed the maximum wellpoint drawdown of 5 to 6 m.

(g) Check the value of h_D from the value of h_0 chosen for wellpoint tip elevation from

$$h_D = h_0 \left(\frac{C_1 C_2}{R_0} (H - h_0) + 1 \right) \quad \text{(see below).} \qquad (16)$$

(h) Compute the total flow Q (in m³/s) from

$$Q = \left[\left(0\cdot73 + 0\cdot27 \frac{(H - h_0)}{H} \right) \frac{kx}{R_0} (H^2 - h_0^2) \right] \qquad (17)$$

for double-sided wellpointing (divide the total flow by two for the flow from a single row of wellpoints).

(i) Estimate spacing, and hence the number of wellpoints, from nomograph for uniform clean sand and gravel or stratified clean sand or gravel (Fig. 2.8).

(j) Calculate flow per wellpoint and check the capacity of the wellpoint from Fig. 2.33.

(k) Check approximate size of header pipe required for flow calculated per side (Fig. 2.34).

(l) Check head losses in the system and calculate loss in the header pipe from Table 2.11. Allow equivalent pipe length for fittings (valves, bends and tees). Calculate the total head loss.

(m) Determine the pump size from total head (required drawdown and head loss) and required capacity (allow at least 50% above calculated capacity per side to achieve initial drawdown). Refer to the pump manufacturer's data for vacuum-assisted pumps (see Fig. 2.35 for typical head capacity and priming time curves). Note that the estimated radius of influence R_0 calculated in this method is the value when equilibrium

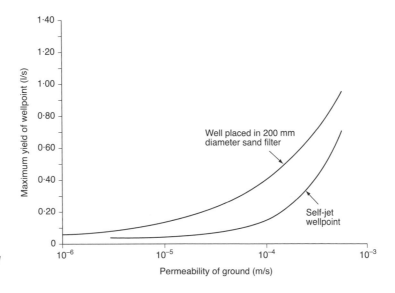

Fig. 2.33. Maximum yield of wellpoints as a function of soil permeability[38]

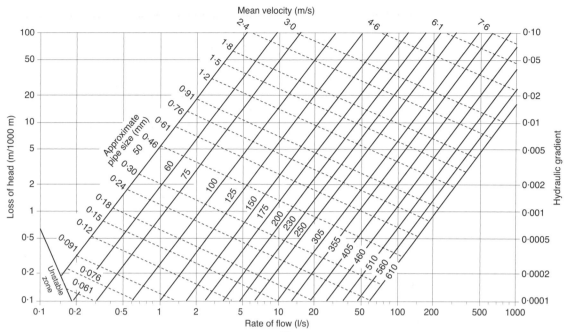

Fig. 2.34. Wellpoints: header pipe capacity and friction losses[38]

drawdown has been established. Before this, during the initial drawdown period, the radius of influence will be reduced and the yield will be greater; both pump and pipework sizes must allow for this.

(*n*) For single- and multi-stage installations to relieve artesian pressure from a contained aquifer, calculate R_0 using appropriate well formulae: h_D from Eq. (5) and Q is twice that for single line sources (Eq. (4)), and follow the design procedure for installation with the gravity flow method above.

Table 2.11 Friction losses in valves and fittings, expressed as a length of straight pipe (in m)[38]

	Type of fitting		Diameter (mm)								
	Open		1·1	1·4	1·7	2·0	2·8	4·3	5·2	6·4	7·6
	$\frac{1}{4}$ closed		6·1	7·9	10·1	12·2	18·3	24·4	30·5	41·2	48·8
1. Gate valve	$\frac{1}{2}$ closed		30·5	39·6	51·8	59·5	91·5	122·0	152·0	213·0	244·0
	$\frac{3}{4}$ closed		122·0	159·0	213·0	244·0	366·0	488·0	610·0	854·0	976·0
2. Standard tee	Flow in line		2·9	4·3	5·0	5·9	9·1	11·9	15·1	22·0	24·7
	Flow to/from branch		9·8	12·8	16·8	19·8	30·5	39·6	50·3	73·2	82·3
3. Standard 90° elbow			4·9	6·4	8·4	9·9	15·2	19·8	25·2	36·6	41·2
4. Medium sweep 90° elbow			4·3	5·5	6·7	7·9	12·2	15·9	21·3	28·0	32·0
5. Long sweep 90° elbow			3·2	4·3	5·3	6·1	9·1	12·2	15·2	21·3	24·4
6. Square (90°) elbow			9·8	12·8	16·8	19·8	30·5	39·6	50·3	73·2	82·3
7. 45° elbow			2·3	3·1	3·7	4·6	6·4	8·5	10·7	15·2	18·3
8. Sudden enlargement	$d/D = \frac{1}{4}$		4·9	6·4	8·4	9·9	15·2	19·8	25·2	36·6	41·2
	$d/D = \frac{1}{2}$		3·2	4·3	5·3	6·1	9·1	12·2	15·2	21·3	24·4
	$d/D = \frac{3}{4}$		2·9	3·7	4·9	5·6	8·4	11·0	13·7	19·8	22·9
9. Sudden contraction	$d/D = \frac{1}{4}$		2·3	3·1	3·7	4·6	6·4	8·5	10·7	15·2	18·3
	$d/D = \frac{1}{2}$		1·7	2·3	2·9	3·4	4·9	6·4	8·2	11·3	12·8
	$d/D = \frac{3}{4}$		1·1	1·4	1·7	2·0	2·8	4·3	5·2	6·4	7·6

Sykes Super UV150/HP is an automatic priming, solids handling centrifugal pump with 150 mm (6") suction and discharge connections. In standard form the pump, which incorporates a bearing housing, is coupled to a Lister HR3 air-cooled diesel engine and is mounted on a four-wheeled chassis with Ackerman steering connected to a towbar.

Suitable for all contractors duties where high performance is the main criterion, the Super UV/150/HP will pump water containing a high proportion of abrasive solids, crude sewage, thick slurries, gaseous sludges and trade effluents. It is ideally suited for wellpoint dewatering applications. Solids up to 75 mm (3") diameter can be passed, the pump will prime and reprime automatically at suction lifts down to 9 m (30 ft) and will deal with intermittent flows under snore conditions.

Head/Capacity Curve

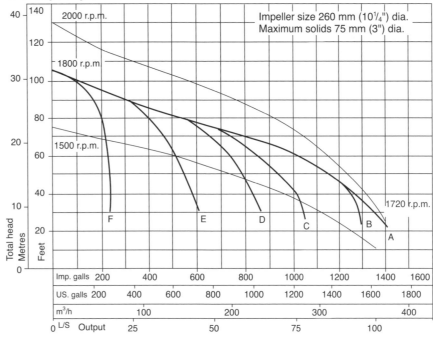

Static Suction Lift

A – 1·5 m   (5 ft) using 3·1 m (10 ft) 150 mm (6") i/d hose
B – 3·1 m (10 ft) using 6·1 m (20 ft) 150 mm (6") i/d hose
C – 4·6 m (15 ft) using 6·1 m (20 ft) 150 mm (6") i/d hose
D – 6·1 m (20 ft) using 9·1 m (30 ft) 150 mm (6") i/d hose
E – 7·6 m (25 ft) using 9·1 m (30 ft) 150 mm (6") i/d hose
F – 9·1 m (30 ft) using 12·2 m (40 ft) 150 mm (6") i/d hose

Priming Time

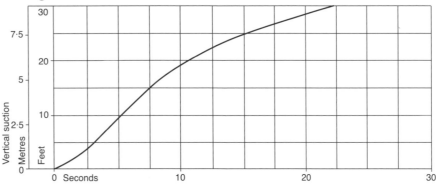

Fig. 2.35. Head/capacity and priming time curves for Sykes Univac pump, 150 mm suction and discharge

Dewatering of square or rectangular plan shape excavation by single- or multi-level wellpoints

(a) Use well formulae for case 5 for opposite sides of the excavation, estimating the radius of influence, drawdown and total flow, as detailed in the section above. Estimate the spacing of wellpoints from the total flow on each side of the excavation using nomographs as before, and determine the header pipe dimensions, head loss and size of pump or pumps, as above.

(b) For multi-stage wellpointing, make successive calculations of drawdown, calculating the radius of influence, drawdown and total flow for each stage.

(c) For artesian conditions use well formulae for case 6, calculating in turn the radius of influence, drawdown, total flow, number of wellpoints, header pipe size, head losses and pump size.

Dewatering of deep square or rectangular plan shape excavation with battered side slopes by deep wells
The following method was described by Hausmann[24].

(a) Make an initial estimate of the total quantity of groundwater to be pumped by replacing the actual excavation with a circular plan shape of approximately equal area. Use the well formula from case 9 (Eq. (14)). If the actual excavation is rectangular with length X and width Y, then

$$a = \left(\frac{XY}{\pi}\right)^{1/2}. \tag{18}$$

Use the radius of influence R_0 from

$$R_0 = 3000(H - h_e)k^{1/2}. \tag{19}$$

(b) Estimate the number of wells needed. For an individual well of radius r_w (in m) the discharge quantity is

$$Q_i = 2\pi r_w h_w k i_e \tag{20}$$

where h_w is the height of well screen (m), and i_e is the average entry gradient. According to empirical findings i_e should not exceed $1/15k^{1/2}$ to avoid turbulence and filter instability for spacings larger than 15 well diameters. Thus, the capacity of an individual well should be limited to

$$Q_i = 2\pi r_w h_w \left(\frac{k^{1/2}}{15}\right) \tag{21}$$

and if h_0, the height of the top of the well screen above the bottom of the aquifer, is set equal to h_w, the height of the well screen, then

$$Q_i = 2\pi r_w h_0 \left(\frac{k^{1/2}}{15}\right). \tag{22}$$

If the number of wells is n, then $n = Q/Q_i$.

(c) Check the original estimate of h_e using

$$Q_{total} = \frac{\pi k(h^2 - h_e^2)}{\log_e R_0 - (1/n)\log_e(x_1, x_2, \ldots, x_n)} \tag{23}$$

where $(x_1, x_2, \ldots, x_n)$ are the radial distances of the wells from the centre of the excavation. Solving for h_e results in a new, improved value for h_e. Using this value, a new R_0 and Q are computed. Steps

(a) to (c) are repeated until h_e assumed is sufficiently close to h_e calculated in step (c).

(d) Return to the original excavation. Distribute the n wells around the perimeter. Check the water level at critical points below the excavation (at the centre and at the corners) using Eq. (22). If the water level is too high, the overall pumping rate Q_{total} has to be increased. This in turn results in a reduced value for h_e and may result in an entry gradient i_e in excess of the maximum recommended of $1/15k^{1/2}$. If so, increase the number of wells and repeat the calculation.

(e) Submersible, centrifugal pumps with one or more impellers driven by an electric motor are used for most deep well installations. The required pump capacity is

$$N = \frac{Qh\gamma_w}{\eta} \ \text{m}^3/\text{s} \tag{24}$$

where γ_w is the density of water to be pumped, and η is the system efficiency. Taking into account friction loss in the delivery pipework, η is usually in the range 0·3 to 0·5. Assuming $\eta = 0·3$ and $\gamma_w = 10 \ \text{kN/m}^3$,

$$N = \frac{Qh}{40} \quad (\text{kW}) \tag{25}$$

where Q is in litres/s and h is in metres.

Dewatering of sheeted excavations where the sheeting does not achieve a seal within an impermeable stratum or horizontal grout cut-off

The design of dewatering systems for sheeted excavations is most conveniently undertaken with the use of two-dimensional flow nets, making provision for the length of the excavation in the calculation to take into account three-dimensional groundwater flow. Where the soil type or depth of excavation vary around the perimeter of the excavation, separate flow net computations can be made for each length and summated.

Flow net construction

The three-dimensional flow of water through a porous media can be represented by the Laplace equation which, when simplified into two dimensions, can be modelled by flow net construction. The flow net consists of flow lines, or stream lines, which represent an almost infinite number of groundwater flow paths and intersecting equipotential lines. The family of curves therefore consists of curvilinear squares. Flow nets can be constructed in four ways: by computer program, by graphical means, by electrical analogy or by physical model. The last two alternatives are both expensive and time-consuming and in practice nowadays can be deleted from the list. On the other hand, computer programs based on the finite element method or finite differences provide the most convenient and fastest solution (standard spreadsheet programs can be used employing finite differences as described by Williams et al.[25]).

The graphical construction of flow nets was described by Taylor[26] and these methods still provide a practical means of determining the base stability of an excavation and the groundwater flow rate into the excavation. Whereas computer programs may indicate improved accuracy, care must be exercised by choice of an appropriate program, understanding its basis, and by correct input of reliable parameters and model geometry.

In earlier times, the electrical analogy method was described by Montague and Thomas[27] and until the widespread introduction of computer programs was used in preference to physical modelling, especially for flow net construction for flow through dams and embankments. The basis of the analogy is that with electricity the current is proportional to the voltage drop, whereas with groundwater flow through soils seepage is proportional to head dissipated; in this analogy, conductivity corresponds to the permeability of the soil.

A flow net may represent flow in plan or in vertical section. In summary, the rules which apply to the graphical solution are as follows.

(a) Flow lines and equipotential lines intersect at right angles and form curvilinear squares.

(b) Where the entire section cannot be divided conveniently into squares, a row of rectangles will remain and the ratio of the lengths of the sides of each rectangle will remain constant.

(c) A discharge face under atmospheric pressure is neither an equipotential nor a flow line; therefore, squares are incomplete and flow lines need not intersect such a boundary at right angles.

(d) In gravity flow systems, equipotential lines intersect the phreatic surface at equal intervals of elevation, each interval being a constant fraction of the total net head.

(e) In sedimentary strata it is not unusual for the horizontal permeability to be greater than the vertical permeability. It is necessary to model this difference in seepage calculations by the graphical construction of flow nets with a deliberate scale distortion (this was described by Taylor[26]). The scale change to the geometry of the vertical section is made prior to drawing the flow net as follows. If the horizontal permeability is k_h, the vertical permeability is k_v and the transformed section of the natural horizontal scale is x, the distorted scale x_1 required to take into account the difference in vertical and horizontal permeability is

$$x_1 = \frac{(k_v/k_h)^{1/2}}{x}. \tag{26}$$

(f) To determine the quantity of seepage, the discharge q per unit width and the head h at any point can be determined by

$$q = kH_1 \frac{N_f}{N_e} = k(H - h_e) \frac{N_f}{N_e}, \qquad h = \frac{n_e}{N_e} H_1 = \frac{n_e}{N_e}(H - h_e) \tag{27}$$

where k is the coefficient of permeability of the soil, H is the total head at entry, h_e is the head at the flow exit, H_1 is the overall net head $(H - h_e)$, N_f is the number of flow channels in the net, N_e is the total number of equipotential drops between the full head H and head h_e at the point of flow exit, and n_e is the number of equipotential drops from the exit to the point at which head h is desired.

A range of flow net constructions is shown in Fig. 2.36. Flow nets can also be used to model flow through strata having two or more different permeabilities; the solution to these composite sections was described by Cedergen[28].

Stability of the base of dewatered sheeted excavations
The risk of failure at the base of a sheeted excavation due to seepage below the sheeting was referred to by Terzaghi and Peck[29] and McNamee[30], and is summarized in BS 8004 and the German Recommendations of the Committee for Waterfront Structures[31].

McNamee referred to local failure by piping or boiling and a general failure of the soil below formation level by heave. BS 8004 concluded that, in order to avoid risk of boiling at formation level in a sheeted excavation in a cohesionless

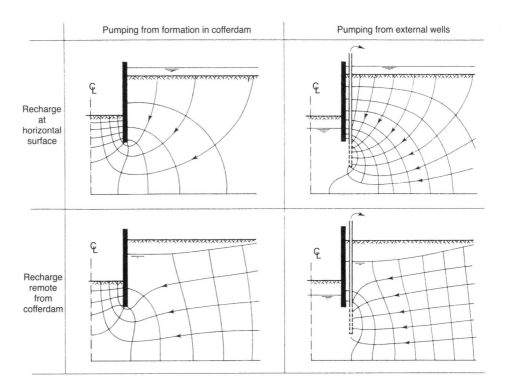

Pumping from formation in cofferdam	Pumping from external wells
Recharge at horizontal surface	
Recharge remote from cofferdam	

Fig. 2.36. Typical flow net construction

stratum, with pumping from sumps at formation level, the minimum penetration depths should be as shown in Fig. 2.37. The German Waterfront Code[31], however, provided more detailed guidance for a similar excavation. It referred to risk of base failure in a cohesionless stratum in two ways, as did McNamee. The following summarizes its recommendations, referring to the specific problem shown in Fig. 2.38. First, the risk of local failure by piping is regarded as a risk which cannot be accurately assessed by analytical

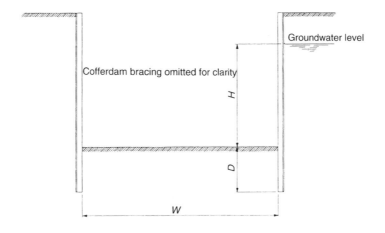

Minimum values for depth of cut-off for cohesionless soils where there is no significant lowering of the external water level

Width of cofferdam, W	Depth of cut-off, D
2H or more	0·4H
1H	0·5H
0·5H	0·7H

H is the height from lowered water level to excavation level.

Fig. 2.37. Minimum values for cut-off depth for cofferdam sheeting in cohesionless soils[2]

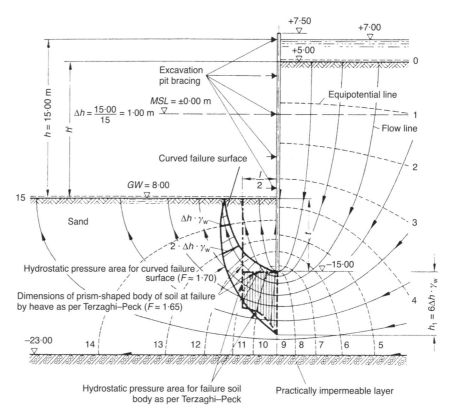

Fig. 2.38. *Factors of safety against failure by heave at formation level calculated using the exit gradient from the flow net with a curved failure surface and a prism-shaped failure soil body*[29]

methods because of the diversity of conditions, including variations in local soil conditions. Where these variations are not excessive, the Waterfront Code concluded that the danger of failure increases in proportion to the overall head difference inside and outside the excavation, and increases in the presence of loose, fine-grained non-cohesive or weakly cohesive material in the subsoil, especially where loose sand lenses occur. The failure risk does not generally occur in strong cohesive soils. Such a failure is first indicated at the formation level by ground swelling and ejection of soil particles in the progressive failure manner shown in Fig. 2.39. An effective preventative measure at an early stage would be to place several thick layers of granular materials, as a graded filter, to retain the subsoil but avoiding excessive restriction of water flow. Only if such measures failed, or were applied too late, would it be necessary to flood the excavated space to equalize the water pressure.

Although the Waterfront Code[31] advised care and observation to counter risk of piping, that is, the local reduction of effective stress to produce quick conditions, it is prudent to check the value of hydraulic gradient at the exit point with the minimum seepage path length. The maximum exit gradient can be calculated by the use of a flow net, from

$$i_{\text{exit}} = \frac{(h/N_{\text{d}})}{a} \tag{28}$$

where a is the length of the flow element at the formation level, and N_{d} is the number of equipotential drops. The factor of safety against piping is $i_{\text{cr}}/i_{\text{exit}}$ where i_{cr} is the critical hydraulic gradient. It can be shown that for zero effective stress

$$i_{\text{cr}} = \frac{G_{\text{s}} - 1}{e + 1} \tag{29}$$

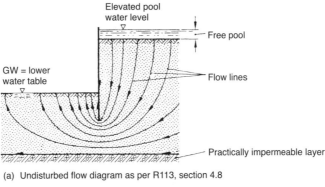

(a) Undisturbed flow diagram as per R113, section 4.8

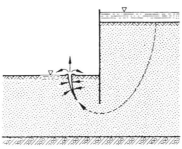

(b) Start of foundation failure by subsurface erosion

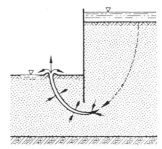

(c) Further stage of foundation failure by subsurface erosion

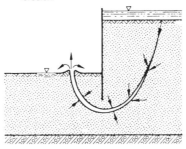

(d) Stage immediately before breakthrough

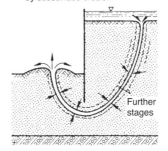

(e) Disaster stage of foundation failure by subsurface erosion

Fig. 2.39. Development of foundation failure by subsurface erosion[31]

where G_s is the specific gravity of the soil grains and e is the voids ratio of the soil. For most soils, i_{cr} lies in the range 0·9 to 1·1, with an average value of 1·0. A minimum factor of safety against piping, i_{cr}/i_{exit}, of 1·5 is advisable.

The Waterfront Code[31] considered failure risk by heave at the base of the excavation and (see Fig. 2.38) recommended examination of the stability in the vertical direction of volumes of soil contained between the inside face of the sheeting and alternative failure planes. One trial failure plane would be that recommended by Terzaghi and Peck, enclosing a rectangular block of soil of depth equal to the sheeting penetration and width equal to half the sheeting penetration. Other failure planes, including those with curved surfaces, would be examined. The vertical stability of the block of soil is assessed as the ratio of the downward force due to the mass of soil w_{ea} above the failure plane to the vertical force c_{fl} caused by the seepage water. A ratio of at least 1·5 is recommended for safety.

The vertical component c_{fl} of the total seepage pressure may be conveniently calculated by flow net. In this method, the residual hydrostatic pressure acting normal to the failure surface is plotted at each intersection of the equipotential lines and the failure surface, the area of the plot representing the total seepage pressure acting on the trial failure surface. The pressure at each intersection point may be computed from $n\Delta h\gamma_w$, where n is the number of equipotentials at the intersection, Δh is the total head difference divided by the number of equipotentials, and γ_w is the density of water.

The risk of failure of the formation to sheeted excavations in soft clays, which is not related specifically to seepage pressures, is described in Chapter 7 on cofferdam design.

The risk of formation heave or local failure by piping changes when deep wells are used to remove groundwater below formation level

Where deep wells are used outside the sheeting, external drawdown is increased and the quantity of water pumped is increased as compared with drawdown and flow quantity where the wells are sited inside the sheeting. It should be noted, however, that where deep wells are installed outside the sheeting, seepage pressures tend to be reduced on the subsoil between the sheeters below formation level, whereas with wells that are sited between the sheeters, seepage pressures tend to increase, and the risk of base instability and heave increases. In the latter case, where the well screen is installed between the sheeters, the closer this is to formation level the higher the seepage pressure and the instability risk, but the drawdown outside the sheeters is less and the quantity of water pumped is smaller. Where deep wells are used between sheeters which do not find a seal (with the toe of the sheeters in an impermeable stratum), the optimum sheeter depth will be defined by five factors: the risk of instability of the soil below formation level by seepage pressure; the risk of drawdown outside the sheeters causing settlement damage to existing structures; the pump resources required (and the pump energy consumed) to obtain and maintain adequate drawdown below formation level; the maximum values of strut or anchor loads, particularly at the lowest frame level; and lastly, the horizontal stability of soil below formation level before the blinding strut or slab is constructed.

Where a cut-off cannot be obtained, the designer frequently defines sheeter depth by the stability requirements of the subsoil below formation level and the lowest bracing loads. The dewatering scheme design is then applied to ensure the necessary drawdown below formation level to obtain dry working conditions with the minimum number of pumps. However, a more refined approach is advisable, with coordinated sheeting depth, formation stability, bracing design and required pumping capacity, and would improve economy.

Development of drawdown with time

Dewatering systems are designed on the basis of a steady-state condition being achieved at the required drawdown. Invariably, construction programmes on site are tight and the period of pre-drainage to achieve this steady state may become critical; indeed, extra pump capacity may be needed to avoid delay. Assessment of the period to achieve drawdown may therefore become important. Hausmann[24] referred to work by Theis[32], later modified by Jacob[33], which gives a solution. Theis provided a non-equilibrium well formula for gravity flow to a single well based on the following assumptions:

(a) the well penetrates a homogeneous, isotropic, horizontal aquifer overlying an impermeable stratum
(b) the Dupuit–Thiem approximation holds; the hydraulic gradient below any point of the drawdown curve is equal to the slope of the drawdown curve at this point
(c) the aquifer is not recharged
(d) water flows out of the pores of the soil simultaneously with the drawdown of the phreatic surface

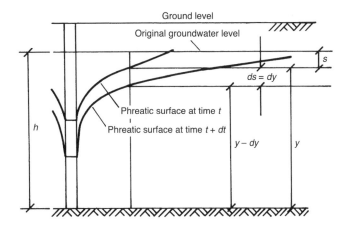

Fig. 2.40. Lowering of phreatic surface with time[24]

(e) the drawdown s is small relative to the aquifer thickness h so that $(h - s)$ is approximately equal to h. This is equivalent to assuming a non-artesian aquifer of thickness $m = h$.

Theis, as reported by Hausmann, equated the water flow through a cylindrical area around the well at a distance x to the volume of water removed from the soil beyond x due to lowering of the phreatic surface, as shown in Fig. 2.40. Theis showed that the drawdown is

$$s = \frac{Q}{4\pi km} W(u) \tag{30}$$

where Q is the quantity of flow, k is the permeability of the soil, m is the thickness of the aquifer, and $W(u)$ is the well function and is defined by

$$W(u) = -0.5772 - \log_e u + u - \frac{u^2}{2 \times 2!} + \frac{u^3}{3 \times 3!} - \frac{u^4}{4 \times 4!} \pm \cdots \tag{31}$$

and

$$u = \frac{x^2 S}{4 t k m}. \tag{32}$$

The function S represents the storage coefficient of the aquifer and is the ratio of the volume of drainable water to total soil volume for an unconfined aquifer, and may be as low as 10^{-5} for confined aquifers which remain saturated during pumping. For unconfined aquifers, it ranges from 0.01 to 0.03. t is the pumping time. $W(u)$ is tabulated in hydrology textbooks (e.g. Driscoll[34]).

Hausmann showed, from Jacob's modification of the work by Theis, that if t is sufficiently large, u is small and for $u < 0.05$ the well function may be approximated by

$$W(u) = -0.577 - \log_e u = \log_e \frac{2.25}{4u} = \log_e \frac{2.25 kmt}{x^2 S}. \tag{33}$$

The drawdown as a function of time is then

$$s = \frac{Q}{4\pi km} \log_e \frac{2.25 kht}{x^2 S}. \tag{34}$$

To apply Jacob's formula (for artesian flow) to unconfined flow, make $m = h$ and use the analogy $2ms$ (artesian) $= h^2 - y^2$ (unconfined), which holds for fully penetrating wells. Thus

$$s = \frac{h^2 - y^2}{2h} \tag{35}$$

and

$$\frac{h^2 - y^2}{2h} = \frac{Q}{4\pi km} \log_e \frac{2 \cdot 25 kht}{x^2 S}.$$ (36)

Drawdown s can therefore be plotted against t and x, using the geometry of the section to obtain h and y and using soil property values for k and S.

The use of the observational method

The foregoing methods of design for dewatering systems are known to be approximate and dependent on soil fabric parameters which themselves vary spatially within the soil and upon their accuracy of measurement. Whilst this may be accepted by the dewatering scheme designer, the subsequent risk at the earliest stages of a construction contract are often mis-judged both in terms of cost of resources and construction delay. The use of the observational method permits a rational approach to these uncertainties particularly in design-and-build contracts where the risks generally are taken by the contractor (and in turn by the specialist dewatering subcontractor). Examples of the observational method applied to dewatering schemes are given in Roberts and Preene[35], Nicholson et al.[36] and Preene et al.[1]

Nicholson explained that the observational method constitutes a way of minimizing costs by modifying design during construction in two basic applications:

(a) *ab initio* from inception of the project
(b) best way out – during construction when unexpected site problems occur.

In the event, it is likely that the method will find application in the second of these two options. When site drawdown fails to be achieved the plant resources can generally be readily increased and the parameters that determine extent of dewatering are easily determined (such as drawdown and discharge flow rate). The matter then becomes the timely application of good engineering sense based on performance.

References

1. Preene M. *et al. Groundwater control.* CIRIA, London, 2000. Publication C515.
2. BS 8004. *Code of practice on foundations.* British Standards Institution, London, 1994.
3. Cashman P.M. and Preene M. *Groundwater lowering in construction.* Spon, London, New York, 2001.
4. Powers J.P. *Construction dewatering.* Wiley, New York, 2nd edition, 1992.
5. Preene M. Case studies of construction dewatering in fine grained Eocene soils. *Ground Engng*, 1993, **26**, Sept., 23–27.
6. Marsland A. Model experiments to study the influence of seepage on the stability of a sheeted excavation in sand. *Géotechnique*, 1953, **3**, No. 6, 223–241.
7. Soubra A.H. and Kestner R. Influence of seepage flow on passive earth pressures. *Proc. Conf. Retaining Structures.* Thomas Telford Ltd., London, 1993, 67–76.
8. Cashman P.M. Groundwater control. *Ground Engng*, 1973, **6**, No. 5, Sept.
9. Ward, W.H. The use of simple relief walls in reducing water pressure beneath a trench excavation. *Géotechnique*, 1957, **7**, 134–146.
10. Ambrasseys N. Cut-off efficiency of grout curtains and slurry trenches. *Proc. Symp. on Grouts and Drilling Muds in Engineering Practice.* Butterworths, London, 1963, 43–46.
11. Brauns J. The effectiveness of imperfect cut-offs beneath hydraulic structures. *National German Conf. on S.M.F.E.*, Nurnburg, 1976 (in German).
12. Telling R.M. *et al.* The effectiveness of jointed cut-off walls beneath dams on pervious soil foundations. *Ground Engng*, 1978, **11**, No. 4, May, 27–37.

13. D'Appolonia D.J. Soil–bentonite slurry trench cut-offs. *ASCE J. Geotech. Engng*, 1980, **106**, Apr., 399–417.

14. Hetherington J. *et al.* A development in slurry trench technique for cut-off construction. *Ground Engng*, 1975, **8**, Nov., 16–20.

15. Caron C. Un nouveau style de perforation; la boue autodurcissable. *Ann. Inst. Tech. Bat Trav. Publ.*, 1973, **311**, Nov., 1–39.

16. Tornaghi R. L'experience italienne dans la domaine des parois souples d'etancheite. *Symp. technologie et organisation de l'execution des parois moulées*, Sofia, 1984.

17. Jefferis S. Effects of mixing on bentonite slurries and grouts. *Proc. ASCE Conf. Grouting in Geotech. Engng*, New Orleans, 1982, 62–76. ASCE, New York, 1982.

18. Anderson M.P. and Woessner W.W. *Applied groundwater modelling*. Academic Press, New York, 1992.

19. Powrie W. and Preene M. Equivalent well analysis of construction dewatering systems. *Géotechnique*, 1992, **42**, No. 4, 635–638.

20. Preene M. and Powrie W. Steady-state performance of construction dewatering systems in fine soils. *Géotechnique*, 1993, **43**, No. 2, 191–205.

21. Mansur C. and Kaufman R. *Dewatering. Foundation engineering*. Ed. G. Leonards, McGraw-Hill, New York, 1962, ch. 3, 241–350.

22. Chapman T.G. Groundwater flow to trenches and wellpoints. *J. Inst. Engrs, Australia*, 1956, Oct.-Nov., 275–280.

23. Forchheimer P. *Uber die Ergiebigkeit von Brunnen-Anlagen*. Des Arch-und-Ing.-Verein zu, Hannover, 1886, 541–547.

24. Hausmann M.R. *Engineering principles of ground modification*. McGraw-Hill, New York, 1990.

25. Williams B. *et al.* Flow net diagrams – the use of finite differences and a spreadsheet to determine potential heads. *Ground Engng*, 1993, **26**, June, 32–36.

26. Taylor D. W. *Fundamentals of soil mechanics*. Wiley, New York, 1948.

27. Montague A. and Thomas A. The use of the Servomex potentiometer to determine pressures, pressure gradients and exit velocities by the method of electrical analogy. *Works on permeable foundations*. Sir M. Macdonald and Partners, London, 1964.

28. Cedergen H. *Seepage, drainage and flow nets*. Wiley, New York, 1977.

29. Terzaghi K. and Peck R.B. *Soil mechanics in engineering practice*. Wiley, New York, 1967.

30. McNamee J. Seepage into a sheeted excavation. *Géotechnique*, 1949, **1**, No. 4, 229–241.

31. EAU 90. *Recommendations of the Committee for Waterfront Structures, Harbours and Waterways*. Ernst and Son, Berlin, 6th English edn, 1993.

32. Theis C.V. The relation between the lowering of the piezometric surface and the rate of discharge of a well using groundwater storage. *Trans. Am. Geophysical Union*, 1935, **16**, 519–524.

33. Jacob C.E. On the flow of water in an elastic artesian aquifer. *Trans. Am. Geophysical Union*, 1940, **21**, 574–586.

34. Driscoll F.G. (ed.) *Groundwater and wells*. Johnson Div., St Paul, Minnesota, 2nd edition, 1986.

35. Roberts T. and Preene M. The design of groundwater control systems using the observational method. *Géotechnique*, **44**, No. 4, 727–734.

36. Nicholson D.P., Tse C.M., and Penny C. *The observational method in ground engineering*. CIRIA, London, 1999, Report C185.

37. Roberts T. and Preene M. Range of application of construction dewatering systems. *Groundwater problems in urban areas*. Thomas Telford Ltd., London, 1994, 415–423.

38. CIRIA. *Control of groundwater for temporary works*. CIRIA, London, 1986, Report 113.

Bibliography

Barron R.A. Consolidation of fine grained soils by drain wells. *Trans. ASCE*, 1948, **73**, 811–835.

Bouwer H. *Groundwater hydrology*. McGraw-Hill, New York, 1962.

Casagrande L. *et al*. Electro-osmatic stabilisation of a high slope in loose saturated silt. *Proc. 5th Int. Conf. S.M.F.E.*, Paris, 1961, Vol. 2, 555–562.

Casagrande A. and Poulos S. On the effectiveness of sand drains. *Canadian Geotech. J.*, 1969, **6**, No. 3.

Darcy H. *Les Fontaines Publiques de la Ville de Dijon*. Dalmont, Paris, 1856.

Dupuit J. *Etudes Théoriques et Pratiques sur le Movement des Eaux*. Dunod, Paris, 1863.

Forchheimer P. *Hydraulik*. Teubner Verlag, Leipzig, 1930.

Gray D. and Mitchell J. Fundamental aspects of electro-osmosis in soils. *ASCE J. S.M.*, 1967, **93**, No. 6, 209–236.

Harr M.E. *Groundwater and seepage*. McGraw-Hill, New York, 1962.

Howden C. and Crawley J.D. Design and construction of the diaphragm wall. *Proc. Instn Civ. Engrs*, 1995, **108**, Feb., 48–62.

Margason E. and Arango L. Sand drain performance on a San Francisco Bay mud site. *ASCE Speciality Conf. Performance of Earth and Earth Supported Structures*, Lafayette, 1972, 181. ASCE, New York 1972.

Powers J. Notes on the design and selection of wellpoint systems. *Short course and seminar on groundwater analysis and design of dewatering systems*, University of Missouri, Rolla, 1976.

Preene M. and Powrie W. Construction dewatering in low permeability soils: some problems and solutions. *Proc. Instn Civ. Engrs, Geotech. Engng*, 1994, **107**, Jan., 17–26.

Roberts T. O. and Preene M. Case studies of construction dewatering in chalk. *Chalk*. Thomas Telford Ltd., London, 1990.

Sanger F. and Golder H.Q. Ground freezing in construction. *S.M.F. Division, ASCE*, 1968, **94**, Jan., 131–157.

US Dept. of the Interior Bureau of Reclamation. *Groundwater manual*. US Government Printing Office, Washington, 1977.

Worth R. and Trenter H. Gravity dock at Nigg Bay for offshore structures. *Proc. Instn Civ. Engrs*, Part 1, 1975, **58**, Aug., 361–376.

3 Open excavation: side slopes and soil retention

This chapter examines the problems of supporting side slopes or cut faces to the periphery of wide, deep excavations and to smaller sites where the soil batters can be accommodated in the available land area. For large cuts associated with heavy earth moving, the scale and size of these cuts means cross-bracing would be quite impractical, whereas for smaller sites the choice between battered or braced excavations is dependent on available space and cost considerations. The wide, open excavations considered may be for permanent use or as part of temporary works for construction. The only criterion for inclusion is that the work is related to civil engineering and not to an industrial process such as mining or quarrying.

Battered excavations

Temporary battered excavations are more economical in direct cost and construction time compared with retention schemes for soil support, and find application where the slopes can be accommodated within the site area and groundwater discharge on to the slopes is small or can be controlled. The decision to omit a support or retention system can only be made on the basis of adequate subsoil knowledge and appropriate stability analyses, however, and should not be made solely on the basis of a cost calculation and an assumed gradient to the batter.

The stability of a cut slope in granular soils can be determined simply from knowledge of the angle of shearing resistance for the soil or the soil layers. In normally consolidated cohesive soils, the stability can be assessed by a repetitive calculation of disturbing and restoring moments for trial potential failure surfaces, the restoring force being based on quick undrained shear strengths of the soil on the failure surface. Where possible, it is usual to avoid the effects of disturbance on the measurement of clay strengths by measuring in situ shear strengths with a vane apparatus rather than relying on laboratory test values.

For cut slopes within over-consolidated clays, it is necessary to relate the method of analysis to the time the cut is to remain exposed, to take account of drainage and the equalization of excess pore pressure generated by the relief of vertical overburden pressure. While an effective stress analysis using drained shear strength parameters would apply to the fully drained condition for permanent works, the designer of temporary batters for construction periods of, say, six months has some difficulty in assessing short-term slope stability without knowing the rate of pore-water pressure dissipation. The choice of slope angle in these clays will depend on the consequences of slope failure. If safety is not endangered by soil slippage, the financial cost of repairs to the slope can be calculated and compared with the actual cost of reducing the slope angle to achieve greater stability.

Vaughan and Chandler[1] calculated soil failure strengths from short-term slope failures in various stiff, over-consolidated clays and concluded that average clay strengths on the failure surface lie in the range 50 to 100% of the undrained shear strength of 38 mm dia. samples. Short-term slope stability in over-consolidated clays in practice depends on the precautions taken to avoid groundwater discharging down the slope (say from permeable strata above the clay) and rainwater falling on to the slope. Harmful effects on stability of the swelling of such clays, due to relief of overburden pressure and the further softening and swelling as groundwater enters fissures, are good reasons to adopt measures to protect the slope. Simple measures such as polythene sheet covers or sprayed concrete blinding can prove beneficial and cost-effective. Slope stability analysis methods were reviewed by Bromhead[2].

Improving the stability of slopes

There are six methods for improving the stability of a cut slope:

(a) regrading the profile of the slope and, for example, weighting the toe of the slope locally with a soil berm to counter the disturbing moment
(b) using tensioned ground or rock anchors to increase the effective stress on the potential failure surface, thereby improving soil strength
(c) intercepting potential failure surfaces with sheet piles, mix-in-place piles, or jet-grouted columns installed from the face or the top of the slope
(d) increasing the effective vertical stress on the potential failure surfaces by reduction of pore-water pressure by drainage
(e) improving composite soil strength by regrading the slope and the inclusion of reinforcement to intercept the potential failure surface, using reinforced soil
(f) driving soil nails through potential failure surfaces.

These methods are well established, enable the engineer to minimize land take at the batters to the periphery of a wide excavation, and may produce a steeper slope with more economy by virtue of reduced excavation quantities. Methods (a)–(d) are described by Bromhead[2], Mitchell[3] and Barley[4]. Methods (e) and (f), reinforced soil and soil nailing, deserve fuller explanation within the context of deep excavations.

In the UK the Department of Transport's manual for reinforced soil and soil nailing[5] defines these techniques as follows.

- Reinforced soil is the technique whereby fill material (frictional or cohesive) is compacted in successive layers on to horizontal placed sheets or strips of geosynthetic or metallic reinforcement.
- Soil nailing is the technique whereby in situ ground (virgin soil or existing fill material) is reinforced by the insertion of tension-carrying soil nails. Soil nails may be of metallic or polymeric material, grouted into a pre-drilled hole or inserted using a displacement technique. They will normally be installed at a slight downward inclination to the horizontal.

In summary, reinforced soil is built-in fill from the base upwards, whereas soil nailing is used for cuts in virgin soils working from the ground surface downwards.

Reinforced soil

Although historically several soil reinforcement methods have been exploited for both civil and military use, the modern form of earth reinforcement was developed and introduced commercially by Henri Vidal in the 1960s. His concept was a composite material of frictional soil and a reinforcing strip which enabled the gravity forces on a wall or slope to be resisted by tensile forces generated in the strip and thence transferred by friction to the soil. The first major structure to be built by this method was a retaining wall near Menton, France, in 1968. By the end of the 1960s, walls were reinforced with galvanized steel strips placed horizontally in layers and connected to a shaped sheet metal member which formed the facing unit. In 1970 a cruciform-shaped precast reinforced concrete member was introduced to replace the sheet metal facing, and this form of wall facing is now widespread and has become the means of identifying Reinforced Earth walls. Over 15 000 structures have been built throughout the world by Vidal's original company, the Reinforced Earth Company Ltd, and many more have been built by competitors using similar methods and, in some cases, alternative reinforcement materials. At the end of 1989 the Reinforced Earth Company listed 9000 retaining wall structures and 2000 bridge abutments in service. Recently, research into the Reinforced Earth wall has centred on the durability of the galvanized steel strips, organic coatings for steel strips in aggressive environments and the effects of seismicity on Reinforced Earth walls. The development of polymer materials in either fabric or grid (geogrid form) in the 1970s allowed the introduction of alternative reinforcement materials in both walls and slopes. Use of these materials, which are visco-elastic, brought the need for further investigation of reinforcement properties, this time into short and long-term creep in addition to durability. A typical reinforced soil wall using polymeric geogrid reinforcement is shown in Fig. 3.1.

A Code of Practice for design and construction of reinforced soil walls was published by the British Standards Institution[6] in 1995 and a draft European Code of Practice for reinforced fill[7] was circulated for comment in mid 2002.

Four types of reinforcement are used in current designs:

(a) a steel strip, typically a galvanized, high-adherence steel strip (by Reinforced Earth Company); other uses of steel reinforcement consist of rods, ladders and rods with anchor plates

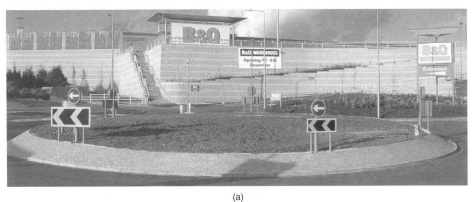

(a)

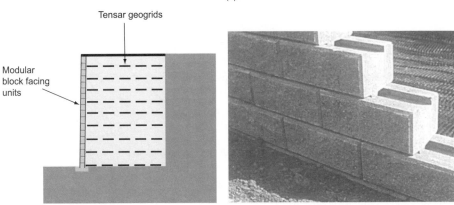

Tensar geogrids

Modular block facing units

(b)   (c)

Fig. 3.1. Modular block retaining wall (courtesy Tensar International Ltd)

(b) polymer geogrids (by Tensar International Ltd and others); cells and meshes are also used

(c) polyester bands known as Parastrip (by Terram Ltd)

(d) synthetic fibres mixed in place with soil, known as Texsol.

The strips are listed in order of use in the UK.

The reinforcement strips must have the following characteristics:

(a) a high resistance to tension, a failure mode which is not brittle and only a very low, limited creep

(b) a high friction coefficient with the backfill material

(c) low deformability under working loads (not exceeding a few percent)

(d) they must be flexible enough not to limit the deformability of the reinforced soil material and to make construction easy

(e) high durability

(f) they must be economical.

The cost of reinforcement in a reinforced soil wall is a relatively high proportion, between 20 and 30% of the total plant labour and material costs, and is therefore a prime issue in terms of overall wall costs.

Types of reinforcement

Metal strip reinforcement

The metallic reinforcing strip currently recommended is galvanized mild steel, generally 5 mm thick and in standard widths of 40 or 60 mm. The surface of the strip is ribbed to improve soil reinforcement friction. The strips are called high-adherence strips. In permanent walls it is usual to allow a sacrificial thickness of the metal to be lost due to corrosion (from 0·5 to 2 mm depending on design life and exposure). It is also usual to place dummy strips through the wall face on aggressive sites in order that strips can be jacked out occasionally to monitor the rate of corrosion. The galvanized steel strip and precast concrete facing panel are competitive for vertically faced walls of medium to large height, due to the high elastic modulus of mild steel and the low creep properties.

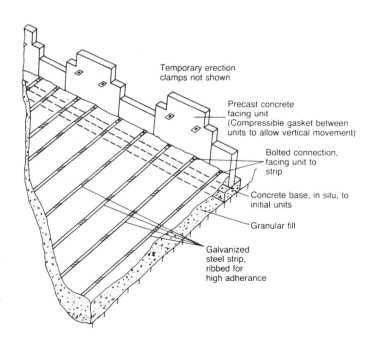

Fig. 3.2. Reinforced Earth wall during construction showing reinforcing strips and precast concrete facing units (courtesy of Reinforced Earth Company Ltd)

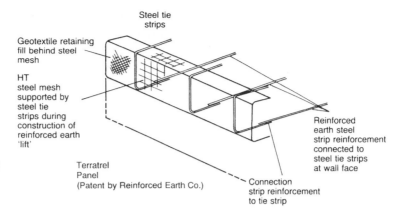

Steel tie
strips

Geotextile retaining
fill behind steel
mesh

HT
steel mesh
supported by
steel tie
strips during
construction of
reinforced earth
'lift'

Terratrel
Panel
(Patent by Reinforced Earth Co.)

Reinforced
earth steel
strip reinforcement
connected to
steel tie strips
at wall face

Connection
strip reinforcement
to tie strip

Fig. 3.3. Terratrel panel for use in steep slope construction (courtesy of Reinforced Earth Company Ltd.)

Figure 3.2 shows a typical cross-section of a Reinforced Earth structure using metal strip reinforcement and precast concrete panel facing. The economics in construction time and cost are determined by a simple and repetitious construction process. After placing the base course of the facing panels on a prepared foundation, each additional panel mechanically interlocks with the previous course. The reinforcing strip and backfill are placed, and compact backfill is then placed in successive layers. Varying shapes of facing panel are available to suit aesthetic requirements. The Reinforced Earth Company developed a technique which has been used in many steep and near-vertical slopes, using steel strip reinforcement and a soft facing of steel mesh backed with geotextile, and suits the requirements of an economic, quick-to-build, soft-faced steep slope able to accept vegetative cover. This technique is called Terratrel[8]. The use of wraparound geotextiles to steepen soil slopes has often been associated with relatively slow construction methods, with excessive amounts of plant and labour. Terratrel uses low-cost steel mesh facing panels in discrete heights between reinforcement levels, allowing a repetitive erection technique without the need for propping of formwork; Fig. 3.3 shows a typical panel. The technique allows high-adherence galvanized steel reinforcing strips to be fixed directly to the steel mesh facing unit, which is sufficiently rigid to support itself as a vertical cantilever, fixed in advance of earth filling. The geotextile used as a backing material behind the steel mesh facing retains the soil and guards against soil wash-out before vegetation can become established. Plant growth can be started by hydroseeding, or turf can be placed behind the mesh as construction proceeds to give an instant green effect. Steep slopes have been built using a coarse stone fill behind the mesh to give a deliberate gabion-type finish. In the UK, an 11 m high, 80° slope of 2000 m² face area has been built at Leeds, and lower slopes have been built at Nottingham (the A52 road improvement), the Elan aqueduct at Birmingham, and the A74 Bogbain bypass in Scotland.

Polymer geogrids

Tensar geogrids are high-strength polymer grids specifically made as tension-resistant inclusions in soils. The manufacturing process begins with an extended sheet of polyethylene or polypropylene which is punched with a regular pattern of circular holes. This sheet is then stretched under controlled heat conditions so that randomly long chain molecules are drawn into an aligned state. This process of stretching increases the tensile strength and stiffness of the polymer. The resulting geogrid structure of ribs and bars produces an effective means of transferring load from soil to geogrid. The prime disadvantage of using a polymer grid is the low elastic modulus and high creep value compared with steel strip. The influence of long-term strength has been the subject of vigorous research[9], and the influence of load capacity on the design life of the geogrid can be predicted by extrapolation from laboratory curves of strain against load with increasing time at various temperatures. Details of characteristic strength derived in this way are shown in Fig. 3.4. The overall effect of this long-term creep feature of the polymer is, however, to

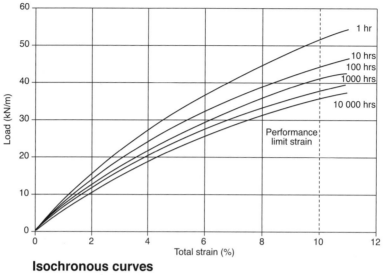

Isochronous curves for Tensar SR80 at 10° ± 1 °C

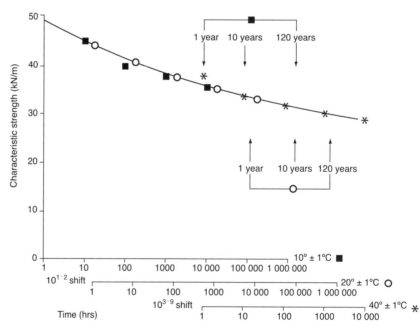

Characteristic strength curve for Tensar SR80. Time–temperature superposition

Fig. 3.4. Derivation of characteristic strength of Tensar geogrid SR80 from short-term stress–strain tests (courtesy of Netlon)

In-soil temperature	Characteristic strength (f_k) of Tensar geogrids (kN/m)		
	SR55	SR80	SR10
10 °C UK (5) and temperate climates	22·0	32·5	45·0
20 °C Warm climates	20·5	30·5	42·0

Characteristic strength of Tensar geogrids for design lives of up to 120 years

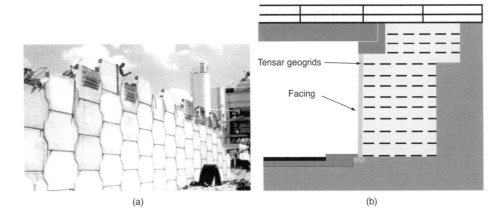

Fig. 3.5. Techniques of wall construction using geogrid reinforcement (courtesy of Tensar International Ltd)

(a) (b)

limit the use of geogrids to relatively modest vertical wall heights (typically 6 to 8 m) in order to remain competitive with metal strip Reinforced Earth walls. The prime advantages of these geogrids are their resistance to attack from all aqueous solutions of acids, alkalis and salts encountered in soils, and high resistance to biological attack. The geogrids are made from polymers formulated to resist ultraviolet light degradation, and when buried or covered by vegetation their life is indefinite. Resistance to corrosion is therefore considerably greater than that of steel strip. In recent years a number of flexible geogrids consisting of a polyester core rib coated in PVC have entered the market. Care should be exercised to ensure that adequate junction and interlock strength and resistance to alkaline environments are provided by such geogrids.

Geogrid reinforced soil walls can be faced with modular concrete block units or can allow a façade of masonry or brickwork to be connected to blockwork with stainless steel ties for aesthetic effect. Full-height or incremental-height reinforced concrete facing units may also be used with a short starter length of the appropriate geogrid cast in at the rear of each unit. A further innovation uses steel stanchions with precast concrete planks secured to a reinforced soil backfill. These techniques of wall construction are shown in Fig. 3.5, courtesy of Tensar International Ltd. Wraparound faces using geogrids may also be used in the same way as metal strip reinforcement to form the face of the structure, using either temporary external formwork or internal bagwork (see Fig. 3.6). In addition, steel mesh panel facings lined with vegetation matting are increasingly used for speed and economy with geogrid reinforcement on steep slopes. A recent example of this technique involved the reinforcement of a 70° slope, 9 m high and 2 km in length for the Channel Tunnel Rail Link. Typical uniaxial geogrid details by Tensar are given in Fig. 3.7.

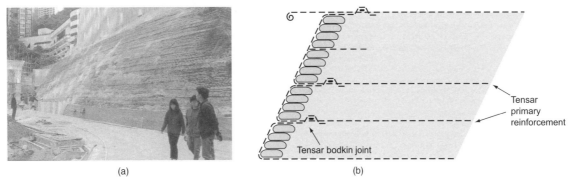

(a) (b)

Fig. 3.6. Geogrid reinforcement used as wraparound reinforcement (courtesy of Tensar International Ltd)

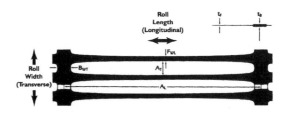

Tensar RE Geogrid specifications

Property	Units	Tensar Geogrid				
		40RE	**55RE**	**80RE**	**120RE**	**160RE**
Polymer (1)		HDPE	HDPE	HDPE	HDPE	HDPE
Minimum carbon black (2)	%	2	2	2	2	2
Roll width	m	1.0 & 1.3	1.0 & 1.3	1.0 & 1.3	1.0 & 1.3	1.0 & 1.3
Roll length	m	50	50	50	50	30
Unit weight	kg/m²	0.29	0.4	0.6	0.94	1.24
Dimensions						
A_L	mm	235	235	235	235	230
A_T	mm	16	16	16	16	16
B_{WT}	mm	16	16	16	16	16
F_{WL}	mm	6	6	6	6	6
t_B	mm	1.8-2.0	2.5-2.7	3.4-3.7	5.5-5.9	7.1-7.7
t_F	mm	0.7	0.9	1.3	2	2.6
Quality control strength						
T_{ult} (3)	kN/m	52.5	64.5	88.0	136.0	173.0
Load at 2% strain (3)	kN/m	12.7	16.1	23.7	38.0	52.5
Load at 5% strain (3)	kN/m	24.7	30.9	45.2	75.5	103.0
Approx strain at T_{ult}	%	11.5	11.5	11.5	11.5	11.5
Long-term creep rupture strength ULS (4)						
P_C or T_{CR} for 10°C	kN/m	23.3	28.7	38.2	54.8	69.4
P_C or T_{CR} for 20°C	kN/m	20.7	25.5	34.0	48.7	61.7
P_C or T_{CR} for 30°C	kN/m	18.8	23.4	30.1	45.3	55.2
Long-term strain limited strength SLS (5)						
T_{CS} for 10°C	kN/m	13.4	17.6	25.0	37.7	48.9
T_{CS} for 20°C	kN/m	11.5	15.4	22.4	34.3	44.8
T_{CS} for 30°C	kN/m	9.8	13.5	20.0	31.3	41.1
Factor for manufacture and extrapolation of data (6)						
f_m		1.0-1.05	1.0-1.05	1.0-1.05	1.0-1.05	1.0-1.05
Installation damage factors for ultimate limit state (7)						
f_d for crushed stone <6mm		1.00	1.00	1.00	1.00	1.00
f_d for crushed stone <37.5mm		1.07	1.07	1.07	1.00	1.00
f_d for crushed stone <75mm		1.25	1.20	1.15	1.06	1.01
f_d for crushed stone <125mm		1.48	1.36	1.25	1.12	1.02
Installation damage factors for serviceability limit state (8)						
f_d for all gradings		1.0	1.0	1.0	1.0	1.0
Environmental factor (9)						
f_e for pH 2.0 to 4.0		1.05	1.05	1.05	1.05	1.05
f_e for pH 4.0 to 12.5		1.00	1.00	1.00	1.00	1.00

(1) HDPE denotes high density polyethylene.

(2) Determined in accordance with BS 2782: Part 4: Method 452B: 1993.

(3) Determined in accordance with ISO 10319 and as a lower 95% confidence limit in accordance with ISO 2602 (BS 2846: Part 2: 1981).

(4) Determined as a lower bound using standard extrapolation techniques to creep rupture data obtained following the test procedure in ISO 13431 for a 120-year design life.

(5) Determined from creep tests carried out following the test procedure in ISO 13431 as the load resulting in 1% strain between 1 month and 120 years after the start of loading.

(6) f_m = 1.0 based on the QA procedures, database, use of lower bound values and extrapolation procedures applied by Tensar International. f_m = 1.05 is given in BBA Certificates No 99/R109 and No 99/R113 for Tensar RE geogrids.

(7) Derived as worst values from site damage trials carried out following the method given in BS 8006: 1995, values as given in BBA Certificate No 99/R113 for Tensar RE geogrids.

(8) Values as given in BBA Certificate No 99/R109 for Tensar RE geogrids.

(9) Values given in BBA Certificate No 99/R113 for Tensar RE geogrids.

Data sheets are also available for the Tensar SR geogrids

Fig. 3.7. Typical uniaxial geogrid details (courtesy of Tensar International Ltd)

Polyester-reinforced thermoplastic webbing
High-strength polyester-reinforced thermoplastic flat webbing also provides a tensile reinforcement material for reinforced soil walls, steepened slopes and mattresses for settlement control. The webbing, known as Paraweb, is manufactured in two forms, either bonded in strips to Terram melded geotextile or woven into mats.

The composite Paraweb and Terram is supplied in rolls 4·5 m wide and up to 150 m long; Paraweb strip is typically 50 to 80 mm wide with centres 240 mm apart within the Terram. Using variable material properties, a range of ultimate tensile strengths are available within the range 95 to 125 kN per metre width.

Polyester and polyaramid bands with a ribbed surface for improved soil-to-band adhesion are also produced in widths of 90 mm and thicknesses of 6, 7 and 8 mm, with breaking loads per strip of 50, 100 and 150 kN, respectively. These strips are used as reinforcement in a similar manner to steel strips in Reinforced Earth walls with precast concrete or metal sheet facing panels. The plastic strips overcome the problems of durability associated with steel strips and the disadvantages of long-term creep associated with polyethylene geogrids. Meshes of these strips are also manufactured under the trade names Paragrid and Paralink.

Synthetic fibre mixed with soil in situ
The use of a fine diameter synthetic fibre mixed in place within the soil to form tensile reinforcement has been patented by the French Bridges and Roads Research Laboratory (LCPC). Contracts have been confined to France, Italy, Holland and Japan, but since 1985 a number of retaining walls have been built using Texsol, with typical heights from 4 m to more than 20 m and front slopes between 45° and 80°. Texsol can only be used to enhance the slope angle to embankments in granular fill materials. Multiple continuous threads are used in the ratio 0·1 to 0·2% by weight of natural soil. The growth of vegetation to walls built in this way is a natural process, although problems of erosion to the wall face may arise at times of heavy rainfall prior to the establishment of the plants.

Application of reinforced soil in excavation works
Retaining walls
Initial projects in the early 1970s for the Reinforced Earth Company were a 23 m high wall on the Nice–Menton highway at Peyronnet, France, the walls to the coal and ore handling facility at Port Dunkirk, major retaining walls to highways in California, Quebec and Bilbao, Spain, and an 11 km long wall built on the Reunion Island in the Indian Ocean.

After transportation works, industrial and commercial sectors are the next largest area for reinforced soil application. These include crushing and screening facilities, sloped wall bunkers for coal and ore storage, safety containment dykes for liquid petroleum gas (LPG) and crude oil tanks, civil and military projects providing protection against explosions, and hydraulic structures such as dam spillways, canal and river walls, coastal defence structures, marine walls and reservoirs.

The use of retaining walls in the UK has been inhibited by patents registered by Vidal in the late 1960s (for the process of Reinforced Earth) and in the early 1970s (for the facings). The Department of the Environment obtained a settlement with the Reinforced Earth Company to build Reinforced Earth walls on public works in the mid 1980s and, more recently, the patent for the wall facing has expired. Prior to this, competitor companies were unable to offer schemes for vertical walls in the UK.

Steep slopes

The economic advantages of steepening soil slopes are self-evident both in terms of construction cost and land take. Geotextile reinforcement is widely used to reinforce fill slopes or regraded slopes in cut. These geotextile layers are placed successively within the slope as the filling is placed and compacted. As deformation within a steep slope is less critical, it is possible to use poorer grades of fill material within steep slopes than vertical wall structures.

For slopes between 45° and 90° a face support will generally be required; if geogrids or Paragrid are being used, the material can be wrapped around successive lifts of fill, thereby making rigid facings unnecessary. Alternatively, soil reinforcement by Texsol synthetic fibres may be considered. For slopes of less than 45° it will not usually be necessary to use wraparound geogrid or Paragrid, and in such cases the use of a Tensar mat pinned to the slope may be necessary to protect seeded slopes from erosion before substantial growth.

Design in reinforced soil

In the UK two principal standards apply to design: BS 8006[6] and the Highways Agency document HA 68/94[5] for highway works. BS 8006 considers both reinforced walls and slopes separately whereas HA 68/94 considers only slopes with a maximum angle to the horizontal of 70°. Both documents use limit state design methods.

The design of walls in reinforced soil is based on one of two available methods known as the two-part wedge (or tie-back wedge) or the coherent gravity system. The two-part wedge method follows design principles used for classical or anchored retaining walls. The coherent gravity method on the other hand is based on monitored behaviour of reinforced soil structures using inextensible reinforcement over a number of walls corroborated by theoretical analysis.

BS 8006 refers to both design methods for internal stability but advises that for inextensible reinforcement (metal strip) the preferred method of design is the coherent gravity method whereas for extensible reinforcement (polymeric) the two-part wedge should be used. The different uses are based on the development of earth pressures within the soil structure; for inextensible reinforcement it is likely that pressure near the top of the wall will remain 'at rest', whereas for extensible reinforcement, active pressure will develop as strain increases. The Highways Agency code HA 68/94 on the other hand prefers the use of the two-part wedge method for all reinforced soil structures. (The French Ministère des Transports specifies the use of the coherent gravity method of design.)

The design (as recommended in BS 8006) requires consideration of both external and internal stability for the reinforced mass of soil.

External stability checks are required for:

- bearing and tilt failure, using a bearing pressure based upon a Meyerhof distribution (see Fig. 3.8)
- sliding along the bases, and sliding forward at the base of the reinforced soil, either soil to soil or soil to reinforcement contact
- external slip surfaces, to the rear and below the reinforced soil structure or through and below it.

Settlement must also be checked of the whole at serviceability state.

Internal stability is concerned with the statical stability of the reinforced block of soil – to ensure that the tensile resistance of each successive layer of reinforced soil has sufficient tensile resistance to counter internal collapse due to its own weight and surcharge loading. Consideration is needed for the local stability of reinforcing elements, sliding on horizontal planes and

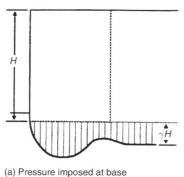

(a) Pressure imposed at base

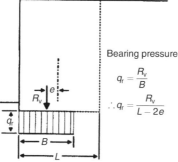

Bearing pressure

$$q_r = \frac{R_v}{B}$$

$$\therefore q_r = \frac{R_v}{L - 2e}$$

Fig. 3.8. Bearing pressure based on a Meyerhof distribution[6]

(b) Idealized bearing pressure

the stability of wedges of reinforced soil. With cohesive frictional fills it will be necessary to consider the effect of pore water pressure on stability.

At ultimate limit state, an expression for the tensile force to be resisted by any element below the top of the structure is used with appropriate safety factors to check the resistance of that element by rupture or failure of adherence.

Wedge stability is considered by examining arbitrary trial wedges at successive depths of elements a, b, c, etc. as shown in Fig. 3.9. For each wedge, the gross tensile force T required to maintain stability is calculated and then compared to the frictional/tensile capacity of the elements anchoring that wedge. The resistance of each reinforcement element layer used is the lesser of its tensile strength or the adherence of that element.

BS 8006 then examines the use of the coherent gravity method as an alternative method of internal stability analysis. The method is based on the following assumptions.

- The reinforced soil block consists of an active zone and a resisting zone separated by a line of maximum tension in the reinforcement, shown in Fig. 3.10. The failure mode is similar to that of a mass of cohesionless soil supported by a rigid wall rotating about the top. BS 8006 assumes the change from at rest pressure to active values occurs at a depth of 6 m from the top of the wall.
- The reinforcement interacts and interlocks with the fill to provide an effective overall resistance against pull-out.

As before, in the coherent gravity method the calculations of the vertical stresses are based on the Meyerhof distribution of pressure. Calculations for the tensile force are made assuming a logarithmic spiral for the locus of maximum tension as shown in Fig. 3.11, with a simplification to the geometry shown in Fig. 3.12 where superimposed strip loads do not apply; consideration of a further maximum tension line is required where strip loads apply. Tensile

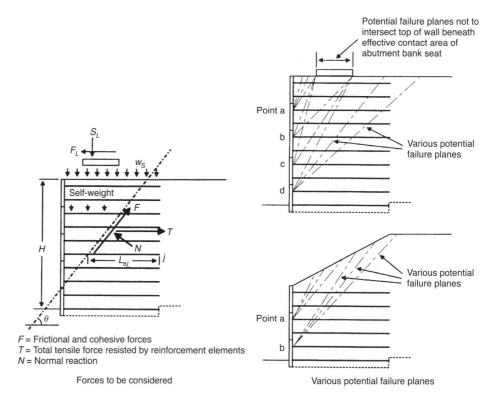

Fig. 3.9. (a) Two part wedge method: wedge stability examined for arbitrary trial wedges[6]

F = Frictional and cohesive forces
T = Total tensile force resisted by reinforcement elements
N = Normal reaction

Forces to be considered

Various potential failure planes

loads are also calculated at the facings. Reinforcement is then provided, with appropriate partial factors applied, for the lesser capacity of the reinforcement element in either tension or adherence. Deformation of the wall face and settlement is calculated at serviceability state.

Design of reinforced slopes

As the angle of the face of the reinforced soil structure declines from the vertical or near-vertical face of walls to those of reinforced slopes, the influence of the retained soil reduces and the proportion of the stability provided by the reinforcement decreases.

The design methods at limit state are based on limit equilibrium methods. In a similar way to wall design both external and internal stability are considered in reinforced slope design. The external stability, as before, is considered for bearing and tilt failure, forwards sliding and slip failure around the reinforced block.

Internal stability may be verified at ultimate limit state either by a two-part wedge analysis (as described in HA 68/94) assuming a bilinear failure surface as shown in Fig. 3.13, circular or non-circular analyses, log spiral failure analyses or the coherent gravity method.

The use of the log spiral analysis and the assessment of moment equilibrium has been described by Leshchinsky and Boedecker[10]. A computer program, ReSlope, has been developed using the method. The use of the log spiral simplifies the analysis procedure as the de-stabilizing moment is determined directly. The restoring moment due to the presence of the reinforcement should equal or be greater than the de-stabilizing moment.

A further failure mode needs to be checked for potential failure surfaces that intersect reinforcement elements but also pass outside the reinforced soil mass (Fig. 3.14). An extension of the analysis method, log spiral or other assumed failure surfaces, is used, and is referred to as 'compound stability' assessment.

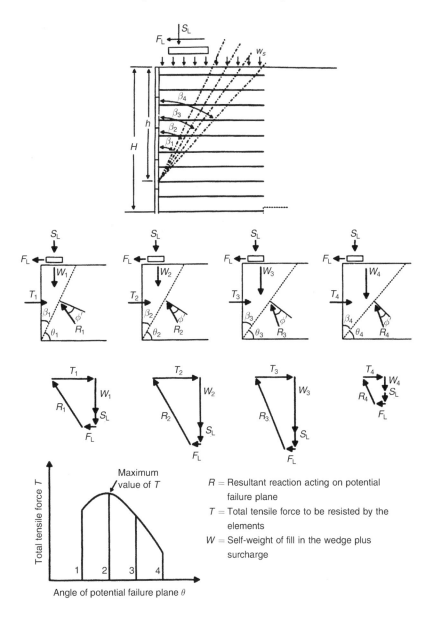

Fig. 3.9. (continued) (b) Internal wedge stability analysis of simple problem[6]

R = Resultant reaction acting on potential failure plane

T = Total tensile force to be resisted by the elements

W = Self-weight of fill in the wedge plus surcharge

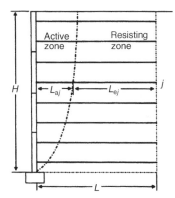

Fig. 3.10. Active and resisting zones separated by a line of maximum tension in the reinforcements; coherent gravity method[6]

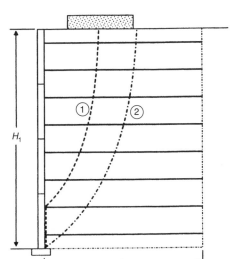

Fig. 3.11. Coherent gravity method: logarithmic spirals used for the basis of calculation of maximum tension in the reinforcement, for strip loading[6]

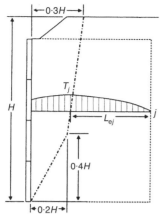

Fig. 3.12. Definition of maximum tension line 2, simplified geometry where superimposed loads do not apply – coherent gravity method[6]

Soil nailing

Soil nailing is the strengthening of existing ground by the introduction of steel reinforcement or more recently carbon fibre rods into the exposed face. There are two particular applications: the retention of a vertical or near-vertical cut soil face, and the stabilization of a soil slope. The soil nailing process is typically a top-downwards operation, whereas reinforced soil construction is usually bottom-upwards.

Steel 'nails' are usually rods 20 to 40 mm in diameter or small steel angle sections typically 50×50 mm (the latter are used in particular in a patented method known as an Hurpinoise wall). The nails are grouted into pre-drilled holes or driven using a percussion drilling device or high-energy firing device. The nails are not prestressed and their density is relatively high (1 bar per 0·5 to 0·6 m²). The nail length is dependent on slope geometry and soil conditions, but would typically be 0·4 to 0·5 times the vertical height of the cut soil face. The soil is progressively excavated in depths of about 1 to 1·5 m and the steep exposed soil face is protected by a layer of sprayed concrete reinforced with high tensile steel mesh. The nails are driven or drilled into the face before or after guniting, depending on risk of soil instability. The process is shown in Fig. 3.15.

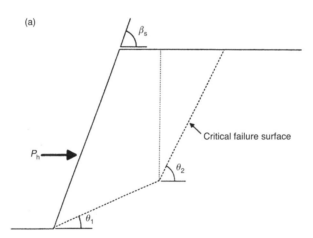

(a)

Two-part wedge approach to reinforced slopes

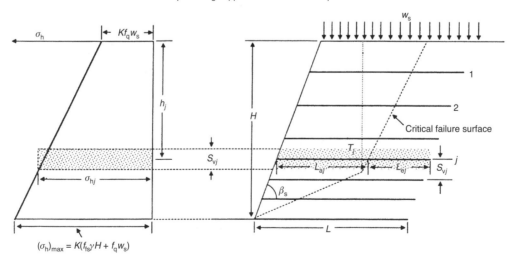

Approximate disturbing stress distribution and reinforcement layout

Fig. 3.13. (a) Reinforced slopes: bilinear failure surface at ultimate limit state in two-part wedge analysis.

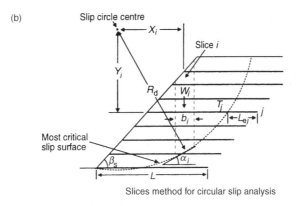

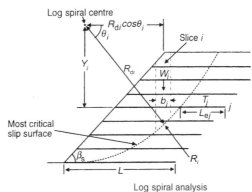

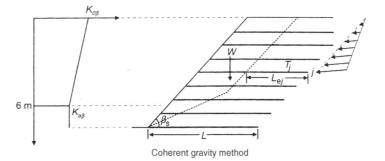

Fig. 3.13. (continued) (b) Reinforced slopes: alternative methods of internal stability analysis, by circular slip analysis, log spiral analysis and coherent gravity method[6]

For nailed slope protection a covering of topsoil secured between galvanized steel mesh layers gives an environmentally friendly finish. Details of a patented system by the Phi Group are shown in Fig. 3.16. Nailed slopes with similar 'green' finishes have recently been used extensively in the UK for steepened slopes, for highway widening schemes.

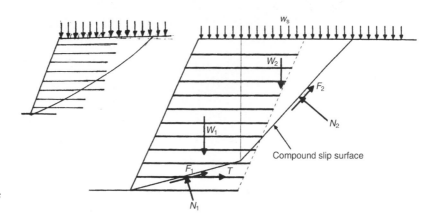

Fig. 3.14. Failure mode with failure surface intersecting reinforcement but passing outside the reinforced soil mass: two-part wedge analysis of compound stability[6]

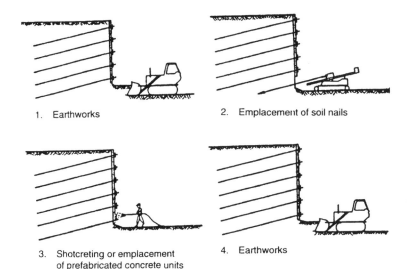

1. Earthworks

2. Emplacement of soil nails

3. Shotcreting or emplacement of prefabricated concrete units

4. Earthworks

Fig. 3.15. Execution phases of soil nailing[11]

The first soil-nailed wall was completed in 1973 in Versailles, France, to retain a cut for a railway (Fig. 3.17). The technique is applied most economically in granular soils and relies on relatively dry ground conditions for practical installation. The growth of the method in Western Europe has centred on France. Figure 3.18 shows the extent of the increasing use of soil nailing, which is explained by its low cost compared with traditional soil support systems.

In the mid 1980s, the use of soil nailing was advancing so quickly in France that the state of site and design work was exceeding theoretical knowledge and proven methods. In part, specialist geotechnical firms found that compared with general contractors there was insufficient expertise in installation and little sophistication in equipment to keep the market to themselves. The use of the process therefore expanded rapidly in the hands of general contractors. In Germany and the UK the method found less favour, possibly due to less favourable ground conditions.

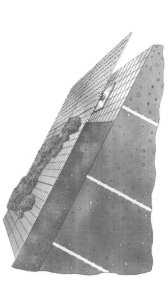

Fig. 3.16. Details of nailed slope protection, patented process (courtesy of Phi Group)

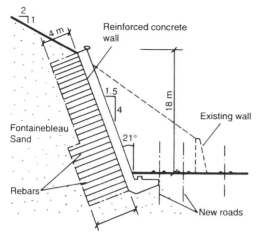

Fig. 3.17. First soil-nailed wall at Versailles, France in 1972/73[11]

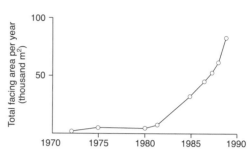

Fig. 3.18. Increase in use of soil-nailing in France, 1972–1989[12]

Following the growth of this method, a four-year national research programme called Clouterre was commissioned by the French Ministry of Transport. Twenty-one firms and research centres collaborated under the technical direction of Professor F. Schlosser. The report incorporates the results of full-scale trials of nailed cuts and includes directives in both design and specification[11].

Design methods

For design purposes, a general stability analysis is applicable with potential failure surfaces either falling outside the volume of reinforced soil, or partly within it. Figure 3.19 shows the location of the potential failure surfaces. The potential failure surface which intersects the reinforcement will cause bending and shear stresses within the reinforcement in addition to the tensile, pull-out forces. The ability of a typical nail to withstand bending and shear is dependent upon its stiffness: the stiffer the nail the greater its resistance to moment and shear in the same way as a pile with an applied horizontal force and moment at its head. Figure 3.20 shows bending and shear forces applied to a stiff nail at the failure surface and the analogy thereto. The failure surface is not the classical Coulomb wedge but the locus of maximum tensile forces in the nails. This potential failure surface is approximately parallel to the wall facing in the upper part of the retained height and separates the soil mass into two zones: the active zone, where shear stresses between soil and nails are directed towards the facing; and the passive zone, where shear stresses are directed towards the inside of the soil mass beyond the potential failure surface.

The stiffness of the nails also modifies the classical Rankine earth pressure distribution against the wall facing. The soil pressures in the upper part are near K_0 earth pressure at rest, but reduce to less than K_a values lower down. For retaining walls, two principal methods have been applied, particularly in France:

(a) 'micropiles', where the nails are relatively long and have considerable tensile strength (200 to 500 kN), grouted in pre-drilled boreholes with relatively wide spacing (about one bar per 3 to 6 m^2)

(b) 'driven or fired nails', where the reinforcing nails are shorter and have less strength in tension (50 to 150 kN), driven or shot into the soil face with a closer spacing (one bar per 0.5 m^2).

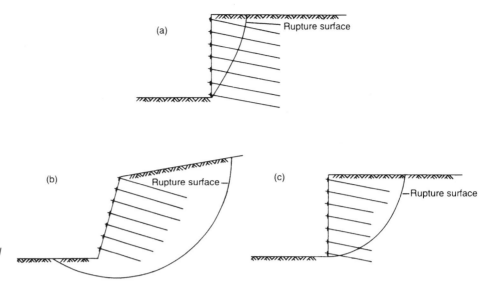

Fig. 3.19. Locations of potential failure surfaces in a nailed wall[11]

The dimensions of soil-nailed walls depend on the strength of the retained soil. An indication of this effect is shown in Figs 3.21 and 3.22. For the micropile solution, the ratio of nail length to the height of vertical facing (L/H) decreases from about 1·7 to 0·5, and the cumulative length of nails from 4·5 to 1·5 m/m² when the soil angle of shearing resistance (ϕ) increases from 25° to 55°. For the driven or fired nails, the L/H ratio and the cumulative length of bars are nearly constant irrespective of the value of ϕ: L/H is approximately 0·5 and the cumulative nail length is from 11 to 12 m/m². The choice between micropile and driven nails depends on cost, available equipment and the nature of the soil (in terms of ease of drilling or driving of the nails and pull-out resistance).

An important aspect of wall design is the development of adequate pull-out resistance to the nail. This resistance, which is the aggregate of friction between retained soil and the surface of the nails, varies according to installation method, grouting technique (with or without pressure) and soil type (cohesive or cohesionless); the optimum conditions are dense granular soils where dilation occurs during shearing. Where such dilatancy is restricted by the dense soil mass, high restraining frictional resistance is set up along the nail. These frictional resistances therefore vary from as high as 600 kPa for dense granular soils to less than 100 kPa for loose sands. For cohesive soils, the maximum soil/nail adhesion is less than that for granular soils and

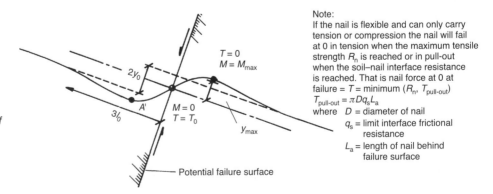

Fig. 3.20. Enlarged distortion of nail at the failure surface with moment and shear applied. Note the analogy of a pile with horizontal load applied at its head[12]

Note:
If the nail is flexible and can only carry tension or compression the nail will fail at 0 in tension when the maximum tensile strength R_n is reached or in pull-out when the soil–nail interface resistance is reached. That is nail force at 0 at failure = T = minimum (R_n, $T_{pull-out}$)
$T_{pull-out} = \pi D q_s L_a$
where D = diameter of nail
q_s = limit interface frictional resistance
L_a = length of nail behind failure surface

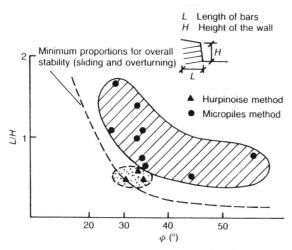

Fig. 3.21. Observed proportions of height of wall to length of nails as a function of retained soil strength[11]

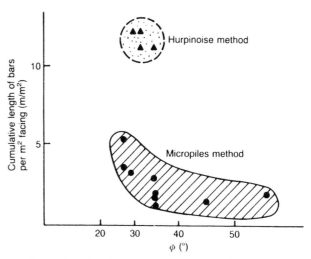

Fig. 3.22. Nailed walls: cumulative length of nails per square metre of wall face as a function of soil strength[12]

ranges from 50 to 100 kPa, reducing as the soil becomes saturated. With the French preference for pressuremeter testing, a large number of pull-out tests were undertaken in the Clouterre research project and limit pressuremeter pressure and soil–nail frictional resistance were correlated (Fig. 3.23). In all cases where economical wall design is necessary, a knowledge of pull-out tests for nails is essential, and before introducing soil nailed walls into previously untried soil conditions there should be a short test programme of nail pull-outs.

Movements which occur in other reinforced soil structures (such as reinforced soil walls) similarly occur in nailed walls and are inherent in the method due to the relatively flexible structure produced by reinforcing soil. Displacements which occur during excavation and are largely complete thereafter vary between $H/1000$ and $H/3000$, where H is the wall height. Figure 3.24 shows some recorded values.

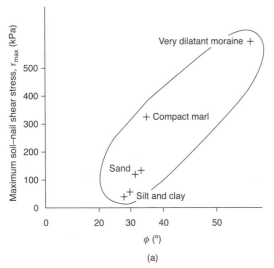

(a)

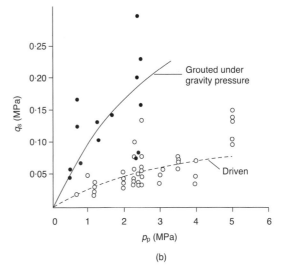

(b)

Fig. 3.23. Values of soil–nail surface friction as a function of soil strength: (a) expressed as angle of soil shearing resistance for various soils; (b) expressed as limit pressure from pressuremeter tests for grouted and driven nails[12]

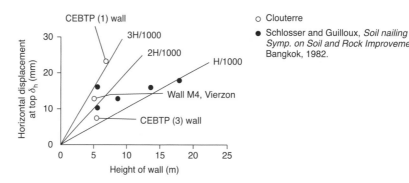

o Clouterre

● Schlosser and Guilloux, *Soil nailing Symp. on Soil and Rock Improvement,* Bangkok, 1982.

Fig. 3.24. Observed range of values of maximum horizontal displacement of nailed walls[12]

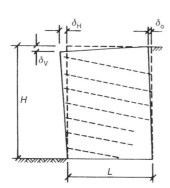

Fig. 3.25. Definitions of displacements δ_H, δ_V and δ_0[12]

Schlosser *et al.*[12] referred to three displacements, δ_H, δ_V, δ_0 (Fig. 3.25), and observed δ_H to be approximately the same as δ_V. The length λ is defined as that minimum distance from the back of the wall to the point where lateral movement δ_0 reduces to zero. The value of λ is a function of soil type (coefficient K), the inclination from the vertical of the wall η, and H, according to the empirical relationship

$$\lambda = K(1 - \tan\eta)H. \qquad (37)$$

The values of δ_H, δ_V and K, from the expression for λ, are summarized in Table 3.1.

Schlosser et al.[12] reported that corrosion should be allowed for in structures with an expected service life of more than 18 months. In France it is usual to allow a sacrificial thickness for corrosion of the nails. The total thickness is calculated so that, given the expected degree of corrosion, an adequate thickness of nail remains at the end of the service life. The Clouterre recommendations specify degrees of corrosion which include resistivity and soil moisture content, and these are included in Table 3.2 showing the recommended extra thicknesses of steel.

The modes of failure of a nailed wall were referred to earlier, and basically can be compared with a classical wedge failure but with modifications. In all cases the overall stability of the wall should be checked, that is, over a potential failure surface which passes to the rear of, and beneath, the nailed volume of soil to emerge at formation level in front of the wall. A conventional

Table 3.1 Displacements in nailed walls

Soil type	Weathered rocks, stiff soils	Sandy soils	Clayey soils
$\delta_H = \delta_V$	$H/1000$	$2H/1000$	$3H/1000$
K	0·8	1·25	1·5

Table 3.2 Sacrificial nail thickness allowed with respect to expected degrees of soil corrosion

Class	Soil character	Service life ≤ 18 months	Service life 1·5 to 30 years	Service life 30 to 100 years
IV	A little corrosive	0	2 mm	4 mm
III	Fairly corrosive	0	4 mm	8 mm
II	Corrosive	2 mm	8 mm	Plastic barrier
I	Strongly corrosive	Compulsory plastic barrier		Compulsory plastic barrier

Bishop, $\phi'c'$ analysis should be used to check that this overall stability is adequate.

The design stages comprise:

(*a*) determination of the critical slip surface and the resisting force or moment to maintain equilibrium
(*b*) determination of the tensile and shear load for an initial spacing and inclination of nails
(*c*) checking at each level for:
  (i)   tension in the nail at the slip surface
  (ii) pull-out of the nail
  (iii) maximum bending and shear in the nail
  (iv) bearing failure of soil against the nail.

BS 8006 recommends that design can be made on the basis of a limit equilibrium approach based on the two-part wedge mechanism or a failure surface using a log spiral.

Although there is some risk of oversimplification, the graphical analysis shown in Fig. 3.26 using the two-part wedge may be used to define the maximum nail force N to preserve equilibrium. Trial failure surfaces for varying values of inclination β of the lower wedge are used to calculate the maximum tension in the nails N_a. An overall factor of safety against pull-out of the soil nails of 1·5 for permanent walls and 1·3 for temporary walls is regarded as adequate where pull-out tests have been performed on a site of known or similar ground conditions.

The design methods recommended by the Clouterre project, summarized by Schlosser[12], comprise an extension of the classical limit equilibrium method (method of slices) to reinforced soils, and take into account the bending

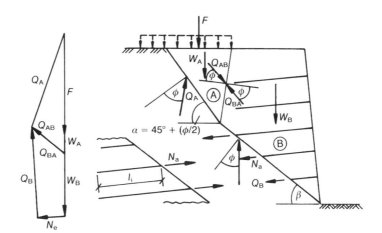

Failure mechanism of nailed wall.

$\Sigma N_a = T_m \times l_i$

where T_m is the friction per unit length of nail and l_i is the nail length beyond the slip surface.

Factor of safety FS $\eta = \dfrac{\Sigma N_a}{N_e}$

where ΣN_a is the sum of maximum available tension arising in the soil nails at the crossing points with failure surface.

N_e is the nail force necessary to the limit equilibrium.

Fig. 3.26. Graphical analysis to determine the factor of safety of wall stability for nail length

stiffness and shear resistance of the nails. It is the mode of failure of the stiff nail system (micropiles, drilled and grouted) which justifies this more sophisticated analysis. Stiffer nails can break in bending or shear at the potential failure surface; the soil below the nail can fail in bearing or the nail can pull out. Schlosser also recommended partial factors of safety to be used in an overall stability analysis.

In addition to these analyses at ultimate limit state the wall should be checked for the risk of movement from site measurements of walls in similar soil conditions. In particular, the proximity of existing structures and services should be noted and estimates made of the lateral distance to the point of zero horizontal soil movement.

The design of the facing depends on the tension in the nails at the facing T_0 and uniform soil pressure acting on the facing. T_0 can be calculated directly using recommended values of T_0/T_{max} given in the Clouterre report, where T_{max} is the maximum tension in the nail in service. The Clouterre report advises the following relationships:

$$\frac{T}{T_{max}} = 0.5 + \frac{(S - 0.5)}{5} \quad \text{for } 1\,\text{m} \leq S \leq 3\,\text{m}$$

$$\frac{T_0}{T_{max}} = 0.6 \quad \text{for } S \leq 1\,\text{m} \tag{38}$$

$$\frac{T_0}{T_{max}} = 1.0 \quad \text{for } S \geq 3\,\text{m}$$

where $S = \max(S_V, S_H)$ in metres and T_{max} may be estimated as the ultimate nail pull-out force used in the design. S_V is nail vertical spacing, S_H is nail horizontal spacing.

Methods of installation and equipment

The stages in construction of the nailed wall are:

(a) excavation at the face of the wall in layers in 1 to 1·5 m deep increments defined by anchor spacing; trimming to face of wall, to line and verticality (or batter)

(b) application of gunite (shotcrete) to the exposed soil face

(c) gunite to be steel mesh reinforced; installation of nails by drilling and grouting or driving; making good gunite perforation by nails (where conditions allow, it may be preferred to install nails prior to gunite application).

Excavation adjacent to the wall face would typically be made by backhoe with the assistance of a wheeled front-end loader to prepare a temporary platform at each successive excavation stage. Where the wall face has a batter (a slight batter of 5° to 10° is not unusual), more work is involved trimming to line and batter with some hand work. The application of gunite (shotcrete) is by hand-held hose from a small portable mixer/compressor unit. Water is applied at the nozzle. Typical gunite thicknesses are 100 to 150 mm applied in successive layers approximately 50 to 75 mm thick. Reinforcement mesh is pinned to the first layer of the hardening concrete. There are two alternative reinforcement methods:

(a) An unprotected metal rod or angle section driven from the soil face (short nails up to 6 m long may be installed by pneumatic 'shot-fired' means). Unprotected nails would only be suitable for temporary or short-term support unless corrosion is allowed for by a sacrificial thickness.

(b) A steel rod section placed within a drilled hole and grouted at gravity, or higher, grout pressure.

Option (b) requires the installation of steel rod nails, typically 32 to 50 mm dia. bars within bores 100 to 150 mm in diameter. The bores would be horizontal or with a small declination, and would be installed using rotary air or water flush. The rig required for drilling the relatively short bores would be a tracked hydraulic rig similar to that used for ground anchor installation such as the Casagrande C6 rig. Depending on soil conditions, it would be necessary to case these relatively short bores, the casing being withdrawn as grout is introduced. Relatively low grout pressures would be used (less than 5 bar). Although the drilled and grouted nail solution uses traditional 'ground anchor' expertise, and the nails are spaced at wider centres than the driven nail option, the cost of drilled and grouted nails is higher than the ungrouted driven nail solution, providing permanent rather than temporary support.

The stages in construction of nailed, steepened soil slopes are similar to those for nailed walls. For slopes of considerable height and depending upon short-term slope stability, the method consists of excavating increments of steepened cut from the crest of the slope, installing the nails by driving (for temporary support) or drilling and grouting (for permanent support) and fixing to the head of each nail a cage of galvanized mesh enclosing either seeded topsoil or geotextile.

Soil retention: further wall constructions

Three further methods of soil retention using flexible wall construction deserve brief mention: ladder walls, gabions and crib walls.

Ladder walls

While soil nailing provides an integral soil and reinforcement mass, an earlier installation, the ladder wall, used a facing tied back into fill with rods transferring their load in friction partly into the fill and partly to an anchorage block forming a composite inclusion. Invented by Andre Coyne in 1926, the method was subsequently used for retaining walls and dam construction in France. Walls up to 20 m high were built using the method for river training walls, to spillway channels and embankment cofferdam structures. The method produced a flexible construction which allowed movements in the wall foundation (for example, due to karstic conditions or due to seismicity) without detriment to the wall itself. Figure 3.27 shows a cross-section of a dam construction by ladder wall where the anchorage forms the protection to the downstream slope of the dam[13].

Gabions

The use of gabions is a traditional method of retaining wall construction which has some advantages over masonry or reinforced concrete wall construction:

(a) gabion construction does not require skilled labour in its construction
(b) the permeability of the gabions allows both free drainage and soil retention
(c) the gabion wall is very flexible and allows considerable distortion before collapse
(d) large walls can be built relatively cheaply where the source of stone is local to the construction site.

The gabion wall can be constructed with a vertical, stepped or sloping front face and is designed as a conventional gravity wall against overturning, sliding

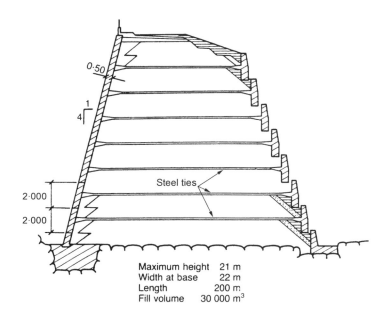

Maximum height   21 m
Width at base   22 m
Length   200 m
Fill volume   30 000 m³

Fig. 3.27. Cross-section of a 'ladder wall' at Conqueyrac, France[13]

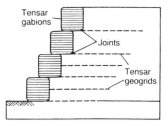

Fig. 3.28. Tailed gabion wall constructed with Tensar polymer grid cages and Tensar geogrid tails to form a Reinforced Earth structure (courtesy of Netlon)

and excessive base pressure. The steel gabion cage itself can be protected either by galvanizing or plastic coating. Typical, economical gabion wall heights range from 5 to 10 m depending on soil conditions. As an aid to stability it is usual to tilt the face of the wall at a batter of approximately 1 in 10. Overall economy may be improved by using a front gabion unit tied to a reinforced soil tendon, in steel or a geogrid of high-strength polymer, as shown in Fig. 3.28.

The Maccaferri company manufactures a patented, combined gabion box and reinforced soil system using either zinc- or PVC-coated wire mesh. The facing units, between 0·5 and 1·0 m thick, can be constructed as a single element and used in either a vertical or stepped face, as shown in Fig. 3.29(a) and (b). The wire mesh units can be filled with soil inside a geotextile and hydroseeded to produce a green face (Fig. 3.29(c)). An example of a stone-filled Maccaferri Terramesh wall to steepen an existing slope for a housing development site in Taiwan is shown in Fig. 3.29(d).

The cost of gabion construction obviously depends on the availability and cost of local stone, since the cost of the gabion cage is a small proportion of total cost. As an indication, for medium height walls where stone cost is limited to £20 per tonne delivered, the unit rate for gabion construction is approximately £80 per m³, excluding the cost of backfill behind the gabion. For walls 8 m high, with stone costing £20 per tonne delivered, and an allowance of £100 per linear metre for backfill, the unit cost of wall face area is approximately £170 per m² (at 2003 prices).

Crib walls

Timber and reinforced concrete crib walls have been used in the UK for soil support for the last 20 years or more. Treated timber cribs, typically up to 10 m in height can provide a life expectancy of 125 years. Reinforced concrete cribs can be used secured to reinforced soil reinforcement to improve the crib wall stability. Alternatively, steel soldiers, universal beams concreted into pre-drilled holes, can be used at intervals within the cribs to improve stability and allow crib wall construction to greater heights, typically up to 12 m.

The crib wall is a flexible construction and can withstand some settlement and movement without detriment. The crib wall is only applicable in dry subsoil conditions or where the rear of the crib can be drained to prevent

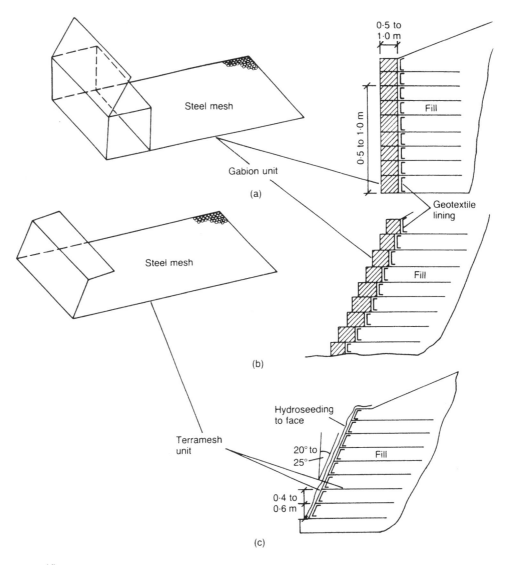

Fig. 3.29. Combined gabion box and reinforced soil system known as Terramesh: (a) vertical face; (b) stepped face; (c) with a hydroseeded face; (d) example of a stone-filled Terramesh wall in Taiwan (courtesy of Maccaferri)

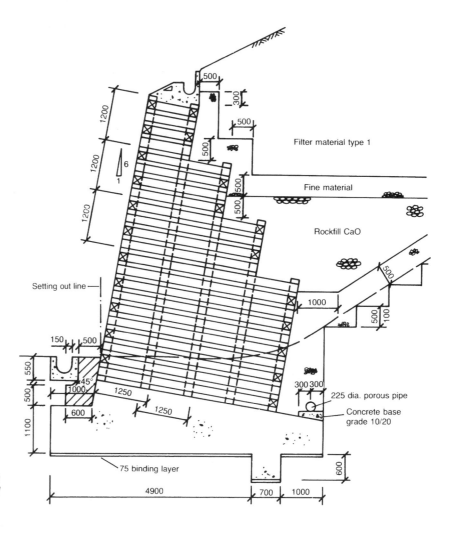

Fig. 3.30. Typical cross-section through four-cell wide crib wall in Tsing Yi, Hong Kong[14]

discharge through the face. The crib itself is backfilled with granular material (old railway ballast is typical), but graded granular material is necessary behind the crib to avoid loss of fines into the crib.

Daley and Thomson[14] described practical design and construction relating to crib walls in Hong Kong, and included a description of a major crib wall constructed at Tsing Yi in the late 1960s. The wall, shown in cross-section in Fig. 3.30, was used to stabilize an existing slope with slope angles varying between 50° and 55°. The crib wall was 75 m long and up to 11 m high. At its highest the wall is concave in plan, but is convex at one end where the fill height is lower. The considerable thickness of the wall is noteworthy.

Approximate current construction costs for the supply and erection near London of a 9 m and 6 m high crib wall in reinforced concrete are £300 per m² and £240 per m² of wall area, respectively.

References

1. Vaughan P.R. and Chandler R.J. *Design of cutting slopes in over-consolidated clay*. Notes for informal discussion. Institution of Civil Engineers, London, 1974.
2. Bromhead E.N. *The stability of slopes*. Blackie, London, 1993.
3. Mitchell R.J. *Earth structures engineering*. Allen and Unwin, Boston, 1983.
4. Barley A.D. Slope stabilization by new ground anchorage systems in rocks and soils. *Proc. Conf. Slope Stability Engineering*, Isle of Wight, UK, 1991, 313–318. Thomas Telford Ltd., London, 1991.

5. *Design methods for the reinforcement of highway slopes by reinforced soil and soil nailing techniques.* Design manual 4, section 1, HA 68/94. UK Department of Transport, 1994.

6. BS 8006. *Code of practice for strengthened/reinforced soils.* British Standards Institution, London, 1995.

7. pr EN 14475. *Execution of special geotechnical works reinforced fill.* British Standards Institution, London, 2002.

8. Smith R.J. The development of Terratrel for the construction of steep slopes. *Int. Reinforced Soil Conf.*, Glasgow, 1990, 135–139. Thomas Telford Ltd., London, 1990.

9. McGown A. *et al.* The load-strain time behaviour of Tensar grids. *Proc. Conf. Polymer Grid Reinforcement*, London, 1984, paper 1.2, 11–17. Thomas Telford Ltd., London, 1985.

10. Leshchinsky D. and Boedeker R.H. Geosynthetic reinforced earth structures. *ASCE J. Geotech. Eng.*, **115**, No. 1, 1459–1478.

11. *Project National Clouterre: recommendations pour la conception, le calcul, l'exécution et le contrôle.* Ponts et Chaussées Presse, Paris, 1991.

12. Schlosser F. *et al.* French research programme, Clouterre on soil nailing. *Proc. Conf. Grouting and Soil Improvement*, New Orleans, 1992, Vol. 2, 739–750. ASCE, New York, 1992.

13. Chabal J.P. A novel reinforced fill dam. *Proc. 8th Euro. Conf. SMFE*, Helsinki, 1983, Vol. 2, 477–480. Balkema, Rotterdam, 1983.

14. Daley P. and Thomson R.R. Some practical aspects associated with the design and construction of crib walls. *Proc. Seminar on Lateral Ground Support Systems*, Hong Kong, 1991, 21–37.

Bibliography

Open Battered Excavations

Skempton A.W. and la Rochelle Pl. The Bradwell slip: a short-term failure in London clay. *Géotechnique*, 1965, **15**, No. 3, 221–242.

Wakeling T.R.M. Discussion: time-dependent behaviour of deep excavations in a stiff fissured clay. *Proc. 6th Euro. Conf. SMFE*, Vienna, 1976, paper 2.2, 29–30. Austrian National Committee, Vienna, 1976.

Reinforced Earth

Exxon Chemical Geopolymers Ltd. *Designing for soil reinforcement*, 1989.

Farrag Kh. and Juran I. Design of geosynthetic reinforced soil structures. *Proc. ASCE Conf. Grouting, Soil Improvement and Geosynthetics*, New Orleans, 1992, 2, 1188–1200. ASCE, New York, 1992.

Ingold T.S. *Reinforced earth.* Thomas Telford Ltd., London, 1982.

Jones C.F. *Earth reinforcement and soil structures.* Thomas Telford Ltd., London, 1996.

Murray R.T. and Farrar D.M. Reinforced earth wall on the M25 at Waltham Cross. *Proc. Instn Civ. Engrs*, 1990, Apr., Vol. 89, 261–282.

Reinforced Earth Co. *Reinforced earth retaining walls.*

Reinforced Earth Co. *Reinforced earth: durability of reinforced earth structures.*

Vidal H. La terre armée. *Ann. de l'Institut Technique du Bâtiment et des Travaux Publics*, 1966, **19**, No. 223–229, 888–938.

Soil nailing

Banyai M. Stabilization of earth walls by soil nailing. *Proc. 6th Conf. S.M.F.E.*, Budapest, 1984, 459–465. Akadémiai Kiado, Budapest, 1984.

Bruce D.A. and Jewell R.A. Soil nailing: application and practice, part 1. *Ground Engng*, 1986, **19**, Nov., 10–15; Soil nailing: application and practice, part 2. *Ground Engng*, 1987, **20**, Jan., 21–33.

Cartier G. and Gigan J.P. Experiments and observations on soil nailing structures. *Proc. 8th Euro. Conf. SMFE*, Helsinki, 1983, 473–476. Balkema, Rotterdam, 1983.

Gässler G. and Gudehus G. Soil nailing – some aspects of a new technique. *Proc. 10th Int. Conf. S.M.F.E.*, Stockholm, 1981, 3, 665–670. Balkema, Rotterdam, 1981.

Gässler G. and Gudehus G. Soil nailing – statistical design. *Proc. 8th Euro. Conf. SMFE*, Helsinki, 1983, 491–494. Balkema, Rotterdam, 1983.

Goulesco N. and Medio J. Soutènement des sols en deblais à l'aide d'une paroi Hurpinoise. *Tunnels et Ouvrages Souterrains*, No. 47, Sept.-Oct., 9–17.

Guilloux A. *et al.* Experiences on a retaining structure by nailing in moraine soils. *Proc. 8th Euro. Conf. S.M.F.E.*, Helsinki, 1983, 499–502. Balkema, Rotterdam, 1983.

Juran I. *et al.* Study of soil-base interaction in the technique of soil nailing. *Proc. 8th Euro. Conf. S.M.F.E.*, Helsinki, 1983, 513–516. Balkema, Rotterdam, 1983.

Juran I. *et al.* Kinematic limit analysis for design of soil nailed structures. *ASCE J. Geotech. Engng*, 1990, **116**, Jan., 54–72.

Medio J. *et al.* Exemples d'applications de soutènements cloués: dix ans de Hurpinoise. *Sols et Fondations*, 1983, Oct., 27–35.

pr EN 14490. *Execution of special geotechnical works: soil nailing.* British Standards Institution, London, June, 2002.

Schlosser F. Analyses et différences de le comportement et le calcul des ouvrages de soutènement en terre armée et par clouage du sol. *Sols et Fondations*, 1983, **184**, Oct., 8–26.

4 Vertical soil support: wall construction

Options for sheeting and walling

While the intended use of a large underground excavation may well define its size, shape and location, and therefore the overall method of construction, the sheeting or walling techniques used at the periphery of these excavations may be common to a number of underground excavation types. Excavations for building basements, cofferdams for land-based industrial facilities, cofferdams for bridge works, cut-and-cover structures and shaft construction frequently share methods for wall construction to support the peripheral subsoil and exclude groundwater. The sheeting or walling selected for a particular project may provide temporary soil support prior to the permanent substructure construction, or it may serve as temporary soil support before being incorporated into the works as the permanent means of soil retention.

The type of peripheral sheeting used will therefore be influenced by the substructure construction method (bottom-up or top-down) and will vary geographically due to soil and groundwater conditions, proximity to the source of materials and the skills and preferences of local contractors. The sheeting or walling should be selected after an accurate comparison in terms of construction time and cost, although it rarely is. Available methods include the following.

- Plate and anchor wall; soil support during construction.
- King post wall, vertical soldiers and horizontal timber or precast concrete laggings or reinforced concrete skin wall; generally only soil support during construction.
- Steel sheet piling, pitched and driven, pressed in, or pitched into a slurry trench excavation; generally only soil support during construction although increased application for permanent walls in car park construction and building basements of modest depth. Sheet piling may be strengthened with steel box pile, I-beam or steel tubes to form combi or high-modulus walls.
- Contiguous bored piling; both temporary support during construction and when lined also a permanent wall. Piles may be formed conventionally or by deep cement–soil mixing methods.
- Secant piling, hard–hard, hard–firm, hard–soft, provides both temporary and permanent support, internal lining sometimes required depending on use. Piles may be drilled and concreted conventionally or by deep cement–soil mixing methods.
- Diaphragm walls
  - reinforced concrete cast in situ; both temporary support during construction and a permanent wall, sometimes with lining.
  - reinforced concrete precast; provides both temporary and permanent soil support.
  - post-tensioned; provides temporary support during construction and a permanent wall, sometimes with lining.
- Soldier pile, tremie concrete (SPTC), previously used in the USA with occasional use elsewhere; providing only temporary soil support during construction.

Table 4.1 Typical applications of embedded walls[31]

Wall type	Typical excavation depth to formation level		Groundwater control		Verticality		Comment
	Cantilever	Propped	Temp	Perm	Typical	Optimum	
King post walls	To 5 m	4·5 to 20 m	No	No	1:100	1:100	Not suitable in water-bearing ground
Sheet piling	To 5 m	4 to 20 m	Yes	Possible	1:75	1:100	Dependent upon soil conditions
Combi wall	To 10 m	8 to 20 m					Hydraulic press installation to limited depth
Contiguous bored piling	To 5 m	4 to 15 m	No	No	1:75	1:125	
Hard–soft secant	To 5 m	4 to 15 m	Yes	No	1:75	1:125	Possible disadvantage of inadequate durability of soft pile
Hard–firm secant	To 6 m	4 to 15 m	Yes	Yes	1:75	1:125	By continuous flight auger – limits depth
Hard–hard secant	To 7 m	7 to 30 m	Yes	Yes	1:75	1:300	Cased installation: increases expense
Soldier pile/tremie concrete	6 m	5 to 15 m	Yes	Yes	1:75	1:100	Method used in USA: lesser extent now
In situ diaphragm wall	Not used	7 to 30 m	Yes	Yes	1:100	1:150	By grab
	Not used	20 to 35 m	Yes	Yes	1:200	1:500	By cutter/mill. High mobilization cost. Wall depth up to 70 m
Precast diaphragm walls	5 m	5 to 12 m	Yes	Yes	1:100	1:150	Depth limited by wall panel weight
Post-tensioned diaphragm walls	5 m	5 to 12 m	Yes	Yes	1:100	1:150	Depth limited by tendon geometry

An indication of the depth of excavation and verticality generally achieved by these methods is given in Table 4.1. In practice, the use of sheet piles is often precluded by the environmental constraints of noise and vibration although the use of hydraulic press equipment allows sheet pile installation of medium length. Piled walls find application particularly in basement construction of medium depth in favourable drilling conditions and diaphragm walls are used for larger excavations of greater depth.

Plate and anchor wall by underpinning

The use of a conventional underpinning method, casting a reinforced concrete wall in short lengths and depths along the perimeter of a basement and securing each individual wall section by ground anchor, is feasible in certain soil conditions. Figure 4.1 shows a site in Madrid where dry, relatively dense sand subsoils allowed the excavation to proceed in short lengths without soil loss on the site boundary, each short length of underpinning being anchored before further excavation. It is not suggested that the underpinning replaces the permanent basement retaining wall.

The use of underpinning to retain soil to a basement excavation has been advanced by the practice of using ground anchors to stabilize a grouted mass or wall of subsoil. Figure 4.2 shows a basement excavation for the Commerz Bank in Frankfurt-am-Main. The adjacent building was underpinned by cement and chemical grouting of the sandy gravel below its

Fig. 4.1. Plate and anchor method used for basement excavation in dense dry sand in Madrid

Fig. 4.2. Basement construction at Frankfurt-am-Main: anchored grouted soil underpinning and anchored Berlin wall used in sandy, gravel subsoil (courtesy of Bauer)

foundations; this block of grouted subsoil was then retained by soil anchors and steel walings below the building. The photograph also shows the use of the king post wall method to retain the subsoil to the site boundary to the street side. A single layer of anchors was used to support the wall of consolidated soil, acting as a propped gravity structure, whereas the sheeted wall was retained by a multi-layer anchor system.

Figure 4.3 shows the combined use of steel strutting and ground anchors to support a grouted subsoil wall on a subway section in Nuremburg in Bavaria. Sodium silicate grouting was used to consolidate the cohesionless quartz sands. The grouted wall was 16 m high and four layers of ground anchors were used with three frames of steel struts and walings. The anchoring of jet-grouted soil masses is an alternative application of the plate and anchor method.

Vertical soldiers and horizontal lagging, king post method

This method owes much of its later popularity to three factors: the comparative cheapness of timber as a structural material; the economy of boring with power augers in certain soils; and the unimpaired access for construction works that anchoring allows. (See Fig. 4.4, showing a basement excavation 20 m deep in Medinah, Saudi Arabia).

The method consists of boring holes on the wall line, typically at 2 to 3 m centres, placing vertical steel universal beam or column soldier piles within the holes and concreting the base of each joist below final formation level. Lean mix concrete is often used for this purpose. In suitable soils the steel soldier pile may be driven. When the soldier pile is to be extracted the base of each joist is supported by gravel backfilled to formation level. As bulk excavation proceeds, horizontal lagging timbers or precast concrete units are wedged between the soldier piles. Steel section walings are placed to take the thrust from the soldier piles to ground anchors drilled at intervals along the length of the waling beam. Alternatively, each soldier pile is anchored and a waling is not needed.

In shallow excavations, the horizontal lagging timbers may be replaced by a reinforced concrete skin wall spanning the soldier piles and cast successively in short lifts as the excavation proceeds. The soldier piles may be cantilevered or propped by raking shores.

In stiff clays, the horizontal skin wall can be curved in plan and cast against a cut face to arch horizontally between the soldier piles.

Use of the king post method is limited to relatively dry ground or dewatered soils which are capable of self-support as each lagging is secured. Where flow of groundwater is limited in granular soils, inclined wellpoints may be tucked between the horizontal timbering. The method is generally only used as temporary soil support and requires construction of the permanent wall by conventional methods. The very big advantage secured by the anchored king post wall is the extent of the clear working space to the permanent works which is unimpeded by rakers, shoring, or soil berms. Nevertheless, the method does occupy a considerable thickness of construction which

Fig. 4.3. Alternate layers of ground anchors and steel strutting used to support deep excavation between chemically consolidated sand walls, Nuremburg (courtesy of Bauer)

Fig. 4.4. King post method: basement excavation in Medinah, Saudi Arabia

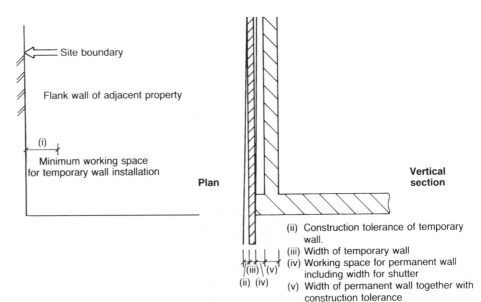

Fig. 4.5. Overall thickness of basement wall construction including means of temporary and permanent soil support, showing proximity to site boundary

(ii) Construction tolerance of temporary wall.
(iii) Width of temporary wall
(iv) Working space for permanent wall including width for shutter
(v) Width of permanent wall together with construction tolerance

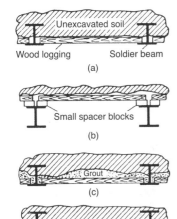

Fig. 4.6. Methods of transferring earth pressure from lagging timbers to soldier piles in Berlin walls: (a) lagging wedged against inside flanges of soldiers; (b) lagging set behind flanges of soldiers; (c) grout or mortar filling between lagging and soil; (d) contact sheeting secured to face of soldiers[1]

remains around the site periphery without contributing to permanent soil support; more important, perhaps, the construction tolerances may be such that it may not be possible, in deep basements, to use the horizontal laggings as a back shutter to the permanent wall works. The method becomes more economical in some urban areas where the soldier piles can be placed temporarily outside the site boundary, behind the laggings, and extracted after use.

The use of the resulting king post wall method may not be economical in terms of the construction width and the plan area occupied. The total width of the temporary and permanent wall becomes the sum of each of the following items:

(*a*) minimum width of the working space between the rear of temporary wall and site boundary; applicable where the site boundary is, for instance, the flank wall of an adjoining property

(*b*) construction tolerance of the temporary wall: typically 1 : 100 verticality tolerance for augered piling

(*c*) width of the temporary wall

(*d*) working space for the permanent wall, where the king post wall is not used as a back shutter

(*e*) width of the permanent wall together with construction tolerance.

Figure 4.5 shows the total width of the construction.

The method realizes the full consequences of poor workmanship in subsidence, excavation and instability risks. Peck[1] showed alternative arrangements for securing lagging to soldiers (Fig. 4.6). Poor contact between laggings and the excavated soil face may induce movement, and Peck recorded that although use of the method shown in Fig. 4.6(b) allows the soldier piles to be incorporated within the permanent wall reinforcement, loss of soil during installation had caused settlements three times those at a basement where the method shown in Fig. 4.6(a) was used in similar conditions. Figure 4.7 shows a good example of very poor construction standards. In the UK, the practice of allowing unsecured laggings to slip between the soldier pile flanges progressively as the bulk excavation continues is a particular example of poor workmanship with an inherent risk of soil movement and subsidence.

Figure 4.8 shows an anchored king post wall with good tolerances and carefully wedged horizontal timber laggings. This excavation, at Raschplatz

Fig. 4.7. Example of poor king post wall construction[29]

Fig. 4.8. Deep excavation through sandy silts and silty sands supported by anchored Berlin wall and dewatered by deep wells, Hannover subway (courtesy of Bauer)

Fig. 4.9. Dual method Berlin wall for multi-storey car park, Zurich (courtesy of Bauer)

subway station in Hannover, was 24 m deep and the subsoil was silty sand varying to a sandy silt. Figure 4.9 also shows the use of anchored soldier piles with horizontal laggings, but with dual methods of construction. The upper part of the walls had steel H-beams placed into pre-drilled holes, with concrete slabs spanning horizontally; the lower part was formed by bored piles by Benoto rig. The maximum depth of the excavation was 28 m, retained by eight layers of anchors. Note the economy in ground anchors achieved by diagonal strutting between soldier piles near the basement corner.

Although the method is only feasible in relatively dry subsoils, if the soils allow economical soil anchoring and dewatering, the king post wall finds

Fig. 4.10. Berlin wall method using steel soldier piles and horizontal timber laggings and wellpoint dewatering for a sewage pumphouse at Al Khobar, Saudi Arabia (courtesy of Bauer)

use in apparently uneconomical conditions. Figure 4.10 shows an excavation for a sewage water pumphouse at Al Khobar, Saudi Arabia. The groundwater drawdown from 1 m below ground level to a depth of 11 m was by three-stage wellpointing and deep wells in a sandy subsoil.

Particular attention is drawn to the risk of failure of anchored king post walls by the vertical component of the anchor force transferring to the base of the soldier pile. Vertical settlements of the wall require consideration. The location of anchorages at re-entrant corners also requires attention where interaction may occur due to the proximity of anchors from adjoining walls at the re-entrant angle.

More recently, in the UK the use of vertical soldiers, raker support and horizontal spanning reinforced concrete skin walls have found favour for shallow basement excavations in London. Excavation by backacter for soldiers and the use of trench boxes followed by backfilling and re-excavation for successive skin wall pours have proved economical where groundwater levels are low and fill or gravel conditions are reasonably dense. In parts of Germany a particularly low price is obtained by the use of shotcrete between and over the vertical soldiers in lieu of horizontal laggings.

Sheet piling

The economical use of sheet piling in basement construction is influenced by five factors.

(a) *The ability to withdraw the piling after use.* Where city sites require maximum occupation of the site area by the basement, it is not unusual for pile extraction to be precluded by the lack of working space for extraction equipment, cranes and handling space. The difficulties of extracting piles at an urban basement site can therefore minimize their re-use despite the use of a back shutter or sheeting lining to separate the permanent wall construction from the sheet piling.

(b) *Depth of the basement.* On urban sites the transporting, handling, pitching and driving of long piles can become onerous tasks. The storage of

Fig. 4.11. Anchored sheet piles in London clay for a telephone switching centre, London

long piles on a typical city site may become a serious logistical problem and costs of storage and moving on site may prove onerous. A typical use of sheet piles for an urban basement construction is shown in Fig. 4.11 for a basement extension to a telephone exchange in North London. Subsoil conditions consisted of London clay from ground level to a considerable depth below final formation level, although the upper 15 m section was weathered. Telecommunications equipment sensitive to vibration was nearby, so hydraulic pile installation by Taywood equipment was specified. This equipment was ideally suited to the subsoil conditions, allowing pile installation to proceed without noise (apart from the power generator) or vibration. The use of ground anchors and temporary embankments allowed construction works to proceed largely unimpeded from strutting and raking shores. Unfortunately, the site working space did not allow the extraction of any of the temporary sheet piles to the basement periphery.

(c) *Soil conditions and the ease of pile installation.* The section of sheet pile to be used will depend on the requirements of flexural strength and the strength to resist driving stresses. Design calculations should therefore be reviewed in the light of anticipated driving conditions. Costs calculated by Potts and Day[2] for sheet piling, diaphragm walls and secant piles designed by modern methods showed favourably for the sheet pile wall used in two underpasses and a basement project. Their comparisons may prove to be inaccurate, however, due to under-estimates of the section required for practicality of driving. Use of high-frequency vibratory equipment to install sheet piles in cohesionless soils and in soft to firm clays and hydraulic pile presses in clays allows reduced noise levels during pile installation, but increased vibration or reduced output result directly from any natural or man-made obstructions. Hard clays or layers of dense sands may require jetting to assist sheeter installation. Where obstructions seriously impede progress, pre-boring may be needed. When hard driving through obstructions occurs there is risk of torn clutches (perhaps occurring below final

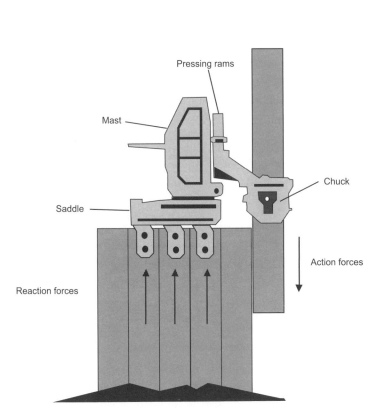

Fig. 4.12. Giken pile press (courtesy of Giken Europe BV)

formation level) causing inadequate groundwater cut-off and severe reduction in pile flexural strength.

(*d*) *Noise and vibration.* These effects have seriously restricted driven sheet pile usage in urban areas in recent years despite the use of acoustic covers to some hammers. The use of high-frequency vibrators to install sheeters reduces the effects of noise pollution and considerable reduction in vibration nuisance has been made by improvements to vibrators by the introduction of a mechanical device, an adjustable eccentric moment which avoids critical frequency vibrations during the start-up and run-down phases. Where vibrators are ineffective, for example in stiff clays, sheet pile installation has been made successfully by hydraulic presses such as the Taywood Pilemaster and more recently by equipment developed by the Japanese company, Giken.

The Giken press, shown in Fig. 4.12, consists of a saddle which clamps on to installed piles and a mast on which hydraulic rams are mounted to apply vertical force through a chuck to push single sheet piles vertically into the subsoil. The service crane is only used to lift the press on to the initial piles and after these reaction piles are pushed in with the assistance of kentledge, successive single piles are installed by the Giken press moving from pile to pile without craneage. The Giken press can install sheet piles through medium dense sands and stiff clays although either lubrication or high-pressure jetting may be needed in the stiffer clays. Some increased difficulty may be experienced in maintaining verticality tolerances compared with conventional installation in panels, first pitched and then driven. Single sheet piles tend to twist whilst being jacked in and modern wide sheet pile sections tend to stretch in their width during installation. The method does, however, allow close installation of sheeters to existing services and foundations and, with the 'Zero-Piler', hard up against projecting obstructions. Minimum sheeter section for installation in stiff clays is LX20 by Corus and using this section sheeters up to 16 m long have been installed in stiff London clay and Gault clay.

The control of noise and vibration due to piling operations is addressed in BS 5228 Part 4, 1992[3], and a useful summary of published work on the matter is contained in a British Steel report[4].

(e) *Incorporation of the sheet pile wall into the permanent works.* Where permanent groundwater levels are low, it may be possible to use the sheeters as part of the permanent wall, with suitable allowance for corrosion risk. The recent use of sealants within the sheet pile interlocks and protective metal covers to protect the sealant during sheeter installation has allowed piling producers to give warranties which guarantee overall permeability of installed walls. Welding of clutches is sometimes resorted to (but of course cannot be carried out below formation level). This development has materially increased the use of sheet piles in permanent construction for basement walls, particularly for car parking use.

Sheet pile seepage resistance is discussed by Sellmeijer and Shouten[6] and in reports by Arbed[7,8].

Available sheet pile sections are shown in Fig. 4.13(a) and (b).

Combined walls

Where soil and groundwater conditions impose high loads on sheet piles, or where permanent construction requires the minimum number of bracing frames, it may be necessary to stiffen and strengthen sheet pile sections to withstand the higher bending moments induced in the sheeting. A number of methods are available.

(a) The use of combined walls. Steel circular tubes ('combi') or sheet pile box sections are introduced at regular intervals along the length of the wall. The combined section is assumed to span vertically and the equivalent section modulus per linear metre of wall is calculated on the basis that the deflections of the king piles and the intermediate sheet piles are similar and the elements work compositely. Combinations of sheet piles, both U and Z sections, with intermediate king piles are shown in Fig. 4.13(c) and (d).

(b) The use of steel sheet pile sections reinforced with steel beams, such as the Peine pile, by Arbed, or the high-modulus pile by Corus, Fig. 4.13(e).

(c) The use of jagged walls: sheet piles with crimped interlocks and joined by double interlock joint units, shown for U and Z pile sections in Fig. 4.14. For walls with anchoring or bracing support, stiffeners are required to the jagged wall units at support levels.

(d) The use of steel sheet piles, either singly or in doubles, at regular intervals with steel tubular piles, in a similar way to the use of box pile sections.

(e) I-beams fitted with clutches on their flanges, such as Arbed (flared flange tips) or Dawson crimped beam (flanges crimped to achieve a flare).

An example of the use of a combined sheet pile and tubular steel section wall is shown in Fig. 4.15. The cofferdam, built on the approach to the River Medway crossing at Rochester, UK, was also used to fabricate the

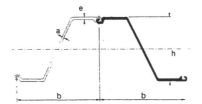 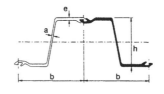

Section	Dimensions				Sectional area	Mass of single pile	Mass per m² of wall	Section modulus	Moment of inertia
	b	h	e	a					
	mm	mm	mm	mm	cm²/m	kg/m	kg/m²	cm³/m	cm⁴/m
AZ 12	670	302	8.5	8.5	126	66.1	99	1200	18140
AZ 13	670	303	9.5	9.5	137	72.0	107	1300	19700
AZ 14	670	304	10.5	10.5	149	78.3	117	1400	21300
AZ 17	630	379	8.5	8.5	138	68.4	109	1665	31580
AZ 18	630	380	9.5	9.5	150	74.4	118	1800	34200
AZ 19	630	381	10.5	10.5	164	81.0	129	1940	36980
AZ 25	630	426	12.0	11.2	185	91.5	145	2455	52250
AZ 26	630	427	13.0	12.2	198	97.8	155	2600	55510
AZ 28	630	428	14.0	13.2	211	104.4	166	2755	58940
AZ 34	630	459	17.0	13.0	234	115.5	183	3430	78700
AZ 36	630	460	18.0	14.0	247	122.2	194	3600	82800
AZ 38	630	461	19.0	15.0	261	129.1	205	3780	87080
AZ 46	580	481	18.0	14.0	291	132.6	229	4595	110450
AZ 48	580	482	19.0	15.0	307	139.6	241	4800	115670
AZ 50	580	483	20.0	16.0	322	146.7	253	5015	121060

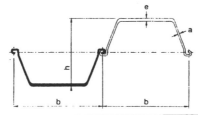

Section	Width	Height	Thickness		Sectional Ares	Mass		Moment of Inertia	Elastic section modulus	Static Moment	Plastic section modulus
	b	h	e	a		kg/m	kg/m2				
	mm	mm	mm	mm	cm2/m	single pile	of wall	cm4/m	cm3/m	cm3/m	cm3/m
AU 14	750	408	10,0	8,3	132	77,9	104	28710	1410	820	1663
AU 16	750	411	11,5	9,3	147	86,3	115	32850	1600	935	1891
AU 17	750	412	12,0	9,7	151	89,0	119	34270	1665	975	1968
AU 18	750	441	10,5	9,1	150	88,5	118	39300	1780	1028	2082
AU 20	750	444	12,0	10,0	165	96,9	129	44440	2000	1157	2339
AU 21	750	445	12,5	10,3	169	99,7	133	46180	2075	1200	2423
AU 23	750	447	13,0	9,5	173	102,1	136	50700	2270	1285	2600
AU 25	750	450	14,5	10,2	188	110,4	147	56240	2500	1420	2866
AU 26	750	451	15,0	10,5	192	113,2	151	58140	2580	1465	2955
PU 6	600	226	7,5	6,4	97	45,6	76	6780	600	335	697
PU 8	600	280	8,0	8,0	91	54,5	91	11620	830	480	983
PU 12	600	360	9,8	9,0	110	66,1	110	21600	1200	715	1457
PU 12 10/10	600	360	10,0	10,0	116	69,6	116	22580	1255	755	1535
PU 16	600	380	12,0	9,0	124	74,7	124	30400	1600	925	1878
PU 20	600	430	12,4	10,0	140	84,3	140	43000	2000	1165	2363
PU 25	600	452	14,2	10,0	156	93,6	156	56490	2500	1435	2899
PU 32	600	452	19,5	10,0	190	114,1	190	72320	3200	1825	3687
L 2 S	500	340	12,3	9,0	177	69,7	139	27200	1600	915	1871
L 3 S	500	400	14,1	10,0	201	78,9	158	40010	2000	1175	2389
L 4 S	500	440	15,5	10,0	219	86,2	172	55010	2500	1455	2956
JSP 3	400	250	13,0	-	191	60,0	150	16800	1340	730	-

Fig. 4.13. (a) Properties of steel sheet piles as provided by Arbed (courtesy Arbed)

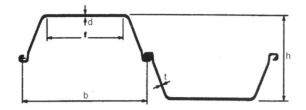

LX and Larssen Steel Sheet Piling

Section	b mm (nominal)	h mm (nominal)	d mm	t mm (nominal)	f Flat of Pan mm	Sectional Area cm²/m of wall	Mass		Combined Moment of Inertia cm⁴/m	Elastic Section Modulus cm³/m	Plastic Section Modulus cm³/m
							kg per linear metre	kg/m² of wall			
LX8	600	310	8.2	8.0	250	116	54.6	91.0	12861	830	1017
LX12	600	310	9.7	8.2	386	136	63.9	106.4	18723	1208	1381
LX16	600	380	10.5	9.0	365	157	74.1	123.5	31175	1641	1899
LX20	600	430	12.5	9.0	330	177	83.2	138.6	43478	2022	2357
LX25	600	450	15.6	9.2	330	200	94.0	156.7	56824	2525	2914
LX32	600	450	21.5	9.8	328	242	113.9	189.8	72028	3201	3703
6W	525	212	7.8	6.4	331	108	44.7	85.1	6459	610	711
GSP2	400	200	10.5	8.6	265	153	48.0	120.0	8740	874	1020
GSP3	400	250	13.0	8.6	271	191	60.0	150.0	16759	1340	1520
GSP4	400	340	15.5	9.7	259	242	76.0	190.0	38737	2270	2652
6 (122.0 kg)	420	440	22.0	14.0	248	370	122.0	290.5	92452	4200	4996
6 (131.0 kg)	420	440	25.4	14.0	251	397	131.0	311.8	102861	4675	5481
6 (138.7 kg)	420	440	28.6	14.0	251	421	138.7	330.2	111450	5066	5924

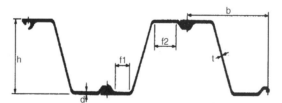

Frodingham Steel Sheet Piling

Section	b mm (nominal)	h mm (nominal)	d mm	t mm (nominal)	f1 mm (nominal)	f2 mm (nominal)	Sectional Area cm²/m of wall	Mass		Combined Moment of Inertia cm⁴/m	Section Modulus cm³/m	Plastic Modulus cm³/m
								kg per linear metre	kg/m² of wall			
1BXN	476	143	12.7	12.7	78	123	166.5	62.1	130.4	4919	688	859
1N	483	170	9.0	9.0	105	137	126.0	47.8	99.1	6048	713	831
2N	483	235	9.7	8.4	97	149	143.0	54.2	112.3	13513	1150	1333
3NA	483	305	9.7	9.5	96	146	165.0	62.6	129.8	25687	1690	1937
4N	483	330	14.0	10.4	77	127	218.0	82.4	170.8	39831	2414	2787
5	425	311	17.0	11.9	89	118	302.0	100.8	236.9	49262	3168	3683

Fig. 4.13. (b) Properties of steel sheet piles produced by Corus (courtesy Corus)

Sheet piles walls with reinforcing box piles

Type of reinforcement

The reinforcement may be :

1. On the wall height :
– over the total height : reinforcing box piles
– partially : forming sheet piles with changing inertia by welding especially prepared shorter piles onto it.

2. In the wall length :
– in total : reinforcement 1/1
– partially : reinforcement 1/2, 1/3, 1/4.

Characteristics of some combinations

Section	1/1 Mass kg/m²	Section modulus cm³/m	1/2 Mass kg/m²	Section modulus cm³/m	1/3 Mass kg/m²	Section modulus cm³/m	1/4 Mass kg/m²	Section modulus cm³/m
PU 12	220	2 795	165	1 580	146	1 645	137	1 440
PU 16	249	3 695	187	2 065	166	2 195	156	1 920
PU 20	281	4 570	211	2 565	187	2 730	176	2 395
PU 25	314	5 645	235	3 145	209	3 395	196	2 980
PU 32	382	7 245	287	3 995	255	4 345	239	3 805
L 2 S	279	3 755	209	2 110	186	2 195	174	1 920
L 3 S	316	4 640	237	2 620	210	2 740	197	2 405
L 4 S	345	5 720	259	3 215	230	3 415	215	2 995

Combinations
Built up U-Box Piles - U-Sections

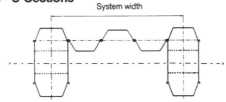

The use of triple intermediary piles is subject to a careful check of the soil conditions.

Section	Combination	Intermediate sheet pile	System width mm	Mass (kg/m²) Length of intermediates 100 %	70 %	Section modulus cm³/m	Moment of inertia cm⁴/m
L 3 S / 600 x 12	1/4	PU 12	2 300	204	178	3 975	208 100
PU 20 / 600 x 12	1/4	PU 12	2 400	200	175	4 130	221 900
L 3 S / 700 x 12	1/4	PU 12	2 300	212	186	4 530	259 600
PU 20 / 700 x 12	1/4	PU 12	2 400	208	183	4 680	275 100
L 4 S / 600 x 12	1/4	PU 12	2 300	210	184	4 400	239 100
PU 25 / 600 x 12	1/4	PU 16	2 400	227	199	5 035	301 500
L 4 S / 800 x 14	1/4	PU 16	2 300	249	220	5 830	375 000
PU 25 / 800 x 14	1/4	PU 16	2 400	245	217	5 805	376 500
PU 32 / 600 x 12	1/4	PU 16	2 400	244	216	6 165	369 500
PU 32 / 800 x 14	1/4	PU 16	2 400	262	234	7 040	457 500

Fig. 4.13. (c) Combination piles: sheet pile properties of combination section walls with box piles using U-shaped sections (courtesy Arbed)

Combinations
AZ Box Piles - AZ Sheet Piles

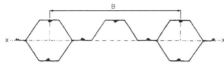

Section	Dimension B mm	Mass Length of intermediates 100% kg/m²	60% kg/m²	Moment of inertia cm⁴/m	Section modulus cm³/m
CAZ 13 / AZ 13	2 680	147	126	60 910	2 000
18 / AZ 13	2 600	156	134	95 900	2 510
18 / AZ 18	2 520	163	139	105 560	2 765
26 / AZ 13	2 600	188	166	151 240	3 530
26 / AZ 18	2 520	196	173	162 660	3 795
36 / AZ 13	2 600	221	199	217 030	4 700
36 / AZ 18	2 520	230	206	230 540	4 990

Combinations
Built up AZ Box Piles - AZ Sheet Piles

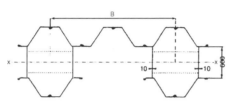

Section	Dimension B mm	Mass Length of intermediates 100% kg/m²	60% kg/m²	Moment of inertia cm⁴/m	Section modulus cm³/m
CAZP 13 / 600 × 10 / AZ 13	2 680	196	175	322 060	5 340
18 / 600 × 10 / AZ 13	2 600	206	184	407 330	5 990
18 / 600 × 10 / AZ 18	2 520	215	191	426 880	6 280
26 / 600 × 10 / AZ 13	2 600	242	220	583 150	8 020
26 / 600 × 10 / AZ 18	2 520	252	228	608 280	8 365
36 / 600 × 10 / AZ 13	2 600	280	257	777 050	10 225
36 / 600 × 10 / AZ 18	2 520	290	267	808 340	10 635

Fig. 4.13. (d) Combination pile walls with box piles using Z-shaped sections (courtesy Arbed)

submerged tube tunnel units for the crossing. The depth of the cofferdam at the river entrance was approximately 17 m, and it was necessary to provide only one cofferdam frame as high as possible to accommodate the height of the units passing under the frame at the time of flooding the cofferdam and floating the units to their final location in the river crossing. Due to the flexural strengths required from the sheet piles, a combined section of Larssen sheeters and 1·2 m dia. steel tubes was used, the pile interlock being continuously welded to the steel tube at its junction with the sheeter. The construction sequence for driving the wall through alluvial deposits into chalk required extremely onerous verticality and positional tolerances for the steel tubes. The tubes, driven by vibrators from either river craft or on land, were installed prior to the sheeters using either leaders or a mechanical template device. Considerable care was required to ensure that the intermediate sheeters, driven later, clutched for this whole length (22·5 m) between the 30 m long tubes.

Contiguous bored piling

The use of low-cost augers and, more particularly, continuous flight auger (CFA) rigs to drill successive but unconnected piles provides an economical wall for both temporary and permanent use for excavations to medium depth where soil conditions are amenable. The contiguous wall can only be used where groundwater is not a hazard or where grouting or jet grouting can be used to prevent leakage between the piles. The risk of 'windows' between adjacent piles can be assessed by applying maximum verticality tolerances quoted for auger and CFA pile installation, typically 1 in 100 with depth, and allowing this maximum tolerance to adjacent piles in opposite directions. Where soil and groundwater conditions are favourable, bored piles can be installed as anchored piles with the space between them shotcreted to provide soil support as excavation proceeds.

The nominal diameters of CFA piles are 300, 450, 600, 750, 900, 1000 and 1200 mm. Since grout or high slump concrete is introduced through the auger

Combination 22/13
Combination 24/11

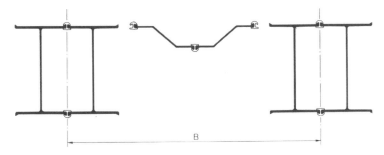

Figure shows HZ 775 A, ZH 9,5/12,0

Section	B cm	Properties per meter of wall [5] Sectional area cm²/m	Moment of inertia cm⁴/m	Section modulus cm³/m	Mass of combination with intermediary sections ZH 9,5 $I_{ZH}=60\%\,I_{HZ}$ kg/m²	ZH 9,5 $I_{ZH}=I_{HZ}$ kg/m²	ZH 12,0 $I_{ZH}=60\%\,I_{HZ}$ kg/m²	ZH 12,0 $I_{ZH}=I_{HZ}$ kg/m²
HZ 575 A	206,5	306,7	145940 *159200*	**5075** *5100*	211	240	218	251
HZ 575 B	206,5	324,5	160910 *174280*	**5560** *5580*	226	255	232	265
HZ 575 C	206,5	348,3	177920 *191400*	**6105** *6125*	244	273	250	284
HZ 575 D	206,5	376,0	197720 *214540*	**6735** *6765*	265	295	271	306
HZ 775 A	206,5	362,3	308380 *334070*	**7960** *8070*	255	284	261	294
HZ 775 B	206,5	380,1	335410 *361240*	**8610** *8715*	269	298	276	309
HZ 775 C	206,5	419,6	376700 *408850*	**9620** *9755*	299	329	305	340
HZ 775 D	206,5	437,5	404370 *436660*	**10275** *10400*	312	343	319	354
HZ 975 A	206,5	400,2	516150 *558370*	**10590** *10800*	285	314	291	324
HZ 975 B	206,5	418,0	558840 *601240*	**11415** *11620*	299	328	306	339
HZ 975 C	206,5	465,2	630290 *683020*	**12825** *13080*	335	365	341	376
HZ 975 D	206,5	483,1	673860 *726770*	**13655** *13900*	348	379	354	389

Combination 26/11

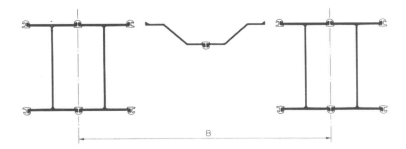

Figure shows HZ 775 A, ZH 9,5/12,0

Section	B cm	Properties per meter of wall [5] Sectional area cm²/m	Moment of inertia cm⁴/m	Section modulus cm³/m	Mass of combination with intermediary sections ZH 9,5 $I_{ZH}=60\%\,I_{HZ}$ kg/m²	ZH 9,5 $I_{ZH}=I_{HZ}$ kg/m²	ZH 12,0 $I_{ZH}=60\%\,I_{HZ}$ kg/m²	ZH 12,0 $I_{ZH}=I_{HZ}$ kg/m²
HZ 575 A	206,5	326,5	177570	**6175**	233	256	239	266
HZ 575 B	206,5	344,3	192580	**6650**	247	270	254	281
HZ 575 C	206,5	368,1	209580	**7190**	266	289	272	299
HZ 575 D	206,5	400,7	237320	**8085**	292	315	298	325
HZ 775 A	206,5	382,1	366110	**9450**	276	299	283	310
HZ 775 B	206,5	399,9	393200	**10095**	291	314	297	324
HZ 775 C	206,5	444,3	448840	**11465**	326	349	332	359
HZ 775 D	206,5	462,1	476550	**12110**	339	362	346	373
HZ 975 A	206,5	419,9	608570	**12485**	306	329	313	340
HZ 975 B	206,5	437,7	651340	**13305**	321	344	327	354
HZ 975 C	206,5	489,9	745700	**15170**	362	385	368	395
HZ 975 D	206,5	507,8	789320	**15995**	375	398	382	409

Fig. 4.13. (e) Peine pile walls: combination pile walls with steel joists, Z-section sheet piles and connectors (courtesy Arbed)

Jagged Wall U

The arrangement into a jagged wall offers economic solutions where high section moduli are needed.

The sheet piles are delivered in doubles, threaded and crimped in the mill alternately to S and Z form.

If the OMEGA 18 section is delivered separately, it has to be threaded on the job site and fixed by welding to every double pile. In this case it is not taken into account for the calculation of the section modulus.

Omega sections threaded in the mill are welded in a way to allow for a respective contribution to the section modulus. See different columns in the table.

For walls with an anchoring or strut system, stiffeners have to be provided at the support levels.

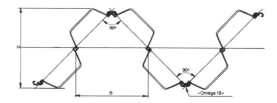

Section	Corner section	Width B cm	Height H cm	Mass kg/m²	Section modulus without Omega cm³/m	With Omega cm³/m	Moment of inertia without Omega cm⁴/m	With Omega cm⁴/m
PU 6	OMEGA 18	92	88	118	2 560	3 460	113 000	158 800
PU 8	OMEGA 18	92	88	138	3 310	4 165	145 000	191 200
PU 12	OMEGA 18	92	88	163	4 285	5 130	189 500	235 400
PU 16	OMEGA 18	92	93	182	4 865	5 855	226 500	272 400
PU 20	OMEGA 18	92	97	202	5 575	6 440	270 600	312 600
PU 25	OMEGA 18	92	101	224	6 310	7 225	319 000	364 900
PU 32	OMEGA 18	92	101	269	7 755	8 665	392 000	437 700
L 2 S	OMEGA 18	78	82	202	4 405	5 240	179 700	213 700
L 3 S	OMEGA 18	78	83	225	5 235	6 070	216 600	251 000
L 4 S	OMEGA 18	78	86	244	5 890	6 695	254 700	289 500

Jagged Wall AZ

Threaded in a reverse position AZ sections may form arrangements at multiple steps for special applications.
The two step arrangement with crimped interlocks on the neutral axis gives an important increase of the moment of inertia. For projects with limited deflection this is an interesting solution.
For sealing screens the O step arrangement represents a most economical solution (reduced height, reliable thickness, low resistance...).

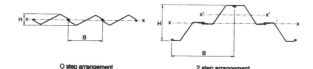

0 step

Section	Dimensions B mm	H mm	Steel section cm²/m	Mass kg/m²	Moment of inertia cm⁴/m	Section modulus cm³/m	Statical moment* cm³	Coating area** m²/m²
AZ 13	718	186	128	100	2 840	305	-	2,28
AZ 18	714	224	133	104	4 280	380	-	2,38
AZ 26	736	238	169	133	6 580	555	-	2,41
AZ 36	753	263	207	162	10 380	790	-	2,45

2 steps

AZ 13	1 340	562	137	107	42 650	1 520	1 190	2,45
AZ 18	1 260	716	150	118	76 660	2 140	1 595	2,70
AZ 26	1 260	807	198	155	126 910	3 145	2 365	2,82
AZ 36	1 260	873	247	194	188 180	4 310	3 215	2,93

* x'-x' about x-x.

** Excludes inside of interlocks.

Fig. 4.14. 'Jagged' pile combination sections. Note the use of an 'Omega' section to join sheet piles delivered to site in double units crimped together (courtesy of Arbed)

Fig. 4.15. Combined tubular steel and steel sheet pile wall, River Medway crossing, UK (courtesy of Carillion)

stem, CFA injected piles do not require top casings during the grouting or concreting process. The depth of wall constructed by this method is, however, limited by the length of reinforcement cage that can be introduced through the cement or grout. A commonly quoted maximum length of 18 to 20 m is dependent upon ground conditions, granular soils detracting from ease of construction of CFA piles of this length. Some risk exists of loss of cement from CFA piles constructed in granular soils. A vibrator can be used with an H-pile mandrel to insert reinforcement cages in piles longer than 12 m and steel joist reinforcement can be used in lieu of reinforcement cages for long piles, although this may prove expensive.

The width of the gap between piles is varied according to ground conditions between 50 and 150 mm, typically 100 mm.

The use of in-cab instrumentation (of machine torque, concrete volume, concrete pressure with depth) is general and is necessary to give confidence in CFA pile construction. At present, concrete pressure is not measured at the critical position of the point of discharge but in time no doubt this will also be corrected. Recent IT developments include the transmission of in-cab readouts to off-site locations in real time.

Inclined pile walls installed by mechanical auger should be mentioned. Sloped sheeting raked towards the centre of the basement may reduce strut loading. Schnabel[9] reported that where sheeting had sloped at an angle of about 10° from the vertical, the measured strut loads were consistently less than two-thirds of the computed strut loads for vertical sheeting in the same ground.

The principal advantages of contiguous pile walls are:

(*a*) low cost and speed of construction for temporary and permanent soil support where drilling conditions are conducive
(*b*) cleanliness and comparative quietness of the installation process; low level of vibration during pile installation
(*c*) for small excavation depths, the ability to minimize the distance between the wall and existing walls
(*d*) the range of soil conditions in which CFA piles can be used is wide: granular soils are suitable with few exceptions; cohesive soils are suitable except where penetrations greater than 8 m into hard clay are required; intermediate c–ϕ soils are suitable; soft clays, where c_u is less than 10 kN/m^2, or weak organic soils, are unsuitable due to shaft bulging; soft rocks, e.g. soft marls and chalk, are suitable (although relatively small penetrations into rock chalk and hard mudstones can cause problems); but hard rocks are not suitable.

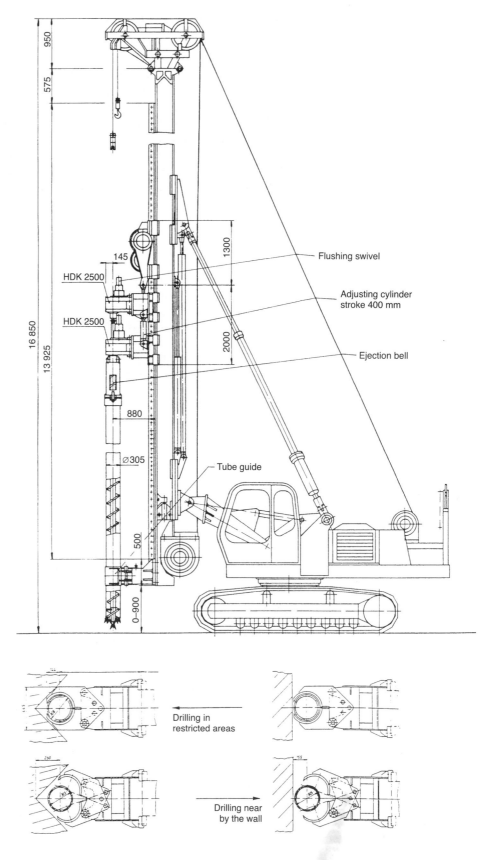

Flushing swivel

Adjusting cylinder stroke 400 mm

Ejection bell

Tube guide

Drilling in restricted areas

Drilling near by the wall

Fig. 4.16. Mini pile rig suitable for contiguous bored pile installation close to existing structures (courtesy of Ingersoll Rand)

The principal disadvantages of contiguous pile walls are:

(a) the risk of groundwater ingress between piles
(b) limitations of the depth of CFA piles: 18 m long cages are the practical limit without special installation measures, although steel joist sections can be used to reinforce deep piles
(c) relatively low efficiency of circular cross-section of pile in bending
(d) where independent lining is not needed, the extent of additional works needed to form an acceptable surface to the wall. A structural reinforced concrete wall, tied to the contiguous piles may be required or, elsewhere, sprayed concrete may suffice to fill the gaps between piles
(e) the minimum distance between the wall and existing structure is large for deeper walls.

So, CFA rigs, without the need for temporary casings, generally provide a cheap wall quickly in granular and clay soils and are not affected during installation by the presence of groundwater. But depths are limited to small to medium depth excavations. Rotary rigs can develop torque greater than 50 T m and with this equipment walls can be built with casings to medium to large depths. Vertical tolerances, however, may limit depth, and layers of harder rock will slow progress and increase cost. The walls are not waterproof since groundwater leakage occurs in the gaps between piles.

The development of mini rotary rigs has permitted the construction of small (up to 300 mm) diameter contiguous pile walls within a minimum axial distance of 250 mm to an existing structure. A typical rig is shown in Fig. 4.16. These rigs are also suitable for pile installation in conditions of low headroom. Large rotary drilling rigs equipped with rock roller core barrels can be used to excavate in hard rock with unconfined compressive strengths of 150 MPa although the rate of drilling will be dependent on rock structure.

Secant piles

The principal disadvantages of contiguous pile walls – the gaps between piles and the resulting problems of lack of waterproofness – are effectively overcome by interlocking or secant piles.

The method consists of boring and concreting primary, or female, piles at centres slightly less than twice the nominal pile diameter. Secondary, or male, piles are then bored at mid-distance between the female piles, the boring equipment cutting a secant section from them. Male piles are bored through female piles before the concrete has achieved its full strength; should this operation be delayed, wear on the auger or the cutting edge to the casing is likely to be much increased. Concrete quality control is therefore important in this respect and deviations in maximum strength may be as important as minimum strength deviation.

As for contiguous pile walls, the secant pile method suffers from the poor efficiency of the circular cross-section in bending. In some instances reinforcement may be bunched at opposite sides of the pile diameter to ensure maximum effectiveness, but the risk of rotation, twist or displacement may preclude this in longer piles. It is usual to reinforce only the male piles, particularly because of the risk of cutting reinforcement in a displaced cage when the male pile is being bored. Some deep walls (in London and elsewhere secant walls have been constructed to depths of 40 m) have utilized steel beam sections placed into the male pile bore as reinforcement, and either rectangular reinforcement cages or steel beam sections may be used in female piles in deep walls where such reinforcement is needed for flexural strength. Weaker grades of concrete can be used in female piles when wall flexural strength is not critical. Advantages are gained in both the higher output of male pile

Fig. 4.17. Hard–soft secant pile wall construction, London

installation allowing rigs of lower torque to bore the female piles. This form of construction, known as hard–soft secant piling, may suffer from lack of durability of the soft piles for permanent construction. Some difficulty may be experienced in the supply of 'soft' concrete from off-site ready mix plants and any slightly lower material cost of the 'soft' concrete is lost if the soft mix has to be mixed on site. The early strength of the female piles requires control in hard–soft secant pile work and this is usually achieved with concrete mixes using cement–bentonite or PFA. A typical hard–soft secant wall used as a car parking basement in London is shown in Fig. 4.17. The wall was temporarily anchored during construction and corner cross-braced. A reinforced concrete lining wall was applied to provide permanent water resistance.

The use of hard–firm secant piles is made to secure durability and particularly to give permanent resistance to water penetration through the female piles. Concrete with a characteristic strength in the range 10 to 20 N/mm^2 at 56 days with retardation is used to allow easier cutting of the secants than for hard–hard piles. CFA rigs normally are used. Pile spacings must allow for adequate secant width to ensure water resistance taking into account pile installation verticality tolerances. Typical hard–firm pile spacings, centre-to-centre of male piles are 900 mm for 600 mm dia. male and female piles and 1150 mm for 750 mm dia. male and female piles.

Hard–hard secant walls are installed using casings with high-torque rigs for deep piles and with CFA rigs for piles of lesser depth. The high-torque rigs use thick temporary casings, jointed with flush mechanical locks, installed and extracted either by the rig itself or by casing oscillators attached to the base of the rig. The maximum depth of installation, in the range 30 m to 40 m (exceptionally) is dependent upon the torque required to rotate the casing and the verticality tolerance needed to ensure the secant depth. Typical spacings of piles to provide adequate secant depth are 650 mm for 750 mm dia. piles, 760 mm for 880 mm dia. piles and 1025 mm for 1180 mm dia. piles.

Typical hard–hard reinforcement details are shown in Fig. 4.18 (after Sherwood *et al.*[10]).

Junctions with floor and raft slabs can be made with secant pile walls in a similar way to diaphragm walls using bend-out bars or bar connectors and

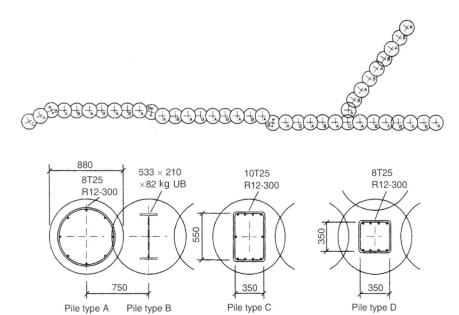

Fig. 4.18. Hard–hard secant pile wall reinforcement details[10]

polystyrene blockwork secured to the reinforcement cage. Where pile re-inforcement cages twist within the bore some difficulty may be experienced in keeping the box-out in the correct position. Where I-beams are used to reinforce female piles, a shear plate can be welded before installation and a shear 'shoe' attached upon exposure.

Inclined walls in secant piling may also be installed at a small inclination to the vertical. In Europe, sloping walls raked away from the basement excavation to increase basement width have been used to dramatic effect. Figure 4.19 shows a typical installation.

The spacing, centre-to-centre, of secant piles remains a matter for judgement by the piling contractor. Figure 4.20 shows support to an excavation for the Piccadilly Line underground railway extension to Heathrow Airport, where 880 mm dia. piles through Thames gravel were spaced initially at 770 mm centres, but in severe groundwater conditions the pile spacing was reduced to 750 mm centres to ensure weatherproofness. Although an internal lining was intended to this wall, the uniformity of finish on the surface of the piles was sufficiently good to leave them exposed without lining in the running tunnels.

The latest rigs, with usable torques in the range 11 to 60 T m, offer the following advantages:

(a) a range of diameters of cased secant piles from 600 to 1800 mm is available with production rates increasing with reducing diameter
(b) difficult conditions including obstructions can be overcome without chiselling
(c) the introduction of CFA construction methods for hard–hard secant walls in the range 410 to 1200 mm in diameter
(d) the use of CFA equipment to bore hard–soft and hard–firm walls.

The secant method therefore provides a waterproof wall which can be built to a considerable depth, in the range 30 to 40 m, and can cope with most types of obstruction. The hard–soft version is limited to shallow excavation depths because of the reduced flexural strength of the wall and some doubt concerning the long-term durability and waterproofness of the soft piles.

Modifications to rotary equipment have minimized the working space required between the rear of the secant pile wall and the site boundary. For relatively shallow walls, up to 12 m deep, Bauer equipment, a modified

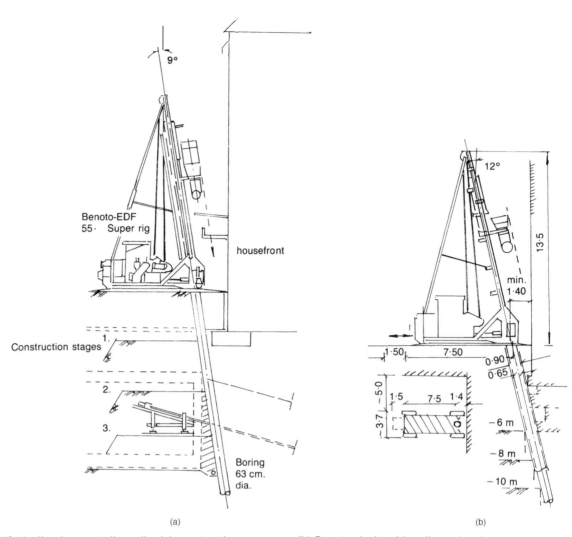

Fig. 4.19. *Inclined secant pile walls: (a) construction sequence; (b) Benoto rig (working dimensions)*

Fig. 4.20. *Secant piles, Piccadilly Line underground railway, Heathrow Airport (courtesy of Lilley)*

Fig. 4.21. Typical guide wall construction for secant pile wall

BG11 rig, permits installation of 410 mm dia. piles with an axial spacing from an existing structure of 305 mm. In 1988 at Staines, UK, Bachy–Bauer installed 410 mm dia. hard–hard walls using such a rig only 100 mm from an existing wall. The pile diameter was restricted and so, therefore, was the excavation depth. The piles were reinforced with universal beam sections.

Guide walls are needed for all forms of secant pile construction, and mention should be made of the cost and time liability this represents. Typical guide wall construction is shown in Fig. 4.21.

Closely spaced anchors, or struts, are used to support secant piling using steel waling members or in situ concrete bearing pads. Secant pile walls may also be used to carry vertical loads. Figure 4.22 shows the method of use of secant piling anchored to deadmen below existing buildings.

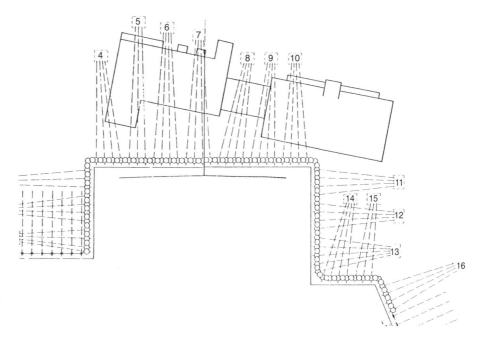

Fig. 4.22. Secant pile wall anchored to deadmen below an existing structure (courtesy of Bauer)

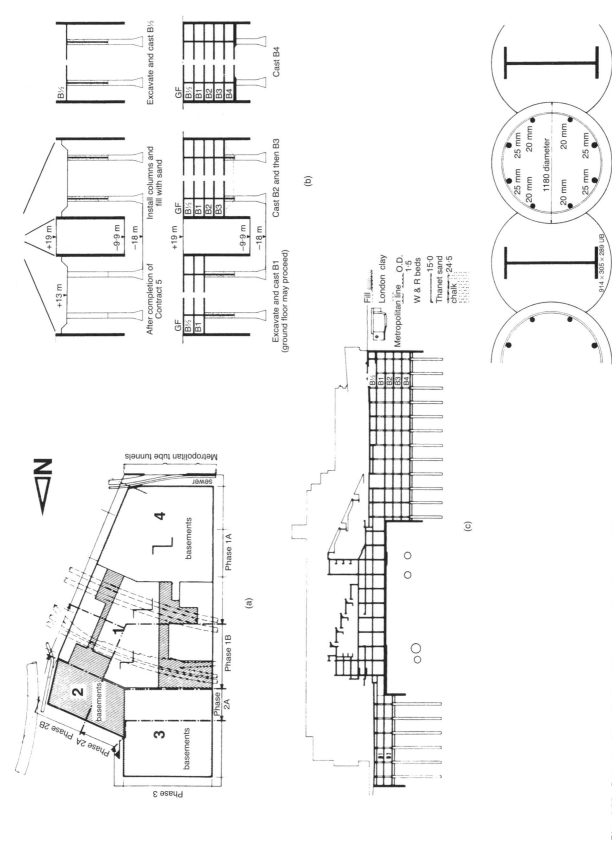

Fig. 4.23. Secant piling, British Library, London: (a) plan; (b) construction sequence; (c) cross-section; (d) typical cross-section of secant wall construction (courtesy of Lilley)

The hard–hard secant pile method has been used successfully in London for the construction of a deep basement to the British Library (Fig. 4.23). The basement extends to four floors, with the maximum depth 24 m below ground level. Underground railway tunnels are bridged by a concrete raft at the centre area of the site where the basement depth is limited to two floors. The maximum depth of the secant pile is 30 m. Due to the high sulphate content in the subsoil and the need to minimize the generated heat of hydration caused by high cement contents, the concrete mix to the piles incorporated 85% cement replacement with a ground granulated furnace slag and an aggregate of maximum size 40 mm. Although a diaphragm wall 1·2 m thick was originally intended for use at the site, the existence of large vertical service ducts at close centres adjacent to the wall caused high design values of shear at the junction of floor slab and wall. The large steel joist sections which reinforce the male piles of the secant wall ideally resist these shear forces.

Diaphragm walls

The first diaphragm walls were tested in 1948 and the first wall was built, using bentonite slurry as a means of support, by Icos in Italy in 1950. That contract was for a cut-off wall on a dam site. Structural walls followed, and in the late 1950s the construction of the Milan Metro allowed Icos to use diaphragm walls extensively in cut-and-cover construction; a method of top-down working known as the Milan method was developed. The first structural diaphragm wall in the UK, at Hyde Park Corner, London, in 1961, was also built by Icos using its then patented process. Many contracts followed for Icos in Europe. These contracts, to build basements, underpasses, marine structures and metro works, were all excavated using rope grabs suspended from tripod rigs and, later, from crawler cranes.

The development of diaphragm walling was encouraged by competition among specialist international firms from the mid 1960s. These firms, including Icos in Europe and the USA, Soletanche and Bachy in France, Trevisani and Rodio in Italy, and Cementation in the UK, all developed excavation systems of their own. Two preferences quickly became evident: rope grabs suspended by rope either from tripod rigs or cranes; or grabs, generally hydraulic powered, mounted on kelly bars mounted on cranes. These two methods of excavation continued into the 1980s. The major problem which these methods failed to solve was the excavation of rock. In the 1970s, rotary percussive tools using reverse circulation were used to excavate, albeit slowly, into hard rock.

In the early 1970s the reverse circulation system was used in Japan for a new generation of rail-mounted rigs, manufactured by the Tone Drill Co. Although these rigs were adequate for excavation in granular soils (but less so in cohesive soils), they were the forerunners of modern reverse circulation rigs and used shaker screens and cyclones to remove cuttings from the slurry in a similar way to the latest Hydrofraise and Trenchcutter rigs. Despite the introduction of these modern reverse circulation rigs, excavation by grab still has its place, on smaller sites and in certain soil conditions, but it is worth noting that kelly-mounted rigs are rarely used and preferences are for heavy 8 tonne rope grabs and hydraulic grabs suspended from cranes.

Incentives to develop excavation equipment (particularly in rock) have come mainly from the need to improve output at the lowest cost; without exception, panel excavation still remains the critical operation in diaphragm wall contracts despite the complexity of all other operations. Minimization of machine downtime is a vital factor in overall excavation production.

In addition to excavation output, increasing wall depths and the requirements of wall verticality tolerance have placed demands on the development of excavation equipment. To a large extent the requirements of depth and tolerance, together with the particular soil or rock type, define the optimum excavation equipment: rope grab or cutter. Modern cutter machines are capable of cutting through rock with a compressive strength of the order of 200 MPa, and of excavation in soils to depths in excess of 100 m. Cutter machines with small roller bits on the outer edge of the cutters were developed for similar tasks. Verticality tolerances of the order of 0·3% can be made to depths of 50 m. The manufacturers of these rigs currently include Soletanche, Bauer, Casagrande, Soilmec and Tone.

Developments in mechanical excavation equipment have radically changed the scale of diaphragm wall contracts that can be undertaken. The Seaforth Dock contract (145 500 m² of wall) and Redcar Ore Terminal (64 680 m², depth 45 m), both excavated by rope grabs, were among the largest projects of their time (1968–1972). The Medinah car park project in Saudi Arabia, completed in two years with three cutter working rigs and five rope grabs, has a total wall area in excess of 320 000 m² and to a maximum depth of 55 m. Wall outputs peaked at almost 30 000 m² per month and consistently averaged almost 20 000 m² per month.

Accompanying these changes in excavation method has been the development of other installation techniques on site:

(a) temporary stop end fabrications which allow water bar installation in panel joints and do not require extraction during, or immediately after, concreting; the CWS joint and similar stop ends
(b) fabricated permanent stop ends which allow the transfer of shear and tensile forces through the panel joints
(c) reusable precast concrete guide walls
(d) improved slurry cleaning equipment, including centrifuges and belt presses
(e) polymers for artificial slurries
(f) improved cage handling methods
(g) smaller reverse circulation rigs for urban sites (City Cutters)
(h) improved cutters such as rock roller bits on Trenchcutter rigs
(i) steerable grabs, hydraulic rope suspended, manufactured by Bauer, Soilmec and Bachy
(j) improved in-cab instrumentation.

While site operations were improving, diaphragm wall designers were also introducing innovations:

(a) structurally efficient plan shapes of diaphragm walls
(b) vertically post-tensioned panels
(c) precast concrete panels
(d) combined slurry cut-off walls, permanent precast concrete diaphragm walls and temporary soil retaining walls
(e) improved wall to slab connection details.

A review of developments in the construction of structural diaphragm walls by Puller and Puller[11] is referred to in greater detail in Chapter 8.

Advantages of diaphragm wall construction
The diaphragm wall is generally efficient in cost and construction time where it is used for both permanent and temporary subsoil retention for walls of medium, and greater, depth.
A previous review of the economics of basement construction[5] by the Author emphasized that cost comparisons between types of basement construction

could only be made after a complete analysis of the unit costs of temporary and permanent walls, the costs of shoring or anchoring and the costs of internal lining walls and basic finishes. The diaphragm wall method compares well for deep walls in a complete analysis of this type. Additional data on cost comparisons are given at the end of this chapter.

In the UK in recent years the number of diaphragm wall contracts has reduced and their size increased as preference has been shown, presumably on the basis of cost, to concrete piled walls, particularly hard–soft secant walls, for many two-storey basements. Diaphragm walls find favour for deeper constructions in the range 3000 to $12\,000\,\mathrm{m^2}$ of wall area. Some of these contracts are part of new metro construction, particularly station box and ventilation shaft construction. In London, in the years 1997 to 2002, works for stations at Canary Wharf on the Jubilee Line, at Westminster Station in Central London and at the Stratford Box and for the Graham Road shaft on the Channel Tunnel Rail Link works have all used diaphragm walls for wall depths in the range 30 to 55 m. The common features for these latest contracts include relatively heavy reinforcement cages (the total cage weights per panel at the Graham Road shaft reached 90 tonnes), CWS joints with water bars in vertical panel joints, extensive use of couplers to splice cages and joints with slab and roof steel, relatively long panels, up to 6·5 m, with large concrete pours despite traffic difficulties in built-up areas, and the extensive use of cutters (the exception being Westminster Station where low-headroom grabs were used). These contracts ranged in size from

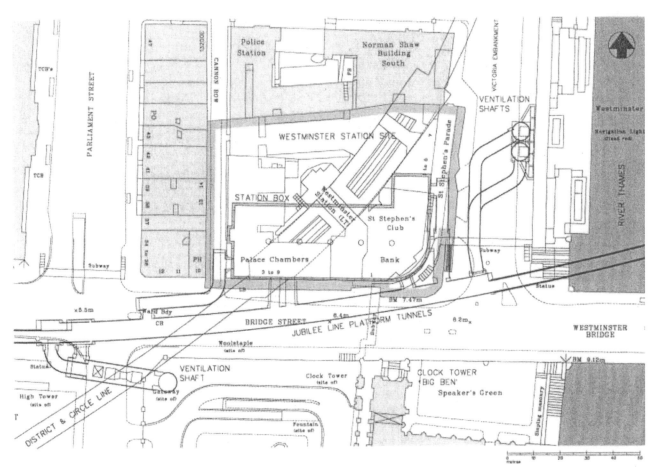

Fig. 4.24 (a) New underground station construction, Westminster, London: plan[30]

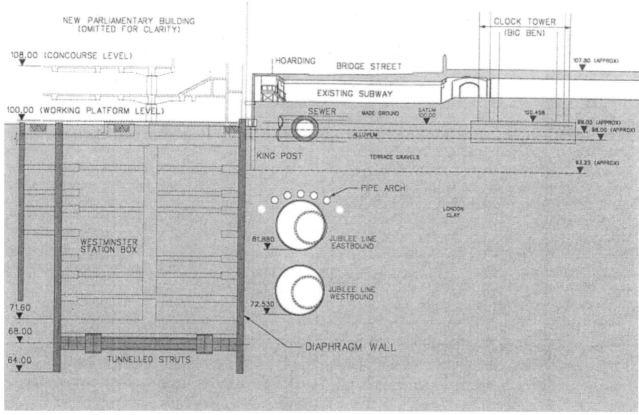

Fig. 4.24 (b) New underground station construction, Westminster, London: cross section of the works[30]

4000 m² at Graham Road to 8000 m² at Westminster Station to 65 000 m² for the Stratford Box.

The construction of the 38 m deep underground escalator hall at Westminster Station was completed alongside very busy thoroughfares, in near proximity to settlement sensitive structures and immediately adjacent to existing Jubilee Line tunnels in frequent use. The works were designed to provide a new ticket hall and access to the new Jubilee Line extension and passenger interchange with the existing District and Circle Line station. Crawley and Glass[12] described the construction works. The plan and section of the works is shown in Fig. 4.24.

The ground conditions were typical of Central London, made ground at the surface, overlying alluvium, Terrace Gravel and London clay. The construction method comprised very large piles, 3 m diameter and 53 m deep to support the existing station and then top-down construction following the 1·5 m thick reinforced concrete underpinning transfer slab within a 1 m thick diaphragm wall installed partly by lower headroom rigs below the existing station platform (see Fig. 4.25). The top-down construction sequence is shown in Fig. 4.26. Temporary retaining walls were necessary for access to support up to 7 m of ground using king post walls with in situ R.C. skin walls, contiguous concrete piles, mini piles combined with cement–bentonite and silicate ester grouting and sheet piles installed by Giken press. This scheme must represent one of the most complex ground engineering schemes completed to date in the United Kingdom.

Elsewhere, in major city centres, large schemes for office and retail use occupy progressively larger and deeper floor space as land values escalate. In Hong Kong in 1994 the LDC H-6 project in Queens Road Central

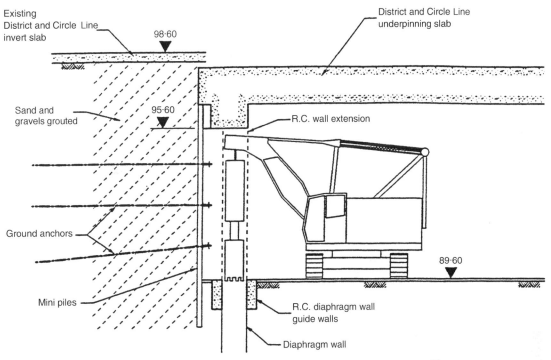

Fig. 4.25. New underground station construction, Westminster, London: construction method[12]

consisted of a perimeter diaphragm wall of $18\,000\,\text{m}^2$, 45 m deep and 1200 mm thick, together with 46 barrettes with a total area of $8500\,\text{m}^2$, to the same depth and thickness. The soil conditions generally consisted of a 15 m depth of fill and alluvium containing cobbles and boulders underlain to a depth of 60 m by completely decomposed granite with SPT values from 50 to more than 240. Within the upper fill and boulder layers, a hydraulic grab was used for pre-excavation to an average depth of 12 m. Within this depth, where no boulders greater than 700 mm were met, an average 7 to $10\,\text{m}^2/\text{h}$ could be achieved, but this was reduced to 30 to 50% of this output where larger boulders were broken by chisel. The pre-excavated trench, backfilled with lean mix concrete, was then excavated using Bauer BG 30 Trenchcutters. The average penetration rate achieved on primary panels was:

- excavation in lean mix concrete: 3 min per metre, $65\,\text{m}^3/\text{h}$;
- excavation in completely decomposed granite, SPT less than 50: 5 min per metre, $45\,\text{m}^3/\text{h}$;
- SPT 50 to 100: 7 min per metre, $30\,\text{m}^3/\text{h}$;
- SPT 100 to 300: 15 min per metre, $13\,\text{m}^3/\text{h}$.

These rates, achieved only during the period of machine operation, do not include breakdown, waiting and working time. The production rate for secondary panels was approximately half that of the primary panels.

Diaphragm walls allow effective transfer of vertical load from the building superstructure to subsoil below basement level.

Early diaphragm walls in the UK did not generally include use of the walls to transfer vertical load from the superstructure. The reluctance of designers to allow such load transfer was due no doubt to lack of published test results. Gradually this situation changed following publication by Fleming and Sliwinski[13] and Xanthakos[14] of reviews of available test data together with their conclusions that there was no evidence that load transfer characteristics

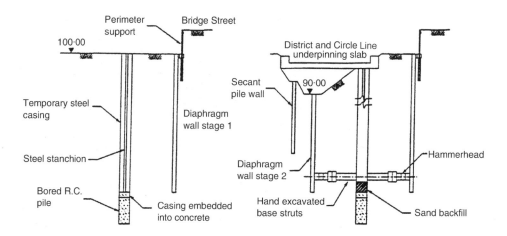

Stage 1
Install perimeter support around site
Install diaphragm walls
Install piles and steel stanchions

Stage 2
Hand excavate struts and hammerheads
Excavate to 90·0 level
Install low height diaphragm wall and secant piles

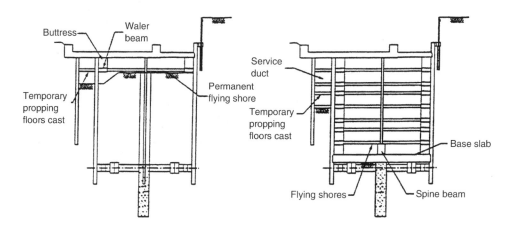

Stage 3
Excavate remainder of site to underside
of first waler level
Install first level of flying shores
Cast slabs, waler beams and buttresses
Continue downwards floor by floor

Stage 4
Repeat stage 3 until all flying shores, floor slabs,
waler beams and buttresses are constructed
Excavate to underside of base slab
Cast base slab and spine beam

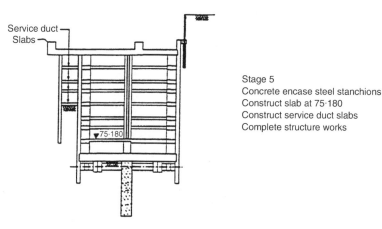

Stage 5
Concrete encase steel stanchions
Construct slab at 75·180
Construct service duct slabs
Complete structure works

Fig. 4.26. New underground
station construction,
Westminster, London: top-down
construction sequence[12]

Fig. 4.27. Cleaning device for removing excessive wall cake thickness

of slurry panels differ materially from those in dry construction. They did recommend, however, that design should be conservative, especially on sites where panel load tests were not justified on cost grounds. Panel tests in the UK have remained few. An early exception was for a load test at a basement construction at Kensington Town Hall in London where Corbett *et al.*[15] concluded that compared with other large bored pile designs, the performance of the test panels was not adversely affected by the bentonite slurry.

Elsewhere, concern has continued to be shown that the slurry has no adverse effect on the ability of surface friction or adhesion to transfer vertical load to the adjacent soil, particularly where an excessively thick wall cake has formed. The maximum time period between completion of panel excavation and any change of slurry and commencement of concreting may be specified with advantage to minimize this build-up. Measures to reduce the effect of a thick wall cake include use of tubes à manchette on the panel face and the use of cleaning devices to remove the wall cake (a typical device is shown in Fig. 4.27).

Diaphragm wall construction causes minimum noise and vibration disturbance
The extent of noise and vibration in diaphragm wall installations is limited to that associated with normal civil engineering plant, cranes, generators, pumps, compressors, power packs etc. for excavation in soils. Obstructions

or rock strata may lead to chiselling and some vibration where conventional grab excavation is used, although the use of modern reverse circulation cutter rigs reduces this (although cutter rigs do not necessarily avoid the need for chiselling boulders). Where such vibrations do occur, soil from the side of the slurry trench may collapse, leading to additional panel overbreak. The extents of chiselling and vibration using conventional grab excavation have been reduced by the successive use of auger coring buckets along the length of the panel excavation.

It should be remembered that even where soil conditions allow relatively quiet plant operation the diaphragm wall process necessitates extraction of stop ends from panels other than secondary panels unless expendable permanent or CWS type stop ends are used, and this operation is only possible some hours after the completion of concreting. Unless expendable reinforced concrete stop ends or CWS type stop ends (which can be extracted at a convenient time) some noise from cranage is inevitable due to out-of-hours stop end extraction.

Quality control of diaphragm wall construction

Considerable skill and care is required on the part of the specialist contractor installing diaphragm walls. Six items within the Author's experience warrant particular attention.

The need for continuous construction

The construction technique is continuous, from commencement of panel excavation to installation of stop end formers and reinforcement cage, concreting and withdrawal of panel stop ends. Any major disruption, whether caused by ineptitude or other circumstances, can cause loss of ground or poor standards of wall construction which may be difficult and expensive to rectify.

It is vital to maintain punctual completion of the construction cycle of excavation, panel preparation for concreting, reinforcement installation, concreting and panel finishing. Factors which can disrupt this operation sequence must be removed. Critical matters include the optimum panel size to ensure compatibility with excavation and concrete outputs; permissible daily working hours allowed in the contract to facilitate daily completion of important stages in the cycle, such as concreting and stop end removal; and high standards of site supervision to ensure the availability of resources of plant, labour and material.

Panel instability

The quality of the work (which is only disclosed when bulk excavation of the site is undertaken) is directly dependent on the subsoil strata since the soil forms a temporary shutter against which the in situ concrete is cast. In terms of wall finish, the smoothness of the diaphragm wall concrete will improve with reducing soil particle size. One would expect to obtain a better surface finish for a diaphragm wall excavated in clay compared with one in sandy gravel. Obstructions in the diaphragm wall excavation, whether man-made or natural, may not only prove difficult to remove from the panel excavation, but their removal may also cause some dislodgement of the soil on the panel face, the resulting void subsequently being filled with concrete overbreak. Where this void is exposed later during site bulk excavation, some remedial work may be needed to remove the excess concrete.

Overbreak on the panel face may be caused, therefore, by removal of obstructions, but more likely by collapses of the panel face caused by instability. Panel stability, reviewed by Xanthakos[14] and Puller[16], was originally studied by several authors including Nash and Jones[17], Muller-Kirchenbauer[18], Piaskowski and Kowalewski[19], Fernandez[20] and Huder[21]. Within the Author's practical experience, panel stability is much dependent on the ability of the soil around the panel effectively to arch during all stages of the panel excavation. In loose sands, sandy gravel and open gravels, large volumes of overbreak frequently occur below guide trench level. Typical overbreak removal operations cause difficulties of access and construction delay. The cost of removal is frequently three or four times that of the original concrete as placed. A differential of at least 1·5 m height between slurry level within the panel excavation and groundwater level within the subsoil adjacent to the panel is necessary to avoid panel instability. The cause of serious panel instability is frequently the neglect of maintaining such a differential height, and in isolated cases the installation of a wellpoint dewatering system has been necessary during the diaphragm wall works to improve the differential height and so increase panel stability. Particular attention is needed where groundwater flows underground or through a closing panel.

Where conventional grab excavation is used there is risk of loss of the panel face, particularly in granular soils, from below guide trench level, by the pumping action during raising and lowering of the excavation grab within the bentonite slurry. Instances of major panel collapse caused by panel instability in very weak clays were reported by Mastikian[22] but fortunately are rare. Some wall face collapses have also been observed in deep panels in highly fissured over-consolidated clays, such as London clay, where fissuring has much reduced the soil strength.

The risk of major panel instability does not appear to increase with greater panel depth, probably due to the relative increase in slurry over pressure with depth. The calculated stability of panels by traditional methods as described in DIN standards and by Xanthakos[14] and others has frequently been shown to be unreliable in both deep and shallow panels. The increase in time spent in the excavation and subsequent preparation of deep panels does not in itself appear to lead to panel instability. Other factors appear to dictate this, including the presence of very soft clays, excessive fluid loss from the slurry, excessive vibration due to construction operations including chiselling, inadequate differential height between slurry and groundwater levels and unstable guide wall construction. Some instability risk particularly applies to shaft construction. Where shaft panels are founded on sloping rockhead it is essential to avoid excessive chiselling. It may be practicable to use multiple reinforcement cages in each panel with a stepped panel toe to minimize this and individual cages for each bite become increasingly important for grab excavation onto sloping rockhead for shafts deeper than 30 to 40 m.

Where shaft excavation is made through permeable strata it is likely that a pumping well within the shaft may be necessary to relieve piezometric pressure and retain the stability of the closing panel excavation. Where such soils are saturated only a small flow of filtrate from the slurry into the soil will cause a rise of pore pressure in the soil. This increase will occur more readily where the permeable stratum is capped above and below by impermeable layers. Relief of any excess pore pressure by pumping ensures an adequate differential head of slurry and allows the closing panel excavation in stable conditions.

Where deep walls are built in tidal conditions it is necessary to monitor groundwater conditions if there is risk of inadequate differential slurry head at high tide. Saline groundwater may lead to flocculation of the slurry and the use of additives is necessary to prevent this. It may be necessary to improve the difference between slurry and groundwater levels by temporary groundwater lowering, by increasing guide wall height or by use of a heavier

slurry. In very weak soils it may be necessary to reduce panel lengths. Any slurry loss from panels left open overnight must be made good regularly.

Inclusions

The combined use of slurry and high-grade concrete within the same wall panel construction requires considerable skill and care to ensure homogeneous finished concrete without deleterious slurry inclusions in the panel.

Bad slurry inclusions, particularly at panel joints, can cause unacceptable standards of structural competence or water resistance of the wall and must be avoided. Cambefort[23] showed examples of poor-quality diaphragm walls caused by inadequate slurry quality amongst other factors. The cause of such inclusions may not necessarily lie with poor-quality slurry; slow, erratic concrete pours with non-cohesive and low-slump concrete may also contribute. The risk of slurry inclusions within wall panels is increased when tremie spacing is too large in long panels and at tee or corner panels.

Fig. 4.28. Large mud inclusion within a diaphragm wall panel

The risk of inclusions in deep diaphragm walls is frequently related to a limited number of causes, principally the use of large, wide box-outs, the excessive density of reinforcement, standards of concrete placement and slurry quality immediately before concreting.

The restriction of wall width by box-outs can seriously impede flow of concrete upwards from tremies in the centre of the wall. Box-outs at the rear of reinforcement should be avoided. Where slurry has an excessive sand content there is risk of slurry inclusions above and below the box-outs and risk of concrete contamination. The risk of inclusions increases rapidly as slurry quality deteriorates and especially so where concrete supply is irregular and flow within the panel is impeded. As an example, Fig 4.28 shows a panel void due to a slurry inclusion. In this case, at a panel joint, the excessively thick slurry failed to be scoured by concrete and fresh concrete from the centre of the panel folded over on the top surface of the heavy slurry leaving a triangular inclusion for the full wall thickness.

For deep walls, particularly those excavated by cutter, it is often advantageous to use separate slurries for excavation and concreting. The 'excavating' slurry is completely replaced in the panel by the 'concreting' slurry immediately prior to placing the cage in the panel. In this way the effect of calcium contamination is restricted and ensures that there is ample time for adequate preparation of slurry for each phase.

For deep walls it is particularly important to ensure that all heavy slurry is removed prior to concreting especially when the cutter rig is used for this purpose. An air lift, used where grab excavation is made, may be preferred for this purpose. Care must be taken to avoid contamination of clean slurry by cleaning cutter wheels and internal pipework if the cutter is used to do this.

To reduce the risk of inclusions the slurry properties must be a balance between adequate filter cake building properties, sufficient shear strength in order to support soil grains without excessive sedimentation, low filter loss, and a viscosity which neither restricts flow of concrete nor requires uneconomic pump energy to circulate it. The slurry will require care to extend its life and fresh slurry may be needed to improve its properties after repeated cleaning. Additives to the slurry include sodium bicarbonate to control high pH and lignosulphinate thinners may be required to reduce viscoscity. Polymers may be added to reduce free water in the slurry or in saline conditions may be used as one measure to prevent flocculation. Recommended values of slurry properties to minimize inclusion risk are shown in Table 4.2.

Before the introduction of cutter rigs, load bearing panels and barrettes excavated to depths of 25 m or so were successfully excavated by grab and concreted without a slurry change, achieving a satisfactory concrete/soil or

Table 4.2 Recommended slurry properties for deep diaphragm walls

	Fresh	Ready for re-use	During excavation	Before concreting
Density (g/m^3)	1·05	Less than 1·15	Less than 1·25	1·10
Marsh value, seconds	30 to 45	30 to 50	30 to 60	30 to 45
Fluid loss (30 mins)	Less than 30 ml	Less than 50 ml	Less than 60 ml	Less than 60 ml
pH	7 to 9·5	7 to 11·0	7 to 11·5	7 to 11·5
Sand content	No spec.	No spec.	No spec.	Less than 3%

Notes.
This chart presumes that the slurry will be changed for the whole panel prior to the installation of the reinforcement cage and subsequent concreting.
For load bearing walls the following values are recommended:
Before concreting: Specific gravity, less than 1·08
Sand content, less than 1%.

rock interface beneath the panel. Deeper panels excavated by grab or cutter require more care, involving a slurry change and including cleaning the base, probably by air lift. Small thicknesses of soft material trapped at the base of the wall are unlikely to affect wall settlement performance at working load, but the effects of sedimentation, loss of debris from the wall cake and increased fluid loss from the slurry accentuate the problem at the base as the panel depth increases. For deep panels which sustain load at their toe it is a wise routine precaution to incorporate 50 mm grout pipes within the panel, staggered in plan, at intervals along the toe to permit toe grouting to reduce the effect of thick basal inclusions. In deep panels where large wall or barrette settlement is unacceptable the following procedure is recommended.

(*a*) On larger sites, construction of a preliminary test panel which can be examined for basal inclusions and, where possible, load tested.
(*b*) Inclusion within random panels of sealed steel tubes to within 300 mm of the panel toe to allow the interface below the panel concrete to be cored. This method is preferred to penetration cone testing next to the panel.
(*c*) Where the panel is founded on rock, acceptance criteria must be defined for the founding depth. Experienced supervisory staff must be on site to verify and agree the base conditions at the bottom of each bite of excavation without delay.
(*d*) Change of the slurry for the whole panel volume is obligatory at the end of the panel excavation.
(*e*) The base of deep load bearing panels should be cleaned by grab and air lift or, for panels excavated by cutter, by the cutter itself or by air lift.
(*f*) Separate slurries should be used for panel excavation by cutter and subsequent panel concreting.
(*g*) Reinforcement spacing should comply with the requirements of DIN 4126.

Tolerances
There is considerable risk of wall construction outside specified tolerances. Tolerances for verticality, concrete protrusions on the inner wall face, positions of box-outs for recesses and locations of reinforcement are detailed in model specifications for diaphragm wall construction; in the UK the ICE *Specification for Piling and Embedded Retaining Walls*[24] lists the following tolerances.

(a) *Guide trench.* Line of finished face nearest to excavation: ±15 mm in 3 m; vertical to within 1:200; minimum clear distance between the faces of the guide walls shall be wall thickness plus 25 mm, and the maximum distance shall be wall thickness plus 50 mm.

(b) *Diaphragm wall.* Exposed wall face and panel ends shall be vertical within a 1:120 tolerance. In addition to verticality tolerance, a further 100 mm shall be allowed for protrusions resulting from irregularities in the ground as excavated.

(c) *Box-outs.* Vertical and horizontal tolerances of ±75 mm and a horizontal tolerance, at right angles to the wall, ±75 mm plus the horizontal tolerance resulting from (b).

(d) *Reinforcement.* Horizontal tolerance of cage head at top guide wall, measured along the trench, ±75 mm; vertical tolerance of cage head relative to the guide wall shall be +150/−50 mm.

(e) *Concrete tolerance.* Where the final trimmed level of the diaphragm wall is up to 1·0 m below the top of the guide wall, the casting tolerance will be 600 mm above the trim level; for each additional 1 m depth of final trim level, or part thereof, allow an additional 150 mm level tolerance.

Similar tolerances are listed in the European Specification for Diaphragm Walls[25].

Concrete quality

The use of larger pours (often in the range 200 to 400 m^3 as required for deeper walls) has placed an increased demand on concrete properties which generally has led to more detailed and stringent concrete specification. The specifiers now require longer periods of retardation, some improvements to 28-day strength, a guarantee of concrete of uniform consistency free from balling of cement and fine sands and pumpable, non-segregating, cohesive mixes. Properties such as bleed of pours assume greater importance as panel depth is increased. Additives such as super-plasticizers have assumed increasing importance and the need to achieve economy in cost has led to an increasing use of ground blast furnace slag in the UK.

The consistency of delivered concrete quality and the rate of delivery remain key factors in the finished quality of diaphragm walls. The concrete mix for deep walls must be cohesive with a high resistance to segregation. The use of cleaner aggregates and the use of crushed angular stone makes this more difficult to achieve and is not identified by traditional quality control tests for consistency, such as the slump test. Improvements to cohesiveness can be made by oversanding or the incorporation of small size rock particles avoiding clay sizes.

The use of the slump test or the flow test to control mix workability on site fails to accurately identify changes in free water content and provides no effective control on bleed of free water from the mix. Bleed is susceptible to variations in water–cement ratio especially when a gap exists at the lower end of the sand grading. The use of ground blast furnace slag in the mix may also increase bleed risk. An example of bleed in deep panels is shown in Fig. 4.29. The depth of the defect is usually limited to the concrete cover thickness but even so may be detrimental to wall durability. Some risk of poor bond between concrete and reinforcement can also occur.

For a particular mix it can be shown experimentally that bleed, a sedimentation effect within concrete, increases rapidly above a critical water–cement ratio and control of free water within the mix quantities by slump testing is often not adequate to prevent excessive bleed in deep panels. The remedy

Fig. 4.29. Example of bleed from concrete on face of diaphragm wall panels

often lies in the more accurate determination of moisture content of aggregates at the mixer.

The need to ensure competent tremie practice in placing concrete is vital as panel depths increase and plan shapes vary. It is essential that the concrete as discharged into the tremie hopper at the beginning of the pour does not mix with the slurry within the tremie pipe as it travels to the bottom of the panel. Several means can be used in an attempt to ensure this. Vermiculite granules and plastic footballs are sometimes used, but full-scale trials have shown that the high concrete velocity within the tremie pipe does not allow adequate separation of concrete and slurry, and a plug of defective concrete is left at the bottom end of the tremie pipe and remains at the base of the panel. The proven procedure to avoid this requires the use of a 'Chinese hat' plug lowered by wire slowly down the tremie pipe with the initial charge of concrete above it. The tremie is then lifted 150 mm to allow the discharge of the uncontaminated concrete across the base of the panel. Figure 4.30 shows the details. The location of tremies within the panel is also important; the ICE Specification recommends a single tremie for panels up to 3·6 m in length, two tremies for panels between 3·6 and 7·2 m long and three tremies for tee panels. This advice appears adequate; it is essential at the commencement of a deep pour that the concrete flows uniformly over the whole of the bottom of the panel and a consistent level across the panel is maintained during the pour. It is a wise precaution to discharge concrete from all tremies simultaneously at the beginning of a pour to cause a rapid flush of concrete and avoid incorporation of a large volume of slurry into the concrete at the wall toe. During the pour accurate records of tremie length and concrete level should be made to avoid splitting tremies either too late or too early.

In summary, the preventative measures to ensure adequate concrete quality depend upon a balance between strength, workability and cohesiveness. It is

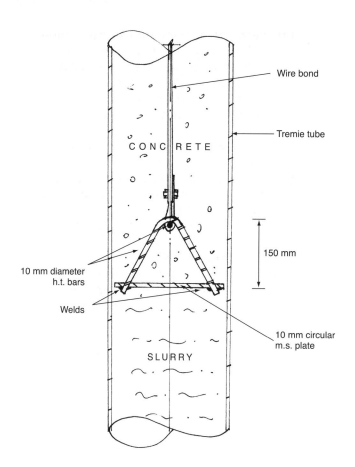

Fig. 4.30. Cross-section through Tremie tube with disposable 'Chinese hat'

important that personnel responsible for specifying and purchasing concrete are also experienced in diaphragm wall construction.

Water-resisting construction

The water resistance of a diaphragm wall structure depends on standards of design and construction. Design methods to achieve high standards include the provision of an integral water bar system between the diaphragm wall panel joints, in the construction joints between the wall and the basement slab and within the basement slab itself. Water resistance of basement construction is discussed more fully in Chapter 8. In general, the following factors affecting water resistance should be noted:

(a) soil and groundwater conditions: the greatest risk occurs with high groundwater in loose granular soils and very weak silts, silty clays and highly fissured over-consolidated clays

(b) compliance with good standards of diaphragm wall excavation, slurry control and concreting: avoid very long periods between excavation and concreting

(c) wall thickness: avoid very thin walls less than 600 mm thick

(d) plan shape of excavation: there is some evidence that leakage at panel joints tends to appear near return angles of wall (joints of panels at the centre of a long length of straight wall also tend to open during bulk excavation and can also cause leakage)

(e) depth to formation level: the greater the basement depth the greater the leakage risk, primarily due to increasing hydraulic head with depth

(f) panel length: shorter panels mean more panel joints but may reduce the risk of inclusions (*g*) means of diaphragm wall excavation: improved verticality tolerance and reduction of vibration with cutter excavation should generate better wall quality than grab excavation and in turn, water resistance standards should be improved

(*h*) extent of reinforcement density in diaphragm wall: high reinforcement density may reduce in situ concrete quality and, in turn, reduce water resistance

(*i*) top-down construction: this is likely to minimize wall movements and improve water resistance, particularly at panel joints

(*j*) the use of water bars in vertical panel joints using the CWS system or similar type of joint is essential; effective design of the joint between the wall and the bottom raft is critical

(*k*) the use of precautionary grouting of vertical panel joints.

Precast diaphragm walls

The disadvantages of using the subsoil face as the shutter for concrete placed within the diaphragm wall panel are obvious. The French firms, Bachy and Soletanche, now united as one firm Bachy–Soletanche, had developed methods of using precast concrete wall panels to overcome these drawbacks. The technique was first introduced in 1970 but has tended to be less popular in recent years. There are no known jobs in the UK using the precast system.

Colas de Francs[26] claimed the following distinct advantages for the precast prefabricated diaphragm over other types:

(*a*) general appearance: no cutting back is required and the finished surface is agreeably clean

(*b*) the shape of the diaphragm can be tailored to form an integral part of the final structure, satisfying technical, aesthetic and economic considerations

(*c*) improved concrete quality and accuracy in placing reinforcement gives considerable savings on materials; prefabricated diaphragms are generally 30% thinner than conventional diaphragm walls

(*d*) the prefabricated diaphragm can be built and installed in the ground to finer tolerances, and openings can be positioned more accurately

(*e*) watertightness at the joints and in the wall itself is better than with conventional diaphragms.

The improved surface finishes can be seen in Fig. 4.31, an example of the Bachy system known as Prefasif walling. Whether the advantages of finish,

Fig. 4.31. Precast diaphragm wall construction: a high standard of wall finish is obtained using the Prefasif system, Schipol, the Netherlands (courtesy of Soletanche–Bachy)

Fig. 4.32. Lifting a precast
diaphragm panel at a
nuclear power station at
Nogent-sur-Seine, France
(courtesy of Soletanche–Bachy)

improved tolerances and reduction in wall thickness offset the cost penalty of
these methods can only be appraised on a job-by-job basis.

Panel widths and lengths are limited by the capacity of mobile lifting equipment suitable for operation on construction sites, and in practical terms this is
of the order of 50 tonnes. The panels are usually cast on site; some additional
site area may be needed to do this although less space is needed to store
reinforcement since prefabrication of reinforcement cages is not necessary
with precasting. Figure 4.32 shows a panel being lifted.

The principal differences between the previous Panosol method by Soletanche and the Prefasif method by Bachy were in the mechanical connection
between panels and the timing of the use of cementitious slurry to surround
the precast unit and support the subsoil. In the Panosol method, the panel
was dug under a cementitious slurry containing retarding and regulating additives, the slurry being removed without difficulty from the smooth face of the
wall during bulk excavation of the site. Slurry between the rear face of the
precast panel and the subsoil remained permanently as an inert filler material
between wall unit and subsoil, the final strength of the set slurry being
designed to exceed neighbouring soil strength. In the Prefasif technique the
slurry was not designed for the dual purpose of a digging slurry and a
medium- or long-term soil support; the panel was dug under a conventional
bentonite mud which was later displaced by the introduction of a cementitious
grout just before the precast unit was positioned in the panel excavation.
Bachy claimed that its process gave flexibility in site operations, allowed a
wide range of grout strengths to be used and was particularly convenient
when large vertical loads were being carried by the panels. The process also
avoided risk of contamination of the grout by soil during the excavation
process. The methods of panel connection for the previous Soletanche
system are shown in Fig. 4.33; Fig. 4.34 shows the technique used originally
by Bachy.

Precast diaphragm panels may be designed to span vertically between
ground anchor levels, taking care to avoid movement caused by the preloading force to the anchors compressing the slurry between wall and subsoil.
Alternatively, soldier panels, themselves anchored, may support panels
spanning horizontally between them. In these cases the soldier wall units
may be extended in depth to improved bearing strata to support vertical
load. Precast diaphragms may also be used in a composite construction of
structural wall and self-hardening slurry cut-off, as shown in Fig. 4.35.

Post-tensioned diaphragm walls

Another innovation originally pioneered by Icos in the late 1960s replaced
vertical reinforcement within the diaphragm wall panel by a pre-stressing
tendon, the reinforcing steel in the cage being used principally to retain the
tendon position during lifting. The use of post-tensioning therefore reduces
steel reinforcement costs to a minimum, although its relatively small use in

Fig. 4.33. Horizontal cross-
section jointing detail for
Panosol diaphragm wall
panels: types (a) and (b) are
standard joints; types (c)–(e)
use temporary metal guides;
types (f) and (g) use pre-formed
water bars (courtesy of
Soletanche–Bachy)

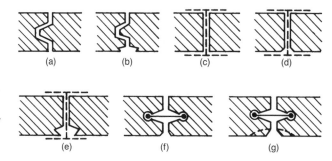

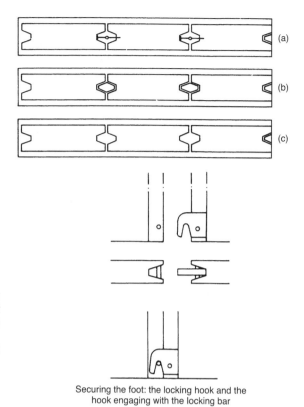

Fig. 4.34. Jointing details for Prefasif diaphragm wall panels – mechanical locking hook joint at the foot of the panel and types of joint in horizontal section: joint type (a) uses a pre-formed water bar, type (b) uses a reinforcing key, and type (c) uses grout only (courtesy of Soletanche–Bachy)

Securing the foot: the locking hook and the hook engaging with the locking bar

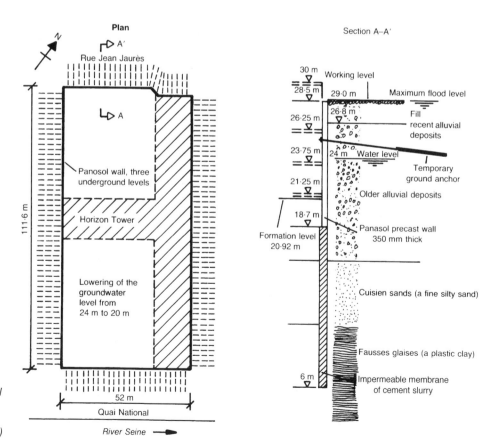

Fig. 4.35. Composite wall construction using precast wall and slurry cut-off, Horizon Tower at Puteaux, Paris (courtesy of Soletanche–Bachy)

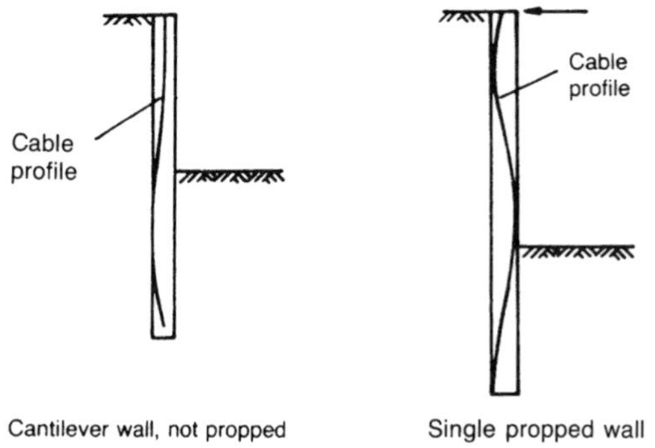

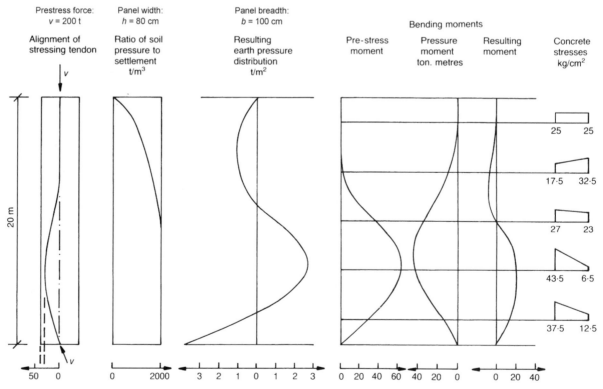

Fig. 4.36. Post-tensioned cantilever and single-propped diaphragm walls showing cable profile and bending moment diagrams for the wall section[27]

Cantilever wall, not propped   Single propped wall

the UK may reflect relatively high cost of tendons and stressing operations, as well as design complexity to cover all stages of construction.

The feature of the method is that stressing of the panel is undertaken before bulk excavation is carried out and while the wall panel is fully embedded. Tendon forces and eccentricities are calculated for loading on the final structure with no tension across the concrete section, the panel movement during stressing being reduced by the surrounding soil, the soil restraint varying between full passive pressure and earth pressure at rest. The cable profiles for a cantilever wall and a propped diaphragm wall are shown in Fig. 4.36. Figure 4.37, taken from Gysi *et al.*[27], shows earth pressure, bending moments and stresses in a typical wall unit before removal of the surrounding soil, the moment applied to the wall section by the pre-stressing force being effectively reduced by the soil stiffness whilst reducing tension developing across the section due to pre-stress.

Fig. 4.37. Earth pressure, bending moments and stresses in a post-tensioned diaphragm wall before excavation in front of the panel[27]

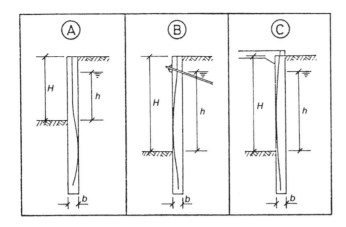

Site	Type	H (m)	h (m)	b (m)	Max pre-stress (N/mm²)
Centrale PTT Bellinzona	A	7·0	2·7	60	3·6
Admiral SA, Paradiso	A	7·6	5·10	80	3·5
German Embassy, London	A	9·6	5·70	90	3·1
ETA-Werke Grenhen	B	13·2	6·2	80	3·7
Propr. Fabriane, Lugano	C	11·6	4·6	60	3·6
Centrale TT, Moralto	C	15·0	—	80	2·1

Fig. 4.38. Examples of post-tensioned walls[27]

Figure 4.38 shows further examples given by Gysi *et al.*[27] The considerable heights of cantilever wall shown, between 7 and 9·6 m, and the relative slenderness of the wall section would appear conducive to excessive soil deformations behind the wall but none are reported. It is possible that the buttressing effect in plan of return walls at the corners of the excavation may have been taken into account in the wall design. In practice, the length of each basement wall section between return angles considerably influences the amount of horizontal movement after bulk excavation at the critical mid-point between corners of any basement.

It should be mentioned that the hoisting and lowering of diaphragm wall cages may cause displacement of steel and, in the case of pre-stressed walls, displacement of the tendon. Checking the tendon position, and correcting if necessary, assumes considerable importance when the tendon force and actual eccentricity are viewed together.

A typical tendon/reinforcement cage detail is shown in Fig. 4.39 after Fuchsberger and Gysi[28]. Although designs have been prepared to use large-diameter high-tensile steel bars of the Lee–McCall type with anchorages cast in to the base of the wall panel, this method has not been used to date, to the Author's knowledge. While the dependence on sound anchorage to each bar is obvious using this method, the compressive stresses and yielding induced in concrete within the anchorage zone of looped tendons at stressing should not be overlooked.

The Author has found that a separately cast capping beam is preferred to house the stressing heads and anchorages of the tendons. Unless this is done the anchorages are founded in the top of the diaphragm wall where concrete quality may not be at its best.

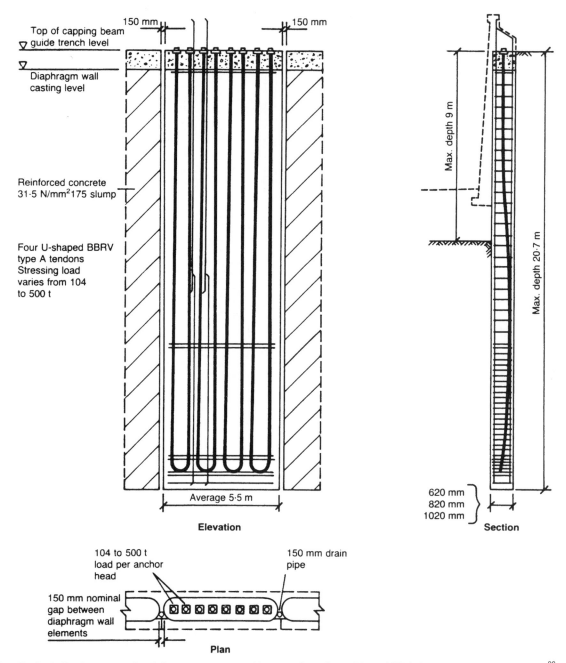

Fig. 4.39. *Typical diaphragm wall reinforcement cage with curved tendons, Irlam O'Heights near Manchester, UK*[28]

Soldier pile tremie concrete (SPTC) method

There have been some variations on the king post method of soil support; by using a mass concrete wall placed under bentonite slurry to replace horizontal lagging timbers, the SPTC method has found favour in the past in the USA. The reinforced concrete walls are of limited span and are dependent on subsoils of low overbreak risk. The method was reported by Peck[1].

Mesh-reinforced gunite has been used successfully to replace the mass concrete walling used in the SPTC method. Figures 4.40 and 4.41 show basement excavations in Stuttgart and Linz, respectively, where gunite over mesh has retained subsoil between anchored vertical steel beams. The absence of groundwater is a prerequisite for the successful use of gunite over mesh.

Fig. 4.40. Composite use of contiguous bored pile walls and gunited steel soldier beams retained by ground anchors, Stuttgart (courtesy of Bauer)

Fig. 4.41. Underpinned walls (left and centre) and walls retained by gunite overmesh between anchored steel soldiers, Linz (courtesy of Bauer)

Construction economics

Previously in this chapter the distinction was drawn between excavation methods and the alternative of peripheral support systems. The permutations of each are considerable. The choice of excavation method may well be constrained by factors other than cost, such as environmental matters like noise, vibration and site traffic, short completion times or the proximity of adjacent structures and services, etc. The choice of peripheral support system may, however, be made with greater freedom. Some constraints other than cost will no doubt still apply (noise and vibration levels vary from one sheeting installation to another, for instance), but within the choice of peripheral support system method lies considerable scope for economy and careful comparisons should be made method by method on each excavation project.

Before this, however, a number of conclusions can be drawn regarding the practical application of the peripheral wall or sheeting methods.

(a) High-torque CFA methods are limited to 35 m depth or so reinforced to 15–18 m depth in medium diameters, less in larger diameters.

(b) Low-torque CFA methods are limited to 20 m depths and pile deviations may prove limiting.

(c) In ground without obstructions or rock, CFA methods generate the least noise and vibration.

(d) In particular cases (e.g. loose sand and gravel over a very stiff clay), CFA methods can cause over-excavation and lead to settlement of adjacent structures. Generally, however, CFA methods are suitable for working close to existing structures.

(e) For temporary works, the hard–soft secant wall constitutes an efficient wall solution. For permanent works, however, durability and strength considerations may limit its application unless a reinforced concrete lining wall is used, designed to withstand groundwater pressure.

(f) Cased secant methods provide a high degree of risk-free excavation in difficult soil or rock conditions or in granular soils near existing foundations.

(g) The water resistance of hard–hard secant piling can reach that of a well-built diaphragm wall. With increasing depth, the risk of gaps between secant piles increases, with resulting lack of water resistance. Improvement of water resistance occurs with closer-centred boring.

(h) For walls greater than 30 m deep, cased secants with high-torque rigs and diaphragm walls are the only methods available. At greater depths, 40 to 45 m, diaphragm walls are the only available method.

(i) Box-outs are more easily accommodated in diaphragm walls than in secant piles.

(j) Construction speed and job size affect wall method selection. Where progress is unimpeded by rock or other obstructions daily production rates vary in the range 50 to 60 m^2 for a high-torque cased secant rig and 70 to 80 m^2 for a CFA secant rig. Diaphragm wall grab units produce 60 to 100 m^2 per day, while hydraulic cutters can produce in excess of 200 m^2 per day (all 12 h day shifts). It is possible to use several rigs on larger sites if a slower technique is chosen.

(k) Sheet pile walls may prove economical for shallow basements in soils free from obstructions: use of Giken press for sheeters of maximum length 20 m in clay. Installation in granular soils by vibrator.

A comparison by Sherwood et al.[10] of relative costs of various walling techniques in different ground conditions and site circumstances is shown in Table 4.3. Bearing in mind that market fluctuations can cause periodic changes in secant pile and diaphragm wall prices, the conclusions that may be drawn from this table are that diaphragms and hard–soft piles are comparable in cost in reasonable soils, sands and fills, where obstructions are few, but high-torque rigs using hard–hard secant methods are necessary where there are heavy obstructions or substantial rock thicknesses. Hydraulic cutters for diaphragm walls are favoured cost-wise for sandy formations with substantial rock layers on large open sites.

Reference should also be made to mobilization costs for walling equipment. A low-torque CFA rig can be mobilized for less than £10 000, while a high-torque cased secant machine can cost £70 000 to £100 000 to mobilize and

Table 4.3 Relative costs of various walling techniques in different ground conditions and site circumstances[10]

Ground conditions and site circumstances	Wall thickness (mm)	CFA hard–soft secant low-torque rigs	CFA hard–hard secant high-torque rigs	Classical cased oscillator hard–hard secant	Cased hard–hard secant high-torque rigs	Grab diaphragm wall	Hydraulic cutter diaphragm wall
Sands and fine-grained fills. No obstructions. Open site	<650	1·0	1·4	–	1·6	1·05	1·1
	650–800	1·0	1·2	–	1·35	1·0	1·1
	850–1000	–	1·25	1·4	1·15	1·0	1·1
	1050–1200	–	–	1·05	1·15	1·0	1·05
	1200–1500	–	–	–	–	1·0	1·1
Clays and fine-grained fills. No obstructions. Open site	<650	1·0	1·3	–	1·5	1·0	–
	650–800	1·0	1·15	–	1·3	1·0	–
	850–1000	–	1·25	1·4	1·15	1·0	–
	1050–1200	–	–	1·1	1·15	1·0	–
	1200–1500	–	–	–	–	1·0	–
Sands and fills containing some wood, bricks, etc. and brickwork. Open site	<650	–	1·0	–	1·2	1·05	1·1
	650–800	–	1·0	–	1·1	1·05	1·1
	850–1000	–	–	1·15	1·0	1·0	1·1
	1050–1200	–	–	1·0	1·0	1·0	1·05
	1200–1500	–	–	–	–	1·0	1·1
Clays and fills containing some wood, bricks, etc. and brickwork. Open site	<650	–	1·0	–	1·25	1·05	–
	650–800	–	1·0	–	1·15	1·05	–
	850–1000	–	–	1·2	1·0	1·0	–
	1050–1200	–	–	1·0	1·0	1·0	–
	1200–1500	–	–	–	–	1·0	–
Sands, clays and fine-grained fills. No obstructions. Small congested site	<650	1·0	1·4	–	1·6	1·25	–
	650–800	1·0	1·2	–	1·35	1·2	–
	850–1000	–	1·05	1·2	1·0	1·0	–
	1050–1200	–	–	1·0	1·0	1·05	–
	1200–1500	–	–	–	–	1·0	–
Sands, clays and fills containing some wood, bricks, etc. and brickwork. Small or congested site	<650	–	1·0	–	1·2	1·25	–
	650–800	–	1·0	–	1·1	1·25	–
	850–1000	–	–	1·5	1·0	1·2	–
	1050–1200	–	–	1·0	1·0	1·2	–
	1200–1500	–	–	–	–	1·0	–
Sands, clays and fills containing heavy obstructions including mass concrete, some steel etc. Open or small congested site	All thicknesses	–	–	–	1·0	–	–
All sandy formations with substantial rock layers. Open site	All thicknesses	–	–	–	1·25	–	1·0
All clayey formations with substantial rock layers	All thicknesses	–	–	–	1·0	–	–
All formations with substantial rock layers. Small or congested site	All thicknesses	–	–	–	1·0	–	–

demobilize on site. Diaphragm wall mobilization costs range from £50 000 for a single rope grab unit with equipment, to more than £100 000 for a single Hydrofraise unit with equipment. Minimum economical job sizes are therefore probably of the order of 1500 to 2000 m² for grab excavation and

5000 m^2 or more for Hydrofraise or Trenchcutter work. A further discussion of the costs of walls for basement construction is included in Chapter 8.

References

1. Peck R.B. Deep Excavations and tunneling in soft ground. *Proc. 7th Int. Conf. S.M.F.E.*, Mexico City, 1969, State of the art volume, 225–290. Sociedad de Mexicana de Suelos, Mexico City, 1969.
2. Potts D.M. and Day R.A. Use of sheet piling retaining walls for deep excavations in stiff clay. *Proc. Instn Civ.Engrs*, 1990, **88**, Dec., 899–927.
3. BS 5228. *Noise control on construction sites.* British Standards Institution, London, 1992.
4. British Steel Corporation. *Control of vibration and noise during piling.* British Steel Corporation, Scunthorpe, 1994.
5. Puller M.J. Economics of basement construction. *Proc. Conf. Diaphragm Walls and Anchorages.* London, 1975, 171–180.
6. Sellmeijer J. and Schouten C. Steel sheet pile seepage resistance. *Proc. 4th Int. Landfill Symposium*, Cagliari, 1993.
7. Arbed Group. *The impervious steel sheet pile wall. Part 1 design.* Arbed, 1998.
8. Arbed Group. *The impervious steel sheet pile wall. Part 2 practical aspects.* Arbed, 1998.
9. Schnabel H. Sloped sheeting. *Civ. Engng*, 1971, **41**, No. 2, 48–50.
10. Sherwood D.E. *et al.* Recent developments in secant bored pile wall construction. *Proc. Conf. Piling and Deep Foundations*, London, 1989, 211–219. DFI, Englewood Cliffs, New Jersey, 1989.
11. Puller M.J. and Puller D.J. Developments in structural slurry walls. *Proc. Conf. Retaining Walls.* Institution of Civil Engineers, London, 1992, 373–384.
12. Crawley J. and Glass P. Westminster Station, London. *Proc. Deep Foundations Conf.*, Vienna, 1998, 5.18.1–5.18.14. DFI, Englewood Cliffs, New Jersey, 1998.
13. Fleming W.K. and Sliwinski Z.J. *Use of bentonite in bored pile construction.* CIRIA, London, 1977, Publication PG3.
14. Xanthakos P. *Slurry walls.* McGraw-Hill, New York, 1979.
15. Corbett, B.O. *et al.* A load bearing wall at Kensington Town Hall, London. *Proc. Conf. Diaphragm Walls and Anchorages*, London, 1975, 57–62. Institution of Civil Engineers, London, 1975.
16. Puller M. J. Slurry trench stability. Theoretical and practical aspects. *Ground Engng*, 1974, 7, Sept., 34–36.
17. Nash J.K. and Jones, G.F. The support of trenches using fluid mud. *Proc. Symp. Grouts and Drilling Muds.* Butterworth, London, 1963, 177–180.
18. Muller-Kirchenbauer H. Stability of slurry trenches. *Proc. 5th Euro. Conf. SMFE*, Madrid, 1972, Vol. 3, 543–553. Sociedad Española de Mechánica del Suelo y Cimentaciones, Madrid, 1972.
19. Piaskowski A. and Kowalewski Z. Applications of thixotropic clay suspensions. *Proc. 6th Int. Conf. S.M.F.E.*, Montreal, 1965, Vol. 2, 526–529. University of Toronto Press, 1965.
20. Fernandez R. Discussion. *Proc. 5th Euro. Conf. S.M.F.E.* Madrid, 1972, Vol. 2, 366–373. Sociedad Española de Mechánica del Suelo y Cimentaciones, Madrid, 1972.
21. Huder J. Stability of bentonite slurry trenches with some experience in Swiss practice. *Proc. 5th Euro Conference. S.M.F.E.*, Madrid, 1972, Vol. 1, 517–522. Sociedad Española de Mechánica del Suelo y Cimentaciones, Madrid, 1972.
22. Mastikian L. Nouveau Port de Bristol. *Proc. 6th Euro. Conf. S.M.F.E.*, Vienna, 1976, Vol. 2.2, 41–44. Austrian National Committee, Vienna, 1976.
23. Cambefort H. *Géotechnique de l'ingeniur.* Editions Eyrolles, Paris, 1972.
24. *Specification for piling and embedded retaining walls.* Institution of Civil Engineers, London, 1996.
25. EN 1538: 2000. *Execution of special geotechnical works: diaphragm walls.* British Standards Institution, London, 2000.
26. Colas des Francs E. Prefasil prefabricated diaphragm walls. *Proc. Conf. Diaphragm Walls and Anchorages*, London, 1975, 81–88. Institution of Civil Engineers, London, 1975.

27. Gysi H.J. *et al.* Prestressed diaphragm walls. *Proc. Euro. Conf. S.M.F.E.*, Vienna, 1976, Vol. 1.1, 141–148. Austrian National Committee, Vienna, 1976.

28. Fuchsberger M. and Gysi H.J. Post tensioned diaphragm wall at Irlams o' th' Height, Manchester. *Proc. 8th Conf. F.I.P.*, London, 1978, supplementary paper. F.I.P., Paris, 1978.

29. Barley A.D. Ten thousand anchorages in rock, part 3. *Ground Engineering*, **8**, Nov. 1988, 35–39.

30. Glass P. and Stones C. Construction of Westminster Station London. *Proc. Instn Civ. Engrs, Structures and Buildings*, 2001, **146**, Aug., 237–252.

31. *Essential guide to the ICE specification.* Federation of Piling Specialists/Institution of Civil Engineers. Thos. Telford, London, 1999.

Bibliography

Banks D.J. *et al.* Construction of Riding Mill Weir. *Proc. Instn Civ. Engrs*, Part 1, 1985, **77**, Feb., 195–216.

Bell A.L. The lateral pressure and resistance of clay and the supporting power of clay foundations. *Proc. Instn Civ. Engrs*, 1915, **199**, Feb., 233–272.

BS 6349. *Code of practice for maritime structures.* British Standards Institution, London, 1984.

BS 8004. *Code of practice for foundations.* British Standards Institution, London, 1986.

BS 8002. *Code of practice for earth retaining structures.* British Standards Institution, London, 1994.

BS EN 12063. Sheet piling. British Standards Institution, London, 1999.

BS EN 1536. Bored piles. British Standards Institution, London, 1999.

Calkin D.W. and Mundy J.K. Temporary works for the pumping stations at Plover Cove reservoir, Hong Kong. *Proc. Instn Civ. Engrs*, Part 1, 1987, **82**, Dec., 1121–1144.

Design manual No. 7. *Soil mechanics, foundations and earth structures.* US Navy, Washington, DC, 1982.

Fenoux G.Y. Le realisation fouilles en site urbain. *Travaux*, Parts 437 and 438, 1971, Aug.–Sept., 18–37.

Puller M.J. The waterproofness of structural diaphragm walls. *Proc. Instn Civ. Engrs, Geotech. Engng*, 1994, **107**, Jan., 47–57.

Sarsby R.W. Noise from sheet piling operations – M67 Denton relief road. *Proc. Instn Civ. Engrs*, Part 1, 1982, **72**, Feb., 15–26.

5 Design of vertical soil support

This chapter addresses the key design items of earth (and water) pressure on a vertical wall and the analysis of the wall to withstand these pressures. Cantilevered, single-propped (or anchored) and multi-propped walls will be considered for both temporary and permanent works.

Geotechnical categories for excavation works are defined in Eurocode 7 (EC7)[1] as follows.

- *Category 1*. Walls that are small and relatively simple structures with a retained height not exceeding 2 m.
- *Category 2*. Conventional structures with no abnormal risks or unusually difficult ground or loading conditions. These walls require site-specific geotechnical data to be obtained and analyses to be made.
- *Category 3*. Walls or parts of structures which fall outside categories 1 and 2 and include very large structures, 'one-off' structures and those involving high risk such as unusual ground conditions or loading (for instance, seismicity).

The design of a typically deep wall for a basement, cofferdam or cut-and-cover structure will require decisions on walling method, use of props or anchors, methods of dewatering/recharge, consideration of repropping during construction, acceptable safety factors and allowable settlement and deformation.

The wall design will require the consideration of both ultimate and serviceability limit states. In practical terms the following matters will need to be addressed.

(*a*) At ultimate limit state:
  (i) overall stability; strut anchor or waling failure, bending stress failure in the sheeting, passive failure of soil below successive stages of excavation, failure by lack of vertical equilibrium of the wall
  (ii) foundation heave – in soft clays, risk of failure by unloading– bearing capacity failure
  (iii) hydraulic failure – piping in cohesionless soils with high external groundwater table.
  Walls should be designed, wherever possible, so that adequate warning is given in advance of collapse by visible signs. The risk of progressive failure of retaining structures needs to be particularly addressed, especially at the temporary works stage.
(*b*) At serviceability limit state:
  (i) deformation of sheeting – avoidance of excessive reduction in working space or space for permanent structure at construction stage
  (ii) excessive soil movements behind the wall or sheeting; vertical settlements not to exceed the permitted settlements of existing structures, services or highways

(iii) unacceptable leakage through or beneath the wall
(iv) unacceptable flexural cracking of the structure
(v) unacceptable cracking in reinforced concrete walls. Crack control requirements in the UK are specified in BS 8110[2] or where more rigorous water resistance is needed in BS 8007[3]. For highway structures in the UK BS 5400[4] and Highways Agency BD 42/00[5] apply.

The following practical points arise concerning wall and soil movement:

- The magnitude of movements in walls and retained soil is dependent in large measure on workmanship standards during wall installation, excavation and wall support works.
- Generally, flexible walls with many propping levels will give similar displacements to stiff walls with few props.
- Wall embedment depth below formation level influences soil deformation, particularly in soft clays.
- Stiffness of propping systems influences soil deformation.
- Top-downwards construction minimizes soil deformation and settlements.
- Installation of a temporary or permanent support of high stiffness at shallow depth in an excavation is an effective control of wall deformation and soil deformation.
- Ground movement cannot be estimated with precision. As a broad indication of movements due to wall installation the following may be helpful.
  In stiff clay: For bored piles: vertical settlement at wall, 0·04% of depth.
                    For diaphragm walls: vertical settlement at wall, 0·05% of wall depth.

The distance behind the wall to negligible settlement is approximately twice wall depth. Similarly, broad indications of patterns of wall deflection and settlements can be obtained from empirical results published by Peck[6], Clough et al.[7], Clough and O'Rourke[8], St John et al.[9], Carder[10], Fernie and Suckling[11], Carder et al.[12] and Long[13].

For excavations in stiff clay, observed soil settlement at the wall due to excavation in front of the wall is generally within the range 0·1% of excavation depth for high-stiffness walls to 0·3% of excavation depth for low-stiffness walls. In sands, a limited number of observations show a similar vertical settlement at the wall of 0·1 to 0·3% of excavation depth. (The Author's experience of several excavations to 20 m depth in medium dense silty sands in Saudi Arabia using anchored king post walls as support shows consistent vertical settlement at the wall of less than 0·1% following excavation to full depth.)

Earth pressures: limiting horizontal pressure

Mohr's circle of stress can be used to illustrate graphically the limiting horizontal soil pressures which can be generated in active or passive states at either side of a retaining wall. The pressures will be considered in terms of effective stress, ignoring, for the time being, the effects of wall friction or wall adhesion.

The problem of assessing earth pressures can be solved using the Coulomb equation for shear strength $\tau' = c' + \sigma' \tan \phi'$, where c' represents effective soil cohesion, σ' represents effective vertical stress and ϕ' represents the angle of shearing resistance in terms of effective stress. Figure 5.1 shows the introduction of effective stress parameters, the total vertical stresses and

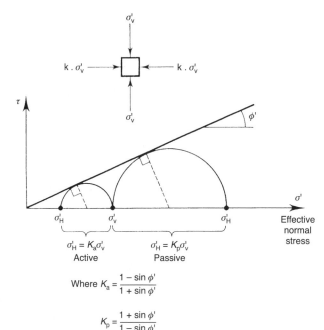

Fig. 5.1. Mohr's circle values of limit pressures and values of K_a and K_p

water pressures (and hence effective vertical stresses) to calculate active and passive earth pressure according to whether horizontal stress is less than or greater than vertical stress. Mohr's circles are seen to touch the failure envelope to give limiting values in the extremes of minimum and maximum horizontal stresses.

Using active and passive earth pressures coefficients,

$$\sigma'_H = K_a \sigma'_v \tag{39}$$

and

$$\sigma'_H = K_p \sigma'_v \tag{40}$$

where

$$K_a = \frac{1 - \sin \phi'}{1 + \sin \phi'} \tag{41}$$

and

$$K_p = \frac{1 + \sin \phi'}{1 - \sin \phi'} \tag{42}$$

The values of ϕ' and c' can be obtained for clay samples from drained triaxial tests or undrained tests with pore-water pressure measurement. The effects of stress level, rate of strain for testing, the degree of weathering and of sample swelling before the test, will all influence the test result. When test results are not available for ϕ', the relationship in Table 5.1 may be used for conservative values. The design parameters ϕ' and c' will cause considerable variation in values of limiting soil pressure, and while it is not unusual to assume $c' = 0$, the effect of this assumption is to reduce to low values the limiting passive pressures immediately below dredge or formation level. In turn, this tends to produce high wall or sheeting moments and increased strut or anchor loads near this level.

The values of ϕ' in cohesionless soils should be based on in situ tests where possible. The relationship between standard penetration resistance and ϕ' is

Table 5.1 Estimation of ϕ' for cohesive soils[17]

Plasticity index	ϕ'
15	30°
20	28°
25	27°
30	25°
40	22°
50	20°
80	15°

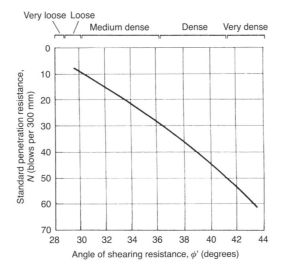

Fig. 5.2. Relationship between standard penetration resistance and ϕ' [17]

Table 5.2 Estimation of ϕ' for weak rocks [19]

Stratum	ϕ'
Chalk	35°
Clayey marl	28°
Sandy marl	33°
Weak sandstone	42°
Weak siltstone	35°
Weak mudstone	28°

Notes. The presence of a preferred orientation of joints, bedding or cleavage in a direction near that of a possible failure plane may require a reduction in the above values, especially if the discontinuities are filled with weaker materials.

Chalk is defined here as unweathered medium-to-hard, rubbly or blocky chalk.

shown in Fig. 5.2. Table 5.2 gives approximate values for the effective angle of shearing resistance of soft rocks considered, somewhat conservatively, as a mass of granular fragments.

Horizontal earth pressure: at rest

In an undisturbed soil mass the horizontal earth pressure, the at rest pressure, is $K_0\sigma'_v$, where K_0 is the coefficient of earth pressure at rest and σ'_v is the effective vertical stress. For normally-consolidated soils K_0 is approximately equal to the empirical expression

$$K_{ONC} = \frac{\sigma'_H}{\sigma'_v} = 1 - \sin\phi'. \tag{43}$$

For normally-consolidated clay K_{ONC} lies in the range 0·55 to 0·65. For over-consolidated clays the removal of considerable overburden pressures within geological time leaves horizontal stress as the major principal stress. The reduction in vertical stress is shown at any depth by the over-consolidation ratio (OCR), which is the ratio of the maximum vertical effective stress ever experienced by the soil to the current vertical effective stress at that depth. The value of σ'_v can be obtained from laboratory consolidation tests and the general relationship between K_0 and the OCR is given in Fig. 5.3 after Brooker and Ireland[14]. The maximum value of K_0 may lie in the range 2 to

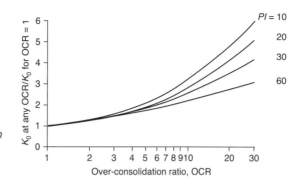

Fig. 5.3. Relationship between coefficient of earth pressure at rest K_0 and over-consolidation ratio[14]

3 for some clays, reducing with depth since OCR reduces with depth. K_0 can also be estimated from pressuremeter test results.

Horizontal earth pressure based on long-term, drained, effective stress values

The limiting horizontal active and passive earth pressures acting on the wall at any depth z are given, respectively, by

$$p'_a = K_a\sigma'_v = K_a(\gamma z + q - u) \tag{44}$$

and

$$p'_p = K_p\sigma'_v = K_p(\gamma z + q - u) \tag{45}$$

and for a soil with a cohesion intercept

$$p'_a = K_a(\gamma z + q - u) - 2c'(K_a)^{1/2} \tag{46}$$

and

$$p'_p = K_p(\gamma z + q - u) - 2c'(K_p)^{1/2} \tag{47}$$

where γ is the bulk soil density (saturated density if below water level), q is the surcharge on ground surface, and u is the pore-water pressure. These values, known as Rankine values, are subject to change when the effects of wall friction and wall adhesion are considered. Walls are not made of perfectly smooth material and wall friction δ and adhesion c_w vary soil stresses proportionately.

The limiting effective active and passive pressures acting horizontally at a depth z are:

$$p'_a = K_a(\gamma z + q - u) - K_{ac}c' \tag{48}$$

and

$$p'_p = K_p(\gamma z + q - u) - K_{pc}c' \tag{49}$$

where

$$K_{ac} = 2\left(K_a\left(1 - \frac{c_w}{c'}\right)\right)^{1/2} \tag{50}$$

and

$$K_{pc} = 2\left(K_p\left(1 - \frac{c_w}{c'}\right)\right)^{1/2} \tag{51}$$

and c' is the effective shear strength.

The pore-water pressure is added to the effective horizontal earth pressure to give the sum of earth and water pressure: $p_a = p'_a + u$ and $p_p = p'_p + u$.

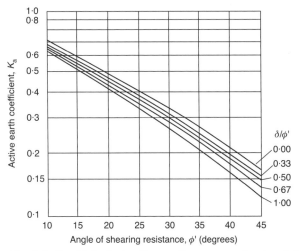

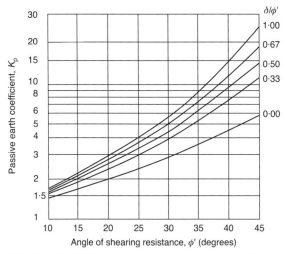

Fig. 5.4. Coefficient of active earth pressure (horizontal component) for a horizontal retained surface[15]

Fig. 5.5. Coefficient of passive earth pressure (horizontal component) for a horizontal retained surface[15]

The earth pressure coefficients K_a and K_p have been calculated for various curved failure surfaces; those frequently used are due to Caquot and Kerisel[15] and are based on a logarithmic spiral surface as shown in Figs. 5.4 and 5.5. The coefficients derived from these figures have been corrected to give horizontal pressures although the actual pressures are inclined at the angle of wall friction δ to the horizontal. Value of K_{ac} and K_{pc} can be calculated from the expressions above.

Horizontal earth pressure based on short-term undrained stress values

In fine-grained soils such as fine silts and clays, the relatively low permeability only allows slow changes in moisture content, pore pressure and overall volume. The instant that load is applied, pore pressure increases and the shear strength of the soil, which depends on the locked-in effective stress, is only able to increase slowly as pore pressures reduce. This immediate shear strength, the undrained value c_u, applies before any volume change and pore pressures alter or, expressed more exactly, the value of c_u can only be used where a new system of boundary stresses is imposed but prior to any dissipation of the new excess pore-water pressures. The undrained shear strength c_u is only correctly used immediately load is applied and it is strictly illogical to use it as soon as pore pressures change. As effective stresses change with pore pressure, shear strength also changes. In clay soils, where the retaining wall structure deforms and attempts to move away from the retained soil bulk, negative pore pressures are generated in the retained soil as excavation proceeds in front of the wall. In highly fissured or laminated clays the reduction in negative pore pressure may proceed relatively quickly and the original value of c_u quickly becomes inapplicable. The use of c_u in such clays can therefore become over-optimistic in retaining wall analysis when the effective stress (on which soil strength depends) reduces as negative pore pressure relaxes.

In soft and very soft homogeneous clays which do not benefit from drainage paths due to fissuring and jointing, low overall permeability of the soil fabric may prevent more efficient change in pore pressure, and the use of c_u, although strictly applicable at the instant of stress change prior to pore pressure change, can be more satisfactorily relied upon. Indeed, for retaining walls founded in soft clays it is prudent to obtain both drained and undrained soil strengths and undertake analysis of both total and effective stress conditions. Temporary works design in these soils, in which the wall structure may have a limited design life, say, of six months, may therefore use total stress methods with some confidence, and the design parameter of undrained shear strength can be conveniently and accurately obtained from in situ shear tests, such as vane tests. Where such short-term conditions do not apply, either by the greater permanence of the temporary wall or due to its role in the permanent structure, analysis of drained effective stress becomes necessary. The choice between the two methods, undrained or drained, depends strictly on the rate of change of pore pressure which, in turn, depends on the permeability of the structure, although it must be restated that the undrained analysis is only strictly applicable immediately before any dissipation commences. In practice, especially for small schemes, sufficient undrained shear measurements may be more readily available than test results from drained samples. However, the availability of test results should not excuse the application of an illogical method of analysis. The short-term undrained method is therefore presented here with the recommendation that its use should be restricted to soft clay conditions for temporary works of short duration. Schemes of longer duration should be checked by both drained and undrained analyses.

In terms of undrained conditions the limiting horizontal active and passive earth pressures acting on the wall at any depth z are given by

$$p_a = K_a \sigma_v - K_{ac} c_u = K_a(\gamma z + q) - K_{ac} c_u \tag{52}$$

and

$$p_p = K_p \sigma_v - K_{pc} c_u = K_p(\sigma_v + q) - K_{pc} c_u. \tag{53}$$

The pressure coefficients are

$$K_{ac} = 2\left(1 + \frac{c_w}{c_u}\right)^{1/2} \tag{54}$$

and

$$K_{pc} = 2\left(1 + \frac{c_w}{c_u}\right)^{1/2}. \tag{55}$$

Tension cracks

The active pressure near ground level will be a minimum for the retaining wall and, in cohesive soils, surface tensions within the clay can cause cracks which can fill with groundwater or rain water. In this case, the water pressure within the potential crack should be allowed as a pressure on the back of the wall. Wall adhesion will not apply over the depth of the crack, which is $(2c_u - q)/\gamma$.

Minimum values of calculated active pressure

In the UK the prolonged use, from 1951 until 1994, of the Civil Engineering Code of Practice for earth-retaining structures[16] indicated both the sound principles on which it was based and the difficulties which have been experienced in agreeing revisions to it. Although the Code was based on calculation of earth pressure in terms of total stress and undrained shear values, it prudently recommended the use of minimum active pressures for design irrespective of those calculated from test values of c_u using the expression $p_{an} = K_a \sigma_v - K_{ac} c_u$.

The Code stated that for cohesive soils the methods of calculation were not final. In the design of structures to retain cohesive soils, a suitable addition should be made to the calculated active pressure of the soil in order to provide for uncertainties. Where, as may be the case with stiffer clays, the total pressure on the wall as calculated according to the Code was small, the value of the total pressure to be assumed for the purposes of design should not be less than that found by assuming the horizontal pressure at any depth to be that due to a fluid with a density of $5\,\text{kN/m}^3$. This safety net for minimum pressure at the active side of the wall was most prudent but did not find mention in some later Codes.

Softening of clays

The process of clay softening is accelerated over time by tension cracks near the ground surface, by the joints and fissures which frequently occur in stiff, over-consolidated clays, and by the laminations of silt or sandy silt partings that can occur in all clays. These routes for easier passage of water not only increase the permeability of the soil fabric but can form failure surfaces themselves of softened planes of clay dividing stiffer, unsoftened blocks of clay bounded by softened, lubricated surfaces. The changes in pore-water pressure as these pressures equalize with hydrostatic groundwater levels are therefore also associated with a loss of clay strength due to softening along surfaces such as joints, fissures, pre-existing shear surfaces, laminations and tensile zones. For this reason it is often prudent to assume a complete loss of cohesive strength in terms of effective stress as the clay softens with time along preferred drainage surfaces.

Wall friction and wall adhesion

The effect of assumptions regarding wall friction in granular soils and adhesion in clay soils on calculated values of active and passive pressure is considerable, and while it is self-evident that wall surfaces are not smooth, design values of friction and adhesion should be chosen carefully. The mobilization of wall friction, to reduce earth pressures on the active side and increase earth pressure on the passive side, necessitates the downwards movement of a soil wedge on the active side and the upwards movement of a similar soil wedge on the opposite, passive side, as shown in Fig. 5.6. Important changes to these relative soil and wall movements are caused by the downwards vertical wall movement due to vertical loads on the wall and the vertical load components of inclined pre-loaded ground anchors, both of which tend to mobilize passive wall friction/adhesion but tend to reduce active friction/adhesion.

Typical values of active wall friction and adhesion as quoted in Codes and values for both active and passive friction and adhesion in the CIRIA report for sheet piled cofferdams[17] are shown in Tables 5.3 and 5.4. These values are all based for wall friction on peak values of ϕ and it is understandable that some conservatism should apply since the peak values themselves may not apply. More logically, it may be prudent to use $\delta_{\text{max}} = \phi'_{\text{crit}}$ if the critical state value is known. If the wall surface texture is less than the typical particle size of the soil (D_{50}), lower values of δ would apply.

The relative movement between wall and soil necessary to generate wall friction or adhesion may not always occur; where the toe of the wall is

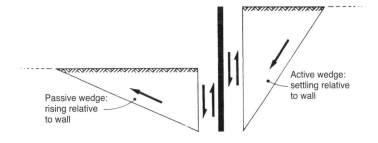

Fig. 5.6. Wall friction acting on active and passive soil wedges[48]

Passive wedge: rising relative to wall

Active wedge: settling relative to wall

Table 5.3 Values of active wall friction angle and adhesion

Construction	Wall friction angle, δ	Wall adhesion
Concrete, brick	20°	Where c_w is less than 50 kN/m² use $c_w = c_u$
Steel piling, tar/bitumen coated	30°	Where walling or sheeting does not penetrate any appreciable depth use $c_w = 0$
Uncoated sheet piles	15°	Where $c_w > 50$ kN/m² use $c_w = 50$ kN/m²

Table 5.4 Active and passive values of wall friction/adhesion

	Wall friction angle, δ	Wall adhesion
Active	0.67ϕ	$0.5c'$ or $0.5c_u \not> 50$ kN/m²
Passive	0.5ϕ	$0.5c'$ or $0.5c_u \not> 25$ kN/m²

founded on hard rock, wall friction/adhesion values quoted in Table 5.4 should be reduced by 50% for dense granular materials and stiff over-consolidated clay. For overlying loose granular soil, where the wall is founded on rock, wall friction/adhesion should be ignored. For anchored walls where there is a tendency for the wall to move downwards relative to the soil, zero wall friction should be allowed.

Neither wall adhesion nor wall friction should be allowed in granular sub-soils where the proximity of machinery, railways or vehicular traffic causes vibrations which could be transmitted through the subsoil to the wall surface.

With cast in situ reinforced concrete diaphragm walls and reinforced concrete piled walls cast under bentonite slurry, values of wall friction/adhesion for active and passive pressure can be assumed to be similar to those for concrete walls given in Table 5.3.

Magnitude of movement needed to mobilize limit pressures

The variation in horizontal pressure, either active or passive, generated by movement of the wall away from or towards the soil mass, is shown in Fig. 5.7. The curve, first derived by Terzaghi and Peck[18] was based on tests in dense sand. Two conclusions are evident:

- the passive coefficient is much higher than the active coefficient
- the deformation needed to fully mobilize the limit passive pressure is much greater than that required to fully mobilize the limit active pressure.

The relative deformation needed to fully mobilize K_a and K_p by means of the stress path followed by a soil element behind the wall in both normally- and

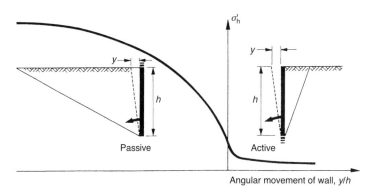

Fig. 5.7. Relationship between strain required to mobilize active and passive pressure for medium dense sand[48]

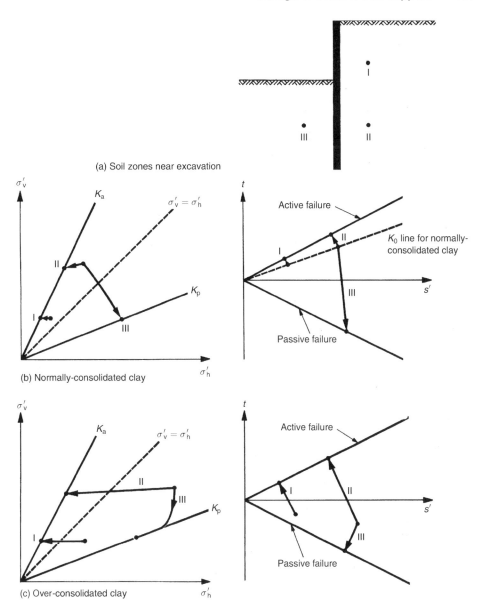

(a) Soil zones near excavation

(b) Normally-consolidated clay

(c) Over-consolidated clay

Fig. 5.8. Stress paths followed for elements behind and in front of a retaining wall in normally- and over-consolidated clays[48]

over-consolidated clay conditions is shown in Fig. 5.8. On the active side there is no change in vertical stress due to excavation, while on the passive side the effective stress path in drained loading may take varying directions depending on the relative importance of the relief of overburden to excavation and the horizontal pressure exerted on the wall.

The stress change needed to fail a normally-consolidated clay in active pressure is much less than that required to fail the same clay in passive pressure. The stress path for over-consolidated clay shows the reverse to be true, however. Terzaghi and Peck's[18] plot of wall movement against mobilized pressure for dense sand may not therefore, accurately show the strains necessary to generate limit active and passive pressures in both normally- and over-consolidated clays.

BS 8002[19] followed the concept of limit state design, with greater emphasis on wall conditions at the serviceability limit state than collapse conditions at the ultimate limit state. The basis of this method is the reduction of soil peak shear strength values on both the active and passive sides of the wall, to values which would be representative of mobilized shear strengths with the permitted wall movement. BS 8002[19] specified that where wall displacements are required to be less than 0·5% of the wall height, the representative undrained shear strength should be divided by a mobilization factor M not less than 1·5. For designs using effective stress values, the value of M was specified to be 1·2 to reduce horizontal wall movements to 0·5% of wall height. For effective stress design, the calculation of wall equilibrium and the structural components of the wall was specified to be based on the lesser of:

(*a*) the representative peak strength of the soil divided by a factor $M = 1·2$

$$\text{design } \tan \phi' = \frac{\text{representative } \tan \phi'_{max}}{M}$$

$$\text{design } c' = \frac{\text{representative } c'}{M}$$

(*b*) the representative critical-state strength of the soil.

The earth pressures on the active side are thus increased and similarly those on the passive side are reduced at serviceability state by the use of the reduced peak shear strength. The Code concludes that structural design of the wall components can then usually be made without the application of partial load factors to bending moments and internal structural forces.

This principle of design using soil strengths that can be mobilized at working conditions in the serviceability limit state is logically extended in BS 8002 to consideration of wall friction and wall adhesion. It recommends that the design value of friction or adhesion at the interface with the wall should be the lesser of either the values obtained from tests or 75% of the design shear strength to be mobilized in the soil itself, that is, using

$$\text{design } \tan \delta = 0·75 \text{ design } \tan \phi'$$

$$\text{design } c_w = 0·75 \text{ design } c_u$$

and since for the soil mass $M = 1·2$

$$\text{design } \tan \phi' = \frac{\text{representative } \tan \phi'}{1·2}$$

this is equivalent to

$$\frac{\text{design } \delta}{\text{representative } \phi'} \simeq \frac{2}{3}$$

and similarly, in total stress analysis

$$\frac{\text{design } c_w}{\text{representative } c_u} = 0·5 \text{ after taking } M = 1·5.$$

The overall effect of reducing peak shear strengths to shear strengths which are mobilized in working conditions by using such M values as are specified in the Code may not be necessary when walls are designed in stiff over-consolidated clays, where relatively small movements are necessary to mobilize limiting active and passive pressures. On the other hand, the recommendation that bending moments and internal forces derived from earth pressures calculated from mobilized soil strengths (peak strengths reduced by the mobilization factor M), without the application of a further partial safety factor on earth pressures allowed in designs based on ultimate structural strengths, may not accurately reflect the variations in load that occur in practice along the length of a wall.

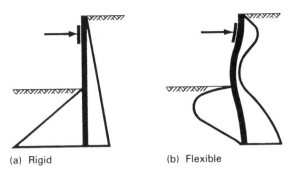

(a) Rigid   (b) Flexible

Fig. 5.9. Influence of wall flexibility on pressure distribution: (a) rigid wall; (b) flexible wall[48]

BS 8002 also specified that in checking the wall stability and soil deformation all walls should be designed for a minimum design surcharge loading of $10 \, kN/m^2$ and a minimum depth of additional unplanned excavation in front of the wall. This additional design depth was specified to be not less than 0·5 m or 10% of the total height retained for cantilever walls or of the height retained below the lowest support level for propped or anchored walls. It should be noted that BS 8002 was originally applicable to walls up to about 8 m high, and no differentiation is made between temporary and permanent walls. A subsequent revision increased this wall depth to 15 m. The imposition of such rules for all walls irrespective of design life would appear to be over-stringent.

Wall flexibility

The stiffer the wall, the greater the earth pressure it attracts and, conversely, the greater flexure of the wall the less pressure (and moment) induced in it by the soil it retains. This phenomenon, originally demonstrated in model tests on an anchored wall by Rowe[20] will be referred to in greater detail later in this chapter.

Consider, however, the difference in deformed shape of a relatively stiff anchored wall and that of an anchored flexible wall, as shown in Fig. 5.9. The flexible wall distorts outwards by a considerable amount at mid-span relative to the stiff wall, causing a reduction in pressure and an effective reduction in vertical span of the wall due to a rise in elevation of the centre of passive support below excavation level. Anchor loads and pressure below excavation level therefore both increase, but bending moment in the wall reduces due to both earth pressure reduction at mid-span and the reduction in the span itself. Due to the movement of the flexible wall away from the soil at mid-span, the soil tends to arch vertically and, providing neither the anchor nor the passive support below formation level yield once mobilized, the abutments to the arch sustain more load and relieve soil pressure from mid-span.

Surcharge loads

The effects of additional loads, surcharging the wall, must be taken into account at both ultimate and serviceability limit states. Loads due to adjacent highways, railways, variations in ground level, storage areas for building materials and plant loads need to be taken into account.

Highway traffic loading
In the UK, guidance on highway traffic loading is given in the publication BD 37/01[21]. Two categories of loading are specified, HA loading that normally occurs on highways and HB loading, corresponding to abnormal

vehicle loads such as industrial loads. The number of HB units is generally specified. The loadings may be summarized as follows.

- HB loading (45 units):   equivalent surcharge $= 20\,\text{kN/m}^2$
- HB loading (37 units):   equivalent surcharge $= 16\,\text{kN/m}^2$
- HB loading (30 units):   equivalent surcharge $= 12\,\text{kN/m}^2$
- HA loading: equivalent surcharge $= 10\,\text{kN/m}^2$

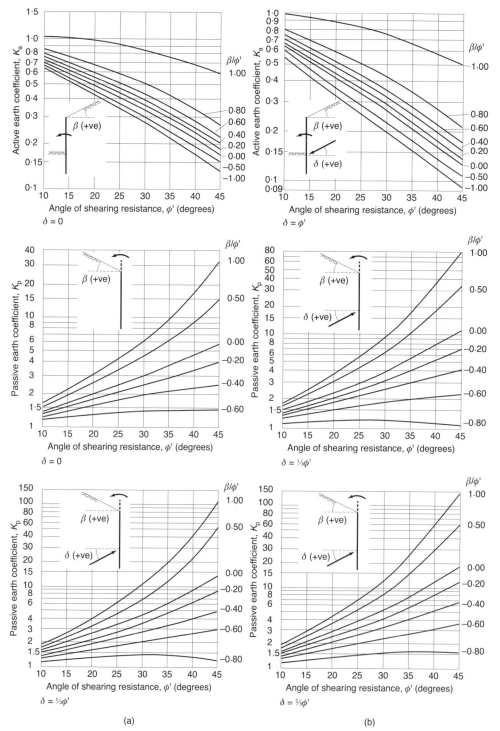

Fig. 5.10. Coefficients of earth pressure (horizontal component) for vertical walls with inclined backfill for varying wall friction δ: (a) active; (b) passive[15]

Railway loading

Railway universal loading (RU) allows for all combinations of rail traffic which currently runs on UK track – or is expected to run in the future. RL is a reduced loading, for lighter traffic, such as in use on underground railways. Both loads are applied over the track width, overall the length of sleepers. The loadings are:

- RU loading: equivalent surcharge $= 50 \, kN/m^2$
- RL loading: equivalent surcharge $= 30 \, kN/m^2$

Surcharge loading: sloping ground

The effect of a sloping ground surface can be taken into account using curves due to Caquot and Kerisel[15] reproduced in Fig. 5.10, giving values of K_a and K_p for vertical walls, inclined backfill and wall friction varying from $\delta = 0$ to $\delta = \phi'$. The effect of layered strata behind the wall should be taken into account in calculations by using modified coefficients for each layer from the curves. The values presented assume that the sloping ground extends a sufficient distance from the wall to exceed the lateral dimension of the potential critical slip plane of the failure wedge (approximately at an angle of $45° + \phi/2$ to the horizontal from the toe of the wall for the active case, and $45° - \phi/2$ for the passive case).

The CIRIA report[17] gives a simple adjustment to the pressure diagrams (Fig. 5.11(a) and (b)) to show the effect of berms, on the active and passive sides of the wall in cohesionless soil. The report notes that the risk for sliding failure should be checked at the base of the berm, especially where the berm soil has a higher angle of shearing resistance than the soil beneath it. Where a gravel berm overlies a stiff clay, the report suggests it may be too optimistic to use the undrained clay strength in checking sliding.

The NAVFAC design manual[22] gives a graphical method for the calculation of passive soil resistance due to an earth berm, as shown in Fig. 5.11(c).

Surcharge loading: point loads and line loads

The CIRIA report[17] reproduced a simple method due to Krey for use in granular soils. The horizontal pressures caused by concentrated point and line loads as estimated by Krey are shown in Fig. 5.12 and should be added to the earth pressure diagram.

An alternative method of computing the effects of point and line loads by Terzaghi was reported in the NAVFAC design manual[22] and was commented upon in the CIRIA report[17]. According to the CIRIA report the method, a modified Boussinesq distribution taking into account field and model measurements, possibly underpredicts the pressure and tends to place the centre of pressure influence too low down the wall. Some caution should be applied, therefore, in the use of the method where the applied loads are high in relation to the weight of soil retained. It should be noted, however, that the method presumes an unyielding rigid wall and the lateral pressures are already approximately double the values obtained from elastic equations. Design charts from NAVFAC[22] for line and point loads are reproduced in Fig. 5.13.

Surcharge loading: uniform rectangular surface load

The NAVFAC design guide also provides the means to estimate the lateral pressure on an unyielding wall due to a uniform rectangular load on the surface at the rear of the wall, after Goldberg et al.[23] (Fig. 5.14). The guide comments that any yield of the wall during application of the load will tend to reduce the pressures calculated from the values given by Goldberg et al.

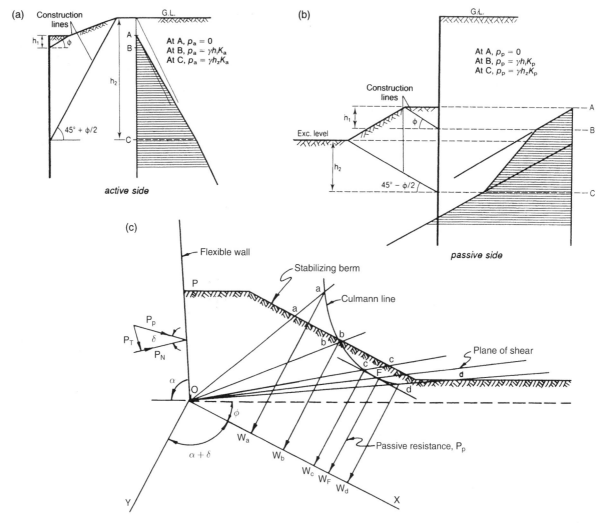

1. Draw berm to scale.
2. Layout OX from point O at angle ϕ below horizontal.
3. Layout OY from point O at angle $(\alpha + \delta)$ below OX.
4. Assume failure surfaces originating at point O and passing through points a, b, c, etc.
5. Compute the weight of each failure wedge.
6. Layout the weight of each failure wedge along OX to a convenient scale.
7. Draw a line parallel to OY for each failure wedge from its weight plotted on OX to its failure plane (extrapolated where necessary).
8. Connect the intersecting points from 7 above with a smooth curve – this is the Culmann curve. Draw a tangent to this curve which is also parallel to OX.
9. Through the tangent point F, draw a line parallel to OY to intersect OX at W_F. Distance FW_F is the value of P_P in the weight scale.
10. Normal component of the passive resistance, $P_N = P_p \cos \delta$.
11. To compute pressure distribution on the wall, assume a triangular distribution.

Fig. 5.11. (a), (b) Pressure diagrams showing the effect of sloping ground on the active and passive sides of the wall[17]. (c) Culmann method for determining passive resistance of earth berm[22]

Wall movement

The effect of wall movement on lateral earth pressures should be restated because of its vital effect on both active and passive pressures. Earth pressures at rest are reduced to limiting active values by movement of the wall away from the soil; much larger movements are needed to increase the at-rest pressure to limiting passive values. The relationship between wall rotation and the coefficient of earth pressure for sands is reproduced in Fig. 5.15. The curve can be used to assess the movement needed to obtain limit pressures in sands of varying compaction state. The NAVFAC guide[22] also suggests

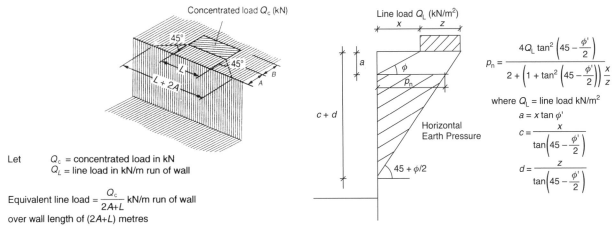

Let Q_c = concentrated load in kN
Q_L = line load in kN/m run of wall

Equivalent line load = $\dfrac{Q_c}{2A+L}$ kN/m run of wall

over wall length of $(2A+L)$ metres

Fig. 5.12. Effect on surcharge loading of point and line loads[17]

that the effects of wall translation on limit pressures can be assessed by assuming the effect of translation is equivalent to the movement at the top of the wall due to rotation, as shown in Fig. 5.15.

The extent of wall movement relative to the retained soil therefore determines the proportion of the limit pressure which applies. This movement may be derived from elastic deflection of the wall or sheeting itself, the compression which occurs in strutting or raking shores (or the curtailment of such movement by pre-loaded supports or anchors), the movement needed to mobilize passive resistance of a soil at an intermediate stage of excavation in front of the wall, or the rotation or translation of a rigid wall.

With the exception of the methods specified in BS 8002[19] the above means of calculating earth pressures have led to designs based on limit pressures where these do not necessarily apply if the extent of proposed wall movements do not justify them. Soil pressures based on the stiffness of the wall, its support and the soil itself are evaluated more realistically by soil/structure analyses based either on the Winkler spring theory or by finite element methods. These methods are referred to again later in this chapter.

Design calculation according to Eurocode 7

Eurocode defines design procedures under four headings:

- by calculation
- by prescriptive measures
- from results of load tests or tests on experimental models
- by observational techniques.

New meanings are given to words within Eurocode 7 as follows.

- *actions* – foundation loadings
- *permanent actions* – dead loads, typically weights of structures and installations
- *variable actions* – imposed loads, typically wind or snow loads
- *accidental actions* – vehicle impacts or explosions
- *transient actions* – a classification related to soil response, for example, wind loading
- *persistent actions* – a classification related to soil response, for example, structural or construction loads.

Eurocode 7 makes use of partial safety factors to allow for uncertainties in the magnitude and combination of loads (actions) and characteristic values of soil and rock parameters obtained from field and laboratory testing.

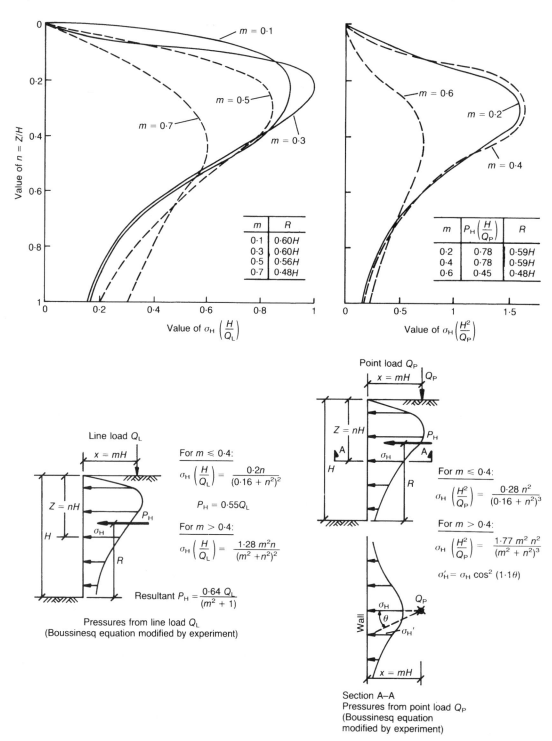

Fig. 5.13. Horizontal pressures on a rigid wall from line loads (left) and point loads (right)[22]

The design values of vertically applied actions V_d to be used in geotechnical design are calculated from the expression $V_d = F_k \times \gamma_F$, where F_k is the characteristic load and γ_F is the partial factor of safety for the applied action.

V_d must be equal to or less than the foundation design bearing resistance R_d. The value of V_d is calculated from characteristic soil strengths also with a partial factor applied. The design value of the material properties X_d is

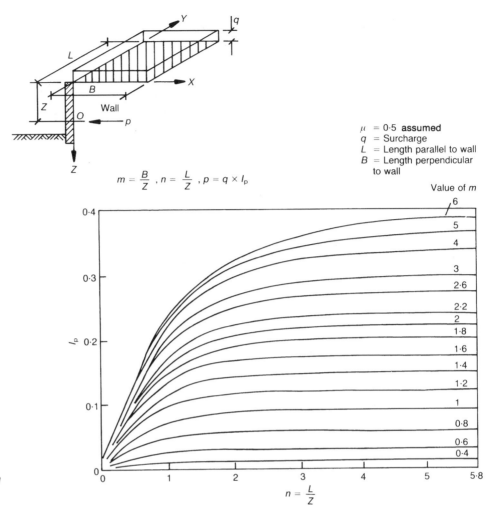

$$m = \frac{B}{Z}, \; n = \frac{L}{Z}, \; p = q \times l_p$$

μ = 0·5 **assumed**
q = Surcharge
L = Length parallel to wall
B = Length perpendicular to wall

Value of m

Fig. 5.14. Lateral pressure on an unyielding wall due to uniform surface load[22]

calculated from the expression $X_d = X_k/\gamma_m$, where X_k is the characteristic value and γ_m is the particular factor of safety for the material properties.

The specified values of these partial factors (γ_m) together with the partial factors γ_F to be applied to the actions are shown in Table 5.5.

The three cases shown in this table refer to the overall stability of the structure, typically buoyancy for an underground structure (case A), the strength of the structural members is the substructure (case B) and the geotechnical design of foundations and earthworks (case C). The partial factors for the ground properties for case C are higher than in cases A and B, allowing for variations in the ground and uncertainties in the analytical work.

Eurocode 7 (EC7) gives some guidance in the choice of characteristic soil properties, defining them as those that give the probability of a more unfavourable value governing the limit state occurrence of not more than 5%, and defines a characteristic value of soil properties as a cautious estimate of mean values within the ground influenced by the foundation loads.

Selection of design parameters

The choice of design parameters in terms of strength and stiffness is particularly important because of the considerable effect on wall design at both ultimate and serviceability states. Three grades of assessment should be considered:

(*a*) moderately conservative soil parameters (case A)

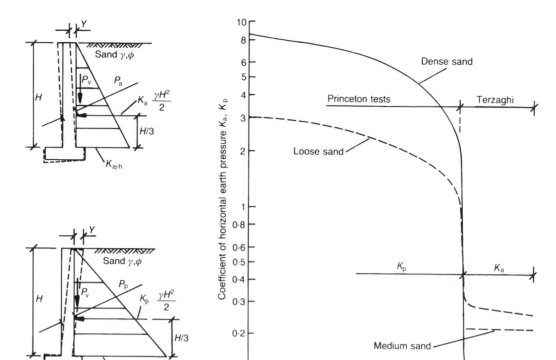

Magnitudes of wall rotation to reach failure

Soil type and condition	Rotation Y/H^*	
	Active	Passive
Dense cohesionless	0·0005	0·002
Loose cohesionless	0·002	0·006
Stiff cohesive	0·01	0·02
Soft cohesive	0·02	0·04

Y = horizontal displacement
$^*H$ = height of the wall

Fig. 5.15. Effect of wall rotation on active and passive pressure in loose and dense sand[22]

(b) worst credible soil parameters (case B)
(c) most probable soil parameters (case C)

The first category, moderately conservative values, is a relatively cautious estimate at the particular limit state. It is a similar value to the representative value as used in BS 8002 and to characteristic values as defined in EC7.

Table 5.5 Partial factors – ultimate limit states in persistent and transient situations[1]

Case	γ_F for actions			γ_M for ground properties			
	Permanent		Variable	$\tan\phi$	c'	c_u	$q_u{}^a$
	Unfavourable	Favourable	Unfavourable				
Case A	1·00	0·95	1·50	1·1	1·3	1·2	1·2
Case B	1·35	1·00	1·50	1·0	1·0	1·0	1·0
Case C	1·00	1·00	1·30	1·25	1·6	1·4	1·4

^{a} Compressive strength of soil or rock.

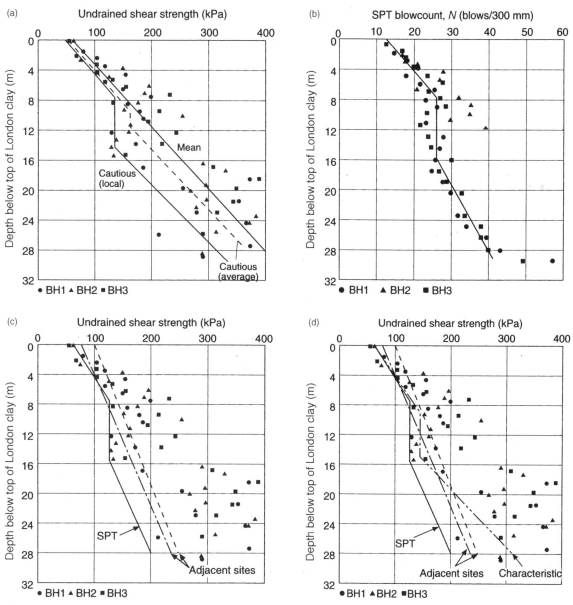

Fig. 5.16. Assessment of moderately conservative strength vs. depth profile for site on London clay. (a) Undrained shear strengths at site; (b) SPT test results from same site; (c) SPT results from (b) and results from adjacent sites compared with the undrained shear strengths; (d) final assessment of all results[24]

Simpson and Driscoll[24] (Fig. 5.16) used a comparison between undrained cohesion values of London clay, SPT values on the same site and plots of undrained strength vs. depth from nearby sites to assess a moderately conservative strength vs. depth profile. The construction is probably best not made on a statistical basis but following a comparison of data from other reliable sources.

The second category, the worst credible value is the worst that can be reasonably assessed could occur, an unlikely circumstance. Simpson and Driscoll[24] suggested that these values can be regarded as 0·1% fractile.

In the third category, the most probable values have a 50% chance of exceedance. It should not be used as the only basis of design but can be used with the observational approach providing the second design approach using worst credible values are used to define contingency measures should trigger values be exceeded.

Certain practical matters arise in preparing a testing schedule which is appropriate to the design on a specific site. These are as follows.

(*a*) An adequate number of classification, moisture content and density tests should be made.

(*b*) Test correlations should be made with other tests, other sites and where possible by back analysis in similar conditions.

(*c*) In stiff clays, care should be exercised in the choice of strength tests, peak, critical state, residual and drained or undrained.

(*d*) Laboratory tests for unconsolidated undrained triaxial values should be made on 100 mm dia. undisturbed samples as single-stage tests.

(*e*) Laboratory tests for drained shear strength should be made on consolidated drained and consolidated undrained triaxial tests and shear box tests (for cohesionless soils) and peak, critical state and residual angles of shearing resistance should be measured. Appropriate rates of shear should ensure complete dissipation of pore pressure.

(*f*) Inspection of the soil fabric should be made visually especially for soft estuarine clays when continuous sampling may prove necessary.

(*g*) Soil stiffness may be measured with the best expectancy of accuracy in self-boring or Menard-type pressuremeter tests in stiff clays and weak to moderately strong rocks.

(*h*) Measurement of groundwater levels should be applied stringently, using standpipes and piezometers to critically assess piezometric levels, their variation and risks associated with changes in groundwater level.

Temporary works

Important differences exist between the design approach to soil-retaining structures for permanent and temporary works. The dissimilarities between temporary works and permanent works design may be summarized as follows.

In temporary works...

(*a*) In clays, negative pore-water pressures are present in the soil. These dissipate with time but while they act they cause the soil to have a greater shear strength than it has in the long term.

(*b*) Support conditions are often different in the temporary works before base slabs, floor slabs or other permanent supports are constructed. Temporary works often rely more on the soil for their support than do permanent works.

(*c*) Loading conditions are often different. Applied surcharges during temporary works construction are often not present in the long term.

(*d*) Ground movements are often a matter of concern during construction, but there is not usually time for long-term movements to develop.

(*e*) A greater proportion of soil strength may be mobilized during temporary works depending on constraints operating during construction. However, the consequences of excessive ground movements or instability can be as severe as for permanent works.

(*f*) Higher stresses may be permitted in the design of the wall in temporary works.

Temporary works may be designed either: by assuming full equilibrium (full drained) pore-water pressures (i.e. long-term strength), the expected loads in the temporary phase and a very low safety factor; or by taking the higher short-term strength and a higher safety factor. (The choice is essentially one of modifying the parameters used and the safety factor adopted in passing from temporary to permanent works phases.)

Mixed total and effective stress design

Since the original ground surface and the soil below it on the active side of the wall are usually more susceptible to softening than the soil below final formation level, a method of calculating earth pressures using effective stress values on the active side and undrained values on the passive side has gained some credibility. The benefit, in terms of calculated earth pressures, is obtained principally from passive pressures based on the limit pressure expression $p_p = \sigma_v + 2c$, that part of the expression relying on cohesion applying at formation level on the passive side. The risk of clay softening on the passive side below formation level can be estimated by reducing the undrained strength/depth profile by 20% to 30% (using 0·7 to 0·8 of the unsoftened design line for c_u) and ignoring the clay strength in the upper 1 m thickness of clay at the surface of the excavation. Overall, the loss of safety for the wall as built will depend on several design matters, which include the choice of parameters, the choice of total or effective design method and the factors of safety that are applied to each component of the wall, the bracing or anchor that supports it, and the extent of embedment of the wall in the soil below formation level. If more optimistic methods are chosen for wall analyses (by using total or mixed total and effective stress methods) these should reflect more stringent factors of safety in the derivation of wall member dimensions. Conversely, if effective stress methods are used throughout, say for temporary works design of limited design life, the final factors of safety in the dimensioning of wall and strutting may be chosen more optimistically. Recommended factors of safety will be reviewed later in this chapter.

Design water pressures

The design of walls to support soil will include consideration of the support of water pressures where there is groundwater above the final excavation level in front of the wall. Where support walls are designed for excavations to cofferdams and shafts below river or sea bed, the pressures from river or sea water levels are evident to the designer and would comprise the major part of pressures on the wall. Where earth support walls are required for excavations on land, the designer has to evaluate the highest ground water levels during the design life of the structure and incorporate these with earth pressures into design pressures for the wall. In excavations on land where groundwater is high, the water pressure will constitute a large proportion of the horizontal force on the active side of the wall, but is a lesser proportion than the earth pressure on the passive side. If water levels rise, the total force on the active side of the wall increases, while if water pressure rise below formation level on the passive side, in most cases total passive resistance from water and soil reduces.

Where vertical soil support walls on land penetrate granular soils with a high water table but obtain a cut-off at depth, the water pressure on each side of the wall is calculated without complication (Fig. 5.17). The hydrostatic pressures on each side of the wall are calculated from $v = \gamma_w x$ where γ_w is the density of water (in fresh water it is 9·81 kN/m³, in salt water it is 10·00 kN/m³), and x is the depth below the groundwater table.

Additional pressures due to heavy rain may need to be considered in defining groundwater levels, and where surfaces are unpaved, full water pressures should be taken in tension cracks in cohesive soils. In cohesionless soils or where drainage is introduced at the rear of the wall, an increase in soil density to its fully saturated value should be allowed for. If the retained cohesionless soil has low permeability but drainage holes through the wall are adequate to discharge the water flow through the retained soil, it is recommended that the effect of the flow of water towards the wall and the increased total active thrust on the wall should be taken into account by calculating total active thrust on a

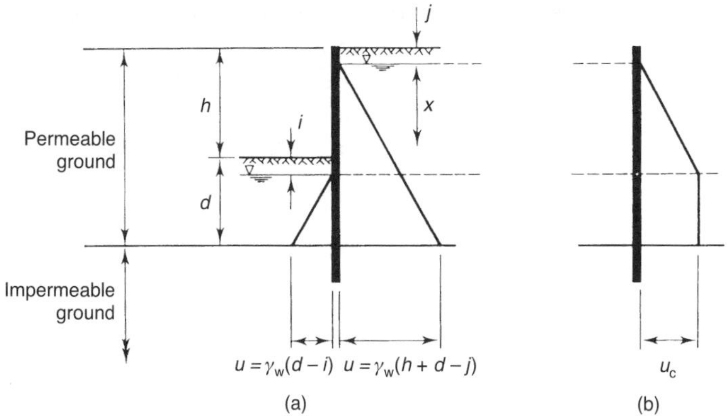

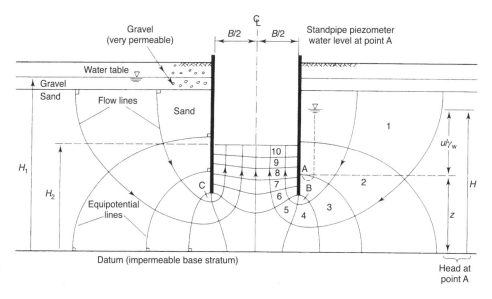

Fig. 5.17. Hydrostatic water pressures on walls in permeable ground with effective cut-off: (a) gross water pressures; (b) net water pressures[17]

vertical wall:

$$P_a = K_a \gamma_b \frac{H^2}{2} + 0 \cdot 5 \gamma_w \frac{H^2}{2} \tag{56}$$

where γ_b is the submerged density of the soil, and H is the vertical height of the earth retained.

It is also prudent to add that where drainage through the wall is not adequate to avoid an increase in head of groundwater in the retained soil during storm conditions, this increase should be allowed for and, if in extreme conditions, the head can reach the top of the wall, this should also be allowed for.

Other conditions that may affect static groundwater levels considered in designs include the effect of waves on retaining walls for marine structures and river and sea cofferdam walls, and the dynamic forces of waves breaking on beaches which can be transmitted to retaining walls for deep excavations below beach level. Some guidance on these matters may be obtained from the work of Sainflou[25] and Minikin[26].

Where walls are situated in tidal conditions the pore pressure will vary with the tide; the effect of rapid drawdown, of cycles of loading and any tidal lag may require special consideration. Guidance is available in reference[27].

Where the vertical wall for soil retention penetrates cohesionless soil but does not secure a cut-off in an impermeable stratum at the toe of the wall,

Fig. 5.18. Flow net: flow into base of a twin-wall cofferdam in sand[17]

the effect of water seepage from the retained soil on the active side of the wall to the passive side should be taken into account. Over time a steady seepage state will develop. In design, the effect on pressure in these conditions may be conveniently assessed by use of flow nets, the construction of which was explained in Chapter 2. A flow net illustrating these conditions is shown in Fig. 5.18. The total head at any point is

$$H = H_1 - (H_1 - H_2)\frac{d}{n_d} \tag{57}$$

where H_1 and H_2 are the heads of groundwater on either side of the wall, d is the number of flow net equipotential drops to the point considered, and n_d is the total number of drops. Also, at any point the total head is

$$H = \frac{u}{\gamma_w} + z \tag{58}$$

where u is the pore-water pressure, and z is the height of point considered above datum. Since H can be calculated by flow net and γ_w and z are known, u can be calculated. The flow net is also used to check the factor of safety against piping (see Chapter 2).

A simple short-cut for calculating pore-water pressure at any point can be made by assuming that the head difference between each side of the wall, active and passive, is dissipated uniformly along the flow path; referring to Fig. 5.19, head difference $= (h + i + j)$ and flow path length is $(2d + h - i - j)$.

Therefore, the head at any point x below the water table on the active side is

$$H_x = \frac{x}{2d + h - i - j}(h + i - j) \tag{59}$$

and since $u = H\gamma_w - z$, pore-water pressure at the toe of the wall is

$$u_{toe} = \frac{2(d + h - j)(d - i)}{2d + h - i - j}\gamma_w. \tag{60}$$

An even simpler first approximation is that in which the water pressure at the toe of the wall is taken as the average at that depth for active and passive sides of the wall. All uses of steady-state flow are best checked by flow net; the reduction of excess head linearly along the length of flow path at the wall can lead to over-optimistic calculated pore pressures in the narrow flow paths that occur between the retaining walls of a narrow cofferdam. In wider cofferdams (where width is greater than four times the differential water head) and single retaining walls where the seepage pressure is free to dissipate horizontally through the passive soils, the first approximation is satisfactory.

The reduction in pore pressure from one side of the wall to the other in the steady-state condition can be assessed by such methods of calculation. More importantly, however, is the effect of preferential drainage paths which can be caused by sand or silt partings in laminated groundwater flow below a vertical wall. Where the pore-water pressure does not reduce gradually because of a horizontal drainage route below the toe of the wall, an excessive pore-water pressure occurs on the passive side, resulting in high net pressures and forces on the wall. Figure 5.20 illustrates this risk.

Where groundwater flow is impeded by the periphery wall to a very large excavation the groundwater level near the wall may rise with time. Where the risk of this increase in pressure exists piezometers should be installed and monitored close to the wall.

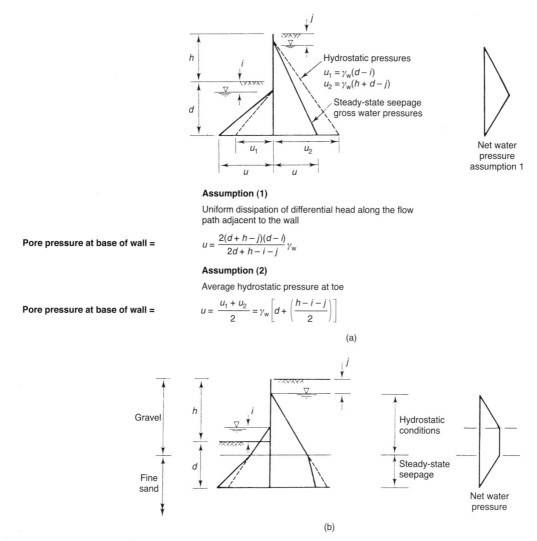

Fig. 5.19. Water pressures – simplifying assumptions for steady-state conditions: (a) uniform ground; (b) layered ground[48]

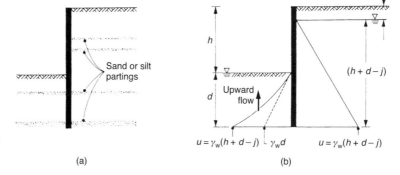

Fig. 5.20. Excessive pore-water pressure on passive side due to underflow: (a) soil cross-section showing pervious interlayers; (b) water pressure diagram[48]

Design methodology

Wall design must satisfy the ultimate limit state and the serviceability limit state with the specified partial safety factors applied.

The partial factor on soil strength at each limit state for both total and effective stress designs for each of the design categories, moderately conservative, worst credible and most probable, is shown in Table 5.6. The design

Table 5.6. Overall stability, cantilever and single-prop walls. Partial factors for use in design calculations[49]

| Design approach | Ultimate limit state | | | Serviceability limit state | | |
| | Effective stress | | Total stress | Effective stress | | Total stress |
	$F_{sc'}$	$F_{s\phi'}$	F_{ssu}	$F_{sc'}$	$F_{s\phi'}$	F_{ssu}
A. Moderately Conservative	1·2	1·2	1·5	1·0	1·0	1·0
B. Worst Credible	1·0	1·0	1·0	Not appropriate	Not appropriate	Not appropriate
C. Most Probable	1·2	1·2	1·5	1·0	1·0	1·0

$$\text{design } \phi'_d = \tan \phi^{-1} \left(\frac{\tan \phi'}{F_{s\phi'}} \right)$$

$$\text{design } c'_d = \frac{c'}{F_{sc'}}$$

$$\text{design } s_{ud} = \frac{s_u}{F_{ssu}}$$

parameters derived from the application of these safety factors are then used to obtain earth pressure coefficients, from charts such as those by Caquot and Kerisel[15].

Either the design approach using moderately conservative parameters (with $F_s = 1·2$ applied to effective stress values c' and ϕ' or $F_s = 1·5$ applied to total stress s_u) or the design approach based on worst credible parameters (with $F_s = 1·0$) is used. An early check of the two sets of calculated design parameters shows which design approach gives the lowest design values. These soil strengths are used with the worst combination of applied loading in both the short term and the long term.

Groundwater conditions which include water pressure and seepage pressure with the most unfavourable values that could occur in the extreme or accidental situation are applied at ultimate limit stage. The accidental situation includes an allowance of 10% of the retained height or 0·5 m, whichever is greater, for unplanned excavation. The most unfavourable values applying in normal conditions are then used to check the serviceability state.

Choice is made then of the analytical method, either based on limiting values of earth pressure or on soil–structure interaction analysis. For simple structures, such as cantilever walls, the limit equilibrium can be applied (with reasonable agreement of the designed wall with more complex soil–structure analysis) although for propped and anchored walls the soil structure analysis will usually show economies in terms of wall penetration, bending moment and prop/anchor loads. These economies may be significant.

For serviceability checks soil structure interaction analysis is necessary to check wall deformation, soil settlements and compliance with crack criteria for R.C. walls.

As a general basis of permanent wall design the following steps are made to establish values of bending moments and shear force, prop/anchor loads and wall penetration.

(a) Establish ultimate limit states (overall stability and wall strength) and serviceability limit states (limiting values of wall deflexion, settlements, crack width criteria).
(b) Collect soil and groundwater data.
(c) Determine wall construction method and wall type.
(d) Determine soil profile and soil parameters.

(e) Determine load case combinations and wall geometry for ultimate limit state (ULS) calculation.

(f) Determine the wall depth for vertical stability. (Check on vertical load carrying capacity or hydraulic cut-off). Check wall friction/adhesion.

(g) Make ULS calculation by limit equilibrium or soil–structure interaction. Check wall penetration for overall stability.

(h) Use the deeper of wall depths for vertical stability (f) or for lateral stability (g) as design depth.

(i) If wall depth is determined by vertical stability (f) recalculate bending moment (BM), and shear force (SF) in wall and prop loads by limit equilibrium or soil-structure interaction method.

(j) If serviceability limit state (SLS) calculations are required, select appropriate soil parameters, groundwater pressures, load case combinations and design geometry.

(k) Carry out SLS calculations to determine wall deflection, BM, SF and prop loads.

(l) Compare calculated wall deflections with initial wall design requirements.

(m) Make assessment of settlement risk to adjacent structures and services.

(n) Check risk of progressive failure.

(o) Determine ULS wall moments and shear force for structural design as the greater of:
    (i) BM and SF from step (g), ULS
    (ii) 1·4 times the BM and SF from step (k), SLS
    (iii) BM and SF from step (n), progressive collapse check

(p) Calculate prop loads, see later this chapter.

Structural design of wall

Ultimate limit state values of bending moments and shear forces for design of the wall section are taken as the greatest of those calculated from application of factored soil strengths (the worst values for case A, moderately conservative or case B, worst credible) or 1·4 times the SLS calculations.

Crack control

The application of both BS and Eurocodes at serviceability state to limiting crack widths in retaining walls due to early age shrinkage and flexure can be most onerous. Although the Eurocodes contain a 'deemed to satisfy' procedure in the absence of detailed calculations this is based on providing sufficient reinforcement to have a greater tensile capacity than the immature concrete whilst limiting the steel stress to a value which limits the crack width to the required width.

The draft I.Struct.E report on basement and cut-and-cover works[51] recommends that different criteria are set for flexural crack widths at various stages and suggests the maximum flexural crack widths shown in Table 5.7.

Table 5.7. Maximum flexural crack widths[51]

Design stage	Suggested maximum flexural crack width (mm)
During construction and recoverable	0·35
In service	0·30
Short-term event	0·35
Drawdown of groundwater to underside of base slab	0·40

Note. Cracking caused by flexure of the entire structure, such as a tunnel built over a patch of soft (or hard) ground or subjected to localized surcharge, passes right through the section and should be limited in width to 0·2 mm at all times.

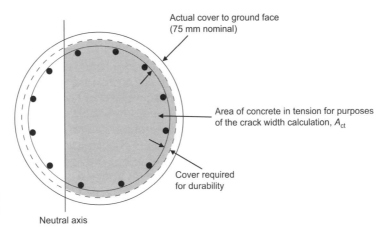

Fig. 5.21. Pile cross-section showing crack width calculation principles to EC2 if tension area in cover thickness is ignored[49]

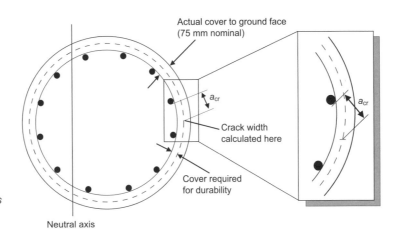

Fig. 5.22. Pile cross-section showing calculation principles for crack width in accordance with BS 8110[49]

The quantity of reinforcement required for crack control may be considerable and strict application of code requirements may be needed to keep steel density to practical levels.

Referring to steel required to resist a defined crack width in bending as calculated according to EC2 (applied to a circular section cast against the ground) the critical parameter is the area of concrete in tension A (EC2 Part 1, 1992, Clause 4.4.2.2. (3)). Figure 5.21 shows the net area in tension which may be used for calculation purposes if the thickness of concrete cover is assumed to be the minimum required for durability.

Referring to crack control requirements in BS 8110: Part I, 1997, the specific items for a typical circular pile section are:

Nominal cover to earth face: 75 mm (Part I Clause 3.3.1.4).
Durability requirements: 35 mm for C35 concrete (Part 1 Table 3.3)
(concrete in moderate exposure Table 3.2, non-aggressive soil).

Crack width (Part 2, section 3.8) should be assessed in accordance with a_{cr}, the distance from the point considered to the surface of the nearest longitudinal bar (Part 1, Clause 3.8.2). Often assessed as the nominal cover required for durability and not the 75 mm cover provided for constructability. Refer to the cross-section shown in Fig. 5.22.

Cantilever walls and single-prop walls

The design of cantilever and single-prop walls requires that the serviceability limit state is considered in terms of wall deformation and soil deformation at the rear of the wall. The ultimate limit state is as follows.

(a) *Overall instability* – the provision of sufficient embedment depth to prevent overturning of the wall. For a single-propped wall the minimum penetration is just sufficient to avoid forward movement of the wall without preventing rotation of the wall at its toe. Such a condition is known as the free earth support condition. As wall penetration is increased beyond this minimum, fixity of the wall is progressively increased until full fixity is obtained and the toe is unable to rotate when earth and water loading is applied to the wall. This state is known as the fixed earth condition. For the cantilever wall without prop support, full fixity must be obtained to prevent rotation and collapse of the wall.

(b) *Foundation failure* – in cohesive soils, the wall penetration depth must be sufficient to prevent basal failure after excavation to formation level in front of the wall.

(c) *Hydraulic failure* – in cohesionless soils, the penetration of the wall must be sufficient to avoid piping in front of the wall after excavation to formation level.

Overall stability

The overall stability of both cantilever and single-prop walls has previously been assessed using limit equilibrium methods in which a factor of safety is applied to an analysis of failure conditions to ensure their avoidance. Such factors of safety were applied in a number of ways and have attracted comment from Potts and Burland[28], and Symons[29]. The various factor methods are as follows.

(a) *Factor on embedment.* A factor of safety is applied to embedment depth. The method is described in references 30 and 31.

(b) *Factor on moments of gross pressure.* This method applies as a factor of safety to moments of gross pressure on the passive side only. Water pressure is not factored. The method is described in references 16 and 22.

(c) *Factors on moments of net pressure.* The net pressure diagram is calculated and the factor of safety is defined as the ratio of moments of the net passive and active forces about the toe of the wall.

(d) Factors on net passive resistance. Potts and Burland[28] developed this method which defines the factor of safety as the ratio of the moment of the net available passive resistance to the moment activated by the retained material including water and surcharge. When using effective stress methods with $c' = 0$ and where there is no surcharge on the passive side, the active pressure diagram is modified so that no active pressure increase occurs below formation level and any such increase as calculated is deducted from the passive pressure diagram. Where total stress or effective stress methods are used, reference should be made to Potts and Burland[28].

(e) *Factor on shear strength on both active and passive sides.* Soil shear strengths are reduced by dividing c' and $\tan \phi'$ by the factor of safety, and the active and passive pressure diagrams are calculated using these reduced values. The reduced values approximate to mobilized values. Bending moments and prop loads derived from the calculation can be used for wall design if they are treated as ultimate limit state values. This method is recommended in BS 8002[19].

(f) Factor on shear strength of passive side only. The passive resistance is factored but no factor is applied to the active side.

Comparative studies show that there is no relationship between factors of safety applied to the methods listed. There is little doubt that the preferred method is really defined by personal use and experience, but some useful observations were made in reference 32 as follows.

(a) The factor on embedment is empirical and should be checked by applying a second method.

(b) The method of factoring moments on gross pressure may give excessive penetration at low angles of shearing resistance ϕ' less than 20° so use varying factors for different ranges of ϕ'.

(c) The factoring of net passive pressure moments tends to give high penetration values.

(d) The factors on modified net passive resistance as recommended by Burland and Potts[28] appear to give consistent results in a reasonable range of soils and wall dimensions.

Factors of safety recommended by Padfield and Mair[48] for use in stiff clays with methods for factoring embedment, moments of gross pressure, net passive resistance and shear strength on both active and passive sides are reproduced in Table 5.8. Two approaches are used: approach A is based on moderately conservative parameters, and approach B uses worst credible soil parameters, geometry and loading in the design. The values in Table 5.8 had been originally intended for walls embedded in stiff clays but were also used for walls in granular or mixed soils.

Table 5.8 Factors of safety for methods of analysing embedment[48]

Method		Design approach A: recommended range for moderately conservative parameters (c', ϕ', or c_u)		Design approach B: recommended minimum values for worst credible parameters ($c' = 0$, ϕ')		Comments
		Temporary works	Permanent works	Temporary works	Permanent works	
Factor on embedment, F_d	Effective stress	1·1 to 1·2 (usually 1·2)	1·2 to 1·6 (usually 1·5)	Not recommended	1·2	This method is empirical. It should always be checked against one of the other methods
	Total stress[a]	2·0	–		–	
Strength factor method, F_s	Effective stress	1·1 to 1·2 (usually 1·2 except for $\phi' > 30°$ when lower value may be used)	1·2 to 1·5 (usually 1·5 except for $\phi' > 30°$ when lower value may be used)	1·0	1·2	The mobilized angle of wall friction δ_m and wall adhesion c_{wm} should also be reduced
	Total stress[a]	1·5	–	–	–	
Factor on moments: CP2 method, F_p	Effective stress	1·2 to 1·5	1·5 to 2·0	1·0	1·2 to 1·5	These recommended F_p values vary with ϕ' to be generally consistent with usual values of F_s and F_r
	$\phi' \geq 30°$	1·5	2·0	1·0	1·5	
	$\phi' = 20$ to 30°	1·2 to 1·5	1·5 to 2·0	1·0	1·2 to 1·5	
	$\phi \leq 20°$	1·2	1·5	1·0	1·2	
	Total stress[a]	2·0	–	–	–	
Factor on moments: Burland–Potts method, F_r	Effective stress	1·3 to 1·5 (usually 1·5)	1·5 to 2·0 (usually 2·0)	1·0	1·5	Not yet tested for cantilevers. A relatively new method with which little design experience has been obtained
	Total stress[a]	2·0	–	–	–	

[a] Speculative, treat with caution.

Note 1. In any situation where significant uncertainty exists, whether design approach A or B is adopted, a sensitivity study is always recommended, so that an appreciation of the importance of various parameters can be gained.

Note 2. Only a few of the factors of safety recommended are based on extensive practice experience, and even this experience is recent. At present, there is no well-documented evidence of the long-term performance of walls constructed in stiff clays, particularly in relation to serviceability and movements. However, the factors recommended are based on the present framework of current knowledge and good practice.

Note 3. Of the four factors of safety recommended, only F_p depends on the value of ϕ'.

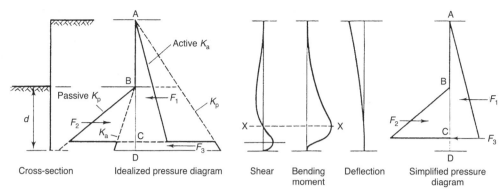

Fig. 5.23. Analysis of cantilevered wall[17]

Calculation can be made by soil–structure interaction analysis or using limit equilibrium methods by program or by hand.

Fixed earth support: cantilevered wall
Certain simplifying assumptions are made due to the relative complexity of the limit equilibrium calculation. Figure 5.23 shows an idealized pressure diagram and typical shear, bending moment and wall deflection diagrams. The simplified procedure is as follows:

- the pressures at the toe of the wall are replaced by a resultant force F_3 acting at C
- forces F_1 and F_2 act through the centres of pressure of their respective areas
- depth BC is found by assuming a level for C and calculating the moments for the forces F_1 and F_2 about level C; repeat until moments balance
- increase the depth BC by 20% to give the design penetration BD
- calculate the maximum bending moment (BM) at the point of zero shear.

This method can be used for layered soils; net water pressures should be included in the active pressure diagram where groundwater occurs. The factor of safety can be applied by using limit pressures and increasing the depth of embedment. The bending moment distribution at limiting equilibrium is assumed to correspond to working conditions. A safety factor of value 2·0 is then applied to these values for design values of BM and shear force (SF). A partial factor of safety is applied to characteristic soil strengths for design of the wall cross-section. Alternatively, for design according to BS 8002[19] a mobilization factor is applied to peak shear strengths to obtain design values of BM and SF. No further safety factor is applied other than the partial factor to material characteristic strength to obtain the design strength.

Bending moment and shear force in the cantilever wall may also be analysed using Winkler spring, finite element or boundary element methods. These methods produce a more realistic soil interaction solution and provide values of lateral wall deformation.

The importance of wall flexibility related to wall deformation and depth of embedment was originally shown by Rowe[20]. The earth distribution was shown by model tests to vary according to the flexibility of the wall. (The wall flexibility was defined by the expression

$$\text{wall flexibility} = EI\frac{d^4y}{dx^4}$$

where E is Young's modulus of the wall material, I is the section modulus of the wall transverse cross-section per unit length, and y and x are horizontal and vertical coordinates of the vertical cross-section of the wall). The reduction in depth to full fixity caused by increasing wall flexibility produced reduced bending moments in the wall section and, according to Rowe, produced savings of up to 20% by weight of the wall compared with design methods based simply on limit pressures. The method was not widely adopted for cantilever pile design but served as an early indicator of the importance of wall and soil interaction.

Free earth support: single-propped walls
The earth pressure, shear and bending moment distribution and wall deflection diagrams which apply to a typical single-propped (or anchored) wall are shown in Fig. 5.24. The method of calculation uses limit pressures or pressures calculated on critical state values of soil parameters or on peak shear strengths reduced by a mobilization factor as defined in BS 8002, and is as follows.

(a) Draw earth pressure diagrams using limiting or mobilized pressures for soil pressure in cohesionless or cohesive homogeneous or layered soils. Include net water pressure, modified to include the effect of steady flow beneath the wall and equalization of pore pressures either side of the wall at the toe. Use tension cracks filled with water where applicable in clays and apply minimum fluid pressures ($5\,\mathrm{kN/m^3}$) when necessary.
(b) Calculate F_1 and F_2 to act through the centre of their respective pressure areas.
(c) Calculate the penetration BD by assuming a trial depth of penetration D and taking moments of forces F_1 and F_2 about the tie rod level. Repeat with trial values of penetration D until these moments balance.

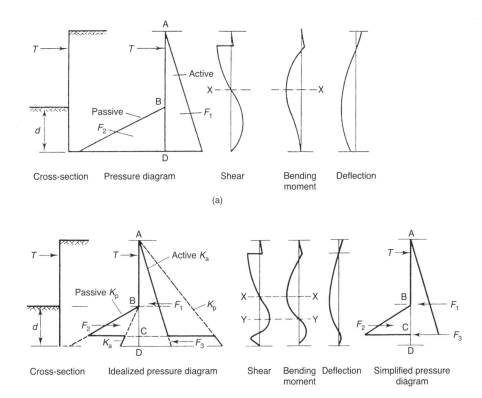

Fig. 5.24. Single-propped or anchored wall with: (a) free earth support; (b) fixed earth support[17]

Cross-section   Pressure diagram   Shear   Bending   Deflection
                                                             moment

(a)

Cross-section   Idealized pressure diagram   Shear   Bending Deflection   Simplified pressure
                                                          moment   diagram

(b)

Angle of shearing resistance ϕ	Depth to zero moment as a proportion of depth from ground surface to formation level H
20°	0·25H
25°	0·15H
30°	0·08H
35°	0·035H
40°	−0·007H

(*d*) The prop load T can then be found by balancing forces $T = F_1 - F_2$.

(*e*) Calculate the bending moment in the wall section at the level of zero shear.

Fixed earth support: single-propped walls

The analysis by hand calculation of the fixed earth, single-propped (or anchored) wall is made less complicated by use of work due to Blum[33] in the 1930s. He approximated the bending moment in a single-anchored wall with fixed earth support by reducing it to zero at the point of zero net earth pressure below formation level. Blum gave approximate depths to this point for relatively uniform soils where the wall is sufficiently deep to ensure fixity; these depths are given in Table 5.9. This support may be solved graphically[16] or by calculation (Fig. 5.24) as follows.

(*a*) Draw earth pressure diagrams using limiting or mobilized pressures for soil pressure in cohesionless, cohesive or layered soils. Include net water pressure modified to include the effect of steady flow beneath the wall and equalization of pore pressures on either side of the wall at the toe. Use tension cracks filled with water where applicable in clays. Apply minimum fluid pressures (5 kN/m^3) where necessary.

(*b*) Draw the net pressure diagram from ground level to the first point of zero pressure below formation level.

(*c*) Calculate active forces F_1 and F_2 from the gross pressure diagram.

(*d*) Take moments of forces F_1 and F_2 and tie rod force T about the first point of zero pressure from the net pressure diagram and equate to zero.

(*e*) Calculate value of force T from this expression.

(*f*) Assume application of passive force F_3 at point C and recalculate F_1 and F_2 to this depth. Take moments of T, F_1 and F_2 about this level and repeat with change in depth to point C until the moments balance. As with the cantilever wall calculation, the calculated depth to point C is increased by 20% to give design penetration depth.

(*g*) Draw the shear force diagram and calculate the maximum bending moment in the wall at the point of zero shear force.

This design procedure, as for free earth support design, is usually made by computer program and where soil deformation prediction is required can be the subject of soil/structure interaction programs or finite element or finite difference computations.

Anchored bulkheads: design development

The description of a propped wall includes within this generic phrase various constructions such as sheet piling, diaphragm walls and reinforced concrete pile walls braced by struts or raking shores, or sheeters and walls of similar construction with tie rods or stressed ground anchors. One of these types of constructions, sheet piling to form a wall or bulkhead tied back by steel rods to an anchor block, known as a deadman, or to anchor piles, was the subject of a historical keynote paper by Terzaghi[34]. This method of construction, which is widespread on waterfronts where it is used to achieve a quay line with reclamation behind it at minimum cost, does not strictly lie within the subject of deep excavations, but no technical discussion on braced sheeting would be complete without reference to the paper and the controversial discussion that followed it. The principal purpose of the paper was to identify and rectify errors in accepted bulkhead design at that time on the basis of tests and observations by Terzaghi and model tests by Rowe[20,35,36]. The paper reached the following principal conclusions.

(a) The identification of the type of soils and fills and their in situ properties of uniformity, relative density and strength are vital matters which are frequently overlooked in anchored bulkhead design.

(b) The distribution of earth pressure on the bulkhead is unlikely to conform to the Coulomb distribution, because of the extent of deformation of the soil structure. This deformation depends on soil and wall stiffness.

(c) If maximum bending moments are calculated on walls in sand assumed to extend to sufficient depth to achieve full fixity irrespective of wall flexibility and sand relative density, errors are likely and these are on the unsafe side.

(d) For sheet piles driven into clay, the assumption of full fixity at depth will probably not apply as time elapses and no reduction in the calculated maximum moment in the wall should be allowed due to wall section flexibility to compensate for this loss.

(e) Anchor tension depends on several factors other than the properties of the backfill material and the flexibility of the wall or sheeting. Therefore, the anchor pull should be computed on the assumption of free earth support. Anchor pull may be greater than that calculated using Coulomb's theory, and may increase due to repetition of loading and unloading from heavy surcharge. An unequal yield of adjacent anchorage produces variations in tie rod pull. Given these risks, more conservative stresses should be used in anchor design than are applied in sheet pile bulkhead design.

These conclusions broadly still apply, although alternative methods of analysis have been developed in which soil, wall and anchor stiffness can be modelled and deformation and induced stress in all three can be calculated. Terzaghi concluded: 'Because of the great variety of subsoil conditions which may be encountered, the subject (anchored bulkheads) does, and always will, leave a wide margin for judgment – and also for misjudgment.'

Anchorage location
Anchorages, deadmen or injected tendons must be located behind potential failure surfaces at the rear of the wall. Figure 5.25 shows the recommended geometry for analysis of deadmen locations (from BS 6349[27]).

Foundation failure
The risk of base failure to an excavation by upward heave applies particularly in very soft and soft clays and silty clays, typically, quick estuarine deposits. The failure is analogous to a bearing capacity failure of foundation, only in reverse; the failure is a shear failure in the soil below formation level, but caused by relief of load (the relief of overburden) and not by the application of load as occurs in a conventional foundation bearing failure.

The methods of Terzaghi[37] and Bjerrum and Eide[38] can be applied to calculate the factor of safety against base failure; these are shown in Fig. 5.26. Terzaghi's method is primarily applicable to shallow or wide excavations,

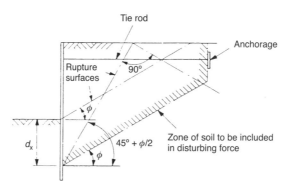

Fig. 5.25. Location of deadman anchorage in granular retained fill[27]

For free earth support d_x is the depth of embedment of sheet piles.
For fixed earth support d_x is ¾ depth of embedment.

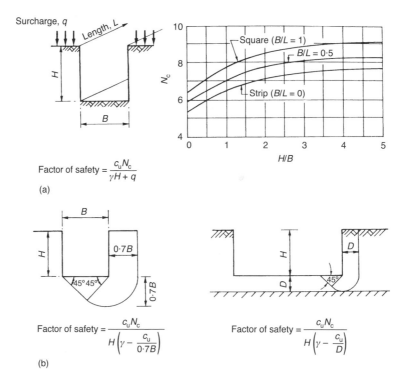

Fig. 5.26. Calculation of factors of safety against basal heave in cohesive soils: (a) deep excavations with $H/B > 1$; (b) for shallow or wide excavations with $H/B < 1$[32]

while the method of Bjerrum and Eide is suitable for deep and narrow excavations with no nearby underlying stiff clay to inhibit failure. Both methods neglect the effect of wall penetration below formation level and therefore results may prove to be conservative, especially where stiffer clays exist with depth. A third method[22] for predicting the basal safety factor where stiff clays exist at depth, is shown in Fig. 5.27.

The factor of safety against basal failure is generally required to be not less than 1·5. If uncorrected values of in situ vane tests are used, the actual factor of safety may be close to 1·0 according to Aas[39]. (A vane correction described by Bjerrum[40] is necessary to obtain more reliable values of safety factor.)

With a factor of safety, based on corrected vane results, which is less than 1·5, substantial soil deformation is likely. If such soil movement is not acceptable, a factor of safety not less than 2·0 is recommended. Increase in movement occurs as the basal factor of safety decreases, and increases rapidly as a factor of safety of 1·0 is approached. Although basal heave is rare within

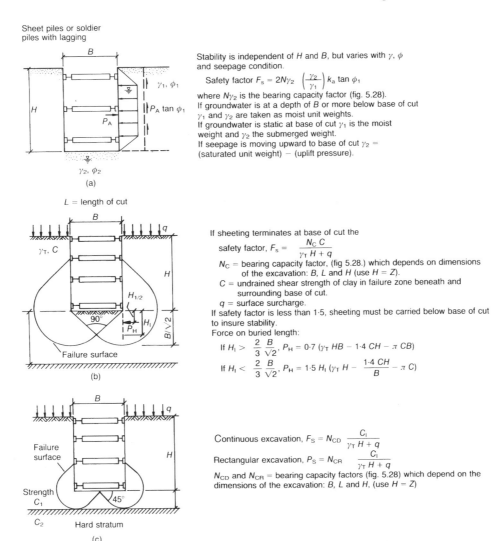

Sheet piles or soldier piles with lagging

(a)

Stability is independent of H and B, but varies with γ, ϕ and seepage condition.

Safety factor $F_s = 2N\gamma_2 \left(\dfrac{\gamma_2}{\gamma_1}\right) k_a \tan \phi_1$

where $N\gamma_2$ is the bearing capacity factor, (fig. 5.28).
If groundwater is at a depth of B or more below base of cut γ_1 and γ_2 are taken as moist unit weights.
If groundwater is static at base of cut γ_1 is the moist weight and γ_2 the submerged weight.
If seepage is moving upward to base of cut $\gamma_2 =$ (saturated unit weight) $-$ (uplift pressure).

L = length of cut

(b)

If sheeting terminates at base of cut the

safety factor, $F_s = \dfrac{N_C C}{\gamma_T H + q}$

N_C = bearing capacity factor, (fig 5.28.) which depends on dimensions of the excavation: B, L and H (use $H = Z$).
C = undrained shear strength of clay in failure zone beneath and surrounding base of cut.
q = surface surcharge.
If safety factor is less than 1·5, sheeting must be carried below base of cut to insure stability.
Force on buried length:

If $H_1 > \dfrac{2}{3}\dfrac{B}{\sqrt{2}}$, $P_H = 0.7\,(\gamma_T HB - 1.4\,CH - \pi\,CB)$

If $H_1 < \dfrac{2}{3}\dfrac{B}{\sqrt{2}}$, $P_H = 1.5\,H_1\left(\gamma_T H - \dfrac{1.4\,CH}{B} - \pi\,C\right)$

(c)

Continuous excavation, $F_S = N_{CD}\,\dfrac{C_1}{\gamma_T H + q}$

Rectangular excavation, $P_S = N_{CR}\,\dfrac{C_1}{\gamma_T H + q}$

N_{CD} and N_{CR} = bearing capacity factors (fig. 5.28) which depend on the dimensions of the excavation: B, L and H, (use $H = Z$)

Fig. 5.27. Calculation of factors of safety against basal heave in: (a) cohesionless soil; (b) cuts in clay of considerable depth; (c) cuts in clay limited by hard stratum[22]

excavations in cohesionless soils, a basal heave analysis is included in Fig. 5.27(a) for completeness, together with basal heave analysis in clay as described in NAVFAC[22] in Fig. 5.27(b) and (c). Figure 5.28 shows the values of bearing capacity factors for use in these analyses. Field and finite element analysis predictions of the correlation between movement and basal failure factor of safety are shown in Fig. 5.29.

Cantilever and single-prop walls, particularly on sloping sites in soft clays and loose granular soils, should always be checked against risk of deep-seated circular slip failure.

Hydraulic failure
The risk of piping failure to the base of an excavation in cohesionless soils was described in Chapter 2. Design charts for penetration of cut-off walls to prevent hydraulic failure in sand and stratified soil are reproduced in Figs 5.30 and 5.31.

Wall flexibility
Rowe's work[20,35,36] in the 1950s and 1960s was initially instrumental in showing the importance of wall stiffness in design. Following a series of

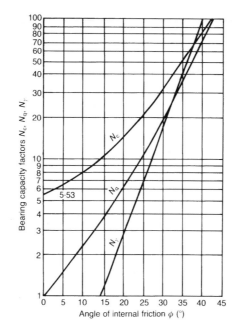

Fig. 5.28. Plot of bearing capacity factors against angle of shearing resistance[22]

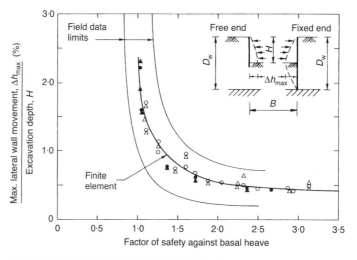

Fig. 5.29. Analytical relationship between maximum lateral wall movement and factor of safety against basal heave from field data, free end and fixed end walls, various sites (note is for finite element analysis data)

model tests on sands of varying relative density in Manchester, UK, Rowe was able to show that interaction between soil and wall was different for steel sheet piles and reinforced concrete sheet piles because of the greater flexibility of the steel sheet pile. This greater flexibility causes a redistribution of earth pressure which differs considerably from the Coulomb distribution, as shown in Fig. 5.32. The flexure of the wall causes reduction in pressure at mid-height and causes the resultant passive force to rise with an increase in fixity for the flexible pile. These changes reduce the design bending moment for a flexible pile, although too often such reductions are not applied in practice to ensure the pile does not crumple during driving.

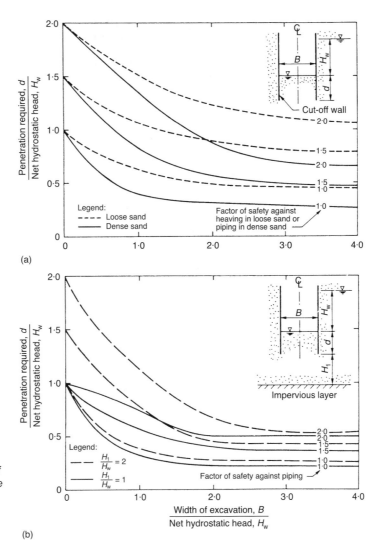

Fig. 5.30. Penetration of cut-off wall to prevent hydraulic failure in homogeneous sand: (a) in sands of infinite depth; (b) in dense sand of limited depth[22]

Materials and stresses

For cantilever and single-propped walls the component parts are designed either from limiting equilibrium hand calculations or computer program outputs using either limiting equilibrium or soil–structure interaction. The input soil parameters are those based on moderately conservative parameters with safety factors at ULS as shown in Table 5.6 (BS 8002 mobilization factors are similar) or at serviceability limit state with a partial safety factor of 1·4 (a check that moderately conservative parameters are more severe, that is lower, than worst credible parameters at ULS being made at the beginning of the design). Crack widths are calculated for serviceability limit state in reinforced concrete walls. Characteristic strengths of steel used for cantilever and single-prop sheet pile walls are given in Table 5.10.

Multi-prop walls

The above description of design methods for cantilever and single-propped (or anchored) walls referred to computations using limit pressures and the application of factors of safety. The methods due to BS 8002[19] have introduced design using earth pressures at the serviceability limit state. Using these methods the bending moment in the walling can be estimated relatively quickly by hand calculation (adopting Blum's methods[33] for cantilever and

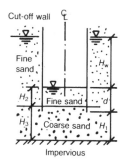

(a) Coarse sand underlying fine sand
Presence of coarse layer makes flow in the fine material more nearly vertical and generally increases seepage gradients in the fine material compared to the homogeneous cross-sections of Fig 5.27.

If top of coarse layer is below toe of cut-off wall at a depth greater than width of excavation, safety factors of Fig. 5.27 (a) for infinite depth apply.

If top of coarse layer is below toe of cut-off wall at a depth less than width of excavation, then uplift pressures are greater than for the homogeneous cross-sections. If permeability of coarse layer is more than ten times that of fine layer, failure head H_w = thickness of fine layer (H_2).

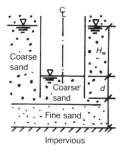

(b) Fine sand underlying coarse sand
Presence of fine layer constricts flow beneath cut off wall and generally decreases seepage gradients in the coarse layer.

If top of fine layer lies below toe of cut-off wall, safety factors are intermediate between those derived from Fig. 5.27 for the case of an impermeable boundary at (i) the top of fine layer, and (ii) the bottom of the fine layer assuming coarse sand above the impermeable boundary throughout.

If top of fine layer lies above toe of cut-off wall, safety factors of Fig. 5.27 are somewhat conservative for penetration required.

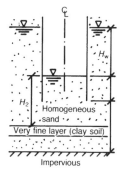

(c) Very fine layer in homogeneous sand
If top of very fine layer is below toe of cut-off wall at a depth greater than width of excavation, safety factors of Fig. 5.27 assuming impermeable boundary at top of fine layer apply.

If top of very fine layer is below toe of cut-off wall at a depth less than width of excavation, pressure relief is required so that unbalanced head below fine layer does not exceed height of soil above base of layer.

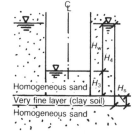

Fig. 5.31. Penetration of cut-off wall to prevent hydraulic failure in stratified soil: (a) coarse sand underlying fine sand; (b) fine sand underlying coarse sand; (c) very fine layer in homogeneous sand[22]

To avoid bottom heave when toe of cut-off wall is in or through the very fine layer ($\gamma_s H_3 + \gamma_c H_s$) should be greater than $\gamma_w H_4$.
  γ_s = saturated unit weight of the sand
  γ_c = saturated unit weight of the clay
  γ_w = unit weight of water
If fine layer lies above subgrade of excavation, final condition is safer than homogeneous case, but dangerous condition may arise during excavation above fine layer and pressure relief is required as in the preceding case.

fixed earth support walls) or even more conveniently using finite element, finite difference or Winkler spring analytical methods. Soil deformation behind the wall may be predicted, if needed by the finite element or finite difference programs. Design requirements and analysis methods for multi-prop walls are a different matter, however. The method of construction for these walls is usually sequential, installing the sheeting or walling and excavation in stages followed by installation of the prop or anchor at each installation stage. The sheeting or walls will, in all likelihood, penetrate the ground below the final excavation level. The extent of wall deformation in this sequence of operations is restricted, although the passive resistance of soil below excavation level at each stage is mobilized to support the wall prior to installation of the bracing or the anchor at that level. Despite the frequent

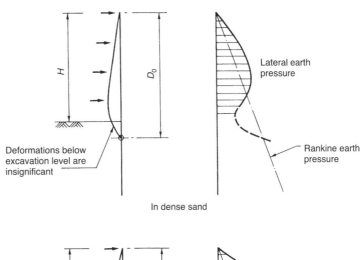

In dense sand

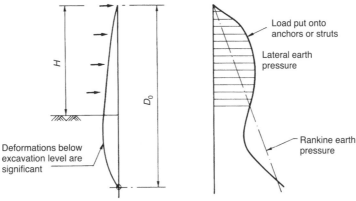

Fig. 5.32. Deflection of a sheet pile and redistribution of active earth pressure[50]

Wide excavations in low modulus soils such as soft clays, silts and loose sands

Table 5.10 Characteristic strengths for steel sheet piling

Designation EN 10027	Minimum yield strength (N/mm²)	Minimum tensile strength (N/mm²)	Minimum elongation on a gauge length of $L_0 = 5.65 S_0$ (A%)
EN 10248 S270 GP	270	410	24
EN 10248 S355 GP	355	480	22

support for the wall, therefore, horizontal deformation of the wall occurs at each passive soil zone prior to installation of the prop or anchor at that level. The wall distorts inwards to mobilize this passive resistance, the wall movement occurring below each stage of excavation. Pore pressure dissipation may occur in cohesive soils during the period needed for strut or anchor installation at successive levels.

The extent of wall movement also depends on the stiffness of the prop or anchor once installed at each level. Where the soil is relatively stiff, say dense sands or gravels, the extent of forward movement of the sheeting at each excavation stage to mobilize soil passive pressure will be relatively small, and active earth pressures on the wall will considerably exceed Coulomb active values above dredge level; redistribution of earth pressure will occur between the lowest strut and formation level. In wide excavations in soils such as soft clays or loose sands where stiffness is low, the successive deformations below excavation level at each propping formation level are considerable. Load is redistributed between the struts, and the sum of the maximum strut loads considerably exceeds the Coulomb values.

Where pre-stressed ground anchors are used at each excavation stage the earth pressure on the wall is determined by the pre-stress levels and subsequent relaxation, and by relative wall and soil stiffnesses. Design methods that have been used for many years have been based on calculations of anchored walls using a Coulomb distribution assuming no pre-stress applied. This non-pre-stress value of anchorage at each excavation stage is subsequently used as the actual value of pre-stress applied to the tendon. This empirical method successfully restricts soil movement but in turn inhibits the Coulomb active earth pressure distribution, on which the calculation is based, from developing, the actual pressures on the retained side of the wall being higher (and nearer K_0 or K_p values) than those calculated. More recent methods using Winkler spring and finite element programs allow an assumed anchor pre-stress load to be introduced to the analysis, from which the actual earth pressures are calculated on the basis of the soil movement permitted by wall and soil stiffness and the extent of the anchor prestress.

The ultimate limit states for multi-prop walls are similar to those for cantilever and single-prop walls:

(a) *overall stability* – risk of strut failure, bending stress failure in sheeting or passive failure of soil below stage excavation level or final formation level

(b) *foundation heave* – in soft clays, risk of failure by unloading; bearing capacity failure

(c) *hydraulic failure* – piping in cohesionless soils with high external groundwater table.

The serviceability limit states are as follows.

(a) *Deformation of sheeting* – the acceptable limits of sheeting deformation will depend on the purpose of the excavation and whether the works are temporary or permanent, or a combination of both. Where walls or sheeting are temporary the deformation must not exceed that which would occupy space required for the permanent works nor cause difficulties with sheeting removal if this is intended. For permanent works, deformation of the wall or sheeting must neither impair the durability of the substructure nor cause visual offence.

(b) *Soil movement behind wall or sheeting; vertical settlements* – the extent of settlement behind the support for the excavation must not exceed the permitted settlement of existing structures, highways or services, unless the consequences of this can be estimated accurately and on re-assessment are acceptable.

(c) *Cracking in reinforced concrete walls* – at the serviceability state, cracking will occur on the tension face of reinforced concrete walls due to application of load, in particular earth and water pressures and surcharge loading, and also on each face of the wall due to early thermal cracking of the concrete. For building substructures the provisions of BS 8110[2] will apply to crack control in walls or, where more rigorous waterproofing is needed, BS 8007[3] may be specified. For highway structures in the UK, design flexural and tension cracks complying with the BS 5400[4] are specified. Design crack widths of 0·25 mm, complying with 'severe' conditions are usual although the pressure of saline or sea water may reduce this value to 0·15 mm. Additional longitudinal steel may therefore prove necessary in diaphragm walls to control crack widths caused by loading, although the application of rules to minimize vertical crack widths due to thermal shrinkage of concrete in panels of limited individual length may prove over-strenuous. Such rules for reinforced concrete works are referred to in the UK Department of Transport's Standard BD 28/87[41]. Eurocodes EC2 and EC7 refer to similar crack control requirements in reinforced concrete walls.

The available methods of design for multi-propped walls are:

(a) empirical methods; based originally on strut load envelopes proposed by Peck for three categories of soil: sands, soft to medium clays and stiff clays. Twine and Roscoe[42] more recently proposed new strut load envelopes for soft to firm clays, stiff to very stiff clays and dry clay or submerged granular soils. The use of empirical methods is recommended as a check on computed strut loads

(b) limit equilibrium programs are a simple solution without addressing all the matters of influence. Programs based on Winkler Spring theory are perhaps nowadays the most widely used methods

(c) full soil–structure interaction analysis by finite element, boundary element or finite difference methods: used where prediction of soil deformation and soil settlement requires calculated estimates

(d) pseudo finite element programs.

Empirical method based on strut load envelopes

The original empirical method, due to Terzaghi and Peck[18], was applied to both temporary works (including piled and diaphragm walls permanently anchored or braced by floor construction, as in top-downwards construction) and permanent works. The strut load envelopes due to Terzaghi and Peck are shown in Fig. 5.33. Note that these diagrams are not intended to represent actual earth pressure or its distribution with depth but load envelopes from which strut loads can be evaluated. Clay is assumed to be undrained and only total stresses are considered. Sands are assumed to be drained (through the sheeting) with zero pore pressure. Where drainage is precluded behind a non-permeable wall, hydrostatically distributed water pressure is added to strut loads. Sheeting or walling was then designed using the Coulomb earth pressure distribution with hydrostatic water pressure added except where drainage occurred through sheeting to relieve water pressure.

In 1969, reviewing his empirical method, Peck pointed out that his recommended method for strut design was less satisfactory in soft to medium clays

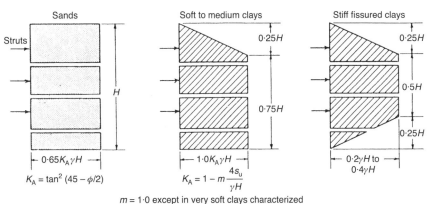

Fig. 5.33. Apparent pressure diagrams for computing strut loads in braced cuts[18]

than for excavation in sands. Peck did point out, however, that the behaviour of clays and the bracing system depends on the stability number

$$N_c = \frac{\gamma D}{c_u} \tag{62}$$

where c_u represents the clay beside and beneath the cut to the depth that would be involved if a general failure were to occur due to the excavation. Peck added that when the depth of excavation corresponds to values of N_c greater than 6 or 7, extensive plastic zones have developed, at least to the bottom of the cut, and the assumption of a state of plastic equilibrium is valid. The movements are essentially plastic and the settlements may be large.

The empirical strut load envelopes reviewed by Peck (Fig. 5.33) do not include the effects of the toe of the sheeting or walling extending below the final formation level, and yet from the point of view of reduction of strut loads in the lower struts (or anchors) and the improvement to ingress of groundwater at formation level, an extension of sheeting vertically below formation level was desirable and often achievable. There were two design methods which allowed this penetration of walling and sheeting to be taken into account in strut load calculation.

The first method assumed that the passive reaction below formation level resisted active pressure below that level together with a portion of the load from the strut load envelope between the lowest strut level and formation level. This method applied to strutted excavations in uniform soil conditions of reasonable strength such as medium-dense to dense granular soils and stiff clays. In less competent soils (loose sands and gravels and soft clays), passive resistance against the sheeting below formation level might be less effective, and in such cases Goldberg et al.[23] advised that the sheeting should penetrate to such depth to avoid piping failure (as discussed in Chapter 2) and the sheeting should be designed as a cantilever from the lowest strut level.

The second empirical method, the source of which is not known, has been used since the mid 1950s by the Author and has been adequately confirmed. The procedure is shown in Fig. 5.34. An additional 'strut' is assumed to act on the strut load envelope to represent the passive resistance acting on the sheeting below formation level. The level of this 'strut' is determined from the net pressure diagram, as shown in Fig. 5.34. The 'strut' load calculated from the strut load envelope is then compared with the available passive resistance using the limiting pressure from the net pressure diagram for the selected penetration depth. The bending moment in the sheeting is calculated from the net pressure diagram.

The strut loads calculated for each successive construction stage are summarized and the highest value at each strut level is used for strut and waling design purposes. Similarly, maximum moment and shear values are calculated for the sheeting or walling for each construction stage from the net pressure diagram and the critical values used for sheeting design.

More recently, empirical data and recommended methods of strut load estimation have been published by Twine and Roscoe[42]. Eighty one case histories, all from the UK, were reviewed. The walls were supported by both timber and steel temporary props, not anchors, and the study did not differentiate between single- and multi-propped walls. Excavations in rock were not considered. The cases were classified according to the ground retained as follows:

- Class A: normally- and slightly over-consolidated clay soils (soft and firm clays)
- Class B: heavily over-consolidated clay soils (stiff and very stiff clays)

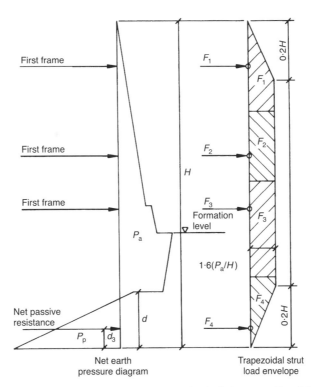

1. Construct net earth pressure diagram, using the limit pressure P_a and P_p
2. Calculate value of P_a, total active pressure
3. Calculate trapezoidal strut load envelope ordinate $1 \cdot 6 (P_a/H)$
4. Calculate strut envelope forces F_1, F_2, F_3, F_4 from shaded areas of strut load envelope (F_4 represents net passive resistance below dredge level and acts at centre of pressure, net passive diagram
5. Calculate factor of safety,

$$\text{mobilized passive resistance} = \frac{\text{Net passive resistance } P_p}{\text{Calculated mobilized passive resistance } F_4}$$

Fig. 5.34. Construction of trapezoidal strut load envelope for braced excavation to take into account passive resistance below formation level

- Class C: granular, cohesionless soils
- Class D: walls retaining both cohesive and cohesionless soils.

Case histories for soft and firm clays (class A) and for stiff clays (class B) were further sub-divided into flexible walls (timber, sheet pile and soldier pile walls) and stiff walls (contiguous, secant pile and diaphragm walls). The characteristic distributed prop load diagrams proposed by Twine and Roscoe are shown in Fig. 5.35.

Twine and Roscoe referred to the range of field measurements compared to values calculated by deformation methods. Field measurements were made on 46 props at four sites. The comparison is shown in Table 5.11. The range of calculated to required values was generally between 1·4 and 10 times. This very wide scatter has been referred to by others for measurements in two deep excavations in London (Batten and Powrie[43] and Richards *et al.*[44]). Both these site measurements of strut loads showed considerable variation with temperature.

Twine and Roscoe concluded that, providing the load–strain behaviour of a prop is ductile, any temperature increase which causes the ultimate capacity of the prop is unlikely to cause sudden prop failure because of plastic deformation of the prop and the transfer of load to nearby props. Because of this, they recommended that the design of steel props should not include temperature effects provided that certain SLS and ULS criteria are satisfied. This serviceability criterion ensures that the temperature effect does not cause

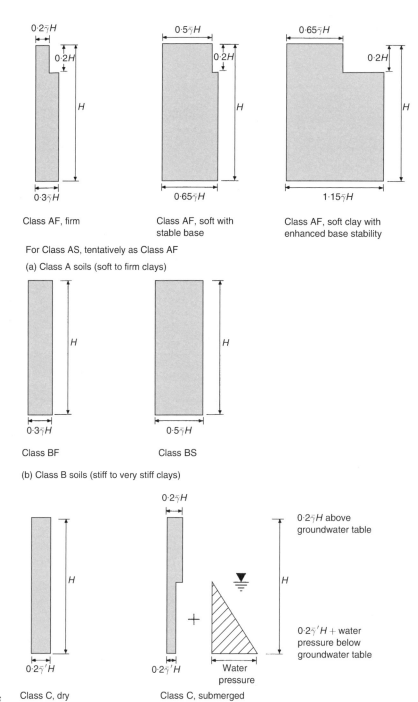

Fig. 5.35. Characteristic distributed prop load diagrams proposed by Twine and Roscoe[42]

yielding of the prop steel and thus avoids permanent deformation and the ULS criterion requires the ultimate capacity of the prop under the temperature effect to be greater than the total ULS design load.

Potts[45] reviewed analysis methods and concluded that all simple methods of analysis were flawed and empirical methods were only of some value if they were verified by observation. These conclusions, in 1992, remain currently valid although the increased use of programs to calculate wall moments, deflections and strut loads has been rapid and empirical methods appear

Table 5.11 Comparison of
measured and calculated prop
loads[42]

Project	No. of monitored props	Range of measured prop loads (tonnes)	Range of ratio: $\dfrac{\text{Measured load}}{\text{Design load}}$
55 Moorgate	6	62·5 to 109	0·16 to 0·28
Almack House, London	15	0 to 118	0·0 to 0·36
A406 Chingford, London			
(i) Piled wall	10	45 to 160	0·28 to 0·82
(ii) Wedge excavation	4	45 to 70	0·19 to 0·39
(iii) Diaphragm wall	6	140 to 220	0·7 to 1·37
A12/M11 Hackney, London	5	623 to 1395	0·51 to 0·83

little used. This change of emphasis appears unfortunate in the Author's view; the equivalent strut load diagnosis of Peck and Twine and Roscoe should still be used as a critical comparison compared with calculated results.

A summary of the advantages and drawbacks of the four types of program is given in Table 5.12, they are based on analytical methods as follows.

(a) *Limit equilibrium (e.g. STAWAL and REWARD)*. A stability analysis in which calculation is made of the statical equilibrium of arbitrary slip surfaces by resolving forces or moments and results in the calculated soil strength mobilized to obtain equilibrium. The internal stress conditions within the soil wedge are not considered.

(b) *Subgrade reaction/beam on springs (e.g. WALLAP, LAWALL)*. Soil behaviour is modelled by a set of unconnected vertical and horizontal springs. Any structural support is modelled by simple springs. In LAWALL the soil is modelled as a simple boundary element using Mindlin's equations for horizontal displacement due to a horizontal force applied within a semi-infinite elastic continuum. Berms are difficult to model; anchors and raking props are difficult to model accurately.

(c) *Pseudo finite elements (e.g. FREW)*. Soil is modelled as an elastic continuum with soil stiffness matrices calculated using a finite element program. Soil model restricted to linear increasing stiffness with depth. Only wall deformation is calculated.

(d) *Finite element and finite differences (e.g. PLAXIS, CRISP, FLAC)*. Full soil–structure interaction with modelled construction sequence. Some programs are now able to model 3D excavations. Wide choice of soil models available; Mohr–Coulomb, and more complicated failure criteria to represent variation of stiffness with strain. Use of low strain values of soil stiffness are necessary.

Comparative analysis using both empirical methods and computer analyses shows a comparatively wide scatter of results for strut loads, wall penetration and wall bending moment. The lack of validation from field observations and the extensive use of programs nowadays gives cause for concern.

Factors of safety: multi-propped wall design

The attention given to comparative methods of applying factors of safety to the overall stability of cantilever and single-prop (or anchored) walls has not extended to multi-prop walls. The design should always consider hydraulic failure by piping from the base of the excavation and the risk of failure of the base of the excavation in soft clays. Overall, stability consideration in a multi-propped wall will rely on three matters: the risk of circular slip instability below the whole excavation in clay conditions on sloping sites;

Table 5.12. Summary of advantages and disadvantages of analytical methods[49]

Method	Basis	Advantages	Disadvantages
Limit equilibrium (Typical programs: STAWAL, REWARD)	Equilibrium conditions used for the failing soil mass. Full mobilization of soil strength, factors of safety applied to lateral stresses at failure	Needs only soil strength parameters. Simple and straightforward. Estimate of deformation possible by relating mobilized strength, soil strength and wall rotation	Does not model soil–structure interaction, wall flexibility or construction sequence. Multi-propped walls, non-uniform surcharges and berms require considerable idealization. Only give an order of wall deformation and surface settlement. Better for cantilever than propped walls
Subgrade reaction/ beam or springs (Typical programs: LAWALL, WALLAP, M. SOILS)	Soil modelled by a set of unconnected vertical and horizontal springs. Alternatively some programs model soil as a simple boundary element using Mindlin's equations for horizontal displacement	Soil–structure interaction taken into account. Wall movements are calculated. Simple to apply. Construction sequence modelled	Soil behaviour idealization is likely to be less than perfect. Results are sensitive to pre-excavation stress state and spring stiffness. Any failure to provide overall stability is usually only shown by a failure to converge
Pseudo finite element (Typical program: FREW)	Soil modelled as an elastic continuum with soil stiffness matrices calculated using a finite element program	Soil–structure taken into account. Wall movements are calculated. Relatively straightforward. Construction sequence modelled	Limited to soil with linearly increasing stiffness at depth. Results sensitive to pre-excavation stress state. Experience shows an overtendency to predict wall deformation
Finite element and finite difference. (Typical programs: OASIS SAFE (FE) PLAXIS (FE) CRISP (FE) FLAC (FD) ABACUS (FE)	Full soil–structure interaction with modelled sequence of construction	Full complex soil models can represent variation of stiffness with strain and anistropy. Can model complex wall and excavation geometry. Can model consolidation at construction stages as soil moves from undrained to drained conditions. Some programs can model 3D conditions	Time-consuming to set up. High quality data required to realise full potential. Use of Mohr–Coulomb soil model may give unrealistic ground deformation

the risk of inadequate prop capacity; wall penetration below final formation level.

The wall penetration depth should always be regarded as a minimum when calculated by methods described in this chapter. Adequate embedment depths will depend on the risk of hydraulic failure as well as passive resistance to the sheeting and relief of load from the lowest frame of bracing. In all multi-propped (or anchored) walls the principal risks of failure in soils other than very soft clays will stem from the adequacy of embedment depth of the wall or sheeting and the sufficiency of strutting or anchoring. To counter these risks in temporary works design requires care and experience.

Other design considerations

Plastic design
Recent work by Kort[46] on sheet pile design for sheet piles has highlighted potential savings in sheet pile tonnage using plastic design methods. Kort's

work includes some validation of the methods by full-scale tests in soft soils and also includes allowance for the phenomenon of oblique bending that may occur in U-shaped, Larrsen sheet piles. Kort's work and its practical application to sheet pile design is referred to in more detail in Chapter 7.

Construction of long walls in short lengths

It has long been realized that safer construction with less wall deformation and reduced strut or anchor loads apply when trenchworks and deep excavations can be taken out in short lengths and the permanent works are built in stages progressively within these lengths. This avoidance of keeping excavations for greater length and greater time with only temporary support than necessary is good construction sense. This method of working in short lengths can particularly apply at the deepest section of cofferdams with short length working during excavation and installation of the bottom frame and then the subsequent replacement of the temporary framing, bottom upwards, by the permanent support. This method is very often most desirable at this depth and in some instances, essential.

Until finite element analysis was applied in three dimensions it was not possible to model short length working and its benefits by calculation. Recently research work by Gourvenec et al.[47] has used the CRISP FE program to compare the deformation of a long embedded cantilevered diaphragm wall excavation using both 3D and plane strain analyses with field measurements of deformation. The wall was 800 m long with a cutting for highway construction. The upslope side of the cutting was supported by diaphragm wall panels 22·85 m deep, 1·5 m thick and 7·5 m long. The downslope wall panels were 12·87 m deep, 1 m thick and 5 m long. An earth berm, 6·36 m in height and 5·17 m wide at its base with a 60 degree face was used to provide temporary support to the upslope wall. The wall height at the upslope side was 7·86 m above formation level. The soil retained was a medium dense sandy silt overlying a stiff overconsolidated fissured clay. Pore pressures were hydrostatic below the sand/clay interface. Both diaphragm wall installation and excavation of the berm were modelled together with realistic construction times for each part of the staged construction.

The wall deformation measured on site compared favourably with the 3D FE analysis deformed wall shape but the plane strain analysis predicted total deformation at the top of the wall as 38 mm, whereas the total from the 3D analysis was 20 mm and broadly agreed with the field measurement. The conclusions reached were as follows.

(a) Reduced ground movements during wall installation were calculated with the 3D analysis compared with the 2D, although the analysis method did not have a significant effect on subsequent wall movements during bulk excavation in front of the wall.

(b) Up to 80% of the post-installation wall movement occurred during bulk excavation to the initial berm profile.

(c) Wall movement when the berm was removed in stages was reduced by about 50% using the 3D analysis compared to that using the plane strain analysis.

(d) Wall movements at the initial base slab prop section during removal of adjacent sections of the berm were very small. Both in the analysis and on site the initial section of base slab prop was effective in restricting wall movement during excavation of the nearby berm sections.

The effect of short length working compared with bulk excavation full length is the reduced rate of dissipation of negative excess pore water pressure induced by bulk excavation. This, in turn, makes for greater safety.

Fig. 5.36. 'Heidelberg' soldier pile and lagging wall allowing extraction of steelwork wallings and soldiers (patented by Bilfinger and Berger)

King post walls

The use of soldier piles, often supported by tiers of ground anchors with horizontal timbers (or laggings) or in situ concrete placed in successive lifts or sprayed as shotcrete, provides an economical form of soil support, particularly in dry subsoils. Care should be taken, however, in assessing the passive resistance below final formation level of such a wall system. The passive

(a)

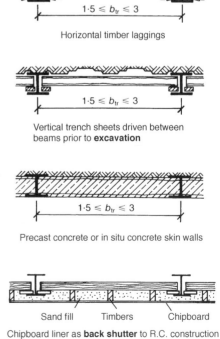

Horizontal timber laggings

$1·5 \leq b_{tr} \leq 3$

Vertical trench sheets driven between beams prior to **excavation**

$1·5 \leq b_{tr} \leq 3$

Precast concrete or in situ concrete skin walls

$1·5 \leq b_{tr} \leq 3$

Sand fill   Timbers   Chipboard

Chipboard liner as **back shutter** to R.C. construction

(b)

Fig. 5.37. King post wall derivatives (dimensions in metres)

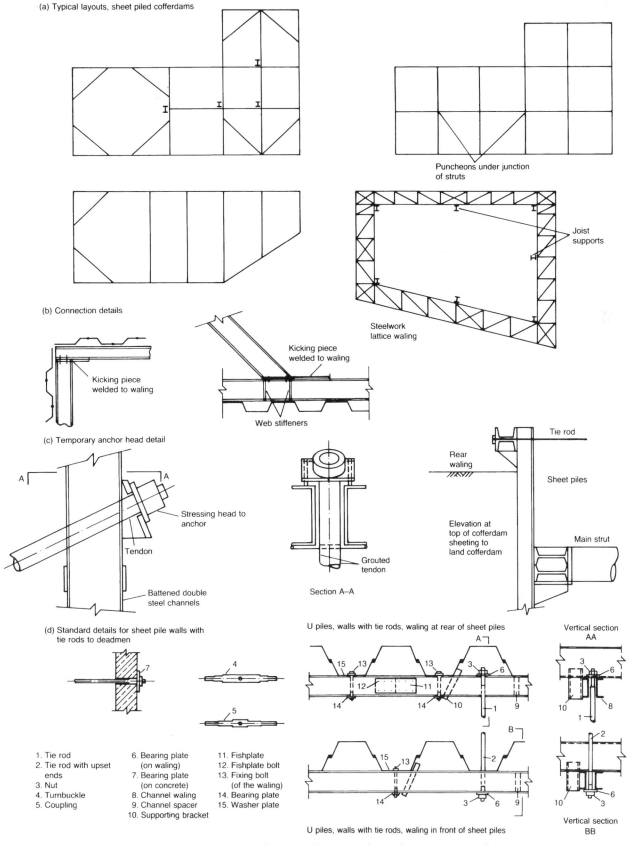

Fig. 5.38. Cofferdam standard construction details: (a) typical layouts, sheet piled cofferdams; (b) connection details; (c) temporary anchor head detail; (d) standard details with tie rods to deadmen

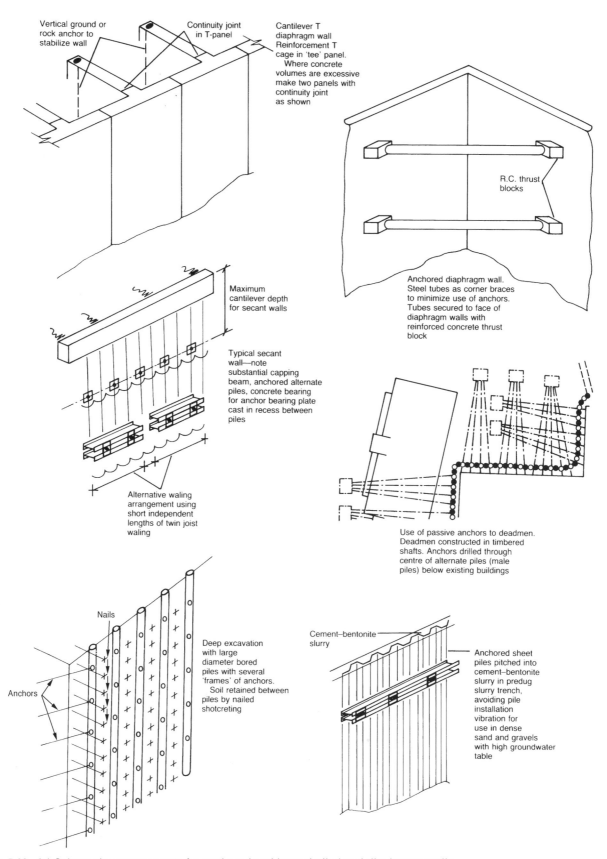

Fig. 5.39. (a) Schematic arrangements for anchored and braced piled and diaphragm walls

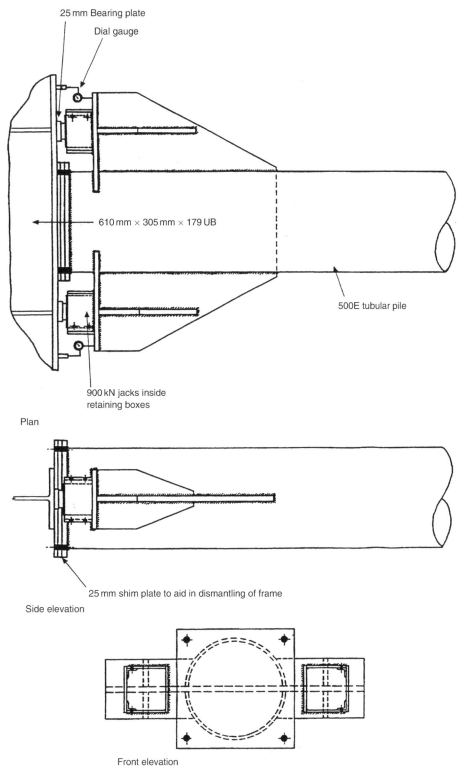

Fig. 5.39. (b) Typical jackable end detail for a tubular (CHS) prop (after Twine and Roscoe[42])

resistance of soil at the front of the soldier piles within their embedment depth can only be mobilized by movement of the soldier pile towards the excavation. Soldier pile walls are relatively flexible constructions, and in relatively dense granular soils and stiff clays this mobilization of passive resistance without

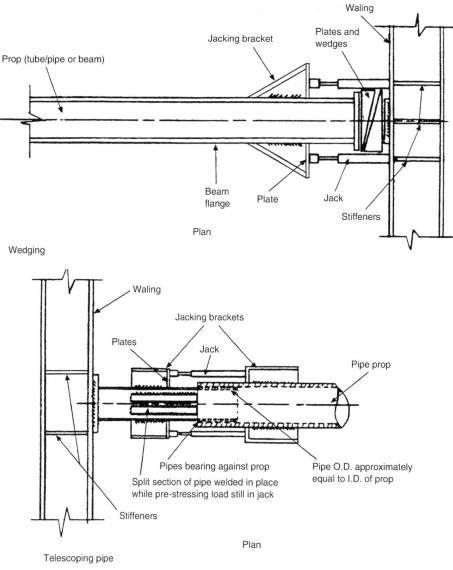

Fig. 5.39. (c) Typical jackable end detail for a UC prop (after Twine and Roscoe[42])

undue lateral movement can reasonably be assumed. In these circumstances it is also reasonable to allow an effective width of soil acting to provide passive resistance in excess of the net width of the steel or reinforced concrete pile acting as the soldier. Where soldier spacing centre-to-centre is greater than four times the net width of the soldier below formation level it is reasonable to assume an effective width of soil to provide passive resistance equal to twice the soldier width below formation level. Where the soldier spacing is less than four times the soldier width below formation level no such increase in calculated passive resistance is permissible because of the risk of overlap of calculated passive zones.

It is essential to check the bearing capacity at the base of such soldiers where inclined anchors are used. The vertical components of all anchors should be summated as they are pre-stressed together with the soldier pile self-weight comprising the vertical load at the soldier base.

Figure 5.36 shows a soldier pile wall constructed by Bilfinger and Berger. Part of the wall is built in a patented form known as a 'Heidelberg' wall where the walings and soldiers can be extracted for reuse.

Construction details

A selection of construction details from the Author's files is given in Figs 5.37 to 5.39. The wall types shown include anchored sheet pile walls, king post walls using timber laggings, cofferdam details and multi-prop walls using secant piles and diaphragm walls. Details of typical end details where jack installation is included are also reproduced from Twine and Roscoe's CIRIA report[42].

References

1. DD ENV 1997–1 Eurocode 7. *Geotechnical design. Part 1: general rules*. British Standards Institution, London, 1995.
2. BS 8110. *Structural use of concrete*. British Standards Institution, London, 1997.
3. BS 8007. *Code of practice for design of concrete structures for retaining aqueous liquids*. British Standards Institution, London, 1981.
4. BS 5400. *Steel, concrete and composite bridges*. British Standards Institution, London, 1990.
5. BD 42/00. *Design manual for roads and bridges,* Vol. 2, section 1, (DMRB 2.1.2), HMSO, London, 2000.
6. Peck R.B. Deep Excavations and tunneling in soft ground. *Proc. 7ʰ Int. Conf. S.M.F.E.*, Mexico City, 1969, State of the art volume, 225–290. Sociedad de Mexicana de Suelos, Mexico City, 1969.
7. Clough G., Smith E. and Sweeney B. Movement control of excavation support systems by iterative design procedure. *ASCE Ground. Engng*, 1989, **1**, 869–884.
8. Clough G. and O'Rourke T. Construction induced movement of insitu walls. ASCE Special Publication No. 15. *Proc. Design and Performance of Earth Retaining Structures*, Cornell University, 1990, 439–470.
9. St John H., Potts D., Jardine R. and Higgins K. Prediction and performance of ground response of a deep basement at 60 Victoria Embankment. *Proc. Wroth Memorial Symposium*, Oxford, 1992. Thomas Telford Ltd., London, 1993.
10. Carder D. *Ground movements caused by different embedded retaining wall construction*. Transport Research Laboratory, Crowthorne, 1995, TRL report 172.
11. Fernie R. and Suckling T. Simplified approach for estimating lateral wall movement of embedded walls in UK ground. *Proc. Int. Symp. Geo. Aspects of Underground Construction in Soft Ground*, City University, 1996, 131–136. City University, London, 1996.
12. Carder D., Morley C. and Alderman G. *Behaviour during construction of a propped diaphragm wall in London clay at Aldershot and road underpass*. Transport Research Laboratory, Crowthorne, 1997, TRL Report 239.
13. Long M. Database for retaining wall and ground movements due to deep excavations. *ASCE J. Geotech. Eng.*, **127**, March 2001, 203–224.
14. Brooker E.W. and Ireland H.O. Earth pressures at rest related to stress history. *Canadian Geotech. J.*, 1965, **11**, Feb., 1–15.
15. Caquot A. and Kerisel J. *Tables for the calculation of passive pressure, active pressure and bearing capacity of foundations*. Gauthier-Villars, Paris, 1948.
16. Civil engineering codes of practice. No. 2. *Earth retaining structures*. Civil Engineering Codes of Practice Joint Committee, London, 1951.
17. CIRIA. *The design and construction of sheet piled cofferdams*. Thomas Telford Ltd., London, 1993, Special publication 95.
18. Terzaghi K. and Peck R.B. *Soil mechanics in engineering practice*. Wiley, New York, 2nd edition, 1967.
19. BS 8002. *Earth retaining structures*. British Standards Institutions, London, 1994.
20. Rowe P.W. Anchored sheet pile walls. *Proc. Instn Civ. Engrs*, Part 1, 1952, **1**, Jan., 27–70.
21. BD 37/01. *Design manual for roads and bridges*, Vol. 1, section 3, (DMRB 1.3). Highways Agency, London, 2001.
22. Design manual 7.2. *Foundation and earth structures*. US Navy, Washington, DC, 1982.

23. Goldberg D.T. *et al. Lateral support systems and underpinning*, Vol. 1, *design and construction*, Vol. 2, *design fundamentals*, Vol. 3, *construction methods*. Federal Highway Administration, Washington, DC, 1976, FAWA-RD-75, 128.

24. Simpson B. and Driscoll R. *Eurocode 7: A commentary*. Building Research Establishment, Watford, 1998.

25. Sainflou M. Essai sur les digues maritimes verticales. *Ann. des Ponts et Chaussées*, 1928, **98**, 5–48, (translated by US Corps of Engineers).

26. Minikin, R. *Wind, waves and maritime structures*. Griffin, London, 1963.

27. BS 6349 (part 1). *Maritime structures*. British Standards Institution, London, 1984.

28. Potts D.M. and Burland J.B. *A parametric study of the stability of embedded earth retaining structures*. Transport Research Laboratory, Crowthorne, 1983, Report 813.

29. Symons, I.F. Assessing the stability of a propped in-situ retaining wall in over-consolidated clay. *Proc. Instn Civ. Engrs*, 1983, **75**, Dec., 617–633.

30. *Piling handbook*. British Steel Corporation, Scunthorpe, 1988.

31. *Sheet piling design manual*. USS Steel, Pittsburgh, 1974.

32. *Review of design methods for excavations in Hong Kong*. Geotechnical Control Office, Hong Kong, 1990.

33. Blum H. *Einspannungsverhaltnisse bei Bohlwerken*. Ernst and Son, Berlin, 1931.

34. Terzaghi K. Anchored bulkheads. *Trans. ASCE*, 1954, **119**, paper 2720, 1243–1324.

35. Rowe P.W. A theoretical and experimental analysis of sheet pile walls. *Proc. Instn Civ. Engrs*, 1955, **4**, Jan., 32–69.

36. Rowe P.W. Sheet pile walls in clay. *Proc. Instn Civ. Engrs*, 1957, **7**, July, 629–654.

37. Terzaghi K. *Theoretical soil mechanics*. Wiley, New York, 1943.

38. Bjerrum L. and Eide O. Stability of strutted excavations in clay. *Géotechnique*, 1956, **6**, 32–47.

39. Aas G. *Stability problems in a deep excavation in clay*. Norwegian Geotechnical Institute, Oslo, 1985, Publication 156.

40. Bjerrum, L. Problems of soil mechanics and construction on soft clays. *Proc. 8th Int. Conf. S.M.F.E.*, Moscow, 1973, Vol. 3, 111–159. USSR National Society for Soil Mechanics and Foundation Engineering, Moscow, 1973.

41. BD 28/87. *Early thermal cracking of concrete*. UK Department of Transport, London, 1987.

42. Twine D. and Roscoe H. *Prop loads: guidance on design*. CIRIA, London, 1996, Funders report.

43. Batten M. and Powrie W. Measurement of temporary prop loads at Canary Wharf. *Proc. ICE Geotech. Eng.*, **143**, 2000, 151–163.

44. Richards D., Homes G. and Beadman D. Measurement of temporary prop walls at Mayfair car park. *Proc. ICE Geotech. Eng.*, **137**, 1999, 165–174.

45. Potts D.M. The analysis of earth retaining structures. *Proc. Conf. Retaining Structures*. Institution of Civil Engineers, London, 1992, 167–186.

46. Kort D.A. *Steel sheet pile walls in soft soil*. DUP Science, Delft, 2002.

47. Gourvenec S., Powrie W. and De Moor E. Three dimensional effects in the construction of a long retaining wall. *Proc. ICE Geotech. Eng.*, 2002, **155,** July, 163–173.

48. Padfield C.J. and Mair R.J. *Design of retaining walls embedded in stiff clay*. CIRIA, London, 1984, report 104.

49. CIRIA. *Embedded retaining walls: guidance for economic design*. Gaba A.R. *et al.* CIRIA, London, 2002.

50. Bjerrum L. *et al.* Earth pressures on flexible structures. *Proc. 5th Euro. Conf. SMFE, Madrid*, 1972, Vol. 2, 169–196.

51. Institution of Structural Engineers, *Design and construction of deep basements including cut-and-cover structures*. Draft, 2003. Inst. Structural Engrs, London.

Bibliography

Bjerrum L. *et al.* Earth pressures on flexible structures. *Proc. 5th Euro. Conf. S.M.F.E.*, Madrid, 1972, Vol. 2, 169–196. Sociedad Española de Mechánica del Suelo y Cimentaciones, Madrid, 1972.

Burland J.B. *et al.* The overall stability of free and propped embedded cantilever retaining walls. *Ground Engng*, 1981, **14**, No. 5, 28–38.

Carder D.R. and Symons L.F. Long term performance of an embedded cantilever retaining wall in stiff clay. *Géotechnique*, 1989, **39**, No. 1, Mar., 55–76.

EAU 90. *Recommendations of the Committee for Waterfront Structures, Harbours and Waterways.* Ernst and Son, Berlin, 6th English edition, 1993.

Egger P. Influence of wall stiffness and anchor prestressing on earth pressure distributions. *Proc. 5th Euro. Conf. S.M.F.E.*, Madrid, 1972, Vol. 1, 259–264. Sociedad Española de Mechánica del Suelo y Cimentaciones, Madrid, 1972.

Garrett C. and Barnes S.J. Design and performance of the Dunton Green retaining wall. *Géotechnique*, 1984, **34**, Dec., 533–548.

Head J.M. and Wynne C.P. Designing retaining walls embedded in stiff clay. *Ground Engng*, 1985, **18**, Apr., 30–38.

McRostie G.C. *et al.* Performance of tied back sheet piling in clay. *Canadian Geotech. J.*, 1972, **9**, 206–218.

Potts D.M. and Burland J.B. *A numerical investigation of the retaining walls of the Bell Common tunnel.* Transport Research Laboratory, Crowthorne, 1983, Supplementary Report 783.

Potts D.M. and Fourier A.B. The effect of wall stiffness on the behaviour of a propped retaining wall. *Géotechnique,* 1984, **34**, Sept. 383–404 (Discussion **35**, 119–120).

Simpson B. *et al.* An approach to limit state calculations in geotechnics. *Ground Engng*, 1981, **14**, No. 6, 21–28.

Symons L.F. *Behaviour of a temporary anchored sheet pile wall on A1(M) at Hatfield.* Transport Research Laboratory, Crowthorne, 1987, Research report 99.

Terzaghi K. Evaluation of coefficients of subgrade reaction. *Géotechnique*, 1955, **5**, No. 4, 297–326.

Winkler, E. *Die lehre von elastizitat und festigkeit*, Prague, 1867.

6 Cofferdam construction

Design and construction responsibilities

Packshaw[1] defined a cofferdam as a temporary structure built to exclude earth and water from a construction area and thus permit the work inside to be carried out in the dry. Nevertheless, he conceded that 'in the dry' should not be taken too literally; seepage upwards through the formation and possibly leakage through the sheeting of the cofferdam walls may bring considerable water quantities into the working space. Packshaw said that to fulfil the purpose of the cofferdam:

(a) the walls of the dam and any internal bracing must withstand the loads and stresses imposed on them
(b) the amount of water entering the dam must be controlled by reasonable pumping and must not interfere with the permanent construction inside it
(c) it must be possible to excavate down to the required level without causing the ground to boil, heave or flow into the dam in an uncontrolled manner
(d) the walls must not deflect inwards so much as to interfere with the permanent construction inside the dam
(e) the cofferdam must have overall stability against unbalanced earth pressure or ground movements such as circular slips.

The responsibility for the safety of cofferdam structures is frequently defined by statutory regulations. In the UK the Construction Regulations[2] and Construction (Design and Management) Regulations stipulate obligations on both designers and contractors. Such regulations require adequate and safe support irrespective of depth. Previous limits of minimum depths requiring timbering no longer apply and all excavations are assessed on a site specific basis. Safety barriers are required where any risk exists and any excavation susceptible to risk of flooding must have adequate means of escape. All excavations require to be regularly inspected by a competent person and adequate precautions are required to avoid the presence of harmful, noxious gases in confined spaces.

In terms of the share of contractual responsibility for cofferdam design and construction, other than health and safety laws, this depends on the nature of the contracts between Employer, Engineer and Contractor. In practice, both design and construction are largely carried out by the Contractor, with whom these responsibilities mainly lie, although not completely so. In the UK for instance, a well used contract form, the ICE Conditions of Contract[3] requires the Engineer's approval to temporary works design, but such approval does not relieve the Contractor from responsibility under contract. It should also be remembered, however, that Engineer and Contractor have duties of care under common law in the UK and damages may be applied to both parties should, for instance, the Engineer be aware of deficiencies in design or construction which result in failure and harm to life or property.

With increasing use of diaphragm wall construction in cofferdam work in both temporary and permanent works phases, it is frequently necessary for Contractor and Engineer to accept responsibility for design in each phase, the Contractor for the temporary works and the Engineer thereafter for the permanent works. Where stresses induced during the temporary works period cause later distress there is every opportunity for dispute between the parties.

Successful cofferdam work implies minimum cost because of its temporary nature. The design is frequently made two or three times: at feasibility stage by the Engineer, at bid stage by the Contractor, and at construction stage by the successful Contractor. The Contractor's design engineer is finally set the task of designing a stable cofferdam that complies with the permanent works requirements at minimum cost in terms of construction, maintenance and final removal. The cofferdam must be safe, and appear so to those who work in it. Normal design criteria for permanent works may not prove economical for temporary construction and factors of safety and soil design parameters may require much care in selection. In particular, the choice of working stresses for construction materials which have been used before and suffered some deterioration will require judgement. Although cofferdam works are frequently considered short-term structures, the period of their use may range from months to years depending on the scale of the contract and any extensions to the contract period. The requirement for structural durability with time therefore depends on assessment of risk and the consequences of failure to 'life and limb' and construction damage. Only the latter may be influenced by insurance cover to temporary and permanent work.

The quality of design data from site investigation should also be referred to. Packshaw[1] stated the following basic rules.

- The site investigation should be deep enough to determine soil and water pressures, especially artesian pressures. A CIRIA report[4] suggested an investigative depth to at least 1·5–2 times the excavation depth, possibly more in weak soils.
- The site investigation should extend around the cofferdam site to a distance equal to its depth to formation level.

As a prerequisite to the investigation, accurate records of existing levels, site history, seasonal variation in groundwater levels, tides and flood frequency are essential. Unless these data are available the cofferdam designer and constructor cannot fulfil their responsibilities irrespective of those defined by statute and contract.

Types of cofferdam

Cofferdams may be divided into three categories:

(a) sheeted types, usually with external shores, anchors or internal bracing
(b) double-skin types, where sheeting is used to form cells, circular in plan shape, or with parallel walls, each containing fill material; the strength of these structures depends on the composite action of fill, sheeting and the underlying soil support
(c) gravity and crib types, where structures made from mass concrete, often precast, or from soil and rock fill resist, by their own weight, disturbing forces of river and sea water flow and groundwater pressure.

Design ingenuity has developed many variations on these types as cofferdam locations, sizes and soil and water depths have demanded. The choice of cofferdam type is wide, and analysis of construction expense and time will frequently be needed for a particular site before a choice can be made. The head of water to be retained, soil properties above and below formation level and depth to rockhead are often critical matters influencing the choice of method. In some instances the principal choice remains between cofferdam and caisson construction, especially where excavation depths are considerable in poor ground. Improvements to construction methods and mechanical equipment have tended to increase use of cofferdam construction to greater depths in recent years. Typically, in the 1960s and 1970s the economical depth of cofferdams would have been in the range 15 to 20 m of water, depending on subsoil type. In later years, however, the economical limit of cofferdam construction frequently extends 30 to 40 m or more, and caisson work continues to decline in popularity.

Sheeted cofferdams

Where space allows, battered excavations may be economical, particularly in clay subsoil or where dewatering is feasible. Where space is confined or groundwater is less easily dealt with, the use of a temporary wall, cantilevered or supported, becomes necessary at the curtilage of the permanent works.

The use of cantilevered sheeting, in steel sheet piling, bored piles or diaphragm walling, will only serve excavations of limited depth, although this depth may be effectively increased by either a short batter at the top of the wall or a temporary berm of soil against the wall at formation level. This berm is removed in short lengths as construction of the permanent wall proceeds. Cantilevered walls are particularly economical where relatively dry cohesionless soils overlie clays of reasonable strength at moderate depth. Such conditions frequently occur in London, with the top surface of London clay occurring at depths of 5 to 7 m. Although the upper horizon of the London clay may be weakened by weathering, a rule of thumb is often used to make the length of pile embedment equal to the depth from ground level to formation level. Excessive horizontal movement at the head of cantilevered walls can be reduced by use of in situ capping beams at the head of diaphragm walls or bored piles. In other instances, the buttressing effect of return angles in plan in the sheeting may limit excessive deformation to allowable values or restrict the plan length, requiring temporary propping at intervals between return angles in the wall.

Where depth to formation level within a large excavation precludes support from cantilever sheeting because of unacceptably high sheeting moments and

Fig. 6.1. Sheet piled excavation supported by raking shores with temporary berm support being removed by tracked excavator, London (courtesy of AMEC)

deflections, the sheeting is temporarily supported by horizontal struts spanning wall-to-wall, by raking shores, spanning where possible from partially completed permanent work or, where space allows and easement is gained, by ground anchors. Figure 6.1 shows a sheet piled excavation supported by raking shores, the temporary berm being removed as the rakers are secured. The relatively high expense of the double-support operation, which is uneconomic for small-scale excavation works, should be noted.

Circular cofferdams

The extent of internal bracing within a sheeted excavation can be reduced by the adoption of a cofferdam that is circular in plan. The plan shape of the permanent works needs either to fit accurately within the circular cofferdam or be reappraised to do so.

The advantages gained by circular structures rest in the comparative economy of structural rings built to resist hoop compression. However, the CIRIA report[4] restated that circular walings used to support sheet piles in circular plan forms require relatively small distortion to reach critical instability, and advised the empirical rule $d \geq D/35$, where d is the difference between outer and inner radii of the ring beam and D is the diameter of the cofferdam to the inner face of the piles.

Stiffness is therefore the essential criteria for circular walings. For this reason reinforced concrete is frequently preferred for circular waling construction. Although steel walings are used more frequently for cofferdams over water, the empirical proportions of $d \geq D/35$ must be observed and care taken to restrain the inner flange of the waling beam to prevent buckling. The CIRIA report gave values for safe waling loads for reinforced concrete waling sections suitable for cofferdams between 5 and 35 m in diameter. Although reinforced concrete waling sections cast against sheet pile, bored pile or diaphragm wall sheeting have the practical advantage of avoiding the use of timber packings between waling and sheeting, they also have disadvantages in the curing time needed before they contribute to cofferdam strength, delaying continuous excavation and possibly impeding extraction of sheet piles for reuse.

In relatively shallow excavations it may prove economical to anchor a square sheet piled enclosure to an outer circumscribing reinforced concrete ring waling, as shown in Fig. 6.2. Deeper excavation will require successive internal ring walings with sheeting of circular plan form. Figure 6.3 shows a land cofferdam with an upper waling cast externally to the sheeting and a lower waling cast inside.

Packshaw[1] stated that the practical limit of a circular cofferdam was of the order of 45 to 60 m in diameter using sheet piling. Developments in piling equipment and the increasing international use of diaphragm walling, often incorporated into the permanent structure, have extended the use of contiguous and secant piles and diaphragm walling into cofferdams of circular plan shape. An example of a large pumping station at the Isle of Grain, UK, is shown in Fig. 6.4. The diaphragm walls, designed to span vertically between circular walings, form a circle of 75 m diameter.

The design and construction of a circular diaphragm wall for a ventilation building at the end of an immersed tube tunnel construction (the Ted Williams) tunnel in Boston, MA was described by Kirmani and Highfill[5]. Soil conditions consisted of 15 m of fill overlying 7·6 m of Boston blue clay overlying glacial till and weathered argillite. Groundwater was 1·8 m below ground level. The cofferdam was almost 80 m in diameter and the depth to formation level was 24 m. The circular cofferdam, consisting of a segmented cylinder of diaphragm wall panels embedded into rock for lateral stability

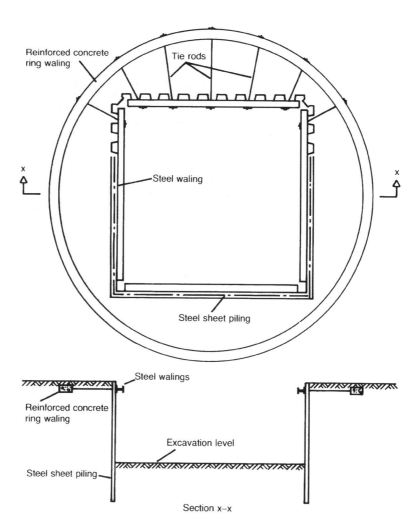

Fig. 6.2. Square sheet piled cofferdam anchored to outer circumscribing reinforced concrete ring waling[1]

was lined with an internal concrete wall cast successively in 2·4 m deep ring beams. The feature of both the design and construction of this cofferdam was the requirement for two large openings at each side of the cofferdam. The following assumptions were made for the load-carrying properties of the cofferdam structure:

(a) hoop stresses would be resisted by the combination of diaphragm wall and lining wall in proportion to their thicknesses
(b) horizontal bending would be resisted by the ring beams
(c) vertical bending would be resisted by the diaphragm wall
(d) buckling of the cylindrical cofferdam would be checked with the combination of both diaphragm and lining wall.

Some indication of the complex steps involved in cofferdam construction are shown in Fig. 6.5. The junction of the immersed tube tunnel and the circular cofferdam is shown in plan in Fig. 6.6. The seal, which had to be watertight, was achieved using two hinged steel gates that spanned between the tunnel and buttresses built in diaphragm walling at the outside of the circular cofferdam. The gates consisted of horizontal steel beams with a continuous vertical steel plate. The beams were spaced at 1·2 m centres and a hinge was made by installing a steel pin through the web of each beam and through a seat bracketed off the tunnel. A continuous vertical rubber seal was attached to the opposite end of the gate and positioned against a steel channel section embedded in each buttress.

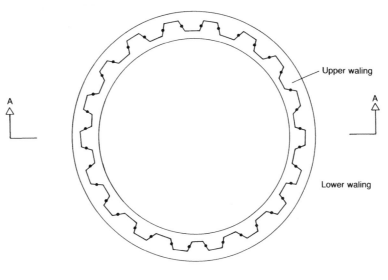

Upper waling

Lower waling

A

A

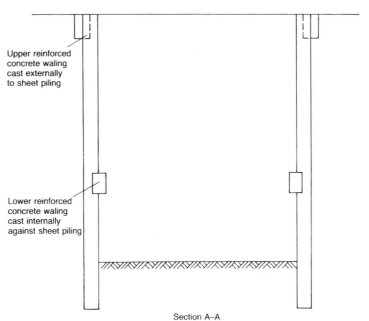

Upper reinforced
concrete waling
cast externally
to sheet piling

Lower reinforced
concrete waling
cast internally
against sheet piling

Section A–A

*Fig. 6.3. Circular cofferdam
with reinforced concrete ring
walings, outer waling
uppermost, inner waling above
formation level*

Fig. 6.4. Circular diaphragm wall with internal reinforced concrete waling, pumping station, Isle of Grain, UK (courtesy of Laing/O'Rourke)

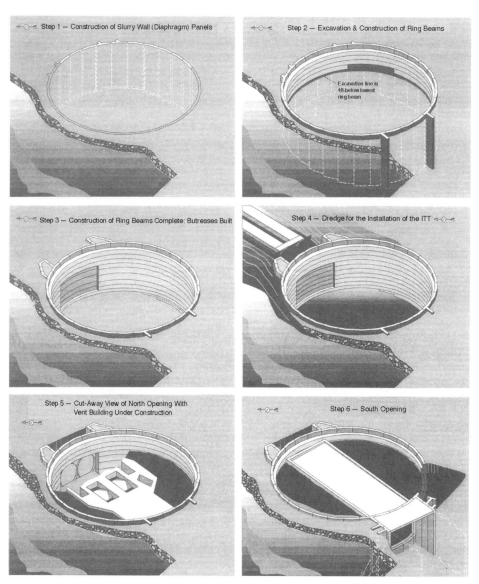

Fig. 6.5. Circular cofferdam for ventilation building, Boston, MA. Stages in construction[5]

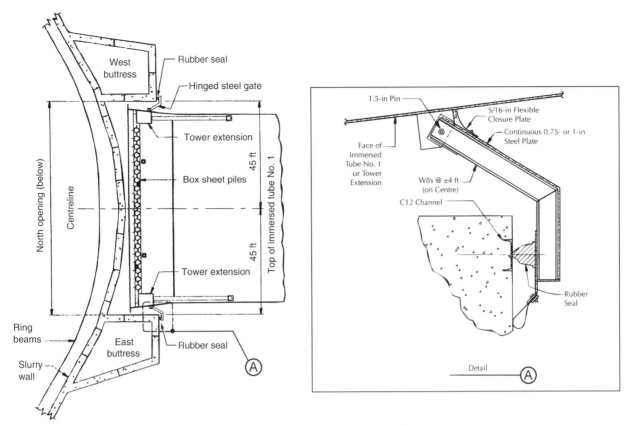

Fig. 6.6. *Plan view of the secondary cofferdam adjacent to the main cofferdam*[5]

A circular cofferdam, also with a lining wall, was constructed as part of recovery works for a collapsed tunnel at Heathrow Airport, London. This cofferdam, 60 m in diameter and 30 m deep to formation level, was constructed in secant piling, 40 m deep; the secant piles extended to a depth of 20 m and below this depth the piles were contiguous. The upper part of the pile over the secant length, was constructed as a 900 mm dia. contiguous pile encased in a soft annulus of cement–bentonite grout as shown in Fig. 6.7. The internal lining wall was constructed against the piles in successive

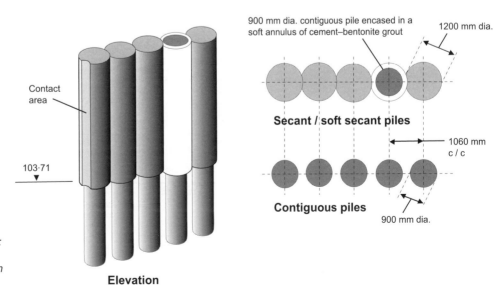

Fig. 6.7. *Circular cofferdam: Heathrow Airport, London, secant pile wall construction (courtesy Mott MacDonald)*

pours 1 m deep. The secant pile construction was noteworthy for its specified verticality tolerance of 1:200; in the event an average tolerance of 1:400 was achieved and the cofferdam was within 50 mm of a perfect circle at a depth of 30 m. It is likely that the adoption of a secant pile solution in preference to use of a diaphragm wall was favoured because of the availability of piling plant on site.

Figure 6.8 shows a vertical section through a deep circular cofferdam built for a pumping station at Weston-Super-Mare, UK, in difficult ground conditions with a high water table. Frodingham No. 4 sheet piles 23 m long were

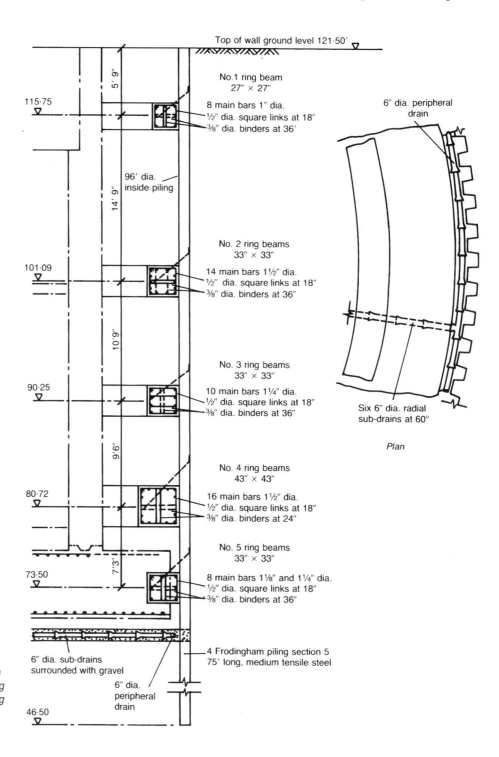

Fig. 6.8. Vertical cross-section of a circular cofferdam showing reinforced concrete ring waling construction, pumping station, Weston-Super-Mare, UK[1]

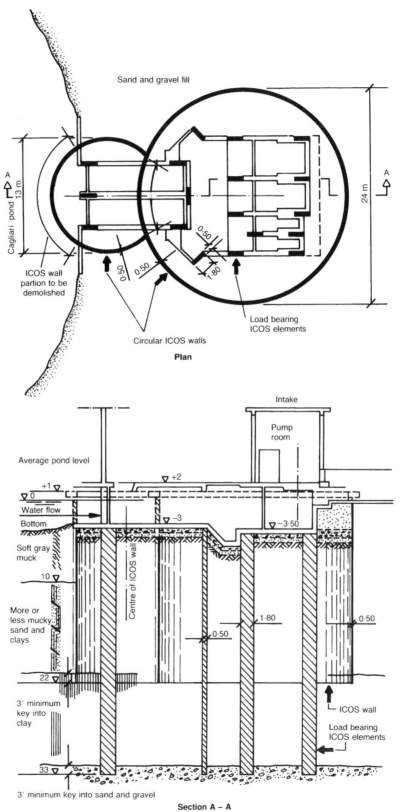

Sand and gravel fill

Cagliari pond 13 m

ICOS wall partion to be demolished

Circular ICOS walls

Plan

Load bearing ICOS elements

24 m

0.50

0.50

0.50

1.80

Intake

Pump room

Average pond level

Water flow

Bottom

Soft gray muck

More or less mucky sand and clays

+1   0   +2   −3   −3.50

Centre of ICOS wall

1.80   0.50   0.50

ICOS wall

Load bearing ICOS elements

10

22

3′ minimum key into clay

33

3′ minimum key into sand and gravel

Section A – A

Soil conditions   0 – 11·9 m loose fill
                   11·9 – 18·3 m sandy silt
                   18·3 – 19·8 m plastic silty clay
                   19·8 – 28·4 m clay
                   28·4 m dense gravel

Fig. 6.9. Figure-of-eight plan shape diaphragm wall water intake, Cagliari, Italy (courtesy of Icos)

supported by five ring walings in a cofferdam 30 m in diameter. Circular cofferdams on land require uniformity of soil and water pressure around the peripheral sheeting. Ground levels should therefore be sensibly level, soil strata relatively level and groundwater pressure constant around the cofferdam.

In a small number of diaphragm wall examples the limited overall diameter of the circular structure and tight control of panel verticality tolerance have allowed the hoop compression to be transferred efficiently from one panel to the next, avoiding ring walings completely. Due to the absence of bending stresses in these wall panels only limited quantities of reinforcement are required when hoop compression can be mobilized in this way.

Some variations on the circular plan shape can be economically used. Icos[6] documented the successful use of elliptical plan shapes for diaphragm wall cofferdams at Palermo, Legano and at the Quero hydroelectric plant, all in Italy. Double circular plan shape diaphragm walls in the form of a figure-of-eight were used by Icos[6] in Cagliari and at Beckton in London. Soil conditions and the general arrangement of the walls at Cagliari are shown in Fig. 6.9.

Two 36 m dia. tanks were recently built at Blackpool in the United Kingdom[7] in close proximity to each other. The tanks are shown in cross-section in Fig. 6.10. A two-dimensional analysis using the FLAC finite difference program was made to assess interaction between the tanks. The interaction analysis was used to estimate the induced additional movements of the diaphragm walls at serviceability limit state, to estimate additional structural forces and bending moments in the diaphragm walls at both serviceability and ultimate states and check the reinforcement design due to these additional forces and moments. The design required tight tolerances for construction of the 40 m deep diaphragm wall. The maximum verticality tolerance allowed was 1 in 300, that is a 133 mm maximum offset allowing guide wall tolerances for each panel over 40 m. This maximum tolerance required the use of a cutter machine although rope-suspended grabs were used for diaphragm wall

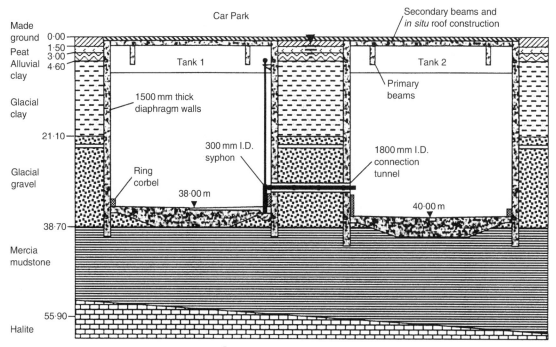

Fig. 6.10. Circular tank construction, Blackpool, UK[7]

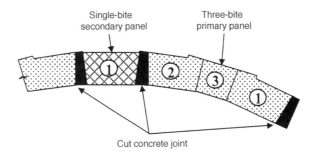

Single-bite secondary panel

Three-bite primary panel

Cut concrete joint

Fig. 6.11. Circular tank construction, Blackpool, UK: panel configuration[7]

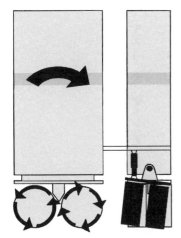

Fig. 6.12. Hydrofraise alignment correction[7]

excavation down to the glacial sands. A three-bite primary panel and a single-bite secondary panel configuration was used with cut joints as shown in Fig. 6.11.

To achieve the required verticality the Hydrofraise machine was equipped with instrumentation that allowed 3D real-time positional monitoring of the cutter head, the alignment being corrected continuously. The Hydrofraise machine has two means of adjusting alignment, by varying the individual cutter drum speeds or the angle of the cutter drums themselves, see Fig. 6.12. The instrumentation used is shown in Fig. 6.13. The maximum inclination of the panels as measured after excavation was 1 in 500 or 80 mm at an excavation depth of 40 m with a measured verticality of 1 in 1000 on most panels.

Excavation for the tanks was made after wall construction by two 16 t 360° excavators of 12 t capacity which were lifted to ground level by hydraulic cranes of 80 t capacity. Using this method, an excavation rate of 1000 m^3/day was achieved on each tank for the full excavation depth.

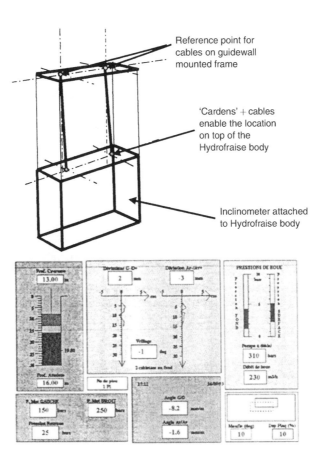

Reference point for cables on guidewall mounted frame

'Cardens' + cables enable the location on top of the Hydrofraise body

Inclinometer attached to Hydrofraise body

Fig. 6.13. Hydrofraise cutter real-time positional monitoring 'Evolution 2' machine[7]

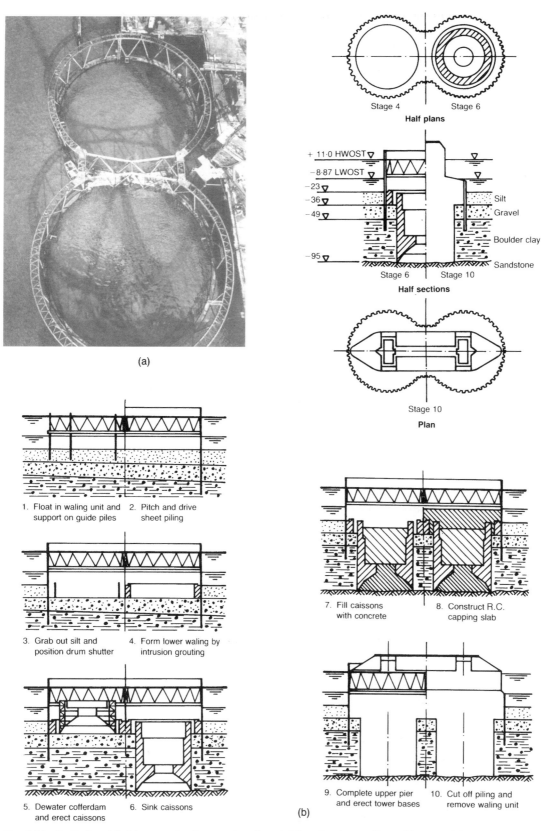

Fig. 6.14. Forth Road Bridge, south pier construction: (a) bracing frame floated into position prior to pitching sheet piles (courtesy of AMEC); (b) construction sequence[25]

On the Forth Road Bridge in Scotland cofferdams for the south main river pier were built in a figure-of-eight, two circular plan forms being connected by cross-bracing. Figure 6.14 shows the bracing frame arrangement and the construction sequence, including the sinking of caissons from the floor of the cofferdams.

Circular cofferdams, in pairs, were built for the east and west piers of the first Severn Bridge, UK. The marl into which the cofferdam sheeters were founded was too hard for pile driving. The toes of the sheet piles were therefore bolted to a concrete anchor ring which had been cast on to the rock surface between tides. In turn, the anchor ring was tied to the marl by dowel rods. The rock was excavated by mechanical loader after blasting with small charges, and a precast concrete segmental lining was grouted into place. The excavation and lining construction were carried out tidally. Excavation continued through the underlying mudstones and when a hard layer was met the cofferdam area was cleaned and covered with blinding concrete. Both ends of the cutwater pier were built to the high tide level within the cofferdams, the sheeting and bracing removed, and the central portion of the pier completed between tides. Figure 6.15 shows the cofferdams and the construction sequence.

Braced cofferdams

The use of cofferdam plan shapes other than circular or elliptical requires structural support to the sheeting by internal bracing for all but shallow excavations. Before considering construction of braced cofferdams over water and land, the most frequent causes of failure should be considered[4]:

(a) failure to make allowance for variation of water levels due to seasonal effect, constriction of flow by the cofferdam itself, and overtopping by high tide or flood conditions

(b) failure to provide and use balancing and/or flooding valves

(c) variations between the ground conditions assumed for design and those revealed by the excavation

(d) failure to control the excavation levels, at all stage of construction, to those indicated in the design

(e) failure to provide adequate support to frames and lateral restraint to compression flanges of waling beams

(f) use of frames to support plant loads, such as pumps and generators, in excess of design allowances

(g) frame members damaged by impact from skips and grabs and inadequately repaired

(h) unauthorized strut removal or substitution

(i) uncontrolled water ingress through separated interlocks into the passive zone below formation level

(j) ill-fitting struts carrying unintentional eccentric loads.

Overall failure is more likely to occur as a result of inadequate strutting or passive soil failure due to inadequate sheeting embedment rather than flexural failure of the sheeting itself. Packshaw[1] examined the reasons for cofferdam failure by soil type and concluded that the cause of failure is almost invariably below formation level; either the soil inside the cofferdam is unable to resist external forces or it undergoes a change in its properties as a result of these forces. Base failure takes several forms as follows.

(a) In permeable ground, if a 'blow' occurs because of inadequate cut-off or excessive pumping from sumps it is likely that the bottom of the piling will be forced inwards due to lack of passive resistance of the soil below

(a)

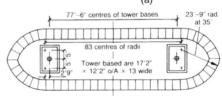

77'–6" centres of tower bases

23'–9" rad. at 35'

83 centres of radii

Tower based are 17'2" × 12'2" o/A × 13 wide

5' 5"

2' 9"

Plan on top of pier
Tower holding-down strands not shown

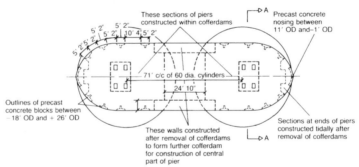

These sections of piers constructed within cofferdams

A

Precast concrete nosing between 11' OD and–1' OD

5' 2" 5' 2"
5' 2" 5' 2" 10' 4" 5' 2"
5' 2" 5' 2"

71' c/c of 60 dia. cylinders

24' 10"

Outlines of precast concrete blocks between –18' OD and + 26' OD

These walls constructed after removal of cofferdams to form further cofferdam for construction of central part of pier

Sections at ends of piers constructed tidally after removal of cofferdams

A

Plant at 10' OD

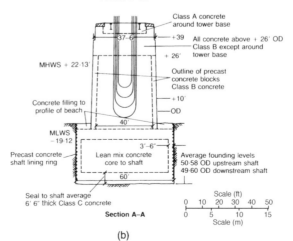

Class A concrete around tower base

37–6"

+39

All concrete above + 26' OD Class B except around tower base

+ 26'

MHWS + 22·13'

Outline of precast concrete blocks Class B concrete

+10'

Concrete filling to profile of beach

OD

40'

MLWS – 19·12

3'–6"

Average founding levels 50·58 OD upstream shaft 49·60 OD downstream shaft

Precast concrete shaft lining ring

Lean mix concrete core to shaft

60'

Seal to shaft average 6' 6" thick Class C concrete

Scale (ft)
0 10 20 30 40 50

Section A–A

Scale (m)
0   5   10   15

Fig. 6.15. Severn Bridge, west pier construction: (a) twin circular cofferdams with segmental ring construction below sheet pile walls (courtesy of AMEC); (b) construction details[26]

(b)

formation level. As excessive load is transferred to the lower frames, progressive collapse follows to the whole structure.

(b) In highly permeable soil, the upward flow of water will reduce the passive resistance of soil below formation level. This may be sufficient to overload the lowest frame even if quick conditions do not develop at the formation.

(c) Variations in loading, say tidal variations, not only test the stiffness and security of the bracing but, by repeated movement, may reduce passive resistance of the subsoil below formation. The lowest frame must be designed to allow for any transfer of load and should be located as near formation level as possible.

(d) In soft clays excavated below a critical depth the piling may deflect inwards.

(e) Uplift due to water pressure may cause base failure. Clay below formation level with artesian water in sand lenses or within a cohesionless substrate are typical risk conditions.

The cause of failure of a major cofferdam on the River Thames did not fall into these categories and deserves mention. The cofferdam, for a river wall improvement, had five frames with one face towards the river and was 15 m deep below high water, 15 m wide and approximately 80 m long. All strutting and walings were of steel section, and standards of workmanship and maintenance were generally above average. One particular strut on the bottom frame was, however, badly fitted; the cut end of the strut was not square to its axis and without shims the eccentric load placed on this strut was sufficient to cause failure at the highest tide after full excavation. The strut bowed badly and, without knowledgeable supervision during a weekend, no remedial action was taken. The next high tide caused progressive failure to the passive soil resistance below formation level and also to each of the four frames in turn above the bottom frame. Bad workmanship, particularly on struts, and avoidance of progressive failure should be added to the above list.

Braced cofferdams over water

In the case of braced cofferdams over water the sheeting is invariably steel piling, and the bracing, of walings, struts, king piles and puncheons, is nowadays usually in structural steel. Only where large quantities of fill material are economically available to build soil islands can diaphragm walling and secant piling be considered for use as cofferdam walls.

The minimum strength of sheet piles for braced cofferdams is the greater strength required either in flexure to resist soil and water pressure or to resist driving stresses. Sheet piles are manufactured in various profiles: the flexural strength of Z-type sheet piling with interlocks at the flanges can be assumed to be the strength of the complete section; those sections clutched on the centre-line (U profile) depend on frictional resistance to shear within the interlocks to develop the full cross-section strength in flexure. Williams and Little[8] considered this matter in depth. BS 8004[9] recommends that where piling is cantilevered substantially above the first frame and passes through very soft clay, or pile cut-off is limited by shallow bedrock, the flexural strength of the whole clutched section should be obtained by welding the clutches. To summarize the advantages and disadvantages of each section, Z profiles tend to have more closely fitting interlocks which are watertight for marine use, and deflections tend to be less when used to cantilever. Z profiles, however, reduce in modulus if they are allowed to rotate during driving. In approximate terms, a rotation of 5° results in a 15% modulus reduction. U profiles, on the other hand, have a greater single section modulus and are less prone to deviate in penetration of dense soils and can be reused more often. The rotation permitted by the interlocks is greater for the U profile than the Z profile (9° compared with 3°), so the U section is better when driving sheeting to a tight radius.

The sheet piles are pitched and driven in panels. Both U or Z section sheet piles should be driven in pairs wherever possible. The toes may need to be strengthened for very hard driving, although this may make extraction difficult at a later stage. Controlled blasting of a narrow trench in the rock may assist where sheet piles need to be driven into strong bedrock.

After pitching in pairs the piles are usually driven in echelon order (1–3–5–2–4–6). In difficult conditions the piles may be driven in two stages, first to part depth and then to full depth with a larger hammer. Piles may also be driven in panels by pitching and driving the first pair to part, but firm, penetration, then pitching the remainder of the panel in pairs. The last pair is fully driven and then the remaining pairs are fully driven successively back to and including the first pair. Jetting and pre-boring may sometimes be used to overcome difficult drilling; jetting should be replaced by conventional driving in the final metre of penetration to avoid loose subsoil at the pile toe.

The initial panel in a cofferdam should begin with the pile pair adjacent to a corner pile, the last panel concluding with the corner pile, all the piles being pitched and interlocked in this last panel before any are driven. For small cofferdams all the piles should be pitched before driving is begun. Cofferdams in water may be built by using the top frame, supported by temporary piles as a template. This template should be built to the design cofferdam dimensions, whereas lower frames should be made to reduced dimensions to allow for sheet pile verticality tolerances. The setting-out line of the top frame should therefore allow:

Table 6.1 Types of pile driving equipment[4]

Type of driver	Soil compatibility	Noise output	Quiet versions	Vibration output	Extract	Rate of penetration	Pairs/single driving
Double-acting air hammer	All soils except stiff clay	High	No	Low	Yes	Medium/low	Both
Single-acting diesel	All soils	High	No	Medium/low	No	Medium	Pairs
Double-acting diesel	All soils	Medium/low	No	Medium/low	No	Medium/low	Pairs
Cable operated drop	All soils	Medium/low	Yes	Medium/low	No	Medium/low	Pairs
Hydraulic drop	All soils	Medium/low	Yes	Medium/low	No	Medium	Both
Vibrator	Granular and soft clays	Medium	N/A	Low	Yes	High	Both
High-speed vibrator	Granular and soft clays	Medium/low	N/A	Low	Yes	High	Both
Hydraulic thrust	Granular with jetting and clays	Low	N/A	Nil	Yes	Slow/ medium	Single/ panel

- total verticality and positional tolerance of sheet piles
- a width dimension to allow cofferdam drainage at formation level
- adequate working space and accommodation for shuttering, where used.

The choice of driving equipment is large and depends on the size and weight of the sheet piles to be driven, embedment length, subsoil conditions, and constraints on noise and vibration. In the UK, legal power is given to local municipalities under the Control of Pollution Act 1974 to impose limits on site noise where this adversely affects the quality of life. BS 5228[10] gives guidance on vibration and noise control due to piling. It is worth remembering that while noise gives rise to complaint, vibration gives rise to structural damage. A summary of pile hammer types and their use is given in Table 6.1.

Impact hammers nowadays are usually hydraulic or diesel; drop hammers and air hammers finding less use than previously. The characteristics of typical current diesel hammers is shown in Table 6.2 and similar characteristics of both small and large hydraulic hammers are listed in Table 6.3. As a general rule, it is best to be on the heavy side with hammer capacity; light hammers tend to spread the top of the pile without achieving increased penetration. A typical hydraulic hammer, a Junttan, is shown mounted on a modern piling rig, with hydraulic leaders in Fig. 6.16.

High-frequency vibrators, see Fig. 6.17, are most effective in loose to medium dense granular soils particularly for sheet pile installation, although

Table 6.2 Characteristics of Delmag diesel hammers. The data listed in this table were obtained from manufacturers' brochures and websites and are current in March 2003. Reference should be made to the manufacturers for up-to-date data and availability before use. Comparative data with other hammer types can be obtained from manufacturers and website www.pilehammerspecs.com. The information is provided to show the range of energy available from modern diesel hammers. Other manufacturers include APE, ICE, HMC, MITSUBISHI, IHI, FEC, BSP and LINKBELT

Model	Mass of ram (kg)	Energy range (m kg)	Striking rate (blows per minute)
D2	220	251–120	60–70
D4	380	503–156	50–60
D5	500	1268	42–60
D6-32	600	1455–873	39–52
D8-22	796	2494–345	38–52
D12	1250	3118	42–60
D15	1500	3867	40–60
D12-32	1282	4323–2170	36–52
D22	2204	5501	42–60
D16-32	1603	5570–2615	36–52
D19-42	1904	5931–2840	37–53
D19-32	1904	5931–2840	37–53
D22-23	2204	6721–3395	38–52
D30	3006	7518–3298	39–60
D25-32	2505	8072–4136	37–52
D30-23	3006	9160–4670	36–52
D30-32	3006	9686–4903	36–52
D36-23	3608	11 516–5266	37–53
D36-32	3608	11 624–5667	36–53
D44	4318	12 056–5958	37–56
D46-23	4610	14 550–6707	37–53
D46-32	4610	14 852–7242	37–53
D55	5512	16 213–8661	36–47
D62-22	6636	22 865–10 942	36–50
D80-23	8863	31 180–17 487	36–45
D100-13	10 732	41 574–21 818	36–45
D200-42	20 029	69 240–43 652	36–52

Note. The hammers listed above are single-acting. Some manufacturers have introduced double-acting hammers incorporating a bounce chamber to increase the blow rate.

Table 6.3 Characteristics of Junttan hydraulic hammers. The data listed in this table were obtained from manufacturers' brochures and websites and are current in March 2003. Reference should be made to the manufacturers for up-to-date data and availability before use. Comparative data with other vibrator types can be obtained from manufacturers and website www.pilehammerspecs.com. The information is provided to show the range of hammer weights, energy and strike rate available from modern hydraulic hammers. Other manufacturers include: IHC, Menck, APE, BSP, Twinwood, Bruce, HPSI, Pilemer, Nissha, HMC, Dawson

Model	Mass of ram (kg)	Maximum energy per blow (m kg)	Strike rate (blows per minute)
HHK-3A	3000	–	40–100
HHK-5A	5000	6000	40–100
HHK-7A	7000	8400	40–100
HHK-9A	9000	10 800	40–100
HHK-12A	12 000	14 400	40–100
HHK-14A	14 000	16 800	40–100
HHK-18A	18 000	21 600	40–100

Note. The hammers listed above have provision of assistance to the ram during its downward travel; the rated energy includes the effect of the motive fluid pressure in addition to the free-fall gravity mass. Other hammers are either single-acting or double-acting. Hydraulic hammers for off-shore operation have been developed with greater energy capacity and for underwater use. Manufacturers of such hammers include Menck.

Fig. 6.16. Modern hydraulic piling hammer mounted on base machine (courtesy of Junttan Piling Equipment)

Fig. 6.17. High-frequency piling
vibrator

penetration of soft to firmer clays can also be achieved for limited penetration depths, as may apply in mixed strata. Characteristics of typical vibratory hammers are listed in Table 6.4.

The detrimental noise and vibratory effect of sheet pile installation in urban areas has for some years restricted their use. A report previously published by the British Steel Corporation[11], gives a review of published recommendations on minimum distances of pile installation to existing structures and services and both BS 5228 (part 4)[10] and the European code of practice on sheet piles EN 12063[12] give advice on noise levels.

Traditionally, acoustic covers have been used to reduce noise from drop and hydraulic piling hammers. The use of acoustic covers has reduced as hydraulic presses have remedied both noise and vibratory objections to sheet piling. A typical hydraulic press, by Giken, is shown in Fig. 6.18.

The hydraulic press installs single sheeters from a clamped reaction to previously installed piles. The system which is virtually vibration-free and noiseless, apart from crane and power-pack noise, allows sheet pile installation immediately adjacent to existing services and allows sheet piling to be installed without environmental problems in city centres. The presses, which can also be used to extract sheet piles, are limited to a downwards thrust of the order of 100 t or so and either lubrication with water introduced through a metal tube welded to the sheeter or water jetting may be needed to assist pile installation in stiff clays. Pile penetration is limited to the order of 15 m or so in stiff clays. A sheet pile of minimum section LX20 is often needed to resist the force inserted on the single pile. There is some tendency for the sheet piles to spread in width and to twist as they are installed. Installation tolerances are somewhat more difficult to control with single-pile installation

Table 6.4 Characteristics of PTC vibratory hammers. The data listed in this table were obtained from manufacturers' brochures and websites and are current in March 2003. Reference should be made to the manufacturers for up-to-date data and availability before use. Comparative data with other vibrator types can be obtained from manufacturers and website www.pilehammerspecs.com. The information is provided to show the range of mass, frequency and power requirements of modern vibrators. Other manufacturers include: Tramac, HMC/Movax, MKT, Dawson, ICE, HPSI, Muller, APE, Vulcan, PVE, Delmag/Tunkers, H and M, Foster

Model	Power of vibrator (kW/hp)	Eccentric moment (m kg)	Max. frequency (Hz/rpm)	Max. amplified (mm)
Excavator mounted				
1HF1	–	0·7	50/3000	6
3HF3	–	3	45/2700	11
7HF4	–	6·5	38/2300	20
10HF5	–	10	35/2100	15
15H2	–	13	28/1680	19
Standard				
7H5	47/63	6·5	33/1980	20
15H1	108/146	15	28/1680	24
25H1A	133/181	23	29/1740	21
30H1A	193/262	30	28/1680	23
50HL	305/414	50	25/1500	31·2
High frequency				
7HF3	92/125	6·5	28/2300	14·5
13HF3	124/169	13·5	38/2300	22
15HF3	167/227	15	38/2300	23
23HF3A	184/250	23	38/2300	20
30HF3A	292/397	27	38/2300	22
46HF3	447/607	46	38/2300	13
Variable frequency				
10HFV	95/129	0–8	38/2300	10·6
15HFV	140/190	0–15	38/2300	15
15HFV5	200/272	0–15	38/2300	15
17HFV	240/326	0–17	38/2300	11
23HFV	222/302	0–23	38/2300	13

by hydraulic press compared with conventional panel installation by diesel or hydraulic hammer.

When pile installation by driven hammer becomes difficult and tearing of the piles and stripped clutches are likely to occur, a strong shoe can be welded to the end of the sheeter to assist penetration and avoid damage (see Fig. 6.19). Pressure water jetting can be incorporated into the shoe to further assist penetration. Pre-boring or pre-augering may also be used along the pile centre-line to overcome difficult driving conditions.

The depth of embedment of cofferdam sheeting is dependent on the need to effect a cut-off in an impermeable strata, to reduce risk of boiling and the quantity of pumping in cohesionless soils, to alleviate risk of base heave where hard strata underlie soft clay and silts, and to generally reduce sheeting movements by mobilizing passive resistance of subsoil below formation level. The height of sheeting driven for tidal works will normally be based on the highest tide levels estimated during the period of the works, with allowance for flood risk. The freeboard will take into account wave action caused by wind and, in navigable rivers, will allow for the wake caused by passing vessels.

In exposed conditions on the sea shore it is at times economical to use half-tide cofferdams, with no works being carried out at peak tides, the cofferdam being pumped out after the tide. As with any cofferdam over water, adequate

Fig. 6.18. Giken hydraulic press for pile installation

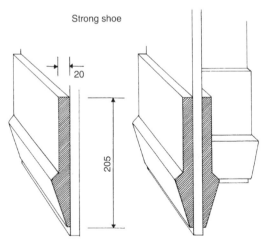

Fig. 6.19. Piling shoe for heavy duty installation of sheet piling (courtesy Dawson Con Plant Ltd)

sluice valves to allow discharge of water are essential when overtopping is considered. In addition, internal bracing must be sufficiently rigid to allow some reverse head and avoid loosening of strutting. Tie rods and external walings are sometimes installed above the top frame, not to resist reverse water heads after overtopping but to give some means of tightening the coffer-dam after dewatering.

The struts of all cofferdams are often made deliberately short to allow wedging or paging with timber wedges, preferably in elm, between sheet piles and the rear face of the walings. This shortening depends on frame depth and the driving accuracy of the sheet piles, which directly depends on quality of workmanship and subsoil conditions. The practice of using short lengths of reinforced concrete to pack the gap between strut ends and the face of walings should be used cautiously since this cube of concrete can be dislodged by accidental blows from excavating plant and time is needed for the concrete to cure before the strutting becomes effective. A well-built and maintained cofferdam in tidal conditions will therefore have each pile pan timber paged against the back of the waling, these wedges being driven tight at each tide, the end-plated struts remaining square to the face of the waling.

The struts, typically from tubular steel, box piles, universal column or battened twin joist sections, are designed at spacings to comply with the overall geometry of the cofferdam. In addition, strut centres must allow lower frame members to be threaded through them and allow excavating grabs and excavation plant to pass vertically without striking the frames. The number of frames will depend on the imposed loading, the strength of the sheeting and the frame material available. The method of excavation within the dam will be controlled directly by the vertical height between frames; efficient excavation equipment such as tracked loading shovels can only be used with reasonable headroom. Frame levels will also condition lift heights of concrete pours for permanent works within the cofferdam. This factor applies particularly where the permanent works are built against the sheeting and where projecting vertical reinforcement lies below walings. Bar couplers may be necessary in these circumstances to reduce the difficulties of excessive or inconvenient reinforcement splice lengths.

The cofferdam frames are supported by steel brackets welded to the sheeting. The use of hanging rods or chains to suspend frames beneath the top frame, which is supported on brackets, is inadvisable; all frames should be supported on an adequate number of brackets welded to the sheeting. Long span struts may require support from king posts which are pre-bored or pre-driven below formation level.

In recent years, increased use has been made of steel bracing walings and struts made to standard sizes and available from construction equipment hire companies. The use of these members is restricted to excavations of only modest depth, although spans of up to 20 m are available for both walings and struts and with adaptation are available for bracing shafts of shallow depth. The struts are usually extended mechanically, although hydraulic struts are also available for higher loads. Typical applications are shown in Fig. 6.20. It should be noted that considerable care is needed to ensure competence of connection between struts and walings in such systems.

The static calculations for the cofferdam structure will take into account soil and water pressures. However, loads due to construction plant such as pumps being placed on the frames, the dynamic effect of waves, accidental collision from vessels and blows caused by excavation grabs and equipment on struts, must also be considered or avoidance measures taken during the construction phase.

The effects of scour on cofferdams in fast flowing rivers will be referred to later. Measures to prevent scour during the construction period include river bed protection by rock fill, precast concrete blocks and tetrapods, rock-filled gabions and grouted mattresses. Routine observation of the depth of scour is essential, particularly where there is risk of under-scour to river bed protection.

In cofferdams built in waters with a high tidal range the sequence of load application and reduction causes movement within the sheeting which is unavoidable and can cause heavy leakage of water into the dam through the pile clutches. Traditional, practical methods of reducing this problem included lead-wool caulking, asbestos-string caulking and, more crudely, the spreading of fly-ash or sawdust on to the water outside the cofferdam as

Code No.	Overall Strut Length(mm)		Weight (kg)
	min	max	
MBS-00	2280	3490	300
MBS-01	3030	4240	370
MBS-02	3780	4990	445
MBS-03	4530	5740	500
MBS-04	5280	6490	570
MBS-05	6030	7240	645
MBS-06	6780	7990	670
MBS-07	7530	8740	740
MBS-08	8280	9490	815
MBS-09	9030	10240	885
MBS-10	9780	10990	960
MBS-11	10530	11740	1015
MBS-12	11280	12490	1070

Code No.	Overall Strut Length(mm)		Weight (kg)
	min	max	
LMBS-00	1890	2690	272
LMBS-01	2390	3190	322
LMBS-02	2890	3690	342
LMBS-03	3390	4190	392
LMBS-04	3890	4690	382
LMBS-05	4390	5190	432
LMBS-06	4890	5690	482
LMBS-07	5390	6190	502
LMBS-08	5890	6690	472
LMBS-09	6390	7190	522
LMBS-10	6890	7690	572
LMBS-11	7390	8190	592

Fig. 6.20. Use of mechanical bracing strut (courtesy of Mabey Ltd)

the tide ebbs. As the dam is pumped out quickly the fine material is taken into the clutch and helps to seal the leak. More recently, durable elastic sealants have been applied to the interlock at site or as a complete filler to the interlock prior to pile despatch from the works.

The construction phase where excavation has been made to a level just below the level at which a frame is to be built was mentioned earlier. The risk factor at the lowest frame level depends on the time taken to build the frame in position, to prop the sheeting and make secure. All materials will therefore be ready to drop into position and weld and page up tightly as the last excavation is taken away. Where conditions are suspect, caution may dictate that this should be done at low tide where possible and also, of course, in short lengths, taking only sufficient excavation to fix one length of waling. Where high bending moments in the sheeting are unavoidable it may be necessary to fix frames, usually after the first frame, below water. Frames may be slung, fixed and packed by divers prior to pumping out the dam.

Code No.	Overall Strut Length(mm)		Weight (kg)
	min	max	
HBS-01	1655	2655	365
HBS-02	2505	3505	433
HBS-03	3355	4355	483
HBS-04	4205	5205	533
HBS-05	5055	6055	583
HBS-06	5905	6905	651
HBS-07	6405	7405	662
HBS-08	7255	8255	730
HBS-09	8105	9105	780
HBS-10	8955	9955	830
HBS-11	9805	10805	880
HBS-12	10655	11655	925
HBS-13	11505	12505	993
HBS-14	12355	13355	1043
HBS-15	13205	14205	1093
HBS-16	14055	15055	1143

Code No. (Shaftbrace)	Code No. (Tankbrace)	Overall Strut Length(mm)		Weight (kg)
		min	max	
SJC-00	MWS-00	490	710	73
SJC-01	MWS-01	710	1150	84
SJC-02	MWS-02	1110	1550	109
SJC-03	MWS-03	1510	1950	124
SJC-04	MWS-04	1910	2350	145
SJC-05	MWS-05	2310	2750	160
SJC-06	MWS-06	2710	3150	180
SJC-07	MWS-07	3110	3550	195
SJC-08	MWS-08	3510	3950	216

Fig. 6.20. Continued (courtesy of Mabey Ltd)

River cofferdams: construction examples
The river cofferdam examples that follow illustrate some of the constructional principles to follow, and the dangers and faults to avoid.

(a) *The Thames Barrier cofferdams* were described by Grice and Hepplewhite[13]. The flood defence barrier was built by the municipal authority, the Greater London Council, to prevent flooding of some 45 square miles of London during critical tides and winds.

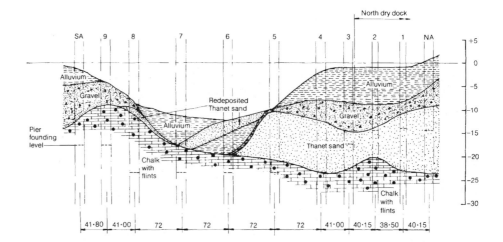

Fig. 6.21. Thames Barrier: geological section across the site[13]

Fig. 6.22. Thames Barrier: general view during cofferdam construction[13]

The geological section across the Thames at the barrier site is shown in Fig. 6.21, and a general view during construction is shown in Fig. 6.22. Eleven deep river cofferdams were built between 1974 and 1980 to house the two abutments and nine piers. Cofferdams 4 to 8 are among the largest river cofferdams built in the UK to date. The seven southern structures were founded on the chalk and the remaining four northern structures were built in the Thanet sand, a very dense grey–green silty fine sand. On the south side, the upper surface of the chalk is about 10 m below datum and dips gently northwards. On the north bank, the chalk is about 25 m below datum and is overlain with the Thanet sand. The chalk, which is fissured and jointed with flints, is classified as upper chalk and is generally unweathered where covered with sand but is moderately to severely weathered elsewhere.

As shipping access was needed through the works, the south side of the river was closed first for construction of piers 6 to 9 and the abutment; construction work then moved to the north-side cofferdams.

The southern cofferdams were built from Larssen No. 6 grade 50B sheet piles 34 m long, fully driven in pairs by piling hammers ranging from the Delmag D44 to the Delmag D62. Final driving sets varied from 400 to 1200 blows per metre. The construction sequence was to install the top frame at level +2·1 OD and then excavate underwater to −18·00 just below bottom frame level. The excavation was completed to −23·75 OD, the formation prepared and the 5 m thick concrete plug placed by tremie. Intermediate frames were installed in cofferdams 6 to 8 after pre-assembly above low water in a position under the top frame. The dams were then dewatered. Access for the south-side cofferdams is shown in Fig. 6.23. The part plan and cross-section of the pier 6 cofferdam is shown in Fig. 6.24. The walings were fabricated from twin 914 × 419 mild-steel universal beams and the struts from beams or tubes. To minimize obstruction to permanent work construction, no vertical bracing was used. The variable gap between the sheet piling and the back of the walings was packed by divers using a grout bag secured on a mild-steel mesh framework hung from the waling. The bag was then grouted with an expanding grout from a surface mixer. A short length of steel beam was used where the gap at the rear of the waling was excessively large. To facilitate removal of the bag at a later stage, a 25 mm hole was left to allow the placing of a small explosive charge.

Fig. 6.23. Thames Barrier: river access to southern cofferdams (courtesy of Carillion)

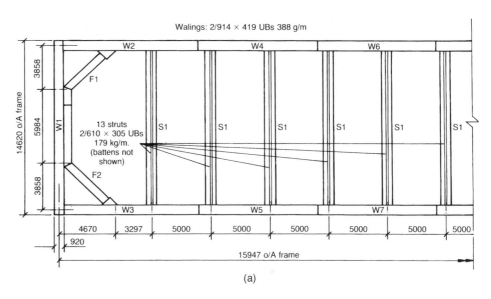

(a)

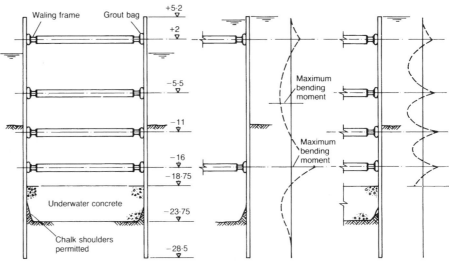

Fig. 6.24 (a) Cofferdam frame at level −5·50, pier 6; (b) bending moments in sheet piles after excavations and dewatering (courtesy of Carillion)

(b)

Fig. 6.24 (c) View of south-side cofferdam showing heavy leakage (courtesy of Carillion)

The construction of all southern cofferdams was slowed by excavation difficulties in the chalk. The alluvium overlying the chalk was removed by rope grabs from cranes, and then kelly-mounted augers and hydraulic grabs were used on the chalk itself. The chalk shoulders left beneath the wide walings were removed with some extra difficulty by kelly-mounted grabs, by chisels and hydrojets. Blasting was also used, with charges of Polar ammon 80% gelignite limited to 250 g of charge per cubic metre of chalk blown. The charges were placed at least 0·5 m from any chalk/water or chalk/pile interface, with separate detonation by Cordtex fuse. After completion the engineers responsible suggested that a cofferdam slightly larger in plan size may have been more economical and would have reduced the difficulty of removing the chalk from under the walings despite the additional excavation and temporary works.

After excavation of the chalk, air lifts were used to sweep and clean the chalk surface to final level, the whole finished surface being inspected and probed by Mackintosh probes from a diving bell.

With the exception of the southern abutment, the concrete plug weight was insufficient to resist the upward pressure and an extensive pressure relief system was needed under each base to achieve a factor of safety against uplift of at least 1·3. Typically the system consisted of 20 tubes, each 865 mm in diameter, temporarily supported from the bottom cofferdam frame. After concreting the plug, and prior to dewatering the cofferdam, the tubes were bored out by auger to 10 m below formation level and filled with gravel. Piezometers and stand-pipes were installed and monitored to check actual uplift pressure.

The cofferdams were pumped in stages with progressive checks on the effectiveness of the pressure relief wells and the integrity of each successive bracing frame. Sluices in the sheeting allowed for reflooding if this was deemed necessary. Considerable leakage through the clutches in all dams was only partly sealed with sawdust and fly-ash. Some split clutches had to be plated over, and water ingress was sufficient to warrant hanging heavy plastic sheets from the walings to reduce nuisance to operatives in the cofferdam (Fig. 6.24(c)).

Additional works were required to the pier 7 cofferdam. One of the fault lines in the chalk crossed pier 7 diagonally, and several split clutches were discovered during diving inspections. After the water in the dam had been pumped out, high readings were obtained for uplift pressures on the bottom of the plug and a fine crack was found across the top of the tremied concrete. The dam was reflooded and a reverse filter installed on the outside of the sheeting, with a grouted cut-off on the far side of the filter to prevent further ingress of water from outside the cofferdam. The solution was successful.

The task of placing the concrete plug by tremie to all cofferdams on the scheme was a major operation. Early trials had established a high slump concrete mix incorporating Pulverized Fuel Ash as half of the cementitious content to reduce the heat of hydration. In each cofferdam pour of $8000\,m^3$ the site-mixed concrete was poured continuously through tremies handled by tracked cranes. The tremies, 300 mm in diameter, were arranged on a 7·5 m grid as shown in Fig. 6.25. The ends of all tremies were submerged in the concrete throughout the pour. Concrete was delivered to the tremies by $3\,m^3$ Trucrete vehicles to 125 mm mobile concrete pumps. The pour was brought up in layers of 2 m maximum thickness, the concrete being built up at one end of the pour and advanced forward on the chalk subsurface to scour any silt remaining to the far end of the dam. The major south-side pours, working night and day, took five days to complete.

The north bank cofferdams required extensive sheet piling through the Thanet sand. Experience at pier 2 showed a large number of split

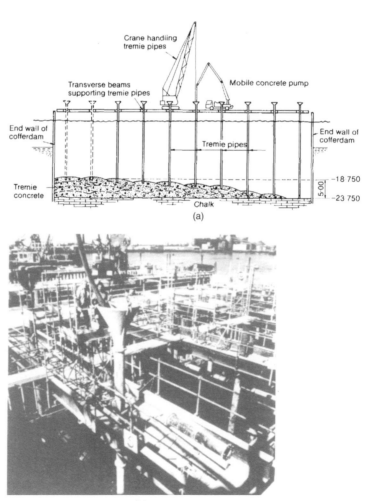

Fig. 6.25. Thames Barrier: (a) longitudinal section through cofferdam showing arrangements for tremie concreting; (b) view of tremie works in progress

clutches in the Larssen No. 6 sheet piles. Pre-boring was used to alleviate the hard driving for the sheet piles on cofferdam 1. For the remaining sheeting at piers 3 to 4, Peine piles made from grade 50 steel, but with clutches of higher grade, were driven into pre-augered secant bores that had been filled with a low-strength Pulverized Fuel Ash–cement–bentonite grout. The clutches of each pile were stitch-welded 10% to prevent slippage during driving the 38·4 m long piles. Each pair weighed 21 t and the toe of each pair was sculpted with toe plates to reduce skin friction during driving.

A part plan and cross-section through the pier 4 cofferdam shows the Peine piles (Fig. 6.26). Their clutches proved very efficient and their double skins gave an open box which permitted filling or grouting as an additional sealing measure if needed. The increased strength of the

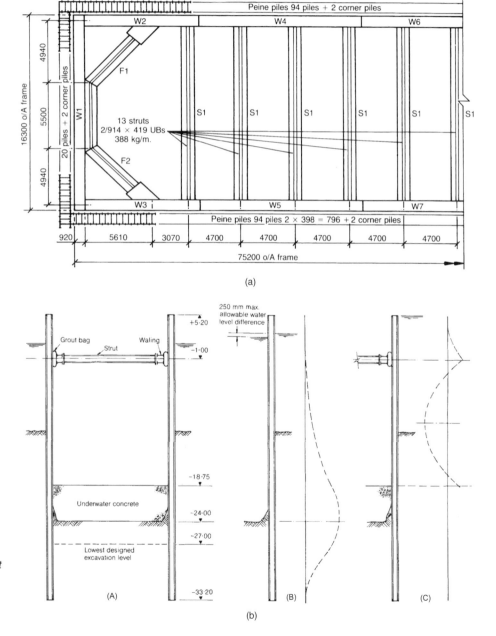

Fig. 6.26. Thames Barrier: (a) general arrangement of frame to pier 4 cofferdam, part plan and cross-section; (b) bending moments in sheet piles after excavation and dewatering[13]

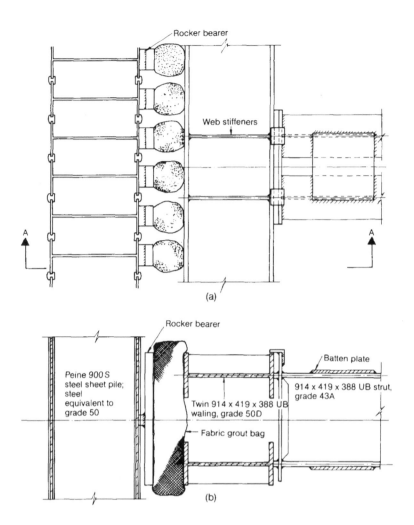

Fig. 6.27. Thames Barrier; pier 4 cofferdam, details of rocker bearing: (a) plan; (b) vertical section[13]

Peine piles allowed the use of only one frame composed of walings and struts from twin 914 × 419 universal beams in high-yield steel.

The maximum design load on the walings was 150 tonnes per metre run, with a maximum axial compressive strut load of 1200 t from the walls. With the risk of cofferdam collapse due to dislodgement of members of the single frame, higher factors of safety were used in the frame design.

Figure 6.27 shows the detail of a rocker bearing that was used to distribute the applied loading from the sheet piling equally to each beam of the twin waling member, the rocker bearing accommodating the deflected form of the sheet piles. A secondary waling with header beams set into the pile heads of 305 × 305 column section was used to smooth out pile deformation during re-strutting of the sheet piles against the permanent works as the main strutting was removed.

For the 9005 section Peine piling, driven using D62 hammers on two Menck MR 60 rigs working 16 hours per day, the period of driving was nine weeks for 235 pairs. The average final blow counts were 600 blows per metre.

With the exception of cofferdam 5, the cofferdams formed from Peine piles were closed with pre-welded Larssen clutches. The seal was then enhanced by grouting within the blister. This precaution was adopted because of the rigidity of the Peine section and the double clutching incorporated in it.

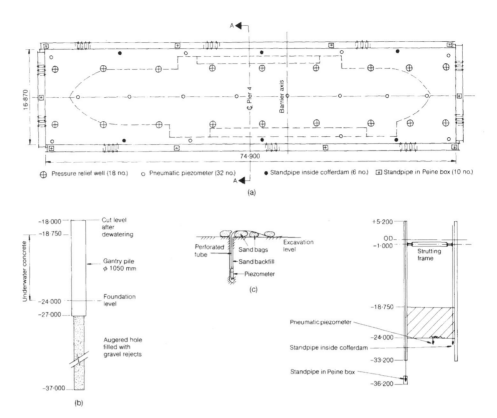

Fig. 6.28. Thames Barrier, north cofferdam construction: (a) plan of cofferdam showing relief well positions; (b) vertical section through relief well; (c) details of piezometer and standpipe installation

Excavation of the northern cofferdams was made easier by the single frame used to support the Peine piles. Pier 3 was founded on Thanet sand, piers 4 and 5 on chalk. In the Thanet sand, excavation was by augering and airlifting. Once into the chalk, augers were used to break up the chalk which was then removed by 500 to 660 mm dia. air lifts aided by a heavy reverse circulation rig. Finally, the chalk surface was cleaned by air lift sweeps. Figure 6.28 shows the plan of the north cofferdam and details of the construction pressure relief system.

(b) *River Hull Barrier.* Flood barriers built across other English rivers in the late 1970s also serve to illustrate construction techniques in river cofferdams. The tidal surge barrier built across the River Hull and completed in 1979 required deep cofferdams for both the monoliths on which the towers were founded and the cills. The works were described by Fleming *et al.*[14]; Fig. 6.29 shows the cofferdams during construction.

The feature of the works (unlike the Thames Barrier) was that the length of the piles was large in relation to the plan area of the cofferdam. The foundation solution for the barrier towers was to found them on mass concrete monoliths within dense glacial sand and gravel approximately 20 m below the river bed level. To avoid disturbance to the subsoil below formation, the contract specified that excavation for the monoliths should be underwater and that the water level in the cofferdam should be maintained at least 0·5 m above the tidal level outside. Mass concrete to a depth of at least 14 m had to be placed by tremie to form the monolith before piping was guaranteed not to occur. A cofferdam sheet piled in two stages was originally considered, but a single-stage cofferdam was constructed with Larssen No. 6 sheeters supported by five bracing frames. The 34 m long sheet piles were the longest rolled by the British Steel Corporation at that time.

(a)

*Fig. 6.29. River Hull tidal surge
barrier: (a) pitching 34 m long
Larssen No. 6 piles to monolith
cofferdam; (b) completed cill
cofferdam*

(b)

(c)

Fig. 6.29. (c) Sheeting and bracing to monolith cofferdam (courtesy of Dawson)

The top three frames were to be fixed above water and the lower two below water, by divers. Due to the small radius of the monolith cofferdam walls it was necessary to reduce the friction in the interlocks during pitching and driving. This was done by crimping every in-pan pile so that interlocks were in line. In addition, it was necessary to ensure that piles were pitched and driven vertically. This was ensured by providing substantial temporary supports at close centres, by instrument checks for verticality and by temporary welding of each in-pan pile to the supports. Driving was carried out in small stages with the toes of the sheeters all at approximately the same depth below ground level. Suspended drop hammers of ram weight 5 t and 7·5 t were used to begin driving, which was completed by a Delmag D46. Excavation was by rope grab, and the two lower frames were suspended from frame 3 before the dam was flooded. The packing from the two lower frames to the sheeters was of pieces of universal column, measured individually by the divers and fitted with a single bolted clamp.

Air lifting was used for the final excavation. During the bottoming-up of the west monolith cofferdam a blow of approximately 80 m³ of loose sand occurred through a split in the intermittent welding of one of the corner piles. The split, about 50 mm wide, started about 2·5 m above formation level. With the risk of further loss of ground if the sand had been removed, it was left in place and later consolidated by grouting after the tremie concrete had been placed. During the final excavation work for the east monolith cofferdam a digging grab impact caused the lower three frames to drop to the bottom of the excavation. The lowest frame was refixed in an intermediate position and there was no inward movement of the sheet piles. Due to the head of water maintained inside the cofferdam, a differential of about 1 m at all times, the net loading in the frames was very small and the two dislodged frames were not refixed.

The monolith was concreted underwater by tremie to a depth of about 16 m. A total of 1550 m³ of ready mix concrete, retarded for 7 h, was placed through four tremies in 34 h continuous pours for each monolith.

Fig. 6.30. View of Fobbing Horse Barrier job site (courtesy of AMEC)

(a)

Fig. 6.31. Fobbing Horse Barrier: (a) south-west pier cofferdam; (b) north-east pier cofferdam (courtesy of AMEC)

(b)

(c) *The Fobbing Horse Barrier.* Figure 6.30 shows an aerial view of works on the Fobbing Horse Barrier in Essex, part of the Thames Flood Defence Works completed in the early 1980s. The bracing details of each cofferdam are shown in Fig. 6.31. The south-west pier is strutted by diagonal steel tube bracing, while the north-east pier uses the alternative method of cross-strutting with box pile sections. Both steel tubes and box pile sections are efficient strut members but suffer the disadvantage of low flexural strength compared with the universal beam and column section.

(d) *Forth Road Bridge.* Successive stages of cofferdam works to a suspension bridge tower construction are shown in Fig. 6.32. The corner braces used to provide horizontal support to each of the three frames are augmented by one cross-strut to each frame on the longer side of the cofferdam. Note the increased structural stiffness provided by relatively light diagonal steel bracing between each of the frames on

(a)

(b)

Fig. 6.32. Forth Road Bridge: (a) south-side tower cofferdam construction (note diagonal bracing); (b) tower base construction within cofferdam (courtesy of AMEC)

(a)

the longer side, and between the puncheon and upper and lower frames across the cofferdam.

(e) *Kingsferry Bridge.* The layout of cross-bracing and diagonal bracing to river cofferdams for a bridge construction at the Isle of Sheppey in Kent is shown in Fig. 6.33. Diagonal braces are used, it will be noted, to give maximum space for the passage of excavation grabs and equipment and to minimize expense in cross-strutting.

Braced cofferdams on land

Cofferdams constructed on land and braced for support include excavation for generating plant, pumping stations and underground facilities for various industrial purposes. The problems that arise with such cofferdams and their method of solution are sometimes common with other deep excavations on land for building basements and cut-and-cover construction for transportation systems. Nevertheless, because building basements and tunnels built in-trench possess some special features they are considered separately in Chapters 8 and 9. The purpose of this section is to describe constructional features of braced land cofferdams, typically those used in pumping stations and similar industrial subsurface structures.

The five main differences between constructional features of land and marine braced cofferdams are as follows.

(a) Land cofferdams require much less work to provide temporary access for plant, labour and materials than many jobs over water.

(b) While the choice of sheeting for schemes over water is often limited to steel sheet piling, a wider range of sheeting and walling methods are available for work on land. The location, depth of excavation, depth to the groundwater table, subsoil conditions and depth to bedrock, if present, will all help to determine the most economical sheeting system. In addition to steel sheet piles, the choice for work on land includes diaphragm walling by in situ reinforced and post-tensioned concrete and precast methods, contiguous piles, secant pile walling using hard–hard, hard–firm and hard–soft methods, and temporary

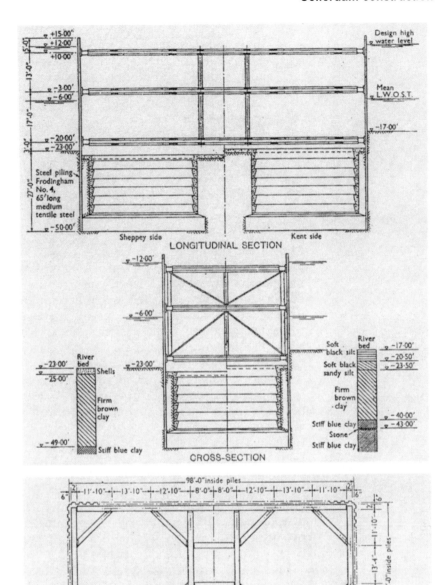

FIG. 4b.—PLAN OF COFFERDAM FOR MAIN PIERS, KINGSFERRY BRIDGE

All frames are similar, and all struts and walings are 24 × 7·5-in. R.S.J.'s in pairs

1. Frames at levels + 10·00 ft and − 3·00 ft to be fixed between tides before closing dam.
2. Dam to be closed at low water and pumping started at once to avoid reversed pressure.
3. Remove all silt, mud, and soft material from bottom: then level and place mass concrete blanket over exposed clay not less than 12 in. thick, leaving working space to construct the first in-situ concrete ring.
4. Excavate for piers in 3 ft 0 in. to 4 ft 0 in. cuts and support sides with in-situ mass concrete rings.
5. Undercut the base to be excavated and concreted in radial segments.
6. Bottom frame may be struck at any time after concrete blanket near river bed level has hardened.
7. Walings from bottom frame slung below second frame and subsequently used as a jury frame strutted from new construction before striking the second frame.
8. Second frame walings lifted and used similarly as a jury frame below the top frame.

Fig. 6.33. (b) Cross-sections through river pier cofferdam and construction sequence[1]

(b)

soil support from soldier walls (with soldier piles and horizontal lagging timbers or concrete skin walls).

(c) The means of bracing land cofferdams includes ground and rock anchors in addition to internal bracing from steel struts and walings.

(d) The proximity of existing structures to the excavation requires greater emphasis on problems of soil deformation around the excavation periphery for cofferdams built on land.

(e) The loads applied to land cofferdams are not likely to include tidally varying groundwater but allowance must be made for superimposed loading from other structures, and from traffic and site plant around the excavation periphery. In addition, in less temperate lands, the effect of freezing soils on soil pressures and bracing loads must be considered.

Choice of sheeting

Whereas methods such as the use of king posts provide temporary soil support to allow construction of the permanent wall, secant or contiguous piling and diaphragm walling allow the temporary walling to be incorporated into the permanent wall structure. The saving in construction time and cost has led to the increased use of these latter systems in land cofferdams.

In other instances, the experience of specialist contractors with diaphragm wall construction has encouraged the introduction of composite sheeting methods. Although only used for temporary support, sheet piles pitched rather than driven into slurry trench excavations have proved attractive cost-wise and avoid the environmental problems of noise and vibration to adjoining structures. It is often necessary to place tremie concrete below formation level to provide sufficient passive resistance to sheet piles pitched in this way.

An example of king post walling is shown in Fig. 6.34. The method, for a pumping station in Jubail, Saudi Arabia, found favour because of a low groundwater table, an essential prerequisite for king post walls unless dewatering is to be employed, and possibly due to lack of competitiveness by specialist diaphragm walling firms for a relatively small job which would be distant from plant and resources.

Figure 6.35 shows the use of sheet piling to the substructure of an ash pit at West Thurrock Generating Station, UK[15]. The works, in difficult ground conditions, were sited adjacent to a reinforced concrete chimney already partly built. The ash pit, founded on the gravel some 16 m below ground level, was built in cofferdam in preference to sinking a caisson because of the risk of undermining the foundations to the chimney if a soil blow were to develop under the cutting edge. The soft marsh clay was comparatively impermeable and had a shear strength of about 30 kN/m^2. The underlying gravel contained an artesian head of groundwater which almost reached ground level and rested in turn on fissured chalk which also contained groundwater. Excavation in the dry would have been very difficult and it was decided to excavate to third frame level only in the dry and take out the remaining 6·4 m depth under water prior to concreting a plug between levels −8·54 and 13·72. Pressure relief wells were also installed to relieve the artesian head in the gravel. These wells consisted of 670 mm dia. bores filled with gravel on a 4·6 m grid, and were installed before the excavation started.

After excavation down to just below second frame level, with top and second frame fixed, sand and silt began to flow from the relief wells which had previously discharged satisfactorily. The cofferdam was immediately flooded and six deep wells with submersible pumps were installed outside the cofferdam and 6·5 m below the clay. The cofferdam was pumped out

Fig. 6.34. Berlin wall method using anchors to scale pit building, depth to formation level 14 m, groundwater table at a depth of 3 m, steel plant, Jubail, Saudi Arabia (courtesy of Bauer)

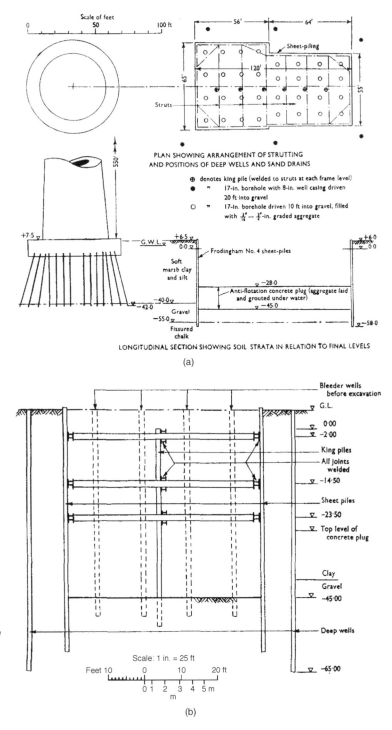

Fig. 6.35. West Thurrock Generating Station: (a) plan and longitudinal section of ash pit disposal cofferdam showing deep wells, sand drains and anti-flotation plug; (b) transverse section of cofferdam[15]

and the third frame fixed in position. The cofferdam was then reflooded to level −1·82 and the excavation completed underwater with the artesian head relieved by the deep wells. The cofferdam was made rigid by welding sheet piles, walings and struts. By taking these measures, diagonal bracing was not needed. The concrete plug was formed by grouting a gravel layer 5·18 m thick underwater using the Intrusion Prepakt method, and after completion the cofferdam was pumped dry. A 380 mm layer of blinding concrete and a 1·2 m reinforced concrete floor slab, both anchored into the anti-flotation plug, completed the ash pit bottom.

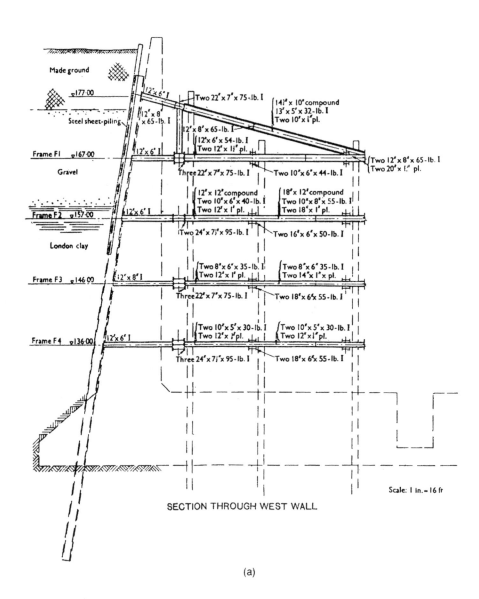

SECTION THROUGH WEST WALL

(a)

Fig. 6.36. (a) Section and (b) plan of cofferdam and framing, Post Office underground station, London[16]

This cofferdam was built just before the introduction of diaphragm walling and secant piling into the UK: in the soil and groundwater conditions that existed at the West Thurrock site it is doubtful whether these alternative methods would have shown any advantage over sheet piling had they been available. However, it is likely that jet-grouting methods would have been used in lieu of the Intrusion Prepakt system.

Measures to reduce settlement around land cofferdams deserve discussion. The extent of such deformation in a stable cofferdam depends on soil bracing and sheeting stiffness and the vertical spacing of bracing frames. Diaphragm wall and reinforced concrete pile sections are stiffer than conventional sheet pile sections and their use is likely to minimize soil deformation adjacent to the excavation. Further precautions may prove necessary, however, and these include installation of frames or other support at frequent vertical centres, pre-loading of struts, use of pre-stressed soil and rock anchors, and the use of jet grouting and pin piling or mix-in-place piles to stiffen artificially the soil and increase passive resistance to the sheeting below formation level.

The use of flat jacks to stress the frames of a land cofferdam to reduce soil movement and the resulting subsidence was reported by Collingridge and

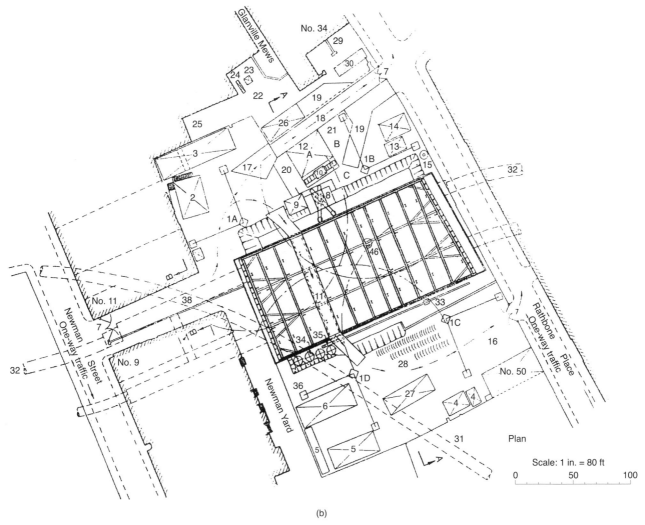

(b)

Fig. 6.36. Continued

Tuckwell[16]. The excavation, in London, was for a new subsurface station for the Post Office. It was 61 m long, 29 m wide and 22·3 m below ground level. At the time it was one of the largest excavations made in Central London.

The contract specified earth pressure at rest in the temporary works design. The ground conditions, typical of London, were made ground and Thames gravel overlying London clay. The specified values of K_0 were 0·75 in the clay and 0·5 in the fill and gravel. To exclude groundwater in the gravel and provide continuous support for all soil above the London clay, a peripheral sheet pile wall was specified to be driven from below basement level of existing buildings to a penetration of 2·5 m into the clay.

The method of excavation support is illustrated in Fig. 6.36. Steel H soldier piles 25 m long were driven to the batter of the outer face of the permanent wall at 1·6 m centres, achieving penetration 4·6 m below formation level of the permanent structure. An intermediate, 0·23 m thick reinforced concrete wall spanned the soldier piles. Four horizontal frames and a top raking frame were used to support the H sections, needle joists being provided between the soldier piles and the walings. Provision was made for jacking each needle joist. As each frame level was reached during bulk excavation, the steelwork was assembled and stressed to a load calculated to retain the subsoil in a state of rest. The aim of needle joists between the main struts

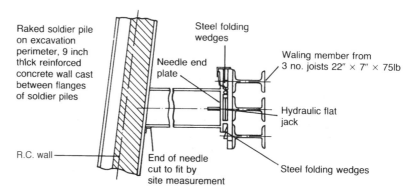

Frame F1

Elevation of jacking system
pre-loading frames: Western District Post Office
London

See section through west wall detail 17

Raked soldier pile on excavation perimeter, 9 inch thick reinforced concrete wall cast between flanges of soldier piles

Steel folding wedges

Needle end plate

Waling member from 3 no. joists 22″ × 7″ × 75lb

Hydraulic flat jack

R.C. wall

End of needle cut to fit by site measurement

Steel folding wedges

By interconnecting hydraulic 'flat jacks', the whole of a frame could be stressed against the ground in four simple operations as soon as it had been assembled — one using sixteen jacks at each end to stress the frame longitudinally — and three operations using twelve jacks on each side to stress the frames transversely. Two sizes of flat jacks were used: 27 cm dia. rated at 64 t, and 35 cm rated at 114 t

Fig. 6.37. System for pre-loading cofferdam frames, Post Office underground station, London[16]

(Fig. 6.37) was to allow a more uniform distribution of pressure to the soil than the application of load to the sheeting at the strut positions. Freyssinet hydraulic flat jacks, with small travel and high capacity, were linked by hydraulic connection and pressure was applied simultaneously in four operations per frame. One operation used 16 jacks at one end to stress the frame longitudinally, and three operations using 12 jacks on each side were used to stress the frame transversely. The two jack sizes used were 27 cm dia. rated at 64 t and 35 cm rated at 114 t. The total jack load was applied in increments of 25%, and a complete jacking operation was completed in half a day. Allowance for temperature stresses avoided overstressing in hot weather, jack load being reduced by 10% for every 5·5°C above 21°C at the time of stressing.

Collingridge and Tuckwell[16] concluded that pre-loading of steel frames with calculated jack loads proved a satisfactory method of preventing ground movements, the uniform transfer of strut load to the soil being very important.

The use of flat jacks to pre-load frames in an attempt to avoid settlement damage has reduced to some extent since the development of ground anchors, which also restrain soil movements. Nevertheless, easement arrangements for anchor installation below neighbouring land and highways frequently experience problems, and it is in these particular sites that pre-loading methods still find application.

The use of pre-tensioned anchors through vertical sheeting or walling to reduce movements caused by large excavations is only effective where the anchorage zone lies outside the soil movement zone associated with the excavation. Long-term soil movement due to consolidation within the anchorage zone limits the application of soil anchors for permanent anchorage to clay soils. Tomlinson[17] has reported a summary of observations of maximum horizontal movement of soil support for excavations in normally-consolidated, over-consolidated clays and gravels. These results

Table 6.5 Observed values of maximum horizontal deflection of sheeting to excavations on land[17]

Soil type	Wall type	Number in sample	Maximum horizontal deflection/excavation depth (%)		Range of excavation depth (m)
			Range	Average	
Soft to firm normally-consolidated clays	Anchored diaphragm wall	3	0·08–0·58	0.30	9 to 24
	Strutted diaphragm wall/secant pile wall	4			
	Strutted sheet pile, soldier pile and concrete infill	5			
Stiff to hard over-consolidated clays	Anchored diaphragm wall	2	0·06–0·30	0·16	10 to 30
	Strutted diaphragm wall/secant pile wall	6			
	Strutted sheet pile, soldier pile and concrete infill	1			
Sands and gravels	Anchored diaphragm wall	2	0·04–0·46	0·19	7 to 20
	Strutted diaphragm wall, secant pile wall	5			
	Strutted sheet pile, soldier pile and concrete infill	1			
	Anchored sheet pile, soldier pile with concrete infill or timbered	4			

are summarized in Table 6.5. The prediction of vertical deformation adjacent to excavations is reviewed in Chapter 11.

An example of pumping station construction using diaphragm walls of varied plan shape is shown in Fig. 6.38. The site, at Redcar, UK, was close to an existing quay wall built in diaphragm wall construction. The groundwater level was high and the subsoil conditions were fine sands overlain by filling composed of broken blast furnace slag. Groundwater was lowered by deep wells in the fine sand located within the cofferdam, and despite large overbreak to the diaphragm walling within the fill material, the works were completed successfully. Figure 6.39 shows the individual panel components of the construction; the action of the heavily reinforced capping beams in limiting movement by any out-of-balance forces on panel units should be noted.

Double-skin cofferdams Double-skin cofferdams built from steel sheet piling and enclosing soil or rock fill divide into two categories.

(a) Double-wall cofferdams. These consist of two parallel lines of sheet piling tied by steel rods at one or more levels between external walings and a fill material, such as sand, gravel, hardcore or broken rock, between the sheet piles. The filling requires adequate drainage which may be maintained by internal sluices or deep wells below the fill. Berms may be used to reduce lateral movements in the pile–fill soil structure and increase stability. If bedrock occurs at shallow depth and the sheeters cannot be driven into it, this type of cofferdam may not prove adequate to resist seepage nor will it be economical because of high moments in the sheet piles.

(b) Cellular cofferdams. These are enclosures, often circular, made from straight web steel sheet piling to contain a filling of sand, gravel and

Fig. 6.38. View of construction of diaphragm wall to pump house, steelworks, Redcar, UK (courtesy of Lilley)

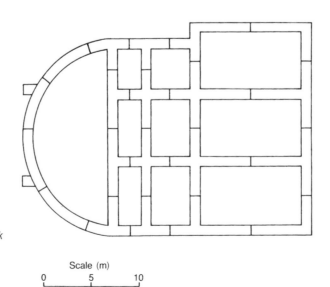

Fig. 6.39. Redcar pumping station: panel layout to 1 m thick diaphragm walls spanning vertically between base slab and capping beam without bracing

Scale (m)

0   5   10

Fig. 6.40. Cellular cofferdam with berm to cut off canal water from a large lock excavation, Canal Albert, Belgium (courtesy of Arbed)

broken rock. The straight piles, which have a high interlock strength, resist pressure from the filling and contained water by circumferential tension in the piling. Adequate drainage of the fill is needed to reduce pressure on the sheeting and to avoid reduction of the shear strength of the filling. The cellular cofferdams are economical for greater water depths, large retained heights, long structures, and where bracing and anchoring is not possible. The additional requirement in sheet pile area is compensated for in the length of piling and pile section and the absence of walings and anchors. The fill quantities may outweigh advantages in pile tonnage, however. An example of the typical use of a cellular cofferdam, to exclude river water from a large excavation, is shown in Fig. 6.40. The works, for a new lock at Kwaasdmechelen on the Canal Albert in Belgium, were completed in the early 1970s.

These two types of double-skin cofferdams are now examined in further detail.

Double-wall cofferdams

Examination of the possible modes of failure of double-wall cofferdams serves to illustrate design and construction precautions.

(a) *Sheet pile flexure; tie rod breakage; passive soil failure at foot of sheet piles.* To avoid overstress in bending or excessive flexural deformation of the sheeters, the pressure from the contained fill and groundwater should be as low as possible. In particular, it is essential that the fill should be drained adequately at all times during the cofferdam life. The drainage system may consist of weep holes or sluices in the inner line of sheet piles, possibly connected to an internal filter layer of gravel within the filling. In addition, deep wells through the filling may be used; these wells, with vertical filters extending upwards into the filling, also serve to reduce the exit gradient of water seepage under the dam. Efficient maintenance of the drainage system is vital, and new weep holes must be cut where migration of fine soil within the fill causes blockage.

The extent of pile penetration into the subsoil or rock beneath the dam and the location of the lowest tie rods determine the passive

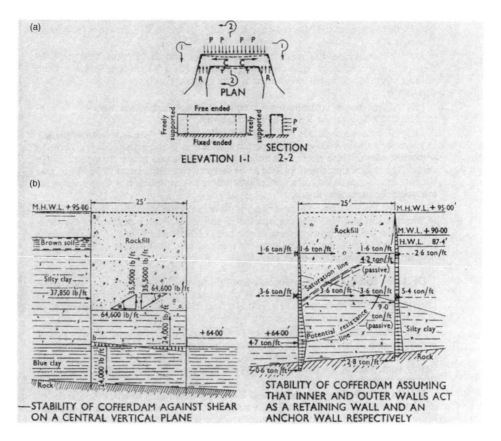

Fig. 6.41. Chola cofferdam, India: (a) plan and assumed support conditions; (b) basis of design, stability considered by shear induced on a vertical plane and assuming inner and outer walls act as a retaining wall and anchor wall[18]

forces mobilized in front of the sheeting. The lowest ties should be installed as low as possible, at low tide level in tidal rivers. Pile penetration will depend on subsoil conditions. Penetration into rock may not be possible; if this can only be achieved by heavy driving, split clutches may occur which in turn could lead to seepage problems and loss of ground. To alleviate problems of piling into rock it may be possible to excavate a trench into rockhead at low tide followed by concreting the pile toe into the trench. In such conditions, construction costs increase and the use of double-wall cofferdams may be uneconomical.

An example of a cofferdam founded on rock at a power station site in India was given by Ellis[18]. The cofferdam, shown in section in Fig. 6.41, was built to allow a dry, unrestricted area for the construction of a cooling water pumphouse at Chola in Southern India. Although a feature of the work was the small penetration of the piles into bedrock, it should be noted that the second row of ties was at a relatively low elevation. Note also the plan shape of the dam, which was such as to buttress the structure substantially at each end, reducing deformation within the dam and stresses in sheet piles and ties.

It is sometimes worth incorporating anchor cells within long lengths of double-wall cofferdams. The cells contribute to construction sequencing but, most importantly, will confine damage to an isolated length of dam should any failure or deformation occur, easing remedial work. A typical arrangement is shown in Fig. 6.42. It may be noted that the cell acts as a strongpoint in the cofferdam and reduces deformation and stresses in piles and soils.

(b) *Sliding.* The total horizontal thrust from river water and ground pressure on the outside of the dam will be resisted by passive resistance

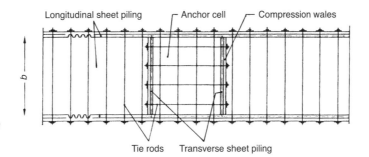

Fig. 6.42. Typical detail in plan of strongpoint in a double-walled cofferdam[27]

of soil below formation level inside the dam and shearing resistance mobilized under the cofferdam due to the weight of fill on cohesionless subsoil or due to the cohesive strength of clay subsoil. The condition is unlikely to dictate cofferdam geometry if pile embedment is sufficient to counter all other modes of failure.

(c) *Shape deformation.* The risk of the rectangular cross-section of the cofferdam adopting a lozenge shape will only be reduced by the following measures:

(i) cofferdam fill of adequate uniform quality placed to ensure resistance to tilting and to shearing forces mobilized within the filling

(ii) adequate drainage within the filling, to ensure maximum shear strength of fill at all times

(iii) adequate penetration of internal and external lines of sheet piles to mobilize reaction to shearing resistance between fill and face of sheet piles.

The height-to-width ratio necessary to avoid tilt may be low, of the order of 1:1. In addition, substantial soil or rock berms may be necessary to avoid unacceptable deformation at the top of the dam. Figure 6.43 shows the cross-section of the double-wall cofferdam used during construction of the outer entrance to Gallions Lock on the Thames in London. It is interesting that despite the extent of the berms and the penetration of the sheeters into the chalk, horizontal deformation of the cofferdam crest at high water reached 0·36 m. Packshaw[1] suggested that the deflection of the cofferdam may have been aggravated by two factors: firstly, the hard-core filling, deposited through water, may have been rather loose; secondly, the rather

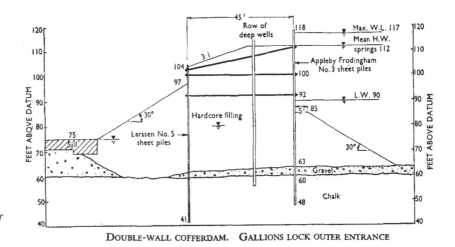

Fig. 6.43. Gallions Lock, double-wall cofferdam at outer entrance showing dimensions in berms, piling and filling[1]

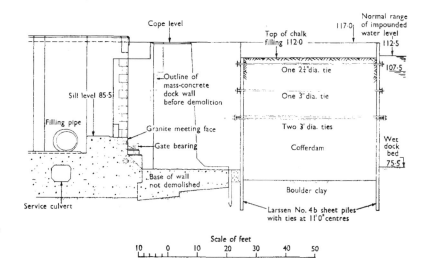

Fig. 6.44. Cross-section of the entrance cofferdam, Immingham dry dock[19]

compressible chalk on which it was built may have contributed to the movement by consolidation of the chalk. The row of deep wells into the chalk should be noted, reducing the piezometric head in the filling and the exit gradient of seepage water under the dam.

Chalk was also used as filling to a double-wall cofferdam during dry construction at Immingham, UK[19]. The cross-section of the dam is shown in Fig. 6.44. There was concern at design stage of the extent of maximum friction which could be mobilized between the chalk fill and the sheet pile face, so tests were made in a large shear box, with a rusted sample of steel in the lower part of the shear box and chalk in varying compaction states in the upper half. A design value for angle of wall friction of 46° was used as a result of the tests.

A cofferdam built across the entrance to St Katherine's Lock in London during replacement of the lock cill had a width-to-height ratio of 0·81. The cross-section and plan of the cofferdam are shown in Fig. 6.45. The dam, founded on Thames gravel, was drained by sluices in the inner line of piling and by two deep wells with submersible pumps in the gravel. The use of puddle clay seals to achieve watertightness against the existing jambs of the lock entrance is a rather outdated method, but proved successful. The seals provided some support to the dam which had very limited length, but deflection at the top of the piling under high water reached 0·3 m.

(d) *Piping.* Like any other cofferdam retaining water or groundwater, double-walled cofferdams founded on granular subsoil are at risk from piping failure by flow beneath the structure into the dewatered area. To avoid piping, the emergent hydraulic gradient can be reduced by adequate embedment of the sheet pile walls; stabilizing berms also increase the length of the drainage path to reduce this gradient.

(e) *Bearing capacity failure.* In very soft clays at the founding level of the cofferdam, the risk of bearing failure may be such to require removal of the clay between the piling to a level where better ground occurs.

(f) *River bed scour.* The risk of scour to the outer sheet piles in swiftly flowing rivers, or where flow is constricted, must be examined in the same way as for any other river cofferdam.

The construction of three double-wall cofferdams at Alton, IL, was described by White and Prentis.[20] At the site, 25 miles north of St Louis, the Mississippi River is about half a mile wide and almost 10 m deep, with a current of just

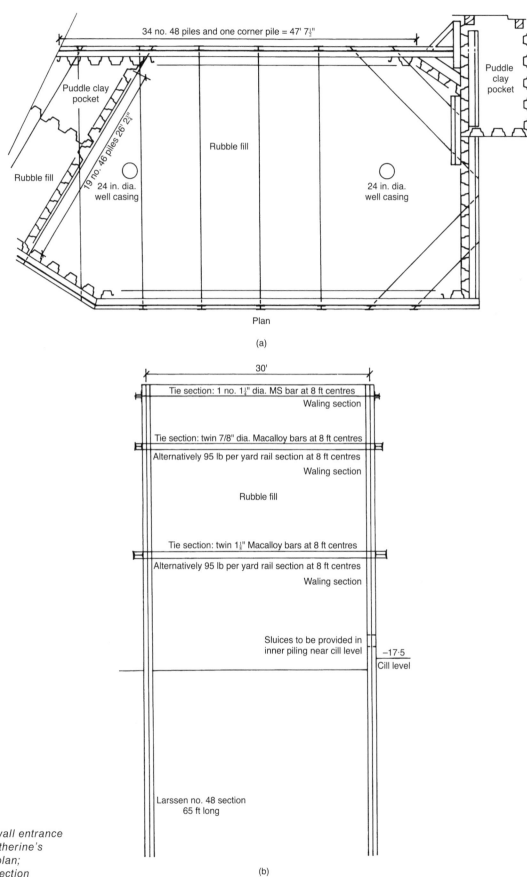

(a)

(b)

Fig. 6.45. Double wall entrance cofferdam at St Katherine's Lock, London: (a) plan; (b) vertical cross-section

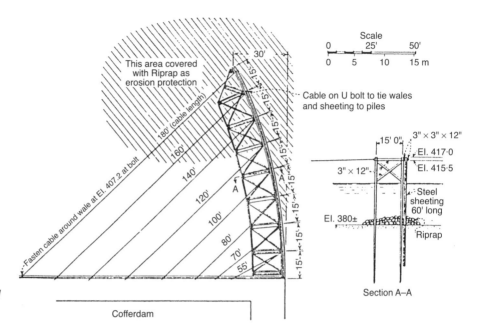

Fig. 6.46. Detail of streamlining fin, dam 26, Mississippi River, Alton, IL[20]

over 2 m/s. Model tests were used to design streamlining lead-in piling to the cofferdams to reduce scour. The streamlining fin to cofferdam 1 is shown in Fig. 6.46. The 18·3 m long steel sheeting piles were pitched and driven from a barge to a timber framework suspended from timber piles previously driven. Added protection was obtained by guying the streamlining fin to the cofferdam and by dumping Riprap at its upstream end. The works were successful in preventing scouring and erosion of the cofferdams without causing harm; sand and silt were deposited along the entire length of the river leg. The cross-section of the double-wall cofferdam is shown in Fig. 6.47.

Cellular cofferdams

Cellular cofferdams are constructed of flat sheet pile sections with high inter-lock tensile strength. They offer the advantage that they can be designed as stable gravity structures even where embedment is difficult, for example where rock occurs at founding level or the subsoil prevents pile penetration.

In plan, cellular cofferdams are typically circular, diaphragm or clover leaf types. Circular types may also be joined together. These four plan forms are shown in Fig. 6.48.

Circular cells have the advantage that they can be individually built and filled; the smaller linking areas are built later. The width of circular structures increases in proportion to their height, and as the diameter increases the inter-lock tension also increases. When the diameter becomes excessive and the interlock tension exceeds permissible limits, flat cells may be used. Individual flat cells are not stable on their own, and unless special measures are taken, cofferdams of this type must be filled in stages. The use of intermediate strong-points is desirable in long lengths of cellular cofferdams built with flat cells, particularly when there is risk of rupture or storm damage. Unless isolated strongpoints are provided, failure in an individual cell can lead to the progressive collapse of several neighbouring cells.

Heights and loadings being equal, flat cell cofferdams require greater weight of steel per linear metre than circular cofferdams. Comparisons based on total pile tonnages can mislead, however, as the total cost of cofferdam construction greatly depends on the cost of fill as placed. While flat cell construction may require larger pile tonnages than circular cells, flat cells are probably

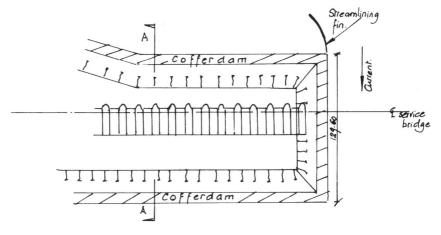

Plan of job site

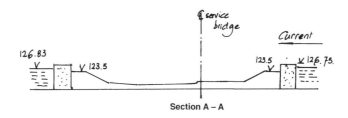

Section A – A

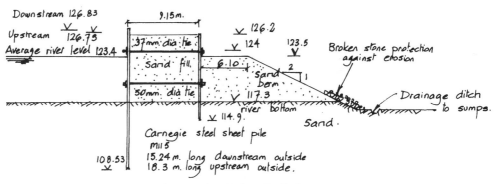

Cross-section of twin-wall cofferdam

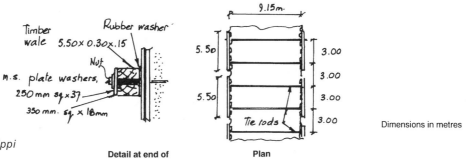

Detail at end of upper tie rod

Plan

Dimensions in metres

Fig. 6.47. Double-wall cofferdam on the Mississippi River, Alton, IL: plan and cross-section[20]

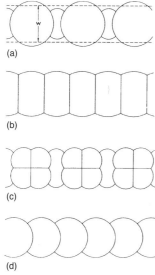

Fig. 6.48. Types of cellular cofferdam plan forms:
(a) circular cells connected by arcs; (b) semi-circular cells with straight diaphragm cross walls; (c) clover leaf cells from four circular arcs of sheeting fixed on two transverse walls perpendicular to each other and connected by small arcs; (d) circular arcs joined to each other

easier and quicker to build and use fewer expensive special connecting piles. The flat cell type also has the advantage that the effective width may be increased without increasing tension in the interlocks.

The earliest cellular cofferdam was built in the early 1900s at Black Rock Harbour, Buffalo, NY. Each of the 27 cells was just over 9 m square in plan, with a similar unsupported height. As all the walls were straight, large deformations were expected, but in one cell an excessive bulge of more than 1 m occurred between cross-walls, although inward movement of the cofferdam crest did not exceed 25 mm. In 1915–1916, the Black Rock Harbour cofferdam was repeated in a dam at Troy, NY. This time the straight outer walls were replaced with curved walls between the cross-walls to form the flat cell type cofferdam.

In 1910, a cellular cofferdam with 20 circular cells was used to raise the battleship Maine from the bottom of Havana Harbour in Cuba. This cofferdam, the first to use circular cells, was built on soft silts and mud overlying medium soft clay; the cell filling was clay. Inward deflections began to occur during pumping out of the cells and it was necessary to build a berm on the inside of the structure. During final stages of dewatering it became necessary to strut the cofferdam from the ship's hull. The cofferdam was, nevertheless, a success and led to the increased use of the cellular cofferdam and steel sheet piling.

Terzaghi[21] stated that the design of cellular cofferdams based on a foundation other than rock requires more judgement than the design of a double-wall cofferdam with a broad inner berm on a similar base. It may also be said that the construction requires more judgement and experience.

Cellular dams may fail in the same way as double-wall types: by sliding or tilting, by failure of the base, by piping failure or by scour. In addition, they may fail by breakage of the interlocks and bursting of the cells. This latter cause, the vulnerability of the interlocks, is the major failure risk, and many of the failures by bursting which have occurred at the time of filling the cells (or immediately afterwards) have been blamed on driving out of lock. Considerable care and diligence must be applied in handling piles and in pitching and driving them to avoid ruptured interlocks.

Before any installation begins, pile dimensional tolerance, pile straightness, quality of fabrication of special piles, cleanliness of interlocks and any possible flaws in steel quality must be thoroughly checked. Careful inspection of welding quality in the fabrication of special piles is essential. These inspections should be made on secondhand piles in particular, but tolerance and quality inspection is always necessary, even on new deliveries. A surplus number of piles must be ordered as a contingency to allow for reject piles if the progress of the works is not to suffer.

One of the most important checks is the gauging of all interlocks. Typical permissible interlock tolerances are summarized in Fig. 6.49. The need for interlocks as delivered to comply strictly with tolerances is self-evident when the large proportion of the mass of the pile section concentrated at the interlock is examined in cross-section. Figure 6.50(a) shows sections of flat web sheet piles manufactured by Arbed with high-strength interlocks. The strict dimensional tolerance necessary to achieve three-point interlock contact is obvious. Figure 6.50(b) shows alternative single- and triple-point interlocks previously available.

The extent of pre-excavation before cofferdam construction begins depends largely on depth of site overburden. The objective of prior excavation is two-fold: to remove shallow obstructions and to minimize the penetration of the driven pile. Where shallow overburden exists, a site strip 1 m deep will be sufficient to remove tree stumps and boulders. If the overburden is deep it

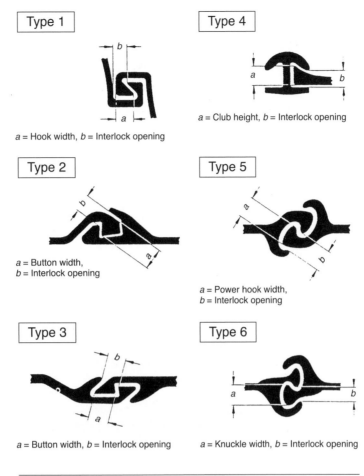

Type 1		Type 4
Type 2		Type 5
Type 3		Type 6

Type 1: *a* = Hook width, *b* = Interlock opening

Type 4: *a* = Club height, *b* = Interlock opening

Type 2: *a* = Button width, *b* = Interlock opening

Type 5: *a* = Power hook width, *b* = Interlock opening

Type 3: *a* = Button width, *b* = Interlock opening

Type 6: *a* = Knuckle width, *b* = Interlock opening

Type	Design dimensions (acc. to section drawings)	Tolerances of design dimensions		
		Designation	plus (mm)	minus (mm)
1	Hook width *a*	Δa	2·5	2·5
	Interlock opening *b*	Δb	2	2
2	Button width *a*	Δa	1	3
	Interlock opening *b*	Δb	3	1
3	Button width *a*	Δa	1·5–2·5*	3
	Interlock opening *b*	Δb	4	0·5
4	Club height *a*	Δa	1	3
	Interlock opening *b*	Δb	2	1
5	Power hook width *a*	Δa	1·5	3·5
	Interlock opening *b*	Δb	3	1·5
6	Knuckle width *a*	Δa	2	3
	Interlock opening *b*	Δb	3	2

Fig. 6.49. Typical permitted interlock tolerances[27]

* Depending on the section

may be advisable to take out 6 to 7 m to reduce driving depth. Where bedrock outcrops it is usual to place 2 m of free-draining fill to provide a toe for the piles during pitching and driving. If overburden consists of very soft silts or clays or soils containing many cobbles and boulders, it must be removed.

An internal template must be used to set the sheet piles to a cellular cofferdam. The templates are usually made with two rings and supported by at least four bearing piles. The template is usually made 200 mm smaller in diameter than the net driving line to allow the piles to rotate slightly and adjust to the correct arc during pitching. Figure 6.51 shows piles pitched to a template.

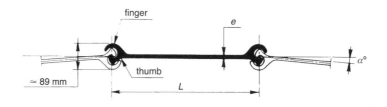

Section	Nominal width L (mm)	Web thickness e (mm)	Deviation angle α°	Perimeter of a single pile (cm)	Steel section of a single pile (cm²)	Mass per m of a single pile (kg/m)	**Mass per m² of wall (kg/m²)**	Section modulus of a single pile (cm³)	Moment of inertia of a single pile (cm⁴)	Coating área* (m²/m)
AS500-12·0	500	12·0	6	138	92·1	72·3	**145**	47	180	1·14
AS500-12·5	500	12·5	6	138	94·8	74·4	**149**	47	180	1·14
AS500-12·7	500	12·7	6	138	95·8	75·2	**150**	47	180	1·14

Note: All the sections interlock together.   * Excludes inside of interlocks.

(a)

PBP one-point contact

Strength of interlock
250 to 350 t/m
14 000 to 19 600 lb/in

ABP three-point contact

Strength of interlock
350 to 500 t/m
19 600 to 28 000 lb/in

Fig. 6.50. Flat pile sections: (a) modern sections with high-strength interlocks; (b) alternative sections previously available showing single-point (left) and three-point contact (right) at interlock (courtesy of Arbed)

(b)

To pitch or set the sheet piles to the template it is usual to use the four special junction piles as 'key piles'. With large cells, and in strong current conditions, additional key piles may be needed to stiffen the sheeting during pitching and subsequent driving. These key piles consist of a straight web pile with a steel joist section welded to the inside of the web. The sheet piles are pitched working away from the key piles, blocking off alternate piles from the template. Guy lines to the tops of evenly spaced piles control verticality, especially in windy conditions and strong currents. Sheeting cannot be accurately pitched in flows faster than 1·2 m/s unless current deflector bulkheads are used, cantilevered from the adjacent completed cell. Closures during pitching should be made mid-way between the key piles; sheeting is then picked up, several piles together, and 'shaken out', especially near the closures. The purpose of shaking out is to ensure that the interlocks run freely and allow some rotation of individual piles to give a smooth arc against the template.

Sheeters should be driven in pairs, ideally with a hammer of energy 12 to 20 kNm. Larger hammers should only be used carefully to avoid split interlocks, especially on long piles. Piles are best driven in increments, the maximum increment of one pile compared with its neighbour not exceeding 2 m. Jetting methods can be used to good effect in sands but should be used simultaneously both inside and outside the cell to maintain verticality. Vibratory hammers are efficient in granular soils.

Where piles have to be spliced because of their length, this is done by driving the bottom section to full penetration and burning a staggered splice line, the stagger being 1·5 to 2·0 m between adjacent sheeters. Driving flat web sheet piles longer than 15 m in one piece is difficult. Where piles are being driven to achieve a cut-off into a sloping rockhead, final penetration should be made on single piles to reduce the risk of 'windows' under the piles.

Fig. 6.51. Cellular cofferdam construction, flat sheet piles pitched and driven to a template (courtesy of Arbed)

After all piles have been driven and released from the template, filling may begin: cell filling should be granular, free-draining material with a reasonable proportion of fines (say, a maximum of 15% passing a 100 sieve and a maximum of 5% passing the 200 size). In large cells, small boulders up to 300 mm would be acceptable. The filling, which in circular cells should be made from the centre of the cell to avoid deformations, may be placed hydraulically, from grabs, by conveyor or by end dumping from trucks. Flat cells are best filled by grab or dragline, and to avoid distortion the differential fill height between adjacent cells should not exceed 1·5 m.

If cellular cofferdams are likely to be overtopped by high tides or flood, the filling must be protected on top. A concrete cap 200 to 300 mm thick is often provided, and this also protects the fill from occasional high waves.

It is essential to provide sufficient flood gates to allow drainage of the enclosed area in the event of flooding. After filling and during dewatering, weep holes should be burnt through the inner sheeting to allow efficient drainage of the fill: 25 mm dia. holes at 2 m centres in every fifth web regularly rodded will suffice. The rate of pumping out should be regulated by the rate of draining the cell fill; in large dams a maximum rate of 1·5 m per 24 hours should apply.

Cell deformation will have occurred during cell filling operations, the cells barrelling at a distance of two-thirds of the cell height from the crest as the slack in the interlocks is taken up. As the cofferdam is pumped dry there is further settlement of the cell fill, and with further flooding and dewatering the total settlement in high cells may reach 150 mm. Horizontal deformation of up to 1% of the unsupported height can be expected at the cofferdam crest after dewatering.

Where a number of circular cells on a curved plan form span-wide openings, the end cells transfer horizontal thrust to an existing wall or natural abutment. Figure 6.52 shows the plan and section of the circular cell cofferdam used on the Bangor–Brewer Bridge, ME, USA. Horizontal bracing was used to strut the tops of four key cells in the structure.

Gravity type cofferdams

The earliest, and simplest form of cofferdam over water was the earth or rock dam, built to isolate a construction area which can then be pumped dry for works and bridge foundations. The design of such cofferdams must take into account the slope stability of the embankment, allowing for seepage forces, the need for scour protection to the river bed and the embankment, and sufficient crest height against overtopping by waves or floods.

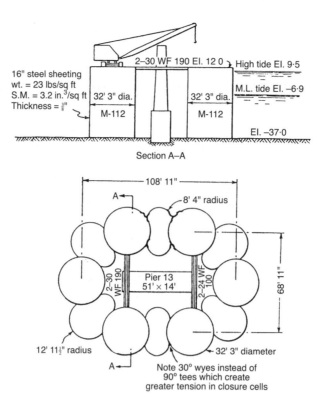

Fig. 6.52. Circular cell cofferdam complex with horizontal bracing, Bangor–Brewer Bridge, ME, USA[23]

The economics of embankment cofferdams obviously depend on the availability of soil and rock for filling and slope protection. In addition, however, pumping costs to keep the enclosure dewatered will depend on the type of soil fill and the permeability of the soil under the embankment. If pumping costs are excessive it may prove economical to install a cut-off through the embankment and into the underlying soil or rock to reduce seepage. Relatively shallow cut-offs may be constructed from sheet piling; deeper walls may be built economically using the slurry trench technique.

During the 1930s several large sand embankment cofferdams were built across the River Nile to allow construction of barrages for irrigation purposes. A major scheme was described by Lee[22] for remodelling works on the Assuit Barrage. The works involved new masonry, sluice gates, lift bridges and improved apron slabs to the original barrage at a site where the Nile is over 800 m wide. Figure 6.53 shows typical sections through the upstream and downstream embankments, known as sudds. The cut-offs were made from Larssen No. 2 sheet piles driven through the pumped sand banks. The sand, impregnated with silt on the upstream face outside the piling, was graded to a batter of 1:3; on the downstream side, where the sand was coarser and cleaner, the gradients were 1:7 or steeper. Dewatering was carried out slowly to allow the sudds to drain gradually, after which there was little seepage through the sudds. The work was carried out in four low-water seasons in successive years, working progressively across the Nile. At the end of each season, the sudds were slowly rewatered and the sheet piles extracted. The greater part of the sand fill to the sudds was removed by the scour of the high river waters.

At sites where timber is cheap, timber cribs can be used to form a gravity cofferdam. The cribs, sometimes shaped to the river bed profile and with pockets up to 3·5 m square, are launched and floated into position and filled with rock and finer material to reduce permeability.

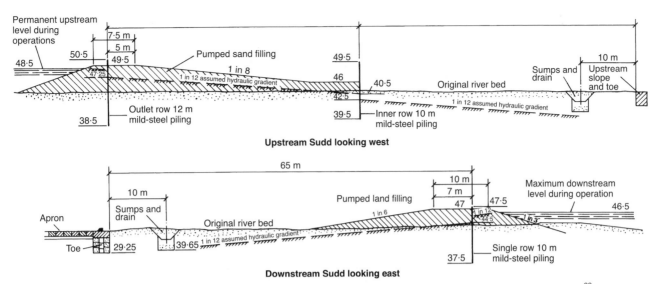

Fig. 6.53. Typical sections, upstream and downstream of sudds for reconstruction of Assuit Barrage, River Nile[22]

Concrete blocks can also be used to form a gravity dam structure to exclude river water from lock and dock constructions. Gabions filled with rock and smaller material to reduce leakage can be used for the same purpose.

One of the most dramatic sequences of work occurs on river or marine construction during closure of a cofferdam to block all flow. This situation occurs typically where a barrage or dam is to be constructed within a cofferdam across a flowing river. Often the dam is built in several stages and as the river flow becomes progressively restricted, scour of the river bed and of the exposed extremes of the cofferdam structure increases rapidly. In the final closure work, time is absolutely critical. White[23] reported some of the measures used in such closures.

(a) On rivers with sandy and silty beds, large dredgers have been used to replace material scoured away.

(b) On swifter flowing rivers with gravelly bottoms, rocks have been dumped from trestle bridges to keep the trestle anchored and stop the flow of the stream. This done, sand and clay are placed against the upstream side of the rock fill to improve watertightness.

(c) Where the depth of the river has been so great as to prohibit access trestles, cableways have been used to drop heavy rocks or concrete blocks into the river.

The second-stage closure of the cofferdam for the Chief Joseph Dam on the Columbia River was only achieved by the retention of large rocks, each weighing from 10 to 30 t, by individual cables, held in place by a large cable spanning upstream of the 15 m closure gap. River flow at the time of closure exceeded 7 m/s.

Mackintosh[24] referred to other closure works for dams on the Columbia River. At the McNary Dam the original 800 m river width had been progressively narrowed to a gap just over 70 m wide between two steel cells. The river level had to be raised 5 m in order to pass through the spillway blocks, and this caused a maximum water velocity of more than 9 m/s. The closure was made over a period of 37 days by dropping a total of 2088 concrete tetrahedra, each weighing 12 t, into the gap from a cableway.

Mackintosh also gave details of the closure of the Dalles Dam, where dumped rockfill, incorporated into a permanent embankment, was used to

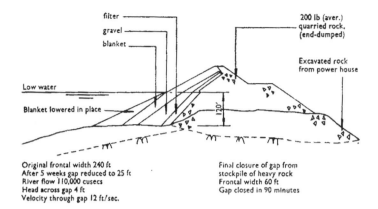

filter
gravel
blanket

200 lb (aver.)
quarried rock.
(end-dumped)

Excavated rock
from power house

Low water

Blanket lowered in place

120'

Original frontal width 240 ft
After 5 weeks gap reduced to 25 ft
River flow 110,000 cusecs
Head across gap 4 ft
Velocity through gap 12 ft/sec.

Final closure of gap from
stockpile of heavy rock
Frontal width 60 ft
Gap closed in 90 minutes

Fig. 6.54. Cross-section of Dalles Dam, Columbia River, USA[24]

close a 150 m wide channel. At the deepest point the river was 55 m below low water and in the first stage the gap was reduced to just over 16 m by dumping rock from barges. To begin the final closure operation, end dumping of rockfill was carried out on a 70 m width, working outwards from the right-hand river bank until the channel was only 7·6 m wide. This last operation took five weeks in a river flow of 3120 m³/s and a velocity through the final channel of 3·7 m/s. Rock mass ranged from 100 to 259 kg. Rock filling was followed by end dumping smaller rock and filter material and then a sand blanket was placed, partly from barges, to form the section shown in Fig. 6.54. The final closure operation, concentrating all resources on a stockpile of heavy rock, was achieved on a width of 18 m in a period of only 1·5 hours.

A spectacular closure on the River Saguency in Canada should also be mentioned. A vast, 28 m high concrete monolith was toppled by blasting into the river. The base of this mass was pre-shaped to conform with river bed soundings and weighed 11 000 t. The river flow was greater than 9 m/s, but the monolith was accurately placed and successful in its purpose.

References

1. Packshaw S. Cofferdams. *Proc. Instn Civ. Engrs*, 1962, **21**, Feb., 367–398.
2. *The Construction Regulations (Health, Safety and Welfare)*. HMSO, London, 1996.
3. *Conditions of contract for civil engineering works*. Institution of Civil Engineers Federation of Civil Engineering Contractors, London, 1955, 1979, 1991, 1999 edns IV, V, VI, VII.
4. CIRIA. *The design and construction of sheet piled cofferdams for temporary works*. Thomas Telford Ltd., London, 1992.
5. Kirmani M. and Highfill S.C. Design and construction of the circular cofferdam for ventilation building no 6 at the Ted Williams Tunnel. *Civ. Engng Practice*, Spring/Summer, 1996, 31–47. Boston Society of Civil Engineers, MA, 1996.
6. *The Icos Company in the underground works*. Icos, Milan, 1968.
7. Wharmby N., Kieren B., Duffy L. and Puller D. Stormwater tank construction at Blackpool. *Proc. Conf. on Underground Construction*. Institute of Mining and Metallurgy, Hemming Group Ltd., London, 2001.
8. Williams S.G. and Little J.A. Structural behaviour of sheet piles interlocked at the centre of gravity of the combined section. *Proc. Instn Civ. Engrs*, 1992, **94**, May, 229–238.
9. BS 8004. *Code of practice for foundations*. British Standards Institution, London, 1986.
10. BS 5228, part 4. *Code of practice for noise control applicable to piling operations*. British Standards Institution, London, 1986.
11. British Steel Corporation. *Report on noise and vibration due to sheet pile installation*. British Steel Corporation, Scunthorpe, 1994.

12. EN 12063. *Code of practice on steel piling*. British Standards Institution, London, 2001.
13. Grice J.R. and Hepplewhite E.A. Design and construction of the Thames Barrier cofferdams. *Proc. Instn Civ. Engrs*, 1983, **74**, May, 191–224.
14. Fleming J.H. *et al*. The River Hull tidal surge barrier. *Proc. Instn Civ. Engrs*, 1980, **68**, Aug., 417–454.
15. Wakeling T.R.M. and Hamilton R.J. Discussion on cofferdams. *Proc. Instn Civ. Engrs*, 1963, **24**, Jan., 106–108.
16. Collingridge V.H. and Tuckwell R.E. Underground station western district post office, construction. *Proc. Instn Civ. Engrs*, 1960, **15**, Feb., 95–104.
17. Tomlinson M.J. *Foundation design and construction*. Longman, Harlow, 1995.
18. Ellis L.G. Discussion on cofferdams. *Proc. Instn Civ. Engrs*, 1963, **24**, Jan., 110–112.
19. Hausser P. *et al*. A comparison of the design and construction of dry docks at Immingham and Jarrow. *Proc. Instn Civ. Engrs*, 1964, **27**, Feb., 291–324.
20. White L. and Prentis E.A. *Cofferdams*. Columbia University Press, New York, 1950.
21. Terzaghi K. Stability and stiffness of cellular cofferdams. *Trans. Am. Soc. Civ. Engng*, 1945, **110**, 1083–1119 and 1120–1202.
22. Lee D. *Deep foundations and sheet piling*. Concrete Publications, London, 1961.
23. White R.E. *Foundation engineering*. Ed. G.A. Leonards, McGraw-Hill, New York, 1962, ch. 10, 894–964.
24. Mackintosh I.B. Discussion on cofferdams. *Proc. Instn Civ. Engrs*, 1963, **24**, Jan., 108–109.
25. Anderson J.K. Forth Road Bridge. *Proc. Instn Civ. Engrs*, 1965, **32**, Nov., 321–512.
26. Gowring G.I. and Hardie A. Severn Bridge, foundations and substructure. *Proc. Instn Civ. Engrs*, 1968, **41**, Sept. 49–67.
27. EAU 90. *Recommendations of the Committee for Waterfront Structures, Harbours and Waterways*. Ernst and Son, Berlin, 6th English edn, 1993.

Bibliography

Banks D.J. *et al*. Construction of Riding Mill weir. *Proc. Instn Civ. Engrs*, Part 1, 1984, **77**, 195–216.
BS 6349 part 1. *Code of practice for maritime structures*. British Standards Institution, London, 2000.
BS 8081. *Code of practice for ground anchorages*. British Standards Institution, London, 1989.
Calkin D.W. and Mundy J.K. Temporary works for the pumping stations at Plover Cove reservoir, Hong Kong. *Proc. Instn Civ. Engrs*, 1987, **82**, Dec., 1121–1144.
Coates R.H. and Slade L.R. Construction of circulating water pump house at Cowes generating station. *Proc. Instn Civ. Engrs*, 1958, **9**, Mar., 217–232.
CIRIA. *Control of groundwater for temporary works*. CIRIA, London, 1986, Report 113.
Dondelinger M. Interlocking H-sections for cofferdams to resist high pressure. *Deep Foundations Inst. J.*, 1985, Spring, 17–28.
Gerrard R.T. *et al*. Barking Creek tidal barrier. *Proc. Instn Civ. Engrs*, Part 1, 1982, **72**, 533–562.
Hutchinson D.G. and Smith R.A. Brecon flood alleviation scheme. *Proc. Instn Civ. Engrs*, Part 1, 1986, **80**, 121–143.
Jessberger H.L. *et al*. Ground freezing. *Geotechnical Engineering Handbook*. Vol. 2. Procedures. Ernst and Son. Berlin, 2003.
Mann T. and Dunn M. Lock construction and realignment on the Sheffield and South Yorkshire navigation. *Proc. Instn Civ. Engrs*, Part 1, 1986, **80**, 1183–1210.
McGibbon J.I. and Booth G.W. Kessock Bridge: construction. *Proc. Instn Civ. Engrs*, Part 1, 1984, **76**, 51–66.
Patterson J.H. Installation techniques for cellular structures. *Proc. Conf. Design and Installation of Pile Foundation and Cellular Structures*. Envo Publishing, Lehigh Valley, USA, 1970.

Piling handbook. British Steel Corporation, Scunthorpe, 1997.

Pokrefke T.J. *et al.* Unique utilization of a physical model to develop a construction sequence of a major cofferdam. *Proc. Hydraulics and Hydrology in the Small Computer Age*, American Society of Civil Engineers, New York, 1985, 1130–1135.

Porter D.L. Innovative repairs to steel sheet pile structures. *Proc. Conf. Innovations in Port Engineering in the 1990s*. American Society of Civil Engineers, New York, 1986, 703–712.

Quinn W.L. Foyle Bridge, construction of foundations and viaduct. *Proc. Instn Civ. Engrs*, Part 1, 1984, **76**, 387–409.

Rossow M.P. Sheetpile interlock tension in cellular cofferdams. *ASCE J. Geotech. Engng*, 1984, **110**, Oct., 1146–1158.

Sarsby R.W. Noise from sheet piling operations – M67 Denton relief road. *Proc. Instn Civ. Engrs*, 1982, **72**, Feb., 15–26.

Schwab J.P. and Howe J.B. Sherman Island hydro cofferdam. *Proc. Conf. Water-power '85*. American Society of Civil Engineers, New York, 1986, 1288–1297.

Skempton A.W. and Ward W.H. Investigations concerning a deep cofferdam in the Thames Estuary clay at Shellhaven. *Géotechnique*, 1952, **3**, Sept., 119–139.

Specification for steel sheet piling. Foundation of Piling Specialists, London, 1991.

Steel sheet piling design manual. Kawasaki Steel Corporation, Tokyo, 1982.

Terzaghi K. Anchored bulkheads. *Trans. Am. Soc. Civ. Engng*, 1954, **119**, 1243–1281.

Townsend G.H. and Greeves I.S. Design and construction of Gallions surface water pumping station. *Proc. Instn Civ. Engrs*, 1979, **66**, Nov., 605–624.

Vasconcelos A.A. and Eigenheer L.P. Xingo rockfill dam. *Proc. Conf. Concrete Face Rockfill Dams*. American Society of Civil Engineers, New York, 1985, 559–565.

7 Cofferdam design

In plan the design must allow for installation tolerances of sheeting or walling and sufficient space to accommodate supporting members such as walings and anchor heads to the sheeting or walling. The design of member sizes will primarily address ultimate limit state conditions, but the serviceability limit state of deformation must be applied to ensure that deformations of the cofferdam members, particularly the sheeting, are not excessive and thus impair construction of the permanent works to the required dimensions and thicknesses.

The design life of the cofferdam will inevitably influence the type of materials used and their durability, but temporary works of very short duration must not be built with inferior materials that are unable to support the construction loads and the earth and water pressures imposed upon them. The sufficiency of secondhand construction materials for cofferdam works is particularly important in this regard.

The cost of the cofferdam must be minimized irrespective of the cost allowance previously made at tender or job negotiation stage. This cost, however, must take into account the efficiency (and cost-effectiveness) of construction works within the cofferdam. For example, cost-effectiveness may be optimized by spending more on an anchored cofferdam than a braced alternative, obtaining permanent works construction unimpaired by bracing and the need to reprop bracing. The construction cost of the cofferdam must include the costs of its removal; extraction and reuse of the materials elsewhere will be influenced by the design. The incorporation of the temporary works into the permanent works should always be considered even if contractual arrangements are not particularly conducive to do so. The obvious example of the application of such a strategy is the use of structural diaphragm or piled walls to provide both temporary soil support during construction and thereafter to form the permanent substructure walls.

Site investigation

The frequent inadequacy of site investigations for heavy civil engineering works has been detailed elsewhere[1], but this shortfall of data for permanent works design often follows the discovery by the temporary works designer of an even greater shortfall in the availability of soils, groundwater and tidal information. The site investigation, conducted to a national code such as BS 5930[2] or DIN 4020[3], requires an initial definition of scope to include number, depth and type of borings and in situ tests, and a laboratory testing programme which satisfies the needs of both temporary and permanent works designers. A CIRIA report on the design and construction of sheet piled cofferdams[4] recommends the following checklist for information required from the investigation:

- location of boreholes with respect to the cofferdam
- date of boring and ground level at boring based on same datum reference as construction drawings

- diameter of boring, drill rig used and whether water was added to the boring
- depth and thickness of all soil strata to at least twice the proposed excavation depth, possibly more in weak soils
- bulk unit weights for each soil type
- standard penetration tests and other relevant in situ tests, such as cone penetrometer tests
- grading curves, Atterberg limits for clay, undrained and, where appropriate, drained shear tests
- vane test results for soft clays, with sensitivity values
- groundwater strike, rate of ingress, standing levels, any permeability test data, casing depth at all stages of boring
- position and detail of piezometers, type and readings
- tidal variations and lag
- site geology
- previous site history
- report interpretation.

The design life of the cofferdam works will also influence the designer's choice of soil strength parameters, based on undrained or drained effective stress values for clay. The prime matters affecting the period of full drainage and effective stress analysis are the drainage path length to permeable strata and the permeability of the consolidating stratum and the permeable drainage strata. Where, for example, an otherwise relatively impermeable clay structure in the active or passive zones is interlayered with permeable sandy beds or laminations, the rate of drainage will increase and pore pressures will return to hydrostatic pressures more rapidly, possibly within the design life of the cofferdam works. For application of total stress, undrained analysis is therefore valid only for a very short period after the application of load to the cofferdam sheeting and support, but the period for full dissipation of excess pore pressure may vary from days to months. In these circumstances the designer's best option will probably lie in the use of undrained analysis in homogeneous clays, particularly soft clays, using effective stress parameters as a check. The use of effective stress analyses without a total stress analysis would then be reserved for areas of good soil drainage, laminated soils or strata of shallow depth, and analyses made at the end of a long construction period or for a later permanent works phase.

Due to the relative cost of drained triaxial tests and their duration it is likely that the number of available test results for a particular clay stratum will be limited and the designer may have little confidence in their statistical average, especially for soils where previous results are not available. This is less likely to be the case for undrained triaxial test results. In this situation the designer may prefer to keep to undrained total stress analyses using higher safety factors.

Design parameters for soil

Earth pressure calculations, as detailed in Chapter 5, rely on parameters for soil density and soil strength in terms of cohesion and the angle of shearing resistance. Preliminary designs may be made using empirical values for a known soil, and some assistance is given in selecting these in the literature[5]. Calculation values are advised in Table 7.1. The angle of shearing resistance in terms of effective stress can be estimated from the clay plasticity index, which is shown in Table 5.1. Note that clays with laminations or seams of silts or sands show lower plasticity values than clay alone, and care must be exercised in tests in such clays. If in doubt, the higher plasticity of those given by testing and from Table 5.1 should be used.

Table 7.1 Preliminary design soil parameters[5]

Type of soil	Density		Final strength		Initial strength* cohesion of undrained soil, cal c_u (kN/m²)	Modulus of volume change, cal E_s (MN/m²)
	Above water, cal γ (kN/m³)	Submerged, cal γ' (kN/m³)	Angle of internal friction, cal ϕ' (degree)	Cohesion cal c' (kN/m²)		
Non-cohesive soils						
Sand, loose, round	18	10	30	–	–	20–50
Sand, loose, angular	18	10	32·5	–	–	40–80
Sand, medium dense, round	19	11	32·5	–	–	50–100
Sand, medium dense, angular	19	11	35	–	–	80–150
Gravel without sand	16	10	37·5	–	–	100–200
Coarse gravel, sharp edged	18	11	40	–	–	150–300
Sand, dense, angular	19	11	37·5	–	–	150–250
Cohesive soils	(Empirical values for undisturbed samples from the North German Area)					
Clay, semi-firm	19	9	25	25	50–100	5–10
Clay, difficult to knead, stiff	18	8	20	20	25–50	2·5–5
Clay, easy to knead, soft	17	7	17·5	10	10–25	1–2·5
Boulder clay, solid	22	12	30	25	200–700	30–100
Loam, semi-firm	21	11	27·5	10	50–100	5–20
Loam, soft	10	9	27·5	–	10–25	4–8
Silt	18	8	27·5	–	10–50	3–10
Soft, org. slightly clayey sea silt	17	7	20	10	10–25	2–5
Soft, very org. strongly clayey sea silt	14	4	15	15	10–20	0·5–3
Peat	11	1	15	5	–	0·4–1
Peat under moderate initial loading	13	3	15	10	–	0·8–2

cal ϕ' = calculation value of the angle of internal friction in cohesive and non-cohesive soils
cal c' = calculation value of the cohesion, corresponding to cal ϕ'
cal c_u = calculation value of the shear strength from undrained tests in saturated cohesive soils
* Appertaining angle of internal friction is to be assumed at cal ϕ'_u

For preliminary calculations, ϕ' for sands and gravels can be estimated from values of standard penetration tests, as shown in Fig. 5.2. Similarly, values of undrained cohesive strength c_u can be estimated from standard penetration tests on over-consolidated clays from the empirical expression $c_u = nf_s$ where n is the test value and f_s is a coefficient which varies with the plasticity index[6]. Values of c_u as a function of effective overburden pressure p_n (for normally-consolidated clays) were given by Skempton[7]:

$$\frac{c_u}{p_n} = 0 \cdot 11 + (0 \cdot 0037 \times \text{plasticity index}). \tag{63}$$

Kenney[8] gave preliminary values for the relationship between ϕ' and plasticity index for normally-consolidated clays based on observations of more than 60 soils (Fig. 7.1).

The value of ϕ' for weak rocks may be estimated for preliminary design purposes from a rock description given in BS 8002[9] (Table 5.2). These indicative values are considered conservative, being based on granular fragments rather than intact rock, taking into account closely jointed rock with a very low value of rock quality designation (RQD).

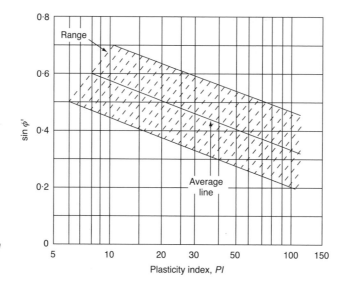

Fig. 7.1. Relationship between plasticity index and angle of shearing resistance[41]

Design of soil support and structural members to the cofferdam

The use of limit equilibrium methods to design cantilever and propped walls for overall stability was described in Chapter 5. A factor of safety is achieved by increasing embedment, decreasing soil strength or factoring moments of pressure diagrams, to give walls of sufficient depth to avoid overturning. The earth pressures on which these analyses have been based are Coulomb values of limit pressures, that is, they are maximum passive pressures and minimum active pressures which are generated by wall movement at failure.

These limit pressures occur, therefore, at the ultimate limit state of wall collapse by overturning. The applied factor of safety, which increases wall embedment, takes into account that in the serviceability condition, when wall and soil deformation is less, the soil passive resistance will be less than that generated in the ultimate limit state and the active pressure will be greater than at failure. Recommended factors of safety for cantilever and propped wall with free earth support are shown in Table 7.2.

For propped walls with fixed earth support the penetration will always be greater than that required for free earth support, and will give an adequate factor of safety against rotation about the prop. If a simplified method is used for the calculation of penetration as explained in Chapter 5, 20% extra penetration is used not as a factor of safety but the additional depth required to correct for the simplification used in the method.

In geotechnical analysis of overall stability of cantilever and propped walls it is customary to apply best estimated values of applied loads, unit weights of soils and water pressure in the calculation of limit pressures. Although contrary to the application of limit state design in its entirety, it is not recommended that partial safety factors greater than 1·0 should be applied to the

Table 7.2 Recommended factors of safety, cantilever and propped walls, free earth support

ϕ'	Effective stress analysis			Total stress analysis
	$\leq 20°$	20–$30°$	$\geq 30°$	
Factor on strength	$F_s = 1·2$		$F_s = 1·2$–$1·1$	$F_s = 1·5$
Factor on moment	$F_p = 1·2$	$F_p = 1·2$–$1·5$	$F_p = 1·5$	$F_p = 2·0$
Factor on net pressure		$(F_{sp}) = 2·0$		Not recommended
Burland–Potts		$F_r = 1·5$		$F_r = 2·0$

various loads on the retaining structure to produce factored bending moments for the wall. As previously stated, unfactored loads with application of increased embedment, factored soil strength or factored moments of the earth diagram should be used according to choice.

The wall, dimensioned according to one of these methods, with an applied factor of safety, will be checked for sliding, basal failure and hydraulic failure, the factor of safety for each being calculated using limit pressures where earth pressure calculation is required. Next is the calculation of the sizes of structural members. Two methods of design are available for the design of the sheeting and its support by walings, struts and anchors: these are the permissible stress method and the limit state method.

- In the permissible stress method, best estimates of load are used. Limit pressure diagrams (or strut load envelopes based on the total pressure from limit earth pressure diagrams) are used to calculate bending moments and shears in the wall/sheeting and in the walings, and thrusts or tensions within the struts or anchors. Permissible stresses based on ultimate stresses reduced by a factor of safety are then calculated from the moments, shears, thrusts and tensions to define the size of these structural members. Permissible stress design is therefore based on limit pressures which do not occur in the serviceability state. Further, the ultimate limit state failure conditions related to these limit pressures, which are based on the monolithic failure of earth masses, may be unrelated to the ultimate limit state conditions (and therefore the earth pressures at these conditions) of collapse of the structural components.
- The limit state method uses conventional methods of design for reinforced concrete, steelwork and timber structural members in which the application of factored loads produces factored bending moments, shears, thrusts and tensions, which are then used with the ultimate or characteristic strength of the material to define their size. Although the logic of this method is flawed when using limit pressures, it appears to be less flawed than using permissible stress design with such pressures. For this reason, and because of the general use in structural design of limit state design, its application is adopted here.

The design procedure is as follows:

(a) Using ULS values for the more onerous of the design approaches, that is either moderately conservative or worst credible parameters and applying the appropriate partial factors thereto (see Table 5.6) calculate the sheeting moments, shears and prop loads.

(b) Calculate values of moment, shears and prop loads for serviceability state using unfactored soil parameters (if serviceability state has been analysed) multiplied by a factor of 1·4.

(c) Adopt greater values for (a) and (b). Consider risk of progressive collapse.

Material stresses
A summary of the properties of materials used in cofferdam construction is given in Table 5.10.

Plastic design of sheet pile walls
Recent developments in the design of sheet piles, particularly sheet piles in soft soil have been described, together with full-scale validation by Kort[10]. The use of plastic design methods for sheet piles has been practised mainly

in Denmark and North Germany since the 1950s following the publication of a method of plastic design for sheet pile walls by Brinch Hansen in 1953.

Kort refers to significant savings that can be obtained using plastic design compared with conventional elastic analysis. Allowing both the full plastic modulus of the pile section but without allowance for development of a plastic hinge may result in a saving of 15 to 20% for a typical anchored wall using a Frodingham type section (without risk of slippage of the clutch). Allowing rotation of the plastic hinge results in a similar saving which can reach a total of 35% or more for plastic design. Some reduction in this saving may be necessary to allow for local buckling of the sheet pile cross-section. The facility to make any reduction will, of course, be dependent on the driveability of the pile section but this would not be likely to be critical in soft soils. Corrosion risk may also need to be assessed in reducing sheet pile thickness.

The recent work by Kort also considers the effect of clutch slippage, which may critically affect the flexural strength of Larssen piles, clutched on the centre line of the sheet pile wall. This aspect of design is referred to as oblique bending and results in a reduction of the saving permitted by plastic design for the Larssen section.

Kort used a subgrade reaction model which allowed moment redistribution and a plastic hinge within the wall height when a certain maximum moment is reached. The development of the plastic hinge would then occur without detriment to wall stability providing embedment depth was sufficient to absorb the increased fixed end moment due to this redistribution. A large wall deflection would result of course. In the event, it does not follow that sheet pile lengths are necessarily longer for plastic designed walls than those elastically designed because the fixed end moment would not always be fully developed. In multi-propped walls the prudent positioning of struts in a plastically designed wall can be of greater effect than the embedment depth.

The effect of a reduction in flexural strength due to slippage at the clutch of Larssen sheet pile sections was investigated by Kort and a design rule was developed to take oblique bending into account. This was done using a subgrade reaction model which in turn was verified by a bending test on two double U-piles and a 3D simulation using the finite element program DIANA.

The progressive development of sheet pile design for both temporary and permanent works design on works other than minor schemes is encapsulated in Kort's work insofar as this may identify more realistic predictions of deformed wall shape; a change of sheet pile section to facilitate economical pile design may follow, together with greater efficiency in design in multi-braced walls for strut levels. All this work would comply with the European Codes, Eurocode 3 (EN 1997) and Eurocode 7 (EN 1997). The value of the original work of Brinch Hansen may finally be realized; the reader is directed to the work of Kort[10].

Overall stability

As has been mentioned, the overall instability of a cofferdam construction should always be checked. Such risk particularly occurs in sloping ground or, typically, in a riverfront cofferdam where the rear wall of the cofferdam supports retained ground and the front face supports tidal river conditions. Where the difference in height is small it may be possible to transfer load from the higher to the lower side by keeping the top frame as low as possible (Fig 7.2). Where the differential height is greater it may be expedient to rake the top frame from one side to the other. Alternatively, anchor the sheeting at the higher side.

Where cohesive soils extend to considerable depths on sloping sites, it is necessary to check that a deep-seated potential slip surface is not a failure

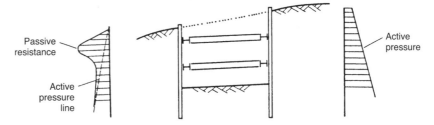

Fig. 7.2. Cofferdam construction in sloping ground[4]

risk. Where such a failure risk exists stability can be increased by driving the sheeting to greater depth to intercept the potential failure surface; jet-grouted columns may be installed below cofferdam formation level before excavation to achieve the same objective.

Bottom failure by piping and basal heave
Repeating earlier advice, the risk of hydraulic failure by piping should be checked for narrow cofferdams that do not achieve a cut-off in cohesionless soils with a high external water table. Risk of basal failure in cofferdams in soft clay should also be checked.

Aggressive site conditions: marine and river cofferdams
The extreme exposures to which cofferdams in both river and sea waters are subjected vary according to geographical location and the size and depth of the cofferdam. Matters to be assessed include the effect of wave forces on the face of the structure, overtopping of the cofferdam walls, scour, protection from vessel impact, and the impact and pressure of ice on the face of the cofferdam.

The effects of wave action on the face of the cofferdam are discussed in BS 6349[11] and in EAU 90[5]. These loads on cofferdams are due to waves in deep water, where waves are reflected, and those in shallower water where waves break on the structure or some distance from it. Sainflou[12] and Minikin[13] determined the forces due to reflected and breaking waves, respectively, referring, to waves on backfilled waterfront structures with standing water within the backfill. These methods should, however, be used cautiously when determining forces on sheeted structures. The very high loads that can be imposed on structures due to breaking waves, with impact pressures of $10\,000\,\text{kN/m}^2$ or more, identify the critical nature of this loading, especially since there is neither a reliable method of calculation nor an empirical solution for determining such loads. BS 6349 refers to breaking wave forces calculated by Minikin's method as high as 18 times those calculated for non-breaking waves. Estimates from computer modelling and measurements from physical models may assist where the scale of the cofferdam works justify such a study.

Waves caused by ship movement may also require consideration. In restricted waters the action of a headwater wave caused by water displacement in front of a vessel may require assessment in determining the maximum head of water on the face of a cofferdam structure; conversely, water drop occurring to the stern of a vessel may also cause variation in loading along the length of a long cofferdam. These matters, together with the action of bow and stern waves, are discussed in reference 5.

Reference should be made to the effect of pressure transmitted through coarse-graded beach deposits to the walls of cofferdams sited between high and low water, and to the dynamic effect on the flow of water below wave-facing cofferdam walls where a cut-off is not obtained by the toe of the walls. In neither case is there guidance from published work and only caution can be advised in the selection of factors of safety on strut or anchor design and on the risk of hydraulic failure at the base of the cofferdam excavation.

The risk of overtopping of the cofferdam sheeting depends on the freeboard allowed to assessments of maximum tide heights, surge and wave heights from natural and man-made causes. It is essential that where there is any risk of the cofferdam flooding from overtopping, the cofferdam sheeting should be tied to prevent it bursting outwards under the action of a water-filled cofferdam. Adequate sluices with safe locations for operating controls are essential to avoid the risk of a cofferdam remaining filled with water on a falling tide.

Scour protection will be needed where cofferdams are sited in fast flowing rivers or tidal conditions. Large cofferdams for bridge piers in fast flowing rivers may benefit from tests using physical models to determine the extent of scour and any increased risk due to obstruction of the flow by adjacent cofferdams. The upstream and downstream ends of a cofferdam may be shaped to reduce scour by providing cutwaters. Where protection is necessary to avoid erosion of the river or sea bed, rock or concrete blocks may be suitable. Grout mattresses, weighted by rockfill, may be adequate for river cofferdams. Where the scour risk is lower it may be sufficient to design the cofferdam sheeting embedment and strutting to ensure that collapse does not follow scour action.

In busy navigable waterways it will be necessary to protect the cofferdam by fendering or strongpoints built into the cofferdam sheeting to avoid damage by vessels. Barge traffic, in particular, appears to cause high collision risk. River authorities frequently define the extent of fendering required for river cofferdam works and specify the signage needed.

Durability of steel sheet pile walls

A report published in 2002 by Corus[14], reviewed corrosion rates in temperate climates for unprotected sheet piles. These rates, shown for each side of both atmospheric and marine locations in Fig 7.3 are based on investigations by British Steel (now Corus) and others. Corrosion rates are quoted as mean values since Corus considers these to be most relevant to design of most structures. Higher values are also quoted based on 95% probability for use where the designer deems necessary.

In their report, Corus refer to the risk of localized corrosion considerably in excess of those shown as mean or 95% probability values (Table 7.3). This local corrosion, known as 'accelerated low water corrosion' or ALWC in the UK and as 'concentrated corrosion' in Japan is not restricted to a particular section or steel manufacturer. The corrosion, based on bacterial growth in colonies, is generally confined to outpans of sheet piles in a zone at the mean water level, or just below. On U-shaped piles, the attack is most severe at the corner of the outpan whilst for Z-shaped piles the attack is concentrated on the corners or legs of the outpans. Corrosion rates within the range of 0·3 to 0·8 mm per year have been observed and in exceptional cases attack has caused local holes and slits in the sheet piles. It must be emphasized that the frequency of occurrence is small, and associated with marine structures; ALWC has not been observed to attack permanent sheet piling used for basement construction in the UK. Papers by Johnson et al.[15], Tsuchida et al.[16] and Fukute et al.[17] should be consulted regarding the risk associated with ALWC.

Methods of increasing the effective life of steel sheet piles are also reviewed in the British Steel *Piling Handbook*[18], and are summarized as follows:

- Use of a heavier section with allowance for a sacrificial thickness.
- Use of high yield steel as an alternative to mild steel, allowing increased bending stresses.

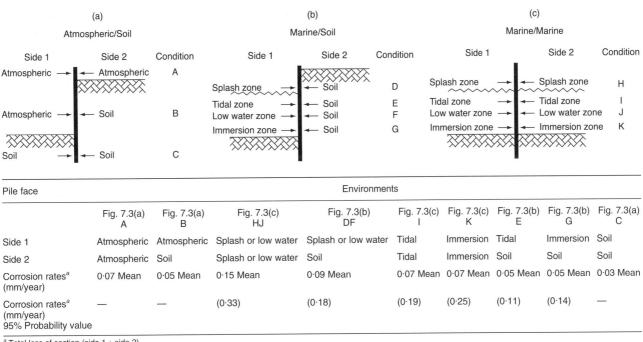

Pile face	Environments								
	Fig. 7.3(a) A	Fig. 7.3(a) B	Fig. 7.3(c) HJ	Fig. 7.3(b) DF	Fig. 7.3(c) I	Fig. 7.3(c) K	Fig. 7.3(b) E	Fig. 7.3(b) G	Fig. 7.3(a) C
Side 1	Atmospheric	Atmospheric	Splash or low water	Splash or low water	Tidal	Immersion	Tidal	Immersion	Soil
Side 2	Atmospheric	Soil	Splash or low water	Soil	Tidal	Immersion	Soil	Soil	Soil
Corrosion rates[a] (mm/year)	0·07 Mean	0·05 Mean	0·15 Mean	0·09 Mean	0·07 Mean	0·07 Mean	0·05 Mean	0·05 Mean	0·03 Mean
Corrosion rates[a] (mm/year) 95% Probability value	—	—	(0·33)	(0·18)	(0·19)	(0·25)	(0·11)	(0·14)	—

[a] Total loss of section (side 1 + side 2)

Notes
1. The corrosion rates quoted are based upon investigations carried out by Corus and others on steel exposed in temperate climates. For most environments mean values are quoted since they are considered to be most relevant to the design and performance of most sheet piling structures. However, in some circumstances the designer may wish to take account of higher values. It is suggested that in these circumstances a reasonable practical upper corrosion rate limit would be that corresponding to a 95% probability value. (Values given in parentheses.)
2. All corrosion rates quoted in the table are measured as total loss of section thickness from both sides, taking into account both environments.
3. For combinations of environments where low water corrosion is involved, in a small number of locations, higher rates than those quoted have been observed at or just below the low water level mark and Corus recommend that periodic inspection is undertaken. In the case of uncertainty, please contact Corus for advice.
4. A maximum value is quoted for soil corrosion and this applies to natural undisturbed soil or well compacted and weathered fill ground where corrosion rates are very low. Recent fill ground or waste tips will require special consideration.
5. Corrosion losses due to fresh water immersion are generally lower than for sea water, however, fresh waters are very variable and no general advice can be given to quantify the increase in life.

Fig. 7.3. Corrosion rates for unprotected sheet piles in temperate climates[18]

Table 7.3. Factors affecting localized corrosion[14]

Mechanism	Cause
1. Macro-cell effect	Potential difference: anodic at low water zone. Macro-cathode within the tidal zone allows available oxygen for the cathodic reduction reaction to cause a corrosive environment. Dependent upon local conditions
2. Removal of the corrosion product by erosion or abrasion	Continual removal of the abrasion product by the action of fendering systems, propellor wash, bow thrusters, waterborne sands and gravels or repeated stresses can lead to localized corrosion. The area where the rust layer is removed becomes anodic to the unaffected areas, particularly in the low water zone where macro-cell effects are strongest
3. Micro-biological activity	Corrosion products from affected structures can contain compounds such as sulphides which stimulate local corrosion
4. Bi-metallic corrosion	Can occur where steel is connected to other steels, metals or alloys. Corrosion is concentrated in the less noble steel often at the junction of the dissimilar materials
5. Fouling by animals/plants	Can cause acceleration of corrosion in localized areas, resulting from the formation of differential aeration cells or possibly by biological processes
6. Stray currents	From improperly grounded DC power sources. Localized damage where current leaves the structure

- Coatings: British Steel (now Corus) recommended tar vinyl and high-build epoxy pitch coatings. Coatings for potable water in the UK must meet byelaw approval and are approved by the Water Research Centre. Most comprise bitumen or two-pack epoxy resin systems.
- Concrete encasements: for marine use.
- Cathodic protection: usually the work of specialist firms.

A review of coating systems for use on sheet piles is made in a publication by a specialist firm, SIGMA Coatings[19].

General layout of the cofferdam

The plan shape of the cofferdam will usually conform approximately to the plan shape of the permanent works to be built within it. In general terms, the cost of cofferdam construction of constant depth is directly proportional to its plan area. Any wastage of space in the choice of cofferdam plan shape therefore will affect cost. The design of circular cofferdams is reviewed later, but in terms of relative economy only square-shaped plan structures or those with circular plan shape storage wells, such as pumping stations, can be accommodated in circular cofferdams cost-effectively.

For rectilinear cofferdam plan shapes the most economical arrangement uses maximum straight runs of piling with the minimum of return angles. The length of strutting across the cofferdam will define the need to support struts by king posts (traditionally known as puncheons) and prop them laterally to reduce the effective lengths of strutting and the risk of buckling. Maximum strut length in steelwork is likely to be of the order of 40 m, and distances in excess of this may need to rely on raking shores from a completed central raft section or support from ground or rock anchors; 45° diagonal corner braces should always be used in frames unless this hinders the permanent construction. Some typical arrangements of framing in plan are shown in Fig. 7.4. The vertical location of frames must be such that the maximum bending stress induced in the sheeting between frames is approximately constant. Overstressing of the sheeting must be avoided, particularly below the lowest frame, which should be located as low as possible to avoid risk of passive failure in the soil. The location of the penultimate frame is also important: the vertical height between final formation level and the penultimate frame should not be excessive in order that sheeting stresses and passive soil stresses are not exceeded immediately prior to placing the bottom frame.

Where soil strengths are low, near or below formation level, and earth and water pressure loading on the sheeting is relatively high, it may be necessary (particularly in river and marine cofferdams) to avoid excessive sheeting stresses and risk of passive failure of the soil below formation level by placing the lowest frame underwater by divers having flooded the cofferdam. The frame levels should generally be chosen to allow concrete lifts to be poured economically. Care may be needed to avoid starter or splice steel reinforcement from one pour being obstructed by the waling of a cofferdam frame. This applies particularly to the lowest frame impeding vertical starter steel in the kicker from the base slab. It may be possible to locate this front and rear starter steel to the wall construction on either side of the temporary waling, or couplers may be needed to extend the steel using the shortened height of the starter steel.

It is essential that load is transferred efficiently from soil to sheeting to waling to strutting, without any doubt as to the direction of the transfer. The principal reasons for failure of sheeted cofferdams are poor workmanship in connections causing insecure transfer of load, inadequate strut sections,

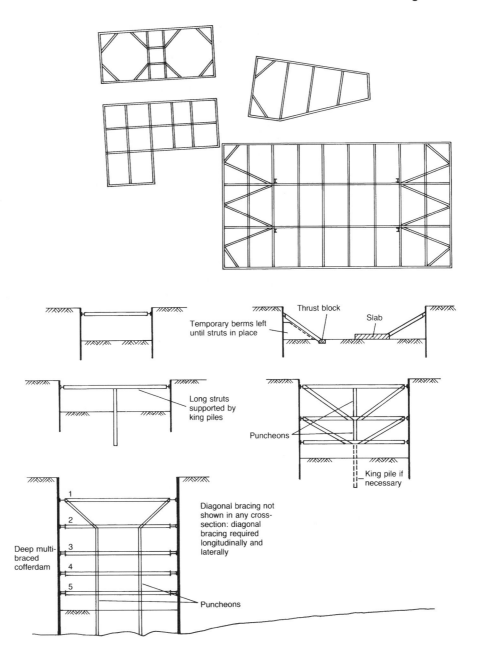

Fig. 7.4. Typical cofferdam framing in plan and in vertical cross-section[4]

inadequate embedment of the sheeting and overload due to inadequate allowance for surcharge loading. These modes of failure should never be forgotten.

Use and design of ground anchors

The economical use of anchors in land cofferdams depends on the strength of the subsoils in which the anchor is to be founded. Dense sands and gravels would be preferred to cohesive subsoils at a similar depth.

The use and design of ground anchors is described in two codes of practice, BS 8081[20] and the European Code BS EN 1537: 2000[21].

The opportunity to use anchors will depend on the ownership of land at the periphery of the cofferdams and on permission to found anchors in neighbouring land. The presence of existing substructures or basements may obstruct anchor installation.

The use of removable anchors may be necessary to avoid obstruction to future use of adjacent sites. Systems which allow removal of the unbonded steel tendon in the face length have been available for some time but only the use of a loop of totally unbonded strand allows the complete removal of the tendon. The method, developed by Keller, requires the pre-bending of plastic-coated strand at its midpoint to an internal diameter as small as 60 mm. The base of the loop complete with a thimble inside the loop is placed at the bottom of the bore. Successive loops at shallower depths may be placed as part of the single-bore multiple-anchor system. The anchor is then grouted. After use the whole looped tendon is destressed and each unbonded strand jacked or winched out of the anchor one by one.

Where internal angles occur in the line of sheeting, anchors from adjacent walls have to be located carefully to avoid anchors obstructing each other (Fig. 7.5).

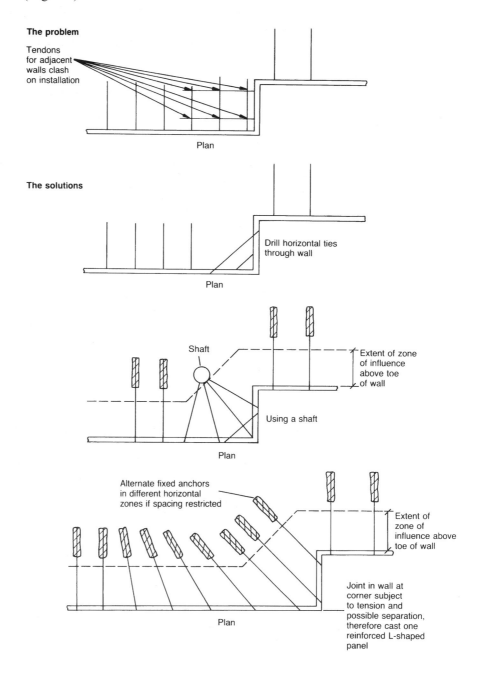

Fig. 7.5. Arrangement of ground anchors at re-entrant angles to retaining walls in plan[20]

Earth pressures acting on an anchor installation in a temporary cofferdam depend not only on soil strengths but also on wall and soil stiffnesses, anchor spacing, anchor yield, the pre-stress locked into the anchors as installed and loss of pre-stress with time. The anchored wall may be designed with active and passive earth pressure diagrams using limiting pressures, as described in Chapter 5 for multi-propped walls. The loads in the anchors can be obtained from the empirical trapezoidal strut load envelope diagrams. Alternatively, methods based on Winkler spring analysis may be used with computer programs in which earth pressures are computed from trial anchor loads input to produce deformed wall profiles, the anchor loads being varied in successive runs to produce acceptable maximum wall deflections.

Temporary anchors used in cofferdam construction have stressing tendons to transfer load from the fixed anchorage on the face of the cofferdam wall to a fixed anchorage within the subsoil outside the potential failure wedge at the rear of the wall. Figure 7.6 shows typical details and geometry. In cohesionless soils the fixed anchorage is formed by pressure-grouted techniques, while in cohesive soils, tremie methods of pouring grout may also be used. BS 8081[20] provides a comprehensive review of the design and construction of both temporary and permanent anchors in soil and rock (it also has an extensive list of references). It depicts five anchor types.

(a) Type A: anchorages consisting of tremie, packer or cartridge-grouted straight shaft boreholes temporarily lined or unlined depending on hole stability.
(b) Type B: anchorages consisting of low pressure (typically injection pressures less than $1000 \, kN/m^2$) grouted boreholes with an increased diameter within the fixed length.
(c) Type C: anchorages consisting of boreholes grouted to high pressure (typically injection pressures more than $2000 \, kN/m^2$). The length of these anchors is enlarged by hydrofracturing of the ground to give a grout fissure system beyond the nominal borehole diameter. Post-grouting using tubes à manchette is frequently used with only a small quantity of secondary grout being required.
(d) Type D: tremie-grouted boreholes consisting of a series of bells or under-reams mechanically formed within the fixed length of the anchor.
(e) Type E: other types of anchor formed by jet grouting or similar techniques.

BS 8081 refers to four items that have to be addressed in the design of these anchors: overall stability, depth of embedment, fixed anchor dimensions, and group effect. To check overall stability in cohesionless soils, several analysis methods are detailed in BS 8081. The simplest method is based on a planar failure surface. The failure wedge may be assumed as based on Coulomb wedge with an angle to the back of the wall of $\beta = 45° + \phi/2$ (Fig. 7.6). A further method, known as the sliding block method, is shown in Fig. 7.7 with a subsequent variation shown as Fig. 7.8. The fixed anchor dimensions based on safety factor methods as detailed below comply with the recommendations of BS 8081. Safety factors for temporary and permanent anchors are reproduced from BS 8081 in Table 7.4. (The relatively high values for temporary anchors compared with those used in Continental Europe may have led to their reduced use in the UK.)

From BS 8081, for fixed anchor design in rock, for type A anchorages, the ultimate load carrying capacity T_f (kN) is estimated from

$$T_f = \pi D L \tau_{ult} \tag{64}$$

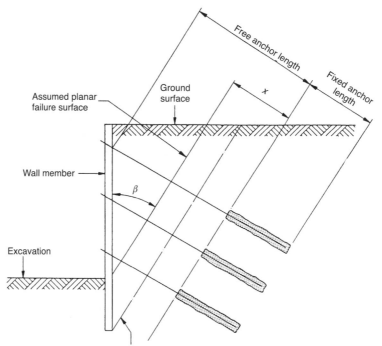

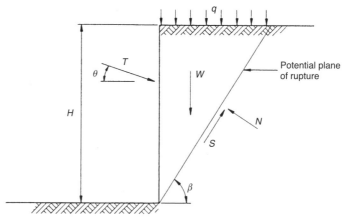

where

 q is the surcharge;
 W is the weight of sliding wedge; $= 0.5\gamma H^2 \cot \beta$;
 γ is the density of wedge;
 H is the depth of excavation;
 T is the anchorage force;
 θ is the angle of inclination of anchorage force;
 β is the angle of inclination of potential plane of rupture;
 ϕ' is the effective angle of shearing resistance of retained ground;
 c' is the effective cohesion of retained ground.

In practice T is expressed in terms of β, and β is then varied and plotted against values of T. The value of β, corresponding to the maximum value of T, defines the critical plane of rupture. The key relationships are

$$T = \frac{(q + \gamma H/2)H \cos \beta (S_f - \cot \beta \tan \phi') - c'H/\sin \beta}{\sin(\theta + \beta) \tan \phi' + S_f \cos(\theta + \beta)}$$

and

$$S_f = \frac{c'H/\sin \beta + [(q + \gamma H/2)H \cos \beta \cot \beta + T \sin(\theta + \beta)] \tan \phi'}{(q + \gamma H/2)H \cos \beta - T \cos(\theta + \beta)}$$

where

 S_f is the required factor of safety (typically 1·5);
 N is the normal force on wedge $= (q + \gamma H/2)H \cos \beta \cot \beta + T \sin (\theta + \beta)$;
 S is the shear resistance of the retained ground $= c'H/\sin \beta + N \tan \phi'$;
 T should not exceed the working load of the anchorage support per unit width.

Fig. 7.6. Ground anchors: wedge method of analysis[20]

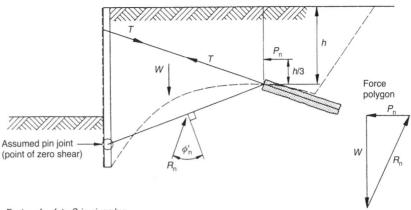

Factor of safety S_f is given by:

$$S_f = \frac{\tan \phi'}{\tan \phi'_n} \geq 1.5$$

where

ϕ'_n is nominal angle of shearing resistance (in degrees).

NOTE. If ϕ'_n has been correctly assumed, the weight W and the forces R_n, and P_n are in equilibrium. If this is not the case ϕ'_n has to be altered.

(a) Modified by Locher (1969)[43] and Littlejohn (1970)[44] and (1977)[45]

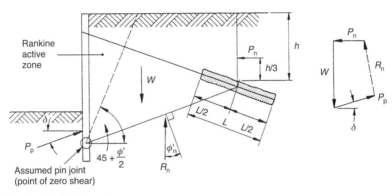

Fig. 7.7. Ground anchors: sliding block method of overall stability analysis[20] (BS 8081): (a) as modified by Locher and Littlejohn; (b) as modified by Ostermayer

Factor of safety S_f is given by:

$$S_f = \frac{\tan \phi'}{\tan \phi'_n} \geq 1.2$$

where

ϕ'_n is the nominal angle of shearing resistance of the soil (in degrees).

(b) Modified by Ostermayer (1977)[24]

where τ_{ult} is the ultimate bond or skin friction at the rock/grout interface (in kN/m^2), D is the diameter of the fixed anchor (in m), and L is the length of the fixed anchor (in m). Bond values recommended for design in rocks and soft rocks are shown in Table 7.5.

For fixed anchor design in cohesionless soils for type B anchorages

$$T_f = Ln \tan \phi' \tag{65}$$

where ϕ' is the effective angle of shearing resistance (degrees) and n is a factor to allow for drilling technique, depth of overburden, fixed anchor diameter and grout pressure. Littlejohn and Bruce[22] suggested that n ranges from 400 to 600 kN/m for coarse sands and gravels, and from 130 to 165 kN/m in fine to medium sands. These values were measured in borehole anchor diameters of approximately 0.1 m. Where the design diameter is larger, n should be increased in linear proportion. Alternatively,

$$T_f = A\sigma'_v \pi DL \tan \phi' + B\gamma h \frac{\pi}{4} (D^2 - d^2) \quad \text{(side shear and end shear)} \tag{66}$$

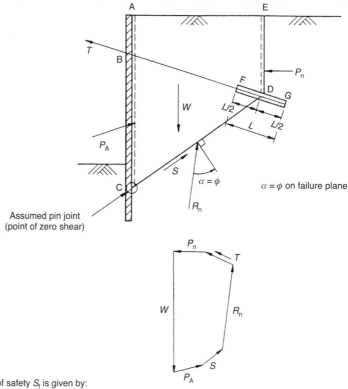

Factor of safety S_f is given by:

$$S_f = \frac{\tan \phi'}{\tan \phi'_n} \geq 1 \cdot 3$$

for non-critical applications.

$$S_f \geq 1 \cdot 5$$

for critical applications (after Kranz (1953)[46] and Ranke and Ostermayer (1968)[47]).

W is the weight of soil mass within the failure surface.
P_n is the design force acting on the surface DE. A driving force due to water must be considered when below the water table. While P_n has been drawn horizontally, it could have been an inclined force.
R_n is the frictional component of soil resistance. This force is applied at an angle, $\alpha = \phi$ (full obliquity) to the normal base of the soil mass. It should be noted that α cannot be greater than the internal friction angle of the soil. Mobilized shear resistance acting along the plane is $(R_n \cos \phi) \tan \phi$.
S is the component of soil resistance due to cohesive soil strength (generally ignored).
P_A is the active earth force between point A and point C. Point C is the point of zero shear.
T is the anchorage force.

(after Cheney 1984[48]).

Fig. 7.8. Ground anchors: revised sliding block method of overall stability analysis[20]

where A is the ratio of contact pressure at the fixed anchor/soil interface to the average effective overburden pressure (it has a value between 1 and 2, depending on construction technique), γ is the unit weight of soil overburden (use submerged weight below water table) (in kN/m^3), h is the depth of overburden to the top of the fixed anchor (in m), σ'_v is the average effective overburden pressure adjacent to the fixed anchor (in kN/m^2), B is the bearing capacity factor and is equivalent to $N_q/1 \cdot 4$ (refer to Berezantzev's curve, Fig. 7.9), d is the diameter of the grout shaft above the fixed anchor (in m) and D is the diameter of the fixed anchor (in m).

For type C anchorages, in cohesionless soils, design methods have relied heavily on field tests in a range of soils rather than load capacity expressions. Figure 7.10 shows load-carrying capacity in sandy gravels and gravelly sands for increasing anchor length. Sherwood and Harris[23] proposed an empirical design method for regroutable anchors which used their experience over 15 years to establish limit shaft friction values in clays and silts and in sands and gravels over the groutable length of the proprietary TMD anchor from Bachy. They argued that while BS 8081 recognizes that pressure-grouted

Table 7.4 Minimum safety factors recommended for design of individual anchorages[20]

Anchorage category	Minimum safety factor			Proof load factor
	Tendon	Ground/grout interface	Grout/tendon or grout/encapsulation interface	
Temporary anchorages where a service life is less than six months and failure would have no serious consequences and would not endanger public safety, e.g. short-term pile test loading using anchorages as a reaction system	1·40	2·0	2·0	1·10
Temporary anchorages with a service life of, say, up to two years where, although the consequences of failure are quite serious, there is no danger to public safety without adequate warning, e.g. retaining wall tieback	1·60	2·5[a]	2·5[a]	1·25
Permanent anchorages and temporary anchorages where corrosion risk is high and/or the consequences of failure are serious, e.g. main cables of a suspension bridge or as a reaction for lifting heavy structural members	2·00	3·0[b]	3·0[a]	1·50

[a] Minimum value of 2·0 may be used if full-scale field tests are available.
[b] May need to be raised to 4·0 to limit ground creep.
Note 1. In current practice the safety factor of an anchorage is the ratio of the ultimate load to design load. The table defines minimum safety factors at all the major component interfaces of an anchorage system.
Note 2. Minimum safety factors for the ground/grout interface generally lie between 2·5 and 4·0. However, it is permissible to vary these, should full-scale field tests (trial anchorage tests) provide sufficient additional information to permit a reduction.
Note 3. The safety factors applied to the ground/grout interface are invariably higher compared with the tendon values, the additional magnitude representing a margin of uncertainty.

anchorages are superior to other types in terms of load capacity, BS 8081 does not differentiate between anchors installed with uniform injection pressure and those with repetitive and selective high-pressure injection. Sherwood and Harris concluded that factors of safety recommended by BS 8081 may be appropriate to less sophisticated ground anchors but are much too conservative for anchor systems which produce more uniform anchorage performance as a result of their installation procedure. They reasoned that preliminary anchor tests should be used as a means of refining design and reducing the factor of safety.

For type D anchorages, BS 8081 does not suggest a design method for cohesionless soils due to lack of published data but warns that if shaft enlargements are required to take all the anchor load, the shear across the interface between the nominal diameter shaft and the enlargements will require examination.

For fixed anchor design in cohesive soils, for type A anchorages, load-carrying capacity may be estimated from

$$T_{\mathrm{f}} = \pi D L \alpha c_{\mathrm{u}} \tag{67}$$

where c_{u} is the undrained shear strength (in kN/m^2) and α is the adhesion factor (in the range 0·28 to 0·36 for stiff clays and 0·48 to 0·6 for stiff to very stiff marls).

For type C anchorages in cohesive soils, BS 8081 reproduces the work by Ostermayer[24] as a design guide for borehole diameters between 0·08 and 0·16 m. The effect of post-grouting pressure on skin friction is shown in Fig. 7.11.

Table 7.5 Rock/grout bond values which have been employed in practice[22]

Rock type	Working bond (N/mm²)	Test bond (N/mm²)	Ultimate bond (N/mm²)	Factor of safety Measured	Factor of safety Design	Source
Igneous						
Basalt	1·93		6·37		3·3	Britain—Parker (1958)
Basalt	1·10	3·60				USA—Eberhardt and Veltrop (1965)
Tuff	0·80					France—Cambefort (1966)
Basalt	0·63	0·72				Britain—Cementation (1962)
Granite	1·56	1·72				Britain—Cementation (1962)
Dolerite	1·56	1·72				Britain—Cementation (1962)
Very fissured felsite	1·56	1·72				Britain—Cementation (1962)
Very hard dolerite	1·56	1·72				Britain—Cementation (1962)
Hard granite	1·56	1·72				Britain—Cementation (1962)
Basalt and tuff	1·56	1·72				Britain—Cementation (1962)
Granodiorite	1·09					Britain—Cementation (1962)
Shattered basalt		1·01				USA—Saliman and Schaefer (1968)
Decomposed granite		1·24				USA—Saliman and Schaefer (1968)
Flow breccia		0·93				USA—Saliman and Schaefer (1968)
Mylontized prophyrite	0·32–0·57					Switzerland—Descoeudres (1969)
Fractured diorite	0·95					Switzerland—Descoeudres (1969)
Granite	0·63	0·81				Canada—Barron *et al.* (1971)
Metamorphic						
Schist	0·31					Switzerland—Birkenmaier (1953)
All types	1·20					Finland—Maijala (1966)
Weathered fractured quartzite	1·56	1·72		1·1		Britain—Cementation (1962)
Blue schist	1·52	1·67		1·1		Britain—Cementation (1962)
Weak meta sediments	1·10	1·23		1·1		Britain—Cementation (1962)
Slate	0·43					Britain—Cementation (1962)
Slate/meta greywacke	1·57	1·73		1·1		Britain—Cementation (1962)
Granite gneiss	0·36–0·69					Sweden—Broms (1968)
Folded quartzite	0·51					Australia—Rawlings (1968)
Weathered meta tuff		0·29				USA—Saliman and Schaefer (1968)
Greywacke	0·34					Germany—Heitfeld and Schaurte (1969)
Quartzite	0·93–1·20	1·02–1·32		1·1		Britain—Gosschalk and Taylor (1970)
Microgneiss	0·95					Italy—Mantovani (1970)
Seridite schist	0·05					Italy—Berardi (1972)
Quartzite/schist	0·10					Italy—Berardi (1972)
Argillaceous and calcareous schist	0·63					Italy—Berardi (1972)
Slate	0·95	1·24		1·3		Switzerland—Moschler and Matt (1972)
Highly metasediments	0·83	1·08		1·3		USA—Buro (1972)
Slate and greywacke	1·08	1·40		1·3		Germany—Anon (1972)
Various metasediments			1·57			Germany—Abraham and Prozig (1973)
Micaschist/biotite gneiss	0·53	0·80		1·5		USA—Nicholson Anchorage Co. Ltd (1973)
Slate	0·60	0·90	1·80	1·5	3·0	Britain—Littlejohn and Truman-Davies (1974)
Sound micaschist	1·74	2·16				USA—Feld and White (1974)
Micaschist	0·52–0·74			1·24		USA—Feld and White (1974)
Very poor gneiss and mud band	0·07					USA—Feld and White (1974)
Carbonate sediments						
Loamy limestone		0·63				Italy—Berardi (1960)
Fissured limestone and intercalations	1·08	1·19		1·1		Britain—Cementation Co. Ltd (1962)
Limestone	0·65					Switzerland—Muller (1966)
Poor limestone	0·32					France—Hennequin and Cambefort (1966)
Massive limestone	0·39–0·78					France—Hennequin and Cambefort (1966)
Karstic limestone	0·54					France—Hennequin and Cambefort (1966)
Tertiary limestone	1·00		2·83		2·8	Switzerland—Losinger and Co. Ltd (1966)

Table 7.5 continued

Rock type	Working bond (N/mm²)	Test bond (N/mm²)	Ultimate bond (N/mm²)	Factor of safety Measured	Factor of safety Design	Source
Limestone			4·55–4·80			Switzerland—Ruttner (1966)
Marly limestone	0·03–0·07 (average) 0·21–0·36 (measured)					Italy—Berardi (1967)
Limestone			0·27			USA—Saliman and Schaefer (1968)
Limestone	0·28					Italy—Berardi (1969)
Dolomitic limestone			1·80			Canada—Brown (1970)
Marly limestone	0·39–0·94					Italy—Berardi (1972)
Limestone	0·26					Italy—Berardi (1972)
Limestone/puddingstone	0·44					France—Soletanche Co Ltd (1968)
Limestone	1·18	1·42		1·2		USA—Buro (1972)
Chalk			0·70			Britain—Associated Tunnelling Co. Ltd (1973)
Dolomite		1·66				Canada—Golder Brawner (1973)
Dolomitic siltstone	0·43					USA—White (1973)
Limestone and marly bands	0·37	0·55		1·5		Italy—Mongilardi (1972)
Arenaceous sediments						
Sandstone	1·44	1·58		1·1		Britain—Morris and Garrett (1956)
Hard sandstone	1·42	1·56		1·1		Britain—Cementation Co. Ltd (1962)
Bunter sandstone	0·95	0·98		1·03		Britain—Cementation Co. Ltd (1962)
Sandstone	0·76	0·84		1·1		Britain—Cementation Co. Ltd (1962)
Sandstone	0·74					Czechoslovakia—Hobst (1968)
Sandstone	0·31	0·40	1·73	1·29	5·6	USA—Drossel (1970)
Sandstone	0·80					USA—Thompson (1970)
Poor sandstone	0·40					Germany—Brunner (1970)
Good sandstone	1·14					Germany—Brunner (1970)
Sandstone and breccia	0·38					France—Soletanche (1968)
Sandstone		0·95				Australia—Williams *et al.* (1972)
Bunter sandstone	0·60	1·20		2·0		Britain—Littlejohn (1973)
Sandstone	1·17					Australia—McLeod and Hoadley (1974)
Argillaceous sediments						
Shale	0·62					Canada—Juergens (1965)
Marl	0·10	0·28		2·8		Italy—Berardi (1987)
Shale	0·30		0·63		2·1	Canada—Hanna and Seaton (1967)
Very weathered shale			0·39			USA—Saliman and Schaefer (1968)
Shale	0·13–0·24					USA—Koziakin (1970)
Grey siltstone	0·62					Britain—Universal Anchorage Co. Ltd (1972)
Clay marl	0·14–0·24	0·21–0·36		1·5		Germany—Schwarz (1972)
Shale	0·62					Canada—McRosite *et al.* (1972)
Argillite	0·82					Canada—Golder Brawner (1973)
Mudstone	0·63	0·88		1·4		Australia—McLeod and Hoadley (1974)
Miscellaneous						
Bedded sandstone and shale	0·20–0·50					Italy—Beomonte (1961)
Porous, sound goassamer	1·57	1·72		1·1		Britain—Cementation Co. Ltd (1962)
Shale and sandstone	0·07	0·10		1·5		USA—Reti (1964)
Soft rocks	0·75					Sweden—Nordin (1966)
Sandstone and shale	1·82					Poland—Bujak *et al.* (1967)
Siltstone and mudstone	1·65					Australia—Maddox *et al.* (1967)
Fractured rock (75% shale)						
Poor			0·24			USA—Saliman and Schaefer (1968)
Average			0·35			USA—Saliman and Schaefer (1968)
Good			0·75			USA—Saliman and Schaefer (1968)
Limestone and clay breccia	0·20–0·23					Italy—Berardi (1972)

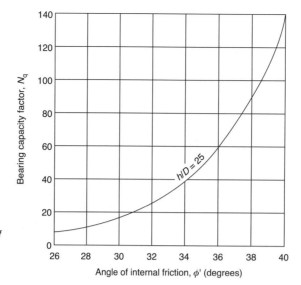

Fig. 7.9. Berezantzev's curve of bearing capacity factor N_q against angle of shearing resistance

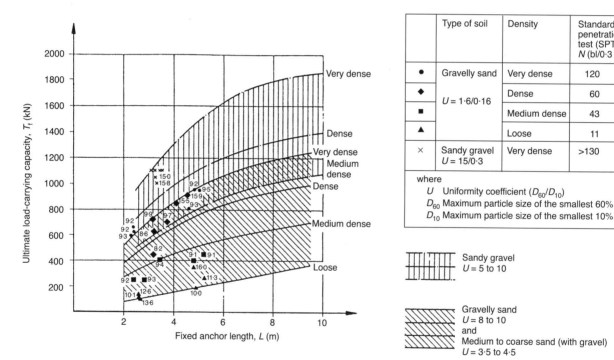

	Type of soil	Density	Standard penetration test (SPT) N (bl/0·3 m)
●	Gravelly sand	Very dense	120
◆	$U = 1·6/0·16$	Dense	60
■		Medium dense	43
▲		Loose	11
×	Sandy gravel $U = 15/0·3$	Very dense	>130

where
U Uniformity coefficient (D_{60}/D_{10})
D_{60} Maximum particle size of the smallest 60%
D_{10} Maximum particle size of the smallest 10%

Sandy gravel
$U = 5$ to 10

Gravelly sand
$U = 8$ to 10
and
Medium to coarse sand (with gravel)
$U = 3·5$ to 4·5

Note 1. Field evidence is limited to a fixed anchor range of 2 m to 5 m approximately.
Note 2. The relationships between soil density and standard penetration test (SPT) values are not in accordance with BS 5930.

Diameter of grouted bodies
$D = 0·1$ m to $0·15$ m

Fig. 7.10. Ultimate load capacity as a function of fixed length in sandy gravels and gravelly sand[42]

For type D anchorages in cohesive soils, the ultimate load capacity of multi-under-reamed anchorages is given by

$$T_f = \pi D L c_u + \frac{\pi}{4}(D^2 - d^2)N_c c_{ub} + \pi d l c_a$$

(side shear + end bearing + shaft resistance)   (68)

where D is the diameter of under-ream (Fig. 7.12) and N_c is the bearing capacity factor (a value of 9·0 is often used), c_{ub} is the undrained shear strength in

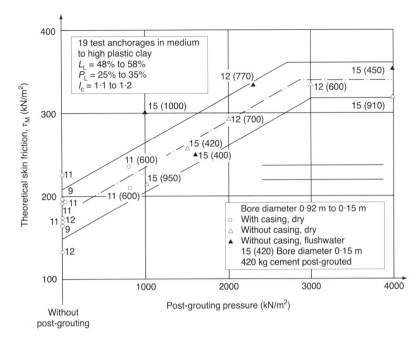

Fig. 7.11. Influence of post-grouting pressure on skin friction in a cohesive soil[24]

Note. The theoretical skin friction is calculated from the borehole diameter and designed fixed anchor length.

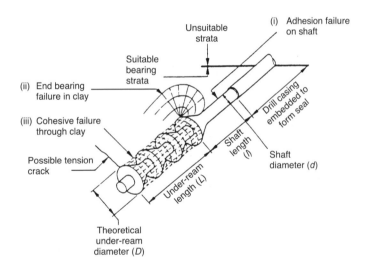

Fig. 7.12. Diagram of multi-under-ream anchorage at ultimate capacity[20]

the clay at the top end of the fixed length, and c_a is the shaft adhesion (in the range 0.3 to $0.35c_u$) (in kN/m^2). BS 8081 comments that under-reaming is best suited to clays with an undrained cohesion c_u greater than $90 \, kN/m^2$. Poor under-reams are likely if this value reduces to 60 to $70 \, kN/m^2$, and under-reaming becomes almost impossible if c_u is less than $50 \, kN/m^2$. Under-reaming is difficult in low plasticity soils where the plasticity index is less than 20.

BS 8081 suggests that to limit interaction between fixed anchors, the spacing between anchors, centre-to-centre, should not be less than four times the enlarged fixed anchor diameter; in practice a minimum spacing of 1·5 to 2·0 m is usual. The tolerances of drilling and borehole enlargement should be considered when anchor spacing is decided, particularly with long anchors.

Table 7.6 Typical sizes and characteristic strengths for pre-stress tendon design[20]

Type of steel	Nominal diameter (mm)	Specified characteristic strength (kN)	Nominal steel area (mm²)
Non-alloy steel			
Wire	7·0	60·4	38·5
7-wire strand	12·9	186	100
	15·2	232	139
	15·7	265	150
7-wire drawn strand	12·7	209	112
	15·2	300	165
	18·0	380	223
Low alloy steel bar			
Grade 1030/835	26·5	568	552
	32	830	804
	36	1048	1018
	40	1300	1257
Grade 1230/1080[a]	25	600	491
	32	990	804
	36	1252	1018
Stainless steel			
Wire	7	44·3	38·5
Bar	25	491	491
	32	804	804
	40	1257	1257

[a] This grade is not covered in BS 4486.

High grout pressures should be avoided for anchors founded at shallow depth where subsoil movement due to these pressures would be detrimental to existing structures or services.

The maximum values of grout/tendon adhesion recommended by BS 8081 for cement grout with a minimum compressive strength of $30\,N/mm^2$ before stressing are:

- $1·0\,N/mm^2$ for clean plain wire or bar
- $1·5\,N/mm^2$ for clean crimped wire
- $2·0\,N/mm^2$ for clean strand or deformed bar
- $3·0\,N/mm^2$ for locally noded strands.

Minimum recommended tendon bond lengths for cement or resin grouted anchorages are $3·0\,m$ where the tendon is homed and bonded in situ, and $2·0\,m$ for tendons bonded under factory-controlled conditions.

For pre-stressed anchors the tendons consist of steel bar, strand or wire, either singly or in groups. Pre-stressing steel is covered in sections 2 (for non-alloy steel wire) and 3 (non-alloy 7-wire strand) of BS 5896[25] and in BS 4486[26] (low alloy steel bar). Typical sizes and specified characteristic strengths from BS 8081[20] are reproduced in Table 7.6. It is usual to proof-load temporary works anchorages to a load equal to 1·25 times the required unfactored working load and then lock-off the anchor at 1·1 times the unfactored working load.

Design of the bearing plate beneath the stressing head requires care. A typical arrangement is shown in Fig. 7.13. The bearing is a thick steel plate, often stiffened to span between wedge-shaped plates which transfer the load from the stressing head through the bearing plate to the steel waling or soldier members. Where the bearing head is bedded on to the concrete wall surface (as for piled or diaphragm walls), BS 8081 recommends that the bedding mortar

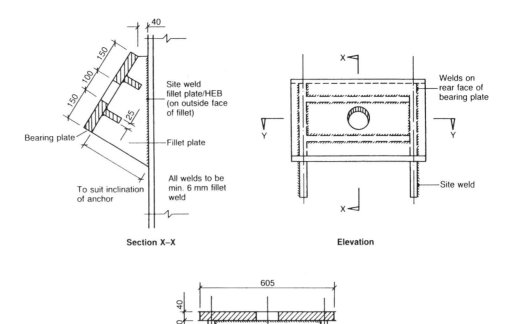

Fig. 7.13. *Anchor bearing plate, detail from Berlin wall installation*

thickness should be limited to 10% of the plate width, with a maximum of 100 mm. The design bearing stress should not exceed 30% f_{cu} (where f_{cu} is the characteristic strength, the 28-day compressive strength) of the grout. Where concrete pads are used to bed the bearing plate on to the wall surface and the depth exceeds 10% of the bearing plate width or 100 mm, the pad should be designed to resist the stresses induced by the bearing plate in the same way as a post-tensioned concrete block is designed as part of a wall.

Methods of improving the load capacity of anchorages in both rock and soil were discussed by Barley[27]. Other developments in anchor construction include the use of removable tendons. This is necessary where further development at the curtilage of site is likely to involve underground excavations that would be impaired by tendons used for temporary support. Specialist anchor firms, including Keller in the UK, have developed systems whereby tendons may be extracted after use with relatively low forces. Keller also originally developed a single-bore multiple-anchorage system, and a typical application in chalk was discussed by Barley *et al.*[28] The system comprises the installation of multiple anchorage units within a single borehole 100 mm to 200 mm in diameter. The anchorages are located at staggered depths in the borehole and each unit anchorage transfers load in a controlled manner to a specific length of borehole. A comparison of the load transfer mechanism of a normal and single-bore multiple anchor is shown in Fig. 7.14. This method, which is particularly suited to anchorage in weak rocks, clays, and mixed cohesive and granular materials rather than non-cohesive soils alone, allows the utilization of a considerable length of borehole as a fixed anchor. As shown, it can materially add to the load capacity of an individual anchor; a limit of approximately 10 m is usual for fixed-length anchors.

The design and installation of 10 000 anchorages in rock was discussed by Barley[29] who gave detailed information regarding anchor dimensions and

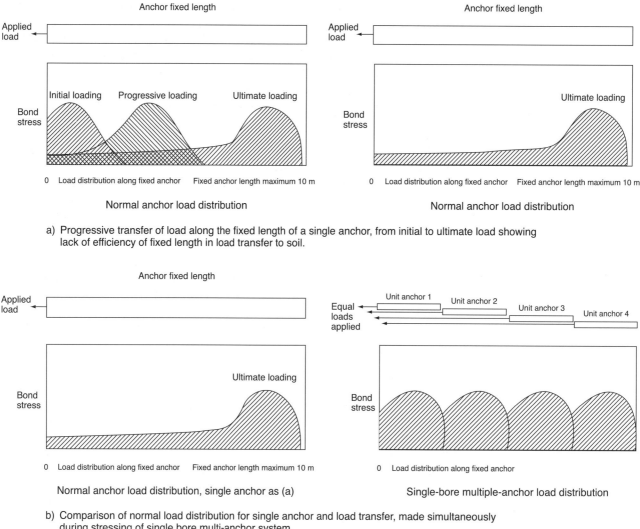

a) Progressive transfer of load along the fixed length of a single anchor, from initial to ultimate load showing lack of efficiency of fixed length in load transfer to soil.

b) Comparison of normal load distribution for single anchor and load transfer, made simultaneously during stressing of single bore multi-anchor system.

Fig. 7.14. Comparison of the load transfer mechanism: normal and single-bore multiple anchors

working and test bond values from a large number of sites in chalk, mudstone, siltstone and marls, sandstone and other rock including strong rocks such as granites. The paper also referred to the hazards of downward movement of sheeting caused by the vertical component of anchor loads and the inadequate transfer of load by poor waling systems. Barley mentioned that inclined twin-channel walings have proved to be the most trouble-free system. Below is the summary of Barley's paper.

Since Littlejohn's initial correlation of standard penetration test (SPT) values with a limited number of bond stress values in chalk some 20 years ago, a steady drive to substantiate and extend this approach and to develop similar correlations in other rocks has continued. However, to allow continual assessment of bond stress/SPT and bond stress/rock strength relationships in order to estimate the safe capacity of rock anchorages, the basic requirement for thorough site investigation operations prior to anchorage design must be satisfied. This requires SPT values, core recovery percentages, RQD values, core logs, unconfined compressive strength (UCS) and point load index values, all to a depth of almost 10 m into the bedrock. In particularly weak and varied rock (that is coal measures) where the presence of good anchorage rock (sandstones) may exist, the full thickness of these bands should be investigated to allow economic design of efficient anchorages.

Chalk, initially considered to be a problematic anchoring rock, has proved to be a very satisfactory founding medium, generally without the requirements of under-reaming. Test anchorages using the described installation techniques have confirmed a reliable correlation between SPT values and ultimate bond stress with F (F = bond stress/SPT value) chalk factors at failure of 20 to 30.

Installation of over 1500 working anchorages, all without failure, has confirmed a reliable guideline for a safe working bond stress of $5 \times$ SPT value to $7 \times$ SPT value. Working loads in the range 400 to 600 kN in medium grade chalks and of the order of 1000 kN in upper grades are generally realistic.

Weak mudstones, siltstones, shales, marls and other weak fine-grained rock continue to be rather unreliable founding strata for straight shaft anchorages, unless particularly low bond stresses are considered. Reasonable correlation exists between SPT and bond stress, albeit at much lower values and over a much broader envelope than those exhibited by chalk anchorages. F mudstone factors at failure generally range from 2·4 to 6·0 with ultimate bond stresses in the 200 to 400 kN/m^2 range. The use of an F mudstone value of unity for permanent straight shaft anchorages, and 1·5 for temporary straight shaft anchorages, is recommended for the initial estimation of working bond stresses. Working loads of shaft anchorages lie in the 150 to 350 kN range. The use of under-reaming techniques to form the positive lock in weak mudstone will allow mobilization of much greater loads and reduce failure rates. Where enlargements are designed and spaced correctly they will reduce the load loss due to creep. In stony mudstones some satisfactory shaft anchorages have been constructed with temporary loads in the 600 to 800 kN range. Sandstones, when their properties and conditions are adequately investigated and reported contribute highly to the success of rock anchorages. Working bond stresses range from 200 to 1000 kN/m^2, depending on particle grading and rock strengths. Although there is very limited data to relate SPT values in very weak sandstones to bond stresses, it is likely that the F sandstone factors will equate to, or be greater than, F chalk values of 20 to 30. The few failures encountered in sandstones have generally been attributed to artesian conditions unknown at the time of anchor installation or to unexpected depths of weathering. Generally, under-reaming is unnecessary in sandstone anchorages and working loads well in excess of 1000 kN have been frequently employed.

BS EN 1537: 2000 was prepared to address the installation, testing and monitoring of permanent and temporary ground anchors where the load capacity is tested. An annex to the standard describes alternative limit state and serviceability limit state design principles in compliance with Eurocode EC7. The Code describes the corrosion protection required for both temporary and permanent anchors. For temporary anchors, the Code requires a protection to the steel components which exhibit corrosion for a minimum design life of two years. In summary this is fulfilled by:

- tendon bond length: a minimum 10 mm cement grout cover to the boreholewall.

- tendon free length: low-friction system to allow movement of the tendon within the borehole by sealed or compound filled plastic or steel sheaths
- transition between anchor head and free length: free length sheath sealed to the bearing plate/anchor head or a metal sleeve or plastic duct may be sealed to the bearing plate
- anchor head where anchor head is accessible, a coating or tape protection; where inaccessible, a metal or plastic cap is required filled with compound for extended use.

A longer period of protection or aggressive conditions require additional protection in order to comply with the Code.

Tremied plugs and grouted bases

Where outer sheeting or walling to a cofferdam fails to achieve a cut-off due to the depth of permeable strata, it may prove economical to seal the cofferdam with a temporary concrete plug installed below the base slab of the permanent works. This concrete plug would be installed below water by tremie methods of placing following the bulk excavation of the cofferdam, with the cofferdam flooded to existing ground level or, for river cofferdams, to the level of the water outside the sheeting. This concrete plug would be designed to withstand the head of water acting as an upward pressure on its underside. The weight of the plug needs to balance or exceed this pressure in order that water within the cofferdam above the plug can be safely pumped out. In wide cofferdams the span of the plug and its effectiveness in withstanding the upward pressure may be improved by the installation of tension piles or anchors which hold the plug down. Figure 7.15 shows typical construction details.

The concrete plug in fact performs a dual role; in addition to preventing the ingress of groundwater into the cofferdam, it also provides an effective prop between the sheeting below formation level prior to the removal of water from the flooded cofferdam, and therefore reduces design bending moments in the outer sheeting or walls and reduces the loads in the lowest and the penultimate frames.

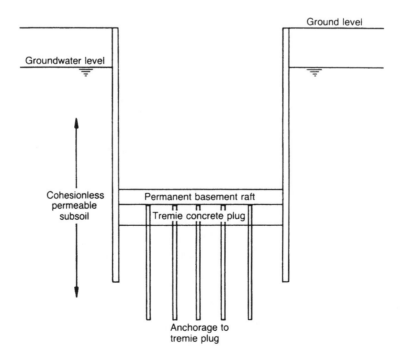

Fig. 7.15. Cross-section of cofferdam showing anchored plug

Some difficulty may be experienced in obtained a completely dry seal to the cofferdam with a tremied plug, and care is needed to avoid a 'blow' through any tremied base concrete of low quality. The concrete plug should wherever possible be placed in one continuous operation without disruption. Any small leakage between the plug and the outer sheeting once detected is remedied by local grouting.

The alternative to placing a concrete plug by tremie is the installation of a horizontal curtain by injection or jet-grouting methods. These curtains can be anchored vertically by tension piles installed prior to grouting, the piles extending to formation level for later incorporation into the basement raft of the permanent works. In a similar way to the concrete plug, the horizontal curtain excludes (or largely excludes) groundwater from the excavation and provides improved passive resistance to the outer sheeting when the excavation within the cofferdam is made to the full depth, reducing the lower strut loads and possibly even reducing the number of cofferdam frames. Typical details are shown in Fig. 7.16.

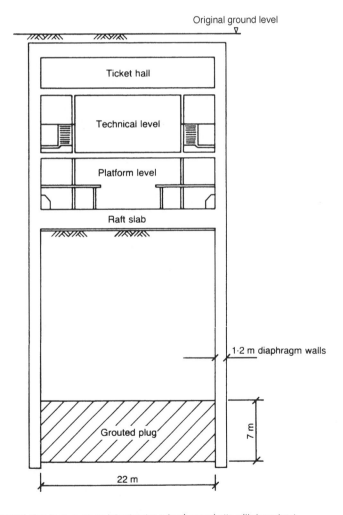

Fig. 7.16. Grouted soil plug to metro station excavation, Cairo Metro, 1994 (from Tunnels and Tunnelling

Grouted plug by two-stage injection by *tube à manchette* with two-stage treatment using cement–bentonite and sodium silicate.
Subsoil conditions consist of shallow fill deposits underlain by approx. 6 m of stiff clay underlain by extensive sand deposit to depth below diaphragm wall construction.
Groundwater generally 3 to 4 m below ground surface: perched water table in fill and confined within aquifer below clay stratum.

Fig. 7.17. Installation of a
horizontal grout curtain,
Leipzig

Drilling in Leipzig for the installation of a horizontal silicate grout curtain
is shown in Fig. 7.17. The subsoils consist of river sands and gravels and two
forms of construction have evolved locally, a deep grouted curtain as shown
or a shallow jet grouted curtain restrained by tension piles.

Sheet piling: selection of section
Steel sheet piling is supplied to comply with EN 10248: 1995 in two grades as
shown in Table 7.7. Where steel sheet piling is used for the outer walls of a
land or marine cofferdam, the choice of section depends both on the flexural
strength needed to resist earth and water pressures and the strength needed to
resist driving stresses. Although these latter stresses may be reduced dramatically by jetting through granular soils, this provision may not necessarily be
available. The CIRIA report[4] provides some assistance to the designer in
assessing the pile section needed for driveability in both cohesionless and
cohesive soils. Table 7.8 from the report is based on experience of sheet
piles, approximately 500 mm wide, driven in panels. The two criteria for
sufficiency of the pile section during driving or vibration are that the head
of the pile should not be damaged unreasonably and the toe of the pile
should not be damaged and become declutched. Resistance to pile penetration
in granular soils is primarily at the toe and the effect of skin friction on a

Table 7.7 Properties of steel used in sheet piling[18]

Designation EN 10027		Classification EN 10020	Minimum yield strength, R_{eH} (N/mm²)[b]	Minimum tensile strength, R_m (N/mm²)[b]	Minimum elongation on a gauge length of $L_0 = 5 \cdot 65 S_0$ (A%)
Steel name	Steel number				
EN 10248 S270GP	1·0023	BS[a]	270	410	24
EN 10248 S355GP	1·0083	BS[a]	355	480	22

[a] BS: Base Steel.
[b] The values in the table apply to longitudinal test pieces for the tensile test.

Table 7.8 Guide for the selection of pile size to suit driving conditions in granular soils[4]

Dominant SPT (N value)	Minimum wall modulus (cm³/m)		Remarks
	BSEN 10 025 Grade 430A, BS 4360 Grade 43A	BSEN 10 025 Grade 510A, BS 4360 Grade 50A	
0–10	450		Grade FE 510A for lengths greater than 10 m
11–20		450	
21–25	850		
26–30		850	Lengths greater than 15 m not advisable
31–35	1300		Penetration of such a stratum greater than 5 m not advisable[a]
36–40		1300	Penetration of such a stratum greater than 8 m not advisable
41–45	2300		
46–50		2300	
51–60	3000		
61–70		3000	Some declutching may occur
71–80	4200		Some declutching may occur with pile lengths greater than 15 m
81–140		4200	Increased risk of declutching. Some piles may refuse

[a] If the stratum is of greater thickness use a larger section of pile.

moving pile is not severe. Pile penetration is therefore a function of the relative density of the soil at the pile toe. In contrast, for cohesive soils, resistance to pile installation is primarily due to soil adhesion to the pile face and little resistance occurs at the pile toe. The resistance to penetration in clay is therefore a function of clay strength c_u and the length of pile within the clay. Damage to the pile toe is unlikely but resistance to pile buckling is necessary when the driving resistance, in terms of clay adhesion, is overcome by a hammer of sufficient capacity. Table 7.9 provides guidance for pile driving in cohesive soils. A review of methods of sheet pile installation has been carried out by the Technical European Sheet Piling Association (TESPA)[30].

The previous use of sheet pile installation equipment such as Taylor Woodrow's 'Pilemaster' machine was particularly suited to pile installations in stiff clays. A more versatile type of machine, developed by Giken presses a single pile from a reaction gained from previously installed piles. This

Table 7.9 Guide to selection of pile size to suit driving conditions in cohesive soils[4]

Clay description	Minimum wall modulus (cm³/m)		Maximum length (m)
	BSEN 10 025 Grade 430A, BS 4360 Grade 43A	BSEN 10 025 Grade 510A, BS 4360 Grade 50A	
Soft to firm	450	400	6
Firm	600–700	450–600	9
Firm to stiff	700–1500	600–1300	14
Stiff	1600–2500	1300–2000	16
Very stiff	2500–3000	2000–2500	18
Hard ($c_u > 200$)	Not recommended	4200–5000	20

Note. The ability of piles to penetrate any type of ground is also a function of attention to good pile driving practice and this table assumes that this will be the case.

press is capable of installing sheeters into some cohesionless soils. Installation in stiff clays is assisted where necessary by lubrication with water or by water jetting. Some risk of loss of soil may occur in the use of jetting in loose soils such as fine sands and silts. During jetting in stiff clays there may be some risk of clay softening, although Giken states that there is no evidence of this in the long term. (Traditional use of jetting in stiff clays to assist sheeter penetration has sometimes been precluded in the last one metre of pile penetration for this reason.)

It should be noted that Giken presses may not be able to install standard corner sheet piles and special corners and junctions need to be fabricated. Corners are installed by the Giken press using two dummy piles, usually shorter piles, which are subsequently extracted.

Design of the bracing

Walings

Where walls or sheeters span vertically, walings are needed to transfer loads from the sheeting to the struts, which provide the bracing, or to the anchors, which retain the sheeting. The walings need not be continuous as, for example, in hammer head struts used against diaphragm wall panels where separate waling reinforcement may be included within the panel reinforcement of the wall. Alternatively, with anchored diaphragm walls it is common to incorporate waling rebar steel to the full panel width without external walings. Where secant pile walls are used in cofferdams, and where every pile or alternate piles are anchored walings may not be necessary. Common waling arrangements are shown in Fig. 7.18.

Where steel walings are used and subjected to heavy loads it may be convenient to use steel beams in pairs in order to provide adequate width on which to seat the bracing struts. It is often convenient to weld end plates to each length of waling to connect them together. It is vital that where rakers or sloping struts are used the tendency for the waling to turn on its support must be resisted. Figures 7.19 and 7.20 show a typical detail. Where anchors are used with walings, the spacing between steel beams must be sufficient to accommodate the inclined tendon between them, or the pair of beams must be inclined, with an adequate gap.

Where steel sheet piling is used it is usual to make the walings continuous over two supports. Unless the piling can be driven to good tolerances in vertical and horizontal alignment it is prudent to allow walings to cantilever mid-way between struts without connecting one to the other. Where tolerances are likely to be well maintained, it is advantageous to connect the ends of walings behind the incoming strut (Fig. 7.21). Where walings are continuous over two spans and joined behind struts the design moment is $WL/10$, but where they cantilever to half span the design moment becomes $WL/8$.

The values of waling load for limit state design as calculated using mobilization factors from BS 8002 or the ULS values using the partial factors applied to soil parameters for moderately conservative parameters, load case A (or the more onerous load case B for the worst credible parameters) as detailed in Chapter 5, are used as design values without further factoring. Comparison should always be made with waling loads calculated by empirical methods.

Where steel sheet piles are braced by steel walings any irregular alignment of the steel piles is rectified by steel packers or hardwood wedges. Where the alignment is particularly poor, concrete infilling can be used between the waling and the sheeters. If diagonal struts transfer longitudinal thrust into the waling, the waling must be designed to take both this thrust and bending

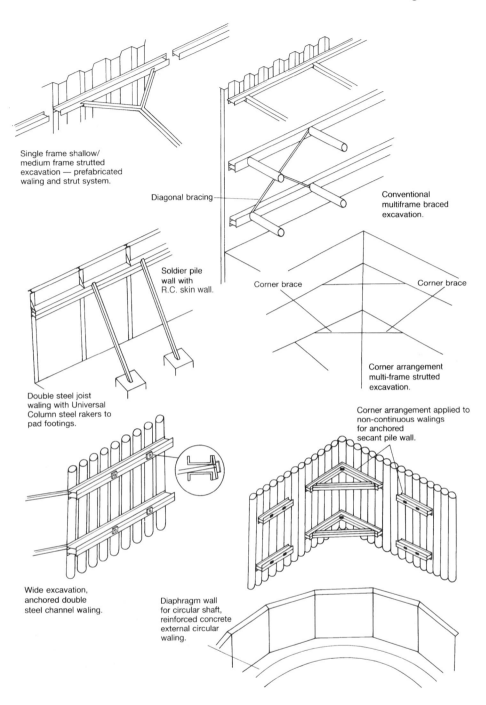

Single frame shallow/
medium frame strutted
excavation — prefabricated
waling and strut system.

Diagonal bracing

Conventional
multiframe braced
excavation.

Soldier pile
wall with
R.C. skin wall.

Corner brace

Corner brace

Corner arrangement
multi-frame strutted
excavation.

Double steel joist
waling with Universal
Column steel rakers to
pad footings.

Corner arrangement applied to
non-continuous walings
for anchored
secant pile wall.

Wide excavation,
anchored double
steel channel waling.

Diaphragm wall
for circular shaft,
reinforced concrete
external circular
waling.

*Fig. 7.18. Typical waling
details, steelwork and
reinforced concrete*

stresses due to the span between struts. It may be necessary to weld steel angles to the back of the walings prior to erection in order that horizontal acting shear keys can be formed by concreting the leg of the angle into the pan of the sheet pile. This will be required if the available length of waling is short and therefore the frictional resistance between waling and sheet pile is insufficient to transfer the thrust (Fig. 7.22). Alternatively steel shear plates occupying the whole pile pan can be welded to the waling and the face of the sheet pile.

Where heavily loaded struts or highly loaded anchors bear on steel walings it will be necessary to use web stiffeners to avoid web buckling of the waling. A typical detail is shown in Fig. 7.23.

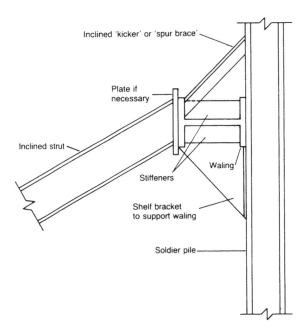

Fig. 7.19. Typical steelwork detail at junction of rakes and waling with bracing to prevent rotation of waling

Inclined 'kicker' or 'spur brace'

Plate if necessary

Inclined strut

Stiffeners

Waling

Shelf bracket to support waling

Soldier pile

Fig. 7.20. Typical connection detail to avoid rotation of waling at junction with strut

Where reinforced concrete diaphragm walls use internal walings within the reinforcement cages, such cages must be reinforced for shear where the anchor or strut bears on the waling but must avoid impeding the passage of tremie tubes through the waling beam reinforcement. Typical arrangements of both steel and reinforced concrete walings are shown in Fig. 7.24.

Walings for use with inclined anchors may themselves be inclined, with the anchor plate bearing directly on the face of the waling. Gusset plates welded to each pile face incline the waling. Alternatively, the waling may bear directly on to the sheeting with the bearing plate inclined. Fig. 7.25 illustrates the arrangements.

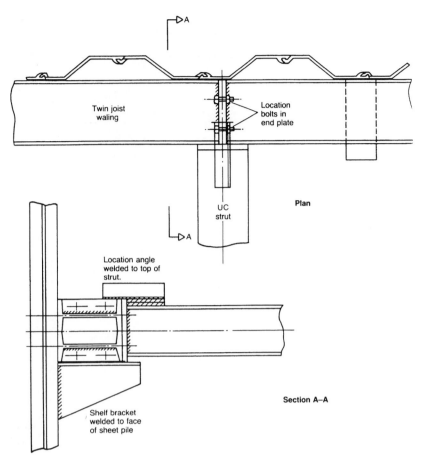

Fig. 7.21. Detail of typical
waling connection behind strut
in light cofferdam steelwork

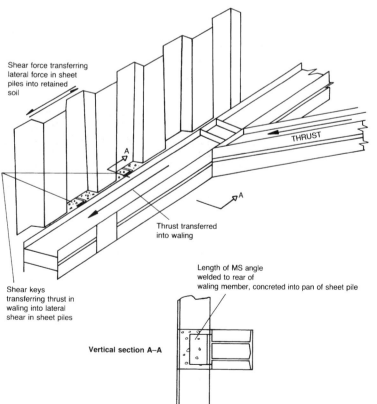

Fig. 7.22. Sheet piled
cofferdam construction: shear
keys at rear of waling transfer
thrust from diagonal strut into
short waling length and through
sheeters into soil at rear of piles

Fig. 7.23. Typical detail of web stiffener in waling to avoid web buckling

Passive anchors

The design of anchored walls is described in Chapter 5. Tie rods from the sheeting wall are anchored to deadmen, an anchor wall or an A-frame of driven piles. Anchor walls are designed on the basis that net available passive resistance is equal to passive pressure less active pressure. No allowance should be made for surcharge being available in front of an anchor wall in this calculation, and wall friction should be ignored because of the risk of vertical movement of the wall to the detriment of this friction. Tie rods, based on a factor of safety of 1·5 to 2·0, are designed using the following working stresses:

- Mild steel (BS 4360 grade 43A or BS EN 10025 grade Fe 430): 110 N/mm^2
- High-yield steel (BS 4360 grade 50B or 50C or BS EN 10025 grade Fe 510): 140 N/mm^2.

Tie rods can be housed in the bottom of pipework to avoid the effects of fill settlement and can be wrapped in Denso tape to reduce corrosion.

Struts

The most likely collapse mechanism of a braced cofferdam is the buckling of its strutting, beginning with the lowest frame and continuing progressively to the highest frame. The collapse of the lowest frame may be associated with inadequate penetration of the sheeting and passive failure below formation level; it may occur during extreme loading, such as high water for a river cofferdam or high waves in storm conditions for a cofferdam in open water. It may also be associated with poor workmanship in bracing or piling, or both. Collapse due to failure of walings or flexural failure of the sheeting

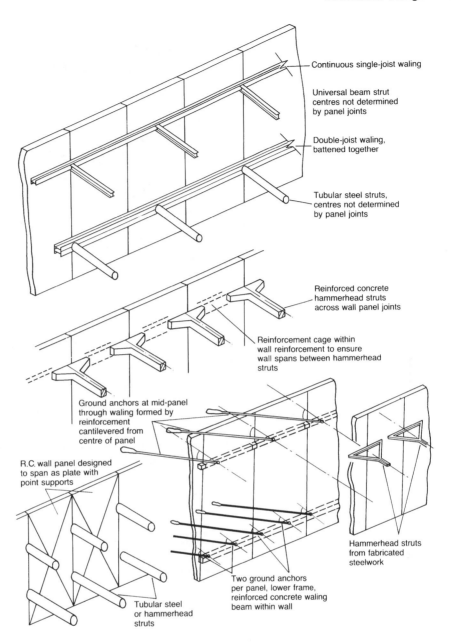

Continuous single-joist waling

Universal beam strut centres not determined by panel joints

Double-joist waling, battened together

Tubular steel struts, centres not determined by panel joints

Reinforced concrete hammerhead struts across wall panel joints

Reinforcement cage within wall reinforcement to ensure wall spans between hammerhead struts

Ground anchors at mid-panel through waling formed by reinforcement cantilevered from centre of panel

R.C. wall panel designed to span as plate with point supports

Two ground anchors per panel, lower frame, reinforced concrete waling beam within wall

Hammerhead struts from fabricated steelwork

Tubular steel or hammerhead struts

Fig. 7.24. Waling systems used with diaphragm walls

itself is much less likely. The extra care that is necessary in the design, detailing fabrication and fixing of cofferdam struts is self-evident. Any economy in the design of struts, especially long struts, can be false. It is essential that a design check is made against progressive collapse. This is best done by removal of any one strut and an analysis of the safety factors against collapse of the remaining structure.

Struts are generally laterally spaced so that excavation grabs may pass safely between them, so that construction materials can be lowered between them, and so that lower frames, when struck, can be threaded out through the frames above. Struts are therefore usually between 4 and 6 m apart. The most versatile strut is the steel tube because of its efficiency in buckling (although less so in bending) and its smooth outline which precludes snagging from muck grabs and construction materials as they are lowered. Other sections used include steel universal column sections, battened pairs of steel beams and box piles. Long tubular struts used in the cofferdam works at

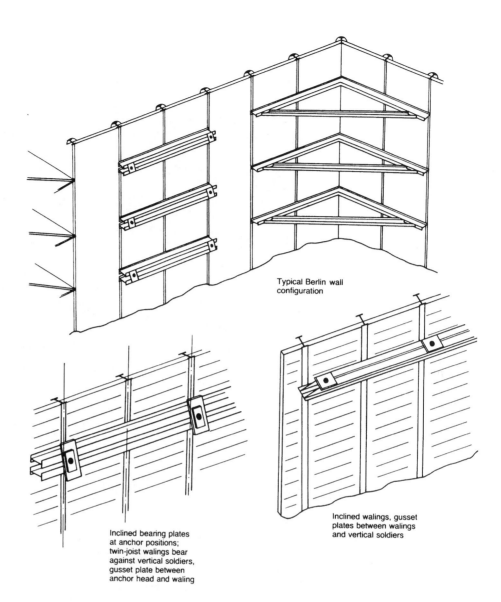

Typical Berlin wall configuration

Inclined bearing plates at anchor positions; twin-joist walings bear against vertical soldiers, gusset plate between anchor head and waling

Inclined walings, gusset plates between walings and vertical soldiers

Fig. 7.25. Waling details with inclined anchors, shown with typical Berlin wall

the Dartford Creek Barrier are shown in Fig. 7.26. Battened steel beams are shown in use on an earlier Thames cofferdam in Fig. 7.27.

Economy in the use of struts in a rectilinear cofferdam can often be achieved by using diagonal compression members in the corners, but care is needed to avoid obstruction to construction plant, such as piling plant, and installing permanent works in the corners.

It is essential to support struts adequately at the walings at each end of the strut. Steel location angles may be usefully welded to the strut end plates prior to bolting or welding into position. It is vital that the struts are square to the walings in plan and the end plates bear uniformly on the walings to avoid eccentric loading. (It is, nevertheless, worth checking the effect of eccentricity of the thrust in the strut by, say, 10% of the strut width or depth in each direction.) The effect of materials and plant loads placed on the strut should be added to the self-weight of the strut in considering the combined effect of compression load and bending.

Design values for struts using limit state design are those similar to walings and are calculated in a similar way. If the mobilization factors are applied as specified in BS 8002 no further factors are required on these values for limit

Fig. 7.26. Tubular steel struts used to brace cofferdam at Dartford Creek, UK (courtesy of AMEC)

Fig. 7.27. Battened steel beams used as struts and braces on River Thames cofferdam, London

state design. If the design process as detailed in Chapter 5 is used, the calculated loads, based on ULS case A moderately conservative values are used without further factoring (if ULS case B, worst credible parameters appropriately factored are more severe than case A these should be used). Comparison should always be made with strut loads calculated by empirical

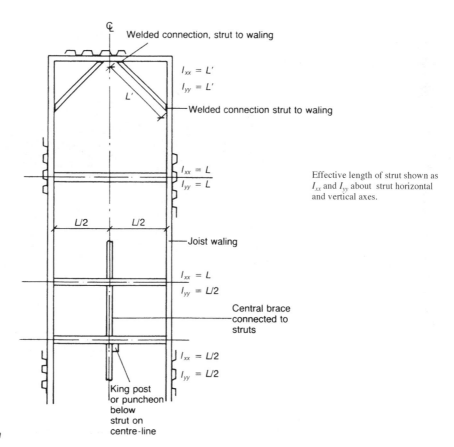

Effective length of strut shown as I_{xx} and I_{yy} about strut horizontal and vertical axes.

Fig. 7.28. Plan of cofferdam construction showing effective lengths of struts used in design

methods. The effective length of the strut is assumed to be equal to its actual length unless braced laterally or vertically at midspan (Fig 7.28). Temperature effects should be considered; the effect of sunlight on long steel struts can be reduced by painting them white.

It is essential that cofferdams are stiffened along their width and length by diagonal bracing to avoid risk of collapse into a lozenge shape. Typical steel-work bracing examples are shown in Fig. 7.29.

The vertical spacing of struts depends on both the strut capacity and the flexural strength of the sheeters or walling. In practical terms, the minimum frame spacing needs to be sufficient to allow mechanical excavation plant to pass under the frame prior to placing the next frame below and to allow sufficient excavation of the cofferdam. The placing of the lowest frame in a multi-frame cofferdam is the period of greatest risk to the bracing. At this stage the excavation is usually close to final formation level. It is likely that the next highest frame will be highly loaded and the factor of safety against passive failure will be at its lowest for all stages of the excavation. The bending stress and deformation of the sheeting will be at their highest values, and although two-dimensional analysis will be unable to show any benefit, it will be a practical advantage to carry out excavations for the lowest frame in short lengths where stresses in the soil, bracing and sheeters are very high at this stage. It is essential that all bracing components are fabricated ready for installation in this bottom frame, to avoid the cofferdam remaining unpropped at the lowest level for any lengthy period, especially at high tides, where these apply. It should be noted that the use of anchors on the bottom frame does not allow the sheeters to be secured speedily at this critical lowest level since the anchor grout requires time to achieve sufficient strength to pre-stress and thus secure the tendons.

(a)

(b)

(c)

Fig. 7.29. Diagonal bracing to cofferdam steelwork: (a) tubular steel bracing between walings, cofferdam to north pier, Forth Road Bridge; (b) light diagonal bracing between walings of circular cofferdam, Severn Bridge west pier; (c) diagonal bracing, Dartford Creek Barrier cofferdam (courtesy of AMEC)

The use of thickened, and where necessary reinforced, blinding slabs to act as props in the period before the base slab or raft is cast, may prove advantageous especially where the span of such props is small.

Where reinforced concrete diaphragm walls are used to retain soil at the curtilage of a cofferdam it is possible to use the strength of the wall panel, designed as a plate, with support from passive soil resistance at the bottom

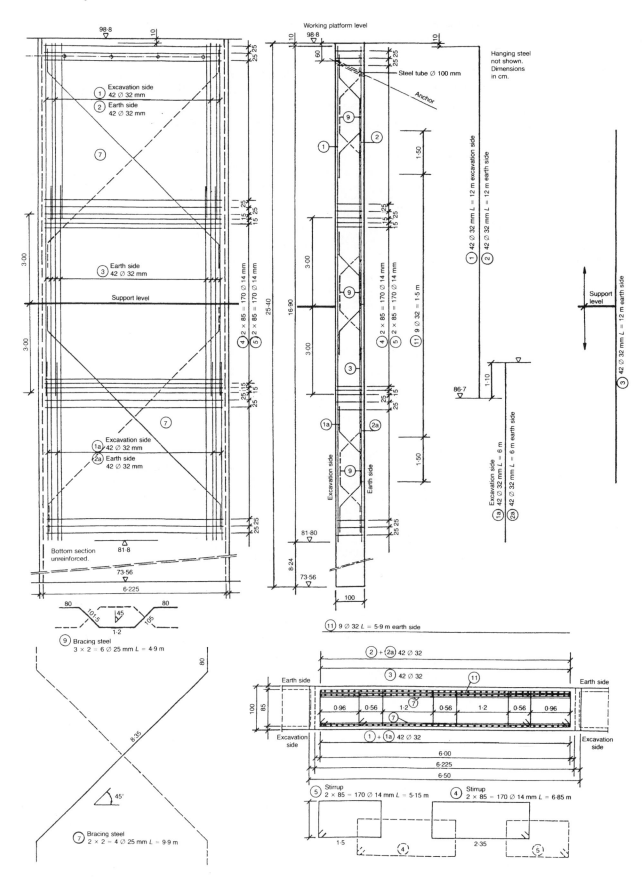

Fig. 7.30. Typical reinforcement detail for diaphragm wall panel (courtesy of Bauer)

of the panel and point supports from hammerhead struts at the vertical joints between panels. This arrangement obviates the need for either external or internal walings, but high shear stresses may occur within the panel near the stub end of the strut and require shear reinforcement. The use of reinforced concrete struts for this arrangement suffers from the comparatively high self-weight of the units, the difficulty of altering the reinforced concrete section for use elsewhere, and the high cost of disposal.

Walling details

A typical reinforcement detail for an anchored diaphragm wall panel is shown in Fig. 7.30. Items that need to be addressed in detailing the wall reinforcement include:

- lifting and bracing steel
- method of joining sections of cages
- method of lifting
- lateral spacing between reinforcement cages of adjacent panels
- type of box-out for junction with floor slabs
- details of starter steel for floor slabs
- access for concreting tremie pipes
- use of couplers
- detail of access through panel for ground anchors
- inclusion of reinforcement for walings
- minimum spacing of reinforcement steel and provision of cover
- consideration of water bars in vertical panel joints.

Sheeting details

Although Larssen U-type sheet piles possess certain advantages over Frodingham Z-types (in stacking, driving, etc.) care is needed with the Larssen section which has clutches along the centre-line, or neutral axis, of the section. In certain conditions, described in BS 8004, insufficient friction may develop within the clutch to develop the full flexural strength of the section. These conditions are:

(a) where the piling passes through very soft clay or other weak material
(b) where the piling is prevented by rock from penetrating to normal cut-off depth
(c) where the piling is used as a cantilever, or if it has a substantial cantilever height above the upper waling
(d) if backfill is placed on one side of the piling after it is driven.

In these circumstances it may be necessary to intermittently weld pile pairs at their interlocks to develop full strength[31].

Circular cofferdams

Circular plan shape cofferdams benefit from the hoop compressive stresses that are induced in waling and walling sections and the ease of providing steel or concrete to resist these stresses. The lack of internal strutting provides unrestricted working space and the circular section improves efficiency in terms of hydraulic performance and scour in river and marine works. It is essential that the induced compressive stresses and earth and groundwater pressures are uniformly applied to the circumference of the cofferdam. These conditions may not apply where ground conditions vary locally, in sloping ground, where local surcharge loading could apply, or where groundwater is flowing swiftly round one side of the cofferdam to the other. As referred to before, the economy of the cofferdam relies on the extent to which the permanent works occupy the circular space provided. Bridge piers and pumping stations can use the circular space particularly well.

Several types of construction can be applied to circular cofferdams: steel sheet piling spanning vertically between circular walings in reinforced concrete or steel, and diaphragm wall units or bored piles also spanning vertically between walings or diaphragm walls spanning vertically or circumferentially.

Although considered as a true circle in theory, some deviation from this shape may occur during construction and subsequent loading of circular walings. Care should be used in the application of the theoretical formula for ring beams due to Timoshenko and Goodier[32]

$$W_u = \frac{KEI}{R^3 \times 10^5} \quad \text{(kN/m)} \tag{69}$$

where W_u is the ultimate radial waling load, K is a coefficient depending on the stiffness of the retained medium, R is the radius of the cofferdam (in m), E is the Young's modulus for the waling material (in N/mm^2), and I is the moment of inertia about the vertical axis (in cm^4). A value of $K = 3$ is used where the retained medium is water, as in a marine cofferdam, and increasing values apply with increasing stiffness, which becomes soil stiffness for land cofferdams. It is common, however, to use a value of $K = 3$ for both land and marine conditions, and applying a factor of safety of 2·0 the safe radial waling load W (in kN/m) becomes

$$W = \frac{1 \cdot 5 \times EI}{R^3 \times 10^5}. \tag{70}$$

Again, the CIRIA report[4] suggests that ring waling stiffness is highly important and recommends the use of the empirical rule for reinforced concrete walings $d = D/35$, where d is the depth of the ring beam (in m) and D is the diameter of the inner face of the cofferdam sheeters (in m). Table 7.10 gives safe loads for reinforced concrete walings of specific size and reinforcement for cofferdams of varying diameter[18]. Care is needed to avoid uneven loading of the waling either at the top or lowest level of the waling due to non-verticality of sheeters. Any uneven distribution of applied load over the depth of the waling could induce torsional stress within it.

Table 7.10 Safe load (in kN/m) in reinforced concrete waling to circular cofferdams[18]

Diameter of cofferdam, D (m)	Size of waling $d \times b$ (mm):				
	450 × 300, six 20 mm dia. bars	600 × 400, ten 20 mm dia. bars	750 × 500, ten 25 mm dia. bars	900 × 600, fourteen 25 mm dia. bars	1050 × 700, twelve 32 mm dia. bars
5	280	500			
10	140	250	390		
15	90	165	260	375	
20		125	195	280	380
25			155	225	305
30				185	255
35					215

Based on: (i) permissible compressive stress in concrete not to exceed 5·2 N/mm^2

(ii) waling load (in kN/m) $= 1 \cdot 5EI/10^5 R^3$; $E =$ Young's modulus, for concrete, $E = 13\,800$ N/mm^2, $I =$ moment of inertia about xy axis (cm^4), $R =$ cofferdam radius (m)

(iii) depth of waling d to be not less that $D/35$

(iv) need to check tension in waling beam if sheet piles distort under load and concentrate load on top and bottom of waling beam.

The design of circular cofferdams with walls that span vertically between walings can therefore be made by considering the walling to span between the circular walings and the usual multi-braced wall analytical methods, spring programs can be used, the circular walings being designed according to the methods of Timoshenko and Goodier or the CIRIA report. For circular cofferdams with walls that are designed to withstand hoop compression, and especially those with large openings in the walls or uneven loading, a more refined approach is necessary. The risk of buckling of the wall panels must be checked. A three-dimensional finite element approach to the design of a large circular cofferdam built with diaphragm wall panels with a reinforced concrete lining wall was described by Kirmani and Highfill[33]. The lining wall was cast as a series of ring beams successively with depth as the excavation proceeded. In the analysis, the load-carrying mechanism of the diaphragm wall-lining wall structure was somewhat arbitrarily divided as follows.

- Hoop compressive stresses would be resisted by the combination of diaphragm wall and lining wall in proportion to their thicknesses.
- Horizontal bending would be resisted by the lining wall.
- Vertical bending would be resisted by the diaphragm wall.
- Buckling of the cylindrical cofferdam would be checked with the combination of the diaphragm wall and the lining wall.

The peripheral walls of circular land cofferdams may be built in contiguous or secant piling or diaphragm walling. Such walls are economical where they are used as temporary support during construction and as permanent walls to the final structure. Secant or contiguous piles, spanning between ring walings in reinforced concrete, are limited to 30 m or so in depth, depending on ground conditions. Maintaining the secant connection between adjacent piles may prove difficult in some ground conditions and require the use of large piling plant and casing oscillators.

Diaphragm walling has advantages and disadvantages over bored pile walls. In depth, for instance, with modern reverse circulation trenchcutters, diaphragm walling can be installed in a range of soils and soft rocks to depths in excess of 50 m. In shafts of small diameter, the length-to-breadth ratio of each wall segmental panel may be such that the wall is kept in hoop compression by earth and groundwater pressures and little or no bending occurs within the wall panel. In these circumstances, the wall requires minimal reinforcement; in fact the concrete strength may be adequate to withstand the hoop compression. In practice, it is best to consider the risk of at least one panel joint failing to transfer all its load to its neighbour because of poor panel verticality. Sufficient vertical steel and space should be allowed for the introduction of an emergency waling.

Where the circular cofferdam diameter is larger, however, the deviation angle between the centre-line of each diaphragm wall panel is reduced and horizontal bending occurs within the panel in addition to hoop compression. In this case it is generally more economical to span the wall vertically and introduce temporary walings. In top-downwards construction, permanent floor slabs provide both temporary and permanent support to allow the wall to span vertically between them. Figure 7.31 shows a simplified method of stress analysis for diaphragm walls without walings designed to span circumferentially.

Care is needed when using temporary circular stop ends to ensure circular walls of limited diameter remain properly connected at the joints. Flat-section temporary stop ends cannot be used. Cut joints are needed below temporary stop ends for deep walls. Full-depth cut joints are suitable but only where the deviation angle between panels is less than 12 to 15°.

1. Design of circular diaphragm walls can be made by considering a unit depth of wall of two adjacent segmental panels assuming the circular panel joints to constitute structural pinned joints, the two panels forming a three-pinned arch. Hoop compression or thrust within the arch and the bending moments within the panel are calculated as follows:

For a three-pinned arch with uniformly distributed load p. Horizontal force at pinned support

$$H = \frac{pl^2}{8f} \quad \text{and axial thrust} \quad N = \frac{H}{\cos \alpha}$$

Bending moment in panel = (Free span moment) − ($H \times$ rise of arch).

2. Consideration should be given, however, to the effect of panel verticality tolerances. If the maximum permitted verticality tolerance is Δ the true shape of the arch may be displaced within the limits AFK to CHM.

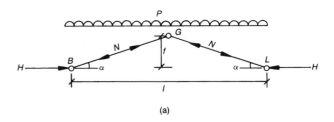

(a)

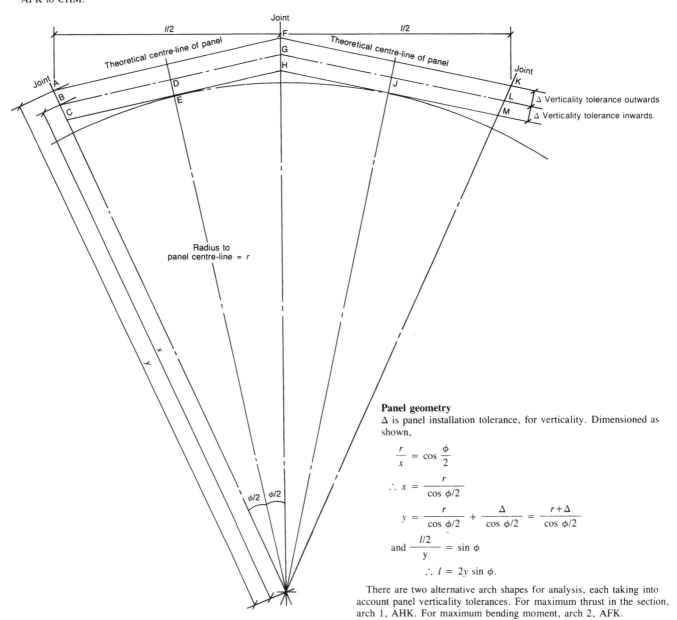

Panel geometry

Δ is panel installation tolerance, for verticality. Dimensioned as shown,

$$\frac{r}{x} = \cos \frac{\phi}{2}$$

$$\therefore x = \frac{r}{\cos \phi/2}$$

$$y = \frac{r}{\cos \phi/2} + \frac{\Delta}{\cos \phi/2} = \frac{r+\Delta}{\cos \phi/2}$$

and $\dfrac{l/2}{y} = \sin \phi$

$$\therefore l = 2y \sin \phi.$$

There are two alternative arch shapes for analysis, each taking into account panel verticality tolerances. For maximum thrust in the section, arch 1, AHK. For maximum bending moment, arch 2, AFK.

(b)

Fig. 7.31. *Circular diaphragm wall design: calculation of hoop compression and bending stress from a three-pinned arch*

Arch 1: for maximum thrust: arch AHK, panel shape AEH.

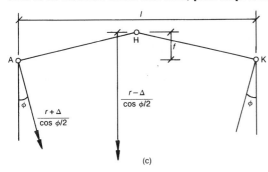

(c)

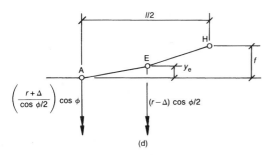

(d)

$$f = \frac{r-\Delta}{\cos \phi/2} - \left(\frac{r+\Delta}{\cos \phi/2}\right) \cos \phi$$

$$= r\left(\frac{1-\cos \phi}{\cos \phi/2}\right) - \Delta\left(\frac{1+\cos \phi}{\cos \phi/2}\right)$$

$$l = 2\left(\frac{r+\Delta}{\cos \phi/2}\right) \sin \phi$$

$$y_c = (r-\Delta) \cos \phi/2 - \left(\frac{1+\Delta}{\cos \phi/2}\right) \cos \phi$$

$$= r\left(\cos \phi/2 - \frac{\cos \phi}{\cos \phi/2}\right) - \Delta\left(\cos \phi/2 + \frac{\cos \phi}{\cos \phi/2}\right)$$

Arch 2: for maximum bending moment in panel, arch AFK panel shape AEF

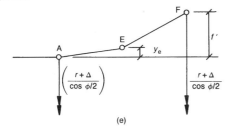

(e)

$$f' = \left(\frac{r+\Delta}{\cos \phi/2}\right) - \left(\frac{r+\Delta}{\cos \phi/2}\right) \cos \phi$$

$$= \frac{r+\Delta}{(\cos \phi/2)} (1 - \cos \phi)$$

Design formulae
(i) For a three-pinned arch with uniformly distributed load.

Horizontal force at pinned support $= H = \dfrac{pl^2}{8f}$

and axial thrust $N = \dfrac{H}{\cos \alpha}$

$\therefore N = \dfrac{pl^2}{8f \cos \alpha}$

(ii) For maximum bending moment use arch 2, AFK with panel shape AEF. Maximum moment will occur in panel at E.

Max. moment M_E = (free span moment at E) $- Hy_e$

$$= \left(0 \cdot 75 \times \frac{pl^2}{8}\right) - Hy_e.$$

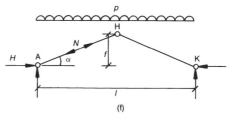

(f)

3. *Design procedure:* select panel width, determine max. verticality tolerance, consider 1 m width of wall at formation level.

(a) Panel geometry: calculate f and l, y_e and f'.
(b) Calculate applied presure p at formation level from active soil pressure and groundwater pressure.
(c) Calculate maximum thrust from arch 1, panel shape AEH by moments about centre joint,

$$H = \frac{pl^2}{8f} \quad \text{and axial thrust} \quad N = \frac{pl^2}{8f \cos \alpha}$$

(d) Calculate maximum bending moment from arch 2, panel shape AEF.

Calculate $H = \dfrac{pl^2}{8f'}$ and max. moment M_E

$$= \text{(free span moment at E)} - Hy_e = \left(0 \cdot 75 \times \frac{pl^2}{8}\right) - Hy_e$$

(e) Check values of thrust and moment, calculated with verticality tolerances allowed, by calculation of thrust and moment for theoretical centreline arch BGL without tolerances.
(f) Repeat calculations (a) to (e) for intermediate depths of shaft.
(g) R.C. design: design horizontal strips of shaft at intermediate depths and at formation level, allowing for thrust and bending moment on the combined section.
(h) Provide anti-crack steel as necessary.
(i) Provide nominal vertical steel, check vertical steel at formation level for stresses due to any embedment of the wall.
(j) For design purposes, shafts may be divided into three categories: (i) ≤ 10 m dia., (ii) $10-40$ m dia. and (iii) >40 m dia.

Practical considerations influence overall design as follows:

(i) Risk of poor connection between panels for the full panel depth increases as the number of panels increase. For this reason it is recommended that category 3 shafts should be designed with circular walings, allowing the wall panels to span vertically irrespective of the quality of the vertical joint between adjacent panels and its structural efficiency.
(ii) Categories 1 and 2 may be designed by the structural methods shown above for bending stress and compressive stress due to hoop compression. For all walls it is recommended that sufficient longitudinal reinforcement is used to ensure that circular walings can be incorporated if inadequate wall joints are revealed after shaft excavation commences. It is further recommended that for walls in category 2 a soil–structure analysis should be made following the initial design. This soil–structure analysis can be made using boundary element or finite element methods.
(iii) Where compressive stresses are induced due to hoop compression or applied vertical load, or both, the reinforced concrete wall panel should be checked for buckling.
(iv) Where embedment of the wall panels is required to obtain a cut-off, care must be taken to provide vertical reinforcement to give sufficient tensile strength to the wall in bending to withstand stresses due to simple support or fixity. It may be practical to avoid these stresses within the structural wall by using a plastic concrete cut-off below the structural wall panels.

Fig. 7.31. Continued

Practical difficulties may also be caused by instability of the last panel where the construction is in water-bearing ground. Groundwater tends to rise within an enclosure and temporary wellpointing may be necessary to avoid a differential head of groundwater between the inside and outside of the closure panel.

Sheet pile walls across dock entrances

There are several means of building a cofferdam across the entrance to lock or dock construction to exclude external river or sea water in order to excavate the floor of the dock or replace existing cills and gates. For new construction, cellular cofferdams or twin, parallel-walled cofferdams may be used. To exclude water from an existing dock, raking struts to the dock floor or walings from the sides of the dock, with diagonal struts to divide the waling span, are useful options. For an existing dock entrance it is often feasible to span walings across the whole entrance width by driving sheet piles to an arc circular in plan, braced by arch walings of steel or reinforced concrete, using the existing walls at the entrance as 'abutments' to the arch walings.

Estimating costs of temporary cofferdams

Many design curves have been published for cantilever and braced cofferdam construction. Those due to Packshaw (Fig. 7.32) show the section modulus of the piling and the number of bracing frames of normal construction in average soil conditions; bending moments induced in cantilever cofferdams for various heights and conditions; and the section moduli, waling loads and maximum penetration depths for one- and two-frame cofferdams in cohesionless soils. The greatest contribution of these graphs may be to prevent serious errors in the estimation of sheeting and bracing requirements during cost estimating by the engineer or contractor.

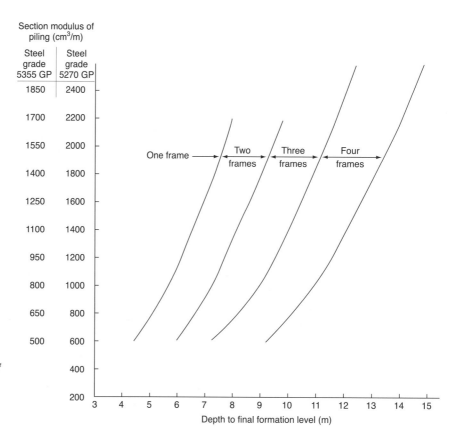

Fig. 7.32. (a) Curves for estimating purposes: number of frames and sheeting section modulus for average cofferdams as depth increases[49]

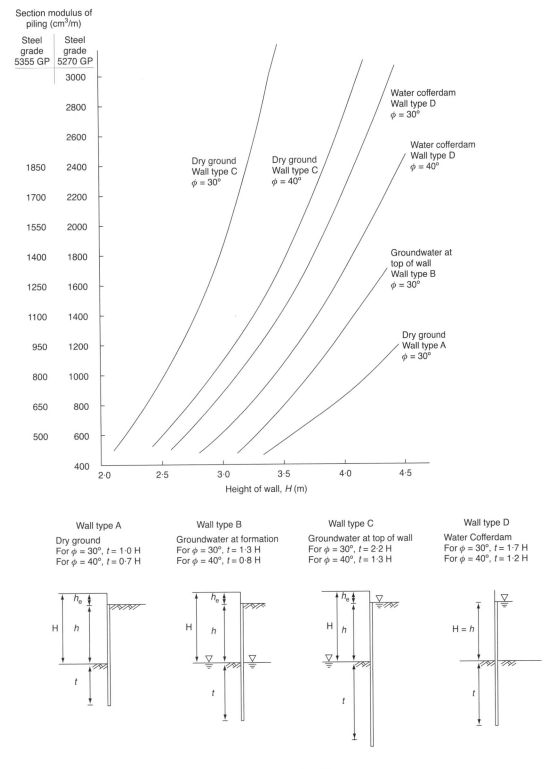

Notes: Penetration t should not be less than h for wall types C and D.
The soil is cohesionless throughout with $\gamma = 18$ kN/m³.

Make $h_e = \dfrac{\text{surcharge}}{\gamma} = \dfrac{\text{surcharge}}{18}$ m.

Fig. 7.32. (b) Section modulus of cantilever sheeting as depth increases for land and water cofferdams in cohesionless soil

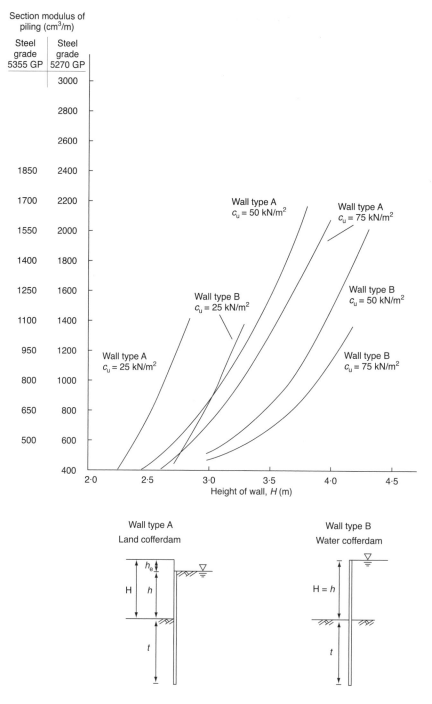

Fig. 7.32. (c) Section modulus of cantilever sheeting as depth increases, cantilever piles in cohesive soil

Notes: For c_u = 25 kN/m^2 t varies between 1·5 H when H = 2·4 m and 2·3H when H = 3·0 m.
For c_u = 50 kN/m^2 and c_u = 75 kN/sq m, t = H

Double-wall cofferdams

Double-wall cofferdams are gravity structures consisting of twin parallel lines of sheeters driven below dredge level, tied together at one or more levels by steel ties and filled with selected material, preferably cohesionless soil. The width-to-height ratio of the structure is at least 0·8, and it is usual to place a berm of granular soil on the inside face to extend the drainage path of water passing beneath the cofferdam and avoid piping near the inside line of sheeters. The stability of a double-wall cofferdam depends on the strength of the sheeters and the ties, on the shear strength of the fill material and the

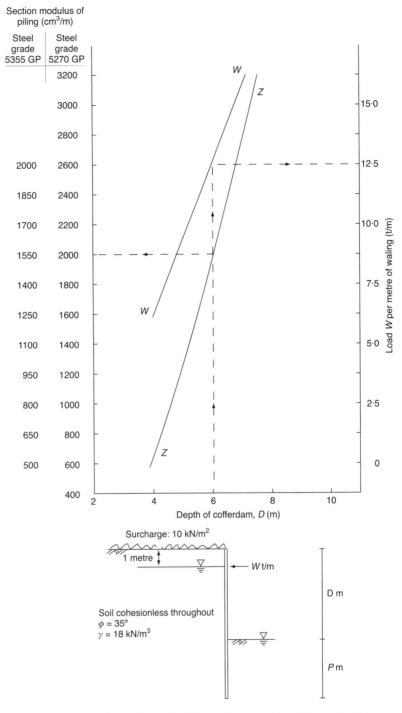

Fig. 7.32. (d) Section modulus, waling load, cofferdams with one bracing frame, cohesionless soil

Notes: Penetration $P = 0.61D$ to give factor of safety of 1.5 against toe failure.
The waling is at groundwater level.

soil at foundation level. This type of cofferdam is not suitable where strong bedrock occurs at shallow depth below formation level as it is necessary for the sheeters to penetrate sufficiently to avoid passive failure in front of them. It may be necessary to reduce the level of water in the fill material between the piles to increase the effective shear strength of the fill and reduce the pressure on the sheeters. Submersible pumps may be needed for this drawdown. In any case, it is essential that sluices are provided on the inner line of piles to reduce the level of the phreatic surface as much as

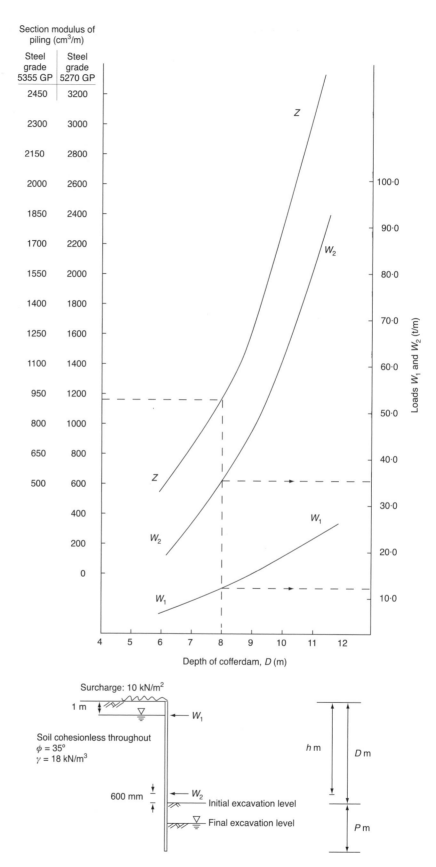

Fig. 7.32. (e) Section modulus, waling load, cofferdams with two bracing frames, cohesionless soil

Notes: Depth to lower waling $h = 0.66$ D. Penetration $P = 0.44$D to give safety factor of 1·5 against toe failure. The upper waling is at groundwater level.

possible. Where the length of the cofferdam exceeds its width by four or five times, it is usual to drive a cross-wall of sheeters to connect the inside and outside line of sheeters. This assists craneage access for construction and reduces the consequences of failure by forming compartments of restricted size.

Cofferdams of this type find application at the entrances to locks and docks, both for new construction and the maintenance of existing structures, such as remedial works on dock gates and cills. The major load on the cofferdam is the head of river water on the outside sheeters. As discussed earlier, wave heights, the effect of water levels caused by passing vessels and the risk of collision by river traffic, must all be considered when assessing this horizontal loading. A concrete slab cover should be provided on the top of the cofferdam where waves can overtop the outside sheeting and increase the water level in the filling.

The possible modes of failure were reviewed in Chapter 6. Each of these failure modes is addressed below for the design of double-wall cofferdams.

(a) *Tie rod design and water pressure.* Where the sheeters do not achieve penetration below the minimum required for free earth support, due to earth and water pressures within the retained fill, the structure will act as a gravity structure when loaded with the outside head of water. In this situation the sheet piles should be designed using at-rest pressures for the fill (using the coefficient for each pressure at rest K_0 for the filling) because deformation of the sheeters is restricted by the ties and it is intended to restrict movement at the head of the cofferdam. Walls should be designed for the most severe assumptions of internal water pressure. Where, for instance, hydraulic filling is used to place sand backfill between the sheeters, the design water level within the cofferdam should be considered vis-à-vis the rate of drainage possible from sluices of flap valves on the inside face. In the worst situation, the water level within the filling may reach the level of the top of the sheeters if the rate of pumping the fill is high and the rate of drainage is low.

(b) *Sliding.* Resistance to sliding is provided by the passive resistance of the soil on the inside face of the cofferdam, the shear strength of the sheeters and the frictional resistance beneath the material filling the cofferdam. Referring to a typical cross-section (Fig. 7.33):

$$\text{resistance to sliding} = P_p + S_1 + S_2 + S_{soil}$$

$$\text{and factor of safety against sliding failure} = \frac{P_p + S_1 + S_2 + S_{soil}}{P_a}.$$

(71)

(c) *Shear failure of the cofferdam filling.* To establish the efficiency of the fill material between the sheeters in resisting any tendency for the top of the

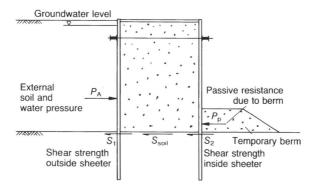

Fig. 7.33. *Sliding and resisting forces in double-wall cofferdam, vertical cross-section*

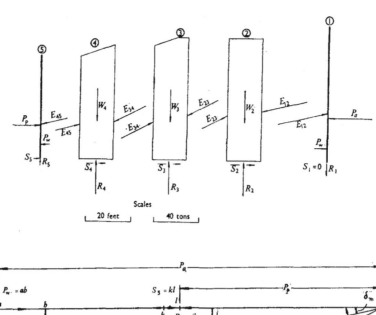

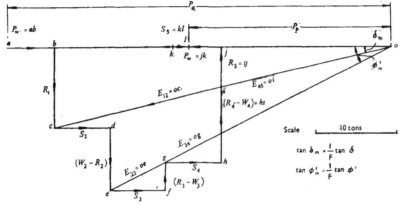

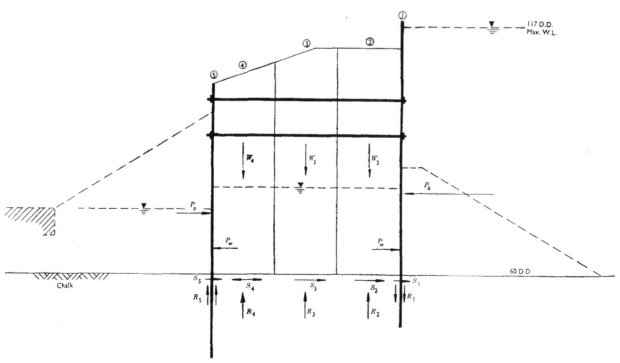

Fig. 7.34. Stability analysis of double-wall cofferdam, Gallions Lock entrance, London[34]

cofferdam to move horizontally, the stability analysis should use a force polygon as suggested by Bishop[34] in the discussion to Packshaw's paper. This analysis was first used for a double-wall cofferdam at the entrance to Gallions Lock in London. The analysis expresses the factor of safety against shear failure between blocks of filling (as shown in Fig. 7.34) as the ratio between the tangents of the angle of shearing resistance for the fill and the mobilized angle of shear on the vertical face of the blocks. Friction between the filling and the internal face of the sheeters is also taken into account, and the factor of safety against slippage between sheeters and fill is expressed as the ratio of the tangents of the angle of wall friction and the mobilized wall friction as shown on the force polygon. Bishop pointed out that the tie-rod pull did not appear as a term in the analysis because its value is small and it was safe to omit it in examining the factor of safety against shear between the vertical elements. There is no other reason, however, for excluding this term, the value from the analysis of the sheet pile walls being included in the force polygon. Factors of safety of the order of 1·5 would be regarded as satisfactory for this stability analysis.

(d) *Overall stability of the cofferdam structure.* A method of checking the overall stability of the double-wall cofferdam is described in reference 5. Figure 7.35 shows the cross-section of a cofferdam founded on soil

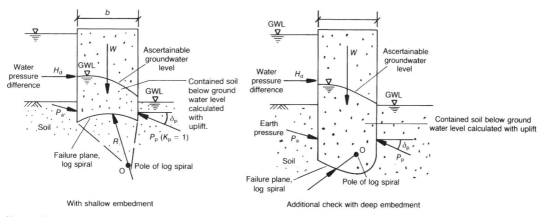

With shallow embedment   Additional check with deep embedment

Note need for effective and completely reliable drainage system to reduce water level in fill.

(a)

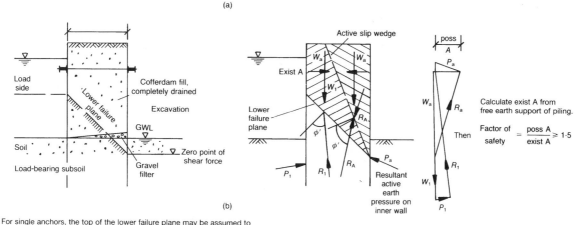

(b)

For single anchors, the top of the lower failure plane may be assumed to be about the elevation of the point of an assumed equivalent free earth support anchor wall. The bottom edge of the lower failure plane lies at the toe of the inner wall if this wall has free earth support but if it has fixed earth support it lies at the zero point of shear force in the fixity zone (as shown above)

Fig. 7.35. Calculation of double-wall cofferdam stability: (a) cofferdam embedded in load-bearing soil, stability analysis; (b) investigation of the anchorage of the inner line of sheet piles[5]

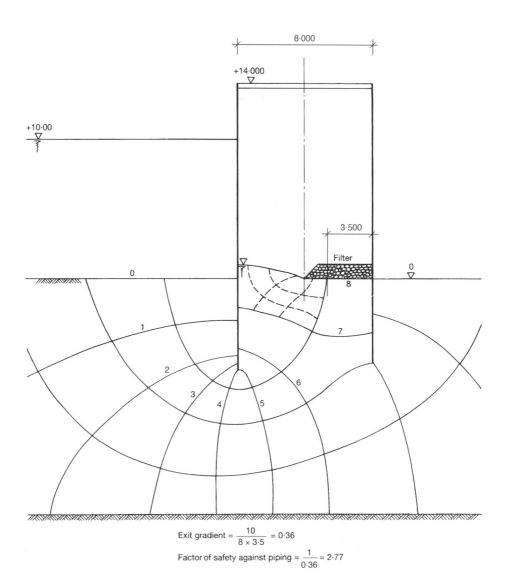

Fig. 7.36. Flow net for double-wall cofferdam, calculation of exit gradient[35]

$$\text{Exit gradient} = \frac{10}{8 \times 3 \cdot 5} = 0 \cdot 36$$

$$\text{Factor of safety against piping} = \frac{1}{0 \cdot 36} = 2 \cdot 77$$

with free earth support to the outside sheeters. The failure plane at the base of the wall is approximated by a logarithmic spiral centred at point 0. The factor of safety against overturning is then the ratio of overturning and resisting moments about the centre of the most unfavourable failure surface. The minimum factor of safety must be at least 1·5. If this is not obtained in the trial, the required stability may be obtained by increasing the width, improving the quality of the fill or deeper driving of the sheeters, or a combination of all three.

(e) *Piping at the inner face of the cofferdam.* Where the cofferdam is founded on relatively permeable material the flow of water from the riverside to the landward side beneath the cofferdam may cause piping failure near the inside line of piling. This condition is examined by use of a flow net, as illustrated in Fig. 7.36[35]. A berm of granular material, including where necessary a blanket of filter material, is effective in increasing the drainage path from the river side and thereby preventing piping.

(f) *Bearing capacity failure at founding level.* The bearing capacity of the soil below the fill placed between the sheeters must be sufficient to support the weight of the filling and resist the lateral force due to the riverside water head and impact forces due to waves and accidental collisions. Where soft clays or silts exist at this level and a stronger soil underlies the soft material, excavation between the sheeters should improve the bearing prior to placing the fill.

(g) *Scour on the outside of the cofferdam.* Where river currents cause risk of scour, the outer face of the cofferdam must be protected to avoid instability of the outer line of piles. This protection may consist of rock or precast concrete blocks placed against the outer face, or grouted mattresses laid on the river bed.

Lateral deformities at the head of a double-wall cofferdam are frequently greater than similar gravity structures when loaded with river water at a high elevation on the outside face. These deformations are associated with mobilization of the shear strength of the cofferdam filling and the friction between the filling and the inside surface of the sheeters. The deflection of the top of the riverside sheeting at the Gallions Lock cofferdam was 350 mm after it had been subjected to the full water load; the height between high water and the inside cill was 12·8 m. A similar displacement was measured at the head of the St Katherine's Lock cofferdam described in Chapter 6. The use of strongpoints, as was shown in Fig. 6.42, minimizes such horizontal movements.

Cellular cofferdams

The construction of cellular cofferdams was described in Chapter 6. Their use extends to piers, dolphins and breakwater structures, but cellular cofferdams also provide economical soil retention temporarily and permanently in deep, wide excavations and exclusion of river and sea water from deep excavations for lock, gravity dock and similar massive, large plan area structures. These gravity structures, depending on the weight of the retained fill and the tensile strength of the sheeters that retain it, are often used where pile driving conditions preclude deeper sheet piling for braced cofferdam construction and where internal bracing or sheeting is unacceptable or impractical. The most popular plan shapes are circular cells with one or two connecting arcs, and diaphragm cells with outer arcs and straight cross-walls. Circular cells consist of independent self-supporting structures, the diameters of which are a function of the interlock strength of the sheet pile secton; the greater the supported height of soil or water, the larger the cell diameter and, in turn, the greater the pile interlock tension. These factors encouraged the development of a straight web pile with three-point contact at the interlock to give increased interlock tensile strength compared with single-point contact interlocks.

Before design can begin the necessary data must be collected. For a cofferdam within a river such data would comprise:

- tidal data and rate of flow, and prediction of both during the design life of the cofferdam
- scour behaviour
- river bed profiles
- soil profile and test data to define strength, permeability and consolidation properties
- borrow areas for suitable filling, and spoil disposal areas
- water quality for cofferdams with a long design life
- previous site use and obstructions
- collision risk from river traffic
- river regulations; permission needed for cofferdam construction.

For maritime works, wind and wave data would be needed, including wave height and period, tide dates and storm risk; also ship collision assessment.

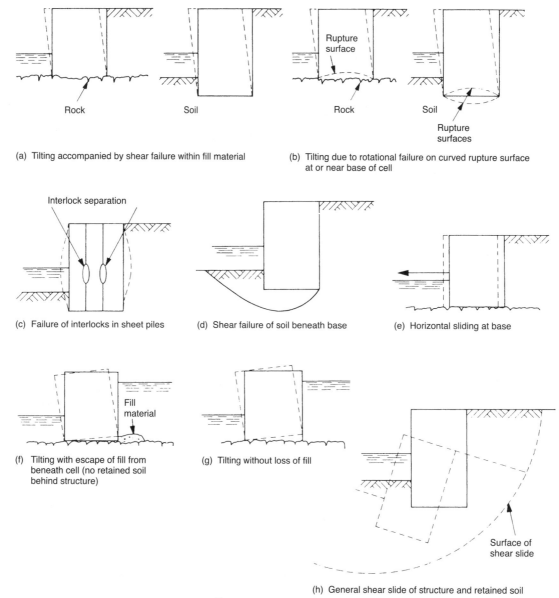

Fig. 7.37. *Modes of failure of cellular cofferdams*[11]

The design of cellular cofferdams was reviewed by Dismuke[36] and summarized in BS 6349[11]. Design of a cellular cofferdam should address the following modes of failure (shown in Fig. 7.37):

(*a*) excessive tilting or rotational failure on a curved rupture surface at or near the base of the cell: internal stability
(*b*) interlock and connection failure
(*c*) instability of base and sliding
(*d*) loss of cell fill due to piling rise
(*e*) overturning.

Each of these failure modes is now addressed in more detail.

Internal stability

The following methods of analysis of cell stability were compared by Dismuke.

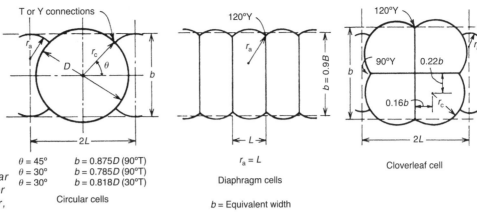

Fig. 7.38. Equivalent rectilinear width and design geometry for cellular cofferdams of circular, diaphragm and cloverleaf cells[36]

Circular cells

$\theta = 45°$　$b = 0.875D$ (90°T)
$\theta = 30°$　$b = 0.785D$ (90°T)
$\theta = 30°$　$b = 0.818D$ (30°T)

b = (Area of cell and arc)/2L

$r_a = L$

Diaphragm cells

b = Equivalent width

b = (Area of one cell)/L

Cloverleaf cell

b = (Area of cell and arc)/2L

(a) The vertical shear method developed in the late 1930s and 1940s, proposed by Terzaghi[37] and later developed by US Tennessee Valley Authority engineers[38].

(b) The horizontal shear method developed by Cummins[39]. This method was introduced because of inconsistencies in the vertical shear method. The method assumes that horizontal shear planes develop within the cell fill and implies that fill on the unloaded side of the cell could be reduced without affecting stability. This conclusion is not practically sound and should not be used in design to reduce fill levels within cells.

(c) Methods due to Brinch-Hansen[40] and described in detail by Ovesen[35]. Two variations, known as the equilibrium and extreme methods, resulted from observations that a circular rupture surface occurred at the base of a model double-wall cofferdam which was loaded to failure: the extreme method is recommended in reference 5 and is the basis of design for cell diameter or width described in the following part of this section.

Before describing the extreme method due to Brinch-Hansen it is necessary to refer to the method of changing a cellular cofferdam plan shape to a rectilinear shape to reduce computation. Figure 7.38 shows how this can be done.

The extreme method assumes that the cell is filled with granular material and is founded on a rock or granular soil base. To simplify the rather complicated calculations of the internal forces on the rupture line at the base of a cofferdam founded on rock, the kinematically true circular rupture line is substituted by a logarithmic spiral satisfying the polar equation $r = r_0 \, e^{\alpha \tan \phi}$. Such a spiral has a characteristic that its radius vector at any point makes an angle ϕ with the corresponding normal. In cohesionless soil, with an angle of shearing resistance ϕ, the resultant of all internal forces within the spiral will thus be directed towards the rotation point of the spiral. This calculation for cofferdams on rock involves the following steps (Fig. 7.39(a)):

(a) generate log spiral locus line

$$r = r_0 \, e^{\alpha \tan \phi} \tag{72}$$

for angle of shearing resistance ϕ with spiral through the feet of the walls.

(b) compute the external and gravity forces ($P, \gamma bH, W_p, W_f$) and reactions (S_h, S_v)

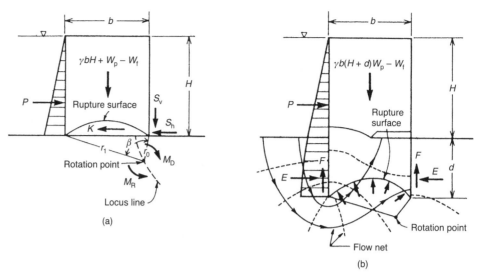

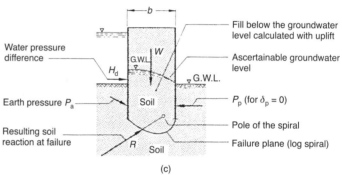

Fig. 7.39. Stability analyses for cellular cofferdams by the extreme method: (a) founded on rock (W_p = weight of piling. W_f = weight of fill below rupture surface); (b) founded on rock overlain by soil; (c) founded on soil, additional check for deep embedment with concave failure surface

(*c*)   take moments about the rotation point of the spiral and find the factor of safety

$$f = \frac{M_{\text{stabilize}}}{M_{\text{disturb}}} \tag{73}$$

(*d*)   Find the critical moment, that is the moment for which f is a minimum, by changing the position of the spiral. If minimum f is greater than unity the cofferdam is stable, although a minimum value of 1·5 is required for design acceptance.

If the cofferdam is founded on rock which is overlain by soil (Fig. 7.39(b)) or if the cofferdam is founded in soil, the disturbing forces are increased by the active earth pressure on the outside of the cofferdam and reduced by the passive earth pressure on the inside. Since deformation will be small it is usual to limit passive pressure to the at-rest value $K_0 = 1$ for sheeting with shallow embedment, and to calculate K_p setting wall friction equal to zero for sheeting with deep embedment.

Where sheeting is driven deep to provide stability, a check for concave failure planes is necessary (Fig. 7.39(c)). The spiral is then located so that its centre of rotation does not lie beyond the line of action of passive force P_p with the angle of wall friction equal to zero.

Interlock and connection failure

The cell hoop force outside the connecting arcs and the hoop stress may be calculated from

$$t_a = p \times r_a \tag{74}$$

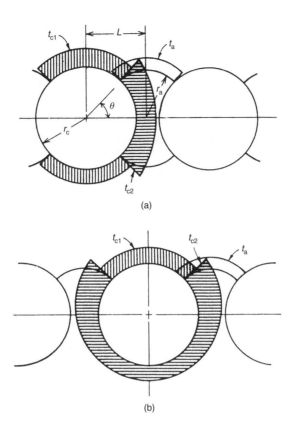

(a)

(b)

Fig. 7.40. Calculation of hoop
forces in circular cofferdam
cells: (a) circular cell
cofferdam; (b) circular cell
bulkhead[36]

and

$$t_{c1} = p \times r_c \tag{75}$$

where t_a is the hoop or interlock force for connecting arcs, t_{c1} is the hoop or interlock force for cells outside arcs, and p is the lateral unit pressure (taken as earth pressures at rest, $K_0 = 1 - \sin\phi$, at the base of the excavation).

Dismuke[36] pointed out that the greatest interlock force, located just inside the arc connection, is frequently overlooked. The cell hoop force at the arc connection is

$$t_{c2} = pL\sec\theta \tag{76}$$

where t_{c2} is the circular cell hoop or interlock force between arcs, L is half the centre-to-centre distance between cells, and θ is the angle between the centre-lines of the cells and a line from centre of a cell to the point on cell periphery where the arc connects.

The relative hoop forces, at any level in the cell, are shown for circular and diaphragm cells in Figs. 7.40 and 7.41, respectively.

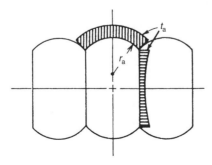

Fig. 7.41. Calculation of hoop
forces in diaphragm cells[36]

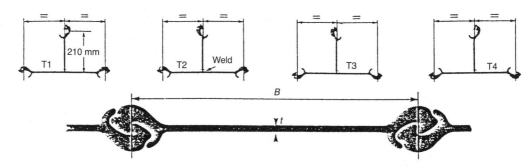

Section	B (mm) (nominal)	t (mm)	Mass		Minimum ultimate strength of interlock (tonnes)			Weights of standard T-junctions (kg/m)
			Per linear metre of pile (kg)	Per square metre of wall (kg)	Grade 43A steel	ASTM-A328 steel	Grade 50A steel	
SW-1	413	9·5	55·3	134·0	285	299	384	83·6
SW-1A	413	12·7	63·8	154·5	285	299	384	96·3

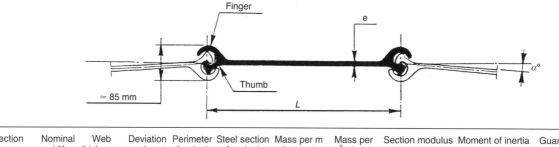

Section	Nominal width, L (mm)	Web thickness, e (mm)	Deviation angle, $\alpha°$	Perimeter of a single pile (cm)	Steel section of a single pile (mm)	Mass per m of a single pile (kg/m)	Mass per m² of wall (kg/m²)	Section modulus of a single pile (cm³)	Moment of inertia of a single pile (cm⁴)	Guaranteed interlock strength (t/m) Steel grade		
										PAE 270	PAE 360	PAE 390
A500-12	500	12·0	6	138	92·1	72·3	145	47	180			
A500-12·5	500	12·5	6	138	94·8	74·4	149	47	180	300	400	500
A500-12·7	500	12·7	6	138	95·8	75·2	150	47	180			

Note: All the sections interlock together

Fig. 7.42. Straight web pile sections and junctions produced in Europe (courtesy of Corus (Frodingham straight web sections, upper figure) and Arbed (Arbed straight web sections, lower figure))

Arc connections between circular cells and diaphragm cells are the most highly stressed part of the sheeting and are the principal point of failure risk. The connections are usually made through T and Y junction piles. Dismuke indicated the theoretical direction of loads acting on T and Y junctions and showed that the formula for t_{c2} gives consistently good results when used to evaluate interlock forces between arcs.

A summary of typical straight web pile sections and junctions produced in Europe with guaranteed interlock strengths is shown in Fig. 7.42.

Stability of base and sliding

For cells not founded on rock it is essential to check the risk of foundation failure; for cofferdams on clay, a bearing capacity failure could be caused by lateral loading on the cofferdam, or pile settlement on the inside line of piles could cause excessive under seepage of water. Where the weight of the cell filling causes excessive settlement slippage of the sheet piles, loss of interlock friction normally maintained by tension at the interlock could occur.

Figure 7.43 gives expressions for assessing the bearing capacity of the soil below the cofferdam, treating the cell as a rigid body. The figure also gives

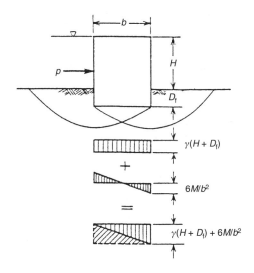

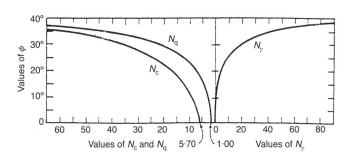

Bearing Capacity Factors (Terzaghi and Peck, 1967)

Ultimate Bearing Capacity

$$q_f = 0.5 b \gamma N_\gamma + C N_c + \gamma D_f N_q$$
for strip loaded area

$$q_f = 0.6 \gamma b N_\gamma + 1.3 N_c + \gamma D_f N_q$$
for circular load areas

where

γ = Unit weight of soil around cell
b = Equivalent cell width
N_γ = Bearing capacity factor
C = Cohesion (psf)
N_c = Cohesive factor
D_f = Ground surface to toe of cell
N_q = Surcharge factor

$$\text{F.S.} = \frac{q_f}{\gamma(H + D_f) + \dfrac{6M}{b^2}} \quad \begin{array}{l} \geq 2.0 \text{ for sand} \\ \geq 2.5 \text{ for clay} \end{array}$$

Factor of safety of internal instability due to settlement of compressible base (for soft and medium clays, q_u = 20 kPa to 50 kPa)

$$\text{F.S.} = \frac{(P_p - P_s)(D/2) f_{ss}(b/L)\left(\dfrac{L + 0.25b}{L + 0.5b}\right)}{M} \quad \begin{array}{l} \geq 1.25 \text{ (temporary)} \\ \geq 1.5 \text{ (permanent)} \end{array}$$

where

P_s = Inboard pressure
P_p = Passive pressure of berm and/or overburden on inside of cofferdam
f_{ss} = Coefficient of friction steel on steel
M = Overturning moment
D = Diameter
b = Equivalent cell width

Fig. 7.43. *Stability of base soils below a cellular cofferdam*[36]

the method for calculating the factor of safety of internal instability due to settlement where the base soil is a compressible clay. The factor of safety against sliding is

$$f = \frac{W \tan \phi' + P_p}{P} \tag{77}$$

where W is the weight of fill and piling, ϕ' is the angle of shearing resistance of cell fillings, P_p is the passive resistance at the inner line of the piling, and P is the lateral force from soil and water on the outer line of the piling.

A value of 1·25 to 1·3 would be considered satisfactory for temporary works. It is not usual for sliding to be a critical mode of failure for cells, except for those founded at shallow depth on rock.

Piling pull-out

There is risk to sheet piles on the outside of cells of pull-out as a result of overturning moment due to lateral loading by soil and water. If this occurs, cell fill may be lost and the cell would fail if the quantity were large. For cells founded on rock, the factor of safety against piling rise is

$$f = b(P_w + P_a)f_{gs} + P_p \frac{H_b}{3} \Big/ \left(P_w \frac{H}{3} + \frac{P_a H_s}{3} \right) \tag{78}$$

where b is equivalent cell width, f_{gs} is the coefficient of friction between the cell filling and sheet piling, H_b is the berm height, P_w is the lateral force due to external water pressure, P_a is the lateral force due to external active soil pressure, P_p is the lateral force due to passive resistance due to the berm, H is the height of the water head above formation level on the outside face, and H_s is the overburden height on the outside face. Values between 1·25 and 1·3 would be acceptable for temporary works.

For cells founded on sands and clay the factor of safety against pile pull-out is

$$f = \frac{\text{resistance to pull-out per unit length of cofferdam}}{\text{pull-out force per unit length of cofferdam}} = \frac{C_p}{F_p}. \tag{79}$$

The pull-out force F_p is

$$F_p = \frac{P_w H + P_a d - P_p H_b}{3b[1 + (b/4L)]} \tag{80}$$

where d is the pile embedment below formation level, and L is the cell module (see Fig. 7.44).

The resistance to pull-out C_p for cells on sand bases is

$$C_p = \tfrac{1}{2} k_a \gamma d^2 \tan \delta \, 2\pi r_c. \tag{81}$$

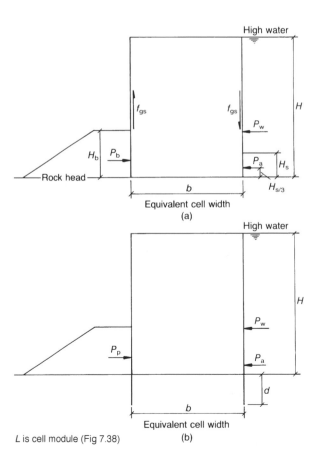

Fig. 7.44. Piling rise and pile pull-out calculations for circular cofferdams: (a) founded on rock; (b) founded in sand and clay

L is cell module (Fig 7.38)

On clay bases

$$C_p = c_a 2\pi r d \qquad (82)$$

where c_a is the adhesion of clay to sheet piles. The factor of safety should not be less than 1·25 for temporary works.

Overturning

If the cell is assumed to rotate about its toe, in a similar way to a gravity wall, the resultant moment due to cell weight and lateral forces should be restricted to the middle one-third of the cell width. The factor of safety against overturning is

$$f = \frac{M_{\text{restoring}}}{M_{\text{disturbing}}} = \frac{(Wb/2)}{(PH/3)}. \qquad (83)$$

The relative complexity of the statical calculations for cellular cofferdams is an opportunity for a finite element approach. This itself would involve similar simplifying assumptions, would have to be made in three dimensions and would only be considered reliable if the results compared with those of the semi-empirical approach of the statical method described above.

Gravity cofferdams

Precast concrete blockwork can provide weight stability for cofferdam structures and is economical in circumstances where the temporary works has a long design life and where alternative means of construction may be unavailable. Blockwork construction is traditional for quay walls and both horizontal and inclined bedding units have been used extensively. Similar construction methods can be used to exclude water from a deep excavation in a river bed. Blockwork cofferdams find particular application at the entrances to docks and locks where excavation and maintenance work is required to the floor of the existing facility. Their use is, of course, limited to sites where adequate load bearing soil is present at reasonably shallow depth, or where the existing soils can be improved in situ at low cost by such methods as vibro-compaction or dynamic consolidation.

The dimensions and weight of the blocks will depend on the head of river water to be excluded from the excavation and the plant, labour and material resources available at the site. Access to the site of the cofferdam and working areas may favour or preclude the use and transport of heavy blockwork. The blocks themselves should be as durable and watertight as possible with a strong dense concrete mix. They may be cuboid or wedge shaped but in all cases should include a key to ensure interlock between adjacent blocks.

The prepared soil bed on which the initial course of blocks is laid should be at least 0·5 m thick, and consist of crushed graded rock accurately levelled with the assistance of divers. In fine-grained subsoil it will be necessary to provide a soil or geotextile filter between the subsoil and the bedding to the units. To improve the stability of the blockwork against overturning and sliding it will frequently be necessary to construct a berm on the inward side of a blockwork wall built to exclude river water. At the same time this reduces the risk of hydraulic failure at the inside of the cofferdam by lengthening the drainage path of water flowing under the blockwork. A filter blanket should be incorporated at the base of the berm.

The design of a blockwork cofferdam, like other traditional gravity structures, consists of checks on sliding, overturning and bearing values, and restricting the resultant moment due to lateral forces and the weight of the blockwork to within the middle-third of the base width to avoid tension on the lowest course of blocks. These checks are made, course-by-course, from the top of the cofferdam to the underside of the initial course of blocks.

The head of water to be supported by the blockwork will be equal to the high tide level at a spring tide plus an allowance for wave height. An allowance for reflected waves due to wind and river craft is required: for reflected waves, this is half the height of the highest wave with reference to the most unfavourable standing water level. Where there is the risk of breaking waves on the cofferdam face (where water depth at the wall is greater than 1·5 times wave height it can be assumed that only reflected waves apply) it is unlikely that a blockwork solution will be adequate to resist the dynamic pressures. It should be noted that wave pressures act not only on the face of the wall but are also transmitted to the joints between blocks. Although this increase in pressure is limited in duration, additional measures to restrict blockwork movement where this force momentarily exceeds the effective block weight should be carefully considered.

References

1. Site Investigation, Steering Group. *Without site investigation ground is a hazard.* Thomas Telford Ltd., London, 1993.
2. BS 5930. *Code of practice for site investigations.* British Standards Institution, London, 1981.
3. DIN Standard 4020. *Geotechnical investigations for construction purposes* (draft). Deutsches Institut fur Normung, Berlin, 2002.
4. CIRIA. *Design and construction of sheet piled cofferdams.* Thomas Telford Ltd., London, 1993, Special publication 95.
5. EAU 90. *Recommendations of the Committee for Waterfront Structures, Harbours and Waterways.* Ernst and Son, Berlin, 6th English edn., 1993.
6. Stroud M.A. and Butler F.G. The standard penetration test and the engineering properties of glacial materials. *Proc. Symp. Engng Behaviour of Glacial Materials,* Birmingham, 1975, 124–135. Midland Soil Mechanics and Foundation Engineering Society, Birmingham, 1975.
7. Skempton A.W. The consolidation of clays by gravitational compaction. *Quart. J. Geol. Soc. Lond.,* 1970, **125**, 373–411.
8. Kenney T.C. Geotechnical properties of glacial lake clays. *ASCE J. S.M.F.E.,* 1959, **85,** June.
9. BS 8002. *Earth retaining structures.* British Standards Institution, London, 1994, (amended 2001).
10. Kort D.A. *Steel sheet pile walls in soft soil.* DUP Science, Delft, 2002.
11. BS 6349. *Maritime structures.* British Standards Institution, London, 2000.
12. Sainflou M. Essai sur les digues maritimes verticales. *Ann. des Ponts et Chaussée,* 1928, **98**, 5–48 (translated by US Corps of Engineers).
13. Minikin R. *Wind, waves and maritime structures.* Charles Griffin, London, 1963.
14. *Durability and protection of steel piling in temperate climates.* Corus, Scunthorpe, 2002.
15. Johnson K. *et al. Low water corrosion of steel piles in marine waters.* EUR 17868en, 1997. European Committee for Standardisation, Brussels, 1997.
16. Tsuchida E. *et al. Studies of the corrosion of steel materials in a marine environment.* Permanent International Association of Navigation Congresses, 1985.
17. Fukute T. *et al. Steel structures in port and harbour facilities.* Permanent International Association of Navigation Congresses, 1990.
18. *Piling handbook.* British Steel Corporation, Scunthorpe, 1997.
19. *Protection of steel sheet piling.* SIGMA coatings, Uithoorn, Holland, 1999.
20. BS 8081. *Ground anchorages.* British Standards Institution, London, 1989.
21. BS EN 1537: 2000. *Execution of special geotechnical work ground anchors.* British Standards Institution, London, 2000.
22. Littlejohn G.S. and Bruce D.A. *Rock anchors: state of the art.* Foundation Publications, Brentwood, 1977.
23. Sherwood D.E. and Harris R.R. Regroutable ground anchors. *Conf. Retaining Structures,* Institution of Civil Engineers, London, 1992, 448–456.

24. Ostermayer H. *Practice in the detail design applications of anchorages*, Institution of Civil Engineers, London, 1976, 55–61 (discussion 62–78).
25. BS 5896. *Specification for high tensile steel wire strand for the prestressing of concrete*. British Standards Institution, London, 1980.
26. BS 4486. *Specification for hot rolled steel bars for the prestressing of concrete*. British Standards Institution, London, 1980.
27. Barley A. Drilling and grouting methods and modes of enhancement of anchorage capacity. *Proc. Ground Modification Seminars*, Sydney, Melbourne, Brisbane, 1992.
28. Barley A. *et al*. Design and construction of temporary ground anchorages at Castle Mall development, Norwich. *Conf. Retaining Structures*. Institution of Civil Engineers, London, 1992, 429–439.
29. Barley A. Ten thousand anchorages in rock. *Ground Engng*, 1988, **21**, No. 6, Sept., 20–20; No. 7, Oct., 24–35; No. 8, Nov., 35–39.
30. *Methods of sheet pile installation*. Technical European Sheet Piling Association (TESPA). Luxembourg, 1995.
31. Williams S.G. and Little J.A. Structural behaviour of sheet piles interlocked at the centre of gravity of the combined section. *Proc. Instn Civ. Engrs*, 1992, **94**, 229–238.
32. Timoshenko S.P. and Goodier J.N. *Theory of elastic stability*. McGraw-Hill, New York, 1970.
33. Kirmani M. and Highfill S.C. Design and construction of the circular cofferdam for ventilation building No. 6 at the Test Williams Tunnel. *Civ. Eng. Practice*, Spring/Summer, 1996, 31–47. Boston Society of Civil Engineers, 1996.
34. Bishop A.W. Discussion on cofferdams. *Proc. Instn Civ. Engrs*, 1963, **24**, 112–116.
35. Ovesen N.K. *Cellular cofferdams: calculation methods and model tests*. Danish Geotechnical Institute, Copenhagen, 1962, Bulletin 14.
36. Dismuke T.D. Cellular structures and braced excavations. *Foundation engineering handbook*. Eds. H.F. Winterkorn and H.Y. Fang, Van Nostrand-Reinhold, Princeton, NJ, 1975, part 14, 445–480.
37. Terzaghi K. Stability and stiffness of cellular cofferdams. *Trans. ASCE*, 1945, **110**, 1083–1119 (discussion 1120–1202).
38. *Steel sheet piling cellular cofferdams on rock*. US Tennessee Valley Authority, 1957, technical monograph No. 75, vol. 1.
39. Cummins E.M. Cellular cofferdams and docks. *Trans. ASCE*, 1957, **125**, 13–34 (discussion 34–45).
40. Brinch-Hansen J. *Earth pressure calculations*. Institution of Danish Civil Engineers, Copenhagen, 1953.
41. Das Braja M. *Principles of Foundation Engineering*, 4th ed, Brooks/Cole, California, 1998.
42. Ostermayer H. and Scheele F. Research and ground anchors in non-cohesive soils. *Rev. Française de Géotechnique*, 1978, No. 3, 92–97.
43. Locher H.G. *Anchored retaining walls and cut-off walls*. Losinger Ltd., Berne, Switzerland, 1969, 1–23.
44. Littlejohn G.S. Soil anchors. *Proc. Conf. on Ground Engineering*, ICE, London, 1970, 33–44.
45. Littlejohn G.S. Ground anchors. *Proc. Review of Diaphragm Walls*, ICE, London, 1977, 93–97.
46. Kranz F. *Uber die Verankesung von Spundwanden*, Ernst and Son, Berlin, 1953, 55–61.
47. Ranke A. and Ostermayer H. Beitrag sur Stabilitatsuntersuchung mehrfach verankerter Bangrubenumschliessugen. *Die Bautechnik*, 45, **10**, 1968, 341–350.
48. Cheney R.S. *Permanent ground anchors*. US Dept of Trans. Federal Highways Admin. Report FHWA/DP/68, 1984.
49. Packshaw S. Cofferdams. *Proc. Instn. Civ. Engrs*, 1962, **21**, Feb., 367–398.

Bibliography

Ayers J.R. and Stokes R.C. Design of flexible bulkheads. *Trans. ASCE*, 1953, paper 2676, 373–383 (discussion 384–402).

Belz C.A. Cellular structure design methods. *Proc. Conf. Design and Installation of Pile Foundations and Cellular Structures*, Envo Publishing, Lehigh Valley, USA, 1970, 319–337.

Boyer W.C. and Lummis H.M. Design curves for anchored steel sheet piling. *Trans. ASCE*, 1953, paper 2689, 639–657.

BS EN 1537. *Ground anchors*. British Standards Institution, London, 1999.

BS EN 12063. *Sheet piling*. British Standards Institution, London, 1999.

Carle R.J. High strength interlock sheet piling in cellular structures. *Proc. Conf. Design and Installation of Pile Foundations and Cellular Structures*, Envo Publishing, Lehigh Valley, USA, 1970, 367–379.

Cedergen H.R. *Seepage, drainage and flow nets*. Wiley, New York, 2nd edition, 1977.

Clayton C.R. and Milititski J. *Earth pressures and earth retaining structures*. Blackie, London, 1993.

Cornfield G.M. Direct reading nomograms for design of anchored sheet pile retaining walls. *Civ. Engng Public Works Rev.*, 1969, **64**, Aug., 753–756.

Dismuke T.D. Stress analysis of sheet piling in cellular structures. *Proc. Conf. Design and Installation of Pile Foundations and Cellular Structures*, Envo Publishing, Lehigh Valley, USA, 1970, 339–365.

Gray H. and Nair K. A note on the stability of soil subject to seepage forces adjacent to a sheet pile. *Géotechnique*, 1967, **17**, Mar., 136–144.

Kaiser P.K. and Hewitt K.J. The effect of groundwater flow on the stability and design of retained excavations. *Canadian Geotech. J.*, 1982, **19**, May, 139–153.

King G.J.W. Design charts for long cofferdams. *Géotechnique*, 1990, **4**, Dec., 647–650.

Manual for the design of reinforced concrete building structures. Institution of Structural Engineers, London, Second edition, 2002.

Manual for the design of steelwork building structures. Institution of Structural Engineers, London, Second edition, 2002.

Patterson J.H. Installation techniques for cellular structures. *Proc. Conf. Design and Installation of Pile Foundations and Cellular Structures*, Envo Publishing, Lehigh Valley, USA, 1970, 393–411.

Potts D.M. and Day R.A. Use of sheet pile retaining walls for deep excavations in stiff clay. *Proc. Instn Civ. Engrs*, 1990, **88**, Dec., 899–927.

Rossow M.P. Sheet pile interlock tension in cellular cofferdams. *ASCE J. Geotech. Engng*, 1984, **110**, No. 10, Oct., 1446–1458.

Schnabel J.R. Sloped sheeting. *ASCE J. Civ. Engng*, 1971, **41**, Feb., 48–50.

Seed H.B. and Whitman R.V. Design of earth retaining structures for dynamic loads. *Proc. Conf. Lateral Stresses in the Ground and Design of Earth Retaining Structures*. American Society of Civil Engineers, New York, 1970, 103–947.

Swatek E.P. Summary – cellular structure design and installation. *Proc. Conf. Design and Installation of Pile Foundations and Cellular Structures*, Envo Publishing, Lehigh Valley, USA, 1970, 413–423.

Terzaghi K. Anchored bulkheads. *Trans. ASCE*, 1954, **119**, paper 1720, 1243–1280 (discussion 1281–1324).

Tomlinson M.J. *Foundations design and construction*. Prentice Hall, Harlow, 7th edition, 2001.

8

Basement construction and design

Engineering an excavation

A number of factors control the relative difficulty of basement construction. Very often these factors cannot be changed by the designer, and include the location of the building, the proximity of existing buildings and services, previous site use, and the proposed use of the basement together with soil and groundwater conditions. The basement structure will be designed to overcome these constraints to transfer the loads from the superstructure to the subsoil. The method of basement construction and the type of peripheral basement wall will be selected to support soils and groundwater at the curtilage of the basement as economically as possible. The permitted soil deformation around the basement construction has to be assessed and complied with. The process was itemized by Lambe[1], as shown in Table 8.1.

Increasingly, clients and architects are demanding larger and deeper basements. This chapter reviews the development of construction methods and the range of basement walling methods available, and describes the design problems that arise.

Construction methods for soil support

Seldom does the location of a basement allow open battered excavations. Particularly on urban sites, space is limited and insufficient to accommodate the cut slopes of battered excavations. Land is expensive and basement constructions inevitably occupy as much of the site as possible. The use of open excavations was reviewed in Chapter 3, although mention will be made here of the need to review soil strength parameters critically for temporary cut slopes.

In certain soils, over-consolidated clays such as London clay for example, the soil strength characteristics are time-dependent, so the period for which the excavation is to be kept open must be carefully assessed. Where space allows the use of battered slopes, the cost penalty of a slope failure should be weighed against the cost of a full soil retention system using temporary walling. It is possible that a compromise solution, using soil nailing or similar ground improvement methods incorporating reinforced soil, may be economically attractive where some horizontal working space is available at the rear of the basement construction but is not sufficient to accommodate a full battered slope. Where some space exists behind the permanent basement wall the choice of method will be determined in permeable soils or granular soils by the extent of groundwater flow and the feasibility and cost of controlling groundwater during basement construction.

An example of a battered basement excavation with a slurry trench cut-off to control groundwater inflow and cut slopes designed on a cost against risk basis was given by Wakeling[2]. The excavation was 130 m × 80 m in plan, to a depth of 5·8 m in soft clay and gravel, extending into stiff fissured silty London clay to a maximum depth of 14·5 m. A bentonite slurry cut-off wall into the London clay contained groundwater in the upper gravels. Groundwater flow from the gravel and the underlying silty sands was controlled by

Table 8.1 Engineering an excavation: a checklist[1]

Step	Activity	Considerations
1	Explore and test subsoil	
2	Select dimensions of excavation	Structure size and grade requirements, depth to good soil, depth to floor requirements; stability requirements
3	Survey adjacent structures and utilities	Size, type, age, location, condition
4	Establish permissible movements	
5	Select bracing, if needed, and construction scheme	Local experience, cost, time available, depth of wall, type of wall, type and spacing of braces, dewater excavation sequence, pre-stress
6	Predict movements caused by excavation and dewatering	
7	Compare predicted with permissive movements	
8	Alter bracing and construction scheme if needed	
9	Instrument – monitor construction and alter bracing and construction as needed	

gravel-filled counterfort drains dug down the slope during bulk excavation. The excavation was battered with side slopes of 1:1 with an intermediate berm at the top of the London clay. A plan and cross-section of the excavation are shown in Fig. 8.1. The method was successful and demonstrates the use of soil parameters based on partially drained soil conditions. Wakeling reported that three slips occurred, all shallow-seated, in the batters within the London clay, reaching their greatest depth between two and five months after excavation. From back analysis on these slopes and using shallow-seated slides reported by Skempton and La Rochelle[3], Wakeling reached a tentative conclusion: for excavations in stiff fissured clays, short-term shallow-seated slips are likely to occur when the computed failure strength exceeds the measured undrained shear strength in the clay by approximately 20%. The point of interest in this example is the cost-effectiveness of a relatively steep slope batter of 1:1 with some risk of minor failure accepted during a relatively short construction time. The use of fully drained parameters in the slope analysis would have led to flatter slopes, albeit with less risk of slippage.

Where compromise solutions to peripheral soil support are required, that is where some space exists at the rear of the permanent basement structure but is insufficient to accommodate a battered slope, crib walls and anchored crib walls can be used. A further solution is the use of soil nailing. These methods were discussed in general terms in Chapter 4, but the relevance of soil nailing to basement construction deserves discussion here.

The soil nailing method developed from the use of fully bonded rock bolts for tunnel support in the 1950s and 1960s. Using the same principles of ground support its use progressed from weaker rocks, such as marls and weak sandstones, into cemented sands, strong clays and, later, to a wider range of granular soils and middle-strength cohesive soils. The range of soils in which nailing can be used is relatively wide (weak clays and loose silts are probably precluded, and the presence of groundwater limits its application in any soil). Although finding widespread application for general soil support in basement schemes in France, Austria, Germany and North America, its application in the UK has been slow.

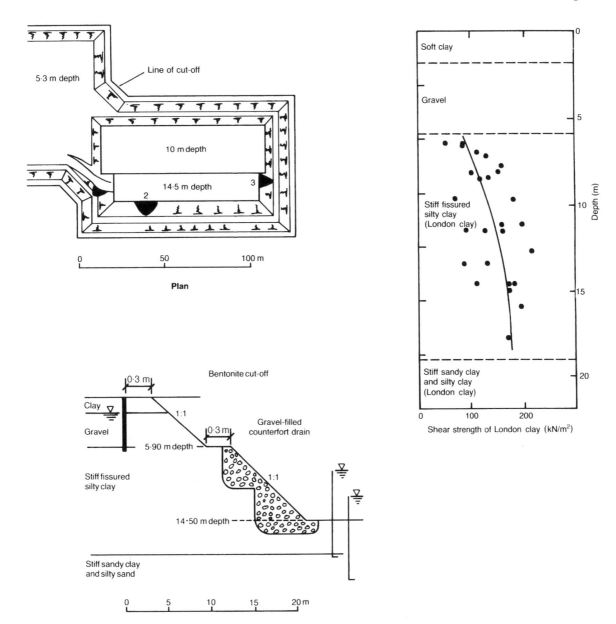

Fig. 8.1. Plan and cross-section of a battered deep excavation into London clay[2]

Soil nailing is in fact a soil-reinforcing technique and uses short tendons, driven or inserted into short bores in the excavated soil face, to improve the shear strength of subsoils. The exposed face is retained and protected by a gunite layer reinforced with a wire mesh. The technique is described by Gässler and Gudehus[4] and Banyai[5], but a complete description of its development – the soil–tendon interaction, design, construction and specification – is given in the report of the French Clouterre project[6]. The UK code of practice BS 8006 Strengthened/Reinforced Soils applies to soil nailing and the draft European code on soil nailing is in course of preparation (Pr EN 14490 at enquiry stage, July 2003).

Typical cross-sections of soil-nailed excavations were reported by Barley[7] and are shown in Fig. 8.2. A soil-nailed excavation support in Pocking, Bavaria, is shown in Fig. 8.3.

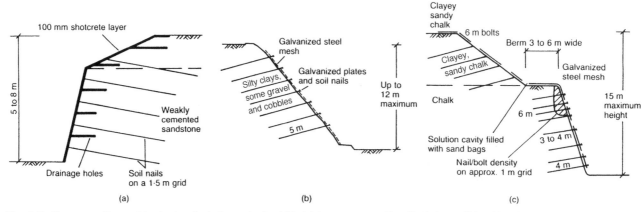

Fig. 8.2. Cross-sections of typical nailed slopes in the UK: (a) temporary soil-nailed slope; (b) soil-nailed slope; (c) rock-bolted

The application of soil nailing to retain excavated slopes at the periphery of basements is referred to here as temporary support, but soil-nailed slopes can also be used for permanent works. Tendon durability and protection was discussed by Barley[7] and in the Clouterre report[6]. The use of alternative reinforcing materials such as stainless steel, carbon fibre and glass-reinforced plastics may lead to an increase in permanently retained soil-nailed excavations. The cost effectiveness of any scheme, the material used and the installation method is much dependent on job size.

The extent of working space at the rear of the permanent retaining wall is likely to reduce the nearer the basement site is to a city centre. In the remainder of this chapter, it is assumed that such space is limited. Soil support systems which incorporate both temporary and permanent support are likely to prove most efficient in minimizing the total width of soil support wall. Alternatively, the construction of sloping sheeting can lead to economies in construction cost where limited working space is available. Schnabel[8] reported that where sheeting sloped at an angle of about 10% from the

Fig. 8.3. Soil-nailed slope at Pocking, Bavaria (courtesy of Bauer)

Fig. 8.4. Plate method being used for a basement extension to the Technical University, Zurich (courtesy of Bauer)

vertical, the measured anchor strut loads were consistently less than two-thirds of the computed anchor loads for vertical sheeting in the same soil. A further study[9] of sloped sheeting supported by ground anchors presented model tests results in sand, confirming Schnabel's recommendations for soil pressures on an inclined anchored wall. It was noted from these model tests that inclined walls require a considerable base width if they are not to suffer a bearing capacity failure.

Underpinning in short lengths may prove necessary to avoid settlement of adjacent structures during basement construction. In dry soil conditions, where the water table lies beneath basement formation level, it may be sufficient, and expedient, to rely on the underpinning to provide horizontal soil support during basement construction in addition to its main purpose of vertical load transfer to depths below the new basement construction. Unless the underpinning is braced or propped from the excavation side its depth will be restricted in either concrete or grouted soil because of horizontal soil pressure at the rear of the underpinning.

Where ground conditions allow successive excavation in the dry, an anchored reinforced concrete plate can be used to provide a continuous reinforcement wall at the periphery of the new basement. These ground conditions may be obtained by grouting in certain soil conditions, given legal consents. Figure 8.4 shows the plate method being used in a base extension in Zurich. Each cast in situ element was retained by ground anchors, excavated alternately at each level. The subsoil was a cohesive silty sandy gravel.

The provision of lateral support to a deep excavation thus turns on six factors: neighbours' rights (reference to the Party Wall Act 1996 in the UK is made in Chapter 1), neighbouring construction, subsoil and groundwater conditions, neighbouring services, and the proposed construction depth and optimization of site area to give the best financial return.

In complying with these factors the majority of urban basements sites will not allow battered open excavations due to space limitations. Vertical peripheral soil support is therefore required, temporarily during construction and as a permanent retaining wall. During construction the simplest form for either sheeting or walling is to cantilever without propping. In typical basement excavations in London the maximum height of cantilever is generally of the order of 5·5 m from formation level. The extent of soil movement during and after bulk excavation, and the presence of delicate services or important highways at the rear of the wall, mitigate against the use of high cantilevers. Temporary berms at the front of the cantilevered wall reduce soil movements effectively but are often uneconomical because of the need to remove the berm successively in short lengths and small volumes. Although propped cantilevers provide more security against excessive wall movement, the cost penalties of providing this support and the impedance to bulk excavation may prove unacceptable. The economical use of peripheral steel sheet pile propped by steel raker tubes from a completed central raft construction with a temporary edge berm was shown in Fig. 6.1. A cost comparison on that particular site showed little difference between propped steel sheet piling with in situ permanent retaining walls and propped diaphragm wall construction.

Figure 8.5 shows why the use of temporary soil berms to reduce cantilever wall movement is unpopular with contractors. The basement, in West London, was large in plan area but limited in depth to 5·625 m from existing ground level. Maximum horizontal wall deformation was specified as 25 mm and ground conditions were medium dense sands and gravels overlying London clay. Two schemes were prepared by a specialist diaphragm contractor, the first with a temporary soil berm and minimum wall depth, the second

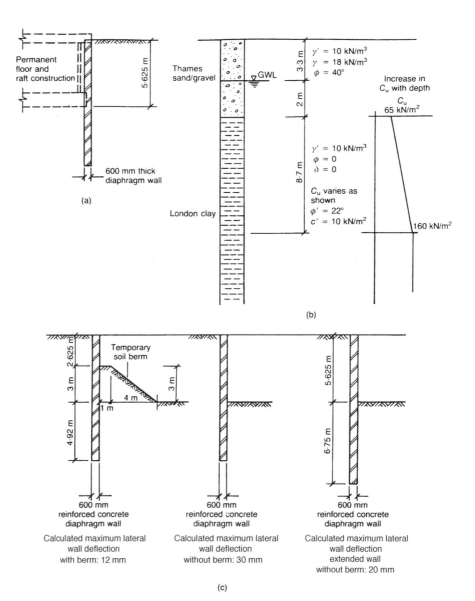

Fig. 8.5. Cantilever wall, West London: (a) wall cross-section; (b) soil profile; (c) calculated maximum deformation with and without soil berm

with a free-standing wall of greater depth. Although the analysis showed a significant beneficial effect on wall deformation of providing a relatively small berm, the main contractor preferred the deeper wall without the berm, shown in Fig. 8.5(c). The cost of the additional walling was significant but avoided later excavation of small soil volumes and impedance to the base raft construction programme. During construction the maximum deformation of the cantilever wall without the berm was 19 mm.

Using finite element methods and assuming linear elastic perfectly plastic soil material (with the effects of enhanced stiffness at small strains), Potts *et al.*[10] reached a number of conclusions on the effectiveness of berms: for berms between 2.5 and 5.0 m high it is the volume of the berm, not its specific geometry, that dictates soil movements adjacent to the excavation wall deformation and bending movements; as the height of the berm reduces below 2.5 m, berms of equal volume, but varying geometry result in different wall deflections and moments – deflections increase and the berm becomes less efficient.

To avoid the obstruction of temporary berms and rakers during construction, soil anchors may be used for soil support to basements of moderate depth. This solution depends on the suitability of soil conditions for anchoring and the legal and practical implications of founding anchors outside the curtilage of the site. The popularity of anchoring in the UK appears to be less than in France and this may depend on cost which in turn may depend on design safety factors. In France a value of 1·5 is usual, whereas in the UK a minimum value of 2·0 has been specified by BS 8001 for temporary works.

Water-resisting basement construction

A complete review of the methods of safeguarding basements against water and dampness was given in the CIRIA report 139[11] in 1995. Later comment on the durability and water resistance of basements is made in the Institution of Structural Engineers report on basements and cut-and-cover construction[12] in draft form in 2003. The British Standard BS 8102[13], published in 1990, serves as a code of practice on the subject.

The whole matter of waterproofness standards is a matter of potential controversy and originates from a false belief that a basement construction in water-bearing ground can be made watertight and completely dry. The requirements of water resistance, a more realistic term, are described in both the CIRIA report 139 and BS 8102 in similar classification. A summary chart of the basic grades of water resistance as defined in both documents is given in Table 8.2. Four performance grades are specified as follows: grade 1 basic utility, grade 2 better utility, grade 3 habitable and grade 4 special.

The water-resisting methods to be adopted to address these performance standards are given in CIRIA report 139 as being one (A, B or C) or a

Table 8.2 Basic grades of water resistance[11]

From Table 1 of BS 8102: 1990				Abbreviated commentary given by CIRIA Report 39
Grade	Basement usage	Performance level[a]	Form of protection	
Grade 1 Basic utility	Car parking plant rooms (excluding electrical equipment); workshops	Some seepage and damp patches tolerable	Type B with RC design to BS 8110	Visible water and BS 8110 crack width may not be acceptable. May not meet Building Regulations for workshops. Beware chemicals in groundwater
Grade 2 Better utility	Workshops and plant rooms requiring drier environment; retail storage	No water penetration but moisture vapour tolerable	Type A or Type B with RC design to BS 8007	Membranes in multiple layers with well lapped joints. Requires no serious defects and higher grade of supervision. Beware chemicals in groundwater
Grade 3 Habitable	Ventilated residential and working, including offices, restaurants, leisure centres	Dry environment	Type A or Type B with RC design to BS 8007, plus Type C with wall and floor cavities and DPM	As Grade 2. In highly permeable ground, multi-element systems (possibly including active precautions, and/or permanent and maintainable under-drainage) probably necessary
Grade 4 Special	Archives and stores requiring controlled environment	Totally dry environment	Type A or Type B with RC design to BS 8007 and a vapour-proof membrane, plus Type C with ventilated wall cavity and vapour barrier to inner skin and floor cavity with DPM	As Grade 3

[a] See CIRIA Report 139[11] for limits on environmental parameters.

combination of two (C + A or C + B); the types being as follows: A, structure requiring the protection of an impervious membrane (i.e. tanked); B, structure without a membrane but with structurally integral protection; C, drained cavity (for use with type A or type B or alone).

Overall, water-resisting reinforced concrete should be used for all the grades together with appropriate design, detailing and construction. Somerville[14], reviewing the durability of R.C. structures referred to the importance of the four 'Cs' in terms of durability; constituents of the mix, cover, compaction and curing. In terms of water resistance it should be recognized that reinforced concrete inevitably cracks as the cement hydrates, through thermal movement and later drying shrinkage. Perhaps, in terms of reinforced concrete basements, the risk of leakage and the management of that leakage to ensure compliance with the required performance standard should be based on four 'Ss': **simplicity** in structural detailing to take into account the intended construction methods and buildability; location of construction joints to receive special attention; **services**: make design provision at an early stage; **spacing** of wall reinforcement and **supervision** of concreting to ensure well compacted dense concrete.

It is inevitable that reinforced concrete walls and rafts will crack, initially due to thermal shrinkage and thence with time due to drying shrinkage. Early age strains due to thermal action are likely to be far greater and more important than strain due to drying shrinkage. The hydration temperatures generated in thick reinforced concrete sections are high and any change to thin sections is likely to generate differential movement and resulting cracking. Similarly, restraint provided by cross-walls or similar structural restraint is likely to cause cracks. These early cracks are important in terms of water resistance because they are likely to pass right through the section. The maximum crack width for early age thermal effects should be limited to 0·2 mm. Cracks due to flexure under load do not generally pass through the section, compressive stresses progressively reducing strains in this zone of the structural section. The maximum flexural crack widths at the surface of the concrete section may be greater than the maximum of 0·2 mm for thermal cracks and typically would be of the order of 0·3 mm. The avoidance of steel congestion in basement R.C. sections to obtain stringent crack control and only secure poorly compacted concrete with risks of bad durability and water leakage cannot be over-emphasized.

A recent paper by Boikan[15] summarized the pitfalls in waterproofing of basements and their prevention. As an introduction, Boikan quoted a legal case in England, *Outwing Construction* vs. *Thomas Weatherald*, when the High Court held that the designer takes responsibility not only for the specification of a waterproofing product, but must also assess the compatibility of that product in conjunction with other parts of the basement design, and the impact of inadequate workmanship and site conditions on the integrity of the design overall. Boikan recommended that particular matters such as the use of incompatible discontinuous products, use of products such as low tolerance to poor workmanship, use of waterproofing products from various sources all required special attention. He further commented that physical barriers, previously asphalt tanking but nowadays polyethylene cast in membranes, or bentonite clay bound into a geotextile required particular attention. These membranes should be assessed in terms of their performance in hard and soft water and contaminants, their gas resistance, their means of bonding to the concrete and the details of bonding one sheet to its neighbour. Boikan included a review of the performance of hydrophilic waterstop systems which are now much preferred to PVC waterstops in in situ R.C. basement construction.

Progressive development of construction methods for deep basements

As basement excavations increase in depth, excavation methods have become more complex, leading to top-downwards techniques which allow simultaneous basement construction and superstructure erection. These techniques became popular in major international city centres in the 1980s and 1990s. This review of the development of these methods in London is largely based on a paper by Zinn[16] and shows the increasing dependence of basement construction methods on progressively larger and more powerful piling and diaphragm wall equipment.

Trench construction

At the beginning of the last century, basement construction in London was restricted to major buildings. Basement walls were built as gravity structures in deep, heavily-timbered trenches at the basement periphery. In later years the walls were built as cantilever reinforced concrete walls in trench. Wall dimensions that resulted from this construction method can be judged from Fig. 8.6, a cross-section of the basement wall to the Shell Centre[17]. The wall, cantilevering for a depth of four basement storeys, was built in pre-stressed concrete within a sheet piled trench with reinforced concrete wallings and struts. Two separate excavation operations were required, the first by

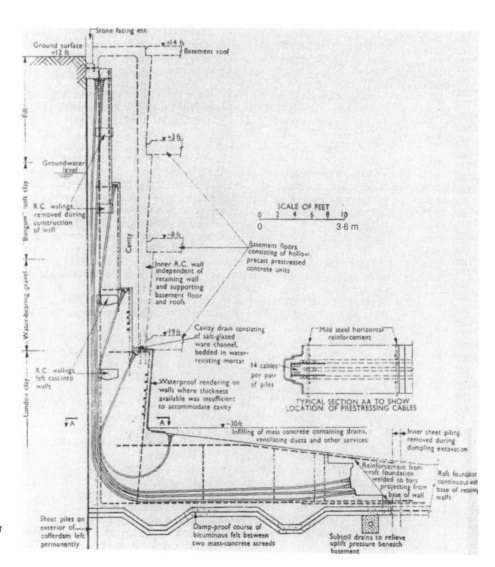

Fig. 8.6. Cross-section of peripheral cantilever prestressed concrete retaining wall in trench, Shell Centre basement, London[17]

grab within the peripheral trench, the second by excavation of the central dumpling after wall completion. The wall construction operations were obstructed by the temporary trench bracing but before it could be removed the inner and outer sheeting to the trench had to be re-strutted against the completed wall; all frame levels, reinforcement splicing levels, concrete lift heights and re-strutting levels were interdependent.

Peripheral walls propped by floor and raft

In the late 1950s the trench method began to be replaced by more efficient basement excavation methods. The changes exploited large-diameter bored piles which were introduced into the UK at that time together with the simple innovation of using the horizontal strength of floors and raft sections as deep beams to span the length of breadth of the excavation. The Fu Centre, Hong Kong (Fig. 8.7) was built with a pile wall, but the base of the cantilever reinforced concrete wall was designed to span horizontally and resist all horizontal earth pressure, allowing the removal of temporary support without inducing purely cantilever moments into the wall.

In the tower block basement of the Hilton Hotel, London (Fig. 8.8) two waling beams, each forming part of a structural floor, were used to temporarily support the outer contiguous bored pile wall. The walings were designed as frames and the upper waling was supported at the bored pile wall and by bored piles inside the wall.

In the third phase of the development of this method, the Royal Garden Hotel site (Fig. 8.9) used diagonal struts, also supported on piles, to reduce the 72 m span of the longest side of the basement. Later, peripheral diaphragm walls propped by successive floors, designed to span as a horizontal frame, were used at Gardiner's Corner, London (Fig. 8.10).

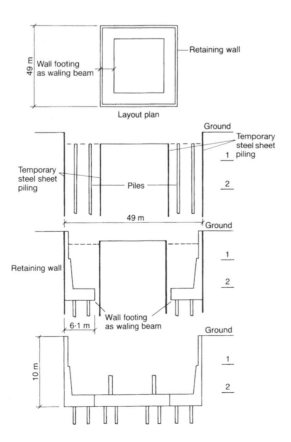

Fig. 8.7. Stages of basement construction, Fu Centre, Hong Kong[16]

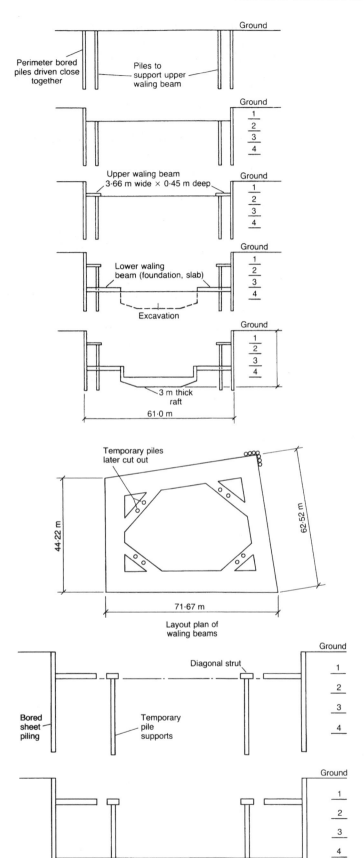

Fig. 8.8. Stages of basement construction, Hilton Hotel, London[16]

Fig. 8.9. Stages of basement construction, Royal Garden Hotel, London[16]

Fig. 8.10. Top-downwards basement construction with floors used as horizontal frame, Gardiners Corner, London (courtesy of Cementation)

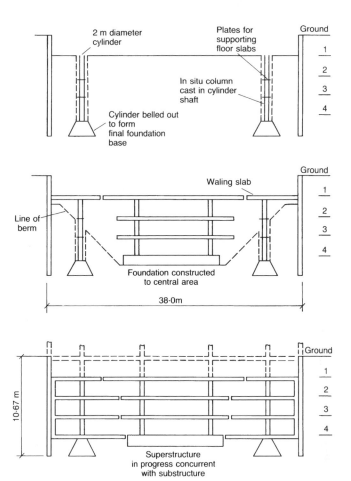

Fig. 8.11. Stages of car park basement construction, Leicester Square, London[16]

Top-downwards construction

The fourth and fifth phases of the development of the basement excavation method are illustrated by a car park at Leicester Square and the Winter Gardens Theatre, both in London.

In the car park works (Fig. 8.11) a 45° berm was used to support the outer bored pile wall while the central area substructure was completed. Floors acting as walings as the berm was removed were supported by reinforced concrete columns, cast in advance of the berm excavation, within pre-bored shafts. Early construction of the central part of the substructure allowed superstructure works to begin before berm excavation and completion of the peripheral wall and slabs.

At the theatre site (Fig. 8.12) the disadvantage of removing the berm subsoil from within the existing work was overcome with temporary steel lattice columns to support the floor sections used as walings at each level.

The top-downwards method was, therefore, at that time almost in place; to achieve maximum economy three criteria had to be achieved by the excavation method:

(a) the retaining wall which supports the width of the excavation should obtain support at each floor level

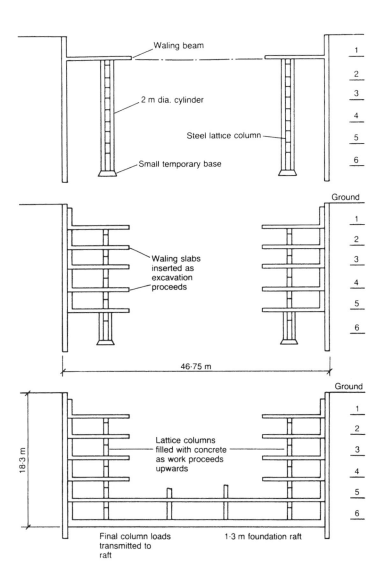

Fig. 8.12. Stages of basement construction, Winter Gardens Theatre, London[16]

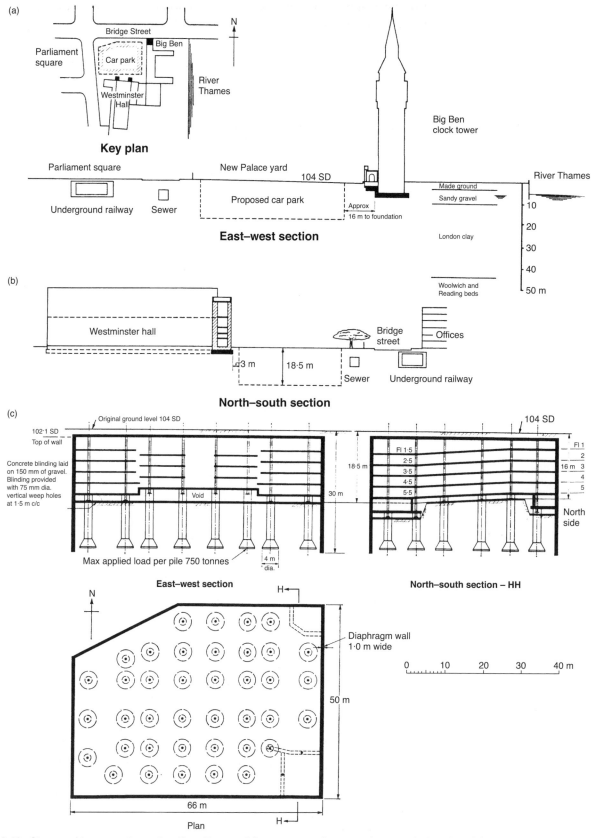

Fig. 8.13. Stages of basement construction, House of Commons underground car park, London: (a) site plan; (b) vertical cross-section showing soil profile; (c) vertical section and plan of car park[19]

(*b*) the ground should act as a temporary soffit 'shutter' to floor construction
(*c*) removal of the excavation must be rapid and continuous.

With the development of diaphragm walling during the 1970s it was logical that bored pile peripheral walls would be replaced with diaphragm walls to act as both temporary and permanent soil support. Fenoux[18] described the construction of a nine-storey basement for car parking in which the superstructure was opened for use before the completion of the substructure. In 1972 the House of Commons underground car park in London was built with peripheral diaphragm walls with temporary support from floor slabs cast successively with continuing excavation. The basement, shown in section in Fig. 8.13, reached a maximum depth of 18·5 m with diaphragm wall 30 m deep. The prime concerns at design stage were to minimize soil movements due to the bulk excavation and limit the effect on nearby historic buildings. The risk of soil heave was more acute since there was no superstructure above the basement. The solution, to build a relatively stiff wall (1 m thick diaphragm) propped at relatively small centres (storey heights) with relatively stiff propping from in situ reinforced concrete floors was, therefore, designed to reduce the risk of settlement of existing structures rather than to reduce construction time. A detailed description was given by Burland and Hancock[19]; details of soil movements, which caused only minor cracking and movement to the adjacent buildings, were given by Burland *et al.*[20]

A more recent deep basement construction in London was described by Marchand[21,22]. This basement, constructed by top-downwards techniques to a depth of 23·9 m from ground level to the lowest basement formation level, was built for car parking below an eight-storey office block superstructure. The basement is one of the deepest in London. Two details are worthy of note: precast concrete stop ends were used in the 1 m thick diaphragm wall construction and, although generally successful, Marchand commented: 'Some of the joints between the precast stop ends and in situ concrete leaked and this was dealt with by grout injection. The sealant used has been specially developed for the mining industry and is pumped in as a fluid which changes to a flexible mass of matted rubber particles. This material can then flex without cracking. In a few places at low level clay had adhered to the stop end, leaving a strip of clay up to 70 mm wide between adjacent panels. This was raked out to a depth of 150 mm and made good in order to provide a waterproof joint.'

Waterproofness of diaphragm wall basements is discussed later in this chapter. Where basement walls built by pile or diaphragm wall techniques remain unlined, the longevity of remedial measures to ensure acceptable waterproofness remains a matter of concern.

The second noteworthy innovation was the use of five rows of pin piles installed in front of the basement wall to stiffen the London clay and prevent softening with time. With increasing groundwater levels the construction would otherwise have required a substantial ground slab to prop the wall and prevent passive failure of the wall. The stiffened soil approach allowed the wall toe to be raised 5 m from the original design, a significant reduction in a very deep wall, originally almost 38 m deep from ground level.

In the 1960s top-downwards construction techniques required the setting of steel columns as part of the superstructure support within pile heads or pile caps at basement formation level. This operation required personnel to trim pile and set precast caps or make bases in situ for the column installation at final basement level. On this contract, a scheme for setting the steel columns directly into the wet pile concrete was investigated but rejected because of the risk of inaccurate placing of the columns. Liners, 21 m long, were used to gain access to each pile head. The operation was costly and time-consuming and was frequently underestimated in terms of construction time.

More recently, specialist firms have developed jigs to enable the steel plunge column to be placed very accurately both in verticality and position within an unlined box supported by bentonite slurry. The development of this jig therefore permits the use of slurry support and allows the steel column to be placed in the wet concrete of the recently concreted pile. The general accuracy of placing plunge columns is of the same order as bored pile construction of the order of 1:75 but with the use of specialist jigs and good site control placing accuracy in the range 1:200 to 1:400 can be maintained. The rolling tolerance of the steel column itself may be critical and should be taken into account in determining likely in situ verticality.

The top-downwards method has obvious advantages in terms of soil movement and completion time, but important disadvantages include the additional cost of excavation and removal of soil from beneath floor slabs in cramped conditions compared with conventional open excavation methods. Also, there is the congestion caused on site by superstructure and substructure contractors working within the same programme period.

A successful application of top-downwards construction was recently made in London on a congested site for the redevelopment of a site in Knightsbridge for use by Harrods department store. The new building consisted of seven storeys above ground and a seven-storey 25 m deep basement. The works are described by Slade and Darling et al.[23], and the control of ground movements and the application of compensation grouting by Fernie[24] and Kenwright et al.[25]

The new structure, built at the rear of the existing Harrods building and connected to it by a new access tunnel, incorporated an existing façade on one elevation. A site plan is shown in Fig. 8.14 and the construction sequence is shown in Fig. 8.15.

The ground conditions on the site are made ground of 3·5 m thickness overlying Terrace Gravel 6·0 m thick which in turn overlie London clay of proven thickness greater than 50 m. The groundwater conditions comprise

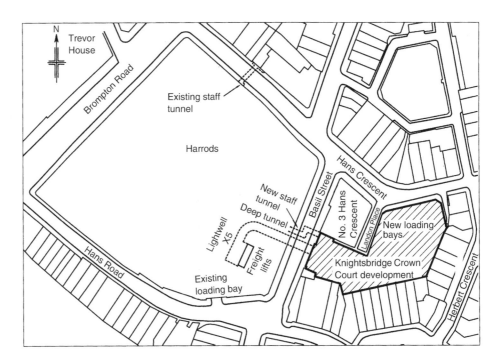

Fig. 8.14. Harrods, Knightsbridge, London. Site plan[23]

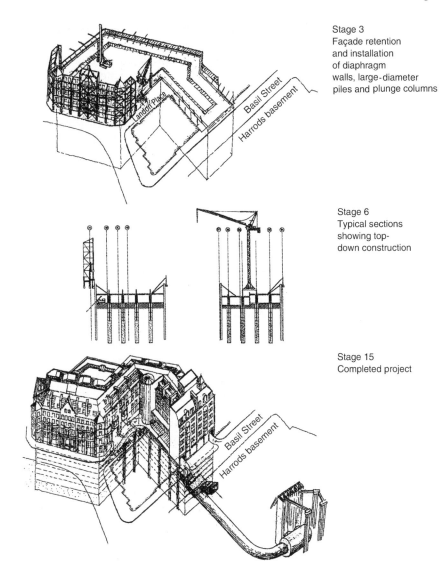

Stage 3
Façade retention
and installation
of diaphragm
walls, large-diameter
piles and plunge columns

Stage 6
Typical sections
showing top-
down construction

Stage 15
Completed project

*Fig. 8.15. Harrods,
Knightsbridge, London.
Construction sequence*[23]

an upper perched water table in the Terrace gravels and a lower aquifer in the Thanet sands and Chalk which underlie the London clay. A hydrostatic pore water pressure distribution was shown by piezometers within the London clay.

The basement construction for parking, plant rooms and workshop use was required to comply with grade 1 of BS 8102 allowing some seepage and damp patches. Due to the demands for basement space the use of a lining wall and drained cavity was not viable and the 800 mm thick diaphragm wall remained unlined. Top-down construction with the ground floor initially built and then excavation in two-storey level increments was possible and shown to be so by finite element analysis. This procedure saved construction time and was monitored during construction by comprehensive instrumentation, collecting data from precise level points, electrolevel beams, in-place inclinometers, water levels, survey targets and base traverse stations. Readings were taken on a 24-hour basis and any change above program supervision trigger levels was sent to the Engineers' terminals. In the event, the trigger levels were not exceeded.

The initial finite element analysis predicted both the deflected shape of the basement walls and the resulting settlement profile outside the basement perimeter. In turn, using these deformation contours, the settlement behaviour of nearby existing buildings was assessed and the classification due to Boscardin and Cording[26] used to make a risk prediction. Maximum settlements due to basement construction were limited to 10 mm and angular distortions to 1 in 750.

The overall stability of the basement in the long term was checked to ensure a minimum factor of safety of 1·4 for the whole basement, taking into account the uplift force due to soil heave and the groundwater pressure resisted by the combination of building weight, the tensile resistance of the piles and the skin friction on the faces of the diaphragm walls. (Skin friction to the lowest basement level was used.) The total assessed long-term uplift pressure over the whole basement area was 340 kN/m².

In the USA, the top-downwards method has been adopted more recently. American practice is described by Fletcher et al.[27] The excavation of a large four-storey deep basement for the Milwaukee Centre, close to historic structures and within 3·5 m of the Milwaukee River, demanded a cut-off and control of groundwater, minimum soil movement and early completion. A major bracing or raker system was judged to be too cumbersome and costly, and a temporary freeze wall system was dismissed because a permanent ground water cut-off would have been necessary. The top-downwards method with a deep diaphragm wall as a cut-off was adopted and proved successful.

Scope for innovation remains. In 1993, a contract for an opera house in Paris used the technique for a 28 m deep basement with anchored support in lieu of lateral support from basement floors as excavation proceeded. Large barrette sections were constructed for superstructure support. A typical cross-section of the basement is shown in Fig. 8.16. Due to the planned construction, after completion of the basement, of a Metro running tunnel on one side of the basement and in close proximity to it, anchor tendons constructed from glass fibre were adopted to avoid obstruction to the Metro tunnelling machine. The brittle, low shear strength of the glass tendons ensured that they would be easily removed by the tunnelling machine.

In Hong Kong, land values have increased demand for larger, deeper basements frequently in unfavourable soil conditions with stringent settlement criteria applied to the basement peripheral subsoils. This market demand has brought about almost an exclusive use of top-downwards construction generally using diaphragm walls. A recent example of the construction of the deep basement for the Dragon Centre in the heart of the Western Kowloon Peninsula was given by Lui and Yau[28]. The site was located on old reclaimed land and the development, for a new retail building, comprised a nine-storey reinforced concrete structure over a five-storey basement for parking use. Historical records showed that the foreshore originally fronted the site. The existing MTR tunnels are within 100 m of the site; the site reclamation was made in 1924. Adjacent existing buildings are either supported on pad footings or driven precast piles. The ground conditions are loose granular fill underlain by marine deposits, generally loose silty clayey fine sand and highly developed granite (dense silty fine to coarse sand) and granite bedrock. Groundwater level is 1·5 m below ground level. A geological section is shown in Fig. 8.17.

The basement structure, 107 m × 67 m in plan was formed from a diaphragm wall box, 1200 mm thick up to 40 m deep installed by cutter with CWS joints to 30 m depth and a cut joint below 30 m. The top-downwards method was used with support of basement floors by steel box stanchions filled with sand–cement grout. Each internal column was supported on a single large-diameter bored pile founded on the bedrock with an allowable bearing pressure of 5 MPa at depths between 45 and 65 m below ground level.

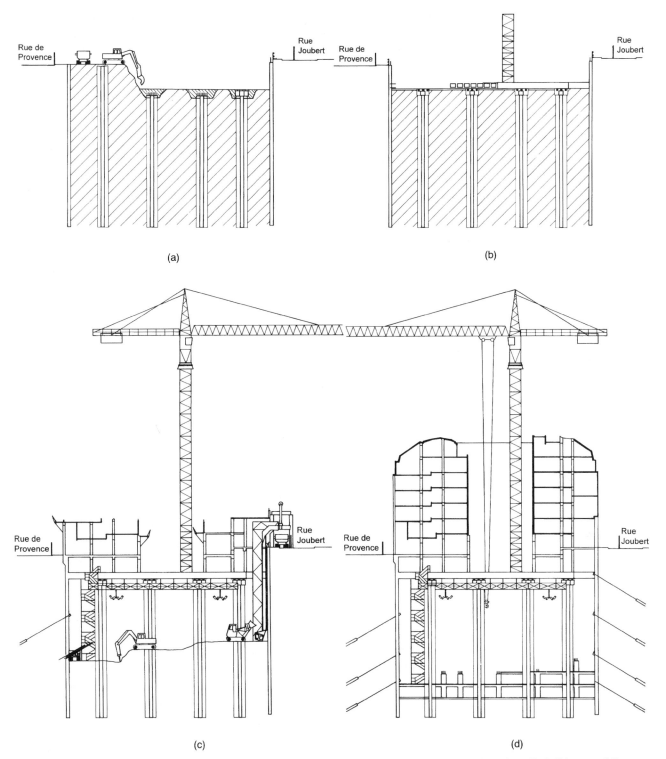

Fig. 8.16. Paris basement construction sequence, Provence Opera, Paris: (a) barrette sections installed; (b) ground floor construction; (c) superstructure construction and excavation below ground floor slab; (d) superstructure and substructure

The basement construction proceeded as the basement floors were cast on grade successively downwards from the ground floor slab. The prime design requirement was to minimize ground movements outside the site. In order to do this, the cut-off effectiveness of the diaphragm wall was improved by grout injection a further 10 m below the wall. A full-scale pumping test was

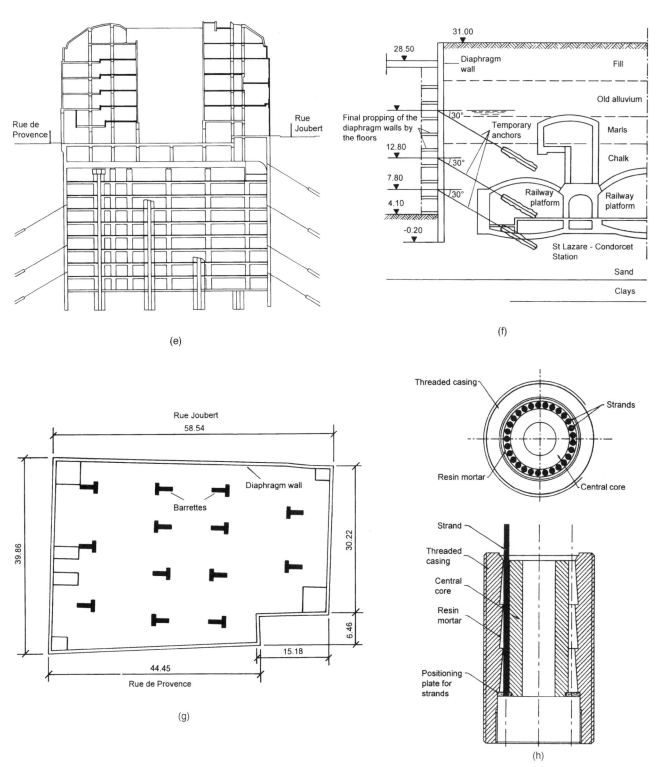

Fig. 8.16. (e) Load transfer of temporary support loads to floors; (f) geological conditions; (g) site plan; (h) anchor head detail for composite soil anchor (courtesy of Soletanche–Bachy)

made and then back analysed. The results were used as design parameters for prediction of ground movements due to full-scale excavation. A further multiple-well pumping test was made after the completion of the diaphragm wall box to simulate the construction dewatering. An array of pumping wells at about 25 m centres was used to lower the water table over the site

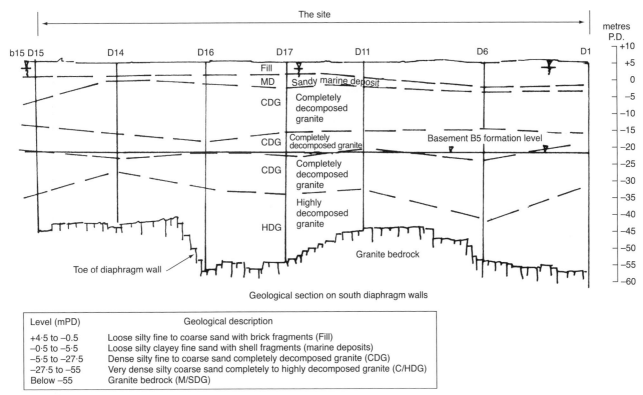

Fig. 8.17. Dragon Centre, Hong Kong. Geological section.

Level (mPD)	Geological description
+4·5 to −0.5	Loose silty fine to coarse sand with brick fragments (Fill)
−0·5 to −5·5	Loose silty clayey fine sand with shell fragments (marine deposits)
−5·5 to −27·5	Dense silty fine to coarse sand completely decomposed granite (CDG)
−27·5 to −55	Very dense silty coarse sand completely to highly decomposed granite (C/HDG)
Below −55	Granite bedrock (M/SDG)

area to the lowest basement level which is about 27 m below ground level. The test was maintained for eleven days until steady-state flow was obtained and then the pumps were switched off and the groundwater allowed to recover to its initial level. The results showed the following.

(a) The total steady rate of flow from the wells was $25\,\mathrm{m}^3$ per hour with measured hydrostatic water pressure on both sides of the wall at steady state.

(b) Readings from piezometers within 5 m distance from the wells showed that the groundwater was lowered to 23·5–29·5 m depth.

(c) With the exception of the eastern corner of the site, the drawdown outside the site was an average 0·5 m at standpipes and 1·5 m at piezometers.

(d) Ground surface settlements were recorded in the range 4 to 16 mm with negligible settlement at adjacent buildings.

(e) The maximum lateral deflections recorded by three inclinometers were in the range 50 to 80 mm at the top of the diaphragm walls, with general wall rotation from the toe.

Following the cessation of pumping, there was negligible recovery to the ground surface settlements and the lateral wall deflections recovered to about half of the maximum wall deflections during the pumping test.

Back analysis using the finite element computer program SEEP was made to vary the rock mass permeability so that calculated pore-water pressures matched those at steady state in the pumping test. The matched calculated value was $1 \times 10^{-8}\,\mathrm{m/s}$.

Further back analyses were made with the computer program FREW, which assumes a linear elastic continuum between active and passive limits on both sides of the wall. With some difficulty the observed wall displacements

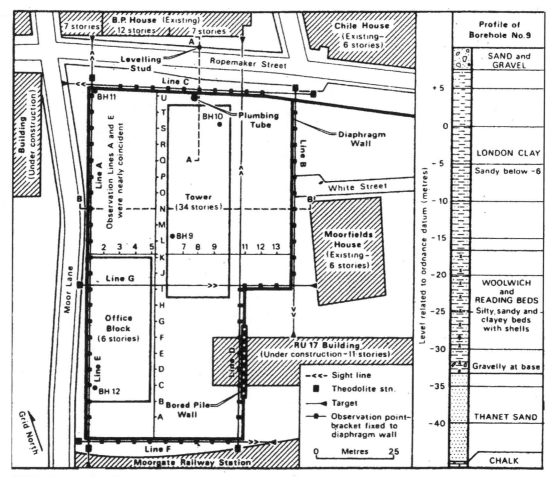

(a) Site plan and soil profile

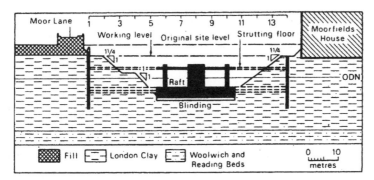

(b) Cross section BB' at tower, showing construction of
tower columns and core bottom upwards and strutting
floor and lower basement below it top downwards

Bulk excavation was carried out to the profiles shown working southwards away from the north
retaining wall. Upon completion and trimming of each excavation slope a thin protective covering
of lightly reinforced concrete was spread to slow down the deterioration of the clay soil. All water
run-off was channelled into sumps and pumped into sewers. Immediately upon completion of
excavation to formation level for the raft, a 0·9 m thick layer of unreinforced concrete was placed
to prevent undue swelling and subsequent reconsolidation of the underlying clay. Construction of
the 3·3 m thick raft then proceeded in alternate bays to allow for shrinkage, the largest pours
being 200 m³. Construction of the tower columns and core then proceeded rapidly so that the
basement floor at +3·3 m AOD could be constructed and used to strut the diaphragm wall.
Upon completion of a section of strutting floor, excavation below the floor was carried out
and the structure in the lower basement floors completed.

Fig. 8.18. Brittanic House, London. Construction sequence[30]

were used to estimate a value of K_0 (0·3 to 0·4) and a relationship between soil modulus EI and SPT value N.

Using these back analysed values, the wall deflections due to the subsequent excavation were analysed and the ground settlements estimated.

Overall, the pumping test and the seepage analysis made thereafter highlighted the importance of achieving a good seal by grouting between the toe of the diaphragm wall and the intact rock. Comparative analyses could be made between a grouted and ungrouted box. The predicted wall deflections reasonably agreed with observed ground movements after basement excavation. In general the maximum ground surface settlement as predicted was approximately 30 to 50% of the maximum wall deflection caused by the pumping test and basement excavation respectively. The vital importance of carrying out pumping tests for deep basements in water-bearing soils was established on this job and continues as standard practice in Hong Kong.

Recharge wells were installed at the Dragon Centre but were not used extensively following observations of settlements outside the basement as excavation progressed.

Semi top-down construction

The use of very large openings in floor slabs that are designed as a frame to provide lateral support to the external walls together with the use of excavators with long dipper arms enables excavation to proceed below the top slab support for considerable depths without intermediate floor support. This method, with only a skeletal structure for the working platform and one intermediate floor was used for a 25 m deep excavation for station construction on the Singapore MRT[29]. Following the construction of the roof, the skeletal plan shape of the roof was used to excavate down to concourse level using backhoes and long arm excavation. The concourse slab was then built with similar large openings to allow further deeper excavation whilst propping the external walls.

Combination of bottom-up and top-down methods

Basements of large plan area can benefit from a combination of both bottom-up and top-down methods. This was used at a very early stage of top-downwards construction in the UK in 1962–1963 at the site of an 18 m deep excavation at Brittanic House in central London. The work, reported by Cole and Burland[30], involved an external diaphragm wall box supported temporarily by an earth berm during construction of the central raft followed by bottom-upwards construction of the central core and tower columns. The outer floors were then constructed top-downwards below an upper strutting floor. The sequence is shown in Fig. 8.18 taken from Cole and Burland's paper. A similar combination of bottom-upwards and top-downwards construction was used for the basement of the Main Tower in Frankfurt[31]. A piled raft was used to support the 198 m high tower on Frankfurt clay, an over-consolidated but rather weak soil. The core of this tower was built bottom-upwards in a conventional four-frame supported excavation in advance of construction, top-downwards of the floors around the core within a peripheral secant pile wall. This combination, shown in sequence in Fig. 8.19, altered superstructure core construction to advance in parallel with basement construction, to the advantage of the overall programme.

Peripheral sheeting or walling

The system adopted to sheet or wall the periphery of the excavation will be influenced by the choice of basement construction method, the suitability of ground and groundwater conditions, the need to build close to site boundaries

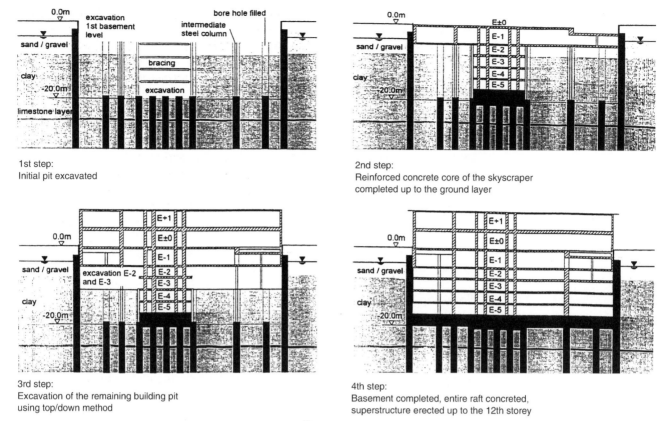

1st step:
Initial pit excavated

2nd step:
Reinforced concrete core of the skyscraper
completed up to the ground layer

3rd step:
Excavation of the remaining building pit
using top/down method

4th step:
Basement completed, entire raft concreted,
superstructure erected up to the 12th storey

Fig. 8.19. Main Tower, Frankfurt. Construction sequence[31]

and minimize wall thicknesses and, not least, by the local availability of materials and specialist plant and equipment. Peripheral sheeting methods are generally the following:

- anchored underpinning: reinforced concrete plates and grouted soil
- king post wall: vertical soldiers and horizontal laggings or reinforced concrete skin wall
- sheet piling
- contiguous bored piling
- secant piling
- soldier pile tremie concrete method (SPTC) – as used previously in the USA.
- diaphragm walls
  - o reinforced concrete cast in situ
  - o precast reinforced concrete
  - o post-tensioned.

The general features of each method were covered in Chapter 4, but their particular application to basement works is reviewed below.

Anchored underpinning

Where the total excavation depth of basement work is typically in the range 8 to 12 m and ground conditions are dry and capable of supporting a face 1·5 to 2 m deep and of similar length, the anchored plate method provides an economical temporary wall support if permission to install anchors outside the curtilage of the site is forthcoming. In conditions where soils lack the strength to stand unsupported to these modest depths, pre-grouting may prove worthwhile in granular soils. Where foundation loads from adjacent structures are such to necessitate transfer of load below the proposed excavation depth, pre-injection of the subsoil below the existing foundations, with anchorage to avoid lateral movement of the grouted soil mass, may prove an economical alternative to conventional mass concrete underpinning.

King post wall

The king post or soldier pile and horizontal timbered wall, previously widely used in North America, has become increasingly popular for basement construction in Europe in recent years. For use in shallow excavations, the king posts may be cantilevered or propped by raking shores or anchored in successive layers as bulk excavation proceeds in deeper basement works. The king posts may be double joist or channel units battened together to allow the anchor to conveniently pass between. Figure 8.20 shows soldier pile walls supported by anchors constructed in basement works in Saudi Arabia to depths exceeding 20 m. Subsoil conditions were layered washdown silts and silty sands, with a groundwater table at formation level or a small height above.

The method requires moderately dry ground conditions with soil of sufficient strength to maintain a vertical face prior to support from the horizontal lagging being placed. King post centres vary from 1·5 to 3·5 m, depending on soil strength, depth of excavation and surcharge loads. A popular innovation is the use of in situ reinforced concrete skin walls cast against the exposed soil face, with thicknesses between 150 and 200 mm. The walls, which span horizontally between king posts, are cast in lifts between 1 and 1·5 m high, depending on the ability of the soil to stand without support.

The king post excavation may be bored by auger rig or, where headroom is limited, low-headroom rigs may be necessary. The toe of the king post is usually concreted to basement formation level, although deeper king posts surrounded by sandy gravel washed in may be preferred if the king posts are to be subsequently extracted. It is economical to use the lined face of the timber laggings or the face of the skin wall as a back shutter to the permanent basement wall, but allowance must be made for tolerances in the king post wall construction.

Due to the width of the king post wall and the permanent wall construction it may be necessary to drill the king post bores close to the site boundary. Where an existing structure is close to this boundary the minimum distance between king post bore and site boundary will be determined by the minimum

Fig. 8.20. Anchored soldier pile walls used in dry layered sand and clayey silt soil for deep basement construction. Note the unimpaired access for plant and site operations, Medinah, Saudi Arabia (courtesy of NCF)

Table 8.3 Minimum distances between soil support system and site boundary for various types of installation plant

Support system	Installation plant	Distance[a]
Underpinning	Conventional bulk excavation plant, e.g. hydraulic excavator with hydraulic grab	Nil
Steel sheet piling	Crane and piling hammer/tracked hydraulic piling machine	500 mm, rear of sheeters to face of boundary wall
Contiguous bored pile wall	Bored pile: tripod equipment typical 600 diameter pile	150 mm
	Large-diameter rig: Hughes CEZ 300 typical 740 pile	385 mm
	Hughes CEZ 450 typical 750 pile	385 mm
	Hughes KCA 100/130 typical 900 pile	450 mm
Contiguous bored pile wall and hard–soft secant wall	CFA rig: Soilmec CM 45 typical 750 pile	350 mm
	Soilmec CM 48E typical 750 pile	350 mm
	Rotary rig CFA: Bauer BG 11 typical 500 pile	400 mm
	Bauer BG 14 typical 600 pile	300 mm
	Bauer BG 26 typical 600 pile	150 mm
	Bauer BG 30 typical 750 pile	100 mm
Hard–hard secant wall	Bauer BG 7 FOW method 254, 273, 305, 343, and 406 mm diameter	Nil
Diaphragm wall	Rope suspended grab	200 mm
	City Cutter	150 mm
	Hydrofraise	150 mm
Berlin walls: soldier piles and horizontal lagging	Rotary piling equipment 600 diameter bore	400 mm
	Manual excavation: hydraulic excavator and trench box	200 mm up to 6 m depth

[a] Minimum distance between outer face of support system and site boundary. Distances quoted are those at ground level; consideration must be given to verticality tolerance of support system.

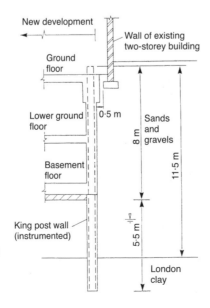

Fig. 8.21. Vertical cross-section through part of a substructure basement, Marylebone, London[32]

overhang of the auger rig from the rear face of the pile bore. Table 8.3 shows the minimum dimension between an existing structure and the outer face of the new wall for various wall types.

It is usual for king post wall construction to be used only as temporary soil support. An exception was described by Mair[32]. In Marylebone, London, a king post wall was used as the permanent peripheral retaining wall in a top-downwards type two-storey basement construction. A cross-section of the construction is shown in Fig. 8.21. King post wall construction was feasible because the whole depth of the basement, to 8 m, was accommodated within dry sands and gravels 11·5 m deep, below which was London clay. The water table in the sands and gravels was below the basement formation level, at a depth of 9·5 m. The king post centres were 1·5 to 1.8 m, and mass concrete infill was placed in 1 m lifts as excavation proceeded. As usual in top-downwards construction, the king post wall was successively propped by ground, lower ground and basement floors.

Sheet piling

The use of sheet piling for temporary soil support to basement construction in urban areas has declined as environmental controls on noise and vibration progressively strengthen. Only where sheet piles can be installed by hydraulic means, particularly in cohesive soils, can the effects of these controls on noise and vibration be avoided. The use of Giken hydraulic press equipment has steadily increased in the UK in a wider range of soils. Typically used in city centres, penetration through stiff clays such as London clay and Gault clay is restricted to a pile length of 16 to 20 m. Water jetting or lubrication of the sheeter surface with water may be necessary to achieve penetration.

Where noise and vibration are critical, as in most city centres, sheet piles for deep basements can be installed by the combined use of slurry trench and sheet piling methods. The sheet piles are pitched into slurry trenches filled with cementitious self-hardening slurry and the toes of the piles concreted in by tremie pipe up to basement formation level. The technique, although uneconomic at first sight, is environmentally friendly. The sheet pile section can be selected on the basis of flexural stress without consideration of driving stresses, and considerable accuracy can be achieved in pitching the sheeters into the slurry trench. The sheeters can obtain support from ground anchors with conventional steel walings or from bracing or raking shores.

Interlocks in sheet piles cannot be assumed to be completely watertight in water-bearing ground unless provision is made for sealing them. Sheet piles sealed by welding at the exposed surface after excavation or prior to installation by a steel contaminant section to allow a bituminous or polymer material seal of the interlock can remedy lack of watertightness. The use of welding may be necessary to augment the sealant compound. This system, now often the subject of contractual guarantees of maximum wall permeability, is becoming more popular in the UK and is further promoting the use of sheet piles for permanent works. Figure 8.22 shows typical joint details between permanent sheet piles and the basement slab.

Contiguous bored piling

The cheapest type of concrete piled wall is the contiguous piled wall. The use of modern continuous flight auger (CFA) rigs allows high output in a wide variety of soils. The depth of pile is limited to the order of 18 to 20 m by the difficulty of inserting reinforcement cages to greater depths through wet concrete and the lack of water resistance in water bearing ground due to the gaps between piles. A structural facing may be applied as sprayed concrete or an in situ reinforced concrete lining.

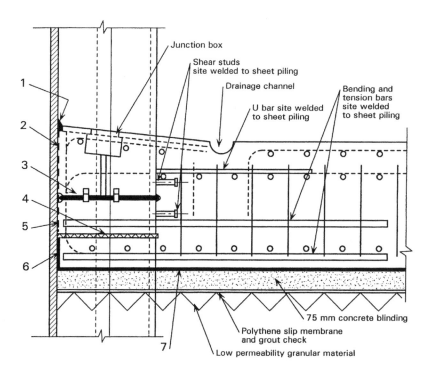

Junction box

Shear studs
site welded to sheet piling

Drainage channel

U bar site welded
to sheet piling

Bending and
tension bars
site welded
to sheet piling

75 mm concrete blinding

Polythene slip membrane
and grout check

Low permeability granular material

Fig. 8.22. Typical joint details between permanent sheet piles and the basement slab

1	10 mm wide x 10 mm deep chase formed in top of slab with pourable sealant.
2	100 mm wide adhesive waterproofing tape membrane with permanent mechanical bond to concrete, bonded to sheet pile at construction joint location.
3	Hose injection waterproofing system clipped to face of sheet piles.
4	20 mm x 5 mm hydrophilic waterstop bonded to sheet piling.
5	Double sided self adhesive rubber/bitumen waterproofing membrane securely bonded to sheet pile, water bar and hydrophilic strip.
6	P.V.C. waterbar returned 125 mm.
7	P.V.C. waterbar with co-extruded hydrophylic elements at construction joints.

Prior to the advent of CFA rigs in these jobs only a short length of top casing was necessary, separating the piles by approximately 50 mm. The piled wall depth was limited to some extent by the verticality tolerance that could be obtained by the augers, typically 1% with depth. In the UK many basement walls were constructed in this way in the 1960s to the 1980s. The walls were anchored temporarily using steel walings or were braced with strutting or rakers. Grouting was used in permeable soils where groundwater entered in the gap between piles. In some instances the intended use of the basement allowed the bored pile wall constructed in this way to remain unlined, while for high-grade basements the piled walls were lined with reinforced concrete or an independent, non-load-bearing blockwork wall.

The advent of CFA piling rigs in the early 1980s, with their ability to operate without casings (even without a top casing), their high output and, for smaller low-torque machines, their ease of transport and erection on site, produced economies which allowed them to replace conventional augers in most soil conditions. CFA piles for wall construction are typically 300, 450, 600, 900, 1000 and 1200 mm in diameter.

Hydraulic auger cleaners, introduced to prevent soil falling on personnel also avoid contamination of new concrete with soil. Other innovations include a projecting tremie pipe from the base of the auger to pump concrete to a lower level than the core of soil progressively lifted by the auger. Standards of quality control for CFA piles are now much improved by in-cab monitoring. Data referring to auger depth, torque applied during pile excavation, rate of withdrawal and concrete pressure are relayed to the rig operator and a more recent IT development enables this data to be transmitted to an off-site terminal such as the contractor's or engineer's office. Further progress is needed to measure concrete pressure near the point of discharge.

CFA rigs operate in a wide range of soil and soft rock conditions, but hard rocks, rock chalk and strong mudstones cause obstruction and make the rigs uneconomic. Minimum distances for rig operation from existing wall boundaries are shown for a range of CFA and rotary rigs in Table 8.3. Some stated dimensions may be reduced by modifying the standard equipment. Bauer, in particular, has introduced a purpose-made rig to operate with reduced minimum distance.

Secant piling

Improvements in rotary rig and equipment design have, as with contiguous pile walls, changed construction methods for secant piles in recent years. Until the 1980s the Benoto rig was the primary method of installing secant pile walls, cutting the concrete of female piles to interlock male piles between them. A heavy-duty hammer grab was used with twin-wall lockable temporary casing equipped with a cutting edge for excavation, the casing being

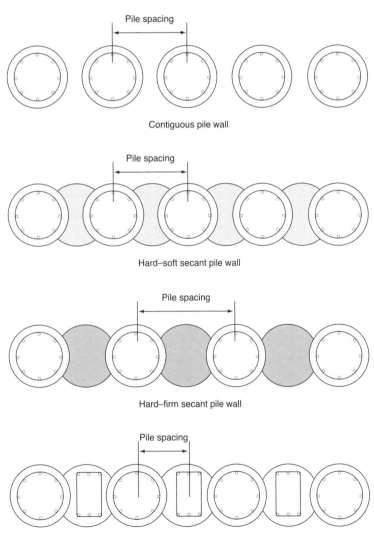

Fig. 8.23. Configuration of reinforcement in contiguous and secant pile walls[62]

oscillated under crowd to achieve penetration. The introduction of powerful rotary machines equipped with CFAs or casing oscillators has enabled much higher output rates than the traditional Benoto rig, which had been used for almost 50 years in Europe and the UK.

Benoto rigs used bores of 880, 1080 and 1180 mm diameter. At present, secant piles installed by CFAs have diameters in the range 450 to 750 mm diameter, whereas cased secant piles typically range from 750 to 1180 mm diameter. Reinforcement, usually limited to male piles, may be from cages or, where required for shear or flexural strength, joist sections may be used. A comparison between contiguous pile and secant pile configuration and re-inforcement is shown in Fig. 8.23. The method provides a near-waterproof wall for both temporary and permanent soil support and, with CFA, rotary or hammer grab excavation, secant walls can penetrate most soils and rock obstructions to maximum depths of 30 to 40 m. The secant pile basement wall is capable of supporting both lateral load from soil and groundwater and vertical load from the curtilage of the superstructure. Vertical loads may be transmitted to the piles by a reinforced concrete capping beam or, for lesser loads, by shear on the vertical contact face between adjacent piles.

Since 1985, the use in the UK of hard–soft and hard–firm secant piles, for depths to 20 m by CFA rigs and for greater depths with high-torque rigs with casing oscillators, has improved production, reduced cost and to some extent reduced the use of diaphragm walling. The unreinforced female piles, cast in the bentonite–cement or bentonite–cement–Pulverized Fuel Ash mix, are cut by the male piles which are reinforced and concreted in the normal way. This type of hard–soft secant wall may not be satisfactory for walls requiring high standards of waterproofness or long-term durability, although internal reinforced concrete lining walls may remedy this situation. Pile rigs used to install secant piles before and after the 1980s are shown in Fig. 8.24.

Other innovations in recent years include mix-in-place piles. This process utilizes cement slurry, pumped through the hollow stem of the auger, mixed with sandy soils during boring and extraction. The unreinforced female piles constructed in this way vary with the sand–cement ratio (with compressive strength of the order of $15 \, N/mm^2$) and can be alternatively spaced with male piles constructed with concrete and reinforced in the normal way.

Fig. 8.24. Piling rigs used for secant pile installation: (a) BG 26 rig (courtesy of Bauer); (b) Benoto rig with hammer grab (courtesy of Lilley)

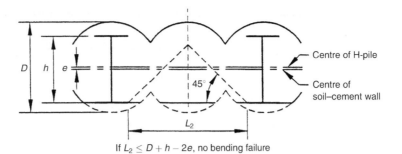

Fig. 8.25. CDSM piles: suggested pile spacing[35]

If $L_2 \leq D + h - 2e$, no bending failure

The use of cement deep soil mixing (CDSM) to produce blocks of overlapping piles for nailed or self-supporting gravity-retaining structures has recently progressed rapidly in the USA after early development in Japan. Yang[33] summarized the use of CDSM for cut-off walls and excavation support in addition to its use in ground stabilization. A later review of deep mixing technology was given by Porbaha *et al.* in 2001.[34] The method, developed in the 1970s from soil–lime mixing methods uses a triple auger machine to produce pile sections in the range 550 to 990 mm in stiffer soils. Steel H sections are installed as flexural reinforcement in retaining walls prior to the hardening of the soil–cement mixture. The soil–cement is designed to arch between adjacent steel H sections. Taki and Yang[35] suggested a spacing of H sections based on empiricism, as shown in Fig. 8.25. Cement deep soil mixed piles reinforced with steel joists for soil support and groundwater control are shown in Fig. 8.26. A soil–cement wall for both groundwater control and for soil retention in highly permeable coralline conditions was used for a two-storey basement at the Marin Tower project in Hawaii. The excavation was only 30 m from the harbour and a high groundwater level. The partial cut-off scheme was achieved by a soil–cement wall of average depth 14 m, using 55 cm soil mix piles installed by triple auger. The coral limestone was ground down to gravel size by the augers without pre-drilling for thorough mixing with the cement grout. Mix designs with cement dosages of 300 to 500 kg/m^3 of in situ soil were used.

The relatively slow take up of soil mixing processes for excavation support in Continental Europe and the UK may be associated with the lack of adequate QA methods. Bruce *et al.*[36] reported current methods in 2000.

Support for piled basement walls by ground and rock anchors
Secant pile walls may be supported by strutting and walings, rakers with walings or ground anchors. Where used, anchors may be taken axially through the piles or through the contact face between the piles. It may be sufficient to use anchors at alternate male piles or every fourth pile, depending on the extent of lateral load, anchor capacity, and the available shear resistance mobilized on the contact face between adjacent piles.

The decision to use ground anchors as a temporary wall support for any wall system will be based on practicality, cost and installation time, which are all influenced by:

- depth of the basement
- groundwater conditions during anchor installation and, thereafter, during basement construction
- subsoil conditions and their suitability for accommodating anchors of adequate capacity economically
- maximum permissible soil and basement wall movements and the plan shape of the basement; the susceptibility of adjacent existing structures to soil movement caused by the basement excavation

Fig. 8.26. Soil–cement wall for excavation support and groundwater control, Tokyo, Japan (courtesy of Raito Inc.)

- the basement construction programme
- the aggressiveness, if any, of groundwater
- the location of existing services
- the location of neighbouring substructures and/or basements
- legal permissions to accommodate anchorages outside the curtilage of the construction site
- the risk of obstruction of future works within the construction site by the presence of anchors.

This list, in no order of priority, may not be exhaustive on any particular site, but indicates those items requiring earliest consideration. Some items are self-explanatory. Subsoil conditions will indicate likely anchor capacities, compact granular soils generally being preferred to cohesive soils in the fixed zone of each tier of anchors. Subsoil and groundwater conditions will dictate drilling costs for anchor installation, and the aggressiveness of groundwater and the period of use of the anchors will dictate the need for corrosion protection.

The location of adjacent substructures and services will determine the practicality of installing anchors at the required elevations, and the plan shape of the basement may determine any difficulties caused by obstructing the drilling of anchors from an adjacent re-entrant basement wall. Above all, legal permissions and licences must be available from owners of adjacent land or highway authorities to allow anchor installation outside the site area. Where anchors are likely to obstruct future construction, a removable-type anchor may be necessary.

Wall movement is likely to be reduced by the use of anchors that are stressed after installation, particularly when fixed-length anchors are founded in competent medium-dense or dense granular soil. When the anchors are founded in stiff cohesive soils only short-term benefit may be gained.

The programme implications of anchor installation also require examination and depend on the timing of bulk excavation following anchor installation. The sequence of drilling, tendon installation, grouting, grout strengthening and stressing for each bank of anchors has to be phased within the overall excavation programme. Comparison with an overall construction programme using alternative forms of wall support may be necessary, taking into account the improved construction outputs obtained by unobtained work areas achieved by anchoring.

The design and construction of ground anchors, described in Chapter 7, is explained in detail in BS 8081[37], which contains an extensive bibliography on ground and rock anchors. Littlejohn and Bruce[38] reviewed the state-of-the-art in rock anchoring and Barley[39] updated this, in particular giving observed bond stress values of both straight shafted and under-reamed anchors in chalk, mudstones, siltstones, shales, marls and sandstones.

Soldier pile tremie concrete method

This North American practice, popular in the 1960s, of modifying the king post wall method by excavating a panel by grab under bentonite slurry between the king posts and filling the panel excavation with unreinforced concrete by tremie, has rarely been used in Europe. In Germany, however, a modification of this method, using mesh-reinforced gunite sprayed between and over the king posts successively as built excavation proceeds, has gained acceptance. Although the construction provides only temporary soil support it is particularly economical in dry granular soils which can be excavated to a vertical face for 2 to 3 m without collapse in shallow to medium-depth basements. The overall thicknesses of temporary and permanent walls and working space at the site boundary are usually not excessive.

Structural diaphragm walls

It may be argued that the most significant advance in recent years in basement construction has been the introduction of the structural diaphragm wall. The principal advantages of this form of construction, introduced into Europe by Icos in the 1950s and 1960s, are: the dual use of the wall to provide both temporary and permanent soil support; the efficiency in bending of the rectangular wall section compared with the circular pile cross-section used previously; the reduction in noise and vibration during installation compared with percussive drilling of sheet piling; the ease of installation of propping, strutting and anchoring against the wall face; the ease of applying finishes to the flat wall face; the ability of the walls to transfer vertical loads; and its use to depths generally in excess of other forms of wall construction.

The dual support provided by the diaphragm wall at construction stage and then during the basement life was often sufficiently economical to justify it on financial savings alone compared with other walling methods. Advantages such as the minimum thickness of construction required by the diaphragm wall for both temporary and permanent soil support were a bonus.

The principal disadvantages of diaphragm walling are the risk of loss or spillage of bentonite slurry, the relatively high cost of cleaning and the disposal of the slurry, the site space needed for large reinforcement cages and the large cranes needed to handle them. Above all, the need for continuity in the construction process from excavation through concreting to removal of temporary stop end formers, is a disadvantage of the method. Structural diaphragm walls still remain the preferred method of walling for deep basements and concrete piled walls, particularly secant walls, have only tended to replace diaphragm walling in basement works of medium depth.

Icos[40] gave details of a wide range of basement constructions. These basements were generally of moderate depth, perhaps two or three basement storeys. The diaphragm walls were all excavated by cable grab mounted on tripods on rails. The wall depth attainable by this equipment was considerable, however – up to 28 m in one example in Paris. The panels used were straight, L- and T-shaped and corrugated in plan. Figure 8.27 shows the diaphragm wall options for basement excavations recommended by Icos.

As patent protection on the Icos wall waned, specialist firms in Europe introduced alternative excavation equipment, although in later years Icos persevered with rope grabs mounted on heavy tracked cranes. In Europe, kelly bar mounted hydraulic grabs became popular in the 1970s and the early 1980s. These grabs, which were capable of excavating wall widths between 500 and 1500 mm, were mounted on single or telescopic kelly bars to maximum depths of approximately 25 m. Panels were dug in a series of grab 'bites' which were typically each 2·8 m long.

Excavation in medium-strong to strong rocks for diaphragm wall works was difficult for all specialist firms at this time. The usual method from the 1950s to the early 1980s was to use a drop chisel progressively along the

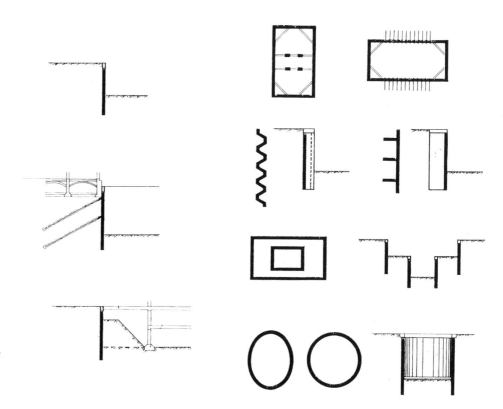

Fig. 8.27. Alternative methods of wall support and plan forms of diaphragm walls for basement construction (courtesy of Icos)

Phase 1   Phase 2   Phase 3   Phase 4   Phase 5

(ii)

(i)

(iii)

(iv)

(v)

(a)

Fig. 8.28. Development of diaphragm wall excavation rigs 1950s–1960s: (a) (i) Icos tripod rig; (ii) action of Else bucket scraper; (iii) excavation with bucket scraper; (iv) hydraulic grab, Kelly mounted; (v) rock chisel

panel under the slurry and alternatively grab the arisings and chisel again. Progress was slow and vibration often quite severe in strong rock. In exceptional cases rotary core barrettes were drilled successively into the rock along each panel under the slurry, and both Icos and Soletanche developed rigs incorporating percussive chiselling with direct or reverse slurry circulation to remove cuttings.

The introduction of a rail-mounted reverse circulation rig for excavation in soil and soft rock by the Tone Boring Company of Japan in the late 1970s was followed by the development of reverse circulation equipment known as the Hydrofraise by Soletanche. In the mid 1980s Bauer and Casagrande produced similar equipment. The Bauer Trenchcutter has been developed into smaller, more manoeuvrable rigs known as City Cutters and more recently, Mini Cutters. In turn, the Hydrofraise has been made more compact for city sites in joint development between Soletanche and Rodio to produce the HL 4000 track-mounted rig. Diaphragm wall rigs developed between the 1950s and 1990s are illustrated in Fig. 8.28. The improved manoeuvrability of the Bauer City Cutter rig is shown in Fig. 8.29.

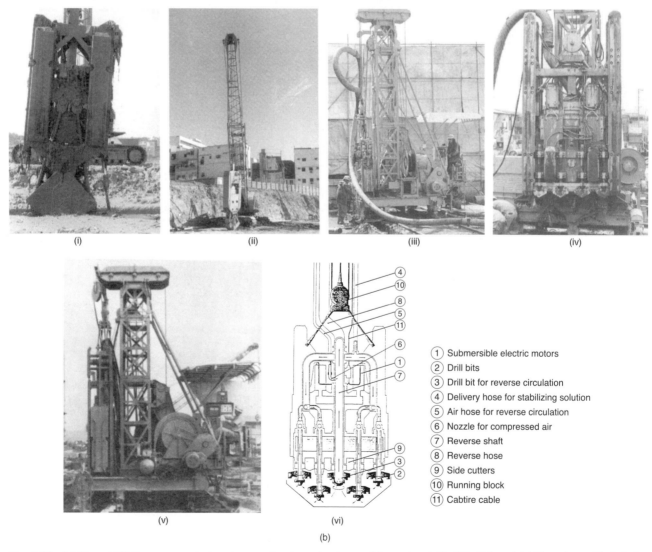

(i)   (ii)   (iii)   (iv)

(v)   (vi)

(b)

1. Submersible electric motors
2. Drill bits
3. Drill bit for reverse circulation
4. Delivery hose for stabilizing solution
5. Air hose for reverse circulation
6. Nozzle for compressed air
7. Reverse shaft
8. Reverse hose
9. Side cutters
10. Running block
11. Cabtire cable

Fig. 8.28. (b) (i) and (ii) Crane-mounted grabs; mechanism of submersible motor drill; (iii), (iv) and (v) Tone Long Wall Drill; (vi) Tone Long Wall Drill: vertical section through cutter

Fig. 8.28. (c) (i) Tone
Electro-Mill Drill; (ii) Bauer BC
30 Trench Cutter rig;
(iii) Bauer MBC 30 Trench
Cutter rig

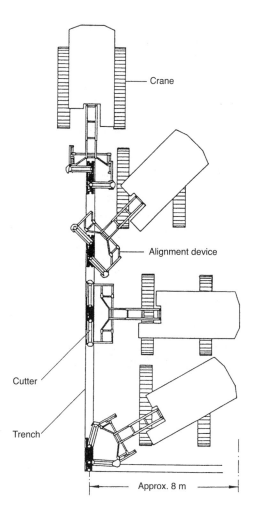

Crane

Alignment device

Cutter

Trench

Approx. 8 m

Fig. 8.29. Bauer City Cutter rig: use of alignment device on small base machine to improve manoeuvrability in limited space

Excavation for diaphragm walls is currently made by a variety of rigs depending on job size, wall depth and soil and rock properties. The reverse circulation machines have the added qualities of silent and vibration-free excavation through a wide range of soils and rocks but, even so, conventional crane-mounted rope grabs are frequently used for walls of moderate depth on small to medium sized jobs. Heavy mechanical grabs up to 9 tonnes in weight are favoured for smaller, shallower basements particularly in cohesive soils. The recent re-introduction of hydraulic grabs by Bauer and others, rope mounted, has accompanied the use of electronic monitoring to improve installation tolerances. The usefulness of rams to allow steerage of these rope suspended hydraulic grabs is less certain.

Cutter reverse circulation rigs saw two significant developments in the early 1990s: the use of rock roller bits on the vertical cutter wheels to allow more efficient excavation in moderately strong and strong rocks, and the construction of a compact, low-headroom rig known as the MBC 30 Trench Cutter. This rig (Fig. 8.30) has its own carrier system mounted on a railway bogie or on crawlers, so a conventional crane is not needed to carry the cutter. The overall dimensions of the complete unit are reduced to 4·7 m long, 4·1 m wide and 5·0 m high (6·0 m high when crawler mounted). Trench widths vary from 640 to 1500 mm; the standard trench length is 2790 mm; and the maximum cutting depth is 55 m.

Excavation in rock for diaphragm walls still remains arduous and expensive. Mention should be made of a practice, typically in Hong Kong, of

Fig. 8.30. Bauer MBC 30 Trench Cutter rig

underpinning deep diaphragm walls where formation level is below rock head, using shear piles drilled through the diaphragm wall, often bundles of T50 rebar, to support the wall in the temporary condition. Figure 8.31 shows a cross section.

The cutters of a modern Soletanche rig, in this instance for a 1500 mm wide wall, are shown in Fig. 8.32.

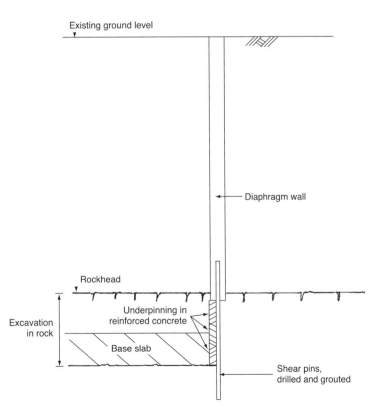

Fig. 8.31. Underpinning of diaphragm wall for excavation of formation level below rockhead; typical Hong Kong practice

Fig. 8.32. Cutters for a modern Soletanche cutter rig (courtesy Soletanche–Bachy)

In a recent paper, Guillaud and Hamelin[41] reviewed the development of diaphragm wall excavation plant during the 1990s and beyond, to 2002. They describe the early sites as cluttered areas, with noisy machines, a liberal covering of slurry over ground surfaces and nearby streets, and long road closures. Such sites should no longer remain; modern, compact low-noise machines and similar slurry treatment equipment have allowed environmentally friendly diaphragm wall excavation to greater depths with greater accuracy. Guillaud and Hamelin review excavation under two headings, cutters for continuous excavation and hydraulic or mechanical grabs, rope or Kelly suspended (or a combination of both). For cutters they refer to recent Soletanche/Bachy cutter developments, referring to the HC03 machine, particularly for confined, city jobs requiring less than 5 m headroom. Despite its 90 tonne weight it can excavate to 50 m depth (see Fig. 8.33(a)). The leading details of this machine are as follows:

- diesel engine delivery 370 kW at 2400 rpm
- max hydraulic pressure 32 MPa
- max depth 50 m
- max torque 80 kNm at 32 MPa
- suction pump: 450 m^3/hr
- max pressure on tool 25 tonnes
- total weight 93 tonnes
- cutter drums 650, 800, 1000 and 1200 mm
- excavated length 2400 mm or 2800 mm.

Regarding noise emissions, the noise from the HC03 is no more than 72 dB in the cab and 80 dB within a hemisphere of 16 m radius.

(a)

(b)

Fig. 8.33. (a) Modern Hydrofraise rig, type HC03 (courtesy Soletanche–Bachy); (b) modern Evolution Hydrofraise rig (courtesy Soletanche–Bachy)

For deep diaphragm walls, the Evolution Hydrofraise rig (see Fig. 8.33(b)) digs to 70 m depth. Other rigs, capable of excavation to more than 100 m display the same accuracy, reliability and ease of erection as the smaller machines. (The Hydrofraise used in 1997 by Obayasti Corp. at Nagoya to build a buried LNG tank inside a circular diaphragm wall, 1·8 m thick weighed 245 tonnes.)

Fig. 8.34. Swivelling hydraulic grab, type KS 3000 (courtesy Soletanche–Bachy)

Developments to grabs are shown in the Soletanche–Bachy KS 3000 (see Fig. 8.34), a swivelling hydraulic grab mounted on a hydraulic crane which also powers the grab. The rig is very compact and can operate very close to existing walls. Steerable grabs are used on the latest variants.

Both grab and Hydrofraise machines benefit from an automatic control and reporting system called SAKSO. This system has three stages of automation: manual (operator in full control); teaching (operator tells the system what movements to make); and automatic (system repeats movements learnt). The movements are fourfold: jib orientation, jib angle, grab orientation, hose winder retract. The real-time monitoring systems of cutters and grabs now include features to include not only deflection on the XX and YY axes, but also rotation about the ZZ axis (corkscrewing) and deviation from the vertical (drift).

Practical design and construction of diaphragm walls

A number of items require consideration in the pre-planning and design of diaphragm wall works.

(a) *Panel size.* The panel length will vary from a minimum of one grab bite to a multiple of grab bites typically 6 to 7 m preferably made up of a number of whole bites with smaller widths between them. Grab bites vary between 2·3 and 2·8 m. The panel length will include two stop ends for the initial (primary) panels, or one stop end for mixed panels dug next to a completed panel. Secondary panels are those dug between two previously concreted panels. Cut joints can be used with cutter rigs, and are particularly advantageous for deep walls. Views of the surfaces of a cut joint from a test panel are shown in Fig. 8.35. The length of the panels must first be assessed on the basis of panel stability (DIN Standard 4126[42] gives methods of assessing panel stability for varying subsoils and surcharge loadings). It is necessary to limit panel length, and hence panel volume, to ensure that concrete outputs are sufficient to fill the panel within a reasonable period taking maximum daily working hours into account. Panels of modest depth can often be dimensioned to ensure excavation of one panel each day (say a 20 m deep panel 4·5 m long dug in stiff clay with no obstructions at an average of 5·5 m^2 per hour, rope grab excavation for 10 hr, one daily

Fig. 8.35. Surfaces of cut joint from test panel

shift). Such an arrangement gives output a rhythm. Panel size is therefore a decision for the specialist contractor.

(*b*) *Excavation sequence.* The sequence of excavation to the basement walls is planned to minimize rig movement and avoid moving pipework from panel to panel. Where stage completions of the peripheral walls are agreed, or where top-downwards construction encourages simultaneous use of the site by both superstructure and substructure contractors, detailed programming must allow access to panels for rigs, muck-away trucks or slurry removal vehicles, service cranes and concrete trucks, and allow curing of concrete in complete panels prior to adjacent mixed or secondary panels.

(*c*) *Panel stability.* Working platform levels must be selected with an awareness of the minimum differential between the head of bentonite slurry in the panel excavation and groundwater level next to the panel. The minimum value to ensure stability is 1·0 m, and many specialists would specify a preference for 1·5 m, especially where groundwater flows in permeable strata.

(*d*) *Guide trench construction.* The standard of diaphragm wall construction is itself influenced by standards of temporary guide wall construction. The guide walls must be sufficiently robust to avoid movement due to loads from excavation rigs, service cranes or reinforcement cages and reaction from stop end jacking systems. Reusable precast concrete guide wall sections have been successfully used on T-shaped panels and cellular walls but each precast unit must be interlocked by a bolted mechanical joint to ensure the same standard of rigidity as in situ concrete walls. It is essential to maintain continuity between in situ guide wall pours by reinforcement passing through the construction joints.

(*e*) *Wall–slab construction joints.* Joints between basement rafts and diaphragm wall, and between intermediate basement floors and wall, can transmit vertical shear or, where necessary, bending moment. Alternative forms of joint construction are shown in Fig. 8.36. Threaded-end couplers (such as Lenton couplers) can be used to develop the full strength of reinforcement bars from within a recess in the face of the

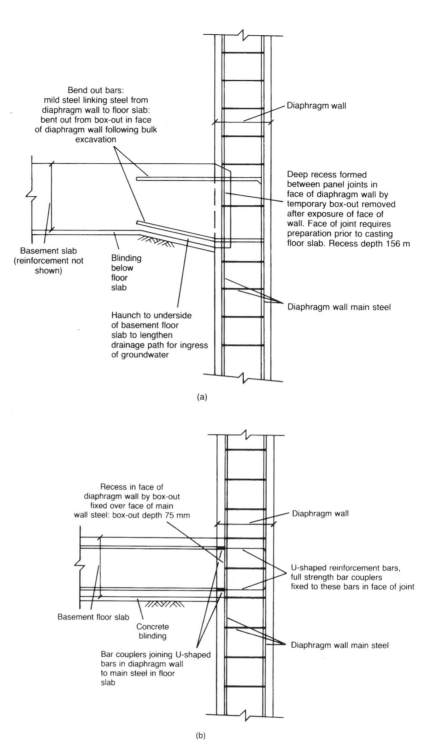

Fig. 8.36. Vertical cross-sections of typical horizontal joints between diaphragm wall and basement floor slab: (a) to achieve resistance to groundwater ingress and transmission of vertical shear; (b) moment connection by couplers

Dimensions of box-out in face of diaphragm wall are dependent upon construction tolerances for location of box-out. If these tolerances are ignored when box-out dimensions are selected, substantial waste may be needed in cutting new box-out shape to house floor slab after exposure of face of diaphragm wall

diaphragm wall at the junction with the slab. Bend out bars can be used instead of couplers, although the closeness of the bar spacing and the diameter of these bars may be limited by the ability to house them in the face of the joint.

(f) *Box-outs.* The depth of box-out will normally be limited to the concrete cover on the main reinforcement. Although polystyrene is used as a

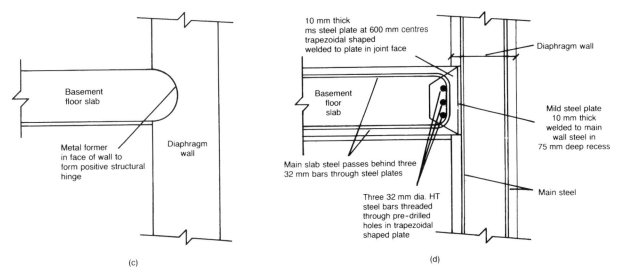

Fig. 8.36. (c) Variation for a structural hinge; (d) Variation for structural continuity

box-out material there is a risk that the box-out will be displaced unless a timber frame with a thin plywood cover secured to the front to ensure its rigidity is used to contain the polystyrene. It is usually a disadvantage to extend the depth of the box-out behind the vertical reinforcement due in part to the difficulty of adequate preparation of this face of the joint but particularly because of the risk of entrapment of heavy slurry below the box out during concreting.

(g) *Reinforcement cage and density.* It is unwise to allow the requirements of calculated shear, moment or crack width to make the spacing of horizontal binders and vertical main steel too small. DIN Standard 4126[42] advises that to ensure no slurry inclusions remain in the concrete, the differences between the flow resistances in adjoining zones in plan in the panel should be kept as small as possible. Minimum spacing of bars for both single- and double-layer vertical steel and horizontal binders is reproduced in Fig. 8.37.

The increasing depth of walls and the higher calculated flexural strengths required from them has led to cages of considerable tonnage. These cages are usually joined in sections over the panel using couplers to join bars in each section. A cage awaiting the arrival of the next section is shown in Fig. 8.38. The vertical bars are staggered to avoid couplers forming a block to concrete flow at one level. Cages are sometimes fabricated off-site in sections and transported to site overnight (see Fig. 8.39). The maximum panel length may be restricted because of transport although multiple cages may be used to allow an economical panel length. Total cage weights of jointed sections for deep walls may demand very large craneage for the final lift into the panel. A 90 tonne weight cage is shown during final insertion into the panel in Fig. 8.40.

(h) *Tremie operation.* Reinforcement cage detailing must allow sufficient vertical access for tremie tubes. Very small single-grab bite panels can only accommodate a single tremie tube, and even with almost continuous concrete supply from truck mixers it is difficult to obtain an average pour rate greater than $40\,m^3$ per hour. For larger panels a second tremie pipe can be used and with continuous concrete delivers a concreting rate between 60 and $80\,m^3$ per hour. In deep, large, T-shaped panels it may be necessary to use three tremies to maintain a uniform upper surface to the concrete as the pour continues, but generally two tremies are sufficient.

Clear flow width e_1 and clear spacing between reinforcing bars e_2 in cm

Line	Maximum liquid limit τ_F, in N/m², during concreting	Clear flow width and clear spacing for a diaphragm wall used as a			
		permanent structure		temporary structure	
		e_1	e_2	e_1	e_2
1	10	5	7	3	5
2	30	7	9	4	6
3	50	10	12	6	8
4	70*	—	—	8	10

* A τ_F value exceeding 50 N/m² is not permitted for permanent structures. The dimensions e_1 and e_2 shall apply in the case of a maximum particle size of the concrete aggregate not exceeding 32 mm; for larger aggregate particles up to 63 mm, the dimensions shall be increased by a factor of 1·5.

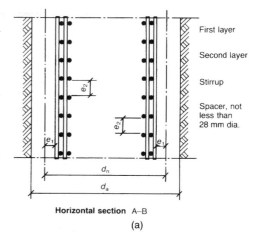

Horizontal section A–B

(a)

Rules from DIN 4126 for cover and reinforcement spacing to diaphragm walls

DIN 4126 states that diaphragm walls shall be designed to ensure that the concrete can flow around the reinforcement and inserts and fill the entire space within the trench. To avoid slurry inclusions it requires that flow resistances in adjoining zones of the wall plan shape should be kept as small as possible.

Concrete cover

To ensure sufficient concrete cover, a minimum clear flow width e_1 (see (a)) shall be maintained between the outer edge of the reinforcement and the outer edge of the excavating tool. Depending on the liquid limit (as defined in DIN 4126) of the slurry intermediate values may be linearly interpolated. The clear distance between the reinforcement and the bottom of the trench shall be not less than 20 cm.

Reinforcement system

Concentration of reinforcement shall be avoided. Minimum clear spacing e_2 between vertical reinforcing bars (see (b)) shall be observed. Where a second layer of reinforcement is used, these bars shall be fitted behind the bars of the first layer in such a way that a free path with a minimum spacing of e_2 is left clear. Spacers not less than 28 mm in diameter shall be provided to form a gap between the first and second vertical reinforcing layer.

At joints between vertical reinforcing bars (see (c)) with a single-layer vertical reinforcement system the minimum spacing e_2 may be reduced by d (diameter of the bar). In the case of a two-layer reinforcement system, the minimum spacing shall be maintained in full. A minimum clear spacing of twice e_2 for horizontal reinforcement shall, as a rule, be maintained. In exceptional cases, such as in the immediate vicinity of concentrated loading, the minimum spacing may be reduced up to $0·7e_2$

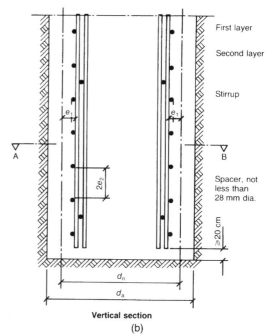

Vertical section

(b)

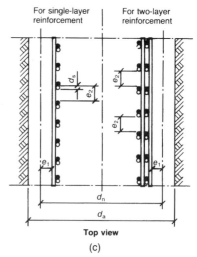

Top view

(c)

Fig. 8.37. Minimum spacing and concrete cover to reinforcement in diaphragm walls as recommended by DIN standard 4126[42]

Fig. 8.38. Reinforcement cage in panel excavation awaiting jointing with a further cage length

Fig. 8.39. Cage transportation

(i) *Concreting rate.* In the Author's view there is considerable risk of poor panel concrete when concreting rates drop below 15 to 20 m³ per hour per tremie. Even when concrete mix quality varies from the optimum, a high rate of concreting may be sufficient to displace the slurry, scour the surface of the reinforcement bars and flow between the reinforcement and around the box-outs. Where the density of reinforcement bar is high, and especially with multi-layers of bars, a high concreting rate and a very workable cohesive concrete are essential.

(j) *Slurry reuse.* The earliest diaphragm wall jobs by Icos did not have the equipment to clean bentonite slurry after excavation and concreting. The slurry was used once and, after storage for much of the pour volume, was carted from site in road tankers or, on the earliest jobs, pumped into public sewers. With the advent of reverse circulation

Fig. 8.40. Heavy cage during final lowering into panel. In this panel, two cages have been used in separate vertical sections

rigs which used large quantities of slurry to excavate each panel, cleaning technology from the oil industry was used to design and build shaker screens, hydrocyclones and at a later date, centrifuges and presses, to clean the slurry. Compact, transportable units were made which could be brought to site and quickly mobilized for use. Nowadays, slurry is cleaned and reused as a matter of routine on virtually all diaphragm wall works to clean bentonite slurry where either grab or reverse circulation rigs are used.

(k) *Stop ends and extraction.* Initially, tubular steel stop ends were used to form semi-circular joints between diaphragm wall panels. This practice, popular with Icos, the originator, and other European firms, gradually changed as rectangular formers gained acceptance. Both types of stop end were extracted as the concrete at the bottom of the panel started to set and gain strength. In very large pours, it was necessary to use high dosages of retarder additive within the concrete to ensure that the set was delayed. Even so, extraction of the stop ends often began before the concrete pour had been completed. Types of vertical panel joints are shown in Fig. 8.41. With the advent of reverse circulation rigs with vertically mounted cutter wheels, it became possible to cut the vertical surface at the end of a concreted panel during excavation of the adjacent panel. This cutting back of the concrete surface avoided the use of temporary formers, and the new concrete in the second panel could be poured against a true vertical surface on the first panel. This procedure has since become less favoured because of the risk of heavy, calcium-contaminated slurry remaining near the cut surface,

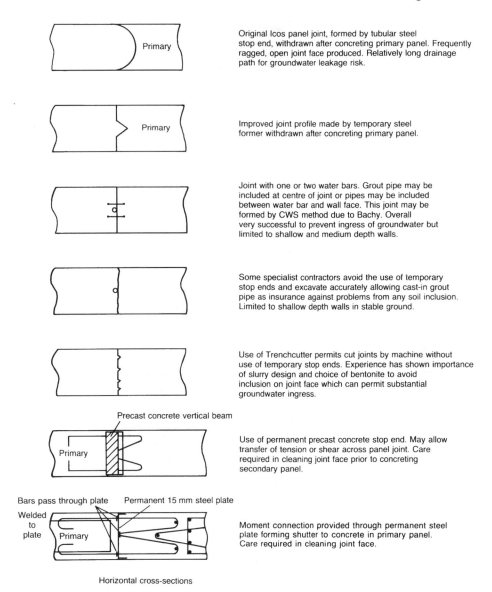

Original Icos panel joint, formed by tubular steel stop end, withdrawn after concreting primary panel. Frequently ragged, open joint face produced. Relatively long drainage path for groundwater leakage risk.

Improved joint profile made by temporary steel former withdrawn after concreting primary panel.

Joint with one or two water bars. Grout pipe may be included at centre of joint or pipes may be included between water bar and wall face. This joint may be formed by CWS method due to Bachy. Overall very successful to prevent ingress of groundwater but limited to shallow and medium depth walls.

Some specialist contractors avoid the use of temporary stop ends and excavate accurately allowing cast-in grout pipe as insurance against problems from any soil inclusion. Limited to shallow depth walls in stable ground.

Use of Trenchcutter permits cut joints by machine without use of temporary stop ends. Experience has shown importance of slurry design and choice of bentonite to avoid inclusion on joint face which can permit substantial groundwater ingress.

Use of permanent precast concrete stop end. May allow transfer of tension or shear across panel joint. Care required in cleaning joint face prior to concreting secondary panel.

Moment connection provided through permanent steel plate forming shutter to concrete in primary panel. Care required in cleaning joint face.

Fig. 8.41. Types of vertical panel joint used in diaphragm waling, shown in horizontal section

which could contaminate the concrete within the second panel, near the vertical joint. This slurry-contaminated concrete often proved to be porous and led to leakage of groundwater into the basement after excavation. The CWS-type stop end former developed by Bachy incorporates single, twin or triple water bars cast into the vertical joint and is released from the vertical surface of the concrete pour after the concrete has hardened during excavation of the second panel. This type of joint (and its derivatives by competing specialist firms) has now gained widespread useage where resistance to groundwater penetration is needed. The CWS joint details are shown in Fig. 8.42. Examples of CWS joint construction for a 1·5 m wide wall, 55 m deep with a double water bar are shown in Fig. 8.43. A temporary plywood former was used on the CWS stop end to facilitate its removal.

Recent developments in diaphragm wall works
Since the conception by Veder of reinforced concrete walls cast into trenches dug under bentonite slurry, and development of the process by Icos and others, there have been many improvements in both application and

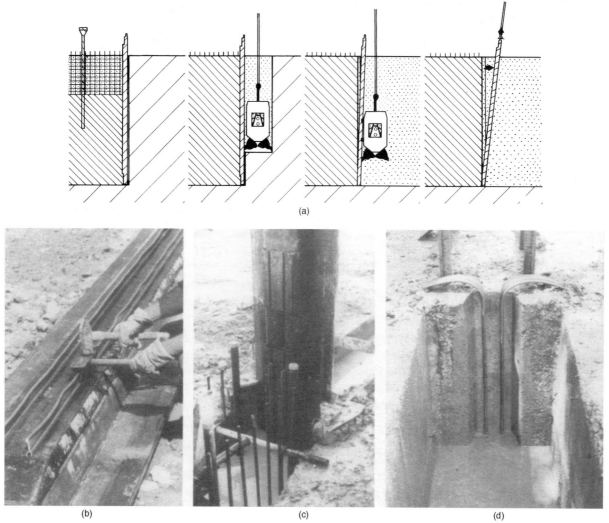

(a)

(b)   (c)   (d)

Fig. 8.42. CWS joint detail: (a) pulling out stop end sideways after excavation of the adjacent panel; (b) stop end blades installed in the CWS joint; (c) CWS joint before concreting; (d) CWS joint with water stop installed (courtesy of Soletanche–Bachy)

mechanical plant. Developments reviewed by Puller and Puller[43] in 1992 and since in terms of plant innovation by Guillaud and Hamelin[41] are as follows:

(*a*) the use of polymeric slurries for excavation support, avoiding effects of some contaminants, reducing pumping energy, avoiding wall cake thickness, reducing slurry disposal costs

(*b*) the development of structurally efficient diaphragm wall plan shapes based on improved joint efficiency between panels

(*c*) the use of post-tensioned diaphragm walls, either precast or cast in situ

(*d*) the use of precast concrete diaphragm walls

(*e*) the use of reverse circulation excavation equipment such as the Hydrofraise and Trenchcutter rigs

(*f*) the development of excavation equipment for work on congested sites

(*g*) improved design of mechanical grabs

(*h*) the development and use of electronic monitoring in grabs and cutters to improve panel excavation tolerances and overall quality control standards

(*i*) the development of improved stearage of cutters and hydraulic grabs

Fig. 8.43. CWS joint fabrication for a 55 m deep panel joint

(*j*)   the development of improved stop end design; use of CWS joints
(*k*)   improved standards of slurry cleaning and quality control of slurry during use.

Items (*a*) and (*b*) are reviewed in more detail below; the remainder are referred to elsewhere in this chapter and in Chapters 4 and 9.

While the original use of bentonite slurry to support diaphragm wall excavations has generally persisted for excavations made by grab, the larger quantities of slurry required for circulation purposes with Hydrofraise and Trenchcutter equipment have brought innovation to slurry design. Using experience from the oil drilling industry, polymeric slurries and mixes of polymeric and bentonite slurries have been used successfully on larger diaphragm wall jobs where the economies of scale have proved beneficial.

Polymeric slurry behaves as a pseudo-plastic fluid and, unlike bentonite slurry, acts in trench support without forming a filter cake. Within the polymeric slurry a molecular lattice structure, which is different from the thixotropic gel structure of a natural clay slurry, is built up after mixing.

The polymeric structure is more efficient in the suspension and transportation of soil particles and leads to reduced energy costs in pumping from excavation to slurry station on the job site. As fluid loss from polymeric slurries is less than that from bentonite slurries, the polymeric slurry can be used with advantage in weak soils where an increase in soil moisture content would cause risk of panel instability. Polymeric slurries cost considerably more than bentonite slurry, but since, with care, the slurry is reusable many times, disposal costs partly compensate for the high initial cost. The rheology of bentonite slurries was discussed by Rogers[44], and the merits of polymeric slurries were reviewed by Beresford *et al.*[45]

Icos began innovations in joint design to enable wall panels to be incorporated into rectilinear and arch plan shapes in the late 1960s. At Redcar, UK, diaphragm wall panels were joined by tension connections to form cellular structures to a new harbour wall. In plan, each of the cells measured 30 m by 15 m. In plan, an inverted arch of diaphragm wall panels was restrained by the tensile resistance of cross-walls, also in panels which, in turn, were anchored to a rear arch of panels. The weight of the soil enclosed within the cells was not used to restrain the wall in overturning because the panel joints could not transmit vertical shear, only tension[46].

Developments by Bachy have led to patented joint forms that develop either full flexural continuity from panel to panel (known as the Teba system) or shear between adjacent panels. The first option, to develop a continuous wall, is based on the use of hydraulic jacks cast within the panel concrete

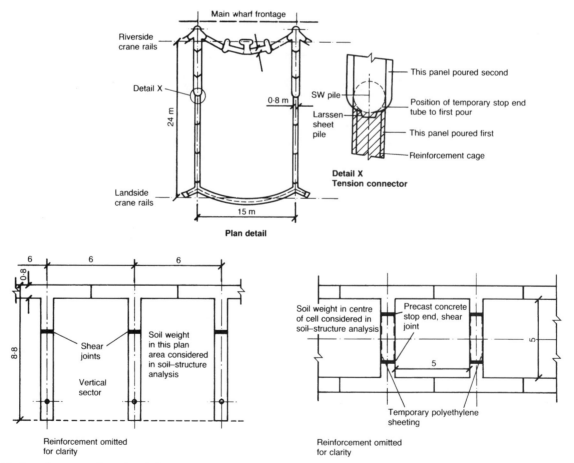

Fig. 8.44. *Development of continuity between diaphragm wall panels to achieve improved, structurally efficient wall plan forms*[43]

and near the panel joint. After concreting, these jacks are actuated and rods are thrust horizontally from the cast concrete to provide continuity with the reinforcement of the adjacent panel subsequent to excavation and concreting. The method is rarely used and only finds application on special projects because of the cost implications of the jack system.

The use of joints to transmit shear, however, has wider application and more scope for development with methods of interactive soil-structure analysis. The construction of walls from large T-shaped and H-shaped diaphragm wall panels joined by shear connection enables the full flexural strength of the multi-panel plan shape to be realized and, in addition, can utilize the stabilizing effect of the weight of soil encapsulated between the legs of the T-units or within the enclosed cellular areas formed by a series of H-panels. The use of such plan shapes to form semi-gravity structures, shown in Fig. 8.44, may only be justified in terms of economy where bracing or anchoring of a basement wall is not possible and single-wall construction has insufficient flexural strength to cope with high imposed cantilever moments and shears. The wall area in T-shaped or cellular panel construction is not cost-effective in terms of the linear wall unless special support constraints apply. Figure 8.45(a) shows development in joint construction to transmit full continuity, shears and tension. The use of shear joints, however, to form a diaphragm wall of varied castellated plan shape can be very cost-effective as a deep unpropped cantilever for a very large basement providing the plan area occupied by this wall can be accommodated in the site space. The flexural efficiency of the castellated shape is shown in Fig. 8.45(b).

The use of semi-gravity structures may be justified where soil and wall movement is critical. Such movements can be effectively minimized by the use of a stiff wall structure and the gravity effect of the weight of soil retained within the cells. One of the largest structural diaphragm wall contracts completed to date utilized semi-gravity cellular plan form jointed diaphragm wall panels for a large underground car park in Medinah, Saudi Arabia, in the

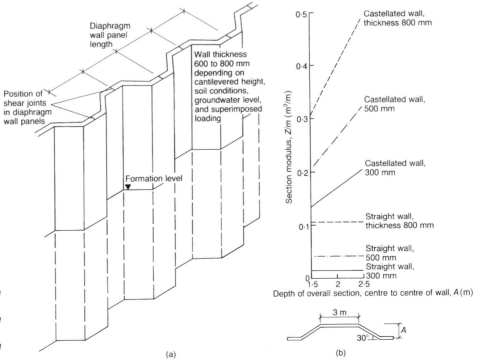

Fig. 8.45. Diaphragm wall built to castellated plan shape: (a) typical layout; (b) plot of section modulus of castellated section against overall depth of section showing improvements to flexural strength compared with a straight wall

Fig. 8.46. Medinah car park: views of unobstructed excavation supported by cellular diaphragm wall

early 1990s. The total area of structural wall exceeded $320\,000\,\mathrm{m}^2$ to provide the exterior walls to an excavation approximately 18 m deep from the ground surface, 100 m wide and more than 1·5 km in total length. Views of the completed diaphragm walls are shown in Fig. 8.46. The site for the car park lies in the centre of a bowl of washdown soils, mainly silty sands and clayey silts from surrounding mountains. The depth to basaltic bedrock over the site area varied from 23 to 55 m. The groundwater level had been monitored over a period of two years prior to construction and showed some variation with time. The average level during construction was 2 m above final excavation level.

The client's brief was to provide a basement construction with a design life of 120 years, which could be excavated without the impediment of cross-bracing, raking shores or temporary berms, and would give the minimum of soil movement behind the walls and, in the long term, below the lowest basement level in the car park. Precious historic structures were sited 20 m from the excavated face of the basement wall and neither noise nor vibration could be tolerated. A cellular diaphragm wall construction was adopted, propped by two basement floors in the permanent condition but acting as a cantilever in the two-year construction period. The cellular wall shown in plan in Fig. 8.47 was adopted using vertical rock anchors into the basalt at the rear of the wall to achieve stability during construction where bedrock was shallow, but where bedrock exceeded 35 m in depth the cellular wall was allowed to cantilever during the construction period.

The use of the cellular wall was justified on the basis of its stiffness to reduce wall and soil movement and the opportunity it gave to undertake unimpeded bulk excavation to the basement with staged handovers of large working areas. Alternative designs using ground anchors, bored piles and T-shaped diaphragm wall panels were considered but were precluded by the predicted soil movement and the relative inefficiency of ground anchoring in the Medinah silts and clays.

To construct the H-shaped cellular diaphragm wall units, three separate panels were excavated and cast using precast concrete permanent stop ends in the construction of the central web panel. Concrete was poured into the central web excavation enclosed within a bag of plastic sheeting to avoid leakage around the stop end which would reduce the effectiveness of the shear and tension bond to the outer panels. The use of plastic sheeting as a temporary measure proved effective in retaining all the concrete within the web panel. The use of projecting reinforcement from one panel to the next had been developed in France and Japan, but its application had been limited;

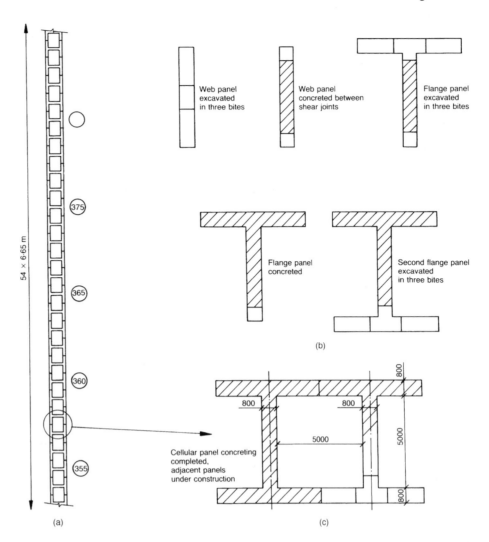

Fig. 8.47. Medinah car park, cellular wall construction: (a) plan of cellular wall construction; (b) construction procedure for single wall unit; (c) wall unit construction adjacent to completed unit

at Medinah, however, the precast joints were used successfully more than 1000 times with only five minor collapses. Construction of the central web panel cage is shown in Figs. 8.48 and 8.49.

The rate of diaphragm wall production on this contract was impressive. The soil conditions, which varied from medium strength silts and clays to stiff and hard clayey silts, were conducive to grab excavation but were less economically excavated by cutter rigs until excavation depths increased below 20 m or so. Three cutter rigs and up to five rope grabs were used on a 24-hour, 6-day week basis. Concreted panel production averaged more than 4000 m^2 per week over much of the two-year wall construction period and reached 7000 m^2 per week over several weeks at peak production.

The Medinah cellular wall was designed using a two-dimensional analysis of the soil–wall structure taking into account non-linear elastic–plastic soil conditions. Soil movement and stress levels in the surrounding soils were predicted for the modelled excavation stages by finite element analysis, taking into account the dissipation of negative pore-water pressure with time for varying depths of rockhead and groundwater. The analysis methods were those described by Jardine et al.[47] The structure deformation results from the two-dimensional analysis were then used with a three-dimensional structural program to predict stress levels and design reinforcement within the cellular wall. This work was incomplete because the analysis did not

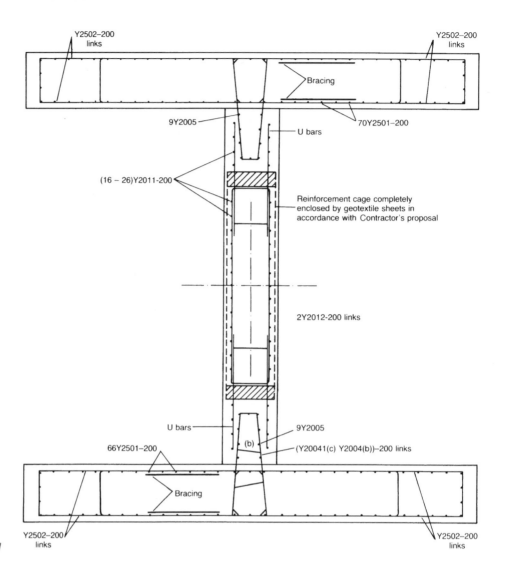

Fig. 8.48. Medinah car park: cellular wall detail showing reinforcement and permanent stop ends to central web panel

include the deformations within the soil and the resulting changes in soil stress levels caused by excavation of the diaphragm wall panel itself. It had been realized prior to the Medinah design that accurate prediction of soil movement and stress adjacent to a completed diaphragm wall basement excavation had to include installation effects of the diaphragm wall panel during panel excavation and concreting. The effects of concreting on in situ soil stress had been shown[48] in measurements which concluded that induced stress caused by the pressure of wet concrete within the diaphragm panel, and the resulting soil deformation, discouraged the use of low earth pressure coefficients in wall design. More recently Lings *et al.*[49] referred to placing temperatures within the concrete as an important influence on wet concrete pressure.

A number of published results of soil movement caused by panel excavation tend to show small horizontal soil movements near the panel, rapidly reducing at short distances equal to the panel length, say, from the panel. Measurements made at Medinah confirm this. (The exception to these generally small movements were those observed during diaphragm wall construction for the Hong Kong Metro. The decomposed granite residual soil conditions in Hong Kong are quite different from those where the other measurements of soil deformation adjacent to panel excavation were made. It was concluded that the cause of the large soil movements in Hong Kong

(a)

Fig. 8.49. Medinah car park:
(a) fabrication of web panel with
permanent precast concrete
stop-ends to cellular wall;

was the presence of a soil with high swell potential, high permeability and a high groundwater table.) Finite element modelling of installation effects by Gunn et al.[50] showed promise in predicting soil movement and stress during panel excavation.

The Medinah soil–structure analysis to predict deformed wall shape and soil movement was only partly successful because of the difficulty of modelling the shear stiffness of a three-dimensional structure in plane strain and the oversimplification of ignoring panel installation movement and stress in the

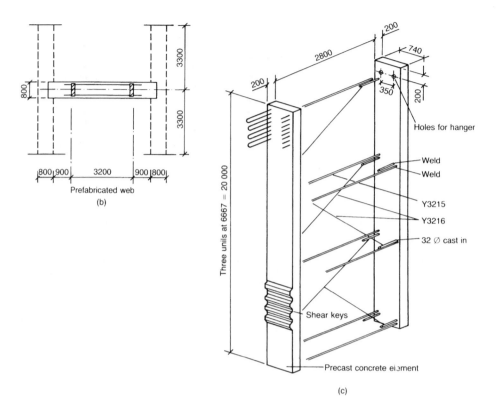

Fig. 8.49. (b) Key plan of one element; (c) isometric of web panel

subsoil. The maximum predicted horizontal soil movement of 27·5 mm after bulk excavation for the deepest cantilever walls was not reached, the total observed maximum horizontal deformation for both panel and bulk excavation for the cellular wall being less than 20 mm, allowing for dissipation of pore pressure with time.

Composite walls and grouting techniques

Mention should be made of the use of diaphragm walls, either precast or in situ concrete construction, as part of a soil retention and groundwater control protection system incorporating non-structural slurry wall cut-offs and horizontal grout plugs over the plan area of the basement. Figure 8.50 shows examples of composite precast diaphragm walls incorporating temporary king post walls cast in the upper section of one wall. The use of jet grouting and intrusion grouting to form a horizontal grout plug to control the inflow of groundwater to excavations was discussed in Chapter 2.

Water resistance of structural diaphragm walls

The difference between expectation and the actual performance of diaphragm walls regarding water resistance has caused disappointment and dispute since the earliest structural walls in the 1950s and 1960s. Then, structural walls generally required the minimum of surface treatment to produce a dry face. Many of the earliest diaphragm wall basements in Paris and London were used for car parking and were either left without finishes or, at most, with an applied sand–cement render. Where leaks occurred these were sealed by application of surface chemical renderings such as Vandex or Xypex to make a crystalline waterproof coating to the wall. These walls, generally 600 or 800 mm thick, were excavated by rope grab or hydraulic grab (rope or Kelly mounted), and temporary tubular steel stop ends were used throughout. Only in basement construction where storage of perishable goods was

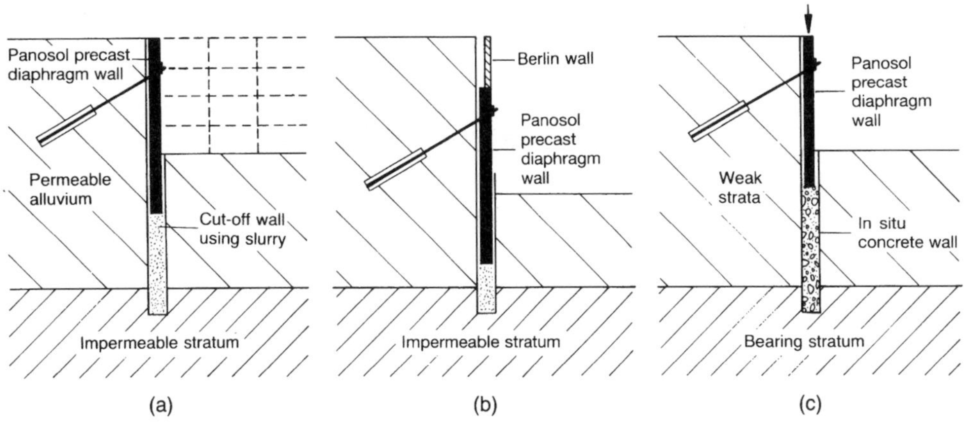

Fig. 8.50. Composite diaphragm wall construction using precast concrete wall sections: (a) anchored Panosol wall with slurry cut-off wall into an impermeable stratum; (b) anchored Panosol wall with temporary Berlin wall above and slurry cut-off wall below; (c) load-bearing anchored Panosol wall with concrete wall below, penetrating a bearing stratum at depth; (d) table of flexural strength of typical Panosol panel sections (courtesy of Soletanche–Bachy)

Thickenss of precast panel (m)	Maximum width of panel excavation (m)	Maximum moment of resistance (ton metre per metre)			
		f_{cu} = 25 MPa	f_{cu} = 27 MPa	f_{cu} = 30 MPa	f_{cu} = 35 MPa
0·20	0·52	6·8	7·5	8·7	10·8
0·25	0·52	12·0	13·3	15·4	19·1
0·30	0·52	18·7	20·8	24·1	29·9
0·40	0·62	36·7	40·7	47·3	58·5
0·50	0·82	60·6	67·3	78·1	96·7
0·60	0·82	90·7	100	117	144

(d)

planned, in shopping areas or office facilities, was a separate lining wall constructed.

In London, the earliest diaphragm walls were built by Icos from 1961 onwards. By 1974 a sufficient number of contracts had been completed to hold a keynote conference on diaphragm walling. At the conference, Sliwinski and Fleming[51] addressed the problem of water resistance:

It is therefore evident that the concrete used for diaphragm walls can for practical purposes be considered impermeable. However, in practice the permeability of a panel must also depend on the formation of cracks and on any local defects in the concrete such as may result from segregation but with normal concrete control and care, such occurrences should be limited to isolated cases. The simple butt joint between panels cannot be claimed to be proof against water entries but significant leakages are rare due to the presence of soil impregnated with bentonite behind the joint, and to the presence of some thin layer of contaminated bentonite at the edges of the joint. Where leaks occur they can usually be ascribed to differential deflexions between wall panels, and these differentials are worse near corners. The whole matter of deflexion differentials (and thereby risk of leakage) between wall panels depends on panel shape in plan, wall height, the use of anchors, excavation procedures and other factors. The present practice for dealing with damp joints is to allow the leak to appear, for the differential wall deflexion, for the most part, to take place, and then to inject cement or chemical grout into the soil at the back of the joint, either vertically or horizontally through drillings depending upon access. Alternatively, steel or other suitable plate, bedded on epoxy-resin mortar, can be bolted to the concrete over the internal face of the joint.

Sliwinski and Fleming continued to refer to panel deviations caused by obstructions due to concrete passing beyond the tubular stop ends, but did not refer to this as a risk of bad water resistance of the wall below basement excavation level. No reference was made to the occurrence of leaks at the junction of diaphragm wall and basement slab in basement or other construction.

The situation described by Sliwinski and Fleming provides a reasonable summary of the opinion of UK specialist firms in the early 1970s. BS 2004[52] stated:

> These joints are usually watertight but minor seepage through leaking joints can be dealt with by grouting or may even be tolerable in certain classes of structure.

Generally the attitude was optimistic, and risk of leakage was only considered after it had happened. The earliest model specification in the UK[53] did not refer to water resistance and typical paragraphs in tender letters by specialist contractors stated:

> The diaphragm walls will be constructed so as to be substantially watertight on initial exposure (free from running leaks but not damp proof) and we only accept responsibility for repairing leaks, within the exposed height, caused by faulty workmanship and/or materials. It should be noted that possible ingress of water into the excavation from below formation level is not prevented by the diaphragm walls.

Overall, specialist firms were relatively optimistic about the likely occurrence of leaks on jobs throughout the UK in a variety of soil conditions and for a range of basement uses. The risk of overbreak, panel collapse, loss of bentonite, displaced box-outs, inadequate excavation rates, etc. were all critical tender risk assessments for the specialist contractor, and wall waterproofness and the cost of associated remedial works were not considered as important as they are today. In the UK in the 1960s and 1970s, specialist firms were usually awarded diaphragm wall contracts on the basis of design-and-construct after technical discussion with a consulting engineer or architect. The contractual risk for waterproofness (apart from damp patches) generally remained firmly with the specialist contractor. By the end of the 1970s most major consultancy firms were designing and specifying diaphragm wall schemes themselves and the contracts were let on a construct-only basis. At this stage, the overall use of the underground structure was clear to the designer, who could incorporate measures such as non-load-bearing blockwork walls and drainage channels to hide any persistent ingress of groundwater.

The use of basement lining walls, cut-and-cover works and underpasses has continued in the UK, France and Germany. In some instances (Lyon Metro 1981, Eastbourne Pumping Station 1993) an in situ reinforced concrete lining has been specified by the engineer or owner to be capable of withstanding the full groundwater pressure acting on the wall.

As referred to previously, the guidance for water resisting design of basements is BS 8102[54] and CIRIA report 139[11]. The use of diaphragm walls in basements can comply with the water-resisting methods defined in documents in terms of method B structural integral protection and method C drained cavity construction. To address method A (an external waterproof membrane) specialist firms have sought over a period of some years to develop a diaphragm wall system to include an outer plastic liner to completely encapsulate the diaphragm wall. The method has had very little application on site and doubts remain regarding its efficiency.

The requirements of BS 8102 to comply with type C (drained protection) have become standard design principles for basement diaphragm wall work in the UK. Most basements are designed with a drained cavity construction and only those used for car parking have the option of exposed unclad diaphragm wall surfaces. Building owners are not prepared to allow unlined diaphragm walls (say for a basement for storage use) where there is reasonable chance of a change of use during the life of the basement. Current practice is therefore to make a drained cavity with a permanent pump provided at a sump at the lowest level. To make this provision, the design volume of the basement is reduced by the volume of the drainage cavity, the volume of the blockwork lining and the volume occupied by the verticality tolerance of the diaphragm walls (say for grabs 1:80 or 1:100), irrespective of whether this tolerance is used by the wall or not. It is widely acknowledged that this solution is uneconomic and often leads to a reduction in car parking spaces in basements where lining is used.

The use of lining walls does not automatically produce protected construction because faulty drainage cavities and drainage between basement floors often lead, over time, to damp blemishes on the exposed face of the lining because of leaks in the hidden diaphragm wall.

The current situation in the UK is this: the specialist contractor generally contracts to leave the exposed diaphragm wall free from running leaks (but not damp patches) and probably has half of the full retention money held against this for, say, twelve months from the end of the main contractor's contract. When leaks arise during this maintenance period the specialist contractor seals them by grouting and trusts that a final inspection at the end of the maintenance period will be the end of leakage responsibility.

The use of non-load-bearing lining walls in basements is similar in both Germany and the USA, although a slightly more optimistic view regarding the water-resisting efficiency of diaphragm walls may remain in France. The water resistance of structural diaphragm walls has been reviewed in some detail[55].

In the Author's experience, basement wall leakages occur at any of five locations:

- in the panel itself
- at vertical panel joints
- at horizontal bottom slab/wall joints
- at the top horizontal joint between panel and capping beam
- below formation level.

Each is now discussed in more detail.

(a) *The panel.* Leaks and damp areas in the panel are caused by soil or slurry inclusions, random cracking perhaps due to shrinkage, or poor quality concrete. Xanthakos[56] concluded:

> It is not difficult to produce walls with permeability of the order of 10^{-10} cm/s. Suppose a wall is 60 cm thick, retains a hydraulic head of 10 m and has a porosity of 15%; if we take into account a suction pressure of 1 atmosphere to assist water flow, the quantity of water percolating through the wall is close to 0·3 litre for 100 m^2 of wall surface over a period of 24 hours.

So if this estimate is correct and the concrete is sound and homogeneous, only very limited dampness should occur on the exposed surface due to concrete permeability.

If soil or slurry inclusions penetrate the full thickness of the wall in water-bearing ground their removal can be difficult and expensive. This matter is a particular risk in water-bearing silts of low strength. The density of reinforcement, the depth of wall, the size of box-outs and the thickness of the wall, concreting continuity and concrete fluidity will all influence the risk of slurry inclusions. The risk is increased by any obstruction to flow or tremied concrete and any disruption, time-wise, to the flow of fluid concrete. These risks are evident in thin, highly reinforced walls with box-outs. Entrapment of heavy slurry below congested, large-diameter reinforcement at slab/wall junctions are particular risk areas for slurry-contaminated concrete and leakage. Random cracking within panels seldom appears, and cracks are not necessarily continuous nor to full wall depth, but where they occur the cracks can cause running leaks. There is a possibility that the size of vertical reinforcing bars may influence shrinkage cracking in relatively thin walls.

There is risk of soil inclusion in weak silts and silty clays and in highly fissured over-consolidated clays, and panel length should be minimized in such soil conditions. Overall, poor water resistance resulting from soil or slurry inclusion may prove to be a high-cost risk because removal of the inclusion throughout the whole wall thickness may be essential for strength, durability and waterproofness requirements. This operation may prove to be costly both in remedial expense and contract delays.

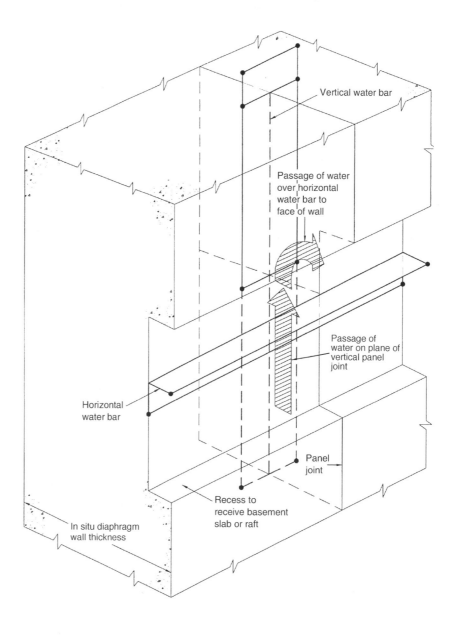

Fig. 8.51. Leakage path of groundwater between water bars at basement slab level, diaphragm wall construction

(b) *Vertical panel joints.* This is the area at greatest risk of leakage. The most likely causes of leakage are panel movement caused by bulk excavation or application of vertical load, or pre-stress of ground anchors, honeycombed concrete and poor concrete near the stop end due to inclusions. Leakages can also occur through slurry contaminated with calcium from concrete cut from the end of the adjacent panels, and through inclusions in joints where precast concrete stop ends are inadequately cleaned before concreting. The use of CWS joints to reduce the risk of leakage at vertical joints by the inclusion of one or more water bars has been shown to be effective. Nevertheless some leakage may occur due to the passage of water between the water bars as shown in Fig. 8.51.

(c) *Horizontal bottom slab/wall joints.* The next highest risk of leakage is the horizontal joint at the basement slab. Although such leaks are possibly a split responsibility between wall and slab constructors, precautions to avoid leakage are necessary in the wall design. The length of the leakage path from the underside to the top of the basement slab will be increased if the underside of the slab is haunched to an increased thickness adjacent to the junction with the wall. Special provision can be made by securing a horizontal L-section flexible water bar to the vertical wall surface within the slab box-out recess and connecting this to the slab water bar system. This precaution is not successful, however, unless the L-section water bar is connected to a water bar within the vertical panel joint. A continuous water bar system between wall and slab, in all horizontal and vertical joints, is expensive and success is not guaranteed. The provision of a continuous water bar system is more easily achieved in precast diaphragm wall construction than conventional in situ walls. The risk of heavy slurry entrapment referred to previously should be noted.

Where a groundwater head exists below the basement floor/diaphragm wall joint, it is essential that design provision is made to resist penetration. The practice of pouring slab concrete into a recess in the wall to receive the floor slab is simply not sufficient to ensure water resistance even if the vertical concrete floor slab surface within the recess is correctly prepared.

(d) *Top horizontal joint between panel and capping beam.* It is not unusual to find leakages in the horizontal joint at the top of a diaphragm wall with a capping beam or other in situ reinforced concrete where a high groundwater occurs or where rain water is allowed to pond in porous backfill to the capping beam/guide wall excavations. Such leakages can occur even when the top of the diaphragm wall is adequately cut down to remove porous concrete and the surface is correctly prepared. Although such work is essential, the provision of a Hydrotite water bar strip in the horizontal joint on the earth face would overcome the risk of water leakage.

(e) *Below formation level.* This risk is often ignored, although the financial consequences of wall leakage or even loss of ground where 'blow' symptoms occur are likely to be very significant. The standard tender clause used by some diaphragm wall specialists in the past has stated:

> We only accept responsibility for repairing leaks, within the exposed height, caused by faulty workmanship and/or materials.

The implication must be that the specialist contractor would not be responsible for faulty workmanship and/or materials below formation level in the area of highest risk. The clause was rarely queried by main contractors or their clients and presumably relieved the specialist contractor of considerable risk.

The obvious preventative measures for leakages all refer to standards of workmanship and quality control during diaphragm wall construction. The importance of design decisions, however, regarding wall thickness, permanent stop end construction and provision of water bars in panel joints, should not be ignored when risk of leakage below formation level is assessed.

Up to the 1990s the general level of acceptance of wall water resistance in the UK was based on the criterion that damp patches on the exposed wall surface would be accepted but running leaks would not, and grout or surface treatment would be accepted as a remedy. Documents such as the DIN standard 4126[42], the British Department of Transport's Specification for Highway Works[57], and the European Code Execution of Special Geotechnical Works: Diaphragm Walls[58], failed to make any reference to acceptable standards of water resistance.

The ICE Specification for Piling and Embedded Walls[59], a widely used standard specification together with a Particular Specification written for the individual contract, makes reference to water resistance, defined as 'water retention' but fails to define unacceptable leakage volumes or areas of dampness. The wording is as follows:

> The Contractor shall be responsible for the repair of any joint, defect or panel where on exposure of the wall visible running water leaks are found which would result in leakage per individual square metre in excess of that stated in the Particular Specifications. Any leak which results in a flow emanating from the surface of the retaining wall shall be sealed.

In France DTU 14.1[60] sets more definitive limits:

> The wall shall comply with the watertightness criteria of a lining wall to a relatively waterproof structure.

> The watertightness of the wall will be such that the flow of seepage and leaks is limited to
> For the whole of the outside walls in their entirety:
> 0.5 litre/m^2/day on yearly average
> 1.0 litre/m^2/day on weekly average
> For all areas of $10\,\text{m}^2$ of wall:
> 2.0 litre/m^2/day on weekly average.

These flows take account of the seepage flows at the joint of the raft to the wall. The limited exactness of the ICE Standard Specification is replaced by precise legal definitions of leakage standards in the French specification, although some difficulty may be experienced in measuring such quantities and applying them accurately.

A useful clause in use in the Middle East appears to strike a realistic specification:

> The diaphragm wall shall be watertight and substantially dry. Remedial measures shall be carried out as directed by the Engineer in areas that do not comply with this requirement. A panel will be considered acceptable if within any area 1 m square the total damp surface does not exceed 10% of that area. The Diaphragm Wall Contractor shall be responsible for the repair of any joint, where, on full exposure of the wall, leaks are found. Running leaks will not be accepted at any location.

It is the Author's opinion that specification clauses for water resistance of diaphragm wall works in general use are inadequate because they do not specify acceptance to adequate standards, they do not specify the method of repair and they do not approach the subject of waterproofness with the considerable importance and detail that it deserves. Several matters are ignored in the latest specifications. As an example, the building owner or tenant's interests are not served by the lack of consideration for leakages occurring after the contractual maintenance period by, say, rising groundwater, the failure of repairs to previous leaks, or movements between panels or basement floor joints due to long-term soil movement such as heave. Current specifications do not relieve the specialist contractor for leakage due to panel movements caused by application of superstructure loading or anchor stressing, matters that are frequently outside his control. The water bar system in the diaphragm wall should be specified by the designer. The wall system should be connected efficiently to the water bar system in the base slab, and should also be specified by the basement designer.

Overall, early optimism among specialist contractors in Italy, France and the UK has now been replaced by a realism that acknowledges that concrete tremied into a slurry in a series of panels will not automatically produce a dry basement. In Europe, internal lining walls are frequently used to avoid the effect of the groundwater ingress. Unfortunately, these internal walls cover up a continuing risk to the building owner and mask the occurrence of further leaks or deterioration in the repairs to the original leaks.

Overall stability: design for uplift

Where hydrostatic groundwater pressures, during construction and within the design life of the structure, are at a higher elevation than the underside of the lowest basement floor level, it is necessary to examine the overall stability of the basement. Failure due to the lack of buoyant self-weight of the basement, and insufficiency of frictional forces to avoid upward displacement of the basement substructure, are fortunately infrequent, but not unknown. Vertical anchoring of the basement raft to rock strata or strong soils below the basement becomes necessary where hydrostatic uplift is severe and such strata exist at economical depth. Drainage of a granular blanket or porous no-fines concrete with permanent pumping may prove necessary where anchoring is not feasible. The rise of groundwater within the design life of the structure should be carefully assessed after consideration of the dead weight of the structure at successive stages of superstructure construction, including final completion; a factor of safety of the order of 1·4 should be obtained for the sum of downward dead weight, total vertical downward anchoring force and frictional resistance to the basement walls compared with upward hydrostatic force on the basement underside. Where most of the downward force consists of dead weight a modified criterion may be used:

$$\text{Upward hydrostatic force} \leq \frac{\text{Dead weight}}{1\cdot1} + \frac{\text{Friction}}{3\cdot0}$$

Where diaphragm walls are used for basement construction, the frictional resistance in cohesionless material or the wall adhesion due to clay strata, should be calculated in the same manner as frictional resistance to bored piles in similar soils, restricting the diaphragm wall surface used in the calculation to the inner and outer surface of the wall below formation level. Further discussion on the overall stability of underground structure is included in Chapter 9.

Construction economics

The relative costs of secant pile and diaphragm walls given by Sherwood et al.,[61] and quoted in Chapter 4, serve only as a comparison between wall costs and do not consider the relative costs of alternative propping systems or the costs of linings to the inside face of the wall. To make a logical choice of wall, propping and lining system on cost grounds, a detailed comparison of the cost of systems should be made for each job site.

A broad cost comparison is reproduced in Fig. 8.52. This comparison includes completed wall construction for two- and three-storey basements

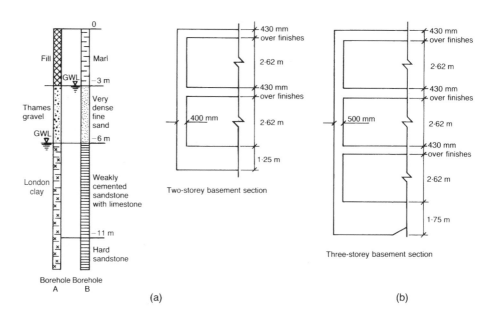

(a)   (b)

Fig. 8.52. Cost comparison of basement walls for temporary and permanent works, two- and three-storey deep cross-sections: (a), (b) for soil profiles shown at boreholes A and B for the constructions described in (c)–(f). A base index of 100 has been used for the lowest cost construction shown in (c).

(c) Two-storey basement construction; soil conditions as borehole A

		Relative cost
(1)	400 mm reinforced concrete basement wall, permanent sheet piles and temporary rakers	159·7
(2)	400 mm reinforced basement concrete wall, temporary sheet piles and temporary rakers	129·5
(3)	400 mm reinforced basement wall, temporary sheet piles and temporary tie-backs	147·8
(4)	400 mm reinforced concrete basement wall, king posts, horizontal lagging timbers and rakers	132·0
(5)	400 mm reinforced concrete basement wall, king posts, horizontal lagging timbers and tie-backs	161·8
(6)	600 mm dia. contiguous bored piles and rakers	100
(7)	600 mm dia. contiguous bored piles and rakers and 100 mm reinforced concrete internal skin	126·0
(8)	600 mm dia. contiguous bored piles and tie-backs	118·4
(9)	600 mm dia. contiguous bored piles and tie-backs and 100 mm reinforced concrete internal skin	144·4
(10)	880 mm secant piles at 750 mm centres and rakers	154·7
(11)	880 mm secant piles at 750 mm centres and rakers and internal skin 112 mm brickwork	164·4
(12)	600 mm thick diaphragm wall and tie-backs	158·7
(13)	600 mm thick diaphragm wall and tie-backs and internal skin 112 mm brickwork	168·4

(d) Three-storey basement construction; soil conditions as borehole A

		Relative cost
(1)	500 mm reinforced concrete basement wall, permanent sheet piles and temporary tie-backs	255·7
(2)	500 mm reinforced concrete basement wall, temporary sheet piles and temporary tie-backs	225·5
(3)	500 mm wall, king posts, timber horizontal laggings and tie-backs	220·2

		Relative cost
(4)	750 mm contiguous bored pile wall and tie-backs	130·6
(5)	750 mm contiguous bored pile wall and tie-backs and internal skin 100 mm reinforced concrete wall	156·6
(6)	880 mm dia. secant piles at 750 mm centres and tie-backs	186·0
(7)	880 mm dia. secant piles at 750 mm centres and tie-backs and internal skin 112 mm brickwork	195·7
(8)	800 mm diaphragm wall and tie-backs	188·5

(e) Two-storey basement; soil conditions as borehole B

		Relative cost
(1)	400 mm reinforced concrete basement wall, permanent sheet piles and temporary rakers	168·7
(2)	400 mm reinforced concrete basement wall, temporary sheet piles and temporary rakers	137·1
(3)	400 mm reinforced concrete basement wall, temporary sheet piles and tie-backs	155·5
(4)	400 mm reinforced concrete basement wall, king posts, horizontal laggings and rakers	134·8
(5)	400 mm reinforced concrete basement wall, king posts, horizontal laggings and tie-backs	164·4
(6)	880 mm secant piles at 750 mm centres and rakers	159·3
(7)	880 mm secant piles at 750 mm centres and rakers and internal skin 112 mm brickwork	169·0
(8)	600 mm thick diaphragm wall and tie-backs	157·8
(9)	600 mm thick diaphragm wall and tie-backs and internal skin 112 mm brickwork	167·5

(f) Three-storey basement; soil conditions as borehole B

		Relative cost
(1)	500 mm reinforced concrete basement wall, king posts, timber horizontal laggings and tie-backs	223·0
(2)	880 mm dia. secant piles at 750 mm centres and tie-backs	169·7
(3)	880 mm dia. secant piles at 750 mm centres and tie-backs and internal skin 112 mm brickwork	179·4
(4)	800 mm diaphragm wall and tie-backs	181·6
(5)	800 mm diaphragm wall and tie-backs and internal skin 112 mm brickwork	191·3

in two particular soil and groundwater conditions. It would be unwise to draw conclusions from this small sample but broadly it showed that, in the UK, contiguous bored pile walls with an internal lining are comparatively inexpensive in good piling ground; secant piling is an economic choice in less conducive soil conditions and for deeper basements; where sheet piling is left in place, an expensive wall results; anchored diaphragm walling is competitive in deeper basements in good soil conditions.

References

1. Lambe T.W. *Proc. Conf. Lateral Stresses and Earth Retaining Structures*, ASCE, New York, 1970, 149–218.
2. Wakeling T.R.M. Discussion, deep excavations. *Proc. 6th Euro. Conf. S.M.F.E.*, Vienna, 1976, Vol. 2.2, 29–30. Austrian National Committee, Vienna, 1976.
3. Skempton A.W. and La Rochelle P. The Bradwell slip, a short term failure in London clay. *Géotechnique*, 1965, **15**, Sept., 221–242.
4. Gässler G. and Gudehus G. Soil nailing, some aspects of a new technique. *Proc. 10th Int. Conf. S.M.F.E.*, Stockholm, 1981, Vol. 3, 665–67. Balkema, Rotterdam, 1981.
5. Banyai M. Stabilization of earth walls by soil nailing. *Proc. 6th Conf. SMFE*, Budapest, 1984, 459–466. Akadémiai Kiado, Budapest, 1984.
6. *Project National Clouterre, recommendations 1991.* Presses de l'Ecole Nationale des Ports et Chaussées, Paris, 1992.
7. Barley A. Soil nailing case histories and developments. *Proc. Conf. Retaining Structures.* Institution of Civil Engineers, London, 1992.
8. Schnabel H. Sloped sheeting. *ASCE J. Civ. Engng*, 1971, **41**, No. 2, 48–50.
9. Hanna T.H. Anchored inclined walls – a study of behaviour. *Ground Engng*, 1973, **6**, 24–33.
10. Potts D.M. *et al.* Use of soil berms for temporary support of retaining walls. *Proc. Conf. on Retaining Structures.* Institution of Civil Engineers, London, 1992, 440–447.
11. CIRIA. *Water resisting basement construction.* CIRIA, London, 1995, Report 139.
12. *Report on basement and cut and cover construction.* Draft. Institute of Structural Engineers, London, 2002.
13. BS 8102. *Protection of structures against water from the ground.* British Standards Institute, London, 1990.
14. Somerville G. The design life of concrete structures. *Struct. Eng.*, **64A**(2), 1986, 60–71.
15. Boikan A. Avoiding pitfalls and risk factors in below ground waterproofing. *Struct. Engr.*, **80**, 2002, 5 June, No. 11, 16–18.
16. Zinn W.V. Economical design of deep basements. *Civ. Engng Public Works Rev.*, 1968, **63**, Mar., 275–280.
17. Measor E. and Williams G. Features in the design and construction of the Shell Centre. *Proc. Instn Civ. Engrs*, 1962, **21**, Mar., 475–502.
18. Fenoux G.Y. Le réalisation fouilles en site urbain. *Travaux*, Parts 437 and 438, 1971, Aug.-Sept., 18–37.
19. Burland, J.B. and Hancock R.J. Underground car park at the House of Commons. *Struct. Engr*, 1977, **55**, Feb. 87–100.
20. Burland J. *et al.* Movements around excavations in London clay. *Proc. 7th Euro. Conf. S.M.F.E.*, Brighton, UK, 1979, Vol. 1, 13–29. British Geotechnical Society, London, 1979.
21. Marchand S.P. A deep basement in Aldersgate Street, London, part 1: contractor's design and planning. *Proc. Instn Civ. Engrs*, 1993, **93**, Feb., 19–26.
22. Marchand S.P. A deep basement in Aldersgate Street, London, part 2: construction. *Proc. Instn Civ. Engrs*, 1993, **97**, May, 67–76.
23. Slade R.E., Darling A. and Sharratt M. Redevelopment of Knightsbridge Crown Court for Harrods. *Struct. Engr*, **80**, 2002, 5 June, 21–27.
24. Fernie R. Movement and deep basement provision at Knightsbridge Crown Court, Harrods, London. *Conf. Response of Buildings to Excavation-induced Ground Movements*, July 2001. CIRIA, 2002.

25. Kenwright J., Dickson R.A. and Fernie R. Structural movement and ground settlement control for a deep excavation within a historic building. *Deep Foundations Institute Conference*, New York, 2000. DFI, Englewood Cliffs, New Jersey, 2000.

26. Boscardin M.D. and Cording E.G. Building response to excavation induced settlement. *ASCE J. Geotech. Eng.*, 1986, **115**, No. 1, 1–21.

27. Fletcher M.S. *et al.* The 'down' of top down. *Civ. Engng*, 1988, **58**, Mar., 58–61.

28. Lui J.Y.H. and Yau P.K.F. The performance of the deep basement for the Dragon Centre. *Proc. of Seminar on Instrumentation in Geotechnical Engineering*, Hong Kong Institution of Engineers, 183–201. Hong Kong, 1995.

29. Mitchell A., Izumi C., Bell B. and Brunton S. Semi top-down construction method for Singapore MRT, NEL. *Proc. Int. Conf. on Tunnels and Underground Structures*, Singapore, 2000. Balkema, Rotterdam, 2000.

30. Cole K.N. and Burland J.B. Observations of retaining wall movements associated with a large excavation. *Proc. of 5th Euro. Conf. S.M.F.E.*, Madrid, 1972.

31. Katzenbach R. and Quick H. A new concept for the excavation of deep building pits in inner urban areas combining top/down method and piled raft foundation. *Proc. 7th Int. Conf. and Exhibition on Piling and Deep Foundations*, Vienna, 1998, 15.17.1–15.17.3. DFI, Englewood Cliffs, New Jersey, 1998.

32. Mair R.J. Developments in geotechnical engineering research: application to tunnels and foundations. *Proc. Instn Civ. Engrs*, 1993, **93**, Feb., 27–41.

33. Yang D.S. Deep mixing. *Proceedings of the Geo-Institute Conference*, ASCE, Logan, Utah, 1997, 130–150. ASCE, New York, 1997.

34. Porbaha A. *et al.* State of the art in construction aspects of deep mixing technology. *Ground Improvement* 5, No. 3, 2001, 123–140.

35. Taki O. and Yang D.S. Soil-cement mixed technique, *Geotechnical Engineering Congress,* ASCE New York. Geotechnical Special Publication 27, Vol. 1, 298–309. ASCE, New York.

36. Bruce D.A. *et al.* Deep mixing: QA/QC and verification methods. *Grouting–Soil Improvement Geosystems including Reinforcement.* Editor, Hans Rathmeyer. 11–22, Finnish Geotechnical Society, Helsinki, 2000.

37. BS 8081. *Code of practice for ground anchorages.* British Standards Institution, London, 1989.

38. Littlejohn G.S. and Bruce D.A. *Rock anchors: state-of-the-art.* Foundation Publications, Brentwood, 1977.

39. Barley A. Ten thousand anchorages in rock. *Ground Engng*, 1988, **21**: No. 6, Sept., 20–29; No. 7, Oct., 24–35; No. 8, Nov. 35–39.

40. *Diaphragm walls.* Icos, Milan, 1968.

41. Guillaud M. and Hamelin J.P. Innovations in diaphragm wall construction plant. *Proc. D.F.I. Conf., Nice*, 2002, 3–8. Presses de l'Ecole Nationale des Ponts et Chaussées, Paris, 2002.

42. DIN Standard 4126. *Cast in-situ concrete diaphragm walls.* Deutsches Institut für Normung, Berlin, 2002.

43. Puller M.J. and Puller D.J. Developments in structural slurry walls. *Proc. Conf. Retaining Structures*, Institution of Civil Engineers, London, 1992, 373–384.

44. Rogers W.F. *Composition and properties of oil wall drilling fluids.* Gulf Publishing, Houston, 1967.

45. Beresford J.J. *et al.* Merits of polymeric fluids as support slurries. *Proc. Conf. Piling and Deep Foundations*, London, 1989. DFI, Englewood Cliffs, New Jersey, 1989.

46. Fisher F.A. Diaphragm wall projects. *Proc. Conf. Diaphragm Walls and Anchorages*, Institution of Civil Engineers, London, 1971, 11–18.

47. Jardine R.J. *et al.* Studies of the influence of non-linear stress-strain characteristics in soil-structure interaction. *Géotechnique*, 1986, **36**, Sept. 377–396.

48. Reynaud P. and Riviere P. Mesure des pressions developpees dans une paroi moulee en cours de betonnage. *Bull. Liaison Lab.*, Ponts et Chausée, Paris, 1981, No. 113, 135–138.

49. Lings M.L. *et al.* The lateral pressure of wet diaphragm wall panels cast over bentonite. *Proc. Instn Civ. Engrs*, 1994, **107**, 163–172.

50. Gunn, M.J. *et al.* Finite element modelling of installation effects. *Proc. Conf. Retaining Structures*, Institution of Civil Engineers, London, 1992, 46–55.

51. Sliwinski Z. and Fleming W.G. Practical consideration affecting the construction of diaphragm walls. *Proc. Conf. Diaphragm Walls and Anchorages*, Institution of Civil Engineers, London, 1975, 1–10.

52. BS 2004. *Code of practice for foundations*. British Standards Institution, London, 1972.

53. *Specification for cast in place concrete diaphragm walling*. Federation of Piling Specialists, London, 1985.

54. BS 8102. *Code of practice for the protection of structures against water from the ground*. British Standards Institution, London, 1990.

55. Puller M.J. Waterproofness of structural diaphragm walls. *Proc. Instn Civ. Engrs, Geotech. Engng*, 1994, **107**, Jan., 47–57.

56. Xanthakos P. *Slurry walls*. McGraw-Hill, New York, 1979.

57. *Specification for highway works*. Department of Transport, London, 1991.

58. EN 1538. *Execution of special geotechnical works: diaphragm walls*. British Standards Institution, London, 1996.

59. *Specification for piling and embedded retaining walls*. Institution of Civil Engineers, London, 1996.

60. Centre Scientifique et Technique de Batiment. DTU No. 14.1. *Travaux de cuvelage*. CSTB, Paris, 1987.

61. Sherwood D.E. *et al*. Recent developments in secant bored pile wall construction. *Proc. Piling and Deep Foundations Conf.*, London, 1989, 211–219. DFI, Englewood Cliffs, New Jersey, 1989.

62. CIRIA. *Embedded retaining walls: guidance for economic design*. Gaba A.R. *et al*. CIRIA, London, 2002.

Bibliography

BS EN 12715: *Grouting*. British Standards Institution, London, 2000.

BS EN 12716: *Jet grouting*. British Standards Institution, London, 2001.

BS EN 12063: *Sheet piling*. British Standards Institution, London, 1999.

Pr EN 14475: *Reinforcement of fills*. CEN, 2002.

BS EN 1538: *Execution of special geotechnical work: Diaphragm walls*. British Standards Institution, London, 2000.

BS EN 1537: *Execution of special geotechnical work: Ground anchors*. British Standards Institution, London, 1999.

BS EN 1536: *Execution of special geotechnical work: Bored piles*. British Standards Institution, London, 1999.

Draft EN 14679: *Execution of special geotechnical work: Deep mixing*. British Standards Institution, London, 2003.

Davies R. and Henkel D. Geotechnical problems associated with construction of Chater Station. *Proc. Conf. Mass Transportation in Asia*, Hong Kong, 1980, 1–31.

Ikuta Y. *et al*. Application of the observational method to a deep basement excavated using the top-down method. *Géotechnique*, 1994, **44**, Dec., 655–664.

Ramaswarmy S.D. Soil anchored tieback system for supporting deep excavations. *J. Instn Engrs Singapore*, 1975, **14**, Dec., 10–33.

Ramaswarmy S.D. and Aziz M.A. Some experiences with ground anchors for substructure construction in Singapore. *Proc. Conf. Geotech.*, Singapore, 1980, 170–180.

Ramaswarmy S.D. and Yong K.Y. Some case studies on problems of substructures of high rise building. *Proc. Conf. Construction Practices in Geotech. Engng*, Surat, India, 1982, 255–260. Oxford and IBH Publishing Co., New Delhi, 1982.

Smoltczyk U. Editor. Geotechnical Engineering Handbook Vol. 2. *Procedures*. 2.5. Ground anchors. Ostermayer H. and Barley T. Ernst and Son, Berlin, 2003.

Washbourne J. The three dimensional stability analysis of diaphragm wall excavations. *Ground Engng*, 1984, **17**, May, 24–39.

Yandzio E. and Biddle A. *Steel intensive basements*. Steel Construction Institute. Ascot 2001.

9 Cut-and-cover construction

Introduction

As the name suggests, cut-and-cover construction consists of tunnel construction by deep excavation in trench, construction of the permanent tunnel structure, and subsequent backfill and reinstatement of the ground surface. The method is economical in comparatively shallow tunnel works and is typically applied in urban highway schemes and for urban metro stations and running tunnel construction. This chapter therefore describes highway and metro schemes and includes the construction of station boxes: sometimes more exactly these stations could be classified as basements, but are included in this chapter with other metro illustrations for completeness.

Historically the method was used as an alternative to bored tunnel construction for underground railway and river-crossing highway schemes in European cities in the second part of the nineteenth century, particularly in London and Paris. Early photographs in 1903 of cut-and-cover works for the Saint-Lazare station on line 3 of the metro in Paris are shown in Figs. 9.1 and 9.2. The photos, taken two weeks apart, show the rapid progress which the method allowed. The station was excavated from below the roof vaults of the station following roof construction. Prior to the Second World War, metro construction in European cities such as Berlin, Paris and London exploited cut-and-cover construction and furthered construction techniques such as the king post method of soil support. Its use provided an alternative to boring for underground tunnels within a range of depths, typically 8 to 10 m. Excavation plant and craneage was largely steam driven, and structural materials were usually timber or steel sheet piling.

The reconstruction of European cities in the 1950s, and the improvements to public transport facilities with progressive urbanization in the 1960s and 1970s, allowed the introduction of improved methods of tunnelling, including cut-and-cover techniques. In particular, improvements to excavation and drilling equipment, the availability of high-quality steel sections and reinforcement and the introduction of ready mixed concrete transformed construction methods. A range of walling methods became available and alternative methods of installation were developed. Reinforced concrete piles were now installed by powerful rotary auger, steel sheet piling was driven by diesel hammer, vibrator or by hydraulic equipment, and new methods of walling such as diaphragm walling and methods of support such as ground and rock anchoring were introduced by innovative contractors and specialists.

In the years following the 1970s many cities invested in new metro systems, further exploiting cut-and-cover methods. In particular, the construction of the Island Line and more recently West Rail in Hong Kong and the Singapore Metro North East line have further used bottom-up, top-down and variant systems and all the walling methods.

While the choice between tunnel or surface construction may be clearly determined by the availability and value of land and the depth of the proposed permanent construction, the choice between bored tunnel and cut-and-cover construction methods may sometimes be less clearly defined. In other

Fig. 9.1. Cut-and-cover works: St Lazare Metro Station, Paris, 1903[30]

Fig. 9.2. As Fig. 9.1. photographed two weeks later[30]

instances, however, the prevalent groundwater conditions, availability of construction site areas or the proximity of existing structures and their foundations, may combine with the available horizontal and vertical alignments to pre-determine the use of either bored tunnels or cut-and-cover construction.

Although the construction methods of cut-and-cover work may appear to be more direct and free from the risks of bored tunnel construction, greater risk of subsidence due to shallow works and the disruption of traffic and services due to large-scale trench works may make cut-and-cover work less attractive. In the early 1980s Megaw and Bartlett[1] listed the disadvantages of cut-and-cover in busy urban areas:

(a) Lengthy occupation of street sites with noise disturbances and disruption to access. This can be mitigated by mining excavation methods below a roof slab constructed at an early stage on the permanent tunnel walls. Roof slab construction allows speedy reinstatement of highways and surface works. In special circumstances tunnelled headings may be used to build the permanent walls with the minimum of surface activity.

(b) In soft clays and silts, excavation in trench may be limited to maintain stability and reduce heave. Short-length working will be necessary and will increase construction and occupation time.

(c) Constraints on alignments by following existing streets may be undesirable, especially where small-radius curves are introduced into metro construction. In some city areas, basements which encroach beyond building lines may worsen the situation.

(d) Progress and cost of cut-and-cover schemes can be badly affected by diversion works to existing services, especially those inaccurately recorded or uncharted and disclosed during trenchworks. These works often require a break in the sequence of trench wall construction to divert the service and then construct the trench wall across the previous alignment of the service.

(e) Ground movement and subsidence of existing structures and services have to be minimized. Methods to reduce subsoil heave, loss of ground, and changes of groundwater level and flow entail cost and construction time penalties. The use of pre-stressed ground anchors, pre-jacking of struts, grouting works and groundwater recharge may all be necessary, particularly where sensitive or old buildings are nearby, and all have cost and time implications for cut-and-cover work.

The construction costs of cut-and-cover works increase significantly with depth, but the effect of construction depth on the cost of bored tunnel works is often much less. The choice of horizontal and vertical alignment for large-scale works such as metro construction additionally involves comparing the capital cost of alternative alignments using varying lengths of bored tunnel and cut-and-cover with the projected energy running costs of trains on those alternative alignments.

Four methods are available for cut-and-cover wall construction:
(a) temporary support from braced or anchored steel sheet piling followed by permanent reinforced concrete wall construction
(b) the soldier wall method of temporary support using soldier piles and horizontal laggings, or sprayed concrete skin walls with bracing or anchoring followed by permanent reinforced concrete wall construction
(c) temporary concrete walls in contiguous, secant reinforced concrete piles or in situ diaphragm wall construction followed by permanent reinforced concrete construction

(*d*) combined temporary and permanent wall construction from walls in reinforced concrete secant piles, or cast in situ or precast diaphragm wall construction.

Bottom-up, top-down or semi-top-down construction

Whilst bottom-up construction was used with timbered or sheet piled earth support for cut-and-cover works until the 1960s and 1970s the use of top-down for building basement construction in those times led to its use in European cities for metro construction, particularly by Soletanche in Paris and Icos in Milan. Every variant of walling method and geotechnical process has been used since then, especially in the Far East, to maximize site development potential, and reduce cost, construction time and disturbance to traffic and urban life.

An example of recent station box construction in Hong Kong has been described by Cook and Paterson[2] for Nam Cheong station on the West Rail work for the Kowloon Canton Railway Corporation. The original contract design used diaphragm walls for the new station, 350 m × 80 m in plan, with an average depth of concourse construction of 15 m below ground level. The new station straddles the existing elevated West Kowloon expressway and the airport expressline railway, as shown in cross-section in Fig. 9.3. The ground conditions comprised approximately 25 m of hydraulic sand overlying a variable thickness of alluvial silt and clay underlain by a weathered granite system. Groundwater varied between 2 m and 5 m below ground level.

The original scheme comprised a diaphragm wall box using the top-down method. In the event, the alternative scheme as built used less materials at less cost to build an in situ structure within a sheet piled cofferdam, the external walls being supported by plunge columns. Detailed vibration studies were undertaken to assess vibration risk in driving the 28 m long sheet piles and only in restricted lengths was this found to be excessive. At these lengths, the sheet piles were pitched into slurry trenches. It is intended to recover all the sheet piles after backfilling behind the permanent walls.

In order to dewater the site, the groundwater was lowered using deep wells. A settlement prediction made prior to the works gave an estimated total settlement below the future high-rise structure over the east box of 35 mm, most of which would occur during construction.

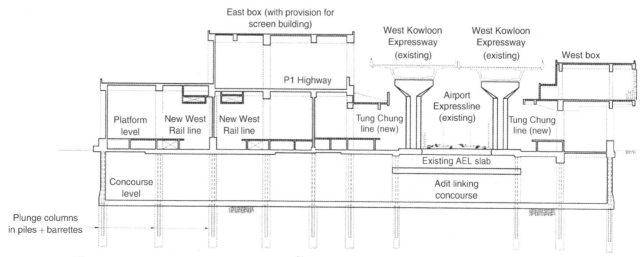

Fig. 9.3. Nam Cheong Station, Hong Kong, cross-section[31]

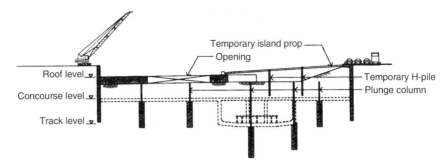

(a) Stage 1: Divert traffic, install diaphragm walls and piles, construct roof

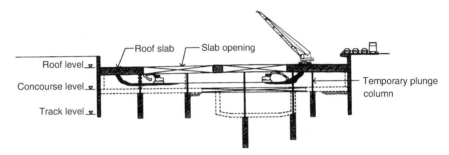

(b) Stage 2: Remove temporary struts, excavate below roof, cast concourse

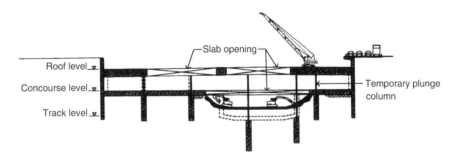

(c) Stage 3: Cast lining walls, excavate and cast track, complete station bottom-up

Fig. 9.4. Station construction sequence, N.E. line, Singapore[25]

The alternative design as built, also built top-down in order to achieve an early handover of the track slab at ground level, minimized time and cost in the use of barrettes with post-grouted shafts to improve load capacity in lieu of bored piles and staged excavation and dewatering to control settlements during construction.

A derivative of top-down construction named semi-top-down has been applied in construction of the stations on the new N.E. line in Singapore. Particularly because of the design requirement for civil defence purposes of a 2 m thick station roof located 3 m below ground level, the roof itself was used as a working platform. The access holes within this roof were large and savings were made by using the smallest skeleton possible of permanent works as temporary works and so the least weight of bracing and propping to be supported by plunge columns, whilst maintaining watertightness and avoiding settlement risk to nearby existing services and buildings. The sequence of top-down and final bottom-up construction is shown in Fig. 9.4.

Choice of wall system

The choice of walling method depends on geology, depth of excavation and the presence of buildings or roads near the excavation. A review by Hulme *et al.*[3] of cut-and-cover walling methods for a large new transportation

Table 9.1 Singapore Metro: construction methods for cut-and-cover stations[3]

Station	Maximum depth of excavation (m)	Typical soil sequence[a]	Retaining system used	Special measures
Braddell	14·9	1F, G4	0·6 and 0·8 m diaphragm walls	
Toa Payoh	13·5	4F, 4K, G	Sheet piles	
Novena	14·7	$\frac{1}{2}$F, 14·2K, G	Sheet piles	
Newton	14·3	3F, 13K, G	0·8 m diaphragm walls	Jet grouting
Orchard	21	$\frac{1}{2}$F, G	Nailed slopes	
Somerset	16·2	2F, 8K, G	0·6 m diaphragm walls or sheet piles	
Dhoby Ghaut	16·1	1F, 10K, S	Sheet piles	
City Hall	22·3	3F, 2K, S3	King piles and shotcrete lagging	
Tanjong Pagar	17·9	$\frac{1}{2}$F, S	Slopes, anchors	
Outram	13·9	2F, 3K, S	8 m deep sheet piles over king piles and timber laggings	
Tiong Bahru	14·1	1F, S	King piles and shotcrete lagging	
Bugis	18·3	1F, 34K, O	1·2/1·0 m diaphragm walls	Lime piles
Lavender	16·5	3F, 20K, O	1·0 m diaphragm walls	
Marina Bay	16·4	12F, 24K, O	Composite H pile/sheet pile	Underwater excavation

[a] Key.   F = fill
G = granite ⎫
S3 = Jurong ⎬ including weathered rock
⎭
K = Kallang
S = boulder bed
O = old alluvium

Example: 3F, 13K, G = 3 m of fill overlying 13 m of Kallang deposit overlying granite (in this case completely weathered granite)

system showed the choices for each station or section of running tunnel on the Singapore MRT. Table 9.1 summarizes the walling methods used for the underground stations on the system. A similar comparison of cut-and-cover station walls on the initial Hong Kong MTR system was presented in the 1980s by McIntosh *et al.*[4] (Table 9.2).

Sheet pile walls
The traditional use of sheet piles in temporary soil support for cut-and-cover construction has been reduced by environmental pressures to avoid noise and vibration due to pile driving in favour of the use of top-downwards techniques which generally favour walling methods that use combined temporary and permanent soil retention. Nevertheless, the use of hydraulic press equipment and jetting to install sheet piles and the monitoring of noise and vibration in less sensitive areas does allow increased sheet pile use. This has been shown particularly in lengths of both the Singapore and Hong Kong metros where excavation depths are limited to the order of 15 to 16 m and where soil conditions allow economical pile driving. Appropriate applications include river crossings, areas where groundwater is high and sites that are some distance from existing structures and services. The lack of flexural stiffness of sheet pile sections, which would normally require frequent propping or the risk of large settlements can be corrected either by stiffening the sheeter sections with soldier piles or tubes, as with the Combi wall, or the stiffening of the retained soil by jet grouting or mix-in-place piles. These latter piles can be drilled in a cellular plan form or as a series of buttresses behind the sheet piles. The adequacy of space to withdraw sheeters from behind the

Table 9.2 Hong Kong Metro stations — adopted construction methods for cut-and-cover works[4]

Station	Depth of excavation (m)	Cover to roof slab (m)	Depth to rock from surface (m)	Engineer's assumed method	Temporary works	Proximity to buildings	Walls	Constructor sequence	Special measures
Choi Hung	20	0-3	a	Temporary Berlin wall with preboring or diaphragm walls	Permanent walls	One end only	Hand-dug interlocking caissons	Top down	Skeletal roof of cross-beams with precast T beam infills
Diamond Hill	22	3	b	Steel I sections king piles and intermediate sheet piles	Permanent walls	No	Hand-dug caissons for steel piles and concrete jack arches	Top down	Walls are to be removable for future widening
Wong Tai Sin	24 max.	3·5-6·5	a	Diaphragm walls	Permanent walls	Medium height housing blocks	Diaphragm walls	Top down	Roof was clear spanning during excavation with concourse suspended from it
Lok Fu	27	2	0-30	Bored tunnel	Berlin wall of steel piles and concrete lagging — ground anchors	High-rise housing block	In situ	Bottom up	Dewatering by ground treatment and wells
Kowtown Tong	18	2	b	Diaphragm walls	Part permanent walls — part Berlin type-ground anchors	No	Part diaphragm wall, part in situ	Bottom up	—
Shek Kip Mei	18-24	1·5-6·5	0-30	Open cut in rock, sheet piling with grouted anchors in soil	Berlin wall, part strutted, part ground anchors	High-rise housing blocks and schools	In situ	Bottom up	Short length of station platforms in bored rock tunnel
Prince Edward	28	2	16-30	Diaphragm walls	Permanent walls	High-rise commercial and residential	Benoto type secant piles and hand-dug caissons	Top down	Extensive grouting was used, plus dewatering and limited recharging
Argyle	25	3-5	b	Diaphragm walls	Permanent walls	High-rise commercial and residential	Benoto type secant piles	Top down	Columns extended to underlying rock and vertically anchored; some areas of slab also anchored; grouting to walls; use of recharge wells
Waterloo	28	2	0-27	Part open cut, part diaphragm walls	Permanent walls	High-rise commercial and residential	Benoto type secant piles to rock, then in situ	Top down	Underpinning to walls
Jordan	18-23	0-4·5	4-20	Diaphragm walls and rock anchors, in situ underpinning	PIP pile walls and 7 levels of steel strutting	High-rise commercial and residential	In situ	Bottom up	Half of station anchored to underlying rock
Tsim Sha Tsui	17-21	3·5-7·5	9·5-13·5	Diaphragm walls and rock anchors, in situ underpinning	PIP pile walls and steel strutting	High-rise commercial and residential	In situ	Bottom up	Part of station anchored to underlying rock
Admiralty	25	0-3	20	Diaphragm walls on rock; rock anchors and in situ underpinning	Combination of open cut, anchored sheet piling and permanent walls, also slurry trenches	No	Part diaphragm wall, part in situ	Bottom up	Part of station anchored vertically to underlying rock: underpinning to diaphragm wall
Chater/ Pedder	28	3	33 c	Diaphragm walls	Permanent walls with struts	High-rise commercial and hotels, low rise historic buildings	Diaphragm walls	Top down	Special measures to construct walls and groundwater recharging

a Not known.   b Not known, large boulders.   c But rock level not proven in some sections.

constructed permanent structure may prove vital in the economic use of sheeters even where good driving conditions exist.

To summarize, the disadvantages of using sheet piles in the continuous walls of cut-and-cover works are as follows.

(a) Noise and vibration during installation: may be overcome by use of Giken type presses for piles of medium depth.

(b) Support is provided only during construction and permanent works are required for tunnel construction.

(c) Obstructions reduce driving efficiency and increase risk of damage due to vibration.

(d) Adequate allowance must be made for installation tolerances. The initial piling line must make allowance for verticality tolerance to ensure adequate width between sheet pile walls to accommodate the permanent works.

(e) Ingress of groundwater through pile clutches and split clutches may cause delay or even local failure. Use of sealed or welded clutches may be feasible.

(f) Future use of sheet piles may determine the cost-effectiveness of the method. Extraction of sheet piles after completion of the permanent works may prove difficult due to soil conditions and lack of working space.

(g) Temporary bracing between sheet pile walls must be replaced as the permanent structure is built with new struts between sheeters and permanent structure. The incomplete and complete permanent structure must be designed to transfer soil and groundwater pressures in this way.

(h) Extension of sheeters for increased cut-off requires welding operations with disruption to overall production.

Where subsoil conditions, environmental restrictions, excavation depths and working space constraints are not severe, sheet piling is still economical for cut-and-cover work. In the 1960s and 1970s, the method was the forerunner of deep secant pile walls and diaphragm walls which now provide alternatives. Reference to these earlier jobs shows some of the difficulties which were experienced.

Historic use of sheet piles in cut-and-cover construction
The second Blackwall Tunnel, a crossing of the River Thames in London, used sheet pile cofferdams for both north and south cut-and-cover approaches[5]. During construction of the north approach, artesian pressures below the cofferdam in a fine dense sand were not sufficiently relieved by pumping from deep wells and pore-water pressures caused spongy patches to develop in the overlying London clay exposed at formation level. The reduction in effective passive pressures supporting the sheet piles below formation level appeared critical as overloading of the cofferdam bracing increased. The formation was hastily reloaded, excavation works were temporarily stopped and the pumps given time to relieve the artesian head. Another feature on the north approach cut-and-cover was a short, 20 m long in situ diaphragm walling built at the junction of the cut-and-cover approach and deep tunnel section to avoid the risk of piling vibration loosening tunnel segments immediately adjacent to the junction.

Two tunnel crossings of the Thames at Dartford used alternative walling systems for each of the cut-and-cover approaches. The first crossing in the early 1960s used sheet piles driven into soft alluvial clays overlying sands and gravels containing an artesian groundwater pressure. The strutting system used to support the sheet piles, shown in Fig. 9.5, allowed secure

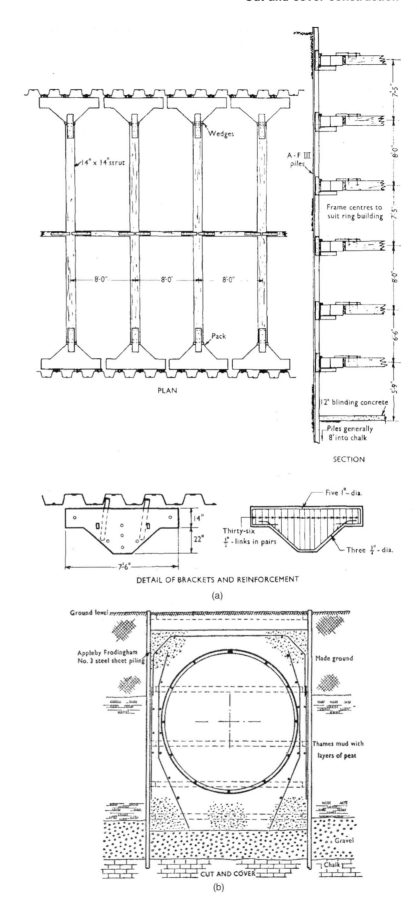

PLAN

SECTION

DETAIL OF BRACKETS AND REINFORCEMENT

(a)

(b)

Fig. 9.5. First Dartford Tunnel,
cut-and-cover construction:
(a) details of bracing frames;
(b) cross-section[32]

frame fixing promptly after excavation to successive depths, preventing yield of the piling and consequent increases in strut loading. The permanent cut-and-cover was built within the trenchworks in tunnel rings, and the sheet piles were left in.

The second Dartford Tunnel was built in 1972 and the walls were built to resist both temporary and permanent soil and groundwater pressures using in situ diaphragm walls.

Neither cut-and-cover sections to the Dartford crossings experienced construction problems, unlike the north approach at Blackwall. There were difficulties, however, with the stability of the formation at the portal of the Clyde Tunnel, completed in the 1960s and built in a sheet piled cofferdam[6,7]. Portal construction within caissons was considered but because of the proximity of nearby buildings and the existence of a boulder clay stratum below formation level which could have affected caisson sinking, a sheet piled cofferdam was preferred. In the event, the boulder clay stratum was found at much greater depth than anticipated. Air bubbles rising within the partly excavated cofferdam showed leakage of compressed air from the tunnel workings and a lack of seal in the sheet piling to the cofferdam. As excavation proceeded through the silt, cofferdam struts were overloaded

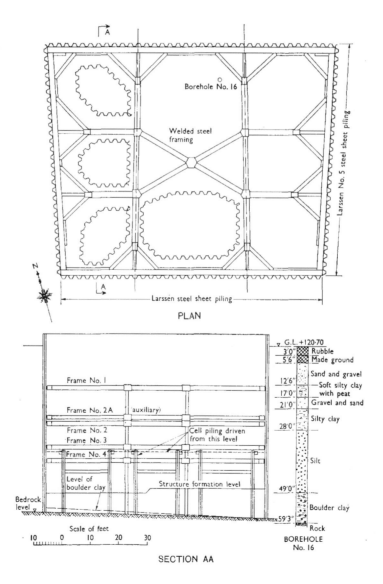

Fig. 9.6. Clyde Tunnel: plan and vertical cross-section of completed partial cofferdam[7]

and the silt below formation level became unstable as pore water pressures increased. A borehole put down within the cofferdam gushed water confirming that groundwater had access to the underside of the silt stratum. A well sunk 3·6 m into the bedrock made some improvement but not enough to allow excavation to continue over the whole base area of the cofferdam. The cofferdam was partly flooded and an auxiliary second frame inserted and pre-loaded. Erection of the third frame was completed in the dry, and the fourth and final frame was built in short trenches where boulder clay did not exist above bedrock, the silt being excavated and replaced by mass concrete within sheet piled cells driven between the upper cofferdam frames. Excavation was completed to formation level over the remainder of the cofferdam (Fig. 9.6).

Anchored or braced king post walls

Although vertical soldier piles or king posts with horizontal poling boards spanning between them had been used most effectively in the sandy subsoils of Berlin in the 1930s, it was the development of powerful mechanical augers, anchoring methods and methods of spraying concrete which promoted its post-war use. Unrestricted, wide, anchored excavations were now possible, and metro schemes, particularly in Germany, adopted the method for temporary soil support. The method is most economical where groundwater is absent or can be reduced by dewatering. Figure 9.7 shows a typical excavation below bracing with reduction of groundwater by pumping.

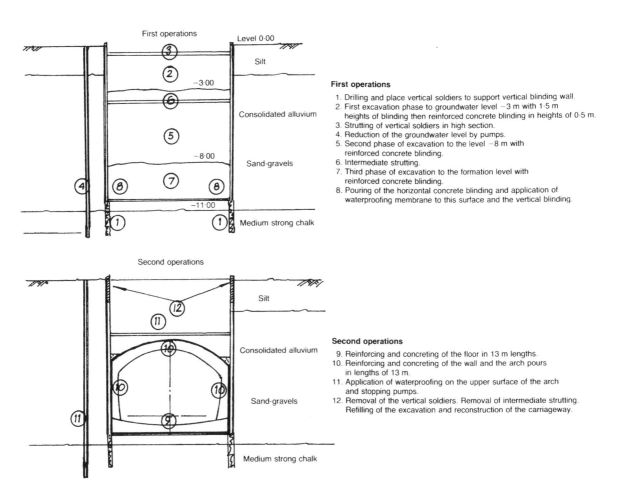

First operations
1. Drilling and place vertical soldiers to support vertical blinding wall.
2. First excavation phase to groundwater level −3 m with 1·5 m heights of blinding then reinforced concrete blinding in heights of 0·5 m.
3. Strutting of vertical soldiers in high section.
4. Reduction of the groundwater level by pumps.
5. Second phase of excavation to the level −8 m with reinforced concrete blinding.
6. Intermediate strutting.
7. Third phase of excavation to the formation level with reinforced concrete blinding.
8. Pouring of the horizontal concrete blinding and application of waterproofing membrane to this surface and the vertical blinding.

Second operations
9. Reinforcing and concreting of the floor in 13 m lengths.
10. Reinforcing and concreting of the wall and the arch pours in lengths of 13 m.
11. Application of waterproofing on the upper surface of the arch and stopping pumps.
12. Removal of the vertical soldiers. Removal of intermediate strutting. Refilling of the excavation and reconstruction of the carriageway.

Fig. 9.7. Cut-and-cover construction using soldier pile walls: sequence of construction using cut-offs and dewatering system[33]

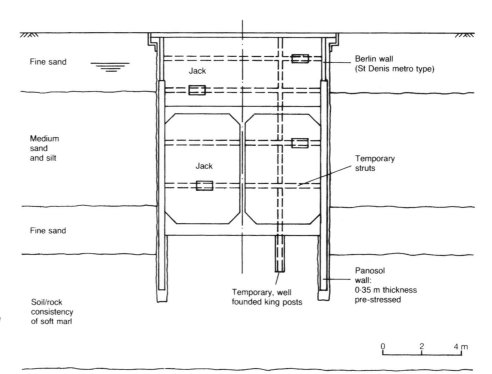

Fine sand

Jack

Medium
sand
and silt

Jack

Fine sand

Berlin wall
(St Denis metro type)

Temporary
struts

Panosol
wall:
0·35 m thickness
pre-stressed

Temporary, well
founded king posts

Soil/rock
consistency
of soft marl

0   2   4 m

*Fig. 9.8. Composite Berlin wall
with pre-stressed precast
diaphragm wall, Fukuoka
Metro, Japan (courtesy of
Soletanche–Bachy)*

The king post wall method is particularly useful as part of a composite wall system, acting as a temporary soil support for shallow depths above a temporary/permanent pile or diaphragm wall at greater depth. A typical composite wall is shown in Fig. 9.8 and is referred to later in this chapter.

Contiguous bored pile walls

Contiguous reinforced concrete piles, installed by either CFA rig or power auger with casing oscillator, are ideally used for cut-and-cover works of moderate excavation depth, say 15 m or so, in cohesive soils with minimal groundwater. Where ingress of heavy groundwater does occur locally through sandy or gravel seams, jet grouting may be used at the rear of the piles to reduce leakage.

An ideal application of the method was the cut-and-cover approach section of the Mersey Kingsway Tunnel in Liverpool in the early 1970s[8]. The cut-and-cover structure was founded on sandstone while the 17·7 m high walls supported boulder clay. To avoid the considerable thickness of cantilevered walls or large overhead propping beam to span the approach width of 26 to 31 m, a continuous arch roof structure was used with backfill over it. The rise of this arch was designed in proportion to the arch span and the depth of backfill so that a balance was obtained between lateral ground pressure from the walls and the outward horizontal arch thrust.

Excavation was initially made to arch springing level between temporary anchored king post walls (Fig. 9.9). From this level, 2·5 m dia. contiguous piles were augered into bedrock. A dumpling between the contiguous bored piles could not be removed until the arch thrust had been developed from the backfill load over the arch. Successive stages of dumpling excavation and filling were carefully sequenced. Two hundred piles were installed at a peak rate of four piles per day.

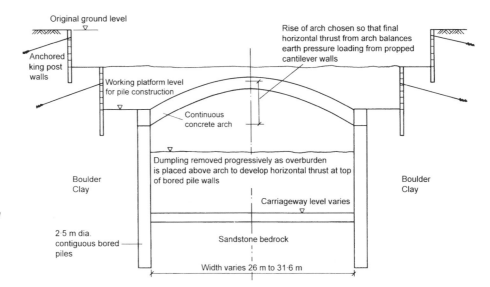

Fig. 9.9. Vertical cross-section of cut-and-cover structure, Liverpool approach to Mersey Kingsway Tunnel; contiguous bored pile walls propped by concrete arch[8]

Secant pile walls

Secant pile construction, alternate male and female piles interlocked to form a hard–hard secant wall, provides an efficient and economical walling system to moderate and greater depths in a wide range of soil and groundwater conditions. A permanent wall is constructed to allow soil support during construction. The principal advantages of the system are as follows.

(*a*) Permanent structural walls are constructed in one operation ahead of excavation.

(*b*) The hard–hard secant pile walls are substantially watertight.

(*c*) Excavation methods using down-the-hole hammers, reverse circulation drills, heavy-duty rotary augers/buckets, or temporary casings with casing oscillators and hammer grabs are highly efficient in hard soil and rock conditions. Excess heads of water or slurry within the temporary pile casing can be used to overcome onerous groundwater conditions. For cut-and-cover structures of modest depth higher production rates can be obtained in less demanding soil conditions with CFA rigs particularly for hard–firm and hard–soft secant pile walls.

(*d*) Good verticality tolerances can be achieved with twin-walled temporary casing, and casing oscillators. Tolerances of the order of 1 in 200 to 1 in 300 may be expected, depending on soil conditions. Little overbreak may be expected and the pile finish is uniform.

(*e*) Pile installation is comparatively noise- and vibration-free although some vibration is inevitable when penetrating through dense granular or rock strata.

(*f*) Loss of ground during excavation is generally small. In soft silts and clays or where sand with a high piezometric head is penetrated, the temporary casing affords continuous lateral support and the stability of the base of the bore within the casing may be continuously retained by a head of water or slurry within the casing to ground level.

(*g*) Vertical loading of secant walls is viable because of the reliability of good soil density below the concreted base of the pile.

(*h*) Temporary gaps may conveniently be left in the secant pile wall to allow service access. Piles are temporarily filled with sand after boring at these locations and are concreted later.

The design and construction of six recent deep stations on the Copenhagen Metro was described by Beadman and Bailey[9]. The design, on the basis

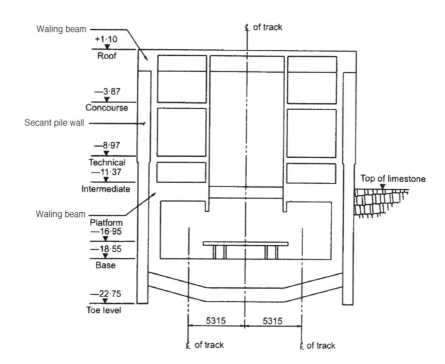

Waling beam
+1·10
Roof

−3·87
Concourse

Secant pile wall

−8·97
Technical
−11·37
Intermediate

Waling beam
Platform
−16·95
−18·55
Base

−22·75
Toe level

₵ of track

Top of limestone

5315   5315

₵ of track   ₵ of track

Fig. 9.10. Copenhagen Metro Station construction: cross-section[9]

of 100-year design life, was made in accordance with the requirements of recently introduced Eurocodes. The six stations were all similar in cross-section and plan shape. The main structure of each is a secant piled box 20 m deep, 20 m wide and 60 m long. The internal structure to the box is shown in cross-section in Fig. 9.10. The support to the box walls is provided by the station roof and floor with a waling beam at approximately mid-height.

The ground conditions consisted of varying depths of well-compacted made ground and over-consolidated sandy clay or clayey sand with bands of water-bearing sands and gravels overlying limestone. The stations all extended into the limestone which was heavily fractured and hard. The permeable sands and gravels contained a secondary aquifer but the main aquifer was within the limestone; the groundwater level was typically 2 m below ground level.

Secant piles were selected in favour of sheet piles (which would not penetrate the limestone) and diaphragm walls (insufficient space on sites for bentonite plant and reinforcement storage). The secant pile solution that was used consisted of hard male piles, 1180 mm dia. with soft female piles 750 mm dia. installed only as far as the intact limestone. CFA and cased techniques were used. The gaps between the male piles in the limestone were sealed with grout.

Most of the stations were built using top-down methods to minimize temporary works and settlements outside the box. The construction sequence was:

(a) construct the secant piles and the station roof
(b) excavate to the waling level and construct the waling beam and the permanent props
(c) hang the inner edge of the waling beam from the roof
(d) excavate to base level and construct the base slab
(e) complete the internal elements, bottom-upwards
(f) remove those hangers that are only required temporarily.

Geotechnical design in accordance with Eurocode EC7 (as detailed in Chapter 4) required three ultimate limits to be considered:

Table 9.3 Soil parameters and partial factors used in construction of the Copenhagen Metro

Soil parameter		SLS	Case B	Case C
Made ground	ϕ'	30/1·0	30/1·0	30/1·25
Glacial till	ϕ'	32/1·0	32/1·0	32/1·25
	c'	25/1·0	25/1·0	25/1·6
Limestone	ϕ'	40/1·0	40/1·0	40/1·25
	c'	50/1·0	50/1·0	50/1·6

- Case A: deals with flotation
- Case B, wall design: deals with the strength of the structural members. Ultimate load factor of 1·35, permanent unfavourable actions (forces)
- Case C, wall design: deals with the geotechnical design: ultimate load factor of 1·0, permanent unfavourable actions (forces).

Soil parameters and partial factors applied to them were as detailed in Table 9.3.

Beadman and Bailey comment that the specified maximum crack width of 0·2 mm (rather than a maximum of 0·3 mm) was most onerous and required substantial increased reinforcement quantities.

Examples of inclined secant pile walls for cut-and-cover works in the late 1960s on the Munich Metro were reported by Weinbold and Kleinlein[10]. The method replaced underpinning in hand-dug pits where space between existing buildings was limited, and in some cases allowed the retention of the existing facades which would otherwise have been rebuilt. Figure 9.11 shows typical cross-sections of the inclined pile walls on metros in Munich and Frankfurt, both bored with a 12° inclination. These piles were installed by Benoto rigs and were continuously supported by temporary casing within the inclined bore at all stages of excavation and concreting. The design of these inclined walls was based on elastic analysis after site experimental verification of the modulus of subgrade reaction. The wall was therefore assumed to be loaded by earth pressure at rest, groundwater pressure and superimposed loads due to buildings, and was to be supported by elastic embedment within the soil and by ground anchors and strutting. Soil conditions, loading and sheeting moments and deflections at successive excavation stages are shown for a typical section in Fig. 9.12.

Hana and Dina[11] carried out a series of model tests on anchored inclined walls. They concluded the following.

(a) The design of an inclined wall supported by rows of pre-stressed anchors should incorporate a rectangular earth pressure envelope.

(b) Walls which tend to undercut the retained soil, inclined away from the excavation (the same direction of inclination as shown in Figs. 9.11 and 9.12), experienced much larger soil subsidence than walls inclined towards the excavation, at all stages of excavation from ground level to final formation. Generally, for walls inclined away from the excavation the largest lateral movements were at the top of the wall, whereas for walls inclined in the opposite direction the largest lateral movements occurred at the base of the wall. There were also vertical movements, particularly for walls inclined away from the excavation. The bearing capacity of the wall base was stated to be very important.

(c) Individual anchor loads changed as construction progressed. In general, for walls inclined towards the excavation, anchor loads reduced from initial values, whereas for walls inclined away from the excavation initial anchor loads increased.

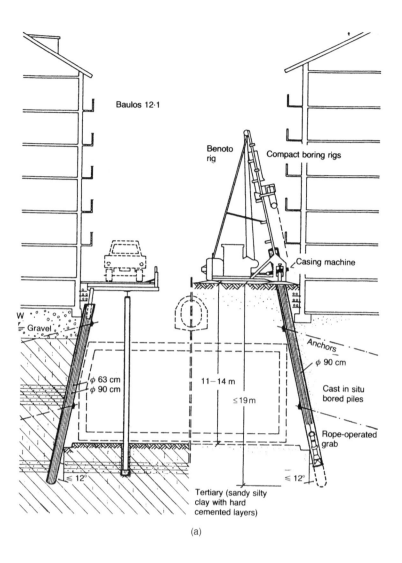

(a)

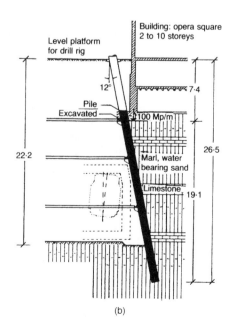

(b)

Fig. 9.11. Inclined secant pile construction for metro construction: (a) cross-section with temporary roadway, pile construction for Benoto rig, Munich Metro; (b) inclined walls, Frankfurt Metro

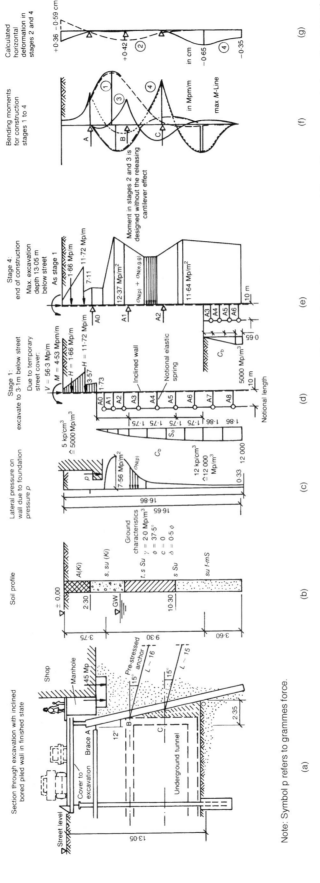

Note: Symbol p refers to grammes force.

Fig. 9.12. Inclined secant wall construction: (a) section; (b) soil profile; (c) lateral pressure on wall due to foundation pressure; (d) earth pressure on wall due to foundation pressure at stage 1 excavation to 3.1 m below street; (e) end-of-construction earth pressure; (f) moment in secant wall for construction stages; (g) deformation during construction stages [10] (*d*) The mechanics of inclined wall behaviour are similar to those of the vertical wall and are controlled by wall and anchor.

Schnabel[12] argued that earth pressure was reduced on walls sloping towards the excavation. Site measurements for sloping walls were compared with calculated pressures for vertical walls, with proposed reduction factors.

Diaphragm walls
Historic use and development

The earliest structural diaphragm walls were built in Italy by Icos in the 1950s. The method was soon used to facilitate cut-and-cover construction for metros in major cities. In Milan, Icos walls were used in a method developed by the firm and shown in Fig. 9.13. The sequence of construction was designed to minimize the disturbance to highway and traffic by early reinstatement of the carriageway above the permanent cut-and-cover roof as excavation and invert construction proceeded beneath it. This method, now familiar as top-downwards construction in both basement and cut-and-cover construction, became the basis of metro construction by Icos in many cities worldwide and, over time, by their competitors. Innovations were introduced by Icos[13] and later by others in Milan, on number 1 and 2 lines, when structural steel column elements were lowered into barrettes, sections of Icos wall, below tunnel invert level, as plunge columns to be used as structural support for reinforced concrete mezzanine floor and roofworks to the tunnel. Details of this construction are shown in Fig. 9.14.

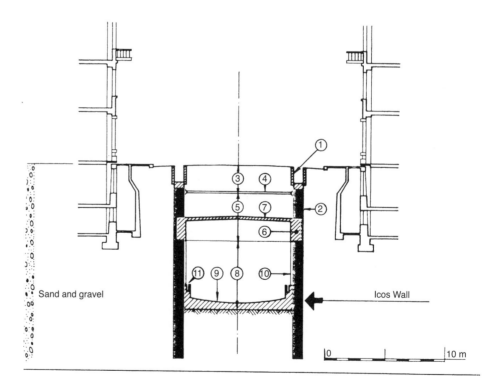

Fig. 9.13. Construction sequence used by Icos in original cut-and-cover works for Milan Metro (courtesy of Icos)

I – Excavation for the guide walls ①.

II – Building of the Icos diaphragm ② forming the permanent side walls of the tunnel.

III – Partial excavation of the soil between the walls ③, placing of the temporary bracing ④, continuation of the excavation ⑤ in order to cut the keys ⑥ for the roof of the tunnel ⑦.

IV – Excavation under cover of the tunnel ⑧: the Icos wall protects the excavation.

V – Construction of the invert ⑨, of the columns, withstanding uplift pressures on the invert, ⑩ and of the utility pipes ⑪.

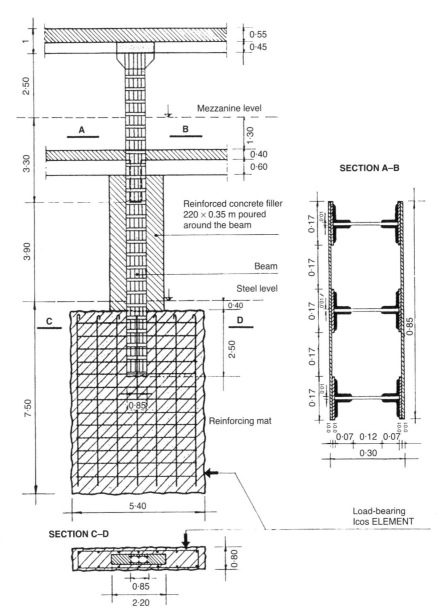

Fig. 9.14. Milan Metro: cross-section of fabricated steel columns cast into reinforced concrete base using diaphragm wall techniques for vertical load-bearing units (courtesy of Icos)

Icos also introduced castellated sections of diaphragm walling on metro construction in Milan (Fig. 9.15). The section, of greater breadth than the straight wall, provides considerably enhanced strength in bending. More recently, panel joints which can transmit vertical shear and tension from one panel to its neighbour have allowed this efficient plan shape to be fully exploited with a continuous wall section.

In the UK, diaphragm walls were introduced in 1962 for use on cut-and-cover construction for a road underpass at Hyde Park Corner in London[14]. The engineer had decided that driven sheet piling could not be used because of installation noise and vibration (a hospital was located nearby), so contiguous bored reinforced concrete piles were specified. Icos diaphragm walls were introduced by the main contractor but neither the contiguous piles of the original scheme nor the alternative of diaphragm walls were considered as part of the permanent subsoil support. This diaphragm wall scheme was also successfully used to underpin the existing hospital walls where the underpass diaphragm wall was built less than 1 m from the main hospital walls and more

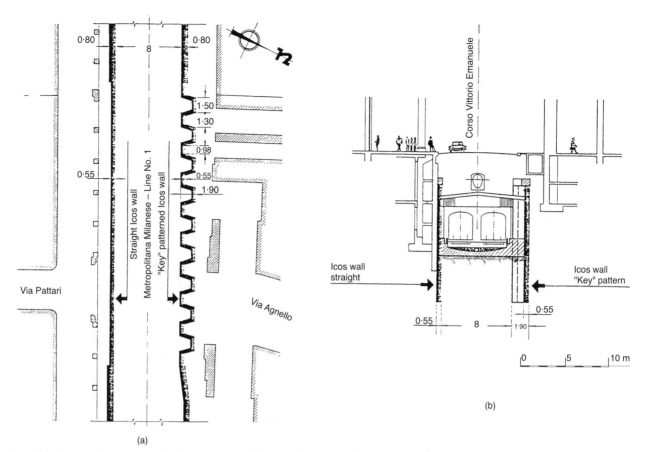

Fig. 9.15. Cut-and-cover construction using castellated plan shape diaphragm walls on one side: (a) plan; (b) cross-section (courtesy of Icos)

than 8 m below it. These measures later became standard practice for such locations. The use of short panels, increased wall reinforcement, pre-loaded struts and reduced open lengths of main excavation limited horizontal and vertical soil movements and wall movements to less than 3 mm.

The reluctance of designers outside Europe to use diaphragm walling as a means of combined temporary and permanent soil support persisted in the 1960s and 1970s. The cut-and-cover for the Calcutta Metro[15] used diaphragm walls only to resist buoyancy under permanent load conditions. A factor of safety of 1·5 was used against flotation with full soil cohesive strength being allowed in calculating wall adhesion to the clay subsoil.

In the UK, diaphragm walls were similarly used to resist buoyancy but with no assumed contribution to flexural strength of the rectangular cut-and-cover box structure housed between the walls. This reluctance to use the flexural strength of the diaphragm wall after construction was evident in the second tunnel crossing of the Thames at Dartford in 1972. By this time, diaphragm wall construction had gained wide acceptance in the UK and the walls at Dartford were extended to depths in excess of 30 m to minimize the length of the driven tunnel. Nevertheless, the flexural strength of the diaphragm walls was ignored for the permanent works design.

The 800 mm and 1 m thick diaphragm walls at Dartford were excavated by kelly-mounted hydraulic grabs through soft alluvial silty clays and dense gravels into hard chalk. Five frames of bracing were necessary to reduce flexural stresses in the wall as bulk excavation proceeded to the deepest sections at the junction with the bored tunnel, almost 30 m from ground level. These high flexural stresses were correctly anticipated by the wall designers who appreciated the relatively large wall movements that would be necessary to mobilize relatively small passive resistance in the soft clays at formation level and immediately below it. Following the innovation used by the contractor for the first Dartford Tunnel, hammerheaded concrete struts were used throughout to brace diaphragm walls in the cut-and-cover length, thus avoiding the need for separate walings.

Shortly after the Dartford Tunnel cut-and-cover works had been constructed by diaphragm walling, the station at Heathrow for the Piccadilly Line extension was built in cut-and-cover box, the diaphragm walls acting as both temporary and permanent soil-retaining walls. Jobling and Lyons[16] said that cut-and-cover construction was chosen in preference to bored tunnelling for three reasons:

(a) the use of station tunnels with space between escalator access tunnels would have used more plan area than the cut-and-cover box and left insufficient space for further station development for surface railways

(b) it was considered very costly to provide foundations for proposed building development over driven tunnels

(c) subsoil strata, flood plain gravels overlying London clay, favoured box construction in diaphragm walling.

The box shown in Fig. 9.16 was typical metro station size at that time, 131·5 m long and 22 m wide with a depth to formation level of 17 m to keep the tunnel drive below the flood plain gravels and within the London clay. The 1 m thick diaphragm walls, propped by three frames, were designed using earth pressures based on a value of $K_a = 0.25$ for the gravel and $K_0 = 0.75$ for the clay and a design groundwater level of 2 m below ground level. The base to the box, between 1·9 and 2·575 m thick, was designed as a beam on

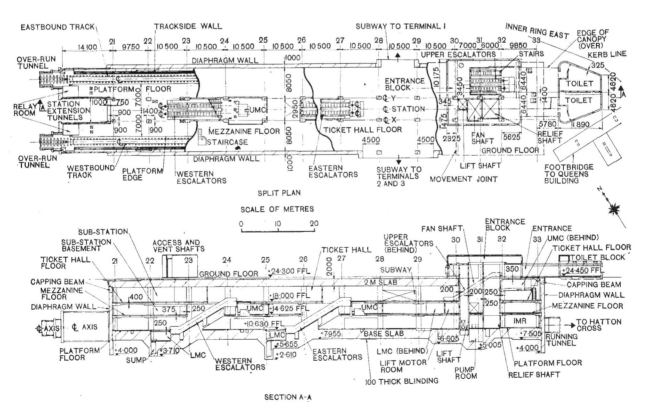

Fig. 9.16. Heathrow Central station, plan and vertical section[16]

an elastic foundation using a modulus of elasticity of $107\,MN/m^2$ for London clay, and a modulus of subgrade reaction of $9055\,kN/m^2$. The design factor of safety against flotation of the box was 1·2 on completion, but a rubble drain beneath the base raft adjacent to the diaphragm walls restricted groundwater pressure on the raft during construction. The raft was not designed to resist hydraulic forces until loaded by the main internal columns.

The walls were temporarily braced by the frames of Rendex No. 6 struts at floor level and by $300\,mm \times 300\,mm$ timber struts at platform level. A maximum deflection of only 5 mm at the top of the diaphragm walls had been specified and pre-loading of the top frame and successive shimming of the second frame was necessary to achieve this. Strut loads were monitored; this showed that middle frame loads exceeded design values prior to the lower frame being placed. This lower frame consisted of timber struts spanning from the central raft section to the walls which were placed as a soil berm $4\,m \times 3\,m$ in section progressively excavated from the face of the walls. Excavation of these berms was uneconomical, being hindered by starter steel from the raft and the strutting itself.

Metro construction in the Far East has utilized diaphragm walling for both station and running tunnel construction in soil conditions generally more demanding than those in Europe. The original contract for the construction of the Hong Kong MTR in the late 1970s[4] comprised running tunnels in bored tunnel and cut-and-cover and the construction of twelve stations. In general, the cut-and-cover tunnels were built within braced sheet pile trenchworks, except in one section close to rather sensitive buildings where a proprietary contiguous (PIP) piling system was used.

The contracts were let as design-and-construct contracts within specifications and layouts prepared by the engineer. Local ground conditions comprised granites in various stages of decomposition, varying from strong intact rock to stiff residual clays containing granite boulders. These ground conditions impose many practical construction difficulties for bored tunnel, large excavations and cut-and-cover work.

Table 9.2 compared those methods of station construction envisaged prior to bidding and those adopted by the successful contractors. Generally, it had been planned that the twelve stations would be built top-down using diaphragm walls, but with three main exceptions: bored tunnel construction for Lok Fu station; top-down construction within sheet pile walls at Diamond Hill; and bottom-upwards construction in open rock cut at Shek Kip Mei. In the event, considerable changes were made as contractors' alternatives for both construction method and walling techniques were considered and then adopted.

Choi Hung and Diamond Hill stations used a locally popular technique at that time, the hand-dug caisson. At Choi Hung (Fig. 9.17) the caissons used were interlocked to form the station walls, and at Diamond Hill (Fig. 9.18) the system was modified for the semi-permanent walls by the use of anchored plates spanning king piles installed within the caissons. Hand-dug caissons were used at both stations to place permanent columns prior to bulk excavation works. More recently the use of family caissons in Hong Kong has declined significantly due to the unacceptable health and safety risks. Only where all other methods are considered inapplicable are hand-dug caissons used in Hong Kong, although at present some use is made of the method in mainland China.

At Argyle station, Hong Kong, one of the largest, with a concourse level, two track levels, 13 entrances and three ventilation shafts, the intensity of street traffic and the proximity of tower blocks, some with piles founded near station formation level, favoured the top-down construction method.

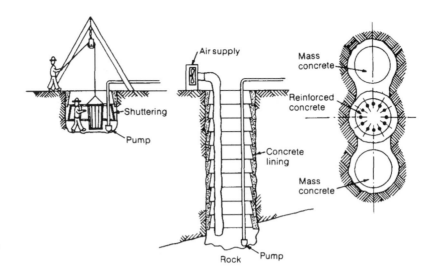

Fig. 9.17. Choi Hung station,
Hong Kong MTR: interlocked
hand-dug caissons[4]

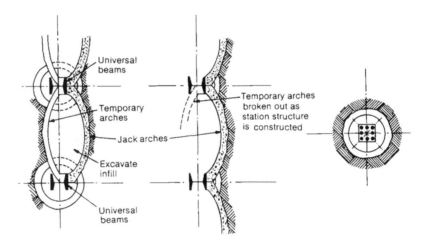

Fig. 9.18. Diamond Hill station,
Hong Kong MTR: jack arches
between soldier piles installed
in hand-dug caissons[4]

Due to difficult subsoil conditions with large granite boulders and the need to penetrate bedrock, secant piles installed by Benoto oscillating rigs were chosen by the contractor. The piles, 1·2 m in diameter and bored at 1 m centres, were reinforced in both male and female piles by 914 mm × 305 mm universal beam sections. Figure 9.19 shows a plan and cross-section of the station and Fig. 9.20 shows a typical cross-section during excavation for the lower track. To reduce settlements due to dewatering and subsidence of adjacent buildings, a bentonite cement and silicate grout curtain was made below the toe of the structural wall to form a cut-off to the box from the high water table where this could not be achieved by the Benoto rigs. This grout curtain produced excellent results, restricting the abstraction rate from the whole box to less than 0·0045 m³/s under a differential head of more than 20 m. Design of the walls during construction and in the permanent case used active and at-rest earth pressures with plastic methods and limit state checks. Station columns, heavily loaded, in some cases up to 15 MN, comprised 1000 mm × 800 mm steel boxes in 50B steel, 20 m long. Figure 9.21 shows a shear shoe and plate arrangement used to transfer high loads from slabs to walls and columns.

At Tsim Sha Tsui station, shown in Fig. 9.22, the bottom-up construction sequence with PIP piles was used by the contractor in preference to the original, pre-bid, top-down method using diaphragm walls, with the following advantages[4].

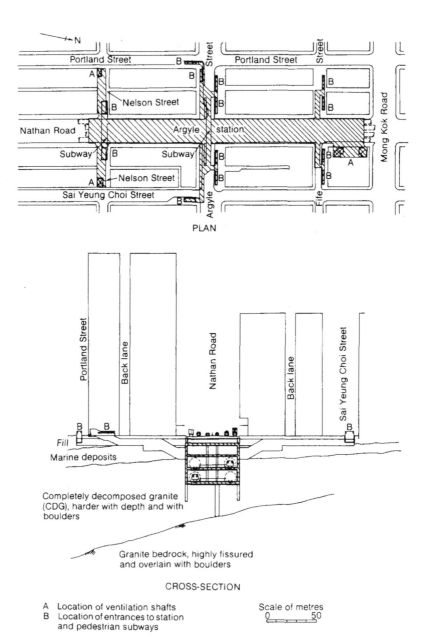

Fig. 9.19. Argyle station, Hong Kong MTR: plan and vertical section showing soil profile and location of existing buildings[4]

(a) Where rock existed above formation level, difficult underpinning work was avoided.

(b) Less noise and vibration was caused by PIP piling.

(c) The PIP wall was narrower than the diaphragm wall.

(d) The PIP wall provided drier conditions in which to build the permanent structural box.

(e) The PIP pile did not require wide, heavy reinforcement cages as used in the diaphragm wall panels.

(f) The work construction period was reduced.

In the event, the method was successful. Figure 9.23 shows the formation of PIP walls, installed by a large continuous flight auger (CFA) with mortar placement through the hollow stem, in a simlar way to CFA piles. The male PIP piles (piles B), however, required a cement paste injection pressure of 200 kg/cm^2 to make a vertical mortar cut-off between adjacent female

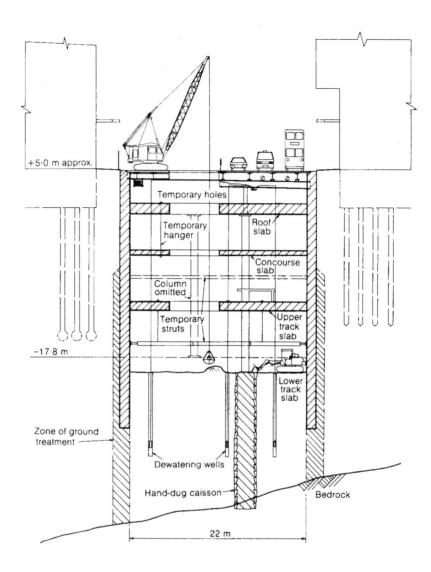

Fig. 9.20. Argyle station, Hong Kong MTR: typical cross-section showing top-down construction for lower track slab using secant pile walls and ground treatment to secure cut-off to bedrock[4]

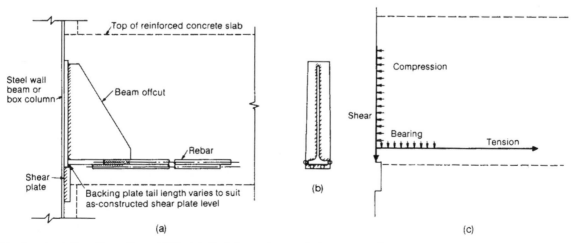

Fig. 9.21. Argyle station, Hong Kong MTR: detail of shear shoe and plate to transfer high loads from slabs to secant pile walls: (a) side view; (b) end view; (c) force transfer[4]

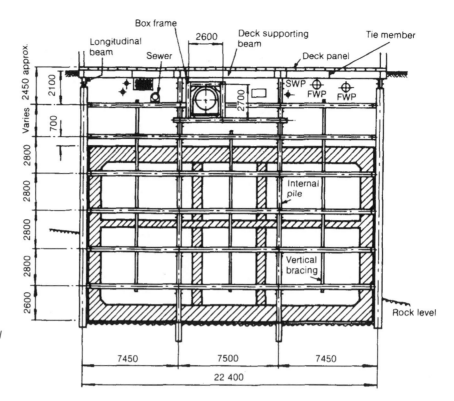

Fig. 9.22. Tsim Sha Tsui station, Hong Kong MTR: typical cross-section of cut-and-cover station constructed by bottom-upwards method showing temporary deck support[4]

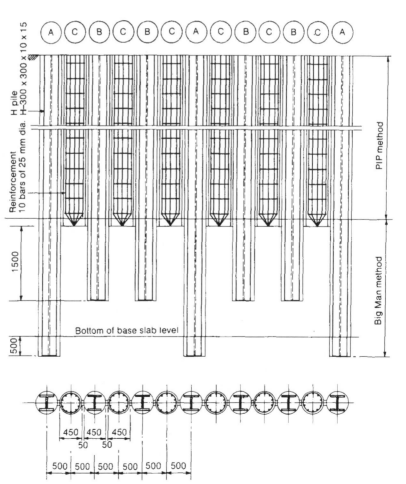

Fig. 9.23. Tsim Sha Tsui station: construction of wall using PIP piles[4]

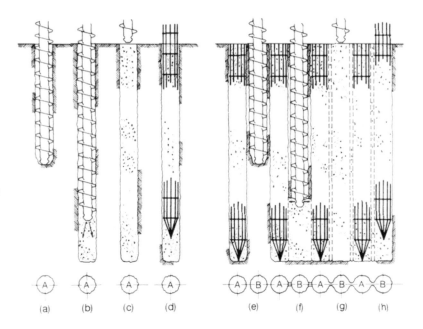

Fig. 9.24. Tsim Sha Tsui station: PIP construction sequence: (a) augering; (b) withdrawing auger and injecting mortar; (c) completing injection; (d) inserting reinforcement cage or steel column section; (e) augering; (f) withdrawing auger then injecting and jetting mortar; (g) completing injection and jetting; (h) inserting reinforcement cage or steel column section[4]

piles. A rock boring machine (typically a Koken N50 Big Man) was used to bore through boulders or into bedrock. Figures 9.23 and 9.24 show the sequence of piles used at Tsim Sha Tsui station: piles A were taken 500 mm below formation level to support the traffic deck at road level; piles B were taken 1·5 m into rock, and the pressure-injected sealing piles C were taken to rockhead.

The following loading and permissible stress values were used in the design:

- wall stiffness per metre width: $EI = 9·40 \times 108\,\mathrm{kN/cm}^2$ per metre
- traffic load: $14·7\,\mathrm{kN/m}^2$
- building load: $353\,\mathrm{kN/m}^2$
- earth pressure: trapezoidal loading, active pressure
- water pressure from 1 m below ground level: fully hydrostatic
- design strength of pile mortar: $23·5\,\mathrm{N/mm}^2$.

The design loading model for the cofferdam is shown in Fig. 9.25. A typical cross-section of the temporary support and the permanent works in Fig. 9.22 shows the six frames of pre-loaded H steel strutting at centres of 2·1 m.

Considerable settlements to existing buildings resulted from the initial Hong Kong MTR construction. Settlement was primarily due to dewatering, diaphragm wall panel installation and bulk excavation, but more importantly the combination of properties of the decomposed granite subsoil and the groundwater regime, unusual for developed city centres, was conducive to high installation deformations.

Davies and Henkel[17] referred to the construction of Chater station and settlements of the existing Courts of Justice building. A section of the construction and soil profile is shown in Fig. 9.26. The permeability of marine deposits was of the order of $10^{-7}\,\mathrm{m/s}$ compared with $10^{-5}\,\mathrm{m/s}$ for the underlying decomposed granite. Wide variations in drawdown were expected due to local variations in the geological profile, and preliminary studies showed unfavourable dewatering settlements could result. Pumping tests had shown that for each 1 m of drawdown a settlement of 4 mm would result. A system of groundwater recharge was used, however, both at the Courts and elsewhere, with beneficial results.

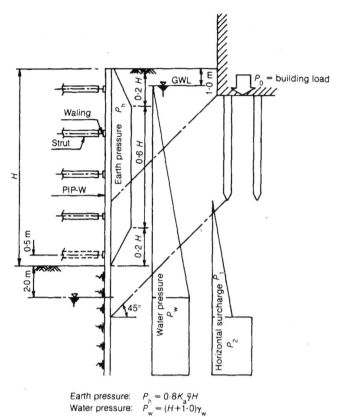

Earth pressure: $P_h = 0.8K_a\bar{\gamma}H$
Water pressure: $P_w = (H+1.0)\gamma_w$

Horizontal surcharge $\begin{cases} P_1 = \frac{1}{2}K_aP_0\text{(pile friction)} \\ P_2 = K_aP_0\text{(building load)} \end{cases}$
from building:

Fig. 9.25. Tsim Sha Tsui station: earth pressure, water pressure and horizontal surcharge loading diagrams[4]

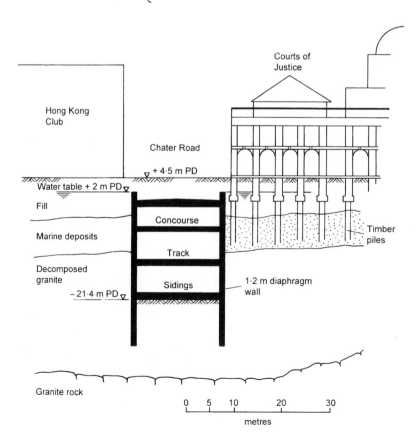

Fig. 9.26. Cross-section of Chater station, Hong Kong, showing soil profile and location of existing structures[17]

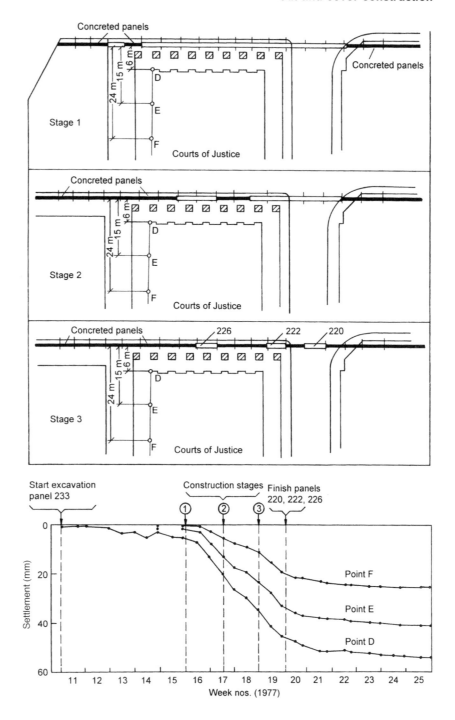

Fig. 9.27. Chater station, settlement record of ground adjacent to diaphragm wall construction[17]

Settlements due to diaphragm wall panel excavation for Chater station had unpredicted and serious consequences. Figure 9.27 shows the extent of movements of three points, D, E and F, spaced 6 m, 15 m and 2 4m, respectively, from the diaphragm wall. The progressive settlement of the points, even as diaphragm wall installation was completed well away from the vicinity of the points, is clear. This is a most unusual phenomenon. Measurements of soil movement due to diaphragm wall installation before and since in widely differing soils, show very small soil movements (a few millimetres) due to panel excavation at points near the panel and very early reduction of soil movement at distances of less than half the panel depth from the panel, as described in references by Farmer and Attewell[18], Uriel and Oteo[19], Clough and O'Rourke[20], Thompson[21], Carder[22] and Carder et al[23]. Generally, vertical settlement at the wall due to diaphragm wall installation in stiff clay is of the order of 0.05% of wall depth and probably becomes negligible at a distance of 1.5 times wall depth from the wall. The progressive movement as panels were excavated at Chater station was therefore unprecedented and unexpected. Morton et al.[24] concluded that this cumulative movement resulted from the combined effect of a relatively high permeability and a medium compressibility of the completely weathered granite. A softened zone of highly compressible soil occurred as the diaphragm panel was excavated due to relaxation of horizontal soil pressures. After the panel was concreted this softened zone compressed due to soil pressures and, in turn, reduced arching action within the soil as further panels were excavated. It may be summarized that such large soil movements only occur as a result of panel excavation in expansive soil with a high permeability and access to a groundwater supply.

In Singapore, metro construction did not proceed until the late 1980s and many organizational and technical lessons learned on the Hong Kong MTR were used to good effect. The works were let mainly on a design-and-construct basis and Table 9.1 showed the wide range of station constructions chosen. The ground conditions in Singapore[3] are predominantly soft clays and loose sands or, from an earlier period, stronger soils and rocks. The soft clays and loose sands have been laid down in valleys eroded into the underlying rocks during periods of low sea level. Where the soft clays and loose sands were virtually absent, cut slopes were used with improvement where necessary by soil nailing, rock bolting or anchoring. Generally, cut-and-cover structures were not supported on these clays; piles or diaphragm walls were used to take loads down to a lower bearing stratum. Where there was any significant depth of soft clay a continuous walling system was used. Sheet piles were used for this purpose, except where existing buildings were particularly vulnerable to soil movement, in which case diaphragm walls were used. A typical cut-and-cover station 15 m deep would generate a net active pressure in the marine clay until the shear strength exceeded about 60 kPa. This strength would only occur at a depth of about 35 m, where the clay persisted to this depth, and would require heavily reinforced diaphragm walls and special construction measures to resist the very high moments and deflections induced in the wall. A thick layer of weak soil above or below formation level poses problems for the designer in coping with these very high wall moments prior to placing the lowest bracing frame.

At Bugis station, 1.2 m thick diaphragm walls were socketed into dense cemented old alluvium up to 14 m to produce walls up to 54 m deep. Where the depth of old alluvium support to the wall was greatest, the marine clay above and below the final excavation level was strengthened with chemico-lime piles. Figure 9.28 shows a cross-section of the station. Seven frame levels were used, but even so, deflections of 150 mm were measured in the diaphragm walls.

Diaphragm walling: recent developments in cut-and-cover works

In recent years, since the end of the 1990s, diaphragm walling has continued to find extensive use in cut-and-cover works for deeper and more heavily loaded walls. In turn, the technique has been improved and varied by competing specialists. These improvements have been applied to excavation plant and diaphragm walling site practice (as referred to in Chapter 8), but specific changes have also been made because of the demands of the plan length

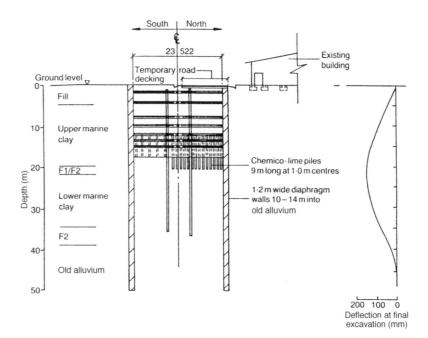

Fig. 9.28. Bugis station, Singapore MRT: cross-section showing seven cofferdam frames used to minimize wall deformation[3]

and depth of cut-and-cover works, both in terms of design and production improvements.

Semi top-down construction
The development of a variation on conventional top-down construction was made, as explained previously in this chapter, on the N.E. line of Singapore MRT system to reduce bracing and strutting, to expedite excavation and still gain the advantages already secured by top-down construction, the minimization of soil and wall deformation to reduce settlements and ground-water leakage. A typical application, described by Mitchell et al.[25], was made on two station boxes on Contract 705, after a tender stage comparison of alternative methods; a summary is shown in Table 9.4, reproduced from this paper. The first decision to use diaphragm walls instead of sheet piling was made to avoid problems with nearby buildings and services. The next decision, the choice of construction method was guided by the disadvantages of large working space and the large props needed to build bottom-up (the box widths were up to 60 m) and the difficulties with conventional top-down due to a very heavy roof structure and a complex internal lay out needed for station operation. These matters were solved by the use of large construction openings in the roof to reduce loading whilst keeping the lateral support of the structure. The roof openings are shown in Fig. 9.29, at Boon Keng station.

The stiffness of this roof (the thickness of 2 m was required for civil defence purposes) compared to the diaphragm walls of the box (not yet lined) meant that a large moment was temporarily transferred to the walls at the junction with the roof. From a crack width consideration, the necessity to comply with a maximum width of 0·2 mm as specified caused considerable design effort to show that in the long term the influence of creep in the diaphragm walls, the influence of the 1 m thick R.C. lining walls and the re-application of water pressure would limit cracks to the 0·2 mm width.

The semi-top-down method also had the advantage that it allowed the base slab to act as a raft before all the weight of the superstructure is applied and thereby reduced settlement.

Table 9.4 N.E. line Singapore MRT; summary of alternative methods at tender stage[25]

Construction method	Main quantities (per station)	Advantages	Disadvantages
Sheet pile	• Sheet pile: 18 000 m² (FSP 4 ~3420 t) • Steel struts and walers: 2900 t (total of 5 or 6 layers) • Decking steel: 1700 t	• Lowest cost • No influence of temp works on station design • Early start on site	• Difficult to install sheet piles in hard ground • Noise and vibration • Sensitive utilities and buildings very close • Ground treatment under utility crossing required • Congestion of site with six layers of struts • Sequence of work affected by strutting • Removal of all temporary works required
D-wall Bottom-up	• Diaphragm wall: 16 000 m² • Steel struts and walers: 2500 t (total of 5 or 6 layers) • Decking steel: 1700 t	• High stiffness and water tightness of retaining wall • D-wall can be installed below utility • D-wall is part of permanent works	• Permanent works design approval needed to start D-wall • Congestion of site with six layers of struts • Sequence of work affected by strutting
D-wall Top-down	• Diaphragm wall: 16 000 m² • Temp props: 1000 t • Steel strut and waler: 400 t (1 layer)	• High stiffness and water tightness of retaining wall • D-wall can be installed below utility • D-wall is part of permanent works • Minimal heavy duty falsework required • Fairly clear working area	• Permanent works design approval needed to start D-wall • All walls have to be under-pinned to soffit • Large number of props to remove at end • All work under roof in confined space
D-wall Semi-top-down	• Diaphragm wall: 16 000 m² • Steel strut and waler: 400 t (1 layer) • Minimal temp props	• High stiffness and water tightness of retaining wall • D-wall can be installed below utility • D-wall is part of permanent works • Very clear working area	• Permanent works design approval needed to start D-wall • Complex design • Some walls have to be underpinned to soffit • Large openings have to be closed later

A precedence network prepared for an example of semi-top-down construction is shown in Fig. 9.30, based on Mitchell *et al.* and prepared by Brian Bell Associates.

Movement joints in box structures

The use of movement joints within the diaphragm walls of cut-and-cover structures has, until now, not been deemed necessary by designers either on the grounds of thermal movement or flexural movement. On the construction of the Stratford station box, part of the Channel Tunnel Rail Link works in London, movement joints have been incorporated in the 1070 m long box, with its width of 50 m and a depth varying between 16 and 22 m. The structure is permanently propped at each end by concrete props at 10 m centres and by road and rail bridges in the middle of the structure. Temporary props are used below the permanent props. The base slab is unreinforced concrete and a

Fig. 9.29. Boon Keng station, semi top-down construction of the N.E. line, Singapore MRT (courtesy of Benaim Consultants)[25]

permanent dewatering scheme will operate by deep wells in the chalk stratum below the box to relieve water pressure on the base slab during its 120-year design life.

The movement joints, shown in Fig. 9.31, were designed to accommodate differential deflections, settlements and in-plane movements. The design requirements for the joint were: $+100\,mm/-0\,mm$ for horizontal deflection, $+10\,mm/-30\,mm$ for horizontal in-plane movement and $\pm10\,mm$ for vertical settlement with joint watertightness for the 120-year design life. The joints are prefabricated off-site in 9 m lengths, in a steel–rubber sandwich construction which is pre-compressed and pinned in the factory. After installation and concreting of the wall each side of the joint the pin system is released following initial concrete shrinkage in the wall, the joint remaining in compression.

Soft tunnel eyes
The Thames tunnel crossing for the Channel Tunnel Rail Link has recently seen the use of a soft eye formed from glass fibre bar reinforced concrete within the end diaphragm wall panels of the reception chamber for the tunnel boring machine (TBM). This innovation was necessary as a replacement for the normal slurry block on the outside of the chamber through which the TBM travels without allowing a 'blow' of groundwater and soil into the reception chamber. The composite cage, made from the conventionally steel reinforced sections and the glass fibre bar section was lifted successfully in one piece (Fig. 9.32). Wider application of 'eyes' of glass fibre reinforcement may be expected to allow permanent access ways through structural diaphragm walls.

Cut-and-cover walls of varied plan form
Where working space allows, the straight walls of cut-and-cover sections can be replaced by walls of varied plan shape to produce walls of improved stiffness and flexural strength. The use of diaphragm walls built to T plan shape and castellated plan shapes with shear joints between panels has been referred to in Chapter 8. A further variation is the use of walls built as horizontal arches with temporary tubular stop ends. The arch shapes span between props or diaphragm cross walls as shown in Fig. 9.33. The improved stiffness and flexural strength of these plan shapes allows reduced vertical propping at increased centres with both cost and programme advantages where working space permits.

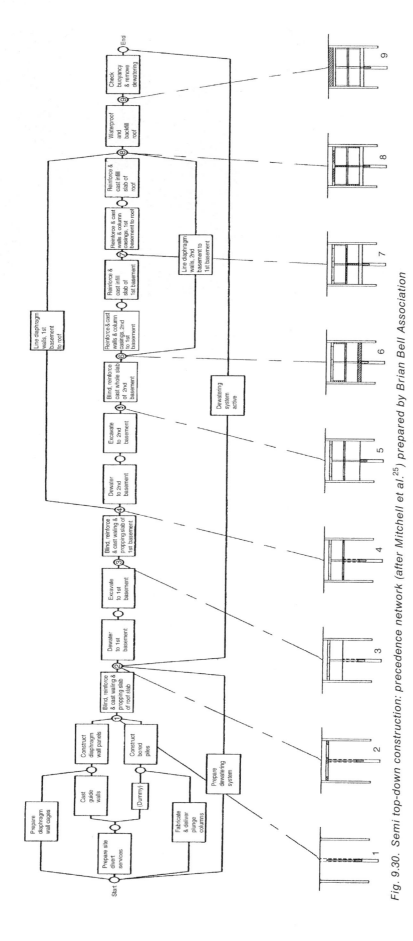

Fig. 9.30. Semi top-down construction: precedence network (after Mitchell et al.[25]) prepared by Brian Bell Association

Fig. 9.31. Movement joint construction: Channel Tunnel Rail Link works, Stratford station box, London

Fig. 9.32. Soft tunnel eye construction: composite reinforcement cage[35]

Observational techniques

The repetitive nature of cut-and-cover construction, in which wall panels are progressively cast, bulk excavation made and bracing frames inserted, allows any observed production or technical improvement in walling or strutting to be introduced at an early stage as the work proceeds. The principles of observational soil mechanics as described by Peck[26] are particularly relevant to cut-and-cover construction. An example of the successful use of this technique is the Limehouse Link highway tunnel in East London which was built in the early 1990s. The original design of the top-downwards construction required temporary 1350 mm dia. steel props between diaphragm walls on each side of the cut-and-cover box below roof level. The props were lifted into place using hoists supported from the soffit of the roof slab (Fig. 9.34). Excavation then continued to formation level below the line of struts. This excavation was slow and costly due to the presence of the struts.

The observational method was applied progressively in a number of stages. Initially, props were destressed and removed one at a time as wall movements were measured. Since wall displacements were small, a new section with 'soft' props was installed with a small gap allowed at the end of the strut prior to load take-up. Since movement again proved to be very small as excavation

Fig. 9.33. Plan of diaphragm wall construction using horizontal arch plan shapes

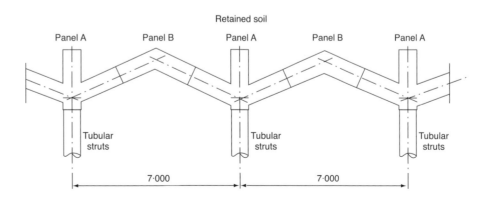

Fig. 9.34. Limehouse link,
London. Heavy props used in
top-down construction[34]

was taken below the props to formation level, the mid-height props were
omitted and excavation was made to full depth prior to the installation of a
strut at blinding level. The monitored wall movements were still very small
and this allowed the continuing omission of the centre struts. Eventually
the blinding struts were also omitted. Contingency struts were always kept
available, but were not needed. The trigger level for maximum wall movement
was defined as 70 mm but the maximum recorded movement was 11 mm, and
generally readings were less than 7 mm. Considerable savings resulted from
avoiding the use of these heavy props.

A similar application of the observational method to reduce the propping to
a cut-and-cover excavation was reported by Beadman et al.[27], for the excavation support (by a secant pile wall) at Norreport station on the Copenhagen
Metro. A system of trigger levels at the various design sections along the
station defined risk and the need to implement contingency measures. The
design calculations were based on most probable soil parameters based on
back analysis of a previous station excavation. Deflection profiles (based on
analysis by the springs program, WALLAP) defined the trigger values. The
green limit was assessed as 70% of the design values, the amber limit used
the most probable soil parameters whilst the red limit, stipulating the stoppage
of excavation was defined as 120% of calculated horizontal deflection values.
This value of 120% of designed deflection still ensured the secant piles
remained within their ultimate capacity.

Precast diaphragm walls
Precast concrete panels were introduced into diaphragm wall works in France
by the firms Bachy and Soletanche during the early 1970s. Each company

Fig. 9.35. Cairo Metro: junction between precast and in situ diaphragm walls

obtained patents for its particular technique. The innovation found early application in cut-and-cover construction and was used in Paris for underpass and metro construction, and in both Lille and Lyon for metro construction. The technique has not been used in the UK, and appears to have found less application in recent years in France. (More recently the two companies have merged to trade internationally together as one.)

In the Far East, in Hong Kong and Thailand, thick, heavily reinforced in situ diaphragm walls are preferred; in Japan there are only a few examples of precast walls; and there are no known precast walls in the USA. This lack of acceptance of a potentially attractive innovation is probably due to a unit cost disadvantage between in situ and precast walls. The introduction of the cutter machine and its use by the largest diaphragm wall contractors may also have detracted from the popularity of precast walls; the reverse circulation process cannot be economically applied when grout is used as the stabilizing fluid during excavation.

The principal feature of the precast diaphragm wall is the absence of any surface finishing subsequent to its exposure after bulk excavation. On bulk excavation the cement–bentonite slurry strips away from the inside surface of the wall to reveal the precast concrete surface, to true alignment. Figure 9.35 shows the junction between in situ and precast diaphragm wall construction on the Cairo Metro.

The use of prefabricated diaphragm walls for metro cut-and-cover construction was described by Namy and Fenoux[28]. They noted two fundamental disadvantages of in situ reinforced concrete diaphragm walls:

(*a*) the surface finish and quality of excavation of the wall depends on subsoil conditions
(*b*) the water resistance of the concrete and the joints may be inadequate.

The development of precast wall methods offers several advantages over in situ diaphragm wall construction.

(a) Site nuisance is reduced by more rapid execution. The sequence of panel excavation is simplified by successive panel excavation, whereas in situ diaphragms frequently use primary, secondary and intermediate panel excavation sequences to allow hardening of concrete. Remedial works in breaking down walls to level or to profile are largely unnecessary.

(b) Site concreting operations and stop end extraction are avoided.

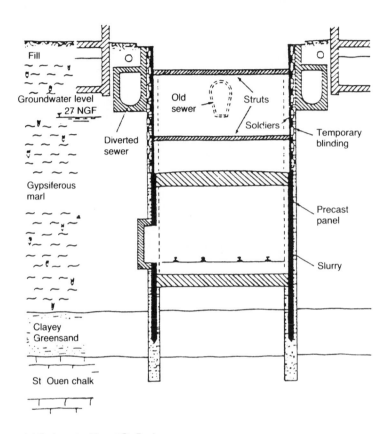

(a) Paris metro Line at St Denis.
Prefabricated diaphragm wall construction.
Top of excavation supported by hardened
slurry and bracing (see below).

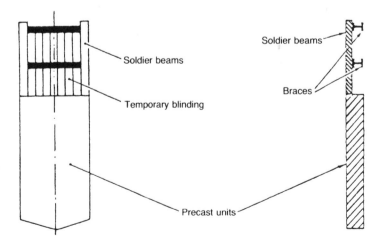

Fig. 9.36. Paris Metro, St Denis, cross-sections of precast diaphragm wall construction: (a) top of excavation supported by hardened slurry and bracing; (b) arrangement of precast concrete elements used in cut-and-cover walls (courtesy of Soletanche–Bachy)

(b) Arrangement of precast element used in
prefabricated diaphragm for cut-and-cover walls.

(*c*) In the permanent phase, constructional thicknesses are reduced by the improved concrete qualities brought by precasting (a 400 mm precast wall can be equivalent to a 600 mm in situ wall panel). By incorporating water bars into the precast panels, good wall finishes and better water resistance are possible.

The use of precast wall panels enables prefabricated units to be made up with soldier beams for temporary soil retention above the precast wall. An example of prefabricated, precast diaphragm construction using the Panosol system is shown in Fig. 9.36 in cross-section. The works, an extension of the Paris Metro in the heart of St Denis, extended 500 m along a confined route, 12 m wide wall-to-wall, bordered by old, delicate buildings.

The subsoils consisted of fill, gypsiferous marls and clayey greensands overlying St Ouen limestone. The marls acted as an upper aquifer close to street level, and the lower aquifer of limestone has its piezometric head near the top of the greensand.

Refuge holes, cross-drainage holes and slab starter bars were incorporated into the precast panels which transferred vertical load through the sealing grout into the limestone. No lining to the precast walls was used in the finished structure although an epoxy resin based treatment was applied to the joints on the inside to provide long-term waterproofness. The wall works, including site set-up, were completed in a period of seven weeks, with a daily output of 30 linear metres of walls complete.

A precast diaphragm wall was also used for metro cut-and-cover construction on the line serving Charles de Gaulle Airport at Sevran. Again, gypsiferous marls and greensands overlying St Ouen marls and limestone contained separate aquifers (shown in Fig. 9.37). Due to the risk of large voids and solution cavities, sometimes several metres deep in the marly limestones, pre-grouting with bentonite–cement grout with a high sand content was carried out under gravity. Smaller cavities in the greensands were injected with bentonite–cement under low pressure. The insertion of the precast panel and the water stop is illustrated in Fig. 9.38. At the base of the panel a blade-shaped plate slides into the vertical groove within the adjacent panel, which serves as a guide as the new unit is lowered. The water stop follows the blade during the lowering. The weight of the panels reached 37 tonnes; the standard panels were 9·50 m high by 3·35 m wide by 0·45 m thick. Extra-thick panels were provided at areas of high loading and at tunnel refuge holes. The site output averaged 30 m of precast panel placed daily, the side walls of the 300 m cut-and-cover section being constructed in less than five months.

New metro construction in Lyon and Lille during the late 1970s provided an opportunity for the use of precast diaphragm walls at two stations, Saxe-Gambetta and Gare de Lille, and on sections of running tunnel in cut-and-over construction.

Saxe-Gambetta station (Fig. 9.39) was built at the junction of two lines in Rhone alluvium 25 m thick underlain by a relatively impermeable sand. The groundwater table was at a depth of only 3·5 m and the alluvium was very permeable. The station incorporated a precast diaphragm wall to support the soil temporarily and provide a cut-off into the sand substratum, together with an in situ reinforced concrete tunnel section. A sandwich-type waterproof membrane was applied to the inside face of the precast wall.

The precast wall was designed to support all loads – soil and groundwater pressure and surcharge loads – during construction. In the permanent condition, the load was divided between soil load on the Panosol wall and water pressure on the reinforced concrete tunnel structure. In the temporary condition the permeable alluvium became impregnated with the cement–bentonite slurry used in the wall excavation, with a resulting reduction in short-term soil pressures and deformation.

The works were built in open trench (Fig. 9.39(b)) with the exception of one section beneath Gambetta Road where traffic could not be diverted (Fig. 9.39(c)). In this latter section, intermediate supports were needed from barette panels. The construction sequence for the works in the open was:

(a) relocate existing utilities
(b) install precast diaphragm wall from street level (economy in the use of materials and panel weight was achieved by making a cut-off at the level of the relocated utilities, an H-beam was set in the top of each panel to allow cantilever support for a temporary roadway for light vehicles)
(c) excavate to groundwater level
(d) concrete between H-beams beneath temporary roadway to support utilities
(e) install temporary ground anchors
(f) complete excavation and station construction (Fig. 9.40).

Gare de Lille station, which was planned to connect with a future line, was built in a larger box 230 m long, 27 m wide and between 14 and 16 m deep. The ground conditions consisted of fill and alluvium overlying chalk with a

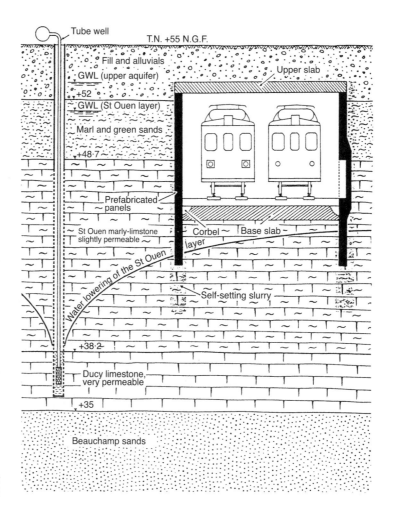

Fig. 9.37. Cross-section of precast diaphragm wall construction for the rail link to Charles de Gaulle Airport, Paris (courtesy of Soletanche–Bachy)

groundwater table at the base of the surface fill material and just below permanent roof level of the tunnel section. As at Lyon Saxe-Gambetta station, the same combination of Panosol precast wall and in situ reinforced concrete tunnel section with a sandwiched waterproof membrane was used. The plan

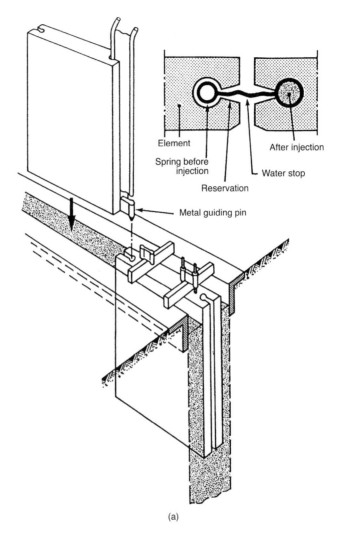

(a)

Fig. 9.38. Rail link to Charles de Gaulle Airport, Paris: (a) view of assembly of precast units in slurry trench; (b) view of completed cut-and-cover tunnel (courtesy of Soletanche–Bachy)

and cross-section of the works is shown in Fig. 9.41. The rate of flow of groundwater into the completed excavation was limited to about $50 \, \text{m}^3$ per hour, demonstrating the effectiveness of the cut-off.

Precast units in both reinforced and pre-stressed concrete were used in sections of the cut-and-cover for the running tunnels of the Lyon Metro, depending on depth to formation. Typical sections are shown in Fig. 9.42, illustrating the use of a grouted base within the walls below formation level and at a depth to balance the groundwater pressure within the alluvium. In some areas, to obtain cut-off within the underlying sandstone it proved more economical to extend the depth of the self-hardening slurry wall where the formation level was deeper.

Ingress of the self-hardening slurry, containing between 150 and 250 kg of slag and cement per cubic metre, into the alluvium at the sides of the excavation was high – estimated at between 1 and $1 \cdot 5 \, \text{m}^3$ per square metre of wall area. The assumed short-term strength properties of the alluvium allowed for this loss and a value of $20 \, \text{kN/m}^2$ was used for cohesion in the design of wall and strutting in the temporary condition. As the water resistance of the permanent structure was achieved with the sandwiched impermeable membrane, the panels were made of rectangular section with

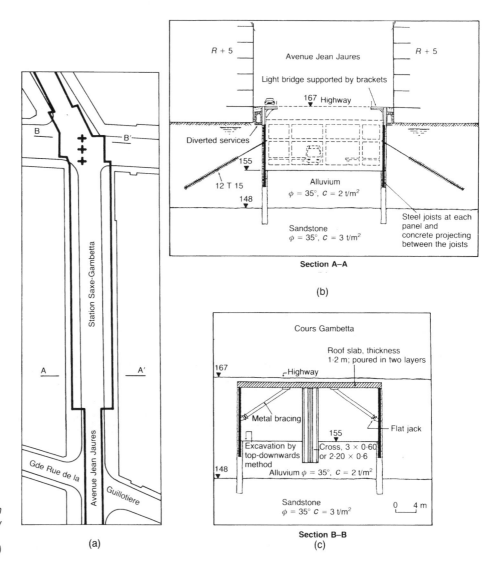

Fig. 9.39. Lyon Metro, Saxe-Gambetta station: (a) plan of site area; (b) section A–A, works in open trench; (c) section B–B, at junction, constructed by top-downwards method (courtesy of Soletanche–Bachy)

(a)

(b)

(c)

Fig. 9.40. Lyon Metro, Saxe-Gambetta station: completed station excavation showing precast diaphragm walls (courtesy of Soletanche–Bachy)

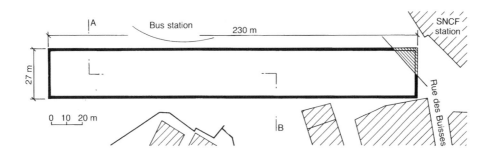

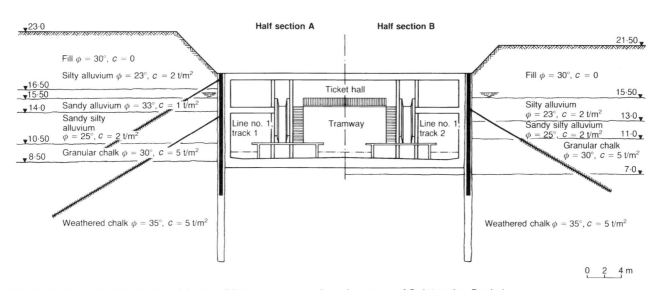

Fig. 9.41. Gare de Lille station: (a) plan; (b) transverse sections (courtesy of Soletanche–Bachy)

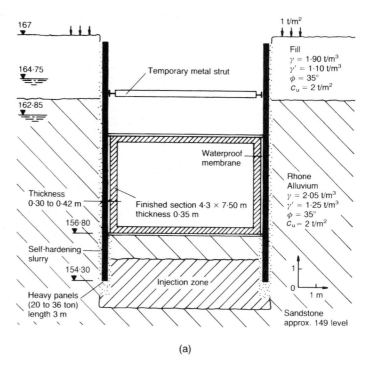

(a)

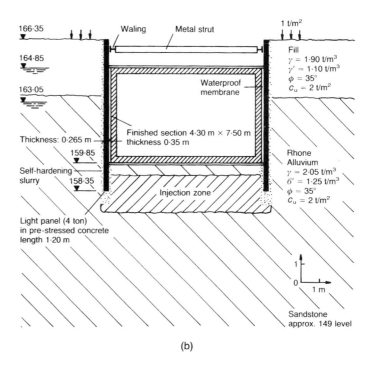

Fig. 9.42. Lyon Metro, typical sections of running tunnel: (a) deep section constructed with precast reinforced concrete units; (b) shallow section using precast pre-stressed concrete units (courtesy of Soletanche–Bachy)

(b)

no special jointing devices, temporary waterproofing being obtained from the self-hardening slurry. Figure 9.43 shows illustrations of the Panosol wall construction applied to the Lyon Metro.

The versatility of precast diaphragm walls in cut-and-cover construction is demonstrated in Figs 9.44 to 9.46. Bachy's method was used to build a culvert at Vitny. Figure 9.44 shows a cross-section of the completed works, which were constructed to high standards of finish, alignment and water

Fig. 9.43. Lyon Metro: two views of exposed precast Panosol panels in running tunnel
(courtesy of Soletanche–Bachy)

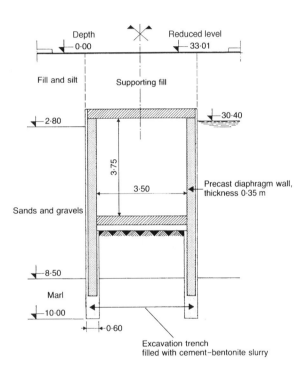

Fig. 9.44. Vitny culvert:
cross-section of completed
works (courtesy of
Soletanche–Bachy)

resistance. The culvert was located in a narrow commercial street in the centre
of the town. The finished culvert, of internal rectangular section, is 3·75 m high
and 3·5 m wide with approximately 3 m depth of cover from existing
carriageway levels, the roof being just below groundwater level. The sequence
of construction was as follows.

(a) Construct a 350 mm thick precast diaphragm wall within an excavated
slurry trench 600 mm wide. The top of the precast wall was carefully
levelled to the soffit level of the roof slab, and the cementitious slurry
within the trench above this level was reinforced with steel mesh.

(b) Excavate between the walls in a strutted excavation, the upper 3 m of
exposed cementitious slurry being protected by sheeting behind vertical

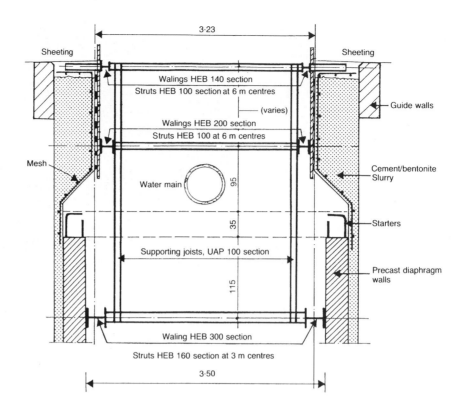

Fig. 9.45. Vitny culvert: cross-section showing temporary soil support above permanent walls (courtesy of Soletanche–Bachy)

runners. The average depth of excavation to the underside of the culvert base slab was 7·3 m from ground level, the precast walls and the slurry securing a cut-off into the marl.

(c) Cast in situ reinforced concrete floor and roof slabs.

(d) Complete waterproofing of joints.

(e) Backfill over roof slab and reinstate carriageway.

The culvert constructed under this contract was 700 m long, used 524 precast concrete wall panels weighing approximately 15 tonnes each. An output of 7·5 linear metres of culvert structure was achieved per day.

Bachy's patented continuous water bar system was used in this work. A perspective view is shown in Fig. 9.47. Vertical sections of PVC water bar are cast into a recess in the face of the prefabricated panel. These are subsequently thermally welded to a third section of water bar in the horizontal plane after exposure of the wall following the main excavation. The horizontal water bar is cast into the in situ floor slab of the culvert. The vertical recess between the panels is finally filled with mortar reinforced with steel mesh.

Overall stability: design for uplift

Cut-and-cover works are frequently constructed in water-bearing soils and in such circumstances it is necessary to consider the risk of failure of the structural box by uplift pressures both during construction and during the design life of the structure. The total downward self-weight of the structure together with the frictional resistance of the external walls, anchors or tension piles is required to exceed the upward hydrostatic force by an acceptable factor of safety at each stage.

In particular, tidal conditions, should they exist, should be considered pessimistically over the design life with allowance for inaccuracy in predicted levels. It would be usual to consider the restoring force in this factor of safety

(a)   (b)

(c)

Fig. 9.46. Vitny culvert, successive stages in construction: (a) excavation by grab;
(b) final stages of excavation and strutting; (c) culvert construction
(courtesy of Soletanche–Bachy)

to be based on:

(*a*) dead weight of structural elements based on minimal dimensions but
the displacement of the structure based on maximum overall
dimensions

(*b*) height of fill above the roof of the cut-and-cover to final finished levels
in permanent condition only

(*c*) frictional resistance due to piled walls or diaphragm walls based on
the inner and outer surface of the walls below the underside of the
base slab

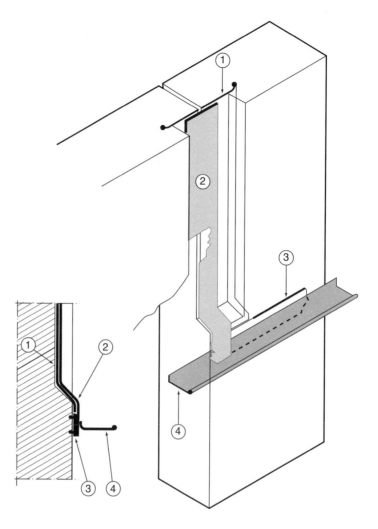

Fig. 9.47. Vitny culvert: water bar system with continuity between vertical and horizontal water bars (courtesy of Soletanche–Bachy)

1. Water bars cast into precast concrete wall units
2. Water bar glued to water bars (1) on face of unit
3. Water bar at horizontal joint cast into units
4. Water bar glued to water bars (3)

(*d*) total resistance from anchors or tension piles based on the ultimate capacity of anchors or piles divided by 2·0, using conservative values of soil or rock parameters, unless the results of pull-out tests are available.

Usually, an overall factor of safety of at least 1·1 on dead weight of the structure and fill over is required. A minimum value of 1·4 is required when the effects of friction and resistance due to anchors or tension piles are included; a further check that upward force does not exceed

$$\left(\frac{\text{dead weight}}{1\cdot1} + \frac{\text{friction}}{3\cdot0}\right)$$

is prudent.

A draft Institution of Structural Engineers report on Basements and Cut and Cover[29] refers to design specifications for buoyancy and flooding

Table 9.5 Typical safety factor requirements, uplift for cut-and-cover structures[29]

Condition	Downward forces D		Upward forces U
	Partial safety factors		Partial safety factor on water density or displacement (γ_f)
	On weights (γ_m)	On friction γ_m, i.e. sides, piles, anchors	
During construction	1·01	2·0	1·01
In service	1·05	3·0	1·05
Extreme event (flooding to 1 m above ground level)	1·03	2·5	1·03

Criterion (for each condition): $\sum \left(\dfrac{D}{\gamma_m} \right) > \sum U \times \gamma_f$

of underground structures for railway clients in Hong Kong, Singapore and London. Typical clauses included a summary of partial safety factors as shown in Table 9.5. Accompanying such a table would be a list of specified material densities. Water density variation of 2% between fresh and sea water was noted, the appropriate density being used in the calculation. These safety factors would be modified if the centre of factored buoyancy did not reasonably correspond to the centre of factored gravity.

The draft report[29] also adds that these metro authorities prudently require the threshold to their underground stations to be not less than 1·0 m above local ground level with no apertures below this level to guard against extensive flooding underground from one source. Similar requirements apply to highway tunnels, particularly approaches to river crossings, in the UK.

References

1. Megaw T.M. and Bartlett J.V. *Tunnels: planning, design, construction.* Ellis Horwood, Chichester, 1981, Vol. 1.
2. Cook R. and Paterson J. Nam Cheong station, Hong Kong. *Struct. Eng.*, 2002, **80**, No. 11, 13–15.
3. Hulme T.W. *et al.* Singapore M.R.T. system: construction. *Proc. Instn Civ. Engrs*, Part 1, 1989, **86**, Aug., 709–770.
4. McIntosh D.F. *et al.* Hong Kong M.T.R. modified initial system: design and construction of underground stations and cut and cover tunnels. *Proc. Instn Civ. Engrs*, Part 1, 1980, **68**, Nov., 599–626.
5. Ridley G. Blackwall Tunnel duplication. *Proc. Instn Civ. Engrs*, 1966, **35**, Oct., 253–274 (discussion 1967, **37**, Jul., 537–555).
6. Morgan H.D. *et al.* Clyde Tunnel design, construction and tunnel services. *Proc. Instn Civ. Engrs*, 1965, **30**, Feb., 291–322.
7. Haxton A.F. and Whyte H.E. Clyde Tunnel construction problems. *Proc. Instn Civ. Engrs*, 1965, **30**, Feb., 323–346 (discussion 1967, **37**, Jul., 511–535).
8. Megaw T.M. and Brown C.D. Mersey Kingsway Tunnel. *Proc. Instn Civ. Engrs*, 1972, **51**, Mar., 479–502.
9. Beadman D.R. and Bailey R.P. Design and construction of the deep stations for the Copenhagen Metro. *Proc. Conf. on Deep Foundations, 2000*, 375–387. Deep Foundations Institute, New York, 2000. DFI, Englewood Cliffs, New Jersey, 2000.
10. Weinbold H. and Kleinlein H. Berechnung und Ausführung einer schrägen Bohrpfahlwand als Gebäudesicherung. *Der Bauingenieur*, 1969, **44**, Jan., 233–239.

11. Hana T.H. and Dina A.O. Anchored inclined walls, a study of behaviour. *Ground Engng*, 1973, **6**, Nov., 24–33.
12. Schnabel J.R. Sloped sheeting. *ASCE J. Civil Engng*, 1971, Feb., 48–50.
13. *The Icos company in the underground works*. Icos, Milan, 1968.
14. Granter E. Park Lane improvement. *Proc. Instn Civ. Engrs*, 1964, **29**, 293–317 (discussion 1966, **33**, 657–664).
15. Dasgupta K.N. *et al*. Calcutta Rapid Transit System and the Park Street underground station. *Proc. Instn Civ. Engrs*, Part 1, 1979, **66**, May, 261–275 (discussion 1980, **68**, 127–129).
16. Jobling D.G. and Lyons A.C. Heathrow Station – Piccadilly Line. *Proc. Instn Civ. Engrs*, 1976, **60**, 212–217.
17. Davies R. and Henkel D.J. Geotechnical problems associated with construction of Chater Station. *Proc. Conf. Mass Transport in Asia*, Hong Kong, 1980, paper J3, 1–31. Concrete Society (HK) Ltd., 1980.
18. Farmer I.W. and Attewell P.B. Ground movements caused by a bentonite-supported excavation in London clay. *Géotechnique*, 1973, **4**, Dec., 576–581.
19. Uriel S. and Oteo C.S. Stress and strain beside a circular trench wall. *Proc. 9th Int. Conf. S.M.F.E.*, Tokyo, 1977, Vol. 1, 781–788. Japanese Society of Soil Mechanics and Foundation Engineering, Tokyo, 1977.
20. Clough G.W. and O'Rourke T.D. Construction induced movements of in situ walls. *Proc. Design and Performance of Earth Retaining Structures*, ASCE Special Publication 15, 439–470. Cornell University, 1989.
21. Thompson P. *A review of the retaining wall behaviour in overconsolidated clay during early stages of construction*. M.Sc. Thesis, Imperial College, 1991.
22. Carder D.R. *Ground movements caused by different embedded retaining wall construction techniques*. Transport Research Laboratory, Crowthorne, 1995. TRL Report 172.
23. Carder D.R. and Darley P. *Long term performance of embedded retaining walls*. Transport Research Laboratory, Crowthorne, 1998. TRL Report 381.
24. Morton K. *et al*. Observed settlements of buildings adjacent to stations constructed for the modified initial system of the M.T.R. Hong Kong. *6th South East Asian Conf. Soil Engng*, Taipei, 1980, 415–429. Organising Committee, Taipei, 1980.
25. Mitchell A., Izumi C., Bell B. and Brunton S. Semi top-down construction method for Singapore MRT, NEL. *Proc. Int. Conf on Tunnels and Underground Structures*, Singapore, 2000. Balkema, Rotterdam, 2000.
26. Peck R.B. Advantages and limitations of the observational method in applied soil mechanics. 9th Rankine Lecture. *Géotechnique*, 1969, **19**, Jun., 169–187.
27. Beadman D. *et al*. The Copenhagen Metro observational method at Norreport station. *Proc. ICE Geotech, Eng.*, 149(4), 231–236.
28. Namy D. and Fenoux G.Y. Tranchées couvertes en parois prefabriquees. *Proc. 6th Euro. Conf. SMFE*, Vienna, 1976, Vol. 1.1, 183–188. Austrian National Committee, Vienna, 1976.
29. Institution of Structural Engineers. *Design and construction of deep basements including cut and cover structures*. Draft, 2002. Institution of Structural Engineers, London, 2002.
30. Tricoire, J. *Le metro de Paris*. Paris Musées, 1999.
31. Nam Cheong station, Hong Kong. *Struct. Engr*, 2002, **80**, June 13–15.
32. Kell J. The Dartford Tunnel. *Proc. Instn Civ. Engrs*, 1963, **24**, Mar. 359–372.
33. Bigey M. *et al. Construction des metros*. Regie Autonome des Transport Parisien, Paris, 1973.
34. Powderham A.J. The observational method learning from projects. *Proc. Instn Civ. Engrs,* Geotechnical Engineering, 2002, **155**, Jan., 59–69.
35. News item. *Ground Engng*, Supplement, 2002.

Bibliography

BS EN 1538: *Diaphragm walls*. British Standards Institution, London, 2000.
BS EN 1537: *Ground anchors*. British Standards Institution, London, 1999.
BS EN 1536: *Bored piles*. British Standards Institution, London, 1999.
BS EN 12063: *Sheet piling*. British Standards Institution, London, 1999.

BS EN 12715: *Grouting*. British Standards Institution, London, 2000.

BS EN 12716: *Jet grouting*. British Standards Institution, London, 2001.

Pr EN 14490: *Soil nailing*. British Standards Institution, London, 2003.

Darling P. The Limehouse Link: two cut and cover techniques. *Tunnels and Tunnelling*, 1991, **23**, Jan., 16–18.

Roy T. Calcutta metro: contract section 16B: *Proc. Instn Civ. Engrs*, Part 1, 1983, **74**, Nov., 871–883.

10 Shafts and caissons: construction and design

Shafts for civil engineering purposes

Shaft construction deserves to be considered separately from both conventional cofferdam and caisson works. Often of small diameter, shafts may be rectangular in plan, or they can obtain maximum benefit from the arching action of soil around the shaft by conforming to a circular or ellipsoid shape. Inclined or vertical shafts may be built for permanent or temporary works. In specialist works such as tunnel construction, a shaft may serve a dual purpose – first, as a means of access to the tunnel drive during construction, and, at a later stage, as a means of ventilation to the completed tunnel.

A comparison of shaft and tunnel construction work shows the particular difficulties that can arise in shaft construction:

(a) groundwater can accumulate on the shaft working face
(b) works and materials have to be transported from the shaft face to ground surface
(c) excavated spoil has to be removed as a dead weight from the shaft face
(d) shaft linings have to be installed progressively downwards.

Although it is beyond the scope of this chapter, a study of installation techniques for deep shafts for mining works can assist in design and construction for shallower shafts for civil engineering purposes. Jones[1] reviewed current methods of shaft sinking and raise boring for mining work. Mechanical mole tunnelling machines were then in use for vertical shaft construction and possessed the twin virtues of increased safety and efficiency. Jones described the purpose of comprehensive investigation prior to sinking to determine the safest and most economical excavation method and best utilization of freezing, grouting and lining techniques. The practice of collaring to support the shaft near the ground surface using sheet piling, diaphragm walling or caisson reconstruction was also described, together with details of drilling jumbos, mucking out, and hoisting and lining methods. Excavation methods using raise boring and raise climbing machines and conventional long hole blasting were also described.

The installation of deep shafts, in the range 100 to 500 m deep was dealt with by Grieves[2] but remains outside the scope of this present volume.

Permanent shafts

In works associated with tunnelling for underground railways and road tunnels, permanent shafts are used for lifts, escalators, staircase access and for ventilation purposes. In sewage disposal schemes, shafts find use in pumping station construction and drop shafts. Some of the deepest shafts are in hydro-electric schemes and pumped storage works.

The vertical connection of tunnel drives to penetrate the sea bed involves shaft work of a special nature. These works are typically necessary for cooling water intakes to power stations and for sewage outfalls. In some cases, offshore jack-up rigs have been used; the procedure is basically to install a bulkhead within a sea bed excavation, to raise a shaft from the tunnel to the underside of the bulkhead and then remove the bulkhead by blasting.

At Wylfa power station[3] a cooling intake was constructed on an exposed coastline through 11 m of water at low tide with a tidal range of 6 m. The headworks to the shaft were constructed from a pit blasted on the sea bed; within the pit were installed a cylindrical shell and bulkhead, concreted into the rock face. The lower section of the 1·2 m dia. shaft was then excavated upwards from the tunnel to meet the bulkhead. This pilot shaft was enlarged to 4 m diameter before removal of the bulkhead.

The Dublin outfall sewer at Howth[4] was raised in sound rock from the end of the tunnel works to just below the sea bed to avoid headworks in expected high seas. After flooding the shaft and tunnel so constructed, the remaining length of shaft was removed by underwater blasting.

The use of concreted shafts and drilled shafts to house steel columns to withstand loads imposed from a superstructure overlaps with the subject of piling. This is inevitable as the size and power of mechanical piling equipment increases. Drilling using rock roller bits, large drag bits, mechanical augers and large diameter down-the-hole hammers, and the support of soil and rock by differential waterhead, drilling slurry or temporary casing, while defined in North America as 'caisson construction', is beyond the scope of this book.

Temporary shafts

Megaw and Bartlett[5] described the use of temporary shafts for tunnel works and stated the principal requirements of all-purpose working shafts for tunnels as follows.

(*a*) They must be available from the earliest stage of construction until tunnel completion.

(*b*) A shaft 4 to 6 m in diameter is typically needed to accommodate hoisting equipment and provide access for workers. Note that in pipe jacking works the shaft diameter may depend on dimensions of precast pipe sections and access clearances; with shield-driven tunnels the shaft dimensions will depend on the size required for hoisting shield components and, unless a separate shield chamber is used, the space needed at the bottom of the shaft to allow shield fabrication. In addition, the shaft diameter, of at least 1·5 times the tunnel drive diameter, must be sufficient to allow break-out from the shaft bottom. For tunnels driven by TBMs the shaft dimensions are directly dependent on TBM dimensions and clearances around it; the break-out eye details and dimensions will depend upon shaft wall construction.

Megaw and Bartlett referred to the spacing of shafts in tunnel works: much earlier, the progress of tunnel works dug by hand was improved by a large number of working shafts. In 1838, eighteen shafts were used to drive the Kilsey Tunnel which was only 2·2 km long. Later, railway works needed a shaft spacing of about 1 km for steam clearance purposes. The location of shafts remains a compromise between optimum tunnel alignment and the availability of adequate space at ground level. This problem was accentuated in earlier times when shield-driven tunnels could only be made in a series of straights. Nowadays, availability of adequate space in urban areas with the requirements of muck-away and construction materials handling and tunnel ventilation often determine shaft spacing.

Sinking methods
The sinking techniques adopted depend on the shaft use, its diameter and depth, soil and rock conditions, groundwater state, the proximity of other structures and their sensitivity to settlement.

Hand-excavated shafts
Although hand excavation would appear to be expensive, where soil is sufficiently stable to stand unsupported for small heights the conditions are relatively dry and moderate labour rates prevail, the method can find economical application. In China, for instance, 'family caissons' are taken down through residual soils where there is risk of boulders that might impair excavation by mechanical plant. These hand-excavated shafts are lined with in situ unreinforced concrete, typically 75 mm thick in small height lifts. Family caissons often were used in Hong Kong until the 1990s but safety legislation since that time has much reduced their use there.

A traditional method of pier construction for foundation support was known as the 'Chicago method' since its introduction on the Chicago Stock Exchange in 1894. Soil support was obtained from vertical poling boards set on the pier periphery and held by steel rings. Hand excavation proceeded in depth increments of 1 to 2 m, depending on conditions, and a further set of boards and rings were placed. At full shaft depth a hand-belling operation was carried out to increase the shaft diameter if soil conditions allowed.

Hand excavation may also be more economical in other circumstances; in weak rocks, for instance, where belling operations may prove difficult for mechanical augers. At Hartlepool Nuclear Power Station, 17 piers, each 2·3 m in diameter, were used as support to the reactor. The boring was taken through 5 m of soft fill, clay and 30 m of glacial fill by rotary auger using bentonite slurry for soil support. Weak bunter sandstone at this depth was then hand-excavated a further 4 m from beneath a casing set into the rockhead and backgrouted throughout its height. The base was belled out by hand to 3·9 m diameter to reduce bearing pressures on the sandstone to $2·9 \, MN/m^2$.

Mechanical excavation
Open shafts have traditionally been excavated by mechanical grabs suspended from cranes or derricks, where space allows, assisted by mechanical loading shovels at excavation level. More recently, hydraulic grabs mounted on cranes or long dipper arms of hydraulic excavators have replaced mechanical grabs and derricks. In rock, shallow shafts are drilled by hand-held rock drills; in deeper works, a shaft jumbo is used with boom-mounted drills mounted on a folding frame. It is usual to pull 1 to 2 m on each round. Beyond a depth of 30 m or so it has been usual to construct a temporary head frame and use muck skips or kibbles to muck out the shaft.

The distinction between piling and shaft construction may only depend on size where the shaft is to be backfilled to form a load-bearing member; mechanical augers are used together with casing, either temporarily or permanently as needed. Bentonite slurry may again be used as a method of soil support; in the reverse circulation process, slurry is used for both soil retention and as a means of transporting the excavated soil cuttings. A temporary top casing is used in these instances to avoid soil disturbance at ground level, to maximize the head of slurry and avoid contamination of concrete during placing of soil fall-ins. Shafts formed in this way are typically 2 to 3 m in diameter and up to 70 to 80 m deep, but much larger diameter and deeper shafts for civil engineering works have been successfully completed using purpose-made reverse circulation equipment.

Soil and rock support

The periphery of the shaft may require no lining in dry, sound rock, but otherwise the following methods are available for soil or rock support:

- *in soils* – timbering; steel sheet piling; precast concrete, cast iron and pressed, welded steel and segmental linings; diaphragm walling; secant piling
- *in rock* – in situ concrete lining; shotcreting; rock dowels and rock bolting.

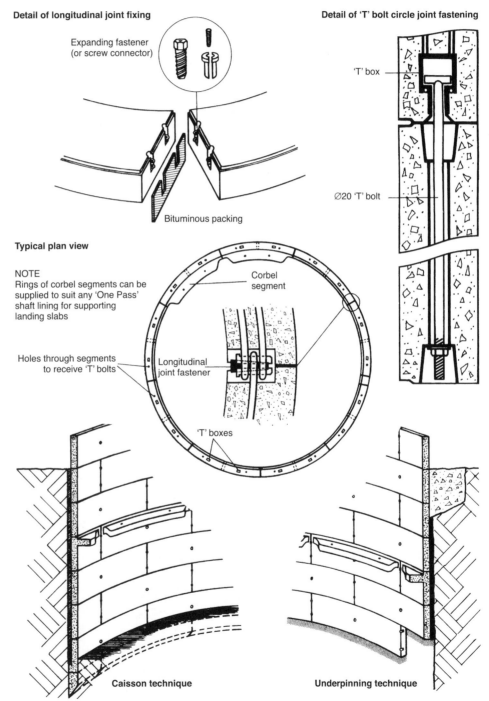

Fig. 10.1. Details of connections to one-pass shaft linings (courtesy of Charcon)

One Pass Shafts can be constructed by caisson or under-pinning techniques and additionally 'chimney fashion' in open excavation.

Each of these methods is now discussed in turn.

(a) *Timbering*. In soft ground, vertical poling boards are driven ahead of excavation and secured by timber walings, strutting and diagonal corner braces. Construction depths are limited with timbering, and the works are labour-intensive by modern standards.

(b) *Sheet piling*. Deeper shafts may be sheet piled, the piles being secured by walings in timber, steel or reinforced concrete. Ground anchors may be used where space outside the shaft allows and space within is confined. Sheet piling may be impeded and pile clutches broken in hard driving caused by boulders or penetration into rockhead. Grouting may be necessary in such cases to avoid ingress of groundwater into the shaft.

(c) *Segmental linings*. Where space and ground conditions allow, the first ring is built a small depth below ground level supported, if the shaft is large, by an external collar to avoid differential settlement around the ring. In dry, sound soil, rings are built successively downwards in an underpinning operation for each ring. After completion of the ring the annular space behind the excavated soil face and the outer segment face is grouted, thus avoiding later loss of ground and subsidence of the ground surface. Where soil conditions are less favourable it may not be possible to complete a whole ring without temporary support for each segment from the central dumpling. In tunnel works segments are in cast-iron or precast concrete. Solid reinforced concrete segments, known as one-pass shaft linings, are available and avoid further in situ lining works. These segments use stressed loop cross-joint connectors (details in Fig. 10.1) and allow the introduction of precast corbels for structural support for landings by bolting to the main lining (Fig. 10.2). Examples of conventional concrete segment and one pass linings are shown in Figs. 10.3 and 10.4. Steel liner plates will themselves be adequate in small diameter shafts, but in larger diameter shafts a curved steel joist is set for every two or three courses of liner.

(d) *Diaphragm walling*. In diaphragm wall shafts a segmental plan shape is used and structural integrity is necessary at each panel joint to transfer hoop compression between panels and retain structural stability. Depths of the order of 30 to 40 m are not unusual for diaphragm wall shafts, and the increasing use of reverse circulation cutter rigs, such

Fig. 10.2. Example of single-pass shaft lining with corbels (courtesy of Charcon)

Fig. 10.3. Conventional bolted precast concrete segment lining (courtesy of Charcon)

Fig. 10.4. Single-pass lining to line tunnel break-out shaft (courtesy of Charcon)

Fig. 10.5. Polygonal plan shape shaft construction using diaphragm walls, Eastern Harbour Crossing, Hong Kong (courtesy of Soletanche–Bachy)

as the Hydrofraise and Trenchcutter rigs, bring improved verticality tolerance to the works and even greater depths. Figure 10.5 shows the use of polygonal plan shaped shafts in Hong Kong for deep access shafts through decomposed granite, constructed by Bachy-Soletanche.

The construction of deep shafts using grab excavation methods was originally made practicable by installing rotary bored piles at the junction of each diaphragm wall panel. The verticality tolerance of pile installation using special equipment was of the order of 1 in 300 or better. The piles were installed before the diaphragm wall panels and acted as a guide to the panel grab, which was shaped to cut soil from the curved pile face. The Icos company used this procedure of interlocked circular units and rectangular panels to build a 4·6 m dia. shaft through fine sands to the very considerable depth of 72 m for mineworks at Speckholzerheide, Holland as long ago as 1954. Improved excavation tolerances achievable with reverse circulation equipment such as the Hydrofraise and Trenchcutter rigs now allow deep shaft construction without the need for bored piles at the junction of each panel. Shafts in excess of 50 m deep can be constructed with this type of equipment, the junction being achieved by cutting the end of the primary panel during excavation of the adjacent secondary panel. Cut joints obviate the need for temporary stop ends in larger diameter shafts.

For a typical small-diameter shaft excavated by grab with an internal diameter of 6 m or so one primary panel is installed and work proceeds successively on two fronts to complete the circle as shown in Fig. 10.6. Verticality of the face of the initial primary panel needs to be measured as excavation proceeds and care should be taken to avoid poor verticality and overdig at the end of the panel which would allow concrete to pass around the stop end tube. With shafts of larger internal diameter,

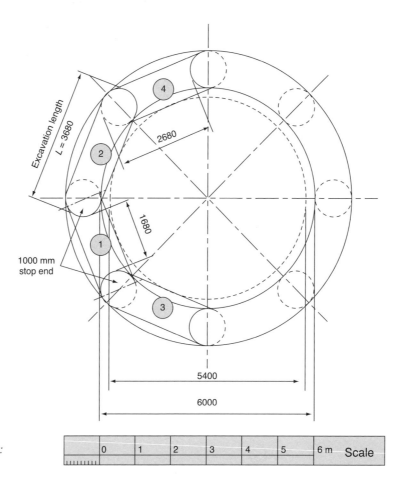

Fig. 10.6. Small-diameter shaft:
a panel configuration

say 10 m or more, two primary starter panels are often preferred to reduce rig standing time. These starters are located opposite each other and it is necessary that only one panel should be open at any one time to ensure stability. Figure 10.7 shows a typical shaft with primary panels within the flat wall sections of the polygonal plan shape. This arrangement avoids the difficulty of cleaning into the curved concrete surface of the panel joint by a grab excavating the adjacent panel.

It is essential to avoid chiselling in shaft panels as much as possible in order to reduce overbreak. Where panels are founded on sloping rockhead it may be practicable to use multiple reinforcement cages with a stepped panel toe to avoid excessive chiselling into bedrock. Individual cages for each bite become necessary with depths greater than 30 to 40 m.

For deep panels reverse circulation cutter rigs prove their value, especially in terms of verticality. Figure 10.8 shows a typical shaft construction in plan using alternative primary and secondary panels with cut joints to a depth of 60 m through marine clays with a high water table onto granite bedrock. Each primary panel concrete volume exceeded 400 m^3.

Some risk of non-verticality to panels exists during the cutting of joints with cutter rigs when the plan deviation between adjacent panels exceeds 12 to 15°.

(e) *Secant piling.* The use of secant piling as a means of shaft construction is limited to depths of the order of 20 m with CFA rigs. Deeper excavation

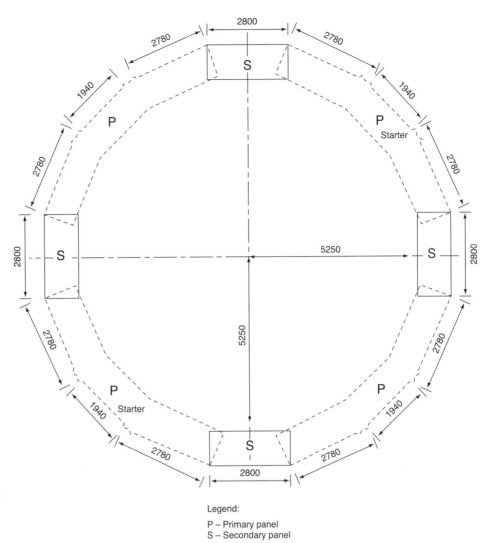

Fig. 10.7. 10 m dia. shaft: panel configuration with two starter panels, panels located within flat wall sections

Legend:

P – Primary panel
S – Secondary panel

(of the order of 40 m or more) can be made by secant piling methods using heavy rotary equipment, powerful casing oscillations and temporary, rigid twin-wall casings. The depth of excavation is limited by the accuracy of installing the temporary casing to maintain the depth of the secant cut with the male secondary piles. A rotary rig with casing oscillator working immediately adjacent to an existing structure is shown in Fig. 10.9.

(*f*) *In situ concrete lining.* In rock excavation where the rock will stand temporarily without support in dry conditions, an in situ lining of mesh-reinforced concrete can be used. Excavation is by drilling and blasting in successive increments of 2 m or more, with concrete pours 6 and 8 m high. Slip-forming methods can be applied in deep shafts. The use of in situ lining overcomes any difficulty in varying amounts of overbreak that occur when using segmental linings. Thermal insulation is necessary when concrete is placed against frozen soil or rock.

(g) *Shotcreting.* In shafts through rock which is relatively stable and dry, sprayed concrete, or shotcrete, may be used to stabilize the face. Applied in layers typically 50 to 60 mm thick, light mesh reinforcement may be pinned to the rock face[6,7].

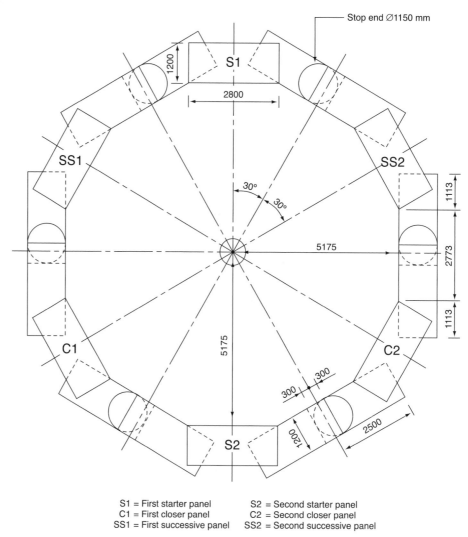

Fig. 10.8. (a) Plan of deep shaft, 10 m minimum internal diameter, two starter panels

S1 = First starter panel   S2 = Second starter panel
C1 = First closer panel   C2 = Second closer panel
SS1 = First successive panel   SS2 = Second successive panel

The construction sequence is S1, S2, SS1, SS2, C1, C2

(h) *Rock dowels and bolts*. Drilled radially from the shaft, dowels and bolts are used as rock reinforcement, and mesh secured to the face of the dowel or bolt may be used to secure the rock face. CIRIA report 101[8] describes rock reinforcement in underground excavations. Rock dowels may be cement- or resin-grouted or may consist of a hollow, high-strength steel tube with a longitudinal slit which compresses radially when driven into a drillhole exerting continuous outward pressure. Another type of dowel uses high-pressure water to expand a steel tube within a drilled hole. Rock bolts are tensioned elements of ultimate capacity in the range 80 to 300 kN. Tensioning is by jack or torque wrench. Several proprietary types are available: bolts in various high-strength steels; more recently, in solid and tubular fibreglass bolts have been developed. Grout may be cement or resin, pumped or encapsulated. Mechanical anchors, also grouted for corrosion protection, are designed for use in hard rocks. The Sure type is an exception, which was specifically developed for soft rocks. Mechanical types are simply driven split-and-wedge types or wedge expansion types such as the duplex anchor. Types of proprietary rock bolts are shown in Fig. 10.10.

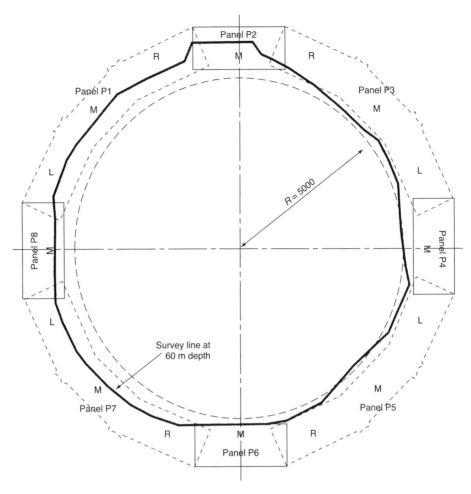

Fig. 10.8 (b) As-built survey of inner face of shaft with cut joints at 60 m depth. Note displacement of panel P2

Primary panels P1 to P8: panels M
Secondary panels: panels L and R

Fig. 10.9. Piled wall construction using a rotary rig with a casing oscillator in close proximity to an existing structure

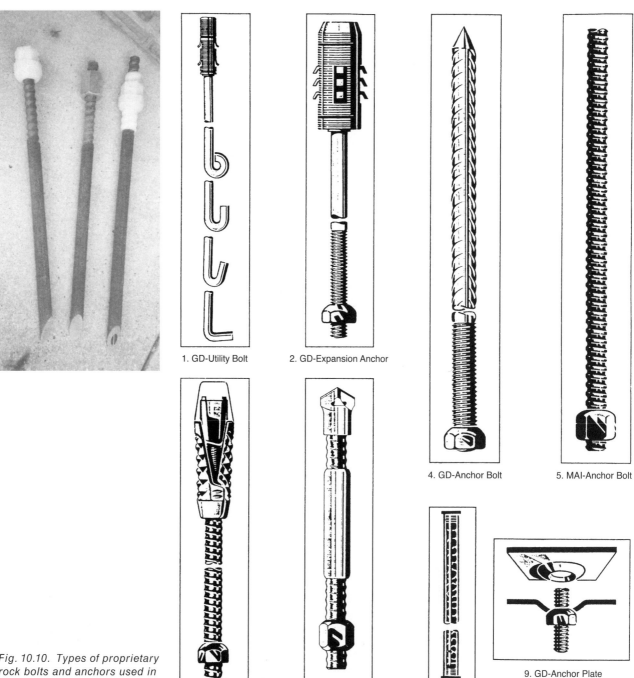

1. GD-Utility Bolt   2. GD-Expansion Anchor

4. GD-Anchor Bolt   5. MAI-Anchor Bolt

6. MAI-Expansion Anchor   7. MAI-Injection Drilling Anchor   8. GD-Topac Cartridge

9. GD-Anchor Plate

Fig. 10.10. Types of proprietary rock bolts and anchors used in shaft construction (courtesy of MAI Systems)

Methods of design for reinforcement of openings in rock are reviewed by Choquet and Hadjigeorgiou[9].

Groundwater control in shafts

Methods of groundwater control were described in detail in Chapter 2. In summary, the methods used in shafts are:

- pumping from sumps in advance of the excavation
- pumping from wellpoints
- pumping from deep wells below or outside the shaft

- grouting of soils and fissures in rock with cement or chemical grouting
- freezing
- compressed air working.

For relatively small shafts the first five items are listed in approximately increasing order of cost. Where compressed air working is needed to drive water from the shaft, an air deck, man and muck lock and compressor installation will be needed. If planned for, this mobilization will fit into the works programme, but if the decision to use air is made during shaft excavation it could be expensive, causing delay and disruption. As described earlier, the depth of compressed air working below water level or ground level is restricted to maximum working air pressures. Groundwater lowering, often by deep wells, may be used to effectively increase this depth. Where compressed air working is necessary and segmental linings are used, all segment joints are caulked. Where cast-iron segments are used, kentledge may be necessary above the air deck to alleviate the low tensile strength of the cast-iron; grouting behind the tubbing reduces risk of circumferential tension within the iron.

Caissons

The maximum practical depth of excavation within cofferdams is of the order of 25 m. To reach founding levels at greater depths, previous generations of engineers have used caissons – either open-well or pneumatic types. Historically, well caissons have been used for bridge foundations in India, Burma and Egypt, using masonry or brick for the caisson walls. Prior to Victorian times these wells were sunk by hand-excavation by divers. The working depth limit was therefore of the order of 6 m or so below water level. It was the British engineer of the late nineteenth century who introduced excavation by grab and sand pump to allow well foundations to much greater depths. The caisson for the Hardinge Bridge on the Lower Ganges reached depths between 32 and 36 m below river level in the late 1870s.

The pneumatic caisson was first used by John Wright in 1851 in foundations to the bridge over the River Medway at Rochester. Brunel used the method on the Saltash Bridge foundations some years later, and pneumatic caissons were used by James B. Eads in 1869 on the St Louis Bridge over the Mississippi

Fig. 10.11. Station floor construction, St Michel station, Paris Metro[10]

River. Eads sank two river piers under air to depths of 26 to 28 m below water level.

Early use of open and pneumatic caissons for metro construction was made at the beginning of the twentieth century for construction of line 4 of the Paris Metro. The construction and sinking of the caissons for the crossing of the Seine and two stations, Cité and St Michel was made by the contracting firm, Chagnaud, in the years 1905 to 1907[10].

The station caissons were much bigger than the pneumatic caissons used in the river. St Michel station is under Rue Danton between Place Saint-Michel and Place Saint-André des Arts. Its 118 m length was made up of three steel caissons, a central unit 66 m long was curved with a radius of 300 m containing the platforms, and one caisson on either side of it, each 26 m long, containing the approaches.

The first construction operation was the excavation of a pit 3 m deep at the station site into which the caisson was built. Figure 10.11 shows the construction of the station floor in the Rue Danton. Figure 10.12 shows the station wall structure (concrete infill is placed between the steel uprights). Figure 10.13 shows the two completed caissons of the three in Saint Michel station. The elliptical caisson sunk at St Michel is in the background. The second elliptical caisson at Place Saint-André des Arts in the front cannot be seen. The third photo gives a good idea of the impressive dimensions of this structure which was subsequently sunk by hand-excavation, with great care to avoid damage to neighbouring buildings.

The caissons at St Michel station are shown at progressive excavation stages in Figs. 10.14 and 10.15. The first photograph shows the caissons, some 11 000 tonnes of steel and concrete ready for sinking. The caissons were sunk, one at a time, to a depth of 20 m below ground level, approximately 13 m below the Seine water level. The second photograph, Fig. 10.15, shows the Place Saint-Michel elliptical caisson and the central caisson during sinking. The other elliptical caisson, still under construction, is in the background.

Two other types of caisson, which are outside the scope of this book, are the box caisson and caissons used to form buoyant foundations. The box caisson, closed at the bottom and open at the top, has been used for quay and breakwater construction at several ports. Little[11] described its use at Rotterdam, where the box caissons, constructed ashore and towed to their location, were founded on prepared sand beds. Similar construction has been used extensively on the River Liffey at the Port of Dublin. These works were described by O'Sullivan[12]; Bruun[13] described caisson quay wall construction in Gdynia, Poland, and at Sheibah, Kuwait, using similar techniques. The method is susceptible to under-scour by current or the erosive action of ship propellers; anti-scour mattresses are sometimes necessary.

A similar technique of floated-in box caissons has found economical use for bridge foundations. The caissons, constructed in dry dock, are towed to site and sunk on prepared foundation soils. The method was used in 1991 for the Queen Elizabeth II Bridge at Dartford in the UK.

Caissons are used to form buoyant foundations to building structures where ground conditions, such as very soft estuarine clays, are inadequate to support the building loads without excessive settlements. An example of this method, designed and built by Soil Mechanics Ltd for sugar mill and preparation buildings in Guyana, was described by Golder[14]. Precast post-tensioned concrete walls were used for these caissons.

Reference must also be made to the use of large caisson structures for offshore foundations described by Hansen and Frode[15]. Typical applications include foundations for lighthouse structures. Caisson techniques also find

Fig. 10.12. Station wall structure, St Michel station, Paris Metro[10]

Fig. 10.13. Two completed caissons at St Michel station, Paris Metro[10]

Fig. 10.14. Caissons at St Michel station, Paris Metro[10]

Fig. 10.15. Caissons at St Michel station, during sinking[10]

application for off-shore oil exploration and storage structures. These matters, however, also fall outside the scope of this book.

Open-well caissons

An open-well caisson consists, in simple terms, of a box open at both top and bottom.

The cutting edge of the caisson is situated at the underside of the curb. Where this is constructed in steelwork, the curb has vertical steel outer skin plates and inner steel cant, or haunch, plates. After the beginning of sinking, concrete is filled between the skin plates. This concrete is termed 'steining'. At the height where the caisson has gained sufficient strength from the composite concrete–steelwork, the caisson walls are frequently cantilevered upwards in reinforced concrete. More recently, reinforced concrete has become an attractive alternative to steelwork in caisson construction as methods of shuttering, slip-forming and concrete placement have developed. The reinforced concrete walls, canted internally, may be lined with steel plate for protection above the steel cutting edge.

Details of steelwork and the cutting edges to the main caisson piers of the Howrah Bridge, Calcutta, are shown in Fig. 10.16. The steel caissons, built in 1937–1938, were designed so that the working chambers within the shafts could be temporarily enclosed by steel diaphragms to allow work under compressed air if required. In the event, the main piers on the Howrah side were sunk by open-well dredging, and only those on the Calcutta side required compressed air to counter running sand.

The sinking of the Howrah caissons were described by Howarth and Smith[16]. The plan size of the main caisson was 55·3 m by 24·9 m, with 21 shafts each 6·25 m square. The two anchorage caissons were each 16·4 m by 8·2 m with two wells 4·9 m square. The Howrah side work site is shown in Fig. 10.17. The caissons were sunk through soft river deposits to a stiff yellow clay 26·5 m below ground level. After penetrating 2·1 m into this clay all the shafts were plugged with concrete after individual dewatering with some 5 m of backfilling in adjacent shafts.

The accuracy of sinking of these large caissons was exceptionally good, within 50 to 75 mm of true plan position. Excavation was efficient, each shaft being of ample size with long, straight cutting edges and thin walls near the cutting edge to allow the grab to work close to it. In very soft soil a number of shafts, symmetrical to the caisson axes, were left unexcavated to allow strict control, while in very stiff clays a large number of the internal walls were completely undercut allowing the whole weight of the caisson to be carried by the outside skin friction and the bearing under the external walls. Skin friction on the outside of the monolith walls was estimated at $29 \, kN/m^2$ while loads on the cutting edge in clay overlying the founding stratum reached 100 tonnes/m.

General rules to help prevent initial tipping of large open caissons were given by Purcell et al.[17] as follows.

(a) Keep the weight of the caisson and its centre of gravity as low as possible by keeping the interior concrete below the waterline during the dangerous stages.

(b) Provide lateral support at as high a level as possible.

(c) Maintain symmetry at the plane of the cutting edge. The removal of false bottoms and dredging in the wells should generally be such as to preserve symmetrical conditions, particularly along the long axis.

(d) Avoid sudden movement of material. Dredge so as to remove mud from the centre, maintaining bearing on the cutting edges.

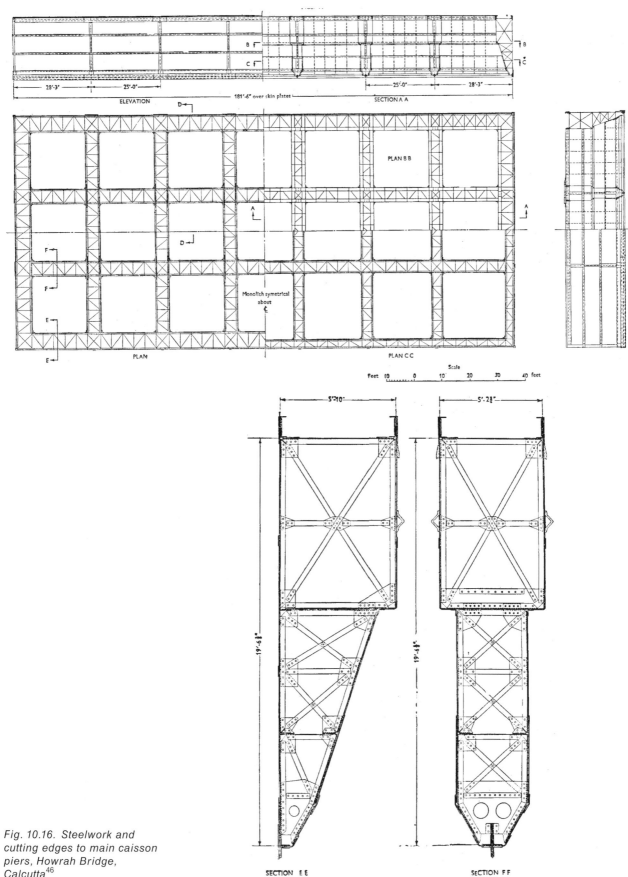

Fig. 10.16. Steelwork and cutting edges to main caisson piers, Howrah Bridge, Calcutta[46]

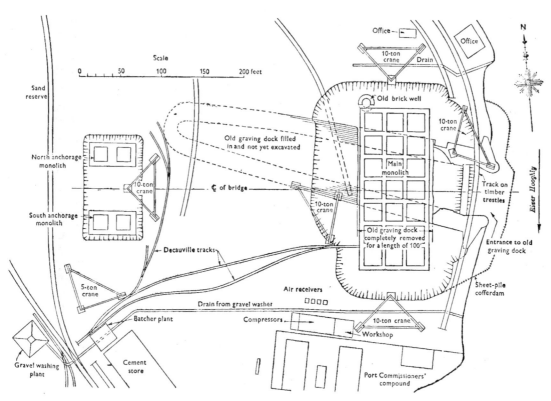

Fig. 10.17. Howrah Bridge work site[16]

(e) Do not dredge below the exterior cutting edges until the caisson is founded. If the caisson will not settle satisfactorily, use jets on the side to reduce skin friction.

(f) In a large, rectangular caisson, sinking may be accomplished by rocking slightly about the short axis, dredging first from one end and then the other. This must never be done about the other axis.

(g) In unstable soils, avoid any action that might tend to make the soil under the cutting edge quick, particularly the use of blasting and pumping down the dredging wells. Jetting on the sides of the caisson, and in the dredge wells if mud plugs tend to form, is usually safe and desirable.

Tomlinson[18] pointed out that caisson proportions, while usually defined in terms of plan shape by the superstructure, are often a compromise. On the one hand, the walls are required to be thick to provide maximum weight for sinking, and on the other, they should be thin to allow the grab to work near the cutting edge. Lightness of weight is desirable to allow a shallow draught during towage from casting yard to mid-river site but this, in turn, is to the detriment of the caisson rigidity, which is essential during early stages of sinking when the caisson may be unevenly supported.

Tomlinson pointed out that the size and layout of the dredging wells depends mainly on the soil type. Dense sands and firm to stiff clays require a minimum number of cross-walls and a minimum outer wall thickness consistent with the weight requirements for sinking and rigidity against distortion. The cross-walls need not extend to cutting edge depth. In sands and soft silts, on the other hand, grabbing below cutting edge level causes soil to move towards the centre of the shaft where the excavation is kept low. Water and air/water jets may be used for excavation and lubrication purposes. The use of bentonite slurry lubrication for caisson sinking will be referred to later.

The use of deep wells, open or pneumatic caissons of relatively small plan size for bridge foundations in rivers is a traditional method in India and Pakistan, and remains currently in use. The following extract from the Indian standard specification for road bridges[19] gives a useful review of precautions to be taken during the sinking of the small wells and basic design criteria for walls built in concrete and brickwork.

710   WELL FOUNDATIONS
710.1   General
While selecting the shape, size and the type of wells for a bridge, the size of pier to be accommodated, need for effecting streamline flow, the possibility of the use of pneumatic sinking, the anticipated depth of foundation, and the nature of strata to be penetrated should be kept in view. Further for the type of well selected, the dredge hole should be large enough to permit easy dredging, the minimum dimension being not less than 2 m. In case there is deep standing water, properly designed floating caissons may have to be used.

710.2   Steining
710.2.1   General
The thickness of the steining shall be fixed from the following considerations:

(i)   It should be possible to sink the well without excessive kentledge.

(ii)   The wells shall not get damaged during sinking.

(iii)   If the well develops tilts and shifts during sinking, it should be possible to rectify the tilts and shifts within permissible limits without damaging the well.

(iv)   The well should be able to resist safely earth pressure developed during a sand blow or during other conditions like sudden drop that may be experienced during sinking.

(v)   Stresses at various levels of the steining should be within permissible limits under all conditions for loads that may be transferred to the well either during sinking or during service.

710.2.2   Design considerations
710.2.2.1   Use of cellular steining with two or more shells or use of composite material in well steining shall not be permitted.

710.2.2.2   In case of plain and reinforced concrete single circular walls, the external diameter of well shall not normally exceed 12 m.

Note: Wells of larger dimensions shall call for supplemental design and construction specifications outside the purview of the code.

710.2.2.3   In case of plain cement concrete wells, the concrete mix for the steining shall not be leaner than 1:3:6. However, in areas subjected to marine or other similar conditions of adverse exposure, the concrete in the steining shall not be leaner than M160 mix with cement content not less than 350 kg per m^3 of concrete and with water cement ratio not more than 0·45.

710.2.2.4   The external diameter of brick masonry wells shall not exceed 6 m. Brick masonry wells for depth greater than 20 m shall not be permitted.

710.2.2.5   For brick masonry wells bricks not less than 70A shall be used in cement mortar not leaner than 1:3 for the steining.

710.2.3   Thickness of well steining

710.2.3.1   The minimum thickness of well steining shall not be less than 500 mm and satisfy the following relationship:

$$h = Kd\sqrt{l}$$

where

h = Minimum thickness of steining in m.
d = External diameter of circular well or dumb bell shaped well in the case twin D wells, the smaller dimension in plan in metres.
l = Depth of well in metres below L.W.L. or ground level whichever is higher.
K = a constant.

The value of K shall be as follows.

(i)   Single Circular or dumb bell shaped well in Cement Concrete
K = 0·030 for predominantly sandy strata.
K = 0·033 for predominantly clayey strata.

(ii)   Twin D wells in Cement Concrete
K = 0·039 for predominantly sandy strata.
K = 0·043 for predominantly clayey strata.

(iii)   Single Circular or dumb bell shaped wells in Brick Masonry
K = 0·047 for predominantly sandy strata.
K = 0·052 for predominantly clayey strata.

(iv)   Twin D wells in Brick Masonry
K = 0·062 for predominantly sandy strata.
K = 0·068 for predominantly clayey strata.

Note: (i)   For boulder strata or for wells resting on rock where blasting may be involved, higher thickness of steining, better grade of concrete, higher reinforcement, use of steel plates in the lower portions etc. may be adopted as directed by the Engineer-In-Charge.

(ii)   For wells passing through very soft clayey strata the steining thickness may be reduced based on local experience and in accordance with the decision of the Engineer-In-Charge, to prevent the well penetrating by its own weight. In such cases, the steining may be adequately reinforced to get sufficient strength.

710.2.3.2   Where nominal steel is provided in the steining as per clause 710.2.4.1 the same shall not be considered in the design for strength.

710.2.4   Reinforcement in well steining

710.2.4.1   For plain concrete wells, vertical reinforcements (either mild steel or deformed bars) in the steining shall not be less than 0·12% of gross sectional area of the actual thickness provided. This shall be equally distributed on both faces of the steining (see Fig. 1). The vertical reinforcements shall be tied up with hoop steel not less than 0·04 per cent of the volume per unit length of the steining.

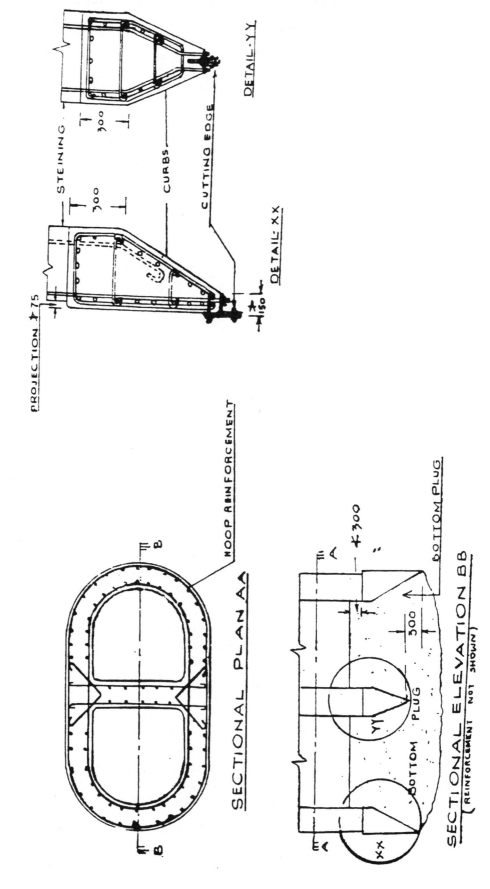

Fig. 1.

710.2.4.2 In case where the well steining is designed as a reinforced concrete element, it shall be considered as a column section subjected to combined axial load and bending. However, the amount of vertical reinforcement provided in the steining shall not be less than 0·2% (for either mild steel or deformed bars) of the actual gross sectional area of the steining. On the inner face a minimum of 0·06% (of gross area) steel shall be provided. The transverse reinforcement in the steining shall be provided in accordance with the provisions for a column but in no case shall be less than 0·04% of the volume per unit length of the steining.

710.2.4.3 The vertical bond rods in brick masonry steining shall not be less than 0·1% of the cross sectional area and shall be encased into cement concrete of 1: M160 mix of size 150 mm × 150 mm. These rods shall be equally distributed along the circumference in the middle of the steining and shall be tied up with hoop steel not less than 0·04% of the volume per unit length of the steining. The hoop steel shall be provided in a concrete band at spacing of 4 times the thickness of the steining or 3 m, whichever is less. The horizontal RCC bands shall not be less than 300 mm wide and 150 mm high, reinforced with bars of diameter not less than 10 mm placed at the corners and tied with 6 mm diameter stirrups at 300 mm centres (see Fig. 2).

710.2.5 Stresses

710.2.5.1 Allowable stresses for different materials used in the construction of wells shall conform to the relevant sections of the IRC Code of Practice for Road Bridges.

710.2.5.2 For piers/abutment fully spanning the well, the steining immediately below it, for a width equal to thickness of pier/abutment after allowing for dispersion shall be checked for any tangential stresses developing in the steining due to the concentration of the load.

710.2.5.3 The stresses in well steining shall be checked at such critical sections where tensile and compressive stresses are likely to be maximum and also where there is change in the area of reinforcement or in the concrete mix.

710.3 Stability of Well Foundations

710.3.1 The stability of well foundations shall be analysed under the most critical combination of loads and forces as per clause 706 allowing for the soil resistance from the sides below scour level by any rational method. The pressure on the foundations shall satisfy the provisions of clause 708.

710.3.2 The stability of the well shall also be checked for the construction stage for following conditions:

(i) In case of pier wells resting on rock without bottom plug and carrying no superstructure, the well being subjected to full pressure due to water current at full design scour.

(ii) Completed abutment well resting on rock and carrying no superstructure. The well being subjected to full designed differential earth pressure.

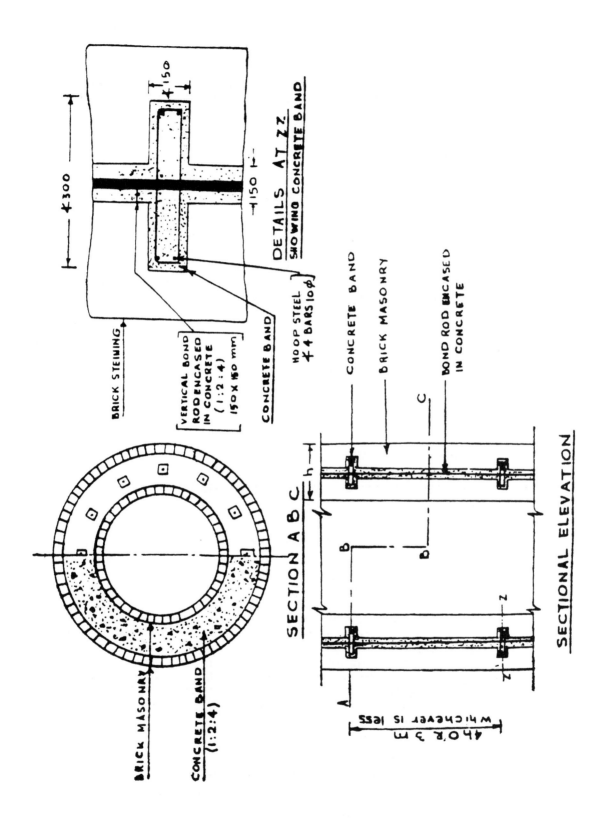

Fig. 2.

Note:

(a)   The seismic force shall not be considered in the above two cases.

(b)   In case it is not stable against overturning and sliding, the safety of the well shall be ensured by suitable methods.

710.3.3   Use of IRC:45 for the design of pier well foundations in cohesionless soil is acceptable. For design of abutment wells in all types of soils and pier wells in cohesive soil guidance may be taken from Appendix 4.

710.3.4   The side earth resistance shall be ignored in case of well foundations resting on rock.

Note: If allowable bearing pressure less than 1 MPa is assigned to the rock strata, the side earth resistance may be taken into account subject to the satisfaction of clause 708.2.1.

710.3.5   If the abutments are designed to retain earth without spillage in front (solid abutment with solid returns) the foundations shall be designed to withstand the earth pressure and horizontal forces for the condition of maximum scour depth in front of 1·27 dsm with approach retained and 2 dsm with scour all around.

710.3.6   However, where earth spilling from the approaches is reliably protected in front, relief due to the spilling earth in front may be considered, assuming that the designed scour extends up to the toe of the protection after launching. However, no passive relief shall be taken for the triangular portion of the earth in front of the abutment up to bottom of well cap, except for its surcharge effect.

710.4   Tilts and Shifts
As far as possible the wells shall be sunk plumb without any tilts or shifts. However, a tilt of 1 in 80 and a shift of 150 mm in a resultant direction shall be considered in the design of well foundations.

Even after resorting to precautionary/remedial measures during execution, if tilts or shifts or both exceed the above limits, their effects on bearing pressure, steining stress, change in span length and shift in the centre line of the bridge shall be examined individually or jointly.

710.5   Cutting Edge
The mild steel cutting edge shall be strong enough and not less than 40 kg/m to facilitate sinking of the well through the types of strata expected to be encountered without suffering any damage. It shall be properly anchored to the well kerb.

When there are two or more compartments in a well, the lower end of the cutting edge of the middle stems of such wells shall be kept about 300 mm above that of the outer wells to prevent rocking as shown in Fig. 1.

710.6   Well Curb
The well curb shall satisfy the following requirements:

(i)   It should have a shape offering the minimum resistance while the well is being sunk.

(ii)   Be strong enough to be able to transmit super-imposed loads from the steining to the bottom plug.

To satisfy the above requirements, the shape and the outline dimensions of the curb shall be as given in Fig. 1. The curb shall invariably be reinforced concrete of mix not leaner than M200: with minimum reinforcement of 72 kg per cu.m. excluding bond rods. This quantity of steel shall be suitably arranged as shown in Fig. 1 to prevent spreading and splitting of the curb during sinking and in service.

(iii) In case pneumatic sinking is indicated, the internal angle of the well curb shall be made steep enough to provide easy access for the pneumatic tools.

(iv) In case blasting is anticipated, the outer faces of the curb shall be protected with suitable steel plates of thickness not less than 6 mm up to half the height of the well curb on the outside and on the inner face not less than 10 mm thick up to top of well curb, suitably reduced to 6 mm to a height of 3 m above the top of the curb. The steel plates shall be properly anchored to the curb and steining. The curb in such a case shall be provided with additional hoop reinforcement of 10 dia. mild steel or deformed bars at 150 mm centres. The latter reinforcement shall also extend up to a height of 3 m into the well steining above the curb, in which portion the mix of concrete in the well steining shall not be leaner than 1:1:3.

710.7   Bottom Plug

The bottom plug shall be provided in all wells and the top shall be kept not lower than 300 mm in the centre above the top of the curb (see Fig. 1). A suitable sump shall be below the level of the culting edge. Before concreting the bottom plug it shall be ensured that its inside faces have been cleaned thoroughly.

The concrete mix used in bottom plug shall have a minimum cement content of 330 kg/m^3 and a slump of about 150 mm to permit easy flow of concrete through tremie to fill up all cavities. Concrete shall be laid in one continuous operation till dredge hole is filled to required height. The concrete shall be placed gently by tremie or skip boxes under still water conditions.

In case grouted concrete e.g. colcrete is used, the grout mix shall not be leaner than 1:2 and it shall be ensured by suitable means such as controlling the rate of pumping that the grout fills up all inter-stices up to the top of the plug.

710.8   Filling the Well

The filling of the well, if considered necessary, above the bottom plug shall be done with sand or excavated material free from organic matter.

710.9   Plug over Filling

A 500 mm thick plug of 1:3:6 cement concrete shall be provided over the filling.

710.10   Well Cap

710.10.1   The bottom of well cap shall preferably be laid as low as possible taking into account the L.W.L.

710.10.2   As many longitudinal bars as possible coming from the well steining shall be anchored into the well cap.

710.10.3   The design of the well cap shall be based on any accepted rational method, considering the worst combination of loads and forces as per clause 706.

710.11   Floating Caissons

710.11.1   Floating caissons may be of steel, reinforced concrete or any suitable material. They should have at least 1·5 m free board above the water level and increased, if considered necessary, in case there is a possibility of caissons sinking suddenly owing to reasons such as scour likely to result from lowering of caissons, effect of waves, sinking in very soft strata etc.

710.11.2   They should be checked for stability against overturning and capsizing while being towed and during sinking for the action of water current, wave pressure, wind, etc.

710.11.3   The floating caisson shall not be considered as part of foundation unless proper shear transfer at the interface is assured.

710.12   Sinking of Wells

The well shall as far as possible be sunk true and vertical through all types of soils. Sinking should not be started till the steining has been cured for at least 48 hours. A complete record of sinking operations including tilt and shifts, kentledge, dewatering, blasting etc. done during sinking shall be maintained at site. For safe sinking of wells necessary guidance may be taken from the precautions as given in Appendix 5.

710.13   Pneumatic Sinking of Wells

710.13.1   Where sub-surface data indicate the need for pneumatic sinking, it will be necessary to decide the method and location of pneumatic equipment and its supporting adaptor.

710.13.2   In cases where concrete steining is provided, it shall be rendered air tight by restricting the tension in concrete which shall not exceed 3/8 of the modulus of rupture. For the circular wells, the tension in steining may be evaluated by assuming it to be a thick walled cylinder.

710.13.3   The steining shall be checked at different sections for any possible rupture against the uplift force and, if necessary, shall be adequately strengthened.

710.14   Sinking of Wells by Resorting to Blasting

PRECAUTIONS TO BE TAKEN DURING SINKING OF WELLS

1.   **Construction of Well Curb and Steining**

1.1   Cutting edge and the top of the well curb shall be placed truly horizontal.

1.2   The methods adopted for placing of the well curb shall depend on the site conditions, and the cutting edge shall be placed on dry bed.

1.3   Well steining shall be built in lifts and the first lift shall be laid after sinking the curb at least partially for stability.

1.4   The steining shall be built in one straight line from bottom to top and shall always be at right angle to the plane of the curb. In no case it shall be built plumb at intermediate stages when the well is tilted.

1.5   In soft strata prone to settlement/creep the construction of the abutment wells shall be taken up after the approach embankment for a sufficient distance near the abutment has been completed.

2.   Sinking

2.1   A sinking history record be maintained at site.

2.2   Efforts shall be made to sink wells true to position and in plumb.

2.3   Sumps made by dredging below cutting edge shall preferably not be more than half the internal diameter.

2.4   Boring chart shall be referred to constantly during sinking for taking adequate care while piercing different types of strata by keeping the boring chart at the site and plotting the soil as obtained for the well steining and comparing it with earlier bore data to take prompt decisions.

2.5   When the wells have to be sunk close to each other and the clear distance is less than the diameter of the wells, they shall normally be sunk in such a manner that the difference in the levels of the sump and the cutting edge in the two wells do not exceed half the clear gap between them (Fig. 3).

2.6   When groups of wells are near each other, special care is needed that they do not foul in the course of sinking and also do not cause disturbance to wells already sunk. The minimum clearance between the wells shall be half the external diameter. Simultaneous and even dredging shall be carried out in the dredging holes of all the wells in the group and plugging of all the wells be done together.

2.7   During construction partially sunk wells shall be taken to a safe depth below the anticipated scour levels to ensure their safety during ensuing floods.

2.8   Dredged material shall not be deposited unevenly around the well.

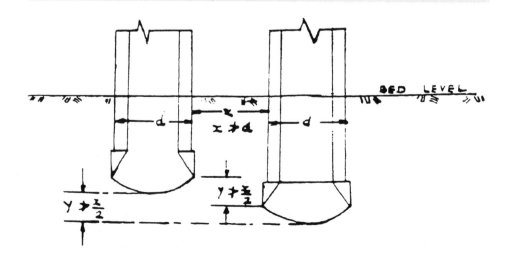

Fig. 3.

3.   **Use of Kentledge**
3.1   Where a well is loaded with kentledge to provide additional sinking effort, such load shall be placed evenly on the loading platform, leaving sufficient space in the middle to remove excavated material.

3.2   Where tilts are present or there is a danger of well developing a tilt, the position of the load shall be regulated in such a manner as to provide greater sinking effort on the higher side of the well.

4.   **Sand Blows in Wells**
4.1   Dewatering shall be avoided if sand blows are expected. Any equipment and men working inside the well shall be brought out of the well as soon as there are any indications of a sand blow.

4.2   Sand blowing in wells can often be minimised by keeping the level of water inside the well higher than the water table and also by adding heavy kentledge.

5.   **Sinking of Wells with Use of Divers**
5.1   Use of divers may be made in well sinking both for sinking purposes like removal of obstructions, rock blasting etc. as also for inspection. All safety precautions shall be taken as per any acceptable safety code for sinking with divers or any statutory regulations in force.

5.2   Only persons trained for the diving operation shall be employed. They shall work under expert supervision. The diving and other equipments shall be of an acceptable standard. It shall be well maintained for safe use.

5.3   Arrangement for ample supply of low pressure clean cool air shall be ensured through an armoured flexible hose pipe. Stand by compressor plant will have to be provided in case of breakdown.

5.4   Separate high pressure connection for use of pneumatic tools shall be made. Electric lights, where provided, shall be at 50 volts (maximum). The raising of the diver from the bottom of wells shall be controlled so that the decompression rate for divers conforms to the appropriate rate as laid down in the regulation.

5.5   All men employed for diving purposes shall be certified to be fit for diving by an approved doctor.

6.   **Blasting**
6.1   Only light charges shall be used under ordinary circumstances and should be fired under water well below the cutting edge so that there is no chance of the curb being damaged.

6.2   There shall be no equipment inside the well nor shall there be any labour in the close vicinity of the well at the time of exploding the charges.

6.3   All safety precautions shall be taken as per IS: 4081 'Safety Code for Blasting and related Drilling Operations', to the extent applicable, whenever blasting is resorted to. Use of large charges,

0·7 kg or above, may not be allowed except under expert direction and with permission from Engineer-In-Charge. Suitable pattern of charges may be arranged with delay detonators to reduce the number of charges fired at a time. The burden of the charge may be limited to 1 m and the spacing of holes may normally be kept at 0·5 and 0·6 m.

6.4   If rock blasting is to be done for seating of the well, the damage caused by the flying debris should be minimised by provisions of rubber mats covered over the blasting holes before blasting.

6.5   After blasting, the steining shall be examined for any cracks and corrective measures shall be taken immediately.

7.   Pneumatic Sinking

7.1   The pneumatic sinking plant and other allied machinery shall not only be of proper design and make, but also be worked by competent and well trained personnel. Every part of the machinery and its fixtures shall be minutely examined before installation and use. Appropriate spares, standbys, safety of personnel as recommended in the IS Code 4188 for working in compressed air must be kept at site. Safety code for working in compressed air and other labour laws and practices prevalent in the country, as specified to provide safe, efficient and expeditious sinking shall be followed.

7.2   Inflammable materials shall not be taken into air locks and smoking shall be prohibited.

7.3   Whenever gases are suspected to be issuing out of dredge hole, the same shall be analysed by trained personnel and necessary precautions adopted to avoid hazard to life and equipment.

7.4   Where blasting is resorted to, it shall be carefully controlled and all precautions regarding blasting shall be observed. Workers shall be allowed inside after blasting only when a competent and qualified person has examined the chamber and steining thoroughly.

7.5   The weight of pneumatic platform and that of steining and kentledge, if any, shall be sufficient to resist the uplift from air inside, skin friction being neglected in this case.

7.6   If at any section the total weight acting downwards is less than the uplift pressure of air inside, additional kentledge shall be placed on the well.

7.7   If it is not possible to make the well heavy enough during excavation, 'blowing down' may be used. The men should be withdrawn and the air pressure reduced. The well should then begin to move with a small reduction in air pressure. 'Blowing down' should only be used where the ground is such that it will not heave up inside the chamber when the pressure is reduced. When the well does not move with a reduction in air pressure, kentledge should be added. Blowing down should be in short stages and the drop should not exceed 0·5 m of any stage. To control sinking during blowing down, use of packs or packings may be made.

8.   **Tilts and Shifts of Wells**

8.1   Tilts and shifts shall be carefully checked and recorded regularly during sinking operations. For the purposes of measuring the tilts along and perpendicular to the axis of the bridge, level marks at regular intervals shall be painted on the surface of the steining of the well.

8.2   Whenever any tilt is noticed adequate preventative measures like putting eccentric kentledge pulling, strutting, anchoring or dredging unevenly and depositing dredge material unequally, putting obstacles below cutting edge, after jetting etc., shall be adopted before any further sinking. After correction the dredged material placed unevenly shall be spread evenly.

8.3   A pair of wells close to each other have a tendency to come closer while sinking. Timber struts may be introduced in between the steining of these wells to prevent tilting.

8.4   Tilts occurring in a well during sinking in dipping rocky strata can be safeguarded by suitably supporting the kerb.

9.   **Sand Island**

9.1   Sand island where provided shall be protected against scour and the top level shall be sufficiently above the prevailing water level so that it is safe against wave action.

9.2   The dimension of the sand island shall not be less than three times the dimension in plan of the well or caisson.

The practical difficulties of sinking small caissons, 12·5 m in diameter in a fast flowing river for the second Bassein Creek bridge at Mumbai, India were described by Deshpande and Patel.[20] The new bridge is supported on nine caissons, three on land and the remaining six were floating caissons sunk through creek water to basalt rock founding stratum. The site conditions are difficult for caisson construction as there are two daily low and high tides with a variation of 4·25 m and an average velocity of 2·4 m/s. The depth of water under the navigation span is 20 m. Occasional wind storms cause high water currents with a velocity of 3 m/s and during the monsoon heavy floods occur.

The floating caissons were initially fabricated at a temporary yard constructed on the creek bank. The cutting edge and steel liners were concreted and fabricated to a height of 8·15 m before launching at high tide.

The anchoring in the creek was difficult due to rapid underwater and surface currents accompanied by eddy formation due to existing piers. At low tide the caisson was positioned and grounded by pouring concrete into the steining. The sinking of the caisson was then continued by excavating the river bed soft marine clay by grab. Severe tilt occurred in sinking caisson P6 due to an obstruction under one side. The tilt was of the order of 1:5 and kentledge and grabbing on one side was needed to correct the tilt to the maximum permissible of 1:60. Generally, tilt in other river caissons was corrected by:

(*a*) grabbing on the opposite side
(*b*) removal of boulder obstructions by divers with hand tools or with water jets
(*c*) use of drop chisel to loosen hard strata and thence by grabbing
(*d*) light blasting

(e) water jetting from the external face on its high side – reducing friction on that side and thereby increasing sinking on that side

(f) applying kentledge on the high side.

A 1 m layer of boulders at caisson P4 had to be removed by drop chisel and water jetting and divers. The penetration of the caisson through the boulder layer took 1 month. At times, it was difficult to sink the caisson through the weathered basalt to founding level. The caisson was moved by filling it with water and making a controlled blast to give it a jerk. The alternative was to fill the caisson with water and then to pump it out fast enough to mobilize and thence reduce the skin friction.

Traditional deep wells, each with one shaft, were specified on two bridges built across the River Ravi in Pakistan as part of the Indus Basin Settlement

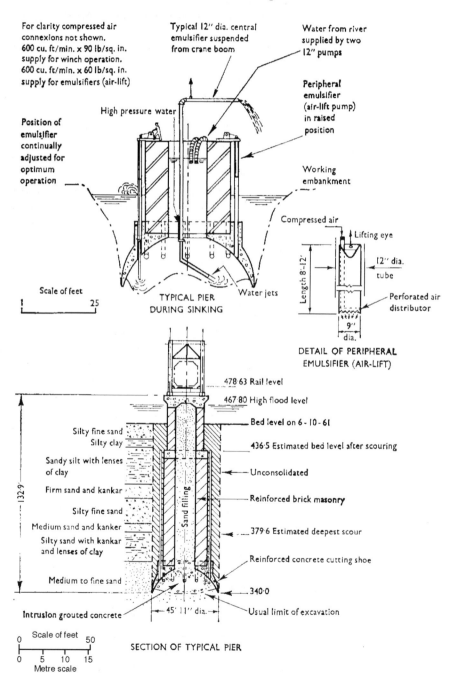

Fig. 10.18. Abdul Hakim railway bridge: well detail during sinking and section of typical pier[21]

Scheme in the 1960s.[21] One of the new bridges replaced a railway bridge where the existing foundations were not deep enough for scour protection with the planned river discharge of 4300 cumecs and modification was not possible.

The wells, 36·6 m below river bed level, were sunk by a method developed in France in 1927 by Cacot. The method reduced side friction and minimized the need for kentledge. Figure 10.18 shows the well dimensions for the railway bridge and the hemispherical shape of the wide well base and the position of airlift pumps, or 'emulsifiers', used to excavate the soil on the well periphery. The reinforced concrete cutting shoe was cast on a form made from rendered dry-stacked bricks. Reinforced brick steining in 3:1 cement mortar was built over the shoe to a height that allowed the initial sinking to be made by crane and clamshell. The following stage of brick steining was then completed and the excavation was undertaken with central air lift. Sinking rates varied from small fractions of a metre to more than 3·5 m per day.

Positional tolerances could only be achieved by sinking at a rake or, more effectively when caught early, by dredging outside the well and surcharging one side of it. In three instances correction could only be made at a considerable depth by divers using water jets cutting below the cutting edge on one side. After completion of sinking, the spherical shoe was plugged with intrusion-grouted aggregate and the well was filled with sand. Savage and Carpenter[21] commented that while the technique was an improvement when kentledge was not available, they considered that well techniques would fall into disuse and be replaced by large-diameter piles as the cost of masonry work increased.

Large caissons for river piers require support in position during lowering. Various methods are used depending on river water depth and soil strength below the river bed and include forming an enclosure, or corral, from pre-driven piles, sinking on a sand island, sinking from within a cofferdam and tethering to anchors on the river bed.

A piled enclosure or corral was formed to support the 46 m by 26·8 m caisson for pier II construction of the Mississippi River Bridge at New Orleans in the mid 1950s. The 6 m high caisson curb, fabricated at Pittsburgh and towed 1900 miles on the Ohio and Mississippi rivers to the job site, was floated into the U-shaped corral formed from 39 90 cm dia. pipe piles, gravel filled and driven 18·3 m into the river bed. Figure 10.19 shows the open-well caisson during fabrication and at pier II reading for sinking. It took one month to sink the caisson to river bed level through 21·3 m of water. The wells were then dredged and the caisson sunk a further 33 m into hard clay when a tremie concrete plug, 6 m thick, was placed. The caisson is shown in plan and section in Fig. 10.20. A total of 27 000 m³ of concrete was used in the construction of the caisson to pier II.

Corrals were also used to retain the caissons for the tower piers to the Mackinac Bridge[22]. Anchors and steel cables were not used because of limited manoeuvring space for floating craft, with risks of fouling and cutting the cables. Four towers, piled with steel tubes into the river bed, were spaced around the caisson perimeter. Each tower was connected horizontally by box-type trusses. The circular caisson was built in steelwork with double walls, with outer diameter 30·5 m and inner diameter 26·2 m. Grouting of discharged aggregate by the Intrusion Prepakt technique was used for all the concrete within the caisson and permitted very high rates of underwater concreting. From a single floating plant, placing reached almost 80 000 m³ in 30 days in caissons and cofferdams to the pier foundations.

Yang[23] described the caisson construction procedure for the Brooklyn pier to the New York City Narrows Bridge. The sand island technique was used for construction of the caisson curb, the island being formed within a

(a)

(b)

Fig. 10.19. Mississippi River Bridge, New Orleans, open-well caisson: (a) during fabrication; (b) about to be launched[11]

continuous chain of steel sheet piled cellular cofferdams. The plan and sectional elevation of the completed caisson is shown in Fig. 10.21. The sand fill within the cofferdam cells was taken to level +3·04 m and the island itself was sand-filled within water to a finished level of −3·65 m. Dewatering was by open pumping aided by a single-stage wellpoint system within the cofferdam enclosure. A clay blanket was placed outside the cofferdam and the enclosed sand island dewatered to −4·88 m. The rate of pumping reduced to 3000 gallons per minute after placing of the clay blanket.

The caisson steel cutting edge, 2·1 m high and 39·3 m by 69·8 m in plan, had internal walls 0·9 m thick and external walls 1·5 m thick. Sixty-six dredging

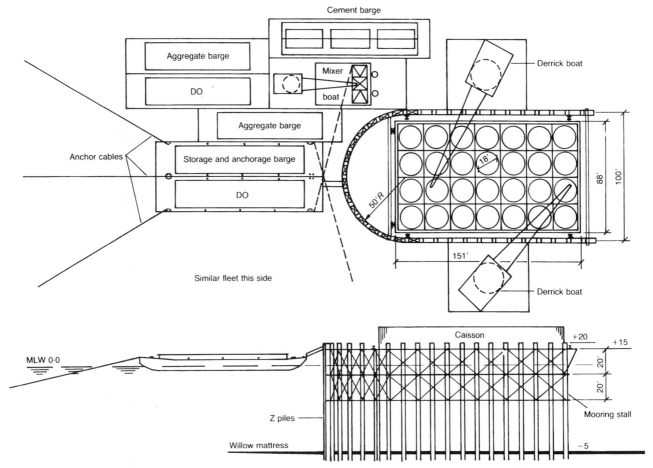

Fig. 10.20. *Mississippi River Bridge, New Orleans: caisson within corral, plan and vertical sections*[11]

wells, each 3·2 m in diameter, were formed in concrete above the cutting edge, being poured in four 3 m lifts in each of the stages of caisson extension. The effective weight of the caisson was 37 000 tonnes at the end of the first stage extension, and 42 000 tonnes was added at each subsequent extension.

Excavation within the shafts started at the caisson centre, working progressively to the edge cells. The excavation, taken through sands and fine gravels into stiff clay, tended to make the caisson sag and the caisson profile was constantly checked to avoid overstressing the structure. The average rate of sinking was 60 cm per day for the first two sinkings stages, the rate depending only on the rate of sand excavation from the cells. The actual volume of excavation barely exceeded the theoretical volume during the early stages. Dredging efficiency was reduced at lower depths into the clay, due in part to the depth effect itself and also because of loss of soil from grabs. At the lowest depths, the daily rate of sinking reduced to 36 cm per day and the actual excavation volume exceeded the theoretical volume by some 27%.

The soil at the cutting edge became more silty and less able to resist excessive pore-water pressure. A differential head between 1 and 2·4 m was maintained between cell water level and mean tide level but several cave-ins occurred. The daily sinking record and the mass diagram during sinking of the Brooklyn caisson are shown in Fig. 10.22.

In the 1970s the Barton tower of the Humber Suspension Bridge was also founded on caissons built on a temporary sand island. The figure-of-eight

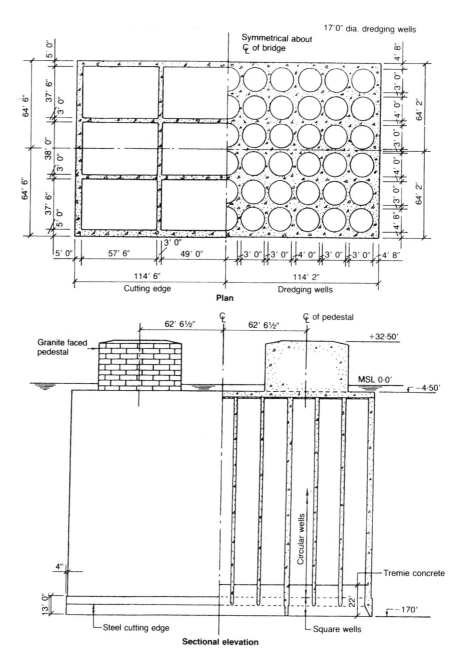

Fig. 10.21. New York City Narrows Bridge, Brooklyn pier: caisson plan and sectional elevation[23]

cofferdam containing the sand fill was subject to considerable scour and some 12 000 tonnes of chalk was needed to remedy this hazard, with much of the cofferdam piling requiring extension and redriving.

The two 24 m diameter caissons consisted of two concentric reinforced concrete cylinders joined by six radial walls to form seven cells. The caissons, extended in 3 m lifts, were excavated by 2 and 4 m^3 grabs, and water jets mounted on jigs and lowered into the cells were used to soften the soil beneath the cutting edge, first at low pressure and later at pressures between 20 and 40 N/mm^2. The excavation was underwater to avoid unloading the Kimmeridge clay. The west caisson penetrated a pocket of ground containing water under artesian pressure during sinking; as a result the bentonite slurry lubricating skin around the caisson was largely flushed away and skin friction greatly increased. The caisson was only sunk to final founding depth with an additional 3000 tonnes of temporary steel kentledge and 4000 tonnes of

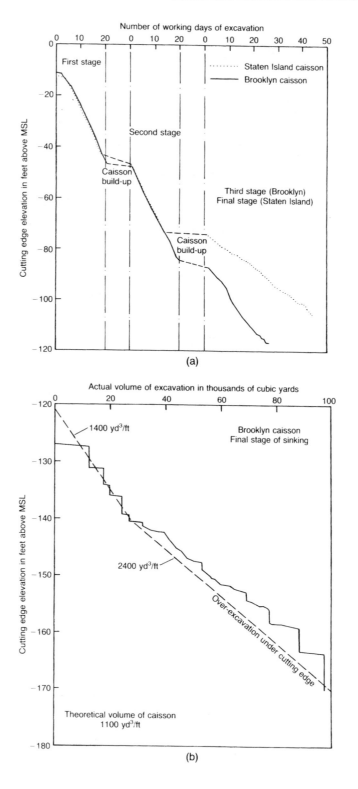

Fig. 10.22. New York City Narrows Bridge: (a) caisson daily sinking record; (b) mass diagram of sinking caisson[23]

permanent concrete to form extended outer walls to the caisson. Views of the caissons during construction are shown in Fig. 10.23.

Mitchell[24] referred to claims for reduction of up to 40% friction with the use of bentonite slurry. This slurry was injected from closely spaced nozzles connected to a header tube cast into the caisson walls, and the injections were regular and in sufficient quantity to keep the annular space next to the

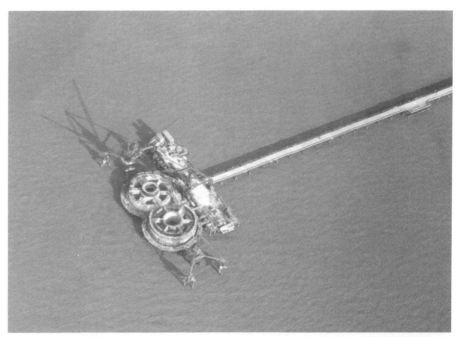

Fig. 10.23. Humber Bridge: two views of caissons during construction. Each of the 24 m diameter caissons had two concentric walls connected by cross-walls (courtesy of AMEC)

caisson full of slurry. Blaine[25], referring to the Baton Rouge Bridge, concluded that the use of water jets from similar nozzles within the caisson wall were, as designed, little value in clay and very dangerous in sands, causing run-ins. At Baton Rouge the two-tier jetting arrangement (Fig. 10.24) was unsuccessful. Fine sand had offered the greatest resistance in caisson sinking, and this situation is common elsewhere. Blaine also concluded that, in sand, blasting was a method of desperation which seldom did any good and caused run-ins.

It should be noted that the obstruction to river flow by sand island construction may well cause excessive bed erosion. Tomlinson[18] noted river bed scour at sand islands formed within steel shells at the Baton Rouge Bridge. The scour, 12 m deep despite the use of woven board anti-scour mattresses,

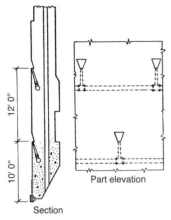

Fig. 10.24. Baton Rouge Bridge: two-tier jetting arrangement[25]

was caused by constriction of the 730 m river width to 97 m wide waterways between the sand islands. The fast flowing Mississippi River removed the whole sand filling to one 37 m diameter island in two to three minutes and caused severe tilt to the partly sunk caisson.

Blaine[25] stated that, irrespective of the detailing of erosion protection at Baton Rouge Bridge, the essential lesson was that the sand island method of caisson sinking is potentially a major erosion hazard. The damage to the caisson referred to by Tomlinson occupied the contractor's entire organization for three months following the accident, in providing further scour protection and plumbing and deepening the displaced caisson.

The south pier to the Forth Road Bridge, built in the early 1960s near the famous railway bridge, was founded on caissons sunk from the bottom of a river cofferdam. The Forth Bridge foundation works were described by Anderson[26]. The south pier foundation was originally designed as two rectangular caissons, floated into position and sunk under compressed air through the boulder clay. The contractor, John Howard and Co. Ltd, produced an alternative design using two circular caissons, which were intended to be driven through the clay as open caissons in the dry. The contractor was confident that the boulder clay would allow sheet piling for the cofferdam to be driven, and also that it would form an adequate seal for caisson excavation in the dry. The construction sequence is shown in Fig. 10.25 with a view of the access to the south pier caisson prior to sinking shown in Fig. 10.26. The site of the pier, a quarter of a mile from the shore, had a steel and timber access jetty which ended with staging enclosing the pier site on three sides.

The cofferdam for the pier, described previously, included a lower ring waling formed successfully underwater by intrusion grouting. After dewatering the cofferdam, the caisson was erected on a 100 mm concrete

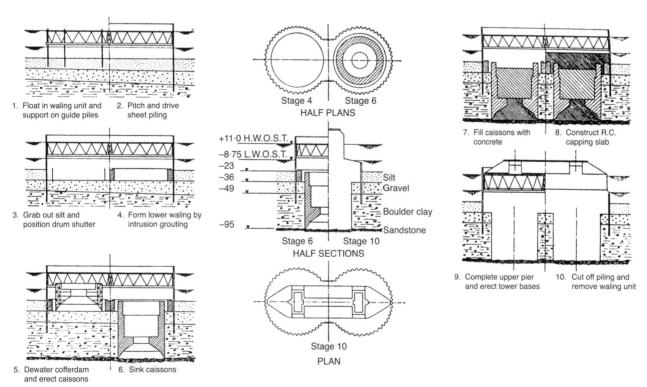

Fig. 10.25. Forth Road Bridge: south pier construction sequence[26]

Fig. 10.26. Forth Road Bridge, south pier caisson: view of river crossing showing extent of access works (courtesy of AMEC)

blinding. The caisson curb consisted of a heavy steel cutting edge mounted on skin plating. The caisson walls extended to a height of 8·5 m in reinforced concrete before sinking. During the erection work the caissons were supported around their internal periphery by concrete blocks at 1·5 m centres, and the space between the blocks was then filled to form a reinforced concrete ring beam of wedge section. After sinking through the gravel, the intermediate sections were removed by blasting and, as the caisson reached the boulder clay, the original concrete stooling was blasted away to allow the caisson to sink on the cutting edge alone.

Although air ducts and locks were ready, the method succeeded in the dry, in 'free air', as the caisson continued downwards at an average rate of 30 cm each day. Mechanical excavation on the caisson floor achieved an average of just less than 100 m³ per day in the solid measure. The downstream caisson was kept 4·5 m lower than its neighbour to ensure that any heavy inflow below the cutting edge did not flood both caissons. There was some seepage but bentonite grouting remedied the situation and, additionally, reduced skin friction during caisson sinking.

The vertical walls extended to a total height of 22·5 m above the cutting edge and the caisson was founded on bedrock. Figure 10.27 shows sections of the caisson and the finished pier. At the end of the sinking both caissons were vertical and less than 150 mm out of position.

The construction of caissons on the Lower Zambezi Bridge was described by Howarth[27]. On this contract both open and pneumatic caissons were used. It was estimated that 16 of the main wells could be sunk from sand banks and from the exposed river bed in the dry season. It was thought that sinking of the remaining wells would likely to be through varying depths of water and it was decided to use floating caisson sinking sets.

The arrangement adopted for the open wells to piers 28 to 32 in the 1932 dry season is shown in Fig. 10.28. This technique minimized the obstruction to river flow and, in turn, the extent of river bed scour. Wire ropes from the craft carrying the caisson curb and its attendant cranes were secured to

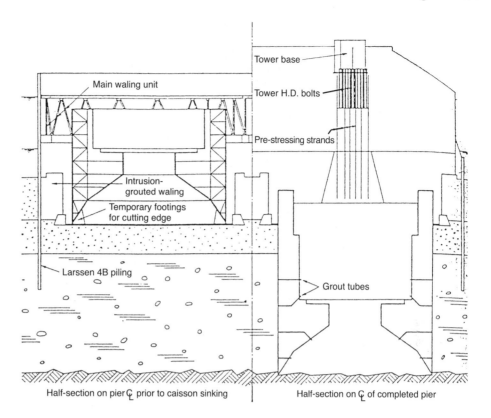

Fig. 10.27. Forth Road Bridge, south pier construction: half-sections showing caissons during sinking and completed pier[26]

heavy concrete or cast-iron anchors. Two 10 t sinkers were laid out upstream and four 5 t sinkers were used as breast moorings. The breast mooring lines from the port-side craft were moored to starboard sinkers and vice versa. One 5 t sinker was laid out downstream.

Caisson buoyancy can be improved by the use of false bottoms to the wells, the temporary bottoms only being removed after the caisson has sunk a small depth into the river bed so that the caisson weight is then supported by outer friction and its cutting edge. In the 'floatation caisson' method devised and patented by Daniel E. Moran for the west bay caissons on the San Francisco–Oakland Bay Bridge in the early 1930s, compressed air was used to regulate the amount of draught and improve control of the caisson

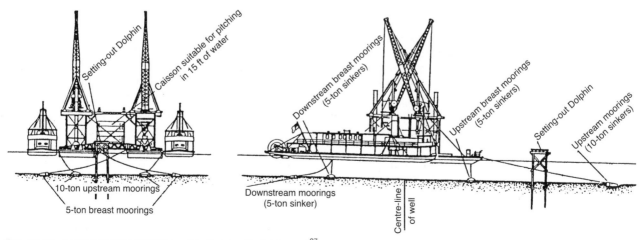

Fig. 10.28. Lower Zambezi Bridge: floating well sinking set[27]

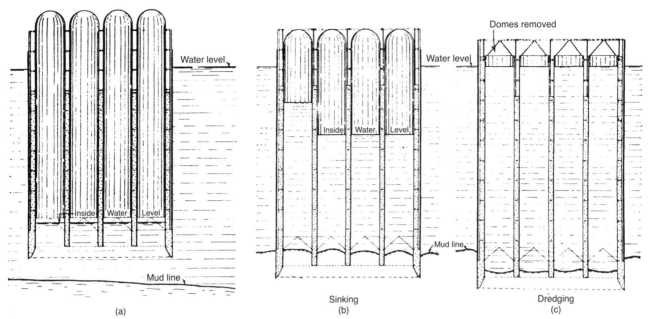

Fig. 10.29. San Francisco–Oakland Bay Bridge, West Bay pier caisson with domed wells, during: (a) floating out; (b) sinking; (c) dredging[11]

during sinking. The technique used a domed-end wall as shown in Fig. 10.29. Figure 10.30 shows the caisson for pier W4 at its final depth. The caisson, described by Little[11], was 28 by 60 m in plan and the 55 cells, each 46 m in diameter, were carried to a height of 23·6 m above the cutting edge before towing to site. The caisson had a draught of 6 m and was positioned with lines to 125 t anchors. Substantial fendering around the caisson was independently anchored. The caisson was sunk by releasing the compressed air from five of the cylindrical shafts, decreasing the buoyancy and concreting the caisson structure progressively from 23·6 m to 35·0 m when the draught was 19·2 m with the cutting edge a small distance above river bed. The air pressure in the cylinders at this stage was 1·5 bar. The air was released from all cylinders, losing 6000 tonnes of buoyancy, and the caisson started to sink into the sandy clay below the river bed under its own weight. The air domes were burnt off to allow dredging to proceed, and finally the caisson was founded on a sloping rockhead 33·5 m below the river bed.

Construction of the Tagus River Bridge in Portugal in the early 1960s similarly used compressed air and steel domes to stabilize caissons for two river piers, the first time this had been done in Europe. Riggs[28] described the methods used by Tudor Engineers, who were retained to design the piers and develop construction procedures for founding caissons on sloping basalt at considerable depth below the river bed. At pier 4, this rockhead slope was defined by no less than 31 borings and an even greater number of jet probings. A sloping rockhead was catered for by constructing the caisson's cutting edge to the same gradient (Fig. 10.31). This created problems in constructing and floating the caisson which were overcome by the use of the air domes. By varying the air pressure in the wells the caisson list was corrected after launching and during sinking.

The open caisson therefore allows permanent pier construction to be taken down through sands, gravels and clays to adequate founding soils or rock at very considerable depths. These depths are often necessary because of very large projections of scour risk in fast flowing rivers, but are not without limit. Mitchell[24] referred to caissons being sunk to the exceptional depth of

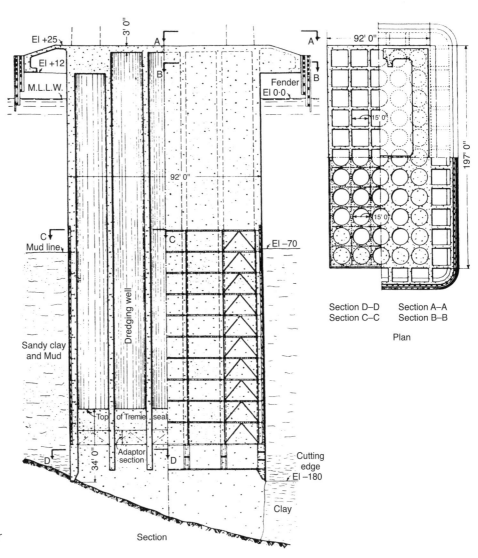

Fig. 10.30. San Francisco–
Oakland Bay Bridge: plan and
cross-section of caisson for pier
W4 at full depth[11]

105 m below the Jamuna River in Bangladesh in the early 1980s. In relatively small caissons, in the dry, excavation may proceed efficiently, but in the majority of cases excavation is only possible underwater and obstructions at shallow depth, such as tree trunks, may only be removed by a diver using small charges; obstructions at greater depths, such as boulders below the cutting edge may produce unavoidable delays in underwater excavation. Inflow of material beneath the cutting edge may occur due to artesian pressure in groundwater, causing subsidence outside the caisson and loss of bentonite seal placed to lubricate the outer skin. As the caisson is founded, sloping bedrock may cause difficulties in achieving uniform bearing for the pier. Unless the caisson is at depths where compressed air working can be used, underwater excavation and diving work may prolong construction.

Hang-ups in caisson sinking sometimes occur unexpectedly and early estimates of skin friction may prove optimistic. Water jetting, air and water jetting, bentonite grouting, and even small charges fired in the contained water, may be used in an attempt to get the caisson moving. The use of extra kentledge is the final resort. It is highly desirable, therefore, that all caissons should be designed to allow extreme weighting by extra kentledge should difficult hang-ups occur.

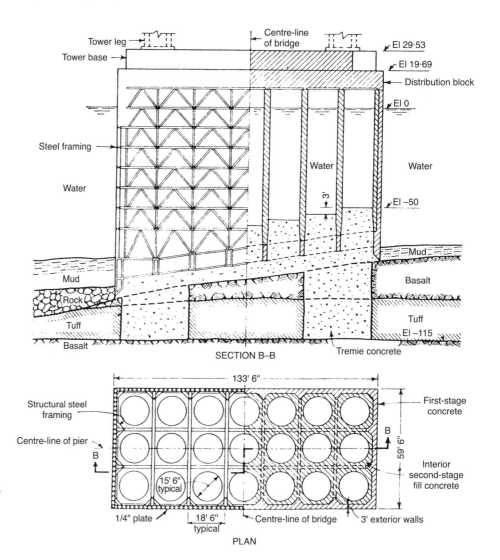

Fig. 10.31. Tagus River Bridge, tower pier 4: plan and cross-section showing sloping rockhead and shaped cutting edge[28]

Difficulties in sinking a large caisson on the Cairo waste water scheme in 1986 were described by Grimes *et al.*[29] The caisson, for a large pumping station at Ameria, had an external diameter of 45 m and was 37 m deep. The ground conditions were 8 m deep silty clay and made ground from ground level overlying dense to very dense sands and gravels together with fine thin hard grey silty clay layers at −10 and −13 below datum. Although the pre-contract design alternatives included the use of a diaphragm wall with a frozen soil base, the two lowest-bidding contractors both opted for a caisson solution.

After sinking the caisson in an open well in the dry at shallow depth, wet caisson sinking continued below groundwater level. Dredging equipment operated from a floating platform which was used subsequently as the permanent base to the dry well of the pumping station. Figure 10.32 shows the sequence of operations prior to casting an underwater plug to the caisson on which the dry well base would be sited. Bentonite was used to assist penetration of the caisson to a total depth of 28 m, but ground loss failures caused considerable difficulty. It became necessary to excavate by grab an annular space outside the caisson walls which was filled with bentonite slurry to achieve final levels.

After a study of the history of open caissons, Gerwick[30] concluded:

(*a*) most cases of initial tipping are caused by attempts to rush the work

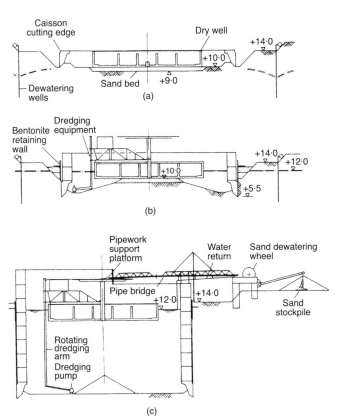

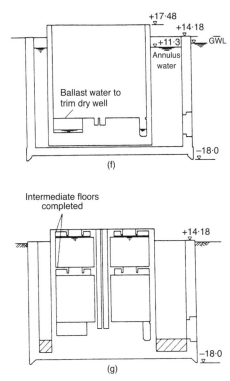

TPS construction: (f) stage 6 – dry well landed on bearings and grouted under base; (g) stage 7 – annulus is dewatered, ballast water added inside the dry well, permanent floor and radial walls added, then dry well dewatered

TPS construction: (a) stage 1 – construction of caisson wall with dry well base inside; (b) stage 2 – wet excavation by dredging from floating dry well; (c) stage 3 – wet excavation and caisson wall pours carried out simultaneously

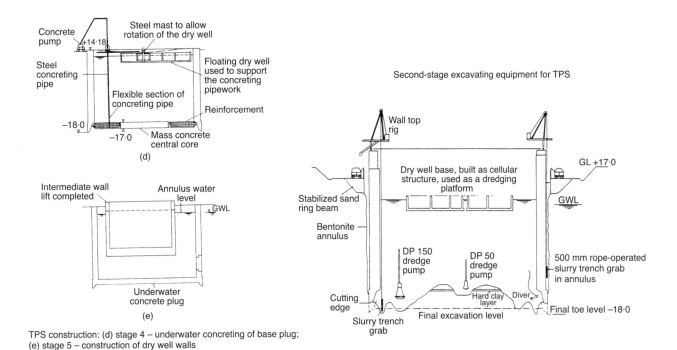

TPS construction: (d) stage 4 – underwater concreting of base plug; (e) stage 5 – construction of dry well walls

Fig. 10.32. Ameria pumping station, Cairo waste water project: sequence of construction stages 1 to 7 and second-stage excavating equipment[29]

(b) most cases of serious tipping occur when the steps taken to correct the minor initial tipping are too radical

(c) false-bottom caissons are the lowest in cost but are the most prone to tip

(d) dome caissons, such as used on the San Francisco–Oakland Bay Bridge, are very expensive and in practice do not give assurance against tipping

(e) false-bottom caissons which permit removal of the false bottom are of major value in preventing tipping

(f) the double-wall caisson, as used on the Mackinac Straits Bridge, is expensive but is unlikely to tip seriously because of its low centre of gravity and high centre of buoyancy

(g) any caisson may act, at times, as a false-bottom type due to soil plugs forming in the wells.

Open caissons in building construction

The use of caissons is not limited to bridge foundations; the technique has found application as a construction method for basements to buildings and for substructures to industrial structures such as pumphouses. In some instances, simultaneous superstructure erection has assisted caisson sinking. Since the 1970s, when slurry trench techniques provided an alternative method of deep basement construction in constricted urban areas, the use of caissons for building foundations has proved progressively less attractive.

The use of the method in Tokyo in 1950 to construct a four-storey basement of very large plan size is shown in Fig. 10.33. Three basement storeys for the

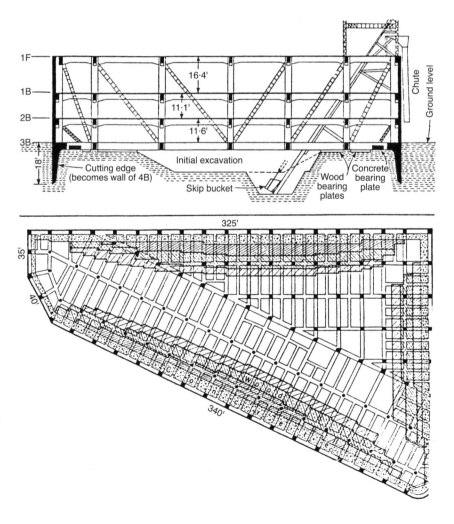

Fig. 10.33. Land caisson for the Nikkatsu building, Tokyo. Bearing plates shown in plan and section were used to control verticality and plan position of the caisson during sinking[31]

Nikkatsu building were constructed above ground. Temporary timber bearing plates beneath internal columns and outer walls were used to control movement as the caisson was sunk. The triangular-shaped caisson had a plan area of about 0·4 hectare and weighed approximately 25 000 tonnes.

After the caisson was founded at its final level, excavation was made in gravel to cutting edge level and a raft constructed to form a fourth basement[31].

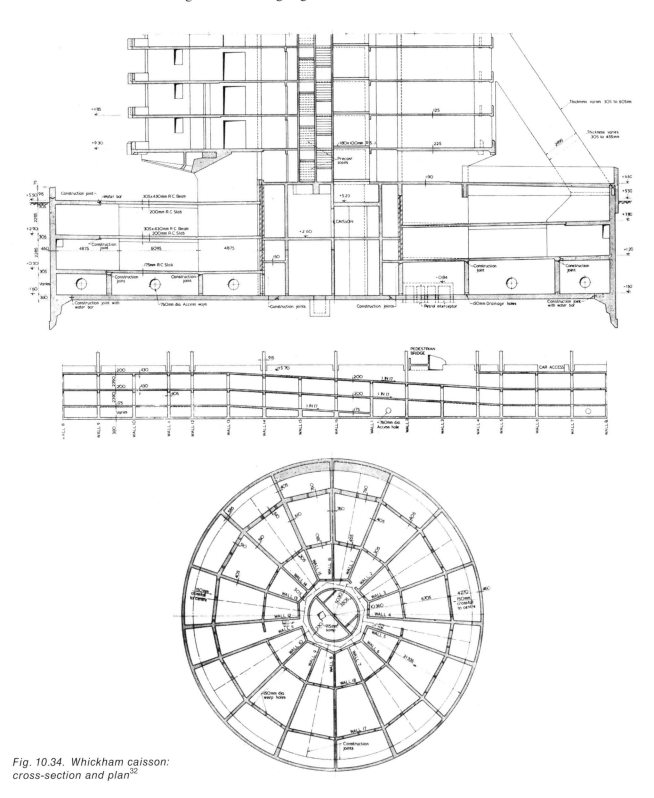

Fig. 10.34. Whickham caisson: cross-section and plan[32]

It was claimed that the cost of temporary diagonal bracing to stiffen the caisson structure during sinking was more than offset by the elimination of large quantities of shoring, strutting and sheet piling. It was noted that footways adjacent to the outside caisson wall subsided uniformly 150 to 175 mm; at a distance of 6 m, street subsidence was about 12 mm.

In the early 1970s a method of caisson construction due to Fehlmann and Lorenz was introduced into the UK. The patented method was based on a caisson curb of special design to allow the caisson to sink under its own weight, the soil adjacent to the cutting edge progressively failing under shear. Bentonite slurry was used as a lubricant. A number of contracts were completed at that time, and 200 contracts had been completed in Europe by 1972.

A 45 m dia. open caisson was sunk using this method through stiff silty clays for a three-storey basement below a 30-storey tower block at Whickham, County Durham, UK. The cross-section and plan of the caisson are shown in Fig. 10.34. The caisson was divided into 16 sections by radial walls, and a floor in the form of a helix was cast prior to sinking to provide horizontal stiffness and act as a permanent access to car parking spaces in the finished basement[32].

At Worthing the same method was used to sink a 26·5 m dia. caisson, 17 m deep, for use as a foul and surface water pumping station; the reinforced concrete curb is shown in Fig. 10.35.

A larger caisson 64 m long and 27 m wide with an overall height of 19 m, sunk on land as an open well, was used for the substructure to a circulating water pumphouse in the Huntly power project[33]. The subsoil conditions consisted of 2 m thick silt overlying a depth of 50 m of pumiceous sand of high permeability interspersed with silt bands, and at 50 m a layer of hard silt of low permeability. Sheet pile cut-off walls were driven around the caisson periphery, which was built to full height before sinking. The sheet piling reduced excavation volume and improved crane access. Water jets cast into the walls were successfully used with sand pumps and air lifts to control excavation. The caisson was supported permanently on bearing piles driven to siltstone to avoid risk of horizontal movement due to liquefaction of the pumiceous sands under seismic conditions.

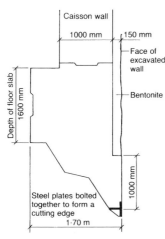

Fig. 10.35. Reinforced concrete curb to caisson for land pumping station, Worthing

Caisson wall
1000 mm
150 mm
Face of excavated wall
Depth of floor slab 1600 mm
Bentonite
1000 mm
Steel plates bolted together to form a cutting edge
1·70 m

Pneumatic caissons

The pneumatic caisson, like the open caisson, is a four-sided box in steel and concrete but with the addition of an air deck so that the caisson bottom is like a diving bell. Compressed air excludes water from this bottom section and enables work under air to carry out the excavation in the dry. The air pressure balances the pore-water pressure at the cutting edge. The maximum depth to which pneumatic caissons can be sunk is therefore directly controlled by the maximum air pressure at which work can proceed. Some labour health laws permit a maximum pressure of 3·4 bar. This pressure balances an external piezometric head of 35 m and, unless a reliable means of reducing the groundwater head is used, is the absolute limit for the pneumatic caisson working[34].

The use of high pressure limits the working hours in the caisson, and both labour and insurance costs become very high. From a health and safety point of view, the whole subject of working under compressed air for sustained periods has been of increasing concern in recent years. The use of pneumatic caissons has therefore declined for reasons other than just cost.

Although there have been experiments with helium/oxygen mixtures, an ordinary oxygen/nitrogen mixture is used in caissons. Air is deliberately allowed to escape beneath the cutting edge, and this is usually sufficient to

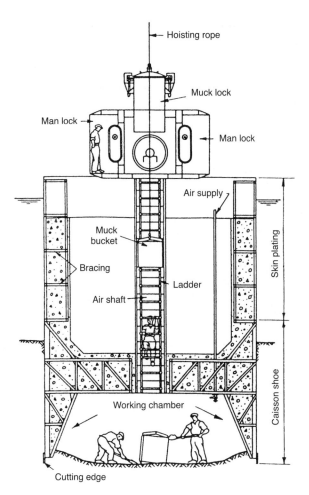

Fig. 10.36. *Typical arrangement of a pneumatic caisson*[36]

ensure adequate ventilation, although exhaust pipes and valves are also provided.

In the open, a caisson may be sunk as deep as possible, the air locks put on, air pumped in, and excavation and sinking continued.

Figure 10.36 shows a typical arrangement of a traditional pneumatic caisson. The caisson has four essential parts: the working chamber; the access shafts; the air locks which allow transfer from working pressure inside the caisson to atmospheric pressure outside, and vice versa; and the air compressor plant.

The working chamber, of the order of 2·5 m high, accommodates between six and eight workers except in the very smallest caissons. Excavation is by hand with the assistance of clay spades and similar compressed air tools, water jets and pumps. In loose sand and silt, a blow pipe may be used to evacuate the material vertically out of the caisson. The blow pipe consists simply of a pipe with a valve at its lower end leading to a T-junction at its upper end, the air pressure in the working platform forcing water and soil up after the valve is opened. Impressive rates of evacuation can be achieved with this method in sands, the soil being excavated from beneath the cutting edge by hand and placed in loose heaps for removal by the blow pipe. The abrasive action of the air/water/sand mixture on steel valves and ends should be noted. More recently, the use of high-pressure water jets with sand pumps has proved advantageous, particularly for dense materials. Water jets with nozzle pressures in the range 20 to 40 N/mm^2 can be used to augment the work of hydraulic bursters to break boulders.

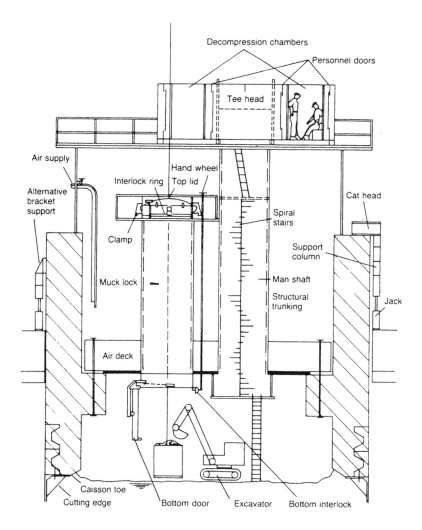

Fig. 10.37. Cairo waste water scheme: cross-section of full-depth caisson showing personnel, mud locks and excavation[35]

Figure 10.37 shows a cross-section through a caisson of later design used on the Cairo waste water system construction in the early 1990s[35]. Excavation, by a Smalley hydraulic excavator into 2·5 m³ muck skips, took six to eight weeks for each shaft from application of compressed air to pouring the concrete plug. On contract 4 of the waste water scheme these shafts were sunk through typical Cairo subsoil conditions of fill overlying silts and sands with a high groundwater table, the excavation finishing in sand or gravel layers. The diameter of the finished structure varied from 6 to 10 m. The caissons were only used for the first 10 m after which a concrete segment-lined underpinning shaft, later lined with in situ reinforced concrete, was used. Air pressure varied with depth of the shafts, from 1·6 to 2·3 bar, and needed between 42 to 340 m³/min free air delivery in the coarser soils.

The shafts are often in a figure-of-eight plan configuration with the muck shaft, usually 1 m in diameter, being placed next to the main access shaft. The shaft sections are usually 3 m lengths to facilitate extension heights to the caisson as sinking proceeds.

For safety reasons, separate air locks for workers and materials, except in the smallest caissons, are sited above maximum water level to allow workers to escape should air pressure fall and the caisson flood. For medium-sized caissons, say up to 100 m² in plan, it is usual to provide two muck locks and one man lock. For high pressures with long lock occupancy times, two man locks may be necessary for medium-sized caissons. Figure 10.38 shows

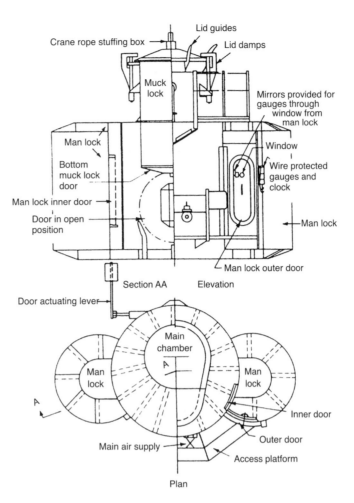

Fig. 10.38. Typical
Gowring-type air lock[36]

the Gowring-type air lock with double man locks accommodating twelve men and a muck lock designed to hold a $1\,m^3$ muck skip.

Compressed air is usually supplied from stationary compressors often driven by variable-speed motors which can increase the supply as caisson sinking proceeds. Compressors must be in duplicate with separate power sources. The compressors are connected to twin air receivers fitted with relief valves. Compressor tools in the caisson are separately supplied with air at operating tool pressure plus working chamber pressure.

The quantity of air supplied and the operation of man locks is under the jurisdiction of local or national health and safety regulations. The air quantity depends on five factors: the caisson size; the number of workers; air leakage from supply lines, stuffing boxes etc.; air loss from under the cutting edge; and air loss through the use of the locks.

Great care is essential in maintaining the true position and verticality of the caisson in the initial 5 to 8 m of sinking. Corrections to caisson position become increasingly difficult with depth. The position and levelling of the caisson should be checked at almost every movement. Howarth[27] commented that after a well had been sunk to a depth exceeding about one and a half times its axis diameter it was a mistake to try to correct position in the plan of that axis; instead, attention should be focused on keeping the well plumb. Small correction to tilt could still be made by careful undercutting.

Where the caisson is a 'floater', that is, handled from floating river craft, some positional error in placing the caisson on the river bed is inevitable. Corrective measures can be taken in the first few metres of sinking; slight tilting of the caisson for a small depth of sinking may bring the caisson back to its true position, after which vertical sinking can be resumed. Alternatively, timber cribbing may be successful, or steel wedge plates can be used under the cutting edge to move the caisson bodily sideways as it sinks. Round caissons, desirable in other respects, such as minimization of overall frictional resistance, are more difficult to control than rectangular plan shapes.

At the start of excavation within the working chamber, in loose granular soils a berm with side slopes of 1:2 horizontal to vertical is left around the periphery of the chamber. As the caisson sinks and the centre area is progressively excavated, the berm drops inwards as the cutting edge penetrates. The berm in the corners is excavated last of all. Where the caisson refuses to move because of high skin friction, 'blowing down' may be used. After the workers have left the working chamber, the air pressure is reduced and the extra effective weight of the caisson allows it to drop. Considerable care is needed to avoid large drops. Run-ins may occur in loose sands and silts, with risk of caisson tilt or movement. The procedure may succeed in hard ground such as stiff clays, but the presence of boulders may cause difficulties.

During sinking in a homogeneous clay, the air pressure is often maintained somewhat less than the theoretical balance, with a reduced air loss below the cutting edge. If such a caisson then penetrates water-bearing granular soil, the air pressure must be increased to achieve a balance against the water head and maintain a stable bottom to the excavation.

As the caisson nears rockhead, forward probing will establish the rockhead shape. Rock may be shot and excavated from the centre of the chamber to allow rock near the cutting edge to be broken out. Control of the drop is essential and 1 m deep holes at 0·5 m centres are drilled to pull about 60 cm depth. Rock pillars are left in the corners of the working chamber and are removed when the material below the remainder of the cutting edge has been cleared away.

When a caisson approaches founding level in soil and is moving without 'blowing down', it is necessary to cast blocks of concrete in small pits at the corners of the chamber on which to seat the caisson. A concreting and grouting procedure seals the caisson at its final level, filling all cavities in the exposed formation and the whole of the working chamber.

After the excavated surface of soil or rock has been levelled and cleaned off, a 60 cm thick pour of fairly workable concrete is made across the chamber floor and worked well below the cutting edge. Concrete of drier consistency can be used to pack the haunches of the curb. Care is needed at this stage because concrete placed in this way forms a seal and prevents air loss below the cutting edge, reducing ventilation and increasing pressure.

Concrete of high workability is then placed by dropping through the bottom door of the muck lock under air pressure to fill the working chamber. Bleeder pipes taken vertically above the chamber show that the filling is complete when grout moves up the pipes.

The whole is then grouted with 1:1 grout placed to fill the lowest section of the air shaft and kept under air pressure of 0·34 to 0·68 bar for 48 hours. The permanent length of the air shaft is then concreted. Figure 10.39 shows typical concreting works in sealing a pneumatic caisson.

The construction details of the caisson, and in particular the caisson curb, deserve comment. Figure 10.40 shows typical pneumatic caisson curbs or shoes. The angle of the haunch above the cutting edge depends on the type of soils to be penetrated. The cutting edge, made from stiffened steel plate, is vulnerable to buckling during caisson sinking and many problems can result. Wilson and Sully[34,36] recorded that the cutting edge shown in Fig. 10.40(c) was used through sand and on to rock on a pumphouse caisson

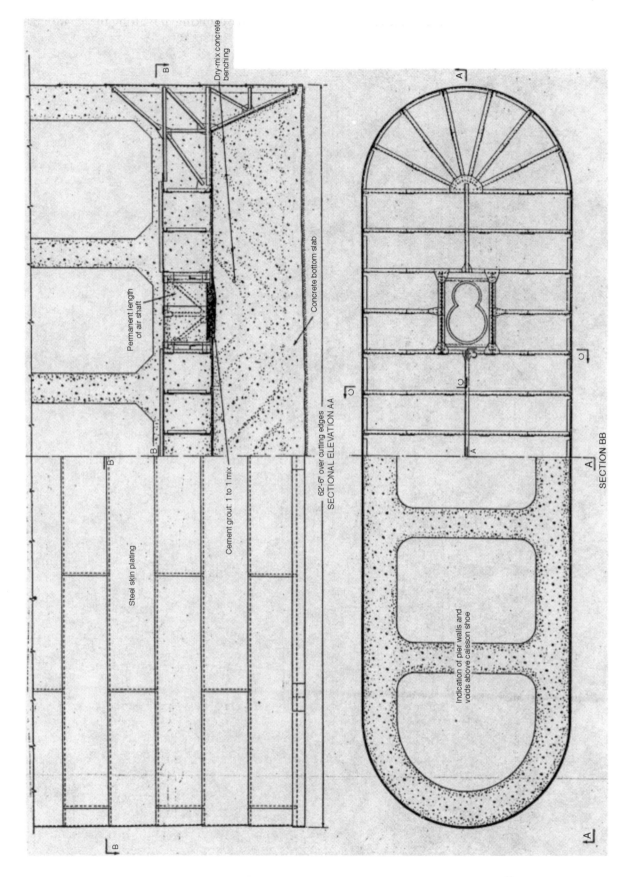

Dry-mix concrete benching

Permanent length of air shaft

Cement grout: 1 to 1 mix

Concrete bottom slab

62'-6" over cutting edges
SECTIONAL ELEVATION AA

Steel skin plating

Indication of pier walls and voids above caisson shoe

SECTION BB

Fig. 10.39. Typical steel caisson for river pier showing deposition of concrete in working chamber[36]

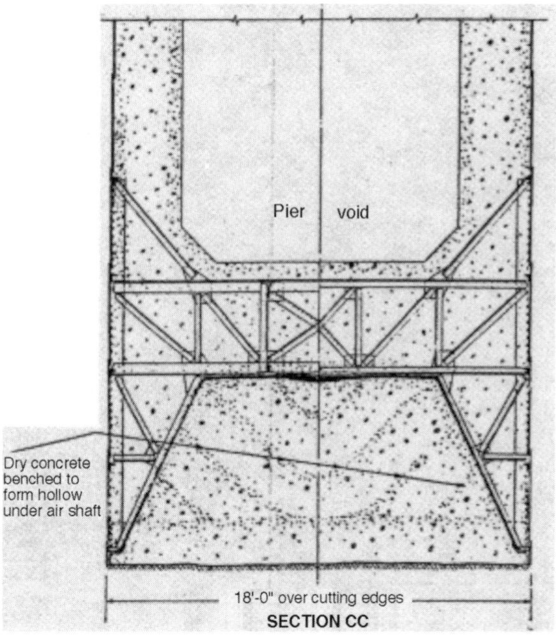

Pier   void

Dry concrete
benched to
form hollow
under air shaft

18'-0" over cutting edges

SECTION CC

Fig. 10.39. Continued

at a steelworks. Considerable excavation was needed under the cutting edge, and pressure from rock not cleared sufficiently from the back of the cutting edge caused the steel plate to be bent inwards as the caisson dropped, causing the concrete to spall on the inside of the haunch and to damage the haunch reinforcement steel.

The cutting edge and haunch detail shown in Fig. 10.40(b) was designed for use in boulder clay, the slight outside slope of the haunch being provided to avoid pincer action in any uneven sinking. In the event, the detail proved less than successful; soft silt overlying the boulder clay and within the small angle of the haunching allowed the caisson to sink quickly and unevenly. Wilson and Sully described troublesome blows caused by loose soil falling and becoming lodged between the outside curb face and the excavated soil surface during sinking. This loose soil formed an inefficient seal and any excess air pressure within the chamber led to rapid air loss and water entry below the cutting edge.

The grain silo caisson curb detail shown in Fig. 10.40(a) was used for sinking predominantly through silty sand with some clay at deeper levels. Note the sloping inner face to the steel cutting edge instead of the usual horizontal lower face. The caisson sinking operation proved quite successful.

Gerwick[30] pointed out that the cutting edge must meet the following requirements.

(a) It must be strong and rugged to resist extremely high localized pressure, such as might be caused by a boulder.

(b) It must be designed to resist twisting, shearing, crushing and particularly the tendency to spread outward because of its sloping inner surface.

(c) Its plates must be adequately stiffened and outside plates must be heavy.

(d) Connection and splice details must be rugged and strong.

(e) There must be provision for ease of concrete placement inside the cutting edge, and provision for seal placement to avoid voids.

(f) There must be sufficient vertical diaphragms to make the cutting edge cross-section act as a whole.

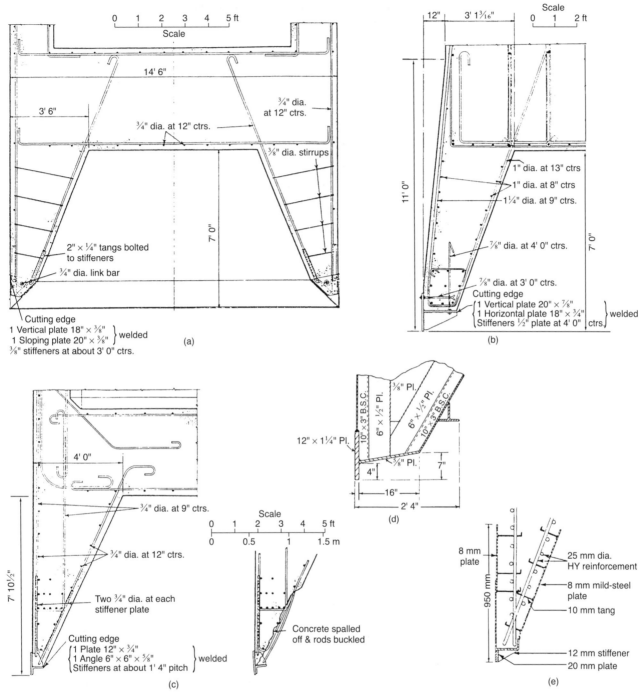

Fig. 10.40. Typical cutting edge and caisson curbs for use in: (a) silty sand with some clay at depth; (b) boulder clay; (c) sand on to rock; (d) soft clay[36]; (e) river deposits, boulder clay, sands, gravels and coal measures, progressively with depth[24]

(g) All cutting edges must be tied together in a rigid frame to resist distortion.

(h) The shoe must be designed for excavation under the cutting edge in greater depths of water.

Wilson and Sully[34] recommended steel caisson curbs in preference to those in reinforced concrete. More recently, however, and particularly for small- to medium-size caissons, the reinforced concrete curb is generally used. Wilson and Sully argued that the lower weight of the steel caisson had advantages of draught during towage and control during the initial sinking when concrete infilling could be adjusted to allow for the presence of soft soils. Wilson and Sully also advised that caisson construction is most economical with the haunches built in trench and the caisson roof shuttering supported from the existing ground.

Above the cutting shoes the caisson walls should be set-in a distance of 25 to 50 mm to assist sinking. The wall thickness is itself dependent on the need to achieve rigidity and resist stresses due to uneven sinking and on the weight requirement to overcome skin friction between caisson and soil during sinking. Adequate vertical reinforcement from the curb to the top of the caisson is necessary to resist any tension in the walls caused by 'hanging up' during sinking.

The plan shape of caissons may be circular, ellipsoid or rectangular. On the Cairo waste water scheme[35], a triple full-depth caisson was constructed to allow the bentonite tunnelling machines for the same working site to break out in opposite directions in close succession. Figure 10.41 shows tunnelling

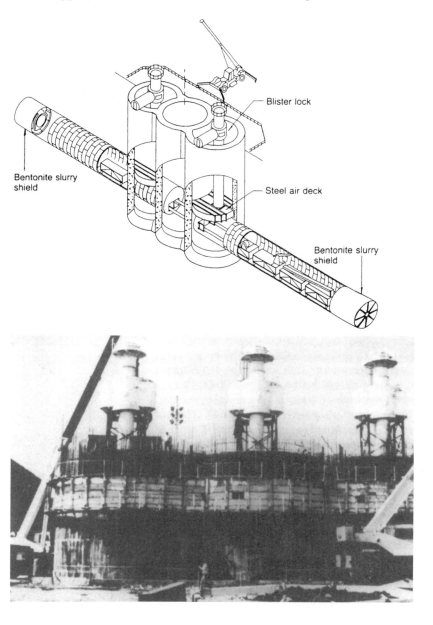

Fig. 10.41. Cairo waste water scheme: triple-cell caisson[35]

Fig. 10.42. Sinking of caisson in a narrow city street, Cairo waste water scheme[35]

from the triple-cell caisson. The caisson was originally sunk in free air to 8·5 m below ground level and sinking continued under compressed air to a depth of 24·5 m using a maximum pressure of 2·07 bar, requiring a maximum air consumption of approximately 113 m^3 per minute. Construction time for sinking was 20 weeks.

A considerable number of caissons were sunk for working shafts during the several phases of the Cairo waste water scheme. In some instances caissons were sunk in very narrow working sites in streets in the residential quarter of the city. Figure 10.42 shows a particular example of a caisson site immediately adjacent to existing buildings. Originally designed, pre-contract, as underpinned caissons of limited depth, on some sections contractors resorted to full-depth caissons (Fig. 10.43). Flint *et al.*[35] concluded that the lack of any distress to very close existing buildings, some of which were very old and probably fragile, was a commendation for the full-depth caisson method in such circumstances.

These caissons were designed on the basis that kentledge would be needed to overcome both skin friction on the outside of the caisson works and the uplift due to compressed air. Resistance was generally greater and more kentledge was used than was anticipated in most cases. Small (75 mm) diameter pipework within the caisson walls introduced bentonite to reduce friction during caisson sinking, but one or two caissons had to be 'blown down' by a sudden reduction of air pressure of up to 25% lasting 30 seconds.

The sinking effort applied to the caisson, that is the effective weight of the caisson plus any kentledge, must be sufficient to overcome the resistance to penetration of the cutting edge and the skin friction between the soil and the outside wall. Stated in these words the equation is somewhat oversimplified; the effective caisson weight is much increased during blowing down when the working chamber pressure is reduced, and resistance at the cutting edge is also much reduced by undercutting. In addition, the use of

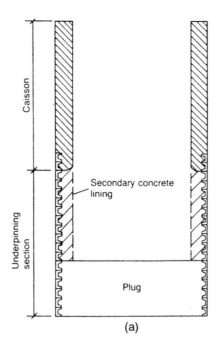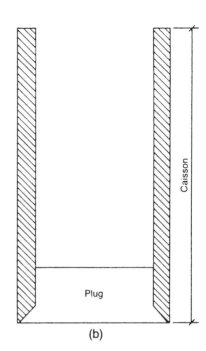

(a)   (b)

Fig. 10.43. Cairo waste water scheme, alternative methods of shaft construction:
(a) Engineer's original design;
(b) Contractor's design[35]

Table 10.1 Values of skin friction during sinking of caissons[37]

Type of soil	Skin friction f_s (kN/m²)
Silt and soft clay	7·2–28·7
Very stiff clay	47·9–191·6
Loose sand	12·0–33·5
Dense sand	33·5–67·0
Dense gravel	47·9–95·8

bentonite slurry to lubricate the outer wall–soil friction is widely practised. On the other hand, distortion or bulges in the outside surface of the caisson wall can substantially increase resistance to penetration. Nevertheless, it is essential that skin friction is never underestimated in considering the weight necessary to sink the caisson nor overestimated in calculating the permanent safe load capacity of the caisson foundation.

Terzaghi and Peck[37] gave indicative values of skin friction (Table 10.1). Values observed during sinking of both pneumatic and open-well caissons in differing soil conditions are quoted in Table 10.2. Comparing these tables leads to the conclusion that there is considerable scatter of skin friction in similarly described soils, and this makes accurate estimation of skin friction before sinking more difficult. Tomlinson[18] pointed out that disturbance of stiff clays by undercutting at the cutting edge is likely to reduce efficient contact between the outer caisson wall surface and soil, and when sinking through soft, sensitive clays and silts, friction generally has been found to be less than the remoulded strength, possibly two-thirds of this value when the caisson is sunk rapidly and continuously. Additionally, in dense sands, grabbing and dragdown during caisson sinking may cause soil disturbance and reduce friction. Nevertheless, a conservative approach is essential and friction should not be underestimated when calculating the minimum effective caisson weight necessary at each increment of depth.

After reviewing eight caisson friction values, Tomlinson concluded that these values were very erratic, ranging from 9·6 to 29 kN/m², with very few higher values, and appeared to vary little with various soil types. Wide variations were due to four factors:

- the presence of boulders
- effects of air escaping below the cutting edge
- 'freezing' effect caused by a stoppage in caisson sinking operations
- the shape of the caisson.

Handman[38] stated that the deeper the designed founding level of a caisson the higher the average sinking effort to bring it to its final level. Wiley[39] observed that the skin friction of the caisson lower section increased directly with depth

Table 10.2 Observed values of skin friction in caissons[18]

Site	Type of caisson	Approximate plan size (m)	Soil conditions	Observed skin friction (kN/m^2)	Remark
Howrah Bridge, Calcutta	Open-well and pneumatic	55 × 25	Soft clays and silty sands	29	Measured value from pneumatic caissons
Baton Rouge Bridge, River Mississippi	Open-well		Caisson 1: Stiff clay.	38·3	
			Tight clay grading to very sandy clay.	40·7	
			Tight clay grading to very sandy clay with lubricating jets	31·0	
			Caisson 3: 9·5 m sand grading to gravel; 4·6 m, clay and sand; 12·2 m stiff clay; 3 m clay and sand; 2 m sand	40·5	
			Caisson 4: 14·3 m sand and clay; 16·1 m sand, sand and clay	35·2	
			Caisson 5: 8·5 m silt; 29·9 m fine sand	53·8	
Lower Zambezi Bridge	Open-well and pneumatic	11 × 6	Mainly sand	22·9	
Uskmouth Power Station	Pneumatic	50 × 33·5	12·2 m soft clay	55·0	
Grangemouth	Open-well	13 × 13	Very soft clay	4·75	
		19·5 × 10	Very soft clay	5·75–10·0	
Kafr-el-Zayat	Pneumatic	15·5 × 5·5	Sand and silt	18·7–26·3	
Grand Tower Mississippi River	Open-well	19 × 8·5	Medium fine sand and silt	Above W.L.: 51 Below W.L.: 29·7	Dewatering from wells shown to effect friction
Verrazano Narrows	Open-well	69·5 × 39	Medium dense to dense sand and fine gravel	84·75–95·4	At lowest stage of sinking to 40 m
Gowtami	Open-well	9 × 6	9·1 m sand 13·7 m stiff clay 7·6 m sand	12·6	
New Redheugh Bridge, Newcastle	Pneumatic	11 m diameter	5·5 m depth below river bed. Hard boulder clay and dense sand at shoe	33	North caisson. Reduction of friction of 20% assumed due to bentonite above point of injection
			10 m depth. Dense sandy gravel and cobbles at shoe	38	
			12 m depth. Top of shoe in gravel, bottom in mudstone	36	
King Edward VII Bridge, Newcastle	Pneumatic	34·6 × 10·7	South caisson. Sand and gravel overlying shale.	31·6	
			Centre caisson 4·9 m sand and gravel overlying 3 m shale.	26·8	
			North caisson sand and gravel overlying shale	35·5	

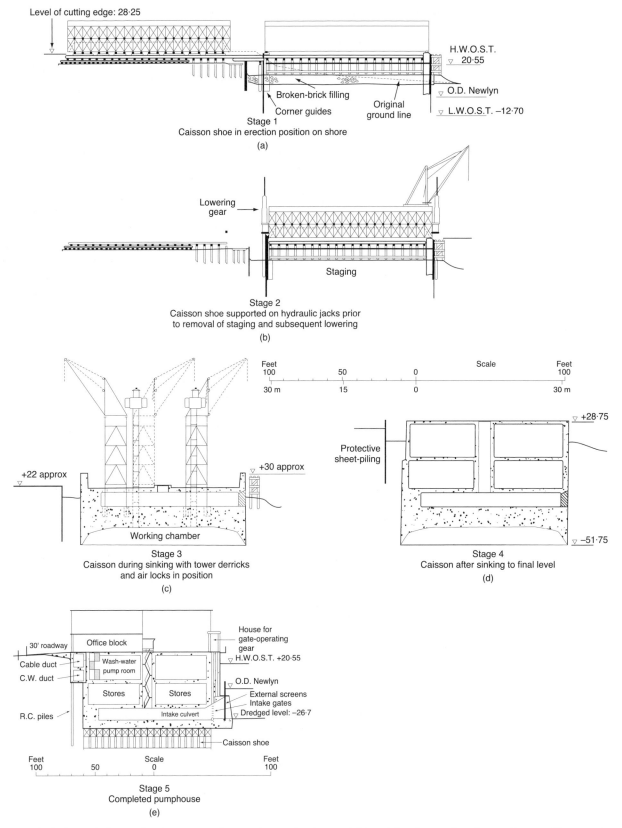

Fig. 10.44. Uskmouth Power Station, stages in erection and caisson sinking: (a) caisson shoe in erection position on shore;
(b) caisson shoe supported on hydraulic jacks prior to removal of staging and subsequent lowering;
(c) caisson during sinking with tower derricks and air locks in position; (d) caisson after sinking to final level;
(e) completed pump house[36]

but the passage of the caisson progressively reduced the friction at any given elevation by lubrication.

Yang[23] described measurements of sinking force made on large open caissons sunk through sands, fine gravel and silty clay for the foundations to the New York City Narrows Bridge. The lower part of the sinking was made with water jet lubrication and, more successfully, with air-water jet lubrication. He concluded the following.

(a) The effective weight of the caisson should always exceed the anticipated resistance without excessive use of a lubricating system.

(b) The bearing capacity of the silty clays at the cutting edge was determined to be 5·9 to 6·5 times the shear strength, which is in good agreement with the theoretical value quoted by Terzaghi and Peck[37].

(c) The skin friction on the caisson could be estimated using Coulomb's active earth pressure. The skin friction on the caisson was a maximum at the very beginning of sinking and reduced to 45% of average overburden pressure. The lower range of skin friction depended on the method and manner of applying water jets and compressed air, but a factor of 40% of average overburden pressure should be considered the practical minimum where a 'built-in' jetting system was installed.

One of the largest caissons sunk in the UK was at the Uskmouth Power Station near Newport, South Wales, in the early 1950s. The construction stages are shown in Fig. 10.44[36]. The caisson, weighing 42 000 t when complete, had a plan size of 50 m by 33·5 m and was 24·4 m deep. The caisson shoe had been fabricated on the river bank and was rolled to its sinking position over a trestle framework. After lowering by hydraulic jacks, the shoe, which weighed 510 t, was weighted further with concrete, allowing it to sink through the river water and into the made up ground. Concreting was continuous and over 5000 m³ was placed in a month, the caisson sinking under its own weight a further depth of 2·4 m without excavation. Compressed air was then applied and the excavated pneumatic caisson sank a total depth of 19·4 m.

The caisson was divided into three working chambers with two air shafts to each chamber. A maximum of 30 men split into five gangs worked in these chambers. Although it was expected that the caisson would tend to drift towards the centre of the river during sinking, the extent of this drift was 1·45 m, further than predicted.

The effects of dewatering in sand from deep wells adjacent to a pneumatic caisson on the Grand Tower pipe bridge spanning the Mississippi River were recorded by Newall[40]. A pneumatic caisson was designed to allow underpinning work from within the land caisson into uneven bedrock. Four deep wells were installed at an early stage to reduce the groundwater table to allow maximum air pressures of 3·4 bar within the caisson. The caisson, built from reinforced concrete with a welded steel cutting edge, is shown in Fig. 10.45. Newall stated that the pumping operation affected the friction on the outer skin; as the well pumps were turned off the caisson began to sink, but during pumping the caisson was effectively held. It was also observed that when pumping was reliably continuous the caisson maintained its theoretical position, but when pumping was discontinued through breakdown, the caisson wandered from position. Newall concluded that it is possible to use dewatering to control the position of land caissons during sinking.

Pneumatic caissons were used successfully for three bridges constructed across the River Tyne at Newcastle, over a period of 80 years[24,41,42]. The plan area of the caissons reduced progressively as each bridge was built, but perhaps the most evident difference between the works is the improved

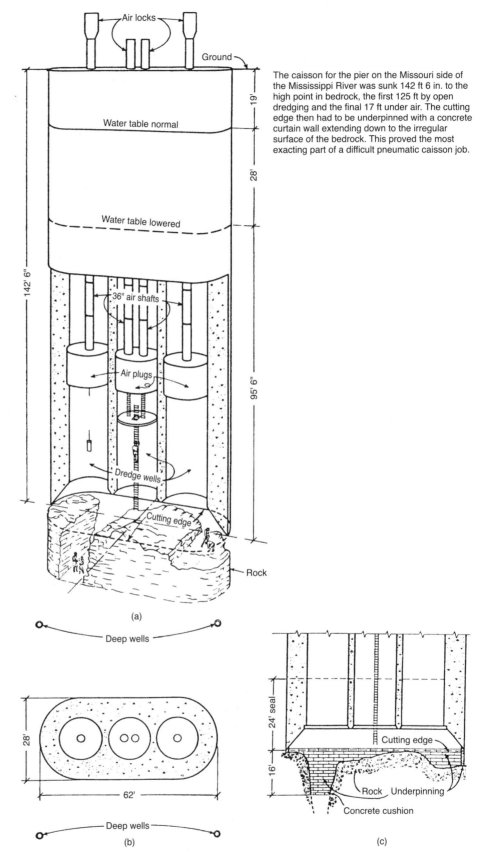

The caisson for the pier on the Missouri side of the Mississippi River was sunk 142 ft 6 in. to the high point in bedrock, the first 125 ft by open dredging and the final 17 ft under air. The cutting edge then had to be underpinned with a concrete curtain wall extending down to the irregular surface of the bedrock. This proved the most exacting part of a difficult pneumatic caisson job.

Fig. 10.45. Pneumatic caisson, Grand Tower Pipe Bridge, River Mississippi: (a) cut-away view; (b) horizontal cross-section; (c) arrangement of underpinning[40]

Table 10.3 Comparison between open well and pneumatic caissons[43]

Open-well caissons	Pneumatic caissons
'Normal' heavy excavating plant only required. No restriction on excavation	Special compressed air plant required. All excavated material has to pass through air locks
No unusual precautions for personnel and normal rates of pay	Special medical precautions, e.g. examination and rejection of unsuitable men — special care during and after decompression — provision of medical locks. Higher rates of pay
No limit of depth so far reached: 240 ft below water level at San Francisco Bay bridge through 200 ft of mud and soft deposits	Practical limit of depth, 120 ft below water level. In some countries restrictions on maximum air pressure
No men working inside caisson except occasional diver's inspection	Men work inside caisson during sinking
Obstacles may hold up sinking and may have to be removed 'blind' by blasting or other means	Obstacles clearly seen and the best method of dealing with them assured
A zone around the inside perimeter of the well (say 2 ft wide) not accessible to the grabs (this is not serious except for small wells)	Whole of the area beneath the caisson accessible to the excavators
Final cleaning up before concreting must be done underwater by grabs. If the depth is not too great, a diver can inspect	Foundation can be thoroughly cleaned and inspected before concrete is placed
Excavation is best suited to soft materials	Excavation can be done in any type of material

health and safety provision for workers in compressed air over the period. The most recent works used the Medical Code of Practice for Work in Compressed Air (1982), in draft form at the time of construction, and the Blackpool Decompression Tables. Examinations, including with X-rays, were regular, in particular to detect a septic necrosis of bone.

The use of pneumatic caissons is reducing in the same way as the use of compressed air to exclude groundwater and stabilize excavation faces is reducing in civil engineering works as a whole. The detrimental physiological effects of working under air have prompted the development of bentonite and earth pressure balanced shields for tunnel works, for example. With greater cost and greater risk in both financial and health terms, the application of compressed air to caisson work is likely to reduce further. Wilson and Smith[43] compared open-well and pneumatic caissons before either financial or health disadvantages became so evident (Table 10.3).

A useful review of German contractors' experience of caisson design and construction in the 1990s was given by Arz et al.[44] The following summary refers to the design aspects within this text, for both open-well and pneumatic caissons.

Plan shape of caissons
Caisson plan shapes which are the most statically efficient are shown in Fig. 10.46. The circular plan shape provides both the minimum cutting edge length and the minimum wall area in contact with the soil in terms of caisson plan area. For this reason large caissons are often circular in plan or nearly so.

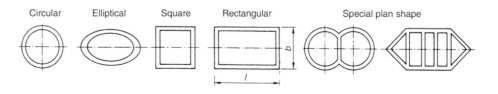

Fig. 10.46. Caisson plan shapes recommended by Arz et al. as statically efficient[44]

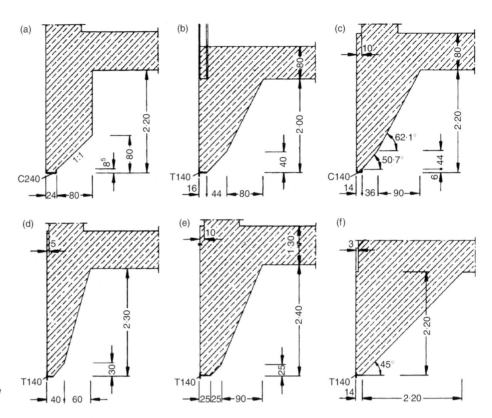

Fig. 10.47. Typical cutting edge profiles[44]

In general, the caisson cross-section is governed by the caisson use and whether it is an open or pneumatic caisson. If the plan shape is rectangular it is often advantageous to use longitudinal or cross-walls to divide the caisson into approximately square plan areas for ease of construction. To reduce the risk of tilt during sinking the ratio of length to width in plan should not exceed 2:1.

Design of walls

The outer surface of the exterior walls is generally set in from the vertical surface of the cutting edge. This is shown in Fig. 10.47. Even a set in distance of 3 cm is sufficient to reduce at-rest earth pressures to active values against the outer wall surface. With open caissons this set-in distance can be larger but certainly with compressed air caissons it needs to be less than 10 cm to avoid excessive air loss.

The thickness of the external walls is determined not only by the applied loads but also by the requirements of minimum self weight. For larger caissons an external wall thickness of 1 m is usually sufficient. The lower level of internal walls may be raised above the cutting edge level to improve sinking (see Fig. 10.48). The thickness of the internal walls is usually 0·6 to 0·8 m. Because of the volume of concrete being placed in these thick external walls it may be necessary to install cooling water pipes to reduce early age thermal cracking in the concrete above the cutting edge.

Design of the cutting edge

The sectional profile of cutting edges varies considerably due to subsoil conditions and the value of the load acting on the cutting edge. The profile must be such that the downward load induces a bearing capacity failure below the cutting edge in order to allow the caisson to sink, although this must be controlled and the rate of sinking must not be excessive. It may be necessary

Fig. 10.48. *View of outer cutting edge to caisson at Bordeaux; showing cutting edge to inner walls at higher level*[44]

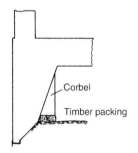

Fig. 10.49. *Temporary corbel above cutting edge used for temporary propping*[44]

to build a corbel above the cutting edge in order to arrest the sinking by temporary vertical propping laid on the excavated surface (Fig. 10.49).

For pneumatic caissons there is a minimum embedment depth of the cutting edge to avoid excessive air loss. The height of the working chamber must be dimensioned to allow sufficient headroom for the safe working of operatives and plant.

In open caissons the cutting edge is generally comparatively slim and the splay angle of the cutting edge is acute. The base of the cutting edge requires protection and steel sections can be used to achieve this. Figure 10.50 shows typical methods of protection.

Deep caissons will usually need bentonite slurry to assist sinking. Alternative means of supplying bentonite, by ring main or through vertical down pipes at 1 m centres cast into the walls are shown in Fig. 10.51.

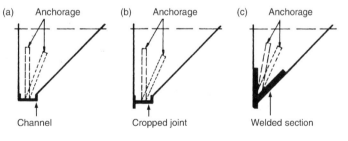

Fig. 10.50. *Protection of cutting edge with steel section*[44]

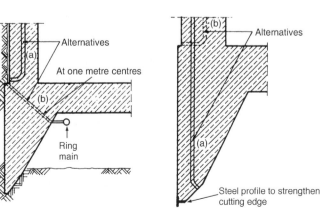

Fig. 10.51. *Alternative slurry ring main locations*[44]

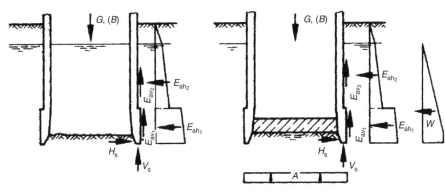

Fig. 10.52. Forces acting on an open caisson during sinking (see Fig. 10.53 for explanation of parameters)[44]

(a) During sinking   (b) Concrete placed into bottom of caisson

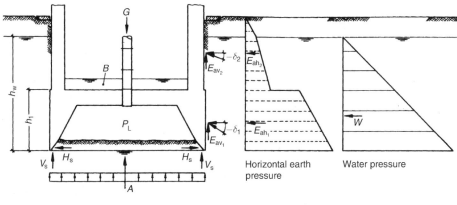

Fig. 10.53. Forces acting on a pneumatic caisson during sinking[44]

G = Self-weight + equipment	V_s = Vertical cutting force
B = Ballast	H_s = Horizontal cutting force
E_{ah} = Horizontal active earth pressure	A = Groundwater uplift
E_{av} = Vertical component of earth pressure	P_L = Compressed air pressure in working chamber
W = Water pressure	

Notation applies to both Figs 10.52 and 10.53

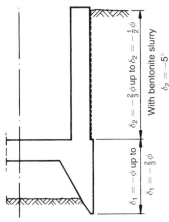

Fig. 10.54. Wall friction resisting caisson sinking – design assumptions[44]

Caisson calculation

The caisson installation phase will generally determine caisson design. For an open caisson, the forces during sinking are shown in Fig. 10.52. The forces acting on a pneumatic caisson during this phase are shown in Fig. 10.53.

The design assumptions regarding wall friction resisting caisson sinking are shown in Fig. 10.54. If bentonite slurry is used a deduction of 5° can be made from the friction angles. The design must consider:

(a) the air pressure at each stage
(b) the weight of the caisson at each stage
(c) the timing and amount of ballasting if required
(d) concreting at each stage.

During construction a minimum of four load cases must be considered:

(a) the caisson must stand unsupported before sinking without air pressure
(b) the stage during sinking when maximum moment occurs on the caisson walls causing tension on the inner face of the external walls
(c) condition at full depth with minimum moment on the external walls
(d) catastrophic case at full depth with complete loss of air pressure (not for open caisson).

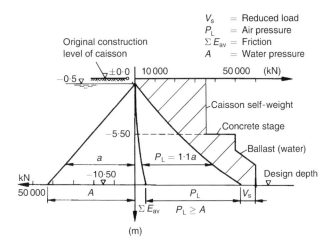

Fig. 10.55. Calculation of net vertical forces at final depth for a pneumatic caisson[44]

Figure 10.55 shows the calculation of net vertical forces at final depth for a pneumatic caisson. Assuming least favourable parameters, a net vertical load of 50 kN/m is likely on the cutting edge although much higher values will occur at the earliest stages of sinking. These values may reach 800 kN/ m. The actual values and distribution of this load on the cutting edge cannot be verified by measurement. Klockner[45] gives average bearing pressure at which cutting edges will come to rest. These may be used in the absence of more accurate data: for gravels, 1·2 to 1·6 MPa; for sands, 0·9 to 1·3 MPa. A check using alternative pressure distributions shown in Fig. 10.55 should be made. A lower acceptable factor of safety would apply to these distributions.

A further condition that should be checked occurs during surges in the rate of sinking and a pendulum effect as correction is made to verticality when increased stresses are induced in the external walls. The resulting indicative earth pressure distribution is shown in Fig. 10.55.

Table 10.4 Open and pneumatic caisson construction in the 1980s–1990s due to Arz et al.[44]

Site	Year of construction	Caisson plan size (m)	Wall thickness (m)	Ground conditions	Founding depth (m)
Compressed air caissons					
Bridge Piers, Kehl	1958–1989	7·00 × 22·00	–	–	18·7
Well shaft, Sturzelberg	1971	Diameter 6·20	–	–	24·5
Four caissons for bridges, Fray-Bentos Uruguay	1974	Diameter 10·00	–	Silt, medium– fine sand	5–7
Contiguous caissons for Baulos Wibaustraat, U-Bahn, Amsterdam	1974–1975	10·00 × 33·00– 66·00	–	Silt, sand	14·0
Pylon foundation, Rotterdam	1977–1979	9·00 × 53·50	–	Clay, sand	12·7
Pumping station, Mannheim	1980	17·80 × 35·40	–	Silt, sand, gravel	11·4
Stormwater pumping station, Berlin-Spandau	1987	8·90 × 9·80	–	Fine–coarse sand	11·5
Pumping station, Bremen-Oslebshausen	1988–1990	Diameter 26·90	–	Silt, fine– medium sand	27·4
Open caissons					
Pipeline shaft, Verbindungskanal, Berlin-Charlottenburg	1982	6·5 × 10·5	1·00	Fine–coarse sand, rock	16·00
Pumping station, Yenikapi, Istanbul	1985–1986	26·80 × 36·50	–	Fill, sand, clay	13·35
Ameria Pumping Station, Cairo	1985–1988	Diameter 44·20	2·50	Clay, hard with depth	28·00
Parking garage, Konstanz	1988–1991	Diameter 52·30	0·65	Marine clay, silt, sand, gravel	16·00

In the final condition, after construction, earth at-rest pressures should be used to check external wall stresses and bearing pressures beneath the caisson (unless there is a more onerous loading).

Typical approximate quantities of reinforcement for preliminary estimating purposes are given as follows:

- in the cutting edge, $250\,\text{kg/m}^3$ of concrete
- in the working chamber roof, $170\,\text{kg/m}^3$ of concrete.

Table 10.4 gives a list of caisson construction examples, open and pneumatic, in the 1980s and 1990s.

References

Shafts

1. Jones M. The ins and outs of uppers and downers. *Tunnels and Tunnelling*, 1984, **16**, Sept., 31–37.
2. Grieves M. Deep shafts. *Tunnelling engineering handbook*. Ed. J. O'Bickell, Chapman and Hall, New York, 1996.
3. Chapman E.J. *et al*. Cooling water intakes at Wylfa power station. *Proc. Instn Civ. Engrs*, 1969, **42**, Feb., 193–216.
4. O'Shee S.F. The construction of the Howth Tunnel. *Trans. Institution of Civil Engineers of Ireland*, Vol. 84, 1957–58, 49–110.
5. Megaw T.M. and Bartlett J.V. *Tunnels: planning, design, construction*. Ellis Horwood, Chichester, Vol. 1, 1981.
6. *Guide to shotcrete*. Report by ACI Committee 506. American Concrete Institute, New York, 1985.
7. *Proc. Conf. Shotcrete for Ground Support*. American Concrete Institute, New York, 1972, SP-54.
8. CIRIA. *A guide to the use of rock reinforcement in underground excavation*. CIRIA, London, 1983, Report 101.
9. Choquet P. and Hadjigeorgiou J. *The design of support for underground excavations in comprehensive rock engineering*. Ed. J.A. Hudson. Pergamon Press, Oxford, 1993, ch. 4, 313–348.

Caissons

10. Tricoire J. *Le Metro de Paris*. Paris Museés, 1999.
11. Little A.L. *Foundations*. Arnold, London, 1961.
12. O'Sullivan. Recent developments in Dublin Port. *Proc. Instn Civ. Engrs*, 1970, suppl., 153–189.
13. Bruun P. *Port engineering*. Gulf Publishing, Houston, TX, 1976.
14. Golder H.Q. Floating foundations, *Foundation engineering handbook*. (Ed. H.F. Winterkorn and H.Y. Fang, Van Nostrand Reinhold, New York, 1974, 537–555.
15. Hansen K. and Frode J. *Proc. Symp. Concrete Sea Structures*, London, 1972, 214–223. F.I.P., London, 1972.
16. Howarth G.E. and Smith S.J. The New Howrah Bridge, Calcutta, construction. *J. Instn Civ. Engrs*, 1947, **28**, May, 211–257.
17. Purcell C.H. *et al*. Difficult problems overcome in sinking deep caissons. *Engn News Record*, 1963, 12 Dec.
18. Tomlinson M.J. *Foundation design and construction*. Longman, Harlow, 1986.
19. Indian Roads Congress. *Standard specifications and code of practice for road bridges: section VII foundations and substructure*. 1988.
20. Deshpande D. and Patel D. Problems encountered for deep caissons. *Proc. Deep Foundations Institute Conf.*, Nice, 2002. DFI, Englewood Cliffs, New Jersey, 2002.
21. Savage C.D. and Carpenter T.G. Indus Basin settlement scheme. TSMB link canal scheme. *Proc. Instn Civ. Engrs*, 1965, **32**, Dec., 549–571 (discussion 1966, **35**, Sept., 184–204).
22. Boynton R.M. Mackinac Bridge. *Civ. Engng*, 1965, **45**, May, 44–49.

23. Yang N.C. Conditions of large caissons during construction. *Highway Res. Rec.*, No. **74**, 1965, 68–84.
24. Mitchell A.J. Caissons. *Handbook of structural concrete*. Ed. F.K. Kong, *et al.* Pitman, London, 1983.
25. Blaine E.S. Practical lessons in caisson sinking from the Baton Rouge Bridge. *Engng News Record*, 1947, 6 Feb., 213–215.
26. Anderson J.K. Forth Road Bridge. *Proc. Instn Civ. Engrs*, 1965, **32**, Nov. 321–512.
27. Howarth G.E. Construction of the Lower Zambezi Bridge. *J. Instn Civ. Engrs*, 1937, **4**, Jan., 369–422.
28. Riggs L.W. Tagus River Bridge tower piers. *Civ. Engng*, 1965, Feb., 41–45.
29. Grimes J.F. *et al.* Greater Cairo waste water project. *Proc. Instn Civ. Engrs*, 1993, **97**, special issue, 34–37.
30. Gerwick B.C. *Handbook of heavy construction*. Eds. J.A. Havers and F.W. Stubbs, McGraw-Hill, New York, 1971.
31. Mason A.C. Open caisson method used to erect Tokyo office building. *Civ. Engng*, 1952, Nov., 46–49.
32. Nisbet R.F. Whickham tower block. *Structural Engr*, 1973, **51**, No. 7, 225–231.
33. Brown A.S. and Cox D.D. Design and sinking of a large concrete caisson at the Huntly power project. *New Zealand Engng*, 1980, **35**, No. 2, 28–32.
34. Wilson W.S. and Sully F.W. *Compressed air caisson foundations.* Institution of Civil Engineers, London, works construction paper No. 13, 3–30, 1949.
35. Flint G.R. *et al.* Greater Cairo waste water project. *Proc. Instn Civ. Engrs*, 1993, **97**, special issue, 18–33.
36. Wilson W.S. and Sully F.W. The construction of the caisson forming the foundations to the circulating water pumphouse for the Uskmouth Generating Station. *Proc. Instn Civ. Engrs*, Part 3, 1952, **1**, 335–356.
37. Terzaghi K. and Peck R.B. Soil mechanics in engineering practice. Wiley, New York, 1967.
38. Handman F.W. Lower Zambezi Bridge. *J. Instn Civ. Engrs*, 1937, **4**, Jan., 325–368.
39. Wiley H.L. Sinking of the piers for the Grand Trunk Pacific Bridge. *Trans ASCE*, 1909, **62**, 132–133.
40. Newall J.N. Pneumatic caisson pier. *Civ. Engng*, 1956, May, 51–55.
41. Davis F.W. and Kirkpatrick G.R. The King Edward VII Bridge, Newcastle on Tyne. *Min. Proc. Instn Civ. Engrs*, 1908, **174**, Apr., 158–221.
42. Anderson D.A. Tyne Bridge, Newcastle. *Proc. Instn Civ. Engrs*, Part 3, 1929–1930, **230**, 167–183.
43. Wilson W.S. and Smith H.S. *Relative methods of sinking bridge foundations.* Institution of Civil Engineers, London, 1950.
44. Arz P. *et al., Grundbau.* Ernst and Son, Berlin, 1994.
45. Klockner, W. *Grundungen BK 1982 Teil II.* Ernst and Son, Berlin, 1982.
46. Ward A.M. and Bateson E. The New Howrah Bridge, Calcutta, construction. *J. Instn Civ. Engrs*, 1947, **28**, May, 167–210.

Bibliography

Shafts

Auld F.A. Design of concrete shaft linings. *Proc. Instn Civ. Engrs*, Part 2, 1979, **67**, Sept., 817–832.
Bills R.F. Developments in shotcrete equipment. *Proc. Engng Foundations Conf. American Concrete Institute*, 1977, SP-54, 201–210. American Concrete Institute, Farmington Hills, Michigan, 1977.
Collins S.P. and Deacon W.G. Shaft sinking by ground freezing. Ely Ouse Essex scheme. *Proc. Instn Civ. Engrs*, 1972, suppl. 7, 129–156.
Design and construction of tunnels and shafts. *Proc. Australian Conf. on Tunnelling*, Australian Institute of Mining and Metallurgy, Melbourne, 1976.
Harding P.G. Fresh air for Frejus: vent shaft excavation in Europe's top tunnel. *Tunnels and Tunnelling*, 1980, **12**, No. 4, May, 25–27.
Lancaster-Jones P.F. Problems of shaft sinking. *Tunnels and Tunnelling*, 1975, **7**, July Aug., 26–28.

Lyons A.C. and Reed A.J. Modern cast iron tunnel and shaft linings. *Proc. 2nd Rapid Excavation and Tunnelling Conf.*, San Francisco, 1974, Vol. 1, 669–689. American Institute of Mining, Metallurgical and Petroleum Engineers, Baltimore, Maryland.

Prater E.G. Examination of some theories of earth pressure on shaft linings. *Canadian Geotech J.*, 1977, **14**, No. 1, Feb., 91–106.

Provost A.G. and Griswold G.G. Shaft sinking considerations and problems. *Proc. 2nd Rapid Excavations and Tunnelling Conf.*, San Francisco, 1974, Vol. 2, 1095–1113. American Institute of Mining, Metallurgical and Petroleum Engineers, Baltimore, Maryland.

Wilson N.E. Designing access shafts for tunnel construction. *Engng J., Montreal*, 1980, **63**, Oct., 12–15.

Caissons

Ameria Pumping Station. *Construct. Ind., Int.*, 1989, **15**, No. 5.

Arz P. *et al. Grundbau Abschnitt B des Beton Kalenders*. Teil II. Ernst and Son, Berlin, 1991.

Chandler J.A. *et al.* Jamuna River 230kV crossing Bangladesh. Construction of foundations. *Proc. Instn Civ. Engineers*, 1984, **76**, Nov., 965–984.

Gales R.R. Hardinge Bridge over the Lower Ganges at Sara. *Min. Proc. Instn Civ. Engineers*, 1917, paper 4200, 18–99.

Hayward D. Humber Bridge. *New Civ. Engnr*, 1975, 10 April, 22–24.

Hayward D. Stubborn caisson sinks under 6500 tons. *New Civ. Engnr*, 1975, 17 July, 16–17.

Hinch L.W. *et al.* Jamuna River 230kV crossing Bangladesh. Design of foundations. *Proc. Instn Civ. Engrs*, 1984, **76**, Nov., 927–949.

Hyatt K.E. and Morley G.W. *The construction of Kafr-el-Zayat railway bridge.* Institution of Civil Engineers, London, 1952, paper No. 19 works construction.

Krauss F.E. Pneumatic technique for buoyant caissons. *J. ASCE Waterways Harbours Coastal Engng Div.*, 1973, **99**, Feb., 19–26.

Lingenfelster H. *Senkkasten Grundbau Taschenbuch Teil 3, 4*. Ernst and Son, Berlin, 1992.

Meldner V. Pneumatic caisson work for the bridge across Lillebaelt. *Baumasch, Bautech.*, 1971, Jul., 289–295.

Pike C.W. and Saurin B.F. Buoyant foundations in soft clay for oil refinery structures at Grangemouth. *Proc. Instn Civ. Engnrs*, Part 3, 1952, **1**, Dec., 301–334.

Porter T.G. *et al.* Shaft excavation in soft clay by caisson construction. *Proc. Conf. Retaining Walls*. Institution of Civil Engineers, London, 1992, 281–290.

Schwald R. and Schneider H. *Tiefgarage Obere Augustinergasse in Konstanz.* Mitteilungsheft der G Baresel, Stuttgart, 1991.

Schwald R. and Schneider H. *Gestarte Absenkung eines offener Vortrage der Baugrundtagung.* DGEG, Dresden Heraasg, 1992.

11

Soil movement due to deep excavations

Introduction

In earlier times the task of the temporary works engineer was to design the peripheral soil support to a deep basement excavation to provide an adequate, but not over-generous, factor of safety against collapse. Risk was identified in terms of the adequacy of the structural strength of strutting, shoring, anchoring, sheeting or walling. Addressing the risk of excessive deformation of sheeting and bracing was frequently not a high priority. Now this has changed and the provision of deep basement accommodation on urban sites has raised to a new importance the serviceability design conditions of acceptable horizontal and vertical soil movement around and below the excavation. As basements are built to greater depths and building developments occupy greater plan areas, the problems of subsidence, heave and horizontal soil movement themselves become priorities. Insurers are no longer prepared to cover risks of property damage which can be recognized, from previous experience, as inevitable. This chapter addresses those factors which cause soil movement around an excavation, typically a large deep basement excavation, the measures which can be taken to alleviate soil movement, and the methods available to the designer to predict movement.

A recent review by Long[1] was made of some 300 case histories of wall and ground movements due to deep excavations worldwide. Generally this data base ignored geographical boundaries, and variations in local standards of specification and workmanship and its limitations in this respect must be acknowledged. Broadly, the collected information was grouped into four categories: predominantly stiff to medium-dense soils; predominantly stiff to medium-dense soils with embedment into a stiff stratum; predominantly stiff to medium-dense soils with a low safety factor against base heave; and cantilever work. Further subdivision was made for internally propped walls, anchored walls, top-down construction and soil strengths. Comparison was made with the charts of Clough et al.[2] and Peck[3] and the regional studies in Oslo (Karlsrud[4]), Taipei, Taiwan (Ou et al.[5]), Singapore (Wong et al.[6]) and the UK (Carder[7], Fernie and Suckling[8]).

The conclusions reached by Long may include the disadvantages of a wide sweep of published data but cannot be disregarded bearing in mind the very large data base collected. Long concluded the following.

For retaining walls in stiff clays with a large safety factor against excavation base heave:

(a) Normalized maximum lateral movement values $\delta_{h\,max}$ are frequently between 0·05%H and 0·25%H where H is the excavation depth.

(b) Normalized maximum vertical settlement values $\delta_{v\,max}$ are usually lower, at values frequently between 0 and 0·20%H.

(c) There is no discernible difference in the performance of propped, anchored or top-down systems.

(d) The values recorded are somewhat less than would be expected from the charts produced by Clough and O'Rourke[9], possibly because the soils in the data base are on average stiffer.

(e) They seem relatively independent of system stiffness and are perhaps controlled by excavation base heave and limited by arching effects in these stiff soils.

(f) The data indicate that less stiff walls may perform adequately in many instances and worldwide design practice may be somewhat conservative.

For retaining walls that retain a significant thickness of soft material (greater than 0·6 of excavation depth) with stiff material at dredge level and where there is a large safety factor against base heave:

(a) The $\delta_{h\,max}$ and $\delta_{v\,max}$ values increase significantly from the stiff soil cases.

(b) The values are close on average to those predicted by Clough and O'Rourke[9].

(c) There is some promise in the use by Addenbrooke[10] of the flexibility number for the analysis of the collected data.

For retaining walls embedded in a stiff stratum that retain a significant thickness of soft material (greater than 0·6 of excavation depth) and have soft material at dredge level but where there is a large safety factor against base heave (determined intuitively):

(a) The $\delta_{h\,max}$ and $\delta_{v\,max}$ values increase significantly from the situation where stiff soil exists at dredge level.

(b) The Clough et al. charts considerably underestimate movements.

In cases where there is a low safety factor against base heave, large movements ($\delta_{h\,max}$ to 3·2% of excavation depth) have been recorded. The data mostly fall within the limited values suggested by Mana and Clough[11] and it is suggested that the relationship between movement, system stiffness and safety factor proposed by Clough et al. form a good starting point for preliminary estimates of system performance.

For cantilever walls, the normalized maximum lateral movements:

(a) are relatively modest and average 0·36% of excavated depth

(b) are surprisingly independent of excavation depth and system stiffness

(c) suggest that less stiff walls would perform adequately in many cases.

To relate these findings to a site-specific assessment of wall displacement may prove difficult or indeed, impossible. The findings by Long represent his conclusions from a wide data base but may not accurately represent risk of wall displacement on a particular site.

Factors that influence soil movement

The principal factors that determine the extent of soil deformation have been listed for conditions in Hong Kong[12]. For wider geographical application the list of factors influencing soil deformation around a deep basement excavation is slightly longer:

(a) effects of stress changes within the subsoil

(b) dimensions of the excavation

(c) soil properties

(d) initial horizontal stresses within the soil

(e) groundwater conditions and changes to them

(f) stiffness of the sheeting and bracing system

(g) effects of pre-load in bracing and anchoring

(h) construction methods

(i) construction workmanship.

This list is not given in any order of priority since the importance of each factor varies from job to job. The list is now examined in more detail.

Effects of stress changes within the subsoil

The complexity of stress changes in four elements in an over-consolidated clay which is supported by a diaphragm wall during excavation are shown in Fig. 11.1 (after Gaba et al.)[13]. The locations of the four elements are:

- Element A: immediately behind the wall
- Element B: immediately in front of the wall
- Element C: beneath the centre of the excavation, some distance from the wall
- Element D: behind the wall and remote from it.

The initial pore pressures, prior to installation of the wall are hydrostatic below an in situ groundwater level.

The changes in the short term during construction and in the long term as steady seepage is established are summarized in Table 11.1. In more detail the progressive changes in stress and pore-water pressure for elements A and B are as follows.

At soil element A
- Over-consolidation of soil in geological time, following deposition and removal of overburden, no further deposition of recent deposits: stress path $0'$ to 0. (K_0 greater than 1.)
- Wall excavation below slurry: reduced lateral total stress, pore-water pressure reduces: stress path 0 to 1.
- Wall concreting: increase in lateral total stress, pore-water pressure increases to approximate in situ values: stress path 1 to 2.
- Excavation in front of wall: wall moves forward, horizontal total stress reduced with reduction in pore-water pressure. Following yield, excessive negative pore-water pressure occurs: stress path 2 to 3.
- Steady-state seepage develops with time (as the permeability of the soil fabric allows). Long-term steady-state seepage pore-water pressure is less than the initial hydrostatic value but probably greater than pore-water

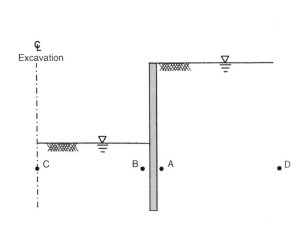

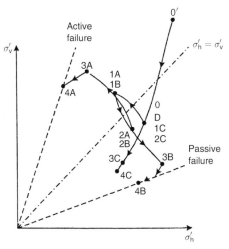

$0'$–0: Overburden removal after deposition (over-consolidation)
0–1: Excavation for wall installation under support fluid
1–2: Concreting of wall
2–3: Excavation of front of wall
3–4: Long-term groundwater seepage conditions

Fig. 11.1. Stress changes in four elements in an over-consolidated clay during excavation[13]

Table 11.1 Changes in the short term during excavation and construction and in the long term as steady state seepage is established[13]

	Element A	Element B	Element C	Element D[a]
Vertical total stress during excavation	Constant	Decreases	Decreases	Unchanged
Horizontal total stress during excavation	Decreases	Decreases due to unloading. Increases due to wall movement	Decreases	Unchanged
Pore-water pressure during excavation	Decreases	Decreases	Decreases	See note[b]
Pore-water pressure in the long term	Probably increases	Increases	Decreases	See note[b]
Undrained shear strength in the long term	Probably decreases	Decreases	Decreases	Unchanged
Strain during excavation	Vertical compression	Vertical extension	Vertical extension	Unchanged
Strain in the long term	Vertical compression	Vertical extension	Vertical extension	Unchanged

Notes
[a] Assumed to be located sufficiently remotely from the wall so as not to be affected by changes in soil stress due to excavation in front of the wall.
[b] Depends on ground permeability.

pressure immediately after excavation. Pore pressure increasing in the long term as steady-state seepage is established: stress path 3 to 4.

Soil element A experiences an overall increase in vertical effective stress and a decrease in horizontal effective stress to bring element A into an active state.

At soil element B
- Excavation makes a large reduction in vertical total stress with a large reduction of pore pressure. Groundwater at formation level.
- Movement of the wall below formation level towards the soil in front of the wall increases horizontal total stress and is likely to result overall in an increase in horizontal effective stress and a reduction in vertical effective stress during excavation.
- Steady-state seepage develops with time, pore pressures increase reducing vertical and horizontal effective stresses: stress path 3 to 4.

The vital factor influencing the horizontal movement of soil below formation level, and therefore the magnitude and extent of vertical settlement is the proximity of the unloading stress path of element B to the failure envelope. If the stress path 2 to 4 is well within the passive failure envelope, this shows that the yield is small and both heave and the resulting horizontal soil movement will also be small. Conversely, if the effective stress points for element B are close to the failure envelope this indicates risk of excessive yield, local passive failure and high lateral movements.

A summary of the stress changes that occur at soil elements A, B, C and D (from reference[13]) is given in Table 11.1.

Dimensions of the excavation
The plan shape, the plan area and the excavation depth all critically influence the extent and distribution of soil movement around and below a basement excavation in given soil conditions. The depth obviously affects movement; Tomlinson[14] referred to unavoidable inward movement in normally strutted

or anchored excavations of the order of 0·25% of excavation depth in soft clays and 0·05% in dense granular soils or stiff clays. It is usual to assume that the volume of horizontal soil movement at the sheeting within a unit length of excavation support is approximately equal to the volume of vertical soil movement at ground level over the same unit length. As a rule of thumb, horizontal soil movements are likely to extend to a maximum lateral dimension of two to three times the excavation depth. The deformed soil profile therefore begins to take shape, although changes with time (due to pore-water pressure dissipation) and the effects of irregular plan shape complicate a simple assessment of settlement risk.

Soil properties

Soil properties were summarized by Peck[3]. Figure 11.2, after Peck, shows smaller wall movements and ground settlements in stiffer soils (such as granular soils and stiff clays) than in softer soils (e.g. soft and medium clays and loose silts).

As reported by Long, soil movements due to excavations in soft clays may prove to be embarrassingly large, particularly where the clays have been assumed incorrectly to be isotropic. Clough *et al.*[15] and Mana and Clough[11] showed the rate and magnitude of lateral wall movement both increase rapidly as the risk of base heave increases and the factor of safety against base failure reaches unity.

Overall deformation in terms of heave below the excavation and vertical settlement around it will depend on many factors including soil stiffness and, in weaker soils, soil strength. In weak clays and loose silts, yield in soil zones may result in providing passive resistance to peripheral sheeting or walling, with large movements resulting. From a practical viewpoint, in loose cohesionless soils with high piezometric pressure due to groundwater, excavation conditions may be close to quick conditions with risk of vertical soil subsidence and loss of ground between timbering, sheet piles or diaphragm wall joints. Soil and groundwater conditions, therefore, pre-empt

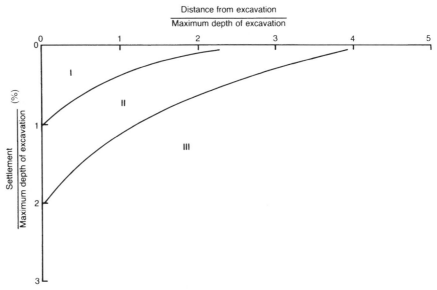

Zone I — sand and soft to hard clay, average workmanship
Zone II — very soft to soft clay
Zone III — very soft to soft clay to a significant depth below bottom of excavation

The data used to derive the three zones were taken from excavations supported by soldier piles or sheet piles with cross-lot struts or tie-backs.

Fig. 11.2. Observed settlements behind excavations[3]

all other factors as the prime critical risk of soil movement around deep excavations.

Initial horizontal stresses within the soil

Where high, locked-in horizontal stresses exist within soils, typically within over-consolidated clays, soil deformations surrounding excavations increase, even at relatively shallow depths. For soils with comparatively low values for coefficient of earth pressure at rest K_0, deformations are much less[16].

Groundwater conditions

The effects of groundwater on soil settlement are varied and occur at different stages of excavation. Where sheeting penetrates a cohesionless stratum but does not achieve a cut-off at depth, a steady groundwater seepage condition will develop whereby flow is established beneath the sheeting and upwards to the formation level of the excavation. This flow causes a decrease in groundwater pressure, an increase in effective stress and settlement outside the periphery of the excavation. At the same time passive resistance reduces due to the upward flow on the inside of the sheeting, and further horizontal movement occurs as sufficient passive resistance is mobilized. The establishment of a steady-state groundwater regime therefore causes both vertical and horizontal soil movement.

Where dewatering of sheeted excavations causes drawdown to the exterior groundwater table, again where the sheeters to the excavation do not make an adequate cut-off at full penetration, effective vertical soil pressure increases, resulting in vertical settlement. Since the drawdown is greatest near the excavation and reduces progressively with increasing distance from it, this settlement profile will be similar in shape to that due to relief of overburden by the excavation itself.

Stiffness of the support system

Parametric studies using Winkler spring or finite element soil–structure interactive programs and observations made on site show that the exterior ground settlement profile surrounding a sheeted excavation reduces as the stiffness of the sheeting and the bracing supporting it increase. The elastic stiffness of the bracing system appears to be most important. The vertical embedment of the sheeting beneath formation level will also materially alter the effective stiffness of the sheeting and influence external soil movement, both vertically and laterally.

A study of the effects of wall stiffness, bracing stiffness, vertical spacing of supports and embedment was reported by Goldberg et al.[17]; a summary of the results is shown in Fig. 11.3 in which the stability number is plotted against the stiffness parameter. The data presented also suggest that sheeting stiffness and support spacing effectively influence external soil movements.

Experience over some years in temporary works design using a Winkler spring program has confirmed site observation that increasing strut stiffness decreases external soil movements, although less effectively at very high values of stiffness. These findings regarding the practical importance of sheeting and strutting stiffness are not confirmed by Clough and Davidson[18] nor by Tomlinson[14]. These authors stated that the amount of yielding for any given depth of excavation is a function of the characteristics of the supported soil and not of the stiffness of the supports. Tomlinson referred to steel structural members, even of heavy section, as being insufficiently stiff to reduce yielding by any significant amount. Reinforced concrete diaphragm walls, he noted, deflect by amounts similar to those experienced with sheet pile walls. This similarity has not been the experience of the

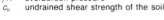

h   vertical distance between support levels or between support
    level and excavation base
E_w modulus of elasticity of wall material
I_w movement of inertia of wall per unit length
γH overburden pressure
c_u undrained shear strength of the soil

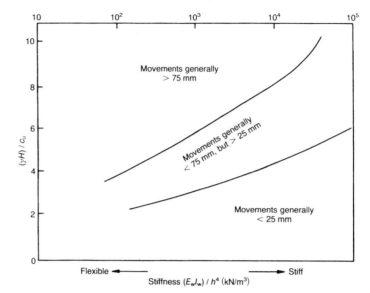

Fig. 11.3. Effects of wall stiffness and support spacing on lateral wall movements[17]

Author and, although it is agreed that soil stiffness should be regarded an important factor, it is considered that both sheeting and strutting stiffness contribute significantly to the extent that soil behind the wall is allowed to move.

In summary, the cross-sectional area of the soil vertical settlement trough outside the basement walls is approximately equal to the cross-sectional area of the horizontal soil deformation curve at the wall relative to the original wall line. The deformed shape of the walls, and of the soil immediately adjacent to it, is made up of deformation between prop levels (and wall deformation prior to the insertion of props) together with inward deformation due to the compression of the props. Prop compression occurs as all forces on the inside and outside of the wall reach equilibrium, earth pressures on the outside face reducing from at-rest earth pressures, and passive pressures on the inside face below dredge level being progressively mobilized as horizontal deformation occurs. The balancing forces mobilized in the props and in the soil below dredge level cause horizontal movement the amount of which depends on the stiffness of the props and the stiffness of the soil in compression below dredge level.

Effects of pre-loading
Within the Author's experience the pre-loading of bracing to deep excavations has been beneficial in reducing settlements outside the excavation in a variety of granular soils and medium–stiff to stiff clays using relatively stiff sheeting and walling such as steel sheet piling and reinforced concrete diaphragm walling. The pre-load tightens the bracing system and thereby reduces one cause of horizontal movement and vertical settlement. Apart from this practical improvement, movement is further reduced due to improving soil stiffness caused by the hysteresis effect on the soil stress–strain curve as the soil is progressively unloaded in shear at each frame level (due to pre-loading) and reloaded for the next bracing frame.

The advantages of reduced soil settlement by pre-loading are not fully accepted by some temporary works designers, although O'Rourke[19] summarized his views by stating that in most instances of cross-lot bracing pre-loaded to 50% of its design load, further movement would be prevented at that frame level, and overstress of the bracing at that frame was unlikely if the pre-load was limited to 50% of the design value.

The pre-loading of bracing can be compared with the pre-stressing of ground anchor tendons. The Author's practice over a long period has been to pre-load anchors to the design load to the completed excavation, calculated on the basis of the trapezoidal strut load envelope recommended by Peck[3] and described in Chapter 7. These loads are applied successively by post-tensioning jacks at each frame level as the excavation reaches that level. A 10% overload is applied at each anchor to allow for slippage and creep within the tendon. Winkler spring analysis is then used to check sheeting stresses and deformations with the applied anchor loads for each stage of the excavation. No excessive movement or overstress has been experienced within this procedure.

The efficiency of pre-loading tendons in reducing vertical settlements outside the periphery of the excavation is related to anchor length. Where the fixed length of the anchor is located within the zone of soil movement caused by the bulk excavation, only a limited reduction in settlement may be expected. This effect is most likely in cohesive strata, while in sands and gravels pre-loaded anchors with a fixed grouted length at least beyond the theoretical Coulomb wedge (at an angle of $45° + \phi/2$ to the horizontal) may be expected to effectively limit horizontal soil movement and vertical settlement.

Construction methods

The choice of overall construction method for the basement, either top-downwards or bottom-upwards, the technique used for walling or sheeting the basement periphery, and the period taken for each excavation stage, all influence the extent of soil movement around the excavation for given groundwater conditions and basement dimensions.

The top-downwards method, using basement floors to successively prop peripheral diaphragm or piled walls, is frequently used to restrict vertical soil settlements. No comparative soil measurements are available to substantiate this view, although certain features of the method would appear to minimize soil movement. These include the regular propping to the exterior wall afforded by the floor at each storey height, the considerable elastic stiffness of this prop, and the avoidance of movement involved in repropping. (The exterior wall is repropped when conventional cross-lot bracing is replaced by temporary supports between the exterior sheeting or walls and the substructure as the permanent works progress in bottom-upwards construction.) Closer examination of a particular site may, however, reveal a less satisfactory situation. The regularity of support provided by the floors to the exterior walling at each storey height would not necessarily provide support at the optimum levels, especially where external surcharge loads are applied from, say, existing foundations to adjacent structures or where the height from the penultimate support to formation level should be minimized, say where soft or weak strata exist immediately below final formation. Again, some contractors prefer to construct the exterior walls and excavate to first basement floor level without casting the ground floor. This procedure loses some advantage of the method in restricting soil movement. Potts et al.[20] showed the results of numerical analysis, concluding that the use of temporary soil berms to support cantilevered external walls from ground floor to first basement floor level only partly reduces the extra settlement caused by excavation to first basement level prior to commencement of floor construction.

The choice of walling or sheeting and its method of installation also influence the extent of vertical soil settlement. With some methods, such as walls from vertical soldier piles and horizontal laggings, the loss of ground caused by the need to have an open face of excavation as the laggings are placed is likely to cause greater settlements than those due to other walling methods. Similarly, where sheet piles are used in granular soils and heavy vibratory or percussive installation methods are chosen in preference to, say, assistance by water jetting, the resulting soil settlement may be significant.

Construction workmanship

Published records of the influence of inadequate construction standards, usually workmanship standards, are numerous and only serve to confirm the common sense knowledge of site staff that short cuts and sloppy attitudes towards workmanship in timbering and excavation support works inevitably lead to support movement, soil subsidence and even local failure and progressive collapse. The designer must bear some responsibility with regard to standards of workmanship. For example, the materials chosen for constructing excavation support should be the best available at site, the chosen method of walling or sheeting should comply with the experience of the supervisors and operatives that are to build it, and construction details such as site-welded connections, reinforcement fixing and stressing works should all be related to the available site skills.

Many causes of additional movements (and failure) of excavations due to bad site practices appear in reference 1. These include late installation of supports, over-excavation, poor pile driving and caisson construction, loss of water through holes for tie-backs and joints or sheet pile interlocks and diaphragm wall joints leading to loss of ground, remoulding and undercutting of clay berms, and excessive surcharge loads from spoil heaps and construction equipment. Many more items of inadequate workmanship or supervision standards that can cause movement, subsidence or collapse can be added to the list. In particular, the lack of rigidity and tightness of shores and braces are important causes of wall and soil movement. Failure to provide or tighten wedges between walling and walings is a significant cause of movement and subsidence. Similarly, with king post walls, failure to efficiently wedge horizontal laggings to vertical soldiers and ensure good uniform contact between soil and laggings is a direct cause of soil subsidence behind the wall. Peck[3] pointed out that the choice of detail of lagging connection to soldier could cause settlements adjacent to the excavation to vary widely; settlements adjacent to walls using the detail in Fig. 4.6(b) were three times those using the detail in Fig. 4.6(a).

Measuring techniques and their accuracy

The measurement of small displacements and angular rotations of surfaces and existing structures has required the development of existing surveying techniques and the use of electronic techniques. A general review of such methods was given by Dunnicliff[21]. More recently, a review of the methods of field measurements made on greenfield sites and existing structures on the extension to the Jubilee Line metro extension was made by Standing et al.[22] Examples of the best accuracies for the different measuring systems were given in this paper and are reproduced in Table 11.2 as a guide to the best expectation of accuracy of measurement for such techniques elsewhere.

Measures to reduce soil movement at the curtilage of a deep excavation

To ensure minimum soil movement horizontally and vertically, around and below a deep excavation of given dimensions in given soil conditions, several measures are necessary. Not all may prove to be financially worthwhile, but they are:

Table 11.2 Examples of the best accuracies for measuring systems[22]

Instrument type (monitoring method)	Building example	Resolution	Precision	Accuracy
Precise level (NA 3003)	Treasury, Palace of Westminster	0·01 mm	0·1 mm	±0·2 mm
Total station (TC 2002)	Ritz: (vertical displacement)	0·1 mm	0·5 mm	±0·5 mm
	Ritz: (horizontal displacement)	0·1 mm	1 mm	±1 mm
	(angular displacement)	0·1 arcsec	2 arcsec	±5 arcsec
Photogrammetry	Elizabeth House	1 mm	1 mm	±2 mm
Tape extensometer	Elizabeth House	0·01 mm	0·03 mm	±0·2 mm
Demec gauge	Palace of Westminster	0·001 mm	0·01 mm	±0·01 mm
Rod extensometer	Elizabeth House	0·001 mm	0·01 mm	±0·2 mm
Electrolevel	Elizabeth House	2 arcsec	10 arcsec	±10 arcsec

(a) provide a wall support which provides both temporary and permanent soil support

(b) make the sheeting or wall support flexurally stiff

(c) avoid installation vibration or other causes of loss of ground

(d) ensure the wall has adequate embedment in a stiff stratum

(e) ensure the wall receives support at frequent vertical centres and reduce these centres progressively with depth

(f) locate the lowest support near formation level

(g) make the bracing stiff in compression

(h) pre-load the bracing or pre-tension the ground anchors

(i) avoid delays in construction of either walling or bracing, avoid keeping diaphragm wall panels open for long periods and avoid delays in bracing works or anchor installation at each support level

(j) avoid any loss of ground by over-excavation or removal of fines during pumping

(k) avoid drawdown caused by dewatering outside the basement

(l) in weak soils, improve ground conditions below formation level to ensure adequate passive resistance inside the sheeting from soil with sufficient strength and high stiffness (such improvement could be made by localized jet grouting, pin piles, mix-in-place piles or vibro-replacement).

For deep basements, where soil conditions permit a cut-off against ground-water ingress, the top-downwards method of construction may prove attractive in meeting some of these criteria to reduce external soil settlement. The method has disadvantages, however, including high excavation costs to remove soil from below basement floor construction, the risk of overall delay caused by any local hold-up in a sequence of interdependent construction activities, and the problems in terms of space and access of several specialist firms working on site at the same time.

In shallower basements the use of top-downwards construction may be prohibitively expensive. In such circumstances, the risk of excessive settlements around the site will be minimized by the above methods. In particular, cantilevered walls and excessively high sheeting are a frequent cause of excessive soil movement outside the excavation and should be avoided where possible by propping the sheeting from temporary bases or from a previously constructed raft at the centre of the basement plan shape. Where walls are cantilevered at any stage individual piles or diaphragm panels

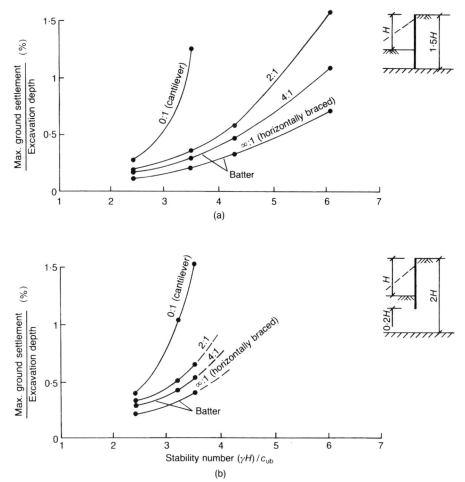

Fig. 11.4. Relationship between maximum ground settlement and stability number at the end of construction after berm excavation for berms of varying batter: (a) fully penetrating, fixed-end MZ-27 sheet pile wall; (b) partially penetrating, free-end MZ-27 sheet pile wall[23]

within the basement wall should be connected by a stiff capping beam in reinforced concrete.

The use of soil berms to minimize lateral movements of walls or sheeters at the periphery of a deep excavation should be noted. The general consensus on the use of berms[23,24] is that the increase in vertical stress using a relatively small volume of soil is often sufficient to reduce lateral movements to walls or sheeters by 50% while the berm is left in place. If the berm is removed in short lengths while rakers or struts are placed, the final lateral movement, and thence the vertical settlement of soil outside the excavation, can be usefully reduced. Numerical studies by Clough and Denby[23] on an excavation in soft to medium clay showed a theoretical relationship (Fig. 11.4) between settlements behind sheet piles with berms and the stability number $\gamma H/c_{ub}$, where c_{ub} is the undrained shear strength at the base of the excavation for the condition after the berm has been removed and the rakers installed. The reduction in ground settlement increases as the stability number increases, and at high stability numbers increasing berm size leads to larger reduction in settlements. This apparent improvement may not be produced, however, where deep-seated movements occur at high-stability numbers with low-strength clays.

Burland *et al.*[24] showed the effect of a soil berm at one stage of a 16 m deep basement excavation in London. The peripheral soils were supported by a diaphragm wall with a depth of embedment 3 m below final formation level. The initial excavation was 10 m deep, at which depth a thick waling slab

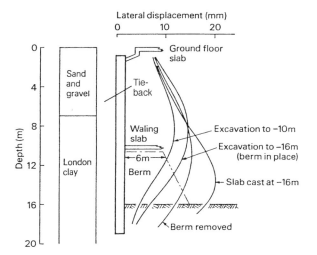

Fig. 11.5. Observations of wall lateral movement; effect of soil berm[24]

was cast on the exposed surface of the London clay. Excavation was then made to the full depth leaving a soil berm below the waling slab, as shown in Fig. 11.5. After the basement raft had been concreted in the central area the berm was removed in short lengths and the raft completed to support the wall. Observations of lateral movement of the wall shown in Fig. 11.5 indicate the efficiency of the berm in reducing wall movement before its removal. Burland *et al.* considered that the weight of berms could be very effective in controlling the softening of the clay, and hence the movements and stability of the toe of the wall. Burland *et al.* also gave the results of a numerical analysis showing the use of berms to reduce movements while excavating the lowest and fourth basement floor spaces to an excavation within London clay. The berm, removed in short lengths and replaced by the propping action of the basement floor, contributes an important shear connection with the diaphragm wall and adds significant surcharge to the soil below final formation level, providing passive resistance to the toe of the wall.

Two recent papers describing strut load measurements, at Mayfair car park[25a] and Canary Wharf underground station[25b], London have highlighted the influence of corner stiffness of walling in rectilinear excavations and the discrepancy between 2D and 3D analyses. The effect of stiffness of corner panels to relieve load from corner brace struts and reduce lateral wall displacements within the plan length of the walling has been long accepted by designers, but field measurements of strut loads and 3D finite element analyses now confirm this. The calculated reduction in displacement of walls due to three-dimensional analysis is also discussed by Simic and French[26].

Where soil movements at the outside of a deep excavation are a vital consideration and space allows a wall thickness substantially greater than usual but the proximity of nearby structures prohibits the use of anchors, a cellular type of wall may be considered. Although not cost-effective in terms of area of diaphragm wall per linear metre of completed wall, the cellular wall, utilizing the self-weight of the enclosed soil for stabilization, is remarkably efficient in limiting horizontal soil movements and vertical settlement behind the wall. Plan forms of a T-panel wall and a double-flange cellular wall were shown in Fig. 8.44.

In Medinah, Saudi Arabia, a cellular diaphragm wall was built to avoid soil deformation at the rear of a 17·5 m deep excavation which was required not to be obstructed by temporary raking shores. The excavation was 100 m wide and more than 1·5 km long. Cross-lot strutting was therefore not practical and ground anchor capacities were uneconomical in the conditions. The excavation was through silty clays and silty sands overlying bedrock up to 55 m deep in close proximity to precious religious shrines. The maximum acceptable lateral soil movement immediately behind the wall, either in the short term or prior to placing permanent props (with basement floors) some 18 months after excavation, was 25 mm. The maximum acceptable lateral soil movement in the proximity of piles to existing substructures within 50 m of the perimeter of the deep excavation was 5 mm. The cellular diaphragm wall, shown in Fig. 11.6, was analysed using finite element methods and measured small strain modulus values with a non-linear finite elastic–plastic numerical model. The combined immediate and drained soil movements were shown to be less than these maximum values. The movement of the wall as-built was significantly less than that predicted, as shown in Fig. 11.7. Difficulties were experienced modelling the effect of the shear stiffness of the cross-walls in the two-dimensional model, and only when this stiffness was reduced was a deformed shape produced by the analysis typical of a cantilever wall.

The proximity of nearby buildings required major temporary works of a different kind during the substructure construction of a large arts centre at the Barbican in London in the 1970s (Fig. 11.8)[27]. Nearby tower blocks, although piled, were susceptible to tilt caused by soil movement during bulk excavation for the theatre, but even more importantly, analyses predicted excessive shear stresses in these piles if significant soil movement were allowed between the piles due to the excavation. Even though cellular diaphragm walls of considerable stiffness were designed at each side of the theatre basement, the predicted horizontal inward movement of these walls below formation level exceeded the maximum that the pile shear could withstand. To prevent this movement below formation level, two props were constructed in tunnels between the cellular walls and pre-loaded with thrusts up to 10 000 kN. The length of the north wall of the theatre exceeds 60 m, with a minimum height of 14 m. The wall was designed to be propped apart by the two diaphragm walls at the east and west sides of the theatre basement and at low level by the two pre-loaded tunnel props, as shown in Fig. 11.8. A horizontal waling was formed by the arch slab at the 6 m level spanning across the whole basement width. The wall itself spans horizontally across the low-level supports and vertically between the arch slab and the prestressed concrete beam within the wall at lower level. Measurements during construction showed that the north theatre wall was moved northwards by a maximum of 10 mm and the south wall moved southwards by 5 mm. The jacks were maintained in an operable state for one year after the basement excavation and were then stabilized by the exchange of hydraulic fluid with epoxy resin grout without loss of pressure. The jacks had therefore fulfilled their purpose and instead of soil movement towards the theatre excavation, the pre-loaded tunnel props caused small movement in the opposite direction. The essential point in this basement design was the risk, avoided by the use of the pre-loaded tunnel props, of progressive wall/soil movement below the excavated level of the theatre basement as it was dug out, the stiffness of the peripheral cellular walls below excavated level being insufficient to reduce it to acceptable levels without the action of the pre-loaded props.

A later, but similar, use of tunnelled struts was made for basement construction at Westminster station, London. Stringent settlement criteria were necessary to avoid damage to the Big Ben clock tower, the adjacent metro tunnels, trunk sewer and nearby parliamentary buildings. Top-downwards construction was used for basement construction but risk of soil deformation below

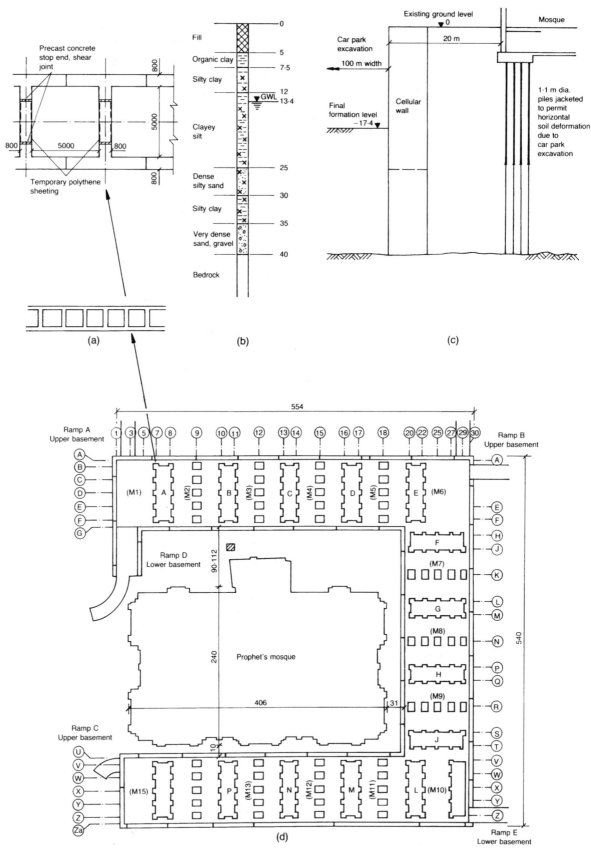

Fig. 11.6. Medinah car park: (a) plan of cellular wall construction; (b) design soil profile; (c) design cross-section; (d) key plan (dimensions are in m)

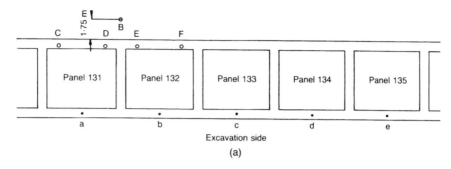

(a)

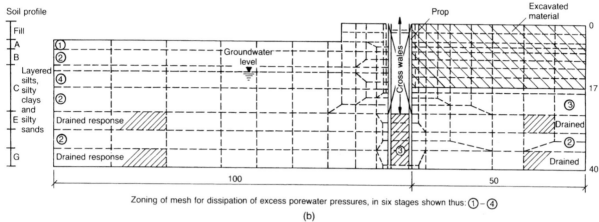

Zoning of mesh for dissipation of excess porewater pressures, in six stages shown thus: ①–④

(b)

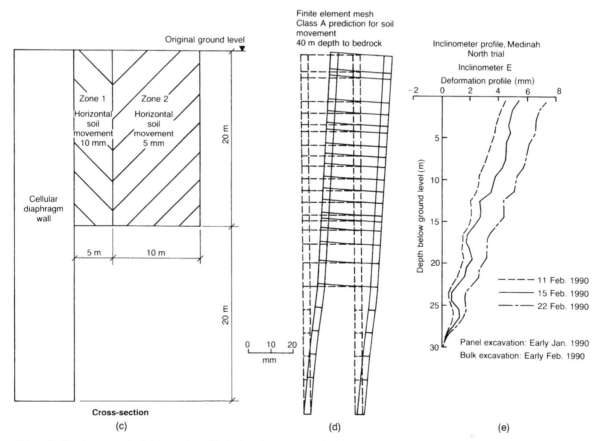

(c)   (d)   (e)

Fig. 11.7. Medinah car park: (a) key plan; (b) finite element mesh; (c) predicted horizontal soil movement due to panel excavation; (d) predicted horizontal soil movement due to bulk excavation; (e) observed horizontal soil movement at rear of wall by inclinometer E

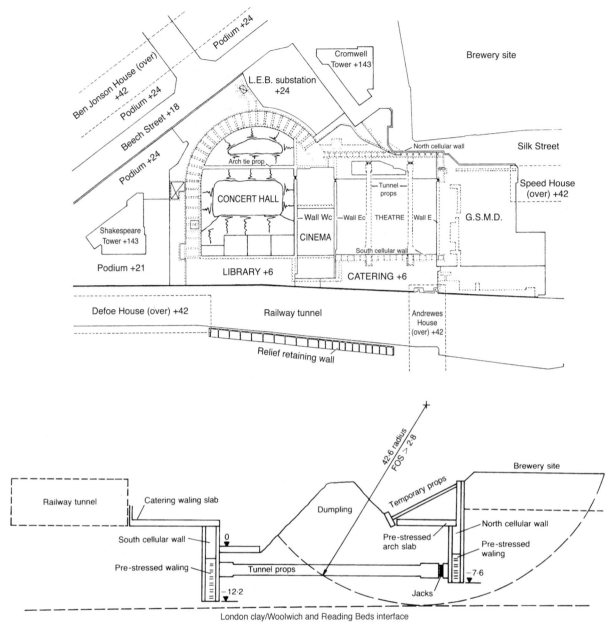

Fig. 11.8. Barbican Arts Centre: site plan and cross-section of site during excavation showing use of pre-loaded tunnel props[27]

the final excavation level required structural support to the diaphragm wall box below that level. A cross-section is shown in Fig. 11.9. Both low-level diaphragm cross-walls and tunnel struts were considered as alternative means of strutting. The low-level tunnel struts were finally adopted because of the risk of poor contact between the outer box diaphragm wall and the diaphragm cross-wall together with the difficulty of installing jacking equipment under 40 m head of bentonite slurry. Three hand-dug tunnel struts, 1770 mm dia. were used, lined with precast concrete segments and filled with reinforced concrete. Hammerhead walings, 1800 mm deep were constructed at the ends of the struts. Access for tunnelling was gained from two 3 m diameter lined pile shafts. At each strut a jacking chamber, 2440 mm dia., was constructed with a jack capacity of 38 000 kN and a stroke of up to 50 mm.

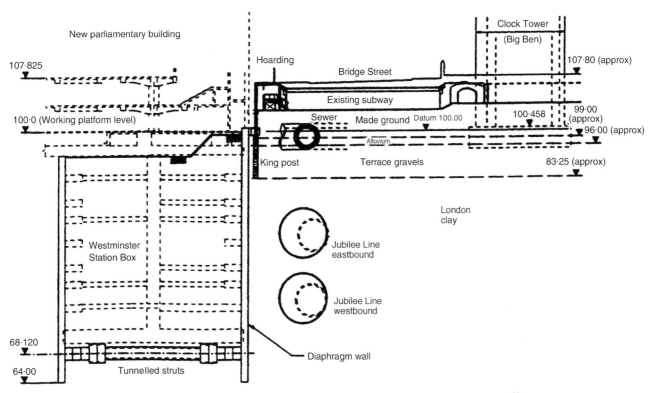

Fig. 11.9. Westminster underground station, London. Use of tunnel struts in top-down construction[33]
(continued p 538)

(continued p 538)

Methods of predicting soil movement

Soil movement behind a supported excavation can be predicted empirically, semi-empirically, by finite element or finite difference methods, or by other methods such as velocity fields.

Empirical methods

The risk of settlements in the vicinity of proposed deep excavations can be assessed, in broad terms, from published data from sites in similar soil conditions. The most useful records include those published by Peck[3], O'Rourke *et al.*[28] and others[29–31].

Peck's work is summarized in Fig. 11.10(a) showing vertical settlement (as a percentage of excavation depth) against distance from the excavation (plotted non-dimensionally as a ratio of excavation depth). Peck used this plot to draw attention to the distances from the cut at which settlement occurs, and to the experience that settlements in plastic clays were likely to be greater than in cohesive soils and stiff clays. Both immediate and consolidation settlements are included in the settlement data in Fig. 11.10. It should be noted that in very soft to soft clays, settlements as great as 0·2% of the excavation depth can occur at distances of three or four times the depth. The critical influence of excavation depth on vertical settlement in shown in Fig. 11.10(b) for basements in Chicago soils, generally supported by sheet piling with small embedment and cross-lot strutting, or more usually with rakers. The upper 5 m of soil in downtown Chicago consists of fill and sand underlain by a soft clay, becoming stiffer with depth until hardpan is met at 23 m. The single-storey basements shown therefore do not penetrate into the soft clays and the recorded settlements were probably caused by the caisson construction on which the basements were founded rather than by the basement excavation. The care required in extrapolating data obtained from one set of soil conditions to another site with an inexact match of soil conditions is self-evident.

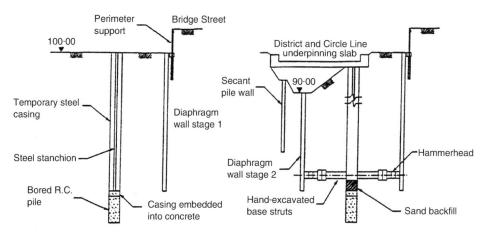

Stage 1
Install perimeter support around site
Install diaphragm walls
Install piles and steel stanchions

Stage 2
Hand-excavate struts and hammerheads
Excavate to 90·0 level
Install low-height diaphragm wall and secant piles

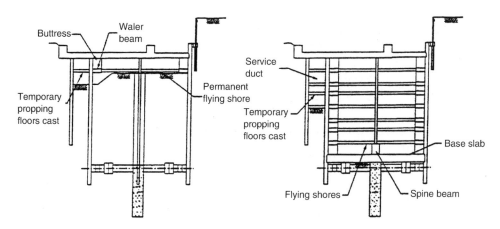

Stage 3
Excavate remainder of site to underside
of first waler level
Install first level of flying shores
Cast slabs, waler beams and buttresses
Continue downwards floor by floor

Stage 4
Repeat stage 3 until all flying shores, floor slabs,
waler beams and buttresses are constructed
Excavate to underside of base slab
Cast base slab and spine beam

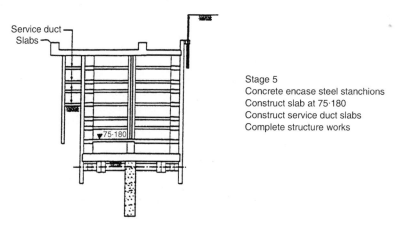

Stage 5
Concrete encase steel stanchions
Construct slab at 75·180
Construct service duct slabs
Complete structure works

Fig. 11.9. Continued

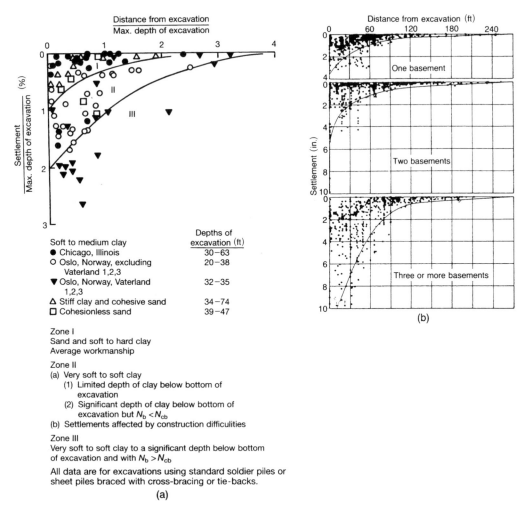

Fig. 11.10. *Summary of settlements adjacent to open cuts in various soils as a function of distance from edge of excavation: (b) settlement associated with foundation construction in Chicago: summary of results and settlements as a function of excavation depth*[3]

The data published by Peck serve only to show the order of settlement and the extent to which such settlements are likely to occur in soft clays.

O'Rourke *et al.*[28] published settlement data for excavations supported by soldier piles and horizontal laggings with cross-lot strutting, in dense sand and interbedded clays in Washington, DC (Fig. 11.11). In these conditions, maximum settlements of the order of 0·3% of excavation depth were recorded immediately to the rear of the sheeting and extended up to twice the excavation depth laterally from the rear of the excavation. O'Rourke *et al.* also published records of settlement readings from Chicago which, while similar to the earlier data by Peck, showed three zones of settlement related to the salient construction characteristics. These plots are shown in Fig. 11.12.

Using these data, O'Rourke[19] published further work on settlement due to braced excavations. He considered the pattern of stress in three stages of excavation and strutting (see Fig. 11.13).

(*a*) *Stage 1, initial excavation before strutting.* The cantilevered sheeting deforms with horizontal soil strains and strain contours of triangular shape, decreasing with depth and distance from the sheeting.

(*b*) *Stage 2, excavation to formation level.* After installation of the top frame support, lateral movement is prevented at that level, but further inward

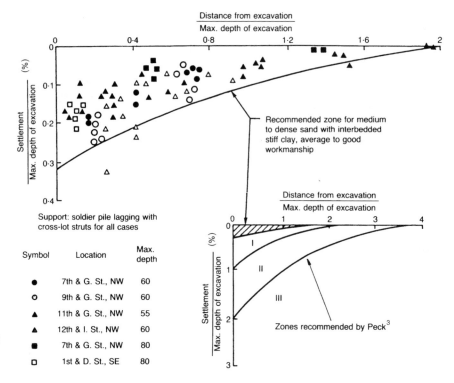

Fig. 11.11. Summary of measured settlements adjacent to strutted excavations in Washington, DC[28]

wall movement at lower levels caused by further excavations produces tensile strains at approximately 45° to the vertical.

(c) *Stage 3, replacement of temporary supports.* As the lower struts are progressively removed to build the permanent structure there is further inward movement of the wall. As the upper supports are removed, the lower part of the sheeting is held by re-strutting to the permanent structure and movement associated with a cantilever wall deflection

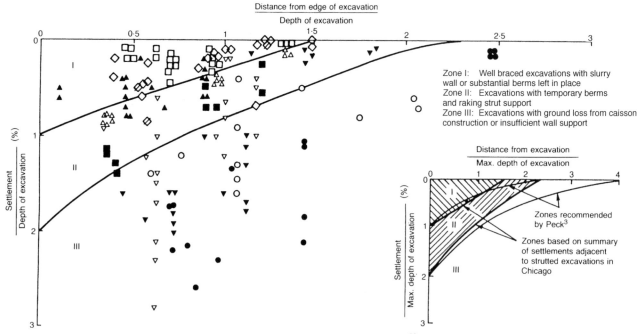

Fig. 11.12. Summary of settlements adjacent to strutted excavations in Chicago[28]

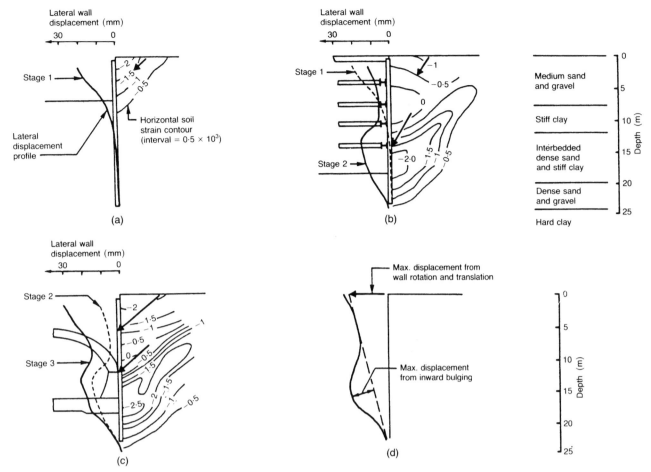

Fig. 11.13. Horizontal strains as measured at successive stages of strutted excavations: (a) stage 1, initial excavation; (b) stage 2, excavation to subgrade; (c) stage 3, removal of struts; (d) principal components of wall movement (bold arrows show movement vectors)[19]

occurs in the upper parts of the wall. The strain contours in this stage are therefore those from a combination of the inward movement of the sheeting at depth and to cantilever action at the higher levels.

O'Rourke[19] developed a relationship between the deformed wall slope and the vertical settlement of the ground at the rear of the wall and defined a coefficient of deformation as the ratio of maximum movement due to the cantilever action of the wall to the maximum total lateral movement of the wall, including elastic bulging of the wall (as shown in Fig. 11.14). These data referred to walls founded in stiff strata and where lateral soil movement below the sheeting towards the excavation was minimal. This relationship could therefore be used to estimate maximum vertical settlement from calculated values of horizontal deformation of the wall. However, no vertical settlement profile results from this computation, and the maximum value of settlement, at the rear of the sheeting, is of limited use on its own.

Clough et al.[32] and Mana and Clough[11] examined data from sheet pile walls and king post walls in clays supported by cross-lot struttings with either free-end or fixed-end support. The results (in Fig. 11.15) show the relationship between maximum lateral wall movement and the factor of safety against basal failure by heave. Lateral movements of sheeting are shown to increase very rapidly below a factor of safety of 2.

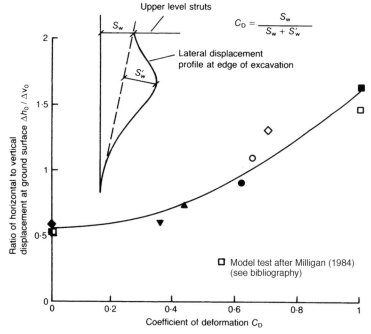

$$C_D = \frac{S_w}{S_w + S_w'}$$

Symbol	Max. depth (m)	Support	Soil	Location
●	18	Soldier piles and lagging, five strut levels	Sand and stiff clay	Washington, DC
▲	13	Soldier piles and lagging, three levels of struts and rakers	Soft to medium clay	Chicago
▼	8	Sheet pile, three raker levels	Soft to medium clay	Chicago
■	13	Slurry wall, two levels of tiebacks and rakers	Soft to medium clay	Chicago
◇	9	Soldier piles and lagging, two raker levels	Soft to medium clay	Chicago
○	8	Sheet pile, two raker levels	Soft to medium clay	Chicago
◆	14	Sheet pile, two levels of struts and rakers	Soft to medium clay	San Francisco

Fig. 11.14. Ratio of horizontal to vertical soil movement as function of the coefficient of deformation[19]

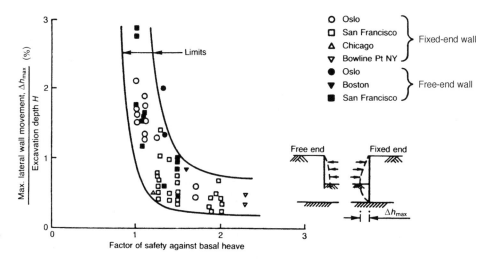

Fig. 11.15. Empirical relationship between the factor of safety against basal heave and non-dimensional maximum lateral wall movement[15]

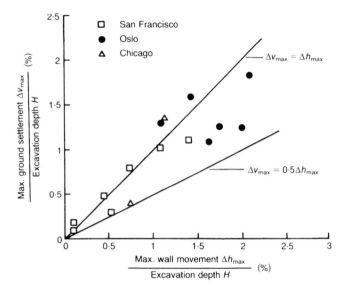

Fig. 11.16. Empirical relationship between maximum ground settlement and maximum lateral wall movements[11]

Mana and Clough[11] produced an empirical relationship between maximum ground settlement and maximum wall movement from data in varied overall ground conditions in clays in San Francisco, Oslo and Chicago (Fig. 11.16). Perhaps the limited conclusion to be drawn from this plot is that maximum vertical settlements appear most likely to be equivalent to maximum horizontal displacements in clays.

Clough had earlier summarized empirical data on anchored sheeting and walls (Fig. 11.17) for subsoils varying from sands and silts to stiff clays and shales to soft clays. Most values of maximum movement remain below 1% of excavated depth and no significant variation is shown with soil type. Clough[31] suggested that the maximum reduction in soil movement using pre-stressed anchors was achieved with pre-stress forces obtained from ground pressures slightly greater than those advised by Terzaghi and Peck[34].

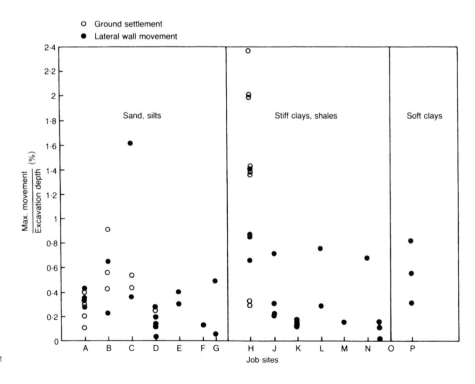

Fig. 11.17. Observed movements of anchored wall systems for varying soil types[31]

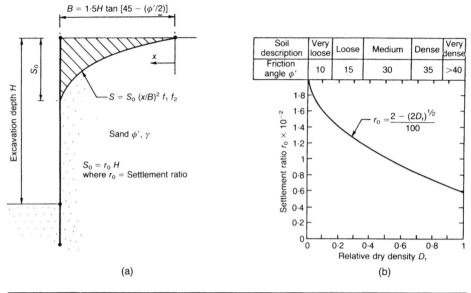

(a)

(b)

Fig. 11.18. *Semi-empirical method to estimate settlement in sands: (a) ground settlement adjacent to wall; (b) variation of settlement ratio with soil properties*[37]

Factor	Workmanship				Factor	Construction difficulty		
	Excellent	Good	Average	Poor		None	Average	Severe
f_1	0·8	0·9	1	1·1	f_2	1	1·02	1·05

Semi-empirical methods

Several methods have been devised which enable the settlement profile at the rear of the wall supporting a deep excavation to be calculated from empirical relationships determined for the lateral movement of the wall. Caspe[35] published a method of analysis which related the settlement profile to the deflected shape of the wall. In this method:

(a) there is a surface behind the wall which defines the limit of soil deformation due to the excavation
(b) a variation in horizontal strain in the soil between this no-strain surface and the wall is assumed
(c) at all locations, vertical strain is assumed to be related to horizontal strain by Poisson's ratio.

Others have commented that for plane strain conditions this last assumption is incorrect and the relationship between vertical and horizontal strain should be expressed by the ratio $v/(1 - v)$. Caspe's method was altered by Bowles[36] to take this into account, with reasonable agreement between the calculated settlement profile and site measurement.

A further semi-empirical method devised by Bauer[37] is shown in Fig. 11.18. This method, applicable to excavation in sands, was claimed to show reasonable fit of settlement profiles with site movements, although the calculated width of settlement influence appears to limit the lateral extent of this zone to less than the excavated depth for practical values of ϕ.

Finite element and finite difference methods

Numerical methods using finite elements or finite differences allow a soil–structure analysis. As mathematical tools these methods provide convenient two-dimensional plane strain solutions (three-dimensional soil–structure solutions are increasingly becoming available) and use commercially available programs (such as PLAXIS and CRISP) or in-house programs developed by academic or professional organizations (such as ICFEP from Imperial

College, London). The methods attempt to address all theoretical requirements with boundary conditions that realistically model the site problem and incorporate, for instance, a stage-by-stage simulation as the excavation progresses, including time-related aspects such as dissipation of excess pore pressure. Displacements are the primary unknown solved by the methods, so prediction of horizontal displacement and vertical settlements fall conveniently to this solution.

Finite element packages generally offer the user a choice of constitutive models, ranging from simple elastic models to sophisticated non-linear elastic–plastic models. The final choice of model will depend on the accuracy required of the prediction and the availability of appropriate input data, particularly with regard to soil parameters. Some of the issues facing the designer in the choice of constitutive model were raised by Woods and Clayton[38] and included two items related to soil stiffness: linearity and small-strain behaviour. Although the solution, using the simple linear model, has been available for many years, it has always been appreciated that most natural soils are of non-linear nature, even at the very low-strain values that occur in wall deformation and settlement profile prediction. In addition, the use of finite element programs to predict movement around excavations has been shown generally to exaggerate deformation unless soil stiffness at very small strain volumes is used in the analysis. To obtain these values, specific measurement procedures have been designed for use in the triaxial test. Even so, choice of a suitable average operational strain level is necessary, particularly for soils from previously undeveloped areas. Where the excavation is near previous sites where measures have been made, back analysis will provide appropriate soil stiffness parameters, providing the excavation and subsoil conditions are similar. Good agreement between the use of small-strain non-linearity to predict settlement behind a strutted excavation and field behaviour was described by Jardine et al.[39]

The Author's experience of use of the PLAXIS model is that soil deformations tend to be overestimated when using the Mohr–Coulomb soil model; more accurate deformation prediction is obtained by use of the PLAXIS soil hardening model, especially in stiff clays. This model is an elastic–plastic type of hyperbolic model handling soil stiffness in terms of stress level and stress path.

In addition to the use of appropriate soil stiffness parameters, the quality of prediction will of course depend on the selection of accurate K_0 values for the particular site. The method of back analysis on its own may not prove sufficiently dependable to obtain these values because of the relatively large variations in at-rest pressures within relatively small distances.

The finite element method was developed by Mana and Clough[11] to formulate a design method for estimating wall deformation and the settlement trough for a strutted excavation in soft to medium clays without resorting to use of a finite element program for a particular design problem. Their procedure was as follows.

(a) At each construction stage where prediction of movement is needed, calculate the minimum factor of safety against basal heave using Terzaghi's method.
(b) Estimate the maximum wall movement Δh_{max} from the relationship between factor of safety against basal heave and maximum wall movement shown in Fig. 11.19. Approximate ground movement Δv_{max} can be estimated by assuming that Δv_{max} lies within the range $0.6\ \Delta h_{max}$ to $1.0 \Delta h_{max}$.

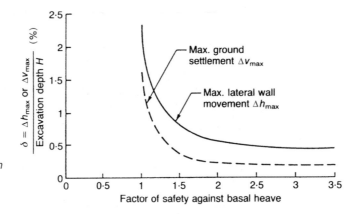

Fig. 11.19. Analytical relationship between maximum lateral wall movement and factor of safety against basal heave[11]

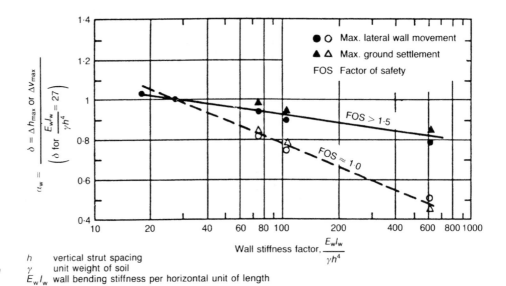

Fig. 11.20. Effect of wall stiffness on maximum lateral wall movement and maximum ground settlement[11]

h vertical strut spacing
γ unit weight of soil
$E_w I_w$ wall bending stiffness per horizontal unit of length

(c) Based on the wall stiffness factor, the strut stiffness factor, the depth to a firm soil layer and the excavation width B, determine the influence coefficients α_w, α_s, α_D, α_B, using Figs. 11.20–11.23.

(d) Determine the influence coefficient for the design strut pre-loading α_p using Fig. 11.24.

(e) Determine the modulus multiplier influence coefficient α_m from Fig. 11.25.

(f) Using the value of Δh_{max} from step (b) and the influence coefficients determined in stages (c)–(e), calculate a revised value for the maximum lateral movement from $\Delta h_{max}^* = \Delta h_{max} \alpha_w \alpha_s \alpha_D \alpha_p \alpha_m$.

(g) Revise the estimate of Δh_{max}^* using the relationship $\Delta v_{max}^* = 0.6 \Delta h_{max}^*$ to $1.0 \Delta h_{max}^*$.

(h) Plot the ground settlement profile using the calculated value Δv_{max}^* and the profile shown in Fig. 11.26.

This method can be used for walls supported by anchors provided the anchors themselves are embedded in a mass of soil or rock which is materially beyond the movement zone.

Other predictive methods

A method originally developed by Roscoe[40] and developed by James et al.[41] and Serrano[42] uses stress and strain fields for increments of structural

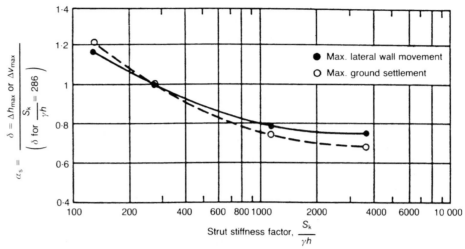

Fig. 11.21. Effect of strut stiffness on maximum lateral wall movement and maximum ground settlement[11]

S_k strut stiffness per horizontal unit of length
h vertical strut spacing
γ unit weight of soil

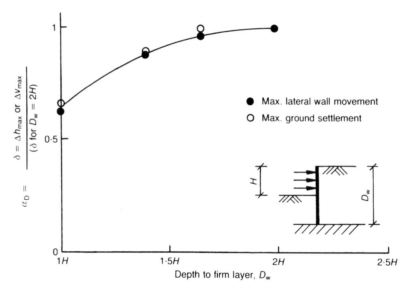

Fig. 11.22. Effect of depth to firm layer on maximum lateral wall movement and maximum ground settlement[11]

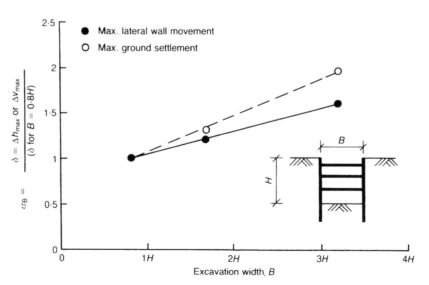

Fig. 11.23. Effect of excavation width on maximum lateral wall movement and maximum ground settlement[11]

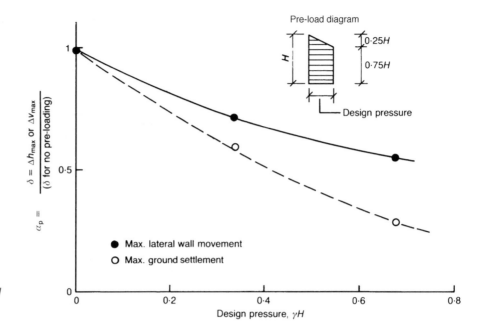

Fig. 11.24. Effect of strut pre-load on maximum lateral wall movement and maximum ground settlement[11]

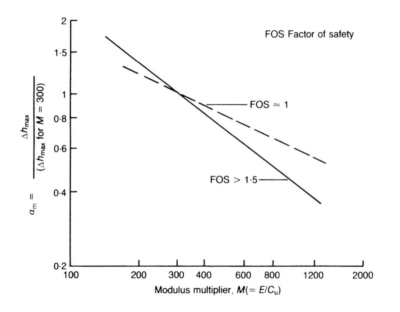

Fig. 11.25. Effect of modulus multiplier on maximum lateral wall movement and maximum ground settlement[11]

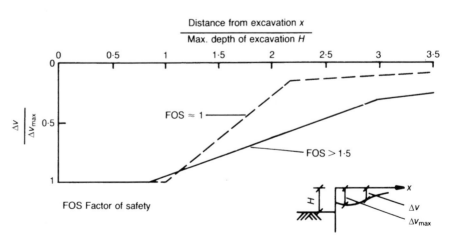

Fig. 11.26. Envelopes to normalize ground settlement profiles[11]

deflection and load. In a series of iterative steps, stress and strain fields are produced which comply with all the parametric values for a particular problem. More recently Maruoka et al.[43] presented a predictive method for vertical settlement in cohesive soils based on the deformed shape of the wall and patterns of zero extension lines in the adjacent soil. They concluded that strain fields consisting of straight lines and circular areas could be used with a rigid body spring model and finite element analysis to give reasonably accurate settlement profile predictions. This method, however, requires the initial prediction of the deformed shape of the wall due to the excavation, and while a solution based on a Winkler spring model could be used to do this, any inaccuracy in this prediction would presumably be reflected in the accuracy of the final settlement profile. A simpler solution based on the kinematics of a mechanism involving soil and wall mass is referred to in Eurocode 7[44].

Soil movement during diaphragm wall and bored pile wall installation

The soil deformations considered in this chapter so far have been due to unloading of the soil surrounding the deep substructure during bulk excavation. The soil structure, however, undergoes several stress changes during installation of the peripheral walling prior to bulk excavation. These changes may be due to dynamic stresses set up by the driving of sheet piles, or the relief of stress due to augering of piles or the excavation of diaphragm wall panels. Each in situ soil stress change has an associated volume change and a resulting vertical settlement. The stress changes and settlements which result from the installation of diaphragm wall panels and bored piles at the periphery of a deep excavation deserve special comment. Soil movements associated with diaphragm wall installation are generally small and limited in lateral extent, but experience with the initial sections of the Island Metro Line in Hong Kong indicated otherwise, and the causes for this difference should be noted.

Stress changes near a diaphragm wall panel excavation occur as a result of unloading due to panel excavation, recharging with bentonite slurry and the subsequent fluid pressures from liquid concrete. (The in situ stresses from the concreting operation were measured in tests by Reynaud[45], which emphasized the relatively high pressures caused by concreting relative to soil values of K_0.) The soil stress changes due to diaphragm wall panel installation are therefore relatively complex and do not stem only from the excavation operation. Similar stress changes occur during bored pile installation.

The extent of soil movement due to excavation of diaphragm wall panels depends on soil properties, groundwater levels, panel width and the length of time between excavation and concreting. There are limited published records of in situ measurements of soil movement due to panel installation: those due to Uriel and Oteo[46] in Seville, Spain; Farmer and Attewell[47] in London; Symons and Carder[48] in London clay; and Humpheson et al.[49], Davis and Henkel[50], Morton et al.[51] and Stroud and Sweeney[52] in Hong Kong, should be referred to. Plots of maximum movement due to the installation of diaphragm walls and bored piles due to Thompson[75] and Carder[7] are reproduced in Figs. 11.27 and 11.28.

Early measurements on the sites in London and Seville within stiff over-consolidated clays confirmed the general opinion of diaphragm wall specialist firms that soil movements are generally small and reduce rapidly at short distances from the panel, say equal to the panel length. Measurements made by the Author at panel excavations in lightly over-consolidated silty clay and silty sand washdown soils in Medinah, Saudi Arabia, also confirm this view. The movements caused by panel excavation in Hong Kong, as

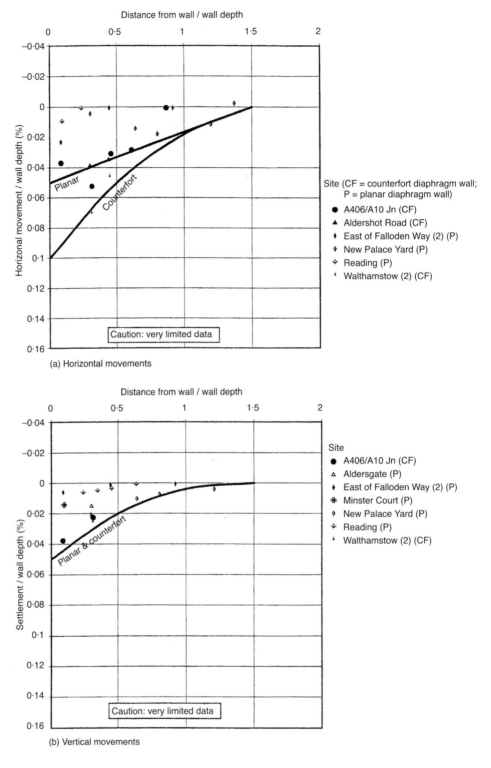

Fig. 11.27. Maximum movement due to installation of planar and counterfort diaphragm walls in stiff clays[75]

described in Chapter 9, were substantial. Measurements made at these sites are compared in Table 11.3. The soil conditions in Hong Kong are materially different from those in London, Seville and Medinah. In the Chater station excavation in Hong Kong, fill and marine deposits to a total depth of 15 m overlie decomposed granite, and the groundwater is only approximately 2·5 m below ground level. Measurements were made during panel excavations up to 35 m deep at three points, 6 m, 15 m and 24 m from the diaphragm wall.

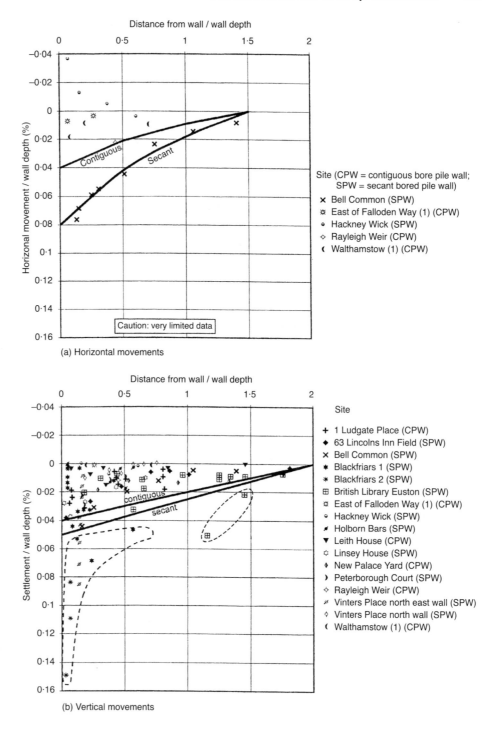

Fig. 11.28. Maximum movement due to contiguous and secant bored pile wall installation in stiff clays[7]

The vertical settlements at these points reached 50 mm, 40 mm and 25 mm, respectively, increasing progressively as the adjacent panels were excavated and concreted.

The following conditions caused these movements in Hong Kong, partly due to the breaking down of soil arch structures spanning panel excavations:

(a) a high groundwater table providing a ready supply of moisture
(b) a relatively high soil permeability (10^{-5} m/s in the completely decomposed granite) which allowed the ready transmission of moisture

Table 11.3 Observed soil deformation due to diaphragm wall panel excavation

Site and reference	Ground conditions	Panel size	Maximum horizontal soil deformation at stated horizontal distance from panel centre line	Remarks
1. London (Farmer and Attwell[47])	London clay: over-consolidated fissured stiff silty clay	15 m deep × 6·1 m long × 0·8 m wide	At 1 m: 16 mm At 2·5 m: 6 mm At 4·5 m: 2·6 mm No movement at 6·1 m from panel	Observations made on one panel only, kept open 7 days before concreting
2. Seville (Uriel and Oteo[46])	Sandy silt up to 13 m overlying Quaternary gravels up to 13 m thickness overlying plastic fissured clay	34 m deep × 3·4 m long × 0·8 m wide	At 2·4 m: 7·5 mm. During panel excavation maximum horizontal deformation 7·5 mm and 7 m depth, 2·4 m from panel centre line	Excavation for circular wall, 25 m dia. measurements made 2·4 m from two panels, diametrically opposite each other
3. Hong Kong (a) (Stroud & Sweeney[52])	Chater Rd/Jackson Rd. 7 m of fill overlying 4 m of marine deposits overlying completely decomposed granite	36 m deep × 6·1 m long	At 1·4 m: 30 mm at 20 m depth. At 6·4 m: less than 10 mm at 20 m depth	Trial panel
(b) (Davis and Henkel[50])	Chater station	17·4 m deep	Maximum movement of about 0·15 to 0·2% depth of excavation movement, some movement at least for horizontal distance equal to panel depths	
4. Medinah Car Park	Layered silty sand and sandy silt overlying basalt bedrock at 30 m depth	30 m deep × 6·8 m long × 0·8 m wide	At 15 m: 8 mm at ground level, reducing linearly with depth to zero at 30 m	Trial panel. Readings made over 11 day period after excavation. No subsequent movement

(*c*) soil with high swell potential which required moisture to cause significant volume change.

The lesson to be learnt from the Hong Kong diaphragm wall excavations is that where these three subsoil conditions occur together, large soil settlements result from diaphragm wall panel installation in advance of bulk excavation in addition to settlements related to bulk excavation.

Mention should also be made of the effects of poor slurry quality control. Where bentonite is subject to prolonged use, vital properties (particularly viscosity) become 'tired' and contamination and pH are inadequately controlled, high fluid loss results. In turn, this leads to less effective lateral support and greater movement.

Researchers have given considerable attention to the installation effects of diaphragm wall panels. Although soil deformation effects may be of limited practical effect (with the exception of the described conditions in Hong Kong) there is likely to be some reduction in in situ earth pressures close to the wall as panel excavation is made. These pressure reductions, likely to be small and only near the wall, may be of the order of 20% for a diaphragm wall panel and about 10% for a bored pile wall. The published analytical work on panel and pile installation includes papers by Tedd *et al.*[53] (finite element data from Bell Common wall), Powrie[54] (elastic stress analysis), Gunn *et al.*[55] (finite element analysis), Ng *et al.*[56] (finite element analyses, Lion Yard Cambridge), Page[57] (centrifuge model tests), de Moor[58] (finite element analyses of a number of panels in sequence), Ng and Yan[59] (3D finite element analysis), Gourvenec and Powrie[60] (3D finite element analysis of panels in sequence), Ng and Yan (3D finite difference analysis of panels in sequence)[61], Powrie and Batten[62] (axisymmetric analysis of a single bored pile), and Cowland and Thorley[63] (Building settlements in Hong Kong due to panel excavation). Lings et al.[64] examined the pressure effect due to wet concrete.

Building response to ground displacement

The earliest published work on the effects of settlement on structures was directed to the tolerance of buildings to settlement and their own weight. Papers by Skempton and MacDonald[65] (1957), Meyerhoff[66,67] (1953, 1956), Polshin and Tokar[68] (1957) and others were based on angular distortion of the structure, or deflection ratio, and horizontal strain was not a prime consideration. Burland and Wroth[69] (1974) and others showed how tensile strains when considered with simple elastic beams could be used to give deflection criteria for the onset of structural damage. Later, in 1977, Burland et al.[70] reproduced 'critical tensile strain' with the concept of 'limiting tensile strain', which could be varied to take account of the properties of differing structural materials and serviceability limit states.

Boscardin and Cording[71] (1989) further developed the relationship between building damage and angular distortion and horizontal strain. A study of eighteen case histories of buildings affected by excavation, either braced excavations or tunnel workings, examined the effects of angular distortion and strain. The classification of visible damage used by Boscardin and Cording is reproduced in Table 11.4. Using this data together with the analysis of a deep beam model they proposed a correlation between angular distortion, horizontal strain and degree of cracking damage as shown in Fig. 11.29. Burland[72] in 2001 progressed the matter further by adopting

Table 11.4 Classification of visible damage to buildings[71]

Class of damage	Description of damage[a]	Approximate width[b] of cracks (mm)
Negligible	Hairline cracks	<0·1
Very slight	Fine cracks easily treated during normal redecoration. Perhaps isolated slight fracture in building. Cracks in exterior brickwork visible upon close inspection	<1
Slight	Cracks easily filled. Redecoration probably required. Several slight fractures inside building. Exterior cracks visible, some repointing may be required for weathertightness. Doors and windows may stick slightly	<5
Moderate	Cracks may require cutting out and patching. Recurrent cracks can be masked by suitable linings. Tuck-pointing and possibly replacement of a small amount of exterior brickwork may be required. Doors and windows sticking. Utility service may be interrupted. Weathertightness often impaired	5 to 15 or several cracks >3 mm
Severe	Extensive repair involving removal and replacement of sections of walls, especially over doors and windows required. Windows and door frames distorted, floor slopes noticeably. Walls lean or bulge noticeably, some loss of bearing in beams. Utility service disrupted	15 to 25 also depends on number of cracks
Very severe	Major repair required involving partial or complete reconstruction. Beams lose bearing, walls lean badly and require shoring. Windows broken by distortion. Danger of instability	usually >25 depends on number of cracks

[a] Location of damage in the building or structure must be considered when classifying degree of damage.
[b] Crack width is only one aspect of damage and should not be used alone as a direct measure of it.
Note. Modified from Burland et al.[70]

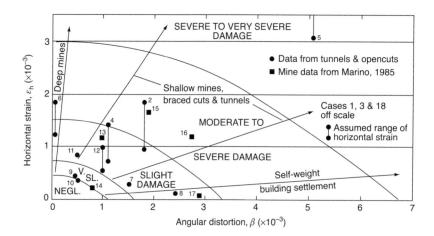

Fig. 11.29. Relationship of damage to angular distortion and horizontal tensile strain[71]

limiting values of tensile strain associated with the Boscardin and Cording categories of damage and showed the derivation of an interaction diagram similar to Fig. 11.29 but for a particular value of the ratio of building length to building height. Burland points out that there are wide gaps in knowledge in these predictions of likely damage, including paucity of observations relating building stiffness to slope and magnitude of structural damage, the effect of piling to these observations, and the effects of time-related soil movement.

The conclusions to Boscardin and Cording[71] are worthy of reiteration.

(*a*) Buildings sited adjacent to excavations are generally less tolerant of differential settlements due to excavation than similar structures settling under their own weight. This is due to the lateral strains that develop in response to most excavations.

(*b*) As a structure is subjected to increasing lateral strains, its tolerance to differential settlement decreases. As a consequence, measures to mitigate excavation-related building damage should include provisions to reduce the lateral strains sustained by the structure.

(*c*) Since the ground movements develop in the form of a travelling wave gradually impinging on a structure, the ratio of the length of the portion of the structure affected by the excavation induced ground movements to height of the structure will initially be very small and grow gradually. Thus, the tolerance of a building to initial deformation will be governed by its tolerance to shearing deformation and horizontal extension.

(*d*) Increasing the ratio of longitudinal stiffness to shear stiffness, E/G, as openings in a wall are assumed to cause, increases the range of deformed length to height ratio, L/H, in which the diagonal strain capacity or shearing resistance is the limiting factor.

(*e*) Points (*c*) and (*d*) suggest that angular distortion, a measure of shearing strain, would be an appropriate parameter to correlate with observed response.

(*f*) If reasonable estimates of ε_{crit} and L/H can be made for a structure in the vicinity of proposed underground construction, the limiting deflection ratio and angular distortion for that structure can be estimated and compared to the estimated ground movement to permit engineers to assess the potential for damage and suitability of possible remedial measures.

(*g*) Frame-type structures, depending on size and other details, can often resist some of the ground movements. Increasing the number of stories creates a structure stiffer in shear that would tend to tilt rather than distort. Conversely, increasing the number of bays typically increases the length of a structure and causes it to distort more to accommodate the ground movements caused by the excavation.

(h) Horizontal ties in the form of reinforced grade beams or similar items are effective means of controlling the strains and distortions in both bearing wall and frame structures adjacent to excavation.

(i) This study only examined cases where the lateral strains are tensile in nature. However, compressive strains may create a critical condition for structures sited over the centre-line of a tunnel or mine. The effects of compressive lateral strain were examined by the National Coal Board[73].

Measures to alleviate the effects of settlement

Whilst use of construction methods such as the top-down system or pre-loading of temporary struts may achieve reductions in settlements below nearby buildings, these measures may not reduce settlements to acceptable levels. Further measures may be needed to reduce risk of cracking or tilt. In summary, these are as follows.

(a) Strengthening the ground by means of grout injection, cement or chemical, or by mix-in-place or pin piles, in order to increase soil stiffness. In extreme cases, freezing of the subsoil may prove an effective solution in granular, water-bearing soils.

(b) Strengthening the affected building by the insertion of improved vertical support by underpinning and horizontal ties to resist horizontal tensile strains imposed by the soil deformation. Shear stiffness of the building can be improved by temporarily filling window and door openings in facades and cross-walls with brickwork or blockwork of requisite strength.

(c) Structural jacking applied progressively as the deep excavation is made to counteract vertical settlement, possibly with improvements of temporary strengthening to the structure.

(d) Compensation and fracture grouting applied progressively as deep excavation is made. Compaction grouting applied to both granular and cohesive subsoils can provide a means of lifting structures to counteract the effects of vertical settlements. The injection of a stiff viscous spherical bulb of grout leads to some compaction and permeation in granular soils, which can be controlled by grout design and control of applied pressures. In cohesive soils neither compaction nor permeation will occur materially and control of grout stiffness and applied pressure will determine the extent of volume of the grout bulb and vertical soil displacement.

Fracture grouting is generally applied to cohesive soils at high pressure, to create thin layers of grout, often of considerable lateral extent. The grout exploits existing planes of weakness at fissures and joints within the soil structure and the extent of this intrusive plane of grout is controlled by grout volume and pressure. Successive injections of compensation and fracture grouting can be made from tubes à manchette, sleeved grout tubes, drilled in arrays from positions both inside and outside the affected structure.

Recently published data and experience associated mainly with tunnelling for the Jubilee Line Extension in London[74] are valuable in the consideration of compensation and fracture grouting as a means to alleviate settlements caused by deep excavations.

References

1. Long M. Database for retaining wall and ground movements due to deep excavations. *ASCE J. Geotech. Eng.* 2001, Mar., 203–224.
2. Clough G., Smith E. and Sweeney B. Movement control of excavation systems by iterative design. *Proc. ASCE Geotech. Eng.*, 1989, **2,** 869–884.
3. Peck R.B. Deep excavations and tunneling in soft ground. *Proc. 7th Int. Conf. S.M.F.E.*, Mexico City, 1969, State of the art volume, 225–290. Sociedad de Mexicana de Mecanica de Suelos, Mexico City, 1969.
4. Karlsrud K. Performance monitoring in deep supported excavations in soft clay. *Proc. 4th Int. Geo. Symp. Field Instrumentation*, Naryang Inst., Singapore, 187–202.
5. Ou C., Hsieh P. and Chiou D. Characteristics of ground surface settlement. *Can. Geotech. J. Ottawa*, **30,** 758–767, 1993.
6. Wong I., Poh T. and Chesah H. Performance of excavation for depressed expressway in Singapore. *ASCE J. Geotech. Eng.*, 1997, **123,** No. 7, 617–625.
7. Carder D. *Ground movements caused by different embedded retaining wall construction techniques.* Transport Research Laboratory, Crowthorne, 1995. TRL report 172.
8. Fernie R. and Suckling T. Simplified approach for estimating lateral movement of embedded walls in UK ground. *Proc. Int. Symp. Geo. Aspects of Underground Construction in Soft Ground.* City University, London, 131–136, 1996.
9. Clough G.W. and O'Rourke T.D. Construction induced movements of in situ walls. *Proc. Design and Performance of Earth Retaining Structures*, ASCE Special Publication 15, 439–470. Cornell University, 1989.
10. Addenbrooke T.I. A flexibility number for the displacement controlled design of multi propped retaining walls. *Ground Eng.* 1994, 41–45.
11. Mana A.I. and Clough G.W. Prediction of movements for braced cuts in clay. *ASCE J. Geotech. Engng*, 1981, **107,** Jun., 759–777.
12. *Review of design methods for excavations.* Geotechnical Control Office, Hong Kong, 1990.
13. CIRIA. *Embedded retaining walls: guidance for economic design.* Gaba A.R. *et al.* CIRIA, London, 2002.
14. Tomlinson M.J. *Foundation design and construction.* Pitman, London, 4th edn., 1980.
15. Clough G.W. *et al.* Prediction of support excavation movements under marginal stability conditions in clay. *Proc. 3rd Int. Conf. Numerical Methods in Geomechanics*, Aachen, 1979, Vol. 4, 1485–1502. Balkema, Rotterdam, 1979.
16. Potts D.M. and Fourie A.B. The behaviour of a propped retaining wall: results of a numerical experiment. *Géotechnique*, 1984, **34,** No. 3, 383–404 (discussion 1986, **35,** No. 1, 119–121).
17. Goldberg D.T. *et al. Vol. 1, Lateral support systems and underpinning; Vol. 2, Design fundamentals; Vol. 3, Construction methods.* Federal Highway Administration, FHWA-RD-75-128, FHWA-RD-75-129, FHWA-RD-75-130. (National Technical Information, 1976 PB 257210, PB 257211, PD 257212.)
18. Clough G.W. and Davidson R.R. Effects of construction on geotechnical performance. *Proc. 9th Int. Conf. S.M.F.E.*, Tokyo, 1977, 15–53. Japanese Society of Soil Mechanics and Foundation Engineering, Tokyo, 1977.
19. O'Rourke T.D. Ground movements caused by braced excavations. *ASCE J. Geotech. Engng*, 1981, **107,** Sept., 1159–1178 (discussion 1983, **109,** Mar., 485–487).
20. Potts D.M. *et al.* The use of soil berms for temporary support of retaining walls. *Proc. Conf. Retaining Structures*, Institution of Civil Engineers, London, 1992, 440–447.
21. Dunicliff J. *Geotechnical instrumentation for monitoring field performance.* J. Wiley, New York, 1988.
22. Standing J.R., Withers A.D. and Nyren R.J. Measuring techniques and their accuracy. *Proc. Conf. Building Response to Tunnelling*, Vol 1, 273–299. CIRIA. Thomas Telford Ltd., London, 2001.
23. Clough G.W. and Denby G.M. Stabilizing berm design for temporary walls in clay. *ASCE J. Geotech. Engng*, 1977, **103,** Feb., 75–90.

24. Burland J.B. *et al.* Movements around excavations in London clay. *Proc. 7th Euro. Conf. S.M.F.E.*, Brighton, 1979, Vol. 1, 13–29. British Geotechnical Society, London, 1979.

25. [a]Richards D., Holmes G. and Beardman, D. Measurement of temporary prop loads at Mayfair car park. *Proc. ICE Geotech. Eng.*, July, 1999, **137**, No. 3, 165–174.

25. [b]Batten M., and Powie W. Measurement and analysis of temporary prop leads at Canary Wharf underground station, East London. *Proc. ICE. Geotech. Eng.*, July, 2000, 151–164.

26. Simic M. and French, D. Three dimensional analysis of deep underground stations. *Proc. Conf. Value of Geotechnics*, Institution of Civil Engineers, London, 1998.

27. Stevens A. *et al.* Barbican Arts Centre. *Structural Engr*, 1977, **55**, No. 11, Nov., 473–485.

28. O'Rourke T.D. *et al. The ground movements related to braced excavation and their influence on adjacent buildings.* US Department of Transport, 1976, DOT-TST76, T-23.

29. Clough G.W. and Tsui Y. Performance of tied back support systems in clay. *ASCE J. Geotech. Engng*, 1974, **100**, Dec., 1259–1273 (discussion 1975, **101**, Aug., 833–836).

30. Clough G.W. Performance of tied back walls. *Proc. ASCE Spec. Conf. Performance of Earth and Earth Supported Structures*, Lafayette, Indiana, 1972, Vol. 3, 259–264. ASCE, New York, 1972.

31. Clough G.W. Deep excavations and retaining structures. *Proc. Symp. Analysis and Design of Founds*, Bethlehem, PA, 1975, 417–465.

32. Clough G.W. *et al.* Prediction of support excavation movements under marginal stability conditions in clay. *Proc. 3rd Int. Conf. Numerical Methods*, Aachen, 1979, Vol. 4, 1485–1502. Balkema, Rotterdam, 1979.

33. Crawley J. and Glass P. Westminster Station, London. *Proc. Deep Foundations Conf.*, Vienna, 1998, 5.18.1–5.18.14. Deep Foundations Institute, Englewood Cliffs, New Jersey, 1998.

34. Terzaghi K. and Peck R.B. *Soil mechanics in engineering practice.* Wiley, New York, 2nd edition, 1967.

35. Caspe M.S. Surface settlement adjacent to braced open cuts. *ASCE J. S.M.F.E.*, 1966, **92**, Jul., 51–59 (discussion 1966, **92**, Nov., 255–256).

36. Bowles J.E. *Foundation analysis and design.* McGraw-Hill, New York, 4th edition, 1988.

37. Bauer G.E. Movements associated with the construction of a deep excavation. *Proc. 3rd Int. Conf. Ground Movements and Structures*, Cardiff, 1984, 694–706 (discussion 870–871 and 876). UWIST, Cardiff, 1984.

38. Woods R.I. and Clayton C.R.I. The application of the Crisp finite element program to practical retaining wall problems. *Proc. Conf. Retaining Structures*, Cambridge. Institution of Civil Engineers, London, 1992, 102–111.

39. Jardine R.J. *et al.* Studies of the influence of non-linear stress-strain characteristics in soil-structure interaction. *Géotechnique*, 1986, **36**, No. 3, 377–396.

40. Roscoe K.H. The influence of strains in soil mechanics. *Géotechnique*, 1970, **20**, No. 1, 129–170.

41. James R.G. *et al.* The prediction of stresses and deformation in a sand mass adjacent to a retaining wall. *Proc. 5th Euro. Conf. S.M.F.E.*, Madrid, 1972, Vol. 1, 39–46. Sociedad Española de Mechanica del Suelo y Cimentationes, Madrid, 1972.

42. Serrano A.A. The method of associated fields of stress and velocity and its application to earth pressure problems. *Proc. 5th Euro. Conf. S.M.F.E.*, Madrid, 1972, Vol. 1, 77–84. Sociedad Española de Mechanica del Suelo y Cimentationes, Madrid, 1972.

43. Maruoka M. *et al.* Ground movements caused by displacements of earth retaining walls. *Proc. Conf. Retaining Structures*, Cambridge. Institution of Civil Engineers, London, 1992, 121–130.

44. Eurocode 7. *Foundations.* British Standards Institution, sixth version, London, 1993.

45. Reynaud P.Y. Mesure des pressions developpées dans une paroi moulée en cours de bétonnage. *Bull. de Liaison des Laboratoires des Ponts et Chaussées*, 1981, May-June, 135–138.

46. Uriel S. and Oteo C.S. Stress and strain beside a circular trench wall. *Proc. 9th Int. Conf. S.M.F.E.*, Tokyo, 1977, Vol. 1, 781–788. Japanese Society of Soil Mechanics and Foundation Engineering, Tokyo, 1977.

47. Farmer I.W. and Attewell P.B. Ground movements caused by a bentonite supported excavation in London clay. *Géotechnique*, 1973, **23**, Dec., 576–581.

48. Symons I.F. and Carder D.R. Field measurement on embedded retaining walls. *Géotechnique*, 1992, **42**, No. 1, 117–126.

49. Humpheson C. *et al.* Basement and substructure for the Hong Kong and Shanghai Bank, Hong Kong. *Proc. Instn Civ. Engrs*, 1986, **80**, Aug., 851–883 (discussion 1987, **82**, Aug., 831–858).

50. Davis R. and Henkel D.J. Geotechnical problems associated with construction of Chater Station. *Proc. Conf. Mass Transport*, Hong Kong, 1980, paper J3.

51. Morton K. *et al.* Observed settlement of buildings for the modified initial system of the mass transit railways, Hong Kong. *Proc. 6th Asian Conf. S.M.F.E.*, Taipei, 1980, Vol. 1, 415–429. Organising Committee, Taipei, 1980.

52. Stroud M.A. and Sweeney D.J. Readings from diaphragm test panel, Chater Road. *A review of diagraphm walls and anchorages*. Institution of Civil Engineers, London, 1977, 142–148.

53. Tedd P. *et al.* Behavior of propped embedded retaining wall in Bell Common Tunnel. *Géotechnique*, 1984, **34**, No. 4, 513–532.

54. Powrie W. Discussion on performance of propped and cantilever rigid walls. *Géotechnique*, 1985, **35**, No. 4, 546–548.

55. Gunn M., Setkunanasthan A. and Clayton C. Finite element modelling of installation effects. *Proc. Conf. on Retaining Structures*, Cambridge, 46–55. Thomas Telford Ltd., London, 1993.

56. Ng C. *et al.* An approximate analysis of the three dimensional effects of diaphragm wall installation. *Géotechnique*, 1995, **45**, No. 3, 497–508.

57. Page J. *Changes in lateral stress during slurry trench installation*. Ph. D. Thesis, Univ. of London, 1995.

58. de Moor E. An analysis of bored pile/diaphragm wall installation effects. *Géotechnique*, 1994, **44**, No. 2, 341–347.

59. Ng C. and Yan R. Stress transfer and deformation mechanisms around a diaphragm wall panel. *ASCE J. Geotech. Eng.*, **1241**, No. 7, 638–648.

60. Gourvenec S. and Powrie W. Three dimensional finite element analysis of diaphragm wall installation. *Géotechnique*, 1999, **49**, No. 6, 801–823.

61. Ng C. and Yan R. Three dimensional modeling of a diaphragm wall construction sequence. *Géotechnique*, 1999, **49**, No. 6, 825–834.

62. Powrie W. and Batten M. *Prop loads in large braced excavations*. CIRIA, London, 2000. Project Report 77.

63. Cowland J. and Thorley C. Ground and building settlement associated with adjacent slurry trench excavation. *Proc. 3rd Int. Conf. on Ground Movements*, Cardiff, 1984, 871–876. UWIST, 1984.

64. Lings M., Ng C. and Nash D. Lateral pressure of wet concrete in diaphragm wall panels cast under bentonite. *ICE Proc. Geotech. Eng.*, 1994, **107**, No. 3, 163–172.

65. Skempton A.W. and MacDonald D.H. The allowable settlement of buildings. *Proc. ICE*, 1957, **III**, No. 5, 727–784.

66. Meyerhoff G.G. Some recent foundation research and its application to design. *Struct. Eng.*, 1953, **31**, 151–167.

67. Meyerhoff G.G. Discussion of Skempton and MacDonald's paper. *Proc. ICE*, 1956, **II**, No. 5, 774.

68. Polshin D. and Tokar R. Maximum allowable non-uniform settlement of structures. *Proc. 4th Int. Conf. S.M.F.E.*, London, 1957, 402–405. Butterworth Scientific Publications, London, 1957.

69. Burland J. and Wroth C. Settlement of buildings and associated damage. *Proc. Conf. on Settlement*, 1974, 611–654. Cambridge, Pentech Press.

70. Burland J. Broms B. and De Mello V. Behavior of foundations and structures. *Proc. Int. Conf. S.M.F.E.*, Tokyo, 1977, Vol. 2, 495–546. Japanese Society of Soil Mechanics and Foundation Engineering, Tokyo, 1977.

71. Boscardin M. and Cording E. Building settlement due to excavation induced settlement. *ASCE J. Geotech. Eng.*, 1989, **115**, No. 1, 1–21.

72. CIRIA. *Building response to tunnelling.* Ed. J. Burland, J. Standing and F. Jardine, Thomas Telford Ltd., London, 2001, 23–41.

73. National Coal Board. *Subsidence engineers' handbook.* National Coal Board Production Dept., London, 1975.

74. CIRIA. *Building response to tunnelling.* Ed. J. Burland, J. Standing and F. Jardine, Thomas Telford Ltd., London, 2001, Vols. 1 and 2.

75. Thompson P. *A review of retaining wall behaviour in overconsolidated clay during the early stages of construction.* M.Sc. Thesis, Imperial College, 1991.

76. Marino G.G. *Subsidence damage to homes over room and pillar mines in Illinois.* PhD Thesis, University of Illinois, 1985.

Bibliography

Chang C.Y. and Duncan J.M. Analysis of soil movement around a deep excavation. *ASCE J. S.M.F.E.*, 1970, **96**, Sept., 1655–1681.

Cole K.W. and Burland J.B. Observation of retaining wall movements associated with a large excavation. *Proc. 5th Euro. Conf. S.M.F.E.*, Madrid, 1972, Vol. 1, 445–453. Sociedad Española de Mechanica del Suelo y Cimentationes, Madrid, 1972.

Cowland J.W. and Thorley C.B. Ground and building settlement associated with adjacent slurry trench excavation. *Proc. 3rd Int. Conf. Ground Movement and Structures*, Cardiff, 1984, 723–738 (discussion 871–876). UWIST, Cardiff, 1984.

Creed M.J. *et al.* Back analysis of the behaviour of a diaphragm wall supported excavation in London clay. *Proc. Int. Conf. Ground Movements and Structures*, Cardiff, 1981, 743–758. UWIST, Cardiff, 1984.

Gumbel J.E. and Wilson J. Observations of ground movement around a trench excavated in London clay. *Proc. Int. Conf. Ground Movements and Structures*, Cardiff, 1981, 841–856.

Jardine R.J. *et al.* Some practical applications of a non-linear ground model. *Proc. 10th Euro. Conf. S.M.F.E.*, Florence, 1991, Vol. 1, 223–228. Balkema, Rotterdam, 1991.

Milligan G.W. Soil deformation behind retaining walls. *Proc. 3rd Int. Conf. Ground Movement and Structures*, Cardiff, 1984, 702–722. UWIST, Cardiff, 1984.

Potts D.M. and Burland J.B. *A numerical investigation of the retaining walls of the Bell Common Tunnel.* Transport Research Laboratory, Crowthorne, 1983, Supplementary Report 783.

Simpson B. *et al.* A computer model for the behaviour of clay. *Géotechnique*, 1979, **29**, No. 2, 149–175 (discussion 1980, **30**, No. 3, 336–339).

Tedd P. *et al.* Behaviour of a propped embedded retaining wall in stiff clay at Bell Common Tunnel. *Géotechnique*, 1984, **34**, No. 4, 513–532.

Wood L.A. and Perrin A.J. Observations of a strutted diaphragm wall in London clay: a preliminary assessment. *Géotechnique*, 1984, **34**, No. 4, 563–579.

Appendix: Selection of typical soil parameters and correlations for initial design purposes

Typical values of soil and rock density

	Density when drained above ground water level (mg/m^3)	Density when submerged below ground water level (mg/m^3)
Gravel	1·60–2·00	0·90–1·25
Hoggin (gravel–sand–clay)	2·00–2·25	1·00–1·35
Coarse to medium sands	1·70–2·10	0·90–1·25
Fine and silty sands	1·75–2·15	0·90–1·25
Loose fine sands	Down to 1·50	Down to 1·90
Stiff clay	1·80–2·15	0·90–1·20
Soft clay	1·60–1·90	0·65–0·95
Peat	1·05–1·40	0·05–0·40
Granite	2·50 (not crushed or broken)	—
Sandstone	2·20 (not crushed or broken)	—
Shale	2·15–2·30	1·20–1·35
Stiff to hard marl	1·90–2·30	1·00–1·35
Chalk	0·95–2·00	0·30–1·00

Atterberg limits

		w_{LL} (%)	w_{PL} (%)	I_p (%)
Sand			Non-plastic	
Silt		30–40	20–25	10–15
Clay		40–150	25–50	15–100
Clay examples	London clay	73	25	48
	Gosport	80	30	50
	Shellhaven	97	32	65

Coefficient of permeability ranges of soils

Soil type	k (cm/s)
Clean gravel	>1.0
Clean sands, clean sands and gravel mixtures	1.0 to 10^{-3}
Fine sands, silts, mixtures of sands, silts and clays	10^{-3} to 10^{-7}
Homogeneous clays	<10^{-7}

Typical values of σ', drained shear strength c' and undrained shear strength c_u

K (m/s $\times 10^{-6}$)	ϕ'	c' (kN/m^2)	c_u (kN/m^2)
Sand loose, round	30°	—	—
Sand loose, angular	32·5°	—	—
Sand medium dense, round	32·5°	—	—
Sand medium dense, angular	35°	—	—
Gravel without sand	37·5°	—	—
Coarse gravel, sharp edged	40°	—	—
Soft normally-consolidated clays	15°–20°	5–10	10–25
Stiff over-consolidated clays	25°–28°	20–25	75–150
Silt	25°–30°	—	10–50
Peat	10°–15°	0–5	—

Typical values of Poisson's ratio

Soil type	Description	ν'
Clay	Soft	0·35–0·4
	Medium	0·3–0·35
	Stiff	0·2–0·3
Sand	Loose	0·15–0·25
	Medium	0·25–0·3
	Dense	0·25–0·35

Typical values of Young's modulus (E) and shear modulus (G). (These values for E are secant values at peak deviatic stress for dense and stiff soils and at maximum deviatic stress for loose, medium and soft soils.)

Soil type	Description	E (MPa)	G (MPa)
Clay	Soft	1–15	0·4–5
	Medium	15–30	5–11
	Stiff	30–100	11–38
Sand	Loose	10–20	4–8
	Medium	20–40	8–16
	Dense	40–80	16–32

Index